Banks on Sentence

Volume 1

14th edition

Banks on Sentence

Volume 1

14th edition

Robert Banks
Member of the Inner Temple

www.banksr.com **book@banksr.com**

Banks on Sentence
First published January 2003 by Butterworths LexisNexis™
Second edition September 2005 published by Robert Banks
Third edition March 2008 published by Robert Banks
Fourth edition June 2009 published by Robert Banks
Fifth edition May 2010 published by Robert Banks
Sixth edition May 2011 published by Robert Banks
Seventh edition 9 May 2012 published by Robert Banks
Eighth edition 30 April 2013 published by Robert Banks
Ninth edition 29 April 2014 published by Robert Banks
Tenth edition 28 April 2015 published by Robert Banks
11th edition 28 April 2016 published by Robert Banks
12th edition 28 April 2017 published by Robert Banks
13th edition 27 April 2018 published by Robert Banks
14th edition 10 May 2019 published by Robert Banks

Production
www.banksr.com
book@banksr.com
Banks on Sentence, PO Box 35, Etchingham, East Sussex TN19 7WS
Sentencing Alert: subscribe at www.banksr.com
Printed in the UK by CPI William Clowes, Copland Way, Ellough, Beccles, Suffolk NR34 7TL
Typeset by Letterpart Ltd, 3 Cricket View, Guards Avenue, Caterham on the Hill, Surrey, CR3 5XL
This book is printed on acid-free paper. The paper is responsibly manufactured and obtained from sustainable forests where at least two trees are planted for each one used in the production of paper.
Every effort is made to ensure that this book is accurate, but due to the way the law changes, computer issues and the complexity of the law, no law book can be without error. Where reliance is placed on an entry, the reader should check the entry is correct.

Photographic credits
Volume 1 © LSE Library on flickr. With thanks.
Volume 2 © Alison Avery Beautiful England Photos. With thanks.

ISBNs:
Volumes 1 and 2: 978-1-9160666-2-5
Volume 1: 978-1-9160666-0-1
Volume 2: 978-1-9160666-1-8

Contents

Volume 1

The sentencing orders with their breach provisions, the sentencing factors that relate to the individual case, and sentencing procedure

Volume 2

The sentencing provisions for the individual offences and the sentencing factors that relate to a defendant

App and Statistics

App

Banks on Sentence 14th edition is available digitally in the following forms:

An app for Apple iPads and Windows 8 and 10 tablets and computers from Banks on Sentence

The app has additional features such as all the Sentencing Council guidelines and the ability to annotate, bookmark, tag and favourite passages of the book, see www.banksr.com for more details.

Statistics

The statistics at the beginning of many of the chapters have been tabulated from the raw data by the MoJ.

This year, the data for most of the statistics tables is no longer made available by the MoJ, so most of the statistics are not up to date.

Committals for sentence are not included in the figures. The 'average length of sentence' column excludes life sentences and indeterminate sentences. In the tables '–' means nil and 0% means less than 0.5%.

Clearly the accuracy of the statistics depends on those who feed the information into the system. Where a defendant is dealt with for a number of offences, the data is entered for the principal offence for which he or she was sentenced.

When a defendant has been found guilty of two or more offences, the principal offence is the offence for which the heaviest penalty was imposed. Where the same disposal is imposed for two or more offences, the offence selected is the offence for which the statutory maximum penalty is the most severe. Statistics for threats to kill and conspiracy to murder are included together, which makes using them very difficult. Similarly, productions of drugs is listed with supply of drugs.

The Ministry of Justice says that the data is subject to inaccuracies inherent in any large-scale recording system. The raw data can be found at www.banksr.com

PREFACE

Then and now

A few days before I wrote this, I retired as a barrister. If all goes to plan, at the end of May 2019 I will cease to be editor of Banks on Sentence. Retirement offers an opportunity to consider how the Bar and the criminal justice system have changed in the 41 years since I became a barrister. I set it out because I think younger readers and others might be surprised by the changes.

1978	2019
In about 1978, a female pupil turned up for the first day of her planned pupillage in Kings Bench Walk and was made to wait a long time. The clerk eventually saw her and said that although she had a pupillage, no member of chambers was prepared to share his room with a woman and so the pupillage had to be terminated.	Women have gained positions in all areas of the Bar and public service.
When you joined an Inn, you didn't need a degree and you had to give a commitment that you intended to practise. If you hadn't obtained a pupillage, the Students' Officer of your Inn arranged a meeting with a Bencher who rang round until a pupillage interview was secured. Few would not help a Bencher. The Bencher was part of a close-knit establishment group.	The current bureaucratic lottery wastes considerable talent. The system favours those who tick a lot of boxes, but does not necessarily pick the best jury advocates.
Officially pupils had to pay the pupil master £50 for a pupillage. It was so unfair that it was invariably waived.	Pupillages are now funded. The number on offer has fallen dramatically.
The Bar had entrenched homophobia and it seemed that all criminal sets of chambers enforced a ban on gay people. After squatting I had to go to a chambers where there was only one other tenant, who had a Mediterranean civil law practice. My solicitors had no prejudice and were loyal.	Whatever the rules, some tenancy applicants have strings pulled for them while others have doors needlessly slammed in their face.
There was little new criminal legislation and most of it was relatively sensible and simple.	Parliament has enacted a torrent of ill-conceived legislation, often in an attempt to please a section of the electorate. The result is a pile of legislative spaghetti which is sometimes in conflict with other sections of legislation and wastes time as it is so confusing. There has also been a plethora of unnecessary new offences.

1978	2019
In the Magistrates' Court cases could be sent to the Crown Court only after sufficient evidence was served. Committals were either agreed or argued on the papers or argued with witnesses being called to give evidence.	This waste of resources has been removed. To save money, except for certain sex cases, the CPS tends not to prosecute weak cases.
In the Magistrates' Court, those remanded into custody awaiting a committal could only be remanded for eight days at a time. This was so the magistrates and the defence could check their health and welfare. Unless the defence agreed, those remanded had to be produced every week and the defence could make a bail application at each hearing without having to prove that there had been a change in circumstances. Police officers normally dealt with remand hearings and the advocates could ask them questions. An officer usually stood in the witness box.	The system has turned into a conveyor belt to save costs. Defendants face long remands without seeing either a Judge or their legal team.
In the Magistrates' Court the prosecution were not obliged to serve the evidence before the trial. Defence counsel needed to write down the evidence as the witness gave it and speak to the defendant over the dock wall to obtain instructions on it. Disclosure was in the discretion of the prosecution.	Although advocates can see the served evidence, police resources mean that they cannot properly consider IT disclosure, which can prove the innocence of defendants. Judges are alive to this issue but if the resources to do the job are not there, they are reluctant to stop a trial being heard. There are also issues about the victims' private material being seen by others. The result is that sometimes a jury will wrongly convict because of the lack of disclosure or will wrongly acquit because of the lack of police investigation.
In the Crown Court, legal aid paid for solicitors to see witnesses, draft defendant statements, comments on the evidence and detailed analysis of the case. In Court, a solicitor's representative or the solicitor involved in the case attended.	The payment for solicitors is so minimal that their involvement in a case where counsel is instructed can be very little.

1978	2019
Being a Judge was a worthwhile and sought-after job. It had status. One problem was that there was virtually no training. Lord Parker, a judge, once said the first summing up he ever heard was his own. The other problem was that selection was within the Lord Chancellor's discretion. One barrister, who for very good reasons had very little work sent to him, went to a dinner which the Lord Chancellor attended. He told the Lord Chancellor about his problem and about two weeks later the barrister became a circuit judge and court staff and advocates considered him to be a dreadful judge.	The attraction of being a judge used to be the generous pension. That has gone. The MoJ cannot fill the High Court vacancies. The main problem today is the unhealthy lifestyle. Judges are expected to read, digest and consider excessive amounts of data on screens which causes large amounts of stress. In business, stress is managed by people working in a team and usually the members of a team discuss the issues and support each other. A Judge sits alone and is often isolated. This causes serious mental health problems. The other main problem is the lack of security in court rooms. Judges feel unsafe and this only adds to the stress. It no surprise that in a survey of judges in 2014, 23% said they would leave their job if there was a viable alternative. In 2016, the figure was 42%. In 2019, the figure must be even higher.
Payment for young barristers at the Magistrates' Court was from solicitors. The solicitor sent the papers to counsel and gave him about £17 for doing a trial. The solicitor then claimed for the barrister's hearing, travel time etc. as if he or she had done the work. Their payment was typically £250+. Members of chambers frequently thought that if solicitors benefited from this rip-off, they would be more likely to brief them in the Crown Court. Many solicitors thought there was nothing wrong in making young barristers wait up to five years for payment. Some solicitors declined to pay at all and when clerks eventually refused to accept any more work from them, the solicitors moved on to cheat another set of chambers. Few in chambers thought these issues were important.	The savage cuts to legal aid mean that most advocates cannot earn a living unless they take on more cases than they should. Large parts of the evidence are simply not read by advocates as they rely on the summaries. When a young barrister burns out and is unable to pay his or her bills, another replaces him or her until they have to give up. It is a scandal.
The aim of barristers was to enhance their reputation. Most tried meticulously hard to perform well.	The overriding consideration of advocates is to do sufficient cases to pay the bills. There is little time to keep up to date with the law or properly reflect on cases.

1978	**2019**
By and large there was competition for work. There were shady deals between some chambers and solicitors, but solicitors and their clients generally chose the advocate on merit.	When a solicitor advocate selects him or herself to conduct the case there is no competition. Their client is frequently represented by someone who lacks the knowledge and ability to do the case properly. With the dreadful pay they receive, some barristers provide poor representation.
Prior to trial the only advance warning that the defence had to give was an alibi notice, if one was required.	There are so many demands for disclosure and skeletons that advocates can be overwhelmed by them. If papers are still being drafted at 11 pm, the advocate cannot be expected to remember everything. This drafting is often after a full day at court and the associated travel. The work is also very unhealthy.
It was almost impossible to mount a child sex case where the witness was a child. Police understandably warned parents about the dangers of their children being involved in trials.	The growth of child sex cases, particularly historical cases, has swamped the courts. In historical cases, the passage of time means that almost all independent evidence has been lost and key witnesses are no longer available.
The law for trials was basically fair. Defendants were protected with rules, many of which were introduced by Victorian judges. These included corroboration, rules on hearsay, the protection from self-incrimination, the jury usually not knowing about the defendant's previous convictions and the right of a defendant to be present.	All these protections have either been removed or whittled away. Some innocent defendants are convicted and sent to prison. Many trials are simply not fair.
The evidence in trials was either: a) evidence of interviews where solicitors were excluded; b) remarks claimed to have been made by defendants; c) items which were said to have been found but there was only the evidence of officers to prove it; or d) eye witness accounts, like police surveillance. London juries tended to reject police evidence while other juries were less keen to do so.	DNA evidence, telephone data, CCTV evidence and tape-recorded interviews are usually incapable of challenge. Such evidence is reliable if the context has been properly disclosed.
Cases were won and lost on the cross-examination of the key witnesses. Juries were regularly swayed by counsel's speeches.	A large proportion of cases are won or lost on the interpretation of the agreed evidence.
The law for sentencing was relatively simple. There were compara type="Table"tively few sentencing orders.	The law for sentencing is now so complex that unlawful procedures are frequently used and unlawful sentences are regularly passed by the Crown Court. Even the Court of Appeal passes unlawful sentences on occasions.

1978	2019
When you visited a prison, a prison officer just ticked your name off the list and there was no search or request for ID. Everything was based on trust. Often, tea or coffee was offered. Counsel were frequently treated as distinguished guests.	Massive security surrounds prison visits, which sometimes makes taking and assessing the evidence difficult. This security is entirely understandable and was brought in because a few legal visitors broke the trust placed in them and smuggled articles in.
Police forces ran the prosecutions, with the DPP being involved only in really serious or important cases. In London it was Scotland Yard who conducted them. There was clearly a conflict of interest but the solicitors at the Yard knew their cases, and the decisions they took that I knew about seemed very sensible at the time. One reason for this was they were selected on merit and properly paid.	The CPS is so starved of resources that it is unable to function properly. The pay to their advocates is a scandal. One advocate who works for the CPS in the Magistrates' Court told me the CPS only prosecutes cases that are easy to prosecute.
The police had suffered a series of PR disasters and were conducting a charm offensive. There was funding for them but the nature of trials produced a low conviction rate. Guilty or not, a lot of defendants took their chances with a not guilty plea.	The underfunding of the police means many if not most fraud incidents do not lead to a jury trial and medium-level and low-level offences, like burglary, are not investigated properly or at all. A vast proportion of the police budget is spent on terrorist detection and prevention and trying to control the proliferation of violent gangs in our cities. The police have had many successes with the former, but if one gang member is caught two youths often take his place. Large numbers of trials collapse because the police are unable to prepare them properly.

It could be said that the problems in 1978 have been replaced by fresh problems today. In fact, many of the problems in 1978 have still not been properly addressed. Perhaps it's a case of some steps forward but more steps back.

I have greatly enjoyed editing this book and I thank those who have contributed to it. I have also appreciated the many invitations that have been extended to me, often to discuss the problems listed above. For four decades I have battled away at court and with those who could change the system. I wish those who are fighting now every success. Lastly, I thank my readers. It is they who have made this book possible.

Robert Banks
5 April 2019

FOREWORD

I am delighted to have been asked to write the Foreword for this latest edition of Robert Banks' excellent book Banks on Sentence. I have used it since it was first published, which I am now horrified to discover was as long ago as 2003. Initially I had it in hard copy, but now it comes as part of an electronic bundle of books provided by a well-known legal publisher. Whilst I never consider an electronic copy to be as satisfying to "leaf through" as a hard copy, it does have the advantage of a search function and has meant that my back has been far better in recent years than it was in 2003 when all criminal practitioners had to carry not only their robes, but also many lever-arch files and numerous books.

So much has changed since 2003, although sadly the fees paid to the criminal practitioner have remained pretty much as they were back then, both for defence and prosecution. This is, to be frank, a disgrace. The £15 million or £23 million increase (depending on your point of view) to the defence advocates' graduated fee scheme (AGFS) at the end of 2018, whilst welcome, can only be seen as the beginning of what must be a far greater investment into the scheme and the criminal justice system generally. This was the first increase since 2007, and it should not be forgotten that from 2007 to 2018 there had been a series of cuts. The initial AGFS scheme, which was intended to apply only to cases lasting up to ten days, was designed at a time when there was no electronic evidence as we know it today, and disclosure and unused material were not the issues they are now. The defence AGFS scheme pre-dates the 2003 Criminal Justice Act (think hearsay and bad character applications) as well as the introduction of defence statements. It is, in short, a creature from another time. Whilst sterling efforts have been made by many at the Bar to make it fit for purpose, clearly it is not, and will remain so, unless and until there is substantial investment in the scheme by the government. It is to be hoped that the government's current 18-month review of criminal legal aid and disclosure will address the issues that all who practise at the criminal Bar are only too well aware of.

Prosecution fees are similarly woeful. The CPS graduated fee scheme A was introduced back in 2001 for cases lasting less than 26 days. This was at the same time as the defence scheme was extended and at that time the schemes seemed to provide parity of funding. CPS scheme B was introduced in 2005 and was extended to cover cases lasting 40 days. The increases to the defence scheme in 2007 were not, however, mirrored in the prosecution scheme and when the CPS scheme C was introduced in 2012, that incorporated cuts of 5%. The government's expressed intention in 2001 to equalise prosecution and defence fees is sadly now a distant dream, best illustrated by the fact that in 2001 the standard appearance fees for both defence and prosecution were £46.50, whereas today they are £91 for the defence and still £46.50 for the prosecution. Proper remuneration of publicly funded practitioners is an absolute priority during my term as Chair of the Bar and I shall press the case at every available opportunity.

The job of the criminal advocate is of course now very different from what it was back in 2003 when Banks on Sentence was first published. Far more is now demanded of the criminal practitioner: hearsay and bad character applications;

skeleton arguments; and opening notes to name but a few. The law seems to be ever more complex, with new statutes adding to or amending legislation, some of which never actually come into force, but lie on the statute books un-repealed, waiting there as a trap for the unwary. The lot of the criminal practitioner has become harder and harder and some of the publications that should be there to help the practitioner are not as helpful as they might be, with incorrect page references or an index that does not seem to be written in the same language as the contents page.

Thankfully, though, Banks on Sentence does not fall into the category of "difficult publication". As a criminal hack who has plied his trade on the Midland Circuit for the past 30 years, I know how valuable a publication this is to anybody who has to deal with criminal sentencing, whether at the Bar, on the Bench, as a practising solicitor or indeed anyone else who has any interest in dealing with criminal offences. The law in relation to sentencing has become particularly complex during my time in practice and in my experience Banks on Sentence has become the "go to" book for anybody dealing with a sentence. In my opinion, anyone who has to deal with a sentence would be well advised to cast their eye over the relevant section of Banks on Sentence before appearing in Court. It had occurred to me that the Sentencing Council's ever-increasing output might mean that Banks on Sentence became less relevant. That is simply not the case. Robert Banks has produced a work that remains on top of the law in an easily digestible form. I commend it to all who have a criminal practice and hope that they find it as much use as I always have.

My aim during my year as Chair of the Bar for 2019 is to make life at the Bar happier and easier for all concerned. If I have half as much success as Robert Banks has had with his book, which I know has made our lives easier, then I will have had a great deal of success.

Richard Atkins QC
Chair of the Bar of England and Wales, 2019

Table of Statutes

References are to paragraph numbers.

Table of Statutory Instruments

References are to paragraph numbers.

Table of Articles of European Convention on Human Rights

References are to paragraph numbers.

Table of Cases

References are to paragraph numbers.

Table of Rules

References are to paragraph numbers.

1 ABSOLUTE DISCHARGE

1.1

Powers of Criminal Courts (Sentencing) Act 2000 s 12

Children and young offenders The order is available whatever the age of the offender.

Court Martial Armed Forces Act 2006 s 185-187 deal with imposing an absolute discharge, the breach of an absolute discharge and the effect of an absolute discharge. The Court may pass this order only for ex-service personnel and civilians, see *Guidance on Sentencing in the Court Martial 2018* Annex B.

Status of an absolute discharge, see the **CONDITIONAL DISCHARGE** ***Status of an absolute or conditional discharge*** para at **19.5**.

History of the order There is a useful history of the power to grant absolute and conditional discharges set out in *R v Clarke* 2009 EWCA Crim 1074, 2010 1 Cr App R (S) 48 (p 296) at para 15.

Victim surcharge There is no surcharge applicable.[1]

Rehabilitation period There is no rehabilitation period.[2]

1.2 *Statistics England and Wales*

Absolute discharges (Aged 21+)

	2014	2015	2016	2017
Crown Court	68	78	76	72
Magistrates' Court	4,379	7,358	3,783	4,271

For explanations about the statistics, see page 1-xii. For more statistics, see www.banksr.com Other Matters Statistics tab.

1.3 *Statutory power to order*

Powers of Criminal Courts (Sentencing) Act 2000 s 12(1) [Except for murder and cases where life or a minimum sentence must be imposed[3]] where a court is of the opinion, having regard to the circumstances including the nature of the offence and the character of the offender, that it is inexpedient to inflict punishment, the court may make an order discharging him [absolutely or conditionally].

Note: The rest of the section is not summarised. Ed.

Combined with other orders

See also the **COMBINING SENTENCES** chapter.

1.4 *Combined with other orders*

Court Martial Only a Service Compensation Order may be combined with an absolute discharge, see Armed Forces Act 2006 s 185(4) and *Guidance on Sentencing in the Court Martial 2018* Annex B.

1.5 *Compensation orders, Combined with*

Powers of Criminal Courts (Sentencing) Act 2000 s 12(7) Nothing in this section shall be construed as preventing a court, on discharging an offender absolutely or conditionally in respect of any offence...from making in respect of the offence an order under Powers of Criminal Courts (Sentencing) Act 2000 s 130 (compensation orders).[4]

---

[1] Criminal Justice Act 2003 s 161A-161B and Criminal Justice Act 2003 (Surcharge) Order 2012 2012/1696

[2] Rehabilitation of Offenders Act 1974 s 5(3)

[3] In Powers of Criminal Courts (Sentencing) Act 2000 s 12(1A) the minimum sentences are listed, Prevention of Crime Act 1953 s 1(2B) and 1A(5) (possessing/threatening with an offensive weapon), Firearms Act 1968 s 51A(2) (certain firearm offences), Criminal Justice Act 1988 s 139(6B), 139A(5B) and 139AA(7) (bladed article offences), Powers of Criminal Courts (Sentencing) Act 2000 s 110(2) and 111(2) (certain class A drug trafficking and dwelling burglary offences), Criminal Justice Act 2003 s 224A, 225(2) and 226(2) (automatic life, CJA 2003 life sentence and detention for life) and Violent Crime Reduction Act 2006 s 29(4) and (6) (using someone to mind a weapon).

[4] As amended by Criminal Justice and Courts Act 2015 Sch 12 paras 8-9

1.6 *Confiscation order, Combined with*

R v Varma 2012 UKSC 42, 2013 1 Cr App R (S) 125 (p 650) The Court of Appeal asked, 'Does the Crown Court have power to make a confiscation order if the defendant receives an absolute or conditional discharge?' Held. [In all cases] the court must proceed under Proceeds of Crime Act 2002 s 6 if section 6(1) and (2) were satisfied. In most cases there was a duty to make an order.

1.7 *Costs, Combined with*

Powers of Criminal Courts (Sentencing) Act 2000 s 12(8) Nothing in this section shall be construed as preventing a court, on discharging an offender absolutely or conditionally in respect of an offence, from…(b) making an order for costs against the offender.[5]

1.8 *Deprivation of property used for crime, Combined with*

Powers of Criminal Courts (Sentencing) Act 2000 s 12(7) Nothing in this section shall be construed as preventing a court, on discharging an offender absolutely or conditionally in respect of any offence…from making in respect of the offence an order under Powers of Criminal Courts (Sentencing) Act 2000 s 143 (deprivation orders).[6]

1.9 *Disqualification, Endorsement etc., Combined with*

Road Traffic Offenders Act 1988 s 46(1) Notwithstanding anything in Powers of Criminal Courts (Sentencing) Act 2000 s 14(3) (rule about disregarding absolute and conditional discharges), a court [when convicting a person involving obligatory or discretionary disqualification orders him to be absolutely or conditionally discharged] may also exercise any power conferred, and must also discharge any duty imposed on the court by Road Traffic Offenders Act 1988 s 34 (obligatory disqualification), section 35 (totting up disqualification), section 36 (disqualification until test is passed) and sections 44-44A (obligation to endorse).

Powers of Criminal Courts (Sentencing) Act 2000 s 12(7) [The court may] on discharging an offender absolutely make an order for disqualification.

Note: The Act does not indicate whether it is road traffic disqualification or not. It is likely to be interpreted as all disqualification orders as that is the natural meaning of the words in the section. Ed.

1.10 *Exclusion Orders, Combined with*

Licensed Premises (Exclusion of Certain Persons) Act 1980 s 1(2)[7] An Exclusion Order may be made… notwithstanding the provisions of Powers of Criminal Courts (Sentencing) Act 2000 s 12 and 14 (the effect etc. of an absolute and conditional discharge) (see **19.5**).

1.11 *Fines, Combined with*

R v Sanck 1990 12 Cr App R (S) 155 LCJ D pleaded to possession of cannabis with intent to supply and was given a conditional discharge and a fine. Held. That was wrong so we quash the conditional discharge.

Note: If it is wrong to combine a conditional discharge with a fine it must also be wrong to combine an absolute discharge with a fine. However, there is nothing wrong with passing a fine on one count/charge and an absolute discharge on a different count/charge. Ed.

1.12 *Referral Orders, Combined with*

Powers of Criminal Courts (Sentencing) Act 2000 s 19(3) The court shall, in respect of any connected offence, either sentence the offender by making a Referral Order or make an order discharging him absolutely.

---

[5] As amended by Criminal Justice and Courts Act 2015 Sch 12 paras 8-9

[6] As amended by Criminal Justice and Courts Act 2015 Sch 12 paras 8-9

[7] This Act was repealed by Violent Crime Reduction Act 2006 Sch 5. This has not been commenced.

1.13 ***Restitution Orders, Combined with***
Powers of Criminal Courts (Sentencing) Act 2000 s 12(7) Nothing in this section shall be construed as preventing a court, on discharging an offender absolutely or conditionally in respect of any offence…from making in respect of the offence an order under Powers of Criminal Courts (Sentencing) Act 2000 s 148 (Restitution Orders).[8]

1.14 ***Serious Crime Prevention Orders, Combined with***
Serious Crime Act 2007 s 19(7) [A Serious Crime Prevention] order must not be made under this section except: a) in addition to a sentence imposed in respect of the offence concerned, or b) in addition to an order discharging the person conditionally.
Serious Crime Act 2007 s 36(5) A Serious Crime Prevention Order may be made in spite of anything in Powers of Criminal Courts (Sentencing) Act 2000 s 12 and 14 (power to make and the effect of an absolute or conditional discharge), see **19.5**.

1.15 ***Unlawful Profit Order, Combined with***
Powers of Criminal Courts (Sentencing) Act 2000 s 12(7) Nothing in this section shall be construed as preventing a court, on discharging an offender absolutely or conditionally in respect of any offence…from making in respect of the offence an Unlawful Profit Order under Prevention of Social Housing Fraud Act 2013 s 4.[9]

1.16 ***Explain sentence, Judge must/Suggested sentencing remarks***
Judicial College's Crown Court Compendium Part II Sentencing June 2018 page 6.1

> **Example**
> You have pleaded guilty to/been convicted of the offence of {specify} but it is neither necessary nor appropriate to impose any punishment because {reason/s}. You will therefore be absolutely discharged. This means that you will hear no more about this: this case is at an end.

2 Anti-Social Behaviour: 2014 Act Orders/Existing ASBOs

2.1
2014 Act orders
Criminal Behaviour Orders The post-conviction ASBO was replaced by the Criminal Behaviour Order on 20 October 2014,[10] see **25.1**.
Civil injunctions The stand-alone ASBO was replaced by the 2014 civil injunctions, Anti-social Behaviour, Crime and Policing Act 2014 s 1-6. Youth Courts, High Courts and County Courts have the power to issue these civil injunctions. There is also the power to issue interim injunctions under section 7. For a Home Office step-by-step guide, see *Anti-social Behaviour, Crime and Policing Act 2014: Reform of anti-social powers: Statutory guidance for frontline professionals* December 2017 page 28. The document also provides guidance for other anti-social behaviour civil orders. These injunctions are available whatever the age of the offender.[11]
Detention Orders Where an offender is in breach of a civil injunction, the Youth Court may make a Detention Order, Anti-social Behaviour, Crime and Policing Act 2014 Sch 2 para 1. Detention is in youth detention accommodation which means a secure training centre, a Youth Offender Institution or secure accommodation, see para 14 of the same schedule. The Youth Justice Board determines which type of accommodation it will be. The applicant or the defaulter may apply to the Youth Court to revoke the order, see para 15 of the same schedule.
Supervision Orders Where an offender is in breach of a civil injunction, the Youth Court may make a Supervision Order, Anti-social Behaviour, Crime and Policing

[8] As amended by Criminal Justice and Courts Act 2015 Sch 12 paras 8-9
[9] As amended by Criminal Justice and Courts Act 2015 Sch 12 paras 8-9
[10] Anti-social Behaviour, Crime and Policing Act 2014 (Commencement No 7, Saving and Transitional Provisions) Order 2014 2014/2590
[11] Anti-social Behaviour, Crime and Policing Act 2014 s 1(1)

Act 2014 Sch 2 para 1. The test to apply and other provisions are in the Schedule. The court may add a supervision requirement, an activity requirement or a curfew requirement.

Closure notices Anti-social Behaviour, Crime and Policing Act 2014 s 76 enables a police officer or local authority to issue a closure notice. The notice prohibits access to premises specified in the notice. These notices last for 24 or 48 hours depending on the rank of the officer signing them. Anti-social Behaviour, Crime and Policing Act 2014 s 80 provides that when a closure notice has been issued, an application must be made to the Magistrates' Court unless the notice has been cancelled. The court may then make a Closure Order prohibiting access, see section 80. The notices may be for up to three months. The orders can be extended, see section 82. In force 20 October 2014.

For more details about closure notices see *Anti-social Behaviour, Crime and Policing Act 2014: Reform of anti-social powers: Statutory guidance for frontline professionals* December 2017 page 57.

Police issue these notices so the details are not listed in this book. For a case on the ASBO closure notices, see *Smith v Snaresbrook Crown Court* 2008 EWHC 1282 (Admin).

Community Protection Notices and Remedial orders Anti-social Behaviour, Crime and Policing Act 2014 s 43 enables police and local authorities to issue Community Protection Notices. In force 20 October 2014. The notices compel individuals aged 16 or over to do 'specific things' and to stop doing 'specific things'. Failure to comply with the order is a criminal offence. Those convicted of breaching a notice can be given a Remedial Order which requires the defendant to carry out specified work, see section 49. Police may give fixed penalty notices for breaches of Community Protection Notices, see section 52.

For more details about Community Protection Notices see *Anti-social Behaviour, Crime and Policing Act 2014: Reform of anti-social powers: Statutory guidance for frontline professionals* December 2017 page 38.

Out-of-court disposals Anti-social Behaviour, Crime and Policing Act 2014 s 102 enables a police officer, an investigating officer and a 'relevant prosecutor' to order an individual to carry out a particular action.

Public Spaces Protection Orders Anti-social Behaviour, Crime and Policing Act 2014 s 59 enables a local authority to issue a Public Spaces Protection Order which prohibits 'specified things' and requires 'specified things' to be done. Failing to comply with the order is a criminal offence, see section 67, and fixed penalty notices can be issued, see section 68.

For more details about Public Spaces Protection Orders see *Anti-social Behaviour, Crime and Policing Act 2014: Reform of anti-social powers: Statutory guidance for frontline professionals* December 2017 page 47.

ASBO, Breach of see the **CRIMINAL BEHAVIOUR ORDERS/ASBOS: BREACH OF** chapter.

Breach of closure notices, Community Protection Notices and Public Spaces Protection Order *Breach Offences Guideline 2018*, see www.banksr.com Other Matters Guidelines tab, in force 1 October 2018 p 56 says, '**Other breach offences** Where an offence is not covered by a sentencing guideline a court is entitled to use, and may be assisted by, a guideline for an analogous offence subject to differences in the elements of the offences and the statutory maxima. In sentencing [for a breach of closure notices, Community Protection Notices and Public Spaces Protection Order], the court should refer to the sentencing approach in step one of the guideline for breach of a Criminal Behaviour Order [see **26.17**] to determine culpability and harm, and determine an appropriate sentence bearing in mind the maximum penalty for the offence.'

Existing ASBOs The repeal does not affect existing ASBOs. This is provided by Anti-social Behaviour, Crime and Policing Act 2014 s 33(1)(b)-(c) and 2(a). Individual Support Orders continue to be in force, Anti-social Behaviour, Crime and Policing Act 2014 s 33(1)(b)-(c) and 2(b).

Varying and discharging ASBOs and Individual Support Orders

2.2 ***Statutory power to vary etc. ASBOs***

Crime and Disorder Act 1998 s 1CA(1) An offender subject to an [ASBO] may apply to the court which made it for it to be varied or discharged.
Crime and Disorder Act 1998 s 1CA(3) The Director of Public Prosecutions may apply to the court which made an [ASBO] for it to be varied or discharged.
(4) A relevant authority may also apply to the court which made an [ASBO] for it to be varied or discharged if it appears to it that:
 (a) in the case of variation, the protection of relevant persons from antisocial acts by the person subject to the order would be more appropriately effected by a variation of the order,
 (b) in the case of discharge, that it is no longer necessary to protect relevant persons from antisocial acts by him by means of such an order.
Note: The section is specifically repealed by Anti-social Behaviour, Crime and Policing Act 2014 Sch 11 para 24 and by Anti-social Behaviour, Crime and Policing Act 2014 (Commencement No 7, Saving and Transitional Provisions) Order 2014 2014/2590 para 3(g)(iii)(dd). However, the saving provisions at para 4 keep the sections in force for orders whose proceedings commenced before the repeal. Ed.

2.3 ***Statutory power to vary etc. Individual Support Orders***

Crime and Disorder Act 1998 s 1AB(6) On an application made by complaint by:
 (a) the person subject to an Individual Support Order, or
 (b) the responsible officer,
the court which made the Individual Support Order may vary or discharge it by a further order.
(7) If the Anti-social Behaviour Order as a result of which an Individual Support Order was made is varied, the court varying the Anti-social Behaviour Order may by a further order vary or discharge the Individual Support Order.

2.4 ***Applications to vary/discharge and service of material***

Procedure The rules are set out in Criminal Procedure Rules 2015 2015/1490 Rule 31.5(2), see **84.105**.
Crime and Disorder Act 1998 s 1CA(2) If [the offender] does [apply to vary the ASBO] he must also send written notice of his application to the Director of Public Prosecutions.
Crime and Disorder Act 1998 s 1CA(5) If the Director of Public Prosecutions or a relevant authority applies for the variation or discharge of an [ASBO], he or it must also send written notice of the application to the person subject to the order.
(6) In the case of an [ASBO] made by a Magistrates' Court, the references in subsections (1), (3) and (4) to the court by which the order was made include a reference to any Magistrates' Court acting in the same local justice area as that court.

2.5 ***Need there be a fresh antisocial act?***

James v Birmingham City Council 2010 EWHC 282 (Admin) There is no basis for saying that a variation requires the establishment of a fresh antisocial act. Frequently, ASBOs will be varied to reflect a change in circumstance which is wholly unrelated to the commission of any fresh antisocial act, such as, say, a defendant may obtain a job in the forbidden area or in circumstances where he will inevitably have contact with someone with whom he should not associate. No antisocial act need be established to justify the variation. There is in principle no basis for treating an extension of duration of the order any differently from any other terms.

3 Appeals: Basic Principles

3.1
Court Martial appeals See the **Court Martial** chapter at **24.18.**
High Court appeals This topic is not dealt with in this book as it is a specialist area that is rarely used for sentence appeals. Ed.

3.2 ***Campaigns, petitions etc.***
Att-Gen's Ref Nos 24 and 45 of 1994 1995 16 Cr App R (S) 583 LCJ The Court considered prosecution appeals in two death by dangerous driving cases. Held. This Court cannot be persuaded by campaigns or by clamour to pass extremely long sentences where the criminality of the offender does not justify it. The Court is primarily concerned with the criminality of the person who has caused the death.

Disparity

3.3 ***Disparity General principles/Test to apply***
R v Weekes and Others 1980 2 Cr App R (S) 377 LCJ Various defendants were convicted of, or pleaded to, robbery and related offences. They received 12, 7 and 6 years in all. One received 12 months. Held. That was 'a ridiculously light sentence'. The court should ask not only whether the defendants labour under a sense of grievance, but whether there is justification for that grievance. In this case, [the difference] forms no basis for an argument based on disparity.
R v Fawcett and Others 1983 5 Cr App R (S) 158 A number of defendants pleaded to robbery and burglary. All but H were sentenced. H's case was put back and he was convicted of another offence and sentenced by a different judge. There was nothing to choose between the defendants in terms of record and H had acted at all material times with C. C received 4 years 9 months and H received 2½ years. Held. The sentences passed upon the defendants excluding H were in principle correct. We apply the *R v Pitson* 1972 56 Cr App R (S) 391 test, "whether right-thinking members of the public would consider that something had gone wrong with the administration of justice", such that a sentence should be reduced. H and C ought plainly to have received the same sentence. That required the other sentences to be reduced also.
R v Lowe 1989 The Times News 14/11/89 Disparity arguments were often misconceived. The correct consideration is not whether the defendant feels aggrieved by his sentence, but whether the public, viewing the various sentences, would perceive that the defendant had suffered an injustice. We uphold the sentence.
R v Martin and Others 2012 EWCA Crim 1908 What is completely clear is that apparent leniency to one offender is no ground for reducing a proper sentence on another.
R v Dyer and Others 2013 EWCA Crim 2114, 2014 2 Cr App R (S) 11 (p 61) Different judges at different times sentenced 28 defendants for street supply of drugs in Soho. Held. Right-thinking members of the public would not expect judges to be bound by out-of-line sentences imposed by other judges.
R v Saliuka 2014 EWCA Crim 1907 D was convicted of possessing class A and B drugs with intent to supply and other charges. Following a *Goodyear* indication D's co-defendant H, on a plea, received "an incredibly lenient" 3 years 7 months. D received 7 years. On appeal the defence relied on disparity. Held. The logical extension to the defendant's argument is that if an unduly lenient sentence was passed upon one [defendant], that requires the court to pass an unduly lenient sentence upon another offender. Right-thinking members of the public would then rightly think that something had gone wrong with the administration of justice. One sentencing error is not cured by making another. Disparity is an argument often deployed in this court but it seldom succeeds. Undue leniency shown to H is no reason for reducing a perfectly proper and otherwise entirely appropriate sentence passed upon D.
R v Wilson 2017 EWCA Crim 1860, 2018 1 Cr App R (S) 25 (p 172) D pleaded to burglary. He was sentenced to 2 years 9 months. Ten days before D was sentenced his

co-defendant, C, pleaded[12] to burglary and received 17 months. D was aged 22 and had 16 convictions but none for burglary. He was in breach of a community order (3 months consecutive, no appeal). C was aged 21 and had convictions for possessing cannabis and being drunk and disorderly. He was in breach of a conditional discharge. Both had pleaded at the pre-trial and preparation hearing. The two Judges described the offending in similar terms. Held. There was nothing to distinguish their roles. Disparity is rarely a successful ground of appeal. The fact that C seems to have received an unexpectedly lenient sentence would not on its own be a ground of appeal for D. A high test has to be met before this Court will intervene but it is met here. We substitute 2 years 3 months.

R v Anderson and Black 2018 EWCA Crim 482 B pleaded to historical sex offences. On appeal it was argued that his sentence was in disparity with those of two other co-defendants, H and M. Held. This Court has frequently indicated its dislike of grounds advanced solely on the basis of disparity, especially disparity with another offender sentenced on another indictment on another occasion by another judge, as in the case of M. The sole statutory test for this Court is whether a sentence was wrong in principle or manifestly excessive.

Note: Disparity arguments are most likely to succeed when both sentences are within the appropriate range and there is nothing to explain the difference between them. Ed.

3.4 *Disparity Cases*

R v Planten 2017 EWCA Crim 1807, 2018 1 Cr App R (S) 24 (p 167) D was convicted of a drugs conspiracy. He was sentenced to 11 years. There were 17 importations of drugs and on one occasion the importation of firearms and ammunition. [There were at least 21 counts on the indictment.] D was involved with six importations. Held. We estimate the weight of cannabis imported was 1,800 kilos. It was argued that the sentence was disparate with the main player. para 30 When sentencing for a number of co-conspirators, all of whom had different roles and not all of whom are to be sentenced for the counts, it is very dangerous for this Court to intervene in a careful calibration of sentences as between counts and as between co-conspirators. That is particularly the case when the judge presided over a long trial. It is [also] very dangerous for this Court to draw inferences from sentences which are passed by the sentencing judge on counts which are not the lead count. We therefore dismiss this appeal.

R v James 2018 EWCA Crim 2724 D was convicted of possession of a firearm and ammunition with intent to endanger life. C was under police surveillance. He took a taxi to a block of flats, which was the address of D's grandmother. He told the taxi to wait, went inside for a few minutes then returned to the taxi, which drove off. The taxi was stopped by police a minute later and C was found to be carrying a .41 Long Colt six-shot single-action army revolver. It was loaded with four rounds of live ammunition. The defence argued that the starting point of 15 years was too high when compared to the 12-year starting point of C's sentence. Held. The disparity point cannot be dismissed on the basis that C was dealt with leniently. 15 years was undoubtedly severe but that does not mean that we would have upheld the complaint that it was manifestly excessive. A person who holds and stores a gun may be (but will not necessarily be) more culpable than a courier. However, we can see no obvious justification for the significantly higher starting point for D. **12 years** not 15.

For more detail, see **262.27** in Volume 2.

3.5 *Disparity Foreign sentences*

R v O'Shea 1985 The Times News 2/12/85 LCJ Where an apparently disparate sentence is imposed in a different jurisdiction, the Court of Appeal could not take it into account when considering an appeal against sentence. The rules about disparity did not apply.

[12] The judgment first says he was convicted of the offence and later it says he pleaded. The first statement must be wrong.

3.6 *Reasons for co-defendant's sentence, Judge not obliged to ascertain*
R v Broadbridge 1983 5 Cr App R (S) 269 D was sentenced subsequent to his co-defendant, E. The Judge refused to familiarise himself with the reasons for E's sentence. Held. The Judge must deal with the person before him allowing such favourable circumstances as there are. The Judge is not obliged to adjourn the case to ascertain the details of the sentence for a co-defendant.

4 APPEALS: COURT OF APPEAL

4.1 *Statistics*

	Oct 2010 to Sep 2011	Oct 2011 to Sep 2012	Oct 2012 to Sep 2013	Oct 2013 to Sep 2014	Oct 2014 to Sep 2015	Oct 2015 to Sep 2016	Oct 2016 to Sep 2017
Applications received	5,481	5,711	5,156	4,706	4,518	4,072	3,788
Granted by single judge	1,063	1,199	1,053	1,213	980	647	668
% granted	18.9%	20.9%	25%	25.8%	21.7%	15.9%	17.6%
Refused by single judge	2,454	2,921	2,868	2,628	2,251	1,774	1,823
Renewed applications	607	735	785	678	614	498	520
Full court allows renewal	425	413	321	9%	9%	n/a	n/a
Appeals allowed	1,386	1,328	1,121	1,016	997	924	797
% of appeals received which were allowed	24.6%	23.3%	32.0%	28.0%	29.0%	22.7%	21.0%
Appeals dismissed	687	673	519	566	427	370	386

For these statistics and for the statistics for conviction appeals, see www.banksr.com Other Matters Statistics tab.

4.2 *Duty of advocate to advise*
Guide to Commencing Proceedings in the Court of Appeal 2018 A1 **Advice and Assistance** A1-1. Provision for advice and assistance on appeal is included in the trial representation order issued by the Crown Court. Solicitors should not wait to be asked for advice by the defendant. Immediately following the conclusion of the case, the legal representatives should see the defendant and advocates should express orally a view as to the prospects of a successful appeal (whether against conviction or sentence or both). If there are reasonable grounds, grounds of appeal should be drafted, signed and sent to instructing solicitors as soon as possible, bearing in mind the time limits that apply to lodging an appeal (see section A6. **Time Limits** [at **4.14**]). Solicitors should immediately send a copy of the documents received from the advocate to the defendant.

4.3 *Duty to advise and costs*
Practice Direction (Costs in Criminal Proceedings) 2015 EWCA Crim 1568 para 8.5 If it appears that the defendant was never given advice, the Crown Court should direct the litigator's attention to this fact and if there is no satisfactory explanation as to why no

advice was sent, the determining officer should bear this in mind when determining the litigator's costs and should draw the litigator's attention to the *Guide to Commencing Proceedings in the Court of Appeal 2008*. [Now with a 2018 edition]
Note: How this can be implemented is far from clear. Ed.

Opportunity to ask for leave to appeal

4.4 ***Opportunity to ask for leave to appeal* Statutory provision**
Appeal against sentence following conviction on indictment.
Criminal Appeal Act 1968 s 9(1) A person who has been convicted of an offence on indictment may appeal to the Court of Appeal against any sentence (not being a sentence fixed by law) passed on him for the offence, whether passed on his conviction or in subsequent proceedings.
(1A) see **4.6**.
(2) A person who on conviction on indictment has also been convicted of a summary offence under Crime and Disorder Act 1998 Sch 3 para 6 (power of Crown Court to deal with summary offence where person sent for trial for indictable-only offence) may appeal to the Court of Appeal against any sentence passed on him for the summary offence (whether on his conviction or in subsequent proceedings) under subsection (7) of that section[13] or sub-paragraph (4) of that paragraph.
Appeal against sentence in other cases dealt with at assizes or quarter sessions.
Criminal Appeal Act 1968 s 10(1) This section has effect for providing rights of appeal against sentence when a person is dealt with by the Crown Court (otherwise than on appeal from a Magistrates' Court) for an offence of which he was not convicted on indictment.
(2) The proceedings from which an appeal against sentence lies under this section are those where an offender convicted of an offence by a Magistrates' Court:
(a) is committed by the court to be dealt with for his offence before the Crown Court, or
(b) having been given a suspended sentence or made the subject of:
(i) an order for conditional discharge,
(ii) a Youth Rehabilitation Order [see **119.1**], or
(iii) a community order [see **15.1**],
appears or is brought before the Crown Court to be further dealt with for the offence.
(3) An offender dealt with for an offence before the Crown Court in a proceeding to which subsection (2) of this section applies may appeal to the Court of Appeal against any sentence passed on him for the offence by the Crown Court.
(4) For the purposes of subsection (3)(a)[14] of this section and section 11, any two or more sentences are to be treated as passed in the same proceeding if:
(a) they are passed on the same day, or
(b) they are passed on different days but the court in passing any one of them states that it is treating that one together with the other or others as substantially one sentence,
and consecutive terms of imprisonment or detention and terms which are wholly or partly concurrent are to be treated as a single term.
(5) [Not listed as it deals with an order which was repealed by Criminal Justice Act 1988.]

4.5 ***Opportunity to ask for leave to appeal* Test to apply**
Criminal Appeal Act 1968 s 11(3) On an appeal against sentence, the Court of Appeal, if they consider that the appellant should be sentenced differently for an offence for which he was dealt with by the court below, may: a) quash any sentence or order which is the subject of the appeal, [and substitute another.]
For the full section, see **4.69**.

[13] Subsection (7) has in fact been repealed. The retention of the phrase 'under subsection 7' appears to be a parliamentary error.
[14] This subsection has been repealed.

Note: It could be argued that the ground of appeal should be 'the applicant should be sentenced differently' with particulars listed. However, the Court of Appeal's approach is to consider whether 'the sentence was wrong in principle or manifestly excessive'. One statement of this principle is at *R v H* 2015 EWCA Crim 1579 para 27. The principle is in tens of thousands of cases. Ed.

4.6 ***Opportunity to ask for leave to appeal Murder***
Criminal Appeal Act 1968 s 9(1) A person who has been convicted of an offence on indictment may appeal to the Court of Appeal against any sentence (not being a sentence fixed by law) passed on him for the offence, whether passed on his conviction or in subsequent proceedings.
(1A) In subsection (1) of this section, the reference to a sentence fixed by law does not include a reference to an order made under Criminal Justice Act 2003 s 269(2) [fixing the minimum term] or (4) [whole life orders] in relation to a life sentence (as defined in section 277 of that Act) that is fixed by law.
R v Lichniak 2001 EWHC 294 (Admin) D and others appealed their mandatory life sentences on the basis that they were incompatible with European Convention on Human Rights arts 3 and 5. Held. It is not easy to see how, in the Court of Appeal, we can have jurisdiction because the sentence is 'fixed by law'. An appeal to the Divisional Court would be barred by Senior Courts Act 1981 s 29(3) as the matter 'relates to trial on indictment'. The most attractive route to jurisdiction is to have resort to Human Rights Act 1998 s 3(1), which requires us to read and give effect to Human Rights Act 1998 s 9(1) in a way which is compatible with Convention rights. If a statutory provision which requires the imposition of a sentence of life imprisonment is incompatible with the Convention then, at least until Parliament has had the opportunity to consider its response to the Court's declaration of incompatibility, the sentence is not for the purposes of section 9(1) of the 1968 Act fixed by law, alternatively the exclusion of sentences fixed by law is itself subject to an implied exception where the statutory provision fixing the sentence is incompatible with the Convention. Accordingly, we hold that this Court, sitting as a division of the Court of Appeal, has jurisdiction to entertain these matters as appeals against sentence, since they raise arguable issues as to the compatibility of section 1 of the 1965 Act with the Convention.
Note: So generally, it is not possible to appeal a mandatory order but it is possible to appeal minimum terms and whole life orders. Ed.

4.7 ***Prosecution ability to appeal***
R v Boggild and Others 2011 EWCA Crim 1928, 2012 1 Cr App R (S) 81 (p 457) The Crown has no general right of appeal against sentence, except where unusually it has been provided by statute.
Note: The prosecution can appeal about the following sentencing matters:[15]

(a) Attorney-General's references (leave required), see the **ATTORNEY-GENERAL'S REFERENCES** chapter.
(b) Confiscation orders (both failure to make and generally) (no leave required[16]), but not reconsideration of benefit and not prison in default orders.[17]
(c) Failure of the Court to make a Football Banning Order (no leave required), see **60.49**.
(d) Serious Crime Prevention Orders[18] (leave required[19]). Ed.

4.8 ***'Sentence'? What is a***
Meaning of "sentence".

[15] There may be others.
[16] Proceeds of Crime Act 2002 s 31
[17] *R v Mills* 2018 EWCA Crim 944, 2 Cr App R (S) 32 (p 231)
[18] Serious Crime Act 2007 s 24(1)(b) with the definition in Serious Crime Act 2007 s 10(4)
[19] Serious Crime Act 2007 s 24(3)

Criminal Appeal Act 1968 s 50(1) In this Act "sentence", in relation to an offence, includes any order made by a court when dealing with an offender including, in particular:

(a) a Hospital Order under Mental Health Act 1983 Part III, with or without a Restriction Order,
(b) an Interim Hospital Order under that Part,
(bb) a hospital direction and a limitation direction under that Part,
(c) a recommendation for deportation,
(ca) a confiscation order under Proceeds of Crime Act 2002 Part 2,
(cb) an order which varies a confiscation order made under Proceeds of Crime Act 2002 Part 2 if the varying order is made under section 21, 22 or 29 of that Act (but not otherwise),
(d) a confiscation order under Drug Trafficking Act 1994 other than one made by the High Court,
(e) a confiscation order under Criminal Justice Act 1988 Part VI,
(f) an order varying a confiscation order of a kind which is included by virtue of paragraph (d) or (e) above,
(g) an order made by the Crown Court varying a confiscation order which was made by the High Court by virtue of Drug Trafficking Act 1994 s 19,
(h) a declaration of relevance, within the meaning of Football Spectators Act 1989 s 23, and
(i) an order under Licensing Act 2003 s 129(2) (forfeiture or suspension of personal licence).

(1A) Powers of Criminal Courts (Sentencing) Act 2000 s 14 (under which a conviction of an offence for which an order for a conditional or absolute discharge is made is deemed not to be a conviction except for certain purposes) shall not prevent an appeal under this Act, whether against conviction or otherwise.

50(2) [see **4.78**].

50(3) An order relating to a requirement to make a payment under regulations under Legal Aid, Sentencing and Punishment of Offenders Act 2012 s 23 or 24[20] is not a sentence for the purposes of this Act.

4.9 *Defendant absconds*

R v Okedare 2014 EWCA Crim 228 D and others absconded either before or during their trials. The Court considered the existing authorities about appeals from defendants who had absconded. Held. There are no different rules for conviction and sentence appeals. para 18 First we consider the **application for leave stage**. para 21 The lawyer, whose duty is to act in the best interests of their client, should not generally advance an appeal on a client's behalf without authority. When he signs a form NG on the applicant's behalf he represents he has authority to appeal (unless he indicates clearly to the contrary). Authority does not have to be express. Authority may be inferred from all the circumstances. para 29 A single judge or the full Court is entitled (but not bound) to conclude that the legal representatives submitting an application for permission have actual or implied authority to do so. Even where the position is clear that an application is launched without instructions, the Court has the power to intervene in the interests of justice. Its most obvious application will be where the court below has imposed an unlawful sentence or lacked jurisdiction. Absconders should not be treated as ineffective *per se*. If the single judge is satisfied there is no authority and the application is not one the Court would wish to entertain, she or he has the power to treat the application as ineffective. However, we would expect orders declaring an application [from an absconder] to be ineffective to be the exception rather than the norm at this stage.

[20] Words substituted by Legal Aid, Sentencing and Punishment of Offenders Act 2012 Sch 5(1) para 3 subject to saving and transitional provisions as specified in SI 2013/534 regs 6-13.

para 36 Next we consider the **renewal stage**. It becomes much harder to infer authority where there is a real risk of [days being added to sentences because the appeal is unmeritorious]. The full Court may well exercise [those] powers or an order for costs. Thus, the lawyer has a duty to his client to advise him of possible, rather than theoretical, consequences of pursuing an application. A lawyer should consider his duties to the client and to the Court very carefully before advancing a renewed application that might have adverse consequences for the client, without clear instructions. However, again, the interests of justice may prevail and there may be cases where the Court is prepared to entertain a renewal application notwithstanding any issue over authority. [But], unless the interests of justice demand a hearing of the merits (for example in the case of an unlawful sentence), the full Court may well treat an application to renew made without instructions as ineffective. Time will continue to run in respect of it. We grant leave in one case, treat another as ineffective, we dismiss three applications on their merits and stay the other one where the defendant might have been trafficked, until the absent defendant can provide certain information.

4.10 *Defendant absconds* *Drafting the grounds*

R v Okedare 2014 EWCA Crim 228 D and others absconded either before or during their trials. Held. para 33 It remains the professional responsibility of the lawyer to highlight the fact that their client has absconded to the Criminal Appeal Office and the single judge. He [or she] must provide a full account of the circumstances of the absconding (with updates if necessary) coupled with an explanation for the basis for the assertion of authority and/or any reason why the Court would wish to entertain the application. The same rules apply for conviction and sentence appeals.
See also the **BAIL OFFENCES** and the **ESCAPE FROM CUSTODY** chapters, and the **CONFISCATION *Defendant absconds*** para at **21.29**.

4.11 *Defendant dies*

Appeals in cases of death.
Criminal Appeal Act 1968 s 44A(1)[21] Where a person has died:

(a) any relevant appeal which might have been begun by him had he remained alive may be begun by a person approved by the Court of Appeal; and

(b) where any relevant appeal was begun by him while he was alive or is begun in relation to his case by virtue of paragraph (a) above or by a reference by the Criminal Cases Review Commission, any further step which might have been taken by him in connection with the appeal if he were alive may be taken by a person so approved.

(2) In this section "relevant appeal" means:

(a) an appeal under section 1, 9, 12 or 15 of this Act; or

(b) an appeal under section 33 of this Act from any decision of the Court of Appeal on an appeal under any of those sections.

(3) Approval for the purposes of this section may only be given to:

(a) the widow or widower or surviving civil partner of the dead person;

(b) a person who is the personal representative (within the meaning of section 55(1)(xi) of the Administration of Estates Act 1925) of the dead person; or

(c) any other person appearing to the Court of Appeal to have, by reason of a family or similar relationship with the dead person, a substantial financial or other interest in the determination of a relevant appeal relating to him.

(4) Except in the case of an appeal begun by a reference by the Criminal Cases Review Commission, an application for such approval may not be made after the end of the period of one year beginning with the date of death.

(5) Where this section applies, any reference in this Act to the appellant shall, where appropriate, be construed as being or including a reference to the person approved under this section.

[21] As inserted by Criminal Appeal Act 1995 s 7(1) and amended by Civil Partnerships Act 2004 Sch 27 para 26.

R v Whelan 1997 Crim LR 659 D was convicted of gross indecency against his daughter. He appealed but then died. His widow sought permission to appeal. Held. The right to ask for the appeal to continue is not limited to where there is a financial interest. The desire to clear someone's name is a legitimate objective, see *R v Kearley* (No 2) 1994 99 Cr App R 335. On the facts, appeal dismissed.
See also: *R v GDM* 2018 EWCA Crim 1287 (An example of approval to continue being granted.)

Which sentences can be appealed?

4.12 ***Sentences imposed on indictment***

Order	Can you appeal?	Authority
Absolute discharge	Yes	Criminal Appeal Act 1968 s 50(1A)
Bind over to come up for judgment	Yes	*R v Williams* 1982 75 Cr App R 378
Bind over to keep the peace	Yes	*R v Atkinson* 1988 10 Cr App R (S) 470[22]
Compensation order	Yes	*R v Thebith* 1970 54 Cr App R 35 and *R v Hayden* 1974 60 Cr App R 304
Conditional discharge	Yes	Criminal Appeal Act 1968 s 50(1A)
Confiscation order Proceeds of Crime Act 2002 Part 2	Yes	Criminal Appeal Act 1968 s 50(1)(ca)
Confiscation order Variation of order if made under POCA 2002 s 21, 22 or 29	Yes	Criminal Appeal Act 1968 s 50(1)(cb)
Confiscation order Criminal Justice Act 1988 Part VI	Yes	Criminal Appeal Act 1968 s 50(1)(e)
Confiscation order Variation of order if made under Criminal Justice Act 1988 Part VI	Yes	Criminal Appeal Act 1968 s 50(1)(f)
Confiscation order Drug Trafficking Act 1994, other than one made by the High Court	Yes	Criminal Appeal Act 1968 s 50(1)(d)
Confiscation order Variation of such order	Yes	Criminal Appeal Act 1968 s 50(1)(f)
Confiscation order Crown Court order varying confiscation order made by High Court under Drug Trafficking Act 1994 s 19[23]	Yes	Criminal Appeal Act 1968 s 50(1)(g)

[22] In this case, the Lord Chief Justice heard an appeal for a defendant who pleaded guilty and appealed his bind over. Further, a bind over would appear to be a sentence for the purposes of Criminal Appeal Act 1968 s 9(1). If one can appeal a bind over to come up for judgment, logically one should be able to appeal a bind over to keep the peace.
[23] This now relates to historical confiscation orders.

Order	Can you appeal?	Authority
Confiscation order Determination of extent of defendant's interest in property[24]	No	Criminal Appeal Act 1968 s 50(1)(ca) as inserted by Serious Crime Act 2015 Sch 4 para 3
Costs, Prosecution order to pay	Yes	*R v Hayden* 1974 60 Cr App R 304
Deferment of sentence	Yes	*R v L (Deferred Sentence)* 1999 2 Cr App R (S) 7
Football Spectators Act 1989 Declaration of relevance	Yes	Criminal Appeal Act 1968 s 50(1)(h)
Deportation, Recommendations for	Yes	Criminal Appeal Act 1968 s 50(1)(c)
Financial Reporting Order	Yes	*R v Adams* 2008 EWCA Crim 914
Football Spectators Act 1989 Declaration of relevance	Yes	Criminal Appeal Act 1968 s 50(1)(h)
Forfeiture order	Yes	*R v Menocal* 1979 69 Cr App R 148
Hospital Order	Yes	Criminal Appeal Act 1968 s 50(1)(a)
Hospital Order, Interim	Yes	Criminal Appeal Act 1968 s 50(1)(b)
Hospital direction and Limitation direction[25]	Yes	Criminal Appeal Act 1968 s 50(1)(bb)
Legal aid contribution, Court order to pay, Legal Aid, Sentencing and Punishment of Offenders Act 2012 s 23-24	No	Criminal Appeal Act 1968 s 50(1)(3)
Life sentences (murder only) (other than minimum term order and whole life orders)	No	Criminal Appeal Act 1968 s 9(1), see **4.6**
Life sentences (discretionary)	Yes	Criminal Appeal Act 1968 s 9(1)
Life sentences (minimum term/whole life orders)	Yes	Criminal Appeal Act 1968 s 9(1) and (1A) *R v Dalton* 1995 2 Cr App R 340
Restitution Order[26]	No Yes[27]	*R v Thebith* 1970 54 Cr App R 35 *R v Hayden* 1974 60 Cr App R 304
Victim surcharge	Yes	*R v Hackney* 2013 EWCA Crim 1156, 2014 1 Cr App R (S) 41 (p 235)

For Criminal Appeal Act 1968 s 50(1) see **4.8**.

Time limits

4.13 *Statutory time limit/Extending time limits*

Initiating procedure.

Criminal Appeal Act 1968 s 18(1) A person who wishes to appeal to the Court of Appeal, or to obtain the leave of that court to appeal, shall give notice of appeal or notice of application for leave to appeal.

---

[24] Inserted by Serious Crime Act 2015 s 1. In force 1/6/15, Serious Crime Act 2015 (Commencement No 1) Regulations 2015 2015/820 para 3.

[25] This is also known as a Hybrid Order, see **67.41**.

[26] Clarification is awaited.

[27] This was said to be because it was dependent on conviction and because of Powers of Criminal Courts (Sentencing) Act 2000 s 149(3)(b).

(2) Notice of appeal etc. shall be given within 28 days from the date on which sentence was passed or, in the case of an order made or treated as made on conviction, from the date of the making of the order.
(3) The time for giving notice under this section may be extended, either before or after it expires, by the Court of Appeal.
Powers of Criminal Courts (Sentencing) Act 2000 s 155(6) For the purposes of:
(a) Criminal Appeal Act 1968 s 18(2) (time limit for notice of appeal or of application for leave to appeal), and
(b) Criminal Justice Act 1988 Sch 3 para 1 (time limit for notice of an application for leave to refer a case under section 36),
the sentence or other order shall be regarded as imposed or made on the day on which it is varied under this section.

4.14 ***Extension of time, Applications for***
Criminal Procedure Rules 2015 2015/1490 Rule 36.4 A person who wants an extension of time within which to serve a notice or make an application must:
(a) apply for that extension of time when serving that notice or making that application, and
(b) give the reasons for the application for an extension of time.
Guide to Commencing Proceedings in the Court of Appeal 2018 A6 **Time Limits** para A6-1. Notice and grounds should be lodged within 28 days from the date of conviction, sentence, verdict, finding or decision that is being appealed (s. 18 Criminal Appeal Act 1968 and CrimPR 39.2(1)). On a reference by the CCRC, Form NG and grounds should be served on the Registrar not more than 28 days after the Registrar has served notice that the CCRC has referred a conviction or sentence (CrimPR 39.2 (2)).
A6-2. Where sentences were passed on different dates there may be two appeals against sentence. For example, there may be an appeal against a custodial term and an appeal against a confiscation order (*R v Neal* 1992 2 Cr App R (S) 352).
A6-3. An application for an extension of the 28 day period in which to give notice of an application must always be supported by details of the delay and the reasons for it (*R v Wilson* [2016] EWCA Crim 65). Often a chronology will assist. It is not enough merely to tick the relevant box on the Form NG.
A6-4. For out of time applications based on a change in law see A5-3. Above [Re convictions mainly not listed] .
A6-5. Applications for an extension of time should be submitted when the application for leave to appeal against either conviction or sentence is made and not in advance. Notwithstanding the terms of s18 (3) Criminal Appeal Act 1968, it has long been the practice of the Registrar to require the extension of time application to be made at the time of service of the notice and grounds of appeal. This practice is now reflected in CrimPR 36.4 and 39.3(2)(h)(ii).
Hamilton and Another v R 2012 UKPC 31, 2013 1 Cr App R 13 (p 205) Privy Council In 2001, D1 and D2 were convicted of murder in Jamaica and were sentenced to life imprisonment, with a 25-year term. In 2003, they sought leave to appeal their convictions and sentences from the Court of Appeal of Jamaica but this was rejected. In 2011, D1 and D2 finally lodged an appeal. [The delay appears primarily due to the difficulty in obtaining pro bono lawyers to act and the restrictions placed on prisoners in using telephones and writing materials.] Held. Imposing time limits does not infringe ECHR, if the very essence of the right to a fair hearing [is] not impaired. The time limit restriction pursued a legitimate aim, and it was proportionate. A flexible approach was seen to be particularly necessary for Caribbean cases. As a general rule, the longer the delay, the more convincing and weighty the explanation will need to be. The test is the interests of justice test. Weight will always be given to the severity of the sentence and the appeal's merit and the more likely it appears that a defendant has suffered a grave

miscarriage of justice, the less likely an application will be rejected as being out of time. Here, because of the very long periods of imprisonment and there being sufficient merit, we grant leave.

R v Bestel and Others 2013 EWCA Crim 1305, 2014 1 Cr App R (S) 53 (p 312) B, R and D applied to appeal their confiscation orders out of time following the decision in *R v Waya* 2012 UKSC 51, 2013 2 Cr App R (S) 20 (p 87). The court considered an extensive selection of precedents. Held. para 9 An extension of time will generally be granted by the single judge when the applicant provides a satisfactory explanation for missing the deadline by a narrow margin and there appears to be merit in the grounds of appeal. This may be because counsel or solicitors were at fault and the applicant personally was not. The court has been more likely in recent times to permit an extension of time where a co-accused's appeal has been allowed on grounds which apply equally to the applicant but the applicant was erroneously advised that no grounds existed. An extension of time is likely to be granted in cases where relevant and cogent fresh evidence admitted under section 23 of the 1968 Act has emerged for the first time well after conviction. Nonetheless, evidence as to the circumstances in which the fresh evidence emerged will be required and prompt action thereafter will be expected, *R v Gogana* 1999 The Times News 12/07/1999 and *R v James* 2000 Crim LR 571. Long periods of delay will require cogent explanation. Because B had applied for an order of rescission and his failure to lodge an appeal against sentence was largely the result of administrative naivety rather than neglect, we grant leave. R and D's applications are refused.

R v Thorsby and Others 2015 EWCA Crim 1, 1 Cr App R (S) 63 (p 443) All the defendants appealed the failure to give them credit, under Criminal Justice Act 2003 s 240A, for half of the time they had spent on a qualifying curfew. All their appeals were out of time, none due to the defendants' fault. The number of days was substantial. As soon as the defendants became aware of the entitlement their legal advisors were told. Held. Neither Criminal Appeal Act 1968 nor the [Criminal Procedure] Rules limit the discretion of the Court on the issue whether an extension of time should be granted. The principled approach to extensions of time is that the Court will grant an extension if it is in the interests of justice to do so. However, there are several components that contribute to the interests of justice. The Court will have in mind finality, the interests of the [parties], the efficient use of resources and good administration. The public interest also critically embraces the justice of the case and the liberty of the individual. In none of these tag cases is it suggested that the interval between discovery and the application for leave was excessive. If a significant number of days was due, it would be right in principle to refuse an extension of time by reason only if the proportion that those days bear to the total sentence imposed.[28] Where there is no good reason why the time limits were not complied with, the Court is unlikely to grant an extension unless injustice would be caused in consequence. The merits of the underlying grounds will be examined. The judgment is judicial and not merely administrative.

In the Court's experience, this Court is likely to extend time limits to correct an error of law once the error is discovered whether the fault lies in the failure of representatives to advise the Court or in the failure of the Court itself. The practice of the Court is generally to refuse a long extension of time unless injustice would be caused by refusal. It is improbable that a long extension of time would be granted on the ground that the sentence imposed was manifestly excessive, particularly when the defendant has already received competent advice to the effect that it was not. The Court will be more likely closely to examine the merits of an out of time appeal when it is argued that some principle of law or legal requirement has been ignored or overlooked.

para 16 In each of the present cases, the Crown Court failed to perform its duty under section 240A (as to which it has no discretion, since the section is mandatory in its terms), partly because of the neglect of the advocates on both sides and partly because it

[28] Perhaps this means that the Court will not grant leave when the sentence to be served is long and tag day figure is small.

failed to obtain or apply the information relevant to the applicant's case. While we embrace the demand that advocates and those instructing them must perform their professional duty to the Court, we do not consider that the failure of the advocates to perform that duty can absolve the Crown Court from its statutory responsibility to give the credit required. It follows, in our view, that when the statutory duty of the Crown Court is not performed, the error in sentencing is not one of judicial assessment but one of law and of principle: a defendant, on whom no statutory duty has been placed, has been deprived of his statutory right to have his days on qualifying curfew and his credit period calculated. In the ordinary way, errors of principle or law in sentencing occur rarely and it is our experience that, when they are clear and the applicant bears no responsibility for the failure, this court is likely to take steps to correct the error even when a significant extension of time is required to achieve it. However, when the applicant, with knowledge of the error, fails to act with due diligence to make the application for an extension of time the position is likely to be different. In those circumstances, the applicant cannot be heard to complain that he has been kept out of his remedy for an error in the performance of the Court's duty that he is entitled to expect will be corrected when discovered.

para 18 Where the passage of time has obscured the entitlement itself, and the problem cannot be solved by drawing appropriate inferences in favour of the applicant, the full court may refuse the extension or grant the extension but refuse leave or dismiss the appeal. One or more of the cases considered by the Court in *R v Leacock and Others* 2013 EWCA Crim 1994, 2014 2 Cr App R (S) 12 (p 72) demonstrates that a substantial passage of time may put the Court in difficulty in resolving whether or not an error has occurred and if so to what extent. In those circumstances, the Court may not be able to conclude that it would be in the interests of justice to intervene.

R v Wilson 2016 EWCA Crim 65 LCJ In 2005, D was convicted of murder. D consulted a number of solicitors about an appeal. In 2015, an application for leave to appeal was lodged. Held. In cases of this kind, this Court must receive details of the delay and an explanation for it. Here, none of the history was set out. That was a clear breach of counsel's duty. This case is a paradigm example of where the process of this Court has been abused. This case has no merit. Application refused.

See also: *R v Hawkins* 1997 1 Cr App R 234 (LCJ The court has traditionally been reluctant [to extend the time limits] save where the extension sought is relatively short and good reason is shown for the failure to apply in time.) *R v Bailey* 2013 EWCA Crim 512 (Defendant received 9-year sentence. Convicted of other matters. Unclear whether the 9 years was an extended sentence. Eleven years later, after the 9-year sentence was served, sentence corrected in line with the sentencing remarks.)

Where the law changes see the **Change in Sentencing Law** ***Case law changes*** para at **12.9**.

Drafting and amending the advice and grounds: General

4.15 ***Advocate/solicitor duties/Must see the defendant at the conclusion of the case***
Guide to Commencing Proceedings in the Court of Appeal Criminal Division 2018 A **Advice and Assistance** para A1-1. Provision for advice and assistance on appeal is included in the trial representation order issued by the Crown Court. Solicitors should not wait to be asked for advice by the defendant. Immediately following the conclusion of the case, the legal representatives should see the defendant and advocates should express orally a view as to the prospects of a successful appeal (whether against conviction or sentence or both). If there are reasonable grounds, grounds of appeal should be drafted, signed and sent to instructing solicitors as soon as possible, bearing in mind the time limits that apply to lodging an appeal (see section A6, [at **4.14**]. **Time Limits**). Solicitors should immediately send a copy of the documents received from the advocate to the defendant.

R v Welsh 2017 EWCA Crim 2471 We emphasise the critical importance that appeal advice is given at the very earliest opportunity, particularly in the case of short custodial sentences. That D did not receive immediate advice to mount an appeal, if such was the legal advice he was receiving, is truly deplorable.
For more detail, see **4.31**.

4.16 ***Appeal notice/Grounds of appeal, Contents and checklist for***
Form of appeal notice
Criminal Procedure Rules 2015 2015/1490 Rule 39.3(1)[29] An appeal notice must:
(a) specify:
(i) the conviction, verdict, or finding,
(ii) the sentence, or
(iii) the order, or the failure to make an order about which the appellant wants to appeal;
(b) identify each ground of appeal on which the appellant relies (and see paragraph (2));
(c) identify the transcript that the appellant thinks the court will need, if the appellant wants to appeal against a conviction;
(d) identify the relevant sentencing powers of the Crown Court, if sentence is in issue;
(e) include or attach any application for the following, with reasons:
(i) permission to appeal, if the appellant needs the court's permission,
(ii) an extension of time within which to serve the appeal notice,
(iii) bail pending appeal,
(iv) a direction to attend in person a hearing that the appellant could attend by live link, if the appellant is in custody,
(v) the introduction of evidence, including hearsay evidence and evidence of bad character,
(vi) an order requiring a witness to attend court,
(vii) a direction for special measures for a witness,
(viii) a direction for special measures for the giving of evidence by the appellant;
(f) identify any other document or thing that the appellant thinks the court will need to decide the appeal.
(2) The grounds of appeal must:
(a) include in no more than the first two pages a summary of the grounds that makes what then follows easy to understand;
(b) in each ground of appeal identify the event or decision to which that ground relates;
(c) in each ground of appeal summarise the facts relevant to that ground, but only to the extent necessary to make clear what is in issue;
(d) concisely outline each argument in support of each ground;
(e) number each ground consecutively, if there is more than one;
(f) identify any relevant authority and:
(i) state the proposition of law that the authority demonstrates, and
(ii) identify the parts of the authority that support that proposition; and
(g) where the Criminal Cases Review Commission refers a case to the court, explain how each ground of appeal relates (if it does) to the reasons for the reference.
Criminal Practice Directions 2015 EWCA Crim 1567 para IX 39C.2[30] Advocates should not settle grounds unless they consider that they are properly arguable. Grounds should be carefully drafted; the court is not assisted by grounds of appeal which are not properly set out and particularised in accordance with para 39C.3 [not listed]. The grounds must:
(i) be concise; and

[29] As amended by Criminal Procedure (Amendment) Rules 2018 2018/132 para 16(a). In force 2/4/18
[30] As inserted by Criminal Practice Directions 2015 Amendment No 6 2018 para 7.

(ii) be presented in A4 page size and portrait orientation, in not less than 12-point font and in 1.5 line spacing.

Appellants and advocates should keep in mind the powers of the court and the Registrar to return for revision, within a directed period, grounds that do not comply with the rule or with these directions, including grounds that are so prolix or diffuse as to render them incomprehensible. They should keep in mind also the court's powers to refuse permission to appeal on any ground that is so poorly presented as to render it unarguable and thus to exclude it from consideration by the court: see Crim P R 36.14. Should leave to amend the grounds be granted, it is most unlikely that further grounds will be entertained.

39C.3 [Re transcripts in conviction appeals Not listed].

Court of Appeal notes on the NG form 2017 page 3 The grounds of appeal must be attached to this notice of application, and should be listed separately for conviction, sentence, or other order, under appropriate headings.

The grounds of appeal must:

(1) Identify each ground of appeal on which the appellant relies, numbering them consecutively (if there is more than one) and concisely outlining each argument in support;

(2) Identify the transcript that the appellant thinks the court will need, if the appellant wants to appeal against conviction (see notes on Transcripts at **4.55**);

(3) Identify the relevant sentencing powers of the Crown Court, if sentence is in issue;

[Note: This should be done in part by the Court of Appeal table, see **4.15**. Ed.]

(4) Where the Criminal Cases Review Commission has referred a case to the court, explain how each ground of appeal relates (if it does) to the reasons for the reference;

(5) Summarise the relevant facts;

(6) Identify any relevant authorities;

(7) Identify any other document or thing that the appellant thinks the court will need to decide the appeal (Please Note: any report relied upon and which was not retained by the Crown Court must be copied and attached to this application form).

NB: (1) Where grounds have been settled by counsel they must be signed by counsel with the name of counsel printed underneath.

(2) If an extension of time is needed, the detailed reasons for the delay must be attached to the grounds of appeal, preferably under a separate heading – grounds for extension of time.

Guide to Commencing Proceedings in the Court of Appeal 2018 para A3-2. [restates Rule 39.3]

In March 2012, the Registrar wrote a letter [see www.banksr.com Other Matters Other Documents Court of Appeal] saying, 'The Court of Appeal (Crim. Div.) will in future strongly recommend any legal representative drafting grounds of appeal against sentence to incorporate within the grounds the table below setting out the details of the sentence passed.'

Count on indictment	**Offence** *(state statutory provision / common law)*	**Pleaded guilty or convicted**	**Sen-tence**	**Consecutive or concurrent**	**Maximum**
Total sentence					
Minimum term if applicable					

Time to count towards sentence under Criminal Justice Act 2003 s 240 or 240A[31]	
Other relevant orders:	

4.17 ***Advice and grounds to be in one document***
Criminal Practice Directions 2015 EWCA Crim 1567 para IX 39C.1 The Court must be provided with an appeal notice as a single document which sets out the grounds of appeal.
Note: This paragraph was repealed in 2018. However, the Court still requires a single document. Ed.
Guide to Commencing Proceedings in the Court of Appeal 2018 para A3-3. The grounds of appeal should set out the relevant facts and nature of the proceedings concisely in one all-encompassing document, not separate grounds of appeal and advice (CPD IX Appeal 39C).

4.18 ***Grounds must be properly arguable/How to draft***
Criminal Practice Directions 2015 EWCA Crim 1567 para IX 39C.2[32] Advocates should not settle grounds unless they consider that they are properly arguable.
Note: This paragraph was repealed in 2018. However, the Court still requires grounds to be properly arguable. Ed.
Guide to Commencing Proceedings in the Court of Appeal 2018 para A3-4. The intended readership of this document is the Court and not the lay or professional client. Its purpose is to enable the single Judge to grasp quickly the facts and issues in the case. In appropriate cases, draft grounds of appeal may be perfected before submission to the single Judge. A separate list of authorities must be provided which should contain the appellant's name and refer to the relevant paragraph numbers in each authority (CPD XII General Application D1) (see section A8-5).
A3-5. Failure to comply with the requirements in CrimPR 39 and the CPD referred to above, will result in a direction from the Registrar that the defects be remedied prior to the case being allocated to a single Judge. Failure to do so may be brought to the attention of the single Judge and/or full Court and legal representatives may be personally required to explain the reasons for non-compliance.
A3-6. Advocates should not settle or sign grounds unless they consider that they are properly arguable. An advocate should not settle grounds they cannot support because they are "instructed" to do so by a defendant.
R v Morson 1976 62 Cr App R 236 I hope that the Bar will act responsibly before making, in the grounds of appeal or in argument, attacks of this general sweeping character upon a summing-up. If they be justified, it is the duty of the Bar to make them. If they be obviously unjustified, it is the duty of the Bar to refrain from making them.

4.19 ***Citing authorities***
Criminal Practice Directions 2015 EWCA Crim 1567 para XII D.1 [This direction applies to the Court of Appeal, the Crown Court and the Magistrates' Court.]
D.2 [There is an extensive extract from *R v Erskine* 2009, see below.]
D.3 Advocates should only cite cases when it is necessary to do so; when the case identifies or represents a principle or the development of a principle. In sentencing appeals, other cases are rarely helpful, providing only an illustration, and this is especially true if there is a sentencing guideline. Unreported cases should only be cited in exceptional circumstances, and the advocate must expect to explain why such a case has been cited.
D.4 [Not about citing authorities Not listed]

[31] Since the Legal Aid, Sentencing and Punishment of Offenders Act 2012 changes, the relevant section is section 240ZA.
[32] As inserted by Criminal Practice Directions 2015 Amendment No 6 2018 para 7.

D.5 When an authority is to be cited, whether in written or oral submissions, the advocate should always provide the neutral citation followed by the law report reference.
D.6 The following practice should be followed:
i) Where a judgment is reported in the Official Law Reports (A.C., Q.B., Ch., Fam.) published by the Incorporated Council of Law Reporting for England and Wales or the Criminal Appeal Reports or the Criminal Appeal Reports (Sentencing) one of those two series of reports must be cited; either is equally acceptable. However, where a judgment is reported in the Criminal Appeal Reports or the Criminal Appeal Reports (Sentencing), that reference must be given in addition to any other reference. Other series of reports and official transcripts of judgment may only be used when a case is not reported, or not yet reported, in the Official Law Reports or the Criminal Appeal Reports or the Criminal Appeal Reports (Sentencing).
ii) If a judgment is not reported in the Official Law Reports, the Criminal Appeal Reports or the Criminal Appeal Reports (Sentencing), but it is reported in an authoritative series of reports which contains a headnote and is made by individuals holding a Senior Courts qualification (for the purposes of Courts and Legal Services Act 1990 s 115), that report should be cited.
iii) Where a judgment is not reported in any of the reports referred to above, but is reported in other reports, they may be cited.
iv) Where a judgment has not been reported, reference may be made to the official transcript if that is available, not the handed-down text of the judgment, as this may have been subject to late revision after the text was handed down.
D.7 In the majority of cases, it is expected that all references will be to the Official Law Reports and the Criminal Appeal Reports or the Criminal Appeal Reports (Sentencing); it will be rare for there to be a need to refer to any other reports. An unreported case should not be cited unless it contains a relevant statement of legal principle not found in reported authority, and it is expected that this will only occur in exceptional circumstances.
D.8 to D.10 [These paras are about how to provide the authorities and are at **4.49**.]

Provision of copies to the Court of Appeal (Criminal Division)

Criminal Practice Directions 2015 EWCA Crim 1567 para XII D.11 Advocates must provide to the Registrar of Criminal Appeals, with their appeal notice, respondent's notice or skeleton argument, a list of authorities upon which they wish to rely in their written or oral submissions. The list of authorities should contain the name of the applicant, appellant or respondent and the Criminal Appeal Office number where known. The list should include reference to the relevant paragraph numbers in each authority. An updated list can be provided if a new authority is issued, or in response to a respondent's notice or skeleton argument. From time to time, the Registrar may issue guidance as to the style or content of lists of authorities, including a suggested format; this guidance should be followed by all parties. The latest guidance is available from the Criminal Appeal Office.
D.12 If the case cited is reported in the Official Law Reports, the Criminal Appeal Reports or the Criminal Appeal Reports (Sentencing), the law report reference must be given after the neutral citation, and the relevant paragraphs listed, but copies should not be provided to the court.
D.13 If, exceptionally, reference is made to a case that is not reported in the Official Law Reports, the Criminal Appeal Reports or the Criminal Appeal Reports (Sentencing), three copies must be provided to the Registrar with the list of authorities and the relevant appeal notice or respondent's notice (or skeleton argument, if provided). The relevant passages of the authorities should be marked or sidelined.
R v Erskine 2009 EWCA Crim 1425, 2 Cr App R 29 LCJ Only an authority which establishes the principle should be cited. References should not be made to authorities which do no more than either a) illustrate a principle or b) restate it. Where a Sentencing Guidelines Council guideline is available there will rarely be any advantage in citing an

authority reached before the issue of the guideline. Where an authority does no more than uphold the sentence imposed at the Crown Court, the advocate must be ready to explain how it can assist the Court to decide that the sentence is manifestly excessive or wrong in principle.

For how to provide the authorities to the Court, see **4.49**.

4.20 ***Grounds must be properly particularised***

Criminal Practice Directions 2015 EWCA Crim 1567 para IX 39C.2[33] Grounds should be carefully drafted; the court is not assisted by grounds of appeal which are not properly set out and particularised in accordance with CrimPR 39.3.

Guide to Commencing Proceedings in the Court of Appeal Criminal Division 2018 para A3-1. Grounds must be settled with sufficient particularity to enable the Registrar, and subsequently the Court, to identify clearly the matters relied upon. A mere formula such as "the conviction is unsafe" or "the sentence is in all the circumstances too severe" will be deemed ineffective.

4.21 ***Advice and grounds Excessively long***

Criminal Practice Directions 2015 EWCA Crim 1567 para IX D.23[34] [This paragraph contains an extract of *R v James and Selby* 2016, see below. The extract is shorter than the one below so is not reproduced. It then says:] In *Standard Bank PLC v Via Mat International* 2013 EWCA Civ 490, 2013 2 All ER (Comm) 1222 the excessive length of court documents prompted: 'It is important that both practitioners and their clients understand that skeleton arguments are not intended to serve as vehicles for extended advocacy and that in general a short, concise skeleton is both more helpful to the court and more likely to be persuasive than a longer document which seeks to develop every point which the advocate would wish to make in oral argument.' No area of law is exempt from the requirement to produce careful and concise documents: *Tchenquiz v Director of the Serious Fraud Office* 2014 EWCA Civ 1333, 2015 1 WLR 838, para 10.

R v James and Selby 2016 EWCA Crim 65 para 49 S, a litigant in person, lodged many hundreds of pages of repetitive handwritten correspondence, grounds and purported fresh evidence. The Registrar directed him to consolidate his grounds into no more than two or three pages. S's response was to lodge a further 50 pages in respect of conviction and to fail to consolidate 150 pages in respect of sentence. Held. Grounds of Appeal in excess of 100 pages are simply not acceptable. Voluminous grounds are not infrequently (but not always) found when the applicant is a litigant in person. They can be unnumbered, handwritten and settled in a large variety of documents. In *R v Clague* 2015 EWCA Crim 284 a litigant in person had lodged over 1,000 pages of grounds of appeal and been ordered to lodge a summary. The court identified the grounds from that summary document only. Lengthy legal documents offer very little assistance to the Court. In *Tombstone Ltd v Raja* 2008 EWCA Civ 1441 it was said, "Practitioners . . . are well advised to note the risk of the court's negative reaction to unnecessarily long written submissions. An unintended and unfortunate side effect of the growth in written advocacy . . . has been that too many practitioners, at increased cost to their clients and diminishing assistance to the court, burden their opponents and the court with written briefs."

4.22 ***Perfection of grounds of appeal General***

Guide to Commencing Proceedings in the Court of Appeal 2018 A8 **Perfection of grounds of appeal** para A8-1. The purpose of perfection is (a) to save valuable judicial time by enabling the Court to identify at once the relevant parts of the transcript and (b) to give the advocate the opportunity to reconsider the original grounds in the light of the

[33] As inserted by Criminal Practice Directions 2015 Amendment No 6 2018 para 7.

[34] As inserted by Criminal Practice Directions 2015 Amendment No 6 2018 para 9.

transcript. Perfected grounds should consist of a fresh document which supersedes the original grounds of appeal and contains inter alia references by page number and letter (or paragraph number) to all relevant passages in the transcript.

A8-2. In conviction or confiscation appeals, the Registrar will almost certainly invite the advocate to perfect grounds to assist the single Judge or full Court. As a general rule, the advocate will not be invited to perfect the grounds of appeal in a sentence case. Where an advocate indicates a wish to perfect grounds of appeal against sentence, the Registrar will consider the request and will only invite perfection where he considers it necessary for the assistance of the single Judge or full Court.

A8-3. If perfection is appropriate, the advocate will be sent a copy of the transcript and asked to perfect the grounds, usually within 14 days. In the absence of any response from the advocate, the existing notice and grounds of appeal will be placed before the single Judge or the Court without further notice. If an advocate does not wish to perfect the grounds, a note to that effect will ensure that the case is not unnecessarily delayed.

A8-4. If, having considered the transcript, the advocate is of the opinion that there are no valid grounds, the reasons should be set out in a further advice and sent to his instructing solicitors. The Registrar should be informed that this has been done, but the advocate should not send the Registrar a copy of that advice. Solicitors should send a copy to the appellant and obtain instructions, at the same time explaining that if the appellant persists with his application the Court may consider whether to make a loss of time order.

A8-5. Advocates should identify any relevant authorities (CrimPR 39.3(2)(g)) and submit a separate list of authorities with the perfected grounds of appeal and include copies of any unreported authorities. the transcript should be returned with a note to that effect.

4.23 ***Perfection of grounds of appeal Confiscation Grounds no longer exist***
Guide to Commencing Proceedings in the Court of Appeal 2018 para A8-2. In conviction or confiscation appeals, the Registrar will almost certainly invite the advocate to perfect grounds to assist the single Judge or full Court. As a general rule, the advocate will not be invited to perfect the grounds of appeal in a sentence case. Where an advocate indicates a wish to perfect grounds of appeal against sentence, the Registrar will consider the request and will only invite perfection where he considers it necessary for the assistance of the single Judge or full Court.

4.24 ***New advocate Duties of new and former lawyers (including where complaint is made)***
Guide to Commencing Proceedings in the Court of Appeal Criminal Division 2018 A4 **Applications by fresh legal representatives** A4-1 In all cases where fresh solicitors or fresh advocates are instructed, who did not act for the appellant at trial, it is necessary for the fresh solicitors or advocate to approach the solicitors and/or advocate who previously acted to ensure that the facts upon which the grounds of appeal are premised are correct, unless there are exceptional circumstances and good and compelling reasons not to do so. Such exceptional circumstances would likely be very rare (*R v McCook* 2014 EWCA Crim 734, 2016 2 Cr App R 30). Where necessary, further steps should be taken to obtain objective and independent evidence to establish the factual basis for the appeal (*R v Lee* 2014 EWCA Crim 2928). The duty to make proper and diligent enquiries of previous representatives is not restricted to cases where criticism is being made of the trial representatives. It extends to all cases where there are fresh representatives acting (*R v McGill and Others* 2017 EWCA Crim 1228).

A4-2. In cases where fresh representatives seek to adduce fresh evidence that was not adduced at trial, not only will the fresh representatives be required to comply with their duties pursuant to McCook; but the Registrar will usually also instigate the "waiver of privilege" procedure or require written reasons as to why the procedure should not be instigated (*R v Singh* 2017 EWCA Crim 466).

A4-3. Where a ground of appeal by fresh representatives criticises trial advocates and/or trial solicitors and in any other circumstance the Registrar considers necessary as set out above, the Registrar will instigate the waiver of privilege procedure. The appellant will be asked to waive privilege in respect of instructions to and advice at trial from legal representatives. If the appellant does waive privilege, the grounds of appeal are sent to the appropriate trial representative(s) and they are invited to respond. Any response will be sent to the appellant and his fresh legal representatives for comment. All of these documents will be sent to the single Judge when considering the application for leave. If the criticism is implicit, the Registrar may still instigate the procedure or he will refer the decision whether to instigate the procedure to a single Judge (*R v JH* 2014 EWCA Crim 2618). The single Judge may draw inferences from any failure to participate in the process. Waiver of privilege is a procedure that should be instigated by the Registrar and not by fresh legal representatives. However, if it is clear that the procedure will need to be instigated, the fresh representatives should lodge a signed waiver of privilege with the grounds of appeal (and any fresh evidence) but go no further.

R v Achogbuo 2014 EWCA Crim 567 LCJ D appealed. It was later admitted that he had appealed before and the first appeal was misconceived. The second made no mention of the first and suggested that his solicitor was incompetent regarding a no comment interview. It was discovered that the solicitor had in fact properly advised D in interview. Held. The Court expects not only the highest levels of disclosure but also the highest standards from advocates and solicitors. In cases where incompetence of trial advocates is alleged, there is a duty to exercise due diligence and make enquiries of trial lawyers and take other steps to obtain evidence before submitting grounds of appeal. Because the second appeal made no mention of the first, we refer this case to the Solicitors Regulation Authority.

Note: It is assumed that the single Judge refused the first application for leave and so it was not formally dismissed. Ed.

R v Singh 2017 EWCA Crim 466 D, using a new legal team, sought to appeal his conviction. Held. "In any case where fresh solicitors or fresh counsel are instructed, it will henceforth be necessary for those solicitors or counsel to go to the solicitors and/or counsel who have previously acted to ensure that the facts are correct, unless there are, in exceptional circumstances, good and compelling reasons not to do so. It is not necessary for us to enumerate such exceptional circumstances, but we imagine that they will be very rare."

4.25 *Service of appeal notice*

Service of appeal notice

Criminal Procedure Rules 2015 2015/1490 Rule 39.2[35]

39.2. The appellant must serve an appeal notice on the Registrar:

(a) not more than 28 days after:

(i) the conviction, verdict, or finding,

(ii) the sentence,

(iii) the order (subject to paragraph (b)), or the failure to make an order, or

(iv) the minimum term review decision under section 274(3) of, or paragraph 14 of Schedule 22 to, the Criminal Justice Act 2003

about which the appellant wants to appeal;

(b) not more than 21 days after the order in a case in which the appellant appeals against a wasted or third party costs order;

(c) not more than 28 days after the Registrar serves notice that the Criminal Cases Review Commission has referred a conviction to the court.

[35] Criminal Procedure (Amendment No 2) Rules 2018 2018/847 para 11 substituted a new Rule 39.2. In force 1/10/18

[Note. The time limit for serving an appeal notice (a) on an appeal under Part 1 of the Criminal Appeal Act 1968 and (b) on an appeal against a finding of contempt of court is prescribed by sections 18 and 18A of the Criminal Appeal Act 1968. It may be extended, but not shortened.
For service of a reference by the Criminal Cases Review Commission, see rule 39.5.]
Criminal Practice Directions 2015 EWCA Crim 1567 para IX 39C.5[36]

Direct Lodgement

para 39C.5 With effect from 1st October 2018, Forms NG and Grounds of Appeal which are covered by Part 39 of the Criminal Procedure Rules (appeal to the Court of Appeal about conviction or sentence) are to be lodged directly with the Criminal Appeal Office and not with the Crown Court where the appellant was convicted or sentenced. This Practice Direction must be read alongside the detailed guidance notes that have been produced to accompany the new forms.[37]

From this date the Crown Court will no longer accept Forms NG and will return them to the sender. Forms NG and Grounds of Appeal should only be lodged once. They should, where possible, be lodged by email. Applications should not be lodged directly onto the Digital Case System. Applications must be lodged at the following address: criminalappealoffice.applications@hmcts.x.gsi.gov.uk

If you do not have access to an email account, you should post Form NG and the Grounds of Appeal to: The Registrar, Criminal Appeal Office, Royal Courts of Justice, Strand, London WC2A 2LL. Once an application has been effectively lodged, the Registrar will confirm receipt within 7 days.

Service

39C.6 Legal representatives should make sure they provide their secure email address for the purposes of correspondence and service of document.[38] The date of service for new applications lodged by email will be the day on which it is[39] sent, if that day is a business day and if sent no later than 2:30pm on that day, otherwise the date of service will be on the next business day after it was sent.

Completing the Form NG

39C.7 All applications must be compliant with the relevant Criminal Procedure Rules, particularly those in Part 39. A separate Form NG should be completed for each substantive application which is being made. Each application (conviction, sentence and confiscation order) has its own Form NG and must be drafted and lodged as a stand-alone application.

Guide to Commencing Proceedings in the Court of Appeal Criminal Division 2018 A2-2. Following a change in procedure, which comes into force on the 1 October 2018, Form NG, signed grounds of appeal and any such accompanying forms must be lodged directly on the Registrar of Criminal Appeals (CrimPR 39.2). A separate Form NG should be completed for each substantive application which is being made. Each application (conviction, sentence and confiscation order) has its own Form NG and must be drafted and lodged as a stand-alone application (CPD IX Appeal 39C).

A2-3. Electronic service at criminalappealoffice.applications@hmcts.x.gsi.gov.uk is encouraged, with large attachments being sent in clearly marked separate emails. Service will be accepted by post at the Criminal Appeal Office, Royal Courts of Justice, Strand, London, WC2A 2LL. Representatives must not lodge Form NG and grounds of appeal on to the Digital Case System (DCS), as this will not alert the Criminal Appeal Office ("CAO") and service will not be effected. However, should the grounds of appeal rely upon trial documents that are already uploaded to the DCS, advocates are encouraged to identify the location of the document on the DCS in their grounds of appeal, which can

[36] As inserted by Criminal Practice Directions 2015 Amendment No 7 2018 EWCA Crim 1760
[37] See www.banksr.com Other Matters Other Documents Criminal Practice Directions and www.banksr.com Other Matters Other Documents Court of Appeal
[38] Perhaps the author meant 'documents'.
[39] Perhaps the author meant 'they are'.

then be obtained by the CAO. If Form NG and grounds of appeal are lodged with the Crown Court on or after the 1 October 2018, service will not be effected and the Crown Court will send the documents back to the representatives.

A2-4. Direct Lodgment on the Registrar of Criminal Appeals applies to all applications to appeal conviction, sentence and confiscation falling within Part 39 of the CrimPR (see Section D. Other Appeals for specific information on where to lodge applications in relation to other types of appeal).

A2.5. It should be noted that Form NG and grounds of appeal are required to be served within the relevant time limit in all cases whether or not leave to appeal is required (e.g. where a trial Judge's certificate has been granted). However, on a reference by the Criminal Cases Review Commission (CCRC), if no Form NG and grounds are served within the required period, then the reference shall be treated as the appeal notice (CrimPR 39.5 (2)).

Note: There is a new Form NG to be used from 1 October 2018, see www.banksr.com Other Matters Other Documents tab Court of Appeal. Ed.

Applying to admit fresh evidence

4.26 *Fresh evidence Statute, Rules and guide*

Criminal Appeal Act 1968 s 23(1) For the purposes of an appeal, or an application for leave to appeal, under this Part of this Act the Court of Appeal may, if they think it necessary or expedient in the interests of justice:

(a) order the production of any document, exhibit or other thing connected with the proceedings, the production of which appears to them necessary for the determination of the case;

(b) order any witness to attend for examination and be examined before the Court (whether or not he was called in the proceedings from which the appeal lies); and

(c) receive any evidence which was not adduced in the proceedings from which the appeal lies.

(1A) The power conferred by subsection (1)(a) may be exercised so as to require the production of any document, exhibit or other thing mentioned in that subsection to:

(a) the Court;

(b) the appellant;

(c) the respondent.

(2) The Court of Appeal shall, in considering whether to receive any evidence, have regard in particular to:

(a) whether the evidence appears to the Court to be capable of belief;

(b) whether it appears to the Court that the evidence may afford any ground for allowing the appeal;

(c) whether the evidence would have been admissible in the proceedings from which the appeal lies on an issue which is the subject of the appeal; and

(d) whether there is a reasonable explanation for the failure to adduce the evidence in those proceedings.

(3) Subsection (1)(c) above applies to any evidence of a witness (including the appellant) who is competent but not compellable.

(4) For the purposes of an appeal, or an application for leave to appeal, under this Part of this Act, the Court of Appeal may, if they think it necessary or expedient in the interests of justice, order the examination of any witness whose attendance might be required under subsection (1)(b) above to be conducted, in manner provided by rules of court, before any judge or officer of the Court or other person appointed by the Court for the purpose, and allow the admission of any depositions so taken as evidence before the Court.

(5) A live link direction under section 22(4) does not apply to the giving of oral evidence by the appellant at any hearing unless that direction, or any subsequent direction of the court, provides expressly for the giving of such evidence through a live link.

(6) In this section, 'respondent' includes a person who will be a respondent if leave to appeal is granted.
Evidence
Criminal Procedure Rules 2015 2015/1490 Rule 39.3(1) An appeal notice must:
(a)-(d) [not listed]
(e) include or attach any application for the following, with reasons:
(i)-(iv) [not listed]
(v) the introduction of evidence, including hearsay evidence and evidence of bad character,
(vi) an order requiring a witness to attend court,
(vii) a direction for special measures for a witness,
(viii) a direction for special measures for the giving of evidence by the appellant.
There are similar provisions for the drafting of respondent's notices at Criminal Procedure Rules 2015 2015/1490 Rule 39.6.
Guide to Commencing Proceedings in the Court of Appeal 2018 para A5-1 **Applications to call fresh evidence** Where grounds of appeal rely upon fresh evidence that was not adduced at trial, an application pursuant to s. 23 Criminal Appeals Act 1968 must be made. If the fresh evidence is provided by a witness, representatives should obtain a statement from the witness in the form prescribed by s9 of the Criminal Justice Act 1967. If the fresh evidence is documentary or real evidence, the representatives should obtain statements from all those involved formally exhibiting the evidence. A Form W should be lodged in respect of each witness dealing with the fresh evidence. The Form W should indicate whether there is an application for a witness order. The Registrar or single Judge may direct the issue of a witness order but only the Court hearing the appeal may give leave for a witness to be called and then formally receive the evidence under s23 of the Criminal Appeal Act 1968.
A5-1.2 A supporting witness statement (in [section] 9 form), or an affidavit from the appellant's solicitor must accompany the fresh evidence and Form W(s), setting out why the evidence was not available at trial and how it has come to light (*R v Gogana* 1999 The Times 12/07/1999). This will implicitly require fresh representatives to comply with *McCook* (see section A4. **Applications by fresh legal representatives**, see **4.24**).
Note: There is a new form W to be used when an application is made for permission to call a witness and/or for a witness order, see www.banksr.com Other Matters Other Documents tab Court of Appeal. Ed.

4.27 ***Fresh evidence*** ***Cases***
R v Erskine 2009 EWCA Crim 1425, 2 Cr App R 29 para 39 Virtually by definition, the decision whether to admit fresh evidence is case- and fact-specific. The discretion to receive fresh evidence is a wide one focusing on the interests of justice. The considerations listed in subsection (2) (a) to (d) are neither exhaustive nor conclusive, but they require specific attention. The fact that the issue to which the fresh evidence relates was not raised at trial does not automatically preclude its reception. However, it is well understood that, save exceptionally, if the defendant is allowed to advance on appeal a defence and/or evidence which could and should have been but were not put before the jury, our trial process would be subverted. Therefore, if they were not deployed when they were available to be deployed, or the issues could have been but were not raised at trial, it is clear from the statutory structure, as explained in the authorities, that unless a reasonable and persuasive explanation for one or other of these omissions is offered, it is highly unlikely that the 'interests of justice' test will be satisfied.
R v Beesley and Others 2011 EWCA Crim 1021, 2012 1 Cr App R (S) 15 (p 71) Where a defendant wished to rely on a medical report to suggest that a Hospital Order should be made because of the requirements in Mental Health Act 1983 s 37, the rules for the admission of fresh evidence under Criminal Appeal Act 1968 s 23 had to be applied, *R v Hughes* 2009 EWCA Crim 841, 2010 1 Cr App R (S) 25 (p 146).

R v Thames Water 2015 EWCA Crim 960, 2 Cr App R (S) 63 (p 439) LCJ D, the defendant company, pleaded to polluting a watercourse with raw sewage. On appeal, the defence tried to dispute certain of the Judge's conclusions by introducing new statements. Held. The Court may receive new evidence when it thinks it is necessary in the interests of justice. This material should have been set out in the basis of plea, as required by the [then] Criminal Practice Direction [now 2015] VII B.11(a) [see **57.42**]. We emphasise the importance of both parties complying strictly with those requirements.
R v Rogers 2016 EWCA Crim 801, 2 Cr App R (S) 36 (p 370) LCJ The Court heard three joined sentence appeals where fresh evidence was sought to be admitted. Held. para 5 The Court must always bear in mind the observations in *R v Erskine* 2009, see above. para 86 An appeal is not an opportunity for a litigant to make good the deficiencies in the way in which their case was prepared or presented before the original court. Applications refused. For more detail see **4.26**.
R v Kelly 2016 EWCA Crim 1505 D's counsel asked to admit bank statements for a confiscation appeal. Application refused because the papers were served late etc. For more detail, see **21.155**.
See also the **Extended Sentences (EDS)** ***Fresh evidence at the Court of Appeal*** para at **56.90**.

4.28 ***Applications to consider fresh issues and submissions***
R v Summerskill 2014 EWCA Crim 2173 D pleaded to sanction busting to Iran. He appealed and, on the day of the hearing, his QC produced a new set of materials and points that had not been raised before. Held. Where a party raises new issues, proper procedures must be followed with a proper application and written explanation. If not, the Court cannot consider matters ahead of time and the prosecution cannot consider the material. Sometimes the Court accepts documents like a prison report at short notice. However, if new evidence is to be put before the Court, a proper application must be made and a written explanation given as to why the material was not put before the judge. What happened here must never happen again.
R v Thames Water 2015 EWCA Crim 960, 2 Cr App R (S) 63 (p 439) LCJ D, the defendant company, pleaded to polluting a watercourse with raw sewage. On appeal, the defence tried to dispute certain of the Judge's conclusions by introducing new statements. Held. It is only in the rarest of circumstances we will allow a party to advance a case not deployed in the court below. The application to admit the evidence is refused.

4.29 ***Post-sentence information about the defendant***
R v Caines and Roberts 2006 EWCA Crim 2915 para 44 The defendants appealed their murder minimum term reviews. Held. From time to time, the Court will be provided with updated information about the offender. This sometimes takes the form of prison reports, sometimes confidential information from the police. The sources vary. The information may serve to show, for example, that the prisoner has provided considerable assistance to the police; sometimes aspects of the mitigation are significantly underlined in a way which may not have been as clear or emphatic in the Crown Court; sometimes the information may indicate that the offender has made significant progress since the sentence began, a feature particularly relevant in cases involving young offenders. The formal procedures for the admission of fresh evidence are not followed. This Court simply considers the evidence before it. So, for example, if a young offender has responded positively to his custodial sentence, and his progress is such that it may be counterproductive for him to serve the sentence actually imposed, it may be reduced on appeal, or changed to a non-custodial disposal, without any implied criticism of the decision of the judge. In short, post-sentence information may impact on, and produce, a reduction in sentence.

R v Beesley and Others 2011 EWCA Crim 1021, 2012 1 Cr App R (S) 15 (p 71) The defendants pleaded to manslaughter. They appealed their IPP sentences and wished to rely on fresh psychiatric evidence. Held. *R v Caines and Roberts* 2006 EWCA Crim 2915 was cited as the basic principle.

R v Rogers 2016 EWCA Crim 801, 2 Cr App R (S) 36 (p 370) LCJ The Court heard three joined sentence appeals where fresh evidence was sought to be admitted. Held. There are circumstances where the Court will consider updates to information placed before the sentencing judge without the conditions in section 23 being applied, but otherwise section 23 is of general application to all sentencing appeals. para 8 The circumstances in which the Court will recognise updated information were described in *R v Caines and Roberts* 2006 EWCA Crim 2915, see above. As was explained in *R v Beesley and Others* 2011 EWCA Crim 1021, 2012 1 Cr App R (S) 15 (p 71) para 33-36, the exception is strictly limited. It will include updated pre-sentence and prison reports on conduct in prison after sentence, but not fresh psychiatric or psychological evidence in support of an argument that a finding of dangerousness ought not to have been made or a hospital order should have been made. para 10 Another limited exception is an updated text, but the circumstances in which this exception will apply are likely to be highly unusual for the reasons explained in *R v AXN and ZAR* 2016 EWCA Crim 590, 2 Cr App R (S) 33 (p 341).[40]

Pre-hearing matters

4.30 *Crown Court judge granting appeal certificate*

Criminal Appeal Act 1968 s 11(1) Subject to subsection (1A) below, an appeal against sentence, whether under section 9(1) or under section 10 of this Act, lies only with the leave of the Court of Appeal.

(1A) If, within 28 days from the date on which the sentence was passed, the judge who passed it grants a certificate that the case is fit for appeal under section 9 or 10 of this Act, an appeal lies under this section without the leave of the Court of Appeal.

Criminal Practice Directions 2015 EWCA Crim 1567 para III 14H.1 The trial or sentencing judge may grant a certificate of fitness for appeal...The judge in the Crown Court should only certify cases in exceptional circumstances.

Criminal Practice Directions 2015 EWCA Crim 1567 para III 14H.3 The first question for the judge is then whether there exists a particular and cogent ground of appeal. If there is no such ground, there can be no certificate; and if there is no certificate there can be no bail. A judge should not grant a certificate with regard to sentence merely in the light of mitigation to which he has, in his opinion, given due weight, nor in regard to conviction on a ground where he considers the chance of a successful appeal is not substantial. The judge should bear in mind that, where a certificate is refused, application may be made to the Court of Appeal for leave to appeal and for bail; it is expected that certificates will only be granted in exceptional circumstances.

14H.4 Defence advocates should note that the effect of a grant of a certificate is to remove the need for leave to appeal to be granted by the Court of Appeal. It does not in itself commence the appeal. The completed Form C will be sent by the Crown Court to the Criminal Appeal Office; it is not copied to the parties. The procedures in the Criminal Procedure Rules Part 39 should be followed.

14H.5 [deals with the power to grant bail with a certificate, see **4.34**.]

14H.6 The length of the period which might elapse before the hearing of any appeal is not relevant to the grant of a certificate; but, if the judge does decide to grant a certificate, it may be one factor in the decision whether or not to grant bail. If bail is granted, the judge should consider imposing a condition of residence in line with the practice in the Court of Appeal (Criminal Division).

[40] Also known as *R v N* 2016 EWCA Crim 590, 2 Cr App R (S) 33

R v Matthews 2014 EWCA Crim 2757 LCJ The Judge granted a certificate. Held. The [then] Criminal Practice Directions 2014 [see the 2015 directions above] embodies the long-standing practice of this court that Crown Court Judges should certify cases only in exceptional circumstances. The paragraphs also make clear that a judge should not grant a certificate with regard to sentence merely in the light of the mitigation to which he has, in his opinion, given due weight. A judge should also bear in mind that applications may always be made to this court for leave to appeal and for bail, or, if bail is not granted, expedition of the hearing of the appeal. If a short sentence is imposed, every effort is made by the Court of Appeal to bring the case on very quickly. Difficulties arise for an appellant if he is granted bail and the court hearing the appeal concludes that there was no basis for the appeal. It is essential that if a judge is to consider granting a certificate and bail, he should set out his reasons for taking such a course. His reasons should explain why the exceptional procedure is being used. This Judge should never have granted a certificate.

4.31 ***Short sentences/Expedited hearings***

R v Welsh 2017 EWCA Crim 2471 On 22 September 2017, D pleaded (full credit) to having an imitation firearm in a public place. D was aged 17 at the time of the offence and he had no previous convictions. The author of the pre-sentence report thought D was showing off and considered him to be immature. On 20 November 2017, a notice of appeal was sent. The Registrar referred the application to the full Court. Held on 1 December 2017. 6 months not 9 was the correct starting point, so with plea, **4 months' YOI** not 6. We emphasise the critical importance that appeal advice is given at the very earliest opportunity, particularly in the case of short custodial sentences. That D did not receive immediate advice to mount an appeal, if such was the legal advice he was receiving, is truly deplorable. Those representing defendants should be aware that this Court is in a position to move swiftly when short sentences are imposed so that appeals [don't become] academic. These circumstances should not arise again.

4.32 ***Abandonment of a ground of appeal or opposition Power to***

Criminal Procedure Rules 2015 2015/1490 Rule 36.14(4)

(4) Paragraph (5) applies where a party wants to abandon:

(a) a ground of appeal on which that party has permission to appeal; or

(b) a ground of opposition identified in a respondent's notice.

(5) Such a party must serve notice on:

(a) the Registrar; and

(b) each other party, before any hearing at which that ground will be considered by the court.[41]

Guide to Commencing Proceedings in the Court of Appeal 2018 A17 **Abandonment**

A17-1. An appeal or application may be abandoned at any time before the hearing without leave by completing and lodging Form A. An oral instruction or letter indicating a wish to abandon is insufficient.

A17-2. At the hearing, an application or appeal can only be abandoned with the permission of the Court (CrimPR 36.13(2)(b)). An appeal or application which is abandoned is treated as being a final determination of the full Court (CrimPR 36.13(4)(c)).

Note: Criminal Procedure Rules 2015 2015/1490 Rule 36.13 sets out how an application should be abandoned. Ed.

4.33 ***Abandonment, Reinstatement of appeal etc. after Rules about***

Guide to Commencing Proceedings in the Court of Appeal 2018 A17 **Abandonment**

A17-1-A17-2. [see **4.32**]

A17-3. A notice of abandonment cannot be withdrawn nor can it be conditional. A person who wants to reinstate an application or appeal after abandonment must apply in

[41] Added by Criminal Procedure (Amendment) Rules 2017 2017/144 para 9

writing to the Registrar with reasons (CrimPR 36.13(5)). The Court has power to allow reinstatement only where the purported abandonment can be treated as a nullity and the applicant must provide the Court with the relevant information to determine the application (*R v Medway* 1976 62 Cr App R 85 and *R v Zabotka* 2016 EWCA Crim 1771).

A17-4. An application to treat the abandonment as a nullity is heard by the full Court. If the Court does agree to treat the abandonment as a nullity, the status of the application is restored as if there had been no interruption.

Note: Rule 36.13(5) states the application should be in writing, with reasons and served on the Registrar. Ed.

R v Smith 2013 EWCA Crim 2388 The defendant abandoned his appeal on legal advice. With new counsel he tried to resurrect the appeal saying the abandonment was based on wrong legal advice. Held. *Since R v Medway* 1976 there have been three recent cases, *R v Offield* 2002 EWCA Crim 1630, *R v Elrayess* 2007 EWCA Crim 2252 and *R v RL* 2013 EWCA Crim 1913. From these cases we derive four propositions.

(i) A notice of abandonment of appeal is irrevocable, unless the Court of Appeal treats that notice as a nullity.

(ii) A notice of abandonment is a nullity if the applicant's mind does not go with the notice which he signs.

(iii) If the applicant abandons his appeal after and because of receiving incorrect legal advice, then his mind may not go with the notice which he signs. Whether this is the case will depend upon the circumstances.

(iv) Incorrect legal advice for this purpose means advice which is positively wrong. It does not mean the expression of opinion on a difficult point, with which some may agree and others may disagree.

If these rules are thought to be too restrictive, then the remedy may lie in the hands of the Criminal Procedure Rule Committee.

R v Livesey 2013 EWCA Crim 1913 D, N and E pleaded to numerous robberies. They applied for leave to appeal. The single Judge refused the applications and stated that the full court should consider making a direction for loss of time prior to the hearing of any renewed application. On a non-counsel application, the full court granted all three leave to appeal and ordered up-to-date prison reports. Eight days before the hearing, D abandoned his appeal based on advice from his solicitor. His solicitor advised him, in strong terms, that he should abandon his appeal because of the risk of losing time. The solicitor wrote to the court in full and frank terms and accepted that he had incorrectly advised D to abandon his appeal. The solicitor accepted that he was unaware that once the full court had granted leave, a direction for loss of time could not be made (Criminal Appeal Act 1968 s 29). D sought to have his abandonment treated as a nullity. Held. The advice was fundamentally flawed and although in the strict sense D knew he was abandoning his appeal, it would be wrong to describe this as a deliberate and informed decision on his part. He had been advised that he was at considerable risk of his sentence being increased in real terms if he persisted with his appeal, a risk that simply did not exist following the grant of leave by the full court. D's decision was based on a wrong view of the law and D's mind did not truly go with the abandonment. Applying the authorities, the act of abandonment was a nullity. Sentence reduced from 32 months to 24.

R v Taylor 2014 EWCA Crim 1208 D was convicted of burglary and counsel wrote grounds of appeal. They were submitted but before they were seen by the single Judge, D signed a Form A abandoning his appeal. He sought to withdraw it. D said the reason why he abandoned the appeal was because he was advised by fellow inmates that he might end up with additional time in custody and he had not received any legal advice about the abandonment. D added that he had acted hastily and should have asked for legal advice. Held. But for the bad advice D would not have abandoned his appeal. That was the sole reason. We allow him to withdraw the abandonment.

R v Chinegwundoh 2015 EWCA Crim 109, 1 Cr App R (S) 61 (p 429) D was unfit to plead but found to have committed fraud and used a false instrument. D was a practising barrister but was disbarred for forging court documents. The Judge made a Supervision Order and a Restraining Order. D appealed, signing the document 'Prince Harold Chinegwundoh, King's Counsel'. He then sought to abandon the appeal. The Registrar instructed counsel. Held. D cannot abandon the appeal as of right. It requires our consent, which we refuse because of our concerns about his mental capacity. The Restraint Order and the Supervision Order (in part) were unlawful.
See also: *R v Medway* 1976 62 Cr App R 85 (LCJ Jurisdiction exists to give leave to withdraw abandonment where circumstances are present which enable the Court to say that the abandonment should be treated as a nullity. The kernel of the 'nullity test' is that the Court is satisfied that the abandonment was not the result of a deliberate and informed decision, in other words that the mind of the applicant did not go with his act of abandonment.)
R v Witter 2016 EWCA Crim 416 (Solicitors wrote to the defendant, D, saying counsel had said the appeal could be reinstated once the evidence they sought had been received. D said he thought the abandonment was in effect a request for an adjournment. Held. The advice was erroneous. We treat the abandonment as a nullity.)
R v Riley 2017 EWCA Crim 243 (An appeal was launched on the basis of non-disclosure. It was then discovered that counsel's clerk had the document, but not counsel. It was argued that the defendant was presented with a fait accompli and was told the abandonment was happening whether he liked it or not. The form was signed by the solicitors. Held. The fact counsel didn't know about the document [was still a live issue]. The notice was a nullity.)
R v Furniss 2018 EWCA Crim 2574 D's counsel drafted grounds of appeal which were rejected by the single Judge. Counsel advised that D should not renew his appeal. D wanted to submit his own grounds of appeal. His solicitors advised him that he would have to abandon his appeal and submit the new grounds. D did so. Held. This advice was wrong. D did not wish to abandon the proceedings. If the correct advice had been given, D would have made clear that he wanted to continue the appeal. D's notice of appeal was a nullity.

4.34 *Bail pending appeal*

Note: Criminal Appeal Act 1968 s 19 provides the power to grant or vary bail. Ed.
Criminal Procedure Rules 2015 2015/1490 Rule 39.8(1) This rule applies where a party wants to make an application to the court about bail pending appeal or retrial.
(2) That party must serve an application in the form set out in the Practice Direction on:
 (a) the Registrar, unless the application is with the appeal notice, and
 (b) the other party.
(3) The court must not decide such an application without giving the other party an opportunity to make representations, including representations about any condition or surety proposed by the applicant.
The rest of Rule 68 is extensive and is not reproduced.
Criminal Practice Directions 2015 EWCA Crim 1567 para III 14H.5 Bail pending appeal to the Court of Appeal (Criminal Division) may be granted by the trial or sentencing judge if they have certified the case as fit for appeal (see Senior Courts Act 1981 s 81(1)(f) and 81(1B)). Bail can only be granted in the Crown Court within 28 days of the conviction or sentence which is to be the subject of the appeal and may not be granted if an application for bail has already been made to the Court of Appeal. The procedure for bail to be granted by a judge of the Crown Court pending an appeal is governed by Criminal Procedure Rules Part 14. The Crown Court judge should use the Criminal Appeal Office Form BC (Crown Court Judge's Order granting bail) which is available to court staff on the HMCTS intranet.
14H.6 The length of the period which might elapse before the hearing of any appeal is not relevant to the grant of a certificate; but, if the judge does decide to grant a

certificate, it may be one factor in the decision whether or not to grant bail. If bail is granted, the judge should consider imposing a condition of residence in line with the practice in the Court of Appeal (Criminal Division).

Guide to Commencing Proceedings in the Court of Appeal 2018 para A13. **Bail pending appeal** (CrimPR 39.8)

A13-1. Bail may be granted (a) by a single Judge or the full Court or (b) by a trial or sentencing Judge who has certified the case fit for appeal. In the latter case, bail can only be granted within 28 days of the conviction or sentence which is the subject of the appeal and may not be granted if an application for bail has already been made to the Court of Appeal (CPD III Custody and bail 14H.5).

A13-2. An application to the Court of Appeal for bail pending appeal must be supported by a completed Form B which must be served on the Registrar and the prosecution. The Court must not decide such an application without giving the prosecution the opportunity to make representations.

A13-3. An application for bail will not be considered by a single Judge or the Court until notice of application for leave to appeal conviction or sentence or notice of appeal has first been given. In practice, Judges will also require the relevant transcripts to be available so they may consider the merits of the substantive application at the same time as the bail application.

A13-4. Where bail is granted pending appeal, the Court may attach any condition that must be met before the party is released, and may direct how such a condition must be met. The Registrar must serve a certificate recording any such condition on the party, the party's custodian and any other person directly affected by the condition (CrimPR 39.9). A condition of residence is always attached.

Note: For the court form, see www.banksr.com Other Matters Other Documents tab Court of Appeal. Ed.

4.35 ***Bail and delay***

R v Golding 2014 EWCA Crim 889 D was sentenced to 14 months for a section 20 assault in August 2011. He appealed his conviction and his sentence. In September 2011, he was granted conditional bail. In May 2014, the full court considered the plea was properly entered and no proper criticism could be made about the 14 months. However, he had lost his job because of the sentence and over the 3 years on bail he had not found another one. Family difficulties caused by that and his period in limbo meant it would be wrong to return him to custody, so 3 months making immediate release was appropriate.

Note: The Court of Appeal is always reluctant to grant bail as it prefers either the *status quo* or an expedited hearing. The case facts here are exceptionally rare and if counsel in a future case indicates that bail should be a factor in not affirming a correct sentence, he or she should expect to be told that the defendant asked for bail and that is the risk he or she takes. Ed.

For more details see para **292.20** in Volume 2.

4.36 ***Case management duties***

A Guide to Commencing Proceedings in the Court of Appeal 2018 A18 **Case Management Duties** A18-1. CrimPR 36.2 gives the Court and parties the same powers and duties of case management as in Part 3 of the Rules. In accordance with those duties, for each application received, the Registrar nominates a case progression officer, (the 'responsible officer'). There is also a duty on the parties to actively assist the Court to progress cases. Close contact between the advocate and solicitors and the responsible officer is encouraged in order to facilitate the efficient preparation and listing of appeals, especially in complex cases and those involving witnesses.

A18-2. Powers under the Criminal Appeal Act 1968 exercisable by the single Judge and the Registrar are contained in s.31 Criminal Appeal Act 1968 (as amended by s.87 Courts Act 2003, s.331 & Sched.32 Criminal Justice Act 2003 and Sched.8 Criminal Justice and Immigration Act 2008). These powers include the power to make procedural

directions for the efficient and effective preparation of an application or appeal and the power to make an order under s.23(1)(a) Criminal Appeal Act 1968 for the production of evidence etc. necessary for the determination of the case.
A18-3. Where the Registrar refuses an application by an appellant to exercise any of the Registrar's case management powers under s.31 Criminal Appeal Act 1968 in the appellant's favour, the appellant is entitled to have the application determined by a single Judge (s. 31A (4) of the Act). There is no provision for any appeal against a procedural direction given by a single Judge and thus such decisions are final.

4.37 ***Case management duties Procedural directions Powers***
Criminal Procedure Rules 2015 2015/1490 Rule 3 sets out the general rules for case management in the Crown Court and Court of Appeal. It is a long rule, most of which is not relevant to sentencing appeals. For reasons of space it is not reproduced.
Criminal Appeal Act 1968 s 31B(1) The power of the Court of Appeal to determine an application for procedural directions may be exercised by:
(a) a single judge, or
(b) the Registrar.
(2) 'Procedural directions' means directions for the efficient and effective preparation of a) an application for leave to appeal, or b) an appeal, to which this section applies.
(3) A single judge may give such procedural directions as he thinks fit:
(a) when acting under subsection (1),
(b) on a reference from the Registrar,
(c) of his own motion, when he is exercising, or considering whether to exercise, any power of his in relation to the application or appeal.
(4) The Registrar may give such procedural directions as he thinks fit:
(a) when acting under subsection (1),
(b) of his own motion.
(5) This section applies to an appeal, and an application to the Court of Appeal for leave to appeal, under:
(a) this Part,
(b) Criminal Justice Act 1987 s 9 [the judicial powers at a preparatory hearing in serious or complex fraud cases], or
(c) Criminal Procedure and Investigations Act 1996 s 35 [appeals from preparatory hearings].

4.38 ***Case management duties Procedural directions Appeals***
Appeals against procedural directions
Criminal Appeal Act 1968 s 31C
(1) and (2) [Repealed]
(3) Subsection (4) applies if the Registrar gives, or refuses to give, procedural directions.
(4) A single judge may, on an application to him under subsection (5):
(a) confirm, set aside or vary any procedural directions given by the Registrar, and
(b) give such procedural directions as he thinks fit.
(5) An application under this subsection may be made by:
(a) an appellant,
(b) a respondent, if the directions:
(i) relate to an application for leave to appeal and appear to need the respondent's assistance to give effect to them,
(ii) relate to an application for leave to appeal which is to be determined by the Court of Appeal, or
(iii) relate to an appeal.
(6) In this section, 'appellant' includes a person who has given notice of application for leave to appeal under any of the provisions mentioned in section 31B(5),
'respondent' includes a person who will be a respondent if leave to appeal is granted.

Guide to Commencing Proceedings in the Court of Appeal 2018 para A18-3. Where the Registrar refuses an application by an appellant to exercise any of the Registrar's case management powers under s.31 Criminal Appeal Act 1968 in the appellant's favour, the appellant is entitled to have the application determined by a single Judge (s. 31A (4) of the Act). There is no provision for any appeal against a procedural direction given by a single Judge and thus such decisions are final.

4.39 ***Court summaries***

Criminal Practice Directions 2015 EWCA Crim 1567 para IX 39G.1 To assist the Court, the Criminal Appeal Office prepares summaries of the cases coming before it. These are entirely objective and do not contain any advice about how the Court should deal with the case or any view about its merits. They consist of two Parts.

68G.2 Part I, which is provided to all the advocates in the case, generally contains:

(a) particulars of the proceedings in the Crown Court, including representation and details of any co-accused,

(b) particulars of the proceedings in the Court of Appeal (Criminal Division),

(c) the facts of the case, as drawn from the transcripts, appeal notice, respondent's notice, witness statements and/or the exhibits,

(d) the submissions and rulings, summing up and sentencing remarks.

68G.3 The contents of the summary are a matter for the professional judgment of the writer, but an advocate wishing to suggest any significant alteration to Part I should write to the Registrar of Criminal Appeals. If the Registrar does not agree, the summary and the letter will be put to the Court for decision. The Court will not generally be willing to hear oral argument about the content of the summary.

68G.4 Advocates may show Part I of the summary to their professional or lay clients (but to no one else) if they believe it would help to check facts or formulate arguments, but summaries are not to be copied or reproduced without the permission of the Criminal Appeal Office. Permission for this will not normally be given in cases involving children, or sexual offences, or where the Crown Court has made an order restricting reporting.

68G.5 Unless a judge of the High Court or the Registrar of Criminal Appeals gives a direction to the contrary, in any particular case involving material of an explicitly salacious or sadistic nature, Part I will also be supplied to appellants who seek to represent themselves before the full court, or who renew to the full court their applications for leave to appeal against conviction or sentence.

68G.6 Part II, which is supplied to the Court alone, contains:

(a) a summary of the grounds of appeal, and

(b) in appeals against sentence (and applications for such leave), summaries of the antecedent histories of the parties and of any relevant pre-sentence, medical or other reports.

68G.7 All the source material is provided to the Court and advocates are able to draw attention to anything in it which may be of particular relevance.

4.40 ***Court targets***

Criminal Practice Directions 2015 EWCA Crim 1567 para IX 39B.5 The following target times are set for the hearing of appeals. Target times will run from the receipt of the appeal by the Listing Officer, as being ready for hearing.

Sentence appeal	Target times
From receipt by Listing Officer to fixing of hearing date:	14 days
From fixing of hearing date to hearing:	14 days
Total time from receipt by Listing Officer to hearing:	28 days

68B.7 Where legal vacations impinge, these periods may be extended. Where expedition is required, the Registrar may direct that these periods be abridged.

68B.8 'Appeal' includes an application for leave to appeal which requires an oral hearing.

4.41 *Late papers*

Note: The Registrar has made it known that 'Many counsel lodge a skeleton or other documents a few days before the hearing thinking that this will give the judges time to read it before the hearing. The Court of Appeal gets through a huge amount of work and the way that is done is by reading ahead. If a court is sitting for a week it will usually have one reading day, often a Monday. Judges' bundles are generally prepared at least two weeks before the hearing and collected by the judges' clerks at least one week before. Skeleton arguments and other documents that come in after the bundles have been collected have to be sent separately as "late papers" and irritate everybody.' Ed.

4.42 *Legal aid*

Legal Aid, Sentencing and Punishment of Offenders Act 2012 s 16(1) Representation for the purposes of criminal proceedings is to be available under this Part to an individual if:

(a) the individual is a specified individual in relation to the proceedings, and

(b) the relevant authority has determined (provisionally or otherwise) that the individual qualifies for such representation in accordance with this Part (and has not withdrawn the determination).

Legal Aid, Sentencing and Punishment of Offenders Act 2012 s 14 In this Part 'criminal proceedings' means:..b) proceedings before a court for dealing with an individual convicted of an offence, including proceedings in respect of a sentence or order,...

(e) proceedings on an appeal brought by an individual under Criminal Appeal Act 1968 s 44A (appeal in case of death of appellant).

Criminal Defence Service (General) (No 2) Regulations 2001 2001/1437 reg 10(1) An application for a representation order in respect of proceedings in the Court of Appeal or the Supreme Court may be made:

(a) orally to the Court of Appeal, or a judge of the court, or

(b) in writing to the Court of Appeal, a judge of the court, or the appropriate officer of the court.

(2) Where an application is made to the court, it may refer it to a judge or the appropriate officer for determination.

(3) Where an application is made to a judge, he may refer it to the appropriate officer for determination.

(4) The appropriate officer may:

(a) grant the application, or

(b) refer it to the court or a judge of the court.

(5) A representation order shall not be granted until notice of leave to appeal has been given in respect of the proceedings which are the subject of the application.

(6) Where a representation order is granted in respect of proceedings in the Court of Appeal, a judge or the appropriate officer may specify the stage of the proceedings at which the representation order shall take effect.

Guide to Commencing Proceedings in the Court of Appeal Criminal Division 2018 **Advice and Assistance** para A1-2. [see **4.15** and **4.43**]

A1-3. Once the Form NG has been lodged, the Registrar is the relevant authority for decisions about whether an individual qualifies for representation for the purposes of criminal proceedings before the Court of Appeal Criminal Division (ss.16(1) & 19(1) Legal Aid, Sentencing and Punishment of Offenders Act 2012 and Reg.8 Criminal Legal Aid (Determinations by a Court and Choice of Representative) Regulations 2013).

A1-4. Where, in order to settle grounds of appeal, work of an exceptional nature is contemplated or where the expense will be great, legal representatives should not contact the LAA for funding but should submit a Form NG with provisional grounds of appeal and with a note to the Registrar requesting a representation order to cover the specific work considered necessary to enable final grounds of appeal to be settled. The Registrar will then consider whether it is appropriate to grant funding for this purpose.

page 10 A14-1. Where the single Judge grants leave or refers an application to the Court, it is usual to grant a representation order for the preparation and presentation of the appeal. This is usually limited to the services of an advocate only. The advocate who settled grounds of appeal will usually be the assigned advocate. If the applicant is a litigant in person, an advocate may be assigned by the Registrar. In such cases the Registrar will provide a brief but does not act as an appellant's solicitor. The Registrar may assign one advocate to represent more than one appellant if appropriate. If it is considered that a representation order for two advocates and/or solicitors is required, the advocate should notify the Registrar and provide written justification in accordance with Criminal Legal Aid (Determinations by a Court and Choice of Representative) Regulations 2013 (S.I. 2013/614).

A14-2. If solicitors are assigned, it should be noted that by virtue of Regulation 12 of the Criminal Legal Aid (Determinations by a Court and Choice of Representative) Regulations 2013, SI 2013/614, a representation order can only be issued to a solicitor if they hold a Standard Crime Contract with the LAA. A solicitor not holding such a franchise may apply to the LAA for an individual case contract (ICC) by virtue of which the solicitor is employed on behalf of the LAA to represent an appellant in a given case.

A14-3. In some circumstances, the Registrar may refer an application to the full Court. This may be because there is a novel point of law, there is fresh evidence to be considered pursuant to s.23 of the Criminal Appeal Act 1968 or because in a sentence case, the sentence passed is very short. A representation order for an advocate is usually granted. The advocate for the prosecution usually attends a Registrar's referral.

4.43 ***Legal aid for new counsel on Crown Court order*** ***Limitations***

Practice Direction (Costs in Criminal Proceedings) 2015 EWCA Crim 1568 LCJ para 8.7 The Crown Court can only amend a representation order in favour of fresh legal representatives if advice on appeal has not been given by trial legal representatives and it is necessary and reasonable for another legal representative to be instructed.

Guide to Commencing Proceedings in the Court of Appeal Criminal Division 2018 **Advice and Assistance** para A1-2. Prior to the lodging of the notice and grounds of appeal by service of Form NG, the Registrar has no power to grant a representation order. The Crown Court can only amend a representation order in favour of fresh legal representatives if advice on appeal has not been given by trial representatives and it is necessary and reasonable for another legal representative to be instructed. Where advice on appeal has been given by trial legal representatives, application for funding prior to the lodging of the notice and grounds of appeal may only be made to the Legal Aid Authority (LAA).

4.44 ***Listing***

Criminal Practice Directions 2015 EWCA Crim 1567 para IX 39B.2 Where possible, regard will be had to an advocate's existing commitments. However, in relation to the listing of appeals, the Court of Appeal takes precedence over all lower courts, including the Crown Court. Wherever practicable, a lower court will have regard to this principle when making arrangements to release an advocate to appear in the Court of Appeal. In case of difficulty, the lower court should communicate with the Registrar. In general an advocate's commitment in a lower court will not be regarded as a good reason for failing to accept a date proposed for a hearing in the Court of Appeal.

4.45 ***Litigants in person***

Equal Treatment Bench Book 2013 www.banksr.com Other Matters Other Documents tab

Chapter 4 page 25 **Key points** Most litigants in person are stressed and worried, operating in an alien environment in what for them is a foreign language. They are trying to grasp concepts of law and procedure about which they may be totally ignorant.
They may well be experiencing feelings of fear, ignorance, frustration, bewilderment and disadvantage, especially if appearing against a represented party. The outcome of the case may have a profound effect and long-term consequences upon their life.
Role of the judge
Judges must be aware of the feelings and difficulties experienced by litigants in person and be ready and able to help them, especially if a represented party is being oppressive or aggressive.
Maintaining patience and an even-handed approach [are] also important where the litigant in person is being oppressive or aggressive towards another party or its representative or towards the court or tribunal. The judge should, however, remain understanding so far as possible as to what might lie behind their behaviour.
Maintaining a balance between assisting and understanding what the litigant in person requires, while protecting their represented opponent against the problems that can be caused by the litigant in person's lack of legal and procedural knowledge, is the key.
Particular areas of difficulty
page 28 para 21 Litigants in person may face a daunting range of problems of both knowledge and understanding.
The judge's role
page 32 para 48 It can be hard to strike a balance in assisting a litigant in person in an adversarial system. A litigant in person may easily get the impression that the judge does not pay sufficient attention to them or their case, especially if the other side is represented and the judge asks the advocate on the other side to summarise the issues between the parties.
a) Explain the judge's role during the hearing.
b) If you are doing something which might be perceived to be unfair or controversial in the mind of the litigant in person, explain precisely what you are doing and why.
c) Adopt to the extent necessary an inquisitorial role to enable the litigant in person fully to present their case (but not in such a way as to appear to give the litigant in person an undue advantage).
Criminal cases
55 Under European Convention on Human Rights art 6(3) (Sch 1, Human Rights Act 1998), everyone charged with a criminal offence has the right to defend him or herself in person or through legal assistance of his or her own choosing or, if he or she has not sufficient means to pay for legal assistance, to be given it free where the interests of justice so require.
56 Those who dispense with legal assistance do so usually because they decline to accept the advice which they have been given, whether as to plea or the conduct of the trial. This, a defendant is entitled to do. However, guidance as to the value of representation may persuade such defendants that they are better advised to retain their representatives. If a defendant decides, notwithstanding advice and guidance, to represent [him] or herself, then the judge must explain the process and ensure proper control over the proceedings is maintained.
Note: This is a heavily edited selection from a fairly long section of the Bench Book. Ed.
R v James and Selby 2016 EWCA Crim 65 para 49 S, a litigant in person, lodged many hundreds of pages of repetitive handwritten correspondence, grounds and purported fresh evidence. The Registrar directed him to consolidate his grounds into no more than two or three pages. S's response was to lodge a further 50 pages in respect of conviction and to fail to consolidate 150 pages in respect of sentence. Held. The Registrar has long acknowledged the difference between applications advanced by counsel and those advanced by a litigant in person and has, for the latter, put in place schemes designed to help as well as to control. The Criminal Appeal Office lawyers give litigants in person

guidance on what the court expects of grounds of appeal (and what it does not want to see) so as if possible to prevent grounds, often in iteration after iteration, becoming too voluminous and thus time consuming for the judiciary and difficult to manage for the Registrar.

4.46 ***Litigants seeking non-qualified people to help them***

R v Conaghan and Others 2017 EWCA Crim 597 Four cases were listed together because all had had someone who was not qualified assisting in the preparation of the appeal. Held. Those who wish to conduct legal activities are subject to stringent requirements. Exercising a right of audience is a reserved legal activity, as is conducting litigation. However, the court has an inherent jurisdiction to grant a right of audience on a case-by-case basis to any person who would not otherwise have a right of audience: see *D v S (Rights of audience)* 1997 1 FLR 724. It is a discretion that should be exercised only in 'exceptional' circumstances. To do otherwise would thwart Parliament's clear intention. para 16 Having considered these developments and the Registrar's Practice Note, it is our view that:

i) The term 'McKenzie friend' is not appropriate in the Court of Appeal Criminal Division. Terms such as 'applicant's friend' or 'applicant's helper' might well be more appropriate, but it would be wrong to express a concluded view pending the results of the consultation in the Civil and Family jurisdictions.

ii) The court will only allow a non-qualified third party to address the court in exceptional circumstances, and this will be decided on a case-by-case basis.

iii) If the Registrar has exceptionally granted permission for a non-qualified third party to act as a litigator, it does not follow that the court will also grant the third party a right of audience. It will only do so in exceptional circumstances.

iv) The Registrar's Practice Note is generally consistent with the current law and best practice in this area.

However, we recommend a number of improvements, including: [1) and 2) not listed] 3) third parties should be put on clear notice that an application should not be advanced beyond the single judge stage, following a refusal, without the applicant being fully advised as to the possible consequences. All applications dismissed with trenchant comments and for some loss of time orders.

4.47 ***Live link directions***

Note: The Court, the single judge and the Registrar can order a live link direction which is a direction that the defendant stays in prison but can see and hear the proceedings through a video link, Criminal Appeal Act 1968 s 22(4). A live link direction may not be given by the Court of Appeal unless the parties to the appeal have had an opportunity to make representations, Criminal Appeal Act 1968 s 22(6). Ed.

4.48 ***Advocate appearing by video***

R v Lane 2017 EWCA Crim 1439 The prosecution counsel was in a trial elsewhere that was overrunning. Held. We are grateful for the arrangements that have been made and grant permission for counsel to appear by video link.

Note: Since this case was heard, the use of the video by advocates has increased. Ed.

4.49 ***Providing authorities to the Court***

Criminal Practice Directions 2015 EWCA Crim 1567 para XII D.8 The paragraphs below specify whether or not copies should be provided to the court. Authorities should not be included for propositions not in dispute. If more than one authority is to be provided, the copies should be presented in paginated and tagged bundles.

D.9 If required, copies of judgments should be provided either by way of a photocopy of the published report or by way of a copy of a reproduction of the judgment in electronic form that has been authorised by the publisher of the relevant series, but in any event:

i) the report must be presented to the court in an easily legible form (a 12-point font is preferred but a 10- or 11-point font is acceptable), and

ii) the advocate presenting the report must be satisfied that it has not been reproduced in a garbled form from the data source.

In any case of doubt the court will rely on the printed text of the report (unless the editor of the report has certified that an electronic version is more accurate because it corrects an error contained in an earlier printed text of the report).

D.10 If such a copy is unavailable, a printed transcript such as from BAILII may be included.

For how to cite the authorities, see para **4.19**.

4.50 ***Registrar of Criminal Appeals, Powers of***

Powers of Court under Part I which are exercisable by registrar.

Criminal Appeal Act 1968 s 31A(1) The powers of the Court of Appeal under this Part of this Act which are specified in subsection (2) below may be exercised by the Registrar.

(2) The powers mentioned in subsection (1) above are the following:

(a) to extend the time within which notice of appeal or of application for leave to appeal may be given,

(aa) to give a live link direction under section 22(4),

(b) to order a witness to attend for examination,

(c) to vary the conditions of bail granted to an appellant by the Court of Appeal or the Crown Court, and

(d) to make orders under section 23(1)(a) (relating to evidence).

(3) No variation of the conditions of bail granted to an appellant may be made by the Registrar unless he is satisfied that the respondent does not object to the variation, but, subject to that, the powers specified in that subsection are to be exercised by the Registrar in the same manner as by the Court of Appeal and subject to the same provisions.

(4) If the Registrar refuses an application on the part of an appellant to exercise in his favour any of the powers specified in subsection (2) above, the appellant shall be entitled to have the application determined by a single judge.

(5) In this section 'respondent' includes a person who will be a respondent if leave to appeal is granted.

Guide to Commencing Proceedings in the Court of Appeal 2018 A10 **Referral by the Registrar** A10-1. Where leave to appeal is required, the Registrar, having obtained the necessary documents, will usually refer the application(s) to a single Judge for a decision (on the papers) under s. 31 Criminal Appeal Act 1968. The Registrar does have the power to refer an application for leave directly to the full Court, in which case he will usually grant the advocate a representation order for the hearing. Where an application is referred because an unlawful sentence has been passed or other procedural error identified, a representation order will ordinarily be granted unless the error is such that the Court could correct it on the papers, but advocates should be aware that the Court may make observations for the attention of the determining officer that a full fee should not be allowed on taxation. A representation order will not be granted where the presence of an advocate is not required, such as where there has been a technical error that the Court can correct without the need for oral argument. An applicant would not have the right to attend the hearing because the appeal is on a point of law only (s.22 Criminal Appeal Act 1968; R v Hyde and Others 2016 EWCA Crim 1031 2 Cr App R (S) 39 (p 416)).

Note: The more commonly used power of the Registrar is the power to give procedural directions under Criminal Appeal Act 1968 s 31B(1)(a) and (b), see **4.37**. For an example of the Registrar hearing from counsel and giving a formal ruling, see *R v Ball* 2015 EWCA Crim 2205. The Registrar is under a duty to provide active case management, see Criminal Procedure Rules 2015 2015/1490 Rule 36.2(2)(a). It is understood that formal hearings are only used as a last resort and where the applicants' lawyers have not been responding properly to correspondence. The case is listed in the Daily Cause list and the directions hearing is heard in open court. Ed.

4.51 ***Removing frivolous or vexatious or unarguable cases from the list Section 20 disposals***
Criminal Appeal Act 1968 s 20 If it appears to the Registrar that a notice of appeal or application for leave to appeal does not show any substantial ground of appeal, he may refer the appeal or application for leave to the Court for summary determination; and where the case is so referred the Court may, if they consider that the appeal or application for leave is frivolous or vexatious, and can be determined without adjourning it for a full hearing, dismiss the appeal or application for leave summarily, without calling on anyone to attend the hearing or to appear for the Crown thereon.
R v Taylor 1979 Crim LR 649 D pleaded guilty to burglary after a ruling on law. He appealed and the Registrar referred the application to the Court for summary disposal, saying the ground of appeal did not show 'any substantial ground of appeal'. Held. The ground of appeal was not arguable. That was sufficient for a section 20 disposal. The section did not just cover foolish and silly cases. The appeal was dismissed without argument.
R v Achogbuo 2014 EWCA Crim 567 LCJ D appealed. It was later admitted that he had appealed before and that the first appeal was misconceived. The second appeal made no mention of the first and suggested that D's solicitor was incompetent regarding a no comment interview. It was discovered that the solicitor had in fact properly advised D. Held. This appeal has no prospect of success and is frivolous and vexatious. The Court will henceforth consider exercising its power under section 20 more frequently if cases of this type occur again. The Court expects not only the highest levels of disclosure but also the highest standards from advocates and solicitors. In cases where incompetence of trial advocates is alleged there is a duty to exercise due diligence and make enquiries of trial lawyers and take other steps to obtain evidence before submitting grounds of appeal. Because the second appeal made no mention of the first, we refer this case to the Solicitors Regulation Authority.
Note: For examples of other applications being dismissed without argument under section 20, see *R v Jones* 2012 EWCA Crim 1789, *R v Davis and Another* 2013 EWCA Crim 2424, *R v McCook* 2014 EWCA Crim 734, 2016 2 Cr App R 30 and *R v Turford and Others* 2014 EWCA Crim 2151. In *R v Davis* 2013, the Court referred the solicitor who drafted the grounds to the Legal Aid Agency so that they could review the basis whereby legal aid had been granted for the appeal. In *R v Ramchelowan* 2018 EWCA Crim 1408, the Court of Appeal held the appeals against conviction and sentence were unmeritorious, frivolous and vexatious. They dismissed the appeal and referred the solicitor advocate to the Solicitors Regulation Authority. Ed.

4.52 ***Removing unarguable cases from the list Full Court***
R v Muller 2014 EWCA Crim 490 D appealed his conviction and sentence. The single Judge refused leave and said there were no arguable grounds. No counsel attended before the full Court. Held. This is not an appeal but a stage in the filter of arguable from unarguable cases. There is absolutely no merit in any of the allegations made by D. Application refused.

4.53 ***Skeleton arguments***
Criminal Practice Directions 2015 EWCA Crim 1567 para IX 39F[42] Advocates should always ensure that the court, and any other party as appropriate, has a single document containing all of the points that are to be argued. The appeal notice must comply with the requirements of Crim P R 39.3. In cases of an appeal against conviction, advocates must serve a skeleton argument when the appeal notice does not sufficiently outline the grounds of the appeal, particularly in cases where a complex or novel point of law has been raised. In an appeal against sentence it may be helpful for an advocate to serve a skeleton argument when a complex issue is raised.

[42] As inserted by Criminal Practice Directions 2015 Amendment No 6 2018 para 8.

39F.3 Paragraphs XII D.17 to D.23 of these Practice Directions set out the general requirements for skeleton arguments. A skeleton argument, if provided, should contain a numbered list of the points the advocate intends to argue, grouped under each ground of appeal, and stated in no more than one or two sentences. It should be as succinct as possible. Advocates should ensure that the correct Criminal Appeal Office number and the date on which the document was served appear at the beginning of any document and that their names are at the end.

Criminal Practice Directions 2015 EWCA Crim 1567 para XII D.17[43] The court may give directions for the preparation of skeleton arguments. Such directions will provide for the time within which skeleton arguments must be served and for the issues which they must address. Such directions may provide for the number of pages, or the number of words, to which a skeleton argument is to be confined. Any such directions displace the following to the extent of any inconsistency. Subject to that, however, a skeleton argument must:

i. not normally exceed 15 pages (excluding front sheets and back sheets) and be concise;
ii. be presented in A4 page size and portrait orientation, in not less than 12-point font and in 1.5 line spacing;
iii. define the issues;
iv. be set out in numbered paragraphs;
v. be cross-referenced to any relevant document in any bundle prepared for the court;
vi. be self-contained and not incorporate by reference material from previous skeleton arguments;
vii. not include extensive quotations from documents or authorities.

D.18 Where it is necessary to refer to an authority, the skeleton argument must:

i. state the proposition of law the authority demonstrates; and
ii. identify but not quote the parts of the authority that support the proposition.

D.19 If more than one authority is cited in support of a given proposition, the skeleton argument must briefly state why.

D.20 A chronology of relevant events will be necessary in most cases.

D.21 [Re applications to stay an indictment on the grounds of abuse of process etc. Not listed.]

D.22 At the hearing the court may refuse to hear argument on a point not included in a skeleton argument served within the prescribed time.

4.54 ***Time estimates***

Criminal Practice Directions 2015 EWCA Crim 1567 para IX 39B.4 The copy of the Criminal Appeal Office summary provided to advocates will contain the summary writer's time estimate for the whole hearing including delivery of judgment. It will also contain a time estimate for the judges' reading time of the core material. The Listing Officer will rely on those estimates, unless the advocate for the appellant or the Crown provides different time estimates to the Listing Officer, in writing, within seven days of the receipt of the summary by the advocate. Where the time estimates are considered by an advocate to be inadequate, or where the estimates have been altered because, for example, a ground of appeal has been abandoned, it is the duty of the advocate to inform the Court promptly, in which event the Registrar will reconsider the time estimates and inform the parties accordingly.

Note: The Registrar has made it known that 'the estimates given are for the whole hearing, not just the [defence advocate's] submissions. It should include time for the judgment.' Ed.

4.55 ***Transcripts, Obtaining/Need for***

Criminal Procedure Rules 2015 2015/1490 Rule 39.3(1)[44] An appeal notice must:

[43] As inserted by Criminal Practice Directions 2015 Amendment No 6 2018 para 9.

[44] As amended by Criminal Procedure (Amendment) Rules 2018 2018/132 para 16(a)(ii). In force 2/4/18

(c) identify the transcript that the appellant thinks the court will need, if the appellant wants to appeal against a conviction…

Note: Although Rule 39.3(2) specifies conviction only, it would be wise to read this rule as including sentence appeals. If counsel requests to listen to the tape of the proceedings, he or she should contact the Crown Court staff, where the hearing was, see Criminal Procedure Rules 2015 2015/1490 Rule 5.5(3). A fee may be charged. Ed.

Guide to Commencing Proceedings in the Court of Appeal 2018 A7 **Transcripts and notes of evidence** para A7-1. [Re conviction appeals Not listed]

A7-2. In sentence cases, transcripts of the prosecution opening of facts on a guilty plea and the Judge's observations on passing sentence are usually obtained. The Registrar will also obtain the relevant transcript in an application for leave to appeal against a confiscation order, an interlocutory appeal from a preparatory hearing or any other appeal providing the application has not been made by the prosecution.

A7-3. A transcript should only be requested if it is essential for the proper conduct of the appeal in light of the grounds. If the Registrar and the advocate are unable to agree the extent of the transcript to be obtained, the Registrar may refer that matter to a Judge.

A7-4. In certain circumstances the costs of unnecessary transcripts may be ordered to be paid by the appellant. Where a transcript is obtained otherwise than through the Registrar, the cost may be disallowed on taxation of public funding.

A7-5. If an appellant is paying privately for his legal representation, an order for transcripts should be placed directly with the transcription company and a copy provided to the Registrar upon receipt. If the Registrar has already obtained transcripts in a private case, the appellant's legal representatives will be required to pay the cost of the transcripts before they are released to them.

The prosecution/respondent

4.56 *Notifying the prosecution*

Criminal Practice Directions 2015 EWCA Crim 1567 para IX 39A.1 When an appeal notice served under [Criminal Procedure Rules 2015] Rule 39.2 is received by the Registrar of Criminal Appeals, the Registrar will notify the relevant prosecution authority, giving the case name, reference number and the trial or sentencing court.

39A.2 If the court or the Registrar directs, or invites, the prosecution authority to serve a respondent's notice under Rule 39.6, prior to the consideration of leave, the Registrar will also at that time serve on the prosecution authority the appeal notice containing the grounds of appeal and the transcripts, if available. If the prosecution authority is not directed or invited to serve a respondent's notice but wishes to do so, the authority should request the grounds of appeal and any existing transcript from the Criminal Appeal Office. Any respondent's notice received prior to the consideration of leave will be made available to the single judge.

39A.3 The Registrar of Criminal Appeals will notify the relevant prosecution authority in the event that:

a) leave to appeal against conviction or sentence is granted by the single judge, or
b) the single judge or the Registrar refers an application for leave to appeal against conviction or sentence to the full court for determination, or
c) there is to be a renewed application for leave to appeal against sentence only.

If the prosecution authority has not yet been served with the appeal notice and transcript, the Registrar will serve these with the notification, and if leave is granted, the Registrar will also serve the authority with the comments of the single judge.

39A.4 The prosecution should notify the Registrar without delay if they wish to be represented at the hearing. The prosecution should note that the Registrar will not delay listing to await a response from the Prosecution as to whether they wish to attend. Prosecutors should note that occasionally, for example, where the single judge fixes a hearing date at short notice, the case may be listed very quickly.

39A.5 If the prosecution wishes to be represented at any hearing, the notification should include details of Counsel instructed and a time estimate. An application by the prosecution to remove a case from the list for Counsel's convenience, or to allow further preparation time, will rarely be granted.
39A.6 There may be occasions when the Court of Appeal Criminal Division will grant leave to appeal to an unrepresented applicant and proceed forthwith with the appeal in the absence of the appellant and Counsel. The prosecution should not attend any hearing at which the appellant is unrepresented, *Nasteska v The former Yugoslav Republic of Macedonia* 2005 No 23152/05. As a Court of Review, the Court of Appeal Criminal Division would expect the prosecution to have raised any specific matters of relevance with the sentencing Judge in the first instance.

4.57 *Respondent's notice*

Criminal Procedure Rules 2015 2015/1490 Rule 39.6(1) The Registrar:
(a) may serve an appeal notice on any party directly affected by the appeal, and
(b) must do so if the Criminal Cases Review Commission refers a conviction, verdict, finding or sentence to the court.
(2) Such a party may serve a respondent's notice, and must do so if:
(a) that party wants to make representations to the court, or
(b) the court or the Registrar so directs.
(3) Such a party must serve the respondent's notice on:
(a) the appellant,
(b) the Registrar, and
(c) any other party on whom the Registrar served the appeal notice.
(4) Such a party must serve the respondent's notice:
(a) not more than 14 days after the Registrar serves:
i) the appeal notice, or
ii) a direction to do so, or
(b) not more than 28 days after the Registrar serves notice that the Commission has referred a conviction.

Guide to Commencing Proceedings in the Court of Appeal 2018 A9 **Respondent's Notice** para A9-1. The Criminal Procedure Rules provide for the service of a Respondent's Notice. Pursuant to CrimPR 39.6(1) the Registrar may serve the appeal notice on any party directly affected by the appeal (usually the prosecution) and must do so in a CCRC case. That party may then serve a Respondent's Notice if it wishes to make representations and must do so if the Registrar so directs (CrimPR 39.6(2)(b)). If directed, the Respondent's Notice should be served within 14 days (CrimPR 39.6(4)(a)). However, unless the case is urgent (in which case the Registrar may impose a deadline shorter than 14 days), 21 days is normally allowed for service. The Respondent's Notice should be served on the Registrar and any other party on whom the Registrar served the appeal notice.
A9-2. The Respondent's Notice must be in the specified Form RN and should set out the grounds of opposition (CrimPR 39.6(5)) including the information set out in CrimPR 39.6(6).
A9-3. In practice, this procedure primarily applies prior to consideration of leave by the single Judge. However, a Respondent's Notice may be sought at any time in the proceedings including at the direction of the single Judge. The Attorney General and the Registrar, following consultation with representatives from the Crown Prosecution Service (CPS) and the Revenue and Customs Prosecution Office (RCPO), have agreed guidance on types of cases and/or issues where the Registrar should consider whether to serve an appeal notice and direct or invite a party to serve a Respondent's Notice before the consideration of leave by the single Judge.
Examples of when the Registrar might direct a Respondent's Notice include:
where the grounds concern matters which were the subject of public interest immunity (PII);

allegations of jury irregularity;
criticisms of the prosecution or the conduct of the Judge;
(iv) complex frauds;
(v) inconsistent verdicts;
(vi) fresh evidence;
(vii) where the grounds claim that the wrong statute, rule or regulation was applied.

The CPS will always be invited to lodge a Respondent's Notice in the following cases:
(i) all conviction and sentence applications involving a fatality;
(ii) all conviction applications involving rape, attempted rape or a serious sexual offence;
(iii) all conviction applications where a CPS Complex Casework Unit dealt with the case;
(iv) all conviction applications where the offence was perverting the course of justice, misconduct in public office and any conspiracy.

A9-4. [Re conviction cases Not listed]

Note: For the court form, see www.banksr.com Other Matters Other Documents tab Court of Appeal. Ed.

4.58 ***Respondent's notice Requirements***

Criminal Procedure Rules 2015 2015/1490 Rule 39.6(5) The respondent's notice must be in the form set out in the Practice Direction.

(6) The respondent's notice must:
(a) give the date on which the respondent was served with the appeal notice,
(b) identify each ground of opposition on which the respondent relies, numbering them consecutively (if there is more than one), concisely outlining each argument in support and identifying the ground of appeal to which each relates,
(c) identify the relevant sentencing powers of the Crown Court, if sentence is in issue,
(d) summarise any relevant facts not already summarised in the appeal notice,
(e) identify any relevant authorities,
(f) include or attach any application for the following, with reasons:
(i) an extension of time within which to serve the respondent's notice,
(ii) bail pending appeal,
(iii) a direction to attend in person a hearing that the respondent could attend by live link, if the respondent is in custody,
(iv) the introduction of evidence, including hearsay evidence and evidence of bad character,
(v) an order requiring a witness to attend court,
(vi) a direction for special measures for a witness, and
(g) identify any other document or thing that the respondent thinks the court will need to decide the appeal.

Single judge

4.59 ***Single judge***

Guide to Commencing Proceedings in the Court of Appeal 2018 A15 **Refusal by the Single Judge** A15-1. Where the single Judge refuses leave to appeal, the Registrar sends a notification of the refusal, including any observations which the Judge may have made, to the appellant, who is informed that he may require the application to be considered by the Court by serving a renewal notice (Form SJ-Renewal) upon the Registrar within 14 days from the date on which the notice of refusal was served on him.

A15-2. A refused application which is not renewed within 14 days lapses. An appellant may apply for an extension of time in which to renew his application for leave (CrimPR 36.3 – 36.5 and s.31 Criminal Appeal Act 1968). The Registrar will normally refer such an application to the Court to be considered at the same time as the renewed application for leave to appeal. An application for an extension of time in which to renew must be supported by cogent reasons.

A15-3. If it is intended that an advocate should represent the appellant at the hearing of the renewed application for leave to appeal, whether privately instructed or on a pro bono basis, such intention must be communicated to the CAO in writing as soon as that decision has been made. Whilst a representation order is not granted by the Registrar in respect of a renewed application for leave, the advocate may apply at the hearing to the Court for a representation order to cover that appearance and any further work done in preparation of the renewal retrospectively. In practice, this is only granted where the application for leave is successful.

For an example of a Lord Justice acting as a single judge, see *R v Adoboli* 2014 EWCA Crim 1204 at para 1.

4.60 ***Single judge, Powers of***

Criminal Appeal Act 1968 s 31(1) There may be exercised by a single judge in the same manner as by the Court of Appeal and subject to the same provisions:

(a) the powers of the Court of Appeal under this Part of this Act specified in subsection (2) below,

(aa) the power to give leave under Criminal Appeal Act 1995 s 14(4B),

(b) the power to give directions under Sexual Offences (Amendment) Act 1976 s 4(4),[45] and

(c) the powers to make orders for the payment of costs under Prosecution of Offences Act 1985 s 16-18 in proceedings under this Part of this Act.

(2) The powers mentioned in subsection (1)(a) above are the following:

(a) to give leave to appeal,

(b) to extend the time within which notice of appeal or of application for leave to appeal may be given,

(c) to allow an appellant to be present at any proceedings,

(ca) to give a live link direction under section 22(4),

(d) to order a witness to attend for examination,

(e) to exercise the powers conferred by section 19,

(f) to make orders under section 8(2) and discharge or vary such orders,

(g) [repealed]

(h) to give directions under section 29(1),

(i) to make orders under section 23(1)(a).

Note: The single judge has power to make the following orders. The subsection number in front denotes where the power is granted in the Act. Ed.

Criminal Appeal Act 1968 s 31(2ZA) renew an Interim Hospital Order made by them by virtue of any provision of this Part,

(2A) suspend a person's disqualification under Road Traffic Offenders Act 1988 s 40(2),

(2B) grant leave of appeal under Criminal Justice Act 1988 s 159,

(2C) under Licensing Act 2003 s 130, to suspend an order under section 129,

(2D) grant leave to appeal under Criminal Justice Act 1987 s 9(11),

(2E) grant leave to appeal under Criminal Procedure and Investigations Act 1996 s 35(1),

(2F) make, discharge or vary a witness anonymity order under Coroners and Justice Act 2009 Part 3, Ch 2.

4.61 ***Single judge Oral hearings***

Guide to Commencing Proceedings in the Court of Appeal 2018 A11 **Oral applications for leave to appeal** All applications for leave (together with any ancillary applications such as for bail, extension of time, or a representation order) are normally considered by a single Judge on the papers, unless it can be demonstrated that there are exceptional reasons why an oral hearing is required. An advocate or solicitors may request an oral

[45] Repealed on 7/10/04 by Youth Justice and Criminal Evidence Act 1999 Sch 6 para 1

hearing, but that request must be supported by written reasons stating why the case is exceptional and any reasons why that hearing should be expedited (expedition will be a matter for the Registrar). That application should be copied to the prosecution. The single Judge determining the substantive application will then decide whether an oral hearing should be arranged. An advocate may make an application for a representation order at the hearing itself. Oral applications for leave and bail are usually heard in Court but in chambers at 9.30am before the normal Court sittings. Advocates appear unrobed. If the advocate considers that an application may take longer than 20 minutes, the Registrar must be notified. If the single Judge declines to hear the application at an oral hearing, the application will then be considered on the papers by that Judge. The single judge may grant the application for leave, refuse it, or refer it to the full court. In conviction cases and in sentence cases where appropriate, the single judge may grant limited leave, i.e. leave to argue some grounds but not others. If the grounds upon which leave has been refused are to be renewed before the full court, counsel must notify the Registrar within 14 days. In the absence of any notification of renewal, it will be assumed that the grounds upon which leave was refused will not be pursued. The single judge may also grant, refuse or refer any ancillary application.

4.62 ***Disclosure***
R v Clarke and Sheppard 2017 EWCA Crim 37 LCJ The Court heard an appeal against conviction where there was no disclosure issue before the trial Judge. The defence made significant disclosure requests about the use of undercover officers. Held. The Court set out the continuing nature of the prosecution's duty to disclose, the relevant powers, the role of the single judge and the procedure generally.
Note: The case is not further summarised as disclosure so rarely arises in appeals against sentence. Ed.
See also the ***Public Interest Immunity hearings*** para at **4.63**.

4.63 ***Disclosure Public interest immunity hearings***
Note: These hearings are more likely to occur in conviction appeals. The procedure can be found in *R v McDonald* 2004 EWCA Crim 2614.

4.64 ***Leave, Who can grant?***
Criminal Appeal Act 1968 s 11(1) Subject to subsection (1A) below, an appeal against sentence, whether under section 9(1) or 10, lies only with the leave of the Court of Appeal.
(1A) If, within 28 days from the date on which the sentence was passed, the judge who passed it grants a certificate that the case is fit for appeal under section 9 or 10 of this Act, an appeal lies under this section without the leave of the Court of Appeal.

4.65 ***Partial leave/Adding a ground of appeal***
Criminal Procedure Rules 2015 2015/1490 Rule 36.14(1)[46] If the court gives permission to appeal then unless the court otherwise directs the decision indicates that:

(a) the appellant has permission to appeal on every ground identified by the appeal notice; and
(b) the court finds reasonably arguable each ground on which the appellant has permission to appeal.

(2) If the court gives permission to appeal but not on every ground identified by the appeal notice the decision indicates that:

(a) at the hearing of the appeal the court will not consider representations that address any ground thus excluded from argument; and
(b) an appellant who wants to rely on such an excluded ground needs the court's permission to do so.

[46] Added by Criminal Procedure (Amendment) Rules 2017 2017/144 para 9

(3) An appellant who wants to rely at the hearing of an appeal on a ground of appeal excluded from argument by a judge of the Court of Appeal when giving permission to appeal must:

(a) apply in writing, with reasons, and identify each such ground;

(b) serve the application on: i) the Registrar, and ii) any respondent;

(c) serve the application not more than 14 days after:

(i) the giving of permission to appeal, or

(ii) the Registrar serves notice of that decision on the applicant, if the applicant was not present in person or by live link when permission to appeal was given.

[For sub-section (4) and (5) see **4.32**]

Criminal Practice Directions 2015 EWCA Crim 1567 para IX 39C.4[47] Where the appellant wants to rely on a ground of appeal that is not identified by the appeal notice, an application under Criminal Procedure Rules 2015 Rule 36.14(5) is required. In *R v James and Others* 2018 EWCA Crim 285 the Court of Appeal identified as follows the considerations that obtain and the criteria that the court will apply on any such application.

(a) as a general rule all the grounds of appeal that an appellant wishes to advance should be lodged with the appeal notice, subject to their being perfected on receipt of transcripts from the Registrar.

(b) the application for permission to appeal under section 31 of the Criminal Appeal Act 1968 is an important stage in the process. It may not be treated lightly or its determination in effect ignored merely because fresh representatives would have done or argued things differently to their predecessors. Fresh grounds advanced by fresh representatives must be particularly cogent.

(c) as well as addressing the factors material to the determination of an application for an extension of time within which to renew an application for permission to appeal, if that is required, on an application under Criminal Procedure Rules Rule 36.14(5) [see **4.32**] the appellant or his or her representatives must address directly the factors which the court is likely to consider relevant when deciding whether to allow the substitution or addition of grounds of appeal. Those factors include (but this list is not exhaustive):

(i) the extent of the delay in advancing the fresh ground or grounds;

(ii) the reasons for that delay;

(iii) whether the facts or issues the subject of the fresh ground were known to the appellant's representatives when they advised on appeal;

(iv) the interests of justice and the overriding objective in Part 1 of the Criminal Procedure Rules.

(d) [Not listed. About *R v McCook* 2014 duties, transcripts and respondent's notices and adding nothing new.]

(e) while an application under Criminal Procedure Rules 36.14(5) will not require "exceptional leave", and hence the demonstration of substantial injustice should it not be granted, the hurdle for the applicant is a high one nonetheless. Representatives should remind themselves of the provisions of paragraph 39C.2 above.

(f) permission to renew out of time an application for permission to appeal is not given unless the applicant can persuade the court that very good reasons exist. If that application to renew out of time is accompanied by an application to vary the grounds of appeal, the hurdle will be higher still.

(g) any application to substitute or add grounds will be considered by a fully constituted court and at a hearing, not on the papers.

(h) on any renewal of an application for permission to appeal accompanied by an application under Criminal Procedure Rules 36.14(5), if the court refuses those applications it has the power to make a loss of time order or an order for costs in line with *R v Gray and Others* 2014 EWCA Crim 2372, 2015 1 Cr App R (S) 27 (p 197). By analogy

[47] As inserted by Criminal Practice Directions 2015 Amendment No 7 2018 EWCA Crim 1760. In force 1/10/18

with *R v Kirk* 2015 EWCA Crim 1764 (where the court refused an extension of time) the court has the power to order payment of the costs of obtaining the respondent's notice and any additional transcripts.
R v Hyde and Others 2016 EWCA Crim 1031, 2 Cr App R (S) 39 (p 416) para 32 The court gave guidance about partial leave:

1) The Single Judge is entitled to grant leave to appeal against sentence on limited grounds or against part of a sentence only.
2) The limited basis on which leave to appeal is granted should be made unambiguously clear on the form SJ.
3) It is a matter for the discretion and evaluation of the Single Judge (where not refusing leave outright on all grounds) as to whether to grant leave to appeal on limited grounds or whether to grant leave to appeal generally.
4) If an applicant desires to pursue those grounds for which leave to appeal has been refused by the Single Judge he is required to renew his application in the usual way within the prescribed time limit.
5) Where the Single Judge has granted leave, either generally or on a limited basis, leave from the Full Court is required to advance a further ground formulated since the Single Judge's decision.
6) If limited leave is granted by the Single Judge together with a Representation Order, that funding is limited to the ground(s) identified as arguable by the single Judge. It will only extend to arguing renewed grounds of appeal if the Full Court subsequently grants leave on the renewed grounds.
7) No different approach is called for where one element of the sentence relates to a Bail Act offence (although of course leave is not required to argue any ground challenging a sentence for a Bail Act offence).
8) Where a sentence requires to be corrected in order to put right an unlawful element of the sentence, but the totality of the sentence will not arguably be affected by correction of such error and there are no other grounds considered arguable and there is no other complexity, the Single Judge ordinarily should grant leave to appeal on that part of the sentence only, withholding a grant of representation order; the matter will then be dealt with by the Full Court as a non-counsel application. If in such a case any other grounds have been raised and rejected by the Single Judge the applicant is then required to renew in the usual way if he wishes to pursue those grounds.

para 21 Where partial leave is granted, no loss of time direction can be made if the Full Court rejects grounds where leave was refused. Limited leave does not preclude the Full Court from restructuring a sentence under Criminal Justice Act 1968 s 11(3). para 25 Where grounds overlap or have a cumulative impact, the Single Judge may well think there is merit in granting leave generally.
Old case: *R v Cox and Thomas* 1999 2 Cr App R 6 (The principles in this case have been incorporated into *R v Hyde and Others* 2016.)

4.66 ***Leave refused by single judge Right to go to the full court, legal aid and time limit***

Criminal Appeal Act 1968 s 31(3) If the single judge refuses an application on the part of an appellant to exercise in his favour any of the powers above specified, the appellant shall be entitled to have the application determined by the Court of Appeal.
Criminal Procedure Rules 2015 2015/1490 Rule 36.5(2) [The party with the right to renew] must:

(a) renew the application in the form set out in the Practice Direction, signed by or on behalf of the applicant,
(b) serve the renewed application on the Registrar not more than 14 days after:
 (i) the refusal of the application that the applicant wants to renew, or
 (ii) the Registrar serves that refusal on the applicant, if the applicant was not present in person or by live link when the original application was refused.

R v Oates 2002 EWCA Crim 1071, 2 Cr App R 39 (p 654) D was refused leave to appeal her conviction for murder. The defence contended she should have legal aid at the full court because of her human rights. Held. There was no breach of European Convention on Human Rights art 6(3)(c). *Monnell and Morris v UK* 1988 10 EHRR 205 held that the interests of justice did not require on an application for leave to appeal that a defendant was entitled to be present or be represented. (The Court referred to a number of other European authorities to support this.)
Guide to Commencing Proceedings in the Court of Appeal 2018 A12 **Powers of the single Judge** The single Judge may grant the application for leave, refuse it or refer it to the full Court. In conviction cases and in sentence cases where appropriate, the single Judge may grant limited leave i.e. leave to argue some grounds but not others. Advocates must notify the Registrar within 14 days whether the grounds upon which leave has been refused are to be renewed before the full Court. If a representation order is granted, in a limited leave case, public funding will only cover grounds of appeal which the single Judge or the full Court say are arguable (*R v Cox and Thomas* 1999 2 Cr App R 6 and *R v Hyde and Others* 2016 EWCA Crim 1031, 2 Cr App R (S) 39 (416)). The single Judge may also grant, refuse or refer any ancillary application.
Note: To renew an application for leave to appeal it is necessary for either the defendant or his legal representative to fill in Part 3 of the single judge's determination sheet, Form SJ. If this is not done, there is no valid renewal. Ed.

4.67 *Leave refused by single judge Fatality cases Prosecution right to attend when application for leave granted in their absence*

Note: I understand that in order to comply with their obligations under the Victim's Code and pursuant to Criminal Procedure Rules 2005 2005/1490 Rule 39A.4, the CPS have notified the Registrar that they would wish to be represented on all sentence appeals which involve a fatality. In renewed applications for leave to appeal sentence (where the prosecution do not normally attend), the following passage now appears in the Criminal Appeal Office Summary in sentence appeals involving a fatality:
'This renewed application is for leave to appeal against a sentence imposed for an offence involving a fatality. The Crown Prosecution Service has indicated that it wishes to be represented at all sentence appeals involving a fatality in order to represent the victim and their family, who will also have the opportunity to attend. In those circumstances, if the court is minded to grant the application for leave to appeal, the Registrar respectfully invites the court to consider adjourning the hearing of the appeal for prosecution counsel to attend.' Ed.
R v Palmer 2017 EWCA Crim 471 D pleaded to murder. Leave to appeal was refused but the appeal was allowed. The case was re-listed because of the protocol [agreed between the CPS and the Court of Appeal] so that the prosecution could attend and the case was re-argued. For more details, see **287.60** in Volume 2.

4.68 *Leave refused by single judge Renewal out of time*

Application for extension of time
Criminal Procedure Rules 2015 2015/1490 Rule 36.4 A person who wants an extension of time within which to serve a notice or make an application must: a) apply for that extension of time when serving that notice or making that application, and b) give the reasons for the application for an extension of time.

The hearing

Costs see the **Costs Appeal** section at **22.65**.
Disqualification For the power of the single judge to suspend disqualification see the ***Single judge, Powers of*** para at **4.60**.

4.69 *Powers of the court*

Criminal Appeal Act 1968 s 11(3) On an appeal against sentence the Court of Appeal, if they consider that the appellant should be sentenced differently for an offence for which he was dealt with by the court below, may:

(a) quash any sentence or order which is the subject of the appeal, and
(b) in place of it pass such sentence or make such order as they think appropriate for the case and as the court below had power to pass or make when dealing with him for the offence,

but the Court shall so exercise their powers under this subsection that, taking the case as a whole, the appellant is not more severely dealt with on appeal than he was dealt with by the court below.

(3A) Where the Court of Appeal exercise their power under paragraph (a) of subsection (3) to quash a confiscation order, the Court may, instead of proceeding under paragraph (b) of that subsection, direct the Crown Court to proceed afresh under the relevant enactment.

(3B) When proceeding afresh pursuant to subsection (3A), the Crown Court shall comply with any directions the Court of Appeal may make.

(3C) The Court of Appeal shall exercise the power to give such directions so as to ensure that any confiscation order made in respect of the appellant by the Crown Court does not deal more severely with the appellant than the order quashed under subsection (3)(a).

(3D) For the purposes of this section:

'confiscation order' means a confiscation order made under:
(a) Drug Trafficking Offences Act 1986 s 1,
(b) Criminal Justice Act 1988 s 71,
(c) Drug Trafficking Act 1994 s 2, or
(d) Proceeds of Crime Act 2002 s 6,

'relevant enactment', in relation to a confiscation order quashed under subsection (3)(a), means the enactment under which the order was made.[48]

(5) The fact that an appeal is pending against an Interim Hospital Order under the Mental Health Act 1983 shall not affect the power of the court below to renew or terminate the order or to deal with the appellant on its termination, and where the Court of Appeal quash such an order but do not pass any sentence or make any other order in its place the Court may, subject to Criminal Justice and Public Order Act 1994 s 25, direct the appellant to be kept in custody or released on bail pending his being dealt with by the court below.

For an example of the Court of Appeal directing that all matters requiring resolution about a substituted confiscation order 'be remitted to the Crown Court' for decision, see *R v Meader* 2011 EWCA Crim 2108.

For the definitions, see Criminal Appeal Act 1968 s 10(4) at **4.4**.

4.70 ***The Court of Appeal is a court of review***

R v A and B 1999 1 Cr App R (S) 52 LCJ at page 56. The Court of Appeal Criminal Division is a court of review. Its function is to review sentences imposed by courts at first instance, not to conduct a sentencing exercise of its own from the beginning.

For more details of the case, see **71.6** and **71.18**.

R v Roberts and Others 2016 EWCA Crim 71, 2 Cr App R (S) 14 (p 98) para 19 It is well established that this court is a court of review. There is no basis for departing from the principle in *R v A and B* 1999. This court considers the material before the sentencing court and any further material admitted before the court under well-established principles. It considers whether the sentence was wrong in principle or manifestly excessive. It does not, years after the sentence, in the light of what has happened over that period, consider whether an offender should be sentenced in an entirely new way because of what has happened in the penal system or because, as in *R v ZTR* 2015 EWCA Crim 1427, the offender has supplied information long after conviction.

Att-Gen's Ref No 79 of 2015 2016 EWCA Crim 448, 2 Cr App R (S) 18 (p 158) D pleaded to attempted GBH with intent and possession of an offensive weapon. He was sentenced on the basis that he had attacked a stranger who was wearing a full burka. The

[48] Sub-paragraphs (a)-(c) have been repealed but the references to them remain in the Criminal Appeal Act 1968.

Attorney-General applied for the sentence to be varied. At some stage, the victim saw D's face in the press and recognised him as someone who had demanded she do something and she had refused. She told the police about that. The Crown Court ordered a further psychiatric report and an addition to the pre-sentence report. The Court purported to vary the sentence outside the time limits. Held. That was unlawful. para 10 The power to declare a sentence unduly lenient depends entirely on what was put before the original sentencing court. It is not open to the Attorney-General to rely upon further evidence not placed before the sentencing court to justify the reference, *Att-Gen's Ref No 19 of 2005* 2006 (see above). para 13 So this court must decide whether a particular sentence is unduly lenient. If it is, it must be quashed whereupon, by virtue of that provision, the court is required to pass 'such sentence as they think appropriate for the case and as the court below have power to pass when dealing with him'. Then it is open for the court to take into account whatever new information is available. We substitute an 11-year extended sentence (7 years' custody 4 years' extended licence) taking into account the new information and reports, which is what the Judge attempted to pass outside the time limits.
R v Rogers 2016 EWCA Crim 801, 2 Cr App R (S) 36 (p 370) LCJ The Court is a court of review. The function of this Court is to review sentences and not to conduct a sentence hearing.
Note: It does not appear that *Att-Gen's Ref No 79 of 2015* 2016 EWCA Crim 448 (see above) was cited in this case. The rule that the Court of Appeal was a court of review was shaped for judicial convenience at a time when sentencing was simple and mistakes hardly happened. It would be unfortunate if prosecutors can put in all material that they wish once it is shown that the sentence was unduly lenient, whereas the defendant is unable to put in relevant material once he or she has established that the sentence was manifestly excessive. Ed.

4.71 ***Right of appellant(s) to attend***

Note: All hearings of the full court are open to the public except where there has been a successful application for the Court to sit in private. Ed.
Right of appellant to be present.
Criminal Appeal Act 1968 s 22(1) Except as provided by this section,[49] an appellant shall be entitled to be present, if he wishes it, on the hearing of his appeal, although he may be in custody.
(2) A person in custody shall not be entitled to be present:
  (a) where his appeal is on some ground involving a question of law alone,[50] or
  (b) on an application by him for leave to appeal, or
  (c) on any proceedings preliminary or incidental to an appeal, or
  (d) where he is in custody in consequence of a verdict of not guilty by reason of insanity or of a finding of disability,
unless the Court of Appeal give him leave to be present.
(3) The power of the Court of Appeal to pass sentence on a person may be exercised although he is for any reason not present.
(4)-(6) [These subsections deal with live link.]
Criminal Procedure Rules 2015 2015/1490 Rule 39.11 A party who is in custody has a right to attend a hearing in public unless:
  (a) it is a hearing preliminary or incidental to an appeal, including the hearing of an application for permission to appeal, or
  (b) that party is in custody in consequence of:
    (i) a verdict of not guilty by reason of insanity, or
    (ii) a finding of disability.

[49] This section also provides the live link provisions.
[50] Since the Criminal Appeal Act 1995, sub-section a) is a relic of no practical application.

R v Martindale 2014 EWCA Crim 1232 D pleaded to landlord Health and Safety offences. A tenant died and another collapsed due to a faulty gas boiler. D was given a Suspended Sentence Order, a £4,000 fine and a £17,500 costs order. She was granted leave to appeal but declined legal aid. The Court of Appeal explained that they were unable to guarantee her travel expenses as they could only be considered at the end of the hearing. She said that as she was unable to afford to attend, the prosecution should not be in a position to attend in order to add anything to the written submissions. Held. We have some sympathy for D but she has chosen not to attend. There is a public interest in the prosecution attending, but we did not invite the prosecution to assist the Court further and the merits of the appeal were considered on the strength of the written submissions.

4.72 ***Ground of appeal found that was not particularised***
R v JB 2017 EWCA Crim 568 D's SHPO was made without objection. He appealed his custodial term for indecent images of his former girlfriend who was then aged 16. Held. We reduce the custodial term and notice that there was no power to make the SHPO, because the condition in Sexual Offences Act 2003 Sch 3 para 13 (the image must be of a person under 16) was not met. As there was no ground of appeal for that and because the prosecution are not represented today, we give them 21 days to notify us that they want to intervene. If no intervention is made, the SHPO will be quashed.
Note: In fact, the condition in Schedule 3 does not apply to the making of an SHPO, see Sexual Offences Act 2003 s 103B(8) and (9), at **101.6**. However, looking at the facts of the case, I consider the 'necessity' test was not made out, see Sexual Offences Act 2003 s 103(2)(b) at **101.3**. Far too many SHPO orders are waved through without proper consideration. For more detail, see **328.26**. Ed.

4.73 ***Court of Appeal can backdate a sentence***
Criminal Appeal Act 1968 s 29(4) The term of any sentence passed by the Court of Appeal under section 3, 4, 5, 11 or 13(4) of this Act shall, unless the Court otherwise direct, begin to run from the time when it would have begun to run if passed in the proceedings from which the appeal lies.
R v Turner 1975 61 Cr App R 67 page 92 D faced two trials. At the end of the first trial D was sentenced to 16 years and his remand time counted against the sentence. At the end of the second trial, D was sentenced to 21 years concurrent. The 21-year sentence started on the day it was passed. Held. We appreciate the difficulty caused. The trial Judge could do nothing about it. 21 years was manifestly excessive, so 18 years. We can solve the start-date difficulty by using section 29(4). We direct that the 18-year sentence shall start at the same time as the other sentence and so have its remand time deducted. The Crown Court cannot backdate a sentence, see **86.54**.

4.74 ***Shall 'not be dealt with more severely', Defendant***
Criminal Appeal Act 1968 s 11(3) On an appeal against sentence the Court of Appeal, if they consider that the appellant should be sentenced differently for an offence for which he was dealt with by the court below may:

(a) quash any sentence or order which is the subject of the appeal; and
(b) in place of it pass such sentence or make such order as they think appropriate for the case and as the court below had power to pass or make when dealing with him for the offence;

but the Court shall so exercise their powers under this subsection that, taking the case as a whole, the appellant is not more severely dealt with on appeal than he was dealt with by the court below.
R v Bennett 1968 52 Cr App R 514 D pleaded to indecent assault. He was sentenced to 3 years' imprisonment when unrepresented. The mental health report could not be used as it did not satisfy the statutory requirements. Held. A Hospital Order with a Restriction Order for an indefinite period is appropriate. A Hospital Order which is a remedial order

designed to treat and cure D cannot be regarded as more severe than imprisonment even though in certain events the Hospital Order may involve detention for a longer period of time than the 3-year sentence. We so order.

R v Sandwell 1985 80 Cr App R 78 D pleaded to two driving whilst disqualified counts. In the past he had been disqualified for 3, 3 and 2 years. He was sentenced to 12 months' disqualification on both counts and 6 months under the totting up provisions, all consecutive to each other. This was unlawful because disqualification cannot be consecutive and the totting up disqualification had to be for 12 months. Held. The 30-month disqualification was entirely justified. 'Taking the case as a whole' in subsection 11(3) means taking the totality of the matters in respect of which D was dealt with by the Crown Court. The first and third disqualification shall be 12 months and the second disqualification shall be 2 years, all concurrent making 2 years.

R v Waters and Young 2008 EWCA Crim 2538 D and Y were given suspended sentences because they had served the appropriate immediate sentence. On appeal counsel argued for an immediate term of imprisonment. Held. The imposition of immediate imprisonment does not offend subsection 11(3) because no ordinary person would consider D and Y were being dealt with more severely.

R v Aldridge and Eaton 2012 EWCA Crim 1456 LCJ E was given a 3-year SOPO. Later the Judge was told the minimum period was 5 years and he varied it to 5 years believing that was the order he made. The application for variation was out of time and no one attended. Held. The order was unlawful. The term could not be extended as that would be treating E 'more severely'. The order must be quashed.

R v Searles 2012 EWCA Crim 2685 D pleaded to robbery. The defence and probation wanted a psychiatric report. The Judge sentenced D to 2 years' YOI without a report. D appealed and a report was obtained. The defence at the first hearing advocated a Hospital Order with a Restriction Order. At the second hearing the oral evidence indicated that a Restriction Order was not necessary. Held. A Hospital Order was the right order. It cannot be regarded as more severe than a sentence of imprisonment or custody, notwithstanding the fact that this appellant will, within a matter of a week or two, be reaching the end of the term of custody imposed in the Court below. The effect of the order which we make today will extend beyond the end date of that custodial term, but its purpose is ameliorative and remedial and not punitive and therefore does not fall foul of the restriction in section 11(3).

R v Thompson and Others 2018 EWCA Crim 639, 2 Cr App R (S) 19 (p 164) (Five-judge court) The Court considered four cases to determine the meaning of 'more severely dealt with'. Held. para 10 When considering section 11(3) the potential impact of a sentence on the offender cannot be ignored. [The cases were reviewed.] Those decisions are case-specific and no general rule can be identified. para 15 Whether a sentence is 'more severe' is not only determined by the period for which an offender might be affected by it but [also] the punitive element of the sentence has to be considered. For an extended sentence pursuant to section 226A or 226B or for an Offender of Particular Concern Order section 11(3) will bite to limit the powers of this court. The authorities based on *R v Round and Dunn* 2009 [and others, see **242.54** in Volume 2] do not provide the appropriate approach. In *R v Bradbury* 2015 EWCA Crim 1176, 2 Cr App R (S) 72 (p 485) it is difficult to see how it could be suggested that he was not being dealt with more severely. That decision does not sit with section 11(3) and should not be followed. *R v Fruen and DS* 2016 EWCA Crim 561, 2 Cr App R (S) 30 (p 271) is not authority for the proposition that if a custodial term is reduced by at least a year, a sentence under Criminal Justice Act 2003 s 236A will necessarily satisfy the requirements of section 11(3). The issue of section 11(3) requires a detailed consideration of the impact of the sentence to be substituted which must involve considerations of entitlement to automatic release, parole eligibility and licence. If a custodial sentence is reduced, the addition of non-custodial orders (such as disqualification from driving or

Sexual Offences Prevention Orders[51]) may be added but, in every case, save where the substituted sentence is 'ameliorative and remedial', that sentence must be tested for its severity (or potential punitive effect) compared to the original sentence.

para 41 For T, who was given Offenders of Particular Concern Orders (in error) (where eligibility for release is after serving one half of the sentence) and should have been given extended sentences (where eligibility for release is after serving two-thirds of the sentence), the date where release becomes unconditional will be of particular importance when assessing comparative severity. We substitute in total a 21½-year extended sentence (17 years' custody 4½ years' extended licence) which will be consecutive to a 2-year determinate term. He will have to be released after serving 18 years whereas previously he had been entitled to be released after 24 years 1 month, so the new sentence is not more severe. para 55 For C, his 12-year determinate sentence should have been an extended sentence but because of section 11(3) we cannot impose that. For F, the Judge was required to pass an Offender of Particular Concern Order but because of section 11(3) we are unable to substitute that. For RF, he was sentenced to consecutive terms totalling 45 years. He was plainly dangerous and should have been given an extended sentence. We substitute a 20-year extended sentence (12 years' custody 8 years' extended licence). He will have to be released after serving 12 years. With the original sentence he would have been released after serving 22½ years. Section 11(3) is [complied with].

Note: I was counsel in the case and during the hearing the phrase 'looking at the worst-case scenario' was frequently used by the Judges. In substituting the terms they did, the approach seems to be making sure that the worst-case scenario for release was not more severe than the previous sentence. Support for this approach is in the phrase 'potential impact of a sentence' at the beginning of the summary and the phrase 'potential punitive effects' near the end of the summary. Ed.

R v Suffi 2018 EWCA Crim 1750 D pleaded to harassment (5 years' extended sentence (2 years' custody 3 years' extended licence)), perverting the course of justice (5 years concurrent) and two driving whilst disqualified offences (4 months concurrent). Held. The extended sentence was unlawful and the [longer] determinate sentence concurrent to an extended sentence was poor sentencing practice. We would wish to make a 5-year extended sentence (4 years' custody 1 year's extended licence), which would be lawful, and a reduced 4 years for the perverting count. Sadly, we can't. Currently D would be released after 2½ years (half the 5-year term) when the custodial term of the extended sentence would have been served. The proposed sentence would release D after 32 months (two-thirds of 4 years). The proposed sentence would treat D more severely. *R v Thompson and Others* 2018 applied.

See also: *R v Thompson* 1978 66 Cr App R 130 (15 months suspended wrong, 9 months immediate right. Not within our power.)

R v Ardani 1983 77 Cr App R 302 (The court had power to add mandatory disqualification as they were reducing the prison term.)

R v Webber 1983 JP 157[52] (Reducing prison and increasing compensation was permissible.)

R v Socratous 1984 6 Cr App R (S) 33 (Can substitute concurrent imprisonment for probation.)

R v Meader 2011 EWCA Crim 2108 (Confiscation order quashed as unlawful. Compensation order for the same sum substituted.)

R v Price 2013 EWCA Crim 1283, 2014 1 Cr App R (S) 36 (p 216) (Given a community order. Had been sentenced for other offences and, but for the instant offence, would have

[51] The Judge presumably meant Sexual Harm Prevention Orders.

[52] This is a report in the JP magazine and not a report in the JP law reports. For a copy of the transcript see www.banksr.com Other Matters Other Documents tab Cases.

been released on licence some 3 months earlier. Appropriate penalty was 6 months, the equivalent of which he had served. Reviewing the authorities, substituting a 6-month sentence would not be treating the defendant 'more severely'.)
R v Pembele 2018 EWCA Crim 128 (D pleaded to dangerous driving and other offences. Held. His appeal is dismissed and there is nothing we can do about the disqualification period which does not comply with the extension provisions.)
Note: The sooner Parliament permits the Court of Appeal to substitute the correct sentence, the better. This provision does not apply to the making or the variation of a Serious Crime Prevention Order, see **99.40**. Ed.

4.75 ***Shall 'not be dealt with more severely', Defendant Unlawful sentences***
R v Duncuft 1969 53 Cr App R 495 LCJ D, a thief, was sentenced to 4 years for dishonesty offences. He had a dreadful record and was a 'complete nuisance'. The Judge declined to pass an extended sentence, [which would not have altered the length of the sentence, but would have ensured release on licence rather than the normal remission.] Held. We cannot do that as it would be treating the defendant 'more severely'.
Note: This is an old case, but it deals with an important point. Ed.
R v Howden 2006 EWCA Crim 1691, 2007 1 Cr App R (S) 31 (p 164) D absconded and was sentenced to 4 years in total. He was unrepresented and had not been sentenced to imprisonment before, so the sentence was unlawful, see **28.19**. The 4 years was not considered excessive. D was represented at the Court of Appeal. Held. It would be a nonsense if we could not quash the unlawful and substitute the same, correct sentence. The words 'sentenced differently' in subsection 11(3) are capable of meaning 'sentenced lawfully instead of unlawfully'. 4 years.
R v Reynolds and Others 2007 EWCA Crim 538, 2 Cr App R (S) 87 (p 553) The Court considered eight cases where the 'dangerousness' provisions had not been applied properly. Held. para 17 Mistakes may go unnoticed by the prosecution. If the defendant appeals and an error is found in favour of the defendant, real difficulties arise. Where a mandatory sentence or an indeterminate sentence should have been imposed, such that the sentence was 'unlawful', we would normally be obliged to correct it. However, that would mean the defendant was being treated more severely. Criminal Appeal Act 1968 s 11(3) must prevail. The only express power to increase the sentence is the 'loss of time' order. para 23 So even where a court has failed to impose a mandatory sentence that does not create a problem. The original sentence, be it an extended sentence when there should have been an indeterminate sentence, is still a lawful sentence. para 57 For H we cannot substitute the mandatory automatic life for an extended sentence.
Note: It could be said that a 'loss of time' order was not an increase in a sentence but only a change to the release provisions. However, the order is treating the defendant 'more severely', but it is authorised by legislation. Ed.
R v Aldridge and Eaton 2012 EWCA Crim 1456 LCJ E was given a 3-year SOPO. Later the Judge was told the minimum period was 5 years and he varied it to 5 years believing that was the order he made. The application for a variation was out of time and no one attended. Held. The order was unlawful. The term cannot be extended as that would be treating E 'more severely'. The order must be quashed.
R v KPR 2018 EWCA Crim 2537 The first Judge failed to pass an Offender of Particular Concern Order, which made the sentence unlawful. D's sex convictions were quashed. The second Judge did pass such an order. Criminal Appeal Act 1968 s 11(3) and Sch 2 para 2(1) provisions require similar consideration. We consider the different release regimes and rearrange the sentences, see **4.88**.
Old case: *R v McGinlay and Ballantye* 1976 62 Cr App R 156 (Sentenced to Borstal when he was unrepresented. The Crown Court had jurisdiction to pass Borstal but acted unlawfully. Court of Appeal can quash or vary the sentence.)
See also the **PROCEDURE, SENTENCING** ***Unlawful orders*** para at **86.60**.

4.76 ***Conviction on related offence quashed Power to increase a sentence***
Criminal Appeal Act 1968 s 4(1) This section applies where:
(a) two or more related sentences are passed,
(b) the Court of Appeal allow an appeal against conviction in respect of one or more of the offences for which the sentences were passed ('the related offences'), but
(c) the appellant remains convicted of one or more of those offences.
(2) Except as provided by subsection (3) below, the Court may in respect of any related offence of which the appellant remains convicted pass such sentence, in substitution for any sentence passed thereon at the trial, as they think proper and is authorised by law.
(3) The Court shall not under this section pass any sentence such that the appellant's sentence (taken as a whole) for all the related offences of which he remains convicted will, in consequence of the appeal, be of greater severity than the sentence (taken as a whole) which was passed at the trial for all the related offences.
(4) For the purposes of subsection (1)(a), two or more sentences are related if:
(a) they are passed on the same day,
(b) they are passed on different days but the court in passing any one of them states that it is treating that one together with the other or others as substantially one sentence, or
(c) they are passed on different days but in respect of counts on the same indictment.
(5) Where:
(a) two or more sentences are related to each other by virtue of subsection (4)(a) or (b), and
(b) any one or more of those sentences is related to one or more other sentences by virtue of subsection (4)(c), all the sentences are to be treated as related for the purposes of subsection (1)(a).
Examples: *R v O'Grady* 1943 (LCJ D was convicted of two offences under Treachery Act 1940 s 1, two offences under Official Secrets Act 1911 and four defence regulation offences. The Judge sentenced her to death, which was the mandatory sentence for the section 1 offences. He passed no sentence on the other offences. The Court of Appeal quashed the section 1 convictions and used its then powers [under Criminal Appeal Act 1907 s 5] (which was re-enacted in section 4) to substitute 14 years' penal servitude on the other offences.)
R v Dolan 1976 62 Cr App R (S) 36 (D pleaded during his trial to receiving stolen goods. The jury convicted him of theft of the same goods. The Judge sentenced him to 5 years for the theft and gave no penalty for the receiving. The Court of Appeal quashed the theft conviction and used its section 4 powers to substitute 3 years for the receiving conviction.)
R v Gnango 2010 EWCA Crim 1691 (D exchanged gunfire in the street with X. X missed and shot V, who died. D was convicted of the murder of V and the attempted murder of X. He was sentenced to detention during HM's pleasure (20 years minimum term) and 12 years' DPP for the attempted murder. The Court of Appeal quashed the murder conviction and used its section 4 powers to increase the attempted murder sentence to 15 years' DPP.)
Note: In this case, the Supreme Court restored the conviction, *R v Gnango* 2011 UKSC 59. The Court of Appeal then reversed its section 4 order and restored the 12-year DPP sentence, *R v Gnango* 2012 EWCA Crim 77. Ed.

4.77 ***Summary and either way offence(s) Appeal is against all***
Criminal Appeal Act 1968 s 11(2A) Where following conviction on indictment a person has been convicted under Criminal Justice Act 1988 s 41[53] of a summary offence, an appeal or application for leave to appeal against any sentence for the either way offence

[53] Section 41 has been repealed, Criminal Justice Act 1988 Sch 37 Part 4.

shall be treated also as an appeal etc. in respect of any sentence for the summary offence and an appeal etc. against any sentence for the summary offence shall be treated also as an appeal etc. in respect of the either way offence.
(2B) If the appellant or applicant was convicted on indictment of two or more either way offences, the references to the either way offence in subsection (2A) above are to be construed, in relation to any summary offence of which he was convicted under Criminal Justice Act 1988 s 41 following the conviction on indictment, as references to the either way offence specified in the notice relating to that summary offence which was given under subsection (2) of that section.

4.78 ***Powers Deportation, Recommendations for***
Criminal Appeal Act 1968 s 50(2) Any power of the Criminal Division of the Court of Appeal to pass a sentence includes a power to make a recommendation for deportation in cases where the court from which the appeal lies had power to make such a recommendation.

4.79 ***Two or more sentences Appeal is against all***
Criminal Appeal Act 1968 s 11(2) Where the Crown Court, in dealing with an offender either on his conviction on indictment or in a proceeding to which section 10(2) applies, has passed on him two or more sentences in the same proceeding,[54] being sentences against which an appeal lies under section 9(1) or 10, an appeal or application for leave to appeal against any one of those sentences shall be treated as an appeal or application in respect of both or all of them.

4.80 ***Direction for loss of time/Unmeritorious appeals***
Criminal Appeal Act 1968 s 29(1) The time during which an appellant is in custody pending the determination of his appeal shall, subject to any direction which the Court of Appeal may give to the contrary, be reckoned as part of the term of any sentence to which he is for the time being subject.
(2) Where the Court of Appeal give a contrary direction under subsection (1) above, they shall state their reasons for doing so, and they shall not give any such direction where:
(a) leave to appeal has been granted, or
(b) a certificate has been given by the judge of the court of trial, or under:
(i) section 1 or 11(1A) of this Act, or
(ii) Senior Courts Act 1981 s 81(1B), or
(c) the case has been referred to them under Criminal Appeal Act 1995 s 9.
Criminal Practice Directions 2015 EWCA Crim 1567 para IX 39E.1...the Full Court may make such a direction whether or not such an indication has been given by the single judge.
Criminal Practice Directions 2015 EWCA Crim 1567 para IX 39E.1[55] Both the Court and the single judge have power, in their discretion, under the Criminal Appeal Act 1968 sections 29 and 31, to direct that part of the time during which an applicant is in custody after lodging his notice of application for leave to appeal should not count towards sentence. When leave to appeal has been refused by the single judge, it is necessary to consider the reasons given by the single judge before making a decision whether to renew the application. Where an application devoid of merit has been refused by the single judge he may indicate that the Full Court should consider making a direction for loss of time on renewal of the application. However, the Full Court may make such a direction whether or not such an indication has been given by the single judge.
39E.2 The case of *R v Gray and Others* 2014 EWCA Crim 2372 makes clear 'that unmeritorious renewal applications took up a wholly disproportionate amount of staff and judicial resources in preparation and hearing time. They also wasted significant

[54] Criminal Appeal Act 1968 s 11(7) For the purposes of this section, any two or more sentences are to be treated as passed in the same proceeding if: a) they are passed on the same day, or b) they are passed on different days but the court in passing any one of them states that it is treating that one together with the other or others as substantially one sentence.
[55] As inserted by Criminal Practice Directions 2015 Amendment No 7 2018 EWCA Crim 1760. In force 1/10/18

sums of public money...The more time the Court of Appeal Office and the judges spent on unmeritorious applications, the longer the waiting times were likely to be...The only means the court has of discouraging unmeritorious applications which waste precious time and resources is by using the powers given to us by Parliament in the Criminal Appeal Act 1968 and the Prosecution of Offenders Act 1985.'

39E.3 Further, applicants and counsel are reminded of the warning given by the Court of Appeal in *R v Hart and Others* 2006 EWCA Crim 3239, 2007 1 Cr App R 31 (p 412) and should 'heed the fact that this court is prepared to exercise its power...The mere fact that counsel has advised that there are grounds of appeal will not always be a sufficient answer to the question as to whether or not an application has indeed been brought which was totally without merit.'

39E.4 Where the Single Judge has not indicated that the Full Court should consider making a Loss of Time Order because the defendant has already been released, the case of *R v Nolan* 2017 EWCA Crim 2449 indicates that the Single Judge should consider what, if any, costs have been incurred by the Registrar and the Prosecution and should make directions accordingly. Reference should be made to the relevant Costs Division of the Criminal Practice Direction.

Guide to Commencing Proceedings in the Court of Appeal 2018 A16 **Directions for loss of time** A16-1. S.29 Criminal Appeal Act 1968 empowers the Court to direct that time spent in custody as an appellant shall not count as part of the term of any sentence to which the appellant is for the time being subject. The Court will do so where it considers that an application is wholly without merit. Such an order may not be made where leave to appeal or a trial Judge's certificate has been granted, on a reference by the CCRC or where an appeal has been abandoned. An appeal is not built into the trial process but must be justified on properly arguable grounds (*R v Fortean* 2009 EWCA Crim 437, Crim LR 798).

A16-2. The only means the Court has of discouraging unmeritorious applications which waste precious time and resources is by using the powers in the Criminal Appeal Act 1968 and the Prosecution of Offences Act 1985. In every case where the Court is presented with an unmeritorious application, consideration should be given to exercising these powers.

A16-3. The mere fact that an advocate has advised that there are grounds of appeal will not be a sufficient answer to the question as to whether or not an application has indeed been brought which was wholly without merit (*R v Gray and Others* 2014 EWCA Crim 2372, 2015 1 Cr App Rep (S) 27 (p 197).

A16-4. The Form SJ, on which the single Judge records his decisions, and the reverse of which is used by appellants to indicate their wish to renew, includes:

• a box for the single Judge to initial in order to indicate that that the full Court should consider loss of time or a costs order if the application is renewed; and

• a box for the applicant to give reasons why such an order should not be made, whether or not an indication has been given by a single Judge.

A16-5. Where the single Judge has not indicated that the full Court should consider making a loss of time order because the applicant is not in custody, the single Judge also has the option of considering whether to make any directions in respect of costs, which could include the prosecution costs (usually in providing a Respondent's Notice). The Practice Direction in relation to costs should be followed.

Declaration in NG from 1 October 2018.

APPELLANTS IN CUSTODY ONLY

I understand that if the single judge and/or the Court is of the opinion that the application for permission to appeal is plainly without merit, an order may be made that time spent in custody as an appellant shall not count towards sentence.

ALL APPELLANTS

I understand that if the court dismisses my appeal or application it may make an order for payment of costs against me, including the cost of any transcript obtained.

[This form should be signed by the appellant but may be signed by his/her legal representative provided the WARNINGS set out above have been explained to him/her. NB if signed by a legal representative, the appellant will be given the opportunity to request a copy of the form.]

Signature Date

(of appellant or legal representative signing on *behalf* of the appellant)

R v Gray and Others 2014 EWCA Crim 2372, 2015 1 Cr App R (S) 27 (p 197) All defendants, G, R, C, H and U, whose cases had been joined together, made renewed appeals against conviction. For G, he was warned by the single Judge and counsel attended. For R and H, the box about loss of time was not initialled. For C and U, the box was initialled or ticked. Held. All applications were hopeless. Unmeritorious renewal applications take up a wholly disproportionate amount of staff and judicial resources in preparation and hearing time. They also waste significant sums of public money, for example in obtaining transcripts, especially in cases against conviction-…waiting times for conviction cases remain at approximately 12 months. The more time the Court of Appeal Office and the judges spend on unmeritorious cases, the longer the waiting times are likely to be. The fact that the single judge has not initialled the box does not deprive the Full Court of the power to make a loss of time order. In *R v Hart and Others* 2006 EWCA Crim 3239, 2007 2 Cr App R (S) 34 (p 192), the Vice President at that time said, "The mere fact that counsel has advised there are grounds of appeal will not always be a sufficient answer to the question as to whether or not an application has indeed been brought which was totally without merit." If [the Full Court] decides to exercise the power, a statement to this effect would suffice: 'Despite being warned of the Court's power to make a loss of time order, the applicant chose to pursue a totally unmeritorious application which has wasted the time of the Court. Such applications hamper the Court's ability to process meritorious applications in a timely fashion.' The following loss of time orders were made: for G, 2 months, for R, C, H and U, 3 months each.

Note: In these conviction appeals, the long list of complaints etc. and the need for transcripts caused the 3-month orders. In sentence appeals, which tend not to generate the same amount of work or expense, the going rate seems to be 28 days. Ed.

R v Saleem 2015 EWCA Crim 955 The single Judge had not ticked the box on the refusal form. A silk came into the case late and made the submissions. Held. The appeal had no merit at all. Failure to tick the box in no way operates as a bar to make a loss of time order. 42-day loss of time order made.

R v O'Leary 2015 EWCA Crim 1706, 2016 1 Cr App R (S) 18 (p 133) D appealed his sentence. The Single Judge ticked the loss of time box. At the hearing D's counsel asked for an indication whether there would be a loss of time order if he pursued the appeal. Held. That was a wholly inappropriate application. The vice to which loss of time orders are intended to be directed had already occurred.

R v Hyde and Others 2016 EWCA Crim 1031, 2 Cr App R (S) 39 (p 416) para 21 Where partial leave is granted, no loss of time direction can be made if the Full Court rejects grounds where leave was refused.

See also: *R v Horne* 2014 EWCA Crim 1253 (This is an utterly hopeless application. The fact that the defendant was represented on a *pro bono* basis did not give him immunity from having time spent in custody disallowed. In deference to counsel's submissions to the court we don't do so.)

R v Fogo and Another 2014 EWCA Crim 1462 (D and F renewed their appeal. The single Judge warned them loss of time would be considered. One had an advocate. Held. The applications were without merit. The advice of a lawyer is a factor but it is not determinate. 42 days not to count.)
R v Lewis 2014 EWCA Crim 1496 (We would have directed loss of time. However, we don't because counsel took a wrong-headed and wholly illogical approach to 'wrong in principle'. The defendant should not be penalised for that.)
Note: When a single judge refuses leave to appeal, there is a warning on the form the judge signs saying that 'if the application is renewed, the Court may make a loss of time order if the application is considered to be wholly without merit, even if it is supported by your legal advisers. The Court certainly will consider doing so if the judge's initials appear in [a box on the form]' but orders can be made when the box is not ticked. Where the Court considers making an order for loss of time, it is usually influenced by whether the box has been ticked. Since the judgment in *R v Gray* 2014 was issued there has been a dramatic increase in these orders. Ed.

4.81 ***Direction for loss of time/Unmeritorious appeals Defendant not in custody***
R v F 2015 EWCA Crim 1852 D was convicted of producing a controlled drug. He grew a cannabis plant. D was convicted and was given a conditional discharge. He appealed and personally addressed the Court. Held. There was no merit in the appeal. We order D to pay the cost of the transcripts (£55).
R v Nolan 2017 EWCA Crim 2449 In 2011, D was convicted of conspiracy to produce a class B controlled drug and other charges. In 2016, the Court of Appeal dismissed his appeal against his confiscation order. D then appealed his conviction. The single Judge said the appeal was without merit. By this time D had been released. D appeared in person at the full court after renewing the application. Held. The appeal, which was almost five years late, was without merit. However, in future where the single judge would have indicated in an unmeritorious case that the full court ought to consider making a loss of time order, but does not do so because the applicant has been released, it is desirable that the single judge orders that:
1 If the Registrar wishes to recover the costs of transcripts he shall notify the [defendant] as soon as practicable and in any event within 21 days of the cost of the transcripts and the [defendant] shall respond as soon as practicable and in any event within 21 days thereafter with a full statement of means if he contends he is unable to pay the costs.
2 If the prosecution wish to recover their costs of dealing with the application, they must provide a schedule of costs incurred as soon as practicable and in any event within 21 days and the applicant must respond as soon as practicable and in any event within 21 days thereafter if he contends that he should not pay the costs with full reasons why he should not pay and if he contends he is unable to pay then he must provide as soon as practicable and in any event within 21 days thereafter a full statement of means.
Then the Court will have the appropriate information to determine whether a costs order should be made and in what amount. Here the costs were £929. D was on benefits but had £140 in the bank. We order £70 costs.

4.82 ***Direction for loss of time Complex cases***
R v Greaves 2008 EWCA Crim 647 Merely because a renewed application involves papers of great bulk and some complexity, the question whether the Court should exercise its powers under section 29 still arises. Bulk and complexity do not operate as some kind of unspoken barrier to an order under section 29. Complexity and bulk do not turn an unarguable application into one which is arguable.

4.83 ***Direction for loss of time European Convention on Human Rights***
Monnell and Morris v UK 1988 10 EHRR 205 Criminal Appeal Act 1968 s 29 did not breach obligations under either European Convention on Human Rights art 6 (right to a fair trial) or art 5 (the right to liberty).

Other matters

4.84 *Recovery of defence costs order Power to order*

Availability The order is not available in the Crown Court or the Magistrates' Court, see Criminal Legal Aid (Recovery of Defence Costs Order) Regs 2013 2013/511 para 7.

Crown Court In the Crown Court the legal aid payments are by contribution orders, see **22.60**.

Commencement 1 April 2013, see Criminal Legal Aid (Recovery of Defence Costs Order) Regs 2013 2013/511 at the introduction.

Young offenders The charge only applies to defendants aged 18 or over at the time an application is made, see Criminal Legal Aid (Recovery of Defence Costs Order) Regs 2013 2013/511 para 7.

Reasons The Court must record reasons for the terms of the order and reasons if no determination is made, see Criminal Legal Aid (Recovery of Defence Costs Order) Regs 2013 2013/511, para 6(2) and 9, below.

Procedure Much of the procedure and the definitions are set out in the Criminal Legal Aid (Recovery of Defence Costs Order) Regs 2013 2013/511 (much of which is not listed here).

Criminal Legal Aid (Recovery of Defence Costs Order) Regs 2013 2013/511 para 5(1) Subject to regulations 7 to 11, at the conclusion of any relevant proceedings involving a represented individual, the relevant court must make a determination that the represented individual is required to pay:

(a) the cost of that individual's representation in such proceedings; or

(b) such proportion of the cost of that individual's representation in the proceedings as the relevant court considers reasonable, having regard in particular to the financial resources of that individual.

(2) The maximum amount payable in respect of a determination made under these Regulations is the full cost of the represented individual's representation in the proceedings before the relevant court.

para 6(1) The relevant court must record a determination made under these Regulations in an RDCO.

(2) When a relevant court makes a determination under these Regulations it must give reasons for the terms of the determination.

(3) A determination under these Regulations may provide for immediate payment of the full amount payable in respect of the determination, or for periodic payment of specified instalments.

(4) Any payment due in respect of a determination made under these Regulations must be made to the Lord Chancellor in accordance with terms of the determination.

Criminal Legal Aid (Recovery of Defence Costs Order) Regs 2013 2013/511 para 8(1) Subject to regulation 17, the relevant court must not make a determination under these Regulations in relation to a represented individual where:

(a) the individual was before the relevant court to appeal against one or more convictions; and (b) in respect of every conviction the relevant court allowed the appeal, unless the relevant court considers it reasonable in all the circumstances of the case to make a determination under these Regulations in relation to the individual.

(2) Where the relevant court makes a determination in relation to a represented individual in accordance with paragraph (1), it must give reasons for doing so.

4.85 *Recovery of defence costs order Required assets/Must not be on qualifying benefits*

Criminal Legal Aid (Recovery of Defence Costs Order) Regs 2013 2013/511 para 9. Subject to regulation 17, the relevant court must not make a determination under these Regulations in relation to a represented individual who is, directly or indirectly, properly in receipt of a qualifying benefit.

para 10(1) Subject to regulation 17, the relevant court must not make a determination under these Regulations in relation to a represented individual who has none of the following:

(a) capital exceeding £3,000;
(b) equity in the individual's main dwelling exceeding £100,000; and
(c) gross annual income exceeding £22,325.

(2) For the purpose of paragraph (1), where an individual resides in more than one dwelling, the court must decide which dwelling is the main dwelling.

4.86 ***Recovery of defence costs order*** ***Order unreasonable/There would be undue hardship***

Criminal Legal Aid (Recovery of Defence Costs Order) Regs 2013 2013/511 para 11(1) Subject to regulation 17, the relevant court must not make a determination under these Regulations if it is satisfied that:

(a) it would not be reasonable to make such a determination, on the basis of the information and evidence available; or
(b) requiring a represented individual to make a payment in respect of the cost of their representation in relevant proceedings would, owing to the exceptional circumstances of the case, involve undue financial hardship.

(2) Where the relevant court, in accordance with paragraph (1), does not make a determination in relation to a represented individual it must give reasons for not making such a determination at the conclusion of the proceedings.

4.87 ***Appeal allowed at renewal hearing*** ***Absent defendant***

Criminal Procedure Rules 2015 2015/1490 Rule 39.12(1) This rule applies where the court decides an appeal affecting sentence in a party's absence.

(2) The court may vary such a decision if it did not take account of something relevant because that party was absent.

(3) A party who wants the court to vary such a decision must:

(a) apply in writing, with reasons,
(b) serve the application on the Registrar not more than 7 days after:
  i) the decision, if that party was represented at the appeal hearing, or
  ii) the Registrar serves the decision, if that party was not represented at that hearing.

R v Spruce and Anwar 2005 EWCA Crim 1090 The two defendants were refused leave but they renewed their applications and their appeals were allowed in their absence. Held. Counsel appearing on a renewal should, if possible, obtain instructions prior to the hearing to proceed in the applicant's absence, if the Court grants leave and proceeds with the appeal. If counsel has no instructions, he or she can normally be expected either to obtain instructions on the day of the hearing, or, if that is impossible, to communicate the result of the appeal to the defendant, together with such advice about the right to re-listing as is appropriate. If, at the defendant's request, the case is re-listed for the defendant to be present, there will only be a full rehearing if there is fresh material with an important bearing on sentence. If there is no such material, the defendant, or counsel on his behalf in his presence, will be invited to comment only on this Court's earlier judgment, a transcript of which will be available for the defendant or his counsel, and the court, prior to the re-listing. Re-listing may or may not be before the same judges who heard the initial application.

In these circumstances, we say that, as the defendant is not present and has not waived any right, the sentence will be reduced as indicated unless within seven days he applies for the matter to be re-listed, but the court does not encourage such an application. If the defendant is unrepresented a letter is normally sent to the defendant which is called a 'do better' letter. It says the defendant a) may ask for the appeal to be restored to the list, to

enable him to be [present], b) that the Court's decision will not be varied unless there is entirely fresh material with an important bearing on sentence, and c) that a request may be made within seven days,[56] setting out such fresh material.
The question of a representation order for counsel at the re-listed hearing will not normally be considered before the conclusion of that hearing, and such an order will not usually be made unless relevant fresh material is present at the re-listed hearing.
R v Furmage 2018 EWCA Crim 433 The Court indicated that it wanted to allow the appeal, but the defendant's advocate had no instructions to allow the application to be treated as a hearing with leave. Held. We grant 14 days to make representations. If none is received, the order indicated will take effect.

4.88 *Defendant retried Limit on sentence*

Criminal Appeal Act 1968 Sch 2 para 2(1) Where a person ordered to be retried is again convicted on retrial, the court before which he is convicted may pass in respect of the offence any sentence authorised by law, not being a sentence of greater severity than that passed on the original conviction.
R v Dobson 2013 EWCA Crim 1416, 2014 1 Cr App R (S) 54 (p 345) D was convicted of two rapes, two indecent assaults and a threat to kill. He received 9 years for the rapes, concurrent sentences for the assaults and 1 year for the threat consecutively making 10 years. He appealed and the sex convictions were quashed. D was retried and reconvicted of one rape and the two assaults. He was acquitted of the second rape. He received 9 years for the rape (and presumably concurrent sentences for the assaults with the threats to kill consecutive. Ed.). The defence were unable to criticise the 9 years save for a breach of Schedule 2. In Schedule 2 the words '[the sentence passed on the] original conviction' could not be construed to mean 'the sentence passed for the total criminality'. Held. D should not legitimately consider he was sentenced for offences which he had not been convicted of, so 8 years not 9, consecutive to the 1 year for the threats.
R v Betts 2017 EWCA Crim 1909, 2018 1 Cr App R (S) 28 (p 201) D was convicted of causing death by dangerous driving. He was sentenced to 3½ years. His conviction was quashed and he was retried and reconvicted. D was then sentenced to 44 months. The Judge was told that he was limited to the 3½ years and he reduced the sentence to 3½ years. The defence argued that because of [presumably] the extra delay and additional other mitigation the sentence should be less than 3½ years. Held. The Judge's task was not to start with the first sentence. His approach to put the first sentence out of his mind was correct. The only relevance of the previous sentence was the second sentence could not be more severe than the first sentence. We reject all the grounds of appeal.
R v KPR 2018 EWCA Crim 2537 D was convicted of rape of a child under 13, two child sex assaults, three indecent image offences and possession of a firearm (1 year consecutive no issue). He abused his partner's daughter when she was aged 11-12. He received 11 years for the rape, 5 years for one of the assaults and 3 years for one of the image counts, consecutive, making for the sex offences 17 years in all. His convictions on the sex offences were quashed and he was convicted again on a re-trial on all counts. The second Judge found D to be dangerous but considered that he was unable to pass a life sentence or an extended sentence because of Schedule 2(2), see above. He passed an Offender of Particular Concern Order on the rape (16 years' custody 1 year's extended licence) with concurrent terms on the other counts. Held. The first rape sentence was unlawful as an Offender of Particular Concern Order was mandatory. The task of the second Judge was to sentence afresh and apply the statutory restriction. Without considering Schedule 2, the Judge would have been entitled to pass an extended sentence. The Judge was obliged to pass an Offender of Particular Concern Order and so are we. Whether a sentence is more severe depends on whether 'an ordinary person' would consider it more severe, R v Maw-Wing 1983 5 Cr App R (S) 347. Criminal Appeal Act 1968 s 11(3) and Sch 2 para 2(1) provisions require similar consideration.

[56] The judgment refers to Form O, which is no longer used.

We need to consider the different release regimes for the initial sentences and the sentences we seek to substitute. We substitute an Offender of Particular Concern Order on the rape (10 years' custody 1 year's extended licence), 4 years on one of the assaults consecutive and [presumably make the 1 year consecutive for the image offence concurrent]. Under the first sentence, D was entitled to be released after 8½ years and under our sentence he may be released after 7 years. That meets the overall justice of the case.

Other matters

4.89 *Can't appeal twice/Repeat appeals*

R v Hughes 2009 EWCA Crim 841, 2010 1 Cr App R (S) 25 (p 146) The words of Criminal Appeal Act 1968 s 9(1) do not explicitly restrict the proceedings to a single appeal. That is, however, their plain effect. Similar words in other statutes in relation to powers of appeal have always been held to have that effect, *R v Pinfold* 1988 87 Cr App R 15.

R v Geraghty 2016 EWCA Crim 1523, 2017 1 Cr App R (S) 10 (p 58) In October 2011 D received 20 years for importing drugs. In February 2013, the same Judge made a confiscation order and Financial Reporting Order (FRO). In July 2013, an application to appeal the FRO was lodged. In December 2013, the application was dismissed. In March 2016, an application to appeal against the 20 years was lodged. Held. para 26 The sentencing Judge expressly treated the terms of the FRO as being inextricably bound up with the length of the prison sentence. The inescapable conclusion is that he was thereby stating that he was treating the terms of the order as substantially one sentence with the sentence of imprisonment. para 29 Both the single judge and the full Court dealing with D's FRO appeal proceeded explicitly and necessarily on the basis that the length of the prison sentence was unchallenged. Thus, we find that the applicant has thereby forfeited any jurisdictional basis upon which he may make any further applications to this Court. para 30 Cases, such as *R v Neal* 1999 2 Cr App R (S) 352, where a second or subsequent order is only made after the appeal against an earlier order has been disposed of, will continue to be capable in appropriate cases of providing an exception to the general rule against repeated applications. Moreover, as this Court recently observed in *R v Yasain* 2015 EWCA Crim 1277, 2016 1 Cr App R (S) 7 (p 34), there is a residual category of cases in which the Court enjoys a very limited jurisdiction to avoid real injustice in exceptional circumstances to exercise an implicit power to reopen a concluded appeal where it is necessary to do so (see **4.91**).

See also: *R v Boughton-Fox* 2014 EWCA Crim 227 (There is no jurisdiction to entertain a second application save in the most exceptional circumstances, which do not remotely arise in this case. Application refused.)

4.90 *Power to rehear concluded appeals* *Procedure rules*

Criminal Procedure Rules 2015 2015/1490 Rule 36.6(5)[57] Where a party wants the court to reopen the determination of an appeal:

(a) the court:

(i) must decide the application without a hearing, as a general rule, but

(ii) may decide the application at a hearing; and

(b) need not announce its decision on such an application at a hearing in public.

Reopening the determination of an appeal

Criminal Procedure Rules 2015 2015/1490 Rule 36.15(1)[58] This rule applies where:

(a) a party wants the court to reopen a decision which determines an appeal or reference to which this Part applies (including a decision on an application for permission to appeal or refer);

(b) the Registrar refers such a decision to the court for the court to consider reopening it.

[57] As inserted by Criminal Procedure (Amendment) Rules 2018 2018/132 para 15(b). In force 2/4/18

[58] Rule 36.15 is inserted by Criminal Procedure (Amendment) Rules 2018 2018/132 para 15(c). In force 2/4/18

(2) Such a party must:
(a) apply in writing for permission to reopen that decision, as soon as practicable after becoming aware of the grounds for doing so; and
(b) serve the application on the Registrar.
(3) The application must:
(a) specify the decision which the applicant wants the court to reopen; and
(b) explain:
(i) why it is necessary for the court to reopen that decision in order to avoid real injustice,
(ii) how the circumstances are exceptional and make it appropriate to reopen the decision notwithstanding the rights and interests of other participants and the importance of finality,
(iii) why there is no alternative effective remedy among any potentially available, and
(iv) any delay in making the application.
(4) The Registrar:
(a) may invite a party's representations on:
(i) an application to reopen a decision, or
(ii) a decision that the Registrar has referred, or intends to refer, to the court; and
(b) must do so if the court so directs.
(5) A party invited to make representations must serve them on the Registrar within such period as the Registrar directs.
(6) The court must not reopen a decision to which this rule applies unless each other party has had an opportunity to make representations.
[Note. The Court of Appeal has power only in exceptional circumstances to reopen a decision to which this rule applies.] [This note appears in the rules.]

4.91 ***Power to rehear concluded appeal Cases***

R v Pedley 2009 EWCA Crim 840, 2010 1 Cr App R (S) 24 (p 132) para 27 There exists a very limited power in this Court to rehear an apparently concluded appeal. It is a power to re-list where by administrative error or otherwise the appellant has been deprived of a proper hearing, so that the apparently concluded appeal can properly be described as a nullity, including cases where the Court failed to follow the rules or well-established procedure. There is no jurisdiction to rehear this case.

R v Yasain 2015 EWCA Crim 1277, 2016 1 Cr App R (S) 7 (p 34) LCJ D was convicted of rape, robbery and kidnap. He appealed the sentence and on 12 June 2014 the Court of Appeal quashed the kidnap conviction because the transcript indicated that the jury never returned a verdict on that count. The trial Judge made enquiries and it was discovered that the transcript was wrong and D had been properly convicted of kidnap. The case was re-listed on 14 May 2015. Held. This Court has, like any other court, an implicit power to revise any order pronounced before it is recorded as an order of the court in the record of the relevant court. If [the relevant court] has recorded the order of this Court, then the power to revise the order is strictly limited. The first question to determine is whether the order made by this Court has been properly recorded. The time at which the record was formally made is when the Crown Court officer amended the record of the Crown Court. para 21 In *R v Blackwood* 2012 EWCA Crim 390, 2012 2 Cr App R 1 (p 1), this Court held that, as the Registrar had sent the order allowing the appeal to the Crown Court with a request that the records held on CREST be updated and the record on CREST had been updated, it was too late to order a retrial. The formal record had recorded an acquittal with no provision for a retrial. para 23 There are two exceptions to this general rule. First, where the previous order is a nullity. An example of this is *R v Majewski* 1976 62 Cr App R 5, where the Court summarily dismissed an appeal when there was a point of substance. The referral had been procedurally invalid. The Court had not performed its function. The second exception is where there was a defect in the procedure that may have led to some real injustice. In *R v Daniel* 1977

64 Cr App R 50, due to an administrative error, the renewed application was listed, heard and dismissed on 14 June 1976 without notice to the applicant's lawyers. The order was recorded by the Crown Court. The Court held that if because of a failure of the court to follow the rules or well-established practice, there is a likelihood that injustice may have been done, then the case should be relisted for hearing. Further, the 'likelihood of an injustice' is for this Court to decide. There may not be a likelihood of injustice if it is clear beyond argument that the application cannot succeed. para 28 In *Taylor v Lawrence* 2002 EWCA Civ 90, the Court of Appeal Civil Division considered the scope of its power to reopen a concluded civil appeal. The defendants in that case appealed on the ground of judicial bias. The appeal was dismissed. The defendants later discovered fresh facts relating to the claimed bias. The Court concluded that, "it has an implicit power to reopen a concluded appeal in exceptional circumstances, where it was necessary to achieve its two principal objectives of correcting wrong decisions and ensuring public confidence in the administration of justice. Further there is a tension between a court having a residual jurisdiction and the need to have finality in litigation. The ability to reopen proceedings after the ordinary appeal process has been concluded can also create injustice." para 38 We can see no basis for any distinction between the Civil Division and the Criminal Division as to the principles applicable. There is the strongest public interest in finality. The jurisdiction to rehear is probably confined to procedural errors, particularly as there are alternative remedies for fresh evidence cases through the Criminal Cases Review Commission.

Here it is far better to determine the matter on the basis that this court's jurisdiction is based on *Taylor v Lawrence* 2002. Although the recording of the order by the Crown Court was highly unsatisfactory, it was recorded. The fact that there was a serious error in the material before it and the Court acted on that error does not make the order a nullity. On the facts we set aside the decision of this Court and dismiss D's two appeals.

R v Powell 2016 EWCA Crim 1539 In 2008, D had his confiscation order reduced. In February 2012, he applied to the CCRC to refer the case back. They thought the appropriate remedy was to apply for a certificate of inadequacy. Although not agreeing with that advice, an application was made and it was refused. It was agreed that the realisable assets figure was nearly £22,900 too much. Held. The CCRC did not understand that the problem was with the confiscation order itself. The original [Crown Court] order was in error. D faces a wrong amount and interest added on the amount too. Unless we correct it there will be an injustice. Enough time and precious resources have already been spent on this. We must end this unhappy saga. Applying *R v Yasain* 2015 (see above), we correct the error.

R v Palmer 2017 EWCA Crim 471 D pleaded to murder. Leave to appeal was refused but at the full court the appeal was allowed. The Registrar pointed out that allowing the appeal where the prosecution had not attended in a fatality case was in breach of the protocol [between the CPS and the Court of Appeal]. An adjournment would have enabled the relatives of the deceased to attend the full hearing. The case was re-listed and re-argued with the prosecution in attendance. For more details, see **287.60** in Volume 2.

R v Hockey 2017 EWCA Crim 742, 2 Cr App R (S) 31 A judge adjourned H's confiscation proceedings *sine die*. The prosecution successfully appealed that decision and a confiscation order was made. Ten years later, H applied to reopen the Court of Appeal decision. Held. The guiding principles must be the interests of the public (including the finality of proceedings), the interests of the defendant and the interests of any victim. The application was without merit.

R v Weekes 2017 EWCA Crim 819 D, aged 17, was convicted of aiding and abetting rape. She appealed the sentence that she was given in November 2014. The single Judge said the victim surcharge was the wrong amount and considered the appeal otherwise to be without merit. She referred the application to the full court on both points. In May 2015, D was told about the full court hearing the day before the hearing. Counsel was

not told. The full court amended the victim surcharge and considered the substantive appeal to be without merit. No one attended. Held. There was a procedural irregularity which led to D being denied the opportunity to be represented before the full court for her application for leave to appeal. We have power to allow the case to be reopened on the ground it was required to avoid a real injustice, but this is subject to our discretion. It cannot be justified to reopen the case because the application to reopen was not sent to the Court until late January 2017. The explanation for the delay was wholly unsatisfactory. The strong interest in finality must prevail. We see little merit in the grounds now sought to be advanced and agree with the single Judge. Appeal dismissed.
Att-Gen's Ref 2017 Re Campbell (No 2) 2017 EWCA Crim 1372[59] D had his sentence increased from a suspended sentence to an immediate prison sentence. The Court asked whether any unpaid work had been done. Counsel said he had no information about the number of hours that had been performed. Three days later the case was relisted and the Court was told that 69 hours had been performed. Held. We have power to vary the sentence, *R v Yasain* 2015 EWCA Crim 1277, 2016 1 Cr App R (S) 7 (p 34). Counsel has a duty to find out the hours done. 30 months not 32.
See also: *R v Procter* 2014 EWCA Crim 162 (D's conviction quashed. Basis for that discovered to be flawed. Eight days later conviction restored.)

4.92 ***Appeals to the Supreme Court***
Right of appeal to Supreme Court.
Criminal Appeal Act 1968 s 33(1) An appeal lies to the Supreme Court, at the instance of the defendant or the prosecutor, from any decision of the Court of Appeal on an appeal to that court under Part I of this Act or Part 9 of the Criminal Justice Act 2003 or section 9 (preparatory hearings) of the Criminal Justice Act 1987 or section 35 of the Criminal Procedure and Investigations Act 1996 or section 47 of the Criminal Justice Act 2003.
(1B) An appeal lies to the Supreme Court, at the instance of the acquitted person or the prosecutor, from any decision of the Court of Appeal on an application under section 76(1) or (2) of the Criminal Justice Act 2003 (retrial for serious offences).
(2) The appeal lies only with the leave of the Court of Appeal or the Supreme Court; and leave shall not be granted unless it is certified by the Court of Appeal that a point of law of general public importance is involved in the decision and it appears to the Court of Appeal or the Supreme Court (as the case may be) that the point is one which ought to be considered by the Supreme Court.
(3) Except as provided by this Part of this Act and section 13 of the Administration of Justice Act 1960 (appeal in cases of contempt of court), no appeal shall lie from any decision of the criminal division of the Court of Appeal.
(4) In relation to an appeal under subsection (1B), references in this Part to a defendant are references to the acquitted person.
When this Part applies
Criminal Procedure Rules 2015 2015/1490 Rule 43.1(1) This Part applies where:

(a) a party wants to appeal to the Supreme Court after:

(i) an application to the Court of Appeal to which Part 27 applies (Retrial following acquittal), or

(ii) an appeal to the Court of Appeal to which applies Part 37 (Appeal to the Court of Appeal against ruling at preparatory hearing), Part 38 (Appeal to the Court of Appeal against ruling adverse to prosecution), or Part 39 (Appeal to the Court of Appeal about conviction or sentence); or

(b) a party wants to refer a case to the Supreme Court after a reference to the Court of Appeal to which Part 41 applies (Reference to the Court of Appeal of point of law or unduly lenient sentencing).

(2) A reference to an 'appellant' in this Part is a reference to such a party.

[59] The judgment is entitled *R v Campbell* 2017 EWCA Crim 1372.

Application for permission or reference

43.2(1) An appellant must:

(a) apply orally to the Court of Appeal:

(i) for permission to appeal or to refer a sentencing case, or

(ii) to refer a point of law immediately after the court gives the reasons for its decision; or

(b) apply in writing and serve the application on the Registrar and every other party not more than:

(i) 14 days after the court gives the reasons for its decision if that decision was on a sentencing reference to which Part 41 applies (Attorney General's reference of sentencing case), or

(ii) 28 days after the court gives those reasons in any other case.

(2) An application for permission to appeal or to refer a sentencing case must:

(a) identify the point of law of general public importance that the appellant wants the court to certify is involved in the decision; and

(b) give reasons why:

(i) that point of law ought to be considered by the Supreme Court, and

(ii) the court ought to give permission to appeal.

(3) An application to refer a point of law must give reasons why that point ought to be considered by the Supreme Court.

(4) An application must include or attach any application for the following, with reasons:

(a) an extension of time within which to make the application for permission or for a reference;

(b) bail pending appeal;

(c) permission to attend any hearing in the Supreme Court, if the appellant is in custody.

(5) A written application must be in the form set out in the Practice Direction.

Note [in the Rules]: For the power of the court or the Registrar to shorten or extend a time limit, see Rule 36.3.

Rule 43.3 deals with detention pending an appeal.

Note: For the court form, see www.banksr.com Other Matters Other Documents tab Court of Appeal. Ed.

R v Stafford and Luvaglio 1969 53 Cr App R 1 The defendant's application for leave was refused. Held. There is no power to certify a question. [The appeal process] only applies when leave to appeal has been granted.

R v Mealey and Sheridan 1975 Crim LR 154 LCJ M and S's application for leave to appeal was refused. Held. There can be no appeal when an application for an appeal has been refused.

R v Cooper 1975 61 Cr App R 215 LCJ The Court does not, when refusing a certificate, give reasons.

R v Cadman-Smith (No 2) 2001 Crim LR 644 The Court of Appeal quashed C's confiscation order and the Customs and Excise wrote ten days later asking the Court to certify a point of law and grant leave to appeal. About a month later, the Court did so but only sent the letter to C's solicitors. About three weeks later, the Customs enquired what had happened and were sent the paperwork. The House of Lords said the [then] 14-day time limit had expired. Held by the Court of Appeal. The Court of Appeal was bound to regulate its procedures so as not to 'impede the right of appeal' by the prosecution. In future the most obvious way is to give the decision in open court after the parties had been notified. They would be able to make oral argument. We do have the power to consider the matter without a hearing, but the decision would be communicated orally and by fax. An injustice has been done so we relist the matter and certify a point of law afresh but refuse leave. [The House of Lords then granted leave, heard the appeal and allowed it, *R v Smith* 2001 UKHL 68, 2002 1 Cr App R 35 (p 466).]

R v Garwood and Others 2017 EWCA Crim 59 LCJ G and H's application for leave to appeal was refused. Held. There can be no appeal when an application for an appeal has been refused. For M, who had leave to appeal, we cannot certify the question posed as leave to appeal related to a different issue.

4.93 ***Appeals to the Supreme Court European Convention on Human Rights art 6***
R v Dunn 2010 EWCA Crim 1823, 2 Cr App R 30 (p 337) D's appeal was dismissed and the Court declined to certify a point of law. He applied for a declaration that that decision was incompatible with his right to a fair trial, based on article 6. Held. The fundamental principle of not being a judge in one's own cause is long established. However, all the Court is doing is determining whether a point of law of general public importance is present. The Supreme Court requires a filtering mechanism or otherwise the Court would be clogged with hopeless cases. Appeal dismissed.

4.94 ***Appeals to the Supreme Court Time limits***
Application for leave to appeal.
Criminal Appeal Act 1968 s 34(1) An application to the Court of Appeal for leave to appeal to the Supreme Court shall be made within the period of 28 days[60] beginning with the relevant date; and an application to the Supreme Court for leave shall be made within the period of 28 days beginning with the date on which the application for leave is refused by the Court of Appeal.
(1A) In subsection (1), "the relevant date" means:
  (a) the date of the Court of Appeal's decision, or
  (b) if later, the date on which the Court of Appeal gives reasons for its decision.
(2) The Supreme Court or the Court of Appeal may, upon application made at any time by the defendant or, in the case of an appeal under section 33(1B), by the prosecutor, extend the time within which an application may be made by him to the Supreme Court or the Court of Appeal under subsection (1) above.
(3) An appeal to the Supreme Court shall be treated as pending until any application for leave to appeal is disposed of and, if leave to appeal is granted, until the appeal is disposed of; and for purposes of this Part of this Act an application for leave to appeal shall be treated as disposed of at the expiration of the time within which it may be made, if it is not made within that time.

5 APPEALS: CROWN COURT APPEALS

Right to appeal and powers of the Crown Court

5.1 ***Right to appeal***
Magistrates' Courts Act 1980 s 108(1) A person convicted by a Magistrates' Court may appeal to the Crown Court:
  (a) if he pleaded guilty, against his sentence,
  (b) if he did not, against the conviction or sentence.
(1A) Powers of Criminal Courts (Sentencing) Act 2000 s 14 (under which a conviction of an offence for which an order for conditional or absolute discharge is made is deemed not to be a conviction except for certain purposes) shall not prevent an appeal under this section, whether against conviction or otherwise.
(2) A person sentenced by a Magistrates' Court for an offence in respect of which…an order for conditional discharge has been previously made may appeal to the Crown Court against the sentence.
(3) In this section 'sentence' includes any order made on conviction by a Magistrates' Court, not being: a) [repealed], b) an order for the payment of costs, c) an order under Animal Welfare Act 2006 s 37(1) (which enables a court to order the destruction of an

[60] This was increased from 14 days on 1/4/05.

animal), or d) an order made in pursuance of an enactment under which the court has no discretion as to the making of the order or its terms, and also includes a declaration of relevance, within the meaning of Football Spectators Act 1989 s 23.
(4) Subsection 3(d) above does not prevent an appeal against a surcharge imposed under Criminal Justice Act 2003 s 161A.

5.2 ***Crown Court powers***

Senior Courts Act 1981 s 48(1) The Crown Court may, in the course of hearing any appeal, correct any error or mistake in the order or judgment incorporating the decision which is the subject of the appeal.
(2) On the termination of the hearing of an appeal the Crown Court:

(a) may confirm, reverse or vary any part of the decision appealed against, including a determination not to impose a separate penalty in respect of an offence, or
(b) may remit the matter with its opinion thereon to the authority whose decision is appealed against, or
(c) may make such other order in the matter as the court thinks just, and by such order exercise any power which the said authority might have exercised.

(3) Subsection (2) has effect subject to any enactment relating to any such appeal which expressly limits or restricts the powers of the court on the appeal.
(4) Subject to Criminal Appeal Act 1995 s 11(6) (power of Criminal Cases Review Commission to refer cases) if the appeal is against a conviction or a sentence, the preceding provisions of this section shall be construed as including power to award any punishment, whether more or less severe than that awarded by the Magistrates' Court whose decision is appealed against, if that is a punishment which that Magistrates' Court might have awarded.
(5) This section applies whether or not the appeal is against the whole of the decision.

5.3 ***Power to vary sentences not subject to appeal***

Senior Courts Act 1981 s 48(5) This section (the powers of the Crown Court on appeal) applies whether or not the appeal is against the whole of the decision.
Dutta v Westcott 1986 8 Cr App R (S) 191 D was sentenced in his absence for driving without insurance and three motoring offences. All the offences arose from the same circumstances. He was given 6 months' disqualification on the insurance matter and no points on the other offences. D arrived afterwards with proof of insurance. He was told by the Court that it was too late and he appealed the insurance matter only. The court quashed the insurance offence and imposed penalty points on one of the other offences. Held. 'The decision which is the subject of the appeal' in section 48 is a wide phrase, so the Crown Court has jurisdiction to consider all matters that were before the Court. However, I emphasise that in the normal way the Crown Court would not need to investigate them. Appeal dismissed.

5.4 ***Power to make any order magistrates could have made***

Senior Courts Act 1981 s 48(1) If the appeal is against a conviction or a sentence, the preceding provisions of this section (the power of the Crown Court) shall be construed as including power to award any punishment, whether more or less severe than that awarded by the Magistrates' Court whose decision is appealed against, if that is a punishment which that Magistrates' Court might have awarded.
R v Birmingham JJs ex parte Wyatt 1975 61 Cr App R 306 LCJ D pleaded at the Magistrates' Court when unrepresented. He had not been sent to prison before and was given 6 months' imprisonment. At the appeal hearing D was represented. The defence said the sentence was unlawful and the Court was restricted to imposing a sentence the Magistrates could have imposed. The Judge said it was a rehearing and because D was now represented the defect was cured. D appealed. Held. The Crown Court could only impose a sentence the Magistrates could have imposed, so we substitute a £50 fine.
R v Inner London Crown Court ex parte Obajuwana 1979 69 Cr App R 125 LCJ D was convicted of overstaying and appealed his recommendation for deportation. The Crown

Court dismissed his appeal and refused through lack of jurisdiction his appeal over his remand in custody pending deportation. Held. The order was one the Magistrates could have made so it was an order the Crown Court could make. The Crown Court is ordered to hear the application.
Barber v Chief Constable of Gwent 1983 5 Cr App R (S) 121 D was convicted of assaulting a PC. The officer lost a front tooth and two other teeth were loosened. D was ordered to perform 240 hours of community service. He appealed the conviction and the appeal was dismissed. The Court also increased the sentence to 6 months. He appealed again. Held. The Crown Court can correct an unlawful sentence. Appeal dismissed.
R v Portsmouth Crown Court ex parte Ballard 1990 154 JP 109 D appealed his sentence of 180 days' imprisonment for unlawful wounding. Before the appeal hearing he was convicted of indecent wounding and sentenced to 180 days' imprisonment. At the appeal hearing the Court made the two sentences consecutive. Held. There was no power to do that as the Magistrates' Court could not have imposed that sentence.

Applications and time limits

5.5 *Contents of appeal notice*

Form of appeal and respondent's notices

Criminal Procedure Rules 2015 2015/1490 Rule 34.3(1)[61] The appeal notice must:

(a) specify:
 (i) the conviction or finding of guilt,
 (ii) the sentence, or
 (iii) the order, or the failure to make an order, about which the appellant wants to appeal;
(b) summarise the issues;
(c) in an appeal against conviction or against a finding of guilt, to the best of the appellant's ability and to assist the court in fulfilling its duty under rule 3.2 (the court's duty of case management):
 (i) identify the witnesses who gave oral evidence in the magistrates' court,
 (ii) identify the witnesses who gave written evidence in the magistrates' court,
 (iii) identify the prosecution witnesses whom the appellant will want to question if they are called to give oral evidence in the Crown Court,
 (iv) identify the likely defence witnesses,
 (v) give notice of any special arrangements or other measures that the appellant thinks are needed for witnesses,
 (vi) explain whether the issues in the Crown Court differ from the issues in the magistrates' court, and if so how, and
 (vii) say how long the trial lasted in the magistrates' court and how long the appeal is likely to last in the Crown Court;
(d) in an appeal against a sentence, order or failure to make an order:
 (i) identify any circumstances, report or other information of which the appellant wants the court to take account, and
 (ii) explain the significance of those circumstances or that information to what is in issue;
(e) in an appeal against a finding that the appellant insulted someone or interrupted proceedings in the magistrates' court, attach:
 (i) the magistrates' court's written findings of fact, and
 (ii) the appellant's response to those findings;
(f) say whether the appellant has asked the magistrates' court to reconsider the case; and
(g) include a list of those on whom the appellant has served the appeal notice.

[61] Criminal Procedure (Amendment No 2) Rules 2018 2018/847 para 8 substituted a new Rule 28.8. In force 1/10/18

Note: For the form, see www.banksr.com Other Matters Other Documents tab Crown Court Appeal. Ed.

5.6 *Service of notice*

Criminal Procedure Rules 2015 2015/1490 Rule 34.2(1) An appellant must serve an appeal notice on:

(a) the Magistrates' Court officer, and

(b) every other party.

Criminal Procedure Rules 2015 2015/1490 Rule 34.10 The Crown Court may:..

(c) direct that an appeal notice be served on any person.

5.7 *Time limits*

Criminal Procedure Rules 2015 2015/1490 Rule 34.2(2) The appellant must serve the appeal notice:

(a) as soon after the decision appealed against as the appellant wants, but

(b) not more than 21 days after:

(i) sentence or the date sentence is deferred, whichever is earlier, if the appeal is against conviction or against a finding of guilt,

(ii) sentence, if the appeal is against sentence, or

(iii) the order or failure to make an order about which the appellant wants to appeal, in any other case.

5.8 *Time limits Extensions*

Criminal Procedure Rules 2015 2015/1490 Rule 34.2(3) The appellant must serve with the appeal notice any application for the following, with reasons:

(a) an extension of the time limit under this rule, if the appeal notice is late,

(b) bail pending appeal if the appellant is in custody,

(c) the suspension of any disqualification imposed in the case, where the Magistrates' Court or the Crown Court can order such a suspension pending appeal.

Criminal Procedure Rules 2015 2015/1490 Rule 34.10 The Crown Court may:

(a) shorten or extend (even after it has expired) a time limit under this Part.

Crown Court Rules 1982 1982/1109 Rule 7(5) The time for giving notice of appeal (whether prescribed under paragraph (3))… may be extended, either before or after it expires, by the Crown Court, on an application made in accordance with paragraph (6).

R v Croydon Crown Court ex parte Smith 1983 77 Cr App R 277 D was summoned for driving matters which took place on 24 September 1980. The summons was dated in April 1981.[62] D acknowledged receipt of a summons with a hearing date on 13 July 1981. He failed to attend. On 12 October 1981, D was convicted in his absence. The matter was adjourned for sentence and a warrant was issued. Nothing appeared to happen for 12 months. He was then arrested and two days later, on 18 October 1982, he was fined and disqualified. On 4 November 1982, D saw a solicitor and on 6 November 1982 he went to the Magistrates' Court to make a statutory declaration. He was told his only option was to appeal. D was told he had 21 days, which expired on 8 November 1982. On 9 November 1982, he saw a solicitor again. On 11 November 1982, the solicitor wrote to the Crown Court applying for an extension to appeal. On 23 November 1982, a written application was refused by a judge. Counsel was briefed to make an oral application. The matter was listed on 20 December 1982. Counsel appeared and was told the Judge had reviewed her decision and the application had been granted only for sentence. D appealed. Held. The reasons for applying for an extension should be set out. There is no right to an oral hearing. The Court may grant an oral hearing using its discretion. Only judges should decide whether there should be an oral hearing. The rules require no written judicial reasons to be given. The court can grant leave for a sentence appeal and refuse leave for a conviction appeal. The refusal to grant the conviction appeal was not perverse. However, because the Court listed the application for an

[62] The report says April 1980, which must be a typo.

extension and then decided the matter without representation, D may well have a sense of grievance. We therefore direct the Court to grant an extension for the conviction appeal.

R (Customs and Excise) v Maidstone Crown Court 2004 EWHC 1459 (Admin) A Crown Court judge hearing an application for an extension of time acts so as to achieve justice for the parties in the case and that will not simply be achieved by granting relief to the party making the application. The judge considering an application must take into account the reasons for the delay and the merits of the proposed appeal. A judge considering whether to give permission to appeal out of time must take into account the merits of the proposed appeal.

R (Birmingham City Council) v Birmingham Crown Court 2009 EWHC 3329 (Admin) The Court heard two joined appeals. Time limits are imposed because of the public interest in finality. It is important that the requirement that a person should appeal within 21 days is not regarded as some form of unimportant formality. The time limit needs to be complied with, and there needs to be some explanation for why it has not been. This public interest has a number of aspects. They include enabling the court to manage its business in a proper manner, see *R v Burley* 1994 The Times News 9/11/94 and to have available the full range of options for a just disposal, *R v Omer-Hassan* 1999 Unreported 2/7/99. They also include the need for those for whose benefit or protection proceedings have been instituted (in this context the victims of antisocial behaviour) to be able to rely on the decision. In the case of a rehearing they include the risk that the memories of witnesses will have faded, and that witnesses who were reluctant to give evidence at the first hearing will refuse to do so when the case comes on again. The cost in time and money to the public authority that will have to reinvestigate the matter, possibly, given the resource implications, at the expense of other important activities, is also a factor relevant to the public interest in finality. Here the Judge was entitled to take into account the age of the person applying for an extension of time, and to do so whether or not this was given as a reason for delay. Courts regularly take account of the age and experience of those before them. Those familiar with even unproblematic teenagers know that they are not always able to appreciate what they should do or it is in their interests to do so as soon as they should. In the case of one applicant the notice refers to the further advice he received, but it would be unduly formalistic to say that age cannot be taken into account in this context save where express reliance is placed on it. I do not consider, moreover, that the only impact of age is on the reasons for delay. Though a civil order, an ASBO exposes the defendant to the risk of criminal sanctions of some significance. It cannot therefore be an unreasonable response for a judge asked to extend time to have regard to the age of the proposed appellant, especially if he is of the age of the two applicants, namely now 14 and 15, given the potential consequences of this particular order. The Judge's discretion in considering the application was a broad one and he was entitled to take account of what he knew of the circumstances of the case.

Note: This is a long and comprehensive case. This summary does not deal with all the guidance given and all the points considered. Since these cases were heard, the obligation on the defendant to provide details for a whole host of matters has greatly increased along with a huge growth in the number of occasions when judges are required to give reasons. It would be sensible for judges to give reasons even if they are short. Ed. For the duty to give reasons at the end of the hearing see the ***Court must give reasons*** para at **5.28**.

5.9 ***Magistrates' Court, Appeals from Extending time limits What the application should contain***

Crown Court Rules 1982 1982/1109 Rule 7(6) An application for an extension of time shall be made in writing, specifying the grounds of the application, and sent to the appropriate officer of the Crown Court.

R (Birmingham City Council) v Birmingham Crown Court 2009 EWHC 3329 (Admin) Those making such applications should provide the following information: a) They should indicate their proposed grounds of appeal briefly and, where possible, indicate the merits of the appeal, also briefly. In doing so they should bear in mind the need not to say so much at an interlocutory stage that the tribunal of fact considering the appeal if permission is granted might be prejudiced. This may be particularly material in small court centres. b) They should say why time should be extended, giving the reasons for delay and, if they are able to, why the proposed respondent would not be prejudiced by an extension of time.

5.10 ***Magistrates' Court, Appeals from Extending time limits Judge should give reasons***

R (Customs and Excise) v Maidstone Crown Court 2004 EWHC 1459 (Admin) As a general rule, it is desirable for a judge to give succinct reasons why an extension of time has either been granted or refused.

R (Birmingham City Council) v Birmingham Crown Court 2009 EWHC 3329 (Admin) The giving of reasons after an application to extend time is not mandatory. It is important to recognise the nature of decisions on interlocutory matters. In *Eagil Trust Co Ltd v Pigott-Brown* 1985 3 AER 119 at 122 it was stated that 'a professional judge should, as a rule, give reasons for his decision. I say as a general rule because in the field of discretion there are well-established exceptions.' The reason for the general rule, both in respect of professional judges and other decision makers is, as has been stated in many cases, so that those affected by a decision will know why it has been made and whether they have any grounds to challenge it, see for example *R v Higher Education Funding Council, ex parte Institute of Dental Surgery* 1994 1 WLR 242 at 256, 258. As to the exceptions to the general rule, in the *Eagil Trust* case Griffiths LJ referred to the exercise of a judge's discretion on costs and to applications to appeal from the decision of an arbitrator. In *R v Harrow Crown Court ex parte Dave* 1994 99 Cr App R 114, 1 WLR 98 at 105 reference is made to procedural and interlocutory decisions as examples of situations in which no reasons are required despite the tendency for appellate courts to expect a judge to give reasons. We do not quash either decision to grant an extension.

See also: *R v Birmingham Crown Court ex parte Sharma* 1988 Crim LR 741 (There is no obligation for the judge to give his or her reasons.)

Matters before the hearing

5.11 ***Duties of Magistrates' Court officer***

Duty of magistrates' court officer

Criminal Procedure Rules 2015 2015/1490 Rule 34.4(2)[63] The magistrates' court officer must:

(a) arrange for the magistrates' court to hear as soon as practicable any application to that court under rule 34.2(3)(c) (suspension of disqualification pending appeal); and

(b) as soon as practicable notify the Crown Court officer of the service of the appeal notice and make available to that officer:

(i) the appeal notice and any accompanying application served by the appellant,

(ii) details of the parties including their addresses, and

(iii) a copy of each magistrates' court register entry relating to the decision under appeal and to any application for bail pending appeal.

(2) [Not listed. Deals with appeals against convictions and findings of guilt.]

(3) Where the appeal is against sentence, the magistrates' court officer must make available to the Crown Court officer as soon as practicable any report received for the purposes of sentencing.

(4) Unless the magistrates' court otherwise directs, the magistrates' court officer:

(a) must keep any document or object exhibited in the proceedings in the magistrates' court, or arrange for it to be kept by some other appropriate person, until at least:

[63] Criminal Procedure (Amendment No 2) Rules 2018 2018/847 para 8 substituted a new Rule 28.8. In force 1/10/18

(i) 6 weeks after the conclusion of those proceedings, or
(ii) the conclusion of any proceedings in the Crown Court that begin within that 6 weeks; but
(b) need not keep such a document if:
(i) the document that was exhibited is a copy of a document retained by the party who produced it, and
(ii) what was in evidence in the magistrates' court was the content of that document.

5.12 ***Duty of person keeping exhibit***
Criminal Procedure Rules 2015 2015/1490 Rule 34.5 A person who, under arrangements made by the Magistrates' Court officer, keeps a document or object exhibited in the proceedings in the Magistrates' Court must:
(a) keep that exhibit until:
(i) 6 weeks after the conclusion of those proceedings, or
(ii) the conclusion of any proceedings in the Crown Court that begin within that 6 weeks,
unless the Magistrates' Court or the Crown Court otherwise directs, and
(b) provide the Crown Court with any such document or object for which the Crown Court officer asks, within such period as the Crown Court officer may require.

5.13 ***Respondent's notice***
Criminal Procedure Rules 2015 2015/1490 Rule 34.3(2)[64] A respondent's notice must:
(a) give the date on which the respondent was served with the appeal notice; and
(b) to assist the court in fulfilling its duty under rule 3.2:
(i) identify the witnesses who gave oral evidence in the magistrates' court,
(ii) identify the witnesses who gave written evidence in the magistrates' court,
(iii) identify the prosecution witnesses whom the respondent intends to call to give oral evidence in the Crown Court,
(iv) give notice of any special arrangements or other measures that the respondent thinks are needed for witnesses,
(v) explain whether the issues in the Crown Court differ from the issues in the magistrates' court, and if so how, and
(vi) say how long the trial lasted in the magistrates' court and how long the appeal is likely to last in the Crown Court.
(3) Paragraph (4) applies in an appeal against conviction or against a finding of guilt where in the magistrates' court a party to the appeal:
(a) introduced in evidence material to which applies:
(i) Part 16 (Written witness statements),
(ii) Part 19 (Expert evidence),
(iii) Part 20 (Hearsay evidence),
(iv) Part 21 (Evidence of bad character), or
(v) Part 22 (Evidence of a complainant's previous sexual behaviour); or
(b) made an application to which applies:
(i) Part 17 (Witness summonses, warrants and orders),
(ii) Part 18 (Measures to assist a witness or defendant to give evidence), or
(iii) Part 23 (Restriction on cross-examination by a defendant).
(4) If such a party wants to reintroduce that material or to renew that application in the Crown Court that party must include a notice to that effect in the appeal or respondent's notice, as the case may be.

5.14 ***Court must give reasonable notice of hearing***
Criminal Procedure Rules 2015 2015/1490 Rule 34.8(2) The Crown Court officer must give as much notice as reasonably practicable of every hearing to:

[64] Criminal Procedure (Amendment No 2) Rules 2018 2018/847 para 8 substituted a new Rule 28.8. In force 1/10/18

(a) the parties,
(b) any party's custodian, and
(c) any other person whom the Crown Court requires to be notified.

Criminal Procedure Rules 2015 2015/1490 Rule 34.8(4) But where a hearing or decision is about a public interest ruling, the Crown Court officer must not:
(a) give notice of that hearing to, or
(b) serve that decision on,

anyone other than the prosecutor who applied for that ruling, unless the court otherwise directs.

5.15 ***Preparatory hearings***

The provisions are listed in Criminal Procedure Rules 2015 2015/1490 Rule 34.7,[65] see www.banksr.com Other Matters Other Documents tab.

5.16 ***Abandoning an appeal***

Criminal Procedure Rules 2015 2015/1490 Rule 34.9(1) The appellant:
(a) may abandon an appeal without the Crown Court's permission, by serving a notice of abandonment on:
(i) the Magistrates' Court officer,
(ii) the Crown Court officer, and
(iii) every other party
before the hearing of the appeal begins, but
(b) after the hearing of the appeal begins, may only abandon the appeal with the Crown Court's permission.
(2) A notice of abandonment must be signed by or on behalf of the appellant.
(3) Where an appellant who is on bail pending appeal abandons an appeal:
(a) the appellant must surrender to custody as directed by the Magistrates' Court officer, and
(b) any conditions of bail apply until then.

Note: After an abandonment both the Crown Court and the Magistrates' Court have power to make a prosecution costs order against that appellant, Senior Courts Act 1981 s 52 and Magistrates' Courts Act 1980 s 109. Ed.

Criminal Procedure Rules 2015 2015/1490 Rule 34.10 The Crown Court may:
(d) allow an appeal notice or a notice of abandonment to be in a different form to one set out in the Practice Direction, or to be presented orally.

Note: For the court form, see www.banksr.com Other Matters Other Documents tab Crown Court Appeal. Ed.

The hearing

5.17 ***Constitution of the Crown Court***

Criminal Procedure Rules 2015 2015/1490 Rule 34.11 On the hearing of an appeal:
(a) the general rule is that the Crown Court must comprise:
(i) a judge of the High Court, a Circuit judge or a Recorder, and
(ii) no less than two and no more than four justices of the peace, none of whom took part in the decision under appeal, and
(b) if the appeal is from a Youth Court:
(i) each justice of the peace must be qualified to sit as a member of a Youth Court, and
(ii) the Crown Court must include a man and a woman, but
(c) the Crown Court may include only one justice of the peace and need not include both a man and a woman if:
(i) the presiding judge decides that otherwise the start of the appeal hearing will be delayed unreasonably, or

[65] Criminal Procedure (Amendment No 2) Rules 2018 2018/847 para 8 substituted a new Rule 34.7. In force 1/10/18

(ii) one or more of the justices of the peace who started hearing the appeal is absent.

5.18 *Hearings to be in open court*

Criminal Procedure Rules 2015 2015/1490 Rule 34.8(1) The Crown Court as a general rule must hear in public an appeal or reference to which this Part applies, but:

(a) may order any hearing to be in private, and

(b) where a hearing is about a public interest ruling, must hold that hearing in private.

5.19 *Appeals are a rehearing*

Senior Courts Act 1981 s 79 The customary practice and procedure with respect to appeals to the Crown Court and in particular any practice as to the extent to which an appeal is by way of rehearing of the case, shall continue to be observed.

R v Knutsford Crown Court ex parte Jones 1985 7 Cr App R (S) 448 D and others pleaded to assault charges. They were given 4-month detention centre orders. They appealed and the Court said that they would have imposed a lesser sentence but the sentences were not so wrong as to justify interfering with them. They appealed again. Held. The Crown Court should take the matter up as from the moment when conviction was announced and proceed to fix the sentence on a rehearing basis. The Crown Court should decide how the defendant should be sentenced, and if that differed from the order of the Magistrates' Court to a significant degree, the appeal should be allowed to that extent. The task of the Crown Court was not the same as the task of the Court of Appeal Criminal Division. 3 months substituted.

R v Swindon Crown Court ex parte Murray 1997 162 JP 36 D pleaded to driving whilst disqualified and was sentenced to 4 months. He appealed to the Crown Court. The Judge affirmed the sentence saying, "there is no reason to disagree with…the Justices". Held. That was the wrong approach. The Court should have considered 'on all the matters that they had heard what in their view was the right sentence'.

5.20 *Crown Court can't commit the case for sentence*

R v Bullock 1963 47 Cr App R 288 LCJ D's appeal against conviction was dismissed. The Court thought his 3-month sentence was inadequate and purported to commit the case to itself and then sentenced D to 12 months. Held. The 12 months was deserved. The Court's action was highly artificial. It would in fact mean there is a further appeal possible to the Court of Appeal. The Crown Court had no power to commit to itself.

Factors during a hearing

5.21 *Judicial indications given at the Magistrates' Court*

R v Isleworth Crown Court ex parte Irvin 1992 RTR 281 D pleaded to disqualified driving and other driving offences. The Magistrates put the case back for social inquiry reports and a community service assessment. They did not, however, say they were keeping all options open. The reports were favourable to D and he was sent to prison for 28 days by a different set of Magistrates. D appealed and the Judge affirmed the imprisonment, saying the Crown Court hearing was a rehearing. Held. That approach was not right. It was a rehearing but the bench had to take account of what had occurred at the first hearing. Imprisonment quashed.

5.22 *Disputes as to the facts*

Shaw v Hamilton 1982 4 Cr App R (S) 80 The prosecution appealed a bind over imposed after D had been acquitted. The Judge declined to allow D to give evidence saying that it was undesirable as that might make it appear that the issue of guilt was being reconsidered. Held. That was wrong. It implied that on an appeal to the Crown Court from a Magistrates' Court against sentence, it is not possible for sworn evidence to be heard. If there is a challenge which does not go to conviction and goes solely to sentence, it is open to the Crown Court to hear evidence.

Williams v R 1983 77 Cr App R 329 D pleaded to section 20 assault and was sentenced to 3 months. He had attacked his partner. He appealed the sentence and the Judge drew counsel's attention to a police account of D saying, "It has happened before, but I just lost my temper." The remark was disputed. The Judge warned the defence he had power to increase the sentence. The Judge asked the defence counsel three times whether she wanted the issue tried. She declined the offer and the sentence was increased to 6 months. D appealed. The prosecution said D had had ample opportunity to give evidence, so the Court had acted properly. Held. That submission is not correct. Whether an issue should be tried does not depend on the consent of the defence. It is a matter for the court. The *R v Newton* 1982 4 Cr App R (S) 388 principles apply, except that it is not possible to ask a jury to try the issue. Where there is a substantial conflict, the court can either a) listen to submissions and proceed on the basis that the defendant's version should, as far as possible, be accepted, or b) to hear evidence. It may be that the evidence, when called, will be very slight, it may be that it will be cross-examined and no evidence will be called in contradiction. But even so, given the sharp divergence or substantial conflict and given the fact that the court is not prepared to proceed on the basis that the defendant's version is substantially correct, the court must hear the evidence before forming its own view in respect of the matter which is in dispute. Sentence quashed and case remitted.

See also the **FACTUAL BASIS FOR SENTENCING Dispute as to facts** section at **57.42**.

5.23 ***Findings of the magistrates on the facts***

R (Tottman) v DPP 2004 EWHC 258 (Admin) D pleaded to drink/driving and the case was adjourned for a special reasons hearing. The reading was 49 μg (14 over the limit). The Magistrates heard from three witnesses for the defence but they were not told about D's recent speeding conviction. The Magistrates found special reasons, decided not to disqualify and awarded 11 penalty points, which was the maximum number. However, with the 3 points for the speeding offence, D became a 'totter' and he was disqualified for 6 months. D appealed contending the Magistrates did not want to disqualify him, so the points should be reduced to 8 or fewer, making fewer than 12 in all. Before the hearing it was agreed by counsel that no witnesses should attend. During submissions the prosecution said they were not going to submit that the special reasons finding was wrong. After submissions, the Judge asked two factual questions that related to the special reasons issue. They were answered. There was no indication that the sentence might be increased. The Court then accepted that special reasons had been found but imposed 12 months' disqualification because of the two answers they had heard and another fact of the case. D appealed. Held. The defence had not conducted their case to answer a suggested discretionary disqualification. The witnesses were not present. The answer to the first question was highly material but D was not there to give an explanation. The defence were never in a position to make submissions. The Court should have given a clear warning about its intentions. It must be queried whether it was open to the Court to elicit further evidence, bearing in mind it was respecting the special reasons finding.

5.24 ***Ability to increase the sentence/Must give a warning***

Senior Courts Act 1981 s 48(4) If the appeal is against a conviction or a sentence, the preceding provisions of this section shall be construed as including power to award any punishment, whether more or less severe than that awarded by the Magistrates' Court whose decision is appealed against, if that is a punishment which that Magistrates' Court might have awarded.

R v Acton Crown Court ex parte Bewley 1988 10 Cr App R (S) 105 The Magistrates bound D over to come up for judgment. This order is not available in Magistrates' Courts. She appealed and was given a total of 6 months' youth custody. She appealed again. Held. The Crown Court can substitute a lawful sentence for an unlawful one. The Judge may have considered that only a substantial sentence would stop her conduct. On the facts, the second sentence was affirmed.

R v Maidstone Crown Court ex parte Litchfield 1992 The Times 30/6/92 D pleaded to speeding and was disqualified for a month. He appealed and the appeal was allowed but without warning the Court increased the fine from £120 to £500. The Court also made a costs order against him because the appeal was successful 'by the skin of his teeth'. He appealed again. Held. The quadrupling of the fine was wrong in principle. It is customary to give a warning so the defendant can consider whether to pursue his or her appeal. There was no inquiry into means. The costs order was manifestly unfair and unjust.

R (Tottman) v DPP 2004 EWHC 258 (Admin) D pleaded to drink/driving and the case was adjourned for a special reasons hearing. The reading was 49 µg (14 over the limit). The Magistrates heard from three witnesses for the defence but they were not told about D's recent speeding conviction. The Magistrates found special reasons, decided not to disqualify and awarded 11 penalty points, which was the maximum number. However, with the 3 points for the speeding offence D became a 'totter' and he was disqualified for 6 months. D appealed contending the Magistrates did not want to disqualify him, so the points should be reduced to 8 or fewer, making fewer than 12 in all. Before the hearing it was agreed by counsel that no witnesses should attend. During submissions the prosecution said they were not going to submit that the special reasons finding was wrong. After submissions, the Judge asked two factual questions that related to the special reasons issue. They were answered. There was no indication that the sentence might be increased. The Court then accepted that special reasons had been found but imposed 12 months' disqualification because of the two answers they had heard and another fact of the case. D appealed. Held. The defence had not conducted their case to answer a discretionary disqualification. The witnesses were not present. The answer to the first question was highly material but D was not there to give an explanation. The defence were never in a position to make submissions. The Court should have given a clear warning about its intentions.

5.25 *Magistrates pass an unlawful sentence*

Senior Courts Act 1981 s 48(1) The Crown Court may, in the course of hearing any appeal, correct any error or mistake in the order or judgment incorporating the decision which is the subject of the appeal.

R v Birmingham JJs ex parte Wyatt 1975 61 Cr App R 306 LCJ D pleaded at the Magistrates' Court when unrepresented. He had not been sent to prison before and was given 6 months' imprisonment. At the appeal hearing, D was represented. The defence said the sentence was unlawful and the Court was restricted to imposing a sentence the Magistrates could have imposed. The Judge said it was a rehearing and because D was now represented the defect was cured. D appealed the committal and the Crown Court decision. Held. The fact a sentence is invalid does not mean the conviction is a nullity. Until the conviction is quashed a defendant can appeal it. The Crown Court could only impose a sentence the Magistrates could have imposed, so we substitute a £50 fine.

R v Acton Crown Court ex parte Bewley 1988 10 Cr App R (S) 105 The Magistrates bound D over to come up for judgment. This order is not available in Magistrates' Courts. She appealed and was given a total of 6 months' youth custody. She appealed again. Held. The Crown Court can substitute a lawful sentence for an unlawful one.

See also the **PROCEDURE, SENTENCING** ***Unlawful orders*** para at **86.60**.

5.26 *Power to make any order magistrates could have made Defendant crosses an age threshold*

Arthur v Stringer 1986 4 Cr App R (S) 329 D was sentenced for assault on a PC and two other offences. When aged 20, he was sentenced to 4 months' detention. He appealed and the Court wished to impose a suspended sentence, adjourned the matter until he was aged 21 and then passed a sentence of suspended imprisonment. They claimed that they were taking a decision that the Magistrates could have taken. The prosecution appealed. Both counsel said the sentence was unlawful. Held. We quash the suspended sentences.

5.27 ***Power to make any order magistrates could have made*** ***Law changes***
R v Ipswich Crown Court ex parte Williamson 1982 4 Cr App R (S) 348 D was given two 6-month sentences, consecutive. He appealed. Before the hearing, the sentence of partly served and partly suspended sentences came into force. The Judge said the Court was thinking of imposing that order but said he couldn't, so the appeal was dismissed. D appealed. Held. The Judge was right because the Magistrates could not impose the sentence. However, we remit the case, so the court can make one sentence immediate and the other sentence suspended.

Other matters

5.28 ***Court must give reasons***
Criminal Justice Act 2003 s 174[66] (2) The court must state in open court, in ordinary language and in general terms, the court's reasons for deciding on the sentence.
R (Aitchison) v Sheffield Crown Court 2012 EWHC 2844 (Admin) D had his appeal against conviction dismissed. She applied to quash the decision on the basis the reasons were inadequate. The prosecution submitted that where a defendant considered the Crown Court's reasons inadequate, they ought to make a request of the court for further reasons, relying on *English v Emery Reimbold & Strick Ltd* 2002 EWCA Civ 605. Held. What is required to fulfil that duty will depend upon the circumstances of the particular case. In an appeal to the Crown Court, a lengthy or elaborate judgment, such as might be given after a civil trial, will not usually be necessary or appropriate. Indeed, where the determinative issue is factual, narrow and straightforward, a short judgment may suffice, *R v Southwark Crown Court ex parte Brooke* 1997 COD 81. Where that issue turns on which witness is telling the truth, it is likely to be enough for the judge simply to say that he believes X rather than Y. Indeed there may be nothing else to say, *Flannery v Halifax Estate Agencies Ltd* 2000 1 WLR 377 at p 382, though it is often helpful to give a fuller explanation. Those comments equally apply to the Crown Court in its appellate capacity. It would usually be entirely inappropriate for a party to apply to the Crown Court for further and better reasons. Here the Crown Court both adequately identified the determinative issue in the appeal and adequately addressed those issues in its reasons.
Old cases: *R v Harrow Crown Court ex parte Dave* 1994 99 Cr App R 114, 1 WLR 98 (Conviction appeal. Must give reasons.) *Pullum v CPS* 2000 Unreported 17/4/00 (LCJ Conviction appeal. Must give reasons.)
See also the **PROCEDURE, SENTENCING** ***Reasons, Judge must give*** para at **86.49**.

5.29 ***Costs*** ***Defence costs***
Prosecution of Offences Act 1985 s 16(3) Where a person convicted of an offence by a Magistrates' Court appeals to the Crown Court under Magistrates' Courts Act 1980 s 108 (right of appeal against conviction or sentence) and, in consequence of the decision on appeal:

(a) his conviction is set aside, or
(b) a less severe punishment is awarded,

the Crown Court may make a defendant's costs order in favour of the accused.
For prosecution costs to be paid by the defendant, see the **COSTS** ***Power to order Crown Court (Indictment and appeals)*** para at **22.31**.
For more detail see the **COSTS** chapter or the back index under Costs.

6 ATTENDANCE CENTRE ORDERS

6.1
Powers of Criminal Courts (Sentencing) Act 2000 s 60
Availability The Attendance Centre Order as a general sentencing order after a conviction was abolished under Powers of Criminal Courts (Sentencing) Act 2000 Sch 12. The Attendance Centre Order is, however, still available for a) fine defaulters,

[66] As substituted by Legal Aid, Sentencing and Punishment of Offenders Act 2012 s 64

and b) offenders who have failed 'to do or abstain from doing anything required to be done or left undone by them', see **6.2**. This enables a court to make an Attendance Centre Order for a young offender judged guilty of contempt of court and those who refuse to be bound over, see **6.2**. In contempt proceedings, the order is not available for those aged under 18.[67]

History and complexity For an excellent analysis of the history and complexity of these orders, see Sentencing News 24 November 2009 Issue 4 page 7. This article states that the apparent reprieve of the abolition of the power to order an Attendance Centre Order in Criminal Justice and Immigration Act 2008 (Commencement No 13 and Transitory Provision) Order 2009 2009/3074 para (2)(f) is ineffective. This is because of para (2)(u)(xix) of the same order. This view has been treated by the authorities as correct.

Revocation, amendment and variation This is provided by Powers of Criminal Courts (Sentencing) Act 2000 Sch 5 para 4 and 5. Applications must comply with Criminal Procedure Rules 2015 2015/1490 Rule 32.3.

Power to order/Making the order

6.2 *Power to order*

Powers of Criminal Courts (Sentencing) Act 2000 s 60(1) Where:

(a) [Repealed]

(b) a court would have power, but for section 89 (restrictions on imprisonment of young offenders and defaulters), to commit a person aged under 21 to prison in default of payment of any sum of money or for failing to do or abstain from doing anything required to be done or left undone, or

(c) a court has power to commit a person aged at least 21 but under 25 to prison in default of payment of any sum of money,

the court may, if it has been notified by the Secretary of State that an attendance centre is available for the reception of persons of his description, order him to attend at such a centre, to be specified in the order, for such number of hours as may be so specified.

(2) An order under subsection (1) is in this Act referred to as an 'Attendance Centre Order'.

Powers of Criminal Courts (Sentencing) Act 2000 Sch 5 para 7(1) References in Schedule 5 to an 'offender' include a person who has been ordered to attend at an attendance centre for such a default or failure as is mentioned in section 60(1)(b) or (c) of this Act.

(2) Where a person has been ordered to attend at an attendance centre for such a default or failure:

(a) Sch 5 paras 2(1)(b), 3(1) and 4(3) shall each have effect in relation to the order as if the words ', for the offence in respect of which the order was made,' and 'for that offence' were omitted, and

(b) Sch 5 paras 2(5)(b) and 3(3)(b) (which relate to custodial sentences for offences) do not apply.

6.3 *Specified attendance centre must be reasonably accessible*

Powers of Criminal Courts (Sentencing) Act 2000 s 60(6) An Attendance Centre Order shall not be made unless the court is satisfied that the attendance centre to be specified in it is reasonably accessible to the person concerned, having regard to his age, the means of access available to him and any other circumstances.

6.4 *Avoid conflict with education, religious beliefs or community orders*

Powers of Criminal Courts (Sentencing) Act 2000 s 60(7) The times at which a person is required to attend at an attendance centre shall, as far as practicable, be such as to avoid:

(a) any conflict with his religious beliefs or with the requirements of any other Community Order to which he may be subject, and

[67] Contempt of Court Act 1981 s 14(2A)

(b) any interference with the times, if any, at which he normally works or attends school or any other educational establishment.

6.5 ***Minimum number of hours Aged under 14***
Powers of Criminal Courts (Sentencing) Act 2000 s 60(3) The aggregate number of hours for which an Attendance Centre Order may require a person to attend at an attendance centre shall not be less than 12 except where:

(a) he is aged under 14, and
(b) the court is of the opinion that 12 hours would be excessive, having regard to his age or any other circumstances.

6.6 ***Maximum number of hours Aged under 16***
Powers of Criminal Courts (Sentencing) Act 2000 s 60(4) The aggregate number of hours shall not exceed 12 except where the court is of the opinion, having regard to all the circumstances, that 12 hours would be inadequate, and in that case:

(a) shall not exceed 24 where the person is aged under 16.

6.7 ***Maximum number of hours Aged 16-20***
Powers of Criminal Courts (Sentencing) Act 2000 s 60(4)(b) shall not exceed 36 where the person is aged 16 or over but under 21 or (where subsection (1)(c) applies) under 25.

6.8 ***Maximum number of hours a day***
Powers of Criminal Courts (Sentencing) Act 2000 s 60(10) A person shall not be required under this section to attend at an Attendance Centre on more than one occasion on any day, or for more than three hours on any occasion.

6.9 ***Defendant already serving an Attendance Centre Order***
Powers of Criminal Courts (Sentencing) Act 2000 s 60(5) A court may make an Attendance Centre Order in respect of a person before a previous Attendance Centre Order made in respect of him has ceased to have effect, and may determine the number of hours to be specified in the order without regard:

(a) to the number specified in the previous order, or
(b) to the fact that [the] order is still in effect.

Combined with other orders

6.10
Note: Some assistance can be found in the **CUSTODY: IMPRISONMENT Combined with other orders** section at **29.5**. Ed.

Matters arising after the hearing

6.11 ***Duties of designated officer***
Powers of Criminal Courts (Sentencing) Act 2000 s 60(11) Where a court makes an Attendance Centre Order, the designated officer for the court shall:

(a) deliver or send a copy of the order to the officer in charge of the attendance centre specified in it, and
(b) deliver a copy of the order to the person in respect of whom it is made or send a copy by registered post or the recorded delivery service addressed to his last or usual place of abode.

6.12 ***Attendance Fixing of times***
Powers of Criminal Courts (Sentencing) Act 2000 s 60(8) The first time at which the person is required to attend at an attendance centre shall be a time at which the centre is available for his attendance in accordance with the notification of the Secretary of State, and shall be specified in the order.
(9) The subsequent times shall be fixed by the officer in charge of the centre, having regard to the person's circumstances.

6.13 ***Effect of payment in part or in whole***
Powers of Criminal Courts (Sentencing) Act 2000 s 60(12) Where a person ('the defaulter') has been ordered to attend at an attendance centre in default of the payment of any sum of money:

(a) on payment of the whole sum to any person authorised to receive it, the Attendance Centre Order shall cease to have effect,
(b) on payment of a part of the sum…the total number of hours for which the defaulter is required to attend at the centre shall be reduced proportionately, that is to say by such number of complete hours as bears to the total number the proportion most nearly approximating to, without exceeding, the proportion which the part bears to the whole sum.

7 ATTENDANCE CENTRE ORDERS: BREACH OF

7.1
Powers of Criminal Courts (Sentencing) Act 2000 Sch 5

7.2 ***Powers of the court on breach***
Powers of Criminal Courts (Sentencing) Act 2000 Sch 5 para 2(1) If it is proved to the satisfaction of the Magistrates' Court before which an offender appears or is brought under paragraph 1 that he has failed without reasonable excuse to attend as mentioned in sub-paragraph (1)(a) of that paragraph or has committed such a breach of rules as is mentioned in sub-paragraph (1)(b) of that paragraph, that court may deal with him in any one of the following ways:
(a) it may impose on him a **fine** not exceeding £1,000,
(b) where the Attendance Centre Order was made by a Magistrates' Court, it may **deal with** him, for the offence in respect of which the order was made, in any way in which he could have been dealt with for that offence by the court which made the order if the order had not been made, or
(c) where the order was made by the Crown Court, it may **commit him to custody or release him on bail** until he can be brought or appear before the Crown Court.

7.3 ***Power to summons/issue warrant for breach***
Powers of Criminal Courts (Sentencing) Act 2000 Sch 5 para 1(1) Where an Attendance Centre Order is in force and it appears on information to a justice that the offender:
(a) has failed to attend in accordance with the order, or
(b) while attending has committed a breach of rules made under Criminal Justice Act 2003 s 221(1)(d) or (e) which cannot be adequately dealt with under those rules,
the justice may issue a summons requiring the offender to appear at the place and time specified in the summons or, if the information is in writing and on oath, may issue a warrant for the offender's arrest.
(2) Any summons or warrant issued under this paragraph shall direct the offender to appear or be brought:
(a) before a Magistrates' Court acting for the local justice area in which the offender resides, or
(b) if it is not known where the offender resides, before a Magistrates' Court acting for the local justice area in which is situated the attendance centre which the offender is required to attend by the order or by virtue of an order under paragraph 5(1)(b) below.
Criminal Procedure Rules 2015 2015/1490 Rule 32.2(1)
This rule applies where:
(a) the responsible officer or supervisor wants the court to:
(i) deal with a defendant for failure to comply with an order to which this Part applies, or
(ii) revoke or amend such an order, or
b) the court considers exercising on its own initiative any power it has to:
(i) revoke or amend such an order, and
(ii) summon the defendant to attend for that purpose.

(2) Rules 7.2 to 7.4, which deal, among other things, with starting a prosecution in a Magistrates' Court,[68] apply:

(a) as if:

(i) a reference in those rules to an allegation of an offence included a reference to an allegation of failure to comply with an order to which this Part applies, and

(ii) a reference to the prosecutor included a reference to the responsible officer or supervisor, and

(b) with the necessary consequential modifications.

7.4 *Procedure*

Criminal Procedure Rules 2015 2015/1490 Rule 32.4(1) Except for Rule 24.8 (written guilty plea: special rules), and 24.9 (Single justice procedure: special rules), the rules in Part 24, which deal with the procedure at a trial in a Magistrates' Court, apply:

(a) as if:

(i) a reference in those rules to an allegation of an offence included a reference to an allegation of failure to comply with an order to which this Part applies,

(ii) a reference to the court's verdict included a reference to the court's decision to revoke or amend such an order, or to exercise any other power it has to deal with the defendant, and

(iii) a reference to the court's sentence included a reference to the exercise of any such power, and

(b) with the necessary consequential modifications.

(2) The court officer must serve on each party any order revoking or amending an order to which this Part applies.

7.5 Breach *Issue to be determined by judge when at a Crown Court*

Powers of Criminal Courts (Sentencing) Act 2000 Sch 5 para 3(4) In proceedings before the Crown Court under this paragraph any question whether there has been a failure to attend or a breach of the rules shall be determined by the court and not by the verdict of a jury.

7.6 *Crown Court powers*

Powers of Criminal Courts (Sentencing) Act 2000 Sch 5 para 3(1) Where by virtue of paragraph 2(1)(c) the offender is brought or appears before the Crown Court and it is proved to the satisfaction of the court:

(a) that he has failed without reasonable excuse to attend as mentioned in paragraph 1(1)(a), or

(b) that he has committed such a breach of rules as is mentioned in paragraph 1(1)(b),

that court may deal with him, for the offence in respect of which the order was made, in any way in which it could have dealt with him for that offence if it had not made the order.

(2) Where the Crown Court deals with an offender under sub-paragraph (1), it shall revoke the Attendance Centre Order if it is still in force.

(3) In dealing with an offender under sub-paragraph (1), the Crown Court:

(a) shall take into account the extent to which the offender has complied with the requirements of the Attendance Centre Order, and

(b) in the case of an offender who has wilfully and persistently failed to comply with those requirements, may impose a custodial sentence notwithstanding anything in Criminal Justice Act 2003 s 152(2) (restrictions on imposing discretionary custodial sentences, see **28.26**).

[68] The words 'by information and summons' were deleted by Criminal Procedure (Amendment) Rules 2018 2018/132 para 14. In force 2/4/18

7.7 *Offender fined Order continues to have effect*

Powers of Criminal Courts (Sentencing) Act 2000 Sch 5 para 2(2) Any exercise by the court of its power under sub-paragraph (1)(a) shall be without prejudice to the continuation of the order.

(3) A fine imposed under sub-paragraph (1)(a) shall be deemed, for the purposes of any enactment, to be a sum adjudged to be paid by a conviction.

7.8 *Offender fined Power to amend order*

Powers of Criminal Courts (Sentencing) Act 2000 Sch 5 para 2(5A) Where a Magistrates' Court dealing with an offender under sub-paragraph (1)(a) would not otherwise have the power to amend the order under paragraph 5(1)(b) below (substitution of different attendance centre), that paragraph has effect as if references to an appropriate Magistrates' Court were references to the court dealing with the offender.

Powers of Criminal Courts (Sentencing) Act 2000 Sch 5 para 5(1) Where an Attendance Centre Order is in force in respect of an offender, an appropriate Magistrates' Court may, on an application made by the offender or by the officer in charge of the relevant attendance centre, by order:..b) substitute for the relevant attendance centre an attendance centre which the court is satisfied is reasonably accessible to the offender, having regard to his age, the means of access available to him and any other circumstances.

7.9 *Part compliance, Must consider*

Powers of Criminal Courts (Sentencing) Act 2000 Sch 5 para 3(2) Where the Crown Court deals with an offender under sub-paragraph (1), it shall revoke the Attendance Centre Order if it is still in force.

(3) In dealing with an offender under sub-paragraph (1), the Crown Court:

(a) shall take into account the extent to which the offender has complied with the requirements of the Attendance Centre Order, and

Powers of Criminal Courts (Sentencing) Act 2000 Sch 5 para 2(4) Where a Magistrates' Court deals with an offender under sub-paragraph (1)(b), it shall revoke the Attendance Centre Order if it is still in force.

(5) In dealing with an offender under sub-paragraph (1)(b), a Magistrates' Court:

(a) shall take into account the extent to which the offender has complied with the requirements of the Attendance Centre Order.

7.10 *Custodial sentences imposed on breach*

Powers of Criminal Courts (Sentencing) Act 2000 Sch 5 para 3(2) Where the Crown Court deals with an offender under sub-paragraph (1), it shall revoke the Attendance Centre Order if it is still in force.

(3) In dealing with an offender under sub-paragraph (1), the Crown Court:

(b) in the case of an offender who has wilfully and persistently failed to comply with those requirements, may impose a custodial sentence notwithstanding anything in Criminal Justice Act 2003 s 152(2) (restrictions on imposing discretionary custodial sentences, see **28.26**).

Powers of Criminal Courts (Sentencing) Act 2000 Sch 5 para 2(4) Where a Magistrates' Court deals with an offender under sub-paragraph (1)(b), it shall revoke the Attendance Centre Order if it is still in force.

(5) In dealing with an offender under sub-paragraph (1)(b), a Magistrates' Court:

(b) in the case of an offender who has wilfully and persistently failed to comply with those requirements, may impose a custodial sentence notwithstanding anything in Criminal Justice Act 2003 s 152(2) (restrictions on imposing discretionary custodial sentences, see **28.26**).

7.11 *Appeal from Magistrates' Court*

Powers of Criminal Courts (Sentencing) Act 2000 Sch 5 para 2(6) A person sentenced under sub-paragraph (1)(b) for an offence may appeal to the Crown Court against the sentence.

7.12 ***Parent/guardian to pay fine etc. for breaches of orders***
Powers of Criminal Courts (Sentencing) Act 2000 s 137(2) Where but for this subsection a court would impose a fine on a child or young person under:..b) Powers of Criminal Courts (Sentencing) Act 2000 Sch 5 para 2(1)(a) (breach of Attendance Centre Order or attendance centre rules), the court shall order that the fine be paid by the parent or guardian of the child or young person instead of by the child or young person himself, unless the court is satisfied:

(i) that the parent or guardian cannot be found, or
(ii) that it would be unreasonable to make an order for payment, having regard to the circumstances of the case.

7.13 ***Parent/guardian to pay fine etc. Offender aged 16-17***
Powers of Criminal Courts (Sentencing) Act 2000 s 137(3) In the case of a young person aged 16 or over, subsections (1) to (2) of this section shall have effect as if, instead of imposing a duty, they conferred a power to make such an order as is mentioned in those subsections.

7.14 ***Parent/guardian must have opportunity of being heard***
Powers of Criminal Courts (Sentencing) Act 2000 s 137(4) Subject to subsection (5), no order shall be made under this section without giving the parent or guardian an opportunity of being heard.

7.15 ***Parent/guardian fails to attend hearing***
Powers of Criminal Courts (Sentencing) Act 2000 s 137(5) An order under this section may be made against a parent or guardian who, having been required to attend, has failed to do so.
For breach proceedings, see the **Community Order: Breach of *Procedure*** para at **16.4**.

7.16 ***Magistrates' Court Sentencing Guidelines 2008***
Magistrates' Court Sentencing Guidelines 2008, see www.banksr.com Other Matters Guidelines tab para 147 When sentencing for the breach of any order for which there is not a specific guideline, the primary objective will be to ensure compliance. Reference to existing guidelines in respect of breaches of orders may provide a helpful point of comparison.

8 Attorney-General's References

8.1
Criminal Justice Act 1988 s 36

8.2 ***Statistics England and Wales***
These statistics are from www.gov.uk/government/statistical-data-sets

	2008	2009	2010	2011	2012	2013	2014	2015	2016	2017
Number of offenders where leave was given	69	102	74	108	73	66	117	127	173	157
Number of offenders whose sentences were unduly lenient	57	77	65	97	65	70	121	102	146	142
Number of offenders whose sentences were increased	52	71	60	94	62	61	106	102	141	137

For further statistics on Attorney-General's References, see www.banksr.com Other Matters Statistics tab.

Considerations at the Crown Court

8.3 *Judicial indications Defence counsel must warn defendant*
R v Goodyear 2005 EWCA Crim 888, 2006 1 Cr App R (S) 6 (p 23) The advocate is personally responsible for ensuring that his client fully appreciates that any sentence indication given by the judge remains subject to the entitlement of the Attorney-General (where it arises) to refer an unduly lenient sentence to the Court of Appeal.
Att-Gen's Ref No 48 of 2006 2006 EWCA Crim 2396, 2007 1 Cr App R (S) 90 (p 558) Defence counsel must advise his client that any sentence indication given by the judge remains subject to the entitlement of the Attorney-General to refer an unduly lenient sentence to the Court of Appeal.

8.4 *Judicial indications Prosecution asserting entitlement to refer*
R v Goodyear 2005 EWCA Crim 888, 2006 1 Cr App R (S) 6 (p 23) It should not normally be necessary for counsel for the prosecution, before the judge gives any indication, to do more than…where it applies, to remind the judge that the position of the Attorney-General to refer any eventual sentencing decision as unduly lenient is not affected. If counsel for the prosecution has addressed his responsibilities, the discretion of the Attorney-General to refer a sentence would be wholly unaffected by the advance sentence indication process. If prosecuting counsel has indicated his support for the indication given, the question whether the sentence should nevertheless be referred to this Court as unduly lenient, and the decision of the Court whether to interfere with and increase it, will be examined on a case-by-case basis, in the light of everything said and done by counsel for the Crown.
Att-Gen's Ref No 48 of 2006 2006 EWCA Crim 2396, 2007 1 Cr App R (S) 90 (p 558) There will be cases where the prosecution should remind the judge that the position of the Attorney-General to refer any sentencing decision as unduly lenient is not affected.

8.5 *Judicial indications No bar to a reference*
Att-Gen's Ref No 40 of 1996 1997 1 Cr App R (S) 357 LCJ D pleaded to ABH, false imprisonment and having a firearm with intent to commit an indictable offence, after an indication was given by the trial Judge that the sentence would be 5 years. He received 4 years for the false imprisonment, and a suspended sentence was activated, making 5 years. D argued that where an indication as to sentence was given, and subsequently a plea was tendered, the Court should be slow to increase a sentence. Held. The sentence was unduly lenient. The Court took account of: a) the fact that it was a reference and D was being sentenced for a second time, and b) there was an indication given by the Judge. Whilst the indication is a matter which the court must take into account, it does not preclude the Court from increasing the sentence. 5 years substituted, making 6.
Att-Gen's Ref No 17 of 1998 1999 1 Cr App R (S) 407 D pleaded to section 18 after the Judge indicated that he was minded to impose a non-custodial sentence. D had attacked V, who was seven months pregnant, with a Stanley knife. Four injuries were caused requiring a total of 52 stitches. D appealed on the basis that effect ought to be given to the indication and the Court ought not to increase the sentence to a custodial penalty. Held. Anyone who pleads guilty to an offence which is, by the terms of that Act, susceptible to an Attorney-General's Reference must be taken to do so in recognition of the risk that, if a lenient sentence is passed, that may give rise to an Attorney-General's Reference to this Court, on which this Court may increase the sentence passed by the sentencing judge. It follows that we do not accept that *Att-Gen's Ref No 40 of 1996* was decided *per incuriam*. It is a factor to take into account, but it will not be a barrier to increasing sentence.
Att-Gen's Ref No 48 of 2006 2006 EWCA Crim 2396, 2007 1 Cr App R (S) 90 (p 558) D pleaded to money laundering offences, following a *Goodyear* indication. The Judge advised that a non-immediate custodial penalty would be imposed on a plea. D received a conditional discharge. Held. Prosecution counsel did not, in accordance with guidelines laid down in *Goodyear*, advise the Judge of the powers of the Attorney-General in

relation to unduly lenient sentences. It may well have had no effect on the proceedings. That, however, cannot in itself preclude this Court from determining that the indication by the Judge that it was appropriate to suspend the sentence of imprisonment was wrong on the facts of the case. Immediate custodial sentences were substituted.

8.6 *Judicial indications If sentence inappropriate prosecution must register dissent*

Att-Gen's Ref Nos 86-87 of 1999 2001 1 Cr App R (S) 141 (p 505) D1 and D2 were convicted of various offences relating to HMRC. The Judge sent for counsel and indicated that he was not minded to impose a custodial penalty. Defence counsel sought clarification and the Judge confirmed that that was his intention irrespective of whether D1 and D2 pleaded or not. Prosecution counsel added only, "unless the evidence changes". In the event, they did not plead and were duly convicted. Held. We consider that where an indication is given by a trial judge as to the level of sentencing and that indication is one which prosecuting counsel considers to be inappropriate…prosecuting counsel should register dissent…otherwise if the offender does act to his detriment on the indication which has been given this Court may well find it difficult to intervene in response to a reference made by the Attorney-General. The fact that the prosecution had acquiesced to the indication was relevant.
R v Goodyear 2005 EWCA Crim 888, 2006 1 Cr App R (S) 6 (p 23) It should not normally be necessary for counsel for the prosecution, before the judge gives any indication, to do more than, first, draw the judge's attention to any minimum or mandatory statutory sentencing requirements and second, where it applies, to remind the judge that the position of the Attorney-General to refer any eventual sentencing decision as unduly lenient is not affected. If counsel for the prosecution has addressed his responsibilities the discretion of the Attorney-General to refer a sentence would be wholly unaffected by the advance sentence indication process. If prosecuting counsel has indicated his support for the indication given, the question whether the sentence should nevertheless be referred to this Court as unduly lenient, and the decision of the Court whether to interfere with and increase it, will be examined on a case-by-case basis, in the light of everything said and done by counsel for the Crown.
Att-Gen's Ref No 48 of 2006 2006 EWCA Crim 2396, 2007 1 Cr App R (S) 90 (p 558) There will be cases where the prosecution should remind the judge that the position of the Attorney-General to refer any sentencing decision as unduly lenient is not affected.
See also: *Att-Gen's Ref No 44 of 2000* 2001 1 Cr App R (S) 132 (p 460) (Prosecution encouraged the Judge to pass a suspended sentence. Defendant entitled to rely on representation. It did lead to a legitimate expectation and the Attorney-General could not resile from it. Leave to refer refused.)
Att-Gen's Ref No 32 of 2015 2015 EWCA Crim 1110 (Court Martial Appeal Court. D pleaded to four sexual activity with a child offences. Counsel told Court he would not refer. Held. Counsel should have just referred relevant authorities to the Court and said the position of the Attorney-General to refer cases was unaffected. As defence counsel had told D the prosecution could still refer, D had no legitimate expectation so there was no bar to hearing case.)

8.7 *Judicial indications Prosecution acquiescence*

Att-Gen's Ref Nos 80-81 of 1999 2000 2 Cr App R (S) 138 LCJ D1 and D2 pleaded to offences relating to the filing of fraudulent invoices, for the company for which D1 was chairman and D2 was managing director. Neither defendant received any benefit. The activities were merely to keep 'a leaking ship afloat'. The Judge had indicated to counsel that he saw no reason for a custodial sentence for D2. This was further discussed in open court and the Judge confirmed that on a plea of guilty, there would be no custodial penalty for D2. D2 then indicated a willingness to give evidence for the prosecution against D1 and pleaded. The Judge indicated that his view on sentence applied equally to D1 whether he pleaded or was convicted. D1 then pleaded. The pleas were accepted. The

Judge sought information as to the defendants' finances. D2 could not pay the level of fine that the Judge deemed appropriate and so he was ordered to contribute to the prosecution costs and was conditionally discharged. D1 was far less criminally culpable and was absolutely discharged with a reduced costs order. Held. There can never be any obligation for the prosecution to acquiesce in an indication given by the judge to which the Crown takes exception. We have regard to the unreserved acquiescence of prosecuting counsel in the line that the Judge was taking and the reliance which the Crown placed on it by accepting the plea of D2 to the more serious offence and taking a statement from him with a view [to him giving evidence against D1]. In fact, D1 pleaded to the less serious offences. Prosecution counsel was instructed by the CPS, who are responsible to the Attorney-General, who was now making the application. Having regard to the unfortunate history of this case, we would consider it almost, if not actually, abusive now to reopen these sentences to the potential detriment of the offenders. We do not grant leave to the Attorney-General.

Att-Gen's Ref No 44 of 2000 2001 1 Cr App R (S) 132 (p 460) D pleaded to eight counts of indecent assault on a girl, five being on a girl under the age of 13, and one count of indecent assault on a male. He received 18 months suspended. D was the deputy headmaster and later the headmaster at a preparatory school. The offences occurred when D was disciplining the children. He denied all offences. Prosecuting counsel enquired as to the possibility of guilty pleas. Defence counsel advised that they were inconceivable if D would receive a custodial sentence. Prosecution counsel informed the Judge that almost all the complainants did not wish D to go to prison. The Judge said to defence counsel that a suspended sentence would be a fair outcome. Defence counsel then saw D but did not warn him about an Attorney-General's Reference. This initiated a joint approach to the Judge, in which prosecution counsel acquiesced and encouraged the Judge to pass a suspended sentence. Brief submissions were made, defence counsel advancing mitigation arguing that this was an exceptional case, prosecution counsel observing that pleas to nine out of 16 counts relating to seven of 11 complainants was satisfactory. The Judge agreed that a suspended sentence was justified. Prosecution counsel at the Court of Appeal tried to argue that the CPS and the Attorney-General were different parts of the system. Held. It was regrettable that such plea bargaining had occurred here. If the Crown, by whatever means they are prosecuting, make representations to a defendant on which he is entitled to rely and on which he acts to his detriment by, as in the present case, pleading guilty in circumstances in which he would not otherwise have pleaded guilty, that can properly be regarded as giving rise to a legitimate expectation on his part that the Crown will not subsequently seek to resile from those representations, whether by way of the Attorney-General exercising his personal statutory duties under section 36 or otherwise. For this purpose the Crown and its agents are indivisible.

R v Goodyear 2005 EWCA Crim 888, 2006 1 Cr App R (S) 6 (p 23) If prosecuting counsel has indicated his support for the indication given, the question whether the sentence should nevertheless be referred to this Court as unduly lenient, and the decision of the Court whether to interfere with and increase it, will be examined on a case-by-case basis, in the light of everything said and done by counsel for the Crown.

See also: *Att-Gen's Ref Nos 8-10 of 2002* 2002 EWCA Crim 1607, 2003 1 Cr App R (S) 57 (p 272) (Unduly lenient sentence left undisturbed as a result of a judicial indication of a non-custodial sentence to which prosecution counsel did not indicate dissent. It would be unjust to alter the inappropriate conditional discharges.)

For occasions when the Attorney-General's position at the Court of Appeal is not asserted in the Crown Court, see the ***Prosecution counsel fails to assert position at Crown Court*** para at **8.44**.

8.8 ***Prosecution tells judge they will not refer case or similar circumstances***
Examples: *Att-Gen's Ref No 44 of 2000* 2001 1 Cr App R (S) 132 (p 460) (Prosecution encouraged the Judge to pass a suspended sentence. Defendant entitled to rely on representation. It did lead to a legitimate expectation and the Attorney-General could not resile from it. Leave to refer refused.)
Att-Gen's Ref No 32 of 2015 2015 EWCA Crim 1110 (Court Martial Appeal Court. D pleaded to four sexual activity with a child offences. Counsel told Court he would not refer. Counsel should have just referred relevant authorities to the Court and said the position of the Attorney-General to refer cases was unaffected. As defence counsel had told D the prosecution could still refer, D had no legitimate expectation so there was no bar to hearing case.)

8.9 ***Judges should administer justice and not fear references***
Att-Gen's Ref No 8 of 2007 2007 EWCA Crim 922, 2008 1 Cr App R (S) 1 (p 1) LCJ D, aged 18, was convicted of possession with intent to supply both cocaine and cannabis. Her co-defendant was convicted of those offences and offences relating to firearms. Prior to conviction, the Judge invited counsel to his room and indicated that he was minded to pass a sentence avoiding immediate custody, and that this could be communicated to D. Subsequently, the Judge passed a custodial sentence of 18 months (after an unfavourable pre-sentence report), after both counsel had erroneously advised the Judge that the offence was one for which the Attorney-General had no power to refer the case. However, when reminded of his indication, he amended the sentence to 12 months' detention suspended for 2 years. Held. It would obviously have been better had the Judge given a full explanation of his amended sentence at the time that he imposed it. Before the verdict the Judge formed the view, on the evidence that he had heard, that if the offender were convicted it would be appropriate to depart from the sentencing guidelines and to impose a sentence that would keep this young woman out of prison. He felt so strongly about this that he took the very unusual step of inviting counsel to his room, informing them of the view that he had formed, and telling counsel for the offender that he could reassure his client that if she were convicted she would not go to prison. We are inclined to think that, in changing his mind and deciding to impose a sentence of detention, the Judge was looking over his shoulder at the possibility that if he followed his initial intention this would lead to a reference by the Attorney-General. The oath taken by a judge to administer justice 'without fear or favour, affection or ill-will' extends to imposing what the judge concludes to be the appropriate sentence, without being deterred by the fear of an Attorney-General's reference. The Judge had every reason for the unusual approach that he adopted to this case. He had every reason for taking a particularly lenient view of this offender and imposing a sentence which, being custodial, emphasised the gravity of the offending, but which, being suspended, reflected the fact that she was unlikely to offend again and that it was not necessary in the circumstances that she should go straight into detention.

Making the application

Article Vincent Scully, former lawyer at the Attorney-General's office, writes about the consequences of the failure to draft a respondent's notice, which in one case acted as a bar to the defence making submissions, see Part 2 of his article in *Archbold Review* Issue 2 March 2018, p 8. The article suggests that the decision was objectional in principle and of questionable validity.

8.10 ***Who can suggest references?***
Attorney-General's statement 2010: Victims, their families, and members of the public can contact the Attorney-General's Office if they think a sentence is much too light.
Contact details: Attorney-General's Office 020 7271 2492
referrals@attorneygeneral.gsi.gov.uk

8.11 ***Power to apply for leave to refer***
Criminal Justice Act 1988 s 36(1) If it appears to the Attorney-General:

(a) that the sentencing of a person in a proceeding in the Crown Court has been unduly lenient, and
(b) that the case is one to which this Part of this Act applies,
he may, with the leave of the Court of Appeal, refer the case to them for them to review the sentencing of that person.

8.12 *Grounds to alter the sentence*
Criminal Justice Act 1988 s 36(2) Without prejudice to the generality of subsection (1) above, the condition specified in paragraph (a) of that subsection may be satisfied if it appears to the Attorney-General that the judge:
(a) erred in law as to his powers of sentencing, or
(b) failed to impose a sentence required by:
(zi) Prevention of Crime Act 1953 s 1A(5),[69]
(i) Firearms Act 1968 s 51A(2),
(ia) Criminal Justice Act 1988 s 139AA(7),
(ii) Powers of Criminal Courts (Sentencing) Act 2000 s 110(2) or 111(2),
(iii) Criminal Justice Act 2003 s 224A, 225(2) or 226(2), or[70]
(iv) Violent Crime Reduction Act 2006 s 29(4) or (6).

8.13 *Power to apply for leave to refer Which offences can be referred?*
Note: There are two types of offence which can be referred to the Court of Appeal under section 36. They are indictable-only matters and offences listed in Criminal Justice Act 1988 (Reviews of Sentencing) Order 2006 2006/1116 Sch 1 listed below. The sooner all these rules are replaced by a simple rule that applications just require leave the better. Ed.
Criminal Justice Act 1988 s 35(3) [Part IV] of this Act (reviews of sentencing) applies to any case:
(a) of a description specified in an order under this section, or
(b) in which sentence is passed on a person:
(i) for an offence triable only on indictment, or
(ii) for an offence of a description specified in an order under this section.
Criminal Justice Act 1988 (Reviews of Sentencing) Order 2006 2006/1116 art 2 Criminal Justice Act 1988 Part IV (reviews of sentencing) shall apply to any case of a description specified in Schedule 1.
Criminal Justice Act 1988 (Reviews of Sentencing) Order 2006 2006/1116 Sch 1
Descriptions of cases to which Criminal Justice Act 1988 Part IV is to apply.
para 1 Any case tried on indictment:
(a) following a notice of transfer given under Criminal Justice Act 1987 s 4 (notices of transfer and designated authorities) by an authority designated for that purpose under section 4(2) of that Act, or
(b) in which one or more of the counts in respect of which sentence is passed relates to a charge which was dismissed under Criminal Justice Act 1987 s 6(1) (applications for dismissal) and on which further proceedings were brought by means of preferment of a voluntary bill of indictment.
para 1A Any case tried on indictment:
(a) following a notice given under Crime and Disorder Act 1998 s 51B (notices in serious or complex fraud cases); or
(b) following such a notice, in which one or more of the counts in respect of which sentence is passed relates to a charge:
(i) which was dismissed under Crime and Disorder Act 1998 Sch 3 para 2 (applications for dismissal); and

[69] Subsections zi) and ia) were inserted by Legal Aid, Sentencing and Punishment of Offenders Act 2012 Sch 26 para 5.
[70] Inserted by Legal Aid, Sentencing and Punishment of Offenders Act 2012 Sch 19 para 2

(ii) on which further proceedings were brought by means of the preferment of a voluntary bill of indictment.[71]

para 2 Any case in which sentence is passed on a person for one of the following offences:

(a) an offence under section 16 of the Offences against the Person Act 1861 (threats to kill);

(b) an offence under section 5(1) of the Criminal Law Amendment Act 1885 (defilement of a girl between 14 and 17);

(c) an offence under section 1 of the Children and Young Persons Act 1933 (cruelty to persons under 16) or section 20 of the Children and Young Persons Act (Northern Ireland) 1968 (cruelty to persons under 16);

(d) an offence under section 6 of the Sexual Offences Act 1956 (unlawful sexual intercourse with a girl under 16),* section 14 or 15 of that Act (indecent assault on a woman or on a man),* section 52 of the Offences against the Person Act 1861 (indecent assault upon a female), or Article 21 of the Criminal Justice (Northern Ireland) Order 2003 (indecent assault on a male);

(e) an offence under section 1 of the Indecency with Children Act 1960* or section 22 of the Children and Young Persons Act (Northern Ireland) 1968 (indecent conduct with a child);

(f) an offence under section 4(2) or (3) (production or supply of a controlled drug), section 5(3) (possession of a controlled drug with intent to supply) or section 6(2) (cultivation of cannabis plant) of the Misuse of Drugs Act 1971;

(g) an offence under section 54 of the Criminal Law Act 1977 or Article 9 of the Criminal Justice (Northern Ireland) Order 1980 (inciting a girl under 16 to have incestuous sexual intercourse);*

(h) an offence under section 50(2) or (3), section 68(2) or section 170(1) or (2) of the Customs and Excise Management Act 1979, insofar as those offences are in connection with a prohibition or restriction on importation or exportation of either:

(i) a controlled drug within the meaning of section 2 of the Misuse of Drugs Act 1971, such prohibition or restriction having effect by virtue of section 3 of that Act; or

(ii) an article prohibited by virtue of section 42 of the Customs Consolidation Act 1876 but only insofar as it relates to or depicts a person under the age of 16;

(i) offences under sections 29 to 32 of the Crime and Disorder Act 1998 (racially or religiously aggravated assaults; racially or religiously aggravated criminal damage; racially or religiously aggravated public order offences; racially or religiously aggravated harassment etc);

(j) an offence under section 4 of the Asylum and Immigration (Treatment of Claimants, etc.) Act 2004 (trafficking people for exploitation);

(k) an offence under section 71 of the Coroners and Justice Act 2009 (slavery, servitude and forced or compulsory labour);

(l) an offence under section 1 (slavery, servitude and forced or compulsory labour), (human trafficking) or 4 (committing an offence with intent to commit a human trafficking offence) of the Modern Slavery Act 2015.

para 3 To the extent that Criminal Justice Act 1988 Part IV does not apply by virtue of section 35(3)(b)(i), any case in which sentence is passed on a person for an offence under one of the following sections of Sexual Offences Act 2003:

(a) s 3 (sexual assault)

(b) s 4 (causing a person to engage in sexual activity without consent)

(c) s 7 (sexual assault of a child under 13)

(d) s 8 (causing or inciting a child under 13 to engage in sexual activity)

[71] Para 1A was inserted by Criminal Justice Act 1988 (Reviews of Sentencing) (Amendment) Order 2012 2012/1833 art 2(2)(a).

(e) s 9 (sexual activity with a child)
(f) s 10 (causing or inciting a child to engage in sexual activity)
(g) s 11 (engaging in sexual activity in the presence of a child)
(h) s 12 (causing a child to watch a sexual act)
(i) s 14 (arranging or facilitating commission of a child sex offence)
(j) s 15 (meeting a child following sexual grooming etc.)
(k) s 25 (sexual activity with a child family member)
(l) s 47 (paying for sexual services of a child)
(m) s 48 (causing or inciting child prostitution or pornography)
(n) s 49 (controlling a child prostitute or a child involved in pornography)
(o) s 50 (arranging or facilitating child prostitution or pornography)
(p) s 52 (causing or inciting prostitution for gain)
(q) s 57 (trafficking into the UK for sexual exploitation)*
(r) s 58 (trafficking within the UK for sexual exploitation)*
(s) s 59 (trafficking out of the UK for sexual exploitation)*
(sa) s 59A (trafficking people for sexual exploitation)[72]
(t) s 61 (administering a substance with intent)

3A(1)[73] Any case in which sentence is passed on a person for an offence under one of the following:

(a) section 11 or 12 of the Terrorism Act 2000 ("the 2000 Act") (offences relating to proscribed organisations);
(b) sections 15 to 18 of the 2000 Act (offences relating to terrorist property);
(ba) sections 19(3) (disclosure of information: duty), 21A(4) (failure to disclose: regulated sector) or 21D(5) (tipping off: regulated sector) of the 2000 Act;[74]
(c) section 38B of the 2000 Act (failure to disclose information about acts of terrorism);
(ca) section 39 of the 2000 Act (disclosure of information);[75]
(d) section 54 of the 2000 Act (weapons training);
(e) sections 57 to 58A of the 2000 Act (possessing things, collecting information and eliciting, publishing or communicating information about members of the armed forces etc for the purposes of terrorism);
(f) section 113 of the Anti-Terrorism, Crime and Security Act 2001 (use of noxious substances or things to cause harm or intimidate);
(g) section 1 or 2 of the Terrorism Act 2006 (encouragement of terrorism);
(h) section 6 or 8 of the Terrorism Act 2006 (training for terrorism);
(i) section 54 of the Counter-Terrorism Act 2008 (offences relating to notification);
(j) section 23 of the Terrorism Prevention and Investigation Measures Act 2011 (offence of contravening a TPIM notice);
(k) section 10 of the Counter-Terrorism and Security Act 2015 (offences of contravening a Temporary Exclusion Order or not complying with a restriction after return).[76]

(2) Any case in which sentence is passed on a person for one of the following:
(a) an offence under section 20 of the Offences Against the Person Act 1861 (inflicting bodily harm);
(b) an offence under the following provisions of the Criminal Damage Act 1971[:]
(i) section 1(1) (destroying or damaging property);

[72] As inserted by Protection of Freedoms Act 2012 (Consequential Amendments) Order 2013 2013/862 Sch 1 para 1
[73] Subsections 3A(1) and (2) were inserted by Criminal Justice Act 1988 (Reviews of Sentencing) (Amendment) Order 2017 2017/751 para 2.
[74] Para 3A(1)(ba) was inserted by Criminal Justice Act 1988 (Reviews of Sentencing) (Amendment No 2) Order 2017 2017/1328 art 2(2)(a). In force 29/1/18
[75] Para 3A(1)(ca) was inserted by Criminal Justice Act 1988 (Reviews of Sentencing) (Amendment No 2) Order 2017 2017/1328 art 2(2)(b). In force 29/1/18
[76] Para 3A(1)(h)-(i) were inserted by Criminal Justice Act 1988 (Reviews of Sentencing) (Amendment No 2) Order 2017 2017/1328 art 2(2)(c). In force 29/1/18

(ii) section 1(1) and (3) (arson);
(iii) section 2 (threats to destroy or damage property);
(c) an offence under sections 1 to 5 of the Forgery and Counterfeiting Act 1981;
where there is jurisdiction in England and Wales by virtue of any of sections 63B to 63D of the 2000 Act (extra-territorial jurisdiction in respect of certain offences committed outside the United Kingdom for the purposes of terrorism etc).

(3) Any case in which sentence is passed on a person for an offence under one of the following:
(a) section 4 of the Aviation Security Act 1982 (offences in relation to certain dangerous articles);
(b) section 114 of the Anti-Terrorism, Crime and Security Act 2001 (hoaxes involving noxious substances or things)
where the court has determined that the offence has a terrorist connection under section 30 of the Counter-Terrorism Act 2008 (sentences for offences with a terrorist connection: England and Wales).

Terrorism Act 2006
(g) s 1 or 2 (encouragement of terrorism),
(h) s 6 or 8 (training for terrorism).

(2)(a) Offences Against the Person Act 1861 s 20 (inflicting bodily harm),
(b) Criminal Damage Act 1971
(i) s 1(1) (destroying or damaging property),
(ii) s 1(1) and (3) (arson),
(iii) s 2 (threats to destroy or damage property),
(c) Forgery and Counterfeiting Act 1981 s 1-5;
where there is jurisdiction in England and Wales by virtue of any of sections 63B to 63D of the [Terrorism Act 2000] (extra-territorial jurisdiction in respect of certain offences committed outside the United Kingdom for the purposes of terrorism etc).

para 4(1)[77] Any case in which sentence is passed on a person for:
(a) attempting to commit a relevant offence,
(b) inciting the commission of a relevant offence, or
(c) an offence under Serious Crime Act 2007 s 44 or 45 (encouraging or assisting an offence) in relation to a relevant offence.

(2) In this paragraph, 'a relevant offence' means an offence set out in paragraph 2(a) to (h) or (j) or (k) or paragraph 3 or 3A[78] [see above].

Note: Offences marked with a * have been repealed. However, it would be possible for the Attorney-General to refer historical offences. Ed.

8.14 ***Power to apply for leave to refer Deferred sentences***

Att-Gen's Ref No 22 of 1992 1993 14 Cr App R (S) 435 LCJ An order deferring sentence is a sentence within the meaning of the statute. It can therefore be referred under section 36.

8.15 ***Power to apply for leave to refer Court Martial***

Review of unduly lenient sentence by Court Martial Appeal Court

Armed Forces Act 2006 s 273(1) If the Attorney-General considers:
(a) that a sentence passed by the Court Martial in respect of an offence under section 42 (criminal conduct) is unduly lenient, and
(b) that condition A or B is satisfied,
he may refer the case to the Court Martial Appeal Court for it to review the sentencing of the offender.

(2) Condition A is that the corresponding offence under the law of England and Wales is under that law an offence which, if committed by an adult, is triable only on indictment.

[77] A new para 4 was substituted by Criminal Justice Act 1988 (Reviews of Sentencing) (Amendment) Order 2012 2012/1833.
[78] As slightly amended by Criminal Justice Act 1988 (Reviews of Sentencing) (Amendment) Order 2017 2017/751 para 2(3)

(3) Condition B is that the case is of a description specified for the purposes of this subsection in an order made by the Secretary of State.
(4) A reference under subsection (1) may not be made without the leave of the Court Martial Appeal Court.
(5) [Powers of the Court, see **8.31**]
(6) For the purposes of subsection (1)(a), the Attorney-General may consider that a sentence passed by the Court Martial is unduly lenient if he considers:

(a) that the Court Martial erred in law as to its powers of sentencing, or

(b) that the sentence is not that required by section 224A, 225(2) or 226(2) of the 2003 Act (the dangerousness provisions) (as applied by section 218A, 219(2) or 221(2) of this Act) or by section 225, 226, 227or 227A[79] of this Act (minimum sentences),[80]

but nothing in this subsection limits subsection (1)(a).
(7) Where a reference under subsection (1) relates to a case in which the Court Martial made an order specified in subsection (7A), the Court Martial Appeal Court may not, in deciding what sentence is appropriate for the case, make any allowance for the fact that the offender is being sentenced for a second time.
(7A) The orders specified in this subsection are:

(a) an order under section 269(2) of the 2003 Act (determination of minimum term in relation to mandatory life sentence);

(b) an order under section 82A(2) of the Sentencing Act (determination of minimum term in relation to discretionary life sentences and certain other sentences).

(8) The reference in subsection (1)(a) to a sentence passed by the Court Martial does not include one passed on an appeal under section 285 (appeal from Service Civilian Court).
(9) In this section and section 274 "sentence" includes any order made by a court when dealing with an offender.

8.16 ***Purpose of references***

R v Reynolds and Others 2007 EWCA Crim 538, 2 Cr App R (S) 87 (p 553) The function of Criminal Justice Act 1988 s 36 is not to provide a general right of appeal to the prosecution. It is a means of ensuring, by judicious selection of cases, that issues of principle in relation to sentencing can be resolved, and sentences corrected, in cases where public confidence in sentencing could otherwise be undermined.

Att-Gen's Ref No 132 of 2001 2002 EWCA Crim 1418, 2003 1 Cr App R (S) 41 (p 190) The purpose of the system of Attorney-General's references is the avoidance of gross error, the allaying of widespread concern at what may appear to be an unduly lenient sentence and the preservation of public confidence in cases where a judge appears to have departed to a substantial extent from the norms of sentencing generally applied by the courts.

Att-Gen's Ref No 79 of 2009 2010 EWCA Crim 187 An Attorney-General's reference is not directly equivalent to an appeal against sentence. It is a different process by which gross errors leading to unduly lenient sentences can be and are repaired.

8.17 ***More than one offence***

Criminal Justice Act 1988 s 36(3) For the purposes of this Part of this Act any two or more sentences are to be treated as passed in the same proceeding if they would be so treated for the purposes of Criminal Appeal Act 1968 s 11 (see para **4.64**).

8.18 ***Duties of the Attorney-General***

Criminal Procedure Rules 2015 2015/1490 Rule 41.2[81]

Service of notice of reference and application for permission

(1) The Attorney[-]General must serve any notice of reference and any application for permission to refer a sentencing case on:

[79] As amended by Legal Aid, Sentencing and Punishment of Offenders Act 2012 Sch 26 para 29.
[80] This subsection is listed as amended by Legal Aid, Sentencing and Punishment of Offenders Act 2012 Sch 22 para 36.
[81] As substituted by Criminal Procedure (Amendment) Rules 2018 2018/132 para 17(a). In force 2/4/18

(a) the Registrar; and
(b) the defendant.
(2) Where the Attorney[-]General refers a point of law:
(a) the Attorney[-General] must give the Registrar details of:
(i) the defendant affected,
(ii) the date and place of the relevant Crown Court decision, and
(iii) the relevant verdict and sentencing; and
(b) the Attorney[-General] must give the defendant notice that:
(i) the outcome of the reference will not make any difference to the outcome of the trial, and
(ii) the defendant may serve a respondent's notice.
(3) Where the Attorney[-]General applies for permission to refer a sentencing case, the Attorney[-General] must give the defendant notice that:
(a) the outcome of the reference may make a difference to that sentencing, and in particular may result in a more severe sentence; and
(b) the defendant may serve a respondent's notice.
(4) [see **8.21**]

8.19 ***Safeguards, The built-in***

Att-Gen's Ref No 14 of 2003 2003 EWCA Crim 1459 When Parliament enacted section 36, it saw fit to introduce a number of safeguards:
(i) the Attorney-General was to consider the matter and decide for himself whether the sentence before him was unduly lenient,
(ii) the Attorney-General was to exercise his discretion whether to seek to refer the matter, Parliament having bestowed upon him a discretion not a duty,
(iii) the Court of Appeal was to decide whether to grant leave to refer the matter,
(iv) the Court of Appeal was to determine whether it considers the sentence unduly lenient,
(v) the Court of Appeal was then to determine whether it was just to interfere with the sentence passed.

The granting of leave to refer a sentence is not to be seen as automatic and here, the Attorney-General had exercised his discretion on a false basis, not being in possession of the full picture as to the nature of the case at the point at which he decided to seek to refer it. Safeguard ii) had not been satisfied.

8.20 ***Contents of a reference***

Form of notice of reference and application for permission

Criminal Procedure Rules 2015 2015/1490 Rule 41.3(1)[82] A notice of reference and an application for permission to refer a sentencing case must give the year and number of that reference or that case.
(2) A notice of reference of a point of law must:
(a) specify the point of law in issue and indicate the opinion that the Attorney-General invites the court to give,
(b) identify each ground for that invitation, numbering them consecutively (if there is more than one) and concisely outlining each argument in support,
(c) exclude any reference to the defendant's name and any other reference that may identify the defendant,
(d) summarise the relevant facts, and
(e) identify any relevant authorities.
(3) An application for permission to refer a sentencing case must:
(a) give details of:
(i) the defendant affected,
(ii) the date and place of the relevant Crown Court decision, and

[82] As amended by Criminal Procedure (Amendment) Rules 2018 2018/132 para 17(b). In force 2/4/18

(iii) the relevant verdict and sentencing,
(b) explain why that sentencing appears to the Attorney-General unduly lenient, concisely outlining each argument in support, and
(c) include the application for permission to refer the case to the court.
(4) A notice of reference of a sentencing case must:
(a) include the same details and explanation as the application for permission to refer the case,
(b) summarise the relevant facts, and
(c) identify any relevant authorities.
(5) Where the court gives the Attorney-General permission to refer a sentencing case, it may treat the application for permission as the notice of reference.
Note: References invariably list the aggravating and mitigating factors of the case. Ed.

8.21 *Time limits*

Criminal Justice Act 1988 Sch 3 para 1 Notice of an application for leave to refer a case to the Court of Appeal under section 36 above shall be given within 28 days from the day on which the sentence, or the last of the sentences, in the case was passed.
Criminal Procedure Rules 2015 2015/1490 Rule 41.2(4)[83] The Attorney-General must serve an application for permission to refer a sentencing case not more than 28 days after the last of the sentences in that case.
The following note appears at the end of the rule. Ed.
Note: The time limit for serving an application for permission to refer a sentencing case is prescribed by Criminal Justice Act 1988 Sch 3 para 1. It may be neither extended nor shortened.
Criminal Procedure Rules 2015 2015/1490 Rule 41.4(3)[84] Such a defendant must serve the respondent's notice:
(a) where the Attorney-General refers a point of law, not more than 28 days after:
(i) the Attorney[-General] serves the reference, or
(ii) a direction to do so,
(b) where the Attorney-General applies for permission to refer a sentencing case, not more than 14 days after:
(i) the Attorney[-General] serves the application, or
(ii) a direction to do so.
Att-Gen's Ref No 112 of 2002 2003 EWCA Crim 676 Defence counsel contended the reference was out of time. Held. It was not. You do not count the day the sentence was passed. *South Staffordshire Tramways* 1991 1 QB 402 applied.
Att-Gen's Ref Nos 59-61 of 2004 2004 EWCA Crim 2488 On 26 March 2004, G and B were sentenced to 9 months suspended. On 19 April 2004, P was sentenced to 3 years. Confiscation and compensation were adjourned. The reference was dated 6 July 2004. On 10 August 2004, the first confiscation order was made. Defence counsel contended the references were out of time. Held. They were not. The sentencing decision was not completed till the judge had dealt with confiscation and compensation. Criminal Appeal Act 1968 s 50 makes plain that 'sentence' extends far beyond the decision whether to impose a custodial or community penalty.

Procedure

8.22 *Procedure*

Note: In 2012 I was told that the procedure was as follows:
a) Where the request originates other than from the Crown Prosecution Service, the Attorney-General's Office will obtain the appropriate papers from the CPS.
b) Where the prosecution advocate suggests a reference should be made, he or she writes an advice within 48 hours of the sentence.
c) The advice is considered by the CPS and if the Chief Crown Prosecutor or their

[83] As amended by Criminal Procedure (Amendment) Rules 2018 2018/132 para 17(a). In force 2/4/18
[84] As amended by Criminal Procedure (Amendment) Rules 2018 2018/132 para 17(d) and (e)(ii). In force 2/4/18

deputy is of the view that the sentence should be referred to the Attorney-General that advice and the relevant case papers are sent to Treasury Counsel or monitoree and to the Attorney-General's Office.

d) Treasury counsel or monitoree sends an advice with a notice of application and a draft reference (headed Draft 1) to the Attorney-General's Office.
e) The draft reference is at the same time sent to the prosecuting advocate for his or her agreement to the factual content.
f) The prosecution advocate agrees or amends the factual content and the document becomes Draft 2.
g) The Attorney-General or Solicitor General makes his or her decision. If the reference is to be made, he or she will sign the notice of application.
h) The draft reference, as amended, is sent to the defendant's solicitors to agree or amend the factual content within 14 days. Any disagreements on the factual basis are to be resolved prior to the hearing at the Court of Appeal. If, exceptionally, disagreement remains, the Court of Appeal will be informed.
i) The Attorney-General or Solicitor General signs the agreed final reference.
j) The document is sent to the Court of Appeal.
k) The Probation Service frequently provides an updated report for the Court. A prison report may also be provided. Ed.

Article Vincent Scully, former lawyer at the Attorney-General's office, writes about the application procedure at Part 1 of his article in *Archbold Review* Issue 2 March 2018, p 6.

8.23 ***Registrar's duties***

Criminal Justice Act 1988 Sch 3 para 2 If the Registrar of Criminal Appeals is given notice of a reference or application to the Court of Appeal under section 36 (see **8.11**), he shall:

(a) take all necessary steps for obtaining a hearing of the reference or application, and
(b) obtain and lay before the Court in proper form all documents, exhibits and other things which appear necessary for the proper determination of the reference or application.

Criminal Procedure Rules 2015 2015/1490 Rule 41.4(1), which once applied, was repealed by Criminal Procedure (Amendment) Rules 2018 2018/132 para 17(c). In force 2/4/18

8.24 ***Duties of the defence***

Criminal Procedure Rules 2015 2015/1490 Rule 41.4(1)[85] A defendant on whom the Attorney-General serves a reference or an application for permission to refer a sentencing case may serve a respondent's notice, and must do so if:

(a) the defendant wants to make representations to the court, or
(b) the court so directs.

(2) Such a defendant must serve the respondent's notice on:
(a) the Attorney-General, and
(b) the Registrar.

(3) Such a defendant must serve the respondent's notice:
(a) where the Attorney-General refers a point of law, not more than 28 days after:
(i) the Attorney[-General] serves the reference, or
(ii) a direction to do so,
(b) where the Attorney-General applies for permission to refer a sentencing case, not more than 14 days after:
(i) the Attorney[-General] serves the application, or
(ii) a direction to do so.

(4) Where the Attorney-General refers a point of law, the respondent's notice must:

[85] As amended by Criminal Procedure (Amendment) Rules 2018 2018/132 para 17(e). In force 2/4/18

(a) give the date on which the respondent was served with the notice of reference;
(b) identify each ground of opposition on which the respondent relies, numbering them consecutively (if there is more than one), concisely outlining each argument in support and identifying the Attorney-General's ground or reason to which each relates,
(c) summarise any relevant facts not already summarised in the reference,
(d) identify any relevant authorities, and
(e) include or attach any application for the following, with reasons:
(i) an extension of time within which to serve the respondent's notice,
(ii) permission to attend a hearing that the respondent does not have a right to attend,
(iii) a direction to attend in person a hearing that the respondent could attend by live link, if the respondent is in custody.

(5) Where the Attorney-General applies for permission to refer a sentencing case, the respondent's notice must:
(a) give the date on which the respondent was served with the application;
(b) say if the respondent wants to make representations at the hearing of the application or reference, and
(c) include or attach any application for the following, with reasons:
(i) an extension of time within which to serve the respondent's notice,
(ii) permission to attend a hearing that the respondent does not have a right to attend,
(iii) a direction to attend in person a hearing that the respondent could attend by live link, if the respondent is in custody.

8.25 ***Registrar's letter to the Judge***

Att-Gen's Ref 2018 Re Bailey and Reece 2018 EWCA Crim 1640, 2018 EWCA Crim 1640 (p 405) The Court dealt with a reference. Held. When the Registrar writes to the Judge involved he is not asking for general comments. He is asking for information that would not be apparent from the papers, such as if the defendant was an informant.
Note: One would have thought the best approach would be to make this clear in the letter that is sent out. Ed.

8.26 ***Up-to-date information on the defendant***

Att-Gen's Ref Nos 31, 42, 43, 45, 50 and 51 of 2004 2004 EWCA Crim 1934, 2005 1 Cr App R (S) 76 (p 377) LCJ It is important that this Court and the Attorney-General are provided with up-to-date information as to the progress which the offender has made since the sentence was passed. This is important because even if the sentence at the time it was passed was not an appropriate sentence, if the offender is responding to the community sentence then that could affect the outcome of the reference. In some cases the progress made by the offender after sentence will undermine the whole purpose of the application and because of this, not later than seven days before the hearing, this Court should not only obtain the reports that are relevant in this category of case but it should make the reports available to the Attorney-General. The Attorney-General can then consider whether it is desirable to withdraw the application.

8.27 ***Varying or withdrawing the notice***

Criminal Procedure Rules 2015 2015/1490 Rule 41.5(1)[86] This rule applies where the Attorney-General wants to vary or withdraw:
(a) a notice of reference, or
(b) an application for permission to refer a sentencing case.
(2) The Attorney-General:
(a) may vary or withdraw the notice or application without the court's permission by serving notice on:

[86] As amended by Criminal Procedure (Amendment) Rules 2018 2018/132 para 17(d). In force 2/4/18

(i) the Registrar, and
(ii) the defendant
before any hearing of the reference or application, but
(b) at any such hearing, may only vary or withdraw that notice or application with the court's permission.

Determining the application

8.28 ***Sentencing judge may not sit on appeal***
Criminal Justice Act 1988 s 36(4) No judge shall sit as a member of the Court of Appeal on the hearing of, or shall determine any application in proceedings incidental or preliminary to, a reference under this section of a sentence passed by himself.

8.29 ***Power to alter the sentence***
Criminal Justice Act 1988 s 36(1) On such a reference the Court of Appeal may…
(i) quash any sentence passed on him in the proceeding, and
(ii) in place of it pass such sentence as they think appropriate for the case and as the court below had power to pass when dealing with him.

8.30 ***Power to alter the sentence Ability to reduce sentence***
R v Hughes 2010 EWCA Crim 1026 LCJ At a reference hearing, the Court has the power not only to uphold or increase the sentence but also to reduce it or to impose a different form of sentence.

8.31 ***Power to alter sentence Court Martial***
Armed Forces Act 2006 s 273(5) On a reference under subsection (1), the Court Martial Appeal Court may:
(a) quash the sentence passed by the Court Martial, and
(b) pass in substitution for it any sentence which the Court Martial Appeal Court thinks appropriate and which is a sentence that the Court Martial had power to pass in respect of the offence.

8.32 ***Test to apply***
Att-Gen's Ref No 4 of 1989 1989 11 Cr App R (S) 517 LCJ The first thing to be observed is that it is implicit in the section that this Court may only increase sentences which it concludes were unduly lenient. It cannot have been the intention of Parliament to subject defendants to the risk of having their sentences increased, with all the anxiety that that naturally gives rise to, merely because in the opinion of this Court the sentence was less than this Court would have imposed. A sentence is unduly lenient where it falls outside the range of sentences which the judge, applying his mind to all the relevant factors, could reasonably consider appropriate. However, it must always be remembered that sentencing is an art rather than a science and that the trial judge is particularly well placed to assess the weight to be given to the competing considerations. Further leniency is not itself a vice.
Att-Gen's Ref 2016 Re Howard 2016 EWCA Crim 1511, 2017 1 Cr App R (S) 8 (p 44) para 27 The Court should only grant leave in exceptional cases and not in borderline cases, see *Att-Gen's Ref No 5 of 1989* 1989 11 Cr App R (S) 489.[87]
Note: The statutory power to amend a sentence does not state a test, see **8.29**. However, the power to refer requires the Attorney-General to consider the sentence was 'unduly lenient', see **8.11**. Ed.
Att-Gen's Ref 2019 Re Guest 2019 EWCA Crim 422 Our role is not to undertake an initial sentencing exercise. We cannot and should not intervene simply because we might ourselves, had we been sitting at first instance, have imposed a different sentence. We are only entitled to intervene if the sentence was not simply lenient but unduly lenient. Those words mean what they say and no gloss should be attempted.

[87] The case reference in the judgment has been corrected.

8.33 ***Defendant's right to be present***

Criminal Justice Act 1988 Sch 3 para 6 Except as provided by paragraphs 7 and 8 below, a person whose sentencing is the subject of a reference to the Court of Appeal under section 36 above shall be entitled to be present, if he wishes it, on the hearing of the reference, although he may be in custody.

Criminal Justice Act 1988 Sch 3 para 7 A person in custody shall not be entitled to be present:

a) on an application by the Attorney-General for leave to refer a case, or

b) on any proceedings preliminary or incidental to a reference, unless the Court of Appeal give him leave to be present.

Criminal Justice Act 1988 Sch 3 para 8 The power of the Court of Appeal to pass sentence on a person may be exercised although he is not present.

Criminal Procedure Rules 2015 2015/1490 Rule 41.6(1)[88] A respondent who is in custody has a right to attend a hearing in public unless it is a hearing preliminary or incidental to a reference, including the hearing of an application for permission to refer a sentencing case.

(2) The court or the Registrar may direct that such a respondent is to attend a hearing by live link.

8.34 ***Evidence What is the factual basis?/Can additional evidence be put in?***

See also the ***Prosecution fail to assert position in the Crown Court/Departing from how case was put by the prosecution*** para at **8.44**.

Att-Gen's Ref No 95 of 1998 1999 The Times 21/4/99 During her trial, D pleaded to causing death by dangerous driving. The prosecution counsel then outlined the facts and said nothing about D being affected by alcohol and nothing about the fatal accident being the culmination of a prolonged piece of bad driving. He did say, "perhaps no one will ever really know why D drove on the wrong side of the road". The Judge said the incident was wholly unexplained. In the reference the Attorney-General sought to revive the issue of alcohol and whether the bad driving had been over some distance. Held. It looks as if the Judge sentenced on the basis of a momentary lapse. Where facts had not been proved or pursued at the Crown Court, the Court of Appeal could not constitute itself as a court of first instance and inquire into those facts. Consideration of whether a sentence was unduly lenient was to be conducted in light of what had been established, not what was alleged. It was doubted whether if the present situation recurred the Court would be prepared to order an adjournment, as in this case, or rather simply to refuse leave on the basis that the case was not sufficiently prepared.

Att-Gen's Ref No 19 of 2005 2006 EWCA Crim 785 D pleaded to sexual offences including seven rapes of children who were intellectually and psychologically disabled. He received 13 years' imprisonment. There were a considerable number of aggravating features. The Attorney-General relied upon two psychiatric reports produced since D had been sentenced. Held. The material which is now before this Court points strongly in the direction of an indeterminate sentence being appropriate. But it is not this Court's function, under Criminal Justice Act 1988 s 36, to substitute, in the light of new material, our view as to what the sentence ought now to be. Our task, under section 36, is to decide whether the Judge's sentence, in the light of the material before him, can properly be characterised as having been unduly lenient.

Note: Section 36(2), which lays down the conditions for increasing the sentence, is about whether the judge erred in law or failed to impose the sentence required. It may be that this was a drafting error but clearly if the judge didn't have the material he cannot be accused of erring in law or failing to impose the sentence required. Presumably victims would prefer the correct sentence to be substituted, rather than one that depended on whether the advocates did their job properly at the sentence hearing.

[88] As amended by Criminal Procedure (Amendment) Rules 2018 2018/132 para 17(d). In force 2/4/18

Notwithstanding this rule the Court of Appeal does not stop defence advocates from relying on favourable prison reports, work performed on community orders etc. Without this information the Court of Appeal would be prevented from properly exercising its discretion whether to use its powers. Ed.

Att-Gen's Ref No 50 of 2008 2009 EWCA Crim 289 LCJ D pleaded to sexual activity with a child family member, V. He received a suspended sentence of 9 months' imprisonment. This was subject to an Attorney-General's reference, which asserted that V was a virgin when D first had sexual intercourse with her. In the Crown Court, the case was not opened on this basis. Held. Such issues must be resolved in the Crown Court. They cannot be advanced as part of the Crown's case on a reference when they have not been advanced in that way before the Crown Court. In relation to any proposed reference, it is also the responsibility of counsel for the offender to examine the reference and to make clear where there is a dispute of fact.

Att-Gen's Ref No 79 of 2009 2010 EWCA Crim 187 The Judge was asked by defence counsel to sentence with full credit for the plea. Defence counsel said the prosecution had served its case late. The prosecution said nothing. The Judge sentenced the defendant with full credit. Counsel for the prosecution sought to argue that the Judge was wrong to give full credit. Held. We should not entertain an application on the basis that the Judge unwittingly proceeded on a wrong factual basis if that factual basis was open to correction by the prosecution at the time and there was no objection.

Att-Gen's Ref No 74 of 2010 2010 EWCA Crim 873 D was convicted of three indecent assaults. He was sentenced to a non-custodial sentence and had performed some unpaid work. Held. Although this Court from time to time looks at material in favour of the offender, in deciding whether a sentence is unduly lenient, material adverse to the offender which was not available to the sentencing judge should be ignored, *Att-Gen's Ref No 19 of 2005* 2006 EWCA Crim 785. We take the view that we do have the power to take into account matters adverse to the offender when deciding what the appropriate sentence is. We note, however, that the point has not been fully argued before us. In any event in deciding whether or not to discount the appropriate sentence for what is called 'double jeopardy', we can take into account matters adverse to the offender. We take into account the supplementary report for us which refers to matters after sentence, namely D's retracting of his admission of guilt, his breach of his SOPO and his showing another registered sex offender his depositions. The starting point was no less than four years. We do not consider a discount for double jeopardy because of these post-sentence matters.

Att-Gen's Ref No 53 of 2013 2013 EWCA Crim 2544, 2014 2 Cr App R (S) 1 (p 1) LCJ D pleaded to numerous sexual offences. Counsel said the victim could be described as 'predatory'. The Judge repeated the word in his sentencing remarks and the prosecution appealed against the imposition of a suspended sentence. The defence contended that three matters in the reference should not be taken into account because they were not before the court. Held. That was right. [Dealing with other evidence.] 'Before the court' means in [the court bundle] or the pre-sentence report. The fact that prosecution counsel does not mention a fact is not generally material. The overriding question is whether something could cause prejudice to the offender. Here it was right to rely on the whole of the interview.

Att-Gen's Ref No 79 of 2015 2016 EWCA Crim 448, 2 Cr App R (S) 18 (p 158) D pleaded to attempted GBH with intent and possession of an offensive weapon. He was sentenced on the basis that he had attacked a stranger who was wearing a full burka. The Attorney-General applied for the sentence to be varied. At some stage, the victim saw D's face in the press and recognised him as someone who had demanded she do something and she had refused. She told the police about that. The Crown Court ordered a further psychiatric report and an addition to the pre-sentence report. The Court purported to vary the sentence outside the time limits. Held. That was unlawful. para 10 The power to declare a sentence unduly lenient depends entirely on what was put before

the original sentencing court. It is not open to the Attorney-General to rely upon further evidence not placed before the sentencing court to justify the reference, *Att-Gen's Ref No 19 of 2005* 2006 (see above). para 13 So this court must decide whether a particular sentence is unduly lenient. If it is, it must be quashed whereupon, by virtue of that provision, the court is required to pass 'such sentence as they think appropriate for the case and as the court below have power to pass when dealing with him'. Then it is open for the court to take into account whatever new information is available. We substitute an 11-year extended sentence (7 years' custody, 4 years' extended licence) taking into account the new information and reports, which is what the Judge attempted to pass outside the time limits.
For the decision about whether the Crown Court could vary the sentence, see **112.12**.

8.35 ***Can the Attorney-General argue that current practice is unduly lenient?***
Att-Gen's Ref No 33 of 1996 1997 2 Cr App R (S) 10 D pleaded to manslaughter and section 20 after initially being arraigned for murder and section 18. Prosecution counsel accepted the pleas and the Judge, at defence counsel's request, gave an indication of sentence. In the event, D received 5 years for manslaughter and 18 months concurrent for the wounding. The Attorney-General argued that the tariff for this offence was unduly lenient and invited the Court of Appeal to amend it. Defence counsel argued that the Court was unable to increase the sentence based on the tariff being unduly lenient. Held. a) The Court can only increase a sentence if it considers it to be unduly lenient, and if there is nothing in the wording of the statute to prevent the Attorney-General from concluding that a tariff as generally accepted is unduly lenient then, as it seems to us, in the absence of express words, it is difficult to see what there is to prevent this Court from coming to the same conclusion. b) Where an offender has entered pleas of guilty having been properly advised as to the sentence which he was likely to receive, that is to say offered advice in accordance with the tariff for the offence as it then stood, it would be wholly wrong for this Court, when reconsidering the tariff, also to increase the sentences. No one could know the value of advice.
Note: If a defendant appeals his or her sentence, the Court of Appeal can decide that the current suggested level of sentencing is too lenient or too severe and introduce what the Court thinks is the correct practice. Further, if the practice is wrong, the sooner it is put right the better. So the rule seems unhelpful. If the Court were to consider a change in the tariff, that would in no way dictate the Court's discretion to alter the sentence. Ed.

8.36 ***Power to alter sentence Life imprisonment***
Att-Gen's Ref No 82 of 2000 2001 2 Cr App R (S) 60 (p 289) On the imposition of a life sentence in substitution for a determinate period, on an Attorney-General's reference, very special considerations apply. Although protection of the public may be relevant to a specified term and to a discretionary life term, no discount can be given from a life sentence if a life sentence is thought to be appropriate in substitution for a determinate term. However, the double jeopardy principle still has some role to play when the Court is called upon to determine whether or not a specified period was unduly lenient. An offender would be entitled to assume, in the light of the specified period passed by the trial judge, that his earliest date for consideration by the Parole Board would be at a particular date in the future, and it may be that he conducts himself by reference to that expectation. Therefore, if he is to be sentenced a second time and the period specified is to be increased, it seems to us that some regard should be paid by this Court to the double jeopardy principle.
Note: Today, the Court just passes a life sentence when it thinks it is correct, with the appropriate minimum term. Ed.
See also: *Att-Gen's Ref No 34 of 1992* 1994 15 Cr App R (S) 167 (LCJ Plea to section 18 and given 8 years. Held. We substitute life.)

8.37 *The discretion whether to increase the sentence*

Att-Gen's Ref No 4 of 1989 1989 11 Cr App R (S) 517 LCJ Even where the Court considers the sentence was unduly lenient, this Court has a discretion as to whether to exercise its powers.

Att-Gen's Ref No 23 of 1992 1993 14 Cr App R (S) 759 LCJ D pleaded to section 18. After an altercation with a reversing van driver, a fight ensued. D stabbed the van driver with a pen knife once in the chest and once in the abdomen. This was a breach of a suspended sentence of 9 months for dishonesty offences. He received 3 months for the section 18 and the suspended sentence was activated in its entirety, making 12 months' imprisonment. There were a number of reports before the trial Judge. One stated that D suffered from a mental disorder, that most likely being schizophrenia, and that D was potentially very dangerous. D was admitted for a period of assessment at the direction of the Home Secretary whilst the instant case was pending. It was observed that he suffered from a mild psychotic illness and that the offence was in no way connected with his mental disorder. Held. The sentence which was passed by this Judge was not merely lenient, it was not merely unduly lenient, it was derisory. Three months' imprisonment for an offence of this kind is simply not a sentence which ought to have been imposed. D was now at liberty and had been so for 8 months, his treatment ongoing. A report urged a non-custodial disposal so as not to undermine his treatment. The balance at the moment is in favour of allowing the medical treatment to continue with D at large. This was an unduly lenient sentence. The course which we are taking is quite exceptional and is due only to the special medical circumstances which have emerged subsequent to not only the trial but also the Attorney-General's reference. It is only in those circumstances that we decline to interfere with the sentence which was passed.

Att-Gen's Ref Nos 31, 42, 43, 45, 50 and 51 of 2004 2004 EWCA Crim 1934, 2005 1 Cr App R (S) 76 (p 377) LCJ The discretion is extremely wide.

Att-Gen's Ref No 24 of 2012 2012 EWCA Crim 1986 Neale Bannon pleaded to section 18. The Judge sentenced him to 12 months suspended. Held. The sentence should have been 2½ years. The man behaving that night was not the true Mr Bannon who was a servant of the community, not a destroyer of it, and a hard-working man, not a thug who threw his weight about. Few here have done such a [high] proportion of their unpaid work. Few here have paid such a [high] proportion of their compensation. Few here [are dealt with after] such a long delay between offence and disposition[89] not attributed to them with such a record of immaculate behaviour from alpha to omega. He could not have done more to demonstrate retrospectively that his remorse was unreserved. There is a place for compassion. A just disposition is to decline to interfere.

Att-Gen's Ref 2018 Re Costa 2018 EWCA Crim 2778 D pleaded (25% discount considered appropriate by the Judge) to conspiracy to supply cocaine. Her partner received 5 years after a full plea discount. D was aged 25 and of good character. She suffered from a disease which causes painful boils. While on a 1-year remand, she was admitted to hospital for an operation. Post-operative care did not take place. The Judge started at 6 years and said that had there been a full discount, D would have just 1 year to serve. He then passed a 2-year suspended sentence with unpaid work. Since the sentence, D had been wholly co-operative and compliant with the order and found part-time employment. Also, her father had been diagnosed with lung cancer and had only a few weeks to live. Held. 4 years was justified. It was wrong to then depart so much from that. The sentence was unduly lenient. The key features are D's conduct since the sentence, the medical hardships if there was a return to prison and the father's illness. The very long wait for the sentence, the miserable time after the operation and her exemplary conduct as a prisoner were relevant factors. With these factors, prison will be significantly harder for her. Returning her to prison would be unduly harsh and not necessary. We do not vary the sentence.

[89] This would be about 11 months later.

See also: *Att-Gen's Ref 2016 Re Susorovs* 2016 EWCA Crim 1856, 2017 1 Cr App R (S) 15 (p 99) (Plea. Street rape. Held. The modern practice is that this court attaches generally little, if any, weight to the fact [that there is another sentencing hearing]. However, the prosecution made submissions which were inconsistent with their submission at the Crown Court, by now placing the case in a higher category. We start at 11 years. With full credit, 7 years 8 months, and because of prosecution unfairness, 6 years 10 months.)
Note: There is in fact a double discretion, both of which are exercised. First there is the discretion whether to grant leave. This can be refused because of delay by the Attorney-General or because of personal circumstances of the defendant.[90] The second is whether to increase the sentence once it is decided that the sentence was unduly lenient. Ed.

8.38 ***Discretion whether to vary sentence Delay***
Att-Gen's Ref Nos 83 and 85 of 2004 2005 EWCA Crim 1537 D, M and B were charged with various supply of drugs offences. They received 4 years, 3 years and 3 years respectively. The Attorney-General submitted the appropriate notices within 28 days as required. There was subsequently a significant delay, between May and December, when sentence was passed and the case was listed. At the hearing in December, the Court asked the Attorney-General to reconsider whether this case was suitable for a reference. In early January of the following year the Attorney-General concluded that it was. The case was then re-listed for June. Held. That is too long after the passing of sentence, at least where a short sentence has been passed. The shorter the sentence the more likely it is that a delay will be viewed as significant. We are being asked to increase M's sentence over a year after it was passed and some four to five months after his release from prison. We take the view, not without some hesitation, that given the delay and given his release from prison it would be wrong of us to now require him to go back to prison. We have no doubt at all that a sentence of 3 years' imprisonment was unduly lenient.

8.39 ***Discretion whether to vary sentence Disparity***
Att-Gen's Ref No 44 of 2005 2005 EWCA Crim 2211 D, aged 18, pleaded to robbery. His co-defendant, T, was charged with robbery but pleaded to section 20, which was accepted (Community Punishment and Rehabilitation Orders imposed for both). D and T asked V to buy them some alcohol, as T was visibly drunk. £20 was given to V and V entered the shop. D and T mistakenly thought that V had taken the money and that they were not going to be provided with the money or the alcohol. They obtained a phone number and attended V's house. T punched V in the face, knocking him to the ground. A glass which V was holding smashed as he attempted to defend himself. D kicked V in the face whilst wearing steel-toe-capped boots. D then snatched a silver chain from around V's neck. D suffered serious damage to two front teeth, amongst other injuries. The Attorney-General argued that the starting point after trial ought to have been near to 3 years, not 18 months as the Judge indicated. The Attorney-General made no reference in relation to T as there was no power under Criminal Justice Act 1988 to refer the case. Held. It would not be appropriate to interfere with the sentence. If an immediate custodial sentence is passed on the offender, there would immediately be a very significant and quite unjust disparity between the offender and T…In these circumstances, it seems to us that it would not be in the public interest to terminate that community penalty and impose a custodial alternative.

8.40 ***Discretion whether to vary sentence Young offenders***
Att-Gen's Ref No 65 of 2012 2012 EWCA Crim 3168 D, aged 17, pleaded to section 18. He received an 18-month Youth Rehabilitation Order. He had served 5 months on remand. Held. The proper sentence for him was 2½-3 years. We are particularly conscious always in cases of this kind of the effect on defendants of their first

[90] For an example see *Att-Gen's Ref No 14 of 2003* 2003 EWCA Crim 1459.

discovering, no doubt to their enormous relief, that they are not to be sent to custody and to have the need to buckle down to comply with the order that has been made, only subsequently to have this court have to say that the original sentence was too lenient and has to be revisited. We think that that is a reason, particularly in the case of a youngster, to modify what otherwise would be the sentence, and for that reason we pass an 18-month DTO.

8.41 ***Double jeopardy reduction, The***

Note: Double jeopardy means the fact the defendant is being sentenced twice for the same offence. Ed.

Att-Gen's Ref Nos 41-42 of 2007 2007 EWCA Crim 1916, 2008 1 Cr App R (S) 77 (p 443) The Court has now made it plain that a significant discount for double jeopardy is likely only to apply where the sentence that was originally imposed was a non-custodial sentence, or was a short custodial sentence which is being increased substantially. In those cases, clearly the element of double jeopardy has a significant effect. The longer the sentence which was originally imposed the less effect double jeopardy can have on the approach of this Court to the ultimate sentence. The proper sentence was 10 years, which we substitute.

Att-Gen's Ref No 79 of 2012 2013 EWCA Crim 197 D was convicted of three rapes on a 6-year-old. Held. The proper sentence was **15 years** not 10. The defence relied on double jeopardy. Where, as here, an offender has been sentenced to a very substantial term the [need to reduce the sentence because of double jeopardy] is much diminished and in certain cases is diminished to vanishing point.

Att-Gen's Ref No 38 of 2013 2013 EWCA Crim 1450 LCJ D pleaded to 14 counts of indecent assault. Held. Double jeopardy did not apply. D was in custody and had been sentenced to an immediate custodial term. He knew that the Attorney-General proposed to refer the sentence to the Court of Appeal.

Att-Gen's Ref Nos 4-8 of 2014 2014 EWCA Crim 651, 2 Cr App R (S) 51 (p 414) para 43 Double jeopardy should not feature to any great extent in cases where significant custodial sentences are imposed.

Att-Gen's Ref No 45 of 2014 2014 EWCA Crim 1566 LCJ D pleaded to two counts of conspiracy to supply and was sentenced to 5 years. D was subsequently convicted of rape and sentenced to 5 years to run concurrently with his 6-year sentence for the drugs offences. Held. The order to make the sentences concurrent made the rape sentence unduly lenient. The principle of double jeopardy remains. [However, sentencing has changed considerably since 2006.] This Court is more conscious of the position of victims. It is entirely proper for the Court not to refer to 'double jeopardy' where there is no reduction for it in sentencing. In future, the Court of Appeal will not refer to 'double jeopardy' where no question of the consideration of double jeopardy arises. The principle does not arise here.

Att-Gen's Ref No 59 of 2014 2014 EWCA Crim 1926 The principle of double jeopardy has little, if any, effect in a case of this kind given it does not fall into the exceptional category identified in *Att-Gen's Ref No 45 of 2014* 2014 EWCA Crim 1566 at para 20. A significant sentence of imprisonment (2½ years) was imposed by the trial Judge in any event, the case was referred speedily to this Court and we are particularly conscious of the consequences of these offences for the victims.

Att-Gen's Ref 2017 Re Phelps 2017 EWCA Crim 2403 D was convicted of perverting the course of justice. D, a detective constable, deliberately coached a drug supply suspect to give a misleading account. D was aged 42 and of good character. He had references from inside and outside the police force. D was dismissed from the police and became unable to support his ex-wife and their children. In 2013, his father died. In 2014, his mother had a chronic illness and he was her sole carer. D was diagnosed with depression. The Judge gave 28 days but as D had 14 days for the tag time no period was served. Held.

para 55 A non-custodial sentence was imposed and considerable anxiety would have been caused by the reference. There was an element of double jeopardy. 11 months substituted.
For more detail, see **302.28** in Volume 2.
Old case: *Att-Gen's Ref Nos 14-15 of 2006* 2006 EWCA Crim 1335, 2007 1 Cr App R (S) 40 (p 215) (LCJ The old rule set out.)
Note: The reductions for double jeopardy are becoming fewer and fewer. Parliament has decided that it cannot apply to certain offences and the last two Lord Chief Justices clearly saw limited application for it. The real impact of double jeopardy is that it is used with delay to persuade the court not to substitute a custodial sentence which originally would have been appropriate especially when community orders or suspended sentences are in place where the requirements have been complied with. In reality there is no real role for double jeopardy when all the factors can be considered when the Court applies its discretion. Ed.

8.42 ***Double jeopardy reduction When not available Murder etc.***
Criminal Justice Act 1988 s 36(3A)[91] Where a reference under this section relates to an order under Criminal Justice Act 2003 s 269(2) (determination of minimum term in relation to mandatory life sentence), the Court of Appeal shall not, in deciding what order under that section is appropriate for the case, make any allowance for the fact that the person to whom it relates is being sentenced for a second time.

8.43 ***Double jeopardy reduction When not available Court Martial***
Armed Forces Act 2006 s 273(7) Where a reference under subsection (1) relates to a case in which the Court Martial made an order specified in subsection (7A), the Court Martial Appeal Court may not, in deciding what sentence is appropriate for the case, make any allowance for the fact that the offender is being sentenced for a second time.
(7A) The orders specified in this subsection are:
(a) an order under section 269(2) of the 2003 Act (determination of minimum term in relation to mandatory life sentence),
(b) an order under section 82A(2) of the Sentencing Act (determination of minimum term in relation to discretionary life sentences and certain other sentences).
For the full section, see **8.15**.

8.44 ***Prosecution fail to assert position in the Crown Court/Departing from how case was put by the prosecution***
See also the ***Evidence What is the factual basis?/Can additional evidence be put in?*** para at **8.34**.
Att-Gen's Ref Nos 25-26 of 2008 2008 EWCA Crim 2665, 2009 1 Cr App R (S) 116 (p 648) The defendants were convicted of murder and other offences and were sentenced to life with minimum terms of 19 and 13 years. At the sentencing hearing, prosecution counsel did not argue for a particular starting point when the issue arose, he merely took the Judge through Criminal Justice Act 2003 Sch 21 (determination of minimum term in relation to mandatory life sentence). The Judge selected a 15-year starting point. Counsel for the Attorney-General argued that due to the sexual motivation present in the killing, the starting point ought to have been 30 years, not 15, for the murder. The defence argued that the prosecution had acquiesced in the selection of the 15-year starting point. Held. It would have been preferable had prosecution counsel advanced positive submissions in the Crown Court. Had counsel adopted a more positive stance in the defendant's favour which they in some way acted upon we might have been persuaded not to interfere with the sentence. We see considerable force in the submission that it could be

[91] Criminal Justice and Immigration Act 2008 s 46 widens this provision to include minimum terms for discretionary 'life sentences and certain other sentences'. This Act refers to orders under Powers of Criminal Courts (Sentencing) Act 2000 s 82A(2), which defines 'life sentence' as a sentence mentioned in Crime (Sentences) Act 1997 s 34. This section defines 'life imprisonment' as 'a sentence of imprisonment for life', 'detention during HM's pleasure', 'custody for life' and the service equivalent sentences. It would seem that the provision includes the 2012 automatic life sentence.

an abuse of the Court's process if prosecution counsel instructed the CPS, for which the Attorney-General is responsible, securing a plea of guilty on one basis and then the Attorney-General instructing fresh counsel to attempt to argue here for a higher penalty and/or starting point. However, that is far from this case. The fact that this was a murder which involved sexual conduct was simply unarguable. 'Acquiescence' was the highest that the defendants could put their case. The prosecution counsel did not adopt a positive stance. The offenders did nothing as a result of the prosecution's acquiescence to the 15-year starting point. Leave would be granted. 24 and 18 years substituted.

Att-Gen's Ref 2016 Re Stewart 2016 EWCA Crim 2238, 2017 1 Cr App R (S) 48 (p 383) An HGV driver received a 4½ year sentence for dangerous driving. The prosecution appealed. The prosecution argument involved a significant departure from the category suggested by the prosecution counsel at the sentencing hearing. She said it was between Levels 2 and 3. Held. It was Category 1. In recent time references have not infrequently involved a departure from what was conceded below. Very often that departure contributed to reason why an application was made. It is not illegitimate for the [law officers] to take that stance. They and we are not bound by such concessions. However, where the Attorney-General or Solicitor General seeks to depart from a concession or acceptance, either on the correct level of categorisation or the existence or absence of aggravating or mitigating factors, this should be clearly flagged up in the text of the final reference.

Att-Gen's Ref 2017 Re Rudd 2017 EWCA Crim 492 D pleaded to four child sex offences. A prosecution sentencing note said the offences were Category 1B. Prosecution counsel presented the case on this basis. Held. The case plainly fell into Category 1A. There is no bar in principle to this Court increasing a sentence because the prosecution acceded to a mistaken category, see *R v Stewart* 2016 EWCA Crim 2238. However, the fact the Solicitor General is departing from a concession as to categorisation made in the Court below may in an appropriate case have an impact on the sentence, *Att-Gen's Ref 2016 Re Susorovs* 2016 EWCA Crim 1856, 2017 1 Cr App R (S) 15 (p 99), see **8.37**.

Att-Gen's Ref 2017 Re Powell 2017 EWCA Crim 2324, 2018 1 Cr App R (S) 40 (p 279) D pleaded to aggravated burglary and common assault (4 months consecutive, no appeal) after a *Goodyear* indication. Both counsel and the Judge said it was a Category 2 case. Prosecution counsel failed to reserve the Attorney-General's position although a reference was mentioned during the hearing. On appeal, the prosecution sought to make the case Category 1. Held. An erroneous categorisation made by prosecution counsel will not normally fetter the Court of Appeal, but counsel will need to explain why the concession should be withdrawn. This case may well be Category 1, but it would not be just to permit the prosecution to go so far behind what was said below about the category. We move this case to the top of Category 2 making the sentence for the aggravated burglary 6 years, not 3 years 9 months.

Att-Gen's Ref 2018 Re McCann and Others 2018 EWCA Crim 132 D and others pleaded to various robberies. The prosecution counsel said all the offences were Category B. The Judge agreed. On appeal the prosecution said the lead robbery should have been Category 1A. Their new counsel said it was an oversight and they should be allowed to withdraw the Category 1B concession. Held. We permit that.

See also: *Att-Gen's Ref 2017 Re Chigariro* 2017 EWCA Crim 1371 (Both counsel at the Crown Court agreed the case was Category 2. Held. The case was Category 1 and there was no bar in applying that category.)

For when the prosecution acquiesce to a judicial indication in the Crown Court, see the ***Judicial indication Prosecution acquiescence*** para at **8.7**.

Other matters

8.45 ***Sentence passed runs from date of sentence unless otherwise stated***
Criminal Justice Act 1988 Sch 3 para 10 The term of any sentence passed by the Court of Appeal or Supreme Court under section 36 shall, unless they otherwise direct, begin to run from the time when it would have begun to run if passed in the proceedings in relation to which the reference was made.
Att-Gen's Ref No 48 of 2014 2014 EWCA Crim 1591 The Court substituted a 3-year term for a community order. At the time of the hearing the defendant was on remand for a fresh matter. Held. We note the rule in para 10 is 'unless they otherwise direct'. We order the sentence should start today.
See also: *Att-Gen's Ref No 52 of 2014* 2014 EWCA Crim 1742 (An example of a 17-year-old being ordered to attend a police station at 4 pm the next day.)

8.46 ***Costs***
Criminal Justice Act 1988 Sch 3 para 11(1)[92] Where on a reference to the Court of Appeal under section 36…or a reference to the Supreme Court under subsection (5) of that section the person whose sentencing is the subject of the reference appears by counsel for the purpose of presenting any argument to the Court of Appeal or the Supreme Court, he shall be entitled to the payment out of central funds of such funds as are reasonably sufficient to compensate him for expenses properly incurred by him for the purpose of being represented on the reference, and any amount recoverable under this paragraph shall be ascertained, as soon as practicable, by the registrar of criminal appeals or, as the case may be, under Supreme Court Rules.
(2) Sub-paragraph (1) has effect subject to:
(a) sub-paragraph (3), and
(b) regulations under Prosecution of Offences Act 1985 s 20(1A)(d) of the (as applied by this paragraph).
(3) A person is not entitled under sub-paragraph (1) to the payment of sums in respect of legal costs (as defined in Prosecution of Offences Act 1985 s 16A) incurred in proceedings in the Court of Appeal.
(4) Prosecution of Offences Act 1985 s 20(1A) to (1C) and (3) (regulations as to amounts ordered to be paid out of central funds) apply in relation to funds payable out of central funds under sub-paragraph (1) as they apply in relation to amounts payable out of central funds in pursuance of costs orders made under section 16 of that Act.

8.47 ***Can the defendant appeal after a reference decision?***
R v Hughes 2009 EWCA Crim 841, 2010 1 Cr App R (S) 25 (p 146) (A directions hearing.) D pleaded to two offences of arson being reckless as to whether life was endangered. He received 5 years on each count, concurrent. The case was subject to an Attorney-General's reference and the sentence was increased to life imprisonment. He was subsequently transferred to a hospital under Mental Health Act 1983. D appealed on the basis that a Hospital Order ought to have been ordered instead of imprisonment. It was questioned whether the Court had the jurisdiction to hear an appeal after having heard the Attorney-General's reference. Held. There is this very important difference between a sentence which has been considered upon an Attorney-General's reference and one which has been the subject of an appeal by the defendant. In the latter case, the defendant has exercised the right of appeal given to him by Criminal Appeal Act 1968 s 9. In the former, that right remains extant and unexercised. It is one thing to say, as this Court has consistently said, that the statutory right of appeal cannot be construed as extending to a right to two (or indeed more) appeals. But it is quite another to say that the statutory right to (a single) appeal given by section 9 is removed when the Attorney-General brings the case to this Court.

[92] The paragraph is listed as amended by Legal Aid, Sentencing and Punishment of Offenders Act 2012 Sch 7 para 11.

R v Hughes 2010 EWCA Crim 1026 LCJ (Same case, final hearing.) There was jurisdiction. Criminal Appeal Act 1968 provides a right to appeal against sentence which was a right which D never exercised until he made the present application. Hospital Order substituted.

Appeals to the Supreme Court

8.48 ***Appeals to the Supreme Court***
Criminal Justice Act 1988 s 36(5) Where the Court of Appeal has concluded its review of a case referred to them under this section the Attorney-General or the person to whose sentencing the reference relates may refer a point of law involved in any sentence passed on that person in the proceeding to the Supreme Court for its opinion, and the Supreme Court shall consider the point and give its opinion on it accordingly, and either remit the case to the Court of Appeal to be dealt with or itself deal with the case.
(6) A reference under subsection (5) shall be made only with the leave of the Court of Appeal or the Supreme Court, and leave shall not be granted unless it is certified by the Court of Appeal that the point of law is of general public importance and it appears to the Court of Appeal or the Supreme Court (as the case may be) that the point is one which ought to be considered by the Supreme Court.
(7) For the purpose of dealing with a case under this section the Supreme Court may exercise any powers of the Court of Appeal.

8.49 ***Appeals Time limits***
Criminal Justice Act 1988 Sch 3 para 4 An application to the Court of Appeal for leave to refer a case to the Supreme Court under section 36(5) shall be made within the period of 14 days beginning with the date on which the Court of Appeal concludes its review of the case, and an application to the Supreme Court for leave shall be made within the period of 14 days beginning with the date on which the Court of Appeal concludes its review or refuses leave to refer the case to the Supreme Court.

8.50 ***Defendant's right to be present Supreme Court***
Criminal Justice Act 1988 Sch 3 para 9 A person whose sentencing is the subject of a reference to the Supreme Court under section 36(5) and who is detained pending the hearing of that reference shall not be entitled to be present on the hearing of the reference or of any proceeding preliminary or incidental thereto except where an order of the Supreme Court authorises him to be present, or where the Supreme Court or the Court of Appeal, as the case may be, gives him leave to be present.

8.51 ***Time served to count***
Criminal Justice Act 1988 Sch 3 para 5 The time during which a person whose case has been referred for review under section 36 above is in custody pending its review and pending any reference to the Supreme Court under section 36(5) shall be reckoned as part of the term of any sentence to which he is for the time being subject.

9 Binding Over to Come Up for Judgment

9.1
This is a derelict power.
Availability The order cannot be made in the Magistrates' Court, *R v Ayu* 1958 43 Cr App R (S) 31 and *R v Acton Crown Court ex parte Bewley* 1988 10 Cr App R (S) 105.
Breach No notice is required and the issue is tried by a judge and not a jury, *R v David* 1940 27 Cr App R 50. There should have been an investigation as to whether there had been a deliberate breach of the condition or whether he had not complied because of lack of means, *R v Philbert* 1973 Crim LR 129.

9.2 ***The common law power***
Senior Courts Act 1981 s 79(1) All enactments and rules of law relating to procedure in connection with indictable offences shall continue to have effect in relation to proceedings in the Crown Court.

(2) Without prejudice to the generality of subsection (1), that subsection applies in particular to:

(b) the release, after respite of judgment, of a convicted person on recognisance to come up for judgment if called on, but meanwhile to be of good behaviour.

9.3 *Need the defendant consent?*

R v Williams 1982 4 Cr App R (S) 239 LCJ Making such an order is certainly very seldom to be done if the defendant does not freely give his consent. It may very well be that the only power the court has if he does not consent is to imprison him.

9.4 *Conditions*

Criminal Practice Directions 2015 EWCA Crim 1567 para VII J.17 If the Crown Court is considering binding over an individual to come up for judgment, the court should specify any conditions with which the individual is to comply in the meantime and not specify that the individual is to be of good behaviour.

R v Hodges 1967 51 Cr App R (S) 361 LCJ D pleaded to office-breaking, larceny and obtaining property and money by false pretences. D, aged 43, had a series of previous convictions. He was sentenced to 5 years' imprisonment. Held. This is one of those cases which the court always looks at with some anxiety in order to see whether the moment may not have arrived when it is opportune to put a man on probation in order to give him a chance, maybe a last chance, to reform rather than spend the rest of his life in prison. The Court has had the benefit of having before them a man who has said his principal in Dublin has arranged, if the court thought fit to free this man, for him to live with his cousin in Ireland who farms and on whose farm this man could be given work. It is quite clearly useless to make a probation order in those circumstances. The Court has come to the conclusion that the proper course here is to bind him over to come up for judgment at common law, it being a condition that he do…today travel to Dublin and that he do not land again in this country for ten years.

R v Williams 1982 4 Cr App R (S) 239 LCJ D was convicted of two counts of theft. He had a number of previous convictions. He was bound over to come up for judgment in his own recognisance of £20 on terms that he was to accompany his mother to Jamaica within ten days and not return to this country for five years. It was suggested by D's counsel that the order be made, as D's mother was Jamaican. D, however, was British. He had been born in this country and lived here ever since. The Judge was minded to acquiesce. Held. Save in exceptional circumstances such as those in *R v Hodges* 1967, it should be used only to ensure that the defendant goes to a country of which he is a citizen or in which he is habitually resident, or where there are very special circumstances in which the receiving country is prepared to take him for his own well-being. This order should not have been made.

See also: *R v Flaherty* 1958 Crim LR 556 (LCJ D We substitute a bind over[93] in the sum of £10 and a condition to return to Ireland.)

Note: Since these cases were decided, the rules for dealing with foreign defendants have been radically altered. Ed.

9.5 *Explain sentence, Judge must/Suggested sentencing remarks*

Criminal Practice Directions 2015 EWCA Crim 1567 para VII J.18 The Crown Court should, if the individual is unrepresented, explain the consequences of a breach of the binding over order in these circumstances.

Judicial College's Crown Court Compendium Part II Sentencing June 2018 page 6-3

[93] It is assumed this was a bind over to come up for judgment although the law report does not make that clear.

> **Example**
> I have been told that you intend to leave this country on {date} and return to {place} and have been shown confirmation of your booking. In these circumstances, as an alternative to sentencing you for this offence, I am going to bind you over to come up for judgment. This means that so long as you leave this country on {date} you will receive no punishment. But if you do not leave you will be brought back before the court for sentence. Do you understand? [Answer] Do you consent? [Answer]"

9.6 ***Appeals***
R v Williams 1982 4 Cr App R (S) 239 LCJ The Judge bound the defendant over to come up for judgment. Held. In one sense the order was not a sentence, it was a respite of judgment. Criminal Appeal Act 1968 s 50(1) defines 'sentence' in the following terms: 'In this Act, "sentence", in relation to an offence, includes any order made by a court when dealing with an offender (including a Hospital Order under Mental Health Act 1959 Part V (now Mental Health Act 1983), with or without an order restricting discharge) and also includes a recommendation for deportation.' Plainly that includes the order that the Judge made in this case, namely, the order of binding over, which was contingent upon the conviction and could not have been made otherwise than upon conviction. There was jurisdiction.

10 Binding Over to Keep the Peace

10.1
This is a very old common law power. It has been suggested that the order may have its origins in Anglo-Saxon times.
Children and young offenders The order is available whatever the age of the offender.
Rehabilitation period The period ends at the expiry of the bind over.[94]
See also the **Rehabilitation of Offenders Act 1974** chapter.

10.2 ***Statistics England and Wales Aged 21+***

Year	2013	2014	2015	2016	2017
Number	147	178	78	578	407

For explanations about the statistics, see page 1-xii. For more statistics, see www.banksr.com Other Matters Statistics tab.

NON-CONVICTION BIND OVERS

Power to order and test to apply

Note: Judges and magistrates are able to use this power: a) for someone who has been acquitted after a trial, see para **10.8**, b) for a witness who gives evidence, see para **10.9**, c) in stand-alone proceedings, and d) for a defendant who the prosecution offers no evidence. Ed.

10.3 ***Statutory power***
Magistrates' Courts Act 1980 s 115(1) The power of a Magistrates' Court on the complaint of any person to adjudge any other person to enter into a recognisance, with or without sureties, to keep the peace or to be of good behaviour towards the complainant shall be exercised by order on complaint.

10.4 ***Extent of power***
Hughes v Holly 1988 86 Cr App R 130 at 138 Magistrates are empowered to bind over a person to be of good behaviour even though he may have committed no offence.

10.5 ***European Convention on Human Rights art 10***
Hashman and Harrup v UK 2000 30 EHRR 241 The appellants were hunt saboteurs. They were bound over to keep the peace and be of good behaviour for 12 months in the

[94] Rehabilitation of Offenders Act 1974 s 5(4)

sum of £100. They admitted their intention to sabotage a hunt. The Court found they had not breached the peace. The applicants contended that their article 10 right of freedom of expression had been interfered with. Held. The bind overs were contrary to article 10.

10.6 *Purpose of order*

Sheldon v Bromfield JJs 1964 2 AER 131 LCJ A charge of assault occasioning ABH was dismissed, with the Judge deciding not only to bind over the defendant, but also two prosecution witnesses, X and Y. Held. The power to bind over is a very important jurisdiction and is in the nature of preventive justice.

Veater v G 1981 3 Cr App R (S) 52 LCJ The powers are exercisable not by reason of any offence having been committed, but as a measure of preventive justice. That is to say where the person's conduct is such as to lead the magistrate to suspect that there may be a breach of the peace, or that he might misbehave.

10.7 *Burden of proof*

Criminal Practice Directions 2015 EWCA Crim 1567 para VII J.8 The court should be satisfied so that it is sure of the matters complained of before a binding over order may be imposed. Where the procedure has been commenced on complaint, the burden of proof rests on the complainant. In all other circumstances, the burden of proof rests upon the prosecution.

10.8 *Defendant acquitted Bind overs should be rare*

R v Middlesex Crown Court ex parte Khan 1997 161 JP 240 D was bound over in the sum of £250 for 12 months. He sought judicial review of the decision. D had been charged with ABH but was acquitted. The Judge proposed to bind D over. When asked whether D consented to the bind over, he replied: "I have no choice." His response angered the Judge, who told D not to answer in such terms. Nothing more was said regarding D's consent. D submitted that: a) the bind over should be quashed as he never consented to it, and b) D ought not to have been bound over at all. Held. a) D's words amounted to, 'I do not want to be bound over but you leave me with no real alternative but consent. So I consent.' b) The Judge should not have done what was done in this case as it was bound to leave D with a feeling that he had not had justice in that court. It is exceedingly rare that it would be appropriate to bind over the defendant who had been acquitted, and this was not a case where it was appropriate.

Emohare v Thames Magistrates' Court 2009 EWHC 689 (Admin) D was arrested after allegedly swinging his head causing it to collide with a police officer who had stopped him to lawfully question him. D was acquitted of assaulting a police officer in the execution of his duty. Despite the acquittal, the justices considered D's actions to be a breach of the peace and bound him over for 2 years in the sum of £500. The Magistrates found that D was aggressive when stopped by the police, and justified the bind over by stating that they had found that D was a man of violence. They also commented to the effect that D was fortunate not to be charged with a public order offence. Held. The justification undermined the justices' finding of fact, and thus there was no proper basis to make the bind over. The rationalisation that D was guilty of a public order offence with which he was not charged, and never had the opportunity to deal with, is an approach which is in wholly inappropriate conflict with the presumption of innocence which should have been applied.

10.9 *Power to bind over complainant, witnesses etc.*

Criminal Practice Directions 2015 EWCA Crim 1567 para VII J.5, www.banksr.com Other Matters Other Documents tab Particularly careful consideration may be required where the individual who would be subject to the order is a witness in the proceedings.

Sheldon v Bromfield JJs 1964 2 AER 131 LCJ A charge of assault occasioning ABH was dismissed, with the Judge deciding not only to bind over the defendant, but also two prosecution witnesses, X and Y. Held. It is well known that the justices have the power pursuant to Justices of the Peace Act 1361. There is jurisdiction to bind over not only the defendant but also the complainant and witnesses who are before the court.

R v Swindon Crown Court ex parte Singh 1983 5 Cr App R (S) 422 D was charged with assaulting V. V was to give evidence for the Crown. The Crown offered no evidence on the agreement that D would submit to being bound over to keep the peace. D agreed. V objected to being bound over. The Judge then bound him over and V appealed. It was submitted that V was not 'a person who or whose case was before the court' as no evidence was called. Accordingly it was submitted that there was no jurisdiction to make the order. Held. V was not a person whose case was before the court within the meaning of Justices of the Peace Act 1968 s 1(7) (see **10.18**). V had not attained or assumed the role of a witness since no evidence was called. He was not a complainant in any technical sense, as the prosecution was brought by the Crown. There was no power to bind him over. It is a serious step to take and should only be taken where facts are proved by evidence before the court which indicate the likelihood that the peace will not be kept. Such cases may occur, but it seems to me that they will be exceedingly rare.

R v Kingston Crown Court ex parte Guarino 1986 Crim LR 325 V was involved in a fight and he was charged with a public order offence. D was charged with Offences Against the Person Act 1861 s 18 in a separate incident. The victim was V. V awaited summary trial and he was a conditionally bound witness for D's case. V attended D's trial and D pleaded to section 20 and the section 18 count was dropped. After D was sentenced the Judge told V that after reading V's statement he intended to bind V over. V made no submissions and was bound over. V appealed saying he was not a person 'who or whose case' was 'before the court' within Justices of the Peace Act 1968 s 1(7), therefore there was no jurisdiction to bind him over. Held. V was not bringing the case, nor had he been a witness. It could make no difference that he was physically present in court. Order quashed on this and other grounds.

R v Lincoln Crown Court ex parte Jones 1990 COD 15 W was a witness and the prosecution decided to bind everyone over and not to have a trial. W was bound over in the sum of £150 for 12 months to be of good behaviour. The others were also bound over. Immediately after the hearing, W consulted solicitors stating that he had been pressurised into consenting by prosecuting counsel and that he had not been advised that he could seek independent legal advice. Held. W was not a person 'who or whose case' was 'before the court' as he had not attained the status of a witness, *R v Swindon Crown Court ex parte Singh* 1984 applied. W could not be considered to be a complainant in any technical sense as it was the Crown who had brought the prosecution.

See also: *R v Ilminster JJs ex parte Hamilton* 1983 The Times 23/6/83 (A party to a fight had been acquitted of behaviour likely to lead to a breach of the peace. He later gave evidence at the trial of another party to that fight. That acquittal should have persuaded the Magistrates not to bind him over to keep the peace.)

Note: Before considering the jurisdiction it might be prudent to decide which Act is being relied upon, see **10.3** and **10.17**. Ed.

10.10 *Standard of proof*

R v Coventry Magistrates' Court ex parte CPS 1996 Crim LR 723 D was brought before the court to show why a bind over order should not be imposed. Held. The standard of proof is a criminal one.

R v Liverpool JJs ex parte Collins 1998 2 Cr App R 108[95] LCJ The standard of proof under Justices of the Peace Act 1361 and Magistrates' Courts Act 1980 s 115 is the criminal standard of proof.

10.11 *Test to apply*

Criminal Practice Directions 2015 EWCA Crim 1567 para VII J.2 Before imposing a binding over order, the court must be satisfied so that it is sure that a breach of the peace involving violence, or an imminent threat of violence, has occurred or that there is a real

[95] Also known as *CPS v Speede* 1998 2 Cr App R 108 and *DPP v Speede* 1998 2 Cr App R 108

risk of violence in the future. Such violence may be perpetrated by the individual who will be subject to the order or by a third party as a natural consequence of the individual's conduct.

R v Liverpool JJs ex parte Collins 1998 2 Cr App R 108[96] LCJ In *Percy v DPP* 1995 3 AER 124, the Court held that a breach of the peace in the context of Magistrates' Courts Act 1980 s 115 had to involve violence or the threat of violence. The violence did not have to be perpetrated by the defendant himself, it was sufficient if his conduct was such that violence from some other third party was a natural consequence of his action, thus giving rise to a real risk, rather than a mere possibility, of some actual danger to the peace. Although the standard of proof under Justices of the Peace Act 1361 or the powers under section 115 is the criminal standard, what has to be proved is different. In considering a complaint under section 115(1) the court must be satisfied that the relevant allegations contained in the complaint have been proved. Under the 1361 Act the court must be sure that there is a risk of a breach of the peace in the future, see *R v Aubrey-Fletcher ex parte Thompson* 1969 53 Cr App R 380.

10.12 ***Power to add sureties***

Magistrates' Courts Act 1980 s 115(1) The power of a Magistrates' Court on the complaint of any person to adjudge any other person to enter into a recognisance, with or without sureties, to keep the peace or to be of good behaviour towards the complainant shall be exercised by order on complaint.

Procedure and other matters

10.13 ***Procedure General***

Note: The Criminal Procedure Rules 2015 2015/1490 behaviour order rules appear to apply, see the note at para **27.2**. Where there is provision for the procedure in the Magistrates' Courts Act 1980 etc., the 1980 Act would take precedence over the 2014 rules. All the rules are at www.banksr.com Other Matters Other Documents tab. Ed.

Magistrates' Courts Act 1980 s 115(1) The power of a Magistrates' Court…to adjudge any other person to enter into a recognisance…shall be exercised by order on complaint.

R v Coventry Magistrates' Court ex parte CPS 1996 Crim LR 723 Procedure by way of complaint was primarily a civil process. The absence of a complaint in Form 98 (see the Magistrates' Courts Rules (Forms) 1981 1981/553) did not invalidate the procedure. The procedure followed could amount to laying an information. The substance of a complaint of the kind contemplated by section 115 was included on the form and a complaint sufficiently identified. There was a presumption that the statutory procedure in section 115 was followed.

R v Liverpool JJs ex parte Collins 1998 2 Cr App R 108[97] LCJ An order under Magistrates' Courts Act 1980 s 115 can only be made after a complaint and after that complaint has been adjudged to be true. A complaint need not be in writing and may be made orally.

See also: *R v Manchester Stipendiary Magistrate ex parte Hill* 1983 AC 328 (A complaint may be made orally.)

10.14 ***Procedure Issuing summons***

Magistrates' Courts Act 1980 s 51 Where a complaint relating to a person is made to a justice of the peace, the justice of the peace may issue a summons to the person requiring him to appear before a Magistrates' Court to answer to the complaint.

10.15 ***Can the court proceed without the defendant?***

Magistrates' Courts Act 1980 s 55(1)-(3)

Magistrates' Courts Act 1980 s 55(1) Where at the time and place appointed for the hearing or adjourned hearing of a complaint the complainant appears but the defendant does not, the court may, subject to subsection (3) below, proceed in his absence.

[96] Also known as *CPS v Speede* 1998 2 Cr App R 108 and *DPP v Speede* 1998 2 Cr App R 108

[97] Also known as *CPS v Speede* 1998 2 Cr App R 108 and *DPP v Speede* 1998 2 Cr App R 108

(2) Where the court, instead of proceeding in the absence of the defendant, adjourns, or further adjourns, the hearing, the court may, if the complaint has been substantiated on oath, and subject to the following provisions of this section, issue a warrant for his arrest.
(3) The court shall not begin to hear the complaint in the absence of the defendant or issue a warrant under this section unless either it is proved to the satisfaction of the court, on oath or in such other manner as may be prescribed, that the summons was served on him within what appears to the court to be a reasonable time before the hearing or adjourned hearing or the defendant has appeared on a previous occasion to answer to the complaint.
R v Liverpool JJs ex parte Collins 1998 2 Cr App R 108[98] LCJ S was arrested for alleged breach of the peace. He appeared before the Magistrates' Court and declined to be bound over. The matter was adjourned. On the adjourned date S failed to attend and the Court heard the matter in his absence and found the case proved. They then issued a warrant for S's arrest. S challenged the order. Held. There are two ways in which the Magistrates' Court can proceed. It can either hear the case in the absence of the defendant or, having substantiated the complaint, it can issue a warrant for the defendant's arrest. The court cannot do either of those unless Magistrates' Courts Act 1980 s 55(3) is satisfied. Being permitted to take either of these courses, it was for the court to choose which course it chose to follow. A factor that should be borne in mind when making that decision is that, if the court hears the case in the absence of the defendant, the section makes it quite clear that it cannot then issue an arrest warrant. That follows from the clear wording of subsection (2) and receives support from the use of the word 'or' in subsection (3). If the court proceeds to hear the case in the absence of the defendant and finds the case proved, then it cannot take the matter further without the defendant being present. He must be present either to enter into a recognisance or to refuse to do so with the consequences that he could go to prison. I should add that I have not considered whether section 122 would allow this to be done by a legal representative on behalf of the defendant. If the court follows this route then the only way that the court can secure the attendance of the defendant is to adjourn. The court is entitled to adjourn, as is made clear by section 54(1). On adjourning, the defendant would have to be given notice of the adjourned hearing. Should he then fail to appear at the adjourned hearing, a warrant may be issued if the court is satisfied that he had adequate notice of the time and place of the adjourned hearing. The alternative route is to hear from the complainant briefly in order only to 'substantiate' the complaint and then proceed to issue a warrant, provided that the circumstances in subsection (3) are satisfied. Here the court could not issue a warrant by virtue of the provisions of subsection (2) and subsection (3). The order is quashed.

10.16 ***Power to remand where complaint is made under section 115(1)***
Magistrates' Courts Act 1980 s 115(2) Where a complaint is made under this section, the power of the court to remand the defendant under subsection (5) of section 55 (non-appearance of the defendant) of this Act shall not be subject to the restrictions imposed by subsection (6) of that section.
Magistrates' Courts Act 1980 s 55(6) The court shall not issue a warrant or remand a defendant under this section or further remand him by virtue of section 128(3) below after he has given evidence in the proceedings.

[98] Also known as *CPS v Speede* 1998 2 Cr App R 108 and *DPP v Speede* 1998 2 Cr App R 108

GENERAL POWERS

Power to order

10.17 ***Statutory power Justices of the Peace Act 1361***
Justices of the Peace Act 1361 s 1 Justices of the Peace…shall have Power…to take of all them that be not of good Fame, where they shall be found, sufficient Surety and Mainprise of their good Behaviour towards the King and his People.[99]

10.18 ***Statutory power to order Justices of the Peace Act 1968***
Justices of the Peace Act 1968 s 1(7) Any court of record having a criminal jurisdiction has, as ancillary to that jurisdiction, the power to bind over to keep the peace, and power to bind over to be of good behaviour, a person who or whose case is before the court, by requiring him to enter into his own recognisances or to find sureties or both, and committing him to prison if he does not comply.
R v Aubrey-Fletcher ex parte Thompson 1969 53 Cr App R 380 LCJ An order can be made at any time during the proceedings.
Percy v DPP 1995 3 AER 124 at 129 Magistrates' Courts Act 1980 s 115 does not affect the justices' power to bind over a person already before the court, whether he be a complainant or a defendant, if the justices consider that it is necessary to do so. Such an order, pursuant to the 1361 Act, can only be made if it emerges that there might be a breach of the peace in the future, see *R v Aubrey-Fletcher ex parte Thompson* 1969 53 Cr App R 380. It can be made at any stage in the proceedings and even if the defendant is acquitted of whatever charge he has faced. It can also be made against a witness. The justices' jurisdiction depends upon the person's presence before them, and, save in the case of a defendant, no order can be made unless that person is warned what the justices intend and is given an opportunity of making representations.

10.19 ***Crown Court has the power to bind over***
Justices of the Peace Act 1968 s 1(7) It is hereby declared that any court of record having a criminal jurisdiction has, as ancillary to that jurisdiction, the power to bind over to keep the peace, and power to bind over to be of good behaviour a person who or whose case is before the court.
R v Liverpool JJs ex parte Collins 1998 2 Cr App R 108[100] LCJ The Act of 1361 does not appear to require any complaint to have been made. Not only does a Magistrates' Court have the power to order a bind over under the 1361 Act but so also does any court of record having a criminal jurisdiction. This is by virtue of Justices of the Peace Act 1968 s 1(7). Thus a Crown Court, like the Magistrates' Court, can bind over a person who has been acquitted or a witness (including a complainant) who has given evidence.

10.20 ***European Convention on Human Rights art 6***
Steel v UK 1999 28 EHRR 603 S and L were both convicted in separate trials of breach of the peace. S was arrested for trying to disrupt a shoot. L was arrested for trying to disrupt motorway building. S argued that 'breach of the peace' was a very general accusation and that consequently this was contrary to article 6(3)(a) (right to be promptly informed of charges). Held. Within 10 hours of S's arrest she was given a charge sheet detailing the charge and the statute under which it was lawful. The sheet included the date and place of the alleged incident. Consequently, there was no breach of article 6(3)(a).

10.21 ***European Convention on Human Rights arts 8, 10 and 11***
Novartis Pharmaceuticals UK Ltd v Stop Huntingdon Animal Cruelty 2009 EWHC 2716 (QB) The defendants, SHAC, were an organisation whose aim was to protect animals by bringing pressure on Huntingdon Life Sciences. An injunction under Protection from Harassment Act 1997 was made restraining them from harassing the claimants, NP, who were connected with Huntingdon Life Sciences. SHAC said it was a

[99] The capitalisation is in the Act.
[100] Also known as *CPS v Speede* 1998 2 Cr App R 108 and *DPP v Speede* 1998 2 Cr App R 108

vehicle for legitimate protest against live animal testing. An injunction was obtained which involved those trading or connected with Huntingdon. NP sought amendments to the injunction. Held. The Court considered the impact of an existing injunction on the article 8, 10 and 11 rights of the defendants. The restrictions on those rights were proportionate.

10.22 ***European Convention on Human Rights art 10***

Steel v UK 1999 28 EHRR 603 S and L were both convicted in separate trials of breach of the peace. S was arrested for trying to disrupt a shoot. L was arrested for trying to disrupt motorway building. Both applicants contended that their article 10 right (right to freedom of expression) was violated. Held. The arrest was not disproportionate. The detention was lawful. There was no breach of article 10.

10.23 ***Common law power***

R v Liverpool JJs ex parte Collins 1998 2 Cr App R 108[101] LCJ There is authority for the existence of a common law power to use a bind over to 'prevent conduct which is contrary to a good way of life', *Percy v DPP* 1995 3 AER 124 at 129. For more detail, see the **Binding Over to Come up for Judgment** chapter.

Test to apply

10.24 ***Test to apply***

Criminal Practice Directions 2015 EWCA Crim 1567 para VII J.2 Before imposing a binding over order, the court must be satisfied so that it is sure that a breach of the peace involving violence, or an imminent threat of violence, has occurred or that there is a real risk of violence in the future. Such violence may be perpetrated by the individual who will be subject to the order or by a third party as a natural consequence of the individual's conduct.

R v Aubrey-Fletcher ex parte Thompson 1969 53 Cr App R 380 LCJ There must emerge during the course of the hearing material from which it may fairly be deduced that there is at least a risk of a breach of peace in the future.

Hughes v Holly 1988 86 Cr App R 130 at 140 Before the magistrates can exercise their power to bind over, they must have some cause to believe that without a binding over order the defendant might repeat his conduct.

R v Middlesex Crown Court ex parte Khan 1997 161 JP 240 If a judge is going to require a man to be bound over in circumstances where he has been acquitted, it is particularly important that he should be satisfied beyond a reasonable doubt that the man poses a potential threat to other persons and that he is a man of violence.

Emohare v Thames Magistrates' Court 2009 EWHC 689 (Admin) A bind over to keep the peace is typically only warranted where there is evidence of likely personal danger to others involving violence or the threat of violence, see, for example, *Percy v DPP* 1995 3 AER 124.

See also: *Lanham v Bernard* 1986 The Times 23/6/86 (It is wrong not to bind over a defendant merely because he indicates he will continue the acts complained of.)

Note: However, the defendant must be made fully aware that the order is proposed. Ed.

10.25 ***Discretionary power, It is a***

Lanham v Bernard 1986 The Times 23/6/86 The Magistrate declined to issue a bind over because the effect was that those who were convicted would be fined and those who were merely bound over would be imprisoned for refusing to consent. Held. We would be loath to say the Magistrate was misguided.

Hughes v Holly 1988 86 Cr App R 130 at 138 Magistrates do have a very wide discretion in deciding whether to bind over.

10.26 ***Burden of proof/Standard of proof***

Criminal Practice Directions 2015 EWCA Crim 1567 para VII J.8 The court should be satisfied so that it is sure of the matters complained of before a binding over order may

[101] Also known as *CPS v Speede* 1998 2 Cr App R 108 and *DPP v Speede* 1998 2 Cr App R 108

be imposed. Where the procedure has been commenced on complaint, the burden of proof rests on the complainant. In all other circumstances, the burden of proof rests upon the prosecution.

Note: This may indicate that the decision is based on judgement and evaluation and not on a formal burden, *R v Crown Court at Manchester ex parte McCann* 2002 UKHL 39 Lords (A case concerning a stand-alone ASBO). Ed.

R v Liverpool JJs ex parte Collins 1998 2 Cr App R 108[102] LCJ The standard of proof under Justices of the Peace Act 1361 or the powers under Magistrates' Courts Act 1980 s 115 is the criminal standard.

10.27 *Defendant under 18*

Conlan v Oxford 1983 5 Cr App R (S) 237 D, a juvenile, was convicted of obstructing a police officer in the execution of his duty. D indicated that he would consent to being bound over. The bench found that they were not able to bind over a juvenile by requiring him to enter into a recognisance and remanded D for a trial before a new bench. Held. Magistrates' Courts Act 1980 s 115 provides for the court to make two separate orders. One is to adjudge a person to enter into a recognisance to keep the peace. The second, which arises under subsection (3), gives a discretion to the justices to commit a person into custody, if he refuses to enter into a recognisance which has been ordered. It is only if there is a refusal to enter into the recognisance that the power to imprison or commit into custody arises. Therefore, the Court was able to make the order as D had indicated his willingness to consent.

For the position when there is no consent, see **10.41**.

Procedure

10.28 *Procedure*

Criminal Practice Directions 2015 EWCA Crim 1567 para VII J.5, www.banksr.com Other Matters Other Documents tab Magistrates' Courts Act 1980 s 51-57 set out the jurisdiction of the Magistrates' Court to hear an application made on complaint and the procedure which is to be followed. This includes a requirement under section 53 to hear evidence and the parties before making any order. This practice should be applied to all cases in the Magistrates' Court and the Crown Court where the court is considering imposing a binding over order. The court should give the individual who would be subject to the order and the prosecutor the opportunity to make representations, both as to the making of the order and as to its terms. The court should also hear any admissible evidence the parties wish to call and which has not already been heard in the proceedings. Particularly careful consideration may be required where the individual who would be subject to the order is a witness in the proceedings.

R v Liverpool JJs ex parte Collins 1998 2 Cr App R 108[103] LCJ The 1361 Act does not appear to require any complaint to have been made. Not only does a Magistrates' Court have the power to order a bind over under the 1361 Act but so also does any court of record having a criminal jurisdiction. This is by virtue of Justices of the Peace Act 1968 s 1(7), 'It is hereby declared that any court of record having a criminal jurisdiction has, as ancillary to that jurisdiction, the power to bind over to keep the peace, and power to bind over to be of good behaviour a person who or whose case is before the Court'.

10.29 *Warn counsel/individual, Court must*

Sheldon v Bromfield JJs 1964 2 AER 131 LCJ A charge of assault occasioning ABH was dismissed, with the Judge deciding not only to bind over the defendant, but also two prosecution witnesses, X and Y. X and Y were not given the opportunity to make representations on the issue of the bind over and were not warned that a bind over was in the Court's contemplation. Held. The Court acted contrary to natural justice and the orders must be quashed.

[102] Also known as *CPS v Speede* 1998 2 Cr App R 108 and *DPP v Speede* 1998 2 Cr App R 108

[103] Also known as *CPS v Speede* 1998 2 Cr App R 108 and *DPP v Speede* 1998 2 Cr App R 108

R v Hendon JJs ex parte Gorchein 1973 1 WLR 1502 LCJ P brought a private prosecution against D arising out of an assault after a near-collision of two cars, one driven by D, the other by E. The justices inquired whether both D and E would consent to being bound over. Both refused. The trial started and P gave evidence. D was convicted and without any warning the Magistrates bound both over to keep the peace. Held. The justices here failed to warn D that they had a binding over in mind. It is high time that this particular error should be eradicated, because it is the easiest thing in the world for justices who contemplate binding over to say what they have in mind and ask the intended recipient what he has to say. They ought to observe that rule.
R v Lincoln Crown Court ex parte Jude 1998 1 Cr App R 130 D was bound over to keep the peace in the sum of £500 for 18 months. Held. A court considering binding over a complainant or a witness in proceedings before it must warn him. It follows that if the Judge failed to warn D of his intention to bind him over or to give him an opportunity to make representations about it, such failure would not necessarily invalidate the order. Much would depend on how familiar he was with the circumstances of the case and whether such circumstances as were not in issue could reasonably justify the order. Here he was warned.
See also: *R v North London Magistrates' Court ex parte Haywood* 1973 3 AER 50 (Disturbance in court. No requirement to inform the parties of the court's intention.)

10.30 ***The court must indicate the reasons why it is minded to bind over***
R v Kingston Crown Court ex parte Guarino 1986 Crim LR 325 The victim, V, was involved in a fight and he was charged with a public order offence. D was charged with section 18 in a separate incident. V awaited summary trial and he was a conditionally bound witness for D's case. V attended D's trial and D pleaded to section 20 and the section 18 count was dropped. After D was sentenced, the Judge told V that after reading V's statement he intended to bind V over. V made no submissions and was bound over. V appealed saying that the proceedings were contrary to natural justice. Held. It was hard to adduce what V's part was. D was unable to challenge the evidence since it was never disclosed. Order quashed on this and other grounds.
R v South Molton JJs ex parte Ankerson 1990 90 Cr App R 158 The court must indicate to the defendant its intention to bind him over and the reasons for being so minded so that he or his representative may make submissions.

10.31 ***Must allow representations to be made***
Criminal Practice Directions 2015 EWCA Crim 1567 para VII J.5 The court should give the individual who would be subject to the order and the prosecutor the opportunity to make representations, both as to the making of the order and as to its terms.
R v South Molton JJs ex parte Ankerson 1990 90 Cr App R 158 The court must indicate to the defendant its intention to bind him over and the reasons for being so minded so that he or his representative may make submissions.
R v Lincoln Crown Court ex parte Jude 1998 1 Cr App R 130 D was bound over to keep the peace in the sum of £500 for 18 months. Held. A court considering binding over a complainant or a witness in proceedings before it must warn him and give him or his representative an opportunity to make representations about it. However, it does not apply to a convicted or acquitted defendant who has come to court knowing and having prepared to meet the nature of the case against him. In the case of an acquitted defendant, the better course is to give him or his representative, if he has one, an opportunity to address the court on the matter. A defendant in respect of whom a Crown Court proposes to direct the indictment to remain on the file is in much the same category for this purpose as a convicted or acquitted defendant, providing that the judge knows enough about the circumstances of the case to enable him to form a judgement as to the need for a binding over order. The Judge gave sufficient warning to D.
Note: A wiser course would be to always give counsel or the individual the opportunity to make representations. Ed.

10.32 ***Evidence, There must be proper***
Criminal Practice Directions 2015 EWCA Crim 1567 para VII J.5 Magistrates' Courts Act 1980 s 51-57 set out the jurisdiction of the Magistrates' Court to hear an application made on complaint and the procedure which is to be followed. This includes a requirement under section 53 to hear evidence and the parties, before making any order. This practice should be applied to all cases in the Magistrates' Court and the Crown Court where the court is considering imposing a binding over order. The court should also hear any admissible evidence the parties wish to call and which has not already been heard in the proceedings. Particularly careful consideration may be required where the individual who would be subject to the order is a witness in the proceedings.
J.6 Where there is an admission which is sufficient to found the making of a binding over order and/or the individual consents to the making of the order, the court should nevertheless hear sufficient representations and, if appropriate, evidence, to satisfy itself that an order is appropriate in all the circumstances and to be clear about the terms of the order.
South West London Magistrates' Court ex parte Brown 1974 Crim LR 313 LCJ The material did not have to be sworn evidence.
Brooks v Nottinghamshire Police 1984 Crim LR 677 High Court Judge at Crown Court A court can only bind over a defendant on admissible evidence and not on counsel's statements or the evidence of an officer about matters of which he did not have personal knowledge. Material relied upon in seeking a bind over must be strictly proved.
Emohare v Thames Magistrates' Court 2009 EWHC 689 (Admin) D was arrested after allegedly swinging his head causing it to collide with a police officer who had stopped him to lawfully question him. D was acquitted of assaulting a police officer in the execution of his duty. Despite the acquittal, the Justices considered D's actions to be a breach of the peace and bound him over for 2 years in the sum of £500. The Magistrates found that D was aggressive when stopped by the police, and justified the bind over by stating that they had found that D was a man of violence. They also commented to the effect that D was fortunate not to be charged with a public order offence. Held. The justification undermined the Justices' finding of fact, and thus there was no proper basis to make the bind over. The rationalisation that D was guilty of a public order offence with which he was not charged, and never had the opportunity to deal with, is an approach which is in wholly inappropriate conflict with the presumption of innocence which should have been applied.
Disputes as to facts see the FACTUAL BASIS FOR SENTENCING ***Same rules apply when imposing ancillary orders*** para at **57.26**.

10.33 ***Evidence, There must be proper Defendant consents***
Criminal Practice Directions 2015 EWCA Crim 1567 para VII J.6 Where there is an admission which is sufficient to found the making of a binding over order and/or the individual consents to the making of the order, the court should nevertheless hear sufficient representations and, if appropriate, evidence, to satisfy itself that an order is appropriate in all the circumstances and to be clear about the terms of the order.
R v Marylebone Metropolitan Stipendiary Magistrate ex parte Okunnu 1988 87 Cr App R 295 The prosecution agreed to drop the case against D if he agreed to be bound over. D agreed. The Magistrate inquired whether D admitted anything. He was told D admitted nothing. The Magistrate then decided there was no evidence to justify a bind over and declined to bind D over. The prosecution then decided to continue with the case. D appealed. Held. There was no evidence to justify an order so the Magistrate could not make the order, even with consent.

10.34 ***Court must decide about bind over before fixing amount of recognisance***
Criminal Practice Directions 2015 EWCA Crim 1567 para VII J.10, www.banksr.com Other Matters Other Documents tab The court must be satisfied on the merits of the case that an order for binding over is appropriate and should announce that decision before

considering the amount of the recognisance. If unrepresented, the individual who is made subject to the binding over order should be told he has a right of appeal from the decision.

Making the order

10.35 ***Drafting the order***
Criminal Practice Directions 2015 EWCA Crim 1567 para VII J.3 In light of the judgment in *R v Hashman and Harrup v UK* 2000 30 EHRR 241 courts should no longer bind an individual over "to be of good behaviour". Rather than binding an individual over to "keep the peace" in general terms, the court should identify the specific conduct or activity from which the individual must refrain.
J.4 When making an order binding an individual over to refrain from specified types of conduct or activities, the details of that conduct or those activities should be specified by the court in a written order, served on all relevant parties. The court should state its reasons for the making of the order, its length and the amount of the recognisance. The length of the order should be proportionate to the harm sought to be avoided and should not generally exceed 12 months.

10.36 ***Conditions, Can't make***
R v Ayu 1958 43 Cr App R (S) 31 LCJ D was committed to be sentenced as an incorrigible rogue. There he was bound over to be accompanied to Nigeria and not to land in this country for 5 years. Held. Conditions can be imposed when binding over to come up for judgment. It could not be made for a binding over to keep the peace.
R v Randall 1986 8 Cr App R (S) 433 LCJ D was a teacher and he was convicted of numerous offences against boys. A Crown Court judge bound him over with a condition not to teach or seek to teach anyone under 18. He breached the order and was ordered to pay £250 and bound over again on the same terms. Counsel for D said although there was power to add conditions to a common law bind over (see the **BINDING OVER TO COME UP FOR JUDGMENT** chapter), there was no power to add a condition to a statutory bind over. The prosecution counsel agreed. Held. We agree. Orders quashed.

10.37 ***The recognisance Fixing the amount of***
Criminal Practice Directions 2015 EWCA Crim 1567 para VII J.10 The court must be satisfied on the merits of the case that an order for binding over is appropriate and should announce that decision before considering the amount of the recognisance. If unrepresented, the individual who is made subject to the binding over order should be told he has a right of appeal from the decision.
J.11 When fixing the amount of recognisance, courts should have regard to the individual's financial resources and should hear representations from the individual or his legal representatives regarding finances.
J.12 A recognisance is made in the form of a bond giving rise to a civil debt on breach of the order.
R v Central Criminal Court ex parte Boulding 1984 79 Cr App R 100 D had very strong views about the manufacture of furs and shouted at employees at a fur shop. Officers approached him and he made threats and was asked to be quiet by police officers. He continued. He was arrested and became very excited. The Magistrates convicted him of using insulting words or behaviour and fined him £10. D appealed to the Crown Court, which also convicted him, affirmed the fine and without warning bound him over in the sum of £500 for two years. D's means were not inquired into. Held. Representations should have been allowed. The present case is a very good example…of a case in which a defendant's means and other personal circumstances should have been inquired into and representations allowed about them. Without such an inquiry and further assistance from him, or his counsel, the Court could not alight upon a proper, just and suitable sum of recognisance. It is one thing to impose a small or trivial sum of money as a recognisance without inquiring and so on, it is quite another to impose, without inquiring into the means of a defendant, a relatively large sum. The order was quashed.

R v Atkinson 1988 10 Cr App R (S) 470 LCJ In this case there was no inquiry into the appellant's means and personal circumstances and no representations were sought from his counsel as to the figure to be included in any bind over. Any proper inquiry would have made it clear that £1,500 was wholly out of proportion to this man's means and circumstances. We quash the bind over.
R v South Molton JJs ex parte Ankerson 1990 90 Cr App R 158 The defendants were bound over to keep the peace in the sum of £150. The defendants appealed and the court in its affidavit said £150 was not an unusual sum and it was quite low. Held. An inquiry must be made into means, however small the figure may appear to the justices.
R v Lincoln Crown Court ex parte Jude 1998 1 Cr App R 130 D was bound over to keep the peace in the sum of £500 for 18 months. D was unemployed and in receipt of £90 a fortnight. Held. An order in the sum of £500 in the circumstances of this case cannot be regarded as so trivial as to dispense with the requirement of an inquiry. The Judge said the amount was relatively moderate. That is not how D would have regarded it with his slender means. For that reason and for that reason alone the order is quashed.
See also: *R v Kingston Crown Court ex parte Guarino* 1986 Crim LR 325 (No inquiry. Order quashed.)

10.38 *On the facts, Judge able/not able to make the order*
R v Inner London Crown Court ex parte Benjamin 1987 85 Cr App R 267 D was arrested for a breach of the peace after police officers had instructed him to stop blowing his conch shell, an instruction which he ignored. It was alleged that he assaulted one of the officers, causing him ABH. He elected for Crown Court trial. He was acquitted. However, the Judge inquired whether D would consent to being bound over. He would not, so the Judge committed him to prison for 7 days or until he agreed to be bound over in the sum of £50 to keep the peace. D was refused bail. Held. There was entirely adequate material before the Judge to found his decision in this case to seek D's consent to the bind over. There was ample material before the Judge to found his view that a consequent breach of the peace was not only possible, but indeed probable, if the applicant did indulge in future unbridled use of his shell trumpet. The result is this: if the applicant will now agree to be bound over, there is nothing simpler than for him to go with his legal adviser to the Inner London Crown Court and say so. To enable him to take this wise course I, for my part, would extend his bail for a further 48 hours. However, if he does not agree, then he must realise that the result must inevitably be his return to prison to serve the remainder of the 7-day term which was imposed by the Judge in the Court below.
Hughes v Holly 1988 86 Cr App R 130 The police had complaints that they did nothing about women being accosted by men in a red light district. As a result a policewoman was asked to walk through a red light district to see if she was accosted by a kerb-crawler. D accosted her. The Magistrates imposed a bind over on D which was affirmed by the Crown Court. The defendant appealed again and claimed he had committed no offence and that the bind over was not legally available. Held. The Crown Court was justified in its conclusions that there was material here upon which the Justices could properly exercise their power to bind over.
R v South Molton JJs ex parte Ankerson 1990 90 Cr App R 158 The Court considered that when the defendants appeared dumb, they showed insolence and displayed a disrespectful and casual attitude. Held. Such behaviour could not possibly justify a bind over because there was no material on which it could be reasonably judged that there was a danger of the defendants committing a breach of the peace if they were not bound over.

10.39 *Bind over should be for a finite period*
R v South Molton JJs ex parte Ankerson 1990 90 Cr App R 158 The binding over should be for a finite period.

10.40 ***Explain sentence, Judge must/Suggested sentencing remarks***
Judicial College's Crown Court Compendium Part II Sentencing June 2018 page 6-4

> **Example**
> I have been told that you are prepared to be bound over to/not to {specify}. Is that right? [Answer] In view of what I have been told about your means, I am going to bind you over to/not to {specify} for (period) in the sum of £... This means that so long as you {specify} you will hear no more about this. But if in the next (period) it is proved to the court that you have {specify}, you will be liable to pay all or part of the sum of £... Do you agree to be bound over on these terms? [Answer]

Consent and committal to custody for refusing to consent

10.41 ***Individual must consent***
Criminal Practice Directions 2015 EWCA Crim 1567 para VII J.13 If there is any possibility that an individual will refuse to enter a recognisance, the court should consider whether there are any appropriate alternatives to a binding over order (for example, continuing with a prosecution). Where there are no appropriate alternatives and the individual continues to refuse to enter into the recognisance, the court may commit the individual to custody. In the Magistrates' Court, the power to do so will derive from Justices of the Peace Act 1968 s 1(7) or, more rarely, from Magistrates' Courts Act 1980 s 115(3), and the court should state which power it is acting under. In the Crown Court, this is a common law power.
J.14 Before the court exercises a power to commit the individual to custody, the individual should be given the opportunity to see a duty solicitor or another legal representative and be represented in proceedings if the individual so wishes. Public funding should generally be granted to cover representation. In the Crown Court this rests with the Judge, who may grant a Representation Order.
J.15 In the event that the individual does not take the opportunity to seek legal advice, the court shall give the individual a final opportunity to comply with the request and shall explain the consequences of a failure to do so.
Veater v G 1981 3 Cr App R (S) 52 LCJ At first sight there is much to be said for the view that an order to keep the peace or be of good behaviour is like any other order of the court. To suggest that such an order requires consent before it is effective is almost a contradiction in terms. However, the authorities convince us the court cannot treat him as bound when he has not bound himself. Where there is a refusal the court's only remedy is to put him in prison until he does.
R v South Molton JJs ex parte Ankerson 1990 90 Cr App R 158 Consent must be obtained from the defendant himself, not his representatives.
R v Lincoln Crown Court ex parte Jude 1998 1 Cr App R 130 D was charged with affray and the prosecution offered him a bind over. The Judge said he was satisfied there was evidence in the papers to do so and said he was proposing to bind D over. He invited defence counsel to make submissions and she appeared to have spoken to D and then made no submissions. The Judge then bound D over. D appealed on a number of grounds including that the order was made without consent. Until the *R v South Molton JJs ex parte Ankerson* 1990 90 Cr App R 158 case the courts appear to have confined the role of consent to that of relieving the court of the obligation to hear and determine the information or complaint before it and/or of its obligation to provide the person concerned with an opportunity to make representations. However, in *ex parte Ankerson* this Court held, seemingly as a generality, that consent is one of several cumulative prerequisites of a binding over. Neither the 1361 Act nor the 1968 Act says anything about consent. It is difficult to identify any logical basis for effectively removing the courts' 1361 Act power to 'require' persons to keep the peace in an otherwise appropriate case by making its exercise conditional on the person concerned's consent. It is equally difficult to see any sensible basis for combining such a condition with the undoubted

obligation in circumstances I have mentioned to provide him with an opportunity to make representations against an order. If his consent were required, there would be no point in providing him with that opportunity.

Given the clear evidence before the Divisional Court and its finding that the consent was given under duress, it does not seem to me to have mattered that each of the defendants, if asked, would have said the same. However, the more important point is that the need for consent appears to have been assumed in the way the matter was presented to the Court, the real issue being whether it was true consent. If the Court in that case had been referred to *R v Woking JJs ex parte Gossage* 1973 2 AER 621 and had had to consider the issue of consent in the sharper focus that it has in this case, not as one of a number of well-founded complaints any one of which was capable of invalidating the order, the Court would not have expressed themselves in such general terms. First, they would have acknowledged that the case before them was an untypical bind over of defendants and that normally the law does not require defendants to give consent or to be warned, and, second, they would have spoken of consent and warning disjunctively rather than conjunctively as requirements for an order in such a case and generally for complainants and witnesses. At all events, for the reasons I have given, that is how I consider the law to be and respectfully disagree with the judgments in *ex parte Ankerson* 1990 to the extent that they suggest the contrary.

Note: The Court implied, but did not state, that consent was not necessary. Ed.

10.42 *Statutory power to commit to custody*

Magistrates' Courts Act 1980 s 115(3) If any person ordered by a Magistrates' Court under subsection (1) (see **10.3**) to enter into a recognisance, with or without sureties, to keep the peace or to be of good behaviour fails to comply with the order, the court may commit him to custody for a period not exceeding 6 months or until he sooner complies with the order.

10.43 *European Convention on Human Rights art 5*

Steel v UK 1999 28 EHRR 603 The first two applicants were both convicted in separate trials of breach of the peace. S was arrested for trying to disrupt a shoot. L was arrested for trying to disrupt motorway building. S was ordered to agree to be bound over and refused. She was committed to prison for 28 days. L similarly refused and was committed to prison for 7 days. The applicants contended that their article 5 rights (right to liberty and security) had been violated. Held. The detention was lawful under English law and, since the applicants could have avoided it by agreeing to be bound over, it was not arbitrary. In the Court's view, both applicants were, therefore, detained for non-compliance with the order of a court, as is permitted by article 5(1)(b), so the detention was permitted by article 5.

10.44 *Legal aid is appropriate*

Criminal Practice Directions 2015 EWCA Crim 1567 para VII J.14 Before the court exercises a power to commit the individual to custody, the individual should be given the opportunity to see a duty solicitor or another legal representative and be represented in proceedings if the individual so wishes. Public funding should generally be granted to cover representation. In the Crown Court this rests with the Judge, who may grant a Representation Order.

J.15 In the event that the individual does not take the opportunity to seek legal advice, the court shall give the individual a final opportunity to comply with the request and shall explain the consequences of a failure to do so.

10.45 *Individual aged under 21 Refusal to consent*

Powers of Criminal Courts (Sentencing) Act 2000 s 60(1)(b) Where a court would have power, but for section 89 below (restrictions on imprisonment of young offenders and defaulters), to commit a person aged under 21 to prison for failing to do or abstain from doing anything required to be done or left undone, the court may, if it has been notified by the Secretary of State that an attendance centre is available for the reception of persons of his description, order him to attend at such a centre, to be specified in the order, for such number of hours as may be so specified.

Powers of Criminal Courts (Sentencing) Act 2000 s 89(1) Subject to subsection (2) below, no court shall:

(a) pass a sentence of imprisonment on a person for an offence if he is aged under 21 when convicted of the offence, or

(b) commit a person aged under 21 to prison for any reason.

(2) Nothing in subsection (1) above shall prevent the committal to prison of a person aged under 21 who is:

(a) remanded in custody,

(b) committed in custody for trial or sentence, or

(c) sent in custody for trial under Crime and Disorder Act 1998 s 51 or 51A.

Veater v G 1981 3 Cr App R (S) 52 LCJ Six youths aged 14-15 were arrested after reports of disorderly behaviour. At some stage all six had been armed with sticks. In interview, it was admitted that their intention was to assault pupils at a nearby school. The facts were admitted and the Magistrates bound them over in their own recognisance of £100 to keep the peace for one year. Each defendant refused to acknowledge himself bound. They took the view that they could not, in law, impose a binding over order unilaterally. Each defendant was released, as the Magistrates felt they had no power to secure compliance with the order. Held. Even if one assumes that the power of magistrates to bind over under the Justices of the Peace Act 1361 is part of their civil, and not their criminal jurisdiction, we would still hold that the prohibition on imprisonment of persons under 17 years of age applies. There is nothing…which suggests that justices have any power to impose an obligation to be bound, except indirectly by threatening imprisonment.

Note: I interpret this as meaning that the court may not detain those aged under 18, but it may order an Attendance Centre Order, see **6.2**. Ed.

For the position generally, see **10.41**.

10.46 *Individual aged 18-20 Refusal to consent*

Powers of Criminal Courts (Sentencing) Act 2000 s 108 In any case where, but for section 89(1) (the restriction on imposing imprisonment for persons under 21) above, a court would have power…c) to commit such a person to prison for contempt of court or any kindred offence.

Howley v Oxford 1985 81 Cr App R 246 A complaint was made against D, aged 19, that he did conduct himself so a breach of the peace was occasioned. The Magistrates found the complaint proved and ordered him to be bound over. D refused to consent to the bind over. Held. A failure to obey an order to enter into a recognisance cannot be dealt with as a contempt of court. To enter into a recognisance is a 'kindred offence' in Criminal Justice Act 1982 s 9(1) (now Powers of Criminal Courts (Sentencing) Act 2000 s 108). Justices were right to commit D…to custody.

Chief Constable of Surrey v Ridley and Steel 1985 Crim LR 725 Two respondents, aged over 17 but under 21, were ordered to be bound over to keep the peace. They refused. The Magistrates, who had not been referred to *Howley v Oxford*, concluded that as a result there was no sanction available to them. The prosecutor appealed, submitting that their refusal constituted a contempt of court punishable by detention. Held. Precisely the same issue had arisen in *Howley v Oxford* and there was no good reason for departing from the reasoning of the Court in that case. What had taken place was a 'kindred offence' to contempt and the Magistrates had been wrong to send the respondents away unpunished. It was inappropriate to consider whether what had happened constituted contempt.

Note: I take it the order was to commit the offender to detention in a Young Offender Institution, though it is not clear. Ed.

Parents and guardians

10.47 ***Parents and guardians Power to bind over***

Availability The order is available when the offender is aged 10-17 and not otherwise, see **10.48**.

Must state reasons There is a duty to state reasons if the order is not made, Powers of Criminal Courts (Sentencing) Act 2000 s 150(1)(b), see **10.47** and Criminal Procedure Rules 2015 2015/1490 Rule 31.2(3)(b).

10.48 ***Parents and guardians Power to order***

Binding over parent or guardian

Powers of Criminal Courts (Sentencing) Act 2000 s 150(1) Where [any person aged under 18] is convicted of an offence, the powers conferred by this section (binding over parents and guardians) shall be exercisable by the court by which he is sentenced for that offence, and where the offender is aged under 16 when sentenced it shall be the duty of that court:

(a) to exercise those powers if it is satisfied, having regard to the circumstances of the case, that their exercise would be desirable in the interests of preventing the commission by him of further offences…

(b) if it does not exercise them, to state in open court that it is not satisfied as mentioned in paragraph a), and why it is not so satisfied,

but this subsection has effect subject to section 19(5) of this Act and paragraph 13(5) of Sch 1 to this Act (cases where referral orders made or extended).

For subsections 150(2)-(4) and (6)-(7) see paras **10.50-10.54**.

For subsection 150(5), see **11.13**.

10.49 ***Parents and guardians Court must specify actions which parent etc. is to take***

Criminal Practice Directions 2015 EWCA Crim 1567 para VII J.19 Where a court is considering binding over a parent or guardian under Powers of Criminal Courts (Sentencing) Act 2000 s 150 to enter into a recognisance to take proper care of and exercise proper control over a child or young person, the court should specify the actions which the parent or guardian is to take.

10.50 ***Parents and guardians Maximum recognisance is £1,000***

Powers of Criminal Courts (Sentencing) Act 2000 s 150(3) An order under this section shall not require the parent or guardian to enter into a recognisance for an amount exceeding £1,000.

10.51 ***Parents and guardians Means Must consider parents'/guardians' means***

Powers of Criminal Courts (Sentencing) Act 2000 s 150(7) The court shall take into account among other things the means of the parent or guardian so far as they appear or are known to the court, and this subsection applies whether taking into account the means of the parent or guardian has the effect of increasing or reducing the amount of the recognisance.

10.52 ***Parents and guardians Maximum length of recognisance***

Powers of Criminal Courts (Sentencing) Act 2000 s 150(4) An order under this section shall not require the parent or guardian to enter into a recognisance:

(a) for a period exceeding three years, and

(b) for a period extending beyond the offender's 18th birthday.

10.53 ***Parents and guardians Duties of parent etc.***

Powers of Criminal Courts (Sentencing) Act 2000 s 150(2) The powers conferred by this section are as follows:

(a) with the consent of the offender's parent or guardian, to order the parent or guardian to enter into a recognisance to take proper care of him and exercise proper control over him, and where the court has passed on the offender a sentence which consists of or includes a Youth Rehabilitation Order, it may include in the recognisance a provision that the offender's parent or guardian ensure that the offender complies with the requirements of that sentence.

Powers of Criminal Courts (Sentencing) Act 2000 s 150(11) For the purposes of this section, taking 'care' of a person includes giving him protection and guidance and 'control' includes discipline.

10.54 ***Parents and guardians*** ***Power to fine where parent etc. refuses to be bound over***

Powers of Criminal Courts (Sentencing) Act 2000 s 150(2) The powers conferred by this section are as follows:

(b) if the parent or guardian refuses consent and the court considers the refusal unreasonable, to order the parent or guardian to pay a fine not exceeding £1,000,

and where the court has passed on the offender a sentence which consists of or includes a Youth Rehabilitation Order, it may include in the recognisance a provision that the offender's parent or guardian ensure that the offender complies with the requirements of that sentence.

Powers of Criminal Courts (Sentencing) Act 2000 s 150(6) A fine imposed under subsection (2)(b) above shall be deemed, for the purposes of any enactment, to be a sum adjudged to be paid by a conviction.

10.55 ***Parents and guardians*** ***Sentencing Children and Young People Guideline 2017***

Sentencing Children and Young People Guideline 2017 www.banksr.com Other Matters Guidelines tab In force 1 June 2017

Section three: Parental responsibilities

3.1 For any child or young person aged under 16 appearing before [the] court there is a statutory requirement that parents/guardians attend during all stages of proceedings, unless the court is satisfied that this would be unreasonable having regard to the circumstances of the case.[104] The court may also enforce this requirement for a young person aged 16 and above if it deems it desirable to do so.

3.2 Although this requirement can cause a delay in the case before the court it is important it is adhered to. If a court does find exception to proceed in the absence of a responsible adult then extra care must be taken to ensure the outcomes are clearly communicated to and understood by the child or young person.

3.3 In addition to this responsibility there are also orders that can be imposed on parents. If the child or young person is aged under 16 then the court has a duty to make a parental bind over or impose a parenting order, if it would be desirable in the interest of preventing the commission of further offences.[105] There is a discretionary power to make these orders where the young person is aged 16 or 17. If the court chooses not to impose a parental bind over or parenting order it must state its reasons for not doing so in open court. In most circumstances a parenting order is likely to be more appropriate than a parental bind over.

3.4 A court cannot make a bind over alongside a referral order. If the court makes a referral order the duty on the court to impose a parenting order in respect of a child or young person under 16 years old is replaced by a discretion.[106]

Combined with other orders

10.56 ***Referral Orders, Combined with***

Powers of Criminal Courts (Sentencing) Act 2000 s 19(1) and (5) Where the court makes a Referral Order, the court may not make an order binding him over to keep the peace or to be of good behaviour.

[104] Children and Young Persons Act 1933 s 34A

[105] Powers of Criminal Courts (Sentencing) Act 2000 s 150 and Crime and Disorder Act 1998 s 8

[106] Crime and Disorder Act 1998 s 9(1A)

10.57 ***Parents and guardians Hospital Orders and Guardianship Orders***
Mental Health Act 1983 s 37(8) Where an order is made under this section (Hospital and Guardianship Orders), the court shall not…make in respect of the offender an order under Powers of Criminal Courts (Sentencing) Act 2000 s 150 (binding over of parent or guardian).

10.58 ***Parents and guardians Referral Orders, Combined with***
Powers of Criminal Courts (Sentencing) Act 2000 s 19(1) and (5)(b) Where the court makes a Referral Order, the court may not make an order binding over the parent or the guardian, under section 150 of this Act.

Other matters

10.59 ***Should the order be entered on the CRO/antecedents?***
Rehabilitation of Offenders Act 1974 s 7(5) No order made by a court with respect to any person otherwise than on a conviction shall be included in any list or statement of that person's previous convictions given or made to any court which is considering how to deal with him in respect of any offence.
Criminal Practice Directions 2015 EWCA Crim 1567 para VII J.16 Courts are reminded of the provisions of Rehabilitation of Offenders Act 1974 s 7(5) which excludes from a person's antecedents any order of the court 'with respect to any person otherwise than on a conviction'.
Note: Presumably when a bind over is made after a conviction, it should be entered following *R v Abrahams* 1952 36 Cr App R 147. Ed.

APPEALS

10.60 ***Appeals Magistrates Court to the Crown Court***
Senior Courts Act 1981 s 29(3)[107] In relation to the jurisdiction of the Crown Court, other than its jurisdiction in matters relating to trial on indictment, the High Court shall have all such jurisdiction to make mandatory, prohibiting or quashing orders as the High Court possesses in relation to the jurisdiction of an inferior court.
R v Inner London Crown Court ex parte Benjamin 1987 85 Cr App R 267 D was acquitted and would not consent to being bound over. He was committed to prison for 7 days or until he agreed to be bound over in the sum of £50 to keep the peace. Held. We have jurisdiction to hear the appeal. It did not relate to trial on indictment.

10.61 ***Appeals Magistrates Court to the Divisional Court***
Emohare v Thames Magistrates' Court 2009 EWHC 689 (Admin) Whilst Magistrates' Courts (Appeals from Binding Over Orders) Act 1956 s 1 provides an ability to appeal to the Crown Court, it does not, of course, preclude an appeal by way of case stated instead.

10.62 ***Appeals Crown Court to the Court of Appeal***
R v Randall 1986 8 Cr App R (S) 433 D, a teacher, was convicted of numerous offences against boys. D was committed for sentence for another indecent assault and the Court made a probation order. D placed an advertisement for tutoring children aged under 18. It was alleged that D had breached the probation order but the prosecution later conceded he had not. The Crown Court Judge dealing with it bound him over with a condition not to teach or seek to teach anyone aged under 18. He breached the order and £250 was estreated and D was bound over again. He appealed contending there was no power to add conditions. Held. The appeal is barred by Criminal Appeal Act 1968 s 10. We therefore reconstitute ourselves as the Divisional Court and dispense with service. There was an error of law and we quash the bind overs and the order estreating £250.

10.63 ***Appeals Crown Court to the Court of Appeal Conviction quashed Bind over substituted***
R v Sharp 1957 41 Cr App R 86 LCJ Court of Appeal quashed the defendants' convictions and as justices of the peace the Court imposed bind overs.

[107] Previously Supreme Court Act 1981 s 29(3)

R v Biffen 1966 Crim LR 111 LCJ The Court quashed the conviction and used its powers as justices of the peace to bind the defendant over.

10.64 ***Appeals Crown Court to the Divisional Court***
R v Liverpool JJs ex parte Collins 1998 2 Cr App R 108[108] LCJ A person made the subject of a bind over may make an application for judicial review.

10.65 ***Procedure for a Crown Court appeal***
Shaw v Hamilton 1982 4 Cr App R (S) 80 D was acquitted of using threatening words and behaviour whereby a breach of the peace was likely to be occasioned. He was bound over and appealed. The Crown Court held that the hearing was analogous to a sentencing hearing and therefore that procedure should be followed. The prosecution should open the evidence from a note taken by the clerk. Held. The Judge fell into the error of trying to equate an appeal against a binding over with either an appeal against conviction or an appeal against sentence. It is, in truth, sui generis (unique). In order to justify making the binding over order in the first instance the Magistrates had to satisfy themselves on admissible material before them that unless steps were taken to prevent it there might be a breach of the peace in the future. A binding over order is a preventive order, but it has to be justified by existing evidence. It should be a rehearing with the same or perhaps improved evidence. The court can hear the evidence and it can be cross-examined.

10.66 ***Parents and guardians Appeals from the Magistrates' Court***
Powers of Criminal Courts (Sentencing) Act 2000 s 150(8) A parent or guardian may appeal to the Crown Court against an order under this section made by a Magistrates' Court.

10.67 ***Parents and guardians Appeals from the Crown Court***
Powers of Criminal Courts (Sentencing) Act 2000 s 150(9) A parent or guardian may appeal to the Court of Appeal against an order under this section made by the Crown Court, as if he had been convicted on indictment and the order were a sentence passed on his conviction.

Power to vary or revoke

10.68 ***Parents and guardians Power to vary or revoke an order on an application by a parent or guardian***
Powers of Criminal Courts (Sentencing) Act 2000 s 150(10) A court may vary or revoke an order made by it under this section if, on the application of the parent or guardian, it appears to the court, having regard to any change in the circumstances since the order was made, to be in the interests of justice to do so.

11 Binding Over to Keep the Peace: Breach

11.1

11.2 ***Statutory power to forfeit etc.***
Magistrates' Courts Act 1980 s 116(2) The Magistrates' Court before which the principal appears or is brought in pursuance of such a summons or warrant as aforesaid may, unless it adjudges the recognisance to be forfeited, order the recognisance to be discharged and order the principal to enter into a new recognisance, with or without sureties, to keep the peace or to be of good behaviour.
Magistrates' Courts Act 1980 s 120(1) This section applies where a recognisance to keep the peace or to be of good behaviour has been entered into before a Magistrates' Court, or
(2) If the recognisance appears to the Magistrates' Court to be forfeited, the court may:
 (a) declare the recognisance to be forfeited, and
 (b) adjudge each person bound by it, whether as principal or surety, to pay the sum in which he is bound,

[108] Also known as *CPS v Speede* 1998 2 Cr App R 108 and *DPP v Speede* 1998 2 Cr App R 108

but in a case falling within subsection (1)(a) above, the court shall not declare the recognisance to be forfeited except by order made on complaint.

Magistrates' Courts Act 1980 s 120(5) A recognisance such as is mentioned in this section shall not be enforced otherwise than in accordance with this section, and accordingly shall not be transmitted to the Crown Court nor shall its forfeiture be certified to that Court.

11.3 *Procedure General*

Magistrates' Courts Act 1980 s 116(1) On complaint being made to a justice of the peace by a surety to a recognisance to keep the peace or to be of good behaviour entered into before a Magistrates' Court that the person bound by the recognisance as principal has been, or is about to be, guilty of conduct constituting a breach of the conditions of the recognisance, the justice may issue a warrant to arrest the principal and bring him before a Magistrates' Court or a summons requiring the principal to appear before such a court, but the justice shall not issue a warrant unless the complaint is in writing and substantiated on oath.

Criminal Practice Directions 2015 EWCA Crim 1567 para VII J.7 Where there is an allegation of breach of a binding over order and this is contested, the court should hear representations and evidence, including oral evidence, from the parties before making a finding. If unrepresented and no opportunity has been given previously, the court should give a reasonable period for the person said to have breached the binding over order to find representation.

11.4 *Procedure Admitting a breach of the peace*

Jackson v Lilley 1982 146 JP 133 D was charged with a public order offence, fined and bound over for one year. He was subsequently charged within that year with assault occasioning ABH. He consented to being bound over. The Magistrates took the view that D's consent to being bound over amounted to proof of a breach of the peace and estreated the recognisance. Held. The most that was involved in agreeing to be bound over was that the Magistrates were justified in fearing that a breach of the peace might take place in future. The mere admission of conduct which justified the making of a bind over was not in itself an admission of a breach of the peace. If the Magistrates were minded to forfeit a recognisance, it was desirable to ask: a) "Do you admit that you entered into a recognisance?" and b) "Do you admit a breach of the peace?" before they proceeded.

11.5 *The breach must be strictly proved*

R v McGarry 1945 30 Cr App R 187 D was bound over under probation for two years. It was alleged he had broken the bind over and a probation officer said in her opinion D had not reported regularly. His probation officer was absent through illness. He was sentenced to 12 months' imprisonment. However, it was not clear whether the order had been reduced to writing, or merely dealt with orally, both being permissible. Held. The sentence of 12 months' imprisonment was bad from the start, because the Court had no material at all on which to form the opinion that he had broken any term of the recognisance which was not before the Court. The breach should be proved just as if the allegation were that D had committed a crime.

11.6 *The proceedings are civil proceedings*

R v Marlow JJs ex parte Sullivan 1983 5 Cr App R (S) 279 The only liability of the applicant if the breach of the recognisance was proved, was the forfeiture of his recognisance. The proceedings which put in issue that liability are, for two reasons, to be regarded as civil, not criminal, proceedings, to which the civil, not criminal, standard of proof applies. The first of those two reasons is that, in our view, proceedings for the forfeiture or estreatment of a recognisance are to be regarded as civil, not criminal, proceedings (see *R v Southampton JJs ex parte Green* 1976 QB 11). Our second reason goes not to the substance of those proceedings, as does our first reason, but to their form. As we understand it, although the words 'complaint and information' are often used interchangeably, as if they were synonymous, a complaint is ordinarily the form which originates a criminal process, so that proceedings begun by complaint are, prima facie, civil not criminal proceedings.

11.7 *Burden and standard of proof*
Criminal Practice Directions 2015 EWCA Crim 1567 para VII J.9 Where there is an allegation of breach of a binding over order, the court should be satisfied on the balance of probabilities that the defendant is in breach before making any order for forfeiture of a recognisance. The burden of proof shall rest on the prosecution.

11.8 *CRO should have details of the order breached*
Criminal Practice Directions 2015 EWCA Crim 1567 para II 8A.7 Where the current alleged offence could constitute a breach of an existing sentence such as a suspended sentence, community order or conditional discharge, and it is known that that sentence is still in force then details of the circumstances of the offence leading to the sentence should be included in the antecedents. The detail should be brief and include the date of the offence.

11.9 *A breach is not an offence*
R v Liverpool JJs ex parte Collins 1998 2 Cr App R 108[109] LCJ A breach of the peace under Justices of the Peace Act 1361 or Magistrates' Courts Act 1980 s 115 is not an offence and does not necessarily involve the proof of an offence.

11.10 *Power to order a reduced sum*
Magistrates' Courts Act 1980 s 120(3) The court which declares the recognisance to be forfeited may, instead of adjudging any person to pay the whole sum in which he is bound, adjudge him to pay part only of the sum or remit the sum.

11.11 *Enforcement*
Magistrates' Courts Act 1980 s 120(4) Payment of any sum adjudged to be paid under this section, including any costs awarded against the defendant, may be enforced, and any such sum shall be applied, as if it were a fine and as if the adjudication were a summary conviction of an offence not punishable with imprisonment and so much of section 85(1) as empowers a court to remit fines shall not apply to the sum but so much thereof as relates to remission after a term of imprisonment has been imposed shall so apply, but at any time before the issue of a warrant of commitment to enforce payment of the sum, or before the sale of goods under a warrant of distress to satisfy the sum, the court may remit the whole or any part of the sum either absolutely or on such conditions as the court thinks just.

11.12 *Costs out of central funds*
Costs in Criminal Cases (General) Regulations 1986 1986/1335 reg 14 Prosecution of Offences Act 1985 s 16 (defence costs out of central funds) shall apply to proceedings in a Magistrates' Court or the Crown Court in which it is alleged that an offender required to enter into a recognisance to keep the peace or be of good behaviour has failed to comply with a condition of that recognisance, as if that failure were an indictable offence.

Practice Direction (Costs in Criminal Proceedings) 2015 EWCA Crim 1568 para 2.1.1 An order [for costs out of central funds] may be made in relation to breach of bind-over proceedings in a Magistrates' Court or the Crown Court.

Parents and guardians

11.13 *Parents and guardians Power to bind over Breach*
Powers of Criminal Courts (Sentencing) Act 2000 s 150(5) Magistrates' Courts Act 1980 s 120 (forfeiture of recognisances) shall apply in relation to a recognisance entered into in pursuance of an order [binding over parents and guardians] under this section as it applies in relation to a recognisance to keep the peace.

[109] Also known as *CPS v Speede* 1998 2 Cr App R 108 and *DPP v Speede* 1998 2 Cr App R 108

12 Change in Sentencing Law

12.1

The rules for dealing with children when they cross an age threshold are complex. For details see the back index under **Children and young offenders** Age.

For the rules on whether to apply a guideline, see the **Guidelines** ***Guidelines issued but not in force/No retrospective application*** para at **64.17**.

See also the **Defendant** ***Historical cases*** paras and the **Sex Offences: Historical** chapter.

12.2 *Presumption against retrospective operation of legislation*

Att-Gen's Ref No 48 of 1994 1995 16 Cr App R (S) 980 LCJ The Court considered a case where the structure of the offence changed along with the maximum sentences. Held. Unless the contrary intention appears, an enactment is presumed not to be intended to have retrospective operation.

Wadstead v Barretto 1994 99 Cr App R 105[110] Master of the Rolls D pleaded to conspiracy to supply cocaine and was subject to a confiscation order. The Judge assessed the amount to be recovered to be £287,603, with a 3-year prison term in default. A receiver was subsequently appointed when part of the sum failed to be paid. New assets were discovered. Between the making of the confiscation order and the appointment of the receiver, Parliament enacted Criminal Justice (International Co-operation) Act 1990, of which section 14 made it an offence to conceal property which represented the proceeds of drug trafficking. Section 15 allowed for interest to be charged on a sum not paid when it was required to be paid, and section 16 allowed the prosecutor or the receiver to make an application for a certificate stating that the realisable amount is greater than the amount taken into consideration when making the confiscation order. The receiver wanted to use these powers. It was argued that the presumption against the retroactive application of statutes did not apply for a number of reasons including: a) it was a procedural step towards liquidating the assets, b) it was not a penal proceeding but simply a procedure to ensure traffickers are stripped of their ill-gotten gains, and c) punishment was not involved. Held. Whether or not such an order is part of the sentence (and it appears not to be for some purposes), it is an unpleasant legal consequence which follows conviction. That brings the presumption into play. A defendant is not to be substantially prejudiced by laws construed as having retroactive effect unless Parliament's intention that they should have that effect is plain. The blackest malefactor is as much entitled to the benefit of the presumption as anyone else.

R v Doherty 2016 UKSC 62, 2017 1 Cr App R (S) 31 (p 234) Supreme Court D was convicted before IPP was abolished and sentenced after. He was sentenced to IPP after the commencement order had been applied. Held. para 17 The general rule of English law, not confined to the criminal law, is that a statute is prospective rather than retrospective in effect unless it distinctly says otherwise, see for example the discussion in a very different context in *Wilson v First County Trust Ltd (No 2)* 2003 UKHL 40 at paras 19, 98, 152 and 186. The presumption against retrospective operation applies equally to repeals, see Interpretation Act 1978 s 16.

12.3 *Commencement of new sentencing orders, Deciding the*

Note: It is important, when considering when new sentencing orders apply, to look at the new piece of legislation, the commencement order if any, and any transitional provisions. New legislation invariably has these written instructions. Ed.

European Convention on Human Rights art 7(1) Nor shall a heavier penalty be imposed than the one that was applicable at the time the criminal offence was committed.

Welch v United Kingdom 1995 20 EHRR 247 European Court D was convicted of cocaine and cannabis importation and other charges. He was imprisoned and made the subject of a confiscation order. Between the commission of the offences and the trial,

[110] Also known as *Re Barretto* 1994 99 Cr App R 105

Drug Trafficking Offences Act 1986 came into force, which the Judge used to make the confiscation order. D claimed that the confiscation order constituted a criminal penalty and therefore breached European Convention on Human Rights art 7(1), being a heavier penalty than was available at the time of the commission of the offence. The Commission held (7 votes to 7, decided on the casting vote of the President) that there had not been a breach of article 7(1). D appealed. Held. The sweeping statutory assumptions in Drug Trafficking Offences Act 1986 s 2(3) that all property passing through the offender's hands over a six-year period is the fruit of drug trafficking unless he can prove otherwise, the fact that the confiscation order is directed to the proceeds involved in drug dealing and is not limited to actual enrichment or profit, the discretion of the trial Judge, in fixing the amount of the order, to take into consideration the degree of culpability of the accused, and the possibility of imprisonment in default of payment by the offender, are all elements which...provide a strong indication of, *inter alia*, a regime of punishment. Taking into consideration the combination of punitive elements outlined above, the confiscation order amounted to a penalty. Accordingly, there had been a breach of article 7(1).

R v Docherty 2014 EWCA Crim 1197, 2 Cr App R (S) 76 (p 601) D pleaded to wounding with intent when IPP was in force. He was sentenced to IPP after the law had been repealed. This applied the relevant commencement order, which made the conviction the determining date. The defence argued that articles 5 and 14 and the international norm of *lex mitior* (if the law relevant to the offence of the accused has been amended, the less severe law should be applied) meant the Judge should have imposed a 2003 extended sentence. The defence also said that it was arbitrary, as if he had pleaded not guilty he would not have been liable to IPP. Held. IPP was clearly suited to this case. Reliance on article 14 failed because a prisoner did not amount to 'other status' in the article, *R (Clift) v Secretary of State for Home Dept* 2006 UKHL 64. The method of introducing the legislation was legitimate. If *lex mitior* applied in the UK, it did not apply here as both before and after the date of legislative change a life sentence was available and it was a real possibility that D would have received a life sentence. The sentence was lawful.

R v Doherty 2016 UKSC 62, 2017 1 Cr App R (S) 31 (p 234) Supreme Court D was convicted before IPP was abolished and sentenced after. He was sentenced to IPP after the commencement order had been applied. The Court considered the defendant's appeal in *R v Docherty* 2014, above. Held. The Court reviewed the principles and the European law. para 64 The several challenges to the sentence fail.

12.4 *Considering enacted law which is not in force*

R v Barry 1983 5 Cr App R (S) 11 LCJ The defendants pleaded to conspiracy to forge banknotes. The conspiracy ended in about April 1981. After the offence, in October 1981, the penalty was reduced from life to 10 years. The Judge, in March 1982, felt he was bound by the new Act. Held. He was correct although the change was not in force at the time.

R v Saunders and Others 2013 EWCA Crim 1027, 2014 1 Cr App R (S) 45 (p 258) LCJ The Court considered the Legal Aid, Sentencing and Punishment of Offenders Act 2012 changes to indeterminate sentences which were not in force when the defendants were sentenced. Held. In the absence of express statutory language, whether the new regime will be more or less draconian than the regime which is being replaced, the sentencing court is not entitled to anticipate new sentencing provisions before they actually come into force, see *Att-Gen's Ref No 55 of 2008* 2008 EWCA Crim 2790, 2009 2 Cr App R (S) 22 (p 142) and *R v I* 2012 EWCA Crim 1792.

12.5 *Maximum sentence increased*

R v Penwith JJs ex parte Casey 1979 1 Cr App R (S) 265 LCJ D and others were convicted of illegal fishing, contrary to a bye-law. Between the commission of the offence and their sentencing hearing, the maximum sentence was increased from a fine

of £50 for a first offence to £1,000. D was fined £250. Held. Legislation which increases penalties is not to be applied to offences committed before the change in the law unless the intention of the statute is clear. Order quashed and case sent back to the Magistrates.
R v Doherty 2016 UKSC 62, 2017 1 Cr App R (S) 31 (p 234) Supreme Court D was convicted before IPP was abolished and sentenced after. He was sentenced to IPP after the commencement order had been applied. Held. para 44 a). If the maximum sentence has been increased by statute since the offence was committed, the English court cannot sentence beyond the maximum which applied at the time of the offence, because that is the sentence to which the defendant was at that time exposed ([the principle being] *lex gravior*).
See also: *R v Dharma* 1905 16 Cr App R 109, 2 KB 335 (LCJ A statute ought not be construed so as to create new obligations in respect of transactions which were complete at the time the Act came into force.)
See also the ***Presumption against retrospective operation of legislation*** para at **12.5**.

12.6 *Maximum sentence reduced*
R v Barry 1983 5 Cr App R (S) 11 LCJ The defendants pleaded to conspiracy to forge banknotes. The conspiracy ended in about April 1981. After the offence, in October 1981, the penalty was reduced from life to 10 years. The Judge, in March 1982, felt he was bound by the new Act. Held. He was correct although the change was not in force at the time.
R v Shaw 1996 2 Cr App R (S) 278 D, a solicitor, stole £3m of clients' money, of which £1m was used for his own means. During the period between the commission of the offence and D's plea of guilty, the maximum sentence was reduced from 10 to 7 years' imprisonment. One offence was committed prior to the reduction. Held. The relevant date is the date of conviction, not sentence or the date of the offence. Therefore, where the sentence is reduced between the date of the offence and date of sentence, it is the reduced maximum which should normally apply.
R v Doherty 2016 UKSC 62, 2017 1 Cr App R (S) 31 (p 234) D was convicted before IPP was abolished and sentenced after. He was sentenced to IPP after the commencement order had been applied. Held. para 44 b) If the maximum sentence has been reduced by statute since the offence was committed, the English court will sentence within the now current maximum. In *R v Shaw* 1996, see above, the statute reducing the maximum sentence (for theft) was held as a matter of construction to apply to past as well as to future offences.
See also: *Att-Gen's Ref No 121 of 2015* 2016 EWCA Crim 173 (para 27 [In historic cases] where the maximum sentence has been reduced, the lower maximum will be applicable.)
R v Anderson 1989 Unreported 27/2/89 (After the offence the maximum disqualification period was reduced to 6 months. Held. As Parliament had indicated that it regarded 6 months as the appropriate maximum it was right to reduce the disqualification from 9 months to 6.)
R v Robertson 1990 Unreported 12/2/90 (*R v Anderson* 1989 applied.)

12.7 *Dates of the offence straddle the date the penalty was increased*
R v S 1992 13 Cr App R (S) 306 D was convicted of indecent assault of girls under the age of 13. The allegations spanned pre-1984 to 1989, with no individual dates specified. During this period, Parliament had enacted Sexual Offences Act 1985 s 3(3), which increased the maximum sentence for the offence to 10 years (from 5 years in the case of a girl aged under 13, otherwise 2 years). The Judge passed a sentence of 5 years' imprisonment in total. Held. Where the particulars of the indictment embrace a period both before and after the operative date, and where in particular the nature of the evidence before the court is such that it is impossible to identify with certainty whether the act in question was indeed perpetrated before or after that date, then the judge is obliged to conclude that his powers are limited to those in force prior to that date.

R v B 1993 14 Cr App R (S) 774 LCJ D pleaded to indecent assault on a female (3 years' imprisonment). His daughter, V, made complaints that D had indecently assaulted her between January 1984 and May 1992. In 1985, the maximum sentence for indecent assault on a female was increased from 2 years to 10 years. It was argued that the sentence was unlawful. Held. If the date of the offence could not otherwise be pinpointed, it might have occurred between January 1984 and September 1985, during a period when the old law left the maximum sentence at 2 years. However, as the whole case was conducted on the common ground that offences against V only began after her seventh birthday, which was in October 1986…it is quite clear that throughout the period of the offending Sexual Offences Act 1985 was in force and accordingly punishment for an offence committed in that period was under the new scale imposed by Parliament. The Judge's power was to sentence for up to 10 years.
R v Cairns 1998 1 Cr App R (S) 434 D pleaded to three counts of indecent assault on a girl under the age of 16, relating to L, M and T. He received 7 years concurrent on each count. The indictment specified three periods of time: a) May 1986 to May 1987, b) 1 January 1985 to 31 December 1987 and c) 1 December 1985 to 31 December 1986 in relation to T, L and M respectively. These periods straddled the date of the increase in the maximum sentence for the offence from 2 years to 10 years. Counsel explained that D had pleaded on the basis that the offences had begun in autumn 1985, after the increase in the maximum sentence. Held. No count should ever charge an offence committed during a period running through an increase in the maximum sentence for an offence. If offences were committed on both sides of the relevant date, the better course would be to prefer two specimen counts, one covering a period ending the 'old' sentencing regime and the other covering a period beginning on the day when the new legislation is operative. This will prevent any uncertainty about the sentencing powers of the court. It should also assist the sentencing judge because it will concentrate his mind on the precise age of the victim at the time the offence was committed if the sentencing process has to take this into account.
R v Hobbs 2002 EWCA Crim 387, 2 Cr App R (S) 93 (p 425) The defendants were convicted of conspiracy to facilitate the illegal entry of immigrants into the UK. During the dates particularised the maximum sentence was raised from 7 to 10 years. The Judge sentenced two of them to 9 and 7½ years. Held. The better course is to prefer distinct counts for the period before and after the date the maximum changed. Defendants should not be affected adversely, with respect to powers of sentence, by changes in the law occurring during the currency of a conspiracy entered into before the changes. A strict, narrow and certain view as to when the offence is complete should be applied and not a more extensive and flexible construction. Conspiracy is complete when the agreement is made. The Judge was restricted to the old maximum.
R v Harries and Others 2007 EWCA Crim 1622, 2008 1 Cr App R (S) 47 (p 255) D had his appeal joined with five others with a common ground. The dates in the indictment straddled the date IPP came into force. Held. para 4 The starting point must be when an offence is charged between two dates which span an increased penalty, the former maximum sentence should apply, see *R v S* 1992 above. However, where the case has been conducted on the basis the offence in question was in fact committed after the date the increase came into force, the new maximum applies, see *R v B* 1993 above. Logically the same approach should be adopted to every legislative provision.
See also: *R v Johnson* 2014 EWCA Crim 1442 (Child cruelty case. Indictment dates for sample offences, 1982-1998, 1983-1999 and 1984-2000. Maximum increased in 1988. Because of the way the case was left to the jury, old maximum applied.)

12.8 ***New offence is different/Structure of law changes***

Att-Gen's Ref No 48 of 1994 1995 16 Cr App R (S) 980 LCJ D was convicted of buggery, Sexual Offences Act 1956 s 12 (12 months' imprisonment suspended for 18 months). There was no consent. D was a nursing assistant to care for the elderly and mentally infirm and had anal intercourse in a lavatory cubicle with a patient suffering from

Alzheimer's disease. Between the commission of the offence and when D came to be sentenced, Parliament amended the legislation relating to buggery. The effect was to redefine non-consensual buggery as rape (thereby raising the maximum sentence from 10 years to life) and to limit section 12 to consensual buggery, for which the maximum sentence was reduced to 2 years. The trial Judge accepted D's submissions that on the date D was sentenced, the maximum sentence for buggery contrary to section 12 was 2 years. Held. Parliament did not intend for the new provisions to be retrospective nor did they intend to reduce the maximum sentence for non-consensual buggery. Plainly, it was not intended that an act of non-consensual buggery committed prior to the change in legislation should be charged as rape. By Sexual Offences Act 1967 s 3(1)(a) the maximum sentence for non-consensual buggery of 10 years applied. There is accordingly no question of imposing a greater sentence for the offence than was available at the time. Sentence increased to **4 years**.

R v BM 2010 EWCA Crim 1454, 2011 1 Cr App R (S) 34 (p 214) D pleaded to unlawful sexual intercourse under the 1956 Act. The offence occurred between 1984 and 1985. The victim was 12 years old at the time. The Judge felt a starting point after a trial would have been 8 years. He considered D's health, and that the offence would have today been charged as rape of a child under 13. Held. That was an incorrect approach. We observe that the offence of unlawful sexual intercourse in the 1956 Act was a different offence from the offence of rape of a child under 13 within the current Act. Considering the relevant case law, **3 years** not 6.

12.9 *Case law changes*

R v Jawad 2013 EWCA Crim 644, 2014 1 Cr App R (S) 16 (p 85) D argued that his confiscation order was disproportionate in the light of *R v Waya* 2012 UKSC 51, 2013 2 Cr App R (S) 20 (p 87). The Court considered the principles in granting leave out of time. Held. Obiter para 29 We should make clear the general approach of this Court, over many years, to change of law cases. An extension of time will not be granted routinely in such a case simply because the law has changed. It will be granted only if substantial injustice would otherwise be done to the defendant, and the mere fact of change of law does not ordinarily create such injustice. Nor is the case where an extension will be refused limited to one where, if the law had been correctly understood at the time of the proceedings in the Crown Court, a different charge or different procedure might well have left the defendant in a similar position to that in which he now finds himself. The line of authority setting out this Court's approach culminates in *R v Cottrell and Fletcher* 2007 EWCA Crim 2016, 2008 1 Cr App R 7 (p 107). The line of authority includes similar pronouncements in *R v Mitchell* 1977 65 Cr App R 185, *R v Ramsden* 1972 Crim LR 547, *R v Gosney* 1971 55 Cr App R 502 (all conviction cases). The Court [in *R v Cottrell and Fletcher* 2007] observed that alarming consequences would flow from permitting the general reopening of old cases on the ground that a decision of a court of authority had removed a widely held misconception as to the prior state of the law on which the conviction which it was sought to appeal had been based.

12.10 *Defendant sentenced years ago*

R v Graham 1999 2 Cr App R (S) 312 The defendant was convicted of importing 665 kilos of cannabis in 1994. He received 12 years. In 1996 his appeal against conviction and sentence was dismissed. The Court of Appeal issued new guidelines for sentencing in cannabis cases in *R v Ronchetti* 1998 2 Cr App R (S) 100. The defendant's case was referred to the Court of Appeal by the Criminal Cases Review Commission and it was argued that the sentence should be 10 years. Held. The Commission was set up to refer possible miscarriages of justice to the Court of Appeal. It has an unfettered power to refer sentencing cases to the Court of Appeal. A defendant sentenced on the prevailing tariff cannot be described as a victim of a miscarriage of justice. An alteration in the statutory maximum or minimum penalties cannot give rise to a legitimate grievance. Changes do not have retrospective effect.

Defendant sentenced years later For the general principles, see the **Defendant** ***Historical cases*** paras at **242.30** and the **Sex Offences: Historical** chapter, both in Volume 2.

13 Children and Young Offenders: General Principles

13.1
History of criminal proceedings for those aged under 18 For a history see *R v Lewis* 1984 6 Cr App R (S) 44.

The orders and procedures

13.2 ***Availability of sentences and orders***
Note: Most of this table will not apply when the sentence is fixed by law (murder), or where there is a minimum sentence applicable. There are also restrictions on many of these orders, the majority of which are not listed. The fact that the order is listed as available does not imply that making the order would be appropriate. Ed.

Sentence or order	**Age**				
	10-12	**13-15**	**16**	**17**	**18-20**
Absolute discharge Powers of Criminal Courts (Sentencing) Act 2000 s 12	Yes				
Attachment of Earnings Order, Detention for failure to comply with Attachment of Earnings Act 1971 s 23	No				Yes[111]
Attendance Centre Order Fine defaulters, those refusing to be bound over Powers of Criminal Courts (Sentencing) Act 2000 s 60	Yes Aged 16+, maximum is 36 hours Aged 14-16, must be for 12-24 hours[112] Aged 10-13, can be less than 12 hours[113]				
Attendance Centre Order[114] Those guilty of contempt of court Powers of Criminal Courts (Sentencing) Act 2000 s 60	No			Yes[115]	
Automatic life/Automatic custody for life Criminal Justice Act 2003 s 224A(2)	No[116]				Yes[117]

[111] Powers of Criminal Courts (Sentencing) Act 2000 s 108(1)-(2)
[112] Unless the court considers 12 hours would be excessive, Powers of Criminal Courts (Sentencing) Act 2000 s 60
[113] Powers of Criminal Courts (Sentencing) Act 2000 s 60(3)-(4)
[114] For an excellent analysis of the history and complexity of these orders, see *Sentencing News* 24 November 2009 Issue 4 page 7. This article states that the apparent reprieve of the abolition of the power to order an Attendance Centre Order in Criminal Justice and Immigration Act 2008 (Commencement No 13 and Transitory Provisions) Order 2009/3074 para (2)(f) is ineffective. This is because of para (2)(u)(xix) of the same order. This view has been treated by the authorities as correct.
[115] Contempt of Court Act 1981 s 14(2A)
[116] Criminal Justice Act 2003 s 224A(1)(a)
[117] These orders are called automatic custody for life.

Sentence or order	Age				
	10-12	13-15	16	17	18-20
Barring (Automatic) Prohibiting regulated activity with children and vulnerable adults Safeguarding Vulnerable Groups Act 2006 s 3	For defendants who become automatically barred on conviction (who must be aged 18 or over), the court is under a duty to tell them they are barred.[118] For those aged under 18, see the note at **117.1**				
Bind over to keep the peace Justices of the Peace Act 1968 s 1(7)	Yes				
Binding over parent or guardian Powers of Criminal Courts (Sentencing) Act 2000 s 150	Yes				No
Community order Criminal Justice Act 2003 s 177	No		Enacted but there will be no commencement		Yes
Committal for contempt of court	Aged under 17 No[119] Aged 17 an Attendance Centre Order[120]				Yes[121]
Committal in default of payment	Attendance Centre Order[122]				Yes[123]
Compensation order Powers of Criminal Courts (Sentencing) Act 2000 s 130	Yes[124]				
Conditional discharge Powers of Criminal Courts (Sentencing) Act 2000 s 12	Yes				
Confiscation order Proceeds of Crime Act 2002 s 6	Only in the Crown Court[125]				
Costs Prosecution of Offences Act 1985 s 18	Yes[126]				

[118] Safeguarding Vulnerable Groups Act 2006 s 2 and Sch 3 and Criminal Procedure Rules 2015 2015/1490 Rule 28(3), see **117.4**.

[119] Contempt of Court Act 1981 s 14(2A) This section is repealed by Criminal Justice and Immigration Act 2008 Sch 4 para 25. Commencement is awaited.

[120] Powers of Criminal Courts (Sentencing) Act 2000 s 60 and *R v Byas* 1995 16 Cr App R (S) 869.

[121] Powers of Criminal Courts (Sentencing) Act 2000 s 108 The section is repealed by Criminal Justice and Court Services Act 2000 s 75 and Sch 8 when and if that part of the Act is in force. There also appears to be a power under Powers of Criminal Courts (Sentencing) Act 2000 s 60 to make an Attendance Centre Order. The power is unlikely ever to be used.

[122] *R v Basid* 1996 1 Cr App R (S) 421

[123] Powers of Criminal Courts (Sentencing) Act 2000 s 108 is repealed by Criminal Justice and Court Services Act 2000 s 75 and Sch 8 when and if that part of the Act is in force.

[124] If the defendant is under 18 the court shall order the parent or guardian to pay the compensation, unless they cannot be found or it would be unreasonable, Powers of Criminal Courts (Sentencing) Act 2000 s 137(1).

[125] Proceeds of Crime Act 2002 s 6(2) Magistrates can commit offenders to the Crown Court under Proceeds of Crime Act 2002 s 70. For an example of a confiscation order being made for an offender aged 17 when sentenced, see *R v Phillips* 2017 EWCA Crim 1514.

[126] If the defendant is aged under 18: a) the amount of prosecution costs shall not exceed the amount of the fine, Prosecution of Offences Act 1985 s 18(5), and b) the court shall order the parent or guardian to pay the prosecution costs unless they cannot be found or it would be unreasonable, Powers of Criminal Courts (Sentencing) Act 2000 s 137(1). When the offender has attained the age of 16 the court's duty changes to a power to so order.

Sentence or order	Age				
	10-12	13-15	16	17	18-20
Criminal Behaviour Orders Anti-social Behaviour, Crime and Policing Act 2014 s 22	Yes[127]				
Criminal Behaviour Orders, Interim Anti-social Behaviour, Crime and Policing Act 2014 s 26	Yes[128]				
Custody for life: Automatic (For those aged 21+ the order is called Life Imprisonment: Automatic) Criminal Justice Act 2003 s 224A[129]	No[130]				Yes
Custody for life (murder only) Powers of Criminal Courts (Sentencing) Act 2000 s 93	No, see Detention at HM's Pleasure				Yes[131]
Custody for life (not murder) Powers of Criminal Courts (Sentencing) Act 2000 s 94(1) and Criminal Justice Act 2003 s 225(2)	No, see Detention for life				Yes
Deferment of sentence Powers of Criminal Courts (Sentencing) Act 2000 s 1-1D	Yes				
Deportation, Recommendations for Immigration Act 1971 s 3(6)	No			Yes[132]	
Deprivation Order Powers of Criminal Courts (Sentencing) Act 2000 s 143(1)	Yes				
Destruction Orders: Animals Animal Welfare Act 2006 s 37(1)	Yes				
Destruction Orders: Dogs Dangerous Dogs Act 1991 s 4(1)(a)	Yes				

[127] This is by implication. It says they can be made for those aged under 18 and, without a prohibited age period, the age should be 10+.
[128] The age limit must be the same as for the full orders.
[129] As inserted by Legal Aid, Sentencing and Punishment of Offenders Act 2012. In force for offences committed on or after 3/12/12
[130] Criminal Justice Act 2003 s 224A(1)(a)
[131] As long as the defendant was aged 18+ when the offence was committed.
[132] Immigration Act 1971 s 3(6) 'if he is convicted after he is of the age of 17'.

Sentence or order	**Age**				
	10-12	**13-15**	**16**	**17**	**18-20**
Detention and Training Order[133] Powers of Criminal Courts (Sentencing) Act 2000 s 100	No for 10-11[134] Yes for 12[135]	Yes[136]	Yes		No
Detention at HM's Pleasure Powers of Criminal Courts (Sentencing) Act 2000 s 90	Yes, if defendant appears to be under the age of 18 at the time of the offence[137]				
Detention for life Criminal Justice Act 2003 s 226(2)	Yes, if: a) it is a serious offence, b) there is a significant risk to members of the public, and c) it is justified etc.				No
Detention in a Young Offender Institution Powers of Criminal Courts (Sentencing) Act 2000 s 96-97	No				Yes[138]
	Where a defendant is in breach of a Suspended Sentence Order or a community order made when he or she was aged 18-21 and the breach hearing is when the defendant is aged 21+, and custody is appropriate, the court must pass a YOI order and not a prison sentence.[139]				
Detention under section 91 Powers of Criminal Courts (Sentencing) Act 2000 s 91	Yes, Crown Court only				No
Disqualification from driving: Obligatory Road Traffic Offenders Act 1988 s 34(1)	Yes[140]				
Disqualification from driving Discretionary Powers of Criminal Courts (Sentencing) Act 2000 s 146-147 Road Traffic Offenders Act 1988 s 34(2)	Yes for the same reasons as in the last footnote but the discretion would be important.				
Disqualification from having custody of a dog order Dangerous Dogs Act 1991 s 4(1)(b)	Yes				

[133] The relevant age is the age at conviction.

[134] For defendants aged under 12, Powers of Criminal Courts (Sentencing) Act 2000 s 100(2)(b)(ii) creates a power to pass the order when the Secretary of State makes an order. The power is not expected to be used.

[135] Defendants aged 12-14 have to be 'persistent offenders', Powers of Criminal Courts (Sentencing) Act 2000 s 100(2)(a)

[136] Defendants aged 12-14 have to be 'persistent offenders', Powers of Criminal Courts (Sentencing) Act 2000 s 100(2)(a)

[137] Powers of Criminal Courts (Sentencing) Act 2000 s 90

[138] Criminal Justice Act 2003 s 225(3)

[139] Criminal Justice Act 2003 Sch 12 paras 10(1)(b), 21(2)(b)(ii) and 23(2)(b)(ii) as interpreted by *R v Aslam* 2015 EWCA Crim 845 para 3. The exception to this rule is when a defendant is in breach of a community order by failing to comply with it and the offence does not carry imprisonment, then where the defendant is aged 21+ at the breach hearing, the court must pass a prison sentence of 6 months or less and not YOI.

[140] I know of no statutory bar and it makes sense for there to be no age limit. If a defendant commits the offence of causing death by driving when aged 18 it must be helpful to the judge sentencing him or her to see on the licence the earlier offences with the appropriate disqualification entered. This is especially so when the period of disqualification for a young offender includes a time in the future when the defendant might otherwise have obtained a driving licence. See also the footnote for Endorsement.

Sentence or order	**Age**				
	10-12	**13-15**	**16**	**17**	**18-20**
Disqualification from keeping an animal order Animal Welfare Act 2006 s 34(1)	Yes				
Endorsement Road Traffic Offenders Act 1988 s 44-49	Yes[141]				
Extended sentences 2012 (EDS) Criminal Justice Act 2003 s 226A-226B	Yes[142]				
Fines Criminal Justice Act 2003 s 163	Yes[143] When aged 10-13, £250 maximum When aged 14-17, £1,000 maximum[144]				
Fine or one day	No				Yes[145]
Football Banning Order Football Spectators Act 1989 s 14A-14B	Yes				
Forfeiture Powers of Criminal Courts (Sentencing) Act 2000 s 143(1) and many other statutes	Yes				
Guardianship Order Mental Health Act 1983 s 37	No[146]		Yes		
Hospital Order/Interim Hospital Order Mental Health Act 1983 s 37-38	Yes[147]				
Hybrid Orders Mental Health Act 1983 s 45A(1)	No[148]				
Imprisonment	No[149]				

[141] Young persons aged under 17 cannot hold a driving licence to drive a car. Young persons aged under 16 cannot hold a driving licence to drive a moped. If the offender does not hold a driving licence, the order for endorsement and penalty points should still be made. It operates as an order that any licence that is obtained should be endorsed and should have listed any penalty points if they have not reached the time for removal. See also the footnote for Disqualification from driving: Obligatory.
[142] Criminal Justice Act 2003 s 226A(1)(a) and 226B(1)(a)
[143] If the defendant is aged under 18 the court shall order the parent or guardian to pay the costs unless they cannot be found or it would be unreasonable, Powers of Criminal Courts (Sentencing) Act 2000 s 137(1). When the offender has attained the age of 16 the court's duty changes to a power to so order.
[144] Magistrates' Courts Act 1980 s 36(1)-(2)
[145] This Magistrates' power in Magistrates' Courts Act 1980 s 135 is repealed by Criminal Justice and Court Services Act 2000 Sch 7 para 67, but that part has not been commenced.
[146] Mental Health Act 1983 s 37(2) provides that the order only applies to those aged 16+.
[147] Mental Health Act 1983 s 43(1) provides that a Magistrates' Court may commit an offender aged 14+ to the Crown Court for the imposition of a Hospital Order with a Restriction Order 'instead of making a Hospital Order'. This implies that the Court can make an order for a child aged 14+ and it appears there is no restriction for offenders aged 10-14.
[148] Powers of Criminal Courts (Sentencing) Act 2000 s 89(1), *Att-Gen's Ref No 54 of 2011* 2011 EWCA Crim 2276, 2012 1 Cr App R (S) 106 (p 635) and *R v Fort* 2013 EWCA Crim 2332, 2014 2 Cr App R (S) 24 (p 167), see **67.42**.
[149] Powers of Criminal Courts (Sentencing) Act 2000 s 89(1)

Sentence or order	Age				
	10-12	13-15	16	17	18-20
Injunctions, Civil Anti-social Behaviour, Crime and Policing Act 2014 s 1	Yes[150]				
Interim Hospital Orders, see Hospital Orders					
Life imprisonment	No, see Detention for life				No[151]
Life imprisonment: Automatic (For those aged 18-20 the order is called Custody for life) Criminal Justice Act 2003 s 224A[152]	No[153]				Yes
Minimum sentences for third Class A drug offence or third domestic burglary Powers of Criminal Courts (Sentencing) Act 2000 s 110-111	No				Yes[154]
Minimum sentences for certain firearm offences Firearms Act 1968 s 51A	No[155]		3 years' detention under section 91[156]		Yes
Notification: Sexual Sexual Offences Act 2003 s 80-92	Yes[157]				
Notification: Sexual Parental Directions Sexual Offences Act 2003 s 89	Yes[158]				No
Offender of Particular Concern Order	No[159]				Yes
Parenting Order[160] With a 2014 injunction Crime and Disorder Act 1998 s 8-9 (as amended)	Yes[161]				No

[150] Anti-social Behaviour, Crime and Policing Act 2014 s 1(1)
[151] See custody for life in this table.
[152] As inserted by Legal Aid, Sentencing and Punishment of Offenders Act 2012. In force for offences committed on or after 3/12/12
[153] Criminal Justice Act 2003 s 224A(1)(a)
[154] Powers of Criminal Courts (Sentencing) Act 2000 s 110(1)(b) and 111(1)(b)
[155] The exception to the rule about detaining persons aged under 18 for possession of prohibited weapons only applies to offenders aged 16 or over at the time of the offence, Powers of Criminal Courts (Sentencing) Act 2000 s 91(1A).
[156] Powers of Criminal Courts (Sentencing) Act 2000 s 91(1A), unless there are exceptional circumstances.
[157] Sexual Offences Act 2003 s 80
[158] Sexual Offences Act 2003 s 89
[159] Criminal Justice Act 2003 s 236A(1)(b)
[160] Parenting Orders may follow: i) a Child Safety Order, ii) a Parental Compensation Order, iii) a Civil Injunction, iv) a Sexual Harm Prevention Order, vi) a conviction of a child or young person, or v) a conviction of a parent of an offence under Education Act 1996 s 443 (failure to comply with school attendance order) or s 444 (failure to secure regular attendance at school of a registered pupil).
[161] For offenders aged 10-15 the court 'must' impose a Parenting Order or provide reasons why they did not do so. For 16 to 17-year-olds the court 'may' impose the order.

Sentence or order	Age				
	10-12	13-15	16	17	18-20
Penalty points Road Traffic Offenders Act 1988 s 28(1)	Yes[162]				
Period of detention in default of payment, Setting a Powers of Criminal Courts (Sentencing) Act 2000 s 108 and 139	No[163]				Yes
Period of detention in default of payment, Passing a Crown Court Powers of Criminal Courts (Sentencing) Act 2000 s 139 Magistrates' Court Magistrates' Courts Act 1980 Sch 4 and Criminal Justice Act 1991 s 22	Power to make Attendance Centre Order[164] No power to order imprisonment[165]				Yes
Referral Order Powers of Criminal Courts (Sentencing) Act 2000 s 16	Youth Court and Magistrates' Court[166] Not in the Crown Court after a conviction (except after an appeal)				
Reparation Order Powers of Criminal Courts (Sentencing) Act 2000 s 73	Yes[167]				No
Restitution Order Powers of Criminal Courts (Sentencing) Act 2000 s 148-149	Yes				
Restraining Order Protection from Harassment Act 1997 s 5	Yes				
Serious Crime Prevention Order Serious Crime Act 2007 s 1 and 19(2)	No[168]				Yes
Service Community Order Armed Forces Act 2006 s 164 and 178	No[169]				Yes
Sexual Harm Prevention Order Sexual Offences Act 2003 s 103A	Yes				

[162] Young offenders aged under 17 cannot hold a driving licence to drive a car. Young offenders aged under 16 cannot hold a driving licence to drive a moped. If the offender does not hold a driving licence, the order for endorsement and penalty points should still be made. It operates as an order that any licence that is obtained should be endorsed and should have listed any penalty points if they have not reached the time for removal.
[163] *R v Joseph* 2009 EWCA Crim 662
[164] Powers of Criminal Courts (Sentencing) Act 2000 s 60
[165] *R v Joseph* 2009 EWCA Crim 662
[166] Powers of Criminal Courts (Sentencing) Act 2000 s 16(1)(a)
[167] Powers of Criminal Courts (Sentencing) Act 2000 s 73(1) grants the power for those 'aged under 18'.
[168] Serious Crime Act 2007 s 6
[169] Armed Forces Act 2006 s 164(5)(a)

Sentence or order	Age				
	10-12	**13-15**	**16**	**17**	**18-20**
Sexual Risk Order Sexual Offences Act 2003 s 122A	Yes				
Suspended Sentence Order Criminal Justice Act 2003 s 189	No,[170] see Suspended Sentences of Detention in a Young Offender Institution below.				
Suspended Sentences of Detention in a Young Offender Institution Criminal Justice Act 2003 s 189	No				Yes
Travel Restriction Order Criminal Justice and Police Act 2001 s 33	Yes				
Victim surcharge Criminal Justice Act 2003 s 161A-161B	Yes[171]				
Violent Offender Order Criminal Justice and Immigration Act 2008 s 98-112	Yes[172]				
Vulnerable groups barring, see Barring (Automatic) in this table					
Young Offender Institution, Detention in Powers of Criminal Courts (Sentencing) Act 2000 s 96-97	No				Yes[173]
Youth Rehabilitation Order Criminal Justice and Immigration Act 2008 s 1-7	Yes[174]				No

13.3 *The age groups*

Note: There are three different age groups.

1 Children under 10, where 'It shall be conclusively presumed that no child under the age of ten years can be guilty of any offence', Children and Young Persons Act 1933 s 50. However, care proceedings can be commenced for these children.

2 Offenders aged 10-13 are known as 'children'.

3 Young offenders aged 14-17 are known as 'young persons', Children and Young Persons Act 1933 s 107. Ed.

13.4 *Basic position*

Note: To determine the maximum sentence and whether an Act applies, it is the date of conviction that matters. This principle, which has a few exceptions, is dealt with at para **13.5** below. To determine the sentence structure and length, the key date is the date of the offence, see **13.12**. To determine whether an offender should be dealt with summarily, see para **13.14**. Ed.

---

[170] Criminal Justice Act 2003 s 189(1)
[171] This is because of the way the legislation is drafted and guidance issued at the time.
[172] Criminal Justice and Immigration Act 2008 s 99(4)(a)(i) lists one of the conditions as 'a sentence of imprisonment or other detention'.
[173] Criminal Justice Act 2003 s 225(3)
[174] Criminal Justice and Immigration Act 2008 s 1(1)

13.5 *Sentencing orders It is the date of conviction, not sentence, that matters*
Note: Acts that provide powers to impose sentencing orders for children and young offenders invariably refer to conviction as the key date. This has been a consistent approach for a long time. 'Convicted' means when the offender pleads guilty or is found guilty. Examples are: a) Detention and Training Order, see Powers of Criminal Courts (Sentencing) Act 2000 s 100(1)(a) and **37.3**, b) detention under section 91, see Powers of Criminal Courts (Sentencing) Act 2000 s 91(1) and **42.3**, c) custody for life, see Powers of Criminal Courts (Sentencing) Act 2000 s 94(1) and **32.3**, and d) extended sentences, see Criminal Justice Act 2003 s 226B(1) and **37.3**. The same approach applies to: a) the ability to impose the adult maximum fine, see Powers of Criminal Courts (Sentencing) Act 2000 s 135(1) and **13.44**, and b) the prohibition on imprisonment for those aged under 21, see Powers of Criminal Courts (Sentencing) Act 2000 s 89(1) and **13.20**. There are exceptions to the rule. The main one is dealing with offenders at the Youth Court who were aged 17 on their first appearance and who turn 18 during the proceedings, see **13.9**. For detention at HM's Pleasure, it is the date of offence that matters, see **287.77**. Ed.

Where an offender is aged under 21 at the date of conviction and aged 21 when sentenced, it is the date of conviction that determines the sentences that apply, see *R v Danga* 1992 13 Cr App R (S) 408. This principle applies to the other age thresholds. Some will be at the Youth Court, e.g. aged 11/12 and aged 14/15 for Detention and Training Orders and aged 13/14 for the maximum fine. In the Crown Court most orders have a minimum age for their imposition. Unless there is a specific legislative bar, it is the date of conviction that matters.

R v Robinson 1993 14 Cr App R (S) 448 LCJ On conviction, D was aged 16 but at sentence he had turned 17. The defence sought to argue that the Court had exceeded its jurisdiction by passing a sentence under section 53(2) (now Powers of Criminal Courts (Sentencing) Act 2000 s 91) on an offender aged 17. Held. D's age for the purposes of sentencing was his age at conviction (see also *R v Danga* 1992 13 Cr App R (S) 408 and *R v Pesapane* 1992 13 Cr App R (S) 438). Accordingly, D was liable to be detained under section 53(2).

R v Morgan 2014 EWCA Crim 2587 D was aged 17 when he pleaded and 18 when he was sentenced. The Judge sentenced him to YOI. Held. It is the age at conviction not sentence that determines the available sentence. The sentence was unlawful.

Procedure

13.6 *Duty to enquire as to age of defendant*
Children and Young Persons Act 1933 s 99(1) Where a person, whether charged with an offence or not, is brought before any court otherwise than for the purpose of giving evidence, and it appears to the court that he is a child or young person, the court shall make due inquiry as to the age of that person, and for that purpose shall take such evidence as may be forthcoming at the hearing of the case.

13.7 *Resolving disputes, How to*
Children and Young Persons Act 1933 s 99(1) Where a person, whether charged with an offence or not, is brought before any court otherwise than for the purpose of giving evidence, and it appears to the court that he is a child or young person, the court shall make due inquiry as to the age of that person, and for that purpose shall take such evidence as may be forthcoming at the hearing of the case, but an order or judgment of the court shall not be invalidated by any subsequent proof that the age of that person has not been correctly stated to the court, and the age presumed or declared by the court to be the age of the person so brought before it shall, for the purposes of this Act, be deemed to be the true age of that person, and, where it appears to the court that the person so brought before it has attained the age of 18 years, that person shall for the purposes of this Act be deemed not to be a child or young person.

Powers of Criminal Courts (Sentencing) Act 2000 s 164(1) For the purposes of any provision of this Act which requires the determination of the age of a person by the court..., his age shall be deemed to be that which it appears to the court...to be after considering any available evidence.

R (B) v London Borough of Merton 2003 EWHC 1689 (Admin) High Court B applied for asylum and the National Asylum Service determined he was not a minor. B went to council offices and claimed he was aged under 18. He was interviewed by a social worker, S, by telephone through an interpreter. S found inconsistencies in B's account and determined that B was not a minor. B brought judicial review proceedings contending the enquiries were inadequate, there should have been a medical examination and S's procedure was unfair. B produced a report from a consultant paediatrician who estimated B's age as 18 plus or minus two years. Held. **The problems** It would be naïve to assume that B is unaware of the advantages of being thought to be a child. B does not produce any reliable documentary evidence of his date of birth or age. There is no reliable medical or other scientific test to determine whether [someone] is over or under 18. The Guidelines for Paediatricians published in November 1999 by the Royal College of Paediatrics and Child Health states, 'In practice, age determination is extremely difficult to do with certainty, and no single approach to this can be relied on. Moreover, for young people aged 15-18, it is even less possible to be certain about age. A young person might be as old as 23 [or] under the age of 18. Age determination is an inexact science and the margin of error can sometimes be as much as five years either side. Anthropometric measuring[175] should not be attempted.' Different people living in the same country, with the same culture and diet, mature physically and psychologically at different rates. A GP is very unlikely to have the knowledge or experience to improve on the accuracy of an intelligent layman. Even paediatricians who have experience in this area can be of limited help.

The appropriate procedure The assessment of age in borderline cases is a difficult matter, but it is not complex. It is not an issue which requires anything approaching a trial. It is a matter which may be determined informally, provided safeguards of minimum standards of inquiry and of fairness are adhered to. The decision maker cannot determine age solely on the basis of the appearance of the [individuals]. In general, the decision maker must seek to elicit the general background of the applicant, including his family circumstances and history, his educational background, and his activities during the previous few years. Ethnic and cultural information may also be important. If there is reason to doubt the applicant's statement as to his age, the decision maker will have to make an assessment of his credibility, and he will have to ask questions designed to test his credibility. It is necessary to take a history from [the individual] with a view to determining whether it is true. The determination of the age of the applicant will depend on the history he gives, on his physical appearance and on his behaviour. However, an untrue history, while relevant, is not necessarily indicative of a lie as to the age of the applicant. Lies may be told for reasons unconnected with the applicant's case as to his age, for example to avoid his return to his country of origin. Furthermore, physical appearance and behaviour cannot be isolated from the question of the veracity of the applicant: appearance, behaviour and the credibility of his account are all matters that reflect on each other. There is no onus of proof on B. A local authority cannot simply adopt a decision made by the Home Office. It must decide itself. If there is an interpreter it is preferable for them to be present during the interview.

Decision Here there was a risk of misunderstandings. The inconsistencies found by S should have been put to B. It cannot be said if that had been done S would have reached the same decision. Last para The reason the Council lost the case was because the

[175] This means measuring the body scientifically.

reasons they gave for their decision originally were wholly inadequate and there was not compliance with fairness. para 58 I set aside S's decision and it must be reconsidered on the information now available.
Note: This guidance is known as the *Merton* guidelines and is referred to in official instructions to magistrates and district judges as the way to proceed when the court is unsure of the age of the defendant. Ed.
For deeming an offender to be a certain age see **13.10**.

13.8 ***The Youth Court Those who turn 18***

Powers of youth courts.
Crime and Disorder Act 1998 s 47(1) Where a person who appears or is brought before a youth court charged with an offence subsequently attains the age of 18, the youth court may, at any time:

(a) before the start of the trial; or [subsection b) repealed] remit the person for trial or, as the case may be, for sentence to a magistrates' court (other than a youth court).

In this subsection "the start of the trial" shall be construed in accordance with Prosecution of Offences Act 1985 s 22(11B).
(2) Where a person is remitted under subsection (1) above:

(a) he shall have no right of appeal against the order of remission;
(b) the remitting court shall adjourn proceedings in relation to the offence; and
(c) subsections (3) and (4) below shall apply.

(3) [deals with remands in custody and bail]
(4) The other court may deal with the case in any way in which it would have power to deal with it if all proceedings relating to the offence which took place before the remitting court had taken place before the other court.
Magistrates' Courts Act 1980 s 24(1) Where a person under the age of 18 years appears or is brought before a Magistrates' Court on an information charging him with an indictable offence he shall, subject to Crime and Disorder Act 1998 s 51 and 51A (sending offenders facing grave crimes etc. to the Crown Court)..., be tried summarily.
Magistrates' Courts Act 1980 s 29(1) Where proceedings in respect of a young person are begun for an offence and he attains the age of 18 before the conclusion of the proceedings, the court may deal with the case and make any order which it could have made if he had not attained that age.
Note: The effect of these two provisions is that if on the first appearance, there is no proposal to send the offender to the Crown Court for trial and the offender is aged under 18, the offender is treated as being aged under 18 during the proceedings. Section 48, below, acts as a safety net in case the decision turns out to be wrong. Ed.
Children and Young Persons Act 1933 s 48(1) A Youth Court sitting for the purpose of hearing a charge against a person who is believed to be a child or young person may, if it thinks fit to do so, proceed with the hearing and determination of the charge, notwithstanding that it is discovered that the person in question is not a child or young person.
Note: Where a suspect aged under 18 is charged, the police should determine what age he or she would be on his or her first appearance at court. If his or her age would be under 18, he or she should appear at the Youth Court. If his or her age would be 18, he or she should appear at the adult court, *R v Amersham Juvenile Court ex parte Wilson* 1981 72 Cr App R 365. If the offender is aged under 18 when jurisdiction/plea is dealt with, the case remains at the Youth Court if he or she turns 18. For details see **13.9**. If the offender has an adjournment (which is now rare) and turns 18 before the jurisdiction/plea determination, the offender appears at an adult court. Ed.
R v Ford 2018 EWCA Crim 1751 D was charged with section 18 and appeared at the Youth Court aged 17. The case was adjourned so the defence could read the papers. On the next appearance D was aged 18. D pleaded to section 18 and possession of an offensive weapon. D was committed for sentence under Powers of Criminal Courts (Sentencing) Act 2000 s 3. At the Crown Court, D received 6½ years in all. Held. We

assume the magistrates purported to commit D under section 3B because that is the section for those who require additional sentencing powers. To use Magistrates' Court Act 1980 s 24 (which enables those who turn 18 to be dealt with in the Youth Court) the defendant must be aged 17 when the court determines mode of trial, see *R v Islington North Juvenile Court ex parte Daley* 1982 75 Cr App R 280 (House of Lords). So, there was no power to take D's plea or commit him to the Crown Court. Everything after that was invalid, so we quash D's sentence, acting as Judges of the Divisional Court. One of the Judges then sat as a District Judge at the Youth Court and committed the matter for trial. The same Judge sat as a Crown Court Judge, took the pleas, heard the case opened, listened to the mitigation, sentenced D to 4 years 8 months and passed some ancillary orders.

13.9 ***Crown Court: Defendant crosses age threshold Those that turn 18 Ability to pass sentences for 17-year-old***

Magistrates' Courts Act 1980 s 29(1) Where proceedings in respect of a young person are begun for an offence and he attains the age of 18 before the conclusion of the proceedings, the court may deal with the case and make any order which it could have made if he had not attained that age.

Note: This section enables a judge to sentence someone who turned 18 to a sentence that was only available to those aged under 18. The power must be exercised rarely. An example might be an offender with a Youth Rehabilitation Order who has to be sentenced for a relatively minor matter after he or she has turned 18. Then another Youth Rehabilitation Order could be imposed. Normally, however, defendants would be sentenced under the provisions for 18-year-olds, which have greater powers. Ed.

13.10 ***Deeming offender is a certain age/Age not agreed***

Criminal Justice Act 1982 s 1(6) For the purposes of any provision of this Act which requires the determination of the age of a person by the court or the Secretary of State his age shall be deemed to be that which it appears to the court or the Secretary of State (as the case may be) to be after considering any available evidence.

R v Brown 1989 11 Cr App R (S) 263 At the time of sentence, D was 20 years and 6 months old. However, on the evidence before the Court D appeared to be 21 years of age. Held. The effect of Criminal Justice Act 1982 s 1(6) and the decision of this Court in *R v Farndale* 1974 58 Cr App R 336 is that provided on the material then before it the Court deems the defendant to be 21 years of age, then for all purposes in terms of sentence thereafter he falls to be so treated.

R v Steed 1990 12 Cr App R (S) 230 D pleaded to theft at the Crown Court. The CRO said he was aged 20. D said he was 21. The police officer was cross-examined by the defence and the Judge asked for the matter to be checked. After an interval, the position hadn't changed and the Judge said he would sentence D on the basis he was 21. In fact he was aged 20 and he appealed. Held. It would have been better if the matter had been adjourned for more detailed enquiries to be made. However, the [deeming] section applies and the sentence of imprisonment was lawful.

Old case: *R v Farndale* 1974 58 Cr App R 336 (D was treated as being aged 21 because of the dates in his antecedents and D did not attempt to dispute it. In fact he was under 21. Held. Parliament had intended [what is now Criminal Justice Act 1982 s 1(6)] to meet the present position precisely. The Court had taken its view on the best possible evidence. The Court applies the section as a very common-sense way out of a difficulty which must arise from time to time in practice.)

For resolving disputes see **13.7.**

13.11 ***Start with the sentence applicable for the date of the offence***

Youths Sentencing Guideline 2009, see www.banksr.com Other Matters Guidelines tab para 5.1 There will be occasions when an increase in the age of the offender will result in the maximum sentence on the date of conviction being greater than that available on the date on which the offence was committed.

5.2 The approach should be, a) The court should take as its starting point the sentence likely to have been imposed on the date on which the offence was committed, b) Where an offender attains the age of 18 after committing the offence but before conviction, Criminal Justice Act 2003 s 142 applies[176] (whilst Crime and Disorder Act 1998 s 37 and Children and Young Persons Act 1933 s 44 apply to those aged under 18), c) It will be rare for a court to have to consider passing a sentence more severe than the maximum it would have had jurisdiction to pass at the time the offence was committed even where an offender has subsequently attained the age of 18, d) However, a sentence at or close to that maximum may be appropriate, especially where a serious offence was committed by an offender close to the age threshold.

Note: There is a replacement guideline, but this information may still be useful. This seems to state the law accurately. Ed.

R v Ghafoor 2002 EWCA Crim 1857, 2003 1 Cr App R (S) 84 (p 428) Where a defendant crosses a relevant age threshold, the starting point is the sentence the defendant would have been likely to receive if he had been sentenced at the date of the commission of the offence. It has been described as a 'powerful factor'...It will rarely be necessary for a court even to consider the passing of a sentence which is more severe than the maximum it would have had jurisdiction to pass at the time of the commission of the offence. Here, where the date of conviction is only a few months after the date of the offence, it would rarely be appropriate to pass a longer sentence than that which would have been passed at the date of the offence.

R v Bowker 2007 EWCA Crim 1608, 2008 1 Cr App R (S) 72 (p 412) D committed an offence two days before his 18th birthday. Held. It is right that those who have committed an offence whilst under the age of 18 should be judged by reference to their age at the time of the offence. Nonetheless, the necessary sentencing disposal has to take account of the matters in Criminal Justice Act 2003 s 142(1) if they are convicted after they have reached 18. If under 18, the court will focus more on their requirements and rehabilitation. This is not a case where delays in investigation or trial resulted in the relevant age watershed being passed. We think it is important to remember that *R v Ghafoor* 2002 EWCA Crim 1857, 2003 1 Cr App R (S) 84 (p 428) envisages flexibility. Here the Judge was right to consider that deterrence was important.

R v G 2010 EWCA Crim 1062 LCJ D pleaded to perverting the course of justice. D engineered an MSN chat room meeting with B, a witness. She then, by cutting and pasting, fabricated a conversation with B, who was giving evidence against a man, C, on trial for serious sexual offences. The doctored conversation purported to be a confession by B that her evidence was false. This was sent to those representing C, causing the witness to be recalled and then the trial to be halted so the matter could be investigated. D subsequently confessed and was committed to the Crown Court. The PCMH, at which she intended to plead guilty, was adjourned because her parents were on trial for drug offences. D was charged in those proceedings but the case against her was dropped. Her perverting the course of justice case was re-listed after her 15th birthday, after which it was possible for the court to impose a DTO (it not being possible before her 15th birthday as she was not a persistent offender). The Judge imposed an 8-month DTO. Held. The offence was a very serious example of perverting the course of justice. It was a cunning and devious plan. Her regret and remorse were genuine. The rule in *R v Ghafoor* 2003 EWCA Crim 1857, 2003 1 Cr App R (S) is not an inflexible rule. Unlike *R v LM* 2002 EWCA Crim 3047 it would have been possible to pass less than 2 years under section 91. However, that would not have been proper. Section 91 is for those who commit grave crimes and is normally available where sentences of 2 years and upwards would be merited. The starting point in such a situation is the likely sentence at the time of the offence. **12-month Supervision Order** substituted.

[176] Accordingly, when sentencing those convicted when aged 18+ who have committed an offence whilst aged under 18, more general public policy considerations may play a greater part.

See also: *R v Egege* 2017 EWCA Crim 2161 D pleaded guilty to a sophisticated online blackmail. He was aged 17 at the time of the offence and aged 20 at the time of the sentence. Held. When an offender crosses a relevant age threshold, the starting point should be the sentence which would have been imposed at the date of the commission of the offence, to avoid a retrospective increase in sentence, see *R v Ghafoor* 2002 [see above], *R v Bowker* 2007 [see above] and the *Sentencing Children and Young People Guideline 2017* section 6 [see **13.15**]. It is of course a well-established principle that children and young persons should be given more lenient sentences than adults for equivalent offences.
For defendants who cross the age threshold, see **13.15**.

13.12 ***Taking into account the age of the defendant at the time of the offence Short gap between offence and age change***

R v Danga 1992 13 Cr App R (S) 408 The broad conceptual approach of sentencing does not undergo a fundamental change simply because the offender passes his 21st birthday. If all factors were identical, an offender aged 21 and a few days is likely to receive in substance much the same sentence punishment as one who is 20 years and 11 months.
R v Robinson 1993 14 Cr App R (S) 448 LCJ D pleaded to burglary and was convicted after trial of rape against an 87-year-old widow. On conviction, D was aged 16 but at sentence had turned 17. The defence sought to argue that the court had exceeded its jurisdiction by passing a sentence under section 53(2)[177] on an offender aged 17. Held. D's age for the purposes of sentencing was his age at conviction (see also *R v Danga* 1992 13 Cr App R (S) 408 and *R v Pesapane* 1992 13 Cr App R (S) 438). Accordingly, D was liable to be detained under section 53(2).
R v Ghafoor 2002 EWCA Crim 1857, 2003 1 Cr App R (S) 84 (p 428) Where the date of conviction is only a few months after the date of the offence, it would rarely be appropriate to pass a longer sentence than that which would have been passed at the date of the offence.
R v Shan 2007 EWCA Crim 1861 D pleaded to section 20. He was aged 17 at the time of the offence and 18 when sentenced. The Judge passed 15 months' detention. The defence argued that he should have received no more than he would have received if he had been sentenced when he was 17. As 15 months would not be available for a Detention and Training Order, the sentence should be reduced. Held. On the face of it there was nothing wrong with the 15 months. The Judge could easily have passed 18 months' detention without criticism. If he had passed that sentence the present argument would evaporate. That demonstrates the absurdity of applying *R v Ghafoor* 2002 EWCA Crim 1857, 2003 1 Cr App R (S) in an inflexible way. If D had pleaded at the first opportunity, that would have been before his 18th birthday. The likelihood is he would have received a shorter sentence. He chose to plead not guilty. It was that choice which meant he was sentenced under a different regime. We dismiss the appeal.

13.13 ***Taking into account the age of the defendant at the time of the offence Significant gap between offence and age change***

R v Cuddington 1995 16 Cr App R (S) 246 Had the matter been discovered and dealt with [promptly], D would have been entitled to be treated as a juvenile and detained for no more than 12 months. Whilst that is not in itself definitive of any sentence which could later be imposed on him, it is a powerful factor to be taken into account.
R v BW 2012 EWCA Crim 3178 D was convicted of ABH. D had been committed to the Crown Court because he had adult co-defendants. D was aged 14 years 4 months at the time of the offence. When sentenced, he was almost 16. The Judge gave him an 8-month DTO. Held. The correct starting point for sentencing is the sentence which would have been appropriate if the sentence had been imposed at the date of the offence. The principle is this: that where an offender has crossed the relevant sentencing threshold

[177] Now Powers of Criminal Courts (Sentencing) Act 2000 s 91

between the date of the offence and the date of conviction, culpability should be judged by reference to the offender's age at the time of the committing of the offence, and it is fair and just to take as a starting point the sentence that the offender would be likely to have received if he had been sentenced at that earlier date, though there is some scope for flexibility. The justification for using that starting point, that which has been described as a 'powerful factor', is that in relation to young persons the philosophy of restricting sentencing powers reflects a) society's acceptance that young offenders are less responsible for their actions and therefore less culpable for their actions, and b) the recognition that, in consequence, sentencing them should place greater emphasis on rehabilitation and less on retribution and deterrence than in the case of adults. It was emphasised in *R v Ghafoor* 2002 EWCA Crim 1857, 2003 1 Cr App R (S) 84 (p 428) that there have to be good reasons for departing from the starting point. For example, in the interim the offender may have been revealed as a dangerous criminal, whereas at the date of the offence that was not so. Taking account of the time spent in custody, a **2-year Youth Rehabilitation Order**, not an 8-month DTO.

13.14 ***Those aged under 18 should be tried summarily*** ***Basic principles***
Magistrates' Courts Act 1980 s 24(1) Where a person under the age of 18 years appears or is brought before a Magistrates' Court on an information charging him with an indictable offence he shall, subject to Crime and Disorder Act 1998 s 51 and 51A (sending adults for trial and sending young offenders for trial for grave crimes) and to sections 24A and 24B below (similar provisions), be tried summarily.
Sentencing Children and Young People Guideline 2017 www.banksr.com Other Matters Guidelines tab. In force 1 June 2017. page 7
2.1 Subject to the exceptions noted below, cases involving children and young people should be tried in the Youth Court. It is the court which is best designed to meet their specific needs. A trial in the Crown Court with the inevitably greater formality and greatly increased number of people involved (including a jury and the public) should be reserved for the most serious cases.[178] The welfare principles in this guideline apply to all cases, including those tried or sentenced in the Crown Court.
This section covers the exceptions to this requirement.[179]
Sentencing Children and Young People Guideline 2017 www.banksr.com Other Matters Guidelines tab In force 1 June 2017. page 9
Charged alongside an adult
2.11 The proper venue for the trial of any child or young person is normally the Youth Court. Subject to statutory restrictions, that remains the case where a child or young person is jointly charged with an adult. If the adult is sent for trial to the Crown Court, the court should conclude that the child or young person must be tried separately in the Youth Court unless it is in the interests of justice for the child or young person and the adult to be tried jointly.
2.12 Examples of factors that should be considered when deciding whether to send the child or young person to the Crown Court (rather than having a trial in the Youth Court) include:

- whether separate trials will cause injustice to witnesses or to the case as a whole (consideration should be given to the provisions of Youth Justice and Criminal Evidence Act 1999 s 27 and 28);
- the age of the child or young person; the younger the child or young person, the greater the desirability that the child or young person be tried in the Youth Court;
- the age gap between the child or young person and the adult; a substantial gap in age militates in favour of the child or young person being tried in the Youth Court;
- the lack of maturity of the child or young person;

[178] *R (H, A and O) v Southampton Youth Court* 2004 EWHC 2912 Admin
[179] Magistrates' Courts Act 1980 s 24

- the relative culpability of the child or young person compared with the adult and whether the alleged role played by the child or young person was minor; and/or
- the lack of previous findings of guilt on the part of the child or young person.

2.13 The court should bear in mind that the Youth Court now has a general power to commit for sentence (as discussed at paragraph 2.9 [not reproduced here]); in appropriate cases this will permit a sentence to be imposed by the same court on adults and children and young people who have been tried separately.

2.14 The court should follow the plea before venue procedure (see flowcharts [not reproduced here]) prior to considering whether it is in the interests of justice for the child or young person and the adult to be tried jointly.

CPS v South East Surrey Youth Court 2005 EWHC 2929 (Admin), 2006 2 Cr App R (S) 26 (p 177) D, then aged 17, allegedly assaulted V in the face with a beer bottle, causing a wound. D was also arrested for an unrelated robbery where it was said a knife was used. The Youth Court sent the robbery to the Crown Court under the 'dangerousness' provisions (before the law was changed requiring that the case had to be sufficiently serious to warrant a 4-year determinate term). On a later date the CPS also asked for the ABH to be sent, under Crime and Disorder Act 1998 s 51A(3)(d). This was on the basis that ABH was a 'specified violent offence': Criminal Justice Act 2003 s 224(3). The Court declined to commit because ABH was not a grave crime, so the provisions of Magistrates' Courts Act 1980 s 24(1) were not met. The CPS appealed. Held. We consider the obligations of a Youth Court when dealing with a potentially dangerous offender. Here the provisions are not merely labyrinthine, they are manifestly inconsistent with each other. Yet again, the courts are faced with a sample of the deeply confusing provisions of Criminal Justice Act 2003 and the satellite statutory instruments to which it is giving stuttering birth. Magistrates' Courts Act 1980 s 24(1) requires summary trial of a person under 18 unless the offence is grave and may require a sentence of long-term detention, in which case the defendant must be committed for trial. Crime and Disorder Act 1998 s 51A requires a child or young person to be sent to the Crown Court for trial if the offence is specified in Sch 15 and if convicted, it appears the criteria for the imposition of an indeterminate sentence or an extended sentence under Criminal Justice Act 2003 s 228[180] would be met. Justices should bear in mind: a) those who are under 18 should, wherever possible, be tried in a Youth Court, which is best designed for their specific needs, *R (H) v Southampton Youth Court* 2004 EWHC 2912 (Admin) and *R (CPS) v Redbridge Youth Court* 2005 EWHC 1390, b) the guidance in *R v Lang* 2005 EWCA Crim 2864, 2006 2 Cr App R (S) 3 (p 13), particularly in para 17(iv) in relation to non-serious specified offences (see **56.26**), c) the need, when dealing with those aged under 18, to be particularly rigorous before concluding that there is a significant risk of serious harm by the commission of further offences. Such a conclusion is unlikely to be appropriate in the absence of a pre-sentence report following assessment by a young offender team, d) in most cases where a non-serious specified offence is charged, an assessment of dangerousness will not be appropriate until after conviction when, if the dangerousness criteria are met, the defendant can be committed to the Crown Court for sentence, and e) when a youth under 18 is jointly charged with an adult, an exercise of judgment will be called for by the Youth Court when assessing the competing presumptions in favour of i) joint trial of those jointly charged, and ii) the trial of youths in the Youth Court. Factors relevant to that judgment will include the age and maturity of the youth, the comparative culpability in relation to the offence and the previous convictions of the [adult and youth], and whether the trial can be severed without either injustice or undue inconvenience to witnesses. Therefore the Justices' approach, in declining to consider Crime and Disorder Act 1998 s 51A(3)(d), was flawed. However, the conclusion that summary jurisdiction should be accepted for the purposes of trial is unimpeachable.

[180] Repealed by Legal Aid, Sentencing and Punishment of Offenders Act 2012 s 123(d), in force 3/12/12

Note: The law has changed since this case was heard. It is listed for the general principles. Following this case, the Youth Court normally delays decisions about dangerousness until after reports have been received. Ed.

13.15 *Defendant crosses age threshold before sentence*

Powers of Criminal Courts (Sentencing) Act 2000 s 7(4) Where, under section 6, a Magistrates' Court commits a person to be dealt with by the Crown Court in respect of an offence triable only on indictment in the case of an adult (being an offence which was tried summarily because of the offender's being under 18 years of age), the Crown Court's powers under subsection (1) in respect of the offender after he attains the age of 18 shall be powers to do either or both of the following:

(a) to impose a fine not exceeding £5,000,

(b) to deal with the offender in respect of the offence in any way in which the Magistrates' Court could deal with him if it had just convicted him of an offence punishable with imprisonment for a term not exceeding 6 months.

Sentencing Children and Young People Guideline 2017 www.banksr.com Other Matters Guidelines tab In force 1 June 2017. page 21

Crossing a significant age threshold between commission of offence and sentence

6.1 There will be occasions when an increase in the age of a child or young person will result in the maximum sentence on the date of *the finding of guilt* being greater than that available on the date on which the offence was *committed* (primarily turning 12, 15 or 18 years old).

6.2 In such situations the court should take as its starting point the sentence likely to have been imposed on the date at which the offence was committed. This includes young people who attain the age of 18 between the *commission* and the[181] *finding of guilt* of the offence[182] but when this occurs the purpose of sentencing adult offenders[183] has to be taken into account, which is:

- the punishment of offenders;
- the reduction of crime (including its reduction by deterrence);
- the reform and rehabilitation of offenders;
- the protection of the public; and
- the making of reparation by offenders to persons affected by their offences.

6.3 When any significant age threshold is passed it will rarely be appropriate that a more severe sentence than the maximum that the court could have imposed at the time the offence was committed should be imposed. However, a sentence at or close to that maximum may be appropriate.

R v Robson 2006 EWCA Crim 1414, 2007 1 Cr App R (S) 54 (p 301) D was aged 17 when he was convicted at the Magistrates' Court of two specified and serious offences. When he came to be sentenced in the Crown Court, he was aged 18. The difference was crucial. Held. The manifest purpose of the provision was to ensure that the sentencing powers of the Crown Court were not limited to those of the Magistrates' Court. It is unnecessary for us to speculate what the word 'just' adds to the exercise. Magistrates' Courts Act 1980 s 29(3) allows the Crown Court to deal with an offender committed by the Magistrates' Court as if he had just been convicted on indictment. The effect of this section merely ensures that the sentencing powers of the Crown Court were not limited to those of the Magistrates' Court. It is sufficient for us to state that, having regard to Criminal Justice Act 2003 s 225-228, it did not require D to be sentenced under the regime applicable to those aged 18 or over solely because he would have been 18 years old on conviction if he had 'just' been convicted on indictment.

R v Egege 2017 EWCA Crim 2161 D pleaded guilty to a sophisticated online blackmail. He was aged 17 at the time of the offence and aged 20 at the time of the sentence. Held.

[181] In the guideline, 'the' is repeated, so one has been removed.

[182] *R v Ghafoor* 2002 EWCA Crim 1857, 2003 1 Cr App R (S) 84 (p 428)

[183] Criminal Justice Act 2003 s 142

When an offender crosses a relevant age threshold, the starting point should be the sentence which would have been imposed at the date of the commission of the offence, to avoid a retrospective increase in sentence, see *R v Ghafoor* 2002 [see **13.11**], *R v Bowker* 2007 [see **13.11**] and the *Sentencing Children and Young People Guideline 2017* section 6. It is of course a well-established principle that children and young persons should be given more lenient sentences than adults for equivalent offences.
For the principle that the starting point is the sentence applicable at the date of the offence, see **13.11**.

13.16 ***Dangerous young offenders***
Powers of Criminal Courts (Sentencing) Act 2000 s 3C(1) This section applies where on the summary trial of a specified offence a person aged under 18 is convicted of the offence.
(2) If, in relation to the offence, it appears to the court that the criteria for the imposition of a sentence under Criminal Justice Act 2003 s 226B[184] would be met, the court must commit the offender in custody or on bail to the Crown Court for sentence in accordance with section 5A(1) (see below).
Powers of Criminal Courts (Sentencing) Act 2000 s 5A(1) Where an offender is committed by a Magistrates' Court for sentence under section 3C (committals for dangerous young offenders) (see above), the Crown Court shall inquire into the circumstances of the case and may deal with the offender in any way in which it could deal with him if he had just been convicted of the offence on indictment before the court.
Sentencing Children and Young People Guideline 2017 www.banksr.com Other Matters Guidelines tab In force 1 June 2017. page 8
Dangerousness
2.5 A 'significant risk' is more than a mere possibility of occurrence. The assessment of dangerousness should take into account all the available information relating to the circumstances of the offence and **may** also take into account any information regarding previous patterns of behaviour relating to this offence and any other relevant information relating to the child or young person. In making this assessment it will be essential to obtain a pre-sentence report.
2.6 Children and young people may change and develop within a shorter time than adults and this factor, along with their level of maturity, may be highly relevant when assessing probable future conduct and whether it may cause a significant risk of serious harm.[185]
2.7 In anything but the most serious cases it may be impossible for the court to form a view as to whether the child or young person would meet the criteria of the dangerous offender provisions without greater knowledge of the circumstances of the offence and the child or young person. In those circumstances jurisdiction for the case should be retained in the Youth Court. If, following a guilty plea or a finding of guilt, the dangerousness criteria appear to be met then the child or young person should be committed **for sentence**.
Sentencing Children and Young People Guideline 2017 www.banksr.com Other Matters Guidelines tab In force 1 June 2017. page 31
6.59 A sentence of detention for life should be used as a last resort when an extended sentence is not able to provide the level of public protection that is necessary. In order to determine this, the court should consider the following factors in the order given:

- the seriousness of the offence;
- the child or young person's previous findings of guilt;
- the level of danger posed to the public and whether there is a reliable estimate of the length of time the child or young person will remain a danger; and
- the alternative sentences available.

[184] Words substituted by Legal Aid, Sentencing and Punishment of Offenders Act 2012 Sch 21 para 9
[185] *R v Lang* 2005 EWCA Crim 2864, 2006 2 Cr App R (S) 3 (p 13)

The court is required to set a minimum term which must be served in custody before parole can be considered.
Dangerous Offenders Guide for Sentencers and Practitioners 2008 para 6.5.3 The Youth Justice Board anticipates that normally the court would find a youth to be a dangerous offender only if he or she was assessed in a pre-sentence report to pose a very high risk of serious harm or, in a small number of cases and due to specific circumstances, a high risk of serious harm. However, the court is not bound by the assessment of risk in the pre-sentence report; it does not follow automatically that, because an offender has been assessed as posing a high risk or very high risk of serious harm, he or she is a dangerous offender.
R (W) v Caernarfon Youth Court 2013 EWHC 1466 (Admin) D, aged 11, was charged with rape of a child under 13 (penetration of V's mouth), sexual assault of a child aged under 13 (×3) and common assault. V was aged 6. The District Judge accepted jurisdiction and the matter was adjourned for trial. Before the trial date D pleaded to all counts. Reports were ordered which revealed: a) a likelihood he had been exposed to adult pornography, b) when aged 5 and 7, he had invited others to lick his penis, and c) at school he had pulled boys' trousers down. The District Judge committed D for sentence under section 3C, because of the significant risk the defendant posed. The defence brought judicial review proceedings claiming that as there had been no trial there could not be a committal under section 3C. Held. We cannot accept that submission. The word 'trial' includes defendants who plead. Here the change of decision about jurisdiction arose because of the report. The District Judge was entitled to exercise his residual powers which are exercisable in very exceptional circumstances to commit D for sentence. Further the acceptance of summary jurisdiction created no legitimate expectation he would be dealt with summarily. However, on the facts, it was not open to the District Judge to commit. Case remitted back to the Youth Court.

13.17 ***Information, school and health reports, Duty to provide***
Children and Young Persons Act 1969 s 9(1) Where a local authority bring proceedings for an offence…it shall be the duty of the authority, unless they are of [the] opinion that it is unnecessary to do so, to make such investigation and provide the court with such information relating to the home surroundings, school report, health and character of the [offender] as appear to the authority likely to assist the court.
(2) If the court requests the authority (in s 9(1) above) to make investigations and provide information or to make further investigations and provide further information…it shall be the duty of the authority to comply with the request.

Reporting restrictions and the press

See also the **Procedure, Sentencing Anonymity/The press etc.** section at **86.6**.

13.18 ***Youth Court General principles***
For the principles see *Judicial College on Reporting Restrictions in the Criminal Courts 2015*, www.banksr.com Other Matters Other Documents Reporting Restrictions pages 14 and 19. Criminal Practice Directions 2015 EWCA Crim 1567 para II 16B specifically refers readers to this publication. Ed.

13.19 ***All courts Vulnerable defendants and the press***
Criminal Practice Directions 2015 EWCA Crim 1567 para I 3G.5 If any case against a vulnerable defendant has attracted or may attract widespread public or media interest, the assistance of the police should be enlisted to try to ensure that the defendant is not, when attending the court, exposed to intimidation, vilification or abuse. Criminal Justice Act 1925 s 41 prohibits the taking of photographs of defendants and witnesses (among others) in the court building or in its precincts, or when entering or leaving those precincts. A direction informing media representatives that the prohibition will be enforced may be appropriate. The court should be ready at this stage, if it has not already

done so, where relevant to make a reporting restriction under Children and Young Persons Act 1933 s 39 or, on an appeal to the Crown Court from a Youth Court, to remind media representatives of the application of section 49 of that Act.
Criminal Procedure Rules 2015 2015/1490 Rule 6 contains the procedure for making or opposing an application. See www.banksr.com Other Matters Other Documents tab.

13.20 ***Youth Court and appeals etc. Automatic anonymity Reporting restrictions***

Restrictions on reports of proceedings in which children or young persons are concerned.

Children and Young Persons Act 1933 s 49(1)[186] No matter relating to any child or young person concerned in proceedings to which this section applies shall while he is under the age of 18 be included in any publication if it is likely to lead members of the public to identify him as someone concerned in the proceedings.
(2) The proceedings to which this section applies are:
(a) proceedings in a youth court;
(b) proceedings on appeal from a youth court (including proceedings by way of case stated);
(c) proceedings in a magistrates' court under Schedule 2 to the Criminal Justice and Immigration Act 2008 (proceedings for breach, revocation or amendment of youth rehabilitation orders);
(d) proceedings on appeal from a magistrates' court arising out of any proceedings mentioned in paragraph (c) (including proceedings by way of case stated).
(3) In this section "publication" includes any speech, writing, relevant programme or other communication in whatever form, which is addressed to the public at large or any section of the public (and for this purpose every relevant programme shall be taken to be so addressed), but does not include an indictment or other document prepared for use in particular legal proceedings.
(3A) The matters relating to a person in relation to which the restrictions imposed by subsection (1) above apply (if their inclusion in any publication is likely to have the result mentioned in that subsection) include in particular:
(a) his name,
(b) his address,
(c) the identity of any school or other educational establishment attended by him,
(d) the identity of any place of work, and
(e) any still or moving picture of him.
(4) For the purposes of this section a child or young person is "concerned" in any proceedings if he is:
(a) a person against or in respect of whom the proceedings are taken, or
(b) a person called, or proposed to be called, to give evidence in the proceedings.
(4A)-(10) [see **13.21**]
(11) In this section: 'programme' and 'programme service' have the same meaning as in Broadcasting Act 1990.

The general prohibition on reporting matters that might lead to identifying any person under the age of 18 involved in the offence before trial is in Youth Justice and Criminal Evidence Act 1999 s 44. The restriction ceases to apply when the individual becomes aged 18.
For the principles about Youth Courts see *Judicial College on Reporting Restrictions in the Criminal Courts 2015*, www.banksr.com Other Matters Other Documents tab Reporting Restrictions pages 11 and 14.

[186] As amended by Youth Justice and Criminal Evidence Act 1999 Sch 2 para 3(2). In force 13/4/15

13.21 ***Youth Court and appeals etc. Automatic reporting anonymity Lifting the reporting restrictions***

Children and Young Persons Act 1933 s 49(4A) If a court is satisfied that it is in the public interest to do so, it may, in relation to a child or young person who has been convicted of an offence, by order dispense to any specified extent with the restrictions imposed by subsection (1) above[187] in relation to any proceedings before it to which this section applies by virtue of subsection (2)(a) or (b) above, being proceedings relating to:

(a) the prosecution or conviction of the offender for the offence,

(b) the manner in which he, or his parent or guardian, should be dealt with in respect of the offence,

(c) the enforcement, amendment, variation, revocation or discharge of any order made in respect of the offence,

(d) where an attendance centre order is made in respect of the offence, the enforcement of any rules made under Criminal Justice Act 2003s 222(1)(d) or (e), or

(e) where a detention and training order is made, the enforcement of any requirements imposed [by] Powers of Criminal Courts (Sentencing) Act 2000 s 103(6)(b).

(4B) A court shall not exercise its power under subsection (4A) above without:

(a) affording the parties to the proceedings an opportunity to make representations, and

(b) taking into account any representations which are duly made.

(5) Subject to subsection (7) below, a court may, in relation to proceedings before it to which this section applies, by order dispense to any specified extent with the requirements of this section in relation to a child or young person who is concerned in the proceedings if it is satisfied:

(a) that it is appropriate to do so for the purpose of avoiding injustice to the child or young person, or

(b) that, as respects a child or young person to whom this paragraph applies who is unlawfully at large, it is necessary to dispense with those requirements for the purpose of apprehending him and bringing him before a court or returning him to the place in which he was in custody.

(6) Paragraph (b) of subsection (5) above applies to any child or young person who is charged with or has been convicted of: a) a violent offence, b) a sexual offence, or c) an offence punishable in the case of a person aged 21 or over with imprisonment for 14 years or more.

(7) The court shall not exercise its power under subsection (5)(b) above:

(a) except in pursuance of an application by or on behalf of the Director of Public Prosecutions, and

(b) unless notice of the application has been given by the Director of Public Prosecutions to any legal representative of the child or young person.

(8) The court's power under subsection (4A) or (5) above may be exercised by a single justice.

(9)[188] If a publication includes any matter in contravention of subsection (1) above, the following persons shall be guilty of an offence and liable on summary conviction to a fine not exceeding level 5 on the standard scale:

(a) where the publication is a newspaper or periodical, any proprietor, any editor and any publisher of the newspaper or periodical;

(b) where the publication is a relevant programme:

(i) any body corporate or Scottish partnership engaged in providing the programme service in which the programme is included; and

(ii) any person having functions in relation to the programme corresponding to those of an editor of a newspaper;

[187] As amended by Youth Justice and Criminal Evidence Act 1999 Sch 2 para 3(5). In force 13/4/15

[188] Subsections (9) to (9E) were added by Youth Justice and Criminal Evidence Act 1999 Sch 2 para 3(7). In force 13/4/15

(c) in the case of any other publication, any person publishing it.

(9A) Where a person is charged with an offence under subsection (9) above it shall be a defence to prove that at the time of the alleged offence he was not aware, and neither suspected nor had reason to suspect, that the publication included the matter in question.

(9B) If an offence under subsection (9) above committed by a body corporate is proved:

(a) to have been committed with the consent or connivance of, or

(b) to be attributable to any neglect on the part of,

an officer, the officer as well as the body corporate is guilty of the offence and liable to be proceeded against and punished accordingly.

(9C) In subsection (9B) above "officer" means a director, manager, secretary or other similar officer of the body, or a person purporting to act in any such capacity.

(9D) If the affairs of a body corporate are managed by its members, "director" in subsection (9C) above means a member of that body.

(9E) Where an offence under subsection (9) above is committed by a Scottish partnership and is proved to have been committed with the consent or connivance of a partner, he as well as the partnership shall be guilty of the offence and shall be liable to be proceeded against and punished accordingly.

For the principles about Youth Courts lifting the restriction, see *Judicial College on Reporting Restrictions in the Criminal Courts 2015*, www.banksr.com Other Matters Other Documents tab Reporting Restrictions page 15.

(10) In any proceedings under Criminal Justice and Immigration Act 2008 Sch 2 (proceedings for breach, revocation or amendment of Youth Rehabilitation Orders) before a Magistrates' Court other than a Youth Court or on appeal from such a court it shall be the duty of the Magistrates' Court or the appellate court to announce in the course of the proceedings that this section applies to the proceedings, and if the court fails to do so this section shall not apply to the proceedings.

(11) In this section:..'sexual offence' means an offence listed in Criminal Justice Act 2003 Sch 15 Part 2, 'specified' means specified in an order under this section, 'violent offence' means an offence listed in Criminal Justice Act 2003 Sch 15 Part 1, and a person who, having been granted bail, is liable to arrest (whether with or without a warrant) shall be treated as unlawfully at large.

13.22 ***Youth Court and appeals etc. Automatic reporting restriction Lifting the reporting restrictions Cases***

Note: Children and Young Persons Act 1933 s 39 enabled courts to direct that certain details of children and young persons should not be published. Criminal Justice and Courts Act 2015 s 79(8) removed the power in the section. Ed.

R v Winchester Crown Court ex parte B 2000 1 Cr App R 11 B, aged 14, who was convicted of the attempted anal rape of a six-year-old boy, sought judicial review of the decision to lift a section 39 order imposing reporting restrictions. Held. The principles to be distilled from the various authorities can be summarised as follows: a) In deciding whether to impose or thereafter to lift reporting restrictions, the court will consider whether there are good reasons for naming the defendant, b) the court will give considerable weight to the age of the offender and to the potential damage to any young person of public identification as a criminal before the offender has the benefit or burden of adulthood, c) by virtue of Children and Young Persons Act 1933 s 44, the court must 'have regard to the welfare of the child or young person', d) the prospect of being named in court with the accompanying disgrace is a powerful deterrent and the naming of a defendant in the context of his punishment serves as a deterrent to others. These deterrents are proper objectives for the court to seek, e) there is a strong public interest in open justice and in the public knowing as much as possible about what has happened in court, including the identity of those who have committed crime, f) the weight to be attributed to the different factors may shift at different stages of the proceedings and, in particular, after the defendant has been found, or pleads, guilty and is sentenced. It may

then be appropriate to place greater weight on the interest of the public in knowing the identity of those who have committed crimes, particularly serious and detestable crimes, and g) the fact that an appeal has been made may be a material consideration.
Note: There is a growing trend to lift the anonymity where juveniles with serious previous convictions commit very serious offences. One example of this is when the President of the Queen's Bench lifted anonymity for a 14-year-old, see *Att-Gen's Ref Nos 21-22 of 2012* 2012 EWCA Crim 1806. The defendant in that case had committed domestic robberies and injured the victim. He and his accomplice also threatened to rape the victim. Ed.
R v Markham and Edwards 2017 EWCA Crim 739 M pleaded to and E was convicted of two murders. They each received a minimum term of 20 years. They were then aged 14 and now aged 15. Before the trial the Judge maintained the section 39 order for both M and E. After the trial, he lifted the order noting that there was now 'a high public interest in identifying' M and E, there was no longer a need for the integrity of the trial process to be preserved and in three years' time (when M and E would be aged 18), the order would no longer apply. Held. [Cases and principles stated and applied.] para 88 The Judge reached the correct conclusion. There was no evidence that the lifting of the reporting restrictions would adversely affect the rehabilitation of M or E. M and E will still be in custody long after the ending of the order. The lifting of the restrictions was a reasonable and proportionate measure balancing the [various principles].
For more details, see **287.27** in Volume 2.
See also: *R (Y) v Aylesbury Crown Court ex parte H* 2000 1 Cr App R 262 (The fact that the defendant's identity is known by local people and the publicity might give him some protection from those who thought he was involved in more arsons were unsatisfactory reasons. Factors listed. Order quashed.)
R v Manchester Crown Court ex parte H 2000 1 Cr App R 262 (The fact that there is an appeal and there might be a retrial was a factor. Other principles considered.)
C v Winchester Crown Court 2014 EWCA Crim 339 (Judicial review of decision to vary a section 39 order. Factors in favour of publication are outweighed by factors such as prisoners and persons in his local area not knowing the defendant's identity and the desire for rehabilitation. Section 39 order to remain in force.)
Note: The Court sat as the Criminal Division of the Court of Appeal to hear the conviction appeal and then reconstituted itself as the Divisional Court to hear the judicial review. Ed.

13.23 *Youth Court and appeals etc. Automatic reporting anonymity Lifting the reporting restrictions Appeals*

R v Manchester Crown Court ex parte H 2000 1 Cr App R 262 H and D were convicted of murdering an elderly woman. The Judge lifted the section 39 anonymity order. H and D appealed. Held after reviewing conflicting authority. There is an appeal to the High Court when the order has been lifted by the judge. On the facts, order quashed.
Note: This case overturns *R v Winchester Crown Court ex parte B* 2000 1 Cr App R 11. Ed.

13.24 *All courts Discretionary reporting restriction*

Note: For the rules to apply see Criminal Procedure Rules 2015 2015/1490 Rule 16 www.banksr.com Other Matters Other Documents tab. The CPS has given guidance to prosecutors, *Guidance on Imposing and Lifting Reporting Restrictions in cases involving Youths who are convicted*, which can be found on its website. Ed.
Power to restrict reporting of criminal proceedings involving persons under 18
Youth Justice and Criminal Evidence Act 1999 s 45(1)[189] This section applies (subject to subsection (2)) in relation to:

[189] In force 13/4/15, Youth Justice and Criminal Evidence Act 1999 (Commencement No 14) (England and Wales) Order 2015 2015/818

(a) any criminal proceedings in any court (other than a service court) in England and Wales or Northern Ireland, and

(b) any proceedings (whether in the United Kingdom or elsewhere) in any service court.

(2) This section does not apply in relation to any proceedings to which Children and Young Persons Act 1933 s 49 (see **13.20**) applies.

(3) The court may direct that no matter relating to any person concerned in the proceedings shall while he is under the age of 18 be included in any publication if it is likely to lead members of the public to identify him as a person concerned in the proceedings.

(4) The court or an appellate court may by direction ('an excepting direction') dispense, to any extent specified in the excepting direction, with the restrictions imposed by a direction under subsection (3) if it is satisfied that it is necessary in the interests of justice to do so.

(5) The court or an appellate court may also by direction ('an excepting direction') dispense, to any extent specified in the excepting direction, with the restrictions imposed by a direction under subsection (3) if it is satisfied:

(a) that their effect is to impose a substantial and unreasonable restriction on the reporting of the proceedings, and

(b) that it is in the public interest to remove or relax that restriction,

but no excepting direction shall be given under this subsection by reason only of the fact that the proceedings have been determined in any way or have been abandoned.

(6) When deciding whether to make:

(a) a direction under subsection (3) in relation to a person, or

(b) an excepting direction under subsection (4) or (5) by virtue of which the restrictions imposed by a direction under subsection (3) would be dispensed with (to any extent) in relation to a person,

the court or (as the case may be) the appellate court shall have regard to the welfare of that person.

(7) For the purposes of subsection (3) any reference to a person concerned in the proceedings is to a person:

(a) against or in respect of whom the proceedings are taken, or

(b) who is a witness in the proceedings.

(8) The matters relating to a person in relation to which the restrictions imposed by a direction under subsection (3) apply (if their inclusion in any publication is likely to have the result mentioned in that subsection) include in particular:

(a) his name,

(b) his address,

(c) the identity of any school or other educational establishment attended by him,

(d) the identity of any place of work, and

(e) any still or moving picture of him.

(9) A direction under subsection (3) may be revoked by the court or an appellate court.

(10) An excepting direction:

(a) may be given at the time the direction under subsection (3) is given or subsequently, and

(b) may be varied or revoked by the court or an appellate court.

(11) In this section 'appellate court', in relation to any proceedings in a court, means a court dealing with an appeal (including an appeal by way of case stated) arising out of the proceedings or with any further appeal.

Note: Criminal Justice and Courts Act 2015 s 78 inserts: a) Youth Justice and Criminal Evidence Act 1999 s 45A, which enables a court to impose lifetime restrictions on reporting for witnesses and victims aged under 18, and b) Children and Young Persons Act 1963 s 39A, which relates to providers of information society services. Ed.

For the principles about discretionary reporting restrictions see *Judicial College on Reporting Restrictions in the Criminal Courts 2015*, www.banksr.com Other Matters Other Documents tab Reporting Restrictions pages 19 and 38.

R v Jolleys ex parte Press Association 2013 EWCA Crim 1135 The Judge imposed an order to shield the son of the defendant. The Press Association appealed. Held. 'Concerned in the proceedings' means 'the person by or against or in respect of whom proceedings are taken or a witness'. It was for the person seeking to derogate from open justice to justify that derogation with clear and cogent evidence, see *R v CCC ex parte W, B and C* 2001 1 Cr App R 2. Other principles considered. There was no power to make the order.

13.25 *All courts Discretionary reporting restrictions for witnesses and victims aged under 18 (life-time orders)*

Power to restrict reporting of criminal proceedings for lifetime of witnesses and victims under 18

Youth Justice and Criminal Evidence Act 1999 s 45A(1)[190] This section applies in relation to:

(a) any criminal proceedings in any court (other than a service court) in England and Wales, and

(b) any proceedings (whether in the United Kingdom or elsewhere) in any service court.

(2) The court may make a direction ("a reporting direction") that no matter relating to a person mentioned in subsection (3) shall during that person's lifetime be included in any publication if it is likely to lead members of the public to identify that person as being concerned in the proceedings.

(3) A reporting direction may be made only in respect of a person who is under the age of 18 when the proceedings commence and who is:

(a) a witness, other than an accused, in the proceedings;

(b) a person against whom the offence, which is the subject of the proceedings, is alleged to have been committed.

(4) For the purposes of subsection (2), matters relating to a person in respect of whom the reporting direction is made include:

(a) the person's name,

(b) the person's address,

(c) the identity of any school or other educational establishment attended by the person,

(d) the identity of any place of work of the person, and

(e) any still or moving picture of the person.

(5) The court may make a reporting direction in respect of a person only if it is satisfied that:

(a) the quality of any evidence given by the person, or

(b) the level of co-operation given by the person to any party to the proceedings in connection with that party's preparation of its case, is likely to be diminished by reason of fear or distress on the part of the person in connection with being identified by members of the public as a person concerned in the proceedings.

(6) In determining whether subsection (5) is satisfied, the court must in particular take into account:

(a) the nature and alleged circumstances of the offence to which the proceedings relate;

(b) the age of the person;

(c) such of the following as appear to the court to be relevant:

(i) the social and cultural background and ethnic origins of the person,

(ii) the domestic, educational and employment circumstances of the person, and

[190] This section was inserted by Criminal Justice and Courts Act 2015 s 78(2). In force 13/4/15

(iii) any religious beliefs or political opinions of the person;
(d) any behaviour towards the person on the part of:
(i) an accused,
(ii) members of the family or associates of an accused, or
(iii) any other person who is likely to be an accused or a witness in the proceedings.

(7) In determining that question the court must in addition consider any views expressed:
(a) by the person in respect of whom the reporting restriction may be made, and
(b) where that person is under the age of 16, by an appropriate person other than an accused.

(8) In determining whether to make a reporting direction in respect of a person, the court must have regard to:
(a) the welfare of that person,
(b) whether it would be in the interests of justice to make the direction, and
(c) the public interest in avoiding the imposition of a substantial and unreasonable restriction on the reporting of the proceedings.

(9) A reporting direction may be revoked by the court or an appellate court.

(10) The court or an appellate court may by direction ("an excepting direction") dispense, to any extent specified in the excepting direction, with the restrictions imposed by a reporting direction.

(11)-(14) [Re Excepting directions. Not listed.]

(15) For the purposes of this section:
(a) criminal proceedings in a court other than a service court commence when proceedings are instituted for the purposes of Part 1 of the Prosecution of Offences Act 1985, in accordance with section 15(2) of that Act;
(b) proceedings in a service court commence when the charge is brought under section 122 of the Armed Forces Act 2006.

(16) In this section:
(a) "appellate court", in relation to any proceedings in a court, means a court dealing with an appeal (including an appeal by way of case stated) arising out of the proceedings or with any further appeal;
(b) "appropriate person" has the same meaning as in section 50;
(c) references to the quality of evidence given by a person are to its quality in terms of completeness, coherence and accuracy (and for this purpose "coherence" refers to a person's ability in giving evidence to give answers which address the questions put to the person and can be understood both individually and collectively);
(d) references to the preparation of the case of a party to any proceedings include, where the party is the prosecution, the carrying out of investigations into any offence at any time charged in the proceedings.

For the principles about life-time orders see *Judicial College on Reporting Restrictions in the Criminal Courts 2015*, www.banksr.com Other Matters Other Documents tab Reporting Restrictions pages 22 and 38.

Note: This is a life-time prohibition, see subsection (2). Ed.

Treatment of offenders under 18 in adult courts

13.26 *Treating children as vulnerable defendants*

Criminal Practice Directions 2015 EWCA Crim 1567 para I 3D.1 …'Vulnerable' includes those under 18 years of age and people with a mental disorder or learning disability, a physical disorder or disability, or who are likely to suffer fear or distress in giving evidence because of their own circumstances or those relating to the case.

Criminal Practice Directions 2015 EWCA Crim 1567 para I 3D.2 …This includes enabling a witness or defendant to give their best evidence, and enabling a defendant to comprehend the proceedings and engage fully with his or her defence. The pre-trial and trial process should, so far as necessary, be adapted to meet those ends. Regard should be

had to the welfare of a young defendant as required by Children and Young Persons Act 1933 s 44 and generally to Criminal Procedure Rules 2015 2015/1490 Parts 1 and 3 (the overriding objective and the court's powers of case management).
Criminal Practice Directions 2015 EWCA Crim 1567 para I 3G.2 It may be appropriate to arrange that a vulnerable defendant should visit, out of court hours and before the trial, sentencing or appeal hearing, the courtroom in which that hearing is to take place so that he or she can familiarise him or herself with it.
3G.3 Where an intermediary is being used to help the defendant to communicate at court, the intermediary should accompany the defendant on his or her pre-trial visit. The visit will enable the defendant to familiarise him or herself with the layout of the court, and may include matters such as: where the defendant will sit, either in the dock or otherwise; court officials (what their roles are and where they sit); who else might be in the court, for example those in the public gallery and press box; the location of the witness box; basic court procedure; and the facilities available in the court.
3G.4 If the defendant's use of the live link is being considered, he or she should have an opportunity to have a practice session.
3G.5 If any case against a vulnerable defendant has attracted or may attract widespread public or media interest, the assistance of the police should be enlisted to try and ensure that the defendant is not, when attending the court, exposed to intimidation, vilification or abuse. Criminal Justice Act 1925 s 41 prohibits the taking of photographs of defendants and witnesses (among others) in the court building or in its precincts, or when entering or leaving those precincts. A direction reminding media representatives of the prohibition may be appropriate. The court should also be ready at this stage, if it has not already done so, where relevant to make a reporting restriction under Children and Young Persons Act 1933 s 39 or, on an appeal to the Crown Court from a youth court, to remind media representatives of the application of section 49 of that Act.
Criminal Practice Directions 2015 EWCA Crim 1567 para I 3G.8 Subject again to the need for appropriate security arrangements, a vulnerable defendant, especially if he is young, should normally, if he wishes, be free to sit with members of his family or others in a like relationship, and with some other suitable supporting adult such as a social worker, and in a place which permits easy, informal communication with his legal representatives. The court should ensure that a suitable supporting adult is available throughout the course of the proceedings.
3G.9 It is essential that at the beginning of the proceedings, the court should ensure that what is to take place has been explained to a vulnerable defendant in terms he or she can understand and, at trial in the Crown Court, it should ensure in particular that the role of the jury has been explained. It should remind those representing the vulnerable defendant and the supporting adult of their responsibility to explain each step as it takes place and, at trial, explain the possible consequences of a guilty verdict and credit for a guilty plea. The court should also remind any intermediary of the responsibility to ensure that the vulnerable defendant has understood the explanations given to him/her. Throughout the trial the court should continue to ensure, by any appropriate means, that the defendant understands what is happening and what has been said by those on the bench, the advocates and witnesses.
Note: This section of the directions deals primarily with trials and the giving of evidence. However, the above edited parts may also assist sentencing hearings although the pressures then are not so protracted or acute. Ed.

13.27 ***Appointment of intermediaries to assist the defendant***
Criminal Practice Directions 2015 EWCA Crim 1567 para I 3F[191] This is the section on intermediaries, which includes: para 3F.3 'A court may use its inherent powers to appoint an intermediary to assist the defendant's communication at trial (either solely when giving evidence or throughout the trial) and, where necessary, in preparation for

[191] As inserted by Criminal Practice Directions 2015 Amendment No 1 2016 EWCA Crim 97 page 6.

the trial.' Relevant cases are listed. para 3F.5 'Assessment should be considered if a child or young person under 18 seems unlikely to be able to recognise a problematic question, or, even if able to do so, may be reluctant to say so to a questioner in a position of authority. … For children aged 11 and under in particular, there should be a presumption that an intermediary assessment is appropriate.'

R v H 2003 EWCA Crim 1209 Courts have an inherent right, indeed a duty, to appoint an intermediary to help a defendant follow the proceedings and to give evidence, if without such assistance he would be unable to have a fair trial.

R (C) v Sevenoaks Youth Court 2009 EWHC 3088 (Admin) When trying a young child, such as this child, with learning difficulties, the Youth Court has a duty under its inherent powers and under the Criminal Procedure Rules to take such steps as are necessary to ensure that he has a fair trial, not just during the proceedings, but beforehand as he and his lawyers prepare for trial. (The Court also dealt with the problem of payment of intermediaries. Ed.)

See also: *SC v UK* 2005 60958/00 and *R v Cox* 2012 EWCA Crim 549, 2 Cr App R (S) 6 (p 63) (LCJ We immediately recognise the valuable contribution made to the administration of justice by the use of intermediaries in appropriate cases.)

R v Holloway 2016 EWCA Crim 2175 (D was indicted with attempted murder of a doctor when an inpatient in a mental hospital. He dismissed his lawyers. Fit to plead. Judge appointed counsel to help him, who helped with advice, cross-examined some witnesses and negotiated with prosecution. Held. Counsel was very helpful to D. Principles considered. There was no power to appoint the counsel.)

R v Biddle 2019 EWCA Crim 86 D was convicted of rape. He was at trial aged 17. He was granted an intermediary. The trial Judge said there was no need for an intermediary for the whole trial, just for the giving of evidence. The intermediary provider declined to attend. Relevant cases were cited. Held. The courts and the MoJ have recognised the important role an intermediary may play in facilitating the proper participation of a vulnerable defendant in their trial. It is not for the provider to dictate the duration of the need for an intermediary. The provider can make a recommendation but it is just that, a recommendation. Ultimately it is for the trial judge to decide, having considered all the material, whether and to what extent an intermediary is necessary. Other Judges might have made a different decision, but the Judge was entitled to rule as he did.

Note: These cases deal with trials. It is possible to stretch the principles to sentence hearings but a grant of intermediaries for sentence hearings seems exceptionally unlikely. Coroners and Justice Act 2009 s 104 inserted Youth Justice and Criminal Evidence Act 1999 s 33BA, which introduced a statutory power for offenders to be examined through intermediaries. Commencement is awaited. Ed.

For an article about intermediaries, see *Dispensing with the 'safety net': Is the intermediary really needed during cross-examination? Archbold Review* 6 July 2017.

13.28 ***Vulnerable children and young offenders Sentencing***

Sentencing Children and Young People Guideline 2017 www.banksr.com Other Matters Guidelines tab In force 1 June 2017. page 7

1.20 When considering a child or young person who may be particularly vulnerable, sentencers should consider which available disposal is best able to support the child or young person and which disposals could potentially exacerbate any underlying issues. This is particularly important when considering custodial sentences as there are concerns about the effect on vulnerable children and young people of being in closed conditions, with significant risks of self harm, including suicide.

1.21 The vulnerability factors that are often present in the background of children and young people should also be considered in light of the offending behaviour itself. Although they do not alone cause offending behaviour – there are many children and young people who have experienced these circumstances but do not commit crime – there is a correlation and any response to criminal activity amongst children and young people will need to recognise the presence of such factors in order to be effective.

13.29 ***Power and duty to remit young offenders to Youth Courts for sentence***
Powers of Criminal Courts (Sentencing) Act 2000 s 8(1) Subsection (2) below applies where a child or young person (that is to say, any person aged under 18) is convicted by or before any court of an offence other than homicide.
(2) The court may and, if it is not a Youth Court, shall unless satisfied that it would be undesirable to do so, remit the case:
(a) if the offender was sent to the Crown Court for trial under Crime and Disorder Act 1998 s 51 or 51A to a Youth Court acting for the place where he was sent to the Crown Court for trial,
(b) in any other case, to a Youth Court acting either for the same place as the remitting court or for the place where the offender habitually resides,
but in relation to a Magistrates' Court other than a Youth Court this subsection has effect subject to subsection (6) below.
(3) Where a case is remitted under subsection (2) above, the offender shall be brought before a Youth Court accordingly, and that court may deal with him in any way in which it might have dealt with him if he had been tried and convicted by that court.
(4) A court by which an order remitting a case to a Youth Court is made under subsection (2) above:
(a) may, subject to Criminal Justice and Public Order Act 1994 s 25 (restrictions on granting bail), give such directions as appear to be necessary with respect to the custody of the offender or for his release on bail until he can be brought before the Youth Court, and
(b) shall cause to be transmitted to the designated officer for the Youth Court a certificate setting out the nature of the offence and stating:
(i) that the offender has been convicted of the offence, and
(ii) that the case has been remitted for the purpose of being dealt with under the preceding provisions of this section.
(5) Where a case is remitted under subsection (2) above, the offender shall have no right of appeal against the order of remission, but shall have the same right of appeal against any order of the court to which the case is remitted as if he had been convicted by that court.
(6) Without prejudice to the power to remit any case to a Youth Court which is conferred on a Magistrates' Court other than a Youth Court by subsections (1) and (2) above, where such a Magistrates' Court convicts a child or young person of an offence it must exercise that power unless the case falls within subsection (7) or (8) below.
(7) The case falls within this subsection if the court would, were it not so to remit the case, be required by section 16(2) below to refer the offender to a youth offender panel (in which event the court may, but need not, so remit the case).
(8) The case falls within this subsection if it does not fall within subsection (7) above but the court is of the opinion that the case is one which can properly be dealt with by means of:
(a) an order discharging the offender absolutely or conditionally, or
(b) an order for the payment of a fine, or
(c) an order (under section 150 below) requiring the offender's parent or guardian to enter into a recognisance to take proper care of him and exercise proper control over him,
with or without any other order that the court has power to make when absolutely or conditionally discharging an offender.
Sentencing Children and Young People Guideline 2017 www.banksr.com Other Matters Guidelines tab In force 1 June 2017. page 10
Remittal from the Crown Court for sentence
2.15 If a child or young person is found guilty before the Crown Court of an offence other than homicide the court must remit the case to the Youth Court, unless it would be

undesirable to do so.[192] In considering whether remittal is undesirable a court should balance the need for expertise in the sentencing of children and young people with the benefits of the sentence being imposed by the court which determined guilt.

2.16 Particular attention should be given to children and young people who are appearing before the Crown Court only because they have been charged with an adult offender; referral orders are generally not available in the Crown Court but may be the most appropriate sentence.

R v Lewis 1984 6 Cr App R (S) 44 Criminal Justice Act 1982 made an alignment of the sentencing powers of the [Crown] Court and the [Magistrates'] Court and the concept of the [Youth] Court being the sole proper forum to deal with juveniles now is out of place. Possible reasons that it would be undesirable [under what is now Powers of Criminal Courts (Sentencing) Act 2000 s 8(2)(a)] to do so are as follows (these of course are by no means comprehensive):

a) that the judge who presided over the trial will be better informed as to the facts and circumstances,
b) that there is, in the sad and frequent experience of this Court, a risk of unacceptable disparity if co-defendants are to be sentenced in different courts on different occasions,
c) that as a result of the remission there will be delay, duplication of proceedings and fruitless expense, and
d) the provisions for appeal [to either the Crown Court or the Court of Appeal].

However, it may become desirable to remit the case where a report has to be obtained and the judge will be unable to sit when the report becomes available, but this situation should be avoided wherever possible.

R v A 1999 163 JP 841 D, aged 16, was committed for trial on the basis that the offences were grave crimes. He pleaded and was remitted to the Youth Court for sentence. He faced an additional offence which was committed for trial. The Youth Court committed the original matters to the Crown Court for sentence under Magistrates' Courts Act 1980 s 6(2). Held. There was no power to do so. However, they did have the power to do so under Magistrates' Courts Act 1980 s 37. We quash the committals and [one of us] sitting as a Magistrate commits the charges to the Crown Court. We then uphold the sentences.

R v Dillon 2017 EWCA Crim 2642, 2019 1 Cr App R (S) 22 (p 155) D was sent to the Crown Court with an adult, AD, on a £102,000 fraud charge. D pleaded guilty and his sentence was adjourned. AD was dealt with at a separate hearing. On D's resumed hearing he was now aged 18. D's role was assessed at the lowest end and he was of good character. The pre-sentence report recommended a Referral Order but it said that order would need a remittal to the Youth Court. The matter was put back and it was suggested the Judge could sit as a district judge. The Judge made a Youth Rehabilitation Order. Held. The pre-sentence report was correct about the Referral Order. The case should have been remitted immediately after the plea (see *R v Lewis* 1984 [above]) because there was no issue of disparity and there was no direct link with AD. The Youth Court is given exclusive competence to make a Referral Order and the Judge could not acquire that by sitting as a district judge. There would have been no extra delay as a pre-sentence report was required. At the Youth Court a Referral Order had to be made. Neither we nor the Crown Court can make a Referral Order. Given the delay, the errors and D's good performance with the Youth Rehabilitation Order, we substitute a conditional discharge. Note: Whether the Judge purported to act as a district judge or just sat as a Crown Court judge is not clear. Ed.

Publicity, see the **Reporting restrictions** section at **13.19**.

[192] Powers of Criminal Courts (Sentencing) Act 2000 s 8

Sentencing principles

13.30 ***Aims and purposes*** ***Statutes***

Crime and Disorder Act 1998 s 37(1) It shall be the principal aim of the youth justice system to prevent offending by children and young persons.

(2) In addition to any other duty to which they are subject, it shall be the duty of all persons and bodies carrying out functions in relation to the youth justice system to have regard to that aim.

Note: Until Criminal Justice Act 2003 s 142A(3)[193] is in force there are no statutory purposes for offenders aged under 18. Section 142A(3) states that for offenders aged under 18 the purposes of sentencing are the punishment of offenders, the reform and rehabilitation of offenders, the protection of offenders and the making of reparation by offenders to persons affected by their offences. (The Act does not apply to minimum sentences for firearm offences, minimum sentences for certain cases of using someone to mind a weapon (Violent Crime Reduction Act 2006 s 29(6)), detention for life for dangerous offenders or to the making of a Hospital Order, an Interim Hospital Order, a hospital direction or a mental health limitation direction order.[194]) Ed.

13.31 ***Sentencing Children and Young People Guideline 2017*** ***Basic principles***

Sentencing Children and Young People Guideline 2017 www.banksr.com Other Matters Guidelines tab In force 1 June 2017. page 4

Sentencing principles

1.1 When sentencing children or young people (those aged under 18 at the date of the finding of guilt) a court must[195] have regard to:

- the principal aim of the youth justice system (to prevent offending by children and young people);[196] and
- the welfare of the child or young person.[197]

1.2 While the seriousness of the offence will be the starting point, the approach to sentencing should be individualistic and focused on the child or young person, as opposed to offence focused. For a child or young person the sentence should focus on rehabilitation where possible. A court should also consider the effect the sentence is likely to have on the child or young person (both positive and negative) as well as any underlying factors contributing to the offending behaviour.

1.3 Domestic and international laws dictate that a custodial sentence should always be a measure of last resort for children and young people and statute provides that a custodial sentence may only be imposed when the offence is so serious that no other sanction is appropriate (see [**13.15** and **14.8**] for more information on custodial sentences).

1.4 It is important to avoid "criminalising" children and young people unnecessarily; the primary purpose of the youth justice system is to encourage children and young people to take responsibility for their own actions and promote re-integration into society rather than to punish. Restorative justice disposals may be of particular value for children and young people as they can encourage them to take responsibility for their actions and understand the impact their offence may have had on others.

1.5 It is important to bear in mind any factors that may diminish the culpability of a child or young person. Children and young people are not fully developed and they have not attained full maturity. As such, this can impact on their decision making and risk taking behaviour. It is important to consider the extent to which the child or young person has been acting impulsively and whether their conduct has been affected by inexperience,

[193] As inserted by Criminal Justice and Immigration Act 2008 s 9. There has been no commencement order for this subsection. It is believed that the Minister for Justice wants deterrence to be a purpose of sentencing for children and young offenders, so that will require new legislation.

[194] Criminal Justice Act 2003 s 142A(4)

[195] This section does not apply when imposing a mandatory life sentence, when imposing a statutory minimum custodial sentence, when imposing detention for life under the dangerous offender provisions or when making certain orders under Mental Health Act 1983.

[196] Crime and Disorder Act 1998 s 37(1)

[197] Children and Young Persons Act 1933 s 44(1)

emotional volatility or negative influences. They may not fully appreciate the effect their actions can have on other people and may not be capable of fully understanding the distress and pain they cause to the victims of their crimes. Children and young people are also likely to be susceptible to peer pressure and other external influences and changes taking place during adolescence can lead to experimentation, resulting in criminal behaviour. When considering a child or young person's age their emotional and developmental age is of at least equal importance to their chronological age (if not greater).

1.6 For these reasons, children and young people are likely to benefit from being given an opportunity to address their behaviour and may be receptive to changing their conduct. They should, if possible, be given the opportunity to learn from their mistakes without undue penalisation or stigma, especially as a court sanction might have a significant effect on the prospects and opportunities of the child or young person and hinder their re-integration into society.

1.7 Offending by a child or young person is often a phase which passes fairly rapidly and so the sentence should not result in the alienation of the child or young person from society if that can be avoided.

1.8 The impact of punishment is likely to be felt more heavily by a child or young person in comparison to an adult as any sentence will seem longer due to their young age. In addition penal interventions may interfere with a child or young person's education and this should be considered by a court at sentencing.

1.9 Any restriction on liberty must be commensurate with the seriousness of the offence. In considering the seriousness of any offence, the court must consider the child or young person's culpability in committing the offence and any harm which the offence caused, was intended to cause or might foreseeably have caused.[198]

1.10 Criminal Justice Act 2003 s 142 sets out the purposes of sentencing for offenders who are over 18 on the date of conviction. That Act was amended in 2008 to add section 142A, which sets out the purposes of sentencing for children and young people, subject to a commencement order being made. The difference between the purposes of sentencing for those under and over 18 is that section 142A does not include as a purpose of sentencing 'the reduction of crime (including its reduction by deterrence)'. Section 142A has not been brought into effect. Unless and until that happens, deterrence can be a factor in sentencing children and young people although normally it should be restricted to serious offences and can, and often will, be outweighed by considerations of the child or young person's welfare.

For more information on assessing the seriousness of the offence see [13.32].

13.32 Section four: Determining the sentence

Sentencing Children and Young People Guideline 2017 www.banksr.com Other Matters Guidelines tab In force 1 June 2017. page 4

4.1 In determining the sentence, the key elements to consider are:

- the principal aim of the youth justice system (to prevent re-offending by children and young people);
- the welfare of the child or young person;
- the age of the child or young person (chronological, developmental and emotional);
- the seriousness of the offence;
- the likelihood of further offences being committed; and
- the extent of harm likely to result from those further offences.

The seriousness of the offence

(This applies to all offences; when offence specific guidance for children and young people is available this should be referred to.)

[198] Criminal Justice Act 2003 s 143(1)

4.2 The seriousness of the offence is the starting point for determining the appropriate sentence; the sentence imposed and any restriction on liberty must be commensurate with the seriousness of the offence.
4.3 The approach to sentencing children and young people should always be individualistic and the court should always have in mind the principal aims of the youth justice system.
4.4 In order to determine the seriousness of the offence the court should assess the culpability of the child or young person and the harm that was caused, intended to be caused or could foreseeably have been caused.
4.5 In assessing **culpability** the court will wish to consider the extent to which the offence was planned, the role of the child or young person (if the offence was committed as part of a group), the level of force that was used in the commission of the offence and the awareness that the child or young person had of their actions and its possible consequences. There is an expectation that in general a child or young person will be dealt with less severely than an adult offender. In part, this is because children and young people are unlikely to have the same experience and capacity as an adult to understand the effect of their actions on other people or to appreciate the pain and distress caused and because a child or young person may be less able to resist temptation, especially where peer pressure is exerted. Children and young people are inherently more vulnerable than adults due to their age and the court will need to consider any mental health problems and/or learning disabilities they may have, as well as their emotional and developmental age. Any external factors that may have affected the child or young person's behaviour should be taken into account.
4.6 In assessing **harm** the court should consider the level of physical and psychological harm caused to the victim, the degree of any loss caused to the victim and the extent of any damage caused to property. (This assessment should also include a consideration of any harm that was intended to be caused or could foreseeably have been caused in the committal of the offence.)

13.33 [Aggravating and mitigating factors]
4.7 The court should also consider any aggravating or mitigating factors that may increase or reduce the overall seriousness of the offence. **If any of these factors are included in the definition of the committed offence they should not be taken into account when considering the relative seriousness of the offence before the court.**

Aggravating factors
Statutory aggravating factors:
Previous findings of guilt, having regard to a) the **nature** of the offence to which the finding of guilt relates and its **relevance** to the current offence; and b) the **time** that has elapsed since the finding of guilt
Offence committed whilst on bail
Offence motivated by, or demonstrating hostility based on any of the following characteristics or presumed characteristics of the victim: religion, race, disability, sexual orientation or transgender identity
Other aggravating factors (non-exhaustive):
Steps taken to prevent the victim reporting or obtaining assistance
Steps taken to prevent the victim from assisting or supporting the prosecution
Victim is particularly vulnerable due to factors including but not limited to age, mental or physical disability
Restraint, detention or additional degradation of the victim
Prolonged nature of offence

Attempts to conceal/dispose of evidence
Established evidence of community/wider impact
Failure to comply with current court orders
Attempt to conceal identity
Involvement of others through peer pressure, bullying, coercion or manipulation
Commission of offence whilst under the influence of alcohol or drugs
History of antagonising or bullying the victim
Deliberate humiliation of victim, including but not limited to filming of the offence, deliberately committing the offence before a group of peers with the intention of causing additional distress or circulating details/photos/videos etc. of the offence on social media or within peer groups
Prolonged nature of offence

Factors reducing seriousness or reflecting personal mitigation (non-exhaustive)
No previous findings of guilt **or** no relevant/recent findings of guilt
Remorse, particularly where evidenced by voluntary reparation to the victim
Good character and/or exemplary conduct
Unstable upbringing including but not limited to: • time spent looked after • lack of familial presence or support • disrupted experiences in accommodation or education • exposure to drug/alcohol abuse, familial criminal behaviour or domestic abuse • victim of neglect or abuse, or exposure to neglect or abuse of others • experiences of trauma or loss
Participated in offence due to bullying, peer pressure, coercion or manipulation
Limited understanding of effect on victim
Serious medical condition requiring urgent, intensive or long-term treatment
Communication or learning disabilities or mental health concerns
In education, work or training
Particularly young or immature child or young person (where it affects their responsibility)
Determination and/or demonstration of steps taken to address addiction or offending behaviour

13.34 ***Discount for the age of the offender***

Age and maturity of the child or young person

page 16 **4.8** There is a statutory presumption that no child under the age of 10 can be guilty of an offence.[199]

4.9 With a child or young person, the consideration of age requires a different approach to that which would be adopted in relation to the age of an adult. Even within the category of child or young person the response of a court to an offence is likely to be very different depending on whether the child or young person is at the lower end of the age bracket, in the middle or towards the top end.

4.10 Although chronological age dictates in some instances what sentence can be imposed (see [**13.15** and **14.8**] for more information) the developmental and emotional age of the child or young person should always be considered and it is of at least equal

[199] Children and Young Persons Act 1933 s 50

importance as their chronological age. It is important to consider whether the child or young person has the necessary maturity to appreciate fully the consequences of their conduct, the extent to which the child or young person has been acting on an impulsive basis and whether their conduct has been affected by inexperience, emotional volatility or negative influences.

R v Ghafoor 2002 EWCA Crim 1857, 2003 1 Cr App R (S) 84 (p 428) The philosophy of restricting sentencing powers for young persons reflects both a) society's acceptance that young offenders are less responsible for their actions and therefore less culpable than adults and b) the recognition that in consequence sentencing them should place greater emphasis on rehabilitation and less on retribution and deterrence than in the case of adults.

R (A) v Leeds Magistrates' Court 2004 EWHC 554 (Admin) The High Court held that where the person against whom the order is sought is a child, the child's best interests are a primary consideration but so are the interests of the public.

R v Adeojo and Mugambwa 2008 EWCA Crim 1552, 2009 1 Cr App R (S) 66 (p 376) The defendants pleaded to robbery. A guard delivering cash was attacked by a four-man gang. Two of the defendants alleged disparity because one of them, a 16-year-old, received a non-custodial sentence. Held. The Court had to have regard to the welfare of the child or young person. He was on the facts less culpable. From time to time the Court is not only encouraged to but entitled to show mercy to a young offender.

R v N, D and L 2010 EWCA Crim 941 LCJ N was convicted of aiding and abetting rape and false imprisonment. D pleaded to rape (×3) and L pleaded to attempted rape and aiding and abetting rape. The victim, V, was aged 13 and started to communicate via computer with D. D and V had not met each other in person. They arranged to meet and D took V to N's flat. L arrived shortly afterwards. D raped V twice, one instance of which involved N and L holding V's legs. D committed oral rape on V. L attempted to rape V. D played with a cigarette lighter and burned some of V's hair. V was not allowed to leave. Some of the activity was filmed by L. D and N were aged 16. L was aged 15. When addressing D, the Judge said, "...in relation to you, no discount for youth is appropriate at all, based on the seriousness of your criminal conduct in this case." Held. It is an old and well-established principle of sentencing that the youth of an offender should normally lead to a lower sentence. It has been repeated time and time again. *Sexual Offences Act 2003 Guideline 2008* para 1.17 states: 'The youth and immaturity of an offender must always be potential mitigating factors for the courts to take into account when passing sentence. However, where the facts of a case are particularly serious, the youth of the offender will not necessarily mitigate the appropriate sentence.' The *Youths Sentencing Guideline 2009* para 1.2, see www.banksr.com Other Matters Guidelines tab, points out that when sentencing an offender aged under 18, a court must have regard to the principal aim of the youth justice system, to prevent offending by children and young persons and the welfare of the offender. Another paragraph states that the youth of the offender is widely recognised as requiring a different approach from that which would be adopted in relation to an adult. There will from time to time be individual offenders whose maturity levels are well in advance of those to be expected of most youths of a similar chronological age. A blanket policy is inappropriate. Even within the category of youth, the response to an offence is likely to be very different, depending on whether the offender is at the lower end of the age bracket, in the middle, or towards the top end. In many cases the maturity of the offender will be at least as important as the chronological age. The Judge was entitled to say what she did. The extended sentence for D (7 years 3 months' custody and 3 years 5 months' licence) upheld.

R v S 2018 EWCA Crim 395 D was convicted of section 18, attempted section 18 and having an offensive weapon. The Judge considered both section 18 offences to be Category 2. She held there were features making them have 'higher culpability'. For an adult the Judge considered that the appropriate sentence was 9 years. Because of D's age that was reduced to 5 years. Held. The 9 years was not wrong. D, like any 14-year-old, simply does not have the maturity to appreciate the consequences of his actions. People of his age change and develop in a way that adults simply [do not]. For a young person of his age, 5 years was a very long time indeed. The sentence did not sufficiently reflect the fact D was aged 14. **4 years'** detention.

For more detail, see **291.46** in Volume 2.

R v JT 2018 EWCA Crim 1942 D pleaded to reckless arson. In May 2016, D was on a bus and when it reached the bus station, he set light to some newspapers and magazines on the floor, and that set fire to the seats. The bus was completely destroyed and very significant damage was done to the fabric of the bus station. The repairs cost about £1.8m. D was aged 15 (now 17), was then of good character but before sentence had been convicted of some offences. His mother had put him into care and he had had a very difficult childhood. The pre-sentence report said D was now a very different young person, focused on making a success of life. Further, this progress would be at risk if there were a custodial sentence. The psychiatric report said D had symptoms consistent with ADHD, a condition which gives rise to impulsive behaviour. The Judge started at 7 years and because of D's youth took one third off, making 56 months, and with plea made that 3 years' detention. Held. The starting point for an adult would not exceed 6 years. The Judge had not followed the detailed advice in the *Sentencing Children and Young People Guideline 2017*. His approach was cursory and inadequate. The one-third discount was an inadequate reflection of what the guideline suggested. Paras 1.2, 1.5 and 1.6 are particularly apposite, see **13.29**. The approach needs to be individualistic. The approach is for a 15-year-old. There was no proper basis for the reduction being one third rather than one half. We would have moved to 3 years and then with plea, 2 years' DTO. The 22-month delay was a significant factor. We recognised the very low culpability involved. This was an exceptional case, so **YRO** with intensive supervision and surveillance.

For a fuller summary, see **209.14** in Volume 2.

Parents and guardians, Enforcing the responsibilities Guidelines see the **PARENTING ORDERS/PARENTAL ORDERS** ***Parents and guardians, Enforcing the responsibilities Guidelines*** para at **82.4**.

13.35 ***Discount for the age of the offender   Offender becomes aged 18+***

R v Mudd 2017 EWCA Crim 1395, 2018 1 Cr App R (S) 7 D pleaded to doing unauthorised acts with intent to impair the operation of computers and other computer-related offences. He was aged 16-18 for the indictment period, aged 19 when he pleaded and aged 20 at his appeal. Held. This was not an easy sentencing exercise. The court must have regard to factors such as youth, the impact of a defendant's medical conditions, where applicable, his [or her] plea and other mitigating factors. In the case of a young offender, there is also the focus on rehabilitation. That is a matter which does not suddenly cease to be of importance the moment the offender reaches his or her 18th birthday. Had D been an adult without difficulties, 6 years would have been appropriate before the plea discount. We grant a full discount for the guilty plea so, **21 months' YOI** not 24 months' YOI.

For the aggravating and mitigating factors and more detail, see **228.10** in Volume 2.

13.36 ***Previous convictions   Sentencing Children and Young People Guideline 2017***

Sentencing Children and Young People Guideline 2017 www.banksr.com Other Matters Guidelines tab In force 1 June 2017. page 22

6.9 The court may also wish to consider any evidence of a reduction in the level of offending when taking into account previous offending behaviour. Children and young people may be unlikely to desist from committing crime in a clear cut manner but there may be changes in patterns of criminal behaviour (e.g. committing fewer and/or less serious offences or there being longer lengths of time between offences) that indicate that the child or young person is attempting to desist from crime.

13.37 ***Guilty plea***
Sentencing Children and Young People Guideline 2017 www.banksr.com Other Matters Guidelines tab In force 1 June 2017. page 17
Note: There is a set of principles which is the same as for adults, see **65.4** onwards, **65.8** and elsewhere, so it is not replicated. Ed.

Welfare

13.38 ***Sentencing Children and Young People Guideline 2017***
Sentencing Children and Young People Guideline 2017 www.banksr.com Other Matters Guidelines tab In force 1 June 2017. page 5
Welfare
1.11 The statutory obligation to have regard to the welfare of a child or young person includes the obligation to secure proper provision for education and training,[200] to remove the child or young person from undesirable surroundings where appropriate[201] and the need to choose the best option for the child or young person taking account of the circumstances of the offence.
1.12 In having regard to the welfare of the child or young person, a court should ensure that it is alert to:
- **any mental health problems or learning difficulties/disabilities;**
- **any experiences of brain injury or traumatic life experience (including exposure to drug and alcohol abuse) and the developmental impact this may have had;**
- **any speech and language difficulties and the effect this may have on the ability of the child or young person (or any accompanying adult) to communicate with the court, to understand the sanction imposed or to fulfil the obligations resulting from that sanction;**
- **the vulnerability of children and young people to self harm, particularly within a custodial environment; and**
- **the effect on children and young people of experiences of loss and neglect and/or abuse.**

1.13 Factors regularly present in the background of children and young people that come before the court include deprived homes, poor parental employment records, low educational attainment, early experience of offending by other family members, experience of abuse and/or neglect, negative influences from peer associates and the misuse of drugs and/or alcohol.
1.14 The court should always seek to ensure that it has access to information about how best to identify and respond to these factors and, where necessary, that a proper assessment has taken place in order to enable the most appropriate sentence to be imposed.
1.15 The court should consider the reasons why, on some occasions, a child or young person may conduct themselves inappropriately in court (e.g. due to nervousness, a lack of understanding of the system, a belief that they will be discriminated against, peer pressure to behave in a certain way because of others present, a lack of maturity etc.) and take this into account.
1.16 Evidence shows that looked after children and young people are over-represented in the criminal justice system.[202] When dealing with a child or young person who is looked

[200] Children and Young Persons Act 1933 s 44
[201] Children and Young Persons Act 1933 s 44
[202] *Department for Education (2014), Outcomes for Children Looked After by Local Authorities in England, as at 31 March 2014*. Statistical First Release 49/2014 [accessed via: www.gov.uk/government/statistics/outcomes-for-children-looked-after-by-local-authorities].

after the court should also bear in mind the additional complex vulnerabilities that are likely to be present in their background. For example, looked after children and young people may have no or little contact with their family and/or friends, they may have special educational needs and/or emotional and behavioural problems, they may be heavily exposed to peers who have committed crime and they are likely to have accessed the care system as a result of abuse, neglect or parental absence due to bereavement, imprisonment or desertion. The court should also bear in mind that the level of parental-type support that a looked after child or young person receives throughout the criminal justice process may vary, and may be limited. For example, while parents are required to attend court hearings, this is not the case for social workers responsible for looked after children and young people. In some instances a looked after child or young person (including those placed in foster homes and independent accommodation, as well as in care homes) may be before the court for a low level offence that the police would not have been involved in, if it had occurred in an ordinary family setting.

1.17 For looked after children and young people who have committed an offence that crosses the custody threshold sentencers will need to consider any impact a custodial sentence may have on their leaving care rights and whether this impact is proportionate to the seriousness of the offence. For other young people who are in the process of leaving care or have recently left care then sentencers should bear in mind any effect this often difficult transition may have had on the young person's behaviour.

1.18 There is also evidence to suggest that black and minority ethnic children and young people are over-represented in the youth justice system.[203] The factors contributing to this are complex. One factor is that a significant proportion of looked after children and young people are from a black and minority ethnic background.[204] A further factor may be the experience of such children and young people in terms of discrimination and negative experiences of authority. When having regard to the welfare of the child or young person to be sentenced, the particular factors which arise in the case of black and minority ethnic children and young people need to be taken into account.

1.19 The requirement to have regard to the welfare of a child or young person is subject to the obligation to impose only those restrictions on liberty that are commensurate with the seriousness of the offence; accordingly, a court should not impose greater restrictions because of other factors in the child or young person's life.

1.20 When considering a child or young person who may be particularly vulnerable, sentencers should consider which available disposal is best able to support the child or young person and which disposals could potentially exacerbate any underlying issues. This is particularly important when considering custodial sentences as there are concerns about the effect on vulnerable children and young people of being in closed conditions, with significant risks of self harm, including suicide.

1.21 The vulnerability factors that are often present in the background of children and young people should also be considered in light of the offending behaviour itself. Although they do not alone cause offending behaviour – there are many children and young people who have experienced these circumstances but do not commit crime – there is a correlation and any response to criminal activity amongst children and young people will need to recognise the presence of such factors in order to be effective.

These principles do not undermine the fact that the sentence should reflect the seriousness of the offence. Further guidance on assessing the seriousness of an offence can be found at [13.32].

See also the **Defendant** ***Custody threshold, Passing the*** para at **242.10** in Volume 2.

[203] www.gov.uk/government/uploads/system/uploads/attachment_data/file/568680/bame-disproportionality-in-the-cjs.pdf

[204] www.gov.uk/government/statistics/children-looked-after-in-england-including-adoption-2015-to-2016 (National table, figure B1)

13.39 *Welfare and the imposition of a custodial sentence*
Sentencing Children and Young People Guideline 2017 www.banksr.com Other Matters Guidelines tab In force 1 June 2017. page 30
6.49 The welfare of the child or young person must be considered when imposing any sentence but is especially important when a custodial sentence is being considered. A custodial sentence could have a significant effect on the prospects and opportunities of the child or young person and a child or young person is likely to be more susceptible than an adult to the contaminating influences that can be expected within a custodial setting. There is a high reconviction rate for children and young people that have had custodial sentences and there have been many studies profiling the effect on vulnerable children and young people, particularly the risk of self harm and suicide, and so it is of utmost importance that custody is a last resort.
6.50 to 6.55 [not listed, see **37.4**, **37.6** and **14.10**]
6.56 It is possible that, following a guilty plea, a two year detention order may be appropriate as opposed to a sentence of section 91 detention, to account for the reduction.

13.40 *Education, training and welfare*
Children and Young Persons Act 1933 s 44(1) Every court in dealing with a child or young person who is brought before it, either as an offender or otherwise, shall have regard to the welfare of the child or young person and shall in a proper case take steps for removing him from undesirable surroundings and for securing that proper provision is made for his education and training.
Children and Young Persons Act 1933 s 107(1) Under this Act, 'child' means a person under the age of 14 years and 'young person' means a person who has attained the age of 14 years and is under the age of 17.
R v H 2009 EWCA Crim 1453 D was convicted of violent disorder. W, aged 16, left a party and had a confrontation with D. D and others followed W to a railway station. D told W he was summoning others by phone who would wait for him at Addlestone station to beat W up. When W reached Addlestone station, W saw a group on the platform and remained on the train. The doors were held open and W was hit by three people. W was picked up by his father, F, and taken home. Afterwards a group of 10-25 youths appeared outside. D kicked and banged the front door. F went out and was punched by D, who was shouting and being aggressive. F hit back and tried to push the group away. The youths backed away to the end of his drive where F was hit with a piece of wood by someone (not D) and bottles. As F went down he heard youths shouting, "Come outside I'm going to kill you". The youths were kicking and screaming at F. A neighbour who came out was also attacked. Whilst F was at hospital, W saw D and another. D was aged 15 at the time and 17 now. He had 11 GCSEs and was studying for an accountancy qualification and for three A levels. There were character references. Held. The key to disposition is his scholastic record. The Judge was entitled to find custody was appropriate. D was a welcome exception to those who have little if any dedication to their education and scant regard for their future. We wish him to start his courses again. Supervision Order with 25 days of specified activities. We hope he will honour this exceptional course.
Note: The judgment does not refer to the injuries and it does not mean pupils keen on school will be able to avoid custody. Ed.

13.41 *The clash between marking the seriousness of the offence and the welfare of the child*
R v W 1999 1 Cr App R (S) 488 D was convicted of indecent assault on a 12-year-old girl. He was acquitted of attempted rape. The victim, V, was walking home in the early evening when D caught up with her and started to kiss her. D, who was aged 13, then put his hand down V's clothes and touched her vaginal area. V pulled his hand away and attempted to escape whereupon D tripped her over, pulled her jogging bottoms down and

simulated sexual intercourse on her. D had no previous convictions. Held. These cases are extremely difficult to deal with. It is extremely important that if any woman, whatever age, and in particular if [the victim is] a child, is sexually assaulted then that is an extremely serious matter and must be dealt with by appropriate punishment. On the other hand, when the attacker is no more than a child, the overriding consideration is to do the best to see what can be done to assist him, but at the same time to mark the seriousness of the offence. Here the two principles clash. It was a gratuitous assault but a **Supervision Order** rather than 8 months was appropriate.

13.42 ***Corrosive effect of custody on young offenders***
Att-Gen's Ref No 65 of 2012 2012 EWCA Crim 3168 D, aged 17, pleaded to section 18. He received an 18-month Youth Rehabilitation Order. Held. The Judge plainly had regard to the risk of counter-productive effects on a young man of custody in a Young Offender Institution, populated very largely by youths with a more entrenched pattern of offending than he has. It may, at the margins, be a reason for not passing a custodial sentence, but it cannot be if the case is plainly one which demands a sentence of custody and with some significance.

Fines etc. for children and young offenders

13.43
Rehabilitation Period 6 months for those aged under 18.[205] See also the **REHABILITATION OF OFFENDERS ACT 1974** chapters.

13.44 ***Fines Children and young offenders Statutes***
Powers of Criminal Courts (Sentencing) Act 2000 s 135(1) Where a person aged under 18 is found guilty by a Magistrates' Court of an offence for which, apart from this section, the court would have power to impose a fine of an amount exceeding £1,000, the amount of any fine imposed by the court shall not exceed £1,000.
(2) Where a person aged under 14 is found guilty by a Magistrates' Court of an offence for which, apart from this section, the court would have power to impose a fine of an amount exceeding £250, the amount of any fine imposed by the court shall not exceed £250.

13.45 ***Fines Children and young offenders Sentencing Children and Young People Guideline 2017***
Sentencing Children and Young People Guideline 2017 www.banksr.com Other Matters Guidelines tab In force 1 June 2017. page 24

Financial order

6.17 The court may impose a fine for any offence (unless the criteria for a mandatory referral order are met). In accordance with statutory requirements, where financial orders are being considered, priority must be given to compensation orders and, when an order for costs is to be made alongside a fine, the amount of the cost must not exceed the amount of the fine. If the child or young person is under 16 then the court has a duty to order parents or guardians to pay the fine; if the young person is 16 or over this duty is discretionary. In practice, many children and young people will have limited financial resources and the court will need to determine whether imposing a fine will be the most effective disposal.

6.18 A court should bear in mind that children and young people may have money that is specifically required for travel costs to school, college or apprenticeships and lunch expenses.

13.46 ***Local authorities No duty to inquire into financial circumstances***
Powers of Criminal Courts (Sentencing) Act 2000 s 138(2) For the purposes of any order under section 137 of this Act made against a local authority, Criminal Justice Act 2003 s 164(1) (fixing of fines) shall not apply.

[205] Rehabilitation of Offenders Act 1974 s 5 Table A

Other matters

Fines see the **Fines etc. for children and young offenders** section at **13.43**.

13.47 ***Breaches of court orders***

Sentencing Children and Young People Guideline 2017 www.banksr.com Other Matters Guidelines tab In force 1 June 2017. page 23

Breaches and the commission of further offences during the period of an order

6.12 If a child or young person is found guilty of breaching an order, or commits a further offence during the period of an order, the court will have various options available depending upon the nature of the order (see Appendix one at page 32 of this guideline [this appendix has been distributed among the relevant chapters]). The primary aim of the court should be to encourage compliance and seek to support the rehabilitation of the child or young person.

For breach of a conditional discharge, see **20.14**.

13.48 ***Gay and lesbian young offenders*** ***Youths Sentencing Guideline 2009***

Youths Sentencing Guideline 2009, see www.banksr.com Other Matters Guidelines tab para 7.6 Particular issues may arise in relation to an offender who is, or who runs the risk of, experiencing familial abuse or rejection on the grounds of sexual orientation. In considering such factors, which may be documented in a pre-sentence report, the court must take care not to disclose facts about an offender's sexual orientation without his or her consent. Similar issues might arise in a family where racial tensions exist.

13.49 ***Black and minority ethnic offenders***

Sentencing Children and Young People Guideline 2017 www.banksr.com Other Matters Guidelines tab In force 1 June 2017. page 6

1.18 There is also evidence to suggest that black and minority ethnic children and young people are over-represented in the youth justice system.[206] The factors contributing to this are complex. One factor is that a significant proportion of looked after children and young people are from a black and minority ethnic background.[207] A further factor may be the experience of such children and young people in terms of discrimination and negative experiences of authority. When having regard to the welfare of the child or young person to be sentenced, the particular factors which arise in the case of black and minority ethnic children and young people need to be taken into account.

For ***Mental health*** issues, see the **Welfare** section at **13.38** and the **DEFENDANT** ***Mentally disordered defendants*** para at **242.39** in Volume 2.

13.50 ***Reasons, Sentencers must give*** ***Children etc.***

Criminal Justice Act 2003 s 174(1)[208] A court passing sentence on an offender has the duties in subsections (2) and (3).

(2) The court must state in open court, in ordinary language and in general terms, the court's reasons for deciding on the sentence.

(3) The court must explain to the offender in ordinary language:

(a) the effect of the sentence,

(b) the effects of non-compliance with any order that the offender is required to comply with and that forms part of the sentence,

(c) any power of the court to vary or review any order that forms part of the sentence, and

(d) the effects of failure to pay a fine, if the sentence consists of or includes a fine.

Criminal Justice Act 2003 s 174(8)[209] Where the offender is under 18 and the court imposes a sentence that may only be imposed in the offender's case if the court is of the opinion mentioned in:

[206] www.gov.uk/government/uploads/system/uploads/attachment_data/file/568680/bame-disproportionality-in-the-cjs.pdf
[207] www.gov.uk/government/statistics/children-looked-after-in-england-including-adoption-2015-to-2016 (National table, figure B1)
[208] As substituted by Legal Aid, Sentencing and Punishment of Offenders Act 2012 s 64
[209] Section 174 was substituted by Legal Aid, Sentencing and Punishment of Offenders Act 2012 s 64.

(a) Criminal Justice and Immigration Act 2008 s 1(4)(a)-(c) and Criminal Justice Act 2003 s 148(1) (Youth Rehabilitation Order with Intensive Supervision and Surveillance or with Fostering), or

(b) Criminal Justice Act 2003 s 152(2) (discretionary custodial sentence),

the court must state why it is of that opinion.

Att-Gen's Ref No 96 of 2009 2010 EWCA Crim 350 LCJ D was convicted of rape. He was aged 14, educationally sub-normal and had an intelligence quotient of 71, well below average. The Judge in his sentencing remarks was mindful of the ability or otherwise of D to comprehend his sentencing remarks and purposely kept them succinct. He informed both counsel that he would reduce his reasons to writing and that they would be made available to both sides within a few days. Held. It would have been better if the Judge had prepared his sentencing remarks in writing, available at the moment when he came to pass sentence. Handing them out later was wrong. We cannot think of any occasion when it can be appropriate for the reasons for a sentencing decision not to be given in open court. In principle, we cannot have sentencing decisions, or the reasons for them, announced behind closed doors. They should be read out publicly.

Parents etc. paying fines etc.

13.51 ***Parent etc. to pay fine, costs, compensation or surcharge***

Powers of Criminal Courts (Sentencing) Act 2000 s 137(1) Where:

(a) any person aged under 18 is convicted of any offence for the commission of which a fine or costs may be imposed or a compensation order may be made, and

(b) the court is of the opinion that the case would best be met by the imposition of a fine or costs or the making of such an order, whether with or without any other punishment, the court shall order that the fine, compensation or costs awarded be paid by the parent or guardian of the child or young person instead of by the child or young person himself, unless the court is satisfied:

(i) that the parent or guardian cannot be found, or

(ii) that it would be unreasonable to make an order for payment, having regard to the circumstances of the case.

13.52 ***Parents etc. paying fine etc. Duty to pay becomes a discretion when offender aged 16+***

Powers of Criminal Courts (Sentencing) Act 2000 s 137(3) In the case of a young person aged 16 or over, subsections (1) to (2) of this section shall have effect as if, instead of imposing a duty, they conferred a power to make such an order as is mentioned in those subsections.

13.53 ***Service parent etc. to pay fine or compensation order Court Martial***

Order for service parent or service guardian to pay fine or compensation

Armed Forces Act 2006 s 268(1) This section applies where:

(a) a person aged under 18 is convicted of an offence by the Court Martial or the Service Civilian Court,

(b) he is a civilian subject to service discipline,

(c) he has a service parent or service guardian, and

(d) the court is of the opinion that the case would best be met by the imposition of a fine or the making of a Service Compensation Order (with or without any other punishment).

(2) The court may, and if the offender is under 16 when convicted must, order that the fine or compensation awarded be paid by the service parent or service guardian instead of by the offender himself, but this is subject to subsection (3).

(3) Where (apart from this subsection) the court would be required by subsection (2) to make an order against a service parent or service guardian, the court need not make such an order if it is satisfied:

a) that no service parent or service guardian can be found, or

b) that it would be unreasonable to make such an order having regard to the circumstances of the case.

(4) No order may be made under this section without giving the parent or guardian an opportunity of being heard, unless the parent or guardian has failed to attend having been required to do so.

(5) For the purposes of Armed Forces Act 2006 s 285 to 287 (appeals from Service Civilian Court) or, as the case may be, Court Martial Appeals Act 1968:

(a) an order under this section is to be treated as a sentence passed on the parent or guardian for the offence, and

(b) the parent or guardian is to be treated for the purpose of enabling him to appeal against the order as if he had been convicted of the offence by the court that made the order.

(6) For the purposes of any appeal against the order, references in Court Martial Appeals Act 1968 s 16A to passing a sentence include making an order.

(7) On an appeal against the order the Court Martial Appeal Court may (as an alternative to exercising its powers under section 16A(2) of that Act) quash the order.

(8) A parent or guardian is a 'service parent' or 'service guardian' for the purposes of this section if he is a person subject to service law or a civilian subject to service discipline.

Fixing of fine or compensation to be paid by parent or guardian

Armed Forces Act 2006 s 269(1) For the purposes of any order under section 268 against the parent or guardian of an offender:

(a) section 249 (fixing of fine) has effect as if any reference to the offender's financial circumstances were to the parent's or guardian's financial circumstances, and as if the reference in subsection (5)(b) to the offender were to the parent or guardian,

(b) section 250(1) (determination of Service Compensation Order) has effect as if any reference to the financial circumstances of the person against whom the Service Compensation Order is made were to the financial circumstances of the parent or guardian,

(c) section 250(2) (preference to be given to compensation if insufficient means to pay both compensation and fine) has effect as if the reference to the offender were to the parent or guardian,

(d) section 267 (power to remit fine) has effect as if any reference to the offender's financial circumstances were to the parent's or guardian's financial circumstances.

(2) Before making an order under section 268 against a parent or guardian, the court may make a Financial Statement Order with respect to him.

(3) In subsection (2) 'Financial Statement Order' has the meaning given by subsection (2), and subsection (3) and (4) of that section apply in relation to a Financial Statement Order made under this section as they apply in relation to such an order made under that section.

13.54 ***Parent etc. to pay fine etc. for breaches of orders***

Powers of Criminal Courts (Sentencing) Act 2000 s 137(2) Where but for this subsection a court would impose a fine on a child or young person under:

(za) Criminal Justice and Immigration Act 2008 Sch 2 para 6(2)(a) or 8(2)(a) (breach of Youth Rehabilitation Order),

(b) Powers of Criminal Courts (Sentencing) Act 2000 Sch 5 para 2(1)(a) (breach of Attendance Centre Order or attendance centre rules),

(d) Powers of Criminal Courts (Sentencing) Act 2000 Sch 8 para 2(2)(a) (breach of Reparation Order),

(e) Powers of Criminal Courts (Sentencing) Act 2000 s 104(3)(b) (breach of requirements of supervision under a Detention and Training Order), or

(f) Criminal Justice and Public Order Act 1994 s 4(3)(b)[210] (breach of requirements of supervision under a secure training order),

[210] Repealed by Crime and Disorder Act 1998 Sch 10 para 1 1/4/2000

…the court shall order that the fine be paid by the parent or guardian of the child or young person instead of by the child or young person himself, unless the court is satisfied:

(i) that the parent or guardian cannot be found, or

(ii) that it would be unreasonable to make an order for payment, having regard to the circumstances of the case.

For ***Parent or guardian paying the victim surcharge*** see **115.13**.

13.55 ***Financial Circumstances Order Parent/guardian***

Powers of Criminal Courts (Sentencing) Act 2000 s 136(1) Before exercising its powers under section 137 (power to order parent or guardian to pay fine, costs, compensation or surcharge) against the parent or guardian of an individual who has been convicted of an offence, the court may make a Financial Circumstances Order with respect to the parent or guardian.

(2) In this section 'Financial Circumstances Order' has the meaning given by Criminal Justice Act 2003 s 162(3) and subsections (4) to (6) of that section shall apply in relation to a Financial Circumstances Order made under this section as they apply in relation to such an order made under that section.

See also the **FINES** ***Financial Circumstances Order*** para at **58.12**.

13.56 ***Financial Circumstances Order Parent/guardian fails to comply etc.***

Powers of Criminal Courts (Sentencing) Act 2000 s 138(3) For the purposes of section 137 of this Act (power to order parent/guardian to pay fine etc.), where the parent/guardian of an offender who is a child or young person:

has failed to comply with an order under section 136 of this Act (power to order statement of financial circumstances), or

a) has otherwise failed to co-operate with the court in its inquiry into his financial circumstances, and

b) the court considers that it has insufficient information to make a proper determination of the parent or guardian's financial circumstances, it may make such determination as it sees fit.

13.57 ***Parent etc. must have opportunity of being heard***

Powers of Criminal Courts (Sentencing) Act 2000 s 137(4) Subject to subsection (5), no order shall be made under this section without giving the parent or guardian an opportunity of being heard.

13.58 ***Consider parents' etc. means***

Powers of Criminal Courts (Sentencing) Act 2000 s 138(1) For the purposes of any order under section 137 of this Act made against the parent or guardian of a child or young person:

za) Criminal Justice Act 2003 s 161A(3) (surcharges) and s 164(4A) (fixing of fines) shall have effect as if any reference in those subsections to the offender's means were a reference to those of the parent or guardian,

a) Criminal Justice Act 2003 s 164 (fixing of fines) shall have effect as if any reference in subsections (1) to (4) to the financial circumstances of the offender were a reference to the financial circumstances of the parent or guardian, and as if subsection (5) were omitted,

b) Powers of Criminal Courts (Sentencing) Act 2000 s 130(11) (determination of compensation order) shall have effect as if any reference to the means of the person against whom the compensation order is made were a reference to the financial circumstances of the parent or guardian, and

c) Powers of Criminal Courts (Sentencing) Act 2000 s 130(12) (preference to be given to compensation if insufficient means to pay both compensation and a fine) shall have effect as if the reference to the offender were a reference to the parent or guardian, but in relation to an order under section 137 of this Act made against a local authority this subsection has effect subject to subsection (2) below.

Sentencing Children and Young People Guideline 2017 www.banksr.com Other Matters Guidelines tab In force 1 June 2017. page 6

1.18 There is also evidence to suggest that black and minority ethnic children and young people are over-represented in the youth justice system.[211] The factors contributing to this are complex. One factor is that a significant proportion of looked after children and young people are from a black and minority ethnic background.[212] A further factor may be the experience of such children and young people in terms of discrimination and negative experiences of authority. When having regard to the welfare of the child or young person to be sentenced, the particular factors which arise in the case of black and minority ethnic children and young people need to be taken into account.

Appeals for parents etc. paying fines etc.

13.59 ***Appeals Parents etc. paying fines etc. Magistrates' Court order***
Powers of Criminal Courts (Sentencing) Act 2000 s 137(6) A parent or guardian may appeal to the Crown Court against an order under this section made by a Magistrates' Court.

13.60 ***Appeals Parents etc. paying fines etc. Crown Court order***
Powers of Criminal Courts (Sentencing) Act 2000 s 137(7) A parent or guardian may appeal to the Court of Appeal against an order under this section made by the Crown Court, as if he had been convicted on indictment and the order were a sentence passed on his conviction.

14 Children and Young Offenders: Custodial Sentences

14.1

This chapter deals with the general principles about custodial sentences for children and young offenders. For the law for the individual orders and general principles, see the following chapters:

Attendance Centre Orders
Custody: General Principles
Custody for Life
Detention and Training Orders
Detention under Powers of Criminal Courts (Sentencing) Act 2000 s 91
Extended Sentences (EDS)
Life Imprisonment chapters and in particular the **Life Imprisonment: Dangerousness, Based on** *Young offenders* para at **74.17**.
Young Offender Institution, Detention in

For detention at HM's Pleasure and mandatory custody for life, see the **Murder** ***Defendant under 21*** paras at **287.77** in Volume 2.

14.2 ***Sentencing children and young offenders***

Order	Aged 10-17	Aged 18-20	Maximum custodial sentence
Life (murder)	Detention at HM's Pleasure[213]	Custody for life[214]	Whole life not available

[211] www.gov.uk/government/uploads/system/uploads/attachment_data/file/568680/bame-disproportionality-in-the-cjs.pdf

[212] www.gov.uk/government/statistics/children-looked-after-in-england-including-adoption-2015-to-2016 (National table, figure B1)

[213] Powers of Criminal Courts (Sentencing) Act 2000 s 90

[214] Powers of Criminal Courts (Sentencing) Act 2000 s 93, unless the defendant was aged under 18 at the time of the offence, when the defendant is detained at HM's Pleasure.

Order	Aged 10-17	Aged 18-20	Maximum custodial sentence
Criminal Justice Act 2003 s 225 Life based on dangerousness	Detention for life[215]	Custody for life[216]	Whole life not available
Criminal Justice Act 2003 s 224A Automatic life	Not available[217]	Automatic custody for life[218]	Whole life not available
Extended sentences (EDS)	Extended sentence of detention[219]	Extended sentence of detention in a Young Offender Institution[220]	Must not exceed the maximum for the offence[221]
Offender of Particular Concern Order Criminal Justice Act 2003 s 236A	Not available[222]	Offender of particular concern order	The custodial term and the one-year extended licence period must not in total exceed the maximum for the offence[223]
Detention in a Young Offender Institution	Not available[224]	Detention in a Young Offender Institution[225]	The maximum for the offence.[226] Life sentences are not available as the sentence is custody for life under Powers of Criminal Courts (Sentencing) Act 2000 s 94 (see above).

[215] Powers of Criminal Courts (Sentencing) Act 2000 s 91(3) and Criminal Justice Act 2003 s 226(2)
[216] Powers of Criminal Courts (Sentencing) Act 2000 s 94(1) and Criminal Justice Act 2003 s 225(2)
[217] Criminal Justice Act 2003 s 224A(1)(a)
[218] Criminal Justice Act 2003 s 224A(2)
[219] Criminal Justice Act 2003 s 226B
[220] Criminal Justice Act 2003 s 226A(4), which is inserted by Legal Aid, Sentencing and Punishment of Offenders Act 2012 s 124. This entitles the order for those aged 18+ as 'an extended sentence of imprisonment'. However, until Criminal Justice and Court Services Act 2000 s 61 is in force, Legal Aid, Sentencing and Punishment of Offenders Act 2012 Sch 21 para 36 applies and Criminal Justice Act 2003 s 226A(12) is inserted. This renames the order an 'extended sentence of detention in a Young Offender Institution'.
[221] Criminal Justice Act 2003 s 226B(7)
[222] Criminal Justice Act 2003 s 236A(1)(b)
[223] Criminal Justice Act 2003 s 236A(2)-(4)
[224] Powers of Criminal Courts (Sentencing) Act 2000 s 96(a)
[225] Powers of Criminal Courts (Sentencing) Act 2000 s 96
[226] Powers of Criminal Courts (Sentencing) Act 2000 s 97(1)

Order	Aged 10-17	Aged 18-20	Maximum custodial sentence
Detention under section 91	Detention under section 91[227]	Not available	The maximum for the offence. If that is life[228] the sentence is detention for life.
Detention and Training Orders[229]	Aged 10-11 No[230] Aged 12-14 Only when a persistent offender[231], see **15.8** Aged 15-17 Yes	Not available	24 months[232]

Note: It is the age at the date of conviction that matters, see **13.5**. Ed.

14.3 ***Maximum summary sentence for offenders aged 10-17 on the date of their conviction***

	Maximum sentence	
	Magistrates Court	**Youth Court**
Either way matters when tried with an adult	Send to Youth Court for sentencing or 6 months DTO For restrictions, see para **37.5**.	n/a
Either way matters	n/a	2 years DTO For restrictions, see para **37.5**.
Summary only offences	n/a	6 months DTO For restrictions, see para **37.5**.

Note: The maximum sentences cannot exceed the statutory maximum for the offence. Ed.

14.4 ***Court Martial***

Guidance on Sentencing in the Court Martial 2018 para 3.1.8 Custodial sentences other than Service detention for young offenders aged between 18 and 21 years need particular care. There are no provisions in Armed Forces Act 2006 for custody in a Young Offender Institution, because it was expected that the provisions in Criminal Justice Act 2003 reducing the minimum age for imprisonment from 21 to 18 years would be in force by the time Armed Forces Act 2006 was brought into force. As at 31 December 2017 those 2003 Act provisions have not been brought into force. However, transitory provisions were made under Armed Forces Act 2006 s 380, Armed Forces Act 2006 (Transitional Provisions etc.) Order 2009 2009/1059 Sch 2 para 4 which enable Service courts to sentence an offender aged over 18 but under 21 years to detention in a Young Offender Institution, until the relevant provisions in the 2003 Act (reducing the minimum age for imprisonment from 21 to 18 years) come into force.

3.1.9 Civilian custodial sentences are also available to Service courts for offenders [aged] under 18.[233] Where a defendant aged under 18 is convicted in the Court Martial of an offence punishable with imprisonment for 14 years or more (including life or where the maximum sentence is not fixed by law), the court may impose a sentence of YOI detention (not Service detention) for any period up to the maximum, Armed Forces

[227] Powers of Criminal Courts (Sentencing) Act 2000 s 91(3)
[228] Powers of Criminal Courts (Sentencing) Act 2000 s 91(3)
[229] Powers of Criminal Courts (Sentencing) Act 2000 s 100
[230] For defendants aged under 12, Powers of Criminal Courts (Sentencing) Act 2000 s 100(2)(b)(ii) creates a power to impose such an order when the Secretary of State makes an order. An order is not expected.
[231] Powers of Criminal Courts (Sentencing) Act 2000 s 100(2)(a)
[232] Powers of Criminal Courts (Sentencing) Act 2000 s 101(1)
[233] Armed Forces Act 2006 Part 8

Act 2006 s 209. In all cases where a defendant aged under 18 is convicted in the Court Martial or the Service Civilian Court of an offence punishable with imprisonment, the court may impose a Detention and Training Order in the same terms as would be available in the civilian courts. A child aged between 12 and 15 may be sentenced to a Detention and Training Order only if the court is of the opinion that he is a persistent offender, and a child [aged] under 12 may be given such a sentence only if the court is of the opinion that he is a persistent offender and only a custodial sentence would be adequate to protect the public from further offending by him, Armed Forces Act 2006 s 211.

Powers and restrictions

14.5 ***Imprisonment is not available for those aged under 21***

Powers of Criminal Courts (Sentencing) Act 2000 s 89(1) No court shall: a) pass a sentence of imprisonment on a person for an offence if he is aged under 21 at the time of conviction, or b) commit a person aged under 21 to prison for any reason.

Note: The custodial sentences that are available are listed in the table at **14.2**. Ed.

14.6 ***Restrictions etc. on passing custody for children and young persons***

There are the following restrictions etc.:

a) The offender who has not received custody before must be legally represented, see the **CUSTODY: GENERAL PRINCIPLES Defendants who have not been previously been sentenced to custody** section at **28.19**.
b) The offence or combination of offences must be so serious that neither a fine nor a community order can be justified, see the **CUSTODY: GENERAL PRINCIPLES** ***Offence must be so serious a fine or a community sentence cannot be justified*** para at **28.26**.
c) The court must have a pre-sentence report unless it is unnecessary because there is a pre-existing report, see the **PRE-SENTENCE REPORTS** chapter.
d) The court must consider the welfare of the offender, see the **CHILDREN AND YOUNG OFFENDERS: GENERAL PRINCIPLES Welfare** section at **13.38**.

14.7 ***Detention for contempt of court or default of payment***

Detention of persons aged at least 18 but under 21 for default or contempt.

Powers of Criminal Courts (Sentencing) Act 2000 s 108(1) In any case where, but for section 89(1) of this Act, a court would have power:

(a) to commit a person aged at least 18 but under 21 to prison for default in payment of a fine or any other sum of money, or

(b) to make an order fixing a term of imprisonment in the event of such a default by such a person, or

(c) to commit such a person to prison for contempt of court or any kindred offence,

the court shall have power, subject to subsection (3) below, to commit him to be detained under this section or, as the case may be, to make an order fixing a term of detention under this section in the event of default, for a term not exceeding the term of imprisonment.

(2) For the purposes of subsection (1) above, the power of a court to order a person to be imprisoned under section 23 of the Attachment of Earnings Act 1971 shall be taken to be a power to commit him to prison.

(3) No court shall commit a person to be detained under this section unless it is of the opinion that no other method of dealing with him is appropriate, and in forming any such opinion, the court:

(a) shall take into account all such information about the circumstances of the default or contempt (including any aggravating or mitigating factors) as is available to it, and

(b) may take into account any information about that person which is before it.

(4) Where a Magistrates' Court commits a person to be detained under this section, it shall:

(a) state in open court the reason for its opinion that no other method of dealing with him is appropriate, and
(b) cause that reason to be specified in the warrant of commitment and to be entered in the register.

(5) Subject to Prison Act 1952 s 22(2)(b) (removal to hospital etc.), a person in respect of whom an order has been made under this section is to be detained:
(a) in a remand centre,
(b) in a Young Offender Institution, or
(c) in any place in which a person aged 21 or over could be imprisoned or detained for default in payment of a fine or any other sum of money,
as the Secretary of State may from time to time direct.

Detention and Training Orders and Youth Rehabilitation Orders with Intensive Supervision and Surveillance or with Fostering

14.8 ***Persistent offenders Who are? Sentencing Children and Young People Guideline 2017***

Sentencing Children and Young People Guideline 2017 www.banksr.com Other Matters Guidelines tab In force 1 June 2017. page 22

Persistent offenders

6.4 Some sentences can only be imposed on children and young people if they are deemed a persistent offender. A child or young person **must** be classed as such for one of the following to be imposed:

- a youth rehabilitation order (YRO) with intensive supervision and surveillance when aged under 15;
- a YRO with fostering when aged under 15; and
- a detention and training order (DTO) when aged 12-14.

6.5 The term persistent offender is not defined in statute but has been considered by the Court of Appeal. In general it is expected that the child or young person would have had previous contact with authority as a result of criminal behaviour. This includes previous findings of guilt as well as admissions of guilt such as restorative justice disposals and conditional cautions.

6.6 A child or young person who has committed one previous offence cannot reasonably be classed as a persistent offender, and a child or young person who has committed two or more previous offences should not necessarily be assumed to be one. To determine if the behaviour is persistent the nature of the previous offences and the lapse of time between the offences would need to be considered.[234]

6.7 If there have been three findings of guilt in the past 12 months for imprisonable offences of a comparable nature (or the child or young person has been made the subject of orders as detailed above in relation to an imprisonable offence) then the court could certainly justify classing the child or young person as a persistent offender.

6.8 When a child or young person is being sentenced in a single appearance for a series of separate, comparable offences committed over a short space of time then the court could justifiably consider the child or young person to be a persistent offender, despite the fact that there may be no previous findings of guilt.[235] In these cases the court should consider whether the child or young person has had prior opportunity to address their offending behaviour before imposing one of the optional sentences available for persistent offenders only; if the court determines that the child or young person has not had an opportunity to address their behaviour and believes that an alternative sentence has a reasonable prospect of preventing re-offending then this alternative sentence should be imposed.

6.9 The court may also wish to consider any evidence of a reduction in the level of offending when taking into account previous offending behaviour. Children and young

[234] *R v M* 2008 EWCA Crim 3329
[235] *R v S* 2000 1 Cr App R (S) 18

people may be unlikely to desist from committing crime in a clear cut manner but there may be changes in patterns of criminal behaviour (e.g. committing fewer and/or less serious offences or there being longer lengths of time between offences) that indicate that the child or young person is attempting to desist from crime.

6.10 Even where a child or young person is found to be a persistent offender, a court is not obliged to impose one of the optional sentences. The approach should still be individualistic and all other considerations still apply. Custodial sentences must be a last resort for all children and young people and there is an expectation that they will be particularly rare for children and young people aged 14 or under.

14.9 *Persistent offenders? Who are Cases*

R v S 2001 1 Cr App R (S) 18 (p 62)[236] D, aged 14 at time of sentence, was convicted of three counts of robbery.[237] On one of the robberies, he had used a kitchen knife. On another robbery, the day after, he threatened to use a kitchen knife when stealing property from a 12-year-old and two 14-year-old boys (3 years' detention under section 53(3)[238] each, concurrent). He was also convicted of two counts of possessing an offensive weapon (3 years' detention under section 53(3), concurrent) and one count of false imprisonment (3 years' detention), which related to one of the counts of robbery. D had no previous convictions. A pre-sentence report and a psychiatric report raised concerns as to his susceptibility to influence from others. Held. D was a persistent offender, in the light of the offences to which he had pleaded guilty. The series of crimes committed qualify him for that category even though he had no previous convictions.

R v D 2001 1 Cr App R (S) 59 (p 202) D pleaded to a residential burglary and was convicted of handling after he was acquitted of another burglary. He was sentenced to a Detention and Training Order after the Judge had found he was a 'persistent offender'. D was aged 14. The Judge took into account a conviction for theft of a cycle (12 hours attendance centre) and three cautions. One caution was in 1997 for criminal damage. Two were in 1998 (on different dates) for theft and common assault. Held. The Judge was entitled to take into account the cautions and we are satisfied D was a 'persistent offender'.

R v B 2001 1 Cr App R (S) 113 (p 389) D was convicted of a residential burglary and sentenced to a Detention and Training Order after the court had found he was a 'persistent offender'. D was aged 12 and had no convictions. The Judge considered the defendant's cautions for criminal damage in 1999, TDA in 2000 (committed one week after the burglary) and cannabis possession in 2000 (two months after the burglary when on bail). Held. Parliament left the question of whether someone was a persistent offender to the good sense of the court. We avoid the temptation to define the term. The offending need not be offences of the same or similar character, nor need the failure to address his offending arise out of a failure to comply with previous orders of the court. The Judge was entirely right to conclude D was a 'persistent offender'. There was nothing wrong with the sentence.

R v C 2001 1 Cr App R (S) 120 (p 415) D, aged 14, pleaded to three counts of burglary and one count of allowing himself to be carried in a vehicle taken without consent. He received a 12-month Detention and Training Order. The Judge stated that he was satisfied that D was a persistent offender for the purposes of the Act. D sought to rely on a definition used by the Home Office for another purpose, which required a number of previous court appearances. Held. D's course of action, including two burglaries whilst he was on bail for a third, was sufficient to properly consider him a persistent offender. The Home Office definition was not appropriate for this Act.

R v L 2012 EWCA Crim 1336, 2013 1 Cr App R (S) 56 (p 317) D pleaded to robbery (×3) and attempted robbery. When aged 14, he with two others approached five boys

[236] The case is also known as *R v AS* 2001 1 Cr App R (S) 18 (p 62).

[237] The judgment refers to counts of burglary. This is presumably a typo.

[238] Now Powers of Criminal Courts (Sentencing) Act 2000 s 91

aged 14 or 15. He had two reprimands, one for theft, and one for possession of an imitation firearm. The Judge imposed a 10-month DTO. Held. Two reprimands and three robberies committed on a single occasion within a minute or so of each other cannot be characterised as 'persistent offending'. The DTO was therefore unlawful.

R v BK 2015 EWCA Crim 1927 D admitted four rapes committed when he was aged between 12 and 13. The victim was his sister, who was then aged 10-11. D, now aged 14, had no findings of guilt. Held. This was an unusual case. D was a persistent offender so we substitute a **Youth Rehabilitation Order with Intense Supervision and Surveillance** with a curfew and tag, not 5 years' detention.

SC (Zimbabwe) v Sec of State 2018 EWCA Civ 929 Court of Appeal (Civil Div) SC pleaded to four offences of using a false instrument and three false representation offences. She was given 7 months. The offending was from 2007 to 2013. The Secretary of State ordered her deportation. She appealed the decision and the crucial issue was whether she was a 'persistent offender' in Immigration Rules Rule 398. Held. We entirely agree with the decision in *Cherge v SSHD* 2016 UKHT 187 (IAC), which said, "Put simply, a 'persistent offender' is someone who keeps on breaking the law. That does not mean that he [or she] has to keep on offending until the date of the relevant decision or up to a certain time before it, or that the continuity of the offending cannot be broken. We do not accept that a 'persistent offender' is a permanent status that can never be lost once it is acquired. An individual can be regarded as a 'persistent offender' even though he may not have offended for some time. Someone can be fairly described as a person who keeps breaking the law even if he is not currently offending. The question whether he [or she] fits that description will depend on the overall picture and pattern of his [or her] offending over his [or her] entire offending history up to that date. Each case will turn on its own facts. Plainly, a persistent offender is not simply someone who offends more than once. There has to be repeat offending but that repetition, in and of itself, will not be enough to show persistence. There has to be a history of repeated criminal conduct carried out over a sufficiently long period to indicate that the person concerned is someone who keeps on re-offending. However, determining whether the offending is persistent is not just a mathematical exercise. How long a period and how many offences will be enough will depend very much on the facts of the particular case and the nature and circumstances of the offending. The criminal offences need not be the same, or even of the same character as each other. Persistence may be shown by the fact that a person keeps committing the same type of offence, but it may equally be shown by the fact that he [or she] has committed a wide variety of different offences over a period of time." SC was a persistent offender. Appeal dismissed.

Note: This case is not binding on a criminal court but it is exactly the approach one would expect the Court of Appeal to approve of. Ed.

For more details see **314.96** in Volume 2.

Proper approach

14.10 ***Sentencing Children and Young People Guideline 2017***

Sentencing Children and Young People Guideline 2017 www.banksr.com Other Matters Guidelines tab In force 1 June 2017. page 28

Custodial sentences

A custodial sentence should always be used as a last resort. If offence specific guidelines for children and young people are available then the court should consult them in the first instance to [assess] whether custody is the most appropriate disposal.

The available custodial sentences for children and young people are:

Youth Court	Crown Court
Detention and training order for the following periods: • 4 months; • 6 months; • 8 months; • 10 months; • 12 months; • 18 months; or • 24 months.	• Detention and training order (the same periods are available as in the Youth Court) • Long-term detention (under Powers of Criminal Courts (Sentencing) Act 2000 s 91) • Extended sentence of detention or detention for life (if dangerousness criteria are met) • Detention at Her Majesty's pleasure (for offences of murder)

6.42 Under both domestic and international law, a custodial sentence must only be imposed as a **'measure of last resort';** statute provides that such a sentence may be imposed only where an offence is "so serious that neither a fine alone nor a community sentence can be justified".[239] If a custodial sentence is imposed, a court must state its reasons for being satisfied that the offence is so serious that no other sanction would be appropriate and, in particular, why a YRO with intensive supervision and surveillance or fostering could not be justified.

6.43 The term of a custodial sentence must be the shortest commensurate with the seriousness of the offence; any case that warrants a DTO of less than four months must result in a non-custodial sentence. The court should take account of the circumstances, age and maturity of the child or young person.

6.44 In determining whether an offence has crossed the custody threshold the court will need to assess the seriousness of the offence, in particular the level of harm that was caused, or was likely to have been caused, by the offence. The risk of serious harm in the future must also be assessed. The pre-sentence report will assess this criterion and must be considered before a custodial sentence is imposed. A custodial sentence is most likely to be unavoidable where it is necessary to protect the public from serious harm.

6.45 Only if the court is satisfied that the offence crosses the custody threshold, and that no other sentence is appropriate, the court may, as a preliminary consideration, consult the equivalent adult guideline in order to decide upon the appropriate length of the sentence.

6.46 When considering the relevant adult guideline, the court **may** feel it appropriate to apply a sentence broadly within the region of half to two thirds of the adult sentence for those aged 15-17 and allow a greater reduction for those aged under 15. This is only a rough guide and must not be applied mechanistically. In most cases when considering the appropriate reduction from the adult sentence **the emotional and developmental age and maturity of the child or young person is of at least equal importance as their chronological age**.

6.47 The individual factors relating to the offence and the child or young person are of the greatest importance and may present good reason to impose a sentence outside of this range. The court should bear in mind the negative effects a short custodial sentence can have; short sentences disrupt education and/or training and family relationships and support which are crucial stabilising factors to prevent re-offending.

6.48 There is an expectation that custodial sentences will be particularly rare for a child or young person aged 14 or under. If custody is imposed, it should be for a shorter length of time than that which a young person aged 15-17 would receive if found guilty of the same offence. For a child or young person aged 14 or under the sentence should normally be imposed in a Youth Court (except in cases of homicide or when the dangerous offender criteria are met).

[239] Criminal Justice Act 2003 s 152(2)

6.49 The welfare of the child or young person must be considered when imposing any sentence but is especially important when a custodial sentence is being considered. A custodial sentence could have a significant effect on the prospects and opportunities of the child or young person and a child or young person is likely to be more susceptible than an adult to the contaminating influences that can be expected within a custodial setting. There is a high reconviction rate for children and young people that have had custodial sentences and there have been many studies profiling the effect on vulnerable children and young people, particularly the risk of self harm and suicide, and so it is of utmost importance that custody is a last resort.

Long-term detention

6.54 A child or young person may be sentenced by the Crown Court to long-term detention under Powers of Criminal Courts (Sentencing) Act 2000 s 91 if found guilty of a grave crime and neither a community order nor a DTO is suitable.

6.55 These cases may be sent for trial to the Crown Court or committed for sentence only[240] (see [**13.14**] for further information).

6.56 It is possible that, following a guilty plea, a two year detention order may be appropriate as opposed to a sentence of section 91 detention, to account for the reduction.

14.11 ***Basic principles and article 3 Offender aged under 18 years Pre-2017 guidelines cases***

Youth Crime Action Plan 2008 (issued by the Home Office) When young people are found guilty of crime, they should receive a sentence which protects the public and punishes the offender but which also tackles their offending with the aim of preventing them [from] doing it again (see www.banksr.com Other Matters Other Documents tab).

R v AM 1998 2 Cr App R (S) 128 LCJ We unreservedly endorse this statement in *R v Fairhurst* 1986. No one should be sentenced to imprisonment or detention unless it is necessary, and the period of imprisonment or detention should be no longer than is necessary. This applies in particular to young offenders. The 24-month limit on sentences of detention in a Young Offender Institution (now detention and training) is intended to ensure that offenders aged 15, 16 or 17 are not sentenced to lengthy periods of detention where this can be avoided. Any sentencer must think long and hard before passing a sentence which exceeds this limit. But the co-existence of the powers contained in section 53(2) and (3) (now Powers of Criminal Courts (Sentencing) Act 2000 s 91) recognises the unwelcome but undoubted fact that some crimes committed by offenders of this age merit sentences of detention in excess of 24 months.

R v Asi-Akram 2005 EWCA Crim 1543, 2006 1 Cr App R (S) 47 (p 260) D pleaded to two rapes and attempting to strangle etc. with intent to commit rape (OAPA 1861 s 21). He was aged 17 when he committed the offences. The Judge said he was a very great danger to women and he looked like a 22-year-old. Held. These were among the very worst examples of this kind of offence. All three women were terrified for their lives. The observation in *R v Millberry* 2002 that in rape cases the sentence for young offenders should be 'significantly shorter' admits of exceptions. It was not designed to be of invariable and inevitable application. Youth will always be a relevant consideration. But the extent to which it calls for a reduction (and specifically a 'significant' reduction) by comparison with adult sentences remains to be assessed by the Court. This is not a case where the youth of the offender played a part in the offences. The sentence of 14 years' detention was justifiably severe.

R v BW 2012 EWCA Crim 3178 The correct starting point for sentencing is the sentence which would have been appropriate if the sentence had been imposed at the date of the offence.

R v Markham and Edwards 2017 EWCA Crim 739 M pleaded to and E was convicted of two murders. Both were then aged 14 and now aged 15. Held. para 49 Crimes committed

240 Powers of Criminal Courts (Sentencing) Act 2000 s 3(b) (as amended)

by children and young persons should be considered in a different light to similar crimes committed by adults. However, that does not mean that punishment in appropriate cases is not an entirely proper approach. In *T v United Kingdom* 2000 30 EHRR 121, this Court said about the appropriate tariff for detention at HM's Pleasure of the two child murderers of James Bulger, "States have a duty under the Convention to take measures for the protection of the public from violent crime. The European Court of Human Rights does not consider that the punitive element inherent in the tariff approach itself gives rise to a breach of Article 3, or that the Convention prohibits States from subjecting a child or young person convicted of a serious crime to an indeterminate sentence allowing for the offender's continued detention or recall to detention following release where necessary for the protection of the public."

For more details, see **287.27** in Volume 2.

Old cases: *R v Storey and Others* 1984 6 Cr App R (S) 104 at 107 *R v Fairhurst* 1986 8 Cr App R (S) 346 *R v Roberts* 1989 11 Cr App R (S) 34 *R v Best* 2006 EWCA Crim 330 (Comments in *R v Storey* 1986 considered but life still upheld.)

Note: These old cases provide little help because the sentencer should concentrate on the guidelines. Ed.

14.12 ***Basic principles Offender under 16 years old Pre-2017 guidelines cases***

R (W) v Thetford Youth Court 2002 EWHC 1252 (Admin), 2003 1 Cr App R (S) 67 (p 323) High Court In two separate cases, Youth Courts declined jurisdiction and committed W and M to the Crown Court. The legislation prevented W, who was aged under 12, from being subject to a Detention and Training Order. M did not satisfy the definition of a 'persistent offender' and could not be subject to a Detention and Training Order. Held. Parliament had recognised that there may be a situation where an offender aged 10-17 might require a custodial sentence and therefore had left available to the courts the power to order detention under section 91. This power must be a long stop reserved for very serious offences. In general, unless the offence merited a sentence of 2 years or more (after considering mitigation), and the criteria for section 91 are satisfied, a court ought to deal with an offender by means of a Detention and Training Order. There may be cases where, despite the fact that the offender is aged under 15 and no Detention and Training Order can be made, the only appropriate sentence is a custodial sentence pursuant to section 91 and possibly for a period of less than 2 years. But I remain of the opinion that the circumstances of the offence and offender will only rarely call for a sentence pursuant to section 91, particularly if the court is dealing with an offender under the age of 12. In expressing my views, as I did in *R (D) v Manchester City Youth Court* 2001 EWHC (Admin) 860, 2002 1 Cr App R (S) 135 (p 573), my use of the expression "very exceptional" may be more restrictive than was strictly necessary or justified. Perhaps it would be better to say that cases involving offenders aged under 15 for whom a Detention and Training Order is not available will only rarely attract a period of detention under section 91, the more rarely if the offender is aged under 12. Both orders declining jurisdiction quashed.

R (W) v Southampton Youth Court 2002 EWCA Civ 1640, 2003 1 Cr App R (S) 87 (p 455) The simple principle underlying the current legislation for sentencing very young offenders is that, generally speaking, first-time offenders aged 13 and 14, and all offenders aged 11 and 12, should not be detained in custody. For 13- and 14-year-olds, where the youth persists in offending, the position changes. Clearly some offences or offending are so serious in themselves that the court has to contemplate the possibility of sending an under 15-year-old for a period in custody, despite the general approach of the legislation. That may be to protect the public or it may be that the long-term interests of the offender require such a drastic course, even though he is aged under 12 or under 15 but not a persistent offender. To cater for this possibility Parliament has left open to the courts the use of Powers of Criminal Courts (Sentencing) Act 2000 s 91. The need in exceptional cases to make use of these powers cannot, however, have been intended to water down the general principle.

14.13 ***Child offenders aged 10-14*** ***Custodial sentences***
R v W 2002 EWCA Crim 2106, 2003 1 Cr App R (S) 95 (p 502) D, now aged 12, was convicted when he was aged 10 of causing GBH with intent. Held. This was a most serious offence. When dealing with a very young person, the Court has to have regard to the length of sentence and the perception of the young of that length. By that we mean that a sentence which may be appropriate for someone older may be crushing for someone who is very young.
R v JT 2004 EWCA Crim 3226 D, aged 10, pleaded to three false imprisonment counts, GBH, two ABHs and two robberies. Held. A custodial sentence will ordinarily be available in the form of a Detention and Training Order. If the Court is prohibited from making such an order by reason of age, in general, detention under section 91 would not be appropriate. There will, however, be rare or exceptional cases, very rare if the offender is aged under 12, when the Court can order section 91 detention for the protection of the public or in the long-term interests of the offender. Here a section 91 detention order was essential for the boy and the public.
R v BK 2015 EWCA Crim 1927 D admitted four rapes committed when he was aged between 12 and 13 with V, his sister, who was then aged 10-11. D, now aged 14, had no findings of guilt. Held. This was an unusual case. D was a persistent offender so we substitute a **Youth Rehabilitation Order with Intense Supervision and Surveillance** with a curfew and tag, not 5 years' detention.
For more details see **314.96** in Volume 2.
Post-2017 guideline case
R v S 2018 EWCA Crim 395 D was convicted of section 18, attempted section 18 and having an offensive weapon. The Judge considered both section 18 offences to be Category 2. She held there were features making them have 'higher culpability'. For an adult the Judge considered that the appropriate sentence was 9 years. Because of D's age that was reduced to 5 years. Held. The 9 years was not wrong. D, like any 14-year-old, simply does not have the maturity to appreciate the consequences of his actions. People of his age change and develop in a way that adults simply [do not]. For a young person of his age, 5 years was a very long time indeed. The sentence did not sufficiently reflect the fact D was aged 14. **4 years'** detention.
For more detail, see **291.46** in Volume 2.
Many of the offence chapters have a paragraph for children and young offenders, see the back index.

15 COMMUNITY ORDERS

15.1
Criminal Justice Act 2003 s 177[241]
Availability Defendant must be aged 18+. For when it is not available, see **15.7.**
Purpose *Imposition of Community and Custodial Sentences Guideline 2017* www.banksr.com Other Matters Guidelines tab page 3 states 'community orders can fulfil all of the purposes of sentencing. In particular, they can have the effect of restricting the offender's liberty while providing punishment in the community, rehabilitation for the offender, and/or ensuring that the offender engages in reparative activities'.
Court Martial This order is not available. The Court Martial can pass a Service Community Order for both service personnel and civilians, see the **Service Community Orders** section at **24.22**.
Historical offences A community order is available for offences committed on or after 4 April 2005. For offences committed before 4 April 2005 (whatever the date of the offence[242]), courts pass a Community Punishment and Rehabilitation Order under

[241] As amended
[242] This is because Powers of Criminal Courts (Sentencing) Act 2000 s 51 came into force without any saving provisions three months after Royal Assent, Powers of Criminal Courts (Sentencing) Act 2000 s 168.

Powers of Criminal Courts (Sentencing) Act 2000 s 51. An unpaid work requirement has to be added. For offences committed on or after 4 April 2005 and before 14 July 2008 the offence has to be imprisonable in order to pass a Community Punishment and Rehabilitation Order.

Victim surcharge The court must impose a victim surcharge, Criminal Justice Act 2003 s 161A-161B and Criminal Justice Act 2003 (Surcharge) Order 2012 2012/1696 as amended. There are exceptions, a) where a compensation order or an Unlawful Profits Order or a Slavery and Trafficking Reparations Order is imposed, when a reduced amount or a nil amount can be ordered, see **17.67**, and b) where the offence was committed before 1 October 2012, when no surcharge can be ordered, see **115.3**. Where the offence was committed on or after that date and before 8 April 2016, the amount to be imposed is the relevant figure in brackets below, see **115.4**. The amount to be imposed is £85 (£60), unless one or more of the offences was committed when the defendant was aged under 18, when the amount is £20 (£15).

Rehabilitation period The rehabilitation period is 12 months beginning with the day provided by or under the order as the last day that the order has effect.[243]

See also the **REHABILITATION OF OFFENDERS ACT 1974** chapter.

15.2 *Statistics England and Wales*

	2014	2015	2016	2017
Total persons sentenced	1,209,202	1,238,917	1,229,511	1,192,337
% given a community sentence	9.3	9.2	8.4	8.0
Community order	90,805	94,150	84,817	78,417
Referral Order	12,858	12,367	11,402	10,611
Reparation Order	198	139	114	83
Total community sentences	112,638	114,284	102,938	95,112

For explanations about the statistics, see page 1-xii. For more detailed statistics, see www.banksr.com Other Matters Statistics tab.

15.3 *Definition*

Criminal Justice Act 2003 s 147(1) In this Part 'community sentence' means a sentence which consists of or includes:

(a) a community order (as defined by section 177),
(b) [repealed],
(c) a Youth Rehabilitation Order.

15.4 *History of the orders*

Order	Applies to those aged[244]	In force
Community order Criminal Justice Act 2003 s 177	18+[245]	4 April 2005

[243] Rehabilitation of Offenders Act 1974 s 5(2)
[244] Ages relate to age at conviction.
[245] Community orders were available for those aged 16+ from 4 April 2005 to 29 November 2009.

<table>
<tr><th>Order</th><th>Applies to those aged[244]</th><th>In force</th></tr>
<tr><td>Requirements</td><td></td><td></td></tr>
<tr><td>Activity[246]
Criminal Justice Act 2003
s 201</td><td>18+</td><td>Repealed[247]</td></tr>
<tr><td>Alcohol abstinence and monitoring[248]
Criminal Justice Act 2003
s 212A</td><td>18+</td><td>Trials from 31 July 2014 to 30 July 2016 in South London local justice area only. The trials have not been extended[249]</td></tr>
<tr><td>Alcohol treatment[250]
Criminal Justice Act 2003
s 212</td><td>18+</td><td rowspan="4">4 April 2005</td></tr>
<tr><td>Attendance centre
Criminal Justice Act 2003
s 214</td><td>18-25</td></tr>
<tr><td>Curfew[251]
Criminal Justice Act 2003
s 204</td><td rowspan="4"></td></tr>
<tr><td>Drug rehabilitation
Criminal Justice Act 2003
s 209</td></tr>
<tr><td>Electronic monitoring[252]
Criminal Justice Act 2003
s 215</td><td>Not yet in force as a stand-alone requirement in a community order. In force as an add-on requirement when certain other requirements are made, see 15.22.</td></tr>
<tr><td>Exclusion
Criminal Justice Act 2003
s 205</td><td>4 April 2005</td></tr>
</table>

[246] Substituted by Criminal Justice Act 2003 Sch 32 para 95. Powers of Criminal Courts (Sentencing) Act 2000 s 60 was commenced by Powers of Criminal Courts (Sentencing) Act 2000 s 168(1).

[247] Offender Rehabilitation Act 2014 s 15(4). Repealed on 1/2/15, Offender Rehabilitation Act 2014 (Commencement No 2) Order 2015 2015/40

[248] Inserted by Legal Aid, Sentencing and Punishment of Offenders Act 2012 s 76

[249] Legal Aid, Sentencing and Punishment of Offenders Act 2012 (Alcohol Abstinence and Monitoring Requirements) Piloting Order 2014 2014/1787. This order was amended by Legal Aid, Sentencing and Punishment of Offenders Act 2012 (Alcohol Abstinence and Monitoring Requirements) Piloting (Amendment) Order 2015 2015/1480. The period was extended by six months by Criminal Justice Act 2003 (Alcohol Abstinence and Monitoring Requirement) (Prescription of Arrangement for Monitoring) (Amendment) Order 2015 2015/1482. The period was further extended to 30 July 2016 by Legal Aid, Sentencing and Punishment of Offenders Act 2012 (Alcohol Abstinence and Monitoring Requirements) Piloting (Amendment) Order 2016 2016/1 and Criminal Justice Act 2003 (Alcohol Abstinence and Monitoring Requirement) (Prescription of Arrangement for Monitoring) (Amendment) Order 2016 2016/10. The ability to add a tag was laid down by Criminal Justice Act 2003 (Alcohol Abstinence and Monitoring Requirement) (Prescription of Arrangement for Monitoring) Order 2016 2016/327. Five of these statutory instruments have been revoked so the trialling is now over, Criminal Justice Act 2003 (Alcohol Abstinence and Monitoring Requirement) (Prescription of Arrangement for Monitoring) Order 2018/210.

[250] Substituted by Criminal Justice Act 2003 Sch 32 para 95. Powers of Criminal Courts (Sentencing) Act 2000 s 60 was commenced by Powers of Criminal Courts (Sentencing) Act 2000 s 168(1).

[251] Still in force for fine defaulters, those refusing to be bound over, and those found to be in contempt of court etc.

[252] The change to a stand-alone requirement is made by Crime and Courts Act 2013 s 44 and Sch 16 para 12(2)(b). There was partial commencement on 17/10/16 for eight local justice areas, Crime and Courts Act 2013 (Commencement No 15, Transitional and Savings Provisions) Order 2016 2016/962 para 2. Originally the provisions were to cease on 13/10/17. This date was put back to 30/6/18 by Crime and Courts Act 2013 (Commencement No 15, Transitional and Savings Provisions) (Amendment) Order 2017 2017/976.

<table>
<tr><th>Order</th><th>Applies to those aged[244]</th><th>In force</th></tr>
<tr><td>Foreign travel prohibition[254]
Criminal Justice Act 2003
s 206A</td><td rowspan="8">18+</td><td>11 December 2013</td></tr>
<tr><td>Mental health treatment[255]
Criminal Justice Act 2003
s 207</td><td>4 April 2005</td></tr>
<tr><td>Programme
Criminal Justice Act 2003
s 202</td><td rowspan="2">4 April 2005</td></tr>
<tr><td>Prohibited activity
Criminal Justice Act 2003
s 203</td></tr>
<tr><td>Rehabilitation activity
Criminal Justice Act 2003
s 200A[256]</td><td>1 February 2015[257]</td></tr>
<tr><td>Residence
Criminal Justice Act 2003
s 206</td><td>4 April 2005</td></tr>
<tr><td>Supervision
Criminal Justice Act 2003
s 213</td><td>Repealed[258]</td></tr>
<tr><td>Unpaid work
Criminal Justice Act 2003
s 199</td><td>4 April 2005</td></tr>
<tr><td>Referral Order
Powers of Criminal Courts (Sentencing) Act 2000 s 16</td><td>10-17</td><td>25 August 2000</td></tr>
<tr><td>Suspended sentence order (with community requirements)
Criminal Justice Act 2003
s 190</td><td>This describes the group of three orders below and is not itself an order. The orders below are stand-alone orders.</td><td>4 April 2005</td></tr>
<tr><td>Youth Rehabilitation Order
Criminal Justice and Immigration Act 2008 s 1</td><td>10-17</td><td>30 Nov 2009[259]</td></tr>
</table>

254 Inserted by Legal Aid, Sentencing and Punishment of Offenders Act 2012 s 72. In force 25/11/13
255 As amended by Legal Aid, Sentencing and Punishment of Offenders Act 2012 s 73
256 As inserted by Offender Rehabilitation Act 2014 s 15
257 Offender Rehabilitation Act 2014 (Commencement No 2) Order 2015 2015/40
258 Offender Rehabilitation Act 2014 s 15(4). Repealed on 1/2/15, Offender Rehabilitation Act 2014 (Commencement No 2) Order 2015 2015/40
259 Commenced by Criminal Justice and Immigration Act 2008 (Commencement No 13 and Transitory Provision) Order 2009 2009/3074 art 2.

Order	Applies to those aged[244]	In force
YRO with Fostering Criminal Justice and Immigration Act 2008 s 1(3)(b)	10-17	30 Nov 2009[260]
YRO with Intensive Supervision and Surveillance Criminal Justice and Immigration Act 2008 s 1(3)(a)	10-17	30 Nov 2009

15.5 ***Power to order***

Criminal Justice Act 2003 s 177(1) Where a person aged 18 or over is convicted of an offence, the court by or before which he is convicted may make an order (referred to as a 'community order') imposing on him any one or more of the following requirements (which are listed in the following paragraphs of the book.)

15.6 ***Offence must carry imprisonment***

Community order available only for offences punishable with imprisonment or for persistent offenders previously fined

Criminal Justice Act 2003 s 150A(1) The power to make a community order is only exercisable in respect of an offence if:

(a) the offence is punishable with imprisonment, or

(b) in any other case, section 151(2)[261] confers power to make such an order.

(2) For the purposes of this section and section 151 an offence triable either way that was tried summarily is to be regarded as punishable with imprisonment only if it is so punishable by the sentencing court (and for this purpose section 148(1) is to be disregarded).

Note: The provision about the order being available for those persistent offenders previously fined is not in force, see **15.11**. Ed.

15.7 ***When is a community order not available?***

Criminal Justice Act 2003 s 150(1) The power to make a community order or Youth Rehabilitation Order is not exercisable in respect of an offence for which the sentence:

(a) is fixed by law,

(b) falls to be imposed under Firearms Act 1968 s 51A(2) (required custodial sentence for certain firearms offences),

(c) falls to be imposed under Powers of Criminal Courts (Sentencing) Act 2000 s 110(2) or 111(2) (requirement to impose custodial sentences for certain repeated offences committed by offenders aged 18 or over),

(ca) falls to be imposed under Violent Crime Reduction Act 2006 s 29(4) or (6) (required custodial sentence in certain cases of using someone to mind a weapon), or

(d) falls to be imposed under section 225(2) or 226(2) of this Act (requirement to impose sentence of imprisonment for life or detention for life).

(2) [where the minimum sentences for offensive weapons or bladed articles under Prevention of Crime Act 1953 s 1A(5) and Criminal Justice Act 1988 s 139AA(7) apply.[262]]

---

260 Commenced by Criminal Justice and Immigration Act 2008 (Commencement No 13 and Transitory Provision) Order 2009 2009/3074 art 2.

261 Commencement is awaited. There is no sign it will ever be in force. However, a new section (2A) has been inserted by Criminal Justice and Immigration Act 2008 Sch 4 para 76(3) which applies to Youth Rehabilitation Orders and permits the court to impose a Youth Rehabilitation Order instead of a fine.

262 As inserted by Crime and Courts Act 2013 Sch 16 para 23. In force 11/12/13 and amended by Criminal Justice and Courts Act 2015 Sch 5 para 13

15.8 *Maximum length of the order*

Criminal Justice Act 2003 s 177(5) A community order must specify a date 'the end date, not more than three years after the date of the order, by which all the requirements in it must have been complied with'.

15.9 *Test to apply*

Criminal Justice Act 2003 s 148(1) and (2)

Criminal Justice Act 2003 s 148(1) A court must not pass a community sentence on an offender unless it is of the opinion that the offence, or the combination of the offence and one or more offences associated with it, was serious enough to warrant such a sentence.

(2) Where a court passes a community sentence:

(b) the restrictions on liberty imposed by the order must be such as in the opinion of the court are commensurate with the seriousness of the offence, or the combination of the offence and one or more offences associated with it.

Criminal Justice Act 2003 s 148(5) The fact that by virtue of any provision of this section:

(a) a community sentence may be passed in relation to an offence, or

(b) particular restrictions on liberty may be imposed by a community order or Youth Rehabilitation Order,

does not require a court to pass such a sentence or to impose those restrictions.

TICs and Totality Guideline 2012: Crown Court, see www.banksr.com Other Matters Guidelines tab

Imposition of Community and Custodial Sentences Guideline 2017 www.banksr.com Other Matters Guidelines tab In force 1 February 2017. page 3 Sentencers must consider all available disposals at the time of sentence; even where the threshold for a community sentence has been passed, a fine or discharge may be an appropriate penalty. In particular, a Band D fine may be an appropriate alternative to a community order. The court must ensure that the restriction on the offender's liberty is commensurate with the seriousness of the offence[263] and that the requirements imposed are the most suitable for the offender.[264]

Sentences should not necessarily escalate from one community order range to the next on each sentencing occasion. The decision as to the appropriate range of community order should be based upon the seriousness of the new offence(s) (which will take into account any previous convictions).

Save in exceptional circumstances at least one requirement must be imposed for the purpose of punishment and/or a fine imposed in addition to the community order.[265] It is a matter for the court to decide which requirements amount to a punishment in each case.

page 14 **Multiple offences attracting community orders: crossing the custody threshold**

If the offences are all imprisonable and none of the individual sentences merit a custodial sentence, the custody threshold can be crossed by reason of multiple offending. If the custody threshold has been passed, the court should refer to the offence ranges in sentencing guidelines for the offences and to the general principles.

Multiple offences, where one offence would merit immediate custody and one offence would merit a community order

A community order should not be ordered to run consecutively to or concurrently with a custodial sentence. Instead the court should generally impose one custodial sentence that is aggravated appropriately by the presence of the associated offence(s). The alternative option is to impose no separate penalty for the offence of lesser seriousness.

---

[263] Criminal Justice Act 2003 s 148(2)(b)

[264] Criminal Justice Act 2003 s 148(2)(a)

[265] Criminal Justice Act 2003 s 177(2A) and (2B)

Offender convicted of more than one offence where a community order is appropriate
A community order is a composite package rather than an accumulation of sentences attached to individual counts. The court should generally impose a single community order that reflects the overall criminality of the offending behaviour. Where it is necessary to impose more than one community order, these should be ordered to run concurrently and for ease of administration, each of the orders should be identical.
Offender convicted of an offence while serving a community order
The power to deal with the offender depends on his being convicted whilst the order is still in force. It does not arise where the order has expired, even if the additional offence was committed whilst it was still current.
If an offender, in respect of whom a community order made by a Magistrates' Court is in force, is convicted by a Magistrates' Court of an additional offence, the Magistrates' Court should ordinarily revoke the previous community order and sentence afresh for both the original and the additional offence.
Where an offender, in respect of whom a community order made by a Crown Court is in force, is convicted by a Magistrates' Court, the Magistrates' Court may, and ordinarily should, commit the offender to the Crown Court, in order to allow the Crown Court to re-sentence for the original offence and the additional offence.
The sentencing court should consider the overall seriousness of the offending behaviour, taking into account the additional offence and the original offence. The court should consider whether the combination of associated offences is sufficiently serious to justify a custodial sentence.
If the court does not consider that custody is necessary, it should impose a single community order that reflects the overall totality of criminality. The court must take into account the extent to which the offender complied with the requirements of the previous order.
Note: There is a similar entry in the *Magistrates' Court Sentencing Guidelines Update March 2012* page 18n. Ed.

15.10 *Pre-sentence reports*

Criminal Justice Act 2003 s 156(3) Subject to subsection (4), a court must obtain and consider a pre-sentence report before:

(a) [Certain custodial sentences, see **56.44**]
(b) in the case of a community sentence, forming any such opinion as is mentioned in section 148(1) or (2)(b) [test for a community order, see **15.9**] or in section 1(4)(b) or (c) of the Criminal Justice and Immigration Act 2008, [the enhanced Youth Rehabilitation Order, see **119.10** and **119.11**] or any opinion as to the suitability for the offender of the particular requirement or requirements to be imposed by the community order or youth rehabilitation order.

(4) Subsection (3) does not apply if, in the circumstances of the case, the court is of the opinion that it is unnecessary to obtain a pre-sentence report.
(5) [For offenders under aged 18, see **83.15**]
(6)-(8) [Failure to have a report and an appeal, see **83.20**]
(9) [Re automatic life and extended sentences]
Imposition of Community and Custodial Sentences Guideline 2017 www.banksr.com Other Matters Guidelines tab In force 1 February 2017. page 6
Pre-sentence reports
In many cases, a pre-sentence report will be pivotal in helping the court decide whether to impose a community order and, if so, whether particular requirements or combinations of requirements are suitable for an individual offender. Whenever the court reaches the provisional view that a community order may be appropriate, it should request a pre-sentence report (whether written or verbal) unless the court is of the opinion that a report is unnecessary in all the circumstances of the case. It may be helpful to indicate to the National Probation Service the court's preliminary opinion as to which of the three

sentencing ranges is relevant and the purpose(s) of sentencing that the package of requirements is expected to fulfil. Ideally a pre-sentence report should be completed on the same day to avoid adjourning the case. If an adjournment cannot be avoided, the information should be provided to the National Probation Service in written form and a copy retained on the court file for the benefit of the sentencing court. However, the court must make clear to the offender that all sentencing options remain open including, in appropriate cases, committal for sentence to the Crown Court.

15.11 ***Community order/Youth Rehabilitation Order for persistent offender previously fined***

Note: Commencement is awaited for Criminal Justice Act 2003 s 151. It has been amended by Domestic Violence, Crime and Victims Act 2004 s 59(1) and Sch 10 para 63, Armed Forces Act 2006 s 378(1) and Sch 16 para 217, Criminal Justice and Immigration Act 2008 s 6(2), 11(2)-(7) and Sch 4 para 71 and 76(1)-(6), Coroners and Justice Act 2009 s 144, 177(1) and Sch 17 para 8 and Sch 21 para 98 and Prevention of Social Housing Fraud Act 2013 s 10 and Sch 1 para 28-29. As the section has not been not in force for so long, it is no longer listed. It can be found in the 12th edition of this book. The provisions for the Court Martial, Armed Forces Act 2006 s 270(7)-(8) have been repealed. Section 151 is a classic example of how not to draft legislation. Ed.

15.12 ***Determining the requirements***

Imposition of Community and Custodial Sentences Guideline 2017 www.banksr.com Other Matters Guidelines tab In force 1 February 2017.

page 4 **Community order levels**

The seriousness of the offence should be the initial factor in determining which requirements to include in a community order. Offence-specific guidelines refer to three sentencing levels within the community order band based on offence seriousness (low, medium and high).

The culpability and harm present in the offence(s) should be considered to identify which of the three sentencing levels within the community order band (low, medium and high) is appropriate.

See below for **non-exhaustive** examples of requirements that might be appropriate in each.

At least one requirement **MUST** be imposed for the purpose of punishment and/or a fine imposed in addition to the community order unless there are exceptional circumstances which relate to the offence or the offender that would make it unjust in all the circumstances to do so.[266]

Low	Medium	High
Offences only just cross community order threshold, where the seriousness of the offence or the nature of the offender's record means that a discharge or fine is inappropriate	Offences that obviously fall within the community order band	Offences only just fall below the custody threshold or the custody threshold is crossed but a community order is more appropriate in the circumstances
In general, only one requirement will be appropriate and the length may be curtailed if additional requirements are necessary		More intensive sentences which combine two or more requirements may be appropriate

[266] Criminal Justice Act 2003 s 177(2A) and (2B)

Suitable requirements might include: • Any appropriate rehabilitative requirement(s) • 40 to 80 hours of unpaid work • Curfew requirement within the lowest range (for example up to 16 hours per day for a few weeks) • Exclusion requirement, for a few months • Prohibited activity requirement • Attendance centre requirement (where available)	Suitable requirements might include: • Any appropriate rehabilitative requirement(s) • Greater number of hours of unpaid work (for example 80 to 150 hours) • Curfew requirement within the middle range (for example up to 16 hours for 2 to 3 months) • Exclusion requirement lasting in the region of 6 months • Prohibited activity requirement	Suitable requirements might include: • Any appropriate rehabilitative requirement(s) • 150 to 300 hours of unpaid work • Curfew requirement up to 16 hours per day for 4 to 12 months • Exclusion order lasting in the region of 12 months
* If order does not contain a punitive requirement, suggested fine levels are indicated below:		
BAND A FINE	**BAND B FINE**	**BAND C FINE**

Old guideline: *New Sentences: Criminal Justice Act 2003 Guideline 2004* paras 1.1.9, 1.1.20, 1.1.25-1.1.29. It appears the guideline has been superseded.

15.13 ***Requirements imposed must be suitable for the offender***
Criminal Justice Act 2003 s 148(2) Where a court passes a community sentence:

(a) the particular requirement or requirements forming part of the community order or, as the case may be, Youth Rehabilitation Order comprised in the sentence must be such as, in the opinion of the court, is, or taken together are, the most suitable for the offender.

(2A) Subsection (2) is subject to Criminal Justice Act 2003 s 177(2A) (community orders: punitive elements)[267] and to Criminal Justice and Immigration Act 2008 Sch 1 para 3(4) (Youth Rehabilitation Order with Intensive Supervision and Surveillance).
Criminal Justice and Immigration Act 2008 Sch 1 para 3(4) A Youth Rehabilitation Order which imposes an extended activity requirement must also impose:

(a) a supervision requirement, and
(b) a curfew requirement (and, accordingly, if so required by paragraph 2, an electronic monitoring requirement).

15.14 ***Order must include a requirement for punishment or a fine***
Criminal Justice Act 2003 s 177(2A)[268] Where the court makes a community order, the court must:

(a) include in the order at least one requirement imposed for the purpose of punishment, or
(b) impose a fine for the offence in respect of which the community order is made, or
(c) comply with both paragraphs (a) and (b).

(2B) Subsection (2A) does not apply where there are exceptional circumstances which:

(a) relate to the offence or to the offender,
(b) would make it unjust in all the circumstances for the court to comply with subsection (2A)(a) in the particular case, and
(c) would make it unjust in all the circumstances for the court to impose a fine for the offence concerned.

[267] As amended by Crime and Courts Act 2013 Sch 16 para 3. In force 11/12/13
[268] Inserted by Crime and Courts Act 2013 Sch 16 para 2. In force 11/12/13

15.15 ***Determining the length of a community order***
R v Odam 2008 EWCA Crim 1087, 2009 1 Cr App R (S) 22 (p 120) D was convicted of exposure and sentenced to a community order with one term only, namely unpaid work of 120 hours. The Judge said he was subject to notification for 5 years. Sexual Offences Act 2003 Sch 3 para 33(b)(c) triggers notification when a defendant 'is made the subject of a community sentence of at least 12 months'. D completed his unpaid work in less than 12 months. Held. Criminal Justice Act 2003 s 200(3) provides that a community order containing an unpaid work requirement comes to an end when the work has been completed. Therefore D had not been sentenced to a community order of at least 12 months so notification did not apply.
R v Davison 2008 EWCA Crim 2795, 2009 2 Cr App R (S) 13 (p 76) D pleaded to two counts of sexual assault. On 27 June 2008, he was sentenced to a community order with 220 hours' unpaid work 'to be completed before 27 June 2009'. The Judge said D was subject to notification requirements. Held. *R v Odam* 2008 was the subject of academic criticism on the basis that the length of such an order must be capable of being determined on the date it is made and cannot depend on how long it takes an offender to carry out the required work. The period specified by the court when imposing a community order is the relevant period for determining the duration of the order however long it takes the offender to carry out the requirements. The opinion in *R v Odam* 2008 is wrong. The date specified by the Judge was 12 months so the Judge was correct to say notification requirements were applicable.
R v Khan 2015 EWCA Crim 835 D pleaded to production of cannabis for his own use. He was given a community order with 100 hours' unpaid work. There was no complaint about that. The Judge said the community order should run for longer than the time the unpaid work was performed so there was some control or power to recall D. She made the order for two years. Held. This order cannot exist other than as a vehicle for the requirement to be performed. The Judge could have imposed a supervision requirement, but she did not. The order cannot be an empty order. It must contain a requirement. The Judge had no power to make the order for 2 years, so 12 months instead.
Note: Legal Aid, Sentencing and Punishment of Offenders Act 2012 s 66[269] made changes to the duration of community orders including a requirement that the order must state the day on which the requirements must end. This is no doubt to cope with the some of the anomalies that have developed with the old wording. Ed.

The requirements that can be made part of a community order/Suspended Sentence Order

15.16 ***Activity requirement***
This requirement was repealed on 1/2/15.[270]

15.17 ***Alcohol abstinence and monitoring requirement***
Criminal Justice Act 2003 s 212A
Legal Aid, Sentencing and Punishment of Offenders Act 2012 s 76[271] substitutes the new section thereby creating this new requirement.
Definition [The requirement is] that the offender must abstain from consuming alcohol or must not consume alcohol more than a specified level (which will be specified by the Secretary of State) during a specified period, Criminal Justice Act 2003 s 212A(1)(a).
Availability [The requirement is available where:] a) i) the consumption of alcohol by the offender is an element of the offence or associated offence, or ii) the consumption of alcohol is a factor that contributed to the commission of the offence or associated offence, b) the offender is not dependent on alcohol, c) the offender is not subject to an

[269] The requirement came into force on 3/12/12
[270] Offender Rehabilitation Act 2014 s 15 and Offender Rehabilitation Act 2014 (Commencement No 2) Order 2015 2015/40
[271] In force 3/12/12

alcohol treatment requirement, and d) there are arrangements for the order in the locality, Criminal Justice Act 2003 s 177(2) and 212A(8)-(11). The Act was only in force for the south London local justice area, until 30 July 2016. For more details see **15.4**.
Monitoring The offender must submit to the monitoring specified in the order, which includes electronic monitoring, Criminal Justice Act 2003 s 212A(1)(b). An electronic monitoring requirement may not be included to monitor compliance, unless it is to monitor another requirement, Criminal Justice Act 2003 s 215(5)-(6).
Maximum length 120 days, Criminal Justice Act 2002 s 212A(2).

15.18 *Alcohol treatment requirement*

Criminal Justice Act 2003 s 212
Definition A requirement that the offender must submit during a period specified in the order to treatment by or under the direction of a specified person having the necessary qualifications or experience with a view to the reduction or elimination of the offender's dependency on alcohol, Criminal Justice Act 2003 s 212(1).
Availability A court may not impose an alcohol treatment requirement in respect of an offender unless it is satisfied:
(a) that he is dependent on alcohol,
(b) that his dependency is such as requires and may be susceptible to treatment, and
(c) that arrangements have been or can be made for the treatment intended to be specified in the order (including arrangements for the reception of the offender where he is to be required to submit to treatment as a resident), Criminal Justice Act 2003 s 212(2).
Defendant must consent A court may not impose an alcohol treatment requirement unless the offender expresses his willingness to comply with its requirements, Criminal Justice Act 2003 s 212(3).
Length The maximum period for which the alcohol treatment requirement has effect (formerly 6 months) was removed by Legal Aid, Sentencing and Punishment of Offenders Act 2012 s 75.[272]
Treatment The treatment required by an alcohol treatment requirement for any particular period must be:
(a) treatment as a resident in such institution or place as may be specified in the order,
(b) treatment as a non-resident in or at such institution or place, and at such intervals, as may be so specified, or
(c) treatment by or under the direction of such person having the necessary qualification or experience as may be so specified,
but the nature of the treatment shall not be specified in the order except as mentioned in paragraph (a), (b) or (c) above, Criminal Justice Act 2003 s 212(5).
Electronic monitoring Where the court makes [this] order it may also impose an electronic monitoring requirement, Criminal Justice Act 2003 s 177(4).

15.19 *Attendance centre requirement*

Criminal Justice Act 2003 s 214
Availability The offender must be aged under 25, Criminal Justice Act 2003 s 214.[273] The court may not impose an attendance centre requirement unless the court is satisfied that the attendance centre is reasonably accessible to the offender concerned, having regard to the means of access available to him and any other circumstances, Criminal Justice Act 2003 s 214(3) and 218(3).
Total hours The aggregate number of hours for which the offender may be required to attend at an attendance centre must not be less than 12 or more than 36, Criminal Justice Act 2003 s 214(2).

[272] In force 3/12/12
[273] This is not in the text of the section but is in the section title.

Hours per day An offender may not be required to attend at an attendance centre on more than one occasion on any day, or for more than three hours on any occasion, Criminal Justice Act 2003 s 214(6).
Electronic monitoring Where the court makes [this] order it may also impose an electronic monitoring requirement, Criminal Justice Act 2003 s 177(4).
Note: Offender Rehabilitation Act 2014 s 17 amends Criminal Justice Act 2003 s 214. The changes are more administrative than substantive. In force 1 February 2015.[274] Ed.

15.20 *Curfew requirement*

Definition A requirement that the offender must remain, for periods specified in the relevant order, at a place so specified, Criminal Justice Act 2003 s 204(1).
Duty to obtain information Before making a relevant order imposing a curfew requirement, the court must obtain and consider information about the place proposed to be specified in the order (including information as to the attitude of persons likely to be affected by the enforced presence there of the offender), Criminal Justice Act 2003 s 104(6).
Number of hours A curfew requirement may specify different places or different periods for different days, but may not specify periods which amount to less than two hours or more than 16[275] hours in any day, Criminal Justice Act 2003 s 204(2).
Electronic monitoring Where the court makes a community order imposing a curfew requirement it must also impose an electronic monitoring requirement unless: a) the court is prevented from doing so by section 215(2) (see **15.22**) or 218(4) (see provision about availability), or b) in the particular circumstances of the case, it considers it inappropriate to do so, Criminal Justice Act 2003 s 177(3).
Length A community order or suspended sentence order which imposes a curfew requirement may not specify periods which fall outside the period of 12[276] months beginning with the day on which it is made, Criminal Justice Act 2003 s 204(3).
R v Henry 2011 EWCA Crim 630 D was convicted of causing death by careless driving. He pulled out of a side road and collided with a van. The driver of the van suffered a fractured spine and died. The Judge described it as a 'momentary inattention' case. D was employed as a salesman, driving 60,000 miles per year. The Judge gave a Curfew Order, among other punishments. It was argued that the Curfew Order was an unusual punishment, given that D was not prone to commit offences at night. Held. The imposition of a 3-month Curfew Order, which had ended by the time of appeal, for an offence that was committed at night, was not wrong in principle. Such an order is designed not simply to prevent night-time offending but is also to be seen as another element in the sentencing process.
R v Ali 2011 EWCA Crim 2747 D pleaded to robbery on the day of trial. The Judge deferred sentence for 6 months, imposing a curfew requirement and other requirements. When D was brought back for sentence, the Judge imposed a community order with supervision and a curfew. It was argued that a 6-month curfew followed by a community order with a curfew was unlawful as the statutory maximum period for a curfew requirement is 6 months. Held. Criminal Justice Act 2003 s 204(3) makes no reference to earlier curfews imposed as conditions for deferment. Had Parliament wished to restrict the period of a curfew, it could and would have done so. The 6-month curfew was history and no more than that. It was to be taken into account when assessing how onerous the community requirements ought to be, but was not a legal obstacle to imposing a curfew requirement at all.
See also: *R v Chesworth* 2014 EWCA Crim 1927 (D pleaded to domestic affray. Suspended sentence with unpaid work and a 12-month curfew between 7 pm and 7 am.

---

[274] Offender Rehabilitation Act 2014 (Commencement No 2) Order 2015 2015/40
[275] This was increased from 12 hours to 16 hours by Legal Aid, Sentencing and Punishment of Offenders Act 2012 s 71. In force 3/12/12
[276] This was increased from 6 months to 12 months by Legal Aid, Sentencing and Punishment of Offenders Act 2012 s 71. In force 3/12/12

Had a terrible record, including 12 shopliftings, several breaches of a court order and drugs offences. Long record of substance abuse but had given birth shortly before sentence. A pre-appeal report noted that the need for a curfew had diminished. Held. The curfew represented a very significant deprivation of D's effective liberty and 12-month curfews are rare. D has now been on curfew for 5 months. Curfew quashed.)

15.21 ***Drug rehabilitation requirement***
Criminal Justice Act 2003 s 209

Definition A requirement that during a period specified in the order ('the treatment and testing period') the offender:

(a) must submit to treatment by or under the direction of a specified person having the necessary qualifications or experience with a view to the reduction or elimination of the offender's dependency on or propensity to misuse drugs, and

(b) for the purpose of ascertaining whether he has any drug in his body during that period, must provide samples of such description as may be so determined, at such times or in such circumstances as may (subject to the provisions of the order) be determined by the responsible officer or by the person specified as the person by or under whose direction the treatment is to be provided, Criminal Justice Act 2003 s 209(1).

Availability A court may not impose a drug rehabilitation requirement unless:

(a) it is satisfied: i) that the offender is dependent on, or has a propensity to misuse drugs, and ii) that his dependency or propensity is such as requires and may be susceptible to treatment,

(b) it is also satisfied that arrangements have been or can be made for the treatment intended to be specified in the order (including arrangements for the reception of the offender where he is to be required to submit to treatment as a resident),

(c) the requirement has been recommended to the court as being suitable for the offender by an officer of a local probation board or an officer of a provider of probation services, and

(d) the offender expresses his willingness to comply with the requirement, see Criminal Justice Act 2003 s 209(2).

Length The requirement that the treatment and testing period must be for at least six months was removed by Legal Aid, Sentencing and Punishment of Offenders Act 2012 s 74.[277]

Treatment The required treatment for any particular period must be:

(a) treatment as a resident in such institution or place as may be specified in the order, or

(b) treatment as a non-resident in or at such institution or place, and at such intervals, as may be so specified,

but the nature of the treatment is not to be specified in the order except as mentioned in paragraph (a) or (b) above, Criminal Justice Act 2003 s 209(4).

Provisions as to samples A community order or suspended sentence order imposing a drug rehabilitation requirement must provide that the results of tests carried out on any samples provided by the offender in pursuance of the requirement to a person other than the responsible officer are to be communicated to the responsible officer, Criminal Justice Act 2003 s 209(6).

Electronic monitoring Where the court makes [this] order it may also impose an electronic monitoring requirement, Criminal Justice Act 2003 s 177(4).

Amendment of, see **15.50**.

Reviews of the order Criminal Justice Act 2003 s 210(1)-(2) deals with this. There is power on a review to amend the order.

[277] In force 3/12/12

15.22 ***Electronic monitoring requirement***
When obligatory Criminal Justice Act 2003 s 177(3) Where the court makes a community order imposing a curfew requirement or an exclusion requirement, the court must also impose an electronic monitoring requirement (as defined by section 215)[278] unless:

(a) it is prevented from doing so by section 215(2) or 218(4), or

(b) in the particular circumstances of the case, it considers it inappropriate to do so.

Availability A court may not include an electronic monitoring requirement in a relevant order…unless the court: a) has been notified by the Secretary of State that electronic monitoring arrangements are available…, and b) is satisfied that the necessary provision can be made under those arrangements (Criminal Justice Act 2003 s 190(3) and 218(9)[279] and Criminal Justice Act 2003 s 218(4)), as amended by Crime and Courts Act 2013 Sch 16 para 18(9).

Availability as a listed requirement rather than an add-on requirement This change was made by Crime and Courts Act 2013 Sch 16 para 12(3). Commencement is awaited.

Need for consent of another person Where…there is a person (other than the offender) without whose co-operation it will not be practicable to secure the monitoring, the requirement may not be included in the order without that person's consent, Criminal Justice Act 2003 s 215(2).

Order must state who is responsible [The] order…must include provision for making a person responsible for the monitoring, and a person who is made so responsible must be of a description specified in an order made by the Secretary of State.

Notification of the order The responsible officer must, before the beginning of [the monitoring] period, notify: a) the offender, b) the person responsible for the monitoring, and c) any person falling within subsection 215(2)(b) (someone whose co-operation is required), of the time when the period is to begin.

15.23 ***Exclusion requirement***
Criminal Justice Act 2003 s 205

Definition 'Exclusion requirement' means a provision prohibiting the offender from entering a place specified in the order for a period so specified, Criminal Justice Act 2003 s 205(1).

Length Where the relevant order is a community order, the period specified must not be more than two years, Criminal Justice Act 2003 s 205(2).

Electronic monitoring Where the court makes a community order imposing an exclusion requirement it must also impose an electronic monitoring requirement unless: a) the court is prevented from doing so by section 215(2) or 218(4), or b) in the particular circumstances of the case, it considers it inappropriate to do so, Criminal Justice Act 2003 s 177(3).

Operational periods An exclusion requirement: a) may provide for the prohibition to operate only during the periods specified in the order, and b) may specify different places for different periods or days, Criminal Justice Act 2003 s 205(3).

R v Jacob 2008 EWCA Crim 2002 D was convicted of exposure. The victim, V, and her 19-month-old daughter, B, were in their kitchen having only recently moved into the house. They waved at D, who was on his driveway, and he waved back. V saw B waving at D again and looked out to see D masturbating and looking directly at her. She contacted the police. V said she was shocked and scared of living in her home. She also said on the day she was an emotional wreck and in a complete shambles for a few days. The Judge imposed a community order with unpaid work, an exclusion order excluding D from his own house for two years and a prohibition order that prohibited him from communicating directly or indirectly with V and B. D had found a house elsewhere but was in desperate financial trouble. Held. There have been no further incidents. The

[278] As amended by Crime and Courts Act 2013 Sch 16 para 12(4). In force 11/12/13
[279] As inserted by Crime and Courts Act 2013 Sch 16 para 18(3). In force 11/12/13

primary purpose of an exclusion requirement is not to punish the offender but to prevent, or at least reduce, the risk of further offending. It was disproportionate to exclude D from his own home when set against the risk of further offences in this case. We take the same view of the prohibited activity requirement, which is also open to the objection that its terms are so broad that it would mean the appellant, once permitted to return to his home, would be in breach of the prohibited activity requirement if he were so much as to say "Good morning" to his next-door neighbours. Requirements quashed.

R (Dragoman) v Camberwell Green Magistrates' Court 2012 EWHC 4105 D, a Romanian, pleaded to theft and going equipped. The District Judge made a community order with a 12-month exclusion requirement, which excluded D from entering the UK for 12 months. Held. In the Magistrates' Courts, a number of persons found guilty of shoplifting or other offences, in order to avoid custody, undertake to go back to the country from which they have come and, to ensure that their undertaking is complied with, judges have made similar orders to D's order. The purpose of the requirement is to exclude the defendant from a particular place where there was a risk of reoffending. In the first and most important respect, it is obvious that there is an entirely separate regime under UK Borders Act 2007 that deals with the power of exclusion. Second, on a much narrower point, it is plain on the construction of Criminal Justice Act 2003 s 205 that it deals with entering an area within the UK. It cannot possibly, on any view, take effect as permitting a judge to exclude someone who is already in the UK from entering the UK. Third, in any event, it is plain from the other terms of the order, which reflects the statutory scheme, that the purpose of exclusion is an inherent part of a community order to reform someone in the UK. Fourth, there is no mechanism in the Act or elsewhere to require someone to be removed from the UK. It was in effect an order for expulsion. The Magistrates' Court has no power to make the order.

R v Blake 2013 EWCA Crim 1884 D pleaded to two burglaries. He entered a property and a shed in the garden during the day whilst the occupier was at work. He took a satellite navigation system, tax discs and DVDs and passed them over the garden fence to an accomplice. D was released on bail with an exclusion condition preventing him from accessing the street where the burglary took place. D lived with his partner and three children in the same street. When sentenced, the Judge imposed an exclusion requirement in the same terms for a period of 2 years. The Judge was concerned that the victims of the burglary would come into contact with D when they had been devastated by the burglary. He also said the exclusion term enabled him to suspend the sentence. He subsequently varied the sentence of his own volition, reducing the exclusion requirement from 2 years to 9 months.[280] D had some convictions. Held. This exclusion term was not wrong in principle. The Judge could take into account the term when considering whether to suspend the imprisonment. He could also take into account the proximity of the victims and that D was too ill to work but not too ill to burgle. Before an exclusion order is imposed, the court must consider carefully the effect on the family, especially any children. There had been a cooling-off period and D would shortly return home. 4 months was the longest term we could impose. As that had passed we quash the order.

15.24 *Foreign travel prohibition requirement*

Criminal Justice Act 2003 s 206A

Criminal Justice Act 2003 s 206A was inserted by Legal Aid, Sentencing and Punishment of Offenders Act 2012 s 72.[281]

Definition [This requirement] means a requirement prohibiting the offender from travelling, on a day or days specified in the order, or for a period so specified to any country or territory specified in the order, Criminal Justice Act 2003 s 206A(1).

[280] The judgment states that in the variation hearing the exclusion requirement was reduced to 9 months, but later states that it was reduced to 12 months. Given the Judge's reasoning, 9 months seems more likely but in any event little turns on it.

[281] In force 3/12/12

Length Maximum of 12 months from the date of the order. If the order prohibits travel on specific days, those days must not be more than 12 months from the date of the community order, Criminal Justice Act 2003 s 206A(2) and (3).
Electronic monitoring Where the court makes [this] order it may also impose an electronic monitoring requirement, Criminal Justice Act 2003 s 177(4).

15.25 *Mental health treatment requirement*

Criminal Justice Act 2003 s 207
Definition Mental health treatment requirement means a requirement that the offender must submit, during a period or periods specified in the order, to treatment by or under the direction of a registered medical practitioner or a registered psychologist (or both, for different periods) with a view to the improvement of the offender's mental condition, Criminal Justice Act 2003 s 207(1).
Availability A court may not include a mental health treatment requirement in a relevant order unless:
(a) the court is satisfied that the mental condition of the offender,[282]
(i) is such as requires and may be susceptible to treatment, but
(ii) is not such as to warrant the making of a Hospital Order or Guardianship Order within the meaning of Mental Health Act 1983,
(b) the court is also satisfied that arrangements have been or can be made for the treatment intended to be specified in the order (including arrangements for the reception of the offender where he is to be required to submit to treatment as a resident patient), and
(c) the offender has expressed his willingness to comply with such a requirement, Criminal Justice Act 2003 s 207(3).
Treatment The treatment required must be one of the following kinds of treatment as may be specified in the relevant order:
(a) treatment as a resident patient in a care home within the meaning of Care Standards Act 2000, or a hospital within the meaning of Mental Health Act 1983, but not in hospital premises where high security psychiatric services within the meaning of that Act are provided,
(b) treatment as a non-resident patient at such institution or place as may be specified in the order,
(c) treatment by or under the direction of such registered medical practitioner or registered psychologist (or both) as may be so specified,
but the nature of the treatment is not to be specified in the order except as mentioned in paragraph (a), (b) or (c), Criminal Justice Act 2003 s 207(2).
Electronic monitoring Where the court makes [this] order it may also impose an electronic monitoring requirement, Criminal Justice Act 2003 s 177(4).
Amendment of, see para **15.48**.

15.26 *Programme requirement*

Criminal Justice Act 2003 s 202
Definition It means a requirement that the offender must participate in an accredited programme specified in the order at a place so specified on such number of days as may be so specified, Criminal Justice Act 2003 s 202(1).
Electronic monitoring Where the court makes [this] order it may also impose an electronic monitoring requirement, Criminal Justice Act 2003 s 177(4).
R v Price 2013 EWCA Crim 1283, 2014 1 Cr App R (S) 36 (p 216) D was given a community order with a 'General Offending Behaviour Programme'. This was contingent on the Probation Service taking the view that this was appropriate. Held. Leaving the programme to the Probation Service was unlawful. The programme must be specified.

---
[282] This condition is listed as amended by Legal Aid, Sentencing and Punishment of Offenders Act 2012 s 72(2).

R v Wilcox 2019 EWCA Crim 192 The Judge imposed a programme requirement but did not specify the number of days. Held. He should have done so. That itself is a good reason to delete the requirement. In any event, we quash it, because D was assessed as unsuitable for it.
Note: In June 2017, the MoJ published the *Impact evaluation of the prison-based Core Sex Offender Treatment Programme*. The authors, who worked with an external advisory panel, compared 2,562 men who had undergone a prison sex offender treatment programme (SOTP) and compared them with 13,219 who had not (for example those held in prisons where SOTPs were not available). Unlike the previous comparative reports, the analysis had extensive statistical checks to ensure the comparisons were reliable. The analysis showed that 10.0% of treated sex offenders committed at least one sexual reoffence during the follow-up period when 8.0% of untreated sex offenders did so. Further, more treated sex offenders committed at least one child image reoffence during the follow-up period when compared with those who did not (4.4% compared with 2.9%). The authors concluded that while the programmes were associated with little or no changes in sexual and non-sexual reoffending, there were some statistically significant differences. For more detail see www.banksr.com Other Matters Other Documents tab. For enquiries e-mail mojanalyticalservices@justice.gsi.gov.uk Ed.

15.27 *Prohibited activity requirement*

Criminal Justice Act 2003 s 203
Availability A court may not include a prohibited activity requirement in a relevant order unless it has consulted an officer of a local probation board or an officer of a provider of probation services, Criminal Justice Act 2003 s 203(2).
Electronic monitoring Where the court makes [this] order it may also impose an electronic monitoring requirement, Criminal Justice Act 2003 s 177(4).
R v Jacob 2008 EWCA Crim 2002 The primary purpose of a [prohibited activity] requirement is not to punish the offender but to prevent, or at least reduce, the risk of further offending. This requirement here was disproportionate. Requirement quashed. For more details of the case see **15.23**.
R v Dunlop 2015 EWCA Crim 1109 D pleaded to violent disorder. After drinking, he and others were fooling about with a taxi and his friend left the taxi and sustained significant injury. He was given a suspended sentence (no complaint). The Judge also made a prohibited activity requirement forbidding 'participating and going into licensed premises' without mentioning it before that. Held. The Judge never consulted an officer of the local probation board (one of the requirements) or if he did he did not inform the parties. Therefore the order is of no effect. In any event the order was not proportionate.

15.28 *Rehabilitation activity requirement*

Criminal Justice Act 2003 s 200A[283]
Definition A requirement that the offender must comply with any instructions given by the responsible officer to attend appointments or participate in activities or both.
Extent of the instructions The responsible officer, when instructing the offender to participate in activities, may require the offender to: a) participate in specified activities and, while doing so, comply with instructions given by the person in charge of the activities, or b) go to a specified place and, while there, comply with any instructions given by the person in charge of the place. The activities include reparative activities such as restorative justice activities.
Purpose The requirement combines the activity requirement and supervision requirement, which are both repealed.

15.29 *Residence requirement*

Criminal Justice Act 2003 s 206

[283] As inserted by Offender Rehabilitation Act 2014 s 15. In force 1/2/15, Offender Rehabilitation Act 2014 (Commencement No 2) Order 2015 2015/40

Definition A requirement that, during a period specified in the relevant order, the offender must reside at a place specified in the order, Criminal Justice Act 2003 s 206(1).
Availability Before making a residence requirement, the court must consider the home surroundings of the offender, Criminal Justice Act 2003 s 206(3).
A court may not specify a hostel or other institution as the place where an offender must reside, except on the recommendation of an officer of a local probation board or an officer of a provider of probation services, Criminal Justice Act 2003 s 206(4).
Electronic monitoring Where the court makes [this] order it may also impose an electronic monitoring requirement, Criminal Justice Act 2003 s 177(4).
Power to enable defendant to reside elsewhere with consent If the order so provides, a residence requirement does not prohibit the offender from residing, with the prior approval of the responsible officer, at a place other than that specified in the order, Criminal Justice Act 2003 s 206(2).

15.30 *Supervision requirement*

Criminal Justice Act 2003 s 213
This requirement was repealed on 1/2/15.[284]

15.31 *Unpaid work requirement*

Criminal Justice Act 2003 s 199-200
Availability The court must be satisfied that the offender is a suitable person to perform the work, see Criminal Justice Act 2003 s 199(3) and 218(1).
Concurrent and consecutive orders These are permissible but the aggregated total must not exceed 300 hours, Criminal Justice Act 2003 s 199(5).
Number of hours Not less than 40 hours and not more than 300 hours, see Criminal Justice Act 2003 s 199(2). Where the requirement is added on breach of the community order the minimum number of hours is 20, see Criminal Justice Act 2003 Sch 8 para 9 (Magistrates' Court) and para 10 (Crown Court).
Period for the hours to be performed The unpaid work must be performed within 12 months, Criminal Justice Act 2003 s 200(2).
Length Unless revoked, a community order imposing an unpaid work requirement remains in force until the offender has worked under it for the number of hours specified in it, Criminal Justice Act 2003 s 200(3).
Electronic monitoring Where the court makes [this] order it may also impose an electronic monitoring requirement, Criminal Justice Act 2003 s 177(4).
Extending the period Criminal Justice Act 2003 Sch 8 para 20(1) Where:

(a) a community order imposing an unpaid work requirement is in force in respect of any offender, and

(b) on the application of the offender or the responsible officer, it appears to the appropriate court that it would be in the interests of justice to do so having regard to circumstances which have arisen since the order was made,

the court may, in relation to the order, extend the period of 12 months specified in section 200(2).
(2) In this paragraph 'the appropriate court' has the same meaning as in para 16(5) (see **15.45**).

General matters

15.32 *Discount for time spent in custody*

Criminal Justice Act 2003 s 149 In determining the restrictions on liberty to be imposed by a community or youth rehabilitation order…, the court may have regard to any period for which the offender has been remanded in custody in connection with the offence or any other offence which was founded on the same facts or evidence.
New Sentences: Criminal Justice Act 2003 Guideline 2004, see www.banksr.com Other Matters Guidelines tab para 1.1.37 The court should seek to give credit for time spent on

[284] Offender Rehabilitation Act 2014 s 15 and Offender Rehabilitation Act 2014 (Commencement No 2) Order 2015 2015/40

remand (in custody or equivalent status) in all cases. It should make clear, when announcing sentence, whether or not credit for time on remand has been given and should explain its reasons for not giving credit when it considers either that this is not justified, would not be practical, or would not be in the best interests of the offender.
1.1.38 Where an offender has spent time in custody on remand, there will be occasions where a custodial sentence is warranted but the length of the sentence justified by the seriousness of the offence would mean that the offender would be released immediately. Under the present framework, it may be more appropriate to pass a community sentence since that will ensure supervision on release.
1.1.39 However, given the changes in the content of the second part of a custodial sentence of 12 months or longer, a court in this situation where the custodial sentence would be 12 months or more should, under the new framework, pass a custodial sentence in the knowledge that licence requirements will be imposed on release from custody. This will ensure that the sentence imposed properly reflects the seriousness of the offence.
1.1.40 Recommendations made by the court at the point of sentence will be of particular importance in influencing the content of the licence. This will properly reflect the gravity of the offence(s) committed.
R v Rakib 2011 EWCA Crim 870, 2012 1 Cr App R (S) 1 (p 1) D was charged with sexual assault and exposure (×2). He was remanded in custody. He received a community order, having spent nearly six months on remand (being the equivalent of an 11- or 12-month sentence). Held. Where an offender has served a significant period on remand, but in light of the duty under Criminal Justice Act 2003 s 142 (purposes of sentencing) a court considers a community order appropriate, the period on remand is not and cannot be (as *R v Hemmings* 2007 EWCA Crim 2413, 2008 1 Cr App R (S) 106 (p 623) suggests) a necessarily determinative factor in deciding what the appropriate sentence is. Section 149 states a court may have regard to any period spent on remand when considering restrictions on liberty to be imposed by a community order. Although Criminal Justice Act 2003 s 149 says 'may have regard to' such periods on remand, a sentencing judge should usually have regard to such periods. It may be that in some cases the significant period spent on remand is sufficient for a court to consider that no further punishment is necessary. Where the offender has served a period on remand equivalent to the maximum custodial sentence, there is still a discretion to impose a community order, even if that includes substantial restrictions. Appeal dismissed.
See also: *R v Page* 2017 EWCA Crim 1015 D pleaded to criminal damage (maximum sentence 3 months). D had already served 4 months in custody. Held. That does not make a community order wrong in principle. There were obvious benefits from making a community order. Community order upheld.
Long periods of remand For situations where the defendant has served a significant part or the whole period of the sentence on remand and a community order is imposed, see **30.19**.
For the rules about where a significant period has been served on remand, see **30.19**.

15.33 *Court must ensure requirements are compatible with each other*

Criminal Justice Act 2003 s 177(6) Before making a community order imposing two or more different requirements, the court must consider whether, in the circumstances of the case, the requirements are compatible with each other.

15.34 *Duty of court to provide copies of the order*

Criminal Justice Act 2003 s 219(1) The court by which any relevant order[285] is made must forthwith provide copies of the order:
(a) to the offender,

[285] A community order is a relevant order, see Criminal Justice Act 2003 s 196.

(b) if the offender is aged 18 or over, to an officer of a local probation board assigned to the court or an officer of a provider of probation services acting at the court,
(c) if the offender is aged 16 or 17, to an officer of a local probation board assigned to the court, an officer of a provider of probation services acting at the court or to a member of a youth offending team assigned to the court, and
(d) where the order specifies a local justice area in which the court making the order does not act, to the local probation board acting for that area, or (as the case may be) a provider of probation services acting in that area.

Note: The Act also places a duty on the court to provide copies of the order to those responsible for the programmes or institutions etc. Where an exclusion order is made, the court must serve the 'person intended to be protected' with a copy of the order, Criminal Justice Act 2003 s 219(2) and Sch 14(3). Ed.

15.35 ***Notification Court must notify the defendant***

Criminal Procedure Rules 2015 2015/1490 Rule 28.2(1) This rule applies where the court:..

(b) imposes a requirement under:
(i) a community order,…

(2) The court officer must notify:..
(b) the defendant and, where the defendant is under 14, an appropriate adult, of:
(i) any requirement or requirements imposed, and
(ii) the identity of any responsible officer or supervisor, and the means by which that person may be contacted:
(c) any responsible officer or supervisor, and, where the defendant is under 14, the appropriate qualifying officer (if that is not the responsible officer), of:
(i) the defendant's name, address and telephone number (if available),
(ii) the offence or offences of which the defendant was convicted, and
(iii) the requirement or requirements imposed, and
(d) the person affected, where the court imposes a requirement:
(i) for the protection of that person from the defendant, or
(ii) requiring the defendant to reside with that person.

(3) If the court imposes an electronic monitoring requirement, the monitor of which is not the responsible officer, the court officer must:
(a) notify the defendant and, where the defendant is under 16, an appropriate adult, of the monitor's identity, and the means by which the monitor may be contacted, and
(b) notify the monitor of:
(i) the defendant's name, address and telephone number (if available),
(ii) the offence or offences of which the defendant was convicted,
(iii) the place or places at which the defendant's presence must be monitored,
(iv) the period or periods during which the defendant's presence there must be monitored, and
(v) the identity of the responsible officer, and the means by which that officer may be contacted.

Combined with other orders

15.36 ***Compensation orders, Combined with***

TICs and Totality Guideline 2012: Crown Court, see www.banksr.com Other Matters Guidelines tab page 16 A compensation order can be combined with a community order. Note: There is a similar entry in the *Magistrates' Court Sentencing Guidelines Update March 2012* page 18p. Ed.

15.37 ***Custody, Combined with Different occasions***

R v Bennett 1980 2 Cr App R (S) 96 D was ordered to perform 200 hours of community work and complied well with the order. He was later dealt with for earlier offences by 18

months' imprisonment. The defence contended that as the order was working well, there should be further community work. Held. That is an alarming proposition. Appeal dismissed.
Fontenau v DPP 2001 1 Cr App R (S) 15 (p 48) LCJ D pleaded to common assault and threatening behaviour. He was sent to a Young Offender Institution for 56 days. He appealed and was released on bail. While on bail he drove whilst disqualified. The Crown Court then dismissed his appeal and he began his detention. He then appeared in custody to be sentenced for the disqualified driving. The Justices questioned whether a consecutive detention sentence or a concurrent sentence which increased the length of detention was justified because the indications were that D's first taste of custody had had a very chastening effect on him and D had a job to go to on his release. The Justices imposed a combination order of 80 hours' community service and probation. Held. Ordinarily it would doubtless be futile and thoroughly undesirable to impose community penalties and custodial sentences on the same occasion. However, the community sentence had a great deal to commend it. There is nothing in statute, authority or principle which precludes the Justices from taking the course they did. Sentence upheld.
For the rule that a community order must include a punishment requirement or a fine, see para **15.14**.

15.38 ***Fine, Combined with***
Note: The power to fine when ordering a Community Order was authorised by Criminal Justice Act 2003 s 177(2A) and (2B), see **15.14**. Ed.

15.39 ***Hospital Orders and Guardianship Orders, Combined with***
Mental Health Act 1983 s 37(8) Where an order is made under this section, the court shall not: a)…make a community order (within the meaning of Criminal Justice Act 2003 Part 12).

15.40 ***Suspended Sentence Order, Combined with***
Criminal Justice Act 2003 s 189(5) A court which passes a suspended sentence on any person may not impose a community sentence in respect of (any other) offence.
R v Robinson 2013 EWCA Crim 199 Rule applied. Community order quashed.

Making the order

15.41 ***Reasons, Must give***
Legal Aid, Sentencing and Punishment of Offenders Act 2012 s 64[286] inserted a new Criminal Justice Act 2003 s 174.
Criminal Justice Act 2003 s 174(1) A court passing sentence on an offender has the duties in subsections (2) and (3).
(2) The court must state in open court, in ordinary language and in general terms, the court's reasons for deciding on the sentence.
(3) The court must explain to the offender in ordinary language:

(a) the effect of the sentence,

(b) the effects of non-compliance with any order that the offender is required to comply with and that forms part of the sentence,

(c) any power of the court to vary or review any order that forms part of the sentence, and

(d) the effects of failure to pay a fine, if the sentence consists of or includes a fine.

Crown Court Bench Book 2013 www.banksr.com Other Matters Other Documents page 37 [Sentencing remarks] example: "[XX] The offence you have committed is sufficiently serious to warrant a community order which will have attached to it the following requirements:

1. You will do [XX] hours of unpaid work which must be carried out when and where you are directed by your supervising officer and in any event within 12 months.

[286] In force 3/12/12

2. You will be subject to and co-operate with supervision by a probation officer for [XX] and that means meeting him as and when he asks and co-operating fully with any instructions which he gives you.
If you fail to complete the unpaid work or do it properly, or fail to co-operate with supervision, you will be breached – that means you will be brought back before this court/the Magistrates' Court and may be made subject to further requirements or re-sentenced for this offence, and that may well result in custody."

15.42 ***Explain sentence, Judge must/Suggested sentencing remarks***
Judicial College's Crown Court Compendium Part II Sentencing June 2018 page 5-3
4. **Passing the sentence**
The court must:
(1) Complete the steps set out in chapter S 3 [in this guide] [determining the seriousness].
(2) State that[:]
(a) the offence, or the combination [of] offences, is serious enough to warrant such a sentence;
(b) the sentence is the least that is commensurate with the seriousness of the offence/s;
(c) (if it is the case) the court has had regard to time spent on remand in imposing the requirement/s attached to the order.
(3) Specify and explain the requirement/s attached to the order including the requirement that the offender keep in touch with the responsible officer in accordance with such instructions as he may be given by that officer.
(4) In the case of offences committed on or after 1st February 2015, specify that it is a requirement of the order that the offender obtains the consent of his supervising officer or the court before any change of residence.
(5) Specify whether any breach of any requirement is to be dealt with in the Crown Court or the Magistrates Court and explain the court's powers in the event of any such breach or conviction of another offence (see chapter S 9-1 [in this guide]).

Example
Your offence is so serious that I must make a community order – and you will be subject to these requirements:
1. You will do 120 hours of unpaid work within the next 12 months which must be done when and where you are directed by your supervising officer;
2. You will be subject to – and co-operate with – supervision/a rehabilitation activity requirement for 12 months. That means you must meet your supervisor when and where you are told to and you must cooperate fully with any instructions that he gives you.
If you fail to complete the unpaid work or to do it properly, or fail to co-operate with supervision/the rehabilitation activity requirement you will be in breach of the order: that means you will be brought back before this Court/the Magistrates' Court and may be given further requirements or resentenced or fined for this offence; and that may well mean custody.

Amending the order

15.43 ***Amendment of requirements***
Criminal Justice Act 2003 Sch 8 para 17(1) The appropriate court may, on the application of the offender or the responsible officer, by order amend a community order:
(a) by cancelling any of the requirements of the order, or
(b) by replacing any of those requirements with a requirement of the same kind, which the court could include if it were then making the order.
(2) The court may not under this paragraph amend a mental health treatment requirement, a drug rehabilitation requirement or an alcohol treatment requirement unless the offender expresses his willingness to comply with the requirement as amended.

(3) If the offender fails to express his willingness to comply with a mental health treatment requirement, drug rehabilitation requirement or alcohol treatment requirement as proposed to be amended by the court under this paragraph, the court may:

(a) revoke the community order, and

(b) deal with him, for the offence in respect of which the order was made, in any way in which he could have been dealt with for that offence by the court which made the order if the order had not been made.

(4) In dealing with the offender under sub-paragraph (3)(b), the court:

(a) must take into account the extent to which the offender has complied with the requirements of the order, and

(b) may impose a custodial sentence (where the order was made in respect of an offence punishable with such a sentence) notwithstanding anything in section 152(2).

15.44 ***Amending the date***

Legal Aid, Sentencing and Punishment of Offenders Act 2012 s 66(5)[287] inserted Criminal Justice Act 2003 Sch 8 para 19A.

Criminal Justice Act 2003 Sch 8 para 19A(1) The appropriate court may, on the application of the offender or the responsible officer, amend a community order by substituting a later date for that specified under section 177(5) (the need to specify a date).

(2) A date substituted under sub-paragraph (1):

(a) may not fall outside the period of six months beginning with the date previously specified under section 177(5) (the need to specify a date),

(b) subject to that, may fall more than three years after the date of the order.

(3) The power under sub-paragraph (1) may not be exercised in relation to an order if it has previously been exercised in relation to that order.

(4) A date substituted under sub-paragraph (1) is to be treated as having been specified in relation to the order under section 177(5) (the need to specify a date).

15.45 ***'Appropriate court', Definition of***

Criminal Justice Act 2003 Sch 8 para 19A(5) In this paragraph 'the appropriate court' has the same meaning as in paragraph 16.

Criminal Justice Act 2003 Sch 8 para 16(5) In this paragraph 'the appropriate court' means:

(a) in relation to any community order imposing a drug rehabilitation requirement which is subject to review, the court responsible for the order,

(b) in relation to any community order which was made by the Crown Court and does not include any direction that any failure to comply with the requirements of the order is to be dealt with by a Magistrates' Court, the Crown Court, and

(c) in relation to any other community order, a Magistrates' Court acting in the local justice area concerned.

15.46 ***Appeal pending, Can't amend when***

Criminal Justice Act 2003 Sch 8 para 24(1) No order may be made under para 16 (amendment by reason of change of residence), and no application may be made under para 13 (magistrates' revocation of order with or without re-sentencing), para 17 (amendment of requirements) or para 20 (extension of unpaid work), while an appeal against the community order is pending.

(2) Sub-paragraph (1) does not apply to an application under para 17 which:

(a) relates to a mental health treatment requirement, a drug rehabilitation requirement or an alcohol treatment requirement, and

(b) is made by the responsible officer with the consent of the offender.

[287] In force 3/12/12

15.47 *Summon defendant, Court must/Power to issue warrant*
Criminal Justice Act 2003 Sch 8 para 25(1) Subject to sub-paragraph (2), where a court proposes to exercise its powers under Sch 8 (amendment) or Sch 5 (powers following subsequent conviction), otherwise than on the application of the offender, the court:
(a) must summon him to appear before the court, and
(b) if he does not appear in answer to the summons, may issue a warrant for his arrest.
(2) This paragraph does not apply to an order cancelling a requirement of a community order or reducing the period of any requirement, or substituting a new local justice area or a new place for the one specified in the order.

15.48 *Amendment Defendant's application*
Criminal Procedure Rules 2015 2015/1490 Rule 33.3(1) This rule applies where:
(a) the defendant wants the court to exercise any power it has to revoke or amend an order to which this Part applies: or
(b) where the legislation allows, a person affected by such an order wants the court to exercise any such power.
(2) That defendant, or person affected, must:
(a) apply in writing, explaining why the order should be revoked or amended, and
(b) serve the application on:
(i) the court officer,
(ii) the responsible officer or supervisor, and
(iii) as appropriate, the defendant or the person affected.

15.49 *Amendment by reason of change of residence*
Criminal Justice Act 2003 Sch 8 para 16(1) This paragraph applies where, at any time while a community order is in force in respect of an offender, the appropriate court is satisfied that the offender proposes to change, or has changed, his residence from the local justice area concerned to another local justice area.
(2) Subject to sub-paragraphs (3) and (4), the appropriate court may, and on the application of the responsible officer must, amend the community order by substituting the other local justice area for the area specified in the order.
(3) The court may not under this paragraph amend a community order which contains requirements which, in the opinion of the court, cannot be complied with unless the offender continues to reside in the local justice area concerned unless, in accordance with paragraph 17 (the amending requirements paragraph), it either:
(a) cancels those requirements, or
(b) substitutes for those requirements other requirements which can be complied with if the offender ceases to reside in that area.
(4) The court may not amend under this paragraph a community order imposing a programme requirement unless it appears to the court that the accredited programme specified in the requirement is available in the other local justice area.
(5) In this paragraph 'the appropriate court' means:
(a) in relation to any community order imposing a drug rehabilitation requirement which is subject to review, the court responsible for the order,
(b) in relation to any community order which was made by the Crown Court and does not include any direction that any failure to comply with the requirements of the order is to be dealt with by a Magistrates' Court, the Crown Court, and
(c) in relation to any other community order, a Magistrates' Court acting in the local justice area concerned.

15.50 *Amendment of mental health, drug and alcohol requirements*
Criminal Justice Act 2003 Sch 8 para 18(1) Where the medical practitioner or other person by whom or under whose direction an offender is, in pursuance of any requirement to which this sub-paragraph applies, being treated for his mental condition or his dependency on or propensity to misuse drugs or alcohol:
(a) is of the opinion mentioned in sub-paragraph (3), or

(b) is for any reason unwilling to continue to treat or direct the treatment of the offender,

he must make a report in writing to that effect to the responsible officer and that officer must apply under paragraph 17 (the amendment paragraph) to the appropriate court for the variation or cancellation of the requirement.

(2) The requirements to which sub-paragraph (1) applies are:

(a) a mental health treatment requirement,

(b) a drug rehabilitation requirement, and

(c) an alcohol treatment requirement.

(3) The opinion referred to in sub-paragraph (1) is:

(a) that the treatment of the offender should be continued beyond the period specified in that behalf in the order [sic],

(b) that the offender needs different treatment,

(c) that the offender is not susceptible to treatment, or

(d) that the offender does not require further treatment.

15.51 ***Consent required for amending mental health, drug and alcohol requirements***
Criminal Justice Act 2003 Sch 8 para 11(2) A court may not amend a mental health treatment requirement, a drug rehabilitation requirement or an alcohol treatment requirement unless the offender expresses his willingness to comply with the requirement as amended.

15.52 ***Amendment to drug rehabilitation requirement***
Criminal Justice Act 2003 Sch 8 para 19 Where the responsible officer is of the opinion that a community order imposing a drug rehabilitation requirement which is subject to review should be so amended as to provide for each subsequent periodic review (required by section 211) to be made without a hearing instead of at a review hearing, or vice versa, he must apply under paragraph 17 to the court responsible for the order for the variation of the order.

For extending the period in an ***Unpaid work requirement,*** see the **Extending the period** section of the ***Unpaid work requirement*** para at **15.31**.

15.53 ***Duties of proper officer when amending a community order***
Criminal Justice Act 2003 Sch 8 para 27(1) On the making of an order revoking or amending a community order, the proper officer of the court must:

(a) provide copies of the revoking or amending order to the offender and the responsible officer,

(b) in the case of an amending order which substitutes a new local justice area, provide a copy of the amending order to:

(i) the local probation board acting for that area, or (as the case may be) a provider of probation services operating in that area, and

(ii) the Magistrates' Court acting in that area,

(c) in the case of an amending order which imposes or amends a requirement specified in the first column of Sch 14 (those in charge of institutions, bodies etc. or those 'intended to be protected by an exclusion requirement'), provide a copy of so much of the amending order as relates to that requirement to the person specified in relation to that requirement in the second column of that Schedule, and

(d) where the court acts in a local justice area other than the one specified in the order prior to the revocation or amendment, provide a copy of the revoking or amending order to a Magistrates' Court acting in the area so specified.

Criminal Justice Act 2003 Sch 8 para 27(3) In this paragraph 'proper officer' means:

(a) in relation to a Magistrates' Court, the designated officer for the court, and

(b) in relation to the Crown Court, the appropriate officer.

Revocation

15.54 ***Revocation of Powers of Crown Court***
Criminal Justice Act 2003 Sch 8 para 14(1) This paragraph applies where:

(a) there is in force a community order made by the Crown Court which does not include a direction that any failure to comply with the requirements of the order is to be dealt with by a Magistrates' Court, and
(b) the offender or the responsible officer applies to the Crown Court for the order to be revoked or for the offender to be dealt with in some other way for the offence in respect of which the order was made.
(2) If it appears to the Crown Court to be in the interests of justice to do so, having regard to circumstances which have arisen since the order was made, the Crown Court may:
(a) revoke the order, or
(b) both:
(i) revoke the order, and
(ii) deal with the offender, for the offence in respect of which the order was made, in any way in which he could have been dealt with for that offence by the court which made the order if the order had not been made.
(3) The circumstances in which a community order may be revoked under sub-paragraph (2) include the offender's making good progress or his responding satisfactorily to supervision or treatment (as the case requires).
(4) In dealing with an offender the Crown Court must take into account the extent to which the offender has complied with the requirements of the order.

15.55 ***Revoking the order Powers of Magistrates' Court***
Criminal Justice Act 2003 Sch 8 para 13(1) This paragraph applies where…it appears to the appropriate Magistrates' Court that, having regard to circumstances which have arisen since the order was made, it would be in the interests of justice:
(a) for the order to be revoked, or
(b) for the offender to be dealt with in some other way for the offence in respect of which the order was made.
(2) The appropriate Magistrates' Court may:
(a) revoke the order, or
(b) both:
(i) revoke the order, and
(ii) deal with the offender, for the offence in respect of which the order was made, in any way in which it could deal with him if he had just been convicted by the court of the offence.
(3) The circumstances in which a community order may be revoked under sub-paragraph (2) include the offender's making good progress or his responding satisfactorily to supervision or treatment (as the case requires).
(4) In dealing with an offender a Magistrates' Court must take into account the extent to which the offender has complied with the requirements of the community order.

15.56 ***Summon the offender, Court must/Power to issue warrant***
Criminal Justice Act 2003 Sch 8 para 14(5) Where the Crown Court proposes to exercise its powers under this paragraph otherwise than on the application of the offender, it must summon him to appear before the court and, if he does not appear in answer to the summons, may issue a warrant for his arrest.
Criminal Justice Act 2003 Sch 8 para 13(6) Where a Magistrates' Court proposes to exercise its powers under this paragraph otherwise than on the application of the offender, it must summon him to appear before the court and, if he does not appear in answer to the summons, may issue a warrant for his arrest.
Criminal Justice Act 2003 Sch 8 para 25(1) Subject to sub-paragraph (2), where a court proposes to exercise its powers under Part 4 (amendment) or 5 (powers following subsequent conviction) of Sch 8, otherwise than on the application of the offender, the court:
(a) must summon him to appear before the court, and

(b) if he does not appear in answer to the summons, may issue a warrant for his arrest.
(2) This paragraph does not apply to an order cancelling a requirement of a community order or reducing the period of any requirement, or substituting a new local justice area or a new place for the one specified in the order.

15.57 ***Revocation Defendant's application***
Criminal Procedure Rules 2015 2015/1490 Rule 32.3(1) This rule applies where:
(a) the defendant wants the court to exercise any power it has to revoke or amend an order to which this Part applies, or
(b) where the legislation allows, a person affected by such an order wants the court to exercise any such power.
(2) That defendant, or person affected, must:
(a) apply in writing, explaining why the order should be revoked or amended, and
(b) serve the application on:
(i) the court officer,
(ii) the responsible officer or supervisor, and
(iii) as appropriate, the defendant or the person affected.

15.58 ***Duties of the court when revoking a community order***
Criminal Justice Act 2003 Sch 8 para 27(1) On the making of an order revoking or amending a community order, the proper officer of the court must:
(a) provide copies of the revoking or amending order to the offender and the responsible officer,
(b) in the case of an amending order which substitutes a new local justice area, provide a copy of the amending order to:
(i) the local probation board acting for that area, or (as the case may be) a provider of probation services operating in that area, and
(ii) the Magistrates' Court acting in that area,
(c) in the case of an amending order which imposes or amends a requirement specified in the first column of Sch 14 (those in charge of institutions, bodies etc. or those 'intended to be protected by an exclusion requirement'), provide a copy of so much of the amending order as relates to that requirement to the person specified in relation to that requirement in the second column of that Schedule, and
(d) where the court acts in a local justice area other than the one specified in the order prior to the revocation or amendment, provide a copy of the revoking or amending order to a Magistrates' Court acting in the area so specified.
Criminal Justice Act 2003 Sch 8 para 27(3) In this paragraph 'proper officer' means:
(a) in relation to a Magistrates' Court, the designated officer for the court, and
(b) in relation to the Crown Court, the appropriate officer.

16 COMMUNITY ORDERS: BREACH OF

16.1
Criminal Justice Act 2003 Sch 8 Part 1
Duty to give a warning Details of the need for a warning can be found in Criminal Justice Act 2003 Sch 8 para 5(1).
Victim surcharge Where a defendant is re-sentenced for breaching a Community Order, there is no power to impose a second victim surcharge for the original offence, *R v George* 2015 EWCA Crim 1096, 2 Cr App R (S) 58 (p 409).
Offenders who become aged 21 at the breach hearing Where a defendant is in breach of a community order made when he or she was aged under 21 and the breach hearing is when the defendant is aged 21+ and custody is appropriate, the court must pass a YOI order and not a prison sentence.[288]

[288] Criminal Justice Act 2003 Sch 12 paras 8(2)(a) and (b), 10(1)(b), 21(2)(b)(ii) and 23(2)(b)(ii). The community order provision was interpreted by *R v Aslam* 2016 EWCA Crim 845, 2 Cr App R (S) 29 (p 267) para 3. The exception to this rule

Preliminary matters

16.2 *What constitutes a breach? Further offences*

Breach Offences Guideline 2018, see www.banksr.com Other Matters Guidelines tab In force 1 October 2018. page 5

Powers of the court following a subsequent conviction

A conviction for a further offence does not constitute a breach of a community order. However, in such a situation, the court should consider the following guidance from the [*TICs and Totality Guideline 2012: Crown Court*]:[289]

> ***Offender convicted of an offence while serving a community order***
> The power to deal with the offender depends on his being convicted whilst the order is still in force; it does not arise where the order has expired, even if the additional offence was committed whilst it was still current.
> For the full guidance, see **16.5**.

16.3 *Breach What is a breach? Non-co-operation*

R v Cassidy 2010 EWCA Crim 3146, 2011 2 Cr App R (S) 40 (p 240) D was sentenced to a Suspended Sentence Order of 34 weeks for possession of amphetamine with intent to supply. He attended a non-enforceable appointment during which an argument developed. D made a number of unpleasant, abusive and threatening remarks to or about the staff. Breach proceedings were initiated. D admitted breaching the earlier order. The Judge, two weeks after the sentence, found that D had misled the court into believing that he would comply with the order, and was therefore not bound by the original order. He imposed 12 months' custody. Held. It is not possible to find on this occasion the court was misled in the way contemplated by *R v Hart* 1983 5 Cr App R (S) 25. The course taken by the Judge was tantamount to sentencing D for an offence of which he had not been convicted. **34 weeks** not 12 months.

16.4 *Procedure*

Power to adjourn and remand The Magistrates' Court has the power to adjourn the hearing and to remand an offender, Criminal Justice Act 2003 Sch 8 para 25A(1). The power may be exercised by a single magistrate, Criminal Justice Act 2003 Sch 8 para 8(5).

Criminal Procedure Rules 2015 2015/1490 Rule 32.1 This Part applies where:

(a) the person responsible for a defendant's compliance with an order to which applies…

(ii) Schedule 8 or 12 to the Criminal Justice Act 2003,…

wants the court to deal with that defendant for failure to comply,

(b) one of the following wants the court to exercise any power it has to revoke or amend such an order:

(i) the responsible officer or supervisor,

(ii) the defendant, or

(iii) where the legislation allows, a person affected by the order, or

(c) the court considers exercising on its own initiative any power it has to revoke or amend such an order.

Criminal Procedure Rules 2015 2015/1490 Rule 32.4(1) Except for Rule 24.8 (written guilty plea: special rules), the rules in Part 24, which deal with the procedure at a trial in a Magistrates' Court, apply:

(a) as if:

(i) a reference in those rules to an allegation of an offence included a reference to an allegation of failure to comply with an order to which this Part applies,

---

is when a defendant is in breach of a community order by failing to comply with it and the offence does not carry imprisonment, then where the defendant is aged 21+ at the breach hearing, the court must pass a prison sentence of 6 months or less and not YOI.

[289] https://www.sentencingcouncil.org.uk/wp-ontent/uploads/Definitive_guideline_TICs__totality_Final_web.pdf p 14

(ii) a reference to the court's verdict included a reference to the court's decision to revoke or amend such an order, or to exercise any other power it has to deal with the defendant, and
(iii) a reference to the court's sentence included a reference to the exercise of any such power, and
(b) with the necessary consequential modifications.
(2) The court officer must serve on each party any order revoking or amending an order to which this Part applies.

Powers of the courts generally

16.5 ***Powers of the courts Defendant commits further offences***
Breach Offences Guideline 2018, see www.banksr.com Other Matters Guidelines tab In force 1 October 2018. page 5
Powers of the court following a subsequent conviction
A conviction for a further offence does not constitute a breach of a community order. However, in such a situation, the court should consider the following guidance from the [*TICs and Totality Guideline 2012: Crown Court*]:[290]

> ***Offender convicted of an offence while serving a community order***
> The power to deal with the offender depends on his being convicted whilst the order is still in force; it does not arise where the order has expired, even if the additional offence was committed whilst it was still current.
> If an offender, in respect of whom a community order made by a magistrates' court is in force, is convicted by a magistrates' court of an additional offence, the magistrates' court should ordinarily revoke the previous community order and sentence afresh for both the original and the additional offence.
> Where an offender, in respect of whom a community order made by a Crown Court is in force, is convicted by a magistrates' court, the magistrates' court may, and ordinarily should, commit the offender to the Crown Court, in order to allow the Crown Court to re-sentence for the original offence and the additional offence.
> The sentencing court should consider the overall seriousness of the offending behaviour taking into account the additional offence and the original offence. The court should consider whether the combination of associated offences is sufficiently serious to justify a custodial sentence.
> If the court does not consider that custody is necessary, it should impose a single community order that reflects the overall totality of criminality. The court must take into account the extent to which the offender complied with the requirements of the previous order.

Crown Court

16.6 ***Issuing a summons/warrant***
Criminal Justice Act 2003 Sch 8 para 8(1) This paragraph applies to a community order made by the Crown Court which does not include a direction that any failure to comply with the requirements of the order is to be dealt with by a Magistrates' Court.
(2) If at any time, while a community order to which this paragraph applies is in force, it appears on information to the Crown Court that the offender has failed to comply with any of the requirements of the order, the Crown Court may:
(a) issue a summons requiring the offender to appear at the place and time specified in it, or
(b) if the information is in writing and on oath, issue a warrant for his arrest.
(3) Any summons or warrant issued under this paragraph must direct the offender to appear or be brought before the Crown Court.

[290] https://www.sentencingcouncil.org.uk/wp-content/uploads/Definitive_guideline_TICs__totality_Final_web.pdf p 14

16.7 *Failure to appear/answer summons*
Criminal Justice Act 2003 Sch 8 para 8(4) Where a summons issued under sub-paragraph (2)(a) requires the offender to appear before the Crown Court and the offender does not appear in answer to the summons, the Crown Court may issue a warrant for the arrest of the offender.

16.8 *Powers of the Crown Court Defendant fails to comply*
Criminal Justice Act 2003 Sch 8 para 10(1) Where…it is proved to the satisfaction of [the] court that [the offender] has failed without reasonable excuse to comply with any of the requirements of the community order, the Crown Court must[291] deal with him in any one of the following ways:

(a) by amending the terms of the community order so as to impose **more onerous requirements** which the Crown Court could impose if it were then making the order,
(aa) by ordering the offender to pay a fine of an amount not exceeding £2,500,[292]
(b) by dealing with him, for the offence in respect of which the order was made, **in any way in which he could have been dealt with** for that offence by the court which made the order if the order had not been made,
(c) where:
(i) the offence in respect of which the order was made was not an offence punishable by imprisonment,
(ii) the offender is aged 18 or over,
(iii) the offender has wilfully and persistently failed to comply with the requirements of the order, by dealing with him, in respect of that offence, by imposing a **sentence of imprisonment** or, in the case of a person aged at least 18 but under 21, detention in a Young Offender Institution for a term not exceeding 6 months.

(2) In dealing with an offender under sub-paragraph (1), the Crown Court must take into account the extent to which the offender has complied with the requirements of the community order.

Criminal Justice Act 2003 Sch 8 para 10(4) In dealing with an offender under sub-paragraph (1)(b), the Crown Court may, in the case of an offender who has wilfully and persistently failed to comply with the requirements of the community order, impose a custodial sentence (where the order was made in respect of an offence punishable with such a sentence) notwithstanding anything in Criminal Justice Act 2003 s 152(2) (restrictions on imposing discretionary custodial sentences, see **28.26**).

(5) Where the Crown Court deals with an offender under sub-paragraph (1)(b) or (c), it must revoke the community order if it is still in force.

Criminal Procedure Rules 2015 2015/1490 Rule 32.2(1) This rule applies where:
(a) the responsible officer or supervisor wants the court to:
(i) deal with a defendant for failure to comply with an order to which this Part applies, or
(ii) revoke or amend such an order, or
(b) the court considers exercising on its own initiative any power it has to:
(i) revoke or amend such an order, and
(ii) summon the defendant to attend for that purpose.

(2) Rules 7.2 to 7.4, which deal, among other things, with starting a prosecution in a Magistrates' Court,[293] apply:
(a) as if:
(i) a reference in those rules to an allegation of an offence included a reference to an allegation of failure to comply with an order to which this Part applies, and

[291] Legal Aid, Sentencing and Punishment of Offenders Act 2012 s 67(5) amended Criminal Justice Act 2003 Sch 8 para 9(1) by deleting the word 'must' and inserting the word 'may', in force 3/12/12. Crime and Courts Act 2013 Sch 16 para 22(1) repealed that amendment and so the word 'must' is reinserted, in force 11/12/13.
[292] Inserted by Legal Aid, Sentencing and Punishment of Offenders Act 2012 s 67(5)(b). In force 3/12/12
[293] The words 'by information and summons' were deleted by Criminal Procedure (Amendment) Rules 2018 2018/132 para 14. In force 2/4/18

(ii) a reference to the prosecutor included a reference to the responsible officer or supervisor, and
(b) with the necessary consequential modifications.

16.9 ***Powers of the Crown Court*** ***Defendant commits further offence(s)***
Criminal Justice Act 2003 Sch 8 para 23(1) This paragraph applies where:
(a) an offender in respect of whom a community order is in force:
(i) is convicted of an offence by the Crown Court, or
(ii) is brought or appears before the Crown Court by virtue of paragraph 22 or having been committed by the Magistrates' Court to the Crown Court for sentence, and
(b) it appears to the Crown Court that it would be in the interests of justice to exercise its powers under this paragraph, having regard to circumstances which have arisen since the community order was made.
(2) The Crown Court may:
(a) revoke the order, or
(b) both:
(i) revoke the order, and
(ii) deal with the offender in any way in which he could have been dealt with for that offence by the court which made the order if the order had not been made.
(3) In dealing with an offender under sub-paragraph (2)(b), the Crown Court must take into account the extent to which the offender has complied with the requirements of the community order.
Criminal Procedure Rules 2015 2015/1490 Rule 32.2(1) (Power stated. For details see para **16.8**.)
For an example of the Court of Appeal reducing a sentence in excess of the Magistrates' Court's maximum sentence, see *R v Brzezinski* 2012 EWCA Crim 198, 2 Cr App R (S) 62 (p 314) (in breach of community order for handling (value around £400) **3 months** not 9).

16.10 ***Amending the order*** ***Crown Court***
Criminal Justice Act 2003 Sch 8 para 10(3)[294] In dealing with an offender under sub-paragraph (1)(a), the court may extend the duration of particular requirements (subject to any limit imposed by Chapter 4 of Part 12 of this Act) but may only amend the order to substitute a later date for that specified under section 177(5) (the need to specify a date) in accordance with sub-paragraphs (3ZA) and (3ZB),
(3ZA) A date substituted under sub-paragraph (3):
(a) may not fall outside the period of six months beginning with the date previously specified under section 177(5),
(b) subject to that, may fall more than three years after the date of the order.
(3ZB) The power under sub-paragraph (3) to substitute a date may not be exercised in relation to an order if that power or the power in paragraph 9(3) to substitute a date has previously been exercised in relation to that order.
(3ZC) A date substituted under sub-paragraph (3) is to be treated as having been specified in relation to the order under section 177(5) (the need to specify a date. Ed.).
Criminal Justice Act 2003 Sch 8 para 10(3A) Where:
(a) the court is dealing with the offender under sub-paragraph (1)(a), and
(b) the community order does not contain an unpaid work requirement,
section 199(2)(a) applies in relation to the inclusion of such a requirement as if for '40' there were substituted '20'.

[294] This sub-paragraph was inserted by Legal Aid, Sentencing and Punishment of Offenders Act 2012 s 66(4). In force 3/12/12

Magistrates' Court

16.11 *Magistrates' Court Laying an information/Issuing of a summons/warrant/ Time limits*

Power to issue a summons in the Magistrates' Court and the time limit The responsible officer has the power to cause an information to be laid where there has been a failure to comply with the order, Criminal Justice Act 2003 Sch 8 para 6(1) and Criminal Procedure Rules 2015 2015/1490 Rule 32.2(1). The time limit is 12 months from the date of the warning, Criminal Justice Act 2003 Sch 8 para 6(1)(b). The power to issue a summons and warrant is listed in Criminal Justice Act 2003 Sch 8 para 7(1).

Criminal Justice Act 2003 Sch 8 para 7(1) This paragraph applies to:

(a) a community order made by a Magistrates' Court, or

(b) any community order which was made by the Crown Court and includes a direction that any failure to comply with the requirements of the order is to be dealt with by a Magistrates' Court.

(2) If at any time while a community order to which this paragraph applies is in force it appears on information to a justice of the peace concerned that the offender has failed to comply with any of the requirements of the order, the justice may:

(a) issue a summons requiring the offender to appear at the place and time specified in it, or

(b) if the information is in writing and on oath, issue a warrant for his arrest.

(3) Any summons or warrant issued under this paragraph must direct the offender to appear or be brought:

(a) in the case of a community order imposing a drug rehabilitation requirement which is subject to review, before the Magistrates' Court responsible for the order, or

(b) in any other case, before a Magistrates' Court acting in the local justice area in which the offender resides or, if it is not known where he resides, before a Magistrates' Court acting in the local justice area concerned.

16.12 *Magistrates' Court Failure to appear/answer summons*

Criminal Justice Act 2003 Sch 8 para 7(4) Where a summons issued under sub-paragraph (2)(a) requires the offender to appear before a Magistrates' Court and the offender does not appear in answer to the summons, the Magistrates' Court may issue a warrant for the arrest of the offender.

16.13 *Magistrates' Court Powers of the court Defendant fails to comply*

Criminal Justice Act 2003 Sch 8 para 9(1) If it is proved to the satisfaction of a Magistrates' Court that (the offender) has failed without reasonable excuse to comply with any of the requirements of the community order, the court must deal with him in any one of the following ways:

(a) by amending the terms of the community order so as to **impose more onerous requirements** which the court could include if it were then making the order,

(aa) by ordering the offender to pay a fine of an amount not exceeding £2,500,[295]

(b) where the community order was made by a Magistrates' Court, by dealing with him, for the offence in respect of which the order was made, **in any way in which the court could deal with him** if he had just been convicted by it of the offence,

(c) where:

(i) the community order was made by a Magistrates' Court,

(ii) the offence in respect of which the order was made was not an offence punishable by imprisonment,

(iii) the offender is aged 18 or over, and

(iv) the offender has wilfully and persistently failed to comply with the requirements of the order, by dealing with him, in respect of that offence, by imposing a

[295] Subsection (aa) was inserted by Legal Aid, Sentencing and Punishment of Offenders Act 2012 s 67(2). In force 3/12/12

sentence of imprisonment or, in the case of a person aged at least 18 but under 21, detention in a Young Offender Institution, for a term not exceeding 6 months.

(2) In dealing with an offender under sub-paragraph (1), a Magistrates' Court must take into account the extent to which the offender has complied with the requirements of the community order.

Criminal Justice Act 2003 Sch 8 para 9(5) Where a Magistrates' Court deals with an offender under sub-paragraph (1)(b) or (c), it must revoke the community order if it is still in force.

16.14 ***Powers of the Magistrates' Court Powers of the court Defendant commits further offences***

Criminal Justice Act 2003 Sch 8 para 21(1) This paragraph applies where:

(a) an offender in respect of whom a community order made by a Magistrates' Court is in force is convicted of an offence by a Magistrates' Court, and

(b) it appears to the court that it would be in the interests of justice to exercise its powers under this paragraph, having regard to circumstances which have arisen since the community order was made.

(2) The Magistrates' Court may:

(a) revoke the order, or

(b) both:

(i) revoke the order, and

(ii) deal with the offender, for the offence in respect of which the order was made, **in any way in which he could have been dealt with** for that offence by the court which made the order if the order had not been made.

16.15 ***Magistrates' Court Amending the terms of the order***

Criminal Justice Act 2003 Sch 8 para 9(3) In dealing with an offender under sub-paragraph (1)(a), the court may extend the duration of particular requirements (subject to any limit imposed by Chapter 4 of Part 12 of this Act) but may only amend the order to substitute a later date for that specified under section 177(5) (the need to specify a date) in accordance with sub-paragraphs (3ZA) and (3ZB),

(3ZA) A date substituted under sub-paragraph (3):

(a) may not fall outside the period of six months beginning with the date previously specified under section 177(5) (the need to specify a date)

(b) subject to that, may fall more than three years after the date of the order.

(3ZB) The power under sub-paragraph (3) to substitute a date may not be exercised in relation to an order if that power or the power in paragraph 10(3) to substitute a date has previously been exercised in relation to that order.

(3ZC) A date substituted under sub-paragraph (3) is to be treated as having been specified in relation to the order under section 177(5) (the need to specify a date).

Criminal Justice Act 2003 Sch 8 para 9(5A) Where a Magistrates' Court dealing with an offender under sub-paragraph (1)(a) would not otherwise have the power to amend the community order under paragraph 16 (amendment by reason of change of residence), that paragraph has effect as if the references to the appropriate court were references to the court dealing with the offender.

16.16 ***Magistrates' Court Re-sentence, Power to***

Criminal Justice Act 2003 Sch 8 para 9(4) In dealing with an offender under sub-paragraph (1)(b), the court may, in the case of an offender who has wilfully and persistently failed to comply with the requirements of the community order, impose a custodial sentence (where the order was made in respect of an offence punishable with such a sentence) notwithstanding anything in section 152(2) (restrictions on imposing custody).

16.17 *Resentencing, Must revoke existing order when*
Criminal Justice Act 2003 Sch 8 para 9(5) Where a Magistrates' Court deals with an offender under sub-paragraph (1)(b) or (c), it must revoke the community order if it is still in force.

16.18 *Committals to Crown Court for re-sentencing etc.*
Criminal Justice Act 2003 Sch 8 para 9(6)[296] Where a community order was made by the Crown Court and a Magistrates' Court would (apart from this sub-paragraph) have the power to deal with the offender under sub-paragraph (1)(a), (aa), (b) or (c), it may instead commit him to custody or release him on bail until he can be brought or appear before the Crown Court.
(7) A Magistrates' Court which deals with an offender's case under sub-paragraph (6) must send to the Crown Court:
(a) a certificate signed by a justice of the peace certifying that the offender has failed to comply with the requirements of the community order in the respect specified in the certificate, and
(b) such other particulars of the case as may be desirable, and a certificate purporting to be so signed is admissible as evidence of the failure before the Crown Court.
Criminal Justice Act 2003 Sch 8 para 22(1) Where an offender in respect of whom a community order made by the Crown Court is in force is convicted of an offence by a Magistrates' Court, the Magistrates' Court may commit the offender in custody or release him on bail until he can be brought before the Crown Court.
(2) Where the Magistrates' Court deals with an offender's case under sub-paragraph (1), it must send to the Crown Court such particulars of the case as may be desirable.

Other matters

16.19 *Question of breach is determined by the judge and not by a jury*
Criminal Justice Act 2003 Sch 8 para 10(6) In proceedings before the Crown Court under this paragraph any question whether the offender has failed to comply with the requirements of the community order is to be determined by the court and not by the verdict of a jury.

16.20 *CRO should have details of the order breached*
Criminal Practice Directions 2015 EWCA Crim 1567 para II 10A.7 Where the current alleged offence could constitute a breach of an existing sentence such as a suspended sentence, community order or conditional discharge, and it is known that that sentence is still in force then details of the circumstances of the offence leading to the sentence should be included in the antecedents. The detail should be brief and include the date of the offence.

16.21 *Appeal is pending isn't a defence*
West Midlands Probation Board v Sadler 2008 EWHC 15 (Admin), 1 WLR 918 The defendants were convicted of affray and each received a 12-month community order with an unpaid work requirement of 240 hours. They lodged notices of appeal. They were required to attend for unpaid work appointments but failed to do so on two occasions on the grounds that they were appealing their convictions. The board did not accept this reason and the defendants were summoned. The Judge dismissed the informations on the grounds that their pending appeals constituted a reasonable excuse. Held. Like any other sentence, a community order takes effect when it is imposed and it remains in full force and effect until and unless it is quashed on appeal or revoked or amended by order of the court. The lodging of an appeal does not of itself have any effect on the enforceability of the order. There is no statutory provision which automatically suspends the operation of a community order pending an appeal against it (or the conviction on which it is founded).

[296] Sub-paragraph 9(6) was inserted by Legal Aid, Sentencing and Punishment of Offenders Act 2012 s 67(4).

16.22 *Defence of entitlement to refuse treatment*
Criminal Justice Act 2003 Sch 8 para 11(1) An offender who is required by any of the following requirements of a community order:
(a) a mental health treatment requirement,
(b) a drug rehabilitation requirement, or
(c) an alcohol treatment requirement,
to submit to treatment for his mental condition, or his dependency on or propensity to misuse drugs or alcohol, is not to be treated for the purposes of paragraph 9 or 10 as having failed to comply with that requirement on the ground only that he had refused to undergo any surgical, electrical or other treatment if, in the opinion of the court, his refusal was reasonable having regard to all the circumstances.
(2) A court may not under paragraph 9(1)(a) or 10(1)(a) amend a mental health treatment requirement, a drug rehabilitation requirement or an alcohol treatment requirement unless the offender expresses his willingness to comply with the requirement as amended.

16.23 *Can the responsible officer set conditions that can trigger breach proceedings?*
Richards v National Probation Service 2007 EWHC 3108 (Admin) D was convicted of possessing a knife or bladed article (3 months' custody, suspended for 12 months, with 100 hours' unpaid work). D was notified of an appointment in accordance with the legislation, but failed to attend. He had informed his responsible officer that he was unable to do so because of an appointment for training for a new job. The Probation Service sent D a letter stating that he must provide written evidence of a failure to attend. The responsible officer was telephoned and informed that D would produce evidence, but only at court. Breach proceedings were commenced. Over one month after the appointment D's legal representatives received a letter from a manager of a public house confirming D had been working at the time of the appointment. The Court found D to be in breach of his order and activated the suspended sentence. Held. In the context of community punishments a responsible officer is entitled to set conditions that require…the offender to inform the officer in advance if he knows he cannot keep an appointment to do work. That plainly must fall within the words 'keep in touch'. It would be entirely reasonable, and within what Parliament intended, that the officer could require that information to be in writing and to be supported by some third party evidence. The service cannot be expected to rely on the oral explanations of a defendant for his failure to attend. It follows, therefore, that where a probation officer requires an offender to inform him in advance of an appointment for which there is a good reason why he cannot attend, and provide that information in writing together with supporting documentation, it is a reasonable requirement well within section 220.

Sentencing for the breach

16.24 *Breach Offences Guideline 2018*
Breach Offences Guideline 2018, see www.banksr.com Other Matters Guidelines tab In force 1 October 2018. page 4

Breach of community order by failing to comply with requirements

Overall compliance with order	Penalty
Wilful and persistent non-compliance	Revoke the order and re-sentence imposing custodial sentence (even where the offence seriousness did not originally merit custody)

Overall compliance with order	Penalty
Low level of compliance	Revoke the order and re-sentence original offence **OR** Add curfew requirement 20 to 30 days* **OR** 30 to 50 hours' additional unpaid work/extend length of order/add additional requirement(s) **OR** Band C fine
Medium level of compliance	Revoke the order and re-sentence original offence **OR** Add curfew requirement 10-20 days* **OR** 20-30 hours additional unpaid work/extend length of order/add additional requirement(s) **OR** Band B fine
High level of compliance	Add curfew requirement 6-10 days* **OR** 10-20 hours additional unpaid work/extend length of order/add additional requirement(s) **OR** Band A fine

* Curfew days do not have to be consecutive and may be distributed over particular periods, for example at weekends, as the court deems appropriate. The period of the curfew should not exceed the duration of the community order and cannot be for longer than 12 months.

For Band A-C fines, see **58.28**.

Technical guidance

a) If imposing more onerous requirements the length of the order may be extended up to 3 years or 6 months longer than the previous length, whichever is longer (but only once).
b) If imposing unpaid work as a more onerous requirement and an unpaid work requirement was not previously included, the minimum number of hours that can be imposed is 20.
c) The maximum fine that can be imposed is £2,500.
d) If re-sentencing, a suspended sentence MUST NOT be imposed as a more severe alternative to a community order. A suspended sentence may only be imposed if it is fully intended that the offender serve a custodial sentence in accordance with the [*Imposition of Community and Custodial Sentences Guideline 2017*].
e) Where the order was imposed by the Crown Court, magistrates should consider their sentencing powers in dealing with a breach. Where the judge imposing the order reserved any breach proceedings[, magistrates should] commit the breach for sentence.

For the Crown Court powers, see para **16.8** and for the powers of the Magistrates' Court see para **16.13**.

16.25 ***Part compliance***

Criminal Justice Act 2003 Sch 8 para 9(2) and 10(2) The court must take into account the extent to which the offender has complied with the community order.

Breach Offences Guideline 2018, see www.banksr.com Other Matters Guidelines tab In force 1 October 2018. page 4

Breach of community order by failing to comply with requirements
The court must take into account the extent to which the offender has complied with the requirements of the community order when imposing a penalty.
In assessing the level of compliance with the order the court should consider:

i) the overall attitude and engagement with the order as well as the proportion of elements completed;
ii) the impact of any completed or partially completed requirements on the offender's behaviour;
iii) the proximity of breach to imposition of order; and
iv) evidence of circumstances or offender characteristics, such as disability, mental health issues or learning difficulties which have impeded [the] offender's compliance with the order.

Pre-2018 guideline cases
R v Poulton 2013 EWCA Crim 1453 D breached his community order by failing to comply with the unpaid work requirement. He had performed only a few hours of work. He had, however, complied with the supervision requirement and the Thinking Skills Programme requirements. Held. D was entitled to a modest reduction so 12 months not 18.
See also *R v Abdille* 2009 EWCA Crim 1195, 2010 1 Cr App R (S) 18 (p 99) (D breached his Suspended Sentence Order. He had attended the courses but had continued to commit offences. It was held that he had learnt nothing from them and there was no unpaid work requirement. Activation in full was correct.)
R v Reynolds 2015 EWCA Crim 1796, 2016 1 Cr App R (S) 33 (p 199) (D failed to attend his unpaid work duties. He had completed 22 out of the 120 hours. The probation report asked for extra hours as it was thought D could continue to be managed in the community. D's explanations for missed appointments etc. were not investigated. A probation officer asked for an adjournment to do that. Held. There should have been an adjournment. We reduce the sentence to immediate release.)
See also the **Suspended Sentence Order: Breach of *Part compliance*** para at **107.18**.

16.26 *Judicial guidance Pre-Guideline cases*
Richards v National Probation Service 2007 EWHC 3108 (Admin) D was sentenced to a suspended sentence with unpaid work. Held. It is well known that community punishments only have a hope of acceptance by the public as real and effective punishment and an effect on the defendant the subject of such orders if they are strictly enforced.
R v Sheppard 2008 EWCA Crim 799, 2 Cr App R (S) 93 (p 524) The defendant breached his suspended sentence. Held. For the public to have any confidence in community orders and suspended sentences they must be properly enforced.
R v Veloz-Parra 2012 EWCA Crim 1065 D breached his community order. Held. It appears that the Judge took the view that the repeated failure to attend for unpaid work was a factor capable of aggravating the original offence. That is not the correct approach. The first task is to identify the appropriate sentence for the original offence and then to give credit for compliance with the order, if appropriate.
R v Aslam 2016 EWCA Crim 845, 2 Cr App R (S) 29 (p 267) D was given an 18-month community order for a robbery. The Judge told D if he breached it he would be listed before her and be given 3 years. There were two failures to report. It was claimed a letter had been forged pretending to be from his employer. D had, however, complied with his curfew for over 40 weeks and completed 115¼ hours of the unpaid work. The probation report said the risk of harm had reduced from medium to low. The report invited the Court to continue the order. It was not suggested that there had been any further offences committed. Held. What is important at a breach hearing is: a) has there been any reoffending? b) Has the risk been reduced? c) Does the Probation Service feel its work

with the offender may usefully continue? The Judge's warning about the likely sentence did not justify a departure from the guideline. As he has served [5 months] we don't continue the order. **7 days'** YOI.

16.27 ***Discount for time spent in custody***
R v Poulton 2013 EWCA Crim 1453 There is no need to deduct the time because as has happened in this case the time is deducted administratively by HM Prison Service.

Appeals

16.28 ***Appeals to Crown Court***
Criminal Justice Act 2003 Sch 8 para 9(8) A person sentenced under sub-paragraph (1)(b) (re-sentencing for breach of requirement order) or (c) (custodial sentence for breach of requirement order) for an offence may appeal to the Crown Court against the sentence.
Criminal Justice Act 2003 Sch 8 para 13(5) A person sentenced under sub-paragraph (2)(b) (order is revoked and offender is re-sentenced) for an offence may appeal to the Crown Court against the sentence.
Criminal Justice Act 2003 Sch 8 para 21(4) A person sentenced under sub-paragraph (2)(b) (revoke order and re-sentence for offence committed in breach of community order) for an offence may appeal to the Crown Court against the sentence.

17 Compensation Orders

17.1
Powers of Criminal Courts (Sentencing) Act 2000 s 130-132
Children and young offenders The order is available whatever the age of the offender. If the offender is aged under 18 the court shall order the parent or guardian to pay the compensation, unless they cannot be found or it would be unreasonable, Powers of Criminal Courts (Sentencing) Act 2000 s 137(1).
Power to search There is a power to search 'a person' when a court is making a compensation order, Powers of Criminal Courts (Sentencing) Act 2000 s 142(1)-(2) and Magistrates' Courts Act 1980 s 80(1). For details see **58.15**.
Victim surcharges Where there are insufficient means to pay a compensation order and a victim surcharge, the victim surcharge can be reduced by up to the full amount, Criminal Justice Act 2003 s 161A(3). For more detail see **115.11**.
For Court Martial orders, see the **Service Compensation Orders** section at **24.39**.

17.2 ***Statistics England and Wales***

Compensation orders[297]

Year		Crown Court	Magistrates' Court	All courts
2015	No of orders	2,585	145,339	147,924
	% of defendants given a compensation order	2.9%	12.6%	11.9%
	Average compensation	£4,099	£169	£238
2016	No of orders	2,315	144,433	146,748
	% of defendants given a compensation order	3.6%	12.3%	11.9%
	Average compensation	£2,426	£141	£177

[297] Excluding motoring offences

Year		Crown Court	Magistrates' Court	All courts
2017	No of orders	2,086	122,686	124,772
	% of defendants given a compensation order	2.7%	11.9%	10.5%
	Average compensation	£3,846	£122	£185

Note: Occasionally the recorded figures for the previous year(s) change when we are supplied with new statistics, so we amend them accordingly.
For explanations about the statistics, see page 1-xii. For more detailed statistics, see www.banksr.com Other Matters Statistics tab.

Preliminary matters

17.3 *Need there be an application?*

Powers of Criminal Courts (Sentencing) Act 2000 s 130(1) The court may on application or otherwise [make a compensation order].
Note: So there is no need for an application. Ed.

Power to order

17.4 *Statutory power to order*

Powers of Criminal Courts (Sentencing) Act 2000 s 130(1)(a) A court by or before which a person is convicted of an offence, instead of or in addition to dealing with him in any other way, may, on application or otherwise, make a compensation order requiring him: a) to pay compensation for any personal injury, loss or damage resulting from that offence or any other offence which is taken into consideration by the court in determining sentence.

17.5 *Sample/specimen counts*

R v Crutchley and Tonks 1994 15 Cr App R (S) 627 C and T pleaded to numerous specimen counts and compensation orders were made for sums representing the entirety of C and T's offending, not just the amounts represented by the counts on the indictment. No offences were taken into consideration. Held. It was not open to the court to make a compensation order in respect of loss or damage arising from admitted offences which had not been charged or taken into consideration, on the ground that the offenders had admitted that the offences charged were sample counts representing a number of other offences.
R v Hose 1995 16 Cr App R (S) 682 Where D was sentenced for specimen counts, a compensation order should only be made for the value represented by the counts with which the defendant has been convicted. Where the evidence clearly shows that, for example, the amount stolen was in excess of what is represented by the specimen counts, this did not mean that the offences had been taken into consideration in the formal meaning of the term (see *Anderson v DPP* 1978 67 Cr App R 185).
Revenue and Customs v Duffy 2008 EWHC 848 (Admin), 2 Cr App R (S) 103 (p 593) D pleaded to four charges under Tax Credits Act 2002 s 35. The first charge was dishonestly completing a tax credit application form for childcare payments. The second charge dealt with a dishonest claim in a letter not leading to any loss because it merely confirmed information that had already been given. The third charge was about a dishonest claim which led to a loss of £149. The fourth charge was about a dishonest claim that led to no loss. D was sentenced on the basis that she had obtained £19,624 dishonestly. No objection was raised about this. The Magistrates limited the compensation order to the loss in the charges, namely £562. The prosecution appealed and contended that the charges were specimen charges. Held. The charges were not specimen charges. However, D's action in completing the application form and in subsequently providing false information to the Revenue together triggered the payment of tax credits over a lengthy period that she was not entitled to. The Magistrates could impose a compensation order in the full amount.

See also the **SAMPLE COUNTS/SPECIMEN COUNTS/REPRESENTATIVE OFFENCES** chapter.

17.6 ***TICs***

Powers of Criminal Courts (Sentencing) Act 2000 s 130(1) A court by or before which a person is convicted of an offence, instead of or in addition to dealing with him in any other way, may, on application or otherwise, make a compensation order requiring him: a) to pay compensation for any personal injury, loss or damage resulting from that offence or any other offence which is taken into consideration by the court in determining sentence.

Powers of Criminal Courts (Sentencing) Act 2000 s 132(5) Where a compensation order is made in respect of a TIC the order shall cease to have effect if the defendant successfully appeals against his conviction or all of the offences in the proceedings in which the order was made. The defendant may appeal against the order as if it were part of the sentence imposed in respect of the offence, or any of the offences he was convicted of.

Magistrates' Court Sentencing Guidelines 2008, see www.banksr.com Other Matters Guidelines tab page 165 Compensation may also be ordered in respect of offences taken into consideration.[298]

CPS Legal Guidance: TICs page 6, see www.banksr.com Other Matters Other Documents tab If a confiscation order is made against the defendant under Proceeds of Crime Act 2002, victims can be compensated using money derived from the confiscated sum. If it is clear that there would otherwise be insufficient means to compensate the victim, the court must order the shortfall to be paid from the confiscated sum. Victims of TIC offences are included in these provisions.

R v Crutchley and Tonks 1994 15 Cr App R (S) 627 C and T pleaded to numerous specimen counts and compensation orders were made for sums representing the entirety of C and T's offending, not just the amounts represented by the counts on the indictment. No offences were taken into consideration. Held. It was not open to the court to make a compensation order in respect of loss or damage arising from admitted offences which had not been charged or taken into consideration, on the ground that the offenders had admitted that the offences charged were sample counts representing a number of other offences.

R v Hose 1995 16 Cr App R (S) 682 LCJ Where D was sentenced for specimen counts, a compensation order should only be made for the value represented by the counts on which the defendant has been convicted. Where the evidence clearly shows that, for example, the amount stolen was in excess of what is represented by the specimen counts, this did not mean that the offences had been taken into consideration in the formal meaning of the term (see *Anderson v DPP* 1978 67 Cr App R 185).

17.7 ***Victim dies***

Holt v DPP 1996 2 Cr App R (S) 314 The death of the person who had suffered the loss does not mean an order cannot be made.

Basic principles

17.8 ***Basic principles***

Powers of Criminal Courts (Sentencing) Act 2000 s 130(2A)[299] provides that the court 'must consider making a compensation order where it is empowered to do so'.

Magistrates' Court Sentencing Guidelines 2008, see www.banksr.com Other Matters Guidelines tab page 165 Subject to consideration of the victim's views, the court must order compensation wherever possible and should not have regard to the availability of other sources such as civil litigation or the Criminal Injuries Compensation Scheme. Any

[298] Powers of Criminal Courts (Sentencing) Act 2000 s 131(2), which is a surprisingly confusing section.

[299] As inserted by Legal Aid, Sentencing and Punishment of Offenders Act 2012 s 63. In force 3/12/12

amount paid by an offender under a compensation order will generally be deducted from a subsequent civil award or payment under the Scheme to avoid double compensation.
Rowlston v Kenny 1982 4 Cr App R (S) 85 QBD D pleaded to benefit fraud. The Magistrates seem to have assumed that they could only make the order if they were satisfied that the loss resulted solely from the offence of the falsely signed initial declaration. Held. The question is not whether the loss results solely from the offence, but whether it can be fairly said to result from the offence. The fact that the defendant might have been charged with another criminal offence but was not [so charged] provides no reason for refusing compensation if the loss can be said fairly to have resulted from an offence of which he was convicted. The whole loss of £179 resulted from the first signed declaration. Compensation order added to sentence.
R v Dorton 1987 9 Cr App R (S) 514 It is not right to consider the compensation order as an additional punishment. It is a speedy method of compensating the victim.
R v Panayioutou 1989 11 Cr App R (S) 536 A compensation order is not a punishment but rather a convenient summary means of putting right all or some of the damage done by a criminal offence. It avoids the necessity for civil proceedings which may be expensive and time-consuming on both sides.
R v Islam 2013 EWCA Crim 2355 The general rule is that compensation orders should not affect the punishment appropriately imposed for the offence. For more details of the case see **17.30**.

17.9 ***Civil law and compensation orders***
Magistrates' Court Sentencing Guidelines 2008, see www.banksr.com Other Matters Guidelines tab page 165 The court should not have regard to the availability of other sources such as civil litigation or the Criminal Injuries Compensation Scheme. Any amount paid by an offender under a compensation order will generally be deducted from a subsequent civil award or payment under the Scheme to avoid double compensation.
R v Chappell 1984 6 Cr App R (S) 214 It is not necessary that the defendant is liable in civil law to the person to whom the order was made.
R v Panayioutou 1989 11 Cr App R (S) 536 A compensation order avoids the necessity for civil proceedings which may be expensive and time-consuming on both sides.
Old case: *R v Thomson Holidays Ltd* 1974 58 Cr App R 429 (Parliament never intended to introduce into the criminal law the concepts of causation which apply to the assessment of damages under the law of contract and tort. The court must do what it can to make a just order on such information that it has.)
Corporate defendants see the **COMPANIES AND PUBLIC BODIES AS DEFENDANTS *Compensation orders*** para at **227.26**.

17.10 ***Victim, Must consider the***
Magistrates' Court Sentencing Guideline 2008, see www.banksr.com Other Matters Guidelines tab page 165 Compensation should benefit, not inflict further harm on, the victim. Any financial recompense from the offender may cause distress. A victim may or may not want compensation from the offender and assumptions should not be made either way. The victim's views are properly obtained through sensitive discussion by the police or witness care unit, when it can be explained that the offender's ability to pay will ultimately determine whether, and how much, compensation is ordered and whether the compensation will be paid in one lump sum or by instalments. If the victim does not want compensation, this should be made known to the court and respected.

17.11 ***Defendants are not able to buy shorter sentences/Those who make reparations should be rewarded***
R v Barney 1989 11 Cr App R (S) 448 D was convicted of obtaining by deception. The Judge said, "Were you in a position to pay compensation, I would reduce your sentence. All I can do is pass the maximum sentence." Held. That was unfortunate. Those words might legitimately give rise to the inference that had the defendant been of some financial substance he would have received a shorter sentence. That cannot be the case.

It must never be thought that the convicted can buy their way out of imprisonment or any part of it. They are wholly independent of the sentencing exercise. We reduce the sentence.

R v Islam 2013 EWCA Crim 2355 D, a doctor, was convicted of numerous indecent assaults. The Judge made compensation orders totalling £38,250. para 33 The defence said the Judge in fixing the prison term had failed to take into account the compensations he made on a later occasion. It was accepted that D had means to pay. Held. The general rule is that compensation orders should not affect the punishment appropriately imposed for the offence. Defendants cannot, as it were, buy their way out of an appropriate custodial sentence.

R v Rahman 2015 EWCA Crim 320, 2 Cr App R (S) 10 (p 106) D and H pleaded to possession of criminal property. They both stole money from the company they worked for. D entered into an agreement to repay the sum stolen. H said he had spent the money gambling and did not enter into an agreement. The Judge sentenced them both to 4 years. Held. Although the two cases had differences, the Judge did not explain how he reached the two identical sentences. We cannot be sure he took the reparations factor into account. As D entered into the agreement we reduce his sentence by 6 months.

Old cases: *R v Mortimer* 1977 Crim LR 624 (The defendant had no means and the compensation order should not have been made. If a judge wished to impose a more lenient sentence with a view that the losers would have some opportunity to get their money back and a compensation order is made, there are two possible courses. Those advising the accused could take steps to ensure that the money is repaid before the hearing or the court could defer sentence for a period to give an opportunity for any representations made to be carried out and see whether they are effective.)

R v Copley 1979 1 Cr App R (S) 55 (It is not open to defendants to buy their way out of prison, or to buy shorter sentences, by offering money in the way of compensation.)

R v Dorton 1987 9 Cr App R (S) 514 (It is not right to consider the compensation order as an additional punishment. It is a speedy method of compensating the victim.)

Proving a loss

17.12 *Must prove a loss*

R v Vivian 1979 68 Cr App R 53 Compensation orders should not be made unless the sum claimed is either agreed or proved.

R v Danvers 1983 5 Cr App R (S) 407 D pleaded to affray. D was ordered to pay compensation of £1,071 for damage caused and loss of business. Evidence was adduced in relation to the damage caused. The Judge said he was satisfied that the loss of business was reduced as a result of the damage inflicted. Held. There was no proper evidence on which to base the award of compensation for loss of business. Compensation orders should not be made where there are disputed issues about liability or amount.

R v Horsham JJs ex parte Richards 1985 7 Cr App R (S) 158 D pleaded to theft and was ordered to pay £164 in compensation. D said the property had been recovered. The prosecution did not introduce any evidence to substantiate the compensation claims. Held. The court had no jurisdiction to make a compensation order without receiving any evidence, where there were real issues raised, as to whether the claimants suffered any, and if so what, loss.

R v Tyce 1994 15 Cr App R (S) 415 A compensation order may not be made unless loss, damage or personal injury has resulted from an offence committed by the offender. There may be cases in which a handler has disposed of goods to others, which means the original loser has not been able to obtain possession of that which was stolen from him. This was not such a case. There was no evidence available to the sentencing Court that anything that the appellant had done had in fact caused loss to the complainant. There may also be cases where the handler is so close to the actual thief that the thief's actions may be treated as the handler's actions. Again, this was not such a case.

R v Godfrey 1994 15 Cr App R (S) 536 D and B pleaded to using threatening words and behaviour. D and B were travelling in a taxi driven by V. A dispute arose between D, B and V which involved racist abuse. The taxi stopped and the doors were opened. During a scuffle all three sustained injuries and the taxi was damaged. V gave no clear evidence as to who had thrown the racist abuse at him. The Judge said even if D had not racially abused V, D could pay more than B because he was in work whereas B was not. D was ordered to pay £350 in compensation to V and B was ordered to pay £250. Held. The Judge should have first determined what compensation should be paid to V before dividing it between D and B. Although a compensation order was appropriate in this case, it was fundamental there should be a secure basis on which compensation could be ordered in terms of an assessment of what V had suffered. The total amount to be paid by D and B should have been fixed at £300. As there was no material on which the Court could distinguish between D and B, D's compensation order would be reduced to £150.
R v Stapylton 2012 EWCA Crim 728, 2013 1 Cr App R (S) 12 (p 68) The court has no jurisdiction to make an order where there are real issues as to whether those to benefit have suffered any and if so, what loss, *R v Horsham JJs ex parte Richards* 1985.
See also: *R v Bateman and Blackwell* 1988 10 Cr App R (S) 240 (No evidence what the loss was.)
R v Watson 1990 12 Cr App R (S) 508 (The property had been returned. The insurers may have suffered a loss but there was no proved loss.)
R v Briscoe 1994 15 Cr App R (S) 699 (There was no evidence of loss and this was not a case where the amount of compensation could be easily ascertained.)

17.13 *Dispute as to loss etc.*
Magistrates' Court Sentencing Guidelines 2008, see www.banksr.com Other Matters Guidelines tab page 165 In cases where it is difficult to ascertain the full amount of the loss suffered by the victim, consideration should be given to making a compensation order for an amount representing the agreed or likely loss. Where relevant information is not immediately available, it may be appropriate to grant an adjournment for it to be obtained.
R v Horsham JJs ex parte Richards 1985 7 Cr App R (S) 158 Where a defendant declines to accept that there is any loss, justice requires that he shall have an opportunity to test the basis and grounds upon which a claim is advanced, and it is for the prosecution to place the appropriate evidence before the court.
R v Clelland 1991 12 Cr App R (S) 697 The prosecution claimed the defendant admitted the damage in interview. At court the defendant disputed that. The Judge made a compensation order. Held. The issue was raised that there should at least have been a hearing before the order was made. Order quashed.
Old cases: *R v Kneeshaw* 1974 58 Cr App R 439 (The majority of the items stolen by the defendant were either recovered or accounted for. The unrecovered items were valued at £114. D was ordered to pay £114 compensation to the victim of the burglary. D said he did not know the whereabouts of the unrecovered items and that V must be mistaken as to what was stolen. Held. Where, in the course of proceedings, the defendant raises the issue that the goods were not stolen at all, unless the applicant can show in evidence that the goods were in fact stolen then a compensation order should not be made.)
R v Cornwall 1979 1 Cr App R (S) 19 (The prosecution relied on the stocktaking discrepancy of £8,600 but that figure may have contained thefts not attributable to the defendant. The defence counsel's figure was £6,000. Held. The order should have been limited to £6,000.)

17.14 *Goods recovered etc.*
R v Hier 1976 Cr App R (S) 233 D was convicted of handling stolen goods. B stole 51 frozen turkeys from P to the value of around £176-180 and left 48 of the turkeys at D's

supermarket. The stolen turkeys were returned to P and resold without any reduction in price. D was ordered to pay £100 compensation to P. Held. There was no loss or damage suffered so the compensation order was quashed.

Specific offences and types of case

17.15 *Complex cases*

R v White 1996 2 Cr App R (S) 58 D was convicted of four counts of handling stolen goods and one of obtaining property by deception. D made an insurance claim of £12,651 in respect of a burglary to his home. The insurers paid £8,473 in settlement of the claim, which included £6,000 for jewellery, which was the maximum payable for jewellery under the policy. A search of D's home revealed a number of the jewellery items he had included in his insurance claim along with a number of other stolen items. The insurance company applied for a compensation order for the full amount paid to D under the claim but D was ordered to pay £3,500 in compensation which was the value of the recovered jewellery. Held. A compensation order should only be made where there is no question of a difficult or complex issue as to liability. No compensation should have been made in this case. It is open to the insurance company to claim the amount paid on the basis that there was a false and fraudulent claim in respect of all the property, but that will be a matter for them.

R v Williams 2001 1 Cr App R (S) 140 (p 500) D was convicted of building work frauds on elderly victims. Some work was not done and some of the bills grossly overvalued the work done. The 'total value of the conviction offences' adjusted for inflation was £141,000. The defence claimed some allowance should be made for the work that was actually done. The Judge said he wanted to strip D of every penny he had fraudulently received and made a confiscation and compensation order for the full amount. Held. The power of the court to make a compensation order is a fairly blunt instrument. Compensation was not intended to be a precise evaluation of loss, such as must take place in a civil court when damages are awarded. It is intended to be speedy, efficacious and cost-free. Inevitably there will be some inequalities in a case of this sort as between one victim and another, but that is not a feature which leads us to conclude that in making no allowance for the value of work in fact performed the Judge fell into any error.

R v James 2003 EWCA Crim 811, 2 Cr App R (S) 97 (p 574) D pleaded to 20 counts of false accounting. D offered to pay £5,000 by way of compensation but was ordered to pay £13,000. D said a full set of invoices had not been recovered which would show that some of the monies he had received were in fact properly paid. Held. It was wrong to make a compensation order as there were difficult and complex issues of liability, and the sum claimed was neither agreed nor proved.

R v Bewick 2007 EWCA Crim 3297, 2008 2 Cr App R (S) 31 (p 184) D pleaded to cheating the revenue. D was ordered to pay compensation of £257,295. Held. There were detailed and complex issues which fell to be decided. There was a headlong conflict between the two competing witnesses. There was of necessity the need to make arbitrary judgments, albeit that they were based on some evidence. The order did not determine D's tax liabilities to HM Revenue and Customs because they were not party to the proceedings. For these reasons in this case compensation proceedings should not have been before the criminal courts. Compensation order quashed.

R v Stapylton 2012 EWCA Crim 728, 2013 1 Cr App R (S) 12 (p 68) para 11 Because compensation orders are for straightforward cases, a court should not embark on a detailed inquiry as to the extent of any injury, loss or damage. If the matter demands such attention it is better left for civil proceedings.

See also: *R v Islam* 2013 EWCA Crim 2355 (Historical sexual abuse with seven victims. Compensation orders should be confined to relatively straightforward cases. Orders quashed. See **17.30**.)

Old cases: *R v Donovan* 1981 3 Cr App R (S) 192 (The defendant hired a car for two days and used and kept it until it was recovered by the owners 4½ months later. The Judge was asked to fix damages on the basis of what might be recovered in a civil claim for loss of use. Held. The amount of such damages is open to argument, so this case is not the kind for which a compensation order is designed. Compensation order quashed. *Hyde v Emery* 1984 6 Cr App R (S) 206 (D was ordered to pay £500 compensation in respect of a false claim for unemployment benefit. It was later discovered that there had been an error in the calculation of the overpayment and the compensation order was reduced to £300. Defence counsel said the order should have been for the difference between the overpayment of unemployment benefit and the amount of supplementary benefit D would have been entitled to had he made a claim. Held. The process of making compensation orders should be a very simple one. The justices should decline to make an order unless it is based upon very simply stated propositions which have been agreed or which are simple to resolve.)

17.16 ***Magistrates' Court Statutory nuisance***

Botross v London Borough of Fulham 1995 16 Cr App R S 622 B was the tenant of a flat owned by L. The flat had widespread dampness which resulted in considerable mould growth and B complained that L was responsible for a statutory nuisance. The Justices were advised by their clerk that, as these were civil proceedings, a finding that the Council had caused or committed a statutory nuisance was not a conviction, therefore there was no power to order compensation. The Justices made an abatement order requiring the Council to remedy and prevent recurrence of the damp at the flat and to replace dilapidated parts within 16 weeks but no order for compensation was made. Held. The legislation replaced by Environmental Protection Act 1990 s 2(1) had been held to be criminal in nature. The parliamentary history of the legislation made it clear that it was the intention of the legislation to preserve the power of the court to make a compensation order on a finding that a statutory nuisance had been committed.
R v Liverpool Crown Court ex parte Cooke 1997 1 Cr App R (S) 7 An aggrieved party is required by statute to give the party responsible for the nuisance 21 days' written notice of the intention to issue proceedings. If the nuisance is remedied before the hearing, no offence is committed. If the nuisance is proved to have existed when proceedings are brought, the court may make a compensation order for any expenses properly incurred by the aggrieved party from the time proceedings were issued until the date of the hearing. The court does not, however, have jurisdiction to make an order for compensation in respect of any period before the expiry of the 21-day statutory notice.

Motor vehicle exception

17.17 ***Motor vehicle exception Basic principles***

Powers of Criminal Courts (Sentencing) Act 2000 s 130(6) A compensation order may only be made in respect of injury, loss or damage (other than loss suffered by a person's dependants in consequence of his death) which was due to an accident arising out of the presence of a motor vehicle on a road, if:

(a) it is in respect of damage which is treated by Powers of Criminal Courts (Sentencing) Act 2000 s 130(5) (see **17.24**) as resulting from an offence under Theft Act 1968 or Fraud Act 2006, or

(b) it is in respect of injury, loss or damage as respects which:

(i) the offender is uninsured in relation to the use of the vehicle, and

(ii) compensation is not payable under any arrangements to which the Secretary of State is a party.

Quigley v Stokes 1977 64 Cr App R 198 D pleaded to TDA. D took a motor vehicle belonging to another and whilst driving collided with two other cars. All three cars were damaged. D was ordered to pay £278 compensation in total for the damage sustained to all three cars. Held. The compensation order was properly made in respect of the damage to the stolen vehicle but there was no power to make a compensation order in respect of the damage to the other vehicles.

R v Ahmad 1992 13 Cr App R (S) 212 D, aged 18, was driving a motor vehicle that had been taken without the owner's consent. Following a high-speed police chase D and his two passengers were arrested. The owner of the car, V, claimed compensation for damage caused to the vehicle, loss of the contents of the car and his personal travelling expenses incurred following the car being taken. D was ordered to pay £518 in compensation to V. Held. Powers of Criminal Courts (Sentencing) Act 2000 s 130(7) provides that in the case of an offence under Theft Act 1968, any damage occasioned to property which was recovered and which occurred while the property was out of the owner's possession would be treated as resulting from the offence, however it was caused. This covered the damage to the car itself, but it could not cover the contents which were not recovered. The amount of compensation should have therefore been limited to the costs of making good the damage to the car and V's travelling expenses. The amount of the order was reduced to £218.

17.18 ***Motor vehicle exception What is the 'arrangement with the Secretary of State'?***

DPP v Scott 1995 16 Cr App R (S) 292 Where an offender is convicted of an offence in connection with the driving of a motor vehicle which has resulted in damage to another person's property, and the damage is treated as being due to an accident arising out of the presence of a motor vehicle on the road, if the offender is uninsured and the damage was not covered by 'arrangements to which the Secretary of State is party' the maximum amount of compensation which the offender may be ordered to pay is limited to £175, or the amount by which the damage exceeds £250,000. (The £175 has since been increased to £300. Ed.)

For a similar decision, see *R v Austin* 1996 2 Cr App R (S) 191.

17.19 ***Motor vehicle exception What is the agreement?***

Note: The Motor Insurers' Bureau (MIB) was set up to provide compensation where motorists suffered loss, death or injury where there was no other body to claim from. The Secretary of State has made a series of agreements with the MIB which can be found at www.banksr.com Other Matters Other Documents tab. Ed.

17.20 ***Motor vehicle exception Defendant is uninsured***

Powers of Criminal Courts (Sentencing) Act 2000 s 130(6) A compensation order may only be made in respect of injury, loss or damage…if:

(b) it is in respect of injury, loss or damage as respects which:

(i) the offender is uninsured in relation to the use of the vehicle, and

(ii) compensation is not payable under any arrangements to which the Secretary of State is a party.

17.21 ***Motor vehicle exception What is an 'accident'?***

Mayor v Oxford 1980 2 Cr App R (S) 280 LCJ M, J and L were charged with taking a lorry without consent and criminal damage. M and J denied the criminal damage charge but pleaded guilty to the taking without consent. M pleaded to careless driving. M, J and L were aged 16 or under and had been drinking. Shortly before midnight M took the keys to his brother's lorry, all three got into it and M began driving. M took a corner too fast and, after swerving to miss a tree, crashed the lorry into a house causing damage to the house and wall of about £600. The Magistrates declined to accept M's plea to the careless driving and said criminal damage arising from the reckless manner in which a motor vehicle has been driven cannot be said to have been caused by an accident arising out of the presence of a motor vehicle on a road. Compensation orders were made against M, J and L. Held. The word 'accident' in English has a variety of meanings. The question to ask is whether, looked at as an ordinary person would look at it, this incident involving a lorry running into a wall can be described properly as an accident arising out of the presence of a motor vehicle on a road. This was plainly, in its ordinary use, an accident. Compensation orders quashed.

R v Stapylton 2012 EWCA Crim 728, 2013 1 Cr App R (S) 12 (p 68) D pleaded to dangerous driving. He took a car and, after travelling at speed in it, he left the road and crashed into a garage. The car needed to be replaced and £5,000 worth of damage was done to the garage. Held. The damage was attributable to an accident, *Mayor v Oxford* 1980 2 Cr App R (S) 280 applied.

Old cases: *Chief Constable of Staffordshire v Rees* 1981 RTR 506 (Driving deliberately at a gate was an accident.) *Bremner v Westwater* 1994 SLT 707 (Forcing a police car off the road without contact was an accident.)

17.22 *Motor vehicle exception Calculating money to be paid*

Powers of Criminal Courts (Sentencing) Act 2000 s 130(7) Where a compensation order is made in respect of injury, loss or damage due to an accident arising out of the presence of a motor vehicle on a road, the amount to be paid may include an amount representing the whole or part of any loss of or reduction in preferential rates of insurance attributable to the accident.

Determining the amount of the loss etc.

17.23 *Determining the loss General principles*

R v Amey, James and Meah 1982 4 Cr App R (S) 410 Care must be taken to ensure that the evidence is sufficient before making an order. The amount of loss should be proved by evidence, not by inference or guesswork. Order reduced.

17.24 *Damaged goods*

Powers of Criminal Courts (Sentencing) Act 2000 s 130(5) In the case of an offence under Theft Act 1968 or Fraud Act 2006, where the property in question is recovered, any damage to the property occurring while it was out of the owner's possession shall be treated for the purposes of compensation as having resulted from the offence, however and by whomever the damage was caused.

17.25 *Goods were insured*

R v Townsend 1981 2 Cr App R (S) 328 The Judge ruled out any evidence that the goods were insured. Held. The Judge was right to do so. The loss has got to fall on someone. It cannot make any significant difference to the amount of penalty whether the loss was to be met by the individual or by his insurer.

What can be included?

17.26 *Funeral expenses*

Powers of Criminal Courts (Sentencing) Act 2000 s 130(1) The court may on application or otherwise make an order requiring him to make payments for funeral expenses or bereavement in respect of a death resulting from an offence other than death due to an accident arising out of the presence of a motor vehicle on a road.

Powers of Criminal Courts (Sentencing) Act 2000 s 130(3) A court shall give reasons if it does not make a compensation order in a case where this section empowers it to do so.

Note: The current specified amount is £12,980.[300] Ed.

R v Williams 1989 Unreported 10/3/89 It is important that sentencers bear in mind the words (which had just been added to the then statute) giving the court power to order compensation for funeral expenses. If the court decides not to order compensation, it must give its reasons.

17.27 *Compensation for general inconvenience*

R v Stapylton 2012 EWCA Crim 728, 2013 1 Cr App R (S) 12 (p 68) D pleaded to dangerous driving. He took a car and, after travelling at speed in it, he left the road and

[300] See Fatal Accidents Act 1976 s 1A(3) and Damages for Bereavement (Variation of Sum) (England and Wales) Order 2013 2013/510 para 2. For deaths before 1/4/13 the figure is £11,800, Damages for Bereavement (Variation of Sum) (England and Wales) Order 2007 2007/3489 para 2.

crashed into a garage. The car needed to be replaced and £5,000 worth of damage was done to the garage. He was aged 19 and out of work. The Judge made an £8,100 compensation order and said he certainly could get work. Part of the order was to compensate the victim for 'general inconvenience'. Held. A compensation order can only be made for injury, loss and damage, not general inconvenience.

Personal injuries

17.28 *Personal injury awards Basic principles*

R v Smith 1998 2 Cr App R S 400 The starting point on making any compensation order in respect of personal injuries must be the extent and severity of those injuries.

17.29 *Suggested personal injury awards*

Magistrates' Court Sentencing Guidelines 2008, see www.banksr.com Other Matters Guidelines tab page 166

Note: These tables are based on the Criminal Injuries Compensation Authority tariff which was adopted by the JSB in its guidance. The JSB was replaced by the Judicial College. The suggested awards were then issued as part of the *Magistrates' Court Sentencing Guidelines 2008*. The MoJ Criminal Injuries Compensation Scheme 2012 reduced many of the awards. However, the guideline figures have not been changed. I would expect sentencers to factor in an uplift to take into account inflation. The MoJ Criminal Injuries Compensation Scheme 2012 can be found at www.justice.gov.uk/victims-and-witnesses/cica. Ed.

Physical injury

Type of injury	Description	Starting point
Abdomen	Injury requiring laparotomy	£3,800
Ankle, Sprained	Disabling for up to 6 weeks	Up to £1,000
	Disabling for 6 to 13 weeks	£1,000
	Disabling for more than 13 weeks	£2,500
Arm	Fractured humerus, radius, ulna (substantial recovery)	£3,300
Brain	Concussion lasting one week	£1,500
Bruise	Depending on size	Up to £100
Cut: no permanent scar	Depending on size and whether stitched	£100-£500
Eye	Blurred or double vision lasting up to 6 weeks	Up to £1,000
	Blurred or double vision lasting for 6 to 13 weeks	£1,000
	Blurred or double vision lasting for more than 13 weeks (recovery expected)	£1,750
Eye, Black		£125
Facial scar	Minor disfigurement (permanent)	£1,500
Finger	Fractured finger other than index finger (substantial recovery)	£1,000
	Fractured index finger (substantial recovery)	£1,750
	Fractured thumb (substantial recovery)	£2,000
Graze	Depending on size	Up to £75
Leg	Fractured tibula (substantial recovery)	£2,500

Type of injury	Description	Starting point
	Fractured femur, tibia (substantial recovery)	£3,800
Nose	Undisplaced fracture of nasal bone	£1,000
	Displaced fracture requiring manipulation	£2,000
	Deviated nasal septum requiring septoplasty	£2,000
Shoulder	Dislocated (substantial recovery)	£1,750
Teeth, Loss of non-front tooth	Depending on cosmetic effect	£1,250
Loss of front tooth		£1,750
Wrist	Dislocated/fractured – including scaphoid fracture (substantial recovery)	£3,300
	Fractured: colles type[301] (substantial recovery)	£4,400
Wrist, Sprained	Disabling for up to 6 weeks	Up to £1,000
	Disabling for 6 to 13 weeks	£1,000
	Disabling for more than 13 weeks	£2,500

Mental injury

Description	Starting point
Temporary mental anxiety (including terror, shock, distress), not medically verified	Up to £1,000
Disabling mental anxiety, lasting more than 6 weeks, medically verified[302]	£1,000
Disabling[303] mental illness, lasting up to 28 weeks, confirmed by psychiatric diagnosis	£2,500

Physical and sexual abuse

Type of abuse	Description	Starting point
Physical abuse of adult	Intermittent physical assaults resulting in accumulation of healed wounds, burns or scalds, but with no appreciable disfigurement	£2,000
Physical abuse of child	Isolated or intermittent assault(s) resulting in weals, hair pulled from scalp etc.	£1,000
	Intermittent physical assaults resulting in accumulation of healed wounds, burns or scalds, but with no appreciable disfigurement	£2,000
Sexual abuse of adult	Non-penetrative indecent physical acts over clothing	£1,000
	Non-penetrative indecent act(s) under clothing	£2,000
Sexual abuse of child (under 18)	Non-penetrative indecent physical act(s) over clothing	£1,000

301 A colles fracture is a distal fracture of the radius in the forearm with dorsal (posterior) displacement of the wrist.

302 In this context, 'disabling' means a person's functioning is significantly impaired in some important aspect of his or her life, such as impaired work or school performance or significant adverse effects on social relationships.

303 Typo corrected.

Type of abuse	Description	Starting point
	Non-penetrative frequent assaults over clothing or non-penetrative indecent act under clothing	£2,000
	Repetitive indecent acts under clothing	£3,000

17.30 *Personal injury awards Approach and quantum*

R v McIntosh 2011 EWCA Crim 951 D pleaded to wounding with intent. He attacked V, causing a large cut to his right hand, a cut to his back near his kidneys, a 7 inch cut to his scalp and a 5 cm superficial cut from mouth to ear. V was permanently disfigured. D was sentenced to 10 years. Held. 7 years and **£6,000 compensation** not £20,000.

R v Stanner 2011 EWCA Crim 1787 D pleaded to a road rage incident. He followed the victim to his home. There was no injury. D was aged 19 and had short-term anxiety. Held. In the guidelines for the assessment of general damages[304] issued by the Judicial Studies Board, the factors to be taken into account for psychiatric damage are: a) the injured person's ability to cope with life and work, b) the effect on the injured person's relationships with family, friends and those with whom he or she comes into contact, c) the extent to which treatment would be successful, d) future vulnerability, e) prognosis, and f) whether medical help has been sought. The level of award for minor psychiatric damage is in the range of £1,000 to £3,875, taking into consideration the length of the period of disability and the extent to which daily activities and sleep were affected. **£250 compensation**, not £1,000.

R v Islam 2013 EWCA Crim 2355 D was convicted of numerous indecent assaults committed between the 1970s and 1990s. He was a doctor and the victims were six female patients aged 13 to mid-20s, and one practice nurse. D preyed on their vulnerability. A 13- or 14-year-old patient visited him having found a lump in her breast and concerned she might have cancer. D used that opportunity to examine her breasts and her vagina. In another, D asked a young woman to see him about a receptionist position. He told her to 'get down', placed his penis in her mouth and ejaculated. He assaulted another young woman aged 14-22 under the guise of performing medical examinations. He touched her breasts and vagina, made lewd remarks and put her hand on his erect penis. The Judge found that substantial psychological problems had been caused by D to his victims. There were no victim impact statements and no psychiatric evidence and the Judge commented that he had formed his own judgement from the victims' evidence. He made compensation orders totalling £38,250, acknowledging that some victims must have had degrees of psychological problems prior to D's offences. It was accepted that D had means. Held. The real point is whether the Judge had sufficient material before him to make the order. First, it is well established that in principle compensation orders should not be made without a proper evidential basis. If there is such a basis, a judge is then certainly able to apply his general knowledge and experience, and to have regard to any relevant guidelines on damages or compensation, in fixing an appropriate sum to be paid by a defendant as compensation, having due regard to his means. A Judge cannot, as it were, simply pluck a figure out of the air. In this case, the Judge had no real evidential basis for assessing the extent of the psychiatric injury (assuming there was such psychiatric injury) caused by D's criminal offending. The Judge was not in a position to make a finding as he did that 'substantial psychological problems' had been caused, in whole or in part, by D's conduct. There were potentially difficult issues of causation and quantification not amenable to the essentially summary procedure appropriate for making compensation awards at the Crown Court. The orders had to be set aside. Such matters are best left to civil proceedings or compensation applications to the CICA.

[304] Unfortunately it appears the Judicial College now restricts this document to judges etc.

17.31 ***Personal injuries Must have evidence***

R v Cooper 1982 4 Cr App R (S) 55 D pleaded to ABH and was ordered to pay £750 in compensation to V. The evidence available in relation to V's injuries was a written statement from the casualty officer at the hospital where V was treated but there was no photographic evidence. Held. Where a substantial sum of money is awarded by way of compensation there should be more detailed evidence of the precise nature of the injuries sustained. An award of compensation is not appropriate where matters such as full details of the injury and matters which may reduce the amount of the compensation are not ascertained and cannot be ascertained. It would be more appropriate for V to bring proceedings in the County Court where the nature and extent of V's injuries could be more fully investigated. Compensation order quashed.

R v Smith 1998 2 Cr App R S 400 D pleaded to ABH and was ordered to pay £4,000 in compensation to V in respect of her injuries. The Judge said V would have a permanent reminder of the attack. Held. The evidence did not make it clear whether V would suffer any long-term effects from her injuries. As such the injuries must be treated as transient. In the absence of evidence of potentially permanent scarring the sum of £4,000 was manifestly wrong, and was reduced to £1,000.

17.32 ***Personal injury awards On the facts, order correct***

R v Pola 2009 EWCA Crim 655, 2010 1 Cr App R (S) 6 (p 32) D was convicted of an offence under Health and Safety at Work etc. Act 1974. V was working at D's premises. V fell and sustained a severe head injury which left him in a severely disabled and dependent state. It was unlikely V would be able to return to work and he would be left in some state of dependency for the rest of his life. The Judge was told that V would not benefit from an insurance policy, he would be unlikely to have an effective civil remedy and he was not entitled to state benefits. The Judge thought that no compensation would be unjust. D was ordered to pay £90,000 compensation to V. The Judge made no order for costs and tailored the fines to take into account the compensation order. The Judge referred to the Judicial Studies Board Guidelines for the assessment of general damages in personal injury cases. Held. The Judge was entitled to make the order and was right to do so. There was a clear and causal link between the conviction and the injury. The Judge had available to him sufficient evidence of the gravity of the injury to demonstrate that it was worth far in excess of anything that he was minded to award. The Judge satisfied himself that there was no more convenient or practicable alternative route of which V might avail himself and that D had sufficient means to satisfy the order. The Judge gave priority to the compensation order over any other financial order and the order was just and proper in the context of the proven culpability of D.

17.33 ***Shock, distress etc. Must have evidence***

Magistrates' Court Sentencing Guidelines 2008, see www.banksr.com Other Matters Guidelines tab page 165 The court should consider the pain and suffering caused by the injury (including terror, shock or distress) and any loss of facility. This should be assessed in light of all factors that appear to the court to be relevant, including any medical evidence, the victim's age and personal circumstances.

R v Vaughan 1990 12 Cr App R (S) 46 D pleaded to one count of burglary and was convicted of one count of criminal damage and two of attempted criminal damage. The charges arose from a disturbance in which D was involved. D was ordered to pay £229 by way of compensation to the victim of the burglary and four witnesses. There was no evidence that any of the witnesses actually suffered distress. Held. There must be either some express evidence or other evidence from which a judge can properly infer distress before he can make such an award. In this case there was no such evidence, express or implied. The compensation orders in favour of the four witnesses cannot stand and must be quashed.

Did the loss 'result from' the offence?

17.34 *General principles*

Powers of Criminal Courts (Sentencing) Act 2000 s 130(1) The court may make a compensation order for any personal injury, loss or damage resulting from that offence.

17.35 *Co-defendant responsible for the loss*

R v Beddow 1987 9 Cr App R (S) 235 D pleaded to TDA. D was a passenger in a van driven by one of his two co-defendants. The van crashed. D was in work and his two co-defendants were unemployed. D was ordered to pay £300, which was the full value of the compensation awarded. On appeal the defence argued that D was asleep at the time of the crash and should not pay the compensation order. Held. The compensation order cannot be criticised.

17.36 *Violent offences Did the injury etc. result from the offence?*

R v Derby 1990 12 Cr App R (S) 502 D pleaded to affray. The prosecution did not press a count on the indictment of GBH with intent and a verdict of not guilty was entered. D, C and others went to B's accommodation during the evening and knocked on his bedroom door. C struck B five or six times with a piece of wood. B sustained bilateral fractures of the ulna of which that on the right side was grossly shattered and dislocated. The Crown said D went with the purpose of frightening B. D was sentenced to 1 year's imprisonment suspended and ordered to pay B compensation of £4,000. Held. It is clear that there must be evidence of causation before the order can be made. Compensation order quashed.

R v Corbett 1993 14 Cr App R (S) 101 D was acquitted of unlawful wounding and pleaded to common assault. D was drinking in a bar with others. Words were exchanged between the group and V, aged 17. V was struck in the face by D's beer glass and suffered injuries which required stitches. D was ordered to pay £250 compensation. The Judge said V's injuries flowed from D's act and offence. D said V's injury did not result from the common assault but accepted it would have done had he been convicted of unlawful wounding. Held. The words of the statute make it clear that some causal connection between the offence and the injury, loss or damage must be established before compensation can be ordered. It was the admitted assault which led to the glass going into V's face. The compensation order was properly made.

R v Taylor 1993 14 Cr App R (S) 276 D pleaded to affray. T, S and others had purchased cans of lager and were in a restaurant waiting for a take-away meal. W, T's brother-in-law, went into the restaurant and asked for one of the cans of lager. The group refused. W grabbed a can of lager and ran outside. When the group left the restaurant T was carrying the cans of lager. W demanded more lager and was joined by D. T continued to refuse and D punched T causing him to drop the cans. T sustained a fractured nose. S and others scrambled to pick up as many cans as they could from the floor. W went behind S and held him whilst another punched S to the ground, where he was kicked. R used a knife to slash at X's neck. The case for the Crown was that D had taken part in a frightening situation but that he did not inflict any actual violence. D was ordered to pay £50 compensation to S and £500 to T. Defence counsel suggested that it is necessary to look in detail at the individual activities of the defendant who is being considered and a compensation order is only properly to be made if the particular damage is attributable fairly to some act by the defendant in question. Held. That puts the interpretation much too narrowly. It may well be that, in particular cases, it is appropriate to separate the different phases of the events relied upon by the prosecution. Where the events take place so close to each other in time and are so linked with each other it would be both artificial and unjust to look narrowly at the physical acts of each defendant relied upon by the prosecution. The chain of events began by D punching T. There was entirely adequate evidential information to justify the inference by the Judge that the injuries to S were caused in part by the participation of this appellant in the offence of affray. Appeal dismissed.

R v Geurtjens 1993 14 Cr App R (S) 280 D pleaded to violent disorder. F hit C in the face and a struggle started. C lost consciousness for a while and was kicked about the face and body. C's brother, K, was threatened and hit by T. K was punched and fell to the ground where he was kicked about the head and body by D. C sustained injuries to his head, hands and face, was detained in hospital overnight and was off work for about five days. K sustained a cut to his forehead, his lips and jaw were swollen and he had marks on his back consistent with having been kicked. D was ordered to pay £200 compensation each to K and C. Defence counsel said the Court should separate C's injuries since they were solely attributable to F. Held. We are satisfied that it was within the power of the Court to make compensation orders against all four defendants in respect of C's injuries.

R v Deary 1993 14 Cr App R (S) 648 D pleaded to affray. An allegation of unlawful wounding was ordered to be left on the file. D was drinking in a pub. B bumped into D and poured beer over her. D became angry and began to throw empty bottles at B. C, an innocent bystander, was hit by a bottle causing a wound to his head which required a large number of stitches. The prosecution said it was one of the bottles thrown by D that hit C. D was ordered to carry out community service and to pay £400 compensation to C. Held. The whole basis of D's plea was that there was no proven causal link between her criminal conduct in the affray and the injury actually suffered by C. The Judge was led into an error which amounts to making an order which he had no jurisdiction to make. Compensation order quashed.

See also: *R v Denness* 1996 1 Cr App R (S) 159 (Affray and injuries. Order upheld.)

17.37 *Did the loss result from the offence? On the facts, order correct*

R v Thomson Holidays Ltd 1974 58 Cr App R 429 The defendant company, D, was convicted of three counts of recklessly making a false statement in the course of its trade or business. D had 2 million copies of a brochure printed bearing descriptions of hotel amenities. Mr and Mrs B chose and booked a holiday based on the information in the brochure but, on arrival at the hotel, they found that the amenities described in the brochure did not exist. A compensation order was made in favour of Mr and Mrs B. D said Mr and Mrs B had not suffered any loss as a result of D's alleged offences. Held. We have no hesitation in saying that on the facts of this case the failure to provide Mr and Mrs B with the amenities which they expected to find available did result from the offences for which D was convicted.

R v Howell 1978 66 Cr App R 179 D pleaded to five counts of handling. S had been guilty of certain acts of burglary and used D as his receiver to dispose of the property. D received a stolen painting from S and sold it to an innocent purchaser, B. A compensation order was made in favour of B. Held. B's loss was as a result of D's offence. A wide meaning is to be given to the words 'resulting from that offence'.

Rowlston v Kenny 1982 4 Cr App R (S) 85 QBD D pleaded to benefit fraud. D falsely signed a declaration that she was entitled to unemployment benefit and signed further declarations on a fortnightly basis confirming her continuing entitlement. R said all payments made to D, £179 in total, were made based on D's initial signed declaration. R applied for an order of compensation in the sum of £179. The Magistrates seem to have assumed that they could only make the order if they were satisfied that the loss resulted solely from the offence of the falsely signed initial declaration. Held. The question is not whether the loss results solely from the offence, but whether it can be fairly said to result from the offence. The fact that the defendant might have been charged with another criminal offence but was not [so charged] provides no reason for refusing compensation if the loss can be said fairly to have resulted from an offence of which he was convicted. The whole loss of £179 resulted from the first signed declaration. Compensation order added to sentence.

17.38 *Did the loss result from the offence? On the facts, order incorrect*
R v Boardman 1987 9 Cr App R (S) 74 D pleaded to theft during his trial. D agreed to buy a boat from K for £1,750 and paid a deposit of £800, with the balance due in eight weeks. A further part of the agreement was that the title of the boat would only pass to D upon payment of the balance. D found the boat to be considerably less sound than he had thought. K agreed to lower the price by £100. Further defects then came to light, in particular that the engine was almost completely useless. D met K to pay the balance due, which was supposed to be £750. D gave K a package marked '£750' and left before K counted the contents. Inside the package were 101 £1 notes wrapped in three £10 notes, giving a total of £131. D moved the boat from its moorings to another destination. D was ordered to pay £619 compensation to K. Held. Whatever the rights and wrongs about the representations which may or may not have been made concerning the vessel's condition, one thing was common ground, and that is that the contract between D and K stipulated that the vessel should remain the property of the seller until the balance of the purchase price had been paid. Thus the seller was still the owner of the boat at the time of the theft and is still the owner of the boat now. There is nothing to suggest that the title has passed since the theft. The seller cannot be said to have lost £619 as a result of the theft. In the normal way a loss can be said to result from a theft of goods if the goods are never returned, or if they are returned damaged, or if the victim has lost the use of the goods and the value of the loss can be estimated, and perhaps in some other cases as well. But here all that has happened is that the seller was tricked into believing for a few moments that he had been paid in full when he had not. Even if that can properly be described as a loss, it is certainly not a loss resulting from the theft.
R v Halliwell 1991 12 Cr App R (S) 692 D pleaded to handling stolen goods and other offences. A motor company's garage was broken into and almost the entire stock of tools and equipment was stolen with a value of approximately £23,000. A car valued at almost £4,000 was also stolen and used to transport equipment to D's premises. A search of D's premises revealed property to the value of about £2,500 whilst property to the value of about £14,000 was recovered through or from D. There was no evidence that D had disposed of any property. D was ordered to pay £9,000 compensation. Held. There was no evidence that D had received all of the goods, nor any evidence that he had received any more than the £14,000 worth of goods which he had returned. Compensation order quashed.
R v Graves 1993 14 Cr App R (S) 790 D pleaded to false accounting. D was the manager of a pub. There was a disparity between a weekly takings sheet and the amount actually banked. The copy of the bank slip filed with the weekly takings sheet had been falsified to conceal a deficiency of £3,000. D was sentenced on the basis that he did not in any way benefit from the missing £3,000. D was ordered to pay £1,500 compensation. Defence counsel said D was trying to conceal the £3,000 loss and the loss did not result from D's offence. Held. *R v Green* 1976 Unreported 20/2/76 applied. Compensation order quashed.

Assessing the defendant's means

17.39 *Means, Must have regard to/The required steps*
Powers of Criminal Courts (Sentencing) Act 2000 s 130(11) The court shall have regard to a defendant's means so far as they appear or are known to the court.
R v York 2018 EWCA Crim 2754 D pleaded to being in charge of a dog which caused injury. She said her outgoings were more than her income, but she just about managed with the help of her sick daughter's [presumed benefits]. The Judge made a £1,000 compensation order with a collection order. Held. Six principles are relevant. 1 An offender must give details of his/her means. 2 A judge must enquire about and make clear findings about the offender's means. 3 The court must take into account an offender's means. 4 A compensation order should not be made unless it is realistic, in the sense the court is satisfied that the offender has or will have the means to pay that order

within a reasonable time. Although a compensation order for as long as 100 months has been upheld, a repayment period of 2-3 years in an exceptional case would not be open to criticism. In general, excessively long repayment periods should be avoided. 5 A court should not make a compensation order on the assumption that the order will be paid by somebody else, e.g. a relative. 6 It is wrong to fix an amount of compensation without regard to the instalments which are capable of being paid and the period over which those instalments should be paid. [It should not be left] for the Magistrates to sort out.

17.40 ***Court must investigate the means of the defendant***

R v Smith 2008 EWCA Crim 164 D was ordered to pay £31,950 by way of compensation, to be paid over 18 months. D was in receipt of income support and had no savings. Held. In imposing the compensation order the Judge failed to carry out an inquiry as to means, failed to consider whether the order he was going to make was in any way realistic, in the sense that it could be satisfied either immediately or within a reasonable space of time, and was wrong in principle.

See also: *R v Wilson* 2010 EWCA Crim 2138 (Judge did not inquire as to D's financial circumstances. Compensation order quashed.)

R v Noble 2015 EWCA Crim 1454 (Here there was no proper investigation so we quash the order. The slip rule hearing in the Crown Court to reassess the compensation order (which had already been arranged) will take place.)

R v Wing 2017 EWCA Crim 633 (£2,000 order and 18 months' imprisonment. No sufficient investigation of the financial position so the order was flawed. Order quashed.)

17.41 ***Court must be satisfied the defendant has the means to pay***

R v Amey, James and Meah 1982 4 Cr App R (S) 410 D pleaded to theft and other charges. He was aged 21, unemployed and on social security. D had £360 in his bank account and it was hoped someone who owed him money could pay him £50 a month. D's counsel said D could pay £100 a month. The Judge ordered him to pay £5,289. Held. The payment of £50 was speculative. Care must be taken to ensure that the evidence is sufficient before making an order. Order reduced.

R v Smith 2008 EWCA Crim 164 D was ordered to pay £31,950 by way of compensation, to be paid over 18 months. D was in receipt of income support and had no savings. Held. In imposing the compensation order the Judge failed to consider whether the order he was going to make was in any way realistic, in the sense that it could be satisfied either immediately or within a reasonable space of time. The order was wrong in principle.

17.42 ***Means, Assessing***

R v Howell 1978 66 Cr App R 179 The court does not need to have a precise calculation of the defendant's assets but rather must take a broad picture.

R v Swann and Webster 1984 6 Cr App R (S) 22 In the new statutory provisions there was nothing to indicate that a trial judge, when considering compensation, should simply pluck a figure out of the air and have no regard to whether or not the offender is in a position to meet all or any of it.

17.43 ***Means, Assessing The defendant must support his account with evidence/ Defence team's duties***

R v Johnson 1982 4 Cr App R (S) 141 The Judge made a compensation order on the basis he was told that a police officer thought there was a possibility of there being money in a suitcase that was coming from Paris. Defence counsel disputed this. After the compensation order was made the police said they were satisfied there was nothing of value in the suitcase. Held. The defendant cannot expect the court simply to accept, without evidence to support it, any statement he makes about his means. Indeed, in this case it would be foolish to accept his statements about his means. The compensation order will be for £500 not £12,000.

R v Roberts 1987 9 Cr App R (S) 275 It is the duty of those who put forward proposals for compensation to ensure that the information placed before the court is not just accurate but that it has been investigated so that [the defence team] are satisfied that the information is correct.
See also: *R v Stewart* 1983 5 Cr App R (S) 320 (D was a juvenile. His counsel said D's car was worth about £900, but expressed doubts about it. D was ordered to pay £223. Held. There is still no valuation. We will not intervene.)

17.44 *Means, Assessing No duty on the prosecution to show the defendant has means*
R v Johnson 1982 4 Cr App R (S) 141 No burden is laid on the prosecution to establish the defendant's means. It is customary for them to pass on a request from the loser that a compensation order be made. The prosecution has no duty to conduct a detailed inquiry into the defendant's means, which clearly must be a matter within his own knowledge.

17.45 *Local authorities No requirement to take account of means*
Powers of Criminal Courts (Sentencing) Act 2000 s 138(2) For the purposes of any order under section 137 of this Act (power to order parents etc. to pay fines etc.) made against a local authority, Powers of Criminal Courts (Sentencing) Act 2000 s 130(11) (duty to have regard to means) shall not apply.

17.46 *Other people's money*
Example: *R v Gray* 2015 EWCA Crim 1345 (Just before sentence, promised a £10,000 banker's draft of money raised by partner and father to pay the victim, her son. In fact not paid. Two months later, compensation for the amount ordered. Order quashed.)

17.47 *Promise of money in the future/Borrowing money to pay order*
R v Mortimer 1977 Crim LR 624 D pleaded to six counts of obtaining property by deception and four counts of obtaining credit as a bankrupt. D was sentenced to 18 months suspended for 2 years and ordered to pay £4,261 compensation over a period of two months. D's wife and a friend were willing to raise second mortgages on their homes to pay the compensation but they were unable to obtain the mortgages. Held. D had no means and the compensation order should not have been made. If a Judge wished to impose a more lenient sentence with a view that the losers would have some opportunity to get their money back and a compensation order is made, there are two possible courses. Those advising the accused could take steps to ensure that the money is repaid before the hearing or the court could defer sentence for a period to give an opportunity for any representations made to be carried out and see whether they are effective.
R v Stapylton 2012 EWCA Crim 728, 2013 1 Cr App R (S) 12 (p 68) D pleaded to dangerous driving. He took a car and, after travelling at speed in it, he left the road and crashed into a garage. The car needed to be replaced and £5,000 worth of damage was done to the garage. He was aged 19 and out of work. The Judge made an £8,100 compensation order and said he certainly could get work. Held. Bearing in mind his means it was not realistic for him to pay the order.
R v Carrington 2014 EWCA Crim 325, 2 Cr App R (S) 41 (p 337) D pleaded to fraud and other charges. At work she made false claims for overtime and petty cash. In all she obtained just under £50,000. Counsel said D was keen to pay the money back as soon as possible. He suggested a £10,000 or £15,000 compensation order based on D and her partner borrowing money. He also said, "Courts really cannot take into account monies that other people are borrowing or monies that they would lend". In fact D was now unemployed, on a very modest pension and relying financially on her partner. With her good character, age etc. the Judge made a suspended sentence order with a £15,000 compensation order. Held. Counsel's statement was not entirely accurate. [Where] the cash flow position of a defendant is not such as to equip him to make an immediate payment for a compensation order, then [funds may be borrowed]. If a judge has

sufficient material to conclude that there were sound prospects that a defendant would be able to repay [such a loan] then a compensation order would not be wrong in principle. However, in this case there was no such material. Order quashed.
For ordering a parent to pay the compensation order for their child, see the **Parents etc. paying fines etc.** section at **58.40**.

17.48 ***Selling assets to pay the order General***
R v Workman 1979 1 Cr App R (S) 335 D was a counter clerk at a post office and committed a series of frauds by manipulating accounts. D obtained a total of £2,118 and used most of the money towards the purchase of a house worth £13,000 and household goods. D lost her job at the post office and was working in low-paid employment. D was ordered to pay £2,118 in compensation. The defence said the compensation would take a long time to discharge and the heavy burden upon D may tempt her to commit further offences in order to meet her obligation under it. Held. D should not be relieved of the burden of the order. That D should go on living in a house which had been bought in part with the proceeds of theft seems not only unacceptable, but contrary to propriety and justice. The compensation should stand but the obligation to meet it should be on the basis of repayment by instalments of £10 per week.

17.49 ***Selling assets to pay the order Matrimonial homes***
R v McGuire 1992 13 Cr App R (S) 332 D was convicted of benefit fraud and an unrelated dishonesty offence. The actual loss to the DHSS was just over £3,450 and two compensation orders were made for just over £1,420. The defence said the orders would require D to sell his sole asset, the matrimonial home. The house was valued at £120,000. The equity was £65,000. D was aged 43. Neither he nor his wife worked. Held. D was clearly capable of working. There is no general principle that a compensation order cannot be made if the order makes the defendant sell his matrimonial home. Here there was no reason why the defendant should not put the house on the market. Appeal dismissed.
R v Gondhia 2008 EWCA Crim 3268 D pleaded to GBH with intent and false imprisonment committed against his wife. D was sentenced to 3½ years and ordered to pay £4,000 to his wife from his share of the sale of the family house. D's wife claimed 100% interest in the house and continued to live there so there were no immediate prospects of realising a sale of the property. Held. The court has to approach the ability of D to meet a compensation order on the assumption that he has, or may have, no assets with which to do so, or no realisable assets with which to do so at such time as they may become available. When also bearing in mind the nature of the very serious substantive penalty to which D has been subject, it is right that the compensation order should be set aside.
R v Parkinson 2015 EWCA Crim 1448, 2016 1 Cr App R (S) 6 (p 24) D pleaded to theft. He stole brass parts worth just over £64,620 from his employer. The prosecution applied for a confiscation order and a compensation order. It was agreed that the benefit was about £39,330 and the available assets were just under £14,690, which was his share of the matrimonial home. The Judge accepted that this order would make it likely that the home would have to be sold. Held. para 22 If a confiscation order alone had been sought, the order could properly [utilise] D's share in the matrimonial home. para 30 A judge, when considering whether or not to make a compensation order, may take the [issue] that the property was a matrimonial home into account. para 38 Crown Court judges should nowadays be a little careful, in the course of confiscation or compensation proceedings, in too readily assuming that the making of a compensation order in such circumstances inevitably will require a jointly owned property to be sold. That may well be the consequence. But under modern jurisprudence there is at least some prospect for a spouse or partner having the remaining beneficial share in the family home, and perhaps also where there are dependent young children, at least raising an opposing argument as to sale or possession: such arguments being potentially available in the

course of enforcement proceedings in the courts which have been subsequently undertaken to realise the value of the defendant's beneficial interest. Such arguments in opposition are capable of placing reliance on the considerations arising under European Convention on Human Rights art 8 or on wider equitable principles. If the enforcing court in subsequent sale and possession proceedings does not consider it unjust or disproportionate to order sale and possession, then that is suggestive of it not having been unjust or disproportionate to have made the original compensation order. para 39 We endorse the judge's approach. Appeal dismissed. For more details see **21.125**.
Old cases: Pre-1992 cases are best ignored.

17.50 ***Selling assets to pay the order Values must be proved***
R v Chambers 1981 3 Cr App R (S) 318 LCJ A motorcycle actually worth £650 was claimed by a police officer, who had custody of the motorcycle, to be worth around £1,600. On that basis it formed £1,600 of a £2,000 compensation order. Held. If there is only tentative agreement as to the value of an article and incomplete investigation into the value of a particular article, then this Court might interfere. Order reduced.
R v Stewart 1983 5 Cr App R (S) 320 A juvenile defendant's counsel said D's car was worth about £900, but expressed doubts about it. D was ordered to pay £223. Held. D has not put before the Court any evidence to suggest the valuation was erroneous. There is still no valuation. We will not intervene.

17.51 ***Defendant has limited means Should an order be made?***
R v Bagga and Others 1989 11 Cr App R (S) 497 D was convicted of ABH and affray. He and others went to a restaurant, were abusive, didn't pay the bill, punched and kicked the proprietor and broke mirrors and bottles. The group said they were going to demolish the restaurant. The cost of the damage was £1,842. The Judge made a compensation order of £200 for each defendant with £200 costs each. Held. A compensation order is sound sentencing policy. We uphold the order made for two of the defendants. However, D had absolutely no money. It was wrong to make a compensation order against a defendant who was in receipt of supplementary benefit. Even if he could afford to pay £2 per week, which the Judge contemplated, the order would take about four years to pay. Order quashed, but the costs order was to remain.

Fixing the amount etc.

17.52 ***Magistrates' Court Limits***
Powers of Criminal Courts (Sentencing) Act 2000 s 131(A1)[305] This section applies if (but only if) a Magistrates' Court has convicted a person aged under 18 ('the offender') of an offence or offences.
(1) The compensation to be paid under a compensation order made by the court in respect of the offence, or any one of the offences, shall not exceed £5,000.
Note: The effect of this is to remove the £5,000 limit for those aged 18+. Ed.

17.53 ***Statute and TICs and Totality Guideline 2012: Crown Court***
Powers of Criminal Courts (Sentencing) Act 2000 s 130(4) Compensation shall be of such amount as the court considers appropriate, having regard to any evidence and to any representations that are made by or on behalf of the accused or the prosecutor.
TICs and Totality Guideline 2012: Crown Court, see www.banksr.com Other Matters Guidelines tab
page 16 **Global compensation orders** The court should not fix a global compensation figure unless the offences were committed against the same victim.[306] Where there are competing claims for limited funds, the total compensation available should normally be apportioned on a pro rata basis.[307]

[305] As amended by Crime and Courts Act 2013 Sch 16 para 8(2) and (3). In force 11/12/13
[306] *R v Warton* 1976 Crim LR 520
[307] *R v Miller* 1976 Crim LR 694

Note: There is a similar entry in the *Magistrates' Court Sentencing Guidelines Update March 2012* page 18p. Ed.

17.54 *Victim provokes the offence*
R v Flinton 2007 EWCA Crim 2322, 2008 1 Cr App R (S) 96 (p 575) D pleaded to ABH and common assault. D was punched by G in a pub. D punched G and threw him to the floor twice, and kicked G on the second occasion. D also pushed a woman, C, who fell over G onto the floor. D was ordered to pay £1,500 to G and £500 to C. Held. Whilst the Court is empowered to make an order for such an amount as it considers appropriate, £1,500 was greater than any award which would have been made in civil proceedings. The largest award that can be made on a full liability basis is £1,000. G's provocative conduct should have led to a reduction in the amount of compensation ordered to be paid to him. But for G's provocative assault the incident would not have occurred. Compensation to G reduced to £750.

17.55 *Multiple losers*
R v Oddy 1974 59 Cr App R (S) 66 A separate compensation order should be made for each loser.

17.56 *Multiple defendants*
R v Grundy 1974 1 AER 292 LCJ A joint and several order has practical disadvantages. Orders should be made severally.

17.57 *Apportioning the loss between the losers*
TICs and Totality Guideline 2012: Crown Court, see www.banksr.com Other Matters Guidelines tab
page 16 **Global compensation orders** The court should not fix a global compensation figure unless the offences were committed against the same victim.[308] Where there are competing claims for limited funds, the total compensation available should normally be apportioned on a pro rata basis.[309]
Note: There is a similar entry in the *Magistrates' Court Sentencing Guidelines Update March 2012* page 18p. Ed.
R v Amey, James and Meah 1982 4 Cr App R (S) 410 Eight individuals were entitled to compensation of £2,022 in total and a bank was entitled to £2,867. Held. Where there are a number of claimants and a defendant's means are insufficient to satisfy all the claims for compensation, the amounts claimed should normally be scaled down and the amount available for compensation apportioned between the claimants on a pro rata basis. It would be open to a Judge to exercise discretion, if there were strong grounds for doing so, to depart from the normal pro rata basis to make such an adjustment as is reasonable. But this discretion should be exercised rarely. It may create more problems than it solves, and what is justice for one may be an injustice for another. As a general rule, apportionment, and not selection, should be the adopted course where there are insufficient means to meet every established claim. If ever there was an instance when the claimants should have been selected, and no orders on a pro rata basis have been made, this was it. It would be a great hardship on the eight individuals to receive only two-fifths of their proved claim and to be forced to resort to civil process for the balance. On the other hand the bank would be far better placed to seek and obtain judgment in the County Court for the amount they were entitled to. It would not be a futile exercise and the judgment debt could properly be met in full over a period of years. By excluding the bank from the order for compensation, it does not mean they are excluded from a proper claim, they are being denied the quick opportunity of getting their money, and that is all. The order in favour of the eight individuals remained and the order in favour of the bank was quashed.

[308] *R v Warton* 1976 Crim LR 520
[309] *R v Miller* 1976 Crim LR 694

R v Beddow 1987 9 Cr App R (S) 235 D pleaded to TDA. D was a passenger in a van driven by one of his two co-defendants. The van crashed. D was in work and his two co-defendants were unemployed. D was ordered to pay £300, which was the full value of the compensation awarded. The defence argued on appeal it was wrong to order D to pay the full amount when the driver was not ordered to pay anything. Held. The compensation order cannot be criticised.
R v Godfrey 1994 15 Cr App R (S) 536 D and B pleaded to using threatening words and behaviour. D and B were travelling in a taxi driven by V. A dispute arose between D, B and V which involved racist abuse. The taxi stopped and the doors were opened. During a scuffle all three sustained injuries and the taxi was damaged. V gave no clear evidence as to who had thrown the racist abuse at him. The Judge said even if D had not racially abused V, D could pay more than B because he was in work whereas B was not. D was ordered to pay £350 in compensation to V and B was ordered to pay £250. Held. The Judge should have first determined what compensation should be paid to V before dividing it between D and B. Although a compensation order was appropriate in this case, it was fundamental there should be a secure basis on which compensation could be ordered in terms of an assessment of what V had suffered. The total amount to be paid by D and B should have been fixed at £300. As there was no material on which the Court could distinguish between D and B, D's compensation order would be reduced to £150.

17.58 *Can interest be added?*
R v Schofield 1978 67 Cr App R 282 D pleaded to theft, obtaining property by deception and 18 TICs. D was ordered to pay £1,243 in compensation which included interest. Held. The court may exercise its discretion as to whether it will include a sum by way of interest or not. Where the amounts are relatively large, where the time is long and where there is no question of any insufficiency of the defendant's means, there is no error in principle in including a sum by way of interest in the award, thereby compensating the victim for the loss of the use of the money as well as for the loss of the money itself.

17.59 *Payment by instalments Maximum period*
Magistrates' Court Sentencing Guidelines 2008, see www.banksr.com Other Matters Guidelines tab page 167 Where the offender has little money, the order may have to be scaled down or additional time allowed to pay. The court may allow compensation to be paid over a period of up to three years in appropriate cases.
Note: For a similar statement, see page 152 in the Guideline. Ed.
R v Yehou 1997 2 Cr App R (S) 48 D was ordered to pay £9,110 compensation. The Judge said he expected it would take D longer to pay than the period usually limited by the courts. Held. The compensation order was far too high and was unlimited in that it could not be paid in a reasonable period of time. Having regard to D's means he could afford to pay £25 per week. Order reduced to £3,900 payable at £25 per week over three years.
R v Kluver 2010 EWCA Crim 3237 D pleaded to theft of a sum of money sent by cheque from one company to another. The sum was £26,000. He was sentenced to 51 weeks suspended and, after careful examination of D's means, the Judge imposed a compensation order in the amount of £23,000 at £120 per month. Held. At that rate, it would have taken D 16 years to pay. The order was too long. Order quashed and replaced with compensation order for £2,880 paid at £120 per month over two years.
R v Ganyo 2011 EWCA Crim 2491, 2012 1 Cr App R (S) 108 (650) D and D1 pleaded to obtaining a money transfer by deception and using a false instrument. Whilst overstayers in 2002, they used false documents to apply for university places and NHS bursaries. D claimed over £25,000 in three years, enabling her to become a qualified mental health nurse. D1 claimed £3,298. D was of good character, whereas D1 had a number of convictions, mainly for driving offences. Both subsequently received indefinite leave to remain and displayed some remorse. The Judge imposed compensation orders for D to pay £10,000 at £100 per month (which would take approximately 8 years) and for D1 to

pay £3,298 at £50 per month (which would take approximately 5½ years). Held. Given that D had gained a professional qualification, which would enable her to be employed in the nursing profession during her career, it is not unrealistic to expect that she can continue to pay over a period of years. The Judge drew an analogy with students and maintenance fees, and this analogy we find attractive. D1 was not as fortunate as D, and did not gain a qualification. However, we are not persuaded that the order was too high or the repayment period too long. Appeals dismissed.
See also the **INSTALMENTS, PAYMENT BY** chapter.

Combined with other orders

17.60 ***Combinations generally***
TICs and Totality Guideline 2012: Crown Court, see www.banksr.com Other Matters Guidelines tab page 16 The court may combine a compensation order with any other form of order.
Note: There is a similar entry in the *Magistrates' Court Sentencing Guidelines Update March 2012* page 18p. Ed.

17.61 ***Absolute or conditional discharges, Combined with***
Powers of Criminal Courts (Sentencing) Act 2000 s 12(7) Nothing in this section shall be construed as preventing a court, on discharging an offender absolutely or conditionally in respect of any offence…from making in respect of the offence an order under Powers of Criminal Courts (Sentencing) Act 2000 s 130 (compensation orders).[310]

17.62 ***Community orders, Combined with***
TICs and Totality Guideline 2012: Crown Court, see www.banksr.com Other Matters Guidelines tab page 16 A compensation order can be combined with a community order.
Note: There is a similar entry in the *Magistrates' Court Sentencing Guidelines Update March 2012* page 18p. Ed.

17.63 ***Confiscation orders, Combined with***
TICs and Totality Guideline 2012: Crown Court, see www.banksr.com Other Matters Guidelines tab page 16 A compensation order can be combined with a confiscation order where the amount that may be realised is sufficient. If such an order is made, priority should be given to compensation.[311]
Note: There is a similar entry in the *Magistrates' Court Sentencing Guidelines Update March 2012* page 18p. Ed.
Proceeds of Crime Act 2002 s 13(5)-(6) Where the Crown Court makes both a confiscation order and a compensation order and believes that there are insufficient means to satisfy both orders in full, the court must direct that so much of the compensation monies as it specifies be recovered under the confiscation order. That amount is the amount the court believes will not be recovered because of insufficiency of the person's means.
For more detail see the **CONFISCATION: PROCEEDS OF CRIME ACT 2002 *Step 15 Compensation orders, combined with*** para at **21.143**.
R v Firmager 2013 EWCA Crim 2756 D was sentenced to 15 months' imprisonment and a compensation order. He appealed before the confiscation hearing. Held. The compensation order was unlawful because it was premature. Order quashed.
For ***Custody, Combined with*** see **28.34**.

17.64 ***Disqualification from being a company director, Combined with***
R v Holmes 1992 13 Cr App R (S) 29 D pleaded to fraudulent trading (9 months' imprisonment suspended, disqualification for 12 months, costs and compensation order). The order was based on defence counsel's belief that significant monies were available. At the Court of Appeal D's affidavit said that the disqualification order had had a serious effect on D's ability to earn a living. Held. When a compensation order is made it is

[310] As amended by Criminal Justice and Courts Act 2015 Sch 12 paras 8-9
[311] *R v Mitchell* 2001 Crim LR 239

generally wrong in principle to inhibit a defendant from freely engaging in business activities which must have been contemplated as necessary for the purpose of fulfilling his obligations under the compensation order. The effect of the disqualification did just that. Compensation order quashed.

17.65 ***Fines, Combined with***

Powers of Criminal Courts (Sentencing) Act 2000 s 130(11) Where the defendant has insufficient means to pay both a fine and a compensation order the court shall give preference to the compensation order.

TICs and Totality Guideline 2012: Crown Court, see www.banksr.com Other Matters Guidelines tab page 16 Priority is given to the imposition of a compensation order over a fine.[312] This does not affect sentences other than fines. This means that the fine should be reduced or, if necessary, dispensed with altogether, to enable the compensation to be paid.

Note: There is a similar entry in the *Magistrates' Court Sentencing Guidelines Update March 2012* page 18p. Ed.

17.66 ***Suspended Sentence Order, Combined with***

TICs and Totality Guideline 2012: Crown Court, see www.banksr.com Other Matters Guidelines tab page 16 A compensation order can be combined with a Suspended Sentence Order.[313]

Note: There is a similar entry in the *Magistrates' Court Sentencing Guidelines Update March 2012* page 18p. Ed.

17.67 ***Victim surcharge, Combined with***

Court's duty to order payment of surcharge

Criminal Justice Act 2003 s 161A(3) Where a court dealing with an offender[314] considers:

(a) that it would be appropriate to make one or more of a compensation order, an Unlawful Profit Order and a Slavery and Trafficking Reparations Order, but

(b) that he has insufficient means to pay both the surcharge and appropriate amounts under such of those orders as it would be appropriate to make, the court must reduce the surcharge accordingly [if necessary to nil].

(4) For the purposes of this section a court does not "deal with" a person if it:

(a) discharges him absolutely, or

(b) makes an order under the Mental Health Act 1983 in respect of him.

(5) In this section "slavery and trafficking reparation order" means an order under section 8 of the Modern Slavery Act 2015, and "unlawful profit order" means an unlawful profit order under section 4 of the Prevention of Social Housing Fraud Act 2013.

Magistrates' Court Sentencing Guidelines 2008, see www.banksr.com Other Matters Guidelines tab page 167 Compensation also takes priority over the victim surcharge where the offender's means are an issue.

Giving reasons

17.68 ***Explain sentence, Judge/Magistrate must***

Criminal Justice Act 2003 s 174(2)[315] The court must state in open court, in ordinary language and in general terms, the court's reasons for deciding on the sentence.

(3) The court must explain to the offender in ordinary language:

(a) the effect of the sentence,

(b) the effects of non-compliance with any order that the offender is required to comply with and that forms part of the sentence,

[312] Powers of Criminal Courts (Sentencing) Act 2000 s 130(12)

[313] Powers of Criminal Courts (Sentencing) Act 2000 s 118(5)

[314] Criminal Justice Act 2003 s 161A(4). For the purposes of this section a court does not 'deal with' a person if it: a) discharges him absolutely, or b) makes an order under Mental Health Act 1983 in respect of him.

[315] As substituted by Legal Aid, Sentencing and Punishment of Offenders Act 2012 s 64

(c) any power of the court to vary or review any order that forms part of the sentence…

17.69 ***Duty to give reasons for not making an order***

Powers of Criminal Courts (Sentencing) Act 2000 s 130(3) A court shall give reasons, on passing sentence, if it does not make a compensation order in a case where this section empowers it to do so.

Criminal Procedure Rules 2015 2015/1490 Rule 28.1(1) This rule applies where the court decides:..

(b) not to make, where it could…

(ii) a compensation order.

(2) The court must explain why it has so decided, when it explains the sentence that it has passed.

Appeals

17.70 ***Can the victim of the loss appeal?***

R (Faithfull) v Ipswich Crown Court 2007 EWHC 2763 (Admin), 2008 3 AER 749 D pleaded to theft of £15,579. She stole the money from V, her employer. The Judge made a confiscation order against D but declined to make a compensation order partly because if both orders were made, the matrimonial home might be at risk. The victim appealed. Held. There was no jurisdiction to hear the appeal because of [what is now Senior Courts Act 1981 s 29(3)].

17.71 ***Court of Appeal and Supreme Court, Powers of***

Powers of Criminal Courts (Sentencing) Act 2000 s 132(3) The Court of Appeal may by order annul or vary any compensation order made by the court of trial, although the conviction is not quashed; and the order, if annulled, shall not take effect and, if varied, shall take effect as varied.

(4) Where the Supreme Court restores a conviction, it may make any compensation order which the court of trial could have made.

(4A) Where an order is made in respect of a person under subsection (3) or (4) above, the Court of Appeal or the Supreme Court shall make such order for the payment of a surcharge under section 161A of the Criminal Justice Act 2003, or such variation of the order of the Crown Court under that section, as is necessary to secure that the person's liability under that section is the same as it would be if he were being dealt with by the Crown Court.

(5) Where a compensation order has been made against any person in respect of an offence taken into consideration in determining his sentence:

(a) the order shall cease to have effect if he successfully appeals against his conviction of the offence or, if more than one, all the offences, of which he was convicted in the proceedings in which the order was made;

(b) he may appeal against the order as if it were part of the sentence imposed in respect of the offence or, if more than one, any of the offences, of which he was so convicted.

17.72 ***Means assessing Defendant says figure given was wrong***

R v Dando 1996 1 Cr App R (S) 155 D was ordered to pay £1,800 in compensation. D gave evidence at trial that he had sufficient means to pay the compensation. D later swore an affidavit claiming he only had £540 available with which to pay compensation. Held. It is an absurdity that D should complain that the trial Judge believed him as to his means. If D does not, or will not pay and is punished as a result then D brought the whole matter on his own head. The CPS should be informed with a view to ensuring D's prosecution for perjury.

Varying or discharging orders

17.73 ***Magistrates' Court***

Review of compensation orders

Powers of Criminal Courts (Sentencing) Act 2000 s 133(1) The magistrates' court for the time being having functions in relation to the enforcement of a compensation order (in this section referred to as "the appropriate court") may, on the application of the person against whom the compensation order was made, discharge the order or reduce the amount which remains to be paid; but this is subject to subsections (2) to (4) below.
(2) The appropriate court may exercise a power conferred by subsection (1) above only:
(a) at a time when (disregarding any power of a court to grant leave to appeal out of time) there is no further possibility of an appeal on which the compensation order could be varied or set aside, and
(b) at a time before the person against whom the compensation order was made has paid into court the whole of the compensation which the order requires him to pay.
(3) The appropriate court may exercise a power conferred by subsection (1) above only if it appears to the court:
(a) that the injury, loss or damage in respect of which the compensation order was made has been held in civil proceedings to be less than it was taken to be for the purposes of the order, or
(b) in the case of a compensation order in respect of the loss of any property, that the property has been recovered by the person in whose favour the order was made, or
(c) that the means of the person against whom the compensation order was made are insufficient to satisfy in full both the order and any or all of the following made against him in the same proceedings:
(i) a confiscation order under Criminal Justice Act 1988 Part 6 or Proceeds of Crime Act 2002 Part 2,
(ii) an unlawful profit order under Prevention of Social Housing Fraud Act 2013 s 4,
(iii) a slavery and trafficking reparation order under Modern Slavery Act 2015 s 8 or
(d) that the person against whom the compensation order was made has suffered a substantial reduction in his means which was unexpected at the time when the order was made, and that his means seem unlikely to increase for a considerable period.
(4) Where the compensation order was made by the Crown Court, the appropriate court shall not exercise any power conferred by subsection (1) above in a case where it is satisfied as mentioned in paragraph (c) or (d) of subsection (3) above unless it has first obtained the consent of the Crown Court.
(5) Where the compensation order has been made on appeal, for the purposes of subsection (4) above it shall be deemed:
(a) if it was made on an appeal brought from a Magistrates' Court, to have been made by that Magistrates' Court,
(b) if it was made on an appeal brought from the Crown Court or from the Criminal Division of the Court of Appeal, to have been made by the Crown Court.

17.74 ***Magistrates' Court Procedure***

Criminal Procedure Rules 2015 2015/1490 Rule 28.5(1) This rule applies where a Magistrates' Court can vary or discharge a compensation order on application by the defendant…
(2) A defendant who wants the court to exercise that power must:
(a) apply in writing as soon as practicable after becoming aware of the grounds for doing so,
(b) serve the application on the Magistrates' Court officer,
(c) where the compensation order was made in the Crown Court, serve a copy of the application on the Crown Court officer, and
(d) in the application, specify the compensation order that the defendant wants the court to vary or discharge and explain (as applicable):
(i) what civil court finding shows that the injury, loss or damage was less than it had appeared to be when the order was made,

(ii) in what circumstances the person for whose benefit the order was made has recovered the property for the loss of which it was made,
(iii) why a confiscation order makes the defendant now unable to pay compensation in full, or
(iv) in what circumstances the defendant's means have been reduced substantially and unexpectedly, and why they seem unlikely to increase for a considerable period.
(3) The court officer must serve a copy of the application on the person for whose benefit the compensation order was made.
(4) [see **17.75**]

17.75 ***Magistrates' Courts varying or discharging Crown Court orders***
Powers of Criminal Courts (Sentencing) Act 2000 s 133(4) Where a compensation order was made in the Crown Court and an issue arises with that order in relation to d) and e) above, the Magistrates Court may only vary or discharge that order with the prior consent of the Crown Court.
Criminal Procedure Rules 2015 2015/1490 Rule 28.5(4) The court must not vary or discharge the compensation order unless:
(a) the defendant, and the person for whose benefit it was made, each has had an opportunity to make representations at a hearing (whether or not either in fact attends), and
(b) where the order was made in the Crown Court, the Crown Court has notified its consent.

17.76 ***Representations, Right to make***
Criminal Procedure Rules 2015 2015/1490 Rule 28.5(4) The court must not vary or discharge the compensation order unless:
(a) the defendant, and the person for whose benefit it was made, each has had an opportunity to make representations at a hearing (whether or not either in fact attends)…

17.77 ***Means change Applying to vary Don't appeal***
R v Palmer 1994 15 Cr App R (S) 550 D pleaded to four counts of theft. D stole frozen food from his employer, a food processing and manufacturing company, to the value of £3,940. The social inquiry report said D was earning about £14,000 from his business. D was ordered to pay £3,940 compensation and prosecution costs. A few weeks after the order was imposed D's business dissolved and he remained unemployed so was unable to make any payments under the compensation order. Held. Parliament had intended that matters of this kind should be dealt with by way of application to the Magistrates' Court. That court may have to make some detailed investigation into the financial means of the applicant. It would not be appropriate, in our view, for this Court to be involved in details of that kind. This appeal is misconceived.
R v Pitt 2014 EWCA Crim 522 The Court of Appeal is not to be used for revisiting compensation orders when those compensation orders were properly made and it is only subsequent events that bring them into question. There are provisions for the Magistrates' Court to direct payment by instalments and where it appears to that court that payment will not be possible, to vary the compensation order with the consent of the Crown Court.
Old case: *R v Slack* 1987 9 Cr App R (S) 65 (The defendant should apply to the Magistrates' Court.)

18 Concurrent and Consecutive Sentences

General principles

18.1
Totality see **242.63** in Volume 2.

18.2 *TICs and Totality Guideline 2012: Crown Court with principles of totality*

TICs and Totality Guideline 2012: Crown Court, see www.banksr.com Other Matters Guidelines tab page 5 The principle of totality comprises two elements:

1 All courts, when sentencing for more than a single offence, should pass a total sentence which reflects all the offending behaviour before it and is just and proportionate. This is so whether the sentences are structured as concurrent or consecutive. Therefore, concurrent sentences will ordinarily be longer than a single sentence for a single offence.

2 It is usually impossible to arrive at a just and proportionate sentence for multiple offending simply by adding together notional single sentences. It is necessary to address the offending behaviour, together with the factors personal to the offender as a whole.

Concurrent/consecutive sentences

There is no inflexible rule governing whether sentences should be structured as concurrent or consecutive components. The overriding principle is that the overall sentence must be just and proportionate. [For custodial sentences]: 1. Consider the sentence for each individual offence, referring to the relevant sentencing guidelines, 2. Determine whether the case calls for concurrent or consecutive sentences.

page 7 **Where consecutive sentences are to be passed**, add up the sentences for each offence and consider if the aggregate length is just and proportionate. If the aggregate length is not just and proportionate, the court should consider how to reach a just and proportionate sentence. There are a number of ways in which this can be achieved.

Examples include:

- when sentencing for similar offence types or offences of a similar level of severity the court can consider:
  - whether all of the offences can be proportionately reduced (with particular reference to the category ranges within sentencing guidelines) and passed consecutively,
  - whether, despite their similarity, a most serious principal offence can be identified and the other sentences can all be proportionately reduced (with particular reference to the category ranges within sentencing guidelines) and passed consecutively in order that the sentence for the lead offence can be clearly identified.
- when sentencing for two or more offences of differing levels of seriousness the court can consider:
  - whether some offences are of such low seriousness in the context of the most serious offence(s) that they can be recorded as 'no separate penalty' (for example, technical breaches or minor driving offences not involving mandatory disqualification),
  - whether some of the offences are of lesser seriousness and are unrelated to the most serious offence(s), that they can be ordered to run concurrently so that the sentence for the most serious offence(s) can be clearly identified.

3 Test the overall sentence(s) against the requirement that they be just and proportionate.

4 Consider whether the sentence is structured in a way that will be best understood by all concerned with it.

Note: There is a similar entry in the *Magistrates' Court Sentencing Guidelines Update March 2012* page 18g. Ed.

18.3 *Judicial guidance Concurrent and consecutive*

Att-Gen's Ref No 28 of 2013 2013 EWCA Crim 1190 D pleaded to seven indecent assaults and sexual activity with a child counts. Held. Courts should impose a total which reflects all offending behaviour, whether the sentences are structured as concurrent or consecutive, as to which there is no inflexible rule. The overriding principle is that the overall sentence must be just and proportionate. Examples of where the overall criminality will not sufficiently be reflected by concurrent sentences include offences committed against different individuals, or offences against the same individual, where one must infer from the text 'more than once'.

18.4 ***Offences arise out of the same incident or facts*** ***TICs and Totality Guideline 2012: Crown Court***

TICs and Totality Guideline 2012: Crown Court, see www.banksr.com Other Matters Guidelines tab page 6 **Concurrent sentences** will ordinarily be appropriate where:

a) offences arise out of the same incident or facts.

Examples include:

- a single incident of dangerous driving resulting in injuries to multiple victims,[316]
- robbery with a weapon where the weapon offence is ancillary to the robbery and is not distinct and independent of it,[317]
- fraud and associated forgery,
- separate counts of supplying different types of drugs of the same class as part of the same transaction.

b) [a series of offences of the same or similar kind, see 18.6]

Where concurrent sentences are to be passed, the sentence should reflect the overall criminality involved. The sentence should be appropriately aggravated by the presence of the associated offences.

Examples include:

- a single incident of dangerous driving resulting in injuries to multiple victims where there are separate charges relating to each victim. The sentences should generally be passed concurrently, but each sentence should be aggravated to take into account the harm caused,
- repetitive fraud or theft, where charged as a series of small frauds/thefts, would be properly considered in relation to the total amount of money obtained and the period of time over which the offending took place. The sentences should generally be passed concurrently, each one reflecting the overall seriousness,
- robbery with a weapon where the weapon offence is ancillary to the robbery and is not distinct and independent of it. The principal sentence for the robbery should properly reflect the presence of the weapon. The court must avoid double-counting and may deem it preferable for the possession of the weapon's offence to run concurrently to avoid the appearance of under-sentencing in respect of the robbery.[318]

Note: There is a similar entry in the *Magistrates' Court Sentencing Guidelines Update March 2012* page 18h. Ed.

18.5 ***Offences arise out of the same incident or facts*** ***Consecutive sentences*** ***Examples***

R v Russell 2013 EWCA Crim 273 D pleaded to possession of cannabis. He was convicted of arson. When arrested for arson he was subjected to a strip search. During the strip search D sat down and upon standing up left behind a bag containing cocaine. A doctor was satisfied that his substance abuse contributed to the arson offence. Held. It is correct that the offence of possession came to light shortly after the arson attack. It is also correct that, on the evidence, his consumption of illicit drugs had contributed to his mental state at the time of the arson offence. However, while the fact of his consumption of drugs was recognised as a contributory factor in sentencing for the arson offence, the fact of his possession of drugs at the same time as he committed the offence of arson was not. That approach by the Judge sentencing for the arson offence was correct

---

[316] *R v Lawrence* 1989 11 Cr App R (S) 580

[317] *R v Poulton and Celaire* 2002 EWCA Crim 2487 and *Att-Gen's Ref Nos 21-22 of 2003* 2003 EWCA Crim 3089, 2004 2 Cr App R (S) 13 (p 63)

[318] *R v Millen* 1980 2 Cr App R (S) 357

because the possession of the cocaine and the carrying out of the arson were separate and distinct criminal acts even if the appellant's prior consumption of illicit drugs had contributed to his committing the arson. A consecutive sentence was correct.

R v AT 2013 EWCA Crim 686 D pleaded to assault by penetration and sexual assault. After a party, V went to W's flat. She was stripped naked, had her breasts bitten and fondled, and made to lie with her legs in the air. W handed D a truncheon and D inserted it into V's vagina, to a depth of around 6½ inches. D was sentenced to consecutive sentences of 5½ years (the assault) and 9 years (the penetration). It was argued that consecutive terms were wrong in principle as the penetration was a gross aggravation of the ongoing sexual assault. Held. The use of the truncheon added greatly to the criminality of the incident. The Judge was fully entitled to pass consecutive sentences. The only live issue was totality. The offences called for a very severe sentence. **14½ years was not manifestly excessive.**

Att-Gen's Ref Nos 74-78 of 2014 2014 EWCA Crim 2535, 2015 1 Cr App R (S) 30 (p 233) L and others pleaded to conspiracy to burgle and attempting to cause or, in the cases of L and G, actually causing an explosion. They tried to steal money from ATMs by creating an explosion using gas cylinders. Held. Offences such as these, which include the use of gas cylinders, and which are increasing across the UK, require deterrent sentences. We would hesitatingly have imposed consecutive terms, not least to emphasise the gravity of the explosion count, and so that any court in future considering previous convictions would find the Court's approach obvious on the face of [the offenders'] antecedent history. For more detail, see **221.48** in Volume 2.

See also: *R v Alexander and Others* 2011 EWCA Crim 89 (Conspiracy to supply cannabis and conspiracy to conceal the proceeds. 18,000 kilos worth £61m. The mere fact that the conduct in concealing the proceeds is an inevitable consequence of the original offence does not lead to the conclusion that further punishment should not be ordered. Concealing the proceeds prevents the authorities from detecting the first offence. Consecutive sentences were justified.)

Note: The reality is that sentencing is an art, not a purely mathematical exercise. Each case is fact-specific. Making sentences concurrent or consecutive is used simply to mark significant features of the offending. Many sets of offences can be equally appropriately sentenced by imposing concurrent or consecutive sentences. It is invariably the total that matters. The old cases have been removed because they add little. They can be found in the 12th edition of this book. Ed.

18.6 *Offences that are of the same or similar kind*

TICs and Totality Guideline 2012: Crown Court, see www.banksr.com Other Matters Guidelines tab page 6 **Concurrent sentences** will ordinarily be appropriate where:

a) [same incident or facts case, see **18.4**]
b) there is a series of offences of the same or similar kind, especially when committed against the same person.

Examples include:

- repetitive small thefts from the same person, such as by an employee;
- repetitive benefit frauds of the same kind, committed in each payment period.

Where concurrent sentences are to be passed the sentence should reflect the overall criminality involved. The sentence should be appropriately aggravated by the presence of the associated offences.

Examples include:

- a single incident of dangerous driving resulting in injuries to multiple victims where there are separate charges relating to each victim. The sentences should generally be passed concurrently, but each sentence should be aggravated to take into account the harm caused;
- repetitive fraud or theft, where charged as a series of small frauds/thefts, would be

properly considered in relation to the total amount of money obtained and the period of time over which the offending took place. The sentences should generally be passed concurrently, each one reflecting the overall seriousness;

- robbery with a weapon where the weapon offence is ancillary to the robbery and is not distinct and independent of it. The principal sentence for the robbery should properly reflect the presence of the weapon. The court must avoid double-counting and may deem it preferable for the possession of the weapon's offence to run concurrently to avoid the appearance of under-sentencing in respect of the robbery.[319]

page 7 **Consecutive sentences** will ordinarily be appropriate where:..

b) offences are of the same or similar kind but where the overall criminality will not sufficiently be reflected by concurrent sentences.

Examples include:

- where offences are committed against different people, such as repeated thefts involving attacks on several different shop assistants,[320]
- where offences of domestic violence or sexual offences are committed against the same individual.

Note: There is a similar entry in the *Magistrates' Court Sentencing Guidelines Update March 2012* page 18i. Ed.

Att-Gen's Ref No 57 of 2009 2009 EWCA Crim 2555, 2010 2 Cr App R (S) 30 (p 190)[321] LCJ D pleaded to possession of two prohibited weapons, five counts of possessing ammunition and possessing an accessory to a firearm. D was minding the articles. The prosecution considered that the sentences should be consecutive to ensure an adequate sentence. Held. That would disapply well-understood sentencing principles and was a step too far. Concurrent terms should normally be imposed for offences which arise out of the same incident or transaction.

Att-Gen's Ref Nos 7-8 of 2013 Re L 2013 EWCA Crim 709, 2014 1 Cr App R (S) 26 (p 140) D was convicted of two conspiracies to defraud. The first was against the Allied Irish Bank and the second the Bank of Scotland. The Judge made the sentences concurrent. The prosecution argued that was inappropriate. Held. We do not accept that a consecutive sentence would have indicated a view that the maximum sentence for conspiracy to defraud was inadequate. On the contrary, the effect of the concurrent sentence is, in our view, to give the impression that the offenders have entirely escaped the consequences of a serious fraud in which substantial loss has resulted. It is true that the nature of the [BoS] fraud was similar and that it overlapped in time with the [AIB] conspiracy but the Bank of Scotland was a separate victim, separately targeted, and, unlike the [AIB] offence, a substantial loss was realised. We have no doubt that a consecutive sentence for the offence was required, subject to the principle of totality.

Note: This paragraph should be read in conjunction with para **18.9**. There is greater use of consecutive sentences than before. This is supported by the *TICs and Totality Guideline 2012*. The earlier cases must be seen in that light. Ed.

18.7 ***Offences that are of the same or similar kind Sexual offences***

R v AD 2013 EWCA Crim 1017 D pleaded (25%) to three indecent assault counts and two other sex offences, each with a maximum of two years. The counts were specimen counts against his niece, V. He admitted a) five digital penetrations when V was aged 12 and 13, b) penile oral penetration on seven occasions when she was aged 12 or 13, and c) placing his erect penis against her naked vagina when she was aged 13. The Judge said that he could not use consecutive sentences to subvert the statutory maximums. For two indecent assaults he received 18 months. He received 9 months for two other counts and 6 months for the third indecent assault. The sentences were made consecutive making **5**

[319] *R v Millen* 1980 2 Cr App R (S) 357

[320] *R v Jamieson and Jamieson* 2008 EWCA Crim 2761, 2009 2 Cr App R (S) 26 (p 199)

[321] This case is sometimes known as *R v Ralphs* 2009 EWCA Crim 2555.

years in all. Held. It was open to the Judge to impose consecutive sentences. He provided an appropriate balance between the competing factors. The sentence was not manifestly excessive.

18.8 ***Different victims***

R v S 2008 EWCA Crim 2827 LCJ D pleaded to two counts of buggery against a boy, an indecent assault against a girl and other sex offences. The Judge passed consecutive sentences for the two victims because D moved from one child to another in strikingly similar circumstances. Held. The Judge was entitled to pass consecutive sentences.

R v Healy 2009 EWCA Crim 2196, 2010 1 Cr App R (S) 105 (p 672) D pleaded to sexual activity in breach of trust with two different schoolgirls. The offending led to consensual full intercourse. One relationship lasted from September 2007 to January 2008 and the other lasted from February to April 2008. Held. Plainly there should be consecutive sentences.

Att-Gen's Ref No 28 of 2010 2010 EWCA Crim 1996, 2011 1 Cr App R (S) 58 (p 374) For a variety of indecent photographs and other sex offences the Judge passed concurrent sentences making 5 years in all. Held. These were all separate offences committed against separate individual children. The Judge fell into error when ordering the sentences to run concurrently. The sentence should have been **4, 4 and 8 years consecutive reduced to 12 years** because of totality.

See also: *R v Islam* 2013 EWCA Crim 2355 (Doctor. Convicted of numerous indecent assaults between 1970s and 1990s against six female patients and an employee. Gross breach of trust. Judge imposed consecutive sentences for each of the victims, totalling 11 years. Aged 71 at appeal. What mattered was the total sentence and 11 years was not manifestly excessive.)

Att-Gen's Ref 2017 Re D 2017 EWCA Crim 2509, 2018 1 Cr App R (S) 47 (p 356) D was convicted of rape and other sexual offences against two victims. Held. We make the counts concerning the different victims consecutive (6 years and 2 years) and consecutive to an 8-year extended sentence (6 years' custody 2 years' extended licence).

18.9 ***Grave cases/Maximum considered inadequate***

TICs and Totality Guideline 2012: Crown Court, see www.banksr.com Other Matters Guidelines tab page 7 **Consecutive sentences** will ordinarily be appropriate where:

b) offences are of the same or similar kind but where the overall criminality will not sufficiently be reflected by concurrent sentences.

Note: There is a similar entry in the *Magistrates' Court Sentencing Guidelines Update March 2012* page 18i. Ed.

R v Jamieson and Jamieson 2008 EWCA Crim 2761, 2009 2 Cr App R (S) 26 (p 199) D pleaded to four offences of administering a poison or noxious substance with intent (OAPA 1861 s 24) and other offences. His brother pleaded to three section 24 offences and seven thefts. They stole from shops and sprayed the security guard with acid etc. causing burns and scarring. The victims were off work for up to three months and were injured and mentally scarred. The maximum for section 24 is 5 years. The Judge imposed consecutive sentences for each of the section 24 offences. Held. The sentence should reflect the overall criminality of D and the course and nature of the offences. The imposition of concurrent sentences may not be appropriate whereas here for the section 24 offences the statutory maximum prevents proper reflection of these matters. Consecutive sentences here were fully justified and total sentences of **9 years** and **6½ years upheld.**

Att-Gen's Ref No 57 of 2009 2009 EWCA Crim 2555, 2010 2 Cr App R (S) 30 (p 190)[322] LCJ D pleaded to possession of two prohibited weapons, five counts of possessing ammunition and possessing an accessory to a firearm. He was minding the articles. The prosecution considered that the sentences should be consecutive to ensure

[322] This case is sometimes known as *R v Ralphs* 2009 EWCA Crim 2555.

an adequate sentence. Held. That would disapply well-understood sentencing principles and was a step too far. Consecutive terms should normally be imposed for offences which arise out of the same incident or transaction.
R v Delucca Re S 2010 EWCA Crim 710 S pleaded to the making etc. of extreme pornography and other offences committed over four years. He was involved in a child pornography network. The Judge started at 12 years for two arranging child pornography offences, 9 years for the making offences (concurrent to each other) and 3 years for the possession offences. She made the 12, 12 and 9 consecutive, making 33 years. The deduction for the plea was 25%, making it 25 years. The result was 12½ years' IPP. Held. To reflect the extreme pornography the terms should be consecutive. It was right to take starting points close to the maximum. The Judge's approach could not be faulted in any way.
Old cases: Best ignored.

18.10 ***Long period, Offences committed over a/Offending continued after an arrest***
Note: Some judges who want to mark the seriousness of committing offences over a long period make the sentences for offences committed during one year or one group concurrent and then make the sentences for each year or group consecutive. Some judges mark the seriousness of continuing to commit the same offences after being arrested by making the post-arrest offences consecutive to the others. If those sentences are appealed, expect the Court of Appeal to concentrate on the total sentence passed. Ed.

Specific offences

Bail offences, see the **BAIL OFFENCES** ***Consecutive or concurrent sentence for the bail and the original offence*** para at **242.3** in Volume 2.
Death by dangerous driving, see the **DEATH BY DRIVING: GENERAL PRINCIPLES** ***Concurrent or consecutive? Should the sentences be?*** para at **237.19** in Volume 2.

18.11 ***Defendant sentenced for two batches of offences at different times***
TICs and Totality Guideline 2012: Crown Court, see www.banksr.com Other Matters Guidelines tab page 9 **Offender serving a determinate sentence** (offence(s) committed before original sentence imposed) Consider what the sentence length would have been if the court had dealt with the offences at the same time and ensure that the totality of the sentence is just and proportionate in all the circumstances. If it is not, an adjustment should be made to the sentence imposed for the latest offence.
Note: There is a similar entry in the *Magistrates' Court Sentencing Guidelines Update March 2012* page 18k. Ed.
R v Hardy 2012 EWCA Crim 3110 D pleaded to child sex offences, and in April 2009 he received 6 years. They related to sex tourist offences in 2004. Following press reports he was charged with more child sex offences. In January 2012 he was convicted of indecent assault and indecency charges. The offences took place in 1988 and 1992. The Judge considered that 10 years was appropriate. He passed 8½ years concurrent to reflect the earlier sentence D would have received if all matters had been heard together in 2009. Held. The correct approach is to work out the sentence for all the offending, which is about 11 years. Now he has served over 2 years we therefore substitute 3½ years consecutive to the 6 years he was currently serving. This would ensure that he serves the equivalent of 11 years.
Note: This case was relisted. The second hearing was *R v Hardy* 2013 EWCA Crim 36. Ed.
R v O'Farrell 2014 EWCA Crim 170 D pleaded to two thefts. The offences were committed over a 3-year period beginning in 2007 but did not come to light until D had been sentenced for fraud offences committed between 2008 and 2010 (6 years 8 months). The two batches of offending were similar. The victims in the second batch reported the matters to the police when they read about the first batch. There was then a long gap before D began to reoffend (presumably in 2007). The Judge considered the 2008-2010 offences and concluded that had the first Judge been sentencing for all

offences, the sentence would have been 8½ years. With 10% credit, he imposed two concurrent sentences of 7½ years. Held. Taking account of the 18 months D had spent in custody for the 2008-2010 offences, D had served the equivalent of a 3-year sentence when the Judge sentenced him to 7½ years. Therefore, the total was 10½ years. The correct approach was to ask whether 10½ years after deductions for the pleas was manifestly excessive. [Although the police did not know about the offences], when sentenced for the 2008-2010 offences, D had the opportunity to ask for the 2007 offences to be taken into consideration. He did not. It was entirely appropriate for a lengthy sentence to be imposed. 10½ years was too long. The sentences for the two counts of theft would be 6½ years not 7½ years, concurrent.
See also: *R v C* 2013 EWCA Crim 1815 (Cases reviewed (but not *R v Hardy* 2012). The approach will vary from case to case.)
For more details see the **THEFT *Victim over 65*** para at **344.45** in Volume 2.

18.12 ***Driving offences***
TICs and Totality Guideline 2012: Crown Court, see www.banksr.com Other Matters Guidelines tab page 6 **Concurrent sentences** will ordinarily be appropriate where: a) offences arise out of the same incident or facts.
Examples include: i) a single incident of dangerous driving resulting in injuries to multiple victims.[323]
Note: There is a similar entry in the *Magistrates' Court Sentencing Guidelines Update March 2012* page 18h. Ed.
R v Hardy 2005 EWCA Crim 3097, 2006 2 Cr App R (S) 4 (p 47) D pleaded at the Magistrates' Court to dangerous driving, failing to provide a specimen and driving while disqualified. A woman had an argument with someone[324] who was drunk, and he drove off in a white van. She flagged down police officers, who found a van outside a kebab shop. Inside the shop D was waving his arms about. That day he had been angry and aggressive and had taken seven of his Valium tablets to control his behaviour. He was also under the influence of alcohol and cannabis. Staff contacted the officers and D drove off with the police in chase with lights and siren on. At one stage they were almost level with him and he swerved at them. He made two severe left turns and drove the wrong way up a one-way street and straight through some red traffic lights without braking. His speed was 60-70 mph in 30 and 40 mph limits. He was caught in a cul-de-sac. A police officer said it was the worst driving he had seen in 18 years' service. At the station D said he was 'pissed' and that he was going to keep on driving until he hurt someone. He refused to supply a specimen. He was aged 39 with convictions dating back to 1986 involving violence. In 2002 he was sentenced to 6 weeks' imprisonment for excess alcohol. Six months later he was convicted of racially threatening words or behaviour. He received **18 months** for the driving, 3 months for the disqualified driving and 3 months for failing to provide a specimen. All were consecutive making **2 years**. The defence argued they should be concurrent. Held. We do not dissent from the general proposition that sentences arising out of the same incident should be concurrent. However, here it would be bizarre if he could drive while disqualified and with excess alcohol without any extra penalty. It is well established that in circumstances of this kind consecutive sentences should usually be imposed, *R v Wheatley* 1983 5 Cr App R (S) 417 and *R v Lawrence* 1989 11 Cr App R (S) 580. We have no hesitation in saying that the sentence was not excessive.
R v Roberts 2012 EWCA Crim 662 D pleaded to aggravated vehicle-taking, dangerous driving, no insurance and no licence. A JCB was stolen and was used to ram the gates of commercial premises to steal an expensive piece of machinery. A short while later the JCB was spotted by police. D was driving it at about 10 mph. When D saw the police he stopped and reversed into the front of a police van. The van was damaged. D drove off,

[323] *R v Lawrence* 1989 11 Cr App R (S) 580
[324] There is no reference to the Judge having found that this person was D. Whether it was D is not clear.

drove over a grass verge and turned the vehicle round so it was facing the police van. D jumped off and the JCB crashed into a parked car and a tree. D was on licence and heavily convicted. Held. Because of the way the particulars were drafted, the vehicle-taking was part of the same incident as the dangerous driving. Consecutive sentences were wrong.

R v Jenkins 2015 EWCA Crim 105, 1 Cr App R (S) 70 (p 491) D pleaded guilty to two counts of causing serious injury by dangerous driving. He collided with a car on the other side of the road and severely injured the two occupants. Held. It was a single act of dangerous driving. The Judge should not have passed consecutive sentences. *R v Noble* 2002 EWCA Crim 1713, 2003 1 Cr App R (S) 65 (p 312) applied.

R v Naeem 2018 EWCA Crim 2938 D pleaded to dangerous driving, disqualified driving, drug driving (four times over the cocaine limit), failing to stop and no insurance. He was sentenced on 26 February 2018. In September 2017, he drove a stolen car and at some stage saw the police. In a police chase, he drove at speeds up to 118 mph and weaved in and out of cars. D only stopped when he crashed into a wall. He fled and was arrested. D was now aged 34 with 51 convictions on 23 occasions. Many of the convictions were for motoring offences including disqualified driving and two drink/drive offences. They included in May 2017, drug driving (fine and 12 months' disqualification); in November 2017, TDA, driving whilst disqualified and no insurance (18 weeks suspended and 28 months' disqualification); and in January 2018, driving whilst disqualified and no insurance (18 weeks plus the 18 weeks suspended sentence activated in full making 36 weeks). The magistrates took a plea to the no insurance and imposed a fine but treated the fine paid because of one day served. The rest of the offences were committed for sentence. The Judge found the driving dangerous in the extreme and considered it lucky that no one was killed. Further the offences were committed shortly after D had been disqualified. The Judge started with the maximum for the three main offences and gave a full plea discount. That made 16 months, 4 months and 4 months. He gave no penalty for the no insurance [although it had not been committed for sentence]. That made 24 months. He made that consecutive to the sentence D was serving. At the invitation of prosecution counsel, he made the disqualification 2 years and 3 years consecutive. Held. The 8 months in total for the two summary only offences was unlawful as the maximum is 6 months. Following the *TICs and Totality Guideline 2012: Crown Court* page 6, as the offences arose out of the same incident all the sentences should be concurrent. The consecutive disqualification was unlawful. The disqualification was not extended. No one at the Crown Court mentioned that two of the offences carried minimum disqualification terms (3 years and 1 year). No one mentioned that an order for disqualification until a test was passed was obligatory for dangerous driving. We impose that order. We are unable to extend the disqualification beyond the 5 years as we cannot rearrange the disqualification without treating D more severely. So, 5 years' disqualification for the drug driving and the dangerous driving and 2 years' disqualification for the driving whilst disqualified, all concurrent. There should have been an endorsement on the no insurance count, so we order that.

Note: I doubt this is an authority for any legal principle except that the application of the law in the courts is in disarray. It is listed to show the pitfalls judges and others can fall into. If the transcript is accurate (which I doubt), there are the following errors. I think TDA or theft of the car should have been charged. The vehicle had false plates and D fled when he saw the police. **Magistrates Court** I can't see why the fine for the serious offence of driving with no insurance was remitted. D could have paid it from savings or applied for time to pay on his release. In any event the Court was obliged to make a collection order. I think the better course would have been to commit the offence for sentence under Powers of Criminal Courts (Sentencing) Act 2000 s 6(2). **Crown Court** 1) The unlawful 4 months and 4 months consecutive which exceeded the maximum sentence. 2) The passing of an order for the no insurance when the matter had not been committed. 3) The failure to pass a sentence for the failing to stop. 4) The failure to address the issue of the two minimum sentences. 5) The failure to extend the disqualification. 6) The failure to pass a disqualification until test is passed order. I think the Court was right to pass consecutive sentences. **Court of Appeal** 1) It is arguable whether the three driving offences arose out of the same incident because two of them started when D began to drive. The dangerous driving is only known to have occurred when D saw the police. But even if it arose out of the same incident, I do not see any reason why the gravity of the three serious offences cannot be marked by consecutive sentences, like armed robbery where the gravity of using a firearm is marked by a consecutive sentence. The guideline only says sentences for matters arising out of the same incident should normally receive concurrent sentences. There is no rule that says you can commit an offence which enables you to commit two more different offences without any extra penalty. The principles are set out at para **18.5** (which deals with the exceptions), para **18.9** (which deals with cases where the maximum is inadequate) and *R v Hardy* 2005, *R v Kirkland* 2004 and *R v Shafi* 2007. The other cases in this paragraph I consider *per incuriam* and should not be followed. 2) The Court misunderstood its powers under section 11(3). They considered that the test was whether the new disqualification orders treated D 'more severely' for the disqualification. They should have considered whether the sentences taken as a whole treated the defendant more severely. 3) They altered the penalty for the no insurance, which had not been committed for sentence. Ed.

See also: *R v Kirkland* 2004 EWCA Crim 2951 (Aggravated vehicle-taking. It is one thing to drive whilst disqualified and another thing to take a vehicle unlawfully. Consecutive sentences were justified.)

R v Shafi 2007 EWCA Crim 2179 (Aggravated vehicle-taking and driving whilst disqualified were properly consecutive.)

R v Aldhain 2018 EWCA Crim 1359 (Dangerous driving and driving whilst disqualified were properly consecutive, because the disobedience of the court's order is separate from the underlying offence.)

Firearms, see the **FIREARM OFFENCES** ***Consecutive or concurrent to other firearm offences*** para at **262.66** in Volume 2.

18.13 ***Historical offending***

R v Clifford 2014 EWCA Crim 2245, 2015 1 Cr App R (S) 32 (p 242) D was convicted of eight indecent assaults against B, C, D and E. The maximum sentence for each was 2 years. D received 4½ years for four offences against B, 6 months for one offence against C, 21 months for two offences against D and 15 months for one offence against E. All were consecutive, making 8 years in all. For two of the offences against B, the maximum was passed on each and they were made concurrent to each other. Held. The Judge could not pass a sentence on a count greater than the then maximum. The Judge was entitled to structure his sentence by imposing consecutive sentences, which would reflect the overall criminality involved according to modern standards and attitudes. Moreover, the use of consecutive sentences was consistent with the *TICs and Totality Guideline 2012*. Passing the maximum for two offences when the offending was not the worst imaginable was permissible as the Judge could have given 1 year on each and made the sentences consecutive. There could be no appeal for that so there is no appeal for the two concurrent sentences. The overall sentence was correct.

See also: *Att-Gen's Ref No 75 of 2015* 2015 EWCA Crim 2116, 2016 1 Cr App R (S) 61 (p 439) (D was convicted of three counts of indecent assault. The offences related to almost 'continuous' oral sex on his partner's daughter aged between 5 and 9. Held. The Judge should not have felt restricted by the 10-year maximum for the offence. We keep the specimen count at 9 years but make the other two offences 5 years consecutive, making 14 years in all.)

Manslaughter, see the **MANSLAUGHTER** ***Concurrent or consecutive sentences Should the sentence be concurrent or consecutive to the sentence for the illegal activity?*** para at **221.29** in Volume 2.

Money laundering, see the **MONEY LAUNDERING** ***Concurrent or consecutive? Should the sentence be*** para at **285.10** in Volume 2.
Rape, see the **RAPE AND ASSAULT BY PENETRATION** ***Series of rapes/Campaign of rape Concurrent or consecutive sentences*** para at **314.63** in Volume 2.
Robbery, see the **ROBBERY** ***Firearm, With Consecutive or concurrent sentences*** para at **319.17** in Volume 2.

Specific sentences

18.14 ***Defendant serving a determinate sentence***
Powers of Criminal Courts (Sentencing) Act 2000 s 154(1) A sentence imposed by the Crown Court shall take effect from the beginning of the day on which it is imposed unless the court otherwise directs.
TICs and Totality Guideline 2012: Crown Court, see www.banksr.com Other Matters Guidelines tab page 9 **Offender serving a determinate sentence** (offence(s) committed before original sentence imposed). Consider what the sentence length would have been if the court had dealt with the offences at the same time and ensure that the totality of the sentence is just and proportionate in all the circumstances. If it is not, an adjustment should be made to the sentence imposed for the latest offence.
Note: There is a similar entry in the *Magistrates' Court Sentencing Guidelines Update March 2012* page 18k. Ed.
R v Sparkes 2011 EWCA Crim 880 D pleaded to two burglaries, aggravated vehicle-taking and two thefts, all of which were committed while he was on bail. With another, he entered two occupied houses and stole the keys to two high-performance cars. D, aged 28, had a number of convictions for burglary. He was then sentenced to 5 years for earlier burglaries. Held. Giving D the appropriate discount for his late pleas of guilty in this and the first cases, the overall sentences should have totalled 6½ years. But unquestionably, the sentences for the instant offences had to be consecutive. If the minimum term were applied consecutively, the totality principle would be breached. Therefore it would be unjust to impose consecutive sentences of 3 years for the instant offences. 18 months concurrent to each other but consecutive to his existing 5-year sentence.
R v Thompson 2012 EWCA Crim 1764 D pleaded to burglary and theft. He received 32 months, in part because of his bad record. He was visited in prison by police and invited to help them 'clear the books'. He admitted stealing motorcycles and pedal cycles. He was charged with six thefts and asked for 68 TICs to be considered. Some were as old as 2007. Two-thirds were old. He pleaded at the first opportunity and was only given a 25% discount. He received 3 years concurrent with the earlier sentence. Held. This called for a significant downward adjustment because he had provided the evidence against himself. The only explanation we can think of is that the Judge was concentrating on a rather difficult back calculation from the eventual release date. D must have at least a 33% discount. The best way is to ask what sentence would have been imposed if all matters were dealt with on the first occasion. That would have been about 3 years 4 months. We consider the release dates and substitute 2 years.
See also: *R v Chaplin* 2015 EWCA Crim 1491, 2016 1 Cr App R (S) 10 (p 63) (Long delay because of co-defendant's trial which stopped both matters being sentenced at the same time. Sentence reduced from 18 months to 9 months consecutive because of totality.)

18.15 ***Defendant serving consecutive sentences already***
Criminal Practice Directions 2015 EWCA Crim 1567 para VII E.2 If a defendant is, at the time of sentence, already serving two or more consecutive terms of imprisonment and the court intends to increase the total period of imprisonment, it should use the expression 'consecutive to the total period of imprisonment to which you are already

subject' rather than 'at the expiration of the term of imprisonment you are now serving', as the defendant may not then be serving the last of the terms to which he is already subject.

R v Holland 2015 EWCA Crim 1753, 2016 1 Cr App R (S) 19 (p 139) D was serving two 9-year concurrent sentences which were made consecutive to a 4-year sentence, making 13 years in all. The Judge sentenced him to a 5-year sentence consecutive 'to the sentence which you are currently serving'. Held. The sentence imposed of 5 years was consecutive not to an overall sentence of 13 years, but rather to the first sentence of 9 years' custody. That means his new sentence would increase the total term to 14 years not 18. Appeal dismissed.

Note: This seems a needless trap for sentencing judges. In most other contexts the authorities treat consecutive sentences as one total term. Ed.

18.16 ***Defendant serving a determinate sentence New offence requires a life sentence***

TICs and Totality Guideline 2012: Crown Court, see www.banksr.com Other Matters Guidelines tab page 11 **Indeterminate sentence** (where the offender is already serving an existing determinate sentence) It is generally undesirable to order an indeterminate sentence to be served consecutively to any other period of imprisonment on the basis that indeterminate sentences should start on their imposition.[325] The court should instead order the sentence to run concurrently but can adjust the minimum term for the new offence to reflect half of any period still remaining to be served under the existing sentence (to take account of the early release provisions for determinate sentences). The court should then review the minimum term to ensure that the total sentence is just and proportionate.

R v Haywood 2000 2 Cr App R (S) 418 LCJ D was sentenced to 8 years for robbery. Two days later he attacked a prison officer and then pleaded to section 18 wounding. That carried automatic life. The Judge considered that 7 years was the notional determinate period and added that to the 8 years, making 15 years. This he halved to make the minimum period to be served. Held. The Judge took a logical and sensible step. Otherwise virtually nothing would have been added to the sentence D was already serving.

R v O'Brien 2006 EWCA Crim 1741 There is no provision which forbids the imposition of an indeterminate sentence to another period of imprisonment. Applying *R v Haywood* 2000 (see above) it is better to increase the notional term rather than the specified minimum term. We share the view expressed in *R v Jones* 1962 (see above) that it is undesirable to impose consecutive indeterminate sentences or order an indeterminate sentence to be served consecutively to another period of imprisonment. Common sense suggests that a sentence of imprisonment or of IPP starts immediately on its imposition. Given the difficulties that may be encountered already in determining when a prisoner must be released or is eligible for parole, it is much easier not to compound those difficulties by making indeterminate sentences consecutive to other sentences or periods in custody.

R v Ashes 2007 EWCA Crim 1848, 2008 1 Cr App R (S) 86 (p 507) D pleaded to aggravated burglary. He served 82 days on remand and was then sentenced to 26 months' imprisonment for dangerous driving and contempt. 128 days later he was sentenced for the aggravated burglary. The Judge took 7 years as the notional term and took into account the amount that was left to serve on the driving matter and sentenced him to 4½ years' IPP and deducted 210 days (i.e. both periods). Held. The court should try to impose a term for a sentence for public protection which is concurrent with the existing determinate sentence but which also takes account of: a) the period still then remaining to be served under the existing determinate term: that should be the period of the sentence still to be served but then halved to take account of the automatic release

325 *R v O'Brien* 2006 EWCA Crim 1741

provisions for determinate sentences, b) the appropriate additional period as the sentence for the offence in respect of which the Court was minded to impose a term of IPP, which should then be halved, and c) the need to ensure that the total of the sentences imposed under a) and b) above does not offend the principle of totality. We stress that the sentencing Judge should bear in mind that the period imposed in the sentence for public protection is the period which the offender must serve before he or she is considered for parole, and that means that the constituent period to be taken into account for ascertaining the determinate sentence at stage a) above is the period remaining to be served (which is now one-half of the sentence) rather than the total sentence imposed. The Judge should have taken the period he had served (128 days) and doubled it to take into account the release provisions. That should then be deducted from the 26-month sentence which would be the amount he has left to serve on the driving matter. We round that down to 17 months left to serve. That should have been added to the 7-year notional term to give 8 years 5 months. That should then be divided in two, making 4 years 2½ months. Only 82 days qualify to be deducted because he was a serving prisoner for the other days. That should then be deducted from the 4 years 2½ months. This is more than was imposed, so the appeal is dismissed.

18.17 *Defendant serving a life sentence New offence requires a determinate sentence*

TICs and Totality Guideline 2012: Crown Court, see www.banksr.com Other Matters Guidelines tab page 11 **Ordering a determinate sentence to run consecutively to an indeterminate sentence** The court can order a determinate sentence to run consecutively to an indeterminate sentence. The determinate sentence will commence on the expiry of the minimum term of the indeterminate sentence and the offender will become eligible for a parole review after serving half of the determinate sentence.[326] The court should consider the total sentence that the offender will serve before becoming eligible for consideration for release. If this is not just and proportionate, the court can reduce the length of the determinate sentence or, alternatively, can order the second sentence to be served concurrently.

Note: There is a similar entry in the *Magistrates' Court Sentencing Guidelines Update March 2012* page 18n. Ed.

Dangerous Offenders Guide see www.banksr.com Other Matters Guidelines tab para 10.1 The Sentencing Guidelines Council has issued a guide to sentencing other counts in IPP and life cases. This is not a definitive guideline.

R v Hills and Others 2008 EWCA Crim 1871, 2009 1 Cr App R (S) 75 (p 441) H was serving DPP and before the minimum term expired he threw hot water in a prison officer's face and hit him with an aluminium flask. He had already received a concurrent sentence for attempting to escape. The Judge considered that 3 years was appropriate and considered that a concurrent sentence would be inappropriate. The Judge passed a consecutive sentence to start on the completion of the minimum term. Held. Where the minimum term has not been served the appropriate guidance is in *R v O'Brien 2006* EWCA Crim 1741 (see the last paragraph). The Judge was entitled to pass the sentence he did.

See also: *R v Taylor* 2011 EWCA Crim 2236, 2012 1 Cr App R (S) 75 (p 421) (D was sentenced to life for murder and when in prison committed three ABHs and three common assaults on officers. It is not unlawful to impose a determinate 3-year sentence consecutive to a mandatory life minimum term of 23 years.)

18.18 *Defendant serving a life sentence New life sentence considered*

TICs and Totality Guideline 2012: Crown Court, see www.banksr.com Other Matters Guidelines tab page 11 **Indeterminate sentence** (where the offender is already serving an existing indeterminate sentence) It is generally undesirable to order an indeterminate

[326] Crime (Sentences) Act 1997 s 28(1B)

sentence to be served consecutively to any other period of imprisonment on the basis that indeterminate sentences should start on their imposition. However, where necessary the court can order an indeterminate sentence to run consecutively to an indeterminate sentence passed on an earlier occasion.[327] The second sentence will commence on the expiration of the minimum term of the original sentence and the offender will become eligible for a parole review after serving both minimum terms.[328] The court should consider the length of the aggregate minimum terms that must be served before the offender will be eligible for consideration by the Parole Board. If this is not just and proportionate, the court can adjust the minimum term.

Note: There is a similar entry in the *Magistrates' Court Sentencing Guidelines Update March 2012* page 18n. Ed.

R v O'Brien 2006 EWCA Crim 1741 There is no provision which forbids the imposition of consecutive indeterminate sentences or the imposition of an indeterminate sentence to another period of imprisonment. Applying *R v Haywood* 2000 (see above) it is better to increase the notional term rather than the specified minimum term. We share the view expressed in *R v Jones* 1962 (see above) that it is undesirable to impose consecutive indeterminate sentences or order an indeterminate sentence to be served consecutively to another period of imprisonment. Common sense suggests that a sentence of imprisonment or of IPP starts immediately on its imposition. Given the difficulties that may be encountered already in determining when a prisoner must be released or is eligible for parole, it is much easier not to compound those difficulties by making indeterminate sentences consecutive to other sentences or periods in custody. Where the judge wants the period left before the defendant can apply for parole to be reflected in the sentence, the judge should increase the term to reflect that period.

R v Ashes 2007 EWCA Crim 1848, 2008 1 Cr App R (S) 86 (p 507) In cases in which the appropriate sentence would be a consecutive sentence to the sentence for public protection, there is a serious problem because a sentencing judge considering imposing such a sentence does not know when the existing sentence for public protection will expire, as the judge cannot predict when the Parole Board will agree to release the offender. A further difficulty is that even if the offender might be safe for release at the end of the sentence for public protection, there is no guarantee that such offender will also be safe to be released at the end of any consecutive determinate sentence. Thus problems arise, first, as to how to shape a sentence that would overcome this difficulty and, second, in ascertaining the date when the sentence for public protection ends and when the determinate sentence starts. There are three possible approaches depending on the circumstances: a) if the subsequent offence is one for which a sentence of imprisonment for public protection is available, then the sentencing judge could pass a new sentence of imprisonment for public protection so as to take account of not only the balance yet to be served of the existing minimum term but also the principle of totality, b) if the offence with which the sentence is concerned is 'associated' with the offence for which the sentence of imprisonment for public protection was passed, one other option might be to adjust the minimum term of the sentence for public protection to reflect the criminality of that extra offence but to give no separate sentence for the new offence (see section 226(1) of the 2003 Act), or c) the judge could order that the determinate sentence be served first and the sentence for public protection be served consecutively, but only if he were dealing with them on the same occasion. Adopting *R v C* 2007 EWCA Crim 680, 2007 2 Cr App R (S) 98 (p 627) in shaping the overall sentence, judges should remember that there is no obligation for the sentences to be expressed in historical date order. There is nothing wrong with stating that the sentence for the first offence in point of time should be served consecutively to a sentence or sentences imposed for any later

[327] *R v Hills and Others* 2008 EWCA Crim 1871, 2009 1 Cr App R (S) 75 (p 441) and *R v Ashes* 2007 EWCA Crim 1848, 2008 1 Cr App R (S) 86 (p 507)

[328] Crime (Sentences) Act 1997 s 28(1B)

offence or offences. Our provisional view is that, when dealing on a subsequent occasion with a further offence, the sentencing court should impose an appropriate concurrent sentence, be it determinate, indeterminate or extended, depending on the circumstances. In any event, the Parole Board would be able to take into consideration the subsequent offence in determining whether to release the offender.
Note: The references to IPP have not been removed in case part of the context is lost. Ed.
R v Hills and Others Re D 2008 EWCA Crim 1871, 2009 1 Cr App R (S) 75 (p 441) D was serving a life sentence and had four years of the minimum term left. He awaited sentence for other sexual offences. The Judge considered 10 years was the appropriate determinate sentence. The Judge passed a life sentence with a minimum term of 9 years made up of half the 10 years and the 4 years outstanding. Held. Where the minimum term has not been served, the appropriate guidance is in *R v O'Brien* 2006 (see above). It is agreed the approach was proper.
R v MJ 2012 EWCA Crim 132, 2 Cr App R (S) 73 (p 416) LCJ The principle established in *R v Smith* 2011 UKSC 37 is that, following the coming into force of the amendments to Criminal Justice Act 2003 s 225 inserted by Criminal Justice and Immigration Act 2008, it is neither unlawful nor wrong in principle for an indeterminate sentence to be imposed on an offender who is already subject to and serving an earlier indeterminate sentence.
See also: *R v Lane* 2010 EWCA Crim 1376 (First IPP term over but no release. Judge ordered 2-year extension for offence in prison but did not say when it should start. Held. It should start on the date of sentence.)
R v Jeter 2015 EWCA Crim 1804 (In 2008 given a 27-year-term for murder. Convicted of two attempted murders on prison staff. Worth 26 years so 13 years minimum term needed to be added to term left to serve. New 34-year minimum term made. Upheld.)

18.19 ***Disqualification from driving***
R v Kent 1983 5 Cr App R (S) 171 Disqualifications cannot be consecutive to one another.
R v Holmes 2018 EWCA Crim 131 D pleaded to dangerous driving and other offences. The Judge sentenced him to 8 months in all and two concurrent periods of disqualification, which he made consecutive to the disqualification he was given on a previous occasion. Held. Disqualification under Road Traffic Offenders Act 1988 s 34 must take effect immediately and cannot be postponed. The order making them consecutive was unlawful, so that part is quashed. The Judge failed to apply the extension rules. There is nothing we can do about that.
For ***Extended sentences*** see the **Extended Sentences** ***Consecutive extended sentences*** paras at **56.78**.

18.20 ***Licence Defendant released on licence***
TICs and Totality Guideline 2012: Crown Court, see www.banksr.com Other Matters Guidelines tab
page 9 **Offender serving a determinate sentence but released from custody**
Approach The new sentence should start on the day it is imposed: Criminal Justice Act 2003 s 265 prohibits a sentence of imprisonment running consecutively to a sentence from which a prisoner has been released. The sentence for the new offence will take into account the aggravating feature that it was committed on licence. However, it must be commensurate with the new offence and cannot be artificially inflated with a view to ensuring that the offender serves a period in custody additional to the recall period (which will be an unknown quantity in most cases).[329] This is so even if the new sentence will, in consequence, add nothing to the period actually served.
Note: There is a similar entry in the *Magistrates' Court Sentencing Guidelines Update March 2012* page 18k. Ed.

[329] *R v Costello* 2010 EWCA Crim 371, 2 Cr App R (S) 94 (p 608)

18.21 ***Licence Defendant serving a sentence for a revoked licence/Defendant's licence would have started by sentence***

Criminal Justice Act 2003 s 265(1) A court sentencing a person to a term of imprisonment may not order or direct that the term is to commence on the expiry of any other sentence of imprisonment from which he has been released:

(a) under this Chapter, or

(b) under Criminal Justice Act 1991 Part 2.[330]

(2) In this section 'sentence of imprisonment' includes a sentence of detention under Powers of Criminal Courts (Sentencing) Act 2000 s 91 or 96,[331] or Criminal Justice Act 2003 s 227 or 228,[332] or a sentence of detention in a Young Offender Institution under Powers of Criminal Courts (Sentencing) Act 2000 s 96 or under Criminal Justice Act 2003 s 226A, 226B, 227,[333] and 'term of imprisonment' is to be read accordingly.

R v Tahid 2009 EWCA Crim 221 D served his custodial sentence for murder and was released on licence. He committed a drug offence and his licence was revoked. D pleaded to supplying heroin and was given 3½ years. The defence asked for the time he had spent in prison before sentence to be taken into account. Held. We reject this suggestion out of hand.

R v Young 2009 EWCA Crim 2077 D pleaded to harassment, was given 3 months' detention and made subject to a Restraining Order prohibiting contact with his former girlfriend. He breached the order and the Judge gave him a 12-month YOI, suspended for 6 months. D was recalled to the Young Offender Institution for 4 months. Held. We bear in mind the recall, which was a direct consequence of the commission of the offence, and consider the sentence was manifestly excessive. 6 months not 12.

R v Costello 2010 EWCA Crim 371, 2 Cr App R (S) 94 (p 608) D was recalled to serve 18 months of his licence. The Judge needed to sentence D for an ABH which he considered merited 12 months. He passed an inflated sentence of 31 months to ensure that D served an extra 6 months. Held by the Vice-President considering all the conflicting authority. If a defendant is returned to prison, he or she can be released before the expiry of the full term. The problem is not so much section 265(1), which was introduced to provide certainty of sentence for the prison authorities, but the repeal of Powers of Criminal Courts (Sentencing) Act 2000 s 116 (the power to order the period of return should be served before the new sentence). That repeal, the uncertainty of the effect of administrative recall and the rule in Criminal Justice Act 2003 s 153(2) (duty to pass the shortest term commensurate) means the Judge is not able to pass an inflated sentence. Sentence reduced to 12 months.

Note: Where a defendant was sentenced before 24 March 2005 and then breaches his or her licence, the court can order licence recall, which can be ordered to run consecutively, Powers of Criminal Courts (Sentencing) Act 2000 s 116-117 and Criminal Justice Act 2003 (Commencement No 8 and Transitional and Saving Provisions) Order 2005 2005/950. For an example and analysis see *R v Smith* 2013 EWCA Crim 167. Ed.

R v Cooney 2013 EWCA Crim 1111 D was recalled to prison and then escaped. He surrendered and was given 3 months consecutive to the recall sentence. The Judge considered that section 265 did not apply as the offence was committed after the recall sentence had started. Held. The section was not so limited. Courts will often be unable to impose any effective penalty. There is an urgent need to reform this section. Appeal allowed.

R v Hookway and Others 2015 EWCA 931, 2 Cr App R (S) 43 (p 337) H, M and J pleaded to a security guard robbery. At the time of the offence, H and M were serving

[330] As substituted by Criminal Justice and Immigration Act 2008 s 20(4)(a)

[331] Words inserted by Legal Aid, Sentencing and Punishment of Offenders Act 2012 s 117(9)(a)

[332] Words inserted by Legal Aid, Sentencing and Punishment of Offenders Act 2012 s 117(9)(b). Criminal Justice and Courts Act 2015 Sch 1 para 24 adds 'or 236A'. In force 13/4/15, Criminal Justice and Courts Act 2015 (Commencement No 1, Saving and Transitional Provisions) Order 2015 2015/778 para 3 and Sch 1 para 72

[333] Words inserted by Legal Aid, Sentencing and Punishment of Offenders Act 2012 Sch 20 para 13

prisoners on day release and J was released on licence. By the time H and M were sentenced, the conditional release date had passed. Had it not been for the fact that the two were remanded into custody prior to sentence, they would have been released from prison. For H and M, the Judge gave sentences consecutive to the sentences they were serving. J was given a concurrent sentence. Held. Because the present offence was committed whilst they were both serving prison sentences, neither of them was subject to administrative recall by the Secretary of State pursuant to Criminal Justice Act 2003 s 254 and, because such recall had not occurred by the time they were sentenced for the present offences, they must be taken to have been released from the earlier sentences. As we see it, the position can be tested in this way. In the absence of any administrative recall, there is no power to detain H and M in prison pursuant to the original sentences until some date in 2017, after which point the present sentences will commence. If there is no such power then H and M can only be held in prison pursuant to the sentences in the present case, so those sentences must run once they are passed. Therefore the Judge was unable to order the sentences to be consecutive.

R v Clancy 2016 EWCA Crim 471 D was given 5 years' extended sentence (4 years' custody 1 year's extended licence) for ABH. He was released and recalled. He then falsely imprisoned a prison officer and pleaded guilty to that offence. The Judge passed a sentence of 32 months, consecutive to the extended sentence. The Judge had been wrongly told the defendant was still serving the custodial term of the sentence. Held. The Judge failed to consider Criminal Justice Act 2003 s 265, which prohibits consecutive sentences to the licence period. The new term will run from the date of sentence.

See also: *R v Carruthers* 2016 EWCA Crim 912 (D was sentenced to 4 weeks consecutive to the recall term. When told that was not possible, the Judge increased it to 24 weeks. Held. That was a commendable approach in terms of overall justice but contrary to the law. 4 weeks restored.)

Earlier cases: Ignore them. Ed.

18.22 *Licence recall and delay/Waiting for co-defendant's trial to end*

R v Phillips and Kalychurn 2015 EWCA Crim 427, 2 Cr App R (S) 9 (p 96) In 2012, P was released on licence for a 4-year robbery sentence. In January 2013, he was charged with an offence and was recalled. In July 2013, he was acquitted of the new offence but remained in custody. In August 2013, he committed an affray in prison because he was upset at not being allowed to attend his grandfather's funeral. Parole was refused because investigations were needed. In January 2014, he was interviewed about the affray. In August 2014, he was charged with the affray. In October 2014, he pleaded to the affray. In December 2014, he was sentenced and the Judge thought 12 months was suitable but reduced the sentence because of the licence problems. The defence argued that the matter he had been recalled for had not been proved and he had been on recall for nearly 2 years and most of that was because of the delay by the prosecution. In September 2013, K was charged with robbery and his licence was revoked. In January 2014, the robbery was dismissed and he pleaded to conspiracy to commit aggravated burglary. He asked to be sentenced straight away but that was refused because of a co-defendant's trial. He waited until August 2014 to be sentenced. When sentenced he had been on recall for nearly one year. Held. A court is able, using its discretion, to reduce an otherwise appropriate sentence to do justice, for example where there has been excessive delay, *R v Kerrigan and Another* 2014 EWCA Crim 2348, 2015 1 Cr App R (S) 29 (p 221). Here the situation was of the defendant's own making. The delay was obviously not excessive.

Note: Many would think the delay was excessive and the injustice clear. Ed.

R v Walker 2018 EWCA Crim 1018 D was serving an IPP sentence. He was released and recalled to prison, so for a new offence the remand period from that date didn't count. He pleaded at an early stage. He could not be sentenced until the co-defendant's trial had taken place, which was 10 months after his plea. Held. It was clearly the intention of

Parliament that periods on recall should not normally count. Had there not been a co-defendant's trial he would have been sentenced earlier. We want to reflect that period so we reduce the 30 month sentence by 20 months [so the sentence was the same as it would have been if he had been sentenced when he pleaded.]

See also the **CONCURRENT AND CONSECUTIVE SENTENCES *Licence Defendant released on licence*** para at **18.20**.

For the approach for remand time in ***Life sentences***, see **74.15**, and in murder cases, see **287.90** in Volume 2.

18.23 *Minimum sentences*

TICs and Totality Guideline 2012: Crown Court, see www.banksr.com Other Matters Guidelines tab page 7 **Consecutive sentences** will ordinarily be appropriate where:

a) [Offences arising out of the same incident or facts, see **18.4**]

b) [Offences of the same or similar kind, see **18.6**]

c) one or more offence(s) qualifies for a statutory minimum sentence and concurrent sentences would improperly undermine that minimum.[334]

However, it is not permissible to impose consecutive sentences for offences committed at the same time in order to evade the statutory maximum penalty.[335]

Note: There is a similar entry in the *Magistrates' Court Sentencing Guidelines Update March 2012* page 18i.

R v Asif 2018 EWCA Crim 2297, 2019 1 Cr App R (S) 26 (p 173) D pleaded to class A drug offences (10½ years), three firearm offences, which carried minimum terms, and possession of ammunition. The firearms were found in D's car and the single round of ammunition was found in D's home. The Judge passed 7 years, 7 years concurrent and 3 years concurrent on the firearm counts. He passed 3 years 4 months consecutive on the ammunition count. He made the three groups of sentences consecutive making 20 years 10 months in all. The defence relied on *Att-Gen's Ref No 57 of 2009* 2009 EWCA Crim 2555, 2010 2 Cr App R (S) 30 (p 190). Held. That case has not been followed where the firearms had been acquired at different times or stored at different locations, see *R v Gibbin* 2014 EWCA Crim 115, 2 Cr App R (S) 28 (229) and *R v Ullah* 2017 EWCA Crim 584. Here we must impose concurrent sentences, making 17 years two months in all. To do otherwise would be an improper attempt to circumvent the maximum stipulated by Parliament.

Note: Suppose a mother stored one firearm, to which a minimum sentence applied, and although she had very powerful mitigation, she was just unable to show exceptional circumstances. If she pleaded very early, she would receive 5 years. Suppose a lifelong criminal, with previous convictions for storing large numbers of prohibited weapons, pleaded to possession of 100 prohibited weapons. Those weapons would inevitably be passed on to criminals. Suppose he too pleaded early and this rule was applied. He would be likely to receive 10 years (the maximum) less the discount, which makes 6 years 8 months on each concurrent. The 1 year 8 months' difference between the two sentences is truly absurd. Frequently two important legal principles clash. Here the suggested clash is between the normal rule about consecutive sentences and the need for adequate sentences for those who supply very dangerous weapons to criminals so they can kill, maim and terrorise others with them. There can be no doubt about which principle Parliament would consider the more important to apply. The Judge's task is to apply his or her oath of office, which is 'do justice'. In fact, I suggest the line of cases at para **262.66** in Volume 2 is wrongly decided, because both the *TICs and Totality Guideline 2012* page 7 and non-firearm past cases show that where the overall criminality is not met by concurrent sentences, consecutive sentences are appropriate, see **18.9**. The guideline only says sentences for matters arising out of the same incident

334 *R v Raza* 2009 EWCA Crim 1413, 2010 1 Cr App R (S) 56 (p 354)

335 *R v Ralphs* 2009 EWCA Crim 2555 This case is usually referred to as *Att-Gen's Ref No 57 of 2009* 2009 EWCA Crim 2555, 2010 2 Cr App R (S) 30 (p 190).

should normally receive concurrent sentences. The Court said that para 5 was qualified by para 7, which must be an example of the Court choosing the wrong alternative and losing sight of justice. In cases like this, the prosecution should draft respondents' notices and be represented. Ed.

18.24 ***Prison in default terms and determinate terms***
Powers of Criminal Courts (Sentencing) Act 2000 s 139(5) Where any person liable for the payment of a fine or a sum due under a recognisance to which this section applies is sentenced by the court to, or is serving or otherwise liable to serve, a term of imprisonment or detention in a Young Offender Institution or a term of detention under section 108 of this Act, the court may order that any term of imprisonment or detention fixed under section 139(2) of this Act shall not begin to run until after the end of the first-mentioned term.

18.25 ***Prison in default terms and determinate terms*** ***Confiscation***
Proceeds of Crime Act 2002 s 38(2) [Where a warrant committing the defendant to prison or detention is issued for a default in payment] the term of imprisonment or of detention under [Powers of Criminal Courts (Sentencing) Act 2000 s 108] (detention of persons aged 18 to 20 for default) to be served in default of payment of the amount does not begin to run until after the term mentioned in subsection (1)(b) above.
PSI 16/2010[336] para 2.7 Early release on a warrant of commitment in default of payment on a confiscation order. Such terms cannot form part of a single term or be aggregated with a sentence of imprisonment. They are always ordered to run consecutively and so will commence on the day after the last custodial day of the sentence of imprisonment.
Suspended Sentence Orders, for the rules about see **106.18**.
For ***Magistrates' Court*** powers, see the **CUSTODY GENERAL PRINCIPLES Magistrates' Court powers and committals** section at **28.5**.

Sentencing remarks

18.26 ***Judge must make it clear whether the sentence is consecutive/Clarity***
Criminal Practice Directions 2015 EWCA Crim 1567 para VII E.1 Where a court passes on a defendant more than one term of imprisonment, the court should state in the presence of the defendant whether the terms are to be concurrent or consecutive. Should this not be done, the court clerk should ask the court, before the defendant leaves court, to do so.
E.2 If a defendant is, at the time of sentence, already serving two or more consecutive terms of imprisonment and the court intends to increase the total period of imprisonment, it should use the expression 'consecutive to the total period of imprisonment to which you are already subject' rather than 'at the expiration of the term of imprisonment you are now serving', as the defendant may not then be serving the last of the terms to which he is already subject.
R v Ketley 1989 Unreported 22/11/89 It is of the greatest importance that a sentencer expresses himself precisely and clearly as to whether sentences are intended to be concurrent or consecutive.

Appeals

18.27 ***It's the total that matters***
R v Lawrence 1989 11 Cr App R (S) 580 It's the (overall) length that matters.
Note: There are three main categories where the defendant appeals his consecutive sentences. They are: a) where the court considers the Judge's approach was correct or within his or her discretion, b) where the court rearranges the sentences as consecutive terms were not appropriate, and c) where the court makes some or all the terms concurrent. Ed.

[336] Prison Service Instructions, see www.banksr.com Other Matters Other Documents tab

19 CONDITIONAL DISCHARGES

19.1

Powers of Criminal Courts (Sentencing) Act 2000 s 12

Availability The order is available for all offences except:

(a) murder,

(b) where automatic life applies,[337]

(c) where there is a minimum sentence (third class A trafficking offence,[338] certain Firearms Act 1968 offences,[339] offensive weapon and bladed article offences when threatening[340] and certain burglary offences[341]),[342]

(d) for breaches of a Criminal Behaviour Order,[343] a Sexual Harm Prevention Order,[344] an Interim Sexual Harm Prevention Order, an ASBO,[345] a Sexual Offences Prevention Order,[346] and an Interim Sexual Offences Prevention Order,

(e) where the defendant has been given a warning under Crime and Disorder Act 1998 s 65 and is convicted of an offence committed within two years of the warning unless [the court] is of the opinion there are exceptional circumstances relating to the offence or the offender,[347]

(f) where the defendant has already served the maximum sentence for that offence before sentence.[348]

Court Martial Armed Forces Act 2006 s 185-187 deal with imposing an absolute and conditional discharge, the breach of those discharges and the effect of those discharges. The Court may pass this order only for civilians, see *Guidance on Sentencing in the Court Martial 2018* Annex B.

History of the order There is a useful history of the power to grant absolute and conditional discharges set out in *R v Clarke* 2009 EWCA Crim 1074, 2010 1 Cr App R (S) 48 (p 296) para 15.

Victim surcharge The court must impose a victim surcharge, Criminal Justice Act 2003 s 161A-161B and Criminal Justice Act 2003 (Surcharge) Order 2012 2012/1696 as amended. There are exceptions, a) where a compensation order or an Unlawful Profits Order or a Slavery and Trafficking Reparations Order is imposed, when a reduced amount or a nil amount can be ordered, see **17.67**, and b) where the offence was committed before 1 October 2012, when no surcharge can be made, see **115.3**. Where the offence was committed on or after that date and before 8 April 2016, the amount to be imposed is the relevant figure in brackets below, see **115.4**. The amount to be imposed is £20 (£15), unless one or more of the offences was committed when the defendant was aged under 18, when the amount is £15 (£10).

[337] This is excluded by Powers of Criminal Courts (Sentencing) Act 2000 s 12(1) as amended by Legal Aid, Sentencing and Punishment of Offenders Act 2012 Sch 19 para 4. In force 3/12/12

[338] See the **Supply of Drugs Minimum sentences** section at **338.71** in Volume 2.

[339] See the **Firearms Minimum sentences** section at **262.53** in Volume 2.

[340] These are excluded by Powers of Criminal Courts (Sentencing) Act 2000 s 12(1) as amended by Legal Aid, Sentencing and Punishment of Offenders Act 2012 Sch 26 para 10.

[341] See the **Burglary Minimum sentences** section at **221.29** in Volume 2.

[342] These are excluded by Powers of Criminal Courts (Sentencing) Act 2000 s 12(1) as amended by Legal Aid, Sentencing and Punishment of Offenders Act 2012 Sch 26 para 10.

[343] Anti-social Behaviour, Crime and Policing Act 2014 s 30(3)

[344] For both types of SHPO it is unavailable, Sexual Offences Act 2003 s 103I(4) inserted by Anti-social Behaviour, Crime and Policing Act 2014 Sch 5.

[345] Crime and Disorder Act 1998 s 1(11) and Anti-social Behaviour, Crime and Policing Act 2014 s 33(1)-(2) (the saving provision)

[346] For both types of SOPO it is unavailable, Sexual Offences Act 2003 s 113(3) and Anti-social Behaviour, Crime and Policing Act 2014 s 114(1)-(2) (the saving provision).

[347] Crime and Disorder Act 1998 s 66(4)

[348] *R v Lynch* 2007 EWCA Crim 2624 (absolute discharge imposed instead), see **30.19**.

Rehabilitation period The rehabilitation period ends on the expiration of the conditional discharge.[349] Where a defendant has breached the conditional discharge and a new sentence is imposed, the longer of the rehabilitation periods applies.[350]
See also the **REHABILITATION OF OFFENDERS ACT 1974** chapter.
Appeals A defendant can appeal a conditional discharge imposed in the Crown Court, see Criminal Appeal Act 1968 s 50(1A), and in the Magistrates' Court, Magistrates' Courts Act 1980 s 108(1) and (1A).

19.2 *Statistics England and Wales*

Conditional discharges

Year	Crown Court	Magistrates' Court	All courts
2015	1,478	54,499	55,977
2016	1,286	45,796	47,082
2017	1,024	39,253	40,277

Note: These statistics have been altered from previous editions. Occasionally the recorded figures for the previous year(s) change when we are supplied with new statistics, so we amend them accordingly. Ed.
For explanations about the statistics, see page 1-xii. For more detailed statistics, see www.banksr.com Other Matters Statistics tab.

19.3 *Statutory power to order/Test to apply*

Powers of Criminal Courts (Sentencing) Act 2000 s 12(1) Where a court by or before which a person is convicted of an offence (not being an offence the sentence for which is fixed by law or falls to be imposed under a provision mentioned in subsection (1A) [minimum sentences] is of the opinion, having regard to the circumstances including the nature of the offence and the character of the offender, that it is inexpedient to inflict punishment, the court may make an order either:
(a) discharging him absolutely; or
(b) if the court thinks fit, discharging him subject to the condition that he commits no offence during such period, not exceeding three years from the date of the order, as may be specified in the order.
For the Court Martial provisions, see Armed Forces Act 2006 s 185.
For ***Effect of an absolute discharge***, see the **CONDITIONAL DISCHARGE** ***Effect of an absolute or conditional discharge*** para at **19.5**.

19.4 *Security for good behaviour*

Powers of Criminal Courts (Sentencing) Act 2000 s 12(6) The court may, if it thinks it expedient for the purpose of the offender's reformation, allow any person who consents to do so to give security for the good behaviour of the offender.[351]
Criminal Practice Directions 2015 EWCA Crim 1567 para VII J.20 Where a court is imposing a conditional discharge under Powers of Criminal Courts (Sentencing) Act 2000 s 12, it has the power, under section 12(6), to make an order that a person who consents to do so give security for the good behaviour of the offender. When making such an order, the court should specify the type of conduct from which the offender is to refrain.

19.5 *Status of an absolute and conditional discharge*

Powers of Criminal Courts (Sentencing) Act 2000 s 14(1) Subject to subsection (2) below, a conviction of an offence for discharge…absolutely or conditionally shall be

[349] Rehabilitation of Offenders Act 1974 s 5(4)
[350] Rehabilitation of Offenders Act 1974 s 6(3)
[351] This will be dealt with under the powers in Magistrates' Courts Act 1980 s 117-120.

deemed not to be a conviction for any purpose other than the purposes of the proceedings in which the order is made and of any subsequent proceedings which may be taken against the offender under section 13 (breach proceedings) (see **20.2**).
(2) Where the offender was aged 18 or over at the time of his conviction of the offence in question and is subsequently sentenced (under section 13, see **20.2**) (breach proceedings) for that offence, subsection (1) above shall cease to apply to the conviction.
(3) Without prejudice to subsections (1) and (2) above, the conviction of an offender who is discharged absolutely or conditionally…shall in any event be disregarded for the purposes of any enactment or instrument which:

(a) imposes any disqualification or disability upon convicted persons, or
(b) authorises or requires the imposition of any such disqualification or disability.

(4) Subsections (1) to (3) above shall not affect:

(a) any right of an offender discharged absolutely or conditionally under section 12 above to rely on his conviction in bar of any subsequent proceedings for the same offence,
(b) the restoration of any property in consequence of the conviction of any such offender,

Powers of Criminal Courts (Sentencing) Act 2000 s 14(6) (rights of appeal are unaffected by this section).
For the Court Martial provisions, see Armed Forces Act 2006 s 187.
R v Patel 2006 EWCA Crim 2689, 2007 1 Cr App R 12 (p 191) D was acquitted of obtaining a pecuniary advantage by deception, namely the opportunity to earn money through employment. D had been conditionally discharged and forced to pay £30 costs for shoplifting, nine years earlier. D completed an application form for a position on the civilian staff of the Metropolitan Police. The form asked, 'Have you ever been convicted of an offence…?' D answered 'No'. The Crown contended that D's answer amounted to a false representation, saying that the distinction sought was between a finding of guilt ('convicted') and the disposal of a criminal matter ('conviction'). The Crown maintained that the question ('Have you ever been convicted of an offence?') amounted to enquiring whether D had been found guilty of an offence, as opposed to having 'previous convictions', which would enquire whether the applicant had been finally disposed in relation to a criminal matter. The Judge ruled there was no case to answer. Held. The distinction drawn by the Crown is not recognised in Powers of Criminal Courts (Sentencing) Act 2000 s 14 (effect of discharge) and therefore the Judge was correct. Appeal dismissed.
See also: *R v Secretary of State ex parte Thornton* 1987 QB 36 ('Found guilty of a criminal offence' is synonymous with 'conviction' or 'finding of guilt').

19.6 ***Notification, A person conditionally discharged is not subject to***
R v Longworth 2006 UKHL 1, 2 Cr App R (S) 62 (p 401) Lords A person conditionally discharged is not subject to notification.

Combined with other orders

19.7 ***Combined with other orders General***
Note: If the court thinks that it is 'inexpedient to inflict punishment' and so orders a conditional discharge, it is wrong to make any other order for the same offence which involves punishment, like a fine. Ed.

19.8 ***Compensation orders, Combined with***
Powers of Criminal Courts (Sentencing) Act 2000 s 12(7) Nothing in this section shall be construed as preventing a court, on discharging an offender absolutely or conditionally in respect of any offence…from making in respect of the offence an order under Powers of Criminal Courts (Sentencing) Act 2000 s 130 (compensation orders).[352]

[352] As amended by Criminal Justice and Courts Act 2015 Sch 12 paras 8-9

Court Martial Only a Service Compensation Order may be combined with a conditional discharge, see *Guidance on Sentencing in the Court Martial 2018* Annex B.

19.9 *Confiscation orders, Combined with*

R v Varma 2012 UKSC 42, 2013 1 Cr App R (S) 125 (p 650) The Court of Appeal asked, 'Does the Crown Court have power to make a confiscation order if the defendant receives an absolute or conditional discharge?' Held. [In all cases] the court must proceed under Proceeds of Crime Act 2002 s 6, if section 6(1) and (2) are satisfied. In most cases there was a duty to make an order.

19.10 *Costs, Combined with*

Powers of Criminal Courts (Sentencing) Act 2000 s 12(8) Nothing in this section shall be construed as preventing a court, on discharging an offender absolutely or conditionally in respect of an offence, from…(b) making an order for costs against the offender.[353]

19.11 *Deportation, Recommendations for, Combined with*

R v Akan 1972 56 Cr App R 716 The Judge decided to make a recommendation for deportation and pass a nominal sentence of imprisonment and suspend it. It was pointed out that if he did that the Judge would not be able to release the defendant on bail. He therefore decided to pass a conditional discharge. On appeal it was argued that as a conditional discharge was deemed not to be a conviction[354] the recommendation for deportation was unlawful. Held. The recommendation for deportation is not to be regarded as a disqualification or a disability,[355] so both orders valid.
Note: In reality it would be rare that a case which warrants a conditional discharge could satisfy the detriment condition, see **33.25**. Ed.

19.12 *Deprivation of property used for crime, Combined with*

Powers of Criminal Courts (Sentencing) Act 2000 s 12(7) Nothing in this section shall be construed as preventing a court, on discharging an offender absolutely or conditionally in respect of any offence…from making in respect of the offence an order under Powers of Criminal Courts (Sentencing) Act 2000 s 143 (deprivation orders).[356]

19.13 *Disqualification, endorsement etc., Combined with*

Road Traffic Offenders Act 1988 s 46(1) Notwithstanding anything in Powers of Criminal Courts (Sentencing) Act 2000 s 14(3) (rule about disregarding absolute and conditional discharges), a court [when convicting a person involving obligatory or discretionary disqualification orders him to be absolutely or conditionally discharged] may also exercise any power conferred, and must also discharge any duty imposed on the court by sections 34 (obligatory disqualification), 35 (totting up disqualification), 36 (disqualification until test is passed) and 44-44A of this Act (obligation to endorse).
Powers of Criminal Courts (Sentencing) Act 2000 s 12(7) [The court may] on discharging an offender absolutely make an order for disqualification.
Note: The Act does not indicate whether it is road traffic disqualification or not. It is likely to be interpreted as all disqualification orders as that is the natural meaning of the words in the section and most disqualification is likely to be seen as for the protection of the public rather than as a simple punishment. Ed.

19.14 *Exclusion Orders, Combined with*

Licensed Premises (Exclusion of Certain Persons) Act 1980 s 1(2)[357] An Exclusion Order may be made…notwithstanding the provisions of Powers of Criminal Courts (Sentencing) Act 2000 s 12 and 14 (the effect etc. of a conditional discharge) (see **19.5**).

[353] As amended by Criminal Justice and Courts Act 2015 Sch 12 paras 8-9
[354] Under the then in force Criminal Justice Act 1948 s 12
[355] This is the expression used in the 1948 Act about disregarding absolute or conditional discharges.
[356] As amended by Criminal Justice and Courts Act 2015 Sch 12 paras 8-9
[357] This Act is repealed by Violent Crime Reduction Act 2006 Sch 5. Commencement is awaited and this provision is unlikely to be enacted soon.

19.15 *Fines, Combined with*
R v Sanck 1990 12 Cr App R (S) 155 LCJ The Judge imposed a fine and a conditional discharge for possession with intent to supply. Held. It is wrong to impose the two orders together. Conditional discharge quashed.

19.16 *Football Banning Orders, Combined with*
Football Spectators Act 1989 s 14A(4)(b) A Football Banning Order may be made under s 14A in addition to an order discharging him conditionally.
(5) A banning order may be made as mentioned by s 14(4)(b) (see above) in spite of anything in Powers of Criminal Courts (Sentencing) Act 2000 s 12 and 14 which relates to orders discharging a person conditionally.

19.17 *Referral Orders, Combined with*
Powers of Criminal Courts (Sentencing) Act 2000 s 19(1)-(4)(d) Where the court makes a Referral Order, the court may not make an order discharging him conditionally.
Powers of Criminal Courts (Sentencing) Act 2000 s 16(1) This section [to make Referral Orders] applies where a Youth Court or other Magistrates' Court is dealing with a person aged under 18 for an offence and:

(c) the court is not proposing to discharge him whether absolutely or conditionally in respect of the offence.[358]

19.18 *Restitution Orders, Combined with*
Powers of Criminal Courts (Sentencing) Act 2000 s 12(7) Nothing in this section shall be construed as preventing a court, on discharging an offender absolutely or conditionally in respect of any offence…from making in respect of the offence an order under Powers of Criminal Courts (Sentencing) Act 2000 s 148 (Restitution Orders).[359]

19.19 *Serious Crime Prevention Orders, Combined with*
Serious Crime Act 2007 s 36(5) A Serious Crime Prevention Order may be made in spite of anything in Powers of Criminal Courts (Sentencing) Act 2000 s 12 and 14 (Power to make and the effect of an absolute or conditional discharge), see **19.3** and **18.8**.
Serious Crime Act 2007 s 19(7)(b) An order must not be made under this section except in addition to an order discharging a person conditionally.

19.20 *Unlawful Profit Order, Combined with*
Powers of Criminal Courts (Sentencing) Act 2000 s 12(7) Nothing in this section shall be construed as preventing a court, on discharging an offender absolutely or conditionally in respect of any offence…from making in respect of the offence an Unlawful Profit Order under Prevention of Social Housing Fraud Act 2013 s 4.[360]
See also the **COMBINING SENTENCES** chapter.

Other matters

19.21 *Explain sentence, Judge must/Suggested sentencing remarks*
Criminal Justice Act 2003 s 174(1) A court passing sentence on an offender has the duties in subsections (2) and (3).
(2) The court must state in open court, in ordinary language and in general terms, the court's reasons for deciding on the sentence.
(3) The court must explain to the offender in ordinary language:

(a) the effect of the sentence,
(b) the effects of non-compliance with any order that the offender is required to comply with and that forms part of the sentence,…[361]

Judicial College's Crown Court Compendium Part II Sentencing June 2018 page 6-2

[358] The parts of this subsection which are underlined are inserted by Legal Aid, Sentencing and Punishment of Offenders Act 2012 s 79(2).
[359] As amended by Criminal Justice and Courts Act 2015 Sch 12 paras 8-9
[360] As amended by Criminal Justice and Courts Act 2015 Sch 12 paras 8-9
[361] In force 3/12/12. For a note about the changing statutes before then, see the 13th edition para **19.23**.

> Example
> You have pleaded guilty to/been convicted of the offence of {specify} but it is neither necessary nor appropriate to impose an immediate punishment and so I propose to discharge you conditionally for a period of…months/years. That means that so long as you commit no further offence there will be no punishment, but if you commit a further offence in that period of…months/years you will be brought back to court and sentenced in respect of this offence and the further offence.

20 CONDITIONAL DISCHARGE: BREACH OF

20.1
Powers of Criminal Courts (Sentencing) Act 2000 s 13
Victim surcharge The amount depends on what sentence was passed for the breach, see **115.4** and **115.6**.
Court Martial The provisions are in Armed Forces Act 2006 s 186.

Preliminary matters

20.2 ***Issuing summons, Power to and effect of***
Powers of Criminal Courts (Sentencing) Act 2000 s 13(1) If it appears to the Crown Court…or to a justice of the peace…that a person in whose case an order for conditional discharge has been made:
(a) has been convicted by a court in Great Britain of an offence committed during the period of conditional discharge, and
(b) has been dealt with in respect of that offence, that court or justice may, subject to subsection (3), issue a summons requiring that person to appear at the place and time specified in it or a warrant for his arrest.
(2) Jurisdiction for the purposes of subsection (1) above may be exercised:
(a) if the order for conditional discharge was made by the Crown Court, by that court,
(b) if the order was made by a Magistrates' Court, by a justice of the peace.
Powers of Criminal Courts (Sentencing) Act 2000 s 13(4) A summons or warrant issued under this section shall direct the person to whom it relates to appear or to be brought before the court by which the order for conditional discharge was made.

20.3 ***Issuing summons Requirements before issue***
Powers of Criminal Courts (Sentencing) Act 2000 s 13(3) A justice of the peace shall not issue a summons under this section except on information and shall not issue a warrant under this section except on information in writing and on oath.

20.4 ***Power to commit for breach of a conditional discharge***
R v Penfold 1995 16 Cr App R (S) 1016 D breached his conditional discharge and was committed for sentence both for the new offence and also for the offence for which he was conditionally discharged. D received consecutive sentences for both offences. The defence contended the committal for the conditional discharge was invalid. Held. The committal was valid.
Note: Although the relevant Acts have been repealed, the principle remains under the new Acts when the new offence is committed for sentence. Ed.

20.5 ***CRO should have details of the order breached***
Criminal Practice Directions 2015 EWCA Crim 1567 para II 10A.7 Where the current alleged offence could constitute a breach of an existing sentence such as a suspended sentence, community order or conditional discharge, and it is known that that sentence is still in force, details of the circumstances of the offence leading to the sentence should be included in the antecedents. The detail should be brief and include the date of the offence.

Power to re-sentence etc.

20.6 ***Power to re-sentence Generally***

Powers of Criminal Courts (Sentencing) Act 2000 s 13(6) Where it is proved to the satisfaction of the court by which an order for conditional discharge was made that the person in whose case the order was made has been convicted of an offence committed during the period of conditional discharge, the court may deal with him, for the offence for which the order was made, in any way in which it could deal with him if he had just been convicted by or before that court of that offence.

(7) [see **20.8**]

(8) [see **20.9**]

(9) [see **20.10**]

(10) The reference in subsection (6) above to a person's having been convicted of an offence committed during the period of conditional discharge is a reference to his having been so convicted by a court in Great Britain.

20.7 ***Crown Court order Magistrates' Court powers***

Powers of Criminal Courts (Sentencing) Act 2000 s 13(5) If a person in whose case an order for conditional discharge has been made by the Crown Court is convicted by a Magistrates' Court of an offence committed during the period of conditional discharge, the Magistrates' Court:

(a) may commit him to custody or release him on bail until he can be brought or appear before the Crown Court, and

(b) if it does so, shall send to the Crown Court a copy of the minute or memorandum of the conviction entered in the register, signed by the designated officer by whom the register is kept.

20.8 ***Magistrates' Court order Crown Court powers***

Powers of Criminal Courts (Sentencing) Act 2000 s 13(7) If a person in whose case an order for conditional discharge has been made by a Magistrates' Court:

(a) is convicted before the Crown Court of an offence committed during the period of conditional discharge, or

(b) is dealt with by the Crown Court for any such offence in respect of which he was committed for sentence to the Crown Court,

the Crown Court may deal with him, for the offence for which the order was made, in any way in which the Magistrates' Court could deal with him if it had just convicted him of that offence.

20.9 ***Magistrates' Court order Different Magistrates' Court***

Powers of Criminal Courts (Sentencing) Act 2000 s 13(8) If a person in whose case an order for conditional discharge has been made by a Magistrates' Court is convicted by another Magistrates' Court of any offence committed during the period of conditional discharge, that other court may, with the consent of the court which made the order, deal with him, for the offence for which the order was made, in any way in which the court could deal with him if it had just convicted him of that offence.

20.10 ***Magistrates' Court order Offender aged under 18***

Powers of Criminal Courts (Sentencing) Act 2000 s 13(9) Where an order for conditional discharge has been made by a Magistrates' Court in the case of an offender under 18 years of age in respect of an offence triable only on indictment in the case of an adult, any powers exercisable under subsection (6), (7) or (8) above by that or any other court in respect of the offender after he attains the age of 18 shall be powers to do either or both of the following:

(a) to impose a fine not exceeding £5,000 for the offence in respect of which the order was made,

(b) to deal with the offender for that offence in any way in which a Magistrates' Court could deal with him if it had just convicted him of an offence punishable with imprisonment for a term not exceeding six months.

Procedure

20.11 *Consider separately Sentence separately from other charge*
R v Webb 1953 37 Cr App R 390 LCJ Merely to take breaches of…conditional discharge into consideration is…undesirable and indeed wrong. They should be separately considered and separate sentences should be passed, so that the original offences may rank as convictions. It is most important that offenders should be made to realise that (conditional discharge) is not a mere formality, and that a subsequent offence committed during the operative period of the order will involve punishment for the crime for which they were originally given the benefit of this lenient treatment.
Note: This is an old case, but this rule is still applied. Ed.
See also: *R v Stuart* 1965 49 Cr App R 17 (A separate sentence should be passed for the original offence, and it should not merely be 'taken into consideration'. *R v Webb* 1953 applied.)

20.12 *Proving the breach*
R v Devine 1956 40 Cr App R 45 LCJ D was placed on probation and breached it. Held. Where a person is brought before a court for breach of a probation order, the alleged breach should be put to him in the clearest possible terms and he should be asked to say whether he admits it or not. The terms in which the matter should be put to him are: a) he should be told where he was originally convicted and what happened to him, b) then he should be told how the breach is alleged to have taken place, if it be by a further conviction, the occasion of that conviction and the adjudication of the court should also be mentioned, c) then he should be asked to say whether he admits those facts, d) if he does, the court can then proceed to deal with him. If he does not, a trial will take place albeit without a jury, he will have to be asked whether he desires to give evidence or call witnesses, and the court will have to pronounce whether it finds that the breach of the probation order has been proved. It is desirable that the proceedings should begin by the matter being put clearly to him and his being asked whether he admits the breach.
R v Long 1960 44 Cr App R 9 LCJ D was placed on probation and breached it. When he appeared at court he was asked if he had been placed on probation and then told, "and having committed a further offence you were produced at these sessions for sentence". Held. Where a person is brought before a court for breach of probation, the breach should be put to him in the clearest possible terms and he should be asked to say whether he admits the breach or not.
Note: The same principle would apply to a breach of a conditional discharge. Ed.

20.13 *New offence carries significant penalty How to sentence*
R v Fry 1954 38 Cr App R 157 LCJ D was convicted of larceny and conditionally discharged. He breached it and was sentenced to Borstal for storebreaking and no penalty was imposed for the breach. Held. The no penalty sentence was wrong. Normally it is not desirable to impose nominal sentences of one day's imprisonment, but in this particular case it was the only way of getting round the difficulty which would otherwise occur. If no sentence at all is passed in respect of the offence for which the applicant was conditionally discharged, the conviction does not rank as a conviction.
Note: Whether the reason remains valid does not affect what is still the normal sentencing policy. A modern reason for this course is that a breach sentence of one day would trigger the imprisonment category in the rehabilitation of offenders procedures whereas no penalty would not. Ed.

20.14 *Children and young offenders*
Sentencing Children and Young People Guideline 2017 www.banksr.com Other Matters Guidelines tab In force 1 June 2017. page 32
Breach of a conditional discharge
7.1 If a child or young person commits an offence during the period of conditional discharge then the court has the power to re-sentence the original offence. The child or

young person should be dealt with on the basis of their current age and not the age at the time of the finding of guilt and the court can deal with the original offence(s) in any way which it could have if the child or young person had just been found guilty.
7.2 There is no requirement to re-sentence; if a court deems it appropriate to do so they can sentence the child or young person for the new offence and leave the conditional discharge in place. If the order was made by the Crown Court then the Youth Court can commit the child or young person in custody or release them on bail until they can be brought or appear before the Crown Court. The court shall also send to the Crown Court a memorandum of conviction.
7.3 If the offender is convicted of committing a new offence after attaining the age of 18 but during the period of a conditional discharge made by a Youth Court then they may be re-sentenced for the original offence by the convicting adult Magistrates' Court. If the adult Magistrates' Court decides to take no action then the Youth Court that imposed the conditional discharge may summon the offender for the breach to be dealt with.

Ancillary orders

20.15 ***After breach sentence ancillary orders of original sentence remain***

R v Evans 1961 45 Cr App R 59 LCJ D was placed on probation and was ordered to pay compensation. He failed to keep in touch with his probation officer and was sentenced to imprisonment. Defence counsel suggested that when the order was breached, the compensation order was nullified. Held. It was not.

21 CONFISCATION: PROCEEDS OF CRIME ACT 2002

21.1

Commencement The 2002 Act does not apply to cases where 'the offence or any offence' was committed before 24 March 2003.[362] Where a defendant faces two separate indictments, the judge will separately determine which confiscation regime applies for each indictment, *R v Moulden* 2008 EWCA Crim 2648, 2009 2 Cr App R (S) 15 (p 84). Where a conspiracy count straddles the commencement date, the conspiracy will be taken to have been completed on the earliest date, for example, the moment the agreement is made, or when the defendant joined the conspiracy, *R v Evwierhowa* 2011 EWCA Crim 572 paras 28-29. For more detail, see **21.14**.

History of confiscation For a brief history of confiscation, see *R v May* 2008 UKHL 28, 2009 1 Cr App R (S) 31 (p 162) House of Lords at paras 7-9. There is another account in *R v Sekhon and Others* 2002 EWCA Crim 2954, 2003 2 Cr App R (S) 38 (p 207) LCJ at paras 6-18.

Children and young offenders The order appears available whatever the age of the offender. For an example of a confiscation order being made for an offender aged 17 when sentenced, see *R v Phillips* 2017 EWCA Crim 1514. For offenders aged 18-20, the Court fixes a detention in default order, not a prison in default order, see Proceeds of Crime Act 2002 s 35(2A), applying Powers of Criminal Courts (Sentencing) Act 2000 s 139(2).

Restraint Orders A Crown Court judge may make a Restraint Order which prohibits a defendant from dealing with any realisable property held by him or her, Proceeds of Crime Act 2002 s 41.

Bankrupts An order can be made against a defendant notwithstanding that his assets are held by a trustee in bankruptcy, *R v Shahid* 2009 EWCA Crim 831, 2 Cr App R (S) 105 (p 687).

Compliance order The court must consider making a compliance order under Proceeds of Crime Act 2002 s 13A[363] to ensure that the compensation order is effective, see **21.148**.

[362] Proceeds of Crime Act 2002 (Commencement No 5, Transitional Provisions, Savings and Amendment) Order 2003 2003/333 para 3(1)
[363] Inserted by Serious Crime Act 2015 s 7. In force 1/6/15

21.2 ***Statistics England and Wales***
Note: The official figures are low and so hard to believe. The MoJ has decided not to publish any more confiscation statistics after 2014. Consequently, the old statistics are not listed. Ed.

21.3 ***Previous confiscation procedures***

Statute	Date
Criminal Justice Act 1988	Where the offence(s) were committed before 1 November 1995.
Criminal Justice Act 1988 with the Proceeds of Crime Act 1995 amendments	For non-drug trafficking offences committed on or after 1 November 1995 and before 24 March 2003.
Drug Trafficking Act 1994	For drug trafficking offences when all of them were committed on or after 3 February 1995 and before 24 March 2003.
Proceeds of Crime Act 2002	For offences when one of them was committed on or after 24 March 2003.

21.4 ***The steps for a Proceeds of Crime Act 2002 s 6 confiscation order***
Step 1 Is one of the following satisfied (Proceeds of Crime Act 2002 s 6(2), see **21.5**)?
(a) The defendant pleaded guilty or was convicted at the Crown Court, or
(b) The defendant was committed to the Crown Court under Powers of Criminal Courts (Sentencing) Act 2000 s 3, 4 or 6, or
(c) The defendant was committed to the Crown Court under Proceeds of Crime Act 2002 s 70 (committal with a view to a confiscation order being considered).
If Yes, go to Step 2, see **21.12**. If No, section 6 confiscation does not apply. Step 1 is at **21.9**.
Step 2 Did the prosecution ask the court to begin confiscation proceedings or did the court of its own motion believe it was appropriate to do so (Proceeds of Crime Act 2002 s 6(3), see **21.13**)? If Yes, go to Step 3, see **21.14**. If No, section 6 confiscation does not apply. Step 2 is at **21.12**.
Step 3 Was the offence committed on or after 24 March 2003? If Yes, go to Step 4, see **21.50**. If No, earlier confiscation regimes will normally apply. These provisions are not dealt with in this book. Step 3 is at **21.14**.
Step 4 Has the defendant a 'criminal lifestyle' (Proceeds of Crime Act 2002 s 6(4)(a), see **21.52**)? A defendant has a criminal lifestyle if, and only if, the offence (or any of the offences) concerned satisfies any of these tests:
(a) it is specified in Sch 2, see **21.53**,
(b) it constitutes conduct forming part of a course of criminal activity (for definition, Proceeds of Crime Act 2002 s 75(3), see **21.52**),
(c) it is an offence committed over a period of at least six months (for meaning, see **21.56**) and the defendant has benefited from the conduct which constitutes the offence, see **21.55**.
In b) and c) the relevant benefit (for definition, Proceeds of Crime Act 2002 s 75(5) and (6), see **21.52**) must be £5,000+, see **21.52**.
If Yes, go to Step 5, see **21.57**. If No, go to Step 6, see **21.63**. Step 4 is at **21.50**.
Step 5 Has the defendant 'benefited from his general criminal conduct' (for definition, Proceeds of Crime Act 2002 s 76(2), see **21.59**)? To answer this, the court must apply the assumptions, Proceeds of Crime Act 2002 s 10, see **21.80**. If Yes, go to Step 7, see **21.65**. If No, section 6 does not apply. Step 5 is at **21.57**.
Step 6 Has the defendant benefited from his 'particular criminal conduct' (for definition, Proceeds of Crime Act 2002 s 76(3), see **21.59**)? If Yes, go to Step 7, see **21.65**. If No, section 6 confiscation does not apply. Step 6 is at **21.63**.

In Steps 4, 5 and 6 when determining whether a defendant has a 'criminal lifestyle' or 'has benefited from his general or particular conduct', the issue must be decided with a 'balance of probabilities' test, Proceeds of Crime Act 2002 s 6(7), see **21.51**.

Step 7 Determine the benefit, applying the assumptions, Proceeds of Crime Act 2002 s 10, see **21.66**. Step 7 is at **21.65**.

Step 8 Determine the extent of the defendant's interest in property under Proceeds of Crime Act 2002 s 10A as inserted by Serious Crime Act 2015 s 1. This is a discretionary step. Step 8 is at **21.110**.

Step 9 Determine the available amount. The available amount is the total 'free property' (for definition, see Proceeds of Crime Act 2002 s 82 and **21.113**) and the 'tainted gifts' (see **21.84**). Step 9 is at **21.112**.

Step 10 Determine whether 'any victim of the conduct has at any time started or intends to start proceedings against the defendant in respect of loss, injury or damage sustained in connection with the conduct'.

If Yes, the court has a discretion to make a confiscation order. The court must make a 'just' order and one that is not more than it would otherwise have ordered (Proceeds of Crime Act 2002 s 7(3)), see **21.133**. If No, go to Step 11. Step 10 is at **21.135**.

Step 11 Determine whether: 'a) a criminal unlawful profit order has been made or b) one is believed to be made or c) it is believed a person has at any time started or intends to start proceedings against the defendant for a civil unlawful profit order'.[364]

If Yes, the court has a discretion to make a confiscation order. The court must make a 'just' order and one that is not more than it would otherwise have ordered (Proceeds of Crime Act 2002 s 7(3)), see **21.133**. If No, the court must make a confiscation order and go to Step 12, see **21.138**. Step 11 is at **21.136**.

Step 12 Has the defendant showed the available amount is less than the benefit? If Yes, go to Step 13. If No, go to Step 14. Steps 12, 13 and 14 are at **21.138**.

Step 13 Make the amount in the confiscation order the 'available amount' or a 'nominal amount'. This is the 'recoverable' amount, see Proceeds of Crime Act 2002 s 6(5)(a) and 7, see **21.133**. Go to Step 15. Step 13 is at **21.138**. For determining the available amount, see Step 9 at **21.112**.

Step 14 Make the amount in the confiscation order the amount the court has assessed to be the benefit. Go to Step 15. Steps 13 and 14 are at **21.138**.

Step 15 Consider time to pay. The order must be paid immediately, unless the defendant needs time to pay, Proceeds of Crime Act 2002 s 9(2). The maximum time is six months, which can later be extended, Proceeds of Crime Act 2002 s 9(3)-(5). Step 15 is at **21.141**.

Step 16 Consider ancillary orders, e.g. costs where the available amount is more than the confiscation order. Step 16 is at **21.142**.

Step 17 Make a prison in default term unless the sum has already been paid. For the table, see **58.50**. Step 17 is at **21.145**.

Step 18 Consider making a compliance order under Proceeds of Crime Act 2002 s 13A to ensure that the compensation order is effective. It is mandatory to consider such an order. Step 18 is at **21.148**.

21.5 *Statutory provisions* *Section 6*

Making of order

Proceeds of Crime Act 2002 s 6(1) The Crown Court must proceed under this section if the following two conditions are satisfied.

(2) The first condition is that a defendant falls within any of the following paragraphs:

(a) he is convicted of an offence or offences in proceedings before the Crown Court,

(b) he is committed to the Crown Court for sentence in respect of an offence or offences under section 3, 3A, 3B, 3C, 4, 4A or 6 of the Powers of Criminal Courts (Sentencing) Act,

[364] As inserted by Prevention of Social Housing Fraud Act 2013 Sch para 12

(c) he is committed to the Crown Court in respect of an offence or offences under section 70 below (committal with a view to a confiscation order being considered).
(3) The second condition is that:
(a) the prosecutor asks the court to proceed under this section, or
(b) the court believes it is appropriate for it to do so.
(4) The court must proceed as follows:
(a) it must decide whether the defendant has a criminal lifestyle,
(b) if it decides that he has a criminal lifestyle it must decide whether he has benefited from his general criminal conduct,
(c) if it decides that he does not have a criminal lifestyle it must decide whether he has benefited from his particular criminal conduct.
(5) If the court decides under subsection (4)(b) or (c) that the defendant has benefited from the conduct referred to it must:[365]
(a) decide the recoverable amount, and
(b) make an order (a confiscation order) requiring him to pay that amount.
Paragraph (b) applies only if, or to the extent that, it would not be disproportionate to require the defendant to pay the recoverable amount.
(6) But the court must treat the duty in subsection (5) as a power if it believes that any victim of the conduct has at any time started or intends to start proceedings against the defendant in respect of loss, injury or damage sustained in connection with the conduct.
(6A) The court must also treat the duty in subsection (5) as a power if:
(a) an order has been made, or it believes an order may be made, against the defendant under Prevention of Social Housing Fraud Act 2013 s 4 (criminal unlawful profit orders) in respect of profit made by the defendant in connection with the conduct, or
(b) it believes that a person has at any time started or intends to start proceedings against the defendant under section 5 (civil unlawful profit orders) of that Act in respect of such profit.[366]
(7) The court must decide any question arising under subsection (4) or (5) on a balance of probabilities.
(8) The first condition is not satisfied if the defendant absconds (but section 27 may apply).
(9) References in this Part to the offence (or offences) concerned are to the offence (or offences) mentioned in subsection (2).

21.6 ***Statutory provisions*** ***Section 7***

Recoverable amount

Proceeds of Crime Act 2002 s 7(1) The recoverable amount for the purposes of section 6 is an amount equal to the defendant's benefit from the conduct concerned.
(2) But if the defendant shows that the available amount is less than that benefit the recoverable amount is:
(a) the available amount, or
(b) a nominal amount, if the available amount is nil.
(3) But if section 6(6) or 6(6A)[367] applies the recoverable amount is such amount as:
(a) the court believes is just, but
(b) does not exceed the amount found under subsection (1) or (2) (as the case may be).
(4) In calculating the defendant's benefit from the conduct concerned for the purposes of subsection (1), any property in respect of which:
(a) a recovery order is in force under section 266, or
(b) a forfeiture order is in force under section 298(2),

[365] The subsection appears as amended by Serious Crime Act 2015 Sch 4 para 19.
[366] Section 6(6A) was inserted by Prevention of Social Housing Fraud Act 2013 Sch para 12.
[367] The phrase 'or 6(6A)' was inserted by Prevention of Social Housing Fraud Act 2013 Sch para 13.

must be ignored.
(5) If the court decides the available amount, it must include in the confiscation order a statement of its findings as to the matters relevant for deciding that amount.

21.7 *Statutory provisions Section 8*
Defendant's benefit
Proceeds of Crime Act 2002 s 8(1) If the court is proceeding under section 6 this section applies for the purpose of:
(a) deciding whether the defendant has benefited from conduct, and
(b) deciding his benefit from the conduct.
(2) The court must:
(a) take account of conduct occurring up to the time it makes its decision,
(b) take account of property obtained up to that time.
(3) Subsection (4) applies if:
(a) the conduct concerned is general criminal conduct,
(b) a confiscation order mentioned in subsection (5) has at an earlier time been made against the defendant, and
(c) his benefit for the purposes of that order was benefit from his general criminal conduct.
(4) His benefit found at the time the last confiscation order mentioned in subsection (3)(c) was made against him must be taken for the purposes of this section to be his benefit from his general criminal conduct at that time.
(5) If the conduct concerned is general criminal conduct the court must deduct the aggregate of the following amounts:
(a) the amount ordered to be paid under each confiscation order previously made against the defendant,
(b) the amount ordered to be paid under each confiscation order previously made against him under any of the provisions listed in subsection (7).
(6) But subsection (5) does not apply to an amount which has been taken into account for the purposes of a deduction under that subsection on any earlier occasion.
(7) These are the provisions:
(a) Drug Trafficking Offences Act 1986,
(c) Criminal Justice Act 1988 Part 6,
(e) Drug Trafficking Act 1994 Part 1,
(h) Part 3 or 4 of this Act.
Paragraphs (b), (d), (f) and (g) relate to Scotland or Northern Ireland.
(8) The reference to general criminal conduct in the case of a confiscation order made under any of the provisions listed in subsection (7) is a reference to conduct in respect of which a court is required or entitled to make one or more assumptions for the purpose of assessing a person's benefit from the conduct.

21.8 *Statutory provisions Section 9*
Available amount
Proceeds of Crime Act 2002 s 9(1) For the purposes of deciding the recoverable amount, the available amount is the aggregate of:
(a) the total of the values (at the time the confiscation order is made) of all the free property then held by the defendant minus the total amount payable in pursuance of obligations which then have priority, and
(b) the total of the values (at that time) of all tainted gifts.
(2) An obligation has priority if it is an obligation of the defendant:
(a) to pay an amount due in respect of a fine or other order of a court which was imposed or made on conviction of an offence and at any time before the time the confiscation order is made, or

(b) to pay a sum which would be included among the preferential debts if the defendant's bankruptcy had commenced on the date of the confiscation order or his winding up had been ordered on that date.

(3) 'Preferential debts' has the meaning given by Insolvency Act 1986 s 386.

For Proceeds of Crime Act 2002 section 10, see **21.66**, section 11, see **21.141**, section 12, see **21.158**, section 13, see **21.143**, section 14, see **21.23**, section 16, see **21.34**, section 17, see **21.35**, section 18, see **21.30**, section 27, see **21.29**, section 70, see **21.11**, section 71, see **21.11**, section 75, see **21.52**, section 77, see **21.84**, section 79, see **21.73**, section 80, see **21.75**, section 84, see **21.73** and Schedule 2, see **21.53**.

Step 1 Has the defendant pleaded guilty, been convicted on indictment, or been committed for sentence?

21.9 ***Step 1***

Step 1 Is one of the following satisfied (Proceeds of Crime Act 2002 s 6(2))?

(a) The defendant pleaded guilty or was convicted at the Crown Court, or

(b) The defendant was committed to the Crown Court under Powers of Criminal Courts (Sentencing) Act 2000 s 3, 4 or 6, or

(c) The defendant was committed to the Crown Court under Proceeds of Crime Act 2002 s 70 (committal with a view to a confiscation order being considered).

If Yes, go to Step 2, see **21.12**. If No, section 6 confiscation does not apply.

21.10 ***Step 1 Statutory provisions***

Proceeds of Crime Act 2002 s 6(1) The Crown Court must proceed under this section if the following two conditions are satisfied.

(2) The first condition is that a defendant falls within any of the following paragraphs:

(a) he is convicted of an offence or offences in proceedings before the Crown Court,

(b) he is committed to the Crown Court for sentence in respect of an offence or offences under Powers of Criminal Courts (Sentencing) Act 2000 s 3, 4 or 6,

(c) he is committed to the Crown Court in respect of an offence or offences under section 70 below (committal with a view to a confiscation order being considered).

For the full section see **21.5**.

21.11 ***Step 1 Committals to the Crown Court***

Proceeds of Crime Act 2002 s 70(1) This section applies if:

(a) a defendant is convicted of an offence by a Magistrates' Court, and

(b) the prosecutor asks the court to commit the defendant to the Crown Court with a view to a confiscation order being considered under section 6 (see **21.13**).

(2) In such a case the Magistrates' Court:

(a) must commit the defendant to the Crown Court in respect of the offence, and

(b) may commit him to the Crown Court in respect of any other offence falling within subsection (3).

(3) An offence falls within this subsection if:

(a) the defendant has been convicted of it by the Magistrates' Court or any other court, and

(b) the Magistrates' Court has power to deal with him in respect of it.

(4) If a committal is made under this section in respect of an offence or offences:

(a) section 6 applies accordingly, and

(b) the committal operates as a committal of the defendant to be dealt with by the Crown Court in accordance with section 71.

(5) If a committal is made under this section in respect of an offence for which (apart from this section) the Magistrates' Court could have committed the defendant for sentence, Powers of Criminal Courts (Sentencing) Act 2000 s 3(2) (offences triable either way), the court must state whether it would have done so.

Proceeds of Crime Act 2002 s 70(6) A committal under this section may be in custody or on bail.

Proceeds of Crime Act 2002 s 71(1) If a defendant is committed to the Crown Court under section 70 in respect of an offence or offences, this section applies (whether or not the court proceeds under section 6).
(2) In the case of an offence in respect of which the Magistrates' Court has stated under section 70(5) that it would have committed the defendant for sentence, the Crown Court:
(a) must inquire into the circumstances of the case, and
(b) may deal with the defendant in any way in which it could deal with him if he had just been convicted of the offence on indictment before it.
(3) In the case of any other offence the Crown Court:
(a) must inquire into the circumstances of the case, and
(b) may deal with the defendant in any way in which the Magistrates' Court could deal with him if it had just convicted him of the offence.
R v Sumal & Sons (Properties) Ltd 2012 EWCA Crim 1840 D was committed under section 70(1) for two summary only matters. The committal was challenged. Held. There was nothing in section 70 to limit its ambit to either way offences.

Step 2 The prosecution must ask, or the Judge must consider, whether confiscation is appropriate

21.12 Step 2

Step 2 Did the prosecution ask the court to begin confiscation proceedings or did the court of its own motion believe it was appropriate to do so (Proceeds of Crime Act 2002 s 6(3), see below)? If Yes, go to Step 3, see **21.14**. If No, section 6 confiscation does not apply.

21.13 ***Step 2 The prosecution must ask the court or the court must consider it appropriate***

Proceeds of Crime Act 2002 s 6(3) The second condition is that:
(a) the prosecutor asks the court to proceed under this section, or
(b) the court believes it is appropriate for it to do so.
For the full section see **21.5**.
R v Meader 2011 EWCA Crim 2108 D pleaded to theft from his employer. He was sentenced to 12 months. The Court adjourned the matter to consider a compensation order. There was no request for a confiscation order and the Court did not say it was appropriate. On 5 October, it was agreed D had benefited by £20,298 and the Judge made a confiscation order without objection. Held. The section 6(3) precondition was not met. Order quashed. Compensation order for the same sum substituted.

Step 3 Was the offence committed on or after 24 March 2003?

21.14 Step 3

Step 3 Was the offence committed on or after 24 March 2003?[368] If Yes, go to Step 4, see **21.50**. If No, earlier confiscation regimes will normally apply. These provisions are not dealt with in this book.
For a list of the earlier confiscation regimes, see **21.3**. For the cases on this issue, see the 12th edition of this book, para **21.14**.

General matters

21.15 ***Purpose of confiscation***

R v May 2008 UKHL 28, 2009 1 Cr App R (S) 31 (p 162) Lords The legislation is intended to deprive defendants of the benefit they have gained from relevant criminal conduct, whether or not they have retained such benefit, within the limits and their available means. It does not provide for confiscation as understood by schoolchildren and others, but nor does it operate by way of a fine.
R v Modjiri 2010 EWCA Crim 829, 2011 1 Cr App R (S) 20 (p 137) D pleaded to possession of cocaine with intent to supply. Held. para 26 We apply [the *dicta* in] *R v*

[368] Proceeds of Crime Act 2002 (Commencement No 5, Transitional Provisions, Savings and Amendment) Order 2003 2003/333 para 3(1)

Glatt 2006 EWCA Crim 605, 'A confiscation order: 1) is a penalty, and is a measure to which [the European Convention on Human Rights] art 1 is applicable, 2) is designed to deter those who consider embarking upon criminal conduct, 3) is designed to deprive a person of profits received from criminal conduct and to remove the value of the proceeds received from criminal conduct from possible use in criminal conduct, 4) is designed essentially to impoverish defendants, not to enrich the Crown'.

R v Waya 2012 UKSC 51, 2013 2 Cr App R (S) 20 (p 87) para 2 Supreme Court The legislative purpose of Proceeds of Crime Act 2002 is to ensure that criminals (and especially professional criminals engaged in serious organised crime) do not profit from their crimes, and it sends a strong deterrent message to that effect. In *R v Rezvi* 2002 UKHL 1, 2 Cr App R 2 (p 300) para 14, it was stated:

'It is a notorious fact that professional and habitual criminals frequently take steps to conceal their profits from crime. Effective but fair powers of confiscating the proceeds of crime are therefore essential. The provisions of the 1988 Act [the forerunner of the 2002 Act] are aimed at depriving such offenders of the proceeds of their criminal conduct. Its purposes are to punish convicted offenders, to deter the commission of further offences and to reduce the profits available to fund further criminal enterprises. These objectives reflect not only national but also international policy.'

These observations have been cited and followed many times, although Lord Steyn's reference in *R v Rezvi* 2002 UKHL 1, 2 Cr App R 2 (p 300) to punishment needs some qualification. Despite the use of the term 'confiscation', which is a misnomer, orders under Proceeds of Crime Act 2002 Part 2 are made in sums of money ('value-based') rather than being directed, as are civil recovery orders under Proceeds of Crime Act 2002 Part 5, at the divestment of specific assets. Nevertheless, a confiscation order is not an additional fine.

21.16 ***Private prosecutors***

R v Zinga (No 2) 2014 EWCA Crim 52, 2 Cr App R (S) 30 (p 240) LCJ Virgin Media brought a private prosecution against the defendant, D, who was convicted of conspiracy to defraud. He enabled people to watch channels without paying Virgin Media. D was convicted and the Judge made an £8.7m confiscation order. The defence contended that private prosecutors could not conduct confiscation proceedings. Held. para 20 Proceeds of Crime Act 2002 s 40(9)(b) says that references in Part 2 of the Act [which includes the making of a confiscation order] to the prosecutor 'are to the person the court believes is to have conduct of any proceedings for the offence'. That makes clear that the term is to be given a wide [meaning]. para 25 We do not agree with the defence. Here the only person who stood to gain from the proceedings was the State. para 36 The Court had a duty to make sure the order was not disproportionate. In the majority of cases the prosecutor will serve the public interest. para 63 Where compensation or recompense is sought, the court must consider whether it requires assistance. Where it does, it should ask the CPS. They can consider whether they wish to take over the case or assist the court.

R v Somaila 2017 EWCA Crim 741 D was convicted of nine counts of obtaining money transfers by deception and received 8 years. The case was prosecuted by the victim. The Judge found that there was about a £20.4m benefit and made a confiscation order under Criminal Justice Act 1988 s 71 for that amount. About £18.2m was directed to be paid as compensation to the victim and about £200,000 to another victim. Held. para 31 Being a prosecutor and a beneficiary does not create an irreconcilable conflict of interest. para 37 It is for the court to judge whether it is appropriate for the private prosecutor to conduct the sentencing, confiscation and compensation stages of the proceedings. The confiscation orders are upheld.

21.17 ***Can order be made? Absolute/conditional discharge, Defendant given***
R v Varma 2012 UKSC 42, 2013 1 Cr App R (S) 125 (p 650) Supreme Court para 12 When the defendant is absolutely or conditionally discharged, there is not only a power to make a confiscation order, there is in most cases a duty to make such an order.

21.18 ***The complexities are a nightmare***
R v Bajwa and Others 2011 EWCA Crim 1093, 2012 1 Cr App R (S) 23 (p 117) The defendants appealed their confiscation order. Held. para 2 Our considerations have made us engage in a long and complicated paper trail in order to answer what ought to be simple questions. The questions raised are not easy to answer and the convoluted process we have felt constrained to go through to reach the answers is bad enough on appeal. But these complications are a nightmare for judges at first instance who regularly have to apply the Proceeds of Crime Act 2002 in confiscation proceedings which result from offences of smuggling tobacco products into this country by sea in containers. It is not in the interests of justice or of the public that the law should be so complicated. It is high time that it was simplified.
For part of the nightmare see **21.101**.
R v Ahmad and Others 2014 UKSC 36, 2 Cr App R (S) 75 (p 580) Supreme Court The President para 35 The 2002 Act has often been described as poorly drafted. That is fair criticism, as can be illustrated by the problems which have had to be faced by the courts in a number of cases. However, in fairness it can be explained in the inherent difficulties in recovering the proceeds of crime.

21.19 ***European Convention on Human Rights Article 1***
Jahn v Germany 2006 42 EHRR 1084 ECtHR para 93 The Court reiterates that an interference with the peaceful enjoyment of possessions must strike a 'fair balance' between the demands of the general interest of the community and the requirements of the protection of the individual's fundamental rights. The concern to achieve this balance is reflected in the structure of [the European Convention on Human Rights] art 1 as a whole, including therefore the second sentence, which is to be read in the light of the general principle enunciated in the first sentence. In particular, there must be a reasonable relationship of proportionality between the means employed and the aim sought to be realised by any measure depriving a person of his possessions. In determining whether this requirement is met, the Court recognises that the State enjoys a wide margin of appreciation with regard both to choosing the means of enforcement and to ascertaining whether the consequences of enforcement are justified in the general interest for the purpose of achieving the object of the law in question, see *Chassagnou v France* 1995 Nos 25088/94, 28331/95 and 28443/95.
R v Waya 2012 UKSC 51, 2013 2 Cr App R (S) 20 (p 87) Supreme Court para 12 It is clear law that [the European Convention on Human Rights] art 1 imports, via the rule of fair balance, the requirement that there must be a reasonable relationship of proportionality between the means employed by the State in, *inter alia*, the deprivation of property as a form of penalty, and the legitimate aim which is sought to be realised by the deprivation. That rule has consistently been stated by the European Court of Human Rights, see for example *Jahn v Germany* 2006 42 EHRR 1084 para 93.
Paulet v UK 2014 No 6219/08 ECtHR Fourth Section D pleaded to three counts of dishonestly obtaining a pecuniary advantage by deception, having a false ID document and other charges. He was an illegal immigrant who obtained jobs by using a false passport. In about four years he earned nearly £73,300. His benefit was assessed at £50,000. He had savings of almost £21,950. The Judge made a confiscation order in that amount. The defence claimed that was disproportionate and oppressive. The Court of Appeal considered the public interest but did not determine whether the requisite balance was maintained in a manner consonant with D's right to 'the peaceful enjoyment of his possessions', within the meaning of Article 1. Held. 6-1 The Court of Appeal's review was too narrow to satisfy the requirement of seeking the fair balance inherent in para 2

of article 1. Therefore article 1 had been violated and it was not necessary to consider the proportionality of the order. The money was not ordered to be returned because of the absence of a proximate causal link between the procedural violation and the financial loss sustained. An award of €2,000 to reflect the anguish suffered, with €10,000 costs and expenses.

Note: So all in all, a disappointing decision, partly because the Judges ducked the real issue. Ed.

R v Parveaz 2017 EWCA Crim 873 D pleaded to producing cannabis. The Judge stopped a confiscation application going to a full hearing. Held. para 32 With regard to the lifestyle provisions, the 2002 Act cannot be said [to be] inherently incompatible with or contrary to the Convention or Article 1 Protocol 1, or inherently disproportionate.

For more detail, see **21.36**.

See also: *R v King* 2014 EWCA Crim 621, 2 Cr App R (S) 54 (p 437) (Car dealer who had 58 sales in breach of regulations and ordered to pay almost £110,000. Said it was in breach of article 1 and to be out of alignment with a sentence of 100 hours' unpaid work. Held. There is a clear distinction between goods provided by lawful contract and those tainted by illegality. This order was not disproportionate.)

21.20 ***European Convention on Human Rights Article 6***

R v Ahmad and Others 2014 UKSC 36, 2 Cr App R (S) 75 (p 580) Supreme Court para 7 Article 6(1) applies to all aspects of the confiscation hearing . . .article 6(2) does not [apply], as the hearing is treated as part of the sentencing process rather than part of the criminal trial, see *Phillips v UK* 2008 ECtHR 41087/98. For more detail see **21.89**.

21.21 ***European Convention on Human Rights Article 6 Confiscation does not amount to bringing of a criminal charge***

R v Bagnall and Sharma 2012 EWCA Crim 677 If the prosecution bring confiscation proceedings, they do not amount to the bringing of a criminal charge within the autonomous meaning under the Convention, *McIntosh v Lord Advocate* 2001 2 Cr App R 27 para 14 and *R v Rezvi* 2002 UKHL 1, 2 Cr App R 2 (p 300) para 30.

Note: Confiscation proceedings are criminal proceedings within the meaning of article 6(1) because they are part of the process of sentencing after a conviction, *R v Briggs-Price* 2009 UKHL 19. It follows that a defendant is entitled to a fair and public hearing within a reasonable time, *R v Gavin and Tasie* 2010 EWCA Crim 2727. However, the right conferred by article 6(2) (the presumption of innocence) is not applicable at the confiscation stage of criminal proceedings (see both the earlier cases). It must logically follow that article 6(3) rights (the minimum rights) are not strictly applicable either (see both the earlier cases). Yet this does not mean that the rights found in article 6(3) are necessarily inapplicable to confiscation proceedings, *R v Gavin and Tasie* 2010 EWCA Crim 2727. Many of the safeguards in article 6(3) will be relevant in the context of determining whether a trial is fair within article 6(1). Ed.

21.22 ***European Convention on Human Rights Article 6 Assessing criminality not subject to a charge***

R v Bagnall and Sharma 2012 EWCA Crim 677 B was convicted of money laundering which related to a bag containing £99,200. D traded in the wholesale distribution of mobile telephones. £50m passed through D's personal bank account. The prosecution decided not to prosecute him for a missing trader intra-community fraud but to rely on that criminality in the confiscation order because it was not worth spending the resources and the criminal benefit could be recovered by confiscation proceedings. It was contended that this was a violation of article 6(1) in that it was unfair to use the confiscation proceedings as a means of imposing the burden on D of having to disprove his involvement in missing trader intra-community fraud. Held. The mere fact that the Crown has accused D of specific offences and adduced evidence to make that accusation good does not amount to the bringing of a new charge. D was not at risk of any further conviction, there was no finding of guilt and the findings reached by the Judge, on the application of the assumptions under Proceeds of Crime Act 2002 s 10, merely went to the amount of the order the Court was obliged to make. The prosecution was obliged to include in its statement of information what was relevant in connection with the making of the assumptions. As a matter of fairness and obligation it set out all it knew and suspected in relation to the source of the assets which it was not disputed had been transferred to the appellant or were held by him. Article 6(1) was no warrant for an assertion that the proceedings were unfair to B.

Pre-hearing matters

21.23 *Postponement* ***Statute***

Time limits The time limits are in bold.

Postponement

Proceeds of Crime Act 2002 s 14(1) The court may:

(a) proceed under section 6 before it sentences the defendant for the offence (or any of the offences) concerned, or

(b) postpone proceedings under section 6 for a specified period.

(2) A period of postponement may be extended.

(3) A period of postponement (including one as extended) must not end after the permitted period ends.

(4) But subsection (3) does not apply if there are exceptional circumstances.

(5) The permitted period is the period of **2 years** starting with the date of conviction.

(6) But if:

(a) the defendant appeals against his conviction for the offence (or any of the offences) concerned, and

(b) the period of 3 months (starting with the day when the appeal is determined or otherwise disposed of) ends after the period found under subsection (5), the permitted period is that period of **3 months**.

(7) A postponement or extension may be made:

(a) on application by the defendant,

(b) on application by the prosecutor,

(c) by the court of its own motion.

(8) If:

(a) proceedings are postponed for a period, and

(b) an application to extend the period is made before it ends,

the application may be granted even after the period ends.

(9) The date of conviction is:

(a) the date on which the defendant was convicted of the offence concerned, or

(b) if there are two or more offences and the convictions were on different dates, the date of the latest.

(10) References to appealing include references to applying under Magistrates' Courts Act 1980 s 111 (statement of case).

(11) A confiscation order must not be quashed only on the ground that there was a defect or omission in the procedure connected with the application for or the granting of a postponement.

(12) But subsection (11) does not apply if, before it made the confiscation order, the court:

(a) imposed a fine on the defendant,

(b) made an order falling within section 13(3) (see above),

(c) made an order under Powers of Criminal Courts (Sentencing) Act 2000 s 130 (compensation orders),

(ca) made an order under Criminal Justice Act 2003 s 161A (orders requiring payment of surcharge),[369]

[369] Subsection (ca) was inserted by Serious Crime Act 2015 Sch 4 para 21. In force 1/6/15

(d) made an order under Prevention of Social Housing Fraud Act 2013 s 4 (unlawful profit orders).[370]

Proceeds of Crime Act 2002 s 15(1) If the court postpones proceedings under section 6 it may proceed to sentence the defendant for the offence (or any of the offences) concerned.

(2) In sentencing the defendant for the offence (or any of the offences) concerned in the postponement period the court must not:

(a) impose a fine on him,

(b) make an order falling within section 13(3),

(c) make an order under Powers of Criminal Courts (Sentencing) Act 2000 s 130 (compensation orders),

(ca) make an order under Criminal Justice Act 2003 s 161A (orders requiring payment of surcharge),[371]

(d) make an order under Prevention of Social Housing Fraud Act 2013 s 4 (unlawful profit orders).[372]

(3) If the court sentences the defendant for the offence (or any of the offences) concerned in the postponement period, after that period ends it may vary the sentence by:

(a) imposing a fine on him,

(b) making an order falling within section 13(3),

(c) making an order under Powers of Criminal Courts (Sentencing) Act 2000 s 130 (compensation orders),

(ca) making an order under Criminal Justice Act 2003 s 161A (orders requiring payment of surcharge),[373]

(d) making an order under Prevention of Social Housing Fraud Act 2013 s 4 (unlawful profit orders).[374]

(4) But the court may proceed under subsection (3) only within the period of 28 days which starts with the last day of the postponement period.

(5) For the purposes of:

(a) section 18(2) of the Criminal Appeal Act 1968 (c. 19) (time limit for notice of appeal or of application for leave to appeal), and

(b) paragraph 1 of Schedule 3 to the Criminal Justice Act 1988 (c. 33) (time limit for notice of application for leave to refer a case under section 36 of that Act),

the sentence must be regarded as imposed or made on the day on which it is varied under subsection (3).

(6) If the court proceeds to sentence the defendant under subsection (1), section 6 has effect as if the defendant's particular criminal conduct included conduct which constitutes offences which the court has taken into consideration in deciding his sentence for the offence or offences concerned.

(7) The postponement period is the period for which proceedings under section 6 are postponed.

21.24 ***Postponement Cases***

Note: It is usual for a judge to postpone the confiscation hearing while the parties serve statements. The defendant will normally be sentenced for the offence before the confiscation hearing. The period of postponement may not exceed two years, Proceeds of Crime Act 2002 s 14(1), (3) and (5), see above. However, this restriction does not apply where there are exceptional circumstances, Proceeds of Crime Act 2002 s 14(4).

R v Soneji and Bullen 2005 UKHL 49, 2006 1 Cr App R (S) 79 (p 430) House of Lords D and B pleaded to money laundering. The defence argued that no confiscation order could be made because the [then] six-month period had expired. The Judge made no

[370] Subsection (d) was inserted by Prevention of Social Housing Fraud Act 2013 Sch para 15.

[371] Subsection (ca) was inserted by Serious Crime Act 2015 Sch 4 para 22(2)(b). In force 1/6/15

[372] Subsection (d) was inserted by Prevention of Social Housing Fraud Act 2013 Sch para 16(2)(b).

[373] Subsection (ca) was inserted by Serious Crime Act 2015 Sch 4 para 22(3)(b). In force 1/6/15

[374] Subsection (d) was inserted by Prevention of Social Housing Fraud Act 2013 Sch para 16(3)(b).

finding that there were exceptional circumstances but he made confiscation orders. The Court of Appeal quashed them because of the failure to find exceptional circumstances. The prosecution appealed. Held. para 24 I would reject the submission that Criminal Justice Act 1993 s 72A (now a re-enacted section 14 with changes) should be given a strict interpretation. Here the prejudice to D and B was not significant. It was decisively outweighed by the countervailing public interest in not allowing a convicted offender to escape confiscation for what are no more than *bona fide* errors in the process. The confiscation orders were restored.

Note: Since this case was heard, the period has been extended from six months to two years. The case went to the European Court, see **21.27**.

R v Neish 2010 EWCA Crim 1011, 2011 1 Cr App R (S) 33 (p 208) LCJ D pleaded to supply of drugs. The Judge postponed confiscation proceedings until 11 December 2009 and set a timetable for it. When the Judge learnt that he would be busy on that day he instructed his listing officer to re-list the case. The case was re-listed before the expiration of the initial postponement period. The case was heard on 4 January 2010 and all agreed there was no valid postponement so no order was made. The prosecution on reflection appealed. Held. If right, this would be absurd. Listing is a judicial function and putting back the date constituted a postponement. Case remitted back to the Judge. In *R v Iqbal* 2010 EWCA Crim 376, 2 Cr App R (S) 72 (p 470),[375] the Court of Appeal held that an application to extend a period of postponement had to be made before the permitted period had expired. If not, there was no jurisdiction to hold confiscation proceedings. Ed.

R v Guraj 2016 UKSC 65, 2017 1 Cr App R (S) 32 (p 261) Supreme Court A forfeiture order was wrongly made at the beginning of the confiscation procedure and then the procedure went to sleep for about 18 months. The Court of Appeal quashed the order because of the delay and the breaches. Held. The Court is under a duty to make a confiscation order unless to do so would be unfair. Legislation and cases considered. There was no unfairness here. Order restored. For more details, see **21.28**.

R v Smith 2018 EWCA Crim 1351 On 14 January 2015, D pleaded to conspiracy to produce cannabis. On 5 August 2015, the court set a confiscation timetable. No criticism was made for this delay. On 8 September 2015, the prosecution served their section 16 statement. On 16 October 2015, the defence reply was received. On 1 December 2015, there was a mention when neither D nor his representative appeared. On 16 March 2016, the prosecution sent their response. On 14 January 2017, the time limit expired. On 16 February 2017, the prosecution asked for a hearing on 17 February. On that day, directions were given about skeleton arguments. On 29 September 2017, at a hearing, the prosecution did not submit there were exceptional circumstances. The Judge held the prosecution had effectively ignored the application and there was nothing exceptional. He refused to extend the time limit. The prosecution appealed. They said a failure to follow the procedure did not deprive the court of jurisdiction and the issue was whether it would be unfair to make an order. Held. From March 2016, there was 9½ months when the prosecution failed to progress the confiscation procedure. para 13 A procedural defect will not necessarily defeat an application for a confiscation order. However, the prosecution is not entitled to ignore the timetable in section 14 and then simply invite the court to consider whether its delay has caused unfairness. That would wholly defeat the legislative intent of section 14. Such an approach would not only encourage delay, which is inherently both undesirable and prejudicial, but would then add a new type of inquiry: what prejudice has been caused by delay. The present case demonstrates a casual and inefficient approach by the prosecution and the Judge was fully entitled to act as he did. We dismiss the application.

[375] This case is also called *Revenue and Customs v Iqbal* 2010 EWCA Crim 376, 2 Cr App R (S) 72 (p 470), because it was a High Court case and a Court of Appeal case.

See also: *R v Sheikh* 2014 EWCA Crim 3057 (The relevant Act was the 1994 Act (6-month limit). Preliminary hearing in 2001. Defendant absconds. Arrested September 2012. Order made February 2014. No explanation for the prosecution delay. Held. 'Exceptional circumstances' has a special meaning. Ask whether the court and the prosecution have made reasonable attempts to meet the timetable, have they acted in good faith, is the extension prejudicial to the defendant, is the defence responsible for any of the delay? If the judge takes those factors into account and the decision is reasonable, we won't interfere. Appeal dismissed.)
R v Jaffery 2016 EWCA Crim 287 (The Court of Appeal quashed a confiscation order and the Crown Court made another one. The defence then argued that the new confiscation order was made outside the 2-year period and there was no postponement order, so the order was a nullity. Held. It wasn't. *R v Iqbal* 2010 EWCA Crim 376, 2 Cr App R (S) 72 (p 470) only applies where an application to postpone confiscation proceedings had been made. No such application had been made.)
Note: As the Court was rightly keen to point out, if the defence were right it would be absurd. When the Court of Appeal quashed the confiscation order it exercised its powers under Criminal Appeal Act 1968 s 11(3A) (see **21.153**) and ordered the proceedings to start afresh. The time limits therefore don't apply because they only apply when the sentencing judge postpones the hearing. Ed.
For ***Procedural errors and the ability to make a confiscation order*** see **21.28**.
See also the ***Human Rights and delay*** para at **21.27**.

21.25 ***Counting the days***
Criminal Procedure Rules 2015 2015/1490 Rule 32.2(1) This rule shows how to calculate any period of time for doing any act which is specified by this Part and Parts 58, 59, 60 and 61 for the purposes of any proceedings under Proceeds of Crime Act 2002 Part 2 or by an order of the Crown Court in restraint proceedings or receivership proceedings.
(2) A period of time expressed as a number of days shall be computed as clear days.
(3) In this rule 'clear days' means that in computing the number of days:
(a) the day on which the period begins, and
(b) if the end of the period is defined by reference to an event, the day on which that event occurs,
are not included.
(4) Where the specified period is five days or less and includes a day which is not a business day, that day does not count.

21.26 ***Delay***
Criminal Practice Directions 2015 EWCA Crim 1567 para XIII G.11 It is important that confiscation hearings take place in good time after the defendant is convicted or sentenced.
R v Soneji and Bullen 2005 UKHL 49, 2006 1 Cr App R (S) 79 (p 430) House of Lords D and B pleaded to money laundering. The defence argued that no confiscation order could be made because the [then] six-month period had expired. The Judge made no finding that there were exceptional circumstances but he made confiscation orders. The Court of Appeal quashed them because of the failure to find exceptional circumstances. The prosecution appealed. Held. para 24 I would reject the submission that Criminal Justice Act 1993 s 72A (now a re-enacted section 14 with changes) should be given a strict interpretation. Here the prejudice to D and B was not significant. It was decisively outweighed by the countervailing public interest in not allowing a convicted offender to escape confiscation for what are no more than *bona fide* errors in the process. The confiscation orders were restored.
R v Guraj 2016 UKSC 65, 2017 1 Cr App R (S) 32 (p 261) Supreme Court A forfeiture order was wrongly made at the beginning of the confiscation procedure and then the procedure went to sleep for about 18 months. The Court of Appeal quashed the order

because of the delay and the breaches. Held. The Court is under a duty to make a confiscation order unless to do so would be unfair. Legislation and cases considered. There was no unfairness here. Order restored. For more details, see **21.28**.

21.27 ***Delay European Convention on Human Rights Article 6***
Minshall v UK 2011 7350/06 ECtHR In February 2000, D pleaded to alcohol duty fraud. In August 2000, the time period was extended. In October 2000, the Judge made a confiscation order for £80,000. D appealed, saying the order was unlawful because it was made after the (then) six-month time limit had expired. In December 2002, the Court of Appeal considered D's case with others on the same point and held the procedural irregularity did not deprive the Crown Court of jurisdiction. Two defendants appealed to the House of Lords and D's case was stayed. On 21 July 2005, the House of Lords affirmed the Court of Appeal's decision. D was then advised against continuing with his appeal and counsel withdrew. D's solicitor drafted two new grounds of appeal. In February 2006, D's application to amend his grounds of appeal was refused and his appeal was dismissed. D then appealed to the European Court of Human Rights. In December 2006, D began judicial review proceedings based on the delay. In November 2008, the judicial review application was dismissed. Held. The eight-month delay before the making of the confiscation order did not deprive the order of its validity or render the proceedings unfair. In appeal proceedings, the time between the lodging of appeal (November 2000) and the granting of leave (July 2001) was not material. However, the four years and seven months between the grant of leave and the determination was material. D's out of time conviction appeal in April 2003 and its dismissal in June 2004 contributed to the delay and the court notes this was against counsel's advice. The staying of the appeal awaiting the House of Lords' decision was reasonable. The overall period was unreasonably long and in breach of the reasonable time requirement of article 6. There was a violation of article 6(1). Taking into account D's contribution to the delay, €2,000 is awarded.
See also: *Bullen and Soneji v UK* 2009 3383/06 (Neither party could be criticised for the adjournment of the confiscation procedure to await a Court of Appeal ruling. However, the delay from then on (December 2000), when taken cumulatively, was in breach of the reasonable time requirement in article 6. The Crown Court orders were made in January and February 2002. There was a delay between a) the lodging of the appeal grounds in February 2002 and the Court of Appeal's judgment in June 2003 and b) the Court's certification for an appeal in July 2003 and the House of Lords' judgment in July 2005.)

21.28 ***Procedural errors and the ability to make a confiscation order***
Proceeds of Crime Act 2002 s 14(11) A confiscation order must not be quashed only on the ground that there was a defect or omission in the procedure connected with the application for or the granting of a postponement.
(12) But subsection (11) does not apply if before it made the confiscation order the court:
(a) imposed a fine on the defendant,
(b) made an order falling within section 13(3),
(c) made an order under the Powers of Criminal Courts (Sentencing) Act 2000 s 130 (compensation orders),
(ca) made an order under the Criminal Justice Act 2003 s 161A (orders requiring payment of surcharge),
(d) made an order under the Prevention of Social Housing Fraud Act 2013 s 4 (unlawful profit orders).
R v Sekhon and Others 2002 EWCA Crim 2954, 2003 2 Cr App R (S) 38 (p 207) LCJ In September 1998, D pleaded to cheating the public revenue. In December 1998, at the sentencing hearing, there was no mention of the postponement of the confiscation proceedings before sentence. After sentence, prosecution counsel raised the issue. The case was adjourned until February 1999. No mention was made of the need for

exceptional circumstances if the case was to be adjourned for more than six months (the then maximum period) from the date of conviction. Held. para 21 Parliament intends that a confiscation order should be made by the court, if a defendant has benefited from his crime, absent any indication to the contrary. The purpose of rules of procedure is not usually to give or take away a court's jurisdiction. What the procedural provisions are doing is to provide a convenient and just machinery enabling the court to exercise its jurisdiction. The procedural provisions can be, but usually are not, conditions that have to be fulfilled to give the court jurisdiction. More usually procedural provisions do no more than: a) enable the court, if they are not complied with, to make orders to require something to be done if it has not been done in accordance with the statutory provisions, or b) in the same circumstances to dismiss the proceedings. Neither a) nor b) above happens automatically in the absence of the proceedings being abandoned. What is required is for the court to come to a decision (usually on the application of the prosecution or defence) to take action a) or b) above. What action the court takes will depend on what is just in all the circumstances. If there is no application made (see above) but the next steps set out in the procedural provisions take place, the step that is not taken as it should have been can usually be ignored. It is no longer relevant even though Parliament has said it 'must' or 'should' be taken. This is because its objective of moving the procedure forward is no longer required. We would not regard this outcome to involve a 'waiver'. It is because of the matters set out above that procedural steps usually do not go to jurisdiction. The difficulty arises because Parliament does not often expressly indicate what procedural steps are to result in proceedings becoming, in effect, a nullity if they are not taken. It may be helpful if it is remembered that a) the use of mandatory terms is far from decisive and b) substantive provisions giving the court its jurisdiction are not to be automatically defeated in the ordinary way by non-compliance with procedural requirements unless this is necessary to achieve the statutory purpose. para 29 We would expect a procedural failure only to result in a lack of jurisdiction, if this was necessary to ensure that the criminal justice system served the interests of justice and thus the public or where there was at least a real possibility of the defendant suffering prejudice as a consequence of the procedural failure. Notwithstanding the actual language of Criminal Justice Act 1993 s 72(1) (now a re-enacted section 14 with changes) which read literally is mandatory in its terms, we would not regard it as likely that Parliament would [have intended to] deprive the court of jurisdiction [when there are] defects in the contents of the written notice.

Note: The Court quashed some of the confiscation orders based on failures to apply the postponement requirements, but those rulings would not now be made because of the decision in *R v Soneji and Bullen* 2005 UKHL 49, 2006 1 Cr App R (S) 79 (p 430) below.

R v Simpson 2003 EWCA Crim 1499, 2004 1 Cr App R (S) 24 (p 158) LCJ and four other judges. D pleaded to VAT tax offences. The Judge made a confiscation order. The defence argued that a court could not make a confiscation order unless a notice which complied with section 72 had been served and *R v Sekhon and Others* 2002 was wrongly decided. Held. It wasn't wrongly decided. We apply it and any defect in the notice[376] did not deprive the Judge of jurisdiction to make the confiscation order.

R v Soneji and Bullen 2005 UKHL 49, 2006 1 Cr App R (S) 79 (p 430) House of Lords D and B pleaded to money laundering. The defence argued that no confiscation order could be made because the [then] six-month period had expired. The Judge made no finding that there were exceptional circumstances but he made confiscation orders. The Court of Appeal quashed them because of the failure to find exceptional circumstances. The prosecution appealed. Held. para 24 I would reject the submission that Criminal Justice Act 1993 s 72A (now a re-enacted section 14 with changes) should be given a strict interpretation. Here the prejudice to D and B was not significant. It was decisively

[376] What the notice defect was is not revealed.

outweighed by the countervailing public interest in not allowing a convicted offender to escape confiscation for what are no more than *bona fide* errors in the process. The confiscation orders were restored.

Note: Once an order has been made, Proceeds of Crime Act 2002 s 14(11) applies. A confiscation order must not be quashed only on the ground that there was a defect or omission in the procedure connected with the application for or the granting of a postponement. Subsection (12) provides some exceptions to this rule. Section 14 is at **21.37**. The case went to the European Court, see **21.27**. Ed.

R v Barnett 2011 EWCA Crim 2936 D was convicted of brothel offences. At court there was a deal struck that the confiscation order should be limited to the amount of cash seized. The Judge made a confiscation order with consent for that amount without there being served any prosecutor's statement. The defence appealed on other grounds. The prosecution sought to contend that the failure to serve the notice meant the confiscation order was invalid. That would have resulted in them being able to recalculate the benefit using a later confiscation order. Held. This was an unattractive argument as it was the prosecution's failure to serve the notice. Applying *R v Sekhon and Knights* 2002 and *R v Simpson* 2003, the confiscation order [was valid].

R v Guraj 2016 UKSC 65, 2017 1 Cr App R (S) 32 (p 261) Supreme Court D pleaded to possession with intent to supply and five other counts. On 16 July 2012, he was sentenced to 5 years 4 months and the Judge made a forfeiture order for the drugs, D's laptop computer, iPhone etc. She postponed confiscation and ordered that D serve an assets statement by 13 August 2012 (which was served on 18 September 2012) and for the prosecution to serve their section 16 statement by 12 October 2012. That did not happen due to claimed staff changes. The Judge also listed a hearing date for 12 November 2012. In October 2013, the prosecution contacted the defence to say they had 'lost sight of the case'. The case was listed on 7 January 2014, when the prosecution asked for an adjournment because counsel was not adequately instructed. The prosecution served their section 16 statement on 15 January 2014. The Judge also made a £500 wasted costs order against the CPS for the failure to serve a statement and the failure of the officer to attend on the day meaning little could be achieved. The prosecution served their section 16 statement on 15 January 2014 with a revised statement on 25 January 2014. The case was listed on 31 March 2014 when no counsel appeared for the prosecution due to a misunderstanding within the CPS. Another wasted costs order was made. On 30 April 2014, the defence served a skeleton argument contending that due to the delay etc. the confiscation proceedings had lapsed. There was a hearing on 2 May 2014, when a special hearing was ordered. On 7 May 2014, a Judge ruled against that submission and set down a new timetable for the proceedings. He also made a wasted costs order against the CPS for the hearing on 31 March 2014. On 9 June 2014, a confiscation order was made on agreed figures. The defence appealed saying the failure to have a postponement order and the error in making a forfeiture order on 12 July 2012 meant no confiscation order could be made. The prosecution said the order was made within the two-year period and confiscation orders should not be struck down on technicalities. The Court of Appeal held that 'the combination of delays and breaches by the prosecution was such as to deprive the court of the power to make a confiscation order'. The court quashed the order. The prosecution appealed. Held. para 11 Section 15(2) is in many cases counter-intuitive and creates a trap into which even the most experienced judges may fall. That is because many forfeiture orders will not be in the least controversial and are inevitable whatever the outcome of confiscation proceedings may be. para 17 Sections 14(11) and (12) are confined to the case of procedural error 'connected with the application for or the granting of a postponement'. They have no application to any other kind of procedural error. para 22 The decisions in *R v Soneji and Bullen* 2005 UKHL 49, 2006 1 Cr App R (S) 79 (p 430) and *R v Knights* 2005 UKHL 50 are not peremptory. But the decisions are also of broader ambit than sections 14(11) and (12). Although the facts of both cases did concern postponements, the reasoning is not confined to that kind of procedural defect. That analysis [in *R v Knight* 2005] holds as good now as then. The court remains under a duty to make a confiscation order. para 29 [Here, the Court of Appeal] overlooked the fact that in a case where the postponements were not criticised, sections 14(11) and (12) had no application. But on the direct question whether section 15(2) mandated invalidity, the application of the principle of Soneji to a non-postponement procedural error was plainly correct. The Court went on to consider ways in which any injustice or unfairness to a defendant arising from making a confiscation order after a premature forfeiture order might be corrected. That was the right approach. para 31 The correct analysis is not that a procedural defect deprives the court of jurisdiction, which would indeed mean that every defect had the same consequence. Rather, [where] a failure to honour the procedure set down by the statute raises the very real possibility that it will be unfair to make an order…an order ought not be made. This is not to deprive section 14(12) of effect; it remains effective to remove the peremptory bar of section 14(11) upon quashing confiscation orders on grounds only of procedural defect connected with postponement. Where section 14(11) applies, no such defect can alone justify quashing. Resulting unfairness, on the other hand, may, but such unfairness cannot be inferred merely from the procedural breach. Where section 14(11) does not apply, a procedural defect, not limited to postponement, will have the effect of making it wrong to make a confiscation order if unfairness to the defendant would thereby ensue. If, however, the defect gives rise to no unfairness, or to none that cannot be cured, there can be no obstacle to the making of the order, and this is what the duty of the court requires. In a few instances, it might be possible to vary an inadvertently imposed sentence within the 56 days period. In others, the correct outcome may be that it is the forfeiture order which ought to be quashed, by way of appeal, rather than the confiscation order; priority for the latter is after all built into [the legislation]. Each case, however, must depend on its own facts. para 32 In the event of a very long period of inactivity, the correct inference may well be that unfairness to the accused has ensued…on the basis that the threat of confiscation had gone away, to the extent that to resume the process is unfair. The statute's intention is clearly that although confiscation may follow sentence, it is to be dealt with promptly. The duty to remove assets falling within the legislation is clearly a legislative priority. para 33 Here the statutory permitted period of two years was not exceeded. para 35 There was no obstacle to the making of [this] confiscation order, and it ought to have been made. Order restored.

For the Court of Appeal decision see the 11th edition of this book at para **22.25a**.

Note: Some of the background to the delay has been taken from the Court of Appeal judgment. Ed.

21.29 ***Defendant absconds***

Proceeds of Crime Act 2002 s 6(1) The Crown Court must proceed under this section if the following two conditions are satisfied.

(2) The first condition is that a defendant falls within any of the following paragraphs:

(a) he is convicted of an offence or offences in proceedings before the Crown Court,

(b) he is committed to the Crown Court for sentence in respect of an offence or offences under section 3, 3A, 3B, 3C, 4, 4A or 6 of the Powers of Criminal Courts (Sentencing) Act,

(c) he is committed to the Crown Court in respect of an offence or offences under section 70 below (committal with a view to a confiscation order being considered).

(3) to (7) [Not listed, see **21.5**]

(8) The first condition is not satisfied if the defendant absconds (but section 27 may apply).

Defendant convicted or committed

Proceeds of Crime Act 2002 s 27(1) This section applies if the following two conditions are satisfied.

(2) The first condition is that a defendant falls within any of the following paragraphs:[377]
(a) he absconds and, either before or after doing so, he is convicted of an offence or offences in proceedings before the Crown Court,
(b) he absconds after being committed to the Crown Court for sentence in respect of an offence or offences under Powers of Criminal Courts (Sentencing) Act 2000 s 3, 3A, 3B, 3C, 4, 4A or 6,
(c) he absconds after being committed to the Crown Court in respect of an offence or offences under Proceeds of Crime Act 2002 s 70 below (committal with a view to a confiscation order being considered).
(3) The second condition is that:
(a) the prosecutor applies to the Crown Court to proceed under this section, and
(b) the court believes it is appropriate for it to do so.
(4) If this section applies, the court must proceed under section 6 in the same way as it must proceed if the two conditions there mentioned are satisfied, but this is subject to subsection (5).
(5) If the court proceeds under section 6 as applied by this section, this Part has effect with these modifications:
(a) any person the court believes is likely to be affected by an order under section 6 is entitled to appear before the court and make representations,
(b) the court must not make an order under section 6 unless the prosecutor has taken reasonable steps to contact the defendant,
(c) section 6(9) applies as if the reference to subsection (2) were to subsection (2) of this section,
(d) sections 10, 16(4), 17 and 18 must be ignored,
(e) sections 19, 20 and 21 must be ignored while the defendant is still an absconder.
(6) Once the defendant ceases to be an absconder:
(a) section 19 has effect as if subsection (1) read:
'(1) This section applies if:
(a) at a time when the first condition in section 27 was satisfied the court did not proceed under section 6,
(b) before the end of the period of six years starting with the day when the defendant ceased to be an absconder, the prosecutor applies to the Crown Court to proceed under section 6, and
(c) the court believes it is appropriate for it to do so.',
b) section 20 has effect as if subsection (4) read:
'(4) The second condition is that:
(a) before the end of the period of six years starting with the day when the defendant ceased to be an absconder, the prosecutor applies to the Crown Court to reconsider whether the defendant has benefited from his general or particular criminal conduct (as the case may be), and
(b) the court believes it is appropriate for it to do so.',
c) section 21 has effect as if subsection (1) read:
'(1) This section applies if:
(a) a court has made a confiscation order,
(b) the prosecutor believes that if the court were to find the amount of the defendant's benefit in pursuance of this section it would exceed the relevant amount,
(c) before the end of the period of six years starting with the day when the defendant ceased to be an absconder, the prosecutor applies to the Crown Court to proceed under this section, and
(d) the court believes it is appropriate for it to do so.',

[377] Subsections (2) and (6) were substituted by Serious Crime Act 2015 s 9. Subsection (7) was removed by the same section. In force 1/6/15

d) the modifications set out in subsection (5)(a) to (d) of this section do not apply to proceedings that take place by virtue of section 19, 20 or 21 (as applied by this subsection).

R (CPS) v Cambridge Crown Court 2010 EWHC 663 (Admin) Divisional Court D pleaded to two offences of managing a brothel. Confiscation proceedings began and D gave evidence. The proceedings were adjourned. D was then given bail from custody, which had been imposed pending her deportation. D then did not attend. The prosecution wanted to continue. The Judge ruled that D had absconded. The prosecution said they did not wish to proceed under section 27 because they could not rely on the assumptions. It appeared that the Judge terminated the proceedings but that was not clear. On appeal to the High Court by the prosecution, the advocate to the Court suggested the proceedings had been abandoned by the prosecution as there had been no order. Held. There is an appeal to the Crown Court. In those circumstances it is wrong for this Court to hear the matter by way of judicial review where an appropriate appeal mechanism is in place.

Note: The reference to the Crown Court must either be a typo for the Court of Appeal or a reference to an opportunity to rehear the matter. It is likely to be the former. What the case decided is far from clear. Ed.

R v Bestel and Others 2013 EWCA Crim 1305, 2014 1 Cr App R (S) 53 (p 312) D pleaded to fraud offences. In confiscation proceedings, he did not file an assets statement. He was sent a draft section 18 statement to sign in prison. He didn't sign it. He did not attend the confiscation hearing. His advocate asked for an adjournment. This was refused and his advocate withdrew. The Judge held the withdrawal was highly likely to frustrate the proceedings. (By this stage D might have been released from prison. Ed.) The prosecution said if this was treated as absconding then everyone who wanted to frustrate confiscation proceedings could just stay at home. Held. para 44 The withdrawal seems unfortunate as the advocate could have helped with the law. In ordinary usage a person who absconds flees, runs away or escapes. In the context of the administration of criminal justice, the phrase 'a defendant absconds' implies that, at least, the defendant has sought to place himself beyond the reach of the court for the purpose of escaping judgment. D did not abscond in this sense. D had deliberately failed to attend hoping that the confiscation hearing would be postponed but knowing of the risk that the court would proceed in his absence. He remained at his known address, had been communicating with his solicitors and with the prosecution, and he had not attempted to escape the reach of the court. He did not abscond within the meaning of section 27.

For an article about the possible difficulty with the provision in section 27(2) above which provides the absconding has to be 'after a conviction', see *Archbold News* Issue 1 2013 page 6.

Note: Proceeds of Crime Act 2002 s 28 deals with defendants who are not acquitted or convicted and Proceeds of Crime Act 2002 s 29 deals with variation of the confiscation order. For an example of the Court of Appeal upholding the making of a confiscation order after a defendant had absconded, see *R v Spearing* 2010 EWCA Crim 2169, 2011 1 Cr App R (S) 101 (p 597). Ed.

R v Okedare 2014 EWCA Crim 1173 D was convicted in his absence of conspiracy to commit benefit fraud. He failed to appear for trial and a warrant was issued. At the confiscation hearing, again in his absence, the Judge ruled that Proceeds of Crime Act 2002 s 6 applied but Proceeds of Crime Act 2002 s 27-28 did not apply. D, still absent, appealed the making of the confiscation order. It was conceded that the Judge was neither entitled to rely upon section 6 alone, nor upon section 27. D contended that he had not been afforded any of the protections under section 28(5), namely: a) an obligation on the prosecution to make reasonable efforts to contact him, b) those potentially affected by the confiscation order have a right to be heard at the hearing, and c) the statutory assumptions under section 10 do not apply. Held. Following the explanatory notes and clear legislative intent, a court is entitled to make a confiscation

order under section 6 [in conjunction with] section 28. We accept this is at variance with the heading of section 28. However, that heading might apply to the time the defendant absconds. Since the original confiscation order in this case was made by the Judge under section 6 alone, and without the protections afforded by section 28(5), we quash it, and remit the matter to the Crown Court.
See also: *R v Nevitt* 2017 EWCA Crim 421 (After D was convicted of conspiracy to defraud, he absconded. Confiscation proceedings commenced in his absence and a confiscation order was made. Held. We apply *R v Spearing* 2010 EWCA Crim 2169, 2011 1 Cr App R (S) 101 (p 597). The order was lawfully made.)
R v Hipwood 2017 EWCA Crim 933 (On 14 March 2013, D was convicted and the prosecution requested confiscation proceedings. After many adjournments, a confiscation order was made in June 2016, when the defendant was not present. In the few hearings between those dates [it appears] the defendant did not attend. The defence argued he had absconded. Held. The confiscation proceedings commenced in March 2013 when the defendant was present. On that date, D had not absconded within section 6(8), so the order was valid.)
See also ***Defendant's qualified right to be present*** at **21.39**.

21.30 ***Defendant ordered to provide information about assets etc.***
Provision of information by the defendant
Proceeds of Crime Act 2002 s 18(1) This section applies if:
(a) the court is proceeding under section 6 in a case where section 6(3)(a) applies, or
(b) it is proceeding under section 6 in a case where section 6(3)(b) applies or it is considering whether to proceed. (For section 6 see para **21.5**.)
(2) For the purpose of obtaining information to help it in carrying out its functions (including functions under section 10A) the court may at any time order the defendant to give it information specified in the order.[378]
(3) An order under this section may require all or a specified part of the information to be given in a specified manner and before a specified date.
(4) If the defendant fails without reasonable excuse to comply with an order under this section the court may draw such inference as it believes is appropriate.
(5) Subsection (4) does not affect any power of the court to deal with the defendant in respect of a failure to comply with an order under this section.
(6) If the prosecutor accepts to any extent an allegation made by the defendant:[379]
(a) in giving information required by an order under this section, or
(b) in any other statement given to the court in relation to any matter relevant to deciding:
(i) the available amount under section 9, or
(ii) whether to make a determination under section 10A, or what determination to make (if the court decides to make one),
the court may treat the acceptance as conclusive of the matters to which it relates.
(7) For the purposes of this section an allegation may be accepted in a manner ordered by the court.
(8) If the court makes an order under this section it may at any time vary it by making another one.
(9) No information given under this section which amounts to an admission by the defendant that he has benefited from criminal conduct is admissible in evidence in proceedings for an offence.

21.31 ***Defendant ordered to provide information*** ***Serious Crime Act 2015 addition***
Provision of information as to defendant's interest in property
Proceeds of Crime Act 2002 s 18A(1) This section applies if the court:[380]

[378] As amended by Serious Crime Act 2015 s 2(2)(a). In force 1/6/15
[379] This subsection was amended by Serious Crime Act 2015 s 2(2)(b)
[380] The section was inserted by Serious Crime Act 2015 s 2(3). In force 1/6/15

(a) is considering whether to make a determination under section 10A of the extent of the defendant's interest in any property, or
(b) is deciding what determination to make (if the court has decided to make a determination under that section).

In this section 'interested person' means a person (other than the defendant) who the court thinks is or may be a person holding an interest in the property.
(2) For the purpose of obtaining information to help it in carrying out its functions under section 10A the court may at any time order an interested person to give it information specified in the order.
(3) An order under this section may require all or a specified part of the information to be given in a specified manner and before a specified date.
(4) If an interested person fails without reasonable excuse to comply with an order under this section the court may draw such inference as it believes is appropriate.
(5) Subsection (4) does not affect any power of the court to deal with the person in respect of a failure to comply with an order under this section.
(6) If the prosecutor accepts to any extent an allegation made by an interested person:
(a) in giving information required by an order under this section, or
(b) in any other statement given to the court in relation to any matter relevant to a determination under section 10A,
the court may treat the acceptance as conclusive of the matters to which it relates.
(7) For the purposes of this section an allegation may be accepted in a manner ordered by the court.
(8) If the court makes an order under this section it may at any time vary it by making another one.
(9) No information given by a person under this section is admissible in evidence in proceedings against that person for an offence.

21.32 *Production orders*

Production orders

Proceeds of Crime Act 2002 s 345(1) A judge may, on an application made to him by an appropriate officer, make a production order if he is satisfied that each of the requirements for the making of the order is fulfilled.
(2) The application for a production order must state that:
(a) a person specified in the application is subject to a confiscation investigation, an exploitation proceeds investigation or a money laundering investigation, or
(b) property specified in the application is subject to a civil recovery investigation or a detained cash investigation.
(3) The application must also state that:
(a) the order is sought for the purposes of the investigation,
(b) the order is sought in relation to material, or material of a description, specified in the application,
(c) a person specified in the application appears to be in possession or control of the material.
(4) A production order is an order either:
(a) requiring the person the application for the order specifies as appearing to be in possession or control of material to produce it to an appropriate officer for him to take away, or
(b) requiring that person to give an appropriate officer access to the material,
within the period stated in the order.
(5) The period stated in a production order must be a period of seven days beginning with the day on which the order is made, unless it appears to the judge by whom the order is made that a longer or shorter period would be appropriate in the particular circumstances.

Requirements for making production orders

Proceeds of Crime Act 2002 s 346(1) These are the requirements for the making of a production order.
(2) There must be reasonable grounds for suspecting that:
(a) in the case of a confiscation investigation, the person the application for the order specifies as being subject to the investigation has benefited from his criminal conduct,
(b) in the case of a civil recovery investigation, the property the application for the order specifies as being subject to the investigation is recoverable property or associated property,
(ba) in the case of a detained cash investigation into the derivation of cash, the property the application for the order specifies as being subject to the investigation, or a part of it, is recoverable property,
(bb) in the case of a detained cash investigation into the intended use of cash, the property the application for the order specifies as being subject to the investigation, or a part of it, is intended by any person to be used in unlawful conduct,
(c) in the case of a money laundering investigation, the person the application for the order specifies as being subject to the investigation has committed a money laundering offence,
(d) in the case of an exploitation proceeds investigation, the person the application for the order specifies as being subject to the investigation is within subsection (2A).
(2A) A person is within this subsection if, for the purposes of Coroners and Justice Act 2009 Part 7 (criminal memoirs etc.), exploitation proceeds have been obtained by the person from a relevant offence by reason of any benefit derived by the person. This subsection is to be construed in accordance with that Part.
(3) There must be reasonable grounds for believing that the person the application specifies as appearing to be in possession or control of the material so specified is in possession or control of it.
(4) There must be reasonable grounds for believing that the material is likely to be of substantial value (whether or not by itself) to the investigation for the purposes of which the order is sought.
(5) There must be reasonable grounds for believing that it is in the public interest for the material to be produced or for access to it to be given, having regard to:
(a) the benefit likely to accrue to the investigation if the material is obtained;
(b) the circumstances under which the person the application specifies as appearing to be in possession or control of the material holds it.
Note: Proceeds of Crime Act 2002 s 347 provides for power to require access. Proceeds of Crime Act 2002 s 348 provides that section 347 does not apply to privileged and excluded material. It also deals with how long the material may be retained for. Ed.
Criminal Practice Directions 2015 EWCA Crim 1567 para XIII G.8 The use of production orders and search warrants involve the use of intrusive state powers that affect the rights and liberties of individuals. It is the responsibility of the court to ensure that those powers are not abused. To do so, the court must be presented with a properly completed application, on the appropriate form, which includes a summary of the investigation to provide the context for the order, a clear explanation of how the statutory requirements are fulfilled, and full and frank disclosure of anything that might undermine the basis for the application. Further directions on the proper making and consideration of such applications will be provided by Practice Direction. However, the complexity of the application must be taken into account in listing it such that the judge is afforded appropriate reading time and the hearing is given sufficient time for the issues to be considered thoroughly, and a short judgment given.

21.33 *Disclosure orders*

Note: A judge has power to make a disclosure order on application by a relevant authority, Proceeds of Crime Act 2002 s 357. The order may require persons to answer questions and provide information. The procedure was considered in *NCA v Simkus and Others* 2016 EWCH 255 (Admin). There is no requirement that the judge should give reasons for making an order, *Nuttall v NCA* 2016 EWHC 1911 (Admin). Ed.

21.34 *Prosecutor's statement*

Statement of information

Proceeds of Crime Act 2002 s 16(1) If the court is proceeding under section 6 in a case where section 6(3)(a) applies, the prosecutor must give the court a statement of information within the period the court orders.

(2) If the court is proceeding under section 6 in a case where section 6(3)(b) applies and it orders the prosecutor to give it a statement of information, the prosecutor must give it such a statement within the period the court orders.

(3) If the prosecutor believes the defendant has a criminal lifestyle, the statement of information is a statement of matters the prosecutor believes are relevant in connection with deciding these issues:

(a) whether the defendant has a criminal lifestyle,

(b) whether he has benefited from his general criminal conduct,

(c) his benefit from the conduct.

(4) A statement under subsection (3) must include information the prosecutor believes is relevant:

(a) in connection with the making by the court of a required assumption under section 10,

(b) for the purpose of enabling the court to decide if the circumstances are such that it must not make such an assumption.

(5) If the prosecutor does not believe the defendant has a criminal lifestyle, the statement of information is a statement of matters the prosecutor believes are relevant in connection with deciding these issues:

(a) whether the defendant has benefited from his particular criminal conduct,

(b) his benefit from the conduct.

(6) If the prosecutor gives the court a statement of information:

(a) he may at any time give the court a further statement of information,

(b) he must give the court a further statement of information if it orders him to do so, and he must give it within the period the court orders.

(6A) A statement of information (other than one to which subsection (6B) applies) must include any information known to the prosecutor which the prosecutor believes is or would be relevant for the purpose of enabling the court to decide:[381]

(a) whether to make a determination under section 10A, or

(b) what determination to make (if the court decides to make one).

(6B) If the court has decided to make a determination under section 10A, a further statement of information under subsection (6)(b) must, if the court so orders, include specified information that is relevant to the determination.

(7) If the court makes an order under this section it may at any time vary it by making another one.

Note: Criminal Procedure Rules 2015 2015/1490 Rule 32.13(1)-(2) and (5) sets down what the statement must contain and is similar to the statute. Ed.

See also the ***Evidential status of the prosecution statement*** at **21.44**.

21.35 *The defendant's reply*

Defendant's response to statement of information

Proceeds of Crime Act 2002 s 17(1) If the prosecutor gives the court a statement of information and a copy is served on the defendant, the court may order the defendant:

(a) to indicate (within the period it orders) the extent to which he accepts each allegation in the statement, and

[381] Subsections (6A) and (6B) were inserted by Serious Crime Act 2015 s 2. In force 1/6/15

(b) so far as he does not accept such an allegation, to give particulars of any matters he proposes to rely on.

(2) If the defendant accepts to any extent an allegation in a statement of information the court may treat his acceptance as conclusive of the matters to which it relates for the purpose of deciding the issues referred to in section 16(3) or (5) (as the case may be).

(3) If the defendant fails in any respect to comply with an order under subsection (1) he may be treated for the purposes of subsection (2) as accepting every allegation in the statement of information apart from:

(a) any allegation in respect of which he has complied with the requirement,

(b) any allegation that he has benefited from his general or particular criminal conduct.

(4) For the purposes of this section an allegation may be accepted or particulars may be given in a manner ordered by the court.

(5) If the court makes an order under this section it may at any time vary it by making another one.

(6) No acceptance under this section that the defendant has benefited from conduct is admissible in evidence in proceedings for an offence.

Criminal Procedure Rules 2015 2015/1490 Rule 33.13(6) A defendant's response notice must:

(a) indicate the extent to which the defendant accepts the allegations made in the prosecutor's statement of information, and

(b) so far as the defendant does not accept an allegation, give particulars of any matters on which the defendant relies,

in any manner directed by the court.

R v Leeming 2008 EWCA Crim 2753 At a mention, the defendant's advocate asked for more time to respond to the prosecution's statement as he was waiting for information from various financial institutions. The Judge refused the application. In the defendant's absence the Judge, believing he had no discretion, accepted the prosecution's invitation to assume their statement was true. Held. A defendant who fails to serve a statement in accordance with an order of the court under Proceeds of Crime Act 2002 s 17(1) does not deprive the judge of his discretion and does not require him to conclude that the defendant is to be treated as accepting every allegation in the prosecutor's statement. [The Judge went beyond the power conferred by section 17(1) by treating the appellant as accepting the allegations that the property he held amounted to benefit from criminal conduct.] The defendant later obtained information which the prosecution accepted disproved the assumptions. A lower and agreed amount substituted.

R v Lowe 2009 EWCA Crim 194, 2 Cr App R (S) 81 (p 544) para 21 There are many complaints that defence statements are inadequate. If identifying the issues is left to the last minute, then insufficient attention is paid to ensuring that any procedural steps needed for the evidence to be admissible are taken.

21.36 *A court has no discretion once proceedings have been started post R v Waya 2012*

Note: Proceedings are not obligatory (see Proceeds of Crime Act 2002 s 6(3) at **21.12**), but once proceedings have been initiated section 6(4) is activated, and the determinations are obligatory. The court is then required to conduct confiscation proceedings. Ed.

R v Waya 2012 UKSC 51, 2013 2 Cr App R (S) 20 (p 87) Supreme Court The Court considered European Convention on Human Rights art 3 and the opportunities to make abuse of process applications. The cases of *R v Morgan and Bygrave* 2008 EWCA Crim 1323, 2009 1 Cr App R (S) 60 (p 333) and *R v Shabir* 2008 EWCA Crim 1809, 1 Cr App R (S) 84 (p 497) were considered. Held. para 18 While these cases are correct, the better analysis of such situations is that orders such as those considered [in those cases] ought to be refused by the judge on the grounds that they would be wholly disproportionate and a breach of article 1. There is no need to invoke the concept of abuse of process.

Note: The principles for abuse of process arguments have to be considered with the principles in *R v Waya* 2012 UKSC 51, 2013 2 Cr App R (S) 20 (p 87). Where an advocate might have submitted there was an abuse of process, he or she would often now rely on the principle of proportionality. Ed.

R v Parveaz 2017 EWCA Crim 873 D pleaded to production of cannabis. In a *Newton* hearing, the Judge said he could not be sure that D had produced cannabis for commercial supply. In their section 16 statement, the prosecution said D had available assets worth at least £178,000. D's section 18 statement gave no explanation as to how he had funded his interest in various properties or explained various cash transactions. The Judge held it was disproportionate and unjust to allow the assumptions to be made, see para 1. He refused to permit the proceedings to continue to a final hearing. The prosecution appealed. Held. It was not open to the Judge to do that in this particular case. The Judge was not sure to the criminal standard that there was production for commercial supply. To focus on the findings at the *Newton* hearing masks the true nature of the exercise before the Judge, which was to focus on the general criminal conduct of D and not the particular criminal conduct. The Judge had not been concerned with the preceding six-year period, and rightly had made no findings in that regard. He was not entitled to address the question of whether or not it was proportionate to embark upon a Proceeds of Crime Act 2002 application. That was for the prosecution. If any challenge could be made to such a decision, it would have to be made by way of judicial review, and such proceedings very rarely can be successfully entertained. para 33 There can be cases where, for example, a particular basis of plea is expressly accepted by the Crown, which may then be wholly inconsistent with pursuit thereafter of confiscation proceedings based on the lifestyle provisions, see *R v Lunnon* 2004 EWCA Crim 1125, 2005 1 Cr App R (S) 24 (p 111). para 36 The Judge seems to have thought that his own conclusions in the *Newton* hearing equated to a finding that there had been no such commercial supply in the preceding six-year period. But it did not. para 41 The Judge's conclusion was both wrong and premature. We set aside the Judge's decision and send the case back to the Crown Court.

21.37 ***A court has no discretion once proceedings have been started/Abuse of process pre-Waya 2012 cases***

R v Lowe 2009 EWCA Crim 194, 2 Cr App R (S) 81 (p 544) D pleaded to fraudulent transfer. He was a director of a company which was being wound up. He moved some property of that company to another company in which he had an interest. That was unlawful. Confiscation proceedings were instituted. The liquidator was able to exercise his powers to treat the transfer as void. Held. para 17 There can be no suggestion of an abuse or oppression. The decision to seek a confiscation order is one that can be seen as simply carrying out the decision of Parliament. D made no offer to restore the property. It would have been restored by operation of the provision of the Insolvency Act if his co-director had not entered into an agreement to restore it. This was not a course of criminal conduct limited to one or more identifiable losers. The fraudulent transfer was made to strip an asset out of his company to the detriment of every creditor.

R (Secretary of State for Work and Pensions) v Croydon Crown Court 2010 EWHC 805 (Admin), 2011 1 Cr App R (S) 1 (p 1) D pleaded to benefit fraud. She obtained income support of just over £25,700 when she had more than one property. The first Judge gave her a Suspended Sentence Order and set the timetable down for a confiscation hearing. At the end he told D that there would be no need for the confiscation hearing if she repaid the money. Prosecution counsel said nothing. About a month later she paid back the whole sum. The prosecution served their statement and at the next hearing the defence said it would be an abuse of process to continue. The first Judge handed the matter over to a second judge. That Judge held that the first Judge had given an unequivocal representation and the prosecution counsel had said nothing. The second Judge held that it would be both oppressive and an abuse to continue. The prosecution appealed saying the prosecution was not responsible for the remarks and the second

Judge was required to conduct confiscation proceedings. Held. The Act acts as a disincentive to make voluntary repayment. Although the prosecution were not responsible for the remark they said nothing to correct it. They could have contacted D to correct the first Judge up until the payment was made. The prosecution had a measure of responsibility for the situation. It would be going too far to suggest the defence should have corrected the error. Stopping confiscation hearings on the ground of abuse of process should be done very sparingly, as the will of Parliament is not to be usurped. A more important issue is the integrity of the administration of justice. Justice must be conducted so it does not undermine public confidence in its own integrity [or] bring the administration of justice into disrepute. Great trust is reposed in the courts, and rightly so. It is of great importance that parties and the public should be able to trust what the court says. It would be damaging to the integrity of the process of criminal justice for the court now to proceed with confiscation. It would involve the court itself in giving the offender an inducement and then reneging on its words after she had acted upon the inducement. Quite simply this would not be a fair process. The prosecution submitted that the words of the statute trump anything the Judge may have said. That is not right. The second Judge was correct to stay the proceedings.

R v Shabir 2008 EWCA Crim 1809, 1 Cr App R (S) 84 (p 497) D, a pharmacist, was convicted of making inflated claims for prescriptions from the Health Service. There were six counts and they were not sample counts. The Judge accepted the total improperly obtained was £464. The prosecution relied on the total amount claimed and said the benefit obtained was nearly £180,000. They asked for a compensation order for over £400,000. The Judge made an order for over £212,000. Held. The Judge was right to find D had obtained the £180,000 figure. The Judge had a discretion to stay the proceedings, *R v Mahmood and Shahin* 2005 EWCA Crim 2168, 2006 1 Cr App R (S) 96 (p 570). This jurisdiction must be exercised with considerable caution, indeed sparingly. It must be confined to cases of true oppression. In particular, it cannot be exercised simply on the grounds that the judge disagrees with the decision of the Crown to pursue confiscation, or with the way it puts its case on that topic. An example which is not sufficient to establish oppression is where the order seeks to extract from the defendant a greater sum than the net profit of his crimes. In this case, the enormous disparity between the [money improperly obtained] and the confiscation order of over £212,000 raises the real likelihood that this order is oppressive. However, such a disparity will not in every case by itself establish oppression. If it is a case in which the criminal lifestyle provisions of the Act can legitimately be applied, and with them the several section 10 assumptions as to the source of assets, it may well be perfectly proper for a confiscation order to be massively greater than the gain from the offences of which the defendant has been convicted. para 29 What was patently oppressive in the present case was to rely on the form of the counts for obtaining a money transfer by deception: i) to bring the criminal lifestyle provisions into operation when they could not have applied if the charges had reflected the fact that the defendant's crimes involved fraud to an extent very much less than the threshold of £5,000, and ii) to advance the contention that the defendant had benefited to the tune of over £179,000 when in any ordinary language his claims were dishonestly inflated by only a few hundred pounds. It was oppressive. If the Judge had been asked to stay the proceedings he would have to have done so. A £464 compensation order substituted.

CPS v Nelson 2009 EWCA Crim 1573, 2010 1 Cr App R (S) 82 (p 530) LCJ Three separate cases were heard together. N pleaded to handling. The Judge stayed the proceedings because although property had been obtained by N, he had received no benefit. P pleaded to deception counts. P had worked unlawfully by deceiving the employer. The Judge found he had paid all his taxes and NI and his wages were truly earned. The Judge made a confiscation order just for some money in some bank accounts and left out the wages. D pleaded to theft. He stole over £131,300 from his employers. The employee refused to support a prosecution and D paid £151,000 for the loss, legal fees and interest. The Judge considered that D would be in a far better position if he had not paid the money. He held that the proceedings were oppressive and an abuse. The CPS appealed the decision for N and D. P also appealed. Held. Orders staying confiscation proceedings are perhaps too readily being made in Crown Courts. An abuse of process argument cannot be founded on the basis that the consequences of the proper application of the legislative structure may produce an 'oppressive' result with which the judge may be unhappy. We adopt the principle in *R v Shabir* 2009 (see above), 'This jurisdiction must be exercised with considerable caution, indeed sparingly. It must be confined to cases of true oppression. In particular, it cannot be exercised simply on the grounds that the judge disagrees with the decision of the Crown to pursue confiscation, or with the way it puts its case on that topic.'

The CPS produced a document entitled 'Guidance for Prosecutors on the Discretion to Instigate Confiscation Proceeds'. It is a useful working document. We are not adopting the guidance in this judgment but it is a fair analysis. The examples given when it may be inappropriate for prosecutors to decide to instigate confiscations are, first, 'where the Crown has reneged on an earlier agreement not to proceed'. Second 'in a simple benefit case, where the defendant has voluntarily paid full compensation to the victim or victims, or is ready, willing and able immediately to repay all of the victims to the full amount of their losses, and has not otherwise profited from his crime'. Third, 'where if the court "were asked to proceed to confiscation" it might be compelled to find that property obtained in the most part legitimately by the defendant, and to which the defendant would have been entitled but for his criminal conduct, must be treated as benefit'. Fourth, 'where a defendant has paid employment by a false representation to his employer' and the extent of his benefit may simply be his wages, it may be that this will have to be re-examined. The confiscation process should not continue for the sake of consistency. It should be discontinued on the emergence of facts which, had they been known at the outset, would have led the prosecutor not to proceed.

For N the decision to stay the proceedings was wrong. For D there was ample evidence to suggest that the benefit far exceeded the loss suffered by his employers and repayments by D. There was no abuse of process. P's appeal is dismissed. There were areas of significant evidence which needed resolution. The proceedings were not an abuse. We remit the case back to the Crown Court.

See also: *R v Morgan and Bygrave* 2008 EWCA Crim 1323, 2009 1 Cr App R (S) 60 (p 333). (Conjoined appeals. Principles considered. One appeal dismissed. The other order varied to a compensation order.) *R v Lowe* 2009 EWCA Crim 194, 2 Cr App R (S) 81 (p 544) (There was no abuse or oppression.)

21.38 *Counsel's duties*

R v Lowe 2009 EWCA Crim 194, 2 Cr App R (S) 81 (p 544) para 21 There are many complaints that defence [responses] are inadequate. Timetables set out in the Criminal Procedure Rules or the court's directions frequently slip. Sometimes it is only at the last minute, either immediately before the court sits or even in the course of a hearing, that some matters are agreed and the real issues emerge, considerably burdening the task of the judge hearing the proceedings. If identifying the issues is left to the last minute, then insufficient attention is paid to ensuring that any procedural steps needed for the evidence to be admissible are taken. In an occasional case, where difficult issues arise, it may be the case that counsel with more experience of such issues is needed. Difficulties are from time to time compounded by the lack of a properly paginated bundle. It is, in the experience of many in this Court, that for reasons such as those we have outlined, it is not always clear from the ruling (or judgment) below what the facts were on which the issues which arose were determined.

The hearing

21.39 ***Defendant's qualified right to be present***

R v Leeming 2008 EWCA Crim 2753 At a mention [where the defendant was not required to attend], the defendant's advocate asked for more time to respond to the prosecution's statement as he was waiting for information from various financial institutions. The Judge refused the application. The Judge proceeded without notice. He treated the prosecutor's statement as being accepted and made the order requested. The defendant later obtained information which the prosecution accepted disproved some of the assumptions. The prosecution conceded that the proceedings were unfair. Held. It was wrong to proceed in the defendant's absence and without notice. A lower and agreed amount substituted.

R v Gavin and Tasie 2010 EWCA Crim 2727 The right to be present at the hearing would be considered to be an aspect of a fair trial within the meaning of article 6(1). The discretion to continue must never be exercised where it is the action of the state itself that causes the defendant to be absent. Here, where the defendant was unable to be present, for example because he had been deported, proceeding against him would be a breach of article 6.

See also: *R v McCormick* 2010 EWCA Crim 1556 (The defendant decided not to attend the confiscation proceedings. Held. He had not absconded. The court should be cautious in proceeding without the defendant but the court can proceed without the defendant.)

R v Bhanji 2011 EWCA Crim 1198 (Defendant chronically ill. Unable to attend or give instructions. The question was whether the hearing was fair. Here, looking at all the circumstances, it was. Order upheld.)

R v Ali 2014 EWCA Crim 1658 (Defendant admitted to a mental hospital a few days before the hearing. The defence said he was very unwell, lacked capacity and was under the jurisdiction of the Court of Protection. They were unable to give a date when he could attend. Their doctor said he was incapable of following the proceedings. The prosecution doctor said there were elements of malingering and he could follow the proceedings. The proceedings had already lasted 18 months. The defence accepted that illness could not be used to stave off proceedings forever. The Judge said on the medical evidence he might never be able to attend and the hearing would be fair. Held. The Judge was able to say he was capable of being present if he wished. The refusal to adjourn and the rejection of the abuse argument was proper.)

R v Hall 2015 EWCA Crim 116 (The defendant, D, did not know about the mention or the full hearing. Solicitors failed to communicate with D properly. Held. He was not an absconder. His case could not be advanced without him. Order quashed. Case remitted to Crown Court.)

R v Place 2015 EWCA Crim 1404 (Defendant in prison absent and claiming illness. Judge entitled to consider that the hearing was fair.)

See also the ***Defendant absconds*** paras at **21.29** and **86.24**.

21.40 ***The stepped approach***

R v May 2008 UKHL 28, 2009 1 Cr App R (S) 31 (p 162) Lords para 48(1) The legislation does not provide for confiscation as understood by schoolchildren and others, but nor does it operate by way of a fine. The benefit gained is the total value of the property or advantage obtained, not the defendant's net profit after deduction of expenses or any amounts payable to co-conspirators. (2) The court should proceed by asking: a) if the defendant has benefited from relevant criminal conduct, b) if so, what is the value of the benefit he has so obtained, and c) what sum is recoverable from him. These questions call for separate answers and must be modified where issues of criminal lifestyle arise. The questions and answers must not be elided.[382] (3) In addressing these questions, the court should, first, establish the facts as best it can on the material available, relying as appropriate on the statutory assumptions. In very many cases the

[382] This means 'skipped over' or 'merged'.

factual findings made will be decisive. (4) The court should focus very closely on the language of the statutory provision in question in the context of the statute and in the light of any statutory definition. Any judicial gloss or exegesis should be viewed with caution. Guidance should ordinarily be sought in the statutory language rather than in the proliferating case law.

21.41 ***Verdict of the jury, Judge making findings of fact and the***
R v Sangha 2008 EWCA Crim 2562, 2009 2 Cr App R (S) 17 (p 94) S, M and Mc were convicted of cheating the public revenue. It was a VAT carousel fraud. The issue before the jury was whether they knowingly played a part in the fraud. For the jury, the role ascribed to each defendant was limited to contributing to the paperwork for the missing fraudsters. VAT was falsely claimed back by others. The Judge found the property obtained in connection with the offence was the VAT falsely claimed and this was not limited by the verdict of the jury. The Judge assessed the benefit at just under £29m and made confiscation orders for S of just over £4.7m, M of just over £970,000 and for Mc of nearly £650,000. Held. para 30 The jury's verdict and the factual basis upon which it was reached will of course have an important part to play in setting the parameters of the confiscation proceedings. It will not be open to the judge to act inconsistently with the verdict or its factual basis when dealing with matters of confiscation. The questions in confiscation proceedings (benefit and the amount recoverable) are distinct from those during the trial. The standard of proof is different. There will normally be evidence additional to that led at the trial. The judge is responsible for making the relevant determinations, not the jury. Whilst the judge must act consistently with the jury's verdict and its factual basis, it is open to him, in the light of the evidence as a whole, to make additional and more extensive findings of fact than those upon which the verdict was based, *R v Threapleton* 2001 EWCA Crim 2892, 2002 2 Cr App R (S) 46 (p 197). The judge should determine the statutory questions on the evidence before him, *R v Olubitan* 2003 EWCA Crim 2940, 2004 2 Cr App R (S) 14 (p 70). para 37 If other misconduct is relevant, the court is not precluded from considering evidence of that other misconduct, even where it amounts to a criminal offence. Appeal dismissed.
See also: *R v Panayi* 2019 EWCA Crim 413 (D was convicted of breaching an Enforcement Notice. The gross rental income was used. Held. As the charge related to 'on or about 18 February 2016', the benefit was the benefit for that day. The order must be for £58 not £95,920.)

Evidence

21.42 ***Evidence Admissibility***
R v Silcock 2004 EWCA Crim 408, 2 Cr App R (S) 61 (p 323) D was convicted of conspiracy to import counterfeit currency and a linked count. During the confiscation proceedings the Judge relied on the co-defendant's statement that: a) the imported currency had a face value of $4.25m which was inadmissible during the trial, and b) witness statements which were not led orally either in the trial or in the confiscation hearing. Held. A confiscation hearing is an extension of the sentencing hearing, and therefore criminal in nature, but by virtue of Criminal Justice Act 1993 the civil procedure is correctly adopted and applied. The Judge was entitled to find as he did, on the basis of material he had derived from the evidence in the trial and the documentary evidence put before him.

21.43 ***Evidence Defence evidence***
R v Walbrook and Glasgow 1994 15 Cr App R (S) 783 D was convicted of supplying amphetamine. During the confiscation proceedings there were issues about a debt owed to D and his beneficial interest under a will. Held. The evidence was vague and unsatisfactory. The burden was on D. Where a defendant has an asset in the form of a debt, the onus is on him to satisfy the court that the realisable value of the debt is less

than its face value. He must do so by producing clear and cogent evidence. Vague and generalised assertions unsupported by evidence will rarely if ever be sufficient to discharge the burden on the defendant. Appeal dismissed.
Note: Although this deals with the assets of a defendant, the CPS regularly and usually successfully rely on this case for evidence in general. Ed.
R v Panesar 2008 EWCA Crim 1643 D pleaded to conspiracy to supply class A drugs. During the confiscation proceedings D in evidence sought to explain cash deposits by saying that his income from being a taxi driver was higher than the amounts declared to the tax authorities. D called a director of the taxi firm to say how hard-working he was. The Judge found that taxi driving was a cash business so he needed to take into account that reprehensibly people do not always declare their full income. The prosecution appealed and attacked this finding relying on *R v Walbrook and Glasgow* 1994 15 Cr App R (S) 783. Held. The Judge was entitled to make this finding. There was, just, an evidential basis for it.

21.44 ***Evidential status of the prosecutor's statement***
R v Dickens 1990 91 Cr App R 164 LCJ D was convicted of conspiracy to supply cannabis resin. During the confiscation proceedings, the Judge said he would act on the prosecution statements without the necessity of the prosecution adducing any evidence in support, despite the fact that D contested the statements. In fact, evidence was called. Held. Where the prosecution statement is not accepted, if the prosecution wish to rely on any of its contents, they must adduce evidence to establish them.
See also the ***Prosecutor's statement*** para at **21.34**.

21.45 ***Evidence Hearsay***
R v Clipston 2011 EWCA Crim 446, 2 Cr App R (S) 101 (p 569) D pleaded to conspiracy to supply class A drugs. D was at the 'top of the conspiracy'. C, D's co-accused, was a 'bagger' of the drugs. The prosecution wished to rely on C's evidence at the confiscation hearing and a warrant was issued for C to be produced at court from prison. C said he had nothing to say. The defence contended that Civil Evidence Act 1995 applied. The Judge admitted evidence of C's out-of-court statements and parts of his counsel's mitigation address, under Criminal Justice Act 2003 s 114(1)(d) (the 'interest of justice' gateway). Held. a) The Civil Evidence Act 1995 hearsay regime has no application to confiscation proceedings. b) The Criminal Justice Act 2003 hearsay regime, while potentially more suitable, can likewise not apply, at least not strictly and directly. c) Our conclusion plainly does not entail that hearsay evidence is inadmissible in confiscation proceedings. Any such outcome would be absurd, having regard to the realities both of confiscation proceedings in particular and the sentencing process more generally. d) Instead, our conclusion does entail that hearsay evidence is admissible in confiscation proceedings. The procedure must be both flexible and fair.
We cannot sensibly be unduly prescriptive but we venture the following broad considerations:

i) In many instances, there will or should be no realistic issue as to the admissibility of the evidence, not least given the focus of Proceeds of Crime Act on 'information'.
ii) There will, however, be occasions where a hearsay statement is of importance and seriously in dispute so that admissibility is, quite properly, a live issue. If so, as it seems to us, the Criminal Justice Act 2003 regime, applied by analogy, will furnish the most appropriate framework for adjudicating on such issues. The vital need is for the judge in such a situation to understand the potential for unfairness and to 'borrow', as appropriate, from the available guidance in Criminal Justice Act 2003 s 114(2) (together with the matters contained in section 116). However, when applying this regime and especially the 'interests of justice' test in section 114(1)(d), it will be of the first importance to keep the post-conviction context in mind. There may well be room for more flexibility than in the trial context.

iii) In many more cases, the real issue will be the weight rather than the admissibility of the evidence or information in question. If so, the 'checklist' contained in Criminal Justice Act 2003 s 114(2) (and the matters set out in section 116), suitably adapted to address weight rather than admissibility, will here too provide a valuable (if not exhaustive) framework of reference. In any event and in every case, a judge must, of course, proceed judicially, having regard to the limitations of the evidence or information under consideration (including, by way of examples, the reliability of the maker, the circumstances in which it came to be made, the reason why oral evidence cannot be given and the absence of cross-examination). Furthermore, care must invariably be taken to ensure that the defendant has a proper opportunity to be heard. There was no basis for a complaint.

R v Weller 2009 EWCA Crim 810 D pleaded to supply. At his house, £1,360 cash was found in his partner's bag. The source and ownership of the cash were disputed. During confiscation proceedings the prosecution sought to adduce a police notebook entry about what was said by the partner to a police officer. The Judge ruled against that. However, the Judge admitted the evidence [from a witness statement]. Held. The Judge was right to disallow the admission of the notebook, as no notice had been served. The issue should have been raised at the confiscation direction hearing. Using [the witness statement] was unfair as the Judge had refused to admit a better source of the same information.

21.46 ***Evidence What is required?***

Criminal Procedure Rules 2015 2015/1490 Rule 33(7) Any witness statement required to be served by this [rule] must be verified by a statement of truth contained in the witness statement.

(2) A statement of truth is a declaration by the person making the witness statement to the effect that the witness statement is true to the best of his knowledge and belief and that he made the statement knowing that, if it were tendered in evidence, he would be liable to prosecution if he wilfully stated in it anything which he knew to be false or did not believe to be true.

(3) and (4) [Not listed as they state the obvious]

21.47 ***Evidence What if there is no evidence for an important matter?***

R v Eddishaw 2014 EWCA Crim 2783 D pleaded to cheating Revenue and Customs of duty payable on alcoholic products. D was the head of an operation producing counterfeit vodka. He purchased large quantities of denatured alcohol, removed the additives and added water. That was bottled with a fake label of a well-known brand. In confiscation proceedings, the Judge said the benefit was the money he had received for selling the counterfeit vodka. The genuine bottles retailed at £8.65 and the counterfeit bottles at £6.80. The wholesale price of the counterfeit bottles was not known. The Judge found on the balance of probabilities that the wholesale black market value was £5. **Issue 1** (Was there a nexus between the offence and the benefit assessed?), see **21.100**. **Issue 2** The defence contended there was no evidence as to what the wholesale value of the counterfeit vodka was. He contrasted this with the expert evidence about the values of illegal drugs. Defence counsel relied on *Lonsdale v Howard & Hallam* 2007 UKHL 32 and *R v Singh* 2005 EWCA Crim 1448. Prosecution counsel said £5 was a fair estimate and D could have given evidence. Held. There is no obligation on the defence to give a value. It was unfortunate the prosecution made no investigation of the distribution network. It would not be proper for this Court to hear evidence. There was simply no evidence to support the £5 figure. para 97 We quash the order and remit the case back to the Crown Court with a direction that the Court shall not assess the benefit or the available amount more than the amounts in the original order. However, the prosecution could apply to increase the available amount under Proceeds of Crime Act 2002 s 22 later this year or next year.

See also: *R v Muddassar and Others* 2017 EWCA Crim 382 (Estimating drug deals. Officer not able to price crack value. Amounts not known. The Judge gave full reasons. Challenges to Judge's findings failed.)

21.48 ***Evidence Companies Piercing/lifting the corporate veil***

R v Seager and Blatch 2009 EWCA Crim 1303 S breached an undertaking not to act as a company director. B contravened a court disqualification from being a company director. In each case the prosecution invited the court to pierce the corporate veil. Held. para 76 This legal principle is that a duly formed and registered company is a separate legal entity from those who are its shareholders and it has rights and liabilities that are separate from its shareholders, *Salomon v A Salomon and Co Ltd* 1897 AC 22 and *Customs and Excise v Hare* 1996 2 All ER 391 at 401F. A court can 'pierce' the carapace of the corporate entity and look at what lies behind it only in certain circumstances. It cannot do so simply because it considers it might be just to do so. Each of these circumstances involves impropriety and dishonesty. The court will then be entitled to look for the legal substance, not just the form. In criminal cases the courts have identified at least three situations when the corporate veil can be pierced. First, if an offender attempts to shelter behind a corporate façade or veil to hide his crime and his benefits from it, see *Customs and Excise v Hare* 1996 2 AER 391, at 402A, *CPS v Compton* 2002 EWCA Civ 1720, paras 44-48, and *R v Grainger* 2008 EWCA Crim 2506, para 15. Second, where an offender does acts in the name of a company which (with the necessary *mens rea*) constitute a criminal offence which leads to the offender's conviction, then 'the veil of incorporation is not so much pierced as rudely torn away', *Jennings v CPS* 2008 UKHL 29 para 16. Third, where the transaction or business structures constitute a 'device', 'cloak' or 'sham', i.e. an attempt to disguise the true nature of the transaction or structure so as to deceive third parties or the courts, *R v Dimsey* 2000 QB 744 at 772. para 84 There was no basis for lifting the veil. For other detail about the case see **21.95**.

Prest v Petrodel Resources and Others 2013 UKSC 34 Supreme Court In divorce proceedings the husband, H, failed to comply with the Court's orders. The Judge found that H, an oil trader, simply treated the cash balances and property of a company, PRL, as his own and drew on them as he saw fit without board control. The management control of PRL was always in H's hands. At the end of the hearing the Judge ordered H to procure the transfer of seven UK properties owned by PRL to his wife in part satisfaction of the lump sum order. The companies appealed. Neither the Judge nor the Court of Appeal believed they could pierce the corporate veil. Held. para 8 Subject to very limited exceptions, most of which are statutory, a company is a legal entity distinct from that of its shareholders. Its property is its own, and not that of its shareholders. That principle applied to a company that was wholly owned and controlled by one man, *Saloman v A Salomon and Co* 1897 AC 22. 'Piercing the corporate veil' means disregarding the separate personality of the company. It is really the exception to the rule in *Saloman v A Salomon and Co*. para 27 The court may be justified in piercing the corporate veil if a company's separate legal personality is being abused for the purposes of some relevant wrongdoing. The difficulty is to identify what is relevant wrongdoing. Two principles lie behind the terms. First, the concealment principle, which enables the court to identify the real actors where they are being concealed. This does not involve piercing the corporate veil. The evasion principle is different and does involve piercing the corporate veil. There is a legal right against a person in control of 'it'[383] which exists independently of the company's involvement, and a company is interposed so the separate legal personality of the company will defeat the right or frustrate its enforcement. (The court then listed case examples.) para 34 The corporate veil may be pierced only to prevent the abuse of corporate legal personality. When a person is under an existing legal obligation or liability or subject to an existing legal restriction which he

[383] Presumably this was the company.

deliberately evades or whose enforcement he deliberately frustrates by interposing a company under his control, the court may pierce the corporate veil. That is only for the purpose of depriving the company or its controller of the advantage that they would otherwise have obtained by the company's separate legal personality. This principle is a limited one. If it is not necessary to pierce the corporate veil it is not appropriate to do so. The Judge was right not to pierce the corporate veil because H was not concealing or evading any legal obligation owed to his wife. The properties were held on a resulting trust by the companies for H. We restore the order for the transfer of the seven properties.

Note: 'No court in this land will allow a person to keep an advantage by fraud', *Lazarus Estates v Beasley* 1956 1 QB 702 at para 712, was affirmed by *Prest v Petrodel Resources and Others* 2013 UKSC 34 para 18. Ed.

R v Sale 2013 EWCA Crim 1306, 2014 1 Cr App R (S) 60 (p 381) D pleaded to corruption and fraud by false representation. D was the managing director and sole shareholder of SS, a company that supplied Network Rail. He provided gifts and hospitality to a Network Rail employee worth just under £7,000. D was given secret tender advice and SS received about £1.9m worth of contracts. A £60,000 invoice was paid twice. D was sentenced on the basis that the work done by SS was 'without criticism as to price or quality'. SS had a turnover of about £9.9m and only in its work with Network Rail was SS dealing illegally. D's benefit in apportioned salary and dividends for Network Rail's contracts was £125,000. SS's gross profit before tax was nearly £200,000. The Judge agreed to lift the corporate veil and found the benefit was £1.9m. The order was made in that sum because of D's assets. Held. The principles in *Prest v Petrodel Resources and Others* 2013 UKSC 34, although strictly *obiter*, apply across the board. This is not a case coming within the evasion principle referred to in *Prest* at para 28. Here there was no legal obligation or liability which was evaded or frustrated by the interposition of the company in this case whereby the interposition of the company would mean that the separate legal personality of the company would defeat the right or frustrate its enforcement. This was a company which existed long before this corrupt conduct and which existed for *bona fide* trading purposes: there was no interposition of the sort described. However, it falls within the concealment principle. D was the sole controller of the company and where there was a very close inter-relationship between the corrupt actions of D and steps taken by the company in advancing those corrupt acts and intentions, the reality is that the activities of both D and the company are so interlinked as to be indivisible. Both entities are acting together in the corruption. The court is entitled to look to see what were the realities of D's criminal conduct. The objectives of Proceeds of Crime Act 2002 are to seek to discover the facts which the existence of the corporate structure would otherwise conceal so as properly to identify the appellant's true benefit. Prior to *R v Waya* 2012 there would have been no fault in finding the benefit figure to be £1.9m. Since then any confiscation order had to bear a proportionate relationship to the purpose of the Proceeds of Crime Act 2002, which is to recover the financial benefit which an offender has obtained from his criminal conduct.

R v McDowell and Singh 2015 EWCA Crim 173, 2 Cr App R (S) 14 (p 137) M's and S's cases were not connected but joined because they shared similar points. M was an arms dealer convicted of two counts of supplying goods subject to a prohibition. S pleaded guilty to carrying on a business as a scrap metal dealer without being entered on the Register. M and S carried on their businesses through a company of which they were sole shareholder and director. para 3 Both said it was inappropriate to lift the corporate veil. Held. Merely because a director had control of funds on behalf of a company, it could not be said that he had 'obtained' those funds save in his capacity as the company's employee. We observe that the need to identify the capacity in which a defendant received and handled the proceeds of crime had been emphasised by the court in *R v Sivaraman* 2008 EWCA Crim 1736, 2009 1 Cr App R (S) 80 (p 469), since approved by the Supreme Court in *R v Ahmad and Others* 2014 UKSC 36, 2 Cr App R (S) 75 (p 580). For M, it is not necessary to lift the corporate veil. M did not attempt to hide his trading behind the cloak of his company. As the Judge put it, he was the *alter ego* of the company. He used it openly as his trading vehicle in the transactions. The Crown Court was entitled to examine the receipts and profits of the company from the criminal conduct of the appellant personally. He was the beneficial owner. For S they were his records so no issue arises.

R v Boyle and Boyle Transport 2016 EWCA Crim 19, 2 Cr App R (S) 11 (p 43) P and M pleaded guilty to conspiracy to make false instruments. They had tampered with tachographs and made false records to defeat the drivers' hours scheme. A confiscation order was made. About two years later, a Judge lifted the corporate veil and appointed an enforcement receiver to obtain the assets to satisfy a confiscation order. The Judge treated the assets of the company as belonging to P and M. P, M and the company appealed about whether the corporate veil should have been lifted. Held. para 88 The test is not simply one of 'justice'. So vague an approach would be unprincipled and would give rise to great uncertainty and inconsistency, see *Salmond v Salomon & Co Ltd* 1897, *R v Seager and Blatch* 2009 and *Prest v Petrodel Resources and Others* 2013. para 89 A Crown Court is of course required in each case to assess the 'reality of the matter'. That is central. But that cannot be permitted in itself to confer a licence on a court to depart from established principles relating to the separate legal status of a limited company. Were it otherwise, courts would simply be circumventing the prohibition on deciding issues relating to the corporate veil through invoking the notion of 'justice' by resorting to a different label, namely the 'reality of the matter'. That is not in itself permissible. The realities are of course essential matters to be taken into account, 'but they do not of themselves provide some principle'. para 90 It is essential to bear in mind that the confiscation process is not of itself aimed at punishment. It is aimed at recovery of benefit. para 91 The actual principles relating to the doctrine of lifting the corporate veil in the confiscation proceedings are the same as in the civil courts. para 92 *Prest v Petrodel Resources and Others* 2013 was of general application. The Crown Court has no inherent jurisdiction of its own and Proceeds of Crime Act 2002 contains no provision purporting to sanction a departure from ordinary principles of company law. para 93 The Crown Courts in confiscation cases should treat with a degree of circumspection, when an issue of lifting or piercing the corporate veil has been raised, tempting invitations to adopt a 'robust' or 'broad brush' approach and to avoid being distracted by 'niceties'. That should not be permitted. [There must be] the proper application of correct legal principles.

para 95 The approach taken in *R v King* 2014 EWCA Crim 621, 2 Cr App R (S) 54 (p 437) is informative. That was not a case concerning the lifting of the corporate veil. The question was, in the context of arguments on proportionality, whether the benefit of an individual should be equated with the turnover or with the net profits of his (unincorporated) business. The Court said at para 42, "The authorities reveal there is a clear distinction to be drawn between a) cases in which the goods or services are provided by way of a lawful contract (or when payment is properly paid for legitimate services) but the transaction is tainted by associated illegality (e.g. the overcharging in *R v Shabir* 2008 EWCA Crim 1809, 1 Cr App R (S) 84 (p 497) or the bribery in *R v Sale* 2013 EWCA Crim 1306, 2014 1 Cr App R (S) 60 (p 381)) and b) cases in which the entire undertaking is unlawful (e.g. a business which is conducted illegally, as in *R v Beazley* 2013 EWCA Crim 567). When making a confiscation order, the court will need to consider the difference between these two types of case. It is to be stressed, however, that this divide is not necessarily determinative because cases differ to a great extent, but it is a relevant factor to be taken into account when deciding whether to make an order that reflects the gross takings of the business." This sort of consideration, whilst not of itself determinative, is likely to be relevant where an issue of lifting the corporate veil is raised. para 96 Even where a company, mixed up in relevant wrong doing, is solely owned and solely controlled by the (criminal) defendant, that does not of itself always necessitate a conclusion in a confiscation case that it is an *alter ego* company, whose turnover and assets are to be equated with being property of the defendant himself. para 101 The Judge based his decision 'fair and square' on the second 'situation' set out in *R v Seager and Blatch* 2009 para 76. In doing so, he clearly considered that the fact that P and M were the 'operating minds' was of paramount importance. He also plainly was influenced by the fact that other shareholders played no active part in the business. That approach was wrong. It cannot be determinative that P and M ran the company and were the 'operating minds'. On the contrary, they were the sole, legally appointed, directors. They were, in substance, executive directors, with very wide general powers and duties. As such directors, it was their delegated responsibility to operate the day-to-day affairs and business of the [first] company (although of course they had no authority to do so unlawfully). Under the companies legislation and conventional Memoranda and Articles of Association shareholders, generally speaking, have no right, as shareholders, to involve themselves in such matters: their ultimate control rests on their voting powers at company meetings. So to say, in the context of this case, that P and M were the 'operating minds' simply does not carry the almost conclusive force which the Judge seems to have ascribed to it. para 106 'The realities of the situation' did not justify the Judge's conclusion. The [first] company was properly set up as a limited company to carry on the family business. It was no sham. It was set up for a legitimate purpose, road haulage. Its substantial operations and assets were used for that purpose. That was its sole activity, over a long period.

We consider the situation for one-man companies. The actual decision in *R v Sale* 2013 is to be explained as one on its own facts, as the court in that case itself made clear. para 119 *R v McDowell and Singh* 2015 EWCA Crim 173, 2 Cr App R (S) 14 (p 137) is not to be taken as an invitation to criminal courts in confiscation cases to regard sole ownership and control of a company as necessarily and always sufficient of itself to justify treating the company as an alter ego of the defendant. To say that is not to provide an open road and a fast car to crooks seeking to conceal their real activities and true benefits behind a one-man limited company. We quash the order to appoint an enforcement receiver. Although the confiscation was made with consent and the extension of time for leave to appeal is 17 months, we quash the confiscation order too.

Note: It is not possible to provide a full summary of this case as the amount of judicial guidance is considerable. To fully take in all the points made it is necessary to read the judgment. Ed.

R v Powell and Westwood 2016 EWCA Crim 1043 P was convicted of environmental permit offences and a waste disposal offence. W pleaded to counts that mirrored P's counts. The Judge refused to lift the corporate veil and the prosecution appealed. Held. para 27 P and W were both well aware of the failure to comply with regulations at the material time and that the reason for non-compliance was out of a desire to increase the company's profitability. But it is important, in looking at the nature of the criminality, to note here that there was no facade or concealment for hiding behind the company's structure in a way which abused the corporate shield. Unlike the situation in *Jennings v CPS* 2008 UKHL 29, 2 Cr App R (S) 29 (p 414), this was not a company being run for an unlawful purpose but rather was a legitimate business which had broken the criminal law through its failure to observe the necessary regulations. P and W's liability depended on consent, connivance or neglect in relation to the company's failures. P and W were not the sole shareholders. Appeal dismissed.

21.49 *Evidence Defendant's right to challenge the evidence*

R v Knaggs 2009 EWCA Crim 1363, 2010 1 Cr App R (S) 75 (p 495) Where a defendant pleads guilty and does not choose to challenge any of the prosecution facts by way of a *Newton* hearing, that does not bar him from challenging the evidence during the confiscation hearing.

Step 4 Does the defendant have a criminal lifestyle?

21.50 ***Step 4***

Step 4 Has the defendant a criminal lifestyle (Proceeds of Crime Act 2002 s 6(4)(a), see **21.52**)? A defendant has a criminal lifestyle if, and only if, the offence (or any of the offences) concerned satisfies any of these tests:

(a) it is specified in Sch 2 (see **21.53**),

(b) it constitutes conduct forming part of a course of criminal activity (for definition, Proceeds of Crime Act 2002 s 75(3), see **21.52**),

(c) it is an offence committed over a period of at least six months and the defendant has benefited from the conduct which constitutes the offence.

In b) and c) the relevant benefit (for definition, Proceeds of Crime Act 2002 s 75(5)-(6), see **21.52**) must be £5,000+, see **21.52**.

If Yes, go to Step 5, see **21.57**. If No, go to Step 6, see **21.63**.

In determining whether a defendant has a 'criminal lifestyle', the issue must be decided with a 'balance of probabilities' test, Proceeds of Crime Act 2002 s 6(7), see below.

21.51 ***Step 4 Statutory provisions***

Proceeds of Crime Act 2002 s 6(4) The court must proceed as follows:

(a) it must decide whether the defendant has a criminal lifestyle (see below),

(b) if it decides that he has a criminal lifestyle it must decide whether he has benefited from his general criminal conduct (see **21.57**),

(c) if it decides that he does not have a criminal lifestyle it must decide whether he has benefited from his particular criminal conduct (see **21.59**).

Proceeds of Crime Act 2002 s 6(7) The court must decide any question arising under subsection (4) or (5) on a balance of probabilities.

For the full section see **21.5**.

21.52 ***Step 4 'Criminal lifestyle', Definition of***

Proceeds of Crime Act 2002 s 75(1) A defendant has a criminal lifestyle if (and only if) the following condition is satisfied.

(2) The condition is that the offence (or any of the offences) concerned satisfies any of these tests:

(a) it is specified in Schedule 2 (see **21.53**),

(b) it constitutes conduct forming part of a course of criminal activity,

(c) it is an offence committed over a period of at least 6 months and the defendant has benefited from the conduct which constitutes the offence.

(3) Conduct forms part of a course of criminal activity if the defendant has benefited from the conduct and:

(a) in the proceedings in which he was convicted he was convicted of three or more other offences, each of three or more of them constituting conduct from which he has benefited, or

(b) in the period of 6 years ending with the day when those proceedings were started (or, if there is more than one such day, the earliest day) he was convicted on at least two separate occasions of an offence constituting conduct from which he has benefited.

(4) But an offence does not satisfy the test in subsection (2)(b) or (c) unless the defendant obtains relevant benefit of not less than £5,000.

(5) Relevant benefit for the purposes of subsection (2)(b) is:

(a) benefit from conduct which constitutes the offence,

(b) benefit from any other conduct which forms part of the course of criminal activity and which constitutes an offence of which the defendant has been convicted,

(c) benefit from conduct which constitutes an offence which has been or will be taken into consideration by the court in sentencing the defendant for an offence mentioned in paragraph (a) or (b).

(6) Relevant benefit for the purposes of subsection (2)(c) is:

(a) benefit from conduct which constitutes the offence,
(b) benefit from conduct which constitutes an offence which has been or will be taken into consideration by the court in sentencing the defendant for the offence mentioned in paragraph (a).

21.53 ***Step 4a Is the offence specified in Schedule 2?***
Proceeds of Crime Act 2002 Sch 2 (lifestyle offences)
Note: These sets of offences have been rearranged. Some of the subsection titles are from Proceeds of Crime Act 2002 Sch 2 and others I have created. The various subsections have been put in alphabetical order. I hope this assists. Ed.

Arms trafficking
Proceeds of Crime Act 2002 Sch 2 para 5(1) An offence under either of the following provisions of Customs and Excise Management Act 1979 if it is committed in connection with a firearm or ammunition:
(a) section 68(2) (exportation of prohibited goods),
(b) section 170 (fraudulent evasion).
(2) An offence under Firearms Act 1968 s 3(1) (dealing in firearms or ammunition by way of trade or business).
(3) In this paragraph 'firearm' and 'ammunition' have the same meanings as in Firearms Act 1968 s 57.

Blackmail
Proceeds of Crime Act 2002 Sch 2 para 9 An offence under Theft Act 1968 s 21 (blackmail).

Copyright etc.
Proceeds of Crime Act 2002 Sch 2 para 7(1) An offence under any of the following provisions of Copyright, Designs and Patents Act 1988:
(a) section 107(1) (making or dealing in an article which infringes copyright),
(b) section 107(2) (making or possessing an article designed or adapted for making a copy of a copyright work),
(c) section 198(1) (making or dealing in an illicit recording),
(d) section 297A (making or dealing in unauthorised decoders).
(2) An offence under Trade Marks Act 1994 s 92(1), (2) or (3) (unauthorised use etc. of trade mark).

Counterfeiting
Proceeds of Crime Act 2002 Sch 2 para 6 An offence under any of the following provisions of Forgery and Counterfeiting Act 1981:
(a) section 14 (making counterfeit notes or coins),
(b) section 15 (passing etc. counterfeit notes or coins),
(c) section 16 (having counterfeit notes or coins),
(d) section 17 (making or possessing materials or equipment for counterfeiting).

Drug etc. trafficking
Proceeds of Crime Act 2002 Sch 2 para 1(1) An offence under any of the following provisions of Misuse of Drugs Act 1971:
(a) section 4(2) or (3) (unlawful production or supply of controlled drugs),
(b) section 5(3) (possession of controlled drug with intent to supply),
(c) section 8 (permitting certain activities relating to controlled drugs),
(d) section 20 (assisting in or inducing the commission outside the UK of an offence punishable under a corresponding law).
1A An offence under any of the following provisions of the Psychoactive Substances Act 2016:
(a) section 4 (producing a psychoactive substance),
(b) section 5 (supplying, or offering to supply, a psychoactive substance),
(c) section 7 (possession of psychoactive substance with intent to supply);

(d) section 8 (importing or exporting a psychoactive substance).[384]

(2) An offence under any of the following provisions of Customs and Excise Management Act 1979 if it is committed in connection with a prohibition or restriction on importation or exportation which has effect by virtue of Misuse of Drugs Act 1971 s 3:

(a) section 50(2) or (3) (improper importation of goods),

(b) section 68(2) (exportation of prohibited or restricted goods),

(c) section 170 (fraudulent evasion).

(3) An offence under either of the following provisions of Criminal Justice (International Co-operation) Act 1990:

(a) section 12 (manufacture or supply of a substance for the time being specified in Sch 2 to that Act),

(b) section 19 (using a ship for illicit traffic in controlled drugs).

Firearms

Proceeds of Crime Act 2002 Sch 2 para 5(2) An offence under Firearms Act 1968 s 3(1) (dealing in firearms or ammunition by way of trade or business).

(3) In this paragraph 'firearm' and 'ammunition' have the same meanings as in Firearms Act 1968 s 57.

Gangmasters

Proceeds of Crime Act 2002 Sch 2 para 9A An offence under Gangmasters (Licensing) Act 2004 s 12(1) or (2) (acting as a gangmaster other than under the authority of a licence, possession of false documents etc.).

Immigration and sexual trafficking

Proceeds of Crime Act 2002 Sch 2 para 4(1) An offence under Immigration Act 1971 s 25, 25A and 25B (assisting unlawful immigration etc.).

(2) An offence under Sexual Offences Act 2003 s 57-59A[385] (trafficking for sexual exploitation).

(3) An offence under Asylum and Immigration (Treatment of Claimants, etc.) Act 2004 s 4 (exploitation).

Note: Section 59A and section 4 offences only apply to offences committed before 31 July 2015.[386] Ed.

Money laundering

Proceeds of Crime Act 2002 Sch 2 para 2 An offence under either of the following provisions of Proceeds of Crime Act 2002:

(a) section 327 (concealing etc. criminal property),

(b) section 328 (assisting another to retain criminal property).

Prostitution and child sex

Proceeds of Crime Act 2002 Sch 2 para 8(1) An offence under Sexual Offences Act 1956 s 33 or 34 (keeping or letting premises for use as a brothel).

(2) An offence under any of the following provisions of Sexual Offences Act 2003:

(a) section 14 (arranging or facilitating commission of a child sex offence),

(b) section 48 (causing or inciting child prostitution or pornography),

(c) section 49 (controlling a child prostitute or a child involved in pornography),

(d) section 50 (arranging or facilitating child prostitution or pornography),

(e) section 52 (causing or inciting prostitution for gain),

(f) section 53 (controlling prostitution for gain).

Note: Serious Crime Act 2015 Sch 4 para 58 renames the offences in paras b), c) and d). The offences become:

---

[384] Inserted by Psychoactive Substances Act 2016 Sch 5 para 2(1) and (2). In force 26/5/16, Psychoactive Substances Act 2016 (Commencement) Regulations 2016 2016/553 para 2

[385] Section 59A only applies to those offences committed on or after 6/4/13, Protection of Freedoms Act 2012 (Commencement No 5 and Savings and Transitional Provisions) Order 2013 2013/470 paras 3 and 8. On the same date s 57-59 were removed from the Act, but the sections continue to apply to offences committed before that date.

[386] Modern Slavery Act 2015 s 7(1) and (3) and Modern Slavery Act 2015 (Commencement No 1, Savings and Transitional Provisions) Regs 2015 2015/1476 para 4

(b) section 48 (causing or inciting sexual exploitation of a child),
(c) section 49 (controlling a child in relation to sexual exploitation),
(d) section 50 (arranging or facilitating sexual exploitation of a child).
Commencement is awaited. Ed.

Slavery, servitude and forced labour[387]

Proceeds of Crime Act Sch 2 para 3A An offence under Modern Slavery Act 2015 s 1 (slavery, servitude and forced or compulsory labour) and para 4(4) an offence under Modern Slavery Act 2015 s 2 (human trafficking).

Terrorism

Proceeds of Crime Act 2002 Sch 2 para 3 An offence under Terrorism Act 2000 s 56 (directing the activities of a terrorist organisation).

Inchoate offences

Proceeds of Crime Act 2002 Sch 2 para 10(1) An offence of attempting, conspiring or inciting the commission of an offence specified in this Schedule,
(1A) An offence under Serious Crime Act 2007 s 44 of doing an act capable of encouraging or assisting the commission of an offence specified in this Schedule (those paragraphs numbered 1-10).
(2) An offence of aiding, abetting, counselling or procuring the commission of such an offence.

21.54 ***Step 4b Does the conduct form part of a course of criminal activity?***

Proceeds of Crime Act 2002 s 75(2) The condition is that the offence (or any of the offences) concerned satisfies any of these tests:..b) it constitutes conduct forming part of a course of criminal activity.
For the full section see **21.52**.

21.55 ***Step 4c Was an offence committed over a period of at least six months?***

Proceeds of Crime Act 2002 s 75(1) A defendant has a criminal lifestyle if (and only if) the following condition is satisfied.
(2) The condition is that the offence (or any of the offences) concerned satisfies any of these tests:..c) it is an offence committed over a period of at least 6 months and the defendant has benefited from the conduct which constitutes the offence.
For the full section see **21.52**.

21.56 ***Step 4c Was an offence committed over a period of at least six months? Meaning of 'at least six months'***

R v Odamo 2013 EWCA Crim 1275, 2014 Cr App R (S) 44 (p 252) D was convicted of conspiracy to defraud and pleaded to two obtaining mortgages by deception counts. Because one of the mortgage offences was committed entirely after the 2002 Act came into force, the prosecution chose to proceed for the confiscation procedure only for that count. The offence was not listed in Proceeds of Crime Act 2002 Sch 2. D had made an application for the mortgage in June 2006. £535,000 was paid into the conveyancer's client account in July 2006. The Judge found D had no gainful employment or legitimate source of income so D must 'have funded the dishonestly obtained mortgage out of the proceeds of the conspiracy to defraud offence'. Accordingly he found the six-month requirement was made out. Held. The transfer occurred when the money was received, applying Theft Act 1968 s 15(2).[388] How the mortgage was serviced was not relevant. The lifestyle provisions did not apply.

R v Bajwa and Others 2011 EWCA Crim 1093, 2012 1 Cr App R (S) 23 (p 117) B, S and H were convicted of conspiracy to evade the duty chargeable on cigarettes. They contended that they had not been involved in the conspiracy for six months. Their first involvement was in March 2004. The Judge said that as the offence was conspiracy the crucial question was whether the offence was committed over at least six months. The defendants appealed. para 22 The prosecution contended that as they did not withdraw

[387] Inserted by Modern Slavery Act 2015 s 7(1)-(3). In force 31/7/15
[388] Repealed by Fraud Act 2006 Sch 3 para 1 on 15/1/07

their involvement, the period was from March to September 2004. Held. The burden of proving fulfilment of the statutory criteria under any of the three paragraphs of section 75(2) must lie on the Crown. The Crown must therefore prove, on a balance of probabilities, that the defendants were involved in the conspiracy alleged for at least six months. para 47 In *R v May* 2008 UKHL 28, 2009 1 Cr App R (S) 31 (p 162) Lord Bingham enjoined all courts and judges to focus very closely on the language of the statutory provision and said "any judicial gloss or exegesis should be viewed with caution". He also emphasised that guidance should be sought in the statutory language rather than the 'proliferating case law'.
Thus in all cases coming within section 75(2)(b) the 'test' focuses on what a particular defendant has done. Thus, both section 75(2)(a) and (b) are focusing on what offences the particular defendant has committed. The words 'it is an offence committed over a period of at least six months' must relate to the particular defendant's part in an offence. These defendants did not come within the provision. para 21 and 56 The Crown accepted S wasn't involved in the conspiracy for at least six months and considering the facts the Crown had failed to show that either B or H were involved in the conspiracy offence for at least six months. Confiscation orders quashed.
See also: *R v Fields* 2013 EWCA Crim 2042, 2014 2 Cr App R (S) 13 (p 84) (*R v Bajwa and Others* 2011 applied.)

Step 5 Has the defendant 'benefited from his general criminal conduct'?

21.57 ***Step 5***
Step 5 Has the defendant 'benefited from his general criminal conduct' (for definition, Proceeds of Crime Act 2002 s 76(2), see **21.59**)? To answer this the court must apply the assumptions, Proceeds of Crime Act 2002 s 10, see **21.66**. If Yes, go to Step 7, see **21.65**. If No, section 6 does not apply.
In determining whether a defendant 'has benefited from his general conduct', the issue must be decided with a 'balance of probabilities' test, Proceeds of Crime Act 2002 s 6(7), see **21.51**.
Standard of proof Any question concerning whether the defendant has benefited from his criminal conduct must be decided on a 'balance of probabilities' standard, Proceeds of Crime Act 2002 s 6(7).

21.58 ***Step 5 Statutory provisions***
Proceeds of Crime Act 2002 s 6(4) The court must proceed as follows:..b) if it decides that he has a criminal lifestyle it must decide whether he has benefited from his general criminal conduct (see below), c) if it decides that he does not have a criminal lifestyle it must decide whether he has benefited from his particular criminal conduct (see **21.59**).
Proceeds of Crime Act 2002 s 6(7) The court must decide any question arising under subsection (4) or (5) on a balance of probabilities.
For the full section see **21.5**.

21.59 ***Step 5 'Conduct, General criminal conduct and particular criminal conduct', Definitions of***
Conduct and benefit
Proceeds of Crime Act 2002 s 76(1) Criminal conduct is conduct which:
(a) constitutes an offence in England and Wales, or
(b) would constitute such an offence if it occurred in England and Wales.
(2) General criminal conduct of the defendant is all his criminal conduct, and it is immaterial:
(a) whether conduct occurred before or after the passing of this Act,
(b) whether property constituting a benefit from conduct was obtained before or after the passing of this Act.
(3) Particular criminal conduct of the defendant is all his criminal conduct which falls within the following paragraphs:
(a) conduct which constitutes the offence or offences concerned,

(b) conduct which constitutes offences of which he was convicted in the same proceedings as those in which he was convicted of the offence or offences concerned,
(c) conduct which constitutes offences which the court will be taking into consideration in deciding his sentence for the offence or offences concerned.

(4) A person benefits from conduct if he obtains property as a result of or in connection with the conduct.
(5) If a person obtains a pecuniary advantage as a result of or in connection with conduct, he is to be taken to obtain as a result of or in connection with the conduct a sum of money equal to the value of the pecuniary advantage.
(6) References to property or a pecuniary advantage obtained in connection with conduct include references to property or a pecuniary advantage obtained both in that connection and some other.
(7) If a person benefits from conduct, his benefit is the value of the property obtained.
For an example of the conduct needing to be a criminal offence, see also: *R v Ali* 2014 EWCA Crim 1658 at **21.102**.

21.60 ***Step 5 'Obtains property as a result of or in connection with the conduct', Meaning of***
Proceeds of Crime Act 2002 s 76(4) A person benefits from conduct if he obtains property as a result of or in connection with the conduct.
For the full section see **21.59**.
R v Sumal & Sons (Properties) Ltd 2012 EWCA Crim 1840 D was convicted of being the owner of a rented property without a licence contrary to Housing Act 2004 s 95(1). The Court found the company had benefited from criminal conduct, namely the rent received whilst the property was unlicensed. The figure was about £6,450. A confiscation order was made. Held. A licence granted under section 88 of the 2004 Act does not operate to confer on a landlord an entitlement lawfully to receive rent which he does not otherwise have. There was no power to make the order.
Note: The case is very hard to follow as the arguments and reasoning are mostly missing and replaced with comment. For a discussion of the meaning of 'in connection with the [criminal conduct]', see *R v Ahmad and Ahmed* 2012 EWCA Crim 391, 2 Cr App R (S) 85 (p 491). Ed.
R v Moss 2015 EWCA Crim 713 LCJ D pleaded to three record-keeping offences and one charge of failing to dispose of a cow's carcass. The prosecution case was that D had unlawfully slaughtered and/or butchered 209 unaccounted-for cattle. His benefit was £1,000 per item. The prosecution suggested that D had a criminal lifestyle because two of the offences were committed over six months and D had benefited by £5,000 or more. The defence said that had not been charged. The Judge found that D had been involved in the unlawful slaughter and butchery of 116 cattle. He calculated the benefit at £83,000, which was less than his realisable assets. Held. Taken in isolation [none] of the offences involved the obtaining of any property or pecuniary advantage. paras 57 and 11 The Judge was wrong to find D had benefited from the offences, so order quashed.
See also: *R v Siaulys and Capital Mastercraft Ltd* 2013 EWCA Crim 2083 (*R v Sumal & Sons (Properties) Ltd* 2012 EWCA Crim 1840 remains good law. Confiscation orders quashed.)
R v Hussain 2014 EWCA Crim 2344 (Landlord who ignored a whole series of enforcement notices. Prosecution claimed nearly £500,000 of housing benefit paid to tenants. The failure to comply with the enforcement notices had caused the obtaining. The order was proportional. The Judge's analysis was not in error. Order upheld.)

21.61 ***Step 5 Statutory provisions for determining benefit***
Defendant's benefit
Proceeds of Crime Act 2002 s 8(1) If the court is proceeding under section 6 this section applies for the purpose of:
(a) deciding whether the defendant has benefited from conduct, and

(b) deciding his benefit from the conduct.

(2) The court must:

(a) take account of conduct occurring up to the time it makes its decision,

(b) take account of property obtained up to that time.

(3) Subsection (4) applies if:

(a) the conduct concerned is general criminal conduct,

(b) a confiscation order mentioned in subsection (5) has at an earlier time been made against the defendant, and

(c) his benefit for the purposes of that order was benefit from his general criminal conduct.

(4) His benefit found at the time the last confiscation order mentioned in subsection (3)(c) was made against him must be taken for the purposes of this section to be his benefit from his general criminal conduct at that time.

(5) If the conduct concerned is general criminal conduct the court must deduct the aggregate of the following amounts:

(a) the amount ordered to be paid under each confiscation order previously made against the defendant,

(b) the amount ordered to be paid under each confiscation order previously made against him under any of the provisions listed in subsection (7).

(6) But subsection (5) does not apply to an amount which has been taken into account for the purposes of a deduction under that subsection on any earlier occasion.

(7) These are the provisions:

(a) Drug Trafficking Offences Act 1986,

(c) Criminal Justice Act 1988 Part 6,

(e) Drug Trafficking Act 1994 Part 1,

(h) Part 3 or 4 of this Act.

Note: Subsections (7) (b), (d), (f) and (g) are Scottish and Northern Irish provisions. Ed.

(8) The reference to general criminal conduct in the case of a confiscation order made under any of the provisions listed in subsection (7) is a reference to conduct in respect of which a court is required or entitled to make one or more assumptions for the purpose of assessing a person's benefit from the conduct.

R v Whittington 2009 EWCA Crim 1641, 2010 1 Cr App R (S) 83 (p 545) D pleaded to money laundering and conspiracy to supply amphetamines. In confiscation proceedings the prosecution relied on a notebook and engaged an accountant who then analysed the figures within it. The accountant said the figures represented £8.8m worth of cocaine dealing. This figure formed part of the Judge's benefit figure. D appealed, saying the accountant's inferences were wrong. Held. Guidance should be found in the statutory language rather than the proliferating case law. Here the question was whether D had obtained property as a result of or in connection with his general criminal conduct, Proceeds of Crime Act 2002 s 76(4). It is vital to bear in mind that it is for the prosecution to prove that the defendant has obtained the property in issue. This issue as to the proof of the existence of property must not be confused with proof of the source of that property. The prosecution must prove the existence of property to the civil standard of proof (except in the confined exception illustrated by *R v Briggs-Price* 2009 UKHL 19, Proceeds of Crime Act 2002 s 6(7)). The prosecution, as the first three assumptions in section 10 indicate, may do so by proving 1) the property has been transferred to the defendant, 2) that he has obtained property, or 3) that he has incurred expenditure after the relevant day (section 10), for only when the prosecution has established that the defendant has held property in one of these three ways does any question of the source of that property arise.

Note: *Serious Organised Crime Agency v Gale* 2010 EWCA Civ 759 provides the opposite result to that in *R v Whittington* 2009. In the *SOCA* case there was only one day of the particulars under the old regime and it was clear that there was no criminal activity during that day. Ed.

21.62 ***Step 5*** ***Statutory provisions for determining benefit*** ***The section 8(4) bar to amendment***

Proceeds of Crime Act 2002 s 8(4) His [the defendant's] benefit found at the time of the last confiscation order mentioned in subsection (3)(c) was made against him must be taken for the purposes of this section to be his benefit from his general criminal conduct at that time.

Note: This subsection makes more sense if you replace the first 'of' with 'when', which is what I think Parliament meant to say. Ed.

For the full section, see **21.61**.

R v Chahal and Another 2014 EWCA Crim 101, 2 Cr App R (S) 35 (p 288) D and C were convicted of money laundering and other counts in 2008. It was a banking fraud exploiting defective banking procedures. In 2010, the Judge made a confiscation order having determined that D's and C's benefit from general criminal conduct was about £140,300. D's order was for nearly £22,700 and C's order was for just over £34,000. In 2011, D was convicted of a missing trader fraud with a loss to the revenue of £22+m. He had been awaiting trial for this fraud when the first confiscation order was made and C had already been convicted of it. The second Judge made confiscation orders which were limited to the benefit determined by the Judge in the first confiscation proceedings. The explanatory notes to the Proceeds of Crime Act 2002 state that section 8(4) 'ensures that a calculation of benefit once made in relation to an offence will apply for the purposes of any subsequent calculation of benefit in respect of general criminal conduct'. The prosecution appealed. Held. Each defendant has engaged in sustained and major criminality. The purpose of section 8(4) is clear enough without referring to the explanatory notes. The earlier findings as to benefit were conclusive as to the benefit from general criminal conduct. If authority was needed it can be found in *R v Barnett* 2011 EWCA Crim 2936. The Judge was right to so limit the benefit. To do otherwise was to drive a coach and horses through the statutory provisions. This result is not attributable to a deficiency in the statutory provisions. It is attributable to the unwise decision of the prosecution to proceed with the first confiscation proceedings and to agree the benefit. Quite why the prosecution didn't adjourn the first confiscation proceeding has not been explained to us.

Step 6 Has the defendant 'benefited from his particular criminal conduct'?

21.63 ***Step 6***

Step 6 Has the defendant benefited from his 'particular criminal conduct' (for definition, Proceeds of Crime Act 2002 s 76(3), see **21.59**)? If Yes, go to Step 7, see **21.65**. If No, section 6 confiscation does not apply.

In determining whether a defendant has 'particular criminal conduct', the issue must be decided with a 'balance of probabilities' test, Proceeds of Crime Act 2002 s 6(7), see below.

21.64 ***Step 6*** ***Statutory provisions***

Proceeds of Crime Act 2002 s 6(4) The court must proceed as follows:.. c) if it decides that he does not have a criminal lifestyle it must decide whether he has benefited from his particular criminal conduct (see **21.59**).

Proceeds of Crime Act 2002 s 6(7) The court must decide any question arising under subsection (4) or (5) on a balance of probabilities.

For the full section see **21.5**.

Step 7 Determining the benefit and applying the assumptions

21.65 ***Step 7***

Step 7 Determine the benefit, applying the assumptions, Proceeds of Crime Act 2002 s 10.

21.66 ***Step 7 Determining the benefit and applying the assumptions Statutory provisions***

Note: The court has no discretion whether to apply the assumptions. The only time the assumptions should not be made is when: a) they are shown to be incorrect, or b) there would be a serious risk of injustice if the assumption were made, see section 10(6) below. The assumptions apply to property transferred by the defendant within six years ending on when the proceedings started. Where there are a number of defendants in a case, the six years run from the earliest date the proceedings started for any defendant, see Proceeds of Crime Act 2002 s 10(8). Ed.

Proceeds of Crime Act 2002 s 6(5) If the court decides under subsection (4)(b) or (c) that the defendant has benefited from the conduct referred to it must:[389]

(a) decide the recoverable amount, and

(b) make an order (a confiscation order) requiring him to pay that amount.

Paragraph (b) applies only if, or to the extent that, it would not be disproportionate to require the defendant to pay the recoverable amount.

Proceeds of Crime Act 2002 s 6(7) The court must decide any question arising under subsection (4) or (5) on a balance of probabilities.

For the full section see **21.5**.

Assumptions to be made in case of criminal lifestyle

Proceeds of Crime Act 2002 s 10(1) If the court decides under section 6 that the defendant has a criminal lifestyle it must make the following four assumptions for the purpose of:

(a) deciding whether he has benefited from his general criminal conduct, and

(b) deciding his benefit from the conduct.

(2) The first assumption is that any property transferred to the defendant at any time after the relevant day was obtained by him:

(a) as a result of his general criminal conduct, and

(b) at the earliest time he appears to have held it.

(3) The second assumption is that any property held by the defendant at any time after the date of conviction was obtained by him:

(a) as a result of his general criminal conduct, and

(b) at the earliest time he appears to have held it.

(4) The third assumption is that any expenditure incurred by the defendant at any time after the relevant day was met from property obtained by him as a result of his general criminal conduct.

(5) The fourth assumption is that, for the purpose of valuing any property obtained (or assumed to have been obtained) by the defendant, he obtained it free of any other interests in it.

(6) But the court must not make a required assumption in relation to particular property or expenditure if:

(a) the assumption is shown to be incorrect, or

(b) there would be a serious risk of injustice if the assumption were made.

(7) If the court does not make one or more of the required assumptions, it must state its reasons.

(8) The relevant day is the first day of the period of six years ending with:

(a) the day when proceedings for the offence concerned were started against the defendant, or

(b) if there are two or more offences and proceedings for them were started on different days, the earliest of those days.

(9) But if a confiscation order mentioned in section 8(3)(c) has been made against the defendant at any time during the period mentioned in subsection (8):

[389] This section appears as amended by Serious Crime Act 2015 Sch 4 para 19. In force 1/6/15

(a) the relevant day is the day when the defendant's benefit was calculated for the purposes of the last such confiscation order;
(b) the second assumption does not apply to any property which was held by him on or before the relevant day.

(10) The date of conviction is:
(a) the date on which the defendant was convicted of the offence concerned, or
(b) if there are two or more offences and the convictions were on different dates, the date of the latest.

21.67 *Step 7* ***Determining the benefit and applying the assumptions*** ***The second assumption***

R v Briggs 2018 EWCA Crim 1135 D pleaded to producing cannabis and abstracting electricity. The Judge made a confiscation order and the defence appealed the inclusion of D's net half share of the property where the police found 20 cannabis plants and 19 cannabis seedlings. Held. The second assumption applies no matter when that property was acquired, because it does not have a 'relevant day' limitation. It applies to a matrimonial home that has been acquired jointly many, many years before the offending in question. Appeal dismissed.

For more details, see **21.81**.

21.68 *Step 7* ***The assumptions*** ***Relevant date, Calculating***

Proceeds of Crime Act 2002 s 10(4) The third assumption is that any expenditure incurred by the defendant at any time after the relevant day was met from property obtained by him as a result of his general criminal conduct.

Proceeds of Crime Act 2002 s 10(8) The relevant day is the first day of the period of six years ending with:
(a) the day when proceedings for the offence concerned were started against the defendant, or
(b) if there are two or more offences and proceedings for them were started on different days, the earliest of those days.

(9) But if a confiscation order mentioned in section 8(3)(c) has been made against the defendant at any time during the period mentioned in subsection (8):
(a) the relevant day is the day when the defendant's benefit was calculated for the purposes of the last such confiscation order;
(b) the second assumption does not apply to any property which was held by him on or before the relevant day.

(10) The date of conviction is:
(a) the date on which the defendant was convicted of the offence concerned, or
(b) if there are two or more offences and the convictions were on different dates, the date of the latest.

For the full section, see **21.66**.

R v Barnett 2011 EWCA Crim 2936 para 31 The Judge considered a confiscation order under the 1988 Act. He calculated the 'relevant day' (in what was then the equivalent of section 10(8)) from the date of arrest. The parties agreed that the date to work back from was the date of the defendant's charge.

Note: This is because of the definition of 'proceedings started', which has been re-enacted in Proceeds of Crime Act 2002 s 85(1). Ed.

21.69 *Step 7* ***Determining the benefit*** ***General matters***

R v May 2008 UKHL 28, 2009 1 Cr App R (S) 31 (p 162) Lords In determining whether the defendant has obtained property or a pecuniary advantage and, if so, the value of it, the court should apply ordinary common law principles. The exercise of this jurisdiction involves no departure from familiar rules governing entitlement and ownership. Determining the recoverable amount calls for inquiry into the financial resources of the defendant at the date of the determination. Determining the benefit calls for a historical inquiry into past transactions.

The defendant ordinarily obtains property if in law he owns it, whether alone or jointly, which will ordinarily connote a power of disposition or control, as where a person directs a payment or conveyance of property to someone else. He ordinarily obtains a pecuniary advantage if (amongst other things) he evades liability to which he is personally subject. Mere couriers or custodians or other minor contributors to an offence, rewarded by a specific fee and having no interest in the property or the proceeds of sale, are unlikely to be found to have obtained that property, although it may be otherwise with money launderers.
The benefit gained is the total value of the property or advantage obtained, not the defendant's net profit after deduction of expenses or any amounts payable to co-conspirators.
CPS v Nelson 2009 EWCA Crim 1573, 2010 1 Cr App R (S) 82 (p 530) LCJ In 2004 EWCA Crim 3188 this Court observed, '...the critical time at which the court looks to ascertain whether a benefit has been obtained is the date when the offence is committed. It is not for the court to have regard to the subsequent consequences of the crime or events which may befall the property.'
Note: This principle has to be read in conjunction with the principles in *R v Waya* 2012 UKSC 51, 2013 2 Cr App R (S) 20 (p 87), see **21.73**. Ed.
R v Harvey 2015 UKSC 73, 2016 1 Cr App R (S) 60 (p 406) Supreme Court In confiscation the benefit was assessed in part on his company's turnover, which included VAT paid. Held (3-2). para 35 The judge trying the benefit issue should be guided by two important factors. First, although the burden may be on the prosecution to establish the gross value of the benefit obtained by the defendant, the burden of establishing that a sum, and if so what sum, should be deducted from that value to reflect VAT accounted for to HMRC lies on the defendant. Second, as in many exercises involved in assessments under Proceeds of Crime Act 2002, a judge should be robust in making such a determination. There is nothing disproportionate about taking a broad-brush approach to questions of what sums were received or paid in the context of criminal activity, where the evidence is confusing, unreliable and/or incomplete. On the contrary: the risk of disproportionality may lie more in spending much time and money pursuing a precise answer which is at best elusive and more frequently unattainable.
For more details see **21.92**.

21.70 ***Step 7 Determining the benefit Prosecution must prove the property was possessed***

R v Whittington 2009 EWCA Crim 1641, 2010 1 Cr App R (S) 83 (p 545) It is vital to bear in mind that it is for the prosecution to prove that the defendant has obtained the property in issue. This issue as to the proof of the existence of property must not be confused with proof of the source of that property. The assumptions have nothing to do with the question whether the defendant has or has had the property in issue. The prosecution must prove the existence of property to the civil standard of proof, Proceeds of Crime Act 2002 s 6(7).
Att-Gen's Ref No 2 of 2008 2008 EWCA Crim 2953[390] D was convicted of two conspiracies to import cocaine. In confiscation proceedings under Drug Trafficking Act 1994, the prosecution relied on cash payments made by D's father, F, in discharge of the mortgage on his home. The monthly payment in the relevant period varied from about £260 to about £330. During that period, sums were paid into F's account. Those payments varied from £40 to £450. For some of that time D was in prison and for some of the time he was in Colombia. F's evidence was read because of his age and state of health. It said that D had not paid any money into the account. Prosecution counsel did not put to D during evidence that he had funded this mortgage. The prosecution relied on F's meagre income to suggest the money had come from D. The Judge found D had no beneficial interest in the house. The prosecution appealed. para 21 They said it was only

[390] As the defendant also appealed, the case is known as *R v Winters* 2008 EWCA Crim 2953 as well.

necessary for them to produce *prima facie* evidence. Held. We disagree. para 19 The burden of proving the benefit is on the prosecution. In the case of expenditure [before the prosecution can rely on it in cases with or without assumptions] the prosecution must prove to the civil standard that the expenditure was incurred by D. Here they had not discharged that burden. That part of the appeal dismissed.
See also: *R v Weller* 2009 EWCA Crim 810 (The Judge relied on the assumptions to prove the defendant possessed the money that was found in his partner's bag. Held. No question of the assumptions arose. Before they could be applied the prosecution had to [prove] the money belonged to the defendant.)
R v Gor 2017 EWCA Crim 3 (The burden of proving the transfer to the defendant's wife was on the prosecution. Until that happened, the assumptions did not apply. Order reduced.)

21.71 *Step 7 Determining the benefit Standard of proof*
Proceeds of Crime Act 2002 s 6(7) The court must decide any question arising under subsection (4) or (5) (Criminal lifestyle and benefit provisions see **21.5**) on a balance of probabilities.
Serious Organised Crime Agency v Gale 2010 EWCA Civ 759 Court of Appeal (Civil) SOCA began recovery proceedings against D. The High Court rejected his arguments and he appealed. On appeal he contended that because the confiscation order depended on establishing criminal conduct, article 6 required the Court to apply the criminal standard of proof. Held. para 29 Article 6 in its criminal dimension is [about] securing a conviction. Confiscation proceedings are significantly different from that. They are not about inflicting punishment but about recovering the proceeds of crime. The cumulative effect of the tests in *Engle v Netherlands (No 1)* 1976 1 EHRR 647 is to make confiscation proceedings civil. para 39 By virtue of Human Rights Act 1998 s 2(8)(a) and 3 the civil standard of proof applies to any question of benefit.

21.72 *Step 7 The assumptions 'Serious risk of injustice'*
Proceeds of Crime Act 2002 s 10(6) But the court must not make a required assumption in relation to particular property or expenditure if: a) the assumption is shown to be incorrect, or b) there would be a serious risk of injustice if the assumption were made.
R v Deprince 2004 EWCA Crim 524 D was convicted of importing class A drugs. During the confiscation proceedings the prosecution relied on assumptions for eight items of income. For five of them there was no obvious explanation. D and his girlfriend gave evidence. D said the income was from an 'off the books property business'. He said this business was extremely successful and that it provided large sums of money. The Judge found D evasive and extremely vague. However, he was prepared to give credence to his girlfriend's evidence. For each of the five items he deducted 25% to avoid injustice. That made for those items £142,142. The defence appealed saying once the Judge found 'a serious risk of injustice' he should not have made any assumption. Held. That is not the law. The Judge's approach was not unlawful or improper. He found that if he deducted the 25% he had eliminated the risk. There was no fault in his very sensible approach.
R v Jones and Others 2006 EWCA Crim 2061 The defendants pleaded to various drug supply offences. The Judge found where they had benefited, they no longer had any assets. Further given their chaotic lifestyles, it was unlikely there would be substantial assets in the future. He considered that if he made the assumptions there would be a serious risk of injustice and it was not of assistance to society (because of the great expense) nor to the defendants and he made no confiscation order. The prosecution appealed. Held. para 13. It is only when considering the appropriateness of applying those assumptions that section 10(6) bites. It is there in order to ensure that assumptions made under section 10 are not so unrealistic or so unjust in relation to a particular defendant that they should not be made. It provides a means of moderating the ultimate calculation of benefit. As far as section 10(6)(b) is concerned, the question will arise, in

relation to any case, as to what will be considered unjust in the circumstances. The prosecution submit that whatever meaning one gives to the phrase 'serious risk of injustice', that cannot include the fact that an order will create hardship. We agree with (the then current) *Blackstone's*, which said: 'The risk of injustice must arise from the operation of the assumptions in the calculation of benefit and not from eventual hardship in the making of a confiscation order, *R v Dore* 1997 2 Cr App R (S) 152, *R v Ahmed* 2004 EWCA Crim 2399, 2005 1 Cr App R (S) 123 (p 703). What is contemplated is some unjust contradiction in the process of assumption (e.g. double counting of income and expenditure), or between an assumption and an agreed factual basis for sentence, see *R v Lunnon* 2004 EWCA Crim 1125, 2005 1 Cr App R (S) 24 (p 111) and *R v Lazarus* 2004 EWCA Crim 2297, 2005 1 Cr App R (S) 98 (p 552).' The purpose of the exercise is to ensure that there is ultimately a sensible calculation of benefit. It is not a discretionary exercise by the judge to determine whether or not it is fair to make an order against a particular defendant. The fact that any benefit was ephemeral, in the sense that it may have been frittered away, perhaps on drugs, is irrelevant to the question. It remained benefit for the purposes of the Act. The Judge was obliged to determine what that benefit was. It is only when the calculation is carried out applying the assumptions that the issues under section 10(6) can arise. We remit the matter to the Crown Court.
R v Rowsell 2011 EWCA Crim 1894 D was convicted of possession with intent to supply class A and C drugs. During the confiscation proceedings D contended that cash and bank deposits were legitimately earned in his music business. No documents were produced to support this. D's laptop was with his sister and D was unable to access it. The Judge refused to rule that there was a serious risk of injustice if the assumptions were drawn. The defence appealed saying the Judge had failed to have regard to the obvious difficulties that D would have in finding details of credits going back to 2002, many of which were comparatively small sums. Held. We unhesitatingly reject this. He had lawyers and he could have asked for time to produce the records.
Note: These cases must be considered with *R v Waya* 2012 UKSC 51, 2013 2 Cr App R (S) 20 (p 87) in mind because *R v Waya* 2012 has changed the law and introduced the principle of proportionality. Ed.

21.73 ***Step 7 Determining the benefit Assessing the value***
Proceeds of Crime Act 2002 s 79(1) This section applies for the purpose of deciding the value at any time of property then held by a person.
(2) Its value is the market value of the property at that time.
(3) But if at that time another person holds an interest in the property its value, in relation to the person mentioned in subsection (1), is the market value of his interest at that time, ignoring any charging order under a provision listed in subsection (4).
(4) The provisions are:
  (a) Drug Trafficking Offences Act 1986 s 9,[391]
  (b) Criminal Justice Act 1988 s 78,[392]
  (d) Drug Trafficking Act 1994 s 27,[393]
Note: paras c) and e) are not listed and relate to Northern Ireland. Ed.
(5) This section has effect subject to section 80 and 81.
Proceeds of Crime Act 2002 s 84(1) Property is all property wherever situated and includes:
  (a) money,
  (b) all forms of real or personal property,
  (c) things in action and other intangible or incorporeal property.
(2) The following rules apply in relation to property:

[391] Repealed by Drug Trafficking Act 1994 Sch 3 para 1
[392] Repealed by Proceeds of Crime Act 2002 Sch 12 para 1 on 24/3/03. The repeal has effect subject to savings specified in SI 2003/333 art 10(1)(a) and art 13(a)).
[393] Repealed by Proceeds of Crime Act 2002 Sch 12 para 1 on 24/3/03. The repeal has effect subject to savings specified in SI 2003/333 art 10(1)(e) and art 13(b)).

(a) property is held by a person if he holds an interest in it,
(b) property is obtained by a person if he obtains an interest in it,
(c) property is transferred by one person to another if the first one transfers or grants an interest in it to the second,
(d) references to property held by a person include references to property vested in his trustee in bankruptcy, permanent or interim trustee (within the meaning of the Bankruptcy (Scotland) Act 1985) or liquidator,
(e) references to an interest held by a person beneficially in property include references to an interest which would be held by him beneficially if the property were not so vested,
(f) references to an interest, in relation to land in England and Wales or Northern Ireland, are to any legal estate or equitable interest or power,
(g) references to an interest, in relation to land in Scotland, are to any estate, interest, servitude or other heritable right in or over land, including a heritable security,
(h) references to an interest, in relation to property other than land, include references to a right (including a right to possession).

R v Sivaraman 2008 EWCA Crim 1736, 2009 1 Cr App R (S) 80 (p 469) D pleaded to conspiracy to evade the duty on hydrocarbons. He was the manager of a service station. The owner purchased diesel fuel with red dye in it, which was for agricultural use and which had a lower excise duty on it. D agreed he had accepted 8-10 deliveries containing 30,000 litres of fuel each and that the right duty had not been paid. He said he had received £15,000. The prosecution claimed the benefit was nine deliveries totalling 270,000 litres and the duty evaded on that was £128,520. D further said he had not received any benefit from the diesel, just his £15,000. The Judge found the benefit was the higher figure and then made an order based on there being less money than that available. Held. para 13 In a joint criminal offence participants may benefit jointly to the same extent by each obtaining the same property or pecuniary advantage, or the value of the benefit received by them may differ as between one and another. The Judge misdirected himself in reaching a decision as to benefit which was contrary to his common-sense view of the true benefit gained by the appellant. £15,000 substituted.

R v Waya 2012 UKSC 51, 2013 2 Cr App R (S) 20 (p 87) Supreme Court para 55 There are four general features of section 80(3) which should be recognised.

(a) Once property has been obtained as a result of or in connection with crime, it remains the defendant's benefit whether or not he retains it. This is inherent in the value-based scheme for post-conviction confiscation.
(b) If, however, the defendant does not retain all or any of the property originally obtained, but does have other property representing it in his hands, then section 80(3) operates. This is an important part of the statutory scheme in cases where, for example, the profits of crime such as drug trafficking are laundered into other assets which are likely to rise in value.
(c) Even in such a case, s 80(3) only bites if the value of the representing property is larger than the value of the property originally obtained. If it is not, the benefit remains the value of what was originally obtained, subject to index-linking under section 80(2)(a).
(d) Where s 80(3) applies, the value of the representing property is an alternative but not an additional or cumulative benefit, see the helpful explanation offered by Toulson LJ in *Pattison*, considered below at paras 59-61.

21.74 ***Step 7 Determining the benefit Assess the value not the profit***

R v May 2008 UKHL 28, 2009 1 Cr App R (S) 31 (p 162) para 48(1) Lords The benefit gained is the total value of the property or advantage obtained, not the defendant's net profit after deduction of expenses or any amounts payable to co-conspirators.

21.75 *Step 7 Determining the benefit Assessing the value of property obtained from conduct*

Proceeds of Crime Act 2002 s 80(1) This section applies for the purpose of deciding the value of property obtained by a person as a result of or in connection with his criminal conduct, and the material time is the time the court makes its decision.

(2) The value of the property at the material time is the greater of the following:

(a) the value of the property (at the time the person obtained it) adjusted to take account of later changes in the value of money,

(b) the value (at the material time) of the property found under subsection (3).

(3) The property found under this subsection is as follows:

(a) if the person holds the property obtained, the property found under this subsection is that property,

(b) if he holds no part of the property obtained, the property found under this subsection is any property which directly or indirectly represents it in his hands,

(c) if he holds part of the property obtained, the property found under this subsection is that part and any property which directly or indirectly represents the other part in his hands.

(4) The references in subsection (2)(a) and (b) to the value are to the value found in accordance with section 79.

R v May 2008 UKHL 28, 2009 1 Cr App R (S) 31 (p 162) Lords para 48(5) In determining whether the defendant has obtained property or a pecuniary advantage and, if so, the value of it, the court should apply ordinary common law principles. The exercise of this jurisdiction involves no departure from familiar rules governing entitlement and ownership. The defendant ordinarily obtains property if in law he owns it, whether alone or jointly, which will ordinarily connote a power of disposition or control, as where a person directs a payment or conveyance of property to someone else. He ordinarily obtains a pecuniary advantage if (amongst other things) he evades liability to which he is personally subject. Mere couriers or custodians or other minor contributors to an offence, rewarded by a specific fee and having no interest in the property or the proceeds of sale, are unlikely to be found to have obtained that property, although it may be otherwise with money launderers.

21.76 *Step 7 Determining the benefit Assessing the value of property Changes in value/Interest*

Proceeds of Crime Act 2002 s 80(1) This section applies for the purpose of deciding the value of property obtained by a person as a result of or in connection with his criminal conduct, and the material time is the time the court makes its decision.

(2) The value of the property at the material time is the greater of the following: a) the value of the property (at the time the person obtained it) adjusted to take account of later changes in the value of money, b) (not listed).

R v Shepherd 2014 EWCA Crim 179 D was convicted of fraudulent trading (×2) and money laundering. D was an online ticket broker. The Judge made a confiscation order, applying the Retail Price Index to adjust the value of the property. The defence contended it should have been the Consumer Price Index. The difference between the two figures was nearly £33,800. Held. No material placed before the court called for any consideration or reconsideration of the established practice in the Crown Court in confiscation proceedings of the reliance upon the RPI (as opposed to the CPI or other method). The RPI remains a more nationally focused yardstick to measure the rise in the cost of living. The Judge applied the RPI in accordance with standard practice and there was no unfairness to D. Subsequently, the SFO and CPS decided to adopt an improved variant of the RPI, known as the RPIJ. The result will be a slightly lower increase in the change in value of money.

21.77 ***Step 7 Determining the benefit Assessing the value 'Market value', Meaning of***
R v Islam 2009 UKHL 30, 2010 1 Cr App R (S) 42 (p 245) Lords D pleaded to importing heroin. Customs seized two consignments of 3.53 and 0.44 kilos of heroin. The issue arose as to what was the market value of the heroin, see Proceeds of Crime Act 2002 s 79(2) at **21.73**. Held. The statute has refrained from defining precisely what is meant by the expression 'market value'. It can be assumed that greater precision was not thought to be necessary. A market, after all, is a place where goods are bought and sold. The market value of goods is the price that they will fetch in that market. Some goods can only be bought and sold in markets that are hard to find or are highly specialised. The nature of the goods is likely to provide the best guide as to where or what this market is. This is a matter which will require to be determined by the court, if there is a dispute. So too is the figure that is to be taken to be the price that the property would fetch in that market. This is a question of fact which is left by the statute for determination by the court as the need arises. The black market is included.

21.78 ***Step 7 Determining the benefit Assessing the value (etc.) Tracing***
R v Waya 2012 UKSC 51, 2013 2 Cr App R (S) 20 (p 87) Supreme Court D pleaded to two counts of obtaining a money transfer by deception. para 36 To obtain a mortgage of £465,000, he made false statements about his employment record and his earnings. With £310,000 of his own, untainted money and the mortgage, a property was obtained. Later the mortgage was paid back with a mortgage from another building society. Held. para 26 It is apparent from the decision in *R v May* 2008 UKHL 28, 2009 1 Cr App R (S) 31 (p 162) that a legitimate and proportionate confiscation order may have one or more of three effects:..
c) it may require a defendant to pay the whole of a sum which he has obtained by crime without enabling him to set off expenses of the crime.
To embark upon an accounting exercise in which the defendant is entitled to set off the cost of committing his crime would be to treat his criminal enterprise as if it were a legitimate business and confiscation a form of business taxation. Although these propositions involve the possibility of removing from the defendant by way of confiscation order a sum larger than may in fact represent his net proceeds of crime, they are consistent with the statute's objective and <u>represent proportionate means of achieving it</u>. para 35 The money was repaid in full. para 28 To make a confiscation order when the defendant has restored to the loser any proceeds of crime which he had ever had <u>is disproportionate</u>. It would not achieve the statutory objective of removing his proceeds of crime but would simply be an additional financial penalty. That it is consistent with the statutory purpose so to hold is moreover demonstrated by the presence of section 6(6). This subsection removes the duty to make a confiscation order, and converts it into a discretionary power, wherever the loser whose property represents the defendant's proceeds of crime either has brought, or proposes to bring, civil proceedings to recover his loss. It may be that the presence of section 6(6) is capable of explanation simply as a means of avoiding any obstacle to a civil action brought by the loser, which risk would not arise if repayment has already been made. But it would be unfair and capricious, and thus disproportionate, to distinguish between a defendant whose victim was about to sue him and a defendant who had already repaid. If anything, an order that the same sum be paid again by way of confiscation is more disproportionate in the second case than in the first. Unlike the first defendant, the second has not forced his victim to resort to litigation.
R v Jawad 2013 EWCA Crim 644, 2014 1 Cr App R (S) 16 (p 85) D argued that his confiscation order was disproportionate in the light of *R v Waya* 2012 UKSC 51, 2013 2 Cr App R (S) 20 (p 87). Held. para 21 *R v Waya* 2012 requires the court to consider whether a Proceeds of Crime Act confiscation order is disproportionate. We are satisfied that it generally will be disproportionate if it will require the defendant to pay for a second time money which he has fully restored to the loser. If there is no additional

benefit beyond that sum, any Proceeds of Crime Act confiscation order is likely to be disproportionate. If there is additional benefit, an order which double counts the sum which has been repaid is likely, to that extent, to be disproportionate, and an order for the lesser sum which excludes the double counting ought generally to be the right order. But, for the reasons explained, we do not agree that the mere fact that a compensation order is made for an outstanding sum due to the loser, and thus that that money may be restored, is enough to render disproportionate a Proceeds of Crime Act confiscation order which includes that sum. What will bring disproportion is the certainty of double payment. If it remains uncertain whether the loser will be repaid, a Proceeds of Crime Act confiscation order which includes the sum in question will not ordinarily be disproportionate.

21.79 ***Determining the benefit*** ***When does the period considered end?***
Proceeds of Crime Act 2002 s 8(1) If the court is proceeding under section 6 this section applies for the purpose of:

(a) deciding whether the defendant has benefited from conduct, and
(b) deciding his benefit from the conduct.

(2) The court must:

(a) take account of conduct occurring up to the time it makes its decision,
(b) take account of property obtained up to that time.

For the full section, see **21.7**.

R v Ali 2014 EWCA Crim 1658 D appealed his confiscation order and the Court reduced the order because some of the benefit figures were wrong. For one benefit item, the Judge made an order for rental profits up to the last day in the particulars in the indictment. Held. We increase that figure to take into account the rental figure up to the day the Judge made his order.

21.80 ***Step 7*** ***Determining the benefit*** ***Increasing the benefit figure because of the change in the value of money***
Proceeds of Crime Act 2002 s 80(2) The value of the property at the material time is the greater of the following: a) the value of the property (at the time the person obtained it) adjusted to take account of later changes in the value of money.

21.81 ***Step 7*** ***Determining the benefit*** ***Benefit figure must be proportionate***
R v Waya 2012 UKSC 51, 2013 2 Cr App R (S) 20 (p 87) Supreme Court D pleaded to two counts of obtaining a money transfer by deception. para 36 To obtain a mortgage of £465,000, he made false statements about his employment record and his earnings. With £310,000 of his own, untainted money and the mortgage, a property was obtained. Later the mortgage was paid back with a mortgage from another building society. Held. para 35 The money was repaid in full. para 28 To make a confiscation order when the defendant has restored to the loser any proceeds of crime which he had ever had is disproportionate. It would not achieve the statutory objective of removing his proceeds of crime but would simply be an additional financial penalty. That it is consistent with the statutory purpose so to hold is moreover demonstrated by the presence of section 6(6). This subsection removes the duty to make a confiscation order, and converts it into a discretionary power, wherever the loser whose property represents the defendant's proceeds of crime either has brought, or proposes to bring, civil proceedings to recover his loss. It may be that the presence of section 6(6) is capable of explanation simply as a means of avoiding any obstacle to a civil action brought by the loser, which risk would not arise if repayment has already been made. But it would be unfair and capricious, and thus disproportionate, to distinguish between a defendant whose victim was about to sue him and a defendant who had already repaid. If anything, an order that the same sum be paid again by way of confiscation is more disproportionate in the second case than in the first. Unlike the first defendant, the second has not forced his victim to resort to litigation.

R v Jawad 2013 EWCA Crim 644, 2014 1 Cr App R (S) 16 (p 85) D pleaded to a money laundering offence which was connected with frauds on Lloyds Bank. The judge made a confiscation order and a compensation order rejecting an argument that that would be double counting. On appeal, D argued that his confiscation order was disproportionate in the light of *R v Waya* 2012 UKSC 51, 2013 2 Cr App R (S) 20 (p 87). Held. para 21 *R v Waya* 2012 requires the court to consider whether a Proceeds of Crime Act confiscation order is disproportionate. We are satisfied that it generally will be disproportionate if it will require the defendant to pay for a second time money which he has fully restored to the loser. If there is no additional benefit beyond that sum, any Proceeds of Crime Act confiscation order is likely to be disproportionate. If there is additional benefit, an order which double counts the sum which has been repaid is likely, to that extent, to be disproportionate, and an order for the lesser sum which excludes the double counting ought generally to be the right order. But, for the reasons explained, we do not agree that the mere fact that a compensation order is made for an outstanding sum due to the loser, and thus that that money may be restored, is enough to render disproportionate a Proceeds of Crime Act confiscation order which includes that sum. What will bring disproportion is the certainty of double payment. If it remains uncertain whether the loser will be repaid, a Proceeds of Crime Act confiscation order which includes the sum in question will not ordinarily be disproportionate.

R v McDowell and Singh 2015 EWCA Crim 173, 2 Cr App R (S) 14 (p 137) M's and S's cases were not connected but joined because they shared similar points. M was an arms dealer convicted of two counts of supplying goods subject to a prohibition. His company was the agent in an aircraft sale to Ghana. para 14 The gross profits of the company were in 2006/07 about £530,000, in 2007/08 about £400,000 and in 2008/09 about £340,000. M had received emoluments of about £170,000 per year. The benefit was assessed as just over £2.55m. The benefit figure included a commission payment of nearly £2m. The available amount was almost £292,500. The confiscation order was made in that sum. M was sentenced to a 2-year suspended sentence. S pleaded guilty to carrying on a business as a scrap metal dealer without being entered on the Register. The Judge based the benefit on the receipts of the company, which totalled nearly £966,000. The available amount was just over £176,000. The confiscation order was made in that sum. S was fined £350. Both M and S argued that the benefit figure was disproportionate and relied on article 1. Held. para 44 The test of proportionality is applied to the benefit. para 51 The application of the proportionality assessment requires examination (as in *R v Sale* 2013 EWCA Crim 1306, 2014 1 Cr App R (S) 60 (p 381)) as to whether the finding of benefit the defendant is liable to repay is a proportionate means of achieving the legitimate objective of depriving him of the proceeds of his criminal conduct. The judge may need to examine both causation under section 76(4) (para 34 of *R v Sale* 2013) and the certainty of double recovery (para 29 of *R v Sale* 2013). We agree with the approach in *R v Sale* 2013, where the underlying transactions producing the appellant's receipts were lawful and not criminal. The cost of those transactions to the defendant may, on the grounds of proportionality, properly be treated as consideration given by the appellant for the benefit 'obtained'. There may be no 'loser' as contemplated in *R v Waya* 2012 and in *R v Jawad* 2013. The underlying principle is the same, the defendant has not gained by his conduct to the extent that he has given value for his receipts. Each case must be decided according to its particular facts. For M it was proportionate. para 64 For S, the Judge determined that the entire business was criminal. S's contentions about the finances of the business were not substantiated. The burden was on S and his argument failed [the test].

R v Briggs 2018 EWCA Crim 1135 D pleaded to producing cannabis and abstracting electricity. The Judge made a confiscation order and the defence appealed the inclusion of D's net half share of the property where the police found 20 cannabis plants and 19 cannabis seedlings, in part, on the basis of proportionality. Held. para 17 This cannot be a complaint. Section 6(5)(b) [see **21.5**] does not relate to the assessment of the benefit. Proportionality applies only when the court has assessed a defendant's benefit and when considering the amount of the confiscation order to be made. It relates [only] to the

recoverable amount. *R v Waya* 2012 paras 24 and 25 stated the concept of proportionality is not akin to the existence of a general discretion not to make, or to reduce, the confiscation order. Further, section 10(6)(b) [see **21.66**] providing [the issue of] serious risk of injustice means that it will only be in extremely unusual circumstances that the court will decline to make a confiscation order on grounds of proportionality, because the assumptions in section 10 will only be applied if they can be applied without serious risk of injustice. The Judge was able to conclude there was no serious risk of injustice under section 10(6)(b) in making the second assumption. Appeal dismissed.
For details about the second assumption and this case, see **21.67**.
See also: *R v King* 2014 EWCA Crim 621, 2 Cr App R (S) 54 (p 437) (Car dealer who had 58 sales in breach of regulations and ordered to pay almost £110,000. Said it was in breach of article 1 and to be out of alignment with sentence of 100 hours' unpaid work. Held. There is a clear distinction between goods provided by lawful contract and those tainted by illegality. This order was not disproportionate.)
R v Awan 2014 EWCA Crim 2496 (Convicted of conspiracy to evade excise duty. The confiscation order was made on a limited basis. Held. No confiscation hearing is complete without some reference to *R v Waya* 2012 and without some citations from the judgments.)

Determining the benefit: Particular situations

21.82 ***Step 7 Determining the benefit Benefit given to another***
R v Frost 2009 EWCA Crim 1737, 2010 1 Cr App R (S) 73 D pleaded to theft and some VAT TICs. He managed his school's budget and submitted false invoices to the County Council. These were paid and he stole the money from the school account. These payments generated VAT and the school was able to claim these as VAT credits. D never received any of these credits. It was claimed that these entries were essential so he could steal the non-VAT element of the false claim. The Judge found that D had disposition or control of the VAT monies. The Judge included in the benefit just over £60,500 for the overpayments of VAT. Held. D never 'got his hands on' the balance of the funds transferred into the school bank account as a result of the VAT fraud. Had he not been caught, he would no doubt have done so or attempted to do so. D never acquired an interest in that part of the fraud so the VAT part should be left out of the benefit figure. Order reduced.

21.83 ***Step 7 Assessing the value (etc.) Asset converted***
R v Dimsey and Allen 2000 1 Cr App R (S) 497 The ordinary and natural meaning of pecuniary advantage must surely include the case where a debt is evaded or deferred.
Note: This interpretation was subsequently adopted by the House of Lords in *R v Cadman-Smith* 2001, see below. Ed.
R v Cadman-Smith 2001 UKHL 68, 2002 2 Cr App R (S) 37 (p 144) Lords The statutory provisions show that when considering the measure of the benefit obtained by an offender, the court is concerned simply with the value of the property to him at the time when he obtained it or, if it is greater, at the material time. In particular, where the offender has property representing in his hands the property which he obtained, the value to be considered is the value of the substitute property 'but disregarding any charging order'.
R v Waya 2012 UKSC 51, 2013 2 Cr App R (S) 20 (p 87) Supreme Court para 60 Toulson LJ in *R v Pattison* 2007 EWCA Crim 1536, 2008 1 Cr App R (S) 51 (p 287) said at para 21: "It is the prosecution's argument that where a defendant acquires property through criminal conduct, and subsequently deals with that property, then any proceeds of that dealing must be benefits which result from the offending and are therefore to be added to the original value of the property. This overlooks the provisions of section 80 (to which the Judge was not referred) but before coming to that section it is worth pausing to consider the implications of the argument. Suppose that after the appellant received the property worth £150,000 he had sold it for that sum and put the money in

the bank. On the prosecution's argument, the benefit that he would then have received and for which he would be amenable to a confiscation order would be £300,000, representing the value of the property (£150,000) plus the sum for which he realised it (£150,000). If he then used the £150,000 to buy a yacht worth £150,000, the benefit would rise to £450,000. If he then tired of sailing and sold the yacht for the same price, the benefit which he would have received and for which he would be liable to a confiscation order would become £600,000. All the while, his true financial position would have remained identical. That offends common sense. Every schoolchild knows that you cannot have the penny and the sweet. If your mother gives you a penny and you buy a sweet with it, your benefit is a penny's worth and not two pennies' worth. It is correct that the provisions of the legislation are draconian, but the effect of the prosecution's argument would not [make] any underlying sense. Fortunately, section 80 addresses the situation where a person subsequently deals with property which has been acquired by him through criminal conduct."

21.84 ***Step 7 Determining the benefit Tainted gifts***
Tainted gifts
Proceeds of Crime Act 2002 s 77(1) Subsections (2) and (3) apply if:
(a) no court has made a decision as to whether the defendant has a criminal lifestyle, or
(b) a court has decided that the defendant has a criminal lifestyle.
(2) A gift is tainted if it was made by the defendant at any time after the relevant day.
(3) A gift is also tainted if it was made by the defendant at any time and was of property:
(a) which was obtained by the defendant as a result of or in connection with his general criminal conduct, or
(b) which (in whole or part and whether directly or indirectly) represented in the defendant's hands property obtained by him as a result of or in connection with his general criminal conduct.
(4) Subsection (5) applies if a court has decided that the defendant does not have a criminal lifestyle.
(5) A gift is tainted if it was made by the defendant at any time after:
(a) the date on which the offence concerned was committed, or
(b) if his particular criminal conduct consists of two or more offences and they were committed on different dates, the date of the earliest.
(6) For the purposes of subsection (5) an offence which is a continuing offence is committed on the first occasion when it is committed.
(7) For the purposes of subsection (5) the defendant's particular criminal conduct includes any conduct which constitutes offences which the court has taken into consideration in deciding his sentence for the offence or offences concerned.
(8) A gift may be a tainted gift whether it was made before or after the passing of this Act.
(9) The relevant day is the first day of the period of 6 years ending with:
(a) the day when proceedings for the offence concerned were started against the defendant, or
(b) if there are two or more offences and proceedings for them were started on different days, the earliest of those days.
Proceeds of Crime Act 2002 s 78(1) If the defendant transfers property to another person for a consideration whose value is significantly less than the value of the property at the time of the transfer, he is to be treated as making a gift.
(2) If subsection (1) applies, the property given is to be treated as such share in the property transferred as is represented by the fraction:
(a) whose numerator is the difference between the two values mentioned in subsection (1), and
(b) whose denominator is the value of the property at the time of the transfer.

(3) References to a recipient of a tainted gift are to a person to whom the defendant has made the gift.

Proceeds of Crime Act 2002 s 81(1) The value at any time (the material time) of a tainted gift is the greater of the following:

(a) the value (at the time of the gift) of the property given, adjusted to take account of later changes in the value of money,

(b) the value (at the material time) of the property found under subsection (2).

(2) The property found under this subsection is as follows:

(a) if the recipient holds the property given, the property found under this subsection is that property,

(b) if the recipient holds no part of the property given, the property found under this subsection is any property which directly or indirectly represents it in his hands,

(c) if the recipient holds part of the property given, the property found under this subsection is that part and any property which directly or indirectly represents the other part in his hands.

(3) The references in subsection (1)(a) and (b) to the value are to the value found in accordance with section 79.

R v Richards 2008 EWCA Crim 1841 D was convicted of money laundering offences which were part of a drugs conspiracy. In that conspiracy was R, who pleaded guilty to drug supply and money laundering offences. D and R were friends. While R was in Holland avoiding the police, he transferred five properties to D which on documents indicated minimal consideration but in reality there was no consideration. There were three other transfers for no consideration. When the confiscation proceedings were heard, four of the properties had been sold and the proceeds were in a solicitor's account. The fifth was on the market. The total value of the five properties was £241,000. The prosecution said they were R's assets. For R the Judge included the property values in the recoverable amount. For D the Judge found the benefit was the £241,000. The defence said if the money was available to R it could not be available to D. Alternatively if the property was his he must be allowed to use it to pay the confiscation order. The Judge said for D the assets were a tainted gift and presumably made a significant confiscation order (the value is not stated in the judgment). Held. It was not stated that the assets were owned jointly. The property could not belong both to R and D. There would be nothing wrong in him making a confiscation order against one defendant based on a valuation at the date of the confiscation order, and against the other defendant based on a valuation at the time of the relevant transaction. If at the time of the order the beneficial interest in the property belonged to R, as both parties contend, how could the beneficial interest in the properties have belonged to D at the time of the transfers? There are different tests to be applied depending on what, if any, determination the court has made as to whether the defendant has a criminal lifestyle. Certain things are clear. First, the tainted gift provisions only apply where there has been a transfer of property. Whether there has been a transfer of property and, if so, what is the nature of the proprietorial interest that has been transferred are matters to be determined by the law of property. In this case the tainted gift provisions cannot determine what interest in the five houses passed to the appellant. Second, if there has been a transfer at a significant undervalue, the consequence in terms of the Act is not to prevent the transfer having such legal effect as it may have as a matter of property law. The effect under the Act is that the value of the property transferred at a significant undervalue is to be included in the valuation of the amount available to the defendant to satisfy the confiscation order. The underlying purpose of the tainted gift provisions of the Act is plain. No self-respecting organised criminal would expect to be caught with high-value property in his own name readily identifiable, particularly since the enactment of legislation which is designed to strip such criminals of their profits. As a matter of standard practice he is likely to have taken steps to transfer high-value assets to nominee companies, offshore trusts or trusted associates who can be looked upon to harbour the assets until such time as he perceives that the danger has passed or he has served any sentence of imprisonment. The scheme adopted by the Act is to enable property transferred at a significant undervalue to be included in the calculation of the available amount. If it transpires that a defendant genuinely cannot recover property (as distinct from having a lack of willingness to do so), section 23 provides for the possibility of a re-assessment. There is nothing in this scheme which supports the contention advanced by the prosecution that the Act operates to re-vest property transferred at an undervalue in the transferor. The order must be quashed.

R v Smith 2013 EWCA Crim 502, 2 Cr App R (S) 77 (p 506) D pleaded to dishonestly making false statements about Housing benefit and Council tax benefit. She had savings, meaning she was not entitled to benefit. The prosecution applied for a benefit of the sum obtained less the amount paid back. In fact she had given money to her family. The Judge found she had no assets. The Judge held that once items were considered to be tainted gifts there was no need to investigate whether there was any prospect of them being recovered. Held. We agree with the Judge for two reasons. First, there is a specific statutory regime governing the valuation of tainted gifts. There is nothing in section 81 which links the value of the gift to its recoverability, even though it contemplates the situation where the recipient of the gift has parted with it. Second, the whole point of including assets which a defendant has given away as one of the components in assessing the amount which a defendant has available was to prevent a defendant dissipating his assets by giving them away. If he is to be able to say that they are of no value because he cannot get them back, that would defeat what the inclusion of tainted gifts in section 9(1) was seeking to achieve. Since you cannot sue the recipient of a gift for its return, there may be many occasions when gifts cannot be recovered. It cannot have been intended for those gifts which the recipient is prevailed upon to return to be included as part of the offender's available assets, but not those which the recipient cannot be persuaded to give up.

R v Lehair 2015 EWCA Crim 1324, 2016 1 Cr App R (S) 2 (p 4) D robbed a bank and on the same day she deposited £1,200 into her account and transferred £1,100 from her account into her husband's account. The Judge found she did not have a criminal lifestyle and the transfer was assessed as a tainted gift. The defence said this was not permissible as Proceeds of Crime Act 2002 s 77(5)(a) required the gift to be made 'at any time after the date on which the offence was committed' when in fact it was made on the same day. Held. A literal translation of the Act is anomalous with the explicit purpose of the Act. It could not have been intended that criminals should have a day's grace to dispose of their assets. Without wishing to define 'date', the order stands.

See also the ***Step 9 Tainted gifts when considering the recoverable amount*** para at **21.115**.

21.85 ***Step 7 Assessing the value Debts/Loans***

R v Ghadami 1998 1 Cr App R (S) 42 D was convicted of a VAT fraud. Two of his assets were houses where the mortgage debt was twice or more than twice the value of the premises. The Judge declined to take into account the debt, saying that mortgage debt should only be regarded as relevant and as having priority to the extent of the value of the security. Held. That was correct. Debts to building societies or banks who have advanced money on security which is no longer adequate have no priority, other than to the extent of the value of the security. That becomes obvious if they choose to exercise their right to sell the property in order to reduce the mortgage debt. They remain creditors of the debtor for the balance, but nothing in Part VI of the 1988 Act gives them any sort of priority when it comes to the making of a confiscation order.

R v McQueen 2001 EWCA Crim 2460 D was convicted of possession with intent to supply MDMA. Police searched his home and found £1,350 in cash which D said was a loan from his sister, S, to set up a business. The Judge for the argument assumed that account was true and treated the money as his realisable assets. On appeal the defence submitted that once the police arrived, the ability to set up a business failed and consequently the money reverted to S. Held. When the police raided D's home the cash was clearly 'property held by the defendant'. Accordingly it formed part of 'the realisable property'. The loan was not an 'obligation having priority at that time'. The Judge had no discretion in the matter and accordingly he was right to make the order.

21.86 ***Step 7 Determining the benefit Assets seized***
R v Crisp and Berry 2010 EWCA Crim 355, 2 Cr App R (S) 77 (p 505) C and B pleaded to evading duty on tobacco. The customs seized £82,000 and about £21,000 cash from their homes. It was forfeited. In assessing the benefit the Judge deducted these sums from the benefit figures. Held. The seizure of the cash did not diminish the loss from the evasion of duty. The deduction was wrong.
Note: This is in line with the principle that when calculating benefit the profit is not the issue. Ed.
R v Waya 2012 UKSC 51, 2013 2 Cr App R (S) 20 (p 87) Supreme Court para 55 a) Once property has been obtained as a result of or in connection with crime, it remains the defendant's benefit whether or not he retains it. This is inherent in the value based scheme for post-conviction confiscation. para 33 In *R v Smith* 2001 UKHL 68, 2002 2 Cr App R (S) 37 (p 144) the defendant had evaded the payment of duty on imported cigarettes by smuggling them past the customs post. The decision in the case was that the pecuniary advantage thus (admittedly) obtained had not retrospectively been undone by the subsequent seizure of the cigarettes. That was plainly correct. Lord Rodger held, at para 23, that the subsequent seizure of the cigarettes was in like case[394] to subsequent loss of or damage to goods obtained in the course of crime. Such loss or damage would not affect the propriety of a confiscation order. Consider for example the case of a burglar who hides the householder's goods in the open air so that they are ruined by the weather or stolen by someone else. The House was not, however, considering the case in which the criminal property obtained has been restored to its owner undamaged. On the contrary, Smith was agreed to have obtained the pecuniary advantage of avoiding payment of the duty, at any rate temporarily.
R v Elsayed 2014 EWCA Crim 333 D pleaded to 'counts of possession of cocaine' with intent to supply. His work locker was searched and 169 grams of cocaine and a small wrap of cocaine (less than 3 grams) were found. No cutting agents or wraps were found at his home. The large amount was at 80% purity and the smaller amount was at 5% purity. D's basis of plea was he was a custodian, which was rejected. The prosecution said he was a street dealer and would have cut the 169 grams into individual wraps of 5% purity. D did not seek a *Newton* hearing to challenge that. In confiscation proceedings D was found to have nearly £246,000 worth of available assets. The prosecution valued the drugs at a street value of £40 a gram, assuming it had been cut to wraps of 5% purity. That made just over £108,000 (169 × 80 ÷ 5 × £40). The Judge agreed because the drugs were going to be cut by D. On appeal, the defence said: a) the benefit should be the actual value when seized, namely the wholesale value, and relied on Proceeds of Crime Act 2002 s 80(2)(a), see **21.75**, and b) using the cut figure of drugs was to an extent speculative. The prosecution said in confiscation proceedings drugs may frequently be valued on a wholesale basis. However, here the Judge was perfectly entitled to adopt the retail valuation. Held. para 25 The *dicta* in *R v Islam* 2009, see above, tells strongly against the defence argument. para 30 The valuation of benefit is essentially a fact-driven exercise. para 20 What D was going to do with the cocaine was not "speculative". D was going to sell it, cut and divided into wraps at 5% purity, as a dealer at street level. It is perfectly consistent with the entire notion of 'market value' that for particular property it may vary, depending for example on the time at which it is obtained or the capacity or role of the person obtaining it. Using the market value here

[394] What this means is not clear. Maybe 'in like case' means 'comparable'. Ed.

flows from a 'fair and purposive' construction of Proceeds of Crime Act 2002 s 79 and 80. It reflects the legislative purpose which was to deprive the defendant of the benefit of his criminal conduct. It was not a disproportionate outcome. Order upheld.

R v Brooks 2016 EWCA Crim 44 D was convicted of conspiracy to import drugs. He was the organiser of boats that would transport drugs from South America to the UK. The Irish Navy seized a yacht with 1,504 kilos of cannabis near the Irish coast. In confiscation proceedings, the Judge included the value of the drugs (worth about £3m) in the benefit figure. Held. para 19 The fact the drugs were seized does not and cannot take the value of the drugs outside the benefit figure. Finding upheld.

Note: For more detail see **21.99**. Different considerations apply when fixing the recoverable amount, see the same case at **21.134**.

21.87 ***Step 7 Determining the benefit Goods restored to the loser***

R v Waya 2012 UKSC 51, 2013 2 Cr App R (S) 20 (p 87) Supreme Court D pleaded to two counts of obtaining a money transfer by deception. para 36 To obtain a mortgage of £465,000, he made false statements about his employment record and his earnings. With £310,000 of his own, untainted money and the mortgage, a property was obtained. Later the mortgage was paid back with a mortgage from another building society. Held. para 35 The money was repaid in full. para 28 To make a confiscation order when the defendant has restored to the loser any proceeds of crime which he had ever had is disproportionate. It would not achieve the statutory objective of removing his proceeds of crime but would simply be an additional financial penalty. That it is consistent with the statutory purpose so to hold is moreover demonstrated by the presence of section 6(6). This subsection removes the duty to make a confiscation order, and converts it into a discretionary power, wherever the loser whose property represents the defendant's proceeds of crime either has brought, or proposes to bring, civil proceedings to recover his loss. It may be that the presence of section 6(6) is capable of explanation simply as a means of avoiding any obstacle to a civil action brought by the loser, which risk would not arise if repayment has already been made. But it would be unfair and capricious, and thus disproportionate, to distinguish between a defendant whose victim was about to sue him and a defendant who had already repaid. If anything, an order that the same sum be paid again by way of confiscation is more disproportionate in the second case than in the first. Unlike the first defendant, the second has not forced his victim to resort to litigation.

R v Harvey 2013 EWCA Crim 1104, 2014 1 Cr App R (S) 46 (p 265) D pleaded to various handling and arson offences. D owned and controlled a plant hire company, JHL. The police searched his property and found 39 stolen 'items of plant'. The total value of stolen goods was £314,700. The value of the plant recovered by police and restored to the losers was £159,800. The defence argued this should be deducted from the benefit. Held. While in D's possession the stolen items had depreciated. *R v Waya* 2012 UKSC 51, 2013 2 Cr App R (S) 20 (p 87) paras 28-29 did not deal with partial restoration. In fact the property appreciated in value. *R v Axworthy* 2012 EWCA Crim 2889, *R v Hursthouse* 2013 EWCA Crim 517, and *R v Jawad* 2013 EWCA Crim 644, 2014 1 Cr App R (S) 16 (p 85) (see **21.81**) dealt with full restoration. There is nothing in the wording of Proceeds of Crime Act 2002 which requires the court to deduct the residual value of chattels after prolonged use. If a defendant steals or otherwise unlawfully obtains someone else's property and uses it for a number of years thereby materially reducing its value, a confiscation order based upon the original value of that property without any deduction is not disproportionate. The Judge was right not to deduct the residual value of the stolen plant after its recovery by the police.

See also: *R v Axworthy* 2012 EWCA Crim 2889 (Stolen property recovered. *R v Waya* 2012 applied. Order quashed.)

21.88 ***Determining the benefit Another confiscation order made within last six years***

Proceeds of Crime Act 2002 s 10(8) The relevant day is the first day of the period of six years ending with:

(a) the day when proceedings for the offence concerned were started against the defendant, or

(b) if there are two or more offences and proceedings for them were started on different days, the earliest of those days.

(9) But if a confiscation order mentioned in section 8(3)(c) has been made against the defendant at any time during the period mentioned in subsection (8):

(a) the relevant day is the day when the defendant's benefit was calculated for the purposes of the last such confiscation order,

(b) the second assumption does not apply to any property which was held by him on or before the relevant day.

(10) The date of conviction is:

(a) the date on which the defendant was convicted of the offence concerned, or

(b) if there are two or more offences and the convictions were on different dates, the date of the latest.

Note: This is the assumptions section. For the full section, see **21.66**. Ed.

R v Barnett 2011 EWCA Crim 2936 On 10 October 2005, D was convicted of brothel offences. It was accepted that the local police gave a measure of tacit approval to the activity in line with a Home Office document which suggested co-operation with the sex industry rather than [driving it underground]. At Court there was a deal struck that the confiscation order should be limited to the amount of cash seized. On 10 October 2005 the Judge gave D an 8-month Suspended Sentence Order and made a confiscation order, as suggested, under Criminal Justice Act 1988 in the sum of just over £21,000. During these proceedings and afterwards, D continued operating his brothels. This was despite warnings. About two months after the order was made, D was arrested again. D pleaded to four counts of keeping a brothel and other charges. The Judge said he was trading in brothels on a breathtaking scale. He was sentenced to 3 years. Proceeds of Crime Act 2002 applied. The Judge calculated the benefit at just over £5m, less the £21,000 figure from the previous hearing. The confiscation order was £4,000. On appeal the defence argued that the assumptions should not have applied to the period before 10 October 2005. Held. The assessment made on 10 October 2005 must be taken as fixed for the purpose of any subsequent assessment of benefit. The relevant day for the second confiscation is that day. We reduce the benefit figure to just over £873,000.

21.89 ***Step 7 Determining the benefit Conspiracies/Joint enterprises/ Apportionment***

R v Byatt 2006 EWCA Crim 904, 2 Cr App R (S) 116 (p 779) D pleaded to conspiracy to rob. A box containing £25,000 was seized from a security guard. His basis of plea was that he withdrew from the conspiracy before the robbery took place. The Judge made a nominal confiscation order of £1. Held. D cannot be said to have been instrumental in obtaining the cash in any realistic way. There was no benefit. Order quashed.

R v May 2008 UKHL 28, 2009 1 Cr App R (S) 31 (p 162) Lords D pleaded to conspiracy to cheat. It was a VAT fraud with a loss to the public of about £11m. Held. There might be circumstances in which orders for the full amount against several defendants might be disproportionate and contrary to [European Convention on Human Rights] art 1, and in such cases an apportionment approach might be adopted, but that was not the situation here and the total of the confiscation orders made by the Judge fell well below the sum of which the Revenue had been cheated. Mere couriers or custodians or other minor contributors to an offence, rewarded by a specific fee and having no interest in the property or the proceeds of sale, are unlikely to be found to have obtained that property, although it may be otherwise with money launderers.

R v Green 2008 UKHL 30, 2009 1 Cr App R (S) 32 (p 182) Lords para 15 Where two or more defendants obtain control of property jointly, each of them has obtained the whole of it within the meaning of the [confiscation legislation].
R v Sivaraman 2008 EWCA Crim 1736, 2009 1 Cr App R (S) 80 (p 469) D pleaded to conspiracy to evade duty for fuel. M, the proprietor of a service station, purchased agricultural diesel, changed the dye in it and sold it for use in road vehicles. D was a cashier there and was promoted to manager. In a basis of plea D said he accepted 8-10 deliveries of diesel each of about 30,000 gallons and he received £15,000 in all. The prosecution contended the benefit was the duty evaded, £128,520. The defence contended it was the £15,000 on the basis that that was the figure D received. Held. Where two or more defendants obtain property jointly, each is to be regarded as obtaining the whole of it. Where property is received by one conspirator, what matters is the capacity in which he receives it, that is whether for his own personal benefit, or on behalf of others, or jointly on behalf of himself and others. This has to be decided on the evidence: *R v Green* 2008, para 15. By parity of reasoning, two or more defendants may or may not obtain a joint pecuniary advantage; it depends on the facts. It follows from the above that participants in a joint criminal offence (including conspiracy) may benefit jointly to the same extent by each obtaining the same property or pecuniary advantage; or the value of the benefit received by them may differ as between one and another. The crucial question was, 'What was D's position in relation to his employer with regard to the purchase and sale of the fuel which generated that pecuniary advantage?' D accepted 8-10 deliveries of fuel, knowing of their illicit nature, which begs the question, in what capacity did he do so? The Judge did not find D was a joint purchaser of the fuel. He believed D was an employee. We substitute a confiscation figure of £15,000.
R v Allpress and Others 2009 EWCA Crim 8, 2 Cr App R (S) 58 (p 399) para 31 A conspiracy is not a legal entity but an agreement or arrangement which people may join or leave at different times. In confiscation proceedings, the court is concerned not with the aggregate benefit obtained by all parties to the conspiracy but with the benefit obtained, whether singly or jointly, by the individual conspirator before the court. It is a misconception that anybody who has taken part in a conspiracy in more than a minor way is to be taken as having a joint share in all benefits obtained from the conspiracy, applying *R v Sivaraman* 2008 EWCA Crim 1736, 2009 1 Cr App R (S) 80 (p 469). In confiscation proceedings, 'the focus of the inquiry is on the benefit gained by the relevant defendant'.
R v Rooney 2010 EWCA Crim 2 D pleaded to importing cannabis resin. Rooney assisted others to move pallets with the boxes of drugs on them. He also recruited a co-defendant and was directing the lorry with the pallets on. He was to be paid £200. Held. The position is: a) if a benefit is shown to be obtained jointly by conspirators, then all are liable for the whole of the benefit jointly obtained, b) if, however, it is not established that the total benefit was jointly received, but it is established that there was a certain sum by way of benefit which was divided between conspirators, yet there is no evidence on how it was divided, then the court making the confiscation order is entitled to make an equal division as to benefit obtained between all conspirators, c) however, if the court is satisfied on the evidence that a particular conspirator did not benefit at all or only to a specific amount, then it should find that is the benefit that he has obtained. Here the Judge was entitled to draw the inference that all the conspirators had obtained benefit.
R v James and Blackburn 2011 EWCA Crim 2991, 2012 2 Cr App R (S) 44 (p 253) J and B were convicted of conspiracy to evade tobacco excise duty. Tobacco was received at a poultry farm where it was treated with chemicals and processed into hand-rolling tobacco. Police raided the premises and B was arrested there. J was arrested elsewhere. For J the prosecution relied on three withdrawals of £10,000 two days after some tobacco was transferred from the farm to a storage area. The Judge held that J was the provider of accommodation and facilities for packing and distribution and this was crucial to the success of the enterprise. He was responsible for causing the tobacco to

arrive at the duty point where indeed he helped. B was a local manager. Held. Only the person or persons who are personally liable to pay the duty will have obtained a pecuniary advantage by evading its payment. Absent that liability, those persons will not have obtained a benefit in accordance with Proceeds of Crime Act 2002 s 76. This was established by the House of Lords in *R v May* 2008 UKHL 28, 2009 1 Cr App R (S) 31 (p 162) and applied in *R v Chambers* 2008 EWCA Crim 2467 and *R v Mitchell* 2009 EWCA Crim 214. However, it does not follow from the fact that a person evades the duty which he personally owes that he has necessarily obtained a benefit by evading it. A person holding the tobacco products at the excise duty point, namely at or shortly after the tobacco emerged from the machine, is the person holding the tobacco products at that time or any person who caused the tobacco products to reach the excise duty point whilst retaining a connection with the goods at that point. (See HMRC *Excise Notice 476: Tobacco Products Duty*.) This was explained in *R v White and Others* 2010 EWCA Crim 978, para 56. There can be more than one person who owes the duty and, under the Regulations, each is liable jointly and severally. However, HMRC can only recover the amount of the duty owed. There can be no double recovery. The word 'holding' has not been authoritatively determined but a person would 'hold' the HRT if he owned it or probably had possession or control. B was in effect the local 'salaried' manager of the factory with no proprietary interest in the tobacco. It might have been agreed or, if not agreed, decided that the £6,960.00 which B spent on miscellaneous expenses was an investment by B in the unlawful enterprise. There was no evidence that B financed the purchase of the raw leaf tobacco. It had to be assumed that B expected to be reimbursed for the expenses, albeit that there was no evidence that he was. The issue was, was B either holding the tobacco or did he cause the tobacco products to reach the excise duty point whilst retaining a connection with the goods at that point of time? In *R v Mitchell* 2009 EWCA Crim 214, a post *R v Chambers* 2008 decision said that they had not heard full argument on the point but that it appeared that the words causing the tobacco products to reach the excise duty point were directed at the person who had real and immediate responsibility for causing the product to reach that point. In para 115, the Court in *R v White and Others* 2010 said that the correctness or otherwise of this *obiter* passage might have to be considered should the point arise. One of the problems for criminal courts in this area is that any interpretation given to the Regulations must be the same as the interpretation that would be given to the Regulations in civil proceedings (court or tribunal) concerning excise duty. Furthermore when construing the word 'cause' in criminal cases, it is normally given a broad meaning, see *R v Williams* 2010 EWCA Crim 2552, applied in *R v H* 2011 EWCA Crim 1508. Whatever the precise meaning of the words 'holding' and 'causing', B as the local manager albeit with no ownership of the tobacco falls into one or both of these categories. The Judge was therefore entitled to find that he caused the tobacco to arrive at the duty point. Next we consider whether B obtained a benefit. In *R v May* 2008 it was said at paragraph 48(6), 'D ordinarily obtains property if in law he owns it, whether alone or jointly, which will ordinarily connote a power of disposition or control, as where a person directs a payment or conveyance of property to someone else. He ordinarily obtains a pecuniary advantage if (among other things) he evades a liability to which he is personally subject. Mere couriers or custodians or other very minor contributors to an offence, rewarded by a specific fee and having no interest in the property or the proceeds of sale, are unlikely to be found to have obtained that property.' B had no interest in the tobacco or the proceeds of sale. On the other hand he was more than a courier or custodian and it would be difficult to categorise him as a very minor contributor to an offence. B, if he had not repaid the £6,960.00, had lost that money and had made no money at all, given that HMRC had intervened before any distribution had effectively taken place.

In the light of *R v Sivaraman* 2008 EWCA Crim 1736, 2009 1 Cr App R (S) 80 (p 469) it seems to us that B's appeal against the confiscation order in so far as it represented the unpaid excise duty must succeed. In these circumstances, we do not need to address the post-hearing submissions that were sent to us on the question of whether or not B had the necessary intent to evade the duty.

R v Lambert and Walding 2012 EWCA Crim 421 The defence submitted that the orders were unlawful because the Judge had failed to apportion between the two defendants. Held. para 9 It is legitimate that the entire realisable assets of a person who embarks on a joint drug-dealing venture should be put at risk, up to the sum of the joint benefit obtained, and not merely his assets up to the limit of his share of that sum. While the present statutory scheme is in place, the refusal to apportion is a legitimate part of it. The scheme does provide some protection to minor contributors who have no interest in the property obtained, see *R v May* 2008 UKHL 28, 2009 1 Cr App R (S) 31 (p 162). Moreover, in the case of drug dealing, unlike, for example, VAT frauds, there is no identifiable financial loser seeking recovery or compensation and the expression 'double recovery' is inapt. The sum subject to the confiscation order is a penalty designed to deprive of benefit and also to deter. The offender has protection to the extent that the amount of the order will not exceed either the joint benefit or his own realisable assets.

R v Ahmad and Others 2014 UKSC 36, 2 Cr App R (S) 75 (p 580) Supreme Court The Court considered two unconnected appeals. The Ahmad defendants had engaged in an MTIC fraud, fraudulently claiming £12.6m of VAT. The Fields defendants were convicted of conspiracy to defraud in relation to goods and services supplied to a company which had forged its accounts. £1.4m was jointly acquired. Neither set of defendants challenged the quantification of the recoverable amounts (£16.1m when adjusted for inflation for the Ahmad defendants and £1.6m for the Fields defendants), or the finding that they obtained that amount jointly. They challenged the decision of the Court of Appeal, relying on *R v May* that each defendant was separately liable for the entire amount, as where a benefit is obtained jointly, each joint beneficiary has obtained the whole of the benefit. The question was, 'when a number of people (whether or not all are before the court) have been involved in the commission of a crime which resulted in property being acquired by them together, what is the proper approach for the court to adopt, and the proper orders for the court to make in confiscation hearings?' Held. As identified in *R v May*, there are three questions to be answered:

a) Has the defendant benefited? para 41 Proceeds of Crime Act 2002 s 76(4) provides that a person benefits from conduct 'if he obtains property as a result of or in connection with the conduct'. In *Jennings*, para 12, Lord Bingham agreed with Laws LJ in the Court of Appeal that the essence of benefit in that phrase is given by the word 'obtains'. para 45 In *Jennings v CPS* 2008 UKHL 29, 2 Cr App R (S) 29 (p 414), para 12, Lord Bingham agreed…that the essence of benefit in that phrase is given by the word 'obtains'. Thus, one is concerned with what the particular defendant obtained, which is by no means necessarily the same as the totality of what was obtained by the criminal enterprise of which he was a party. para 46 Accordingly, where property is obtained as a result of a joint criminal enterprise, it will often be appropriate for a court to hold that each of the conspirators 'obtained' the whole of that property. However, that will by no means be the correct conclusion in every such case. para 50 There has sometimes been a tendency to equiparate[395] joint involvement in the crime with joint ownership of the fruits of the crime. But the fact that the defendants were jointly responsible for the crime in question does not automatically justify a conclusion that they jointly obtained the resulting property.

para 51 Judges in confiscation proceedings should be ready to investigate and make findings as to whether there were separate obtainings. Sometimes of course this is too difficult or impossible. In many cases the court will not have before it all the conspirators for a variety of reasons. A court should never make a finding that there has been joint obtaining from convenience, or worse from laziness. para 56 In many cases it

[395] This means compare.

is often completely unclear how many people were involved in the crime, what their roles were, and where the money went. As a result, if the court could not proceed on the basis that the conspirators should be treated as having acquired the proceeds of the crime together, so that each of them 'obtained' the 'property', it would often be impossible to decide what part of the proceeds had been 'obtained' by any or all of the defendants. It is one thing for the court to have to decide whether a defendant obtained any property, which the 2002 Act requires. It is another thing for the court to have to adjudicate on the respective shares of benefit jointly obtained, which the Act does not appear to require.

para 58 [In relation to the Ahmad defendants] it would be logically incoherent to hold the two Ahmad defendants each liable for half of the 'property' simply on the basis that it would be oppressive for each to be liable for the whole. If an argument based on oppression were right, then no order could be made unless the number of participants and the role of every participant in the fraud could be ascertained.

b) What is the value of the benefit? para 61 A defendant who steals property or obtains it by deception does not, as explained above, acquire ownership of that property. In such a case the court takes the market value of the goods, not because that represents the value of the thief's legal interest in the goods, which would be nil, but, as explained in *R v Rose* 2008 EWCA Crim 239, approved in *R v Waya* 2012, the market value of the property, because that is the value of what the thief has misappropriated, namely what it would cost anyone to acquire it on the open market.

para 62 In the light of [Lord Bingham's] observation [in *R v May* 2008], it seems clear that the 'interests' of a defendant's co-conspirators are not to be taken into account when valuing the property for the purpose of assessing the value of the property which the defendant 'obtained'.

para 66 [The] argument [to treat the Ahmad defendants as having acquired an interest equal in value to half the £12.6m] has the attraction of being consistent with the ordinary cases of beneficial joint ownership, but it would have to be very persuasive before we were justified in departing from [the] clear and consistent [line of authority].

para 67 The position of joint obtainers under Proceeds of Crime Act 2002 *inter se* is very different from that of two lawful joint owners or joint debtors, and it is unsurprising if their rights and obligations under the 2002 Act do not follow those of such owners and debtors.

para 70 It therefore [followed] that the Court of Appeal was right to conclude that each of the Ahmad defendants 'obtained' £16.1m (after adjusting for inflation) as 'property', and that that was the value of their benefit. In the second appeal…there was no appeal against the Judge's finding that the Fields defendants jointly obtained a benefit worth £1.6m. [Consequently it] was right to hold that the benefit…in respect of each defendant was the whole amount of the property obtained.

c) What is the sum payable? (See para **21.114**.)

R v Sayers and Sayers 2014 EWCA Crim 2157 D and K pleaded to 'cash for crash' fraud. A benefit figure was based on the total obtained by three claimants from one bogus accident. Held. *R v Ahmad and Others* 2014 UKSC 36, 2 Cr App R (S) 75 (p 580), which was heard after the order was made, meant that was incorrect. The benefit figure for each defendant was their insurance payout with the order for costs made.

R v Dad and Others 2014 EWCA Crim 2478 D and others were convicted of conspiracy to defraud and money laundering. They made a series of bogus insurance claims. The Judge found although the defendants held separate bank accounts and assets, the assets were regarded by the defendants as all part of a family pot. Nevertheless he apportioned the benefit equally because otherwise it would be disproportionate and unfair. Held. It is easy to see why the Judge did that but *R v Waya* 2012 UKSC 51, 2013 2 Cr App R (S) 20 (p 87) had not displaced *R v May* 2008 UKHL 28, 2009 1 Cr App R (S) 31 (p 162) about apportionment. The Judge was wrong to do so, so prosecution appeal allowed. Where the Judge had not apportioned, appeal dismissed.

R v Smith 2014 EWCA Crim 2707, 2015 1 Cr App R (S) 43 (p 315) D pleaded to conspiracy to defraud. He made a false insurance claim for a claimed collision of his car and a Range Rover driven by W. D accepted liability and both made claims. D received £5,800 and W £17,028. Experts discovered the accident was staged. The prosecution in confiscation proceedings added the two payouts together for the benefit figure and adjusted that for inflation. The Judge agreed. D's assets were £28,000. D claimed his benefit should be assessed at £5,800. Held. para 23 The fraud was undoubtedly joint. That does not necessarily mean the benefit was joint. That there must have been a pre-concert is obvious. But there were separate claims. On the evidence neither received the full sum. There was no evidence of pooling. There were separate payments made. There is an inference that D and W made an adjustment because if D just received payment for his car then he had little or nothing to gain. However, a 'kick back' would not have been sufficient for a finding of the joint figure for the benefit. As prosecution counsel concedes the Judge's reasoning was unsatisfactory and as counsel was not able to make any concession, we accept the proper course is to quash the order and remit the matter to the Crown Court for the matter to be properly explored.
See also: *R v Strange* 2018 EWCA Crim 118 (LCJ D pleaded to conspiracy to supply drugs. D's role was limited to dealing with the money. P, a co-defendant, handed over 1.18 kilos of cocaine to a courier. P met D in a car park. About £124,000 was placed in P's car. D claimed he was returning cash to P. The Judge said the benefit was the 9 kilos of cocaine seized in all (£378,000). Held. All conspirators are to be taken to [have] obtained property that any of them obtain, subject to the clear exceptions of those taking only a small or insignificant role. Order upheld.)
See also the ***Step 9 The available amount Conspiracies/Joint enterprises*** para at **21.114**.

21.90 ***Step 7 Determining the benefit Conspiracies/Joint enterprises Expenses***
R v Mahmood 2013 EWCA Crim 325 D pleaded to a conspiracy to import heroin. D was placed in a leading role. In confiscation proceedings, the Judge included the conspirator's expenditure in the benefit figure. Held. The joint liability of members of a conspiracy does not assist in identifying which member of it may have incurred expenditure in the course of its operation. Nor does the statutory assumption in section 10(4) help. It is an assumption about the source of expenditure, once it has been established that a defendant incurred it. What is required is evidence about the identity of the particular member of the conspiracy who actually incurred the expenditure. The section 10(4) assumption does not mean that, unless he can prove otherwise, each conspirator is treated as having incurred all of the expenditure. It may be that in the circumstances of a particular case the court can draw inferences that a particular member of the conspiracy met an expense of its operation. In other, and perhaps many, cases, the natural inference will be that the conspirators will have contributed equally to such expenses. But without a finding that the defendant in question spent something, the section 10(4) assumption is not triggered. Here there was no finding about D's expenditure, so the expenses cannot be attributed to him.

21.91 ***Determining the benefit Directors of companies***
R v Powell and Westwood 2016 EWCA Crim 1043 P was convicted of environmental permit offences and a waste disposal offence. W pleaded to counts that mirrored P's counts. Both were directors and shareholders of the offending company. Both were involved in the management and finances of the offending site. The clean-up costs paid by the Ministry of Defence and the public purse were about £1.125m. The prosecution said that by abandoning the site P and W had avoided the costs of a clean-up and therefore had a pecuniary advantage. The Judge made a limited confiscation order. The Judge had refused to lift the corporate veil and the prosecution appealed. Held. para 27 P and W were both well aware of the failure to comply with regulations at the material time and that the reason for non-compliance was out of a desire to increase the

company's profitability. But it is important, in looking at the nature of the criminality, to note here that there was no facade or concealment for hiding behind the company's structure in a way which abused the corporate shield. Unlike the situation in *Jennings v CPS* 2008 UKHL 29, 2 Cr App R (S) 29 (p 414), this was not a company being run for an unlawful purpose but rather was a legitimate business which had broken the criminal law through its failure to observe the necessary regulations. P and W's liability depended on consent, connivance or neglect in relation to the company's failures. P and W were not the sole shareholders. para 29 There needs to be a legal right against the person controlling the company which exists independently of the company's involvement. We find it hard to identify [any] legal right, liability, obligation or restriction for P or W which existed independently of the company. It was the company which had incurred obligations to comply with the relevant environmental laws by obtaining the permit. The prosecution's approach would risk making every company director liable in the confiscation proceedings whenever a company broke the criminal law. para 31 As *Prest v Petrodel Resources and Others* 2013 UKSC 34, para 35 makes plain, the court is concerned with abuse of the corporate veil to evade or frustrate the law. The facts point away from showing that this is the sort of case in which a benefit obtained by a company should be treated as a benefit obtained by the individual criminal. para 34 Neither P or W had a personal liability for the costs of cleaning up the company's polluted site.

21.92 ***Step 7* Determining the benefit VAT considerations**

R v Harvey 2015 UKSC 73, 2016 1 Cr App R (S) 60 (p 406) Supreme Court D was convicted of five counts of arson and nine counts of handling. He ran a hire business. D arranged an arson attack on a competitor and police found he had stolen property on his premises. In confiscation proceedings it was a 'criminal lifestyle' case. D's benefit was assessed as just over £2,275,000, based on a) his company's turnover, which included VAT paid, b) the stolen items, and c) 'general criminal conduct'. The Court of Appeal dismissed his appeal, *R v Morgan* 2013 EWCA Crim 1104, see the 9th edition of this book at para **25.89**. The Supreme Court considered whether the VAT was rightly included in the benefit. Held (3-2). para 25 In a number of respects VAT for which a defendant had to account, and has accounted, to HMRC is in a different category from either income or corporation tax, and, *a fortiori*, from expenses incurred in connection with acquiring money or an asset. para 27 Where money is paid to a defendant as a result of a transaction which is liable to VAT, the defendant is regarded under EU law as collecting the VAT element on behalf of HMRC. The defendant will have paid VAT in the form of input tax to its suppliers. It would seem particularly harsh, even penal, in a case where a defendant has accounted for all the VAT for which he is liable, not to allow him credit for that sum. para 30 That gives rise to a powerful argument that, at least when the VAT has been accounted for to HMRC, it, or a sum equivalent to it, has not been 'obtained' by the defendant as a matter of ordinary domestic statutory construction. para 32 Any provision which entitles the executive to effect double recovery from an individual, although not absolutely forbidden by European Convention on Human Rights art 1, is clearly at risk of being found to be disproportionate. That proposition would seem to apply in relation to any sum payable pursuant to Proceeds of Crime Act 2002, which, while intended to be deterrent, is not intended to be punitive. para 35 The judge trying the issue should be guided by two important factors. First, although the burden may be on the prosecution to establish the gross value of the benefit obtained by the defendant, the burden of establishing that a sum, and if so what sum, should be deducted from that value to reflect VAT accounted for to HMRC lies on the defendant. Second, as in many exercises involved in assessments under Proceeds of Crime Act 2002, a judge should be robust in making such a determination. There is nothing disproportionate about taking a broad-brush approach to questions of what sums were received or paid in the context of criminal activity, where the evidence is confusing, unreliable and/or incomplete. On the contrary: the risk of disproportionality may lie more in spending much time and money pursuing a precise answer which is at best elusive and more frequently unattainable. para 36 So it would be disproportionate, at least when VAT output tax has been accounted for to HMRC (either by remittance or by its being set off against input tax), to make a confiscation order calculated on the basis that that tax, or a sum equivalent to it, has been 'obtained' by the defendant for the Act. We leave open the position in relation to VAT for which the defendant is liable, but in respect of which he has not accounted, to HMRC. Appeal allowed.

For how to consider benefit for VAT offences, see the ***Step 7 Determining the benefit VAT frauds*** para at **21.109**.

Determining the benefit: Particular offences

21.93 *Step 7 Determining the benefit Administrative offences*

R v Moss 2015 EWCA Crim 713 LCJ D pleaded to three record-keeping offences and one charge of failing to dispose of a cow's carcass. The prosecution case was that D had unlawfully slaughtered and/or butchered 209 unaccounted-for cattle. His benefit was £1,000 per item. The prosecution suggested that D had a criminal lifestyle because two of the offences were committed over six months and D had benefited by £5,000 or more. The defence said that had not been charged. The Judge found that D had been involved in the unlawful slaughter and butchery of 116 cattle. He calculated the benefit at £83,000, which was less than his realisable assets. Held. Taken in isolation [none] of the offences involved the obtaining of any property or pecuniary advantage. paras 57 and 11 The Judge was wrong to find D had benefited from the offences, so order quashed.

21.94 *Step 7 Determining the benefit Benefit fraud*

R v Richards 2005 EWCA Crim 491, 2 Cr App R (S) 97 (p 583) D was sentenced for specimen charges of falsely obtaining benefit. The defence considered the benefit should be reduced by the amount she could have obtained lawfully. Held. Section 71(4) bites at the moment the property is obtained. [No allowance should be made for the amount that could have been obtained lawfully.] Appeal dismissed.

R v Jacques 2014 EWCA Crim 1922 D pleaded to benefit fraud offences. Her confiscation order was made by agreement on the day judgment was given in *R v Waya* 2012 UKSC 51, 2013 2 Cr App R (S) 20 (p 87). The confiscation order was based on the amount she had received and not on the amount she had been overpaid. On appeal the defence argued that she had been entitled to a very significant part of the money she had received. Further that following *R v Waya* 2012, the calculation was disproportionate. Held. para 22 We do not accept that the principle in *R v Waya* 2012 ensured that the benefit figure had to be confined to the incremental gain which had flowed from the unlawful behaviour.

21.95 *Step 7 Determining the benefit Corruption*

R v Sale 2013 EWCA Crim 1306, 2014 1 Cr App R (S) 60 (p 381) D pleaded to corruption and fraud by false representation. D was the managing director and sole shareholder of SS, a company that supplied Network Rail. He provided gifts and hospitality to a Network Rail employee worth just under £7,000. D was given secret tender advice and SS received about £1.9m worth of orders. A £60,000 invoice was paid twice. D was sentenced on the basis that the work done by SS was 'without criticism as to price or quality'. SS had a turnover of about £9.9m and only in its work with Network Rail was SS dealing illegally. D's benefit in apportioned salary and dividends for Network Rail's contracts was £125,000. SS's gross profit before tax was nearly £200,000. The Judge agreed to lift the corporate veil and found the benefit was £1.9m. Because of D's assets the order was made in that sum. Held. para 46 Prior to *R v Waya* 2012 there would have been no fault in finding the benefit figure to be £1.9m. Since then any confiscation order had to bear a proportionate relationship to the purpose of the Proceeds of Crime Act 2002, which is to recover the financial benefit which an offender has obtained from his criminal conduct. Corruption of this nature clearly impacts on others. The company obtained contracts with a client with whom it had had no previous business relationship. Existing contractors with Network Rail were cheated out of the tendering process. The substantial market in Network Rail contracts of this type was distorted, with the company gaining a market share to the detriment of others. Tendering costs were avoided. para 56 Had this been an offence whose only criminal effect was upon Network Rail which had been provided with value for money achieved by the performance of a contract which required the company to expend monies in the ordinary course of business, it would have seemed to us proportionate to limit the confiscation order to the profit made, and to treat the full value given under the contract as analogous to full restoration to the loser. However, the pecuniary advantage gained by obtaining market share, excluding competitors, and saving on the costs of preparing proper tenders means a proportionate confiscation order would need to reflect those additional pecuniary advantages. An order for profit gained under these contracts, together with the value of pecuniary advantage obtained, would represent a proportionate order which would avoid double counting. There is no difficulty in attributing these items to D as proportionately representing his benefit since he was the sole shareholder in the company. But we do not have the [information] to make a confiscation order on this basis. There has been no analysis done in relation to pecuniary advantage. We are therefore obliged to substitute the nearly £200,000 figure.

21.96 ***Step 7 Determining the benefit Couriers***

R v May 2008 UKHL 28, 2009 1 Cr App R (S) 31 (p 162) Lords In determining whether the defendant has obtained property or a pecuniary advantage and, if so, the value of it, the court should apply ordinary common law principles. The exercise of this jurisdiction involves no departure from familiar rules governing entitlement and ownership. Determining the recoverable amount calls for inquiry into the financial resources of the defendant at the date of the determination. Determining the benefit calls for a historical inquiry into past transactions.

The defendant ordinarily obtains property if in law he owns it, whether alone or jointly, which will ordinarily connote a power of disposition or control, as where a person directs a payment or conveyance of property to someone else. He ordinarily obtains a pecuniary advantage if (amongst other things) he evades liability to which he is personally subject. Mere couriers or custodians or other minor contributors to an offence, rewarded by a specific fee and having no interest in the property or the proceeds of sale, are unlikely to be found to have obtained that property, although it may be otherwise with money launderers.

See also: ***Determining the benefit Money launderers/Money custodians*** para at **21.106**.

21.97 ***Step 7 Determining the benefit Businessmen obtaining money when not registered***

R v May 2008 UKHL 28, 2009 1 Cr App R (S) 31 (p 162) Lords In determining whether the defendant has obtained property or a pecuniary advantage and, if so, the value of it, the court should apply ordinary common law principles. The exercise of this jurisdiction involves no departure from familiar rules governing entitlement and ownership. Determining the recoverable amount calls for inquiry into the financial resources of the defendant at the date of the determination. Determining the benefit calls for a historical inquiry into past transactions.

The defendant ordinarily obtains property if in law he owns it, whether alone or jointly, which will ordinarily connote a power of disposition or control, as where a person directs a payment or conveyance of property to someone else. He ordinarily obtains a pecuniary advantage if (amongst other things) he evades liability to which he is personally subject. Mere couriers or custodians or other minor contributors to an offence, rewarded by a specific fee and having no interest in the property or the proceeds of sale, are unlikely to be found to have obtained that property, although it may be otherwise with money launderers.

R v McDowell and Singh 2015 EWCA Crim 173, 2 Cr App R (S) 14 (p 137) M's and S's cases were not connected but joined because they shared similar points. M was an arms

dealer convicted of two counts of supplying goods subject to a prohibition. His company was the agent in an aircraft sale to Ghana. S pleaded guilty to carrying on a business as a scrap metal dealer without being entered on the Register. Held. para 32 This Court has held that trading in criminal breach of a prohibition is criminal conduct from which benefit can be derived, *R v Del Basso* 2010 EWCA Crim 1119, 2011 1 Cr App R (S) 41 (p 268). That case and *R v Sumal & Sons (Properties) Ltd* 2012 EWCA Crim 1840 demonstrate the importance of identifying the criminal conduct of the offender at the first stage of the assessment. It is not sufficient to treat 'regulatory' offences as creating a single category of offence to which POCA is uniformly applied. There is a narrow but critical distinction to be made between an offence that prohibits and makes criminal the very activity admitted by the offender or proved against him (as in *R v Del Basso* 2010) and an offence comprised in the failure to obtain a licence to carry out an activity otherwise lawful (*R v Sumal & Sons (Properties) Ltd* 2012). para 53 For M the underlying transactions were prohibited and unlawful. It is not arguable that he did not benefit from his criminal conduct. Neither is it arguable that, because commission payments were received after a licence was applied for or granted, they did not comprise benefit from criminal conduct under the Act. para 60 For S, his trading activity was not criminal conduct from which benefit accrued. The criminal conduct was the failure to register before carrying on business. However, S's trading receipts were obtained as a result of or in connection with trading activity that was lawful in itself and not from the failure to register the particulars of the business that comprised the criminal offence. We derive some support for our identification of the nature of the criminal conduct from the alternative means by which the offence may be committed: failing to notify a change of circumstances in breach of section 1(5). It would be an odd and inconsistent result if one means of committing the offence attracted a POCA benefit finding while the other did not. Confiscation order quashed.
See also: *R v Shim* 2016 EWCA Crim 576 (D pleaded to supplying unlicensed security staff. Held. The benefit was the gross receipts not the net profit, applying *R v McDowell and Singh* 2015. It wasn't just failure to register, D had supplied staff in direct breach of prohibition.)

21.98 Step 7 ***Determining the benefit Disqualified from being a company director Breach of***
R v Seager and Blatch 2009 EWCA Crim 1303 S breached an undertaking not to act as a company director. B contravened a court disqualification from being a company director. In each case the Judge considered the benefit figure was the turnover in their companies, namely £1.5m and just over £940,000. The orders were made before *R v May* 2008 UKHL 28, 2009 1 Cr App R (S) 31 (p 162) was heard. Held. para 68 This offence is no different from other crimes. The three questions are the same: a) Has the defendant benefited? b) What is the value of the benefit? and c) What sum is recoverable from him? para 75 What the benefit is is a question of fact, and turnover might be relevant. Considering these issues and that there was no basis to 'pierce the corporate veil' the benefit cannot be the turnover. For B there was no finding that he had benefited in connection with the offence. There was no other 'real' benefit. The benefit and confiscation order for B was his agreed income, just over £221,000. For S there was no investigation what [any other] benefit [besides the turnover] he had received so the order was simply quashed.
Piercing the corporate veil see **21.48**.

21.99 ***Step 7 Determining the benefit Drugs, Unlawful***
R v Islam 2009 UKHL 30, 2010 1 Cr App R (S) 42 (p 245) House of Lords D pleaded to importing 3.53 and 0.44 kilos of heroin on separate occasions. The goods were seized. In confiscation proceedings the Judge relied on the wholesale value of the drugs, and assessed that part of the benefit figure at nearly £71,500. The Court of Appeal felt bound by an earlier case and ruled the drugs had no lawful market so no market value, see *R v*

Islam 2008 EWCA Crim 1740. The Court felt unable to assess the money used to purchase the drugs because the Judge had not relied on that assessment. They deducted the drugs figure from the confiscation figure. The prosecution appealed. Held (3-2). para 33 There is no rule that Parliament does not concern itself with black market values. para 34 When assessing benefit, the heroin is to be valued by reference to the market value 'at the time the person obtains it', applying Proceeds of Crime Act 2002 s 79(2) and 80(2)(a). para 48 In *R v Rose* 2008 EWCA Crim 239, the Court of Appeal held that the thief or handler was to be regarded as obtaining a benefit in the amount of their market value by obtaining possession of them, even though they were liable to be and were restored to their legitimate owner (and any attempt to sell them would no doubt have involved further wrong-doing). A distinction of this nature, between the benefit from obtaining stolen goods and from obtaining drugs – one moreover putting drug offenders on a more favourable basis as regards confiscation than thieves or handlers – is not convincing. para 17 It is not out of place to give a different meaning to market value when considering the benefit than the meaning given to the phrase when considering the 'available amount', see **21.117**. We overrule the earlier case and restore the sentencing Judge's confiscation figure.

R v Elsayed 2014 EWCA Crim 333 D pleaded to 'counts of possession of cocaine' with intent to supply. His work locker was searched and 169 grams of cocaine and a small wrap of cocaine (less than 3 grams) were found. No cutting agents or wraps were found there or at his home. The large amount was at 80% purity and the smaller amount was at 5% purity. D's basis of plea was he was a custodian, which was rejected. The prosecution said he was a street dealer and would have cut the 169 grams into individual wraps of 5% purity. D did not seek a *Newton* hearing to challenge that. In confiscation proceedings D was found to have nearly £246,000 worth of available assets. The prosecution valued the drugs at a street value of £40 a gram, assuming it had been cut to wraps of 5% purity. That made just over £108,000 (169 × 80 ÷ 5 × £40). The Judge agreed because the drugs were going to be cut by D. On appeal, the defence said: a) the benefit should be the actual value when seized, namely the wholesale value, and relied on Proceeds of Crime Act 2002 s 80(2)(a), see **21.75**, and b) using the cut figure of drugs was to an extent speculative. The prosecution said in confiscation proceedings drugs may frequently be valued on a wholesale basis. However, here the Judge was perfectly entitled to adopt the retail valuation. Held. para 25 The *dicta* in *R v Islam* 2009, see above, tells strongly against the defence argument. para 30 The valuation of benefit is essentially a fact-driven exercise. para 20 What D was going to do with the cocaine was not 'speculative'. D was going to sell it, cut and divided into wraps at 5% purity, as a dealer at street level. It is perfectly consistent with the entire notion of 'market value' that for particular property it may vary, depending for example on the time at which it is obtained or the capacity or role of the person obtaining it. Using the market value here flows from a 'fair and purposive' construction of Proceeds of Crime Act 2002 s 79-80. It reflects the legislative purpose, which was to deprive the defendant of the benefit of his criminal conduct. It was not a disproportionate outcome. Order upheld.

R v Brooks 2016 EWCA Crim 44 D was convicted of conspiracy to import drugs. He was the organiser of the boats that would transport drugs from South America to the UK. The Irish Navy seized a yacht with 1,504 kilos of cannabis near the Irish coast. In confiscation proceedings, the Judge included the value of the drugs (worth about £3m) in the benefit figure. The Judge found that D had contributed to the purchase of the drugs. On appeal, the prosecution accepted that they had never contended that D had purchased the drugs. Held. para 17 It is clear that the word 'obtain' [in Proceeds of Crime Act 2002 s 76(4)] is to be given a broad, normal meaning, in which the role of a particular conspirator may be relevant. On the basis of the extensive role of D in the drugs conspiracy and, in particular, his central involvement in the transportation and proposed delivery of the drugs with significant managerial and operational control over the exercise, [means] D 'obtained criminal property' and thus has benefited from his

criminal conduct in respect of the drugs. para 16 There was ample evidence of that, even if he had not contributed to their purchase. para 19 Once property has been obtained as a result of or in connection with crime, it remains the defendant's benefit whether or not he retains it. This is inherent in the value based scheme for post-conviction confiscation, see *R v Waya* 2012 UKSC 51, 2013 2 Cr App R (S) 20 (p 87) para 55 a). para 19 The fact the drugs were seized does not and cannot operate so as to take the value of the drugs outside the benefit figure.
See also: *R v Strange* 2018 EWCA Crim 118 (LCJ D pleaded to conspiracy to supply drugs. D's role was limited to dealing with the money. P, a co-defendant, handed over 1.18 kilos of cocaine to a courier. P met D in a car park. About £124,000 was placed in P's car. D claimed he was returning cash to P. The Judge said the benefit was the 9 kilos of cocaine seized in all (£378,000). Held. All conspirators are to be taken to [have] obtained property that any of them obtain, subject to the clear exceptions of those taking only a small or insignificant role. Order upheld.)

21.100 ***Step 7 Determining the benefit Duty evasion (alcohol smuggling etc.)***
R v Eddishaw 2014 EWCA Crim 2783 D pleaded to cheating Revenue and Customs of duty payable on alcoholic products. D was the head of an operation producing counterfeit vodka. He purchased large quantities of denatured alcohol, removed the additives and added water. That was bottled with a fake label of a well-known brand. In confiscation proceedings, the Judge said the benefit was the money he had received for selling the counterfeit vodka. The genuine bottles retailed at £8.65 and the counterfeit bottles at £6.80. The wholesale price of the counterfeit bottles was not known. The Judge found on the balance of probabilities that the wholesale black market value was £5. The Court considered Alcoholic Liquor and Duties Act 1979 s 4 and 78 and Finance Act 1995 s 5. **Issue 1** The Judge found that there was sufficient nexus between the cheat offence and the value of the vodka D was selling. The defence argued no duty was ever due. Held. para 33 This case is on all fours with *R v Louca* 2013 EWCA Crim 2090, 2014 2 Cr App R (S) 9 (p 49) (see **21.101**). para 30 One cannot take too narrow a view of Proceeds of Crime Act 2002 s 76(4) (see **21.60**). When *bona fide* vodka is sold in the shops a very large part of the purchase price is referable to duty. The whole objective was to produce something very similar to vodka and to evade the payment of any duty. The vodka was indeed obtained as a result of or in connection with the conspiracy to cheat Revenue and Customs. **Issue 2** (Guessing an amount for the wholesale value of the counterfeit vodka), see **21.47**.

21.101 ***Step 7 Determining the benefit Duty evasion (tobacco smuggling etc.)***
Note: For all Customs and Excise Management Act 1979 s 50(2) or (3), 68(2) and 170 offences,[396] once the confiscation proceedings are triggered (see **21.12**), the court must follow the Proceeds of Crime Act 2002 confiscation provisions. The categories of persons liable to pay tobacco duty are set out in HMRC *Excise Notice 476: Tobacco Products Duty*. The result is that it is more difficult to make confiscation orders for those defendants who were not holding the tobacco products at an excise duty point or caused the tobacco products to reach such a point, *R v Khan and Others* 2009 EWCA Crim 588. The expression 'cigarettes of that description' includes both genuine goods and counterfeit goods of substantially the same type made up to resemble them. Therefore the prosecution can calculate from the duty on genuine cigarettes, *R v Varsani* 2010 EWCA Crim 1938. Ed.
R v Bajwa and Others 2011 EWCA Crim 1093, 2012 1 Cr App R (S) 23 (p 117) The defendants pleaded to or were convicted of conspiracy to evade the duty chargeable on cigarettes. The defendants were arrested on 13 and 14 September 2004. On 13 September one of the bills of lading was seized. On 21 September 2004, a container containing 7 million counterfeit cigarettes arrived at Felixstowe. The bill of lading said

[396] Proceeds of Crime Act 2002 s 75 and Sch 2 para 1(2)

the goods were patio heater parts. On 22 September 2004, the cigarettes were seized by customs. In confiscation proceedings the defendants denied that they had obtained any 'pecuniary advantage' within Proceeds of Crime Act 2002 s 76(5), see **21.59**. They claimed that they had never become liable to pay any duty on the cigarettes and so could not be said to have evaded any duty on the cigarettes. The Judge held this was a question of fact for each defendant. He said the pecuniary advantage was that they were working together in the conspiracy. On appeal the defendants argued:

(a) none of them was ever liable to pay the duty on the counterfeit cigarettes, because:
 (i) none of them is a person who is liable to pay the duty within the terms of the 2001 Regulations, and
 (ii) none of the conspirators could be 'holding' the cigarettes at the excise duty point, because none possessed the bill of lading, which was 'the key to the goods' and none had any other right to obtain possession of the cigarettes any more,
(b) they were arrested, which meant that they must have impliedly ceased to have any further interest in the goods,
(c) none of them could have 'caused' the tobacco to reach the excise duty point, and
(d) neither did they retain a sufficient connection with the goods at the duty excise point.

Held. This issue about 'pecuniary advantage' is relevant to two aspects of these confiscation proceedings. First, it is relevant to the question of whether the conditions in section 75(2)(c) (see **21.55**) are fulfilled by determining whether the defendant has a 'criminal lifestyle'. In this case that 'benefit' is said by the Crown to take the form of evading the duty payable on the counterfeit cigarettes, thereby obtaining a 'pecuniary advantage' within section 76(5), see **21.59**. Second, the question of whether the defendants have obtained a 'pecuniary advantage' is relevant to what, if any, 'benefit' each of the defendants have obtained, either from his 'general criminal conduct' or his 'particular criminal conduct', for the purposes of Proceeds of Crime Act 2002 s 6(4) (see **21.58**). Some principles are:[397]

(1) A person 'obtains a pecuniary advantage' within Proceeds of Crime Act 2002 s 76(5), see **21.59**, if he evades or defers a debt that is then due and owing.[398]
(2) Duty is payable on tobacco imported by sea in ships when the ship enters the limits of the port where the goods are to be imported.[399]
(3) Duty will be 'evaded' when the duty becomes payable but it is not paid. The precise point at which evasion occurs is, however, controversial.[400]
(4) If goods are smuggled into the UK past the 'excise duty point' and excise duty is thereby evaded, a 'pecuniary advantage' to the extent of the duty evaded will be obtained even if the goods are thereafter seized by HMRC or are lost or destroyed.[401]
(5) A person is only liable to pay excise duty on tobacco imported by sea in a ship if:
 (a) he is 'holding' the goods at the excise duty point, or
 (b) he caused the goods to reach the excise duty point and he retained a sufficient connection with the goods at that point.[402]
(6) The Crown must prove, on a balance of probabilities, that a particular defendant has:

[397] The footnotes in this summary are in the judgment.

[398] *R v Smith* 2001 UKHL 68, 2002 2 Cr App R (S) 37 (p 144) at para 18, approving *R v Dimsey and Allen* 2001 UKHL 46, 2002 1 Cr App R (S) 17 (p 187). *R v Smith* 2001 concerned the provisions in Criminal Justice Act 1988 s 71(5). But the principle was followed in *R v Varsani* 2010 EWCA Crim 1938 in relation to Proceeds of Crime Act 2002 s 76(5).

[399] See para 32 of this judgment.

[400] *R v Mitchell* 2009 EWCA Crim 214 at para 26. When precisely the excise duty is 'evaded' when tobacco is imported by sea appears to be a point on which two divisions of the Court of Appeal have given conflicting views. In *R v Mitchell* 2009, at para 26, Toulson LJ said that 'evasion' occurs only when the importer 'ought to declare'. In *R v White and Others* 2010 EWCA Crim 978, Hooper LJ said, at para 46, that this statement was not right and that the evasion takes place when the ship carrying the tobacco enters the limits of the port because that is when the duty is payable. We discuss this later in the judgment.

[401] *R v Smith* 2001 UKHL 68, 2002 2 Cr App R (S) 37 (p 144) and *R v Varsani* 2010 EWCA Crim 1938

[402] See paras 35 and 36 of this judgment (not summarised). As noted, the qualification on '*caused*' suggested by Toulson LJ in *R v Mitchell* 2009 is *obiter* but may not add too much in any case.

(a) evaded the duty payable, so that
(b) a 'pecuniary advantage' within section 76(5) has been 'obtained by him' and that defendant has thus obtained a 'benefit' to the extent of the monetary value of that pecuniary advantage.[403]

The first question is whether any appellant was '*holding*' the counterfeit cigarettes at the time that it entered the port of Felixstowe. As the law currently stands, that depends on whether any of them had possession or control of the cigarettes at that point. Obviously, none of them was physically in possession of the cigarettes at the time. However, it is elementary commercial law that if a person is the lawful holder of a bill of lading then he has 'symbolic' or 'constructive' possession of the goods that are identified in the bill of lading, such that he can demand their delivery up by the ship owner at the completion of the contractual voyage. We are prepared to assume a person who is the lawful holder of a bill of lading for the goods in respect of which he intends to import will be 'holding' those goods, whether or not he is the consignor or consignee named in the bill of lading. Here the bill of lading identified the right container but it did not identify the cigarettes as being within the container. More importantly, at the time the ship entered the port of Felixstowe none of the appellants was the lawful holder of the one bill of lading we know about because it had been seized by customs on 13 September 2004. There was no evidence before the Judge about who possessed the other bills of lading. So there is no basis on which if any of the appellants actually held one of the other bills of lading at the relevant time. There are no findings of fact which enable us to reach a conclusion that one of the eight had another bill of lading. For similar reasons we must reach the conclusion that none of the appellants had 'control' over the cigarettes at the time that they entered the port of Felixstowe. Therefore we conclude that it is not established that any of the appellants was 'holding' the cigarettes when they entered the port of Felixstowe.

Next we consider whether any of the appellants 'caused' the cigarettes to reach the excise duty point. If so, then we must consider whether that person has also 'retained a connection with the goods at that point' [see para 39 in this judgment (not summarised)]. It was open to the Judge to find that each of the defendants '*caused*' the counterfeit cigarettes to reach the relevant excise duty point, the limit of the port of Felixstowe. In addition, we think that on those facts it would also have been open to the Judge to conclude that each of the appellants was a person who had 'real and immediate responsibility for causing' the cigarettes to reach the excise duty point. As the Crown pointed out in argument, there was nothing more that any of the conspirators needed to do for the container and the cigarettes to sail past the limits of the port of Felixstowe and it was as a result of their actions that the container and the goods got onto the quayside at Felixstowe.

The next question is 'Did any of the appellants "retain a connection" with the cigarettes at the excise duty point?' The combined effect of the seizure of the bill of lading by customs on 13 September 2004 and the arrest and questioning of the appellants on 13/14 September 2004 is that: a) the appellants must, by inference, have ended their common understanding to carry out the conspiracy and b) it was no longer possible to achieve the object of the conspiracy. That must have an impact on whether any of the appellants retained a connection with the cigarettes by the time they passed the excise duty point. It is impossible for us to conclude that the Crown could prove, on a balance of probabilities, that any of the appellants had retained a connection with the cigarettes by the time the vessel passed the excise duty point. The conspiracy was impossible of completion and the basis of the common understanding had come to an end. The obvious inference is that the appellants had abandoned any connection they had with the cigarettes by 21 September 2004. None of the defendants were persons who were liable

[403] *Jennings v CPS* 2008 UKHL 29, 2 Cr App R (S) 29 (p 414) at paras 13 and 14 applied in *R v Middlecote* 2011 EWCA Crim 548 at para 14.

to pay the excise duty on the cigarettes at the moment that the vessel, loaded with the container, passed within the limits of the port of Felixstowe on 21 September 2004. We quash the confiscation order.

R v Bell 2011 EWCA Crim 6 D1, D2, D3 and D4 pleaded to fraudulently evading duty chargeable on cigarettes. All were involved in different ways in handling smuggled cigarettes after they had been imported. They appealed their confiscation order to which they had consented. Held. It would be a grave injustice if we didn't intervene. In general terms a person is not liable for excise duty on smuggled tobacco products unless he has a connection with the smuggled goods at the time of the importation. When the goods arrive by sea, that is when the ship enters the port of destination in this country. Held. Unfortunately no one applied their mind to whether the defendant had obtained a pecuniary advantage either directly because he was liable for the duty himself or indirectly because he had a causal link with the non-payment of the duty by another. It is not disputed none of the defendants were liable to pay the duty either directly or indirectly. For D1 and D2 we reduce the order to the amount of the money they were given to hire van(s) and their rewards which totalled for D1 £950 and for D2 £420. For D3 and D4 we reduce the order to represent the value of the cigarettes sold and the VAT which ought to have been paid.

Note: The defendant Louca, below, was a co-defendant in the case. Ed.

R v Louca 2013 EWCA Crim 2090, 2014 2 Cr App R (S) 9 (p 49) D pleaded to being knowingly concerned in the fraudulent evasion of excise duty. D and two others were seen unloading items into a warehouse. 1.3 million cigarettes with a payable excise duty and VAT of just over £204,000 were found in the warehouse. D paid D4 (see above) £10,000 for some cigarettes with a value of just over £36,000. On appeal the defence argued there was no real benefit as the goods had been seized. Held. The goods have not been restored. Smuggled cigarettes are of no value to customs. We take into account *R v Waya* 2012 UKSC 51, 2013 2 Cr App R (S) 20 (p 87). Confiscation order a little over £36,000 (value of the smuggled cigarettes). That was not disproportionate.

R v Hussain 2014 EWCA Crim 1181 D pleaded to being concerned in keeping goods with intent to defraud. A confiscation order was made by valuing the goods on their lawful market value. The goods were Russian-made tobacco which could not be sold in the UK because there was no assessment of the quality and safety of the product. The prosecution agreed with the defence that the value should have been the value of the goods if sold on the black market. Held. To determine whether the agreed view was correct, there were two critical questions: a) What, if anything, did D obtain as a result of or in connection with his admitted criminal conduct? b) What was the value of [the goods] which he obtained? In Proceeds of Crime Act 2002 s 80(2) (see **21.75**) the value of the property at the material time is the greater of the value of the property at the time the person obtained it, adjusted to take account of the later changes in the value of money and the value at the time that person obtained the property. In this case the value of the property obtained was the market value of the tobacco products at the time he obtained them. As none of the products could be lawfully purchased because: a) they did not bear the relevant duty marks, and b) the relevant market is the unlawful black market [price], that is the figure we substitute.

See also: *R v Middlecote* 2011 EWCA Crim 548 (After the tobacco was imported, it was delivered to D's industrial unit. He assisted in unloading the containers and loading the tobacco into smaller lorries and vans. Held. He had not caused the tobacco to reach the point of duty. D was not holding the tobacco at the point of duty. He was not liable for any of the duty. Duty element of confiscation order quashed. Order based on his rewards and the price of the loads which provided the cover for the smuggling.)

R v Tatham 2014 EWCA Crim 266 (Order made under Criminal Justice Act 1988 s 71. Under the old regime and the 2002 regime, for a confiscation order to be made, the offender would have to be personally liable for the import duty. Review of current law. Order upheld when applying the correct test.)

21.102 ***Step 7 Determining the benefit Solicitors' costs***
R v Wright 2014 EWCA Crim 382 D was convicted of a 'crash for cash' insurance fraud. During confiscation proceedings, the prosecution contended that the £2,258 costs paid to the solicitor for processing the claim were part of the benefit. The Judge included those costs. On appeal the defence contended the money had never been handled by him. Held. We accept that D did not obtain the property. The fee paid was for work done. The solicitors were not a knowing party. In consequence of the claim there was a chain of events which created the payment to the solicitors. In ordinary litigation D, as client, would have been liable for the solicitor's fees had the insurers not paid them. Consequently he had obtained a pecuniary advantage. D as a direct result of this fraud avoided what would otherwise have been his liability for the solicitor's costs. The order was correct.
See also: *R v Sayers and Sayers* 2014 EWCA Crim 2157 (Pleas to 'crash for cash' fraud. Order varied to include solicitor's costs, following *R v Wright* 2014 EWCA Crim 382 (above).)

21.103 ***Step 7 Determining the benefit Enforcement notice offences***
R v Ali 2014 EWCA Crim 1658 D was convicted of failing to comply with an enforcement notice and was committed for sentence. He bought four properties and converted them into 38 flats. He was served with enforcement proceedings and took no notice of them. The Judge included in the amount the rent and housing benefit obtained before the enforcement notices were issued. The defence challenged that. Held. This issue is of practical importance because breaches of the planning laws may not be discovered for some time. Proceeds of Crime Act 2002 s 76(1)(a) and (b) define criminal conduct as 'conduct which…constitutes an offence in England and Wales'. Proceeds of Crime Act 2002 s 75(2) requires the relevant conduct to comprise an offence or offences. D's conduct did not constitute an offence until an enforcement notice was actually effective, which meant the relevant notice period had expired. We reduce the order to reflect that.
See also: *R v Del Basso* 2010 EWCA Crim 1119, 2011 1 Cr App R (S) 41 (p 268) (D ran an illegal car park and ignored an enforcement notice. Held. The money had clearly been obtained. These enforcement offences were within the confiscation scheme. Benefit (the parking revenue) of £1.881m upheld.)
R v Panayi 2019 EWCA Crim 413 (D was convicted of breaching an Enforcement Notice. The gross rental income was used. Held. As the charge related to 'on or about 18 February 2016', the benefit was the benefit for that day. The order must be for £58 not £95,920.)

21.104 ***Step 7 Determining the benefit Environmental offences***
R v Rory J Holbrook Ltd 2015 EWCA Crim 1908 D pleaded to operating a waste operation and depositing waste without permits. D agreed to construct and landscape a golf course. No permits were obtained notwithstanding D had a conviction in 2008 for operating without a waste management licence. The total fine was £30,000. D's turnover was about £5m. The Judge found D was significantly reckless. She assessed the benefit as the cost of depositing the 94,010 tonnes of waste at a site, which was about £97,500, the £3,530 permit fees which were avoided and the income generated, £146,180. A confiscation order for £247,278 was made. The defence argued that the order was disproportionate and should be confined to profits, relying on *R v King* 2014 EWCA Crim 621, 2 Cr App R (S) 54 (p 437). Further it was a legitimate company and its undertakings were lawful. Held. The submission misunderstood the decision in *R v King* 2014. The depositing and the treatment of the waste were unlawful in their entirety. The order was not disproportionate. We uphold it.
For the appeal about the fine see **251.11** in Volume 2.

21.105 ***Step 7*** ***Determining the benefit*** **Loan sharks**
R v Chapman 2015 EWCA Crim 694 D pleaded to eight counts of breaching Consumer Credit Act 1974 s 39(1) by carrying on an unlicensed money-lending business. He charged interest well above standard rates. He loaned a total of about £137,000 and received repayments of about £221,000. The defence said the repayments were from lawful loan agreements and if that failed the benefit should just be the profit. The Judge took the £221,000 figure as the benefit and made a confiscation order for about £177,500. On appeal the defence said the confiscation order was a penalty within Consumer Credit Act 1974 s 170 and so barred. Also that confiscation did not apply because all D had done was not to obtain a licence. Held. Section 170 was limited in scope so did not apply. Relying on *Hampshire CC v Beazley* 2013 EWCA Crim 567, the order was entirely proportionate.

21.106 ***Step 7*** ***Determining the benefit*** **Money launderers/Money custodians**
R v May 2008 UKHL 28, 2009 1 Cr App R (S) 31 (p 162) Lords D pleaded to conspiracy to cheat. It was a VAT fraud with a loss to the public of about £11m. On appeal the issue was how benefit should be determined which required analysis of whether D had obtained property. Held. He ordinarily obtains a pecuniary advantage if (among other things) he evades a liability to which he is personally subject. para 48(6) D ordinarily obtains property if in law he owns it, whether alone or jointly, which will ordinarily connote a power of disposition or control, as where a person directs a payment or conveyance of property to someone else. Mere couriers or custodians or other minor contributors to an offence, rewarded by a specific fee and having no interest in the property or the proceeds of sale, are unlikely to be found to have obtained that property, although it may be otherwise with money launderers.

R v Allpress and Others 2009 EWCA Crim 8, 2 Cr App R (S) 58 (p 399) SA, DS, MC pleaded to assisting another to retain the benefit of drug trafficking. PM was convicted of that offence. SM was convicted of three offences of possessing criminal property. Their cases were joined together as a similar point arose in each. SA, DS and MC were couriers of money who received rewards and expenses. PM was a solicitor and was involved in transferring cash through bank accounts he controlled as client accounts. SM stored his brother's drug money at his shop. On appeal the issue was what benefit each had obtained. Held by a five-judge court. para 48 If a shopper in a supermarket gives money to a till operator at the checkout, which the till operator puts in the till, nobody would ordinarily think of the till operator benefiting from that sum of money or of the money being under the till operator's power of disposition or control in the [confiscation regime] sense. The [cash] would be the shop's money from the moment that the till operator took it from the customer. It may be that the till operator would have physical power to dispose of the money elsewhere. It may be that he or she could put it in their pocket undetected, but that is no different from the physical power of any bailee to use the property for a different purpose from that of the bailment. Moreover, one would not ordinarily regard the till operator's physical possession of the money as a benefit to the till operator, or as the possession of money which was theirs to control or dispose of, merely because if the operator were to misappropriate and spend it, an innocent recipient would obtain good title. It is a fallacy to argue that because the recipient would obtain a valid title, therefore the money was the till operator's. It is difficult to see why the nature of a custodian's interest in money should be different merely because the custodian knows or suspects that it is tainted by crime. If a criminal asks D for a reward to deliver stolen property to a professional receiver and to collect an envelope containing the price which the receiver has agreed to pay, and D does so, we do not see why as a matter of general principle D should be regarded as having an interest in the money which he collects (any more than in the property which he delivers to the receiver), simply because he knows or suspects that the property was stolen, or simply because if D had instead spent the money in a shop, the shopkeeper would have obtained a good title to it.

para 78 [The Judges in *R v May* 2008 were] no doubt aware that there might be cases where it might be said that D had a limited interest in goods. D might, for example, use criminal proceeds to pay for the charter of a yacht etc. In such cases, D would have a right to possession and the interest could be of substantial value. But the fact that Proceeds of Crime Act 2002 s 84(2) and 79(3) contain provisions for cases where an offender obtains a limited interest in property, and for the means of valuing such an interest, is beside the point in the ordinary case where no suggestion is being advanced that the offender obtained a limited interest in the relevant property. We reject the argument that the observations in *R v May* 2008 and *Jennings v CPS* 2008 UKHL 29, 2 Cr App R (S) 29 (p 414) were incorrect or inapplicable in relation to POCA 2002, either in cases involving other forms of property or in cases involving money. If D's only role in relation to property connected with his criminal conduct, whether in the form of cash or otherwise, was to act as a courier on behalf of another, such property does not amount to property obtained by him within the meaning of Proceeds of Crime Act 2002 s 80(1). For SA, DS and MC we reduce the confiscation order to the amounts of the rewards and expenses. For SM we quash the confiscation order. For PM, payment of monies into [the] account gave rise to a thing in action in favour of PM (jointly with his partners). The starting point (as in *R v Sharma* 2006 EWCA Crim 16, 2006 2 Cr App R (S) 63 (p 416)) is that this was therefore his property. In *Sharma* the defendant caused the proceeds of a fraud in which he was engaged to be paid into a company account of which he was the sole signatory. It was held that the money in the account was money held for his benefit as the sole signatory on the account, and that decision was approved by the House of Lords in *R v May* 2008 (para 34). In this case the account was not only in the name of the firm of which PM was a partner, so that he had a thing in action against the bank, but he also had in fact sole operational control over the account.
para 86 We do not exclude the possibility of a case where money is paid into a bank account in the name of D, but which is in reality operated entirely by P for the benefit of P, and where it would be wrong, unusually, to conclude that D obtained monies paid into the account. This is more likely to arise in a domestic than a commercial context. We have in mind, for example, the possibility of a husband or father operating an account in the name of his wife or child, which he treats entirely as his own and in respect of which the wife or child is a mere nominee. But in the present case the judge was not satisfied on the evidence that PM was a bare trustee or nominee in relation to the funds in the account. It is true that the offences of which PM was convicted all contained the ingredient of assisting RW (a VAT fraudster) to retain control of the proceeds of his criminal conduct, but with that ultimate objective PM received funds, in respect of which he had legal ownership and also practical control. The case was no different in principle than if a dishonest money changer had been paid £1m and had agreed to transfer an equivalent amount to an offshore account in a different currency. The £1m received by the money changer would have been money obtained by him. In this case PM received funds in his account in England in exchange for which he remitted funds to the USA and Spain. His appeal is dismissed.
Note: D and P are initials used by the Court of Appeal. These remarks are subject to the decision in *R v Waya* 2012 UKSC 51, 2013 2 Cr App R (S) 20 (p 87), see **21.73**. Ed.
R v Sander 2013 EWCA Crim 690 D was convicted of assisting another to retain the benefit of criminal conduct. He controlled the flow of money into an account, although the account was not in his name and he did not pay the money in. The total was just over £6.95m. Defence counsel conceded that that was the benefit figure. On appeal another counsel asked to withdraw that concession, saying D would only have received a small proportion of that figure. Held. The concession was properly made. He had obtained the money because he controlled it.
See also: *R v Mehmet* 2015 EWCA Crim 797 (The defendant withdrew money from a bank account in a fraud offence. Cases considered. Held. He was assuming the rights of the owner. He had obtained the benefit. Appeal dismissed.)

21.107 ***Step 7 Determining the benefit Mortgages obtained by deception***
R v Waya 2012 UKSC 51, 2013 2 Cr App R (S) 20 (p 87) Supreme Court D was convicted of obtaining a money transfer by deception. In about 2003, D purchased a property with £310,000 from his own resources and £465,000 from a mortgage company. To obtain the money he made false statements about his employment history and earnings. The borrowed money was paid to a solicitor, who paid the vendor. A charge in favour of the lender was placed on the property. In April 2005, the mortgage was redeemed on payment of the full sum secured together with a fee of £58,000 for early redemption. The flat was remortgaged to secure the sum of £838,943. There is no clear evidence as to what happened to the balance (which must have been of the order of £360,000) in excess of the redemption money but the Judge accepted that D spent up to £150,000 on the flat during his period of ownership.

It was not a criminal lifestyle case. The value of the house rose from £775,000 to £1,850,000. The Judge deducted £310,000 from the current value of the house and arrived at £1,540,000 benefit. The Court of Appeal reduced the figure to £1,110,000. Held. The first issue is the identification of the property that D obtained (in the language of Proceeds of Crime Act 2002 s 76(4)), 'as a result of or in connection with' the criminal conduct for which he was convicted, Theft Act 1968 s 15A.[404] The contention that D obtained the whole leasehold interest in the flat by his dishonest conduct would completely ignore his down-payment, out of untainted funds, of £310,000. That would not be a fair or purposive application of section 76(4), and it would also be disproportionate for the purposes of Human Rights Act 1998. The submission that D obtained £465,000 calls for close examination. In the case of an ordinary loan induced by fraud, there is no doubt that the defendant does obtain the loan sum advanced. The fact that he is under an obligation to repay it, and even intends to repay it, does not mean that he does not obtain it. Indeed the obligation (and intention) to repay both assume an initial obtaining; if there had not been an initial obtaining, there would be nothing to repay. Nor does the fact that repayment is secured mean that he does not obtain it. A loan may often be secured on property belonging to the borrower. The security means that the lender has a much better prospect of being repaid, but once again there can be no doubt that the borrower obtains the sum advanced. It is paid to him and he can use it either as he wishes, or maybe for the particular purposes for which it is advanced. In either case, it has come into his possession and control; he has obtained it. If a borrower does in fact repay a fraudulently induced loan, secured or unsecured, a confiscation order which requires him to pay the same sum again is (lifestyle considerations apart) likely to be disproportionate and wrong. But that, likewise, does not mean that he did not obtain the loan sum advanced in the first place. para 49 The difference in the present case lies in the legal machinery by which the loan advance is made. The appeal has proceeded on the agreed or assumed factual basis that the same solicitor was acting for D and the mortgage lender; that the mortgage advance was paid to the solicitor to be held in the solicitor's client account, until completion, in trust for and to the order of the mortgage lender; and that on completion the jointly instructed solicitor transferred the advance to the vendor's solicitor, receiving instead an executed transfer of the lease. D would already have executed a charge of the lease in favour of the mortgage lender. para 50 In the eyes of the law all these events occurred simultaneously. That is established by the decision of the House of Lords in *Abbey National Building Society v Cann* 1991 1 AC 56. There is a full explanation in the speech of Lord Oliver at page 92-93. After referring to 'the proposition that, at least where there is a prior agreement to grant the charge on the legal estate when obtained, the transactions of acquiring the legal estate and granting the charge are, in law as in reality, one indivisible transaction', Lord Oliver analysed the position in detail and concluded:

[404] Repealed by Fraud Act 2006 Sch 3 para 1 (15/1/07: repeal has effect subject to savings specified in 2006 Sch 2 para 3)

'The reality is that the purchaser of land who relies upon a building society or bank loan for the completion of his purchase never in fact acquires anything but an equity of redemption, for the land is, from the very inception, charged with the amount of the loan without which it could never have been transferred at all and it was never intended that it should be otherwise. The "*scintilla temporis*" is no more than a legal artifice.'

In this case the mortgage advance was paid to the vendor's solicitor at D's behest. But he had no control over its disposal in the recipient's hands; the sole and predetermined purpose of the payment was to form part of the purchase price of the flat, with the mortgage lender having security for its repayment from the moment of completion. D never in fact acquired anything but an equity of redemption (as Lord Oliver put it in *Cann*), the equity of redemption corresponding in value (at that point) to his untainted down-payment of £310,000. The prosecution submission that D obtained £465,000 is a legally inaccurate account of the transaction, because the loan sum never became his or came into his possession. Under the tripartite contractual arrangements between vendor, purchaser and mortgage lender D obtained property in the form of a thing in action which was an indivisible bundle of rights and liabilities, and it cannot be correct to fasten onto the rights and ignore the liabilities (the analysis would of course be different if the loan had ever been at the defendant's free disposal: see paras 48 and 49 above). In short, what D obtained was the right to have the mortgage advance applied in the acquisition of his flat, subject from the moment of completion to the mortgage lender's security, which ensured the repayment of the advance. This thing in action had no market value at or immediately after completion, as the equity of redemption (or in everyday speech, the equity) represented D's down-payment. There will no doubt be other mortgage fraud cases in which this thing in action does have a value. One example would be the common case where false representations as to income and status of the borrower are accompanied by a dishonestly inflated valuation of the property which is being purchased. In such a case the fraud may not only have induced a larger loan than would otherwise have been made, but may well have induced a loan which is not fully secured as the lender believes. Another example might be the case where the property which the defendant is purporting to purchase does not exist, or is not really being purchased at all. In both these cases the thing in action has a real value to the defendant. The prosecution submitted that [the property held by D] was a 60% interest in the flat. That submission can be accepted so far as it goes, but it does not address the incidence of the mortgage. The property representing the original chose in action was a fractional part of D's total interest in the flat, the fraction corresponding to the part of the original purchase price financed by the dishonestly obtained mortgage (that is, 60%). But fairness requires that the mortgage liability (deductible under section 79(3)) should be matched to this 60% interest, so that the benefit obtained by D was initially nil. Otherwise 60% of his untainted contribution of £310,000 would, irrationally, be treated as proceeds of crime. The interest which fairly represented his original chose in action was 60% of the open market value of the flat from time to time, less the whole of the mortgage liability (£465,000). In other words it was 60% of any increase in the flat's market value over its acquisition price. That represents the reality of what he obtained from his crime and is, moreover, a proportionate order to make by way of confiscation, subject only to the re-mortgage, considered below. para 71 So, for example, if the confiscation day had occurred before the remortgage and if the flat had then been worth £1.2m, the value of the property obtained by D as a result of his dishonesty would have been computed under section 80(2) and (3) as follows:

Market value £1,2m. Mortgage £465,000. Equity = £735,000.

Equity £735,000. Original equity £310,000. Appreciation = £425,000.

Appreciation £425,000. 60% thereof = £255,000.

The remortgage para 74 By the remortgage D realised additional liquid funds of about £360,000 (after payment-off of the original mortgage and the fee for early repayment). Up to £150,000 of the £360,000 is assumed to have been spent on the flat and was no doubt reflected, to some extent, in its market value at the confiscation day. There is no evidence of what happened to the balance of £210,000. It cannot therefore be caught by section 80(3), since there are only two possible valuation dates that can be relevant: the date when property is first obtained, and the confiscation day. That is spelled out in section 80(2), together with the definition of 'material time' in section 80(1). If this £210,000 were known still to be in the bank, or to have been converted into some other identifiable asset, then section 80(3)(b) would catch it, but there are no findings that either has occurred, rather than the money simply being consumed in living expenses. The statute does not provide for any assumption adverse to the defendant to be made on that point. We must assume (in Toulson LJ's homely phrase) that D decided to consume the sweet.

para 75 The prosecution (para 126) disputes this analysis. The prosecution would apply an extended principle derived from *CPS v Rose* 2008 EWCA Crim 239, 2 Cr App (S) 80 (p 445) to the remortgage as well as to the original mortgage. They supplement this submission by pointing out that otherwise ill-gotten gains could easily be laundered, and the effectiveness of the confiscation regime undermined. That cannot, however, be a good reason for disregarding the reasonably plain terms of the statute. It is inherent in the scheme of section 80(3)(b) that it can operate only where the defendant still possesses the representing property. If he previously created it, and then liquidated it and spent the money, section 80(3)(b) cannot apply. In most cases (though not here) section 80(2)(a) will provide a satisfactory alternative basis for an order, and in some cases (though not here) money raised by a remortgage will be traceable into more valuable assets held at the confiscation day.

Early payments to reduce mortgage para 76 D paid £23,400 of the mortgage out of untainted funds. para 77 Once the repayment of capital was made, the representing property in the hands of D was no longer 60% of the market value less mortgage and untainted contribution but was the lesser percentage which £465,000 less £23,400 yields. Thus the effect of repayment of principal out of untainted funds is not to have the paradoxical effect of diminishing the section 79(3) deduction and so increasing the severity of the confiscation order. In this case, where the repayment was relatively small and seems to have been made at a time when most of the capital appreciation had already taken place, justice can be done by the simple adjustment of adding the amount of the repayment to the amount of the original down-payment. But in the case of a long-term instalment mortgage under which principal was repaid throughout the term, it might be more accurate (and fairer) to adjust the percentages of the original down-payment and the original mortgage advance so that a smaller proportion of the capital appreciation is treated as benefit. Elaborate and precise calculations would not be called for; in many cases experienced counsel would be able to agree on the appropriate adjustment and invite the judge to adopt it.

Conclusion para 78 The benefit obtained by D from his criminal behaviour was a thing in action with no immediate market value. It was an item of property but it had a very short life, since on completion it immediately came to be represented by a fractional 60% share of the leasehold interest in the flat, subject to (the whole of) the mortgage, with the remaining 40% representing the untainted contribution. In economic terms, his benefit was so much of any appreciation in value as was attributable to the mortgage obtained by his dishonesty. Immediately after completion this value was nil, but as the market value of the flat increased the benefit came to have a significant value, that is 60% of the appreciation in the net value of the flat, subject to the mortgage.

para 79 Here the amount raised and secured by the remortgage had three elements. The first, £465,000 plus the early repayment fee of £58,000, had no significant economic effect since it merely substituted one mortgage lender for another (possibly at a different rate of interest). No new, untainted money of D was used to redeem the original mortgage. The next element, not exceeding £150,000 at most, was recycled into the flat and probably produced some increase, but not a pound for pound increase, in its market

value. The third element, the balance, must be supposed to have been consumed in expenditure of one sort or another so as to fall outside the ambit of section 80(3). para 80 A small adjustment needs to be made for the repayment of the principal sum of £23,400. The adjusted figures are:
Market value £1,850,000. Mortgage £862,000. Equity = £987,400.
Equity £987,400. Original equity and repayment £333,400. Appreciation = £654,000.
Appreciation £654,000. 60% thereof = £392,400.
para 81 We substitute a confiscation order in the sum of £392,400. That is a substantial sum, but the order is not disproportionate.
R v Oyebola 2013 EWCA Crim 1052, 2014 1 Cr App R (S) 58 (p 359) D was convicted of four counts of furnishing false information and other counts. He lied about his identity and his personal situation to obtain mortgages on properties which he then let out on a multi-occupancy basis. The Judge found the benefit to be just over £1.5m and made an order for just under £667,000. Held. *R v Waya* 2012 has not changed the principle that rental income from such a property does constitute benefit.
R v Mahmood 2014 EWCA Crim 2208 D fraudulently obtained a remortgage advance and a confiscation order of £90,000 was made, with nearly £480,000 of realisable assets. D argued it was disproportionate. Held. The existence of a mere obligation to repay does not make the confiscation order disproportionate. It is only if the debt has been repaid, or there is a certainty of repayment, then, following *R v Waya* 2012 UKSC 51, 2013 2 Cr App R (S) 20 (p 87) an issue of proportionality may arise. We do not consider there is any merit in this ground.

21.108 *Step 7 Determining the benefit Thieves*
R v Allpress and Others 2009 EWCA Crim 8, 2 Cr App R (S) 58 (p 399) Four defendants were sentenced for assisting another to retain the benefit of drug trafficking. Held. *Obiter* para 63 A thief cannot be heard to say in confiscation proceedings that the relevant value is not the market value of the stolen property, but the value of his interest subject to the interest of the true owner, which would result in a nil or nominal valuation on the part of the thief. By stealing the property, the thief has assumed the rights of the true owner, and his benefit is what it would have cost him to acquire the property lawfully, i.e. its open market value: *CPS Nottinghamshire v Rose* 2008 EWCA Crim 239. Note: These remarks are subject to the decision in *R v Waya* 2012 UKSC 51, 2013 2 Cr App R (S) 20 (p 87), see **21.73**.
For the confiscation section of the *Theft and Burglary in a Building other than a Dwelling Guideline 2008*, see **344.3** in Volume 2.

21.109 *Step 7 Determining the benefit VAT frauds*
R v Chahal and Another 2015 EWCA Crim 816 C and S were convicted of cheating the public revenue in a missing trader VAT fraud. The total trading exceeded £181.5m. C was a director and 50% shareholder of Letting Solutions, which was largely a buffer company. S was a director/manager of another such company. Each were party to the making of false claims. Held. para 23 It is an important matter that the fraud operated by the presentation of apparently genuine claims for inputs which were actually part and parcel of the fraud. para 38 The buffer and export traders' receipt of a credit or payment in respect of the input claims amounts to a pecuniary advantage within the terms of Proceeds of Crime Act 2002 s 76(5); see *R v Dimsey and Allen* 2000 1 Cr App R (S) 497. Indeed, if the input claims had not been made, the relevant trader would have owed HMRC a very substantial sum indeed for output tax charged on its sales. para 39 The total turnover of the transactions (i.e. upon which VAT was calculated) represented the benefit obtained. It was appropriate that the Crown limit its claim to the amounts of VAT which had been claimed. para 40 For the VAT inputs, i) the court is not concerned under the POCA code to determine the amount of profit made, as calculated in an accounting exercise. It is no less a benefit received because he has not, in the event, seen the full fruits of it because he elected to use it in the next part of the fraud, ii) equally, the

exercise is not concerned with limiting the benefit obtained by reference to the loss caused to another. The effect of the Code is not to limit the recovery of benefit generated by criminal conduct by reference to whether it is equivalent to the actual loss caused to another: see *R v Dimsey and Allen* 2000 at p 501. The offender cannot set off his expenses. There was no need to moderate the application of Proceeds of Crime Act 2002 s 10(6). Appeal dismissed.
For how to consider VAT in commercial transactions, see the ***Step 7 Determining the benefit VAT*** para at **21.92**.

Step 8 Determine the extent of the defendant's interest in property

21.110 ***Step 8***
Step 8 Determine the extent of the defendant's interest in property.
Note: This applies to property where third parties have an interest in it, like matrimonial homes. Ed.

21.111 ***Step 8 The statutory power***
Determination of extent of defendant's interest in property
Proceeds of Crime Act 2002 s 10A(1) Where it appears to a court making a confiscation order that:[405]

(a) there is property held by the defendant that is likely to be realised or otherwise used to satisfy the order, and
(b) a person other than the defendant holds, or may hold, an interest in the property, the court may, if it thinks it appropriate to do so, determine the extent (at the time the confiscation order is made) of the defendant's interest in the property.

(2) The court must not exercise the power conferred by subsection (1) unless it gives to anyone who the court thinks is or may be a person holding an interest in the property a reasonable opportunity to make representations to it.
(3) A determination under this section is conclusive in relation to any question as to the extent of the defendant's interest in the property that arises in connection with:

(a) the realisation of the property, or the transfer of an interest in the property, with a view to satisfying the confiscation order, or
(b) any action or proceedings taken for the purposes of any such realisation or transfer.

(4) Subsection (3):

(a) is subject to section 51(8B), and
(b) does not apply in relation to a question that arises in proceedings before the Court of Appeal or the Supreme Court.

(5) In this Part, the 'extent' of the defendant's interest in property means the proportion that the value of the defendant's interest in it bears to the value of the property itself.
There is no appeal from this order, see Serious Crime Act 2015 Sch 4 para 3.

Step 9 Determining the available amount

21.112 ***Step 9***
Step 9 Determine the available amount. The available amount is the total 'free property' (for definition, see Proceeds of Crime Act 2002 s 82) and the 'tainted gifts' (for definition, see **21.84**).

21.113 ***Step 9 The available amount Statutory provisions***
Determining the extent of the defendant's interest in property Proceeds of Crime Act 2002 s 10A, which was inserted by Serious Crime Act 2015 s 1, provides the power to do this. It would appear that this could be done either when the order is being made or after, but it is far from clear. This power is listed as **Step 8**, see **21.110**.
Available amount
Proceeds of Crime Act 2002 s 9(1) For the purposes of deciding the recoverable amount, the available amount is the aggregate of:

[405] Section inserted by Serious Crime Act 2015 s 1. In force 1/6/15

(a) the total of the values (at the time the confiscation order is made) of all the free property then held by the defendant minus the total amount payable in pursuance of obligations which then have priority, and
(b) the total of the values (at that time) of all tainted gifts.
(2) An obligation has priority if it is an obligation of the defendant:
(a) to pay an amount due in respect of a fine or other order of a court which was imposed or made on conviction of an offence and at any time before the time the confiscation order is made, or
(b) to pay a sum which would be included among the preferential debts if the defendant's bankruptcy had commenced on the date of the confiscation order or his winding up had been ordered on that date.
(3) 'Preferential debts' has the meaning given by Insolvency Act 1986 s 386.
Proceeds of Crime Act 2002 s 83 Realisable property is: a) any free property held by the defendant, b) any free property held by the recipient of a tainted gift.
Note: Property is free unless there is: a) a forfeiture or deprivation order made in respect of it, or b) an application has been made for detention, seizure etc. of it under Proceeds of Crime Act 2002 s 82. The available amount is the value of a) the 'free property' less certain obligations which have priority (like court orders), and b) the value of the tainted gifts, Proceeds of Crime Act 2002 s 77, see **21.84**. Fines or other court orders are obligations having priority made after a conviction and before the confiscation order is made, Proceeds of Crime Act 2002 s 9(2) above. The defendant's debts are not obligations having priority. Ed.

21.114 ***Step 9 The available amount Conspiracies/Joint enterprises***
R v Ahmad and Others 2014 UKSC 36, 2 Cr App R (S) 75 (p 580) Supreme Court The Court considered two unconnected appeals. The Ahmad defendants had engaged in an MTIC fraud, fraudulently claiming £12.6m of VAT. The Fields defendants were convicted of conspiracy to defraud in relation to goods and services supplied to a company which had forged its accounts. £1.4m was jointly acquired. Neither set of defendants challenged the quantification of the recoverable amounts (£16.1m when adjusted for inflation for the Ahmad defendants and £1.6m for the Fields defendants), or the finding that they obtained that amount jointly. They challenged the decision of the Court of Appeal, relying on *R v May* 2008, that each defendant was separately liable for the entire amount, as where a benefit is obtained jointly, each joint beneficiary has obtained the whole of the benefit. The question was, 'when a number of people (whether or not all are before the court) have been involved in the commission of a crime which resulted in property being acquired by them together, what is the proper approach for the court to adopt, and the proper orders for the court to make in confiscation hearings?' Held. As identified in *R v May* 2008, there are three questions to be answered.
a) Has the defendant benefited?
b) What is the value of the benefit? (See para **21.89**.)
c) What is the sum payable?
para 72 To take the same proceeds twice over would not serve the legitimate aim of the legislation and, even if that were not so, it would be disproportionate. The violation of article 1 would occur at the time when the state sought to enforce an order for the confiscation of proceeds of crime which have already been paid to the state. The appropriate way of avoiding such a violation would be for the confiscation order made against each defendant to be subject to a condition which would prevent that occurrence. para 73 This approach may appear to risk producing inequity between criminal conspirators, on the basis that some of them may well obtain a 'windfall' because the amount of the confiscation order will be paid by another. However, that is an inherent feature of joint criminality. para 74 Accordingly, where a finding of joint obtaining is made, whether against a single defendant or more than one, the confiscation order should be made for the whole value of the benefit thus obtained, but should provide that

it is not to be enforced to the extent that a sum has been recovered by way of satisfaction of another confiscation order made in relation to the same joint benefit. para 78 Appeals allowed.

See also the ***Step 7 Determining the benefit Conspiracies/Joint enterprises/ Apportionment*** para at **21.89**.

21.115 ***The available amount Step 9 Tainted gifts when considering the recoverable amount***

R v Duncan Smith 1996 2 Cr App R 1 D was convicted of fraudulent trading. The prosecution included some guns worth £49,000 as a tainted gift. The Judge accepted that the son had disposed of the guns to pay for family expenses. Held. page 24 A judge does have power to make a confiscation order against a defendant in relation to a gift made by him, notwithstanding that at the time of the making of the order the donee no longer has realisable assets resulting from the disposal by him of that gift. In other words, although a judge cannot make an order against a defendant in relation to assets which he does not have, it is open to him to make an order against a defendant in relation to a disposal by way of gift, even though, at the time the order is made, the donee has, by whatever route, disposed of the gift.

R v Liverpool Magistrates' Court ex parte A 1997 Unreported 5/12/97 D was convicted of transferring the proceeds of drug trafficking. The Judge made a £15,000 confiscation order[406] which was based on agreed assets. A property in D's wife's name was sold for £8,000 to pay the confiscation order. The proceeds were paid to his son, who used most of the money to pay for a wedding. The money was not paid and a Magistrate heard an application for D to be committed to prison. D applied for judicial review and also for a certificate of inadequacy. Held. page 10 'Realisable property', including gifts caught by the Act, necessarily means that circumstances may arise where gifts which a defendant has made may be practically, even legally, irrecoverable. But they are nevertheless still regarded as realisable property under this draconian Act. The purpose is obvious. They are intended to make it as difficult as possible for those who traffic in drugs to get away with the proceeds of that traffic. Both applications dismissed.

R v Usoro 2015 EWCA Crim 1958 D pleaded to conspiracy to defraud. It was an advance fee fraud. The benefit was agreed at £41,000. The Judge found that the money D had given due to a court order to support his children was a tainted gift. The defence appealed, saying that D was under a legal and moral duty to pay the money. The prosecution said that if the payments were not regarded as a tainted gift, people could give their offspring the proceeds of crime without fear of a confiscation order. Held. It is clear that the policy of Proceeds of Crime Act 2002 in relation to gifts is to prevent criminals from dissipating the proceeds of crime by distributing them and then resisting confiscation proceedings on the basis that gifts had been made. para 18 In other confiscation contexts the prosecution authorities have accepted the principle that bringing up children and looking after the family home should be considered adequate consideration to displace the suggestion that the application of the proceeds of crime were gifts[407] and caught by the provisions of the relevant confiscation legislation, *Gibson v Revenue and Customs* 2008 EWCA Civ 645. The Judge fell into error. He heard no evidence as to the value of maintaining the children and whether that value was significantly less than the amount of the payments which was crucial to his finding that section 78(1) applied.[408] He did not hear any evidence because the issue was not contested. para 21 Moreover, his focus on whether the payments were tainted gifts deflected his consideration from the prior question of whether they were gifts. It is only after one concludes that the payment has been made for a consideration of value

[406] The transcript says £15,000 'by way of compensation', which is assumed to be an error.

[407] The Judge clearly didn't mean to say this as an application cannot be a gift, but precisely what he did mean to say is not clear.

[408] This again is not clear.

significantly less than the amounts of the payment that section 78(1) requires the payments to be treated as a gift. The payments thus wholly or partly discharge his legal duty to or in respect of his children. We adjust the confiscation order accordingly.

R v Johnson 2016 EWCA Crim 10, 2 Cr App R (S) 38 para 2 D pleaded guilty to 16 counts of fraud. She was given a Suspended Sentence Order. The Judge found the benefit to be £45,000 and accepted D's affidavit which said she had sold her property to her daughter for £140,000 but gifted her £20,000 in the conveyance. That was taken to mean the property was worth £140,000 and there was a gift of £20,000 to the daughter. At the date of the hearing the gift was valued at £0. There were no other assets. The Judge made a finding that it was a tainted gift and she made a confiscation order for £20,000. The Judge ordered any money collected to be paid to the victim. The money was not paid and D applied for a variation order. The application was refused. D then appealed the order out of time. D was sent to prison in default. The defence argued the order was unjust. Held. Although there can be no appeal against the variation we consider the Judge was right to refuse the application. We are not asked to determine the issue about the compensation order so we don't. para 31 A judge should consider the following when considering a tainted gift which is worthless.

(i) The robustness of the evidence of the value of the tainted gift.

(ii) The proportionality of making an order in the sum sought. This requires the court to appreciate the distinction between this exercise and the exercise of a general discretion to avoid hardship, applying *R v Waya* 2012 UKSC 51, 2013 2 Cr App R (S) 20 (p 87) para 20-21, summarised in part at **21.107**.

(iii) The appropriate term of imprisonment to be imposed in default. The stipulated scale provides for maximum sentences relating to various amounts payable under the order. Although there is an obligation to impose a term of imprisonment in default when making a confiscation order (Powers of Criminal Courts (Sentencing) Act 2000 s 139(2)), the court is required to consider all of the circumstances of the case when doing so in accordance with *R v Castillo* 2011 EWCA Crim 3173, 2012 2 Cr App R (S) 36 (p 201). There is no minimum term which must be imposed. The purpose of the term is enforcement not further punishment, and where the court is affirmatively satisfied that enforcement is impossible that may be a reason to make a substantial reduction in the term imposed in default. This will inevitably be a wholly exceptional course because the court will usually have limited confidence that an asset which has been apparently given away cannot be recovered by the offender or that the offender cannot satisfy the order by other means.

The Judge's decision was not wrong. Had she conducted a proportionality exercise considering *R v Waya* 2012 UKSC 51, 2013 2 Cr App R (S) 20 (p 87) (see **21.107**), *R v Jawad* 2013 EWCA Crim 644, 2014 1 Cr App R (S) 16 (p 85) (see **21.81**) and *R v Harvey* 2015 UKSC 73, 2016 1 Cr App R (S) 60 (p 406) (see **21.92**) she would have come to the same decision. Appeal dismissed.

R v Box 2018 EWCA Crim 542 D pleaded to nine frauds and two counts of making a false instrument. She caused a loss of about £4,085,000 to many people by abusing her position as a solicitor and chancellor of a diocese. She received 7 years' imprisonment. In confiscation proceedings, D called no evidence. The Judge reduced the prosecution's tainted gifts figure by considering whether there was some legal or moral basis on which D could recover the gift. The prosecution appealed. Held. All cases are different but it is hard to conceive a case where it would be proper to reduce the tainted gifts figure without hearing evidence. para 15 Section 81(1) operates to require the court to take the greater of the value of the property given at the date of the gift or the value of property 'found', as defined in section 81(2). Once it is clear that the value of the property at the time of the gift is greater than any 'found' property it is not necessary to consider further what property may exist which in any way represents the original gift. The order could not be held to be disproportionate. The Judge was persuaded to embark on a process almost akin to tracing the stolen assets, and to find that if no assets could be found which represented the gift then that gift should not be included in the recoverable amount. This is not the way the tainted gifts scheme works. It operates as an incentive for him or her to recover the proceeds of her crime from persons to whom she has passed them by whatever means are available to her. What those persons have done with them, or whether they received them knowing of their criminal origin, are likely to be largely irrelevant factors. We increase the tainted gifts figures to the prosecution's original amounts.

See also the ***Step 9 Determining the benefit Tainted gifts*** para at **21.84**.

21.116 ***The available amount Step 9 Tainted gifts when considering the recoverable amount and matrimonial property***

R v Hayes 2018 EWCA Crim 682, 2 Cr App R (S) 27 (p 239) D was convicted of various counts of conspiracy to defraud. He agreed to manipulate the Yen LIBOR system for illegal profit. In 2007, D met his wife, W. They lived together and in 2010 she gave up her job. Later that year, they married and D paid £995,000 for a home in Shoreditch and it was placed in their joint names. W made no contribution to the purchase price. In December 2011, D bought a second home outright in Surrey for just over £1.2m and put it in their joint names. A declaration of trust was made that they were joint beneficial tenants. D also paid for major renovation works. The Shoreditch home was sold (at no profit). W looked after the house and their baby. In December 2012, D was arrested in the UK. He had earlier been investigated in the US and in December 2012 he was charged there with similar offences to the ones he had just been arrested for. In May 2013, W returned to work. In June 2013, D was charged in the UK. In July 2013, D transferred to W his entire interest (legal and beneficial) in their house, for £250,000. W took out a mortgage on the property for £350,000 of which it seems that £250,000 was then paid to D to assist with his large legal bills. In 2015, D was convicted and sentenced [see **267.26** in Volume 2]. In 2016, in confiscation proceedings, the Judge found that: a) the acquisition of the home where W obtained a joint beneficial interest, and b) the 2013 disposal to W, were both tainted gifts. The first ruling was challenged on appeal. D's benefit was assessed at just over £850,000. The available amount was assessed at just over £1,760,000, which included the value of their Surrey home. A confiscation order for just over £850,000 was made. Later the house was sold for about £1.6m. From the sale proceeds about £780,000 was paid out for the confiscation order. After the mortgage was paid off the rest was given to W. Held. para 25 The wide reach of these tainted gifts provisions is explained by Parliament's evident determination that: a) convicted criminals should be required, by all practicable means, to disgorge the proceeds of their criminality, and b) [the need] to deter attempts to gift away assets. Section 77(2) is capable of applying to gifts both of property which [themselves were] obtained from criminal conduct and also (if made after the relevant day) of property which was not. para 34 The 2002 Act provides no definition, as such, of the word 'gift' or the word 'consideration'. It is plain from section 78(1): a) that the value of the property is to be assessed at the time of transfer; b) that the consideration must have value and must have value in the sense of being capable of being assessed in money terms in a way which can then, as necessary, be utilised in accordance with the mathematical approach stipulated in section 78(2); and c), that while at common law the adequacy of any consideration provided under an agreement is rarely to be investigated by the courts, such a matter is precisely the subject of focus for the purpose of section 78(1). If the consideration is of a value significantly less than the value of the property transferred then section 78(1) deems there to have been a 'gift'.

para 42 The essential question was: what was the consideration provided in this case? The consideration must be at a value not being significantly less than the value of the property at the time of transfer, so the tainted gift provisions require an investigation into that. In short, they are drafted in terms of money or money's worth, to be objectively assessed. para 47 Aspects of the defence arguments as to 'value' seemed at stages to reflect arguments of a kind that might perhaps be raised in the Family Court but [those] arguments have no part to play in deciding tainted gifts issues. The Family Court is concerned to decide as to what is the fair and just division of assets and the needs of any children and so on. That, most emphatically, is not the function of the Crown Court in making its assessment under sections 77 and 78. para 48 Nor is there any great assistance in considering cases relating to proprietary or equitable interests. The court is not concerned to ascertain from the parties' conduct what the shared intention was with regard to ownership of the house at the time of transfer. That is because the parties have in the transfer expressly declared their shared intention and agreement: that is, of joint legal and beneficial entitlement. As between themselves, therefore, that is decisive. Since no one could allege, or has alleged, that the acquisition of the house involved a sham, it follows that D and W were, legally and beneficially, joint owners. On any sale, they would together have been entitled to the net proceeds. It is irrelevant for that purpose that W had made no financial contribution to the original acquisition. It is irrelevant, as a matter of property law, just because that is what the two of them had intended and agreed: as evidenced by the written declaration of trust. para 49 In determining the impact of section 78 of the 2002 Act *Gibson v Revenue and Customs* 2008 EWCA Civ 645 [see **21.115**] is readily distinguishable from this case. So too is *R v Usoro* 2015 EWCA Crim 1958 [see **21.115**], where the payments were for the children's maintenance and support. para 55 It is clear from the statutory wording that such valuation has to be made objectively and in monetary terms, on an evidential basis. Each case was 'fact sensitive'. What 'family services' (itself a rather open-ended phrase) actually involve can vary between cases. In this context, it would be wrong to commit to a wholly inflexible purported statement of principle. In any event, *Gibson v Revenue and Customs* 2008 is one illustration, albeit on its own facts, that there is no inflexible principle. *R v Usoro* 2015 is another illustration. Moreover, we note that in *R v Thompson* 2015 EWCA Crim 1820 [see **21.125**], the Judge had apparently made an allowance of 10% "in respect of family life" (not further defined or explained in the judgment). That was a finding which, albeit not debated in the Court of Appeal, attracted no adverse comment from the Court. On the facts, disappointment in not having children and the giving up of employment by the wife did not constitute valuable consideration for the purposes of section 78(1).

para 58 In this difficult area of tainted gifts, we suggest (without intending in any way to be either exhaustive or prescriptive):

(1) The approach required under section 78(1) involves the following steps:

(i) place a value upon the property transferred, at the time of transfer;

(ii) assess whether consideration has been provided by the recipient of the property and (if it has) assess the value of the consideration provided;

(iii) assess whether the value (if any) of that consideration (if any) is significantly less than the value of the property transferred, at the time of transfer; and

(iv) if there is found to be a significant difference apply the calculation prescribed in section 78(2); thereafter also applying the provisions of section 81 as appropriate.

(2) Each of steps (i), (ii) and (iii) above must always be undertaken objectively and on an evidence based approach. There is no room, in this context, for 'plucking a figure out of the air' or anything like that.

(3) Where the consideration which is asserted to have been provided by the recipient of the property is not in the form of a direct financial contribution or contributions, then it is necessary to examine the evidence rigorously and closely to see if the asserted consideration (whether by way of 'services' or otherwise) is capable of being assessed as consideration of value and (if it is) to what extent.

(4) Any consideration which is asserted to have been provided must be attributable to the transfer of property in question.

(5) Any consideration which is asserted to have been provided must, for the purposes of section 78(1), be capable of being ascribed a value in monetary terms.

(6) Each case, ultimately, will depend on its own facts and circumstances.

para 59 Here W made no financial contributions at all, directly or indirectly, towards the purchase [of the house]. Their marriage for around a year,[409] and their son's birth in October 2011, cannot of [themselves] involve 'consideration' of 'value' which could to any extent, let alone the asserted 50%, come within section 78(1). When the house in Surrey was purchased the family continued to live in Shoreditch, a property jointly owned. Furthermore, everything that W did as wife and mother at that time is also to be put into the context of D paying all the household expenses and other outgoings: and so what she did, as the Judge found, can properly be attributed to, and set against, that in any event. The prosecution, very fairly, never sought to argue that payment by D of all the household expenses and other 'regular' outgoings constituted a tainted gift within the ambit of section 78(1). The Judge's conclusion was wholly justified.
para 35 The defence was right to abandon the suggestion that W had no interest to transfer to W. He only acquired such an interest at exactly the same time as W: that being their shared intent.
Note: The date of sentence in the summary was taken from D's earlier Court of Appeal case, *R v Hayes* 2015 EWCA Crim 1944, 2016 1 Cr App R (S) 63 (p 449), see **267.26** in Volume 2. The date of D's arrest and the charges in the US were taken from Wikipedia. Ed.

21.117 ***Step 9 The available amount Debts***
Proceeds of Crime Act 2002 s 9(2)
An obligation has priority if it is an obligation of the defendant:..

(b) to pay a sum which would be included among the preferential debts if the defendant's bankruptcy had commenced on the date of the confiscation order or his winding up had been ordered on that date.

(3) 'Preferential debts' has the meaning given by Insolvency Act 1986 s 386.
For the full section see **21.8**.
R v Najafpour 2009 EWCA Crim 2723, 2010 2 Cr App R (S) 38 (p 245) A confiscation order was made against D. The available amount included a debt of £40,400 which was owed by Z, who was the ringleader of a drug gang. The Judge accepted that 'this is money which on any likelihood D is not going to get'. The Judge included the debt because 'D had entered the agreement with his eyes open, which meant he must take the consequence of entering into agreement with criminals'. D appealed, saying the debt was arising out of an illegal contract and it could not be enforced in any court. Held. If it was impossible to recover the debt, it would be quite inconsistent to trigger the default sentence. A defendant is not to be imprisoned if he satisfies the court that he simply does not have the assets available. So if an asset is of no financial value, it must be assessed as such. Order varied to exclude the debt.
R v Islam 2009 UKHL 30, 2010 1 Cr App R (S) 42 (p 245) House of Lords D pleaded to importing 3.53 and 0.44 kilos of heroin on separate occasions. The goods were seized. Held (3-2). para 33 When assessing the available amount, the market value is taken 'at the time the confiscation order is made' of any 'free property then held by the defendant', applying Proceeds of Crime Act 2002 s 9(1) and 79(1) and (2). Where HMRC have seized goods, forfeiture is automatic, and in that case the goods will no longer be property held by the defendant at the time of the confiscation order within Proceeds of Crime Act 2002 s 84(2), see *R v Dore* 1997 2 Cr App R (S) 152, at p 158. But, in other cases, the confiscation order will precede any order for forfeiture under Misuse of Drugs Act 1971 s 27. The heroin may then continue in law to be 'free property then held by the defendant' at the time of the confiscation order within the meaning of section 84(2), although physically [it was] in the possession of the authorities. In such circumstances, it would, however, be impossible to regard it as having any market value for the purposes of assessing the available amount. It would not, because it could not,

[409] The year seems to refer to how long the marriage had lasted before the transfer, not that the marriage was only a year long. There were difficulties with the marriage which would not have impacted on the decision.

ever be bought or sold on any market. The assessment of market value for the purpose of determining 'the available amount' at the time when the confiscation order is made, raises different considerations. Leaving aside the special position arising from tainted gifts, the purpose of restricting the recoverable amount to the lesser of 'the defendant's benefit from the conduct concerned' and 'the available amount' under Proceeds of Crime Act 2002 s 7(1)-(2)(a), and 9(1) is to ensure that confiscation orders are not made against defendants in an amount beyond that which they can meet at the time of the confiscation order. The court is in this context therefore concerned with the value of property which the defendant can actually be required or expected to realise on the market. It would defeat this purpose if a black market value were put on drugs which would never conceivably be sold. Where, at the time of the confiscation order, drugs were still held by the defendant and potentially realisable on a black market here or abroad, a further consideration arises. As a matter of general policy, the court will not enforce or condone the doing of an illegal act here or abroad. The 'integrity of the justice process' must be preserved, see *Hall v Hebert* 1993 2 SCR 159. On the same principle contracts for the performance of illegal acts abroad are unenforceable. A confiscation order requires the defendant to realise his available assets, on pain of serving the additional period of imprisonment specified by the court when making the order. If the court took account of black market value in fixing the value of the defendant's available property, it could itself be regarded as requiring or encouraging, or imprisoning for failure to effect, an unlawful realisation of the drugs by the defendant. The court is not, however, implicated in any similar way if, when assessing the defendant's benefit from illegally obtained drugs, it recognises the fact that such drugs had a real and intended black market value.

R v Smith 2013 EWCA Crim 502, 2 Cr App R (S) 77 (p 506) D pleaded to dishonestly making false statements about Housing benefit and Council tax benefit. The prosecution applied for a benefit of the sum obtained less the amount paid back. In fact she had given money to her family. The Judge found she had no assets. The Judge held that once items were considered to be tainted gifts there was no need to investigate whether there was any prospect of them being recovered. Held. We agree with the Judge for two reasons. First, there is a specific statutory regime governing the valuation of tainted gifts. There is nothing in section 81 which links the value of the gift to its recoverability, even though it contemplates the situation where the recipient of the gift has parted with it. Second, the whole point of including assets which a defendant has given away as one of the components in assessing the amount which a defendant has available was to prevent a defendant dissipating his assets by giving them away. If he is to be able to say that they are of no value because he cannot get them back, that would defeat what the inclusion of tainted gifts in section 9(1) was seeking to achieve. Since you cannot sue the recipient of a gift for its return, there may be many occasions when gifts cannot be recovered. It cannot have been intended for those gifts which the recipient is prevailed upon to return to be included as part of the offender's available assets, but not those which the recipient cannot be persuaded to give up.

See also: *R v Burkus* 2012 EWCA Crim 1090 (Defence sought to take into account a genuine private loan. Held. Under Proceeds of Crime Act 2002 s 9, the only loans excluded from the 'recoverable amount' are those having priority. The loan, if it ever existed, did not have priority.)

21.118 ***Step 9 The available amount Expenses***

R v Yu and Another 2015 EWCA Crim 1076, 2 Cr App R (S) 75 (p 500) D and his wife pleaded to four trade mark offences. During the confiscation hearing the Judge was unable to accept their account due to inconsistencies. She found the pair had failed to satisfy her that the available amount was less than the benefit. The main issue on appeal was how the court should deal with expenses when considering the available amount. Held. para 30 Dating back certainly to *R v Comiskey* 1991 93 Cr App R 227, expenses are capable of being taken into account when calculating the available amount. It was said at page 233 that "the court cannot close its eyes to the obvious and cannot ignore the fact that some expenses must have been incurred" and that must be read subject to the burden of proof on the defendant contained in Proceeds of Crime Act 2002 s 7(2), see **21.133**. A defendant who fails to satisfy that burden will not succeed in reducing the recoverable amount beneath the value of his benefit. Appeal dismissed.

21.119 ***Step 9 The available amount Defendant is not truthful Is that fatal?***
R v McIntosh and Marsden 2011 EWCA Crim 1501, 2012 1 Cr App R (S) 60 (p 342) D and M were convicted of conspiracy to cheat the public revenue between 31 December 2001 and 23 July 2002. They had obtained over £3.6m from a missing trader fraud. D and M contended they had no realisable assets. The Judge disbelieved them. He found they had concealed their assets. He considered that that compelled him to make an order for the full sum. Held. There is no principle that a court is bound to reject a defendant's case that his current realisable assets are less than the full amount of the benefit, merely because it concludes that the defendant has not revealed their true extent or value, or has not participated in any revelation at all. The court must answer the statutory question in Criminal Justice Act 1988 s 71(6) (now replaced) in a just and proportionate way. The court may conclude that a defendant's realisable assets are less than the full value of the benefit on the basis of the facts as a whole. A defendant who is found not to have told the truth or who has declined to give truthful disclosure will inevitably find it difficult to discharge the burden imposed upon him. But it may not be impossible for him to do so. Other sources of evidence, apart from the defendant himself, and a view of the case as a whole, may persuade a court that the assets available to the defendant are less than the full value of the benefit.

R v John 2014 EWCA Crim 1240, 2 Cr App R (S) 73 (p 568) D was convicted of conspiracy to steal vehicles. In confiscation proceedings in 2007, his benefit was assessed at £200,000. A £7,200 confiscation order was made reflecting his then assets. In 2009, he had a road accident and received compensation of £21,000 for his injuries and £5,400 for the loss of his vehicle. The payment for the injuries was £13,000 for general damages (for pain and suffering etc.) and £10,000 for special damages (payment for a scan, physiotherapy, therapy and hearing aids). In 2014, the prosecution applied for a reconsideration of the confiscation order. The Judge considered it "more than just" that D should forgo the insurance payments which were awaiting payment. D appealed. The prosecution said D had an ongoing right to NHS care. Held. It is important for judges to assess carefully what course is truly just. In cases such as this not involving a windfall gain, the consideration [of a defendant's assets] should be particularly anxious. It would not be fair for the special damages to be included. However, the general damages should be included.

Note: The test for the recoverable amount at a confiscation hearing is (amongst other matters) the amount that 'the court believes is just', Proceeds of Crime Act 2002 s 7(3). The test on a reconsideration is (amongst other matters) the amount the court 'believes is just', Proceeds of Crime Act 2002 s 22(4). The Court is not saying here that one type of damage is to be included and the other is not. It is saying that on these facts this was the appropriate decision. Ed.

21.120 ***Step 9 The available amount Insurance payouts***
R v John 2014 EWCA Crim 1240, 2 Cr App R (S) 73 (p 568) D was convicted of conspiracy to steal vehicles. In confiscation proceedings in 2007, his benefit was assessed at £200,000. A £7,200 confiscation order was made reflecting his then assets. In 2009, he had a road accident and received compensation of £21,000 for his injuries and £5,400 for the loss of his vehicle. The payment for the injuries was £13,000 for general damages (for pain and suffering etc.) and £10,000 for special damages (payment for a scan, physiotherapy, therapy and hearing aids). In 2014, the prosecution applied for a reconsideration of the confiscation order. The Judge considered it "more than just" that D should forgo the insurance payments which were awaiting payment. D appealed. The prosecution said D had an ongoing right to NHS care. Held. It is important for judges to

assess carefully what course is truly just. In cases such as this not involving a windfall gain, the consideration [of a defendant's assets] should be particularly anxious. It would not be fair for the special damages to be included. However, the general damages should be included.
Note: The test for the recoverable amount at a confiscation hearing is (amongst other matters) the amount that 'the court believes is just', Proceeds of Crime Act 2002 s 7(3). The test on a reconsideration is (amongst other matters) the amount the court 'believes is just', Proceeds of Crime Act 2002 s 22(4). The Court is not saying here that one type of damage is to be included and the other is not. It is saying that on these facts this was the appropriate decision. Ed.

21.121 ***Step 9 The available amount Joint assets***

R v Gangar and White 2012 EWCA Crim 1378, 2013 1 Cr App R (S) 67 (p 372) G and W were convicted of Ponzi-type investment fraud. The defendants' benefit was agreed as £60,750,000 in each case. They were arrested in 2002 so the Act applying was Criminal Justice Act 1988. G had available over £1.7m. W had available over £185,000. Apart from these assets the Judge held G and W had over £971,000 which they held jointly. He held that those assets should be treated as available to each of them. That raised G's assets to about £2,750,000 and W's assets to £1.2m. The defence contended they could not be counted twice. Held. The 2002 provisions substantially follow the 1988 provisions. The essential feature when determining the available assets is, as explained in *R v May* 2008 UKHL 28, 2009 1 Cr App R (S) 31 (p 162), that no one is to be penalised for not paying what he has not got. If G were to realise the asset, W could not, by definition, also realise it. It may be that in a case where there are several co-owners all alleged by the Crown to be conspirators in the crime, but only one or few of whom are before the court, the court must find that in making confiscation orders the beneficial interests of other alleged accomplices fall to reduce the confiscation order which can be made against those present. That is, however, the inevitable consequence of the fact that such persons have a beneficial interest. That ought not to lead to any identified asset being left available to any person who is alleged to have been guilty of the offence, since a [restraint] order will ordinarily be available to freeze it until the missing criminal is apprehended. Moreover, in cases arising since 2002, any traceable proceeds of crime can be recovered by the civil recovery process under Proceeds of Crime Act 2002 Part 5 whether or not anyone is prosecuted for the crime. As to unidentified assets, the judge will, if the evidence justifies it, find against the defendants who are present that there are hidden assets, whether identified or not. Order reduced accordingly.
R v Ahmad and Others 2014 UKSC 36, 2 Cr App R (S) 75 (p 580) Supreme Court The Court considered two unconnected appeals. The Ahmad defendants had engaged in an MTIC fraud, fraudulently claiming £12.6m of VAT. The Fields defendants were convicted of conspiracy to defraud in relation to goods and services supplied to a company which had forged its accounts. £1.4m was jointly acquired. Neither set of defendants challenged the quantification of the recoverable amounts (£16.1m when adjusted for inflation for the Ahmad defendants and £1.6m for the Fields defendants), or the finding that they obtained that amount jointly. The Court considered whether it was right that the state could claim the same benefit for a number of defendants because they were each held to be responsible for the whole benefit. Held. para 72 We accept to take the same proceeds twice over would not serve the legitimate aim of the legislation and, even if that were not so, it would be disproportionate. The violation of [European Convention on Human Rights art 1] would occur at the time when the state sought to enforce an order for the confiscation of proceeds of crime which have already been paid to the state. The appropriate way of avoiding such a violation would be for the confiscation order made against each defendant to be subject to a condition which would prevent that occurrence. para 73 This approach may appear to risk producing inequity between criminal conspirators, on the basis that some of them may well obtain a 'windfall' because the amount of the confiscation order will be paid by another.

However, that is an inherent feature of joint criminality. If the victim of a fraud were to sue the conspirators and to obtain judgments against them, he would be entitled to enforce against whichever defendant he most easily could. The losses must lie where they fall, and there is nothing surprising, let alone wrong, in the criminal courts adopting that approach. Where a finding of joint obtaining is made, whether against a single defendant or more than one, the confiscation order should be made for the whole value of the benefit thus obtained, but should provide that it is not to be enforced to the extent that a sum has been recovered by way of satisfaction of another confiscation order made in relation to the same joint benefit. A subsequent confiscation order made against a later-tried defendant in relation to the same benefit may well be such an order. In theory a court might therefore need to consider whether to stay the enforcement of a confiscation order made against one or more defendants to await the outcome of a later criminal trial against other defendants in respect of the same criminal conspiracy. However, except perhaps when a second trial is imminent, this would not normally be appropriate bearing in mind the purpose of the 2002 Act and the statutory stipulation for a speedy hearing (see para 10 of this judgment). Orders made on the basis of lifestyle assumptions will require special consideration on their facts. Confiscation orders amended accordingly. For more detail see **21.89**.

R v Dad and Others 2014 EWCA Crim 2478 D and others were convicted of conspiracy to defraud and money laundering. They made a series of bogus insurance claims. The Judge found although the defendants held separate bank accounts and assets, the assets were regarded by the defendants as all part of a family pot. Nevertheless he apportioned the benefit equally because otherwise it would be disproportionate and unfair. Held. It is easy to see why the Judge did that but *R v Waya* 2012 UKSC 51, 2013 2 Cr App R (S) 20 (p 87) had not displaced *R v May* 2008 UKHL 28, 2009 1 Cr App R (S) 31 (p 162) about apportionment. The Judge was wrong to do so, so the prosecution appeal was allowed. Where the Judge had not apportioned, the appeal was dismissed.

The Court also considered whether the adjustment for the available amount in *R v Ahmad and Others* 2014 UKSC 36, 2 Cr App R (S) 75 (p 580) (see above) applied. Held. para 56 The last sentence of para 74 of the case makes clear that [an adjustment] may not be required in cases of lifestyle assumption. It all depends on the circumstances. No such adjustment is required here as [the individual confiscation orders do not equal the total of the benefit and we can discount a lottery win adjustment occurring.]

21.122 ***Step 9 The available amount Legal costs***

R v Martin and White 1998 Unreported 20/2/98 www.banksr.com Other Matters Other Documents tab M was convicted of alcohol duty evasion and VAT fraud. In confiscation proceedings M asked for his legal expenses of £750,000 to be deducted from the total. Held. An obligation may only be taken into account in reduction of the amount which might be realised if it has priority at the time of the making of the order. Thus, there can be no question of any reduction being made for legal costs at the time this order [was made].

Piercing the corporate veil see **21.48**.

21.123 ***Step 9 The available amount Pension policies***

R v Chen 2009 EWCA Crim 2669, 2010 2 Cr App R (S) 34 (p 221) D pleaded to conspiracy to obtain property by deception. The benefit was assessed as £68,000+. D had virtually no assets. There was a car worth £100 and two pension policies due to mature in 2018. He had no right to access until then. The policies could not be assigned or sold. There was no surrender value. There was, however, an underlying value based on the number of units in the fund. The Judge held that the policies were 'free property' and he could treat the asset value as the current value of the fund. The defence said the value was nil and the prosecution could apply when the funds became available. Held. The policies were free property. In neither *R v Cornfield* 2006 EWCA Crim 2909, 2007 1 Cr App R (S) 124 (p 771) nor *R v Ford* 2008 EWCA Crim 966, 2009 1 Cr App R (S)

13 (p 68) was it possible for the prosecution to return to court when assets became available. That was a highly material distinction. It was wrong to say that the current market value of the policies was the current value of the underlying fund. We do not include the value of the pensions in the confiscation figure. Order varied.

21.124 ***Step 9 The available amount Property, Assessing the value of General principles***

R v Hedges 2004 EWCA Crim 2133 D's only relevant asset was his house, which was owned jointly by his wife. The market value was assessed as £230,000. The Judge deducted the outstanding mortgage of £50,000 and £5,000 for anticipated sale costs, making £175,000. The Judge then divided that by two, making £87,500. A confiscation order for that amount was made. D appealed saying that because D was jointly and severally liable to repay the mortgage, the mortgage figure should be deducted after his share of the house was assessed. Held. The whole of the mortgage will be deducted out of the proceeds of sale so the approach of the Judge properly reflected what the Act was aiming to achieve. Appeal dismissed.

Larkfield Ltd v Revenue and Customs 2010 EWCA Civ 521 Raymond May (see below) appealed his confiscation order and the case went to the House of Lords, see **21.69**. Revenue and Customs began enforcement proceedings in the High Court. The parties appealed about whether a third party was the beneficial owner of the property which was alleged to be 'realisable property'. Held. The dispute is to be resolved in accordance with ordinary principles of property law, save where the [confiscation legislation] provides otherwise.

For the case at first instance see *Revenue and Customs v May and Others* 2009 EWHC 1826 (QB) at **21.132**.

R v Sheidu 2014 EWCA Crim 1671 D pleaded to five counts of acquiring criminal property. In confiscation proceedings, the prosecution relied on photographs of him on a partially built house with crude wooden scaffolding. In it, D was making a gesture of triumph with his arm. D denied it was him. The Judge accepted the prosecution value of £250,000 and included it in the calculations. The Judge looking at a photograph of a house with someone in it was able to say with facial mapping (a comparison technique) that the someone was D. Held. It seems likely the house was in Nigeria. However, without knowing where it was, a vital element in the valuing of it was missing. £250,000 was a totally arbitrary figure. The better course was to leave the house out of the confiscation calculations.

R v Gor 2017 EWCA Crim 3 When assessing the value of the property, defence counsel argued that as there was only three months to pay, the Court should select the lower of the house valuations as it was a forced sale. Held. The defendant will be given time for an orderly realisation of his assets and if the property has not achieved its market price within the time period, it is inconceivable a court would not grant an extension. Courts should use the proper open market valuation. This was especially true here as there were substantial hidden assets.

21.125 ***Step 9 The available amount Property Matrimonial property***

Webber v Webber 2006 EWHC 2893 (Fam) President of the Family Division D faced confiscation proceedings. His wife applied for ancillary relief in her divorce proceedings. She sought more than a 50% share of the matrimonial home. The Court considered how the Crown Court would approach the asset. Held. para 44 The Crown Court has no regard to, and makes no allowance for, any possible adverse consequences for a former spouse and her child when deciding the amount to be confiscated. The court's function is simply to conduct an arithmetical exercise to determine the assets available for confiscation, see *R v Ahmed and Qureshi* 2004 EWCA Crim 2599.

Re B 2008 EWHC 690 (Admin) High Court D pleaded to an excise fraud. Just before his plea, he transferred his half share of his house to his wife for no consideration. The Judge made a confiscation order based on his half share in the house. D's wife appealed contending she had been financing the family while her husband had been unemployed. Bank account records confirmed she paid the mortgage payments. Held. I accept the house was put in her name to put the finances in order and not to avoid the confiscation order as the prosecution contend. However, I don't accept D contributed little to the mortgage payments. D's incapacity payments would have reflected the payments. The wife has demonstrated care for her ill husband. However, the transfer is treated as a [tainted] gift so caught by the Act. The house had to be sold.

Gibson v Revenue and Customs 2008 EWCA Civ 645 D was convicted of conspiracy to import cocaine. In confiscation proceedings his benefit was assessed at over £38m. The confiscation order included £5m for hidden assets. His assets included his matrimonial home which after deducting the mortgage was worth over £51,000. The house was in joint names with his wife, W. Proceedings were started to enforce the order. W was joined to the proceedings and argued 50% of the equity was hers. W gave evidence and the Judge found her evidence about the mortgage payments not credible and that she had guilty knowledge that those payments were not legitimately earned. He found that tainted money was used to fund the mortgage payments and decided W's share was 12.5%. Held. There were legitimate funds which might have been sufficient to support the mortgage. There were also large cash sums which were paid into accounts from which mortgage payments were made. It is the prosecution who have to establish a public policy jurisdiction entitling the court to confiscate her assets, when she was not convicted and when no confiscation order has been made against her. In fact there is no power to violate her rights protected by [European Convention on Human Rights] art 1. W was entitled to 50% of the equity.

R v Beaumont 2014 EWCA Crim 1664, 2015 1 Cr App R (S) 1 (p 1) D pleaded to two counts of fraud. She assisted in a fraud on a company. The confiscation order of just over £17,500, which was the money she had received, was agreed. D had lost her job. Her only savings were a jointly held bank account with her share now at £4,500. She did have a £50,000 share of her family home jointly owned by her long-term partner. The house also housed her two adult sons and their children from time to time. The Judge made an identical compensation order. Held. *R v Hackett* 1988 10 Cr App R (S) 388, *R v Holah* 1989 11 Cr App R (S) 282 and other [older cases] provide support for the proposition that where a compensation order is likely to require the matrimonial or family home to be sold, it is not generally appropriate to take into account the value of that home. We consider a similar approach is justified when considering Proceeds of Crime Act 2002 s 13(5)-(6). The house should not be sold. Applying *R v Morgan and Bygrave* 2008 EWCA Crim 1323, 2009 1 Cr App R (S) 60 (p 333), as the only way of satisfying the order is through the sale of the matrimonial home, we order the compensation order to be paid from the confiscation order sum.

R v Parkinson 2015 EWCA Crim 1448, 2016 1 Cr App R (S) 6 (p 24) D pleaded to theft. He stole brass parts worth just over £64,620 from his employer. The prosecution applied for a confiscation order and a compensation order. It was agreed that the benefit was about £39,330 and the available assets were just under £14,690, which was his share of the matrimonial home. The Judge accepted that this order would make it likely that the home would have to be sold. Held. para 21 D's share in the matrimonial home constituted free property and part of the available amount for the purposes of section 9. Further, [the fact] that another person may also have a beneficial interest in such property has no impact, for the purposes of a confiscation order, on that outcome. para 22 If a confiscation order alone had been sought, the order could properly [utilise] D's share in the matrimonial home. para 30 A judge, when considering whether or not to make a compensation order, may take the [fact] that the property was a matrimonial home into account. para 32 Making both orders might raise issues of proportionality, applying *R v Waya* 2012 UKSC 51, 2013 2 Cr App R (S) 20 (p 87) and *R v Jawad* 2013 EWCA Crim 644, 2014 1 Cr App R (S) 16 (p 85) (see **21.81**). para 36 *R v*

Beaumont 2014 (see above) is a decision on its own facts. Whilst a potential consequential forced sale of the family home is a matter to be taken into account, it is not to be taken as some kind of trump card in resisting the making of a compensation order or a section 13(6) direction, let alone with regard to the making of the confiscation order itself. para 38 Crown Court judges should nowadays be a little careful, in the course of confiscation or compensation proceedings, in too readily assuming that the making of a compensation order in such circumstances inevitably will require a jointly owned property to be sold. That may well be the consequence. But under modern jurisprudence there is at least some prospect for a spouse or partner having the remaining beneficial share in the family home, and perhaps also where there are dependent young children, at least raising an opposing argument as to sale or possession: such arguments being potentially available in the course of enforcement proceedings in the courts which have been subsequently undertaken to realise the value of the defendant's beneficial interest. Such arguments in opposition are capable of placing reliance on the considerations arising under article 8 of the Convention or on wider equitable principles. If the enforcing court in subsequent sale and possession proceedings does not consider it in any particular case to be unjust or disproportionate to order sale and possession, that is suggestive of it not having been unjust or disproportionate to have made the original compensation order. para 39 We endorse the judge's approach. Appeal dismissed.
See also: *Stack v Dowden* 2007 UKHL 17 as explained and clarified in *Jones v Kernott* 2011 UKSC 53 and *CPS v Piper* 2011 EWHC 3570 (Admin).
R v Thompson 2015 EWCA Crim 1820 (Two homes. Each purchased as a matrimonial home. Second home purchased from funds of the defendant, D, a fraudster. D paid the mortgage until the time he was investigated, when his wife, with no job, provided some of the money. Held. It was an investment property. The prosecution were able to show that the wife was unable to satisfy the rule in matrimonial law about quantifying disappointment in family life etc. Order that 90% of the equity was available for confiscation upheld.)
R v Flynn 2016 EWCA Crim 201 (The Judge deducted the defendant's legal aid charge on the property from the valuation figure. That was disproportionate as that would mean the defendant's wife would pay half the legal aid figure. The figure should have been deducted from the defendant's share of the property.)
For ***Matrimonial property and tainted gifts*** see **21.116**.

21.126 ***Step 9 The available amount Property owned outright***
The value is the market value, see Proceeds of Crime Act 2002 s 79(2) at **21.73**.

21.127 ***Step 9 The available amount Property not owned outright Procedure***
Criminal Procedure Rules 2015 2015/1490 Rule 32.13 (1) This rule applies where:

(a) the court can make a confiscation order; and
(b) the prosecutor asks the court to make such an order, or the court decides to make such an order on its own initiative.

Criminal Procedure Rules 2015 2015/1490 Rule 32.13(3) Where it appears to the court that a person other than the defendant holds, or may hold, an interest in property held by the defendant which property is likely to be realised or otherwise used to satisfy a confiscation order:

(a) the court must not determine the extent of the defendant's interest in that property unless that other person has had a reasonable opportunity to make representations; and
(b) the court may order that other person to give such information, in such manner and within such a period, as the court directs.

21.128 ***Step 9 The available amount Property not owned outright The beneficial interest Cases***
Jones v Kernott 2011 UKSC 53 Supreme Court In 1981, C bought a mobile home and in 1983, D moved in with her. The couple never married and their income was similar. The

next year they had a child and the year after that they bought a house for £30,000 in their joint names. There was no declaration of trust as to how the beneficial interest was to be held. The purchase was funded from the sale of the mobile home (£6,000) and a mortgage supported by their joint income. In 1986, they had a second child and, with a loan of £2,000, an extension was built. D did some of the work and a Judge found the value was increased from £30,000 to £44,000. In 1986, a second child was born. In 1993, D moved out and stopped making payments towards the mortgage and contributed little to the children's expenses. In 1995, C and D tried to sell the house for £69,995 but were unsuccessful. They cashed in their insurance policy, which was in both their names. From £2,800 of the proceeds and a mortgage, D bought his own home. In 2006, C applied to the County Court for a declaration that she was entitled to the entire beneficial interest of their home. The Judge found D was able to buy the next house because of his lack of support for his former home and children and held C was entitled to 90% of their home. The High Court dismissed D's appeal and the Court of Appeal (2-1) allowed his further appeal, saying the parties owned the property as tenants in common in equal shares. Held. para 19 There are two reasons why a challenge to the presumption of beneficial joint tenancy is not to be lightly embarked on. The first is implicit in the nature of the enterprise. If a couple in an intimate relationship (whether married or unmarried) decide to buy a house or flat in which to live together, almost always with the help of a mortgage for which they are jointly and severally liable, that is on the face of things a strong indication of emotional and economic commitment to a joint enterprise. That is so even if the parties, for whatever reason, fail to make that clear by any overt declaration or agreement.

para 22 The second reason is that the notion that in a trusting personal relationship the parties do not hold each other to account financially is underpinned by the practical difficulty, in many cases, of taking any such account, perhaps after 20 years or more of the ups and downs of living together as an unmarried couple.

para 25 Where a house or flat is in joint names for joint occupation by a married or unmarried couple, where both are responsible for any mortgage, there is no presumption of a resulting trust arising from their having contributed to the deposit (or indeed the rest of the purchase) in unequal shares. The presumption is that the parties intended a joint tenancy both in law and in equity. But that presumption can of course be rebutted by evidence of a contrary intention, which may more readily be shown where the parties did not share their financial resources.

para 31 The search is primarily to ascertain the parties' actual shared intentions, whether expressed or to be inferred from their conduct. However, there are at least two exceptions. The first, which is not this case, is where the classic resulting trust presumption applies. Indeed, this would be rare in a domestic context, but might perhaps arise where domestic partners were also business partners, see *Stack v Dowden* 2007 UKHL 17 at para 32. The second is where it is clear that the beneficial interests are to be shared, but it is impossible to divine a common intention as to the proportions in which they are to be shared. In those two situations, the court is driven to impute an intention to the parties which they may never have had.

para 32 Once the court was satisfied that it was the parties' common intention that the beneficial interest was to be shared in some proportion or other, the court might have to give effect to that common intention by determining what in all the circumstances was a fair share (see *Gissing v Gissing* 1971 AC 886 at p 909). *Stack v Dowden* 2007 gave qualified approval to the proposition that 'the answer is that each is entitled to that share which the court considers fair having regard to the whole course of dealing between them in relation to the property'.

para 46 The primary search must always be for what the parties actually intended, to be deduced objectively from their words and their actions. It cannot impose a solution upon them which is contrary to what the evidence shows that they actually intended. But if it cannot deduce exactly what shares were intended, it may have no alternative but to ask what their intentions as reasonable and just people would have been had they thought about it at the time. This is a fallback position.

para 51 In summary, the following are the principles applicable where a family home is bought in the joint names of a cohabiting couple who are both responsible for any mortgage, but without any express declaration of their beneficial interests.

(1) The starting point is that equity follows the law and they are joint tenants both in law and in equity.

(2) That presumption can be displaced by showing a) that the parties had a different common intention at the time when they acquired the home, or b) that they later formed the common intention that their respective shares would change.

(3) Their common intention is to be deduced objectively from their conduct.

(4) In those cases where it is clear either a) that the parties did not intend joint tenancy at the outset, or b) had changed their original intention, but it is not possible to ascertain by direct evidence or by inference what their actual intention was as to the shares in which they would own the property, 'the answer is that each is entitled to that share which the court considers fair having regard to the whole course of dealing between them in relation to the property'. The whole 'course of dealing…in relation to the property' should be given a broad meaning, enabling a similar range of factors to be taken into account as may be relevant to ascertaining the parties' actual intentions.

(5) Each case will turn on its own facts. Financial contributions are relevant but there are many other factors which may enable the court to decide what shares were either intended (as in case (3)) or fair (as in case (4)).

para 53 The assumptions as to human motivation, which led the courts to impute particular intentions by way of the resulting trust, are not appropriate to the ascertainment of beneficial interests in a family home. Whether they remain appropriate in other contexts is not the issue in this case.

para 48 Here at the outset, C and D's intention was to provide a home for themselves and their progeny. D would not have been able to do this had he still had to contribute towards the mortgage, endowment policy and other outgoings on the property. The logical inference is that they intended that his interest in it should crystallise then (sic).

para 17 The claimant whose name is not on the proprietorship register has the burden of establishing some sort of implied trust, normally what is now termed a 'common intention' constructive trust. The claimant whose name is on the register starts (in the absence of an express declaration of trust in different terms, and subject to what is said below about resulting trusts) with the presumption (or assumption) of a beneficial joint tenancy.

para 52 This case is not concerned with a family home which is put into the name of one party only. The starting point is different. The first issue is whether it was intended that the other party have any beneficial interest in the property at all. If he does, the second issue is what that interest is. There is no presumption of joint beneficial ownership. But their common intention has once again to be deduced objectively from their conduct. If the evidence shows a common intention to share beneficial ownership but does not show what shares were intended, the court will have to proceed as at [sub] para 4) and 5) above.

para 49 The value of the property was £60,000 in late 1993 and £245,000 in 2008. The share of the £60,000 was equal between the parties. Leaving the balance to C, that gives D £30,000 and her £215,000 roughly so 12% and 88% respectively. This calculation ignores the mortgage, which may be the correct approach, as in 2008 the mortgage debt was almost fully covered by the endowment policy which was always meant to discharge it. Introducing the mortgage liability in 1993 into the calculation would be to

D's disadvantage, because at that stage the endowment policy would not have been sufficient to discharge the debt, so the equity would have been less. This is so close to that which the first Judge found that it would be wrong to interfere.
Note: In confiscation proceedings I have noticed that judges are not very interested in the finer points of civil law and prefer a broad brush approach. They also have to deal with where the purchase or the mortgage was paid for by criminal property. In those cases expect the judge to include as much as he or she feels they can include. As this chapter is about confiscation, other property law cases have not been included. Ed.
Where the property is subject to trusts, see **21.132**.

21.129 ***Step 9 The available amount Property Mortgages and other encumbrances***
R v Ghadami 1998 1 Cr App R (S) 42 D was convicted of a VAT fraud. Two of his assets were houses where the mortgage debt was twice or more than twice the value of the premises. The Judge declined to take into account the debt, saying that mortgage debt should only be regarded as relevant and as having priority to the extent of the value of the security. Held. That was correct. Debts to building societies or banks which have advanced money on security that is no longer adequate have no priority, other than to the extent of the value of the security. That becomes obvious if they choose to exercise their right to sell the property in order to reduce the mortgage debt. They remain creditors of the debtor for the balance, but nothing in Part VI of the 1988 Act gives them any sort of priority when it comes to the making of a confiscation order.
R v Hedges 2004 EWCA Crim 2133 D was convicted of handling stolen goods. The Judge made a confiscation order. The only relevant asset was D's share in a house, which he jointly owned with his wife. Held. Although in theory the defendant is liable to discharge the whole mortgage, the mortgage and the sale costs are taken out of the sale price before there is any division.

21.130 ***Step 9 The available amount Money subject to forfeiture proceedings***
R v Weller 2009 EWCA Crim 810 D pleaded to supply. In confiscation proceedings, D's counsel argued that certain cash was not 'free property' within the meaning of Proceeds of Crime Act 2002 s 82 because it was subject to a forfeiture application under Proceeds of Crime Act 2002 s 298(4). Held. Section 82 does not exclude property subject to section 298(4) applications. The money can be included.

21.131 ***Step 9 The available amount Property Sale expenses***
R v Cramer 1992 13 Cr App R (S) 390 D pleaded to drug supply offences. The principal asset for confiscation was his house. The Judge made no allowance for costs of the sale of the house. The defence said the estate agent's charges, the solicitor's costs, other legal costs, the VAT, search certificates expenses etc. should be deducted. Held. The market value of the house must mean its net market value after the inevitable costs have been deducted. We reduce the order to take into account all the costs.

21.132 ***Step 9 The available amount Trusts/contracts, Assets bound by***
Revenue and Customs v May and Others 2009 EWHC 1826 (QB) High Court D appealed his confiscation order and the case went to the House of Lords, see **21.69**. Revenue and Customs began enforcement proceedings in the High Court. Held. Once assets have been identified as relevant realisable property they may be recovered, subject to the protection afforded by Criminal Justice Act 1988 s 80(8) and 82(4).[410] They may be recovered from any trust or company irrespective of any legal obstacles or protections for the direct or indirect benefit of the defendant which would otherwise arise under company or trust law…If the position were otherwise a master criminal, before embarking on a serious financial crime, would be able to protect his assets, other than

[410] Repealed by Proceeds of Crime Act 2002 Sch 12 para 1 (24/3/03: repeal has effect subject to savings specified in SI 2003/333 art 10(1)(a) and art 13(a)).

those directly obtained from the crime he was about to commit, by placing them all in trust. It cannot have been the intention of Parliament to make that possible leaving the victims with only the potential weapon of the law of insolvency to rely upon.
Note: The parties appealed and the order was overturned but the above principles were not challenged, *Larkfield Ltd v Revenue and Customs* 2010 EWCA Civ 521. Ed.
R v Modjiri 2010 EWCA Crim 829, 2011 1 Cr App R (S) 20 (p 137) D pleaded to possession of cocaine with intent to supply. His benefit figure was assessed at nearly £84,000. D's sister, S, purchased a long lease of a flat from her own funds. Out of familial duty she conveyed it to D and another sibling with a Declaration of Trust declaring the lease was held on trust for themselves beneficially at 50% for S and 25% for the brothers. It stated that the lease shall not be assigned, nor shall any mortgage charge or lease be granted without the consent of all of them. The Judge regarded Proceeds of Crime Act 2002 s 79(3), which says, 'But if at that time another person holds an interest in the property its value…is the market value of his interest at that time, ignoring any charging order'. The prosecution appealed. Held. We readily accept that it would be difficult to sell a part beneficial interest in a flat or house. There is no market in such interests. We doubt too whether it would be possible to borrow moneys from a bank or other lending institution on the security of such a beneficial interest. The Judge's error was to assume that Proceeds of Crime Act 2002 s 79(3) is concerned with the realisation of property as well as its valuation. It is not. It does not require the court to assume that a beneficial interest has to be sold separately as such. The court must proceed on the basis that D can obtain an order under Trusts of Land and Appointment of Trustees Act 1996 s 14 for the sale of the property as a whole, and that he will on a sale receive his due proportion of the proceeds of sale. We agree with *Revenue and Customs v May and Others* 2009 EWHC 1826 (QB). The possibility that D will not obtain an order for the sale of the property as a whole does not affect or diminish its market value (although the costs of obtaining the order may be relevant). If D could show that he had no other means of satisfying the confiscation order, the court would order the sale of the lease notwithstanding the provisions of the declaration of trust. The 25% share should be included.
See also: *R v Dad and Others* 2014 EWCA Crim 2478 (Applying section 79(3), the Judge was wrong to include a property which was placed in the defendant's name on trust for his brother who had mental issues, *R v Harriot* 2012 EWCA Crim 2294.)

21.133 ***Step 9 The available amount The recoverable amount***
Proceeds of Crime Act 2002 s 6(5) If the court decides under subsection (4)(b) or (c) (see **21.51**) that the defendant has benefited from the conduct referred to, it must:
(a) decide the recoverable amount, and
(b) make an order (a confiscation order) requiring him to pay that amount.
Paragraph (b) applies only if, or to the extent that, it would not be disproportionate to require the defendant to pay the recoverable amount.[411]
For the full section see **21.5**.
Recoverable amount
Proceeds of Crime Act 2002 s 7(1) The recoverable amount for the purposes of section 6 is an amount equal to the defendant's benefit from the conduct concerned.
(2) But if the defendant shows that the available amount is less than that benefit, the recoverable amount is:
(a) the available amount, or
(b) a nominal amount, if the available amount is nil.
(3) But if section 6(6) (victim starting proceedings) applies the recoverable amount is such amount as:
(a) the court believes is just, but

[411] As inserted by Serious Crime Act 2015 Sch 4 para 3. In force 1/6/15

(b) does not exceed the amount found under subsection (1) or (2) (as the case may be).
(4) In calculating the defendant's benefit from the conduct concerned for the purposes of subsection (1), any property in respect of which:
(a) a recovery order is in force under section 266, or
(b) a forfeiture order is in force under section 298(2),
must be ignored.
(5) If the court decides the available amount, it must include in the confiscation order a statement of its findings as to the matters relevant for deciding that amount.

Other orders If the court makes a confiscation order it must take that into account before it imposes a fine, costs order, forfeiture, unlawful profit order[412] and deprivation orders. However, it must leave the confiscation order out of account in deciding the appropriate sentence for the defendant, Proceeds of Crime Act 2002 s 13.[413]
For appeals over agreed assets see para **21.154**.

21.134 ***Step 9 The available amount Hidden assets***
Note: The starting point is Proceeds of Crime Act 2002 s 7(1)-(2) at **21.133**. Ed.
R v McIntosh and Marsden 2011 EWCA Crim 1501, 2012 1 Cr App R (S) 60 (p 342) D and another were sentenced for a missing trader fraud. Held. The court may conclude that a defendant's realisable assets are less than the full value of the benefit on the basis of the facts as a whole. A defendant who is found not to have told the truth or who has declined to give truthful disclosure will inevitably find it difficult to discharge the burden imposed upon him. But it may not be impossible for him to do so. Other sources of evidence, apart from the defendant himself, and a view of the case as a whole, may persuade a court that the assets available to the defendant are less than the full value of the benefit. The judge concluded that he was not satisfied that D no longer held such property there or elsewhere. He found that the value of what he had abroad was totally unknown. This was a crucial finding. Once the Judge had reached that conclusion, there was no basis on which he could conclude that the value of D's realisable property was less than the value of his benefit, in the light of D's role in so lucrative a conspiracy. There was no justification for valuing his available assets as less than the full value of the benefit, even accepting the modest style in which he lived.
R v Lee and Another 2013 EWCA Crim 657 L was a career criminal involved in large-scale theft or handling. His wife ran a shop. Her account was agreed to be an entirely unrealistic picture of its activity. The Judge found they lived off crime. On appeal, the defence said the Judge illegitimately moved directly from rejection of the cases advanced by the defendants to the conclusion that, not only were there unrevealed assets, but that they must be in the sum of the whole of the benefit. Held. The starting point is section 7 of the Act, which provides that the realisable or available amount is to be taken to be the benefit figure unless the contrary is shown on the balance of probabilities. Both defendants understandably rely on the decision of this court in *R v McIntosh and Marsden* 2011 EWCA Crim 1501, 2012 1 Cr App R (S) 60 (p 342) and its subsequent endorsement by *R v Ahmad and Ahmed* 2012 EWCA Crim 391, 2 Cr App R (S) 85 (p 491). para 21 Those cases show that when the court is addressing the question of undisclosed or, as they are often called, hidden assets which have to be included in the available amount, the judge is not bound simply because he disbelieves a defendant, to decide that his hidden assets must be the full amount of the benefit. We agree with what is said in those judgments, that it may be a legitimate conclusion for the judge to reach that the defendant clearly has hidden assets, but not as much as the statute calculates as benefit. Indeed it may be possible. We also agree that the mere fact that a defendant gives evidence which the judge cannot believe does not necessarily mean that the only

412 As inserted by Prevention of Social Housing Fraud Act 2013 Sch para 14
413 Serious Crime Act 2015 Sch 4 para 89 repeals para 14 of this Schedule. As with the other changes, it is no longer required. In force 1/6/15, Serious Crime Act 2015 (Commencement No 1) Regulations 2015 2015/820 para 3

conclusion is that the amount of hidden assets is the full amount of the benefit. It is clearly possible to have a case in which everything the defendant says about his assets is rightly disbelieved, but there is the clearest possible evidence from elsewhere that he is destitute and there simply is not any money anywhere.

R v Yu and Another 2015 EWCA Crim 1076, 2 Cr App R (S) 75 (p 500) D and his wife, W, pleaded to four trade mark offences. During the confiscation hearing the Judge was unable to accept their account due to inconsistencies. She found the pair had failed to satisfy her that the available amount was less than the benefit. Held. para 35 The Judge did not move directly from disbelieving D and W to finding not only that they had hidden assets but that these were necessarily in the same amount as their benefit. The Judge was amply entitled to reject the various tangled and inconsistent explanations offered by D and W. If there was nothing other than the evidence which was disbelieved, there was no or no proper basis for the Judge concluding that the value of the appellants' realisable property was less than the value of their benefit. Having regard to the burden of proof resting on the appellants and once having disbelieved them, there was no proper evidential foundation for the Judge [to accept the defence's suggestions about the finances]. The Judge was both entitled and bound to reach the conclusion to which she came. Confiscation order upheld.

R v Brooks 2016 EWCA Crim 44 D was convicted of conspiracy to import drugs. He was the organiser of the boats that would transport drugs from South America to the UK. The Irish Navy seized a yacht with 1,504 kilos of cannabis near the Irish coast. In confiscation proceedings, the Judge included in the benefit the value of the drugs (worth about £3m), the value of a villa and other property which came to just over £3.6m. The Judge repeatedly noticed the absence of documentary evidence to support D's claims and considered that D avoided leaving a financial trail for his dealings. He also found that D led a cash lifestyle with purchases of cars, property in Thailand, boats, expensive watches and stays at expensive hotels. From that he inferred that D had significant amounts of cash available to him. The only identifiable assets were a share in a Spanish villa worth just less than £300,000, and premium bonds and other small items totalling £1,400. The Judge found that D had not disclosed his assets and had failed to discharge the burden of showing that his assets were less than the benefit. He then held that the recoverable amount was the same as the benefit at just over £3.6m. Held. para 24 *R v McIntosh and Marsden* 2011 [provides] the correct approach. It was wrong for the Judge to make a leap from rejecting D's account as to his assets to concluding necessarily that the available amount should equate to the amount of benefit. Where the drugs had been seized, the Judge should have looked for evidence to show that D had available assets. However, the Judge could conclude that there were hidden assets. After rejecting D's evidence, the Judge was entitled to take a broad brush approach. There was evidence of an affluent lifestyle which could have justified a finding of hidden assets, but the Judge had failed to assess the matter on the whole of the evidence which had led to an overstatement of an appropriate benefit figure.[414] para 27 In *R v Thacker* 1995 16 Cr App R (S) 461 the Court held that where drugs had been seized from a defendant by Customs and Excise they were not property held by a defendant for the purposes of calculating the recoverable amount. In *R v Islam* 2009 UKHL 30, 2010 1 Cr App R (S) 42 (p 245) the House of Lords made plain at paras 34, 37 and 44 that a clear distinction was to be drawn between the assessment of value for the purpose of calculating benefit and the assessment of value for the purpose of calculating the available or recoverable amount. para 28 More recently this court in *R v Kakkad* 2015 EWCA Crim 385 said at para 32 "Self-evidently, property seized and forfeited would no longer be part of the available amount. Its value would not be part of all the free property held by the appellant, as was pointed out in *R v Islam* 2009."

[414] I think the Court meant 'recoverable amount' not 'benefit figure'.

para 29 We note that at para 34 of *R v Islam* 2009, it was said that where HMRC have seized goods, forfeiture is automatic, and in that case the goods will no longer be property held by the defendant at the time of a confiscation order. [Further] that in other cases the confiscation order would precede any order for forfeiture under the Misuse of Drugs Act so that the drugs would continue in law to be 'free property then held by the defendant' at the time of the confiscation order, even though physically in the possession of the authorities and destined to be the subject of a forfeiture order. Here the drugs were seized by the Irish Navy and thus do not fall within the first part of these comments. However, the situation does not cause difficulty since, as was pointed out, in such circumstances it would be impossible to regard the drugs as having any market value for the purpose of assessing the available amount. They would not ever be bought or sold on any market, legal or otherwise.
para 30 The Judge moved too precipitately from a rejection of D's evidence to including the value of the drugs in the available amount. para 41 We accept the Judge's finding about D's cash lifestyle. We take the tainted gifts for the mortgage payments on the Spanish property (£135,000), the cash and consider the fair and proportionate recoverable amount is £0.5m.
See also: *Att-Gen's Ref No 8 of 2009* EWCA Crim 732[415] (D pleaded to conspiracy to produce cannabis. The benefit was assessed at about £1.97m. D did not give evidence at the confiscation hearing. The Judge decided there were £0.5m of hidden assets. The prosecution appealed. Held. Unless there was other evidence so the Judge could be satisfied that D's realisable assets were less than the benefit, the Judge was obliged to make a confiscation order for the £1.97m. D was allowed to give evidence and the Court found he had so satisfied the test and made an order for £215,000.)
Note: Since 2009, the prisons have filled up with defendants with claimed hidden assets for which there was no prospect of their orders being paid. Today, judges appear to be more judicial and less draconian in how they approach the amount to be recovered. Ed.

Step 10 The victim's court proceedings exception

21.135 Step 10

Step 10 Determine whether 'any victim of the conduct has at any time started or intends to start proceedings against the defendant in respect of loss, injury or damage sustained in connection with the conduct'. If Yes, the court has a discretion to make a confiscation order. The court must make a 'just' order and one that is not more than it would otherwise have ordered (Proceeds of Crime Act 2002 s 7(3)). If No, the court must make a confiscation order and go to Step 12.
Proceeds of Crime Act 2002 s 6(5) [If the court decides that the defendant has benefited, it must decide the recoverable amount and make an order that he pay that amount.]
(6) But the court must treat the duty in subsection (5) as a power if it believes that any victim of the conduct has at any time started or intends to start proceedings against the defendant in respect of loss, injury or damage sustained in connection with the conduct.
Proceeds of Crime Act 2002 s 7(3) But if section 6(6) (victim starting proceedings) applies, the recoverable amount is such amount as:
(a) the court believes is just, but
(b) does not exceed the amount found under subsection (1) or (2) (as the case may be).
For the full sections see **21.5**.
Revenue and Customs v Crossman 2007 EWHC 1585 (Ch) D was sentenced for a VAT fuel fraud. The benefit was fixed at nearly £490,000. In February 2004, the order was made for nearly £56,000. In July,[416] D paid the sum. In April 2005, Revenue and Customs served a statutory demand for over £343,000. D began County Court action to

[415] The judgment refers to this case as *R v McMillan-Smith* 2009 EWCA Crim 732 in error.
[416] The judgment states D paid the sum in 'mid-2005…probably July', but in the context of the judgment it is likely that the sum was paid in mid-2004.

set the demand aside. The application was dismissed with costs. In 2006, Revenue and Customs issued a bankruptcy petition for D for the £343,000+ sum. The prosecution documents in part were untrue. D served his opposition relying on the confiscation order saying it was in part double recovery. Held. para 36 At the time of the confiscation proceedings, Revenue and Customs intended to bring civil proceedings. They should have disclosed that to the Court. However, there is no injustice in making a bankruptcy order.

R v Lowe 2009 EWCA Crim 194, 2 Cr App R (S) 81 (p 544) D's benefit was assessed as just over £191,300. The assets were assessed as just under £42,000, which was a significant proportion of his home. The defence said the order would amount to a double penalty. The Judge made an order for the assets figure. Held. para 9 If section 6(5) applies then under section 7(3), the court can fix the amount as that which the court considers just, subject to the maximum that the court would have fixed had it been under the mandatory duty to make the order. para 11 Here, section 6(6) did not operate as the remedy to recover the land lay against the company and not against D.

CPS v Nelson 2009 EWCA Crim 1573, 2010 1 Cr App R (S) 82 (p 530) LCJ The section 6(6) concession does not appear to apply where a defendant has voluntarily repaid a victim for loss and damage before the victim has started or expressed an intention to start civil proceedings against him.

R v Silvester 2009 EWCA Crim 2182 D, a bank manager, pleaded to stealing £166,000 from elderly customers of his bank. In confiscation proceedings the benefit and realisable assets were agreed. The prosecution told the Judge that he did not seek a compensation order. He did not tell the Judge or the defence that the bank was intending to take civil proceedings against D. The Judge made an order for just short of £183,000 taking into account inflation. D paid the confiscation order and received the bank's civil claim for just over £288,000, which included interest and costs. D went through a divorce and said he had no realisable assets. His home was sold. The defence appealed saying that the Judge was not given the full facts and had he been he would have been able to exercise a discretion about confiscation. The prosecution put forward a variety of punitive and unfair options. Held. para 28 There are three highly relevant features. First, the benefit figure was known to be the entire value of all D's offending. It was not a criminal lifestyle case. Second, there was a single loser and third, that loser was intending to extract recovery. We quash the confiscation order and it shall not be returned to D for 42 days so the bank can [intervene to recover it].

Step 11 The unlawful profit order exception

21.136 ***Step 11***

Step 11 Determine whether a) a criminal unlawful profit order has been made or b) one is believed to be made or c) it is believed a person has at any time started or intends to start proceedings against the defendant for a civil unlawful profit order.[417]

If Yes, the court has a discretion to make a confiscation order. The court must make a 'just' order and one that is not more than it would otherwise have ordered (Proceeds of Crime Act 2002 s 7(3)), see **21.133**. If No, the court must make a confiscation order and go to Step 12, see **21.138**.

21.137 ***Step 11 Statute***

Proceeds of Crime Act 2002 s 6(6A) The court must also treat the duty in subsection (5) as a power if:

(a) an order has been made, or it believes an order may be made, against the defendant under Prevention of Social Housing Fraud Act 2013 s 4 (criminal unlawful profit orders) in respect of profit made by the defendant in connection with the conduct, or

[417] As inserted by Prevention of Social Housing Fraud Act 2013 Sch para 12

(b) it believes that a person has at any time started or intends to start proceedings against the defendant under section 5 (civil unlawful profit orders) of that Act in respect of such profit.

Proceeds of Crime Act 2002 s 7(3) But if section 6(6) or 6(6A) (victim starting proceedings) applies the recoverable amount is such amount as:

(a) the court believes is just, but

(b) does not exceed the amount found under subsection (1) or (2) (as the case may be).

For the full sections see **21.5**.

Steps 11-13 Fixing the amount

21.138 ***Steps 11-13***

Step 12 Has the defendant showed the available amount is less than the benefit? If Yes, go to Step 13. If No, go to Step 14.

Step 13 Make the amount in the confiscation order the 'available amount' or a 'nominal amount'. This is the 'recoverable' amount, see Proceeds of Crime Act 2002 s 6(5) and 7, see **21.133**. Go to Step 15, see **21.141**.

Step 14 Make the amount in the confiscation order the amount the court has assessed to be the benefit. Go to Step 15, see **21.141**.

Proceeds of Crime Act 2002 s 7(1) The recoverable amount for the purposes of section 6 is an amount equal to the defendant's benefit from the conduct concerned.

(2) But if the defendant shows that the available amount is less than that benefit, the recoverable amount is:

(a) the available amount, or

(b) a nominal amount, if the available amount is nil.

For the full section see **21.5**.

Note: For an example of an order being made for a nominal amount after the Law Society (which was treated as a victim) had obtained a High Court order for the defendant to pay £6.3m, see *R v Matthews* 2012 EWCA Crim 321. Ed.

21.139 ***Step 12 Defendant to show available amount is less than the benefit***

R v Ilsemann 1990 12 Cr App R (S) 398 D was convicted of importing cannabis resin. The benefit was fixed at over £396,000. The prosecution found a little less than £215,000. D did not give evidence or put in evidence any statement. The Judge made an order for the full benefit figure. Held. That was perfectly proper. If D wished to say that [the £215,000 figure] was all that was realisable, then it was for him to satisfy the court to that effect.

R v Barwick 2001 1 Cr App R (S) 129 D pleaded to 21 counts of theft and one deception offence. The benefit figure adjusted for inflation was just over £600,000. The police were unable to find any significant assets or trace where the stolen money had gone. D claimed he had lost a lot in gambling. The casinos D named only recorded a low value of gambling by him. There was no evidence of D living an extravagant lifestyle. D gave evidence and the Judge found him to be about the most unconvincing witness it would be possible to imagine. The Judge acknowledged that some of the money would have gone and reduced the benefit figure by £150,000. He made the confiscation order for £450,000. Held. para 28 It is likely that an offender may take steps to make the proceeds of crime difficult to trace. Once it is proved that he has received the benefit, it is pragmatic, and entirely fair to the defendant, to place upon him the onus of showing (to the civil standard) that he no longer has the proceeds or that their extent or value has diminished. para 37 Once the benefit has been proved, it is permissible, and ought normally to be the approach of the court, to conclude that the benefit remains available until the defendant proves otherwise, subject to the issue of changes in the value of money.

Grayson and Barnham v UK 2008 23/12/2008 ECtHR D was convicted of possession of 28 kilos of heroin with intent to supply. The Judge found D had failed to rebut the assumption that his assets were less than the benefit figure. D appealed and the Court dismissed his appeal. He and another with a similar point appealed to the European Court. Held. It was not unreasonable to expect D to explain what had happened to all the money shown by the prosecution to have been in his possession, any more than it was unreasonable at the first stage of the procedure to expect them to show the legitimacy of the source of such money or assets. The rights of the defence were protected by the safeguards built into the system, namely that it was a public hearing, there was advance disclosure, the defence could adduce documentary evidence and call evidence. The placing of the onus on the defendant was not incompatible with article 6.

R v Summers 2008 EWCA Crim 872, 2 Cr App R (S) 101 (p 569) D contested his confiscation order and the Judge held that D had not shown that he didn't have hidden assets. The defence made a number of submissions seeking to weaken the burden on the defence of showing the assets were less than the benefit figure. Held. It was not for the prosecution to establish that D had undisclosed assets, more particularly where the case from the outset was clearly that he had such assets, but [it was] for D to satisfy the court to the appropriate standard and on the basis of evidence that he had no such assets. The Judge properly concluded that D had failed to discharge that burden.

Att-Gen's Ref No 8 of 2008 2009 EWCA Crim 732[418] D was convicted of conspiring to produce cannabis. He did not give evidence in his confiscation proceedings. The benefit was just over £1.97m. The Judge found hidden assets of £50,000 but gave no reasons for the figure. The prosecution appealed his confiscation order saying the Judge should have made the order for the £1.97m benefit figure. The Court indicated the Judge should have found that there were hidden assets. D then sought to appeal. He waived privilege. Held in the prosecution appeal. Given that D appeared to have a history of concealing assets, the Judge ought not to have concentrated just on what assets he might still have. It was for D to satisfy the Judge that his realisable assets were less than the benefit figure. This he had singularly failed to do. We quash the confiscation order made and substitute one of just over £1.97m. Held in the defence appeal. D had been advised not to give evidence and had not been fully advised that the Judge would be obliged to find he had not shown his assets were less than the benefit. Also his reply failed to deal with the allegation of hidden assets. We give him leave to give evidence. We approach the evidence of D with considerable caution. He had lied in his trial, he accepted that he had tried to obtain a mortgage by deception and he had not given to the court the account which he was now giving us. Having examined the documents about bailiffs etc., although D is a proven liar and criminal we believed his account that he had an extravagant lifestyle. We are satisfied he had no assets. We make the confiscation order for £215,000, the value of his realisable assets.

See also: *R v Pigott* 2009 EWCA Crim 2292, 2010 2 Cr App R (S) 16 (p 91) (About £27.4m benefit. Nearly £0.5m assets. Nothing wrong with finding £1m hidden assets.)

R v Majid 2012 EWCA Crim 1023 (Over £46m benefit. £70,000 assets. No evidence from defendant. £3½m for hidden assets was sensible, fair and proportionate.)

21.140 ***Defendant to show available amount is less than the benefit Judge can take into account the real world realities***

R v Hartshorne 2010 EWCA Crim 1283 D was convicted of importing cannabis resin. There were 303 crates of cannabis imported containing an average of 100 kilos of cannabis. The benefit was assessed at £60m. D gave evidence and his evidence was largely rejected. The gross profits were agreed at £15m. The Judge identified costs in the operation of warehousing, transport, packaging, the preparation of false documents, shipping, wages and the like. The prosecution proposed a figure of 25% of gross profit for the overheads. The Judge said he was going to err on the side of caution and made the deduction 33%. He found the net profit was £10m. Second, he considered the intercepted telephone calls and considered that it would be safer to proceed on the basis

[418] The judgment lists the case as *Att-Gen v McMillan-Smith* 2009 EWCA Crim 732 in error.

that there was a more senior person involved, making the number of key organisers five, not four as suggested by the prosecution. Next, the Judge considered that an equal division would not be right as they were of different seniority. He assessed D's percentage as 10%. The prosecution appealed saying there was no evidence to support the first part and the Judge was too generous for the second part. Third, the Judge, having found hidden assets, decided the available amount was the difference between £1m and the money spent, which he rounded down to £½m. He therefore made a £½m order. Held. The two separate and alternative approaches to the problems created by placing the burden upon the offender were considered in *R v Versluis* 2004 EWCA Crim 3168, 2005 2 Cr App R (S) 26 (p 144), where the Court noted the *R v Comiskey* 1991 93 Cr App R 227 and *R v Cukovic* 1996 1 Cr App R (S) 131 approach, and at page 147, "If we are correct in believing that it is the actual property that we ought to have regard to, then it seems to us that draconian though the provisions of the Act may be, the court cannot close its eyes to the obvious and cannot ignore the fact that some expenses must have been incurred. There can be no question of carrying out an accountancy exercise, but it does seem to us that some acknowledgement ought to be made of the realities of the situation. We reduce the sum here." We consider the Judge was applying that interests of justice test. Once the Judge embarked on the exercise to which he was invited, he was not bound to accept without question any proposition advanced to him by the prosecution. The Judge's duty was to make his own judgment. It is quite true that there will often in the assessment of hidden assets be a dearth of evidence but the judge is required to do his best upon the evidence which is available and by the application of the burden of proof. The prosecution's own assertion of 25% for overheads was itself unsupported either by expert evidence or by the evidence of any conspirator. The Judge had a feel for the case. The prosecution advanced no reasoned basis for substituting their view for that of the Judge. For the second part, the Judge made perfectly legitimate conclusions.

Step 15 Consider time to pay

21.141 ***Step 15***

Step 15 Consider time to pay. The order must be paid immediately, unless the defendant needs time to pay, Proceeds of Crime Act 2002 s 11(2), see below. The maximum time is six months, which can later be extended, Proceeds of Crime Act 2002 s 11(3)-(5), see below.

Time for payment

Proceeds of Crime Act 2002 s 11(1) Unless subsection (2) applies, the full amount ordered to be paid under a confiscation order must be paid on the day on which the order is made.[419]

(2) If the court making the confiscation order is satisfied that the defendant is unable to pay the full amount on that day, it may make an order requiring whatever cannot be paid on that day to be paid:

(a) in a specified period, or

(b) in specified periods each of which relates to a specified amount.

(3) A specified period:

(a) must start with the day on which the confiscation order is made, and

(b) must not exceed three months.

(4) If: a) within any specified period the defendant applies to the Crown Court for that period to be extended, and

(b) the court is satisfied that, despite having made all reasonable efforts, the defendant is unable to pay the amount to which the specified period relates within that period, the court may make an order extending the period (for all or any part or parts of the amount in question).

[419] The section was substituted for section 11 by Serious Crime Act 2015 s 5. In force 1/6/15

(5) An extended period:
(a) must start with the day on which the confiscation order is made, and
(b) must not exceed six months.
(6) An order under subsection (4):
(a) may be made after the end of the specified period to which it relates, but
(b) must not be made after the end of the period of six months starting with the day on which the confiscation order is made.
(7) Periods specified or extended under this section must be such that, where the court believes that a defendant will by a particular day be able:
(a) to pay the amount remaining to be paid, or
(b) to pay an amount towards what remains to be paid,
that amount is required to be paid no later than that day.
(8) The court must not make an order under subsection (2) or (4) unless it gives the prosecutor an opportunity to make representations.
R v City of London JJs ex parte Chapman 1998 162 JP 359 The court should normally set a specific date by which the sum is to be paid.
Note: In calculating the time period, it is necessary to count the day the order was made, because that is the natural meaning of the words of the Act. For the application of the rule in a similar statutory provision (Extradition Act 2003 s 99(2)), see *R (Zaporozhchenko) v City of Westminster Magistrates' Court* 2011 EWHC 34 (Admin). The opposite method of calculating the days in confiscation proceedings is in Criminal Procedure Rules 2015 2015/1490 Rule 33.2. The provision in this paragraph is not under those rules. Ed.

Step 16 Consider ancillary orders

21.142 ***Step 16***
Step 16 Consider ancillary orders, e.g. costs, where the available amount is more than the confiscation order.

21.143 ***Step 16 Compensation, fines, forfeiture, victim surcharge and deprivation orders***
Confiscation and victim surcharge orders
Proceeds of Crime Act 2002 s 13(1) If the court makes a confiscation order it must proceed as mentioned in subsections (2) and (4) in respect of the offence or offences concerned.
(2) The court must take account of the confiscation order before:
(a) it imposes a fine on the defendant, or
(b) it makes an order falling within subsection (3).
(3) These orders fall within this subsection:
(a) an order involving payment by the defendant, other than an order under Prosecution of Offences Act 1985 s 21A (criminal courts charge) or a priority order,
(b) an order under Misuse of Drugs Act 1971 s 27 (forfeiture orders),
(c) an order under Powers of Criminal Courts (Sentencing) Act 2000 s 143 (deprivation orders),
(d) an order under Terrorism Act 2000 s 23 or 23A (forfeiture orders).
(3A) In this section 'priority order' means any of the following:[420]
(a) a compensation order under Powers of Criminal Courts (Sentencing) Act 2000 s 130,
(b) an order requiring payment of a surcharge under Criminal Justice Act 2003 s 161A,
(c) an unlawful profit order under Prevention of Social Housing Fraud Act 2013 s 4,
(d) a slavery and trafficking reparation order under Modern Slavery Act 2015 s 8.[421]

[420] This subsection was inserted by Serious Crime Act 2015 s 6(3). In force 1/6/15
[421] Inserted on 17/3/16 by Modern Slavery Act 2015 Sch 5 para 15. Modern Slavery Act 2015 (Consequential Amendments) Regulations 2016/244 substituted a new Schedule 5 para 15 on 25/2/16.

(4) Subject to subsection (2), the court must leave the confiscation order out of account in deciding the appropriate sentence for the defendant.
(5) Subsection (6) applies if:

(a) the Crown Court makes both a confiscation order and an order for the payment of compensation under Powers of Criminal Courts (Sentencing) Act 2000 s 130 against the same person in the same proceedings, and

(b) the court believes he will not have sufficient means to satisfy both the orders in full.[422]

(6) In such a case the court must direct that so much of the amount payable under the priority order (or orders) as it specifies is to be paid out of any sums recovered under the confiscation order; and the amount it specifies must be the amount it believes will not be recoverable because of the insufficiency of the person's means.[423]

Effect of postponement

Proceeds of Crime Act 2002 s 15(1) If the court postpones proceedings under section 6 it may proceed to sentence the defendant for the offence (or any of the offences) concerned.

(2) In sentencing the defendant for the offence (or any of the offences) concerned in the postponement period the court must not:

(a) impose a fine on him,

(b) make an order falling within section 13(3) [forfeiture, deprivation or an order involving payment by the defendant],

(c) make an order for the payment of compensation under Powers of Criminal Courts (Sentencing) Act 2000 s 130, or

(ca) make an order for the payment of a surcharge under Criminal Justice Act 2003 s 161A,[424] or

(d) make an unlawful profit order under Prevention of Social Housing Fraud Act 2013 s 4.[425]

TICs and Totality Guideline 2012: Crown Court, see www.banksr.com Other Matters Guidelines tab page 16 (*Magistrates' Court Sentencing Guidelines Update March 2012* page 18p) A compensation order can be combined with a confiscation order where the amount that may be realised is sufficient. If such an order is made, priority should be given to compensation.[426]

R v Williams 2001 1 Cr App R (S) 140 (p 500) D was convicted of building work frauds on elderly victims. The Judge said he wanted to strip D of every penny he had fraudulently received and made a confiscation and compensation order each for the full amount. Held. That course was entirely appropriate.

For the compensation order decision see **17.15**.

R v Paivarinta-Taylor 2010 EWCA Crim 28, 2 Cr App R (S) 64 (p 420) D was convicted of obtaining property by deception. Sentence was postponed. About a month later she was fined £1,000. Confiscation proceedings were postponed until about a month after that when the Judge made a confiscation order of about £35,560. The defence contended the failure to comply with the statute meant either the fine or the confiscation order should be quashed or both. Held. The authorities reached different conclusions. As the House of Lords made clear in *R v Soneji and Bullen* 2005 UKHL 49, 2006 1 Cr App R (S) 79 (p 430), the purpose of the sequence set out in section 71(1) of the 1988 Act is to ensure the effectiveness of the sentencing procedure overall, and the purpose behind section 72A(9) is to maintain the primacy of confiscation orders by prohibiting the Court from imposing a fine or other financial order until after the making of a confiscation order, even though the Court may impose other types of sentence or order before making

[422] As inserted by Serious Crime Act 2015 s 6(4)
[423] As amended by Serious Crime Act 2015 s 6(5)
[424] Serious Crime Act 2015 Sch 4 para 22. In force 1/6/15
[425] Subsection d) was inserted by Prevention of Social Housing Fraud Act 2013 Sch para 16(2).
[426] *R v Mitchell* 2001 Crim LR 239

a confiscation order. Sections 72(5) and 72(9A) are clearly further reflections of the same purposes. Parliament cannot be taken to have intended total invalidity. Parliament did not intend that the imposition of a fine before making a confiscation order should render the fine itself invalid, nor did it intend that the Court could no longer proceed to consider the making of a confiscation order, and nor did it intend that the resultant order should be invalid. Appeal dismissed.

R v Constantine 2010 EWCA Crim 2406 Section 13(2) and (3) means that the costs order cannot effectively be made until the court has determined all matters necessary for the confiscation.

R v Jawad 2013 EWCA Crim 644, 2014 1 Cr App R (S) 16 (p 85) D pleaded to a money laundering offence which was connected with frauds on Lloyds Bank. The Judge made a confiscation order and a compensation order rejecting an argument that that would be double counting. On appeal, D argued that his confiscation order was disproportionate in the light of *R v Waya* 2012 UKSC 51, 2013 2 Cr App R (S) 20 (p 87). Held. para 21 *R v Waya* 2012 requires the court to consider whether a Proceeds of Crime Act confiscation order is disproportionate. We are satisfied that it generally will be disproportionate if it will require the defendant to pay for a second time money which he has fully restored to the loser. If there is no additional benefit beyond that sum, any Proceeds of Crime Act confiscation order is likely to be disproportionate. If there is additional benefit, an order which double counts the sum which has been repaid is likely, to that extent, to be disproportionate, and an order for the lesser sum which excludes the double counting ought generally to be the right order. But, for the reasons explained, we do not agree that the mere fact that a compensation order is made for an outstanding sum due to the loser, and thus that that money may be restored, is enough to render disproportionate a Proceeds of Crime Act confiscation order which includes that sum. What will bring disproportion is the certainty of double payment. If it remains uncertain whether the loser will be repaid, a Proceeds of Crime Act confiscation order which includes the sum in question will not ordinarily be disproportionate.

R v Firmager 2013 EWCA Crim 2756 D was sentenced to 15 months' imprisonment and a compensation order. He appealed before the confiscation hearing. Held. The compensation order was unlawful because it was premature. Order quashed.

R v Beaumont 2014 EWCA Crim 1664, 2015 1 Cr App R (S) 1 (p 1) D pleaded to two counts of fraud. She assisted in a fraud on a company. The confiscation order of just over £17,500, which was the money she had received, was agreed. The Judge made an identical compensation order. Held. Applying *R v Morgan and Bygrave* 2008 EWCA Crim 1323, 2009 1 Cr App R (S) 60 (p 333), as the only way of satisfying the order is through the sale of the matrimonial home, we order the compensation order to be paid from the confiscation order sum.

R v Davenport 2015 EWCA Crim 1731, 2016 1 Cr App R (S) 41 (p 248) D was convicted of conspiracy to defraud. He ran companies which purported to offer finance but in fact just extracted fees from the victims. The benefit was agreed at £12m. The available amount was about £13.94m. The Judge made a confiscation order for £12m and a compensation order for £1.94m, the difference between the two amounts. The defence said that was disproportionate. Held. [The Judge had failed to properly apply] the principles in *R v Waya* 2012 and *R v Jawad* 2013. The confiscation order was disproportionate. para 66 One of the essential points of *R v Jawad* 2013 is that restitution to the victims must be 'assured' or 'certain'. The making of a compensation order does not in itself ensure restitution. Moreover, the availability of (ostensibly) sufficient assets may not necessarily give such assurance: for example, those (not infrequent) cases where the defendant is adjudged to have hidden assets but where their whereabouts are unknown and their nature nebulous. Further, Micawberish promises of 'money tomorrow' will, as Jawad makes clear, likely be disregarded. But here D had assets [with the

sale of a property more than the Judge had estimated]. The Judge had given too much weight to what defence counsel called 'a temporal requirement' and insufficient weight to the reality of forthcoming restitution in full. We quash the order.
para 75 Where the Crown seeks both a compensation order and a confiscation order in circumstances where sections 13(5) and (6) are not applicable, we think that judges may wish, irrespective of whether or not they are proceeding under section 6(6), to bear in mind the following points:

(1) The Court is empowered to make both a confiscation order and a compensation order.

(2) However, the court should be alert to any risk of double counting inherent in such a combination of orders and should be alert to the risk of making a confiscation order which is disproportionate.

(3) The court ordinarily should not make both a compensation order and a confiscation order representing the full amount of the benefit where there has been actual restitution to the victims prior to the date of the confiscation hearing, see *R v Waya* 2012 and *R v Jawad* 2013.

(4) Where it is asserted by a defendant that there will be restitution made after the date of the hearing, the court should scrutinise very carefully and critically the evidence and arguments raised in support of such assertion.

(5) If the court remains uncertain whether the victims will be repaid under the compensation order, a confiscation order which includes that amount will not ordinarily be disproportionate, see *R v Jawad* 2013.

(6) However, mathematical certainty of restitution is not required. The court should approach matters in a practical and realistic way in deciding whether restitution is assured.

(7) Restitution to the victims in the future is capable of being properly assessed as assured, depending on the particular circumstances, notwithstanding that such restitution will not be immediate, or almost immediate, at the time of the confiscation hearing. Obviously the longer the time frame the greater force there will be to an argument that restitution is not assured: but a prospective period of delay in realisation is not of itself necessarily a conclusive reason for proceeding to make a combination of such orders without adjusting the amount of the confiscation order.

(8) Whilst a defendant who is truly intent on making restitution in full to his victims ordinarily should be expected to have arranged such restitution prior to the date of the confiscation hearing, there may sometimes be cases where that is not possible. If, in such a case, the court has firm and evidence-based grounds for believing that restitution may nevertheless be forthcoming, albeit that cannot be taken as 'assured' at the time of the hearing, the court has power in its discretion to order an adjournment to enable matters to be ascertained.

R v Guraj 2016 UKSC 65, 2017 1 Cr App R (S) 32 (p 261) Supreme Court The forfeiture order was wrongly made at the beginning and procedure went to sleep for about 18 months. The Court of Appeal quash the confiscation order. Held. para 11 Section 15(2) is in many cases counter-intuitive, and creates a trap into which even the most experienced and skilled trial judges may fall. That is because many forfeiture orders will not be in the least controversial and are inevitable whatever the outcome of confiscation proceedings may be, like the forfeiture of the drugs in this case. Sections 14(11) and (12) are confined to the case of procedural error 'connected with the application for or the granting of a postponement'. They have no application to any other kind of procedural error. Confiscation order restored, see **21.28**.

R v Sachan 2018 EWCA Crim 2592 D pleaded to fraud. In his basis of plea, D promised to pay £51,450 in confiscation. He was sentenced to 3 years 3 months and ordered to pay the promised amount in compensation. It was known that confiscation proceedings would follow. Over 18 months later, a confiscation order was made for nearly £19,000. The prosecution asked for it to be paid in compensation and it was. D appealed the

second confiscation order, which was refused. He than applied to appeal the first compensation order. The defence said the first order was unlawful, because of section 72A(9), so it should be quashed. Held. para 16 Parliament did not intend that non-compliance with section 15(2) would render a compensation order invalid because a [premature] compensation order was made. There was no reason to set the order aside or vary it. The Crown has undertaken not to enforce more than the £51,450.
See also: *R v Donohoe* 2006 EWCA Crim 2200, 2007 1 Cr App R (S) 88 (p 548) (In a supply case, the Judge passed a 5-year sentence and a forfeiture order for the drugs. Confiscation was postponed. The breach of section 15(2) did not prohibit the Court from making a confiscation order.)

21.144 ***Step 16 Custody, Combined with***
Proceeds of Crime Act 2002 s 13(4) The court shall leave the confiscation order out of account in determining the appropriate sentence (except for fines, drug forfeiture orders and Deprivation Orders etc.[427]).
R v Rogers 2001 EWCA Crim 1680, 2002 1 Cr App R (S) 81 (p 338). The decision in *R v Andrews* 1997 1 Cr App R (S) 279 was without reference to section 72(5) (the repealed but similar Criminal Justice Act 1988 section. Ed.) and the court cannot reduce a custodial sentence because of the confiscation order.
For custody and prison in default terms see the ***Step 17 Prison in default terms and determinate terms*** para at **21.147**.

Step 17 Make a prison in default order

21.145 ***Step 17 Prison in default orders***
Step 17 Make a prison in default order unless the sum has already been paid.
Note: The judge must fix a term of imprisonment to be served in default of payment. The periods are set out at **58.50**. Ed.
Children and young offenders For offenders aged 18-20, the court fixes a detention in default order, not a prison in default order, see Proceeds of Crime Act 2002 s 35(2A) applying Powers of Criminal Courts (Sentencing) Act 2000 s 139(2).
Appeals The prosecution cannot appeal a prison in default order, *R v Mills* 2018 EWCA Crim 944, 2 Cr App R (S) 32 (p 231).
R v Ellis 1996 2 Cr App R (S) 403 A confiscation order and a prison in default order are two separate orders. Failure to make a prison in default order does not invalidate a confiscation order.
R v Castillo 2011 EWCA Crim 3173, 2012 2 Cr App R (S) 36 (p 201) D was convicted of conspiracy to cheat the public revenue and was sentenced to 10 years' imprisonment. The conspiracy in question was a massive missing trader intra-community fraud which ran from May 2001 to August 2003. It involved trade in mobile phones purchased VAT-free in other member states of the EU, engineered to make bogus claims for the refund of millions of pounds of VAT. The estimated loss was over £250 million. The investigation led to 45 arrests; 96 sets of premises were searched; 260 computers and 500,000 documents were seized. 529 trading chains were identified. D lived in Barcelona and over £300m went through his company's bank accounts. He was at the centre of the fraud. In the confiscation proceedings under Criminal Justice Act 1988, the benefit figure was agreed at over £30m. The Judge was satisfied that D's minimum profit was £4 million and that there were £3m hidden assets. He made a £3m confiscation order. The Judge heard submissions on the appropriate sentence in default and said, "D's approach has been, for all material purposes, wholly untruthful and it is plain to me that the present purpose of his untruthfulness is to preserve his remaining criminal assets of at least £3 million." The Judge made a confiscation order for £3 million with 10 years' imprisonment consecutive in default.
The principles are:

[427] For details of the limited exceptions, see Proceeds of Crime Act 2002 s 13(2) and (3).

(1) All the circumstances of the case have to be considered.
(2) The purpose of the default term is to secure payment of the confiscation order.
(3) It is not the court's function to find an arithmetical match between the amount of the order and the length of the term. For any given band or bracket prescribed in the statute an order at the bottom of the band should attract a default term[428] at the bottom of the band, an order in the middle of the band should attract a term in the middle or an order at the top should attract a term at the top.
(4) The court is not to be influenced by the overall totality of the sentence passed for the crime plus the default term.
(5) But for any given band the court should have regard to the maxima: the maximum amount of a confiscation order within the band and the maximum default term within the band.
(6) Given principle 5, and especially in a case such as this falling within the top band where there is no maximum confiscation order but only a maximum default term, regard must be had to the requirement of proportionality. Thus in *R v Whiteway-Wilkinson* 2010 EWCA Crim 35 the court accepted at para 19 that for a confiscation order of £2-3m a default term of 7-8 years would have been appropriate.

The requirement of proportionality has to be respected, but bearing in mind the purpose is to secure payment. Therefore the demands of proportionality are much weaker than where the court is punishing the offender. Its first condition is effectiveness. However, proportionality commands some attention especially in the top bracket where there is no maximum amount for the confiscation order. A sum of £2-3m is not far above the top bracket's floor of £1 million when one considers that the same bracket would contain an order for, say, £100 million. In setting the default term for an order of £2-3m, some heed should be paid to the fact that the maximum would be the same for an order five times as great or more; and consideration should be given to fixing a somewhat shorter period, otherwise the court's process looks and therefore is capricious and unjust. But in this context proportionality does not define the right order. It merely adjusts what would otherwise be a wrong one. In *R v Whiteway-Wilkinson* 2010 EWCA Crim 35 a default term of 10 years was reduced to 8 for a confiscation order of about £2.1m. The effect of the proportionality principle, although it needs to be respected, is very weak in this case but **9 years** not 10.

R v Hussain 2014 EWCA Crim 1181 The Court reduced a confiscation order to below the sum already paid by the defendant. Held. The Act does not require a prison in default term to be made where there is no question of the State not having had [the] penalty met in full.

21.146 *Step 17 Default periods Maximum terms and appropriate length*

Default sentences

Proceeds of Crime Act 2002 s 35(2A)[429] Where a court is fixing a term of imprisonment or detention under the [Powers of Criminal Courts (Sentencing) Act 2000 s 139(2)] (as applied by subsection (2) above) in respect of an amount ordered to be paid under a confiscation order, the maximum terms are those specified in the second column of the Table for amounts described in the corresponding entry in the first column.

Amount	Maximum term
£10,000 or less	6 months
More than £10,000 but no more than £500,000	5 years
More than £500,000 but no more than £1m	7 years
More than £1m	14 years

[428] To assist the reader, the grammar has been tidied up.
[429] As inserted by Serious Crime Act 2015 s 10. In force 1/6/15

R v Morrisey 2019 EWCA Crim 244 D pleaded to benefit fraud. The Judge gave him a 16-month suspended sentence and made a confiscation for just over £69,000 with just over £27,000 of it payable to the victim, Brighton and Hove Council. She made a 5-year default term. The defence said the length was outside the appropriate range. Held. The court has a discretion up to the maximum amount. The term will fall between the maximum amount and that at the top of the lower band, in this case 6 months. The court has to consider all the circumstances and is not bound to follow an arithmetical approach. It must have particular regard to the purpose of the imposition of a period of imprisonment in default, which is to secure the payment of the amount ordered. The Judge was entitled, indeed obliged, to take into account the circumstances of D's offending and his subsequent behaviour. It was a sophisticated fraud over many years. He had concealed his ownership of a property in Ireland during the course of the confiscation proceedings and had transferred it into his daughter's name after the sentence. The only inference was that he was trying to ensure that it was not seen as his asset in the proceedings. We note that 7 months on, this confiscation order has not been paid. **4 years** substituted.

See also: *R v Pettitt* 2010 EWCA Crim 1884,

R v Young 2011 EWCA Crim 1176.

R v Laval 2017 EWCA Crim 883 (About £72,000 to be paid over 5 years. The single Judge said, "It was not a precise arithmetical exercise, but a term towards the lower end of the bracket may often be appropriate for an amount towards the lower end. A factor is the need to make it clear that nothing will be gained by a failure to pay. A balancing exercise was required." We agree. 3 years not 5.)

Old cases: *R v Szrajber* 1994 15 Cr App R (S) 821, *R v French* 1995 16 Cr App R (S) 841, *R v Cox* 2008 EWCA Crim 3007 (Order of just over of £400,000. Seriousness of the offending is not a factor, so 4 years not 5.) *R v Smith* 2009 EWCA Crim 344, *R v Pigott* 2009 EWCA Crim 2292, 2010 2 Cr App R (S) 16 (p 91) (Order of just short of £1.5m. Because there were orders greatly exceeding this amount it should be less than the maximum, so 8 years not 10.)

21.147 ***Step 17 Prison in default terms and determinate terms***

Proceeds of Crime Act 2002 s 38(2) [Where a warrant committing the defendant to prison or detention is issued for a default in payment] the term of imprisonment or of detention under [Powers of Criminal Courts (Sentencing) Act 2000 s 108] (detention of persons aged 18-20 for default) to be served in default of payment of the amount does not begin to run until after the term mentioned in subsection (1)(b) above.

PSI 16/2010[430] para 2.7 Early release on a warrant of commitment in default of payment on a confiscation order. Such terms cannot form part of a single term or be aggregated with a sentence of imprisonment. They are always ordered to run consecutively and so will commence on the day after the last custodial day of the sentence of imprisonment.

R v Pigott 2009 EWCA Crim 2292, 2010 2 Cr App R (S) 16 (p 91) D pleaded to cheating the public revenue and was sentenced to 8 years' imprisonment. He was ordered to pay a £1.4m confiscation order with a 10-year prison in default term. D challenged the prison in default term. Held. In determining the default sentence, the Judge was entitled to take into account what she had learnt of D's offending during the trial. However, she should also have borne in mind the 10-year term was also applicable to an amount of money greatly exceeding D's. The appropriate term was 8 years.

R v Price 2009 EWCA Crim 2918, 2010 2 Cr App R (S) 44 (p 283) D was convicted of importing cocaine. He was sentenced to 28 years' imprisonment and a 10-year prison in default term for his confiscation order. D was aged 64. In 1997, he suffered a stroke and was now suffering from multiple sclerosis. It was argued no one should receive 38 years for D's offence and the principles of totality should be considered. Held. The purpose of default terms was that individuals should pay the sum owing. The decision to pay is the

[430] Prison Service Instructions, see www.banksr.com Other Matters Other Documents tab

defendant's choice. If totality applied it would undermine the purpose of ordering prison in default terms. With the benefit of fresh reports we can reduce the 28 years which was appropriate to 25 years. The 10-year term is upheld.

R v Aspinwell 2010 EWCA Crim 1294, 2011 1 Cr App R (S) 54 (p 346) D pleaded to money laundering offences. He deceived old people by selling them equipment for their burglar alarms that wasn't needed and was at a vastly inflated price. D paid the cheques into the bank. A confiscation order for £297,600 was made with a 3-year prison in default term. The Judge considered there were hidden assets. D, who was aged 78, appealed his 12-month sentence. In February 2008, considering his ill-health and with mercy, the Court of Appeal reduced his sentence to 9 months and suspended it. In 2010, one doctor assessed his life expectancy as around 4½ years and another doctor at 1-2 years. Reports indicated his current health condition could be managed in prison. Held. The purpose of prison in default is not to punish but to secure payment, *R v Price* 2009 applied. We are bound to assume there are sums available.

Step 18 The Judge must consider making a compliance order

21.148 *Step 18*

Step 18 Must consider making a compliance order

Note: A compliance order was created by the Serious Crime Act 2015 s 7, which inserted Proceeds of Crime Act 2002 s 13A. The section came into force on 1 June 2015. The court is obliged to consider making an order but it is not a mandatory order.

Orders for securing compliance with confiscation order

Proceeds of Crime Act 2002 s 13A[431]

(1) This section applies where the court makes a confiscation order.

(2) The court may make such order as it believes is appropriate for the purpose of ensuring that the confiscation order is effective (a "compliance order").

(3) The court must consider whether to make a compliance order:

(a) on the making of the confiscation order, and

(b) if it does not make a compliance order then, at any later time (while the confiscation order is still in effect) on the application of the prosecutor.

(4) In considering whether to make a compliance order, the court must, in particular, consider whether any restriction or prohibition on the defendant's travel outside the United Kingdom ought to be imposed for the purpose mentioned in subsection (2).

(5) The court may discharge or vary a compliance order on an application made by:

(a) the prosecutor;

(b) any person affected by the order.

R v Pritchard 2017 EWCA Crim 1267, 2 Cr App R (S) 54 D's confiscation order was for about £93,000. The benefit figure was about £246,240. D had lived in Spain until 2011. His ex-wife and his two non-dependent daughters lived there. The Judge found £88,920 worth of hidden assets. The Judge made a compliance order which ordered a travel[432] restriction order, which prohibited D from leaving the UK and made him surrender his passports etc. Held. para 20 The Act says the order is made not when 'it is necessary' but when the court 'believes it is appropriate' to ensure that the confiscation order is effective. para 25 The word 'appropriate' does not require any gloss. However, the making of the order must be justified. Such an order therefore can only be made if there is proper reason for so doing. Proportionality must be involved in the decision-making process. A travel restriction involves a restriction on freedom of movement, an important right in itself. The court has to strike a balance between the need to ensure that the confiscation order in question is effective and the risk of that confiscation order being rendered ineffective if no travel restriction is made, on the one hand, and the impact upon the individual defendant if a travel restriction is made, on the other hand. Here the decision to make the order was unassailable. The order was indefinite in time. Those

[431] Inserted by Serious Crime Act 2015 s 7. In force 1/6/2017

[432] The judgment says the Judge made a traffic restriction order. I assume that was a typo.

orders should be considered the exception rather than the rule. The circumstances to consider on deciding the length are, amongst others, the length of time of the custodial sentence to be served and what is a reasonable period of time to ensure enforcement and to ensure the effectiveness of the confiscation order. In all such orders where made it would be good practice expressly to write in that the travel restriction will expire on satisfaction in full of the confiscation order in question and to refer also to the liberty to apply to vary or discharge and vary the length of the order.

Sentencing remarks and appeals

21.149 ***Reasons, Judge must give/A judgment is essential***
R v Martin and White 1998 Unreported 20/2/98 www.banksr.com Other Matters Other Documents tab M was convicted of alcohol duty evasion and VAT fraud. In confiscation proceedings the prosecution stated the profits amounted to £3.23m but were only able to identify assets of £1.1m. They therefore believed that monies had been salted away and asked for an order to be made for the full £3.23m. M did not give evidence but produced two accountant's reports. The Judge said she did not accept those figures and made the order £3.32m. Held. That appears a slip for £3.23m. We accept she did not explain her reasons for rejecting the criticisms in the reports. Therefore we must consider the material ourselves and exercise our own discretion. The defence made some modest inroads into the figure. We substitute £3m.
R v Summers 2008 EWCA Crim 872, 2 Cr App R (S) 101 (p 569) D contested his confiscation order and the Judge said in a short judgment, "I am not in a position to determine every item individually and make a ruling on each one. I have the information before me. D's evidence does not satisfy me that there are no hidden assets. On the other hand, I am unable to be more precise than to take an overall view of what he has kept back and hidden for himself. The combination of all the evidence that I have heard and read, together with the amounts listed, allows me to say that of the benefit of just over £11m the defendant has been able to satisfy me that £7m of that is no longer available to him in the form of realisable assets." Held. The ruling was defective in that it failed to indicate the basis, even in general terms, of how the Judge had reached the figures concerned and simply stating that he had taken all the evidence into account is no substitute for indicating, even if briefly, his conclusions and the basis on which those conclusions were reached including in this case the important figures of £7m and £4m.
R v Lowe 2009 EWCA Crim 194, 2 Cr App R (S) 81 (p 544) para 21 It is essential that the court hearing the proceedings finds and sets out all the relevant facts in its judgment, including the facts that are agreed before it. It is not always clear from the judgments given by the Crown Court what the facts were, on which issues arose and which issues were determined. As the task of the court hearing the confiscation proceedings is to apply the statutory provisions to the facts (as agreed or found), it is essential that the ruling (or judgment) sets out all the relevant facts, as agreed and as found.

21.150 ***Appeals***
Prosecution The prosecutor can appeal the order, Proceeds of Crime Act 2002 s 31. Guidance is at *Guide to Commencing Proceedings in the Court of Appeal 2018* section **D**.
For the court form, see www.banksr.com Other Matters Other Documents Forms.
The prosecution cannot appeal a prison in default order, *R v Mills* 2018 EWCA Crim 944, 2 Cr App R (S) 32 (p 231).
Court of Appeal The Court of Appeal's powers on an appeal are laid down by Proceeds of Crime Act 2002 s 32.
Power to make fresh assessment For an example of the Court of Appeal quashing a confiscation, and on a different date determining the facts, giving the defendant the opportunity of giving evidence and making a fresh confiscation, see *R v Middlecote* 2011 EWCA Crim 548.

21.151 ***Counsel's written work and the NG and respondent's notice forms***
R v Lowe 2009 EWCA Crim 194, 2 Cr App R (S) 81 (p 544) para 21 ii) Too many authorities are cited to courts. Advocates should bear the observations in *R v May* 2008 UKHL 28, 2009 1 Cr App R (S) 31 (p 162) House of Lords at para 48(4) (see **21.37**) clearly in mind before any authority is cited to the judge hearing the proceedings or in this Court. We were provided with a large bundle of authorities which were unnecessary.
Note: There is a confiscation NG form and a respondent's notice form to be used from 1 October 2018, see www.banksr.com Other Matters Other Documents Forms. Ed.

21.152 ***Appeals after a change in the case law***
R v Jawad 2013 EWCA Crim 644, 2014 1 Cr App R (S) 16 (p 85) D argued that his confiscation order was disproportionate in the light of *R v Waya* 2012 UKSC 51, 2013 2 Cr App R (S) 20 (p 87). The Court considered the principles in granting leave out of time. Held. *Obiter* para 29 We should make clear the general approach of this Court, over many years, to change of law cases. An extension of time will not be granted routinely in such a case simply because the law has changed. It will be granted only if substantial injustice would otherwise be done to the defendant, and the mere fact of change of law does not ordinarily create such injustice. Nor is the case where an extension will be refused limited to one where, if the law had been correctly understood at the time of the proceedings in the Crown Court, a different charge or different procedure might well have left the defendant in a similar position to that in which he now finds himself. The line of authority setting out this Court's approach culminates in *R v Cottrell and Fletcher* 2007 EWCA Crim 2016, 2008 1 Cr App R 7 (p 107). The line of authority includes similar pronouncements in *R v Mitchell* 1977 65 Cr App R 185, *R v Ramsden* 1972 Crim LR 547 and *R v Gosney* 1971 55 Cr App R 502. (All conviction cases. Ed.) The Court [in *R v Cottrell and Fletcher*] observed that alarming consequences would flow from permitting the general reopening of old cases on the ground that a decision of a court of authority had removed a widely held misconception as to the prior state of the law on which the conviction which it was sought to appeal had been based. para 28 and 30 Here only an extension of a few days was required. In the event, D did not require an extension of time. We doubt very much that if an extension of time had been required in the present case, we should have granted it.
para 31 The principle of finality that decisions made under the law as it was then understood should not be disturbed unless substantial injustice would follow is well recognised and we must apply it. The relevant date is the date of the confiscation order and not of the enforcement proceedings. Within the criminal jurisdiction, the enforcement proceedings and their consequences are a relevant factor in a consideration whether a substantial injustice might follow should an extension of time be refused. So, also, is the availability of an application to the Crown Court under section 23. In particular, where the 'available amount' is represented by the value of the very property which the tainted loans enabled the applicant to acquire, it must follow that when at the enforcement stage it is known that the property is subject to a charge in favour of the lender, that charge must be brought into account so as to reduce the available amount if it has not already been considered. Equally, if the market value of the property has decreased since the making of a confiscation order based on the market value of the property, section 23 would enable the Crown Court to reflect that fact. Where, however, as a result of an erroneous assessment of benefit, a defendant has been required to meet a confiscation order from assets which can be clearly demonstrated to be untainted, the availability of the section 23 application may not, in our view, act to ameliorate the stringency of the principle.
R v Chapman 2013 EWCA Crim 1370 The defence submitted their grounds of appeal. The Supreme Court then gave its judgment in *R v Waya* 2012 UKSC 51, 2013 2 Cr App R (S) 20 (p 87). The defence then sought to amend their grounds. It was agreed that applying the principles of *R v Waya* 2012 the benefit should have been just over

£1,557,800 and not nearly £2,535,400 as the Judge found. The prosecution opposed the appeal because of the need for finality and the fact that even if the benefit figure was reduced it would have no effect on the actual confiscation amount, which was just over £152,100. Held. None of the original grounds had merit but the appeal notice was within the prescribed time. para 24 A distinction has to be drawn between that and where a notice was not filed in time. There is a public interest in not allowing final decisions to be reopened, except where necessary to avoid substantial injustice. Once an appeal has been constituted, however, either by filing a notice of appeal in time or by obtaining an extension of time from the court, the order of the court below, although not formally provisional, is subject to review. In practical terms it is not final and there is no comparable public interest in refusing to reopen it, since that is the very purpose of the appeal procedure. For the court to refuse to allow an appellant to take advantage of a change in the law occurring between the date of the order below and the filing of the notice of appeal would be inconsistent with the appeal process; but if that is so, it is difficult to see how it could justify refusing to allow him to take advantage of a change in the law occurring between the filing of the notice of appeal and the hearing itself. This approach is borne out by the observations of the court in *R v Jawad* 2013. Here the principle of finality did not apply. We therefore substitute the correct benefit figure.
See also: *R v Bestel and Others* 2013 EWCA Crim 1305, 2014 1 Cr App R (S) 53 (p 312) at **4.14**.

21.153 ***Appeals Power of Court of Appeal to remit case back to the Crown Court***
Criminal Appeal Act 1968 s 11(3A) Where the Court of Appeal exercise their power under paragraph (a) of subsection (3) (power to quash a sentence or order. Ed.) to quash a confiscation order, the Court may, instead of proceeding under paragraph (b) of that subsection, direct the Crown Court to proceed afresh under the relevant enactment.
(3B) When proceeding afresh pursuant to subsection (3A), the Crown Court shall comply with any directions the Court of Appeal may make.
(3C) The Court of Appeal shall exercise the power to give such directions so as to ensure that any confiscation order made in respect of the appellant by the Crown Court does not deal more severely with the appellant than the order quashed under subsection (3)(a).
See also: *R v Adams* 2014 EWCA Crim 2926.
R v Jaffery 2016 EWCA Crim 287 (The Court of Appeal quashed a confiscation order and the Crown Court made another one. The defence then argued that the new confiscation order was made outside the 2-year period and there was no postponement order, so the order was a nullity. Held. It wasn't. *R v Iqbal* 2010 EWCA Crim 376, 2 Cr App R (S) 72 (p 470) only applies where an application to postpone confiscation proceedings had been made. No such application had been made.)
Note: As the Court was rightly keen to point out, if the defence was right it would be absurd. When the Court of Appeal quashed the confiscation order it exercised its powers under Criminal Appeal Act 1968 s 11(3A) (see **21.153**) and ordered the proceedings to start afresh. The time limits therefore don't apply because they only apply when the sentencing Judge postpones the hearing. Ed.

21.154 ***Appeals Defendant claims agreed assets/figures are wrong***
R v Hirani 2008 EWCA Crim 1463 D pleaded to cheating the public revenue involving a £185,000 benefit fraud. The benefit figure was assessed as £161,023. D claimed, partly because of his divorce, that he had very few or no assets. There was significant evidence to disprove that. At court, D signed a document to his legal team agreeing the benefit figure and a £110,000 realisable figure. A memorandum of agreement was then signed by prosecution and defence counsel containing those figures. The Judge then made a confiscation order based on those figures. D paid no money. Two years later enforcement proceedings began. D appealed the order and waived privilege claiming that he was told he could avoid prison by saying he had inadequate funds. He said he was wrongly advised. Held. In other jurisdictions consent orders may be set aside on very narrow

grounds. We do not exclude the possibility in confiscation proceedings that such circumstances might conceivably arise. They do not arise when the essence of the complaint is that in seeking the best deal available, erroneous advice was given, save in the most exceptional circumstances. The whole process would need to be unfair. This case does not come close to that. Counsel's assessment of D's prospect of success (namely he was unlikely to be believed) was accurate.

R v Yew 2013 EWCA Crim 809 D contested his confiscation order. The defence provided a copy of the Land Registry's copy of title which showed the registered owners of a property were D and his wife. Both counsel agreed the value of a property without considering D's wife's interest. D appealed and D's solicitor said that was a mistake on their part. The prosecution conceded the interest should have been taken into account. Held. We reduce the value of the property.

R v Mackle and Others 2014 UKSC 5, 2014 2 Cr App R (S) 33 (p 265) Supreme Court D and others consented to a confiscation order in a tobacco smuggling case. Later it was discovered that the order was based on a false belief of their liability for duty. D and the others appealed and the Court of Appeal in Northern Ireland said the defendants were bound by their consent. Held. para 48 We apply *R v Emmett* 1998 AC 773 and *R v Bell* 2011 EWCA Crim 6. para 50 A defendant's consent could not confer jurisdiction to make a confiscation order. para 54 A defendant is not precluded from appealing a confiscation order made by consent when the consent was based on a mistake of law or wrong legal advice.

R v Yaxley-Lennon 2018 EWCA Crim 244, 2 Cr App R (S) 23 (p 214) D pleaded to two mortgage frauds. In confiscation proceedings, his counsel agreed a £125,000 benefit figure, but argued the proposed order was disproportionate. The Judge and the single Judge rejected that argument. Two years later, new counsel sought to renew the appeal saying the benefit figure was £30,000 too much. The new prosecution counsel conceded that the correct approach had not been adopted in the confiscation procedure. Held. This court will not readily depart from agreements as to benefit and realised assets by properly advised and experienced counsel. We do not accept that a substantial injustice would be caused by refusing to extend the time limits. Substantial injustice is not judged just by the amount of money in issue. The fact the rents obtained were not included in the benefit figure reinforces our view that the application for an extension of time needs to be refused.

R v Yaqob 2018 EWCA Crim 1728 D pleaded to supplying class A drugs as a courier. The case was adjourned. The prosecution said there was a £200,000 benefit. D had a new counsel who thought that that figure had been agreed. The figure was formally agreed. Held. It is only in very exceptional circumstances that this Court will go back on an agreed figure. However, here the prosecution say the figure was wrong, it should not have been agreed and the appropriate figure is what the defence say it is. There are exceptional circumstances, so we substitute £2,000, the correct figure.

See also: *R v Ayankoya* 2011 EWCA Crim 1488 (*R v Hirani* 2008 applied. Agreed figure. Defendant misled or may have been misled about the possibility of having an adjournment. Documents indicate there was force in some of the defendant's concerns. It was wholly exceptional, so order varied.)

21.155 ***Appeals Fresh evidence***

R v Halliday 2014 EWCA Crim 620 D pleaded to Tax Credit fraud (×5). The prosecution said D had fraudulently misstated her income on application forms for mortgages. On appeal, D sought to adduce fresh evidence that was available at the Crown Court and which contradicted a concession made by defence counsel. The Court heard from six witnesses including the defendant, witnesses from the mortgage companies and the then defence counsel. Held. The fresh evidence is admitted as it clearly goes towards establishing whether or not the mortgage advances would have been as a result of

'general criminal conduct'. On the balance of probabilities, the assumption that D obtained criminal benefit from the mortgage advances is incorrect and there is a serious risk of injustice to D, if any such assumption was made. Confiscation order reduced.
R v Kelly 2016 EWCA Crim 1505 D appealed his confiscation order and sought to admit in evidence some bank statements and some information about loans. The defence contended the material was not fresh evidence. Held. An application to admit the evidence was necessary. The Court may admit evidence if it thinks it is necessary or expedient in the interests of justice to admit it. It wasn't either here. The documents were not sent to the Court or the prosecution until last week. The prosecution has had no opportunity to consider them properly. It would not be proper to adjourn the matter. Application refused. Appeal dismissed.
See also the **APPEALS: COURT OF APPEAL** ***Fresh evidence*** paras at **4.26**.

21.156 ***Appeals Conflict between Crown Court and High Court***
R v Hackett 2013 EWCA Crim 1273 D pleaded to two counts of duty evasion. In confiscation proceedings, the Judge found that there were further trips to France to avoid duty. She made a confiscation order for just over £645,000. D appealed and his appeal was dismissed. The prosecutor applied for a receiver to be appointed. The Judge heard new evidence and the prosecution conceded that records were kept of journeys across the Channel and there was no evidence to support the Judge's assertion. The application was dismissed with costs. With consent the High Court issued a certificate of inadequacy and the realisable property was assessed at £425,000.[433] Meanwhile D had paid over £0.5m. He could not recover the overpayment from the Crown Court. The CCRC referred the case to the Court of Appeal. Held. The conflict between the two courts cannot be allowed to persist. We allow the appeal. We give 28 days for the parties to agree the true figure.

21.157 ***Mistakes discovered after an appeal***
R v Powell 2016 EWCA Crim 1539 In 2008, D had his confiscation order reduced. In February 2012, he applied to the CCRC to refer the case back. They thought the appropriate remedy was to apply for a certificate of inadequacy. Although not agreeing with that advice, an application was made and it was refused. It was agreed that the realisable assets figure was nearly £22,900 too much. Held. The CCRC did not understand that the problem was with the confiscation order itself. The original order was in error. D faces a confiscation order with the wrong amount and interest added on the amount too. Unless we correct it there will be an injustice. Enough time and precious resources have already been spent on this issue. We must end this unhappy saga. Applying *R v Yasain* 2015 (see above), we correct the error.

Matters after an order has been made

Note: Almost all the matters that occur after the confiscation order is made are not listed, as this book deals with sentence and not recovery etc. Ed.

21.158 ***Interest on unpaid sums***
Interest on unpaid sums
Proceeds of Crime Act 2002 s 12(1) If any amount required to be paid by a person under a confiscation order is not paid when it is required to be paid, he must pay interest on the amount for that period for which it remains unpaid.[434]
(2) The rate of interest is the same rate as that for the time being specified in Judgments Act 1838 s 17 (interest on civil judgment debts).
(3) For the purposes of this section no amount is required to be paid under a confiscation order if:
 (a) an application has been made under section 11(4),
 (b) the application has not been determined by the court, and

[433] The figure in the judgment is £425,50.57, which is clearly a typo. Further, to make any sense, the benefit and not the realisable property would need to have been re-assessed.
[434] As amended by Serious Crime Act 2015 Sch 4 para 20. In force 1/6/15

(c) the period of 12 months starting with the day on which the confiscation order was made has not ended.
(4) In applying this Part the amount of the interest must be treated as part of the amount to be paid under the confiscation order.
Variation There is power to vary the order, Proceeds of Crime Act 2002 s 29.
Reconsideration The court may increase the order if, within six years from the date of the conviction, the prosecutor applies to the court to consider evidence which was not available at the relevant time, Proceeds of Crime Act 2002 s 21-22.
Discharge There is power to discharge the order, Proceeds of Crime Act 2002 s 30.

22 COSTS

22.1

Power to search There is a power to search 'a person' when a court is making etc. a costs order under Administration of Justice Act 1970 Sch 9 paras 3, 4 and 9 (orders for costs), Powers of Criminal Courts (Sentencing) Act 2000 s 142(1)-(2) and Magistrates' Courts Act 1980 s 80(1). For details see **58.15**.
This book does not deal with the following because they do not relate to sentence:
a) wasted costs order, Prosecution of Offences Act 1985 s 19A and Costs in Criminal Cases (General) Regulations 1986 1986/1335 reg 3A-3D, Practice Direction (Costs in Criminal Proceedings) 2015 EWCA Crim 1568 para 4.2, and
b) cost orders for unnecessary acts or omissions under Prosecution of Offences Act 1985 s 19(1) and Costs in Criminal Cases (General) Regs 1986 1986/1335 reg 3.
c) third party costs, Prosecution of Offences Act 1985 s 19B, Criminal Procedure Rules 2015 2015/1490 Rule 45.10, Costs in Criminal Cases (General) Regulations 1986 1986/1335 paras 3E-I and Practice Direction (Costs in Criminal Proceedings) 2015 EWCA Crim 1568 para 4.7.
See also the **INSTALMENTS, PAYMENT BY** chapter.
For ordering a parent to pay a costs order for their child, see the **CHILDREN AND YOUNG OFFENDERS: GENERAL PRINCIPLES Parents etc. paying fines etc.** section at **13.51**.

General matters

Note: This general matters section applies to all costs orders. Ed.

22.2 ***Making representations (in court and/or in writing)***

Criminal Procedure Rules 2015 2015/1490 Rule 45.2(1) The court must not make an order about costs unless each party and any other person directly affected:
(a) is present; or
(b) has had an opportunity:
(i) to attend, or
(ii) to make representations.
(2) The court may make an order about costs:
(a) at a hearing in public or in private; or
(b) without a hearing.

22.3 ***Test to apply***

Criminal Procedure Rules 2015 2015/1490 Rule 45.2(3) In deciding what order, if any, to make about costs, the court must have regard to all the circumstances, including:
(a) the conduct of all the parties; and
(b) any costs order already made.
(4) [see **22.5**]
(5) [see **22.6**]
(6) If the court makes an order for the payment of costs:
(a) the general rule is that it will be for an amount that is sufficient reasonably to compensate the recipient for costs:
(i) actually, reasonably and properly incurred, and
(ii) reasonable in amount.

b) [see **22.18**]
(7) [see next para]

22.4 ***Relevant factors when assessing costs***

Criminal Procedure Rules 2015 2015/1490 Rule 45.2(7) On an assessment of the amount of costs, relevant factors include:

(a) the conduct of all the parties,
(b) the particular complexity of the matter or the difficulty or novelty of the questions raised,
(c) the skill, effort, specialised knowledge and responsibility involved,
(d) the time spent on the case,
(e) the place where and the circumstances in which work or any part of it was done, and
(f) any direction or observations by the court that made the costs order.

22.5 ***Contents of the order***

Criminal Procedure Rules 2015 2015/1490 Rule 45.2(4) If the court makes an order about costs, it must:

(a) specify who must, or must not, pay what, to whom, and
(b) identify the legislation under which the order is made, where there is a choice of powers.

22.6 ***Duty to give reasons if application refused or representations rejected***

Criminal Procedure Rules 2015 2015/1490 Rule 45.2(5) The court must give reasons if it:

(a) refuses an application for a costs order, or
(b) rejects representations opposing a costs order.

22.7 ***Delegate the amount of costs, Can't***

Practice Direction (Costs in Criminal Proceedings) 2015 EWCA Crim 1568 para 1.2.4 Where the court is required to specify the amount of costs to be paid it cannot delegate the decision, but may require the appropriate officer of the court to make enquiries to inform the court as to the costs incurred, and may adjourn the proceedings for enquiries to be made if necessary.

22.8 ***When the order takes effect***

Criminal Procedure Rules 2015 2015/1490 Rule 45.2(9) An order for the payment of costs takes effect when the amount is assessed, unless the court exercises any power it has to order otherwise.

22.9 ***When can you apply?***

Note: In *Quayum v DPP* 2015 EWHC 1660 the Court of Appeal held that the Crown Court was right to refuse to make a wasted costs order two working days after a case was concluded. The reason was that Costs in Criminal Cases (General) Regulations 1986 1986/1335 Rule 3 provides that applications can be made 'at any time during criminal proceedings'. The same phrase does not appear in the regulations for other costs orders (as far as I can see). Ed.

Defendant's Costs Order (Central Funds)

22.10 ***Defendant's Costs Order Application for***

Criminal Procedure Rules 2015 2015/1490 Rule 45.4(4) Where a person wants the court to make an order that person must:

(a) apply as soon as practicable, and
(b) outline the type of costs and the amount claimed, if that person wants the court to direct an assessment, or
(c) specify the amount claimed, if that person wants the court to assess the amount itself.

Re Patel 2012 EWCA Crim 1508 In November 2007 D changed his plea following a legal ruling. In October 2009, the Court of Appeal quashed D's conviction (*R v Patel and*

Hussain 2009 EWCA Crim 2311) and D applied for costs. In January 2009, the Court granted a Defendant's Costs Order and his solicitors submitted a bill for about £3.5m. The determining officer asked for documents and it was discovered that in January 2007, D and his solicitors agreed to cap D's liability for profit costs at £275,000. In July 2008, D paid £275,000 to solicitors for fees and it was said 'there [was] no other payment outstanding'. In October 2009, a deed was drawn up which raised the original fee levels and removed the cap. No mention was made of this when counsel applied for costs. D in an affidavit said the cap was imposed for financial reasons and by March 2009, as the appeal was approaching, he was in a much better state and he wanted to recompense his solicitors at the standard commercial rate. Held. If we had known about the cap, its purported removal and the retrospective increase in fees, we would have been required either to determine the issue whether the applicant had properly incurred [extra] fees or direct the determining officer to consider the matter. para 36 We do not accept the argument that we have no jurisdiction to reconsider the application for a Defendant's Costs Order. Without needing to consider the 'exceptional circumstances' test under *Taylor v Lawrence* 2002 EWCA Civ 90, the solicitors failed (whether deliberately or otherwise) in their duty to make disclosure in an *ex parte* hearing of information solely within their own knowledge. Costs in Criminal Cases (General) Regulations 1986 1986/1335 reg 14(4) requires that, when making a claim, 'Where there are any special circumstances which should be drawn to the attention of the appropriate authority, the applicant shall specify them'. The solicitors failed to comply with this requirement. We draw the attention of the Registrar to this ruling and invite him to make such enquiries as he deems appropriate.

22.11 ***Defendant's Costs Order Application not necessary***
Criminal Procedure Rules 2015 2015/1490 Rule 45.4(3) The court may make an order:
(a) on application by the person who incurred the costs, or
(b) on its own initiative.

22.12 ***Defendant's Costs Order Power to order Supreme Court***
Prosecution of Offences Act 1985 s 16(5) Where…
(b) the Supreme Court determines an appeal, or application for leave to appeal, from such a Divisional Court in a criminal cause or matter,
(c) the Court of Appeal determines an application for leave to appeal to the Supreme Court under Criminal Appeal Act 1968 Part II, or
(d) the Supreme Court determines an appeal, or application for leave to appeal, under Part II of that Act,
the court may make a Defendant's Costs Order in favour of the accused.
Practice Direction (Costs in Criminal Proceedings) 2015 EWCA Crim 1568 para 2.4.2 On determining an application for leave to appeal to the Supreme Court under Criminal Appeal Act 1968 Part II, whether by prosecutor or by defendant, the court may make a defendant's costs order.
2.4.3 In considering whether to make such an order, the court will have in mind the principles applied by the Crown Court in relation to acquitted defendants (see para 2.2.1 and 2.2.2 (see **22.19**)).
Court of Appeal powers see the **APPEALS: COURT OF APPEAL** ***Costs Power to order*** para at **22.64**.

22.13 ***Defendant's Costs Order Power to order Crown Court***
Prosecution of Offences Act 1985 s 16(2) Where:
(a) any person is not tried for an offence for which he has been indicted or sent for trial, or
(aa) a notice of transfer is given under a relevant transfer provision but a person in relation to whose case it is given is not tried on a charge to which it relates, or
(b) any person is tried on indictment and acquitted on any count in the indictment,
the Crown Court may make a defendant's costs order in favour of the accused.

Prosecution of Offences Act 1985 s 16(12) In subsection (2)(aa) 'relevant transfer provision' means:
(a) Criminal Justice Act 1987 s 4, or
(b) Criminal Justice Act 1991 s 53.
Practice Direction (Costs in Criminal Proceedings) 2015 EWCA Crim 1568 para 2.2.4 In respect of proceedings in the Crown Court commenced on or after 1 October 2012, legal costs (sums paid for advocacy, litigation services or experts' fees) may only be allowed under a defendant's costs order to a defendant who is an individual and only 1) in respect of appeals against conviction or sentence from a Magistrates' Court; or 2) after 27 January 2014 in other relevant Crown Court proceedings provided that the Director of Legal Aid Casework has made a determination of financial ineligibility in relation to the defendant. The relevant proceedings are those in which the accused has been sent by a Magistrates' Court to the Crown Court for trial, where a bill of indictment has been preferred (under Administration of Justice (Miscellaneous Provisions) Act 1933 s 2(2)(b)) or following an order for a retrial made by the Court of Appeal or the Supreme Court. Where legal costs may be allowed, if the court fixes the amount to be paid under section 16(6C) of the Act it must calculate any amounts allowed in respect of legal costs in accordance with the rates and scales prescribed by the Lord Chancellor. If the court does not fix the amount of costs to be paid out of central funds, the costs will be determined by the appropriate authority in accordance with the General Regulations and any legal costs allowed will be calculated at the prescribed rates and scales.
Crown Court on Appeal powers see the **APPEALS: CROWN COURT** ***Costs Power to order*** para at **5.29**.

22.14 ***Defendant's Costs Order Power to order Magistrates' Court***
Prosecution of Offences Act 1985 s 16(1) Where:
(a) an information laid before a justice of the peace for any area, charging any person with an offence, is not proceeded with,
(b) a Magistrates' Court inquiring into an indictable offence as examining justices determines not to commit the accused for trial,
(c) a Magistrates' Court dealing summarily with an offence dismisses the information,
that court or, in a case falling within paragraph (a) above, a Magistrates' Court for that area may make an order in favour of the accused for a payment to be made out of central funds in respect of his costs (a 'defendant's costs order').
For ***Making representations (in court and/or in writing)***, see para **22.2**.
For ***Relevant factors when assessing costs***, see para **22.4**.

22.15 ***Defendant's Costs Order Test to apply***
Prosecution of Offences Act 1985 s 16(6) A defendant's costs order shall, subject to the following provisions of this section, be for the payment out of central funds, to the person in whose favour the order is made, of such amount as the court considers reasonably sufficient to compensate him for any expenses properly incurred by him in the proceedings.
Prosecution of Offences Act 1985 s 16(10) Subsection (6) above shall have effect, in relation to any case falling within subsection (1)(a) or (2)(a) above, as if for the words 'in the proceedings' there were substituted the words 'in or about the defence'.
Practice Direction (Costs in Criminal Proceedings) 2015 EWCA Crim 1568 para 1.3.1 Where a court orders that the costs of a defendant, appellant or private prosecutor should be paid from central funds, the order will be for such amount as the court considers sufficient reasonably to compensate the party for expenses incurred by him in the proceedings, unless the court considers that there are circumstances that make it inappropriate to allow the full amount, in which event it will allow such lesser sum as it considers just and reasonable. This will include the costs incurred in the proceedings in

the lower courts unless for good reason the court directs that such costs are not included in the order, but it cannot include expenses incurred which do not directly relate to the proceedings themselves, such as loss of earnings.
para 2.1.1 (for the Magistrates' Court) and 2.2.1 (for the Crown Court) Whether to make such an order is a matter in the discretion of the court in the light of the circumstances of each particular case. A Defendant's Costs Order should normally be made[435] unless there are positive reasons for not doing so, for example, where the defendant's own conduct has brought suspicion on himself and has misled the prosecution into thinking that the case against him was stronger than it was.
For the general test to apply see the ***Test to apply*** para at **22.3**.

22.16 ***Defendant's Costs Order Court may decline to make an order***
Criminal Procedure Rules 2015 2015/1490 Rule 45.4(5) The general rule is that the court must make an order, but:
(a) the court may decline to make a defendant's costs order if, for example:
(i) the defendant is convicted of at least one offence, or
(ii) the defendant's conduct led the prosecutor reasonably to think the prosecution case [was] stronger than it was, and
(b) the court may decline to make a prosecutor's costs order if, for example, the prosecution was started or continued unreasonably.
Prosecution of Offences Act 1985 s 16A(1)[436] A defendant's costs order may not require the payment out of central funds of an amount that includes an amount in respect of the accused's legal costs, subject to the following provisions of this section.
(2) Subsection (1) does not apply where condition A, B or C is met.
(3) Condition A is that the accused is an individual and the order is made under:
(a) section 16(1) (the power of the Magistrates' Court),
(b) section 16(3) (the power of the Crown Court on appeal), or
(c) section 16(4)(a)(ii) or (iii) or (d) (the power of the Court of Appeal).
(4) Condition B is that the accused is an individual and the legal costs were incurred in proceedings in a court below which were:
(a) proceedings in a Magistrates' Court, or
(b) proceedings on an appeal to the Crown Court under Magistrates' Courts Act 1980 s 108 (right of appeal against conviction or sentence).
(5) Condition C is that the legal costs were incurred in proceedings in the Supreme Court.
Prosecution of Offences Act 1985 s 16A(8)[437] Where a court makes a defendant's costs order requiring the payment out of central funds of an amount that includes an amount in respect of legal costs, the order must include a statement to that effect.
(9) Where, in a defendant's costs order, a court fixes an amount to be paid out of central funds that includes an amount in respect of legal costs incurred in proceedings in a court other than the Supreme Court, the latter amount must not exceed an amount specified by regulations made by the Lord Chancellor.

22.17 ***Defendant's Costs Order Refusal to order Court must explain there is no suggestion of guilt***
Practice Direction (Costs in Criminal Proceedings) 2015 EWCA Crim 1568 para 2.1.1 (for the Magistrates' Court) and 2.2.1 (for the Crown Court) The court when declining to

[435] In the Crown Court paragraph (2.2.1) there is inserted here, 'whether or not an order for costs between the parties is made'.
[436] As inserted by Legal Aid, Sentencing and Punishment of Offenders Act 2012 Sch 7 para 2. The Schedule was in force from 1/10/12, Legal Aid, Sentencing and Punishment of Offenders Act 2012 (Commencement No 2 and Specification of Commencement Date) Order 2012 2012/2412.
[437] As inserted by Legal Aid, Sentencing and Punishment of Offenders Act 2012 Sch 7 para 2. The Schedule was in force from 1/10/12, Legal Aid, Sentencing and Punishment of Offenders Act 2012 (Commencement No 2 and Specification of Commencement Date) Order 2012 2012/2412.

make a costs order should[438] explain, in open court, that the reason for not making an order does not involve any suggestion that the defendant is guilty of any criminal conduct but the order is refused because of the positive reason that should be identified.[439]

Minelli v Switzerland 1983 5 EHRR 554 The presumption of innocence will be violated if, without the accused having previously been proved guilty and notably without his having had the opportunity of exercising his rights of defence, a judicial decision concerning him reflects an opinion that he is guilty. This may be so in the absence of any formal finding. It suffices that there is some reasoning suggestive that the court regards the accused as guilty.

22.18 *Defendant's Costs Order Awarding partial costs*

Prosecution of Offences Act 1985 s 16(6A)[440] Where the court considers that there are circumstances that make it inappropriate for the accused to recover the full amount mentioned in subsection (6), a defendant's costs order must be for the payment out of central funds of such lesser amount as the court considers just and reasonable.

(6B) Subsections (6) and (6A) have effect subject to:

(a) section 16A, and

(b) regulations under section 20(1A)(d).

(6C) When making a defendant's costs order, the court must fix the amount to be paid out of central funds in the order if it considers it appropriate to do so and:

(a) the accused agrees the amount, or

(b) subsection (6A) applies.

(6D) Where the court does not fix the amount to be paid out of central funds in the order:

(a) it must describe in the order any reduction required under subsection (6A), and

(b) the amount must be fixed by means of a determination made by or on behalf of the court in accordance with procedures specified in regulations made by the Lord Chancellor.

Criminal Procedure Rules 2015 2015/1490 Rule 45.2(6) If the court makes an order for the payment of costs:

(a) the general rule is that it must be for an amount that is sufficient reasonably to compensate the recipient for costs:

(i) actually, reasonably and properly incurred, and

(ii) reasonable in amount; but

b) the court may order the payment of:

(i) a proportion of that amount,

(ii) a stated amount less than that amount,

(iii) costs from or until a certain date only,

(iv) costs relating only to particular steps taken, or

(v) costs relating only to a distinct part of the case.

Practice Direction (Costs in Criminal Proceedings) 2015 EWCA Crim 1568 para 2.1.1 Magistrates' Court Where the defendant has been acquitted on some counts but convicted on others the court may make an order that only part of the costs be paid, see paras 2.2.1 and 2.2.2 below. Where the court considers that it would be inappropriate that the defendant should recover all of the costs properly incurred, either the amount allowed must be specified in the order or the court may describe to the appropriate authority the reduction required.

---

438 Although the Practice Direction says 'should', judges will interpret this as meaning 'shall' rather than introducing 'best practice'.

439 *Hussain v UK* 2006 43 EHRR 22 (p 437)

440 As inserted by Legal Aid, Sentencing and Punishment of Offenders Act 2012 Sch 7 para 2 (in force from 1/10/12), Legal Aid, Sentencing and Punishment of Offenders Act 2012 (Commencement No 2 and Specification of Commencement Date) Order 2012 2012/2412

2.2.1 Crown Court Where the court considers that it would be inappropriate that the defendant should recover all of the costs properly incurred, either the lesser amount must be specified in the order, or the court must describe to the appropriate authority the reduction required.
2.2.2 Where a person is convicted of some count(s) in the indictment and acquitted on other(s) the court may exercise its discretion to make a defendant's costs order but may order that only a proportion of the costs incurred be paid. The court should make whatever order seems just having regard to the relative importance of the charges and the conduct of the parties generally. The proportion of costs allowed must be specified in the order.

22.19 ***Defendant's Costs Order*** ***Defendant acquitted/No trial took place***
Practice Direction (Costs in Criminal Proceedings) 2015 EWCA Crim 1568 para 2.2.1 Where a person is not tried for an offence for which he has been indicted, or in respect of which proceedings against him have been sent for trial or transferred for trial, or has been acquitted on any count in the indictment, the court may make a defendant's costs order in his favour. Whether to make such an order is a matter for the discretion of the court in the light of the circumstances of the particular case. A defendant's costs order should normally be made whether or not an order for costs between the parties is made, unless there are positive reasons for not doing so, for example, where the defendant's own conduct has brought suspicion on himself and has misled the prosecution into thinking that the case against him was stronger than it was. The court when declining to make a costs order should explain, in open court, that the reason for not making an order does not involve any suggestion that the defendant is guilty of any criminal conduct but the order is refused because of the positive reason that should be identified.[441]
2.2.2 Where a person is convicted of some count(s) in the indictment and acquitted on other(s) the court may exercise its discretion to make a defendant's costs order but may order that only part of the costs incurred be paid. The court should make whatever order seems just having regard to the relative importance of the two charges and the conduct of the parties generally. Where the court considers that it would be inappropriate that the defendant should recover all of the costs properly incurred, the amount must be specified in the order.
Practice Direction (Costs in Criminal Proceedings) 2015 EWCA Crim 1568 para 2.4.1 A successful appellant under Criminal Appeal Act 1968 Part I may be awarded a defendant's costs order. Orders may also be made on an appeal against an order or ruling at a preparatory hearing (section 16(4A), to cover the costs of representing an acquitted defendant in respect of whom there is an Attorney-General's reference under Criminal Justice Act 1972 s 36 (see Criminal Justice Act 1972 s 36(5) and (5A)) and in the case of a person whose sentence is reviewed under Criminal Justice Act 1988 s 36 (see Criminal Justice Act 1988 s 36 and Sch 3 para 11).
2.4.2 On determining an application for leave to appeal to the [Supreme Court] under Criminal Appeal Act 1968 Part II, whether by prosecutor or by defendant, the court may make a defendant's costs order.
2.4.3 In considering whether to make such an order the court will have in mind the principles applied by the Crown Court in relation to acquitted defendants (see para 2.2.1 (see above) and 2.2.2 (see above)).
Emohare v Thames Magistrates' Court 2009 EWHC 689 (Admin) D was tried for assaulting a PC. The prosecution said the assault was deliberate but the Magistrates were not sure and acquitted him. However, the Magistrates bound him over. He applied for a defendant's costs order and the Magistrates said that his behaviour was reprehensible and he had brought the case on himself. They recognised this was not one of the exceptions listed in the [then current] Practice Direction. But they did comment that D was fortunate not to be charged with an offence under Public Order Act 1986 s 4 to

[441] *Hussain v UK* 2006 43 EHRR 22 (p 437)

which he would have had no defence. Held. We quash the bind over as there was no proper basis for it to have been made. The breadth of the discretion is circumscribed by Practice Direction (Costs: Criminal Proceedings) 2004 2 AER 1070,[442] and in particular by paragraphs II.1.1, 1.2 and 2.1. Whilst the example given in paragraph II.1.1 is only an example, it is narrowly drawn in conjunctive terms because of the need to respect the presumption of innocence both at common law and under European Convention on Human Rights art 6. That need is emphasised in cases such as *R v South West Surrey Justices ex parte James* 2000 Crim LR 690. The Magistrate's reasons why costs should not be awarded is wholly contrary to the reasons why the exceptions to the general rule that a defendant's costs order should be awarded after an acquittal should be narrowly drawn. Such thinking flies in the face of the decisions of the European Court of Human Rights such as *Minelli v Switzerland* 1983 5 EHRR 554. In any event, he had never had the opportunity to defend the Public Order Act 1986 offence. Costs granted.
See also: *R (Pluckrose) v Snaresbrook Crown Court* 2009 EWHC 1506 (Admin) (Liable for disqualification via the totting up procedure. D unsuccessfully argued exceptional hardship and appealed to the Crown Court. The appeal was allowed. A defendant's costs order was refused. It was open to the Court to refuse the application for costs, under their broad discretion.)

22.20 ***Defendant's Costs Order*** ***What costs are included?***
Criminal Procedure Rules 2015 2015/1490 Rule 45.4(1) This rule applies where the court can order the payment of costs out of central funds.
(2) In this rule, costs:
(a) include:
(i) on an appeal, costs incurred in the court that made the decision under appeal, and
(ii) at a retrial, costs incurred at the initial trial and on any appeal, but
(b) do not include costs met by legal aid.

22.21 ***Defendant's Costs Order*** ***Assessment of costs***
Criminal Procedure Rules 2015 2015/1490 Rule 45.4(6) If the court makes an order:
(a) the court may direct an assessment under, as applicable:
(i) Costs in Criminal Cases (General) Regulations 1986 1986/1335 Part III, or
(ii) Serious Crime Act 2007 (Appeals under Section 24) Order 2008 2008/1863 Part 3,
(b) the court may assess the amount itself in a case in which either:
(i) the recipient agrees the amount, or
(ii) the court decides to allow a lesser sum than that which is reasonably sufficient to compensate the recipient for expenses properly incurred in the proceedings;
(c) an order for the payment of a defendant's costs which includes an amount in respect of fees payable to a legal representative, or disbursements paid by a legal representative, must include a statement to that effect.
(7) If the court directs an assessment, the order must specify any restriction on the amount to be paid that the court considers appropriate.
(8) If the court assesses the amount itself, it must do so subject to any restriction on the amount to be paid that is imposed by regulations made by the Lord Chancellor.
Note: The procedure is laid out in Costs in Criminal Cases (General) Regulations 1986 1986/1335 reg 4-13. Ed.
For ***Contents of the order***, see para **22.5**.
For ***Duty to give reasons if application refused or representations rejected***, see para **22.6**.

[442] Now Practice Direction (Costs in Criminal Proceedings) 2015 EWCA Crim 1568

22.22 ***Defendant's Costs Order Attorney-General's references***
Criminal Justice Act 1988 Sch 3 para 11 Where on a reference to the Court of Appeal under section 36 or a reference to the Supreme Court under section 36(5) the person whose sentencing is the subject of the reference appears by counsel for the purpose of presenting any argument to the Court of Appeal or the Supreme Court, he shall be entitled to his costs…out of central funds of such funds as are reasonably sufficient to compensate him for expenses properly incurred by him for the purpose of being represented on the reference, and any amount recoverable under this paragraph shall be ascertained, as soon as practicable, by the Registrar of Criminal Appeals or, as the case may be, under Supreme Court Rules.

22.23 ***Defendant's Costs Order Explain sentence, Judge/Magistrate must***
Criminal Justice Act 2003 s 174(2)[443] The court must state in open court, in ordinary language and in general terms, the court's reasons for deciding on the sentence.
(3) The court must explain to the offender in ordinary language:

(a) the effect of the sentence,

(b) the effects of non-compliance with any order that the offender is required to comply with and that forms part of the sentence,

(c) any power of the court to vary or review any order that forms part of the sentence…

Practice Direction (Costs in Criminal Proceedings) 2015 EWCA Crim 1568 para 2.1.1 Magistrates' Court and Practice Direction (Costs in Criminal Proceedings) 2015 EWCA Crim 1568 para 2.2.1 Crown Court…The court when declining to make a costs order should explain, in open court, that the reason for not making an order does not involve any suggestion that the defendant is guilty of any criminal conduct but the order is refused because of the positive reason that should be identified.[444]
Note: Whether a costs order is part of the sentence is open to debate. Ed.

22.24 ***Taxation etc.***
Note: The procedure is laid down in Practice Direction (Costs in Criminal Proceedings) 2015 EWCA Crim 1568 para 5.1.1 and onwards. Ed.
For ***When the order takes effect***, see para **22.8**.

Prosecution (private) costs out of central funds

For ***Making representations (in court and/or in writing)***, see para **22.2**.

22.25 ***Prosecution costs out of central funds Power to order and test to apply***
Prosecution of Offences Act 1985 s 17(1)[445] Subject to subsection (2) (see **22.26**) and (2A) (see **22.28**), the court may:

(a) in any proceedings in respect of an indictable offence, and

(b) in any proceedings before a Divisional Court of the Queen's Bench Division or the Supreme Court in respect of a summary offence,

order the payment out of central funds of such amount as the court considers reasonably sufficient to compensate the prosecutor for any expenses properly incurred by him in the proceedings.
Prosecution of Offences Act 1985 s 17(5) Where the conduct of proceedings to which subsection (1) above applies is taken over by the Crown Prosecution Service, that subsection shall have effect as if it referred to the prosecutor who had the conduct of the proceedings before the intervention of the Service and to expenses incurred by him up to the time of intervention.
Note: The same test to apply is at Practice Direction (Costs in Criminal Proceedings) 2015 EWCA Crim 1568 para 1.3.1, see **22.15**. Other provisions are at paragraph 2.6. Ed.
For the general test see the ***Test to apply*** para at **22.3**.

443 As substituted by Legal Aid, Sentencing and Punishment of Offenders Act 2012 s 64
444 *Hussain v UK* 2006 43 EHRR 22 (p 437) ECtHR
445 The phrase 'and (2A)' was inserted by Legal Aid, Sentencing and Punishment of Offenders Act 2012 Sch 7 para 4(2).

22.26 ***Prosecution costs out of central funds Authorities that cannot claim costs***
Prosecution of Offences Act 1985 s 17(2) No order under this section may be made in favour of:
(a) a public authority, or
(b) a person acting:
(i) on behalf of a public authority, or
(ii) in his capacity as an official appointed by such an authority.
Prosecution of Offences Act 1985 s 17(6) In this section 'public authority' means:
(a) a police force within the meaning of section 3 of this Act,
(b) the Crown Prosecution Service or any other government department,
(c) a local authority or other authority or body constituted for purposes of:
(i) the public service or of local government, or
(ii) carrying on under national ownership any industry or undertaking or part of an industry or undertaking, or
(d) any other authority or body whose members are appointed by Her Majesty or by any Minister of the Crown or government department or whose revenues consist wholly or mainly of money provided by Parliament.
For ***Relevant factors when assessing costs***, see para **22.4**.

22.27 ***Prosecution costs out of central funds The general rule for awarding***
Criminal Procedure Rules 2015 2015/1490 Rule 45.4(5) The general rule is that the court must make an order, but:..b) the court may decline to make a prosecutor's costs order if, for example, the prosecution was started or continued unreasonably.

22.28 ***Prosecution costs out of central funds Awarding partial costs***
Prosecution of Offences Act 1985 s 17(2A)[446] Where the court considers that there are circumstances that make it inappropriate for the prosecution to recover the full amount mentioned in subsection (1), an order under this section must be [made] for the payment out of central funds of such lesser amount as the court considers just and reasonable.
(2B) When making an order under this section, the court must fix the amount to be paid out of central funds in the order if it considers it appropriate to do so and:
(a) the prosecutor agrees the amount, or
(b) subsection (2A) applies.
(2C) Where the court does not fix the amount to be paid out of central funds in the order:
(a) it must describe in the order any reduction required under subsection (2A), and
(b) the amount must be fixed by means of a determination made by or on behalf of the court in accordance with procedures specified in regulations made by the Lord Chancellor.
Criminal Procedure Rules 2015 2015/1490 Rule 45.2(6) If the court makes an order for the payment of costs:
(a) the general rule is that it must be for an amount that is sufficient reasonably to compensate the recipient for costs:
(i) actually, reasonably and properly incurred, and
(ii) reasonable in amount, but
(b) the court may order the payment of:
(i) a proportion of that amount,
(ii) a stated amount less than that amount,
(iii) costs from or until a certain date only,
(iv) costs relating only to particular steps taken, or
(v) costs relating only to a distinct part of the case.
For ***Contents of the order***, see para **22.5**.
For ***Duty to give reasons if application refused or representations rejected***, see para **22.6**.

[446] Subsections (2A)-(2C) were inserted and subsections (3) and (4) were repealed by Legal Aid, Sentencing and Punishment of Offenders Act 2012 Sch 7 para 4(3) and (4).

For ***When the order takes effect***, see para **22.8**.

PROSECUTION COSTS PAID BY THE DEFENDANT

22.29

Children and young offenders The order is available whatever the age of the offender. If the offender is aged under 18: a) the amount of prosecution costs shall not exceed the amount of the fine, Prosecution of Offences Act 1985 s 18(5), and b) the court shall order the parent or guardian to pay the prosecution costs unless they cannot be found or it would be unreasonable, Powers of Criminal Courts (Sentencing) Act 2000 s 137(1). When the offender has attained the age of 16 the court's duty changes to a power to so order.

Power to order

22.30 ***Prosecution costs paid by the defendant Power to order Court of Appeal***

Prosecution of Offences Act 1985 s 18(2) Where the Court of Appeal dismisses:

(a) an appeal or application for leave to appeal under Criminal Appeal Act 1968 Part I,

(b) an application by the accused for leave to appeal to the Supreme Court under Part II of that Act,

(c) an appeal or application for leave under Criminal Justice Act 1987 s 9(11), or

(d) an appeal or application for leave to appeal under Criminal Procedure and Investigations Act 1996 s 35(1),

it may make such order as to the costs to be paid by the accused, to such person as may be named in the order, as it considers just and reasonable.

(2A) Where the Court of Appeal reverses or varies a ruling on an appeal under Criminal Justice Act 2003 Part 9, it may make such order as to the costs to be paid by the accused, to such person as may be named in the order, as it considers just and reasonable.

Prosecution of Offences Act 1985 s 18(6) Costs ordered to be paid under subsection (2) or (2A) may include the reasonable cost of any transcript of a record of proceedings made in accordance with rules of court made for the purposes of Criminal Appeal Act 1968 s 32.

Practice Direction (Costs in Criminal Proceedings) 2015 EWCA Crim 1568 para 3.3 The Court of Appeal (Crim Div) may order an unsuccessful appellant to pay costs to such person as may be named in the order. Such costs may include the costs of any transcript obtained for the proceedings in the Court of Appeal, Prosecution of Offences Act 1985 s 18(2) and (6).

22.31 ***Prosecution costs paid by the defendant Power to order Crown Court (Indictment and appeals)***

Prosecution of Offences Act 1985 s 18(1) Where:..b) the Crown Court dismisses an appeal against such a conviction or against the sentence imposed on that conviction, or c) any person is convicted of an offence before the Crown Court, the court may make such order as to the costs to be paid by the accused to the prosecutor as it considers just and reasonable.

22.32 ***Prosecution costs paid by the defendant Power to order Committals***

Costs in Criminal Cases (General) Regulations 1986 1986/1335 reg 14(1) Prosecution of Offences Act 1985 s 17-18 shall apply to proceedings in the Crown Court in respect of a person committed by a Magistrates' Court to that Court:

(a) with a view to his being sentenced for an indictable offence in accordance with Powers of Criminal Courts Act 1973 s 42, or

(b) with a view to his being sentenced by the Crown Court under Bail Act 1976 s 6(6) or 9(3), or

(c) with a view to the making of a Hospital Order with an order restricting his discharge under Mental Health Act 1983 Part 3,

as they apply where a person is convicted in proceedings before the Crown Court.

(2) Prosecution of Offences Act 1985 s 18 shall apply to proceedings in the Crown Court:

(a) in respect of a person sent by a Magistrates' Court as an incorrigible rogue under Vagrancy Act 1824 s 5 as if he were committed for trial before the Crown Court, and

(b) in respect of an appeal under Vagrancy Act 1824 s 14 as if the hearing of the appeal were a trial on indictment.[447]

Note: It has been announced that the government intend to repeal Vagrancy Act 1824 s 4. It may be some time before there is a repeal. Ed.

(3) Prosecution of Offences Act 1985 s 18 shall apply to proceedings in a Magistrates' Court or the Crown Court for dealing with an offender:

(a) under any of the following provisions of Powers of Criminal Courts (Sentencing) Act 2000:

(i) section 13 (commission of further offence by person conditionally discharged),

(ii) section 119(1) or 123 (power of court on conviction of further offence to deal with suspended sentence and breach of requirement of suspended sentence supervision order),

(iii) Sch 1 para 5 (power of court on referral back from panel),

(iv) Sch 3 Part II (breach of requirement of certain community orders),

(v) Sch 5 paras 1-3 (breach etc. of attendance centre order),

(vi) Sch 7 paras 2-4 (breach of requirement of supervision order),

(vii) Sch 8 paras 2-4 (breach of requirement of Action Plan Order or Reparation Order), and

b) under any of the following provisions of Criminal Justice Act 2003:[448]

(ai) section 256AC (breach of supervision requirements imposed under section 256AA),

(i) Sch 8 Part 2 (breach of requirement of community order),

(ii) Sch 12 Part 2 (breach of community requirement of suspended sentence order or conviction of further offence),

(iii) paragraphs 7 to 9 of Schedule 19A (breach, revocation or amendment of supervision default orders),

as if the offender had been tried in those proceedings for the offence for which the order was made or the sentence passed.

22.33 ***Prosecution costs paid by the defendant Power to order Magistrates' Court***

Prosecution of Offences Act 1985 s 18(1) Where any person is convicted of an offence before a Magistrates' Court the court may make such order as to the costs to be paid by the accused to the prosecutor as it considers just and reasonable.

22.34 ***Prosecution costs paid by the defendant No costs order where fine does not exceed £5***

Prosecution of Offences Act 1985 s 18(4) Where any person is convicted of an offence before a Magistrates' Court and:

(a) under the conviction the court orders payment of any sum as a fine, penalty, forfeiture or compensation, and

(b) the sum so ordered to be paid does not exceed £5,

the court shall not order the accused to pay any costs under this section unless in the particular circumstances of the case it considers it right to do so.

Prosecution costs Procedure

22.35 ***There must be a proper enquiry***

R v Wilson-Jones 2015 EWCA Crim 1266 D pleaded to theft. She elected to be tried in the Crown Court and then pleaded. She was given a conditional discharge and the

[447] As amended by Costs in Criminal Cases (General) (Amendment) Regulations 2013 2013/2526 para 2

[448] As amended by Costs in Criminal Cases (General) (Amendment) Regulations 2015 2015/12 para 2

prosecution asked for £500 costs. The Judge heard she was not in work and received disability allowance. Held. Although there was some enquiry about her means, there was no basis for her paying £500.

22.36 ***Prosecution costs paid by the defendant*** ***Prosecution should serve full details of costs early*** ***Defence should give notice of objections***

Practice Direction (Costs in Criminal Proceedings) 2015 EWCA Crim 1568 para 3.6 The prosecution should serve upon the defence, at the earliest time, full details of its costs so as to give the defendant a proper opportunity to make representations upon them if appropriate. If a defendant wishes to dispute all or any of the prosecution's claim for costs, the defendant should, if possible, give proper notice to the prosecution of the objections proposed to be made or at least make it plain to the court precisely what those objections are. There is no provision for assessment of prosecution costs in a criminal case. Such disputes have to be resolved by the court, which must specify the amount to be paid.[449]

22.37 ***Prosecution costs paid by the defendant*** ***Principles are the same in Crown Court and Magistrates' Court***

R v Macatonia 2009 EWCA Crim 2516 D pleaded to trade mark offences. The prosecution were granted their costs. Held. The principles set out in *R v Northallerton Magistrates' Court ex parte Dove* 2000 1 Cr App R (S) 136 by Bingham LJ (concerning a Magistrates' Court hearing) apply to the Crown Court as they do to the Magistrates' Court. Two principles were relevant here, proportionality and the sum must not exceed the sum actually and reasonably incurred.

Note: These principles are distributed in the relevant paragraphs in this chapter. Ed.

For ***Making representations (in court and/or in writing)***, see para **22.2**.

22.38 ***Prosecution costs paid by the defendant*** ***Disputes must be resolved by the court***

Practice Direction (Costs in Criminal Proceedings) 2015 EWCA Crim 1568 para 3.6 There is no provision for assessment of prosecution costs in a criminal case. Such disputes have to be resolved by the court, which must specify the amount to be paid, see *R v Associated Octel Ltd* 1996 EWCA Crim 1327, 1997 1 Cr App R (S) 435.

For the rule when a ***confiscation order*** is made, see **21.143**.

Prosecution costs Means

22.39 ***Prosecution costs paid by the defendant*** ***Means, Must consider***

Practice Direction (Costs in Criminal Proceedings) 2015 EWCA Crim 1568 para 3.4 An order should be made where the court is satisfied that the defendant or appellant has the means and the ability to pay. The order is not intended to be in the nature of a penalty which can only be satisfied on the defendant's release from prison.

R v Northallerton Magistrates' Court ex parte Dove 2000 1 Cr App R (S) 136 LCJ An order to pay costs to the prosecutor should never exceed the sum which, having regard to D's means and any other financial order imposed upon him, D is able to pay and which it is reasonable to order D to pay. A court which proposes to make any financial order against a defendant must give the defendant a fair opportunity to adduce any relevant financial information and make any appropriate submissions.

R v Brown 2013 EWCA Crim 2023 D was on benefits and was sentenced to 12 months' imprisonment. The Judge made a costs order for £450. The defence said he would be released from prison after 6 months. D was without means. The Judge said that was why he had given D 12 months to pay. Held. In *R v Jenkins* 2005 EWCA Crim 6, it was said, "It is a well-established principle that financial penalties should be imposed and financial orders made only where there is some clear prospect of means available to satisfy them. We well understand the…Judge's wish to ensure some contribution from the appellant towards the costs of his prosecution, but there was no or no sufficiently

[449] See *R v Associated Octel Ltd* 1996 EWCA Crim 1327, 1997 1 Cr App R (S) 435.

clear prospect in the appellant's case of the necessary available means to satisfy the order. It was wrong that the order should have been made." The order against D was wrong in principle.

22.40 ***Prosecution costs paid by the defendant   Can the order be based on the defendant's capital?***
R (Gray) v Crown Court at Aylesbury 2013 EWHC 500 (Admin) High Court W, the wife of the main defendant, D, was convicted of two Animal Welfare Act 2006 offences. The police and the RSPCA searched a farm and 115 equines were seized. Witnesses described the shocking condition some animals were in. The trial lasted 52 days. The prosecution said their costs were just over £732,000 of which just over £43,200 was expert fees which had been paid out of central funds. W was given a community order and ordered to pay £750. The defendants appealed and the hearing lasted 34 days. W's convictions and the costs orders were upheld. W was ordered to pay £200,000 extra costs. W and D both appealed to the High Court. Held. para 68 There was no rule which prevented a court making a costs order based solely on capital. It was very easy to envisage cases in which a retired person with no income but large amounts of capital could be ordered to pay very substantial costs out of capital. If there was a rule prohibiting this, then it would be difficult to make costs orders against prisoners as they had no income while they might have substantial amounts of capital.
For more detail see **22.62**.

22.41 ***Prosecution costs paid by the defendant   Means   Duty of defendant to provide information***
R v Northallerton Magistrates' Court ex parte Dove 2000 1 Cr App R (S) 136 LCJ It is for the defendant facing a financial penalty by way of fine or an order to pay costs to a prosecutor to disclose to magistrates information as will enable justices to assess what he can reasonably afford to pay. In the absence of such disclosure, justices may draw reasonable inferences as to D's means from evidence they have heard and from all the circumstances of the case.

22.42 ***Prosecution costs paid by the defendant   Defence information rejected***
R v Rance 2012 EWCA Crim 2023, 2013 1 Cr App R (S) 123 (p 636) D, a property developer, was convicted of a planning offence at the Magistrates' Court. He was committed for sentence. He appealed the conviction, which was unsuccessful. The prosecution applied for confiscation, which was also unsuccessful. The prosecution applied for £130,000 costs. They said they considered he had the means to pay. The Judge rejected the defence assertions and asset documents. D did not give evidence. The defence said that D's means were never subject to oral evidence. The witnesses were unavailable. Further, there was no proper enquiry. Held. It must have been obvious to D and his legal advisers that any account he gave of his means [would] be subject to close scrutiny by the Judge. His assertions as to his means had been challenged by the prosecution throughout the confiscation proceedings. It was up to D and his legal advisers to decide whether he should give oral evidence and whether he should call witnesses. No application to call evidence or adjourn the matter was made. The Judge's approach was fair and appropriate.

22.43 ***Prosecution costs paid by the defendant   Means   No information supplied***
R v Northallerton Magistrates' Court ex parte Dove 2000 1 Cr App R (S) 136 LCJ It was for D to put forward relevant financial details to guide the decision of the justices. He no doubt knew that he faced a potential fine of up to £5,000 on conviction and, as soon as the prosecutor made application for costs, he knew of the sum which he could be ordered to pay under that head. He had a full opportunity to adduce any information or make any submissions that he wished, and he was notably unforthcoming. He gave inaccurate details as to his income, he produced no accounts for his business, he gave no indication

of the value of the farm or what he paid for it, he gave no indication of any sort as to his assets. There was nothing which could be calculated to surprise the applicant or catch him off his guard. He cannot complain.

R v Bodycote Hip 2010 EWCA Crim 802, 2011 1 Cr App R (S) 6 (p 38) The defendant company was prosecuted under Health and Safety legislation. It was fined £533,000 and ordered to pay the agreed sum of £200,000 in costs. Held. The appellant provided no information as to its resources. The appellant's ability to pay was not therefore a limiting factor which the Judge had to consider. The quantification of costs was agreed at £200,000. It was not therefore necessary for the Judge to investigate whether costs in that sum had been actually or reasonably incurred.

22.44 ***Prosecution costs paid by the defendant Means Insufficient means to pay both fines and costs***

R v Northallerton Magistrates' Court ex parte Dove 2000 1 Cr App R (S) 136 LCJ If, when the costs sought by the prosecutor are added to the proposed fine, the total exceeds the sum which, in the light of the defendant's means and all other relevant circumstances, the defendant can reasonably be ordered to pay, it is preferable to reduce the sum of costs rather than reduce the fine.

22.45 ***Prosecution costs paid by the defendant Means Third party not to pay costs***

Practice Direction (Costs in Criminal Proceedings) 2015 EWCA Crim 1568 para 3.4 An order should not be made on the assumption that a third party might pay.

22.46 ***Prosecution costs paid by the defendant Means The defendant has debts***

Practice Direction (Costs in Criminal Proceedings) 2015 EWCA Crim 1568 para 3.4…Whilst the court should take into account any debt of the appellant or defendant, where the greater part of those debts relates to the offence itself, the court may still make an order for costs.

Prosecution costs Making the order General matters

For ***Relevant factors when assessing costs***, see para **22.4**.

22.47 ***Prosecution costs paid by the defendant The court's discretion/Test to apply***

Prosecution of Offences Act 1985 s 18(1)(c) Where any person is convicted of an offence before the Crown Court, the court may make such order as to the costs to be paid by the accused to the prosecutor as it considers just and reasonable.

Criminal Procedure Rules 2015 2015/1490 Rule 45.4(5) The general rule is that the court must make an order, but:

(a) the court may decline to make a defendant's costs order if, for example:

(i) the defendant is convicted of at least one offence, or

(ii) the defendant's conduct led the prosecutor reasonably to think the prosecution case stronger than it was, and

(b) the court may decline to make a prosecutor's costs order if, for example, the prosecution was started or continued unreasonably.

R v Kravchenko 2016 EWCA Crim 1446 D elected trial for theft of £9.89 from Tesco. He was convicted and the Judge gave him a conditional discharge, £2,800 costs and a court charge of £120. At the time of the sentence he was a paid carer for his partner. Now he was hoping to be in receipt of Employment Support Allowance. The defence said the costs were disproportionate to the loss. Held. Justice is done by enabling the prosecution a fair and reasonable amount of costs when a person elects trial. Looking at the appropriate table the figure was fair and reasonable. Order reduced to £350 due to D's lack of means.

See also: *R v Maidstone Crown Court ex parte Litchfield* 1992 The Times 30/6/92 (Disqualification appeal allowed at Crown Court. Fine increased. Costs order made against D because the appeal was successful 'by the skin of his teeth'. Held. The costs order was manifestly unfair and unjust.)

For the general test see the ***Test to apply*** para at **22.3**.

22.48 *Prosecution costs paid by the defendant Costs should not be used as a punishment*

Practice Direction (Costs in Criminal Proceedings) 2015 EWCA Crim 1568 para 3.4…The order is not intended to be in the nature of a penalty which can only be satisfied on the defendant's release from prison.

R v Hayden 1974 60 Cr App R 304 LCJ It would be clearly wrong to penalise a man, that is to say increase the punishment suffered by a man, merely because he had taken the advantage of his constitutional right of trial by jury. But, on the other hand, it is perfectly right to say of a man who has elected to go for trial that if the case is one in which the costs of the prosecution should fall on the defendant in the events which happen, then, by going to the Crown Court, he must inevitably suffer a higher financial penalty, if that is the right word, because he has chosen to go to the court where the costs, for reasons which we all understand, are bound to be higher.

R v Northallerton Magistrates' Court ex parte Dove 2000 1 Cr App R (S) 136 LCJ An order should never exceed the sum which the prosecutor has actually and reasonably incurred. The purpose of such an order is to compensate the prosecutor and not to punish the defendant. Where the defendant has, by his conduct, put the prosecutor to avoidable expense he may, subject to his means, be ordered to pay some or all of that sum to the prosecutor. But he is not to be punished for exercising a constitutional right to defend himself.

R v Rahal 2017 EWCA Crim 1779 para 10(2) The purpose of the costs order is to compensate the prosecution for the costs it has incurred, not to penalise the defendant.

22.49 *Discount for time spent in custody and costs*

R v Rakib 2011 EWCA Crim 870, 2012 1 Cr App R (S) 1 (p 1) D was convicted of two counts of exposure and sentenced to a 3-year community order with requirements. He had served 173 days on remand. At trial he disputed the accuracy of the identification made by the victim. Following the conviction, he accepted that it was correct. The Judge imposed a costs order of £2,800 at £500 per month. D was employed (when not on remand) earning nearly £15,000 per year and had no dependants. Held. Usually we would have no difficulty in saying such an order is correct. However, although there is no necessary correlation between sentence and an order for costs, we consider it was incumbent upon the Judge to take account of the time spent on remand over and above the eventual community order. The order was wrong in principle.

22.50 *Prosecution costs paid by the defendant Defendant acquitted of some of charges*

R v B&Q 2005 EWCA Crim 2297 The defendant company was convicted of three counts and acquitted of five counts. Held. An allowance should have been made for the acquittals on the direction of the trial Judge.

R v Splain 2010 EWCA Crim 49 D stood trial for 17 trade mark offences. He was convicted of three, acquitted of eight and the remaining six were withdrawn by the Judge. He was fined £2,000 on each count, and ordered to pay £22,045 in costs, which represented the full amount. Held. The Judge remarked in his sentencing observations that what D was really doing for commercial purposes was to test the regulations, as found by the jury, to beyond the limits of the criminal law. The prosecution and the trial were clearly in the public interest. It was wrong in principle for the Judge to make an order for the totality of the costs against D when he was only convicted on three of the counts. It does not follow that a mathematical approach should be taken. This was not a case of a sledgehammer being used to crack a nut. Our approach accords with the approach generally taken in civil proceedings. Costs reduced to £10,000.

See also: *R v Foley* 2014 EWCA Crim 894 (D offered to plead to handling. The prosecution rejected the offer. Nearly eight months later the trial started. When a discharge looked likely, the prosecution accepted the handling offer and D was ordered to pay all their costs. £250 not £1,000 costs.)

22.51 ***Prosecution costs paid by the defendant Apportioning costs between defendants***

Practice Direction (Costs in Criminal Proceedings) 2015 EWCA Crim 1568 para 3.5 Where co-defendants are husband and wife, the couple's means should not be taken together. Where there are multiple defendants the court may make joint and several orders, but the costs ordered to be paid by an individual should be related to the costs in or about the prosecution of that individual. In a multi-handed case where some defendants have insufficient means to pay their share of the costs, it is not right for that share to be divided among the other defenders.

R v Harrison 1993 14 Cr App R (S) 419 D pleaded to trade description offences. The Judge considered that the first defendant was the principal defendant and stood to gain financially from the offence. Further, he had the means to pay, whereas the second defendant, who was his son, had little to do with running the business. He therefore made the principal defendant pay all the costs. Held. Where there are several defendants it will usually be appropriate when making a costs order to look to see what would be a reasonable estimate of the costs if each defendant were tried alone. However, the Judge's approach was proper.

R v Fresha Bakeries Ltd 2002 EWCA Crim 1451, 2003 1 Cr App R (S) 44 (p 202) The defendant company, FB Ltd, its sister company, H Ltd, the Chief Executive of the group (CE), the chief engineer at the plant (E), and the production director (PD) pleaded to offences under Health and Safety at Work etc. Act 1974 s 2-3. The companies and E pleaded at the first appearance. CE and PD pleaded the day before the trial was fixed. Two workmen were burnt to death trying to repair a bread oven when major breaches of Health and Safety procedures took place. It was agreed by the prosecution, the defence and the Judge that the Judge should fix the overall financial penalty as if it were a single company and apportion the fine and costs elements between the companies. The companies were able to pay a significant fine. The pre-tax profits of FB Ltd were £250,000, and H Ltd's profits were £400,000. The Judge distinguished *R v Ronson and Parnes* 1992 13 Cr App R (S) 153 (where costs were adjusted so that they were what they would have been if the defendant had been tried alone) and calculated the costs to include the work up and until sentence, notwithstanding their early plea. FB Ltd was fined £250,000 with costs of £175,000, H Ltd was fined £100,000 with £75,000 costs, CE was fined £10,000 with £5,000 costs, PD was fined £1,000 and E was fined £2,000 (neither with a costs order). The revised figure for the costs when the companies pleaded was £108,451. The revised figure when the other defendants pleaded was £283,307. The companies appealed. Held. It was a very bad case. There was no basis for holding that the fines totalling £350,000 were manifestly excessive. It may be appropriate to order the defendant who is more responsible to pay a greater share of the costs than he would pay if he were tried alone. The Judge was entitled to conclude that the corporate defendants bore a greater responsibility than the individual defendants. However, the Judge took too little account of the fact that the companies had no control over the proceedings against CE and PD. If they had pleaded when the companies did, the costs would have been significantly less. Taking into account the costs incurred for the proposed trial after the corporate defendants had pleaded and the reduced costs figure now available, FB Ltd's costs should be **£105,000** and H Ltd's costs should be **£45,000**.

R v Rahal 2017 EWCA Crim 1779 para 10(4) Where there is more than one defendant, a defendant is generally to be held liable only for the proportion of the costs attributable to the prosecution against him. In that regard the court should consider what would be the amount of costs if the defendant had been tried alone, see *R (Gray) v Crown Court at Aylesbury* 2013 EWHC 500 (Admin).

Prosecution costs Making the order Fixing the amount

22.52 ***Prosecution costs paid by the defendant Fixing the amount***
Practice Direction (Costs in Criminal Proceedings) 2015 EWCA Crim 1568 para 3.7 The principles to be applied in deciding on the amount of costs are those set out by the Court of Appeal in *Neville v Gardner Merchant* 1983 5 Cr App R (S) 349. The court when awarding prosecution costs may award costs in respect of time spent in bringing the offences to light, even if the necessary investigation was carried out, for example, by an environmental health official.[450] Generally it will not be just or reasonable to order a defendant to pay costs of an investigation which the prosecutor itself will not satisfy. In *Balshaw v CPS* 2009 EWCA Crim 470, 2 Cr App R (S) 109 (p 712), the Court of Appeal considered the circumstances in which the CPS may be able to recover costs associated with the investigation incurred by the police. The Divisional Court has held that there is a requirement that any sum ordered to be paid by way of costs should not ordinarily be greatly at variance with any fine imposed. Where substantial research is required in order to counter possible defences, the court may also award costs in respect of that work if it considers it to be justified.
R v Rahal 2017 EWCA Crim 1779 para 10(1) The order to pay costs should not exceed the sum which it is reasonable to expect the defendant to be able to pay, having regard to his means and any other financial order imposed upon him.

22.53 ***Prosecution costs paid by the defendant The court should take an overall view***
R v Splain 2010 EWCA Crim 49 D stood trial for 17 trade mark offences. He was convicted of three, acquitted of eight and the remaining six were withdrawn by the Judge. He was fined £2,000 on each count, and ordered to pay £22,045 in costs, which represented the full amount sought by the prosecution. Held. We consider that it is right to take an overall view. £10,000 substituted.

22.54 ***Prosecution costs paid by the defendant Costs limited to amount incurred***
R v Northallerton Magistrates' Court ex parte Dove 2000 1 Cr App R (S) 136 LCJ An order should never exceed the sum which the prosecutor has actually and reasonably incurred.
R v Rahal 2017 EWCA Crim 1779 para 10(3) The order should not exceed the costs that the prosecution had actually incurred. Those costs may include costs incurred in relation to the court hearing and the costs of the investigation, see *R v Associated Octel Ltd* 1996 EWCA Crim 1327, 1997 1 Cr App R(S) 435.

22.55 ***Prosecution costs paid by the defendant Costs of the investigation etc.***
R v F Howe and Son (Engineers) Ltd 1999 2 Cr App R (S) 37 The power permits an order to include the cost of the prosecuting authority carrying out investigations with a view to prosecution, see *R v Associated Octel Ltd* 1996 EWCA Crim 1327, 1997 1 Cr App R (S) 435.
R v Balshaw v CPS 2009 EWCA Crim 470, 2 Cr App R (S) 109 (p 712) D was ordered to pay prosecution costs of £22,600, of which £13,600 represented the cost of a report by KPMG LLP commissioned by the police. The prosecution was brought by the CPS. D appealed against the payment of prosecution costs. The defence said as the CPS had incurred no liability to pay for the report it was not just and reasonable for the defence to pay for it. Held. The issue was whether the order was 'just and reasonable'. To order an accused to pay costs to a prosecutor for which it is not liable is neither just nor reasonable. But the proposition must not be taken too far. Provided that the order does not lead to a windfall in favour of the prosecutor or to a disguised fine or penalty we see no reason why it would not be just and reasonable to make an order to the prosecutor in respect of sums which the court is satisfied are part of those costs of investigation which the prosecutor will itself satisfy. There is no principle that an order is proscribed where

[450] *Neville v Gardner Merchant* 1983 5 Cr App R (S) 349

the costs are designed to compensate a third party. The CPS's disbursements to professionals, such as a barrister or a pathologist, are recoverable. Nor is there any principle that the CPS may only recover those costs which it has directly incurred. The statute does not necessarily prevent the recovery by a prosecutor of fees which it will pay to another body which has itself incurred liability to pay those fees. The report was an important analysis of the sources of income in the banks of two of the conspirators. Since the CPS said it would pay the police the Judge was correct to say it was just and reasonable. The costs were relevant costs. Appeal dismissed.
R v Rahal 2017 EWCA Crim 1779 para 10(3) The prosecution costs may include costs incurred in relation to the court hearing and the costs of the investigation: see *R v Associated Octel Ltd* 1996 above.

22.56 ***Prosecution costs paid by the defendant CPS scale of average costs, Using the***
R v Dickinson 2010 EWCA Crim 2143, 2011 1 Cr App R (S) 93 (p 554) D pleaded on rearraignment to possession of cocaine (2.5 grams at 5%). The prosecution sought costs. A figure of £1,500 was provided, which was the average figure taken from the CPS scale of costs, which the Judge was told was used nationally. The lower figure was £1,200 and the upper £1,800. The Judge chose the lower figure and also fined D £200. It was argued it was disproportionate to the actual costs, unjustifiable and that as D was of limited means, was not just or reasonable. D was to pay the entire sum at £20 per week. Held. In principle the Judge was entitled to rely on the costs scales as a fair and reasonable guide to the costs that the CPS incurred in bringing and concluding this prosecution. Of course, in each case, the Judge as well as the prosecutor must be alert to the possibility that, having regard to the particular features of the case, the costs scale is not a fair and reasonable guide to actual costs incurred. Order upheld.
R v Thelwall 2016 EWCA Crim 1755 LCJ D had his Health and Safety appeal dismissed. The prosecutor, the Health and Safety Executive (HSE), asked for their costs from the defendant, which included a solicitor at Court and a counsel's fee vastly in excess of what the CPS would pay. Held. para 27 HSE's position on appeal is no different from that of the CPS. In any event D had no money.)
R v Rahal 2017 EWCA Crim 1779 D was prosecuted by Southwark Borough Council for obtaining a council flat by pretending she had a child when she had no child. She was convicted. Held. para 14 It was said that the Crown Court should have used the CPS scale of costs. The Judge was not required to do that. If the costs incurred are ones reasonably incurred, they are in principle recoverable. We uphold the order except the council cannot claim for two counsel to prosecute the case as that was not a just or reasonable expense.
For costs against corporate defendants, see the **Companies and Public Bodies as Defendants** ***Costs orders*** para at **227.27** in Volume 2.

22.57 ***Prosecution costs paid by the defendant On the facts, order correct/ incorrect***
R v Dickinson 2010 EWCA Crim 2143, 2011 1 Cr App R (S) 93 (p 554) D pleaded on rearraignment to possession of cocaine (2.5 grams at 5%). The prosecution sought costs. A figure of £1,500 was provided, which was the average figure taken from the CPS scale of costs, which the Judge was told was used nationally. The lower figure was £1,200 and the upper £1,800. The Judge chose the lower figure and also fined D £200. It was argued it was disproportionate to the actual costs, unjustifiable and, as D was of 'limited means', was not just or reasonable. D was to pay the entire sum at £20 per week. Held. The costs scales are generally known, or should be known. D was represented from the time of his first appearance in the Magistrates' Court. It was plain, or should have been plain, that if D elected trial in the Crown Court he would be exposed, if convicted, to a substantial order for costs. The total financial penalty would be a strain on D. However, it was not suggested to the Judge that it would be unduly and unfairly onerous.

R v Wogui 2013 EWCA Crim 1483 D pleaded to theft. He was given a 16-month sentence and £1,200 cash found on his person was used to offset some of the prosecution costs. He was also ordered to pay £800 in costs at £5 per week. Held. The order for costs should have had regard to D's means and such orders should be payable within a reasonable period of time. Once D is released, he will have to find employment. Even if he is successful, the order would take three years to pay off. It is unduly burdensome and the £1,200 payment was sufficient. Order quashed.

22.58 ***Prosecution costs paid by the defendant What the order must contain/Must specify the amount***

Prosecution of Offences Act 1985 s 18(3) The amount to be paid by the accused in pursuance of an order under this section shall be specified in the order.

Criminal Procedure Rules 2015 2015/1490 Rule 45.2(4) If the court makes an order about costs, it must:

(a) specify who must, or must not, pay what, to whom, and

(b) identify the legislation under which the order is made, where there is a choice of powers.

For ***Contents of the order***, see para **22.5**.

22.59 ***Prosecution costs paid by the defendant Reasons, Must give***

Criminal Justice Act 2003 s 174(2)[451] The court must state in open court, in ordinary language and in general terms, the court's reasons for deciding on the sentence.

(3) The court must explain to the offender in ordinary language:

(a) the effect of the sentence,

(b) the effects of non-compliance with any order that the offender is required to comply with and that forms part of the sentence…

Note: Whether costs are part of a sentence is open to debate. Ed.

For ***Duty to give reasons if application refused or representations rejected***, see para **22.6**.

For ***When the order takes effect***, see para **22.8**.

Other orders

22.60 ***Contribution Orders (Crown Court)***

Crown Court In proceedings to which Criminal Legal Aid (Contribution Orders) Regulations 2013 2013/483 apply, namely proceedings in the Crown Court, the represented defendant may be liable to make payments under an Income Contribution Order. If the defendant is convicted or if the representation order is withdrawn, the defendant may be required to pay the whole or part of the cost of the representation under a capital contribution order, Practice Direction (Costs in Criminal Proceedings) 2015 EWCA Crim 1568 para 6.1.1.

Crown Court: acquitted defendant If the trial judge considers that there are exceptional reasons, a defendant who is acquitted may nevertheless be required to pay the whole or part of the costs of the representation in the Crown Court [under Criminal Legal Aid (Contribution Orders) Regulations 2013 2013/483 reg] 25(b), Practice Direction (Costs in Criminal Proceedings) 2015 EWCA Crim 1568 para 6.1.2.

Crown Court: partial acquittals Where a defendant is convicted of one or more, but not all offences, he may apply in writing to the trial judge (or a judge nominated for that purpose by the resident judge) for an order that he pay a proportion only of the costs of the representation in the Crown Court on the ground that it would be manifestly unreasonable that he pay the whole amount [under Criminal Legal Aid (Contribution Orders) Regulations 2013 reg] 26. An application must be made within 21 days of the date on which the individual is dealt with. The judge may refuse the application or make an order specifying the proportion of costs which the defendant must pay, Practice Direction (Costs in Criminal Proceedings) 2015 EWCA Crim 1568 para 6.1.3.

[451] As substituted by Legal Aid, Sentencing and Punishment of Offenders Act 2012 s 64

Procedure: The procedure and the rules are set out in Criminal Legal Aid (Contribution Orders) Regs 2013 2013/483.

Combined with other orders

22.61 ***Absolute and conditional discharge, Combined with***

Powers of Criminal Courts (Sentencing) Act 2000 s 12(8) Nothing in this section shall be construed as preventing a court, on discharging an offender absolutely or conditionally in respect of an offence, from a) making an order under Prosecution of Offences Act 1985 s 21A (Criminal Courts Charge) or b) making an order for costs against the offender.[452]

22.62 ***Fines, Combined with/The costs order must not be disproportionate to fine***

Prosecution of Offences Act 1985 s 18(5) Where any person under the age of 18 is convicted of an offence before a Magistrates' Court, the amount of any costs ordered to be paid by the accused under this section shall not exceed the amount of any fine imposed on him.

Magistrates' Court Sentencing Guidelines, January 2004 page 175 The costs ordered to be paid should not be grossly disproportionate to any fine imposed for the offence. This principle was affirmed in *BPS Advertising Limited v London Borough of Barnet* 2006 EWHC 3335 (Admin)[453] in which the Court held that, while there is no question of an arithmetical relationship, the question of costs should be viewed in the context of the maximum penalty considered by Parliament to be appropriate for the seriousness of the offence.

Note: Although this guideline has been replaced, this principle is still followed. Ed.

Practice Direction (Costs in Criminal Proceedings) 2015 EWCA Crim 1568 para 3.7…The Divisional Court has held that there is a requirement that any sum ordered to be paid by way of costs should not ordinarily be greatly at variance with any fine imposed.

R v Northallerton Magistrates' Court ex parte Dove 2000 1 Cr App R (S) 136 LCJ The Magistrates imposed costs of £4,624, which were four and a half times greater than the fine of £1,000. Held. While there is no requirement that any sum ordered by justices to be paid to a prosecutor by way of costs should stand in any arithmetical relationship to any fine imposed, the costs ordered to be paid should not in the ordinary way be grossly disproportionate to the fine. Justices should ordinarily begin by deciding on the appropriate fine to reflect the criminality of the defendant's offence (bearing in mind his means) and then consider what, if any, costs he should be ordered to pay. If, when the costs sought by the prosecutor are added to the proposed fine, the total exceeds the sum which, in the light of the defendant's means and all other relevant circumstances, the defendant can reasonably be ordered to pay, it is preferable to reduce the sum of costs rather than reduce the fine. It is very hard to resist the conclusion that the costs were disproportionate. Matter remitted to the Magistrates for them to reconsider the issue.

R v Splain 2010 EWCA Crim 49 D stood trial for 17 trade mark offences. He was convicted of three, acquitted of eight and the remaining six were withdrawn by the Judge. He was fined £2,000 on each count, and ordered to pay £22,045 in costs, which represented the full amount sought by the prosecution. Held. The fact that the amount of the costs was disproportionate to the amount of the fines is not, in our judgment, the crucial factor. There may well be cases in which in the totality of the sentencing process the court is justified in weighting the penalty onto the costs more than onto the fine.

R v Dickinson 2010 EWCA Crim 2143, 2011 1 Cr App R (S) 93 (p 554) D pleaded on rearraignment to possession of cocaine (2.5 grams at 5%). The prosecution sought costs. A figure of £1,500 was provided, which was the average figure taken from the CPS scale of costs, which the Judge was told was used nationally. The lower figure was £1,200 and the upper £1,800. The Judge chose the lower figure and also fined D £200. It was argued

[452] As amended by Criminal Justice and Courts Act 2015 Sch 12 paras 8-9

[453] The case reference in the guideline is in error.

it was disproportionate to the actual costs, unjustifiable and that as D was of 'limited means', was not just or reasonable. D was ordered to pay the entire sum at £20 per week. Held. D was represented from the time of his first appearance in the Magistrates' Court. It was plain, or should have been plain, that if D elected trial in the Crown Court he would be exposed, if convicted, to a substantial order for costs. The total financial penalty would be a strain on D. However, it was not suggested to the Judge that it would be unduly and unfairly onerous. Order upheld.

Middleton v Cambridge Magistrates' Court 2012 EWHC 2122 (Admin) High Court The Conservators of the River Cam brought a private prosecution against D for breach of bye-laws. Two charges were dropped and D pleaded to two. D was on benefits. He was fined £75 on each charge. His only asset was his houseboat, which was his home. The prosecution asked for nearly £6,900 costs and these were awarded. Held. D could pay the costs but whether it is reasonable to make him pay is a different matter. The maximum fine for each offence was Level 1, which is £200. There is no requirement for any mathematical relationship between the fine and the costs. The costs were grossly disproportionate and not just and reasonable. Case remitted to the Magistrates for reconsideration.

R (Gray) v Crown Court at Aylesbury 2013 EWHC 500 (Admin) High Court D, a horse trader, was convicted of 11 Animal Welfare Act 2006 offences. The police and the RSPCA searched a farm and 115 equines were seized. Witnesses described the shocking condition some animals were in. The trial, involving D's wife, W, and three other members of his family lasted 52 days, including 34 days of evidence. The prosecution said their costs were just over £732,000 of which just over £43,200 was expert fees which had been paid for out of central funds. D received 24 weeks' imprisonment and was ordered to pay £400,000 costs. W, who was convicted of two counts, was given a community order and ordered to pay £750. The defendants appealed and the hearing lasted 34 days. The Court ordered two counts against D to be dismissed. The rest of the convictions and the costs orders were upheld. D was ordered to pay £400,000 extra costs and W was ordered to pay £200,000 extra costs. They both appealed to the High Court. Held. The normal rule is that costs should not be grossly disproportionate to a fine imposed for the same offence, but in appropriate cases there could be exceptions where justice requires it. Applying the [then] Criminal Procedure Rules, the Judge on appeal was entitled to depart from the normal rule that the costs should not be grossly disproportionate because of the complexity of the matter (including 34 days of evidence) and the conduct of the defence, which involved taking every legal argument that could be taken. D's costs orders upheld. In W's case the Court had not considered what the costs order should have been if she had been tried alone. We remit her case back to the Court for the Court to reconsider the order after performing that exercise.

See also: *R v Owen* 2011 EWCA Crim 2419 (Convicted of driving without due care and attention. Acquitted of dangerous driving. He was prepared to admit the lesser offence at the outset, but at trial denied both offences. The £225 fine could not be criticised. Costs should not be grossly disproportionate to the fine, so £360 costs, not £775.)

22.63 ***Fines, Combined with Offender under 18***

Prosecution of Offences Act 1985 s 18(5) Where any person under the age of 18 is convicted of an offence before a Magistrates' Court, the amount of any costs ordered to be paid by the accused under this section shall not exceed the amount of any fine imposed on him.

Appeals

22.64 ***Court of Appeal Power to order***

Prosecution of Offences Act 1985 s 16(4) Where the Court of Appeal:

(a) and (b) [Not listed. Re conviction appeals]

(c) on an appeal under that Part against sentence, exercises its powers under section 11(3) of that Act (powers where the court considers that the appellant should be sentenced differently for an offence for which he was dealt with by the court below), or

(d) allows, to any extent, an appeal under section 16A of that Act (appeal against order made in cases of insanity or unfitness to plead),

the court may make a defendant's costs order in favour of the accused.

(4A) The court may also make a defendant's costs order in favour of the accused on an appeal under Criminal Justice Act 1987 s 9(11) or Criminal Procedure and Investigations Act 1996 s 35(1) (appeals against orders or rulings at preparatory hearings) or under Criminal Justice Act 2003 Part 9.

(5) Where…the Court of Appeal determines an application for leave to appeal to the Supreme Court under Criminal Appeal Act 1968 Part II, the court may make a defendant's costs order in favour of the accused.

Prosecution of Offences Act 1985 s 16(6A)[454] Where the court considers that there are circumstances that make it inappropriate for the accused to recover the full amount mentioned in subsection (6), a defendant's costs order must be for the payment out of central funds of such lesser amount as the court considers just and reasonable.

(6B) Subsections (6) and (6A) have effect subject to:

(a) section 16A, and

(b) regulations under section 20(1A)(d).

(6C) When making a defendant's costs order, the court must fix the amount to be paid out of central funds in the order if it considers it appropriate to do so and:

(a) the accused agrees the amount, or

(b) subsection (6A) applies.

(6D) Where the court does not fix the amount to be paid out of central funds in the order:

(a) it must describe in the order any reduction required under subsection (6A), and

(b) the amount must be fixed by means of a determination made by or on behalf of the court in accordance with procedures specified in regulations made by the Lord Chancellor.

Practice Direction (Costs in Criminal Proceedings) 2015 EWCA Crim 1568 para 2.4.1 A successful appellant under Criminal Appeal Act 1968 Part I may be awarded a defendant's costs order. Orders may also be made…in the case of a person whose sentence is reviewed under Criminal Justice Act 1988 s 36 (see Criminal Justice Act 1988 s 36 and Sch 3 para 11).

2.4.3 In considering whether to make such an order, the court will have in mind the principles applied by the Crown Court in relation to acquitted defendants (see paras 2.2.1 and 2.2.2 (see **22.18**)).

R v Zinga (No 3) 2014 EWCA Crim 1888 LCJ Virgin Media (VM) brought a successful private prosecution, see *R v Zinga (No 1)* 2012 EWCA Crim 2357, the conviction appeal, and *R v Zinga (No 2)* 2014 EWCA Crim 52, 2 Cr App R (S) 30 (p 240), the confiscation order appeal. VM was awarded both trial and appeal costs (excluding the confiscation appeal) totalling almost £1m under Prosecution of Offences Act 1985 s 17. VM then applied for £93,000 costs relating to the confiscation order appeal which was for the work of a partner, a trainee and two junior experienced counsel. VM argued that they had no specialist knowledge of criminal law and the hourly charging rates for the partner, trainee and two counsel (£445, £145, £300 and £200 respectively) were justified. Held. There is no good reason not to apply the same approach to identical language in s 17 as to s 16(6) (the provision regarding Defendant's Costs Orders). We adopt an approach similar to the Court's approach in *R v Dudley Magistrates' Court*

[454] As inserted by Legal Aid, Sentencing and Punishment of Offenders Act 2012 Sch 7 para 2 (commencement 1/10/12), Legal Aid, Sentencing and Punishment of Offenders Act 2012 (Commencement No 2 and Specification of Commencement Date) Order 2012 2012/2412

ex parte Power City Stores 1990 154 JP 654 to s 16(6), albeit that that case is not binding. However, since that was decided, the legal services market has moved on. The approach to be adopted is therefore:

(a) in determining whether a person, whether it be a corporate body or private individual, has acted reasonably and properly in instructing the solicitors and advocates instructed, the court will consider what steps were taken to ensure that the terms on which the solicitors and advocates were engaged were reasonable.

(b) the private prosecutor is expected properly and reasonably to examine the competition in the relevant market, test it and seek tenders or quotations before selecting the solicitor and advocate instructed. Rarely, if ever, will it be reasonable to instruct the solicitors and advocates without taking such steps.

(c) in determining whether the costs which are charged are proper and reasonable in a criminal case, the court will also have regard to the relevant market and the much greater flexibility in the way in which work is done.

(d) the court will also have regard to the guidance given by the Ministry of Justice.

The counsel for the trial needed very specialist knowledge of copyright law and European directives. In this case, it was reasonable to instruct the same legal team for the appeal as at trial. It not the practice of the Court of Appeal where the issues are of law for solicitors to assist in preparation or for them to attend, except in special circumstances. No special circumstances existed and therefore the significant solicitors' costs were unreasonable. The only costs reasonably incurred were those of formally instructing counsel, and attendances on and correspondence with the parties to this appeal, including VM. The hourly rates are adjusted to those of the Senior Court Costs Office guide, accounting for the fact that the rates were fixed in 2010. Therefore, we allow £320 and £125 for the partner and trainee respectively. The response to this appeal could reasonably have been prepared by one advocate alone and conferences and discussions with the solicitor were unreasonable. The proper approach is to consider the brief fee that should properly and reasonably have been charged for one experienced counsel to cover preparation, a skeleton argument and attendance at the hearing. An hourly rate is neither appropriate nor reasonable for this type of appeal. In this case, following the table of fees for the Administrative Court, which may provide a helpful starting point for judges, a brief fee of £10,500 for counsel of 20 years' seniority for the two hearings in total is reasonable.

22.65 *Crown Court No appeal about costs from Magistrates' Court*

Magistrates' Courts Act 1980 s 108(1) A person convicted by a Magistrates' Court may appeal to the Crown Court:

(a) if he pleaded guilty, against his sentence,

(b) if he did not, against the conviction or sentence.

Magistrates' Courts Act 1980 s 108(3) In this section 'sentence' includes any order made on conviction by a Magistrates' Court, not being:..b) an order for the payment of costs.

22.66 *Court of Appeal Appellant in person*

Prosecution of Offences Act 1985 s 19(4) The Court of Appeal may order the payment out of central funds of such sums as appear to it to be reasonably sufficient to compensate an appellant who is not in custody and who appears before it on, or in connection with, his appeal under Criminal Appeal Act 1968 Part I.

22.67 *Court of Appeal Don't appeal the details*

R v Macatonia 2009 EWCA Crim 2516 The defence contended that the prosecution charged at too high a rate and the time claimed was too high. Held. It would be a sad day if it was thought that orders for costs made, as this order was, on the basis of limited information, at the close of proceedings, should be appealed to this court on anything other than a decision which was effectively manifestly excessive, or was wrong in principle. We cannot be concerned with points of detail.

22.68 ***Costs in Court of Appeal Transcripts***
Prosecution of Offences Act 1985 s 18(6) Costs ordered to be paid under subsection (2) or (2A) may include the reasonable cost of any transcript of a record of proceedings made in accordance with rules of court made for the purposes of Criminal Appeal Act 1968 s 32.
Practice Direction (Costs in Criminal Proceedings) 2015 EWCA Crim 1568 para 3.3 The Court of Appeal (Crim Div) may order an unsuccessful appellant to pay costs to such person as may be named in the order. Such costs may include the costs of any transcript obtained for the proceedings in the Court of Appeal, Prosecution of Offences Act 1985 s 18(2) and (6).

Solicitors paying costs: Inherent jurisdiction

22.69 ***Solicitors paying costs Inherent jurisdiction***
Practice Direction (Costs in Criminal Proceedings) 2015 EWCA Crim 1568 para 1.2.3 The Senior Courts also have the power under their inherent jurisdiction over officers of the court to order a solicitor personally to pay costs thrown away. The inherent jurisdiction of the court should be invoked only to avoid a clear injustice.[455] Where the legislature has stepped in with particular legislation in a particular area (e.g. the wasted costs provisions) then, within that particular area, the existing inherent jurisdiction will be ousted or curtailed, at any rate in so far as the particular legislation is negative in character.[456] Given the present provisions relating to costs, the exercise of the inherent jurisdiction will occur only in the rarest of circumstances.
4.6.2 No such order may be made unless reasonable notice has been given to the solicitor of the matter alleged against him and he is given a reasonable opportunity of being heard in reply.
4.6.3 This power should be used only in exceptional circumstances not covered by the statutory powers: see para 1.2.3.

23 COUNSEL/ADVOCATES, DUTIES OF

General

23.1 ***Barristers Code of Conduct***
BSB Handbook May 2018
The Conduct Rules: You and the court
rC3 You owe a duty to the court to act with independence in the interests of justice. This duty overrides any inconsistent obligations which you may have (other than obligations under the criminal law). It includes the following specific obligations…

.1 you must not knowingly or recklessly mislead or attempt to mislead the court;
.2 you must not abuse your role as an advocate;
.3 you must take reasonable steps to avoid wasting the court's time;
.4 you must take reasonable steps to ensure that the court has before it all relevant decisions and legislative provisions;
.5 you must ensure that your ability to act independently is not compromised.

rC4 Your duty to act in the best interests of each client is subject to your duty to the court.
rC5 Your duty to the court does not require you to act in breach of your duty to keep the affairs of each client confidential.

23.2 ***Solicitor-advocates Code of Conduct***
Solicitors Regulation Authority Code of Conduct 2011 Version 20 1 October 2018 Chapter 5

[455] *Symbol Park Lane Ltd v Steggles Palmer* 1985 1 WLR 668
[456] *Shiloh Spinners Ltd v Harding* 1973 AC 691, *Harrison v Tew* 1989 QB 307

This chapter is about your duties to your client and to the court if you are exercising a right to conduct litigation or acting as an advocate. The outcomes apply to both litigation and advocacy but there are some indicative behaviours which may be relevant only when you are acting as an advocate.
You must achieve these outcomes:

O(5.1) you do not attempt to deceive or knowingly or recklessly mislead the court,
O(5.2) you are not complicit in another person deceiving or misleading the court,
O(5.3-5.8) [Not listed]
Acting in the following way(s) may tend to show that you have achieved these outcomes and therefore complied with the Principles:
IB(5.1) advising your clients to comply with court orders made against them, and advising them of the consequences of failing to comply,
IB(5.2) drawing the court's attention to relevant cases and statutory provisions, and any material procedural irregularity.
IB(5.3-5.13) [Not listed]

23.3 ***Duties of counsel/advocate Assist the judge/Know the court's sentencing powers***

R v Komsta and Murphy 1990 12 Cr App R (S) 63 It cannot be too clearly understood that there is a positive obligation on counsel (not just counsel for defendants but counsel who represent the prosecution) to ensure that no order is made that the court has no power to make. That is something which should be fully understood by all members of the bar. Counsel should not hesitate to invite the Court to exercise [powers to vary an unlawful sentence] in appropriate cases.
R v Hartrey 1993 14 Cr App R (S) 507 It is the duty of both prosecuting and defence counsel to inform themselves of the extent of the court's powers in any case in which they are instructed, to know what options are open to the trial judge and to correct him if, as it is unfortunately only too easy to do in the morass of legislation which governs the subject, he should make a mistake. Prosecuting counsel, in particular, is not there merely to recite a brief résumé of the facts, to produce the antecedent history of the defendant, and thereafter to take no further interest in the proceedings.
R v Johnstone 1996 The Times 18/6/96 LCJ No judge is to be criticised when confronted with such a catalogue of offending if, from time to time, he lost sight of the technical nuances of his sentencing powers. It was to be profoundly hoped that, assisted by counsel on both sides, he would be put back on track and thus spare the Registrar of Criminal Appeals or the full court from having to interfere on a wholly academic but nonetheless important basis when dealing with important sentences.
R v Blight 1999 2 Cr App R (S) 196 LCJ It is difficult to see how those who mitigate can do so properly without having in the very front of their minds the powers within which the judge must exercise his duty. Counsel is not performing his own duty merely by having a copy of *Archbold* to hand. Whether or not the judge asks for assistance, he should immediately be able to draw the judge's attention to any unlawful sentence or similar oversight.
R v Cain 2006 EWCA Crim 3233, 2007 2 Cr App R (S) 25 (p 135) LCJ The duty (to be aware of maximum sentences etc.) is not restricted to defence advocates. We emphasise the fact that advocates for the prosecution also owe a duty to assist the judge at the stage of sentencing. It is not satisfactory for a prosecuting advocate, having secured a conviction, to sit back and leave sentencing to the defence. Nor can an advocate, when appearing for the prosecution for the purpose of sentence on a plea of guilty, limit the assistance that he provides to the court to the outlining of the facts and details of the defendant's previous convictions.
The advocate for the prosecution should always be ready to assist the court by drawing attention to any statutory provisions that govern the court's sentencing powers. It is the duty of the prosecuting advocate to ensure that the judge does not, through inadvertence,

impose a sentence that is outside his powers. The advocate for the prosecution should also be in a position to offer to draw the judge's attention to any relevant sentencing guidelines or guideline decisions of this Court.
There is nothing novel about these propositions. They were clearly stated in *Att-Gen's Ref No 52 of 2003* 2003 EWCA Crim 3731 and *R v Pepper and Others* 2005 EWCA Crim 1181, 2006 1 Cr App R (S) 20 (p 111). What causes us particular concern is that, as the appeals before us demonstrate, there appears to be a widespread disregard of these judicial admonitions. It may be that the only way of achieving an acceptable standard of practice is to require the prosecuting advocate to prepare a schedule or memorandum that identifies the matters relevant to sentence to which we have referred above. We are aware that such a requirement has been imposed by a Practice Note dated 21 May 2003 in New Zealand.

23.4 *Prosecution duty to assist the judge with authorities, guidelines and statutory requirements*

Attorney-General's Guidelines on the Acceptance of Pleas and the Prosecutor's Role in the Sentencing Exercise (revised 2009), www.banksr.com Other Matters Guidelines tab para D4 Before the judge gives the indication, the prosecution advocate should draw the judge's attention to any minimum or mandatory statutory sentencing requirements. Where the prosecution advocate would be expected to offer the judge assistance with relevant guideline cases or the views of the Sentencing Guidelines Council, he or she should invite the judge to allow them to do so. Where it applies, the prosecution advocate should remind the judge that the position of the Attorney-General to refer any sentencing decision as unduly lenient is unaffected. In any event, the prosecution advocate should not say anything which may create the impression that the sentence indication has the support or approval of the Crown.
R v Richards 1993 The Times 1/4/93 LCJ The Judge had specifically asked for the assistance of counsel in relation to sentencing indecent assault but was unfortunately misinformed. Held *obiter*. Counsel, particularly counsel for the Crown, had a duty to the court to inform himself or herself of the maximum sentence for any of the offences for which the court was going to have to sentence and to make sure that if the judge made any error he was reminded of his powers. See *R v Nunes* 1991 The Times 31/7/91.
Att-Gen's Ref No 7 of 1997 1998 1 Cr App R (S) 268 at 272 LCJ It is pertinent to observe that the practice of reticence during the sentencing process developed in days before the Attorney-General had power to refer unduly lenient sentences to this Court, at a time when sentencing provisions were very much less complex than they are today, and at a time before sentencing decisions were as fully reported as they now are. Judges should not, we suggest, be slow to invite assistance from prosecuting counsel in these matters, and counsel should be ready to offer assistance if asked. We further hope that judges will not be affronted if prosecuting counsel do offer to give guidance to the relevant provisions and appropriate authorities when these difficult matters fall to be considered.
Att-Gen's Ref Nos 80-81 of 1999 2000 2 Cr App R (S) 138 LCJ It is clearly understood the duty of prosecution counsel is to draw the judge's attention to authority which in the prosecution submission the judge should be aware of.
R v Cain 2006 EWCA Crim 3233, 2007 2 Cr App R (S) 25 (p 135) LCJ The duty (to be aware of maximum sentences etc.) is not restricted to defence advocates...It may be that the only way of achieving an acceptable standard of practice is to require the prosecuting advocate to prepare a schedule or memorandum that identifies the matters relevant to sentence to which we have referred above. We are aware that such a requirement has been imposed by a Practice Note dated 21 May 2003 in New Zealand.
R v G 2014 EWCA Crim 1221 LCJ D was convicted of rape and other sex offences. Before the verdict the Judge warned counsel he was considering a life sentence. Some of the offences were committed before the 2003 changes. Others were not. The Judge received no assistance from prosecution counsel. Counsel said the Judge was experienced and did not need any help. Held. Bearing in mind the time span over which the

offences were committed and the significant changes made by legislation, a judge needs help. It is incumbent on the prosecution to assist the Judge about his powers and remind him of the relevant authorities. The amendments to the legislation needed to be carefully analysed by the Judge. We will ask the DPP to make sure [that] Crown counsel are reminded in cases of this gravity [that] assistance must be provided whatever view may be taken of the experience of the judge.

23.5 ***Duty of legal representatives to tell the court of other matters awaiting sentence***
R v Bennett 1980 2 Cr App R (S) 96 D was ordered to perform 200 hours of community work and later dealt with for earlier offences by 18 months' imprisonment. Held. It needs to be said, as firmly and as strongly as possible, that there is an obligation on solicitors, counsel and judges alike to do all within their power to ensure that as far as possible all outstanding charges against a defendant are dealt with in the same court, by the same judge upon a single occasion. This will enable a consistency in the sentencing of an individual person to be achieved and the kind of unsatisfactory situation such as now confronts this Court to be eliminated.
So we wish to make it plain that when a solicitor and a member of the Bar know that there are other charges against him to be dealt with than those before the Court they should ensure that an application is made to the judge to have the defendant they represent put back to be dealt with later at that Crown Court centre or be transferred to another Crown Court centre where the other outstanding charges lie. Since they are more likely than anyone else to have this kind of knowledge, solicitors especially should be alert to achieving this conclusion.
See also the **Attorney-General's References** ***Judicial indications Defence counsel must warn defendant*** para at **8.3** and the **Factual Basis for Sentencing** ***Duty of defence counsel to raise issue/write to the prosecution*** para at **57.45**.
See also the **Attorney-General's References** ***Judicial indications If sentence inappropriate prosecution must dissent*** para at **8.6** and the ***Judicial indication Prosecution acquiescence*** para at **8.7**.

23.6 ***Press notices, Prosecution involved in***
R v Innospec Ltd 2010 Lloyd's Rep FC 462 www.banksr.com Other Matters Other documents Crown Court decisions Southwark Crown Court Thomas LJ The defendant company pleaded to conspiracy to corrupt where approximately $8m in bribes were paid. There were concurrent criminal proceedings in other jurisdictions. There was a suggestion that the company should issue a press notice in an approved form. This is not a practice which should be adopted in England and Wales…It would be inconceivable for a prosecutor to approve a press statement [for] a person convicted of burglary or rape. Companies who are guilty of corruption should be treated no differently [from] others who commit serious crimes.

Dangerous offender provisions

23.7 ***Dangerous offender provisions, Duty to be aware of***
R v Reynolds and Others 2007 EWCA Crim 538, 2 Cr App R (S) 87 (p 553) The fact that so many mistakes are still being made means that we must reinforce what this Court has said time and time again, and the Lord Chief Justice has recently underlined in *R v Cain* 2006, see **23.3**, about the duty of both prosecuting and defence counsel to ensure that they are fully aware themselves of the potential impact of the dangerousness provisions of Criminal Justice Act 2003 on their case, are prepared to assist the judge in that respect, and are alert to any mistakes that the judge makes in passing sentence, so that any problem can be resolved before it is too late. As far as judges themselves are concerned, we would recommend that they have the statute itself available so that its provisions can be readily referred to.
Court of Appeal, see the **Appeals: Court of Appeal** chapter.

24 Court Martial

24.1

The courts Military offences can be dealt with either: a) summarily by a commanding officer, Armed Forces Act 2006 s 131, or b) by a Court Martial, Armed Forces Act 2006 s 50 and 154. A Court Martial is presided over by a judge advocate and military lay members make up the board, which performs the role of a jury, Armed Forces Act 2006 s 155. Deliberations are in private. Where there is an equality of votes, the judge advocate has the casting vote.

This book does not deal with summary proceedings due to lack of space. The majority of the entries for Court Martial in this book are next to the comparable entry for the civilian courts.

R v Love 1998 1 Cr App R 458 Court Martial sentences are concerned at one and the same time to achieve two things. First, to punish service personnel for the criminality of their conduct, second, to deal with them also on a disciplinary basis. In that they are unique. Members of other professions and occupations who transgress the law of the land are dealt with quite separately: a) by the civilian criminal courts, followed b) if appropriate, by disciplinary proceedings before their own professional bodies. This would be so, for example, in the case of lawyers, doctors, nurses, architects and police officers. These considerations [are] of some importance when it comes to determining what should be this Court's approach to these appeals.

Venues The Military Court Service (MCS) is part of the Ministry of Defence, and maintains five staffed Military Court Centres at Bulford (Wiltshire), Catterick (Yorkshire), Colchester (Essex), Portsmouth (Hampshire) and Sennelager (Germany).

Maximum penalties These are listed in the *Guidance on Sentencing in the Court Martial 2018* Annex A.

Civilians The jurisdiction to deal with civilians (whether they are ex-servicemen or not) is at *Guidance on Sentencing in the Court Martial 2018* para 4.1. The range of sentences that can be imposed is at para 4.3.

Disciplinary offences These are dealt with in the *Guidance on Sentencing in the Court Martial 2018* paras 6.1 to 6.20.

24.2 *Statistics*

Number of hearings

	2008	2009	2010	2011	2012	2013	2014	2015	2016	2017
Number	741	705	485	643	404	540	514	342	435	400

For an explanation about the statistics, see page 1-xxii. For more statistics, see www.banksr.com Other Matters Statistics tab.

Procedure

24.3 *Reporting restrictions*

Practice in the Court Martial: Collected Memoranda 2011 para 11.1 contains directions about reporting restrictions in the Court Martial.

24.4 *The purposes of sentencing*

Armed Forces Act 2006 s 237(1) A court or officer dealing with an offender for a service offence must have regard to the following purposes of sentencing:

(a) the punishment of offenders,

(b) the maintenance of discipline,

(c) the reduction of service offences and other crime (including reduction by deterrence),

(d) the reform and rehabilitation of offenders,

(e) the protection of the public,

(f) the making of reparation by offenders to persons affected by their offences.

(2) If the offender is aged under 18 the court or officer must also have regard to his welfare.
(3) This section does not apply in relation to:
(a) an offence the sentence for which is fixed by law,
(b) an offence the sentence for which, as a result of subsection (2) of Armed Forces Act 2006 s 218A, 219, 221 and 225-227[457] (required custodial sentences) falls to be imposed under:
Criminal Justice Act 2003 s 224A, 225(2) or 226(2)[458] [the dangerousness provisions],
Powers of Criminal Courts (Sentencing) Act 2000 s 110(2) or 111(2) [minimum sentences], or
Firearms Act 1968 s 51A(2) [minimum sentences],
(c) an offence the sentence for which falls to be imposed under Armed Forces Act 2006 s 227A(2) [offences of threatening with a weapon in public or on school premises].[459]
(4) In this section 'sentencing' includes the making of any order when dealing with an offender in respect of his offence.

24.5 *Statutory approach to sentencing*

Armed Forces Act 2006 s 238(1) A court or officer dealing with an offender for a service offence ('the current offence') must in considering the seriousness of the offence:
(a) consider the offender's culpability in committing the offence and any harm which the offence caused, was intended to cause or could foreseeably have caused,
(b) if the offender has one or more previous convictions, treat as an aggravating factor each previous conviction that the court or officer considers can reasonably be so treated,
(c) if the offender committed the current offence while:
(i) charged with another service offence and released from service custody, or
(ii) on bail,
treat the fact that it was committed in those circumstances as an aggravating factor.
(2) In considering whether a previous conviction can reasonably be treated as an aggravating factor the court or officer must have regard (in particular) to:
(a) the nature of the offence to which the conviction relates and its relevance to the current offence, and
(b) the time that has elapsed since the conviction.
(3) Any reference in subsection (1) or (2) to a previous conviction is to be read as a reference to:
(a) a previous conviction of a service offence,
(b) a previous conviction by a court in the British Islands of an offence other than a service offence,
(c) a previous conviction by a court in a member State other than the United Kingdom of a relevant offence under the law of that State, or
(d) a finding of guilt in respect of a member State service offence.
(4) Nothing in this section prevents the court or officer from treating:
(a) a previous conviction by a court outside both the British Islands and any member State, or
(b) a previous conviction by a court in any member State (other than the United Kingdom) of an offence which is not a relevant offence or a member State service offence,
as an aggravating factor in any case where the court or officer considers it appropriate to do so.

[457] 'Section 218A' was inserted by Legal Aid, Sentencing and Punishment of Offenders Act 2012 Sch 22 para 31(a).
[458] 'Section 224A' was inserted by Legal Aid, Sentencing and Punishment of Offenders Act 2012 Sch 22 para 31(b).
[459] 'Section 237(3)(c)' was inserted by Legal Aid, Sentencing and Punishment of Offenders Act 2012 Sch 26 para 25.

(5) For the purposes of this section:
(a) an offence is 'relevant' if the offence would constitute an offence under the law of any part of the United Kingdom if it were done in that part at the time of the conviction in respect of the current offence,
(b) 'member State service offence' means an offence which:
(i) was the subject of proceedings under the service law of a member State other than the United Kingdom, and
(ii) would constitute an offence under the law of any part of the United Kingdom, or a service offence, if it were done in any part of the United Kingdom, by a member of Her Majesty's forces, at the time of the conviction of the defendant for the current offence, and
(c) 'service law', in relation to a member State other than the United Kingdom, means the law governing all or any of the naval, military or air forces of that State.

24.6 ***The approach to sentencing***

Guidance on Sentencing in the Court Martial 2018 para 1.1 (edited) Sentencing is a complex and difficult exercise and whilst it must not be reduced to a rigid or mechanistic process, consistency of approach is essential to maintain public confidence. Those who sentence have a discretion to reflect the gravity of the offence, the effect on the victim, the circumstances of the offender, and the public and Service interest.

para 2.7 (edited) The close-knit structure of the Armed Forces means the sentences are more widely disseminated than civilian sentences and thus deterrence is a more important factor in Court Martial sentencing.

R v Cooney and Others 1999 2 Cr App R 428 Courts-Martial Appeal Court The Court Martial in sentencing may helpfully ask itself:
(a) Is this a case where the offence merits loss of liberty, taking into account:
(i) the touchstone of what might occur in a civilian court,
(ii) any issue of service context rendering it the more serious,
(iii) the length and nature of service and record of the defendant?
(b) What are the financial consequences of dismissal?
(c) Is imprisonment necessary?
(d) Is service detention, if available for the defendant, appropriate, taking into account the nature of the offence, the less serious nature of that punishment compared with imprisonment and the lower remission available?
(e) Is dismissal merited despite (if such be the case) the recommendation of a commanding officer that the defendant should be retained and notwithstanding the financial consequences of such dismissal?
(f) If custody is necessary and service detention is available, and there would be severe financial consequences attendant on dismissal, should service detention be imposed, notwithstanding that imprisonment would be imposed in a civilian court?
(g) If service detention is appropriate, what should be its duration bearing in mind the different consequences in relation to dismissal of a sentence of a year or more?

R v Heslop 2016 EWCA Crim 1951 Court Martial Appeal Court D was convicted of assault by penetration. Held. para 18 Sentencing is not just a matter of applying the guideline as there are the additional military principles to consider that include the maintenance of discipline and the reduction in service offending.

24.7 ***Court of Appeal judgments, Applying***

Guidance on Sentencing in the Court Martial 2018 para 3.1.1 (edited) The Court Martial has the same regard as civilian courts to judgments of the Court of Appeal which give guidance as to sentencing, and to guidelines of the Sentencing Council to the extent that they are applicable.

24.8 *Majority and tied decisions*
Guidance on Sentencing in the Court Martial 2018 para 2.4 (edited) The judge and board members often achieve consensus, but if it is necessary for them to vote on sentence only a simple majority is required with the judge having the casting vote.

24.9 *Separate or global sentences*
Guidance on Sentencing in the Court Martial 2018 para 2.13 The Court Martial is required to pass a separate sentence in respect of each offence (see Armed Forces Act 2006 s 255), except where the trial was at the election of the defendant, in which case one global sentence for all offences is passed (see Armed Forces Act 2006 s 131(5) and 165). Where the court considers that the totality of the offending should be marked by a disciplinary sanction (such as dismissal, reduction in rank etc.) the relevant sentence may either be attached to each charge or to a more serious charge with 'No Separate Penalty' recorded against the others.

24.10 *Parity with sentences at civilian courts*
R v Cooney and Others 1999 2 Cr App R 428 Courts-Martial Appeal Court The three defendants were sentenced for indecent assault, causing death by dangerous driving and false accounting. All were considered very highly by their superiors. Held. Although parity and consistency in sentencing are important, there are a variety of reasons why sentences in military and civilian contexts may differ. Some offences in a service context may be treated more severely, but others may be treated apparently more leniently, because of the availability as an alternative to imprisonment of service detention, with its own objectives and different rules of remission, or because of the serious financial consequences. In a closely knit and inherently hierarchical organisation such as the armed services, there may be a particular need to mark criminal conduct that is inimical to trust or to discipline with a substantial form of punishment. Further, especially where the offender enjoys senior NCO or officer rank, the question of an exemplary or deterrent sentence may fall for consideration. The issue of whether there is a service context must always be considered by this Court when exercising its jurisdiction. Although, in relation to drugs offences, the supply of drugs may be more serious in a service context, one-off possession may call for similar treatment in a military and civilian context. Violence and sexual offences may call for similar treatment, whether in a military or civilian context, but, in the services the need for deterrence may be more significant if, for example, violence is used by a superior officer, or seniority in rank is abused when committing a sexual offence. Dishonesty may be treated similarly in both contexts, but breaches of trust by officers or senior NCOs may be more serious because of the risk of setting a bad example to lower ranks. We take into account the recommendation from C's commanding officer and the financial consequences with the longer than necessary punishments and reduce them.

24.11 *Preserving an army career*
Att-Gen's Ref No 18 of 2016 2016 EWCA Crim 522 D pleaded at the Crown Court to three threats to kill, inflicting grievous bodily harm (section 20), assault by beating and damaging property. A Major from his unit spoke of D's superb performance in the field. The Judge gave him a suspended sentence. Held. This court does what it properly can to preserve a soldier's career and by doing so produces an outcome which is most beneficial for both society and the offender. However, this was not such a case.
For more details see **292.17** in Volume 2.

24.12 *Combat stress*
R v Blackman 2014 EWCA Crim 1029, 2 Cr App R 18 (p 244) Court Martial Appeal Court LCJ D was convicted of murder. He was a sergeant in the Royal Marines and calmly shot an unarmed, badly injured, Afghan insurgent. D had spent 15 years in the Royal Marines and character witnesses commented on his exceptional qualities as an outstanding commander in his post. He had completed six tours of duty. A medical report produced two years after the incident noted that D suffered from accumulated frustration

and could have suffered from combat stress disorder, though it was not possible to say with any certainty. Held. para 68 In mitigation, D had an outstanding service record. para 69 The effects on him of the nature of the conflict and the command he exercises were mitigating factors. The most serious [effect] was the stress. para 70 It is self-evident that forces sent to combat insurgents will be placed under much greater stress than forces sent to fight a regular army. para 72 D was under considerable stress dealing with insurgency and significant further stress because of the remote location of his command post. He had had little face-to-face contact with those commanding him and they could not assess the effect of the conditions upon him.
para 73 The Court Martial was correct that a very substantial reduction from the starting point was required. para 75 D's mental welfare had not been assessed in the ordinary way. The combat stress should have been accorded greater weight. **8 years,** not 10. For more detail see the **MURDER** para at **287.68** in Volume 2.

24.13 ***Reasons Judge must give reasons Court Martial***

Duty to give reasons and explain sentence

Armed Forces Act 2006 s 252(1) Any court or officer passing sentence on an offender for a service offence:

(a) must state in open court, in ordinary language and in general terms and in accordance with section 253, its (or his) reasons for deciding on the sentence passed, and

(b) must explain to the offender in ordinary language:

(i) the effect of the sentence,

(ii) where the offender is required to comply with any order forming part of the sentence, the effects of non-compliance with the order,

(iii) any power, on the application of the offender or any other person, to vary or review any order forming part of the sentence, and

(iv) where the sentence consists of or includes a fine, the effects of failure to pay the fine.

(2) Subsection (1)(a) does not apply:

(a) to an offence the sentence for which is fixed by law, or

(b) to an offence the sentence for which, as a result of subsection (2) of section 225, 226 or 227 of this Act (required custodial sentences), falls to be imposed under Sentencing Act s 110(2) or 111(2) or Firearms Act 1968 s 51A(2) (minimum sentences).

(3) The Secretary of State may by order:

(a) prescribe cases in which subsection (1)(a) or (b) does not apply,

(b) prescribe cases in which the statement referred to in subsection (1)(a) or the explanation referred to in subsection (1)(b) may be made in the absence of the offender, or may be provided in written form.

(4) In this section and section 253 'sentence' includes any order made when dealing with the offender in respect of his offence.

Note: Sentencers would be wise to ignore section 252(2) as it is contrary to Criminal Justice Act 2003 s 174(1). For the case law, see **86.49**. This area is one of the most important for the defendant and the lawyers to hear. The lawyers need the reasons to determine whether the sentence was lawful and within the court's discretion. The Court Martial Appeal Court would also need to know the reasons. Ed.

Particular offences

Note: Particular offences are normally listed in the relevant chapter. Assistance can be found in the back index. Ed.

24.14 ***Absent without leave***

R v Owen 2013 EWCA Crim 2385 Court Martial Appeal Court D, a private, pleaded to three charges of being absent without leave. He joined the Army aged 16. D was absent for 184 days, 28 days and 26 days. He was given 2 months, 3 months and 4 months, making a total of 9 months. He and his family suffered a number of personal problems for which he absented himself to provide support. They included sexual abuse on a relative which caused severe effects and marital problems. He raised these concerns through the chain of command and D felt the response was inadequate. He was told he would have to be on duty on Christmas Day and that caused his first absence. He was contacted two and three months later and told to ask for welfare support. Arrangements were made for a return but he didn't turn up. He was then arrested by the police for a violent offence which ended the first period of absence. No evidence was offered against him and he was ordered to return and failed to do so. This failure started the second period of absence (four days after the end of the first period). He said he wouldn't return. After four weeks he was militarily detained in the UK. He was released on condition he flew to his unit. He failed to do so. The absence caused him to miss training. D, now aged 21, had had several disciplinary findings along with two civilian convictions. The Judge passed 2-month, 3-month and 4-month sentences all consecutive. Held. We have in mind the effect on military discipline of absences like this. The three periods could not be treated as one course of conduct owing to D twice failing to return to his unit when given the opportunity to do so. We note, notwithstanding the problems, he was told he would have to be on duty on Christmas Day. He must have found it extremely difficult to cope with his problems. The weight given to his personal problems was insufficient so **7 months** in all.

24.15 ***Assaults***

Guidance on Sentencing in the Court Martial 2018 **Offences of Violence (Assault, Battery, ABH, GBH, Wounding)** para 5.9.1 [edited] Unlawful violence displays a lack of discipline and can corrode unit cohesiveness and operational effectiveness, particularly when directed towards service colleagues. Deterrent sentences are often necessary particularly where violence is associated with excess alcohol. The starting points for more serious offences of violence are those provided in the [Sentencing Council] guidelines, but factors resulting from operational considerations may amount to mitigation justifying a lower sentence than in the guidelines.

For the aggravating and mitigating factors, and the starting points for ABH, see paras 5.9.2 to 5.9.5.

R v L 2017 EWCA Crim 709 D, a Lance Corporal in the Royal Military Police (RMP), was convicted of one count of battery. D, V and other members of their RMP unit had been at a bowling alley. D and V had had a lot to drink and they continued to drink when they got back to their accommodation. D banged on V's door in an aggressive manner. They got into an argument and it was suggested that V said to D, "Get out, you Fenian bastard." D then punched V to the left side of his face and an exchange of blows took place. A witness entered the room and saw V sitting on the floor with D standing over him. D punched V three times in the face. The witness intervened and stopped a fourth punch before ushering D from the room. In interview, D could not remember why he was in V's room. The insult from V was said to be particularly provocative because D was a Roman Catholic from Northern Ireland who, despite consequences to him and his family, had had the courage to join the British Army. The author of the pre-sentence report proposed a fine and/or a severe reprimand as being a suitable punishment. The Judge Advocate, upon hearing that the defence was hoping to dissuade him from ordering D's dismissal, said "Police officers are trusted. They are given rank and powers. Unfortunately, when something goes wrong and they behave in the way that your client did, consequences follow." That the attack was on a fellow serviceman and in his own private quarters were aggravating factors. In mitigation, D had an exemplary four-year record and was of previous good character. He was reduced to the ranks, dismissed from the service and ordered to serve 60 days' detention. A reduction to the ranks would end D's career in the RMP. Held. The offence must be seen in the military context. Court Martial Guidance for sentencing is explicit: regard should be had to the Sentencing Council guidelines. The only reference the Judge Advocate made to the guidelines was to say that they would not be helpful. Had this offence been committed in a civilian context by a man of previous good character, it is highly unlikely he would have received a custodial sentence. The sentencing process was flawed. D has already served 60 days' detention. Therefore, we quash the order for dismissal, detention and reduction to the ranks and in their place impose a **severe reprimand.** If the detention had not been served we would have imposed a fine and/or a compensation order.

24.16 ***Motoring offences***

Guidance on Sentencing in the Court Martial 2018 para 5.11.1 **Motoring Offences** [edited] Motoring offences within military establishments, if committed on roads that are as a matter of law public roads, are dealt with in the same way as motoring offences on public roads in England and Wales but are subject to a different sentencing regime because the Court Martial has no power to impose penalty points on driving licences or disqualify from driving. Driving offences are often charged as breaches of standing orders.

For details of overseas cases and serious and alcohol-related motoring offences, see paras 5.11.1 to 5.11.3.

24.17 ***Unfitness or misconduct through alcohol***

Guidance on Sentencing in the Court Martial 2018 www.banksr.com Other Matters Guidelines tab para 6.14 **Service policy** [Not listed. Mitigating and aggravating factors and starting points set out.]

R v Rabouhi 2014 EWCA Crim 1517 D was convicted of misconduct through alcohol. D had been out at a US base with other NCOs for drinks and a meal. Returning in the early hours, D was talking to V, a senior NCO, and other colleagues when three officers came in. A verbal altercation followed and D later admitted to behaving obnoxiously, though one officer conceded that his own behaviour may have led D to lash out. V tried to prevent D returning to the scene and there was physical contact. D punched V three times. V fell to the ground. V accepted he was at fault. D eventually went to his room but then returned and threatened one of the officers with assault. In interview, D said he had drunk four or five units of alcohol and was 'quite merry'. He also admitted to pushing an officer in the first exchange but said he acted in self-defence (no assault offence was proved). D, aged 34, was a corporal with almost ten years' service and was of exemplary character. He could have had the matter dealt with by his commanding officer but chose not to. Held. Although striking a senior NCO is capable of fortifying a charge, D's commanding officer valued him and was likely to have disposed of the matter more leniently. **Reprimand**, not £1,000 fine.

Appeals

24.18

The appeal courts The appeal from a summary hearing is to the Summary Appeal Court. The appeal from a Court Martial is to the Court Martial Appeal Court, Armed Forces Act 2006 s 272. The Judges are normally Court of Appeal judges. The Court normally sits at the Royal Courts of Justice in London.

R v Martin 2017 EWCA Crim 648, 2 Cr App R (S) 28 (p 226) LCJ para 15 The Court of Appeal and Court Martial Appeal Court have a materially identical review role, with no significant difference between their practice and procedure with regard to the way in which post-sentence matters are treated. para 26 Extraordinarily, it is open to this Court to consider post-sentencing matters [which we do here].

24.19 ***Powers of the Court Martial Appeal Court***

Court Martial Appeals Act 1968 s 16A(1) Where, on a single occasion, the Court Martial passes two or more sentences on a person, an appeal or application for leave to appeal against any of those sentences is to be treated as an appeal or application in respect of both or all of them.

(2) On an appeal against sentence the Appeal Court may quash the sentence passed by the Court Martial and pass in substitution for it any sentence that:

(a) they think appropriate, and

(b) is a sentence that the Court Martial had power to pass in respect of the offence.

(3) But the Court may not exercise their powers under subsection (2) in such a way that, taking the case as a whole, the appellant is dealt with more severely on appeal than he was dealt with by the Court Martial.

24.20 ***Court Martial Appeal Court Practice and Procedure***

R v Martin 2017 EWCA Crim 648, 2 Cr App R (S) 28 (p 226) LCJ para 15 The Court of Appeal and Court Martial Appeal Court have a materially identical review role, with no significant difference between their practice and procedure with regard to the way in which post-sentence matters are treated. para 26 Extraordinarily, it is open to this Court to consider post-sentencing matters [which we do here].

24.21 ***Appeals Deference to Court Martial***

R v Birch 2011 EWCA Crim 46 Court Martial Appeal Court As a matter of principle a Court Martial is a specialist court. It has an ability to assess the likely effect on a service which depends upon mutual confidence of a person's continued service which it is difficult for this Court as an appeal court to reproduce. For those reasons there are, as is well known, a number of observations to that effect in the decided cases and we treat them as axiomatic. A Court Martial is entitled to a level of deference from this Court. That said, this Court exists to interfere with sentences when they are wrong.

Service Community Orders

24.22

Armed Forces Act 2006 s 164 and 178

Availability The Court may pass service detention for all ranks and civilians if: a) the offender is aged over 18 and will reside in the UK when the order is in force, and b) they have been dismissed from the Armed Forces, see Armed Forces Act 2006 s 164 and *Guidance on Sentencing in the Court Martial 2018* Annex B.

Service Supervision and Punishment Order This is a lesser alternative order to a Service Community Order. It was designed to place restrictions on an offender whilst ensuring that he or she remains available to his or her unit for normal work. It is not available for officers, warrant officers, NCOs, ex-service personnel or civilians, see *Guidance on Sentencing in the Court Martial 2018* Annex B.

Requirements are made in the order and one-sixth of an offender's gross pay is forfeit, Armed Forces Act 2006 s 173(1). The order must be for 90, 60 or 30 days, beginning with the day the order was made, Armed Forces Act 2006 s 173(2). There are certain restrictions in terms of the rank of the offender and the length of the order and discretionary elements of the punishment may be varied by the commanding officer. The order cannot be nullified by the offender's commanding officer.

Overseas Community Order This order is only available for civilians dealt with by the Court Martial who will reside outside the UK when the order is in force. There are significant restrictions on its operation, see Armed Forces Act 2006 s 182-183 and *Guidance on Sentencing in the Court Martial 2018* Annex B.

Service Supervision and Punishment Order For more guidance, see *Guidance on Sentencing in the Court Martial 2018* para 3.10.1.

24.23 ***Definition***

Armed Forces Act 2006 s 178(1) A service community order is an order:

(a) imposing on the offender one or more of the requirements mentioned in section 177(1) of the 2003 Act (community orders under that Act), and

(b) specifying the local justice area in England and Wales…where the offender resides or will reside.

24.24 ***Power to order***

Armed Forces Act 2006 s 164(1) [The court may make a service community order] only if the person being sentenced is on the same occasion sentenced to dismissal or dismissal with disgrace and subsection (5) permits.

Armed Forces Act 2006 s 164(5) The court may not make a service community order unless:

(a) the offender is aged 18 or over when convicted, and

(b) it appears to the court that he will reside in the United Kingdom when the order is in force.

Note: A civilian may be sentenced to a Service Community Order. Ed.

24.25 ***Guidance***

Guidance on Sentencing in the Court Martial 2018 para 3.8

Service Community Order (only in combination with dismissal) 3.8.1 This is an order providing Service courts with almost the full range of community punishment options available to civilian courts when the offender is sentenced to dismissal or dismissal with disgrace, and provided he is aged over 18 and will reside in the United Kingdom, Armed Forces Act 2006 s 164 and 178. The court may sentence an offender to any Community Order listed in Criminal Justice Act 2003 s 177.[460]

3.8.2 The court may attach community requirements to a suspended sentence of imprisonment, Armed Forces Act 2006 s 200, but would not normally do so unless the offender was also sentenced to dismissal (see para 3.1.7, see **106.5**). A pre-sentence report is usually available to the court which advises as to the usefulness of any proposed order, and an order is in the same terms as in the civilian courts.

3.8.3 As SCOs may be awarded only in combination with dismissal, their supervision is undertaken by the probation service in the area where the offender is to reside after he has left the Service. Before a court imposes an SCO it must be satisfied that arrangements are in place for the supervision to be carried out. It is, therefore, helpful for the judge to give an early indication to the pre-sentence report writer that dismissal and an SCO is a possible sentence, so that the writer can undertake the necessary checks before making any recommendation.

3.8.4 Breaches of Service Community Orders are dealt with by the civilian courts in the United Kingdom.

24.26 ***Test to apply***

Armed Forces Act 2006 s 270(1) A court must not award a community punishment in respect of an offence unless it is of the opinion that the offence, or the combination of the offence and one or more offences associated with it, was serious enough to warrant such a punishment.

Armed Forces Act 2006 s 270(3) In forming any such opinion as is mentioned in subsection (1), a court must take into account all such information as is available to it about the circumstances of the offence and any associated offence, including any aggravating or mitigating factors.

Armed Forces Act 2006 s 270(6A) The fact that by virtue of any provision of this section:

(a) a community punishment may be awarded in respect of an offence, or

(b) particular restrictions on liberty may be imposed by a community punishment,

does not require a court to award such a punishment or to impose those restrictions.

24.27 ***Imposing requirements***

Armed Forces Act 2006 s 178(2) The power to include in the order one or more of the requirements mentioned in section 177(1) of the 2003 Act is subject to:

(a) any restriction that section 177(1) imposes in relation to a particular requirement,

(b) the provisions of the 2003 Act mentioned in the paragraphs of section 177(2) of that Act, and

(c) section 218 of that Act.

See the **COMMUNITY ORDERS** ***The requirements that can be made part of a community order*** section at **15.16** for details of the requirements which can be imposed.

[460] But see Armed Forces Act 2006 s 178(5) relating to certain minor technical differences.

24.28 ***Requirements must be suitable for the offender***

Armed Forces Act 2006 s 270(2) Where a court awards a community punishment:

(a) the particular requirement (or requirements) included in the order must be such as the court considers the most suitable for the offender, and

(b) the restrictions on liberty imposed by the order must be such as in the opinion of the court are commensurate with the seriousness of the offence, or the combination of the offence and one or more offences associated with it.

(3) In forming any such opinion as is mentioned in subsection (2)(b), a court must take into account all such information as is available to it about the circumstances of the offence and any associated offence, including any aggravating or mitigating factors.

(4) In forming an opinion for the purposes of subsection (2)(a) the court may take into account any information about the offender which is before it.

24.29 ***Discount for time spent in custody***

Armed Forces Act 2006 s 270(5) In determining the restrictions on liberty to be imposed by a community punishment in respect of an offence, the court may have regard to any period for which the offender has, since being charged with the offence or any related offence, been kept in service custody in connection with the offence or any related offence.

(6) In subsection (5) 'related offence' has the meaning given by section 247.

Service Community Orders: Breach of

24.30

Armed Forces Act 2006 Sch 5 and Criminal Justice Act 2003 Sch 8

The rules for breaches of the order are the same as the civilian ones save for the paragraphs listed at **24.33**.

For details see the **COMMUNITY ORDER: BREACH OF** chapter.

24.31 ***Warnings and laying of information***

Armed Forces Act 2006 Sch 5 para 2 Criminal Justice Act 2003 Sch 8 para 5(1)(b) and 6(1) (warning and laying of information) have effect in relation to a service community order under CJA 2003 as if the references to a justice of the peace were to the Crown Court. For the civilian rules, see **16.1**.

General

24.32 ***Civilian rules apply to Service Community Orders***

Armed Forces Act 2006 Sch 5 para 1(1) In Criminal Justice Act 2003 Sch 8 (breach, revocation or amendment of community order), 'community order' includes a Service Community Order under this Act.

24.33 ***Civilian requirements etc. which cannot be imposed on breach***

Armed Forces Act 2006 Sch 5 para 1(2) In its application to such an order, Criminal Justice Act 2003 Sch 8 has effect as if:

para 2(b) (interpretation for community order with drug rehabilitation requirement)

para 4 (orders made on appeal)

para 5(4) (failure to comply dealt with by Crown Court where no contrary order made)

para 6(2) (breach after warning dealt with by Crown Court where no contrary order made)

para 7 (issue of summons or warrant by justice of the peace)

para 9 (breach: powers of Magistrates' Courts)

para 13 (revocation of order with/without re-sentencing: powers of Magistrates' Court)

para 16(5) (amendment by reason of change of residence: 'appropriate court')

para 17(6) (amendment of requirement of order: 'appropriate court')

para 18(4) (amendment of treatment requirements of community order on report of practitioner: 'appropriate court')

para 19A(5) (substituting a later date in a community order)[461]
para 20(2) (extension of unpaid work requirement: 'appropriate court')
para 21 (powers of Magistrates' Court following subsequent conviction)
para 25A (hearings in relation to offender under Sch 8 of this Act)
para 27(1)(b)(ii) (provide a copy of the order to the local Magistrates' Court when revoking or amending order)
para 27(1)(d) (provide copy of order to local Magistrates' Court where court acts in local justice area other than the one specified in the order)
para 27(2) [(provision of documents to the court)]
para 27(3)(a) ('proper officer' in Magistrates' Court is designated officer)

were omitted.

24.34 ***Powers to re-sentence offenders***

Armed Forces Act 2006 Sch 5 para 8(1) This paragraph applies for the purposes of construing the powers conferred on the Crown Court by Criminal Justice Act 2003 Sch 8 para 10(1)(b), 14(2)(b)(ii), 17(3)(b) and 23(2)(b)(ii) to deal with the offender, for the offence in respect of which the order was made, in any way in which he could have been dealt with for that offence by the court which made the order. (The powers conferred are the powers of the Crown Court (see **16.8**), revocation (see **15.54**) and amendment (see **15.43** and **16.10**).)

(2) Each of those powers shall be construed in relation to a Service Community Order under this Act as a power to deal with the offender, for the offence in respect of which the order was made:

(a) if that offence is an offence punishable with imprisonment, in any way in which the Crown Court could deal with him if he had just been convicted before that court of an offence punishable with imprisonment,

(b) if it is not an offence punishable with imprisonment, in any way in which the Crown Court could deal with him if he had just been convicted before that court of an offence not punishable with imprisonment.

(3) A term of imprisonment or fine imposed by virtue of this paragraph:

(a) must not exceed the maximum permitted for the offence in respect of which the order was made, and

(b) where the order was made by the Service Civilian Court, must not exceed:

(i) in the case of a term of imprisonment, 6 months,

(ii) in the case of a fine, the prescribed sum.

24.35 ***Committal on subsequent conviction***

Armed Forces Act 2006 Sch 5 para 7 Criminal Justice Act 2003 Sch 8 para 22 (committal to Crown Court on subsequent conviction by Magistrates' Court in England or Wales) has effect as if the reference to a community order included a Service Community Order. For the civilian powers, see **16.18**.

24.36 ***Amending***

Armed Forces Act 2006 Sch 5 para 5 In Criminal Justice Act 2003 Sch 8 Part 4 (amendment of order) as it applies to a Service Community Order under CJA 2003, 'the appropriate court' means the Crown Court. For the civilian rules, see **15.43** and **16.10**.

Armed Forces Act 2006 Sch 5 para 6 In Criminal Justice Act 2003 Sch 8 para 19 (amendment in relation to review of drug rehabilitation requirement) as it applies to such an order, 'the court responsible for the order' means the Crown Court. For the civilian rules, see **15.50**.

[461] 'para 19A(5)' was inserted by Legal Aid, Sentencing and Punishment of Offenders Act 2012 s 78(6).

24.37 ***Revocation***
Armed Forces Act 2006 Sch 5 para 4 Criminal Justice Act 2003 Sch 8 para 14 (Crown Court's powers of revocation) has effect as if the reference in sub-paragraph (1)(a) to a community order as there mentioned included a Service Community Order under this Act. For the civilian rules, see **15.55**.

24.38 ***Appeals***
Armed Forces Act 2006 Sch 5 para 9 Where a sentence is passed by virtue of Armed Forces Act 2006 Sch 5 para 8 above, Criminal Appeal Act 1968 s 9 (appeal against sentence) applies as if the offender had been convicted on indictment of the offence for which the sentence was passed.

Service Compensation Orders

24.39
Availability The Court may pass this order for all ranks, ex-servicemen and women, and civilians, see Armed Forces Act 2006 s 164 and *Guidance on Sentencing in the Court Martial 2018* Annex B.
Limits on use Armed Forces Act 2006 s 175 places limitations on ordering compensation.
Motor vehicle exception No Service Compensation Order may be made in respect of injury, loss or damage due to an accident arising out of the presence of a motor vehicle on a road unless certain exceptions apply, Armed Forces Act 2006 s 175(5)-(7), see para **24.40**.
Offender's means A court or officer must have regard to a person's financial circumstances so far as they appear or are known to the court or officer, Armed Forces Act 2006 s 250(1).
Insufficient means to pay fine and compensation order Where the court or officer considers that the offender has insufficient means to pay both an appropriate fine and appropriate compensation, the court or officer must give preference to compensation, Armed Forces Act 2006 s 250(2).
Funeral expenses No Service Compensation Order may be made in respect of: a) bereavement, b) funeral expenses, or c) loss of any other kind suffered by the dependants of a person in consequence of his death, Armed Forces Act 2006 s 175(4), see para **24.40**.
For general guidance, see the **COMPENSATION ORDERS** chapter.

24.40 ***Statutory provisions***
Service compensation orders
Armed Forces Act 2006 s 175(1) A Service Compensation Order is an order that requires the offender to pay compensation for any personal injury, loss or damage resulting from:
(a) the offence of which he has been convicted, or
(b) where any other offence is taken into consideration in determining his sentence, any offence so taken into consideration.
(2) A Service Compensation Order must be of such amount as the court considers appropriate, having regard to any evidence and to any representations that are made by or on behalf of the offender or the prosecutor.
(3) In the case of an offence of unlawfully obtaining any property (whether by stealing it, handling it or otherwise), where the property in question is recovered, any damage to the property occurring while it was out of the owner's possession is to be treated for the purposes of this section as having resulted from the offence, however and by whomever the damage was caused.
(4) No Service Compensation Order may be made in respect of:
(a) bereavement,
(b) funeral expenses, or
(c) loss of any other kind suffered by the dependants of a person in consequence of his death.

(5) No Service Compensation Order may be made in respect of injury, loss or damage due to an accident arising out of the presence of a motor vehicle on a road unless:

(a) it is in respect of damage treated by subsection (3) as resulting from an offence of unlawfully obtaining any property, or

(b) it is in respect of injury, loss or damage as respects which:

(i) the offender is uninsured in relation to the use of the vehicle, and

(ii) compensation is not payable under any arrangements to which the Secretary of State is a party.

(6) Where a Service Compensation Order is made in respect of injury, loss or damage due to an accident arising out of the presence of a motor vehicle on a road, the amount to be paid may include an amount representing the whole or part of any loss of or reduction in preferential rates of insurance attributable to the accident.

(7) For the purposes of subsection (5) a person is not uninsured in relation to the use of a vehicle if:

(a) the vehicle is in the public service of the Crown, or

(b) the use of the vehicle is exempted from insurance by Road Traffic Act 1988 s 144.

(8) The court must give reasons, on passing sentence, if it does not make a Service Compensation Order in a case where it has power to do so.

(9) References in this section to 'the court' are references to the court or officer sentencing the offender.

24.41 ***Duty to consider***

Note: Armed Forces Act 2006 s 175(7A)[462] provides that the court 'must consider making a compensation order where it is empowered to do so'. Ed.

24.42 ***Duty to give reasons***

Armed Forces Act 2006 s 175(8) The court must give reasons, on passing sentence, if it does not make a Service Compensation Order in a case where it has power to do so.

Combined with other orders

24.43 ***Absolute and conditional discharge, Combined with***

Only a Service Compensation Order may be combined with an absolute or conditional discharge, see *Guidance on Sentencing in the Court Martial 2018* Annex B.

Service Detention

24.44

Armed Forces Act 2006 s 164

Availability The Court may pass service detention on warrant officers, NCOs, ex-servicemen (but not ex-officers) and other ranks, see *Guidance on Sentencing in the Court Martial 2018* Annex B.

Maximum term 2 years, Armed Forces Act 2006 s 164(1) and 244(1), see **24.48**.

Licence On release, detainees are not subject to a licence.

Remission There is automatic remission for those serving 24+ days. Where the sentence is less than 28 days the amount is the number of days served more than 24 days. Otherwise it is one third unless that would mean the detainee would serve less than 24 days. A commandant may award good conduct remission if the detainee is serving more than 90 days. The maximum amount is one sixth of the sentence. A Judge Advocate can also make awards of up to 28 days. For more detail see Service Custody and Service of Relevant Sentences Rules 2009 2009/1096 and *Practice in the Court Martial: Collected Memoranda 2011* para 6.1.

Suspended Sentence of Service Detention See the SUSPENDED SENTENCE OF SERVICE DETENTION chapter.

Rehabilitation period 12 months for those aged 18+. 6 months for those aged under 18.[463]

[462] As inserted by Legal Aid, Sentencing and Punishment of Offenders Act 2012 s 63(2)

[463] Rehabilitation of Offenders Act 1974 s 5 Table A

Place of detention Most sentences of detention are served at the Military Corrective Training Centre in Colchester (very short sentences may be served in unit guardhouses). Detainees are not paid during their sentence and are reduced to the lowest rank possible for the duration of the sentence.
Statistics The statistics that are available are too incomplete to be worth listing.

24.45 ***Offence must be 'serious enough' to warrant detention***
Service detention: general restriction
Armed Forces Act 2006 s 242(1) A court may not pass a sentence of service detention in respect of an offence unless it is of the opinion that the offence, or the combination of the offence and one or more offences associated with it, was serious enough to warrant such a sentence.
(2) In forming any such opinion as is mentioned in subsection (1) or section 243(2) (length of sentence), a court must take into account all such information as is available to it about the circumstances of the offence and any associated offence, including any aggravating or mitigating factors.
(3) In subsections (1) and (2) 'court' does not include the Summary Appeal Court.
(4) A sentence of service detention may not be:
(a) passed by an officer at a summary hearing, or
(b) passed or confirmed by the Summary Appeal Court,
unless the officer or court is of the opinion that the offence it is in respect of (or, if it is in respect of two or more offences, the combination of them) was serious enough to warrant such a sentence.
(5) In forming any such opinion as is mentioned in subsection (4) or section 243(3) (length of sentence), an officer or the Summary Appeal Court must take into account all such information as is available to him or it about the circumstances of the offence (or offences), including any aggravating or mitigating factors.

24.46 ***Guidance and details of what service detention entails***
Guidance on Sentencing in the Court Martial 2018 para 3.4.1 Service Detention in all but short sentences of less than 14 days should normally be served at the Military Corrective Training Centre (MCTC) Colchester. Service detention is available only for Warrant Officers and below, and an offender sentenced to detention in the Court Martial may also be reduced in rank or rate – there is no automaticity as there used to be before Armed Forces Act 2006 came into force. If he is not reduced or disrated by the court to the lowest rank or rate he can be, he is treated as an able seaman, private or airman for the duration of the sentence of detention. On completion of the sentence he regains his original rank (or any lower rank specified by the court). See also para 3.6.4 [not listed].
[3.4.2 not listed] 3.4.3 Service personnel are not paid any salary whilst serving a sentence of detention in Service Custody premises; they are provided with a small allowance to meet their immediate needs. An allowance may also be paid to help meet the needs of their dependent family. The time in detention does not count towards qualification for Service pension entitlement.
3.4.4 Offenders who are not sentenced also to dismissal serve sentences in A Company MCTC where the regime is not dissimilar to basic military training. The aim is to return retrained Service personnel to their Service to continue their career. The MCTC can achieve their objectives of retraining, rehabilitation and addressing offending behaviour only if the length of the term of detention is sufficient to enable a full programme of training to be completed, and in this respect detention has some similarities with certain community orders in civilian life.
3.4.5 Offenders who are sentenced also to dismissal (or who are to be discharged) serve sentences in D Company MCTC where the regime has less military training and contains a significant element of pre-release training aimed at rehabilitation and resettlement, thereby assisting the Service person to make a successful transition to civilian life.

3.4.6 The regime at MCTC is not primarily intended for those who have been convicted of serious criminal offences. However, even for a fairly serious offence an offender (including a sex offender) might be ordered to serve a period of detention where the court considers there is a better chance of rehabilitation for him in the Service environment than in a civilian penal institution. Such a course is not usual but it is available to the Court Martial as a real alternative to imprisonment. Whilst convicted sex offenders are subject to licensing conditions MCTC does not treat sex offenders. Therefore, in the case of a serious offender (including a sex offender), the likelihood of re-offending and the impact and harm that this would have should be considered both before and during sentencing. The pre-sentence report should help the sentencing court in this consideration. Those concerned with sentencing sex offenders should understand that the MOD cannot license, order community requirements nor recall serious offenders once they have been released from Service detention.
3.4.7 The [Court Martial Appeal Court] has equated detention with imprisonment in terms of loss of liberty[464] although in *R v Holmes* 2004 EWCA Crim 3180 at para 12 and *R v Birch* 2011 EWCA Crim 46 at para 11, the Court acknowledged that imprisonment and detention are different notwithstanding the loss of liberty.
3.4.8 It is wrong to consider a sentence of Service detention to be a more severe punishment than a sentence of imprisonment of the same length on the grounds that remission in a sentence of detention is one-third (unless the detainee earns extra remission) whereas for a determinate sentence of imprisonment of the same length it is one-half. Detention does not carry the stigma that having served a sentence of imprisonment does, and when released from detention an offender is not subject to licence as a released prisoner is. Detainees at MCTC routinely sleep in barrack rooms, and can earn a half-day's leave per week at a certain stage of their sentence. Service personnel are used to certain restrictions on their liberty and the regime in A Company MCTC is no more demanding than most basic military training regimes. The crucial issue is that a sentence must be of sufficient length to enable retraining and rehabilitation to be completed, whilst also allowing the regime at the MCTC to address any prevalent offending behaviour. This has worked well in the past and rates of recidivism among those who have served sentences of Service detention at MCTC are very low, with many former detainees going on to have highly successful careers including subsequent promotion.
3.4.9 Thus when calculating the appropriate length of a sentence of Service detention, it would not be appropriate for the court to reduce sentences artificially to reflect the length of time an offender in a civilian prison would actually serve before being released on licence.

R v Griffin 2018 EWCA Crim 267 D pleaded to a sexual assault. The prosecution counsel said, "Service detention is not the same as imprisonment. It is essentially a kind of basic training which involves the defendant staying in Colchester and attending a welding course. It also involves serving approximately two thirds of the term which can be reduced slightly by the Commandant." Held. Given the sexual assault was unpleasant and because of the conditions under which the detention will be served, we dismiss the appeal.

24.47 *Sentence must be for the shortest term*

Length of term of service detention: general provision

Armed Forces Act 2006 s 243(1) This section applies where a sentence of service detention is passed in respect of a service offence.
(2) Where the detention is imposed by a court other than the Summary Appeal Court, it must be for the shortest term (not exceeding the permitted maximum) that in the opinion of the court is commensurate with the seriousness of the offence or the combination of the offence and one or more offences associated with it.

464 *R v Ball and Rugg* 1998 The Times 17/2/98

(3) Where the detention is imposed by an officer at a summary hearing or by the Summary Appeal Court, it must be for the shortest term (not exceeding the permitted maximum) that in the opinion of the officer or court is commensurate with the seriousness of the offence (or, if it is imposed in respect of two or more offences, the seriousness of them taken together).

24.48 *Maximum sentence is two years*

Limit on combined term of sentences of service

Armed Forces Act 2006 s 244(1) A court or officer may not:

(a) pass a sentence of service detention,

(b) make a direction under section 189 (consecutive terms of service detention), or

(c) make an order under section 191 or 193 (activation of suspended sentence of service detention),

whose effect would be that a person would (at the relevant time) be subject to sentences of service detention the combined term of which exceeds two years.

(2) In subsection (1) 'the relevant time' is the time immediately after the passing of the sentence or the making of the direction or order.

(3) For the purposes of this section, the combined term of sentences of service detention is:

(a) if none of the sentences overlap, the aggregate of the terms of the sentences,

(b) otherwise, the aggregate of:

(i) the period (or periods) during which any of the sentences overlaps any other of them, and

(ii) the period (or periods) for which none of the sentences overlap.

(4) Where subsection (1) is contravened, any part of any sentence of service detention which would (apart from this subsection) have effect after the end of the permitted period is remitted by virtue of this subsection.

(5) In subsection (4) 'permitted period' means the period:

(a) beginning with the date of contravention, and

(b) equal in length to the longest sentence of service detention that could have been passed on that date without contravening subsection (1).

(6) For the purposes of the reference in subsection (4) to a part of a sentence which would have effect after the end of the permitted period, any prospect of early release is to be disregarded.

(7) In subsection (1)(a) 'sentence of service detention' does not include a suspended sentence of service detention.

Section 244: supplementary

Armed Forces Act 2006 s 245(1) Subsections (2) to (5) apply for the purposes of section 244.

(2) A person is to be regarded as not subject to any sentence from which he has been released early.

(3) A person is to be regarded as not subject to a suspended sentence of service detention unless an order that the sentence shall take effect has been made.

(4) Subject to subsection (3), a person is to be regarded as subject to any sentence of service detention that has been passed on him but:

(a) has not taken effect, or

(b) as a result of section 290(5) or (6) or 291(6) or (7), has ceased to have effect and has not resumed effect.

(5) A person who has been detained continuously pursuant to two or more sentences of service detention is to be regarded as subject to all of those sentences (whether or not any of them has been served in full).

(6) For the purposes of subsection (5), any periods of detention which would be continuous but for section 290(3), (5) or (6) or 291(5), (6) or (7) are to be treated as continuous.

Note: The 2-year maximum sentence can also be found in the table in Armed Forces Act 2006 s 164(1).

25 Criminal Behaviour Orders

25.1

Anti-social Behaviour, Crime and Policing Act 2014 s 22

This order is a post-conviction order and is one of the replacements for the ASBO.[465]

Availability The order is available whatever the age of the offender, see **25.10**. By implication an Interim Order must be similarly available.

Step-by-step guide For a Home Office step-by-step guide, see Anti-social Behaviour, Crime and Policing Act 2014: Reform of anti-social powers Statutory guidance for frontline professionals December 2017 page 28.

Interim Orders There is power to make an Interim Order, Anti-social Behaviour, Crime and Policing Act 2014 s 26. There is no need to specify the length of the order and there is no maximum or minimum term. The same powers exist.

Principles The majority of the principles and the suggested terms are in the **Preventive Orders** chapter.

Statistics There are no statistics currently available.

Variation and discharge The provisions are in Anti-social Behaviour, Crime and Policing Act 2014 s 27. For the form to vary or revoke an order, see www.banksr.com Other Matters Other Documents Criminal Behaviour Orders.

A Crown Court has no power to vary a Magistrates' Court order, even where the defendant is being sentenced for breaching the order. The Judge can't vary it by sitting as District Judge under Courts Act 2003 s 66, because the judge is still sitting as a Crown Court judge, *R v Potter* 2019 EWCA Crim 461.

Reviews The provisions are in Anti-social Behaviour, Crime and Policing Act 2014 s 28 and 29.

General principles about ordering

25.2 ***Statutory provisions***

Power to make orders

Anti-social Behaviour, Crime and Policing Act 2014 s 22(1) This section applies where a person ('the offender') is convicted of an offence.

(2) The court may make a Criminal Behaviour Order against the offender if two conditions are met.

(3) The first condition is that the court is satisfied, beyond reasonable doubt, that the offender has engaged in behaviour that caused or was likely to cause harassment, alarm or distress to any person.

(4) The second condition is that the court considers that making the order will help in preventing the offender from engaging in such behaviour.

(5) A Criminal Behaviour Order is an order which, for the purpose of preventing the offender from engaging in such behaviour:

(a) prohibits the offender from doing anything described in the order,

(b) requires the offender to do anything described in the order.

(6) The court may make a Criminal Behaviour Order against the offender only if it is made in addition to:

(a) a sentence imposed in respect of the offence, or

(b) an order discharging the offender conditionally.

(7) The court may make a Criminal Behaviour Order against the offender only on the application of the prosecution.

[465] In force 20/10/14 Anti-social Behaviour, Crime and Policing Act 2014 (Commencement No 7, Saving and Transitional Provisions) Order 2014 2014/2590

(8) The prosecution must find out the views of the local youth offending team before applying for a Criminal Behaviour Order to be made if the offender will be under the age of 18 when the application is made.
(9) Prohibitions and requirements in a Criminal Behaviour Order must, so far as practicable, be such as to avoid:
(a) any interference with the times, if any, at which the offender normally works or attends school or any other educational establishment,
(b) any conflict with the requirements of any other court order or injunction to which the offender may be subject.
R v D 2005 EWCA Crim 3660 The Court considered a SOPO. Held. The focus of the [statute for making SOPOs] must be the risk of further offending.

Procedure

25.3 *Who may apply for an order?*
Anti-social Behaviour, Crime and Policing Act 2014 s 22(7) The court may make a Criminal Behaviour Order against the offender only on the application of the prosecution.

25.4 *Youth offending team, Must consult*
Anti-social Behaviour, Crime and Policing Act 2014 s 22(8) The prosecution must find out the views of the local youth offending team before applying for a Criminal Behaviour Order to be made if the offender will be under the age of 18 when the application is made.
Anti-social Behaviour, Crime and Policing Act 2014 s 22(10) In this section 'local youth offending team' means:
(a) the youth offending team in whose area it appears to the prosecution that the offender lives, or
(b) if it appears to the prosecution that the offender lives in more than one such area, whichever one or more of the relevant youth offending teams the prosecution thinks appropriate.

25.5 *Application for*
Criminal Procedure Rules 2015 2015/1490 Rule 31.3(1) This rule applies where:
(a) a prosecutor wants the court to make:..iii) a Criminal Behaviour Order.
(2) Where paragraph (1)(a) applies (order on application), the prosecutor must serve a notice of intention to apply for such an order on:
(a) the court officer,
(b) the defendant against whom the prosecutor wants the court to make the order, and
(c) any person on whom the order would be likely to have a significant adverse effect,
as soon as practicable (without waiting for the verdict).
(3) A notice under paragraph (2) must:
(a) summarise the relevant facts,
(b) identify the evidence on which the prosecutor relies in support,
(c) attach any written statement that the prosecutor has not already served, and
(d) specify the order that the prosecutor wants the court to make.
Note: There is a note at the bottom of this rule which says the form for making an application is in a Criminal Practice Direction. It isn't in the current directions, 2015 EWCA Crim 1567. It can, however, be found at www.justice.gov.uk/courts/procedure-rules/criminal/formspage Part 50 or see www.banksr.com Other Matters Other Documents tab Criminal Behaviour Orders. Ed.
R v W and F 2006 EWCA Crim 686 Two defendants were convicted of robbery and the Judge made ASBOs as requested. Held. The case summary attached to the application for the ASBOs did not set out the particular facts which the CPS relied on other than the facts constituting the robbery offence. Instead the application set out only a vague 'Overview of the problem' and some 'Reasoning'. Therefore there was no summary of facts that the Judge could put to the offenders to see, quickly and easily, whether or not

the facts were disputed by them. It was unfortunate that the prosecution did not assist the Judge or the defence in summarising the facts at the hearing when the ASBO was sought. The result was that the Judge was in no position to make findings of particular facts to support his general conclusion that the defendants had been guilty of antisocial behaviour, other than the facts of the robbery offence. ASBOs quashed.

Note: For the Criminal Behaviour Order application form, see www.banksr.com Other Matters Other Documents Criminal Behaviour Orders. Ed.

25.6 *Defendant's response*

Criminal Procedure Rules 2015 2015/1490 Rule 31.3(4) A defendant served with a notice under paragraph (2) must:

(a) serve notice of any evidence on which the defendant relies on: i) the court officer, and ii) the prosecutor, as soon as practicable (without waiting for the verdict), and[466]

(b) in the notice, identify that evidence and attach any written statement that has not already been served.

Note: There is a note at the bottom of this rule which says the form for the reply is in a Criminal Practice Direction. It isn't in the current directions, 2015 EWCA Crim 1567. It isn't at www.justice.gov.uk/courts/procedure-rules/criminal/formspage. It appears to have been withdrawn. Ed.

25.7 *Specified supervisory person, Evidence from*

Anti-social Behaviour, Crime and Policing Act 2014 s 24(1) A Criminal Behaviour Order that includes a requirement must specify the person who is to be responsible for supervising compliance with the requirement. The person may be an individual or an organisation.

(2) Before including a requirement, the court must receive evidence about its suitability and enforceability from:

(a) the individual to be specified under subsection (1), if an individual is to be specified,

(b) an individual representing the organisation to be specified under subsection (1), if an organisation is to be specified.

Anti-social Behaviour, Crime and Policing Act 2014 s 24(4) It is the duty of a person specified under subsection (1):

(a) to make any necessary arrangements in connection with the requirements for which the person has responsibility (the 'relevant requirements'),

(b) to promote the offender's compliance with the relevant requirements.

25.8 *Adjourning the hearing/Hearing the case in the defendant's absence*

Anti-social Behaviour, Crime and Policing Act 2014 s 23(3) The court may adjourn any proceedings on an application for a Criminal Behaviour Order even after sentencing the offender.

(4) If the offender does not appear for any adjourned proceedings the court may:

(a) further adjourn the proceedings,

(b) issue a warrant for the offender's arrest, or

(c) hear the proceedings in the offender's absence.

(5) The court may not act under paragraph (b) of subsection (4) unless it is satisfied that the offender has had adequate notice of the time and place of the adjourned proceedings.

(6) The court may not act under paragraph (c) of subsection (4) unless it is satisfied that the offender:

(a) has had adequate notice of the time and place of the adjourned proceedings, and

(b) has been informed that if the offender does not appear for those proceedings the court may hear the proceedings in his or her absence.

R v Khan 2018 EWCA Crim 1472, 2 Cr App R (S) 53 (p 426) D pleaded to dangerous driving, cannabis supply and two drug possession counts. The offences related to a road

466 Criminal Procedure (Amendment No 2) Rules 2016 2016/705 para 11(b)(iii) removes the requirement that the notice had to be in writing. In force 3/10/16

rage incident in January 2016. The supply related to D giving someone a lift. The possession counts were small amounts of cannabis found in D's car. In December 2016, shortly before D was sentenced, the prosecution applied for a Criminal Behaviour Order. D received a 16-month suspended sentence. The Criminal Behaviour Order hearing was in August 2017. The delay was partly because the prosecution was considering whether to pursue confiscation proceedings. Held. para 22 It was most unsatisfactory that the hearing was more than seven months after the main sentencing hearing. A delay of several months (save in the most exceptional circumstances) is wholly unacceptable.

25.9 ***Evidence***
Anti-social Behaviour, Crime and Policing Act 2014 s 23(1) For the purpose of deciding whether to make a Criminal Behaviour Order the court may consider evidence led by the prosecution and evidence led by the offender.
(2) It does not matter whether the evidence would have been admissible in the proceedings in which the offender was convicted.
Anti-social Behaviour, Crime and Policing Act 2014 s 33(5) In deciding whether to make a Criminal Behaviour Order a court may take account of conduct occurring up to 1 year before the commencement day.
(6) In this section 'commencement day' means the day on which this Part comes into force [20 October 2014].

25.10 ***Children and young offenders***
Anti-social Behaviour, Crime and Policing Act 2014 s 23(7) Subsection (8) applies in relation to proceedings in which a Criminal Behaviour Order is made against an offender who is under the age of 18.
(8) In so far as the proceedings relate to the making of the order:
(a) Children and Young Persons Act 1933 s 49 (restrictions on reports of proceedings in which children and young persons are concerned) does not apply in respect of the offender,
(b) Children and Young Persons Act 1933 s 39 of that Act (power to prohibit publication of certain matters) does so apply.

Making the order

25.11 ***Test to apply***
Anti-social Behaviour, Crime and Policing Act 2014 s 22(2) The court may make a Criminal Behaviour Order against the offender if two conditions are met.
(3) The first condition is that the court is satisfied, beyond reasonable doubt, that the offender has engaged in behaviour that caused or was likely to cause harassment, alarm or distress to any person.
(4) The second condition is that the court considers that making the order will help in preventing the offender from engaging in such behaviour.
DPP v Bulmer 2015 EWHC 2323 (Admin), 2016 1 Cr App R (S) 12 (p 74) para 22 B had a long record of anti-social behaviour offences and breaches of court orders, but she was unable to manage her chronic alcoholism. The District Judge refused to make a Criminal Behaviour Order because there was no positive requirement to assist her with her alcoholism and an order would not prevent her anti-social behaviour, partly because the proposed order did not give her assistance with alcoholism. Held. para 22 The removal of the requirement of necessity was designed to reduce the hurdle required before an Order can be made. para 21 The legislative language is a shade less clear than it was under the purely prohibitory regime of the 1998 Act. The addition of a power to impose positive requirements has not changed the emphasis from 'necessity and protection' to 'help and prevention'. para 23 There is no obligation to order a positive requirement. para 24 The wording of section 22(4) of the 2014 Act does not mean that, where an offender's problem, whether it is a disease, alcoholism or drug addiction, means that he or she is totally unresponsive to an order and where it is not possible for the underlying cause of the behaviour to be tackled by a positive requirement, the

condition in section 22(4) of the 2014 Act is not met. The District Judge erred by focusing on these elements. para 30 Section 22(4) makes no reference to the burden or standard of proof. It is concerned whether, once the gateway in section 22(3) has been passed, the court 'considers' that making the order will 'help in preventing' anti-social behaviour which caused or was likely to cause harassment, alarm or distress to any person. Had Parliament wished the criminal standard to apply, it could have used the appropriate language. The inquiry under section 22(3) is a factual one whereas that under section 22(4) is one of judgment and evaluation. para 35 The court should proceed with a proper degree of caution and circumspection because such orders are not lightly to be imposed. Satisfaction to the criminal standard is not required in what is an evaluative exercise. para 41 The fact that a person has not responded to orders and other disposals in the past is not in itself a reason for deciding not to make an order. para 44 Relying on the ordinary power of the police to arrest on reasonable suspicion may be insufficient to provide pre-emptive protection from a person with a history of anti-social behaviour to those who are or are likely to be affected by the behaviour. An order imposed on a person who causes criminal damage by spraying graffiti preventing him or her from being in possession of spray paint in a public place gives the police the opportunity to take action in advance of the actual spraying or acts of preparation. para 47 Had the District Judge concluded that the condition in section 22(4) of the 2014 Act was met, he would have had to consider its proportionality.

R v Khan 2018 EWCA Crim 1472, 2 Cr App R (S) 53 (p 426) para 12 The Court of Appeal considered a Criminal Behaviour Order. Held. This Court noted in *R v Browne-Morgan* 2016 EWCA Crim 1903, 2017 1 Cr App R (S) 33 (p 279) that the court is not required to be satisfied beyond reasonable doubt that making the order will help in preventing the offender from engaging in such behaviour. para 18 We note that the Home Office has issued the updated *Anti-social Behaviour, Crime and Policing Act 2014: Anti-social behaviour powers: Statutory guidance for frontline professionals* Dec 2017, which states that the [Criminal Behaviour Order] "is intended for tackling the most serious and persistent offenders where their behaviour has brought them before a criminal court", [see page 29]. para 20 Criminal behaviour orders should not become a mere matter of box-ticking routine. Such orders are not lightly to be imposed; the court should proceed with a proper degree of caution and circumspection; the order must be tailored to the specific circumstances of the person on whom it is to be imposed; and assessments of proportionality are intensively fact-sensitive. Here, we quash the order.

25.12 *Special measures*

Note: These provisions are listed at Anti-social Behaviour, Crime and Policing Act 2014 s 31. Ed.

25.13 *Order may have mandatory as well as prohibitive terms*

Anti-social Behaviour, Crime and Policing Act 2014 s 22(5) A Criminal Behaviour Order is an order which, for the purpose of preventing the offender from engaging in such behaviour:

(a) prohibits the offender from doing anything described in the order,
(b) requires the offender to do anything described in the order.

25.14 *Drafting the terms*

Note: The specimen terms and principles are in the **PREVENTIVE ORDERS The wording of the order and drafting the prohibitions** section and the following sections at **84.35**. Ed.

Anti-social Behaviour, Crime and Policing Act 2014 s 22(5) A Criminal Behaviour Order is an order which, for the purpose of preventing the offender from engaging in such behaviour:

(a) prohibits the offender from doing anything described in the order,
(b) requires the offender to do anything described in the order.

Anti-social Behaviour, Crime and Policing Act 2014 s 22(9) Prohibitions and requirements in a Criminal Behaviour Order must, so far as practicable, be such as to avoid:

(a) any interference with the times, if any, at which the offender normally works or attends school or any other educational establishment,

(b) any conflict with the requirements of any other court order or injunction to which the offender may be subject.

Anti-social Behaviour, Crime and Policing Act 2014 s 24(1) A Criminal Behaviour Order that includes a requirement must specify the person who is to be responsible for supervising compliance with the requirement. The person may be an individual or an organisation.

Anti-social Behaviour, Crime and Policing Act 2014 s 24(3) Before including two or more requirements, the court must consider their compatibility with each other.

25.15 *Consecutive orders*

Anti-social Behaviour, Crime and Policing Act 2014 s 25(2) If on the day a Criminal Behaviour Order ('the new order') is made the offender is subject to another Criminal Behaviour Order ('the previous order'), the new order may be made so as to take effect on the day on which the previous order ceases to have effect.

25.16 *Terms included by the Act*

Anti-social Behaviour, Crime and Policing Act 2014 s 24(6) An offender subject to a requirement in a Criminal Behaviour Order must:

(a) keep in touch with the person specified under subsection (1) in relation to that requirement, in accordance with any instructions given by that person from time to time,

(b) notify the person of any change of address.

These obligations have effect as requirements of the order.

25.17 *Maximum and minimum terms*

Anti-social Behaviour, Crime and Policing Act 2014 s 25(3) A Criminal Behaviour Order must specify the period ('the order period') for which it has effect.

(4) In the case of a Criminal Behaviour Order made before the offender has reached the age of 18, the order period must be a fixed period of:

(a) not less than 1 year, and

(b) not more than 3 years.

(5) In the case of a Criminal Behaviour Order made after the offender has reached the age of 18, the order period must be:

(a) a fixed period of not less than 2 years, or

(b) an indefinite period (so that the order has effect until further order).

(6) A Criminal Behaviour Order may specify periods for which particular prohibitions or requirements have effect.

25.18 *How long should the order last?*

R v Janes 2016 EWCA Crim 676, 2 Cr App R (S) 27 (p 256) D was convicted of fraud. He overcharged a man aged in his 80s for gardening work. D was aged 43 and in 2009 was given 2 years for consumer credit offences and money laundering. He was sentenced to 18 months and was given a Criminal Behaviour Order which had the effect of preventing him from touting for business. Held. **3 years** not 10 met the needs of the case.

25.19 *Start of the order*

Anti-social Behaviour, Crime and Policing Act 2014 s 25(1) A Criminal Behaviour Order takes effect on the day it is made, subject to subsection (2).

(2) If on the day a Criminal Behaviour Order ('the new order') is made the offender is subject to another Criminal Behaviour Order ('the previous order'), the new order may be made so as to take effect on the day on which the previous order ceases to have effect.

Matters after an order is made

25.20 ***Duties of the person subject to an order***
Anti-social Behaviour, Crime and Policing Act 2014 s 22(6) An offender subject to a requirement in a Criminal Behaviour Order must:

(a) keep in touch with the person specified under subsection (1) in relation to that requirement, in accordance with any instructions given by that person from time to time,

(b) notify the person of any change of address.

These obligations have effect as requirements of the order.

26 CRIMINAL BEHAVIOUR ORDERS/ASBOS: BREACH OF

26.1
Anti-social Behaviour, Crime and Policing Act 2014 s 30
Crime and Disorder Act 1998 s 1(10)
Modes of trial Both offences are triable either way.
Maximum sentences Both offences On indictment 5 years. Summary 6 months and/or an unlimited fine.[467] There are maximum fines for those aged under 18, see **13.44**.
Conditional discharge This order may not be passed for either offence, Anti-social Behaviour, Crime and Policing Act 2014 s 30(3) and Crime and Disorder Act 1998 s 1(11).
The repeal of ASBOs does not affect existing orders This is provided by Anti-social Behaviour, Crime and Policing Act 2014 s 33(1)(b).
Parenting Orders For offenders aged under 16, the court may make a Parenting Order for a breach of an ASBO by those aged under 16 unless there are exceptional circumstances.[468]
ASBO procedure As the ASBO has been replaced, the procedure section has been substantially reduced. For full details, see the 9th edition of this book.

General matters

26.2 ***Nature of the proceedings***
R v Crown Court at Manchester ex parte McCann 2002 UKHL 39 Lords It is common ground that proceedings for breach of an Anti-social Behaviour Order are criminal in character under domestic law and fall within the autonomous concept of 'a criminal charge' under European Convention on Human Rights art 6.
Note: The same principles would no doubt apply to breaches of Criminal Behaviour Orders. As the breach is a specific offence, the triable either way procedure is used, see Magistrates' Courts Act 1980 s 17A-21. Ed.

26.3 ***What constitutes a breach?***
R v Evans 2004 EWCA Crim 3102, 2005 1 Cr App R 32 (p 546) D, aged 78, was given a Restraining Order which prohibited her from being 'abusive by words or actions towards X, Y and Z and their respective families'. A plumber who came to do repairs for Mrs Z parked his van close to Mrs Z's car. D's car was parked in the same street. D drove her car close up behind the van, blocking it in. Breach proceedings were brought. D was convicted and the defence said driving a car could not be 'an abusive action'. Held. Looking at the meaning of words in a criminal context is no reason for giving them a narrow or strained meaning. The application of that meaning to the facts should be left to the fact-finding tribunal. It can make no difference that the offence in this case was being by action contrary to the terms of a Restraining Order, rather than contrary to a statutory provision which specifically prohibits such conduct. Either way, the approach

[467] Legal Aid, Sentencing and Punishment of Offenders Act 2012 s 85(1) and (4) and Legal Aid, Sentencing and Punishment of Offenders Act 2012 (Commencement No 11) Order 2015 2015/504
[468] Crime and Disorder Act 1998 s 8 as amended by Crime and Security Act 2010 s 41. No commencement order has been issued.

elucidated in cases such as *Brutus v Cozens* 1972 56 Cr App R (S) 799 and *R v Associated Octel Ltd* 1996 EWCA Crim 1327, 1997 1 Cr App R (S) 435 should apply. The Judge was right to leave the case to the jury.
Note: Although this was for a breach of a different order, the case may provide assistance. Ed.

Preliminary matters Breach of a Criminal Behaviour Order

26.4 *Duty of specified person to inform prosecution*

Anti-social Behaviour, Crime and Policing Act 2014 s 24(1) A Criminal Behaviour Order that includes a requirement must specify the person who is to be responsible for supervising compliance with the requirement. The person may be an individual or an organisation.
Anti-social Behaviour, Crime and Policing Act 2014 s 24(4) It is the duty of a person specified under subsection (1)(c) if the person considers that the offender:
(i) has complied with all the relevant requirements, or
(ii) has failed to comply with a relevant requirement,
to inform the prosecution and the appropriate chief officer of police.

26.5 *Reporting restrictions*

Anti-social Behaviour, Crime and Policing Act 2014 s 30(5) In relation to any proceedings for an offence under this section that are brought against a person under the age of 18:
(a) Children and Young Persons Act 1933 s 49 (restrictions on reports of proceedings in which children and young persons are concerned, see **13.20**) does not apply in respect of the person,
(b) Youth Justice and Criminal Evidence Act 1999 s 45 (power to restrict reporting of criminal proceedings involving persons under 18, see **13.24**) does so apply.
(6) If, in relation to any proceedings mentioned in subsection (5), the court does exercise its power to give a direction under Youth Justice and Criminal Evidence Act 1999 s 45, it must give its reasons for doing so.

26.6 *Special measures*

Note: Special measures for witnesses for ASBO cases are at Crime and Disorder Act 1998 s 11(2)-(5). Special measures for Criminal Behaviour Orders are at Anti-social Behaviour, Crime and Policing Act 2014 s 31. Ed.

26.7 *Evidence*

Anti-social Behaviour, Crime and Policing Act 2014 s 30(4) In proceedings for an offence under this section, a copy of the original Criminal Behaviour Order, certified by the proper officer of the court which made it, is admissible as evidence of its having been made and of its contents to the same extent that oral evidence of those things is admissible in those proceedings.
Anti-social Behaviour, Crime and Policing Act 2014 s 33(5) In deciding whether to make a Criminal Behaviour Order a court may take account of conduct occurring up to one year before the commencement day.
(6) In this section 'commencement day' means the day on which this Part comes into force.

Procedure and evidence Breach of an ASBO

26.8 *Who may initiate the proceedings?*

Crime and Disorder Act 1998 s 1(10A) The following may bring proceedings for [a breach]: a) a council which is a relevant authority, b) the council for the local government area in which the person (subject to the ASBO) resides or appears to reside, and c) Transport for London [when made on their application].

26.9 *Magistrates' Courts' time limits*

Crime and Disorder Act 1998 s 1(7) Nothing in this section shall affect the operation of Magistrates' Courts Act 1980 s 127 (time limits for laying informations or complaints).

26.10 *Duplicity, Breach and*

S v Doncaster Youth Offending Team 2003 EWHC 1128 (Admin) High Court S was convicted of failing to comply with a Detention and Training Order. S had failed to reside where the YOT had instructed him to, and he had failed to report for four consecutive weeks. It was submitted that the information was bad for duplicity. Held. Sometimes it is difficult to distinguish between separate offences on the one hand and different features of committing the same offence on the other. There were two quite separate licence conditions of which the appellant was in breach. These were failing to keep in touch with his supervising officer and failing to live at the address approved by his supervising officer. These were two separate offences that should not have been tried on the same information.

Note: Although this case deals with a breach of a different order, the principles may be of assistance. Ed.

26.11 *Reporting restrictions*

Crime and Disorder Act 1998 s 1(10D) Children and Young Persons Act 1933 s 49 (reporting restrictions) does not apply in respect of the child or young person against whom the proceedings are brought. Youth Justice and Criminal Evidence Act 1999 s 45 (power to restrict reporting of criminal proceedings involving persons under 18) does apply.

(10E) [Where,] in such proceedings, the court does exercise its power to give a direction under Youth Justice and Criminal Evidence Act 1999 s 45 it shall give its reasons for so doing.

For the principles see *Judicial College on Reporting Restrictions in the Criminal Courts 2015*, www.banksr.com Other Matters Other Documents Reporting Restrictions page 31.

26.12 *Prosecutors, Guidance to*

See *CPS Breach of ASBO Guidance* on its website.

26.13 *Criminal records should have details of the order breached*

Criminal Practice Directions 2015 EWCA Crim 1567 para II 10A.7 Where the current alleged offence could constitute a breach of an existing sentence such as a suspended sentence, community order or conditional discharge, and it is known that that sentence is still in force, then details of the circumstances of the offence leading to the sentence should be included in the antecedents. The detail should be brief and include the date of the offence.

Proving the breach

26.14 *Statutory offences Criminal Behaviour Orders*

Anti-social Behaviour, Crime and Policing Act 2014 s 30(1) A person who without reasonable excuse:

(a) does anything he or she is prohibited from doing by a Criminal Behaviour Order, or

(b) fails to do anything he or she is required to do by a Criminal Behaviour Order,

commits an offence.

Crime and Disorder Act 1998 s 1(10) If without reasonable excuse a person does anything which he is prohibited from doing by an ASBO [he or she commits an offence].

26.15 *Is there a defence that the term was invalid?*

R (W) v DPP 2005 EWHC 1333 (Admin) High Court W's ASBO prohibited him from 'committing any criminal offence'. Breach proceedings were conducted and the issue arose whether the validity of the term affected the breach issue. Held. An Anti-social Behaviour Order is to be treated as a valid order unless and until it is varied. It is only if it is invalid, as opposed to an order which might have been made in some other form, that any question arises as to whether the court considering an allegation of breach of the order can take into account submissions relating to its validity. *Boddington v British Transport Police* 1999 2 AC 143 is authority for the proposition that if an order of this type is plainly invalid, then the Magistrates can consider submissions to that effect in the same way as they can consider submissions that a bye-law was *ultra vires* without the necessity of prior proceedings or concurrent proceedings in the High Court for the purpose of identifying and declaring the invalidity. This would only apply to an order as plainly invalid as one which contains a restraint preventing a defendant from committing any criminal offence. There will be a danger of opening floodgates if challenges to ASBOs could be made in breach proceedings, but in all these cases there are exceptions which are as plain as the exception in this case. This prohibition was unenforceable.

DPP v T 2006 EWHC 728 (Admin)[469] Proceedings were started for breach of a term, 'not to act in an antisocial manner in Manchester'. The District Judge who made the order found the term was so wide and the behaviour in the prohibition was not specified, so it was unenforceable and therefore invalid. The prosecution appealed. Held. The normal rule in relation to an order of the court is that it must be treated as valid and be obeyed unless and until it is set aside. Even if the order should not have been made in the first place, a person may be liable for any breach of it committed before it is set aside. Secondly, the person against whom an ASBO is made has a full opportunity to challenge that order on appeal or to apply to vary it. There is no obvious reason why the person against whom the order was made should be allowed to raise that issue as a defence in subsequent breach proceedings rather than by way of appeal against the original order. It does not follow that the District Judge lacked any means of giving effect to the concerns he had about the width and uncertainty of the order. It was open to him to consider whether the relevant provision lacked sufficient clarity to warrant a finding that the respondent's conduct amounted to a breach of the order, whether the lack of clarity provided a reasonable excuse for non-compliance with the order, and whether, if a breach was established, it was appropriate in the circumstances to impose any penalty for the breach. It was not open to the District Judge, as a matter of jurisdiction, to rule that the original order was invalid.

R v Bestel and Others 2013 EWCA Crim 1305, 2014 1 Cr App R (S) 53 (p 312) D sought to appeal his confiscation order in the light of the decision in *R v Waya* 2012 UKSC 51, 2013 2 Cr App R (S) 20 (p 87). Held. para 26 It is a long-established principle that an order of the court is to be obeyed unless and until it is subsequently rescinded or invalidated, see *McGrath v Chief Constable of The Royal Ulster Constabulary* 2001 UKHL 39. On the other hand, we recognise that when enforcement proceedings are taken in respect of breaches of obligations arising after a change in the law, the enforcing authority may well need to judge the justice of the case against the changed circumstances and to ameliorate the penalty which would otherwise be imposed.

R v JB 2015 EWCA Crim 599 LCJ Divisional Court and Court of Appeal. D was sentenced to IPP for an offence that was committed before the provisions came into force. He applied for Habeas Corpus. Held in the Divisional Court. Only the Court of Appeal can set the order aside. The position is clear, 'An order of a court of competent jurisdiction must be obeyed unless and until it is set aside on appeal. It cannot be ignored as a suspected nullity,' *Niblett v Sec of State* 2009 EWHC 2851 (Admin). Order refused. Held in the Court of Appeal. We quash the order and substitute a determinate term.

26.16 *Mental element for the offence (mens rea) and forgetfulness*

R v Nicholson 2006 EWCA Crim 1518 D attended a demonstration and was in breach of her ASBO prohibiting her for a period of not less than two years or until further order from going within 500 m of a number of premises (five) scheduled to the order. She sought to raise a reasonable excuse defence saying she had no recollection of ever having heard before, or at the demonstration, of any reference to one of the named premises she was prohibited from going to in her ASBO. The Judge ruled the offence was a strict liability offence where the prosecution does not have to prove any sort of *mens rea* (the mental element of the offence), but where there is a statutory provision for a defence or an evidential issue to be raised based on the presence or absence of some

[469] This case is also known as *DPP v T* 2006 EWHC 728 (Admin).

state of mind on the part of the defendant. The prosecution do not as part of their case have to prove a knowing breach of the order. Held. It is not helpful to characterise an offence as one of 'strict liability'. The fact that the prosecution do not as part of their case have to prove a knowing breach of such order means that there is not the same tension between proof by the prosecution of its case triggering considerations of an evidential issue of reasonable excuse (if it is raised) and acceptance of forgetfulness or misunderstanding as such an excuse. If a jury were to accept forgetfulness or misunderstanding in the circumstances as genuine and reasonable, say, because of chronic absent-mindedness or pressing distractions, we do not consider that it is necessary to combine it with another reason or to look for another one, 'in which forgetfulness plays its part', in the different statutory context of offences of possession of offensive weapons and possession of bladed articles.

Sentencing guidelines and judicial guidance

26.17 ***Breach Offences Guideline 2018***

Breach Offences Guideline 2018, see www.banksr.com Other Matters Guidelines tab In force 1 October 2018 page 27

Breach of a criminal behaviour order (also applicable to breach of an anti-social behaviour order)

Anti-Social Behaviour, Crime and Policing Act 2014 s 30

STEP ONE **Determining the offence category**

The court should determine the offence category with reference only to the factors listed in the tables below. In order to determine the category the court should assess **culpability** and **harm**.

Culpability

A	• Very serious or persistent breach
B	• Deliberate breach falling between A and C
C	• Minor breach • Breach just short of reasonable excuse

Harm

The level of **harm** is determined by weighing up all the factors of the case to determine the harm that has been caused or was at risk of being caused. In assessing any risk of harm posed by the breach, consideration should be given to the original offence(s) or activity for which the order was imposed and the circumstances in which the breach arose.

Category 1	• Breach causes **very** serious harm or distress • Breach demonstrates a continuing risk of serious criminal and/or anti-social behaviour
Category 2	• Cases falling between Categories 1 and 3
Category 3	• Breach causes little or no harm or distress • Breach demonstrates a continuing risk of minor criminal and/or anti-social behaviour

26.18

STEP TWO **Starting point and category range**

Having determined the category at step one, the court should use the corresponding starting point to reach a sentence within the category range from the appropriate sentence table below. The starting point applies to all offenders irrespective of plea or previous convictions.

	Culpability		
Harm	**A**	**B**	**C**
Category 1	**Starting point** 2 years' custody	**Starting point** 1 year's custody	**Starting point** 12 weeks' custody
	Category range 1 to 4 years' custody	**Category range** High-level community order to 2 years' custody	**Category range** Medium-level community order to 1 year's custody
Category 2	**Starting point** 1 year's custody	**Starting point** 12 weeks' custody	**Starting point** High-level community order
	Category range High-level community order to 2 years' custody	**Category range** Medium-level community order to 1 year's custody	**Category range** Low-level community order to 26 weeks' custody
Category 3	**Starting point** 12 weeks' custody	**Starting point** High-level community order	**Starting point** Medium-level community order
	Category range Medium-level community order to 1 year's custody	**Category range** Low-level community order to 26 weeks' custody	**Category range** Band B fine to high-level community order

NOTE: A conditional discharge **MAY NOT** be imposed for breach of a criminal behaviour order.

For the meaning of a high-level, medium-level and a low-level community order, see **15.12**. For a band B fine, see **58.28**.

26.19 [Aggravating and mitigating factors]

Page 30 The table below contains a **non-exhaustive** list of additional factual elements providing the context of the offence and factors relating to the offender. Identify whether any combination of these, or other relevant factors, should result in an upward or downward adjustment from the starting point.

In some cases, having considered these factors, it may be appropriate to move outside the identified category range.

Factors increasing seriousness
Statutory aggravating factors:
Previous convictions, having regard to a) the **nature** of the offence to which the conviction relates and its **relevance** to the current offence; and b) the **time** that has elapsed since the conviction
Offence committed whilst on bail
Other aggravating factors:
Offence is a further breach, following earlier breach proceedings
Breach committed shortly after order made
History of disobedience of court orders or orders imposed by local authorities

Breach constitutes a further offence (where not separately prosecuted)
Targeting of a person the order was made to protect or a witness in the original proceedings
Victim or protected subject of order breached is particularly vulnerable due to age, disability, culture, religion, language, or other factors
Offence committed on licence or while subject to post sentence supervision
Factors reducing seriousness or reflecting personal mitigation
Genuine misunderstanding of terms of order
Breach committed after long period of compliance
Prompt voluntary surrender/admission of breach or failure
Age and/or lack of maturity where it affects the responsibility of the offender
Mental disorder or learning disability
Sole or primary carer for dependent relatives

STEP THREE to STEP EIGHT These are: Consider assistance to the prosecution, Reduction for guilty plea, Totality principle, Ancillary orders, Duty to give reasons and Consider time spent on bail with a tag.

26.20 ***Suggested approach to the guideline***
Note: I have listed a few old cases in the book, because they deal with legal principles. Those cases should be treated with care as the new guideline must be applied. The old cases should not determine the length of the sentence. That is determined by the guideline. Ed.

26.21 ***Judicial guidance*** ***Pre-2018 guideline cases***
R v Braxton 2003 EWCA Crim 1037 A sentence close to the maximum must be reserved for cases of persistent and prolonged breaches or where the behaviour was truly intimidating.
R v Dickinson 2005 EWCA Crim 289, 2 Cr App R (S) 78 (p 489) It is important that offenders committing breaches of an ASBO are sternly dealt with. Such people must understand that the courts will endeavour to ensure that teeth are given to the orders.
R v Lamb 2005 EWCA Crim 3000, 2006 2 Cr App R (S) 11 (p 84) We prefer the approach in *R v Tripp* 2005 EWCA Crim 2253 and *R v Braxton* 2004 (see above) to the approach in *R v Morrison* 2006 1 Cr App R (S) 85 (p 488). The sentence is for the breach. The sentence must be proportionate and commensurate. If the conduct which constitutes the breach is a distinct criminal offence with a maximum of say 6 months that is a feature to be borne in mind in the interests of proportionality. It cannot be right that the court's power is limited to the 6 months. We do not consider that it is wrong in principle for the Judge to impose custody for the instant offence (here drunkenness). However, sentences should not be imposed as a kind of device to circumvent maximum penalties which are believed to be too modest.
R v Stevens 2006 EWCA Crim 255 *R v Morrison* 2006 had been wholly undermined by *R v Lamb* 2006. The sentence had to be proportionate but the sentence was not limited to the maximum available for the distinct criminal offence. 9 months for the breach for when he was drunk and incontinent upheld.
Note: Although these cases related to ASBOs, they may be of assistance when considering Criminal Behaviour Orders. Ed.

Sentencing cases etc.

26.22 ***Previous breach appearances, Defendant has*** ***Pre-2018 guideline cases***
Breach Offences Guideline 2018, see www.banksr.com Other Matters Guidelines tab In force 1 October 2018 page 30 includes 'Offence is a further breach, following earlier breach proceedings' as an aggravating factor.

R v Savage 2012 EWCA Crim 1678 D pleaded to breach of an ASBO. He was prohibited from, among other things, entering any NHS building unless he was in need of genuine medical attention, and providing false names, DOBs, addresses or symptoms to NHS staff. He was taken to hospital by ambulance. He told staff he was HIV positive, had been coughing up blood, had a partner who had untreated TB and was multi-resistant to drugs. He was X-rayed and his blood was checked. There were no signs of active infections. He was deemed medically fit for discharge. A psychiatrist's report stated that D did not suffer from a mental illness. D was aged 42 and had used 93 aliases and 45 false DOBs. He had 52 convictions for 95 offences, the majority of which were for burglary and theft. This was D's fifth breach of his ASBO. Held. Although the breaches may have not caused harassment to a particular individual, they are far from being inconsequential. Personnel and resources had to be diverted from genuine cases within the already overstretched NHS. Previous custodial sentences have not prevented offending. A substantial custodial sentence was justified, however **12 months** not 18 months (representing 27 months after trial).

R v Henry 2014 EWCA Crim 1892 D was convicted of breaching his ASBO (×5 counts). A 5-year ASBO was imposed following a year-long pattern of worsening antisocial behaviour including threats to kill, harassment and criminal damage towards D's neighbours. D was prohibited, amongst other things, from harrying the neighbourhood. Eight months after it was made, D breached the ASBO on more than five occasions. He intimidated his neighbours, made abusive comments at them, and pushed his clothed bottom towards one victim. The Judge noted that, on one occasion, D had abused the same person as before the ASBO was imposed. D was aged 47 on appeal and had convictions for similar behaviour dating back almost a decade. Held. The harm caused was not easily found within the guideline's definition of 'serious harm'. Nevertheless, D's behaviour was uncontrolled and he engendered real and persistent alarm in the minds of his neighbours. However, **2 years**, not 30 months.

R v Gough 2015 EWCA Crim 1079 D refused to wear any clothes in Court. He wanted to represent himself. The Judge refused to permit him to appear in Court naked. He was tried and convicted of breaching his ASBO in his absence. D had conducted a campaign to be allowed to be naked in public. He had already spent about 8 years in prison mostly for breaches of court orders about being naked. After serving a prison sentence, he was released naked save for socks and boots. D had declined the offer of clothing. He was met by waiting police officers who arrested him for breaching his ASBO. D was aged 55. He was given 16 months for the last breach of his ASBO. Held. The conviction was safe because to allow him naked in Court would be permitting a breach of his ASBO. No guideline was likely to assist the Judge. **30 months** was justified.

27 Criminal Procedure Rules: Behaviour Rules

27.1

Criminal Procedure Rules 2015 2015/1490 Rule 31

For details about the making etc. of preventive orders, see the **Preventive Orders** chapter.

27.2 ***Orders to which these rules apply***

Criminal Procedure Rules 2015 2015/1490 Rule 31.1(1)[470] [Rule 50] applies to the Crown Court and Magistrates' Courts where the court could decide to make, vary or revoke a civil order: a) as well as, or instead of, passing a sentence, and b) that requires someone to do, or not to do, something.

[Explanatory] Note: In the circumstances set out in the Acts listed, the court can make a behaviour order:

(a) on conviction, under:

(i) Football Spectators Act 1989 s 14A (Football Banning Orders),

[470] As amended by Criminal Procedure (Amendment) Rules 2015 2015/13 para 9

(ii) Protection from Harassment Act 1997 s 5 (Restraining Orders),
(iii) Crime and Disorder Act 1998 s 1C and 1D (Anti-social Behaviour Orders and Interim Anti-social Behaviour Orders),
(iv) Crime and Disorder Act 1998 s 8 and 9 (Parenting Orders),
(v) Sexual Offences Act 2003 s 103A (Sexual Harm Prevention Orders),
(vi) Serious Crime Act 2007 s 19 or 21 (Serious Crime Prevention Orders),
(vii) Anti-social Behaviour, Crime and Policing Act 2014 s 22 (Criminal Behaviour Orders).
(viii) Modern Slavery Act 2015 s 14 (Slavery and Trafficking Prevention Orders),

(b) on acquittal, under:
(ix) Psychoactive Substances Act 2016 s 19 (prohibition orders),
(x) Immigration Act 2016 s 20 (labour market enforcement orders)[471]

Protection from Harassment Act 1997 s 5A (Restraining Orders on acquittal), and
(c) on the making of a finding of i) not guilty by reason of insanity, or ii) disability, under Sexual Offences Act 2003 s 104 (Sexual Offences Prevention Orders), and
(d) in proceedings for a genital mutilation offence, under paragraph 3 of Schedule 2 to the Female Genital Mutilation Act 2003 s 9 (female genital mutilation protection orders).

In the circumstances set out in Criminal Justice (European Protection Order) Regulations 2014 214/3300, which give effect to Directive 2011/99/EU of the European Parliament and of the Council of 13 December 2011, on the European protection order:
(a) a Magistrates' Court, and in some cases the Crown Court, may make a European Protection Order to supplement a protection measure ordered by a court in England and Wales, where the protected person has decided to reside or stay in another European Union member State or is already residing or staying there (see also rule 31.9), and
(b) a Magistrates' Court may make a Restraining Order to give effect in England and Wales to a European Protection order made by a competent authority in another European Union member State (see also rule 31.10).

Note: The details of European Protection Orders are not dealt with in this book as they are so rare. Ed.

27.3 *Prosecution's application*

Criminal Procedure Rules 2015 2015/1490 Rule 31.3(1) This rule applies where:
(a) a prosecutor wants the court to make one of the following orders if the defendant is convicted:
(i) an anti-social behaviour order (but this rule does not apply to an application for an interim anti-social behaviour order),
(ii) a Serious Crime Prevention Order,
(iii) a Criminal Behaviour Order, or
(iv) a prohibition order;
(b) a prosecutor proposes, on the prosecutor's initiative or at the court's request, a Sexual Harm Prevention Order if the defendant is convicted;
(c) a prosecutor proposes a Restraining Order whether the defendant is convicted or acquitted.

(2) Where paragraph (1)(a) applies (order on application), the prosecutor must serve a notice of intention to apply for such an order on:
(a) the court officer,
(b) the defendant against whom the prosecutor wants the court to make the order, and
(c) any person on whom the order would be likely to have a significant adverse effect,
as soon as practicable (without waiting for the verdict).

(3) A notice under paragraph (2) must:

[471] Added by Criminal Procedure (Amendment) Rules 2017 2017/144 para 6

(a) summarise the relevant facts,
(b) identify the evidence on which the prosecutor relies in support,
(c) attach any written statement that the prosecutor has not already served, and
(d) specify the order that the prosecutor wants the court to make.

27.4 ***Evidence Hearsay***

Criminal Procedure Rules 2015 2015/1490 Rule 31.1(3) A reference to 'hearsay evidence' in this Part of the rules is a reference to evidence consisting of hearsay within the meaning of Civil Evidence Act 1995 s 1(2).

Criminal Procedure Rules 2015 2015/1490 Rule 31.6(1) A party who wants to introduce hearsay evidence must:
(a) serve notice on:[472]
(i) the court officer, and
(ii) every other party directly affected, and
(b) in that notice:
(i) explain that it is a notice of hearsay evidence,
(ii) identify that evidence,
(iii) identify the person who made the statement which is hearsay, or explain why if that person is not identified, and
(iv) explain why that person will not be called to give oral evidence.
(2) A party may serve one notice under this rule in respect of more than one notice and more than one witness.

27.5 ***Evidence Hearsay Applications to cross-examine***

Criminal Procedure Rules 2015 2015/1490 Rule 31.7(1) This rule applies where a party wants the court's permission to cross-examine a person who made a statement which another party wants to introduce as hearsay.
(2) The party who wants to cross-examine that person must:
(a) apply in writing, with reasons, not more than 7 days after service of the notice of hearsay evidence, and
(b) serve the application on:
(i) the court officer,
(ii) the party who served the hearsay evidence notice, and
(iii) every party on whom the hearsay evidence notice was served.
(3) The court may decide an application under this rule with or without a hearing.
(4) But the court must not:
(a) dismiss an application under this rule unless the applicant has had an opportunity to make representations at a hearing (whether or not the applicant in fact attends), or
(b) allow an application under this rule unless everyone served with the application has had at least seven days in which to make representations, including representations about whether there should be a hearing.

27.6 ***Evidence Hearsay credibility and consistency***

Credibility and consistency of maker of hearsay statement

Criminal Procedure Rules 2015 2015/1490 Rule 31.8(1)[473] This rule applies where a party wants to challenge the credibility or consistency of a person who made a statement which another party wants to introduce as hearsay.
(2) The party who wants to challenge the credibility or consistency of that person must:
(a) serve notice of intention to do so on:
(i) the court officer, and
(ii) the party who served the notice of hearsay evidence,
not more than seven days after service of that hearsay evidence notice, and
(b) in the notice, identify any statement or other material on which that party relies.

---

[472] Criminal Procedure (Amendment No 2) Rules 2016 2016/705 para 11(e) removes the requirement that the notice had to be in writing. In force 3/10/16

[473] As amended by Criminal Procedure (Amendment No 2) Rules 2016 2016/705 para 11(f)(i) and (ii)

(3) The party who served the hearsay notice:
(a) may call that person to give oral evidence instead, and
(b) if so, must serve notice of intention to do so on:
(i) the court officer, and
(ii) every party on whom he served the hearsay notice,
not more than seven days after service of the notice under paragraph (2).

27.7 ***Representations, Right to make***
Criminal Procedure Rules 2015 2015/1490 Rule 31.2(1)[474] The court must not make a behaviour order unless the person to whom it is directed has had an opportunity:
(a) to consider:
(i) what order is proposed and why, and
(ii) the evidence in support, and
(b) to make representations at a hearing (whether or not that person in fact attends).
(2) That restriction does not apply to making an interim behaviour order, but unless other legislation otherwise provides, such an order has no effect unless the person to whom it is directed:
(a) is present when it is made, or
(b) is handed a document recording the order not more than seven days after it is made.

Disputes as to facts see the **FACTUAL BASIS FOR SENTENCING** ***Same rules apply when imposing ancillary orders*** para at **57.26**.

27.8 ***Duty to explain if order not made when it could be***
Criminal Procedure Rules 2015 2015/1490 Rule 31.2(3)[475] Where the court decides not to make, where it could:
(a) a Football Banning Order,
(b) a Parenting Order, after a person under 16 is convicted of an offence,
the court must announce, at a hearing in public, the reasons for its decision.

28 CUSTODY: GENERAL PRINCIPLES

28.1
See also the **CUSTODY: IMPRISONMENT** chapter.
Rehabilitation period The rehabilitation period depends on which custodial sentence is imposed and for what length. The periods were changed by Legal Aid, Sentencing and Punishment of Offenders Act 2012 s 139, see **89.6**.
For the release provisions see the first paragraph of the particular custody order, such as **CUSTODY: IMPRISONMENT** para **29.1**.
Concurrent or consecutive sentences For rules see the **CONCURRENT OR CONSECUTIVE SENTENCES** chapter.

28.2 ***Statistics England and Wales***
Custodial sentences

		2012	2013	2014	2015	2016	2017
Detention and Training Orders	Males	2,545	1,921	1,562	1,454	1,342	1,244
	Fem.	172	109	103	68	42	48
	All	2,758	2,057	1,684	1,522	1,384	1,341
Detention under s 91	Males	289	255	240	265	223	292
	Fem.	10	8	6	7	10	3
	All	299	263	246	274	233	295

474 As amended by Criminal Procedure (Amendment) Rules 2015 2015/13 para 9
475 As amended by Criminal Procedure (Amendment) Rules 2015 2015/13 para 9

		2012	2013	2014	2015	2016	2017
Immediate imprisonment	Males	77,718	74,730	74,676	74,464	74,433	70,535
	Fem.	7,017	6,668	7,103	7,001	7,047	6,946
	All	85,152	81,830	82,188	81,465	81,480	77,875
Young Offender Institution	Males	9,266	7,522	6,235	5,649	5,346	5,906
	Fem.	510	327	308	232	202	228
	All	9,838	7,894	6,560	5,881	5,548	6,159
Total immediate custody	Males	89,818	85,170	83,343	82,485	81,993	78,571
	Fem.	7,709	7,125	7,525	7,323	7,313	7,236
	All	98,047	92,799	91,313	89,808	89,306	86,275
Total persons sentenced	Males	878,475	827,170	846,709	849,792	839,805	806,907
	Fem.	294,392	283,025	303,350	314,175	309,362	292,409
	All	1,223,252	1,169,727	1,215,695	1,163,967	1,149,167	1,192,337
Percentage of persons sent to custody	Males	10.2%	10.3%	9.8%	9.7%	9.8%	9.7%
	Fem.	2.6%	2.5%	2.5%	2.3%	2.4%	2.4%
	All	8.0%	8.0%	7.5%	7.7%	7.8%	7.2%

These figures are continually being revised. Many of the totals do not add up correctly, mainly due to where the sex of a person was not specified. Therefore, the 'All' figures sometimes contain male, female and unspecified persons.

Persons sentenced to immediate custody at all courts by length[476]

Magistrates' Courts	**2014**	**2015**	**2016**	**2017**
Total persons sentenced	1,123,102	1,152,006	1,147,732	1,116,442
Number given immediate custody	43,935	43,087	43,452	41,992
Percentage given immediate custody	3.9%	3.7%	3.8%	3.7%
Crown Courts				
Total persons sentenced	86,100	86,911	81,779	75,915
Number given immediate custody	47,378	47,261	46,360	44,283
Percentage given immediate custody	55%	54%	56%	58%
Less than 12 months	15,058	14,869	14,248	13,022
12 months to 3 years	21,551	21,295	20,779	22,041
Over 3 years to 5 years	5,691	5,797	5,920	3,753
Over 5 years to 10 years	3,417	3,814	3,909	3,978
Over 10 years	983	1,117	1,097	1,127
Life, Discretionary	442	369	407	362

476 The figures given in the table relate to persons for whom these offences were the principal offences for which they were dealt with. When a defendant has been found guilty of two or more offences, it is the offence for which the heaviest penalty is imposed. Where the same disposal is imposed for two or more offences, the offence selected is the offence for which the statutory maximum penalty is the most severe. The compilers say that every effort is made to ensure that the figures presented are accurate and complete. However, it is important to note that these data have been extracted from large administrative data systems generated by the courts and police forces. As a consequence, care should be taken to ensure that data collection processes and their inevitable limitations are taken into account when those data are used.

Note: These statistics have been altered from previous editions. Occasionally the recorded figures for the previous year(s) change when we are supplied with new statistics, so we amend them accordingly. For explanations about the statistics, see page 1-xii.

Guidelines

28.3 ***Imposition of Community and Custodial Sentences Guideline 2017***

Imposition of Community and Custodial Sentences Guideline 2017 www.banksr.com Other Matters Guidelines tab In force 1 February 2017 page 7

The approach to the imposition of a custodial sentence should be as follows:

1) Has the custody threshold been passed?

- A custodial sentence must not be imposed unless the offence or the combination of the offence and one or more offences associated with it was so serious that neither a fine alone nor a community sentence can be justified for the offence.
- There is no general definition of where the custody threshold lies. The circumstances of the individual offence and the factors assessed by offence-specific guidelines will determine whether an offence is so serious that neither a fine alone nor a community sentence can be justified. Where no offence specific guideline is available to determine seriousness, the harm caused by the offence, the culpability of the offender and any previous convictions will be relevant to the assessment.
- The clear intention of the threshold test is to reserve prison as a punishment for the most serious offences.

2) Is it unavoidable that a sentence of imprisonment be imposed?

- Passing the custody threshold does not mean that a custodial sentence should be deemed inevitable. Custody should not be imposed where a community order could provide sufficient restriction on an offender's liberty (by way of punishment) while addressing the rehabilitation of the offender to prevent future crime.
- For offenders on the cusp of custody, imprisonment should not be imposed where there would be an impact on dependants which would make a custodial sentence disproportionate to achieving the aims of sentencing.

3) What is the shortest term commensurate with the seriousness of the offence?

- In considering this the court must NOT consider any licence or post sentence supervision requirements which may subsequently be imposed upon the offender's release.

4) Can the sentence be suspended?

- A suspended sentence **MUST NOT** be imposed as a more severe form of community order. A suspended sentence is a custodial sentence. **Sentencers should be clear that they would impose an immediate custodial sentence if the power to suspend were not available.** If not, a non-custodial sentence should be imposed.

page 8

The following factors should be weighed in considering whether it is possible to suspend the sentence:

Factors indicating that it would not be appropriate to suspend a custodial sentence	**Factors indicating that it may be appropriate to suspend a custodial sentence**
Offender presents a risk/danger to the public	Realistic prospect of rehabilitation
Appropriate punishment can only be achieved by immediate custody	Strong personal mitigation
History of poor compliance with court orders	Immediate custody will result in significant harmful impact upon others

The imposition of a custodial sentence is both punishment and a deterrent. To ensure that the overall terms of the suspended sentence are commensurate with offence seriousness, care must be taken to ensure requirements imposed are not excessive. A court wishing to impose onerous or intensive requirements should reconsider whether a community sentence might be more appropriate.

Pre-sentence report

Whenever the court reaches the provisional view that:

- the custody threshold has been passed; and, if so
- the length of imprisonment which represents the shortest term commensurate with the seriousness of the offence;

the court should obtain a pre-sentence report, whether verbal or written, unless the court considers a report to be unnecessary. Ideally a pre-sentence report should be completed on the same day to avoid adjourning the case.

28.4 *Magistrates' Court Sentencing Guidelines 2008*

Magistrates' Court Sentencing Guidelines 2008, see www.banksr.com Other Matters Guidelines tab page 163 para 1 A custodial sentence must not be imposed unless the offence 'was so serious that neither a fine alone nor a community sentence can be justified for the offence'.[477] Guidance regarding this threshold and the approach to the imposition of custodial sentences is set out in the Sentencing Guidelines Council's definitive guideline *Overarching Principles: Seriousness 2004*, www.banksr.com Other Matters Guidelines tab.

2 The guideline emphasises that:

(a) the clear intention of the threshold test is to reserve prison as a punishment for the most serious offences,

(b) passing the custody threshold does not mean that a custodial sentence should be deemed inevitable; custody can still be avoided in light of offender mitigation or where there is a suitable intervention in the community which provides sufficient restriction (by way of punishment) while addressing the rehabilitation of the offender to prevent future crime. However, where the offence would otherwise appear to warrant a term of imprisonment within the Crown Court's jurisdiction, it is for the Crown Court to make that judgment,

(c) the approach to the imposition of a custodial sentence should be as follows:

(i) Has the custody threshold been passed?

(ii) If so, is it unavoidable that a custodial sentence be imposed?

(iii) If so, can that sentence be suspended? (Sentencers should be clear that they would have imposed a custodial sentence if the power to suspend had not been available.)

(iv) If not, impose a sentence which takes immediate effect for the shortest term commensurate with the seriousness of the offence.

Magistrates' Court powers and committals

28.5 *Magistrates' Court powers   Maximum term*

Powers of Criminal Courts (Sentencing) Act 2000 s 78(1) A Magistrates' Court shall not have power to impose imprisonment, or detention in a Young Offender Institution, for more than 6 months in respect of any one offence.

(2) Unless expressly excluded, subsection (1) above shall apply even if the offence in question is one for which a person would otherwise be liable on summary conviction to imprisonment or detention in a Young Offender Institution for more than 6 months.

(3) Subsection (1) above is without prejudice to Magistrates' Courts Act 1980 s 133 (consecutive terms of imprisonment).

[477] Criminal Justice Act 2003 s 152(2)

(4) Any power of a Magistrates' Court to impose a term of imprisonment for non-payment of a fine, or for want of sufficient distress to satisfy a fine, shall not be limited by virtue of subsection (1) above.

28.6 ***Magistrates' Court powers Consecutive sentences***
Consecutive terms of imprisonment
Magistrates' Courts Act 1980 s 133(1) Subject to Criminal Justice Act 2003 s 265, a Magistrates' Court imposing imprisonment or youth custody on any person may order that the term of imprisonment or youth custody shall commence on the expiration of any other term of imprisonment or youth custody imposed by that or any other court; but where a Magistrates' Court imposes two or more terms of imprisonment or youth custody to run consecutively the aggregate of such terms shall not, subject to the provisions of this section, exceed 6 months.
(2) If two or more of the terms imposed by the court are imposed in respect of an offence triable either way which was tried summarily otherwise than in pursuance of [Magistrates' Courts Act 1980] s 22(2) above, the aggregate of the terms so imposed and any other terms imposed by the court may exceed 6 months but shall not, subject to the following provisions of this section, exceed 12 months.
(2A) In relation to the imposition of terms of detention in a young offender institution subsection (2) above shall have effect as if the reference to an offence triable either way were a reference to such an offence or an offence triable only on indictment.
(3) The limitations imposed by the preceding subsections shall not operate to reduce the aggregate of the terms that the court may impose in respect of any offences below the term which the court has power to impose in respect of any one of those offences.
(4) Where a person has been sentenced by a Magistrates' Court to imprisonment and a fine for the same offence, a period of imprisonment imposed for non-payment of the fine, or for want of sufficient goods to satisfy the fine, shall not be subject to the limitations imposed by the preceding subsections.
(5) For the purposes of this section a term of imprisonment shall be deemed to be imposed in respect of an offence if it is imposed as a sentence or in default of payment of a sum adjudged to be paid by the conviction or for want of sufficient goods to satisfy such a sum. Where a Magistrates' Court imposes two or more terms of imprisonment or youth custody to run consecutively the aggregate of such terms shall not, subject to the provisions of this section, exceed 6 months.

28.7 ***Magistrates' Court powers Consecutive sentences Triable either way offences***
Magistrates' Courts Act 1980 s 133(2) If two or more of the terms imposed by the court are imposed in respect of an offence triable either way which was tried summarily otherwise than in pursuance of Magistrates' Courts Act 1980 s 22(2) (certain triable either way offences), the aggregate of the terms so imposed and any other terms imposed by the court may exceed 6 months but shall not, subject to the following provisions of this section, exceed **12 months**.
(3) The limitations imposed by the preceding subsections shall not operate to reduce the aggregate of the terms that the court may impose in respect of any offences below the term which the court has power to impose in respect of any one of those offences.
For the full section, see **28.6**.

28.8 ***Magistrates' Court powers Consecutive to another term being served***
Magistrates' Courts Act 1980 s 133(1) Subject to Criminal Justice Act 2003 s 265 (restriction on consecutive sentences for released prisoners), a Magistrates' Court imposing imprisonment or youth custody on any person may order that the term of imprisonment or youth custody shall commence on the expiration of any other term of imprisonment or youth custody imposed by that or any other court.
For the full section, see **28.6**.

28.9 *Magistrates' Court powers Consecutive terms Either way offence*
Magistrates' Courts Act 1980 s 133(2) If two or more of the terms imposed by the court are imposed in respect of an offence triable either way which was tried summarily otherwise than in pursuance of section 22(2) of this Act, the aggregate of the terms so imposed and any other terms imposed by the court may not exceed 12 months.

28.10 *Summary only matters Consecutive activated suspended sentences*
R v Chamberlain 1992 13 Cr App R (S) 525 The Magistrates' Courts Act 1980 s 133 limit on sentencing powers for consecutive sentences did not apply when activating a suspended sentence.
R v Hester-Wox 2016 EWCA Crim 1397, 2 Cr App R (S) 43 We apply the rule in *R v Chamberlain* 1992.

28.11 *Magistrates' Court powers Consecutive terms Prison in default*
Magistrates' Courts Act 1980 s 133(4) Where a person has been sentenced by a Magistrates' Court to imprisonment and a fine for the same offence, a period of imprisonment imposed for non-payment of the fine, or for want of sufficient distress to satisfy the fine, shall not be subject to the limitations imposed by the preceding subsections.

28.12 *Magistrates' Court powers Occasions where restrictions don't apply*
Magistrates' Courts Act 1980 s 133(5) For the purposes of this section a term of imprisonment shall be deemed to be imposed in respect of an offence if it is imposed as a sentence or in default of payment of a sum adjudged to be paid by the conviction or for want of sufficient distress to satisfy such a sum.

28.13 *Legitimate expectation of non-custodial sentence raised*
Allocation Guideline 2016, see www.banksr.com Other Matters Guidelines tab In force 1 March 2016
page 36 Where the court decides that the case is suitable to be dealt with in the Magistrates' Court, it must warn the defendant that all sentencing options remain open and, if the defendant consents to summary trial and is convicted by the court or pleads guilty, the defendant may be committed to the Crown Court for sentence.
R v Gillam 1980 2 Cr App R (S) 267 On 2 May 1980, D pleaded to two counts of dwelling burglary, which were committed in November 1979, and reckless driving. He had 13 previous convictions. The Judge read a social inquiry report which was not unfavourable to D and adjourned the case for a community service assessment. In March 1980 he had been sent to prison for one month with a 3-month suspended sentence activated in full. In June 1980 he was released from prison. The Judge had ensured he was released on bail. On the next appearance, the second social enquiry report found D was suitable for community service and recommended that. Without asking for representations, the Judge imposed two concurrent 6-month sentences. Held. Burglary is a very serious offence. D's record was in some respects appalling. D does not merit beneficial consideration of this court. He should have been sent to prison for at least 15 months. However, there was an important sentencing principle here. There was created in D's mind an expectation that he would be given community service if the report was disposed to such a course. When that happens and an alternative to prison is found to be satisfactory, the court should adopt that alternative. Otherwise a feeling of injustice will be aroused. We substitute community service.
R v Rennes 1985 7 Cr App R (S) 343 D pleaded to two handling charges and four other charges at the Magistrates' Court. The Stipendiary Magistrate adjourned for a community service assessment. At the next hearing, there was a favourable community service assessment but she committed the case to the Crown Court, which imposed 12 months' imprisonment. It was not suggested that sentence was manifestly excessive. Held. It makes no difference that the expectation was at the Magistrates' Court and the sentence was made at the Crown Court. The defendant's legitimate expectations should not be defeated. If they were, he suffers an injustice. Therefore it all depends on what the

defendant was led to expect. If there had been a warning there would be no sense of injustice, so it would be wise to give one. We quash the sentence and due to time served impose a conditional discharge.

R v Gutteridge v DPP 1987 9 Cr App R (S) 279 D pleaded to TDA and three associated driving matters. He had 'rather a bad character'. The Magistrate said he would give D a suspended sentence or remand him for reports if there was reason to do so. After the defence made their representations he remanded the case for reports, saying that that should not be construed as an indication that any recommendation would be followed. The next Magistrate declined to deal with the case and then lay justices gave D 6 months. D appealed. The Crown Court dismissed his appeal saying the sentence was fully justified, the first Magistrate had not given a promise and the appeal was a rehearing so they could look at the matter afresh. Held. The paramount consideration is that when D was before the Crown Court he still had a legitimate grievance. The words used by the first Magistrate were a clear indication that nothing more severe than a suspended sentence would be passed. D therefore did have a legitimate grievance. It makes not the slightest difference that the appeal was a rehearing. Sentence quashed.

R v Chamberlain 1995 16 Cr App R (S) 473 D pleaded to burglary and was remanded for reports (which were then a court requirement). On the next hearing, the probation report said D was depressed and the most appropriate way of dealing with that was he should attend a PACT course. A further report about that was requested. On the next hearing, D was assessed as suitable to attend that programme but D was given, by a third judge, 12 months and some breach sentences. Held. Although the sentence was entirely suitable, the course contemplated by the second Judge must be followed. This case underlines yet again the necessity for sentencers to explain clearly what the position is when they order adjournments for further assessments. Defendants should invariably be told in clear terms they must not assume from the adjournment that a particular form of sentence has been ruled out. We substitute probation.

R v CD 2018 EWCA Crim 571 D pleaded to sexually assaulting a child. A psychiatrist recommended a sex offender treatment programme. The Judge asked the probation officer whether there was any reason why he should not pass a community order. The officer asked for an adjournment to liaise with the sex offender programme providers and the Judge agreed saying, "I am minded to think that the case could be dealt with without a loss of liberty. I will adjourn without promises for a pre-sentence report." D co-operated with probation and their report recommended a community order or a suspended sentence with a community sex offender programme. At the next hearing, D received 2 years. Held. The remarks were conveying mixed messages. Although the Judge said, "no promises" it was clear he was minded to give a non-custodial sentence. At the last hearing there was no new information. D could reasonably believe that if a suitable course was proposed, he would not receive immediate custody. There was a legitimate sense of injustice aroused, so we suspend the 2-year sentence with a condition of an attendance on a sex offender programme.

See also: *R v Horton and Alexander* 1985 7 Cr App R (S) 155 (Judge remanded case for reports and community service assessment, saying, "even though I consider an immediate custodial sentence is likely to be the conclusion". There was no legitimate expectation.)

R v Woodin 1994 15 Cr App R (S) 307 (Judge remanded case for reports and later passed an immediate custodial sentence. No warning was given and bail was granted. There was no legitimate expectation, because the Judge was obliged to obtain a report as (then) there was a requirement to do so when considering whether a custodial sentence was justified.)

28.14 ***Overcrowding, Prison***

Note: The sentencing principle about the problem of overcrowded prisons has rightly fallen out of favour. I think the best approach is to ignore this factor and simply apply the 2017 guideline at **28.3**. Ed.

The maximum for the offence

28.15 ***Maximum must be reserved for the most serious cases***

R v Pinto 2006 EWCA Crim 749, 2 Cr App R (S) 87 (p 579) It is well established that the maximum sentence should be passed only in the most truly exceptional cases, which are so serious that it is difficult to imagine a yet more serious example of the offence. Sentence therefore reduced.

R v Bright 2008 EWCA Crim 462, 2 Cr App R (S) 102 (p 578) The maximum sentence permitted by statute is, of course, very rarely imposed, and nowadays when there has been a guilty plea, effectively never…It is sometimes loosely said that the maximum sentence should be reserved for the worst case of its kind, and from this imaginative counsel for the defendant will urge examples of cases of greater criminality than the offence established against his client. The argument, however, is founded on the misapprehension that if a realistically more serious case can be imagined, the imposition of the maximum is precluded. That is why we repeat, the maximum sentence permitted by statute is reserved not for the worst possible case which can realistically be conceived, but for cases which in the statutory context are truly identified as cases of the utmost gravity.

R v Khan 2017 EWCA Crim 2248 D pleaded at the Magistrates' Court to dangerous driving. He drove at up to 98 mph in a built-up area. He also went through red lights. He had three previous convictions for dangerous driving and seven for driving whilst disqualified. He also had other serious previous convictions. The Judge gave him 16 months for the dangerous driving and 4 months for disqualified driving, making 20 months in all. D said the Judge should not have started at the maximum for each offence. Held. The maximum sentence should be reserved for the most serious criminality. However that does not mean the Judge has to imagine the worst possible case. The Judge should ask whether the case comes within the broad band of [the most serious cases]. Where the maximum is relatively low that band may be wide. Here we uphold the sentences but make them concurrent.

Note: Why these two separate offences, for which D had significant previous convictions, should be concurrent is not explained. I doubt there could be an explanation. Ed.

R v Saxton 2018 EWCA Crim 1976 D pleaded to a section 20 assault. He punched and kicked a sex offender, V, in a medical centre of a prison with another. The two called him a 'dirty Paki rapist'. V was seriously injured. D had 90 previous offences, many of which were relevant. The Judge started at 5 years (the maximum). The defence said the case did not justify the maximum sentence. Held. It is well established that the maximum sentence is reserved not for the worst possible case which can realistically be conceived, but for cases which are truly identified as being of the utmost gravity. This can be because of one single stand-out feature or a series of features. Where the maximum sentence is relatively low there may indeed be a broad range of cases that require sentences [at][478] or approaching the maximum. The maximum here was justified.

See also: *R v Butt* 2006 EWCA Crim 47, 2 Cr App R (S) 59 (p 364) (*R v Ambler and Hargreaves* 1976 applied.)

See also the **CONCURRENT AND CONSECUTIVE SENTENCES** ***Grave cases/Maximum considered inadequate*** para at **18.9.**

28.16 ***Maximum must be reserved for the most serious cases   Total sentence above the maximum***

R v Nelson and Shaibu 2016 EWCA Crim 1517, 2017 1 Cr App R (S) 11 (p 68) N was convicted of possessing a prohibited weapon and assisting his co-defendant, S. N controlled, in a gang, a number of drug runners. Following two shooting incidents, in one of which a police community support officer was shot at but not injured, N hid the Scorpion sub-machine gun involved in a loft. The assisting offence was based on N knowing that S had put the gun to active use and N assisted in concealing the gun, to

[478] The judgment says 'another', which must be a typo.

impede the prosecution of S. The Judge passed 8 years for the firearm offence (maximum 10 years) and 4 years for the assisting count (maximum 7 years) consecutive making 12 years in all. Held. In principle it is not wrong to impose a [total] sentence which exceeds the maximum for the highest of the offences charged. But where this happens we would expect an explanation of exactly which facts and/or other considerations justified this course. The possession and the assisting are interlinked on the facts and even if (to test the argument) this case was treated as an aggravated and serious case of possession (to take account of the concealment of the weapon to assist an offender), the sentence should have fallen short of the maximum 10 years' custody. There is no doubt that the offending was indeed grave; but it is possible to imagine many much worse scenarios, for instance when weapons caused actual injury or even death or are proven to have been used in repeated violent criminality over a long period. Bearing in mind the degree of overlap between the two counts and the statutory maximums, 5 years and 4 years making 9 years in all.

28.17 ***Maximum given with plea of guilty/Maximum sentence considered inadequate***

Reduction in Sentence for a Guilty Plea Guideline 2007, see www.banksr.com Other Matters Guidelines tab para E 5.3 The sentencer cannot remedy perceived defects (e.g. an inadequate charge or maximum penalty) by refusal of the appropriate discount.

Note: There is a new guideline but this statement would appear to reflect current sentencing practice. Ed.

R v Barnes 1983 5 Cr App R (S) 368 D pleaded to attempted rape and going equipped. He received a maximum 7 years' imprisonment for the attempted rape and a concurrent 9-month sentence for going equipped. The victim, V, was the 15-year-old female friend of D's daughters. D took all three girls to his house, sent his daughters to bed and forced V to drink alcohol. He then approached her with an eight-inch knife, grabbed her hair and throat and told her to remove her lower garments. One of D's daughters approached D and V immediately ran away. Held. There should have been more credit for D's guilty plea, considering he saved the girl the ordeal of going into the witness box and giving an account of the horrifying events…D is clearly entitled to some reduction below the maximum sentence. Clearly the reduction cannot be a substantial one because the offence itself was very serious.

R v Greene 1993 14 Cr App R (S) 682 Once the maximum has been set by Parliament and a plea of guilty has been proffered at an early stage, then it was incumbent on the Judge to reflect that willingness to plead guilty in the sentence that he felt obliged to pass.

R v March 2002 EWCA Crim 551, 2002 2 Cr App R (S) 98 (p 448) D, aged 16, with others, pleaded to one count of conspiracy to cause ABH, three counts of ABH, one count of threats to kill and one count of incitement to steal. He received a maximum 24-month Detention and Training Order. Two counts of indecent assault, which attracted section 91 detention, were left to lie on file. The Judge described the case as the most disgusting case he had ever had to deal with. The Judge criticised the prosecution for accepting pleas to the offences and allowing the indecent assault charges to lie on the file, indicating that he would have passed a higher sentence had he been able to. The Judge gave no discount for the plea, stating that "in the acceptance of the pleas to lesser offences, and the counts to lie on file, D had had all the discount he could hope for". Credit was not given for the 8 months served on remand either. Held. The Judge was only entitled to sentence for the offence of which D had been convicted. He should have loyally applied the Act. We are concerned not to undermine the advice given that pleas of guilty attract discounts. What he could not do was to go behind the compromise between defence and prosecution and sentence on a basis which the Crown could have pursued, but chose not to pursue. 6 months' discount allowed.

R v Bogoslov 2008 EWCA Crim 676 D pleaded to four counts of possession of a false identity document (max 2 years). The Judge passed 2 years concurrent, saying the plea

was reflected in the sentences not being consecutive and the maximum sentence was restrictive. Held. D was entitled to credit for the plea. Starting at 18 months, so on a plea 12 months.
R v Simpson 2009 EWCA Crim 423, 2 Cr App R (S) 69 (p 492) Sentence reduced to reflect plea.
Old cases: *R v Carroll* 1995 16 Cr App R (S) 488 (Whatever the Judge's view, the maximum sentence must be reserved for the most serious examples, and any appropriate discount must be given.)
R v Sherif and Others 2008 EWCA Crim 2653, 2009 2 Cr App R (S) 33 (p 235) (We are bound by the maximum sentences laid down by Parliament.)
See also the **CUSTODY: GENERAL PRINCIPLES** ***Maximum sentence already served*** para at **30.19**, the **DETENTION AND TRAINING ORDERS** ***Discount for guilty plea Maximum sentence given*** para at **37.16** and the **CONCURRENT AND CONSECUTIVE SENTENCES** ***Grave cases/Maximum considered inadequate*** para at **18.9**.

28.18 ***There is a maximum sentence for another offence of the same crime which is lower***

R v Hinton 1995 16 Cr App R (S) 523 LCJ D pleaded to indecent assault on a female. However, the original charge was unlawful sexual intercourse with a child, V, who was D's stepdaughter. There was a delay between the commission of the offence and D's arrest and, because of the statutory time bar in relation to that offence, the charge had to be substituted. D had indicated he would plead to unlawful sexual intercourse (maximum 2 years), and subsequently pleaded to indecent assault (maximum 10 years). He received 3 years' imprisonment. Held. The only reason why the Judge was able to pass a sentence of 3 years was because the offence charged originally was time-barred and, accordingly, there was substituted for it what might seem the lesser offence of indecent assault, rather than unlawful sexual intercourse. An offence of indecent assault, since 1985, carries a maximum sentence of 10 years. Accordingly, the Judge's sentence was strictly lawful in terms of the maxima imposed by Parliament, but the unfairness of the situation is clear: had it not been for the time bar, D could not have been sentenced to more than 2 years' imprisonment. It would be unfair that he should be sentenced to more than that, simply because the case had been delayed in coming to court.
R v I 1998 2 Cr App R (S) 63 D was convicted of indecent assault (maximum 10 years). He was acquitted of rape. Held. We approach sentence on the basis that the Court was dealing with an act of unlawful sexual intercourse (maximum 2 years). That charge could not be indicted because of the one-year time limit. Consequently relying on *R v Hinton* 1995 16 Cr App R (S) 523 we regard the maximum as 2 years.
R v Jones 2002 EWCA Crim 2983, 2003 1 WLR 1590 D was charged with indecent assault against a female, Sexual Offences Act 1956 s 14,[479] where the incident was essentially unlawful sexual intercourse with a girl under the age of 16, Sexual Offences Act 1956 s 6.[480] The maximum sentences were 10 years and 2 years respectively. D was charged with indecent assault in order to avoid the statutory bar in bringing prosecutions for unlawful sexual intercourse with a girl under the age of 16 taking effect and preventing a prosecution. D alleged this was an abuse of process. Held. In such cases, it has consequently become a not-infrequent practice to charge indecent assault under section 14, thereby avoiding the 12-month restriction on prosecution for an offence under section 6. This practice has been noted without adverse comment, and indeed with implied approval, in a number of sentence appeals in this Court. Given the clear provision in section 14(2), which precludes the defence of consent, the substantive offence of indecent assault is plainly apt to cover the act of penile penetration involved in sexual intercourse and of the various acts of fondling and foreplay which precede it, whether or not such acts amount to an attempt at such intercourse. There is nothing in

[479] Repealed on 1/5/2004 by Sexual Offences Act 2003 Sch 7 para 1
[480] Repealed on 1/5/2004 by Sexual Offences Act 2003 Sch 7 para 1

the statutory history of the offence, or the content of the 1956 Act, to require a contrary construction. Thus the overlap between section 6 and section 14 is plain and inevitable. Leaving aside the question of limitation, the bringing of a prosecution and the selection of an appropriate charge lies within the discretion and the responsibility of the Crown and, in the event of a charge being brought under one or other of sections 6 and 14, it is *prima facie* the duty of the Court to decide the matter according to whether or not the ingredients of the substantive offence have been proved.

R v Figg 2003 EWCA Crim 2751, 1 Cr App R (S) 68 (p 409) D was convicted of indecent assault. He was acquitted of rape. Held. Unfortunately the Judge in *R v Isles* 1999 did not point to the significance in *R v Hinton* 1999 that in that case the prosecution was prepared to accept a plea to unlawful sexual intercourse, which itself gave rise to the unfairness. The fact of the anomaly between sexual intercourse and indecent assault is not itself decisive. There are other anomalies in the law. It is ludicrous to say that the existence of earlier legislation thwarts the intention of Parliament in the later legislation and superimposes a maximum sentence of 2 years' imprisonment under whichever Act the offence is charged. In this case a justifiable choice to prosecute indecent assault does not carry with it the limitation imposed by *R v Hinton* 1999. The Judge in this case was not constrained by a 2-year maximum. However, nothing we have said should detract from the now settled policy of treating 2 years' imprisonment as the maximum sentence appropriate to a charge of indecent assault brought in circumstances where, but for the expiry of the 12-month time limit, the charge would have appropriately have been laid as unlawful sexual intercourse.

R v Dosanjh and Others 2013 EWCA Crim 2366, 2014 2 Cr App R (S) 25 (p 191) D was convicted of conspiracy to cheat the Revenue where the Revenue lost £39m. The Judge sentenced him to 15 years. The defence relied on *R v Rimmington and Goldstein* 2005 UKHL 63 to suggest that it was wrong to pass a longer term than was available for an equivalent statutory offence which would have a 7- or 10-year maximum. Held. para 29 It is for Parliament to decide the maximum sentences. Where Parliament has set maximum sentences for particular conduct, it is not for the courts and the executive to decide that those sentences are not enough, and that the statutory limits should be evaded. para 33 [The offence of] conspiracy to cheat the public revenue is used to supplement the statutory framework and is recognised as the appropriate charge for the small number of the most serious revenue frauds, where the statutory offences will not adequately reflect the criminality involved and where a sentence at large is more appropriate than one subject to statutory restrictions. These are not 'ordinary' cases. para 34 The House of Lords recognised that the general approach may not apply where there was good reason for charging the common law offence. In this case there was good reason.

Defendants who have not been previously been sentenced to custody

28.19 *Statutory provisions*

Restriction on imposing custodial sentences on persons not legally represented.

Powers of Criminal Courts (Sentencing) Act 2000 s 83(1) A magistrates' court on summary conviction, or the Crown Court on committal for sentence or on conviction on indictment, shall not pass a sentence of imprisonment on a person who:

(a) is not legally represented in that court, and

(b) has not been previously sentenced to that punishment by a court in any part of the United Kingdom,

unless he is a person to whom subsection (3) below applies.

(2) A magistrates' court on summary conviction, or the Crown Court on committal for sentence or on conviction on indictment, shall not:

(a) pass a sentence of detention under section 90 or 91 below,

(b) pass a sentence of custody for life under section 93 or 94 below,

(c) pass a sentence of detention in a young offender institution, or

(d) make a detention and training order,

on or in respect of a person who is not legally represented in that court unless he is a person to whom subsection (3) below applies.

(3) This subsection applies to a person if either:

(a) representation was made available to him for the purposes of the proceedings under Part 1 of the Legal Aid, Sentencing and Punishment of Offenders Act 2012 but was withdrawn because of his conduct or because it appeared that his financial resources were such that he was not eligible for such representation;

(aa) he applied for such representation and the application was refused because it appeared that his financial resources were such that he was not eligible for such representation; or

(b) having been informed of his right to apply for such representation and having had the opportunity to do so, he refused or failed to apply.[481]

(4) For the purposes of this section a person is to be treated as legally represented in a court if, but only if, he has the assistance of counsel or a solicitor to represent him in the proceedings in that court at some time after he is found guilty and before he is sentenced.

(5) For the purposes of subsection (1)(b) above a previous sentence of imprisonment which has been suspended and which has not taken effect under section 119 below or under section 19 of the Treatment of Offenders Act (Northern Ireland) 1968 shall be disregarded.

(6) In this section "sentence of imprisonment" does not include a committal for contempt of court or any kindred offence.

28.20 ***Service detention/Imprisonment Need for legal representation Court Martial***

Restriction on imposing custodial sentence or service

Armed Forces Act 2006 s 263(1) A sentence of:

(a) imprisonment, or

(b) service detention,

must not be passed by the Court Martial or the Service Civilian Court, or passed or confirmed by the Summary Appeal Court, in respect of an offender who is not legally represented in that court.

(2) Subsection (1) does not apply if the offender:

(a) having been informed of his right to apply for legal representation and having had the opportunity to do so, refused or failed to apply, or

(b) was aged 21 or over when convicted, and has previously been sentenced to imprisonment by a civilian court in any part of the United Kingdom or for a service offence, or sentenced to detention by a court in any other member State or for a member State service offence.

(3) The Court Martial or the Service Civilian Court must not:

(a) pass a sentence of detention under section 209 or 218 (young offenders' detention), or

(b) make an order under section 211 (detention and training),

on or in respect of an offender who is not legally represented in that court unless the offender, having been informed of his right to apply for legal representation and, having had the opportunity to do so, refused or failed to apply.

(4) For the purposes of this section an offender is 'legally represented' in the Court Martial or the Service Civilian Court only if he has the assistance of counsel or a solicitor to represent him in the proceedings in that court at some time after he is found guilty and before he is sentenced.

(5) For the purposes of this section an offender is 'legally represented' in the Summary Appeal Court:

[481] This section has been amended by Criminal Justice and Court Services Act 2000 s 74 and Sch 7 para 178, but it looks unlikely that commencement will ever occur.

(a) in a case where his appeal was only against punishment, if he has the assistance of counsel or a solicitor to represent him at some time during the proceedings in that court,

(b) in any other case, only if he has the assistance of counsel or a solicitor to represent him in the proceedings in that court at some time after the court confirms or substitutes the finding and before it confirms or passes sentence.

(6) For the purposes of subsection (2)(b):

(a) a previous sentence of imprisonment which has been suspended and has not taken effect is to be disregarded,

(b) 'sentence of imprisonment' does not include a committal for contempt of court or any kindred offence,

(c) 'member State service offence' means an offence which:

(i) was the subject of proceedings under the service law of a member State other than the United Kingdom, and

(ii) at the time it was done, would have constituted an offence in any part of the United Kingdom, or a service offence, if it had been done in any part of the United Kingdom by a member of Her Majesty's forces,

(d) 'service law', in relation to a member State other than the United Kingdom, means the law governing all or any of the naval, military or air forces of that State.

28.21 ***Need for legal representation Cases***

R v Hollywood 1991 12 Cr App R (S) 325 D pleaded guilty when he was represented. But neither counsel nor a solicitor were present when D was given a suspended sentence. Held. The sentence of imprisonment was invalid. However, the Court of Appeal could cure the defect. Appeal dismissed.

R v Wilson 1995 16 Cr App R (S) 997 After conviction and before sentencing D sacked her lawyer. D was sentenced to 7 years' imprisonment. Held. D's legal aid had not been withdrawn so she was still entitled to representation. To sentence her without representation was unlawful.

R v Howden 2006 EWCA Crim 1691, 2007 1 Cr App R (S) 31 (p 164) (D absconded and was sentenced to 4 years in total. He was unrepresented and had not been sentenced to imprisonment before, so the sentence was unlawful.)

R v Henry 2013 EWCA Crim 1415, 2014 1 Cr App R (S) 55 (p 347) (The defendant's sentence was unlawful. The Court of Appeal can replace an unlawful sentence with a lawful one.)

See also: *McC v Mullan and Others* 1984 81 Cr App R 54 (The Lords dealing with a civil action against the Magistrates. Northern Irish Divisional Court held sentence unlawful.)

28.22 ***Need for legal representation Suspended sentences don't count as a 'previous sentence'***

Powers of Criminal Courts (Sentencing) Act 2000 s 83(5) For the purposes of (the requirement the defendant must be legally represented) a previous sentence of imprisonment which has been suspended and which has not taken effect…shall be disregarded.

Criminal Justice Act 2003 s 189(6) Subject to any provision to the contrary contained in Criminal Justice Act 1967, Powers of Criminal Courts (Sentencing) Act 2000 or any other enactment passed or instrument made under any enactment after 31 December 1967, a suspended sentence which has not taken effect under paragraph 8 of Schedule 12 is to be treated as a sentence of imprisonment (or in the case of a person aged at least 18 but under 21, a sentence of detention in a Young Offender Institution) for the purposes of all enactments and instruments made under enactments.

New Sentences: Criminal Justice Act 2003 Guideline 2004, see www.banksr.com Other Matters Guidelines tab para 2.2.6 A suspended sentence is a sentence of imprisonment. It is subject to the same criteria as a sentence of imprisonment which is to commence immediately.

R v Hollywood 1991 12 Cr App R (S) 325 D pleaded guilty when he was represented. But neither counsel nor a solicitor were present when D was handed a suspended sentence. Held. The sentence of imprisonment was invalid. However, the Court of Appeal could cure the defect and the appeal was dismissed.

28.23 ***Need for legal representation Suspended sentences don't qualify for 'previous sentence' Court Martial***

Armed Forces Act 2006 s 263(6) For the purposes of subsection (2)(b):

(a) a previous sentence of imprisonment which has been suspended and has not taken effect is to be disregarded.

28.24 ***Need for legal representation Contempt of court***

Powers of Criminal Courts (Sentencing) Act 2000 s 83(6) In this section (which deals with the need for legal representation) 'sentence of imprisonment' does not include a committal for contempt of court or any kindred offence.

Criminal Procedure Rules 2015 2015/1490 Rule 48.5(1) This rule applies where the court observes, or someone reports to the court:

(a) in the Court of Appeal or the Crown Court, obstructive, disruptive, insulting or intimidating conduct, in the courtroom or in its vicinity, or otherwise immediately affecting the proceedings,

(b) in the Crown Court, a contravention of:

(i) Criminal Procedure (Attendance of Witnesses) Act 1965 s 3 (disobeying a witness summons),

(ii) Juries Act 1974 s 20 (disobeying a jury summons),

(iii) [Deleted[482]]

(c) in a Magistrates' Court, a contravention of:

(i) Magistrates' Courts Act 1980 s 97(4) (refusing to give evidence), or

(ii) Contempt of Court Act 1981 s 12 (insulting or interrupting the court, etc.),

(d) a contravention of Contempt of Court Act 1981 s 9 (without the court's permission, recording the proceedings, etc.),

(e) any other conduct with which the court can deal as, or as if it were, a criminal contempt of court, except failure to surrender to bail under Bail Act 1976 s 6.

(2) Unless the respondent's behaviour makes it impracticable to do so, the court must:

(a) explain, in terms the respondent can understand (with help, if necessary):..

(vi) that the respondent may take legal advice; and

(b) allow the respondent a reasonable opportunity to reflect, take advice, explain and, if he or she so wishes, apologise.

Old cases: They included draconian powers which were contrary to this new rule and good court management. Ed.

28.25 ***Need for legal representation Curing defect at the Court of Appeal***

R v Howden 2006 EWCA Crim 1691, 2007 1 Cr App R (S) 31 (p 164) D absconded and was sentenced to 4 years in total. He was unrepresented and had not been sentenced to imprisonment before, so the sentence was unlawful. The 4 years was not considered excessive. D was represented at the Court of Appeal. Held. It would be a nonsense if we could not quash the unlawful and substitute the same, correct sentence. The words, 'sentenced differently' in subsection 11(3) are capable of meaning 'sentenced lawfully instead of unlawfully'. 4 years.

Old case: *R v Hollywood* 1991 12 Cr App R (S) 325 (The Court of Appeal could cure the defect and the appeal was dismissed.)

Custody possible because community sentence/fine cannot be justified

28.26 ***Offence must be so serious a fine or community sentence cannot be justified***

General restrictions on imposing discretionary custodial sentences

482 Criminal Procedure (Amendment No 3) Rules 2017 2017/755 para 11(a)

Criminal Justice Act 2003 s 152(1) This section applies where a person is convicted of an offence punishable with a custodial sentence other than one:

(a) fixed by law, or

(b) falling to be imposed under a provision mentioned in subsection (1A).[483]

(1A) [This contains a list of sections setting out minimum sentences.]

Note: These provisions relate to minimum sentences and dangerous offenders. Ed.

(2) The court must not pass a custodial sentence unless it is of the opinion that the offence, or that offence and one or more offences associated with it, was so serious that neither a fine alone nor a community sentence can be justified.

(3) Nothing in subsection (2) prevents the court from passing a custodial sentence on the offender if:

(a) he fails to express his willingness to comply with a requirement which is proposed by the court to be included in a community order and which requires an expression of such willingness, or

(b) he fails to comply with an order under Criminal Justice Act 2003 s 161(2) (pre-sentence drug testing).

R v Howells 1999 1 Cr App R (S) 335 LCJ It would be dangerous and wrong for this Court to lay down prescriptive rules governing the exercise of judgement about whether a case is so serious that only a custodial sentence can be justified. Any guidance we give, however general, will be subject to exceptions and qualifications in some cases. We do, however, think that in approaching cases which are on or near the custody threshold, courts will usually find it helpful to begin by considering the nature and extent of the defendant's criminal intention and the nature and extent of any injury or damage caused to the victim. Other things being equal, an offence which is deliberate and premeditated will usually be more serious than one which is spontaneous and unpremeditated or which involves an excessive response to provocation. An offence which inflicts personal injury or mental trauma, particularly if permanent, will usually be more serious than one which inflicts financial loss only. The approach is:

(a) The court will have regard to an offender's admission of responsibility for the offence, particularly if reflected in a plea of guilty tendered at the earliest opportunity and accompanied by hard evidence of genuine remorse, as shown, for example, by an expression of regret to the victim and an offer of compensation. Attention is drawn to Criminal Justice and Public Order Act 1994 s 48.[484]

(b) Where offending has been fuelled by addiction to drink or drugs, the court will be inclined to look more favourably on an offender who has already demonstrated (by taking practical steps to that end) a genuine, self-motivated determination to address his addiction.

(c) Youth and immaturity, while affording no defence, will often justify a less rigorous penalty than would be appropriate for an adult.

(d) Some measure of leniency will ordinarily be extended to offenders of previous good character, the more so if there is evidence of good character (such as a solid employment record or faithful discharge of family duties) as opposed to a mere absence of previous convictions. It will sometimes be appropriate to take account of family responsibilities, or physical or mental disability.

(e) While the court will never impose a custodial sentence unless satisfied that it is necessary to do so, there will be even greater reluctance to impose a custodial sentence on an offender who has never before served such a sentence.

(f) Courts should always bear in mind that criminal sentences are in almost every case intended to protect the public, whether by punishing the offender or reforming him, or

[483] As amended by Criminal Justice and Courts Act 2015 Sch 5 para 14

[484] Repealed on 5/8/00 by Powers of Criminal Courts (Sentencing) Act 2000 Sch 12 para 1

deterring him and others, or all of these things. Courts cannot and should not be unmindful of the important public dimension of criminal sentencing and the importance of maintaining public confidence in the sentencing system.

(g) Where the court is of the opinion that an offence, or the combination of an offence and one or more offences associated with it, is so serious that only a custodial sentence can be justified and that such a sentence should be passed, the sentence imposed should be no longer than is necessary to meet the penal purpose which the court has in mind.

28.27 ***Custodial sentences only where justifiable*** **Court Martial**

Discretionary custodial sentences: general restrictions

Armed Forces Act 2006 s 260(1) This section applies where a court is dealing with an offender for a service offence punishable with a custodial sentence, other than an offence the sentence for which:

(a) is fixed by law, or

(b) falls to be imposed under Criminal Justice Act 2003 s 224A, 225(2) or 226(2) (as applied by Armed Forces Act 2006 s 218A, 219(2) or 221(2)) or as a result of any of Armed Forces Act 2006 s 225 to 227A.[485]

(2) The court must not pass a custodial sentence unless it is of the opinion that the offence, or the combination of the offence and one or more offences associated with it, was so serious that no less severe sentence can be justified for the offence.

(3) Nothing in subsection (2) prevents the court from passing a custodial sentence where:

(a) the court had proposed to award a community punishment, and

(b) the offender failed to express his willingness to comply with a requirement which the court proposed to include in the community punishment and which required an expression of such willingness.

(4) In forming any such opinion as is mentioned in subsection (2) or section 261(2) (length of sentence), a court must take into account all such information as is available to it about the circumstances of the offence and any associated offence, including any aggravating or mitigating factors.

(5) For the purposes of this section a sentence falls to be imposed as a result of subsection (2) of section 225, 226 or 227 (of this Act) if it is required by that subsection and the court is not of the opinion there mentioned.

28.28 ***Explain sentence, Judge must/Suggested sentencing remarks***

Judicial College's Crown Court Compendium Part II Sentencing June 2018 page 4-18

Passing a sentence

2. Passing the sentence

(1) [The court must for] all determinate sentences of imprisonment[:]

(a) Set out findings in relation to those matters described in paras 1–3 of chapter S3 [of this guide] [determining the seriousness etc.].

(b) The offence by itself or in combination with other offences must be so serious that neither a fine alone nor a community sentence can be justified [Criminal Justice Act 2003 s 152(2)] or the offender refuses to express his willingness to comply with a requirement of a community order proposed by the court for which his willingness to comply is necessary i.e. a drug rehabilitation requirement, an alcohol treatment requirement or a mental health treatment requirement.

(c) The sentence must be the shortest term that is commensurate with the seriousness of the offence, either by itself or in combination with others [Criminal Justice Act 2003 s 153(2)].

(d) All offenders are released having served no more than half their sentence. This is the 'requisite custodial period': see Criminal Justice Act 2003 s 244(3). Many

[485] As amended by Legal Aid, Sentencing and Punishment of Offenders Act 2012 Sch 22 para 34(2) and Sch 26 para 27

offenders are released earlier on Home Detention Curfew or other early release provision but such earlier release is at the discretion of the Secretary of State exercised through the Prison Governor and not the court and no reference should be made to the likelihood or otherwise of such release.

> **Example**
> The offence is so serious that only a custodial sentence can be justified and the least possible sentence I can impose having regard to the aggravating and mitigating factors of the case is one of ……months'/years' imprisonment.

28.29 ***Judge explaining the release provisions]***

3 Spelling out the effect of the sentence.

(1) **Unconditional release** applies to:

(a) a prisoner serving a sentence of one day;

(b) a prisoner serving a term of less than 12 months who is aged under 18 on the last day of the requisite custodial period; and

(c) a prisoner serving a sentence of less than 12 months imposed for an offence committed before 1 February 2015 [Criminal Justice Act 2003 s 243A].

> **Example**
> You will serve up to half of your sentence in custody and then you will be released.

(2) **Licence and post-sentence supervision** will generally apply for sentences under two years. First, there will generally be a licence period (the second half of the custodial sentence) and second, there will be a post-sentence supervision period which in combination will run for 12 months from the defendant's release. This is to ensure that there is an appropriate period of engagement with probation services on the expiry of the custodial element of a short sentence.

The period of licence plus post-sentence supervision will be 12 months from release if an offender sentenced between one day and less than two years is:

(a) aged 18+ on the last day of the requisite custodial period;

(b) not serving sentences under [Criminal Justice Act 2003 s 226A, 226B and 236A];

(c) not serving sentences for offences committed before 1 February 2015 [Criminal Justice Act 2003 s 256AA].

The period of licence plus post-sentence supervision will be 3 months from release if an offender sentenced between one day and less than two years is:

(a) aged under 18 on the last day of the requisite custodial period, serving a sentence under [Powers of Criminal Courts (Sentencing) Act 2000 s 91] of less than 12 months;

(b) serving a sentence of detention under [Powers of Criminal Courts (Sentencing) Act 2000 s 91 or 96]of less than 12 months for an offence committed before 1 February 2015 [Criminal Justice Act 2003 s 256B].

Release on licence with post-sentence supervision

> **Example**
> You will serve up to one half of your 12 month sentence in custody before you are released on licence. When you are released, you will be on licence and then postsentence supervision for a total of 12 months after that. You must comply with the terms of the licence and supervision and commit no further offence or you will be liable to serve a further period in custody.

(3) Release on **licence** applies to prisoners serving determinate sentences of two years duration or longer, other than sentences under [Criminal Justice Act 2003 s 226A, 226B or 236A]:

Release on licence with no post-sentence supervision

> **Example**
> You will serve up to one half of your five year sentence in custody. You will serve the remainder on licence. You must keep to the terms of your licence and commit no further offence or you will be liable to be recalled and you may then serve the rest of your sentence in custody.

(4) Concurrent and consecutive sentences

(a) Where D is to be sentenced for more than one offence, sentences should be imposed in respect of each offence of which D has been convicted (unless the offence is to be marked with "no separate penalty").

(b) Sentences may be ordered to run concurrently or consecutively. In the absence of express order, sentences will be served concurrently.

(c) A determinate sentence of imprisonment may be ordered to run consecutively to any other custodial sentence (including a minimum term of an indeterminate sentence): [Powers of Criminal Courts (Sentencing) Act 2000 s 154].

(d) A sentence cannot be ordered to be served consecutively to a sentence from which D has already been released: [Criminal Justice Act 2003 s 265].

(e) When passing consecutive sentences the sentencer must have regard to the principle of totality, applying the SC Guideline: Offences Taken into Consideration and Totality.

> **Example: Court has to sentence for two offences**
> On count 1 of this indictment, the charge of wounding {name} on {date}, the sentence will be two years' imprisonment. On count 2, the charge of assaulting {name} on {date}, the sentence will be one year's imprisonment. The sentence on count 2 will run consecutively to the sentence on count 1, making a total sentence of three years in all. That is the least sentence that I can impose to mark the totality of your offending. You will serve up to half of your total sentence in custody and then .....

> **Example: where D is already serving a life sentence with a minimum of 10 years**
> For this offence of wounding you will serve a sentence of 18 months' imprisonment. This sentence will be served consecutively to the minimum term of 10 years which you are currently serving. This means that when you have completed the minimum term of 10 years you will then serve this sentence of 18 months and you will not be eligible to be considered for parole until you have served up to half of this new sentence.

Other matters

For ***Corrosive effect of custody***, see the **CHILDREN AND YOUNG OFFENDERS: GENERAL PRINCIPLES** ***Corrosive effect of prison on young offenders*** para at **13.42**.

28.30 ***Global sentences***

Note: It is standard judicial practice to pass a sentence on the most serious offence to reflect the offending on all the counts. The alternative is to pass one or more consecutive sentences.

R v Lindo 2015 EWCA Crim 735 D pleaded to possession of cannabis with intent to supply, no insurance and driving otherwise than in accordance with a licence. D had not passed his test and only had a learner's licence but still drove alone in a car with the cannabis. The Judge said that the driving matters put people's lives at risk and said that compounded the offence. He imposed no penalty on the driving matters but said the offending could be properly reflected in the sentence for the cannabis. He started at 12 months and increased that to 18 months to reflect the driving matters before the plea discount. Held. As neither of the offences carried imprisonment, that was wrong. Sentence reduced accordingly.

For using a global sentence when passing an extended sentence, see para **56.76**.

28.31 ***Consecutive sentences Summary only matters Sentencing at the Crown Court***
R v James 2007 EWCA Crim 1906, 2008 1 Cr App R (S) 44 (p 238) D pleaded to three common assault counts. The first plea had been an alternative to ABH. The other two had been committed to the Crown Court with the ABH count. The Judge sentenced D to 4, 2 and 3 months' imprisonment, making 9 months. The Judge said the Magistrates' Court limitation did not apply to the Crown Court. Held. It did apply.
R v Tuplin 2009 EWCA Crim 1572 D pleaded to criminal damage, common assault and using threatening words or behaviour with intent. D was committed for trial for a matter that was not proceeded with. The first two matters were added to the indictment. A count of affray was also added and D pleaded to the threatening words and behaviour count as an alternative. The sentencing Judge accepted that the charges of criminal damage and common assault were before him pursuant to Criminal Justice Act 1988 s 40 (power to join in indictment count for common assault etc.) but rejected the submission that his sentencing powers were restricted by Magistrates' Courts Act 1980 s 133(1) (6 months maximum). There was an application under the 'slip rule' for the Judge to adjust the sentences, which was rejected. Held. Magistrates' Courts Act 1980 s 133(1), in addition to section 22(2) (triable either way offences to be treated as summary offences), applied to limit the Crown Court when sentencing for offences before it under Criminal Justice Act 1988 s 40. This criminal damage count was a summary only matter as far as sentence was concerned. Common assault was a summary only matter. The Public Order Act 1986 s 4 offence was also summary only when added at the Crown Court and so fell within this restriction. So the maximum for these consecutive sentences was 6 months.

28.32 ***Custody must be for the shortest term***
Criminal Justice Act 2003 s 153(1) This section applies where a court passes a custodial sentence other than one fixed by law or imposed under Criminal Justice Act 2003 s 225 or 226.[486] [These provisions relate to life sentences.]
(2) Subject to the provisions listed in subsection (3).
(3) [This contains a list of sections setting out minimum sentences.]
R v Ollerenshaw 1999 1 Cr App R (S) 65 When a court is considering imposing a comparatively short period of custody, that is of about 12 months or less, it should generally ask itself, particularly where the defendant has not previously been sentenced to custody, whether an even shorter period might be equally effective in protecting the interests of the public, and punishing and deterring the criminal. For example, there will be cases where, for these purposes, six months may be just as effective as nine, or two months may be just as effective as four.

28.33 ***Custodial sentence must be for the shortest term Court Martial***
Armed Forces Act 2006 s 261(1) This section applies where a court passes a custodial sentence for a service offence, other than a sentence fixed by law or imposed under Criminal Justice Act 2003 s 225 or 226 (as applied by section 219(2) or 221(2) of this Act).
(2) The custodial sentence must be for the shortest term (not exceeding the permitted maximum) that in the opinion of the court is commensurate with the seriousness of the offence or the combination of the offence and one or more offences associated with it.
(3) Subsection (2) is subject to Armed Forces Act 2006 s 220, 222, 225-227 and 227A[487] (sentences that may or must be imposed for certain offences).

[486] As amended by Criminal Justice and Courts Act 2015 Sch 5 para 15
[487] As amended by Legal Aid, Sentencing and Punishment of Offenders Act 2012 Sch 26 para 28

Combined with other orders

28.34 ***Compensation orders, Combined with***
TICs and Totality Guideline 2012: Crown Court, see www.banksr.com Other Matters Guidelines tab page 16 (Magistrates' Court guideline update page 18p) A compensation order can be combined with a sentence of immediate custody where the offender is clearly able to pay or has good prospects of employment on his release from custody.
R v Jorge 1999 2 Cr App R (S) 1 The passing of a sentence of imprisonment is very relevant to the defendant's means in at least three commonly encountered ways and maybe in others. First, it will deprive him of his earning power whilst in prison. Second, it may very well make it difficult for him to find work when he comes out. Third, it will often mean that by the time he comes out he will be in financial difficulty, especially if he has dependants.
R v Coppola 2010 EWCA Crim 2758 D pleaded to possession of 98 tablets of ecstasy with intent to supply and possession of cocaine and ketamine. D was stopped when driving and the drugs were found. He was bailed and absconded to Italy. About three years later, D was arrested at an airport on his return to the UK. He had with him €2,400. There was a short *Newton* hearing as D asserted that he was purely a social supplier. This was not accepted by the Judge. D was imprisoned for 4½ years and fined £1,800. Held. It is clear from the transcript that the Judge was considering depriving D of the money that he brought into the country, or the greater part of it, as part of confiscation or forfeiture proceedings, along with the drugs and the car. It is apparent that he was not entitled to do that, as there was no evidence which would justify the necessary inferences or conclusions so far as this money was concerned. In those circumstances, it is wrong in principle to try to achieve by fine what was not available by the initially chosen route. In those circumstances, we think it right that the fine should be set aside. It may be that the Judge could have reached his conclusion by other routes, for example, by the making of costs orders, but we do not think it would be right for this Court to second guess what might have been done on that occasion.
A compensation order may well be appropriate despite an immediate prison sentence if either the defendant has assets from which to pay it, especially no doubt the proceeds of his crime, or he is reasonably assured of income when he comes out from which it is reasonable to expect him to pay. Otherwise, a compensation order is not appropriate and indeed in some cases may operate as an incentive to further crime on release.
R v Islam 2013 EWCA Crim 2355 D was convicted of numerous indecent assaults committed between the 1970s and 1990s. Held. It was accepted that D had means. The fact that a defendant has been sentenced to a substantial custodial sentence is not necessarily a bar in itself to the court also making a compensation order in an appropriate case, see *R v Martin* 1989 11 Cr App R (S) 424. The argument that because of the 11-year sentence imposed on D, the Judge was wrong to make a compensation order at all, cannot succeed.
Old cases: They add little. If required, they can be found in the 10th edition of this book. Ed.

28.35 ***Costs, Combined with***
Practice Direction (Costs in Criminal Proceedings) 2015 EWCA Crim 1568 para 3.4 The [costs] order is not intended to be in the nature of a penalty which can only be satisfied on the defendant's release from prison.

28.36 ***Deportation, Automatic liability for, Combined with***
R v Gebru 2011 EWCA Crim 3321 The provisions described as 'automatic deportation' in fact do not necessarily lead to the automatic deportation of an offender. The provisions lead to liability for deportation. Judges should not, therefore, pass a shorter sentence or a sentence different in nature from one they would otherwise have passed on the basis they have been informed that the offender is liable to automatic deportation.

Extended sentences see the **Extended sentences (EDS)** ***Extended sentences and determinate sentences*** para at **56.79**.
Disqualification, Combined with see **41.16**.

28.37 *Fines, Combined with*
TICs and Totality Guideline 2012: Crown Court, see www.banksr.com Other Matters Guidelines tab page 13 (Magistrates' Court guideline update page 18m) A fine should not generally be imposed in combination with a custodial sentence because of the effect of imprisonment on the means of the defendant. However, exceptionally, it may be appropriate to impose a fine in addition to a custodial sentence where: a) the sentence is suspended, b) a confiscation order is not contemplated and there is no obvious victim to whom compensation can be awarded, and the offender has, or will have, resources from which a fine can be paid.[488]
Magistrates' Court Sentencing Guidelines 2008, see www.banksr.com Other Matters Guidelines tab page 15 The guideline applies to the Magistrates' Court and to the Crown Court hearing appeals or sentencing for summary only offences.
page 152 A fine and a custodial sentence may be imposed for the same offence although there will be few circumstances in which this is appropriate, particularly where the custodial sentence is to be served immediately. One example might be where an offender has profited financially from an offence but there is no obvious victim to whom compensation can be awarded. Combining these sentences is most likely to be appropriate only where the custodial sentence is short and/or the offender clearly has, or will have, the means to pay.
Care must be taken to ensure that the overall sentence is proportionate to the seriousness of the offence and that better-off offenders are not able to 'buy themselves out of custody'.
Note: The section of the guideline is of general application. Ed.
R v Garner 1985 7 Cr App R (S) 285 It is wrong to impose a fine either as punishment or confiscation if a defendant is unable to pay it. Where a sentencer is imposing a term of imprisonment which he considers is itself adequate punishment for the offence, he will not add to the imprisonment a punitive fine. In most cases, if the sentence of imprisonment is the maximum permitted, that will be thought adequate in itself, but there may be exceptional cases where even the maximum permitted sentence of imprisonment is considered to be inadequate, and in such rare cases a punitive fine could properly be added to the term of imprisonment. Such a possibility is, we think, specifically contemplated by Finance Act 1972 s 38(1).[489] On the other hand, we see nothing wrong in adding a fine to any sentence of imprisonment if the sentencer is satisfied that the defendant has made a profit from his wrongdoing, and believes on reasonable grounds that he has the means to pay back that or some of that profit. In such circumstances it is wrong to look at the imprisonment to be served in default of payment of the fine as additional punishment. It is not being used as a punishment, but as a means of coercing the offender into surrendering the proof of his wrongdoing. The offender can choose whether to pay up or spend further time in prison.
R v Coppola 2010 EWCA Crim 2758 D pleaded to possession of 98 tablets of ecstasy with intent to supply and possession of cocaine and ketamine. D was stopped when driving and the drugs were found. He was bailed and absconded to Italy. About three years later, D was arrested at an airport on his return to the UK. He had with him €2,400. There was a short *Newton* hearing as D asserted that he was purely a social supplier. This was not accepted by the Judge. D was imprisoned for 4½ years and fined £1,800. Held. It is clear from the transcript that the Judge was considering depriving D of the money that he brought into the country, or the greater part of it, as part of confiscation or forfeiture proceedings, along with the drugs and the car. It is apparent that he was not

[488] This guidance is also provided by the *Fraud Guideline 2009* page 12.
[489] Repealed by Value Added Tax Act 1983 Sch 11

entitled to do that, as there was no evidence which would justify the necessary inferences or conclusions so far as this money was concerned. In those circumstances, it is wrong in principle to try to achieve by fine what was not available by the initially chosen route. In those circumstances, we think it right that the fine should be set aside. It may be that the Judge could have reached his conclusion by other routes, for example, by the making of costs orders, but we do not think it would be right for this Court to second guess what might have been done on that occasion.
R v M 2014 EWCA Crim 2384 D pleaded to making (×3, which was downloading) and distributing indecent photos of children. The Judge imposed a £500 fine because he said D had a share of a second property. Held. The significant and exceptional mitigation made it **16 months** concurrent, not 21. A fine may be combined with an immediate custody, where the term imposed is inadequate and additional punishment is required. That is not the case here, so we quash the fine.
See also: *R v Hutson* 2017 EWCA Crim 561 (D pleaded to theft and dangerous driving (2 years and 8 months consecutive). He was in breach of a Criminal Behaviour Order (£700 fine, based on the amount found on D). Held. No one has complained about the fine and we don't alter it.)
For more details, see **344.27** in Volume 2.

28.38 ***Hospital and Guardianship Orders, Combined with***
Mental Health Act 1983 s 37(8) Where an order is made under this section, the court shall not:..pass a sentence of imprisonment.
Note: It can be inferred that the court cannot pass other forms of custody. However, the court can pass a Hybrid Order, see **67.41**. Ed.

28.39 ***Preventive orders, Combined with***
R v P 2004 EWCA Crim 287, 2 Cr App R (S) 63 (p 343) LCJ The conduct primarily envisaged as triggering these orders was for a less grave offence than street robbery, namely graffiti, abusive and intimidating language, excessive noise, fouling the street with litter, drunken behaviour and drug dealing. Doubtless, in drafting that report, the Home Office had in mind that courts have considerable powers to restrain robbers. We do not go so far as to suggest that ASBOs are necessarily inappropriate in cases with characteristics such as [this case where the offence was robbery etc. and 3 years' detention was appropriate]. But where custodial sentences in excess of a few months are passed, and offenders are liable to be released on licence, circumstances in which there is demonstrable necessity to make ASBOs are likely to be limited.

28.40 ***Sexual Harm Prevention Orders, Combined with***
R v Smith and Others 2011 EWCA Crim 1772, 2012 1 Cr App R (S) 82 (p 468) The Court gave guidance about SOPOs. Held. para 14 A SOPO may plainly be necessary if the sentence is a determinate term or an extended term. In each of those cases, whilst conditions may be attached to the licence, that licence will have a defined and limited life. The SOPO by contrast can extend beyond it and this may be necessary to protect the public from further offences and serious sexual harm as a result.
Note: There is good reason to believe that this principle would apply to Sexual Harm Prevention Orders. Ed.

28.41 ***Prison in default of payment, Combined with***
Powers of Criminal Courts (Sentencing) Act 2000 s 139(5) Where a court orders a prison in default term it may be consecutive to a term being served.
Magistrates' Courts Act 1980 s 133(4) Where a person has been sentenced by a Magistrates' Court to imprisonment and a fine for the same offence, a period of imprisonment imposed for non-payment of the fine, or for want of sufficient distress to satisfy the fine, shall not be subject to the limitations imposed by the preceding subsections (the 6-month and 12-month maximum consecutive terms).

(5) For the purposes of this section a term of imprisonment shall be deemed to be imposed in respect of an offence if it is imposed as a sentence or in default of payment of a sum adjudged to be paid by the conviction or for want of sufficient distress to satisfy such a sum.

R v Price 2009 EWCA Crim 2918, 2010 2 Cr App R (S) 44 (p 283) D was convicted of importation of cocaine, having pleaded to assisting the commission of an offence punishable under corresponding law, namely exporting cocaine from Ghana. He was sentenced to 28 years and 11 years concurrent. A confiscation order was also made for £2.34m, with 10 years in default of payment. D had arranged three 'dummy runs' using palletised drums of molasses. These had been bought under an assumed name. D then attempted to import 693.9 kilos (equivalent to 526 kilos at 100% purity) of cocaine. The Judge regarded him as the prime mover in the operation and described the crime as "a major sophisticated attempt to bring a huge quantity of cocaine into the United Kingdom". D argued that no one could expect a sentence of 38 years considering the totality of his offending. Held. We do not agree. The purpose of the period in default is designed to ensure that nothing is to be gained by the defendant if he fails to comply with the order. The fundamental objection to allowing a defendant to say that in the light of his own sentence he should suffer a lesser period of default is that it remains his own choice, in his hands, as to whether he serves the period of imprisonment in default or not. The period in default is a quite distinct and separate justification. It must be borne in mind that the Judge, particularly one sitting through six weeks of a trial, as it was in this case, is in the best position to determine what period of imprisonment is most likely to persuade the defendant to pay over the sums of money it has been found that he can realise. Sentence reduced on the basis that the Judge had not taken account of D's health problems.

Suspended sentence, Combined with, see the **CUSTODY: IMPRISONMENT *Suspended sentence, Combined with*** para at **29.5**.

Post-sentence supervision

28.42 *Post-sentence supervision and Supervision default orders*

Defendants aged 18+ on release, who have committed an offence on or after 1 February 2018 (subject to a few exceptions) and finish a determinate sentence of less than 2 years, will be released on post-sentence supervision, Criminal Justice Act 2003 s 256AA. The supervision lasts for 12 months, Criminal Justice Act 2003 s 256AA(4). The only requirements that can be imposed are listed in Criminal Justice Act 2003 s 256AB. The breach procedure is in Criminal Justice Act 2003 s 226AC. The penalties are (see Criminal Justice Act 2003 s 256AC(4): a) committal to a prison or detention in a YOI for not more than 14 days, b) a fine not exceeding level 3, a supervision default order (which has an unpaid work requirement or a curfew with a tag), see Criminal Justice Act 2003 Sch 19A.

Note: The title 'post-sentence supervision' is odd as the licence period is very much part of the sentence imposed. Ed.

28.43 *Post-sentence supervision, Breach of Breach Offences Guideline 2018*

Breach Offences Guideline 2018, see www.banksr.com Other Matters Guidelines tab In force 1 October 2018 page 13

Breach of post-sentence supervision

Criminal Justice Act 2003 s 256AC and Sch 19A

Where the court determines a penalty is appropriate for a breach of a post-sentence supervision requirement it must take into account the extent to which the offender has complied with all of the requirements of the post-sentence supervision or supervision default order when imposing a penalty.

In assessing the level of compliance with the order the court should consider:

i) the offender's overall attitude and engagement with the order as well as the proportion of elements completed;

ii) the impact of any completed or partially completed requirements on the offender's behaviour;
iii) the proximity of the breach to the imposition of the order; and
iv) evidence of circumstances or offender characteristics, such as disability, mental health issues or learning difficulties which have impeded [the] offender's compliance with the order.

Level of compliance	Penalty
Low	Up to 7 days' committal to custody **OR** Supervision default order in range of 30-40 hours' unpaid work **OR** 8-12 hour curfew for minimum of 20 days
Medium	Supervision default order in range of 20-30 hours' unpaid work **OR** 4-8 hour curfew for minimum of 20 days **OR** Band B fine
High	Band A fine

For a band A-C fine, see **58.28**.
Breach of supervision default order

Level of compliance	Penalty
Low	Revoke supervision default order and order up to 14 days' committal to custody
Medium	Revoke supervision default order and impose new order in range of 40-60 hours' unpaid work OR 8-16 hour curfew for minimum of 20 days
High	Band B fine

i) A supervision default order must include either:
an unpaid work requirement of between 20 hours and 60 hours
OR
a curfew requirement for between 2 and 16 hours for a minimum of 20 days and no longer than the end of the post-sentence supervision period.
ii) The maximum fine which can be imposed is £1,000.

29 Custody: Imprisonment

29.1

Court Martial The Court may pass imprisonment for all ranks, ex-servicemen and women, and civilians, see *Guidance on Sentencing in the Court Martial 2018* Annex B. *Guidance on Sentencing in the Court Martial 2018* para 3.1 provides the powers and principles for imposing imprisonment in the Court Martial, see **29.2**.
Offenders serving detention in a Young Offender Institution and who turn 21 For the power to pass such detention, see **118.4**.
Victim surcharge The court must impose a victim surcharge, Criminal Justice Act 2003 s 161A-161B and Criminal Justice Act 2003 (Surcharge) Order 2012 2012/1696 as amended. There are exceptions, a) where a compensation order or an Unlawful Profits Order or a Slavery and Trafficking Reparations Order is imposed, when a reduced amount or a nil amount can be ordered, see **17.67**, and b) where the offence was

committed before 1 October 2012, when no surcharge can be made, see **115.3**. In the Magistrates' Court no victim surcharge can be made for offences committed before 1 September 2014. In the Crown Court where the offence was committed on or after 1 October 2012 (1 September 2014 in the Magistrates' Court) and before 8 April 2016, the amount to be imposed is the relevant figure in brackets below, see **115.4**. The amount is: for a sentence of 6 months or less, £115 (£80), more than 6 months to 24 months, £140 (£100), and more than 24 months, £170 (£120). For defendants who are now aged 21+ but were aged under 18 when the offence was committed, the amount is £30 (£20), see **115.4**.

The rules about imprisonment are mostly in the **CUSTODY: GENERAL PRINCIPLES** chapter because the rules are of general application.

Rehabilitation periods Over 48 months: excluded from rehabilitation.[490] More than 30 months but not more than 48 months, 7 years. More than 6 months but not more than 30 months: 4 years. 6 months or less: 2 years.[491] Legal Aid, Sentencing and Punishment of Offenders Act 2012 s 139 changed the periods, see **89.6**.

Release A prisoner is usually released after serving half their sentence. There are exceptions, namely life sentences, IPP, DPP, extended sentences and the sentences below.[492]

Release and supervision (Certain offences committed before 4 April 2005) Prisoners sentenced to determinate sentences of 4 years or more for a Criminal Justice Act 2003 Sch 15 offence committed prior to 4 April 2005 and sentenced prior to 3 December 2012 are eligible to be considered for discretionary release by the Parole Board at the halfway point. They are automatically released at the two-thirds point. They remain on licence until the three-quarters point of the sentence.

Release and supervision (Extended licences) Prisoners convicted prior to 3 December 2012 of an offence committed prior to 30 September 1998 who received an extended licence under Powers of Criminal Courts (Sentencing) Act 2000 s 86 (sexual cases) of 4 years or more are eligible for discretionary release by the Parole Board at the halfway point. They are automatically released at the two-thirds point and remain on licence until the end of the sentence.

Supervision Normally after release, a prisoner is on licence until the end of term. Again, there are exceptions. Where a determinate sentence is for less than 12 months or determinate sentences total less than 12 months, release at the halfway point is unconditional.

For associated chapters, see the beginning of the previous chapter.

For statistics see the **CUSTODY: GENERAL PRINCIPLES** ***Statistics*** para at **28.2**.

See also the **CHILDREN AND YOUNG OFFENDERS: CUSTODIAL SENTENCES** chapter.

29.2 *Court Martial*

Guidance on Sentencing in the Court Martial 2018 para 3.1.1 (edited) Sentences of imprisonment are not normally imposed by the Court Martial for a criminal conduct offence unless the same offence would attract a sentence of imprisonment in the civilian courts. However, and exceptionally, if the conduct is more serious within a Service context imprisonment might be appropriate. The same principles apply when determining the length of the sentence of imprisonment; this should follow the general civilian guidance unless there is some special Service justification for departure.

3.1.2 (edited) Any sentence of imprisonment imposed upon a warrant officer or non-commissioned officer when passed with dismissal or dismissal with disgrace, Armed Forces Act 2006 s 295(4), involves automatic reduction in rank or disrating to the

[490] Rehabilitation of Offenders Act 1974 s 5(1b)

[491] Rehabilitation of Offenders Act 1974 s 5 Table A

[492] Criminal Justice Act 2003 s 244(1) and (3)

lowest level that could be awarded in the Court Martial, and can also have the effect of preventing immediate payment of a pension; this means that some differences in practice are inevitable.

3.1.3 Where the criminal conduct offence is so serious that it would inevitably warrant a sentence of imprisonment in a civilian court, considerations related to the disciplinary issues of the Services become less significant and the accepted practice of the civilian courts is always followed unless there are exceptional Service-related circumstances that justify a departure. (See also para 3.4.12.)

Guidance on Sentencing in the Court Martial 2018 para 3.4.16 The calculation for credit for time spent in pre-trial custody (or on remand) is carried out administratively at the MCTC [Military Corrective Training Centre] or at the civilian prison, where the offender is informed of his expected release date. Where an offender has been held in Service custody after charge pending trial, the time thus served is allowed against the time to be served under the sentence passed. The offender's pay may be forfeited for any time in detention allowed against the sentence but that is an administrative decision not part of the sentence. Judges in the civilian courts are no longer required to direct that time spent on remand should count towards sentence. However, as a matter of good practice in the Court Martial when dealing with sentences of Service detention the judge states the time to be taken into account when calculating the release date. The judge announces the full length of the sentence of Service detention without deductions, and explains that the offender will be released after he has served ⅔ of the sentence of detention less the time already served in custody, subject to the restrictions of credit in paragraph 3.4.2 above or any further credit he may receive for good behaviour in sentences of over 90 days.

29.3 *Statutory provisions Children and young offenders*

Restriction on imposing imprisonment on persons under 21.

Powers of Criminal Courts (Sentencing) Act 2000 s 89(1) Subject to subsection (2) below, no court shall:

(a) pass a sentence of imprisonment on a person for an offence if he is aged under 21 when convicted of the offence, or

(b) commit a person aged under 21 to prison for any reason.

(2) Nothing in subsection (1) above shall prevent the committal to prison of a person aged under 21 who is:

(a) remanded in custody,

(b) committed in custody for trial or sentence, or

(c) sent in custody for trial under Crime and Disorder Act 1998 s 51 or 51A.

29.4 *Five-day minimum term*

Powers of Criminal Courts (Sentencing) Act 2000 s 78(7) Magistrates' Courts Act 1980 s 132 contains provision about the minimum term of imprisonment which may be imposed by a Magistrates' Court.

Magistrates' Courts Act 1980 s 132 A Magistrates' Court shall not impose imprisonment for less than 5 days.

R v Hourigan 2003 EWCA Crim 2306 D was on bail with a condition he should attend half an hour before the court sat. His case was in a warned list and then listed for 10.30. At 11.40, D's counsel said D would be at court within the hour. At 2.30 pm, D attended and the Court was told there had been a misunderstanding. D was sentenced to 2 days' imprisonment. Held. Because the correct procedures were not followed, we quash the conviction. Magistrates are expressly prohibited from imposing a sentence of less than 5 days. On the face of it, that prohibition ought also to apply in practice in the ordinary run of cases in the Crown Court. It is difficult to see what justification there could be for imposing such a short sentence.

Note: The Magistrates' Court has power to detain an offender who has committed an imprisonable offence to detention within the precincts of the court-house or any police station up until no later than 8 pm, Magistrates' Courts Act 1980 s 135. Ed.

Combined with other orders

For the bulk of the orders, see the **CUSTODY: GENERAL PRINCIPLES *Combined with other orders*** section at **28.34**.

29.5 *Suspended sentence, Combined with*

R v Sapiano 1968 52 Cr App R 674 LCJ The Court passed a 9-month term of imprisonment and a 9-month term of imprisonment suspended for three counts of handling. Held. This was a wrong sentence as it went against the intention of the Act, which was to avoid immediate custody, and was potentially impractical. We suspend all sentences.

R v Butters and Fitzgerald 1971 55 Cr App R 515 The defendants were subject to immediate imprisonment and suspended sentences at the same time. Held. That was undesirable as a matter of sentencing practice, although there is no statutory bar to doing that. In general courts should avoid mixing up sentences which fall into different categories. The sentences were rearranged so it was one or the other.

30 CUSTODY: TIME ON REMAND/TAG AND CURFEW DISCOUNT

30.1

Criminal Justice Act 2003 s 240ZA

Overview Days spent in custody awaiting sentence are deduction from the sentence by the Prison Service. The exception to this is life sentences with their minimum terms (see **74.15** and for murder cases see **287.90** in Volume 2). Judge and magistrates should explain deduction in their sentencing remarks, see the **PROCEDURE, SENTENCING *Explain sentence, Sentencer must Time on remand/curfew*** para at **86.50**. The court, however, still has to work out the time spent on tag with and a curfew and make the necessary deductions to the sentence, see **30.21**.

Extended disqualification *R v Needham and Others* 2016 EWCA Crim 455, 2 Cr App R (S) 26 (p 219) states that 'it was the clear intention of Parliament that time spent on remand would not count when considering the 2015 extended disqualification provisions, under Road Traffic Offenders Act 1988 s 35A. *R v Harkins* 2011 EWCA Crim 2227 (see **41.10**) para 16 points to the correct approach to the question of time spent on remand under s 35A. If the time spent on remand would lead to a disproportionate result in terms of the period of disqualification, then the court has power in fixing the discretionary element to adjust that period to take account of time spent on remand. The court should take a broad-brush approach to the question of adjustment.' For more detail see **41.16**.

Community orders and ***Youth Rehabilitation Orders*** For making allowance for time spent in custody before a community order is passed, see **15.32** and before a YRO is passed, see **119.33**.

Breach of a community order For deducting time, see **16.27**.

Costs see the **COSTS *Discount for time spent in custody and costs*** para at **22.49**.

Detention and Training Orders for deducting the time, see **37.12**.

Suspended Sentence Orders see the **SUSPENDED SENTENCE ORDERS *Time served on remand*** paras at **106.19**. When activating them, see the **SUSPENDED SENTENCE ORDERS: BREACH OF *Time served on remand*** para at **107.27**.

Time on remand awaiting sentence

30.2 *Statutory provisions*

Time remanded in custody to count as time served: terms of imprisonment and detention

Criminal Justice Act 2003 s 240ZA(1)[493] This section applies where:

(a) an offender is serving a term of imprisonment in respect of an offence, and

(b) the offender has been remanded in custody (within the meaning given by section 242) in connection with the offence or a related offence.

[493] As amended by Legal Aid, Sentencing and Punishment of Offenders Act 2012 s 108

(2) It is immaterial for that purpose whether, for all or part of the period during which the offender was remanded in custody, the offender was also remanded in custody in connection with other offences (but see subsection (5)).
(3) The number of days for which the offender was remanded in custody in connection with the offence or a related offence is to count as time served by the offender as part of the sentence. But this is subject to subsections (4) to (6).
(4) If, on any day on which the offender was remanded in custody, the offender was also detained in connection with any other matter, that day is not to count as time served.
(5) A day counts as time served:
(a) in relation to only one sentence, and
(b) only once in relation to that sentence.
(6) A day is not to count as time served as part of any period of 28 days served by the offender before automatic release (see section 255B(1)).

30.3 *Statutory provisions Definitions etc.*
Criminal Justice Act 2003 s 240ZA(7) For the purposes of this section a suspended sentence:
(a) is to be treated as a sentence of imprisonment when it takes effect under paragraph 8(2)(a) or (b) of Schedule 12, and
(b) is to be treated as being imposed by the order under which it takes effect.
(8) In this section 'related offence' means an offence, other than the offence for which the sentence is imposed ('offence A'), with which the offender was charged and the charge for which was founded on the same facts or evidence as offence A.[494]
(9) For the purposes of the references in subsections (3) and (5) to the term of imprisonment to which a person has been sentenced (that is to say, the reference to the offender's 'sentence'), consecutive terms and terms which are wholly or partly concurrent are to be treated as a single term if:
(a) the sentences were passed on the same occasion, or
(b) where they were passed on different occasions, the person has not been released at any time during the period beginning with the first and ending with the last of those occasions.
(10) The reference in subsection (4) to detention in connection with any other matter does not include remand in custody in connection with another offence but includes:
(a) detention pursuant to any custodial sentence,
(b) committal in default of payment of any sum of money,
(c) committal for want of sufficient distress to satisfy any sum of money,
(d) committal for failure to do or abstain from doing anything required to be done or left undone.
(11) This section applies to a determinate sentence of detention under section 91 or 96 of the Sentencing Act or section 227 or 228[495] of this Act as it applies to an equivalent sentence of imprisonment.
Criminal Justice Act 2003 s 242(2) References in sections 240ZA and 241 to an offender's being remanded in custody are references to his being: a) remanded in or committed to custody by order of a court, b) remanded to Youth Detention accommodation under Legal Aid, Sentencing and Punishment of Offenders Act 2012 s 91(4), or c) remanded, admitted or removed to hospital under Mental Health Act 1983 s 35, 36, 38 or 48.

[494] The grammar is Parliament's.
[495] Criminal Justice and Courts Act 2015 Sch 1 para 16 adds 'or 236A', which relates to Offenders of Particular Concern Orders. In force 13/4/15, Criminal Justice and Courts Act 2015 (Commencement No 1, Saving and Transitional Provisions) Order 2015 2015/778 para 3 and Sch 1 para 72.

30.4 *Court Martial*

Crediting of time in service custody: terms of imprisonment and detention

Armed Forces Act 2006 s 246(1)[496] This section applies where:

(a) a court or officer sentences an offender to a term of imprisonment or service detention in respect of a service offence ('the offence in question'), and

(b) the offender has been kept in service custody, in connection with the offence in question or any related offence, for any period since being charged with the offence in question or any related offence.

(2) The number of days for which the offender was kept in service custody in connection with the offence in question or any related offence since being so charged is to count as time served by the offender as part of the sentence. But this is subject to subsections (2A) to (2C).

(2A) If, on any day on which the offender was kept in service custody, the offender was also detained in connection with any other matter, that day is not to count as time served.

(2B) A day counts as time served:

(a) in relation to only one sentence, and

(b) only once in relation to that sentence.

(2C) A day is not to count as time served as part of any automatic release period served by the offender (see section 255B(1) of the 2003 Act).[497]

(3)-(5) [These subsections have been repealed]

(6) This section applies to:

(a) a determinate sentence of detention under Armed Forces Act 2006 s 209,

(b) a sentence of detention under Criminal Justice Act 2003 s 226B or 228 passed as a result of Armed Forces Act 2006 s 221A or 222,

(c) a determinate sentence of Detention in a Young Offender Institution,

as it applies to an equivalent sentence of imprisonment.

(7) References in this section to 'the court' are to the court or officer mentioned in subsection (1).

Guidance on Sentencing in the Court Martial 2018 para 3.1.6 (edited) The Court Martial is informed whether an offender has been held in custody prior to trial. If so, this period counts towards the time the offender will serve, see para 5.2.

Armed Forces Act 2006 s 270(5) In determining the restrictions on liberty to be imposed by a community punishment in respect of an offence, the court may have regard to any period for which the offender has, since being charged with the offence or any related offence, been kept in service custody in connection with the offence or any related offence.

(6) In subsection (5) 'related offence' has the meaning given by section 247.

30.5 *Judicial powers/judicial discretion*

R v Prenga 2017 EWCA 2149, 1 Cr App R (S) 17 (p 287) The discretion to modify a lawful sentence is exceptional jurisdiction. The rules for credit for remand time are intended to lay down a comprehensive scheme. Parliament has made clear that remand time in cases unrelated to the instant case should not warrant any adjustment in sentence.

Att-Gen's Ref 2018 Re Rushworth 2018 EWCA Crim 2196 D pleaded to robbery. The Judge imposed a suspended sentence. He ordered that the time served on remand should not count if the order was breached. Held. There was no power to so order, *Archer v Governor of HMP Low Newton* 2014 EWHC 240 (Admin). If the sentence was activated, the time would be deducted automatically.

[496] As amended by Legal Aid, Sentencing and Punishment of Offenders Act 2012 Sch 13 para 2 and Sch 22 para 32

[497] This subsection was amended by Offender Rehabilitation Act 2014 Sch 6 para 3. In force 1/2/15

Particular situations

30.6 ***Attorney-General's references***

Criminal Justice Act 1988 Sch 3 para 5 The time during which a person whose case has been referred for review under section 36 [see **8.29**] is in custody pending its review and pending any reference to the Supreme Court under section 36(5) shall be reckoned as part of the term of any sentence to which he is for the time being subject.

30.7 ***Bail hostels***

R v Watson 2000 2 Cr App R (S) p 301 D was released on bail with a condition that he resided at a bail hostel. He was not permitted to go into the garden or leave, except when supervised. He only left to collect his benefit. He was there 11 months before sentence. For 5 months he had been tagged. Held. A bail hostel was not to be equated with imprisonment. However, the loss of liberty should be taken into account. More credit for that should have been given.

Note: I see no reason why this principle should not continue to apply. Ed.

30.8 ***Defendant earlier in custody for charge not proceeded with etc.***

R v Jarvis 2002 EWCA Crim 885, 2 Cr App R (S) 123 (p 558) D pleaded to escaping. He was charged with aggravated burglary and remanded in custody. He appeared in the Crown Court and he leapt over the dock and was caught. Later the prosecution dropped the burglary charge because a witness had died. The Judge refused to give him credit for the time he was in custody for the other matter. Held. The Judge was right not to give him credit.

R v Taylor 2008 EWCA Crim 465 Defence counsel asked the Court of Appeal for remand time served for an offence for which he was acquitted. Held. A judge is not bound to make that decision. In an appropriate case the judge should reflect that time. Here it won't affect our conclusion about the reduction required.

R v Defreitas 2011 EWCA Crim 1254 D pleaded to handling stolen goods, having been charged with burglary. He was remanded some 11 months prior to the offence on a charge of robbery. That prosecution was discontinued. It was submitted that that period should be taken into consideration and treated as mitigation. Counsel relied on *R v Roberts* 2000 1 Cr App R (S) 569 and *R v Governor of Wandsworth Prison ex parte Sorhaindo* 1999 The Times 5/1/99, 1999 96(4) LSG 38. Held. Neither of the two cases provide D with any assistance. Neither a general principle nor the specific circumstances of this case require or would justify an adjustment to the sentence. Sentence unaltered.

R v Prenga 2017 EWCA 2149, 1 Cr App R (S) 17 (p 287) The defendant, D, was released on bail and then remanded in custody when a European arrest warrant was issued in Italy. The warrant was withdrawn. The defence said the failure of the advocate to ask for a remand in custody was an error. Held. Parliament has made clear that remand time in cases unrelated to the instant case should not warrant any adjustment in sentence. We don't know whether if D had asked for a remand that would have affected the remand time in Italy. No point was taken at the sentencing hearing. The system does not ordinarily allow a second bite of the cherry.

R v Cowlbeck 2018 EWCA Crim 219 D received 16 months for ABH. Initially he was granted bail. He failed to attend a hearing and a warrant was issued which was executed. On that day, D was arrested for robbery and remanded in custody for that. Either the Court failed to deal with the execution of the warrant or failed to inform the Prison Service that he was also in custody for the ABH matter. D was acquitted of the robbery and the Judge was invited to deduct the time served. He refused to do so. Held. In the unusual circumstances we do, so 7 months.

30.9 ***Defendant earlier in custody for a conviction which was later quashed***

R v Roberts 2000 1 Cr App R (S) 569 D was remanded in custody for drugs offences. Eighteen days later he was sentenced at the Magistrates' Court to 5 months' imprisonment. After he had served his sentence the Crown Court sentenced him to 42 months for the drugs offences. Later a different Crown Court quashed the sentence of 5 months and

substituted a conditional discharge. Held. The 42 months was a perfectly proper sentence. Considering *R v Governor of Wandsworth Prison ex parte Sorhaindo* 1999 The Times 5/1/99, 1999 96(4) LSG 38 it would be appropriate to reduce the sentence by 5 months.
Note: As in the previous paragraph, with the change of law, I expect the judicial discretion to reduce the sentence slightly will remain, but it will rarely be exercised. Ed.

30.10 ***Extradition, Time in custody awaiting***

Time remanded on bail to count towards time served: terms of imprisonment and detention

Criminal Justice Act 2003 s 243(1)[498] A fixed-term prisoner is an extradited prisoner for the purposes of this section if:

(a) he was tried for the offence in respect of which his sentence was imposed or he received that sentence

(i) after having been extradited to the United Kingdom, and

(ii) without having first been restored or had an opportunity of leaving the United Kingdom, and

(b) he was for any period kept in custody while awaiting his extradition to the United Kingdom as mentioned in paragraph (a).

(2) In the case of an extradited prisoner, the court must specify in open court the number of days for which the prisoner was kept in custody while awaiting extradition.

(2A) Criminal Justice Act 2003 s 240ZA (see **30.2**) applies to days specified under subsection (2) as if they were days for which the prisoner was remanded in custody in connection with the offence or a related offence.

Powers of Criminal Courts (Sentencing) Act 2000 s 101(12A) Criminal Justice Act 2003 s 243 (persons extradited to the United Kingdom) applies in relation to a person sentenced to a Detention and Training Order as it applies in relation to a fixed-term prisoner, with the reference in subsection (2) of that section to Criminal Justice Act 2003 s 240ZA being read as a reference to subsection (8) (see **30.2**).

Anti-social Behaviour, Crime and Policing Act 2014 s 171 inserted two subsections into Prison Act 1952 s 49.[499]

Prison Act 1952 s 49(3A) Where:

(a) a person is extradited to the United Kingdom from a Category 1 territory for the purpose of serving a term of imprisonment or another form of detention mentioned in subsection (2) of this section, and

(b) the person was for any time kept in custody in that territory with a view to the extradition (and not also for any other reason),

the Secretary of State shall exercise the power under that subsection to direct that account shall be taken of that time in calculating the period for which the person is liable to be detained.

(3B) In subsection (3A) of this section 'Category 1 territory' means a territory designated under Extradition Act 2003 for the purposes of Part 1 of that Act.

R v Eastham 2013 EWCA Crim 625 Criminal Justice Act 2003 s 243(1) requires the court in the case of an extradited prisoner to specify in open court the number of days which the prisoner was kept in custody while awaiting extradition. Those days are then treated as if they were days for which the prisoner was remanded in custody and fall to be taken into account administratively towards the sentence.

R v Chalk 2013 EWCA Crim 2084 D was arrested in Spain under a European Arrest Warrant. He spent 68 days in custody before he was extradited. The Judge sentenced D and said that the sentence would not reflect the fact D had spent "something over two months" in custody, but in reflecting his early plea, the sentence would be reduced from 60 months to 40 months. Held. The Judge did not comply with Criminal Justice

[498] This section is as amended by Legal Aid, Sentencing and Punishment of Offenders Act 2012 s 110(8).
[499] In force 21/7/14

Act 2003 s 243(2) which requires the number of days to be specified in court (so they can be deducted administratively later). The application of that section is mandatory. The words used by the Judge were too imprecise to allow the correction to be done administratively. We specify 68 days spent in custody count under section 243.
See also: *R v Johnson* 2014 EWCA Crim 2073 (Judge erroneously thought deduction for remand abroad treated in same way as remand in England. Court of Appeal specified days on foreign remand to count.)
R (Shields-McKinley) v Sec of State and Others 2017 EWHC 658 (Admin), 2 Cr App R (S) 17 (p 113) (Judge failed to make D's time awaiting extradition count because no one asked him to. Days in custody abroad known very much later. D starts judicial review. Held. Appeal refused partly because it was the wrong court to apply to, no days were specified by the Crown Court and the sentence was lawful.)

30.11 ***Deportation, Time in custody awaiting***
R v Grynhaus 2016 EWCA Crim 942 D went to Israel in breach of his bail and was arrested there. He contested his deportation but was returned to the UK. D received 8 months for his bail offence. The Judge gave 18 months' credit for the 18 months spent in Israel in custody. The defence contended it would be unfair not to double the figure to equate with time served in the UK. Held. D was not extradited. The sentencing Judge had a discretion about the 18 months served in custody in Israel. It was not irrelevant that while D was fighting deportation his victims were waiting to give evidence. The Judge acted impeccably.
R v Keeley 2018 EWCA Crim 2089 D pleaded to two notification offences. In 2013, D, in breach of his notification requirements, went on a circuitous route to the Philippines. In 2017, he was arrested there and was deported for posing a risk to children. The Judge started at 5 years and with plea moved to 40 months. He reduced that by 4 months to 36 months because of the time D had spent in custody in the Philippines. Held. There is no automatic right for time spent in custody pending deportation to be taken into account. The Judge exercised his discretion perfectly properly.
Note: It isn't clear what the defence was asking for except that they wanted D to be treated as if he had been extradited. The effect of that is that he would serve 16 months (20 months less 4 months counting as time served) instead of 18 months (half of 36 months). Ed.
For details of the 2013 case, see *R v Keeley* 2013 EWCA Crim 1014 at **242.7** in Volume 2.

30.12 ***Extradition etc., Time in custody awaiting Life sentences***
Criminal Justice Act 2003 s 269(1) This section applies…a court passes a life sentence in circumstances where the sentence is fixed by law.
Criminal Justice Act 2003 s 269(3) The part of his sentence is to be such as the court considers appropriate taking into account:..b) the effect of Criminal Justice Act 2003 s 240ZA (crediting periods of remand in custody) or of any direction which it would have given under Criminal Justice Act 2003 s 240A (crediting periods of remand on certain types of bail) if it had sentenced him to a term of imprisonment.
(3A) The reference in subsection (3)(b) to section 240ZA includes Armed Forces Act 2006 s 246 (crediting periods in service custody).
Note: Cases under the old law where there was a discretion whether to count days spent awaiting extradition include the following. That same law applies to life sentences (so the minimum term is or is not adjusted to take that into account. Ed.
R v Khyam and Others 2008 EWCA Crim 1612, 2009 1 Cr App R (S) 77 (p 455) para 147 LCJ The defendant was convicted of terrorism. The Judge declined to make any allowance for time in custody in Pakistan because his detention was of direct importance to the authorities in Pakistan. Held. His detention there arose directly from his suspected involvement in this conspiracy. The period should count.

R v Noye 2013 EWCA Crim 510 LCJ In 2000, D was convicted of murder. After the murder D fled to Spain. He spent 9 months fighting his extradition 'every inch of the way'. The trial Judge said there was no reason to include the 9-month period, because D had tried to avoid extradition. In 2010, when his sentence was reviewed, no allowance was made for the 9 months. The minimum term was set (as before) at 16 years. The cases were reviewed. Held. The court was and is now vested with a discretion. D not only contested the extradition, he fled the country in a well-organised, sophisticated plan to evade justice. When contesting the extradition he put up a false story which was not relied on at his trial. We agree that no allowance should be made.
Old cases: *R v Simone* 2000 2 Cr App R (S) p 332 (Sentence reduced) *R v Andre and Burton* 2002 1 Cr App R (S) 24 (p 98) (Sentence not reduced.)

30.13 ***Honouring the judge's plan for release/how the sentence would apply***
R v Johnson 2013 EWCA Crim 908 D pleaded to two burglaries and three aggravated vehicle-takings. In May 2007 and September and October 2008, D stole keys from houses and then with them stole the cars. They were committed when he was aged 16 and 17. In March 2010, D was sentenced to 6 years' YOI for robbery. Whilst in custody, he admitted these offences. The Judge adjourned the sentence for almost 12 months, on the promise that if D made 'very real' progress whilst in custody, it was likely he would receive a concurrent sentence. The Judge remarked that there was no evidence save for D's admissions and that he clearly wanted to 'wipe the slate clean'. In January 2012, he imposed 15 months for the two burglaries and 3 months for the aggravated vehicle-taking, all concurrent to his sentence for robbery. The Judge said that the release date would be the same as for his robbery sentence. Held. The problem with that course was that in order for the release dates to be the same, the sentence imposed for the burglary and aggravated vehicle-taking offences would have to be 21 weeks, not 15 months. The Judge's clear intention was that D would not stay in custody any longer than he would have done for the robbery offence. Effect must be given to the legitimate expectation that was created by the Judge's comments. 21 weeks, not 15 months.
R v Babiak 2017 EWCA Crim 160, 1 Cr App R (S) 52 (p 407) The Judge wanted the defendant's 13½-year sentence to run concurrently and start at the same time as the 7-year sentence that was imposed in 2013. He so ordered. In fact, the new sentence started on the day it was passed. Held. To reflect the clear intentions of the Judge, we reduce the new sentence to 10 years 9 months.

30.14 ***Hospitals***
Criminal Justice Act 2003 s 242(2) References in sections 240ZA and 241 to an offender's being remanded in custody are references to his being:..c) remanded, admitted or removed to hospital under Mental Health Act 1983 s 35, 36, 38 or 48.
Note: Where a defendant is sentenced to a Detention and Training Order a 'remand in custody' includes 'a reference to his being remanded, admitted or removed to hospital under Mental Health Act 1983 s 35, 36, 38 or 48', Powers of Criminal Courts (Sentencing) Act 2000 s 101(11). Ed.
Old case: *R v Bryan* 2006 EWCA Crim 379, 2 Cr App R (S) 66 (p 436) (LCJ Here it would not be appropriate to make an allowance for time spent on remand. The Court does not appear to have had the relevant section drawn to its attention.)

30.15 ***Licence revoked, Defendant has his or her***
R v Tahid 2009 EWCA Crim 221 D served his custodial sentence for murder and was released on licence. He committed a drug offence and his licence was revoked. D pleaded to supplying heroin and was given **3½ years**. The defence asked for the time he had spent in prison before sentence to be taken into account. Held. We reject this suggestion out of hand.
R v Kerrigan and Another 2014 EWCA Crim 2348, 2015 1 Cr App R (S) 29 (p 221) K pleaded to robbing a man, V, in the street. D punched V repeatedly and stole V's phone, keys and wallet. In a separate case, W pleaded to attempted robbery. He provided a large

hunting knife and transport for the main assailant. Both had been on licence and appealed against orders preventing time spent in custody on recall counting towards sentence. For K this was 7 months and for W it was 11 months. K was aged 26 and W aged 22 on appeal and both had multiple previous convictions, including recent ones. Held. K and W did not qualify for any automatic reduction in their sentences. They breached their licence. They were recalled to serve the balance, or part of the balance, of an existing sentence and they were, therefore, detained pursuant to a custodial sentence. Unless K and W can bring themselves within the Judge's general discretion to do justice, the periods they spent on remand which coincided with time spent in custody on recall should not be counted twice. They didn't, so appeal dismissed.
For the bar on making a new sentence consecutive to a licence recall, see **Concurrent and Consecutive Sentences** ***Licence Defendant serving a sentence for a revoked licence*** at **18.21**.

30.16 ***Local authority care, Remanded to***
R v Anderson 2017 EWCA Crim 2604, 2018 2 Cr App R (S) 21 D pleaded to robbery. He had spent 28 weeks in local authority accommodation prior to his sentence. D asked for that time to count towards his sentence. Held. Time counts when the offender has been remanded in custody, see Criminal Justice Act 2003 s 240ZA(1) [and **30.2**]. Criminal Justice Act 2003 s 242(2) [see **30.3**] says that 'remanded into custody' refers to 'remanded to Youth Detention accommodation'. It does not include time spent in 'local authority accommodation'. If the Judge thought it would count, it still does not count, *R v Bright* 2008 EWCA Crim 462, 2 Cr App R (S) 102 (p 578) applied. However, for 98 days of D's time in local authority accommodation he was on a tag and curfew. We are entitled to make and do make a direction that that time should count, see *R v D and H* 2016 EWCA Crim 1807. That case pointed out that there was an anomaly and so counsel should raise this time on a tag with the judge so that he or she may adjust the sentence.

30.17 ***Police detention***
Note: Criminal Justice Act 2003 s 240ZA(1)(b) refers to 'a remand in custody' as did its forerunner. This means that days in police custody continue not to be counted. There is, however, an exception. Where a defendant is sentenced to a Detention and Training Order, a 'remand in custody' includes 'being held in police detention', Powers of Criminal Courts (Sentencing) Act 2000 s 101(11). Ed.

30.18 ***Retrials***
Criminal Appeal Act 1968 Sch 2 para 2(4)[500] Criminal Justice Act 2003 s 240ZA and 240A (crediting of periods of remand in custody or on bail subject to certain types of condition: terms of imprisonment and detention) shall apply to any sentence imposed on conviction on retrial as if it had been imposed on the original conviction.
R v Hudson 2011 EWCA Crim 906, 2 Cr App R (S) 116 (p 666) D was convicted of rape and his conviction was quashed. He was reconvicted and the Judge considered 6 years was appropriate. At first the Judge believed that the time before the first conviction would not count. Held. That was erroneous.

30.19 ***Significant/whole period served on remand/curfew Non-custodial sentence imposed***
New Sentences: Criminal Justice Act 2003 Guideline 2004, see www.banksr.com Other Matters Guidelines tab para 1.1.37 The court should seek to give credit for time spent on remand (in custody or equivalent status) in all cases. It should make clear, when announcing sentence, whether or not credit for time on remand has been given and should explain its reasons for not giving credit when it considers either that this is not justified, would not be practical, or would not be in the best interests of the offender.
1.1.38 Where an offender has spent time in custody on remand, there will be occasions where a custodial sentence is warranted but the length of the sentence justified by the

[500] Legal Aid, Sentencing and Punishment of Offenders Act 2012 Sch 13 para 6 substitutes '240ZA' for '240'.

seriousness of the offence would mean that the offender would be released immediately. Under the present framework, it may be more appropriate to pass a community sentence since that will ensure supervision on release.

R v Hemmings 2007 EWCA Crim 2413, 2008 1 Cr App R (S) 106 (p 623) D pleaded to battery and criminal damage and was sentenced to a community order. More serious counts were not proceeded with. Before sentence he had spent 99 days in custody. The defence argued that the 99 days was the equivalent of the maximum sentence that would have been imposed if he had been on bail. The Judge considered he posed a real risk, particularly to his partner, and imposed a community order. Held. No doubt D and the community would benefit from him undergoing a period of supervision. However, the order is a form of punishment and wrong in principle. Conditional discharge substituted.

R v Lynch 2007 EWCA Crim 2624 D pleaded to common assault. V saw what he thought was D assaulting his partner and went to assist her. D swung a punch at V and V fell. There was a scuffle for about 30 seconds. V sustained bruising and a minor abrasion. D was charged with ABH on V and ABH on his partner and remanded in custody. The partner twice failed to attend court. D was aged 39 and had 29 previous convictions including five robberies, section 18, three GBHs, three ABHs and two common assaults. The prosecution accepted a plea to common assault on V (maximum sentence 6 months). D had been in custody for 5 months and 22 days, the equivalent of nearly 12 months. The Judge imposed a conditional discharge, saying the courts needed to retain some control over him and D should view himself as effectively being under a suspended sentence. Held. We entirely sympathise with the proper and understandable desire of the Judge to keep some form of control over D, particularly as the likelihood of further violent offences was high. However, it was inappropriate to impose a sentence which exposed D to the risk of further punishment when he had served more than the maximum sentence. We would have wished to impose a 5-month prison sentence but, as the Court of Appeal cannot impose a more severe sentence than the original sentence, absolute discharge instead.

R v Rakib 2011 EWCA Crim 870, 2012 1 Cr App R (S) 1 (p 1) D was convicted of two counts of exposure and sentenced to a 3-year community order with requirements. He had served 173 days on remand, i.e. nearly 6 months. That was equivalent to an 11- or 12-month sentence, given the mandatory Criminal Justice Act 2003 s 240[501] direction for remand time to count against a resulting sentence of imprisonment. The defence relied upon *R v Hemmings* 2007 EWCA Crim 2413, 2008 1 Cr App R (S) 106 (p 623), which was substantially similar to D's case, in which a community order was substituted for a conditional discharge expiring immediately. Held. The punishment of the offender is one purpose of any sentence. It is not the only purpose. Judges must have regard to rehabilitation of offenders and protection of the public, which are other purposes under Criminal Justice Act 2003 s 142(1). Periods spent on remand cannot be a necessarily determinative factor in deciding what the appropriate sentence is, Criminal Justice Act 2003 s 149. Had the court in *Hemmings* been referred to Criminal Justice Act 2003 s 149 (discretion to have regard to time on remand when imposing community order etc.), we have no doubt they would have approached the appeal differently. The community sentence was neither manifestly excessive nor wrong in principle.

R v Gaynor 2016 EWCA Crim 1629 D was convicted of sexual assault. He was acquitted of assault by penetration and ABH. The Judge thought the equivalent of 10 months he had served awaiting trial was sufficient and passed 10 months. The defence pointed out that if the sentence had been less than 6 months the notification period would be 7 years not 10. Held. It was not right to make the sentence the same as time served. **3 months** was appropriate for the offence.

For more detail, see **323.8** in Volume 2.

[501] Repealed by Legal Aid, Sentencing and Punishment of Offenders Act 2012 s 108(1) on 3/12/12. The repeal has effect subject to transitional and transitory provisions specified in SI 2012/2906 Sch 15.

R v Pereira-Lee 2016 EWCA Crim 1705, 2017 1 Cr App R (S) 17 D pleaded to ABH on a police officer and possession of cannabis (no penalty). He was aged 30, with 16 sentencing hearings for 29 offences, including assault with intent to resist arrest, possession of offensive weapons and bladed articles and drug offences. The pre-sentence report said there was a high risk of reoffending. D was on a curfew and there was a 15-month delay before sentence.[502] The Judge started at 12 months which with the plea discount gave 10 months. The Judge considered that [because of the curfew allowance], prison or a Suspended Sentence Order would not be in the public interest or in D's interest. The Judge said he wanted to provide some structure to secure rehabilitation. He gave D a community order with 50 hours' unpaid work (now done), a 2-year curfew and 25 Resolve Programme sessions. The defence said that due to the curfew he should have been given the appropriate prison sentence, meaning immediate release. Held. The credit for tag time must be deducted, Criminal Justice Act 2003 s 240A(2). There is a distinction in credit. It must be given for remand time/tag time for custodial sentences (including suspended ones). The starting point for community orders is a discretion as to whether it is to be taken into account. The different approach is often adopted for community orders to rehabilitate the offender through participation in activities/ programmes. The Resolve Programme was in D's interest. The Judge was fully justified in passing a community order. Although we would not have imposed the curfew or the unpaid work, we will not interfere with them.

R v Sutherland 2017 EWCA Crim 2259 D was acquitted of GBH with intent after spending 4 months 20 days in custody. He pleaded to racially aggravated harassment, for which he had been remanded into custody. He was abusive to an Asian police officer. The Judge considered that the offence did not pass the custodial threshold and considered any custodial sentence to be wrong in principle. He was asked to pass a conditional discharge. Held. The only sentencing options were a conditional discharge or a community order with unpaid work. We apply *R v Rakib* 2011 EWCA Crim 870, 2012 1 Cr App R (S) 1 (p 1). The time spent on remand was taken into account when the Judge ordered 40 hours' unpaid work, which was the minimum that could be ordered.

Note: *R v Rakib* 2011 was a case where the community order was said to be helping rehabilitation and protecting the public. Those issues did not apply here as D was said to be remorseful and posed a low-risk of re-conviction. The other difference was that in *R v Rakib* 2011, there was no unpaid work requirement, which is a real punishment. The rule used to be that if you had served more punishment in prison than the offence warranted, any further punishment was wrong in principle. This rule would make both a community order with unpaid work and a conditional discharge (where the defendant could be re-punished if the order was breached) wrong in principle. The only order that would be just is a fine or 1 day's custody, which still appears to be available. Ed.

For the rules when a defendant is given a community order after a long period in custody, see **30.19**.

See also: *R v Bell* 2010 EWCA Crim 1075.

R v Kennedy 2010 EWCA Crim 3064 (Plea. Common assault. He had been remanded in custody for 143 days before he was sentenced and that time spent in custody was equivalent to just over 9 months' custody. The statutory maximum is 6 months. He received 3 months suspended. Held. Therefore were he to reoffend he would serve longer than permissible by law.)

R v Blake 2011 EWCA Crim 2152 (Sex offender who had served whole of maximum sentence on remand. Propriety of community sentence indicated.)

30.20 ***Whole sentence served on remand Is there a licence period?***

R (Galiazia) v Governor of Hewell Prison and Others 2014 EWHC 3427 (Admin), 2015 1 Cr App R (S) 13 (p 100) High Court D was sentenced to 12 months. He had served 411 days on remand. The Judge thought that would wholly extinguish the sentence and there

[502] The length of time the curfew lasted is not revealed.

was nothing more to serve. The Secretary of State considered the time could not be set off against the licence. D refused to co-operate with his licence as it was unjust. He was recalled to prison. D challenged the licence and the recall. Held. The key phrase is 'is to count as time served by the offender as part of the sentence', in Criminal Justice Act 2003 s 240ZA(3).[503] If D's interpretation was correct, section 240ZA(6) could never bite. D's appeal fails.

Bail, tag and curfew

30.21 ***Tags Statutory provisions***

Criminal Justice Act 2003 s 240A(1) This section applies where:

(a) a court sentences an offender to imprisonment for a term in respect of an offence committed on or after 4 April 2005,

(b) the offender was remanded on bail by a court in course of or in connection with proceedings for the offence, or any related offence, after the coming into force of Criminal Justice and Immigration Act 2008 s 21, and

(c) the offender's bail was subject to a qualifying curfew condition and an electronic monitoring condition ('the relevant conditions').

(2) Subject to subsections (3A) and (3B), the court must direct that the credit period is to count as time served by the offender as part of the sentence.

(3) The credit period is calculated by taking the following steps.

Step 1

(a) the day on which the offender's bail was first subject to the relevant conditions (and for this purpose a condition is not prevented from being a relevant condition by the fact that it does not apply for the whole of the day in question), and

(b) the number of other days on which the offender's bail was subject to those conditions (but exclude the last of those days if the offender spends the last part of it in custody).

Step 2

Deduct the number of days on which the offender, whilst on bail subject to the relevant conditions, was also:

(a) subject to any requirement imposed for the purpose of securing the electronic monitoring of the offender's compliance with a curfew requirement, or

(b) on temporary release under rules made under Prison Act 1952 s 47.

Step 3

From the remainder, deduct the number of days during that remainder on which the offender has broken either or both of the relevant conditions.

Step 4

Divide the result by 2.

Step 5

If necessary, round up to the nearest whole number.

(3A) A day of the credit period counts as time served:

(a) in relation to only one sentence, and

(b) only once in relation to that sentence.

(3B) A day of the credit period is not to count as time served as part of any period of 28 days served by the offender before automatic release (see section 255B(1)).

Note: This section is listed as amended by Legal Aid, Sentencing and Punishment of Offenders Act 2012 s 109. The 2012 Act repealed subsections (4)-(7) and (9) of this section and so removed the discretion to order the remand time to count. There is a duty to state the days counted in open court, see subsection (8) at **86.50**. Ed.

30.22 ***Tags Step by step guide***

Crown Court Bench Book 2013 www.banksr.com Other Matters Other Documents page 33 The five steps [are]:

[503] The judgment refers to the wrong section so it has been corrected.

1. Calculate the days on bail with the relevant conditions (viz. a) curfew for 9 hours or more and b) electronic monitoring) beginning on the day on which the conditions were imposed and ending on the day before the day of sentence.
2. Deduct any days where the offender has been subject, at the same time, to:
   (a) Community Order, Youth Rehabilitation Order or requirement of a suspended sentence with a similar qualifying curfew, or
   (b) release on Home Detention Curfew or other temporary release with a similar qualifying curfew.
3. Deduct any days on which he has been in breach of any part of the relevant conditions.
4. Divide the resultant days by 2.
5. Round up if there is a half day.

R v Thorsby and Others 2015 EWCA Crim 1, 1 Cr App R (S) 63 (p 443) All the defendants appealed the failure to give credit, under Criminal Justice Act 2003 s 240A, for half the time they spent on qualifying curfew. All their appeals were out of time, none due to the defendants' fault. Held. The credit period is calculated as follows:

Step 1 Add up the days spent on **qualifying** curfew including the first, but not the last if on the last day the defendant was taken into custody.

Step 2 Deduct days on which the defendant was at the same time **also**: i) being monitored with a tag for compliance with a curfew requirement and/or ii) on temporary release from custody.

Step 3 Deduct days when the defendant has broken the curfew or the tagging condition.

Step 4 Divide the result by 2.

Step 5 If necessary, round up to the nearest whole number.

The decisions in *R v Leacock and Others* 2013 EWCA Crim 1994, 2014 2 Cr App R (S) 12 (p 72) make clear that there is a duty on the court imposing a qualifying curfew to complete the appropriate form, for court officials to ensure that the form travels with the defendant from court to court and for those representing the defendant to ensure that they have all the necessary details to hand at the time of sentence. It is for the parties to make the calculations, agree the result and inform the judge. In the unlikely event of a dispute, the judge must decide whether it is necessary and proportionate to resolve the dispute and, if so, how the dispute is to be resolved.

30.23 *Tags General principles*

R v Barrett 2009 EWCA Crim 2213, 2010 1 Cr App R (S) 87 (p 572) For 126 days the defendant was on bail with a 12-hour night-time curfew. He was visited almost every day by police and complied with the curfew. He was not entitled to a section 240A discount because he was not electronically tagged. The Judge gave him no discount. Held. It was not for the courts to rewrite a statute so the condition about tagging was removed. In an appropriate case a judge could give some allowance for a lengthy curfew outside the statute. However, the Judge was right not to do so here.

R v Monaghan and Others 2009 EWCA Crim 2699, 2010 2 Cr App R (S) 50 (p 343) Section 240A applies only to offences committed after 4 April 2005. It does not apply to a period of bail before 3 November 2008. If on bail on 3 November 2008, the period after that date counts. No reduction should normally be given for a night-time curfew.

30.24 *Tags Procedure*

R v Irving and Squires 2010 EWCA Crim 189, 2 Cr App R (S) 75 (p 492) Solicitors and counsel must ask their defendants whether they have been tagged. When passing sentence, every judge should employ the formula suggested in *R v Gordon* 2007 EWCA Crim 165, 2 Cr App R (S) 66 (p 400). The formula is: 'The defendant will receive full credit for the full period of time spent in custody on remand and half the time spent under curfew if the curfew qualified under the provisions of section 240. On the information before me the total period is [XX] days but if this period is mistaken, this Court will order an amendment of the record for the correct period to be recorded.' Applications must be lodged promptly but we make a deduction here.

Note: As a result of time spent in custody being deducted administratively by the prison, the reference to 'time in custody on remand' in the suggested formula in *R v Irving and Squires* 2010 should be ignored. Ed.

R v Hoggard 2013 EWCA Crim 1024, 2014 1 Cr App R (S) 42 (p 239) The Judge made no order for time spent on curfew as he believed the deduction was done automatically. Held. para 23

1 In contrast to [time on remand] there is no automatic deduction of days spent on bail subject to a curfew condition and an electronic monitoring condition.

2 The discretion, formerly provided by the combination of subsections 4(b), (5) and (7), not to give a direction at all, or to give a direction as to a period of days less than the credit period, has gone.

3 Instead, there is now a requirement under subsection (2) that, subject to subsections (3A) and (3B), the court must direct that the credit period is to count as time served.

4 Subsection (3A) prevents the same remand time counting several times against two or more sentences (whether they are to be served concurrently or consecutively).

5 Subsection (3B) prevents remand time shortening any 'fixed term recall' under section 255B (which was introduced by the 2008 Act).

6 Step 2 in subsection (3) prevents credit for tagged bail counting towards a subsequent sentence for such time as the defendant was also subject to an electronically monitored curfew requirement in connection with any other sentence (which includes being released on Home Detention Curfew) or had been temporarily released from prison in relation to another sentence.

7 Step 3 in subsection (3) prevents credit for days on which the defendant breached either the qualifying curfew condition or the electronic monitoring condition.

8 Under subsection (8), when a direction is given the court must state in open court the number of days on which the offender was subject to the relevant conditions, and the number of days (if any) which it has deducted under Steps 2 and 3.

Against that background and in view of the guidance previously given in *R v Irving and Squires* 2010 EWCA Crim 189, 2 Cr App R (S) 75 (p 492):

(i) It remains essential that every court which imposes a curfew and tagging condition uses the Court Service form entitled 'Record of Electronic Monitoring of Curfew Bail' (or its up-to-date equivalent) which is required to follow the defendant from court to court. When a defendant is sent or committed to the Crown Court then the form (properly completed) must go with the papers to the Crown Court. If the defendant has never been subject to curfew and tagging the magistrates are required to say so, or to send a copy of his bail conditions. If on receipt of a case involving a defendant on bail there is no such form and the question of his status is not clear, then the Crown Court must ask the magistrates for clarification and get hold of the form if it exists.

(ii) Solicitors and, if they have not done it, counsel are required to ask the defendant whether he has been subject to curfew and tagging. If he says that he has, they are required to find out, from the court record, for which periods. It is also the responsibility of the CPS to have a system for ensuring that such information is available.

(iii) The consideration of Steps 1-3 will be part of the post-conviction proceedings and thus not subject to the invariable application of strict rules of evidence. The approach to admissibility, particularly in relation to hearsay evidence, should be that identified in *R v Clipston* 2011 EWCA Crim 446, 2 Cr App R (S) 101 (p 569) with emphasis upon the procedures adopted to deal with Steps 1-3 being both flexible and fair.

(iv) Nevertheless, if there is a dispute under, in particular, Step 2 and/or Step 3, then the prosecution must prove to the criminal standard that the days sought to be deducted from the number of days identified under Step 1 are caught by the relevant step.
(v) However, if the court is of the opinion that the resolution of the dispute, or part of it, would be likely to amount to the disproportionate use of time and expense then (without more) the dispute, or the relevant part of it, should be resolved in the defendant's favour and no deduction made from the number of days identified under Step 1. The court is only likely to be of such an opinion if the number of days involved is relatively modest.

The court will then deal with the maths required by Steps 4 and 5 and will thereafter give a direction, complying in the process with subsection (8).

R v Huggins 2013 EWCA Crim 1524 D pleaded to going equipped. He had been subject to a 10-hour night-time non-qualifying curfew for 37 weeks. The Judge said he could not take that into account as a matter of law. He started the sentence at 10 months and with a late plea reduced it to 9. Held. The Judge was not under a duty to make an allowance for time with a non-qualifying curfew, but in an appropriate case with a lengthy period a judge could make an allowance for it. Here an allowance should have been made, so 4 months substituted.

30.25 ***Tags*** ***Procedure*** ***Disputes***

R v Hoggard 2013 EWCA Crim 1024, 2014 1 Cr App R (S) 42 (p 239) The Judge made no order for time spent on curfew as he believed the deduction was done automatically. H had spent 38 days on a curfew and tag. At the Court of Appeal, the Probation Service said H had breached the terms of the curfew and/or tag on 8 days. H denied this. Held. The net credit in dispute was thus 4 days. In the particular circumstances of this case resolution of the dispute would have required an adjournment, the attendance of the prosecution, and the likely calling of evidence. We concluded that such further proceedings would be likely to amount to a disproportionate use of time and expense. Accordingly we resolved the dispute in the appellant's favour and, having applied Steps 4 and 5, ordered (as indicated above) that 47 days should count towards the service of his sentence.

30.26 ***Tags*** ***Bail terms, Onerous*** ***Period did not qualify***

R v Glover, Cox and Issitt 2008 EWCA Crim 1782 G was convicted of conspiracy to cheat the revenue. He was sentenced 123 days later. It was argued that the time he had spent on bail should have been taken into consideration because although he was allowed bail after becoming seriously ill, he had stringent conditions. He was subject to tagging and was not allowed to leave his small house for a month. After that he was allowed two ½-hour outings per day. Held. The Judge was entitled to say that even bail with stringent conditions is different from being in prison. It is possible that a judge may be persuaded by the facts of a particular case to make some modest adjustment to sentence in circumstances of this kind, but it is a question to be assessed by the judge in each case. We are satisfied that in this case the Judge's reasoning for making no adjustment was proper and open to him.

R v Sherif and Others 2008 EWCA Crim 2653, 2009 2 Cr App R (S) 33 (p 235)[504] The defendants were released on bail awaiting their terrorist trial. For some of them their terms included a 24-hour curfew i.e. house arrest. The rest had a shorter curfew. Applying *R v Glover* 2008 there may be a modest credit given. But that should not apply to those with a night-time curfew. Here we give for 16 months of house arrest 3 months' credit.

Note: As in the previous paragraph, I see no reason why this principle should not continue to apply. Ed.

[504] The commencement date given for section 240A in the judgment is incorrect.

30.27 *Bail terms Avoiding double accounting*
Remand on Bail (Disapplication of Credit Period) Rules 2008 2008/2793 These rules provide that there should be no double accounting when the defendant is tagged as a released prisoner or tagged as part of a suspended sentence etc.

30.28 *Tags Judge's sentencing remarks*
Judicial College's Crown Court Compendium Part II Sentencing June 2018 page 4-35

> **Example**
> I certify that you have spent 47 days on remand subject to a qualifying curfew and I direct that 24 days will count towards your sentence. If this calculation is later found to be wrong it will be put right by correcting the record administratively without any further hearing.

R v Hoggard 2013 EWCA Crim 1024, 2014 1 Cr App R (S) 42 (p 239) Save in a case where it is clear that there is no possibility of crediting a period of remand on bail, the order of the court should, in accordance with *R v Nnaji* 2009 EWCA Crim 468, 2 Cr App R (S) 107 (p 700), be along the following lines:
'The defendant will receive full credit for half the time spent under curfew if the curfew qualified under the provisions of [section] 240A. On the information before me the total period is [XX] days (subject to the deduction of [XX] days that I have directed under Step(s) 2 and/or 3 making a total of [XX] days), but if this period is mistaken, this Court will order an amendment of the record for the correct period to be recorded.'

30.29 *Tags Appeals*
R v Hoggard 2013 EWCA Crim 1024, 2014 1 Cr App R (S) 42 (p 239) It remains the case that it ought not to be expected that [the Court of Appeal] will routinely grant long extensions of time to correct errors when no one has applied his mind to the issue until long after the event.
R v Leacock and Others 2013 EWCA Crim 1994, 2014 2 Cr App R (S) 12 (p 72) M pleaded to two counts of fraud. His advocate made no enquiries as to the tag time. On 12 December 2012, M was sentenced and no discount was made for the 43 days on a tag. An appeal was lodged on 5 April 2013. Counsel accepted that the failure to mention the days was his error. Held. It is the duty of the advocate to check carefully [what the position was]. The Court will not correct errors unless an application is promptly made. The Court will apply the time limits strictly. Exceptionally here the Court was prepared to direct 21 days to count.
Note: The problem is that it must be unjust to punish a defendant for an error, made by their counsel, of which the defendant was not aware. Ed.
R v Sinclair 2013 EWCA Crim 2567 D was serving a sentence for rape. His release date was calculated and it was discovered that the days on a qualifying curfew were not taken into account by the prison. The appeal was lodged 2 years and 11 months out of time. Held. Anxious consideration was required in determining whether to depart from the Lord Chief Justice's clear direction in *R v Leacock and Others* 2013 (see above). As a matter of fairness to D, and bearing in mind the substantial difference (126 days) it will make to his release date, leave was granted. This was an exceptional case and does not detract from the guidance in *Leacock.*
R v Thorsby and Others 2015 EWCA Crim 1, 1 Cr App R (S) 63 (p 443) All the defendants appealed the failure to give them credit for half the time they had spent on a qualifying curfew. All their appeals were out of time, none due to the defendants' fault. The number of days was substantial. As soon as the defendants became aware of the entitlement their legal advisors were told. Held. Neither the Criminal Appeal Act nor the [Criminal Procedure] Rules limit the discretion of the Court on the issue whether an extension of time should be granted. The principled approach to extensions of time is that the Court will grant an extension if it is in the interests of justice to do so. In none of the cases is it suggested that the interval between discovery and the application for leave was excessive. If a significant number of days was due, it would be right in principle to

refuse an extension of time by reason only if the proportion that those days bear to the total sentence imposed (sic).[505] In future we expect defendants' representatives to send the Court of Appeal office the notice and grounds, either with agreement with the prosecution, or with the necessary documentary evidence to support: a) that he or she is entitled to the tag credit and b) the number of those days. The Court of Appeal office will not routinely become the investigator for the applicant. It is the responsibility of his legal representatives to make the necessary enquiries.

For more details about this case and applications for an extension of time to appeal, see **4.14**.

For more details about this case and the principles of ordering curfew and tag time, see **30.22**.

R v Marshall and Others 2015 EWCA Crim 1999, 2016 1 Cr App R (S) 45 (p 282) Various defendants asked for their tag time to be credited. Held. para 12 The advice in *R v Thorsby and Others* 2015 could not be clearer, yet still applications are being lodged without agreement from the Crown on the number of days spent on qualifying curfew, and with no accompanying statement from the applicant's solicitor setting out why an extension of time should be granted. They are being lodged late, so that they demand an urgent response from the Court of Appeal Office. Further, some local Crown Prosecution Units are not responding to requests from the defence solicitors for an agreement. As a result, the Court of Appeal Office is spending a disproportionate amount of time and resources on correcting errors. para 13 In future, if the requirements in *R v Thorsby and Others* 2015 have not been complied with, the Criminal Appeal Office will no longer progress applications. The Registrar will notify the applicant's solicitor of the duty to comply with *R v Thorsby and Others* 2015 before anything can happen. The CPS Appeals Unit has undertaken to assess the number of days. If the calculations are agreed, the single judge will be able to give leave and send the matter to the full court for a formal declaration without any need for representation. If the calculations are not agreed, the single judge may prefer simply to refer the matter to the full court for resolution, without giving leave or making a representation order. If the Registrar is satisfied that the Crown Court has used the appropriate words, allowing them to amend the days administratively, he will notify the parties that the Crown Court retains jurisdiction and that initially he intends to treat the application as ineffective. The applicant can then ask the Crown Court to re-list the matter and resolve the issue. para 14 Practitioners must appreciate that there may come a time when, in the case of serious misconduct, the court will be forced to report any offender to their professional body for a failure to comply with their professional obligations and/or consider making a costs order. The liberty of the subject is at stake and this issue is not to be taken lightly.

30.30 ***Appeal hearing, Bailed after sentence passed awaiting***

R v Robertson 2012 EWCA Crim 609 D was released on bail with a tag after he was sentenced. Held. The language of section 240A(1)(b) is broad enough to cover this period. Time ordered to count.

Note: The language concerned has not been changed. Ed.

30.31 ***Appeals (both remand time and tag time)***

R (Shields-McKinley) v Sec of State and Others 2017 EWHC 658 (Admin), 2 Cr App R (S) 17 (p 113) It is not appropriate to seek judicial review of a decision of HM Prison Service when the mistake was made by the Crown Court.

31 Custody for Life

31.1

This chapter does not deal with custody for life in murder cases.

Powers of Criminal Courts (Sentencing) Act 2000 s 94

[505] Perhaps this means the Court will not grant leave when the sentence to be served is long and the number of tag days owed is small.

Availability The sentence is only available for those ages 18-20 on the date of their conviction when the conditions are met, see **31.2**.
Custody for life based on dangerousness This is passed under Criminal Justice Act 2003 s 255(1) and (2)(b), see para **76.2**.
Mandatory custody for life Mandatory custody for life is only available for those convicted of murder who are aged 18-20 and not subject to be detained during HM's Pleasure (i.e. aged 10-17 at time of the offence), see **287.77** in Volume 2.
HM's Pleasure, Detention at, see the **MURDER *Defendant under 21 Statutes*** para at **287.77** in Volume 2.
General principles For details, see the **CUSTODY: GENERAL PRINCIPLES** chapter.
Victim surcharge The court must impose a victim surcharge of £170[506] (£30) in non-mandatory life cases unless one or more of the offences was committed when the defendant was aged under 18, when the amount is £30, Criminal Justice Act 2003 s 161A-161B and Criminal Justice Act 2003 (Surcharge) Order 2012 2012/1696 as amended. There are exceptions, a) where a compensation order or an Unlawful Profits Order or a Slavery and Trafficking Reparations Order is imposed, when a reduced amount or a nil amount can be ordered, see **17.67**, and b) where the offence was committed before 1 October 2012, when no surcharge can be made, see **115.3**. Where the offence was committed on or after that date and before 8 April 2016, the amount to be imposed is £120 (£20), see **115.4**. Where the defendant is aged under 18 when the offence was committed, the amount is the relevant figure in brackets above.[507]
For the statistics for this order, see the **LIFE IMPRISONMENT: BASIC PRINCIPLES/ DISCRETIONARY LIFE *Statistics*** para at **74.2**.

31.2 *Power to order*

Power to impose custody for life in certain other cases where offender at least 18 but under 21
Powers of Criminal Courts (Sentencing) Act 2000 s 94(1) Where a person aged at least 18 but under 21 is convicted of an offence other than murder, the court shall, if it considers that a sentence for life would be appropriate, sentence him to custody for life.
(2) Subsection (1) is subject to section 79 and 80.[508]
For the rules about ordering see the **LIFE IMPRISONMENT: DISCRETIONARY LIFE** chapter.

31.3 *Test to apply*

Powers of Criminal Courts (Sentencing) Act 2000 s 94(1) The court shall, if it considers that a sentence for life would be appropriate, sentence him to custody for life.

32 DEFERRED SENTENCES

32.1

Powers of Criminal Courts (Sentencing) Act 2000 s 1
Children and young offenders The order is available whatever the age of the offender.
The disadvantages of the order Many believe that it is an ineffectual sentence. The order has a number of disadvantages and no advantages when compared with a sentence with a community element. The major problem is that if the defendant commits a further offence within the deferred period, it is unlikely that his guilt for that offence will be established before the end of the deferred period. A defendant can, if necessary, elect trial for either way offences and plead not guilty, which will usually ensure that the breach will not be proved before the deferred hearing. The general view is that it is better

[506] Criminal Justice Act 2003 (Surcharge) Order 2012 2012/1696 and Criminal Justice Act 2003 (Surcharge) (Amendment) Order 2016 2016/398 Table 2 for defendants aged 18+ when the offence was committed
[507] Criminal Justice Act 2003 (Surcharge) Order 2012 2012/1696 and Criminal Justice Act 2003 (Surcharge) (Amendment) Order 2016 2016/398 both provide in Table 1 a £30 (or £20 for offences committed before 8/4/16) penalty for offences specified in Powers of Criminal Courts (Sentencing) Act 2000 s 76. Custody for life is so specified in section 76(1)(c).
[508] Both these sections have been repealed. They were general restrictions which have been re-enacted.

to give a community sentence or a Suspended Sentence Order so that there is a supervision element in the sentence and unpaid work orders can be attached to the sentence.
Victim surcharge The order does not apply.[509]

32.2 *Statistics England and Wales*

Deferred sentences

Year	2012	2013	2014	2015	2016
Sentences given	1,669	1,583	1,476	1,135	1,066

For explanations about the statistics, see page 1-xii. The MoJ no longer provides Banks on Sentence with these statistics. For more statistics, see www.banksr.com Statistics tab.

Power to order and general principles

32.3 *Power to defer*

Powers of Criminal Courts (Sentencing) Act 2000 s 1(1) The Crown Court or a Magistrates' Court may defer passing sentence on an offender for the purpose of enabling the court, or any other court to which it falls to deal with him, to have regard in dealing with him to:

(a) his conduct after conviction (including, where appropriate, the making by him of reparation for his offence), or
(b) any change in his circumstances,

but this is subject to subsections (3) and (4) below.
Powers of Criminal Courts (Sentencing) Act 2000 s 1(3) The power conferred by subsection (1) above shall be exercisable only if:

(a) the offender consents,
(b) the offender undertakes to comply with any requirements as to his conduct during the period of the deferment that the court considers it appropriate to impose, and
(c) the court is satisfied, having regard to the nature of the offence and the character and circumstances of the offender, that it would be in the interests of justice to exercise the power.

32.4 *Power to defer for a restorative justice requirement*

Powers of Criminal Courts (Sentencing) Act 2000 s 1ZA(1)[510] Without prejudice to the generality of paragraph (b) of section 1(3), the requirements that may be imposed under that paragraph include restorative justice requirements.
Note: The rest of the section is not reproduced. Ed.
In May 2014, the MoJ issued guidance entitled *Pre-sentence Restorative Justice (RJ)*, see www.banksr.com Other Matters Other Documents tab, which sets out a definition of RJ, an explanation of RJ, the legislation about RJ, the procedure to be used for RJ, the types of RJ activity, a process overview of RJ, the task of an RJ facilitator and the sentencing of defendants involving RJ.

32.5 *Procedure and principles*

R v George 1984 6 Cr App R (S) 211 LCJ The purpose of deferment is…to enable the court to take into account the defendant's conduct after conviction or any change in circumstances and then only if it is in the interests of justice to exercise the power. The principles are:

(a) The power is not to be used as an easy way out for a court which is unable to make up its mind about the correct sentence, see *R v Burgess* 1974 Unreported 18/7/74.
(b) The court should make it clear to the defendant what the particular purposes are which the court has in mind under section 1(1) of the Act and what conduct is

[509] Criminal Justice Act 2003 s 161A and Criminal Justice Act 2003 (Surcharge) Order 2012 2012/1696
[510] Inserted by Crime and Courts Act 2013 Sch 16 para 5, in force 11/12/13

expected of him during deferment. The failure to do so, or more often the failure on the part of the defendant or his representatives to appreciate what those purposes are or that conduct is, has been a fruitful source of appeals to this Court.
(c) It is essential that the deferring court should make a careful note of the purposes for which the sentence is being deferred and what steps, if any, it expects the defendant to take during the period of deferment. Ideally the defendant himself should be given notice in writing of what he is expected to do or refrain from doing, so that there can be no doubt in his mind what is expected of him.

32.6 ***New Sentences: Criminal Justice Act 2003 Guideline 2004***

New Sentences: Criminal Justice Act 2003 Guideline 2004, see www.banksr.com Other Matters Guidelines tab para 1.2.6 Under the new framework, there is a wider range of sentencing options open to the courts, including the increased availability of suspended sentences, and deferred sentences are likely to be used in very limited circumstances. A deferred sentence enables the court to review the conduct of the defendant before passing sentence, having first prescribed certain requirements. It also provides several opportunities for an offender to have some influence as to the sentence passed: a) it tests the commitment of the offender not to reoffend, b) it gives the offender an opportunity to do something where progress can be shown within a short period, c) it provides the offender with an opportunity to behave or refrain from behaving in a particular way that will be relevant to sentence.

32.7 ***When is it appropriate? Guideline***

New Sentences: Criminal Justice Act 2003 Guideline 2004, see www.banksr.com Other Matters Guidelines tab para 1.2.7 Given the new power to require undertakings and the ability to enforce those undertakings before the end of the period of deferral, the decision to defer sentence should be predominantly for a small group of cases at either the custody threshold or the community sentence threshold where the sentencer feels that there would be particular value in giving the offender the opportunities listed because, if the offender complies with the requirements, a different sentence will be justified at the end of the deferment period. This could be a community sentence instead of a custodial sentence or a fine or discharge instead of a community sentence. It may, rarely, enable a custodial sentence to be suspended rather than imposed immediately.
The use of deferred sentences should be predominantly for a small group of cases close to a significant threshold where, should the defendant be prepared to adapt his behaviour in a way clearly specified by the sentencer, the court may be prepared to impose a lesser sentence.

Combined with other orders

32.8 ***Combined with other orders Generally***

Note: The fact that the court is deferring sentence would inevitably preclude the court from imposing most sentencing orders. Ed.

32.9 ***Interim disqualification, Combined with***

Road Traffic Offenders Act 1988 s 26(2) Where a court defers passing sentence under Powers of Criminal Courts (Sentencing) Act 2000 s 1 it may, where the offence carries obligatory or discretionary disqualification, order [interim disqualification].

32.10 ***Referral Orders, Combined with***

Powers of Criminal Courts (Sentencing) Act 2000 s 19(7) Where the court makes a Referral Order, the court may not defer passing sentence on him.

32.11 ***Restitution Orders, Combined with***

Powers of Criminal Courts (Sentencing) Act 2000 s 148(2) The court may on conviction (whether or not the passing of the sentence is in other respects deferred) exercise any of the following powers [restitution etc.].

Other matters

32.12 ***Adding conditions New Sentences: Criminal Justice Act 2003 Guideline 2004***

New Sentences: Criminal Justice Act 2003 Guideline 2004, see www.banksr.com Other Matters Guidelines tab para 1.2.8 A court may impose any conditions during the period of deferment that it considers appropriate.[511] These could be specific requirements as set out in the provisions for community sentences,[512] or requirements that are drawn more widely. These should be specific, measurable conditions so that the offender knows exactly what is required and the court can assess compliance. The restriction on liberty should be limited to ensure that the offender has a reasonable expectation of being able to comply whilst maintaining his or her social responsibilities.

32.13 ***Attorney-General's references***

Att-Gen's Ref No 22 of 1992 1993 14 Cr App R (S) 435 LCJ An order deferring sentence is a sentence within the meaning of the statute. It can therefore be referred under Criminal Justice Act 1988 s 36.

32.14 ***Explain sentence, Judge must/Provide details of alternative sentence/ Suggested sentencing remarks***

New Sentences: Criminal Justice Act 2003 Guideline 2004, see www.banksr.com Other Matters Guidelines tab para 1.2.9 Given the need for clarity in the mind of the offender and the possibility of sentence by another court, the court should give a clear indication (and make a written record) of the type of sentence it would be minded to impose if it had not decided to defer and ensure that the offender understands the consequences of failure to comply with the court's wishes during the deferral period.

Judicial College's Crown Court Compendium Part II Sentencing *June 2018* page 6-6

Example

As you have heard, I am thinking about deferring sentence: that means, in this case, putting it off for a period of 4 months. The reason I would do so is that {e.g. although your offence qualifies for a custodial sentence you have e.g. moved away from the area where these offences were committed/ ceased to associate with the people you committed this offence with/renewed your relationship with your father/got a job/agreed to take part in the restorative justice programme with your victim/s}. Because of this I am thinking of putting you to the test. But if I am to defer sentence I need you to agree and undertake to do these things;

1. To stay away from {place – e.g. as shown on a map};
2. To do your best to keep your job at {employer};
3. To take part in the restorative justice programme.

I know that your advocate has said that you would agree to this but I need to hear this from you. Do you undertake to do all of these things? [Answer]

In addition, I would make it a condition firstly that you continue to live with your father at {place} and secondly that you co-operate fully with your supervising probation officer.

Do you agree to sentence being deferred – that is put off – on these terms? [Answer]

[Assuming D's consent] I will defer sentence for 4 months: that is until {date} and on that date you will either come back to this court or to another court where I shall be and I shall sentence you. In the meantime you must do all of the things which you have agreed to do and comply with the conditions which I have imposed. If you have succeeded, then I will not sentence you to an immediate term of imprisonment. If you have not succeeded, or if you have been convicted of any further offence, I will have no alternative but to send you to prison. Your supervising officer will prepare a short report about your progress before we meet again; and I also direct that a transcript of what I have just said to you must be prepared by {date} and provided to you (through your solicitors), to your supervising officer and to the court.

---

[511] Powers of Criminal Courts (Sentencing) Act 2000 s 1(3)(b)

[512] Criminal Justice Act 2003 s 177

The deferred hearing

32.15 ***Procedure at a deferred hearing***

R v George 1984 6 Cr App R (S) 211 LCJ The task of the court which comes to deal with the offender at the expiration of the period of deferment is as follows:

(a) the purpose of the deferment and any requirement imposed by the deferring court must be ascertained,

(b) the court must determine if the defendant has substantially conformed or attempted to conform with the proper expectations of the deferring court, whether with regard to finding a job [or similar expectation].

32.16 ***Custody not appropriate if order complied with***

R v George 1984 6 Cr App R (S) 211 LCJ If the defendant has substantially conformed or attempted to conform with the proper expectations of the deferring court, whether with regard to finding a job [or similar expectation]…then the defendant may legitimately expect that an immediate custodial sentence will not be imposed. If he has not, then the court should be careful to state with precision in what respects he has failed.

33 Deportation, Recommendations for

33.1

Immigration Act 1971 s 6

Availability The defendant must be a foreign national and be aged 17+.[513] (There are restrictions, see the **Statutory powers/Power to order** section at **33.2** below.)

The need to make recommendations has been greatly reduced by the liability for automatic deportation procedure, see **33.14**.

Statutory powers/Power to order

33.2 ***Power to deport when a recommendation is made***

Immigration Act 1971 s 3(6) A person who is not a British citizen shall also be liable for deportation from the United Kingdom if, after he has attained the age of 17, he is convicted of an offence for which he is punishable with imprisonment and on his conviction is recommended for deportation.

Immigration Act 1971 s 6(1) Where under section 3(6) (see above) a person convicted of an offence is liable to deportation on the recommendation of a court, he may be recommended for deportation by any court having the power to sentence him for the offence.

33.3 ***Requirement that defendant be convicted of an imprisonable offence***

Immigration Act 1971 s 6(3)(b) The question whether an offence is one for which a person is punishable with imprisonment shall be determined without regard to any enactment restricting the imprisonment of young offenders or persons who have not previously been sentenced to imprisonment.

33.4 ***Defendant must be aged 17+***

Immigration Act 1971 s 3(6) A person who is not a British citizen shall also be liable for deportation from the United Kingdom if, after he has attained the age of 17…

Immigration Act 1971 s 6(3)(a) A person shall be deemed to have attained the age of 17 at the time of his conviction if, on consideration of any available evidence, he appears to have done so to the court making or considering a recommendation.

33.5 ***Human Rights Act 1998***

R v Carmona 2006 EWCA Crim 508, 2 Cr App R (S) 102 (p 662) There is now no need for a sentencing court to consider the Convention rights of an offender whose offence justifies a recommendation for deportation. His Convention rights will be considered if the Home Secretary makes a deportation order against which the offender appeals to the Tribunal.

---

[513] Immigration Act 1971 s 3(6)

Specific individuals

33.6 ***British citizen, Proof of being a/Exemptions, Proof of***

Immigration Act 1971 s 3(8) When any question arises whether or not a person is a British citizen or is entitled to any exemption under this Act, it shall lie on the person asserting it to prove that he is.

33.7 ***Commonwealth citizens and Irish citizens***

Immigration Act 1971 s 7(1) A Commonwealth citizen or a citizen of the Republic of Ireland who is ordinarily resident in the United Kingdom:

(a) shall not be liable to deportation if at the time of the Secretary of State's decision he had at all times since the coming into force of this Act been ordinarily resident in the United Kingdom,

(b) shall not be liable to deportation if at the time of the Secretary of State's decision he had been ordinarily resident in the United Kingdom for the last five years,

(c) shall not on conviction of an offence be recommended for deportation if at the time of conviction he had been ordinarily resident in the United Kingdom for the last five years.[514]

(2) A person who has at any time become ordinarily resident in the United Kingdom or in any of the Islands shall not be treated for the purposes of this section as having ceased to be so by reason only of his having remained there in breach of immigration law.

(3) The 'last five years' is to be taken as a period amounting in total to five years, exclusive of any time during which the person claiming exemption under this section was undergoing imprisonment or detention by virtue of a sentence passed of six months or more for an offence on a conviction in the United Kingdom and Islands.

33.8 ***Diplomats and their families***

Immigration Act 1971 s 8(2) and (3) This Act shall not apply to any person who is a member of a mission (within the meaning of Diplomatic Privileges Act 1964), is a member of the family and forms part of the household of that member, or a person otherwise entitled to a like immunity from jurisdiction as is conferred by that Act on a diplomatic agent. If a member of a mission is not a diplomatic agent he does not count as a member of a mission if he was resident outside the United Kingdom and was outside the United Kingdom when he was offered the post and he has not ceased to be such a member after having taken up the post.

33.9 ***EU citizens*** ***The Directive***

European Union Directive 2004/38/EC art 27

1 Member States may restrict the freedom of movement and residence of Union citizens and their family members, irrespective of nationality, on grounds of public policy, public security or public health. These grounds shall not be invoked to serve economic ends.

2 Measures taken on grounds of public policy or public security shall comply with the principle of proportionality and shall be based exclusively on the personal conduct of the individual concerned. Previous criminal convictions shall not in themselves constitute grounds for taking such measures. The personal conduct of the individual concerned must represent a genuine, present and sufficiently serious threat affecting one of the fundamental interests of society. Justifications that are isolated from the particulars of the case or that rely on considerations of general prevention shall not be accepted.

3 In order to ascertain whether the person concerned represents a danger for public policy or public security, when issuing the registration certificate or, in the absence of a registration system, not later than three months from the date of arrival of the person concerned on its territory or from the date of reporting his/her presence within the territory, as provided for in art 5(5), or when issuing the residence card, the host Member State may, should it consider this essential, request the Member State of origin and, if

---

[514] Two or more sentences for consecutive or partly consecutive terms shall be treated as a single sentence, Immigration Act 1971 s 7(4)(b).

need be, other Member States to provide information concerning any previous police record the person concerned may have. Such enquiries shall not be made as a matter of routine. The Member State consulted shall give its reply within two months.

4 The Member State which issued the passport or identity card shall allow the holder of the document who has been expelled on grounds of public policy, public security, or public health from another Member State to re-enter its territory without any formality even if the document is no longer valid or the nationality of the holder is in dispute.

33.10 ***EU citizens Cases***

R v Bouchereau 1978 66 Cr App R 202 ECJ In the case of EU nationals, and in order to comply with EC law, a recommendation for deportation on public policy grounds cannot be made based on a person's conviction alone. It is also necessary to justify the deportation by demonstrating that the presence or conduct of the person concerned constitutes a genuine and sufficiently serious threat to the requirements of public policy or public security. A recommendation can be made if the conditions of the EEC Treaty article 48 64/221 (now 2004/38/EC) are satisfied.

R v Escauriaza 1988 87 Cr App R 344 Under EEC law, a valid recommendation for deportation can only be made if at least two conditions are fulfilled: first, that there exists a genuine and sufficiently serious threat to the requirements of public policy affecting one of the fundamental interests of society. In our judgement, that is simply a somewhat fuller way of saying that the defendant's continued presence in the United Kingdom would be to its detriment. Second, that the reasons are given to the defendant for making the recommendation. The EEC law here simply mirrors the law and practice of this country.

R v Carmona 2006 EWCA Crim 508, 2 Cr App R (S) 102 (p 662) Citizens of the EU have additional rights under article 48 of the Treaty. The present position is that a recommendation for deportation may be made only if the conditions specified in Directive 64/221 are satisfied. This is because, as stated above, a recommendation is a 'measure' concerning expulsion from a Member State, see *R v Bouchereau* 1978 66 Cr App R 202. However, the Directive permits expulsion on the ground of public policy, and it adds little if anything to our domestic requirements that a recommendation for deportation should be made by a judicial authority, only if the conduct of the offender justifies it (in the sense that deportation is a proportionate response to his offending), and adequate reasons should be given: *cf.* European Union's Directive 2004/38/EC arts 3, 6 and 9, see the helpful summary in *B v Secretary of State for the Home Department* 2002 HRLR 439.

In the case of non-EU citizens, sentencing courts should consider only whether the offence committed by the offender, in the light of the information before the court, justifies the conclusion that his continued presence in this country is contrary to the public interest. Different considerations will arise in relation to EU citizens once Directive 2004/38/EC is in force.

Note: The directive is now in force. Ed.

Bulale v Secretary of State for the Home Dept 2008 EWCA Civ 806 D was a citizen of the Netherlands and appealed against his order for deportation. He had been resident in the UK for a continuous period of five years, albeit the majority of that time had been spent in custody for offences of robbery and burglary. D's pre-sentence report said he posed, and would continue to pose, a high likelihood of committing further offences. In considering D's deportation, his previous convictions could only be taken into account so far as they were evidence of 'personal conduct constituting a present threat to the fundamental interests of society'. As such, D's propensity to commit robbery threatened the fundamental interest of protecting members of society from violent crime of a sufficiently serious nature. Held. Whilst it should be difficult to expel an EU citizen on the basis of crimes of dishonesty, violence is a different matter. Guidance by the Secretary of State suggests that a serious violent or other offence which carries a penalty of 10 years' imprisonment or more might constitute serious grounds of public policy.

The type of offence committed by D accordingly fell within that guideline. The tribunal was therefore entitled to decide that D represented a genuine and sufficiently serious threat to the public and there were serious grounds for deporting him. D was an unmarried man of 21. There was no dependency between him, his mother and siblings who were also resident in the UK, he could speak Dutch, and he had spent 14 years in the Netherlands including the whole of his school career. As such, it was not disproportionate to require him to return there.

R v Kluxen 2010 EWCA Crim 1081, 2011 1 Cr App R (S) 39 (p 249) This Court, when dealing only with EU citizens, said that the court must consider whether the offender's conduct (including the instant offence and any earlier ones) constituted 'a genuine and sufficiently serious threat to the requirements of public policy affecting one of the fundamental interests of society'. These were the cases of *R v Kraus* 1982 4 Cr App R (S) 113, *R v Compassi* 1987 9 Cr App R (S) 270 and *R v Escauriaza* 1988 87 Cr App R 344. In all of these cases the Court adopted the reasoning of the European Court of Justice in *R v Bouchereau* 1978 66 Cr App R 202, which has survived the replacement of Directive 64/221 by Directive 2004/38.

On first reading, the *Bouchereau* test might seem to be more exacting than the *Nazari* test, resulting in a higher threshold for offenders who are EU citizens than for those who are not. However, in a number of cases, this Court has accepted that for all practical purposes the tests are the same.

In *R v Spura* 1988 10 Cr App R (S) 376, the Court referred to the *Bouchereau* test and continued: 'In *R v Escauriaza* 1988 87 Cr App R 344 the Court concluded that EEC law simply mirrored the law and practice of the United Kingdom. On that basis, one goes back to the test originally laid down in *Nazari* where the test was said to be "does the potential detriment to this country justify the recommendation for deportation of this Appellant?…The overall test, as distilled by the European Court in *Bouchereau*, is whether a full inquiry into the circumstances reveals that a genuine and sufficiently serious threat to the requirements of public policy has affected the fundamental interests of society".' This was adopted in *R v Cravioto* 1990 12 Cr App R (S) 71.

Thus there is a consistent line of authority from this Court to the effect that the *Nazari* and *Bouchereau* tests are substantially the same, and thus that a court considering recommending an offender's deportation should apply substantially the same test whether the offender is or is not a citizen of the EU. This Court has not yet been required to decide whether this approach should be varied, given that article 27(2) of Directive 2004/38 includes the concept of proportionality not expressly referred to either in article 3 of Directive 64/221 or in the case of *Bouchereau*. In any event, both the *Nazari* and the *Bouchereau* tests set at a high level the bar that must be cleared before a recommendation for deportation can be made. Lawton LJ did not go so far as to say in *Nazari* that it was only defendants convicted of serious crimes or having long criminal records whose continued presence in the United Kingdom would be to its detriment, but he clearly had such persons particularly in mind. The terms in which the *Bouchereau* test is expressed themselves indicate its demanding nature.

33.11 *EU citizens Secretary of State's policy*

R v Kluxen 2010 EWCA Crim 1081, 2011 1 Cr App R (S) 39 (p 249) para 30 The Secretary of State's policy is that no EU citizen should be deported unless the prison term is 2+ years.

33.12 *Illegal immigrant, Defendant is an*

R v Benabbas 2005 EWCA Crim 2113 D pleaded to using a false instrument. He attempted to use a forged French passport to obtain a UK National Insurance number. The passport was in his name. There was no sign of anyone living at the address he gave police. D was an Algerian who had no right to be in the UK. The Judge sentenced him to 7 months and recommended deportation. Held, after reviewing the authorities extensively. The illegality or irregularity of D's immigration status can vary from the case of a lawful entrant who overstays his permit to the unlawful entrant who gains entry by fraudulent means, but also because the illegality or irregularity can either be the essence of the offence for which the defendant is sentenced (see *R v Uddin* 1971 Unreported 27/7/71, *R v Akan* 1972 56 Cr App R 716, *R v Nazari* 1980 (the case of *Anyanwu*), *R v Bei Bei Wang* 2005 EWCA Crim 293), or can be entirely irrelevant to it (*R v Kandhari* 1979 Unreported 24/3/79, *Miller v Lenton* 1981 3 Cr App R (S) 171, *R v Nunu* 1991 12 Cr App R (S) 752, *R v Okelola* 1992 13 Cr App R (S) 560). In the latter class of case, the general principle has been that such incidental illegality or irregularity in the status of the defendant is irrelevant, as Bridge LJ stated it to be in *Kandhari*. In our judgement this is not because of the *Nazari* detriment principle, since it will be recalled that in *Nazari* itself this court said, of the case of *Anyanwu*, an overstayer, that if his appeal had not been abandoned, it would have been dismissed. This appears to have been overlooked. It is because the defendant is to be sentenced for the offence of which he has been convicted and not for his incidental status under the Immigration Act. Even so, we would have thought that the defendant's status, if indeed it was clear, was not entirely irrelevant: it is part of the defendant's personal conduct which, as a matter of the public interest, could be taken into account as part of the balancing exercise. What the cases of *R v Kandhari* 1979, *Miller v Lenton* 1981, *R v Nunu* 1991 and *R v Okelola* 1992 appear rather to be concerned with is the rejection of the idea, focused on by the sentencing court in that category of case, that a recommendation for deportation could properly be made simply because of the illegality or irregularity of status and not as a result of a reasoned balance based on the detriment approach. Whether that view of that class of case is correct or not, however, we do not think that the *R v Kandhari* 1979 approach applies at all to the category where the essential gravamen of the offence for which the defendant is being sentenced is itself an abuse of this country's immigration laws. While we would be reluctant ourselves to go as far as Lawton LJ did in *R v Nazari* 1980 in suggesting that a recommendation for deportation should be automatic in the case of every overstayer, and the case of *R v Akan* 1972 supports us in that view, we do think that the public interest in preventing the fraudulent use of passports to gain entry or support residence is of considerable importance and deserves protection. Moreover, in such a case, the issue of *R v Nazari* 1980 detriment is intimately bound up with the protection of public order afforded by confidence in a system of passports. We therefore think it is correct to distinguish between the case of a person who enters the UK by fraudulent means and the case of a person who is in the country unlawfully and is convicted of an offence unconnected with his status and the circumstances in which he entered the country.

In this connection, *R v Bei Bei Wang* 2005 is instructive. That case differed from the present in at least two respects. First, the defendant there was not charged with use of a forged passport: her offence was that of entering without a passport. Second, she entered solely for the purpose of claiming asylum, which she did immediately. That was the context in which Fulford J there applied the *Kandhari* test. The balance of authority as well as the reason of the thing suggest that the *Kandhari* approach is inappropriate in connection with the offence of entering without a passport, but may well, for entirely different reasons, nevertheless be necessary in a case where the entrant immediately claims asylum. In such a situation, the claim for asylum can only be assessed by the Secretary of State, and he is probably best left to consider it without any possible complication arising from a recommendation for deportation.

R v Chirimimanga and Others 2007 EWCA Crim 1684 P, E and C pleaded to using a forged instrument with intent and obtaining a pecuniary advantage by deception. P also pleaded to three counts of possessing an identity document relating to another. All three defendants had applied for work using passports that were fraudulently stamped with 'leave to remain' and 'no time limit'. The Judge said it was undesirable that they should remain in this country a moment longer than was necessary and recommended that they be deported immediately on their release from custody. Held. The gravamen of these offences was an abuse of this country's immigration laws. The defendants may have entered this country legally but none of them had a right to remain at the time of the offences. They plainly intended to use, and did use, the forged stamps in their passports dishonestly to represent that the opposite was the case. There were good grounds for the Judge to make the recommendations that he did. It would have been better if he had spelled out in more detail why, having regard to the defendants' offences, their continued presence in the United Kingdom was to its detriment. But the Judge's failure to give full reasons is not a ground for quashing the recommendations that he made. Deportation recommendation upheld.

33.13 ***Refugee status, Defendant has applied for***
R v Villa and Villa 1993 14 Cr App R (S) 34 A person with refugee status is not exempt from deportation. If a defendant receives a sentence that does not involve immediate custody, or is likely to be eligible for release before a decision on deportation is made, the sentencing judge should consider giving a direction for release pending the Secretary of State's decision on the deportation order.
R v Kibunyi 2009 EWCA Crim 9 We would not wish anything that we say in any way to indicate a prohibition upon a court, in an appropriate case, making a recommendation for deportation, even where it is said that an asylum application has been made or is to be made.
Trafficked victim, Defendant was a see the **DEFENDANT** ***Trafficked victim, Defendant was a*** para at **242.64** in Volume 2.

Automatic liability for deportation and recommendations

33.14 ***Automatic liability for deportation Statutory provisions***
UK Borders Act 2007 s 32(5) The Secretary of State must make a deportation order in respect of a foreign criminal (subject to section 33, see para **33.19**).
UK Borders Act 2007 s 32(1)[515] In this section a 'foreign criminal' means a person:
(a) who is not a British citizen,[516]
(b) who is convicted in the United Kingdom of an offence,[517] and
(c) to whom Condition 1 or 2 applies.
(2) Condition 1 is that the person is sentenced to a period of imprisonment of at least 12 months (for definition see below).
(3) Condition 2 is that:
(a) the offence is specified by order of the Secretary of State under Nationality, Immigration and Asylum Act 2002 s 72(4)(a) (serious criminal), and
(b) the person is sentenced to a period of imprisonment (for definition see **33.16**).
UK Borders Act 2007 s 32(6) When certain conditions apply, the Secretary of State may revoke a section 32(5) deportation order.

33.15 ***Automatic liability for deportation Definition of 12 months' imprisonment***
UK Borders Act 2007 s 38(1) In section 32(2) the reference to a person who is sentenced to a period of imprisonment of at least 12 months:
(a) does not include a person who receives a suspended sentence (unless a court subsequently orders that the sentence or any part of it (of whatever length) is to take effect),
(b) does not include a person who is sentenced to a period of imprisonment of at least 12 months only by virtue of being sentenced to consecutive sentences amounting in aggregate to more than 12 months,

[515] This section has been summarised.
[516] 'British citizen' has the same meaning as in Immigration Act 1971 s 3(5), UK Borders Act 2007 s 38(3). The burden of proof in Immigration Act 1971 s 3(8) shall apply.
[517] Persons subject to an order of Criminal Procedure (Insanity) Act 1964 s 5 (insanity etc.) are not treated as being convicted, UK Borders Act 2007 s 38(3).

(c) includes a reference to a person who is sentenced to detention, or ordered or directed to be detained, in an institution other than a prison (including, in particular, a hospital or an institution for young offenders) for at least 12 months, and
(d) includes a person who is sentenced to imprisonment or detention, or ordered or directed to be detained, for an indeterminate period (provided that it may last for 12 months).

33.16 ***Automatic liability for deportation Definition of imprisonment in section 32(3)(b)***
UK Borders Act 2007 s 38(2) In UK Borders Act 2007 s 32(3)(b) the reference to a person who is sentenced to a period of imprisonment:
(a) does not include a person who receives a suspended sentence (unless a court subsequently orders that the sentence or any part of it is to take effect), and
(b) includes a person who is sentenced to detention, or ordered or directed to be detained, in an institution other than a prison (including, in particular, a hospital or an institution for young offenders).

Deportation, Recommendation for

33.17 ***Automatic liability for deportation applies Don't make a recommendation***
R v Kluxen 2010 EWCA Crim 1081, 2011 1 Cr App R (S) 39 (p 249) Rule stated. No useful purpose would be served in doing so.

33.18 ***Recommendations should now be rare***
R v Kluxen 2010 EWCA Crim 1081, 2011 1 Cr App R (S) 39 (p 249) It will be rare for the test to be satisfied where no offences merit a custodial sentence of 12+ months. An offender who repeatedly commits minor offences could conceivably do so, as could a person who commits a single offence involving, for example, the possession or use of false identity documents for which he receives a custodial sentence of less than 12 months. We observe that even if a court makes no recommendation for an offender's deportation, the Secretary of State may nevertheless deport him if he deems this conducive to the public good.

33.19 ***Automatic liability for deportation Exceptions***
UK Borders Act 2007 s 32(5) The Secretary of State must make a deportation order in respect of a foreign criminal (subject to section 33).
UK Borders Act 2007 s 33(1) Section 32(4) and (5):
(a) do not apply where an exception in this section applies (subject to subsection (7) below), and
(b) are subject to Immigration Act 1971 s 7 and 8 (Commonwealth citizens, Irish citizens, crew and other exemptions).
(2) Exception 1 is where removal of the foreign criminal in pursuance of the deportation order would breach:
(a) a person's Convention rights, or
(b) the United Kingdom's obligations under the Refugee Convention.
(3) Exception 2 is where the Secretary of State thinks that the foreign criminal was under the age of 18 on the date of conviction.
(4) Exception 3 is where the removal of the foreign criminal from the United Kingdom in pursuance of a deportation order would breach rights of the foreign criminal under the EU treaties.
(5) Exception 4 is where the foreign criminal:
(a) is the subject of a certificate under Extradition Act 2003 s 2 or 70,
(b) is in custody pursuant to arrest under section 5 of that Act,
(c) is the subject of a provisional warrant under section 73 of that Act,
(d) is the subject of an authority to proceed under Extradition Act 1989 s 7 or an order under paragraph 4(2) of Schedule 1 to that Act, or
(e) is the subject of a provisional warrant under section 8 of that Act or of a warrant under paragraph 5(1)(b) of Schedule 1 to that Act.

(6) Exception 5 is where any of the following has effect in respect of the foreign criminal:

(a) a hospital order or guardianship order under Mental Health Act 1983 s 37,
(b) a hospital direction under section 45A of that Act,
(c) a transfer direction under section 47 of that Act,
(d) a compulsion order under Criminal Procedure (Scotland) Act 1995 s 57A,
(e) a guardianship order under section 58 of that Act,
(f) a hospital direction under section 59A of that Act,
(g) a transfer for treatment direction under Mental Health (Care and Treatment) (Scotland) Act 2003 s 136, or
(h) an order or direction under a provision which corresponds to a provision specified in paragraphs (a) to (g) and which has effect in relation to Northern Ireland.

(6A) Exception 6 is where the Secretary of State thinks that the application of section 32(4) and (5) would contravene the United Kingdom's obligations under the Council of Europe Convention on Action against Trafficking in Human Beings (done at Warsaw on 16 May 2005).

(7) The application of an exception:

(a) does not prevent the making of a deportation order,
(b) results in it being assumed neither that deportation of the person concerned is conducive to the public good nor that it is not conducive to the public good,

but section 32(4) applies despite the application of Exception 1 or 4.

Att-Gen's Ref No 20 of 2013 2013 EWCA Crim 1188 Section [32] obliges the Secretary of State to deport unless such a course would breach Convention rights or treaties. That is not the same as deportation itself being automatic, that is an automatic liability to deportation. The Court said in *R v Gebru* 2011 EWCA Crim 3321, 'The provisions described as "automatic deportation" in fact do not necessarily lead to the automatic deportation of an offender. The provisions lead to a liability for deportation.'

33.20 ***Rearranging the sentences to avoid automatic liability for deportation***

R v Hakimzadeh 2009 EWCA Crim 959, 2010 1 Cr App R (S) 10 (p 49) D pleaded to 14 counts of theft. The Court of Appeal considered that the appropriate sentence was 12 months. The defence asked for the sentences to be consecutive in part so no sentence was of 12+ months so automatic disqualification was not triggered. Held. Having regard to the age (they had been finished by 2000) of these offences, D's very substantial period of residence here and the fact that deportation was never in the Judge's mind, we do as suggested.

R v Gebru 2011 EWCA Crim 3321 The provisions described as 'automatic deportation' in fact do not necessarily lead to the automatic deportation of an offender. The provisions lead to a liability for deportation. Judges should not, therefore, pass a shorter sentence or a sentence different in nature from one they would otherwise have passed on the basis they have been informed that the offender is liable to automatic deportation.

R v Mintchev 2011 EWCA Crim 499 D was sentenced to 12 months for a section 20 wounding. He was in the final year of his law degree and of impeccable character. Held. The sentence could not be criticised. As a matter of principle, it would not be right to reduce an otherwise appropriate sentence so as to avoid the provisions of the UK Borders Act, because: a) sentences are intended to be commensurate with the seriousness of the offence, b) when passing sentence a judge is neither entitled nor obliged to reach a contrived result so as to avoid the operation of a statutory provision, and c) automatic deportation provisions are not a penalty included in the sentence. They are, instead, a consequence of the sentence so that Criminal Justice Act 116(3)[518] has no application. Authority points to the same conclusion. In *Att-Gen's Ref No 50 of 1997* 1998 2 Cr App R (S) 155, it was held that it was not appropriate for a sentence to be reduced to

[518] The judgment does not refer to a year. The only statute I know that would fit the context is Criminal Appeal Act 1968 s 11(3).

limit the extent of an offender's obligation to register under Sex Offenders Act 1997. Rose LJ said (at page 157), "[s]uch an approach cannot conceivably have been intended by Parliament because it would lead inevitably to a partial circumventing of the provisions of the Act itself..." It is difficult to see why the observations of Rose LJ should not apply with equal force in the present context. While it may be difficult to reconcile the decision in *R v Hakimzadeh* 2010 (above) with the approach suggested by the observations of Rose LJ, that decision can be explained as doing no more than approving the adjustment in the structure of an otherwise appropriate sentence in order to avoid the automatic liability for deportation provisions. There is no warrant for widening the ratio of *R v Hakimzadeh* 2010 and, thus explained, it does not bear on the issues in this case. It cannot be right to reduce the sentence simply to avoid automatic liability for deportation.

See also: *R v Turner* 2010 EWCA Crim 2897, 2011 2 Cr App R (S) 18 (p 102) (Speaking for ourselves, but without wishing to express a concluded view, we doubt whether it can be right to defeat the intention of Parliament by adjusting what would otherwise be a perfectly proper sentence.)

Note: I would expect the last three cases to be applied, rather than the first case. Ed.

33.21 ***Don't use other court powers to remove defendants from UK***

R (Dragoman) v Camberwell Green Magistrates' Court 2012 EWHC 4105 D, a Romanian, pleaded to theft and going equipped. The District Judge made a community order with a 12-month exclusion requirement, which excluded D from entering the UK for 12 months. Held. It was in effect an order for expulsion. The Magistrates' Court has no power to make the order. For more details about the case see **15.23**.

Procedure

33.22 ***Notice requirement***

Immigration Act 1971 s 6(2) A court may not recommend a person for deportation unless he has been given at least 7 days' notice in writing stating that a person is not liable for deportation if he is a British citizen, describing the persons who are British citizens and stating, so far as material, the effect of section 3(8) and section 7.

R v Omojudi 1992 13 Cr App R (S) 346 The court made a recommendation for deportation without giving the defendant the required notice of seven days or more prior to his court appearance and without inviting counsel to assist or to address the court. Held. It is of great importance that the statutory requirements of the Immigration Act 1971 and the guidelines in *R v Nazari and Others* 1980 71 Cr App R 87 are followed. Appeal allowed.

R v Abdi 2007 EWCA Crim 1913 Defence counsel said there was no evidence that D had been served notice of the impending recommendation for deportation. Held. We do not believe that the court should impute to Parliament an intention that failure to serve notice should necessarily render a recommendation for deportation invalid. No complaint can properly be made about the recommendation for deportation in this case. Appeal dismissed.

33.23 ***Judge must warn defence counsel***

R v Carmona 2006 EWCA Crim 508, 2 Cr App R (S) 102 (p 662) The judge should warn the advocate that he is considering making a recommendation for deportation in order for the advocate to be able to make such submissions and to put before the court such material as he thinks fit.

R v Haq 2013 EWCA Crim 1478, 2014 Cr App R (S) 52 (p 307) The Judge did not warn counsel. Held. The failure of a Judge to spell out that he was considering a recommendation is not necessarily fatal to the recommendation. Order considered and upheld.

33.24 ***There must be a full inquiry***

R v Nazari and Others 1980 71 Cr App R 87 It is clear that Parliament intended that there should be a full inquiry into a case before any recommendation for deportation is made.

R v Omojudi 1992 13 Cr App R (S) 346 The court made a recommendation for deportation without giving the defendant the required notice of seven days or more prior to his court appearance and without inviting counsel to assist or to address the court. Held. It is of great importance that the statutory requirements of the Immigration Act 1971 and the guidelines in *R v Nazari and Others* 1980 71 Cr App R 87 are followed. Appeal allowed.

R v Frank 1992 13 Cr App R (S) 500 D was sentenced to 2 years 9 months. The Judge then paused and said, "One moment. I also intend to recommend you for deportation." Held. Both the European Directive and the principles of natural justice require that before a recommendation is made there should be a full inquiry into the circumstances and reasons should be given for the recommendation. The addition of the words which followed the pause do not in any way comply with that which is required by law. Recommendation for deportation quashed.

R v Bozat and Others 1997 1 Cr App R (S) 270 It is imperative for the judge to spell out the reasons for making a recommendation and should not make such a recommendation as a matter of course. A recommendation should only be made after careful consideration of the guidelines in *R v Nazari and Others* 1980 71 Cr App R 87. Recommendation for deportation quashed.

R v Kibunyi 2009 EWCA Crim 9 Defence counsel said she was under the impression that D had applied for asylum. The Judge said D's account was stretching credulity but that he did not want the recommendation for deportation to stand if she was granted asylum. Held. We would not wish anything that we say in any way to indicate a prohibition upon a court, in an appropriate case, making a recommendation for deportation, even where it is said that an asylum application has been made or is to be made. The Judge, however, was clearly in two minds in relation to making a recommendation for deportation. The appropriate course would have been to conduct some form of *Newton* hearing after which a decision could have been made based on fact whether or not to make a recommendation for deportation.

Disputes as to facts see the **FACTUAL BASIS FOR SENTENCING** ***Same rules apply when imposing ancillary orders*** para at **57.26**.

Test to apply

33.25 ***Basic test Detriment requirement***

R v Nazari and Others 1980 71 Cr App R 87 Courts should keep in mind the following when considering whether to make a recommendation for deportation. These are guidelines and not rigid rules of law. There may be exceptions depending on the evidence.

The court must consider whether the offender's continued presence in the United Kingdom is to its detriment. This country has no use for criminals of other nationalities, particularly if they have committed serious crimes or have long criminal records. The more serious the crime and the longer the criminal record, the more obvious it is that there should be an order recommending deportation. A first offence, or a minor offence of shoplifting, may not normally justify a recommendation for deportation. However, a series of shoplifting offences, or a first offence of shoplifting carried out as part of a gang in a planned raid on a department store, might merit such a recommendation.

R v Benabbas 2005 EWCA Crim 2113 D pleaded to using a false instrument. He attempted to use a forged French passport to obtain a UK National Insurance number. The passport was in his name. There was no sign of anyone living at the address he gave to the police. D was an Algerian who had no right to be in the UK. The Judge sentenced him to 7 months and recommended deportation. Held, after reviewing the cases extensively. The statutory discretion is in itself unfettered, but, answering the purpose of its context, the *Nazari* approach of looking to the detriment of the defendant's presence in this country is well established as providing the rationality which informs the discretion. Where the defendant's presence in this country is lawful and regular, the

Nazari approach involves a relatively straightforward exercise of balancing the aggravation of the defendant's wrongdoing, present, past and potential, against the mitigation which he can pray in aid, which includes the interests of his family. That balance may on occasions be a difficult one to find (see *R v Altawel* 1981 3 Cr App R (S) 281, *R v Cravioto* 1990 12 Cr App R (S) 71), but the test and the elements in it are plain and, subject to the interests of the family, personal to the defendant (see *R v Nazari* 1980, *R v David* 1980, *R v Altawel* 1981, and *R v B* 2001 EWCA Crim 765, 2 Cr App R (S) 104 (p 464)). We say personal to the defendant, but of course the detriment still has to be judged by reference to the public interest and the requirements of public policy. As the ECJ put it in *Bouchereau* (at para 29), what the courts are concerned with is 'evidence of personal conduct constituting a present threat to the requirements of public policy'.

R v Carmona 2006 EWCA Crim 508, 2 Cr App R (S) 102 (p 662) The first question to be considered is whether the continued presence of the offender is to the detriment of this country, see Lawton LJ in the guideline case of *R v Nazari* 1980 2 Cr App R (S) 84. We do not think there is any difference of substance between this [detriment] test and the formulation whether it is in the public interest for the offender to be deported, or against the public interest for him to remain in this country. We [rely on] *N (Kenya) v Secretary of State for the Home Department* 2004 EWCA Civ 1094 at para 83, 'The "public good" and the "public interest" are wide-ranging but undefined concepts. The broad issues of social cohesion and public confidence in the administration of the system by which control is exercised over non-British citizens who enter and remain in the United Kingdom are engaged. They include an element of deterrence, to non-British citizens who are already here, even if they are genuine refugees, and to those minded to come, so as to ensure that they clearly understand that, whatever the circumstances, one of the consequences of serious crime may well be deportation.'

The question for the court is whether the offence and other material before the court lead to the conclusion that the continued presence of the offender is detrimental to this country. One serious offence is liable to lead to that conclusion, see, for example, *Kouyoumdjian* 1990 12 Cr App R (S) 35. In that connection, we refer to *N (Kenya) v Secretary of State for the Home Department* 2004 EWCA Civ 1094, para 64 and 65. Where a person who is not a British citizen commits a number of very serious crimes, the public interest side of the balance will include importantly, although not exclusively, the public policy need to deter and to express society's revulsion at the seriousness of the criminality. The risk of reoffending is a factor in the balance, but, for very serious crimes, a low risk of reoffending is not the most important public interest factor.

On the other hand, an offence that is not in itself so serious, such as shoplifting, against a history of previous offences, leading to a conclusion of likely reoffending, may justify a recommendation for deportation. We do not exclude the possibility of a first offence that is not in itself serious justifying a recommendation for deportation if the material before the court cogently leads to the conclusion that the offender is likely to continue repeatedly to reoffend.

R v Kluxen 2010 EWCA Crim 1081, 2011 1 Cr App R (S) 39 (p 249) The rights of the offender under European Convention on Human Rights arts 2, 3 and 8 should not be taken into account on the rare occasions when a recommendation for deportation is being considered. This is for the reasons explained in *R v Carmona* 2006 2 Cr App R (S) 102 (p 662) paras 15-22, namely that the Secretary of State and, in the event of an appeal against a deportation order, the Asylum and Immigration Tribunal, are able and better placed than a sentencing court to consider the offender's Convention rights.

33.26 ***Detriment requirement judged by the length of the sentence***

R v Carmona 2006 EWCA Crim 508, 2 Cr App R (S) 102 (p 662) The sentence imposed by the sentencing court is an indication of the seriousness of the offence, but no more than that. It is not appropriate to lay down a mathematical test for seriousness or for the making of a recommendation for deportation based on the length of the custodial sentence imposed by the court. We were told that the Home Secretary applies an unpublished rule of thumb where a recommendation for deportation has been made. He will not normally order deportation unless the offender has received a sentence of at least 1 year's imprisonment if he is not an EU national, and of at least 2 years if he is an EU national. This should not prevent sentencing judges making a recommendation for deportation when passing a lower sentence, provided that they are satisfied that the continued presence of the offender is against the public interest, but they should be cautious in doing so in such cases. We reject the submission that the court should never make a recommendation in such cases because it will not result in deportation. We bear in mind that the practice of the Home Secretary is subject to exceptions: he has not, as we understand it, fettered his discretion, and indeed he could not lawfully do so. We also bear in mind that the difference between a sentence that is less than, say, 2 years' imprisonment and one that is greater may result from factors that do not bear on the seriousness of the offence itself and which may not have a significant effect on the issue of public interest. For example, a plea of guilty by an offender may result in a sentence below the 2-year level, as may facts indicating that a period of custody may bear particularly hard on the offender for reasons personal to him or her. Indeed, these considerations should lead the Home Secretary to be cautious in the application of the rule of thumb to which we have referred.

33.27 ***Basic test Oppression in home country***

R v Nazari and Others 1980 71 Cr App R 87 Courts should keep in mind the following when considering whether to make a recommendation for deportation. These are guidelines and not rigid rules of law. There may be exceptions depending on the evidence.

The courts are not concerned with the political systems which operate in other countries. They may be harsh, they may be soft, they may be oppressive, and they may be the quintessence of democracy. The court has no knowledge of those matters over and above that which is common knowledge and it would be undesirable for any court to express its views about regimes which exist outside the UK. It is for the Home Secretary to determine in each case whether an offender's return to his country of origin would have consequences which would make his compulsory return unduly harsh. No doubt he will take into account the personal circumstances of each person and will consider the political situation in their country. These are matters for him and not for the courts.

R v Benabbas 2005 EWCA Crim 2113 D pleaded to using a false instrument. He attempted to use a forged French passport to obtain a UK National Insurance number. The passport was in his name. There was no sign of anyone living at the address he gave police. D was an Algerian who had no right to be in the UK. The Judge sentenced him to 7 months and recommended deportation. Held, after reviewing the cases extensively. The court generally does not embark and is in no position to embark on any assessment of what would happen to the defendant on return to his country of origin, *R v Nazari* 1980, *R v Altawel* 1981 3 Cr App R (S) 281 and *R v B* 2001 EWCA Crim 765, 2 Cr App R (S) 104 (p 464). Whether an order for deportation is made or not is ultimately for the Secretary of State.

R v Kluxen 2010 EWCA Crim 1081, 2011 1 Cr App R (S) 39 (p 249) The political situation in the country to which the offender may be deported (see *R v Nazari* 1980 at p 95 and *R v Carmona* 2006 2 Cr App R (S) 102 (p 662) at paragraphs 18 and 19) should not be taken into account on the rare occasions when a recommendation for deportation is being considered. This is for the reasons explained in *R v Carmona* 2006 paras 15-22, namely that the Secretary of State and, in the event of an appeal against a deportation order, the Asylum and Immigration Tribunal, are able and better placed than a sentencing court to consider the offender's Convention rights.

33.28 *Basic test Hardship and family considerations etc.*

R v Nazari and Others 1980 71 Cr App R 87 Courts should keep in mind the following when considering whether to make a recommendation for deportation. These are guidelines and not rigid rules of law. There may be exceptions depending on the evidence.

The court should consider the effects of a recommendation for deportation upon others not before the court. The court has no wish to break up families or impose hardships on innocent people.

R v Carmona 2006 EWCA Crim 508, 2 Cr App R (S) 102 (p 662) In *R v Nazari and Others* 1980 71 Cr App R 87, this Court stated that the effect that an order recommending deportation will have upon others who are not before the Court and who are innocent persons etc. had to be considered. It is to be noted that the Court of Appeal in *Nazari* did not suggest that hardship to the offender himself should be considered by the Court as a factor pointing against a recommendation for deportation. In subsequent cases this Court has quashed recommendations on the ground of the harm that would be suffered by innocent members of the offender's family, see *R v Cravioto* 1990 12 Cr App R (S) 71 and *R v Shittu* 1993 14 Cr App R (S) 283, but we have been referred to no case in which this Court has quashed a recommendation for deportation on the ground that deportation would harm the interests of the offender himself. Indeed, in *R v B* 2001 EWCA Crim 765, 2 Cr App R (S) 104 (p 464), this Court held that a sentencer should not consider difficulties of a personal nature that will affect the offender if he returns to his country of origin. In this case the offender, if deported, would have been returned to Kosovo. The Court reached its conclusion because, 'We have no means of assessing the appellant's likely personal circumstances in Kosovo'.

It should also be noted that the statement in *R v Nazari* that '[this] Court and all other Courts would have no wish to break up families or impose hardship on innocent people' was not intended and has not been understood literally. In appropriate cases this Court has upheld a recommendation for deportation even though its implementation would or might lead to the break-up of the offender's family, as in *R v Oddendaal* 1992 13 Cr App R (S) 341.

R v Kluxen 2010 EWCA Crim 1081, 2011 1 Cr App R (S) 39 (p 249) The rights of the offender under European Convention on Human Rights arts 2, 3 and 8 are not to be taken into account. This is for the reasons explained in *R v Carmona* 2006 2 Cr App R (S) 102 (p 662) paras 15-22, namely that the Secretary of State and, in the event of an appeal against a deportation order, the Asylum and Immigration Tribunal, are able and better placed than a sentencing court to consider the offender's Convention rights.

33.29 *Don't speculate about the Secretary of State's decision*

R v Yeboah 2010 EWCA Crim 2394 D pleaded to possessing a false identity document with intent. He was a Ghanaian national who came to the UK on a six-month visitor visa to visit his half-brother. He subsequently applied for an EU residence card on the basis that he was dependent on his half-brother, who was an EU citizen. That application was refused and was renewed. He obtained a job at Planet Hollywood by providing a forged letter from the Home Office stating that he had leave to remain, and a false National Insurance number. D was sentenced to 6 months, and therefore the Court had a discretion to recommend him for deportation. Held. The Judge, after a review of D's immigration history and status, concluded that it was likely that he would be removed irrespective of any decision made by the Judge. Whether a foreign national is to be deported is a matter for the Secretary of State, subject to an appeal to the Immigration Appeal Tribunal. Speculation as to its likely decision is an irrelevant consideration when judges are passing sentence in criminal cases.

On the facts, deportation recommendation correct/incorrect

33.30 *General*

Note: It is important to remember that following *R v Kluxen* 2010 EWCA Crim 1081, 2011 1 Cr App R (S) 39 (p 249), see **33.18**, deportation orders are not made where automatic liability for deportation applies. The following cases have to be read with that in mind. Ed.

33.31 *On the facts, recommendation correct/incorrect*

R v Halili 2009 EWCA Crim 25 D pleaded to two counts of possession of false identification with intent, fraud, and obtaining a pecuniary advantage by deception. D, an Albanian national, attempted to open a bank account using a Finnish passport. He had used a Belgian passport to obtain employment. A search of his home revealed several bank cards and other documents bearing the names in the passports. D, aged 21, was of previous good character. The pre-sentence report said D presented a low risk of reoffending and there was no evidence that he posed a risk of harm. The Judge said that there was an overarching public policy despite D's previous good character that a recommendation for deportation be made. Held. Taking into account the number and nature of the offences, we do not accept that the documents were for a legitimate purpose so the recommendation was properly made. Appeal dismissed.

R v Maya 2009 EWCA Crim 2427, 2010 Cr App R (S) 14 (p 85) D was convicted of using a false instrument, obtaining a pecuniary advantage by deception and two counts of fraud. D was a Congolese national and had used a false South African passport to enter the UK. He claimed asylum but his application was refused. D was in receipt of asylum seeker's benefits, including vouchers and accommodation, and was not entitled to work because of his immigration status. D used false identity documents and fabricated education and employment history to obtain work, earning almost £27,000 at the same time as receiving £15,000 in asylum benefits. D, aged 35, was of previous good character and the pre-sentence report said D posed no risk of reoffending. Held. This is a case where on numerous occasions D told lies, not only in the use of his passport but in his application for employment. He fabricated his education and employment history and earned good wages whilst enjoying benefits simultaneously. The trial Judge was correct in his assessment that D will represent a potential detriment to the United Kingdom if he remains in this country. Appeal dismissed.

R v Brown 2010 EWCA Crim 1807, 2011 1 Cr App R (S) 79 (p 482) D was convicted of dishonestly failing to disclose information (×2) and possession of a false identity document (×2). A recommendation for deportation was made. D was a Jamaican national who was given leave to remain contingent on her maintaining herself and any dependants without recourse to public funds. She subsequently applied for income support, housing and council tax benefits, using her passport with a counterfeit Home Office stamp and a counterfeit letter purporting to grant unrestricted entry and indefinite leave to remain. D received £4,748. The Judge sentenced D to 10 months and therefore she was not liable to be automatically deported. D was a single mother with one dependent child and no income and was of good character. She had travelled to the USA and Jamaica and returned to the UK with the false stamp in her passport. Held. She was not charged with using a false passport but the position was similar to that in *Benabbas*. She entered legally and has begun to repay the money obtained at £20 per month. The recommendation for deportation was correctly made.

R v Yeboah 2010 EWCA Crim 2394 D pleaded to possessing a false identity document with intent. He was a Ghanaian national who came to the UK on a six-month visitor visa to visit his half-brother. He subsequently applied for an EU residence card on the basis that he was dependent on his half-brother, who was an EU citizen. That application was refused and was renewed. He obtained a job at Planet Hollywood by providing a forged letter from the Home Office stating that he had leave to remain, and a false National Insurance number. D was sentenced to 6 months, and therefore the Court had a discretion to recommend D for deportation. Held. This case has no aggravating features. There is no persistent offending. D was of good character. We think that the recommendation for deportation was therefore wrong in principle.

R v Rajeswaran 2011 EWCA Crim 789 D pleaded to possession of a false identity document with intent. The Court also made a recommendation for deportation. Held. This case bears similarities to *R v Ovieriakhi*. However, there were additional aggravating factors. A reduction from 12 months to 8 results in automatic deportation no longer applying. The Court decided to make a recommendation for deportation as the offence was committed in order to circumvent immigration control.

R v Haq 2013 EWCA Crim 1478, 2014 Cr App R (S) 52 (p 307) D was convicted of four sexual assaults and an outraging public decency count. D targeted lone women. On the London Underground he: a) touched a woman's bottom with his hand, b) groped and pinched another, c) twice he forced his groin against a woman and continually pressed his erect penis against a woman's buttocks and d) for 20 minutes he masturbated under his clothing sitting opposite a woman. D received 12 months in all. His Oyster card showed a pattern of random travel on the Underground. He was in the UK illegally. Held. The Judge was right to say he was a sexual predator. There was a series of offences. The Judge was right to make the order.

See also: *R v Okhotnikov* 2008 EWCA Crim 1190, 2009 1 Cr App R (S) 33 (p 188) (Supplying false passports.)

R v Junab 2012 EWCA Crim 2660, 2013 2 Cr App R (S) 23 (p 159) (Overstayer obtained work in breach of her original entry condition. Used false passport and driving licence to obtain NI number. Plea to using false documents. Then absconded with her children. Given 6 months plus 1 month consecutive for breach of bail. Expert said deportation would have profound effect on children. We are obliged to ignore that. The Judge's approach was not wrong.)

33.32 *Explain sentence, Judge/Magistrate must Judge must give reasons*

Criminal Justice Act 2003 s 174(2)[519] The court must state in open court, in ordinary language and in general terms, the court's reasons for deciding on the sentence.

(3) The court must explain to the offender in ordinary language:

(a) the effect of the sentence,

(b) the effects of non-compliance with any order that the offender is required to comply with and that forms part of the sentence,

(c) any power of the court to vary or review any order that forms part of the sentence…

R v Bozat and Others 1997 1 Cr App R (S) 270 The sentencing Judge recommended that all the defendants be deported without giving reasons for doing so. Held. It is imperative for the judge to spell out the reasons for making a recommendation and should not make such a recommendation as a matter of course. A recommendation should only be made after careful consideration of the guidelines in *R v Nazari and Others* 1980 71 Cr App R 87. Recommendation for deportation quashed.

R v Carmona 2006 EWCA Crim 508, 2 Cr App R (S) 102 (p 662) The judge must give reasons for making a recommendation for deportation, which need not be lengthy but must show that the material issues have been addressed, *R v Rodney* 1996 2 Cr App R (S) 230. A failure to give adequate or any reasons will not necessarily lead to its being quashed, but will require this Court to reconsider the recommendation.

R v Chirimimanga and Others 2007 EWCA Crim 1684 A judge's failure to give full reasons is not a ground for quashing the recommendations that were made.

See also: *R v Rodney* 1996 2 Cr App R (S) 230 (We stress the crucial importance of giving reasons.)

R v Belaifa 1996 Unreported 26/2/96 (It is imperative for the judge to spell out his reasons. Recommendations without reasons are liable to be quashed.)

[519] As substituted by Legal Aid, Sentencing and Punishment of Offenders Act 2012 s 64

Status etc. and appeals against the recommendation

33.33 ***The recommendation is not part of the punishment of the offender***
R v Carmona 2006 EWCA Crim 508, 2 Cr App R (S) 102 (p 662) A recommendation for deportation is not part of the punishment imposed on the offender.

33.34 ***Deportation does not justify a reduction in sentence***
R v Carmona 2006 EWCA Crim 508, 2 Cr App R (S) 102 (p 662) The making of a recommendation for deportation does not justify a reduction in the sentence otherwise appropriate.
Att-Gen's Ref 2018 Re Abdoule 2018 EWCA Crim 1758 D was convicted of rape. Held. The possibility of deportation is irrelevant to the sentence and should have no effect on it, *Att-Gen's Ref 41 of 2013* 2013 EWCA Crim 1729, 2014 1 Cr App R (S) 80 (p 493).

33.35 ***Appealing/Challenging the recommendation***
Immigration Act 1971 s 6(5) Where a court recommends or purports to recommend a person for deportation, the validity of the recommendation shall not be called into question except on an appeal against the recommendation or against the conviction on which it is made. Thus the recommendation shall be treated as a sentence for the purpose of any enactment providing an appeal against sentence.
Note: So defendants can apply for leave to appeal against recommendations. Ed.

33.36 ***Appeals from the Magistrates' Court to the Crown Court***
Senior Courts Act 1981 s 48(2) The Crown Court may during any appeal confirm, reverse or vary any part of the decision appealed against.
Senior Courts Act 1981 s 48(4) If the appeal is against conviction or sentence [the power granted in this section] shall be construed as including power to award any punishment, whether more or less severe than that awarded in the Magistrates' Court.
Senior Courts Act 1981 s 48(6)(b) In this section 'sentence' includes any order made by the court including a recommendation for deportation.

33.37 ***Appeals No deportation order to be made while appeal is pending***
Immigration Act 1971 s 6(6) A deportation order shall not be made on the recommendation of a court so long as an appeal or further appeal is pending against the recommendation or against the conviction on which it was made. For this purpose an appeal or further appeal shall be treated as pending until the expiration of the time for bringing that appeal.

Combined with other orders

Automatic liability for deportation, Combined with, see **33.18**.

33.38 ***Conditional discharge, Combined with***
R v Akan 1972 56 Cr App R 716 The Judge decided to make a recommendation for deportation and pass a nominal sentence of imprisonment and suspend it. It was pointed out that if he did that he would not be able to release the defendant on bail. The Judge therefore decided to pass a conditional discharge. On appeal it was argued that, as a conditional discharge was deemed not to be a conviction,[520] the recommendation for deportation was unlawful. Held. The recommendation for deportation [can be made with a conditional discharge].
Note: In reality it would be rare that a case which warrants a conditional discharge could satisfy the detriment condition, see **33.25**. Ed.

33.39 ***Extradition, Combined with***
Old case: *R v Bow Street Magistrates' Court ex parte Van Der Holst* 1986 83 Cr App R 114 (A Magistrates' Court made a recommendation for deportation. Held. Extradition and deportation are very different creatures. The procedures are different. The objectives are different even though the consequences may be the same. There is nothing to suggest they are inconsistent with each other. Order for extradition upheld.)

[520] Under the then in force Criminal Justice Act 1948 s 12

33.40 ***Imprisonment, Combined with***

R v Gebru 2011 EWCA Crim 3321 The provisions described as 'automatic deportation' in fact do not necessarily lead to the automatic deportation of an offender. The provisions lead to a liability for deportation. Judges should not, therefore, pass a shorter sentence or a sentence different in nature from one they would otherwise have passed on the basis they have been informed that the offender is liable to automatic deportation.

33.41 ***Life imprisonment, Combined with***

Immigration Act 1971 s 6(4) A recommendation for deportation may be made with a sentence of imprisonment for life.

Note: However, after the introduction of automatic deportation it should not be made. Ed.

34 Derogatory Assertion Orders

34.1

Offences Breach of an order is a summary only offence.[521] The maximum sentence is an unlimited fine.[522] There are maximum fines for those aged under 18, see **13.44**.

Newspapers As the Derogatory Assertion Order can be made in the Crown Court, it seems inconceivable that the prosecution would consider summary proceedings suitable for a major national newspaper which made a great deal of money flouting an order. It seems likely that for those offences, contempt of court proceedings would be commenced. For assistance with the penalties and cases, see the **Perverting the Course of Justice/Contempt of Court/ Perjury etc.** chapter.

The definitions are listed in Criminal Procedure and Investigations Act 1996 s 59(2)-(3). How corporations should be prosecuted is determined by Criminal Procedure and Investigations Act 1996 s 60(4)-(6). The defences are set out in Criminal Procedure and Investigations Act 1996 s 60(3).

Purpose The measures contained in Criminal Procedure and Investigations Act 1996 s 58-61 are said to protect persons referred to in a speech in mitigation of sentence or a submission relating to sentence (for example, a victim or witness) by allowing judges and magistrates to impose reporting restrictions on derogatory assertions made during such a speech or submission, see *Home Office Circular 11/1997* para 26.

Advocates' responsibilities

34.2 ***Counsel's Code of conduct***

The Bar Standards Board Handbook May 2018

rC7 Where you are acting as an advocate, your duty not to abuse your role includes the following obligations:

rC7.1 you must not make statements or ask questions merely to insult, humiliate or annoy a witness or any other person,

rC7.2 you must not make a serious allegation against a witness whom you have had an opportunity to cross-examine unless you have given that witness a chance to answer the allegation in cross-examination,

rC7.3 you must not make a serious allegation against any person, or suggest that a person is guilty of a crime with which your client is charged unless:

a) you have reasonable grounds for the allegation, and
b) the allegation is relevant to your client's case or the credibility of a witness, and
c) where the allegation relates to a third party, you avoid naming them in open court unless this is reasonably necessary.

[Rest omitted.]

rC20 Where you are a BSB authorised individual, you are personally responsible for your own conduct and for your professional work. You must use your own professional

[521] Criminal Procedure and Investigations Act 1996 s 60(1)

[522] Legal Aid, Sentencing and Punishment of Offenders Act 2012 s 85(1) and (4) and Legal Aid, Sentencing and Punishment of Offenders Act 2012 (Commencement No 11) Order 2015 2015/504

judgement in relation to those matters on which you are instructed and be able to justify your decisions and actions. You must do this notwithstanding the views of your client, professional client, employer or any other person.

34.3 *Attorney-General's guidelines*

Attorney-General's Guidelines on the Acceptance of Pleas and the Prosecutor's Role in the Sentencing Exercise 2012 www.banksr.com Other Matters Guidelines tab

page 5 **E. Pleas in mitigation**

E1. The prosecution advocate must challenge any assertion by the defence in mitigation which is derogatory to a person's character (for instance, because it suggests that his or her conduct is or has been criminal, immoral or improper) and which is either false or irrelevant to proper sentencing considerations. If the defence advocate persists in that assertion, the prosecution advocate should invite the court to consider holding a Newton hearing to determine the issue.

E2. The defence advocate must not submit in mitigation anything that is derogatory to a person's character without giving advance notice in writing so as to afford the prosecution advocate the opportunity to consider their position under paragraph E1. When the prosecution advocate is so notified they must take all reasonable steps to establish whether the assertions are true. Reasonable steps will include seeking the views of the victim. This will involve seeking the views of the victim's family if the victim is deceased, and the victim's parents or legal guardian where the victim is a child. Reasonable steps may also include seeking the views of the police or other law enforcement authority, as appropriate. An assertion which is derogatory to a person's character will rarely amount to mitigation unless it has a causal connection to the circumstances of the offence or is otherwise relevant to proper sentencing considerations.

E3. Where notice has not been given in accordance with paragraph E2, the prosecution advocate must not acquiesce in permitting mitigation which is derogatory to a person's character. In such circumstances, the prosecution advocate should draw the attention of the court to the failure to give advance notice and seek time, and if necessary, an adjournment to investigate the assertion in the same way as if proper notice had been given. Where, in the opinion of the prosecution advocate, there are substantial grounds for believing that such an assertion is false or irrelevant to sentence, he or she should inform the court of their opinion and invite the court to consider making an order under Criminal Procedure and Investigations Act 1996 s 58(8), preventing publication of the assertion.

E4. Where the prosecution advocate considers that the assertion is, if true, relevant to sentence, or the court has so indicated, he or she should seek time, and if necessary an adjournment, to establish whether the assertion is true. If the matter cannot be resolved to the satisfaction of the parties, the prosecution advocate should invite the court to consider holding a Newton hearing to determine the issue.

34.4 *CPS guidance*

CPS Legal Guidance: Derogatory or Defamatory Mitigation Prosecuting advocates should be proactive in ensuring that derogatory or defamatory statements in mitigation are handled robustly.

[Unlike the requirement for counsel, there is] no similar express requirement in the Solicitors' Code of Conduct, and so prosecuting advocates should be alert to ensure as far as possible to challenge inappropriate assertions made in mitigation and that the court is reminded of its power to resolve issues by hearing evidence, in accordance with the Attorney-General's Guidelines.

Availability and test to apply

34.5 ***When do the provisions apply?***

Criminal Procedure and Investigations Act 1996 s 58(1) This section applies where a person has been convicted of an offence and a speech in mitigation is made by him or on his behalf before:

(a) a court determining what sentence should be passed on him in respect of the offence, or

(b) a Magistrates' Court determining whether he should be committed to the Crown Court for sentence.

(2) This section also applies where a sentence has been passed on a person in respect of an offence and a submission relating to the sentence is made by him or on his behalf before:

(a) a court hearing an appeal against or reviewing the sentence, or

(b) a court determining whether to grant leave to appeal against the sentence.

Home Office Circular 11/1997 para 27 A sentencing court, a Magistrates' Court considering committal to the Crown Court for sentence, a court hearing an appeal against or reviewing the sentence, or a court determining an application for leave to appeal against sentence may make an order under section 58(7) (interim order) or section 58(8) (full order) of the Act in relation to an assertion which is made during a mitigation speech or in a submission following sentence.

34.6 ***Power to make/Test to apply***

Criminal Procedure and Investigations Act 1996 s 58(4) Where there are substantial grounds for believing:

(a) that an assertion forming part of the speech or submission is derogatory to a person's character (for instance, because it suggests that his conduct is or has been criminal, immoral or improper), and

(b) that the assertion is false or that the facts asserted are irrelevant to the sentence,

the court may make an order under subsection (8) in relation to the assertion.

Criminal Procedure and Investigations Act 1996 s 58(3) Where it appears to the court that there is a real possibility that an order under subsection (8) will be made in relation to the assertion, the court may make an order under subsection (7) in relation to the assertion.

34.7 ***Test to apply Assertion previously made***

Criminal Procedure and Investigations Act 1996 s 58(5) An order under subsection (7) or (8) must not be made in relation to an assertion if it appears to the court that the assertion was previously made:

(a) at the trial at which the person was convicted of the offence, or

(b) during any other proceedings relating to the offence.

34.8 ***Full orders Availability etc.***

Criminal Procedure and Investigations Act 1996 s 58(6) Section 59 has effect where a court makes an order under subsection (7) (see **34.9**) or (8).

Criminal Procedure and Investigations Act 1996 s 58(8) An order under this subsection:

(a) may be made at any time before the court has made a determination with regard to sentencing, but only if it is made as soon as is reasonably practicable after the making of the determination,

(b) may be revoked at any time by the court,

(c) subject to paragraph (b), shall cease to have effect at the end of the period of 12 months beginning with the day on which it is made,

(d) may be made whether or not an order has been made under subsection (7) with regard to the case concerned.

34.9 ***Interim orders Availability etc.***

Criminal Procedure and Investigations Act 1996 s 58(6) Section 59 has effect where a court makes an order under subsection (7) or (8) (see **34.8**).

Criminal Procedure and Investigations Act 1996 s 58(7) An order under this subsection:

(a) may be made at any time before the court has made a determination with regard to sentencing,

(b) may be revoked at any time by the court,

(c) subject to paragraph (b), shall cease to have effect when the court makes a determination with regard to sentencing.

34.10 ***The order does not affect other orders***

Criminal Procedure and Investigations Act 1996 s 61(3) Nothing in section 58 or 59 affects any prohibition or restriction imposed by virtue of any other enactment on a publication or on matter included in a programme.

34.11 ***'Makes a determination with regard to sentencing', Definition of***

Criminal Procedure and Investigations Act 1996 s 58(9) For the purposes of subsection (7) and (8) the court makes a determination with regard to sentencing:

(a) when it determines what sentence should be passed (where this section applies by virtue of subsection (1)(a)), see **34.5**,

(b) when it determines whether the person should be committed to the Crown Court for sentence (where this section applies by virtue of subsection (1)(b)), see **34.5**,

(c) when it determines what the sentence should be (where this section applies by virtue of subsection (2)(a)), see **34.5**,

(d) when it determines whether to grant leave to appeal (where this section applies by virtue of subsection (2)(b)), see **34.5**.

34.12 ***The order must not be made if the assertion was made at trial etc.***

Criminal Procedure and Investigations Act 1996 s 58(5) An order under subsection (7) or (8) must not be made in relation to an assertion if it appears to the court that the assertion was previously made:

(a) at the trial at which the person was convicted of the offence, or

(b) during any other proceedings relating to the offence,

(c) when it determines what the sentence should be (where this section applies by virtue of subsection (2)(a)),

(d) when it determines whether to grant leave to appeal (where this section applies by virtue of subsection (2)(b)).

34.13 ***The orders Reporting restrictions***

Criminal Procedure and Investigations Act 1996 s 58(6) Section 59 has effect where a court makes an order under subsection (7) or (8).

Criminal Procedure and Investigations Act 1996 s 59(1) Where a court makes an order under section 58(7) or (8) in relation to any assertion, at any time when the order has effect the assertion must not:

(a) be published in Great Britain in a written publication available to the public, or

(b) be included in a relevant programme for reception in Great Britain.

(2) In this section:

'relevant programme' means a programme included in a programme service, within the meaning of Broadcasting Act 1990,

'written publication' includes a film, a soundtrack and any other record in permanent form but does not include an indictment or other document prepared for use in particular legal proceedings.

(3) For the purposes of this section an assertion is published or included in a programme if the material published or included:

(a) names the person about whom the assertion is made or, without naming him, contains enough to make it likely that members of the public will identify him as the person about whom it is made, and

(b) reproduces the actual wording of the matter asserted or contains its substance.

Other matters

34.14 ***Guidance***

Home Office Circular 11/1997 para 28 The court may have to complete some enquiries before making a full order and so the power to make interim orders exists.

Note: Criminal Practice Directions 2015 EWCA Crim 1567 para I 6B.1 provides guidance about open justice and reporting restrictions can be found in *Reporting Restrictions in the Criminal Courts 2014*, which was issued by the Judicial College, the Newspaper Society, the Society of Editors and the Media Lawyers Association. Ed.

34.15 ***Notice to be given to the press***

Home Office Circular 11/1997 para 31 It will be important to ensure that the order which prohibits publication of the specific derogatory assertion under section 59 of the Act is brought to the attention of the press and other media representatives, for example radio and television broadcasters. It will be for the court to take steps promptly to inform the appropriate sections of the media of the order, and to decide whether the information needs to be circulated beyond the local media to the national media, for example the Press Association. If there is any doubt about whether or not the national media are likely to be interested, they should be notified of the order. (The reporting restrictions relate to written publications which are published in Great Britain and to programmes for reception in Great Britain. "National" media should be construed accordingly for these purposes.)

33 It will also be appropriate to display a copy of the notice in some prominent position within the court complex to which the public has access. The notice should be displayed for at least 28 days from the date on which it was made.

34 Your attention is also drawn to Practice Direction 1983 76 Cr App R 78 in relation to reporting restrictions. This says that, where a court makes an order that publication of any report of proceedings may be postponed or prohibited, courts will normally give notice to the press in some form that an order has been made and court staff should be prepared to answer any query about a specific case. But as far as the media are concerned it is, and will remain, the responsibility of those reporting cases, and their editors, to ensure that no breach of any order occurs and the onus rests with them to make enquiries in any case of doubt.

34.16 ***Appeals from the Crown Court***

Criminal Justice Act 1988 s 159(1) A person aggrieved may appeal to the Court of Appeal, if that court grants leave, against:

(aa) an order made by the Crown Court under Criminal Procedure and Investigations Act 1996 s 58(7) or (8) in a case where the Court has convicted a person on a trial on indictment.

35 Destruction Orders: Animals

35.1

Animal Welfare Act 2006 s 37(1)

Children and young offenders The order is available whatever the age of the offender.

Destruction in the interests of the animal

35.2 ***Power to order***

Animal Welfare Act 2006 s 37(1) The court by or before which a person is convicted of an offence under:

section 4 (unnecessary suffering),
section 5 (mutilation),
section 6(1) and (2) (docking of dogs' tails),
section 7 (administration of poisons etc.),
section 8(1) and (2) (fighting etc.), and
section 9 (failure to ensure welfare of animal responsible for),

may order the destruction of an animal in relation to which the offence was committed[523] if it is satisfied, on the basis of evidence given by a veterinary surgeon, that it is appropriate to do so in the interests of the animal.
Animal Welfare Act 2006 s 37(6) In subsection (1), the reference to an animal in relation to which an offence was committed includes, in the case of an offence under section 8(1) or (2), an animal which took part in an animal fight in relation to which the offence was committed.

35.3 ***Destruction of the animal, The administration of the***
Animal Welfare Act 2006 s 37(3) Where a court makes an order under subsection (1) (see **35.2**), it may:
(a) appoint a person to carry out, or arrange for the carrying out of, the order,
(b) require a person who has possession of the animal to deliver it up to enable the order to be carried out,
(c) give directions with respect to the carrying out of the order (including directions about how the animal is to be dealt with until it is destroyed),
(d) confer additional powers (including power to enter premises where the animal is being kept) for the purpose of, or in connection with, the carrying out of the order,
(e) order the offender or another person to reimburse the expenses of carrying out the order.

35.4 ***Representations, Right to make Restrictions on making the order***
Animal Welfare Act 2006 s 37(2) A court may not make an order under subsection (1) (see **35.2**), unless:
(a) it has given the owner of the animal an opportunity to be heard, or
(b) it is satisfied that it is not reasonably practicable to communicate with the owner.

Destruction after conviction for fighting etc.

35.5 ***Power to destroy***
Animal Welfare Act 2006 s 38(1) The court by or before which a person is convicted of an offence under section 8(1) or (2) (fighting etc.) may order the destruction of an animal in relation to which the offence was committed[524] on grounds other than the interests of the animal.
Animal Welfare Act 2006 s 38(5) In subsection (1), the reference to an animal in relation to which the offence was committed includes an animal which took part in an animal fight in relation to which the offence was committed.

35.6 ***Representations, Right to make***
Animal Welfare Act 2006 s 38(2) A court may not make an order under subsection (1) (see **35.2**), unless:
(a) it has given the owner of the animal an opportunity to be heard, or
(b) it is satisfied that it is not reasonably practicable to communicate with the owner.
Disputes as to facts see the **Factual basis for Sentencing** ***Same rules apply when imposing ancillary orders*** para at **57.26**.

35.7 ***Destruction of the animal, The administration of the***
Animal Welfare Act 2006 s 38(3) Where a court makes an order under subsection (1) (see **35.2**), it may:
(a) appoint a person to carry out, or arrange for the carrying out of, the order,
(b) require a person who has possession of the animal to deliver it up to enable the order to be carried out,
(c) give directions with respect to the carrying out of the order (including directions about how the animal is to be dealt with until it is destroyed),

[523] Animal Welfare Act 2006 s 37(6) In subsection (1), the reference to an animal in relation to which an offence was committed includes, in the case of an offence under section 8(1) or (2), an animal which took part in an animal fight in relation to which the offence was committed.
[524] Animal Welfare Act 2006 s 38(5) In subsection (1), the reference to an animal in relation to which the offence was committed includes an animal which took part in an animal fight in relation to which the offence was committed.

(d) confer additional powers (including power to enter premises where the animal is being kept) for the purpose of, or in connection with, the carrying out of the order,
(e) order the offender or another person to reimburse the expenses of carrying out the order.

Appeals

35.8 *Appeals*

Magistrates' Courts Act 1980 s 108(1) A person convicted by a Magistrates' Court may appeal to the Crown Court:
(a) if he pleaded guilty, against his sentence;
(b) if he did not, against the conviction or sentence.

Magistrates' Courts Act 1980 s 108(3) In this section 'sentence' includes any order made on conviction by a Magistrates' Court, not being:..c) an order under Animal Welfare Act 2006 s 37(1) (which enables a court to order the destruction of an animal, see **35.2**).

Animal Welfare Act 2006 s 37(4) Where a court makes an order under subsection (1) (see **35.2**), each of the offenders and, if different, the owner of the animal may:
(a) in the case of an order made by a Magistrates' Court, appeal against the order to the Crown Court,
(b) in the case of an order made by the Crown Court, appeal against the order to the Court of Appeal.

(5) Subsection (4) does not apply if the court by which the order is made directs that it is appropriate in the interests of the animal that the carrying out of the order should not be delayed.

Note: The purpose of these two different sections is far from clear. Ed.

Animal Welfare Act 2006 s 41(1) Nothing may be done under an order under section 33, 35, 37 or 38 with respect to an animal or an order under section 40 unless:
(a) the period for giving notice of appeal against the order has expired,
(b) the period for giving notice of appeal against the conviction on which the order was made has expired, and
(c) if the order or conviction is the subject of an appeal, the appeal has been determined or withdrawn.

(2) Subsection (1) does not apply to an order under section 37(1) if the order is the subject of a direction under subsection (5) of that section.

35.9 *Appeals Directions pending an appeal*

Animal Welfare Act 2006 s 41(3) Where the effect of an order is suspended under subsection (1):
(a) no requirement imposed or directions given in connection with the order shall have effect, but
(b) the court may give directions about how any animal to which the order applies is to be dealt with during the suspension.

(4) Directions under subsection (3)(b) may, in particular:
(a) authorise the animal to be taken into possession,
(b) authorise the removal of the animal to a place of safety,
(c) authorise the animal to be cared for either on the premises where it was being kept when it was taken into possession or at some other place,
(d) appoint a person to carry out, or arrange for the carrying out of, the directions,
(e) require any person who has possession of the animal to deliver it up for the purposes of the directions,
(f) confer additional powers (including power to enter premises where the animal is being kept) for the purpose of, or in connection with, the carrying out of the directions,
(g) provide for the recovery of any expenses in relation to removal or care of the animal which are incurred in carrying out the directions.

(5) Any expenses a person is directed to pay under subsection (4)(g) shall be recoverable summarily as a civil debt.

35.10 ***Appeals*** ***Restriction on the right of appeal***

Animal Welfare Act 2006 s 37(5) Subsection (4) (see **35.8**) does not apply if the court by which the order is made directs that it is appropriate in the interests of the animal that the carrying out of the order should not be delayed.

Animal Welfare Act 2006 s 41(2) Subsection (1) (see **35.8**) does not apply to an order under section 37(1) (see **35.2**) if the order is the subject of a direction under section 37(5).

35.11 ***From the Magistrates' Court*** ***Fighting offences***

Animal Welfare Act 2006 s 38(4)(a) Where a court makes an order under subsection (1) in relation to an animal which is owned by a person other than the offender, that person may:

(a) in the case of an order made by a Magistrates' Court, appeal against the order to the Crown Court.

35.12 ***From the Crown Court*** ***Fighting offences***

Animal Welfare Act 2006 s 38(4)(b) Where a court makes an order under subsection (1) (see **35.2**), in relation to an animal which is owned by a person other than the offender, that person may:

(b) in the case of an order made by the Crown Court, appeal against the order to the Court of Appeal.

35.13 ***Pending appeals etc.*** ***Suspension of order***

Animal Welfare Act 2006 s 41(1) Nothing may be done under an order under section 33, 35, 37 or 38 with respect to an animal or an order under section 40 unless:

(a) the period for giving notice of appeal against the order has expired,

(b) the period for giving notice of appeal against the conviction on which the order was made has expired, and

(c) if the order or conviction is the subject of an appeal, the appeal has been determined or withdrawn.

35.14 ***Pending appeals etc.*** ***Suspension of order*** ***Effect***

Animal Welfare Act 2006 s 41(3) Where the effect of an order is suspended under subsection (1) (see **35.2**):

(a) no requirement imposed or directions given in connection with the order shall have effect, but

(b) the court may give directions about how any animal to which the order applies is to be dealt with during the suspension.

(4) Directions under subsection (3)(b) may, in particular:

(a) authorise the animal to be taken into possession,

(b) authorise the removal of the animal to a place of safety,

(c) authorise the animal to be cared for either on the premises where it was being kept when it was taken into possession or at some other place,

(d) appoint a person to carry out, or arrange for the carrying out of, the directions,

(e) require any person who has possession of the animal to deliver it up for the purposes of the directions,

(f) confer additional powers (including power to enter premises where the animal is being kept) or the purpose of, or in connection with, the carrying out of the directions,

(g) provide for the recovery of any expenses[525] in relation to removal or care of the animal which are incurred in carrying out the directions.

[525] Animal Welfare Act 2006 s 41(5). Any expenses a person is directed to pay under subsection (4)(g) shall be recoverable summarily as a civil debt.

36 Destruction Orders: Dogs

36.1

Dangerous Dogs Act 1991 s 4, 4A and 4B

Children and young offenders The order is available whatever the age of the offender.

Offences Failure to deliver up a dog for destruction is an offence under Dangerous Dogs Act 1991 s 4(8) and is a summary only offence. Maximum sentence is an unlimited fine.[526] There are maximum fines for those aged under 18, see **13.44**).

Civil power For the civil power to order destruction of a dog, see para **36.9**.

Statutory provisions

36.2 ***Destruction Orders Statutory power to order***

Dangerous Dogs Act 1991 s 4(1)(a) Where a person is convicted of an offence under section 1 or 3(1) (see **245.1** in Volume 2) or of an offence under an order made under section 2, the court may order the destruction of any dog in respect of which the offence was committed and, subject to subsection (1A) below, shall do so in the case of an offence under section 1 or an aggravated offence under section 3(1).[527]

Dangerous Dogs Act 1991 s 4(1A) Nothing in subsection (1)(a) above shall require the court to order the destruction of a dog if the court is satisfied that the dog would not constitute a danger to public safety.

Anti-social Behaviour, Crime and Policing Act 2014 s 107(3) inserted a new section 4(1B).[528]

Dangerous Dogs Act 1991 s 4(1B) For the purposes of subsection (1A)(a), when deciding whether a dog would constitute a danger to public safety, the court:

(a) must consider:

(i) the temperament of the dog and its past behaviour, and

(ii) whether the owner of the dog, or the person for the time being in charge of it, is a fit and proper person to be in charge of the dog, and

(b) may consider any other relevant circumstances.

36.3 ***Destruction Orders Restrictions on the destruction of the dog***

Dangerous Dogs Act 1991 s 4(3) A dog shall not be destroyed pursuant to an order under subsection (1)(a):

(a) until the end of the period for giving notice of appeal against the conviction or against the order, and

(b) if notice of appeal is given within that period, until the appeal is determined or withdrawn,

unless the offender and, in a case to which subsection (2) above applies, the owner of the dog, give notice to the court that made the order that there is to be no appeal.

(4) Where a court makes an order under subsection (1)(a) it may:

(a) appoint a person to undertake the destruction of the dog and require any person having custody of it to deliver it up for that purpose, and

(b) order the offender to pay such sum as the court may determine to be the reasonable expenses of destroying the dog and of keeping it pending its destruction.

(5) Any sum ordered to be paid under subsection (4)(b) above shall be treated for the purposes of enforcement as if it were a fine imposed on conviction.

36.4 ***Dangerous Dog Offences Guideline 2016 Dog dangerously out of control***

Note: This guidance applies to all the four different ways to commit the Dangerous Dogs Act 1991 s 3(1) offence. For each of the four sections for this offence in the guideline the

[526] Legal Aid, Sentencing and Punishment of Offenders Act 2012 s 85(1) and (4) and Legal Aid, Sentencing and Punishment of Offenders Act 2012 (Commencement No 11) Order 2015 2015/504

[527] Anti-social Behaviour, Crime and Policing Act 2014 s 106(3) removed the 'or (3)' which was at the end of the subsection.

[528] In force 13/5/14, Anti-social Behaviour, Crime and Policing Act 2014 (Commencement No 2, Transitional and Transitory Provisions) Order 2014 2014/949 para 7

guidance is the same, except that: a) where death or injury is caused or an assistance dog is killed or injured, para A applies, and b) where there is no injury or death, para B applies. Ed.

Dangerous Dog Offences Guideline 2016, see www.banksr.com Other Matters Guidelines tab pages 7, 13, 19 and 25. In force 1 July 2016

Destruction order/contingent destruction order

In any case where the offender is not the owner of the dog, the owner must be given an opportunity to be present and make representations to the court.

If the dog is a prohibited dog, refer to the guideline for possession of a prohibited dog in relation to destruction/contingent destruction orders, see **36.5**.

[Para A Where death or injury is caused or an assistance dog is killed or injured] The court **shall** make a destruction order unless the court is satisfied that the dog would not constitute a danger to public safety.

[Para B Where there is no injury or death] If the dog is not prohibited and the court is satisfied that the dog would constitute a danger to public safety the court **may** make a destruction order.

In reaching a decision, the court should consider the relevant circumstances which **must** include:

- the temperament of the dog and its past behaviour;
- whether the owner of the dog, or the person for the time being in charge of it, is a fit and proper person to be in charge of the dog;

and **may** include:

- other relevant circumstances.

If the court is satisfied that the dog would not constitute a danger to public safety and the dog is not prohibited, it **may** make a contingent destruction order requiring the dog be kept under proper control. A contingent destruction order may specify the measures to be taken by the owner for keeping the dog under proper control, which include:

- muzzling;
- keeping on a lead;
- neutering in appropriate cases; and
- excluding it from a specified place.

Where the court makes a destruction order, it **may** appoint a person to undertake destruction and order the offender to pay what it determines to be the reasonable expenses of destroying the dog and keeping it pending its destruction.

Fit and proper person

In determining whether a person is a fit and proper person to be in charge of a dog the following non-exhaustive factors may be relevant:

- any relevant previous convictions, cautions or penalty notices;
- the nature and suitability of the premises that the dog is to be kept at by the person;
- where the police have released the dog pending the court's decision whether the person has breached conditions imposed by the police; and
- any relevant previous breaches of court orders.

36.5 *Sentencing Council guidelines Possession of/Breeding/selling etc. a prohibited dog*

Dangerous Dog Offences Guideline 2016, see www.banksr.com Other Matters Guidelines tab. In force 1 July 2016

page 31 Possession of a prohibited dog/Breeding, selling etc. a prohibited dog, Dangerous dogs Act 1991 s 1(7)

Destruction order/contingent destruction order

In any case where the offender is not the owner of the dog, the owner must be given an opportunity to be present and make representations to the court.

The court **shall** make a destruction order unless the court is satisfied that the dog would not constitute a danger to public safety.

In reaching a decision, the court should consider the relevant circumstances which must include:

- the temperament of the dog and its past behaviour;
- whether the owner of the dog, or the person for the time being in charge of it, is a fit and proper person to be in charge of the dog;

and **may** include:

- other relevant circumstances.

If the court is satisfied that the dog would not constitute a danger to public safety, it shall make a contingent destruction order requiring that the dog be exempted from the prohibition on possession or custody within the requisite period.

Where the court makes a destruction order, it **may** appoint a person to undertake destruction and order the offender to pay what it determines to be the reasonable expenses of destroying the dog and keeping it pending its destruction.

Fit and proper person

In determining whether a person is a fit and proper person to be in charge of a dog the following non-exhaustive factors may be relevant:

- any relevant previous convictions, cautions or penalty notices;
- the nature and suitability of the premises that the dog is to be kept at by the person;
- where the police have released the dog pending the court's decision whether the person has breached conditions imposed by the police; and
- any relevant previous breaches of court orders.

Note: the court must be satisfied that the person who is assessed by the court as a fit and proper person can demonstrate that they are the owner or the person ordinarily in charge of that dog at the time the court is considering whether the dog is a danger to public safety. Someone who has previously not been in charge of the dog should not be considered for this assessment because it is an offence under the Dangerous Dogs Act 1991 to make a gift of a prohibited dog.

36.6 *Destruction Orders Test to apply*

Note: For how to approach the test, see the *Dangerous Dog Offences Guideline 2016* at **36.4**. Ed.

Kelleher v DPP 2012 EWHC 2978 (Admin) High Court D pleaded to two counts of being in charge of a dog dangerously out of control and two counts of failing to comply with a control order.[529] D's two dogs were subject to control orders arising from previous incidents, neither of which had involved any injury to the public. In September 2009, one of D's dogs, which was muzzled, escaped and went for another dog. D's second dog, which was unmuzzled, then managed to get free and bit the other dog, whose owner was extremely upset and distressed by the incident. An expert indicated controls which would, in his view, ensure that the dogs were not a danger to the public. A destruction order was nonetheless made against both dogs and D appealed to the Crown Court. Since the first hearing, D's living arrangements had changed and two years had passed, during which there were no problems with the dogs. The Judge in the Crown Court purportedly applied the test in section 4(1A) but went on to uphold the order. He also found that since the move was recent there was no opportunity to assess the new arrangements and the dogs' dangerousness. Held. In an aggravated case there must be a destruction order unless the dog would not constitute a danger to public safety. The burden is on the defendant to show that the dog is not a danger to public safety. In a non-aggravated case the court will not make a destruction order unless, on the material, the court takes a view that it is necessary. Destruction order quashed and case remitted for reconsideration.

Note: In sentencing, burdens of proof are out of fashion. The Court of Appeal considers that decisions should be made by evaluating the factors in the case. Ed.

[529] The Court said this was what was charged and so it is assumed that is what D pleaded to.

36.7 ***Contingent Destruction Orders Statutory provisions***
Dangerous Dogs Act 1991 s 4A(1) Where:

(a) a person is convicted of an offence under section 1 or an aggravated offence under section 3(1) or (3),[530]
(b) the court does not order the destruction of the dog under section 4(1)(a), and
(c) in the case of an offence under section 1, the dog is subject to the prohibition in section 1(3).[531]

the court shall order that, unless the dog is exempted from that prohibition within the requisite period, the dog shall be destroyed.
(2) Where an order is made under subsection (1) in respect of a dog, and the dog is not exempted from the prohibition in section 1(3) within the requisite period, the court may extend that period.
(3) Subject to subsection (2) above, the requisite period for the purposes of such an order is the period of two months beginning with the date of the order.
(4) Where a person is convicted of an offence under section 3(1) or (3)[532] above, the court may order that, unless the owner of the dog keeps it under proper control, the dog shall be destroyed.
(5) An order under subsection (4) above:

(a) may specify the measures to be taken for keeping the dog under proper control, whether by muzzling, keeping on a lead, excluding it from specified places or otherwise, and
(b) if it appears to the court that the dog is a male and would be less dangerous if neutered, may require it to be neutered.

(6) Subsections (2) to (4) of section 4 shall apply in relation to an order under subsection (1) or (4) as they apply in relation to an order under subsection (1)(a) of that section.
Kelleher v DPP 2012 EWHC 2978 (Admin) High Court D pleaded to two counts of being in charge of a dog dangerously out of control in a public place and two counts of failing to comply with a control order.[533] D challenged a Destruction Order. Held. Subsection 4A(1) makes no sense, and is only concerned with section 1 (dogs bred for fighting), so the only sensible way to read it is to omit 'or an aggravated offence under section 3(1) or (3)'. It is singularly ill-drafted.

36.8 ***Contingent Destruction Orders Burden and standard of proof***
R v Davies 2010 EWCA Crim 1923 D was convicted of being in charge of a dangerously out-of-control dog. Held. Applying normal principles, the burden of satisfying the court falls on the party making the assertion to the civil standard. It is the defendant who is seeking to displace a mandatory consequence and it is the defendant who will normally be the owner of the dog, and he or she will be best placed to know about and adduce evidence of the dog's characteristics.
For more details, see **36.11**.

36.9 ***Statutory power to destroy otherwise than on a conviction***
Note: This is a power to order a dog to be destroyed when there has been no conviction. It is a civil power exercised by magistrates. Ed.
Dangerous Dogs Act 1991 s 4B(1) Where a dog is seized under section 5(1) or (2) below or in exercise of a power of seizure conferred by any other enactment[534] and it appears to a justice of the peace:

530 Anti-social Behaviour, Crime and Policing Act 2014 s 106(4)(a) removed the 'or (3)' which was at the end of the subsection.
531 The punctuation is Parliament's. Ed.
532 Anti-social Behaviour, Crime and Policing Act 2014 s 106(4)(a) removed the 'or (3)' which was at the end of the subsection.
533 The Court said this was what was charged and so it is assumed that is what D pleaded to.
534 As amended by Anti-social Behaviour, Crime and Policing Act 2014 s 107(4)(a)

(a) that no person has been or is to be prosecuted for an offence under this Act or an order under section 2 in respect of that dog (whether because the owner cannot be found or for any other reason), or

(b) that the dog cannot be released into the custody or possession of its owner without the owner contravening the prohibition in section 1(3) above,

he may order the destruction of the dog and, subject to subsection (2) below, shall do so if it is one to which section 1 above applies.

(2) Nothing in subsection (1)(b) shall require the justice to order the destruction of a dog if he is satisfied:

(a) that the dog would not constitute a danger to public safety, and

(b) where the dog was born before 30 November 1991 and is subject to the prohibition in section 1(3) above, that there is a good reason why the dog has not been exempted from that prohibition.

(2A) For the purposes of subsection (2)(a), when deciding whether a dog would constitute a danger to public safety, the justice or sheriff:

(a) must consider:

(i) the temperament of the dog and its past behaviour, and

(ii) whether the owner of the dog, or the person for the time being in charge of it, is a fit and proper person to be in charge of the dog, and

(b) may consider any other relevant circumstances.[535]

(3) Where in a case falling within subsection (1)(b) the justice does not order the destruction of the dog, he shall order that, unless the dog is exempted from the prohibition in section 1(3) within the requisite period, the dog shall be destroyed.

(4) Subsections (2) to (4) of section 4 shall apply in relation to an order under subsection (1)(b) or (3) above as they apply in relation to an order under subsection (1)(a) of that section.

(5) Subsections (2) and (3) of section 4A above shall apply in relation to an order under subsection (3) above as they apply in relation to an order under subsection (1) of that section, except that the reference to the court in subsection (2) of that section shall be construed as a reference to the justice.

R v Walton Street JJs ex parte Crothers 1992 Crim LR 875 A prosecution was discontinued against D for three offences under Dangerous Dogs Act 1991. The Magistrates had heard an application by the police for the destruction of D's dog and made the order. D asserted that there was no jurisdiction and that he had not been given a chance to make representations. Held. A person who has been summoned but against whom proceedings have been discontinued has nonetheless been prosecuted (see section 4B(1)(a)). The rules of natural justice require that an owner of property should be given an opportunity to be heard in any case involving the destruction of that property. Order quashed.

R v Walton Street JJs ex parte Crothers (No 2) 1996 160 JP 427 A previous Destruction Order had been quashed (see above). F gave the dog to C, who requested its release from the police. The police handed the dog over but immediately re-seized him. Another Destruction Order was sought under section 4B. Held. If the prosecution was discontinued the dog must be released to the owner but could lawfully be re-seized and subjected to a Destruction Order in civil proceedings.

See also: *R v Haringey Magistrates' Court ex parte Cragg* 1997 161 JP 61 (It was an abuse of process to bring fresh proceedings under section 5(4) (a Destruction Order when no one had been prosecuted etc., now repealed). Order quashed.)

Webb v Chief Constable of Avon 2017 EWHC 3311 D was prosecuted for [presumably] possession of a prohibited dog. [The case is factually and legally complicated.] A

[535] As inserted by Anti-social Behaviour, Crime and Policing Act 2014 s 107(4). In force 13/5/14

contingency order was made. The case eventually reached the High Court. Held. Someone who wished to be the registered keeper could not apply for a certificate of exemption. [The complexities of this case are not listed.]

36.10 ***Must inform the owner***

Dangerous Dog Offences Guideline 2016, see www.banksr.com Other Matters Guidelines tab pages 7, 13, 19 and 25 In any case where the offender is not the owner of the dog, the owner must be given an opportunity to be present and make representations to the court.

R v Trafford Magistrates' Court ex parte Riley 1996 160 JP 418 R owned an Alsatian dog which, whilst under the control of T, broke free and bit a policeman. T was convicted of an offence under Dangerous Dogs Act 1991 s 3 and the Magistrates were bound to make a Destruction Order. R was not given notice of the hearing. Held. The failure to give R notice of the hearing was a breach of natural justice.

See also: *R v Ealing Magistrates' Court ex parte Fanneran* 1996 160 JP 409 (It was a breach of natural justice not to inform the defendant of the hearing in which the Destruction Order was made.)

Disputes as to facts see the **FACTUAL BASIS FOR SENTENCING** ***Same rules apply when imposing ancillary orders*** para at **57.26**.

Making the order

36.11 ***Contingent Destruction Order or Destruction Order?***

Note: For how to approach the issue, see the *Dangerous Dog Offences Guideline 2016* at **36.4**. Ed.

R v Flack 2008 EWCA Crim 204, 2010 2 Cr App R (S) 70 (p 395) D pleaded, on rearraignment, to being the owner of a dog which had caused injury while dangerously out of control in public, and to being the owner of another dog dangerously out of control in public (Destruction Order and Contingent Destruction Order). V and her husband were walking through a park when V's husband noticed D's two dogs running towards them. He remarked that V should take care. However, before V could take evasive action, the dogs attacked her lower left leg. One of the dogs bit her leg, ripping her trousers and causing a severe wound which bled profusely. D's partner subsequently visited V's home and admitted that the dogs were hers. V's husband visited D's home and identified which of the two dogs was responsible for causing the injury. D pleaded on a specific basis, namely that an unknown third party had opened the gate behind which the dogs were secured, thereby allowing them to escape. An animal behaviour consultant reported that, in a two-hour assessment, the dogs displayed no signs of aggression. The Judge noted this report but in his view the Court could not assume that the dog which had caused the injuries would not constitute a danger to public safety. Held. The relevant principles that can be made in respect of a dog whose owner has been convicted under s 3(1) of the 1991 Act of failing to keep a dog under control in a public place are that:

(a) The court is empowered under section 4(1) of the 1991 Act to order the destruction of the dog.

(b) Nothing in that provision shall require the court to order destruction if the court is satisfied that the dog would not constitute a danger to public safety: section 4(1)(a) of the 1991 Act.

(c) The court should ordinarily consider, before ordering immediate destruction, whether to exercise the power under section 4A(4) of the 1991 Act to order that, unless the owner of the dog keeps it under proper control, the dog shall be destroyed (known 'as a suspended order of destruction').

(d) A suspended order of destruction under that provision may specify the measures to be taken by the owner for keeping the dog under control, whether by muzzling, keeping it on a lead, or excluding it from a specified place or otherwise: see section 4A(5) of the 1991 Act.

(e) A court should not order destruction if satisfied that the imposition of such a condition would mean the dog would not constitute a danger to public safety.

(f) In deciding what order to make, the court must consider all the relevant circumstances, which include the dog's history of aggressive behaviour and the owner's history of controlling the dog concerned in order to determine what order should be made.

In this case, the Judge does not appear to have considered whether to impose a suspended Destruction Order in relation to the dog which caused the injury. He made no order disqualifying him from owning or being in control of dogs. We are not surprised by that conclusion. Suspended Destruction Order, not Destruction Order.

R v Harry 2010 EWCA Crim 673 D pleaded to being in charge of a dog which caused injury while dangerously out of control. D's parents were having building work carried out on their house. The builders had been instructed to keep the garden gate closed. D arrived at his parents' house and let their two dogs, Snoopy and Millie, into the garden. Snoopy was a male English bull terrier and Millie was a female Staffordshire bull terrier. The garden gate had been left open and the dogs got out into the street. V left his girlfriend's house. As he walked towards a car parked outside, the two dogs ran towards him. The dogs appeared friendly, but as they met V, Snoopy jumped up and bit V on the penis, the top of his legs, his stomach and back. V ran back to his girlfriend's house but it was locked so he ran to a neighbour's home. The dogs followed, biting him on his back. V threw his jacket at the dogs but they kept up the chase. A resident of another house let him in. V was taken to hospital and had multiple bite wounds and scratches, a deeper wound on his buttock and a superficial graze on his penis. D had no convictions. It was accepted that the gate had been left open by builders and D had let the dogs out without checking the gate. D and his parents were conscientious dog owners who cared for their animals and had an excellent record of animal ownership. Neither dog had done anything of this nature before, nor shown any propensity to do so. The veterinary report said neither dog displayed any aggressive attributes as normal behavioural characteristics. Millie did not represent an individual danger to anyone and Snoopy was unlikely to behave aggressively, but he was boisterous. Held. Contingent Destruction Order, not a Destruction Order.

R v Davies 2010 EWCA Crim 1923 D was convicted of being in charge of a dangerously out of control dog. The dog in question, an Alsatian, was subject to an immediate Destruction Order. D was walking two dogs, neither of which were restrained or controlled in any way, when he encountered his neighbour, also walking a dog. D's dogs attacked the neighbour's dog, which was restrained, and when the neighbour intervened, one of D's dogs caused a deep laceration over her finger. The Judge found that it was the Alsatian that had caused the injury and ordered its immediate destruction. The defence argued that it should have been suspended. D appealed. Held. The Judge was not referred to the relevant case law, providing that prior to considering immediate destruction, the court should consider a suspended Destruction Order. Suspended order substituted.

R v Baballa 2010 EWCA Crim 1950 D pleaded to being the owner of a dog which caused injury whilst dangerously out of control (section 3) and three possession of pit bull charges. No evidence was offered on three other section 3 offences. D was also committed for sentence for another possession of a pit bull terrier charge. D was walking through a park with his four dogs. One dog, Crystal, approached V. V tried to shield himself using D. All four dogs were barking at V and jumping up at him. In the event, he was bitten by Crystal. D's dogs were examined, Crystal was identified as a mongrel and the other three had pit bull terrier characteristics within the meaning of the 1991 Act. An expert concluded that the three dogs did not constitute a danger to the public. Crystal was destroyed. D appealed against Destruction Orders in respect of the other three dogs. Held. The guidance given in *R v Flack* 2008 EWCA Crim 204 in relation to section 3(1) offences (dangerously out of control) applies to section 1(3) offences (possession of a pit

bull). Applying those principles to the present case, we consider that, before ordering the immediate destruction of the three dogs, the Judge should have considered whether to exercise his power under section 4A(1) of the 1991 Act to make a Contingent Destruction Order. He should have considered whether he could be satisfied that the imposition of the conditions which would be attached to a certificate of exemption would be sufficient to ensure that the dog would not constitute a danger to public safety. For the three dogs, Contingent Destruction Order with conditions, not Destruction Order.
Kelleher v DPP 2012 EWHC 2978 (Admin) High Court D pleaded to two counts of being in charge of a dog dangerously out of control in a public place and two counts of failing to comply with a control order.[536] D challenged a destruction order. Held. *R v Flack* 2008 para e) (see above) only applies to aggravated offences. The decision in *R v Davies* 2010 (see above) was an aggravated offence case and his comments about non-aggravated offences were erroneous.
R v Singh 2013 EWCA Crim 2416 D was convicted of being the owner of a dog which caused injury whilst dangerously out of control. D took Ace, his 5-year-old German Shepherd, with him to a local Sikh centre on regular occasions. The centre contained within its grounds a school and a gym. There was a garden area immediately adjacent to the car park, which was enclosed by a fence. D had installed a large dog kennel there and it was his practice to keep Ace chained up in, or adjacent to, the kennel. When Ace wasn't chained up, he was on a lead. V, aged 12, regularly used the gym. One evening, V and his father were walking past the garden area on their way out to the car park when Ace ran out of the garden area and attacked V, knocking him to the floor. Ace bit V on the arm, back and leg. It caused a deep penetrating wound to the thigh and V had to undergo surgery. Eight stitches were inserted and V was kept in hospital overnight. V also suffered bruising and scratches. Seven weeks after the incident, V continued to suffer pain and difficulty in walking. There was obvious scarring and he had developed a fear of dogs. Ace was taken into the care of the police. D said Ace had been chained up in his kennel and that V must have entered the garden area and untied Ace. The jury rejected that assertion. D, aged 33, regularly acted as a volunteer at the Sikh centre. He had no previous convictions. He expressed regret for what had happened, but maintained that his account was true. An expert assessed Ace and found that he responded well to being handled by a stranger, accepted wearing a muzzle and could not be incited to attack another. The conditions in which D kept Ace were found to be satisfactory. He considered that Ace could be returned to D so long as he was kept muzzled in public, castrated and walked on a lead. Held. The sentencing remarks did not reveal the Judge's reasons for finding that D was not a fit and proper person to have custody of a dog. It was likely that this was an act of momentary carelessness in leaving the gate to the enclosed area open. There was no evidence that such an incident had occurred previously. D had proper facilities to prevent him from coming into contact with members of the public. Disqualification of having custody of a dog would be quashed. Immediate destruction was manifestly excessive, considering the measures recommended by the expert. Contingent destruction order substituted.

36.12 *Contingent Destruction Orders Conditions, Imposing*

R (Sandhu) v Isleworth Crown Court 2012 EWHC 1658 (Admin) The Judge made a Contingent Destruction Order for two pit bull-type dogs, which were prohibited dogs. It was then necessary for DEFRA to issue 'a certificate of exemption' or the dogs had to be destroyed. The details are set out in Dangerous Dogs Compensation and Exemption Schemes Order 1991 1991/1744. The period for one to be issued was two months, which can be extended. The owner was sentenced to a substantial prison term so the defence were concerned about who was to keep the dogs in the meantime. His cousin applied for a certificate of exemption. The defence complained that the Judge had not listed the conditions that were to apply. Held. DEFRA is obliged to issue a certificate of exemption

[536] The Court said this was what was charged and so it is assumed that is what D pleaded to.

when the requirements in article 9 of the Order are made out. It is not open to the Court to impose conditions. The conditions in Dangerous Dogs Act 1991 s 4A(5) do not apply to prohibited dogs. It is not for this court to consider the accommodation of a dog. Claim dismissed.
Note: If the Contingency Order followed a Crown Court conviction, it is not explained why the High Court action was not barred as it related to 'trial on indictment'. The fact that the claimant was not the defendant did not affect the issue of whether the Contingency Order related to trial on indictment. If the case was an appeal from the Magistrates' Court, that is not explained. Ed.

Appeals

36.13 ***Appeals Statutory provision***
Dangerous Dogs Act 1991 s 4(2) Where a court makes an order under subsection (1)(a) (see **36.2**) above for the destruction of a dog owned by a person other than the offender, the owner may appeal to the Crown Court against the order.

37 DETENTION AND TRAINING ORDERS

37.1
Powers of Criminal Courts (Sentencing) Act 2000 s 100-102
Availability The order is not available for those aged 10-11.[537] The order is available for those aged 12-14, if they are deemed to be 'persistent offenders'.[538] The order is available for those aged 15-17.[539] The age to apply is age at the date of conviction, see **13.5**.
Court Martial The Court may pass a Detention and Training Order for those who are not officers, warrant officers or NCOs, see *Guidance on Sentencing in the Court Martial 2018* Annex B.
Disqualification from driving Where the court passes a Detention and Training Order with either obligatory disqualification, discretionary disqualification or disqualification under the totting up provisions, the court is required to select the appropriate period of disqualification and extend it by half the length of the Detention and Training Order.[540] The section was designed to prevent offenders serving most of their disqualification periods in custody. The sections were amended by Criminal Justice and Courts Act 2015 s 30. For more detail see **41.16**.
Victim surcharge The court must impose a victim surcharge of £30, Criminal Justice Act 2003 s 161A-161B and Criminal Justice Act 2003 (Surcharge) Order 2012 2012/1696 as amended. There are exceptions, a) where a compensation order or an Unlawful Profits Order or a Slavery and Trafficking Reparations Order is imposed, when a reduced amount can be ordered or a nil amount can be ordered, see **17.67**, and b) where the offence was committed before 8 April 2016. For details of older offences, see para **37.1** in the 12th edition of this book.
Release and supervision Release is automatic at the halfway point. The Secretary of State has the power, where exceptional circumstances exist, to release on compassionate grounds at any stage, Powers of Criminal Courts (Sentencing) Act 2000 s 102(3). The Secretary of State also has a power of early release. This may be exercised one month before the halfway point for orders of 8-18 months' duration and either one or two months before the halfway point for orders in excess of 18 months, Powers of Criminal Courts (Sentencing) Act 2000 s 102(4). On release, the prisoner is supervised and the

[537] For offenders aged under 12, Powers of Criminal Courts (Sentencing) Act 2000 s 100(2)(b)(ii) creates a power to pass the Detention and Training Order when the Secretary of State makes an order. This power is not expected to be used.
[538] Powers of Criminal Courts (Sentencing) Act 2000 s 100(2)(a)
[539] Powers of Criminal Courts (Sentencing) Act 2000 s 100(1)(a)
[540] Road Traffic Offenders Act 1988 s 35A(1)-(3) and (4)(b) and Powers of Criminal Courts (Sentencing) Act 2000 s 147A(1)-(3) and (4)(b) inserted by Coroners and Justice Act 2009 s 2 and Sch 16 paras 2 and 5. Schedule 16 is in force from 13/4/15.

supervision lasts until the end of the period that he or she was sentenced to. An offender subject to a DTO is not released on licence. The supervision period is a separate part of the term, *R v McGeechan* 2019 EWCA Crim 235 para 23.

Rehabilitation period Where the sentence is 6 months or less, the rehabilitation period is 18 months. Where the sentence is over 6 months, the rehabilitation period is 2 years.[541]

See also the **REHABILITATION OF OFFENDERS ACT 1974** chapter.

37.2 *Statistics England and Wales*

Detention and Training Orders

	2009	2010	2011	2012	2013	2014	2015	2016	2017
Males	4,101	3,480	3,381	2,545	1,921	1,562	1,454	1,342	1,244
Females	351	251	234	172	109	103	68	42	48
All	4,479	3,757	3,646	2,758	2,057	1,684	1,554	1,408	1,341

For explanations about the statistics, see page 1-xii. For more detailed statistics, see www.banksr.com Other Matters Statistics tab

Power to order and the statutory provisions

37.3 *Statutory provisions*

Offenders under 18: detention and training orders.

Powers of Criminal Courts (Sentencing) Act 2000 s 100(1) Subject to sections 90 and 91 [the duty to pass detention at HM's Pleasure and the power to order long-term detention] above, and [Criminal Justice Act 2003] s 226 [detention for life] and 226B[542] [Extended Determinate Sentence for those under 18] [the minimum sentences for threatening with an offensive weapon or bladed article], and subsection (2), where:

(a) a child or young person (that is to say, any person aged under 18) is convicted of an offence which is punishable with imprisonment in the case of a person aged 21 or over, and

(b) the court is of the opinion that Criminal Justice Act 2003 s 152(2) [offence is so serious that a community sentence cannot be justified] applies, or the case falls within subsection (3) [supplementary to section 152(2)] of that section,

the sentence that the court is to pass is a detention and training order.

(1A)[543] Subsection (1) applies with the omission of paragraph (b) in the case of an offence the sentence for which falls to be imposed under these provisions:

(a) section 1(2B) or 1A(5) of the Prevention of Crime Act 1953 (minimum sentence for certain offences involving offensive weapons),

(b) section 139(6B), 139A(5B) or 139AA(7) of the Criminal Justice Act 1988 (minimum sentence for certain offences involving article with blade or point or offensive weapon).

(2) A court shall not make a detention and training order:

(a) in the case of an offender under the age of 15 at the time of the conviction, unless it is of the opinion that he is a persistent offender;

(b) in the case of an offender under the age of 12 at that time, unless:

(i) it is of the opinion that only a custodial sentence would be adequate to protect the public from further offending by him; and

(ii) the offence was committed on or after such date as the Secretary of State may by order appoint.

---

541 Rehabilitation of Offenders Act 1974 s 5(2) and (8)

542 As amended by Legal Aid, Sentencing and Punishment of Offenders Act 2012 Sch 21 para 13

543 As inserted by Legal Aid, Sentencing and Punishment of Offenders Act 2012 Sch 26 para 11

(3) A detention and training order is an order that the offender in respect of whom it is made shall be subject, for the term specified in the order, to a period of detention and training followed by a period of supervision.
Note: As there has been no appointment by the Secretary of State, section 100(2)(b) has no application. Ed.

37.4 ***Sentencing Children and Young People Guideline 2017***
Sentencing Children and Young People Guideline 2017, see www.banksr.com Other Matters Guidelines tab In force 1 June 2017 page 30
6.50 A court can only impose a DTO if the child or young person is legally represented unless they have refused to apply for legal aid or it has been withdrawn as a result of their conduct.
6.51 If it is determined that the offence is of such seriousness that a custodial sentence is unavoidable then the length of this sentence must be considered on an individual basis. The court must take into account the chronological age of the child or young person, as well as their maturity, emotional and developmental age and other relevant factors, such as their mental health or any learning disabilities.

Persistent offenders

37.5 ***Persistent offender, Offender aged 12-14 must be a***
Powers of Criminal Courts (Sentencing) Act 2000 s 100(2)(a) A court shall not make a Detention and Training Order in the case of an offender under the age of 15 at the time of conviction unless it is of the opinion that he is a persistent offender.
For the full section, see **37.3**.
R (W) v Thetford Youth Court 2002 EWHC 1252 (Admin), 2003 1 Cr App R (S) 67 (p 323)[544] It is accepted that where an offender aged under 15, who is not a persistent offender, and a custodial sentence is appropriate so a Detention and Training Order is not available, a sentence under section 91 may be appropriate and a term of less than 2 years is available. This would only be in 'very exceptional' cases.
R v Jahmarl 2004 EWCA Crim 2199, 2005 1 Cr App R (S) 96 (p 534) D was convicted of attempted robbery. At the time of the offence he was aged 14 and at the conviction and sentence hearing he was aged 15. D was of good character. The Judge thought the sentencing options were either 2 years' detention under section 91 or a non-custodial sentence. Held. The rules about when it is appropriate to commit youths for trial do not restrict the Crown Court's sentencing powers. The Court was not faced with that stark choice. The proper sentence length was 1 year. We do not agree he did not qualify for a Detention and Training Order. With the probation officer's assistance we think a 1-year DTO would be the better order.
Note: The key point was that he was aged 15+ at the time of his conviction. Ed.
For the principles about who is a ***Persistent offender*** and further guidelines, see **14.8**.

37.6 ***Sentencing Children and Young People Guideline 2017***
Sentencing Children and Young People Guideline 2017, see www.banksr.com Other Matters Guidelines tab In force 1 June 2017 page 30
6.52 A DTO cannot be imposed on any child under the age of 12 at the time of the finding of guilt and is only applicable to children aged 12-14 if they are deemed to be a persistent offender. (See [**14.8**].)
6.53 A DTO can be made only for the periods prescribed: 4, 6, 8, 10, 12, 18 or 24 months. Any time spent on remand in custody or on bail subject to a qualifying curfew condition should be taken into account when calculating the length of the order. The accepted approach is to double the time spent on remand before deciding the appropriate

[544] Also known as *R (M) v Waltham Forest Youth Court* 2002 EWHC 1252, 2003 1 Cr App R (S) 67 (p 323)

period of detention, in order to ensure that the regime is in line with that applied to adult offenders.[545] After doubling the time spent on remand the court should then adopt the nearest prescribed period available for a DTO.

37.7 *Offender aged 10-14*

R (W) v Thetford Youth Court 2002 EWHC 1252 (Admin), 2003 1 Cr App R (S) 67 (p 323)[546] It is accepted that: a) where an offender is aged under 12, b) a custodial sentence is appropriate, and c) a Detention and Training Order is not available, a sentence under section 91 may be appropriate and a term of less than 2 years is available. This would only be in 'very exceptional' cases.

37.8 *Length of order The fixed terms and maximum term*

Powers of Criminal Courts (Sentencing) Act 2000 s 101(1) Subject to subsection (2) below, the term of a Detention and Training Order shall be 4, 6, 8, 10, 12, 18 or 24 months.

(2) The term of a Detention and Training Order may not exceed the maximum term of imprisonment that the Crown Court could (in the case of an offender aged 21 or over) impose for the offence.

(3) and (4) see **37.9**

(5) Where the term of the Detention and Training Order…exceeds 24 months, the excess shall be treated as remitted.

R v Norris 2001 1 Cr App R (S) 116 (p 401) Where the court wishes to impose, either on separate occasions or on the same occasion, a Detention and Training Order consecutive to a Detention and Training Order, the aggregate total does not have to equal the terms specified in the Act, namely 4, 6, 8, 10, 12, 18 or 24 months.

For consecutive DTOs, see **37.9**.

37.9 *Consecutive sentences and maximum term*

Powers of Criminal Courts (Sentencing) Act 2000 s 101(3) Subject to subsections (4) and (6) below, a court making a Detention and Training Order may order that its term shall commence on the expiry of the term of any other Detention and Training Order made by that or any other court.

(4) A court shall not make in respect of an offender a Detention and Training Order the effect of which would be that he would be subject to Detention and Training Orders for a term which exceeds 24 months.

(5) [see **37.8**].

(6) [see **37.17**].

R v Norris 2001 1 Cr App R (S) 116 (p 401) Where the court wishes to impose, either on separate occasions or on the same occasion, a Detention and Training Order consecutive to a Detention and Training Order, the aggregate total does not have to equal the terms specified in the Act, namely 4, 6, 8, 10, 12, 18 or 24 months. To do otherwise would create serious anomalies when two defendants are sentenced at the same time. Such a restriction on sentencing powers would oblige the court to impose unfair sentences. It would create injustices so manifest that Human Rights Act 1998 s 3 would oblige the court not to so restrict the sentencing.

C v DPP 2001 EWHC 453 (Admin), 2002 1 Cr App R (S) 45 (p 189) LCJ D, aged 16, appeared before the Court on eight matters including three offences of driving whilst disqualified (4 months, 6 months consecutive, 6 months concurrent DTO), affray (4-month DTO) and four other offences (no separate penalty). D contended that the sentences were unlawful as there was no jurisdiction to pass consecutive DTOs on the same occasion which exceeds 6 months in total. Held. The intention of section 101(2) is simply to restrict the power given by Powers of Criminal Courts (Sentencing) Act 2000 s 101(1) to impose a term of up to 24 months for an individual offence to the maximum which the Crown Court can impose on an adult for the same individual offence. The

[545] *R v Eagles* 2006 EWCA Crim 2368, 2007 1 Cr App R (S) 99 (p 612)

[546] Also known as *R (M) v Waltham Forest Youth Court* 2002 EWHC 1252, 2003 1 Cr App R (S) 67 (p 323)

Crown Court could impose the maximum term of 6 months' imprisonment for the offence of driving while disqualified for an offender aged 21+. Section 101(3) of the 2000 Act enabled the court to order that that term should commence on the expiry of the 4-month Detention and Training Order for the driving whilst disqualified offence.
R v Philips 2017 EWCA Crim 15147 D was sentenced to 10 months and 4 months consecutive making 14 months. Held. This was lawful as the constituent parts of the sentence (10 months and 4 months) were of the permitted length even if 14 months was not.
R v Okugbeni 2018 EWCA Crim 2638 D was sentenced to 14 months' DTO, which was made consecutive to a 10-month DTO. When told the total was in excess of the maximum, the Judge used the slip rule to make the sentence 14 months consecutive. Held. The second sentence was unlawful too as 14 months was not one of the prescribed terms. We substitute a 12-month term, which would make a 22-month sentence which is lower than the maximum.

37.10 ***Consecutive sentences Supervision has started***

Powers of Criminal Courts (Sentencing) Act 2000 s 101(6) A court making a Detention and Training Order shall not order that its term shall commence on the expiry of the term of a Detention and Training Order under which the period of supervision has already begun (under s 103(1) [not listed]).
Powers of Criminal Courts (Sentencing) Act 2000 s 103(1)-(2) The period of supervision of an offender who is subject to a Detention and Training Order: a) shall begin with the offender's release, whether at the halfway point of the term of the order or otherwise, and b) shall end when the term of the order ends, unless the Secretary of State orders that the period of supervision shall end at such a point during a term of detention and training.

The restrictions on imposing this order

Justified, Must be see the **CUSTODY: GENERAL PRINCIPLES** ***Offence must be so serious a fine or a community sentence cannot be justified*** para at **28.26**.
Legally represented, Offender must be see the **CUSTODY: GENERAL PRINCIPLES Defendants who have not been previously sentenced to custody** section at **28.19**.
Pre-sentence report, Must have see **PRE-SENTENCE REPORT** ***Pre-sentence report, Court must have Those under 18*** para at **83.15**.
Mentally disordered defendants see the **DEFENDANT** ***Mentally disordered defendants*** para at **242.39** in Volume 2.
Sentence must be for the shortest term see the **CUSTODY: GENERAL PRINCIPLES** ***Must be for the shortest term, Custody*** para at **28.32**.

Sentencing principles

37.11 ***Basic principles***

For general principles see the **CHILDREN AND YOUNG OFFENDERS: CUSTODIAL SENTENCES** ***Basic principles offender aged under 18 years old*** para at **14.11**.
R v Fairhurst 1986 8 Cr App R (S) 346 LCJ On the one hand there exists the desirability of keeping youths under the age of 17 out of long terms of custody. On the other hand it is necessary that serious offences committed by youths of this age should be met with sentences sufficiently substantial to provide both the appropriate punishment and also the necessary deterrent effect, and in certain cases to provide a measure of protection to the public. A balance has to be struck between these objectives.
R v AM 1998 2 Cr App R (S) 128 LCJ We unreservedly endorse this statement in *R v Fairhurst* 1986 (see above). No one should be sentenced to imprisonment or detention unless it is necessary, and the period of imprisonment or detention should be no longer than is necessary. This applies in particular to young offenders. The 24-month limit on sentences of detention in a Young Offender Institution (now detention and training) is intended to ensure that offenders aged 15, 16 or 17 are not sentenced to lengthy periods of detention where this can be avoided. Any sentencer must think long

and hard before passing a sentence which exceeds this limit. But the co-existence of the powers contained in section 53(2) and (3) (now Powers of Criminal Courts (Sentencing) Act 2000 s 91) recognises the unwelcome but undoubted fact that some crimes committed by offenders of this age merit sentences of detention in excess of 24 months. In the case of an offender aged 15, 16 or 17 the 24-month limit for detention in a Young Offender Institution should not be exceeded unless the offence is clearly one calling for a longer sentence. The court should not exceed the 24-month limit for detention in a Young Offender Institution (now detention and training) without much careful thought, but if it concludes that a longer sentence, even if not a much longer sentence, is called for, then the court should impose whatever it considers the appropriate period of detention under section 53(2) and (3) (now section 91).
For the discretion whether to impose custody and the principles of sentencing young offenders, see the **Children and Young Offenders** chapters.
Welfare of the offender, Must consider see the **Children And Young Offenders: General Principles** ***Welfare of young offenders*** paras at **13.38**.

37.12 ***Discount for time spent in custody/on a tag and curfew Statute***
Powers of Criminal Courts (Sentencing) Act 2000 s 101(8) In determining the term of a detention order for an offence, the court shall take into account any period for which the offender has been remanded, a) in custody, or b) on bail subject to a qualifying curfew condition and an electronic monitoring condition (within the meaning of Criminal Justice Act 2003 s 240A) in connection with the offence, or any other offence the charge for which was founded on the same facts or evidence.
(9) Where a court proposes to make Detention and Training Orders in respect of an offender for two or more offences:

(a) subsection (8) (discount for time on bail/curfew) shall not apply, but
(b) in determining the total term of the Detention and Training Orders...the court shall take account of the total period (if any) for which he has been remanded in connection with any of those offences, or any other offence the charge for which was founded on the same facts or evidence.

Powers of Criminal Courts (Sentencing) Act 2000 s 101(11) Any reference in subsection (8)...above to an offender's being remanded in custody is a reference to his being: a) held in police detention, b) remanded in or committed to custody by an order of a court, c) remanded to youth detention accommodation under Legal Aid, Sentencing and Punishment of Offenders Act 2012 s 91(4)[547] or d) remanded, admitted or removed to hospital under Mental Health Act 1983 s 35, 36, 38 or 48.

37.13 ***Discount for time spent in custody/on a tag and curfew Cases***
R v Ganley 2001 1 Cr App R (S) 17 (p 60) Time spent in custody on remand will not be automatically deducted from a period to be served under a Detention and Training Order. It has to be taken into account.
R v B 2001 1 Cr App R (S) 89 (p 303) D had spent 3½ months in custody. The defence asked for twice the time spent in custody to be deducted from the sentence. The Judge refused to do so. He passed a sentence which took into account all the factors. Held. Taking into account the period in custody or secure accommodation for the purposes of [what is now section 101(8)] does not involve a one-to-one, day-for-day or month-for-month reduction in sentence, let alone a two-to-one reduction. The reason for that is that the periods to which the court is entitled to sentence a young defendant to Detention and Training Orders are specified in blocks and deducting precise amounts of time is inconsistent with that provision. Doubling up is not available.
R v Fieldhouse and Watts 2001 1 Cr App R (S) 104 (p 361) No rule of general application can be devised to cover the infinitely various situations which may arise. However, the proper approach can perhaps best be illustrated by taking by way of

[547] Substituted by Legal Aid, Sentencing and Punishment of Offenders Act 2012 Sch 12 para 43(a)

example a defendant who has spent four weeks on remand, which is the equivalent of a 2-month term. The court is likely to take such a period into account in different ways according to the length of the Detention and Training Order, which initially seems appropriate. If that period is 4 months, the court may conclude a non-custodial sentence is appropriate. If that period is 6, 8, 10 or 12 months, the court is likely to impose 4, 6, 8 or 10 months respectively. If that period is 18 or 24 months, the court may well conclude that no reduction can properly be made, although the court will, of course, bear in mind for juveniles the continuing importance of limiting the period in custody to the minimum necessary. The observations to this effect in *R v Mills and Others* 1998 2 Cr App R (S) 128 at 131 still hold good. For those offenders for whom long-term detention under [what is now Powers of Criminal Courts (Sentencing) Act 2000 s 91] might otherwise be appropriate, a Detention and Training Order of 24 months may be a proper sentence even on a plea of guilty and even when a significant period has been spent in custody.

R v Pitt 2001 EWCA Crim 1295, 2002 1 Cr App R (S) 46 (p 195) D, then aged 17, pleaded to unlawful wounding and received 18 months. He had spent four months awaiting trial. The maximum was 24 months. Held. Taking the plea and the four months into account, 15 months was appropriate. That wasn't available, as it was either 18 or 12 months. This Act puts the courts in a straitjacket. Therefore 12 months substituted.

R v Norman Re W 2006 EWCA Crim 1792, 2007 1 Cr App R (S) 82 (p 509) para 41 A Detention and Training Order is not a sentence of imprisonment for the purposes of [what is now Criminal Justice Act 2003 s 240ZA] so the period on remand remains a period which is required to be taken into account. Here, the defendant's remand meant that he could not be granted early release. That is a relevant consideration.

R v Eagles 2006 EWCA Crim 2368, 2007 1 Cr App R (S) 99 (p 612) Because the period is deducted before sentence, it is necessary to double the time spent on remand before deducting that from the appropriate sentence. Then the judge has to fit that into the 4, 6, 8, 10, 12, 18 and 24-month (rigid) periods. The judge should generally settle on the nearest permissible period. We do not say that he has to settle on the next lowest permissible period.

R v J 2012 EWCA Crim 1570, 2013 1 Cr App R (S) 74 (p 412) D was convicted of possession of cocaine and heroin with intent to supply. The Judge started at 2 years. D had been on a qualifying curfew for 231 days which, because D was going to receive a DTO, had to be taken into account in full. That was equivalent to eight months. The Judge imposed an 18-month DTO, thereby crediting six months for the curfew. Held. The approach taken by the Judge was entirely consistent with the decision in *R v Eagles* 2006 EWCA Crim 2368, 2007 1 Cr App R (S) 99 (p 612) and she could not be faulted for imposing an 18-month DTO, that being the nearest permissible period for which such an order could be imposed.

37.14 ***Discount for time spent in custody/on a tag and curfew Cases Short periods***

R v Inner London Crown Court ex parte I 2000 The Times 12/5/00 D had spent less than 24 hours in custody. Held. The duty under [what is now section 101(8)] is to take account of the time spent. It is not to reflect inevitable time spent in some specific way in the sentence passed.

R v Inner London Crown Court ex parte P, N and S 2001 1 Cr App R (S) 99 (p 343). The defendants had spent three days in custody. Held. I would not regard it as appropriate or desirable that any precise reflection should be sought to be given, in making a Detention and Training Order, of a day or two. It is impossible to fine-tune by reference to a day or two the sentence which is appropriate.

R v Fieldhouse and Watts 2001 1 Cr App R (S) 104 (p 361) No rule of general application can be devised to cover the infinitely various situations which may arise. The weekend spent in custody in this case could not sensibly be reflected in the sentence.

See also the **Custody: Time on Remand/Curfew Discount** chapter.

37.15 ***Discount for time spent on bail subject to a curfew***
Powers of Criminal Courts (Sentencing) Act 2000 s 101(8)(b) In determining the term of a detention order for an offence, the Court shall take into account any period for which the offender has been remanded on bail subject to a qualifying curfew condition and an electronic monitoring condition (within the meaning of Criminal Justice Act 2003 s 240A) in connection with the offence, or any other offence the charge for which was founded on the same facts or evidence.
For more detail about the tag see the **CUSTODY: TIME ON REMAND/CURFEW DISCOUNT *Bail, tag and curfew*** section at **30.21**.

37.16 ***Discount for guilty plea Maximum sentence given***
Reduction in Sentence for a Guilty Plea Guideline 2007, see www.banksr.com Other Matters Guidelines tab para 5.6. A Detention and Training Order of 24 months may be imposed on an offender aged under 18 if the offence is one which would but for the plea have attracted a sentence of long-term detention in excess of 24 months under Powers of Criminal Courts (Sentencing) Act 2000 s 91.
Note: There is a new guideline but this statement would appear to reflect current practice. Ed.
R v Marley 2001 EWCA Crim 2779, 2 Cr App R (S) 21 (p 73) D pleaded to one count of damaging property and on a separate occasion to violent disorder. After reports he was sentenced to a 24-month Detention and Training Order for the violent disorder, with no separate penalty for the damaging property. The Judge expressly stated he had taken into account D's plea and that credit would be given. Held. Powers of Criminal Courts (Sentencing) Act 2000 s 91 did not apply to violent disorder (having a maximum sentence of less than 14 years) and therefore the maximum Detention and Training Order available to the Judge was 24 months. Therefore D had not received credit for his guilty plea. This was as a result of the Judge being under the false impression that section 91 did apply. Sentence reduced.
R v Kelly 2001 EWCA Crim 1030, 2002 1 Cr App R (S) 11 (p 40) D, aged 15, pleaded to causing GBH and received a 24-month Detention and Training Order. D's co-defendant also pleaded and received the same sentence. D and his co-defendant initiated an attack on another man in a chip shop. Despite the efforts of a local shop owner, the attack was prolonged and violent. The victim suffered very serious injuries. D was of previous good character. As it was a section 20 case, detention under section 91 was not available. Held. D ought to have been given credit for his guilty plea. The rule of credit for guilty pleas is not inflexible but it is well established. 18 months not 24.
R v M 2002 EWCA Crim 551, 2 Cr App R (S) 98 (p 448) D, aged 16, with others, pleaded to one count of conspiracy to cause ABH, three counts of ABH, one count of threats to kill and one count of incitement to steal. He received a maximum 24-month Detention and Training Order. Two counts of indecent assault, which attracted section 91 detention, were left to lie on file. The Judge described the case as the most disgusting case he had ever had to deal with. The Judge criticised the prosecution for accepting pleas to the offences and allowing the indecent assault charges to lie on the file, indicating that he would have passed a higher sentence had he been able to. The Judge gave no discount for the plea, stating that, "in the acceptance of the pleas to lesser offences, and the counts to lie on file, D had had all the discount he could hope for". Credit was not given for the 8 months served on remand either. Held. The Judge was only entitled to sentence for the offence of which D had been convicted. There is no invariable rule to the effect that the maximum sentence cannot be imposed where there is a guilty plea. There are a number of well-established exceptions to the general rule and the list is not closed. However, it will rarely be appropriate to impose a maximum sentence where there has been a guilty plea. The exceptions include at least the following: a) where the imposition of the maximum term is necessary for the protection of the public, b) where the plea was of a technical nature, c) cases where a plea is practically speaking inevitable, and d) where the count is a specimen count. The Judge

should have loyally applied the Act. All circumstances fall to be considered. None of the recognised exceptions to the general principle apply here. We are concerned not to undermine the advice given that pleas of guilty attract discounts. What the Judge could not do was to go behind the compromise between defence and prosecution and sentence on a basis which the Crown could have pursued, but chose not to pursue. Sentence reduced to the next step down, namely 18 months. Any greater discount would reduce the sentence to the next step down, which is 12 months. That would be unconscionable. Therefore we restricted the discount to 6 months. We are not obliged to give any credit for the time on remand. The scheme of the DTO legislation must be considered as a whole.

Note: This case was applied in *R v T* 2011 EWCA Crim 2345, so the passages about the exceptions are treated as valid. Ed.

See also: *R v Dalby and Berry* 2005 EWCA Crim 1292, 2006 1 Cr App R (S) 38 (p 216) (*R v M* 2002 applied.)

See also the **Custody: General Principles** ***Maximum given with plea of guilty*** para at **28.17** and the **Guilty Plea, Discount for** ***Maximum given with plea of guilty*** para at **65.15**.

37.17 ***Consecutive sentences Supervision has started***

R v McGeechan 2019 EWCA Crim 235 The breach sentence had to start on the day it was passed and could not be consecutive to the fresh DTO sentence, Powers of Criminal Courts (Sentencing) Act 2000 s 106(1)(a), see **38.2**.

Note: The real source of the prohibition is in fact Powers of Criminal Courts (Sentencing) Act 2000 s 101(6), see **37.9**. Ed.

37.18 ***Detention and Training Order, Offender serving sentence on remand***

R v Norman Re W 2006 EWCA Crim 1792, 2007 1 Cr App R (S) 82 (p 509) para 41 W was remanded into custody while awaiting sentence. At the time he was serving a Detention and Training Order. During his period on remand he became eligible for release but, as he was remanded for the new offence, he was not released. W was sentenced to 3 years 7 months' detention under section 91. The Judge made an order saying that 182 remand days should count, which was the whole period. The prison service drew the Judge's attention to the fact that for some of these days he was serving the Detention and Training Order. It appears the Judge did not amend the order. He granted a certificate for leave to appeal. Held. A Detention and Training Order is not a sentence of imprisonment for the purposes of Criminal Justice Act 2003 s 240(4)(a)(i)[548] so it remains a period which is required to be taken into account unless the judge exercises his discretion under Criminal Justice Act 2003 s 240(4)(b). Here, W's remand meant that he could not be granted early release. That is a relevant consideration. It is therefore a matter for the judge to determine using his discretion. The right order was made.

Note: This case is factually unclear and the summary above is based on an inference. I suspect most judges would consider it 'just' not to count the period a defendant was serving the custodial part of a DTO. Ed.

37.19 ***Licence period/Supervision***

Note: There are two parts to a Detention and Training Order. After the period in detention the offender is released subject to supervision. Ed.

The period of supervision.

Powers of Criminal Courts (Sentencing) Act 2000 s 103(1) The period of supervision of an offender who is subject to a detention and training order:

(a) shall begin with the offender's release, whether at the half-way point of the term of the order or otherwise; and

(b) subject to subsection (2) below, shall end when the term of the order ends.

[548] Repealed by Legal Aid, Sentencing and Punishment of Offenders Act 2012 s 108(1). In force 3/12/12

(2) Subject to subsection (2A), the Secretary of State may by order provide that the period of supervision shall end at such point during the term of a detention and training order as may be specified in the order under this subsection.

(2A) An order under subsection (2) may not include provision about cases in which:

(a) the offender is aged 18 or over at the half-way point of the term of the detention and training order, and

(b) the order was imposed in respect of an offence committed on or after the day on which section 6(4) of the Offender Rehabilitation Act 2014 came into force.

(3) During the period of supervision, the offender shall be under the supervision of:

(a) an officer of a local probation board or an officer of a provider of probation services; or

(c) a member of a youth offending team;

and the category of person to supervise the offender shall be determined from time to time by the Secretary of State. Combined with other orders

(4)-(7) [Not listed Re the provision of supervision]

37.20 ***Defendant serving sentence for breach of Detention and Training Order***

Powers of Criminal Courts (Sentencing) Act 2000 s 104B(1)[549] Where a court makes a Detention and Training Order in the case of an offender who is subject to a period of detention under section 104(3)(a) (breach of supervision), the Detention and Training Order takes effect:

(a) at the beginning of the day on which it is made, or

(b) if the court so orders, at the time when the period of detention under section 104(3)(a) above ends.

(2) Where a court orders an offender who is subject to a Detention and Training Order to be subject to a period of detention under section 104(3)(a) (detention for breach of order) above for a failure to comply with requirements under a different Detention and Training Order, the period of detention takes effect as follows:

(a) if the offender has been released by virtue of subsection (2), (3), (4) or (5) of section 102 (ordinary DTO), at the beginning of the day on which the order for the period of detention is made, and

(b) if not, either as mentioned in paragraph (a) above or, if the court so orders, at the time when the offender would otherwise be released by virtue of subsection (2), (3), (4) or (5) of section 102.

37.21 ***Detention and Training Order, Combined with (passed on separate occasions)***

Powers of Criminal Courts (Sentencing) Act 2000 s 101(7) Where a Detention and Training Order ('the new order') is made in respect of an offender who is subject to a Detention and Training Order under which the supervision period has begun ('the old order'), the old order shall be disregarded in determining:

(a) for the purposes of subsection (4), whether the effect of the new order would be that the offender would be subject to Detention and Training Orders for a term which exceeds 24 months, and

(b) for the purposes of subsection (5), whether the term of the Detention and Training Orders to which the offender would be subject exceeds 24 months.

37.22 ***Detention under section 91, Combined with (sentenced on one occasion)***

R v Fairhurst 1986 8 Cr App R (S) 346 LCJ As this Court has said in the case of *R v Gaskin* 1985 7 Cr App R (S) 28, it is undesirable that sentences of section 53(2) detention (now section 91 detention) and of youth custody should be passed to run either consecutively to or concurrently with each other. It is not, however, always possible to avoid this. The only way out of the problem in general may be to impose no separate

[549] As inserted by Legal Aid, Sentencing and Punishment of Offenders Act 2012 s 80(7). In force 3/12/12

penalty for the offences for which section 53(2) (now section 91) detention is not available. Although that solution is not altogether satisfactory, it provides fewer difficulties than any other possible method.
R v Mills and Others 1998 2 Cr App R (S) 128 at 134 LCJ We consider it generally undesirable to impose concurrent sentences under both Children and Young Persons Act 1933 s 53(2)-(3) (now section 91) and Criminal Justice Act 1982 s 1B (detention in a Young Offender Institution, now replaced by detention and training). They should be particularly avoided for offenders under the age of 16. Where there are multiple offences, the court should pass sentences under section 53(2) and (3) for the offences for which it is available, and subsequently impose no separate penalty for the other offences.
R v Reynolds and Others Re S 2007 EWCA Crim 538, 2 Cr App R (S) 87 (p 553) paras 66-70 D was convicted of section 18 in which he was said to have played a part in an attack on an innocent passer-by. He also pleaded to a section 47 charge against the same victim. The Judge found that D was not dangerous within the meaning of the 2003 Act but imposed detention under section 91 for both offences, 6 years on the section 18 and 1 year concurrent on the section 47. Held. The Judge was not entitled to impose detention under section 91 for the section 47. The only practicable course was to impose no separate penalty.

37.23 ***Detention under section 91 Offender serving a Detention and Training Order***

Powers of Criminal Courts (Sentencing) Act 2000 s 106A(7) Subject to subsection (9) below, where at any time an offender is subject concurrently:

(a) to a detention and training order, and

(b) to a sentence of detention,

he shall be treated for the purposes of the provisions specified in subsection (8) below as if he were subject only to the sentence of detention.

(8) Those provisions are:

(a) sections 102 to 105 above,

(b) section 92 above, section 235 of the 2003 Act and section 210 of the Armed Forces Act 2006 (place of detention etc.),

(c) Chapter 6 of Part 12 of the 2003 Act, and

(d) section 214 of the Armed Forces Act 2006 (offences committed during a detention and training order under that Act).

(9) Nothing in subsection (7) above shall require the offender to be released in respect of either the order or the sentence unless and until he is required to be released in respect of each of them.
R v S and N 2017 EWCA Crim 2208 On 21 March 2017, S pleaded to two rapes and in May 2017 he was sentenced to 11 years' detention (reduced to 9 years on appeal). On 7 March 2017, D had been sentenced to a Detention and Training Order. The Judge revoked that order. Held. The Judge had no power to revoke the order because of Powers of Criminal Courts (Sentencing) Act 2000 s 106A(7).

37.24 ***Hospital and Guardianship Orders, Combined with***

Mental Health Act 1983 s 37(8) Where an order is made under this section, the court shall not: pass a sentence of imprisonment…and for the purposes of this subsection 'sentence of imprisonment' includes any sentence or order for detention.

37.25 ***Young Offender Institution, Detention in, Offender serving Detention and Training Order***

Powers of Criminal Courts (Sentencing) Act 2000 s 106(1) Where a court passes a sentence of detention in a Young Offender Institution in the case of an offender who is subject to a Detention and Training Order, the sentence shall take effect as follows:

(a) if the offender has been released…, at the beginning of the day on which it is passed,

(b) if not, either as mentioned in paragraph (a) above or, if the court so orders, at the time when the offender would otherwise be released.

Powers of Criminal Courts (Sentencing) Act 2000 s 106(4) Where at any time an offender is subject concurrently:

(a) to a Detention and Training Order, and

(b) to a sentence of detention in a Young Offender Institution,

he shall be treated for the purposes of sections 102 to 105 and of section 98 of this Act (place of detention), Chapter IV of this Part (return to detention) and Criminal Justice Act 1991 Part II (early release) as if he were subject only to the one of them that was imposed on the later occasion.

(5) Nothing in subsection (4) above shall require the offender to be released in respect of either the order or the sentence unless and until he is required to be released in respect of each of them.

Note: Criminal Justice and Courts Act 2015 s 15(3) substitutes 'Criminal Justice Act 2003 Part 12 Chapter 6 (release, licences, supervision and recall)' for 'Criminal Justice Act 1991 Part II (early release)'.[550] Ed.

Other matters

37.26 *Explain sentence, Judge must/Suggested sentencing remarks*

Judicial College's Crown Court Compendium Part II Sentencing June 2018 page 4-32

7. **Passing the sentence**

The court must:

(1) Complete the steps set out in chapter S3 [of this guide] [determining the seriousness].

(2) State that it has had regard to[:]

(a) the welfare of the offender; and, if appropriate, that it is taking steps to remove him from undesirable surroundings and/or secure proper provision for his education and training;

(b) the need to prevent him from further offending.

(3) Also state that[:]

(a) the seriousness of the offence is such that a fine or a youth rehabilitation order cannot be justified; and that[:]

(b) the sentence is the least that can be passed to mark the seriousness of the offence/s;

(4) In relation to time spent on remand in custody/secure accommodation/qualifying curfew, as there is no power to order this to count towards the sentence, the court must take this into account when fixing the term. This has not been affected by the provisions of Legal Aid, Sentencing and Punishment of Offenders Act 2012.

(5) Explain that up to one half of the sentence – the 'detention' part of the sentence – will be served in custody and the remainder – the 'training' part – will be served on supervision.

(6) If the offence is committed on or after 1 February 2015 and the offender is aged 18 at the time of the expiry of half the sentence (the requisite custodial period) he will be subject to supervision for 12 months from the date of the end of the requisite custodial period.

(7) Explain the consequences of[:]

(a) Reoffending during the currency of the supervised term of the order – if the offence is punishable with imprisonment, he may be ordered to be detailed for the period outstanding,

(b) Failing to co-operate with supervision – he may be taken before the Youth Court and either fined or ordered to serve the remainder of the order or 3 months, whichever is less,

[550] In force 13/4/15, Criminal Justice and Courts Act 2015 (Commencement No 1, Saving and Transitional Provisions) Order 2015 2015/778 para 3 and Sch 1 para 11

(c) Failing to co-operate with any further supervision period (age 18: see above) – a sentence of curfew, unpaid work or up to 14 days in a Young Offender Institution.

Example
I have had regard to your welfare and to the need to provide for your education and training and I am satisfied that your offence is so serious that only a custodial sentence can be justified.
But for your plea of guilty and the fact that you have spent 76 days on remand in custody I would have sentenced you to a term of 2 years' Detention and Training, this being the least sentence which I could have imposed to mark the seriousness of your offence. Giving you full credit for your prompt plea of guilty and taking account of the time which you have spent on remand I reduce that term to one of 12 months' Detention and Training.
Either: Of this sentence you will spend up to one half in detention – that is custody – and then you will be released to serve the other half of the sentence – the training part – on supervision in the community.
Or – if the offender is 18 by the time that the requisite custodial period expires:
Of this sentence you will spend up to one half in detention – that is custody – and then you will be released and then be supervised in the community for 12 months.
In any case: If, once you have been released and while you are on supervision, you commit any offence punishable with imprisonment or if you fail to co-operate with your supervising officer you will be liable to be returned to custody.

38 Detention and Training Orders: Breach of Supervision

38.1
Release The period of detention imposed for breach of a DTO must be served in full. There is no provision for early release, *R v McGeechan* 2019 EWCA Crim 235 para 23.

Statutory provisions

38.2 ***Statutory provisions Offender commits another offence***
Powers of Criminal Courts (Sentencing) Act 2000 s 105(1) This section applies to a person subject to a Detention and Training Order if:

(a) after his release and before the date on which the term of the order ends, he commits an offence punishable with imprisonment in the case of a person aged 21 or over ('the new offence'), and

(b) whether before or after that date, he is convicted of the new offence.

(2) Subject to section 8(6) of this Act (duty of adult Magistrates' Court to remit young offenders to Youth Court for sentence), the court by or before which a person to whom this section applies is convicted of the new offence may, whether or not it passes any other sentence on him, order him to be detained in such youth detention accommodation as the Secretary of State may determine for the whole or any part of the period which:

(a) begins with the date of the court's order, and

(b) is equal in length to the period between the date on which the new offence was committed and the date mentioned in subsection (1) above.

(3) The period for which a person to whom this section applies is ordered under subsection (2) above to be detained in youth detention accommodation:

(a) shall, as the court may direct, either be served before and be followed by, or be served concurrently with, any sentence imposed for the new offence, and

(b) in either case, shall be disregarded in determining the appropriate length of that sentence.

Interaction with sentences of detention in a young offender institution.
Powers of Criminal Courts (Sentencing) Act 2000 s 106(1) Where a court passes a sentence of detention in a young offender institution in the case of an offender who is subject to a detention and training order, the sentence shall take effect as follows:

(a) if the offender has been released by virtue of subsection (2), (3), (4) or (5) of section 102 above, at the beginning of the day on which it is passed;

(b) if not, either as mentioned in paragraph (a) above or, if the court so orders, at the time when the offender would otherwise be released by virtue of subsection (2), (3), (4) or (5) of section 102.

(4) Subject to subsection (5) below, where at any time an offender is subject concurrently:

(a) to a detention and training order, and

(b) to a sentence of detention in a young offender institution,

he shall be treated for the purposes of sections 102 to 105 above and of section 98 above (place of detention), Chapter IV of this Part (return to detention) and Chapter 6 of Part 12 of the Criminal Justice Act 2003 (release, licences, supervision and recall) as if he were subject only to the one of them that was imposed on the later occasion.

(5) Nothing in subsection (4) above shall require the offender to be released in respect of either the order or the sentence unless and until he is required to be released in respect of each of them.

(6) Where, by virtue of any enactment giving a court power to deal with a person in a way in which a court on a previous occasion could have dealt with him, a detention and training order for any term is made in the case of a person who has attained the age of 18, the person shall be treated as if he had been sentenced to detention in a young offender institution for the same term.

Section 106A deals with definitions and 106B is about further supervision.

38.3 *Statutory provisions Breach of supervision requirements*

Powers of Criminal Courts (Sentencing) Act 2000 s 104(1) Where it appears on information to a justice of the peace that the offender has failed to comply with the requirements under section 103(6)(b) above, the justice:

(a) may issue a summons requiring the offender to appear at a place and time so specified, or

(b) if the information is in writing and on oath, may issue a warrant for the offender's arrest.

(2) Any summons or warrant issued under this section shall direct the offender to appear or be brought:

(a) before a youth court acting in the local justice area in which the offender resides, or

(b) if it is not known where the offender resides, before a youth court acting in the same local justice area as the justice who issued the summons or warrant.

(3) If it is proved to the satisfaction of the youth court before which an offender appears or is brought under this section that he has failed to comply with requirements under section 103(6)(b), that court may:

(a) order the offender to be detained, in such youth detention accommodation as the Secretary of State may determine, for such period, not exceeding the maximum period found under subsection (3A) below, as the court may specify,

(aa) order the offender to be subject to such period of supervision, not exceeding the maximum period found under subsection (3A) below, as the court may specify, or[551]

(b) impose on the offender a fine not exceeding level 3 on the standard scale.

(3A) The maximum period referred to in subsection (3)(a) and (aa) above is the shorter of:

(a) three months, and

(b) the period beginning with the date of the offender's failure and ending with the last day of the term of the Detention and Training Order.

(3B) For the purposes of subsection (3A) above a failure that is found to have occurred over two or more days is to be taken to have occurred on the first of those days.

---

[551] Section 104(3)(a)-(aa) substituted for section 104(3)(a) by Legal Aid, Sentencing and Punishment of Offenders Act 2012 s 80(2)

(3C) A court may order a period of detention or supervision, or impose a fine, under subsection (3) above before or after the end of the term of the Detention and Training Order.

(3D) A period of detention or supervision ordered under subsection (3) above:

(a) begins on the date the order is made, and

(b) may overlap to any extent with the period of supervision under the Detention and Training Order.[552]

(4) An offender detained in pursuance of an order under subsection (3)(a) above shall be deemed to be in legal custody.

(4A) Where an order under subsection (3)(a) above is made in the case of a person who has attained the age of 18, the order has effect to require the person to be detained in prison for the period specified by the court.

(5) A fine imposed under subsection (3)(b) above shall be deemed, for the purposes of any enactment, to be a sum adjudged to be paid by a conviction.

(5A) Sections 104A and 104B below make further provision about the operation of orders under subsection (3) above.

(6) An offender may appeal to the Crown Court against any order made under subsection (3)(a), (aa) or (b) above.

Note: Subsection (4A) above says a person who has 'attained the age of 18' is required to be detained in 'prison'. It should read 'a person who has attained the age of 18-20' should be required to be detained in a 'Young Offender Institution'. Those who abscond and who are arrested after they have 'attained the age of 21' should be required to be detained in 'prison'. Ed.

38.4 *Explanation of breach sentence*

R v McGeechan 2019 EWCA Crim 235 D was released on supervision and committed further offences. Held. para 23 An offender subject to a DTO is not released on licence. The supervision period is a separate part of the term. The commission of an offence during the supervision period does not permit the court to reactivate any part of the detention and training period. The detention period which the court has power to impose is not limited to the specified terms for which a DTO may be ordered set out in section 101 of the Act. The breach sentence is not part of the [first] DTO but a discrete form of detention. It follows that a period of detention under section 105 is not in itself a DTO.

38.5 *Concurrent and consecutive terms after breach of supervision*

Powers of Criminal Courts (Sentencing) Act 2000 s 104(3C)[553] A court may order a period of detention or supervision, or impose a fine, under subsection (3) above before or after the end of the term of the Detention and Training Order.

(3D) A period of detention or supervision ordered under subsection (3) above:

(a) begins on the date the order is made, and

(b) may overlap to any extent with the period of supervision under the Detention and Training Order.

Powers of Criminal Courts (Sentencing) Act 2000 s 104B(1)[554] Where a court makes a Detention and Training Order in the case of an offender who is subject to a period of detention under section 104(3)(a) (breach of supervision), the Detention and Training Order takes effect:

(a) at the beginning of the day on which it is made, or

(b) if the court so orders, at the time when the period of detention under section 104(3)(a) above ends.

[552] Added by Legal Aid, Sentencing and Punishment of Offenders Act 2012 s 80(3)
[553] As inserted by Legal Aid, Sentencing and Punishment of Offenders Act 2012 s 80(3), in force 3/12/12
[554] As inserted by Legal Aid, Sentencing and Punishment of Offenders Act 2012 s 80(7), in force 3/12/12

(2) Where a court orders an offender who is subject to a Detention and Training Order to be subject to a period of detention under section 104(3)(a) (detention for breach of order) above for a failure to comply with requirements under a different Detention and Training Order, the period of detention takes effect as follows:

(a) if the offender has been released by virtue of subsection (2), (3), (4) or (5) of section 102 (ordinary DTO), at the beginning of the day on which the order for the period of detention is made, and

(b) if not, either as mentioned in paragraph (a) above or, if the court so orders, at the time when the offender would otherwise be released by virtue of subsection (2), (3), (4) or (5) of section 102.

Sentencing principles

38.6 *Sentencing Children and Young People Guideline 2017*

Sentencing Children and Young People Guideline 2017, see www.banksr.com Other Matters Guidelines tab In force 1 June 2017 page 35

Breach of a detention and training order (DTO)

7.21 If a child or young person is found to have breached a supervision requirement after release from custody then the court may:

- impose a further period of custody of up to three months or the length of time from the date the breach was committed until the end of the order, **whichever is shorter**;
- impose a further period of supervision of up to three months or the length of time from the date the breach was committed until the end of the order, **whichever is shorter**;
- impose a fine of up to £1,000; or
- take no action.

Even if the offender has attained the age of 18, proceedings for breach of the supervision requirements must be dealt with in the Youth Court.

Commission of further offences during a DTO

7.22 If a child or young person is found guilty of a further imprisonable offence committed during the currency of the order then the court can impose a further period of detention. This period of detention cannot exceed the period between the date of the new offence and the date of when [sic] the original order would have expired.

7.23 This period can be served consecutively or concurrently with any sentence imposed for the new offence and this period should not be taken into account when determining the appropriate length of the sentence for the new offence.

38.7 *Magistrates' Court Sentencing Guidelines*

Magistrates' Court Sentencing Guidelines 2008, see www.banksr.com Other Matters Guidelines tab page 147 When sentencing for the breach of any order for which there is not a specific guideline, the primary objective will be to ensure compliance. Reference to existing guidelines in respect of breaches of orders may provide a helpful point of comparison.

38.8 *Duplicity, Breach and*

S v Doncaster Youth Offending Team 2003 EWHC 1128 (Admin) S was convicted of failing to comply with a Detention and Training Order. S had failed to reside where the YOT had instructed him to, and he had failed to report for four consecutive weeks. It was submitted that the information was bad for duplicity. Held. Sometimes it is difficult to distinguish between separate offences on the one hand and different features of committing the same offence on the other. There were two quite separate licence conditions of which the defendant was in breach. These were failing to keep in touch with his supervising officer and failing to live at the address approved by his supervising officer. These were two separate offences that should not have been tried on the same information.

Parents and guardians

38.9 ***Parent/guardian to pay fine etc. for breaches of orders***

Powers of Criminal Courts (Sentencing) Act 2000 s 137(2) Where but for this subsection a court would impose a fine on a child or young person under:..e) Powers of Criminal Courts (Sentencing) Act 2000 s 104(3)(b) (breach of requirements of supervision under a Detention and Training Order)…the court shall order that the fine be paid by the parent or guardian of the child or young person instead of by the child or young person himself, unless the court is satisfied:

(i) that the parent or guardian cannot be found, or

(ii) that it would be unreasonable to make an order for payment, having regard to the circumstances of the case.

(3) In the case of a young person aged 16 or over, subsections (1) to (2) of this section shall have effect as if, instead of imposing a duty, they conferred a power to make such an order as is mentioned in those subsections.

(4) Subject to subsection (5), no order shall be made under this section without giving the parent or guardian an opportunity of being heard.

(5) An order under this section may be made against a parent or guardian who, having been required to attend, has failed to do so.

Combined with other orders

38.10 ***Detention and Training Orders, Combined with***

R v McGeechan 2019 EWCA Crim 235 The breach sentence had to start on the day it was passed and could not be consecutive to the fresh DTO sentence, Powers of Criminal Courts (Sentencing) Act 2000 s 106(1)(a), see **38.2**.

Note: The real source of the prohibition is in fact Powers of Criminal Courts (Sentencing) Act 2000 s 101(6), see **37.17**. Ed.

The principles can be found in the **DETENTION AND TRAINING ORDERS Combined with other orders** section at para **37.20**.

39 DETENTION UNDER POWERS OF CRIMINAL COURTS (SENTENCING) ACT 2000 S 91

39.1

Powers of Criminal Courts (Sentencing) Act 2000 s 91

Availability The order is available for offenders aged 10-17 on the date of their conviction when the conditions are met, see **39.3**.

Victim surcharge The court must impose a victim surcharge of £30, Criminal Justice Act 2003 s 161A-161B and Criminal Justice Act 2003 (Surcharge) Order 2012 2012/1696 as amended. There are exceptions, a) where a compensation order or an Unlawful Profits Order or a Slavery and Trafficking Reparations Order is imposed, when a reduced amount or a nil amount can be ordered, see **17.67**, and b) where the offence was committed before 1 October 2012, when no surcharge can be made, see **115.3**. Where the offence was committed on or after that date and before 8 April 2016, the amount to be imposed is £20, see **115.4**.

Release and supervision Release is at the halfway point or earlier if the HDC provisions apply. There must be a minimum period of 3 months' supervision following immediately on release, Criminal Justice Act 2003 s 256B.[555] If the sentence is of 12 months or more, then licence will be until sentence expiry.

Rehabilitation periods Over 48 months: excluded from rehabilitation.[556] More than 30 months but not more than 48 months: 3½ years. More than 6 months but not more than 30 months: 2 years. 6 months or less: 18 months.[557] Legal Aid, Sentencing and Punishment of Offenders Act 2012 s 139 changed the periods, see **89.6**.

[555] As inserted by Legal Aid, Sentencing and Punishment of Offenders Act 2012 s 115

[556] Rehabilitation of Offenders Act 1974 s 5(1b)

[557] Rehabilitation of Offenders Act 1974 s 5 Table A

See also the **REHABILITATION OF OFFENDERS ACT 1974** chapter.

39.2 ***Statistics England and Wales***

Detention under section 91

	2008	2009	2010	2011	2012	2013	2014	2015	2016	2017
Males	490	389	404	380	289	255	240	265	223	292
Females	20	28	7	22	10	8	6	7	10	3
All	510	417	411	406	299	263	246	272	233	295

For explanations about the statistics, see page 1-xii. These figures may contain individuals whose sex was not recorded, therefore some figures may not reconcile. For more detailed statistics, see www.banksr.com Statistics tab.

Power to order

39.3 ***Statutory provisions***

Powers of Criminal Courts (Sentencing) Act 2000 s 91(1) Subsection (3) below applies where a person aged under 18 is convicted on indictment of:

(a) an offence punishable with imprisonment for 14 years or more, not being an offence the sentence for which is fixed by law,

(b) an offence under Sexual Offences Act 2003 s 3 (sexual assault),

(c) an offence under Sexual Offences Act 2003 s 13 (child sex offences committed by children or young persons),

(d) an offence under Sexual Offences Act 2003 s 25 (sexual activity with a child family member), and

(e) an offence under Sexual Offences Act 2003 s 26 (inciting a child family member to engage in sexual activity).

Powers of Criminal Courts (Sentencing) Act 2000 s 91(3) If the court is of the opinion that neither a Youth Rehabilitation Order nor a Detention and Training Order is suitable, the court may sentence the offender to be detained for such a period, not exceeding the maximum term of imprisonment with which the offence is punishable, as may be specified in the sentence.

R v AM 2015 EWCA Crim 2272 D pleaded to GBH with intent. She was aged 14 when convicted and was sentenced to 20 months' detention under section 91. Held. There is no substance in the suggestion she had to be a persistent offender to be so sentenced.

39.4 ***Assessing seriousness Associated offences***

R v AM 1998 2 Cr App R (S) 128 LCJ The court could now, when considering the seriousness of an offence falling within section 53(2) and (3) (now section 91), take account of an associated offence even if it were not part and parcel of the main offence and did not fall within section 53(2) and (3).

39.5 ***Appropriate length Is it restricted?***

R (D) v Manchester City Youth Court 2001 EWHC (Admin) 860, 2002 1 Cr App R (S) 135 (p 573) High Court There is no statutory restriction on a court passing a section 91 sentence of less than 2 years. But it will only be in very exceptional and restricted circumstances that it will be appropriate to do so, rather than make a Detention and Training Order. The fact that an offender, as here, does not qualify for a Detention and Training Order because he is not a persistent offender is not such an exceptional circumstance as to justify the passing of a period of detention of less than 2 years under section 91.

R (W) v Southampton Youth Court 2002 EWCA Civ 1640, 2003 1 Cr App R (S) 87 (p 455) para 13 LCJ The power of the Crown Court in section 91 is not restricted either to a period of more than 2 years' detention or less than 2 years' detention.

R v Jahmarl 2004 EWCA Crim 2199, 2005 1 Cr App R (S) 96 (p 534) D was convicted of attempted robbery. At the time of the offence he was aged 14 and at the sentence

hearing he was aged 15. D was of good character. The Judge thought the sentencing options were either a 2-year detention under section 91 or a non-custodial sentence. Held. The rules about when it is appropriate to commit youths for trial do not restrict the Crown Court's sentencing powers. The Court was not faced with that stark choice. The proper sentence length was 1 year. D could have been sentenced to detention under section 91 for less than 2 years. We do not agree he did not qualify for a Detention and Training Order. With the probation officer's assistance, we think a 1-year DTO would be the better order.
Note: Support for the principle that less than 2 years can be passed is that Parliament set the old rehabilitation periods for periods of section 91 detention at 'less than 6 months' and '6 months to 30 months', see the 8th edition of this book. Ed.

39.6 ***Offender aged under 12***

Powers of Criminal Courts (Sentencing) Act 2000 s 100(2)(b) A court shall not make a Detention and Training Order in the case of an offender under the age of 12 at the time of conviction, unless i) it is of the opinion that only a custodial sentence would be adequate to protect the public from further offending by him, and ii) the offence was committed on or after such a date as the Secretary of State may by order appoint.
R (W) v Thetford Youth Court 2002 EWHC 1252 (Admin), 2003 1 Cr App R (S) 67 (p 323)[558] High Court In the case of an offender aged under 12, the appropriate sentence will usually be a non-custodial sentence. It is accepted that: a) where an offender is aged under 12, b) a custodial sentence is appropriate, and c) a Detention and Training Order is not available, a sentence under section 91 may be appropriate and a term of less than 2 years is available. This would only be in 'very exceptional' cases.

39.7 ***Offender aged under 15***

R (W) v Thetford Youth Court 2002 EWHC 1252 (Admin), 2003 1 Cr App R (S) 67 (p 323)[559] High Court In the case of an offender aged under 15 who is not a persistent offender, the appropriate sentence will usually be a non-custodial sentence. It is accepted that where: a) an offender aged under 15 who is not a persistent offender, b) a custodial sentence is appropriate, and c) a Detention and Training Order is not available, a sentence under section 91 may be appropriate and a term of less than 2 years is available. This would only be in 'very exceptional' cases.

The restrictions on imposing this order

Justified, must be see the **CUSTODY: GENERAL PRINCIPLES Offence must be so serious a fine or a community sentence cannot be justified** section at **28.26**.
Legally represented, Offender must be see the **CUSTODY: GENERAL PRINCIPLES Defendants who have not been previously sentenced to custody** section at **28.19**.
Sentence must be for the shortest term see the **CUSTODY: GENERAL PRINCIPLES** ***Must be for the shortest term, Custody*** at para at **28.27**.

Sentencing principles

39.8 ***Basic principles***

For general principles see the **CHILDREN AND YOUNG OFFENDERS: CUSTODIAL SENTENCES** ***Basic principles*** para at **14.11**.
R v Fairhurst 1986 8 Cr App R (S) 346 LCJ Considering detention under Children and Young Persons Act 1933 s 53(2) (now section 91). It was not necessary that the crime committed should be one of exceptional gravity, such as attempted murder, manslaughter, wounding with intent, armed robbery or the like [to impose section 91 detention].
R v JR and G 2001 1 Cr App R (S) 109 (p 377) Sentencing young men or boys of this age (14) is always a difficult exercise. The court has to perform a balancing act between the interests of the public and the victim and the interests of the young offender. *R v Ganley* 2001 1 Cr App R (S) 17 (p 60) was not intended to create a principle that no

[558] Also known as *R (M) v Waltham Forest Youth Court* 2002 EWHC 1252, 2003 1 Cr App R (S) 67 (p 323)
[559] Also known as *R (M) v Waltham Forest Youth Court* 2002 EWHC 1252, 2003 1 Cr App R (S) 67 (p 323)

offender under the age of 15 can be detained if they are of previous good character. Its purpose was to remind sentencers of their duty to avoid imposing lengthy sentences on very young offenders where possible without removing from them a power given by statute.
R (W) v Southampton Youth Court 2002 EWCA Civ 1640, 2003 1 Cr App R (S) 87 (p 455) The simple principle underlying the current legislation for sentencing very young offenders is that, generally speaking, first-time offenders aged 13 and 14, and all offenders aged 11 and 12, should not be detained in custody. For 13- and 14-year-olds, where the youth persists in offending, the position changes. Clearly some offences or offending are so serious in themselves that the court has to contemplate the possibility of sending an under 15-year-old for a period in custody, despite the general approach of the legislation. That may be to protect the public or it may be that the long-term interests of the offender require such a drastic course, even though he is under 12 or under 15 but not a persistent offender. To cater for this possibility, Parliament has left open to the courts the use of Powers of Criminal Courts (Sentencing) Act 2000 s 91. The need in exceptional cases to make use of these powers cannot, however, have been intended to water down the general principle.
Note: The *Sentencing Children and Young People Guideline 2017*, see www.banksr.com Other Matters Guidelines tab (at **13.31**), takes precedence over these cases. Ed.
Pre-sentence report must have see the **PRE-SENTENCE REPORTS** ***Pre-sentence report, Court must have Those aged under 18*** para at **83.15**.
Mentally disordered offenders see the **DEFENDANT** ***Mentally disordered defendants*** para at **242.39** in Volume 2.
Welfare of the offender, Must consider see the **CHILDREN AND YOUNG OFFENDERS: GENERAL PRINCIPLES Welfare** section at **13.38**.

39.9 ***Sentences for offences where section 91 orders are unavailable***
R v Mills and Others 1998 2 Cr App R (S) 128 at 134 LCJ Where some of the offences fall within section 53(2) and (3) (now section 91) and other offences are 'associated' but do not fall within the section, it will usually be preferable to impose a term under section 53(2) and (3) which takes account of the associated offence or offences which do not fall within that section. In such a case the practice recommended by the Court in *R v Fairhurst* 1986 8 Cr App R (S) 346 of imposing no separate penalty for the lesser offence should be adopted.
R v Reynolds and Others Re S 2007 EWCA Crim 538, 2 Cr App R (S) 87 (p 553) paras 66-70 D was convicted of section 18 and pleaded to a section 47 charge against the same victim. The Judge imposed detention under section 91 for both offences, 6 years on the section 18 and 1 year concurrent on the section 47. Held. The Judge was not entitled to impose detention under section 91 for the section 47. The only practicable course was to impose no separate penalty.
R v Y 2016 EWCA Crim 442 D, then aged 17, pleaded to possession of a prohibited weapon and possession of ammunition without a certificate. Section 91 applied to the first offence but not the second. The Judge gave D 4 years and 1 year consecutive. Held. We pass a global sentence of 4 years. We apply that to the first count and impose no penalty on the second count.
See also: *R v S* 2017 EWCA Crim 1821 D pleaded to two robberies, possession of a bladed article and assault by beating. The Judge gave 24 months and 8 months consecutive on the robberies and concurrent detention on the other counts. Held. Detention under section 91 was not available for the non-robbery counts so the sentence should be 'no penalty'.

39.10 ***Explain sentence, Judge must/Suggested sentencing remarks***
Judicial College's Crown Court Compendium Part II Sentencing June 2018 page 4-30
3. **Passing the sentence**
The court must:

(1) Complete the steps set out in chapter S3 [in this guide] [determining the seriousness].
(2) State that it has had regard to the welfare of the offender and the need to prevent the offender from further offending.
(3) (In an appropriate case) state that it is taking steps to remove him from undesirable surroundings and/or secure proper provision for his education and training.
(4) Also state that[:]

(a) the seriousness of the offence is such that only a sentence under s 91 can be justified;

(b) the sentence is the least that can be passed to mark the seriousness of the offence/s.

5) Explain that up to one half of the sentence will be served in custody and on release D will be on licence/supervision (as appropriate) and if D reoffends or does not co-operate with the terms of licence/supervision D will be liable to be returned to custody.

Example
In deciding what is the right sentence in your case I have had regard to your welfare and the need to prevent you from committing any more offences and I am satisfied that the best way of achieving these things is to sentence you to a term of detention under section 91* and that despite your age your offence is so serious that nothing but a substantial custodial sentence can be justified. The least sentence that I can pass is one of 3 years' detention.
You will serve up to half this sentence in custody and then you will be released on licence. Your licence will be subject to a number of conditions and if you break any of those conditions your licence may be revoked and you will be liable to serve the rest of the sentence in custody.
*Reference to section 91 is not for the benefit of D (although he may already have had this possibility explained to him and understand what it means) but so that there is no ambiguity in the minds of all other parties, including the CACD [Court of Appeal Criminal Division], about the provision under which the sentence has been imposed.

Detention for life

39.11
Availability The order is available for offenders who are 10-17 years of age on the date of their conviction when the statutory conditions are met.
Murder When the offence is murder, the sentencing order is called Detention at HM's Pleasure, see the **MURDER** ***Defendant aged under 21*** paras at **287.77** in Volume 2.
Note: It can be inferred that the criteria for detention for life are a mixture of the principles for imposing life sentences, see the **LIFE SENTENCES: CJA 2003 S 225 AND 226/DISCRETIONARY LIFE** chapter, and the principles for sentencing children and young offenders, see the **CHILDREN AND YOUNG OFFENDERS** chapter. Ed.
Victim surcharge The amount is £30, Criminal Justice Act 2003 s 161A-161B. For more detail see **39.1**.
Detention for life or detention for public protection for serious offences committed by those under 18

39.12 ***Detention for life Statutory provisions***
Criminal Justice Act 2003 s 226(1) This section applies where:

(a) a person aged under 18 is convicted of a serious offence committed after the commencement of this section, and

(b) the court is of the opinion that there is a significant risk to members of the public of serious harm occasioned by the commission by him of further specified offences.

(2) If:

(a) the offence is one in respect of which the offender would apart from this section be liable to a sentence of detention for life under Powers of Criminal Courts (Sentencing) Act 2000 s 91, and

(b) the court considers that the seriousness of the offence, or of the offence and one or more offences associated with it, is such as to justify the imposition of a sentence of detention for life,

the court must impose a sentence of detention for life under that section.
(3) In a case not falling within subsection (2), the court may impose a sentence of Detention for Public Protection if the notional minimum term is at least two years.
(3A) The notional minimum term is the part of the sentence that the court would specify under section 82A(2) of the Sentencing Act (determination of tariff) if it imposed a sentence of Detention for Public Protection but was required to disregard the matter mentioned in section 82A(3)(b) of that Act (crediting periods of remand).
(4) A sentence of Detention for Public Protection is a sentence of detention for an indeterminate period, subject to the provisions of Crime (Sentences) Act 1997 Part 2 Chapter 2 as to the release of prisoners and duration of licences.
(5) An offence the sentence for which is imposed under this section is not to be regarded as an offence the sentence for which is fixed by law.
See also the **LIFE IMPRISONMENT: DISCRETIONARY LIFE** chapter.

Combined with other orders

39.13 ***Detention and Training Orders, Combined with***
R v Fairhurst 1986 8 Cr App R (S) 346 LCJ As this Court has said in the case of *R v Gaskin* 1985 7 Cr App R (S) 28, it is undesirable that sentences of section 53(2) detention (now section 91 detention) and of youth custody should be passed to run either consecutively to or concurrently with each other. It is not, however, always possible to avoid this. The only way out of the problem in general may be to impose no separate penalty for the offences for which section 53(2) (now section 91) detention is not available. Although that solution is not altogether satisfactory, it provides fewer difficulties than any other possible method.
R v Mills and Others 1998 2 Cr App R (S) 128 at 134 LCJ We consider it generally undesirable to impose concurrent sentences under both Children and Young Persons Act 1933 s 53(2)-(3) (now section 91) and Criminal Justice Act 1982 s 1B (detention in a Young Offender Institution, now replaced by detention and training). They should be particularly avoided for offenders under the age of 16. Where there are multiple offences, the court should pass sentences under section 53(2) and (3) for the offences for which it is available, and subsequently impose no separate penalty for the other offences.
R v Reynolds and Others Re S 2007 EWCA Crim 538, 2 Cr App R (S) 87 (p 553) paras 66-70 The defendant was convicted of section 18 in which he was said to have played a part in an attack on an innocent passer-by. He also pleaded to a section 47 charge against the same victim. The Judge found that D was not dangerous within the meaning of the 2003 Act but imposed detention under section 91 for both offences, 6 years on the section 18 and 1 year concurrent on the section 47. Held. The Judge was not entitled to impose detention under section 91 for the section 47. The only practicable course was to impose no separate penalty.
For imposing section 91 detention when an offender is subject to a Detention and Training Order, see **37.23**.

39.14 ***Hospital and Guardianship Orders, Combined with***
Mental Health Act 1983 s 37(8) Where an order is made under this section, the court shall not: pass a sentence of imprisonment…and for the purposes of this subsection 'sentence of imprisonment' includes any sentence or order for detention.
For assistance for the position with other orders, see the **CUSTODY, IMPRISONMENT Combined with other orders** section at **28.34**.

40 DISMISSAL FROM HM'S SERVICE

40.1
Armed Forces Act 2006 s 164

Availability The Court may make this order for all ranks and ex-servicemen and women (but only if they are members of the reserve forces), see *Guidance on Sentencing in the Court Martial 2018* Annex B.
Statistics The statistics are so incomplete, they are no longer listed in this book.
Rehabilitation period 12 months for those aged 18+, 6 months for those under 18.[560] Legal Aid, Sentencing and Punishment of Offenders Act 2012 s 139 amended the periods, see **89.6**.

40.2 *Test to apply*

Armed Forces Act 2006 s 265 A court may not pass a sentence of dismissal or dismissal with disgrace in respect of an offence unless it is of the opinion that the offence, or the combination of the offence and one or more offences associated with it, was serious enough to warrant such a sentence.

40.3 *Guidance*

Guidance on Sentencing in the Court Martial 2018 para 3.2
Dismissal and Dismissal with disgrace from Her Majesty's Service 3.2.1 Dismissal is a sentence imposed by a court; discharge is an administrative action resulting in the ending of employment. Although the effects may appear similar, there are significant differences. Dismissal either with or without disgrace can have far-reaching consequences on an ex-Service person in civilian life. The primary consideration for the Court Martial is whether the offence is serious enough that the offender should be dismissed as a sentence, Armed Forces Act 2006 s 265(1). In *R v Downing* 2010 EWCA Crim 739 at para 13, [the Lord Chief Justice] said, "The question whether the criminal activities of a member of the military require dismissal from the Service is pre-eminently, although not exclusively, a decision for the Court Martial. For this purpose, for the assessment of the impact of the applicant's convictions on his ability to continue to serve in the relevant force, the Court Martial must be regarded as an expert tribunal, entitled to the same level of respect to which any such tribunal is entitled when an appeal court is considering its decision."
3.2.2 It is, therefore, well established that dismissal should not be imposed as a matter of mere expediency. It would be wrong in principle to dismiss purely because the offender is, for some extraneous reason, not fitted for Service life, or states that he does not wish to remain in the Service. In those circumstances administrative discharge may be appropriate, and that is not a matter within the power of the court. Dismissal can be awarded with or without either imprisonment or detention, and in combination with any other punishment. Dismissal and dismissal with disgrace remains on an offender's record for 12 months from the date of sentence before becoming spent[561] (6 months for offenders sentenced when under 18 years).
3.2.3 Where dismissal is an option, particularly in cases where the Services' policy in relation to the particular type of offending is that it is incompatible with further Service (for example some forms of drug abuse), but the court decides not to dismiss, it should give its reasons fully. The court should state that the decision not to dismiss is made on the basis of all the information before it. It is important for the court's reasons for non-dismissal to be clear to the Services when considering whether to discharge the offender subsequently. It would arguably be executive interference in the judicial process (and therefore unfair) for the Services to discharge the offender solely for the same matter for which the court decided not to dismiss, not least because the court is likely to have imposed a heavier sentence of detention, designed to re-train and rehabilitate, to offset the non-dismissal. There might, however, be separate additional reasons for discharge which were not considered by the court and which must remain a matter for the Services; the court cannot prevent or restrain the Services from discharging. See paras 2.18.1 to 2.18.4 and also 3.4.13 to 3.4.15 [Not listed. Ed.].

[560] Rehabilitation of Offenders Act 1974 s 5 Table A
[561] Legal Aid, Sentencing and Punishment of Offenders Act 2012 s 139, in force 10/3/14

3.2.4 An offender who is dismissed from the Service must also be reduced to the ranks, Armed Forces Act 2006 s 295(4) (except in the case of a commissioned officer, whose commission is forfeit) and has no right to a resettlement course or terminal leave. There is inevitably a financial effect on the offender of losing his job, and added effects, which may be more significant, if he has not yet qualified for a pension in immediate payment, see para 3.3 at **40.5**. Although reduction in rank is automatic, the court should always state in sentencing remarks that reduction is part of the sentence.
3.2.4 The Court Martial does not as a matter of course hear whether an offender's Commanding Officer wishes to retain him (as used to be the case). The offender may introduce evidence from his superior officers in mitigation or as a character reference, and the prosecutor can address the Court Martial on Service policy regarding the relevant offence. In that way, operational effectiveness can be taken into account as a relevant consideration. The future employability of the offender is a relevant consideration. In *R v Bywater* 2010 EWCA Crim 483 at para 20, the [Court Martial Appeal Court] said, "…there is a sound basis for concluding that, given the particular features of military service referred to elsewhere in the Guidance, 'employability' may be a relevant consideration when a Court Martial is considering the question of dismissal, even if not the only or primary factor."
3.2.6 The Board should be reminded that an officer called by the defence to give the character of the accused may not necessarily be expressing the views of the Commanding Officer.
3.2.7 Dismissal with disgrace is an exceptional form of punishment for use when the nature and circumstances of the offence make a sentence of dismissal inadequate to reflect the displeasure with which the court regards the defendant's conduct. It marks the fact that the defendant's conduct has disgraced the Service in the sense that it has been dishonoured, shamed, discredited or brought the Service into disrepute. The offence itself need not necessarily be disgraceful. It is used sparingly to avoid diluting its effect, and when the offending conduct is such that the court wishes to draw attention to its gravity. When considering whether dismissal with disgrace is appropriate the court takes into account: i) The nature of the offence, ii) Its surrounding circumstances, iii) The rank of the offender and the degree of responsibility that should therefore be expected of him, and iv) Whether the sentence is in the interests of the Service.
3.2.8 The Court Martial should always consider dismissal with disgrace where an offender is sentenced for a serious offence committed on operations where the offence is likely to tarnish the reputation of other members of the British Armed Forces involved in that operation. In the case of R v Blackman, where a Royal Marine Sergeant was filmed executing an injured enemy combatant and then telling those under his command not to report it, the court of first instance correctly concluded that dismissal with disgrace was appropriate. (The point was not fully argued before the CMAC, which, as a matter of clemency substituted dismissal for dismissal with disgrace.)

Principle

3.3.12 Any court in sentencing must take account of the effect of the sentence passed, and particularly the financial effect. In *R v Cooney, Allam and Wood* 1999 3 AER 173, the [Court Martial Appeal Court] reinforced this principle and, on the facts of one of the cases (Allam), stated at page 183e that dismissal and the ensuing loss of an immediate pension was too severe for a single charge of causing death by dangerous driving, particularly because there was no aggravating feature arising from the Service context. Sometimes, however, the issue of loss of pension and gratuity has been exaggerated and misinterpreted by advocates seeking to use this point to argue against dismissal. In civilian life a professional person convicted of serious offences would inevitably lose his employment. He would retain contributions conferring entitlement to a pension which he would be due to receive when reaching pensionable age (normally 65), and he would most likely suffer financial loss by not being able to earn as much money in any subsequent employment. In the Service context, the dismissed individual retains a preserved pension which fully reflects the years already served, but he may lose the opportunity to qualify for an immediate pension (AFPS75) or Early Departure Payment (AFPS05) – in effect that future loss is no different from future loss of earnings in the civilian context. It is, therefore, a flawed argument to suggest that someone who has committed an offence meriting dismissal should be retained in the Service solely on the basis that he otherwise would lose the opportunity to qualify for an immediate pension by serving for a further period. Nevertheless, any potential loss should be one of the factors which is relevant when considering dismissal.

3.3.14 The [Court Martial Appeal Court] has accepted this proposition in a number of cases, for example *R v Peters* 2005 EWCA Crim 3096. In *R v Birch* 2011 EWCA Crim 46, Hughes LJ said, "Courts Martial are extremely familiar with the financial consequences of what they do. Any calculation of loss of income in any event proceeds upon the wholly hypothetical basis that the defendant is not going to be employed anywhere else and as a fit young man he almost certainly would be employed elsewhere. We agree with the general proposition that in this case, as in some others, the impact of the loss of income is readily susceptible to over-statement. We also bear in mind that a person in a civilian occupation who behaved as this defendant did would at least be at serious risk of losing a civilian job."

40.4 ***Assessing loss of income***

R v Birch 2011 EWCA Crim 46 D was a corporal with nine years' service. When drunk, he entered a barrack room and assaulted two of its occupants. He punched one man four times and threw a chair at him and head-butted or attempted to head-butt another. He was sentenced to 6 months' detention, demoted to the ranks and dismissed from service. The victims were recruits under his care. Held. The Court Martial is extremely familiar with the financial consequences of what it does. Any calculation of loss of income in any event proceeds upon the wholly hypothetical basis that D is not going to be employed anywhere else and as a fit young man he almost certainly would be employed elsewhere. The impact of the loss of income is readily susceptible to over-statement. We also bear in mind that a person in a civilian occupation who behaved as this defendant did would at least be at serious risk of losing a civilian job.

40.5 ***Assessing loss of income Pensions (dismissal and reduction in rank)***

Guidance on Sentencing in the Court Martial 2018 para 3.3.1 The Armed Forces have three pension schemes for the Regular Forces. It is important that the court knows which scheme applies to a defendant where dismissal is being considered. Those who are susceptible to the greatest financial loss are those with higher ranks or those who have been in the Services for a long time. Whilst it is necessary to consider the financial implications of sentences passed on such Service personnel, seniority and maturity in an offender are aggravating factors and it would be wrong to sentence a high-ranking offender to a significantly lower sentence than a junior or low-ranking one for the same offence solely in order to preserve his financial advantages.

3.3.2 Entitlement to a pension or Early Departure Payment (EDP), without having to wait until scheme pension age, is a valuable benefit. Early departure as a result of dismissal from the Armed Forces before the member reaches their entitlement point will cause the member to lose this benefit and instead leave with a deferred pension and, if they have served long enough, potentially a resettlement grant. Members who leave after passing their entitlement point will receive an immediate pension or EDP, based on service up to the last day of reckonable or qualifying service in the Armed Forces.

3.3.3 Those who are nearing a qualification point for an immediate pension or EDP would be the most affected by the financial effects of dismissal, which can amount to the loss of a significant sum accrued over many years. The loss of opportunity to have the remaining years of an engagement count towards a pension calculation has an additional effect. As dismissal is not automatic (as used to be the case when a person was sentenced to imprisonment, for example) the decision to dismiss will always be made having considered all of the consequences of the sentence.

More detail can be found at paras 3.3.4 to 3.3.11.

R v Wright-Stainton 2011 EWCA Crim 2131 D pleaded to four counts of fraud. He was a Financial Systems Administrator in the Army, after almost 22 years of service. He was responsible for payroll and allowances and had access to the Army's personnel computer system. Using this privileged access, D submitted false claims and credited his account with money to which he was not entitled. He benefited to the sum of £3,699.10. D, aged 39 at appeal, was of good character and had received four medals. He had incurred debts of £20,000 and suffered from a serious depressive illness. D would have received a total retirement package of £292,536 unless he was discharged. Upon discharge, in consequence of the sentence imposed, he would lose £239,442 of those benefits. Held. He was in gross breach of trust. It must be recognised that the loss of benefit is a consequence of dismissal. Dismissal was an excessive punishment.

See also: *R v Cooney* 1999 2 Cr App R 428 (CMAC Here dismissal with pension loss for causing death by dangerous driving was too severe a penalty. Principles considered.)

R v Martin 2017 EWCA Crim 648, 2 Cr App R (S) 28 (p 226) (LCJ Rules considered for reductions in rank and pension entitlement. Held. The consequences of a reduction in rank are far from straightforward. [Some of the entitlements are protected. Due to the ability to regain rank etc., the factor here does not have much weight so we do not disturb the sentence.])

Note: The problem appears to be that neither the court nor the pension authority can adjust the retained proportion of a dismissed defendant's pension. Ed.

40.6 *On the facts, dismissal correct/within court's discretion*

R v Bailey 2019 EWCA Crim 372 D, a Flight Lieutenant, pleaded to Armed Forces Act 2006 s 42, namely theft. He found a set of keys to the RAF station's gym and kept them for about a year. At a weekend, D entered a storeroom at the gym and stole a women's ski jacket for use by his wife on a holiday. After the holiday he said he tried to return the jacket but the locks had been changed. D was aged 43 with 22 years' service and was of exemplary good character. He had medals and decorations. There were five RAF references. The starting point for any offence of dishonesty was dismissal. The Court Martial said the keys should have been returned at the earliest opportunity and trust and integrity were essential for maintaining discipline. Further those guilty of theft could not realistically continue serving. Held. This is a very sad case. Dismissal would have a significant financial impact on him and his family. Most of the listed mitigating factors were present. We understand why a grave view is taken of dishonesty in service life. As outsiders we struggle to see how D could continue to exercise authority. Dismissal was not wrong.

Old cases: *R v Downing* 2010 EWCA Crim 739, *R v Ingram* 2010 EWCA Crim 1645 and *R v Gibson* 2010 EWCA Crim 2813

For a summary of these cases, see the 13th edition of this book.

40.7 *On the facts, dismissal incorrect*

R v Birch 2011 EWCA Crim 46 D was a corporal with nine years' service. When drunk, he entered a barrack room and assaulted two of its occupants. He punched one man four times and threw a chair at him and head-butted or attempted to head-butt another. The victims were recruits under his care. D was sentenced to 6 months' detention, demoted to the ranks and dismissed from service. His Platoon Commander described him as hard-working, talented and trustworthy with a good future in the Army. Held. It is clear that the Court Martial attached a good deal of significance to D's conduct during the trial. He denied the offence. His assertion was that he could not remember anything at all about the evening, but he nevertheless had the several recruit witnesses who were called challenged and, it would appear, quite directly challenged. The accusation in effect was that it was all a 'put-up job'. That behaviour at trial did him no credit at all. It deprived him of what would have been easily his best mitigation, which was that he got very drunk and now wished he had not. Courts which have to deal with trials of that kind are used to having to remind themselves that, although the conduct during the trial deprives the defendant of mitigation, it does not make the offence any worse. The sentence was too severe. The dismissal will be quashed. The other sentences remain.

R v Robinson 2014 EWCA Crim 1601 D was convicted of battery. D, who had been drinking, hitched a lift with three on-duty army colleagues in a taxi, driven by V. There was an unpleasant argument over the fare and everyone but D left the vehicle. "Turbulence developed into physicality" opposite the Military Police station. D was told by his colleagues to stay in the taxi but left and involved himself in the 'struggle'. He bit[562] V on the head. V played an active and willing part in the 'struggle' and didn't want a prosecution. D was a corporal in the Royal Military Police. He was aged 35 and had over 14 years' service. He was on heavy medication and had no convictions. He had five children, two with medical needs. The pre-sentence report said: a) D should remain in the Royal Military Police, b) he posed a low risk of serious harm and reoffending, and c) dismissal would severely affect his pension. The Judge Advocate said, like civilian police, D was expected to adhere to higher standards of discipline. Held. D's mistake was to leave the car and join the fight. We are not convinced that if D was a civilian policeman he would be sacked. We assume V, accustomed to delivering soldiers back to Colchester, had a mature attitude to their behaviour. V's attitude to the case assists in assessing culpability and harm. D's commanding officer's efforts to retain D were important. **Severe reprimand** and the loss of ten days' pay, not dismissal.

R v L 2017 EWCA Crim 709 D, a Lance Corporal in the Royal Military Police (RMP), was convicted of one count of battery. D, V and other members of their RMP unit had been at a bowling alley. D and V had had a lot to drink and they continued to drink when they got back to their accommodation. D banged on V's door in an aggressive manner. They got into an argument and it was suggested that V said to D, "Get out, you Fenian bastard." D then punched V to the left side of his face and an exchange of blows took place. A witness entered the room and saw V sitting on the floor with D standing over him. D punched V three times in the face. The witness intervened and stopped a fourth punch before ushering D from the room. In interview, D could not remember why he was in V's room. The insult from V was said to be particularly provocative because D was a Roman Catholic from Northern Ireland who, despite consequences to him and his family, had had the courage to join the British Army. The author of the pre-sentence report proposed a fine and/or a severe reprimand as being a suitable punishment. The Judge Advocate, upon hearing that the defence was hoping to dissuade him from ordering D's dismissal, said "Police officers are trusted. They are given rank and powers. Unfortunately, when something goes wrong and they behave in the way that your client did, consequences follow." That the attack was on a fellow serviceman and in his own private quarters were aggravating factors. In mitigation, D had an exemplary four-year record and was of previous good character. He was reduced to the ranks, dismissed from the service and ordered to serve 60 days' detention. A reduction to the ranks would end D's career in the RMP. Held. The offence must be seen in the military context. Court Martial Guidance for sentencing is explicit: regard should be had to the Sentencing Council guidelines. The only reference the Judge Advocate made to the guidelines was to say that they would not be helpful. Had this offence been committed in a civilian context by a man of previous good character, it is highly unlikely he would have received a custodial sentence. The sentencing process was flawed. D has already served 60 days' detention. Therefore, we quash the order for dismissal, detention and reduction to the ranks and in their place impose a **severe reprimand.** If the detention had not been served we would have imposed a fine and/or a compensation order.

[562] 'Bit' may be a typo for 'hit'.

R v Price and Bell 2014 EWCA Crim 229 (Staff Sergeant, D1, convicted of negligently performing duties in relation to a live firing exercise. Corporal, D2, pleaded to negligently performing duties whilst handling a weapon. D2's weapon had jammed. D1, who was supervising the exercise, failed to stop the exercise knowing the weapon was unsafe, and failed to warn the officer attempting to clear the jam that he was pointing the weapon at a colleague. D2 attempted to clear the jam and the weapon discharged and killed the colleague. D2's training had been deficient. It was a failure to respond to the unusual demands of a live firing exercise. Unblemished character with genuine integrity and professionalism. Army wanted D2 to remain in service. Dismissal was not necessary for either. **Reduction to ranks** substituted.)
R v Coleman 2017 EWCA Crim 2346 (D pleaded to Public Order Act 1986 s 5. He banged on a cubicle in a ladies' lavatory and exposed his penis to a woman, V, when she came out. V's husband was in the same army unit. D's commanding officer wanted to retain him because of his distinguished service record. Held. Minor sex offences are more serious in the services because they undermine unit cohesion. However, a **reduction in rank** from Corporal to Lance Corporal, not dismissal.)
R v Townsend 2018 EWCA Crim 430 (D pleaded to negligently performing a duty. He flew an RAF aeroplane with nearly 200 passengers and crew. His camera (which he was discouraged from having in the cockpit) fell and jammed the control slide stick. This caused the plane to go into a steep dive and fall about 4,400 feet in half a minute. The loss of gravity caused 32 physical and 'a number' of psychological injuries. His co-pilot suffered serious spinal injuries. The cost to the RAF was 'many millions of pounds'. D was aged 49 and had a long and 'unblemished' career with a good future ahead of him. His superiors wanted him to stay. Held. We are not satisfied a suspended sentence (no appeal) and dismissal was necessary. It was a heavy combination with no reasons to justify it. Dismissal quashed.)
Old cases: *R v Wright-Stainton* 2011 EWCA Crim 2131 and *R v Smart* 2011 EWCA Crim 2738

41 Disqualification from Driving: Basic Principles

41.1

Children and young offenders The order is available whatever the age of the offender.[563]
Court Martial Motoring offences within military establishments, if committed on roads that are as a matter of law public roads, are dealt with in the same way as motoring offences on public roads in England and Wales but are subject to a different sentencing regime because the Court Martial has no power to impose penalty points on driving licences or disqualify from driving. Driving offences are often charged as breaches of standing orders, *Guidance on Sentencing in the Court Martial 2018* para 5.11.1. There is also no power to endorse a licence.
Compulsory extended periods The rules for imposing all types of driving disqualification (except interim disqualification) were radically altered from 13 April 2015 by Road Traffic Offenders Act 1988 s 35A[564] (as amended), which requires the court to add an extended period to the disqualification period. For more details, see **41.16**.
Rehabilitation period The rehabilitation period begins at the date of conviction and ends on the last day of the disqualification period.[565]
See also the **Rehabilitation of Offenders Act 1974** chapter.
There are the following other chapters:

[563] I know of no statutory bar and it makes sense for there to be no age limit. If a defendant commits the offence of causing death by driving when aged 18 it must be helpful to the judge sentencing him or her to see on the licence the earlier offences with the appropriate disqualification entered. This is especially so when the period of disqualification for a young offender includes a time in the future when the offender might otherwise have obtained a driving licence.
[564] As inserted by Coroners and Justice Act 2009 s 2 and Sch 16 paras 2 and 5
[565] Rehabilitation of Offenders Act 1974 s 5(8)

Disqualification from Driving: Discretionary: General Power
Disqualification from Driving: Discretionary: Road Traffic
Disqualification from Driving: Interim
Disqualification from Driving: Obligatory
Disqualification from Driving: Totting Up

For young drivers who lose their licence when they accumulate six penalty points, see the **Revocation of New Drivers' Licences** chapter.

There is also the **Endorsement** chapter. Penalty points are dealt with in the **Disqualification from Driving: Totting Up Penalty points** section at **46.6**.

41.2 *Statistics England and Wales*

Disqualification from driving: Number of orders

	Crown Court			Magistrates' Court		
	2014	**2015**	**2016**	**2014**	**2015**	**2016**
Endorsements without disqualification	5,603	6,792	8,190	383,995	426,480	447,559
Total number of disqualifications	4,613	5,458	6,028	58,078	59,984	62,361
Driving test requirement imposed	3,075	3,589	4,115	1,248	1,428	1,784
Disqualified until test is passed (stand-alone)	2,226	2,794	2,997	39	39	38
Periods of disqualification						
Under 6-month period	48	35	40	6,467	6,944	6,811
6-month period	100	113	117	2,660	2,548	2,786
Over 6 months and under 1 year	20	20	27	506	521	632
1 year	781	798	736	12,812	13,953	13,918
Over 1 year and under 2	337	372	499	20,206	20,677	21,755
2 years and under 3	547	621	711	5,927	6,119	7,137
3 years	415	467	379	5,947	5,498	5,356
Over 3 years and under 4	18	30	180	1,542	1,772	1,938
4 years and under 5	81	88	135	1,167	1,084	1,232
5 years and under 10	113	103	166	766	793	720
10 years and less than life	15	14	20	36	33	33
Life	2	3	21	2	2	5

For an explanation about the statistics, see page 1-xii. The MoJ no longer provide Banks on Sentence with these statistics.

Disqualification in the defendant's absence

41.3 *Statutory power*

Magistrates' Courts Act 1980 s 11(4) [Where the defendant fails to attend] the court shall not in a person's absence impose any disqualification on him, except on resumption of the hearing after an adjournment under section 10(3) (of this Act), and where a trial is adjourned…the notice required by section 10(2) (of this Act) shall include notice of the reason for the adjournment.

41.4 *Magistrates' Court Sentencing Guidelines*

Magistrates' Court Sentencing Guidelines 2008, see www.banksr.com Other Matters Guidelines tab page 186 para 23 The guideline applies to the Magistrates' Court and to the Crown Court hearing appeals or sentencing for summary only offences.[566]

A court is able to disqualify an offender in absence provided that he or she has been given adequate notice of the hearing and that disqualification is to be considered.[567] It is recommended, however, that the court should avoid exercising this power wherever possible unless it is sure that the offender is aware of the hearing and the likely imposition of disqualification. This is because an offender who is disqualified in absence commits an offence by driving from the time the order is made, even if he or she has not yet received notification of it, and, as a result of the disqualification, is likely to be uninsured in relation to any injury or damage caused.

Matters prior to the hearing

41.5 *Defendant must produce licence*

Road Traffic Offenders Act 1988 s 27(1) Where a person who is the holder of a licence is convicted of an offence involving obligatory or discretionary disqualification, and a court proposes to make an order disqualifying him or [to endorse his licence] the court must, unless it has already received it, require the licence to be produced to it.

Road Traffic Offenders Act 1988 s 27(3) If the holder of the licence has not caused it to be delivered etc. unless he satisfies the court that he has applied for a new licence and has not received it, he is guilty of an offence.

Note: Although this section (not all of which is listed) remains in force, courts rely on the DVLA record, see **41.6**. For an additional power for the court to require a licence in disqualification cases under section 146, see **44.4**. Ed.

Making the order

41.6 *Basic principles*

Driving licence From 8 June 2015, the counterpart of a driving licence (which was used at court in addition to the photocard) has been replaced by the electronic driving record maintained by the DVLA, Road Safety Act 2006 Sch 3.

R v Crew 2009 EWCA Crim 2851, 2010 2 Cr App R (S) 23 (p 149) D pleaded to causing death by careless driving. Held. The definitive guideline provides no guidance as to the length of disqualification and so it is important to bear in mind, first, the risk represented by the offender is reflected by the level of culpability which attaches to his driving, and second, the main purpose of disqualification is forward looking and preventive rather than backward looking. In that regard, D's previous unblemished driving record is clearly an important factor as is the absence of aggravating factors such as speed.

R v Rasul 2013 EWCA Crim 1458 D was convicted of dangerous driving. He drove at a police officer. Held. There is a basic public protection purpose intending to punish misuse and deter the offender and others from indulging in dangerous driving. The court has a wide discretion.

R v Acton 2018 EWCA Crim 2410 D pleaded to causing death by careless driving. A lorry driver indicated that D would have to drive out of a junction first to let the lorry turn right. D did so and a car hit him. The driver died. Held. A 6-month suspended

[566] See page 15 of the Guidelines.

[567] Magistrates' Courts Act 1980 s 11(4)

sentence was well within the guideline range. In *R v Cooksley* 2003 EWCA Crim 996, 2004 1 Cr App R (S) 1 (p 1), Lord Woolf said: "The main purpose of disqualification is, 'forward looking and preventive rather than backward looking and punitive'." However, the *Causing Death by Driving Guideline 2008* para 30 makes clear that disqualification is an important element of the overall punishment for the offence. 2 years not 3.
See also the **DEATH BY DRIVING: GENERAL PRINCIPLES *Disqualification*** paras at **237.21** in Volume 2.
For ***How long should the disqualification be relative to the custodial term?*** see the ***The defendant's livelihood and loss of licence/Order must be proportionate*** para at **41.10**.
Disputes as to facts see the **FACTUAL BASIS FOR SENTENCING *Same rules apply when imposing ancillary orders*** para at **57.26**.

41.7 ***Two or more offences with discretionary disqualification***
TICs and Totality Guideline 2012: Crown Court, see www.banksr.com Other Matters Guidelines tab page 15 (Magistrates' Court guideline update page 18o)
Other combinations involving two or more offences involving discretionary disqualification As orders of disqualification take effect immediately, it is generally desirable for the court to impose a single disqualification order that reflects the overall criminality of the offending behaviour.

41.8 ***Long periods are counter-productive***
Compulsory extended periods The rules for imposing all types of driving disqualification (except interim disqualification) have been radically altered from 13 April 2015 by Road Traffic Offenders Act 1988 s 35A[568] (as amended), which requires the court to add an extended period to the disqualification period. For more details, see **41.16**.
R v Ziad 2011 EWCA Crim 209 D pleaded early to dangerous driving and failing to stop. D drove behind V's car. He then passed V on her near side, pulled in front of her car and braked, causing her to perform an emergency stop. V pulled into the slow lane. D's car slowed down so that it was level with V. He pulled over and collided with V's car. He also forced her into a kerb at a roundabout. He then drove off at speed. The incident was witnessed by an off-duty police officer. D contended that the damage caused was unintentional. He had previous convictions, but none for driving offences. Held. He has a family to support. The 5-year period would result in [about 3 years' disqualification after his release]. That bears too heavily upon him. 3 years' disqualification, not 5. 8 months for dangerous driving was not the subject of the appeal.
See also: *R v Tantrum* 1989 11 Cr App R (S) 348 (Normally the disqualification should not inhibit too much the rehabilitation of the offender. Very long disqualifications tend to do just that and cause further crimes to be committed.)
R v Collins 2010 EWCA Crim 1342, 2011 1 Cr App R (S) 35 (p 218) (Plea to dangerous driving and section 20 GBH. Atrociously dangerous, irresponsible and stupid driving. Victim of crash sustained very serious injuries. Because long periods can be counter-productive, 5 years, not 8.)
R v Wasik 2010 EWCA Crim 1427 (Plea to possession of a false identity document, driving whilst disqualified, making a false statement for insurance and driving without insurance. Subject to a 3-year ban. So he can support his family on release, 12-month ban not 5 years, which made it only 2 months extra to the 3 years.)

41.9 ***Need to protect the public/Purpose of***
R v Backhouse and Others 2010 EWCA Crim 111 The four defendants were convicted of dangerous driving and acquitted of causing death by dangerous driving. Three of them drove very powerful motorbikes. They all drove at excessive speeds. The Judge gave them suspended sentences and 4 years' disqualification. One defendant needed his licence to work as a newsagent. Another lost his job because of the disqualification.

[568] As inserted by Coroners and Justice Act 2009 s 2 and Sch 16 paras 2 and 5

Held. Disqualification has the purpose of protecting the public. Disqualification is also intended to punish and deter offenders and others. The Judge was justified in having regard to protecting the public.
R v Cook 2018 EWCA Crim 124 D pleaded to dangerous driving and was given 10 months' detention. He drove at speed and dangerously for over ten minutes. D was aged 18, had attempted suicide and had self-harmed. Held. Disqualification is not only a protective measure. Gross LJ said in *R v Mohammed* 2016 EWCA Crim 1380, "Disqualification has the purpose of protecting the public. Disqualification is also intended to punish and deter offenders and others. A balance, however, has to be struck and the court should not disqualify for a period that is longer than necessary and should bear in mind the effects of a ban on employment or employment prospects."
For more details, see **234.7** in Volume 2.
See also the **Life disqualification** section at **41.13**.

41.10 ***The defendant's livelihood and loss of licence/Order must be proportionate***
Compulsory extended periods The rules for imposing all types of driving disqualification (except interim disqualification) were radically altered from 13 April 2015 by Road Traffic Offenders Act 1988 s 35A[569] (as amended), which requires the court to add an extended period to the disqualification period. For more details, see **41.16**.
R v Bowling 2008 EWCA Crim 1148, 2009 1 Cr App R (S) 23 (p 122) D pleaded to engaging in sexual activity in the presence of a child (kerb crawling). He was a self-employed roofer and received 22 months. Held. The general rule is that if a defendant is given a custodial sentence, and the court imposes a period of disqualification from driving under section 147, it will do so for a period equal to, or slightly in excess of, the period of custody. The policy behind this general rule is that the court should not impose a period of disqualification that will inhibit the offender from rehabilitating himself. This is particularly so in cases where the offender is dependent on the ability to drive for his livelihood. The period depends very much on the facts of the case. The principle applies here so 2 years, not 4 years.
R v Backhouse and Others 2010 EWCA Crim 111 The four defendants were convicted of dangerous driving and acquitted of causing death by dangerous driving. Three of them drove very powerful motorbikes. They all drove at excessive speeds. The Judge gave them suspended sentences and 4 years' disqualification. One defendant needed his licence to work as a newsagent. Another lost his job because of the disqualification. Held. Disqualification has the purpose of protecting the public. Disqualification is also intended to punish and deter offenders and others. The Judge was justified in having regard to protecting the public.
R v Docherty and Davis 2011 EWCA Crim 1591, 2012 1 Cr App R (S) 48 (p 282) D1 and D2 pleaded (20% credit) to conspiracy to rob. D1 was the ringleader and D2 was his lieutenant. The car was bought and insured to perform a reconnaissance trip and the subsequent robbery. Held. Bearing in mind all the factors, including future employment [and] the punitive effect of a disqualification in relation to totality, **4 years'** disqualification, not 6, in addition to 5½ and 5 years' custody.
R v Harkins 2011 EWCA Crim 2227 D pleaded to three burglaries and other offences. He was given 3 years' detention and a 3-year disqualification under PCC(S)A 2000 s 147. Held. When the Court in *R v Bowling* 2008 (see above) referred to 'a period of custody', it was referring to the nominal sentence passed by the court rather than the precise period of time for which an appellant would be held in custody by virtue of various early release arrangements and the credit to be given in respect of periods spent remanded in custody. The point of the disqualification under this particular section is to punish and to deter, by removing access to a lawful use of a vehicle used in commission of the offences for which the sentences were passed. Thus, if the disqualification is to be effective at all, it is implicit that it must apply after release from custody and normally

[569] As inserted by Coroners and Justice Act 2009 s 2 and Sch 16 paras 2 and 5

that will be a proportionate result provided it does not seriously impair rehabilitation, for example, because the offender has work to go to and for which he needs to drive, such that that important element in rehabilitation would be thwarted by the period of disqualification. There is no evidence of any substance that that is the case here. Furthermore, proportionality is preserved by the general practice of keeping the period of disqualification broadly commensurate with the custodial sentence. That is not the same, however, as requiring the judge to fine tune the period of disqualification in order to accord with the precise calculation of release dates and periods spent on licence. Furthermore it does not require the judge to have regard to any direction he has made for credit against the sentence for time spent on remand[570] unless it would result in a gross disparity between the sentence passed and the period of disqualification.

R v Knight and Others 2012 EWCA Crim 3019, 2013 2 Cr App R (S) 45 (p 297) D and three others pleaded to conspiracy to burgle. The Judge imposed a blanket 4-year ban irrespective of the length of the custodial sentences. Held. para 14 That is a flawed approach and the Judge should have had regard to the issue of proportionality and should have considered whether the driving disqualification was broadly commensurate with the custodial sentence being imposed.

R v Yohans 2013 EWCA Crim 882 D was convicted of conspiracy to steal. He drove a van in convoy with another van and was stopped by police. Around 40 men jumped out wearing balaclavas etc. D was a self-employed driver. D was aged 32 at his appeal and had convictions for robbery, assault, cannabis possession and waste depositing. He had not previously been in custody. He was sentenced to 2 years' custody and a 3-year disqualification. The van was forfeited. Held. This was organised looting of high-value goods. Being a driver aggravated the offence. The disqualification should have been more than the custodial period but less than 3 years. **2-year disqualification** not 3.

41.11 *Disqualification should be passed at the same time as the sentence for the offence*

R v Talgarth JJs ex parte Bithell 1973 RTR 546 LCJ D was charged with driving without insurance and driving without an MOT certificate. D failed to attend court on numerous occasions and finally pleaded guilty by letter, neglecting to include his driving licence, as was necessary, for the Justices to exercise their powers of endorsement. They proceeded in his absence and fined him, but adjourning the decision on disqualification. The case was repeatedly adjourned and eventually a warrant was issued for D's arrest. Finally, D appeared, having been arrested, and produced his licence. D was disqualified for 6 months. D appealed on the basis that the Justices were *functus officio* when they fined D at the earlier hearing. Held. Disposing with different elements on different occasions was bad sentencing practice. But a decision would not be quashed merely because it was bad sentencing practice. The Justices went beyond their powers in adjourning part of the sentencing hearing because of the statutory provisions about adjourning. This was because: a) they did not adjourn sentence, they sentenced in part and adjourned in part, and b) they did not observe the four-week maximum period for adjournment.[571] Disqualification quashed.

41.12 *Disqualification orders may not be consecutive*

R v Kent 1983 5 Cr App R (S) 171 Disqualification periods cannot be consecutive to one another.

R v Holmes 2018 EWCA Crim 131 D pleaded to dangerous driving and other offences. The Judge sentenced him to 8 months in all and two concurrent periods of disqualification, which he made consecutive to the disqualification he was given on a previous occasion. Held. Disqualification under Road Traffic Offenders Act 1988 s 34 must take

[570] Credit for time on remand is no longer subject to an order by the court. Since 3/12/12 it is deducted administratively by the prison. However, the principle remains relevant.

[571] This case perhaps would not be decided the same way today.

effect immediately and cannot be postponed. The order making them consecutive was unlawful, so that part is quashed. The Judge failed to apply the extension rules. There is nothing we can do about that.

For ***Reduced periods of disqualification for attendance on courses***, see the **DISQUALIFICATION FROM DRIVING: OBLIGATORY** ***Reduced periods of disqualification for attendance on courses*** para at **43.8**.

41.13 ***Life disqualification On the facts, correct/incorrect***

R v McCluskie 1992 13 Cr App R (S) 334 D pleaded to careless driving. He was driving a minibus and collided with a police car intending to enter the road from which D was exiting. The police car followed D, who had failed to stop, and eventually managed to get D's attention, instructing him to pull over. D was drunk, and gave a specimen of blood reading 93 mg. D had previous convictions for driving offences: in 1978 TDA, in 1979 driving above the prescribed limit and driving without insurance (fine and disqualified), in 1982 TDA, driving whilst disqualified (fine and disqualified), in 1985 excess alcohol (fine and disqualified), in 1990 failing to stop after an accident and driving whilst unfit (fines and disqualifications), driving whilst disqualified, excess alcohol and failure to provide a specimen (3 months and disqualified). D was disqualified for life. Held. The record was appalling. It is correct that a protracted period of disqualification has to be imposed. However, it is unreasonable to assume that after such a period of time, D would be unable to drive a car without excess alcohol. 10 years' disqualification, not life.

R v Rivano 1993 14 Cr App R (S) 578 D was convicted of driving whilst disqualified and driving with no insurance. He subsequently pleaded to driving whilst disqualified, excess alcohol and driving with no insurance. By virtue of those convictions he was in breach of a sentence of 7 months' imprisonment, suspended for 2 years. D received 13 months' imprisonment and was disqualified for life. D was seen by an off-duty policeman driving a blue Mini, and the following day another policeman attempted to stop D in the same Mini. D drove on but later abandoned the car. He was arrested and breathalysed, with a reading of 102 µg. He denied driving the car on both occasions. D, aged 30, had been disqualified on a previous occasion for a period of 10 years. D appealed on the basis that disqualification for life was wrong in principle and manifestly excessive. It was argued that it would prevent D's rehabilitation. Held. D was an absolute menace, but disqualification for life was not an appropriate penalty to impose for a man of 30. 10 years' disqualification, not life.

R v Buckley 1994 15 Cr App R (S) 695 D was convicted of burglary (9 months) and pleaded to reckless driving (21 months consecutive), driving whilst disqualified (6 months consecutive), possessing an offensive weapon (3 months concurrent), and handling stolen goods (9 months consecutive). Those offences put D in breach of a partially suspended sentence of 2 years' imprisonment (9 months immediate, the balance suspended) for offences including driving whilst disqualified. The balance of 15 months was restored in full. D was also disqualified for life. D had previous convictions: 20 TDA, 21 driving whilst disqualified and five reckless driving. Held. Six convictions for reckless driving by the age of 32 demonstrate an astonishing readiness to imperil the public. Distinguished *R v Rivano* 1993 (see previous para) on the basis that the habit of driving with excess alcohol appears not to pose such a long-term risk to the public as in the instant case. Appeal dismissed.

41.14 ***Explain sentence, Judge/Magistrate must***

Criminal Justice Act 2003 s 174(1) A court passing sentence on an offender has the duties in subsections (2) and (3).

(2) The court must state in open court, in ordinary language and in general terms, the court's reasons for deciding on the sentence.

(3) The court must explain to the offender in ordinary language:

(a) the effect of the sentence,

(b) the effects of non-compliance with any order that the offender is required to comply with and that forms part of the sentence,

(c) any power of the court to vary or review any order that forms part of the sentence…

Note: This paragraph applies to both the general power to disqualify (dealt with in this chapter) and the road traffic power to disqualify (see the next chapter). Ed.

R v Needham and Others 2016 EWCA Crim 455, 2 Cr App R (S) 26 (p 219) The Court considered the new section 35A provisions about extending disqualification. para 47 It is important that there is a degree of clarity in judges' sentencing remarks so that others may identify the correct extension period pursuant to section 35A and any uplift pursuant to section 35B. para 48 Accordingly, the judge in sentencing under section 35A should state the total period of disqualification but breaking that period down into the discretionary and extension periods. He [or she] should also give brief reasons for the length of the discretionary disqualification. When sentencing under section 35B the court should state the total period of disqualification imposed but then explain how the legislative steer of this section has been taken into account by indicating what the period of disqualification would have been but for section 35B and then indicating the period added by way of upward adjustment for the purposes of section 35B. Again, brief reasons should be given for the imposition of both these elements.

R v Goode 2017 EWCA Crim 2432 D pleaded to section 18, kidnapping, threats to kill and dangerous driving. He was sentenced to 10 years' YOI in all. D was disqualified from driving for 10 years. There was a year on remand, and for the disqualification a need for a minimum term and an extended term. The Judge did not explain why he thought 5 years after D's release was appropriate. Held. The Judge must briefly explain the reasons for the length of disqualification.

For more detail, see **234.8**.

Combined with other orders

41.15 *Absolute and conditional discharge, Combined with*

Road Traffic Offenders Act 1988 s 46(1) Notwithstanding anything in Powers of Criminal Courts (Sentencing) Act 2000 s 14(3) (rule about disregarding absolute and conditional discharges), a court [when convicting a person involving obligatory or discretionary disqualification orders him to be absolutely or conditionally discharged] may also exercise any power conferred, and must also discharge any duty imposed on the court by sections 34 (obligatory disqualification), 35 (totting up disqualification), 36 (disqualification until test is passed) and 44-44A of this Act (obligation to endorse).

Powers of Criminal Courts (Sentencing) Act 2000 s 12(7) [The court may] on discharging an offender absolutely or conditionally impose any disqualification.

Note: The Act does not indicate whether the 'disqualification' is driving disqualification or not. It is likely to be interpreted as all disqualification orders, as that is the natural meaning of the words in the subsection. Ed.

For ***Imprisonment, Combined with*** and the not-yet-in-force extension of the disqualification, see **41.1**.

41.16 *Custody, Combined with extended periods Statute*

Note: Coroners and Justice Act 2009 s 2 and Sch 16 paras 2 and 5 inserted Road Traffic Offenders Act 1988 s 35A and Powers of Criminal Courts (Sentencing) Act 2000 s 147A. These provisions provide that where defendants are disqualified under Road Traffic Offenders Act 1988 s 34 or 35 (obligatory disqualification or totting up) or Powers of Criminal Courts (Sentencing) Act 2000 s 146 or 147 (disqualification for any offence or when a motor vehicle was used for the purposes of crime) there must be an extension period added to the term selected. Section 147A is almost identical to section 35A so is not included. The only difference between the two sections is that they apply to different types of disqualification (see above).

The extension period is calculated to be the period the defendant would be in custody. The section was designed to prevent offenders serving most of their disqualification periods in prison. The sections were amended by Criminal Justice and Courts Act 2015 s 30.[572] Ed.

Extension of disqualification where custodial sentence also imposed

Road Traffic Offenders Act 1988 s 35A(1) This section applies where a person is convicted in England and Wales of an offence for which the court:

(a) imposes a custodial sentence, and

(b) orders the person to be disqualified under section 34 [obligatory and discretionary disqualification] or 35 [totting up].

(2) The order under section 34 or 35 must provide for the person to be disqualified for the appropriate extension period, in addition to the discretionary disqualification period.

(3) The discretionary disqualification period is the period for which, in the absence of this section, the court would have disqualified the person under section 34 or 35.

(4) The appropriate extension period is:

(a) where an order under Powers of Criminal Courts (Sentencing) Act 2000 s 82A(2) (life sentence: determination of tariffs) is made in relation to the custodial sentence, a period equal to the part of the sentence specified in that order,

(b) in the case of a detention and training order under section 100 of that Act (offenders under 18: detention and training orders), a period equal to half the term of that order,

(c)-(d) [Repealed]

(e) where Criminal Justice Act 2003 s 226A (extended sentence for certain violent, sexual offences or terrorism[573]: persons 18 or over) applies in relation to the custodial sentence, a period equal to two-thirds of the term imposed pursuant to section 226A(5)(a) of that Act,

(f) where section 226B of that Act (extended sentence for certain violent, sexual offences or terrorism[574]: persons under 18) applies in relation to the custodial sentence, a period equal to two-thirds of the term imposed pursuant to section 226B(3)(a) 10 of that Act,

(fa) in the case of a sentence under section 236A of that Act (special custodial sentence for certain offenders of particular concern), a period equal to half of the term imposed pursuant to section 236A(2)(a) of that Act,

(g) where an order under section 269(2) of that Act (determination of minimum term in relation to mandatory life sentence: early release) is made in relation to the custodial sentence, a period equal to the part of the sentence specified in that order,

(h) in any other case, a period equal to half the custodial sentence imposed.

(5) If a period determined under subsection (4) includes a fraction of a day, that period is to be rounded up to the nearest number of whole days.

(7) This section does not apply where:

(a) the custodial sentence was a suspended sentence,

(b) the court has made an order under Criminal Justice Act 2003 s 269(4) (determination of minimum term in relation to mandatory life sentence: no early release) in relation to the custodial sentence, or

(c) the court has made an order under Powers of Criminal Courts (Sentencing) Act 2000 s 82A(4) (determination of minimum term in relation to discretionary life sentence: no early release) in relation to the custodial sentence.

(8)-(10) [Secretary of State's regulatory powers]

---

572 Section 35A is in force from 13/4/15, Criminal Justice and Courts Act 2015 (Commencement No 1, Saving and Transitional Provisions) Order 2015 2015/778 para 3 and Sch 1 para 25.

573 As amended by Counter-Terrorism and Border Security Act 2019 Sch 4 para 6(a) In force 12 April 2019, Counter-Terrorism and Border Security Act 2019 s 27(3).

574 As amended by Counter-Terrorism and Border Security Act 2019 Sch 4 para 6(a) In force 12 April 2019, Counter-Terrorism and Border Security Act 2019 s 27(3).

(11) In this section:..
'custodial sentence' has the meaning given by Powers of Criminal Courts (Sentencing) Act 2000 s 76;
'suspended sentence' has the meaning given by Criminal Justice Act 2003 s 189.

Effect of custodial sentence in other cases

Road Traffic Offenders Act 1988 s 35B (1) This section applies where a person is convicted in England and Wales of an offence for which a court proposes to order the person to be disqualified under section 34 or 35 and:

(a) the court proposes to impose on the person a custodial sentence (other than a suspended sentence) for another offence, or

(b) at the time of sentencing for the offence, a custodial sentence imposed on the person on an earlier occasion has not expired.

(2) In determining the period for which the person is to be disqualified under section 34 or 35, the court must have regard to the consideration in subsection (3) if and to the extent that it is appropriate to do so.

(3) The consideration is the diminished effect of disqualification as a distinct punishment if the person who is disqualified is also detained in pursuance of a custodial sentence.

(4) If the court proposes to order the person to be disqualified under section 34 or 35 and to impose a custodial sentence for the same offence, the court may not in relation to that disqualification take that custodial sentence into account for the purposes of subsection (2).

(5) In this section 'custodial sentence' and 'suspended sentence' have the same meaning as in section 35A.

41.17 ***Custody, Combined with extended periods*** ***Judicial guidance***

R v Needham and Others 2016 EWCA Crim 455, 2 Cr App R (S) 26 (p 219) The Court considered the new section 35A provisions.

Commencement para 13 Coroners and Justice Act 2009 (Commencement No 17) Order 2015 2015/819 para 29 has the effect that the new sections do not apply to offences committed wholly or partly before 13 April 2015. An offence is partly committed before that date if a 'relevant event' occurred before commencement. 'Relevant event' means any act or other event (including any consequence of an act) proof of which is required for conviction of the offence. A clear example of this would be a case of causing death by dangerous driving where the driving took place before 13 April 2015, but the victim did not die of his injuries until some days after that date. For an offence of driving whilst disqualified on 14 April where the offender had been disqualified on 12 April 2015, para 29(3) means the offence falls within the new sections [because the relevant act is the driving]. Where offences attracting disqualification are dealt with a non-motoring offence committed before the commencement date it is only the dates of the offences attracting disqualification that matter.

It is the whole custodial term that matters para 21 Where part of the custodial term is for offences that disqualification does not apply to, it is the global term that matters. para 25 Where other offences are involved, section 35B comes into play in addition to section 35A. This section does not use the mechanism of a discretionary period and an extension period of disqualification as section 35A does. Instead, where this section applies, the effect of section 35A(2) and (3) is that in determining the length of disqualification, the court 'must have regard…if and to the extent that it is appropriate to do so' to the diminished effect of disqualification as a distinct punishment on a person who is also detained pursuant to a custodial sentence. Where this section is engaged the phrase 'must have regard' appears to give a greater degree of latitude to the sentencer in fixing the term of disqualification than that which is achieved by the extension period mechanism under section 35A. para 27 Section 35B should be regarded as a means of increasing what would otherwise be a disqualification under section 35A so as to cater for the other offence or offences. In this respect section 35B should be regarded as complementary to section 35A rather than something distinct from it. [The interaction of sections 35A and 35B is listed at para 28 and is not listed here]. para 29 Parliament in using the phrases 'must have regard' and 'if and to the extent that it is appropriate' has clearly entrusted some measure of discretion to the court as to whether to adjust the disqualification under the section to any extent or at all.

Check list para 31 **Step 1** Does the court intend to impose a 'discretionary' disqualification under section 34 or 35 for any offence? If Yes, go to Step 2.

Step 2 Does the court intend to impose a custodial term for that same offence? If Yes, section 35A applies and the court must impose an extension period (see section 35A(4)(h)) for that same offence and consider Step 3. If No, section 35A does not apply at all. Go on to consider section 35B and Step 4.

Step 3 Does the court intend to impose a custodial term for another offence (which is longer or consecutive) or is the defendant already serving a custodial sentence? If Yes, consider what increase ('uplift') in the period of 'discretionary disqualification' is required to comply with section 35B(2) and (3). In accordance with section 35B(4) ignore any custodial term imposed for an offence involving disqualification under section 35A.

Discretionary period + extension period + uplift = total period of disqualification

If No, [there is] no need to consider section 35B at all.

Discretionary period + extension period = total period of disqualification

Step 4 Does the court intend to impose a custodial term for another offence or is the defendant already serving a custodial sentence? If Yes, consider what increase ('uplift') in the period of 'discretionary disqualification' is required to comply with section 35B(2) and (3).

Discretionary period + uplift = total period of disqualification

Credit for curfew or remand, see **4.20**.

Minimum periods of disqualification para 39 The minimum period relates to the discretionary period alone [see the step-by-step guide above] and not to the discretionary period plus the extension period. To hold otherwise would run counter to the intention of the legislation and to the provisions of section 35A(3).

Early release arrangements para 40 The length of the custodial term for calculating the appropriate extension period relates to the term of custody and does not take account of the possibility of early release for example under the Home Detention Curfew Scheme.

Start of disqualification para 42 Disqualification does not commence upon release. Disqualification starts from the day upon which it is pronounced by the court.

Reduction for courses in drink drive cases para 44 Where there is a reduced disqualification period for drink drive offenders who have attended a special course, any reduction would come off the entire disqualification including the extension period under section 35A.

Impact on sentencing guidelines para 45 Where *Causing Death by Dangerous Driving Guideline 2008* para 31 gives guidance about disqualification, courts should focus on the legislation rather than para 31 of the guideline. The court's approach should be to fix the discretionary term taking account of relevant factors including the need for protection of the public. There will often be close correlation between that factor and the levels of harm and culpability involved in the offence of causing death by dangerous driving.

Sentencing remarks para 47 It is important that there is a degree of clarity in judges' sentencing remarks so that others may identify the correct extension period pursuant to section 35A and any uplift pursuant to section 35B. para 48 Accordingly, the judge in sentencing under section 35A should state the total period of disqualification but breaking that period down into the discretionary and extension periods. He [or she] should also give brief reasons for the length of the discretionary disqualification. When sentencing under section 35B the court should state the total period of disqualification imposed but then explain how the legislative steer of this section has been taken into account by indicating what the period of disqualification would have been but for section 35B and then indicating the period added by way of upward adjustment for the purposes of section 35B. Again, brief reasons should be given for the imposition of both these elements.

41.18 ***Custody, Combined with Extended periods Cases***
R v Axford 2017 EWCA Crim 2651 D pleaded to possessing cocaine, heroin and cannabis with intent and aggravated vehicle-taking (no appeal). He tried to throw drugs into a prison. The sentence for the vehicle offence was 1 year consecutive, making 6 years in all. The Judge considered 2 years' disqualification appropriate and extended it by 3 years (which was half the 6 years). Held. We reduce the drugs sentence from 5 years to 4 years 3 months, and the vehicle-taking offence makes the sentence 5 years 3 months. para 21 Pursuant to Road Traffic Offenders Act 1988 s 35A(2) the appropriate extension period is half of the 12 months imposed for the aggravated taking away which is the offence in respect of which he was disqualified. In addition, we are required by Road Traffic Offenders Act 1988 s 35B(2) to consider the custodial term for the drugs. Half of that period [4 years 3 months] is now 25 months and 15 days. The [extended] disqualification will be 2 years plus 6 months under section 35A plus 25 months and 15 days under section 35B making 4 years 7 months and 15 days. The time served during the interim suspension should be deducted from the discretionary proportion of the disqualification period as an administrative act.
Note: A more absurd way to calculate disqualification is hard to imagine. There is no reason why disqulaifiacation should not start from the date of release, with the prison authorities informing the DVLA of the relevant dates. Unfortunately that is not how the legislation was drafted. Ed.
R v Raja 2019 EWCA Crim 298 D pleaded to drug offences (total sentence 7½ years) and dangerous driving (14 months).[575] The total sentence was 8 years 8 months. The Judge imposed 3 years' discretionary disqualification for the dangerous driving and 3 years 9 months' disqualification (half the 7½-year term) as an extension under section 35A. Held. That was unlawful. The Judge was obliged to pass the 3 years' disqualification with a 7-month (half the 1 year 2 months) extension under section 35A for the dangerous driving and [then an extension under section 35B]. We pass 3 years 2 months, under section 35B,[576] as an extension on the drug counts making the same 3 years 9 months' disqualification.
For more detail about the drugs case, see **338.37**.

41.19 ***Custody, Combined with extended periods Long custodial sentence Short disqualification***
R v Needham and Others 2016 EWCA Crim 455, 2 Cr App R (S) 26 (p 219) para 29 In a case where a very lengthy custodial sentence is to be served for 'another offence' which is not motoring related, it might be anomalous or run counter to considerations of rehabilitation to impose an extremely long period of disqualification under section 35B in order that a comparatively short period of disqualification should take place after release from custody. Examples might include a motoring offence combined with a non-motoring related homicide attracting a life sentence with a long minimum term, or a case involving a very long extended sentence passed for sexual offending.
See also: *Att-Gen's Ref 2018 Re Scott* 2018 EWCA Crim 1336, 2 Cr App R (S) 37 (Attempted murder on four young children. Life with 24-year not 14-year minimum term. 2 years' disqualification suitable. New 26-year disqualification imposed, see **288.5** in Volume 2).

41.20 ***Custody, Combined with extended periods Time on remand***
R v Needham and Others 2016 EWCA Crim 455, 2 Cr App R (S) 26 (p 219)

[575] The sentence is not clear but I infer that D received two concurrent sentences for driving matters.
[576] There is a greater discretion under section 35B than 35A and the Court of Appeal could not pass a longer term of disqualification than the Crown Court Judge.

Credit for curfew or remand? para 32 Where someone is subject to a curfew prior to sentence there is no question of credit in respect of that [when considering the extended term]. para 34 By removing the provisions that related to remand time by Criminal Justice and Courts Act 2015 s 30, it was the clear intention of Parliament that time spent on remand would not count. para 35 This has the potential to produce injustice. To avoid such injustice a court may take into account a significant remand period in determining the appropriate discretionary period under section 35A. Many of the offences to which section 35A applies involve obligatory minimum periods of disqualification. There can be no question of such a minimum period being reduced to take account of time spent on remand, but there may be scope for some reduction if the sentencer has in mind a longer period than the statutory minimum. para 38 *R v Harkins* 2011 EWCA Crim 2227 (see **41.10**) para 16 points to the correct approach to the question of time spent on remand under s 35A. If the time spent on remand would lead to a disproportionate result in terms of the period of disqualification, then the court has power in fixing the discretionary element to adjust that period to take account of time spent on remand. We do not envisage a precise arithmetical calculation taking place. The court should take a broad-brush approach to the question of adjustment.

R v Abbassi 2017 EWCA Crim 779 D was convicted of causing serious injury by dangerous driving. The Judge gave 28 months' custody and 5 years' disqualification, which he extended by 14 months. He reduced the 14 months to 10 months because of time on remand. Held. That was wrong. The adjustment should have been made to the 5-year term and not the extension period, under the general discretion under Road Traffic Offenders Act 1988 s 35B. We consider 16 months' custody and 2 years' disqualification is appropriate. We reduce the extension period to 8 months to take into account the time on remand.

Note: It appears the Court of Appeal made the same error as the sentencing Judge by purporting to reduce the extension period. However, the Court of Appeal's approach seems to be wrong as the extension period before a reduction would be 8 months (being half of the 16-month custodial sentence), so it could not be 8 months after a reduction. The 2-year disqualification could not be reduced as that is the minimum term that can be imposed and there was no discretionary disqualification to be reduced. The case shows the injustice that can be caused by the poorly drafted 2015 Act to those with long periods of remand in custody facing obligatory disqualification. For more details of the case, see **235.5** in Volume 2. Ed.

R v Young 2019 EWCA Crim 332 LCJ D pleaded to four burglaries, theft, dangerous driving, driving whilst disqualified and failing to provide a specimen (with 3 years' minimum disqualification). The Judge passed 3 years 10 months' custody and 3 years' disqualification extended by 23 months. D had spent 139 days on remand. There was 25 days' tag time. Held. The Court in *R v Needham and Others* 2016 recognised that if time spent on remand in custody was not credited against the total term of disqualification, that could lead to an unfair disadvantage to an offender who had been remanded against someone else who had not. It is important to draw attention to limitations on that possible allowance. The scope for such an adjustment arises only where: a) there has been no interim disqualification, b) the period of time on remand was of such a nature that the term of disqualification would otherwise be disproportionate, and c) adjustment did not reduce the disqualification below the statutory minimum period attracted by any of the offences concerned. In *R v Needham* the period of 102 days on remand was described as 'substantial', but a failure to allow for that period was not considered disproportionate. As the disqualification was the minimum required, there was no scope for a reduction. We adjust the sentence to comply with the statute.

41.21 *Endorsement, Combined with*

R v Usaceva 2015 EWCA Crim 166, 2 Cr App R (S) 7 (p 90) D pleaded to causing death by dangerous driving. She was sentenced to 6 years' imprisonment and was disqualified for 10 years. The Judge also endorsed her licence with 11 points, at the invitation of the prosecution advocate. Held. Looking at Road Traffic Offenders Act 1988 s 44(1) it is clear [that] when disqualification is ordered only the conviction and the disqualification should be recorded. The rule in *R v Kent* 1983 5 Cr App R (S) 171 should be applied. The licence should not be endorsed.

41.22 ***Penalty points, Combined with***

R v Kent 1983 5 Cr App R (S) 171 If a court disqualifies an offender from driving, it may not on the same occasion order penalty points to be endorsed on the licence.

Att-Gen's Ref 2017 Re Abbas 2017 EWCA Crim 2015, 2018 1 Cr App R (S) 33 (p 237) D pleaded to driving whilst disqualified. The Court disqualified him for 6 months and gave him 6 penalty points. Held. That was wrong. Penalty points quashed.

Deceiving the court

41.23 ***Court deceived regarding the circumstances***

Road Traffic Offenders Act 1988 s 49(1) This section applies where in dealing with a person convicted of an offence involving obligatory endorsement a court was deceived regarding any circumstances that were or might have been taken into account in deciding whether or for how long to disqualify him.

(2) If:

(a) the deception constituted or was due to an offence committed by that person, and

(b) he is convicted of that offence,

the court by or before which he is convicted shall have the same powers and duties regarding an order for disqualification as had the court which dealt with him for the offence involving obligatory endorsement but must, in dealing with him, take into account any order made on his conviction of the offence involving obligatory endorsement.

Note: This section appears needlessly restricted. There is no mention of court time limits and an offender has to have been convicted of an offence when the deception took place. So if the offender or someone acting on his or her behalf deceives a court that the offender was not the driver, the section cannot be used to impose an endorsement or a period of disqualification. Ed.

Appeals

41.24 ***Ability to appeal***

Road Traffic Offenders Act 1988 s 38(1) A person disqualified by an order of a Magistrates' Court under section 34 [obligatory and discretionary disqualification] or 35 [totting up] of this Act may appeal against the order in the same manner as against a conviction.

41.25 ***Suspend the disqualification pending appeal, Power to***

Road Traffic Offenders Act 1988 s 39(1) Any court in England and Wales [whether a Magistrates' Court or another] which makes an order disqualifying a person may, if it thinks fit, suspend the disqualification pending an appeal against the order.

Road Traffic Offenders Act 1988 s 40(1) and (2) Where a person [who] has been convicted and disqualified (either obligatory or discretionary) a) appeals to the Crown Court, or b) appeals or applies for leave to appeal to the Court of Appeal, against his conviction or his sentence, the Crown Court or, as the case may require, the Court of Appeal may, if it thinks fit, suspend the disqualification.

(3) Where a person ordered to be disqualified has appealed or applied for leave to appeal to the Supreme Court:

(a) under Administration of Justice Act 1960 s 1 from any decision of a Divisional Court of the Queen's Bench Division which is material to his conviction or sentence, or

(b) under Criminal Appeal Act 1968 s 33 from any decision of the Court of Appeal which is material to his conviction or sentence,

the Divisional Court or, as the case may require, the Court of Appeal may, if it thinks fit, suspend the disqualification.

(4) Where a person ordered to be disqualified makes an application in respect of the decision of the court in question under Magistrates' Courts Act 1980 s 111 (statement of case by Magistrates' Court) or Senior Courts Act 1981 s 28 (statement of case by Crown Court) the High Court may, if it thinks fit, suspend the disqualification.
(5) Where a person ordered to be disqualified:
(a) applies to the High Court for an order of certiorari to remove into the High Court any proceedings of a Magistrates' Court or of the Crown Court, being proceedings in or in consequence of which he was convicted or his sentence was passed, or
(b) applies to the High Court for leave to make such an application, the High Court may, if it thinks fit, suspend the disqualification.
Note: Where there is an appeal to the Court of Appeal, the power to suspend a disqualification order may be exercised by the single judge, Criminal Appeal Act 1968 s 31(2A).

41.26 ***Suspending the disqualification pending an appeal*** ***Adding terms***
Road Traffic Offenders Act 1988 s 40(6) Any power of a court under this section to suspend the disqualification of any person is a power to do so on such terms as the court thinks fit.

41.27 ***Suspending the disqualification pending an appeal*** ***Appeal fails***
Road Traffic Offenders Act 1988 s 37(2) Where the holder of the licence appeals against the order and the disqualification is suspended under section 39 of this Act, the period of disqualification shall be treated for the purpose of subsection (1) above as beginning on the day on which the disqualification ceases to be suspended.
Road Traffic Offenders Act 1988 s 43 In determining the expiration of the period for which a person is disqualified by an order of a court made in consequence of a conviction, any time after the conviction during which the disqualification was suspended or he was not disqualified shall be disregarded.

Removal of disqualification

41.28 ***Removal of disqualification*** ***Statutory power***
Road Traffic Offenders Act 1988 s 42(1)-(2) Subject to the provisions of this section, a court may remove the disqualification as from such date as may be specified in the order.

41.29 ***Removal of disqualification*** ***When can an application be made?***
Road Traffic Offenders Act 1988 s 42(3) No application shall be made under subsection (1) [see **41.28**] above for the removal of a disqualification before the expiration of whichever is relevant of the following periods from the relevant date,[577] that is:
(a) two years, if the disqualification is for less than four years (disregarding any extension period),[578]
(b) one half of the period of disqualification (disregarding any extension period), if the disqualification is (disregarding any extension period),[579] for less than ten years but not less than four years,
(c) five years in any other case,
and in determining the expiration of the period after which under this subsection a person may apply for the removal of a disqualification, any time after the conviction during which the disqualification was suspended or he was not disqualified shall be disregarded.
(3A)[580] In subsection (3) 'the relevant date' means:
(a) the date of the order imposing the disqualification in question, or

[577] 'the relevant date' was substituted by Coroners and Justice Act 2009 Sch 21 para 90 (1) and (8)(a)(i). In force 16/7/18, Coroners and Justice Act 2009 (Commencement No 18) Order 2018 2018/733 para 2(c)
[578] Inserted by Coroners and Justice Act 2009 Sch 21 para 90 (1) and (8)(a)(ii). In force 16/7/18, Coroners and Justice Act 2009 (Commencement No 18) Order 2018 2018/733 para 2(c)
[579] Words substituted by Coroners and Justice Act 2009 Sch 21 para 90 (1) and (8)(a)(iii). In force 16/7/18, Coroners and Justice Act 2009 (Commencement No 18) Order 2018 2018/733 para 2(c)
[580] Inserted by Coroners and Justice Act 2009 Sch 21 para 90 (1) and (8)(b). In force 16/7/18, Coroners and Justice Act 2009 (Commencement No 18) Order 2018 2018/733 para 2(c)

(b) if the period of the disqualification is extended by an extension period, the date in paragraph (a) postponed by a period equal to that extension period, and

(3B)[581] Extension period means an extension period added pursuant to:

(a) section 35A or 35C,

(b) section 248D of the Criminal Procedure (Scotland) Act 1995, or

(c) section 147A of the Powers of Criminal Courts (Sentencing) Act 2000.

41.30 ***Removal of disqualification Defendant's application***

Criminal Procedure Rules 2015 2015/1490 Rule 29.2(1) This rule applies where, on application by the defendant, the court can remove a disqualification from driving.

(2) A defendant who wants the court to exercise that power must:

(a) apply in writing, no earlier than the date on which the court can exercise the power,

(b) serve the application on the court officer, and

(c) in the application:

i) specify the disqualification that the defendant wants the court to remove, and

ii) explain why.

(3) The court officer must serve a copy of the application on the chief officer of police for the local justice area.

[Note. For the circumstances in which the court may remove a disqualification from driving imposed under section 34 or 35 of Road Traffic Offenders Act 1988 (a), see section 42 of the Act (b). The court may not consider an application made within 2 years of the disqualification, in any case; or, after that, before a specified period has expired.]

41.31 ***Removal of disqualification Matters to have regard to***

Road Traffic Offenders Act 1988 s 42(2) The court may, as it thinks proper having regard to:

(a) the character of the person disqualified and his conduct subsequent to the order,

(b) the nature of the offence, and

(c) any other circumstances of the case,

either by order remove the disqualification as from such a date as may be specified…or refuse the application.

41.32 ***Removal of disqualification Further applications***

Road Traffic Offenders Act 1988 s 42(4) Where an application is refused, a further application shall not be entertained if made within three months after the date of the refusal.

42 DISQUALIFICATION FROM DRIVING: INTERIM

42.1

Road Traffic Offenders Act 1988 s 26

For the general rules about disqualification and a list of the different disqualification chapters, see the **DISQUALIFICATION FROM DRIVING: BASIC PRINCIPLES** chapter.

42.2 ***Power to order***

Road Traffic Offenders Act 1988 s 26(1) Where a Magistrates' Court:

(a) commits an offender to the Crown Court under Powers of Criminal Courts (Sentencing) Act 2000 s 6 or any enactment mentioned in subsection (4) of that section,[582] or

(b) remits an offender to another Magistrates' Court under Powers of Criminal Courts (Sentencing) Act 2000 s 10,

[581] Inserted by Coroners and Justice Act 2009 Sch 21 para 90 (1) and (8)(c). In force 16/7/18, Coroners and Justice Act 2009 (Commencement No 18) Order 2018 2018/733 para 2(c)

[582] These are Vagrancy Act 1824, committal of offences triable either way (Powers of Criminal Courts (Sentencing) Act 2000 s 3-4A), breaches of conditional discharges (Powers of Criminal Courts (Sentencing) Act 2000 s 13(5)) and those with convictions during their suspended sentences (Criminal Justice Act 2003 Sch 12 para 11(2)).

to be dealt with for an offence involving obligatory or discretionary disqualification, it may order him to be disqualified until he has been dealt with in respect of the offence.
(2) Where a court:

(a) defers passing sentence on an offender under Powers of Criminal Courts (Sentencing) Act 2000 s 1 in respect of an offence involving obligatory or discretionary disqualification, or

(b) adjourns after convicting an offender of such an offence but before dealing with him for the offence,

it may order the offender to be disqualified until he has been dealt with in respect of the offence.

42.3 ***Maximum length of the order***
Road Traffic Offenders Act 1988 s 26(4) An order under this section shall cease to have effect at the end of the period of six months beginning with the day on which it is made, if it has not ceased to have effect before that time.
Road Traffic Offenders Act 1988 s 26(6) Where a court orders a person to be disqualified under this section ('the first order'), no court shall make a further order under this section in respect of the same offence or any offence in respect of which an order could have been made under this section at the time the first order was made.

42.4 ***Don't endorse the licence***
Road Traffic Offenders Act 1988 s 26(10) Where a court makes an order under this section, section 44(1) (endorsement of the licence) shall not apply.

42.5 ***The automatic reduction to the final disqualification by length of interim disqualification***
Road Traffic Offenders Act 1988 s 26(12) Where on any occasion a court deals with an offender…any period of disqualification which is on that occasion imposed under section 34 (obligatory and discretionary disqualification) or 35 (totting up) of this Act shall be treated as reduced by any period during which he was disqualified (with an interim order).
(13) Any reference in this or any other Act to the length of a period of disqualification shall, unless the context otherwise requires, be construed as a reference to its length before any reduction under this section.
R v Cooper 2018 EWCA Crim 1958 The Judge ordered the period of the interim disqualification to be deducted from the final disqualification. Held. That was wrong. It is done automatically, see section 26(12).

Combined with other orders

42.6 ***Deferred sentence, Combined with***
Road Traffic Offenders Act 1988 s 26(2) Where a court defers passing sentence under Powers of Criminal Courts (Sentencing) Act 2000 s 1 it may where the offence carries obligatory or discretionary disqualification order [interim disqualification].

43 Disqualification from Driving: Obligatory

43.1
Road Traffic Offenders Act 1988 s 34(1)
There are the following other chapters:

Disqualification from Driving: Basic Principles
Disqualification from Driving: Discretionary: General Power
Disqualification from Driving: Discretionary: Road Traffic
Disqualification from Driving: Interim
Revocation of New Drivers' Licences

Extended disqualification The rules for imposing all types of driving disqualification (except interim disqualification) were from 13 April 2015 radically altered by Road Traffic Offenders Act 1988 s 35A[583] (as amended), which requires the court to add an extended period to the disqualification period. For more details, see **41.16**.

For young drivers who lose their licence when they accumulate six penalty points, see the **Revocation of New Drivers' Licences** chapter.

There is also an **Endorsement** chapter. Penalty points are dealt with in the **Disqualification from Driving: Totting Up Penalty points** section at **46.6**.

For the general rules about disqualification, see the **Disqualification from Driving: Basic Principles** chapter.

For ***Reduced periods of disqualification for attendance on courses***, see the **Disqualification from Driving: Obligatory** ***Reduced periods of disqualification for attendance on courses*** para at **43.8**.

43.2 *Statutory obligation to disqualify*

Road Traffic Offenders Act 1988 s 34(1) Where a person is convicted of an offence involving obligatory disqualification, the court must order him to be disqualified for such period not less than 12 months as the court thinks fit unless the court for special reasons thinks fit to order him to be disqualified for a shorter period or not to order him to be disqualified.

(2) [see **45.2**]

(3) [see **43.6**]

(4B) Where a person convicted of an offence under Road Traffic Act 1988 s 40A (using a vehicle in dangerous condition etc.) has within the three years immediately preceding the commission of the offence been convicted of any such offence, subsection (1) above shall apply in relation to him as if the reference to 12 months were a reference to six months.

For subsections (4), (4A), (4AA), (5) and (6) see **43.5**.

For ***special reasons***, see the **Special Reasons** chapter.

43.3 *Obligatory disqualifications*

Offence	Act	Statutory source of the obligation	Minimum length
Causing death by careless driving (simple)	Road Traffic Act 1988 s 2B	Road Traffic Offenders Act 1988 s 34(1) and Sch 2 Part I	1 year
Causing death by careless driving (drink or drugs etc.)	Road Traffic Act 1988 s 3A	Road Traffic Offenders Act 1988 s 34(4)(a)	2 years (3 years for repeat offenders)
Causing death by dangerous driving	Road Traffic Act 1988 s 1	Road Traffic Offenders Act 1988 s 34(4)(a)	2 years
Causing death by driving (unlicensed or uninsured)[584]	Road Traffic Act 1988 s 3ZB	Road Traffic Offenders Act 1988 s 34(1) and Sch 2 Part I	1 year

[583] As inserted by Coroners and Justice Act 2009 s 2 and Sch 16 paras 2 and 5

[584] Before 13/4/15, the offence included causing death whilst disqualified from driving, see **241.1** in Volume 2.

Offence	Act	Statutory source of the obligation	Minimum length
Causing death by driving when disqualified	Road Traffic Act 1988 s 3ZC[585]	Road Traffic Offenders Act 1988 s 34(4)	2 years
Causing serious injury by dangerous driving	Road Traffic Act 1988 s 1A[586]	Road Traffic Offenders Act 1988 s 34(4)	2 years
Causing serious injury when disqualified	Road Traffic Act 1988 s 3ZD[587]	Road Traffic Offenders Act 1988 s 34(4)	2 years
Dangerous driving	Road Traffic Act 1988 s 2	Road Traffic Offenders Act 1988 s 34(1) and Sch 2 Part I	1 year
Driving or attempting to drive while unfit	Road Traffic Act 1988 s 4(1)	Road Traffic Offenders Act 1988 s 34(1) and Sch 2 Part I	1 year (3 years for repeat offenders, see **43.6** in Volume 1)
Driving or attempting to drive with excess alcohol	Road Traffic Act 1988 s 5(1)(a)	Road Traffic Offenders Act 1988 s 34(1) and Sch 2 Part I	1 year (3 years for repeat offenders, see **43.6** in Volume 1)
Driving with concentration of specified drug above limit	Road Traffic Act 1988 s 5A[588]	Road Traffic Offenders Act 1988 s 34(1) and Sch 2 Part I	1 year (3 years for repeat offenders, see **43.6** in Volume 1)
Failing to provide a specimen (when not in charge etc.)	Road Traffic Act 1988 s 7	Road Traffic Offenders Act 1988 s 34(1) and Sch 2 Part I	1 year (3 years for repeat offenders, see **43.6** in Volume 1)
Failing to allow a specimen to be subjected to a laboratory test (when not in charge etc.)	Road Traffic Act 1988 s 7A	Road Traffic Offenders Act 1988 s 34(1) and Sch 2 Part I	1 year (3 years for repeat offenders, see **43.6** in Volume 1)
Manslaughter by the driver of a motor vehicle	Common law	Road Traffic Offenders Act 1988 s 34(4)(a) and Sch 2 Part II	2 years

585 As inserted by Criminal Justice and Courts Act 2015 s 29(1). In force 13/4/15

586 As inserted by Legal Aid, Sentencing and Punishment of Offenders Act 2012 s 143, in force 3/12/12 by Legal Aid, Sentencing and Punishment of Offenders Act 2012 (Commencement No 3 and Saving Provision) Order 2012 2012/2770 para 2

587 As inserted by Criminal Justice and Courts Act 2015 s 29(1). In force 13/4/15

588 As inserted by Crime and Courts Act 2013 s 56

Offence	Act	Statutory source of the obligation	Minimum length
Motor racing and speed trials on public ways	Road Traffic Act 1988 s 12	Road Traffic Offenders Act 1988 s 34(1) and Sch 2 Part I	1 year
Using a vehicle in a dangerous condition etc.	Road Traffic Act 1988 s 40A	Road Traffic Offenders Act 1988 s 34(1), 34(4B) and Sch 2 Part I	6 months when committed within 3 years of a conviction for section 40A

A 'repeat offender' is someone who has, within ten years immediately preceding the commission of the offence, been convicted of any of the offences marked with the repeat offending in brackets.[589]

The reference in the table to '(when not in charge etc.)' means the obligatory disqualification does not apply to those offenders who are merely 'in charge'.[590]

43.4 *Drink/drive and drug/drive prescribed limits*

		Breath µg (micrograms)	Blood mg (milligrams)	Urine mg (milligrams)
Magistrates' Court England and Wales		35	80	107
Scotland from 5/12/14		22	50	67
Service personnel performing a regulated duty, see **247.15** in Volume 2	Reg 4 duty	35	80	107
	Reg 5 duty	9	20	27

Note: The information is taken from the Directgov Think! website http://think.direct.gov.uk/drink-driving.html. Ed.

Drug Driving (Specified Limits) (England and Wales) Regulations 2014 2014/2868 para 2

	Blood µg (micrograms)
Amphetamine[591]	250
Benzoylecgonine [the human body converts cocaine into this]	50
Clonazepam	50
Cocaine	10
Delta-9-Tetrahydrocannabinol [the main active ingredient in cannabis]	2
Diazepam	550
Flunitrazepam [commonly known as Rohypnol]	300
Ketamine	20
Lorazepam	100

[589] The power to endorse and disqualify in manslaughter cases only arises when the manslaughter is 'by the driver of a motor vehicle', Road Traffic Offenders Act 1988 Sch 2 Part II.

[590] Road Traffic Offenders Act 1988 Sch 2 Part I Column 4

[591] Added by Drug Driving (Specified Limits) (England and Wales) (Amendment) Regulations 2015 2015/911. In force 14/4/15

Lysergic acid diethylamide [commonly known as LSD]	1
Methadone	500
Methylamphetamine [commonly known as amphetamine]	10
Methylenedioxymethamphetamine [commonly known as ecstasy]	10
6-Monoacetylmorphine [the human body converts heroin into this and morphine]	5
Morphine	80
Oxazepam	300
Temazepam	1,000

43.5 *Statutory duty to disqualify for 2+ years*

Road Traffic Offenders Act 1988 s 34(4) [The obligation to disqualify shall apply to the following offences/persons but the disqualification period shall be] two years:

(a) In relation to a person convicted of:

(i) manslaughter,[592]

(ii) an offence under Road Traffic Act 1988 s 1 (causing death by dangerous driving), or

(iia) an offence under Road Traffic Act 1988 s 1A (causing serious injury by dangerous driving),[593] or

(iib)[594] an offence under section 3ZC of that Act (causing death by driving: disqualified drivers), or

(iic) an offence under section 3ZD of that Act (causing serious injury by driving: disqualified drivers), or

(iii) an offence under Road Traffic Act 1988 s 3A (causing death by careless driving while under the influence of drink or drugs), and

(b) in relation to a person on whom more than one disqualification for a fixed period of 56 days or more has been imposed within the three years immediately preceding the commission of the offence.

(4A) For the purposes of subsection (4)(b) above there shall be disregarded any disqualification imposed under section 26 of this Act [interim disqualification] or of Powers of Criminal Courts (Sentencing) Act 2000 s 147 [disqualification where vehicle used for the purposes of crime] and any disqualification imposed in respect of an offence of stealing a motor vehicle, an offence under Theft Act 1968 s 12 or 25 [taking motor vehicles etc. and going equipped to steal], or an attempt to commit such an offence.

(4AA) For the purposes of subsection (4)(b), a disqualification is to be disregarded if the period of disqualification would have been less than 56 days but for an extension period added pursuant to: (a) section 35A or 35C, (b) section 248D of the Criminal Procedure (Scotland) Act 1995, or (c) section 147A of the Powers of Criminal Courts (Sentencing) Act 2000.[595]

(5) The preceding provisions of this section shall apply in relation to a conviction of an offence committed by aiding, abetting, counselling or procuring, or inciting to the commission of, an offence involving obligatory disqualification as if the offence were an offence involving discretionary disqualification.

(5A) [Not listed. Re Scotland]

---

592 The power to endorse and disqualify in manslaughter cases only arises when the manslaughter is 'by the driver of a motor vehicle', Road Traffic Offenders Act 1988 Sch 2 Part II.

593 Subsection (iia) was inserted by Legal Aid, Sentencing and Punishment of Offenders Act 2012 s 143, in force 3/12/12 by Legal Aid, Sentencing and Punishment of Offenders Act 2012 (Commencement No 3 and Saving Provision) Order 2012 2012/2770 para 2.

594 Subsections (iib) and (iic) were inserted by Criminal Justice and Courts Act 2015 Sch 6 para 4. In force 13/4/15

595 Inserted by Coroners and Justice Act 2009 Sch 21 para 90 (1) and (2). In force 16/7/18, Coroners and Justice Act 2009 (Commencement No 18) Order 2018 2018/733 para 2(c).

(6) This section is subject to section 48 of this Act [which relates to the exemptions from disqualification and endorsement for certain construction and use offences].

43.6 *Statutory duty to disqualify for 3+ years*

Road Traffic Offenders Act 1988 s 34(3) Where a person convicted of an offence under the following provisions of Road Traffic Act 1988:

(a) section 4(1) (driving or attempting to drive while unfit),
(aa) section 3A (causing death by careless driving when under the influence of drink or drugs),
(b) section 5(1)(a) (driving or attempting to drive with excess alcohol),
(ba) section 5A(1)(a) and (2) (driving or attempting to drive with concentration of specified controlled drug above specified limit),[596]
(c) section 7(6) (failing to provide a specimen) where that is an offence involving obligatory disqualification,[597]
(d) section 7A(6) (failing to allow a specimen to be subjected to laboratory test) where that is an offence involving obligatory disqualification,[598]

has within the ten years immediately preceding the commission of the offence been convicted of any such offence, subsection (1) above shall apply in relation to him as if the reference to 12 months were a reference to three years.

43.7 *Previous conviction had special reasons, Magistrates found*

Bolliston v Gibbons 1984 6 Cr App R (S) 134 D pleaded to excess alcohol. He had a previous conviction about nine years before the commission of the current offence, where special reasons had been found. The Magistrate was sympathetic to D's position but considered she had to disqualify for the 3-year minimum period. Held. We too are sympathetic to D but the Magistrate was right to disqualify for 3 years. Special reasons had to relate to the current offence to apply. D's only remedy was at a later date to apply for the removal of the disqualification.

43.8 *Reduced periods of disqualification for attendance on courses*

Reduced disqualification for attendance on courses

Road Traffic Offenders Act 1988 s 34A(1)[599] This section applies where:

(a) a person is convicted of a relevant drink offence or a specified offence by or before a court, and
(b) the court makes an order under section 34 of this Act disqualifying him for a period of not less than 12 months (disregarding any extension period added pursuant to section 35A or 35C).

(2) In this section 'relevant drink offence' means:

(a) an offence under paragraph (a) of subsection (1) of section 3A of the Road Traffic Act 1988 (causing death by careless driving when unfit to drive through drink) committed when unfit to drive through drink,
(b) an offence under paragraph (b) of that subsection (causing death by careless driving with excess alcohol),
(c) an offence under paragraph (c) of that subsection (failing to provide a specimen) where the specimen is required in connection with drink or consumption of alcohol,
(d) an offence under section 4 of that Act (driving or being in charge when under influence of drink) committed by reason of unfitness through drink,
(e) an offence under section 5(1) of that Act (driving or being in charge with excess alcohol),

[596] As inserted by Crime and Courts Act 2013 Sch 22 para 12
[597] Obligatory disqualification means that the defendant was driving etc. rather than being in charge.
[598] Obligatory disqualification means that the defendant was driving etc. rather than being in charge.
[599] As inserted by Road Traffic Act 2006 s 34, in force 24/6/13, Road Safety Act 2006 (Commencement No 9 and Transitional Provisions) Order 2012 2012/2938 para 2(b). As amended by Coroners and Justice Act 2009 Sch 22 para 31 (a), (d) and (e). In force 13/4/15

(f) an offence under section 7(6) of that Act (failing to provide a specimen) committed in the course of an investigation into an offence within any of the preceding paragraphs, or

(g) an offence under section 7A(6) of that Act (failing to allow a specimen to be subjected to a laboratory test) in the course of an investigation into an offence within any of the preceding paragraphs.

(3) In this section 'specified offence' means:

(a) an offence under Road Traffic Act 1988 s 3 (careless, and inconsiderate driving),

(b) an offence under section 36 of that Act (failing to comply with traffic signs),

(c) an offence under Road Traffic Regulation Act 1984 s 17(4) (use of special road contrary to scheme or regulations), or

(d) an offence under section 89(1) of that Act (exceeding speed limit).

(3A) 'The reduced period' is the period of disqualification imposed under section 34 of this Act (disregarding any extension period added pursuant to section 35A or 35C) as reduced by an order under this section.

(4) [About the power to amend regulations]

(5) Where this section applies, the court may make an order that the period of disqualification imposed under section 34 of this Act ('the unreduced period') shall be reduced if, by the relevant date, the offender satisfactorily completes an approved course specified in the order but including any extension period added pursuant to section 35A or 35C.

(6) In subsection (5) above:

'an approved course' means a course approved by the appropriate national authority for the purposes of this section in relation to the description of offence of which the offender is convicted, and

'the relevant date' means such date, at least two months before the last day of the period of disqualification as reduced by the order, as is specified in the order.

(7) The reduction made in a period of disqualification by an order under this section is a period specified in the order of:

(a) not less than three months, and

(b) not more than one quarter of the unreduced period,

(and, accordingly, where the unreduced period is 12 months, the reduced period is nine months).[600]

(8) A court shall not make an order under this section in the case of an offender convicted of a specified offence if:

(a) the offender has, during the period of three years ending with the date on which the offence was committed, committed a specified offence and successfully completed an approved course pursuant to an order made under this section or section 30A of this Act on conviction of that offence, or

(b) the specified offence was committed during his probationary period.

(9) A court shall not make an order under this section in the case of an offender unless:

(a) the court is satisfied that a place on the course specified in the order will be available for the offender,

(b) the offender appears to the court to be of or over the age of 17,

(c) the court has informed the offender (orally or in writing and in ordinary language) of the effect of the order and of the amount of the fees which he is required to pay for the course and when he must pay them, and

(d) the offender has agreed that the order should be made.

Note: Coroners and Justice Act 2009 Sch 22 para 31(b) and (c) attempts to make amendments to sections 34A(2) and (3) by directing that '(disregarding any extension period added pursuant to sections 35A or 35C)' be inserted after the words 'section 34', which do not appear in either subsection. I have ignored these amendments. Ed.

[600] The brackets are in the Act.

43.9 *Reduced periods of disqualification for attendance on courses When not applicable*

Road Traffic Offenders Act 1988 s 34A(8) A court shall not make an order under this section in the case of an offender convicted of a specified offence if:

(a) the offender has, during the period of three years ending with the date on which the offence was committed, committed a specified offence and successfully completed an approved course pursuant to an order made under this section or section 30A of this Act (reduced penalty points for attendance on courses) on conviction of that offence, or

(b) the specified offence was committed during his probationary period.

(9) A court shall not make an order under this section in the case of an offender unless:

(a) the court is satisfied that a place on the course specified in the order will be available for the offender,

(b) the offender appears to the court to be of or over the age of 17,

(c) the court has informed the offender (orally or in writing and in ordinary language) of the effect of the order and of the amount of the fees which he is required to pay for the course and when he must pay them, and

(d) the offender has agreed that the order should be made.

43.10 *More than one offence carrying obligatory disqualification*

TICs and Totality Guideline 2012: Crown Court, see www.banksr.com Other Matters Guidelines tab page 15 (Magistrates' Court guideline update page 18o)

Offender convicted of two or more obligatory disqualification offences, Road Traffic Offenders Act 1988 s 34(1) The court must impose an order of disqualification for each offence unless for special reasons it does not disqualify the offender.[601]

All orders of disqualification imposed by the court on the same date take effect immediately and cannot be ordered to run consecutively to one another.

The court should take into account all offences when determining the disqualification periods and should generally impose like periods for each offence.

43.11 *Special reasons found but defendant has 12+ penalty points*

TICs and Totality Guideline 2012: Crown Court, see www.banksr.com Other Matters Guidelines tab page 15 (Magistrates' Court guideline update page 18o)

Offender convicted of two or more offences involving…b) obligatory disqualification but the court for special reasons does not disqualify the offender and the penalty points to be taken into account number 12 or more, Road Traffic Offenders Act 1988 s 28 and 35.

Where an offender is convicted on the same occasion of more than one offence to which Road Traffic Offenders Act 1988 s 35(1) applies, only one disqualification shall be imposed on him.[602] However, the court must take into account all offences when determining the disqualification period. For the purposes of appeal, any disqualification imposed shall be treated as an order made on conviction of each of the offences.[603]

43.12 *Magistrates' Court Sentencing Guidelines*

Magistrates' Court Sentencing Guidelines 2008, see www.banksr.com Other Matters Guidelines tab page 186 para 17 The guideline applies to the Magistrates' Court and to the Crown Court hearing appeals or sentencing for summary only offences.[604]

Where an offender is disqualified for 12 months or more in respect of an alcohol-related driving offence, the court may order that the period of disqualification will be reduced if the offender satisfactorily completes an approved rehabilitation course.[605]

---

[601] Road Traffic Offenders Act 1988 s 34(1)
[602] Road Traffic Offenders Act 1988 s 34(3)
[603] Road Traffic Offenders Act 1988 s 34(3)
[604] See page 15 of the guidelines.
[605] Road Traffic Offenders Act 1988 s 34A

18 Before offering an offender the opportunity to attend a course, the court must be satisfied that an approved course is available and must inform the offender of the effect of the order, the fees that the offender is required to pay, and when he or she must pay them.
19 The court should also explain that the offender may be required to satisfy the Secretary of State that he or she does not have a drink problem and is fit to drive before the offender's licence will be returned at the end of the disqualification period.[606]
20 In general, a court should consider offering the opportunity to attend a course to all offenders convicted of a relevant offence for the first time. The court should be willing to consider offering an offender the opportunity to attend a second course where it considers there are good reasons. It will not usually be appropriate to give an offender the opportunity to attend a third course.
21 The reduction must be at least three months but cannot be more than one-quarter of the total period of disqualification: a period of 12 months' disqualification must be reduced to nine months, in other cases, a reduction of one week should be made for every month of the disqualification so that, for example, a disqualification of 24 months will be reduced by 24 weeks.
22 When it makes the order, the court must specify a date for completion of the course which is at least two months before the end of the reduced period of disqualification.

43.13 ***The minimum term is not the tariff period***

R v Bagshawe 2013 EWCA Crim 127, 2 Cr App R (S) 62 (p 393) D pleaded to causing death by careless driving (simple). He pulled out at a junction causing a motorcyclist to hit him. It was a middle category case. D was aged 86. The Judge considered a custodial sentence could not be justified but considered the minimum disqualification was insufficient. D received a community penalty with unpaid work and a 3-year disqualification. Held. The minimum disqualification period was not the normal or standard period. Disqualification has a dual role or function. First it is a penalty. Second it has a preventative element, *R v Crew* 2009 EWCA Crim 2851, 2010 2 Cr App R (S) 23 (p 149). The Court looks backwards as well as forwards. The Judge was entitled to sentence as he did.

See also: *R v Sharman* 1974 RTR 213 (The widely held belief that 12 months is the tariff is wrong.)

43.14 ***Reasons Must give reasons if not disqualifying***

Criminal Procedure Rules 2015 2015/1490 Rule 28.1(1)(c)(iii) This rule applies where the court decides…

(c) not to order, where it could…

(iii) the defendant's disqualification from driving, for the usual minimum period or at all…

(2) The court must explain why it has so decided, when it explains the sentence that it has passed.

For the general principles for sentencing remarks, see **86.47**.

44 Disqualification from Driving: Discretionary: General Power

44.1

Powers of Criminal Courts (Sentencing) Act 2000 s 146-147

This power to disqualify generally derives from two sections: Powers of Criminal Courts (Sentencing) Act 2000 s 146 'for any offence' (see **44.2**) and section 147 'where vehicle used for purposes of crime' (see **44.3**).

Conspiracy Under Powers of Criminal Courts Act 1973 s 44, there was authority that there was a restricted power to pass disqualification from driving when there was a

[606] Road Traffic Act 1988 s 94 and Motor Vehicles (Driving Licences) Regulations 1999 1999/2864 reg 74

conspiracy count. The wording in section 44 was not re-enacted in section 146 and there is now no such difficulty. The Court of Appeal has confirmed that there is a power to disqualify in conspiracy cases, *R v Langley* 2014 EWCA Crim 1284.

Compulsory extended periods The rules for imposing all types of driving disqualification (except interim disqualification) were from 13 April 2015 radically altered by Road Traffic Offenders Act 1988 s 35A[607] (as amended), which requires the court to add an extended period to the disqualification period. For more details, see **41.16**.

Other chapters For a list of the disqualification chapters, see the start of the previous chapter.

For the general rules about disqualification, see the **DISQUALIFICATION FROM DRIVING: BASIC PRINCIPLES** chapter.

44.2 *Power to order 'Any offence'*

Any offence

Powers of Criminal Courts (Sentencing) Act 2000 s 146(1) The court [where] a person is convicted of an offence may, instead of or in addition to dealing with him in any other way, order him to be disqualified, for such period as it thinks fit, for holding or obtaining a driving licence.

R v Cliff 2004 EWCA Crim 3139, 2005 2 Cr App R (S) 22 (p 118) D was convicted of affray. He was a residential caretaker in student accommodation. He developed a relationship with V. D, after consuming alcohol, had his advances towards V rejected. He left but returned shortly after and took a ball bearing gun (BB gun) from his room. He subsequently took another BB gun from his room. V had been warned about D's guns and had locked herself in the bathroom. D fired the guns at the door, eventually kicking the door and gaining entry. After a few minutes, D left. D, aged 24, had previous convictions for dishonesty and offences connected with motor cars. He had recently sought treatment for a cocaine addiction. The Judge said, "It is often said in the court that drugs ruin lives and you are an example of that. I order disqualification because you admitted during the course of your evidence that you drove a vehicle that night and it is clear that you were heavily influenced by either drink or drugs, or more likely a combination of both. A potent and very risky cocktail." D was sentenced to 15 months' imprisonment and 2 years' disqualification. The defence said there is no nexus between the offence and D's driving. Held. Section 146 is wide in its ambit. The editors of *Archbold* state, 'section 146 is significantly wider than section 147 in that it is available to both the Crown Court and to Magistrates' Courts. It is not limited to any particular offence and it is not necessary that the offence should be connected in any way with the use of a motor vehicle.' We agree with that observation. It is not necessary for the offence to be connected to the use of the motor car. The section provides an additional punishment available to the court. That is not to say that a court can impose a period of disqualification arbitrarily. There must be a sufficient reason for the disqualification. The Judge was not only entitled to disqualify, but right to do so.

R v Sofekun 2008 EWCA Crim 2035, 2009 1 Cr App R (S) 78 (p 460) D pleaded to possessing cannabis with intent, driving without a licence and no insurance. Police stopped his car and 68 self-sealed bags containing herbal cannabis were found. Some were hidden in the car and some were in his underpants. The Judge sentenced him to 8 months' YOI and disqualified him for 15 months under section 146. Held. Section 146 is an additional punitive power, available to the court whether or not the defendant has committed a driving-related offence. The judgment in *R v Cliff* 2004 (see above) should not be taken to have created any restrictions on the exercise of the use of that power, which cannot otherwise be found in the statutory provision itself. The car was undoubtedly being used for the purpose of committing or facilitating the possession of this cannabis with intent to supply. Here the order was plainly justified.

[607] As inserted by Coroners and Justice Act 2009 s 2 and Sch 16 paras 2 and 5

44.3 Power to order *'Used for purposes of crime' power*

Driving disqualification where vehicle is used for purposes of crime

Powers of Criminal Courts (Sentencing) Act 2000 s 147(1) This section applies where a person:

(a) is convicted before the Crown Court of an offence punishable on indictment with imprisonment for a term of two years or more, or

(b) having been convicted by a Magistrates' Court of such an offence, is committed under section 3 (committals for triable either way offences, see **13.16**) to the Crown Court for sentence.

(2) This section also applies where a person is convicted by or before any court of common assault or of any other offence involving an assault (including an offence of aiding, abetting, counselling or procuring, or inciting to the commission of, an offence).

(3) If, in a case to which this section applies by virtue of subsection (1) above, the Crown Court is satisfied that a motor vehicle was used (by the person convicted or by anyone else) for the purpose of committing, or facilitating the commission of, the offence in question, the court may order the person convicted to be disqualified, for such period as the court thinks fit, [from] holding or obtaining a driving licence.

(4) If, in a case to which this section applies by virtue of subsection (2) above, the court is satisfied that the assault was committed by driving a motor vehicle, the court may order the person convicted to be disqualified, for such period as the court thinks fit, [from] holding or obtaining a driving licence.

Powers of Criminal Courts (Sentencing) Act 2000 s 147(6) Facilitating the commission of an offence shall be taken for the purposes of this section to include the taking of any steps after it has been committed for the purpose of disposing of any property to which it relates or of avoiding apprehension or detection.

R v Patel 1995 16 Cr App R (S) 756 D pleaded to wounding with intent. There was a contretemps between him and the driver of another car. The passenger in the other car, V, made some gestures at D. The cars stopped at a traffic light and D went over to the passenger side of V's car, hit the window of the car and, when V got out, hit V with an anti-theft device. The Judge disqualified D for 3 years. The defence (appear to have) claimed that the vehicle was not 'used for the purpose of committing, or facilitating the commission of, the offence in question'. Held. The vehicle was not used for the purposes of committing the offence. However, the vehicle could be said to have been used 'for the purpose [of] facilitating the commission of the offence', so there was power to make the order.

R v Suffi 2018 EWCA Crim 1750 D pleaded to harassment and the conduct straddled the date when the maximum penalty for the offence was increased. Held. The offence was a continuing offence so the maximum was the new higher maximum. *R v Harries and Others* 2007 applied.

Note: In *R v Gorry and Coulson* 2018 EWCA Crim 1867 the Court of Appeal held that Powers of Criminal Courts (Sentencing) Act 2000 s 147(3) could not be used for conspiracy to burgle and steal. If this is correct, in conspiracy cases courts should use the general disqualification powers, see **44.1**. Ed.

44.4 *Power to require licence*

Powers of Criminal Courts (Sentencing) Act 2000 s 146(4) A court which makes an order under this section disqualifying a person [from] holding or obtaining a driving licence shall require him to produce:

(a) any such licence held by him together with its counterpart,

(b) in the case where he holds a Community licence (within the meaning of Road Traffic Act 1988 Part III, his Community licence and its counterpart (if any)).

Powers of Criminal Courts (Sentencing) Act 2000 s 147(5) A court which makes an order under this section disqualifying a person [from] holding or obtaining a driving licence shall require him to produce:

(a) any such licence held by him together with its counterpart,

(b) in the case where he holds a Community licence (within the meaning of Road Traffic Act 1988 Part III, his Community licence and its counterpart (if any)).

Note: From 8 June 2015, the counterpart of a driving licence (which was used at court in addition to the photocard) has been replaced by the electronic driving record maintained by the DVLA, Road Safety Act 2006 Sch 3. For the power for the court to require a licence generally, see **41.5**. Ed.

44.5 ***Two or more offences with discretionary disqualification***

TICs and Totality Guideline 2012: Crown Court, see www.banksr.com Other Matters Guidelines tab (Magistrates' Court guideline update page 18o)

page 15 **Other combinations involving two or more offences involving discretionary disqualification** As orders of disqualification take effect immediately, it is generally desirable for the court to impose a single disqualification order that reflects the overall criminality of the offending behaviour.

44.6 ***Discretionary disqualification does not erase penalty points***

Magistrates' Court Sentencing Guidelines 2008, see www.banksr.com Other Matters Guidelines tab page 185 Totting up disqualifications, unlike other disqualifications, erase all penalty points.

Judicial approach to discretionary disqualification

For **Basic principles** see the **Disqualification from Driving: Basic principles** chapter

44.7 ***Must warn defence advocate***

R v Ireland 1988 10 Cr App R (S) 474 D pleaded to TDA, two burglaries and other offences. He and others stole a Transit van and used the vehicle to transport stolen goods from the burglaries. He had been before the Court before for theft and driving offences. Without any prior indication, the Judge disqualified D for 18 months. Held. The Judge should have given counsel an opportunity to address him on the issue of disqualification, especially because of D's work as a motor-cycle mechanic.

R v Docherty and Davis 2011 EWCA Crim 1591, 2012 1 Cr App R (S) 48 (p 282) The judge should invite submissions before making such orders.

44.8 ***Burglars/Thieves***

R v Knight and Others 2012 EWCA Crim 3019, 2013 2 Cr App R (S) 45 (p 297) K, G, U and MV pleaded to conspiracy to burgle. Seven properties were burgled during two nights and keys stolen for cars to be taken. The Judge gave them all a 3-year disqualification. Held. We apply *R v Harkins* 2011 (see **41.10**). The Judge's approach was flawed and he should have had regard to the issue of proportionality and whether the driving disqualification was broadly commensurate with the custodial sentence being imposed. K was aged 20, was not the organiser and received 30 months' detention. With the 74 days remand time counting, 27 months' disqualification. G was aged 30, of effective good character and worked as a mechanic. He was involved only on the second night (four burglaries), had one conviction (community order) and received 2 years. With the 117 days curfew credit time, an 18-month disqualification was appropriate. U was aged 23, was involved in onward sale of the vehicles and was not present when the houses were burgled. He had nine previous court appearances, had been to custody before and was given 40 months. With no remand time, a 40-month disqualification was appropriate. MV was aged 21 and was the driver but not the organiser. He had seven previous court appearances, no evidence of employment prospects and received 34 months. With no remand time, a 34-month disqualification was appropriate.

R v Penson 2014 EWCA Crim 602 D pleaded to theft. D drove to various B&Q stores in different parts of the country, stealing mechanical and electrical items worth nearly £3,000. D, aged 60, had in excess of 50 convictions for shoplifting. He was disqualified from driving for 5 years. The Judge said D was a determined and professional thief.

Held. The Judge was fully justified to disqualify D. While the primary purpose of disqualification may be prevention, it also has a punitive purpose and should be seen as part of the total sentence. **3 years'** disqualification not 5.

44.9 *Sexual cases*

Examples: *R v Bowling* 2008 EWCA Crim 1148, 2009 1 Cr App R (S) 23 (p 122) (Plea to kerb crawling. 2 years not 4), *R v Fielding* 2011 EWCA Crim 1188 (Exposure on motorway while driving ×2. 1 year not 2) and *R v Ketteridge* 2014 EWCA Crim 1962, 2015 1 Cr App R (S) 11 (p 89) (Exposure (×2). D exposed his penis, masturbating and staring at girls: a) aged 17-18 and b) 13-16, whilst driving slowly or stationary. Danger to road users. **9 months' custody** in all and **1-year disqualification** upheld.)

44.10 *On the facts, disqualification appropriate/not appropriate*

R v Cooper 1983 RTR 183 D pleaded to burglary, theft and allowing himself to be carried in a conveyance taken without authority (9 months' concurrent, disqualified for 2 years). His younger brother, aged 19 and without a licence, stole a car and crashed it into the gatepost of a nearby house. He then met D, and proceeded to show D that he could drive. Both D and his brother had been drinking. The car was stopped by police and D was breathalysed. D, aged 44, had two minor driving convictions in 1976 and appealed against the disqualification. Held. The offence plainly did not call for disqualification, especially a substantial period of 2 years. Disqualification, as a general rule, should be reserved for cases involving bad driving, persistent motoring offences, or for cases involving the use of a vehicle for the purposes of crime. The courts should think very carefully before imposing a disqualification which might deprive a man of his livelihood, except in cases of bad driving.

R v Gilder 2011 EWCA Crim 1159, 2012 1 Cr App R (S) 4 (p 16) D pleaded to theft. He, with others, stole diesel from a depot. The team went by truck, twice on the first night and three times on the second night. D was a passenger in the truck used. The loss was £9,116 worth of diesel. D had five previous convictions for theft and similar offences. The prosecution said they did not believe the truck belonged to D. W was sentenced to 15 months for the theft and one month consecutive for an unrelated handling charge. Held. It was a highly sophisticated and planned operation by professional criminals. The fact that D was a passenger was no bar to disqualification. The Judge was fully entitled to impose disqualification. However, bearing in mind he was aged 27, 18 months' disqualification not 3 years.

See also: *R v Stokes* 2012 EWCA Crim 1148 (Plea to stealing petrol from a petrol station. 18 months not 2 years)

45 DISQUALIFICATION FROM DRIVING: DISCRETIONARY: ROAD TRAFFIC

45.1

Road Traffic Offenders Act 1988 s 34(2)

Compulsory extended periods The rules for imposing all types of driving disqualification (except interim disqualification) were from 13 April 2015 radically altered by Road Traffic Offenders Act 1988 s 35A[608] (as amended), which requires the court to add an extended period to the disqualification period. For more details, see **41.16**.

For a list of the various disqualification chapters, see the beginning of the next chapter.

For ***Reduced periods of disqualification for attendance on courses***, see the **DISQUALIFICATION FROM DRIVING: OBLIGATORY** ***Reduced periods of disqualification for attendance on courses*** para at **43.8**.

For the general rules about disqualification, see the **DISQUALIFICATION FROM DRIVING: BASIC PRINCIPLES** chapter.

[608] As inserted by Coroners and Justice Act 2009 s 2 and Sch 16 paras 2 and 5

45.2 *Power to disqualify/Test to apply*

Road Traffic Offenders Act 1988 s 34(2) Where a person is convicted of an offence involving discretionary disqualification…the court may order him to be disqualified for such period as the court thinks fit.

45.3 *Magistrates' Court Sentencing Guidelines*

Magistrates' Court Sentencing Guidelines 2008, see www.banksr.com Other Matters Guidelines tab The guideline applies to the Magistrates' Court and to the Crown Court hearing appeals or sentencing for summary only offences.[609]

page 185 para 10 Whenever an offender is convicted of an endorsable offence or of taking a vehicle without consent, the court has a discretionary power to disqualify instead of imposing penalty points. The individual offence guidelines above indicate whether the offence is endorsable and the number or range of penalty points it carries.

11 The number of variable points or the period of disqualification should reflect the seriousness of the offence. Some of the individual offence guidelines above include penalty points and/or periods of disqualification in the sentence starting points and ranges. However, the court is not precluded from sentencing outside the range where the facts justify it. Where a disqualification is for less than 56 days, there are some differences in effect compared with disqualification for a longer period, in particular, the licence will automatically come back into effect at the end of the disqualification period (instead of requiring application by the driver) and the disqualification is not taken into account for the purpose of increasing subsequent obligatory periods of disqualification.[610]

12 In some cases in which the court is considering discretionary disqualification, the offender may already have sufficient penalty points on his or her licence that he or she would be liable to a 'totting up' disqualification if further points were imposed. In these circumstances, the court should impose penalty points rather than discretionary disqualification so that the minimum totting up disqualification period applies (see para 7 at **46.11**).

Judicial approach, see the **DISQUALIFICATION FROM DRIVING: DISCRETIONARY: GENERAL POWER Judicial approach to discretionary disqualification** section at **44.7**.

45.4 *Defendant liable to both discretionary and totting up disqualification*

TICs and Totality Guideline 2012: Crown Court, see www.banksr.com Other Matters Guidelines tab (*Magistrates' Court Sentencing Guidelines Update March 2012* page 18o[611])

page 15 Offender convicted of two or more offences involving discretionary disqualification and obligatory endorsement from driving but the court for special reasons does not disqualify the offender and the penalty points to be taken into account number 12 or more, Road Traffic Offenders Act 1988 s 28 and 35.

Where an offender is convicted on the same occasion of more than one offence to which Road Traffic Offenders Act 1988 s 35(1) applies, only one disqualification shall be imposed on him.[612] However, the court must take into account all offences when determining the disqualification period. For the purposes of appeal, any disqualification imposed shall be treated as an order made on conviction of each of the offences.[613]

Magistrates' Court Sentencing Guidelines 2008, see www.banksr.com Other Matters Guidelines tab page 185 para 12 In some cases in which the court is considering discretionary disqualification, the offender may already have sufficient penalty points on his or her licence that he or she would be liable to a 'totting up' disqualification if further

609 See page 15 of the Guidelines.
610 Road Traffic Offenders Act 1988 s 34(4), 35(2), 37(1A)
611 This is how the page is numbered.
612 Road Traffic Offenders Act 1988 s 34(3)
613 Road Traffic Offenders Act 1988 s 34(3)

points were imposed. In these circumstances, the court should impose penalty points rather than discretionary disqualification so that the minimum totting up disqualification period applies (see para 7 at **46.11**).
Jones v DPP 2001 RTR 8 (p 80) D pleaded to speeding. He drove at between 94 and 101 mph. He had three speeding endorsements on his licence with 11 penalty points. He was therefore liable to discretionary disqualification and 'totting up' disqualification. The issue arose as to which type of disqualification the Magistrates should consider first. Held. The court is obliged to consider discretionary disqualification first before 'totting up'. However, the court is not limited to considering that issue in isolation. The court can in its discretion decide not to impose discretionary disqualification because it is conscious that the result will be the imposition of 'totting up' disqualification.

Combined with other orders

45.5 ***Penalty points, Combined with***
Magistrates' Court Sentencing Guidelines 2008, see www.banksr.com Other Matters Guidelines tab page 185 para 12 In some cases in which the court is considering discretionary disqualification, the offender may already have sufficient penalty points on his or her licence that he or she would be liable to a 'totting up' disqualification if further points were imposed. In these circumstances, the court should impose penalty points rather than discretionary disqualification so that the minimum totting up disqualification period applies (see para 7 at **46.11**).
Disqualification from Driving: New Drivers see the **Revocation of New Drivers' Licences** chapter.

46 Disqualification from Driving: Totting Up

46.1
Road Traffic Offenders Act 1988 s 28-30 and 35
There are the following other chapters:

- **Disqualification from Driving: Basic Principles**
- **Disqualification from Driving: Discretionary: General Power**
- **Disqualification from Driving: Discretionary: Road Traffic**
- **Disqualification from Driving: Obligatory**
- **Disqualification until Test is Passed**

Revocation of New Drivers' Licences For young drivers who lose their licence when they accumulate six penalty points, see the **Revocation of New Drivers' Licences** chapter.
There is also an **Endorsement** chapter.
Compulsory extended periods The rules for imposing all types of driving disqualification (except interim disqualification) were from 13 April 2015 radically altered by Road Traffic Offenders Act 1988 s 35A[614] (as amended), which requires the court to add an extended period to the disqualification period. For more details, see **41.16**.
Reduced periods of disqualification for attendance on courses There is a power to order reduced periods of disqualification where the offender completes a course, see the **Disqualification from Driving: Obligatory** ***Reduced periods of disqualification for attendance on courses*** para at **43.8**.
Rehabilitation The rehabilitation period ends on the last day of the disqualification period.[615]
See also the **Rehabilitation of Offenders Act 1974** chapter.

[614] As inserted by Coroners and Justice Act 2009 s 2 and Sch 16 paras 2 and 5
[615] Rehabilitation of Offenders Act 1974 s 5(8)

Step-by-step guide to totting up

46.2 ***The totting up steps***

Step 1 Does obligatory disqualification apply? (For details, see **43.2**.) If it does, totting up does not apply.

Step 2 Do the defence assert there are special reasons for not endorsing the licence? If yes, the application is determined. If the application is successful, totting up does not apply. However, discretionary disqualification can be considered (see the **SPECIAL REASONS** ***Special reasons found Court can still disqualify*** para at **104.11**) but it would be unlikely. If the application is unsuccessful, go to Step 3.

Step 3 What are the total penalty points?

(a) Where some of the new offences have a range, determine the number in that range.

(b) Consider whether any of the offences were committed on the same occasion, see **46.12**. For those that are, select the offence which carries the largest number of penalty points and then just consider penalty points for that offence,[616] unless the court thinks it fit not to apply this rule.[617]

(c) Add the points for the new offence(s) to those of any on the licence whose date of commission is within 3 years.

Step 4 Consider whether there are 12 or more points in total or not.

Step 5 If there are 12 or more points, consider whether there are 'grounds for mitigating the normal consequences of the conviction' (also known as 'exceptional hardship').

Step 6 If not, the court must consider previous periods of disqualification (excluding interim disqualification, disqualification when the vehicle is used for the purposes of crime and disqualification for stealing a vehicle[618]). Although disqualification under the totting up rules 'wipes the licence clean', obligatory and discretionary disqualification do not.[619]

Step 7 The court must determine whether the defendant had a period of disqualification of 56 days or more within the three years preceding the commission of the latest offence in respect of which penalty points were awarded. If not, disqualify for at least 6 months. If there are, disqualify for at least 12 months and at least 2 years if there is more than one such period, see para **46.4**.

Step 8 Where the defendant faces both discretionary disqualification and totting up for the same offence, the court should consider the following:[620]

(a) Whether discretionary disqualification is appropriate for the case before the court. This issue should be decided by considering the defendant's whole driving record.

(b) Where:

(i) it is decided the defendant ought to be disqualified,

(ii) the number of points in the totting up procedure number 12 or more, and

(iii) the period of disqualification under discretionary disqualification is shorter than totting up (taking into account the minimum term),

the court should disqualify through the totting up method as opposed to the discretionary disqualification method. This is so that the minimum term of disqualification applies.

(c) If the court decides to disqualify under the discretionary power, the points for that offence do not count and totting up does not apply. Any points on the licence remain.

(d) If the court decides not to use the discretionary power, then the court adds the penalty points to the previous points and disqualifies him or her under the totting up provisions.

---

[616] *R v Kent* 1983 5 Cr App R (S) 171

[617] Road Traffic Offenders Act 1988 s 28(5)

[618] Road Traffic Offenders Act 1988 s 35(1A) limits the disqualifications to take into account obligatory and discretionary disqualification so excluding these disqualifications.

[619] Road Traffic Offenders Act 1988 s 29(1)(b)

[620] The bulk of the material in Step 8 is taken from *Jones v DPP* 2001 RTR 8 (p 80).

The court should then disqualify for the relevant period.
Note: Although the *Magistrates' Court Sentencing Guidelines 2008* (see **46.5**) approach could be taken to be in conflict with the last step based on *Jones v DPP* 2001 RTR 8 (p 80), it is intended to discourage short periods of discretionary disqualification when the defendant should be subject to the totting up procedure.
Where the court orders disqualification, no penalty points should be entered on the licence.[621] Ed.
Step 9 Consider whether it would be appropriate to order disqualification until the defendant has passed a driving test, see the **DISQUALIFICATION UNTIL TEST IS PASSED** chapter. This order is available whether or not the defendant has passed a test already.

46.3 *Flow chart*

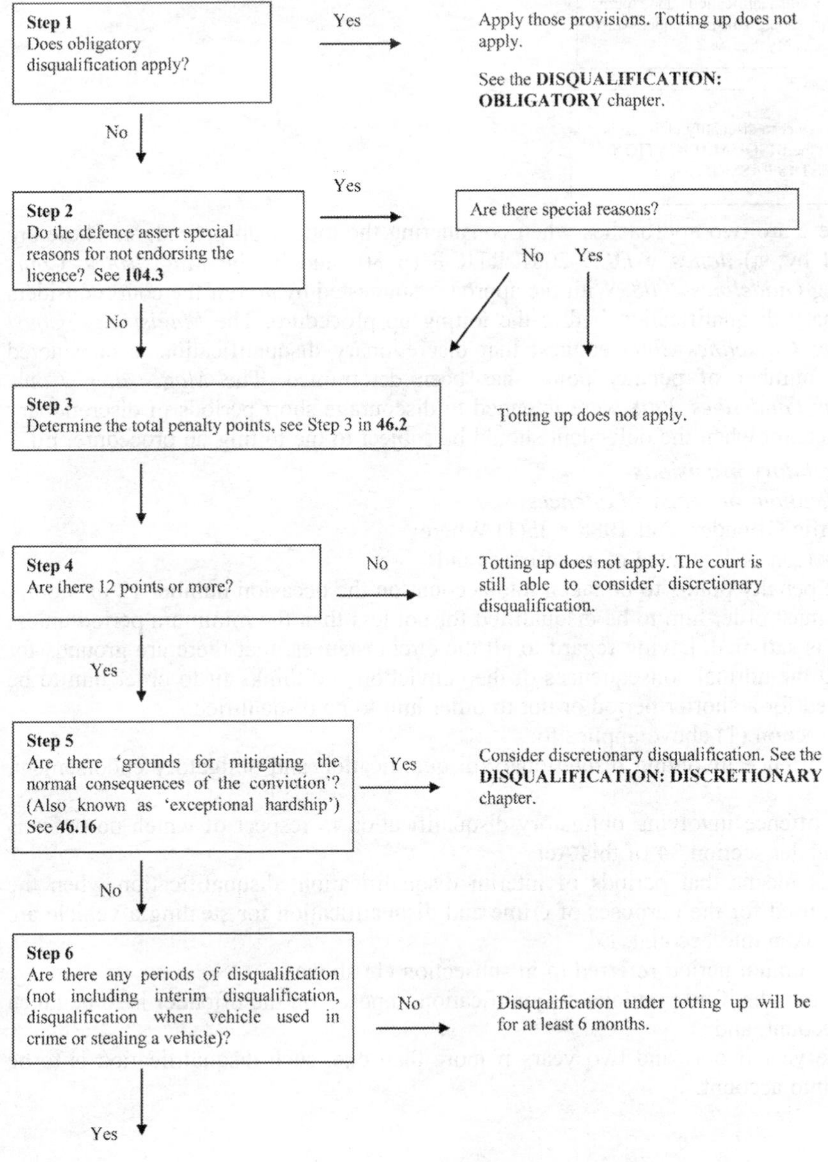
Step 1
Does obligatory disqualification apply?
Yes
Apply those provisions. Totting up does not apply.
See the DISQUALIFICATION: OBLIGATORY chapter.
No
Step 2
Do the defence assert special reasons for not endorsing the licence? See 104.3
Yes
Are there special reasons?
No
Yes
No
Step 3
Determine the total penalty points, see Step 3 in 46.2
Totting up does not apply.
Step 4
Are there 12 points or more?
No
Totting up does not apply. The court is still able to consider discretionary disqualification.
Yes
Step 5
Are there 'grounds for mitigating the normal consequences of the conviction'? (Also known as 'exceptional hardship') See 46.16
Yes
Consider discretionary disqualification. See the DISQUALIFICATION: DISCRETIONARY chapter.
No
Step 6
Are there any periods of disqualification (not including interim disqualification, disqualification when vehicle used in crime or stealing a vehicle)?
No
Disqualification under totting up will be for at least 6 months.
Yes

[621] *R v Kent* 1983 5 Cr App R (S) 171

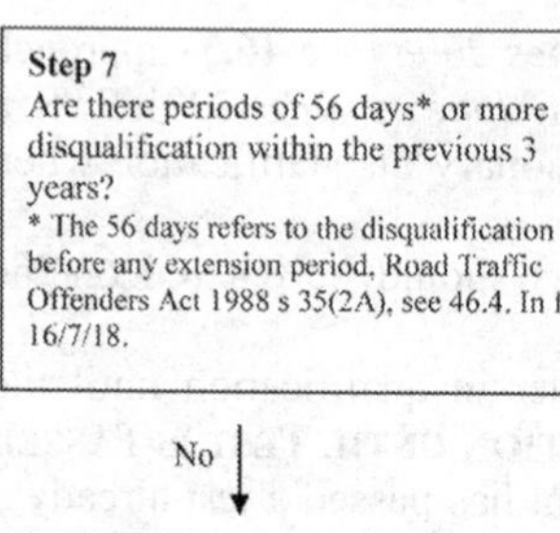

Step 7
Are there periods of 56 days* or more disqualification within the previous 3 years?
* The 56 days refers to the disqualification before any extension period, Road Traffic Offenders Act 1988 s 35(2A), see 46.4. In force 16/7/18.
Yes
If there is one period, disqualification under totting up will be for at least 12 months.
If there are two periods, disqualification under totting up will be for at least 2 years.
No

Step 8
Where the defendant faces both discretionary disqualification and totting up, the court should consider under which power to disqualify. See **46.2**

Step 9
Consider whether to disqualify until test is passed. See the **DISQUALIFICATION UNTIL TEST IS PASSED** chapter.

Note: There are two approaches when considering the totting up procedure. These are suggested by: a) *Jones v DPP* 2001 RTR 8 (p 80) and b) the *Magistrates' Court Sentencing Guidelines 2008*. With the approach suggested by *Jones*, the court considers discretionary disqualification before the totting up procedure. The *Magistrates' Court Sentencing Guidelines 2008* suggest that discretionary disqualification is considered once the number of penalty points has been determined. The *Magistrates' Court Sentencing Guidelines 2008* were intended to discourage short periods of discretionary disqualification when the defendant should be subject to the totting up procedure. Ed.

46.4 *Statutory provisions*

Disqualification for repeated offences

Road Traffic Offenders Act 1988 s 35(1) Where:

(a) a person is convicted of an offence, and

(b) the penalty points to be taken into account on the occasion number 12 or more,

the court must order him to be disqualified for not less than the minimum period unless the court is satisfied, having regard to all the circumstances, that there are grounds for mitigating the normal consequences of the conviction and thinks fit to order him to be disqualified for a shorter period or not to order him to be disqualified.

(1A) Subsection (1) above applies to:

(a) an offence involving discretionary disqualification and obligatory endorsement, and

(b) an offence involving obligatory disqualification in respect of which no order is made under section 34 of this Act.

Note: This means that periods of interim disqualification, disqualification when the vehicle is used for the purposes of crime and disqualification for stealing a vehicle are not to be taken into account. Ed.

(2) The minimum period referred to in subsection (1) above is:

(a) six months if no previous disqualification imposed on the offender is to be taken into account, and

(b) one year if one, and two years if more than one, such disqualification is to be taken into account,

and a previous disqualification imposed on an offender is, subject to subsection (2A),[622] to be taken into account if it was for a fixed period of 56 days or more and was imposed within the three years immediately preceding the commission of the latest offence in respect of which penalty points are taken into account under section 29 of this Act.
(2A) A previous disqualification imposed on an offender for a fixed period is not to be taken into account for the purposes of subsection (2) if that period would have been less than 56 days but for an extension period added pursuant to:
(a) section 35A or 35C,
(b) section 248D of the Criminal Procedure (Scotland) Act 1995, or
(c) section 147A of the Powers of Criminal Courts (Sentencing) Act 2000.[623]
(3) Where an offender is convicted on the same occasion of more than one offence to which subsection (1) above applies:
(a) not more than one disqualification shall be imposed on him under subsection (1) above,
(b) in determining the period of the disqualification the court must take into account all the offences, and
(c) for the purposes of any appeal, any disqualification imposed under subsection (1) above shall be treated as an order made on the conviction of each of the offences.
(4) No account is to be taken under subsection (1) above of any of the following circumstances:
(a) any circumstances that are alleged to make the offence or any of the offences not a serious one,
(b) hardship, other than exceptional hardship, or
(c) any circumstances which, within the three years immediately preceding the conviction, have been taken into account under that subsection in ordering the offender to be disqualified for a shorter period or not ordering him to be disqualified.
(5) References in this section to disqualification do not include a disqualification imposed under section 26 of this Act or Powers of Criminal Courts (Sentencing) Act 2000 s 147 (offences committed by using vehicles) or a disqualification imposed in respect of an offence of stealing a motor vehicle, an offence under Theft Act 1968 s 12 or 25, an offence under Road Traffic Act 1988 s 178, or an attempt to commit such an offence.
(5A) The preceding provisions of this section shall apply in relation to a conviction of an offence committed by aiding, abetting, counselling, procuring, or inciting to the commission of, an offence involving obligatory disqualification as if the offence were an offence involving discretionary disqualification.
Road Traffic Offenders Act 1988 s 35(7) This section is subject to section 48 of this Act (exemptions from disqualification and endorsement for certain construction and use offences).

46.5 *Magistrates' Court Sentencing Guidelines*

Magistrates' Court Sentencing Guidelines 2008, see www.banksr.com Other Matters Guidelines tab The guideline applies to the Magistrates' Court and to the Crown Court hearing appeals or sentencing for summary only offences.[624]

page 184 An offender must be disqualified for at least two years if he or she has been disqualified two or more times for a period of at least 56 days in the three years preceding the commission of the offence.[625] The following disqualifications are to be

[622] Inserted by Coroners and Justice Act 2009 Sch 21 para 90 (1) and (6)(a). In force 16/7/18, Coroners and Justice Act 2009 (Commencement No 18) Order 2018 2018/733 para 2(c)
[623] Inserted by Coroners and Justice Act 2009 Sch 21 para 90 (1) and (6)(b). In force 16/7/18, Coroners and Justice Act 2009 (Commencement No 18) Order 2018 2018/733 para 2(c)
[624] See page 15 of the Guidelines.
[625] Road Traffic Offenders Act 1988 s 34(4)

disregarded for the purposes of this provision: a) interim disqualification, b) disqualification where vehicle used for the purpose of crime, c) disqualification for stealing or taking a vehicle or going equipped to steal or take a vehicle.
Disputes as to facts see the **FACTUAL BASIS FOR SENTENCING** ***Same rules apply when imposing ancillary orders*** para at **57.26**.

PENALTY POINTS

Determining the number of points to attribute

Driving licence From 8 June 2015, the counterpart of a driving licence (which was used at court in addition to the photocard) has been replaced by the electronic driving record maintained by the DVLA, Road Safety Act 2006 Sch 3.

46.6 ***Statutory duty to attribute penalty points***

Road Traffic Offenders Act 1988 s 28(1) Where a person is convicted of an offence involving obligatory endorsement, then, subject to the following provisions of this section, the number of penalty points to be attributed to the offence is:

(a) the number shown in relation to the offence in the last column of Part I or Part II of Schedule 2 to this Act, or

(b) where a range of numbers is shown, a number within that range.

Note: The number of points is listed at the start of the relevant chapters for the offences in Volume 2 of this book. For the list of offences and their penalty points, see **54.5**. Ed.

46.7 ***Aiding, abetting etc., Offence is Disqualification is obligatory***

Road Traffic Offenders Act 1988 s 28(2) Where a person is convicted of an offence committed by aiding, abetting, counselling or procuring, or inciting to the commission of, an offence involving obligatory disqualification, then, subject to the following provisions of this section, the number of penalty points to be attributed to the offence is ten.

Note: This only applies when special reasons are found because otherwise penalty points would not be ordered. Ed.

46.8 ***Fixed penalty offences***

Road Traffic Offenders Act 1988 s 28(3) [When the court is determining the points without a hearing etc.] the number of penalty points to be attributed to an offence is:
a) [The fixed penalty number] shown in the last column of Part 1 of Schedule 2 to this Act in relation to the offence (see **54.5**),
b) where a range of numbers followed by the words 'or appropriate penalty points [fixed penalty]' is shown there in relation to the offence, the appropriate number of penalty points for the offence, and
c) where only a range of numbers is shown there in relation to the offence [in that Schedule], the lowest number in the range.

46.9 ***European Convention on Human Rights art 6***

Miller v DPP 2004 EWHC 595 (Admin), 2005 RTR 3 (p 44) High Court D pleaded by post to three speeding offences. The offences were committed in February 1999 and the Magistrates issued a warrant backed with bail. In May 2001 police phoned D, who was asked to attend the police station. D did so and was bailed to attend the Magistrates' Court. At the first hearing, the case was adjourned to July 2001 because of lack of time. On that day, the prosecution asked for an adjournment because of a CPS failure to send counsel the defence skeleton argument in time. The case was put off until August 2001. At that hearing, D contended the delay was an infringement of his article 6 rights and asked to change his plea. The Magistrates rejected this but, because there was insufficient time for the sentencing procedure, the case was adjourned. The defence said this was the fault of the Court for ignoring the defence time estimate. In September 2001, D was fined and disqualified under the totting up procedure. Some of the penalty points had been accrued since this case was first before the Magistrates' Court. The Magistrates then made a wasted costs order against the CPS. D next asked the

Magistrates to state a case for an appeal and the Magistrates refused to do so. D then sought judicial review and in March 2002, D's disqualification was suspended pending the appeal. The matter was heard in the Divisional Court in July 2002. The Court ordered the Magistrates to state a case. In October 2002, the Magistrates stated a case and in March 2003 the appeal was heard. D's counsel's main point was that for a case as simple as three speeding offences the two-year delay until sentence was a breach of his article 6 rights. All parties agreed that part of the argument should be adjourned until after the House of Lords had determined an appeal. The House of Lords determined that case, *Att-Gen's Ref No 2 of 2001* 2003 UKHL 68, 2004 1 Cr App R 25 (p 317)[626] in December 2003 and no further argument was necessary. D, in light of the case, asked for a reduced sentence, namely that the disqualification should be reduced to the period already served. Held in March 2004. The delay was excessive. The delay could not be a special reason. The suggested reduction would be a just and appropriate remedy for the breach of D's article 6 rights. To make the period easy to apply, the period will be reduced to 5 months so enabling no further period to be served.

Determining the number of penalty points to be taken into account

46.10 ***Statutory provisions***

Road Traffic Offenders Act 1988 s 29(1) Where a person is convicted of an offence involving obligatory endorsement, the penalty points to be taken into account on that occasion are:

(a) any that are to be attributed to the offence or offences of which he is convicted, disregarding any offence in respect of which a (totting up order) under section 34 of this Act is made, and

(b) any that were on a previous occasion ordered to be endorsed on his driving record,[627] unless the offender has since that occasion and before the conviction been disqualified under section 35 of this Act.

(2) If any of the offences was committed more than three years before another, the penalty points in respect of that offence shall not be added to those in respect of the other.

(3) [Repealed]

46.11 ***Magistrates' Court Sentencing Guidelines***

Magistrates' Court Sentencing Guidelines 2008, see www.banksr.com Other Matters Guidelines tab The guideline applies to the Magistrates' Court and to the Crown Court hearing appeals or sentencing for summary only offences.[628]

page 185 para 7 Disqualification for a minimum of six months must be ordered if an offender incurs 12 penalty points or more within a three-year period.[629] The minimum period may be automatically increased if the offender has been disqualified within the preceding three years. Totting up disqualifications, unlike other disqualifications, erase all penalty points.

The period of a totting up disqualification can be reduced or avoided for exceptional hardship or other mitigating circumstances. No account is to be taken of hardship that is not exceptional hardship or circumstances alleged to make the offence not serious. Any circumstances taken into account in the preceding three years to reduce or avoid a totting up disqualification must be disregarded.[630]

46.12 ***Two or more offences on the same occasion***

Road Traffic Offenders Act 1988 s 28(4) Where a person is convicted (whether on the same occasion or not) of two or more offences committed on the same occasion and

[626] It would appear that the court gave the title *Att-Gen's Ref No 2 of 2001* to two cases. This case should not be confused with *Att-Gen's Ref No 2 of 2001* 2001 2 Cr App R (S) 121 (p 524).

[627] As amended by Road Safety Act 2006 Sch 7 para 1.

[628] See page 15 of the Guidelines.

[629] Road Traffic Offenders Act 1988 s 35

[630] Road Traffic Offenders Act 1988 s 35

involving obligatory endorsement, the total number of penalty points to be attributed to them is the number or highest number that would be attributed on a conviction of one of them (so that if the convictions are on different occasions the number of penalty points to be attributed to the offences on the later occasion or occasions shall be restricted accordingly).
(5) The court may if it thinks fit determine that subsection 28(4) shall not apply to the offences (or, where three or more offences are concerned, to any one or more of them).
(6) Where a court makes such a determination it shall state its reasons in open court and, if it is a Magistrates' Court, shall cause them to be entered in the register of its proceedings.
R v Kent 1983 5 Cr App R (S) 171 All disqualifications now run concurrently.

46.13 ***Two or more offences Definition of 'same occasion'***

Johnson v Finbow 1983 RTR 363 D was sentenced for failing to stop and failing to report. She had an accident and failed to stop and give her name. She also failed to report the accident within the required 24 hours. The Magistrates treated the offences as being on different occasions. Held. It can be said these offences were not committed at the same moment. They might have been committed on different days. However, it is sensible to look at the matter more broadly. The offences arose out of the same accident. It can be said that the lapse of time, although significant, is not sufficiently great to be able to say, as a matter of common sense, that those offences were committed on different occasions. When one sees how closely they are connected with the accident, and how similar, in fact, the two offences are in their nature, then the proper conclusion is that when arising out of the same accident these two offences were committed 'on the same occasion'.
Johnston v Over 1985 RTR 240 D pleaded to using a van without insurance and using a caravanette without insurance. Both vehicles were parked outside his home. D was stripping parts from one to use on the other vehicle. The Magistrates gave four penalty points for each offence. Held. It could not be said the offences were committed other than on the same occasion, namely when the police officer discovered the vehicles were not covered by insurance. Each case will depend on the facts. It is not a question of law. Common sense dictates that having regard to the use which was made of the vehicle at the material time, the offences were committed on the same occasion.
Note: These are old cases, but there have been no reported cases since. Ed.

46.14 ***Where a defendant was disqualified, those penalty points don't count***

Road Traffic Offenders Act 1988 s 29(1)(a) [When the court is determining how many penalty points there are on a licence it shall] disregard any offence in which an order under Road Traffic Offenders Act 1988 s 34 (namely obligatory and discretionary disqualification) was made.
Note: The effect of this is that when the court is totting up the penalty points, the offences where the defendant was disqualified don't count. Ed.

Defence establishing 'exceptional hardship'

46.15 ***Statutory provisions and Magistrates' Court Sentencing Guidelines***

Road Traffic Offenders Act 1988 s 35(4) No account is to be taken of any of the following circumstances:..b) hardship, other than exceptional hardship.
Magistrates' Court Sentencing Guidelines 2008, see www.banksr.com Other Matters Guidelines tab page 185 No account is to be taken of hardship that is not exceptional hardship or circumstances alleged to make the offence not serious.

46.16 ***Exceptional hardship, Definition of***

Fay v Fay 1982 AC 835 Lords The House of Lords considered the meaning of 'hardship, other than exceptional hardship' in Matrimonial Causes Act 1973 s 3(2). Held. It was not possible to define with any precision what is meant by 'exceptional' hardship. The imprecision of this concept with the resultant impossibility of definition must have been deliberately accepted as appropriate by the legislature and is itself an indication that the determination of what is exceptional is essentially a matter for the judge. The hardship suffered by the applicant must be shown to be something out of the ordinary. Any attempt to define a meaning would be a betrayal of the deliberate imprecision favoured by Parliament. A judge's finding would not be disturbed unless it was clearly wrong. Note: Although this is a family law case, the editors of *Wilkinson's Road Traffic Offences* rightly believe the same approach may be broadly applied when considering the meaning of 'exceptional hardship' in Road Traffic Offenders Act 1988 s 35(4)(b). Ed.

Brennan v McKay 1997 SLT 603 Scottish High Court of Justiciary D, a taxi driver, was liable for totting up and claimed 'exceptional hardship'. He said he would be likely to lose his job as a taxi driver, which he had had for eight years. Further, he would be likely to find it difficult to obtain other work, which would substantially affect him and his family. D was disqualified. Held. To contend 'exceptional hardship' flowing from the loss of a licence, it will be necessary to demonstrate not only that D may lose his employment, but that associated with that loss of employment are other circumstances which may involve reflected hardship of a serious kind upon his business or his family or his long-term prospects. In *Howdle v Davidson* 1994 SCCR 754 the Court pointed out that the question is ultimately one of fact and degree, and that while it cannot be asserted as an invariable rule that exceptional hardship will only be established where persons other than the accused and his immediate family will suffer, nevertheless the hardship does require to be exceptional. Here there is nothing which takes D's case out of the ordinary where somebody requires to have a licence to carry on his employment and the loss of his licence will cause hardship to him and to his immediate family. What is missing from this case is that additional element. Appeal dismissed.

Note: Although this is a Scottish case, these principles have been widely applied in England since this case was reported. Ed.

46.17 *Defendant must prove his or her mitigating circumstances*

R v Sandbach JJs ex parte Pescud 1983 5 Cr App R (S) 177 D was convicted of driving without due care and attention and, at a later date, of driving at an excessive speed. He was prosecuted first for the excess speed and at a later date for the due care charge. The Magistrates were obliged to disqualify D, unless they were satisfied that there were grounds for mitigating the consequences of the conviction. Such grounds were argued and D was not disqualified. On the second prosecution, for the first (chronological) offence, D was at risk of being disqualified through the 'totting up' system. Transport Act 1981 s 19(2)[631] precluded reliance upon any matters relied upon as grounds for mitigating the consequences of the conviction in the previous three years. D's representative was unable to assure the Court that the mitigating circumstances were different from the previous occasion. The Magistrates were advised not to allow the advancement of the mitigating circumstances. D accepted that the mitigating circumstances were the same, but appealed against the decision not to hear the mitigating circumstances on the second occasion. Held. Where D states that although mitigating grounds have been relied upon before another court within the preceding three years, there are other and different mitigating grounds, it is for him to establish the fact. He can do so by calling evidence or by ensuring a copy of the register of the court is present. If he does not do either of these things, there is no onus on the court to assume that the grounds are not the same.

Owen v Jones 1988 RTR 102 D, a CID officer, was convicted of excess alcohol. He received a fine, a costs order and ten penalty points on his licence. D was discovered at 4 am in charge of a car in a public place. His blood alcohol level was 176 mg. The Justices heard that D's licence had three penalty points prior to this conviction. D successfully argued that disqualification would result in exceptional hardship and was unnecessary. D asserted that it was the policy of his police force to request the resignation of, or actively dismiss, officers disqualified from driving. He argued that a

[631] Repealed on 15/5/89 by Road Traffic (Consequential Provisions) Act 1988

disqualification would result in the loss of his job and house (which was owned by the police force). No evidence was heard on this point. The prosecution appealed. Held. There is no reason why justices should not be allowed to say to a defendant that they are fully apprised of the fact sought to be asserted by him and therefore do not require evidence of it. Justices should not come to this conclusion easily. It was not necessary on this occasion to hear evidence.

46.18 ***Totting up erases penalty points***

Road Traffic Offenders Act 1988 s 29(1) Where a person is convicted of an offence involving…endorsement, the penalty points to be taken into account on that occasion are…any that were on a previous occasion ordered to be endorsed…unless the offender has since that occasion and before the conviction been disqualified.

Magistrates' Court Sentencing Guidelines 2008, see www.banksr.com Other Matters Guidelines tab page 185 Totting up disqualifications, unlike other disqualifications, erase all penalty points.

R v Brentwood JJs ex parte Richardson 1992 95 Cr App R 187 The relevant date for the purposes of wiping the slate clean was the date of sentence and not the date of the verdict.

46.19 ***Absolute and conditional discharges, Offences dealt with by Do they count?***

Road Traffic Offenders Act 1988 s 46(2)(b) A conviction in respect of which particulars have been endorsed on the counterpart of any licence held by him or on[632] his driving record is to be taken into account notwithstanding anything in Powers of Criminal Courts (Sentencing) Act 2000 s 14(1) (disregarding absolute and conditional discharges) in determining his liability to punishment or disqualification for any offence involving obligatory or discretionary disqualification in subsequent proceedings.

Combined with other orders

46.20 ***Absolute and conditional discharges, Combined with***

Road Traffic Offenders Act 1988 s 46(1) Notwithstanding anything in Powers of Criminal Courts (Sentencing) Act 2000 s 14(3) (rule about disregarding absolute and conditional discharges), a court [when convicting a person involving obligatory or discretionary disqualification orders him to be absolutely or conditionally discharged] may also exercise any power conferred, and must also discharge any duty imposed on the court by section 35 of this Act (totting up disqualification).

Powers of Criminal Courts (Sentencing) Act 2000 s 12(7) [The court may] on discharging an offender absolutely or conditionally impose any disqualification.

Note: The Act does not indicate whether 'the disqualification' is driving disqualification or not. It is likely to be interpreted as all disqualification orders, as that is the natural meaning of the words in the subsection. Ed.

Custody, Combined with see **41.16**.

46.21 ***Discretionary disqualification and penalty points, Combined with***

Magistrates' Court Sentencing Guidelines 2008, see www.banksr.com Other Matters Guidelines tab page 185 para 12 In some cases in which the court is considering discretionary disqualification, the offender may already have sufficient penalty points on his or her licence that he or she would be liable to a 'totting up' disqualification if further points were imposed. In these circumstances, the court should impose penalty points rather than discretionary disqualification so that the minimum totting up disqualification period applies [see para 7 at **46.11**].

[632] As amended by Road Safety Act 2006 Sch 3 and 7. In force 8/6/15

46.22 ***Disqualified until test is passed, Combined with***
Magistrates' Court Sentencing Guidelines 2008, see www.banksr.com Other Matters Guidelines tab page 185 para 15 An offender disqualified as a 'totter' under the penalty points provisions may also be ordered to retake a driving test. In this case, the extended test applies.

46.23 ***Revocation of a probationary driver's licence, Combined with***
Note: When a probationary driver has his or her licence revoked because of six penalty points those points remain on his or her licence. Consequently, the totting up procedure will remain applicable at any time the licence accumulates 12 points. Ed.
See also the **COMBINING SENTENCES** chapter.

Other matters

46.24 ***How long does an endorsement last?***
Road Traffic Offenders Act 1988 s 45(5) Endorsements remain on a licence for:
11 years from the date of conviction for offences relating to drink/drugs and driving, causing death by careless driving whilst under the influence of drink/drugs, and causing death by careless driving then failing to provide a specimen for analysis.
4 years from date of conviction for reckless/dangerous driving and offences resulting in disqualification.
4 years from the date of offence in all other cases.

47 DISQUALIFICATION UNTIL TEST IS PASSED

47.1
Road Traffic Offenders Act 1988 s 36
For a list of the disqualification chapters, see the first paragraph of the previous chapter.

47.2 ***Statistics England and Wales***
Disqualification until driving test is passed[633, 634]

	Crown Court			Magistrates' Court		
	2014	**2015**	**2016**	**2014**	**2015**	**2016**
With disqualification	3,127	3,589	4,115	1,248	1,428	1,784
Stand-alone	2,318	2,794	2,997	39	39	38

For explanations about the statistics, see page 1-xii. The MoJ no longer provide Banks on Sentence with these statistics. For more statistics, see www.banksr.com Other Matters Statistics tab

47.3 ***Obligatory orders Power to order***
Disqualification until test is passed
Road Traffic Offenders Act 1988 s 36(1) Where this subsection applies to a person the court must order him to be disqualified until he passes the appropriate driving test.
(2) Subsection (1) above applies to a person who is disqualified under section 34 of this Act on conviction of:
(a) manslaughter by the driver of a motor vehicle,
(b) an offence under Road Traffic Act 1988 s 1 (causing death by dangerous driving),[635]
(c) an offence under Road Traffic Act 1988 s 1A (causing serious injury by dangerous driving),

[633] Excludes disqualifications with a set length and a driving test requirement, disqualifications without a driving test requirement and disqualifications imposed solely under the penalty points system.
[634] The figures given in the table relate to all motoring offences for which defendants are sentenced. When a defendant has been sentenced for two or more offences, each of the two or more offences is counted. Disqualifications for non-motoring offences are excluded.
[635] Section 36(2)(b) was amended by and 36(c)-(f) was inserted by Criminal Justice and Courts Act 2015 Sch 6 para 5(3). In force 13/4/15

(d) an offence under Road Traffic Act 1988 s 2 (dangerous driving),
(e) an offence under Road Traffic Act 1988 s 3ZC (causing death by driving: disqualified drivers), or
(f) an offence under Road Traffic Act 1988 s 3ZD (causing serious injury by driving: disqualified drivers).

(3) Such persons as the Secretary of State may by order prescribe. [Subsection summarised]

Driving Licences (Disqualification until Test Passed) (Prescribed Offence) Order 2001 2001/4051 An offence under Road Traffic Act 1988 s 3A (causing death by careless driving under the influence of drink or drugs) [is] prescribed for the purposes of s 36(1).

47.4 *Discretionary orders Power to order*

Road Traffic Offenders Act 1988 s 36(4) Where a person to whom subsection (1) above does not apply (obligatory disqualification till test is passed) is convicted of an offence involving obligatory endorsement, the court may order him to be disqualified until he passes the appropriate driving test (whether or not he has previously passed any test).

47.5 *Discretionary orders Test to apply*

Road Traffic Offenders Act 1988 s 36(6) In determining whether to make an order under subsection (4) above, the court shall have regard to the safety of road users.

Magistrates' Court Sentencing Guidelines 2008, see www.banksr.com Other Matters Guidelines tab page 185 para 16 The discretion to order a retest is likely to be exercised where there is evidence of inexperience, incompetence or infirmity, or the disqualification period is lengthy (that is, the offender is going to be 'off the road' for a considerable time).

R v Bannister 1991 12 Cr App R (S) 314 LCJ D was convicted of reckless driving. He drove with his full beam headlights on. D overtook a police officer, who flashed him to indicate his lights were on full beam. He braked fiercely causing the officer to brake very sharply. D's car was almost stationary. The officer overtook and could see D's car accelerating towards him with his headlights on full beam as well as two large driving lamps. D drove his car about 1-2 feet behind the officer's car. At the end D accelerated into the officer's car. D was aged 34. The Judge ordered D to be disqualified until he had passed a test. The defence said that he had been driving for most of his adult life and there were no offences recorded against him indicating either ineptitude, carelessness or dangerous driving prior to this event and there had been no criticism in the past of the quality of his driving. Held. This was deliberate dangerous driving, driving which carried with it a manifest risk with a potentially lethal vehicle. The dangers from this sort of behaviour are twofold. There is the obvious inherent danger of driving in this particular manner. There is no evidence that this young man is an incompetent driver, nor is there any evidence of lack of experience in driving. Apart from the ability to control the car, to steer it, and drive it competently, there is another component to good driving: it is that the driver shall have a proper regard for other road users. That is the lesson which D has to be taught again. No doubt it is that which the Judge had in mind when he decided to impose this additional order requiring D to take a test before he resumes driving. Appeal dismissed.

47.6 *Magistrates' Court Sentencing Guidelines*

Magistrates' Court Sentencing Guidelines 2008, see www.banksr.com Other Matters Guidelines tab page 185 para 13 Where an offender is convicted of dangerous driving, the court must order disqualification until an extended driving test is passed.

14 The court has discretion to disqualify until a test is passed where an offender is convicted of any endorsable offence.[636] Where disqualification is obligatory, the extended test applies. In other cases, it will be the ordinary test.

[636] Road Traffic Offenders Act 1988 s 36(4)

15 An offender disqualified as a 'totter' under the penalty points provisions may also be ordered to retake a driving test. In this case, the extended test applies.
16 The discretion to order a retest is likely to be exercised where there is evidence of inexperience, incompetence or infirmity, or the disqualification period is lengthy (that is, the offender is going to be 'off the road' for a considerable time).
Reduced period of disqualification for completion of rehabilitation course
17 Where an offender is disqualified for 12 months or more in respect of an alcohol-related driving offence, the court may order that the period of disqualification will be reduced if the offender satisfactorily completes an approved rehabilitation course.[637]
18 Before offering an offender the opportunity to attend a course, the court must be satisfied that an approved course is available and must inform the offender of the effect of the order, the fees that the offender is required to pay, and when he or she must pay them.
19 The court should also explain that the offender may be required to satisfy the Secretary of State that he or she does not have a drink problem and is fit to drive before the offender's licence will be returned at the end of the disqualification period.[638]
20 In general, a court should consider offering the opportunity to attend a course to all offenders convicted of a relevant offence for the first time. The court should be willing to consider offering an offender the opportunity to attend a second course where it considers there are good reasons. It will not usually be appropriate to give an offender the opportunity to attend a third course.
21 The reduction must be at least three months but cannot be more than one-quarter of the total period of disqualification: a period of 12 months' disqualification must be reduced to nine months. In other cases, a reduction of one week should be made for every month of the disqualification so that, for example, a disqualification of 24 months will be reduced by 24 weeks.
22 When it makes the order, the court must specify a date for completion of the course which is at least two months before the end of the reduced period of disqualification.

47.7 ***Judicial guidance***

R v Gordon 2012 EWCA Crim 772, 2013 1 Cr App R (S) 9 (p 52) The essential consideration when considering whether to order a retest is the safety of other road users. It is not an additional punishment. It is to ensure competence when the defendant resumes his or her driving.

47.8 ***Passengers Is the order appropriate for passengers?***

R v Bradshaw 2001 RTR 4 (p 41) When dealing with passengers this order does not seem appropriate.

R v Roberts 2013 EWCA Crim 785 LCJ D pleaded to aggravated vehicle-taking. After drinking he was a passenger in a car which, while being driven at speed, crashed and overturned. The owner's 13-year-old son died. The Judge disqualified D until he had passed a test. Held. Each case depends upon its own facts. In this case, on his own account D was behind the wheel for a period earlier on when he should not have been. The Judge was fully entitled to order an extended driving test. For more details see the **AGGRAVATED VEHICLE TAKING *Death is caused Cases*** para at **204.9**.

R v Beech and Others 2016 EWCA Crim 1746 LCJ H and T pleaded to conspiracy to steal and were also sentenced for aggravated vehicle taking. A team broke into a cash machine at a supermarket. Police gave chase by helicopter and the escaping car reached speeds of up to 150 mph. H and T were passengers. H and T were sentenced to 3 years, 2 years' disqualification and disqualification until a test was passed. Held. *R v Bradshaw* 2001 and *R v Wiggins* 2001 RTR 3 (p 37) turned on their particular facts. We take into account the egregious nature of the driving, the journey was to escape a serious professional criminal attempt on a cash machine, the speeds reached, the manner of the

[637] Road Traffic Offenders Act 1988 s 34A
[638] Road Traffic Act 1988 s 94 and Motor Vehicles (Driving Licences) Regulations 1999 1999/2864 reg 74

driving and that the public were put at risk. H and T both had a conviction for dangerous driving. They were participating in the dangerous driving. The Judge was right to make the order.

47.9 *Can't have two 'test' orders at the same time*

Road Traffic Offenders Act 1988 s 36(7) Where a person is disqualified until he passes the extended driving test:

(a) any earlier order under this section shall cease to have effect, and

(b) a court shall not make a further order under this section while he is so disqualified.

An example: *R v Edwards* 2014 EWCA Crim 2662 (Rule applied. Second test disqualification quashed.)

47.10 *What test has to be passed?*

Road Traffic Offenders Act 1988 s 36(5) In this section, 'appropriate driving test' means:

(a) an extended driving test, where a person is convicted of an offence involving obligatory disqualification or is disqualified under section 35 of this Act (totting up),

(b) a test of competence to drive,[639] other than an extended driving test, in any other case.

Magistrates' Court Sentencing Guidelines 2008, see www.banksr.com Other Matters Guidelines tab page 185 para 14 Where disqualification is obligatory, the extended test applies. In other cases, it will be the ordinary test.

15 An offender disqualified as a 'totter' under the penalty points provisions may also be ordered to retake a driving test. In this case, the extended test applies.

47.11 *Defendant has never passed a test*

Road Traffic Offenders Act 1988 s 36(4) Where a person to whom subsection (1) [an obligatory order for disqualification until a driving test has been passed] above does not apply is convicted of an offence involving obligatory endorsement, the court may order him to be disqualified until he passes the appropriate driving test (whether or not he has previously passed any test).

R v Miller 1994 15 Cr App R (S) 505 D pleaded to careless driving. A reckless driving count was dropped. D had never passed his test. He was aged 23 and had 10 previous convictions for driving whilst disqualified. The Judge found that D had shown a wanton disregard for other road users and ordered that he be disqualified until he had passed a driving test. Held. There was evidence that his driving was grossly incompetent. The order may achieve the desired aim that he passes his test. It is impossible to say that the Judge erred.

47.12 *Ability to drive when disqualified until test is passed*

Road Traffic Offenders Act 1988 s 37(3) A person disqualified (until he passes a test) is (unless he is also disqualified otherwise than by virtue of such an order) entitled to obtain and to hold a provisional licence and to drive a motor vehicle in accordance with the conditions subject to which the provisional licence is granted.

R v Miller 1994 15 Cr App R (S) 505 The effect of such disqualification is to permit him to go on the road, properly displaying L-plates and accompanied by a competent driver.

47.13 *On the facts, order correct/incorrect*

R v Bannister 1991 12 Cr App R (S) 314 LCJ D was convicted of reckless driving. He drove with his full beam headlights on. D overtook a police officer, who flashed him to indicate his lights were on full beam. He braked fiercely causing the officer to brake very sharply. D's car was almost stationary. The officer overtook and could see D's car accelerating towards him with his headlights on full beam as well as two large driving lamps. D drove his car about 1-2 feet behind the officer's car. At the end D accelerated into the officer's car. D was aged 34. The Judge ordered D to be disqualified until he had

[639] This is defined in Road Traffic Offenders Act 1988 s 36(4) as a test prescribed by virtue of Road Traffic Act 1988 s 89(3), i.e. the normal driving test.

passed a test. The defence said that he had been driving for most of his adult life and there were no offences recorded against him indicating either ineptitude, carelessness or dangerous driving prior to this event and there had been no criticism in the past of the quality of his driving. Held. This was deliberate dangerous driving, driving which carried with it a manifest risk with a potentially lethal vehicle. The dangers from this sort of behaviour are twofold. There is the obvious inherent danger of driving in this particular manner. There is no evidence that this young man is an incompetent driver, nor is there any evidence of lack of experience in driving. Apart from the ability to control the car, to steer it, and drive it competently, there is another component to good driving: it is that the driver shall have a proper regard for other road users. That is the lesson which D has to be taught again. No doubt it is that which the Judge had in mind when he decided to impose this additional order requiring D to take a test before he resumes driving. Appeal dismissed.

R v Gordon 2012 EWCA Crim 772, 2013 1 Cr App R (S) 9 (p 52) D pleaded to causing death by careless driving. At about 6.30 pm he drove his flatbed truck across the central reservation of a dual carriageway to turn right into the southbound carriageway. It was in January and the road was unlit. He waited there but the back of the lorry protruded into the northbound carriageway by 1.8 metres. A number of motorists saw the hazard and avoided it. V in his car did not and hit the lorry. V sustained very serious head injuries and died. It was accepted that D did not know the junction. D was aged 49 with no relevant convictions. He had an unblemished motoring record. Held. Given D's long driving experience and good motoring record the order was not necessary. For more detail see the **DEATH BY DRIVING: CARELESS DRIVING (SIMPLE)** ***HGV/coach drivers*** para at **239.11** in Volume 2.

Combined with other orders

47.14 ***Absolute and conditional discharge, Combined with***

Powers of Criminal Courts (Sentencing) Act 2000 s 12(7) [The court may] on discharging an offender absolutely or conditionally make an order for disqualification.

Road Traffic Offenders Act 1988 s 46(1) Notwithstanding anything in Powers of Criminal Courts (Sentencing) Act 2000 s 14(3) (rule about disregarding absolute and conditional discharges), a court [when convicting a person involving obligatory or discretionary disqualification orders him to be absolutely or conditionally discharged] may also exercise any power conferred, and must also discharge any duty imposed on the court by section 36 of this Act (obligation to order disqualification until test is passed).

Powers of Criminal Courts (Sentencing) Act 2000 s 12(7) [The court may] on discharging an offender absolutely or conditionally impose any disqualification.

Note: The Act does not indicate whether the 'disqualification' is driving disqualification or not. It is likely to be interpreted as all disqualification orders, as that is the natural meaning of the words in the subsection. Ed.

47.15 ***Revocation of probationary driver's licence, Combined with***

Road Traffic (New Drivers) Act 1995 s 4(5) Subsections (1) and (1A) do not apply to a person whose licence has been revoked under section 3 if, before he passes a relevant driving test, an order is made in relation to him under Road Traffic Offenders Act 1988 s 36 (disqualification until test is passed).

Note: The presumed purpose of this section is to ensure that a driver is not subject to two orders to pass a driving test. If a driver has his licence revoked because he has six penalty points on his licence and is then convicted of causing death by dangerous driving, he or she must be ordered to be disqualified till he or she has passed the test. The effect of this section ensures that the sole order is the disqualification order. Ed.

47.16 ***Totting up, Combined with***
Magistrates' Court Sentencing Guidelines 2008, see www.banksr.com Other Matters Guidelines tab page 185 para 15 An offender disqualified as a 'totter' under the penalty points provisions may also be ordered to retake a driving test. In this case, the extended test applies.

48 Disqualification from Being a Director of a Company etc.

48.1
(Including managing a company when bankrupt)
Company Directors Disqualification Act 1986 s 1(1)
There are extensive powers of the civil courts to make these orders. Those powers are not dealt with in this book.
This order imposes more restrictions than simply disqualification from being a company director. One of the restrictions is that the person may not in any way…be concerned or take part in the promotion, formation or management of a company without leave of the court, see **55.4**.
Availability The power is available in the Crown Court and the Magistrates' Court, after the defendant has been convicted of an offence 'in connection with the promotion, formation, management, liquidation or striking off of a company with the receivership of a company's property or with his being an administrative receiver of a company', see **48.4**.
Maximum lengths The summary maximum is 5 years and the Crown Court maximum is 15 years, see **48.11** and **48.12**.

48.2 ***Statistics*** ***England and Wales***
Director disqualifications[640]

	2011-12	2012-13	2013-14	2014-15	2015-16	2016-17	2017-18
Criminal matters	102	54	62	58	47	97	243
Other	1,113	960	1,211	1,151	1,161	1,117	988
Total	1,215	1,014	1,273	1,209	1,208	1,214	1,231

For more statistics, see www.banksr.com Other Matters Statistics tab.

48.3 ***Rationale of the order***
R v Edwards 1998 2 Cr App R (S) 213 The rationale behind the power to disqualify is the protection of the public from the activities of persons who, whether for reasons of dishonesty, or of naivety or incompetence in conjunction with the dishonesty of others, may use or abuse their role and status as a director of a limited company to the detriment of the public.

Power to order and test to apply

48.4 ***Power to order*** ***Indictable offences***
Disqualification orders: general
Company Directors Disqualification Act 1986 s 1(1) In the circumstances specified below in this Act a court may…make against a person a disqualification order. That is to say an order that for a specified period:

(a) he shall not be a director of a company, act as receiver of a company's property or in any way, whether directly or indirectly, be concerned or take part in the promotion, formation or management of a company unless (in each case) he has the leave of the court, and
(b) he shall not act as an insolvency practitioner.

[640] According in part to each year's *Insolvency Service Annual Report and Accounts.*

Company Directors Disqualification Act 1986 s 2(1) The court may make a disqualification order against a person where he is convicted of an indictable offence (whether on indictment or summarily) in connection with the promotion, formation, management, liquidation or striking off of a company with the receivership of a company's property or with his being an administrative receiver of a company.
(2) 'The court' for this purpose means:
(a) any court having jurisdiction to wind up the company in relation to which the offence was committed, or
(b) the court by or before which the person is convicted of the offence, or
(c) in the case of a summary conviction in England and Wales, any other Magistrates' Court acting in the same local justice area.

48.5 ***Power to order Summary offences***
Company Directors Disqualification Act 1986 s 5(2) Where a person is convicted of a summary offence counting for those purposes, the court by which he is convicted (or, in England and Wales, any other Magistrates' Court acting in the same local justice area) may make a disqualification order against him if the circumstances specified in the next subsection are present.
(3) Those circumstances are that, during the 5 years ending with the date of the conviction, the person has had made against him, or has been convicted of, in total not less than three default orders and offences counting for the purposes of this section, and those offences may include that of which he is convicted as mentioned in subsection (2) and any other offence of which he is convicted on the same occasion.

48.6 ***Test to apply/Judicial guidance***
R v Chandler 2015 EWCA Crim 1825, 2016 1 Cr App R (S) 37 D pleaded to three offences under Consumer Protection from Unfair Trading Regulations 2008 2008/1277. D was sentenced on the basis that he was unaware of the offences and a sacked employee was to blame. Held. *Re Sevenoaks Stationers (Retail) Ltd* 1991 Ch 164 was a civil appeal over a director's disqualification where there was misconduct by a relevant officer. The statutory provision there was Company Directors Disqualification Act 1986 s 6, which [shows] that disqualification turns on 'the conduct of the director (either taken alone or taken together with his conduct as a director of any other company or companies) makes him unfit to be concerned in the management of a company'. The judgment then points out that guidance on what is unfit was given long ago in *Re Lo-Line Electric Motors Ltd* 1988 Ch 477 at p 486, 'Ordinary commercial misjudgement is in itself not sufficient to justify disqualification. In the normal case, the conduct complained of must display a lack of commercial probity, although I have no doubt in an extreme case of gross negligence or total incompetence disqualification could be appropriate. [It must be shown that the director in question] behaved in a commercially culpable manner in trading through limited companies.'
Note: I am unaware of any judicial guidance about the test to apply in criminal proceedings except for the above case. There are authorities from civil proceedings. I have not listed them. I would expect that judges in the criminal courts would consider the primary consideration was the protection of the public. In *R v Steel* 2014 EWCA Crim 787, the Court of Appeal considered the factors relevant when deciding the appropriate length of an order. They are (para 10): the duration of the offending, whether the offender had been dishonest throughout or had traded for a considerable period legitimately, the amount involved, the previous character of the offender and whether there had been a prompt admission of guilt. When considering whether to impose an order, the two key factors in that list would appear to be the scale of the dishonesty and the overall loss. Ed.
R v Young 1990 12 Cr App R (S) 262 D pleaded to managing a company as an undischarged bankrupt. He was conditionally discharged and ordered to pay costs. He was also disqualified for 2 years. Held. Disqualification of Company Directors Act 1986

s 2 provides that the court may make a disqualification order against a person when he is convicted of an indictable offence (whether on indictment or summarily) in connection with the promotion, formation, management or liquidation of a company or with the receivership or management of a company's property. This is a completely general and unfettered power given by Parliament to courts on the occasion when a person is convicted of an indictable offence of that type. It is a different power from that exercised in the Chancery Division.

R v Cobbey 1993 14 Cr App R (S) 82 LCJ D had pleaded to fraudulent trading. He was the director of a company for a short period of time and in that period incurred liabilities of around £68,000. Held. The fact that he was a director for only a short time signifies little when it is appreciated how much harm he managed to do in that short time. The fact that he may have derived little or no personal benefit from his dishonesty has little relevance to the losses he caused and might cause again to others until he has learnt the importance of straight and careful business dealings. The order is upheld.

48.7 ***In connection with the management of a company Factor satisfied/Not satisfied***

R v Cobin 1984 6 Cr App R (S) 17 D pleaded, after a seven-day trial, to a number of counts of obtaining property by deception. He and his father, F, were involved with three businesses concerned with selling yachts. Through these companies, by various deceptions, D obtained property to finance his business. He was imprisoned and disqualified from being a director of a company for 5 years. It was argued that, as the deceptions involved third parties, there was no jurisdiction to make the disqualification as the acts were not 'in connection with the management of a company'. Held. The legislature could have chosen to say 'in respect of the management of a company'. They did not. They chose the words 'in connection with the management of a company' and in the judgment of this Court the offences committed were in connection with the management of a company.

R v Austen 1985 7 Cr App R (S) 214 D pleaded to nine specimen counts relating to the dishonest raising of finance by entering into hire purchase agreements in the names of companies that he owned. He was disqualified for 10 years among other punishments. Held. The words of the section when they refer to 'the management of the company' refer to the management of the company's affairs and there is no reason in language for differentiating between internal affairs and external affairs. Indeed, as a matter of policy, it may be thought appropriate that management should extend to both internal and external affairs. The section should cover activity in relation to the birth, life and death of a company. That, in the judgment of this Court, would accord with the legislature's intent.

R v Georgiou 1988 10 Cr App R (S) 137 Carrying on an insurance business through a limited company is a function of management and if that function is performed unlawfully in any way which makes a person guilty of an indictable offence it can properly be said that that is in connection with the management of the company.

R v Goodman 1993 14 Cr App R (S) 147 D pleaded to an offence under Company Securities (Insider Dealing) Act 1985. He received 18 months' imprisonment (9 months of which was suspended) and was disqualified for 10 years. He was the chairman of a public company and withheld information when selling shares in that company. The question was whether the offence of insider trading was connected with the management of the company. Held. The correct test is whether the offence had some relevant factual connection with the management of the company. 10-year disqualification order upheld.

R v Creggy 2008 EWCA Crim 394 D pleaded to money laundering. He was a solicitor and he assisted in the retention of the proceeds of criminal conduct of clients, suspecting them to be such. The sum was just under £1m. It was accepted that D was not involved in the fraud which led to the offence of money laundering, nor was it suggested that D received or retained any money for his involvement. D was given a suspended sentence and disqualified from acting as a company director for 7 years. It was argued that the Judge had no power to disqualify D as his act of assisting in the retention of the money was not an offence in connection with the management of a company. Held. D made available his client account as a private banking facility for the assets of the company so that those who managed it could manage its affairs by placing its funds there rather than in the bank. The assets were in fact criminal proceeds. He suspected that they were and he received them in circumstances in which no further disbursement of them could be made without his participation. That is quite sufficient relevant factual connection between the financial management of the company and the offence which D committed. The Judge was entitled to disqualify.

48.8 ***Procedure/Notice must be given of proposal and the misconduct relied on***
R v Chandler 2015 EWCA Crim 1825, 2016 1 Cr App R (S) 37 D pleaded to three offences under Consumer Protection from Unfair Trading Regulations 2008 2008/1277. D was sentenced on the basis that he was unaware of the offence and a sacked employee was to blame. The defence were unaware that the Judge was considering a disqualification from being a company director order. Held. It appears the order to disqualify was something of an afterthought. The Judge should have indicated that he was considering disqualification. The Judge needed to ensure that D had proper notice of what allegations of misconduct he was having to face and had an opportunity to make informed submissions about it. Because that was not done, order quashed.

Making the order

48.9 ***Can a judge pick which disqualifications apply?***
R v Cole, Lees and Birch 1998 BCC 87[641] The disqualification order made by the Judge attempted to specify the consequences of disqualification. Held. In our judgment it is plain from Disqualification of Company Directors Act 1986 s 1 that the Act envisages one disqualification with a number of different consequences. It does not envisage five different types of disqualification. The Judge could order disqualification or not. The order was therefore incomplete and imperfect. Order amended.
R v Ward 2001 EWCA Crim 1648, 2002 BCC 953 W and H were convicted of conspiracy to defraud and theft of company funds. After an Attorney-General's Reference, they received terms of imprisonment and disqualification orders. When drawn up, they referred to '...a directorship of a public company' whereas the Court of Appeal purported to disqualify them from acting as directors of 'a company'. Held. There is no jurisdiction to limit a disqualification order to the holding of a directorship in a public company. Disqualification under section 1 applies to all categories listed in section 1. Judges and justices should make it clear that their order under section 1 applies to all the categories which are identified in section 1.

48.10 ***Power to make Company offences***
Company Directors Disqualification Act 1986 s 5(1) An offence counting for the purposes of this section is one of which a person is convicted (either on indictment or summarily) in consequence of a contravention of, or failure to comply with, any provision of the companies legislation requiring a return, account or other document to be filed with, delivered or sent, or notice of any matter to be given, to the registrar of companies (whether the contravention or failure is on the person's own part or on the part of any company).

48.11 ***Maximum period of disqualification Indictable offences***
Company Directors Disqualification Act 1986 s 2(3) The maximum period of disqualification under this section is:
(a) 5 years by a court of summary jurisdiction, and
(b) in any other case, 15 years.

[641] Since this case was reported, section 1 has been amended, but it would appear that the rule that there can be only one order remains.

48.12 *Maximum period of disqualification Summary offences*
Company Directors Disqualification Act 1986 s 5(5) The maximum period of disqualification under this section is 5 years.

48.13 *On the facts How long should the order be? Judicial guidance*
R v Steel 2014 EWCA Crim 787 D pleaded guilty to fraud. Held. para 10 The factors relevant when deciding the appropriate length of an order are the duration of the offending, whether the offender had been dishonest throughout or had traded for a considerable period legitimately, the amount involved, the previous character of the offender and whether there had been a prompt admission of guilt.
R v Millard 1994 15 Cr App R (S) 445 D was convicted of nine counts of fraudulent trading (30 months' imprisonment on each, concurrent, 15-year disqualification). The deficiency was £728,189 in respect of six companies for which D was the decision maker. Held. Adopting the approach in *Re Sevenoaks Stationers (Retail) Ltd* 1991 Ch 164: Upper bracket of 10 years+ should be reserved for the most serious cases. Middle bracket of 6-10 years for serious cases which do not merit the upper bracket and lower bracket of 2-5 years where, though disqualification is mandatory, the case is not serious. Here it is the middle bracket, so 8 years not 15.

48.14 *On the facts How long should the order be? On the facts correct/ incorrect*
R v Randhawa and Randhawa 2008 EWCA Crim 2599 D1 and D2, a married couple, were convicted of being involved in the formation, promotion or management of a company while being undischarged bankrupts, and contravening an order disqualifying them from being company directors. They both received terms of imprisonment and were disqualified for a period of 12 years, thereby extending the current period of disqualification under the undertaking procedure by 6 years. After giving undertakings, they were disqualified from being company directors after a company entered into voluntary liquidation with an estimated deficiency of £853,826. Subsequently, D1 and D2 were involved in the promotion, formation or management of two companies. The prosecution was complicated by allegations made by D1 against counsel, and by judicial review proceedings in relation to a bad character application. An appeal against conviction was abandoned and subsequently D1 and D2 accepted that they were guilty of the offences charged, after previously denying any wrongdoing. Held. It was important that the disqualifications reflected the gravity of the criminality. Equally, it was appropriate to recognise the defendants' acceptance of the position, the sensible abandonment of the appeals against conviction and the way in which the defendants presented themselves to this Court. Terms of disqualifications reduced to **10 years** and **8 years**.
R v Steel 2014 EWCA Crim 787 D pleaded to fraud. He and his wife ran a company providing holidays. D falsely claimed that his company was a member of ABTA, that he had a bonding arrangement with his bank and that the purchasers' money was safe. The money obtained was not put in a company account but in their personal account. When the company became insolvent he carried on, which caused a 'large' number of people to lose money. D was aged 43. He was sentenced to 2½ years with a confiscation order of just over £180,500 and a compensation order of nearly £41,800 to the victims. Held. Fortunately the victims had been compensated. There were no previous convictions for flouting orders. The company was not set up for fraud. The case fell into the middle bracket so **7 years** not 15.
R v McGrath 2017 EWCA Crim 1945 D was convicted of conspiracy to blackmail and controlling prostitutes for gain. Held. D did use his company as a front for criminal activities, but **10 years** not 15.
See also: *R v Connolly* 2012 EWCA Crim 477 (Plea to unfair commercial practice (×2) and engaging in aggressive commercial practice. Breach of a conditional discharge, imposed in 2010 for engaging in an unfair commercial practice. In dispute with clients

over the nature or quality of window work provided. D instructed his employees to remove the windows of one, and the door and door frame of another, unless the customers paid the invoice in full. Both duly paid. The defence said in the end the work was done satisfactorily. 5 months' custody and a **5-year** director's disqualification was tough and intentionally so.)
R v Cadman 2012 EWCA Crim 611, 2 Cr App R (S) 88 (p 525) (Cases about the order listed. **7 years** would have been appropriate.)
R v Clayton 2017 EWCA Crim 49 (Plea. D, a director of a company, forged a resolution of his company which authorised loans of about £1m. Company for sale for £7.75m. D had 77% of the shares of the company. **7 years** was within the Judge's discretion.)
Note: There are different judicial views on whether the civil approach is helpful. Practitioners should expect each case to be dealt with on its own facts. Ed.

Combined with other orders

48.15 ***Absolute and conditional discharges, Combined with***
Powers of Criminal Courts (Sentencing) Act 2000 s 12(7) [The court may] on discharging an offender absolutely or conditionally make an order for disqualification.
Note: The Act does not indicate whether it relates to orders for disqualification from being a company director or not. It may be interpreted as all disqualification orders, as that is the natural meaning of the words in the section. Also, the Divisional Court does not like interpreting statutes to limit proper exercise of discretion. Ed.
R v Young 1990-91 12 Cr App R (S) 262 D pleaded to managing a company as an undischarged bankrupt. He was conditionally discharged and ordered to pay costs. He was also disqualified for 2 years. Held. As disqualification is unquestionably a punishment, it would be quite inappropriate for a disqualification to be linked with a conditional discharge.

48.16 ***Compensation orders, Combined with***
R v Holmes 1992 13 Cr App R (S) 29 D pleaded to fraudulent trading (9 months' imprisonment suspended, disqualification for 12 months, costs and compensation order). The order was based on defence counsel's belief of significant monies being available. At the Court of Appeal D's affidavit said that the disqualification order had had a serious effect on his ability to earn a living. Held. When a compensation order is made it is generally wrong in principle to inhibit a defendant from freely engaging in business activities which must have been contemplated as necessary for the purpose of fulfilling his obligations under the compensation order. The effect of the disqualification did just that. Compensation order quashed.
See also the COMBINING SENTENCES chapter.

Managing a company when bankrupt

48.17
Company Directors Disqualification Act 1986 s 11
Mode of trial Triable either way
Maximum sentence On indictment 2 years. Summary 6 months and/or unlimited fine.[642] There are maximum fines for those aged under 18, see **13.44**.

48.18 ***Judicial guidance Pre-2018 guideline case***
R v Theivendran 1992 13 Cr App R (S) 601 LCJ The underlying purpose of the Acts (Insolvency Act 1986 and Company Directors Disqualification Act 1986) is to rationalise the law of insolvency and in general to enable those who have suffered business failure to get back on their feet as rapidly as may be consistent with fairness to the creditors. If the contravention has been flagrant…a custodial sentence would in principle be appropriate. If, on the other hand, there are no aggravating features, such as previous

[642] Legal Aid, Sentencing and Punishment of Offenders Act 2012 s 85(1) and (4) and Legal Aid, Sentencing and Punishment of Offenders Act 2012 (Commencement No 11) Order 2015 2015/504

offences of the same kind or personal profit gained in the fraud of creditors, that may be taken into account as justifying suspension of the sentence. (The need for exceptional circumstances to suspend sentences was in force shortly after the judgment.)

49 Disqualification from Being a Director of a Company etc.: Breach of

49.1

Company Directors Disqualification Act 1986

s 11 (acting as a director of a company or directly or indirectly taking part in or being concerned in the promotion, formation or management of a company…when an undischarged bankrupt etc.)

s 13 (acting in contravention of a disqualification order or in contravention of s 11, 12(2), 12A or 12(B) [of this Act])

Modes of trial Triable either way

Maximum sentences On indictment 2 years. Summary maximum 6 months and/or an unlimited fine.[643] There are maximum fines for those aged under 18, see **13.44**.

Confiscation In breach proceedings courts should approach confiscation in the same way as they do with other offences, see **21.98**.

49.2 ***Breach Offences Guideline 2018***

Breach Offences Guideline 2018, see www.banksr.com Other Matters Guidelines tab In force 1 October 2018 page 45

Company Directors Disqualification Act 1986 (section 13)

STEP ONE **Determining the offence category**

The court should determine the offence category with reference only to the factors listed in the tables below. In order to determine the category the court should assess **culpability** and **harm**.

Culpability

A	• Breach involves deceit/dishonesty in relation to actual role within company • Breach involves deliberate concealment of disqualified status
B	• All other cases

Harm

The level of **harm** is determined by weighing up all the factors of the case to determine the harm that has been caused or was at risk of being caused. In assessing any risk of harm posed by the breach, consideration should be given to the original offence(s) for which the order was imposed and the circumstances in which the breach arose.

Category 1	Breach results in significant risk of or actual serious financial loss **OR** Breach results in significant risk of or actual serious non-financial harm to company/organisation or others
Category 2	Cases falling between Categories 1 and 3
Category 3	Breach results in very low risk of or little or no harm (financial or non-financial) to company/organisation or others

[643] Legal Aid, Sentencing and Punishment of Offenders Act 2012 s 85(1) and (4) and Legal Aid, Sentencing and Punishment of Offenders Act 2012 (Commencement No 11) Order 2015 2015/504

49.3

STEP TWO **Starting point and category range**

Having determined the category at step one, the court should use the corresponding starting point to reach a sentence within the category range from the appropriate sentence table below. The starting point applies to all offenders irrespective of plea or previous convictions. The court should then consider further adjustment within the category range for aggravating or mitigating features.

	Culpability	
Harm	**A**	**B**
Category 1	**Starting point** 1 year's custody	**Starting point** 12 weeks' custody
	Category range 26 weeks' to 1 year 6 months' custody	**Category range** High-level community order to 36 weeks' custody
Category 2	**Starting point** 26 weeks' custody	**Starting point** High-level community order
	Category range 12 weeks' to 36 weeks' custody	**Category range** Medium-level community order to 26 weeks' custody
Category 3	**Starting point** 12 weeks' custody	**Starting point** Medium-level community order
	Category range Medium-level community order to 26 weeks' custody	**Category range** Band C fine to high-level community order

For the meaning of high-level and medium-level community orders, see **15.12**. For a Band C fine, see **58.28**.

49.4 [Aggravating and mitigating factors]
Page 48 The table below contains a **non-exhaustive** list of additional factual elements providing the context of the offence and factors relating to the offender. Identify whether any combination of these, or other relevant factors, should result in an upward or downward adjustment from the starting point.
In some cases, having considered these factors, it may be appropriate to move outside the identified category range.

Factors increasing seriousness
Statutory aggravating factors:
Previous convictions, having regard to a) the **nature** of the offence to which the conviction relates and its **relevance** to the current offence; and b) the **time** that has elapsed since the conviction
Offence committed whilst on bail
Other aggravating factors:
Breach committed shortly after order made
Breach continued after warnings received
Breach is continued over a sustained period of time
Breach involves acting as a director in multiple companies

Breach motivated by personal gain
Offence committed on licence or while subject to post sentence supervision
Factors reducing seriousness or reflecting personal mitigation
Breach not motivated by personal gain
Breach committed after long period of compliance
Genuine misunderstanding of terms of disqualification
Evidence of voluntary reparation/compensation made to those suffering loss
Breach activity minimal or committed for short duration
Age and/or lack of maturity where it affects the responsibility of the offender
Mental disorder or learning disability where linked to the commission of the offence
Sole or primary carer for dependent relatives

STEP THREE to STEP EIGHT These are: Consider assistance to the prosecution, Reduction for guilty plea, Totality principle, Ancillary orders, Duty to give reasons and Consider time spent on bail with a tag.

49.5 ***Suggested approach to the guideline***

Note: I consider the old cases add little and sentencers should simply apply the guideline. Ed.

50 Disqualification from Keeping an Animal

50.1

Animal Welfare Act 2006 s 34(1)

This is a separate power from the disqualification from having a dog. For that power, see the **Disqualification from Having Custody of a Dog** chapter.

Children and young offenders The order is available whatever the age of the offender.

General matters

50.2 ***Statutory power to disqualify***

Animal Welfare Act 2006 s 34(1) If a person is convicted of an offence to which this section applies, the court by or before which he is convicted may, instead of or in addition to dealing with him in any other way, make an order disqualifying him under any one or more of subsections (2) to (4) for such period as it thinks fit.

Animal Welfare Act 2006 s 34(5) Disqualification under subsection (2), (3) or (4) may be imposed in relation to animals generally, or in relation to animals of one or more kinds.

Animal Welfare Act 2006 s 34(10) This section applies to an offence under any of [the following] sections:

section 4 (unnecessary suffering),
section 5 (mutilation),
section 6(1) and (2) (docking of dogs tails),
section 7 (administration of poisons etc.),
section 8 (fighting etc.),
section 9 (duty of persons responsible for animals to ensure welfare), and
section 13(6) and (9) (regulations under this Act).

50.3 ***Extent of the disqualification***

Animal Welfare Act 2006 s 34(2) Disqualification under this subsection disqualifies a person:

(a) from owning animals,
(b) from keeping animals,
(c) from participating in the keeping of animals, and

(d) from being party to an arrangement under which he is entitled to control or influence the way in which animals are kept.

(3) Disqualification under this subsection disqualifies a person from dealing in animals.

(4) Disqualification under this subsection disqualifies a person:

(a) from transporting animals, and

(b) from arranging for the transport of animals.

50.4 *Duty to give reasons and explain the order*

Animal Welfare Act 2006 s 34(8) Where a court decides not to make an order under subsection (1) in relation to an offender, it shall:

(a) give its reasons for the decision in open court, and

(b) if it is a Magistrates' Court, cause them to be entered in the register of its proceedings.

50.5 *Power to seize the animals*

Animal Welfare Act 2006 s 35(1) Where:

(a) a court makes an order under section 34(1), and

(b) it appears to the court that the person to whom the order applies owns or keeps any animal contrary to the disqualification imposed by the order,

it may order that all animals he owns or keeps contrary to the disqualification be taken into possession.

50.6 *Suspension of the order for alternative arrangements to be made*

Animal Welfare Act 2006 s 34(7) The court by which an order under subsection (1) is made may:.. where it appears to the court that the offender owns or keeps an animal to which the order applies, suspend the operation of the order, and of any order made under section 35 in connection with the disqualification, for such period as it thinks necessary for enabling alternative arrangements to be made in respect of the animal.

50.7 *Judicial guidance*

Barker and Williamson v RSPCA 2018 EWHC 880 (Admin), 2 Cr App R (S) 13 (p 92) B and W pleaded at the Magistrates' Court to two charges of failing to ensure the needs of their dogs were met (section 9). An RSPCA inspector visited their 'utterly squalid and utterly chaotic home' and found a 10-year-old King Charles spaniel and her five offspring. The dogs had a heavy flea infection and were let out from their crates for 2-3 hours a day. The inspector gave advice. Later a vet called to neuter and spay the dogs and the RSPCA refused to return the dogs as the treatment advised had not been effective. B and W had disability and mobility issues. [There was significant mitigation and the full facts are not listed.] The Court imposed a 7-year animal disqualification order only. The two appealed the orders at the Crown Court, which upheld them save that B and W could keep terrapins. B and W then appealed to the High Court. Held. para 48 There can be an 'all animals' order. A person's treatment of a dog may, in principle, shed light on his or her likely treatment of a cat or a parrot. There can be an order covering some kinds of animal but not others. There can be an exclusory order, that is to say an order prohibiting the ownership etc. of all animals except those of certain kinds, which is the order the Crown Court made. para 51 Under Animal Welfare Act 2006 s 34(5) it is not permissible to prohibit the ownership etc. of individual animals; e.g. owning animals except for one particular terrapin. The prohibition must be framed by reference either to all animals or to kinds of animal, by reference to their genus or species. para 52 The disqualification orders were not oppressive or harsh. 7 years was not too long. Appeal dismissed.

Terminating and varying the order

50.8 *Terminating or varying the order Statutory provisions*

Animal Welfare Act 2006 s 43(1) A person who is disqualified by virtue of an order under section 34…may apply to the appropriate court for the termination of the order.

Animal Welfare Act 2006 s 43(7) In subsection (1), the reference to the appropriate court is to:

(a) the court which made the order under section 34…, or
(b) in the case of an order made by a Magistrates' Court, to a Magistrates' Court acting for the same local justice area as that court.

Animal Welfare Act 2006 s 43(3) On an application under subsection (1), the court may:
(a) terminate the disqualification,
(b) vary the disqualification so as to make it less onerous, or
(c) refuse the application.

50.9 ***Terminating or varying the order Time restrictions***

Animal Welfare Act 2006 s 43(2) No application under subsection (1) may be made:
(a) before the end of the period of one year beginning with the date on which the order is made,
(b) where a previous application under that subsection has been made in relation to the same order, before the end of the period of one year beginning with the date on which the previous application was determined, or
(c) before the end of any period specified under section 34(6) (see below),…or subsection 43(5) below in relation to the order.

Animal Welfare Act 2006 s 34(6) The court by which an order under subsection (1) is made may specify a period during which the offender may not make an application under section 43(1) for termination of the order.

Animal Welfare Act 2006 s 43(5) Where the court refuses an application under subsection (1), it may specify a period during which the applicant may not make a further application under that subsection in relation to the order concerned.

50.10 ***Terminating or varying the order Procedure***

Criminal Procedure Rules 2015 2015/1490 Rule 28.6(1) This rule applies where, on application by the defendant, the court can remove, revoke or suspend a disqualification or restriction included in a sentence (except a disqualification from driving).
(2) A defendant who wants the court to exercise such a power must:
(a) apply in writing, no earlier than the date on which the court can exercise the power;
(b) serve the application on the court officer; and
(c) in the application:
(i) specify the disqualification or restriction, and
(ii) explain why the defendant wants the court to remove, revoke or suspend it.
(3) The court officer must serve a copy of the application on the chief officer of police for the local justice area.

50.11 ***Terminating or varying the order Test to apply and costs***

Animal Welfare Act 2006 s 43(4) When determining an application under subsection (1), the court shall have regard to the character of the applicant, his conduct since the imposition of the disqualification and any other circumstances of the case.

Animal Welfare Act 2006 s 43(6) The court may order an applicant under subsection (1) to pay all or part of the costs of the application.

50.12 ***Terminating or varying the order Appeal, Order suspended awaiting an***

Animal Welfare Act 2006 s 34(7) The court by which an order under subsection (1) is made may:.. suspend the operation of the order pending an appeal.

51 Disqualification from Keeping an Animal: Breach of

51.1

Animal Welfare Act 2006 s 34(9)
Mode of trial Summary only

Maximum sentence 6 months or an unlimited fine.[644] There are maximum fines for those aged under 18, see **13.44**.

51.2 ***Statutory offence***
Animal Welfare Act 2006 s 34(9) A person who breaches a disqualification imposed by an order under subsection (1) commits an offence.

51.3 ***Breach Offences Guideline 2018***
Breach Offences Guideline 2018, see www.banksr.com Other Matters Guidelines tab In force 1 October 2018 page 51
Breach of disqualification from keeping an animal
Animal Welfare Act 2006 (section 32)

STEP ONE **Determining the offence category**

The court should determine the offence category with reference only to the factors listed in the tables below. In order to determine the category the court should assess **culpability** and **harm**.

Culpability

A	Serious and/or persistent breach
B	All other cases

Harm

The level of **harm** is determined by weighing up all the factors of the case to determine the harm that has been caused or was at risk of being caused. In assessing any risk of harm posed by the breach, consideration should be given to the original offence(s) for which the order was imposed and the circumstances in which the breach arose.

Category 1	• Breach causes or risks death or very serious harm or suffering to animal(s) • Breach results in risk of or actual serious harm to individual(s)
Category 2	• Cases falling between Categories 1 and 3
Category 3	• Breach causes or risks little or no harm or suffering to animal(s) • Breach results in very low risk of or little or no harm to individual(s)

51.4

STEP TWO **Starting point and category range**

Having determined the category at step one, the court should use the corresponding starting point to reach a sentence within the category range from the appropriate sentence table below. The starting point applies to all offenders irrespective of plea or previous convictions. The court should then consider further adjustment within the category range for aggravating or mitigating features.

[644] Legal Aid, Sentencing and Punishment of Offenders Act 2012 s 85(1) and (4) and Legal Aid, Sentencing and Punishment of Offenders Act 2012 (Commencement No 11) Order 2015 2015/504

Harm	Culpability A	Culpability B
Category 1	**Starting point** 16 weeks' custody	**Starting point** 8 weeks' custody
	Category range 6 weeks' to 26 weeks' custody	**Category range** Medium-level community order to 16 weeks' custody
Category 2	**Starting point** 8 weeks' custody	**Starting point** Medium-level community order
	Category range Medium-level community order to 16 weeks' custody	**Category range** Band C fine to high-level community order
Category 3	**Starting point** Medium-level community order	**Starting point** Band A fine
	Category range Band C fine to high-level community order	**Category range** Discharge to Band B fine

For the meaning of high-level and medium-level community orders, see **15.12**. For a Band A-C fine, see **58.28**.

51.5 [Aggravating and mitigating factors]

Page 54 The table below contains a **non-exhaustive** list of additional factual elements providing the context of the offence and factors relating to the offender. Identify whether any combination of these, or other relevant factors, should result in an upward or downward adjustment from the starting point.

In some cases, having considered these factors, it may be appropriate to move outside the identified category range.

Factors increasing seriousness
Statutory aggravating factors:
Previous convictions, having regard to a) the **nature** of the offence to which the conviction relates and its **relevance** to the current offence; and b) the **time** that has elapsed since the conviction
Offence committed whilst on bail
Other aggravating factors:
Breach committed immediately or shortly after order made
History of disobedience to court orders
Breach conducted in commercial context
Breach involves deceit regarding ownership of/responsibility for animal
Harm risked or caused to multiple animals (where not taken into account at step one)
Offence committed on licence or while subject to post sentence supervision
Factors reducing seriousness or reflecting personal mitigation
Breach committed after long period of compliance
Genuine misunderstanding of terms of order
Prompt voluntary surrender/admission of breach or failure
Age and/or lack of maturity where it affects the responsibility of the offender

Mental disorder or learning disability where linked to the commission of the offence
Sole or primary carer for dependent relatives

STEP THREE to STEP EIGHT These are: Consider assistance to the prosecution, Reduction for guilty plea, Totality principle, Ancillary orders, Duty to give reasons and Consider time spent on bail with a tag.

51.6 ***Seizure of the animals Statutory provisions***

Section 35: supplementary

Animal Welfare Act 2006 s 35(1) Where:

(a) a court makes an order under section 34(1), and

(b) it appears to the court that the person to whom the order applies owns or keeps any animal contrary to the disqualification imposed by the order,

it may order that all animals he owns or keeps contrary to the disqualification be taken into possession.

(2) Where a person is convicted of an offence under section 34(9) because of owning or keeping an animal in breach of disqualification under section 34(2), the court by or before which he is convicted may order that all animals he owns or keeps in breach of the disqualification be taken into possession.

(3) An order under subsection (1) or (2), so far as relating to any animal owned by the person subject to disqualification, shall have effect as an order for the disposal of the animal.

(4) Any animal taken into possession in pursuance of an order under subsection (1) or (2) that is not owned by the person subject to disqualification shall be dealt with in such manner as the appropriate court may order.

(5) A court may not make an order for disposal under subsection (4) unless:

(a) it has given the owner of the animal an opportunity to be heard, or

(b) it is satisfied that it is not reasonably practicable to communicate with the owner.

(6) Where a court makes an order under subsection (4) for the disposal of an animal, the owner may:

(a) in the case of an order made by a Magistrates' Court, appeal against the order to the Crown Court,

(b) in the case of an order made by the Crown Court, appeal against the order to the Court of Appeal.

(7) In subsection (4), the reference to the appropriate court is to:

(a) the court which made the order under subsection (1) or (2), or

(b) in the case of an order made by a Magistrates' Court, to a Magistrates' Court for the same local justice area as that court.

(8) In this section, references to disposing of an animal include destroying it.

51.7 ***Seizure of animals Test to apply***

Animal Welfare Act 2006 s 36(3) In determining how to exercise its powers under section 35 and this section, the court shall have regard, amongst other things, to:

(a) the desirability of protecting the value of any animal to which the order applies, and

(b) the desirability of avoiding increasing any expenses which a person may be ordered to reimburse.

51.8 ***Appointment of persons to carry out seizure and directions***

Animal Welfare Act 2006 s 36(1) The court by which an order under section 35 is made may:

(a) appoint a person to carry out, or arrange for the carrying out of, the order,

(b) require any person who has possession of an animal to which the order applies to deliver it up to enable the order to be carried out,

(c) give directions with respect to the carrying out of the order,

(d) confer additional powers (including power to enter premises where an animal to which the order applies is being kept) for the purpose of, or in connection with, the carrying out of the order,

(e) order the person subject to disqualification, or another person, to reimburse the expenses of carrying out the order.

(2) Directions under subsection (1)(c) may:

(a) specify the manner in which an animal is to be disposed of, or

(b) delegate the decision about the manner in which an animal is to be disposed of to a person appointed under subsection (1)(a).

Animal Welfare Act 2006 s 36(4) In determining how to exercise a power delegated under subsection (2)(b), a person shall have regard, amongst other things, to the things mentioned in subsection (3)(a) and (b).

(5) If the owner of an animal ordered to be disposed of under section 35 is subject to a liability by virtue of subsection (1)(e), any amount to which he is entitled as a result of sale of the animal may be reduced by an amount equal to that liability.

52 Disqualification from Having Custody of a Dog

52.1

Dangerous Dogs Act 1991 s 4(1)(b)

This is a separate power from the disqualification from keeping an animal. For that power, see the **Disqualification from Keeping an Animal** chapter.

Children and young offenders The order is available whatever the age of the offender.

Offences The offence is summary only with an unlimited fine,[645] Dangerous Dogs Act 1991 s 4(8). There are maximum fines for those aged under 18, see **13.44**.

Breach Offences Guideline 2018, see www.banksr.com Other Matters Guidelines tab In force 1 October 2018 page 56 says, **'Other breach offences** Where an offence is not covered by a sentencing guideline a court is entitled to use, and may be assisted by, a guideline for an analogous offence subject to differences in the elements of the offences and the statutory maxima.'

52.2 ***Statutory power to disqualify***

Dangerous Dogs Act 1991 s 4(1) Where a person is convicted of an offence under section 1 or 3(1)[646] above or of an offence under an order made under section 2 above the court:..b) may order the offender to be disqualified, for such period as the court thinks fit, from having custody of a dog.

Dangerous Dogs Act 1991 s 4(1B)[647] For the purposes of subsection (1A)(a), when deciding whether a dog would constitute a danger to public safety, the court:

(a) must consider:

(i) the temperament of the dog and its past behaviour, and

(ii) whether the owner of the dog, or the person for the time being in charge of it, is a fit and proper person to be in charge of the dog, and

(b) may consider any other relevant circumstances.

52.3 ***Can the disqualification have conditions?***

R v Haynes 2003 EWCA Crim 3247, 2004 2 Cr App R (S) 9 (p 36) D was convicted of three aggravated offences of dogs injuring a person in a public place. The Judge decided to make a disqualification order for a period of 3 years. Held. The statutory framework does not permit the making of an order incorporating the provisions recommended by the expert. However, here we have the defendant's signed undertaking to the Court and we quash the disqualification order.

[645] Legal Aid, Sentencing and Punishment of Offenders Act 2012 s 85(1) and (4) and Legal Aid, Sentencing and Punishment of Offenders Act 2012 (Commencement No 11) Order 2015 2015/504

[646] Anti-social Behaviour, Crime and Policing Act 2014 s 106(3) removed the 'or (3)' which was here.

[647] Inserted by Anti-social Behaviour, Crime and Policing Act 2014 s 107(3). In force 13/5/14

52.4 *Test to apply*

R v Flack 2008 EWCA Crim 204, 2010 2 Cr App R (S) 70 (p 395) D appealed a destruction order. Held. para 11 The relevant principles that can be made in respect of a dog whose owner has been convicted under section 3(1) of the 1991 Act of failing to keep a dog under control in a public place are that: (6) In deciding what order to make, the court must consider all the relevant circumstances which include the dog's history of aggressive behaviour and the owner's history of controlling the dog concerned in order to determine what order should be made.

Note: This was the test used in *R v Singh* 2013 EWCA Crim 2416. Ed.

52.5 *On the facts, order inappropriate*

R v Haynes 2003 EWCA Crim 3247, 2004 2 Cr App R (S) 9 (p 36) D was convicted of three aggravated offences of dogs injuring persons in a public place. D owned three dogs. He took the three dogs to a dog play area, near his flat. D left the dogs in the play area, which was fenced and gated, so he could talk to a neighbour. The dogs appear to have escaped the play area and focused their attention on a 7-year-old girl. The dogs knocked her off her bike and surrounded her. D returned to the play area and was very apologetic. The girl suffered multiple superficial grazes on her abdomen, superficial wounds to the front of one thigh and a small graze below the right eye. The dogs were assessed by a specialist in animal behaviour who observed no signs of aggression. He described them as a 'delight'. He recommended a series of conditions including: a) D may have one dog returned to him, b) the dog was to be kept on a two-metre lead at all times, and c) the dog was not to be in the play area where the incident occurred. The Judge decided to make a disqualification order for a period of 3 years. Held. There is no statutory power to disqualify a person from having custody of more than one dog, nor is there any statutory power to make a qualified disqualification order or to specify conditions which must be met if the offender is to be permitted to retain one or more dogs. In deciding whether to make a disqualification order and whether to order the forfeiture of any or all of the dogs, the Judge was entitled to have regard to any voluntary undertaking offered by D as to his future conduct. It would follow that in the event of any further offence being committed by D and it being found that he was in breach of his undertaking, that breach would be treated as a serious aggravating factor and would almost certainly lead to the loss of the dog or dogs in question. As the Judge was satisfied by the expert that none of the dogs constituted a danger to the public, both types of destruction orders were inappropriate. However, here we have D's signed undertaking to the Court and we quash the disqualification order.

R v Singh 2013 EWCA Crim 2416 D was convicted of being the owner of a dog which caused injury whilst dangerously out of control. D took Ace, his 5-year-old German Shepherd, with him to a local Sikh centre on regular occasions. The centre contained within its grounds a school and a gym. There was a garden area immediately adjacent to the car park, which was enclosed by a fence. D had installed a large dog kennel there and it was his practice to keep Ace chained up in, or adjacent to, the kennel. When Ace wasn't chained up, he was on a lead. V, aged 12, regularly used the gym. One evening, V and his father were walking past the garden area on their way out into the car park when Ace ran out of the garden area and attacked V, knocking him to the floor. Ace bit V on the arm, back and leg. It caused a deep penetrating wound to the thigh and V had to undergo surgery. Eight stitches were inserted and V was kept in hospital overnight. V also suffered bruising and scratches. Seven weeks after the incident, V continued to suffer pain and difficulty in walking. There was obvious scarring and he had developed a fear of dogs. Ace was taken into the care of the police. D said Ace had been chained up in his kennel and that V must have entered the garden area and untied Ace. The jury rejected that assertion. D, aged 33, regularly acted as a volunteer at the Sikh centre. He had no previous convictions. He expressed regret for what had happened, but maintained that his account was true. An expert assessed Ace and found that he responded well to being handled by a stranger, accepted wearing a muzzle and could not be incited to attack another. The conditions in which D kept Ace were found to be entirely satisfactory. He considered that Ace could be returned to D so long as he was kept muzzled in public, castrated and walked on a lead. Held. The sentencing remarks did not reveal the Judge's reasons for finding that D was not a fit and proper person to have custody of a dog. It was likely that this was an act of momentary carelessness in leaving the gate to the enclosed area open. There was no evidence that such an incident had occurred previously. D had proper facilities to prevent him from coming into contact with members of the public. Disqualification of having custody of a dog would be quashed. Immediate destruction was manifestly excessive, considering the measures recommended by the expert. Contingent destruction order substituted.

52.6 ***Disqualification for how long?***

Example: *R v Shallow* 2011 EWCA Crim 1443, 2012 1 Cr App R (S) 33 (p 197) (Plea. Staffordshire bull terrier bit 9-year-old girl on the thigh. Held on for 30 seconds, causing a nasty gash. Scarring. Previous concerns regarding the dog's temperament. Dog was loosely muzzled. **10 years'** disqualification upheld.)

52.7 ***Termination of the order***

Dangerous Dogs Act 1991 s 4(6) Any person who is disqualified from having custody of a dog by virtue of an order under subsection (1)(b) above may, at any time after the end of the period of one year beginning with the date of the order, apply to the court that made it (or a Magistrates' Court acting in the same local justice area as that court) for a direction terminating the disqualification.

(7) On an application under subsection (6) above the court may:

(a) having regard to the applicant's character, his conduct since the disqualification was imposed and any other circumstances of the case, grant or refuse the application, and

(b) order the applicant to pay all or any part of the costs of the application,

and where an application in respect of an order is refused no further application in respect of that order shall be entertained if made before the end of the period of one year beginning with the date of the refusal.

53 Drug Orders: Non-Co-operation

53.1

Note: There are two offences, one under Drugs Act 2005 s 12 and one under Police and Criminal Evidence Act 1984 s 63B. Ed.

53.2 ***Failing to attend an initial assessment etc.***

Drugs Act 2005 s 12 (failing to attend an initial assessment or failing to remain for its duration)

Mode of trial Summary only

Maximum sentence Level 4 fine (£2,500) and/or 3 months[648]

A drug order is issued by a police officer at a police station, Drugs Act 2005 s 9.

53.3 ***Magistrates' Court Sentencing Guidelines Class A Revised 2017***

Magistrates' Court Sentencing Guidelines 2008, see www.banksr.com Other Matters Guidelines tab. (no page or para number) In force 24 April 2017. The guidelines apply to the Magistrates' Court and to the Crown Court hearing appeals or sentencing for summary only offences.[649]

Drugs–class A–fail to attend/remain for initial assessment and fail/refuse to provide a sample (Revised 2017)

Drugs Act 2005 s 12

Police and Criminal Evidence Act 1984 s 63B

[648] Drugs Act 2005 s 12(7)

[649] See page 15 of the guidelines

Step 1. Determining the offence category

The Court should determine the offence category using the table below.

Category 1 Higher culpability **and** greater harm

Category 2 Higher culpability **and** lesser harm **or** lower culpability **and** greater harm

Category 3 Lower culpability **and** lesser harm

The court should determine the offender's culpability and the harm caused with reference **only** to the factors below. Where an offence does not fall squarely into a category, individual factors may require a degree of weighting before making an overall assessment and determining the appropriate offence category.

CULPABILITY demonstrated by one or more of the following:

Factors indicating higher culpability

- Deliberate failure to attend/remain

Factors indicating lower culpability

- All other cases

HARM demonstrated by one or more of the following:

Factors indicating greater harm

- Aggressive, abusive or disruptive behaviour

Factors indicating lesser harm

- All other cases

Step 2. Starting point and category range

Having determined the category at step one, the court should use the starting point to reach a sentence within the appropriate category range in the table below. The starting point applies to all offenders irrespective of plea or previous convictions.

Offence Category	**Starting Point**	**Range**
Category 1	Medium-level community order	Low-level community order to high-level community order
Category 2	Band C fine	Band B fine to low-level community order
Category 3	Band B fine	Band A fine to Band C fine

The court should then consider adjustment for any aggravating or mitigating factors. The following is a **non-exhaustive** list of additional factual elements providing the context of the offence and factors relating to the offender. Identify whether any combination of these, or other relevant factors, should result in an upward or downward adjustment from the sentence arrived at so far.

Factors increasing seriousness

Statutory aggravating factors:

- Previous convictions, having regard to a) the nature of the offence to which the conviction relates and its relevance to the current offence; and b) the time that has elapsed since the conviction
- Offence committed whilst on bail
- Offence motivated by, or demonstrating hostility based on any of the following characteristics or presumed characteristics of the victim: religion, race, disability, sexual orientation or transgender identity

Other aggravating factors:

- Failure to comply with current court orders
- Offence committed on licence or post sentence supervision
- Offender's actions result in a waste of resources

Factors reducing seriousness or reflecting personal mitigation

- No previous convictions **or** no relevant/recent convictions
- Remorse
- Good character and/or exemplary conduct

- Serious medical condition requiring urgent, intensive or long-term treatment
- Age and/or lack of maturity where it affects the responsibility of the offender
- Mental disorder or learning disability
- Sole or primary carer for dependent relatives
- Determination and/or demonstration of steps having been taken to address addiction or offending behaviour

Band C fine is 150% of weekly take home pay/weekly benefit payment, see **58.28**.
For the meaning of a low, medium and high-level community order see **15.12**.

53.4 ***Failure to give sample for testing***
Police and Criminal Evidence Act 1984 s 63B(8) (failure to give sample for testing)
Mode of trial Summary only
Maximum sentence Level 4 fine (£2,500) and/or 3 months
A police officer may require a sample at the police station, Police and Criminal Evidence Act 1984 s 63B(1).

54 ENDORSEMENT

54.1
Road Traffic Offenders Act 1988 s 44-49
Children and young offenders The order and penalty points are available whatever the age of the offender.[650]
Driving licence The counterpart is no longer required as the courts use the electronic driving record (maintained by the DVLA), Road Traffic Offenders Act 1988 s 7(10) as amended by Road Safety Act 2006 Sch 3 para 31.[651]
Totting up See the **DISQUALIFICATION FROM DRIVING: TOTTING UP** chapter.
Rehabilitation period 5 years,[652] 2½ years if the defendant is aged under 18.[653] If there is more than one endorsement, the rehabilitation period is whichever is the longer period.[654] However, the endorsement remains on the licence for 4 years (see **54.9**) and should where appropriate be taken into account, see **54.7**.
See also the **REHABILITATION OF OFFENDERS ACT 1974** chapter.
See also the **DISQUALIFICATION FROM DRIVING: GENERAL PRINCIPLES** chapter.

54.2 ***Statistics England and Wales***
[Defendants who have] endorsements without disqualifications Aged 21+[655]

	Crown Court	Magistrates' Court
2014	5,603	383,995
2015	6,792	426,480
2016	8,190	447,559

For explanations about the statistics, see page 1-xii. The MoJ no longer provides Banks on Sentence with these statistics.

[650] Young persons aged under 17 cannot hold a driving licence to drive a car. Young persons aged under 16 cannot hold a driving licence to drive a moped. If the offender does not hold a driving licence, the order for endorsement and penalty points should still be made. This means that any licence that is obtained should be endorsed and should list any penalty points if they have not reached the time for removal.
[651] Road Safety Act 2006 (Commencement No 11 and Transitional Provisions) Order 2015 2015/560. In force 8/6/15
[652] This figure is not affected by Legal Aid, Sentencing and Punishment of Offenders Act 2012 s 139, see Legal Aid, Sentencing and Punishment of Offenders Act 2012 (Commencement No 9, Saving Provision and Specification of Commencement Date) Order 2014 2014/423 para 3 and Explanatory Note.
[653] Rehabilitation of Offenders Act 1974 s 5 Table A. For a case about declaring a conviction, see *Power v Provincial Insurance* 1998 RTR 60 Court of Appeal.
[654] Rehabilitation of Offenders Act 1974 s 6(2)
[655] The figures given in the table relate to all motoring offences for which a defendant is sentenced. When a defendant has been sentenced for two or more offences, each of the two or more offences is counted. Endorsements for non-motoring offences are excluded.

54.3 *Obligation to endorse*

Orders for endorsement

Road Traffic Offenders Act 1988 s 44(1) Where a person is convicted of an offence involving obligatory endorsement, the court must order there to be endorsed on his driving record particulars of the conviction and also:

(a) if the court orders him to be disqualified, particulars of the disqualification, or

(b) if the court does not order him to be disqualified:

(i) particulars of the offence, including the date when it was committed, and

(ii) the penalty points to be attributed to the offence.

(2) Where the court does not order the person convicted to be disqualified, it need not make an order under subsection (1) above if for special reasons it thinks fit not to do so.

(3) [Scotland]

(4) This section is subject to section 48 of this Act. [The defence of reasonable cause not to suspect the vehicle involved was not a danger]

R v Kent 1983 5 Cr App R (S) 171 All offences attracting obligatory or discretionary disqualification must be endorsed on the defendant's driving licence unless there are special reasons.

54.4 *Court Martial*

Guidance on Sentencing in the Court Martial 2018 para 5.11.1 (edited) Motoring offences within military establishments, if committed on roads that are as a matter of law public roads, are dealt with in the same way as motoring offences on public roads in England and Wales but are subject to a different sentencing regime because the Court Martial has no power to impose penalty points on driving licences or disqualify from driving. Driving offences are often charged as breaches of standing orders.

Note: There is no power to endorse either. The absence of these powers is absurd. Ed.

54.5 *Penalty points/Interpreting endorsement codes*

Code	Offence	Penalty points	Years on licence[656]
Accident offences			
AC10	Failing to stop after an accident	**5-10**	**4**
AC20	Failing to give particulars or to report an accident within 24 hours	**5-10**	**4**
AC30	Undefined accident offences	**4-9**	**4**
Disqualified driver			
BA10	Driving whilst disqualified by order of court	**6**	**4**
BA30	Attempting to drive while disqualified by order of court	**6**	**4**
Careless driving			
CD10	Driving without due care and attention	**3-9**	**4**
CD20	Driving without reasonable consideration for other road users	**3-9**	**4**
CD30	Driving without due care and attention or without reasonable consideration for other road users	**3-9**	**4**
CD40	Causing death through careless driving when unfit through drink	**3-11**	**11**

[656] The time period runs from the date of the offence.

Code	Offence	Penalty points	Years on licence[656]
CD50	Causing death by careless driving when unfit through drugs	**3-11**	**11**
CD60	Causing death by careless driving with alcohol level above the limit	**3-11**	**11**
CD70	Causing death by careless driving then failing to supply a specimen for analysis	**3-11**	**11**
CD80	Causing death by careless or inconsiderate driving	**3-11**	**4**
CD90	Causing death by driving: unlicensed, disqualified or uninsured drivers	**3-11**	**4**
Construction and Use offences			
CU10	Using a vehicle with defective brakes	**3**	**4**
CU20	Causing or likely to cause danger by reason of use of unsuitable vehicle or using a vehicle with parts or accessories (excluding brakes, steering or tyres) in a dangerous condition	**3**	**4**
CU30	Using a vehicle with defective tyre(s)	**3**	**4**
CU40	Using a vehicle with defective steering	**3**	**4**
CU50	Causing or likely to cause danger by reason of load or passengers	**3**	**4**
CU80	Using a mobile phone while driving a motor vehicle	**3**	**4**
Reckless/Dangerous driving			
DD10	Causing serious injury by dangerous driving	**3-11**	**4**
DD40	Dangerous driving	**3-11**	**4**
DD60	Manslaughter or culpable homicide while driving a vehicle	**3-11**	**4**
DD80	Causing death by dangerous driving	**3-11**	**4**
DD90	Furious driving	**3-9**	**4**
Drink or drugs			
DR10	Driving or attempting to drive with alcohol level above limit	**3-11**	**11**
DR20	Driving or attempting to drive while unfit through drink	**3-11**	**11**
DR30	Driving or attempting to drive then failing to supply a specimen for analysis	**3-11**	**11**
DR31	Driving or attempting to drive then refusing to give permission for analysis of a blood sample that was taken without consent due to incapacity	**3-11**	**11**
DR40	In charge of a vehicle while alcohol level above limit	**10**	**4**
DR50	In charge of a vehicle while unfit through drink	**10**	**4**

Code	Offence	Penalty points	Years on licence[656]
DR60	Failure to provide a specimen for analysis in circumstances other than driving or attempting to drive	**10**	**4**
DR61	Refusing to give permission for analysis of a blood sample that was taken without consent due to incapacity in circumstances other than driving or attempting to drive	**10**	**11**
DR70	Failing to provide specimen for breath test	**4**	**4**
DR80	Driving or attempting to drive when unfit through drugs	**3-11**	**11**
DR90	In charge of a vehicle when unfit through drugs	**10**	**4**
Insurance offences			
IN10	Using a vehicle uninsured against third party risks	**6-8**	**4**
Licence offences			
LC20	Driving otherwise than in accordance with a licence	**3-6**	**4**
LC30	Driving after making a false declaration about fitness when applying for a licence	**3-6**	**4**
LC40	Driving a vehicle having failed to notify a disability	**3-6**	**4**
LC50	Driving after a licence has been revoked or refused on medical grounds	**3-6**	**4**
Miscellaneous offences			
MS10	Leaving a vehicle in a dangerous position	**3**	**4**
MS20	Unlawful pillion riding	**3**	**4**
MS30	Play street offences	**2**	**4**
MS40	Driving with uncorrected defective eyesight or refusing to submit to a test	**3**	**4**
MS50	Motor racing on the highway	**3-11**	**4**
MS60	Offences not covered by other codes	**3**	**4**
MS70	Driving with uncorrected defective eyesight	**3**	**4**
MS80	Refusing to submit to an eyesight test	**3**	**4**
MS90	Failure to give information as to identity of driver etc.	**6**	**4**
Motorway offences			
MW10	Contravention of Special Roads Regulations (excluding speed limits)	**3**	**4**
Pedestrian crossings			
PC10	Undefined Contravention of Pedestrian Crossing Regulations	**3**	**4**
PC20	Contravention of Pedestrian Crossing Regulations with moving vehicle	**3**	**4**
PC30	Contravention of Pedestrian Crossing Regulations with stationary vehicle	**3**	**4**

Code	Offence	Penalty points	Years on licence[656]
Speed limits			
SP10	Exceeding goods vehicle speed limits	**3-6**	**4**
SP20	Exceeding speed limit for type of vehicle (excluding goods or passenger vehicles)	**3-6**	**4**
SP30	Exceeding statutory speed limit on a public road	**3-6**	**4**
SP40	Exceeding passenger vehicle speed limit	**3-6**	**4**
SP50	Exceeding speed limit on a motorway	**3-6**	**4**
Traffic direction and signs			
TS10	Failing to comply with traffic light signals	**3**	**4**
TS20	Failing to comply with double white lines	**3**	**4**
TS30	Failing to comply with 'Stop' sign	**3**	**4**
TS40	Failing to comply with direction of a constable/warden	**3**	**4**
TS50	Failing to comply with traffic sign (excluding: 'Stop' signs, traffic lights or double white lines)	**3**	**4**
TS60	Failing to comply with a school crossing patrol sign	**3**	**4**
TS70	Undefined failure to comply with a traffic direction sign	**3**	**4**
Special code			
TT99	To signify a disqualification under totting up procedure. If the total of penalty points reaches 12 or more within three years, the driver is liable to be disqualified.		**4**
Theft or unauthorised taking			
UT50	Aggravated taking of a vehicle	**3-11**	**4**
Mutual recognition codes[657]			
MR09	Reckless or dangerous driving (whether or not resulting in death, injury or serious risk)		**4**
MR19	Wilful failure to carry out the obligation placed on driver after being involved in a road accident (hit or run[658])		**4**
MR29	Driving a vehicle while under the influence of alcohol or other substance affecting or diminishing the mental and physical abilities of a driver		**4**
MR39	Driving a vehicle faster than the permitted speed		**4**
MR49	Driving a vehicle whilst disqualified		**4**
MR59	Other conduct constituting an offence for which a driving disqualification has been imposed by the state of offence		**4**

[657] An 'MR' code appears on a licence when the driver is disqualified in Northern Ireland, the Isle of Man or the Republic of Ireland. The disqualification period will be valid in Great Britain and will stay on your licence for 4 years from the date of conviction.

[658] Presumably this means 'hit and run'.

Aiding, abetting, counselling or procuring: Offences as coded, but with the end 0 changed to 2
Causing or permitting: Offences as coded, but with the end 0 changed to 4
Inciting: Offences as coded, but with the end 0 changed to 6
Period of time: Periods of time are signified as follows: D = Days, M = Months, Y = Years
Obsolete codes: BA20, CU60, DD30, DD70, DD80, LC10, MS40, PL10, Pl20, PL30, PL40, PL50, SP60, UT10, UT20, UT30 and UD40 are obsolete.
Period offence is on a licence The legislation is at **54.9**.

54.6 *Sentence codes on driving licences*

A Imprisonment
B Detention in a place specified by the Secretary of State
C Suspended Prison Sentence
D Suspended Sentence Supervision Order
E Conditional discharge (maximum 3 years)
F Bound over
J Absolute discharge
K Attendance Centre (minimum 12 hours, maximum 24 hours)
M Community Service Order (minimum 40 hours, maximum 240)
N Cumulative Sentences (Scottish Courts only)
P Youth Custody Sentence
Q Parent or Guardian Order
S Compensation Orders (Scottish Courts)
T Hospital Guardian
U Admonition (Scottish Courts only)
V Young Offender Institution (Scottish Courts only)

54.7 *Can the court consider spent endorsements?*

Chief Constable of West Mercia v Williams 1987 RTR 188 D was charged with using a false instrument, a driving licence. He produced a driving licence at court which he had created and from which he had removed his endorsements. However, there were no effective endorsements on his licence. All parties agreed the case depended on whether the Justices were entitled to take into consideration previous convictions evidenced by endorsements which were no longer effective. Held. Justices were entitled to do so. The Justices were wrong to find no case to answer.
Note: This principle about admissibility at trial has been applied to sentencing hearings. Ed.

54.8 *Reasons* *Must give reasons if not endorsing*

Criminal Procedure Rules 2015 2015/1490 Rule 28.1(1) This rule applies where the court decides:…

(c) not to order, where it could:

(ii) the endorsement of the defendant's driving record….

(2) The court must explain why it has so decided, when it explains the sentence that it has passed.
For the general principle about giving reasons, see **86.47**.

54.9 *How long do endorsements remain on a licence*

Effect of endorsement on driving records
Road Traffic Offenders Act 1988 s 45A(1) An order that any particulars or penalty points are to be endorsed on a person's driving record shall operate as an order that his driving record is to be so endorsed until the end of the period for which the endorsement remains effective.
(2) At the end of the period for which the endorsement remains effective the Secretary of State must remove the endorsement from the person's driving record.

(3) An endorsement ordered on a person's conviction of an offence remains effective (subject to subsections (4) and (5) below):

(a) if an order is made for the disqualification of the offender, until four years have elapsed since the conviction, and

(b) if no such order is made, until either:

(i) four years have elapsed since the commission of the offence, or

(ii) an order is made for the disqualification of the offender under section 35 of this Act.

(4) Where the offence was under one of the following sections of Road Traffic Act 1988, the endorsement remains effective until four years have elapsed since the conviction:

(a) section 1 (causing death by dangerous driving),

(b) section 1A (causing serious injury by dangerous driving),

(c) section 2 (dangerous driving),

(d) section 3ZC (causing death by driving: disqualified drivers), or

(e) section 3ZD (causing serious injury by driving: disqualified drivers).

(5) Where the offence was one:

(a) under section 3A, 4(1), 5(1)(a) or 5A(1)(a) and (2) of that Act (driving offences connected with drink or drugs),

(b) under section 7(6) of that Act (failing to provide a specimen) involving obligatory disqualification, or

(c) under section 7A(6) of that Act (failing to allow a specimen to be subjected to a laboratory test),

the endorsement remains effective until 11 years have elapsed since the conviction.

Combined with other orders

54.10 ***Absolute and conditional discharges, Combined with***

Road Traffic Offenders Act 1988 s 46(1) Notwithstanding anything in Powers of Criminal Courts (Sentencing) Act 2000 s 14(3) (rule about disregarding absolute and conditional discharges) (see **19.5**) a court, [when convicting a person involving obligatory or discretionary disqualification, orders him to be absolutely or conditionally discharged,] may also exercise any power conferred, and must also discharge any duty imposed on the court by section 44 of this Act (obligation to endorse).

54.11 ***Disqualification, Combined with***

R v Usaceva 2015 EWCA Crim 166, 2 Cr App R (S) 7 (p 90) D pleaded to causing death by dangerous driving. She was sentenced to 6 years' imprisonment and was disqualified for 10 years. The Judge also endorsed her licence with 11 points, at the invitation of the prosecution advocate. Held. Looking at Road Traffic Offenders Act 1988 s 44(1) it is clear when disqualification is ordered only the conviction and the disqualification should be recorded. The rule in *R v Kent* 1983 5 Cr App R (S) 171 should be applied. The licence should not be endorsed.

55 Exclusion From Licensed Premises Order

55.1

Licensed Premises (Exclusion of Certain Persons) Act 1980 s 1

Repeal This order is repealed by Violent Crime Reduction Act 2006 Sch 5. No commencement order has been issued. The intention was to repeal this power when Drinking Banning Orders came into force but that did not happen.

Breach of the order A person who enters a premises in breach of an Exclusion Order commits a summary only offence. The maximum sentence is one month's imprisonment and/or a Level 4 fine (£2,500), Licensed Premises (Exclusion of Certain Persons) Act 1980 s 2.

55.2 ***Statistics England and Wales***

Exclusion Orders

Year	2012	2013	2014	2015	2016
Without electronic monitoring	34	16	20	11	15
With electronic monitoring	5	3	3	1	2

For explanations about the statistics, see page 1-xii. The MoJ no longer provides Banks on Sentence with these statistics.

55.3 ***Statutory power to order***

Licensed Premises (Exclusion of Certain Persons) Act 1980 s 1[659] Where a court before which a person is convicted of an offence committed on licensed premises is satisfied that in committing that offence he resorted to violence or offered or threatened to resort to violence, the court may…make an order prohibiting him from entering those premises or any other specified premises, without the express consent of the licensee of the premises or his servant or agent.

55.4 ***Test to apply***

Licensed Premises (Exclusion of Certain Persons) Act 1980 s 1 [The offence] was committed on licensed premises [and the court] is satisfied that in committing that offence he resorted to violence or offered or threatened to resort to violence.

55.5 ***Explain sentence, Judge must/Suggested sentencing remarks***

Judicial College's Crown Court Compendium Part II Sentencing June 2018 page 7.11

> **Example**
> In addition to the sentence of {specify} for the offence of {specify} I make an Exclusion from Licensed Premises Order, which means that you must not go into {specify public houses}. This order will last for {period} from today.
> If you disobey this order you will be committing a further offence, which is punishable with a fine or imprisonment.

Combined with other orders

55.6 ***Absolute and conditional discharges, Combined with***

Licensed Premises (Exclusion of Certain Persons) Act 1980 s 1(2)[660] An exclusion order may be made…notwithstanding the provisions of Powers of Criminal Courts (Sentencing) Act 2000 s 12 and 14 (the effect etc. of an absolute and conditional discharge) (see **19.5**).

56 EXTENDED SENTENCES (EDS)

56.1

Criminal Justice Act 2003 s 226A-226B

Availability/Commencement A court may pass this sentence 'whatever the date of the offence'.[661]

Children and young offenders The order is available whatever the age of the offender.[662]

Court Martial Armed Forces Act 2006 s 219A and 221A are corresponding sections for this extended sentence for servicemen and women aged 18+ and under 18, and are inserted by Legal Aid, Sentencing and Punishment of Offenders Act 2012 Sch 22 para 2. The Court may pass an extended sentence for all ranks, ex-servicemen and women, and civilians, see *Guidance on Sentencing in the Court Martial 2018* Annex B.

Disqualification from driving Where the court passes an extended sentence with either obligatory disqualification, discretionary disqualification or disqualification under the

[659] This Act is repealed by Violent Crime Reduction Act 2006 Sch 5. No commencement order has been issued.
[660] This Act is repealed by Violent Crime Reduction Act 2006 Sch 5. No commencement order has been issued.
[661] In force where the conviction was on or after 3 December 2012, Criminal Justice Act 2003 s 226A(1)(a) and 226B(1)(a) and Legal Aid, Sentencing and Punishment of Offenders Act 2012 (Commencement No 4 and Saving Provisions) Order 2012 2012 /2906 para 2 and 6.
[662] Criminal Justice Act 2003 s 165(2)

totting up provisions, the court is required to select the appropriate period of disqualification and extend it by two-thirds of the length of the custodial term of the extended sentence.[663] The section was designed to prevent offenders serving most of their disqualification periods in custody. The sections were amended by Criminal Justice and Courts Act 2015 s 30. For more detail see **41.16**.

The order is not a replacement for IPP 'For offenders who will continue to represent a significant risk to the safety of the public for an indefinite period, the new extended sentence cannot be treated as a direct replacement for the old IPP', *R v Saunders and Others* 2013 EWCA Crim 1027, 2014 1 Cr App R (S) 45 (p 258) LCJ.

History Sexual and violent offences and extended sentences are dealt with under six different sets of rules. For offences committed:

(a) On 1 October 1967, preventive detention and corrective training were abolished. On the same date, there was power to pass an extended sentence, which enabled the courts to exceed the maximum for an offence when the defendant had three prison sentences for 2+ years since he or she was aged 21. It was rarely used. There was no statutory power to increase the sentences for sexual or violent offences other than when based on the previous offending. Criminal Justice Act 1967 s 37 introduced these changes.

(b) On 1 July 1974, the above provisions were re-enacted by Powers of Criminal Courts Act 1973 s 28. The provisions lasted until 30 September 1992.

(c) From 1 October 1992 to 29 September 1998, there was a power to pass a sentence to protect the public from serious harm, Criminal Justice Act 1991 s 2(2)(b).

(d) From 30 September 1998 to 3 April 2005 there was power to pass a 'longer than commensurate' and an extended sentence, which were re-enacted by Powers of Criminal Courts (Sentencing) Act 2000 s 80(2) and 85.

(e) From 4 April 2005 to 2 December 2012, there were the Dangerous Offender provisions created by Criminal Justice Act 2003 s 227-228. These extended sentences replaced both the 'longer than commensurate' sentence and the old extended sentence. These provisions were amended by Criminal Justice and Immigration Act 2008 s 15-17.

(f) From 3 December 2012, Legal Aid, Sentencing and Punishment of Offenders Act 2012 s 124, which inserted Criminal Justice Act 2003 s 226A-226B, enacted the extended sentence 2012 (EDS).

Passing an extended sentence Sentencers should: a) decide the appropriate determinate term after considering all the relevant factors and all the appropriate discounts, b) determine the appropriate length of the licence 'necessary to protect members of the public from serious harm' etc., c) express the sentence as a single period (by adding the custodial part and the extended licence together), and d) state the custodial period and the extension period of the sentence.

Victim surcharge The court must impose a victim surcharge of £170, Criminal Justice Act 2003 s 161A-161B and Criminal Justice Act 2003 (Surcharge) Order 2012 2012/1696 as amended, unless one or more of the offences was committed when the defendant was aged under 18, when the amount is £30.[664] There are exceptions, a) where a compensation order or an Unlawful Profits Order or a Slavery and Trafficking Reparations Order is imposed, when a reduced amount or a nil amount can be ordered,

[663] Road Traffic Offenders Act 1988 s 35A(1)-(3) and (4)(e) and (f) and Powers of Criminal Courts (Sentencing) Act 2000 s 147A(1)-(3) and (4)(e) and (f) inserted by Coroners and Justice Act 2009 s 2 and Sch 16 paras 2 and 5. Schedule 16 is in force from 13/4/15.

[664] Criminal Justice Act 2003 (Surcharge) Order 2012 2012/1696 and Criminal Justice Act 2003 (Surcharge) (Amendment) Order 2016 2016/398 both provide in Table 1 a £30 (or £20 for offences committed before 8/4/16) penalty for offences specified in Powers of Criminal Courts (Sentencing) Act 2000 s 76. An extended sentence under Criminal Justice Act 2003 s 226B is so specified.

see **17.67**, and b) where the offence was committed before 1 October 2012, when no surcharge can be made, see **115.3**. Where the offence was committed on or after that date and before 8 April 2016, the amount to be imposed is £120 for an adult, see **115.4**.

Rehabilitation period The period is not specifically dealt with in the legislation. The period may depend on the length of the term of custody, see **89.6**. Alternatively the period may depend on the total length of the extended sentence (including the licence) and treating that as the custodial term. This is how the length is determined in notification, see **78.8**.

Release and licence 2012 EDS sentences Sentence passed 3 December 2012 to 12 April 2015

Criminal Justice Act 2003 s 246A provides that whatever the age of the prisoner, the prisoner is put into one of two categories.

Category 1 applies to all prisoners unless they are in Category 2. Release occurs automatically at the two-thirds point of the 'requisite custodial period'.

Category 2 is where a prisoner has either: a) a custodial term of 10 years or more or b) a sentence which was imposed in respect of a Criminal Justice Act 2003 Sch 15B offence. For Category 2 prisoners, their case is referred to the Parole Board at the two-thirds point, Criminal Justice Act 2003 s 246A(4). If the application to the Parole Board is unsuccessful, the 'long stop' for the next review by the Parole Board is 24 months, Criminal Justice Act 2003 s 246A(4)(b). The test for the Parole Board is 'protection of the public', Criminal Justice Act 2003 s 246A(6)(b). Release on licence is automatic at the expiry of the custodial term, Criminal Justice Act 2003 s 246A(7).

Release and licence 2012 EDS sentences Sentence passed on or after 13 April 2015

All prisoners (whatever their age) are subject to Category 2 rules, above.[665] Category 1 ceases to exist.

When released, the defendant remains on licence for the remaining licence period and the extended licence. For more detail see the ***Automatic and Parole Board release*** para at **56.92**.

Release and supervision (CJA 2003 s 227 and 228)

Offence committed prior to July 2008 Prisoners sentenced prior to 14 July 2008 to an extended sentence under Criminal Justice Act 2003 s 227 or 228 in relation to an offence committed on or after 4 April 2005 are eligible for discretionary release by the Parole Board at the halfway point of the custodial period and are automatically released at the end of the custodial period. They remain on licence until the end of the sentence.

56.2 *Statistics England and Wales*

Extended sentences

	Aged 10-17		Aged 18-20		Aged 21+		All		Total
	Male	**Fem.**	**Male**	**Fem.**	**Male**	**Fem.**	**Male**	**Fem.**	**Both**
2014	12	0	64	1	554	4	630	5	635
2015	17	1	47	2	589	12	653	15	668
2016	21	0	46	0	548	10	615	10	625
2017	16	1	50	0	499	9	565	10	575

For explanations about the statistics, see page 1-xii. For more detailed statistics, see www.banksr.com Other Matters Statistics tab.

665 Criminal Justice Act 2003 s 246A as amended by Legal Aid, Sentencing and Punishment of Offenders Act 2012 s 125

Step-by-step guide

56.3 ***A step-by-step guide for the 2012 extended sentences (EDS)***

The court can only impose an extended sentence if it is not required to impose discretionary life or automatic life,[666] or detention for life or custody for life.[667] The steps are as follows:

Step 1 Is the current offence a 'specified offence', i.e. is it listed in Criminal Justice Act 2003 Sch 15?[668]

If No, go to Step 2. For Step 1 see **56.17**.

If Yes, go to Step 4. Step 1 is in Criminal Justice Act 2003 s 226A(1)(a) and 226B(1)(a), see **56.17**.

Step 2 Was the offence abolished before 4 April 2005?[669]

If No, the court can pass an extended sentence.

If Yes, go to Step 3. Steps 2 and 3 are in Criminal Justice Act 2003 s 226A(10) and 226B(8). For Step 2, see **56.22**.

Step 3 Would the offence have constituted a 'specified offence' if committed on the day the offender was convicted of the offence?[670] For Step 3 see **56.22**.

If Yes, go to Step 4.

If No, the court cannot pass an extended sentence.

Step 4 Is there 'a significant risk to members of the public of serious harm occasioned by the commission of further specified offences by the offender'? Criminal Justice Act 2003 s 226A(1)(b) and 226B(1)(b) sets out Step 4, see **56.24**. 'Serious harm' means 'death or serious personal injury, whether physical or psychological', Criminal Justice Act 2003 s 224(3), see **56.25**. For Step 4 see **56.23**.

If Yes, and the defendant is aged 18+, go to Step 5.

If Yes and the defendant is aged under 18, go to Step 6. Step 4 is at **56.23**.

If No, the court may not pass an extended sentence.

Step 5 Did the defendant at the date of the offence have a conviction listed in Criminal Justice Act 2003 Sch 15B?[671]

If Yes, the court can pass an extended sentence. The requirement that an extended sentence must be 4+ years long does not apply to an extended sentence where the defendant has a Sch 15B previous conviction.

If No, go to Step 6. Step 5 is at **56.59**.

Step 6 Does the offence justify a custodial term of 4 years or more, which can be a global term for all the offending allocated to one count. Step 6 is in Criminal Justice Act 2003 s 226A(3) and 226B(1)(d), see **56.64** and **56.65**. Step 6 is at **56.63**.

If Yes, the court may pass an extended sentence with a custodial term of at least 4 years. The court is not obliged to pass the sentence.

If No, the court must pass a determinate sentence or a non-custodial sentence.

The statutory provisions

56.4 ***Statutory definitions***

Meaning of 'specified offence' etc.

Criminal Justice Act 2003 s 224(1) An offence is a 'specified offence' for the purposes of this chapter if it is a specified violent offence or a specified sexual offence.

Criminal Justice Act 2003 s 224(3) In this chapter:

'serious harm' means death or serious personal injury, whether physical or psychological,

[666] Criminal Justice Act 2003 s 226A(1)(c)
[667] Criminal Justice Act 2003 s 226B(1)(c)
[668] Criminal Justice Act 2003 s 226A(1)(a) and 226B(1)(a) make this requirement.
[669] Criminal Justice Act 2003 s 226A(10)(a) and 226B(8)(a) make this requirement.
[670] Criminal Justice Act 2003 s 226A(10)(b) and 226B(8)(b) make this requirement.
[671] Criminal Justice Act 2003 s 226A(2) makes this requirement, as inserted by Legal Aid, Sentencing and Punishment of Offenders Act 2012 Sch 18 para 1.

'specified violent offence' means an offence specified in Part 1 of Schedule 15 [see **56.19**],
'specified sexual offence' means an offence specified in Part 2 of that Schedule [see **56.20**],
'specified terrorism offence' means an offence specified in Part 3 of that Schedule [see **56.21**].[672].

56.5 ***Extended sentences (EDS) for those aged 18+***

Extended sentence for certain violent, sexual offences or terrorism[673]*: persons 18 or over*

Criminal Justice Act 2003 s 226A(1) This section applies where:

(a) a person aged 18 or over is convicted of a specified offence (see **56.17**) (whether the offence was committed before or after this section comes into force),

(b) the court considers that there is a significant risk to members of the public of serious harm occasioned by the commission by the offender of further specified offences (see **56.30**),

(c) the court is not required by section 224A [see the **Life Sentence: Automatic** chapter) or 225(2) (see the **Life Sentence: Dangerousness, Based on** chapter] to impose a sentence of imprisonment for life [or] custody for life,[674] and

(d) condition A or B is met.

(2) Condition A is that, at the time the offence was committed, the offender had been convicted of an offence listed in Schedule 15B [see **56.61**].

(3) Condition B is that, if the court were to impose an extended sentence of imprisonment, the term that it would specify as the appropriate custodial term would be at least 4 years (see **56.62**).

(4) The court may impose an extended sentence of imprisonment on the offender.

(5) An extended sentence of imprisonment is a sentence of imprisonment the term of which is equal to the aggregate of:

(a) the appropriate custodial term, and

(b) a further period (the 'extension period') for which the offender is to be subject to a licence.

(6) The appropriate custodial term is the term of imprisonment that would (apart from this section) be imposed in compliance with Criminal Justice Act 2003 s 153(2) (the requirement that the sentence should be for the shortest term, see **28.32**).

(7) The extension period must be a period of such length as the court considers necessary for the purpose of protecting members of the public from serious harm occasioned by the commission by the offender of further specified offences, subject to subsections (7A) and (9) (see the next paragraph).[675]

(7A)-(9) [Maximum and minimum extensions, see **56.6**]

(10) In subsections (1)(a) and (8) (see above and **56.6**), references to a specified offence, a specified violent offence and a specified sexual offence include an offence that:

(a) was abolished before 4 April 2005, and

(b) would have constituted such an offence if committed on the day on which the offender was convicted of the offence.

(11) Where the offence mentioned in subsection (1)(a) was committed before 4 April 2005:

[672] As inserted by Counter-Terrorism and Border Security Act 2019 s 9(2)(b) In force 12 April 2019, Counter-Terrorism and Border Security Act 2019 s 27(3).

[673] As amended by Counter-Terrorism and Border Security Act 2019 s 9(3)(a)In force 12 April 2019, Counter-Terrorism and Border Security Act 2019 s 27(3).

[674] The phrase in Criminal Justice Act 2003 s 226A(1)(c), inserted by Legal Aid, Sentencing and Punishment of Offenders Act 2012 s 124, is 'imprisonment for life'. However, until Criminal Justice and Court Services Act 2000 s 61 is in force, Legal Aid, Sentencing and Punishment of Offenders Act 2012 Sch 21 para 36 applies and 'custody for life' is substituted for those aged 18-20.

[675] As amended by Offender Rehabilitation Act 2014 s 8(2)

(a) subsection (1)(c) has effect as if the words 'by section 224A or 225(2)' (automatic life and the 2003 life sentence provisions) were omitted, and
(b) subsection (6) has effect as if the words 'in compliance with section 153(2)' (the requirement that the sentence should be for the shortest term, see **28.32**) were omitted.

(12) In the case of a person aged at least 18 but under 21, this section has effect as if:
(a) the reference in subsection (1)(c) to imprisonment for life were to custody for life, and
(b) other references to imprisonment (including in the expression 'extended sentence of imprisonment') were to detention in a young offender institution.

56.6 ***Extended sentence 2012 for those aged 18+ Maximum and minimum extensions***

Criminal Justice Act 2003 s 226A(7A)[676] The extension period must be at least a year.
Criminal Justice Act 2003 s 226A(8) The extension period must not exceed:
(a) 5 years in the case of a specified violent offence, and
(b) 8 years in the case of a specified sexual offence or specified terrorism offence[677].

(9) The term of an extended sentence of imprisonment imposed under this section in respect of an offence must not exceed the term that, at the time the offence was committed, was the maximum term permitted for the offence.

R v Pinnell and Joyce 2010 EWCA Crim 2848, 2011 2 Cr App R (S) 30 (p 168) P pleaded to two counts of section 20 and one count of ABH. He received a 3½-year extended sentence (2 years' custody 18 months' extended licence) on each section 20 consecutive to each other. He received 8 months determinate on the ABH concurrent. This made a 7-year extended sentence in total (4 years' custody 3 years' licence). Held. This was unlawful (see the ***What are the maximum and minimum extension periods?*** para at **56.12**). The combination of the custodial term and extension period cannot exceed the maximum statutory sentence for the offence to which the extended sentence is attached. If the maximum period for the offence is 5 years, the extension period is therefore limited to a year. For more detail see **56.78**.

56.7 ***Extended sentences (EDS) for those aged under 18***

Extended sentence for certain violent, sexual offences or terrorist offence[678]: persons under 18

Criminal Justice Act 2003 s 226B(1) This section applies where:
(a) a person aged under 18 is convicted of a specified offence (see **56.17**) (whether the offence was committed before or after this section comes into force),
(b) the court considers that there is a significant risk to members of the public of serious harm occasioned by the commission by the offender of further specified offences (see **56.23**),
(c) the court is not required by section 226(2) (see **74.4**) to impose a sentence of detention for life under Powers of Criminal Courts (Sentencing) Act 2000 s 91, and
(d) if the court were to impose an extended sentence of detention, the term that it would specify as the appropriate custodial term would be at least 4 years (see **56.61**).

(2) The court may impose an extended sentence of detention on the offender.

Criminal Justice Act 2003 s 226B(3) An extended sentence of detention is a sentence of detention the term of which is equal to the aggregate of:
(a) the appropriate custodial term, and
(b) a further period (the 'extension period') for which the offender is to be subject to a licence.

---

[676] As inserted by Offender Rehabilitation Act 2014 s 8(2). In force 1/2/15, Offender Rehabilitation Act 2014 (Commencement No 2) Order 2015 2015/40

[677] As amended by Counter-Terrorism and Border Security Act 2019 s 9(3)(b) In force 12 April 2019, Counter-Terrorism and Border Security Act 2019 s 27(3).

[678] As amended by Counter-Terrorism and Border Security Act 2019 s 9(4)(a) In force 12 April 2019, Counter-Terrorism and Border Security Act 2019 s 27(3).

(4) The appropriate custodial term is the term of detention that would (apart from this section) be imposed in compliance with section 153(2).
(5) The extension period must be a period of such length as the court considers necessary for the purpose of protecting members of the public from serious harm occasioned by the commission by the offender of further specified offences, subject to subsections (5A) and (7) (see next paragraph).[679]
(5A)-(7) [Maximum and minimum extensions, see **56.8**]
(8) In subsections (1)(a) and (6), references to a specified offence, a specified violent offence and a specified sexual offence include an offence that:
(a) was abolished before 4 April 2005, and
(b) would have constituted such an offence if committed on the day on which the offender was convicted of the offence.
(9) Where the offence mentioned in subsection (1)(a) was committed before 4 April 2005:
(a) subsection (1) has effect as if paragraph (c) were omitted, and
(b) subsection (4) has effect as if the words 'in compliance with section 153(2)' were omitted.
Criminal Justice Act 2003 s 226B(5A)[680] The extension period must be at least a year.
Criminal Justice Act 2003 s 226B(6) The extension period must not exceed:
(a) 5 years in the case of a specified violent offence, and
(b) 8 years in the case of a specified sexual offence.
(7) The term of an extended sentence of detention imposed under this section in respect of an offence may not exceed the term that, at the time the offence was committed, was the maximum term of imprisonment permitted for the offence in the case of a person aged 21[681] or over.

56.8 *Extended sentence for those under 18 Maximum and minimum extension period*

Criminal Justice Act 2003 s 226B(5A)[682] The extension period must be at least a year.
Criminal Justice Act 2003 s 226B(6) The extension period must not exceed:
(a) 5 years in the case of a specified violent offence, and
(b) 8 years in the case of a specified sexual offence or a specified terrorist offence[683].
(7) The term of an extended sentence of detention imposed under this section in respect of an offence may not exceed the term that, at the time the offence was committed, was the maximum term of imprisonment permitted for the offence in the case of a person aged 21[684] or over.

56.9 *Section 229 Assessment of dangerousness*

The assessment of dangerousness

Criminal Justice Act 2003 s 229(1)[685] This section applies where:
(a) a person has been convicted of a specified offence, and

[679] As amended by Offender Rehabilitation Act 2014 s 8(2)
[680] As inserted by Offender Rehabilitation Act 2014 s 8(2). In force 1/2/15, Offender Rehabilitation Act 2014 (Commencement No 2) Order 2015 2015/40 para 2
[681] The number in Criminal Justice Act 2003 s 226B(7) (which was inserted by Legal Aid, Sentencing and Punishment of Offenders Act 2012 s 124) is '18'. However, until Criminal Justice and Court Services Act 2000 s 61 is in force, Legal Aid, Sentencing and Punishment of Offenders Act 2012 Sch 21 para 36 applies and '21' is substituted for '18'.
[682] As inserted by Offender Rehabilitation Act 2014 s 8(3). In force 1/2/15, Offender Rehabilitation Act 2014 (Commencement No 2) Order 2015 2015/40 para 2
[683] As amended by Counter-Terrorism and Border Security Act 2019 s 9(4)(b) In force 12 April 2019, Counter-Terrorism and Border Security Act 2019 s 27(3).
[684] The number in Criminal Justice Act 2003 s 226B(7) (which was inserted by Legal Aid, Sentencing and Punishment of Offenders Act 2012 s 124) is '18'. However, until Criminal Justice and Court Services Act 2000 s 61 is in force, Legal Aid, Sentencing and Punishment of Offenders Act 2012 Sch 21 para 36 applies and '21' is substituted for '18'.
[685] Sections 229-230 were moved under a new heading entitled 'Extended sentences' by Legal Aid, Sentencing and Punishment of Offenders Act 2012 Sch 19 para 18. In force 3/12/12

(b) it falls to a court to assess under any of sections 225 to 228 whether there is a significant risk to members of the public of serious harm occasioned by the commission by him of further such offences.

(2) The court in making the assessment referred to in subsection (1)(b):

(a) must take into account all such information as is available to it about the nature and circumstances of the offence,

(aa) may take into account all such information as is available to it about the nature and circumstances of any other offences of which the offender has been convicted by a court anywhere in the world,

(b) may take into account any information which is before it about any pattern of behaviour of which any of the offences mentioned in paragraph a) or (aa) forms part, and

(c) may take into account any information about the offender which is before it.

(2A) The reference in subsection (2)(aa) to a conviction by a court includes a reference to:

(a) a conviction of an offence in any service disciplinary proceedings, and

(b) a conviction of a service offence within the meaning of Armed Forces Act 2006 ('conviction' here including anything that under section 376(1) and (2) of that Act is to be treated as a conviction).

(2B) For the purposes of subsection (2A)(a) 'service disciplinary proceedings' means:

(a) any proceedings under Army Act 1955, Air Force Act 1955 or Naval Discipline Act 1957 (whether before a [Court Martial] or any other court or person authorised under any of those Acts to award a punishment in respect of any offence), and

(b) any proceedings before a Standing Civilian Court,

and 'conviction' includes the recording of a finding that a charge in respect of the offence has been proved.

56.10 *Section 232A Certificates of conviction*

Certificates of conviction

Criminal Justice Act 2003 s 232A[686] Where:

(a) on any date after the commencement of Schedule 15B a person is convicted in England and Wales of an offence listed in that Schedule, and

(b) the court by or before which the person is so convicted states in open court that the person has been convicted of such an offence on that date, and

(c) that court subsequently certifies that fact,

that certificate is evidence, for the purposes of section 224A,[687] that the person was convicted of such an offence on that date.

Preliminary matters

56.11 *What are the extended sentences called?*

Order	Aged 10-17	Aged 18-20	Aged 21+
Extended sentences (EDS)	Extended sentence of detention[688]	Extended sentence of detention in a Young Offender Institution[689]	Extended sentence of imprisonment[690]

[686] As inserted by Legal Aid, Sentencing and Punishment of Offenders Act 2012 Sch 19 para 21

[687] Criminal Justice and Courts Act 2015 s 5(2) amends 'section 224A' to 'sections 224A and 226A'. In force 13/4/15, Criminal Justice and Courts Act 2015 (Commencement No 1, Saving and Transitional Provisions) Order 2015 2015/778 para 3 and Sch 1 para 5

[688] Criminal Justice Act 2003 s 226B(2) inserted by Legal Aid, Sentencing and Punishment of Offenders Act 2012 s 124

[689] Criminal Justice Act 2003 s 226A(4) inserted by Legal Aid, Sentencing and Punishment of Offenders Act 2012 s 124 entitles the order for those aged 18+ as 'an extended sentence of imprisonment'. However, until Criminal Justice and Court Services Act 2000 s 61 is in force, Legal Aid, Sentencing and Punishment of Offenders Act 2012 Sch 21 para 36 applies and Criminal Justice Act 2003 s 226A(12) is inserted. This renames the order as 'extended sentence of detention in a Young Offender Institution'.

[690] Criminal Justice Act 2003 s 226A(4) as inserted by Legal Aid, Sentencing and Punishment of Offenders Act 2012 s 124

56.12 ***What are the maximum and minimum extension periods?***

Order	Aged 10-17	Aged 18+
Extended sentences (EDS) for specified violent offences	The extension period must not exceed 5 years[691]	The extension period must not exceed 5 years[692]
Extended sentences (EDS) for specified sexual offences or terrorism offence[693]	The extension period must not exceed 8 years[694]	The extension period must not exceed 8 years[695]

Minimum terms: The extension period must be for at least one year, Offender Rehabilitation Act 2014 s 8. In force 1 February 2015.[696] For more detail, see **56.6** and **56.8**.

56.13 ***Dangerous Offenders Guide***

Note: This guide is not a definitive guideline. It was written for the 2003 extended sentences but the information may be helpful. Ed.

Sentencing Guidelines Council Dangerous Offenders Guide 2008, www.banksr.com Other Matters Guidelines tab

para 9.3 Extended sentence Criminal Justice Act 2003

9.3.1 When passing an extended sentence, the court must fix the custodial term for the offence. This must be for the shortest term commensurate with the seriousness of the offence(s).[697]

9.3.2 The appropriate custodial term must be at least 4 years unless the offender has a previous conviction for an offence listed in Criminal Justice Act 2003 Sch 15A. (This would be Sch 15B under the 2012 extended sentences and this now only applies to those aged 18+. Ed.) Where a court exercises its discretion to impose an extended sentence where there is such a previous conviction and the appropriate custodial term would have been less than 12 months, the court is nonetheless required to set that term at 12 months.[698]

9.3.5 When passing an extended sentence, in addition to fixing the custodial term, the court must fix the extension period. The length of the extension period is such as the court considers necessary for the purpose of protecting members of the public from serious harm caused by the offender committing further specified offences, Criminal Justice Act 2003 (s 227(2)(b) and s 228(2)(b)). [This would be s 226A(7) and s 226B(5) for the 2012 extended sentences (EDS).]

The extension period must not exceed 5 years for a specified violent offence or 8 years for a specified sexual offence (s 227(4) and s 228(4)) [this would be s 226A(8) and s 226B(6) for the 2012 extended sentences (EDS)]. Further, the aggregate of the custodial term and the extension period must not exceed the maximum penalty for the offence (s 227(5) and s 228(5)) [this would be s 226A(9) and s 226B(7) for the 2012 extended sentences (EDS)].

9.3.6 The length of the extension period is not intended to reflect the seriousness of the offence, it is designed to provide greater protection for the public from the commission

[691] Criminal Justice Act 2003 s 226B(6)(a) as inserted by Legal Aid, Sentencing and Punishment of Offenders Act 2012 s 124

[692] Criminal Justice Act 2003 s 226A(8)(a) as inserted by Legal Aid, Sentencing and Punishment of Offenders Act 2012 s 124

[693] As amended by Counter-Terrorism and Border Security Act 2019 s 9(3)(b) In force 12 April 2019, Counter-Terrorism and Border Security Act 2019 s 27(3).

[694] Criminal Justice Act 2003 s 226B(6)(a) as inserted by Legal Aid, Sentencing and Punishment of Offenders Act 2012 s 124

[695] Criminal Justice Act 2003 s 226A(8)(b) as inserted by Legal Aid, Sentencing and Punishment of Offenders Act 2012 s 124

[696] Offender Rehabilitation Act 2014 (Commencement No 2) Order 2015 2015/40

[697] Criminal Justice Act 2003 s 153(2) and 227(3)

[698] Criminal Justice Act 2003 s 227(2)-(3)(b)

of further offences. Therefore, proportionality with the seriousness of the offence is not a primary factor in determining the length of the extension period. Rather, the objective should be to fix the length of the extension period by reference to what realistically can be achieved within it to secure the offender's rehabilitation and prevent reoffending.
In some cases, the court may be able to tailor the extension period to the availability and length of treatment or other programmes. In all cases the court should consider whether the length of the extension period can be justified by the evidence available.[699]
9.3.7 The extension period commences at the end of the custodial term, not the point at which the offender has been released on licence during the custodial term.[700]

56.14 ***Committals Youth Courts***

Powers of Criminal Courts (Sentencing) Act 2000 s 3C(1) This section applies where on the summary trial of a specified offence a person aged under 18 is convicted of the offence.
(2) If, in relation to the offence, it appears to the court that the criteria for the imposition of a sentence under Criminal Justice Act 2003 s 226B would be met, the court must commit the offender in custody or on bail to the Crown Court for sentence in accordance with section 5A(1) (see **13.16**).
R v Robson 2006 EWCA Crim 1414, 2007 1 Cr App R (S) 54 (p 301) D was aged 17 when he was convicted at the Magistrates' Court of two specified and serious offences. When he came to be sentenced in the Crown Court, he was aged 18. The difference was crucial. Held. Magistrates' Courts Act 1952 s 29(3) allows the Crown Court to deal with an offender committed by the Magistrates' Court as if he had just been convicted on indictment. The effect of this section merely ensures that the sentencing powers of the Crown Court were not limited to those of the Magistrates' Court and does not require D to be sentenced under the regime applicable to those aged 18 or over solely because he would have been 18 years old on conviction if he had 'just' been convicted.
CPS v South East Surrey Youth Court 2005 EWHC 2929 (Admin), 2006 2 Cr App R (S) 26 (p 177) High Court D, then aged 17, allegedly assaulted V in the face with a beer bottle, causing a wound. D was also arrested for an unrelated robbery where it was said a knife was used. The Youth Court sent the robbery to the Crown Court and on a later date the CPS also asked for the ABH to be sent, under Crime and Disorder Act 1998 s 51A(3)(d). This was on the basis that ABH was a 'specified violent offence', Criminal Justice Act 2003 s 224(3). The Court declined to commit because ABH was not a grave crime, so the provisions of Magistrates' Courts Act 1980 s 24(1) were not met. The CPS appealed. Held. We consider the obligations of a Youth Court when dealing with a potentially dangerous offender. Here the provisions are not merely labyrinthine, they are manifestly inconsistent with each other. Yet again, the courts are faced with a sample of the deeply confusing provisions of Criminal Justice Act 2003 and the satellite statutory instruments to which it is giving stuttering birth. Magistrates' Courts Act 1980 s 24(1) requires summary trial of a person under 18 unless the offence is grave and may require a sentence of long-term detention, in which case the defendant must be committed for trial. Crime and Disorder Act 1998 s 51A requires a child or young person to be sent to the Crown Court for trial if the offence is specified in Criminal Justice Act 2003 Sch 15 and if convicted, it appears that the criteria for the imposition of an indeterminate sentence or an extended sentence under section 228 would be met. Justices should bear in mind: a) those who are under 18 should, wherever possible, be tried in a Youth Court, which is best designed for their specific needs, *R (H) v Southampton Youth Court* 2004 EWHC 2912 (Admin) and *R (CPS) v Redbridge Youth Court* 2005 EWHC 1390, b) the guidance in *R v Lang* 2005 EWCA Crim 2864, 2006 2 Cr App R (S) 3 (p 13), particularly in para (iv) in relation to non-serious specified offences (see **56.25**), c) the need, when dealing with those under 18, to be particularly rigorous before concluding

[699] *R v Nelson* 2001 EWCA Crim 2264, 2002 1 Cr App R (S) 134 (p 565) paras 19 and 21-22
[700] *R v S* 2005 EWCA Crim 3616, 2006 2 Cr App R (S) 35 (p 224) para 18

that there is a significant risk of serious harm by the commission of further offences. Such a conclusion is unlikely to be appropriate in the absence of a pre-sentence report following assessment by a young offender team, d) in most cases where a non-serious specified offence is charged, an assessment of dangerousness will not be appropriate until after conviction, when, if the dangerousness criteria are met, the defendant can be committed to the Crown Court for sentence, and e) when a youth under 18 is jointly charged with an adult, an exercise of judgement will be called for by the Youth Court when assessing the competing presumptions in favour of: 1) joint trial of those jointly charged and 2) the trial of youths in the Youth Court. Factors relevant to that judgement will include the age and maturity of the youth, the comparative culpability in relation to the offence and the previous convictions of the two and whether the trial can be severed without either injustice or undue inconvenience to witnesses. Therefore the Justices' approach in declining to consider section 51A(3)(d) was flawed. However, the conclusion that summary jurisdiction should be accepted for purposes of trial is unimpeachable.

56.15 ***Defendant has crossed an age threshold since offence***
R v Robson 2006 EWCA Crim 1414, 2007 1 Cr App R (S) 54 (p 301) As a matter of statutory construction, we conclude that the age of the offender for the purpose of determining which of the statutory regimes under the 2003 Act (the dangerousness provisions) applies to him is the offender's age at the date of conviction.
See also the **Children And Young Offenders: Custodial Sentences** ***Defendant crosses age threshold before sentence*** para at **13.15**.

56.16 ***Comparing the release provisions with life sentences***
Att-Gen's Ref No 27 of 2013 2014 EWCA Crim 334[701] LCJ para 35-39 It was suggested that there was an anomaly between life sentences and EDS extended sentences because of the different release provisions. If the appropriate determinate sentence is 10 years, a life prisoner receives a minimum term of 5 years and would be eligible for release after the expiration of that period, whereas an EDS prisoner would become entitled to be released at two-thirds of the 10-year period, namely after 7½ years. Held. It is not for the Court to correct the anomaly, if anomaly it be, by reducing the appropriate term to take account of the early release provisions. That would offend general principle[s] and undermine the purpose of Criminal Justice Act 2003 s 246A, which is to ensure that those subject to the new extended sentences serve one third more of the appropriate custodial term than those sentenced under the old regime.

Step 1 Is the current offence a specified offence?

56.17 ***Step 1 Is the current offence a specified offence?***
Step 1 Is the current offence a 'specified offence', i.e. is it listed in Criminal Justice Act 2003 Sch 15?[702] For the definition of a specified offence see the next paragraph.
If No, go to Step 2. See **56.22**.
If Yes, go to Step 4, at **56.23**.

56.18 ***Specified offences Statutory definition***
Criminal Justice Act 2003 s 224(1) An offence is a 'specified offence' for the purposes of this Chapter if it is a specified violent offence or a specified sexual offence.
Criminal Justice Act 2003 s 224(3) 'Specified violent offence' means an offence specified in Sch 15 Part 1 (of this Act). 'Specified sexual offence' means an offence specified in Sch 15 Part 2 (of this Act).

56.19 ***Specified offences Violent offences***
Criminal Justice Act 2003 Sch 15 Part 1
Note: The statutes are listed in chronological order. Ed.
Common law offences:

[701] This case is also known as *R v Burinskas* 2014 EWCA Crim 334.
[702] Criminal Justice Act 2003 s 226A(1)(a) and 226B(1)(a) make this requirement.

Manslaughter
Kidnapping
False imprisonment

Offences Against the Person Act 1861
- s 4 (soliciting murder)
- s 16 (threats to kill)
- s 18 (wounding with intent to cause grievous bodily harm)
- s 20 (malicious wounding)
- s 21 (attempting to choke, suffocate or strangle in order to commit or assist in committing an indictable offence)
- s 22 (using chloroform etc. to commit or assist in the committing of any indictable offence)
- s 23 (maliciously administering poison etc. so as to endanger life or inflict grievous bodily injury)
- s 27 (abandoning children)
- s 28 (causing bodily injury by explosives)
- s 29 (using explosives etc. with intent to do grievous bodily harm)
- s 30 (placing explosives with intent to do bodily injury)
- s 31 (setting spring guns etc. with intent to do grievous bodily harm)
- s 32 (endangering the safety of railway passengers)
- s 35 (injuring persons by furious driving)
- s 37 (assaulting officer preserving wreck)
- s 38 (assault with intent to resist arrest)
- s 47 (assault occasioning actual bodily harm)

Explosive Substances Act 1883
- s 2 (causing explosion likely to endanger life or property)
- s 3 (attempt to cause explosion, or making or keeping explosive with intent to endanger life or property)
- s 4 (making or possession of explosives under suspicious circumstances)[703]

Infant Life (Preservation) Act 1929 s 1 (child destruction)

Children and Young Persons Act 1933 s 1 (cruelty to children)

Infanticide Act 1938 s 1 (infanticide)

Firearms Act 1968
- s 16 (possession of firearm with intent to endanger life)
- s 16A (possession of firearm with intent to cause fear of violence)
- s 17(1) (use of firearm to resist arrest)
- s 17(2) (possession of firearm at time of committing or being arrested for offence specified in Schedule 1 to that Act)
- s 18 (carrying a firearm with criminal intent)

Theft Act 1968
- s 8 (robbery or assault with intent to rob)
- s 9 (burglary with intent to: a) inflict grievous bodily harm on a person, or b) do unlawful damage to a building or anything in it)
- s 10 (aggravated burglary)
- s 12A (aggravated vehicle-taking)

Criminal Damage Act 1971
- s 1 (arson)
- s 1(2) (destroying or damaging property (other than an offence of arson))

Taking of Hostages Act 1982 s 1 (hostage-taking)

Aviation Security Act 1982
- s 1 (hijacking)

[703] As inserted by Criminal Justice and Courts Act 2015 s 2(1)-(2). In force 13/4/15, Criminal Justice and Courts Act 2015 (Commencement No 1, Saving and Transitional Provisions) Order 2015 2015/778 para 3 and Sch 1 para 2

s 2 (destroying, damaging or endangering safety of aircraft)
s 3 (other acts endangering or likely to endanger safety of aircraft)
s 4 (offences in relation to certain dangerous articles)
Mental Health Act 1983 s 127 (ill-treatment of patients)
Prohibition of Female Circumcision Act 1985 s 1[704] (prohibition of female circumcision)
Public Order Act 1986
s 1 (riot)
s 2 (violent disorder)
s 3 (affray)
Criminal Justice Act 1988 s 134 (torture)
Road Traffic Act 1988
s 1 (causing death by dangerous driving)
s 3A (causing death by careless driving when under influence of drink or drugs)
Aviation and Maritime Security Act 1990
s 1 (endangering safety at aerodromes)
s 9 (hijacking of ships)
s 10 (seizing or exercising control of fixed platforms)
s 11 (destroying fixed platforms or endangering their safety)
s 12 (other acts endangering or likely to endanger safe navigation)
s 13 (offences involving threats)
s 3ZC (causing death by driving: disqualified drivers)[705]
Channel Tunnel (Security) Order 1994 1994/570 (offences relating to Channel Tunnel trains and the tunnel system)
Protection from Harassment Act 1997 s 4 or 4A[706] (putting people in fear of violence and stalking involving fear of violence or serious alarm or distress)
Crime and Disorder Act 1998
s 29 (racially or religiously aggravated assaults)
s 31(1)(a) or (b) (racially or religiously aggravated offences under Public Order Act 1986 s 4 or 4A)
Terrorism Act 2000
s 54 (weapons training)
s 56 (directing terrorist organisation)
s 57 (possession of article for terrorist purposes)
s 59 (inciting terrorism overseas)
[From 12 April 2019, terrorist offences are listed in Part 3, see **56.21** and repealed.[707]]
International Criminal Court Act 2001
s 51 or 52 (genocide, crimes against humanity, war crimes and related offences (other than one involving murder))
Anti-terrorism, Crime and Security Act 2001
s 47 (use etc. of nuclear weapons)
s 50 (assisting or inducing certain weapons-related acts overseas)
s 113 (use of noxious substance or thing to cause harm or intimidate)
Female Genital Mutilation Act 2003
s 1 (genital mutilation)
s 2 (assisting a girl to mutilate her own genitalia)
s 3 (assisting a non-UK person to mutilate overseas a girl's genitalia)

704 Repealed, but still available for historical offences
705 Criminal Justice and Courts Act 2015 Sch 6 para 11 adds this entry. In force 13/4/15, Criminal Justice and Courts Act 2015 (Commencement No 1, Saving and Transitional Provisions) Order 2015 2015/778 para 3 and Sch 1 para 75
706 'or 4A' and 'and stalking involving fear of violence or serious alarm or distress' were inserted by para 147.
707 see Counter-Terrorism and Border Security Act 2019 s 9 and Sch 4 para 9(1)-(2) In force 12 April 2019 by Counter-Terrorism and Border Security Act 2019 s 27(3).

Domestic Violence, Crime and Victims Act 2004 s 5[708] (causing or allowing the death of a child or vulnerable adult or cause them to suffer serious physical harm[709])
Terrorism Act 2006
s 5 (preparation of terrorist acts)
s 6 (training for terrorism)
s 9 (making or possession of radioactive device or material)
s 10 (use of radioactive device or material for terrorist purposes etc.)
s 11 (terrorist threats relating to radioactive devices etc.)
[From 12 April 2019, terrorist offences are listed in Part 3[710], see **56.21**]
Modern Slavery Act 2015[711]
s 1 (Slavery, servitude and forced or compulsory labour)
s 2 (Human trafficking [when not a sexual offence listed in Part 2 of this schedule, see **56.20**])
An offence of:
(a) aiding, abetting, counselling, procuring or inciting the commission of an offence specified in this Part of this Schedule,
(b) conspiring to commit an offence so specified, or
(c) attempting to commit an offence so specified.[712]
An attempt to commit murder or a conspiracy to commit murder.[713]

56.20 ***Specified offences Sexual offences***
Criminal Justice Act 2003 Sch 15 Part 2
Note A * has been added to show the section or Act has been repealed. The entry remains for historical offences.
Sexual Offences Act 1956
s 1 (rape)*
s 2 (procurement of woman by threats)*
s 3 (procurement of woman by false pretences)*
s 4 (administering drugs to obtain or facilitate intercourse)*
s 5 (intercourse with girl under 13)*
s 6 (intercourse with a girl under 16)*
s 7 (intercourse with a defective)*
s 9 (procurement of a defective)*
s 10 (incest by a man)*
s 11 (incest by a woman)*
s 14 (indecent assault on a woman)*
s 15 (indecent assault on a man)*
s 16 (assault with intent to commit buggery)*
s 17 (abduction of woman by force or for the sake of her property)*
s 19 (abduction of unmarried girl under 18 from parent or guardian)*
s 20 (abduction of unmarried girl under 16 from parent or guardian)*
s 21 (abduction of defective from parent or guardian)*
s 22 (causing prostitution of women)*

[708] This offence was inserted by Domestic Violence, Crime and Victims Act 2004 Sch 10 para 59(2).
[709] This description was amended by the Schedule to Domestic Violence, Crime and Victims (Amendment) Act 2012 para 6. In force 2/7/12, Domestic Violence, Crime and Victims (Amendment) Act 2012 (Commencement) Order 2012 2012/1432
[710] see Counter-Terrorism and Border Security Act 2019 s 9(5) and Sch 4 para 12(3) In force 12 April 2019, Counter-Terrorism and Border Security Act 2019 s 27(3).
[711] Inserted by Modern Slavery Act 2015 s 6(1)-(2). No commencement order has been issued.
[712] Criminal Justice and Courts Act 2015 s 2(1) and (3) amended this paragraph to include: a) aiding and abetting, counselling or procuring [listed] offences, incitement to commit [listed] offences, and b) a Serious Crimes Act 2007 Part 2 offence where the person intended or believed [a listed offence] would be committed. In force 13/4/15, Criminal Justice and Courts Act 2015 (Commencement No 1, Saving and Transitional Provisions) Order 2015 2015/778 para 3 and Sch 1 para 2
[713] Criminal Justice and Courts Act 2015 s 2(1) and (4) amend this sentence to include: a) incitement to commit murder and b) a Serious Crimes Act 2007 Part 2 offence where the person intended or believed murder would be committed. In force 13/4/15, Criminal Justice and Courts Act 2015 (Commencement No 1, Saving and Transitional Provisions) Order 2015 2015/778 para 3 and Sch 1 para 2

s 23 (procuration of girl under 21)*
s 24 (detention of woman in brothel)*
s 25 (permitting girl under 13 to use premises for intercourse)*
s 26 (permitting girl under 16 to use premises for intercourse)*
s 27 (permitting defective to use premises for intercourse)*
s 28 (causing or encouraging the prostitution of, intercourse with or indecent assault on girl under 16)*
s 29 (causing or encouraging prostitution of defective)*
s 32 (soliciting by men)*
s 33 (keeping a brothel)[714]
s 92A (keeping a brothel used for prostitution)[715]

Mental Health Act 1959 s 128 (sexual intercourse with patients)*
Indecency with Children Act 1960 s 1 (indecent conduct towards young child)*
Sexual Offences Act 1967
s 4 (procuring others to commit homosexual acts)*
s 5 (living on earnings of male prostitution)*

Theft Act 1968 s 9 (burglary with intent to commit rape)*
Criminal Law Act 1977 s 54 (inciting girl under 16 to have incestuous sexual intercourse)*
Protection of Children Act 1978 s 1 (indecent photographs of children)
Customs and Excise Management Act 1979 s 170 (fraudulent evasion of duty etc. in relation to goods prohibited [from importation] under Customs Consolidation Act 1876 s 42 (indecent or obscene articles))
Criminal Justice Act 1988 s 160 (possession of indecent photograph of a child)
Sexual Offences Act 2003
s 1 (rape)
s 2 (assault by penetration)
s 3 (sexual assault)
s 4 (causing a person to engage in sexual activity without consent)
s 5 (rape of a child under 13)
s 6 (assault of a child under 13 by penetration)
s 7 (sexual assault of a child under 13)
s 8 (causing or inciting a child to engage in sexual activity)
s 9 (sexual activity with a child)
s 10 (causing or inciting a child to engage in sexual activity)
s 11 (engaging in sexual activity in the presence of a child)
s 12 (causing a child to watch a sexual act)
s 13 (child sex offences committed by children or young persons)
s 14 (arranging or facilitating commission of a child sex offence)
s 15 (meeting a child following sexual grooming)
s 15A (sexual communication with a child)
This entry was inserted by Serious Crime Act 2015 Sch 4 para 68(2). In force 3 April 2017.
s 16 (abuse of position of trust: sexual activity with a child)
s 17 (abuse of position of trust: causing or inciting a child to engage in sexual activity)
s 18 (abuse of position of trust: sexual activity in the presence of a child)
s 19 (abuse of position of trust: causing a child to watch a sexual act)
s 25 (sexual activity with a child family member)
s 26 (inciting a child family member to engage in sexual activity)

---

[714] Criminal Justice and Courts Act 2015 s 2(1)-(5) delete this entry. In force 13/4/15, Criminal Justice and Courts Act 2015 (Commencement No 1, Saving and Transitional Provisions) Order 2015 2015/778 para 3 and Sch 1 para 2

[715] As inserted by Criminal Justice and Courts Act 2015 s 2(1) and (6). In force 13/4/15, Criminal Justice and Courts Act 2015 (Commencement No 1, Saving and Transitional Provisions) Order 2015 2015/778 para 3 and Sch 1 para 2

s 30 (sexual activity with a person with a mental disorder impeding choice)
s 31 (causing or inciting a person with a mental disorder impeding choice to engage in sexual activity)
s 32 (engaging in sexual activity in the presence of a person with a mental disorder impeding choice)
s 33 (causing a person with a mental disorder impeding choice to watch a sexual act)
s 34 (inducement, threat or deception to procure sexual activity with a person with a mental disorder)
s 35 (causing a person with a mental disorder to engage in or agree to engage in sexual activity by inducement, threat or deception, of a person with a mental disorder)
s 36 (engaging in sexual activity in the presence, procured by inducement, threat or deception, of a person with a mental disorder)
s 37 (causing a person with a mental disorder to watch a sexual act by inducement, threat or deception)
s 38 (care workers: sexual activity with a person with a mental disorder)
s 39 (causing or inciting sexual activity)
s 40 (care workers: sexual activity in the presence of a person with a mental disorder)
s 41 (care workers: causing a person with a mental disorder to watch a sexual act)
s 47 (paying for sexual services of a child)
s 48 (causing or inciting child prostitution or pornography)
s 49 (controlling a child prostitute or child involved in pornography)
s 50 (arranging or facilitating child prostitution or pornography)
Note: Serious Crime Act 2015 Sch 4 para 68(3)-(5) renames the section 48-50 offences.
The offences become:
s 48 (causing or inciting sexual exploitation of a child),
s 49 (controlling a child in relation to sexual exploitation),
s 50 (arranging or facilitating sexual exploitation of a child).[716]
s 52 (causing or inciting prostitution for gain)
s 53 (controlling prostitution for gain)
s 57 (trafficking into the UK for sexual exploitation)
s 58 (trafficking within the UK for sexual exploitation)
s 59 (trafficking out of the UK for sexual exploitation)
s 59A (trafficking out of the UK for sexual exploitation)[717]
s 61 (administering a substance with intent)
s 62 (committing an offence with intent to commit a sexual offence)
s 63 (trespass with intent to commit a sexual offence)
s 64 (sex with an adult relative: penetration)
s 65 (sex with an adult relative: consenting penetration)
s 66 (exposure)
s 67 (voyeurism)
s 69 (intercourse with an animal)
s 70 (sexual penetration of a corpse)

Modern Slavery Act 2015[718]

s 2 (Human trafficking when committed with a view to exploitation that consists of or includes behaviour within Modern Slavery Act 2015 s 3(3))[719]

[716] In force 1/6/15, Serious Crime Act 2015 (Commencement No 1) Regulations 2015 2015/820 para 3
[717] As inserted by para 139
[718] Inserted by Modern Slavery Act 2015 s 6(1) and (3). In force 31/7/15, Modern Slavery Act 2015 (Commencement No 1, Savings and Transitional Provisions) Regs 2015 2015/1476 para 2(a)
[719] Modern Slavery Act 2015 s 3(3) Something is done to or in respect of the person: a) which involves the commission of an offence under: i) Protection of Children Act 1978 s 1(1)(a) (indecent photographs of children), or ii) Sexual Offences Act 2003 Part 1 (sexual offences), as it has effect in England and Wales, or b) which would involve the commission of such an offence if it were done in England and Wales.

An offence of:[720]

(1) Aiding, abetting, counselling or procuring the commission of an offence specified in this Part of this Schedule.
(2) An attempt to commit such an offence.
(3) Conspiracy to commit such an offence.
(4) Incitement to commit such an offence.
(5) An offence under Serious Crime Act 2007 Part 2 in relation to which an offence specified in this Part of this Schedule is the offence (or one of the offences) which the person intended or believed would be committed.

56.21 ***Specified offences*** ***Terrorist offences***
Criminal Justice Act 2003 Sch 15 Part 3[721]
Specified Terrorism Offences
Terrorism Act 2000
s 11 (membership of a proscribed organisation)
s 12 (inviting support for a proscribed organisation)
s 54 (weapons training)
s 56 (directing a terrorist organisation)
s 57 (possession of article for terrorist purposes)
s 58 (collection of information likely to be of use to a terrorist)
s 58A (publishing information about members of the armed forces etc.)
s 58B (entering or remaining in a designated area)
s 59 (inciting terrorism overseas).
Anti-terrorism, Crime and Security Act 2001
s 47 (use etc. of nuclear weapons)
s 50 (assisting or inducing certain weapons-related acts overseas)
s 113 (use of noxious substance or thing to cause harm or intimidate)
Terrorism Act 2006
s 1 (encouragement of terrorism)
s 2 (dissemination of terrorist publications)
s 5 (preparation of terrorist acts)
s 6 (training for terrorism)
s 8 (attendance at a place used for terrorist training)
s 9 (making or possession of radioactive device or material)
s 10 (misuse of radioactive device or material for terrorist purposes etc.)
s 11 (terrorist threats relating to radioactive devices etc.)
(1) Aiding, abetting, counselling or procuring the commission of an offence specified in the preceding paragraphs of this Part of this Schedule.
(2) An attempt to commit such an offence.
(3) Conspiracy to commit such an offence.
(4) Incitement to commit such an offence.
(5) An offence under Part 2 of the Serious Crime Act 2007 [encouraging or assisting offences, see **212.1** in Volume 2] in relation to which an offence specified in the preceding paragraphs of this Part of this Schedule is the offence (or one of the offences) which the person intended or believed would be committed.

56.22

Steps 2 and 3

Step 2 Was the offence abolished before 4 April 2005?[722]
If No, the court can pass an extended sentence. If Yes, go to Step 3.

[720] As substituted by Criminal Justice and Courts Act 2015 s 2(1) and (7). In force 13/4/15, Criminal Justice and Courts Act 2015 (Commencement No 1, Saving and Transitional Provisions) Order 2015 2015/778 para 3 and Sch 1 para 2
[721] As inserted by Counter-Terrorism and Border Security Act 2019 s 9(5) In force 12 April 2019, Counter-Terrorism and Border Security Act 2019 s 27(3).
[722] Criminal Justice Act 2003 s 226A(10)(a) and 226B(8)(a) make this requirement.

Steps 2 and 3 are in Criminal Justice Act 2003 s 226A(10) and 226B(8).
Step 3 Would the offence have constituted a 'specified offence' if committed on the day the offender was convicted of the offence?[723] For the list of specified offences see **56.18**. If Yes, go to Step 4. If No, the court cannot pass an extended sentence.

Step 4 Is there a 'significant risk of serious harm'?

Statutory provisions and general principles

56.23 ***Step 4***

Step 4 Is there 'a significant risk to members of the public of serious harm occasioned by the commission of further specified offences by the offender'? Criminal Justice Act 2003 s 226A(1)(b) and 226B(1)(b) sets out Step 4. 'Serious harm' means 'death or serious personal injury, whether physical or psychological', Criminal Justice Act 2003 s 224(3), see **56.25**.

If Yes, and the defendant is aged 18+, go to Step 5, at **56.59**. If Yes and the defendant is aged under 18, go to Step 6, at **56.63**. If No, the court may not pass an extended sentence.

Note: The following cases primarily deal with IPP but the principles are likely to be applied when the courts consider extended sentences. Ed.

56.24 ***Significant risk of serious harm Statutory provisions***

Criminal Justice Act 2003 s 226A(1) This section applies where:

(a) a person aged 18 or over is convicted of a specified offence (see **56.17**) (whether the offence was committed before or after this section comes into force),

(b) the court considers that there is a <u>significant risk to members of the public of serious harm</u> occasioned by the commission by the offender of further specified offences (see **56.23**).

Criminal Justice Act 2003 s 226B(1) This section applies where:

(a) a person aged under 18 is convicted of a specified offence (see **56.17**) (whether the offence was committed before or after this section comes into force),

(b) the court considers that there is a <u>significant risk to members of the public of serious harm</u> occasioned by the commission by the offender of further specified offences (see **56.30**).

Note: The underlining is added for emphasis. Ed.

R v Abdallah and Others 2016 EWCA Crim 1868, 2017 1 Cr App R (S) 29 (p 204) LCJ G was convicted of terrorist offences. para 9 The Judge found there was no risk of significant harm to members of the public in the UK. He found there was such a risk in Syria. Held. para 14 The phrase must be intended to include the public in other countries. It will, nevertheless, only be relevant to consider the risk of harm to such persons where the further specified offences in contemplation are offences which, in view of their territorial scope, are capable of causing harm abroad. G's extended sentences upheld.

56.25 ***'Serious harm', Definition of***

Criminal Justice Act 2003 s 224(3) 'Serious harm' means death or serious personal injury, whether physical or psychological.

R v Lang 2005 EWCA Crim 2864, 2006 2 Cr App R (S) 3 (p 13) para 17(i) The risk identified must be significant. This is a higher threshold than mere possibility of occurrence and in our view can be taken to mean (as in the Oxford Dictionary) 'noteworthy, of considerable amount or importance'.

para 19 The risk to be assessed is to 'members of the public'. This seems to be an all-embracing term. It is wider than 'others', which would exclude the offender himself. We see no reason to construe it so as to exclude any particular group, for example prison officers or staff at mental hospitals, all of whom, like the offender, are members of the public. In some cases, particular members of the public may be more at risk than members of the public generally, for example when an offender has a history of violence

[723] Criminal Justice Act 2003 s 226A(10)(b) and 226B(8)(b) make this requirement.

to cohabitees or of sexually abusing children of cohabitees, or, as in one of the cases before us, where the offender has a particular problem in relation to a particular woman. *R v Pedley* 2009 EWCA Crim 840, 2010 1 Cr App R (S) 24 (p 132) In *R v Lang* 2005 the Court noted that the dictionary definition of 'significant' is 'noteworthy, of considerable amount or importance'. That was not to substitute a different expression for the statute, but was and remains a helpful indication of what kind of risk is in issue. It is wholly unhelpful to redefine 'significant risk' in terms of numerical probability, whether as 'more probable than not' or by any other percentage of likelihood. No attempt should be made by sentencers to attach arithmetical values to the qualitative assessment which the statute requires of them. Such would, moreover, be inconsistent with the degree of flexibility inherent in the word 'significant'. However, In *R v Lang* 2005 at para 17 the Court had said that a 'significant risk' presented a higher threshold than a mere possibility of occurrence. Some risk is not enough. It must be significant.

56.26 *Significant risk How to assess General principles*

R v Lang 2005 EWCA Crim 2864, 2006 2 Cr App R (S) 3 (p 13) para 7 and 11 Significant risk must be shown in relation to two matters: first, the commission of further specified, but not necessarily serious, offences, and second, the causing thereby of serious harm to members of the public. Serious harm is defined in section 224(3) as meaning 'death or serious personal injury, whether physical or psychological'. It is a concept familiar since Criminal Justice Act 1991 s 2(2)(b)[724] and previous decisions of this Court will continue to be relevant to its assessment. For example, as was said in *R v Bowler* 1994 15 Cr App R(S) 78, sexual assaults which are relatively minor physically may lead to serious psychological injury, and downloading indecent images of children may cause serious psychological injury to a child arising not only from what the child has been forced to do but also from the knowledge that others will see what they were doing (see *R v Collard* 2004 EWCA Crim 1664, 2005 1 Cr App R (S) 34 (p 155)).

para 17 The following factors should be borne in mind when a sentencer is assessing significant risk:

i) The risk identified must be significant. This is a higher threshold than mere possibility of occurrence and in our view can be taken to mean (as in the Oxford Dictionary) 'noteworthy, of considerable amount or importance'.

ii) In assessing the risk of further offences being committed, the sentencer should take into account the nature and circumstances of the current offence, the offender's history of offending including not just the kind of offence but its circumstances and the sentence passed, details of which the prosecution must have available, and whether the offending demonstrates any pattern, social and economic factors in relation to the offender including accommodation, employability, education, associates, relationships and drug or alcohol abuse, and the offender's thinking, attitude towards offending and supervision and emotional state. Information in relation to these matters will most readily, though not exclusively, come from antecedents and pre-sentence probation and medical reports. The guide for sentence for public protection issued in June 2005 for the National Probation Service affords valuable guidance for probation officers. The guidance in relation to assessment of dangerousness in paragraph 5 is compatible with the terms of this judgment.

iii) If the foreseen specified offence is serious, there will clearly be some cases, though not by any means all, in which there may be a significant risk of serious harm. For example, robbery is a serious offence. But it can be committed in a wide variety of ways many of which do not give rise to a significant risk of serious harm. Sentencers must therefore guard against assuming there is a significant risk of serious harm merely because the foreseen specified offence is serious. A pre-sentence report should usually be obtained before any sentence is passed

[724] Repealed by Powers of Criminal Courts (Sentencing) Act 2000 Sch 12 para 1

which is based on significant risk of serious harm. In a small number of cases, where the circumstances of the current offence or the history of the offender suggest mental abnormality on his part, a medical report may be necessary before risk can properly be assessed.

iv) If the foreseen specified offence is not serious, there will be comparatively few cases in which a risk of serious harm will properly be regarded as significant. The huge variety of offences in Schedule 15 includes many which, in themselves, are not suggestive of serious harm. Repetitive violent or sexual offending at a relatively low level without serious harm does not of itself give rise to a significant risk of serious harm in the future. There may, in such cases, be some risk of future victims being more adversely affected than past victims but this, of itself, does not give rise to significant risk of serious harm.

v) (No longer relevant. Ed.)

vi) In relation to offenders under 18 and adults with no relevant previous convictions at the time the specified offence was committed, the court's discretion under section 229(2) [evidence provisions, see **56.41**] is not constrained by any initial assumption such as, under section 229(3) [the repealed presumption provision], applies to adults with previous convictions. It is still necessary, when sentencing young offenders, to bear in mind that, within a shorter time than adults, they may change and develop. This and their level of maturity may be highly pertinent when assessing what their future conduct may be and whether it may give rise to significant risk of serious harm.

R v Pedley 2009 EWCA Crim 840, 2010 1 Cr App R (S) 24 (p 132) The question whether the risk of serious harm is, in any individual case, significant so as to justify an IPP sentence is highly fact-sensitive. It must remain a decision for the careful assessment of the judge before whom the case comes. He will need to consider all the information about the defendant. In addressing the question whether the risk of serious harm is significant, the judge is entitled to balance the probability of harm against the nature of it if it occurs. The harm under consideration must of course be serious harm before the question even arises. But we agree that within the concept of significant risk there is built in a degree of flexibility which enables a judge to conclude that a somewhat lower probability of particularly grave harm may be significant and conversely that a somewhat greater probability of less grave harm may not be.

R v Brook 2012 EWCA Crim 136, 2 Cr App R (S) 76 (p 433) D was convicted of manslaughter on the basis of provocation. The attack was ferocious and relentless. D had no convictions. The pre-sentence report concluded that D was a 'dangerous' offender. Held. para 14 The Judge was bound to make the assumption that D's loss of control was reasonable in all the circumstances. It is therefore difficult to see how loss of control could provide the basis for a 'significant risk'. The analysis in the pre-sentence report was compelling but in critical respects it was wholly inconsistent with the jury's verdict. IPP quashed.

R v Ali 2016 EWCA Crim 1335 D pleaded to GBH with intent, ABH and dangerous driving. He drove at the doorman of a club, V, and continued to drive when V was underneath his car. V had catastrophic brain injuries. D also drove at two other people, one of whom was injured. D's alcohol reading was 102 μg and there was cocaine in his blood. D was aged 19 and when aged 14, he was convicted of two batteries. The pre-sentence report said the offences were out of character and D had good victim empathy. The psychiatric report said there was no evidence of mental illness and considered the most likely explanation for the offence was intoxication. Neither report supported a finding of dangerousness. The Judge said the authors of the reports were not lawyers and the facts of the offending showed he was dangerous. The Judge started at 15 years and passed a 15-year extended sentence (11 years' custody 4 years' extended licence). Held. A judge is not bound by the findings in reports. We do not say a judge cannot find dangerousness solely on the facts of the offence. However, there must be a

proper basis for such a finding. It is not sufficient simply to say that the offending was truly appalling and given the background history as set out in the pre-sentence report [or] the psychiatric report, dangerousness was made out. Judges must be careful when finding dangerousness for young offenders, especially when there is no pattern of offending. The Judge did not explain why he rejected the findings in the two reports. Nor did he explain how the offence gave rise to the required risk. The sentencer must explain how he reached his finding. There was no proper basis for the finding of significant risk. The court has a discretion whether to pass an extended sentence when dangerousness is found. para 32 Here, had a finding of dangerousness been justified, the appropriate sentence would still have been a determinate sentence.
Note: This last finding appears to have been based on the pre-sentence finding that D will address his risks and the safeguards built into the Parole Board's discretion whether to release a prisoner, see para 31 of the judgment. Ed.

56.27 ***Significant risk How to assess Risk must be a future risk***
R v Johnson and Others 2006 EWCA Crim 2486, 2007 1 Cr App R (S) 112 (p 674) IPP is concerned with future risks and public protection. Although punitive in effect, with far-reaching consequences for the offender on whom it is imposed, strictly speaking, it does not represent punishment for past offending: when the information before the court is evaluated, for the purposes of this sentence, the decision is directed not to the past, but to the future, and the future protection of the public.
Note: Courts are likely to consider this guidance applies to extended sentences as well as IPP. Ed.
See also: *Att-Gen's Ref No 56 of 2006* 2006 EWCA Crim 2296, 2007 1 Cr App R (S) 96 (p 558) (Knife used in Post Office robbery. No harm was done. Held. The court must look to the future risk.)

56.28 ***Significant risk How to assess Children and young offenders***
Sentencing Children and Young People Guideline 2017, see www.banksr.com Other Matters Guidelines tab page 8 In force 1 June 2017
Dangerousness
2.5 A 'significant risk' is more than a mere possibility of occurrence. The assessment of dangerousness should take into account all the available information relating to the circumstances of the offence and **may** also take into account any information regarding previous patterns of behaviour relating to this offence and any other relevant information relating to the child or young person. In making this assessment it will be essential to obtain a pre-sentence report.
2.6 Children and young people may change and develop within a shorter time than adults and this factor, along with their level of maturity, may be highly relevant when assessing probable future conduct and whether it may cause a significant risk of serious harm.[725]
2.7 In anything but the most serious cases it may be impossible for the court to form a view as to whether the child or young person would meet the criteria of the dangerous offender provisions without greater knowledge of the circumstances of the offence and the child or young person. In those circumstances jurisdiction for the case should be retained in the Youth Court. If, following a guilty plea or a finding of guilt, the dangerousness criteria appear to be met then the child or young person should be committed **for sentence**.
Sentencing Children and Young People Guideline 2017, see www.banksr.com Other Matters Guidelines tab page 31 In force 1 June 2017
6.59 A sentence of detention for life should be used as a last resort when an extended sentence is not able to provide the level of public protection that is necessary. In order to determine this, the court should consider the following factors in the order given:

[725] *R v Lang* 2005 EWCA Crim 2864, 2006 2 Cr App R (S) 3 (p 13)

- the seriousness of the offence;
- the child or young person's previous findings of guilt;
- the level of danger posed to the public and whether there is a reliable estimate of the length of time the child or young person will remain a danger; and
- the alternative sentences available.

The court is required to set a minimum term which must be served in custody before parole can be considered.

R v Lang 2005 EWCA Crim 2864, 2006 2 Cr App R (S) 3 (p 13) para 7 and 11. The following factors should be borne in mind when a sentencer is assessing significant risk: i)-v) [not listed, see **56.26**]

vi) In relation to offenders under 18 and adults with no relevant previous convictions at the time the specified offence was committed, the court's discretion under section 229(2) [evidence provisions, see **56.41**] is not constrained by any initial assumption. It is still necessary, when sentencing young offenders, to bear in mind that, within a shorter time than adults, they may change and develop. This and their level of maturity may be highly pertinent when assessing what their future conduct may be and whether it may give rise to significant risk of serious harm.

Dangerous Offenders Guide 2008, see www.banksr.com Other Matters Guidelines tab para 6.5.1 The court should be particularly rigorous before concluding that a youth is a dangerous offender. When assessing likely future conduct and whether it may give rise to a significant risk of serious harm, the court should consider the offender's level of maturity and that he or she may change and develop in a shorter period of time than an adult.

6.5.2 When assessing the risk of the offender committing further specified offences, a young person is less likely than an adult to have an extensive criminal record. Accordingly, when preparing a pre-sentence report, the youth offending team looks not only at the offender's previous convictions but also at any evidence of violence or sexual aggression at home, at school or amongst the offender's peer group that may not have resulted in a conviction. Subject to paras 6.2.3 and 6.3.3.4, the court may have regard to this information.

6.5.3 The Youth Justice Board anticipates that normally the court would find a youth to be a dangerous offender only if he or she was assessed in a pre-sentence report to pose a very high risk of serious harm or, in a small number of cases and due to specific circumstances, a high risk of serious harm (see para 6.4.5 above). However, as noted at para 6.1.4 above, the court is not bound by the assessment of risk in the pre-sentence report; it does not follow automatically that, because an offender has been assessed as posing a high risk or very high risk of serious harm, he or she is a dangerous offender (see, for instance, para 6.5.6).

Note: This is not a definitive guideline. Ed.

R v Chowdhury 2016 EWCA Crim 1341, 2 Cr App R (S) 41 (p 452) D, who was aged 18 at the date of the offence, pleaded to assault by penetration. Held. Sentencers should be careful when reaching a finding of dangerousness in relation to young people, especially when there is no pattern of offending. Young people are more likely to act impulsively, more likely to be responsive to any sentence imposed, and more likely to effect change, especially when any sentence is likely to be long.

56.29 *Significant risk How to assess Few women face the risk*

R v Robson 2006 EWCA Crim 1414, 2007 1 Cr App R (S) 54 (p 301) D was convicted of sexual assault. He was aged 17 and had breached a supervision order for exposure. He pinned a girl against a wall and slid his hand up her skirt. Held. We doubt whether it would be right to say that an offender represents a significant risk that women would be caused serious harm if only a relatively small proportion of women would be susceptible to severe psychological injury as a result of what the offender might do.

Note: This is a surprising result as the interpretation does not follow the simple words in section 225(1) (now section 226A(1)(b)) and fails to provide the necessary protection for these women. Ed.

Step 4 Is there a 'significant risk of serious harm'? Offence considerations

56.30 ***Significant risk How to assess No intent to cause harm***
Criminal Justice Act 2003 s 143(1) In considering the seriousness of any offence, the court must consider the offender's culpability in committing the offence and any harm which the offence caused, was intended to cause or might foreseeably have caused.
R v Johnson and Others 2006 EWCA Crim 2486, 2007 1 Cr App R (S) 112 (p 674) It does not automatically follow, from the absence of actual harm caused by the offender to date, that the risk that he will cause serious harm in the future is negligible. Where the facts of the instant offence or indeed any specified offences for the purposes of section 229(3) are examined, it may emerge that no harm actually occurred. That may be advantageous to the offender, and some of the cases examined in *R v Lang* 2005 EWCA Crim 2864, 2006 2 Cr App R (S) 3 (p 13) exemplify the point. Another such example is *R v Isa* 2005 EWCA Crim 3330, 2006 2 Cr App R (S) 29 (p 192). On the other hand the absence of harm may be entirely fortuitous. A victim cowering away from an armed assailant may avoid direct physical injury or serious psychological harm. Faced with such a case, the sentencer considering dangerousness may wish to reflect, for example, on the likely response of the offender if his victim, instead of surrendering, resolutely defended himself. It does not automatically follow from the absence of actual harm caused by the offender to date that the risk that he will cause serious harm in the future is negligible.
R v Hogan 2006 EWCA Crim 2691, 2007 1 Cr App R (S) 110 (p 665) D pleaded to manslaughter. He had been drinking throughout the day, and had consumed about 14 pints of beer in a pub. He had become agitated and irritating. V was also drinking in the local pub and went to put some music on the jukebox. D took offence to V's choice of music, marched towards V aggressively and punched V once in the face. The punch was strong and powerful. V fell to the floor. There was blood coming from V's mouth and swelling to his face and forehead. D continued to act aggressively and shouted at V. He threatened to punch V again if he got up from the floor. V also suffered an undetected injury, a fracture across the floor of his skull. Complications arose which resulted in the development of meningitis and encephalitis from which V subsequently died. D did not intend to cause any serious harm. He was aged 28 and had served a total of 3 years' detention for robbery, affray, theft and criminal damage. Held. Although the index offence did not involve any intention to cause really serious harm, it was a remarkable display of aggression and lack of self-control. This was an entirely unprovoked attack on an inoffensive man. The single blow was one of considerable force. Moreover, it was preceded and accompanied by aggressive behaviour over a period of time.
Att-Gen's Ref No 55 of 2008 2008 EWCA Crim 2790, 2009 2 Cr App R (S) 22 (p 142) LCJ We are troubled by what the Judge described as his reluctance "to impose an indefinite sentence for a crime which, though obviously of the gravest kind in its category, is not one in which harm was desired or intended". That approach influenced him on the element of proportionality. Our reservations arise in part from the terms of Criminal Justice Act 2003 s 143 and in part because, as we have emphasised, the issue remains the risk to the public, not simply what the offender desired or intended. Thus, for example, a reckless offender, or an offender with little or no insight into the consequences of his actions, may represent a significant risk to the public. In short, an order of IPP may be fully justified notwithstanding that, in the broadest sense, the offender did not intend or desire the outcome of his actions. Moreover, the proportionality issue is at least in part addressed by conditions 3A and 3B themselves, and by the removal of the previous statutory assumption relating to the assessment of dangerousness in section 229. If the harm consequent on any individual offence was not intended

or desired by the offender, then, in the context of condition 3B, a determinate sentence of 4 years' or more imprisonment is less likely to be appropriate. On the other hand, a relatively minor offence may well reignite concern about the element of public danger posed by a defendant who has already committed one of the very serious offences identified in condition 3A. These considerations are all relevant to the court's decision.
R v Pedley 2009 EWCA Crim 840, 2010 1 Cr App R (S) 24 (p 132) The requirement that there must be a significant risk not only of reoffending, but of harm that can properly be called serious, must not be watered down. That emerges very clearly from the practical advice to sentencers contained in *R v Lang* 2005, all of which we endorse. We do not agree that it follows that there is any justification for attempting a redefinition of the plain English expression 'significant risk…of serious harm'.

56.31 *Significant risk How to assess No harm done*
R v Islam 2006 EWCA Crim 1523, 2007 1 Cr App R (S) 43 (p 244) There is no general requirement for the purpose of an assessment of dangerousness either in considering the serious offence in respect of which sentence is being passed or in considering any previous relevant offence which may bring into operation the assumption specified in section 229(3) that actual serious harm, physical or psychological, has in fact been caused. The risk may be established where the instant serious offence of antecedent relevant offences happened not to have caused serious harm, either physical or psychological.
Note: Although the assumption has been repealed, the principle is in line with other cases that the real issue is the future prediction and not the actual results of the offence that is to be sentenced for. Ed.
R v Pedley 2009 EWCA Crim 840, 2010 1 Cr App R (S) 24 (p 132) There is a commonly advanced submission that because the defendant has not yet caused serious harm, it *necessarily* follows that there cannot be a significant risk that he will do so in future, and thus that offences which did not cause serious harm should be ignored. That commonly made submission is wrong.
See also: *R v McGrady* 2006 EWCA Crim 1547, 2007 1 Cr App R (S) 45 (p 256) (Aggressive bag snatch leaving woman in distress. Previous for section 20. Insufficient proof of significant risk.)
R v Logan 2006 EWCA Crim 3007, 2007 2 Cr App R (S) 7 (p 259) (Defendant used syringe with needle to threaten women at ATM robberies. No harm done. This was a classic case for IPP.)

56.32 *Significant risk How to assess Risk not based on current offence*
R v Green 2007 EWCA Crim 2172, 2008 1 Cr App R (S) 97 (p 579) D pleaded to causing death by careless driving, aggravated vehicle-taking and section 20 wounding. The prosecution dropped a section 18 charge because they had witness difficulties and accepted an offer of a plea to section 20. When driving at speed on a motorway he lost control of his car and killed one of his passengers. About five months later, he stabbed someone twice in the neck. It was accepted that the Judge was entitled to find the dangerousness criteria were made out but the defence suggested that the Judge could not 'deploy that finding for the causing death offence'. Held. Criminal Justice Act 2003 s 225 does not require any kind of *nexus* between the particular facts of the particular offence and the finding of dangerousness. Once a defendant has been convicted of a serious offence within the meaning of the Act, whatever the facts and nature, it is perfectly possible for a finding of dangerousness to be made on the basis of material which has no close relationship to the actual offence for which sentence is being passed.

56.33 *Significant risk How to assess Was the offence(s) an isolated incident?*
R v Bailey 2006 EWCA Crim 144, 2 Cr App R (S) 50 (p 323) D pleaded to ABH (3 years' imprisonment with an extension period of 2 years). D, with others fuelled by drink, repeatedly and relentlessly attacked V, kicking, punching and stamping on him. The Judge said the attack was "like hyenas to the kill". V suffered multiple bruises and

grazes to his head and body, a nosebleed and blood in his urine. They were not serious or long-lasting. D, aged 19, had two convictions. In 2004, there was an assault in which the victim was kicked to the ground. In 2005, there was a theft of a mobile. Held. This was a terrible, vicious and really sustained attack and this Court has rarely, if ever, seen a worse case of street violence. It was appalling. D was fortunate that V's injuries were not significantly graver. There was no reasonable basis of determining that a risk of significance had been demonstrated that D would either kill someone or cause them serious injury in the foreseeable future. His previous convictions did not reveal a pattern of behaviour that leads to this grave conclusion. It was no more than ABH which falls short of serious personal injury. The conviction and the conviction for battery both stand as essentially isolated incidents neither of which involved infliction of serious harm to another. The criteria had not been satisfied. His behaviour had not yet reached the stage where it can properly be concluded that he poses a significant risk of serious harm to others. The extension period is quashed.

Att-Gen's Ref No 5 of 2011 2011 EWCA Crim 1244, 2012 1 Cr App R (S) 20 (p 103) D was convicted of wounding with intent, GBH and sexual assault. He had attacked a woman walking home at night, with gross violence. There were splits, cuts and tears to the genitalia. He was of good character and the offence was unexplained and out of character. Held. The assessment of risk for the future was an exceptionally difficult task. The offender had committed an offence which was out of character. For that reason, an IPP sentence had to be imposed as a long determinate sentence was not sufficient to deal with the future risk.

See also: *R v Veseli* 2008 EWCA Crim 2965 (The fact that the offence was a cold-blooded and near-fatal stabbing was relevant to future risk but by itself was not capable of supporting a finding of dangerousness. A finding of dangerousness may be made even where there had been no previous convictions to establish a pattern of violence. 15 years' determinate not IPP.)

Step 4 Is there a 'significant risk of serious harm'? Defendant's situation

56.34 *Significant risk How to assess Defendant on licence*

R v Smith 2011 UKSC 37, 2012 1 Cr App R (S) 83 (p 489) Supreme Court (*R v Smith* 2010 EWCA Crim 246 on appeal) D was on licence from a life sentence. He reoffended and he was recalled. He later received an IPP sentence. He argued that he could not be released from his licence until he no longer posed a significant risk of serious harm. He would no longer pose such a risk so IPP would not be made out. Held. To ask a judge to consider whether a defendant will pose such a risk to the public, for example after he has served 6 years, places an unrealistic burden on him or her. The risk must be considered on the premise that he is at large when the sentencing exercise is conducted.

Note: For a critical analysis of the decision in *R v Smith* 2011, see 2011 Crim LR 892 and *Criminal Law Week* 28 July 2011 para 16. Ed.

R v MJ 2012 EWCA Crim 132, 2 Cr App R (S) 73 (p 416) LCJ We do not share the concerns expressed in *Criminal Law Week* about the impact of [the observations in *R v Smith* 2011 UKSC 37]. As a matter of principle and practice, the decision in *R v Smith* 2011 underlines that the decision whether IPP should be ordered is made, and can only be made, at the date of the sentencing hearing.

56.35 *Significant risk How to assess Defendant drunk*

R v Chapman 2007 EWCA Crim 2593, 2008 1 Cr App R (S) 103 (p 607) D pleaded to manslaughter. The victim, V, aged 78, saw D and T urinating against a wall at the entrance of a supermarket. Both had consumed a considerable amount of alcohol. V remonstrated with them. T swore at V and V aimed a few weak punches at T. D grabbed V by the shoulders and pulled him to the ground with considerable force. V's ribs were fractured, pneumonia was caused and he died. D had a large number of previous convictions, including five offences against the person, two of which were for ABH. In

passing sentence the Judge said that he had to take into account both the circumstances of this offence and his previous record. The Judge said the offence had been caused by him becoming blind drunk and behaving appallingly in public. Held. It may well be that because of his drunken state D did not realise that he might cause serious harm by acting as he did and did not appreciate the age of his victim, but there is an obvious public risk if D gets himself so drunk as to behave in such a way without realising the potential consequences. Nor can this be regarded as being simply a one-off piece of behaviour. He is somebody with a propensity to violence when drunk. 2 years' IPP affirmed.
Note: This is a very fact-specific case. Ed.

56.36 ***Significant risk How to assess Defendant is or will be undergoing treatment***

Att-Gen's Ref No 134 of 2006 2007 EWCA Crim 309, 2 Cr App R (S) 54 (p 332) D pleaded to rape of a 12-year-old child and other sex offences in relation to children. Held. The Judge fell into error by saying D was not dangerous because he was suitable for a sex offender treatment programme and that he was willing to participate in such a programme. That is to speculate that he will successfully complete the programme, of which there is no guarantee. IPP with an increased minimum term substituted.

R v Nurthen 2014 EWCA Crim 83 D pleaded to wounding with intent and false imprisonment. For some weeks he failed to take his medication. On Christmas Day, D drank a bottle of champagne and became highly delusional and psychotic. He seized V, a stranger in the street, and held a knife to his throat saying at first he wanted it all and later saying he was fed up with his life and was going to kill V. Police arrived and asked a question whereupon D cut V. V was absolutely terrified. D suffered from a delusional disorder. He self-harmed when he was under high levels of distress and anxiety. A psychiatrist said D would be dangerous in the future if he failed to take his medication and/or took alcohol. Held. The sentencing Judge was perfectly entitled, indeed bound to consider the risk posed by D when he is released into the community. It is unhelpful to refer to this as a 'contingent risk'. It is simply a risk of the individual committing further specified offences in the future, and serious harm resulting. Whether such harm is in fact done is of course dependent upon the circumstances in which the offender finds himself in the future, and the choices he makes. It is one thing for D to maintain his drug regime and alcohol abstinence whilst in prison, and quite another as to whether he will continue to do so upon release without the discipline of the prison regime, albeit with the supervision of the probation service during the licence period. Extended sentence upheld.

See also: *R v Brennan* 2015 EWCA Crim 1449 and 2014 EWCA Crim 2387 (D pleaded to manslaughter based on diminished responsibility. The Court of Appeal quashed his murder conviction. The victim was killed in May 2013. The Court of Appeal assessed the case in July 2015. Held. This was a shocking and savage murder on a defenceless man. D was a deeply troubled and damaged young man. Since his remand there had been a profound improvement. Two psychiatrists said because of the treatment his risk to others was low. D was not [now] dangerous whatever the position was in 2013. For more detail see **283.61** in Volume 2.)

56.37 ***Significant risk How to assess Is the relevant time the date of the offence or the sentence or the release?***

R v Smith 2011 UKSC 37, 2012 1 Cr App R (S) 83 (p 489) Supreme Court It would place an unrealistic burden on the sentencing judge if the correct construction of Criminal Justice Act 2003 s 225(1)(b) was that the judge must consider whether he will pose a significant risk when he has served his sentence. Imagine, as in this case, that the defendant's conduct calls for a determinate sentence of 12 years. It is asking a lot of a judge to expect him to form a view as to whether the defendant will pose a significant risk to the public when he has served 6 years. We do not consider that section 225(1)(b) requires such an exercise. Rather it is implicit that the question posed by section 225(1)(b) must be answered on the premise that the defendant is at large. It is at the moment that he imposes the sentence that the judge must decide whether, on that premise, the defendant poses a significant risk of causing serious harm to members of the public.

Note: For a critical analysis of the decision in *R v Smith*, see 2011 Crim LR 892 and *Criminal Law Week* 28 July 2011 para 16. Ed.

R v MJ 2012 EWCA Crim 132, 2 Cr App R (S) 73 (p 416) LCJ We do not share the concerns expressed in *Criminal Law Week* about the impact of [the observations in *R v Smith* 2011 UKSC 37]. As a matter of principle and practice, the decision in *Smith* underlines that the decision whether IPP should be ordered is made, and can only be made, at the date of the sentencing hearing. That is the date when the sentencing court is required to form its opinion whether there is a significant risk to members of the public, which includes police custody officers, prison officers and fellow prisoners.

R (Sturnham) v Parole Board and Another (Nos 1 and 2) 2013 UKSC 47 Supreme Court D was sentenced to IPP and after the expiry of his minimum term he was refused parole. He brought a civil action against the Parole Board. An issue arose as to whether there was a different test for 'significant risk' at the time of imposition of the sentence and at the time of release. Additionally, the correctness of *R v Smith* 2011 (see above) was considered. Held. (*Obiter* in relation to the test on imposition of IPP) para 29 The equation of 'substantial' risk with any risk that is 'not merely perceptible or minimal' tends to change the focus or starting point in a way which might influence the conclusion. It is preferable to concentrate on the statutory language and not to paraphrase. para 33 [We are] far from satisfied that *R v Smith* 2011 is the last word. In a number of other cases, the predictive approach appears to have been assumed to be correct for the imposition of IPP. In *R v Johnson and Others* 2006 EWCA Crim 2486, 2007 1 Cr App R (S) 112 (p 674), it was said that "It does not automatically follow from the absence of actual harm caused by the offender to date [i.e. to the date of sentencing], that the risk that he will cause serious harm in the future is negligible". para 36 The reasoning in *R v Smith* 2011 does not address the relationship between discretionary life sentences and IPP or consider what basis there could be for requiring a different approach to the assessment of risk under the latter, when compared with the former. para 38 [We] have grave reservations about the reasoning in *R v Smith* 2011 para 15. However, as it was not challenged on this appeal [we] can say no more.

R v Atkinson 2018 EWCA Crim 1612 D pleaded to attempted robbery and having a bladed article. In November 2017, D entered a newsagent's brandishing a knife and demanded money. In interview he made full admissions. In early 2017, D's alcohol consumption had escalated and he was abusing drugs. That had led to D resigning from his job the week before the robbery. The pre-sentence report said, 'D had accumulated debts and had been subject to various personal crises. D's personal circumstances were very different at the date of the sentence. There was less stress and he was capable of acting and thinking rationally.' The Judge passed an 8½-year extended sentence (4½ years' custody 4 years' extended licence). Held. The time to assess dangerousness is at the date of sentence, not the date of the offence. We quash the extended sentence as there was no basis for such a finding at the date of sentence.

See also: *R v Brennan* 2015 EWCA Crim 1449 and 2014 EWCA Crim 2387 (Plea to manslaughter based on diminished responsibility. Murder conviction quashed. Killing May 2013. Court of Appeal assessment July 2015. Held. This was a shocking and savage murder on a defenceless man. D was a deeply troubled and damaged young man. Since his remand there had been a profound improvement. Two psychiatrists said because of the treatment his risk to others was low. D was not [now] dangerous whatever the position was in 2013. For more detail see **283.61** in Volume 2.)

56.38 *Significant risk How to assess Defendant aged under 18*
Dangerous Offenders Guide 2008, see www.banksr.com Other Matters Guidelines tab para 6.5.1 The court should be particularly rigorous before concluding that a youth is a dangerous offender.[726] When assessing likely future conduct and whether it may give rise to a significant risk of serious harm, the court should consider the offender's level of maturity and that he or she may change and develop in a shorter period of time than an adult.[727]
6.5.2 When assessing the risk of the offender committing further specified offences, a young person is less likely than an adult to have an extensive criminal record. Accordingly, when preparing a pre-sentence report, the youth offending team looks not only at the offender's previous convictions but also at any evidence of violence or sexual aggression at home, at school or amongst the offender's peer group that may not have resulted in a conviction.[728] Subject to paras 6.2.3 and 6.3.3.4, the court may have regard to this information.
6.5.3 The Youth Justice Board anticipates that normally the court would find a youth to be a dangerous offender only if he or she was assessed in a pre-sentence report to pose a very high risk of serious harm or, in a small number of cases and due to specific circumstances, a high risk of serious harm (see para 6.4.5 above).[729] However, as noted at para 6.1.4 above, the court is not bound by the assessment of risk in the pre-sentence report; it does not follow automatically that, because an offender has been assessed as posing a high risk or very high risk of serious harm, he or she is a dangerous offender (see, for instance, para 6.5.6).[730]
Note: This is not a definitive guideline. Ed.
R v Ali 2016 EWCA Crim 1335 D pleaded to GBH with intent. D was aged 19. Held. Judges must be careful when finding dangerousness for young offenders, especially when there is no pattern of offending. Here there was no proper basis for the finding of significant risk.
For more detail, see **56.10**.

56.39 *Significant risk How to assess No explanation for offending*
R v Groombridge 2013 EWCA Crim 274 D pleaded (at the PCMH) to attempting to choke, suffocate or strangle under Offences Against the Person Act 1861 s 21, and two thefts. He left home and was unable to pay rent/board whilst staying with various friends. He visited his great-grandmother, strangled her and smothered her with a cushion. She was vulnerable, aged 92 and soiled herself. D, aged 16, was of previous good character. Held. An extended sentence was necessary. There was no reason for, or understanding of, how and why D came to act so violently towards his great-grandmother. If he was provoked to act in that way because he was upset or worried by the possibility of not being able to pay for his keep, then there must have been a significant risk of serious harm.
See also: *Att-Gen's Ref 2017 Re Smith* 2017 EWCA Crim 252, 2 Cr App R (S) 2 (p 5) (D pleaded to two rapes (vaginal and oral) and an assault by penetration. He raped a 14-year-old girl using threats and holding a Stanley knife. Girl badly affected. D then aged 31 and now aged 37 with a good character. Held. There was planning and premeditation. The Judge gave too much weight to the fact it was an isolated incident and not enough weight to the absence of an explanation for the rape. Extended sentence substituted.)

[726] *CPS v South East Surrey Youth Court* 2005 EWHC 2929 (Admin), 2006 2 Cr App R (S) 26 (p 177) at 17(iii), see **56.14**.
[727] *R v Lang* 2005 EWCA Crim 2864, 2006 2 Cr App R (S) 3 (p 13) at para 17(vi)
[728] *Youth Justice Board, Criminal Justice Act 2003, 'Dangerousness' and the New Sentences for Public Protection, Guidance for youth offending teams*, 2006, p 9
[729] *Youth Justice Board, Criminal Justice Act 2003, 'Dangerousness' and the New Sentences for Public Protection, Guidance for youth offending teams*, 2006, p 10
[730] *Youth Justice Board, Criminal Justice Act 2003, 'Dangerousness' and the New Sentences for Public Protection, Guidance for youth offending teams*, 2006, p 11

56.40 ***Significant risk How to assess Parents of victim at risk***
R v Farrar 2006 EWCA Crim 3261, 2007 2 Cr App R (S) 35 (p 202) D pleaded to abducting a child and sexually assaulting the same child. The Judge decided that there was a significant risk of serious harm to boys and their parents, describing the incident as "every parent's worst nightmare". Held. We regard his opinion about harm to parents as speculative. If correct, it would mean that in every case in which a young child was the subject of a sexual offence punishable with 10 years' imprisonment or more, a significant risk of serious harm would be found to exist, and an indefinite sentence imposed. That cannot be right.

Step 4 The evidence Basic principles

56.41 ***Evidence Statutory provisions***
Criminal Justice Act 2003 s 229(2) The court in making the assessment referred to in subsection (1)(b) (the serious risk subsection):

(a) must take into account all such information as is available to it about the nature and circumstances of the offence,
(aa) may take into account all such information as is available to it about the nature and circumstances of any other offences of which the offender has been convicted by a court anywhere in the world,
(b) may take into account any information which is before it about any pattern of behaviour of which any of the offences mentioned in paragraph (a) or (aa) forms part, and
(c) may take into account any information about the offender which is before it.

56.42 ***Evidence Statutory provisions Service convictions***
Criminal Justice Act 2003 s 229(2A)[731] The reference in subsection (2)(aa) above to a conviction by a court includes a reference to:

(a) a conviction of an offence in any service disciplinary proceedings, and
(b) a conviction of a service offence within the meaning of Armed Forces Act 2006 ('conviction' here including anything that under section 376(1) and (2) of that Act is to be treated as a conviction).

(2B) For the purposes of subsection (2A)(a) 'service disciplinary proceedings' means:

(a) any proceedings under Army Act 1955, Air Force Act 1955 or Naval Discipline Act 1957 (whether before a [Court Martial] or any other court or person authorised under any of those Acts to award a punishment in respect of any offence), and
(b) any proceedings before a Standing Civilian Court, and 'conviction' includes the recording of a finding that a charge in respect of the offence has been proved.

56.43 ***Evidence, Need for***
R v Xhelollari 2007 EWCA Crim 2052 D was convicted of rape. He was aged 35 with two theft convictions (both conditionally discharged). The pre-sentence report said there was a high risk of reoffending which was based on the 'extremely serious offence' and the fact that he had been 'unable to take any responsibility for his actions'. The Judge found there was a 'significant risk'. Held. The imposition of a sentence of IPP in this case was wrong in principle. The pre-sentence report did not identify factors which led to a conclusion that there was a significant risk of serious harm posed by D. The risk assessment of the report was based entirely upon the perceived vulnerability of the victim and the unwillingness of D to acknowledge guilt. It recognised, however, the absence of any relevant pattern of offending behaviour and that the final decision was for the Court. The imposition of a sentence in this case seems to us to lead to a conclusion that such sentences would always be passed on a first conviction for rape where, as is always the case, there must have been some psychological harm to the victim and where the offender refuses to admit guilt. That…is an inadequate basis on

[731] Sections 229-230 are moved under a new heading entitled 'Extended sentences' by Legal Aid, Sentencing and Punishment of Offenders Act 2012 Sch 19 para 18 as of 3/12/12.

which to impose an indeterminate sentence on a necessary hypothesis that there is a significant risk of serious harm from future offending. Such a conclusion must be founded upon evidence rather than speculation or mere apprehension of some risk of future harm.

Step 4 The evidence Pre-sentence reports

56.44 ***Statutory provisions***

(These provisions also apply to life sentences based on the dangerousness provisions.)

Pre-sentence reports and other requirements

Criminal Justice Act 2003 s 156(3)[732] Subject to subsection (4), a court must obtain and consider a pre-sentence report before:

(a) in the case of a custodial sentence, forming any such opinion as is mentioned in [Criminal Justice Act 2003] section 152(2) [requirement not to pass a custodial sentence unless the offence was so serious that a fine or community order could not be justified], see **28.26**, section 153(2) [requirement that the sentence should be for the shortest term], see **28.32**, section 225(1)(b) [the significant risk in the dangerousness provisions], see **56.9**, section 226(1)(b) [the significant risk in the dangerousness provisions for those aged under 18], see **56.24**, section 226A(1)(b) [the significant risk in the dangerousness provisions for 2012 extended sentences], see **56.24**, or section 226B(1)(b)] 4 [the significant risk in the dangerousness provisions for the 2012 extended sentences for those aged under 18], see **76.3**, or

(b) [about community sentences, not listed]

(4) Subsection (3) does not apply if, in the circumstances of the case, the court is of the opinion that it is unnecessary to obtain a pre-sentence report.

(5) In a case where the offender is aged under 18, the court must not form the opinion mentioned in subsection (4) unless:

(a) there exists a previous pre-sentence report obtained in respect of the offender, and

(b) the court has had regard to the information contained in that report, or, if there is more than one such report, the most recent report.

56.45 ***Pre-sentence reports Children and young offenders***

On 15 October 2014, the Youth Justice Board set out its instructions to youth offending teams and managers about how to draft reports for courts (referral panel reports and pre-sentence reports), see www.banksr.com Other Matters Other Documents tab. It is an exceptionally focused document giving a wealth of detailed instructions. Paragraph 2.12 prohibits a recommendation either way about the dangerousness of the offender.

56.46 ***Pre-sentence reports Cases***

R v Lang 2005 EWCA Crim 2864, 2006 2 Cr App R (S) 3 (p 13) para 17(i) The sentencer will be guided, but not bound by, the assessment of risk in such reports. A sentencer who contemplates differing from the assessment in such a report should give both counsel the opportunity of addressing the point.

R v Johnson and Others 2006 EWCA Crim 2486, 2007 1 Cr App R (S) 112 (p 674) at para 23 The Judge was not bound to follow the report. It was for him to reach whatever conclusions he deemed appropriate.

Att-Gen's Ref No 145 of 2006 2007 EWCA Crim 692 LCJ D pleaded to sex offences. The Judge did not obtain a pre-sentence report. Held. The Judge ought to have ordered a pre-sentence report. The sentencing court has an obligation under Criminal Justice Act 2003 s 156(3) (see above) to obtain a report before considering this issue unless it is of the opinion that it is unnecessary so to do. At each extreme of the spectrum of sexual offending, it may be that the answer to the question of risk is so clear that no report need be obtained. However, in most cases the court will need help from the Probation Service who use such risk assessment tools as OASys and Risk Matrix 2000 which can provide valuable help to the sentencer in taking this crucial sentencing decision.

---

[732] This section is listed as amended by Legal Aid, Sentencing and Punishment of Offenders Act 2012 Sch 21 para 22.

Note: The Court of Appeal obtained a report so the requirement was met. Ed.
R v Xhelollari 2007 EWCA Crim 2052 D was convicted of rape. He was aged 35 with two theft convictions (both conditionally discharged). The pre-sentence report said there was a high risk of reoffending which was based on the 'extremely serious offence' and the fact he had been 'unable to take any responsibility for his actions'. The Judge found there was a 'significant risk'. Held. The imposition of a sentence of Imprisonment for Public Protection in this case was wrong in principle. The pre-sentence report did not identify factors which led to a conclusion that there was a significant risk of serious harm posed by the appellant. The risk assessment of the report was based entirely upon the perceived vulnerability of the victim and the unwillingness of the appellant to acknowledge guilt. It recognised, however, the absence of any relevant pattern of offending behaviour and that the final decision was for the court. The imposition of a sentence in this case seems to us to lead to a conclusion that such sentences would always be passed on a first conviction for rape where, as is always the case, there must have been some psychological harm to the victim and where the offender refuses to admit guilt. That, in our judgement, is an inadequate basis on which to impose an indeterminate sentence on a necessary hypothesis that there is a significant risk of serious harm from future offending. Such a conclusion must be founded upon evidence rather than speculation or mere apprehension of some risk of future harm.
R v Griffin 2008 EWCA Crim 119, 2 Cr App R (S) 61 (p 357) The risk assessment tools OASys and Risk Matrix 2000 were used in an assessment of D, who had been convicted of manslaughter. The probation officer had criticised the use of Risk Matrix 2000 as it was primarily designed for use with sex offenders. Held. The use of risk assessment tools by the Probation Service is clearly necessary for them because risk assessment is an extremely difficult task and the use has been approved by this Court in *R v Boswell* 2007 EWCA Crim 1587. There was no evidence placed before the Judge in this case, as opposed to criticisms made by counsel, to justify the claim that the probation officer had made inappropriate use of the Risk Matrix 2000 system. The Judge had in mind the criticisms made by defence counsel of that particular risk assessment tool and he heard from her the dangers of the use of it. In any event, it is perfectly clear that the Judge made his own assessment, as is required by statute, no doubt making use of the contents of the report but attaching such weight to them as he thought fit in the light of the criticisms that were made, but it is, as required by statute, the Judge who had to make the assessment.
R v Pedley 2009 EWCA Crim 840, 2010 1 Cr App R (S) 24 (p 132) As this Court was to say in *R v Lang* 2005, there ordinarily should be a report before an IPP sentence is passed, unless of course the point is conceded. Moreover, Criminal Justice Act 2003 s 156 requires such a report before an indeterminate sentence is passed unless the judge considers it unnecessary. If such is not obtained, then on appeal this Court is under a duty to obtain a report unless it concludes either that the judge was right to decide it was not necessary or that it is not now necessary.

56.47 ***Judge rejecting findings of the pre-sentence report***
R v Rocha 2007 EWCA Crim 1505 D pleaded to robbery. The Judge must have, by his assessment of the risk factor, disagreed with the psychiatrist. Held. He was of course not bound by that finding. However, we do not know his reasoning for that rejection. A defendant wants to know what his sentence is and does not want to hear a long speech from the judge, but an indeterminate sentence is a very serious matter and both the appellant and this Court need to be able to understand the judge's reasoning process. Sometimes that may be obvious, but if part of the process involves rejecting the opinion of a suitably qualified expert, as it may be perfectly proper for the judge to do, the Court needs to be able to understand the reason for the sentencing judge not accepting it. Considering the matter again, we quash the IPP.
For the defence cross-examining the author of the report, see **83.12**.

See also the **PRE-SENTENCE REPORTS** chapter and the ***Evidence Bad behaviour with no conviction for it Using reports*** para at **56.57**.

Step 4 The evidence Previous convictions, good character and TICs

56.48 ***Convictions, Using Basic principles***

Criminal Justice Act 2003 s 143(2) In considering the seriousness of an offence ('the current offence') committed by an offender who has one or more previous convictions, the court must treat each previous conviction as an aggravating factor if (in the case of that conviction) the court considers that it can reasonably be so treated having regard, in particular, to:

(a) the nature of the offence to which the conviction relates and its relevance to the current offence, and

(b) the time that has elapsed since the conviction.

Criminal Justice Act 2003 s 143(4) Any reference in subsection (2) to a previous conviction is to be read as a reference to:

(a) a previous conviction by a court in the United Kingdom,

(aa) a previous conviction by a court in another member State of a relevant offence under the law of that State,

(b) a previous conviction of a service offence within the meaning of Armed Forces Act 2006 ('conviction' here including anything that under section 376(1) and (2) of that Act is to be treated as a conviction),

(c) a finding of guilt in respect of a member State service offence.

(5) Subsections (2) and (4) do not prevent the court from treating:

(a) a previous conviction by a court outside both the United Kingdom and any other member State, or

(b) a previous conviction by a court in any member State (other than the United Kingdom) of an offence which is not a relevant offence,

as an aggravating factor in any case where the court considers it appropriate to do so.

(6) For the purposes of this section:

(a) an offence is 'relevant' if the offence would constitute an offence under the law of any part of the United Kingdom if it were done in that part at the time of the conviction of the defendant for the current offence,

(b) 'member State service offence' means an offence which:

i) was the subject of proceedings under the service law of a member State other than the United Kingdom, and

ii) would constitute an offence under the law of any part of the United Kingdom, or a service offence (within the meaning of Armed Forces Act 2006), if it were done in any part of the United Kingdom, by a member of Her Majesty's forces, at the time of the conviction of the defendant for the current offence . . .

(d) 'service law', in relation to a member State other than the United Kingdom, means the law governing all or any of the naval, military or air forces of that State.

R v Lang 2005 EWCA Crim 2864, 2006 2 Cr App R (S) 3 (p 13) Criminal Justice Act 2003 s 143(2) requires the court, when considering the seriousness of an offence committed by an offender who has previous convictions, to treat each previous conviction as an aggravating factor if, in the case of that previous conviction, the court considers that it can reasonably be so treated, having regard in particular to the nature of the offence to which the conviction relates and its relevance to the current conviction and the time that has elapsed since the conviction. This provision requires the court to look beyond the instant offence (and any offences associated with it) in order to see whether there are aggravating factors which it should have in mind when assessing the seriousness of that instant offence. Section 143(3) requires the court to consider commission of an offence on bail as an aggravating factor, when considering the seriousness of that offence.

R v Johnson and Others 2006 EWCA Crim 2486, 2007 1 Cr App R (S) 112 (p 674) D pleaded to manslaughter and affray. He was sentenced to IPP and appealed. Held. We address a number of issues:

(i) The existence of previous convictions for specified offences does not compel a finding of dangerousness.

(ii) Previous offences, not in fact specified for the purposes of section 229, are not disqualified from consideration. Thus, for example, as indeed the statute recognises, a pattern of minor previous offences of gradually escalating seriousness may be significant.

(iii) It does not automatically follow from the absence of actual harm caused by the offender to date, that the risk that he will cause serious harm in the future is negligible.

(iv) The inadequacy, suggestibility, or vulnerability of the offender may bear on dangerousness. Such characteristics may serve to mitigate the offender's culpability. In the final analysis, however, they may also serve to produce or reinforce the conclusion that the offender is dangerous.

(v) There is no reason why the prosecution's failure to comply with their duty to provide details of previous specified offences, even when it can and should, should either make an adjournment obligatory, or indeed preclude the imposition of IPP etc., when appropriate.

(vi) It is not obligatory for the sentencer to spell out all the details of the earlier specified offences. But, the requirement is that the sentencing remarks should explain the reasoning which has led the sentencer to the conclusion.

56.49 ***Convictions, Using Prosecution should provide the judge with details***

R v Isa 2005 EWCA Crim 3330, 2006 2 Cr App R (S) 29 (p 192) D pleaded to sexual assault (6 months' IPP). He had approached a 13-year-old girl in Oxford Street, held her arm and touched her breast with his other hand. He had a number of previous convictions including indecent assaults on both girls aged under 14 and older women. The Judge had available to him the fact of D's previous convictions. Held. D was a persistent low-level sex offender. Regrettably the Judge did not have any details about those convictions, something that prosecution authorities must now obtain as a matter of course in any case where consideration will be required as to the appropriateness or otherwise of IPP etc. IPP quashed.

R v Bryan and Bryan 2006 EWCA Crim 1660, 2007 1 Cr App R (S) 53 (p 296) para 11 It is incumbent on the prosecution in cases such as these to make sure that the judge is furnished with the fullest possible material in relation to previous offences. It is no good for the prosecution to complain of failures properly to implement these statutory provisions, if those for whom they are responsible do not provide the material by which it can be done.

56.50 ***Convictions, Using Dispute as to details etc.***

R v Bryan and Bryan 2006 EWCA Crim 1660, 2007 1 Cr App R (S) 53 (p 296) There were no full details of the relevant convictions. The Judge said that either defendant could come back to him within 28 days so that he could reduce the sentence should facts emerge to suggest it was wrong. Held. para 12 That was a sensible, practical course for the saving of public money, but it was wrong. If there was insufficient material on the basis of which a proper view in relation to Criminal Justice Act 2003 s 225 could be reached, then the Judge should have adjourned until that material was forthcoming.

56.51 ***Old convictions***

R v Halliwell 2015 EWCA Crim 1134, 2 Cr App R (S) 64 (p 454) D pleaded to section 18 and ABH. D stabbed his daughter in the shoulder area and in the back. D was now aged 45 and between 1982 and 2005 he had 13 sentencing hearings for 29 offences. He had two section 47 offences in 1984 (a fine and 21 days' detention). In 1987, he had a section 20 wounding (community order). He also had a long history of alcohol abuse.

Held. The 1984 and 1987 offences were historical and [could not be used] to assess dangerousness. There had been no violence on his record for 25 years. We quash the extended sentence. For details see **291.31** in Volume 2.

56.52 ***Convictions, Using*** ***The sentence does not represent additional punishment***
R v Johnson and Others 2006 EWCA Crim 2486, 2007 1 Cr App R (S) 112 (p 674) D pleaded to manslaughter and affray. He was sentenced to IPP and appealed. Held. para 3 Although punitive in its effect, with far-reaching consequences for the offender on whom it is imposed, strictly speaking, [IPP] does not represent punishment for past offending. As any such assessment of future risk must be based on the information available to the court when sentence is passed, the potential for distraction from the real issue is obvious. When the information before the court is evaluated, for the purposes of this sentence, the decision is directed not to the past, but to the future, and the future protection of the public.
For convictions used to found extended sentences which are quashed on appeal, see **56.89**.

56.53 ***Persons of good character***
R v Lang 2005 EWCA Crim 2864, 2006 2 Cr App R (S) 3 (p 13) para 17(vi) In relation to offenders under 18 and adults with no relevant previous convictions at the time the specified offence was committed, the court's discretion under section 229(2) is not constrained by any initial assumption such as, under section 229(3), applies to adults with previous convictions. It is still necessary, when sentencing young offenders, to bear in mind that within a shorter time than adults, they may change and develop. This and their level of maturity may be highly pertinent when assessing what their future conduct may be and whether it may give rise to significant risk of serious harm.
Note: The statutory assumption has been repealed. Ed.
R v Clarke 2007 EWCA Crim 2580 D pleaded to section 18 wounding on his wife, V. When she said the relationship was over he punched V, bit her, poured bleach over her and ultimately cut her throat with a significant strike with a knife. He then drank some bleach and tried to cut his throat. The injury to V was life-threatening and the doctor said it was only good luck that a major organ was not severed and she hadn't died. D was of good character. A psychiatrist said, "When domestic tensions arose, D did not have the cognitive and social skills to understand and articulate his feelings and to problem solve. He therefore became irrational and started exhibiting impulsive and self-harming behaviour." Held. It is unusual to pass a sentence of IPP on a man of good character. However, section 225 not only clearly contemplates that that might be so, but requires if the dangerousness provision is made out that such a sentence be passed in the absence of a life sentence. There is no doubt this was a serious offence. The Judge after considering the psychiatric evidence was eminently entitled to find IPP made out.
Note: This case, like many in this chapter, is fact-specific. It is a mere illustration of how one case was dealt with. It is not a precedent. Ed.
R v Newland 2016 EWCA Crim 351, 1 Cr App R (S) 74 (p 453) D pleaded to robbery and possession of an imitation firearm. He committed a terrible domestic armed robbery which put the victims aged 90 and 86 in hospital. D was aged 23, of good character, married and from a settled background. The pre-sentence report assessed D as having a low risk of reoffending. The Judge found the dangerousness provisions satisfied and gave detailed reasons for that and for not accepting the conclusions in the pre-sentence report and in the psychologist's report (finding not given). Held. The Judge's analysis of the evidence cannot be faulted. His conclusions are reasoned. It was open to him to pass an extended sentence.
See also: *R v Veseli* 2008 EWCA Crim 2965 (A finding of dangerousness may be made even where there had been no previous convictions to establish a pattern of violence. Although this was a cold-blooded and near-fatal stabbing, that by itself could not support IPP. 15 years' determinate not IPP.)

Att-Gen's Ref 2017 Re Smith 2017 EWCA Crim 252, 2 Cr App R (S) 2 (p 5) (D pleaded to two rapes (vaginal and oral) and an assault by penetration. He raped a 14-year-old girl using threats and holding a Stanley knife. Girl badly affected. D then aged 31 and now aged 37 with a good character. Held. There was planning and premeditation. The Judge gave too much weight to the fact it was an isolated incident and not enough weight to the absence of an explanation for the rape. Extended sentence substituted.)

56.54 *Repetitive low-level offending*

R v Lang 2005 EWCA Crim 2864, 2006 2 Cr App R (S) 3 (p 13) para 17(iv) Repetitive violent or sexual offending at a relatively low level without serious harm does not of itself give rise to a significant risk of serious harm in the future. There may, in such cases, be some risk of future victims being more adversely affected than past victims but this, of itself, does not give rise to significant risk of serious harm. 17(viii) It cannot have been Parliament's intention, in a statute dealing with the liberty of the subject, to require the imposition of indeterminate sentences for the commission of relatively minor offences. On the contrary, Parliament's repeatedly expressed intention is to protect the public from serious harm (compare the reasoning of the Court in relation to automatic life sentences in *R v Offen and Others* 2001 2 Cr App R (S) 10 (p 44) paras 96-99).

R v Isa 2005 EWCA Crim 3330, 2006 2 Cr App R (S) 29 (p 192) D pleaded to sexual assault (6 months' IPP). He had approached a 13-year-old girl in Oxford Street, held her arm and touched her breast with his other hand. He had a number of previous convictions, including indecent assaults on both girls aged under 14 and older women. The Judge had available to him the fact of D's previous convictions. Held. D was a persistent low-level sex offender. The level of sentences in the past was incompatible with a suggestion that serious harm had been caused. 12 months' imprisonment substituted.

See also: *R v Swinscoe* 2006 EWCA Crim 2412 (It is important to have regard to the gravity of the crime to which the dangerousness provisions relate.)

Note: There are two routes for an extended sentence for defendants aged 18+. They are: a) the offence justifies a 4+ year term of imprisonment and b) the Schedule 15B route. Ed.

56.55 *TICs*

R v Lavery 2008 EWCA Crim 2499 D pleaded to robbery and asked for five offences to be taken into consideration. Held. It is open to a judge to refuse to take an offence into consideration if he forms the view that to do so would be to distort the sentencing exercise and to lead to an unjust result and that the public interest requires that the offence be charged. There is no reason in principle why an offence to be taken into consideration and which is of a more serious nature than the index offence or offences should not result in a higher sentence than would otherwise have been the case, as the sentence will reflect the defendant's overall criminality. It is open to the court to take those TICs into account when considering the 'significant risk'. Here, there was no alternative but to find the dangerousness provisions were made out.

Step 4 The evidence Bad character (where there is no conviction)

56.56 *Bad behaviour with no conviction for it*

R v Considine 2007 EWCA Crim 1166, 2008 1 Cr App R (S) 41 (p 215) C was convicted of two counts of making threats to kill and possession of a bladed article. C was acquitted of ABH and criminal damage. His former partner gave evidence, detailing a number of incidents which had not resulted in criminal convictions. The Judge described her evidence as "serious violence towards her going back many years" which, if made the subject of trial and convictions, would have filled those 10 years with 'specified offences'. It was submitted to the Judge that these matters were unsubstantiated. In passing an IPP sentence, the Judge took account of the facts of the offences and C's previous convictions. He also considered his own assessment of C and the pre-sentence report. Held. para 37 We decline to lay down any hard and fast rules about how the court should approach the resolution of disputed facts when making the section 229 assessment. para 26 The breadth of the material which may be used to enable the court to make the assessment is emphasised by reference to 'all' the information available to the court about the offence and its circumstances, and 'any' information about the offender and 'any' information about 'any pattern of behaviour' of which the offence forms part. An assessment based on 'information' is not restricted to 'evidence', and the information to be taken into account when making the assessment is not limited to the offender's previous convictions or a pattern of behaviour established by them, or indeed information about the offender which is limited to them. If it were otherwise, section 229(2)(b) would not have been made to apply to the offender without previous convictions. Accordingly, as a matter of statutory construction, relevant information bearing on the assessment of dangerousness may take the form of material adverse to the offender which is not substantiated or proved by criminal convictions. There can be no logical reason for distinguishing between formal evidence adduced before a jury and evidence or information which comes before the court through some different route. It would be quite inconsistent to adopt different approaches to such information on the basis of its source, or to exclude it from consideration because it formed no part of the material before the jury, or was not properly described as 'evidence' at all. Considering *R v Farrar* 2006 EWCA Crim 3261, 2007 2 Cr App R (S) 35 (p 202), it did not decide that, absent a conviction, a court making the section 229 decision was precluded from considering evidence of previous misconduct which would amount to a criminal offence. The judge should not rely on a disputed fact unless it could be resolved 'fairly' to [the defendant]. One example of unfairness would arise if, notwithstanding the availability of evidence to justify prosecution for a serious offence, the defendant was undercharged on the basis that if convicted of the less serious offence, the prosecution could then supply the court with all the 'information' relating to the more serious offence. If the defendant were then treated as if he had been convicted of the offence, that would be unfair to him just because he might end up convicted, or effectively convicted in the course of the sentencing decision, in effect, without due process. If the judge were to exclude evidence [relevant to the issue of dangerousness] from the trial, either on the basis that it was of insufficient relevance, or that, for whatever reason, it would be unfair for it to be admitted, the same conclusion would follow.

In reality, there will be very few cases in which a fair analysis of all the information in the papers prepared by the prosecution, events at the trial, if there has been one, the judicial assessment of the defendant's character and personality (always a critical feature in the assessment), the material in mitigation drawn to the attention of the court by the defendant's advocate, the contents of the pre-sentence report, and any psychiatric or psychological assessment prepared on behalf of the defendant, or at the behest of the court itself, should not provide the judge with sufficient appropriate information on which to form the necessary judgment in relation to dangerousness.

R v JW 2009 EWCA Crim 390, 2 Cr App R (S) 94 (p 623)[733] D, aged 14, was convicted of attempted murder and possession of a firearm with intent to endanger life. The Judge noted the applicant's school report and said: a) it was a depressing one with evidence of disruptive behaviour, truancy and violence, b) the applicant had been excluded after a fellow pupil had been injured, but he had not been convicted of that incident, c) D would not be treated as someone who was guilty of that attack, d) the fact that he had been permanently excluded from school could not be ignored. It was noted that he was doing well educationally whilst in custody. Held. The Judge indicated that he could not ignore the fact of the applicant's expulsion from school and yet, in the same breath, he indicated that he was not treating the applicant as guilty of the incident alleged to have taken place

[733] The Cr App R (S) list this case as 2009 EWCA Crim 107, which is an error.

at the school. Given that the main reason for the expulsion was the untested and unproven allegation made against the applicant, which was denied by him, it was inappropriate for the Judge to place any weight on the fact of expulsion.

56.57 ***Evidence Bad behaviour with no conviction for it Using reports***
R v Considine 2007 EWCA Crim 1166, 2008 1 Cr App R (S) 41 (p 215) D was convicted of two counts of making threats to kill. Held. *R v Farrar* 2006 EWCA Crim 3261, 2007 2 Cr App R (S) 35 (p 202) clearly did not decide that, absent a conviction, the court making the section 229 decision is precluded from considering evidence of previous misconduct which would amount to a criminal offence. Arguments advanced on the basis that it did so decide are ill-founded. The contrary is true, and in *R v Farrar* 2006, the end result was that material directly related to the earlier incident did in fact contribute to the conclusion that Farrar himself should properly be assessed as dangerous. For this purpose no conviction was necessary. Provided the judge could resolve the issue fairly, it was sufficient for the information to be contained in a psychiatric report.
R v JW 2009 EWCA Crim 390, 2 Cr App R (S) 94 (p 623)[734] D, aged 14, was convicted of attempted murder and possession of a firearm with intent to endanger life. The Judge had a pre-sentence report and a psychological report. Both authors of the reports considered D was not dangerous. The Judge considered the facts of the offences to be enough to conclude that D posed a significant risk. In his sentencing remarks he mentioned both reports and their conclusions but did not analyse those conclusions. Held. The court is not bound by the assessments made in reports. However, if the court asks for the assistance of experts, and having read their assessments is minded to reject their conclusions, the court should set out in some detail the reasons for so doing. That was not done here.
R v LE 2014 EWCA Crim 1939 D pleaded to having sex with an adult relative (×7) and perverting the course of justice and was given an EDS. The pre-sentence report said D posed a risk to children and vulnerable adults. It was based, at least partially, on V's reports by the complainant which were the basis of the trial and when she was much younger but the earlier abuse was not accepted. The report also relied on reports of abuse from former partners of D which were again denied. Held. It would not be right for this Court to take account of an assessment which was based, in part at least, on such disputed factors that had not been either admitted or been the subject of convictions. Pre-appeal report set aside. However without that material, we conclude the 'dangerousness' test was made out.
R (S) v Leicestershire & Rutland Probation Trust 2014 EWHC 3154 (Admin), 2015 1 Cr App R (S) 12 (p 95) High Court D was convicted of raping his stepdaughter (×5) and indecently assaulting another girl. D appealed asking (amongst other matters) for references in the report to the facts for an offence for which a Judge directed an acquittal to be removed and the report to record that D was acquitted of raping his ex-wife. D's concern was the use of the report at Parole Board hearings. After a High Court hearing the report was redrafted. D asserted that the new report should not refer to a) his ex-wife as a victim (because he was acquitted of this matter) and b) a police claim that there were indecent images on his computer when no charges were brought. Held. The OASys[735] assessment in the report must contain all relevant facts, including those relating to an unpursued allegation, provided it is clearly and unequivocally stated that no charges were brought and no conviction ensued. A mere recitation of facts, however vigorously denied, is permissible. The same approach is adopted to the dropped rape charge as it is clear that the judge rejected it as there was no case to answer, a strong finding in favour of D. There is nothing in the report to suggest these matters were treated as correct [or relied on for their recommendations]. If the Parole Board draws an

[734] The Cr App R (S) list this case as 2009 EWCA Crim 107, which is an error.
[735] Offender Assessment System

incorrect inference from this, judicial review proceedings could be pursued at least in theory. I reject this application as the inclusion of these matters is neither irrational nor unreasonable. D is able to raise matters of concern with the authorities.

56.58 ***Evidence Judge should not hear evidence to determine guilt***
R v Farrar 2006 EWCA Crim 3261, 2007 2 Cr App R (S) 35 (p 202) D pleaded to abducting a child and sexual assault of the same child. The police had been called on three other occasions in relation to D's behaviour with children. He was not charged with these offences. D was of good character. The writer of the pre-sentence report relied on these incidents to suggest that D posed a very high risk of sexual harm to boys. The Judge heard evidence from one of the alleged victims, a 7-year-old boy, a police officer and D. The Judge accepted the victim's evidence and rejected D's evidence. He considered that D was guilty of indecent assault on the boy. The other incidents were not investigated and the Judge said he would disregard them. Held. It is neither a matter of express language and logic, nor is it compellingly clear, that Criminal Justice Act 2003 s 229(2)(b) has the effect of permitting a judge alone to decide that a defendant is guilty of a discrete offence unconnected with that for which he is to be sentenced. A 'pattern of behaviour' constituted by discrete offences can just as well be established by conviction by a jury or Magistrates' Court of the offences as by the finding of a judge alone. Hence, 'language and logic' do not require the implication. Further, it is not 'compellingly clear' that Parliament can be taken to have intended to deprive a defendant of the right to a trial by judge and jury or Magistrates' Court of a discrete offence by implication. It was wrong of the Judge to undertake such an exercise. The principle must not be taken too far. As the Court in *R v Canavan and Others* 1998 1 Cr App R (S) 243 recognised, full account can be taken of 'acts done in the course of committing that offence or offences even when such acts might have been separately charged'. In cases of sexual offences against children, evidence about the offences charged may demonstrate a pattern of behaviour before their commission which includes other criminal conduct, for example conduct which is an offence contrary to Sexual Offences Act 2003 s 14-15. We therefore reconsider the issue and, using an admission in a pre-sentence report prepared for us, we affirm the IPP sentence.
R v Considine 2007 EWCA Crim 1166, 2008 1 Cr App R (S) 41 (p 215) D was convicted of two counts of making threats to kill. Held. It is inappropriate to embark on a *Newton* hearing to decide whether or not the defendant has committed a discrete but similar offence to those already before the court, solely for making the assessment of dangerousness.
See also the FACTUAL BASIS FOR SENTENCING ***Newton hearing Must not be a substitute for a jury trial*** para at **57.60**.

Step 5 Does the defendant have a previous conviction for a Criminal Justice Act 2003 Sch 15B offence?

56.59 ***Step 5***
Step 5 Did the defendant, at the date of the offence, have a conviction listed in Criminal Justice Act 2003 Sch 15B?
If Yes, the court can pass an extended sentence. The requirement that an extended sentence need not be 4+ years long does not apply to a Sch 15B extended sentence. If No, go to Step 6, see **56.63**.
Offenders aged under 18: This route to order a 2012 extended sentence only applies to defendants aged 18+, as the condition is not included in Criminal Justice Act 2003 s 226B, which deals with defendants aged under 18.

56.60 ***Statutory provisions***
Criminal Justice Act 2003 s 226A(1) This section applies where: d) condition A or B is met.
(2) Condition A is that, at the time the offence was committed, the offender had been convicted of an offence listed in Schedule 15B.

56.61 ***Schedule 15B Part 1 offences***

Criminal Justice Act 2003 Sch 15B Part 1[736] The following offences to the extent that they are offences under the law of England and Wales:

para 1 Manslaughter

2-3B Offences Against the Person Act 1861

section 4 (soliciting murder)

section 18 (wounding with intent to cause grievous bodily harm)

section 28 (causing bodily injury by explosives)

section 29 (using explosives etc. with intent to do grievous bodily harm)[737]

3C-3E Explosive Substances Act 1883

section 2 (causing explosion likely to endanger life or property)

section 3 (attempt to cause explosion, or making or keeping explosive with intent to endanger life or property)

section 4 (making or possession of explosive under suspicious circumstances)[738]

4-6 Firearms Act 1968

section 16 (possession of a firearm with intent to endanger life)

section 17 (use of a firearm to resist arrest)

section 18 (carrying a firearm with criminal intent)

7 Robbery under Theft Act 1968 s 8 where, at some time during the commission of the offence, the offender had in his possession a firearm or an imitation firearm within the meaning of Firearms Act 1968.

For determining the issue when there is no firearm count, see **ROBBERY** ***Firearm, With No firearm count*** at **319.18** in Volume 2.

8 Protection of Children Act 1978 s 1 (indecent images of children)

9-11 Terrorism Act 2000

section 54 (weapons training)[739]

section 56 (directing terrorist organisation)

section 57 (possession of article for terrorist[740] purposes)

section 59 (inciting terrorism overseas) if the offender is liable on conviction on indictment to imprisonment for life

12-14 Anti-terrorism, Crime and Security Act 2001

section 47 (use etc. of nuclear weapons)

section 50 (assisting or inducing certain weapons-related acts overseas)

section 113 (use of noxious substance or thing to cause harm or intimidate)

15 Sexual Offences Act 2003

section 1 (rape)

section 2 (assault by penetration)

section 4 (causing a person to engage in sexual activity without consent) if the offender is liable on conviction on indictment to imprisonment for life

section 5 (rape of a child under 13)

section 6 (assault of a child under 13 by penetration)

section 7 (sexual assault of a child under 13)

section 8 (causing or inciting a child under 13 to engage in sexual activity)

section 9 (sexual activity with a child)

section 10 (causing or inciting a child to engage in sexual activity)

section 11 (engaging in sexual activity in the presence of a child)

---

736 As inserted by Legal Aid, Sentencing and Punishment of Offenders Act 2012 s 122. In force for offences committed on or after 3/12/12

737 Sections 28-29 were inserted by Criminal Justice and Courts Act 2015 s 3(1)-(2). In force 13/4/15, Criminal Justice and Courts Act 2015 (Commencement No 1, Saving and Transitional Provisions) Order 2015 2015/778 para 3 and Sch 1 para 3

738 Sections 2-4 were inserted by Criminal Justice and Courts Act 2015 s 3(1)-(2). In force 13/4/15, Criminal Justice and Courts Act 2015 (Commencement No 1, Saving and Transitional Provisions) Order 2015 2015/778 para 3 and Sch 1 para 3

739 Section 54 was inserted by Criminal Justice and Courts Act 2015 s 3(1) and (3). In force 13/4/15, Criminal Justice and Courts Act 2015 (Commencement No 1, Saving and Transitional Provisions) Order 2015 2015/778 para 3 and Sch 1 para 3

740 Presumably Parliament meant 'terrorism'.

section 12 (causing a child to watch a sexual act)
section 14 (arranging or facilitating commission of a child sex offence)
section 15 (meeting a child following sexual grooming etc.)
section 25 (sexual activity with a child family member) if the offender is aged 18 or over at the time of the offence
section 26 (inciting a child family member to engage in sexual activity) if the offender is aged 18 or over at the time of the offence
section 30 (sexual activity with a person with a mental disorder impeding choice) if the offender is liable on conviction on indictment to imprisonment for life
section 31 (causing or inciting a person with a mental disorder to engage in sexual activity) if the offender is liable on conviction on indictment to imprisonment for life
section 34 (inducement, threat or deception to procure sexual activity with a person with a mental disorder) if the offender is liable on conviction on indictment to imprisonment for life
section 35 (causing a person with a mental disorder to engage in or agree to engage in sexual activity by inducement etc.) if the offender is liable on conviction on indictment to imprisonment for life
section 47 (paying for sexual services of a child) against a person aged under 16
section 48 (causing or inciting child prostitution or pornography)
section 49 (controlling a child prostitute or a child involved in pornography)
section 50 (arranging or facilitating child prostitution or pornography)
Note: Serious Crime Act 2015 Sch 4 para 69(2)-(4) renames the section 48-50 offences.[741] Ed.
The offences become:
s 48 (causing or inciting sexual exploitation of a child),
s 49 (controlling a child in relation to sexual exploitation),
s 50 (arranging or facilitating sexual exploitation of a child).
section 62 (committing an offence with intent to commit a sexual offence) if the offender is liable on conviction on indictment to imprisonment for life

39 Domestic Violence, Crime and Victims Act 2004 s 5 (causing or allowing the death of a child or vulnerable adult)[742]

40 Terrorism Act 2006
section 5 (preparation of terrorist acts)
section 6 (training for terrorism)[743]
section 9 (making or possession of radioactive device or materials)
section 10 (misuse of radioactive devices or material and misuse and damage of facilities)
section 11 of that Act (terrorist threats relating to radioactive devices, materials or facilities)

43 Modern Slavery Act 2015[744]
s 1 (Slavery, servitude and forced or compulsory labour)
s 2 (Human trafficking)

44 (1) An attempt to commit an offence specified in the preceding paragraphs of this Part of this Schedule ('a listed offence') or murder
(2) Conspiracy to commit a listed offence or murder
(3) Incitement to commit a listed offence or murder

[741] In force 1/6/15, Serious Crime Act 2015 (Commencement No 1) Regulations 2015 2015/820 para 3
[742] Section 5 now includes victims who suffer serious injury. The description in this schedule is not the same as the name of the offence in the 2004 Act because the 2004 Act has been amended. I would expect the court to rely on the offence created by the section and not the now-inaccurate description of the offence. However, there are competing arguments either way.
[743] Section 6 was inserted by Criminal Justice and Courts Act 2015 s 3(1) and (5). In force 13/4/15, Criminal Justice and Courts Act 2015 (Commencement No 1, Saving and Transitional Provisions) Order 2015 2015/778 para 3 and Sch 1 para 3
[744] Inserted by Modern Slavery Act 2015 s 6(1) and (4). In force 31/7/15, Modern Slavery Act 2015 (Commencement No 1, Savings and Transitional Provisions) Regs 2015 2015/1476

(4) An offence under Part 2 of the Serious Crime Act 2007 in relation to which a listed offence or murder is the offence (or one of the offences) which the person intended or believed would be committed
(5) Aiding, abetting, counselling or procuring the commission of a listed offence

56.62 ***Schedule 15B Part 2 offences***
Criminal Justice Act 2003 Sch 15B Part 2, 3 and 4[745] The following offences to the extent that they are offences under the law of England and Wales:
45 Murder
46(1) Any offence that:
(a) was abolished (with or without savings) before the coming into force of this Schedule, and
(b) would, if committed on the relevant day, have constituted an offence specified in Part 1 of this Schedule.
(2) 'Relevant day', in relation to an offence, means:
(a) for the purposes of this paragraph as it applies for the purposes of Criminal Justice Act 2003 s 246A(2), the day on which the offender was convicted of that offence, and
(b) for the purposes of this paragraph as it applies for the purposes of Criminal Justice Act 2003 s 224A(4) and 226A(2), the day on which the offender was convicted of the offence referred to in Criminal Justice Act 2003 s 224A(1)(a) or 226A(1)(a) (as appropriate).
47 An offence under Army Act 1955 s 70, Air Force Act 1955 s 70 or Naval Discipline Act 1957 s 42 as respects which the corresponding civil offence (within the meaning of the Act in question) is an offence specified in Part 1 or 2 of this Schedule.
48(1) An offence under Armed Forces Act 2006 s 42 as respects which the corresponding offence under the law of England and Wales (within the meaning given by that section) is an offence specified in Part 1 or 2 of this Schedule.
(2) Armed Forces Act 2006 s 48 (attempts, conspiracy etc.) applies for the purposes of this paragraph as if the reference in subsection (3)(b) of that section to any of the following provisions of that Act were a reference to this paragraph.
49 An offence for which the person was convicted in Scotland, Northern Ireland or a member State other than the United Kingdom and which, if committed in England and Wales at the time of the conviction, would have constituted an offence specified in Part 1 or 2 of this Schedule.

Step 6 Does the count justify a 4-year sentence?

56.63 ***Step 6***
Step 6 Does the offence justify a custodial term of 4 years or more, which can be a global term for all the offending allocated to one count. Step 6 is in Criminal Justice Act 2003 s 226A(3) and 226B(1)(d), see **56.64** and **56.65**.
If Yes, the court may pass an extended sentence with a custodial term of at least 4 years. The court is not obliged to pass the sentence. If No, the court must pass a determinate sentence or non-custodial sentence.
Note: Step 6 does not apply to those with a Sch 15B conviction, see **56.59**.

56.64 ***Statutory provisions Defendant aged 18+***
Criminal Justice Act 2003 s 226A(1) This section applies where:..d) condition A or B is met.
(2) Condition A is that the offender had been convicted of a Schedule 15B offence (see **56.59**).
(3) Condition B is that, if the court were to impose an extended sentence of imprisonment, the term that it would specify as the appropriate custodial term would be at least 4 years.

[745] As inserted by Legal Aid, Sentencing and Punishment of Offenders Act 2012 s 122

56.65 ***Statutory provisions Defendant aged under 18***
Criminal Justice Act 2003 s 226B(1) This section applies where: d) if the court were to impose an extended sentence of detention, the term that it would specify as the appropriate custodial term would be at least 4 years.

56.66 ***The offence must justify a custodial term of at least four years***
R v Pinnell and Joyce 2010 EWCA Crim 2848, 2011 2 Cr App R (S) 30 (p 168) P pleaded to two counts of section 20 and one count of ABH. He received a 3½-year extended sentence (2 years' custody 18 months' extended licence) on each section 20 consecutive to each other. He received 8 months determinate on the ABH concurrent. This made a 7-year extended sentence in total (4 years' custody 3 years' extended licence). Held. This was unlawful. If no one offence would justify a 4-year custodial term, the seriousness of the aggregate offending must be considered. If a 4-year custodial term results from aggregating the shortest terms commensurate with the seriousness of each offence, then that 4-year term can be imposed in relation to the specified offence. If there is more than one specified offence, that aggregate term should be passed for the lead specified offence, or, if appropriate, concurrently on more than one specified offence. If appropriate, a concurrent determinate term may be imposed for other offences. The combination of the custodial term and extension period cannot exceed the maximum statutory sentence for the offence to which the extended sentence is attached. If the maximum period for the offence is 5 years, the extension period is therefore limited to a year.
Note: The aggregate rule means you can aggregate the offending and load it onto one of the sentences so it is 4 years or more. It does not mean you can make the sentences consecutive and if the total is over 4 years the sentence is lawful. This is unless the Criminal Justice Act 2003 Sch 15B exception applies, see **56.59**, where there is no 4-year maximum. Ed.
R v Casbolt 2016 EWCA Crim 1377 D pleaded with full credit to blackmail (not a specified offence), stalking and two harassment counts. The Judge gave him a 5-year extended sentence (4 years' custody 1 year's extended licence). This would have given a starting point of 6 years, which was above the 5-year maximum for the offence. The prosecution said that [an aggregate sentence for the other offences] justifies the 4 years' custody relying on *R v Pinnell and Joyce* 2010 (see above). Held. That approach might have been legitimate if any of the other offences were specified but they weren't. The sentence had to be reduced, making an extended sentence not possible.

56.67 ***Don't create longer terms to satisfy the criteria***
Att-Gen's Ref No 55 of 2008 2008 EWCA Crim 2790, 2009 2 Cr App R (S) 22 (p 142) LCJ IPP under Criminal Justice Act 2003 s 225(3B) may not be imposed unless the offence justifies the 2+ years even if there is a significant risk of serious harm. In such cases courts will ensure that longer than appropriate sentences are not imposed in order to avoid the restrictions created by condition 3B. Criminal Justice Act 2003 s 153(2) remains in force and any custodial sentence must 'be for the shortest term…that in the opinion of the court is commensurate with the seriousness of the offence, or the combination of the offence and one or more offences associated with it'.
R v Hackett 2018 EWCA Crim 2563 D pleaded to sexual assault. The Judge found the offence was Category 1B (starting point 2½ years, range 2-4 years). She moved to 5 years and with plea credit made an 8-year 1 month extended sentence (4 years 1 month's custody 4 years' extended licence). Held. With the location, timing, circumstances and the previous conviction, the Judge was entitled to go to the top of the range. The Judge appears to have adjusted the sentence so she could pass an extended sentence. We start at 4 years, so with 25% and not 20% plea credit, **3 years**.
For more detail, see **323.10** in Volume 2.
See also: *R v Nsumbu* 2017 EWCA Crim 1046, 2 Cr App R (S) 51 (D pleaded to robbery on the second hearing, which was the first hearing with an indictment. A report was

ordered about fitness to plead. The Judge started at 5 years. He said that with plea that makes 4 years, enabling him to make an extended sentence. Held. The Judge was able to conclude the defendant had not pleaded at the first opportunity. However, no reason was given why the discount was ⅕ and not ¼. Making an extended sentence is not one of them.)

The procedure, guilty plea, making the order and giving reasons

56.68 ***Warn counsel, Judge must***

R v G 2014 EWCA Crim 1302 The Judge failed to warn counsel he was about to pass an extended sentence. Held. There was a clear obligation on Judges to give an indication where there is consideration of dangerousness so that both counsel could address that matter. Here the lack of warning was a failure of the Judge. Sentence reconsidered and varied.

See also: *R v Pithiya* 2010 EWCA Crim 1766 (Counsel might have inferred the Judge was not considering IPP when he proceeded without a pre-sentence report. That created a clear unfairness, so we consider the matter afresh.)

R v Parry and Another 2016 EWCA Crim 1822 (LCJ para 26 In the usual course of events, a sentencing judge should indicate if he or she is considering an extended sentence, and invite submissions on that question. Here the pre-sentence report said the required risk was established and near the end, counsel did make a submission. Appeal dismissed.)

R v Gillings 2018 EWCA Crim 832 D, aged 16, pleaded to aggravated burglary and other offences. There was no mention in the pre-sentence report or in the prosecution sentencing note or during the hearing of the issue of dangerousness. The Judge passed an extended sentence. Held. D was clearly 'dangerous'. para 28 The Judge should have given the defence a specific opportunity to address that issue. On a different ground, determinate sentence substituted.

R v Chapman 2019 EWCA Crim 324 The Judge passed an extended sentence without warning counsel. Held. The lack of warning could not of itself be a reason for allowing this appeal. [The circumstances were considered.] Appeal dismissed.

Note: It is a pity the Court did not mention how disadvantaged a defendant is if his or her counsel has not been warned. Ed.

56.69 ***Guilty plea, Discount for***

Reduction in Sentence for a Guilty Plea Guideline 2007, see www.banksr.com Other Matters Guidelines tab para 2.6 A reduction in sentence should only apply to the punitive elements of a penalty, para 5.1, see www.banksr.com Other Matters Guidelines tab. Where a sentence for a 'dangerous offender' is imposed under the provisions in Criminal Justice Act 2003…[and] is an extended sentence, the approach will be the same as for any other determinate sentence.

Note: This guideline has been replaced but the guidance remains in force. Consequently, there are discounts for the custodial element but not the extended licence. Ed.

R v B and Others 2012 EWCA Crim 1272 Counsel submitted that the effect of para 5.1 of the guideline was that there should be a reduction in the licence period for a guilty plea in just the same way as there is for the custodial element. Held. We do not accept that. If a judge concludes that somebody is dangerous and that an extended sentence is necessary, then it is appropriate for the judge to ask what period of extension ought to be imposed in order to provide proper protection for the public. para 5.1 only refers to the custodial element.

R v Casbolt 2016 EWCA Crim 1377 D pleaded with full credit to blackmail (not a specified offence), stalking and two harassment counts. The Judge gave him a 5-year extended sentence (4 years' custody 1 year's extended licence). This would have given a starting point of 6 years, which was above the 5-year maximum for the offence. The prosecution said that [an aggregate sentence for the other offences] justifies the 4 years' custody relying on *R v Pinnell and Joyce* 2010 EWCA Crim 2848, 2011 2 Cr App R (S)

30 (p 168). Held. That approach might have been legitimate if any of the other offences were specified but they weren't. The sentence had to be reduced, making an extended sentence not possible.

56.70 *The order is discretionary*

Att-Gen's Ref No 27 of 2013 2014 EWCA Crim 334[746] LCJ para 25 It should not be overlooked that Criminal Justice Act 2003 s 226A(4) makes the imposition of [an extended] sentence discretionary. As was the case under the previous regime, even where there is a finding of dangerousness, an ordinary determinate sentence is sometimes appropriate.

R v Ali 2016 EWCA Crim 1335 D pleaded to GBH with intent, ABH and dangerous driving. The Judge started at 15 years and passed a 15-year extended sentence (11 years' custody 4 years' extended licence). Held. The court has a discretion whether to pass an extended sentence when dangerousness is found. para 32 Here, had a finding of dangerousness been justified, the appropriate sentence would still have been a determinate sentence.

Note: This last finding appears to have been based on the pre-sentence finding that D would have addressed his risks and the safeguards built into the Parole Board's discretion whether to release a prisoner, see para 31 of the judgment. Ed.

For more detail, see **56.10**.

R v Gardener 2019 EWCA Crim 170 D pleaded to two section 16A offences. He sent three videos showing D holding a shotgun and a pistol. D could be heard saying, "I am going to ruin your fucking life" and other threats. Held. The decision to impose an extended sentence was unimpeachable. It was a little unfortunate that the Judge ending with his remarks about the risk D posed and did not add something like, "The risk is such that it cannot adequately be met by a determinate sentence."

For more detail, see **262.30** in Volume 2.

See also: *R v BD* 2015 EWCA Crim 1415 (Convicted of two rapes and a sex assault. Victim was his stepdaughter, aged 6 or 7. One rape was with a punch. Also raped a family friend, aged 14, who was babysitting. No previous sexual convictions. Held. It was unfortunate that neither counsel dealt with the interaction of the extended sentence and the SOPO. Here we think the SOPO would provide sufficient protection so we quash the extended sentence.)

56.71 *Judicial discretion Children and young offenders*

R v Gillings 2018 EWCA Crim 832 D, aged 16, pleaded to aggravated burglary (which involved three youths, two knives and a machete) and other offences. He was aged 15 at the time of the offence. D had a conviction for a knife-point robbery, two possession of knife offences and had dishonesty offences on his record. He was into gang activity and his school attendance was very poor. D had never been to custody before. The Judge passed a 5-year extended sentence. Held. D was clearly 'dangerous'. However, D could be sufficiently punished and the public sufficiently protected by a determinate sentence. 5 years' detention.

56.72 *Calculating the determinate term*

Coroners and Justice Act 2009 s 126(4) In this section references to the notional determinate term are to the determinate sentence that would have been passed in the case if the need to protect the public and the potential danger of the offender had not required the court to impose a life sentence (in circumstances where the sentence is not fixed by law) or, as the case may be, an extended sentence of imprisonment or detention.

For the rest of the section see **64.12**.

TICs and Totality Guideline 2012: Crown Court, see www.banksr.com Other Matters Guidelines tab

[746] This case is also known as *R v Burinskas* 2014 EWCA Crim 334.

page 10 Extended sentences: using multiple offences to calculate the requisite determinate term

Approach In the case of extended sentences imposed under Criminal Justice Act 2003, providing there is at least one specified offence, the threshold requirement under Criminal Justice Act 2003 s 227(2B) (now Criminal Justice Act 2003 s 226A(1) and 226B(1). Ed.) is reached if the total determinate sentence for all offences (specified or not) would be four years or more.[747] The extended sentence should be passed either for one specified offence or concurrently on a number of them. Ordinarily either a concurrent determinate sentence or no separate penalty will be appropriate to the remaining offences.[748] The extension period is such as the court considers necessary for the purpose of protecting members of the public from serious harm caused by the offender committing further specified offences.[749] The extension period must not exceed 5 years (or 8 for a sexual offence). The whole aggregate term must not exceed the statutory maximum. The custodial period must be adjusted for totality in the same way as determinate sentences would be. The extension period is measured by the need for protection and therefore does not require adjustment.

56.73 ***Determining the licence period***

Sentencing Guidelines Council Dangerous Offenders Guide 2008, see www.banksr.com Other Matters Guidelines tab

Note: This guide is not a definitive guideline. It was written for the old 2003 extended sentences but the information may be helpful. Ed.

Extended sentence

para 9.3.5 When passing an extended sentence, in addition to fixing the custodial term, the court must fix the extension period. The length of the extension period is such as the court considers necessary for the purpose of protecting members of the public from serious harm caused by the offender committing further specified offences, Criminal Justice Act 2003 (s 227(2)(b) and s 228(2)(b)) (this would be s 226A(7) and s 226B(5) for the 2012 extended sentences (EDS)).

The extension period must not exceed 5 years for a specified violent offence or 8 years for a specified sexual offence (s 227(4) and s 228(4)) (this would be s 226A(8) and s 226B(6) for the 2012 extended sentences (EDS)). Further, the aggregate of the custodial term and the extension period must not exceed the maximum penalty for the offence (s 227(5) and s 228(5)) (this would be s 226A(9) and s 226B(7) for the 2012 extended sentences (EDS)).

9.3.6 The length of the extension period is not intended to reflect the seriousness of the offence, it is designed to provide greater protection for the public from the commission of further offences. Therefore, proportionality with the seriousness of the offence is not a primary factor in determining the length of the extension period. Rather, the objective should be to fix the length of the extension period by reference to what realistically can be achieved within it to secure the offender's rehabilitation and prevent reoffending.

In some cases, the court may be able to tailor the extension period to the availability and length of treatment or other programmes. In all cases the court should consider whether the length of the extension period can be justified by the evidence available.[750]

R v Terry 2012 EWCA Crim 1411, 2013 1 Cr App R (S) 51 (p 285) D was convicted of attempted murder. The Judge passed a 23-year extended sentence (18 years' custody 5 years' extended licence). The defence (surprisingly) contended that 23 years was outside the figures in the guideline. Held. Applying Criminal Justice Act 2003 s 227(3) the extension period is a different creature [from] a custodial term. It is imposed for a different reason, namely to enhance the protection of the public in view of the special

[747] This would not apply to the 2012 extended sentences under the Sch 15B route.

[748] *R v Pinnell and Joyce* 2010 EWCA Crim 2848, 2011 2 Cr App R (S) 30 (p 168)

[749] *R v Cornelius* 2002 EWCA Crim 138

[750] *R v Nelson* 2001 EWCA Crim 2264, 2002 1 Cr App R (S) 134 (p 565) at paras 19 and 21-22

risk which the offender has been found to pose. There is nothing wrong in principle in the extension period taking the total term of the extended sentence outside the figures in the guideline.

Att-Gen's Ref No 27 of 2013 2014 EWCA Crim 334[751] LCJ para 26 An extended sentence does not involve the imposition of a custodial term longer than is commensurate with the seriousness of the offence. The extension is to the period of licence which is of the length the court considers necessary for the purpose of protecting the public from serious harm, subject to the maximums. Inherent in those provisions is the principle that it is the extended period of licence that provides protection to the public.

56.74 ***Licence extension How long should it be?***

R v KA 2013 EWCA Crim 1264 D pleaded to sex offences on his children and indecent image counts. The probation report said a 3-year extension was necessary for the relevant work to be carried out. He was given a 16-year sentence with an 8-year extension for three of the offences. Two were made under Powers of Criminal Courts (Sentencing) Act 2000 s 85.[752] One was made under Criminal Justice Act 2003 s 227.[753] There were determinate sentences for the rest and all the sentences were concurrent. The Judge gave no reason for the 8-year extension. Held. 12 years was not appealable. A 4-year extension, not 8, was appropriate.

R v Williams 2016 EWCA Crim 1506 D was convicted of burglary with intent to commit GBH and ABH. He was in breach of a suspended sentence. D was with his former partner and she went home without him after some bad behaviour from him. D followed her home and smashed a window to get in and he punched and kicked her. She had multiple bruises. D had numerous convictions for violence. Held. There was nothing wrong with the 6-year custodial term of the extended sentence. Although D had a history of domestic abusive and violent behaviour, a 5-year extension, which was the maximum, was too long. 3 years' extended licence instead.

R v ARB 2017 EWCA Crim 1882, 2018 1 Cr App R (S) 23 (p 163) D pleaded to assault by penetration. He was aged 25 and had no previous convictions. D was sentenced to a 12-year extended sentence (7½ years' custody 4½ years' extended licence). One ground of appeal was that the extended licence should be 4 years not 4½. Held. The length of any extension period is based on the time that a judge concludes that supervision in addition to that which follows on from any custodial sentence is required to reduce the future danger posed by a particular defendant. "The length of the extension period is not to be determined by the age of the defendant or his lack of previous conviction save in so far as they are indicators as to the degree of harm he posed into the future and for how long he will pose that harm." Appeal dismissed.

R v Hale 2018 EWCA Crim 813 LCJ D pleaded to 24 child sex and child-image offences. D was then aged 16-19 and the four known female victims were aged 14 or 15. Other victims could be seen on the sex images. There was consensual vaginal intercourse. One girl was plied with alcohol to assist him having sex with her. The images included oral and vaginal penetration of children aged 5-8. D was now aged 20 with no convictions. He was sentenced to a 14-year extended sentence (10 years' custody 4 years' extended licence). Held. para 41 The 4-year extension does not reflect D's age and the availability of treatment on his release, and is disproportionate. **2 years** instead.

R v Philips 2018 EWCA Crim 2008 D pleaded to three offences of attempting sexual activity with a child. In breach of his SOPO, D set up a Facebook account pretending to be 14-year-old boy. This led to messages with someone who said she was a 14-year-old girl. D wrote to her about taking her virginity with pictures of his penis. The girl was fictional. D was aged 28. In 2014, he had a conviction for inciting a female aged 16 to engage in penetrative sex (2 years). In 2017, D breached his SHPO (15 months). D was

[751] This case is also known as *R v Burinskas* 2014 EWCA Crim 334.

[752] Repealed by Criminal Justice Act 2003 Sch 37 para 1 (3/12/12)

[753] Repealed by Legal Aid, Sentencing and Punishment of Offenders Act 2012 s 123 on 3/12/12

sentenced to a 14-year extended sentence (6 years' custody 8 years' extended licence). D appealed only the extended licence, which was the maximum. The defence said D was relatively young and had not been able to complete a sex offending course, the pre-sentence report appeared to say that D would address his desires and the Judge did not give the crushing effect of the sentence enough weight. Held. We see merit in those points. The licence is not tied to the seriousness of the offending. It should not be longer than necessary and should be just and proportionate. It should not crush the defendant. The Judge paid insufficient attention to the section about offender rehabilitation in the *Dangerous Offenders Guide*, www.banksr.com Other Matters Guidelines tab, at para 9.3.6, see **56.73**. **4 years'** extended licence not 8.

56.75 ***Some offences 'specified', some not***

R v Lang 2005 EWCA Crim 2864, 2006 2 Cr App R (S) 3 (p 13) When offenders are to be sentenced for several offences only some of which are specified, the court which imposes an indeterminate sentence under sections 225 or 226 or an extended sentence under sections 227 or 228 for the principal offences should generally impose a shorter concurrent sentence for the other offences.

Note: This case was about IPP. The same principle would apply to the 2012 extended sentences (EDS). Ed.

56.76 ***Must consider a global term***

R v O'Brien 2006 EWCA Crim 1741 paras 3 and 68 D pleaded to robbery and assault with intent to rob. Held. Take the most serious offence and work out the notional determinate term to reflect the totality of the offending. So the robbery term should reflect the need to punish for the assault. We increase the robbery sentence's notional term.

R v O'Halloran 2006 EWCA Crim 3148 D pleaded to section 20 GBH and four robberies. The Judge calculated the notional term with 2½ years for the section 20 and 2½ years for the robberies taking into account totality. He then passed IPP. The defence argued that the term should not be based in part on the section 20 offence because that was not a 'serious offence' so could not attract an IPP sentence. Held. Where the judge has a specified but not a serious offence of some gravity, at the same time as a serious offence which would attract a sentence of Detention or Imprisonment for Public Protection, he should: i) impose a sentence of IPP for the serious offence, and ii) impose a concurrent extended sentence for the specified non-serious offence (see *R v Lang* 2005 EWCA Crim 2864, 2006 2 Cr App R (S) 3 (p 13) para 20). However, in fixing the notional determinate term for the IPP, the judge is entitled to take account of the circumstances of the specified non-serious offence. To hold otherwise would give an uncovenanted bonus to the offender and would short-change the victims and the public.

R v Lunkov 2008 EWCA Crim 1525 D pleaded to aggravated burglary, two dwelling house burglaries and a sexual assault. The aggravated burglary and the sexual assault were on the same occasion. The sentence for the aggravated burglary was unclear and there was no separate penalty for the burglaries. D had in 4 weeks entered three apartments of lone women, at night. The Judge started at 6 years for the sex offence and with the burglaries arrived at a notional term of 10 years. The Judge sentenced D to 5 years' IPP. The defence said the term should not include the simple burglaries, emphasising that those offences were not specified. Held. It is essential to regard the whole of the offender's behaviour. The offences demonstrated an emerging pattern of offending.

Note: The references to IPP have not been removed in case part of the context is lost. Ed.

R v Stannard and Others 2008 EWCA Crim 2789, 2009 2 Cr App R (S) 21 (p 128) LCJ It is now well established that the totality of the offending may be reflected in the assessment of the notional term when an indeterminate sentence is imposed on one or more counts of the indictment.

See also: *R v Edwards* 2006 EWCA Crim 3362, 2007 1 Cr App R (S) 106 (p 646) (We uphold the Judge's approach in setting the minimum term for the totality of the offending including those which were not 'serious offences'.)
R v Johnston 2014 EWCA Crim 2909 (Convicted of two sex assaults by penetration (3 years) and attempted rape (8 years). Judge made an extended sentence with a global custodial term of 11 years. Held. There was no appeal on the sex assault counts because on their own they may not have caused the defendant to be assessed as dangerous. Sentence reduced on other grounds.)
See also the ***Consecutive extended sentences*** para at **56.78**.

56.77 ***Custodial term must be for the shortest term***
Sentencing Guidelines Council Dangerous Offenders Guide 2008, www.banksr.com Other Matters Guidelines tab
Note: This guide is not a definitive guideline. It was written for the old 2003 extended sentences but the information may be helpful. Ed.
Extended sentence
para 9.3.1 When passing an extended sentence, the court must fix the custodial term for the offence. This must be for the shortest term commensurate with the seriousness of the offence(s).[754]
For the basic principle, see **28.32**.
Note: Although the Act has been amended the principle remains the same. Ed.

56.78 ***Consecutive extended sentences, Avoid***
TICs and Totality Guideline 2012: Crown Court, see www.banksr.com Other Matters Guidelines tab page 10
Extended sentences for public protection: using multiple offences to calculate the requisite determinate term
page 10 **Approach** In the case of extended sentences imposed under Criminal Justice Act 2003, providing there is at least one specified offence, the threshold requirement under Criminal Justice Act 2003 s 227(2B) (now Criminal Justice Act 2003 s 226A(1) and 226B(1). Ed.) is reached if the total determinate sentence for all offences (specified or not) would be four years or more.[755] The extended sentence should be passed either for one specified offence or concurrently on a number of them. Ordinarily either a concurrent determinate sentence or no separate penalty will be appropriate to the remaining offences.[756] The custodial period must be adjusted for totality in the same way as determinate sentences would be. The extension period is measured by the need for protection and therefore does not require adjustment.
R v Lang 2005 EWCA Crim 2864, 2006 2 Cr App R (S) 3 (p 13) para 20 It will not usually be appropriate to impose consecutive extended sentences.
R v Brown and Butterworth 2006 EWCA Crim 1996 The court does have power to pass consecutive extended sentences. However, when release provisions are factored in, difficulties may very well arise in respect of the calculation of dates for release and the start of the period on licence. Consecutive extended sentences should be avoided.
R v C 2007 EWCA Crim 680, 2007 2 Cr App R (S) 98 (p 627) It seems to us that, in the first instance, we should not disturb the consistent advice that has been given in relation to the provisions of Crime and Disorder Act 1998 and Powers of Criminal Courts (Sentencing) Act 2000, as exemplified in particular in *R v Nelson* 2001 EWCA Crim 2264, 2002 1 Cr App R (S) 134 (p 565) and *R v Pepper and Others* 2005 EWCA Crim 1181, 2006 1 Cr App R (S) 20 (p 111). Where these provisions apply a court should not, as a matter of good practice, and save in exceptional circumstances, impose consecutive extended sentences, or consecutive sentences of any other nature with an extended sentence. But there is nothing unlawful in doing so and in some cases it may be

[754] Criminal Justice Act 2003 s 153(2) and 227(3)
[755] This would not apply to the 2012 extended sentences under the Sch 15B route.
[756] *R v Pinnell and Joyce* 2010 EWCA Crim 2848, 2011 2 Cr App R (S) 30 (p 168)

necessary. Consecutive sentences under the 1998 and 2000 Acts do not, in themselves, impose insuperable difficulties to those seeking to administer them. Consecutive sentences under the 2003 Act should be approached with great caution. Nonetheless they can be valuable tools in the sentencer's armoury. One particular example is where a defendant is charged with repeated affrays. In such a case, the sentencer has to work within the confines of a maximum sentence of three years' imprisonment. In such circumstances, consecutive sentences may be the only way to impose an appropriate custodial punishment and provide for a realistic extended period on licence. Judges should try to avoid consecutive sentences if that is at all possible and adjust the custodial term or minimum period within concurrent sentences to reflect the overall criminality if that is possible within other sentencing constraints.

R v Pinnell and Joyce 2010 EWCA Crim 2848, 2011 2 Cr App R (S) 30 (p 168) In two separate cases, P pleaded to two counts of section 20 and one ABH (all specified offences with a maximum of 5 years). He received a 3½-year extended sentence (2 years' custody 18 months' extended licence) on each section 20 consecutive to each other. He received 8 months determinate on the ABH concurrent. This made a 7-year extended sentence in total. J pleaded to ABH, theft and possession of an offensive weapon. The last two offences were not specified offences. J received a 5-year extended sentence for the ABH (4 years' custody 1 year's extended licence) but the Judge did not say to which offence it related. Held. Criminal Justice Act 2003 s 227(3) (now repealed and replaced by section 226A(6)) refers to Criminal Justice Act 2003 s 153, which contains the general provision as to the length of discretionary custodial sentences. Under section 153, custodial sentences must be for the shortest term, commensurate with the seriousness of the offence, or the combination of the offence and one or more offences associated with it, see **28.32**. As a result of Criminal Justice Act 2003 s 305(1), 'associated' is to be read in accordance with Powers of Criminal Courts (Sentencing) Act 2000 s 161(1), see **56.79** or **108.24**. That section provides that an offence is associated with another offence if the offender is convicted of it or has it taken into consideration. That principle can be applied to extended sentences. para 22 Section 153 points to the court being able to aggravate a specified offence with a non-specified offence. However, the language of section 227(2B) is such that the custodial term for each extended sentence must be at least 4 years. Separate consecutive sentences, each shorter than 4 years, cannot be extended even if their total is more than 4 years. para 35 The aggravated total can be more than the offence to which it is attached justifies. It is not possible by passing shorter consecutive sentences to constitute a single custodial term so as to qualify for the 4+ year rule, *R v Langstone* 2001 EWCA Crim 710, 2 Cr App R (S) 98 (p 439). para 47 If no one offence would justify a 4-year custodial term, the seriousness of the aggregate offending must be considered. If a 4-year custodial term [is suitable], then a 4-year term can be imposed for the specified offence. If there is more than one specified offence, that aggregate term should be passed for the lead specified offence, or, if appropriate, concurrently on more than one specified offence. If the maximum sentence for the offence is 5 years, the extension period is therefore limited to a year. para 48 There is no objection to imposing an extended sentence consecutive to another sentence, or to imposing consecutive extended sentences, although we suggest that it should be done only where there is a particular reason for doing so. The extension periods in the case of consecutive extended sentences will themselves be consecutive. In a case of consecutive extended sentences, each offence for which such a sentence is imposed must itself be a specified offence. Most importantly, each offence for which an extended sentence is imposed must also justify, on ordinary principles, including the aggregation of associated offences, a custodial term of at least 4 years. It is not possible to pass separate sentences of less than 4 years to meet this condition to the imposition of an extended sentence, even if their total is more than 4 years. para 37 and 41 For P the Judge was wrong to make the two extended sentences consecutive to each other. It was unlawful. None of the sentences met the 4-year condition. It should have been 4 years' custody for one offence and a 1-year extended licence (which was the maximum extension because the offence has a 5-year maximum). J's sentence would be rearranged by aggravating the offences and making the ABH 5 years' extended sentence (4 years' custody 1 year's licence).

R v Francis 2014 EWCA Crim 631 On 5 December 2012, D was convicted of section 18 and a firearm offence. He was sentenced to an 18-year extended sentence (13 years' custody 5 years' licence). About six months later, D was convicted of arson with intent and sentenced to a 16-year extended sentence (11 years' custody 5 years' licence). The Judge made the custodial sentences consecutive and the licence periods concurrent. This made the custodial period 24 years and the total period 29 years. Held. Consecutive extended sentences are not unlawful, but where possible, judges should avoid them by structuring their sentences in a different way. It was not lawful for the Judge to make the sentences partly consecutive and partly concurrent. The total custodial period was too long so 21 years not 24. The licence extension periods should be 3 years and 2 years consecutive which would be the sentence the Judge intended.

R v S 2014 EWCA Crim 968 D pleaded and was convicted of various sex abuse offences against four members of his extended family. For V1 the abuse started when she was aged 5. For three offences of indecency with a child, D was sentenced to 20 months on each, consecutive, making **5 years**. (Note: The maximum would appear to be 2 years on each.[757] Ed.) For an indecent assault on V1, D received **3 years** consecutive. (Note: The maximum would appear to be 10 years.[758] Ed.) For sexual assault on V2, which carried a maximum of 14 years, D received **3 years** on each of the two counts, concurrent with one another. For V3 the abuse started when she was aged 15. The maximum again was 14 years and D received **2 years** on each concurrent. V4 was aged between 25 and 32 when the abuse occurred. The maximum was 2 years and D received 1 year concurrent. This sentence was not part of the extended sentence. The Judge passed a total of 13 years (5 + 3 + 3 + 2 all consecutive, the constituent parts are in bold in this summary) and said that was an extended sentence of 18 years (13 years' custody 5 years' licence). Held. The sentence was fully justified. We adopt the headnote in *R v Pinnell* 2010 (for the case see above), where it was explained that short sentences can be aggravated by an associated offence to create a sentence that satisfies the 4-year requirement. Whilst consecutive sentences were appropriate because the offences were against different victims, it would have been proper to pass a concurrent sentence of 4+ years so an extended sentence could be passed. The sentences for V1 (8 years in all) remained the same. The sentences for V2 (3 years × 2) and V3 (2 years) would be increased to 5 years. The overall sentence was therefore the same.

Note: The problem here is that the amended sentence is still unlawful. The 20-month sentences which are part of the 5-year term could not form part of an extended sentence because they were less than 4 years in length. The same is true for the 3-year sentence for the offence against V1. It is also unlawful because an extended licence has to be passed for each offence. When the extended licences are made consecutive, the total is far in excess of the permitted 5-year maximum. Ed.

See also:*R v G* 2013 EWCA Crim 1302 (D was given 12 months, 12 months, 16 months and 8 months, all consecutive, making 4 years. The appropriate custodial term must be a single 4-year term, not the aggregate of successive consecutive sentences. One sentence was made 4 years and the rest were made concurrent.)

Note: This area of law lends itself to argument. The low maximum sentences for historical offences, the need for a guilty plea discount, the desire for adequate sentences, the traps in fixing extended licences and the needlessly complex legislation provide an explosive mix. Ed.

[757] This is because V1 was said to be aged 5 in 1985. Therefore the offence must have been committed before 1997, when the penalty was increased to 10 years. Ed.

[758] If V1 was aged 5 in 1985 and the offences were committed when she was aged 8-10, the offence must have been committed after 1985, when the penalty was increased. Ed.

R v Watkins and P 2014 EWCA Crim 1677, 2015 1 Cr App R (S) 6 (p 41) D pleaded to attempted oral and anal rape, two conspiracies to rape and 19 other sex assault and image offences. The Judge said he passed a 35-year extended sentence made up of two 15-year terms (concurrent) and two 14-year terms (concurrent) but consecutive to each other and each with a 6-year extended licence. Held. The Judge must have been well aware that he could not pass extended sentences which had consecutive custodial terms and concurrent extended licence periods. The 15-year sentences were determinate.)
Note: It was agreed that D satisfied the dangerousness criteria. The Judge would clearly have wanted the more serious offending (the two offences with a 15-year custodial term) to be the subject of an extended sentence rather than the other less serious offences (the offences with the 14-year custodial term). The only proper inference was that he wanted all the sentences to be extended. That is confirmed by the fact the Judge told the defendant he would serve two-thirds of the 29-year term. He clearly wanted a 6-year extended licence period but forgot to divide the period by two so giving all the sentences a 3-year extended licence. That would mean that when the pairs of sentences were made consecutive, there would be a 6-year licence period. Ed.

56.79 ***Consecutive extended sentences Associated offences***
Criminal Justice Act 2003 s 305(1) In this Part, 'associated', in relation to offences, is to be read in accordance with Powers of Criminal Courts (Sentencing) Act 2000 s 161(1).
Powers of Criminal Courts (Sentencing) Act 2000 s 161(1) An offence is associated with another if:

(a) the offender is convicted of it in proceedings in which he is convicted of the other offences, or (although convicted of it in earlier proceedings, is sentenced for it at the same time as he is sentenced for that offence), or
(b) the offender admits the commission of it in the proceedings in which he is sentenced for the other offence and requests the court to take it into consideration when sentencing him for that offence.

Note: The significance of this section can be found in *R v Pinnell and Joyce* 2010 EWCA Crim 2848, 2011 2 Cr App R (S) 30 (p 168) at **56.78**. The word 'associated' does not appear in any of the sections of Criminal Justice Act 2003 dealing with either the 2003 or the 2012 EDS extended sentences. It appears in sections 148, 152, 153, 156, 166, 207, 208, 225, 226 and 269 both in their original and in their substituted versions. These sections deal with community sentences, the requirement that custodial sentences must be 'so serious' a fine or a community sentence cannot be justified, pre-sentence reports, provisions for mentally disordered defendants, life sentences, detention for life sentences, remand time and the repealed IPP and DPP. It appears the legislation creates more problems than it solves. Ed.

56.80 ***Consecutive extended sentences Extended sentences and determinate sentences***
R v Brown and Butterworth 2006 EWCA Crim 1996 The court has the power to pass an extended sentence consecutive to a determinate sentence. It may very well be that the court has power to pass a determinate sentence consecutive to an extended sentence. Nothing in the statutory provisions forbids this. However, when release provisions are factored in, difficulties may very well arise in respect of the calculation of dates for release and the start of the period on licence. A determinate sentence consecutive to an extended sentence should be avoided. However, we [do not believe] that such problems will arise if an extended sentence is made consecutive to a determinate sentence. There is no reason to suppose that an extended sentence concurrent with a determinate sentence will cause insuperable difficulties. However, where the determinate sentence is longer than the custodial element of an extended sentence this may well have the effect of the extension being subsumed in the longer determinate sentence. It is sensible to avoid that combination since it would defeat the purpose of the mandatory extended sentence.

R v C 2007 EWCA Crim 680, 2007 2 Cr App R (S) 98 (p 627) If an extended sentence is ordered to run consecutively to a determinate sentence, the logical solution would be that the prisoner would be released when he has served one-half of the determinate term and then such part of the custodial term of the extended sentence as is required by Criminal Justice Act 2003 s 247(2) and (4) (now section 246A). The prisoner is then on licence until the end of the custodial term (if released early) plus one-half of the determinate sentence plus the extension period. As we understand it this is the practice adopted by the Secretary of State. This, however, would appear to be in conflict with Criminal Justice Act 2003 section 264(2). However, section 264(2) is in discretionary terms and the above practice is the practice of the Secretary of State. More difficult questions arise if a determinate sentence is expressed to be consecutive to an extended sentence. The answer is to impose the determinate sentence first, and the extended sentence should be consecutive to that. In shaping the overall sentence, judges should remember that there is no obligation for the sentences to be expressed in historical date order. There is nothing wrong with stating that the sentence for the first offence in point of time should be served consecutively to a sentence or sentences imposed for any later offence or offences.

R v Prior 2014 EWCA Crim 1290 It is generally undesirable to pass a determinate sentence consecutive…to an extended sentence. The best way [to sentence] is to treat the extended sentence as a lead sentence and expressly increase the custodial term on the other offending. The departure from best practice…did not, however, in this instance render these sentences unlawful or provide a ground of appeal.

R v McAllister 2014 EWCA Crim 2069 The Judge passed a 7½-year sentence and a 3-year sentence and made them consecutive. He then made that a 15-year extended sentence (10½ years' custody 4½ years' extended licence). Held. That was wrong because the extended licence has to apply to one sentence and not the total, and the 3-year sentence could not be extended as it was too short. Sentence reduced as manifestly excessive and rearranged.

R v Clancy 2016 EWCA Crim 471 D was sentenced for ABH to a 5-year extended sentence (4 years' custody 1 year's extended licence). He was released and recalled. He then falsely imprisoned a prison officer and pleaded guilty to that offence. The Judge passed a sentence of 32 months, consecutive to the extended sentence. The Judge had been wrongly told the defendant was still serving the custodial term of the sentence. Held. The Judge failed to consider Criminal Justice Act 2003 s 265 which prohibits consecutive sentences to the licence period. The new term will run from the date of sentence.

R v PE 2016 EWCA Crim 1373 The Judge passed determinate sentences, then an extended sentence, and then passed more determinate sentences. Held. It is generally advisable to make the extended sentence consecutive to the determinate sentence(s) as there is certainty as to the date upon which the consecutive sentence will start.

R v Ulhaqdad 2017 EWCA Crim 1216, 2 Cr App R (S) 46 (p 397) D was sentenced to an extended sentence with six determinate sentences consecutive to it. The Prison Service told the Court that for calculating the release date it did not really matter which way round the sentences were imposed. Held. It appears the Prison Service simply aggregate the terms. It remains better practice if the determinate sentences are passed first followed by the extended sentences.

Att-Gen's Ref 2017 Re D 2017 EWCA Crim 2509, 2018 1 Cr App R (S) 47 (p 356) In August 2017, D was convicted of rape and other sexual offences against two victims. In February 2017, he was sentenced to an 8-year extended sentence (6 years' custody 2 years' extended licence) for robbery and assault with intent to rob. Held. We make the counts concerning the different victims consecutive (6 years and 2 years) and consecutive to the extended sentence.

56.81 ***Consecutive extended sentences Consecutive licences***
R v Thompson and Others 2018 EWCA Crim 639, 2 Cr App R (S) 19 (p 164) (Five-judge court) para 29 The court can pass consecutive extended sentences where the total extended licence is in excess of the maximum permitted for a single term.

56.82 ***Consecutive extended sentences Extended sentences Release***
R v Hibbert 2015 EWCA Crim 507, 2 Cr App R (S) 15 (p 159) In 2013, D was sentenced to a 16-year extended sentence (12 years 9 months' custody 3 years 3 months' extended licence) for a firearm offence. In 2014, he was sentenced to 4 years for drug supply. Held. There was a clear need for an additional penalty for the drug offence. D will only be eligible to apply to the Parole Board after he has served ⅔ of the custodial term of the extended sentence. Here he can apply to the Parole Board after 10½ years ((12 years 9 months × 2/3) + (4 years ÷ 2)).

56.83 ***Explain sentence, Judge must/Suggested sentencing remarks***
Judicial College's Crown Court Compendium Part II Sentencing June 2018 page 4-11
4C **Extended sentences**
(26) Where the court passes such a sentence, it must set the custodial term and the (licence) extension period. These must not, in total, exceed the maximum sentence permitted for the offence and any extension period must not exceed 5 years (specified violent offence) or 8 years (specified sexual offence).
(27) In setting the custodial term the usual principles of sentencing apply. The extension period is a further period of licence necessary to protect members of the public from the significant risk of serious harm caused by D's commission of further specified offences.
(28) In respect of offences committed on or after 1 February 2015: there is a minimum extension period of 1 year: Criminal Justice Act 2003 s 226A and 226B as amended by [Offender Rehabilitation Act 2014] s 8.
(29) Any extended sentence must be attached to an individual offence or individual offences. It cannot be imposed as a global sentence. It is not possible to make multiple extended sentences partly consecutive and partly concurrent, e.g. by imposing the custody consecutively but the licence periods concurrently, see *R v Francis* 2014 EWCA Crim 631; *R v DJ* 2015 EWCA Crim 563, 2 Cr App R (S) 16 (p 164).
4D Passing an extended sentence:
32 The court must:
(1) Set out findings in relation to those matters described in paragraphs 1-3 of [this guide] [determining the seriousness etc.].
(2) Set out the reasons for finding that D is dangerous within the meaning of Criminal Justice Act 2003 Part 12 Chapter V [the dangerousness provisions].
(3) Set out the reasons for passing an extended sentence.
(4) Explain that the sentence is an extended sentence of imprisonment/detention in a Young Offender Institution, which has two parts: a custodial term and an extended licence period.
(5) Fix the custodial term. In doing so, credit should (almost invariably) be given for any plea of guilty and this should be spelt out clearly.

Example
But for your plea of Guilty the custodial term of your sentence would have been 6 years. Giving you [full] credit for your plea of Guilty, I reduce this to 4 years.

(33) Give credit for time spent on remand subject to a qualifying electronically monitored curfew: time spent on remand in custody counts automatically. For a full explanation of the provisions relating to time on remand, see chapter S4-9 [in this guide].

(34) Where the court makes a direction in relation to time spent on remand subject to a qualifying electronically monitored curfew it should also state that if the calculation of days is not correct, a correction will be made administratively without the need for a further hearing.

(35) Fix the extension period. This is to be such period as the court thinks appropriate having regard to the risk posed.

(36) Explain the consequences:

(1) Every D subject to an extended sentence will serve at least two thirds of the custodial term in custody before his case is referred to the Parole Board for them to consider his release. D will not serve more than the whole of the custodial term (unless they are recalled once on licence).

(2) On release D will be on licence, which will last until the end of the custodial term, and D will then serve the extended period of licence: this begins when the licence period of the custodial term ends and lasts until the end of the extended licence period.

(3) D's licence will be subject to conditions; and if any of the conditions are broken, they would be liable to have the licence revoked and be returned to custody to serve the rest of the total sentence in custody.

Example (offender does not have a previous Sch.15B conviction)

Because you have been convicted of a specified offence I am required to consider the issue of dangerousness, that is, whether you present a significant risk of causing serious harm by committing further specified offences. I am satisfied that you do present such a risk, as I have already told your advocate, because (…) (if this is also a serious offence – i.e. max sentence life or 10 years+ – and a life sentence is not considered necessary or appropriate, explain why.)

I have considered whether a standard determinate sentence is appropriate. If imposing such a sentence the least period of imprisonment I could have imposed in all the circumstances of your case (including credit for plea) would have been one of 6 years.

Such a sentence would not fully address the risk you represent and I do consider it necessary to impose an extended sentence in order to protect the public in the future.

The extended sentence is made up of two parts: a custodial period, which will be no longer than the 6 year period I mentioned, and an extended licence period of 4 years making an extended sentence of 10 years duration in total.

You will serve 2/3 of the custodial period in prison before the Parole Board will consider whether it is safe to release you, and if so on what terms.

Once released, you will serve on licence any part of the custodial period which remains, and you will then be subject to an extended licence for a further period of 4 years, making 10 years in all.

If, when you are subject to licence, you commit another offence or fail to comply with the terms of your release, you are liable to be recalled to custody and may serve the entire sentence in custody.

[**Where time spent on remand in custody:** The days which you have spent on remand in custody will automatically count towards the custodial term of your sentence.]

[**Where time spent on qualifying electronically monitored curfew:** I certify that you have spent 47 days on a qualifying curfew and I direct that 24 days will count towards the custodial term of your sentence. If this calculation is later found to be wrong it will be put right by correcting the record administratively without any further hearing.]

[Mention notification requirements if the offence is a sexual offence to which the notification regime under the SOA 2003 applies]

Example (offender does have a previous Sch.15B conviction)
Because you have been convicted of a specified offence I am required to consider the issue of dangerousness, that is, whether you present a significant risk of causing serious harm by committing further specified offences. I am satisfied that you do present such a risk, as I have already told your advocate, because… (if this is also a serious offence – i e max sentence life or 10 years+ – and a life sentence is not considered necessary or appropriate, explain why.)
I have considered whether a simple determinate sentence is appropriate. If imposing such a sentence the least period of imprisonment I could have imposed in all the circumstances of your case (including your guilty plea) would have been one of 3 years.
However you have a previous conviction for [section 18 GBH with intent], an offence listed within Sch.15B to the Criminal Justice Act 2003. Accordingly I must consider whether to impose a standard determinate sentence or an extended sentence.
I do not consider that a sentence of three years imprisonment would fully address the risk you represent and so it is necessary to impose an extended sentence in order to protect the public in the future.
The extended sentence is made up of two parts: a custodial period, which will be no more than the 3 years I mentioned, and an extended licence period of 2 years making an extended sentence of 5 years duration in total.
You will serve 2/3 of the custodial period in prison before the Parole Board will consider whether it is safe to release you, and if so on what terms.
Once released, you will serve on licence any part of the custodial period which remains, and you will then be subject to an extended licence for a further period of 2 years, making 5 years in all.
If, when you are subject to licence, you commit another offence or fail to comply with the terms of your release, you are liable to be recalled to custody and may serve the entire sentence in custody.
[**Where time spent on remand in custody:** The days which you have spent on remand in custody will automatically count towards the custodial term of your sentence.]
[**Where time spent on qualifying electronically monitored curfew:** I certify that you have spent 47 days on a qualifying curfew and I direct that 24 days will count towards the custodial term of your sentence. If this calculation is later found to be wrong it will be put right by correcting the record administratively without any further hearing.]
[Mention notification requirements if the offence is a sexual offence to which the notification regime under the SOA 2003 applies.]

R v Lang 2005 EWCA Crim 2864, 2006 2 Cr App R (S) 3 (p 13) para 17(ix) Sentencers should usually, and in accordance with Criminal Justice Act 2003 s 174(1)(a) (now section 174(2)-(3)[759]), give reasons for all their conclusions. In particular, that there is or is not a significant risk of further offences or serious harm, and for not imposing an extended sentence under sections 227 and 228. Sentencers should, in giving reasons, briefly identify the information which they have taken into account.
R v Rocha 2007 EWCA Crim 1505 D pleaded to robbery. The Judge must by his assessment of the risk factor have disagreed with the psychiatrist. Held. He was not bound by that finding. However, we do not know his reasoning for that rejection. A defendant wants to know what his sentence is and does not want to hear a long speech from the judge, but an indeterminate sentence is a very serious matter and both the appellant and this Court need to be able to understand the judge's reasoning process. Sometimes that may be obvious, but if part of the process involves rejecting the opinion of a suitably qualified expert, as it may be perfectly proper for the judge to do, the court needs to be able to understand the reason for the sentencing judge not accepting it. Considering the matter again we quash the IPP.
R v Gardener 2019 EWCA Crim 170 D pleaded to two section 16A offences. He sent three videos showing D holding a shotgun and a pistol. D could be heard saying, "I am going to ruin your fucking life" and other threats. Held. The decision to impose an

[759] As substituted by Legal Aid, Sentencing and Punishment of Offenders Act 2012 s 64. In force 3/12/12

extended sentence was unimpeachable. It was a little unfortunate that the Judge ending with his remarks about the risk D posed and did not add something like, "The risk is such that it cannot adequately be met by a determinate sentence."
For more detail, see **262.30** in Volume 2.
For the rules about giving explanations/reasons in custody cases, see the **PROCEDURE, SENTENCING Sentencing remarks** section at **86.49**.

Combined with other orders

56.84 ***Extended sentences and defendant already on a licence***
R v Ceolin 2014 EWCA Crim 526 D was given an extended sentence when he was already subject to a licence from an earlier IPP sentence. Held. That was not wrong in principle. The criteria for an extended sentence were well satisfied. The sentence can be justified even though it achieves no actual benefit in terms of public protection, *R v Smith and Others* 2011 EWCA Crim 1772, 2012 1 Cr App R (S) 82 (p 468). It can be justified by the need to emphasise to the Parole Board both the risk that D still presents and that he offended while subject to his licence.

56.85 ***Defendant expected to be deported***
Att-Gen's Ref Nos 9-10 of 2011 2011 EWCA Crim 1953 D was convicted of an unspecified number of rapes, assaults and witness intimidation. There was callous exploitation and brutality of five victims tricked into coming to the UK. Two were repeatedly raped. D was convicted of assaulting all five. One victim had objects inserted into her anus to prepare her for anal intercourse. D tried to trick another girl to come to the UK during his trial when he was in custody. The Judge considered the IPP criteria made out, but exercised his discretion not to impose it. Held. 21 years was in the right bracket. D will undoubtedly be deported. As a matter of law his situation is identical to any other prisoner subject to IPP. para 16 In assessing danger to the public we are concerned with residents in this country and elsewhere. para 14 In the case of a domestic prisoner the planning for possible release is a carefully thought-out process. The programme for release typically involves: a) not only work with the prisoner in custody, but planning for progressive release into the community, b) progressive posting to a less secure prison and eventually to an open prison and…brief periods and gradually longer periods of home release in order to see whether he can cope and whether he remains a risk, and c) a conditions of residence. It will always involve carefully formulated licence conditions designed to control the prisoner's behaviour, monitored by probation officers and others. None of that is in practice possible for a foreign national prisoner who is going to be deported more or less immediately on release. [Releasing D on] licence is impossible and planning for the kind of progressive stage release is [therefore] also impossible. Those realities are relevant considerations for any court which is asking itself whether as a matter of discretion a sentence of IPP ought to be imposed. In some cases the answer will be [it should not be imposed], because the effect of those practicalities may be that if it is imposed the prisoner will in practice scarcely be available for release and may at the very least spend very much longer in custody than would an equivalent domestic prisoner. However, such is the danger that D presents it would be wrong not to impose IPP here. 10½ years' DPP substituted.
Att-Gen's Ref No 30 of 2013 2013 EWCA Crim 1188 D pleaded to rape and an unrelated section 20. He blocked the victim's windpipe and threatened to kill her. She was affected physically and emotionally. The pre-sentence report said the dangerousness criteria were satisfied but it wasn't warranted as D would be deported. Counsel told the Judge that deportation would follow automatically. The Judge concluded that an extended sentence was pointless. Held. *Att-Gen's Ref Nos 9-10 of 2011* 2011 EWCA Crim 1953 applied. The appropriate course was for the sentencing court to ask itself a pure question of sentencing. An extended sentence was inevitable. We substitute a 10-year extended sentence (6 years' custody 4 years' extended licence).

See also: *Att-Gen's Ref No 41 of 2013* 2013 EWCA Crim 1729, 2014 1 Cr App R (S) 80 (p 493) (Judge believed the defendant would be deported. Extended sentence still required. One substituted.)
For combining extended sentences and determinate sentences consecutively see **56.80**.
See also the **CUSTODY Combined with other orders** section at **28.34**.
For ***Extended sentences and determinate sentences***, see **56.80**.

Combined with other orders

56.86 ***Offender of Particular Concern Order, Combined with***
Criminal Justice Act 2003 s 236A(1) Subsection (2) [the imposition of the an Offender of Particular Concern Order] applies where:..(c) the court does not impose one of the following for the offence:
(i) a sentence of imprisonment for life, or
(ii) an extended sentence under section 226A.
(2)-(4) [Not listed]
(5) The references in subsections (1)(c) and (2) to a sentence imposed for the offence include a sentence imposed for the offence and one or more offences associated with it.
For the full section, see **81.2**.
R v Fruen and DS 2016 EWCA Crim 561, 2 Cr App R (S) 30 (p 271)[760] para 127 The checklist is as follows:.. (d) Criminal Justice Act 2003 s 236A cannot apply if the court imposes life or an extended sentence for the offence or an associated offence.
R v Powell 2018 EWCA Crim 1074, 2 Cr App R (S) 34 (p 303) D was sentenced to three extended sentences, two Offender of Particular Concern Orders and 10 determinate sentences. Held. Having imposed an extended sentence, the Court was precluded from passing an Offender of Particular Concern Order on other counts, see section 236A(1)(c) and (5). *R v Fruen and DS* 2016 applied. We quash the Offender of Particular Concern Order.

56.87 ***Sexual Harm Prevention Order, Combined with***
Example: *R v BD* 2015 EWCA Crim 1415 (Convicted of two rapes and a sex assault. Victim was his stepdaughter, aged 6 or 7. One rape was with a punch. Also raped a family friend, aged 14, who was babysitting. No previous sexual convictions. Held. It was unfortunate that neither counsel dealt with the interaction of the extended sentence and the SOPO. Here we think the SOPO would provide sufficient protection so we quash the extended sentence.)

Appeals

56.88 ***Court of Appeal will not normally interfere if the judge applies the correct principles etc.***
R v Johnson and Others 2006 EWCA Crim 2486, 2007 1 Cr App R (S) 112 (p 674) This Court will not normally interfere with the conclusions reached by a sentencer who has accurately identified the relevant principles and applied his mind to the relevant facts. We cannot too strongly emphasise that the question to be addressed in this Court is not whether it is possible to discover some words used by the sentencer which may be inconsistent with the precise language used *in R v Lang* 2005 EWCA Crim 2864, 2006 2 Cr App R (S) 3 (p 13), or indeed some failure on his part to deploy identical language to that used in *R v Lang* 2005, but whether the imposition of the sentence was manifestly excessive or wrong in principle. Notwithstanding the 'labyrinthine' provisions of sections 224-229, and the guidance offered by *R v Lang* 2005, these essential principles are not affected. They apply with equal force to references by the Attorney-General. In such cases the question is whether the decision not to impose the sentence, in the circumstances, was unduly lenient. In particular: in cases to which section 229(3) applies, where the sentencer has applied the statutory assumption, to succeed the appellant should demonstrate that it was unreasonable not to disapply it. Equally, where

[760] Also known as *R v LF* 2016 EWCA Crim 561, 2 Cr App R (S) 30 (p 271)

the Attorney-General has referred such a case because the sentencer has decided to disapply the assumption, the reference will not succeed unless it is shown that the decision was one which the sentencer could not properly have reached.

56.89 ***Convictions used to found an extended sentence are quashed on appeal***
Criminal Justice Act 2003 s 231(1)[761] Subsection (2) also applies where:

(a) a sentence has been imposed on any person under section 225(3), 226A, or 227(2),
(b) the condition in section 225(3A) or (as the case may be) 226A(2) or 227(2A) was met but the condition in section 225(3B) or (as the case may be) or 226A(3) or 227(2B) was not, and
(c) any previous conviction of his without which the condition in section 225(3A) or (as the case may be) 226A(2) or 227(2A) would not have been met has been subsequently set aside on appeal.

(2) Notwithstanding anything in Criminal Appeal Act 1968 s 18, notice of appeal against the sentence may be given at any time within 28 days from the date on which the previous conviction was set aside.
(3) Subsection (4) applies where:

(a) a sentence has been imposed on a person under section 224A,
(b) a previous sentence imposed on that person has been subsequently modified on appeal, and
(c) taking account of that modification, the previous offence condition in section 224A(4) would not have been met.

(4) Notwithstanding anything in Criminal Appeal Act 1968 s 18, notice of appeal against the sentence mentioned in subsection (3)(a) may be given at any time within 28 days from the date on which the previous sentence was modified.
Note: There is a corresponding section for Court Martial, see Armed Forces Act 2006 s 228. Ed.

56.90 ***Fresh evidence at the Court of Appeal***
Criminal Justice Act 2003 s 229(2) The court in making the assessment referred to in subsection (1)(b) (the serious risk subsection):..b) may take into account any information which is before it about any pattern of behaviour of which any of the offences mentioned in paragraph (a) or (aa) forms part, and c) may take into account any information about the offender which is before it.
For the full section see **56.9**.
R v Beesley and Others 2011 EWCA Crim 1021, 2012 1 Cr App R (S) 15 (p 71) The defendants pleaded to manslaughter. They appealed their IPP sentences and wished to rely on fresh psychiatric evidence. Held. As the provisions in relation to dangerousness require the court to take into account all information, and in the light of the practice set out in *R v Caines and Roberts* 2006, we do not consider that section 23 constrains this Court from receiving further information about the offender where it is right to do so. The Court will be rarely assisted by psychological assessments that attempt to assess the risk other than the risk assessment using OASys contained in the pre-sentence report. It will therefore only be in an exceptional case that this Court will be prepared to consider further psychological assessments in relation to the dangerousness provisions. If there is an application and the material is disputed such that a witness has to be called then directions will have to be given and the provisions of section 23 may be applied. In this case we have heard the defence doctor. The position of the Parole Board is different as it is assessing not only the actual conduct of the defendant which led him to commit the offence, but [also] whether the work undertaken by the defendant in custody has changed the risk posed by the defendant.

[761] Amended by Legal Aid, Sentencing and Punishment of Offenders Act 2012 Sch 19 para 20

56.91 ***Court of Appeal isn't helped by reference to fact-specific cases***
R v Johnson and Others 2006 EWCA Crim 2486, 2007 1 Cr App R (S) 112 (p 674) This Court is normally not assisted by reference to previous individual cases where there appears to be some similarity with the instant case. We remind advocates that individual sentencing decisions are fact-specific, and that it is rare for reports of sentencing cases to provide guidance about principle, or indeed to treat all the details of the information before the court which are no more than summarised.

Release

56.92 ***Automatic and Parole Board release***
Release on licence of prisoners serving extended sentence under section 226A or 226B
Criminal Justice Act 2003 s 246A(1)[762] This section applies to a prisoner ('P') who is serving an extended sentence imposed under section 226A or 226B.
(2) It is the duty of the Secretary of State to release P on licence under this section as soon as P has served the requisite custodial period for the purposes of this section if:
(a) the sentence was imposed before the coming into force of Criminal Justice and Courts Act 2015 s 4,
(b) the appropriate custodial term is less than 10 years, and
(c) the sentence was not imposed in respect of an offence listed in [Criminal Justice Act 2003] Sch 15B Parts 1 to 3 of or in respect of offences that include one or more offences listed in those Parts of that Schedule.
(3) In any other case, it is the duty of the Secretary of State to release P on licence in accordance with subsections (4) to (7).
(4) The Secretary of State must refer P's case to the Board:
(a) as soon as P has served the requisite custodial period, and
(b) where there has been a previous reference of P's case to the Board under this subsection and the Board did not direct P's release, not later than the second anniversary of the disposal of that reference.
(5) It is the duty of the Secretary of State to release P on licence under this section as soon as:
(a) P has served the requisite custodial period, and
(b) the Board has directed P's release under this section.
(6) The Board must not give a direction under subsection (5) unless:
(a) the Secretary of State has referred P's case to the Board, and
(b) the Board is satisfied that it is no longer necessary for the protection of the public that P should be confined.
(7) It is the duty of the Secretary of State to release P on licence under this section as soon as P has served the appropriate custodial term, unless P has previously been released on licence under this section and recalled under Criminal Justice Act 2003 s 254 (provision for the release of such persons being made by s 255C).
(8) For the purposes of this section:
'appropriate custodial term' means the term determined as such by the court under Criminal Justice Act 2003 s 226A or 226B (as appropriate),
'the requisite custodial period' means:
a) in relation to a person serving one sentence, two-thirds of the appropriate custodial term, and
b) in relation to a person serving two or more concurrent or consecutive sentences, the period determined under Criminal Justice Act 2003 s 263(2) and 264(2).
R (Stott) v Secretary of State 2018 UKSC 59 Supreme Court (3-2) para 152 The aim of the EDS provisions is in general terms legitimate. para 154 The early release provisions have to be seen as part of the chosen sentencing regime, and the question of whether there is an objective justification for the differential treatment of prisoners in relation to

[762] As inserted by Legal Aid, Sentencing and Punishment of Offenders Act 2012 s 125 and amended by Legal Aid, Sentencing and Punishment of Offenders Act 2012 s 125(3). Amendment in force 3/12/12

earlier release [needs to be] considered in that wider context. para 155 EDS prisoners cannot be said to be in an analogous situation to other prisoners. Rather than focusing entirely upon the early release provisions, the various sentencing regimes have to be viewed as whole entities, each with its own particular, different, mix of ingredients, designed for a particular set of circumstances. The provisions are not incompatible with European Convention on Human Rights art 5 and 14.
For more detail see the **Release and supervision** note at **56.1**.

57 Factual Basis for Sentencing

57.1
For the opening and many other procedural matters, see the **Procedure, Sentencing** chapter.

Background and burdens of proof

57.2 ***Avoiding problems with factual issues***
Note: The Court of Appeal has indicated that the prosecution should avoid problems with jury verdicts by careful drafting of the indictment to avoid factual disputes. Ed.
R v Gandy 1989 11 Cr App R (S) 564 D and 24 others were charged with affray after an incident in a restaurant where glasses and stools were thrown. One man lost an eye. D pleaded to violent disorder on the basis that he had not used a weapon in the disturbance. An eye-witness identified D at a photo parade as the person throwing a glass during the incident. The prosecution accepted there were six breaches of the ID Code of Practice. The Judge conducted a *Newton* hearing and sentenced D on the basis that he threw the glass which resulted in the loss of another's eye (3 years' imprisonment). D appealed. Held. The Judge was not to be criticised for holding a *Newton* hearing although there was some regret that the prosecution had not seen fit to include a specific count charging D with wounding, either with intent or maliciously.
See also: *R v Allan and Others* 2011 EWCA Crim 1022 (The failure of the prosecution to prefer charges which accurately reflected the evidence led the Judge to select a starting point of 12 years which, whilst it might have been appropriate for the case advanced by the Crown, was too high for a conspiracy. Sentences reduced.)

57.3 ***Defendant should have the benefit of any doubt***
R v Finch 1993 14 Cr App R (S) 226 D was convicted of possessing amphetamine sulphate with intent. D was found in possession of a bag containing a white substance (246 grams at 6% purity) and a wallet containing £1,071. He claimed the police were aware of his activities and that he had stolen £21,000 from a dealer and that was where the £1,071 had come from. D was a police informant. The Judge rejected D's contention that the £21,000 and the possession of drugs were to do with his activities as a police informant. A police officer who D claimed to have dealt with was unavailable to give evidence and D declined to give evidence. The Judge did not hold a *Newton* hearing. Held. D's account was not inconsistent with the jury's verdict. The Judge was obliged to sentence on the most favourable basis to D and he was not entitled to reject D's account without having held a *Newton* hearing. With considerable reluctance, sentence reduced from 5 to 3 years.
R v Tovey 1993 14 Cr App R (S) 766 D was found not guilty of wounding with intent, but guilty of unlawful wounding and not guilty of murder but guilty of manslaughter. He received 7 years' imprisonment. D and V had entered into an argument in a pub. A fight ensued which left V with 12 stab wounds, two of which were fatal, D with one stab wound and a cut to his finger, and a third man, S, with a stab wound to the hand. D's account was that it was V who brought the knife to the pub, whereas the prosecution alleged that it was D who produced the knife. D requested that in light of the jury's verdict, proceedings should continue on the basis that D did not produce the knife. The Judge rejected this request, stating that he would be faithful to the jury's verdict. However, he stated that he was not bound to proceed on that basis as their verdict did not

make it clear that they had accepted D's account that he had not produced the knife. The Judge sentenced D on the basis that he had produced the knife. Held. The issue as to who produced the knife and how it got there remained obscure and as it was on the evidence, the benefit of the doubt arising from that obscurity or confusion should be given to D. Sentence reduced.

Old cases: *R v Stosiek* 1982 4 Cr App R (S) 205 (The court has to be extremely astute to give the benefit of the doubt to the defendant about the basis on which the jury have convicted.)

R v Ahmed 1984 6 Cr App R (S) 391 (The defence version must be accepted unless the judge is sure that it is wrong.)

57.4 *Burden and standard of proof for facts adverse to the defendant (incl. Newton hearings)*

R v Kerrigan 1993 14 Cr App R (S) 179 The Judge held a *Newton* hearing and the defence appealed saying the Judge had not directed himself according to the criminal standard of proof. Held. It is far better if a judge does openly direct himself to the relevant onus and standard of proof. Much depends on the way in which the judge expresses himself on the facts. A failure to do so is not fatal in every case. We find it difficult to conclude that this experienced Judge did not appreciate the onus and standard of proof he had to apply.

R v Bertram 2003 EWCA Crim 2026, 2004 1 Cr App R (S) 27 (p 185) The judge is not bound to accept the most favourable version to the defence. The judge should carefully apply the criminal standard of proof and give the defendant the benefit of any doubt.

R v Davies 2008 EWCA Crim 1055, 2009 1 Cr App R (S) 15 (p 79) LCJ The standard of proof for the judge when determining the aggravating features that establish the starting point is the criminal standard.

R v Lashari 2010 EWCA Crim 1504, 2011 1 Cr App R (S) 72 (p 439) D pleaded to possession of a prohibited firearm. Police found a 12-bore shot pistol and cartridges. The pistol was in working order. D gave evidence that he had found them in a bag in a car park and stored them in the boot of the car, with the intention of handing them to the police. He claimed he forgot about the pistol, and was initially nervous about taking it to the police station as he was a Muslim and was unsure how the police would react. The Judge treated D's account as extraneous mitigation and, applying the civil standard of proof, rejected it. He did not make a specific finding on the issue, though he noted it was more likely that D was keeping the weapon for another person. It was submitted that D's account was not extraneous mitigation but was relevant to the facts of the offence. It was therefore for the prosecution to disprove, on the criminal standard of proof, that D's account was false. Held. D's claims could not properly be categorised as extraneous mitigation. They were directly related to the circumstances of the offence itself and were facts that were directly relevant to the sentence for the offence committed by D. The Judge should therefore have applied the criminal standard of proof and asked whether the Crown had proved that the version of events put forward by D did not occur. However, looking at the facts overall, there were no 'exceptional circumstances' to enable the minimum sentence not to be passed.

Old cases: *R v Ahmed* 1984 6 Cr App R (S) 391 (The defence version of the facts must be accepted, unless the judge is sure that it is wrong.)

R v Mirza 1993 14 Cr App R (S) 64 (LCJ The judge must direct himself in accordance with the normal criminal burden and standard of proof. There is every indication that that is what he did and he was entitled to form the view he did.)

57.5 *Burdens of proof for matters raised by defendant*

R v Guppy 1995 16 Cr App R (S) 25 A civil burden of proof rests on D where he puts forward extraneous issues in mitigation of doubtful validity, and he should be afforded the opportunity to call evidence in support. Ordinarily, a court would accept the accuracy of counsel's statement.

Bad character etc. for which there is no conviction

57.6 ***Judge must sentence for the offences the defendant(s) had pleaded to/been convicted of***

Att-Gen's Ref Nos 32-35 of 2010 2010 EWCA Crim 2900, 2011 2 Cr App R (S) 32 (p 200)[763] C was convicted of conspiracy to rob. He was acquitted of murder and manslaughter. The victim died of a stab wound inflicted by a co-defendant who was convicted of murder. The prosecution said the offence was aggravated by the death. Held. Criminal Justice Act 2003 s 143(1), see **56.30**, provides three ways in which the seriousness of an offence may be affected in the context of the harm caused by the offence. This includes death. It would be an injustice for C to receive an additional punishment for an offence of which he had been acquitted. It was not a foreseeable consequence of C's offence that the victim would be stabbed, let alone fatally stabbed. C was to be sentenced for just the conspiracy to rob.

R v Stone 2011 EWCA Crim 1602 There is nothing inherently wrong in principle or unfair about a trial judge expressing his or her own conclusions of the facts, based on the evidence as called, even if the jury have not been called upon to make their own findings. However, a trial judge must always exercise great care to ensure that he or she does not appear to go behind the verdicts of a jury and make findings of fact which are inconsistent with those verdicts and [any] findings of [fact] the jury were called upon to make. Here, the Judge may have given the appearance of doing so whatever his intention. 5 months not 12.

R v Oakes and Others Re R 2012 EWCA Crim 2435, 2013 2 Cr App R (S) 22 (p 132) para 61 LCJ D was convicted of the murder of V. He killed V in 2002. To prove the murder the prosecution called evidence about the murder of V2 in Italy in 1993. D knew both victims. D was the last person to see both victims. The murders had the following similarities: a) remnants of their hair were left with the body, b) their bras were broken in the same way, and c) their trousers were damaged and disarranged in the same way. D denied both murders. V2's body was found in 2010. At the trial in Italy, D was not convicted of V2's murder. Later he was convicted of it in his absence, but that did not constitute a final conviction. The Judge said it was proved without doubt that D killed V2 but he was not sentencing D for it. Held. D did not fall to be sentenced as someone previously convicted of murder under Criminal Justice Act 2003 Sch 21 para 4(2)(d) [see para **287.87** in Volume 2]. There was no conviction. The sentencing Judge is required to reflect on and balance all the relevant aggravating and mitigating features including the judge's findings of fact on disputed points. Such findings may well include that in the course of the offence of which he has been convicted, the defendant committed other offences. The indictment is not required to be overloaded with charges. Where for example the conviction is for an offence of conspiracy, the judge may need to make findings for the purpose of sentence about which of the overt acts the defendant has been shown to have committed. There will be other situations in which it is conceded that sentence should be passed which reflects offences beyond those charged: the indictment may contain charges which have been treated by consent as samples of a course of conduct, or the defendant may ask the court to take into consideration other specific offences. However, it is equally axiomatic that, situations such as these apart, a defendant cannot simply be sentenced for offences of which he has not been convicted, or on the basis that he has in fact committed them. The ability of the judge to make findings that other offences have been committed does not extend to reaching a non-jury verdict about allegations put before the jury by way of similar fact evidence, at least unless the jury must have been satisfied that they were proved, or unless the defendant has been convicted of them in the past.

para 84 The principle is clear. Even when evidence which serves to establish the defendant's guilt of an offence charged on the indictment is deployed as similar fact

[763] The transcript lists the case as *R v Jumah and Others* 2010 EWCA Crim 2900, which is in error.

evidence, the sentencing decision cannot proceed on the basis that he is guilty of a distinct and separate offence of which he has not been convicted and which he denies. Although we sympathise with the judge's approach, it was inconsistent with [these principles].

R v Stone and Moore 2012 EWCA Crim 186 LCJ S and M pleaded to offences under Unfair Trading Regulations 2008. They pleaded not guilty to a conspiracy to defraud count and that was left on the file. The Judge said it was an affront to justice and common sense to sentence them on the basis that they did not know perfectly well what was going on. The defence argued that the Judge erred in treating S and M as dishonest when dishonesty was neither an element of the offences nor the basis upon which the appellants had entered their pleas of guilty. Held. This was a thoroughly disreputable business. S and M were perhaps fortunate that the prosecution chose not to pursue the charge of conspiracy to defraud, but they fell to be sentenced for offences of neglect of duty only. Dishonesty was not a component of the regulatory offences. The Judge was wrong to sentence them upon the basis of dishonesty. The Judge was also plainly wrong to seek guidance from the Fraud Guideline, which is also predicated upon dishonesty. S and M could only be sentenced for what was alleged against them in the particulars of the offence.

See also: *R v Allan and Others* 2011 EWCA Crim 1022 (The failure of the prosecution to prefer charges which accurately reflected the evidence led the Judge to select a starting point of 12 years which, whilst it might have been appropriate for the case advanced by the Crown, was too high for a conspiracy. Sentences reduced.)

R v Gonaciu 2014 EWCA Crim 2051, 2015 1 Cr App R (S) 19 (p 148) (The Judge was wrong to assume the defendant and other gang members had gone round Europe stealing from vulnerable members of the public, when there were no foreign convictions admitted or proved. For more detail, see **344.27** in Volume 2.)

R v S 2015 EWCA Crim 52 (The Judge was wrong to use an acquittal as support for a finding of 'dangerousness' and to fix the length of the custodial term. However, if we ignore the acquittal, neither the 'dangerousness' finding nor the length of the imprisonment were wrong.)

R v M(A) 2015 EWCA Crim 792 (Convicted. One count of voyeurism. Victim said D had done this many times before. Judge said it would be unrealistic and unjust to ignore the earlier incidents. Should have been sentenced for one incident, so **6 months** not 9.)

If old cases are required, see para **72.5** in the 8th edition of this book.

57.7 ***Judge must sentence for the offence(s) the defendant(s) had pleaded to/been convicted of   Ancillary orders***

Anderson v DPP 1978 67 Cr App R 185 Lords D was convicted of 13 counts involving dishonesty of over £7,000. There was a schedule of 20 similar cases involved to the value of £19,600. The Court made a Criminal Bankruptcy Order for £26,754. Held. The extra allegations had not been subject to any charge, D had never pleaded to them and nor had he been convicted of them. It was not right to take them into consideration.

R v Brammer and Others 1982 4 Cr App R (S) 247 The defendants pleaded to damaging property. They dug material from the bank of a river and used it to build a dam. That enabled them to net trout on the gravel bed. Staff at a fish farm became suspicious and took some photographs. As a result the defendants, who were taking fish out of the river, tipped them back into the water and removed the dam. To some extent they restored the river bank. The prosecution estimated the repairs at £198. The defence estimated them at £40. The Judge said, "You were there to slaughter whatever fish you could lay your hands on" and ordered each of the four defendants to pay £10 compensation. Held. The defendants were being sentenced for the wrong offence. The compensation order was quashed.

57.8 *Judge must sentence for the offence(s) the defendant(s) had pleaded to/been convicted of   Using other incidents to show offence was not an isolated incident*

R v U 2011 EWCA Crim 2094 D was convicted of a single exposure. The prosecution supported the case with two similar incidents. The Judge took the other two incidents into account to show the offence was not an isolated incident. Held. That was not appropriate.

Att-Gen's Ref No 80 of 2009 2010 EWCA Crim 470 D pleaded to section 18. The victim, V, was his wife. V and D had a turbulent marriage, with D often violent to V. Police were called and her injuries were noted. On each occasion, V declined to give evidence against D. Both sides complained that the other drank to excess and was overly jealous. D was aged 36 with two spent convictions. There were references saying that he was caring, hard-working and contributed to the community. The prison report said that he was pleasant and well behaved. Held. Where there is a documented, albeit unproven, history of violence towards the victim the offender cannot have the benefit of positive good character. But where allegations of assault are denied and remain unproven the violence cannot be an aggravating feature. D stood to be sentenced for this offence alone.

R v Connors and Others 2013 EWCA Crim 1165 LCJ T and his son, P, were convicted of conspiracy to hold a person in servitude and conspiracy to require forced labour. T's daughter, JC, and her husband were convicted of holding a person in servitude and requiring a person to perform forced labour. T, P and C were convicted of three different ABHs. The four recruited vulnerable adults on the pretence that they would be paid, fed and housed. The victims, once caught, had no means of escape. They were forced to perform forced labour for extensive hours without payment. They suffered actual violence and threats of violence. The victims were held against their will at travellers' sites. The main offences only became an offence on 6 July 2010. The Judge took into account offending 'over very many years involving hundreds of workers'. He treated the pre-2010 offending as aggravating the offences. Held. To ignore the earlier history would be unrealistic. Because the victims had been subjected to ill-treatment when the offence came into force meant they were more vulnerable not less.

For more details see para **346.7** in Volume 2.

See also: *R v Burrowes* 2014 EWCA Crim 1401 (The Judge took into account one of the bad character incidents, which she said showed that D was part of a paedophile ring. The prosecution on appeal said the incident showed the indicted offence was not an isolated incident. Held. It should not have been used to aggravate this offence.)

See also the ***Judge must accept the jury's verdict*** para at **57.11**.

57.9 *Non-criminal behaviour/Permitted uses of bad character*

R v Thomas 2009 EWCA Crim 904, 2010 1 Cr App R (S) 14 (p 75) It has always been open to a judge, when assessing the culpability of the defendant, to have regard to the defendant's antecedent behaviour not all of which is necessarily evidenced by previous convictions. Pre-sentence reports frequently refer to attitude and behaviour etc. so that the court can determine whether the use of violence reveals an entrenched disregard for others or is a one-off.

R v Khan 2009 EWCA Crim 389, 2010 1 Cr App R (S) 1 (p 1) D pleaded to a drugs matter and was interviewed by a probation officer. D asked for a 'good report' and said, "I've got[764] a grand here." D indicated a bag of cash. The interview was stopped. Three days later the officer phoned D to tell him the case had been re-assigned. D said, "I am not happy with the things you said. Do you not like Asians? Are you a racist? I could have seen you right. I'm going to have a hit on you. A hit on you." The officer took the remarks very seriously and moved home and office. D was charged with perverting the course of justice, and the prosecution put the telephone call to rebut D's defence that the earlier conversation was a joke. The Judge treated the later conversation as an

[764] The judgment says, "I've to a grand here", which I assume was a typo.

aggravating factor. The defence contended that he should be sentenced just for what he had been convicted of. Held. Where the aggravating conduct is not disputed there can be no objection to it being taken into account. Similarly after a *Newton* hearing, a court may have regard to conduct which aggravates the offence. However, there are limits to a *Newton* hearing in relation to conduct capable of sustaining a separate charge on which a verdict from a jury could be sought. Here the relevant conduct (the threats) was deployed before the jury, and D was able to challenge the evidence. It would have been most unlikely that the jury would have convicted him unless they had accepted the threats were made. But that might have happened. The Judge had every opportunity to evaluate the evidence. Nothing in this judgment is intended to cast doubt that no one should be sentenced for criminal conduct in respect of which he has not been convicted. Similarly such conduct (should not) be established in a *Newton* hearing. Nevertheless, where the conduct has been subject to specific scrutiny in a trial then unless reliance on the conduct is inconsistent with a verdict, a judge should be able to take that conduct into account if it has been established to the criminal standard.

Note: The problem with this approach is that it does replace a jury's verdict with a judge's decision for what was considered a separate incident. It would have been a lot fairer if the indictment was drafted so as to include the telephone call rather than using the incident as supporting evidence. Ed.

See also the ***Judge must sentence for the offences the defendant(s) had pleaded to/been convicted of*** para at **57.6**.

57.10 ***Previous violent behaviour Domestic violence***

Domestic Violence Guideline 2006, see www.banksr.com Other Matters Guidelines tab page 3 para **C Aggravating and mitigating factors**

3.1 The history of the relationship will often be relevant in assessing the gravity of the offence. Therefore, a court is entitled to take into account anything occurring within the relationship as a whole, which may reveal relevant aggravating or mitigating factors.

Note: This guideline has been replaced by the 2018 guideline.[765] However, this extract may be useful. Ed.

Domestic Abuse Guideline 2018, see banksr.com Other Matters Guidelines tab page 3 para 9. In force 24 May 2018. The following list of non-exhaustive aggravating and mitigating factors are of particular relevance to offences committed in a domestic context, and should be considered alongside offence specific factors.

Aggravating Factors

- A proven history of violence or threats by the offender in a domestic context

[For the rest of the factors, see **246.2** in Volume 2.]

Att-Gen's Ref No 80 of 2009 2010 EWCA Crim 470 D pleaded to section 18. The victim, V, was his wife. V and D had a turbulent marriage, with D often violent to V. Police were called and her injuries were noted. On each occasion, V declined to give evidence against D. Both sides complained that the other drank to excess and was overly jealous. D was aged 36 with two spent convictions. There were references saying that he was caring, hard-working and contributed to the community. The prison report said that he was pleasant and well behaved. Held. Where there is a documented, albeit unproven, history of violence towards the victim the offender cannot have the benefit of positive good character. But where allegations of assault are denied and remain unproven the violence cannot be an aggravating feature. D stood to be sentenced for this offence alone.

For using earlier incidents of violence in the sentencing procedure, see the **Murder** ***Bad character with/without a conviction/Background of violence*** para at **287.76** in Volume 2.

[765] See the Sentencing Council press release 22/2/18.

Determining the factual basis and jury's verdicts etc.

For the basic position, see the ***Judge must not sentence for offences the defendant(s) had not pleaded to/been convicted of*** para at **57.6**.

57.11 ***Judge must accept the jury's verdict***

R v Baldwin 1989 11 Cr App R (S) 139 D was found not guilty of murder but guilty of manslaughter. The Judge asked the foreman to clarify on what grounds the jury had found D not guilty of murder. The foreman informed the Judge it was on the basis of lack of intent. This was logically incomprehensible as the facts disclosed a deliberate blow with a knife, yet it was said to be struck without intent. Held. Perplexing as this view was, the sentence should have given effect to the verdict. Sentence reduced.

R v McGlade 1991 12 Cr App R (S) 105 at 109 There is clear authority that if the verdict of a jury leads inexorably to one version of the facts being found and only one version, the Judge is bound to sentence upon that basis. But if the verdict of a jury leaves open some important issue which may affect sentence, then the Judge, having heard all the evidence himself in the course of the trial, is free and indeed, it is his duty to come to a conclusion, if he can, upon where the truth lies.

Old cases: *R v Hudson* 1979 1 Cr App R (S) 130 (The Judge should have adopted the factual implications of the jury's verdict and sentenced D on his account of the incident. Sentence reduced.)

R v Singh 1981 3 Cr App R (S) 180 (D was convicted of unlawful wounding and acquitted on section 18. His defence of self-defence was rejected by the jury. Held. The Judge appears to have sentenced D as if he were convicted of section 18. Clearly this was wrong.)

57.12 ***Jury riders and jury answers***

R v Matheson 1958 42 Cr App R 145 LCJ It may happen that on an indictment for murder the defence may ask for a verdict of manslaughter on the grounds of diminished responsibility and also on some other ground such as provocation (now loss of control). If the jury return a verdict of manslaughter, the judge may, and generally should, then ask them whether their verdict is based on diminished responsibility or on the other ground or on both.

R v Solomon and Triumph 1984 6 Cr App R (S) 120 The only instance that we have been able to find in which it might be said to be common practice to go behind the general verdict and to enquire from the jury the basis upon which it was reached is in the case of a verdict of manslaughter, when the jury may have reached their decision on alternative grounds which have been left to them by the judge.

57.13 ***Jury opinions etc. Judge not bound by them***

R v Ekwuyasi 1981 Crim LR 574 D was convicted of importing cannabis. The foreman of the jury attempted to tell the Judge something to qualify the view which the jury had apparently taken of D's participation. The Judge silenced him. Outside court the foreman told defence counsel, "We appear to have done the wrong thing." Held. The Judge was not bound by a rider from the jury.

R v Cairns and Others 2013 EWCA Crim 467, 2 Cr App R (S) 73 (p 474) para 8 After conviction following a trial, the judge is bound to honour the verdicts of the jury but, provided he does so, is entitled to form his [or her] own view of the facts in the light of the evidence. This is so even if the jury express an opinion on a matter going only to sentence: see *R v Mills* 2004 1 Cr App R (S) 57 (p 332).

Old cases: *R v Warner* 1967 51 Cr App R 437 (Even if the jury do express their opinion, the judge having heard the evidence is still entitled, where the evidence supports it, to reach his own view of the facts.)

R v Solomon and Triumph 1984 6 Cr App R (S) 120 (*R v Warner* 1967 applied)

R v Wilcox 1984 6 Cr App R (S) 276 (*R v Warner* 1967 applied)

57.14 ***Uncertainty over jury's verdict***

R v Finch 1993 14 Cr App R (S) 226 D was convicted of possessing amphetamine sulphate with intent. D was found in possession of a bag containing a white substance (246 grams with 6% purity) and a wallet containing £1,071. He claimed the police were aware of his activities and that he had stolen £21,000 from a dealer and that was where the £1,071 had come from. D was a police informant. The Judge rejected D's contention that the £21,000 and the possession of drugs were to do with his activities as a police informant. This was not inconsistent with the jury's verdict. A police officer who D claimed to have dealt with was unavailable to give evidence and D declined to give evidence. The Judge did not hold a *Newton* hearing. Held. The Judge was obliged to sentence on the most favourable basis to D and he was not entitled to reject D's account without having held a *Newton* hearing. With considerable reluctance, sentence reduced from 5 years to 3.

R v Byrne 2002 EWCA Crim 1979, 2003 1 Cr App R (S) 68 (p 338) The defence case in the defendant's murder trial was lack of intent. The Judge left the issue of provocation to the jury. The jury convicted of manslaughter, and the Judge decided it was not appropriate to ask them for the basis of their verdict. Held. The Judge was entitled not to ask, and decided that the basis of the verdict was provocation. The Judge has a duty to explain his decision, and it would have been better if he had gone into greater detail. Sentence upheld.

R v King 2017 EWCA Crim 128, 2 Cr App R (S) 6 (p 25) D was convicted of manslaughter. On appeal the defence disputed the way the Judge approached the factual basis and the findings he made. Held (after considering a large number of authorities). If there was only one possible interpretation of a jury's verdict(s), the judge had to sentence on that basis. When there was more than one possible interpretation, the judge had to make up his or her own mind, to the criminal standard, as to the factual basis on which to pass sentence. If there was more than one possible interpretation, and the judge was not sure of any of them, the judge was obliged to pass sentence on the basis of the interpretation (whether in whole or in relevant part) most favourable to the defendant.

See also **MANSLAUGHTER** ***Uncertainty over jury's verdict*** para at **283.12** in Volume 2.

Evidence

There is a separate section dealing with oral evidence in a *Newton* hearing, see the ***Newton*** **hearings and the evidence** section at **57.67**.

57.15 ***Evidence Basic principles, There must be proper evidence***

R v Smith 1988 10 Cr App R (S) 271 LCJ When the judge decides the factual situation (for sentence) he is not bound by the rules of admissibility which would be applicable in a trial. He can take into account the contents of witness statements or depositions. He can take into account evidence he may have heard in the trial of co-defendants. He must, however…bear in mind the danger of self-serving statements which are likely to be untrue, that such statements have as a rule not been subjected to cross-examination and that the particular defendant whom he is sentencing may not have had the opportunity to put forward his version of events. The last danger can be avoided by giving the defendant the opportunity to give evidence if he wishes. As in the *Newton* case, the aim is to provide the judge with the fullest information possible, whilst at the same time ensuring that the particular defendant has every opportunity to present his side of the picture.

R v Hobstaff 1993 14 Cr App R (S) 605 It is wholly improper for the Crown to inform the court of the effects of an indecent assault upon the complainant without submitting supporting evidence to the court in the appropriate form. The evidence had to be made available in a proper form such as an expert's report or a witness statement. This serves two essential purposes: a) the evidence had to be served in advance to the defence, allowing defence counsel to deal with it as he saw fit, b) the evidence had to form part of the judge's papers, allowing the judge to be fully informed, and his judgment would not be influenced by prosecution information alone.

R v O'S 1993 14 Cr App R (S) 632 The Judge sentenced D saying, "The damage to these girls is incalculable. It could be they will be marked for the rest of their lives." Held. It does not appear that there was any evidence to justify those comments. We underline the observations in *R v Hobstaff* 1993 14 Cr App R (S) 605. The danger is that a case can be opened in a florid way on material which has not been made available to the defence. If that was to be accepted by the judge or the judge made assumptions not based on the evidence but perhaps based on his experience, then the defence may be put at a disadvantage. Sentences reduced.

57.16 *Evidence must be served by the prosecution in advance*

R v Hobstaff 1993 14 Cr App R (S) 605 It is wholly improper for the Crown to inform the court of the effects of an indecent assault upon the complainant without submitting supporting evidence to the court in the appropriate form. The evidence had to be made available in a proper form such as an expert's report or a witness statement. This serves two essential purposes: a) the evidence had to be served in advance to the defence, allowing defence counsel to deal with it as he saw fit, b) the evidence had to form part of the judge's papers, allowing the judge to be fully informed, and his judgment would not be influenced by prosecution information alone.

57.17 *Evidence When matters have to be strictly proved/Hearsay*

Criminal Justice Act 2003 s 114(1) In criminal proceedings a statement made not in oral evidence in the proceedings is admissible as evidence of any matter stated…if [certain provisions apply].

Note: The details about hearsay evidence are not dealt with as this book is primarily about sentencing. Ed.

Criminal Justice Act 2003 s 134 'Criminal proceedings' means criminal proceedings in which the strict rules of evidence apply.

Flewitt v Horvath 1972 RTR 121 D was convicted of driving with excess alcohol. In evidence, he asserted that "someone" had told him that a third party had put vodka in his drink. Held. That evidence is hearsay evidence and not admissible. Any evidence called must not infringe the rule against hearsay evidence.

Pugsley v Hunter 1973 1 WLR 578 The strict rules of evidence apply to special reasons.

Note: It appears the effect of the 2003 Act is to make hearsay evidence admissible in sentencing hearings where: a) the conditions of the Act are satisfied and the court grants permission, or b) both parties agree it can be admitted, or c) the evidence falls into the rare category of automatically admissible hearsay evidence such as public documents. Ed.

57.18 *Evidence Civil court judgments*

R v DF 2017 EWCA Crim 2058 D was convicted of child rape and other child sex offences. Although it did not form part of the evidence against D, the Judge was told about abuse allegations against D, made by other complainants. The charges were 'withheld for lack of sufficient evidence'. The Judge was told that one of the complainants had given evidence in care proceedings and the Court had found D had sexually abused her. The Judge used that finding in considering whether D was dangerous. The Judge also found that the social service records showed D had a complete disregard for a prohibition order made about his access to the family address and to [specified] children. Held. The Judge was right to take into account the findings in the family proceedings when assessing dangerousness and D's culpability. He was correct to remind himself that the finding was to a lesser standard of proof.

57.19 *Counsel's statements*

R v Guppy 1995 16 Cr App R (S) 25 Ordinarily, a court would accept the accuracy of counsel's statement.

Note: This case deals with mitigation material raised by the defence. Entirely different considerations arise when the prosecution wish to assert matters of significance. That material should be in writing and, if this is not possible because the prosecution have only just heard about it, the defence should be told about it prior to the hearing. Also the judge may want an explanation why the prosecution or the defence have only just been told about it. 'Ordinarily' in the reported case does not mean the judge will always accept it. All defence material is better served in writing in advance so that: a) it carries more weight, and b) the prosecution have time, if they wish, to make enquiries. This may also mean it is agreed between the parties. Ed.

57.20 *Evidence Need the originals be at court?*
R v Tower Bridge Magistrates' Court ex parte DPP 1988 86 Cr App R 257 D pleaded to driving with excess alcohol. The Magistrates asked for the original print-out from the breath machine. The original was not available but a copy was. They were unwilling to proceed without it and adjourned the case for a day. The next day, the stipendiary Magistrate was told the original had not arrived. He said it was unfair to D to adjourn the case again and was unhappy to proceed with a guilty plea. He asked D whether he wanted to change his plea and D did so. The Magistrate asked the prosecution to proceed or offer no evidence. The prosecution was not in a position to proceed and was not prepared to offer no evidence so the Magistrate dismissed the case for want of prosecution. In an affidavit the Magistrate said the print-out was required to check that the calibration was accurate, that the readings were correct and to see if there was a vast discrepancy between the readings. Held. There was no need for the original. D had admitted the offence. This was an improper use of the Magistrate's discretion. There may be cases where it is right that the magistrate should look at some of the evidence when a person pleads guilty but that should only be necessary when the defendant is unrepresented. The Magistrate's decision was quashed.

57.21 *Evidence Using evidence from co-defendant's trial*
R v Michaels and Skoblo 1981 3 Cr App R (S) 188 M and S, two doctors, were convicted of conspiracy to defraud. The co-defendant was then tried and convicted. The Judge was not prepared to accept the defence account that they had not committed the offence for gain. He heard evidence from M, S and others to determine the issue. During the doctors' evidence the Judge frequently remarked that he had been trying the co-defendants' case and during the trial other explanations were given which were inconsistent with the doctors' evidence. The Judge said he was impressed with that other evidence. Counsel pointed out that he had not been able to cross-examine those witnesses. The Judge rejected the doctors' evidence and sentenced them on the prosecution's version of events. Held. Clearly that was something he could not do. It was quite wrong to take into account other evidence. The only proper course for this Court is to sentence on the defence version of events.
R v Smith 1988 10 Cr App R (S) 271 LCJ D and P pleaded to conspiracy to steal. Their co-conspirators, C and J, were convicted at trial. C and J alleged that they had been forced to participate in the conspiracy by D's threats of violence and that D was the ringleader. C, J and P all gave evidence at trial to that effect. The conspiracy concerned stolen credit cards used to conceal thefts from a petrol station at which C, J and P were employed. D asserted that it was he who had been forced to participate in the conspiracy through the threat of violence from C and J. The Judge rejected this assertion after considering the evidence in C and J's trial. He reminded himself that C and J had good reason to exaggerate D's role. The Judge invited D to give evidence on five occasions, which D declined to do. D appealed on the basis that the Judge was wrong to pay regard to evidence presented during C and J's trial and that he was wrong to accept the versions provided by C and J at trial as they had been disbelieved by the jury. Held. It was the Judge's task to decide the facts of the conspiracy which involved the various defendants. He was not obliged, nor would it have been proper for him to sentence one conspirator

on the basis of facts advanced by him and then to sentence the others on a totally disparate version of events advanced by them. In doing so he is not bound by the rules of admissibility. However, he should bear in mind the danger of relying on self-serving statements. This evidence has not been tested in cross-examination and clearly presents a danger. This can be avoided by resolving the issue following the *Newton* case. *R v Taggart* 1979 and *R v Depledge* 1979 were correctly decided. They are to be preferred to the other decisions in this judgment which are inconsistent with them. *R v Michaels and Skoblo* 1981 not followed.

R v Murray 2014 EWCA Crim 195 D pleaded to conspiracy to import drugs. There was a basis of plea. L was convicted of the same count. The prosecution said in effect the basis of plea was a matter for the Judge. The Judge relied on L's evidence for D's sentence. Held. That evidence may have had self-serving aspects. If the Judge was not going to hold a *Newton* hearing he should not have relied on the evidence. Sentence reduced.

R v Marsh and Cato 2018 EWCA Crim 986, 2 Cr App R (S) 28 paras 6 and 44 A judge should not make findings of fact based on evidence called in a trial conducted without the defendant present or represented which run counter to the mitigation or a basis of plea without informing the defence of their intention to do so, so that the defence can make submissions.

Pre-sentence reports, see the **PRE-SENTENCE REPORTS** chapter.

Judge/Magistrate making factual decisions

57.22 ***Judge/Magistrate does not have to accept the mitigation***

R v Taggart 1979 1 Cr App R (S) 144 The judge is entitled to determine the matter on the information before him but he will resolve any doubt in favour of the defendant.

R v Depledge 1979 1 Cr App R (S) 183 D was convicted of ABH amongst other offences. The prosecution said that D had assaulted V, a police officer, with a six-inch nail or some nails taken from his pocket. The defence hotly contested this assertion, submitting that D pleaded guilty not on the basis that he was not the aggressor, but on the basis that he, having been attacked by the police officer, over-reacted and had retaliated with excessive violence. The prosecution said that the attack was wholly from D. It was common ground that D had taken a nail or some nails from his pocket at some point during the incident. However, it would have been D's case that his intention was merely to divest himself of any offensive weapon that might have been in his possession. Held. Where there is such a conflict between prosecution and defence, the only thing a court can do…unless it is minded, as some courts are, to hear the conflicting evidence on each side and make up its mind where the truth lies, is to form the best picture it can of the circumstances of the offence. It is in no way bound to accept as gospel truth everything that is said in mitigation on behalf of D.

57.23 ***Judge should make it clear that the defence account is not accepted***

R v Tolera 1999 1 Cr App R (S) 25 LCJ D pleaded to possession of heroin with intent to supply. Held. Where the defendant, having pleaded guilty, advances an account of the offence: a) which the prosecution does not accept, or feels it cannot challenge, but which b) the court feels unable to accept, whether because it conflicts with the facts disclosed in the Crown case or because it is incredible and defies common sense, it is desirable that the court should make it clear that it does not accept the defence account and why. There is an obvious risk of injustice if the defendant does not learn until sentence is passed that his version of the facts is rejected, because he cannot then seek to persuade the court to adopt a different view. The court should therefore make its views known so a hearing can be held and the matter resolved. We don't feel the Judge was entitled to reject the defence version given during the hearing.

R v Whiting 2013 EWCA Crim 1085 D pleaded to ABH. He submitted a defence case statement saying he did not touch the victim, V, with a bottle. The prosecution in opening said there were a number of competing versions and suggested the bottle had

actually struck a fence rather than V. The Judge said, "D either threw or hit V with a bottle or glass. The evidence was not clear but it was clear you used a weapon." Held. The Judge should have alerted the defence that he was minded to make this finding. We will interfere. 6 months' detention not 9 months.
See also: *R v Anderson* 2002 EWCA Crim 1850, 2003 1 Cr App R (S) 82 (p 421) (The defence should have been told the mitigation was not accepted. Sentence reduced.)

57.24 ***Factual basis for sentencing clear, Judge must make***
R v McFarlane 1995 16 Cr App R (S) 315 D pleaded to ABH. The prosecution case was that he assaulted his partner with a fork, punched her repeatedly in the head and placed his hands around her neck threatening to strangle her. D alleged he had only slapped her around the face. When sentencing, the Judge did not state upon which factual basis he was sentencing D. Held. The confusion had stemmed from trial counsel failing to specifically state that there was a significant difference in the prosecution's allegations and D's account. Held. This Court has difficulty in determining the factual basis on which the Judge sentenced D. The Court of Appeal would be greatly assisted if it was clearly recorded on the transcript the factual basis on which D was sentenced when there was a substantial difference between D's account and the prosecution's allegations. Sentence reduced.
R v McFeeley and Others 1998 2 Cr App R (S) 26 The defendants, D, T and M, pleaded to conspiracy to commit robbery and received 15 years' imprisonment. The count related to a series of robberies and attempted robberies in the Greater Manchester area. There were seven defendants. D and T had their bases of plea accepted, namely that they had only taken part in two robberies. The prosecution did not suggest the others were involved in the same robberies. The sentencing Judge remarked that he did not feel it necessary to draw any distinction between the defendants and that all were conspirators who had played vital parts. Held. In conspiracy cases, it is vital to make clear to the court whether a basis of plea is either: a) guilty to involvement in the overall conspiracy but only to an active role in a limited number of robberies, or b) guilty to an active involvement in a limited number of robberies, and limited involvement in the conspiracy, joining late or leaving early. This was unclear in this case. Sentences reduced.
R v Cairns and Others 2013 EWCA Crim 467, 2 Cr App R (S) 73 (p 474) para 3 The judge has to determine the gravity of the offending and is both entitled and required to reach his or her own assessment of the facts. The conclusions must be clear and unambiguous not least so that both the offender and the wider public will know the facts which have formed the basis for the sentencing exercise. They also [let us know the facts if there is an appeal].

57.25 ***Judge determining roles played Better to give counsel notice before deciding***
R v B and J 2015 EWCA Crim 11, 1 Cr App R (S) 56 (p 396) D1 and D2 were convicted of a section 18 assault. D1 and D2 were, between them, armed with one or two knives. D1, D2 and another pushed V over a wall and pursued him down the street whereupon V collapsed between two parked cars. He had been stabbed three times, which led to blood loss and poisoning, causing all V's limbs to be amputated, and he now uses a colostomy bag. At trial, no particular roles were ascribed but nonetheless the Judge principally ascribed the stabbing to D2. Held. para 8 It may have been better for the Judge to have given counsel notice of the findings he was proposing to make.
For more details see **291.48** in Volume 2.

57.26 ***Same rules apply about factual basis when imposing ancillary orders***
R v Irving and Irving 2013 EWCA Crim 1932, 2014 2 Cr App R (S) 6 (p 32) The Judge was asked to make a Football Banning Order and without giving the defence the opportunity to deal with an adverse finding, he 'rubber-stamped' the draft order. Held. para 11 Without holding a *Newton* hearing the Judge was bound to sentence on the basis

put forward by the defence. The proceedings were fatally flawed. This case is a further illustration of the need for a careful scrutiny before an order of this sort is made. Order quashed.

57.27 ***Judge misstates factual basis***
R v Warren 2017 EWCA Crim 226, 2 Cr App R (S) 5 After the Judge had passed sentence, the prosecution told the Judge he had misstated the facts for D. The Judge said he would not increase the sentence. Later the Judge learnt the prosecution were preparing to appeal the sentence. The Judge then listed the case and increased the sentence. Held. Where an error occurs in the factual basis of sentence it should be pointed out to the court as soon as possible and consideration should be given to correcting it at the earliest opportunity, preferably by revisiting sentence on the same day rather than a subsequent day.
For more detail see **112.3**.

BASIS OF PLEA

Basis of plea   Drafting the document

57.28 ***Basis of plea   Basic principles***
Criminal Practice Directions 2015 EWCA Crim 1567 para VII B.7 The prosecution may reach an agreement with the defendant as to the factual basis on which the defendant will plead guilty, often known as an 'agreed basis of plea'. It is always subject to the approval of the court, which will consider whether it is fair and in the interests of justice.
para B.8 *R v Underwood and Others* 2004 EWCA Crim 2256, 2005 1 Cr App R (S) 90 (p 478) outlines the principles to be applied where the defendant admits that he or she is guilty, but disputes the basis of offending alleged by the prosecution.
R v Marsh and Cato 2018 EWCA Crim 986, 2 Cr App R (S) 28 The defence served a basis of plea and the prosecution counsel said they took no issue with it and 'it wasn't contrary to their evidence'. The prosecution counsel then opened the case contrary to the basis of plea and the Judge departed from it too. The defence appealed. Held. We don't understand how it could be said the basis of plea wasn't contrary to the evidence. Had the prosecution not been prosecuting 18 defendants they would have sorted it out. The basis of plea was not signed by the advocates, as it should have been if agreed, so the Judge was free to ignore it. The prosecution made their case crystal clear in their opening. In our view, the defence had sufficient notice of the case that they had to meet. This ground of the appeal is dismissed.
Note: This seems contrary to the basic principles of sentencing. Defendants should not receive extra imprisonment because agreed documents are not signed. It is important that parties should be able to rely on what the prosecution say. A basis of plea should be checked in the same way whether there is one or 18 defendants. The excuse given that counsel didn't have time is no real excuse. Once the opening had been given, the Judge or the defence should have intervened. The fact that the defence knew when the opening was given what the case was is not the crucial issue. What was important is that the defence were denied an opportunity to have a *Newton* hearing (as the time for having one had passed) because they trusted what the prosecution said. If a judge wants to depart from an agreed basis of plea, the defence should be told, see **57.56**. If the prosecution are: a) told what the defence case is, b) the difference between the accounts is significant, c) the prosecution don't ask for a *Newton* hearing, and d) the judge does not raise the issue, the defendant is entitled to be sentenced on his or her version of the facts, see **57.57**. Ed.

57.29 ***Prosecution may only accept fair and accurate bases of plea***
Criminal Practice Directions 2015 EWCA Crim 1567 para VII B.8…a) The prosecution may accept and agree the defendant's account of the disputed facts or reject it in its entirety. If the prosecution accepts the defendant's basis of plea, it must ensure that the basis of plea is factually accurate and enables the sentencing judge to impose a sentence

appropriate to reflect the justice of the case, b) in resolving any disputed factual matters, the prosecution must consider its primary duty to the court and must not agree with or acquiesce in an agreement which contains material factual disputes.

R v Beswick 1996 1 Cr App R (S) 343 D pleaded to unlawful wounding after kneeing a man in the face and biting off the top of his ear. D pleaded on an agreed basis that he had not thought about the consequences and had acted as he did in order to free himself from the fracas that he had found himself embroiled in. At sentence, the Judge indicated he did not accept the basis of plea and prosecution counsel submitted in a *Newton* hearing that D was the aggressor. D was sentenced on the basis that he had intentionally bitten V's ear but had not intentionally bitten part of it off. Held. It is axiomatic that whenever a court has to sentence an offender it should seek to do so on a basis which so far as is relevant to the determination of the correct sentence is true. It follows from this that the prosecution should not lend itself to any agreement whereby a case is presented to the sentencing judge to be dealt with so far as that basis is concerned on an unreal and untrue set of facts concerning the offence to which a plea of guilty is to be tendered.

R v Daniels and Smith 2012 EWCA Crim 532, 2 Cr App R (S) 89 (p 532) D and S put forward a favourable basis of plea which was not disputed. Held. It behoves both prosecutors, and indeed judges, to view critically bases of plea proffered to the court in circumstances where further enquiry might show that they are unrealistic.

R v Cairns and Others 2013 EWCA Crim 467, 2 Cr App R (S) 73 (p 474) para 5 A basis of plea must not be agreed on a misleading or untrue set of facts and must take proper account of the victim's interests. para 5 ii) The written basis of plea must be scrutinised by the prosecution with great care.

57.30 ***Contents***

Criminal Practice Directions 2015 EWCA Crim 1567 para VII B.14 A basis of plea should not normally set out matters of mitigation but there may be circumstances where it is convenient and sensible for the document outlining a basis to deal with facts closely aligned to the circumstances of the offending which amount to mitigation and which may need to be resolved prior to sentence. The resolution of these matters does not amount to a *Newton* hearing properly so defined and in so far as facts fall to be established the defence will have to discharge the civil burden in order to do so. The scope of the evidence required to resolve issues that are purely matters of mitigation is for the court to determine.

R v Underwood and Others 2004 EWCA Crim 2256, 2005 1 Cr App R (S) 90 (p 478) para 4 The Crown may accept and agree the defendant's account of the disputed facts. If so, the agreement should be reduced into writing and signed by both advocates. It should then be made available to the judge before the start of the Crown's opening, and, if possible, before he is invited to approve the acceptance of any plea or pleas. If, however, pleas have already been accepted and approved, then it should be available before the sentencing hearing begins. If the agreed basis of plea is not signed by the advocates for both sides, the judge is entitled to ignore it. Similarly, if the document is not legible [he or she should ignore it]. The Crown may reject the defendant's version. If so, the areas of dispute should be identified in writing and the document should focus the court's attention on the precise fact or facts which are in dispute.

57.31 ***Contents must be agreed***

Criminal Practice Directions 2015 EWCA Crim 1567 para VII B.8 d), www.banksr.com Other Matters Other Documents tab An agreed basis of plea that has been reached between the parties must not contain any matters which are in dispute and any aspects upon which there is not agreement should be clearly identified.

See also: *R v Cairns and Others* 2013 EWCA Crim 467, 2 Cr App R (S) 73 (p 474) para 5 iii).

See also the ***GOODYEAR*** **INDICATIONS** ***Basis of plea Must have one and it must be agreed*** **para at 63.13.**

57.32 ***Conspiracy cases Basis must be clear***
R v McFeeley and Others 1998 2 Cr App R (S) 26 The defendants, D, T and M, pleaded guilty to conspiracy to commit robbery and received 15 years' imprisonment. The count related to a series of robberies and attempted robberies in the Greater Manchester area. There were seven defendants. D and T had their bases of plea accepted, which stated that they had only taken part in two robberies. The prosecution did not suggest the others were involved in the same robberies. The sentencing Judge remarked that he did not feel it necessary to draw any distinction between the defendants and that all were conspirators who had played vital parts. Held. In conspiracy cases, it is vital to make clear to the court whether a basis of plea [indicates that the defendant][766] is either a) guilty to involvement in the overall conspiracy but only to an active role in a limited number of robberies, or b) guilty to an active involvement in a limited number of robberies, and limited involvement in the conspiracy, joining late or leaving early. This was unclear in this case. Sentences reduced.

57.33 ***Matters outside the knowledge of the prosecution***
Criminal Practice Directions 2015 EWCA Crim 1567 para VII B.12 Where the disputed issue arises from facts which are within the exclusive knowledge of the defendant and the defendant is willing to give evidence in support of his case, the defence advocate should be prepared to call the defendant. If the defendant is not willing to testify, and subject to any explanation which may be given, the judge may draw such inferences as appear appropriate.
Criminal Practice Directions 2015 EWCA Crim 1567 para VII B.14 A basis of plea should not normally set out matters of mitigation but there may be circumstances where it is convenient and sensible for the document outlining a basis to deal with facts closely aligned to the circumstances of the offending which amount to mitigation and which may need to be resolved prior to sentence. The resolution of these matters does not amount to a *Newton* hearing (*R v Newton* 1982 4 Cr App R (S) 388, see **57.42**) properly so defined and in so far as facts fall to be established the defence will have to discharge the civil burden in order to do so. The scope of the evidence required to resolve issues that are purely matters of mitigation is for the court to determine.
R v Underwood and Others 2004 EWCA Crim 2256, 2005 1 Cr App R (S) 90 (p 478) para 5 The…most difficult situation arises when the Crown may lack the evidence positively to dispute the defendant's account. In many cases an issue raised by the defence is outside the knowledge of the prosecution. The prosecution's position may well be that they had no evidence to contradict the defence assertions. That does not mean that the truth of matters outside their own knowledge should be agreed. In these circumstances, particularly if the facts relied on by the defendant arise from his personal knowledge and depend on his own account of the facts, the Crown should not normally agree the defendant's account unless it is supported by other material. There is, therefore, an important distinction between assertions about the facts which the Crown is prepared to agree, and its possible agreement to facts about which, in truth, the prosecution is ignorant. Neither the prosecution nor the judge is bound to agree facts merely because, in the word currently in vogue, the prosecution cannot 'gainsay' the defendant's account. Again, the court should be notified at the outset in writing of the points in issue and the Crown's responses. We need not address those cases where the Crown occupies a position which straddles two, or even all three, of these alternatives.
Generally speaking, matters of mitigation are not normally dealt with by way of a *Newton* hearing. It is, of course, always open to the court to allow a defendant to give evidence of matters of mitigation which are within his own knowledge. From time to time, for example, defendants involved in drug cases will assert that they were acting

[766] I assume this is what the transcript meant to say.

under some form of duress, not amounting in law to a defence. If there is nothing to support such a contention, the judge is entitled to invite the advocate for the defendant to call his client rather than depend on the unsupported assertions of the advocate.

R v Milson 2010 EWCA Crim 2189 D pleaded to possession of cocaine and cannabis with intent to supply. The defence put forward a basis of plea which said there was 'no commercial basis or profit of any description'. The document was countersigned 'This can't be gainsaid' by prosecuting counsel. Held. The use of the word 'gainsaid' is one which is frequently seen in cases where insufficient consideration has been given by prosecuting counsel to the basis of plea which has been tendered. It frequently represents a lazy way of justifying a failure properly to analyse the circumstances of a particular case. The root problem lies in the acceptance of the basis of plea without proper consideration and on a basis which on any sensible examination turns out to be unrealistic. Be that as it may, D will enjoy the benefit of that basis of plea. This case has again demonstrated the continued use of the word 'gainsay' as a substitute for analysis.

R v Cairns and Others 2013 EWCA Crim 467, 2 Cr App R (S) 73 (p 474) para 5 If a defendant seeks to mitigate on the basis of assertions of fact outside the prosecutor's knowledge (for example as to his state of mind), the judge should be invited not to accept this version unless given on oath and tested in cross-examination as set out in Consolidated Criminal Practice Direction 2011 para IV.45.14 (now Criminal Practice Directions 2015 EWCA Crim 1567 para VII B.12. Ed.). If evidence is not given in this way, the judge might draw such inferences as he thought fit from that fact.

See also: *Att-Gen's Ref No 23 of 2011* 2011 EWCA Crim 1496, 2012 1 Cr App R (S) 45 (p 266) LCJ (D pleaded to murder. At the sentencing hearing, the Crown had said they could not gainsay D's denial of an intention to kill. Held. When issues of fact relevant to sentence arose, the combination of the words 'not' and 'gainsay' as an answer to a direct question, or as an indication of the position taken by the Crown, was meaningless. It was an answerless answer, bereft of content.)

For ***Goodyear indications***, see the ***GOODYEAR*** **INDICATIONS** ***Basis of plea*** paras at **63.13**.

Basis of plea Judicial approach

57.34 ***Prosecution accept basis of plea That is only conditional***

R v Beswick 1996 1 Cr App R (S) 343 The prosecution and the defence agreed on a basis of plea and D pleaded to section 20. A count of section 18 was not pursued. The case was put over for reports. When it was relisted a different Judge rejected the basis of plea and ordered a *Newton* hearing. The *Newton* ruling was adverse to D and he lost credit for his plea. The defence appealed, saying prosecution counsel did not stand by an earlier agreement but actively pursued and advanced a different and more serious case against D. Held. If the agreement was to be binding on the prosecution, that might hamper the process of ascertaining the true facts. It must be considered as being conditional upon the approval of the judge and the defence cannot without that approval seek to hold the prosecution to it. Since the prosecution should not have lent itself to such an agreement, it would offend and obstruct the doing of justice were the prosecution to be bound by it so as to hamper the judge in his task of ascertaining the truth.

R v Underwood and Others Re K 2004 EWCA Crim 2256, 2005 1 Cr App R (S) 90 (p 478) at para 58 D pleaded to robbery. He signed a basis of plea and the prosecution did not sign it. The Judge made a note that the prosecution said a trial of the issues was not necessary. He sentenced D on a later date. Held. There were important distinct factual issues in the basis of plea, including whether the weapons carried were a broomstick or a machete and baton as asserted by the victim. The prosecution decision to let the sentencing process proceed because of the reluctance of the victim to give evidence was entirely understandable. D should be sentenced on the basis of plea. 4 years not 6.

See also: *CPS v Mattu* 2009 EWCA Crim 1483 (D was acquitted in Case 1. Nine days later, D was arrested for what became Case 2. Later, D was charged in what became Case 3, pleaded and was sentenced on his basis of plea. The Judge found in Case 2 that that trial would be an abuse. The prosecution appealed. Held. The prosecution in Case 2 was wholly inconsistent with the accepted basis of plea in Case 3. Whether Case 2 was prosecuted because of pique over the acquittals does not matter. The Case 2 evidence was available for Case 3. The prosecution attempt to go behind the basis of plea was an abuse of process. If the trial went ahead it would be fundamentally unfair. A change of venue and counsel does not remedy the abuse. The Judge was right.)
Basis of plea Goodyear indications, see also the ***GOODYEAR*** **INDICATIONS** ***Basis of plea*** paras at **63.13**.

57.35 ***Basis of plea Multi-handed cases***
R v Underwood and Others 2004 EWCA Crim 2256, 2005 1 Cr App R (S) 90 (p 478) para 10(b) At the end of the *Newton* hearing the judge cannot make findings of fact and sentence on a basis which is inconsistent with the pleas to counts which have already been accepted by the Crown and approved by the court. Particular care is needed in relation to a multi-count indictment involving one defendant, or an indictment involving a number of defendants, and to circumstances in which the Crown accepts, and the court approves, a guilty plea to a reduced charge.
c) Where there are a number of defendants to a joint enterprise, the judge, while reflecting on the individual bases of plea, should bear in mind the relative seriousness of the joint enterprise on which the defendants were involved. In short, the context is always relevant. He should also take care not to regard a written basis of plea offered by one defendant, without more, as evidence justifying an adverse conclusion against another defendant.
para 41 The Judge seems to have treated the written bases of plea of two co-defendants, who did not give any evidence before him, as relevant to support the conclusions he reached adverse to D. We reduce the sentence.
R v Cairns and Others 2013 EWCA Crim 467, 2 Cr App R (S) 73 (p 474) para 5 In cases involving multiple defendants, the bases of plea for each defendant must be factually consistent with each other.
For ***Fraud*** cases, see the **FRAUD AND FINANCIAL SERVICES OFFENCES** ***Complex fraud, Plea discussion in*** paras at **267.11** in Volume 2.
See also ***Newton hearings Multi-handed cases*** para at **57.64**.

Basis of plea Judge rejects it

57.36 ***The judge can reject the basis of plea***
Criminal Practice Directions 2015 EWCA Crim 1567 para VII B.7 The prosecution may reach an agreement with the defendant as to the factual basis on which the defendant will plead guilty, often known as an 'agreed basis of plea'. It is always subject to the approval of the court, which will consider whether it adequately and appropriately reflects the evidence as disclosed on the papers, whether it is fair and whether it is in the interests of justice.
Criminal Practice Directions 2015 EWCA Crim 1567 para VII B.9 *R v Underwood and Others* 2004 EWCA Crim 2256, 2005 1 Cr App R (S) 90 (p 478) emphasises that, whether or not pleas have been 'agreed', the judge is not bound by any such agreement and is entitled of his or her own motion to insist that any evidence relevant to the facts in dispute (or upon which the judge requires further evidence for whatever reason) should be called. Any view formed by the prosecution on a proposed basis of plea is deemed to be conditional on the judge's acceptance of the basis of plea.
B.10 A judge is not entitled to reject a defendant's basis of plea absent a *Newton* hearing unless it is determined by the court that the basis is manifestly false and as such does not

merit examination by way of the calling of evidence or alternatively the defendant declines the opportunity to engage in the process of the *Newton* hearing whether by giving evidence on his own behalf or otherwise.

R v Beswick 1996 1 Cr App R (S) 343 D pleaded to unlawful wounding after kneeing a man in the face and biting off the top of his ear. D pleaded on an agreed basis that he had not thought about the consequences and had acted as he did in order to free himself from the fracas that he had found himself embroiled in. At sentence, the Judge indicated he did not accept the basis of plea and prosecution counsel submitted in a *Newton* hearing that D was the aggressor. D was sentenced on the basis that he had intentionally bitten V's ear but had not intentionally bitten part of it off. Held. a) The prosecution should not lend itself to any agreement whereby a case is presented to the sentencing judge to be dealt with so far as that basis is concerned on an unreal and untrue set of facts concerning the offence to which a plea of guilty is to be tendered. b) When this happens the judge is entitled to direct the trial of an issue so that he may determine consistently with the offence to which the plea of guilty has been tendered the true factual basis on which he has to sentence.

R v Underwood and Others 2004 EWCA Crim 2256, 2005 1 Cr App R (S) 90 (p 478) para 6 After submissions from the advocates the judge should decide how to proceed. If not already decided, he will address the question whether he should approve the Crown's acceptance of pleas. Then he will address the proposed basis of plea. We emphasise that whether or not the basis of plea is 'agreed', the judge is not bound by any such agreement and is entitled of his own motion to insist that any evidence relevant to the facts in dispute should be called before him. No doubt, before doing so, he will examine any agreement reached by the advocates, paying appropriate regard to it, and any reasons which the Crown, in particular, may advance to justify him proceeding immediately to sentence. At the risk of stating the obvious, the judge is responsible for the sentencing decision and he may therefore order a *Newton* hearing to ascertain the truth about disputed facts.

R v Lucien 2009 EWCA Crim 2004 D pleaded to unlawful wounding on the first day of his trial. His plea was tendered on a specific written basis and sentence was adjourned. Three weeks later he pleaded to kidnapping and robbery. Those pleas, following an abuse of process application, were tendered on a specific written basis. D asserted that he was unaware of the existence of a knife and did not brandish a knife himself. The Judge rejected that claim. When sentencing, the Judge proceeded to reject other aspects of D's basis of plea. Held. The Judge was entitled to reach the conclusion that he did and to sentence on that basis. Whilst the defence had notice of the Judge's disagreement with that part of the basis of plea, they had no notice that the Judge did not accept other aspects of it. If a judge does not accept an important and relevant part of the basis of plea, he or she should make that clear so that the defence can decide how they wish to proceed. Here, the defence could have called the defendant to give evidence on that topic, or simply made submissions on the evidence as it stood. Before the trial of the issue is embarked upon, it may in some cases be appropriate for the judge to be invited to consider whether there are any of the matters agreed upon which do not offend the first of these principles (see **57.42**) and to which therefore the prosecution should continue to be bound.

R v ATE Trucks 2018 EWCA Crim 752, 2 Cr App R (S) 29 (p 265) D pleaded to a risk assessment offence under the Health and Safety regulations. A contractor was killed while a lorry was being dismantled. The prosecution and the defence agreed a basis of plea and the application guideline decisions. Held. There is much to be said for sensible agreement. The Judge significantly disagreed with the basis of plea as to level of culpability and the likelihood of harm arising. No agreements can bind the Judge or determine the sentence.

57.37 ***First judge makes no comment about basis of plea, new judge rejects it***
R v Beswick 1996 1 Cr App R (S) 343 The prosecution and the defence agreed on a basis of plea and D pleaded to section 20. A count of section 18 was not pursued. The case was put over for reports. When it was relisted a different Judge rejected the basis of plea and ordered a *Newton* hearing. The *Newton* ruling was adverse to D and he lost credit for his plea. The defence appealed, saying prosecution counsel did not stand by an earlier agreement but actively pursued and advanced a different and more serious case against D. Held. If the agreement was to be binding on the prosecution, that might hamper the process of ascertaining the true facts. It must be considered as being conditional upon the approval of the judge and the defence cannot without that approval seek to hold the prosecution to it. Since the prosecution should not have lent itself to such an agreement, it would offend and obstruct the doing of justice were the prosecution to be bound by it so as to hamper the judge in his task of ascertaining the truth.
R v Robotham 2001 2 Cr App R (S) 69 (p 323) D pleaded to possession of amphetamine and was found guilty of two counts of possession of ecstasy with intent to supply (4 years 6 months' imprisonment). D was searched in a nightclub and found to have 0.45 grams of amphetamine, 56 ecstasy tablets and the fragments of approximately five ecstasy tablets. A further 32 ecstasy tablets were found at D's home. He pleaded guilty on a specific basis: a) He was not a commercial dealer. b) He was merely a custodian for the drugs found at his home and had intended, as instructed, to pass the drugs back to their owner after a very brief period. c) In the nightclub he was holding on to the drugs for a very short period. d) There was no intention to supply them commercially. The Crown accepted this plea and the Judge agreed to adjourn the sentencing. At sentence, a different Judge rejected the basis of plea and conducted a *Newton* hearing. D was subsequently sentenced on the basis that D was involved in commercial supply. It was submitted that D had a legitimate expectation that he would be sentenced on the basis upon which he pleaded. Held. The basis of plea was plainly fanciful. The actions of the trial Judge were passive and nothing in them can be said to give rise to a legitimate expectation that D would be sentenced on the basis upon which he pleaded. The situation was caused by the failure of prosecuting counsel to address the basis of plea properly in accordance with his duty. Appeal dismissed.

57.38 ***The judge rejects the basis of plea Can the defendant change his or her plea?***
R v Beswick 1996 1 Cr App R (S) 343 Where the judge rejects an agreed basis of plea and directs a trial of an issue, this does not create a ground upon which the defendant should be allowed to vacate his plea of guilty when it is clear that, unreal though the agreed facts may be, he does admit his guilt of the offence to which he has pleaded guilty. We say that because in this case when the Judge decided there should be a trial of issues there was an application, which he rejected, that the appellant should be allowed to vacate his plea.

57.39 ***The judge rejects the basis of plea Role of prosecuting counsel***
Criminal Practice Directions 2015 EWCA Crim 1567 para VII B.13...Whatever view has been taken by the prosecution, the prosecutor should not leave the questioning to the judge, but should assist the court by exploring the issues which the court wishes to have explored.
R v Beswick 1996 1 Cr App R (S) 343 Where the judge rejects an agreed basis of plea and directs a trial of an issue, he is entitled to expect prosecuting counsel to assist him by the presentation of the prosecution evidence and in testing any evidence called on behalf of the defence. In so far as the agreement, were it on the trial of the issue to be binding on the prosecution, might hamper the process of ascertaining the true facts, it must be considered as being conditional upon the approval of the judge and the defence cannot without that approval seek to hold the prosecution to it. Since the prosecution should not

have lent itself to such an agreement, it would offend and obstruct the doing of justice were the prosecution to be bound by it so as to hamper the judge in his task of ascertaining the truth.

57.40 ***The judge rejects the basis of plea Defence must be told***

R v Underwood and Others Re K 2004 EWCA Crim 2256, 2005 1 Cr App R (S) 90 (p 478) at para 58 (Conclusions at para 72) We think it probable the Judge passed sentence on the basis that the written basis of plea in relation to premeditation was nonsense. Unfortunately he did not say so. There is therefore a distinct possibility that the defendant was sentenced on the basis that this was a premeditated offence without the Judge either giving the defendant the opportunity to give evidence in support of his basis of plea, or, through his counsel, the chance to persuade the Judge that it represented a tenable view of the facts. The defendant should be sentenced on the facts in his basis of plea.

R v Lucien 2009 EWCA Crim 2004 D pleaded to unlawful wounding on the first day of his trial. His plea was tendered on a specific basis and sentence was adjourned. Three weeks later he pleaded to kidnapping and robbery. Those pleas, following an abuse of process application, were tendered on a specific basis. D asserted that he was unaware of the existence of a knife and did not brandish a knife himself. The Judge rejected that claim. When sentencing, the Judge proceeded to reject other aspects of D's basis of plea. Held. The Judge was entitled to reach the conclusion that he did and to sentence on that basis. Whilst the defence had notice of the Judge's disagreement with that part of the basis of plea, they had no notice that the Judge did not accept other aspects of it. If a judge does not accept an important and relevant part of the basis of plea, he or she should make that clear so that the defence can decide how they wish to proceed. Here the defence could have called D to give evidence on that topic, or simply made submissions on the evidence as it stood.

Basis of plea Other matters

57.41 ***Prosecution don't challenge the account Defence call evidence***

Criminal Practice Directions 2015 EWCA Crim 1567 para VII B.8 e) On occasion the prosecution may lack the evidence positively to dispute the defendant's account, for example, where the defendant asserts a matter outside the knowledge of the prosecution. Simply because the prosecution does not have evidence to contradict the defendant's assertions does not mean those assertions should be agreed. In such a case, the prosecution should test the defendant's evidence and submissions by requesting a *Newton* hearing (*R v Newton* 1982 4 Cr App R (S) 388).

R v Guppy 1995 16 Cr App R (S) 25 Where D relies upon extraneous matters in mitigation which are completely unrelated to the facts or circumstances of the offence, this would clearly fall outside the scope of a *Newton* hearing.

R v Tolera 1999 1 Cr App R (S) 25 LCJ D pleaded to possession of heroin with intent to supply. Held. Where the defendant, having pleaded guilty, advances an account of the offence which: a) the prosecution does not accept, or feels it cannot challenge, but which b) the court feels unable to accept, whether because it conflicts with the facts disclosed in the Crown's case or because it is incredible and defies common sense, a hearing can be held and evidence called to resolve the matter. That will ordinarily involve calling the defendant and the prosecutor should ask appropriate questions to test the defendant's evidence, adopting for this purpose the role of *amicus*, exploring matters which the court wishes to be explored. It is not generally desirable that the prosecutor, on the ground that he has no evidence to contradict [the account] of the defendant, should simply fold his hands and leave the questioning to the judge.

DISPUTE AS TO FACTS

Power to determine and counsel's duty

57.42 ***Basic principles***

Criminal Practice Directions 2015 EWCA Crim 1567 para VII B.11 Where the defendant pleads guilty, but disputes the basis of offending alleged by the prosecution, and agreement as to that has not been reached, the following procedure should be followed:

a) The defendant's basis of plea must be set out in writing, identifying what is in dispute and must be signed by the defendant;
b) the prosecution must respond in writing setting out their alternative contentions and indicating whether or not they submit that a *Newton* hearing is necessary;
c) the court may invite the parties to make representations about whether the dispute is material to sentence; and
d) if the court decides that it is a material dispute, the court will invite such further representations or evidence as it may require and resolve the dispute in accordance with the principles set out in *R v Newton* 1982 4 Cr App R (S) 388.

R v Newton 1982 4 Cr App R (S) 388 LCJ D appealed against sentence on the basis that there was a substantial dispute of fact between the defence and prosecution and that D was sentenced on the prosecution's version, despite the Judge acknowledging that he was bound to take D's version where there was substantial conflict between the two. Held. The Judge had three options open to him: a) put the issue to the jury, b) he himself could have heard evidence from both sides and come to his own conclusion, c) he could have heard submissions only from both sides and then come to a conclusion. However, if he does so, and there is a substantial conflict of facts, he must, so far as it is possible, come down on the side of D.

57.43 ***Magistrates' Court It is the same procedure***

R v Telford JJs ex parte Darlington 1988 87 Cr App R 194 A factual dispute arose in relation to the value, amount and description of goods taken in a burglary. Held. Where D has entered a plea of guilty and it appears to the Justices that that guilty plea amounts to an acceptance of the whole of the ingredients of the offence charged, D has thereby made an unequivocal plea which the Justices must accept and enter onto the record. Held. Factual disputes in the Magistrates' Court should be dealt with in the same way they are in the Crown Court, hearing evidence upon any disputed facts which it is necessary to resolve themselves, and subsequently proceeding to sentence.

R v Waltham Forest JJs ex parte Barton 1990 RTR 49 In the Magistrates' Court, the procedure outlined in *Newton* is perfectly appropriate when determining factual disputes.

57.44 ***Committals for sentence***

Shaw v Hamilton 1982 4 Cr App R (S) 80 The prosecution appealed a bind over imposed after D had been acquitted. The Judge declined to allow D to give evidence saying that it was undesirable as that might make it appear that the issue of guilt was being reconsidered. Held. That was wrong. It implied that on an appeal to the Crown Court from a Magistrates' Court against sentence, it is not possible for sworn evidence to be heard. If there is a challenge which does not go to conviction and goes solely to sentence, it is open to the Crown Court to hear evidence.

Munroe v DPP 1988 152 JP 657[767] High Court D pleaded to ABH on a PC. D was committed for sentence. The Court was told that at the Crown Court, the plea version was materially different from the prosecution's case. D claimed one punch with an open hand and the prosecution claimed four punches with a clenched fist. D said he had told the Magistrates about his version. Enquiries revealed that the Magistrates' Court had no record of the disagreement. The defence asked the Crown Court to remit the case to the Magistrates' Court to determine the factual basis and to consider again whether a

[767] The case is also called *Munroe v CPS* 1988 152 JP 657.

committal was needed. The Crown Court said they had no power to do that. They considered the factual issue should be determined by the Crown Court. D appealed. Held. The Crown Court did have power to remit the case to find the correct version, *R v Mutford and Lothingland JJs ex parte Harber* 1971 55 Cr App R (S) 57. The Crown Court also has the jurisdiction to determine the issue itself. Which is appropriate depends on when the dispute arises. Where the dispute occurs in the Magistrates' Court they should hear the evidence and determine the issue. If they commit they must ensure the Crown Court is told of their findings. The Crown Court should then sentence on the facts as found by the magistrates and not allow the case to be reopened. If the dispute arises at the Crown Court they should determine the issue.
See also the ***Magistrates' Court It is the same procedure*** para at **57.43**.

57.45 ***Duty of defence counsel to raise issue/write to the prosecution***

R v Underwood and Others 2004 EWCA Crim 2256, 2005 1 Cr App R (S) 90 (p 478) para 3 The starting point has to be the defendant's instructions. His advocate will appreciate whether any significant facts about the prosecution evidence are disputed and the factual basis on which the defendant intends to plead guilty. If the resolution of the facts in dispute may matter to the sentencing decision, the responsibility for taking any initiative and alerting the prosecutor to the areas of dispute rests with the defence. The Crown should not be taken by surprise, and if it is suddenly faced with a proposed basis of plea of guilty where important facts are disputed, it should, if necessary, take time for proper reflection and consultation to consider its position and the interests of justice. In any event, whatever view may be formed by the Crown on any proposed basis of plea, it is deemed to be conditional on the judge's acceptance of it.

R v Mohun 1993 14 Cr App R (S) 5 It is the responsibility of solicitors and counsel acting for a defendant to notify the prosecution that a plea of guilty is going to be put forward in circumstances where the defendant disputes the prosecution's version of the facts of the offence so that steps can be taken to ensure that necessary witnesses are available at court to enable a *Newton* hearing to proceed. If there is a pre-trial review, it is elementary that appropriate notice should be given in the course of that pre-trial review.

R v Gardener 1994 15 Cr App R (S) 667 Where there is a dispute about relevant facts which may affect the sentencing decision, counsel for the defence should make that fact clear to the prosecution and the court should be informed at the outset of the hearing, if not by counsel for the prosecution, then by counsel for the defence. The judge can then consider whether it is appropriate or necessary to conduct a *Newton* hearing. If for some reason the procedure is overlooked at the very outset of the case, then counsel for the defence should ensure that during the course of the mitigation the judge is made aware not merely that there is a dispute, but that there is an issue of fact which the defence wishes to resolve in a *Newton* hearing. In this case the first reference to a *Newton* hearing appeared in the advice on appeal. This is far too late. This Court will not normally consider an argument that the judge failed to order a hearing into disputed facts unless the possibility of such a hearing is raised expressly and unequivocally at the Crown Court for the judge to consider. There are huge disadvantages if that procedure is not followed. To take an example: it would put this Court into an impossible position if it was invited to accept the defendant's version of events without the victim having any opportunity to be heard and when the Crown's case throughout is that the victim's version is correct. Appeal dismissed.

Att-Gen's Ref Nos 3-4 of 1996 1997 1 Cr App R (S) 29 If there is to be a challenge to important facts in the prosecution case and these were very important facts, it must be made crystal clear to the sentencing judge. If it can be avoided it is very undesirable that the sentence should be passed on an artificial basis either in the Crown Court or in the Court of Appeal.

R v Tolera 1999 1 Cr App R (S) 25 D pleaded to possession of heroin with intent to supply (5 years' imprisonment, forfeiture order and recommendation for deportation). A minicab driver was called to a pub where he collected D and two others. He drove them to a block of flats. D entered the flats and returned after 20 minutes. D then asked to be taken to another address. During this journey the cab passed a police van, causing D to 'slump down' in his seat. The officers noticed this and decided to stop the cab. They witnessed D place something in his trousers. D was searched and a bag was found under his waistband. It was later discovered that the bag contained 55.8 grams of heroin at 51% purity. A search of D's premises yielded £1,500 in cash. D claimed that under the threat of violence he had been forced to be a courier but had not been dealing in the drugs. The Judge did not accept this account. The Judge ordered a *Newton* hearing. In passing sentence, the Judge declined to treat D as a mere courier of drugs. In his view D was a distributor of drugs for those who were engaged in a substantial way in dealing heroin. Held. If D wishes to ask the Court to pass sentence on any other basis than that disclosed in the Crown's case, it is necessary for D to make that quite clear. If the Crown does not accept the defence account, and if the discrepancy between the two accounts is such as to have a potentially significant effect on the level of sentence, then consideration must be given to the holding of a *Newton* hearing. The initiative rests on the defence.

R v Cairns and Others 2013 EWCA Crim 467, 2 Cr App R (S) 73 (p 474) para 4 If, however, the offender seeks to challenge the [prosecution] account, the onus is on him to do so and to identify the areas of dispute in writing, first with the prosecution and then with the court.

R v Marsh and Cato 2018 EWCA Crim 986, 2 Cr App R (S) 28 Parties to a sentencing exercise must ensure that the factual basis for sentence is properly established. Where there is any dispute that may have a significant impact upon the nature or length of any sentence imposed, the dispute should be resolved, if necessary by holding a *Newton* hearing. If a defendant decides to plead guilty but does not submit a basis of plea, the defence advocate should ensure that the prosecutor is aware of any differences in the case as presented by the prosecution and the defendant's instructions as to be advanced in mitigation, so that the prosecutor is not taken by surprise.

For prosecution roles in *Newton* hearings, see **57.63**.

Disputes as to facts Determining the dispute

57.46 ***Court should consider whether there is a substantial diversion***

R v Hall 1985 6 Cr App R (S) 321 D pleaded to inflicting GBH, causing GBH, damaging property, theft and attempted theft (3 years' imprisonment). Two offences of criminal damage were taken into consideration. They alleged that D entered his mother-in-law's house intending to seize his child. D lost his temper and his mother-in-law turned her back to D. He then attempted to gouge out her right eye, and knocked her to the floor. He proceeded to kick her in the stomach and aimed a kick towards her face. She was able to block the kick but in doing so suffered a fractured arm. D's version was that he intended to 'win back' his wife and was emotional and very upset. His mother-in-law had intervened, he pushed her out of the way and took his child. He then pushed his mother-in-law a second time after she had approached him and argued with him. He pushed her to the floor and kicked her once. He alleged this was how she suffered a fractured arm. The sentencing Judge in his remarks recited the prosecution's version of the incident. D appealed. Held. In such circumstances it is for the judge to consider whether there is a substantial divergence or conflict of fact which might materially affect his sentence. After making his assessment (see *R v Newton*) the judge should then consider whether the conflict was such as to materially affect the sentence he wished to impose. Where the sentence upon the prosecution version is likely to be the same as the sentence imposed if D's version is accepted, it is undesirable that a judge should be seen to adopt the prosecution's version. In such a situation, the court should specifically proceed on D's version to avoid any sense of grievance.

57.47 ***Dispute between prosecution and defence not substantial***
R v Underwood and Others 2004 EWCA Crim 2256, 2005 1 Cr App R (S) 90 (p 478) para 10(e) Where the impact of the dispute on the eventual sentencing decision is minimal, the *Newton* hearing is unnecessary. The judge is rarely likely to be concerned with minute differences about events on the periphery. 10(f) The judge is entitled to decline to hear evidence about disputed facts if the case advanced on the defendant's behalf is, for good reason, to be regarded as absurd or obviously untenable. If so, however, he should explain why he has reached this conclusion.
R v Hall 1985 6 Cr App R (S) 321 After making his assessment (see *R v Newton* 1982) the judge should then consider whether the conflict was such as to materially affect the sentence he wished to impose. Where the sentence upon the prosecution version is likely to be the same as the sentence imposed if D's version is accepted, it is undesirable that a judge should be seen to adopt the prosecution's version. In such a situation, the court should specifically proceed on D's version to avoid any sense of grievance.
R v Bent 1986 8 Cr App R (S) 19 D pleaded to theft (3 months) and common assault (6 months consecutive). He had stolen a packet of Scotch eggs from a supermarket and was chased by a security guard. The prosecution alleged that D punched the security guard in the face and struck him with a stick. D suggested that he pushed the security guard and threatened him with a stick. In his sentencing remarks the Judge had accepted the prosecution's version. D appealed on the basis that the Judge should have resolved the issue in line with the guidance provided by *R v Newton* 1982 4 Cr App R (S) 388. Held. This was not a case where there was a substantial conflict between prosecution and defence. It is impossible for the court to say that the sentences imposed were excessive or wrong in principle. A *Newton* hearing was not necessary. Appeal dismissed.
Note: Many practitioners are likely to consider that the decision in *R v Bent* 1986 was a judicial 'fudge'. The difference was substantial and 6 months consecutive would not normally be imposed for just a threat to strike. Ed.
R v Bilinski 1987 9 Cr App R (S) 360 D pleaded to importing heroin with a street value of around £600,000 (12 years' imprisonment). A ship, of which D was a senior member of the crew, was searched by customs officers. Packages were discovered which were later found to contain heroin. D's fingerprints were on the packages. D admitted importing the drugs for a sum of £3,500 but asserted that he was informed that the packages contained cannabis, not heroin. The Judge stated that D's belief as to the type of drug which the package contained was irrelevant. D appealed. Held. D's belief as to the type of drug imported is relevant, and in some instances it will be necessary to conduct a *Newton* hearing. However, in cases which accord with *R v Hawkins* 1985 7 Cr App R (S) 351, where D's assertion is manifestly false, the judge is entitled to reject it without hearing any evidence. In D's case, a small degree of curiosity or enquiry would have revealed the true nature of the drug in this case and accordingly the mitigating effect of the belief, if held, was small. The sentence was reduced on other grounds.
See also: *R v Sweeting* 1982 4 Cr App R (S) 388 (Dispute about how a victim came to sustain a stab wound. We do not regard it as a significant difference. No need to hold a *Newton* hearing.)

57.48 ***Account obviously false so Newton not required/Issue can be dealt with on the papers***
Criminal Practice Directions 2015 EWCA Crim 1567 para VII B.10 A judge is not entitled to reject a defendant's basis of plea absent a *Newton* hearing unless it is determined by the court that the basis is manifestly false and as such does not merit examination by way of the calling of evidence…
R v Mudd 1988 10 Cr App R (S) 22 D pleaded to burglary (3 years' youth custody) and reckless driving (6 months' youth custody, concurrent and disqualified from driving for 2 years.) One offence of theft was taken into consideration. D, with others, broke into a working men's club causing £800 worth of damage. They stole cash to the value of £3,500. When driving home in the early hours after the burglary had been committed, D

was signalled to stop by a police car. D failed to stop and a chase ensued. That formed the basis of the reckless driving charge. D asserted that he was asked to meet some acquaintances at the working men's club at 4.30 am to collect a parcel. He did not know that stolen property would be involved. He met an acquaintance in the club's car park and upon returning to the car, he discovered several money bags and a tin on the back seat. He then drove off. D denied entering the building. The Judge rejected D's account and explained his reasons and D was sentenced accordingly. Held. It is clear that the Judge thought D's account was incredible and as such it was not necessary for him to hold a *Newton* hearing.

R v Taylor 2006 EWCA Crim 3132, 2007 2 Cr App R (S) 24 (p 129) D pleaded to two counts of importation of cannabis and one count of transferring criminal property (5 years' imprisonment). Customs officers observed D getting out of a Mercedes car and talking with the driver of a Vauxhall car. The Vauxhall driver opened the boot of his car and D was seen taking a plastic carrier bag and a holdall and placing them in the Mercedes. The men were arrested and £216,640 in cash together with a quantity of euro currency was found. A search of premises indicated that those premises were a major centre for the storage and distribution of cannabis with a turnover of hundreds of thousands of pounds. D pleaded to transferring criminal property and one count of importation with a basis of plea. It was maintained that D would deliver and fetch on a total of five occasions, at his friend's request, bags which he believed contained money and which he suspected was connected with crime. D claimed that he received between £100 and £200 for each delivery or collection. It was claimed about once a month D had been involved in the delivery of about 1 kilo of cannabis. This occurred on approximately ten occasions and D received £100 for each delivery. D had also purchased 1 kilo of cannabis on two occasions to supply to friends. He had never supplied to the public. The Crown did not accept the basis of plea. The Judge declined to hold a *Newton* hearing. D appealed. Held. If the Judge reached the conclusion that evidence was unnecessary because the basis of plea was absurd or manifestly untenable, he did not in fact explain why he had reached that conclusion. However, there was ample evidence which allowed the Judge to reject the full force of D's basis of plea. The judge should in such circumstances deal with the arguments on full submissions from both sides and give a reasoned decision so that the basis upon which mitigation is to take place can be entirely clear to all concerned. Appeal allowed. 4 years not 5.

If old cases are required they can be found in the 10th edition of this book.

57.49 ***No dispute between prosecution and defence Judge can form different view***
Criminal Practice Directions 2015 EWCA Crim 1567 para VII B.9 *R v Underwood and Others* 2004 EWCA Crim 2256, 2005 1 Cr App R (S) 90 (p 478) emphasises that whether or not pleas have been 'agreed' the judge is not bound by any such agreement and is entitled of his or her own motion to insist that any evidence relevant to the facts in dispute (or upon which the judge requires further evidence for whatever reason) should be called. Any view formed by the prosecution on a proposed basis of plea is deemed to be conditional on the judge's acceptance of the basis of plea.

R v Kerr 1980 2 Cr App R (S) 54 D pleaded to importing cannabis resin (18 months' imprisonment). D had attempted to carry 10 kilos of cannabis resin through customs at Heathrow Airport. It was estimated that the street value of the drugs was £10,000. D claimed that he was unaware that the packages he had carried were in fact cannabis. He realised only that the packages were, or were likely to have been, cannabis when he collected his baggage from the carousel at Heathrow Airport. Prior to trial, D outlined his defence and the prosecution stated that they were in no position to refute what was being said. D wished to give evidence on oath: he had received the slabs of what turned out to be cannabis from a man in Pakistan, whose son was a dealer in marble. The Judge rejected this story as 'improbable'. D appealed. Held. The Judge listened to the evidence on oath, directed himself as it were on the matter that he had to decide and came to a conclusion that was supported by the evidence in the case. The Judge was entitled to sentence D on the basis that he did. The facts fully supported the view taken by the Judge.

R v Ghandi 1986 8 Cr App R (S) 391 D pleaded to one count of possession of a controlled drug with intent to supply. D flew in to Heathrow Airport from Bombay and his movements were monitored by customs officers, along with his co-accused. Upon returning to Heathrow the following morning, D withdrew a holdall from the luggage deposit, and both men were arrested when D met with his co-accused with the holdall. The holdall contained almost 10 kilos of heroin. D asserted that his co-accused had given him the ticket to withdraw the holdall from the luggage deposit. However, subsequently he admitted that he had brought the holdall into the UK and claimed he had been offered £7,000 to do so. D pleaded on the basis: a) that he believed the packages to be cannabis, and b) that that issue would be determined by the Judge. The trial of his co-accused proceeded, and D gave evidence for the Crown. The Judge then tried the issue of D's knowledge of the contents of the packages. D was not cross-examined by the Crown as they had called him and relied upon his evidence in his co-accused's trial, which understandably would have placed them in some difficulty. The Judge commented on this, noting that in relation to the *Newton* hearing he had not had the benefit of seeing D under cross-examination. The Judge did not accept D's account and accordingly sentenced on the basis that D knew that the packages contained heroin and not cannabis. D appealed on the basis that the Judge was wrong to try the issue of D's belief. Held. There was an issue to be tried and the Judge was right not to put it to the jury. The Judge was also entitled to reject D's account on the evidence presented to him. Where the Crown calls a defendant in a co-accused's trial, the trial of such an issue at present relating to the defendant should be postponed until the conclusion of the co-accused's trial. Further, even where the prosecution feel unable to advance any evidential challenge to the account given by D, counsel should still consider to what extent he can assist the court to determine the issue by exploring in cross-examination any issues which require explanation.

57.50 ***Defendant convicted Judge can form own view***

R v Wood 1992 13 Cr App R (S) 207 D was convicted of buggery and ABH. It was alleged that D had assaulted V and forced her to have anal intercourse. She had 23 injuries. There was a gaping tear to her anus. D asserted that the Judge directed the jury that the issue of consent was not relevant for the offence of buggery, thereby leaving him without the knowledge of the view that the jury had formed as to whether V had, or had not, consented. The Judge decided that V did not consent and proceeded to sentence on that basis. Held. This was a finding which the Judge was entitled to make. It is perhaps unsurprising that the Judge refused to accept, even as a real possibility, the proposition that having already been beaten up, this woman would nevertheless herself go to the lengths suggested and encourage him into an act of anal intercourse causing much damage.

See also: *R v Ellis* 2004 EWCA Crim 1355, 2005 1 Cr App R (S) 31 (p 142) (Convicted of violent disorder. Sentenced on the basis he delivered a particular kick. The Judge was entitled to come to his own conclusion on the facts as he had heard the evidence.)

R v Griffin 2008 EWCA Crim 119, 2 Cr App R (S) 61 (p 357) (Convicted of manslaughter. Court satisfied that there was more than one available interpretation of the jury's verdict. The Judge was therefore entitled and obliged to formulate his own view.)

57.51 ***Defence decline a Newton hearing/to give evidence***

R v Moss 1987 9 Cr App R (S) 91 D pleaded to importation of cocaine. His account that he was a courier and believed the goods were cannabis was not accepted by the Judge. The Judge gave the defence the chance to have the prosecution witnesses called and for the defendant to give evidence. The offer was declined on the basis that the Judge had all the necessary evidence before him. On appeal the defence argued that the Judge should have taken a more active role in sentencing. They relied on *R v Williams* 1983 5 Cr App R (S) 134 and *R v Smith* 1986 8 Cr App R (S) 169. Held. We are quite unable to see what else the Judge could have done. The Judge was entitled to draw the inferences he did.

57.52 ***Plea during the trial Defendant not finished his evidence***

R v Mottram 1981 3 Cr App R (S) 123 D was convicted, following a change of plea, of corruption (6 months' imprisonment and fined £1,000 plus costs). Three co-defendants, B, T and L, pleaded guilty at various points during the trial. B received 6 months' imprisonment suspended for 12 months and was ordered to pay £2,000 to Conmot Developments plus costs. T received 12 months' imprisonment suspended for 12 months and ordered to pay a £2,000 fine plus costs. L was fined £250 and ordered to pay £250 costs. B and T were employed by Fram Gerrard, a company engaged in building work for Salford City Council. B was T's superior in the quantity surveying department. Fram Gerrard subcontracted foundation work to Conmot Developments. D was the managing director of Conmot and acted as quantity surveyor of the Salford building site. Towards the end of the contract it became necessary to issue a final certificate for the work which had been completed by Conmot. T, witness for the Crown, met D and B. It was agreed then that the final and accurate account figure for the subcontract work carried out was £510,000. T alleged that subsequently the three met again, where D said he would write down the figure of £510,000 to £450,000 and that the difference, £51,000,[768] would be divided, with some money going to Conmot and £17,000 being divided between the three men. T alleged that D stated that he would convince his fellow directors that the amount due was £450,000 but in order to obtain £510,000 it would be necessary to pay T and L £17,000. T alleged that D said he would split the £17,000 with them if they would support his story. They were, in effect, being paid to keep quiet. T and B received £2,000 each. D received £1,000 but informed T that he did not want any more money. T received a further £1,000 but D did not receive any of it. The prosecution alleged that either: a) the true value had been increased to £510,000, or b) the true value was £510,000 and B and T falsely pretended it was worth £450,000. D gave evidence that he was trying to obtain certification from Fram Gerrard for £510,000 in order to obtain payment sooner than it would otherwise have been paid if there had been a protracted dispute. D gave evidence and during his evidence-in-chief, the Judge sent the jury out and discussed with counsel how to put his case. He stated that he intended to instruct the jury that on D's version there was no defence in law to the charge of corruption. D then pleaded guilty. He appealed against sentence on the basis that he was not sentenced on the basis upon which he pleaded. Held. D was sentenced on the evidence of T, that the corrupt scheme originated from D. The Judge rejected D's account without hearing his evidence-in-chief in full and without hearing him cross-examined. The Judge ought not to have sentenced on that basis. Appeal allowed.

57.53 ***Mitigation which does not contradict prosecution case***

Criminal Practice Directions 2015 EWCA Crim 1567 para VII B.8 e) On occasion the prosecution may lack the evidence positively to dispute the defendant's account, for example, where the defendant asserts a matter outside the knowledge of the prosecution. Simply because the prosecution do not have evidence to contradict the defendant's assertions does not mean those assertions should be agreed. In such a case, the prosecution should test the defendant's evidence and submissions by requesting a *Newton* hearing (*R v Newton* 1982 4 Cr App R (S) 388), following the procedure set out in paragraph IV.45.13, below.

Criminal Practice Directions 2015 EWCA Crim 1567 para VII B.14 Where the disputed issue arises from facts which are within the exclusive knowledge of the defendant and the defendant is willing to give evidence in support of his case, the defence advocate

[768] The judgment states that the difference between £510,000 and £450,000 is £51,000. Either the original figure of £510,000 is correct and the difference should be £60,000, or the original figure of £510,000 is incorrect and should read £501,000.

should be prepared to call the defendant. If the defendant is not willing to testify, and subject to any explanation which may be given, the judge may draw such inferences as appear appropriate.

R v Broderick 1994 15 Cr App R (S) 476 D pleaded to importation. She initially admitted knowledge that the bags involved contained cocaine. D later alleged she thought they contained cannabis. D also claimed some duress. The Judge indicated scepticism about this. Held. The Judge's scepticism was justified. The alleged duress was not a contradiction of the prosecution case, but an extraneous mitigation purporting to explain the background of the offence. It went to matters outside the knowledge of the prosecution and a *Newton* hearing was not necessary.

R v Underwood and Others 2004 EWCA Crim 2256, 2005 1 Cr App R (S) 90 (p 478) para 10(g) Generally speaking, matters of mitigation are not normally dealt with by way of a *Newton* hearing. It is, of course, always open to the court to allow a defendant to give evidence of matters of mitigation which are within his own knowledge. From time to time, for example, defendants involved in drug cases will assert that they were acting under some form of duress, not amounting in law to a defence. If there is nothing to support such a contention, the judge is entitled to invite the advocate for the defendant to call his client rather than depend on the unsupported assertions of the advocate.

57.54 *Judge directing a jury to decide the issue*

Criminal Practice Directions 2015 EWCA Crim 1567 para VII B.8 f) If it is not possible for the parties to resolve a factual dispute when attempting to reach a plea agreement under this part, it is the responsibility of the prosecution to consider whether the matter should proceed to trial, or to invite the court to hold a *Newton* hearing as necessary.

R v Newton 1982 4 Cr App R (S) 388 LCJ D appealed against sentence on the basis that there was a substantial dispute of fact between the defence and prosecution and that D was sentenced on the prosecution's version, despite acknowledging that he was bound to take D's version where there was substantial conflict between the two. Held. The Judge had three options open to him. The first was to put the issue to the jury.

R v Cranston 1993 14 Cr App R (S) 103 D was charged with one count of indecent assault and one count of buggery. He indicated that he wished to plead to buggery but not to the indecent assault. The indecent assault charge was intended to cover the alleged actions prior to the act of buggery, but both counsel agreed that it could and should be used to obtain from the jury their decision as to whether or not D had forced V to submit to the act of buggery. The Judge initially agreed to this but later discharged the jury after considering the case law. Held. The decision to discharge the jury was correct. If the jury had been invited to give a verdict on the indecent assault on the basis that the alleged conduct included the act of buggery, consent could have been no defence and the verdict would have had to be one of guilty. *R v Young* 1990-91 12 Cr App R (S) 279 was not disapproving of a properly drawn count if a verdict on that count would indicate a jury's decision on a factual issue which was relevant to sentencing.

R v Eubank 2001 EWCA Crim 891, 2002 1 Cr App R (S) 4 (p 11) LCJ D pleaded to robbery. There was a dispute as to the facts of the robbery as D insisted he was not carrying a firearm, whereas the shop assistant insisted that D was carrying a firearm and displayed it to her. He then conducted a *Newton* hearing in relation to the issue of the firearm. He concluded that although there may not have been a 'real' gun, he was satisfied that D was at least carrying an imitation weapon which he used in the course of the robbery in order to induce the shop assistant into opening the till. Held. If the Crown is going to invite the judge to come to the conclusion that the offence was committed with a firearm, then the appropriate course is to include a count on the indictment to make that position clear. Before a defendant is convicted of such a grave offence, he is entitled to have the verdict of a jury. Sentence reduced.

R v Underwood and Others 2004 EWCA Crim 2256, 2005 1 Cr App R (S) 90 (p 478) para 10(a) There will be occasions when the *Newton* hearing will be inappropriate. Some issues require a verdict from the jury. To take an obvious example, a dispute whether the necessary intent under Offences Against the Person Act 1861 s 18 has been proved should be decided by the jury. Where the factual issue is not encapsulated in a distinct count in the indictment when it should be, then, again, the indictment should be amended and the issue resolved by the jury. We have in mind, again for example, cases where there is a dispute whether the defendant was carrying a firearm to commit a robbery. In essence, if the defendant is denying that a specific criminal offence has been committed, the tribunal for deciding whether the offence has been proved is the jury.

Note: This is not a derelict power. When a defendant falls to be sentenced in a murder case when the prosecution and the defence don't agree whether the murder was for 'gain', judges frequently invite the prosecution to add a count of robbery etc. Then a jury decides that important matter which is likely to determine whether the starting point is a 15-year or a 30-year minimum term. Ed.

57.55 *Judge to direct a jury to decide the issue, No need for*

R v Ribas 1976 63 Cr App R 147 D was charged with importation of 161 grams of cocaine. Much of it was 'almost 100%' pure. D, a Brazilian national, entered the UK from Paris with the cocaine and the evidence suggested that it would be diluted and sold to the general public, producing over 300 grams of the drug, with a street value of approximately £8,000. D claimed the quantity was for his personal use only, with the explanation being that it was for consumption during his trip to Europe, which would last a few months. With the prosecution not accepting this, the defence argued the issue should be decided by the addition of a count of possession with intent to supply and a jury empanelled. The Judge rejected that and each side called evidence before the Judge. The Judge rejected the 'own use' account as incredible. Held. D's account was an incredible story and it was not in the least surprising that the Judge rejected it. We do not accept a jury should be sworn.

R v Young 1990-91 12 Cr App R (S) 279 D was originally charged with one count of rape and one count of buggery. He indicated that he would be pleading guilty to buggery but not guilty to rape. The Crown applied to amend the indictment to include a third count to allow the resolution of the issue of consent in relation to the buggery charge. D was convicted of buggery without consent, found not guilty of rape and the jury were discharged from returning a verdict on the third count. D received 4 years' imprisonment. It was D's account that V had consented. Held. Consent is not an issue in a case of buggery. The course followed by the Judge was not justified in law. The jury were left to consider an issue which it was not for them to consider. In such circumstances it is for the judge himself to decide the question of consent if that is in issue. The issue is not for the court to decide, therefore it will be resolved on the version most favourable to D. The sentence was reduced from 4 years to 18 months.

R v Dowdall and Smith 1992 13 Cr App R (S) 441 D was indicted with theft of a pension book and an attempted theft three days later. There was a dispute as to whether D stole the book from the victim's handbag in a supermarket or had found the book. To resolve the issue the Judge split the count into two, one for each version. D pleaded to one and was convicted of the other. D appealed on the basis that the Judge should not have added the count but should have held a *Newton* hearing. Held. The Judge was in error to split the counts. He should either have accepted D's account or have tried the issue. It would not be appropriate to proliferate alternative accounts. The golden rule is to 'keep it short and simple'. The result was that D and his co-defendant on the last count were prejudiced on the attempted theft. All convictions quashed, leaving just the one count D pleaded to.

57.56 *Judge does not hold Newton hearing Defence must be told and be given reasons*

R v Underwood and Others 2004 EWCA Crim 2256, 2005 1 Cr App R (S) 90 (p 478) para 10(e) Where the impact of the dispute on the eventual sentencing decision is minimal, the *Newton* hearing is unnecessary. The judge is rarely likely to be concerned

with minute differences about events on the periphery. 10(f) The judge is entitled to decline to hear evidence about disputed facts if the case advanced on the defendant's behalf is, for good reason, to be regarded as absurd or obviously untenable. If so, however, he should explain why he has reached this conclusion.
R v Gandy 1989 11 Cr App R (S) 564 D and 24 others were charged with affray after an incident in a restaurant where glasses and stools were thrown. One man lost an eye. D pleaded to violent disorder on the basis that he had not used a weapon in the disturbance. An eye-witness identified D at a photo parade as the person throwing a glass during the incident. The prosecution accepted there were six breaches of the ID Code of Practice. The Judge conducted a *Newton* hearing and sentenced D on the basis that he threw the glass which resulted in the loss of another's eye (3 years' imprisonment). D appealed. Held. The Judge was not to be criticised for holding a *Newton* hearing although there was some regret that the prosecution had not seen fit to include a specific count charging D with wounding, either with intent or maliciously. Where there was a *Newton* hearing, it was important that the judge approached the issue as if he were a jury, and direct himself as if he were a jury.
R v Taylor 2006 EWCA Crim 3132, 2007 2 Cr App R (S) 24 (p 129) D pleaded to two counts of supply of cannabis and one count of transferring criminal property (5 years' imprisonment). Customs officers observed D getting out of a Mercedes car and talking with the driver of a Vauxhall car. The Vauxhall driver opened the boot of his car and D was seen taking a plastic carrier bag and a holdall and placing them in the Mercedes. The men were arrested and £216,640 in cash, together with a quantity of euro currency, was found. A search of premises indicated that those premises were a major centre for the storage and distribution of cannabis with a turnover of hundreds of thousands of pounds. D pleaded to transferring criminal property and one count of importation with a basis of plea. It maintained that D would deliver and fetch on a total of five occasions, at his friend's request, bags which he believed contained money and which he suspected was connected with crime. D claimed that he received between £100 and £200 for each delivery or collection. It was claimed that about once a month D had been involved in the delivery of about 1 kilo of cannabis. This occurred on approximately 10 occasions and D received £100 for each delivery. D had also purchased 1 kilo of cannabis on two occasions to supply to friends. He had never supplied to the public. The Crown did not accept the basis of plea. The Judge declined to hold a *Newton* hearing. D appealed. Held. If the Judge reached the conclusion that evidence was unnecessary because the basis of plea was absurd or manifestly untenable, he did not in fact explain why he had reached that conclusion. However, there was ample evidence which allowed the Judge to reject the full force of D's basis of plea. The judge should in such circumstances deal with the arguments on full submissions from both sides and give a reasoned decision so that the basis upon which mitigation is to take place can be entirely clear to all concerned. Appeal allowed on other grounds.
See also: *R v Bolt* 1999 2 Cr App R (S) 202 (The Judge should have given an indication. Sentence reduced.)
Old case: *R v Mackenzie* 1986 7 Cr App R (S) 441 (The Judge ought not to have sentenced D without more ado even though she might have wanted to spare the victim giving evidence. She could have avoided this by hearing D's evidence first and only calling the victim in the unlikely event D's version proved in the slightest degree credible.)

57.57 *Judge declines to hold a Newton hearing Judge must sentence on defendant's account*

R v McCreesh and Lennon 2010 EWCA Crim 314 D in a basis of plea claimed not to be involved in the organisation of a diesel duty fraud. The prosecution rejected this assertion. The Judge declined to hold a *Newton* hearing. Held. If: a) the defendant pleads guilty on a written basis setting out his version on matters of fact which go to the nature of the offending as distinct from matters merely amounting to personal mitigation, b) the prosecution disagrees with the defendant's version, and c) the difference is material, i.e. it will affect the judge's decision on sentence, fairness to the prosecution and the defence requires that there should be a *Newton* hearing unless the judge has formed the view from his reading of the papers that the defendant's version is incredible. In that case, he is entitled to indicate the view which he has formed at that stage but fairness requires that he should give the defendant the opportunity, if he chooses, to advance evidence or argument in support of the defendant's version. If the defendant does so, the judge must give a ruling to explain, however succinctly, his reasons for accepting or rejecting the defendant's version. If the judge takes the view at the outset that no *Newton* hearing is needed because the difference will not affect his sentence, he should say so in unambiguous terms and he must then sentence the defendant on the written basis put forward by the defendant.

R v Cairns and Others 2013 EWCA Crim 467, 2 Cr App R (S) 73 (p 474) para 11 D pleaded to possession of MDMA with intent. Police found 11 wraps containing 4 grams of MDMA, messages on D's mobile indicating drug dealing and just over £306. D was not in employment. A basis of plea said he was a user of class A and B drugs and supplied MDMA to friends and associates. Neither counsel signed it. The prosecution counsel said they accepted the basis of plea and were not seeking a *Newton* hearing. The Judge asserted he was sentencing D according to his basis of plea and sentenced him as a Category 3 street dealer. Held. Both the prosecution and the Judge could have rejected the basis of plea but they didn't. The Judge could not treat him as a street dealer. Sentence reduced.

See also: *R v Dudley* 2011 EWCA Crim 2805, 2012 2 Cr App R (S) 15 (p 61) D pleaded guilty and lodged a basis of plea. His co-defendants were tried and the prosecution ascribed a much more serious role to D than was in the basis of plea. The Judge sentenced D on this aggravated basis. Held. That decision was flawed. He could have rejected the basis and held a *Newton* hearing. As he did not, we sentence D on the basis of plea version.

57.58 *Reasons Judge must give reasons after a factual dispute*

Criminal Justice Act 2003 s 174(1)[769] A court passing sentence on an offender has the duties in subsections (2) and (3).

(2) The court must state in open court, in ordinary language and in general terms, the court's reasons for deciding on the sentence.

For the duty to give reasons after a *Newton* hearing, see **57.66**.

Newton hearings Basic principles

57.59 *Power to order*

R v Newton 1982 4 Cr App R (S) 388 LCJ D appealed against sentence on the basis that there was a substantial dispute of fact between the defence and prosecution and that D was sentenced on the prosecution's version, despite the Judge acknowledging that he was bound to take D's version where there was substantial conflict between the two. Held. The Judge had three options open to him: a) put the issue to the jury, b) he himself could have heard evidence from both sides and come to his own conclusion, c) he could have heard submissions only from both sides and then come to a conclusion. However, if he does not hear evidence, and there is a substantial conflict of facts, he must, so far as it is possible, come down on the side of D.

57.60 *Newton hearings Must not be a substitute for jury trial*

R v Druce 1993 14 Cr App R (S) 691 D pleaded to unlawful sexual intercourse (count 2) and indecent assault of a female (count 5). He received 3 years' imprisonment. V, aged 14, was living in an adolescent unit of a hospital. She ran away. She met D, aged 46, and he invited her to spend the night with him. D took her to his mother's house, which he knew to be empty. It was alleged that D forced V to take her knickers off, fingered her

[769] As substituted by Legal Aid, Sentencing and Punishment of Offenders Act 2012 s 64. In force 3/12/12

and had sexual intercourse without her consent over a period of 2 hours. D alleged that V had badgered him for money and had consented to intercourse. D drove V back to the hospital unit. V alleged that D threatened her and forced her to give him oral sex, for which he gave her £20. D stated that she continued to ask him for money and suggested she give him oral sex. The Judge held a *Newton* hearing. His conclusions were that the suggestion of oral sex came from D and not V, and that intercourse was with V's 'reluctant consent'. He sentenced D on this basis. Held. It was the prosecution's case in the course of the *Newton* inquiry that V had not consented. That is not an appropriate attitude for the prosecution to adopt on a *Newton* inquiry in a case where a man was charged with unlawful sexual intercourse and not with rape. If it was the prosecution's case that V had not consented, D should have been charged with rape. It cannot be right for a judge to be asked as part of a *Newton* inquiry to find a man guilty of a more serious offence than he has been charged with. It was for the jury and not the Judge to decide if this man had been guilty of the offence of rape. We must give D the benefit of the doubt and proceed on the basis that she did consent. Sentence reduced.
See also: *R v Stocks* 1986 Unreported 28/1/86 (The Judge heard evidence as to whether D had a gun. He was wrong to do so as it was another indictable offence that should be tried by a jury.)
Old case: *R v Huchison* 1972 56 Cr App R 307 (LCJ The course adopted by the Judge to determine whether it was one incident was wrong. D should be sentenced on his version, so 2 years not 4.)
See also the ***Judge must not sentence for the offences the defendant had not pleaded to/been convicted of*** para at **57.6**.

57.61 ***Newton hearings Judge deciding issues***
Criminal Practice Directions 2015 EWCA Crim 1567 para VII B.13 The decision whether or not a *Newton* hearing is required is one for the judge. Once the decision has been taken that there will be a *Newton* hearing, evidence is called by the parties in the usual way and the criminal burden and standard of proof apply. Whatever view has been taken by the prosecution, the prosecutor should not leave the questioning to the judge, but should assist the court by exploring the issues which the court wishes to have explored. The rules of evidence should be followed as during a trial, and the judge should direct himself appropriately as the tribunal of fact. Paragraphs 6 to 10 of *Underwood* provide additional guidance regarding the *Newton* hearing procedure. (See paras **57.35**, **57.36**, **57.53**, **57.54**, **57.56**, **57.62** and **57.69**.)
R v Underwood and Others 2004 EWCA Crim 2256, 2005 1 Cr App R (S) 90 (p 478) para 8 The judge must then make up his mind about the facts in dispute. He may, of course, reject evidence called by the prosecution. It is sometimes overlooked that he may equally reject assertions advanced by the defendant, or his witnesses, even if the Crown does not offer positive contradictory evidence.
R v Gandy 1989 11 Cr App R (S) 564 D and 24 others were charged with affray after an incident in a restaurant where glasses and stools were thrown. One man lost an eye. D pleaded to violent disorder on the basis that he had not used a weapon in the disturbance. An eye-witness identified D at a photo parade as the person throwing a glass during the incident. The prosecution accepted there were six breaches of the ID Code of Practice. The Judge conducted a *Newton* hearing and sentenced D on the basis that he threw the glass which resulted in the loss of another's eye (3 years' imprisonment). D appealed. Held. The Judge was not to be criticised for holding a *Newton* hearing although there was some regret that the prosecution had not seen fit to include a specific count charging D with wounding, either with intent or maliciously. Where there was a *Newton* hearing, it was important that the judge approach the issue as if he were a jury, and direct himself as if he were a jury. The Court was also concerned that the Judge had not adhered to the identification guidance in *Turnbull*. It was incorrect to admit the evidence of the witness which breached the ID Code of Practice.

57.62 *Newton hearings Burdens and standard of proof*
R v Underwood and Others 2004 EWCA Crim 2256, 2005 1 Cr App R (S) 90 (p 478) para 9 The judge must, of course, direct himself in accordance with ordinary principles, such as the burden and standard of proof. In short, his self-directions should reflect the relevant directions he would have given to the jury.
For the basic rules about the burden and standard of proof see **57.4**.

57.63 *Newton hearings Role of prosecution counsel*
R v Underwood and Others 2004 EWCA Crim 2256, 2005 1 Cr App R (S) 90 (p 478) para 7 During a *Newton* hearing, the prosecuting advocate should assist the judge by calling any appropriate evidence and testing the evidence advanced by the defence. The defence advocate should similarly call any relevant evidence and, in particular, where the issue arises from facts which are within the exclusive knowledge of the defendant and the defendant is willing to give evidence in support of his case, be prepared to call him. If he is not, and subject to any explanation which may be proffered, the judge may draw such inferences as he thinks fit from that fact. An adjournment for these purposes is often unnecessary. If the plea is tendered late when the case is due to be tried, the relevant witnesses for the Crown are likely to be available. The *Newton* hearing should proceed immediately. In every case, or virtually so, the defendant will be present. It may be sufficient for the judge's purpose to hear the defendant. If so, again, unless it is impracticable for some exceptional reason, the hearing should proceed immediately.

57.64 *Newton hearings Multi-handed cases*
R v Underwood and Others 2004 EWCA Crim 2256, 2005 1 Cr App R (S) 90 (p 478) para 10 b) At the end of the *Newton* hearing the judge cannot make findings of fact and sentence on a basis which is inconsistent with the pleas to counts which have already been accepted by the Crown and approved by the court. Particular care is needed in relation to a multi-count indictment involving one defendant, or an indictment involving a number of defendants, and to circumstances in which the Crown accepts, and the court approves, a guilty plea to a reduced charge. 10 c) Where there are a number of defendants to a joint enterprise, the judge, while reflecting on the individual bases of plea, should bear in mind the relative seriousness of the joint enterprise on which the defendants were involved. In short, the context is always relevant. He should also take care not to regard a written basis of plea offered by one defendant, without more, as evidence justifying an adverse conclusion against another defendant.
See also ***Basis of plea Multi-handed cases*** at **57.35**.

57.65 *Newton hearings Judge should not compel defendant to give evidence*
R v Robinson 1989 Unreported 9/10/89 D pleaded to burglary where the occupier apprehended him. The Judge did not accept his claim that he believed the house was unoccupied. The occupier was unavailable. The Judge said that D should be called and then he found D had told a pack of lies. Held. The *Newton* hearing was unnecessary. D had a justified sense of grievance because his sentence had been increased. Sentence reduced.

57.66 *Newton hearings There must be a judgment/Judge must give reasons*
Criminal Justice Act 2003 s 174(1)[770] A court passing sentence on an offender has the duties in subsections (2) and (3).
(2) The court must state in open court, in ordinary language and in general terms, the court's reasons for deciding on the sentence.
R v Underwood and Others 2004 EWCA Crim 2256, 2005 1 Cr App R (S) 90 (p 478) para 9 Having reached his conclusions [in the *Newton* hearing], the judge should explain them in a judgment.

[770] As substituted by Legal Aid, Sentencing and Punishment of Offenders Act 2012 s 64. In force 3/12/12

R v Cairns and Others 2013 EWCA Crim 467, 2 Cr App R (S) 73 (p 474) para 7 At the conclusion of a [*Newton*] hearing, in order to meet the requirements of the defendant and the wider public, the judge should provide a reasoned decision as to his [or her] findings of fact.
For the duty to give reasons generally see **57.58**.

Newton hearings and the evidence

57.67 ***Judge should seek agreement on evidence***
R v Beswick 1996 1 Cr App R (S) 343 Before the trial of the issue is embarked upon, it may in some cases be appropriate for the judge to be invited to consider whether there are any of the matters agreed upon which do not offend the first of these principles (prosecution accepting false bases of plea) and to which therefore the prosecution should continue to be bound. It is also important that the issues to be tried are clearly identified and that there is agreement on which of the prosecution witnesses' statements bear on those issues and whether these witnesses are to be called or whether their statements can be read.

57.68 ***Defence dispute a significant witness statement***
R v Gass 2000 1 Cr App R (S) 475 D pleaded to supplying ecstasy. The prosecution relied on the finances to rebut the defence plea that this was social supply. The defence wanted a key witness called. He wasn't. The Judge held a *Newton* hearing, ruling against the defence. On appeal, the defence submitted that as the Judge made an explicit reference to a witness statement it was fair to conclude he must have used it in reaching his conclusions adverse to the defendant. Further the Judge should not have placed any reliance on the witness statement. Held. We accept both those submissions.

57.69 ***The calling of evidence***
R v Underwood and Others 2004 EWCA Crim 2256, 2005 1 Cr App R (S) 90 (p 478) para 7 [During a *Newton* hearing], the prosecuting advocate should assist the judge by calling any appropriate evidence and testing the evidence advanced by the defence. The defence advocate should similarly call any relevant evidence and, in particular, where the issue arises from facts which are within the exclusive knowledge of the defendant and the defendant is willing to give evidence in support of his case, be prepared to call him. If he is not, and subject to any explanation which may be proffered, the judge may draw such inferences as he thinks fit from that fact. An adjournment for these purposes is often unnecessary. If the plea is tendered late when the case is due to be tried the relevant witnesses for the Crown are likely to be available. The *Newton* hearing should proceed immediately. In every case, or virtually so, the defendant will be present. It may be sufficient for the judge's purpose to hear the defendant. If so, again, unless it is impracticable for some exceptional reason, the hearing should proceed immediately.

57.70 ***Sparing the victim giving evidence***
R v Mackenzie 1986 7 Cr App R (S) 441 D pleaded to ABH. The victim said that he had a bicycle tyre with him. In interview D said his motive was theft. Both facts were part of the prosecution case. At Court the defence version was that D did not have a bicycle tyre with him and D had no intention of committing any offence. Held. Not only was the conflict not resolved, but the Judge sentenced D on the prosecution case. The defence version was clearly absurd. However, the Judge ought not to have sentenced D without more ado even though she might have wanted to spare the victim giving evidence. She could have avoided this by hearing D's evidence first and only calling the victim in the unlikely event D's version proved in the slightest degree credible. Alternatively she could have reminded counsel that causing the victim to relive her experience of the attack would largely nullify any discount to be gained for D's plea. However, the course taken cannot be justified, so D had to be sentenced on his version of events.

57.71 ***Judge knowing defendant's previous convictions***
R v Eubank 2001 EWCA Crim 891, 2002 1 Cr App R (S) 4 (p 11) LCJ D pleaded to robbery. There was a dispute as to whether D had a firearm. D insisted he was not

carrying a firearm, whereas the shop assistant insisted that D was carrying a firearm and displayed it to her. The Judge was aware of D's antecedents prior to passing sentence. He then conducted a *Newton* hearing in relation to the issue of the firearm. Held. The fact that a judge knows of a defendant's antecedents does not disqualify him from conducting a *Newton* hearing.

57.72 ***Identification evidence***

R v Gandy 1989 11 Cr App R (S) 564 D and 24 others were charged with affray after an incident in a restaurant where glasses and stools were thrown. One man lost an eye. D pleaded to violent disorder on the basis that he had not used a weapon in the disturbance. An eye-witness identified D at a photo parade as the person throwing a glass during the incident. The prosecution accepted there were six breaches of the ID Code of Practice. The Judge conducted a *Newton* hearing and sentenced D on the basis that he threw the glass which resulted in the loss of another's eye (3 years' imprisonment). D appealed. Held. The Judge was not to be criticised for holding a *Newton* hearing although there was some regret that the prosecution had not seen fit to include a specific count charging D with wounding, either with intent or maliciously. Where there was a *Newton* hearing, it was important that the judge approach the issue as if he were a jury, and direct himself as if he were a jury. We are concerned that the Judge did not adhere to the guidance in *Turnbull*. Some breaches were technical. Others were of substance. It was incorrect to admit the evidence of the eye-witness where there had been breaches of the ID Code of Practice. There remained a reasonable doubt whether D had thrown the glass. Sentence reduced.

57.73 ***Judge's role in questioning***

R v McGrath and Casey 1983 5 Cr App R (S) 460 During their trial, M and C pleaded to one count of theft and one count of assault occasioning ABH, with one count of robbery and one count of inflicting GBH left to lie on file. The victim, V, gave evidence. M and C had dined at a restaurant and had met V. V gave M and C a lift home. V stopped the car and M and C got out. A fight ensued. V suffered lacerations to the scalp, a nose bleed, two broken teeth and an undisplaced fracture of the tip of his nose. There was a difference between M and C, and V as to the facts. The Judge indicated during defence mitigation that he wished to hear evidence on the dispute. M and C gave evidence and prosecution counsel said that he did not propose to cross-examine them. The Judge himself cross-examined M and C. Held. It was unfortunate that the Judge was left in the position that he himself had to cross-examine and that he did in fact do so. If there has been a trial and a verdict, then the sentencer should sentence on the verdict, but on the version of events most favourable to the accused consistent with that verdict. Where there has been a plea of guilty, *R v Taggart* 1979 1 Cr App R (S) 144 suggests the approach that should be taken. Consequently, where the judge wishes to hear evidence, *R v Newton* 1982 4 Cr App R (S) 388 provides guidance for such a situation. That investigation should be conducted by counsel appearing for the defendant, on one hand, and for the Crown on the other. It is not an investigation in which a judge should embark upon a cross-examination of the accused person. In this case, the Court's approach fell between the *Taggart* and *Newton* approaches. Sentences varied.

R v Myers 1996 1 Cr App R (S) 187 D pleaded to possession of ecstasy with intent to supply. He was searched at a nightclub and found to have 14 ecstasy tablets on his person. He admitted intending to sell the tablets. However, this was limited to 'two or three' friends. Between counsel advancing and the Crown accepting the basis of plea, D enlarged the number of people he intended to sell the tablets to. The Judge made it clear that he did not accept D's account. The Judge ordered a *Newton* hearing on this issue and when sentencing stated that he did not believe D's account. The defence said the Judge intervened prematurely and in a harsh way when D gave his evidence. Held. The Judge is entitled to make his concerns known about any matter that is revealed by the state of the evidence in front of him when a defendant is pleading guilty. The Judge was entitled to insist on...a *Newton* hearing. He was further entitled in the *Newton* hearing...to question the defendant, especially if the Crown had, in the Judge's view, taken a mistaken view of the facts of the case. The question, of course, for the Judge is when and how he is properly to do that. Here he was premature in his interruptions. He should have waited until the defence counsel had finished his questions and D had been cross-examined. Then he should have asked questions to clear matters up. We are left with the unmistakable impression that he publicly conveyed the impression that he had made up his mind on the papers and without regard to D's evidence. In view of the unhappy way the Judge conducted the *Newton* hearing, sentence reduced.

57.74 ***Findings must not be inconsistent with the pleas***

R v Underwood and Others 2004 EWCA Crim 2256, 2005 1 Cr App R (S) 90 (p 478) para 10(b) At the end of the *Newton* hearing the judge cannot make findings of fact and sentence on a basis which is inconsistent with the pleas to counts which have already been accepted by the Crown and approved by the court. Particular care is needed in relation to a multi-count indictment involving one defendant, or an indictment involving a number of defendants, and to circumstances in which the Crown accepts, and the court approves, a guilty plea to a reduced charge.

para 40 It is difficult to avoid the conclusion that D was sentenced on a basis that went beyond the counts to which he had pleaded.

57.75 ***On the facts, there should have been a Newton hearing***

R v Meah and Marlow 1991 12 Cr App R (S) 461 The defendants pleaded to importing heroin in different cases. Meah had 83 condoms of heroin weighing 60 grams in his shoes. He also had swallowed 67 condoms of heroin. The total with seven others was 150 packages with 136 grams at 37% worth on the street £16,930. Marlow had 39 condoms in his shoes and 32 in his bowels. His total was 57 grams at 40% with a £6,806 street value. They both suggested the drugs were for their own use. In both cases the Judge found this difficult to accept. Held. We are not surprised that the Judge was suspicious. When a suggestion of this sort is made, the judge should hold a *Newton* inquiry unless the suggestion is so absurd it can be rejected out of hand. Once the Judge declined to hold a *Newton* inquiry he should have sentenced the defendants on the basis that the drugs were for their own consumption. Sentences were reduced.

R v Archer 1994 15 Cr App R (S) 387 D, aged 15, pleaded not guilty to rape of a girl aged 14. During trial, the prosecution amended the indictment to include indecent assault and unlawful sexual intercourse, to which D pleaded guilty. He received 12 months' detention in a Young Offender Institution on both, concurrent (the maximum possible sentence). The girl gave evidence to the effect that she did not consent. The Judge did not allow D to give evidence. However, it was known that his pleas were on the basis that the girl did consent. The Judge proceeded to sentence on the basis that the girl did not consent and that D had used violence during the incident, in accordance with the girl's evidence. Held. The Judge came to a conclusion about D's state of mind which he should not have reached without, at least, having heard from D. The sentence was reduced.

R v Yorkshire Water Services Ltd 1995 16 Cr App R (S) 280 The defendant company pleaded to two counts of causing sewage effluent to enter controlled waters and was fined a total of £75,000. Scarborough Borough Council was similarly charged but the Crown offered no evidence. In mitigation on behalf of the defendant company, it was said that though strictly liable, the defendant company was morally blameless and that the fault lay with Scarborough. The Judge made it clear in his sentencing remarks that he would not accept what was said in mitigation and viewed that they were blameworthy. Held. The Judge erred in his approach. The offences were strict liability offences and therefore the issue of moral blameworthiness was irrelevant to the plea and so the Judge was not entitled to form his own view on it.

R v Winter, Colk and Wilson 1997 1 Cr App R (S) 331 C pleaded to conspiracy to cause GBH. D and W were convicted of the same count. Each received 6 years' imprisonment. A man recruited a team of five men to exact rough justice upon a man believed to have stolen a large quantity of tools from his shed. The conspirators gained entry to V's home and attacked him. The attack included the use of a baseball bat, although various versions of events were recounted in Court. W admitted receiving £100 for his involvement. D subsequently admitted that he had also received £100. V suffered a devastating head injury and suffered permanent brain damage. C pleaded on the specific basis that he did not personally use violence against the victim. The prosecution opened the case on the basis that C had used violence but it was made clear that reliance was placed on inferences from the victim's case and not the evidence of D and W. The Judge stated that he proposed to sentence on the evidence he had heard at trial, including evidence to the effect that C had used violence against V. The Judge refused to hear any evidence in relation to C in a *Newton* hearing. Held. C should have been given the opportunity to give evidence if he had so wished. This was not done. C had a genuine grievance. A discount was necessary to reflect that.
See also: *R v Steele* 2010 EWCA Crim 2069 (Defence did not expressly ask for a *Newton* hearing. The Judge did indicate he was not minded to accept the defence version. As the Judge was responsible for the sentencing we will sentence on the defence version.)
Note: If old cases are required, see the 10th edition of this book. Ed.

Newton hearings and loss of credit for the plea

57.76 ***Basic principles***

Reduction in Sentence for a Guilty Plea Guideline 2017, see www.banksr.com Other Matters Guidelines tab In force 1 June 2017. page 7

F. EXCEPTIONS

F1. [not relevant]

F2. Newton hearings and special reasons hearings In circumstances where an offender's version of events is rejected at a Newton hearing[771] or special reasons hearing,[772] the reduction which would have been available [when] the plea was indicated should normally be halved. Where witnesses are called during such a hearing, it may be appropriate [to make a further] reduction.[773]

R v Underwood and Others 2004 EWCA Crim 2256, 2005 1 Cr App R (S) 90 (p 478) para 11 The principles are clear. If the issues at the *Newton* hearing are wholly resolved in the defendant's favour, the credit due to him should not be reduced. If, however, the defendant is disbelieved, or obliges the prosecution to call evidence from the victim, who is then subjected to cross-examination, which, because it is entirely unfounded, causes unnecessary and inappropriate distress, or if the defendant conveys to the judge that he has no insight into the consequences of his offence and no genuine remorse for it, these are all matters which may lead the judge to reduce the discount which the defendant would otherwise have received for his guilty plea, particularly if that plea is tendered at a very late stage. Accordingly, there may even be exceptional cases in which the normal entitlement to credit for a plea of guilty is wholly dissipated by the *Newton* hearing. In such cases, again, the judge should explain his reasons.

Att-Gen's Ref Nos 102-103 of 2006 2006 EWCA Crim 3247 The defendants, T and E, pleaded to robbery. T had approached the victim, V, in the street and asked him for

[771] A *Newton* hearing is held when an offender pleads guilty but disputes the case as put forward by the prosecution and the dispute would make a difference to the sentence. The judge will normally hear evidence from witnesses to decide which version of the disputed facts to base the sentence on.

[772] A special reasons hearing occurs when an offender is convicted of an offence carrying mandatory licence endorsement or disqualification from driving and seeks to persuade the court that there are extenuating circumstances relating to the offence that the court should take into account by reducing or avoiding endorsement or disqualification. This may involve calling witnesses to give evidence.

[773] The extract has been amended so that it is easily understood.

money. T produced a small lock knife and threatened him, holding the knife against his throat. The defendants then took him to his home address and forced him to let them in. They searched and ransacked the premises, stealing a quantity of DVDs, CDs, a mobile phone and a PlayStation. During the course of the robbery T punched V twice in the mouth, causing a cut lip. The defendants were arrested shortly afterwards. There was a *Newton* hearing at which V and others were called. T did not give evidence. T disputed possession of the knife and the violence used in V's home. The Judge found against him on those issues. Held. For T, the issue is whether any credit can be given for his plea. Two very substantial elements of the offence were disputed by him. The consequence was that the victim had to give evidence. But he did admit presence and was prepared to admit the thefts. Some small credit can be given for his plea.
R v Abodunde 2007 EWCA Crim 3092 The Judge started at 12 years and would have reduced it to 8 years for the plea. Because of the defendant's lies at the one-hour *Newton* hearing, he gave 11 years. Decision upheld.
Note: I suspect many would consider a 'punishment' of 1 year's custody for every 20 minutes of a *Newton* hearing to be totally disproportionate and wrong. Ed.
R v Caley and Others 2012 EWCA Crim 2821, 2013 2 Cr App R (S) 47 (p 305) para 27 It is neither necessary nor possible to attempt to lay down a rule as to what (if any) reduction for plea should survive an adverse *Newton* finding. It will depend, as it seems to us, on all the circumstances of the case, including the extent of the issue determined, on whether lay witnesses have to give evidence and on the extra public time and effort that has been involved. Some cases involve little more than an assertion in mitigation which the judge is not minded to accept at face value, so that the defendant is given an opportunity to give evidence about it, often (sensibly) there and then. In that case, the reduction ought normally to be less than it would have been if the (false) assertion had not been made, but significant reduction for a plea of guilty will, we anticipate, normally survive. Other cases may be ones where something akin to a full trial has to take place, with full preparation by the Crown, lay witnesses having to be called and considerable court time taken up. In such a case, the reduction for plea of guilty which survives is likely, we suggest, to be very small, and may be none at all. In between there may be a considerable range of situations. These must be left to the informed judgment of the sentencing judge.
para 53 There will be some cases where after an adverse *Newton* determination, no reduction for plea of guilty will survive.

57.77 *Newton hearing abandoned Loss of guilty plea credit*

Att-Gen's Ref Nos 118-119 of 2007 2007 EWCA Crim 121 The defendants pleaded and the case was adjourned for a *Newton* hearing. The hearing became unnecessary. The Judge gave a full discount. The prosecution said that, because of the subsequent preparation, that was inappropriate. Held. The discount is very much a matter for the Judge. His decision was entirely appropriate.
R v Dooley 2007 EWCA Crim 2748, 2008 1 Cr App R (S) 109 (p 637) D pleaded to possession of heroin with intent to supply at the PCMH. She claimed that she believed that the drugs were cannabis. She did not persist in a *Newton* hearing. The Judge reduced the discount because D had put forward a false story to try to reduce her sentence. Held. The credit is rightly tempered by the proposed but abandoned *Newton* hearing.
R v Gravesande 2009 EWCA Crim 314 D pleaded and took part in a *Newton* hearing that was abandoned after it became hopeless. The Judge considered the case as overwhelming and gave no discount. Held. The Judge should have given him in the region of 10%, so 4 years not 4½.
R v Devine 2010 EWCA Crim 1305 D pleaded to possession of cocaine with intent. The Judge disbelieved D in a *Newton* hearing about whether he knew it was cocaine and reduced the plea credit to 10%. Held. D could not have complained about a 10-year starting point. 10% discount for the plea was too little. With that and because of the co-defendant's sentence, 8 years not 9.

R v Duggan 2014 EWCA Crim 1368 D pleaded at the earliest opportunity to causing serious injury by dangerous driving. D and V had been involved in an altercation in a pub with D offering to 'take the matter outside'. Bystanders subsequently intervened and escorted D to her car, which she got into. V then approached D and there was a verbal altercation. D refused to get out of her car and instead tried to drive out of her parking space. She manoeuvred two to four times in an attempt to get out, but on the last occasion D crushed V against a parked car. V had a fractured femur but suffered no continuing disability. During sentencing, D interrupted the Judge as he described the dangerous driving as involving "three reversing manoeuvres" and shouted, "It didn't". The Judge immediately decided to hold a *Newton* hearing. The matter was adjourned and about two months later at the intended hearing two witnesses turned up. D accepted the facts and a hearing was no longer needed. Subsequently, the Judge only awarded D 10% credit. Held. It was unnecessary to adjourn for a *Newton* hearing as the matter could have been clarified then. D should therefore receive a full one third credit.

57.78 *Newton hearings* *Loss of all guilty plea credit*

R v Underwood and Others 2004 EWCA Crim 2256, 2005 1 Cr App R (S) 90 (p 478) para 11 If the defendant is disbelieved, or obliges the prosecution to call evidence from the victim, who is then subjected to cross-examination, which, because it is entirely unfounded, causes unnecessary and inappropriate distress, or if the defendant conveys to the judge that he has no insight into the consequences of his offence and no genuine remorse for it, these are all matters which may lead the judge to reduce the discount which the defendant would otherwise have received for his guilty plea, particularly if that plea is tendered at a very late stage. Accordingly, there may even be exceptional cases in which the normal entitlement to credit for a plea of guilty is wholly dissipated by the *Newton* hearing. In such cases, again, the judge should explain his reasons.

R v Elicin and Moore 2008 EWCA Crim 2249, 2009 1 Cr App R (S) 98 (p 561) D pleaded where the case was overwhelming. He lied at a *Newton* hearing and was disbelieved. The Judge gave no credit for the plea. Held. The judge is entitled to refuse a discount where there is an overwhelming case and lies during a *Newton* hearing.

R v Caley and Others 2012 EWCA Crim 2821, 2013 2 Cr App R (S) 47 (p 305) para 53 There will be some cases where, after an adverse *Newton* determination, no reduction for plea of guilty will survive.

R v Jackson 2013 EWCA Crim 1635 D said he would plead guilty in a significant drugs conspiracy but only on various bases. One week before his trial he pleaded. There was a two-day *Newton* hearing and his account was rejected in its entirety. The Judge refused to give him any credit. Held. The Judge was entitled to withhold a substantial part of the discount but D should have a modest discount. **9 years** not 10.

R v Abdollahi 2015 EWCA Crim 1265 D pleaded to drug offences five months before he was sentenced. There was a *Newton* hearing when the defence contentions were not accepted. The Judge gave D no credit for his plea. Held. That was in error. It would be rare for an unsuccessful *Newton* to mean there was no credit. We give 10%.

Old case: *R v Hassall* 2000 1 Cr App R (S) 67 (The Judge said he gave no discount for the plea. Held. The Judge was wrong to give D no credit for his plea so 12 months not 15.)

Appeals

57.79 *Defence fail to notify the prosecution and the court that there is a dispute*

R v Gardener 1994 15 Cr App R (S) 667 Where there is a dispute about relevant facts which may affect the sentencing decision, counsel for the defence should make that fact clear to the prosecution and the court should be informed at the outset of the hearing, if not by counsel for the prosecution then by counsel for the defence. The judge can then consider whether it is appropriate or necessary to conduct a *Newton* hearing. If for some reason the procedure is overlooked at the very outset of the case, then counsel for the defence should ensure that during the course of the mitigation the judge is made aware not merely that there is a dispute, but that there is an issue of fact which the defence wishes to resolve in a *Newton* hearing. In this case the first reference to a *Newton* hearing appeared in the advice on appeal. This is far too late. This Court will not normally consider an argument that the judge failed to order a hearing into disputed facts unless the possibility of such a hearing is raised expressly and unequivocally at the Crown Court for the judge to consider. There are huge disadvantages if that procedure is not followed. To take a simple example: this Court is likely to be put into an impossible position, as in the present case, where we are invited to accept the defendant's version of events and therefore to reject the victim's account of what happened without the victim having had any opportunity to be heard and when the Crown's case throughout is that the victim's version is correct. Appeal dismissed.

57.80 ***Findings of fact not made It is for the Court of Appeal to decide***

R v Bowen 2001 1 Cr App R (S) 82 (p 282) D was convicted of manslaughter. The jury was not asked what their basis for the verdict was. The Judge did not indicate whether it was provocation or lack of sufficient intent. Held. It was for the Court of Appeal to decide.

57.81 ***Can the Court of Appeal hold a Newton hearing?***

R v Guppy 1995 16 Cr App R (S) 25 By virtue of section 11(3), the Court, being clothed with the powers to make "such order as they think appropriate for the case and as the court below had power to make when dealing with him for the offence" has, in our judgment, and as was common ground, power to order a Newton hearing in appropriate cases. However here it would not be appropriate as the sentencing Judge indicated that he accepted the defendant's evidence on this disputed fact.

Att-Gen's Ref Nos 3-4 of 1996 1997 1 Cr App R (S) 29 This Court can hold a *Newton* hearing. We offer the defence a *Newton* [hearing]. (Offer declined.) We have no hesitation in considering the defence version was manifestly false.

R v Kennedy 2017 EWCA Crim 654 The Judge failed to hold a *Newton* hearing and failed to explain why she had not done so. The Court of Appeal was invited to hold one itself. Held. It is not for this Court to hold a *Newton* hearing. The holding of a *Newton* hearing and the calling of evidence, even the appellant alone, would appear to fall foul of the provisions of Criminal Appeal Act 1968 s 23, see **4.26**. Even if it were permissible, the taking of such a course would also preclude any appeal were this Court to make assailable findings of fact. On the facts the Judge would have inevitably rejected part of the basis of plea but not the other two parts. Due to the lack of a reasoned approach and the two arguable parts of the basis of plea, we reduce the sentence.

Note: The Court in *R v Kennedy* 2017 made no reference to *R v Guppy 1995* or *Att-Gen's Ref Nos 3-4 of 1996*, where it was said the Court of Appeal can hold a *Newton* hearing. The Court can admit material that should have been admitted at the lower court, like medical reports in Hospital Order cases. Criminal Appeal Act 1968 s 23 provides a filter process, not a bar to admitting evidence. Further, the fact that there is no appeal from a new finding of fact by the Court of Appeal does not prevent the Attorney-General from presenting a more serious factual basis than the one presented at the Crown Court, see **8.34**. It is time the powers and duties of the Court of Appeal were reformed so that the key factor was justice and what the defendant had done and was not bound by Crown Court judges mistakes. Ed.

57.82 ***Overturning the findings made by the judge***

R v Druce 1993 14 Cr App R (S) 691 D pleaded to unlawful sexual intercourse and indecent assault of a female. He received 3 years' imprisonment. V, aged 14, was living in an adolescent unit of a hospital. She ran away. She met D, aged 46, and he invited her to spend the night with him. D took her to his mother's house, which he knew to be empty. It was alleged that D forced V to take her knickers off, fingered her and had sexual intercourse without her consent over a period of 2 hours. D alleged that V had badgered him for money and had consented to intercourse. D drove V back to the

hospital unit. V alleged that D threatened her and forced her to give him oral sex, for which he gave her £20. D stated that she continued to ask him for money and suggested she give him oral sex. The Judge held a *Newton* hearing. His conclusions were that the suggestion of oral sex came from D and not V, and that intercourse was with V's 'reluctant consent'. He sentenced D on this basis. Held. It was the prosecution's case in the course of the *Newton* inquiry that V had not consented. That is not an appropriate attitude for the prosecution to adopt on a *Newton* inquiry in a case where a man was charged with unlawful sexual intercourse and not with rape. If it was the prosecution's case that V had not consented, D should have been charged with rape. It cannot be right for a judge to be asked as part of a *Newton* inquiry to find a man guilty of a more serious offence than he has been charged with. It was for the jury and not the Judge to decide if this man had been guilty of the offence of rape. We must give D the benefit of the doubt and proceed on the basis she did consent. Sentence reduced.
R v Cairns and Others 2013 EWCA Crim 467, 2 Cr App R (S) 73 (p 474) para 10 This Court will not interfere with a finding of fact made following a *Newton* hearing provided that the judge has properly directed himself [unless] the Court is satisfied that no reasonable finder of fact could have reached that conclusion.
For an example of the Court of Appeal overturning a Judge's finding, see *R v Gandy* 1989 11 Cr App R (S) 564 at **57.61**.

57.83 ***Evidence, Receiving***
R v Guppy 1995 16 Cr App R (S) 25 The Court of Appeal can receive evidence under Criminal Appeal Act 1968 s 11(3) and 23. However, it cannot order defendants to swear an affidavit of means. The Court can also order a *Newton* hearing but cannot order the defendant to give evidence.
See also the **APPEALS: COURT OF APPEAL Drafting the advice and grounds: Evidence** section at **4.26**.
FINANCIAL REPORTING ORDERS This order has been repealed, see **99.1**.

58 FINES

58.1
Availability The order where appropriate can be passed whatever the age of the offender.
For children and young offenders, see the **CHILDREN AND YOUNG OFFENDERS: GENERAL PRINCIPLES Fines etc. for children and young offenders** section at **13.43**.
Enforcement of fines Enforcement of fines in the Magistrates' Courts is not dealt with for reasons of space.
Court Martial The Court may fine all ranks, ex-servicemen and women, and civilians, see Armed Forces Act 2006 s 164 and *Guidance on Sentencing in the Court Martial 2018* Annex B. For more detail, see **58.5**.
Victim surcharge The court must impose a victim surcharge. The amount is 10% of the fine, rounded up or down to the nearest pound, which must be no less than £30 (£20) and not more than £170 (£120), Criminal Justice Act 2003 s 161A-161B and Criminal Justice Act 2003 (Surcharge) Order 2012 2012/1696 as amended. Where the offence was committed after 1 October 2012 but before 8 April 2016, the amount is the relevant figure in brackets above, see **115.4**. For offences committed by those aged under 18 between those dates, the amount is £15.Where one or more of the offences was committed when the defendant was aged under 18, the amount is £20. There are exceptions, a) where a compensation order or an Unlawful Profits Order or a Slavery and Trafficking Reparations Order is imposed, when a reduced amount can be ordered or no victim surcharge need be imposed, see **17.67**, and b) where the offence was committed before 1 April 2007, when no surcharge can be made, see **115.3**. Where the offence was committed on or after that date and before 1 October 2012, the amount is £15.

Rehabilitation period 12 months, 6 months for those under 18.[774]
See also the **REHABILITATION OF OFFENDERS ACT 1974** chapter.
For corporate defendants and public bodies as defendants, see the **COMPANIES AND PUBLIC BODIES AS DEFENDANTS** chapter, the *Fraud, Bribery and Money Laundering: Corporate Offenders Guideline 2014* at **227.18** in Volume 2 and the note about the *Environmental Offences Guideline 2014* at **251.3** in Volume 2.

58.2 ***Statistics England and Wales***
Fines Aged 21+

		Crown Court			Magistrates' Court		
		2015	**2016**	**2017**	**2015**	**2016**	**2017**
Offenders sentenced	Males	1,560	1,212	1,059	553,635	531,929	489,645
	Females	185	168	116	257,785	249,312	219,018
	Companies and public bodies	287	323	300	7,613	8,096	9,139
	All	2,032	1,703	1,475	819,033	789,337	717,802

For explanations about the statistics, see page 1-xii.

Power to order and maximum fines

58.3 ***General power of Crown Court to fine offender***
Criminal Justice Act 2003 s 163 Where a person is convicted on indictment of any offence for which the sentence is not fixed by law and does not fall to be imposed under Powers of Criminal Courts (Sentencing) Act 2000 s 110(2) [minimum 7 years for third class A drug trafficking offence] or 111(2) [minimum 3 years for third domestic burglary] or under s 224A[775] [automatic life], s 225(2) [life sentences] or s 226(2) [detention for life], the court, if not precluded from sentencing an offender by its exercise of some other power, may impose a fine instead of or in addition to dealing with him in any other way in which the court has power to deal with him, subject however to any enactment requiring the offender to be dealt with in a particular way.

58.4 ***All Crown Court fines have an unlimited maximum***
Criminal Law Act 1977 s 32(1) Where a person convicted on indictment of any offence (whether triable only on indictment or either way) would, apart from this subsection, be liable to a fine not exceeding a specified amount, he shall by virtue of this subsection be liable to a fine of any amount.

58.5 ***Court Martial***
Fixing of fines
Armed Forces Act 2006 s 249(1) A court or officer fixing a fine to be imposed on an offender in respect of a service offence must, before fixing the amount of the fine, inquire into the offender's financial circumstances.
(2) The amount of any fine fixed by a court or officer in respect of a service offence must be such as, in the opinion of the court or officer, reflects the seriousness of the offence.
(3) In fixing the amount of any fine to be imposed on an offender in respect of a service offence, a court or officer must take into account the circumstances of the case including, among other things, the offender's financial circumstances so far as they are known, or appear, to the court or officer.
(4) Subsection (3) applies whether taking into account the offender's financial circumstances has the effect of increasing or reducing the amount of the fine.
(5) Where:

[774] Rehabilitation of Offenders Act 1974 s 5 Table A
[775] Section '224A' is inserted by Legal Aid, Sentencing and Punishment of Offenders Act 2012 Sch 19 para 14.

(a) the court has inquired into the offender's financial circumstances as required by this section,
(b) the offender has failed to co-operate with the court in its inquiry (whether by failing to comply with a financial statement order under section 266 or otherwise), and
(c) the court considers that it has insufficient information to make a proper determination of the offender's financial circumstances,

the court may make such determination of his financial circumstances as it considers appropriate.

(6) References in subsection (5) to 'the court' are to the court or officer fixing a fine in respect of a service offence.

58.6 *Court Martial Guidance and paying by instalments*

Guidance on Sentencing in the Court Martial 2018 3.7.1 The court may award a fine up to the maximum prescribed by statute for the offence. There is no limit on the level of fine to be awarded for a Service disciplinary offence, except where the defendant elected trial and the court is therefore limited to the powers of a commanding officer. In those circumstances the maximum fine for a Service offence is a sum equivalent to 28 days' pay, Armed Forces Act 2006 s 136. Pay for these purposes means basic pay, not including allowances. A fine is expressed as an amount of money, rather than numbers of days' pay.

3.7.2 If an offender is retained in the Service, a fine will normally be recovered through the offender's pay account and the court should specify the time by which the fine should be recovered. The court may order the fine to be paid by instalments; [at] the end of each month, the court should specify the dates of the instalments correspondingly. Generally if a fine cannot reasonably be recovered within 12 months it may be at too high a level. If the offender has been dismissed or discharged from the Service, a fine can be enforced through the use of a Financial Penalty Enforcement Order (FPEO), Armed Forces Act 2006 s 322. FPEOs are also used where the person against whom the financial penalty was awarded is neither subject to Service law nor subject to Service discipline, Armed Forces Act 2006 s 9(3).[776]

3.7.3 Like a civilian court, the Court Martial has regard to the means of the offender when assessing the level of a fine and is provided with details of the offender's gross pay.[777] The court may allow time for the fine to be paid, or direct that it be paid in instalments, Armed Forces Act 2006 s 251, but there are administrative instructions capping deductions from pay which are designed to ensure that every Service person has sufficient money left each month for living expenses.

3.7.4 The Court Martial can impose a term of imprisonment in default of payment of a fine in the same way as in the civilian courts. If a defendant is serving a sentence of imprisonment (or detention in a YOI) the judge may order the sentence in default to run consecutively.[778] Periods in custody for default are contained in the Powers of Criminal Courts (Sentencing) Act 2000 s 139(4).

58.7 *Unlimited fines at Magistrates' Court/Committal for sentence*

Note: Legal Aid, Sentencing and Punishment of Offenders Act 2012 s 85(1)-(2) provide for unlimited fines at a Magistrates' Court for offences:
(a) which are either way offences, or
(b) where no maximum fine is specified, or
(c) where the specified maximum fine is £5,000+, and

[776] See *Manual of Service Law* Chapter 16.
[777] Armed Forces (Court Martial) Rules 2009 2009/2041 Rule 114(2)(g)
[778] See Armed Forces Act 2006 s 269A (inserted by Armed Forces Act 2001 s 16) and 3.12.3 [not listed] below in relation to setting a period of imprisonment in default.

(d) which are Level 5 offences, unless they are listed in Legal Aid, Sentencing and Punishment of Offenders Act 2012 (Fines on Summary Conviction) Regulations 2015 2015/664 para 2 and Schedule. For the details of which these offences are, see the first paragraph of the chapter for the relevant offences in Volume 2.

This section is in force for offences committed on or after 12 March 2015[779] by those aged 18+ at the date of conviction. For those aged under 18, see **16.26**. Ed.

Criminal Practice Directions 2015 EWCA Crim 1567 para XIII Annex 3:

Magistrates' Court: Very large fine involved

1. This Annex applies when Legal Aid, Sentencing and Punishment of Offenders Act 2012 s 85 comes into force and the Magistrates' Court has the power to impose a maximum fine of any amount.

2. An authorised DJ (MC) must deal with any allocation decision, trial and sentencing hearing in the following types of cases which are triable either way:

a) cases involving death or significant, life-changing injury or a high risk of death or significant, life-changing injury,
b) cases involving substantial environmental damage or polluting material of a dangerous nature,
c) cases where major adverse effect on human health or quality of life, animal health or flora has resulted,
d) cases where major costs through clean-up, site restoration or animal rehabilitation have been incurred,
e) cases where the defendant corporation has a turnover in excess of £10 million but does not exceed £250 million, and has acted in a deliberate, reckless or negligent manner,
f) cases where the defendant corporation has a turnover in excess of £250 million,
g) cases where the court will be expected to analyse complex company accounts,
h) high-profile cases or ones of an exceptionally sensitive nature.

3-5. [These paragraphs deal with the assignment of the DJ and preliminary hearings etc.]

6. When dealing with sentence, Powers of Criminal Courts (Sentencing) Act 2000 s 3 can be invoked where, despite the Magistrates' Court having maximum fine powers available to it, the offence or combination of offences make it so serious that the Crown Court should deal with it as though the person had been convicted on indictment.

7. An authorised DJ (MC) should consider allocating the case to the Crown Court or committing the accused for sentence.

58.8 *Triable either way offences*

Magistrates' Courts Act 1980 s 32(1) On summary conviction of any of the offences triable either way listed in Sch 1 to this Act, a person shall be liable to imprisonment for a term not exceeding 6 months or to a fine not exceeding the prescribed sum or both, except that a) a Magistrates' Court shall not have power to impose imprisonment for an offence so listed if the Crown Court would not have that power in the case of an adult convicted of it on indictment.

Note: This only applies to offences committed before 12 March 2015, see **58.7**. The offences in Schedule 1 can be found in the 9th edition of this book at para 73.8. Ed.

58.9 *The standard scale of fines for summary offences*

Criminal Justice Act 1982 s 37 There shall be a standard scale of fines for summary offences, which shall be known as 'the standard scale'.

[779] Legal Aid, Sentencing and Punishment of Offenders Act 2012 (Commencement No 11) Order 2015 2015/504

Level on the scale	1	2	3	4	5 Offence before 12/3/15	5 Offence on or after 12/3/15
Amount of fine	£200	£500	£1,000	£2,500	£5,000	Unlimited

Note: The power to pass unlimited fines does not apply where the power has been disapplied by Legal Aid, Sentencing and Punishment of Offenders Act 2012 (Fines on Summary Conviction) Regulations 2015 2015/664 para 2 and Schedule. To determine whether the summary maximum is unlimited, see the entry in the book for the particular offence. Ed.

58.10 ***Offence committed for 'commercial' benefit Guidelines***

Magistrates' Court Sentencing Guidelines 2008, see www.banksr.com Other Matters Guidelines tab page 150 para 26 Some offences are committed with the intention of gaining a significant commercial benefit. These often occur where, in order to carry out an activity lawfully, a person has to comply with certain processes which may be expensive. They include, for example, 'taxi-touting' (where unauthorised persons seek to operate as taxi drivers) and 'fly-tipping' (where the cost of lawful disposal is considerable).

27 In some of these cases, a fine based on the standard approach set out above may not reflect the level of financial gain achieved or sought through the offending. Accordingly: a) where the offender has generated income or avoided expenditure to a level that can be calculated or estimated, the court may wish to consider that amount when determining the financial penalty, b) where it is not possible to calculate or estimate that amount, the court may wish to draw on information from the enforcing authorities about the general costs of operating within the law.

See also the **COMPANIES AND PUBLIC BODIES AS DEFENDANTS** chapter.

Obtaining information and searches

58.11 ***Means Duty of defendant to provide information***

R v Northallerton Magistrates' Court ex parte Dove 2000 1 Cr App R (S) 136 LCJ It is for the defendant facing a financial penalty by way of fine or an order to pay costs to a prosecutor to disclose to magistrates information as will enable justices to assess what he can reasonably afford to pay. In the absence of such disclosure, justices may draw reasonable inferences as to the defendant's means from evidence they have heard and from all the circumstances of the case.

58.12 ***Financial Circumstances Orders***

Powers to order statement as to offender's financial circumstances

Criminal Justice Act 2003 s 162(1) Where an individual has been convicted of an offence, the court may, before sentencing him, make a Financial Circumstances Order with respect to him.

(2) Where a Magistrates' Court has been notified in accordance with Magistrates' Courts Act 1980 s 12(4) that an individual desires to plead guilty without appearing before the court, the court may make a Financial Circumstances Order with respect to him.

(3) In this section 'a Financial Circumstances Order' means, in relation to any individual, an order requiring him to give to the court, within such period as may be specified in the order, such a statement of his financial circumstances as the court may require.

(4)-(6) [see **58.13**]

R v Day 2014 EWCA Crim 2683, 2015 1 Cr App R (S) 53 LCJ D pleaded to carrying out an operation to an SSSI without giving notice to Natural England, Wildlife and Countryside Act 1981 s 28E. D was one of the richest men in England. Held. para 50 In future, courts should make wealthy defendants detail their assets and their income over a five-year period, under Criminal Justice Act 2003 s 162. For more detail see **58.32**.

See also the **Children and Young Offenders: General Principles** ***Financial Circumstances Order Parents/Guardian*** paras at **13.55**.

58.13 ***Financial Circumstances Orders Failure to comply with***

Criminal Justice Act 2003 s 162(4) An individual who without reasonable excuse fails to comply with a Financial Circumstances Order is liable on summary conviction to a fine not exceeding Level 3 [£1,000] on the standard scale.

(5) If an individual, in furnishing any statement in pursuance of a financial circumstances order:

(a) makes a statement which he knows to be false in a material particular,
(b) recklessly furnishes a statement which is false in a material particular, or
(c) knowingly fails to disclose any material fact,

he is liable on summary conviction to a fine not exceeding Level 4 [£2,500] on the standard scale.

(6) Proceedings in respect of an offence under subsection (5) may, notwithstanding anything in Magistrates' Courts Act 1980 s 127(1) (limitation of time), be commenced at any time within two years from the date of the commission of the offence or within six months from its first discovery by the prosecutor, whichever period expires the earlier.

See also the **Children and Young Offenders** ***Financial Circumstances Order Parents/Guardian fails to provide*** paras at **13.19**.

58.14 ***Financial Statement Orders Court Martial***

Financial statement orders

Armed Forces Act 2006 s 266(1) Before sentencing a person who has been convicted of a service offence, a court may make a Financial Statement Order, but this does not apply to the Summary Appeal Court.

(2) A Financial Statement Order is an order requiring the person to give to the court, within such period as may be specified in the order, such a statement of his financial circumstances as the court may require.

(3) A person who without reasonable excuse fails to comply with a Financial Statement Order commits an offence and is liable to a fine not exceeding Level 3 on the standard scale.

(4) A person who in providing any statement in pursuance of a Financial Statement Order:

(a) makes a statement which he knows to be false in a material particular,
(b) recklessly provides a statement which is false in a material particular, or
(c) knowingly fails to disclose any material fact, commits an offence and is liable to a fine not exceeding Level 4 on the standard scale.

58.15 ***Searching persons at the Crown Court (for fines and other orders)***

Power of Crown Court to order search of persons before it.

Powers of Criminal Courts (Sentencing) Act 2000 s 142(1) Where:..

(za) the Crown Court orders a person to pay a surcharge under Criminal Justice Act 2003 s 161A,
(a) the Crown Court imposes a fine on a person or forfeits his recognisance,
(b) the Crown Court makes against a person any such order as is mentioned in Administration of Justice Act 1970 Sch 9 paras 3, 4 or 9 (orders for the payment of costs),..
(c) the Crown Court makes a compensation order against a person,
(d) the Crown Court makes against a person an order under section 137 of this Act (order for parent or guardian to pay fine, costs compensation or surcharge), or
(e) on the determination of an appeal brought by a person under Magistrates' Courts Act 1980 s 108 a sum is payable by him, whether by virtue of an order of the Crown Court or by virtue of a conviction or order of the Magistrates' Court against whose decision the appeal was brought, then, if that person is before it, the Crown Court may order him to be searched.

(2) Any money found on a person in a search under this section may be applied, unless the court otherwise directs, towards payment of the fine or other sum payable by him, and the balance, if any, shall be returned to him.
Magistrates' Courts Act 1980 s 80(1) Where a Magistrates' Court has adjudged a person to pay a sum by a conviction or has ordered the enforcement of a sum due from a person under a Magistrates' Court maintenance order, the court may order him to be searched.

Relating the fine to the offence

58.16 ***A fine must reflect the seriousness and the circumstances of the case***
Criminal Justice Act 2003 s 164(2) The amount of any fine fixed by a court must be such as, in the opinion of the court, reflects the seriousness of the offence.
(3) In fixing the amount of any fine to be imposed on an offender (whether an individual or other person), a court must take into account the circumstances of the case including, among other things, the financial circumstances of the offender so far as they are known, or appear, to the court.

Means: General approach

58.17 ***Means Duty to inquire into offender's financial situation***
Criminal Justice Act 2003 s 164(1) Before fixing the amount of any fine to be imposed on an offender who is an individual, a court must inquire into his financial circumstances.

58.18 ***Means Duty to inquire into offender's financial situation Court Martial***
Armed Forces Act 2006 s 249(1) A court or officer fixing a fine to be imposed on an offender in respect of a service offence must, before fixing the amount of the fine, inquire into the offender's financial circumstances.

58.19 ***Means Assessment of financial circumstances***
Magistrates' Court Sentencing Guidelines 2008, see www.banksr.com Other Matters Guidelines tab page 150 para 15 While the initial consideration for the assessment of a fine is the offender's relevant weekly income, the court is required to take account of the offender's financial circumstances more broadly. Guidance on important parts of this assessment is set out below.
16 An offender's financial circumstances may have the effect of increasing or reducing the amount of the fine. However, they are not relevant to the assessment of offence seriousness. They should be considered separately from the selection of the appropriate fine band and the Court's assessment of the position of the offence within the range for that band.

58.20 ***Means Determining fine in defendant's absence or without financial circumstances statement***
Criminal Justice Act 2003 s 164(5) Where:
(a) an offender has been convicted in his absence in pursuance of Magistrates' Courts Act 1980 s 11 or 12 (non-appearance of accused), or
(b) an offender:
(i) has failed to furnish a statement of his financial circumstances in response to a request which is an official request for the purposes of Criminal Justice Act 1991 s 20A (offence of making false statement as to financial circumstances),
(ii) has failed to comply with an order under section 162(1) of this Act, or
(iii) has otherwise failed to co-operate with the court in its inquiry into his financial circumstances,
and the court considers that it has insufficient information to make a proper determination of the financial circumstances of the offender, it may make such determination as it thinks fit.
See also the **PROCEDURE, SENTENCING Absent defendants** section at **86.24**.

58.21 *Means Fines must be within offender's means*

Magistrates' Court Sentencing Guidelines 2008, see www.banksr.com Other Matters Guidelines tab page 150 para 22 Where the household of which the offender is a part has more than one source of income, the fine should normally be based on the income of the offender alone.

23 However, where the offender's part of the income is very small (or the offender is wholly dependent on the income of another), the court may have regard to the extent of the household's income and assets which will be available to meet any fine imposed on the offender.[780]

R v Chelmsford Crown Court ex parte Birchall 1989 11 Cr App R (S) 510 D, a lorry driver, was fined £7,600 for a series of offences relating to the overloading of his lorry. The Magistrates applied a rigid formula relating to the level of fine for each offence. There was £400 for each offence with £20 for each 1% the lorry was over the permitted weight. Payment was to be at £300 a month if he was in employment and £25 a month if not. D's contract was over and he was now unemployed. Held. The fine was imposed without regard to whether D had the capacity to pay. If he remained out of work it would take 25 years to pay the fine. The sentence was truly astonishing. It offended three principles of sentencing: a) it should reflect the gravity of the offence, b) it must be within D's capacity to pay, otherwise it will just drive him to prison, and c) payment should be completed within a reasonable time. Fine reduced.

Old case: *R v Maund* 1980 2 Cr App R (S) 289 (Fine of £5,000 and 2 years' imprisonment for five counts of theft. No evidence that D had benefited personally or had the means to pay the fine. Therefore fine was wrong.)

For the rule in the Court Martial, see Armed Forces Act 2006 s 249(3) at **58.5**.

Means: Individual circumstances

For corporate defendants and public bodies as defendants, see the **COMPANIES AND PUBLIC BODIES AS DEFENDANTS** chapter.

58.22 *Means Can the fine be based on the defendant's capital/savings?*

Magistrates' Court Sentencing Guidelines 2008, see www.banksr.com Other Matters Guidelines tab page 150 para 20 Where an offender has savings these will not normally be relevant to the assessment of the amount of a fine although they may influence the decision on time to pay.

21 However, where an offender has little or no income but has substantial savings, the court may consider it appropriate to adjust the amount of the fine to reflect this.

R (Gray) v Crown Court at Aylesbury 2013 EWHC 500 (Admin) High Court W, the wife of the main defendant, D, was convicted of two Animal Welfare Act 2006 offences. The police and the RSPCA searched a farm and 115 equines were seized. Witnesses described the shocking condition some animals were in. The trial lasted 52 days. The prosecution said their costs were just over £732,000 of which just over £43,200 was expert fees which had been paid out of central funds. W was given a community order and ordered to pay £750. The defendants appealed and the hearing lasted 34 days. W's convictions and the costs orders were upheld. W was ordered to pay £200,000 extra costs. W and D both appealed to the High Court. Held. para 68 There was no rule which prevented a court making a costs order based solely on capital. It was very easy to envisage cases in which a retired person with no income but large amounts of capital could be ordered to pay very substantial costs out of capital. If there was a rule prohibiting this, then it would be difficult to make costs orders against prisoners as they had no income while they might have substantial amounts of capital.

Note: Costs orders are of course different from fines, but there are similarities. I can see no reason why the same principles should not apply to fines as well. Ed.

[780] *R v Engen* 2004 EWCA Crim 1536

58.23 *Means Potential earning capacity*
Magistrates' Court Sentencing Guidelines 2008, see www.banksr.com Other Matters Guidelines tab page 150 para 24 Where there is reason to believe that an offender's potential earning capacity is greater than his or her current income, the court may wish to adjust the amount of the fine to reflect this.[781] This may apply, for example, where an unemployed offender states an expectation to gain paid employment within a short time. The basis for the calculation of the fine should be recorded in order to ensure that there is a clear record for use in variation or enforcement proceedings.

58.24 *Means Third party money*
R v Curtis 1984 6 Cr App R (S) 250 A lorry driver was convicted of evading the duty on half a ton of tobacco. He was a courier and refused to name who he was working for. The duty evaded was £23,000. The Judge imposed a suspended sentence and a fine of £10,000 with a period of 12 months' imprisonment in default. He said, "It will be interesting to see whether those who put you up to this are prepared to back you when they are told that you, who were the courier, have been caught." Held. Endorsing *R v Burke* 1982 Unreported 30/11/82, it is wrong in principle to impose a fine on an assumption that others will pay the fine…and to impose a prison sentence in default of payment of the fine. D is not in a position to pay any fine at all as he is in serious financial plight. Fine quashed.

58.25 *Means Household has more than one source of income*
Magistrates' Court Sentencing Guidelines 2008, see www.banksr.com Other Matters Guidelines tab page 150 para 22 Where the household of which the offender is a part has more than one source of income, the fine should normally be based on the income of the offender alone.
23 However, where the offender's part of the income is very small (or the offender is wholly dependent on the income of another), the court may have regard to the extent of the household's income and assets which will be available to meet any fine imposed on the offender.[782]

58.26 *Means No reliable information*
Criminal Practice Directions 2015 EWCA Crim 1567 para VII Q.6 In the case of an individual, the court is entitled to conclude that the defendant is able to pay any fine imposed unless the defendant has supplied financial information to the contrary. It is the defendant's responsibility to disclose to the court such information relevant to his or her financial position as will enable it to assess what he or she reasonably can afford to pay. If necessary, the court may compel the disclosure of an individual defendant's financial circumstances. In the absence of such disclosure, or where the court is not satisfied that it has been given sufficient reliable information, the court will be entitled to draw reasonable inferences as to the offender's means from evidence it has heard and from all the circumstances of the case.
Magistrates' Court Sentencing Guidelines 2008, see www.banksr.com Other Matters Guidelines tab page 149 para 11 Where an offender has failed to provide information, or the court is not satisfied that it has been given sufficient reliable information, it is entitled to make such determination as it thinks fit regarding the financial circumstances of the offender.[783] Any determination should be clearly stated on the court records for use in any subsequent variation or enforcement proceedings. In such cases, a record should also be made of the applicable fine band and the court's assessment of the position of the offence within that band based on the seriousness of the offence.
12 Where there is no information on which a determination can be made, the court should proceed on the basis of an assumed relevant weekly income of £350. This is

[781] *R v Little* 1976 Unreported 14/4/76
[782] *R v Engen* 2004 EWCA Crim 1536
[783] Criminal Justice Act 2003 s 164(5)

derived from national median pre-tax earnings. A gross figure is used as, in the absence of financial information from the offender, it is not possible to calculate appropriate deductions.[784]

13 Where there is some information that tends to suggest a significantly lower or higher income than the recommended £350 default sum, the court should make a determination based on that information.

14 A court is empowered to remit a fine in whole or part if the offender subsequently provides information as to means.[785] The assessment of offence seriousness and, therefore, the appropriate fine band and the position of the offence within that band are not affected by the provision of this information.

R v Northallerton Magistrates' Court ex parte Dove 2000 1 Cr App R (S) 136 LCJ It was for the defendant, D, to put forward relevant financial details to guide the decision of the Justices. D no doubt knew that he faced a potential fine of up to £5,000 on conviction and, as soon as the prosecutor made an application for costs, he knew of the sum which he could be ordered to pay under that head. He had a full opportunity to adduce any information or make any submissions that he wished, and he was notably unforthcoming. He gave inaccurate details as to his income, he produced no accounts for his business, he gave no indication of the value of the farm or what he paid for it, and he gave no indication of any sort as to his assets. There was nothing which could be calculated to surprise D or catch him off his guard. He cannot complain.

58.27 *Means Unusually low outgoings*

Magistrates' Court Sentencing Guidelines 2008, see www.banksr.com Other Matters Guidelines tab page 149 para 19 Where the offender's living expenses are substantially lower than would normally be expected, it may be appropriate to adjust the amount of the fine to reflect this. This may apply, for example, where an offender does not make any financial contribution towards his or her living costs.

Magistrates' Court band system

58.28 *Fine bands*

Magistrates' Court Sentencing Guidelines 2008, see www.banksr.com Other Matters Guidelines tab page 148

Fine band	Starting point	Range
A	50% of relevant weekly income	25-75% of relevant weekly income
B	100% of relevant weekly income	75-125% of relevant weekly income
C	150% of relevant weekly income	125-175% of relevant weekly income

58.29 *Fine bands D and E*

para 36 Two further fine bands are provided to assist a court in calculating a fine where the offence and general circumstances would otherwise warrant a community order (Band D) or a custodial sentence (Band E) but the court has decided that it need not impose such a sentence and that a financial penalty is appropriate.

37 The following starting points and ranges apply:

Fine band	Starting point	Range
D	250% of relevant weekly income	200-300% of relevant weekly income
E	400% of relevant weekly income	300-500% of relevant weekly income

38. In cases where these fine bands apply, it may be appropriate for the fine to be of an amount that is larger than can be repaid within 12 months.

[784] For 2011-2012, the median pre-tax income of all taxpayers was £390 per week, *HMRC Survey of Personal Incomes*. This figure has been increased to take account of inflation.

[785] Criminal Justice Act 2003 s 165(2)

58.30 ***Magistrates' Court Sentencing Guidelines 2008 Applying them***
Magistrates' Court Sentencing Guidelines 2008, see www.banksr.com Other Matters Guidelines tab page 148 para 7 The offender's financial circumstances are taken into account by expressing that position as a proportion of the offender's relevant weekly income.
8 Where an offender is in receipt of income from employment or is self-employed and that income is more than £100 per week after deduction of tax and National Insurance (or equivalent where the offender is self-employed), the actual income is the relevant weekly income.
9 Where an offender's only source of income is state benefit (including where there is relatively low additional income as permitted by the benefit regulations) or the offender is in receipt of income from employment or is self-employed but the amount of income after deduction of tax and National Insurance is £100 or less, the relevant weekly income is deemed to be £100.
10 In calculating relevant weekly income, no account should be taken of tax credits, housing benefit, child benefit or similar.

58.31 ***Magistrates' Court Sentencing Guidelines 2008 Applying them Out of the ordinary expenses***
Magistrates' Court Sentencing Guidelines 2008, see www.banksr.com Other Matters Guidelines tab page 149 para 17 In deciding the proportions of relevant weekly income that are the starting points and ranges for each fine band, account has been taken of reasonable living expenses. Accordingly, no further allowance should normally be made for these. In addition, no allowance should normally be made where the offender has dependants.
18 Outgoings will be relevant to the amount of the fine only where the expenditure is out of the ordinary and substantially reduces the ability to pay a financial penalty so that the requirement to pay a fine based on the standard approach would lead to undue hardship.

Rich and poor defendants

58.32 ***Wealthy defendants Statutes and guidelines***
Criminal Justice Act 2003 s 164(3) In fixing the amount of any fine to be imposed…a court shall take into account…the financial circumstances of the defendant so far as they are known, or appear, to the court (previously Powers of Criminal Courts (Sentencing) Act 2000 s 128(3)).
(4) Subsection (3) applies whether taking into account the financial circumstances has the effect of increasing or reducing the amount of the fine (previously Powers of Criminal Courts (Sentencing) Act 2000 s 128(4)).
Magistrates' Court Sentencing Guidelines 2008, see www.banksr.com Other Matters Guidelines tab page 150 para 25 Where the offender is in receipt of very high income, a fine based on a proportion of relevant weekly income may be disproportionately high when compared with the seriousness of the offence. In such cases, the court should adjust the fine to an appropriate level. As a general indication, in most cases the fine for a first-time offender pleading not guilty should not exceed 75% of the maximum fine.
Fraud Guideline 2009, see www.banksr.com Other Matters Guidelines tab para 49 When sentencing for fraud and the exceptional case where a fine is imposed with custody, courts must ensure that the fine does not enable wealthy offenders to 'buy themselves out of custody'.

58.33 ***Wealthy defendants Cases***
R v Jerome 2001 1 Cr App R (S) 92 (p 316) D was convicted of handling. A computer and other equipment worth in all about £2,739 were stolen in a burglary. D was traced when a message was sent from the computer through the Internet. His flat was searched and the equipment was found. He was an antiques dealer and his turnover was about £100,000. The Judge said he was minded to imprison D but was concerned that his business might be permanently wrecked. He was fined £10,000. Held. It is permissible

to increase a fine for a wealthy or relatively wealthy offender. However, there must be some proportionality between the scale of the offence and the fine imposed. In handling, the value of the goods must be taken into consideration. **£6,000** fine not £10,000.
Note: Many will consider the sentencing Judge's proportionality of just under four times the value is more realistic than the Court of Appeal's proportionality of just over twice the value. Ed.
R v Day 2014 EWCA Crim 2683, 2015 1 Cr App R (S) 53 LCJ D pleaded after a court ruling to carrying out an operation to an SSSI without giving notice to Natural England, Wildlife and Countryside Act 1981 s 28E. He felled 43 trees, constructed a track to take vehicles, constructed banks and stripped flora to assist a pheasant shoot. Threats were made to those who complained. D was one of richest men in England. para 35 The Judge said for a large company the fine should be substantial enough to have a real economic impact so with the attendant bad publicity there is sufficient pressure on management and shareholders to tighten regulatory compliance and change company policy. Similar considerations should apply to wealthy individuals. Held. para 50 In future, courts should make wealthy defendants detail their assets and their income over a five-year period, under Criminal Justice Act 2003 s 162. The fine had to be of such a size to punish D and fulfil the other objectives of sentencing. A fine significantly greater than £450,000 would have been amply justified. Seven figures should not in these cases be regarded as inappropriate. para 51 For large companies, a fine should, as a matter of course, be paid either immediately or within a single number of days. The same principles should apply to individuals of enormous wealth.

58.34 ***Poor defendants Statute and Magistrates' Court Sentencing Guidelines 2008***

Criminal Justice Act 2003 s 164(3) In fixing the amount of any fine to be imposed…a court shall take into account…the financial circumstances of the defendant so far as they are known, or appear, to the court.
(4) Subsection (3) applies whether taking into account the financial circumstances has the effect of increasing or reducing the amount of the fine.
Magistrates' Court Sentencing Guidelines 2008 tab, see www.banksr.com Other Matters Guidelines page 155 para 1 An offender whose primary source of income is state benefit will generally receive a base level of benefit (e.g. Jobseeker's Allowance, a relevant disability benefit or income support) and may also be eligible for supplementary benefits depending on his or her individual circumstances (such as child tax credits, housing benefit, council tax benefit and similar).
2 If relevant weekly income were defined as the amount of benefit received, this would usually result in higher fines being imposed on offenders with a higher level of need. In most circumstances that would not properly balance the seriousness of the offence with the financial circumstances of the offender. While it might be possible to exclude from the calculation any allowance above the basic entitlement of a single person, that could be complicated and time consuming.
3 Similar issues can arise where an offender is in receipt of a low earned income since this may trigger eligibility for means-related benefits such as working tax credits and housing benefit depending on the particular circumstances. It will not always be possible to determine with any confidence whether such a person's financial circumstances are significantly different from those of a person whose primary source of income is state benefit.
4 For these reasons, a simpler and fairer approach to cases involving offenders in receipt of low income (whether primarily earned or as a result of benefit) is to identify an amount that is deemed to represent the offender's relevant weekly income.
5 While a precise calculation is neither possible nor desirable, it is considered that an amount that is approximately halfway between the base rate for Jobseeker's Allowance and the net weekly income of an adult earning the minimum wage for 30 hours per week

represents a starting point that is both realistic and appropriate. This is currently £110.[786] The calculation is based on a 30-hour working week in recognition of the fact that many of those on minimum wage do not work a full 37-hour week and that lower minimum wage rates apply to younger people.

58.35 ***Poor defendants Other guidance***

JSB Equal Treatment Bench Book 2010 para 1.4.5, see banksr.com Other Matters Other Documents tab Self-evidently, the impact of a £100 fine is greater for someone whose weekly income is £60 than for someone whose weekly income is £600. The majority of people on low incomes have no savings or access to cheap credit. Attempting to pay fines, legal costs or compensation from limited resources can result in problematic levels of debt, a failure to meet other financial commitments such as rent (resulting in a risk of homelessness), utility bills (with the attendant risk of disconnection), or child support payments (increasing child poverty). Payment may also create pressure to acquire resources by illegal means. Financial hardship is likely to affect not only the offender but also any children or other dependants.

1.4.6 The most commonly used threshold of low income is 60% of median income. In 2006-07, the 60% threshold was worth £112 per week for a single adult with no dependent children, £193 per week for a couple with no dependent children, £189 per week for a single adult with two dependent children under 14, and £270 per week for a couple with two dependent children under 14. These sums of money are measured after income tax, council tax and housing costs have been deducted, where housing costs include rents, mortgage interest (but not the repayment of principal), buildings insurance and water charges. They therefore represent what the household has available to spend on everything else it needs, from food and heating to travel and entertainment. Around 13 million people in the UK were living in households below this low-income threshold. This is around a fifth (22%) of the population. At 30%, disabled adults are twice as likely to live in low-income households as non-disabled adults. The number of children living in low-income households was 3.9 million in 2006-07. Health inequalities associated with class, income or deprivation are pervasive and can be found in all aspects of health, from infant death to the risk of mental ill-health. The limited information on progress over time (infant death, low birth weight) shows no sign that they are shrinking.

(Sources: www.poverty.org.uk, www.cpag.org.uk, www.shelter.org.uk)

Making the order

58.36

Collection order Courts must make a collection order when imposing a fine, a compensation order, an unlawful profits order or a sum under a Slavery and Trafficking Reparations Order unless it is impracticable or inappropriate to do so.[787] In particular the court must state the sum involved, determine whether the individual is an existing defaulter, and state if an attachment of earnings or an application for benefit deduction has been made. The reason why these orders are mandatory is that once made, there can be enforcement without a need for a court hearing.

Attachment of earnings order A court must make an attachment of earnings order 'where it appears the [defendant is aged 18+ and liable to pay a fine, or a compensation

---

[786] With effect from 1/10/11, the minimum wage was £6.08 per hour for an adult aged 21 or over. Based on a 30-hour week, this equated to approximately £173 after deductions for tax and national insurance. To ensure equivalence of approach, the level of Jobseeker's Allowance for a single person aged 22 was used for the purpose of calculating the mid-point; this was £53.45. [Note: From April 2019, the minimum wage per hour increased as follows: aged 25+, £8.21; aged 21-24, £7.70; aged 18-20, £6.15; aged under 18, £4.35 and for apprentices, £3.90. Ed.]

[787] Courts Act 2003 Sch 5 para 12(1)

order, or an Unlawful Profits Order, or a sum under a Slavery and Trafficking Reparations Order[788]] and a) is in employment and b) it is not impracticable or inappropriate to make the order'.[789]

Benefit deductions order A court must make a benefit deductions order 'where it appears the [defendant is aged 18+ and liable to pay a fine, or a compensation order, or an Unlawful Profits Order, or a sum under a Slavery and Trafficking Reparations Order[790]] and a) is entitled to a relevant benefit and b) it is not impracticable or inappropriate to make the order'.[791]

58.37 ***Fine must reflect the offence seriousness Must consider circumstances***

Criminal Justice Act 2003 s 164(2) The amount of any fine fixed by a court must be such as, in the opinion of the court, reflects the seriousness of the offence.

(3) In fixing the amount of any fine to be imposed on an offender (whether an individual or other person), a court must take into account the circumstances of the case including…the financial circumstances of the offender so far as they are known, or appear, to the court.

(4) Subsection (3) applies whether taking into account the financial circumstances of the offender has the effect of increasing or reducing the amount of the fine.

(4A) In applying subsection (3), a court must not reduce the amount of a fine on account of any surcharge it orders the offender to pay under section 161A of this Act, except to the extent that he has insufficient means to pay both.

For dealing with means in the Court Martial, see Armed Forces Act 2006 s 249 at **58.5**.

58.38 ***Fixing the fine Magistrates' Court Sentencing Guidelines 2008***

Magistrates' Court Sentencing Guidelines 2008, see www.banksr.com Other Matters Guidelines tab page 148 The guideline applies to the Magistrates' Court and to the Crown Court hearing appeals or sentencing for summary only offences.[792]

para 2 The Court must also take into account the financial circumstances of the offender. This applies whether it has the effect of increasing or reducing the fine.[793] Normally a fine should be of an amount that is capable of being paid within 12 months.

3 The aim is for the fine to have an equal impact on offenders with different financial circumstances. It should be a hardship but should not force the offender below a reasonable 'subsistence' level.

The guidance aims to establish a clear, consistent and principled approach to the assessment of fines that will apply fairly in the majority of cases. However, it is impossible to anticipate every situation that may be encountered and in each case the court will need to exercise its judgement to ensure that the fine properly reflects the seriousness of the offence and takes into account the financial circumstances of the offender.

Note: There is a structured approach to applying a fine at page 153 of the Guidelines. Ed.

58.39 ***Fines must be proportionate***

R v Lamont 2013 EWCA Crim 215 D was convicted of making indecent photographs (×4) and possession of extreme pornographic images (×4). In June 2010, his wife found a magazine dating back to the 1970s which contained indecent images. D and his wife were in the throes of an acrimonious divorce. The police were notified in November and they seized his two computers. Indecent images were found on the old computer, as well as around 18,000 images involving animals. It was not possible to ascertain when those images were accessed. D admitted accessing pornographic websites prior to June 2010. D had accessed a bestiality website in June 2010 and D's wife remembered seeing a pornographic image on the old computer in 2008. In 2010, the new computer was

788 Courts Act 2003 Sch 5 para 2
789 Courts Act 2003 Sch 5 para 7A(2)
790 Courts Act 2003 Sch 5 para 2
791 Courts Act 2003 Sch 5 para 7A(3)
792 See page 15 of the Guidelines.
793 Criminal Justice Act 2003 s 164(1) and (4)

purchased and material transferred from the old computer. There were 27 images at Level 4 and the Judge described them as being just short of sadistic. D was aged 54 and of good character. He was a Conservative councillor in Kensington and Chelsea. He had very poor eyesight, such that he would not have been able to view thumbnail images on a computer. The Judge imposed a 6-month suspended sentence and a £20,000 fine. There was no complaint about the suspended sentence. Held. The principle that a fine should reflect the seriousness of the offence must mean that a sense of proportion must be maintained even in the case of an unusually affluent offender, see *R v Fairburn* 1980 2 Cr App R (S) 315. There comes a point where what is substantial and proportionate having regard to the means of the offender becomes disproportionate in relation to the seriousness of the offence. **£5,000 fine** not £10,000 on one count. The other £10,000 fine remains, making total fines of £15,000.

58.40 ***Multiple fines for non-imprisonable offences***
TICs and Totality Guideline 2012: Crown Court, see www.banksr.com Other Matters Guidelines tab page 12 (*Magistrates' Court Sentencing Guidelines Update March 2012* page 181) **Offender convicted of more than one offence** where a fine is appropriate
Approach The total fine is inevitably cumulative. The court should determine the fine for each individual offence based on the seriousness of the offence[794] and taking into account the circumstances of the case including the financial circumstances of the offender so far as they are known, or appear, to the court.[795] The court should add up the fines for each offence and consider if they are just and proportionate. If the aggregate total is not just and proportionate the court should consider how to reach a just and proportionate fine. There are a number of ways in which this can be achieved. For example: a) Where an offender is to be fined for two or more offences that arose out of the same incident or where there are multiple offences of a repetitive kind, especially when committed against the same person, it will often be appropriate to impose for the most serious offence a fine which reflects the totality of the offending where this can be achieved within the maximum penalty for that offence. No separate penalty should be imposed for the other offences. b) Where an offender is to be fined for two or more offences that arose out of different incidents, it will often be appropriate to impose a separate fine for each of the offences. The court should add up the fines for each offence and consider if they are just and proportionate. If the aggregate amount is not just and proportionate the court should consider whether all the fines can be proportionately reduced. Separate fines should then be passed.
Where separate fines are passed, the court must be careful to ensure that there is no double-counting.[796] Where compensation is being ordered, that will need to be attributed to the relevant offence, as will any necessary ancillary orders.
Multiple offences attracting fines: crossing the community threshold
If the offences being dealt with are all imprisonable, the community threshold can be crossed by reason of multiple offending when it would not be crossed for a single offence.[797] However, if the offences are non-imprisonable (e.g. driving without insurance) the threshold cannot be crossed.[798]

Payment by instalments (including costs and compensation payments)

58.41 ***Instalments, Payment by Fines Statutory power***
Powers of Criminal Courts (Sentencing) Act 2000 s 139(1) Subject to the provisions of this section, if the Crown Court imposes a fine on any person or forfeits his recognisance, the court may make an order:

[794] Criminal Justice Act 2003 s 164(2)
[795] Criminal Justice Act 2003 s 164(3)
[796] *R v Pointon* 2008 EWCA Crim 513
[797] Criminal Justice Act 2003 s 148(1)
[798] Criminal Justice Act 2003 s 150A restricts the power to make a community order by limiting it to cases where the offence is punishable with imprisonment.

(a) allowing time for the payment of the amount of the fine or the amount due under the recognisance, or

(b) directing payment of that amount by instalments of such amounts and on such dates as may be specified in the order.

Magistrates' Courts Act 1980 s 75(1) A Magistrates' Court by whose conviction or order a sum is adjudged to be paid may, instead of requiring immediate payment, allow time for payment, or order payment by instalments.

(2) Where a Magistrates' Court has allowed time for payment, the court may, on application by or on behalf of the person liable to make the payment, allow further time or order payment by instalments.

58.42 ***Instalments, Payment by*** ***Costs and compensation,*** ***Statutory powers***

Powers of Criminal Courts (Sentencing) Act 2000 s 141(1) Where the Crown Court makes any such order as is mentioned in Administration of Justice Act 1970 Sch 9 Part 1 (orders against accused for the payment of costs or compensation), the court may: a) allow time for the payment of the sum due under the order, b) direct payment of that sum by instalments of such amounts and on such dates as the court may specify.

58.43 ***Instalments, Payment by*** ***Fines and Service Compensation Orders*** ***Court Martial***

Power to allow payment of fine or service compensation order by instalments

Armed Forces Act 2006 s 251(1) A court or officer awarding a fine or service compensation order in respect of a service offence may make an order under this section.

(2) An order under this section is an order:

(a) allowing time for payment of the amount due in respect of the fine or service compensation order ('the amount due'), or

(b) directing payment of that amount by instalments of such amounts and on such dates as may be specified in the order.

(3) If no order under this section is made when the fine or service compensation order is imposed, at any later time the appropriate court may make such an order on the application of the person by whom the amount due is payable ('the relevant person').

(4) The appropriate court may on the application of the relevant person vary an order made under this section.

(5) In this section 'the appropriate court' means:

(a) if the fine or service compensation order was imposed by an officer and subsection (6) applies, the commanding officer of the relevant person,

(b) if the fine or service compensation order was imposed by a court and subsection (6) or (7) applies, the Court Martial.

(6) This subsection applies if the relevant person is for the time being:

(a) subject to service law,

(b) a member of a volunteer reserve force, or

(c) a member of an ex-regular reserve force who is subject to an additional duties commitment.

(7) This subsection applies if the relevant person is for the time being a civilian subject to service discipline.

58.44 ***Instalments, Payment by*** ***How long should the period be?***

Magistrates' Court Sentencing Guidelines 2008, see www.banksr.com Other Matters Guidelines tab page 148 The guideline applies to the Magistrates' Court and to the Crown Court hearing appeals or sentencing for summary only offences.[799]

para 2 Normally a fine should be of an amount that is capable of being paid within 12 months.

R v Chelmsford Crown Court ex parte Birchall 1989 11 Cr App R (S) 510 D was convicted of 10 offences of using a goods vehicle whose gross weight exceeded the

[799] See page 15 of the Guidelines.

permitted limit. The most serious offence was when his lorry was about 25% over the permitted weight. The Magistrates applied the relevant guideline and imposed a fine of £7,600 payable over two years (£300 per month) if he was in employment. If not in work it would take 25 years (£25 a month) to pay. D, aged 45, was a man of good character and would be 70 years old when the fine was paid off if he remained unemployed. The fine was upheld by the Crown Court. Held. As the Lord Chief Justice said in *R v Olliver and Olliver* 1989 11 Cr App R (S) 10, if it causes hardship, so it should, but it should not create a situation where the applicant is in a position either that he cannot pay or that in order to pay he has to be under a burden of paying instalments over a period of 25 years. A fine of £1,300 will ensure that it can be paid within a period of about two years. I appreciate that it will cause hardship, but it is intended to do so.
R v Boyle 1995 16 Cr App R (S) 927 If the Judge thought all the defendant could afford to pay was £5 a week it was not appropriate to quantify the costs in an amount which, when added to the fine, would take as long as five years to pay. She should have regarded two years or, more exceptionally, three years as the period within which payment should be achieved and have scaled down the order for costs appropriately.
R v S & S Scaffolding Ltd 2014 EWCA Crim 264 The company, S, pleaded (full credit) to failing to discharge a duty under Health and Safety at Work etc. Act 1974 s 2(1). V died when he fell through a skylight. The only appeal issue was the rate of payment for the £75,000 fine. S was ordered to pay at £5,000 per month. There were £31,500 costs payable on top. S appealed on the basis that the Judge failed to give sufficient consideration to the impact of the £75,000 fine on the business. Held. It was anticipated that there would be a discussion [as to the ability of S to pay the sum selected by the Judge] towards the end of the proceedings. That did not take place. There can be sympathy for the submission that insufficient regard was had to the basic figures of the turnover and viability of S. Having re-examined the figures, the matter can be properly dealt with by the sums being paid at £25,000 per annum.
Old case: *R v Olliver and Olliver* 1989 11 Cr App R (S) 10 (LCJ There is nothing wrong in principle in the period of payment being longer, indeed much longer than one year, providing it is not an undue burden. Certainly, a two-year period will seldom be too long and in an appropriate case three years will be unassailable, depending on the case details.)
See also the **Companies and public bodies as Defendants** ***Fines Time to pay single payment*** para at **227.24** in Volume 2.

58.45 ***Instalments, Payment by Prison in default of payment***
R v Aitchison and Bentley 1982 4 Cr App R (S) 404 LCJ D and E were convicted of possession of cannabis and fined £150, payable in instalments. The Judge also imposed a term of imprisonment in default 'of any one payment'. Held. The vice was this, if D or E defaulted on any one payment, it would appear they would serve the entire term in default, without any consideration given to the instalments already paid. Where fines are imposed with terms of imprisonment in default, and payments are to be made in instalments, it is preferable for the court to fix a period of imprisonment in default, and then make any order as to instalments without mentioning a default sentence in that context.

58.46 ***Instalments, Payment by Varying time to pay***
Magistrates' Courts Act 1980 s 75(2) Where a Magistrates' Court has allowed time for payment, the court may, on application by or on behalf of the person liable to make the payment, allow further time or order payment by instalments.

Prison in default of payment

58.47
Companies Obviously, prison in default orders should not be imposed. If confirmation is needed, see *Judicial College's Crown Court Compendium Part II Sentencing June 2018* page 5.8.

58.48 ***Prison in default of payment Statutory power***
Powers of Criminal Courts (Sentencing) Act 2000 s 139(2) If the Crown Court imposes a fine on any person, the court shall make an order fixing a term of imprisonment or of detention under section 108 of this Act (detention of persons aged 18 to 20 for default) which he is to undergo if any sum which he is liable to pay is not duly paid or recovered.
Mandatory orders The section makes it clear the order is mandatory when a fine is imposed.
Rehabilitation period There is no period.[800]
For those paying by instalments, see **58.45**.

58.49 ***Prison in default of payment Court Martial***
For the Court Martial terms, see Armed Forces Act 2006 s 269A as inserted by Armed Forces Act 2011 s 16 and the table at Armed Forces Act 2006 s 139(4).
Guidance on Sentencing in the Court Martial 2018 para 3.7.4 The Court Martial can impose a term of imprisonment in default of payment of a fine in the same way as in the civilian courts. If a defendant is serving a sentence of imprisonment (or detention in a YOI) the judge may order the sentence in default to run consecutively.[801] Periods in custody for default are contained in the Powers of Criminal Courts (Sentencing) Act 2000 s 139(4).
For ***Fine enforcement*** in the Court Martial see **58.60**.

58.50 ***Prison in default of payment Maximum periods***
Powers of Criminal Courts (Sentencing) Act 2000 s 139(4)

An amount not exceeding £200	7 days
An amount exceeding £200 but not exceeding £500	14 days
An amount exceeding £500 but not exceeding £1,000	28 days
An amount exceeding £1,000 but not exceeding £2,500	45 days
An amount exceeding £2,500 but not exceeding £5,000	3 months
An amount exceeding £5,000 but not exceeding £10,000	6 months
An amount exceeding £10,000 but not exceeding £20,000	12 months
An amount exceeding £20,000 but not exceeding £50,000	18 months
An amount exceeding £50,000 but not exceeding £100,000	2 years
An amount exceeding £100,000 but not exceeding £250,000	3 years
An amount exceeding £250,000 but not exceeding £1 million	5 years
An amount exceeding £1 million	10 years

Note: The terms for non-payment of confiscation were increased on 1 June 2015, see **21.146**.

58.51 ***Prison in default of payment and prison terms, 12-month Magistrates' Court maximum does not apply***
Powers of Criminal Courts (Sentencing) Act 2000 s 139(5) Where a court orders a prison in default term it may be consecutive to a term being served.
Magistrates' Courts Act 1980 s 133(4) Where a person has been sentenced by a Magistrates' Court to imprisonment and a fine for the same offence, a period of imprisonment imposed for non-payment of the fine, or for want of sufficient distress to satisfy the fine, shall not be subject to the limitations imposed by the preceding subsections (the 6-month and 12-month maximum consecutive terms).

800 Rehabilitation of Offenders Act 1974 s 1(3)(a)
801 See Armed Forces Act 2006 s 269A (inserted by Armed Forces Act 2001 s 16) and 3.12.3 [not listed] below in relation to setting a period of imprisonment in default.

(5) For the purposes of this section a term of imprisonment shall be deemed to be imposed in respect of an offence if it is imposed as a sentence or in default of payment of a sum adjudged to be paid by the conviction or for want of sufficient distress to satisfy such a sum.
R v Price 2009 EWCA Crim 2918, 2010 2 Cr App R (S) 44 (p 283) D was convicted of importing cocaine, having pleaded to assisting the commission of an offence punishable under corresponding law, namely exporting cocaine from Ghana. He was sentenced to 28 years and 11 years, concurrent. A confiscation order was also made for £2.34m, with 10 years in default of payment. D had arranged three 'dummy runs' using palletised drums of molasses. These had been bought under an assumed name. D then attempted to import 693.9 kilos (equivalent to 526 kilos at 100% purity) of cocaine. The Judge regarded him as the prime mover in the operation and described the crime as "a major sophisticated attempt to bring a huge quantity of cocaine into the United Kingdom". D argued that no one could expect a sentence of 38 years considering the totality of his offending. Held. We do not agree. The purpose of the period in default is designed to ensure that nothing is to be gained by the defendant if he fails to comply with the order. The fundamental objection to allowing a defendant to say that in the light of his own sentence he should suffer a lesser period of default, is that it remains his own choice, in his hands as to whether he serves the period of imprisonment in default or not. The period in default is a quite distinct and separate justification. It must be borne in mind that the judge, particularly a judge sitting through six weeks of a trial, as it was in this case, is in the best position to determine what period of imprisonment is most likely to persuade the defendant to pay over the sums of money it has been found that he can realise. Sentence reduced on the basis that the Judge had not taken account of D's health problems.

58.52 ***Prison in default of payment Payment by instalments***
R v Aitchison and Bentley 1982 4 Cr App R (S) 404 LCJ D and E were convicted of possession of cannabis and fined £150, payable in instalments. The Judge also imposed a term of imprisonment in default "of any one payment". Held. The vice was this, if D or E defaulted on any one payment, it would appear they would serve the entire term in default, without any consideration given to the instalments already paid. Where fines are imposed with terms of imprisonment in default, and payments are to be made in instalments, it is preferable for the court to fix a period of imprisonment in default, and then make any order as to instalments without mentioning a default sentence in that context.

Combined with other orders

58.53 ***Community Order, Combined with***
Note: The power to fine when ordering a Community Order is authorised by Criminal Justice Act 2003 s 177(2A) and (2B), see **15.14**. Ed.

58.54 ***Compensation orders, Combined with***
Powers of Criminal Courts (Sentencing) Act 2000 s 130(11) Where the defendant has insufficient means to pay both a fine and a compensation order the court shall give preference to the compensation order.
TICs and Totality Guideline 2012: Crown Court, see www.banksr.com Other Matters Guidelines tab page 16 (*Magistrates' Court Sentencing Guidelines Update March 2012* page 18p) Priority is given to the imposition of a compensation order over a fine.[802] This does not affect sentences other than fines. This means that the fine should be reduced or, if necessary, dispensed with altogether, to enable the compensation to be paid.

[802] Powers of Criminal Courts (Sentencing) Act 2000 s 130(12)

58.55 ***Conditional discharges, Combined with***
R v Sanck 1990 12 Cr App R (S) 155 LCJ The Judge imposed a fine and a conditional discharge for possession with intent to supply. Held. It is wrong to impose the two orders together. Conditional discharge quashed.
Note: If the court thinks that it is 'inexpedient to inflict punishment' so it orders a conditional discharge, it would appear unsuitable to impose any other order for the same offence which involves punishment. Ed.
Confiscation order, Fines must be ordered after the see **21.143**.

58.56 ***Court Martial, Fines combined with other sentences***
Guidance on Sentencing in the Court Martial 2018 para 3.7.5 **Combination of financial penalties with other sentences** Normally a financial penalty should not be imposed where other elements of the sentence (such as dismissal, detention or reduction in rank) carry significant financial consequences and reduce the offender's means. In exceptional cases a financial penalty can be added to these punishments, for example if the offender is leaving the Service immediately after trial and the reduction in rank would have no practical effect. However, a Service Compensation Order can be awarded with other sentences carrying financial consequences, but the court should have in mind the offender's ability to pay. See para 3.12 [not listed. Ed.].
For ***Custody, Combined with*** see **28.37**.

58.57 ***Hospital and Guardianship Orders, Combined with***
Mental Health Act 1983 s 37(8) Where an order is made under this section, the court shall not:..impose a fine.
For ***Prison in default of payment and prison terms***, see **58.51**.

58.58 ***Referral Order, Combined with***
Powers of Criminal Courts (Sentencing) Act 2000 s 19(1)-(4) Where the court makes a Referral Order, the court may not deal with the offender by ordering him to pay a fine.

58.59 ***Unlawful profit orders, Combined with***
Prevention of Social Housing Fraud Act 2013 s 4(8)-(9) [Where] the offender has insufficient means to pay 'an appropriate sum under an unlawful profit order and an appropriate sum under a fine', the court must give preference to making an unlawful profit order (though it may impose a fine as well).
See also the **COMBINING SENTENCES** chapter.

Other matters

58.60 ***Court must state the effect of the sentence and of non-compliance***
Criminal Justice Act 2003 s 174(3)[803] The court must explain to the offender in ordinary language:

(a) the effect of the sentence,

(b) the effects of non-compliance with any order that the offender is required to comply with and that forms part of the sentence,

(c) any power of the court to vary or review any order that forms part of the sentence, and

(d) the effects of failure to pay a fine, if the sentence consists of or includes a fine.

For parents etc. paying fines, see the **CHILDREN AND YOUNG OFFENDERS: GENERAL PRINCIPLES Parents etc. paying fines etc.** section at **58.40**.

58.61 ***Suggested sentencing remarks***
Judicial College's Crown Court Compendium Part II Sentencing June 2018 page 5.8 [Suggested sentencing remarks]

803 As inserted by Legal Aid, Sentencing and Punishment of Offenders Act 2012 s 64. In force 3/12/12

Example 1 D is a limited company
D is a limited company For this offence the company will be fined the sum of £250,000. This will be paid through the Magistrates' Court and must be paid within 28 days.
Example 2: D is an individual
For this offence you will be fined the sum of £250. This will be paid through the Magistrates' Court and you will receive a notice telling you where and how to make payment. The first instalment will be paid by {date}. If you fail to pay the fine, or any instalment of it, you will go to prison for 10 days.

Note: This is clearly incomplete. The sentencer in each case should say they make a collection order or why they don't make a collection order. For details see **58.36**.

58.62 ***Fine enforcement Court Martial***
Guidance on Sentencing in the Court Martial 2018 para 3.7.2 If an offender is retained in the Service, a fine will normally be recovered through the offender's pay account and the court should specify the time by which the fine should be recovered. The court may order the fine to be paid by instalments; in that event, given that Service pay is monthly at the end of each month, the court should specify the dates of the instalments correspondingly. Generally if a fine cannot reasonably be recovered within 12 months it may be at too high a level. If the offender has been dismissed or discharged from the Service, a fine can be enforced through the use of a Financial Penalty Enforcement Order (FPEO), Armed Forces Act 2006 s 322. FPEOs are also used where the person against whom the financial penalty was awarded is neither subject to Service law nor subject to Service discipline, Armed Forces Act 2006 s 309(3).[804]

58.63 ***Appeals Court of Appeal can't suspend them pending an appeal***
R v Day 2014 EWCA Crim 2683, 2015 1 Cr App R (S) 53 LCJ para 57 D appealed a £450,000 fine. Neither this Court nor the Magistrates' Court had power to suspend fines pending an appeal. The payments unit could decide not to enforce the fine. There is good reason for strict observance of the obligation to pay a fine when an appeal is brought. This fine should have been paid within days.

58.64 ***Varying time to pay***
Magistrates' Courts Act 1980 s 75(2) Where a Magistrates' Court has allowed time for payment, the court may, on application by or on behalf of the person liable to make the payment, allow further time or order payment by instalments.

59 Fixed Penalties and Financial Penalty Deposits

59.1
Road Traffic Offenders Act 1988 s 51-90F
Fixed penalty notices were introduced as a quicker and cheaper alternative to court proceedings. There are two main groups. The first is for road traffic offences[805] and the second is for disorderly behaviour,[806] which is a wide group including theft. Once a notice has been issued the alleged offender has a set number of days to pay the penalty or request an appeal.

Endorsements and penalty points Since 1997, the notices are able to include endorsements and penalty points, Road Traffic Offenders Act 1988 s 57-57A.

Financial penalty deposits Since 2009, where the offender does not have a satisfactory address in the UK, a police officer or a vehicle examiner may ask for a financial penalty deposit.

Deposits are payable when the offender: a) is issued with a fixed penalty notice, or b) is to be summoned for the offence. The deposit is paid to the officer. Where an offender will be summoned and he or she has no satisfactory address, a police officer or VOSA

[804] See *Manual of Service Law* Chapter 16.
[805] Road Traffic Offenders Act 1988 Sch 2 and Fixed Penalty Order 2000 2000/2792 Sch 1 and 2 as amended
[806] Penalties for Disorderly Behaviour (Amount of Penalty) Order 2002 2002/1837 Sch as amended

vehicle examiner may require the offender to pay a deposit of £300. That is higher than for any fixed penalty offence, Road Traffic Offenders Act 1988 s 90A-90F and Road Safety (Financial Penalty Deposit) (Appropriate Amount) Order 2009 2009/492 as amended.
There is a policy that the fixed penalty should be the same as the financial penalty deposit.
The Act gives the recipient the ability to contest the allegation, see section 90C(3). For an explanatory memorandum about the system for Road Traffic fixed penalties and the 2013 increases, see the Explanatory Memorandum to the Road Safety (Financial Penalty Deposit) (Appropriate amount) (Amendment) Order 2013 2013/2025.
Vehicle prohibitions and immobilisation Where the recipient of a notice fails to make immediate payment, a police officer or vehicle examiner may prohibit him or her immediately from driving any vehicle of which he or she was in charge, Road Traffic Offenders Act 1988 s 90D. Under certain conditions the vehicle may be immobilised, Traffic Management Act 2004 s 79 and Road Safety Act 2006 Sch 4.
Victim surcharge Half the relevant victim surcharge is added to all penalties, Criminal Justice and Police Act 2001 s 3(2) and (2A) as amended by Domestic Violence, Crime and Victims Act 2004 s 15[807]

60 Football Banning Orders

60.1

Football Spectators Act 1989 s 14A
Children and young offenders The order is available whatever the age of the offender.
Breaches of the order Failure to comply with the order is a summary only offence with a maximum sentence of 6 months and/or a Level 5 fine, Football Spectators Act 1989 s 14J (an unlimited fine.[808] There are maximum fines for those aged under 18, see **13.44**).
Breach Offences Guideline 2018, see www.banksr.com Other Matters Guidelines tab In force 1 October 2018 page 56 says, '**Other breach offences** Where an offence is not covered by a sentencing guideline a court is entitled to use, and may be assisted by, a guideline for an analogous offence subject to differences in the elements of the offences and the statutory maxima. In sentencing [for a breach of a Football Banning Order], the court should refer to the sentencing approach in step one of the guideline for breach of a Criminal Behaviour Order [see **26.17**] to determine culpability and harm, and determine an appropriate sentence bearing in mind the maximum penalty for the offence.'

60.2 *Statistics England and Wales*

Football Banning Orders

Year	2012	2013	2014	2015	2016
Number	348	582	341	328	311

For explanations about the statistics, see page 1-xii. The MoJ no longer provides Banks on Sentence with these statistics.

60.3 *Definition*

Football Spectators Act 1989 s 14(4) 'Banning order' means an order made by the court under this Part which:

(a) in relation to regulated football matches in the United Kingdom prohibits the person who is subject to the order from entering any premises for the purpose of attending such matches, and

807 Domestic Violence, Crime and Victims Act 2004 (Commencement No 15) Order 2012 2012/1697
808 Legal Aid, Sentencing and Punishment of Offenders Act 2012 s 85(1) and (4) and Legal Aid, Sentencing and Punishment of Offenders Act 2012 (Commencement No 11) Order 2015 2015/504

(b) in relation to regulated football matches outside the United Kingdom, requires that person to report at a police station in accordance with this Part.

60.4 ***Stand-alone orders***

Applications for An application for a banning order may be made by the relevant chief officer[809] or the DPP, by complaint to a Magistrates' Court, Football Spectators Act 1989 s 14B(1)-(3).

Procedure The Criminal Procedure Rules 2015 2015/1490 behaviour order rules apply, see the **CRIMINAL PROCEDURE RULES: BEHAVIOUR RULES** chapter. All the rules are at www.banksr.com Other Matters Other Documents tab.

Test to apply The test is whether a) the applicant has proved that the [other party] at any time caused or contributed to violence or disorder in the UK or elsewhere, and b) the court is satisfied that there are reasonable grounds to believe that the making of a banning order would help to prevent violence or disorder at or in connection with any regulated football matches, Football Spectators Act 1989 s 14B(4). If those conditions are made out, the court must make an order.

Appeals An appeal lies to the Crown Court over a making and a refusal to make an order, Football Spectators Act 1989 s 14D(1) and (1A).

POST-CONVICTION ORDERS

60.5

Note: These orders have three serious flaws. First, the orders have a 3-year minimum term when custody is not imposed or 6 years when custody is imposed (see **60.32**), so it is difficult to use the order for low-level offending. Courts are therefore often faced with the choice between making no order or making a draconian order. Second, the orders cannot be suspended, which would, on occasions, encourage offenders to behave. Third, the orders lack flexibility as they impose a blanket ban on attending all regulated matches, which cannot be altered. The result is that courts use another preventive order or more usually use requirements that can be imposed with community orders and suspended sentences, such as an exclusion requirement which prevents someone from entering certain places for a set period. Ed.

60.6 ***Purpose of the order***

R v Doyle and Others 2012 EWCA Crim 995, 2013 1 Cr App R (S) 36 (p 197) para 6 The order is not designed as a punishment, although it will have that effect. It is designed as a preventative measure.

60.7 ***Human Rights Act 1998***

Commissioner of Police v Thorpe 2015 EWHC (Admin) 2016 1 Cr App R (S) 46 Police applied for a stand-alone Football Banning Order. The Magistrates granted one and added that the order was only to apply to matches between Fulham and either Brentford or Chelsea football clubs. The police appealed. Held. No convention right was engaged and [even] if it was, it [would be] a qualified right which [has been decided by] Parliament. The qualification to the order was unlawful.

Power to order/Test to apply

60.8 ***Statutory power to order***

Football Spectators Act 1989 s 14A(1) Section 14A applies where a person (the offender) is convicted of a relevant offence (listed in section 14A(2)), see **60.12**.

(2) Once convicted of a 'relevant offence' (see **60.9**), the court must make a banning order in respect of the offender if it is satisfied there are reasonable grounds to believe that making a banning order would help to prevent violence[810] or disorder[811] at or in connection with any regulated football matches (see **60.11**).

[809] . 'Relevant officer' means the chief officer of police of any police force maintained for a police area, or the chief constable of the British Transport Police.

[810] Football Spectators Act 1989 s 14C(1) 'Violence' means violence against persons or property and includes threatening violence and doing anything which endangers the life of any person.

Football Spectators Act 1989 s 14C(3) 'Violence' and 'disorder' are not limited to violence and disorder in connection with football.
R v Doyle and Others 2012 EWCA Crim 995, 2013 1 Cr App R (S) 36 (p 197) para 7 The two conditions [for making a Football Banning Order] are these:

(i) There must be a conviction for a relevant offence, Football Spectators Act 1989 s 14A(1). The offences which are relevant are listed in Schedule 1. For the most part they become relevant not simply when a particular offence is committed, such as affray, but only when it is committed in the circumstances stipulated in Schedule 1. If the offence falls within Schedule 1, then the second condition must also be met.

(ii) The Judge must be satisfied that there are reasonable grounds to believe that making a banning order would help to prevent violence or disorder at or in connection with any regulated football matches: s 14A(2). Moreover by s 14A(3) if the court is not so satisfied, it must in open court state that fact and give its reasons.

Once both conditions are satisfied, a Football Banning Order must be made (see section 14A(2) above).

60.9 *Relevant offences What are they?*

Football Spectators Act 1989 s 14(8) and Sch 1 The relevant offences for this section are:

Note: The offences listed with a * are offences which enable a declaration of relevance to be made. For more detail, see **60.19**. The order of the list of offences has been rearranged to assist the reader. Ed.

Statutory offences Alcohol and drugs offences

* (g) any offence under Licensing Act 1872 s 12 (persons found drunk in public places, etc.) of being found drunk in a highway or other public place committed while the accused was on a journey to or from a football match to which this Schedule applies being an offence as respects which the court makes a declaration that the offence related to football matches,

* (h) any offence under Criminal Justice Act 1967 s 91(1) of [disorderly behaviour while drunk in a public place] committed in a highway or other public place while the accused was on a journey to or from a football match to which this Schedule applies being an offence as respects which the court makes a declaration that the offence related to football matches,

* (l) any offence under Road Traffic Act 1988 s 4, 5 or 5A [driving etc. when under the influence of drink or drugs or with an alcohol concentration above the prescribed limit] or with a concentration of a specified controlled drug about the specified limit[812] committed while the accused was on a journey to or from a football match to which this Schedule applies being an offence as respects which the court makes a declaration that the offence related to football matches.

Statutory offences Football offences

(a) any offence under Football Spectators Act 1989 s 14J(1), 19(6), 20(10) or 21C(2),

(b) any offence under Sporting Events (Control of Alcohol etc.) Act 1985 s 2 or 2A (alcohol, containers and fireworks) committed by the accused at any football match to which this Schedule applies or while entering or trying to enter the ground,

* (j) any offence under Sporting Events (Control of Alcohol etc.) Act 1985 s 1 (alcohol on coaches or trains to or from sporting events) committed while the accused was on a journey to or from a football match to which this Schedule applies being an offence as respects which the court makes a declaration that the offence related to football matches,

(p) any offence under Football (Offences) Act 1991.

[811] Football Spectators Act 1989 s 14C(2) 'Disorder' includes a) stirring up hatred against a group of persons defined by reference to colour, race, nationality (including citizenship) or ethnic or national origins, or against any individual as a member of such a group, b) using threatening, abusive or insulting words or behaviour or disorderly behaviour, or c) displaying any writing or other thing which is threatening, abusive or insulting.

[812] As amended by Crime and Courts Act 2013 Sch 22 para 15

Statutory offences Public Order Act 1986 offences

(c) any offence under Public Order Act 1986 s 4A or 5 (harassment, alarm or distress) or any provision of Public Order Act 1986 Part 3 or 3A (hatred by reference to race etc.) committed during a period relevant to a football match to which this Schedule applies at any premises while the accused was at, or was entering or leaving or trying to enter or leave, the premises,

* (k) any offence under Public Order Act 1986 s 4A or 5 (harassment, alarm or distress) or any provision of Public Order Act 1986 Part 3 or 3A (hatred by reference to race etc.) committed while the accused was on a journey to or from a football match to which this Schedule applies being an offence as respects which the court makes a declaration that the offence related to football matches,

* (q) any offence under Public Order Act 1986 s 4A or 5 (harassment, alarm or distress) or any provision of Public Order Act 1986 Part 3 or 3A (hatred by reference to race etc.):

(i) which does not fall within paragraph c) or k) above,

(ii) which was committed during a period relevant to a football match to which this Schedule applies, and

(iii) as respects which the court makes a declaration that the offence related to that match or to that match and any other football match which took place during that period.

Statutory offences Tickets

(u) any offence under Criminal Justice and Public Order Act 1994 s 166 (sale of tickets by unauthorised persons) which relates to tickets for a football match.

Violence and threats Persons, Against

(d) any offence involving the use or threat of violence by the accused towards another person committed during a period relevant to a football match to which this Schedule applies at any premises while the accused was at, or was entering or leaving or trying to enter or leave, the premises,

* (m) any offence involving the use or threat of violence by the accused towards another person committed while one or each of them was on a journey to or from a football match to which this Schedule applies being an offence as respects which the court makes a declaration that the offence related to football matches,

* (r) any offence involving the use or threat of violence by the accused towards another person:

(i) which does not fall within paragraph d) or m) above,

(ii) which was committed during a period relevant to a football match to which this Schedule applies, and

(iii) as respects which the court makes a declaration that the offence related to that match or to that match and any other football match which took place during that period.

Violence and threats Property, Against

(e) any offence involving the use or threat of violence towards property committed during a period relevant to a football match to which this Schedule applies at any premises while the accused was at, or was entering or leaving or trying to enter or leave, the premises,

* (n) any offence involving the use or threat of violence towards property committed while the accused was on a journey to or from a football match to which this Schedule applies being an offence as respects which the court makes a declaration that the offence related to football matches,

* (s) any offence involving the use or threat of violence towards property:

(i) which does not fall within paragraph e) or n) above,

(ii) which was committed during a period relevant to a football match to which this Schedule applies, and

(iii) as respects which the court makes a declaration that the offence related to that match or to that match and any other football match which took place during that period.

Weapons etc. Possession of etc.

(f) any offence involving the use, carrying or possession of an offensive weapon or a firearm committed during a period relevant to a football match to which this Schedule applies at any premises while the accused was at, or was entering or leaving or trying to enter or leave, the premises,

* (o) any offence involving the use, carrying or possession of an offensive weapon or a firearm committed while the accused was on a journey to or from a football match to which this Schedule applies being an offence as respects which the court makes a declaration that the offence related to football matches,

* (t) any offence involving the use, carrying or possession of an offensive weapon or a firearm:

(i) which does not fall within paragraph f) or o) above,

(ii) which was committed during a period relevant to a football match to which this Schedule applies, and

(iii) as respects which the court makes a declaration that the offence related to that match or to that match and any other football match which took place during that period.

60.10 ***Relevant offence? What is a*** ***Cases***

R v O'Keefe 2003 EWCA Crim 2629, 2004 1 Cr App R (S) 67 (p 402) D pleaded to threatening behaviour contrary to Public Order Act 1986 s 4. After a football match between Norwich and Chelsea, a fight broke out in a pub between Chelsea supporters and local residents. Two of the Chelsea supporters were persuaded to leave the pub. Ten minutes later a group of Norwich supporters entered the same pub, with one person shouting "Come on Chelsea" and beckoning the entire pub. The two Chelsea supporters who had left the pub returned and a violent altercation ensued. The defence argued that D's offence, Public Order Act 1986 s 4, was not included in the list of offences in Football Spectators Act 1989 Sch 1. Held. The offence fell within the general 'threatening and violence' categories within the Schedule. Any other interpretation would be absurd.

R v Doyle and Others 2012 EWCA Crim 995, 2013 1 Cr App R (S) 36 (p 197) para 10 The relevant offences are listed in Schedule 1.

(i) There are some offences listed in para (a) and (p) which are *ipso facto* relevant. Those are, in essence, offences which of their nature are concerned with football.

(ii) Offences listed under paragraph (b) must have been committed whilst entering or trying to enter the ground.

(iii) Offences listed under paragraphs (c) to (f) must have been committed during the period relevant to a football match (which means 24 hours either side of the match, see Sch 1 para 4(2)(b)) and when D was at, or entering or leaving, premises, although it would seem that the premises can be any premises and are not confined to football grounds; they might well, for example, be a public house).

(iv) Offences listed under paragraphs (g) to (o) and (q) will be relevant if they are 'related to football matches'; this calls for a judgment of the court declaring this to be so. The decision is called in the Act a 'declaration of relevance'; see section 23.

The judgment which is required in relation to offences listed under (g) to (o) and (q) is therefore not an assessment of the legal character of the offence. It is a determination whether on the particular facts of the offence as it was committed on the occasion in question, the offence was 'related to football matches'.

Although the test is expressed in terms of 'matches' in the plural,…it would suffice if the behaviour was, on the particular facts, related to a single match. But it is clear that what the Act is targeting is those offences which have a connection with football, generally with the defendant's following of the game.

Paragraphs (g) to (o), although not (q), are all concerned with offences committed when the defendant was on a journey to or from a football match at the stipulated level (essentially Blue Square North or South[813] or above). It is obvious that football disorder and violence can often occur on such journeys. Equally, because the Act requires the judgment of the court whether the particular offence was 'related to football matches' it is clear that the *mere* fact that the defendant was on a journey to or from a match is not enough. There must be another connection. The offence must be 'related to football matches'.

The Act offers no definition of when this condition will be met. It is (no doubt deliberately) left to the judgment of the judge on the particular facts before him. It would be wrong to attempt to define when the condition will be met. The facts which may occur will vary too much. It is not difficult to say that a pitched battle between opposing fans as they walk away from the ground is 'related', or that a defendant who, when on his own 20 miles away from the ground on his journey home meets a rival for a woman's affections and hits him, is not committing an offence related to football matches. But in between there will be infinite graduations of conduct, and they must be left to the judge in each case. In one or two reported cases the court has taken into account whether what was described as the 'spark' for an offence of violence was a football factor, such as a dispute with opposing fans, but this is only an example of the kind of matter which may be relevant and must not be taken as a substitute test. If a football-related 'spark' is present that will no doubt be likely to lead to the conclusion that the offence was related to football matches. But it is all too notorious that the 'spark' for offences of violence may sometimes be illusory, or minimal, or simply irrelevant. If the offence be one committed by a group of football fans clearly acting as such, in a group whose identity is clearly football-oriented, their violence may well justify the expression 'related to football matches' even if the particular *casus belli* is that exception is taken to another person for no particular reason. We offer only the observation that it will not by itself be enough to make an offence 'related to football matches' that it would not have occurred 'but for' the fact that D was *en route* to or from a match. If that by itself was enough, then every offence of the listed kind which was committed on a journey to or from a match would automatically qualify and the additional test of relation to football matches would be unnecessary and meaningless.

60.11 ***Regulated football match, Definition of***

Football Spectators Act 1989 s 14(2) A 'regulated football match' means an association football match in England and Wales, or elsewhere, which is a prescribed match or a match of prescribed description.

Football Spectators (Prescription) Order 2004 2004/2409 art 3(1) An association football match (in England and Wales) described in paragraphs (2) or (3) shall be a regulated football match for the purposes of Part II of the 1989 Act.

Football Spectators (Prescription) Order 2004 2004/2409 art 3(2) A regulated match is an association football match in which one or both of the participating teams represents:

(a) a club which is for the time being a member (whether a full or associate member) of the Football League, the Football Association Premier League, the Football Conference, the Welsh Premier League, the Scottish Premier League or the Scottish Football League,

(b) a club whose home ground is for the time being situated outside England and Wales, or

(c) a country or territory.[814]

Football Spectators (Prescription) Order 2004 2004/2409 art 3(3) A regulated football match is an association football match played in the Football Association Cup (other than in a preliminary or qualifying round).

---

[813] These were non-league football club divisions.

[814] As amended by Football Spectators (Prescription) (Amendment) Order 2006 2006/761

Test to apply

60.12 ***Test to apply/Order is mandatory***
Football Spectators Act 1989 s 14A(2) Once convicted of a 'relevant offence' (see **60.9**), the court must make a banning order in respect of the offender if it is satisfied there are reasonable grounds to believe that making a banning order would help to prevent violence or disorder, at or in connection with, any regulated football matches (see **60.11**).
Football Spectators Act 1989 s 14C(3) 'Violence'[815] and 'disorder'[816] are not limited to violence and disorder in connection to football.

60.13 ***Reasonable grounds that an order would prevent violence, Test for***
R v Doyle and Others 2012 EWCA Crim 995, 2013 1 Cr App R (S) 36 (p 197) para 15 Whether the condition [of reasonable grounds that an order would prevent violence etc.] is met will in some cases be the key question. No doubt the more the offence is linked to football grievances or the group 'culture' of a set of fans linked by their support for a team, the more likely it will be that a Football Banning Order will help prevent violence or disorder. The more there is a history of football-related offending, the greater will be the likelihood that the condition will be met. However, it is clear that it is possible for this condition to be met by the commission of a single offence, of which the defendant has just been convicted. What it is important to remember is that this condition clearly contemplates that there must be a risk of repetition of violence or disorder at a match before it is met. The test of reasonable grounds to believe that a Football Banning Order will help prevent violence or disorder at regulated matches does not set a high hurdle, but it is clear that it is not automatically satisfied just because the instant offence was football-related. If that were so, the condition would add nothing and would not be needed. Many football-related offences will give rise to exactly this risk, but not all will. *R v Boggild and Others* 2011 EWCA Crim 1928, 2012 1 Cr App R (S) 81 (p 457) (see para **60.36**) was an example of one which the judge determined did not.

60.14 ***Banning orders must be proportionate***
R (White) v Blackfriars Crown Court 2008 EWHC 510 (Admin), 2 Cr App R (S) 97 (p 542) High Court D pleaded to common assault, possession of a class C drug and entering a playing area at a football match. A banning order was made which was upheld on appeal. D referred to *Gough v Chief Constable of Derbyshire Constabulary* 2002 QB 1213 arguing that the requirement to surrender D's passport was contrary to EC law and the need for proportionality. Reference was also made to the European Convention on Human Rights and the need to satisfy the test of proportionality. Held. The Court concluded that if operated properly, banning orders will be proportionate. It is proportionate to require those who have demonstrated a real risk of participation in football hooliganism to obtain permission to travel abroad while matches are taking place, *R v Gough* 2002. *R v Gough* 2002 is distinguishable from cases under section 14A. It is plain that in a normal case, the legislature intended that the conviction for the relevant offence would be sufficient to satisfy section 14A(2) (see **60.12**), *R v Hughes* 2005 EWCA Crim 2537, 2006 1 Cr App R (S) 107 (p 632). The Court is bound by *R v Hughes* 2006. Order upheld.

60.15 ***Standard of proof***
R v Hughes 2005 EWCA Crim 2537, 2006 1 Cr App R (S) 107 (p 632) D was convicted of affray. He punched a football fan with a fist whilst leaving a football match. A banning order was made for a period of 3 years. The defence appealed arguing that the Judge failed to apply the criminal standard of proof when considering a statement by a police officer regarding a separate incident with other football fans the same day, which

[815] Football Spectators Act 1989 s 14C(1) 'Violence' means violence against persons or property and includes threatening violence and doing anything which endangers the life of any person.

[816] Football Spectators Act 1989 s 14C(2) 'Disorder' includes a) stirring up hatred against a group of persons defined by reference to colour, race, nationality (including citizenship) or ethnic or national origins, or against any individual as a member of such a group, b) using threatening, abusive or insulting words or behaviour or disorderly behaviour, or c) displaying any writing or other thing which is threatening, abusive or insulting.

D disputed. Held. Under section 14A, the first element (conviction of a relevant offence) is already made out to the criminal standard. It is clear that the legislature intended for the conviction itself to satisfy section 14A(2) (see **60.12**). If there were something in the particular case that meant that the judge was not so satisfied then he should explain what it was in open court.
Note: Increasingly judges simply apply judicial evaluation after considering all the relevant factors. That is a far better approach than the Victorian burden and standard of proof approach. Ed.

60.16 ***A single relevant offence may be sufficient***
R v Smith 2003 EWCA Crim 2480, 2004 1 Cr App R (S) 58 (p 341) D pleaded to threatening words. He travelled to, but was unable to gain entry into, Kidderminster Harriers' football stadium. He was put on a train by the police with others and was described as drunk and abusive. With permission, the group stopped at various pubs *en route* to Shrewsbury. At one station, police instructed the train operators not to open the doors of the train. It was submitted on D's behalf that it was this which led to the threatening behaviour and therefore the incident was not related to the earlier football match. D received a 60-hour Community Punishment Order and a Football Banning Order for a term of 3 years. Held. There may well be circumstances within the commission of one offence that properly give rise to reasonable grounds to believe that a banning order would help [prevent violence or disorder in relation to football matches]. It is not right to say as a matter of law that the mere fact that the reasonable grounds for such a belief are based on the commission of one offence is necessarily an inadequate basis for such reasonable grounds.
R v Hughes 2005 EWCA Crim 2537, 2006 1 Cr App R (S) 107 (p 632) D was convicted of affray. He punched a football fan with a closed fist whilst leaving a football match. A banning order was made for a period of 3 years. D appealed on the basis that the incident involved 'simply one punch' and was not a case of general hooliganism. Held. There is no requirement for repetition or propensity under section 14A.
R v Boggild and Others 2011 EWCA Crim 1928, 2012 1 Cr App R (S) 81 (p 457) The defendants pleaded to affray. The Judge declined to make a Football Banning Order, instead opting for a prohibited activity requirement preventing the defendants from attending away matches. Held. It is palpably not the scheme of the Act to make a Football Banning Order the inevitable consequence of a football-related conviction. Judges ought to address their minds to the differences between the consequences of a Football Banning Order on the one hand and a prohibited activities requirement attached either to a Suspended Sentence Order or a community order. They are not to be treated as equivalents.

60.17 ***Deterrence is an important factor***
R (White) v Blackfriars Crown Court 2008 EWHC 510 (Admin), 2 Cr App R (S) 97 (p 542) High Court D pleaded to common assault, possession of a class C drug and entering a playing area at a football match. D entered the playing area at the conclusion of a match between Millwall and Tranmere Rovers, ran at the assistant referee and shouted at him. The assistant referee had scratches as a result of raising his hands to defend himself. A banning order was made which was upheld on appeal. D argued that the imposition of an order was disproportionate considering the offence was an isolated incident. Held. The Court was right to take into account and give great weight to deterrence when considering the banning order.
R v Curtis 2009 EWCA Crim 1225, 2010 1 Cr App R (S) 31 (p 193) D pleaded to an offence under Public Order Act 1986 s 4. D was fined and subject to a banning order for a period of 5 years. D was involved in shouting, chanting and taunting police officers after a match between Birmingham City and Aston Villa, a well-known flash-point. D was not involved in the throwing of missiles aimed at police, nor in the criminal damage to police vehicles. D's image was captured on video and placed in a newspaper

requesting assistance with his identification. He voluntarily attended the police station. D was aged 22 with no previous convictions but had a caution for common assault. It was argued on D's behalf that there was no evidence to justify the conclusion that the order would help prevent violence or disorder at subsequent matches, alternatively, the order was excessive in its length. Held. D's behaviour warranted the making of a banning order, despite the fact that the behaviour was an isolated incident. The Judge was entitled to take into account the deterrent nature of such orders. However, not every case of a football-related offence of this type is suitable for a banning order. Each case will turn on its facts. However, 3 years not 5.

Declarations of relevance

60.18 ***Declarations of relevance*** ***Judge making declarations of relevance***
Football Spectators Act 1989 s 23(5) In this section 'declaration of relevance' means a declaration by a court for the purposes of Football Spectators Act 1989 Sch 1 that an offence related to football matches, or that it related to one or more particular football matches.
Football Spectators Act 1989 Sch 1 para 1 (g)-(o), (q)-(t)…(g) any offence…committed while the accused was on a journey to or from a football match to which this Schedule applies, being an offence as respects which the court made a declaration that the offence related to football matches.
Note: The other sub-paragraphs have either the same wording or similar. For the list of offences, see **60.9**. Ed.
Football Spectators Act 1989 s 23(1) Subject to subsection (2) below, a court may not make a declaration of relevance as respects any offence unless it is satisfied that the prosecutor gave notice to the defendant, at least five days before the first day of the trial, that it was proposed to show that the offence related to football matches, to a particular football match or to particular football matches (as the case may be).
(2) A court may, in any particular case, make a declaration of relevance notwithstanding that notice to the defendant as required by subsection (1) above has not been given if he consents to waive the giving of full notice or the court is satisfied that the interests of justice do not require more notice to be given.
R v Elliot and Others 2007 EWCA Crim 1002, 2 Cr App R (S) 68 (p 430) D was convicted of violent disorder and affray. He received a custodial sentence and a Football Banning Order. D was among a group of Wolverhampton Wanderers supporters who had travelled to London. Some had travelled to London with the intention of attending the match, some had travelled to London knowing that, because of the match, there would be Wolverhampton supporters in London. D was involved in violence in Leicester Square. The Judge found that the violence was participated in purely by Wolverhampton fans and the people subjected to the attack had no connection with Wolverhampton Wanderers or West Ham United, who were Wolverhampton's opponents that day. The Judge also found that the violence began after a disparaging remark made about a female who was not a Wolverhampton fan, but was with D's group. Held. The issue was whether the Judge could and should make the declaration, that is to say, whether the violent disorder or affray related to that match or any other match which took place in that period. Clearly the presence of D in London related to the football match that had taken place earlier. But it is not their presence or allegiance which is the touchstone of the declaration, it is the relationship between the offence and the match. The spark was unconnected with the match and although those participating in the violence were Wolverhampton supporters, the incident had nothing else to do with the football match. It was wrong to make the declaration. Order quashed.
R v Mabee 2007 EWCA Crim 3230 D pleaded to violent disorder. D travelled to London with his friends to watch his football team play, and was waiting in a pub after the game for a train to arrive which would take him home. A group of people who supported a different team, and not one involved in the earlier match which D had attended, entered

the pub. A fight ensued. The investigating officer acknowledged in evidence that the incident had nothing to do with the earlier football matches. Another officer said he believed a racist comment had started the incident. D received 12 months' detention and a banning order. Held. It was not right to make the declaration that the violent disorder related to the football match. The instant case was indistinguishable from *R v Elliot* 2007. Banning order quashed.

R v Boggild and Others 2011 EWCA Crim 1928, 2012 1 Cr App R (S) 81 (p 457) *Obiter* Nobody present has been able to identify any purpose in a declaration of relevance in the present state of the legislation and those who are responsible for looking at the Act may wish to consider whether there is any continued usefulness in that provision.

60.19 ***Declarations of relevance Relevant offences What are they?***

Football Spectators Act 1989 Sch 1 para 1 (g)-(o), (q)-(t)…(g) any offence… committed while the accused was on a journey to or from a football match to which this Schedule applies, being an offence as respects which the court made a declaration that the offence related to football matches.

Note: The offences are in the list of offences at **60.19** with a *. Ed.

60.20 ***Declarations of relevance 'Offence related to football matches', Definition of***

Football Spectators Act 1989 s 23(5) In this section 'declaration of relevance' means a declaration by a court for the purposes of Football Spectators Act 1989 Sch 1 that an offence related to football matches, or that it related to one or more particular football matches.

R v Smith 2003 EWCA Crim 2480, 2004 1 Cr App R (S) 58 (p 341) D pleaded to threatening words. He travelled to, but was unable to gain entry inside, Kidderminster Harriers' football stadium. He was put on a train by the police with others and was described as drunk and abusive. With permission, the group stopped at various pubs *en route* to Shrewsbury. However, at one station, police instructed the train operators not to open the doors of the train. It was submitted on D's behalf that it was this which led to the threatening behaviour and therefore the incident was not related to the earlier football match. D received a 60-hour Community Punishment Order and a Football Banning Order for a term of 3 years. Held. There is no definition of 'related to football matches' in the Act. On the facts, the incident was not related to football matches. We can well envisage instances of offences being committed at considerable physical removal from football matches and considerable removal in time which could be an offence related to football matches. Order quashed.

DPP v Beaumont 2008 EWHC 523 (Admin), 2 Cr App R (S) 98 (p 549) High Court D pleaded to an offence under Public Order Act 1986 s 5, with no evidence being offered on charges of criminal damage. A group of Manchester United supporters behaved in a rowdy manner and caused substantial damage to the interior of the train. A banning order was made by the Magistrates' Court, which was subsequently quashed by the Crown Court on the basis that 'related to football matches' had the same meaning as 'relevant to' (certain periods are 'relevant to' a designated football match, with the period in question being one hour after the end of the match, Football Spectators Act 1989 s 1(8)). There was no evidence to suggest that the offence had been committed within this period and therefore the order was quashed. The DPP appealed by way of case stated on the basis that 'related to football matches' was not defined in the Act, nor governed by Football Spectators Act 1989 s 1(8), and should be given its ordinary meaning. Held. There is no reference to any period relevant to a football match in the paragraphs concerning offences committed on a journey to or from a football match. To treat the two expressions ('…offence related to a football match' and '…period relevant to a football match') as the same would be plainly a mistaken interpretation of the provision.

R v Parkes and Cartwight 2010 EWCA Crim 2803, 2011 2 Cr App R (S) 10 (p 54) P and C pleaded to threatening words and behaviour. Both were supporters of Wolverhampton

Wanderers, known as Wolves. Owing to bad weather, their match was cancelled. On the same day West Bromwich Albion played Peterborough. After that match some Albion supporters went to a pub and police received information that there was going to be disorder. P, C and three others went to the pub and Albion supporters climbed over a fence and started to sing and chant at the five. Within seconds bottles and beer glasses were thrown. Albion supporters swelled to about 40, and 50 more Wolves supporters arrived and tried to provoke Albion supporters. At sentence, the defence accepted that the incident related to football. On appeal they took the point that it didn't relate to football. Held. We ask, "Can the spark which caused the violence be something wholly unrelated to football?" The fact that the match was never played was of little substance. The spark was football. Judged individually, the offences clearly related to the Albion–Peterborough match. The offences were related to football.
See also: *R v Smith* 2004 1 Cr App R (S) 58 (p 341) (Incidents committed at considerable physical removal from football matches and considerable removal in time could well be offences related to football matches.)

60.21 ***Declarations of relevance Failure to make a declaration of relevance***
DPP v Beaumont 2008 EWHC 523 (Admin), 2 Cr App R (S) 98 (p 549) High Court D pleaded to an offence under Public Order Act 1986 s 5, with no evidence being offered on charges of criminal damage. A group of Manchester United supporters behaved in a rowdy manner and caused substantial damage to the interior of the train. A banning order was made by the Magistrates' Court, which was subsequently quashed by the Crown Court on the basis that 'related to football matches' had the same meaning as 'relevant to' (certain periods are 'relevant to' a designated football match, with the period in question being one hour after the end of the match, Football Spectators Act 1989 s 1(8)). There was no evidence to suggest that the offence had been committed within this period and therefore the order was quashed. The DPP appealed by way of case stated on the basis that 'related to football matches' was not defined in the Act, nor governed by Football Spectators Act 1989 s 1(8) and should be given its ordinary meaning. Held. It is true that the statute requires a court to make a declaration of relevance. D was entitled to raise the issue of failing to make a declaration of relevance. However, the failure to make a declaration of relevance does not render the banning order invalid.

60.22 ***Declarations of relevance Right of appeal***
Note: There is an appeal against the making of the declaration of relevance in the Crown Court, Criminal Appeal Act 1968 s 10(3)(c) and 50(h) and the Magistrates' Court, Magistrates' Courts Act 1980 s 108(3). Ed.

The procedure and the evidence

60.23 ***Bail Power to add terms***
Football Spectators Act 1989 s 14A(4BB) A person who is remanded on bail (see section 14A(4BA)) may be required by the conditions of his bail:

(a) not to leave England and Wales before his appearance before the court, and

(b) if the control period relates to a regulated football match outside the United Kingdom or to an external tournament which includes such matches, to surrender his passport to a police constable, if he has not already done so.

60.24 ***Power to remand after an adjournment***
Football Spectators Act 1989 s 14A(4BA) If the court adjourns or further adjourns the proceedings under section 14A(4A) or (4B), the court may remand the offender.

60.25 ***Power to adjourn and to issue a warrant for arrest***
Football Spectators Act 1989 s 14A(4A) The court may adjourn proceedings in relation to an order under section 14A even after sentencing the offender.
(4B) If the offender does not appear for any adjourned proceedings, the court may further adjourn the proceedings or may issue a warrant for his arrest.

(4C) The court may not issue a warrant under section 14A(4B) for the offender's arrest unless it is satisfied that he or she has had adequate notice of the time and place of the adjourned proceedings.

60.26 ***Evidence Duty to serve***
Criminal Procedure Rules 2015 2015/1490 Rule 31.4(2) A party who wants the court to take account of evidence not already introduced must:
(a) serve notice on:[817]
(i) the court officer, and
(ii) every other party,
as soon as practicable (without waiting for the verdict), and
(b) in the notice, identify that evidence, and
(c) attach any written statement containing such evidence.

60.27 ***Evidence Admissibility***
Football Spectators Act 1989 s 14A(3B) It is immaterial whether evidence presented to the court for the purposes of deciding whether to make an order under section 14A would have been admissible in the proceedings in which the offender was convicted.
Procedural rules, see the **CRIMINAL PROCEDURE RULES: BEHAVIOUR RULES** chapter.

60.28 ***Court may hear evidence from prosecution and defence***
Football Spectators Act 1989 s 14A(3A) For the purposes of deciding whether to make an order under section 14A, the court may consider evidence led by the prosecution and the defence.
Disputes as to facts see the **FACTUAL BASIS FOR SENTENCING** ***Same rules apply when imposing ancillary orders*** para at **57.26**.

60.29 ***There must be careful scrutiny before an order is made***
R v Irving and Irving 2013 EWCA Crim 1932, 2014 2 Cr App R (S) 6 (p 32) The Judge was asked to make a Football Banning Order and without giving the defence the opportunity to deal with an adverse finding he 'rubber-stamped' the draft order. Held. The proceedings were fatally flawed. This case is a further illustration of the need for a careful scrutiny before an order of this sort is made. Order quashed.

Making the order

60.30 ***Ban must be with a sentence***
Football Spectators Act 1989 s 14A(4)(a) A banning order may only be imposed under section 14A in addition to a sentence imposed in respect of the relevant offence or in addition to an order discharging him conditionally.

60.31 ***Start date for the order***
Football Spectators Act 1989 s 14F(1) A banning order has effect for the period specified by the court beginning on the day on which the order is made.

60.32 ***Maximum and minimum terms***
Football Spectators Act 1989 s 14F(3) Where the order is made under section 14A (see **60.8**) in addition to a sentence of imprisonment taking immediate effect, the maximum is 10 years and the minimum is 6 years. In section 14F(3) 'imprisonment' includes any form of detention.
(4) In any other case where the order is made under section 14A (see **60.8**), the maximum is 5 years and the minimum is 3 years.
(5) Where the order is made under section 14B (stand-alone orders) (see **57.5**) the maximum is 5 years and the minimum is 3 years.
Note: There is, however, a power to replace or omit any requirements in the order. There is also a power to terminate the order (see **60.45**). Ed.

[817] Criminal Procedure (Amendment No 2) Rules 2016 2016/705 para 11(c) removes the requirement that the notice had to be in writing. In force 3/10/16

60.33 *Can't limit the extent of the order*

R v Doyle and Others 2012 EWCA Crim 995, 2013 1 Cr App R (S) 36 (p 197) para 4(2) It is not possible to make an order limited to particular matches or particular teams.

Commissioner of Police v Thorpe 2015 EWHC (Admin) 2016 1 Cr App R (S) 46 Police applied for a stand-alone Football Banning Order. The Magistrates granted one and added that the order was only to apply to matches between Fulham and either Brentford or Chelsea football clubs. The police appealed. Held. No convention right was engaged and [even] if it was, it [would be] a qualified right which [was decided by] Parliament. The limitation to the order was unlawful.

60.34 *How long should the order be?*

R v Curtis 2009 EWCA Crim 1225, 2010 1 Cr App R (S) 31 (p 193) D pleaded to Public Order Act 1986 s 4. D was fined and subject to a banning order for a period of 5 years. D was involved in shouting, chanting and taunting police officers after a match between Birmingham City and Aston Villa, a well-known flash-point. D was not involved in the throwing of missiles aimed at police, nor in the criminal damage to police vehicles. D's image was captured on video and placed in a newspaper requesting assistance with his identification. He voluntarily attended the police station. D was aged 22 with no previous convictions but had a caution for common assault. It was argued on D's behalf that there was no evidence to justify the conclusion that the order would help prevent violence or disorder at subsequent matches, alternatively, the order was excessive in its length. Held. D's behaviour warranted the making of a banning order, despite the fact that the behaviour was an isolated incident. The Judge was entitled to take into account the deterrent nature of such orders. However, not every case of a football-related offence of this type is suitable for a banning order. Each case will turn on its facts. However, **3 years** not 5.

See also: *R v Wiggins and Others* 2014 EWCA Crim 1433, 2 Cr App R (S) 72 (p 560) (Pub violent disorder. For about 4 minutes glasses were thrown, then Lincoln supporters left. They regrouped and attacked the other team's supporters outside the pub. Furniture and punches were thrown. Kicks were delivered. Extreme danger to the public. Held. **6-year** order not 10 for four defendants. 10-year order upheld for two defendants.)

For more detail see **203.12** in Volume 2.

60.35 *On the facts, order correct/incorrect*

R (White) v Blackfriars Crown Court 2008 EWHC 510 (Admin), 2 Cr App R (S) 97 (p 542) High Court D pleaded to common assault, possession of a class C drug and entering a playing area at a football match. D entered the playing area at the conclusion of a match between Millwall and Tranmere Rovers, ran at the assistant referee and shouted at him. The assistant referee had scratches as a result of raising his hands to defend himself. A banning order was made which was upheld on appeal. D argued that the imposition of an order was disproportionate considering the offence was an isolated incident. Held. The Court was right to take into account and give great weight to deterrence when considering the banning order.

R v Doyle and Others 2012 EWCA Crim 995, 2013 1 Cr App R (S) 36 (p 197) The defendants were convicted of affray. They travelled home to Reading from a football match at West Ham. They were foul-mouthed, rowdy and drunk. A passenger asked them to stop their behaviour and they assaulted him. The defence challenged the Football Banning Order. Held. para 25 As to the first condition, that the offence be 'related to football matches', the Judge's statement that watching the football match was a direct cause of the behaviour amounted to a conclusion that, but for the match, they would not have been where they were, and perhaps not drunk. That may be so, and in some circumstances that might be enough to justify a declaration that the offence was 'related to football matches', for example if the affray were fuelled by the tribal identity of a group of football fans. Such a decision would, however, at the least involve a conscious conclusion that it was the football and its tribal excitement which had led to the unpleasant behaviour. In the present case the Judge did not so determine and the evidence showed only that the offence arose out of the fact that the defendants were drunk, rather than that it had any connection to football. As to the second condition, the Judge clearly did not address it at all. Order quashed.

60.36 ***On the facts, Judge entitled to refuse to make an order***
R v Boggild and Others 2011 EWCA Crim 1928, 2012 1 Cr App R (S) 81 (p 457) Civil Division[818] The defendants pleaded to affray. 15 minutes after a Wolverhampton Wanderers v Everton match had ended, Everton fans, including the defendants, were looking for the coach which was to take them home. It was not where they expected it to be, and they wandered around the stadium in search of it. They came across a large group of Wolverhampton supporters outside a pub. A brief skirmish ensued, started by the Wolverhampton supporters. It lasted one minute and glasses, traffic cones, punches and kicks were thrown. The defendants then found their transport. Suspended sentences or community orders were imposed with a condition that the defendants not attend any professional football match in the UK except for matches at Everton's home ground, Goodison Park. No defendants had any convictions relating to football violence. The Judge said that an element of the sentence was to deter others from behaving as the defendants had behaved. He relied on the facts that the defendants were not looking for trouble and the disturbance was started by the other supporters. He took into account the good character or lack of non-minor convictions of the defendants. The prosecution appealed against the failure to make a Football Banning Order. Held. It is palpably not the scheme of the Act to make a Football Banning Order the inevitable consequence of a football-related conviction. Further, deterrence is not the determinative factor when deciding whether the test for imposing an order has been met. The Judge was entitled to reach the conclusion that the test wasn't satisfied. The appeal was dismissed.

60.37 ***Explain sentence, Judge/Magistrate must***
Criminal Justice Act 2003 s 174(2)[819] The court must state in open court, in ordinary language and in general terms, the court's reasons for deciding on the sentence.
(3) The court must explain to the offender in ordinary language:
(a) the effect of the sentence,
(b) the effects of non-compliance with any order that the offender is required to comply with and that forms part of the sentence,
(c) any power of the court to vary or review any order that forms part of the sentence…

60.38 ***Duty to explain if order not made when it could be***
Football Spectators Act 1989 s 14A(3) If the court is not satisfied that the grounds are made out for making an order, then it must state that fact and give its reasons.
Criminal Procedure Rules 2015 2015/1490 Rule 31.2(3) Where the court decides not to make, where it could:
(a) a Football Banning Order . . .
the court must announce, at a hearing in public, the reasons for its decision.

60.39 ***Alternatives when test not satisfied***
R v Doyle and Others 2012 EWCA Crim 995, 2013 1 Cr App R (S) 36 (p 197) para 8 If the second condition [of reasonable grounds to believe an order would prevent violence etc.] is not made out, but the judge wants to impose an order which will, by way of punishment, keep the defendant away from a football match for a while, he has power to do so in a number of ways, for example by making it a requirement of a community order or suspended sentence that he does not attend matches, either generally or limited to a particular team or teams. Since immediate sentences of imprisonment were imposed,

[818] This case was heard by a Court sitting both in the Criminal Division and the Civil Division. However, only the Civil Division had the power to hear the appeal.
[819] As substituted by Legal Aid, Sentencing and Punishment of Offenders Act 2012 s 64

there was no other order available to the Judge except perhaps an ASBO, but the test for the making of such an order is necessity, significantly higher than the second condition for a Football Banning Order.

After the hearing

60.40 ***Duties of the individual subject to a banning order***

Football Spectators Act 1989 s 14E(2A) A banning order must require the person subject to the order to give notification of the events mentioned in section 14E(2B) (see below) to the enforcing authority.[820]

(2B) The events of which the subject of the order must inform the enforcing authority are:

(a) a change of any of his names,

(b) the first use by him after the making of the order of a name for himself that was not disclosed by him at the time of the making of the order,

(c) a change of his home address,[821]

(d) his acquisition of a temporary address,[822]

(e) a change of his temporary address[823] or his ceasing to have one,

(f) his becoming aware of the loss[824] of his travel authorisation,

(g) receipt by him of a new[825] travel authorisation,

(h) an appeal made by him in relation to the order,

(i) an application made by him under section 14H(2) for termination of the order,

(j) an appeal made by him under section 23(3) against the making of a declaration of relevance in respect of an offence of which he has been convicted.

(2C) A notification required by section 14E(2A) must be given before the end of the period of 7 days beginning with the day on which the event in question occurs, and:

(a) in the case of a change of a name or address or the acquisition of a temporary address,[826] must specify the new[827] name or address,

(b) in the case of the first use of a previously undisclosed name, must specify that name, and

(c) in the case of a receipt of a new[828] travel authorisation, must give details of that travel authorisation.

R v Doyle and Others 2012 EWCA Crim 995, 2013 1 Cr App R (S) 36 (p 197) para 4 The consequences of an order are:

(a) The order prohibits the defendant from attending any regulated football match anywhere in the UK (section 14(4)(a)). That means all league matches at Blue Square North and South[829] level or above, plus cup matches except for preliminary rounds. It is not possible to make an order limited to particular matches or particular teams.

(b) It requires him to report within five days to the police station, and to provide the police with all the names he uses, any address where he lives for more than 4 weeks and his passport details (section 14E).

(c) It then enables the enforcing authority (currently the UK Football Banning Order Authority) at its entire discretion, to direct him via the police as to how he must comply with the order.

---

820 The enforcing authority is the authority empowered to grant exemptions under Football Spectators Act 1989 s 20, which refers to an organisation established by the Secretary of State under .

821 'Home address' means the address of sole or main residence, Football Spectators Act 1989 s 14E(8).

822 'Temporary address' in relation to any person means the address (other than his home address) of a place at which he intends to reside, or has resided, for a period of at least four weeks, Football Spectators Act 1989 s 14E(8).

823 'Temporary address' in relation to any person means the address (other than his home address) of a place at which he intends to reside, or has resided, for a period of at least four weeks, Football Spectators Act 1989 s 14E(8).

824 'Loss' includes theft or destruction, Football Spectators Act 1989 s 14E(8).

825 'New' includes replacement, Football Spectators Act 1989 s 14E(8).

826 'Temporary address' in relation to any person means the address (other than his home address) of a place at which he intends to reside, or has resided, for a period of at least four weeks, Football Spectators Act 1989 s 14E(8).

827 'New' includes replacement, Football Spectators Act 1989 s 14E(8).

828 Football Spectators Act 1989 s 14E(8). 'New' includes replacement.

829 These were football club divisions.

(d) It also enables the authority, again at its discretion, to order him to report to a police station when told to do so, and to surrender his passport, in order to prevent him from travelling abroad to a regulated football match outside the UK (section 14(4)(b) and 19).

(e) During what is termed the control period for any foreign football match or tournament, the authority may prohibit the defendant from travelling out of the country at all (section 19). This applies to all matches or tournaments in which a British team (national or club) has an interest, whether it is playing in any particular match or not. The control period starts 5 days before the match or tournament and ends only when the whole tournament ends.

para 8 If a Football Banning Order is mandatory, its prohibitions must be the wholesale ones, see a)-e) above.

60.41 ***Report within five days of banning order, Duty to***

Football Spectators Act 1989 s 14E(2) The person who is the subject of the banning order must report initially at a police station specified within the order within the period of 5 days beginning with the day on which the order is made.

60.42 ***Exemptions from reporting requirements***

Football Spectators Act 1989 s 20(1) A person who is subject to a banning order may:

(a) as respects a particular regulated football match, or

(b) as respects regulated football matches played during a period,

apply to the exempting authority[830] to be exempt from the requirements imposed by Football Spectators Act 1989, as respects a match or matches played during that period.

R v Doyle and Others 2012 EWCA Crim 995, 2013 1 Cr App R (S) 36 (p 197) para 4 If the defendant wishes to avoid any of the [court] prohibitions, the defendant has to persuade the authority to grant an exemption, Football Spectators Act 1989 s 20. That includes the case where he needs to travel abroad for a reason completely unconnected with football, such as work or a family wedding, to a country many miles away from the place where the match is happening. In this case also he must get special permission to go. There is a right of appeal to the magistrates if he is refused.

60.43 ***Justification for exemption***

Football Spectators Act 1989 s 20(4) The exempting authority shall exempt the applicant from the requirements imposed by or under Football Spectators Act 1989, as respects any match or matches to which the application relates if he shows to the authority's satisfaction:

(a) that there are special circumstances which justify the exemption, and

(b) that, because of those circumstances, he would not attend the match or matches if he were so exempted.

Football Spectators Act 1989 s 20(5) In making a decision under section 20(4) the exempting authority shall have regard to any guidance issued by the Secretary of State under section 21.

Combined with other orders

For the need for the order to be combined with another sentencing order, see **60.30**.

60.44 ***Absolute discharge and conditional discharge, Combined with***

Football Spectators Act 1989 s 14A(4) A banning order may be made under this section:

(a) in addition to a sentence imposed in respect of the relevant offence, or

(b) in addition to an order discharging him conditionally.

Football Spectators Act 1989 s 14A(5) A banning order may be made as mentioned by section 14(4)(b) in spite of anything in Powers of Criminal Courts (Sentencing) Act 2000 s 12 and 14 (which relates to orders discharging a person absolutely or conditionally and their effect).

[830] The exempting authority is the authority empowered to grant exemptions under Football Spectators Act 1989 s 20, which refers to an organisation established by the Secretary of State under Police Act 1996 s 57.

Termination and variation of the order

60.45 *Termination of orders*

Football Spectators Act 1989 s 14H(1) If a banning order has had effect for at least two-thirds of the period determined under section 14F (see **60.30** and **60.32**), the person subject to the order may apply to the court[831] by which it was made to terminate it.
(2) On an application under section 14H(1) the court may terminate the banning order from a specified date or refuse the application. In exercising the power to terminate an order, the court must have regard to the person's character, his conduct since the banning order was made, the nature of the offence or conduct which led to it and any other circumstances which appear to be relevant.
Football Spectators Act 1989 s 14H(4) Where an application under section 14H(1) is refused, no further application may be made within the period of six months beginning on the day of the refusal.
(5) A court may order the applicant to pay all or part of the costs of an application under this section.

60.46 *Procedure*

Note: Criminal Procedure Rules 2015 2015/1490 Rule 31.5(2) applies, see **84.14**. Ed.

60.47 *Power to include additional requirements*

Football Spectators Act 1989 s 14G(1) A banning order may, if the court making the order thinks fit, impose additional requirements on the person subject to the order in relation to any regulated football matches.
R v Doyle and Others 2012 EWCA Crim 995, 2013 1 Cr App R (S) 36 (p 197) The defendants were convicted of affray. They travelled home to Reading from a football match at West Ham. They were foul-mouthed, rowdy and drunk. A passenger asked them to stop their behaviour and they assaulted him. para 22 There were two additional prohibitions, namely: a) not to be in any town or city where either West Ham or England are playing for a period running from 4 (not 3) hours before to 4 hours after the match, and b) not to be within 1 mile of any stadium where either West Ham or England are playing during that same period. The defence challenged the Football Banning Order. Held. para 5 Football Supporters Act 1989 s 14G permits additional requirements to be added by the court. These can be tailor-made, but they must be requirements 'in relation to any regulated football matches'. There were some in this case, as we shall show. These additional requirements are the only part of a banning order which is in the control of the court. Given the extent of the controls provided by the standard terms of a banning order, careful consideration ought to be given to whether any additional requirements sought are indeed required.
It is perhaps technically possible for the second ban to add to the first, but only if the stadium in question is right at the edge of a town or city, and it is difficult to see what the justification for it could ever have been. An order in this form meant, for example, that the defendants would have had to move out of their homes if West Ham came to play at Reading. These conditions had not been canvassed before the judge and it remains a mystery how they came to be contained in the order as served on the defendants. On any view, the first was wrongly stated and the inclusion of the second was simply unlawful.

60.48 *Power to vary, replace or omit additional requirements*

Football Spectators Act 1989 s 14G(2) The court[832] by which a banning order was made may, on application made by a) the person subject to the order, or b) the person who applied for the order or who was the prosecutor in relation to the order, vary the order so as to impose, replace or omit any such requirements.

[831] Reference to the court includes any Magistrates' Court in the same local justice area, Football Spectators Act 1989 s 14H(6).
[832] In the event that the order was made by a Magistrates' Court, the reference to the 'court' includes any Magistrates' Court in the same local justice area, Football Spectators Act 1989 s 14G(3).

Appeals

60.49 ***Prosecution right of appeal***

Football Spectators Act 1989 s 14A(5A) The prosecution have a right of appeal against a failure by the court to make a banning order under section 14A: a) where the failure is by a Magistrates' Court, to the Crown Court, and b) where it is by the Crown Court, to the Court of Appeal.

Guidance for prosecution appeals can be found at *Guide to Commencing Proceedings in the Court of Appeal 2018* section **D19**.

R v Boggild and Others 2011 EWCA Crim 1928, 2012 1 Cr App R (S) 81 (p 457) After a conviction, the judge declined to make a Football Banning Order. The prosecution appealed. Held. The Court of Appeal Criminal Division has no jurisdiction to hear an appeal by the prosecution against the failure to make a Football Banning Order, Senior Courts Act 1981 s 53(2). The Court of Appeal Civil Division does have jurisdiction to hear such an appeal, by virtue of Senior Courts Act 1981 s 53(3).

Note: For appeals over the making of the declaration of relevance, see para **60.22**. Ed.

61 Foreign Travel Orders

61.1

Sexual Offences Act 2003 s 114-119

This was a stand-alone preventive order. It was repealed on 8 March 2015,[833] Anti-social Behaviour, Crime and Policing Act 2014 Sch 5 para 3(1). It has been replaced by the Sexual Harm Prevention Order.

The repeal does not affect existing orders This is provided by Anti-social Behaviour, Crime and Policing Act 2014 s 114(1)(b) and (2)(b).

Discharge There is power to discharge an order.[834]

Vary There is power to vary the terms of an order[835] but no power to extend the length of the order.[836]

Breach offences If a person without reasonable excuse a) does anything which he is prohibited under the order from doing, or b) fails to surrender his or her passport, he or she commits an offence.[837] The offence is an either way offence with a maximum sentence on indictment of 5 years or on summary conviction 6 months and/or an unlimited fine.[838] There are maximum fines for those aged under 18, see **13.44**.

Guideline for breach offences The relevant sentencing guideline is at **102.5**.

62 Forfeiture/Deprivation orders

62.1

Powers of Criminal Courts (Sentencing) Act 2000 s 143

Children and young offenders The orders are available whatever the age of the offender.

The different powers A section 143 order is one of a large number of forfeiture orders. The section 143 order is also known as a forfeiture order although the Act calls the order a Deprivation Order. There are forfeiture orders which deal with counterfeit currency and anything for making of such currency, Forgery and Counterfeiting Act 1981 s 24(1), drugs and anything relating to drug offences, Misuse of Drugs Act 1971 s 27, firearms and ammunition, Firearms Act 1968 s 52, knives, Knives Act 1997 s 6 and terrorist material, Terrorism Act 2000 s 23A.

[833] Anti-social Behaviour, Crime and Policing Act 2014 (Commencement No 8, Saving and Transitional Provisions) Order 2015 2015/373

[834] Sexual Offences Act 2003 s 118

[835] Sexual Offences Act 2003 s 118

[836] Anti-social Behaviour, Crime and Policing Act 2014 s 114(1)(b) and (4)

[837] Sexual Offences Act 2003 s 122

[838] Legal Aid, Sentencing and Punishment of Offenders Act 2012 s 85(1) and (4) and Legal Aid, Sentencing and Punishment of Offenders Act 2012 (Commencement No 11) Order 2015 2015/504

Destruction orders Articles forfeited under Powers of Criminal Courts (Sentencing) Act 2000 s 143 which are in the possession of the police or National Crime Agency may be destroyed or otherwise disposed of if it is in the opinion of the Chief Officer of Police or the Director General of SOCA that it is not in the public interest that it should be sold or retained, Police (Property) Regulations 1997 1997/1908 reg 8.
Many of the forfeiture powers also contain a power to destroy the forfeited article/substance, e.g. Misuse of Drugs Act 1971 s 27(1) (drugs and anything relating to an offence under that Act), Firearms Act 1968 s 52(1) (firearms and ammunition in relation to an offence under that Act) and counterfeiting currency, Forgery and Counterfeiting Act 1981 s 24(3) (anything relating to the offence under Part II of that Act).

62.2 ***Statistics England and Wales***
Forfeiture orders[839] Number of orders Aged 21+

	2013	2014	2015	2016
Forfeiture orders for property	60,410	52,393	46,941	46,964
Forfeiture orders for vehicle/ship/aircraft	171	137	147	211

For explanations about the statistics, see page 1-xii. The MoJ no longer provides Banks on Sentence with these statistics. For more detailed statistics, see www.banksr.com Other Matters Statistics tab

Power to order

62.3 ***Statutory provisions***
Powers of Criminal Courts (Sentencing) Act 2000 s 143(1) Where a person is convicted of an offence and the court is satisfied that any property which has been lawfully seized from him, or which was in his possession or under his control at the time when he was apprehended for the offence, or when a summons in respect of it was issued:
(a) has been used for the purposes of committing, or facilitating[840] the commission of, any offence, or
(b) was intended by him to be used for that purpose, the court may, subject to subsection (5) [see **62.7**], make an order under this section in respect of that property.
(2) Where a person is convicted of an offence and the offence, or an offence which the court has taken into consideration in determining his sentence, consists of unlawful possession of property which: a) has been lawfully seized from him, or b) was in his possession or under his control at the time when he was apprehended for the offence of which he has been convicted or when a summons in respect of that offence was issued, the court may subject to subsection (5) [see **62.7**] make an order under this section in respect of that property.
(3) [Re the effect of the order, see **62.11**]
(4) Any power conferred on a court by subsection (1) or (2) above may be exercised:
(a) whether or not the court also deals with the offender in any other way in respect of the offence of which he has been convicted; and
(b) without regard to any restrictions on forfeiture in any enactment contained in an Act passed before 29th July 1988.
(5) [Re matters that can be considered, see **62.7**]
(6)-(7) [Re motor vehicles, see **62.4**]

839 Excluding motoring offences
840 Facilitating the commission of an offence shall be taken for the purposes of subsection (1) to include the taking of any steps after it has been committed for the purpose of disposing of any property to which it relates or of avoiding apprehension or detection, Powers of Criminal Courts (Sentencing) Act 2000 s 143(8).

(8) Facilitating the commission of an offence shall be taken for the purposes of subsection (1) above to include the taking of any steps after it has been committed for the purpose of disposing of any property to which it relates or of avoiding apprehension or detection.

62.4 *Motor vehicles Statutory provisions*

Powers of Criminal Courts (Sentencing) Act 2000 s 143(6) Where a person commits an offence to which this subsection applies by:

(a) driving, attempting to drive, or being in charge of a vehicle, or

(b) failing to comply with a requirement made under Road Traffic Act 1988 s 7 or 7A (failure to provide a specimen for analysis or laboratory test or to give permission for such a test) in the course of an investigation into whether the offender had committed an offence while driving, attempting to drive or being in charge of a vehicle, or

(c) failing, as the driver of a vehicle, to comply with Road Traffic Act 1988 s 170(2) or (3) (duty to stop and give information or to report an accident),

the vehicle shall be regarded for the purposes of the section as used for the purpose of committing the offence (and for the purpose of committing any offence of aiding, abetting, counselling or procuring the commission of the offence).

(7) Subsection (6) (see above) applies to: a) an offence under Road Traffic Act 1988 which is punishable with imprisonment, b) an offence of manslaughter, and c) an offence under Offences Against the Person Act 1861 s 35 (wanton and furious driving).

The rest of the section is set out at **62.3**.

Test to apply

62.5 *Statutory provisions*

Powers of Criminal Courts (Sentencing) Act 2000 s 143(5) When considering passing a deprivation order, a court must have regard to the value of the property and the likely financial and other effects on the offender of the making of any order [taken together with any other order that the court contemplates making].

The rest of the section is set out at **62.3**.

62.6 *Prosecution must prove application is made out*

R v Pemberton 1982 4 Cr App R (S) 328 D pleaded to three counts of burglary. A deprivation order for five cars was made. (There is no reference in the report as to the connection between the five cars, D and the burglary. It is likely that the Court did not have this information either. Ed.) Held. It is not sufficient for the prosecution to state that they seek a deprivation order without any evidence. The judge should put them to proof. The prosecution must justify their application. There should have been a proper investigation. This was not done. Order quashed.

62.7 *Failure to apply statutory considerations*

Trans Berckx v North Avon Magistrates and Others 2011 EWHC 2605 (Admin) High Court An employee committed tachograph offences when driving two different lorries. Both lorries were forfeited. The owner of the lorries appealed and the Magistrates said that they forfeited the lorries because of the number of times drivers of lorries from that company had been convicted of 'this type of offence' (ten times in 3 years). Held. As the Magistrates had not considered the statutory test [see para **62.7**] the orders were invalid.

62.8 *Magistrates' Court Sentencing Guidelines 2008 Deprivation Orders*

Magistrates' Court Sentencing Guidelines 2008, see www.banksr.com Other Matters Guidelines tab page 169 The court has the power to deprive an offender of property used for the purpose of committing or facilitating the commission of an offence, whether or not it deals with the offender in any other way.[841]

Before making the order, the court must have regard to the value of the property and the likely financial and other effects on the offender.

[841] Powers of Criminal Courts (Sentencing) Act 2000 s 143

Without limiting the circumstances in which the court may exercise the power, a vehicle is deemed to have been used for the purpose of committing the offence where the offence is punishable by imprisonment and consists of:

(1) driving, attempting to drive, or being in charge of a motor vehicle,
(2) failing to provide a specimen, or
(3) failing to stop and/or report an accident.[842]

Basic principles

62.9 *There must be a proper investigation*

R v Pemberton 1982 4 Cr App R (S) 328 D pleaded to three counts of burglary. A deprivation order for five cars was made. (There is no reference in the report as to the connection between the five cars and D and the burglary. It is likely that the Court did not have this information either. Ed.) Held. It is not sufficient for the prosecution to state that they seek a deprivation order without any evidence. The judge should put them to proof. The prosecution must justify their application. There should have been a proper investigation. This was not done. Order quashed.

R v Joyce and Others 1989 11 Cr App R (S) 253 Deprivation orders were made in respect of three members of the Joyce family in respect of their cars, after guilty pleas to a number of specimen counts of obtaining money by deception. The offences involved large-scale fraud upon the DHSS, with a large number of false claims being made for statutory benefits. Held. No one appeared to have explored the ownership of the cars, nor their value, nor the extent to which they were used to transport the family to the various DHSS offices. None of the defendants were in the dock to hear the order being made, nor in the course of sentence did the Judge allude to the question of confiscation. He did not give any indication that he was mitigating the penalty of imprisonment to reflect the financial penalty which the confiscation represented.

R v Highbury Corner Magistrates' Court ex parte Di Matteo 1991 92 Cr App R 263 D was convicted of driving whilst disqualified and driving without insurance. He drove a car whilst disqualified and a deprivation order for his car, amongst other penalties, was made. Held. The Magistrate did not have sufficient information to make the order. Regard should have been had to the value of the property and to the likely financial and other effects on D of making a forfeiture order, taken together with all other orders which he had in contemplation. If the effect of such an order taken with any other penalties would be to create an excessive criminal penalty the order should not be made. Order quashed.

R v Jones 2017 EWCA Crim 2192, 2018 1 Cr App R (S) 35 (p 248) D pleaded to possession of 4.54 grams of crack cocaine. The Judge found that because of what was found at D's home, D was a commercial dealer. The Judge forfeited £4,600 in cash. During mitigation, D's counsel gave an explanation for the money, saying a 'lot of the money' had come from cards/roulette. Held. It is not clear whether there was a formal application for forfeiture of the money. The procedure seemed to be extremely lax. The Judge should have taken a much firmer and more formal grip on the matter. There must be a proper investigation. The Judge never expressly said he rejected D's account for the cash. As the Judge had not applied his mind properly, we quash the order.

See also: *R v Hall* 2014 EWCA Crim 2413 (The Judge, without an application, made a deprivation order. We quash the order because the Judge failed to investigate the situation properly.)

62.10 *Dual purposes of the order*

R v Highbury Corner Magistrates' Court ex parte Di Matteo 1991 92 Cr App R 263 D was convicted of driving whilst disqualified and driving without insurance. Held.

[842] Powers of Criminal Courts (Sentencing) Act 2000 s 143(6)-(7)

[Forfeiture] can serve a dual purpose: the removal from public circulation of an article which has been used to commit or facilitate the commission of an offence and as part of the punishment of the offender.

62.11 ***Effect of the order***

Powers of Criminal Courts (Sentencing) Act 2000 s 143(3) An order under section 143 shall deprive the offender of his rights, if any, in the property to which it relates, and the property shall (if not already in their possession) be taken into the possession of the police.

The rest of the section is set out at **62.3**.

62.12 ***Judicial guidance***

R v Troth 1979 1 Cr App R (S) 341 D pleaded to theft of coal. The Court made a forfeiture order for the lorry that was used to transport the coal. D co-owned the lorry with his cousin, who knew nothing of the theft. Held. Orders should not be made unless they are simple orders and there are no complicating factors. Order quashed.

O'Leary International v Chief Constable of North Wales and CPS 2012 EWHC 1516 (Admin) para 14(x) The guidance [about ownership] in *R v Troth* 1979 should be followed.[843]

R v Thomas 2012 EWCA Crim 1159 As a general principle, deprivation orders should not be made except in cases which were simple and uncomplicated.

62.13 ***Can't forfeit a house***

R v Khan 1983 76 Cr App R 29 The Judge made a deprivation order in respect of D's house. Held. Deprivation orders do not apply to real property. By virtue of Police Property Act 1897 s 1, property is confined to personal property and not real property. A house was not included in the word 'anything', *R v Beard* 1974 1 WLR 1549. The words of the statute are to enable a person authorised by the court to destroy or deal with forfeited property in a manner which the court sees fit. The words are only apt to deal with things that are tangible. To extend the ambit of the section would lead to difficulties and uncertainties and would place a strained construction on the language used, *R v Cuthbertson* 1980 71 Cr App R 148. The Judge had no jurisdiction to make the order. Order quashed.

R v Pearce 1996 2 Cr App R (S) 316 D pleaded to producing cannabis. He purchased a house and converted the upstairs so cannabis could be grown there. 180 plants were seized. The Judge forfeited the house. Held. Misuse of Drugs Act 1971 s 27 was considered in *R v Beard* 1974 1 WLR 1549, where it was decided 'anything' did not include a house. Order quashed.

Note: Houses are now dealt with by confiscation. Ed.

62.14 ***Defendant must possess the property***

Powers of Criminal Courts (Sentencing) Act 2000 s 143(1)…that any property…which was in his possession or under his control at the time when he was apprehended for the offence, or when a summons in respect of it was issued.

The rest of the section is set out at **62.3**.

R v Rana 1998 2 Cr App R (S) 288 D pleaded to conspiracy to obtain property by deception. D used his car when he went to the Companies Registry (now Companies House) to obtain information for the offence. Later his brother was arrested in the car after he had presented a forged authority to a bank. The Judge made a forfeiture order for the car. D appealed saying the car was not in his possession or control at the time the car was seized. Held. The brother was using the car on his and D's behalf. The car was seized from D, so order affirmed.

Old case: *R v Hinde* 1977 64 Cr App R 213 (Order quashed applying a slightly differently worded section.)

[843] The judgment is poorly indented. In the judgment it looks as if this section is from another case. It isn't.

62.15 ***Immigration and asylum cases***

UK Borders Act 2007 s 25(1) A court making a forfeiture order under Powers of Criminal Courts (Sentencing) Act 2000 s 143 may order that the property be taken into the possession of the Secretary of State (and not of the police) where the court thinks that the offence in connection with which the order is made either related to immigration or asylum or was committed for a purpose connected with immigration or asylum.

62.16 ***Must be used for the purpose of committing etc. any offence***

Powers of Criminal Courts (Sentencing) Act 2000 s 143(1) …any property that…a) has been used for the purposes of committing, or facilitating[844] the commission of, any offence, or b) was intended by him to be used for that purpose.
The rest of the section is set out at **62.3**.

R v Lidster 1976 RTR 240 D was convicted of two counts of handling stolen goods. He transferred the stolen goods using his Jaguar car and a deprivation order was made for his car. The defence submitted that it was an extreme and excessive penalty. Held. The use of the car was integral to the commission of the offence. The order was entirely appropriate.

R v Slater 1986 8 Cr App R (S) 217 D pleaded to conspiracy to supply drugs and two counts of handling. The Judge made a deprivation order for £1,136 which he found was in his possession on the basis that the money was the product of a dishonest action. The Crown argued that [property] 'used for the purpose of committing any offence by anyone' was to be widely construed and as such the offence was the purchase of drugs which provided D with the sum of money. Held. There is no power within the section to order forfeiture of the sum of money on the basis it was the product of dishonest action. To enable such a power would place far too wide a construction on the statute. The test is 'has [the property] been used for the purpose of committing any offence by the defendant'. Order quashed.

62.17 ***Property owned by others wholly or partly/on HP***

R v Troth 1979 1 Cr App R (S) 341 D pleaded to theft of coal. The Court made a forfeiture order for the lorry that was used to transport the coal. D co-owned the lorry with his cousin, who knew nothing of the theft. Held. Orders should not be made unless they are simple orders and there are no complicating factors. Order quashed.

R v Kearney 2011 EWCA Crim 826, 2 Cr App R (S) 106 (p 608) D pleaded to six offences of making off without payment and two thefts. Driving an Audi, he filled up with diesel at petrol stations and didn't pay. He changed the plates on the car to avoid detection. The value of the fuel was £450. The Audi was the subject of HP. The outstanding balance was £13,004. To pay off the HP needed £9,113. The value was estimated to be £10,000. The Judge ordered the forfeiture of the car and ordered the car to be sold and £450 of the proceeds to be paid to the losers. Later, D used the car as part payment for another car. Held. In law the vehicle was owned by the finance company. D was only a bailee. Deprivation orders should only be made in simple and uncomplicated cases. The order only affects the rights of the offender and cannot affect the rights of others in the property. Order quashed with a fresh compensation order made instead.

O'Leary International v Chief Constable of North Wales and CPS 2012 EWHC 1516 (Admin) High Court Four lorry drivers driving for the same company were stopped for driving offences and some charged with producing false letters of attestation. Some were sent to prison. In each case their lorry was forfeited. The company wrote to the Magistrates' Court about the orders and was told that the Court could not accept that the company did not know about their drivers' activities. One driver appealed to the Crown Court and the Judge did not allow the company to make any representations as they were not a party to the proceedings. The orders there were upheld. The company applied to

[844] Powers of Criminal Courts (Sentencing) Act 2000 s 143(8). Facilitating the commission of an offence shall be taken for the purposes of subsection (1) (see **62.4**) to include the taking of any steps after it has been committed for the purpose of disposing of any property to which it relates or of avoiding apprehension or detection.

the Magistrates' Court for the return of the property under Police Property Act 1897 s 1(1). The company claimed they did not know about their drivers. They called evidence and the District Judge found that the company did know what was going on. The company applied to the High Court by case stated. The company also brought a claim for conversion in the High Court. The CPS attended as an interested party and said that Powers of Criminal Courts (Sentencing) Act 2000 s 143 only operated to deprive the offender of his rights in the property and not any other person. Held. Section 143 could not deprive the owner of property when they were not an offender prosecuted. It only deprived the offender of his rights. There is nothing in section 143 which suggests the power can affect any rights of the owner. That would offend the fundamental principle that to be deprived of your rights you have to be a party to the proceedings. We cannot quash the orders but we order the lorries should be delivered to the company. The District Judge should have declined jurisdiction.
Note: The reason the Court could not quash the orders was that the appeal was not made by the offenders who were subject to the order. None of these problems would have arisen if the company had been prosecuted as well. The Court listed a series of helpful authorities on this point. Ed.

62.18 *'Used for the purposes', Definition of*

Powers of Criminal Courts (Sentencing) Act 2000 s 143(1) Where a person is convicted of an offence…and the court is satisfied that any property which has been lawfully seized from him that has been used for the purposes of committing, or facilitating[845] the commission of, any offence, the court may make an order in respect of that property.
The rest of the section is set out at **62.3**.
R v Slater 1986 8 Cr App R (S) 217 D contended that the Judge had no power to make the order on the basis that the Judge had found that the £1,136 seized at his house was the proceeds of a dishonest action, and not used for the purposes of committing or facilitating an offence. Held. The proper construction of the section is '…has been used for the purpose of committing an offence by D'. Construing the section to read '…has been used for the purpose of committing any offence by anyone' was too wide. Order quashed.
R v Coleville-Scott 1991 12 Cr App R (S) 238 LCJ D was convicted of importation of cannabis, for which he received sums of money, and was subject to a deprivation order in respect of £125,000. D contended that this was unlawful, citing *R v Slater* 1986 (see above). In *R v Slater* 1986, it was never considered whether the money passed from customer to supplier had been used to facilitate the commission of an offence, only that the money was used by the customers to commit an offence when purchasing drugs from the supplier. Held. A distinction is necessary between a person who uses property to commit or facilitate the commission of an offence, and the person who commits the offence. There is nothing in section 143 which requires the user and the offender to be one and the same. The question was, 'were the sums of money paid to D to facilitate the commission of the offence by him?' Those payments were made to D in order to facilitate the commission of the offence and therefore the Judge had the power to make an order under section 143.

62.19 *Onerous total financial penalties/Penalties must be proportionate*

R v Scully 1985 7 Cr App R (S) 119 D was employed as a driller for oil and received, after tax, £24,000 per annum, £500 per week. The Judge imposed a fine of £5,000 to be paid at a rate of £500 per month in addition to a sentence of imprisonment, which was suspended. The Judge also imposed a deprivation order for his car, which was purchased for approximately £10,000. Held. The overall penalty should be commensurate with the

[845] Facilitating the commission of an offence shall be taken for the purposes of subsection (1) (see **62.3**) to include the taking of any steps after it has been committed for the purpose of disposing of any property to which it relates or of avoiding apprehension or detection, Powers of Criminal Courts (Sentencing) Act 2000 s 143(8).

offence. Considering the offence and the nature of the property recovered, the overall financial penalty of £15,000 was too heavy a burden. Deprivation order quashed. Fine upheld.

R v Joyce and Others 1989 11 Cr App R (S) 253 Deprivation orders were made in respect of three members of the Joyce family in respect of their cars, with all three receiving custodial sentences. Held. The Judge had failed to reflect their effect when determining the custodial sentences. The effect of a deprivation order must be taken into account when determining the sentence as a whole. Terms of imprisonment reduced. Orders upheld.

R v Highbury Corner Magistrates' Court ex parte Di Matteo 1991 92 Cr App R 263 The forfeiture of D's car was ordered, against which D applied for leave to judicially review that decision. D drove his car whilst disqualified, uninsured and on bail for those same two offences. Held. If the effect of an order, taken with any other sentence(s) or order(s) made, would be to create an excessive criminal penalty the forfeiture order should not be made. An order should not be made if the effect of that order would be to subject D to undue hardship, see *R v Taverner* 1974 Unreported 4/4/74 and *R v Buchholz* 1974 Unreported 10/5/74. A court considering making a deprivation order must consider whether in conjunction with any other sentence(s) or order(s) the court wishes to make, a forfeiture order would inflict too great a burden on D, and must look at the total effect of the penalties imposed and measure that against the totality of his offending.

R v De Jesus 2015 EWCA Crim 1118, 2 Cr App R (S) 44 (p 343) D and S pleaded to two robberies. D's mother died as a result of medical negligence and D used part of his share of the damages paid to buy a car which was worth just under £14,000. Using the car, D and S drove to a dimly lit site. One took a baseball bat out of the car and the two used that in a robbery of two students. The Judge gave them both 28 months and he forfeited D's car. The defence argued that there was an unreasonable disparity between D and S. Held. The Judge was right to give the two the same sentence. Deprivation Orders are not in the nature of confiscation orders which deprive the offender of the proceeds of this offending. Proportionality is an important factor. We quash the order.

See also: *R v Priestly* 1996 2 Cr App R (S) 144 (see **62.17**).

Theft In theft cases, see the **THEFT *Sentencing Guidelines Council guideline* Deprivation Orders** section at **344.3** in Volume 2.

The hearing

62.20 *On the facts, order correct/incorrect*

R v Connelly 2012 EWCA Crim 2049 D pleaded to six counts of taking indecent photos of a child, V. D's computer was examined and there were six photos of the same 7-year-old child clearly taken on two different days. Her poses for the camera were clearly sexualised. In one, V had pulled down her underclothes and exposed her genitalia. D was a keen amateur photographer. He had many thousands of innocent pictures of his family, family occasions, his grandchildren and his military career. The photos of V had been deleted. The Judge made a SOPO which restricted D's possession and use of photographic equipment with a police inspection requirement. The Judge also made a deprivation order after hearing that V's family wanted complete confidence that the images would not resurface. Held. We take judicial notice of the fact that an expert with sophisticated software can always retrieve deleted files. But that is not a risk that we consider is sufficiently real to deprive him of the computer and its legitimate contents. The SOPO provided sufficient checks on D and his computer.

See also: *R v Kearney* 2011 EWCA Crim 826, 2 Cr App R (S) 106 (p 608) (A car was used to steal plates and make off without payment. However, as the car was subject to HP and had been sold after the hearing, compensation orders to the victims made instead.)

R v Lee 2012 EWCA Crim 2658, 2013 2 Cr App R (S) 18 (p 79) (Van used in kidnapping and beating of victim. Family on benefits so loss of van claimed to be significant and that it would make it more difficult to find work. Deprivation order not wrong.)
R v Hamlett 2015 EWCA Crim 1412 (Plea to dangerous driving. Police chase over two miles and 80 mph speeding in 30 mph zone. Red lights crossed. Prosecution asked for an order. Defence said why it was unsuitable and there was no mention in the sentencing remarks until the Judge was prompted by the prosecution. Held. It was something of an afterthought. The car was worth £10,000. The suspended sentence, unpaid work, £500 fine and disqualification were sufficient.)

62.21 ***Using proceeds to pay victim etc.***
Powers of Criminal Courts (Sentencing) Act 2000 s 145(1) Where a court makes an order under section 143 in a case where:

(a) the offender has been convicted of an offence which has resulted in a person suffering personal injury, loss or damage, or
(b) any such offence is taken into consideration by the court in determining sentence, the court may also make an order that any proceeds which arise from the disposal of the property and which do not exceed a sum specified by the court shall be paid to that person.

(2) The court may only make an order under section 145(1) if it is satisfied but for the inadequacy of the offender's means it would have made a compensation order under which the offender would have been required to pay compensation of an amount not less than the specified amount.

62.22 ***Explain sentence, Judge/Magistrate must***
Criminal Justice Act 2003 s 174(2)[846] The court must state in open court, in ordinary language and in general terms, the court's reasons for deciding on the sentence.
(3) The court must explain to the offender in ordinary language:

(a) the effect of the sentence,
(b) the effects of non-compliance with any order that the offender is required to comply with and that forms part of the sentence,
(c) any power of the court to vary or review any order that forms part of the sentence…

Combined with other orders

62.23 ***Combined with other orders General***
Powers of Criminal Courts (Sentencing) Act 2000 s 143(4) The court may pass a deprivation order:

(a) whether or not the court also deals with the offender in any other way in respect of the offence of which he or she has been convicted, and
(b) without regard to any restrictions on forfeiture in any enactment contained in an Act passed before 29 July 1988.

62.24 ***Absolute and conditional discharges, Combined with***
Powers of Criminal Courts (Sentencing) Act 2000 s 12(7) Nothing in this section shall be construed as preventing a court, on discharging an offender absolutely or conditionally in respect of any offence…from making in respect of the offence an order under Powers of Criminal Courts (Sentencing) Act 2000 s 130 (compensation orders).[847]

62.25 ***Imprisonment, Combined with***
R v Priestly 1996 2 Cr App R (S) 144 D was convicted of two offences of conspiracy concerning trademarks. He received 4 years' imprisonment. He was also convicted of 11 counts of using trademarks contrary to Trademarks Act 1938 (2 years each, concurrent). The conspiracy was of considerable size. A confiscation order under Criminal Justice

[846] As substituted by Legal Aid, Sentencing and Punishment of Offenders Act 2012 s 64
[847] As amended by Criminal Justice and Courts Act 2015 Sch 12 paras 8-9

Act 1988 s 71[848] was made in the sum of £94,000 (to serve a further 2 years' imprisonment in default of payment). A deprivation order in respect of a sewing machine, a computer and two sums of cash totalling £35,255 was also made. The total financial penalty was £129,255. It was argued that when ordering deprivation, the Judge had failed to take account of the total penalty imposed and that had breached the principle in *R v Joyce and Others* 1989 11 Cr App R (S) 253. It is in that light that it was argued that a sentence of 4 years' imprisonment was excessive. Held. The Judge had failed to consider the effect of the order. Order upheld. 3 years' imprisonment, not 4.

63 *GOODYEAR* INDICATIONS

Non-*Goodyear* indications/Plea bargaining is not permitted

63.1 *Basic principles*

R v Turner 1970 54 Cr App R 352 D was charged with theft. During his trial defence counsel gave strong views about the dangers of continuing with his not guilty plea. The clerk of the court said he told counsel that the Judge would not allow much more time and that he was authorised to say that whether D pleaded guilty or not guilty, the result would be the same and there would not be a term of imprisonment. Defence counsel got the impression that the message the clerk was authorised to give was that if at this stage there was a plea then there would be a fine. Held. Once D felt that this was an intimation emanating from the Judge, it is really idle to think that D really had a free choice in the matter. Counsel must be completely free to do what is his duty, namely to give the accused the best advice he can and, if need be, advise in strong terms. It is of course imperative that so far as is possible justice must be administered in open court. A statement that on a plea of guilty [such a] sentence would be imposed but that on conviction following a plea of not guilty [the offence] would attract a severer sentence is one that should never be made. This could be taken to be undue pressure on the accused, thus depriving him of that complete freedom of choice which is essential. The only exception to this rule is that it should be permissible for a judge to say that whatever happens, whether the accused pleads guilty or not guilty, the sentence will or will not take a particular form, e.g. a probation order, or a fine, or a custodial sentence. Finally, where any such discussion on sentence has taken place between judge and counsel, counsel for the defence should disclose this to the accused and inform him of what took place. New trial ordered.

R v Grice 1978 66 Cr App R 167 D was charged with unlawful sexual intercourse. The Judge formed the view that it would be unfortunate if the victim had to go into the witness box to give evidence and be cross-examined, so asked counsel for the prosecution and defence to come and see him. The Judge indicated that he was not minded to impose an immediate sentence if D pleaded guilty and said one of the matters he had in mind was that the victim had attempted suicide over the affair between her and D. D decided to plead guilty. The Judge in sentencing said "This must never happen again with either this girl or the other girl. I want you to promise that you will never go near those two girls again. Are you willing to make that promise?" D replied, "Yes." D was sentenced to 2 years suspended. The following week, D went to a house where the younger victim was visiting. When that information was brought to the notice of the Judge, he issued a warrant and committed D to prison for a weekend for contempt of court. D was later sentenced to 2 years' immediate imprisonment. The Judge said the previous suspended sentence was what is colloquially known among lawyers as a 'plea bargain' in that if D pleaded guilty the sentence would be suspended. Held. It was clearly 'plea bargaining'. The Judge disregarded *R v Turner* 1970 54 Cr App R 352. The occasions when the judge should discuss sentence with counsel should be rare indeed

[848] Repealed by Proceeds of Crime Act 2002 Sch 12 para 1

and where there is such a discussion the judge should take the utmost pains to comply with the directions in *R v Turner* 1970. The original sentence of 2 years suspended was restored.

Att-Gen's Ref No 44 of 2000 2001 1 Cr App R (S) 132 (p 460) D pleaded to eight counts of indecent assault on a girl, five being on a girl under the age of 13, and one count of indecent assault on a male. He received 18 months' suspended. D was the deputy headmaster and later the headmaster at a preparatory school. The offences occurred when D was disciplining the children. He denied all offences. Prosecuting counsel enquired as to the possibility of guilty pleas. Defence counsel advised that they were inconceivable if D would receive a custodial sentence. Prosecution counsel said almost all the complainants did not wish D to go to prison. He said to defence counsel that a suspended sentence would be a fair outcome. Defence counsel then saw D but did not warn him about the prosecution being able to make an Attorney-General's reference. This initiated a joint approach to the Judge, in which prosecution counsel acquiesced and encouraged the Judge to pass a suspended sentence. Brief submissions were made: defence counsel advancing mitigation arguing that this was an exceptional case, prosecution counsel observing that pleas to nine out of 16 counts relating to seven of 11 complainants was satisfactory. The Judge agreed that a suspended sentence was justified. Prosecution counsel at the Court of Appeal tried to argue that the CPS and the Attorney-General were different parts of the system so the Attorney-General was not bound by what had happened at the Crown Court. Held. It was regrettable that such plea bargaining had occurred here. In our judgement, if the Crown, by whatever means they are prosecuting, make representations to a defendant on which he is entitled to rely and on which he acts to his detriment by, as in the present case, pleading guilty in circumstances in which he would not otherwise have pleaded guilty, that can properly be regarded as giving rise to a legitimate expectation on his part that the Crown will not subsequently seek to resile from those representations, whether by way of the Attorney-General exercising his personal statutory duties under section 36 or otherwise. For this purpose the Crown and its agents are indivisible. Leave to appeal refused.

R v Goodyear 2005 EWCA Crim 888, 2006 1 Cr App R (S) 6 (p 23) para 67 LCJ The judge should never be invited to give an indication on the basis of what would be, or what would appear to be, a 'plea bargain'. He should not be asked to be involved, nor become involved, in discussions linking the acceptability to the prosecution of a plea or basis of plea, and the sentence which may be imposed. He is not conducting or involving himself in any plea bargaining. In short, he is not to be asked to indicate levels of sentence which he may have in mind depending on possible different pleas. Thus, for example, he should refuse to give an indication based on the possibility that the defendant might plead guilty to section 18, alternatively section 20, alternatively section 47.

R v Nightingale 2013 EWCA Crim 405 CMAC D, a Sergeant in the SAS, was charged with possession of a prohibited firearm and possession of ammunition. The offences triggered the minimum sentence provisions. D's counsel did not seek an indication of sentence. In Court there was a discussion about another case the Judge had dealt with on a plea meriting a 2-year sentence, and noted that D had not pleaded to both counts. The Judge then stated that if D was to be found guilty, and exceptional circumstances were not present, there could be no reduction from the minimum sentence. In a further conference with D, D's counsel explained that the Judge had given an indication 'in legal speak' that if D was found guilty, he would receive 5 years. If he were to plead guilty, there was a strong possibility he would not receive custody. D subsequently pleaded guilty and received 18 months' detention, reduced to 12 months suspended on appeal. Held. It was reasonably expected that following a guilty plea in exceptional circumstances, D's sentence would be less than 2 years. The significance of a sentence of less than 2 years was that it would be served in military detention, not a civilian prison. It was also significant that notwithstanding the conviction, D may have been able to continue his military career. The observations [in *R v Turner* 1970] do not mean that in a case where imprisonment is inevitable it is permissible for the judge on his own initiative, uninvited, to give an indication to the defendant that a very long sentence of imprisonment will be the consequence of conviction by the jury or by the Court Martial, and a relatively short one will follow if the defendant decides to plead guilty. D's freedom of choice was improperly narrowed. The plea was a nullity. Conviction quashed. Retrial ordered.

Att-Gen's Ref No 85 of 2014 2014 EWCA Crim 2088, 2015 1 Cr App R (S) 14 (p 111) On the day set for D's trial, there was a discussion with counsel in the Judge's chambers where the Judge indicated that, if D pleaded, he was minded not to impose immediate custody. A *Goodyear* indication in open court was made with the Judge stating that a guilty plea would lead to the offending being put in Category 1B and a non-immediate custodial sentence. D pleaded to sexual activity with a child under 16 (×3). The Judge imposed a suspended sentence following the indication. Held. The procedure was similar to that criticised in *R v Turner* 1970 54 Cr App R 352 and revisited in *R v Goodyear* 2005 EWCA Crim 888, 2006 1 Cr App R (S) 6 (p 23). There should have been no discussion in the Judge's chambers and there should have been no indication that a plea could make the difference between a custodial and a non-custodial sentence. **2 years**, not 9 months suspended for 12.

63.2 ***Defendants must have a free choice for their pleas***

R v Goodyear 2005 EWCA Crim 888, 2006 1 Cr App R (S) 6 (p 23) para 30 LCJ The defendant is personally and exclusively responsible for his plea. When he enters it, it must be entered voluntarily, without improper pressure.

63.3 ***Prosecution has no duty to acquiesce***

Att-Gen's Ref Nos 80-81 of 1999 2000 2 Cr App R (S) 138 LCJ There can never be any obligation for the prosecution to acquiesce in an indication given by the judge to which the prosecution takes exception.

THE *GOODYEAR* PROCEDURE

Preliminaries

63.4 ***Reasons for giving Goodyear indications***

R v Goodyear 2005 EWCA Crim 888, 2006 1 Cr App R (S) 6 (p 23) para 53 LCJ The objective of these Guidelines is to ensure common process and continuing safeguards against the creation or appearance of judicial pressure on the defendant. The potential advantages include, first and foremost, that the defendant himself would make a better informed decision whether to plead or not. Experience tends to suggest that this would result in an increased number of early guilty pleas, with a consequent reduction in the number of trials, and the number of cases which are listed for trial, and then, to use current language, 'crack' at the last minute, usually at considerable inconvenience to those involved in the intended trial, and in particular, victims and witnesses. Properly applied, too, there may be a reduced number of sentences to be considered by the Attorney-General and, where appropriate, referred to this Court as unduly lenient. In short, an increase in the efficient administration of justice will not impinge on the defendant's entitlement to tender a voluntary plea.

63.5 ***Objective of the Goodyear procedure***

Criminal Practice Directions 2015 EWCA Crim 1567 para VII C.2 The objective of the *Goodyear* guidelines is to safeguard against the creation or appearance of judicial pressure on a defendant.

63.6 ***Court Martial***

Guidance on Sentencing in the Court Martial 2018 para 2.22 In appropriate cases the judge may give a *Goodyear* indication at an Initial Hearing, or at a subsequent hearing, if requested by the defence. This sets a ceiling on the sentence, in the event that the defendant pleads guilty, and is given on the record. If a *Goodyear* indication is given and a guilty plea is entered on that basis, the sentencing court is bound by that indication (even if there is a different judge) and a court may not pass a sentence which is more severe than the indication given by the judge. The judge will advise the Board at the beginning of the sentencing process if an indication has been given.

63.7 *Magistrates' Court, Goodyear indication not available in*

R v Goodyear 2005 EWCA Crim 888, 2006 1 Cr App R (S) 6 (p 23) para 78 LCJ It would be impracticable for these new arrangements to be extended to proceedings in the Magistrates' Court. Accordingly, for the time being, magistrates should confine themselves to the statutory arrangements in Criminal Justice Act 2003 Sch 3 (Allocation of cases triable either way and committing cases to the Crown Court etc.).

63.8 *Confiscation proceedings etc.*

R v Goodyear 2005 EWCA Crim 888, 2006 1 Cr App R (S) 6 (p 23) para 65(d) LCJ Any indication which may be given relates only to the matters about which an indication is sought. Thus, certain steps, like confiscation proceedings, follow automatically, and the judge cannot dispense with them or, by giving an indication of sentence, create an expectation that they will be dispensed with.

63.9 *Attorney-General's right to seek a reference*

R v Goodyear 2005 EWCA Crim 888, 2006 1 Cr App R (S) 6 (p 23) para 65(a) and 71 LCJ Any sentence indication given by the judge remains subject to the entitlement of the Attorney-General (where it arises) to refer an unduly lenient sentence to the Court of Appeal. We do not envisage a process by which the judge should give some kind of preliminary indication, leading to comments on it by counsel for the Crown, with the judge then reconsidering his indication, and perhaps raising it to a higher level, with counsel for the defendant then making further submissions to persuade the judge, after all, to reduce his indication. If nothing else, such a process would smack of precisely the kind of bargaining process which should be avoided. If counsel for the prosecution has addressed his responsibilities in accordance with paragraph 69 of this judgment, see **63.12**, the discretion of the Attorney-General to refer a sentence would be wholly unaffected by the advance sentence indication process. We do not anticipate that counsel for the Crown will have said or done anything which may indicate or convey support for or approval of the sentence indication. If, however, he has done so, the question whether the sentence should nevertheless be referred to this Court as unduly lenient, and the decision of the Court whether to interfere with and increase it, will be examined on a case-by-case basis, in the light of everything said and done by counsel for the Crown.

Att-Gen's Ref No 48 of 2006 2006 EWCA Crim 2396, 2007 1 Cr App R (S) 90 (p 558) The trial Judge said after a request for a *Goodyear* indication that he did not think it appropriate or necessary to impose a custodial sentence other than a suspended sentence of imprisonment. Held. Any indication must be subject to the Attorney-General's right to refer the case to the Court of Appeal. Defence counsel must advise their clients that any request for an indication is subject to the entitlement of the Attorney-General to refer cases to the Court of Appeal. The least sentence that could have been properly imposed for these offences would have been one of 2 years' imprisonment. The indication cannot preclude this Court from saying a suspended sentence was wrong. When taking into account that D had been given an indication that a custodial sentence would not be imposed and that he has been at liberty until today, the right sentence to impose is one of 18 months' immediate imprisonment.

See also: *Att-Gen's Ref No 30 of 2014* 2014 EWCA Crim 1248 (An example of the Court of Appeal increasing a sentence given after a *Goodyear* indication and the Court not mentioning the indication as a factor.)

Advocates' responsibilities and basis of plea

63.10 ***Defendant advocate must have written authorisation to apply***

R v Goodyear 2005 EWCA Crim 888, 2006 1 Cr App R (S) 6 (p 23) para 64 LCJ The defendant's advocate should not seek an indication without written authority, signed by his client, that he, the client, wishes to seek an indication.

63.11 ***Defence advocates' responsibilities***

R v Goodyear 2005 EWCA Crim 888, 2006 1 Cr App R (S) 6 (p 23) para 65. LCJ The advocate is personally responsible for ensuring that his client fully appreciates that:

(a) he should not plead guilty unless he is guilty,

(b) any sentence indication given by the judge remains subject to the entitlement of the Attorney-General (where it arises) to refer an unduly lenient sentence to the Court of Appeal,

(c) any indication given by the judge reflects the situation at the time when it is given, and that if a 'guilty plea' is not tendered in the light of that indication the indication ceases to have effect,

(d) any indication which may be given relates only to the matters about which an indication is sought. Thus, certain steps, like confiscation proceedings, follow automatically, and the judge cannot dispense with them, nor, by giving an indication of sentence, create an expectation that they will be dispensed with.

63.12 ***Prosecution advocates' responsibilities***

R v Goodyear 2005 EWCA Crim 888, 2006 1 Cr App R (S) 6 (p 23) paras 69 and 70 LCJ As the request for indication comes from the defence, the prosecution is obliged to react, rather than initiate the process. The advocate for the prosecution is responsible for the following specific matters:

(a) If there is no final agreement about the plea to the indictment, or the basis of plea, and the defence nevertheless proceeds to seek an indication, which the judge appears minded to give, prosecuting counsel should remind him of this guidance, that normally speaking an indication of sentence should not be given until the basis of the plea has been agreed, or the judge has concluded that he can properly deal with the case without the need for a *Newton* hearing.

(b) If an indication is sought, the prosecution should normally enquire whether the judge is in possession of or has had access to all the evidence relied on by the prosecution, including any personal impact statement from the victim of the crime, as well as any information of relevant previous convictions recorded against the defendant.

(c) If the process has been properly followed, it should not normally be necessary for counsel for the prosecution, before the judge gives any indication, to do more than, first, draw the judge's attention to any minimum or mandatory statutory sentencing requirements, and where he would be expected to offer the judge assistance with relevant guideline cases, or the views of the Sentencing Guidelines Council, to invite the judge to allow him to do so, and second, where it applies, to remind the judge that the position of the Attorney-General to refer any eventual sentencing decision as unduly lenient is not affected.

(d) In any event, counsel should not say anything which may create the impression that the sentence indication has the support or approval of the Crown.

R v Kulah 2007 EWCA Crim 1701, 2008 1 Cr App R (S) 85 (p 494) *R v Goodyear* 2005 already imposes an obligation on the prosecution to draw the attention of the judge to any minimum or mandatory sentencing requirements. That obligation includes a duty to inform the judge that the offence charged is a specified offence and of the requirement to undertake a risk assessment required by each of the relevant subsections.

63.13 ***Basis of plea Must have an agreed basis of plea***

Criminal Practice Directions 2015 EWCA Crim 1567 para VII C.3 Such [*Goodyear*] indications should normally not be given if there is a dispute as to the basis of plea unless the judge concludes that he or she can properly deal with the case without the need for a *Newton* hearing.

R v Goodyear 2005 EWCA Crim 888, 2006 1 Cr App R (S) 6 (p 23) para 62 LCJ Where appropriate, there must be an agreed, written basis of plea. Unless there is, the judge should refuse to give an indication, otherwise he may become inappropriately involved in negotiations about the acceptance of pleas, and any agreed basis of plea. An indication should not be sought while there is any uncertainty between the prosecution and the defence about an acceptable plea or pleas to the indictment, or any factual basis relating to the plea.

R v Martin 2013 EWCA Crim 2565, 2014 2 Cr App R (S) 21 (p 144) D pleaded to theft and possession of MDMA. D's basis of plea stated that he sold drugs to friends at cost and made no profit. That was rejected by the prosecution. A second basis of plea was entered, stating that he supplied drugs to others making no gain save for benefiting from bulk purchasing for his friends and himself. The question of a *Newton* hearing arose and the Judge told D that if he found that there was no financial gain, the sentence would be 21 months, but if he found that D was making money, the sentence would start at 40 months and, after credit for the plea (not entered at the first opportunity), be reduced to 30 months. A *Newton* hearing was held and the Judge rejected D's evidence. The Judge then realised that he had fallen into error in that he had indicated credit for the guilty plea would remain at 25% in the event that D was disbelieved in the *Newton*. The Judge said that as he had rejected D's evidence, D had therefore wrongly had a *Newton* and that he would lose half of the 25% credit as a consequence. The Judge honoured the starting point of 40 months but gave a 12.5% discount, namely 5 months, resulting in a 35-month sentence. Held. The sentencing process was flawed from the outset. The Judge ought not to have given an indication of the sentence he would pass given alternative findings in the *Newton* hearing. To do so offends against *R v Goodyear*. We have difficulty thinking of any circumstances in which a judge ought to give an indication of sentence in advance of a *Newton* hearing, not only because the judge will find it hard to predict what basis he would be sentencing upon, but because he will not know to what extent he will need to reduce the amount of credit given for the plea. The indication given by the Judge would be honoured. 30 months not 35.

Note: This was not a *Goodyear* indication but an informal indication. The principles apply to both. Ed.

63.14 ***Basis of plea must be written***

Criminal Practice Directions 2015 EWCA Crim 1567 para VII C.3...If there is a basis of plea agreed by the prosecution and defence, it must be reduced into writing and a copy provided to the judge.

R v Goodyear 2005 EWCA Crim 888, 2006 1 Cr App R (S) 6 (p 23) para 66 LCJ Any agreed basis should be reduced into writing before an indication is sought. Where there is a dispute about a particular fact which counsel for the defendant believes to be effectively immaterial to the sentencing decision, the difference should be recorded, so that the judge can make up his or her own mind.

For more information about bases of plea, see the **FACTUAL BASIS FOR SENTENCING Basis of plea** section at **57.28**.

63.15 ***What indications can be asked for?***

R v Omole 2011 EWCA Crim 1428, 2012 1 Cr App R (S) 41 (p 240) D pleaded to possession of false identity documentation. Prior to pleading to numerous fraud offences, his counsel sought an indication as to whether the fraud offences fell in the top bracket or second bracket of the Sentencing Guidelines Council's guideline. The Judge gave a clear indication that the offences were within the second bracket. Held. The indication did not conform to the guidelines given in *Goodyear*. In this case, the Judge ought to a) have treated the request for an indication as if he was being asked to indicate the maximum sentence at that stage and b) have considered whether at that stage he was in an appropriate position to give such an indication as to the maximum sentence.

The application and the hearing

63.16 *When can an application be made?*

R v Goodyear 2005 EWCA Crim 888, 2006 1 Cr App R (S) 6 (p 23) para 73 LCJ We anticipate that any sentence indication would normally be sought at the plea and case management hearing. We do not rule out the entitlement of a defendant to seek an indication at a later stage, or even, in what we know would be a rare case, during the course of the trial itself.

63.17 *Reporting restrictions*

R v Goodyear 2005 EWCA Crim 888, 2006 1 Cr App R (S) 6 (p 23) para 77 LCJ The fact that the case may yet proceed as a trial, and that if it does so, no reference may be made to the request for a sentence indication, leads to the conclusion that reporting restrictions should normally be imposed, to be lifted if and when the defendant pleads or is found guilty.

63.18 *The hearing must be in open court*

Criminal Practice Directions 2015 EWCA Crim 1567 para VII C.8 A *Goodyear* indication should be given in open court in the presence of the defendant but any reference to the hearing is not admissible in any subsequent trial, and reporting restrictions should normally be imposed.

63.19 *Procedure*

Application for indication of sentence

Criminal Procedure Rules 2015 2015/1490 Rule 3.23(1) This rule applies where a defendant wants the Crown Court to give an indication of the maximum sentence that would be passed if a guilty plea were entered when the indication is sought.

(2) Such a defendant must:
- (a) apply in writing as soon as practicable; and
- (b) serve the application on:
  - (i) the court officer, and
  - (ii) the prosecutor.

(3) The application must:
- (a) specify:
  - (i) the offence or offences to which it would be a guilty plea, and
  - (ii) the facts on the basis of which that plea would be entered; and
- (b) include the prosecutor's agreement to, or representations on, that proposed basis of plea.

(4) The prosecutor must:
- (a) provide information relevant to sentence, including:
  - (i) any previous conviction of the defendant, and the circumstances where relevant,
  - (ii) any statement of the effect of the offence on the victim, the victim's family or others; and
- (b) identify any other matter relevant to sentence, including:
  - (i) the legislation applicable,
  - (ii) any sentencing guidelines, or guideline cases, and
  - (iii) aggravating and mitigating factors.

(5) The hearing of the application:
- (a) may take place in the absence of any other defendant;
- (b) must be attended by:
  - (i) the applicant defendant's legal representatives (if any), and
  - (ii) the prosecution advocate.

Criminal Practice Directions 2015 EWCA Crim 1567 para VII C.1 The defence should notify the court and the prosecution of the intention to seek an indication in advance of any hearing.
C.3 The judge should not become involved in negotiations about the acceptance of pleas or any agreed basis of plea, nor should a request be made for an indication of the different sentences that might be imposed if various different pleas were to be offered.
C.4 There should be no prosecution opening nor should the judge hear mitigation. However, during the sentence indication process the prosecution advocate is expected to assist the court by ensuring that the court has received all of the prosecution evidence, any statement from the victim about the impact of the offence, and any relevant previous convictions. Further, where appropriate, the prosecution should provide references to the relevant statutory powers of the court, relevant sentencing guidelines and authorities, and such other assistance as the court requires.
C.5 Attention is drawn to paragraph 70(d) of *Goodyear* which emphasises that the prosecution 'should not say anything which may create the impression that the sentence indication has the support or approval of the Crown'. This prohibition against the Crown indicating its approval of a particular sentence applies in all circumstances when a defendant is being sentenced, including when joint sentencing submissions are made.
R v Goodyear 2005 EWCA Crim 888, 2006 1 Cr App R (S) 6 (p 23) para 75 LCJ The hearing should normally take place in open court, with a full recording of the entire proceedings, and both sides represented, in the defendant's presence.

63.20 *Unrepresented defendants*

R v Goodyear 2005 EWCA Crim 888, 2006 1 Cr App R (S) 6 (p 23) para 68 LCJ In the unusual event that the defendant is unrepresented, he would be entitled to seek a sentence indication of his own initiative. There would be difficulties in either the judge or prosecuting counsel taking any initiative, and informing an unrepresented defendant of this right. That might too readily be interpreted as or subsequently argued to have been improper pressure.

63.21 *Judge may remind the defence of the ability to ask for an indication*

Criminal Practice Directions 2015 EWCA Crim 1567 para VII C.2…The judge should only give a *Goodyear* indication if one is requested by the defendant, although the judge can, in an appropriate case, remind the defence advocate of the defendant's entitlement to seek an advance indication of sentence.
R v Goodyear 2005 EWCA Crim 888, 2006 1 Cr App R (S) 6 (p 23) para 56 LCJ The judge is entitled in an appropriate case to remind the defence advocate that the defendant is entitled to seek an advance indication of sentence.

63.22 *Indication must be sought by the defendant*

Criminal Practice Directions 2015 EWCA Crim 1567 para VII C.2…Any advance indication given should be the maximum sentence if a guilty plea were to be tendered at that stage of the proceedings only. The judge should not indicate the maximum possible sentence following conviction by a jury after trial.
R v Goodyear 2005 EWCA Crim 888, 2006 1 Cr App R (S) 6 (p 23) para 55 LCJ The judge should not give an advance indication of sentence unless one has been sought by the defendant. Subject to the judge's power to give an appropriate reminder to the advocate for the defendant the process of seeking a sentence indication should normally be started by the defendant.

63.23 *Complex cases*

R v Goodyear 2005 EWCA Crim 888, 2006 1 Cr App R (S) 6 (p 23) paras 74 and 76 LCJ The judge is most unlikely to be able to give an indication, even if it is sought, in complicated or difficult cases, unless issues between the prosecution and the defence have been addressed and resolved. Therefore in such cases, no less than seven days' notice in writing of an intention to seek an indication should normally be given to the prosecution, and the court. If an application is made without notice when it should have been given, the judge may conclude that any inevitable adjournment should have been avoided and that the discount for the guilty plea should be reduced accordingly. The fact that notice has been given, and any reference to a request for a sentence indication, or the circumstances in which it was sought, would be inadmissible in any subsequent trial.

63.24 ***The judicial discretion whether to give an indication***

R v Goodyear 2005 EWCA Crim 888, 2006 1 Cr App R (S) 6 (p 23) para 57 LCJ Where an advance indication of sentence is sought, the judge retains an unfettered discretion to refuse to give one. It may indeed be inappropriate for him to give any indication at all. For example, he may consider that for a variety of reasons the defendant is already under pressure (perhaps from a co-accused), or vulnerable, and that to give the requested indication, even in answer to a request, may create additional pressure. Similarly, he may be troubled that the particular defendant may not fully have appreciated that he should not plead guilty unless in fact he is guilty. Again, the judge may believe that if he were to give a sentence indication at the stage when it is sought, he would not properly be able to judge the true culpability of the defendant, or the differing levels of responsibility between defendants. In a case involving a number of defendants, he may be concerned that an indication given to one defendant who seeks it may itself create pressure on another defendant. Yet again, the judge may consider that the application is no less than a 'try on' by a defendant who intends or would be likely to plead guilty in any event, seeking to take a tactical advantage of the changed process envisaged in this judgment. If so, he would probably refuse to say anything at all, and indeed, a guilty plea tendered after such tactical manoeuvrings may strike the judge as a plea tendered later than the first reasonable opportunity for doing so, with a consequent reduction in the discount for the guilty plea.

See also: *R v Kulah* 2007 EWCA Crim 1701, 2008 1 Cr App R (S) 85 (p 494) (Principle restated.)

63.25 ***The content of a Goodyear indication***

R v Goodyear 2005 EWCA Crim 888, 2006 1 Cr App R (S) 6 (p 23) para 54 LCJ Any advance indication of sentence to be given by the judge should normally be confined to the maximum sentence if a plea of guilty were tendered at the stage at which the indication is sought. For the judge to indicate his view of the maximum possible level of sentence following conviction by the jury, as well as its level after a plea of guilty, would have disadvantages.

See also: *R v Omatseye* 2014 EWCA Crim 2973 (Judge indicated an 8-month Suspended Sentence Order. D given that with an unpaid work requirement. D had a legitimate expectation. Requirement quashed. In future it would be better to say [that such terms] are a possibility.)

63.26 ***Plea discount***

R v Hackney 2013 EWCA Crim 1156, 2014 1 Cr App R (S) 41 (p 235) The Judge was wrong to take into account the *Goodyear* indication when considering the plea discount.

Goodyear indications and extended sentences

63.27 ***Extended sentences Basic principles***

Criminal Practice Directions 2015 EWCA Crim 1567 para VII C.7 If the offence is a specified offence such that the defendant might be liable to an assessment of 'dangerousness' in accordance with Criminal Justice Act 2003 it is unlikely that the necessary material for such an assessment will be available. The court can still proceed to give an indication of sentence, but should state clearly the limitations of the indication that can be given.

Note: The cases below are listed for completeness only. The ordering of an IPP sentence is different from the ordering of an extended sentence. Ed.

R v Kulah 2007 EWCA Crim 1701, 2008 1 Cr App R (S) 85 (p 494) It is not necessarily inappropriate to seek or to give a *Goodyear* indication merely because a defendant is charged with a specified offence. However, there may be dangers in undertaking this course and it is necessary to warn of them. If an indication is improperly given, a sentencing judge may find himself bound by the 'dangerous offender' provisions to impose a sentence which is qualitatively different from the indication he has given. In the alternative, he may consider himself bound by his prior indication to impose a sentence which does not accord with mandatory statutory provisions. It is axiomatic that a *Goodyear* indication will be sought before plea. At that time, it will often be the case that the sentencing judge will not be in possession of the information necessary to enable him or her to make the assessment of risk required. The great majority of cases will not, however, be clear-cut. Pre-sentence and other appropriate reports will not be available. In such cases, it remains a matter for the judge to decide whether it is appropriate to give an indication.

R v Seddon 2007 EWCA Crim 3022, 2008 2 Cr App R (S) 30 (p 174) D was charged with wounding with intent. The basis of plea was accepted. The Judge did not have a pre-sentence report, nor did he have a psychiatric report. The Judge was asked to give a *Goodyear* indication and said that he would be surprised if it turned out to be a case in which the dangerousness provisions of Criminal Justice Act 2003 were to bite, but he made it quite clear that he could not say what the position would be until he had seen all the material on the defendant. The Judge also said a determinate sentence would be up to 5 years, possibly as much as 6 or 7, but on this plea it would certainly be below 4. D pleaded guilty. On sentencing, the Judge had the full pre-sentence report and also the psychiatric report. The Judge gave notice to new counsel for the defence that whatever he had or had not said on the previous occasion, the present material caused him to arrive at the provisional conclusion that this was a man who was within the dangerousness provisions. Prosecution counsel agreed that the Judge had previously said it would be a determinate sentence of 4 years or less, but that the Judge would have to see a pre-sentence report. The Judge concluded that there was a significant risk from the defendant and the statute made a sentence of IPP obligatory. IPP was passed. Held. When giving an indication of sentence, the Judge was not attempting any determination of the question of dangerousness at that point and counsel made it absolutely clear that she understood that that was the position. On sentencing, we would not expect the Judge to remember precisely the words he had uttered on the previous occasion and he was put in a difficult position without a transcript. The Judge had not given an unqualified indication. He had expressly and wisely qualified what he had said and was clearly and precisely understood in the reservations he had expressed. If the dangerousness condition is met, then IPP is mandatory. Judges should be cautious about giving a *Goodyear* direction where the question of whether the defendant meets the dangerousness test or not has yet to be determined. If a judge has made a determination of whether the defendant is dangerous or not based on sufficient material, then no doubt the sentencing judge will regard that question as having been resolved once and for all on the previous occasion. If the evidence indicates that the dangerousness condition is met, the mandatory sentence of IPP or an extended sentence must be passed notwithstanding any previous indication. The indication, in short, cannot relieve the judge of the statutory obligation to pass an indefinite or extended sentence if the statutory conditions for doing so are met.

R v Newman 2010 EWCA Crim 1566, 2011 1 Cr App R (S) 68 (p 419) Particular caution is warranted where a *Goodyear* indication is sought in the case of a specified offence which might attract an extended sentence or a sentence of Imprisonment for Public Protection. In such cases, although a judge retains a discretion to give such an indication, there are obvious dangers involved. There is scope, additionally, for a judge to give what might be termed a qualified *Goodyear* indication, depending on the ultimate conclusion as to dangerousness, and applicable only if a determinate sentence was ultimately imposed.

Note: The Sentencing Guidelines Council issued a *Guide to Dangerous Offenders*. It is not a definitive guideline. At page 13 of that guideline, there is a section about giving an indication when the dangerousness provision will/may apply. Ed.

63.28 ***Extended sentences Too little information Better to defer indication***
R v Kulah 2007 EWCA Crim 1701, 2008 1 Cr App R (S) 85 (p 494) We doubt that it was open for the Judge to make an assessment of the dangerousness of the defendant on the basis of the material then before him. We do not consider that this case falls into the category of very clear cases. If the judge thinks it desirable to give an indication of sentence, the more appropriate course would be to give that indication subject to the important qualifications we have set out and to defer the assessment of dangerousness until the court is in possession of the material it needs to enable it to make that decision.
Note: This decision will not help judges who want to encourage a plea but face a trial about to start or need the sort of material which is usually only available after conviction. There would seem no objection to the judge indicating what a determinate sentence or a notional minimum term would be. However, the suggestion that the judge was considering an extended sentence is likely to encourage defendants to take their chances and have a trial. Ed.

63.29 ***Extended sentences Indeterminate sentence not indicated so sentence quashed***
R v McDonald 2007 EWCA Crim 1117, 2008 1 Cr App R (S) 20 (p 91) D pleaded to burglary and making a threat to kill following a *Goodyear* indication of 5 years in custody. Prosecuting counsel confirmed to the sentencing Judge that it was an IPP case. Defence counsel did not say anything to the Judge nor did he remind him of the indication that the Judge had given. D was sentenced to 4½ years' IPP. Held. Had the Judge been reminded of the indication he would not have imposed a sentence of IPP and would quite rightly have felt himself bound by the indication that he had previously given. It would be unjust for the sentence of IPP to remain. 4½ years not 4½ years' IPP.

63.30 ***Extended sentences Potentially dangerous offenders Terms of indication***
R v Kulah 2007 EWCA Crim 1701, 2008 1 Cr App R (S) 85 (p 494) If the judge decides to give an indication where an assessment of future risk remains to be made, he should make the following matters clear:

(a) The offence (or one of them) is a specified offence listed in Criminal Justice Act 2003 Sch 15, bringing into operation the 'dangerous offender' provisions contained in Part 12, Chapter 5 of that Act.

(b) The information and materials necessary to undertake the assessment of future risk which is required by those provisions are not available and that assessment remains to be conducted.

(c) If the defendant is later assessed as 'dangerous', the sentences mandated by the provisions, an indeterminate or extended sentence, will be imposed.

(d) If the defendant is not later assessed as 'dangerous', the indication relates in the ordinary way to the maximum determinate sentence which will be imposed.

(e) If the offender is later assessed as 'dangerous', the indication can only relate to the notional determinate term which will be used in the calculation of the minimum specified period the offender would have to serve before he may apply to the Parole Board to direct his release, or, in a case where an extended sentence is the only lawful option, it will relate to the appropriate custodial term within the extended sentence (that is, the indication does not encompass the length of any extension period during which the offender will be on licence following his release).

(f) If an indeterminate sentence is mandated by the provisions, the actual amount of time the offender will spend in custody is not within the control of the sentencing judge, only its minimum.

Nevertheless, it seems to us that judges may, understandably, feel a reluctance to give a *Goodyear* indication in circumstances where they do not yet know how dangerous the defendant really is.

Events after an application for a *Goodyear* indication

63.31 ***Judge is bound by indication Later judges bound by indication***
Criminal Practice Directions 2015 EWCA Crim 1567 para VII C.6 An indication, once given, is, save in exceptional circumstances (such as arose in *R v Newman* 2010 EWCA Crim 1566, 2011 1 Cr App R (S) 68 (419)), binding on the judge who gave it, and any other judge, subject to overriding statutory obligations such as those following a finding of 'dangerousness'. In circumstances where a judge proposes to depart from a *Goodyear* indication this must only be done in a way that does not give rise to unfairness (see *R v Newman* 2010).

R v Goodyear 2005 EWCA Crim 888, 2006 1 Cr App R (S) 6 (p 23) para 61 LCJ Once an indication has been given, it is binding and remains binding on the judge who has given it, and it also binds any other judge who becomes responsible for the case. We recognise that a new judge has his own sentencing responsibilities, but judicial comity as well as the expectation aroused in a defendant that he will not receive a sentence in excess of whatever the first judge indicated, requires that a later sentencing judge should not exceed the earlier indication.

R v Transco Plc 2006 EWCA Crim 838, 2 Cr App R (S) 111 (p 740) LCJ The defendant company pleaded to an offence under Health and Safety legislation in which a man died in an explosion. The company asked for a *Goodyear* indication and was told that the Judge was not thinking of a fine as high as one with six noughts. The company was fined £1m. Held. The Judge gave no reason for his change. We can only assume his indication had slipped his memory. The Judge should have imposed a fine significantly below £1m. In any event the correct fine was £250,000.

R v McDonald 2007 EWCA Crim 1117, 2008 1 Cr App R (S) 20 (p 91) D pleaded to burglary and making a threat to kill following a *Goodyear* indication of 5 years in custody. Prosecuting counsel confirmed to the sentencing Judge that it was an IPP case. Defence counsel did not say anything to the Judge nor remind him of the indication that the Judge had given. D was sentenced to 4½ years' IPP. Held. Had the Judge been reminded of the indication he would not have imposed a sentence of IPP and would quite rightly have felt himself bound by the indication that he had previously given. It would be unjust for the sentence of IPP to remain. 4½ years not 4½ years' IPP.

R v Kulah 2007 EWCA Crim 1701, 2008 1 Cr App R (S) 85 (p 494) We accept that it will not always be possible for a judge who has given a *Goodyear* indication to impose the sentence. We suggest that it would be desirable that whenever possible the judge who has given a *Goodyear* indication should himself sentence the defendant. If it is unavoidable, the sentencing judge should be provided with a transcript of the *Goodyear* indication. There is scope for misunderstanding if a *Goodyear* indication is merely relayed to the sentencing judge by counsel.

R v Newman 2010 EWCA Crim 1566, 2011 1 Cr App R (S) 68 (p 419) D pleaded to section 18 wounding. The Judge indicated a 3-year sentence after a *Goodyear* indication and D pleaded guilty. At the sentencing hearing about 6 weeks later, the Judge said he had been wrong to give the indication. He said the indication was incorrect for two reasons. First, it was a case which conceivably merited an indeterminate sentence and second, he had not seen the pre-sentence report. Now he had read the report he considered 3 years wholly inadequate. He offered to let D change his plea. The defence said D did not wish to. The Judge passed a 6-year extended sentence (4 years' detention and 2 years' extended licence). The defence did not suggest that the sentence was excessive but said that the Judge was not able to pass a sentence in excess of the indication. Held. The attractions of *Goodyear* and its practical importance are manifest. *Goodyear* indications will only serve their purpose if indications once given can be relied upon. Accordingly, and at least save exceptionally, indications thus given are binding in as far as they go, hence the need for circumspection before they are given.[849] It goes without saying that revisions to *Goodyear* indications should be very much the exception, and, as it seems to us, they can only be made in a manner which is fair to the defendant: in other words, where the matter can be revised without the defendant sustaining any prejudice other than mere disappointment. Had the Judge left the matter as set out in the *Goodyear* indication, first there would have been the unfortunate consequence of an inadequate sentence being passed contrary to the public interest and, second, there would have been the risk of an Attorney-General's reference to the benefit of no one. The offer to the defendant to change his plea was entirely fair. We are not persuaded any injustice resulted.

Note: Many judges and practitioners may consider that it is not unusual for a defendant to receive a lenient sentence. There are of course some principles that have to be applied even if it means a defendant receives a low sentence. The principle that a defendant can only be sentenced for the offences he or she pleaded to or was convicted of is one. That principle is not open to exceptions, however wrong the sentence appears to be on the facts. Therefore it could be argued that the public interest for defendants to know: a) that the word of the judge can always be relied upon, and b) that the integrity of the *Goodyear* system should be maintained, would outweigh the desirability of increasing the sentence. Further, "My word is my bond" followed by, "Please ignore my word. My undertaking is worthless" is not very judicial. In future, practitioners may consider asking the judge before he or she gives a *Goodyear* indication to indicate that if he or she had second thoughts, the undertaking would remain. It does not appear that *R (Secretary of State for Work and Pensions) v Croydon Crown Court* 2010 EWHC 805 (Admin), 2011 1 Cr App R (S) 1 (p 1) (see **21.37**) was cited to the Court as it had only just been decided. Ed.

R v Martin 2013 EWCA Crim 2565, 2014 2 Cr App R (S) 21 (p 144) D pleaded to theft and possession of MDMA. D's basis of plea stated that he sold drugs to friends at cost and made no profit. That was rejected by the prosecution. A second basis of plea was entered, stating that he supplied drugs to others making no gain save for benefiting from bulk purchasing for his friends and himself. The question of a *Newton* hearing arose and the Judge told D that if he found that there was no financial gain, the sentence would be 21 months, but if he found that D was making money, the sentence would start at 40 months and, after credit for the plea (not entered at the first opportunity), be reduced to 30 months. A *Newton* hearing was held and the Judge rejected D's evidence. The Judge then realised that he had fallen into error in that he had indicated credit for the guilty plea would remain at 25% in the event that D was disbelieved in the *Newton*. The Judge said that as he had rejected D's evidence, D had therefore wrongly had a *Newton* and that he would lose half of the 25% credit as a consequence. The Judge honoured the starting point of 40 months but gave a 12.5% discount, namely 5 months, resulting in a 35-month sentence. Held. The sentencing process was flawed from the outset. The indication given by the Judge would be honoured. 30 months not 35.

Note: This was not a *Goodyear* indication but an informal indication. The principles apply to both. Ed.

Att-Gen's Ref 2017 Re Parish and Redford 2017 EWCA Crim 2064 P and R pleaded not guilty to various firearm counts. They denied possession of the firearms. On the day of trial a new count of conspiracy to transfer prohibited firearms was added. Defence counsel asked for a full discount if there was a plea and without any input from prosecution counsel, the Judge agreed. Counsel discussions continued and later the two pleaded. A full discount was given. In a sentencing note P's counsel asked for a full discount. The prosecution note said nothing about the plea discount. Held. The procedure was highly unsatisfactory. A full discount was not appropriate. The Judge has

[849] This sentence is written *verbatim*.

a discretion but the plea discount cannot here be 'greater than 20% or at the very most 25%'. However, the plea was after the indication was given which provided some incentive to plead. The new count did not suggest an intent to endanger life. With some reluctance we consider that to deprive P and R of the full discount would be unjust.
For more detail, see **262.20** in Volume 2.
See also: *R v Williams-Bell* 2015 EWCA Crim 1284 (Judge said before trial there would be a shortish non-immediate suspended sentence. Later the Judge was told about another matter. Judge said that aggravates it and passed two consecutive immediate prison sentences (10 and 11 months). The sentence was entirely appropriate but the Judge fell into error, so sentences concurrent.)

63.32 ***Defendant absconds***
Example: *R v Davies* 2015 EWCA 930, 2 Cr App R (S) 57 (p 404) (D given a *Goodyear* indication. D pleads. Case put back for 15 minutes. D absconds. A departure from the *Goodyear* indication can only be done when it does not give rise to unfairness. The indication was binding.)

63.33 ***No plea entered The indication has no effect***
R v Goodyear 2005 EWCA Crim 888, 2006 1 Cr App R (S) 6 (p 23) para 61 LCJ If, after a reasonable opportunity to consider his position in the light of the indication, the defendant does not plead guilty, the indication will cease to have effect.
R v Patel 2009 EWCA Crim 67, 2 Cr App R (S) 67 (p 475) D sought a *Goodyear* indication and was told that the sentence would be 7 years after a trial and 6 years 3 months on a plea. D did not plead and was convicted. After conviction the Judge said that he thought his *Goodyear* indication was slightly generous but not necessarily so. The Judge gave D an 8-year sentence. It was submitted that there was no basis for the Judge to depart from his *Goodyear* indication. Held. We are prepared to accept the evidence did not get any worse. The worsening of the evidence was not the only circumstance in which a Judge might conclude that the right sentence was not the one he had in mind for the *Goodyear* indication. If D did not plead, the indication lapsed and was irrelevant. We do not accept the post-conviction remark was an indication of the sentence, but given that opinion after the trial, we think his second thoughts were better than his third. Sentence reduced to 7 years.

63.34 ***Further indications***
R v Goodyear 2005 EWCA Crim 888, 2006 1 Cr App R (S) 6 (p 23) para 60 LCJ If at any stage the judge refuses to give an indication (as opposed to deferring it), it remains open to the defendant to seek a further indication at a later stage. However, once the judge has refused to give an indication, he should not normally initiate the process, except, where it arises, to indicate that the circumstances had changed sufficiently for him to be prepared to consider a renewed application for an indication.
R v Kulah 2007 EWCA Crim 1701, 2008 1 Cr App R (S) 85 (p 494) para 33 The defence asked for a *Goodyear* indication and the Judge declined to give one. When the case was listed before another Judge, the defence re-applied. Held. It is a matter of great concern that an application was made to the second Judge without that Judge being told of the earlier application, its outcome or the reasons for the refusal to give an indication. If it is the case that a practice of forum shopping is developing, it is to be deprecated.

63.35 ***Defendant's right of appeal***
R v Goodyear 2005 EWCA Crim 888, 2006 1 Cr App R (S) 6 (p 23) para 72. The defendant's entitlement to apply for leave to appeal against sentence if, for example, insufficient allowance has been made for matters of genuine mitigation, is unaffected.

64 GUIDELINES

64.1 ***Outline***
There are three types of guideline:

(a) Guidelines from the Sentencing Council. The guidelines need to be constructed according to Coroners and Justice Act 2009 s 120-121. The Act requires the court to follow/have regard to the relevant sentencing guidelines, see **64.5** and **64.14**.
(b) Guidelines from the Sentencing Guidelines Council. The proper approach to them is described at **64.14**.
(c) Guidelines issued by the Court of Appeal. Year by year the number of guideline cases has reduced. Firearms is the only major one left. As the name implies, these are only a guide. However, the guideline remarks continue to be important. For more details see **64.20**.

Consultation On 28 February 2019, the Sentencing Council issued a consultation paper which invited comments about increasing the amount of information in its online versions. The consultation closes on 23 May 2019.

64.2 *What duty applies?*

	Offence committed	
Which guideline applies?	**Before 6 April 2010**	**On or after 6 April 2010**
Sentencing Guidelines Council guideline applies	Duty to have regard	Duty to have regard, see **64.14**
Sentencing Council guideline applies	Duty to have regard[850]	Duty to follow

Note: Since 2010, I have not noticed the courts making any distinction between guidelines where there is a 'duty to follow' and guidelines where there is 'a duty to have regard'. Judges sensibly concentrate on working out the correct sentence. Ed.
For the duty to have regard, see **64.14** and for the duty to follow, see **64.5**.

64.3 *Applying the guidelines*

Magistrates' Court Sentencing Guidelines 2008, see www.banksr.com Other Matters Guidelines tab

Note: Although this appears in the *Magistrates' Court Sentencing Guidelines 2008*, it is of general application because these terms cannot have different meanings in different courts. Ed.

page 145 **Meaning of 'range', 'starting point' and 'first-time offender'**

These guidelines are for a first-time offender convicted after a trial. They provide a starting point based on an assessment of the seriousness of the offence and a range within which the sentence will normally fall in most cases.

They are explained in a format that follows the structured approach to the sentencing decision which identifies first those aspects that affect the assessment of the seriousness of the offence, then those aspects that form part of personal mitigation and, finally, any reduction for a guilty plea.

In practice, the boundaries between these stages will not always be as clear cut but the underlying principles will remain the same.

Assessing the seriousness of the offence

1 a) These guidelines apply to an offence that can be committed in a variety of circumstances with different levels of seriousness.

[850] This is because of Coroners and Justice Act 2009 (Commencement No 4, Transitional and Saving Provisions) Order 2010 2010/816 art 7(2), as amended by Coroners and Justice Act 2009 (Commencement No 4, Transitional and Saving Provisions) (Amendment) (Order) 2011 2011/72 art 2(2), which negates the repeal of Criminal Justice Act 2003 s 172 (duty to have regard to the guidelines).

They apply to a first-time offender who has been convicted after a trial.[851] A first-time offender is a person who does not have a conviction which by virtue of Criminal Justice Act 2003 s 14(2) must be treated as an aggravating factor.
c) The expected approach is for a court to identify the description that most nearly matches the particular facts of the offence for which sentence is being imposed. This will identify a starting point from which the sentencer can depart to reflect aggravating or mitigating factors affecting the seriousness of the offence (beyond those contained in the description itself) to reach a provisional sentence.
d) The range is the bracket into which the provisional sentence will normally fall after having regard to factors which aggravate or mitigate the seriousness of the offence. The particular circumstances may, however, make it appropriate that the provisional sentence falls outside the range.
2 Where the offender has previous convictions which aggravate the seriousness of the current offence, that may take the provisional sentence beyond the range given particularly where there are significant other aggravating factors present.
Offender mitigation
3 Once the provisional sentence has been identified (by reference to the factors affecting the seriousness of the offence), the court will take into account any relevant factors of offender mitigation. Again, this may take the provisional sentence outside the range.
R v Healey and Others 2012 EWCA Crim 1005, 2013 1 Cr App R (S) 33 (p 176) A reader might think the categories which are in the guideline boxes are mutually exclusive. They are not. There is an inevitable overlap between the scenarios which are described in adjacent boxes. We wholeheartedly endorse the approach of one counsel who said one defendant fell somewhere between the two boxes.

64.4 *Judicial approach*

Note: Many Crown Court judges see their role as passing the correct sentence to reflect all the factors rather than treating the Sentencing Council guidelines as a master plan to determine the sentence. They 'stand back' at the end of the sentencing exercise and consider whether a particular sentence was appropriate. After they have arrived at the correct sentence they weave the relevant guideline into their sentencing remarks. There are exceptions. The *Drug Offences Guideline 2012* is treated like a flow chart. Some judges give too much importance to the starting points and insufficient weight to the aggravating and mitigating factors. Ed.
R v Millberry 2002 EWCA Crim 2891, 2003 2 Cr App R (S) 31 (p 142) para 34 LCJ We would emphasise that guidelines can produce sentences which are inappropriately high or inappropriately low if sentencers merely adopt a mechanistic approach to the guidelines. It is essential that having taken the guidelines into account, sentencers stand back and look at the circumstances as a whole and impose the sentence which is appropriate having regard to all the circumstances. Double accounting can be the result of guidelines if they are applied indiscriminately and must be avoided. Guideline judgments are intended to assist the judge to arrive at the correct[852] sentence. They do not purport to identify the correct sentence. Doing so is the task of the trial judge.
R v Last 2005 EWCA Crim 106, 2 Cr App R (S) 64 (p 381) para 15 LCJ The Court considered the guilty plea sentencing guideline in a murder case. Held. The guideline is no more than a guideline. It does not affect the court's powers of sentencing set out in the legislation. It merely indicates how those powers can be exercised. They are to assist the judge. The fact that 'every court must have regard to the relevant guideline' does not mean that it has to be followed. Neither the guidelines for murder in Criminal Justice

[851] Coroners and Justice Act 2009 (Commencement No 4, Transitional and Saving Provisions) Order 2010 2010/816 art 2 and Sch 1 para 22(b)(iv)
[852] The judgment says 'current', which presumably is a typo.

Act 2003 Sch 21 nor the guilty plea guideline removes the judge's discretion. The court is only to have regard to the guidelines. The court may, where appropriate, depart from them but the court must state the reasons for not following a guideline.[853]

R v Martin 2006 EWCA Crim 1035, 2007 1 Cr App R (S) 3 (p 14) The sentencing decision does not represent a mathematical exercise, nor does it result from an arithmetical calculation.

Att-Gen's Ref No 126 of 2006 2007 EWCA Crim 53, 2 Cr App R (S) 59 (p 362) D, aged 14, murdered a fellow schoolboy. The sentencing starting points were from Criminal Justice Act 2003 Sch 21. Held. It is clear that the appropriate sentence remains fact-specific. It is trite law that irrespective of the 'starting point', the end result may be a minimum term of 'any length', well below or well above the defined starting point. The court must take account of every aggravating and mitigating feature. These lists are not exhaustive. The same holds good [for the] definitive guidelines issued by the Sentencing Guidelines Council/Sentencing Council, or guideline decisions of this Court.

Att-Gen's Ref Nos 7-9 of 2009 2009 EWCA Crim 1490 LCJ A judge has to do justice. Regard must be had to the guideline but a judge is entitled to disregard it, if by following it an injustice would result.

R v Charles and Others 2011 EWCA Crim 2153, 2012 1 Cr App R (S) 74 (p 414) The difficulty with the guidelines is that they are designed to ensure consistency in sentencing and reflect the public perception and Parliament's perception of the gravity of the offences. But that objective is inept where the facts are wholly different from those envisaged in the guideline.

Att-Gen's Ref No 74 of 2011 2011 EWCA Crim 2855 Because of the way in which the guideline categories have had to be drafted, there is sometimes a temptation to rely too strictly on the precise physical nature of the act and to pay insufficient attention to all the circumstances.

R v Healey and Others 2012 EWCA Crim 1005, 2013 1 Cr App R (S) 33 (p 176) The Judge considered that the guideline was woefully inadequate. Held. Very few judges are fortunate enough to go through life without encountering rare occasions when they would prefer the law to be otherwise to that which it is. The judge's duty is nevertheless to apply it, at first instance or in this Court, just as it is the duty of the citizen to obey the law. There is deliberately built into the Sentencing Council's guidelines a good deal of flexibility which is appreciable. It does not, however, extend to deliberately disregarding the guidelines, not on the grounds that the case has particular facts which warrant distinguishing it from the general level, but because the judge happens to take a different view about where the general level ought to be. The latter approach is demonstrably unlawful. Here it was not open to the Judge to use an earlier authority rather than just applying the Sentencing Council guideline.

R v Marcantonio 2012 EWCA Crim 1279 There will be cases where the record of the offender, combined with his inability or unwillingness to rehabilitate himself and respond to non-custodial options, are factors which will entitle a sentencing judge not just to depart from the relevant sentencing guidelines, but to depart radically from those guidelines so that there can be no doubt that the protection of the public is being considered first and foremost. Burglary worth 18 months but with his record etc. we start at 7½ years.

R v Brooke 2012 EWCA Crim 1642 The Definitive Guideline does not remove from a sentencing judge the discretion to do justice. D was a recidivist burglar. D's appeal over a 12-year starting point for one burglary failed.

[853] Criminal Justice Act 2003 s 174(6)(b), see para **64.18**, inserted by Legal Aid, Sentencing and Punishment of Offenders Act 2012 s 64. In force 3/12/12

R v Myers 2013 EWCA Crim 622 A 16-year-old received a 12-month DTO for a nasty unprovoked attack (ABH). The defence argued that the starting point for an adult was 18 months. Held. Every case [after] having regard to the guidelines has to be dealt with on its own facts. Appeal dismissed. For more detail see **201.8** in Volume 2.
R v Venclovas and Another 2015 EWCA Crim 138 D1 and D2 pleaded on rearraignment to ABH and threatening with an offensive weapon. The Judge sentenced them outside the guideline. Held. The guideline does allow a judge to move outside the sentencing range but the Judge did not explain in his sentencing remarks that he was considering a sentence outside the range…and indeed, if he was doing so, why he was taking that view. The possibility of the matter being dealt with outside the range was not mentioned during the hearing, and…counsel did not have an opportunity to address the Court on that matter. We reduce the sentence.
For more details see **201.17** in Volume 2.
R v Surgenor 2018 EWCA Crim 357, 2 Cr App R (S) 9 (p 71) D pleaded to aggravated burglary. The Judge placed the offence in Category 1 and started at 9 years. Held. On a strict mechanistic application of the relevant guideline this case is in Category 1. But the guideline also contains a non-exhaustive list of additional factual elements which enables a court to adjust upwards or downwards the starting point. A tariff is a tariff for the general and the sentencer is sentencing the particular individual for the particular offence, which requires a close assessment and analysis of the culpability and harm occasioned against the personal mitigation available. In this case there was considerable personal mitigation. Ultimately the sentencer, in making that analysis of culpability and harm against the personal mitigation, must ensure that a just and proportionate sentence is imposed. A strict mechanistic application of the guideline would result here in a sentence which would be contrary to the interests of justice. We start at 5 years, so with plea, 3 years 4 months' YOI, not 6 years.
For more detail, see **222.7** in Volume 2.
Note: A summary of the principles might be: a) look at all the relevant factors, b) move from the starting point up and down to arrive at a just provisional sentence, then c) apply the plea discount. Ed.

Duty to follow the guideline

64.5 ***Duty to follow the guidelines Statutory provisions and cases***
Sentencing guidelines: duty of court
Coroners and Justice Act 2009 s 125(1) Every court:
(a) must, in sentencing an offender, follow any sentencing guidelines which are relevant to the offender's case, and
(b) must, in exercising any other function relating to the sentencing of offenders, follow any sentencing guidelines which are relevant to the exercise of the function,
unless the court is satisfied that it would be contrary to the interests of justice to do so.
(2) Subsections (3) and (4) apply where:
(a) a court is deciding what sentence to impose on a person ('P') who is guilty of an offence, and
(b) sentencing guidelines have been issued in relation to that offence which are structured in the way described in section 121(2) to (5) ('the offence-specific guidelines').
(3) The duty imposed on a court by subsection (1)(a) to follow any sentencing guidelines which are relevant to the offender's case includes:
(a) in all cases, a duty to impose on P, in accordance with the offence-specific guidelines, a sentence which is within the offence range, and
(b) where the offence-specific guidelines describe categories of case in accordance with section 121(2), a duty to decide which of the categories most resembles P's case in order to identify the sentencing starting point in the offence range,

but nothing in this section imposes on the court a separate duty, in a case within paragraph (b), to impose a sentence which is within the category range.

R v Blackshaw and Others 2011 EWCA Crim 2312 LCJ The Court considered a consolidated set of appeals arising from the August 2011 public disorder. The Court considered the need to pass sentences outside the guidelines. Held. The court should approach the sentencing decision by reference to any relevant guidelines (which effectively apply the legislative requirement to consider culpability and harm even when not necessarily expressed in those terms). This provides the starting point and it produces the desirable consistency of approach to sentencing decisions up and down the country without sacrificing the obligation to do justice in the individual and specific case. The often quoted aphorism, that sentencing guidelines are guidelines not tramlines, continues to be fully reflected in the present legislative framework. The legislation does not constrain the proper exercise of individual judgement on the specific facts of the case and the provision in section 125(1)(a) that the court 'must follow…any sentencing guidelines' does not require slavish adherence to them. This follows not only from the fact that the latitude given by the legislation to sentence anywhere within the offence range (see section 125(3) and (4)) but, more generally, because of the specific provisions of section 125(1), which expressly removes any obligation to follow the guidelines where 'the court is satisfied that it would be contrary to the interests of justice to do so'. An inflexible approach would be inconsistent with the terms of the statutory framework-…even when the approach to the sentencing decision is laid down in an apparently detailed and on the face of it intentionally comprehensive scheme, the sentencing judge must achieve a just result. Nothing in the 2009 Act has diminished the jurisdiction of this court, where necessary, to promulgate judgments relating to the principles and approach to be taken to sentencing decisions. They bind sentencing courts. In this case none of the [relevant] guidelines contemplated these offences. Therefore sentences beyond the ranges in the guidelines were not only appropriate, but inevitable.

Note: Nothing in the legislation alters the maximum sentences as laid down by Parliament. Also the new provisions do not override the requirement that 'custodial sentences must be for the shortest term commensurate with the seriousness of the offence'.[854] It appears that courts must follow the approach set out in the guidelines. However, the resulting sentence must reflect the fact-specific circumstances of the offence, which involves the exercise of judicial discretion, which is fully preserved by the statute. Ed.

R v Dyer and Others 2013 EWCA Crim 2114, 2014 2 Cr App R (S) 11 (p 61) The Court considered sentences imposed for offences of class A drug supply to test purchasers in Soho. They considered the *Drug Offences Guideline 2012* (where there is a duty to follow the guideline). Held. para 13 A definitive guideline sets out the approach which the court must follow. Subsequent decisions of this court may help to interpret the guidance contained within the guideline and provide illustrations of the circumstances in which it operates and, of equal importance, when the interests of justice might justify departure from it. [A definitive] guideline is intended to encapsulate the approach to the vast majority, but [not][855] necessarily all, the cases that come before the court. The interests of justice permit departure from the guidelines in appropriate cases.

R v Whittaker 2018 EWCA Crim 701 D pleaded to possession of crack cocaine with intent to supply and class B and C supply counts. He was found with 0.8 grams of crack and small amounts of other drugs when visiting a friend of his in prison. The Judge declined to place the offence in Category 4, saying he did not want to be constrained by the guidelines. Held. The Judge may have misconstrued the guideline. We start in

[854] Coroners and Justice Act 2009 s 125(6)(c)

[855] I suspect that the transcript is missing the word 'not'.

Category 4. Section 125 does not impose a duty to impose a sentence within the category range. There is a considerable discretion given to the sentencing Judge. With plea and good character, 2 years 8 months not 4 years.
For more detail, see **338.36** in Volume 2.

64.6 ***Sentencing Guidelines Council's guidelines Status***
Coroners and Justice Act 2009 (Commencement No 4, Transitional and Saving Provisions) Order 2010 2010/816 art 7(1) Existing guidelines which have effect immediately before the coming into force of the 2009 Act (sentencing guidelines: duty of court) are to be treated as guidelines issued by the Sentencing Council for England and Wales.[856]

64.7 ***Duty to follow Not applicable to pre-April 2010 offences***
Coroners and Justice Act 2009 Sch 22 para 27(1) Nothing in Coroners and Justice Act 2009 s 125 or 126 has effect in relation to the sentencing of persons for offences committed before the commencement of the section in question.
(2) Where an offence is found to have been committed over a period of two or more days, or at some time during a period of two or more days, it must be taken for the purposes of sub-paragraph (1) to have been committed on the last of those days.
Coroners and Justice Act 2009 (Commencement No 4, Transitional and Saving Provisions) Order 2010 2010/816 art 7(2) The repeal of Criminal Justice Act 2003 s 172 (which is the duty of the court to have regard to sentencing guidelines) shall have no effect where a court is sentencing an offender for, or exercising any other function relating to the sentencing of offenders in respect of, an offence committed before 6 April 2010.

64.8 ***Duty to follow Exceptions No category resembles the case***
Coroners and Justice Act 2009 s 125(4) Subsection (3)(b) (see **64.5**) does not apply if the court is of the opinion that, for the purpose of identifying the sentence within the offence range which is the appropriate starting point, none of the categories sufficiently resembles P's case.

64.9 ***Duty to follow Pleas, informants and totality***
Coroners and Justice Act 2009 s 125(5) Subsection (3)(a) is subject to:
(a) Criminal Justice Act 2003 s 144 (reduction in sentences for guilty pleas), see **65.2**,
(b) Serious Organised Crime and Police Act 2005 s 73-74 (assistance by defendants: reduction or review of sentence) and any other rule of law by virtue of which an offender may receive a discounted sentence in consequence of assistance given (or offered to be given) by the offender to the prosecutor or investigator of an offence (see **71.7**), and
(c) any rule of law as to the totality of sentences (see **242.62** in Volume 2).

64.10 ***Duty to follow Other sentencing rules***
Coroners and Justice Act 2009 s 125(6) The duty imposed by subsection (1) (see **64.5**) is subject to the following provisions:
(a) Criminal Justice Act 2003 s 148(1)-(2) (restrictions on imposing community sentences) (see **15.9**),
(b) Criminal Justice Act 2003 s 152 (restrictions on imposing discretionary custodial sentences) (see **28.26**),
(c) Criminal Justice Act 2003 s 153 (custodial sentence must be for shortest term commensurate with seriousness of offence) (see **28.32**),
(d) Criminal Justice Act 2003 s 164(2) (fine must reflect seriousness of offence, see **58.16**), or
(da) Criminal Justice Act 2003 s 224A (life sentence for second listed offence for certain dangerous offenders) (see **75.2**).[857]

[856] This is what it says. I think it means that pre-2009 guidelines are to be treated the same as post-2009 guidelines.
[857] Section 125(6)(da) was inserted by Legal Aid, Sentencing and Punishment of Offenders Act 2012 Sch 19 para 23.

Coroners and Justice Act 2009 s 125(7) Nothing in this section or section 126 is to be taken as restricting any power (whether under Mental Health Act 1983 or otherwise) which enables a court to deal with a mentally disordered offender in the manner it considers to be most appropriate in all the circumstances.

64.11 ***Duty to follow Minimum sentences***

Coroners and Justice Act 2009 s 125(6) The duty imposed by subsection (1) (see **64.5**) is subject to the following provisions:

(ea) Prevention of Crime Act 1953 s 1(2B) and 1A(5) (minimum sentence for certain offences involving offensive weapons),[858]

(f) Firearms Act 1968 s 51A (minimum sentence for certain offences under section 5 etc.),

(fa) Criminal Justice Act 1988 s 139(6B), 139A(5B) and 139AA(7) (minimum sentence for certain offences involving article with blade or point or offensive weapon),[859]

(g) Powers of Criminal Courts (Sentencing) Act 2000 s 110(2) and 111(2) (minimum sentences for certain drug trafficking and burglary offences),

(h) Violent Crime Reduction Act 2006 s 29(4) and (6) (minimum sentences for certain offences involving firearms).

64.12 ***Duty to follow Life and extended sentences***

Coroners and Justice Act 2009 s 125(6) The duty imposed by subsection (1) (see **64.5**) is subject to the following provisions:..

(e) Criminal Justice Act 2003 s 269 and Sch 21 (determination of minimum term in relation to mandatory life sentence) . . .

Coroners and Justice Act 2009 s 126(1) Section 125(3) (except as applied by virtue of Criminal Justice Act 2009 s 126(3)) is subject to any power a court has to impose:

(a)-(b) [repealed],

(c) an extended sentence of imprisonment by virtue of Criminal Justice Act 2003 s 226A[860] (see **56.5**),

(d) an extended sentence of detention by virtue of Criminal Justice Act 2003 s 226B[861] (see **56.7**).

(2) Subsection (3) applies where a court determines the notional determinate term for the purpose of determining in any case:

(a) the order to be made under Powers of Criminal Courts (Sentencing) Act 2000 s 82A (life sentence: determination of tariffs) (see **74.4**),

(c) the appropriate custodial term for the purposes of Criminal Justice Act 2003 s 226A(6)[862] (extended sentence for certain violent, sexual or terrorism offences[863]: persons 18 or over) (see **56.5**), or

(d) the appropriate term for the purposes of Criminal Justice Act 2003 s 226B(4)[864] (extended sentence for certain violent, sexual or terrorism offences[865]: persons under 18) (see **56.7**).

[858] Section 125(6)(ea) was inserted by Legal Aid, Sentencing and Punishment of Offenders Act 2012 Sch 26 para 31(2) and amended by Criminal Justice and Courts Act 2015 Sch 5 para 17(1) and (2).

[859] Section 125(6)(fa) was inserted by Legal Aid, Sentencing and Punishment of Offenders Act 2012 Sch 26 para 31(3) and amended by Criminal Justice and Courts Act 2015 Sch 5 para 17(1) and (3).

[860] Legal Aid, Sentencing and Punishment of Offenders Act 2012 Sch 21 para 34(2)(b) substitutes '226A' for 227. In force 3/12/12

[861] Legal Aid, Sentencing and Punishment of Offenders Act 2012 Sch 21 para 34(2)(c) substitutes '226B' for 228. In force 3/12/12

[862] Legal Aid, Sentencing and Punishment of Offenders Act 2012 Sch 21 para 34(3)(b) substitutes '226A(6)' for 227(3). In force 3/12/12

[863] As amended by Counter-Terrorism and Border Security Act 2019 Sch 4 para 12(2)(a) In force 12 April 2019, Counter-Terrorism and Border Security Act 2019 s 27(3).

[864] Legal Aid, Sentencing and Punishment of Offenders Act 2012 Sch 21 para 34(3)(c) substitutes '226B(4)' for 228(3). In force 3/12/12

[865] As amended by Counter-Terrorism and Border Security Act 2019 Sch 4 para 12(2)(b) In force 12 April 2019, Counter-Terrorism and Border Security Act 2019 s 27(3).

(3) Coroners and Justice Act 2009 s 125(2)-(5) apply for the purposes of determining the notional determinate term in relation to an offence as they apply for the purposes of determining the sentence for an offence.[866]
(4) In this section references to the notional determinate term are to the determinate sentence that would have been passed in the case if the need to protect the public and the potential danger of the offender had not required the court to impose a life sentence (in circumstances where the sentence is not fixed by law) or, as the case may be, an extended sentence of imprisonment or detention.
(5) In subsection (4) 'life sentence' has the same meaning as in Crime (Sentences) Act 1997 Part 2, Chapter 2.[867]

64.13 ***Judicial approach Assaults***

R v Channer 2010 EWCA Crim 1753, 2011 1 Cr App R (S) 75 (p 464) D pleaded to section 20. Held. This Court has frequently stressed, sentencing guidelines are just that, guidelines, particularly in relation to assaults, where circumstances are infinitely variable and seriousness may be reflected in various criteria. It is wrong and may lead to error to attempt to force a specific case into a particular guideline box on the basis of the limited criteria by which cases may be categorised in the guidelines. Any sentence must take into account all relevant matters, and thereby reflect the justice of the particular case.
R v Dodds 2013 EWCA Crim 22, 2 Cr App R (S) 54 (p 358) *R v Channer* 2010 applied.

Duty to have regard to the guideline

64.14 ***Statutory provisions***

Duty of court to have regard to sentencing guidelines

Criminal Justice Act 2003 s 172(1) Every court must:

(a) in sentencing an offender, have regard to any guidelines which are relevant to the offender's case, and
(b) in exercising any other function relating to the sentencing of offenders, have regard to any guidelines which are relevant to the exercise of the function.

(2) In subsection (1) 'guidelines' means sentencing guidelines issued by the Council under section 170(9) as definitive guidelines, as revised by subsequent guidelines so issued.
Note: This section was repealed on 6 April 2010.[868] However, it continues to apply to offences committed before the November date, Coroners and Justice Act 2009 Sch 22 para 27 and the guidelines for the Sentencing Council, see **64.2**. Ed.
R v Forbes and Others 2016 EWCA Crim 1388 LCJ The Court considered eight historical sex case appeals and the guidelines. Held. para 9 The phrase 'have regard to' (which was intended to have the same meaning as 'by measured reference to') was intended to make it clear that the judge should not simply apply the relevant guideline applicable at the date of sentence, subject to any lower statutory maximum sentence applicable at the date the offence was committed, but use the guideline in a measured and reflective manner to arrive at the appropriate sentence. It is therefore important for the sentencing judge to guard against too mechanistic an approach, either in terms of an equivalent offence or in adopting the figures in the guideline without having regard to the fact that generally higher maxima are provided for some of the modern-day offences.

64.15 ***Court Martial***

Sentencing guidelines

Armed Forces Act 2006 s 259(1) A court must:

[866] This subsection is written *verbatim*.
[867] Legal Aid, Sentencing and Punishment of Offenders Act 2012 Sch 21 para 34(4) tries to amend this subsection but inserts text in the wrong subsection. Commencement would be ineffective as the text has to follow a 'has' when the subsection does not contain one.
[868] This includes offenders who are tried in their absence.

(a) in sentencing an offender for a service offence, have regard to any guidelines that are relevant to the offender's case, and
(b) in exercising any other function relating to the sentencing of offenders for service offences, have regard to any guidelines which are relevant to the exercise of the function.

(2) However, the court may depart from the guidelines mentioned in subsection (1)(a) or (b) if in its opinion the departure is justified by any features of service life or of the service disciplinary system that are relevant to the case.

(3) Subsection (2) does not limit any power existing apart from that subsection to depart from guidelines.

(4) References in subsection (1)(a) and (b) to sentencing an offender for a service offence include making any order when dealing with an offender in respect of such an offence.

(5) In this section 'guidelines' means sentencing guidelines issued by the Sentencing Council for England and Wales under Coroners and Justice Act 2009 s 120 as definitive guidelines, as revised by any subsequent guidelines so issued.

Note: Coroners and Justice Act 2009 s 125 does not apply to the Court Martial. Ed.

R v Heslop 2016 EWCA Crim 1951 Court Martial Appeal Court D was convicted of assault by penetration. Held. para 18 Sentencing is not just a matter of applying the guideline as there are the additional military principles to consider that include the maintenance of discipline and the reduction in service offending.

Note. *Guidance on Sentencing in the Court Martial 2018* para 2.15 sets out the position in a little more detail. Ed.

Other matters

64.16 *Draft guidelines Proper approach*

R (DPP) v Camberwell Youth Court 2004 EWHC 1805 (Admin) High Court The advice from the Sentencing Guidelines Panel has no legal force but it is helpful as an indication of a considered response to the sentencing problem posed in cases such as this.

R v Doidge 2005 EWCA Crim 273 It will not, in general, be appropriate for advice of the Sentencing Advisory Panel to be cited to this Court. Advice from the Sentencing Advisory Panel may well be useful for sentencers and advocates as background material, but it cannot found a ground of appeal.

R (W) v Brent Youth Court 2006 EWHC 95 (Admin) High Court In cases where there is no guidance from the Sentencing Guidelines Council, it is permissible and helpful for the court to consider any relevant publication of the Sentencing Advisory Panel.

R v Abbas 2008 EWCA Crim 1897, 2009 RTR 3 (p 23) The defence referred to draft guidelines produced by the Sentencing Advisory Panel. Held. Those are not guidelines to which it is appropriate for this Court to have any reference at all, given that they are what they say they are, namely draft guidelines, which may or may not be implemented.

R v Valentas 2010 EWCA Crim 200, 2 Cr App R (S) 73 (p 477) LCJ Although the proposals of the Sentencing Advisory Panel are of considerable interest as part of the background which sentencing judges may wish to bear in mind, the proposals themselves do not constitute guidance to sentencers which serve to displace, or amend or in any way undermine the authority of the guidance issued by the Court of Appeal. They therefore provide no justifiable basis for interfering with a sentencing decision in which the sentencing judge applied the existing guidance of the court.

R v Connelly 2017 EWCA Crim 1569, 2018 1 Cr App R (S) 19 (p 127) D pleaded to manslaughter. The Judge used a draft guideline which had been used to road-test a proposed guideline. It was written at the very early stages in the drafting of the proposed guideline. Held. Draft guidelines should not be used. Only definitive guidelines should be used.

64.17 ***Guidelines Guideline issued but not in force/No retrospective application/ Which do you use?***

R v Bao 2007 EWCA Crim 2781, 2008 2 Cr App R (S) 10 (p 61) D pleaded to managing a brothel. It was accepted that the sentence had been increased by the new guidelines. Held. The Judge was right to consider the sentencing guidelines even though they had not been published at the time of the offence.

Note: This rule is particularly important when sentencing historical sex offences. Ed.

R v Boakye and Others 2012 EWCA Crim 838, 2013 1 Cr App R (S) 2 (p 6) Whenever there is a change of tariff, and whether it is the result of parliamentary or other intervention, there is inevitably potential for different outcomes between offenders sentenced before the change and those sentenced after it. We do not, however, agree that this creates an injustice towards those who were perfectly properly sentenced before the change. On the contrary, to apply the guideline retrospectively would carry a greater risk of injustice. The injustice would then be to those who were sentenced under the same regime as offenders who now seek retrospective alteration, but whose sentence, because it has been served, cannot be adjusted. The reality is that any change has to start at some point.

See also: *R v Fascina* 2012 EWCA Crim 2473 (D, a vulnerable drug courier, pleaded to importation shortly before the guidelines were in force. *R v Boakye* 2012 was correctly decided.)

This means the following:

Offence	**Guideline**	**Which guideline?**
Historical offence		The guideline in force at the time of sentence, while remembering the maximum sentences available when the offence was committed, see **242.30** in Volume 2. Care must be taken when attempting to match historical offences and offences in the guideline. The ingredients of the old and new offences are frequently not the same.
Offence committed before new guideline published/in force	New guideline published but not in force	The judge can consider the factors and principles mentioned in the new guideline but the new guideline should not be applied, see **64.16** and *R v Boakye and Others* 2012 above. There is no appeal based on retrospective application of the guideline, *R v Boakye and Others* 2012 above.
	New guideline in force at the time of the sentence hearing	The guideline in force at the time of sentence is applied.
	Old guideline in force on the date of conviction but new guideline in force at time of sentence.	The guideline in force at the time of sentence is applied, see *R v Boakye and Others* 2012 EWCA Crim 838, 2013 1 Cr App R (S) 2 (p 6) at para 23.
	Some defendants to be sentenced before and some after the guideline is in force	Note: Better to sentence all at the same time as a legitimate grievance could develop between defendants. An exception would be where separate sentencing is desirable and it would not create a disparity, e.g. a mother who is being given a suspended sentence could be sentenced before the others. Ed.
	Sentence before new guideline in force and tariff will be less under new guideline	As above. Note: Defence counsel look for valid reasons to ask for reports/references etc. to ensure sentence is under new guideline. With the *Drug Offences Guideline 2012*, sensible judges were sympathetic while others were not. Ed.

64.18 ***Reasons Judge must explain how guideline was applied etc.***
Criminal Justice Act 2003 s 174(6)[869] The court must identify any definitive sentencing guidelines relevant to the offender's case and:

(a) explain how the court discharged any duty imposed on it by Coroners and Justice Act 2009 s 125 (duty to follow guidelines unless satisfied it would be contrary to the interests of justice to do so),

(b) where the court was satisfied it would be contrary to the interests of justice to follow the guidelines, state why.

For subsections 174(1)-(3) see **86.49**.

Criminal Procedure Rules 2015 2015/1490 Rule 28.1(1) This rule applies where the court decides:

(a) not to follow a relevant sentencing guideline…

(2) The court must explain why it has so decided, when it explains the sentence that it has passed.

Att-Gen's Ref 2018 Re Doherty and Others 2018 EWCA Crim 1924 D was convicted and T, E and S pleaded to conspiracy to import farmed puppies and sell them as home-bred puppies. Despite repeated requests, the Judge failed to explain how he had applied the guideline. Held. This was regrettable. It created difficulties for one of the defendants who was sentenced later and for this Court. The Judge failed to apply the guideline or applied it in a wholly inappropriate fashion.

For more detail, see **267.43** in Volume 2.

64.19 ***Reasons No need to refer to every part of sentencing decision***
R v Messent 2011 EWCA Crim 644 LCJ We must make it clear that in sentencing remarks, a judge is not normally expected to refer to a whole series of fact-specific sentencing decisions which have been drawn to his attention and address them one by one, taking each of the individual decisions and demonstrating how and why they do or do not assist him, in relation to the decision in the individual case. In other words, these decisions do not constitute binding precedents which he must apply or distinguish. The system would collapse if judges were required to do that.

Court of Appeal guidance/guidelines

64.20 ***Power to issue guidance/guidelines***
Coroners and Justice Act 2009 s 124(8) This section [which deals with the power of the Court of Appeal and the Lord Chancellor to propose to the Sentencing Council that sentence guidelines be prepared or revised] is without prejudice to any power of the appeal court to provide guidance relating to the sentencing of offenders in a judgment of the court.

Att-Gen's Ref Nos 73 and 75 of 2010 and 3 of 2011 Re P 2011 EWCA Crim 633[870] LCJ D was convicted of two counts of rape and two counts of assault by penetration. He broke into V's bedsit through a kitchen window. V, aged 37, was alone and asleep. The sentencing Judge said he was following the guideline and said for multiple rape the starting point was 8 years. Held. That is questionable as it stands. In any event guidelines are no more than guidelines. Sexual offences committed by a burglar should be approached as if they were among the most serious offences of their kind, as the culpability of the criminal is at its highest and the harm done to the victim is at its most grave. As it happens, [these offences] are not dealt with directly in the current Sentencing Guidelines Council's Definitive Guideline. We emphasise [that] the jurisdiction of the Court of Appeal to amplify, to explain or to offer a definitive sentencing guideline of its own, to issue guidelines if it thinks fit is undiminished. The relevant statutory provisions emphasise the obvious truth that no sentence should be an unjust sentence and that no guidance can require that an unjust sentence should be imposed.

869 As substituted by Legal Aid, Sentencing and Punishment of Offenders Act 2012 s 64
870 In some reports this is listed as 73, 75 and 3 of 2010.

Dealing with the matter very generally, in a case where rape has been committed after or in the course of burglary in a home, even if there are no additional features beyond the rape and the burglary, the starting point will rarely be less than 12 years' imprisonment. As these cases show, in many such cases where rape or serious sexual assault is perpetrated in the course of a burglary, several additional aggravating features are usually present. In such cases, where there are aggravating features, the starting point for consideration will increase to 15 years' imprisonment and beyond. Here 15 years not 8. For more detail, see **314.43** in Volume 2.

Note: The suggestion that the Court of Appeal can issue its own guidelines runs counter to the belief of many in Parliament and elsewhere that the modern legislation was to replace the Court of Appeal's role with a suggested broad-based Council to issue guidance and guidelines. However, this re-affirmation is exceptionally welcome. Ed.

R v Dyer and Others 2013 EWCA Crim 2114, 2014 2 Cr App R (S) 11 (p 61) The Court considered sentences imposed for offences of class A drug supply to test purchasers in Soho and the *Drug Offences Guideline 2012*. Held by Leveson LJ. para 15 What Lord Judge in *Att-Gen's Ref Nos 73 and 75 of 2010 and 3 of 2011* was not saying was that this court could issue its own guideline in conflict with a Definitive Guideline issued by the Council. Neither was he suggesting that it is appropriate to go back to the pre-guideline authorities and seek to argue that they, rather than the guideline, provide the approach that the court should follow. Amplification and explanation is precisely the function of this court as is issuing guidelines in areas or circumstances not covered by a Definitive Guideline. If the interests of justice demonstrate that a guideline requires revision, the court will undoubtedly identify that fact: it will then be for the Council, pursuing its statutory remit, to revisit the guideline and undertake the necessary consultation which precedes the issue of all guidelines. Given the composition of the Council, we doubt that substantial differences of approach are likely ever to emerge.

The overarching principles

64.21 *Aggravating factors* *Overarching Principles: Seriousness Guideline 2004*

Overarching Principles: Seriousness Guideline 2004 para 1.20, see www.banksr.com Other Matters Guidelines tab **(i) Aggravating factors**

1.20 Sentencing guidelines for a particular offence will normally include a list of aggravating features which, if present in an individual instance of the offence, would indicate either a higher than usual level of culpability on the part of the offender, or a greater than usual degree of harm caused by the offence (or sometimes both).

1.21 The lists below bring together the most important aggravating features with potential application to more than one offence or class of offences. They include some factors (such as the vulnerability of victims or abuse of trust) which are integral features of certain offences; in such cases, the presence of the aggravating factor is already reflected in the penalty for the offence and **cannot be used as justification for increasing the sentence further**. The lists are not intended to be comprehensive and the aggravating factors are not listed in any particular order of priority. On occasions, two or more of the factors listed will describe the same feature of the offence and care needs to be taken to avoid "double counting".

* Those factors marked with an asterisk are statutory aggravating factors where the statutory provisions are in force.

1.22 Factors indicating higher culpability:

- Offence committed whilst on bail for other offences*
- Failure to respond to previous sentences
- Offence was racially or religiously aggravated*
- Offence motivated by, or demonstrating, hostility to the victim based on his or her sexual orientation (or presumed sexual orientation)
- Offence motivated by, or demonstrating, hostility based on the victim's disability (or presumed disability)

- Previous conviction(s), particularly where a pattern of repeat offending is disclosed
- Planning of an offence
- An intention to commit more serious harm than actually resulted from the offence
- Offenders operating in groups or gangs
- 'Professional' offending
- Commission of the offence for financial gain (where this is not inherent in the offence itself)
- High level of profit from the offence
- An attempt to conceal or dispose of evidence
- Failure to respond to warnings or concerns expressed by others about the offender's behaviour
- Offence committed whilst on licence
- Offence motivated by hostility towards a minority group, or a member or members of it
- Deliberate targeting of vulnerable victim(s)
- Commission of an offence while under the influence of alcohol or drugs
- Use of a weapon to frighten or injure victim
- Deliberate and gratuitous violence or damage to property, over and above what is needed to carry out the offence
- Abuse of power
- Abuse of a position of trust

Note: The guideline has boxes instead of bullet points and a # symbol which deals with legislation which had not then been enacted but now has. Ed.

64.22 ***Factors indicating a more than usually serious degree of harm*** **Guidelines**
Overarching Principles: Seriousness Guideline 2004, see www.banksr.com Other Matters Guidelines tab para 123 Factors indicating a more than usually serious degree of harm [are:] 1 Multiple victims, 2 An especially serious physical or psychological effect on the victim, even if unintended, 3 A sustained assault or repeated assaults on the same victim, 4 Victim is particularly vulnerable, 5 Location of the offence (for example, in an isolated place), 6 Offence is committed against those working in the public sector or providing a service to the public, 7 Presence of others e.g. relatives, especially children or partner of the victim, 8 Additional degradation of the victim (e.g. taking photographs of a victim as part of a sexual offence) and 9 In property offences, high value (including sentimental value) of property to the victim, or substantial consequential loss (e.g. where the theft of equipment causes serious disruption to a victim's life or business).

64.23 ***Factors indicating significantly lower culpability*** **Guidelines**
Overarching Principles: Seriousness Guideline 2004, see www.banksr.com Other Matters Guidelines tab para 125 Factors indicating significantly lower culpability [are:] 1 A greater degree of provocation than normally expected, 2 Mental illness or disability, 3 Youth or age, where it affects the responsibility of the individual defendant, and 4 The fact that the offender played only a minor role in the offence.
For ***Personal mitigation***, see **DEFENDANT** ***Personal mitigation*** at **242.48** in Volume 2.

64.24 ***Prevalence of the offence in the locality***
Overarching Principles: Seriousness Guideline 2004, see www.banksr.com Other Matters Guidelines tab para 1.39 There may be exceptional local circumstances which lead a court to decide that prevalence should influence sentencing levels. The pivotal issue in such cases will be the harm being caused to the community. It is essential that sentencers both have supporting evidence from an external source (for example the local Criminal Justice Board) to justify claims and are satisfied that there is a compelling need to treat the offence more seriously than elsewhere.
R v Stockdale 2005 EWCA Crim 1582 The Court considered the above guideline. Held. With respect to the Council, we entertain very great difficulty in accepting that a local

judge is not entitled to go on his local knowledge and must have evidence of conditions. The crime in the locality may be notorious. The Judge may be extremely well placed to have an informed view of it. He may have had hundreds of cases before him displaying time and again the criminality in the area. We seriously question this approach by the Sentencing Council.

R v Oosthuizen 2005 EWCA Crim 1978, 2006 1 Cr App R (S) 73 (p 385) Criminal Justice Act 2003 s 172(1)(a)[871] says, 'Every court must have regard to any guidelines which are relevant'. It is not open to judges to disregard what the Council says. It does not necessarily follow that in every case a guideline will be followed. If, in any particular town or city, there are statistics available to the CPS, the Local Criminal Justice Board or otherwise, which demonstrate a prevalence of a particular offence, those statistics can and should be made available to the Court. In the absence of such statistics or other evidence identifying particular prevalence, a judge, however experienced, should not make the assumption that the offence is more marked in his or her area than it is nationally.

R v Chambers and Others 2005 EWCA Crim 1160, 2006 1 Cr App R (S) 23 (p 135) The seven defendants each pleaded at the first opportunity to offences relating to the supply of class A drugs. Held. These sentences simply disregard what was said in *R v Afonso* 2004 EWCA Crim 2342, 2005 1 Cr App R (S) 99 (p 560). It is plain that the Judge does not agree with and does not feel bound by that guidance. That is not a sustainable position. In principle sentencing in Leicester should not be out of line with sentencing in Liverpool, Leeds or London. Local inconsistency is inherently unjust.

R v Williamson 2007 EWCA Crim 44 D was convicted of murder. He shot the victim. The Judge mentioned the locality, Nottingham, when considering the aggravating circumstances. (He did not mention it as a separate aggravating factor. Ed.) Held. It is justified in principle to include in appropriate cases a deterrent element to reflect local circumstances and needs, where these are either proved by evidence or well known to the Judge from local or regional knowledge. It is important that any increase in sentence to reflect this element is proportionate. (There is no reference to the SGC guideline in the judgment. Ed.)

R v Bondzie 2016 EWCA Crim 552, 2 Cr App R (S) 28 (p 261) D was sentenced for street drug dealing. The Judge was given a statement about the harm caused by drug dealing in the Thanet area. The Judge said the drug problem was a desperately serious problem in the area. The Single Judge gave leave because he thought the starting point had been increased because of this. Held. Sentencing levels set in guidelines such as the *Drug Offences Guideline 2012* take account of collective social harm. In the case of drugs supply this will cover the detrimental impact of drug dealing activities upon communities. Accordingly, offenders should normally be sentenced by straightforward application of the guidelines without aggravation for the fact that their activity contributes to a harmful social effect upon a neighbourhood or community. It is not open to the judge to increase sentence for prevalence in ordinary circumstances or in response to his own personal view that there is "too much of this sort of thing going on in this area". para 11 [When considering this principle], there must be evidence provided to the court by a responsible body or by a senior police officer. That evidence must be before the court in the specific case being considered with the relevant statements or reports having been made available to the Crown and defence in good time so that meaningful representations about that material can be made. Even if such material is provided, a judge will only be entitled to treat prevalence as an aggravating factor if, a) he [or she] is satisfied that the level of harm caused in a particular locality is significantly higher than that caused elsewhere (and thus already inherent in the guideline levels), b) that the circumstances can properly be described as exceptional, and c) that it is just and proportionate to increase sentence for such a factor in the particular case before him.

[871] Repealed by Coroners and Justice Act 2009 Sch 23(4) para 1

para 19 If the Crown intends to invite the court to consider that matter, it must expressly say so at the hearing, identifying the materials upon which it relies as evidence and referring the judge to the relevant guideline. If a judge of his or her own motion is contemplating prevalence as a factor, he or she should clearly identify that as a matter to be addressed in submissions to the court. Any sentence imposed should then identify if prevalence has been a factor and provide reasoning so that the parties, and possibly this court, may understand how it has influenced the sentencing decision. The Thanet situation does not reveal a picture significantly different from other parts of the country. Sentence reduced.

R v Khalid 2017 EWCA Crim 592 (The Judge said: "There is too much of this sort of behaviour and I hope that this message reaches people like you and this sort of driving comes to an end in this city." Held. para 11 It is now well established that courts should be hesitant before increasing a sentence because of prevalence. Principles stated. para 13 Where a judge of his or her own motion contemplated prevalence as a relevant consideration, that should be identified as a matter to be addressed in submissions to the court and any sentence then imposed should identify whether prevalence had been a factor in the decision and reasons should be provided therefor.)

Note: This provision has created nothing but problems since it was issued. Sensible judges refer to the awful consequences of certain offences and decline to specify that their area has a particular problem. Ed.

R v Ali 2018 EWCA Crim 2359, 2019 1 Cr App R (S) 27 (p 182) D pleaded to death by dangerous driving. The Judge took into account a statement from a Detective Inspector comparing the fatalities in Bradford to other local authorities. [The statement did refer to road traffic matters but the extract did not.] The Judge appeared to make the fact that the offence was committed in Bradford a reason to increase the sentence. The statement was not served before the hearing. Held. This deprived the defence of sufficient time to prepare submissions. The evidence was too general. It needed to be specific to a particular offence. The information should not have been an aggravating factor.

See also: *R v Lanham and Willis* 2008 EWCA Crim 2450, 2009 1 Cr App R (S) 105 (p 592).

64.25 ***No guideline for an offence Judge may consider analogous guideline***

R v Kavanagh 2008 EWCA Crim 855, 2 Cr App R (S) 86 (p 493) D pleaded to public nuisance. He called women at a gym on a telephone and asked them about their underwear and proceeded to ask about more explicit matters. It became clear that he was able to watch them during the call. D made hundreds of calls. There was no definitive guideline for public nuisance but there was a guideline about sexual offences. Held. Where an offence is of a sexual nature, and there is no doubt that this offending was, we ought to try as best as possible to relate it to the Guideline. It is impossible to contemplate fitting every offence into the guidelines issued by the Sentencing Guidelines Council, but it is important that where an offence is not within the guidelines but is an offence similar to those within the guidelines, an attempt should be made to see how best to relate that offence to those within the guidelines. We take two different starting points. The first is to look at the guidelines in respect of sexual assaults, and in particular the bracket of offending for contact between naked genitalia of the offender and another part of the victim's body, where the range is 6 to 24 months, and [second] voyeurism, which on the basic offence would attract a community service order but with aggravating features can attract a sentence of up to 24 months.

R v Lewis 2012 EWCA Crim 1071, 2013 1 Cr App R (S) 23 (p 121) D pleaded to possessing pornographic images of a female adult engaging in sexual activities with horses and a dog. The Judge had regard to the guidelines for possession of child pornography as they were of a 'similar kind'. Held. When a case concerns an offence for which there is no guideline, the judge may well consider analogous guidelines. While in broad terms this is legitimate, the Judge in *R v Rowe* 2010 EWCA Crim 357, 2 Cr App R (S) 89 (p 561) at para 4 stated that the judge's task is "to assess each case individually"

by "the essential exercise of judgment". He further stated that it is not to be expected that the provision of guidelines will provide a substitute for this in every possible situation.
Note: The Court of Appeal has suggested courts use the *Causing Death by Driving Guideline 2008* for the offence of causing serious injury by dangerous driving, *R v Smart* 2015 EWCA Crim 1756 at **235.7** in Volume 2. Ed.

Appeals

64.26 *The Court of Appeal is not interested in cases about the guidelines*
R v Balazs 2014 EWCA Crim 937 LCJ Counsel put before the Court a number of authorities purporting to show how the [sex offences] guideline is operated. We repeat yet again that authorities on how the guidelines operate are of no assistance to this Court and must not be cited.
Note: Although these cases were of no assistance to the then Lord Chief Justice, they remain of interest to practitioners and no doubt to judges sitting in the Crown Court. Ed.

65 Guilty Plea, Discount for

65.1
Criminal Justice Act 2003 s 144
For ***Detention and Training Orders, see*** the **Detention and Training Orders *Discount for guilty plea Maximum sentence given*** para at **37.16**.
For ***Life sentences***, see the **Life Sentence: Basic Principles/Discretionary Life *Guilty plea Discount for*** para at **74.10**.

Statute, Court Martial and purpose

65.2 *Statutory provisions*
Reduction in sentences for guilty pleas
Criminal Justice Act 2003 s 144(1) In determining what sentence to pass on an offender who has pleaded guilty to an offence in proceedings before that or another court, a court must take into account:
(a) the stage in the proceedings for the offence at which the offender indicated his intention to plead guilty, and
(b) the circumstances in which this indication was given.
(2) In the case of an offender who:
(a) is convicted of an offence the sentence for which falls to be imposed under a provision mentioned in subsection (3), and
(b) is aged 18 or over when convicted,
nothing in that provision prevents the court, after taking into account any matter referred to in subsection (1) of this section, from imposing any sentence which is not less than 80 per cent of that specified in that provision.[872]
(3) The provisions referred to in subsection (2) are: Prevention of Crime Act 1953 s 1(2B) or 1A, Powers of Criminal Courts (Sentencing) Act 2000 s 110(2) and 111(2) and Criminal Justice Act 1988 s 139(6B), 139A(5B) or 139AA(7).[873]
(4) In the case of an offender who:
(a) is convicted of an offence the sentence for which falls to be imposed under a provision mentioned in subsection (5), and
(b) is aged 16 or 17 when convicted,
nothing in that provision prevents the court from imposing any sentence that it considers appropriate after taking into account any matter referred to in subsection (1) of this section.[874]

[872] As amended by Legal Aid, Sentencing and Punishment of Offenders Act 2012 Sch 26 para 18(2)(b)
[873] Subsections (3)-(5) were inserted by Legal Aid, Sentencing and Punishment of Offenders Act 2012 Sch 26 para 18(2)(3), and Criminal Justice and Courts Act 2015 Sch 5 para 12(3).
[874] As amended by Criminal Justice and Courts Act 2015 Sch 5 para 12(4)

(5) The provisions referred to in subsection (4) are: Prevention of Crime Act 1953 s 1(2B) or 1A(5) [and] Criminal Justice Act 1988 s 139(6B), 139A(5B) or 139AA(7).[875]

65.3 *Court Martial*

Reduction in sentences for guilty pleas

Armed Forces Act 2006 s 239(1) This section applies where an offender:

(a) has pleaded guilty to a service offence in proceedings before a court, or

(b) at a summary hearing in respect of a service offence, has admitted the offence.

(2) In determining what sentence to pass on the offender, the court or officer dealing with him for his offence must take into account:

(a) the stage in the proceedings for the offence at which he indicated his intention to plead guilty or his intention to admit the offence at a summary hearing, and

(b) the circumstances in which this indication was given.

(3) In subsection (2) 'sentence' includes any order made when dealing with the offender in respect of his offence.

(4) Subsection (5) applies in the case of an offence the sentence for which, as a result of Armed Forces Act 2006 s 225(2) or 226(2) (required custodial sentences), falls to be imposed under Powers of Criminal Courts (Sentencing) Act 2000 s 110(2) and 111(2) (minimum sentences).

(5) Nothing in Powers of Criminal Courts (Sentencing) Act 2000 s 110(2) and 111(2) prevents the court, after taking into account any matter mentioned in subsection (2) above, from imposing any sentence which is at least 80% of that specified in Powers of Criminal Courts (Sentencing) Act 2000 s 110(2) and 111(2).

(6) Nothing in section 227A(2) prevents the court, after taking into account any matter mentioned in subsection (2) of this section, from imposing any sentence which is at least 80% of that specified in section 227A(2).[876]

Guidance on Sentencing in the Court Martial 2018, see www.banksr.com Other Matters Documents tab para 2.21.1 The Court Martial follows the statutory provisions relating to reduction in sentence for a guilty plea [Armed Forces Act 2006 s 239], and approaches reductions in accordance with the [Sentencing Council guidelines]. For sentences based on numerical values, such as lengths of custody or amounts of fines, the level of reduction is a proportion of the total sentence would otherwise be imposed, with the proportion being on a sliding scale depending upon the stage in the proceedings at which the guilty plea was entered or indicated. The first reasonable opportunity attracts the maximum ⅓ reduction; after the trial date is set, a ¼ reduction; and at the door of the court/after the trial has begun a ⅒ reduction.

2.21.2 Defendants are normally reminded of the reductions for a plea of guilty at the Initial Hearing (IH) if their counsel has not already done so. Reduction may be withheld in certain circumstances,[877] but the normal sliding scale applies even where the offender has been "caught red-handed". As sentences of Service detention include a large element of retraining the success of which depends upon minimum periods at MCTC, the mathematical approach to reduction is not appropriate for short sentences of detention where the reduction would be only a few days.[878] For non-numerical sentences such as dismissal this approach has no applicability but it is possible to reduce a sentence (for example fewer steps in reduction of rank) to reflect a guilty plea.

Calculating the discount

65.4 *Reduction in Sentence for a Guilty Plea Guideline 2017/Purpose of the discount*

Reduction in Sentence for a Guilty Plea Guideline 2017, see www.banksr.com Other Matters Guidelines tab In force 1 June 2017 page 4

[875] As amended by Criminal Justice and Courts Act 2015 Sch 5 para 12(5)

[876] Subsection (6) is inserted by Legal Aid, Sentencing and Punishment of Offenders Act 2012 Sch 26 para 26.

[877] See Sentencing Council Definitive Guideline on Reduction in Sentence for a Guilty Plea.

[878] See also 4.7.2 below [not listed in the book] in relation to calculating credit for time spent in post-charge custody.

The purpose of this guideline is to encourage those who are going to plead guilty to do so as early in the court process as possible. Nothing in the guideline should be used to put pressure on a defendant to plead guilty.

Although a guilty person is entitled not to admit the offence and to put the prosecution to proof of its case, an acceptance of guilt:

(a) normally reduces the impact of the crime upon victims;
(b) saves victims and witnesses from having to testify; and
(c) is in the public interest in that it saves public time and money on investigations and trials.

A guilty plea produces greater benefits the earlier the plea is indicated. In order to maximise the above benefits and to provide an incentive to those who are guilty to indicate a guilty plea as early as possible, this guideline makes a clear distinction between a reduction in the sentence available at the first stage of the proceedings and a reduction in the sentence available at a later stage of the proceedings.

The purpose of reducing the sentence for a guilty plea is to yield the benefits described above. The guilty plea should be considered by the court to be independent of the offender's personal mitigation.

- Factors such as admissions at interview, co-operation with the investigation and demonstrations of remorse should **not** be taken into account in determining the level of reduction. Rather, they should be considered separately and prior to any guilty plea reduction, as potential mitigating factors.
- The benefits apply regardless of the strength of the evidence against an offender. The strength of the evidence should **not** be taken into account when determining the level of reduction.
- The guideline applies only to the punitive elements of the sentence and has no impact on ancillary orders including orders of disqualification from driving.

page 5

C. THE APPROACH

Stage 1: Determine the appropriate sentence for the offence(s) in accordance with any offence specific sentencing guideline.
Stage 2: Determine the level of reduction for a guilty plea in accordance with this guideline.
Stage 3: State the amount of that reduction.
Stage 4: Apply the reduction to the appropriate sentence.
Stage 5: Follow any further steps in the offence specific guideline to determine the final sentence.

D. DETERMINING THE LEVEL OF REDUCTION

The maximum level of reduction in sentence for a guilty plea is one-third

D1. Plea indicated at the first stage of the proceedings

Where a guilty plea is indicated at the first stage of proceedings a reduction of one-third should be made (subject to the exceptions in section F). The first stage will normally be the first hearing at which a plea or indication of plea is sought and recorded by the court.[879]

D2. Plea indicated after the first stage of proceedings – maximum one quarter – sliding scale of reduction thereafter

After the first stage of the proceedings the maximum level of reduction is **one-quarter** (subject to the exceptions in section F).

The reduction should be decreased from **one-quarter** to a maximum of **one-tenth** on the first day of trial having regard to the time when the guilty plea is first indicated to the

[879] In cases where (in accordance with the Criminal Procedure Rules) a defendant is given the opportunity to enter a guilty plea without attending a court hearing, doing so within the required time limits will constitute a plea at the first stage of proceedings.

court relative to the progress of the case and the trial date (subject to the exceptions in section F). The reduction should normally be decreased further, even to zero, if the guilty plea is entered during the course of the trial.
For the purposes of this guideline a trial will be deemed to have started when pre-recorded cross-examination has begun.
page 6
E. APPLYING THE REDUCTION
E1. Imposing one type of sentence rather than another
The reduction in sentence for a guilty plea can be taken into account by imposing one type of sentence rather than another; for example:
- by reducing a custodial sentence to a community sentence, or
- by reducing a community sentence to a fine.

Where a court has imposed one sentence rather than another to reflect the guilty plea there should normally be no further reduction on account of the guilty plea. Where, however, the less severe type of sentence is justified by other factors, the appropriate reduction for the plea should be applied in the normal way.
E2.-E3. [matters at the Magistrates' Court], see **65.8**.
page 7
F. EXCEPTIONS
F1. Further information, assistance or advice necessary before indicating plea
Where the sentencing court is satisfied that there were particular circumstances which significantly reduced the defendant's ability to understand what was alleged or otherwise made it unreasonable to expect the defendant to indicate a guilty plea **sooner than was done**, a reduction of one-third should still be made.
[For when the defendant requires advice, see **65.16**.]
F2. *Newton* hearings and special reasons hearings, see 57.76.
F3. Offender convicted of a lesser or different offence, see **65.27**.
F4. Minimum sentence under section 51A of the Firearms Act 1968, see **262.44** in Volume 2.
F5. Appropriate custodial sentences for persons aged 18 or over when convicted under the Prevention of Crime Act 1953 and Criminal Justice Act 1988 and prescribed custodial sentences under the Power of Criminal Courts (Sentencing) Act 2000
In circumstances where:
- an appropriate custodial sentence of at least six months falls to be imposed on a person aged 18 or over who has been convicted under sections 1 or 1A of the Prevention of Crime Act 1953; or sections 139, 139AA or 139A of the Criminal Justice Act 1988 (certain possession of knives or offensive weapon offences) **or**
- a prescribed custodial sentence falls to be imposed under section 110 of the Powers of Criminal Courts (Sentencing) Act 2000 (drug trafficking offences) or section 111 of the Powers of Criminal Courts (Sentencing) Act 2000 (burglary offences),

the court may impose any sentence in accordance with this guideline which is not less than 80 per cent of the appropriate or prescribed custodial period.[880]
The rest of the guideline is distributed in this chapter.

65.5 ***The Judge must not start higher than the maximum***
R v Gregory and Butler 2017 EWCA Crim 1297 G and B pleaded to conspiracy to burgle. They were involved in 48 burglaries of commercial and club premises. The benefit figure was about £212,000 and the damage caused was about £½m. The Judge said he bore in mind the sentence that would have been appropriate had he been able to pass consecutive sentences. For G, he considered that the proper sentence was 14 years

[880] In accordance with Criminal Justice Act 2003 s 144(2)-(3)

and gave 25% for the plea, making 10½ years. He then reduced that to 10 years as that was the maximum sentence. Held. That was not permissible. The Judge should have started with the maximum and reduced that with the plea to 7½ years.

65.6 *Judicial discretion*

R v Last 2005 EWCA Crim 106, 2 Cr App R (S) 64 (p 381) para 9 and 17 LCJ Prior to the guidelines there was no guidance but it was generally assumed that the reduction should be approximately one-third. That was no more than a rule of thumb, and judges exercised a broad discretion to vary the reduction. The guidelines do not remove the judge's discretion. If the judge does not follow the guidelines he retains a discretion as long as he gives valid reasons.
R v Bowering 2005 EWCA Crim 3215, 2006 2 Cr App R (S) 10 (p 80) The defendant pleaded guilty to a very bad piece of driving in crowded, narrow, built-up streets (maximum 2 years). He had convictions in relation to cars. The Judge gave him 21 months without an explanation for the small discount. The sole issue was whether the discount for the plea was sufficient. Held. The judge is not bound to follow the guidelines, but if he does not, it is incumbent on him to explain why. There was no alternative but to reduce the sentence to 18 months.
R v Caley and Others 2012 EWCA Crim 2821, 2013 2 Cr App R (S) 47 (p 305) para 28 The general approach which we have endeavoured to set out is essential to an understanding by defendants and their advisers. But it does not altogether remove the scope of the judge to treat an individual case individually. We make no attempt to anticipate the great variety of circumstances which might arise.
R v Hussain 2018 EWCA Crim 780, 2 Cr App R (S) 12 (p 89) D pleaded to being concerned with the supply of cannabis and other offences. The Judge said the credit for pleading would be that he would suspend the sentence. Held. The Judge should select the [provisional] sentence, then deduct the credit and then determine whether the sentence should be suspended. The starting point of 12 months was appropriate. So, with 25% plea credit, 9 months, which we suspend, not 12 months suspended.
Note: The discretion in *R v Last* 2005 should be exercised very carefully or else sentencing will become inconsistent. Ed.

65.7 *Late plea*

Reduction in Sentence for a Guilty Plea Guideline 2017, see www.banksr.com Other Matters Guidelines tab In force 1 June 2017 page 5
D. DETERMINING THE LEVEL OF REDUCTION
D1. Plea indicated at the first stage of the proceedings [not relevant]
D2. Plea indicated after the first stage of proceedings – maximum one quarter – sliding scale of reduction thereafter
After the first stage of the proceedings the maximum level of reduction is **one-quarter** (subject to the exceptions in section F [see **65.4**].
The reduction should be decreased from **one-quarter** to a maximum of **one-tenth** on the first day of trial having regard to the time when the guilty plea is first indicated to the court relative to the progress of the case and the trial date (subject to the exceptions in section F). The reduction should normally be decreased further, even to zero, if the guilty plea is entered during the course of the trial.
For the purposes of this guideline a trial will be deemed to have started when pre-recorded cross-examination has begun.
R v Dallimore and Others 2013 EWCA Crim 1891, 2014 1 Cr App R (S) 31 (p187) M pleaded on the day set for his trial. That was about 9 months after the prosecution case statement was served. Five days before the plea, the defence had e-mailed saying that M accepted his guilt and negotiations started. The Judge gave him a 5% discount for his plea. Held. There is no ironclad rule that a deduction of at least 10% must be granted in circumstances where a plea of guilty is tendered at the door of the court, at or around the

time of the start of the trial. The guideline is exactly what it says, and the percentage is a recommendation. However, so lawyers can advise their clients properly in the future, in these circumstances, M should receive 10% credit.

R v Redhead 2013 EWCA Crim 1997 In December 2012, D pleaded not guilty to robbery at his PCMH. The case was put in the warned list for 2 April 2013. On 21 March 2013, D's solicitors wrote a letter to the CPS saying D would plead guilty. The witnesses were de-warned. On 3 April 2013, D pleaded and the Judge ordered a *Newton* hearing. On 15 May 2013, the witness was not sure which robber kicked him so the *Newton* hearing was not required. On 13 June 2013, D was given only 10% for his plea. Held. The amount of credit is a matter for the Judge. Although the plea indication was a week before the trial date, it was not a court-door plea. There are good policy reasons for encouraging pleas before the date of trial. The discount should have been 20%.

R v S 2016 EWCA Crim 2058, 2017 1 Cr App R (S) 41 (p 332) D pleaded not guilty to historical sex offences. The trial was estimated to last for four or five days and on the second day D pleaded. There was further prosecution evidence to follow, including evidence from D's wife and his daughter. The victims had given evidence on the first day of the trial. The Judge declined to give D any plea credit. She described D as controlling and manipulative. Held. In general, some plea credit should be given, save perhaps in exceptional circumstances, even if the plea is entered at such a late stage. We apply *R v Carew* 2015 EWCA Crim 437, 'It takes some courage to plead guilty at a late stage and there should be encouragement to all offenders to recognise their offending and to own up to it.' The amount of credit must be looked at by reference to the facts of the case. Different considerations may apply in, for example, sexual cases such as the present, where one of the objectives of the giving of credit is to spare the victims from the ordeal of having to give evidence. The appellant's victims in this case had to go through that ordeal and to re-live in that way the abuse[,] which is likely to have had a much greater effect on them than it would have done to the victims of the robbery and wounding in the *R v Carew* 2015 case, while being accused of making the whole thing up. That would inevitably have been a traumatic experience.

The *Reduction in Sentence for a Guilty Plea Guideline 2007* does not distinguish between a plea which is entered at the door of the court and a plea entered after the trial has begun. Sentencing judges should not feel constrained by this guideline to give 10% credit for a guilty plea entered after the commencement of trial in all circumstances. A judgement is required as to what credit is appropriate. That will require careful assessment of the facts of the particular case, including (particularly in sex cases) the extent to which witnesses have been spared from giving evidence on the one hand, or have been required to go through that ordeal on the other, as well as consideration of the amount of time and costs which have been saved as a result of the defendant's plea at that stage. The strength of the case against the defendant may also be relevant. That is not intended to be a definitive or exhaustive list. All the circumstances of the case will need to be taken into account and it may be that there will be some exceptional cases where no reduction is appropriate. Here there appears to have been a strong case against D, but he did save at least some prosecution witnesses from what would have been an ordeal for them, in particular D's wife. Several days of court time were saved. We start at 22 years and deduct 1 year for the plea.

Note: This case was heard before the new guideline applied, which indicates that pleas during a trial can warrant a zero discount. The major advantage of a late plea is that it ensures there will be no jury disagreement and no retrial. For the prosecution, it ensures there will be no acquittal. If a week of court time is saved, that can be very important to the court and others. I consider there are elements of this case that will be helpful despite the change of wording in the new guideline. Ed.

R v McDougall 2017 EWCA Crim 179 In July 2015, when the trial was about to start, D pleaded to child sex offences on an amended indictment. A rape count was dropped.[881] Before that D had not indicated any pleas or accepted any guilt. D then applied to vacate his pleas and his case was put back. The case was heard in February 2016, when D's application was not pursued. The Judge gave him no plea discount, citing the extra trauma to the victims and the lack of merit in the application. The defence said the pleas were maintained and the plea avoided the cost of a trial. Held. We agree with that. There are sound policy reasons why some credit should be given. We give an 8% discount.

See also the ***Evidence served late*** para at **65.12** and the ***Complex case*** para at **65.9**.

Magistrates' Court

65.8 ***Magistrates' Court***

Reduction in Sentence for a Guilty Plea Guideline 2017, see www.banksr.com Other Matters Guidelines tab In force 1 June 2017 page 6.

E. APPLYING THE REDUCTION

E1. [not relevant]

E2. More than one summary offence

When dealing with more than one summary offence, the aggregate sentence is limited to a maximum of six months. Allowing for a reduction for each guilty plea, consecutive sentences might result in the imposition of the maximum six-month sentence. Where this is the case, the court **may** make a modest additional reduction to the overall sentence to reflect the benefits derived from the guilty pleas.

E3. Keeping an either way case in the Magistrates' Court to reflect a guilty plea

Reducing a custodial sentence to reflect a guilty plea may enable a magistrates' court to retain jurisdiction of an either way offence rather than committing the case for sentence to the Crown Court. In such cases a magistrates' court should apply the appropriate reduction to the sentence for the offence(s) arrived at in accordance with any offence specific sentencing guideline and if the resulting sentence is then within its jurisdiction it should go on to sentence.

Particular sentencing orders and offences

For ***Burglary Minimum sentences for third domestic burglary***, see the **BURGLARY** ***Minimum 3 years' custody Plea of guilty*** para at **221.29** in Volume 2.

65.9 ***Complex cases***

R v Western and Others 2011 EWCA Crim 290 The defendants pleaded on the first and second day that the case was fixed. The Judge said the defendants had had plenty of opportunity to plead and gave 15% discount. The defence said they only received the graphic material shortly before the trial which was the first time the prosecution case had coalesced. The prosecution said that only when the vast amount of data was brought together was the case against each defendant clarified. Held. There is substance in these arguments. As a general proposition, in a case of complexity, a defendant is entitled to know the full nature of the case against him before he enters his plea. Here the advocates could not properly advise earlier. All defendants should be given full credit.

R v Caley and Others 2012 EWCA Crim 2821, 2013 2 Cr App R (S) 47 (p 305) para 28 A case which is sometimes treated as meriting exceptional treatment is the exceptionally long and complex trial, whether in fraud or otherwise (such as people trafficking, complex drug cases and serial sex abuse cases with many complainants). Since the rationale of reduction for plea is the public benefit which we have described, we leave open the possibility that in some such cases, unusually, some considerable benefits may well ensue from a plea of guilty even at a late stage. Care must, however, be taken with such a proposition so that it does not become routine. If it does, the incentive to focus on plea at an early stage is lost, and it becomes impossible to maintain proper parity between late-pleading defendants and those who indicate their guilt at the right time.

[881] It may be that more than one count was dropped.

See also the ***Evidence served late*** para at **65.12**.

65.10 ***Disqualification, penalty points and ancillary orders***

Reduction in Sentence for a Guilty Plea Guideline 2017, see www.banksr.com Other Matters Guidelines tab In force 1 June 2017 page 4 para B The guideline applies only to the punitive elements of the sentence and has no impact on ancillary orders including orders of disqualification from driving..

Fraud, see the **Fraud and Financial Services Offences** ***Guilty plea, Late*** para at **267.14** in Volume 2.

65.11 ***Historical cases***

R v H 2011 EWCA Crim 2753, 2012 2 Cr App R (S) 21 (p 88) para 47 g) Early admissions and a guilty plea are of particular importance in historical cases. Because [historical cases] relate to facts which are long past, the defendant will inevitably be tempted to lie his way out of the allegations. It is greatly to the defendant's credit if he makes early admissions. Even more powerful mitigation is available to the offender who, out of a sense of guilt and remorse, reports himself to the authorities. Considerations like these provide the victim with vindication, often a feature of great importance to them.

Importation of drugs, see the **Importation/Exportation of Drugs (Class A, B and C)** ***Minimum sentences Plea of guilty*** para at **338.75** in Volume 2.

Murder, see the **Murder Guilty plea** section at **287.25** in Volume 2.

Rape, see the **Rape and Assault by Penetration** ***Guilty plea*** para at **314.11** in Volume 2.

Perverting the course of Justice, see the **Perverting the Course of Justice etc.** ***Mitigation, bogus*** para at **302.22** in Volume 2.

Supply Minimum sentences for third class A drug trafficking offence, see the **Supply of Drugs.** ***Minimum 7 years' for class A suppliers Plea of guilt*** para at **338.75** in Volume 2.

Terrorism, see the **Terrorism** ***Guilty plea*** para at **343.5** in Volume 2.

Special situations

65.12 ***Evidence served late***

R v Atkinson and Smith 2004 EWCA Crim 3223, 2005 2 Cr App R (S) 34 (p 206) After S had pleaded not guilty at a PDH, the Judge indicated to him that if evidence was served which caused him to change his plea he would not hold the not guilty plea against him. Important fingerprint and forensic evidence was later served. S pleaded guilty on the first day of his trial. Held. He was entitled to the full discount for his plea.

Att-Gen's Ref No 79 of 2009 2010 EWCA Crim 187 On 24 July 2009, at his PCMH, D pleaded to unlawful wounding and not guilty to rape. The case was adjourned for trial on 11 August 2009. On 4 August 2009, the defence indicated that there would be a guilty plea to rape. The prosecution had served crucial DNA evidence on 30 June 2009, along with transcripts of the interview which did not contain critical passages. Further transcripts were served on 23 July 2009. On the day of sentence, the defence said that if they had had the information earlier, more rapid progress might have been made, as D claimed amnesia for the incident. The Judge gave D full credit for the plea. The prosecution appealed, and the defence said that the duty of those defending a man charged with this kind of offence means that it may well be necessary to explore scientific evidence. Held. We unhesitatingly accept that. We are some way from accepting that every judge would have taken that view but it cannot be said this Judge was wrong to do so.

R v Thompson 2012 EWCA Crim 1431 D pleaded not guilty and his co-defendant pleaded guilty. Six weeks later D pleaded. Held. At the first hearing, all the relevant documents had not been served. On the facts of this case he did so at what was the first reasonable opportunity. We must stress how important it is for a judge carrying out a sentencing exercise to carry out the exercise that ascertains whether or not the plea was in fact entered at the first reasonable opportunity. It cannot be an invariable rule that that must be when the defendant is interviewed at the police station, because in many cases that will be at a later time, depending on when documents have been served and a number of other factors. Sentence reduced.

65.13 ***New count/charge added***

R v Wacha 2013 EWCA Crim 1108 D pleaded to damaging property and not guilty to arson with intent and damaging property reckless whether life was endangered. D wanted to scare V and threw a brick through V's kitchen window. V then saw D outside holding a bottle with a lit rag in the neck. V shouted a warning and D dropped the bottle and ran off. At D's trial, V did not turn up and the prosecution added a count of having an article with intent to destroy property. D pleaded to that and asked for a full discount as it had only just been drafted. Held. At the PCMH, D denied throwing the bottle confirmed by his Defence Case Statement. Applying *R v Caley and Others* 2012 he was not entitled to more than the 10% given.

R v Hearn 2014 EWCA Crim 110 D pleaded to handling stolen goods. The indictment initially alleged burglary and theft. At the PCMH, D offered to plead to handling but that was rejected. On the day of trial, the handling count was added and D pleaded. The first two counts were dropped. Held. The credit for the plea should be approaching the maximum. Sentence reduced.

Att-Gen's Ref 2017 Re Parish and Redford 2017 EWCA Crim 2064 P and R pleaded not guilty to various firearm counts. They denied possession of the firearms. On the day of trial a new count of conspiracy to transfer prohibited firearms was added. Defence counsel asked for a full discount if there was a plea and without any input from prosecution counsel, the Judge agreed. Counsel discussions continued and later the two pleaded. A full discount was given. In a sentencing note P's counsel asked for a full discount. The prosecution note said nothing about the plea discount. Held. The procedure was highly unsatisfactory. A full discount was not appropriate. The Judge has a discretion but the plea discount cannot here be 'greater than 20% or at the very most 25%'. However, the plea was after the indication was given which provided some incentive to plead. The new count did not suggest an intent to endanger life. With some reluctance we consider that to deprive P and R of the full discount would be unjust. For more detail, see **262.20** in Volume 2.

65.14 ***Maximum considered too low***

Reduction in Sentence for a Guilty Plea Guideline 2007, see www.banksr.com Other Matters Guidelines tab para E 5.3 The sentencer cannot remedy perceived defects (e.g. an inadequate charge or maximum penalty) by [a] refusal of the appropriate discount.

Note: There is a new guideline, but this guidance remains in force. Ed.

R v Greene 1993 14 Cr App R (S) 682 Once the maximum has been set by Parliament and a plea of guilty has been proffered at an early stage, it was incumbent on the Judge to reflect that willingness to plead guilty in the sentence that he felt obliged to pass.

R v M 2002 EWCA Crim 551, 2 Cr App R (S) 98 (p 448) D, aged 16, with others, pleaded to one count of conspiracy to cause ABH, three counts of ABH, one count of threats to kill and one count of incitement to steal. He received a maximum 24-month Detention and Training Order. Two counts of indecent assault which attracted section 91 detention were left to lie on file. The Judge described the case as the most disgusting case he had ever had to deal with. The Judge criticised the prosecution for accepting pleas to the offences and allowing the indecent assault charges to lie on the file, indicating that he would have passed a higher sentence had he been able to. The Judge gave no discount for the plea, stating that "in the acceptance of the pleas to lesser offences, and the counts to lie on file, D [had] had all the discount he could hope for". Credit was not given for the 8 months served on remand either. Held. The Judge was only entitled to sentence for the offence of which D had been convicted. He should have loyally applied the Act. We are concerned not to undermine the advice given that pleas of guilty attract discounts. What he could not do was to go behind the compromise between defence and prosecution and sentence on a basis which the Crown could have pursued, but chose not to pursue. 6 months' discount allowed.

R v Bogoslov 2008 EWCA Crim 676 D pleaded to four counts of possession of a false identity document (maximum 2 years). The Judge passed 2 years concurrent saying the plea was reflected in the sentences not being consecutive and the maximum sentence was restrictive. Held. D was entitled to credit for the plea. Starting at 18 months, so with a plea 12 months.

See also: *R v Simpson* 2009 EWCA Crim 423, 2 Cr App R (S) 69 (p 492) (Sentence reduced to reflect plea.)

65.15 ***Maximum given with a plea of guilty***

Reduction in Sentence for a Guilty Plea Guideline 2007, see www.banksr.com Other Matters Guidelines tab para E 5.3 The sentencer cannot remedy perceived defects (e.g. an inadequate charge or maximum penalty) by [a] refusal of the appropriate discount.

Note: Although there is a new guideline, this statement is in force as this subject is not dealt with in the new guideline. Ed.

R v Bogoslov 2008 EWCA Crim 676 D pleaded to four counts of possession of a false identity document (maximum 2 years). The Judge passed 2 years concurrent saying the plea was reflected in the sentences not being consecutive and the maximum sentence was restrictive. Held. D was entitled to credit for the plea. Starting at 18 months, so on a plea 12 months.

R v Higham 2016 EWCA Crim 2314 D pleaded to dangerous driving, disqualified driving and no insurance. He was involved in a police chase with other people in his car. The Judge said the case had pretty well all the aggravating factors you can possibly get. D's driving record was 'appalling'. The Judge said he stopped counting at 11 disqualified driving offences on his record. He gave D the maximum (2 years and 6 months consecutive) saying D had no alternative but to plead. Held. Anyone who pleads guilty at the earliest opportunity is entitled to as a general rule a one third discount, *R v Caley and Others* 2012 EWCA Crim 2821, 2013 2 Cr App R (S) 47 (p 305). It is not a reason to reduce the discount because the maximum penalty is inadequate or because the defendant could have been charged with something different. Despite the overwhelming nature of the evidence [which was then a reason for a reduced discount] there was no proper ground to reduce the discount, so 16 months and 4 months consecutive.

See also: *R v Simpson* 2009 EWCA Crim 423, 2 Cr App R (S) 69 (p 492) (Sentence reduced to reflect plea.)

R v Sullivan 2014 EWCA Crim 292 (**18 months** not 2 years for the dangerous driving and 5 months not 6 for disqualified driving, see **234.12** in Volume 2.)

See also the **Detention and Training Order** ***Discount for plea Maximum given*** para at **37.16**.

Particular situations relating to the defendant

65.16 ***Advice Defendant requires advice/Defence needs investigating***

Att-Gen's Ref No 79 of 2009 2010 EWCA Crim 187 On 24 July 2009, at his PCMH, D pleaded to unlawful wounding and not guilty to rape. The case was adjourned for trial on 11 August 2009. On 4 August 2009, the defence indicated that there would be a guilty plea to rape. The prosecution had served crucial DNA evidence on 30 June 2009, along with transcripts of the interview which did not contain critical passages. Further transcripts were served on 23 July 2009. On the day of sentence, the defence said that if they had had the information earlier, more rapid progress might have been made, as D claimed amnesia for the incident. The Judge gave D full credit for the plea. The prosecution appealed, and the defence said that the duty of those defending a man charged with this kind of offence means that it may well be necessary to explore scientific evidence. Held. We unhesitatingly accept that. We are some way from accepting that every judge would have taken that view but it cannot be said this Judge was wrong to do so.

R v Caley and Others 2012 EWCA Crim 2821, 2013 2 Cr App R (S) 47 (p 305) para 14 There will certainly be cases where a defendant genuinely does not know whether he is guilty or not and needs advice and/or sight of the evidence in order to decide. They might, however, include cases where even if the facts are known there is a need for legal advice as to whether an offence is constituted by them, or cases where a defendant genuinely has no recollection of events. There may be other cases in which a defendant cannot reasonably be expected to make any admission until he and his advisers have seen at least some of the evidence. Such cases aside, however, whilst it is perfectly proper for a defendant to require advice from his lawyers on the strength of the evidence (just as he is perfectly entitled to insist on putting the Crown to proof at trial), he does not require it in order to know whether he is guilty or not, he requires it in order to assess the prospects of conviction or acquittal, which is different. Moreover, even though a defendant may need advice on which charge he ought to plead guilty to, there is often no reason why uncertainty about this should inhibit him from admitting, if it is true, what acts he did. If he does so, normally the public benefits to which we have referred will flow. para 28 The general approach does not altogether remove the scope of the judge to treat an individual case individually. We make no attempt to anticipate the great variety of circumstances which might arise, but give three examples. One is the case of murder where there is real necessity for advice on the availability of a defence, whether self-defence, lack of intent, or the partial defences of diminished responsibility or of loss of control. This Court recognised this in *R v Peters* 2005 EWCA Crim 605, 2 Cr App R (S) 101 (p 627), but only in the context of a defendant who accepts, and makes clear early that he accepts, responsibility for the killing, see para 19…A third case which is sometimes treated as meriting exceptional treatment is the exceptionally long and complex trial, whether in fraud or otherwise (such as people trafficking, complex drug cases and serial sex abuse cases with many complainants). Since the rationale of reduction for plea is the public benefit which we have described, we leave open the possibility that in some such cases, unusually, some considerable benefits may well ensue from a plea of guilty even at a late stage. Care must, however, be taken with such a proposition so that it does not become routine. If it does, then the incentive to focus on plea at an early stage is lost, and it becomes impossible to maintain proper parity between late-pleading defendants and those who indicate their guilt at the right time.

R v Creathorne 2014 EWCA Crim 500, 2 Cr App R (S) 48 (p 382) D pleaded to death by careless driving. He was interviewed three months after the accident. D said he was suffering from amnesia but made no comment. He pleaded not guilty at his PCMH and was treated later as still suffering from amnesia. He pleaded shortly after, following the service of the collision report, toxicology evidence and a report on D's tyres. The Judge decided that D was only entitled to a 25% discount. D appealed, arguing he was entitled to a full discount as he had been suffering from amnesia and had thus pleaded at the first opportunity having received legal advice. Held. In *R v Caley* 2012 EWCA Crim 2821 it was held that, against the backdrop of a need for consistency in sentencing discounts, the determination of the 'first reasonable opportunity' was a matter for the sentencing judge and he or she had a residual discretion to treat cases individually. The Court in *R v Caley* also recognised the need to avoid an investigation into every case and slow down the administration of justice. Following this approach, the Judge determined that the first reasonable opportunity was at the PCMH. The central question is therefore at what point in time was the advice given to D? D's amnesia at his PCMH meant his ability to form a considered decision as to his plea depended upon the ability of his legal advisers to review sufficient evidence to proffer sensible advice. In cases such as this, legal advisors should ordinarily be entitled to see all the material evidence before advising their client. What the material evidence will be will vary from case to case. In this case, the Judge did not analyse what evidence was available to D's legal advisers. A court should also normally be slow to go against the professional judgment of legal advisers where they say there is relevant evidence they have not had sight of. D should have received a full one-third discount.

R v Evans 2014 EWCA Crim 1916 D pleaded to murder and was sentenced to a minimum term of 22 years. A number of psychiatric reports were prepared on D, who pleaded guilty after the PCMH but three weeks before trial. D never denied the facts surrounding the offence, the only issue was the availability of the defence of diminished responsibility. As soon as it was confirmed following the medical evidence that D could not run that defence, he pleaded guilty. The Judge began with a starting point of 25 years and afforded D credit of 3 years. Held. There was no good reason to deny D the full credit for his plea, which he had intimated as soon as he was advised he had no diminished responsibility defence. Full one-sixth credit given.

R v Markham and Edwards 2017 EWCA Crim 739 Double murder case. For M, a report which arrived shortly before the day the case was listed for trial said he had no defence based on diminished responsibility. E's report, which said she did have such a defence, was rejected by the jury. Both were aged 14. Held. It is hard to see why they should have different sentences. One-sixth off (3½ years) not 1 year.

For more details, see **287.27** in Volume 2.

See also the ***Defence request reports*** para at **65.18**.

65.17 *Co-defendant, Giving evidence to help a*

R v Lawless 1998 2 Cr App R (S) 176 D pleaded to affray and his co-defendant was convicted of the same offence. D gave evidence for him. The Judge sentenced them both to 21 months, saying that D had thrown his credit away because the jury must have found his evidence to be lies and it was wholly discredited. Held. It is important that a co-defendant should not be inhibited from giving evidence. He was entitled to a discount, so 15 months instead.

R v Hickman 2000 2 Cr App R (S) 171 (p 176) D made a late plea of guilty to robbery and his co-defendant pleaded not guilty and was convicted of the same offence. D gave evidence for him. The Judge took his lies into account and sentenced them both to the same sentence. Held. The principle in *R v Lawless* 1998 has to be applied. 3½ years not 4.

R v Abdul and Others 2013 EWCA Crim 926 M and Ab were convicted of robbery and possession of a firearm with intent to commit robbery. H pleaded guilty to the same. H later gave evidence in support of M and Ab for which the Judge reduced his credit from ⅓ to ¼. Held. H's sentence was factually based on the Crown's case and when he pleaded, he had not tendered a basis of plea nor any mitigation with an intention mendaciously to reduce his culpability and avoid being sentenced on a full facts basis. The later evidence given was not designed to reduce his sentence, but to assist his co-defendants at their trial. If H was guilty of perjury, then the appropriate course was to deal with that allegation separately and not to reduce credit for a plea which would have otherwise attracted a maximum discount.

R v Wilson 2018 EWCA Crim 449, 2 Cr App R (S) 7 (p 55) D pleaded to class A drug supply offences. The Judge said D was entitled to a full plea discount, but because he had given lying evidence for his drug dealing co-defendant, D was going to receive no plea discount. Held. The authorities establish that: i) as a matter of principle it is wrong to reduce or remove credit for plea solely because the defendant has given lying evidence in support of another in a trial, and ii) that may be different if the evidence is relied upon by way of a dishonest pre-sentence attempt to reduce the defendant's own culpability. We agree that this case falls into principle i). That would normally mean we would reduce the sentence from 6 years to 4 years. However, the Judge should have made the sentence concurrent to the sentence D was serving, so we don't reduce the sentence as that would be unjust. Appeal dismissed.

See also: *R v Mohammed* 2017 EWCA Crim 655 (D pleaded and gave evidence for his co-defendant. Held. D did not try to reduce his role. The fact he was disbelieved is no reason to reduce the full discount for his plea.)

65.18 *Defence requests reports*
R v Murphy 2013 EWCA Crim 1951 D changed his plea to guilty to reckless arson. He set fire to his ex-partner's home. At the hearings on 21 December 2012 and 28 February 2013 a psychiatrist's report about D's fitness to plead was not available. On 5 March 2013, at the adjourned PCMH, D changed his plea. The Judge reduced D's discount to reflect the fact that the plea was made at the PCMH. Held. There were real issues as to whether he was fit to plead. It was only after the report was served that an informed view about D's fitness to plead could be taken. The PCMH was the first reasonable opportunity for a plea to be entered. Full discount substituted.
R v Port 2013 EWCA Crim 2668, 2014 2 Cr App R (S) 26 (p 203) D pleaded (at his PCMH) to ABH and possession of an offensive weapon. The Judge gave him reduced credit as he considered that the PCMH was not the earliest opportunity. The defence appealed contending that D had wished to see CCTV footage before entering his plea, so the PCMH was the first reasonable opportunity. Held. The Early Guilty Plea Scheme does not permit a defendant to delay admitting his guilt in order to see whether or not his criminality is revealed in film footage. D knew he had delivered an unlawful blow and was carrying an offensive weapon. Therefore to suggest that he was entitled to delay entering his plea so as to watch the film of the incident in which he had participated is an untenable suggestion.

65.19 *Defendant accepts guilt but challenges the offence particulars*
R v Papworth 2019 EWCA Crim 61 D 'admitted five charges' at the Magistrates' Court. For two he accepted guilt but said the dates were wrong. He did not plead. The matter was committed for trial. The Judge gave D only 25% credit for the two he had not pleaded to at the Magistrates' Court. Held. D was right not to plead, as the dates were wrong. D was entitled to full credit for all the counts.
Note: As one of the counts was rape, I am not sure the judgment properly distinguishes between an indication of guilt and a plea. Ed.

65.20 *Defendant changes his plea*
R v Collins 2018 EWCA Crim 2238 In October 2017, a week before his trial for sex offences, D pleaded guilty. The victim, V, was aged 12 when the offences were committed in 2015. D then changed his legal representatives and sought to vacate his pleas. The case had to be transferred to another Crown Court where a judge did not know his former legal representatives. His plea application was refused. In June 2018, D was sentenced to 8 years. V explained in her impact statement the roller-coaster of emotions and prolonged agony that D's plea application had caused her. The Judge said he would have given 10% for the pleas but because of the application, the discount would have been negligible, so he gave no discount. Held. The 10% discount was correct. We do not underestimate the effect the plea application had on V, but D should have had some discount. We give 5%.

65.21 *Defendant could have admitted matter earlier*
R v G 2016 EWCA Crim 541, 2 Cr App R (S) 17 (p 152) D pleaded to three historical rapes and other sex offences committed against his daughter, V. With a full discount the Judge gave him 16 years. Later the Judge varied the sentence to 18 years by reducing the discount for the guilty plea because D could have admitted the matter earlier. V had made complaints against D in 1987 (D denied it, no proceedings), in 1996 (plea to lesser sex offence than rape) and in 1999 (when she tried to make D admit it). Held. The Judge was not entitled to increase the sentence because D had refused to admit his offending earlier. Original sentence restored.

65.22 *What is the first reasonable opportunity to indicate a plea/Offence admitted in interview*

Reduction in Sentence for a Guilty Plea Guideline 2017, see www.banksr.com Other Matters Guidelines tab In force 1 June 2017 page 4

The guilty plea should be considered by the court to be independent of the offender's personal mitigation.

- Factors such as admissions at interview, co-operation with the investigation and demonstrations of remorse should **not** be taken into account in determining the level of reduction. Rather, they should be considered separately and prior to any guilty plea reduction, as potential mitigating factors.

page 5 **D. DETERMINING THE LEVEL OF REDUCTION**

D1. Plea indicated at the first stage of the proceedings

Where a guilty plea is indicated at the first stage of proceedings a reduction of one-third should be made (subject to the exceptions in section F). The first stage will normally be the first hearing at which a plea or indication of plea is sought and recorded by the court.[882]

For the full section, see **65.4**.

R v Price 2018 EWCA Crim 1784, 2019 1 Cr App R (S) 24 (p 166) LCJ D pleaded to burglary and other offences. In interview he admitted the burglary. At the Magistrates' Court, D gave no indication of plea. He pleaded at the PTPH and was given a 25% discount. The Judge thought much of the defendant's account at the interview was a "complete cock 'n' bull story". Held. The first available opportunity to indicate the plea was at the Magistrates' Court. That wasn't done. We apply the guideline. The admission in interview could be taken into account with the personal mitigation, but the Judge was entitled to ignore it because of his comments. Appeal dismissed.

65.23 *Defendant makes pre-plea applications/appeals*

R v Ward 2005 EWCA Crim 1926, 2006 1 Cr App R (S) 66 (p 356) D was involved in a missing trader VAT fraud. He maintained a not guilty plea to cheating the public revenue while his counsel argued a point of law. The legal point failed and he pleaded guilty. Held. He was not entitled to full credit for his plea, which was late, even though he was being advised in relation to matters of law.

See also: *R v Chaytor* 2011 EWCA Crim 929 (LCJ MP's false expenses claims. Plea after appeal to Court of Appeal and Supreme Court and abuse application. No indication given before or during appeal and application. The discount could have been less than the 25% given.)

65.24 *Defendant seeks Goodyear indication*

R v Hackney 2013 EWCA Crim 1156, 2014 1 Cr App R (S) 41 (p 235) The Judge was wrong to take into account the *Goodyear* indication when considering the plea discount.

65.25 *Defendant's limited plea rejected Defendant pleads*

R v Gunning 2013 EWCA Crim 179 D pleaded to ABH (×2) and criminal damage. He offered a basis of plea which was rejected. He subsequently abandoned the basis of plea and pleaded on full facts. The Judge gave him 25% credit. Held. The Judge did not have the benefit of the decision in *R v Caley and Others* 2012 EWCA Crim 2821, 2013 2 Cr App R (S) 47 (p 305) as to the first reasonable opportunity. D did all that was required of him under the provisions of the Early Guilty Plea Scheme and was therefore entitled to expect to receive full credit.

Note: The part relied on in *R v Caley* 2012 is at para 18, which states that the important time is when you indicate your plea. Ed.

R v James 2015 EWCA Crim 2124 D pleaded to wounding with intent and other offences. He put forward a basis of plea nearly four months later and withdrew it 17 days

[882] In cases where (in accordance with the Criminal Procedure Rules) a defendant is given the opportunity to enter a guilty plea without attending a court hearing, doing so within the required time limits will constitute a plea at the first stage of proceedings.

later. About a month later he was sentenced. The Judge said the basis of plea was wholly unfounded once the evidence was given. He gave 20% for the plea. Held. Here witnesses were not inconvenienced and very little time and effort [was spent on this]. We don't say the service and withdrawal of a basis of plea should never be taken into account, but here D should have received a maximum discount.
See also: *R v Stokes and Stokes* 2012 EWCA Crim 612, 2 Cr App R (S) 92 (p 55) (The opposite result to the above case, which can be taken to have been superceded because the case was decided before the recent changes.)

65.26 *Defendant's personal mitigation*
Reduction in Sentence for a Guilty Plea Guideline 2017, see www.banksr.com Other Matters Guidelines tab In force 1 June 2017 page 4 para B The guilty plea should be considered by the court to be independent of the offender's personal mitigation. Factors such as admissions at interview, co-operation with the investigation and demonstrations of remorse should not be taken into account in determining the level of reduction. Rather, they should be considered separately and prior to any guilty plea reduction, as potential mitigating factors.

65.27 *Offer to plead rejected Convicted of that count/Plea later accepted*
Reduction in Sentence for a Guilty Plea Guideline 2017, see www.banksr.com Other Matters Guidelines tab In force 1 June 2017 page 7
See also: *R v Ali* 2018 EWCA Crim 111, 1 Cr App R (S) 53 (p 413) (On the first day of D's murder trial, the prosecution added a manslaughter count. D offered to plead to it as an alternative to murder. The offer was rejected. D pleaded not guilty to it. He was aged 16. D was acquitted of murder and convicted of manslaughter. The Judge held the refusal to plead was a tactical decision. Held. There is a discretion to give credit. There was no good reason not to plead. The Judge was entitled to give no credit.)
F. EXCEPTIONS
F1.-F2. [not relevant]
F3. Offender convicted of a lesser or different offence
If an offender is convicted of a lesser or different offence from that originally charged, and has earlier made an unequivocal indication of a guilty plea to this lesser or different offence to the prosecution and the court, the court should give the level of reduction that is appropriate to the stage in the proceedings at which this indication of plea (to the lesser or different offence) was made taking into account any other of these exceptions that apply. In the Crown Court where the offered plea is a permissible alternative on the indictment as charged, the offender will not be treated as having made an unequivocal indication unless the offender has entered that plea.
Att-Gen's Ref Nos 33-34 of 2001 2001 EWCA Crim 1908, 2002 1 Cr App R (S) 92 (p 400) Before their murder trial the defendants offered to plead to manslaughter. The offer was rejected and there was no plea to manslaughter. They contested the trial on the basis of presence. Held. The Judge was right to have regard to that, but he could not give as much credit to it as he would have been able to do had it in fact been tendered.
R v Bertram 2003 EWCA Crim 2026, 2004 1 Cr App R (S) 27 (p 185) D offered to plead to manslaughter, and the prosecution rejected the offer. His defence put forward at his trial for murder was inconsistent with a plea to manslaughter. The jury convicted him of manslaughter. The Judge refused to give him any credit for his offer. Held. He should have some credit for his offer. It was unrealistic for him to plead guilty to manslaughter at the beginning of the trial.
R v Dickinson 2009 EWCA Crim 2119, 2010 1 Cr App R (S) 93 (p 596) D offered to plead to section 20 at the PCMH but the offer was not accepted for about 4 months. The Judge declined to give D full credit. Held. He should have been given full credit.
R v Birt 2010 EWCA Crim 2823 D offered to plead to manslaughter but the offer was rejected. The jury acquitted her of murder and convicted her of manslaughter. The Judge gave no credit for the offer to plead. Held. If in a homicide case a) the defendant offers

to plead guilty to manslaughter, b) that offer is rejected by the prosecution, c) the defendant pleads not guilty to any offence before the jury, and d) the defendant is ultimately convicted of manslaughter, then it is a matter for the discretion of the judge whether to give any and, if so, what credit for the earlier offer of a plea. If there was good reason for the defendant not to renew his plea of guilty before the jury then, generally, some credit should be given for the earlier offer. If there was no good reason for the defendant's failure to renew his plea of guilty before the jury, then generally no credit should be given for the earlier offer. Here D had no viable defence to manslaughter. Her defence to the murder would not have been undermined by a plea to manslaughter. There was no good reason for her not to renew her plea before the jury so she was not entitled to a discount.

R v Ahmad 2010 EWCA Crim 2882 D pleaded to a complex fraud indictment. Early on D indicated a willingness to plead to substantive counts but not to the conspiracy counts. The offer was rejected. On the day of trial the offer was repeated and accepted. The Judge gave 20% for the plea. Held. [In essence] they pleaded at the first opportunity so a full discount substituted.

R v Rainford 2010 EWCA Crim 3220, 2011 2 Cr App R (S) 15 (p 88) D was convicted of manslaughter by reason of provocation. D offered a plea to manslaughter by reason of provocation, but the plea was rejected by the Crown. D advanced a defence of self-defence. Held. When a plea is offered, rejected and not entered, the court has to ask itself whether there was a good reason for not entering the plea. If there is an issue of causation which can only be solved by medical evidence, that would be a good reason for putting the prosecution to proof and not entering the plea. If, however, a defendant is faced with an overwhelming case on murder and seeks to put the prosecution to proof of all the ingredients of the offence, in the hope that he may be acquitted altogether or may have a tactical advantage in the trial of the real issue, provocation, he may well find himself in a position where the judge is entitled to afford him no credit for the offered plea. Here the only issue was provocation. There was no good reason for not entering a plea so no credit was due.

R v Rawson 2013 EWCA Crim 9, 2 Cr App R (S) 59 (p 379) D offered to plead to manslaughter at his PCMH. The offer was rejected then and again later. On the first day of trial the offer was repeated and again rejected. D had still not entered a plea. The trial for murder started on the basis of self-defence and was aborted because some new information was produced. Next day the prosecution accepted the earlier offer and D pleaded to manslaughter based on loss of control. The Judge said he could have pleaded earlier and had chosen not to do so and gave no plea discount. Held. D was keeping all options open. There was therefore no good reason why the plea was not entered before. The Judge was entitled not to give credit for the early offer to plead. However, D was entitled to credit for the plea when made. 7 years not 8.

See also: *R v Wilson* 2013 EWCA Crim 830, 2014 1 Cr App R (S) 19 (p 110) (Convicted of alternative count of ABH. Acquitted of attempted section 18. Always offered to plead if more serious charge dropped. Guilt on lesser charge not contested. Held. We discourage tactical not guilty pleas. Those who conduct cases like this should expect no credit.)

For ***Newton hearing, Defendant takes part in etc.***, see the **FACTUAL BASIS FOR SENTENCING** ***Newton hearing Loss of guilty plea credit*** para at **57.77**.

65.28 *False mitigation*

R v Martin 2006 EWCA Crim 1035, 2007 1 Cr App R (S) 3 (p 14) When mitigating, counsel claimed in a class A importation case that the defendant thought that the drug was cannabis at the time of importation. This was contrary to what was said in the pre-sentence report. Counsel declined the offer of a *Newton* hearing to decide the issue. There was nothing to suggest that the Judge made a reduction for the suggestion. Held. The Judge was entitled to make a slight reduction for the rejected mitigation plea.

R v Burns 2010 EWCA Crim 1413 D pleaded at an early stage and gave a false account to the probation service. He put forward a basis of plea which had to be amended. The Judge gave him 20% not 33%. Held. He was entitled to full credit.

R v Wendt 2015 EWCA Crim 2241, 2016 1 Cr App R (S) 53 (p 339) D pleaded to harassment. He had a series of relevant and recent harassment and public order offence previous convictions. The pre-sentence report said that D had told the writer he had been in the Royal Marines and had been discharged on health grounds due to shrapnel in his leg and post-traumatic stress disorder (PTSD) following an incident when his fellow Marines had been killed. Further he had undergone counselling through the armed forces but his alcohol consumption had escalated. In light of these factors, the Court deferred sentence. At the deferred hearing, D did not attend. The Court heard that D had not completed his basic training with the Marines and did not suffer from PTSD. As a result of misleading the Court, his credit for his plea would be reduced. Held. If the Court had known the truth it would not have deferred sentence. There should be no reflection in the punishment for the instant offence for D's deception, just a reduction in the credit for the plea.

See also: *R v Roach* 2015 EWCA Crim 1490 (Plea by D given at preliminary hearing. Judge reduced credit to 25% because he did not believe D had been beaten by others as he had claimed and he had gone on the run. Full credit given.)

See also the **Perverting the Course of Justice** ***Mitigation, Bogus*** para at **302.22** in Volume 2.

65.29 ***False mitigation Minimising culpability/Lying to the court causing adjournments etc.***

R v Duncan 2005 EWCA Crim 3594, 2006 2 Cr App R (S) 28 (p 189) D pleaded early to causing death by dangerous driving. At Court he invented a favourable factual background which had to be checked. The doctor attended and his account was found to be untrue. The Judge reduced the discount for the plea to 12.5% because of the untruths and lack of candour. Held. The doctor had been hampered by D's lack of disclosure. The 12.5% discount was entirely justified. He had embarked on a thoroughly discreditable attempt to minimise his culpability.

R v Robinson 2009 EWCA Crim 450, 2 Cr App R (S) 79 (p 532) D indicated a plea to causing death by dangerous driving early. When arrested 7 hours after the offence he said that he had not drunk since the offence. In interview he repeated that account twice. With backtracking,[883] the expert thought D had drunk more than four pints of lager. According to the pre-sentence report, he said that he had drunk four pints before the accident and two after. The Judge said that he did not accept that and considered that he had drunk more than four pints before the accident. He offered D a *Newton* hearing. D declined the offer. The Judge said that he was giving 25% discount rather than full credit because "There has been a contest as to the facts and I have rejected it. You sought to minimise the amount of alcohol that you drank." Held. We do not say that a judge cannot take account of a change in story advanced in a pre-sentence report, nor do we say that the Judge was not entitled to take the view he did. Bearing in mind the change of account was not persisted in and was expressly abandoned, there should be full credit.

65.30 ***Overwhelming prosecution case/Defendant caught red-handed***

Reduction in Sentence for a Guilty Plea Guideline 2017, see www.banksr.com Other Matters Guidelines tab page 4 para B The benefits [of an early guilty plea] apply regardless of the strength of the evidence against an offender. The strength of the evidence should not be taken into account when determining the level of reduction.

---

[883] 'Backtracking' is calculating the alcohol level at the time of the accident by using the alcohol reading with an estimate for how much the body absorbs alcohol in between the two times.

The judicial decision

65.31 *Judge must determine when plea entered*

R v Thompson 2012 EWCA Crim 1431 We must stress how important it is for a judge to ascertain whether or not the plea was in fact entered at the first reasonable opportunity.

65.32 *Judicial indications must be kept*

R v Schofield 2013 EWCA Crim 1452 D pleaded to possession with intent at his second PCMH. There was no indication of plea in interview or at the Magistrates' Court. At the first appearance at the Crown Court, D asked for an adjournment so DNA evidence could be analysed. At the next appearance, he pleaded and the Judge said D would receive the maximum credit for the plea. The case was adjourned for reports. At the sentence hearing, the Judge held that his plea was not at the first opportunity and gave D only 25% credit. Held. D was not entitled to the full discount. However, because of the unequivocal statement about discount by the first Judge, D should receive it, so 28 months not 32.

See also: *R v Hankey and Owen* 2012 EWCA Crim 2766 (Pleas to cannabis production and possession with intent to supply. First Judge at time of plea indicated that full credit would be given. Second Judge gave one full credit and the other 20%. Fairness dictates that the indication is adhered to. Full credit given.)

See also: *R v Claydon and Another* 2015 EWCA Crim 140, 1 Cr App R (S) 71 (p 496) (We honour the indication given by the first Judge to C. D is not in as good a position as C. However, so there is no sense of grievance, full discount for him as well.)

65.33 *Judge should warn if reducing discount for guilty plea*

R v Wasden and Others 2010 EWCA Crim 2423 Twelve defendants pleaded to violent disorder involving a fight on a train between two groups. The incident was clearly shown on CCTV. At the PCMH, the Judge offered a full discount. A different Judge gave only 10-15%. Held. para 49 It is important where a judge is considering a reduced discount that counsel are told so submissions can be made. Substantial reductions to the sentences made.

65.34 *State that the sentence has been discounted, Judge must*

Criminal Justice Act 2003 s 174(7)[884] Where, as a result of taking into account any matter referred to in Criminal Justice Act 2003 s 144(1) (guilty pleas), the court imposes a punishment on the offender which is less severe than the punishment it would otherwise have imposed, the court must state that fact.

Reduction in Sentence for a Guilty Plea Guideline 2007, see www.banksr.com Other Matters Guidelines tab para 3.1 The court should usually state what the sentence would have been if there had been no reduction.

Note: This guideline has been replaced, but the guidance remains in force. Ed.

R v P 2004 EWCA Crim 287, 2 Cr App R (S) 63 (p 343) It has been said more than once, see *R v Fearon* 1996 2 Cr App R (S) 25 and *R v Aroride* 1999 2 Cr App R (S) 406, that it is highly desirable that a sentencing judge in every case makes it absolutely plain to a defendant that he has been given credit for his plea. Otherwise there is a possibility that the plea will not have been taken into consideration.

See also: *R v Bishop* 2000 1 Cr App R (S) 89 (p 432)

65.35 *State that the sentence has been discounted, Judge fails to*

R v Joyce 2017 EWCA Crim 647, 2 Cr App R (S) 24 (p 186) D pleaded to manslaughter. It was unclear what the discount for the plea was. Held. That was unfortunate. There has been a large degree of speculation about that. We will conduct the sentencing exercise afresh. 27 years was the right figure before plea discount. With a full discount that makes a 9-year minimum term, as the Judge ordered.

---

[884] As amended by Legal Aid, Sentencing and Punishment of Offenders Act 2012 s 64

65.36 ***Counsel can ask what the discount was***

R v Webb and Clark 2011 EWCA Crim 882 D pleaded to supplying cocaine and other counts. The evidence was from undercover officers. There were nine days of disclosure, anonymity for witnesses, entrapment etc. arguments. They failed and the defendant pleaded. The Judge said he was going to give a reduced discount for the plea. After the sentence one counsel for the defendants asked how much the discount had been reduced by. The Judge declined to say. Held. That was a legitimate request which the Judge should have responded to.

65.37 ***Exactly the right discount, Entitlement to***

R v Clough 2009 EWCA Crim 1669, 2010 1 Cr App R (S) 53 (p 334) D pleaded to conspiracy to export 337 kilos of cocaine. The Judge started at 26 years. D received 18 years. Held. Had the Judge not explicitly promised a full one-third discount we would not have amended the sentence by a small amount. As he did, we amend it to 17 years 4 months.

R v Payne 2010 EWCA Crim 1823 D pleaded at the first available opportunity. The Judge said had he not pleaded she would have given him 24 months. She then gave D 18 months. Held. D was entitled to a full discount so 16 months not 18.

R v High 2018 EWCA Crim 499 (9½ years' extended sentence (5½ years' custody 4 years' extended licence) given. In fact, with full discount the custodial term should have been 5 years 4 months. Fresh counsel spotted the error nearly two years after sentence. Prosecution conceded the point. Almost three years after the sentence was imposed, with no counsel attending, the correct sentence was substituted.[885])

R v Paul and Others 2019 EWCA Crim 476 The Judge gave 7% plea discount. He made the discount 1 month whereas it should have been 3 months. Held. This Court does not normally make such a small adjustment, but it is appropriate to do so.

See also: *R v Goodale* 2013 EWCA Crim 1144, 2014 1 Cr App R (S) 37 (p 220) (Given 7 years as a minimum sentence in a drugs case with the full 20% off for plea. The defendant was entitled to the exact figure even if it was expressed in days, so 5 years and 219 days not 5 years and 8 months, which was 24 days more.)

R v Gould 2013 EWCA Crim 1434 (As the Judge said 14 years with full discount, the defendant was entitled to 9 years 4 months not 9½ years.)

Appeals

65.38 ***Advice Poor advice about discount and appeals***

R v Caley and Others 2012 EWCA Crim 2821, 2013 2 Cr App R (S) 47 (p 305) para 28 We consider appeals based on the defendant receiving poor advice. Poor advice, if clearly demonstrated, might be relevant to the issue of first reasonable opportunity, especially in the case of a young or inexperienced defendant in need of advice. It is, however, likely that before a defendant could satisfy the judge that it was right to proceed on the basis of poor advice, he would have to consider optional full waiver of privilege. That is because the question may well be raised what (if anything) he was telling his lawyers about his actions.

66 Home Detention Curfew Scheme

66.1

Criminal Justice Act 2003 s 246, 250 and 253 as amended

Home Detention Curfew (HDC) enables prisoners to be released early with a curfew and whilst wearing a tag. Not all prisoners are eligible (see **66.3** to **66.5**). Some prisoners are 'presumed unsuitable' (see **66.6**), but they can be released on HDC if they show there are exceptional circumstances. Release, which is discretionary, is also dependent on there

885 I was counsel in the case. I have added facts that are not included in the judgment.

being a residence with electricity. The prisoner is subject to the scheme until he or she would have been released from prison under Criminal Justice Act 2003 s 243A(2) and Criminal Justice Act 2003 s 244(1).

Court Martial Those serving a sentence of imprisonment imposed by a Court Martial may be eligible for HDC. However, if they have not been dismissed from the armed forces, they cannot nominate service quarters as a suitable address for release because there will not be 24-hour access to those supervising the scheme.

Extended disqualification When determining extended disqualification, the Home Detention Curfew Scheme should not be a factor, see *R v Needham and Others* 2016 EWCA Crim 455, 2 Cr App R (S) 26 (p 219) at **41.16**.

66.2 *Statutory provisions*

Criminal Justice Act 2003 s 246(1) Subject to subsections (2) to (4), the Secretary of State may:

(a) release on licence under this section a fixed-term prisoner at any time during the period of 135 days ending with the day on which the prisoner will have served the requisite custodial period.

66.3 *Eligibility Length of sentence*

Criminal Justice Act 2003 s 246(2) Subsection (1)(a) does not apply in relation to a prisoner unless:

(a) the length of the requisite custodial period is at least 6 weeks…

Note: The requisite custodial period for both sentences of less than 12 months and 12 months or more is one half, see Criminal Justice Act 2003 s 243A(3) and Criminal Justice Act 2003 s 244(3). Therefore for a prisoner to be eligible for release on HDC, the minimum length of sentence is 12 weeks. Ed.

66.4 *Eligibility Minimum period to be served*

Criminal Justice Act 2003 s 246(2) Subsection (1)(a) does not apply in relation to a prisoner unless:…

(b) he has served:

(i) at least 4 weeks of [the requisite custodial] period, and

(ii) at least one-half of [the requisite custodial] period.

Note: Therefore, the minimum period in all cases is 28 days and will in most cases be half of the requisite custodial period. Ed.

66.5 *Those not eligible for release on HDC*

Criminal Justice Act 2003 s 246(4)[886] Subsection (1) does not apply where:

(a) the sentence is imposed under section 226A, 227 or 228 [extended sentences],

(aa) the sentence is for a term of 4 years or more,

(b) the sentence is for an offence under Prisoners (Return to Custody) Act 1995 s 1,

(c) the prisoner is subject to a hospital order, hospital direction or transfer direction under Mental Health Act 1983 s 37, 45A or 47,

(d) the sentence was imposed by virtue of Schedule 8 para 9(1)(b) or (c) or 10(1)(b) or (c) in a case where the prisoner has failed to comply with a curfew requirement of a community order,

(e) the prisoner is subject to the notification requirements of Sexual Offences Act 2003 Part 2,

(f) the prisoner is liable to removal from the United Kingdom,

(g) the prisoner has been released on licence under this section at any time, and has been recalled to prison under section 255(1)(a) (and the revocation has not been cancelled under section 255(3)),

[886] As amended by Legal Aid, Sentencing and Punishment of Offenders Act 2012 s 110(9), 112, Sch 10 para 23 and Sch 14 para 7

(ga) the prisoner has at any time been released on licence under Criminal Justice Act 1991 s 34A and has been recalled to prison under Criminal Justice Act 2003 s 38A(1)(a) (and the revocation of the licence has not been cancelled under Criminal Justice Act 2003 s 38A(3)),[887]
(h) the prisoner has been released on licence under section 248 during the currency of the sentence, and has been recalled to prison under section 254,
(ha) the prisoner has at any time been returned to prison under Criminal Justice Act 1991 s 40 or Powers of Criminal Courts (Sentencing) Act 2000 s 116, or
(i) in the case of a prisoner to whom section 240ZA applies or a direction under section 240A relates, the interval between the date on which the sentence was passed and the date on which the prisoner will have served the requisite custodial period is less than 14 days.

66.6 *Those 'presumed unsuitable' for release on HDC*

Note: There is a list in prison instructions PSI 43/2012 Annex B of examples of current offences for which prisoners will be presumed unsuitable for release on HDC. Annex B replaces the list in PSI 3½003 Annex A. Where a prisoner is serving sentences for more than one offence, and one of the offences attracts the presumption, the prisoner will be presumed unsuitable for HDC. Prisoners presumed unsuitable must show that there are exceptional circumstances in order to be considered for release. Ed.

66.7 *Two or more terms of imprisonment*

Criminal Justice Act 2003 s 246(4) Subsection (1) does not apply where:.. aa) the sentence is for a term of 4 years or more.
Criminal Justice Act 2003 s 246(4ZA) Where subsection (4)(aa) applies to a prisoner who is serving two or more terms of imprisonment, the reference to the term of the sentence is:
(a) if the terms are partly concurrent, a reference to the period which begins when the first term begins and ends when the last term ends,
(b) if the terms are to be served consecutively, a reference to the aggregate of the terms.

66.8 *Licence conditions*

Criminal Justice Act 2003 s 250(4) Any licence under this chapter in respect of a prisoner serving a sentence of imprisonment or detention in a Young Offender Institution (including a sentence imposed under Criminal Justice Act 2003 s 226A or 227) or any sentence of detention under Powers of Criminal Courts (Sentencing) Act 2000 s 91 (detention) or 96 (detention in YOI) or Criminal Justice Act 2003 s 226A or 226B (new extended sentences) or section 227 or 228 (old extended sentences):
(a) must include the standard conditions, and
(b) may include:
(i) any condition authorised by Criminal Justice and Court Services Act 2000 s 62 or 64, and
(ii) such other conditions of a kind prescribed by the Secretary of State for the purposes of this paragraph as the Secretary of State may for the time being specify in the licence.
Note: For full details see PSI 40/2012, which details the three licence templates: (a) all-purpose for 12 months or more, (b) under 12 months for those aged 18+, and (c) under 12 months for those aged under 18. Ed.

66.9 *Curfew*

Criminal Justice Act 2003 s 250(5) A licence under section 246 must also include a curfew condition complying with section 253.

[887] As inserted by Criminal Justice and Courts Act 2015 s 15(4). In force 13/4/15, Criminal Justice and Courts Act 2015 (Commencement No 1, Saving and Transitional Provisions) Order 2015 2015/778 para 3 and Sch 1 para 11

Criminal Justice Act 2003 s 253(1) For the purposes of this chapter, a curfew condition is a condition which:

(a) requires the released person to remain, for periods for the time being specified in the condition, at a place for the time being so specified (which may be premises approved by the Secretary of State under Offender Management Act 2007 s 13), and
(b) includes requirements for securing the electronic monitoring of his whereabouts during the periods for the time being so specified.

(2) The curfew condition may specify different places or different periods for different days, but may not specify periods which amount to less than 9 hours in any one day (excluding for this purpose the first and last days of the period for which the condition is in force).
(3) The curfew condition is to remain in force until the date when the released person would (but for his release) fall to be released unconditionally under section 243A or on licence under section 244.
Criminal Justice Act 2003 s 253(5) The curfew condition must include provision for making a person responsible for monitoring the released person's whereabouts during the periods for the time being specified in the condition; and a person who is made so responsible shall be of a description specified in an order made by the Secretary of State.

66.10 ***Foreign nationals who are not eligible***
R v Al-Buhairi 2003 EWCA Crim 2922, 2004 1 Cr App R (S) 83 (p 496) There is no certainty as to the release of any defendant. This is far too speculative an area. We are not persuaded that any allowance should be made.

66.11 ***Don't consider HDC when determining the sentence***
R v Alkazraji 2004 2 Cr App R (S) 55 (p 291) LCJ The Judge wanted the defendant released before she had her baby. He thought that there was every prospect that she would be tagged. However, in prison she tested positive for drugs. Held. In general it is inappropriate for a judge to take into account the possibility, the likelihood or the almost certainty that the defendant will be released under a tagging or residential order. There is always a degree of uncertainty. Pass the appropriate sentence and do not take into account administrative arrangements.
R v Round and Dunn 2009 EWCA Crim 2667, 2010 2 Cr App R (S) 45 (p 292) The Court considered the various anomalies of the curfew scheme, HDC, which depended on how the sentence was constructed. In particular, there is a problem when the defendant has two consecutive sentences, which means there is a different release date depending on which sentence is served first. Held. The general principle that early release, licence and their various ramifications should be left out of account is of some importance. There is another problem if the HDC rules change during the sentence. It is not incumbent on sentencers to alter the ordinary manner of expressing their sentences to maximise the uncertain possibilities of HDC. It is not wrong in principle for a judge to refuse to consider early release possibilities when calculating his sentence or framing the manner or order in which they are expressed to be imposed. It is neither necessary nor practicable to undertake such examinations, although there may be particular cases in which an unusual course is justified.
See also: *R v Dale* 2004 2 Cr App R (S) 58 (p 308) (Principle restated).
See also the **DEFENDANT** ***Release Don't take release into account when sentencing*** para at **242.54** in Volume 2.

67 HOSPITAL AND GUARDIANSHIP ORDERS

67.1
Mental Health Act 1983 s 37(1)
Availability, see the ***Power to order*** paras at **67.3** (Hospital Orders) and **67.40** (Guardianship Orders) below.

Children and young offenders The two orders and the interim orders are only available for those aged 16+, Mental Health Act 1983 s 37(2).
Description The Lord Chief Justice has given a comprehensive description of the various orders that are available when an offender suffers from a mental disorder, see *R v Vowles and Others* 2015 EWCA Crim 45, 2 Cr App R (S) 6 (p 39) para 9.
Victim surcharge There is no surcharge applicable for either a Hospital Order or a Guardianship Order.[888]
Release The First-tier Mental Health Tribunal determines release. The tribunal has a legal member, a medical member and a lay person. Application for release can be heard after six months from the date the order was made and every 12 months thereafter. Patients will automatically be referred to the tribunal if they have not applied within three years from the making of the order. For release from a Restriction Order, see **67.25**, for a Guardianship Order, see **67.39** and for a Hybrid Order, see **67.46**.
Rehabilitation period The rehabilitation period ends when the Hospital Order ceases to have effect.[889] Where a Hospital Order is made without a conviction under Mental Health Act 1983 s 37(3) (see **67.7**) the order is not subject to Rehabilitation of Offenders Act 1974 and so there is no rehabilitation period.[890]
See also the **REHABILITATION OF OFFENDERS ACT 1974** chapter.

HOSPITAL ORDERS

67.2 *Statistics England and Wales*

Hospital and Guardianship orders

Year	2012	2013	2014	2015	2016	2017
Hospital	415	440	424	392	389	341
Guardianship	7	6	4	1	5	4

For explanations about the statistics, see page 1-xii.

Power to order

67.3 *Power to order*

Mental Health Act 1983 s 37(1) Where a person is convicted of an offence punishable with imprisonment other than an offence the sentence for which is fixed by law, and the conditions mentioned in subsection (2) (see **67.8**) are satisfied, the court may by order authorise his admission to and detention in such hospital as may be specified in the order.
Mental Health Act 1983 s 37(8) For the purposes of this subsection 'sentence of imprisonment' includes any sentence or order for detention.
For ***Interim Hospital Orders***, see the **HOSPITAL ORDERS: INTERIM** chapter.

67.4 *Nature of a Hospital Order*

R v Vowles and Others 2015 EWCA Crim 45, 2 Cr App R (S) 6 (p 39) LCJ para 46 The Court in *R v Birch* 1989 11 Cr App R (S) 202 with great clarity set out the characteristics of a Hospital Order without a Restriction Order: "A Hospital Order is not a punishment. Questions of retribution and deterrence, whether personal or general, are immaterial. The offender who has become a patient is not kept on any kind of leash by the court, as he is when he consents to a probation order with a condition of inpatient treatment. The sole purpose of the order is to ensure that the offender receives the medical care and attention which he needs in the hope and expectation of course that the result will be to avoid the commission by the offender of further criminal acts."

[888] Criminal Justice Act 2003 s 161A-161B and Criminal Justice Act 2003 (Surcharge) Order 2012 2012/1696
[889] Rehabilitation of Offenders Act 1974 s 5(8)(d)
[890] *R (Singh) v Stratford Magistrates' Court* 2007 EWHC 1582 (Admin), 2008 1 Cr App R 2 (p 36) para 30

67.5 *European Convention on Human Rights*

R v Drew 2003 UKHL 25, 2004 1 Cr App R (S) 8 (p 65) Lords An order for implementing automatic life when a section 37 Hospital Order was wanted by the Judge was not incompatible with European Convention on Human Rights arts 3 and 5.

R (Singh) v Stratford Magistrates' Court 2007 EWHC 1582 (Admin), 2008 1 Cr App R 2 (p 36) High Court D pleaded not guilty to assaulting a police officer even though he had formally admitted the facts. A Hospital Order was made. Held. The making of a Hospital Order does not breach European Convention on Human Rights art 6.

For more details of the case, see **67.7**.

See also: *R v Vowles and Others* 2015 EWCA Crim 45, 2 Cr App R (S) 6 (p 39) (LCJ The fact that a prisoner transferred to hospital under Mental Health Act 1983 s 47 had to satisfy a hospital and a prison body before he or she could be released was compatible with art 5(4).)

67.6 *Minimum sentences, Hospital Orders and*

Powers of courts to order hospital admission or guardianship

Mental Health Act 1983 s 37(1A) In the case of an offence the sentence for which would otherwise fall to be imposed under:

(za) Prevention of Crime Act 1953 s 1(2B) or 1A(5),[891] [minimum sentences for threatening with an offensive weapon].

(a) Firearms Act 1968 s 51A(2) [minimum sentences for certain firearm offences],

(aa) Criminal Justice Act 1988 s 139(6B), 139A(5B) or 139AA(7),[892] [minimum sentences for threatening with a bladed article].

(b) Powers of Criminal Courts (Sentencing) Act 2000 s 110(2) [minimum sentences for third domestic burglary] or 111(2) [third class A trafficking offence],

(ba) Criminal Justice Act 2003 s 224A[893] [automatic life],

(c) Criminal Justice Act 2003 s 225(2) or 226(2) [dangerous offenders], or

(d) Violent Crime Reduction Act 2006 s 29(4) or (6) [minimum sentences in certain cases of using someone to mind a weapon],

nothing in those provisions shall prevent a court from making an order under subsection (1) above for the admission of the offender to a hospital.

(1B) References in subsection (1A) above to a sentence falling to be imposed under any of the provisions mentioned in that subsection are to be read in accordance with Criminal Justice Act 2003 s 305(4) [interpretation of Part 12, Sentencing section].

Criminal Justice Act 2003 s 305(4) For the purposes of this Part:

(za) a sentence falls to be imposed under Prevention of Crime Act 1953 s 1 (2B) or 1A(5) if it is required by that provision and the court is not of the opinion there mentioned,[894]

(a) a sentence falls to be imposed under Firearms Act 1968 s 51A(2) if it is required by that subsection and the court is not of the opinion there mentioned,

(aa) a sentence falls to be imposed under Criminal Justice Act 1988 s 139(6B), 139A(5B) or 139AA(7) if it is required by that provision and the court is not of the opinion there mentioned,[895]

(b) a sentence falls to be imposed under Powers of Criminal Courts (Sentencing) Act 2000 s 110(2) or 111(2) if it is required by that provision and the court is not of the opinion there mentioned,

---

[891] Inserted by Legal Aid, Sentencing and Punishment of Offenders Act 2012 Sch 26 para 2(2) and amended by Criminal Justice and Courts Act 2015 Sch 5 para 1(a)

[892] Inserted by Legal Aid, Sentencing and Punishment of Offenders Act 2012 Sch 26 para 2(3) and amended by Criminal Justice and Courts Act 2015 Sch 5 para 1(b)

[893] As inserted by Legal Aid, Sentencing and Punishment of Offenders Act 2012 Sch 19 para 1

[894] As amended by Criminal Justice and Courts Act 2015 Sch 5 para 16 (2)

[895] As amended by Criminal Justice and Courts Act 2015 Sch 5 para 16 (3)

(ba) a sentence falls to be imposed under Violent Crime Reduction Act 2006 s 29(4) or (6) if it is required by that provision and the court is not of the opinion there mentioned,
(bb) a sentence falls to be imposed under Criminal Justice Act 2003 s 224A if the court is obliged by that section to pass a sentence of imprisonment for life[896] or, if the person is aged at least 18 but under 21, custody for life,[897]
(c) a sentence falls to be imposed under Criminal Justice Act 2003 s 225(2) if the court is obliged to pass a sentence of imprisonment for life or, in the case of a person aged at least 18 but under 21, a sentence of custody for life under that subsection,
(d) a sentence falls to be imposed under Criminal Justice Act 2003 s 226(2) if the court is obliged to pass a sentence of detention for life under that subsection.

Mental Health Act 1983 s 37(8) For the purposes of this subsection 'sentence of imprisonment' includes any sentence or order for detention.

67.7 *Power to order at the Crown Court without a conviction*

Mental Health Act 1983 s 37(3) Where a person is charged before a Magistrates' Court with any act or omission as an offence and the court would have power, on convicting him of that offence, to make an order under subsection (1) above, then, if the court is satisfied that the accused did the act or made the omission charged, the court may, if it thinks fit, make such an order without convicting him.

R (Singh) v Stratford Magistrates' Court 2007 EWHC 1582 (Admin), 2008 1 Cr App R 2 (p 36) High Court D pleaded not guilty to assaulting a police officer even though he had formally admitted the facts. There was evidence of cognitive impairment and D's solicitor indicated that a defence of insanity would be advanced. The District Judge adjourned the trial for a psychiatric report with a view not to investigating the issue of insanity, but with a view to proceeding under section 37(3) (making of a Hospital or Guardianship Order without convicting the accused). D sought judicial review. Held. Both in cases of alleged insanity at the time of the offence and of apparent unfitness to stand trial, the magistrates have the power to abstain from either conviction or acquittal but rather to make a Hospital or Guardianship Order, if such be justified medically, and provided only that it is shown that the accused did the act or made the omission charged. That is a medical rather than a penal disposal. The Magistrates' Court has the power, in an appropriate case, to try the issue of insanity and pronounce its conclusion upon it, without convicting or acquitting the accused, provided that the conditions for making a Hospital or Guardianship Order under section 37(3) are met. Equally, however, if satisfied that there is no purpose in resolving the issue of insanity, and if a section 37(3) order is going to be made, the court can deal with the case without trying that issue. There is no entitlement to the trial of the issue of insanity, rather the interests of justice and of the accused must be considered individually in each case. In all cases where section 37(3) is a possibility, the court should determine the fact-finding exercise first. So the defendant does not have a veto upon the exercise of the power to order a Hospital Order. The fact-finding issue may be concluded on admissions or may involve hearing evidence. If the court is not satisfied that the act/omission was done/made, an unqualified acquittal must follow, whatever the anxieties may be about the accused's state of health. Before embarking on a case in which a section 37(3) order may be applied, magistrates should make it clear that there is a possibility that the order may be made and invite submissions upon the course to be adopted. In particular, careful consideration must be given to any reason advanced why the issue of insanity should be tried. Such an application should be resolved having regard to the interests of justice, which include, but are not limited to, justice to the accused. The making of a section 37(3) order need not be predicated on the determination of the issue of fitness to plead but may be based

[896] Subsection 305(4)(bb) was inserted by Legal Aid, Sentencing and Punishment of Offenders Act 2012 Sch 19 para 22.
[897] Until Criminal Justice and Court Services Act 2000 s 61 is in force, Legal Aid, Sentencing and Punishment of Offenders Act 2012 Sch 19 para 24(3) applies and the phrase underlined is inserted.

more broadly upon the mental state of the accused, provided that the acts/omissions are proved. The flexibility of the section 37(3) procedure was emphasised in *R (P) v Barking Youth Court* 2002 EWHC 734 (Admin), 2 Cr App R 19 (p 294). If section 37(3) does not arise, then the court should proceed to trial. The making of the order does not breach European Convention on Human Rights art 6. The District Judge was entitled to conclude that a section 37(3) order might be appropriate.
See also: *R v Lincoln (Kesteven) JJs ex parte O'Connor* 1983 1 AER 901 LCJ (The circumstances in which it will be appropriate to exercise this unusual power are bound to be very rare.)
Note: There are of course the civil powers to make Hospital Orders without a conviction. Ed.

Test to apply

67.8 ***Test to apply***
Mental Health Act 1983 s 37(2) The conditions referred to in subsection (1) (see **67.3**) are that:
(a) the court is satisfied, on the written or oral evidence of two registered medical practitioners, that the offender is suffering from mental disorder and that either:
(i) the disorder is of a nature or degree which makes it appropriate for him to be detained in a hospital for medical treatment and appropriate medical treatment is available for him, or
(ii) in the case of an offender aged 16 years or over, the disorder is of a nature or degree which warrants his reception into guardianship under this Act, and
(b) the court is of the opinion, having regard to all the circumstances including the nature of the offence and the character and antecedents of the offender, and to the other available methods of dealing with him, that the most suitable method of disposing of the case is by means of an order under this section.
R v Birch 1989 11 Cr App R (S) 202 The judge should: a) decide whether a period of compulsory detention is apposite. If no, the possibility of a probation order with a condition of in- or out-patient treatment should be considered, b) consider whether the conditions in section 37(2)(a) are met, c) consider whether the further condition in section 41(1) is satisfied.

67.9 ***General judicial guidance/Step-by-step guide***
R v Vowles and Others 2015 EWCA Crim 45, 2 Cr App R (S) 6 (p 39) LCJ para 51 The judge must carefully consider all the evidence in each case and not, as some of the early cases have suggested, feel circumscribed by the psychiatric opinions. A judge will invariably have to have regard to: 1) the extent to which the offender needs treatment for the mental disorder from which the offender suffers, 2) the extent to which the offending is attributable to the mental disorder, 3) the extent to which punishment is required, and 4) the protection of the public including the regime for deciding release and the regime after release. There must always be sound reasons for departing from the usual course of imposing a penal sentence and the judge must set these out. In the light of the amendments to Mental Health Act 1983 s 45A, a judge must now pay very careful attention to the different effect in each case of the conditions applicable to and after release. As is shown in *R v Teasdale* 2012 EWCA Crim 2071, this consideration may be one matter leading to the imposition of a Hospital Order under sections 37 [Hospital Orders] and 41 [Restriction Orders]. para 53 The fact that two psychiatrists are of the opinion that a Hospital Order with [a Restriction Order] is the right disposal is therefore never a reason on its own to make such an order. The judge must first consider all the relevant circumstances, including the four issues we have set out [above] and then consider the alternatives as follows. A court should, in a case where: 1) the evidence of medical practitioners suggests that the offender is suffering from a mental disorder, 2) that the offending is wholly or in significant part attributable to that disorder and 3)

treatment is available, and it considers in the light of all the circumstances to which we have referred, that a Hospital Order (with or without a restriction) may be an appropriate way of dealing with the case, consider the matters in the following order:
i) As the terms of section 45A(1) require, before a Hospital Order is made, whether or not with a Restriction Order, a judge should consider whether the mental disorder can appropriately be dealt with by a hospital and limitation direction [also called a Hybrid Order] under section 45A see (**67.41**).
ii) If [he or she] can, the judge should make such a direction under section 45A(1). This consideration will not apply to a person under the age of 21 at the time of conviction as there is no power to make such an order (see **67.42**).
iii) If such a direction is not appropriate the court must then consider if the medical evidence satisfies the condition in section 37(2)(a) and (b) (see **67.8**). It is essential that [the] judge gives detailed consideration to all the factors encompassed within section 37(2)(b). For example, where the court is considering a life sentence under Criminal Justice Act 2003 as amended in 2012 (following the guidance given in *Att-Gen's Ref No 27 of 2013* 2014 EWCA Crim 334), if: 1) the mental disorder is treatable, 2) once treated there is no evidence he [or she] would be in any way dangerous, and 3) the offending is entirely due to that mental disorder, a Hospital Order under sections 37 and 41 [with a Restriction Order][898] is likely to be the correct disposal.
iv) The language of section 37(2)(b) makes clear [that] the court must also have regard to the question of whether other methods of dealing with him are available, [including] transfer from prison to hospital for treatment, under section 47.
If a Hospital Order is [appropriate] it will generally be [undesirable] to make an interim order.
R v Przybylski 2016 EWCA Crim 506 For the problems of Hybrid Orders which do not give lifetime protection to the public and are therefore wrong, see **67.41**.
R v Edwards and Others 2018 EWCA Crim 595, 2 Cr App R (S) 17 (p 120) para 12 Mental Health Act 1983 s 45A could have been better drafted but the position is clear. Section 45A and the judgment in *R v Vowles* 2015, see above, do not provide a 'default' setting of imprisonment, as some have assumed. The sentencing judge should first consider if a Hospital Order may be appropriate under section 37(2)(a). If so, before making such an order, the court must consider all the powers at its disposal including a section 45A order. Consideration of a section 45A order must come before the making of a Hospital Order. This is because a disposal under section 45A includes a penal element and the court must have 'sound reasons' for departing from the usual course of imposing a sentence with a penal element. Sound reasons may include the nature of the offence and the limited nature of any penal element (if imposed) and the fact that the offending was very substantially (albeit not wholly) attributable to the offender's illness. However, the graver the offence and the greater the risk to the public on release of the offender, the greater the emphasis the judge must place upon the protection of the public and the release regime.
para 13 The reason for the court's emphasis on the penal element of any sentence in *R v Vowles* 2015 is to be found in the purposes of sentencing set out in Criminal Justice Act 2003 s 142. They are: a) the punishment of offenders, b) the reduction of crime (including its reduction by deterrence), c) the reform and rehabilitation of offenders, d) the protection of the public, and e) the making of reparation by offenders to persons affected by their offences.
para 14 It follows that, as important as the offender's personal circumstances may be, rehabilitation of offenders is but one of the purposes of sentencing. The punishment of offenders and the protection of the public are also at the heart of the sentencing process. In assessing the seriousness of the offence, Criminal Justice Act 2003 s 143(1) provides that the court must consider the offender's culpability in committing the offence and any

[898] It is not entirely clear but I think this is what the Judge meant.

harm caused, intended or foreseeable. Hence the structure adopted by the Sentencing Council in the production of its definitive guidelines and the two pillars of sentencing: culpability and harm. Assessing the culpability of an offender who has committed a serious offence but suffers from mental health problems may present a judge with a difficult task.

The steps are:

i) Consider whether a Hospital Order may be appropriate.
ii) If [it is], the judge should then consider all his sentencing options including a section 45A order.
iii) In deciding on the most suitable disposal the judge should remind him or herself of the importance of the penal element in a sentence.
iv) To decide whether a penal element to the sentence is necessary the judge should assess (as best he or she can) the offender's culpability and the harm caused by the offence. The fact that an offender would not have committed the offence but for their mental illness does not necessarily relieve them of all responsibility for their actions.
v) A failure to take prescribed medication is not necessarily a culpable omission; it may be attributable in whole or in part to the offender's mental illness.
vi) If the judge decides to impose a Hospital Order under section 37/41, he or she must explain why a penal element is not appropriate.
vii) The regimes on release of an offender on licence from a section 45A order and for an offender subject to section 37/41 orders are different but the latter do not necessarily offer a greater protection to the public, as may have been assumed in *R v Ahmed* 2016 EWCA Crim 670 and/or or by the parties in the cases before us. Each case turns on its own facts.
viii) and ix) [Not listed. Restatement about the rules for grounds of appeal and fresh evidence.]

67.10 *Discretion, There is a*

Mental Health Act 1983 s 37(1) Where a person is convicted of an offence…the court may by order authorise his admission to and detention in such hospital as may be specified in the order.

R v Nafei 2004 EWCA Crim 3238, 2005 2 Cr App R (S) 24 (p 127) There is a discretion whether to make a Hospital Order which was not wrongly applied here.

R v Khelifi 2006 EWCA Crim 770, 2 Cr App R (S) 100 (p 650) There is no presumption that where the conditions in section 37(2) are made out, a Hospital Order will be made. The appellant's welfare, while always relevant, cannot be treated as an overriding consideration. Defendants with all kinds of illnesses have sometimes to be sentenced to substantial prison terms.

67.11 *Need there be a link between the offence and the illness?*

R v McBride 1972 Crim LR 390 D pleaded to two counts of handling. Two doctors' reports stated that D was suffering from a mental illness. A third stated that as D had pleaded, his law breaking could not be attributed to his psychiatric disability. He received 2½ years. Held. The fact that D pleaded guilty did not preclude his counsel from arguing that D's depression was causally connected with the commission of the offences and even if there were no such connection it would not necessarily follow that an order ought not to be made.

67.12 *Minor offences*

R v Eaton 1976 Crim LR 390 D was convicted of criminal damage. She smashed two panes of glass in a telephone kiosk. D had been discharged from a non-secure hospital eight days before and her behaviour was described as being antisocial. It was reported that she was suffering from a psychopathic disorder and required treatment in a secure or special hospital, but no place was available. After the sentence was imposed a place did become available. Held. It was not right for the courts to be asked to deal with persons like D within the penal system. They should be dealt with by the social services and health authorities. The fact that the offence was a minor offence did not preclude the making of a Hospital Order, as D clearly needed treatment. Here, on the facts, Hospital Order with a Restriction Order.

67.13 *Serious offending Not proper to impose custody to prevent release*

R v Howell 1985 7 Cr App R (S) 360 LCJ D was convicted of two counts of rape. He had a number of court appearances, one of which was for indecent assault. He had previously been transferred to hospital during that sentence. D suffered from schizophrenia and a serious personality disorder with deviant sexual overtones. The Judge passed life imprisonment. Held. The object of that plainly was to try and ensure that if this man were ever to be released by the Mental Health Review Tribunal, he would return to prison rather than be set free. We understand the reason but that course was not a proper one. In such circumstances, where medical opinion is unanimous and there is a bed available, a Hospital Order should be made.

R v Mitchell 1997 1 Cr App R (S) 90 D pleaded to manslaughter after absconding from a hospital where he was subject to a Hospital Order. There was substantial evidence of D's schizophrenia and another Hospital Order was recommended. The Judge passed concurrent sentences of life imprisonment. Held. *R v Fleming* 1993 14 Cr App R (S) 151 was incorrectly decided on a misunderstanding in the law. The 'additional safeguard' of a life sentence is erroneous: the discretionary lifer panel is analogous to the Mental Health Review Tribunal. *Fleming* is better disregarded. The principle is clearly established that when the preconditions for a Hospital Order are satisfied and a bed is available in a secure hospital, a Hospital Order, with the appropriate protection of a section 41 order, is the appropriate disposal, rather than a life sentence.

See also: *R v Moses* 1996 2 Cr App R (S) 407 (There was unanimous medical opinion that a Hospital Order was appropriate. Hospital Order substituted for life imprisonment. *R v Howell* applied.)

R v Hutchinson 1997 2 Cr App R (S) 60 (Following *R v Mitchell* 1997, Hospital Order substituted for life sentences.)

Note: These cases must be considered with the later cases in the next two paragraphs. In *R v Fleming* 1993 14 Cr App R (S) 151, the defendant had been previously given a Hospital Order. The Court considered it was a different case from *R v Howell* 1985. Because of his previous history that would not be safe. There were additional safeguards provided by a life sentence in that the Home Secretary would consider release. The Judge was entitled to pass a sentence of life imprisonment for a plea to manslaughter where a Hospital Order had been recommended. Ed.

67.14 *Serious offending Deterrent sentences are required*

R v Nafei 2004 EWCA Crim 3238, 2005 2 Cr App R (S) 24 (p 127) D pleaded to importation of 30 kilos of cocaine, equivalent to 15.38 kilos at 100% purity. The street value was estimated at £1.8m. During an interview it was noted that D may have suffered from a mental illness. Reports were prepared and stated that he suffered from schizophrenia. Two doctors recommended a Hospital Order under section 37. The Judge said: "There is no causal link between mental condition and the offence here, much less so in an offence of basic or specific intent…I must sentence for the offence and that necessarily means that I must pass the usual sentence irrespective of the defendant's mental capacity or incapacity. I do not believe that any other sentence or order can be justified." He passed 12 years. D submitted that the Judge erred in not imposing a Hospital Order. Held. Mental Health Act 1983 s 37 confers a discretion which may be exercised where (as here) the statutory preconditions are met. The appellant knew at the time of the offending what he was doing. We would not go so far as to say that where, as here, there is no causal connection between the mental illness and the offence of drug importation, and where, as here, the offence of drug importation was committed by the offender knowingly with his eyes wide open, a Hospital Order can *never* be justified.

But what we would say is that, in circumstances such as the present, we at present find it difficult to envisage a case where the discretion to make a Hospital Order will be likely to be exercised. Sentence affirmed.
R v Khelifi 2006 EWCA Crim 770, 2 Cr App R (S) 100 (p 650) D pleaded to conspiracy to defraud, in what was described as 'a well-organised and elaborate bank fraud' which netted some £800,000. With others, false bank accounts were set up and cheques from the accounts were used to pay for goods. The goods were subsequently returned in exchange for cash. The fraud continued for 18 months. D had for several years suffered from episodes of paranoid schizophrenia and had a history of treatment. During proceedings he was subject to an Interim Hospital Order to facilitate the assessment of his condition. D was confirmed as suffering from paranoid schizophrenia and recommended for a Hospital Order. The Judge disagreed stating, "I have reluctantly come to the conclusion that justice cannot be done here…by a Hospital Order." Held. There is no presumption that where the conditions in section 37(2) are made out, a Hospital Order will be made. The appellant's welfare, while always relevant, cannot be treated as an overriding consideration. Defendants with all kinds of illness have sometimes to be sentenced to substantial prison terms and there is nothing unique about schizophrenia. The need to assess the personal circumstances of the offender in the light of the seriousness of the offence is a feature of all sentencing and it will not only be in cases of drug crime that it may be necessary to sentence ill patients to a prison term. The approach in *R v Nafei* 2004 extends beyond drug importation cases.

67.15 ***Serious offending Public protection is paramount/Hospital Order suitable***
R v IA 2005 EWCA Crim 2077, 2006 1 Cr App R (S) 91 (p 521) D, aged 19, pleaded on rearraignment to rape (custody for life), eight counts of indecent assault on a male (8 years on each, concurrent and concurrent with the rape) and three counts of having an offensive weapon (12 months on each, concurrent and concurrent with the rape). The total sentence was custody for life with a minimum specified term of 6 years and 9 months. The Judge said, "Because I cannot say when you will be safe to be released, the only sentence that I can properly impose is one of custody for life." He expressed a hope that D could be transferred to a secure hospital unit, but that there was no guarantee. A report stated that D suffered from the pervasive development disorder of autistic spectrum disorder combined with a significant learning disability. A subsequent report recommended a Hospital Order. D was placed in a YOI which a subsequent report stated was an inappropriate setting for D's disabilities and mental illness. A transfer under section 47 was not possible due to the minimum term. It was pointed out that under a Hospital Order the Mental Health Review Tribunal would be required to direct the absolute discharge of the patient if it was satisfied that he was not then suffering from mental illness or that it was not necessary for the health or safety of the patient or for the protection of other persons that he should receive medical treatment. Held. Judges are not required to ignore, but should, on the contrary, give some appropriate weight to, such differences as there are between the regime of custody for life, with the Parole Board's role after the expiry of the minimum period, and the regime of a Hospital Order with indefinite restriction, with the Mental Health Review Tribunal's role under Mental Health Act 1983 s 73. This does not mean assuming that the latter regime, which has the advantage of guaranteeing hospital treatment, will in any particular case necessarily afford significantly less protection to the public than the former. On the one hand, this was very serious offending. On the other, D is someone with diverse and unusual problems, who the doctors unanimously advise would benefit by treatment in a psychiatric hospital. The Judge ought to have weighed the seriousness of the offending and the fact that a life sentence affords the most security to the public against the unanimous view of the doctors that a Hospital Order was most suitable. The fact that there was no guarantee that D would be transferred from prison to a secure hospital was relevant. The right order was a Hospital Order with indefinite restrictions.

R v Simpson 2007 EWCA Crim 2666, 2008 1 Cr App R (S) 111 (p 658) D pleaded to attempted murder and received life imprisonment with a minimum term of 6 years. In 1993 there was a relatively minor incident between D and M, a colleague of D's. It triggered a series of delusional beliefs in D's mind which subsequently developed into a persistent delusional disorder. D then left his job and moved away. His mental state deteriorated and he attributed his unhappiness to M, building up a series of delusional beliefs focused on him. He harboured them over a number of years and it led him to plan revenge. He decided to return to the area where he had been employed and track down M. He forced his way into M's home and discovered that M was not in, but M's wife and child were. D engaged in a savage and persistent attack on M's wife. D said, "I walked in and like stuck the screwdriver in her stomach to begin with and then it was like a frenzy and she was strong…and I just kept going on at her with the screwdriver." M's wife suffered 13 separate wounds to her head, face and neck, 25 separate wounds to other parts of her body, including defence wounds to her hands and arms, a dislocated finger, black eye and many abrasions. D had no previous convictions. Two medical practitioners concluded that the disorder had significantly affected his life and that D showed very little remorse, being more concerned with his own mental torture. They recommended a Hospital Order rather than imprisonment as D would be able to be treated more effectively in the former. The doctors did not consider that D was likely to fill the criteria for admission to a high security hospital. The Judge rejected a Hospital Order because of the wider interests of public protection. The Court was told that the possibility of escape had troubled the Judge particularly. Held. The Judge justifiably regarded protection as paramount in relation to the actual and potential victims of D's current delusional symptoms. We understand and fully endorse the Judge's view that public protection is and will remain a crucial consideration. We also have regard to the risk of escape. We have been reassured by oral evidence that escape was very rare. The danger emanates substantially from a deep-seated mental illness and it is treatment for that illness accompanied by secure conditions which give the best chance of eliminating or minimising the risk. Hospital Order substituted.

R v Hughes 2010 EWCA Crim 1026 LCJ D pleaded to two offences of arson being reckless as to whether life was endangered. D started two fires in his flat, resulting in the emergency services being called on two consecutive days. An accelerant was used on the second occasion. D admitted to both fires. D, aged 40, had a long history of offending, mainly for offences of dishonesty but with some incidents of violence. In 1999 he had received 4½ years for arson, reckless as to endangering life. A psychiatric report diagnosed depressive disorder, but no issue of a Hospital Order was raised. Two months before the instant offences, he was admitted to hospital but a psychiatrist saw no evidence of depression or psychosis. The new report stated that D required continuing hospital treatment and talked in terms of years. The theme of D's paranoid illness had changed with the passage of time. D received 5 years on each count, concurrent. The case was subject to an Attorney-General's reference and the sentence was increased to life imprisonment, with a minimum term of 3 years 9 months. However, after 2½ years of his sentence, D was transferred to Ashworth Hospital by order of the Home Secretary under Mental Health Act 1983 s 47 and had been there since. D was diagnosed with paranoid schizophrenia coupled with a personality disorder. In 2008 a report stated that D was suffering from paranoid schizophrenia at the time of the offences. The Crown did not seek to challenge the evidence in the new report. Held. There were strong reasons why a Hospital Order would be more suitable. It will provide continuity of care by forensic psychiatrists in a secure hospital for as long as is necessary, *R v Beatty* 2006 EWCA Crim 2359, MHLR 333. There is clear authority that where the conditions for a Hospital Order are met at time of sentence, a Hospital Order rather than a discretionary life sentence should be imposed. We take the view that this is a clear case, albeit a rare one, in which it has been found that the mental illness present now must have been present then. Hospital Order substituted for life sentence.

R v Welsh 2011 EWCA Crim 73 D pleaded to manslaughter based on diminished responsibility. He took a knife to a party and for no reason stabbed the victim in the neck. D had convictions for violence. Both the prosecution and the defence doctors recommended a Hospital Order. The issue was whether his responsibility for his actions was sufficient to justify a life sentence. Held. An important factor is public confidence when choosing between a Hospital Order with a Restriction Order and life imprisonment. That confidence can only be satisfied by ensuring that the issue is resolved in a way which best protects the public and reflects the gravity of the offence. A life prisoner with a minimum term order may not be released unless the Parole Board is satisfied that 'it is no longer necessary for the protection of the public that the prisoner should be confined', Crime (Sentences) Act 1997 s 28(6)(b). By contrast, the First-tier Tribunal must discharge a patient absolutely if it is not satisfied that he is suffering from mental disorder of a nature or degree which makes it appropriate for him to be liable to be detained in a hospital for medical treatment, Mental Health Act 1983 s 72(1)(b)(i), and is satisfied that it is not appropriate for the patient to remain liable to be recalled to hospital for further treatment, Mental Health Act 1983 s 73(1)(a) and (b). If it is not satisfied that the defendant is suffering from a mental disorder [as we have just] described, but [it] is [satisfied that it is] appropriate for the patient to remain liable to be recalled to hospital for further treatment, the Tribunal is required to direct a conditional discharge (section 73(2)). We bear in mind *R v Drew* 2003 UKHL 25, 2004 1 Cr App R (S) 8 (p 65) para 21, 'Defendants made subject to Hospital Orders, whether restricted or not, are entitled to release when the medical conditions justifying their original admissions cease to be met…further, they are liable to recall only on medical grounds. They may be a source of danger to the public even though these medical conditions are not met.' A Hospital Order with a Restriction Order would not maintain public confidence. **Life imprisonment**.

Att-Gen's Ref No 54 of 2011 2011 EWCA Crim 2276, 2012 1 Cr App R (S) 106 (p 635) D was sentenced to a Hospital Order with restrictions. The Judge said if he had not passed that sentence he would have passed a 12-year notional term. The Judge's primary concern was to achieve continuity of treatment at Broadmoor. He feared a highly disrupted treatment or a hiatus in the treatment. He thought that was not in the public interest. The prosecution appealed. Held. The DPP regime and the Hospital Order regime have features in common. Both have discretionary release. In neither case is there an absolute right to release. Under both regimes the release is conditional and the defendant is subject to recall. Under DPP, release is dependent upon the responsible authority being satisfied that the defendant is no longer a danger to the public for <u>any</u> reason and principally not at risk of relapsing into dangerous crime. Under the Hospital Order regime release is dependent upon the responsible authority being satisfied that the defendant no longer presents any danger which arises from his medical condition. The licence can be revoked if the defendant shows that he remains a danger to the public from crime. Under the Hospital Order regime, recall is available but only if the defendant's medical condition relapses. Simple crime does not trigger a recall under the Hospital Order regime. This sentencing decision simply left out the vital consideration [about release]. We agree with the Judge about the highly undesirable interruption to the treatment. We propose to adjourn the matter so that arrangements are put in place for D to be immediately transferred to Broadmoor under section 47. That would mean that D would go straight back to Broadmoor. 6 years' DPP will later be substituted.

R v Fort 2013 EWCA Crim 2332, 2014 2 Cr App R (S) 24 (p 167) D pleaded to manslaughter on the basis of diminished responsibility. He had a secure childhood but did not socialise. D lived with his parents and his sister. One evening in July 2008, he read a book and then went downstairs to see if anyone was watching TV and in D's own words "it just happened". He stabbed his mother 35 times with a large kitchen knife while his father and sister were asleep upstairs. D dialled 999 to call an ambulance and he said he had killed his mother but he could not say why. The police arrived. D was arrested, remanded into custody and later transferred from a YOI to a psychiatric clinic. He had for some time suffered from violent thoughts which could be treated in hospital as opposed to a YOI. D was aged 18 and had no convictions. The medical reports had varied opinions in the two years five months before D's appeal. In April 2011, a doctor gave his primary diagnosis as 'obsessive compulsive disorder'. The final agreed reports said D was suffering from 'schizoid personality disorder with a long-standing history of thoughts of violence'. He had killed his mother during an episode of 'disassociative disorder'. There was no medication to treat the dissociative episodes. The Judge found that the three [main] psychiatrists concluded: a) D was best managed in a hospital environment, b) he was 'very dangerous', and c) he presented a very severe risk of significant violence to other people. They proposed a Hospital Order. However, the Judge was concerned that there might be a time when it was no longer appropriate for him to be detained in a hospital and he was then a danger to the public. She considered it would be better if the Parole Board determined his release. D was sentenced to life (which was treated as custody for life) with a minimum term of 4 years. A medical report for the appeal said D's symptoms had consistently been worsened by stress such as examinations and moves to prison. That was not possible to control and in a custodial setting he posed a risk to officers, other inmates and healthcare staff. It was very unlikely that D would be returned to prison as he was likely to break down very quickly with very serious injuries to others. Held. para 54 In manslaughter cases based on diminished responsibility the judge had to assess the seriousness of the offence by reference to the defendant's culpability and the harm consequent upon his actions. But these two considerations are neither the paramount nor the exclusive considerations. para 54 D did not have much, if any, mental responsibility for his actions in the killing. D would not continue to pose a significant risk of serious harm to members of the public occasioned by the commission of serious offences <u>once</u> his mental disorder had been cured or substantially alleviated such as to enable him to be discharged (albeit conditionally) from a Hospital Order with a Restriction Order. That order was appropriate, not custody for life.

R v Vowles and Others 2015 EWCA Crim 45, 2 Cr App R (S) 6 (p 39) In what is now the leading case, the LCJ gave guidance on when to impose Hospital Orders and this is listed at **67.15** and other paragraphs. The Court also considered six appeals on their merits. In V's appeal, at para 90, in B's appeal, at para 100, and DI's appeal, at para 161 the Court held that new psychiatric evidence did not show that V and B's IPP sentences and DI's life sentence were wrong in principle. In C's appeal, at para 114, JO's appeal at para 134 and M's appeal at para 200, the Court held that the new evidence showed that the evidence at the sentencing hearing was wrong and substituted a Hospital Order with a Restriction Order for C and M's IPP and JO's custody for life.

For the duty of the court to consider the protection of the public, see **67.9**.

Reports

67.16 *Power to request information*

Mental Health Act 1983 s 39(1) Where a court is minded to make a Hospital Order or Interim Hospital Order in respect of any person it may request:

(a) the Primary Care Trust or Local Health Board for the area in which that person resides or last resided, or

(b) the National Assembly for Wales or any other Primary Care Trust or Local Health Board that appears to the court to be appropriate,

to furnish the court with such information as they have or can reasonably obtain with respect to the hospital or hospitals (if any) in their area or elsewhere at which arrangements could be made for the admission of that person in pursuance of the order.

(1A) In relation to a person who has not attained the age of 18 years, subsection (1) above shall have effect as if the reference to the making of a Hospital Order included a reference to a remand to hospital under section 35 or 36 above or the making of an order under section 44 (committal to hospital under section 43) (see **67.27**).
(1B) Where the person concerned has not attained the age of 18 years, the information which may be requested under subsection (1) above includes, in particular, information about the availability of accommodation or facilities designed so as to be specially suitable for patients who have not attained the age of 18 years.

67.17 ***Obtaining reports Magistrates' Courts Power to obtain reports and Remand time limits***

Powers of Criminal Courts (Sentencing) Act 2000 s 11(1) If, on the trial by a Magistrates' Court of an offence punishable with imprisonment, the court:
(a) is satisfied that the accused did the act or made the omission charged, but
(b) is of the opinion that an inquiry ought to be made into his physical or mental condition before the method of dealing with him is determined,
the court shall adjourn the case to enable a medical examination and report to be made, and shall remand him.
Powers of Criminal Courts (Sentencing) Act 2000 s 11(2) An adjournment under subsection (1) above shall not be for more than three weeks at a time where the court remands the accused in custody, nor for more than four weeks at a time where it remands him on bail.

67.18 ***Obtaining reports Magistrates' Courts Bail terms***

Powers of Criminal Courts (Sentencing) Act 2000 s 11(3) Where on an adjournment under subsection (1) above the accused is remanded on bail, the court shall impose conditions under Bail Act 1976 s 3(6)(d) and the requirements imposed as conditions under that paragraph shall be or shall include requirements that the accused:

(a) undergo medical examination by a registered medical practitioner or, where the inquiry is into his mental condition and the court so directs, two such practitioners, and
(b) for that purpose attend such an institution or place, or on such practitioner, as the court directs and, where the inquiry is into his mental condition, comply with any other directions which may be given to him for that purpose by any person specified by the court or by a person of any class so specified.

Court requested medical reports For the rules about and for what they should contain see **77.4**.

67.19 ***Reports, Duty to serve***

Mental Health Act 1983 s 54(3) Where, in pursuance of a direction of the court, any such report is tendered in evidence otherwise than by or on behalf of the person who is the subject of the report, then:

(a) if that person is represented by an authorised person, a copy of the report shall be given to that authorised person,
(b) if that person is not so represented, the substance of the report shall be disclosed to him or, where he is a child or young person, to his parent or guardian if present in court, and
(c) except where the report relates only to arrangements for his admission to a hospital, that person may require the signatory of the report to be called to give oral evidence, and evidence to rebut the evidence contained in the report may be called by or on behalf of that person.

67.20 ***Instructions to doctors***

Mental Health Act 1983 s 12(1) The recommendations required for an application for the admission of a patient under this Part of this Act or a guardianship application (in this Act referred to as 'medical recommendations') shall be signed on or before the date of the application, and given by practitioners who have personally examined the patient either together or separately, but where they have examined the patient separately, not more than five days must have elapsed between the days on which the separate examinations took place.

Procedure

67.21 *Court requiring oral evidence*

Mental Health Act 1983 s 54(2A) But the court may require the signatory of any such report (those for the courts) to be called to give oral evidence.

67.22 *Magistrates committal for sentence Committal to hospital*

Committal to hospital under s. 43

Mental Health Act 1983 s 44(1) Where an offender is committed under section 43(1) (see **67.27**), and the Magistrates' Court by which he is committed is satisfied on written or oral evidence that arrangements have been made for the admission of the offender to a hospital in the event of an order being made under this section, the court may, instead of committing him in custody, by order direct him to be admitted to that hospital, specifying it, and to be detained there until the case is disposed of by the Crown Court, and may give such directions as it thinks fit for his production from the hospital to attend the Crown Court by which his case is to be dealt with.

(2) The evidence required by subsection (1) above shall be given by the approved clinician (see section 12) who would have overall responsibility for the offender's case or by some other person representing the managers of the hospital in question.

(3) The power to give directions under section 37(4) (see **67.23**), section 37(5) (see **67.61**) and section 40(1) (see **67.59**) shall apply in relation to an order under this section as they apply in relation to a Hospital Order, but as if references to the period of 28 days mentioned in section 40(1) were omitted, and subject as aforesaid an order under this section shall, until the offender's case is disposed of by the Crown Court, have the same effect as a Hospital Order together with a Restriction Order.

67.23 *Evidence required for Hospital Order*

Mental Health Act 1983 s 37(4) An order for the admission of an offender to a hospital (in this Act referred to as 'a Hospital Order') shall not be made under this section unless the court is satisfied on the written or oral evidence of the approved clinician who would have overall responsibility for his case or of some other person representing the managers of the hospital that arrangements have been made for his admission to that hospital, and for his admission to it within the period of 28 days beginning with the date of the making of such an order and the court may, pending his admission within that period, give such directions as it thinks fit for his conveyance to and detention in a place of safety.

Mental Health Act 1983 s 54(2) For the purposes of any provision of this Part of this Act under which a court may act on the written evidence of any person, a report in writing purporting to be signed by that person may, subject to the provisions of this section, be received in evidence without proof of the following:

(a) the signature of the person, or

(b) his having the requisite qualifications or approval or authority or being of the requisite description to give the report.

67.24 *Explain sentence, Judge must/Suggested sentencing remarks*

Judicial College's Crown Court Compendium Part II Sentencing June 2018 page 6-10

Example
[Having set out the facts of the case] Having heard the medical evidence which has been given in court today by Dr…and having read the reports prepared by Dr…and Dr…all of whom are approved by the Secretary of State under the Mental Health Act 1983 s 12(2):
I am satisfied that[:]
- You are suffering from a mental disorder, namely {disorder}[;]
- This disorder is of a nature which makes it appropriate for you to be detained in a hospital for medical treatment; and
- Appropriate medical treatment is available for you at {place}.

I am of the opinion that[:]
- because of all the circumstances of your case including[:]
  - o the nature of the offence of {offence} to which you have pleaded guilty/of which you have been convicted/of which you have been found not guilty by reason of insanity/the act which you are found to have done}; and
  - o your character and your past [antecedents], which includes a longstanding and complicated history of mental illness;
- and having considered all the other available ways in which I might deal with you the most suitable method of dealing with your case is by making an order under the Mental Health Act 1983 s 37.

I therefore make an order that you will be {re-}admitted to and detained at {place}. I am satisfied that arrangements have been made for you to be {re-}admitted within 28 days to this hospital {where you have already been for many months}.
[In some cases it may be appropriate to add: I make it clear that the order which I have made is not a punishment but is for your own wellbeing and that of the public.]

Restriction Orders

67.25
Discharge from order Restriction Orders have no time limit. A Restriction Order can be discharged either by the Ministry of Justice after a request by a registered clinician or by a Mental Health Tribunal granting an absolute discharge. If the tribunal is satisfied to the civil standard that a) there is no longer a risk, and b) the patient is no longer suffering from a mental disorder or no longer requires further treatment, it would be contrary to the European Convention on Human Rights art 5 to detain a patient.

67.26 ***Restriction Orders Power to make and test to apply***
Power of higher courts to restrict discharge from hospital
Mental Health Act 1983 s 41(1) Where a Hospital Order is made in respect of an offender by the Crown Court, and it appears to the court, having regard to the nature of the offence, the antecedents of the offender and the risk of his committing further offences if set at large, that it is necessary for the protection of the public from serious harm so to do, the court may, subject to the provisions of this section, further order that the offender shall be subject to the special restrictions set out in this section, and an order under this section shall be known as 'a Restriction Order'.
R v Birch 1989 11 Cr App R (S) 202 D pleaded to manslaughter. She suffered from a depressive illness and had received psychiatric treatment in the past. Three doctors gave evidence at trial and stated that a Restriction Order was not necessary. Held. When assessing whether section 41(1) is satisfied, the court must assess not the seriousness of the risk that D will reoffend, but the risk that if he does so, the public will suffer serious harm. The harm in question need not, in our view, be limited to personal injury. Nor need it relate to the public in general, for it would suffice if a category of persons, or even a single person, were adjudged to be at risk. The category of person so protected would no doubt exclude the offender himself. Nevertheless the potential harm must be serious, and a high possibility of a recurrence of minor offences will no longer be sufficient. It would, however, be a mistake to equate the seriousness of the offence with the probability that a Restriction Order will be made. This is only one of the factors which section 41(1) requires to be taken into account. A minor offence by a man who proves to be mentally

disordered and dangerous may properly leave him subject to a restriction. In theory the converse is also true. A sentencer should not impose a restriction to mark the gravity of the offence. The court need not follow the course which the doctor recommends.
R v Nwohia 1996 1 Cr App R (S) 170 One should not impose a Restriction Order simply to ensure that medication is taken.
R (Jones) v Isleworth Crown Court 2005 EWHC 662 (Admin) High Court D was charged with burglary and attempted burglary. A jury found he had committed the acts. The Judge admitted him to hospital pursuant to Criminal Procedure (Insanity) Act 1964 and made a Restriction Order. The decision was based on the offender's previous convictions for a substantial number of residential burglaries, two ABHs and threatening behaviour. Held. It must be always recalled in the context of cases such as this that it is necessary for the judge to look to the future. Of course the evidence as to what had happened in the past provides a guide to the future, but it does not determine the nature of the risk. The Judge was bound to consider the risk in the future and the nature of that risk, having regard to the past, but he was not bound to determine that risk solely by reference to the nature of the violence in the past. It was necessary to consider the escalating violence coupled with the abuse of drugs revealed not only in the history of the previous convictions but in the descriptions of his behaviour when detained in hospital. The decision was amply warranted.
See also: *R v Chowdhury* 2011 EWCA Crim 936 (An example of the Court of Appeal arranging for undertakings about passports to be given so that a Restriction Order could be quashed. The Judge was concerned about problems if the defendant went abroad and stopped taking his medication.)
R v Goucher 2011 EWCA Crim 2473 (Reports suggested a risk of harm but not a risk of serious harm, as required by section 41. Hospital Order remains but Restriction Order quashed.)

67.27 *Magistrates' power to commit for sentence*

Power of Magistrates' Courts to commit for restriction order
Mental Health Act 1983 s 43(1) If in the case of a person aged 14 or over who is convicted by a Magistrates' Court of an offence punishable on summary conviction with imprisonment:

(a) the conditions which under section 37(1) above are required to be satisfied for the making of a Hospital Order are satisfied in respect of the offender, but

(b) it appears to the court, having regard to the nature of the offence, the antecedents of the offender and the risk of his committing further offences if set at large, that if a Hospital Order is made a Restriction Order should also be made,

the court may, instead of making a Hospital Order or dealing with him in any other manner, commit him in custody to the Crown Court to be dealt with in respect of the offence.
(2) Where an offender is committed to the Crown Court under this section, the Crown Court shall inquire into the circumstances of the case and may,

(a) if that court would have power so to do under the foregoing provisions of this Part of this Act upon the conviction of the offender before that court of such an offence as is described in section 37(1) above, make a Hospital Order in his case, with or without a Restriction Order,

(b) if the court does not make such an order, deal with the offender in any other manner in which the Magistrates' Court might have dealt with him.

(3) The Crown Court shall have the same power to make orders under sections 35, 36 and 38 above in the case of a person committed to the court under this section as it has under those sections in the case of an accused person within the meaning of section 35 or 36 or of a person convicted before that court as mentioned in section 38.
(4) The power of a Magistrates' Court under Powers of Criminal Courts (Sentencing) Act 2000 s 3 (which enables such a court to commit an offender to the Crown Court where the court is of the opinion that greater punishment should be inflicted for the

offence than the court has power to inflict) shall also be exercisable by a Magistrates' Court where it is of the opinion that greater punishment should be inflicted…on the offender unless a Hospital Order is made in his case with a Restriction Order.
(5) The power of the Crown Court to make a Hospital Order, with or without a Restriction Order, in the case of a person convicted before that court of an offence may be exercised by such a court in the case of a person committed to the court under Vagrancy Act 1824 s 5 (committals to the Crown Court of incorrigible rogues).
Note: The Home Office has announced that it intends to repeal Vagrancy Act 1824 s 4. The officials are taking their time to do so. Ed.

67.28 ***Evidence What incidents may the psychiatrists rely on?***
R v M 2014 EWCA Crim 2642 D pleaded to common assault and was committed to the Crown Court under section 43(1)(b), see **67.27**, so a Restriction Order could be made. He attacked a care worker in a psychiatric hospital. The victim received an injury to his eye. The two doctors disagreed about the need for a Restriction Order. The doctor who advocated a Restriction Order, P, relied on incidents which D disputed. The Judge made a Restriction Order. Without determining any principle of law, the Court of Appeal directed the prosecution to serve any evidence of the disputed incidents. At a directions hearing, the prosecution indicated that there was no CPS or police material to assist. The Court held that the medical records were created in the course of a profession, and therefore statements within them were admissible as evidence subject to the conditions in Criminal Justice Act 2003 s 117(2) and (7). The prosecution were unable to identify from those records two of the allegations referred to by the psychiatrists in their reports. Two other allegations failed to identify 'the relevant person' who had supplied the professional or office holder with the information, and so the conditions in section 177(2)(b) were not met. The Court directed that P should disregard those four incidents in reconsidering her opinion. At the full hearing, P gave evidence and still recommended a Restriction Order. The Court considered that it needed to validate the findings [on which the Restriction Order was made]. Held. The Judge was well aware of the care required when making a Restriction Order. The term 'antecedents' in section 41 does not only refer to previous criminal convictions or cautions. The Court is not precluded from taking into account established factual incidents suggestive of the risk presented by the offender. That said, it is irrefutable that an offender should not be sentenced for offences or on the basis of offences neither admitted nor proved. Public protection does not trump due process. For disputed entries in the medical records, the conflict almost inevitably will be decided judicially. The offender is not entitled to demand one method of factual resolution over another. The appropriate procedure will be a matter of judicial evaluation for the particular case. If there has been a trial and the offender has given evidence, the judge may be able to form a view as to the risk of danger to the public in the context of the medical opinion as to the nature and degree of his mental disorder. The absence of previous criminal convictions or offending behaviour will not determine the outcome. The offender should be entitled to examine the records and make representations accordingly. Allegations of behaviour within psychiatric units may not lend themselves to live evidence, nor should there necessarily be live evidence. Where a complainant may not be able to give evidence by reason of mental incapacity, the hearsay provisions in Criminal Justice Act 2003 s 116 would [apply]. The judge will need to exercise caution in attributing weight or credence to the disputed events and also manage satellite litigation. para 35 In assessing serious harm the court is not bound by the index offence, see *R v K* 2000 MHLR 9. Neither is it necessary to refer to the nature of past harm, see *R v Golding* 2006 EWCA Crim 1965, 2007 1 Cr App R (S) 79 (p 486) and *R (Jones) v Isleworth Crown Court* 2005 EWHC 662 (Admin). We do bear in mind that D disputes part of the medical records. Although the procedure adopted by the Judge may have been defective, we agree with P. Appeal dismissed.

67.29 ***Restriction Orders Summary only matters at the Crown Court***
R v Avbunudje 1999 2 Cr App R (S) 189 A charge of common assault was added to an indictment charging assault with intent to rob. D pleaded to the former, while the latter was left on the file. It was argued that the Crown Court did not have the jurisdiction to make a Restriction Order as by statute it was restricted to the Magistrates' Court's powers of sentencing. Held. If the submission is correct then that would be a significant lacuna in this field. That approach would not assist the offender. The Crown Court can notionally commit the matter to itself and then impose a Restriction Order. Order affirmed.
Note: The Crown Court could not commit the matter to itself (if the committal was under the general powers) because common assault is a summary only offence. If the committal was to be under section 43(1), see **67.27**, it would be invalid as the section only applies to defendants who are convicted in the Magistrates' Court. D pleaded at the Crown Court. Ed.

67.30 ***Restriction Orders What do they mean?***
Mental Health Act 1983 s 41(3) The special restrictions applicable to a patient in respect of whom a Restriction Order is in force are as follows:

(a) none of the provisions of Part II of this Act relating to the duration, renewal and expiration of authority for the detention of patients shall apply, and the patient shall continue to be liable to be detained by virtue of the relevant Hospital Order until he is duly discharged under the said Part II or absolutely discharged under sections 42, 73, 74 or 75,

(aa) none of the provisions of Part II of this Act relating to community treatment orders and community patients shall apply,

(b) no application shall be made to the appropriate tribunal in respect of a patient under section 66 or 69(1) (applications to tribunals) below,

(c) the following powers shall be exercisable only with the consent of the Secretary of State, namely:

(i) power to grant leave of absence to the patient under section 17 (leave of absence) above,

(ii) power to transfer the patient in pursuance of regulations under section 19 (transfer of patients) above or in pursuance of subsection (3) of that section, and

(iii) power to order the discharge of the patient under section 23 (discharge of patients) above,

and if leave of absence is granted under the said section 17 power to recall the patient under that section shall vest in the Secretary of State as well as the responsible clinician, and

(d) the power of the Secretary of State to recall the patient under the said section 17 and power to take the patient into custody and return him under section 18 (return and readmission of patients absent without leave) above may be exercised at any time,

and in relation to any such patient section 40(4) above shall have effect as if it referred to Part II of Schedule 1 to this Act instead of Part I of that Schedule.

(4) A Hospital Order shall not cease to have effect under section 40(5) above if a Restriction Order in respect of the patient is in force at the material time.

Mental Health Act 1983 s 41(6) While a person is subject to a Restriction Order the responsible clinician shall at such intervals (not exceeding one year) as the Secretary of State may direct examine and report to the Secretary of State on that person, and every report shall contain such particulars as the Secretary of State may require.

67.31 ***Restriction Orders Judge can make an order against medical advice***
R v Royse 1981 3 Cr App R (S) 58 D was convicted of manslaughter by reason of diminished responsibility. She was assessed as suffering from a paranoid psychosis

which was a form of *folie-à-deux*[899] communicated by her husband. She began to recover after his death. However, a Hospital Order was made against the advice of medical practitioners. They all believed she was recovering and not deluded. Held. Whether or not medical practitioners recommend that a Restriction Order should be made, the responsibility lies with the judge to assess whether an order is appropriate, providing the necessary requirements are satisfied. He was quite entitled to form his own view. We can understand why the Judge made the order, but in light of the new evidence, we quash the order.

R v Talarico 2013 EWCA Crim 2798 D pleaded to three counts of attempting to cause ABH. He carried out three random, unprovoked attacks on members of the public who were unknown to him. In a pub, D approached V1 from behind. He wrapped a cable round her neck and choked her. When the cable snapped he ran off laughing. Within minutes he made a similar attack on V2, a six-year-old, with a belt. When V2's mother pulled her away the belt slipped off. A few minutes later D put a washing line around V3's neck. The line was pulled and V3 could not breathe. V3 managed to struggle free. D was arrested and transferred to a secure hospital. D was aged 42 at appeal and had two common assault convictions in 2004 and 2006. He received a penalty notice for domestic violence and was cautioned for putting his hand over a woman's mouth in the street. D was assessed as having a depressive psychosis. D said he heard voices telling him to choke or suffocate someone or even kill them. A Hospital Order was agreed. Two doctors considered a Restriction Order was not necessary as his illness was under control. The Judge said the offences were extremely serious and potentially dangerous and made a Restriction Order. Held. We agree with the Judge's comment about the offences. He was perfectly entitled to consider the risk that D may relapse if he reverted to alcohol and/or drugs and failed to take his medicine. The Judge was able to make a Restriction Order. However, because of the latest medical report, the order could be removed.

67.32 ***Restriction Orders Need for oral evidence***

Mental Health Act 1983 s 41(2) A Restriction Order shall not be made in the case of any person unless at least one of the registered medical practitioners whose evidence is taken into account by the court under section 37(2)(a) above has given evidence orally before the court.

R v Birch 1989 11 Cr App R (S) 202 D pleaded to manslaughter. She lured her husband to her flat under false pretences, shot him with a shotgun and then stabbed him five times. D suffered from a depressive illness and had received psychiatric treatment in the past. Three doctors gave evidence at trial and stated that a Restriction Order was not necessary. A Hospital Order with a Restriction Order with no limit of time was imposed. Held. Before a Hospital Order can be made, the court must be satisfied of the stated conditions 'on the written or oral evidence of two practitioners'. But where a Restriction Order is in question, section 41(2) requires no more than that the court shall hear the oral evidence of one of the medical practitioners. It need not follow the course which he recommends.

R v Safi 2007 EWCA Crim 1392 D pleaded to exposure, having exposed his erect penis to two women on two occasions, whilst running toward them fondling himself. Two doctors prepared reports which concluded that D was suffering from a psychotic illness, most likely schizophrenia. Two further reports were prepared by a third doctor. D stated that he planned to discontinue his medication. The third doctor's conclusion was that D posed a significant risk of committing another sexual offence. In his view a Restriction Order was required and subsequently recommended that it should be without limit of time. D was resistant to medication. D's counsel asked for an adjournment based on the fact that the legislation requires the court to have before it two reports, both of which, it was argued, were 'stale'. Refusing the application, the Judge relied on the earlier reports

[899] This is a medical condition.

and imposed a Restriction Order with no limit. Subsequently, there was a considerable improvement in D's condition, but a fourth doctor felt it highly likely that D's schizophrenia would re-emerge if he ceased taking his medication and engaged in recreational drug use, which he had done in the past. Held. There may be some cases where it is appropriate to rely on a report which was compiled a little while previously, and other cases in which it may not. In this case, there was a not insignificant lapse of time between the earlier reports and the hearing, but we think that it was open to the Judge to rely on the up-to-date report from the third doctor and at least one of the earlier reports to enable him to consider whether at the time of sentence the appellant was suffering from mental illness.

67.33 ***Restriction Orders Need for oral evidence Telephone evidence***
(including the giving of evidence by live link and telephone generally)
R v Clark 2015 EWCA Crim 2192, 2016 1 Cr App R (S) 52 (p 332) D pleaded to affray and criminal damage. The defendant consented to be absent when the psychiatrists were to give evidence by live link. The link did not work and both counsel agreed after a considerable time had been wasted that the doctors could give evidence by telephone. Held. We note the definition of 'live link' in Criminal Procedure Rules 2015 2015/1490 Rule 2.2. It applies to telephone live links and to internet-based live links. However, evidence cannot be heard by telephone in a criminal case even where there is consent, *R v Diane* 2009 EWCA Crim 1494, 2010 2 Cr App R (S) 1 (p 1) and *R v Hampson* 2012 EWCA Crim 1807, 2014 1 Cr App R 4 (p 28). The rules are not as consistent or comprehensive as they might be. A defendant cannot give evidence by live link. Criminal Justice Act 2003 s 51 provides the evidence can be heard after 'a plea of guilty'. Consequently, if D had been convicted by a jury, live link could not have been used at all. Parliament should consider repealing the piecemeal legislation enabling new rules to be drafted.
In any event the evidence in D's hearing was not sworn. We therefore consider the matter afresh. After hearing from both doctors on live link that a Restriction Order was not necessary, we agreed with them and quash the order.
Note: In *R v Diane* 2009 trial evidence from a witness in Belgium was received by telephone. In *R v Hampson* 2012 an essential witness could not attend as he was on an oil rig. His evidence was also given by telephone. In both cases the conviction was quashed. Ed.

67.34 ***Restriction Orders Time limit***
R v Gardiner 1967 51 Cr App R 187 LCJ D was convicted of indecent assault on a boy and inciting two others to commit indecency. Held. We do not suggest that Restriction Orders should be made in every case, but it is very advisable that they should be made in all cases where it is thought that the protection of the public is required. Since in most cases the prognosis cannot be certain, the safer course is to make any Restriction Order unlimited in point of time. The only exception is where the doctors are able to assert confidently that recovery will take place within a fixed period when the Restriction Order can properly be limited to that period.
R v Haynes 1981 3 Cr App R (S) 330 LCJ D was made subject to a Hospital Order after he pleaded to manslaughter. He appealed the Restriction Order, which was without limit of time. Held. *R v Gardiner* 1967 affirmed. A Restriction Order without limit of time is not analogous to a determinate sentence.
R v Nwohia 1996 1 Cr App R (S) 170 D pleaded to ABH. There were other incidents of offending behaviour, including the production, but not use, of knives. He had not seriously hurt anyone in the past. D had been admitted to mental hospitals on previous occasions. Of three doctors, only one recommended a Restriction Order. The Judge imposed a Hospital Order and a Restriction Order without limit of time. Held. Making predictions about the future of this type of case is very difficult. In a case such as this,

unless there is some foundation in the medical evidence for saying that the patient can be cured within a particular period, it would be indeed unwise to put a limit on the Restriction Order.

67.35 *Restriction Orders On the facts, order correct/Judge able to make the order*
R v Nwohia 1996 1 Cr App R (S) 170 D pleaded to ABH. There were other incidents of offending behaviour, including the production, but not use, of knives. He had not seriously hurt anyone in the past. D had been admitted to mental hospitals on previous occasions. Of three doctors, only one recommended a Restriction Order. The Judge imposed a Hospital Order with a Restriction Order without limit of time. Held. It is not necessary to wait until someone is actually seriously injured before making a Restriction Order.
R v Safi 2007 EWCA Crim 1392 D pleaded to exposure, having exposed his erect penis to two women on two occasions, whilst running toward them fondling himself. D claimed there were voices telling him that these women wanted sexual relationships with him. Two doctors prepared reports which concluded that D was suffering from a psychotic illness, most likely schizophrenia. Two further reports were prepared by a third doctor. D stated that he planned to discontinue his medication. The third doctor's conclusion was that D posed a significant risk of committing another sexual offence. In his view a Restriction Order was required and subsequently recommended that it should be without limit of time. D was resistant to medication. Subsequently, there was a considerable improvement in D's condition, but a fourth doctor felt it highly likely that D's schizophrenia would re-emerge if he ceased taking his medication and engaged in recreational drug use, which he had done in the past. Held. We do not think the Judge can be faulted for concluding that there was a real risk of members of the public suffering serious harm from the appellant. Even if his reoffending did not go beyond the level of his previous offending, the Judge understandably thought that some people might be seriously affected by it. The Restriction Order was justified.
See also: *R v Golding* 2006 EWCA Crim 1965, 2007 1 Cr App R (S) 79 (p 486) (Plea to burglary. Restriction Order imposed. D had one conviction for assault in 1985. Judge was correct to impose a Restriction Order based on the risk of D committing further acquisitive offences which may lead to violence.)
R v Chiles 2012 EWCA Crim 196 (D pleaded to simple arson. He dialled 999 saying he had set fire to his curtains and told a fireman he wanted to be arrested. He suffered from psychotic illness and claimed to be suffering from harassment. He stated he started the fire to require the authorities to relocate him, but with no intention of destroying the building or causing injury. Neither doctor asked for a Restriction Order. There was ample material to make one.)
R v MS 2015 EWCA Crim 680 (Plea to voyeurism. Held camera in changing room used by a 13-year-old. 2004 conviction for voyeurism. Needed hospital treatment and had a history of non-co-operation with staff. With the evidence from the doctor, the Judge was entitled to make the order.)

67.36 *Restriction Orders On the facts, order incorrect*
Example: *R v Aden-Hassan* 2013 EWCA Crim 1252 (Two doctors said it was not necessary. We are slow to criticise the Judge but she did not identify why the wide powers otherwise available were not sufficient. Order quashed.)

67.37 *Restriction Order Explain sentence, Judge must/Suggested sentencing remarks*
Judicial College's Crown Court Compendium Part II Sentencing June 2018 page 6-11

> **Example**
> I have also considered whether this order should be subject to special restrictions {which are specified in section 41 of the Act}. Having heard the evidence of Dr…I am satisfied that because of the nature of your offence/act and also having regard to your past (including your history of mental illness) and to the risk that you will commit further offences if you are not detained, it is necessary to protect the public from serious harm and it is not possible to say for how long that will be so.
> Accordingly I order that you will be subject to the special restrictions set out in the Mental Health Act 1983 s 41 without limit of time.

67.38 ***Restriction Orders Termination of***

Powers of Secretary of State in respect of patients subject to restriction orders

Mental Health Act 1983 s 42(1) If the Secretary of State is satisfied that in the case of any patient a Restriction Order is no longer required for the protection of the public from serious harm, he may direct that the patient shall cease to be subject to the special restrictions, and where the Secretary of State so directs, the Restriction Order shall cease to have effect, and section 41(5) shall apply.

(2) At any time while a Restriction Order is in force in respect of a patient, the Secretary of State may, if he thinks fit, by warrant discharge the patient from hospital, either absolutely or subject to conditions. Where a person is absolutely discharged under this subsection, he shall thereupon cease to be liable to be detained by virtue of the relevant Hospital Order, and the Restriction Order shall cease to have effect accordingly.

Guardianship orders

67.39

Discharge A Guardianship Order can be discharged by the responsible clinician, the responsible local social services authority or by the nearest relative of the patient.[900] The order must be in writing.

Statistics

England and Wales Guardianship Orders Aged 21+

Year	2012	2013	2014	2015	2016	2017
Orders	7	6	5	1	5	4

For explanations about the statistics, see page 1-xii. For more detailed statistics, see www.banksr.com Other Matters Statistics tab

67.40 ***Power to order***

Mental Health Act 1983 s 37(1) Where a person is convicted of an offence punishable with imprisonment other than an offence the sentence for which is fixed by law, and the conditions mentioned in subsection (2) (see **67.8**) are satisfied, the court may place him under the guardianship of a local social services authority or of such other person approved by a local social services authority as may be so specified.

Mental Health Act 1983 s 37(8) For the purposes of this subsection 'sentence of imprisonment' includes any sentence or order for detention.

Mental Health Act 1983 s 37(6) An order placing an offender under the guardianship of a local social services authority or of any other person (in this Act referred to as 'a Guardianship Order') shall not be made under this section unless the court is satisfied that that authority or person is willing to receive the offender into guardianship.

Mental Health Act 1983 s 39A Where a court is minded to make a Guardianship Order in respect of any offender, it may request the local social services authority for the area in which the offender resides or last resided, or any other local social services authority that appears to the court to be appropriate:

[900] Mental Health Act 1983 s 23(1) and (2)

(a) to inform the court whether it or any other person approved by it is willing to receive the offender into guardianship, and

(b) if so, to give such information as it reasonably can about how it or the other person could be expected to exercise in relation to the offender the powers conferred by section 40(2) below,

and that authority shall comply with any such request.

Mental Health Act 1983 s 40(2) A Guardianship Order shall confer on the authority or person named in the order as guardian the same powers as a guardianship application made and accepted under Part II of this Act (see section 7-10).

Hybrid Orders

67.41 *Hybrid Orders (Hospital and limitation directions meaning imprisonment and a Hospital Order)*

Note: These orders are officially called hospital and limitation directions orders, Mental Health Act 1983 s 45A. A hospital direction means a direction that the patient shall be transferred to hospital. A limitation direction means a restriction direction, Mental Health Act 1983 s 45B. Ed.

Power of higher courts to direct hospital admission

Mental Health Act 1983 s 45A(1) This section applies where, in the case of a person convicted before the Crown Court of an offence the sentence for which is not fixed by law:

(a) the conditions mentioned in subsection (2) below are fulfilled, and

(b) the court considers making a Hospital Order in respect of him before deciding to impose a sentence of imprisonment ('the relevant sentence') in respect of the offence.

(2) The conditions referred to in subsection (1) above are that the court is satisfied, on the written or oral evidence of two registered medical practitioners:

(a) that the offender is suffering from mental disorder,

(b) that the mental disorder from which the offender is suffering is of a nature or degree which makes it appropriate for him to be detained in a hospital for medical treatment, and

(c) that appropriate medical treatment is available for him.

(3) The court may give both of the following directions, namely:

(a) a direction that, instead of being removed to and detained in a prison, the offender be removed to and detained in such hospital as may be specified in the direction (in this Act referred to as a 'hospital direction'), and

(b) a direction that the offender be subject to the special restrictions set out in section 41 above (in this Act referred to as a 'limitation direction').

(4) A hospital direction and a limitation direction shall not be given in relation to an offender unless at least one of the medical practitioners whose evidence is taken into account by the court under subsection (2) above has given evidence orally before the court.

(5) A hospital direction and a limitation direction shall not be given in relation to an offender unless the court is satisfied on the written or oral evidence of the approved clinician who would have overall responsibility for his case, or of some other person representing the managers of the hospital that arrangements have been made:

(a) for his admission to that hospital, and

(b) for his admission to it within the period of 28 days beginning with the day of the giving of such directions,

and the court may, pending his admission within that period, give such directions as it thinks fit for his conveyance to and detention in a place of safety.

(6) If within the said period of 28 days it appears to the Secretary of State that by reason of an emergency or other special circumstances it is not practicable for the patient to be

received into the hospital specified in the hospital direction, he may give instructions for the admission of the patient to such other hospital as appears to be appropriate instead of the hospital so specified.
(7) Where such instructions are given:
(a) the Secretary of State shall cause the person having the custody of the patient to be informed, and
(b) the hospital direction shall have effect as if the hospital specified in the instructions were substituted for the hospital specified in the hospital direction.
(8) Section 38(1) and (5) and section 39 above shall have effect as if any reference to the making of a hospital order included a reference to the giving of a hospital direction and a limitation direction.
(9) A hospital direction and a limitation direction given in relation to an offender shall have effect not only as regards the relevant sentence but also (so far as applicable) as regards any other sentence of imprisonment imposed on the same or a previous occasion.
For subsection 45A(3) see para **67.43**.
R v Drew 2003 UKHL 25, 2004 1 Cr App R (S) 8 (p 65) Lords Where both an order under Mental Health Act 1983 s 37 and a term of imprisonment are unsuitable in isolation, a section 45A order will be appropriate.
R v Staines 2006 EWCA Crim 15, 2 Cr App R (S) 61 (p 376) It is not necessarily wrong to impose an order under Mental Health Act 1983 s 45A where the offender suffers from a psychopathic disorder and a mental illness. The oddity is that it is not available for a mental illness alone. An order under Mental Health Act 1983 s 45A carries with it the distinct advantage that both sets of criteria, those that focus on medical grounds and those that focus upon the safety of the public, can be taken into account.
For a discussion about this order, see *R v Staines* 2006 2 Cr App R (S) 61 (p 376).
R v Poole 2014 EWCA Crim 1641, 2015 1 Cr App R (S) 2 (p 7) The Judge made a hybrid order with a limitation direction. The defence argued that it was inappropriate to make a limitation direction unless the conditions under section 41 were met. The Judge rejected this. Held. The Judge was right. If the conditions were made out for a hybrid order a limitation direction must be made. It is necessary to enable a transfer to prison.
R v Przybylski 2016 EWCA Crim 506 D was found unfit to plead and after treatment was judged fit to plead and changed his plea to guilty of wounding with intent and possession of an offensive weapon. D walked along a road with a broken and an unbroken bottle. When a cyclist, V, stopped at a traffic light, D smashed the unbroken bottle and repeatedly struck V with the bottles. Members of the public came to V's aid. V suffered multiple wounds. A psychiatrist said that D suffered from schizo-affective disorder and recommended a Hospital Order with a Restriction Order. The Judge passed a 10-year extended sentence (6 years' custody 4 years' extended licence) with a section 45A direction. At the appeal, the psychiatrist said that D was at a higher risk than many other patients of relapsing into a psychotic condition in the future. He was a person who is likely to need ongoing anti-psychotic medication, probably for the rest of his life, and will require very close supervision for many years to come in order to ensure that he remains mentally stable. Held. The culpability was reduced by D's mental illness. D was likely to continue presenting a danger to the public for more than 10 years. In our view a determinate prison sentence accompanied by a section 45A order does not provide sufficient protection for the public and accordingly the appellant's offences cannot appropriately be dealt with by means of the directions under section 45A. The only way to provide proper protection for the public is by means of a Hospital Order with a Restriction Order.

67.42 *Hybrid Orders Defendant aged under 21*

R v Fort 2013 EWCA Crim 2332, 2014 2 Cr App R (S) 24 (p 167) D pleaded to manslaughter on the basis of diminished responsibility. The Judge varied the sentence from life imprisonment to a Hybrid Order. D was aged under 21 when he pleaded. The Court assessed the position as if D had been sentenced to custody for life. Held. para 76

We agree with the conclusion in *Att-Gen's Ref No 54 of 2011* 2011 EWCA Crim 2276, 2012 1 Cr App R (S) 106 (p 635). Because D was aged under 21 when convicted, he could not be sentenced to imprisonment, even if he became 21 when sentenced, Powers of Criminal Courts (Sentencing) Act 2000 s 89 and *R v Danga* 1992 13 Cr App R (S) 408. Custody for life is not a sentence of imprisonment, Powers of Criminal Courts (Sentencing) Act 2000 s 94. Mental Health Act 1983 s 45A(1)(b) refers to a sentence of imprisonment. There is nothing in section 45A which refers to detention. The definition section at Mental Health Act 1983 s 55 which refers to section 47(5) means the power to order Hybrid Orders cannot be extended to those aged under 21.

67.43 ***Hybrid Orders The directions***
Mental Health Act 1983 s 45A(3) The court may give both of the following directions, namely:

(a) a direction that, instead of being removed to and detained in a prison, the offender be removed to and detained in such hospital as may be specified in the direction (in this Act referred to as a 'hospital direction'), and

(b) a direction that the offender be subject to the special restrictions set out in section 41 (in this Act referred to as a 'limitation direction', see **67.26**).

(4) A hospital direction and a limitation direction shall not be given in relation to an offender unless at least one of the medical practitioners whose evidence is taken into account by the court under subsection (2) has given evidence orally before the court.

(5) A hospital direction and a limitation direction shall not be given in relation to an offender unless the court is satisfied on the written or oral evidence of the approved clinician who would have overall responsibility for his case, or of some other person representing the managers of the hospital that arrangements have been made:

(a) for his admission to that hospital, and

(b) for his admission to it within the period of 28 days beginning with the day of the giving of such directions,

and the court may, pending his admission within that period, give such directions as it thinks fit for his conveyance to and detention in a place of safety.

For ***Hospital directions/limitation directions***, see the **Restriction Orders** section at **67.26**.

67.44 ***Hybrid Orders On the facts incorrect***
Att-Gen's Ref No 91 of 2014 2014 EWCA Crim 2891 (Hammer attack by defendant now aged 21 who was suffering from schizophrenia. The sentence should have been an extended sentence to give the public greater protection, see **288.11** in Volume 2.)

67.45 ***Explain sentence, Judge must/Suggested sentencing remarks***
Judicial College's Crown Court Compendium Part II Sentencing June 2018 page 6-12

> **Example**
> For the offence of {specify} I sentence you to {specify term} imprisonment and I direct, under the provisions of the Mental Health Act 1983 s 45A, that in the light of the psychiatric evidence namely {specify} the criteria for a hospital order are met; and so instead of being removed to and detained in a prison, you will be removed to and detained in {specify hospital}. You will be subject to the special restrictions set out in the Mental Health Act 1983 s 41 without limit of time.
> What this means is that you will be detained in hospital for as long as necessary. If and when it is no longer necessary and if your sentence has not expired you will be transferred to prison. Once in prison you will serve the remainder of the sentence which I have imposed. [Here explain the prison sentence and release provisions as appropriate, but add: On release from prison, in addition to the conditions on your licence you will also be subject to the conditions of your release from hospital.]

Combined with other orders

67.46 *Hybrid Orders Release*

R v Thompson and Others 2018 EWCA Crim 639, 2 Cr App R (S) 19 (p 164) (Five-judge court) para 5 If an offender, subject to a Hybrid Order (with a determinate or an extended sentence), has been returned to prison as treatment is no longer required, eligibility for release is the same as if he had received the determinate or extended sentence alone. If the offender remains in hospital, the limitation direction (or Restriction Order) expires on the date that the offender would have been released on licence (i.e. directed by the Parole Board in the case of an extended or indeterminate sentence) but he will remain in hospital until considered well enough to be discharged following the normal procedures.

R v Edwards and Others 2018 EWCA Crim 595, 2 Cr App R (S) 17 (p 120) The Court stated the guidance in *R v Thompson and Others* 2018 EWCA Crim 639 above and added: *Indeterminate sentences* para 9 If a section 45A patient's health improves such that his responsible clinician or the Tribunal notifies the Secretary of State that he [or she] no longer requires treatment in hospital, the Secretary of State will generally remit the patient to prison under Mental Health Act 1983 s 50(1). On arrival in prison, the section 45A order would cease to have any effect. Release would be considered by the Parole Board in the usual way. para 10 If a section 45A patient has passed their tariff date and the Tribunal then notified the Secretary of State that he is ready for conditional discharge, the Secretary of State could notify the Tribunal that he should be so discharged (Mental Health Act 1983 s 74(2)). In that case, the offender would be subject to mental health supervision and recall in the usual way. However, the Secretary of State would, in practice, refer the offender to the Parole Board.

67.47 *Combined with other orders General position*

Mental Health Act 1983 s 37(8) Where an order is made under this section, the court shall not:..(pass imprisonment, make a community order or impose a fine etc.) but the court may make any other order which it has power to make apart from this section and for the purposes of this subsection 'sentence of imprisonment' includes any sentence or order for detention.

67.48 *Bind overs of parents and guardians, Combined with*

Mental Health Act 1983 s 37(8) Where an order is made under this section, the court shall not:..make in respect of the offender an order under Powers of Criminal Courts (Sentencing) Act 2000 s 150 (binding over of parent or guardian).

67.49 *Community orders, Combined with*

Mental Health Act 1983 s 37(8) Where an order is made under this section, the court shall not:..make a community order (within the meaning of Criminal Justice Act 2003 Part 12) but the court may make any other order which it has power to make apart from this section and for the purposes of this subsection 'sentence of imprisonment' includes any sentence or order for detention.

67.50 *Detention, Combined with*

Mental Health Act 1983 s 37(8) Where an order is made under this section, the court shall not:..pass sentence of imprisonment…and for the purposes of this subsection 'sentence of imprisonment' includes any sentence or order for detention.

67.51 *Existing Hospital Orders or Guardianship Orders*

Mental Health Act 1983 s 40(5) Where a patient is the subject of a Hospital Order or Guardianship Order, any previous application, Hospital Order or Guardianship Order by virtue of which he was liable to be detained in a hospital or subject to guardianship shall cease to have effect, but if the first-mentioned order, or the conviction on which it was made, is quashed on appeal, this subsection shall not apply and section 22 (special provisions as to patients sentenced to imprisonment) shall have effect as if during any period for which the patient was liable to be detained or subject to guardianship under the order, he had been detained in custody as mentioned in that section.

67.52 ***Fines, Combined with***
Mental Health Act 1983 s 37(8) Where an order is made under this section, the court shall not:..impose a fine.

67.53 ***Imprisonment, Combined with***
Mental Health Act 1983 s 37(8) Where an order is made under this section, the court shall not:..pass a sentence of imprisonment.
See also the ***Hybrid Orders*** paras at **67.40**.

67.54 ***Referral Orders, Combined with***
Mental Health Act 1983 s 37(8) Where an order is made under this section, the court shall not:..make a Referral Order (within the meaning of Powers of Criminal Courts (Sentencing) Act 2000) in respect of the offence.

67.55 ***Serious Crime Prevention Orders, Combined with***
R v Dunning 2018 EWCA Crim 3018 D pleaded to three threats to kill involving a particular school and the Judge passed a Hospital Order and a Serious Crime Prevention Order (SCPO) banning D from the area where the school was and schools generally. D told mental health staff he harboured plans to launch a Dunblane-style gun attack on the primary school's children. The defence said as there was a Restriction Order in place and the SCPO was wrong it principle. The prosecution said a mere breach of the condition of release from the Hospital Order would not itself justify recall and D might benefit from clear boundaries. There was nothing wrong with the Judge's conclusions.

67.56 ***Youth Rehabilitation Orders, Combined with***
Mental Health Act 1983 s 37(8) Where an order is made under this section, the court shall not:..pass a Youth Rehabilitation Order (within the meaning of Criminal Justice and Immigration Act 2008 Part 1) in respect of the offence.

Matters arising after the order is made

67.57 ***Determining which hospital***
R v Marsden 1968 52 Cr App R 301 It is not necessary for a court to order admission to a hospital in the part of the country where he is normally resident. However, a transfer may later be appropriate if beds become available etc.

67.58 ***Information to be supplied to the hospital/guardian***
Criminal Procedure Rules 2015 2015/1490 Rule 28.9(1) This rule applies where the court:
(a) orders the defendant's detention and treatment in hospital, or
(b) makes a Guardianship Order.
(2) Unless the court otherwise directs, the court officer must, as soon as practicable, serve on (as applicable) the hospital or the guardian:
(a) a record of the court's order,
(b) such information as the court has received that appears likely to assist in treating or otherwise dealing with the defendant, including information about:
i) the defendant's mental condition,
ii) the defendant's other circumstances, and
iii) the circumstances of the offence.

67.59 ***Time limit to transfer individual to hospital***
Mental Health Act 1983 s 40(1) A Hospital Order shall be sufficient authority for a constable, an approved mental health professional or any other person directed to do so by the court to convey the patient to the hospital specified in the order within a period of 28 days.
R (DB) v Nottingham Healthcare NHS Trust 2008 EWCA Civ 1354, 2009 PTSR 547 High Court D was convicted of affray and initially sentenced to a Community Rehabilitation Order. He was then, and continued to be, a patient of the community mental health team and received anti-psychotic medication. Before returning to court, he was assessed by a forensic psychiatrist who recommended a Hospital Order. A second

confirmed that view, both recommending Arnold Lodge. About three and a half months later the Judge made a Hospital Order[901] directing his admission within 28 days to Wells Road. The mistake was noticed and on 21 December the Judge varied the order and required D's transfer to Arnold Lodge within 28 days of 21 December. D was admitted there on 17 January. It was common ground that the varied order ran from 17 December and not 21 December, therefore D was transferred after the 28-day period had expired. Held. The effect of a Hospital Order is set out in section 40, which expressly limits the authority conferred by an order made under section 37 to the period of 28 days from the date of the making of the order. It follows that, once the period of 28 days from 17 December 2004 had expired, the Hospital Order relating to the claimant ceased to have effect. It would be preferable for the standard form of order to specify the date when the 28-day period expires. In addition, it would be sensible for orders made under section 37 to include a direction or recommendation (for it has no statutory force) on the lines of that set out in the circular. The direction 'that pending admission to a hospital within the 28-day period, the defendant should be conveyed to and detained in a place of safety, namely…' had been, in each case, deleted. The result was that there was no lawful authority for his detention during that period.

67.60 ***Hospital Orders What do they entail?***

R v Drew 2003 UKHL 25, 2004 1 Cr App R (S) 8 (p 65) at para 9 adopting a passage in *R v Birch* 1989 11 Cr App R (S) 202, 'Once the offender is admitted to hospital pursuant to a Hospital Order or transfer order without restriction on discharge, his position is almost exactly the same as if he were a civil patient. In effect he passes out of the penal system and into the hospital regime. Neither the court nor the Secretary of State has any say in his disposal. Thus, like any other mental patient, he may be detained only for a period of 6 months, unless the authority to detain is renewed, an event which cannot happen unless certain conditions, which resemble those which were satisfied when he was admitted, are fulfilled. If the authority expires without being renewed, the patient may leave. Furthermore, he may be discharged at any time by the hospital managers or the "responsible medical officer". In addition to these regular modes of discharge, a patient who absconds or is absent without leave and is not retaken within 28 days is automatically discharged at the end of that period (section 18(5)) and if he is allowed continuous leave of absence for more than 6 (now 12) months, he cannot be recalled (section 17(5)).

Another feature of the regime which affects the disordered offender and the civil patient alike is the power of the responsible medical officer to grant leave of absence from the hospital for a particular purpose, or for a specified or indefinite period of time: subject always to a power of recall (except as mentioned above).

There are certain differences between the positions of the offender and of the civil patient, relating to early access to the Review Tribunal and to discharge by the patient's nearest relative, but these are of comparatively modest importance. In general the offender is dealt with in a manner which appears, and is intended to be, humane by comparison with a custodial sentence. A Hospital Order is not a punishment. Questions of retribution and deterrence, whether personal or general, are immaterial. The offender who has become a patient is not kept on any kind of leash by the court, as he is when he consents to a probation order with a condition of in-patient treatment. The sole purpose of the order is to ensure that the offender receives the medical care and attention which he needs in the hope and expectation of course that the result will be to avoid the commission by the offender of further criminal acts.'

67.61 ***Power to amend order Secretary of State***

Mental Health Act 1983 s 37(5) If within the said period of 28 days it appears to the Secretary of State that by reason of an emergency or other special circumstances it is not

[901] It is likely that this was because he had breached his order, but the judgment does not say this.

practicable for the patient to be received into the hospital specified in the order, he may give directions for the admission of the patient to such other hospital as appears to be appropriate instead of the hospital so specified, and where such directions are given:

(a) the Secretary of State shall cause the person having the custody of the patient to be informed, and

(b) the Hospital Order shall have effect as if the hospital specified in the directions were substituted for the hospital specified in the order.

67.62 ***Power to amend order Secretary of State Hybrid Orders***

Mental Health Act 1983 s 45A(6) If within the said period of 28 days it appears to the Secretary of State that by reason of an emergency or other special circumstances it is not practicable for the patient to be received into the hospital specified in the hospital direction, he may give instructions for the admission of the patient to such other hospital as appears to be appropriate instead of the hospital so specified.

(7) Where such instructions are given:

(a) the Secretary of State shall cause the person having the custody of the patient to be informed, and

(b) the hospital direction shall have effect as if the hospital specified in the instructions were substituted for the hospital specified in the hospital direction.

(8) Section 38(1) (see **68.1**) and (5) (see **68.5**) and section 39 (see **71.18**) shall have effect as if any reference to the making of a Hospital Order included a reference to the giving of a hospital direction and a limitation direction.

(9) A hospital direction and a limitation direction given in relation to an offender shall have effect not only as regards the relevant sentence but also (so far as applicable) as regards any other sentence of imprisonment imposed on the same or a previous occasion.

See also the ***Hybrid orders*** para at **67.41**.

67.63 ***Defendant absconds from hospital***

Mental Health Act 1983 s 40(6) Where:

(a) a patient admitted to a hospital in pursuance of a Hospital Order is absent without leave,

(b) a warrant to arrest him has been issued under Criminal Justice Act 1967 s 72, and

(c) he is held pursuant to the warrant in any country or territory other than the United Kingdom, any of the Channel Islands and the Isle of Man,

he shall be treated as having been taken into custody under section 18 (return and readmission of patients absent without leave) above on first being so held.

Appeals

67.64 ***Magistrates' Court, Appeals from***

Mental Health Act 1983 s 45(1) Where on the trial of an information charging a person with an offence a Magistrates' Court makes a Hospital Order or Guardianship Order in respect of him without convicting him, he shall have the same right of appeal against the order as if it had been made on his conviction, and on any such appeal the Crown Court shall have the same powers as if the appeal had been against both conviction and sentence.

(2) An appeal by a child or young person with respect to whom any such order has been made, whether the appeal is against the order or against the finding upon which the order was made, may be brought by him or by his parent or guardian on his behalf.

67.65 ***No hospital available and an appeal***

R v Jones 1977 Crim LR 158 LCJ Where Hospital Orders are suitable but not practicable because no hospital is available, it is not appropriate for such cases to come before the Court of Appeal as the only purpose to be served is to give the issue publicity. There is no reason to suppose the court will be able to make a Hospital Order.

Note: This is an old case, but the principles still make sense. Ed.

67.66 *Fresh evidence for the requirements*
R v Beesley and Others 2011 EWCA Crim 1021, 2012 1 Cr App R (S) 15 (p 71) Where a defendant wished to rely on a medical report to suggest that a Hospital Order should be made because of the requirements in Mental Health Act 1983 s 37, the rules for the admission of fresh evidence under Criminal Appeal Act 1968 s 23 had to be applied, *R v Hughes* 2009 EWCA Crim 841, 2010 1 Cr App R (S) 25 (p 146).
R v Fort 2013 EWCA Crim 2332, 2014 2 Cr App R (S) 24 (p 167) D pleaded to manslaughter on the basis of diminished responsibility. The Judge sentenced him to life, which was treated as custody for life. He appealed and relied on new medical reports. Held. para 64 The aim of any 'fresh evidence' pursuant to Criminal Appeal Act 1968 s 23 must be to assist in satisfying the burden upon him that: i) at the time of sentence he was suffering from a mental disorder that was susceptible to treatment, ii) the reason for the offence was D's mental disorder, iii) the appellant does not pose a significant risk of serious harm to members of the public occasioned by the commission of serious offences if his mental disorder were to be cured or substantially alleviated, so that iv) the sentence of custody for life was wrong in principle.
Note: Recent decisions show that the Court of Appeal is keen to receive evidence which helps them understand the defendant's mental condition, especially if there are re-assessments and uncertainty as to which assessments are correct. Ed.

67.67 *Appeal with new assessments suggesting the earlier assessments were wrong*
R v Beatty 2006 EWCA Crim 2359, MHLR 333 In 1991, D was sentenced to discretionary life, having pleaded to rape, kidnapping and making threats to kill. The minimum term was an unconfirmed 8 years. Originally a Hospital Order was thought by the Judge to be appropriate and an Interim Hospital Order was made so that D could be assessed. Evidence before the Judge showed that the statutory conditions were not made out. An assessment stated that D could not be treated and that D was an 'extremely and very dangerous man' who constituted a grave and immediate danger to the public. The Judge had no option but to pass an indeterminate sentence. In 1976 D was given a Hospital Order for the rape, attempted murder, wounding with intent and assault of a young girl. After D's life sentences his appeal was dismissed. D was admitted to Broadmoor for treatment under sections 47 and 49. There was evidence that he may be amenable to treatment. He was given 'technical lifer status'[902] (D was treated as if he were the subject of a Hospital Order). There was no restriction and D was subsequently discharged to a hostel and remained unsupervised in the community. The Home Office wrote a letter saying the new information that was available cast doubt on the medical evidence available to the Judge. The CCRC referred the case to the Court of Appeal. The Court of Appeal then considered fresh evidence. Held. There is an important distinction to be drawn between a life sentence prisoner who develops a mental illness or disorder post sentence and who is transferred to hospital under sections 47 and 49 of the 1983 Act and one whose condition was such at the time of sentence that the judge should have made a Hospital Order with a restriction under sections 37 and 41 of the 1983 Act. The present case falls fairly and squarely within the latter category. It is not as if some treatment or drug has come into existence subsequently that was not available or known about at the time of sentence. If the Judge had had the evidence before him that we have had it is inevitable that he would have made a Hospital Order with a Restriction Order. Hospital Order substituted.
R v Hughes 2010 EWCA Crim 1026 LCJ D pleaded to two offences of arson being reckless as to whether life was endangered. At sentence there was a psychiatric report which diagnosed depressive disorder. However, no issue of a Hospital Order was raised. Two months before the instant offences, he was admitted to hospital but a psychiatrist saw no evidence of depression or psychosis. The new report stated that D required continuing hospital treatment and talked in terms of years. The theme of D's paranoid

[902] This status was abolished by the Home Office in 2005, see para 58 of the judgment.

illness had changed with the passage of time. D received 5 years on each count, concurrent. The case was subject to an Attorney-General's reference and the sentence was increased to life imprisonment, with a minimum term of 3 years 9 months. However, after 2½ years of his sentence, D was transferred to Ashworth Hospital by order of the Home Secretary under Mental Health Act 1983 s 47 and has been there since. D was diagnosed with paranoid schizophrenia coupled with a personality disorder. In 2008 a report stated that D was suffering from paranoid schizophrenia at the time of the offences. The Crown did not seek to challenge the evidence in the new report. Held. There were strong reasons why a Hospital Order would be more suitable. It will provide continuity of care by forensic psychiatrists in a secure hospital for as long as is necessary, *R v Beatty* 2006 EWCA Crim 2359, MHLR 333. We take the view that this is a clear case, albeit a rare one, in which it has been found that the mental illness present now must have been present then. Hospital Order substituted for life sentence.

R v Vowles and Others 2015 EWCA Crim 45, 2 Cr App R (S) 6 (p 39) In what is now the leading case, the LCJ gave guidance on when to impose Hospital Orders and this is listed at **67.15** and other paragraphs. The Court also considered six appeals on their merits. In V's appeal, at para 90, in B's appeal, at para 100, and DI's appeal at para 161 the Court held that new psychiatric evidence did not show that V and B's IPP sentences and DI's life sentence were wrong in principle. In C's appeal, at para 114, JO's appeal at para 134 and M's appeal at para 200, the Court held that the new evidence showed that the evidence at the sentencing hearing was wrong and substituted a Hospital Order with a Restriction Order for C and M's IPP and JO's custody for life.

R v Kitchener 2017 EWCA Crim 937 In 2002, D pleaded to attempted murder. He stabbed a stranger, V, in the neck and tried to strangle her. V thought she was going to die but managed to raise the alarm. D walked away and then returned to kick her. D later admitted the attack. He said he was responding to hallucinations and intended to kill and torture V. It was D's 20th birthday and he was of good character. When aged 4, D witnessed a serious assault on his mother by his father. When aged 16, he was sexually abused. A medical report said, a) D did not suffer from any psychotic illness, b) D suffered from a number of psychiatric problems, and c) these problems did not amount to a serious mental illness. The Judge was satisfied that D had an unstable character, presented a serious danger to the public and was likely to commit violent offences in the future. D was sentenced to custody for life with a 4-year 8-month minimum term. In June 2007, D attempted suicide. He was assessed and transferred to Rampton Hospital. Medical reports before the Court said at the time of his sentence, D was suffering from a severe personality disorder. In particular he had 'depressive episodes', emotionally unstable personality disorder and dependent personality disorder. Another report agreed and said the disorder was intimately associated with the offence. Further, a) if D were to return to prison that would cause a deterioration to his condition, b) a personality disorder is difficult to detect in a 20-year-old, and c) it was in the public interest for a Hospital Order to be made. Held. Very considerable caution should be exercised before a Judge decides a Hospital Order is the appropriate disposal where a dangerous offender has committed a very violent crime and the offender is suffering from a personality disorder. The new evidence could not be obtained in 2002. Our task is not to conduct a re-sentencing exercise but to consider whether the sentence was wrong in principle or manifestly excessive. D needs hospital treatment. Prison is counter-productive to the treatment needed, which can only be provided in a hospital setting. That will provide the public with greater public protection by gradually securing D's successful return to the community. We substitute a Hospital Order with a Restrictions Order.

See also: *R v Colborne* 2014 EWCA Crim 286 (D was sentenced to 18 months' IPP in 2006. He was transferred to a hospital. Held. The evidence from two new doctors shows he was at the time suffering from paranoid schizophrenia. Hospital Order with a Restriction Order substituted.)

R v Janaway 2014 EWCA Crim 2244 (Another example where a Hospital Order with a Restriction Order was substituted for IPP, because the full picture was not before the sentencing Judge.)
R v Turner 2015 EWCA Crim 1249 (In 2007, report at Crown Court did not propose a Hospital Order. All those since did. Held. This was not an attempt to revisit an issue, not challenged at the right time. *R v Vowles and Others* 2015 considered. Hospital Order not 18 months' IPP.)
R v Hoppe 2016 EWCA Crim 2258 (Over 12 years out of time. Five new doctors. Consensus now and at the time of the sentence that the defendant suffered from mental illness. The risks to the public are best served with a Hospital Order and not with life. (The minimum term was served long ago.))

68 Hospital Orders, Interim

68.1 *Power to order*

Mental Health Act 1983 s 38(1) Where a person is convicted of an offence punishable with imprisonment (other than an offence the sentence for which is fixed by law) and the court before or by which he is convicted is satisfied, on the written or oral evidence of two registered medical practitioners:

(a) that the offender is suffering from mental disorder, and

(b) that there is reason to suppose that the mental disorder from which the offender is suffering is such that it may be appropriate for a Hospital Order to be made in his case,

the court may, before making a Hospital Order or dealing with him in some other way, make an order (in this Act referred to as 'an Interim Hospital Order') authorising his admission to such hospital as may be specified in the order and his detention there in accordance with this section.

68.2 *Judicial guidance*

R v Vowles and Others 2015 EWCA Crim 45, 2 Cr App R (S) 6 (p 39) LCJ para 56 A judge should [think] long and hard before making an interim order. Although there are now a number of private providers to the NHS who have facilities at which offenders who are the subject of interim orders can now be held, the making of such an order has the consequence that [for] the victim of the crime there is no closure until the final order is made, there are significant costs to the general administration of justice in bringing a case back to court and there is acute pressure on the availability of secure beds.

68.3 *Evidence required*

Mental Health Act 1983 s 38(3) At least one of the registered medical practitioners whose evidence is taken into account under subsection (1) above shall be employed at the hospital which is to be specified in the order.
For the ***Power to request information*** para see **67.16**.

68.4 *Test to apply*

Mental Health Act 1983 s 38(4) An Interim Hospital Order shall not be made…unless the court is satisfied, on the written or oral evidence…that arrangements have been made for his admission to that hospital and for his admission to it within the period of 28 days beginning with the date of the order, and if the court is so satisfied the court may, pending his admission, give directions for his conveyance to and detention in a place of safety.

68.5 *Maximum length of each order*

Mental Health Act 1983 s 38(5)(a) An Interim Hospital Order shall be in force for such period, not exceeding 12 weeks, as the court may specify when making the order.

68.6 *Attendance of the defendant subject to an Interim Hospital Order*
Mental Health Act 1983 s 38(2) In the case of an offender who is subject to an Interim Hospital Order, the court may make a Hospital Order without his being brought before the court if he is represented by an authorised person who is given an opportunity of being heard.

68.7 *Renewed, Interim order may be*
Mental Health Act 1983 s 38(5)(b) An Interim Hospital Order may be renewed for further periods of not more than 28 days at a time if it appears to the court, on the written or oral evidence of the responsible clinician, that the continuation of the order is warranted, but no such order shall continue in force for more than 12 months in all and the court shall terminate the order if it makes a Hospital Order in respect of the offender or decides after considering the written or oral evidence of the responsible clinician to deal with the offender in some other way.

68.8 *Renewals and the defendant's attendance*
Mental Health Act 1983 s 38(6) The power of renewing an Interim Hospital Order may be exercised without the offender being brought before the court if he is represented by counsel or a solicitor and his counsel or solicitor is given an opportunity of being heard.

68.9 *Duty to terminate Interim Order*
Mental Health Act 1983 s 38(5)(a) The court shall terminate the (Interim) order if it makes a Hospital Order in respect of the offender or decides after considering the written or oral evidence of the responsible clinician to deal with the offender in some other way.

69 HYGIENE PROHIBITION ORDERS

69.1
Food Safety and Hygiene (England) Regulations 2013 2013/2996 reg 7
There are two orders. One is a prohibition in the management of any food premises (regulation 7(4)), and the other imposes prohibitions (regulation 7(1)-(3)).
Availability The order is only available when a food business operator is convicted of an offence contrary to Food Safety and Hygiene (England) Regs 2013 reg 7.
Emergency notices and orders An enforcement authority may serve a Hygiene Emergency Prohibition notice. A Magistrates' Court may make a Hygiene Emergency Prohibition Order. For both powers see Food Safety and Hygiene (England) Regs 2013 reg 8.
Requirement to serve etc. a copy of the order The enforcement authority may serve a copy of the order on the food business operator and for reg 7(1) cases affix a copy of the order on the premises, Food Safety and Hygiene (England) Regs 2013 2013/2996 reg 7(5).
Revocation of the order Where an enforcement authority is satisfied that the food business operator has taken sufficient measures to secure that the health risk condition in a reg 7(1) case is no longer fulfilled it may [revoke] the order. For both powers see Food Safety and Hygiene (England) Regs 2013 2013/2996 reg 7.

Prohibition on the participation in the management of any food business

69.2 *Power to order*
Food Safety and Hygiene (England) Regulations 2013 2013/2996 reg 7(4) If:
(a) a food business operator is convicted of an offence under these Regulations, and
(b) the court by or before which he is so convicted thinks it proper to do so in all the circumstances of the case,
the court may, by an order, impose a prohibition on the food business operator participating in the management of any food business, or any food business of a class or description specified in the order.

69.3 *Test to apply*
Food Safety and Hygiene (England) Regulations 2013 2013/2996 reg 7(4)…b) the court thinks it proper to do so in all the circumstances of the case.

R v Crestdane Ltd 2012 EWCA Crim 958, 2013 1 Cr App R (S) 19 (p 102) LCJ The power to impose a prohibition is not limited to cases where closure of the premises is necessary in the interests of public health, nor should such a limitation be put upon those very general words which the regulations omit. Protection of the public against a present or future risk of injury is but one of the relevant considerations. Even if by the time of the hearing conditions in the kitchen have improved and the immediate danger to the public has passed with the result that the Hygiene Emergency Prohibition Order has been lifted, the court might conclude that there is such a risk of some future breach of the regulations, carrying with it such obvious dangers to the public health, that the court should prohibit the operator from future management of a food business. If a company cannot be trusted to be a food business operator without creating a serious risk to public health, then a Hygiene Prohibition Order will be necessary. However, regardless of the future risks, the facts of any particular offence might alone justify the imposition of a Hygiene Prohibition Order. There should be a sharp focus on the number, nature and extent of the offences proved against a defendant. The series of long-standing breaches accepted or condoned by the management plainly present a greater risk of future incidents than an isolated lapse by a particular individual; but then some single incident may have been so serious and can have had such disastrous consequences that the court may think it proper to impose the prohibition in all the circumstances of that case. The history of convictions or a failure to heed warnings or advice are plainly highly significant factors.

Improvements made after the event are obviously relevant, but protestations of future good conduct should be regarded with caution and even scepticism if there is a long history of previous breaches. Furthermore, in sentencing any particular offender for such offences the court should always have in mind that the imposition of, or the upholding of, a Hygiene Prohibition Order is likely to send out a powerful message to others working in the food industry that they must strictly comply with the requirements of rigorous food hygiene. If they fail to do so and serious breaches of the regulations result, then a conviction might be visited with an order preventing the defendant from future involvement in running food businesses. In an appropriate case such an order might follow even if the defendant has belatedly complied with the regulations. In sentencing for these offences, therefore, deterrence should always be an important consideration.

69.4 *On the facts, order correct*

R v Crestdane Ltd 2012 EWCA Crim 958, 2013 1 Cr App R (S) 19 (p 102) LCJ D pleaded early to 18 food hygiene offences. The restaurant seated 400 customers. Improvement notices were served in 2007. In 2010, D pleaded to nine food safety offences (£13,500 fine). Filth, mouse droppings and poor hygiene were found. In 2010 and 2011, three pest control reports detailed mouse problems. The recommendations in the last report went unheeded. In 2011, health officers found a widespread lack of compliance with food safety legislation. There were: a) ingrained dirt and there were mouldy vegetables on the floor in the chiller, b) a build-up of dirt and grease around the door architrave, c) thick deposits of grease and debris underneath the cookers and two service trolleys, d) the plastic cladding on the wall beneath the sink was dirty, e) the lid of a large plastic food container was covered in deposits of flour, dirt and mouse droppings, f) a heavy build-up of grease beneath the cooking range, g) widespread dirt, including a dirt-covered thermometer which was used to take the temperature of food, h) a serious mouse infestation which posed a very real risk of food contamination, and i) mouse droppings on the outside of rice containers, inside a roll of Clingfilm, and adjacent to cutlery and plates. A Hygiene Emergency Prohibition Order was served, which was later lifted. The annual turnover was about £2m and the profit was £840,000+. The Court imposed a £51,000 fine (no appeal) and made a Hygiene Prohibition Order. The company was now in breach of its lease. Each day there were 52 staff who had all been laid off. Held. The state of the premises was shocking. The remedial action was taken too late. We cannot now trust what the company says. There is an obvious risk to public safety if they continue to operate the business. Having regard to the sustained and serious nature of the breaches, the previous conviction and the company's failure to heed the previous warnings and advice, the order was entirely proportionate to the facts found.

Imposing prohibitions

69.5 *Power to order prohibitions*

Food Safety and Hygiene (England) Regulations 2013 2013/2996 reg 7(1) If:

(a) a food business operator is convicted of an offence under these Regulations, and

(b) the court by or before which he is so convicted is satisfied that the health risk condition is fulfilled with respect to the food business concerned,

the court shall by an order impose the appropriate prohibition.

(2) The health risk condition is fulfilled with respect to any food business if any of the following involves risk of injury to health (including any impairment, whether permanent or temporary), namely:

(a) the use for the purposes of the business of any process or treatment,

(b) the construction of any premises used for the purposes of the business, or the use for those purposes of any equipment, and

(c) the state or condition of any premises or equipment used for the purposes of the business.

69.6 *Test to apply*

Food Safety and Hygiene (England) Regulations 2013 2013/2996 reg 7(1) If …the court…is satisfied that the health risk condition is fulfilled with respect to the food business concerned, the court shall…impose the appropriate prohibition.

Note: For the full regulation, see **69.5**.

69.7 *What prohibition should be ordered?*

Food Safety and Hygiene (England) Regulations 2013 2013/2996 reg 7(3) The appropriate prohibition is:

(a) in a case falling within paragraph (2)(a) (see **69.5**), a prohibition on the use of the process or treatment for the purposes of the business,

(b) in a case falling within paragraph (2)(b) (see **69.5**), a prohibition on the use of the premises or equipment for the purposes of the business or any other food business of the same class or description, and

(c) in a case falling within paragraph (2)(c) (see **69.5**), a prohibition on the use of the premises or equipment for the purposes of any food business.

IMPRISONMENT see the **CUSTODY: GENERAL PRINCIPLES** and **CUSTODY: IMPRISONMENT** chapters.

70 IMPRISONMENT FOR PUBLIC PROTECTION (REPEALED)

70.1

Criminal Justice Act 2003 s 224-235

The repeal of IPP Legal Aid, Sentencing and Punishment of Offenders Act 2012 s 123-124, which came into force on 3 December 2012,[903] abolished: a) IPP, b) DPP, and c) Criminal Justice Act 2003 first set of extended sentences. Parliament's intention was to substitute the new extended sentences (see the **EXTENDED SENTENCES (EDS)** chapter) for IPP and DPP. The extended sentence is often called EDS (Extended Determinate Sentence).

The repeals are limited to Criminal Justice Act 2003 s 225(3)-(4) (IPP), s 226(3)-(4) (DPP), s 227 (extended sentences for those aged 18+) and s 228 (extended sentences for those aged under 18). The dangerousness provisions have been retained and continue to apply to life sentences and to the new extended sentences.

[903] Legal Aid, Sentencing and Punishment of Offenders Act 2012 (Commencement No 4 and Saving Provisions) Order 2012 2012/2906

These provisions will not affect those given IPP before the commencement date.
Release Release for prisoners serving IPP and DPP is via the Parole Board on expiry of the minimum term. The test is whether 'the prisoner's confinement is no longer necessary for the protection of the public', Crime (Sentences) Act 1997 s 28(6)(b) and 34(2)(d). On release, the prisoner is subject to supervision.
Appeals On 18 March 2016, the Lord Chief Justice heard 13 joined appeals where it was submitted that IPP had been imposed wrongly between five and nine years previously. All the appeals were rejected and the Court stressed the need for appeals to be brought within the 28-day time limit, *R v Roberts and Others* 2016 EWCA Crim 71, 2 Cr App R (S) 14 (p 98). There was nothing in the judgment to help those trapped in prison with wrongly imposed IPP sentences.
Rehabilitation period All the IPP, DPP and extended sentences are excluded from rehabilitation.[904]
See also the **REHABILITATION OF OFFENDERS ACT 1974** chapter.

71 INFORMANTS/GIVING EVIDENCE FOR THE PROSECUTION

71.1

The courts can make sentence reductions when the defendant is subject to a written agreement under Serious Organised Crime and Police Act 2005 s 73 or when the defendant does not sign such an agreement.
Crown Court judges tend to give substantial discounts to those giving very significant help to the authorities a) to encourage others, b) perhaps because judges consider the chance of their reoffending may be less than that of other career criminals, and c) perhaps because holding them in prison can be problematic.

71.2 *Court Martial*

Note: Armed Forces Act 2016 s 7-12 inserts Armed Forces Act 2006 s 304(B)-(H), which introduces immunity to prosecutions, undertakings as to the use of evidence, reductions in sentence and reviews of sentence for informants. No commencement order has been issued. Ed.

General principles

71.3 *The proper approach*

R v King 1985 7 Cr App R (S) 227 LCJ One then has to turn to the amount by which the starting figure should be reduced. The quality and quantity of the material disclosed by the informer is one of the things to be considered, as well as accuracy and the willingness or otherwise of the informer to confront other criminals and to give evidence against them in due course if required in court. Another aspect to consider is the degree to which he has put himself and his family at risk by reason of the information he has given, in other words the risk of reprisal. The reasoning behind this practice is expediency. It is to the advantage of law-abiding citizens that criminals should be encouraged to inform upon their criminal colleagues. They know that if they do so they are likely to be the subject of unwelcome attention, to say the least, for the rest of their lives. They know that their days of living by crime are probably at an end. Consequently, an expectation of substantial mitigation of what would otherwise be the proper sentence is required in order to produce the desired result, namely the information. The amount of that mitigation, it seems to us, will vary from about one-half to two-thirds reduction according to the circumstances.
R v P 2007 EWCA Crim 2290, 2008 2 Cr App R (S) 5 (p 16) [The discount for helping the authorities] is a long-standing and entirely pragmatic convention. The stark reality is that without it major criminals who should be convicted and sentenced for offences of the utmost seriousness might, and in many cases certainly would, escape justice. Moreover, the very existence of this process, and the risk that an individual for his own

[904] Rehabilitation of Offenders Act 1974 s 5(1)(f)

selfish motives may provide incriminating evidence, provides something of a check against the belief, deliberately fostered to increase their power, that gangs of criminals, and in particular the leaders of such gangs, are untouchable and beyond the reach of justice. The greatest disincentive to the provision of assistance to the authorities is an understandable fear of consequent reprisals. Those who do assist the prosecution are liable to violent ill-treatment by fellow prisoners generally, but quite apart from the inevitable pressures on them while they are serving their sentences, the stark reality is that those who betray major criminals face torture and execution. Sentences should reflect all the relevant circumstances rather than mathematical computations. It is only in the most exceptional case that the appropriate level of reduction would exceed **three-quarters** of the total sentence which would otherwise be passed, and the normal level will continue, as before, to be a reduction of somewhere **between one-half and two-thirds** of that sentence.
R v Bevans 2009 EWCA Crim 2554, 2010 2 Cr App R (S) 31 (p 199) LCJ The essential principle is that no hard-and-fast rules can be laid down for this fact-specific decision.
R v AXN and ZAR 2016 EWCA Crim 590, 2 Cr App R (S) 33 (p 341)[905] LCJ We were told far greater use is made of the system established under the common law than the statutory scheme.

71.4 *Police practice and responsibilities*
R v AXN and ZAR 2016 EWCA Crim 590, 2 Cr App R (S) 33 (p 341)[906] LCJ para 7 Police currently follow the following practice. The text will set out:
(i) The offender's status and whether he is a Covert Human Intelligence Source (CHIS) under the Regulation of Investigatory Powers Act 2000.
(ii) The details of the assistance provided, the information or intelligence provided and whether he is willing to be a witness.
(iii) The effort to which the offender had gone to obtain the information.
(iv) Any risk to the offender or his family.
(v) An assessment of the benefit derived by the police, including any arrests or convictions or any property recovered.
(vi) Any financial reward the offender has already received for the assistance provided.
(vii) A statement as to whether the offender will be of future use to the police.

71.5 *Foreign criminals, Information about*
Att-Gen's Ref 2017 Re Orr 2017 EWCA Crim 1639 D pleaded to 17 child sex and image offences. The Judge took into account his informing. Since that sentence D helped with identifying a serious sex offender in Australia resulting in his being arrested and pleading guilty. Held. For that we discount the appropriate figure by 20%.

71.6 *Discount How great should it be?*
R v A and B 1999 1 Cr App R (S) 52 LCJ Where defendants co-operate with the prosecuting authorities, not only by pleading guilty but by testifying or expressing willingness to testify, or making a witness statement which incriminates a co-defendant, they will ordinarily earn an enhanced discount, particularly where such conduct leads to the conviction of a co-defendant or induces a co-defendant to plead guilty. It has been the long-standing practice of the courts to recognise by a further discount of sentence the help given, and expected to be given, to the authorities in the investigation, detection, suppression and prosecution of serious crime: see e.g. *R v Sinfield* 1981 3 Cr App R (S) 258, *R v King* 1985 7 Cr App R (S) 227 and *R v Sivan* 1988 10 Cr App R (S) 282. The extent of the discount will ordinarily depend on the value of the help given and expected to be given. Value is a function of quality and quantity. If the information is accurate,

[905] Also known as *R v N* 2016 EWCA Crim 590, 2 Cr App R (S) 33
[906] Also known as *R v N* 2016 EWCA Crim 590, 2 Cr App R (S) 33

particularised, useful in practice, and hitherto unknown to the authorities, enabling serious criminal activity to be stopped and serious criminals brought to book, the discount may be substantial.

R v P 2007 EWCA Crim 2290, 2008 2 Cr App R (S) 5 (p 16) Sentences should reflect all the relevant circumstances rather than mathematical computations. It is only in the most exceptional case that the appropriate level of reduction would exceed **three-quarters** of the total sentence which would otherwise be passed, and the normal level will continue, as before, to be a reduction of somewhere **between one-half and two-thirds** of that sentence.

R v Patel 2007 EWCA Crim 3159 The starting point for all in this tax fraud was 12 months. The co-defendants who were equally involved received 8 months after a late plea. Held. It was in the highest degree important in fraud cases of this kind that defendants should be given every encouragement to break ranks with co-defendants and make a statement implicating them. Sentence reduced from 4 months to **1 month** to enable immediate release.

R v Bevans 2009 EWCA Crim 2554, 2010 2 Cr App R (S) 31 (p 199) LCJ D pleaded to murder after Derek Blackburn, an informer, had given evidence. (For details of Blackburn's appeal after pleading to assisting an offender, see *R v P and Blackburn* 2007 EWCA Crim 2290, 2008 2 Cr App R (S) 5 (p 16).) He also pleaded to conspiracy to supply drugs (7 years concurrent). V was shot dead in a gangland execution. F fired the shots. D was the driver. V's income was largely from drugs. Before D's trial he had agreed to enter into a statutory agreement. However, he refused to be interviewed, and then after he had been interviewed he refused to give evidence. But D did say he would provide information about a corrupt DC's relationship with F. The DC was on a retainer to provide information about F on police computers. The Judge started at 27 years and gave 1 year off for the plea, making 26. Then eight months after D's plea, D entered into a statutory agreement which was silent about F's part in the murder. When the investigation into the DC started, the corrupt relationship was over. D gave evidence which was considered truthful. He was strenuously cross-examined and did not exaggerate his evidence. D was a career criminal. His sentence was reviewed and his term was reduced by 5 years. He asked for a greater discount. Held. The essential principle is that no hard-and-fast rules can be laid down for this fact-specific decision. D's level of co-operation was completely calculated. It was far from full. 5 years was sufficient, as that equated to a 10-year determinate term.

R v Dougall 2010 EWCA Crim 1048, 2011 1 Cr App R (S) 37 (p 227) LCJ D pleaded to conspiracy to corrupt. Over 4 years D's company was involved in nearly £20m sales of medical equipment. There were also others higher up who were involved. Corrupt payments of 20% were made to doctors and intermediaries. D gave very significant international help under a statutory agreement. He was given 12 months. Held. Where the appropriate sentence for a defendant whose level of criminality and features of mitigation, combined with a guilty plea and full co-operation with the authorities investigating a major crime involving fraud or corruption, with all the consequent burdens of complying with his part of the SOCPA agreement, would be 12 months' imprisonment or less, the argument that the sentence should be suspended is very powerful. This result will normally follow. This seems to us to face the practical realities and produce a pragmatic answer to the problem. We are not to be misunderstood as saying that in circumstances like those we have outlined here, a suspended sentence must always be ordered. The sentence should have been suspended.

R v K 2013 EWCA Crim 627 D pleaded to cultivation of cannabis. The Judge started at 4½ years. He reduced the sentence by a third for his plea and a further 18 months because of his assistance, making 18 months. D on appeal asked for that to be suspended. Held. After *R v Dougall* 2010 was decided, suspended sentences can be 2 years long. The same argument made in that case can be made here. The proper approach here is to suspend the sentence.

R v Campbell 2018 EWCA Crim 802, 2 Cr App R (S) 24 (p 222) D pleaded to possession with intent to supply of cocaine (40 months) and of cannabis (no penalty). D was a drug dealer. He was the victim of an attempted murder and a robbery at his home address. He was shot and received physical and psychological injuries. He spent three weeks in hospital and had bullets remaining in his stomach and thigh. His recovery was estimated to take 12 months. D and his wife gave evidence at the attempted murder trial. The Judge gave a discount for D's injury and his trauma but declined to give evidence for D's co-operation with the police and his giving of evidence. Held. That was wrong in principle. For this issue everything will depend on the degree of the assistance and the extent the assistance contributed to a successful co-operation. Here the prosecution had other evidence to prove the identity of the robbers so the assistance was very limited. On these facts we decline to reduce the sentence.
Note: A defendant is entitled to be considered for a discount even if the prosecution decide not to use his or her assistance. The problem here is that it is difficult to persuade criminals to give evidence against their assailants. At the time D chose to assist he would not know what the strength of the evidence against the robbers was. The failure to give a clear discount will discourage other criminals from giving assistance. The fear of retribution in prison and to criminals' families remains whether the evidence is very useful or not. That is why most Judges use their sentencing power to encourage other people to provide assistance. Ed.
See also: *R v Nshuti* 2012 EWCA Crim 1530 (Plea (full credit) to conspiracy to supply heroin and crack. Found with five wraps of heroin and one of crack. Thereafter, test purchases made. Dealing £900 of drugs at street value three times per week for three to four months. Assisted police by implicating the manager of the operation. Because of the assistance given, we start at **4½ years**, not 7½. With full credit for the plea, **3 years' detention** not 4 years 3 months, representing a total 60% discount.)
R v Hankin 2013 EWCA Crim 749 (D pleaded to conspiracy to supply MDMA (class A). Police were watching a friend of D who allowed him to stay at his flat. D was asked to store MDMA. 30 kilos at 100% purity. Stored for four to five weeks. Custodian. No benefit or reward. Aged 69 at appeal. Previous good character. Remorseful. Gave evidence against a co-accused. No formal agreement. Suffered threats. 50% discount for police assistance. Starting at 10 years, reduced to 5. Full credit. **3 years 4 months** not 5 years.)
See also the ***Formal agreements What is the proper discount?*** para at **71.10**.

Formal agreements

71.7 *Formal agreements General principles*

Serious Organised Crime and Police Act 2005 s 73(1)-(2) provides that where a defendant has, pursuant to a written agreement, assisted or offered to assist the investigator or prosecutor, the court may take into account the extent and the nature of the assistance offered. Serious Organised Crime and Police Act 2005 s 73(4) provides that where the court passes a lesser sentence in such cases the court shall state that it has done so and what the greater sentence would have been, unless it would not be in the public interest to disclose it.
R v P 2007 EWCA Crim 2290, 2008 2 Cr App R (S) 5 (p 16) The process is not confined to offenders who provide assistance in relation to crimes in which they were participants, or accessories, or with which they were otherwise linked. At the end of this process the sentence actually imposed may be appealed to this Court in the usual way. Where the review arises from a defendant's failure or refusal to provide assistance in accordance with the written agreement, the sentencing Judge will already have in mind the sentence which would have been passed 'but for the assistance given or offered'. This sentence should be readily ascertained from the sentencing remarks where the judge, in compliance with section 73(3)(b), has identified, as he normally should, the sentence which would have been imposed but for the assistance given or offered. We doubt whether,

save exceptionally, it would be right for the sentence indicated at that stage to be subject to any reduction, but equally, as section 73(5) provides, it should not be increased by way of punishment for a defendant who has backed away from the agreement. Non-compliance is not a separate crime, nor indeed an aggravating feature of the original offence, the penalty is that the defendant will be deprived of the reduction of sentence which would have been allowed if he had complied with the agreement. Instead he will normally serve the appropriate sentence for his criminality in full. The review itself is not an appeal against sentence, whether imposed in the Crown Court or this Court. It is a fresh process which takes place in new circumstances. Accordingly the process of review is not inhibited by the fact that this Court has already heard and decided an appeal against the original sentence, whether the sentence is varied on appeal or not. The existing 'text' system, verified in the usual way (as to which see *R v X* 1999 2 Cr App R (S) 294, *R v R* 2002 EWCA Crim 267) may still be used, where appropriate, either before sentence is imposed in the Crown Court, or indeed at the hearing of an appeal against sentence. In summary, pragmatism still obtains. SOCPA 2005 does not include any direct provision suggesting the level of discount appropriate to be provided to a defendant who enters into and performs the SOCPA 2005 agreement. The general principles are well established in a series of decided cases. These include *R v Sinfield* 1981 3 Cr App R (S) 258, *R v King* 1985 7 Cr App R (S) 227, *R v Sivan* 1988 10 Cr App R (S) 282, *R v Debagg and Izzet* 1991 12 Cr App R (S) 733, *R v X* 1994 15 Cr App R (S) 750, *R v Sehitoglu and Ozakan* 1998 1 Cr App R (S) 89, *R v A and B* 1999 1 Cr App R (S) 52, *R v K* 2002 EWCA Crim 927, 2003 1 Cr App R (S) 6 (p 22), *R v R* 2002 EWCA Crim 267, *R v A* 2006 EWCA Crim 1803, 2007 1 Cr App R (S) 60 (p 347) and *R v Z* 2007 EWCA Crim 1473. The first principle is obvious. No hard-and-fast rules can be laid down for what, as in so many other aspects of the sentencing decision, is a fact-specific decision. The first factor in any sentencing decision is the criminality of the defendant, weight being given to such mitigating and aggravating features as there may be. Thereafter, the quality and quantity of the material provided by the defendant in the investigation and subsequent prosecution of crime falls to be considered. Addressing this issue, particular value should be attached to those cases where the defendant provides evidence in the form of a witness statement or is prepared to give evidence at any subsequent trial, and does so, with added force where the information either produces convictions for the most serious offences, including terrorism and murder, or prevents them, or which leads to disruption to or indeed the break-up of major criminal gangs. Considerations like these then have to be put in the context of the nature and extent of the personal risks to and potential consequences faced by the defendant and the members of his family. In most cases the greater the nature of the criminality revealed by the defendant, the greater the consequent risks. The vast majority of the earlier authorities were decided before the arrangements for calculating the discounts for a guilty plea were formalised, as they now have been by statute and the Sentencing Guidelines Council. When it applies, the discount for the guilty plea is separate from and additional to the appropriate reduction for assistance provided by the defendant, *R v Wood* 1997 1 Cr App R (S) 347. Accordingly, the discount for the assistance provided by the defendant should be assessed first, against all other relevant considerations, and the notional sentence so achieved should be further discounted for the guilty plea. In the particular context of the SOCPA 2005 arrangements, the circumstances in which the guilty plea indication was given, and whether it was made at the first available opportunity, may require close attention. Finally, we emphasise that in this type of sentencing decision a mathematical approach is liable to produce an inappropriate answer, and that the totality principle is fundamental. In this Court, on appeal, focus will be on the sentence, which should reflect all the relevant circumstances, rather than its mathematical computation. It is only in the most exceptional case that the appropriate level of reduction would exceed

three-quarters of the total sentence which would otherwise be passed, and the normal level will continue, as before, to be a reduction of somewhere **between one-half and two-thirds** of that sentence.

R v H and Others 2009 EWCA Crim 2485, 2010 2 Cr App R (S) 18 (p 104) LCJ The statutory regime does not extinguish the text regime or alter the text principles. There is no potential conflict between them. The statutory regime offers greater potential benefit to the public interest, so the text discount will be less.

R v Dougall 2010 EWCA Crim 1048, 2011 1 Cr App R (S) 37 (p 227) LCJ The SFO cannot enter into an agreement about the penalty. The constitutional position is that, save in minor matters like motoring offences, the imposition of the sentence is a matter for the judiciary. There may be discussion and agreement about the basis of plea, the court must rigorously scrutinise in open court in the interest of transparency and good governance the basis of plea and see whether it reflects the public interest. This statement from the SFO was advancing submissions. It should have simply and objectively drawn the Court's attention to potential mitigation. A 12-month sentence does not have to be suspended. However, here, taking into account the release in half the sentence and the early release provisions (curfew and tag), it would be appropriate to suspend it.

R v D 2010 EWCA Crim 1485, 2011 1 Cr App R (S) 69 (p 424) LCJ D was charged with importing class A drugs. He absconded and was subsequently arrested. He pleaded not guilty and 'played the system' until he changed his plea shortly before trial. He was sentenced. He then expressed willingness to provide intelligence to SOCA. In the meantime, leave to appeal against sentence was refused. He provided information, but refused to give evidence against an individual who was subsequently convicted. D then entered into a Serious Organised Crime and Police Act 2005 s 73 agreement (a SOCPA agreement). He did not agree to give evidence. At the time of appeal, no arrests had taken place. Following the SOCPA agreement, the case was restored to the list to be reviewed, under the legislation. The Judge discounted the sentence "in the region of 25 per cent". Held. a) Where an individual provides information of considerable value, does everything asked of them by SOCA and fulfils their end of the 'contract' in entirety, they are not entitled to the 'normal' discount of 50-66% of the sentence that would have been passed after a trial. b) It is not necessarily the case that because the individual has given information which is not of a nature which could readily be converted into admissible evidence to be given from a witness box, and he is accordingly not asked to give evidence, the reduction in sentence should be less than 50%. As we explained in *R v P* 2007 EWCA Crim 2290, 2008 2 Cr App R (S) 5 (p 16) 'what the defendant has earned by participating in the written agreement system is an appropriate reward for the assistance provided for the administration of justice'. That, in the end, is always fact-specific. c) There may be cases when information and intelligence may be offered which will be of inestimable value to the administration of justice, and about which, for example, the defendant cannot, even if he wished, provide admissible evidence at any subsequent trial. Again, it does not necessarily follow that the absence of any arrest consequent on the provision of information automatically renders it less valuable than it might reasonably be expected to be. d) The mere fact of delay does not result in an automatic reduction of discount. In the present case the information or intelligence provided by the applicant was provided after he had sought, unsuccessfully, to manipulate the system to his advantage. His co-operation only began after sentence had been imposed on him and he had been in custody for over a year. Naturally he could not be blamed for the delays which arose after he decided to co-operate, but the delay for which he was responsible diminished the value of the information he provided. To the extent that it has, then the level of discount must be reduced proportionately.

71.8 ***Formal agreements Exclusion of the public etc.***

R v P 2007 EWCA Crim 2290, 2008 2 Cr App R (S) 5 (p 16) No new powers in relation to publicity arise in relation to sentences imposed in the context of a written agreement under section 73. The publicity provisions in Serious Organised Crime and Police

Act 2005 s 75 are directed to reviews under section 74. While it is crucial to the entire process that the identity of those who provide assistance should, so far as practicable, be concealed, it is simultaneously fundamental to our criminal justice system that sentences should be imposed in open court, after public hearings. As reviews produce a decision of the court relating to sentence, unless absolutely necessary, the normal principle that sentences must not be imposed or reduced or altered after private hearings, privately ordered, should as far as possible be applied to them. In the review process section 73(4) and (7) allow the court first, not to disclose, save to the prosecutor and the defendant, that a sentence has been discounted, and second, allow the court to disapply Criminal Justice Act 2003 s 174, which requires the court to explain the reasons for its sentences. Reality must be faced. Professional criminals appreciate the likely range of sentence if they are convicted, and more important, they will quickly discover the purpose of any review process. A post-sentence reduction following a section 74 review will convey, at the very least, that something very unusual has happened, and criminals are perfectly well able to ask themselves why a reduction has been ordered, and then form their own conclusions. That said, actual knowledge will turn suspicion into confirmed fact. By section 75 the court is empowered to exclude the media and their representatives from the review. The power should be used with great caution, particularly where the review arises under section 74(2) following failure to fulfil an agreement to provide assistance. In any event where practicable alternatives are available, they should, if possible, be adopted. For example, it may be possible to anonymise the proceedings. It may also be possible to admit authorised representatives of the media subject to an order prohibiting publication of the whole or any specific aspect of the proceedings without the approval of the court. Alternatively, if the media have been excluded from any part of the hearing, the court may be able to provide information about the outcome of the review, together with a brief summary of the reasons for the decision, sufficient, even if brief, to enable the public to understand it, without disclosing any relevant identities. To the fullest extent it can, it should. In any event a full transcript of the entire hearing of the proceedings should be prepared immediately after its conclusion, and retained in appropriate conditions of secrecy by the specified prosecutor, and kept available for further directions by the court in relation to publicity if and when the public interest so requires, at least until further order by the court, and in any event until the end of the sentence.

71.9 *Formal agreements Minimum sentences*

Serious Organised Crime and Police Act 2005 s 73(5) Nothing in any requirement which a) requires that a minimum sentence is passed, or b) where the sentence is fixed by law, requires the court to take into account certain matters etc., affects the power of the court to act under section 73(2) (power to take into account assistance given where there is a written agreement). (Section summarised. Ed.)

71.10 *Formal agreements What is the proper discount?*

R v D 2010 EWCA Crim 1485, 2011 1 Cr App R (S) 69 (p 424) LCJ D was charged with importing class A drugs. He absconded and was subsequently arrested. He pleaded not guilty and 'played the system' until he changed his plea shortly before trial. He was sentenced. He then expressed willingness to provide intelligence to SOCA. In the meantime, leave to appeal against sentence was refused. He provided information, but refused to give evidence against an individual who was subsequently convicted. D then entered into a Serious Organised Crime and Police Act 2005 s 73 formal agreement (a SOCPA agreement). He agreed to provide, among other information, details of everything within his knowledge or belief about the drug trafficking activities of some 32 individuals and similar details in relation to the criminal activities of four individuals suspected of involvement in money laundering and the investment of the proceeds of crime in property. He did not agree to give evidence. At the time of appeal, no arrests had taken place. Following the SOCPA agreement, the case was restored to the list to be reviewed under the legislation. The Judge discounted the sentence "in the region of 25 per cent". Held. D performed his agreement, and provided valuable information, but nevertheless it was a limited agreement. He did not describe his own full criminality. He was not prosecuted for it. He did not agree or offer to give evidence against anyone. He declined to give evidence against the criminal he identified when he first approached the authorities with a view to acting as a possible informant. In short, as he was entitled, the agreement he entered into was much less comprehensive than it might have been. The Judge's 25% discount should not be interfered with.

R v Hood 2012 EWCA Crim 1260, 2013 1 Cr App R (S) 49 (p 273) D pleaded to murder. He entered into a formal agreement and then gave evidence against his girlfriend. She was convicted of the same murder. The prosecution considered his evidence as significant. The Judge held: a) D had not exposed himself to a serious risk, b) D had not told the whole truth, c) D had lied when he said that he had given evidence because he wanted the victim's family to have closure, and d) D's motive was the statutory discount. The Judge factored in that the crime was of the gravest kind. Held. We endorse that approach. Cases of assistance involve assessing both the gravity of the offence which the defendant has committed and also the gravity of the offence which he is giving evidence about. There is no tariff for the appropriate reduction to reflect assistance given to the Crown, whether including the giving of evidence or not. Every case depends upon its facts. The 'normal' level of discount is something in the region of half to two-thirds of what the sentence would otherwise have been [because a defendant] who gives evidence against dangerous people puts himself at considerable risk. The judge in the present case rightly distinguished this case from that. On the facts, 7 years discount not 5.

See also: *R v McGarry* 2012 EWCA Crim 255, 2 Cr App R (S) 60 (p 354) (Late pleas (25%). Classic mortgage fraud. £50m defrauded. Formal agreement with prosecution just before plea. Interviewed extensively but not asked to give evidence because of value and questions about 'good faith'. Witness statement was served as unused material on co-defendants. One, with an overwhelming case, pleaded. Judge had grave doubts about its value and started at 11 years. 20% not 10% credit for the assistance, so 6½ years not 7.)

71.11 ***Formal agreements Information given after sentence Review of the sentence***

Serious Organised Crime and Police Act 2005 s 74(1) This section applies if:
(a) the Crown Court has passed a sentence on a person in respect of an offence, and
(b) the person falls within subsection (2).

(2) A person falls within this subsection if:
(a) he receives a discounted sentence in consequence of his having offered in pursuance of a written agreement to give assistance to the prosecutor or investigator of an offence but he knowingly fails to any extent to give assistance in accordance with the agreement,
(b) he receives a discounted sentence in consequence of his having offered in pursuance of a written agreement to give assistance to the prosecutor or investigator of an offence and, having given the assistance in accordance with the agreement, in pursuance of another written agreement gives or offers to give further assistance,
(c) he receives a sentence which is not discounted but in pursuance of a written agreement he subsequently gives or offers to give assistance to the prosecutor or investigator of an offence.

(3) A specified prosecutor may at any time refer the case back to the court by which the sentence was passed if:
(a) the person is still serving his sentence, and
(b) the specified prosecutor thinks it is in the interests of justice to do so.

For the cases see **71.18**.

71.12 ***Formal agreements Varying the sentence upwards***
Serious Organised Crime and Police Act 2005 s 74(2) A person falls within this subsection if:

(a) he receives a discounted sentence in consequence of his having offered in pursuance of a written agreement to give assistance to the prosecutor or investigator of an offence but he knowingly fails to any extent to give assistance in accordance with the agreement,

(b) he receives a discounted sentence in consequence of his having offered in pursuance of a written agreement to give assistance to the prosecutor or investigator of an offence and, having given the assistance in accordance with the agreement, in pursuance of another written agreement gives or offers to give further assistance,

(c) he receives a sentence which is not discounted but in pursuance of a written agreement he subsequently gives or offers to give assistance to the prosecutor or investigator of an offence.

(3) A specified prosecutor may at any time refer the case back to the court by which the sentence was passed if:

(a) the person is still serving his sentence, and

(b) the specified prosecutor thinks it is in the interests of justice to do so.

Note: For the procedure, see Criminal Procedure Rules 2015 2015/1490 Rule 28.11. Ed.
See also the ***Future help*** paras at **71.18**.

71.13 ***Formal agreements Discretion of the authorities to refer the case back for resentence***
Re Loughlin 2017 UKSC 63, 2018 1 Cr App R (S) 21 (p 135) Supreme Court S and his brother, D, gave assistance to the police in Northern Ireland with a formal agreement. They pleaded guilty to murder and other offences. The normal penalty would have been life with a minimum term of 22 years. The Judge gave S and D a 75% reduction for their assistance and with the plea discount gave them life with a minimum term of 3 years. Various people were put on trial using S and D's evidence. All were acquitted except one, who was convicted on other evidence. The trial Judge found that S and D had lied to the police and to the Court. He also found that S and D had understated their role and exaggerated the role of others. Held. para 12 Where offenders fail to give assistance in accordance with their agreement, the specified prosecutor must consider whether it is in the interest of justice to refer the case back to court. That [issue should not be determined by asking] whether there is a necessity. para 33 Here the official in her report had demonstrated a careful, perfectly legitimate investigation into the question of the interest of justice and her conclusion cannot be impeached.[907]

Different informant situations

71.14 ***Danger, The defendant exposes himself or herself to***
R v A and B 1999 1 Cr App R (S) 52 LCJ Where by supplying valuable information to the authorities, a defendant exposes himself or his family to personal jeopardy, it will be ordinarily recognised in the sentence passed.

71.15 ***Defendant pleads not guilty and gives evidence***
R v A and B 1999 1 Cr App R (S) 52 LCJ If a defendant denies guilt and is convicted without supplying valuable information or expressing a willingness to do so, the Court of Appeal will not ordinarily reduce the sentence to reflect information given after sentence. The reason is the Court is a court of review. In such a situation the defendant must address representations to the Home Office or the Parole Board.
R v A 2006 EWCA Crim 1803, 2007 1 Cr App R (S) 60 (p 347) D was convicted of harbouring etc. heroin. He was stopped when driving his car, and five 1-kilo packets of heroin were found. Twenty-two 1-kilo packets were found at his home. He accepted guilt

[907] I'm not sure whether Lord Kerr meant that a decision in principle cannot be impeached or whether this particular decision could not be impeached.

and identified two men, K and W. His defence was duress. Both were arrested. K absconded after bail and W was tried and convicted. D gave evidence at that trial. The prosecution said that they considered that W would not have been convicted without D's evidence. Held. The assistance was at the highest end of the spectrum. The general rule in *R v A and B* 1999 1 Cr App R (S) 52 that the court is precluded from taking into account material that has arisen subsequently by those who plead not guilty remains valid. However, it is subject to exceptions as here. D has always maintained the same account. We make a very substantial reduction. 5 years resulting in his relatively early release not 13.

Drugs cases see the **Importation of Drugs** ***Assisting the prosecution*** para at **274.43** in Volume 2.

71.16 ***Giving evidence in the first trial but not in the retrial***

R v Guy 1999 2 Cr App R (S) 24 The defendant gave evidence in the first trial and the co-defendant was convicted. The Court of Appeal quashed the conviction and the defendant did not give evidence at the retrial. The co-defendant was acquitted. Held. The appropriate discount here is 50%. His failure to give evidence in the second trial should not be held against him. If he had given evidence, a further slight reduction might have been justified.

For ***Family informing on the defendant***, see the **Supply of Drugs** ***Informing on the defendant, Defendant's family*** para at **338.29** in Volume 2.

71.17 ***Events might have been created to falsely claim a discount***

R v M 2013 EWCA Crim 620 Before D was sentenced he indicated he would provide information about the location of a substantial quantity of arms and ammunition. It was agreed that no application to adjourn the case should be made because it might put him in danger. He was sentenced and D provided the information. As a result the arms and ammunition were found. The prosecution said that was insufficient as they had evidence that the guns were probably planted and that they could call evidence about that. They also said if D gave evidence they would want to cross-examine him. D refused to give evidence. Held. If the Court were to accept D's account a substantial discount would be made. The situation is similar to a *Newton* hearing. D knows if he gives evidence he is at risk of being charged with attempting to pervert the course of justice. As the matter stands the evidence was insufficient and we agreed to let D give evidence. He declined. The evidence was consistent with both being strong mitigation and the guns being planted. The burden of proof was on D. This appeal must fail.

Note: If the police had reasonable cause to believe he was involved either on his own or in a joint enterprise to plant guns and ammunition to falsely claim a discount, D could be arrested and charged with both possession of the firearms and ammunition, and attempting to pervert the course of justice. Ed.

71.18 ***Future help/Information given after the sentence***

R v A and B 1999 1 Cr App R (S) 52 LCJ A and B pleaded to importing ecstasy. The sentencing Judge was told they were already assisting Customs. At the Court of Appeal the police said that there was additional information given which related to a major, mostly international crime. This information was found to be correct. Also there was further information which was described as high in the scale of valuable intelligence. Held. Account will be taken of help given and reasonably expected to be given in the future. If a defendant is sentenced following a contested trial without supplying valuable information before sentence or expressing willingness to do so, the Court of Appeal will not ordinarily reduce a sentence to take account of information supplied by the defendant after sentence. So much is made clear by *R v Waddingham* 1983 5 Cr App R (S) 66 at 68-69, with commentary at 1983 Crim LR 492, *R v Debagg and Izzet* 1991 12 Cr App R (S) 733 at 736-737 and *R v X* 1994 15 Cr App R (S) 750 with commentary at 1994 Crim LR 469. The reason for this general rule is that the Court of Appeal is a court of review. Its function is to review sentences imposed at first instance, not to conduct a sentencing exercise of its own from the beginning. Thus it relies entirely, or almost entirely, on material before the sentencing court. A defendant who has denied guilt and withheld all co-operation before conviction and sentence cannot hope to negotiate a reduced sentence in the Court of Appeal by co-operating with the authorities after conviction. In such a situation a defendant must address appropriate representations to the Parole Board or the Home Office. To this general rule there is one apparent, but only partial exception. It sometimes happens that a defendant pleads guilty and gives help to the authorities, for which help credit is given, explicitly or not, when sentence is passed. In such a case the sentencing court will do its best to assess and give due credit for information already supplied and information which, it is reasonably hoped, will thereafter be supplied. But it may be that the value of the help is not at that stage fully appreciated, or that the help greatly exceeds, in quantity or quality or both, what could reasonably be expected when sentence was passed, so that in either event the credit given did not reflect the true measure of the help in fact received by the authorities. In such cases this Court should review the sentence passed, adjusting it, if necessary. Applying those principles, A and B are entitled to some additional credit. Therefore A's sentence reduced from 13 to 11 years and B's from 14 to 12 years.

R v R 2002 EWCA Crim 267 LCJ The defendant provided significant information in relation to the offence to which he pleaded guilty. He did this after he had been sentenced. Held. He was entitled to rely on it. However, it would not have the same weight as it would have carried if it were given before sentence.

R v K 2002 EWCA Crim 927, 2003 1 Cr App R (S) 6 (p 22) The defendant was sentenced and after that gave assistance and promised to give more. Held. The Court cannot criticise the sentence imposed on the material the Judge had before him. It would normally follow that the Court cannot interfere with the sentence passed. It may well be appropriate for the prison authorities and the Parole Board to consider what has transpired since the sentence was passed. The sentence was upheld.

R v Jackson 2009 EWCA Crim 1695 D pleaded to various burglaries and was sentenced to 5½ years. It was a proper sentence. However, the Judge did not know that D was going to give evidence in a murder trial. D did give helpful evidence at the trial. Held. D's evidence was important. He was entitled to two-thirds off. Taking 9 years as the starting point, 3 years.

Note: Crucially here the information was given before the defendant was sentenced, although the evidence was given afterwards. Ed.

R v H and Others 2009 EWCA Crim 2485, 2010 2 Cr App R (S) 18 (p 104) LCJ H revealed his willingness to provide information at an early stage. H was not seen before the trial because a) he was pleading not guilty, b) a meeting was considered difficult because he was in very close proximity to a co-accused and c) the Source Unit was short of resources. His lawyers and the CPS were unaware of the offer when H was sentenced. After sentence he passed information on a regular basis. A text was supplied to the Court of Appeal. Held. These cases fell within the exceptional cases permitting flexibility identified by *R v A and B* 1999.

See also: *R v Z* 2007 EWCA Crim 1473 (Some information given before and some after sentence. This is not a case which fits into the *R v A and B* 1999 exception, so no reduction) and the ***Future help*** para at **71.18**.

71.19 *Giving evidence in major cases*

R v Sehitoglu and Ozakan 1998 1 Cr App R (S) 89 S and O made early guilty pleas to conspiracy to possessing heroin. S gave information and evidence in a linked murder case, in which his part had been crucial. He had also given information and assistance in a significant drugs conspiracy. He was due to give evidence in that case and he was described as the lynchpin in both cases. He and his family were very seriously at risk. The police were satisfied that his account was true and accurate. The Judge started at 25 years for S and reduced it to 15 because of the assistance he had given. Held. The case falls into the highest category of drug trafficking. On a trial the sentence for O and

S would be in the region of 24 years. The information, assistance, evidence given and the risks to S and his family mark this as a case where the maximum possible reduction should be made. Applying *R v King* 1985 7 Cr App R (S) 227 the approach should be to decide the appropriate sentence if the matter had been contested. Here we give maximum credit, so the reduction is two-thirds. So from 24 years it becomes **8 years**.

R v Guy 1999 2 Cr App R (S) 24 D pleaded to importing cocaine. D, his then girlfriend and her child were stopped by Customs officers at Gatwick airport after a flight from Jamaica when they were en route to Manchester. A search of their luggage revealed packages of 3.95 kilos of cocaine (2.29 kilos at 100% purity). The packages were replaced with dummies. D and his girlfriend were arrested, and he was frank with the Customs officers and co-operated with them. Later that day different Customs officers met D in Manchester. The co-accused was expected to meet D there, and he too was arrested. His co-accused was tried and convicted and received 12 years. D gave evidence against him. He also gave significant information to Customs. D received 8 years. The co-accused's conviction was quashed on appeal and he was acquitted at the retrial. D did not give evidence in that trial. He was aged 26 and was a person of positive good character. Held. The sentence originally given by the Judge for the co-accused was entirely appropriate. D was significantly less involved than him. The starting point ought to have been 10 years. He was entitled to 50% discount, so **5 years** instead.

R v Dawes 2008 EWCA Crim 1652 While the defendant was in custody police approached him about being a witness. Initially he said that he was willing to provide information but would not make a witness statement. Following his conviction he agreed to make a statement about the murder. He said that he had received threats to his life from drug dealers while he was in prison warning him not to help the police. In a statement he described the threats to his life as being real and causing him fear. He did give evidence in the murder trial saying he had witnessed it. It was important evidence in securing a conviction. Held. The assistance in the murder trial produced a conviction for the most serious of offences. This is not a case where the defendant has come clean about other offending in which he or others had been involved. The police were well aware of his existence as a witness and sought him out. Here the appropriate discount for the assistance is one-third from what would otherwise have been the appropriate sentence. 3 years' discount was appropriate.

See also: *R v BA* 2008 EWCA Crim 1701 (Judge said that 22-24 years was appropriate for this offence of conspiracy to supply drugs. Held. There was exceptional assistance. Taking 22 years and giving two-thirds discount for the assistance and then one-third for the plea, **4½ years** not 7.)

71.20 ***Information not known by the Judge***

R v Emsden 2015 EWCA Crim 2092, 2016 1 Cr App R (S) 62 (p 444) D pleaded guilty to various dishonesty offences. During the hearing D shouted remarks about having given evidence. Unbeknown to the Judge, D had given evidence for the prosecution in an attempted rape case before his sentence. He gave evidence in the case again after his sentence. The evidence was of a cell confession. The single Judge was unaware of the assistance given as well. Held. This Court will always look carefully at any attempts to rely on mitigation arising post-sentence, as explained in *R v A and B* 1999 1 Cr App R (S) 52. Since this Court is a court of review, assistance given to the police or the Crown post-sentence will normally be too late, subject to certain exceptions. In *R v H and Others* 2009 EWCA Crim 2485, 2010 2 Cr App R (S) 18 (p 104), the Court said that where assistance had been given by an offender but, by some oversight or misadventure, the judge was ignorant of it, this Court would consider mitigation which should have been before the Crown Court and take it into consideration on appeal. It would be in the interest of justice to receive this fresh evidence. **30 months** not 33.

71.21 ***Late information and requests for adjournments***
R v AXN and ZAR 2016 EWCA Crim 590, 2 Cr App R (S) 33 (p 341)[908] LCJ para 32 An offender, if he wishes to assert that he has provided assistance, should make clear his position at the earliest opportunity. As *R v Debagg and Izzet* 1991 12 Cr App R (S) 733 emphasised, 'where the offer of assistance is made late in the day and proves to be of no value, there must always be some difficulty for the Court in determining how genuine the offer and the remorse are'. A court should not readily contemplate granting an adjournment, unless the request to the police has been made in a timely manner and the delay has arisen because the police have been unable to provide the information despite every effort on their behalf. A court should not ordinarily grant an adjournment because a request has been made late.

71.22 ***Life sentences***
R v Bevans 2009 EWCA Crim 2554, 2010 2 Cr App R (S) 31 (p 199) LCJ Given 26 years after plea, minimum term was reduced by 5 years. This was appropriate, see **71.6**.

71.23 ***Offer to assist rejected/Information not used/Value of information disputed***
R v Miller and Henry 2004 EWCA Crim 3323, 2005 2 Cr App R (S) 43 (p 257) H pleaded to robbery. H had been willing to provide a statement to the police implicating M and to give evidence against him. Held. It is important to emphasise that those who are prepared to assist the prosecuting authorities against others are entitled to anticipate that that will be reflected in a reduced sentence, even if the authorities have not taken advantage of the offer.
R v E 2009 EWCA Crim 541 D pleaded to importing cocaine. He arrived at Heathrow airport with 0.689 kilos of cocaine at 100%. He gave full details of the others involved when questioned at Heathrow. It was not acted upon because of lack of resources. The prosecution accepted that he was a courier. Held. We see no distinction between where the offer to assist is rejected and where for other reasons the offer of assistance is not taken up. There should be a 2-year reduction on top of the discount for the plea, for all the mitigating factors including the assistance which might put him and his family at risk, the remorse and the good character, so **5 years 4 months**.
R v J 2014 EWCA Crim 1264 D pleaded to class A drug supply conspiracies. During the investigation D made an offer to the police to provide information, which was declined. Prosecution counsel told the Judge that there were 'good reasons' the offer was declined. Held. The court will not normally engage in an investigation into the value of the assistance which has been provided. There are many practical difficulties for the court to overcome when confronted with an offer of information that has not been accepted. The information may be unreliable, unverifiable, untruthful or unusable. The police may already be in possession of this information. Would the police have to give evidence as to their view? Would the interests of justice require J's attendance at this hearing? This was not a case in which D was able to show that the police have acted perversely or have misconducted themselves. The offer could be relied upon in mitigation but nothing else. Here no credit would be given.
R v AXN and ZAR 2016 EWCA Crim 590, 2 Cr App R (S) 33 (p 341) LCJ Two defendants appealed their sentences saying not enough credit had been given for their offer/actual assistance. For one defendant the police provided no text. For the other, the police said some of the information was false. Held. para 18 The obligation of the police [to provide a text] is a very limited one. There can be cases where, if the police were obliged to answer assertions made, the answer, even if a simple denial, could reveal information that might have been sought by the offender for use in his own or another's criminal enterprise. The police simply may not wish to deal with the offender for operational or other reasons. Although the court will always expect the police to inform the court of the fact that the police have made a decision not to provide a text as matter

[908] Also known as *R v N* 2016 EWCA Crim 590, 2 Cr App R (S) 33

of case management, it is sufficient if the police merely state that they will not provide any information to the court in relation to the offender's assertions of assistance. The police are not required to give any explanation of their reasons for the decision (for example they decline to engage or have engaged and wish to take the matter no further), or the stage at which they decided not to provide any information. The police need do no more than say that the police will not provide any information to the court. Such a statement to the court can generally be provided by letter. para 21 Where the police consider the information is of no value it is for the police to decide the extent of the information they wish to provide to the court. On occasion they may wish to tell the court [that] their assessment is that it is of no value. That [decision] is for their judgement to be exercised in the public interest and the interests of justice. A response [giving reasons why the information is of no value] might provide the offender with information of matters that might endanger others or which might assist the offender in his own or a colleague's criminal enterprise. It is not for a court to inquire further. The safeguard is [that] law enforcement agencies will invariably provide information by way of text where they have initiated the engagement with the offender. Further there are appropriate bodies that can investigate any failure. para 30 The need for an officer to give an explanation to the judge will be highly unusual, as the court will not go behind or question the content of a text.

71.24 ***Poor information***

R v A and B 1999 1 Cr App R (S) 52 LCJ If the information given is unreliable, vague, lacking in practical utility or already known to the authorities, no identifiable discount may be given or, if given, any discount will be minimal.

Procedure

71.25 ***Document handed to the judge about an informant***

R v X 1999 2 Cr App R (S) 294 The defendant pleaded to a number of burglaries. A confidential document indicating that the defendant had given information to the police was prepared by a police officer at a high level and passed to the Judge. Prosecution counsel began a public interest immunity application before the Judge concerning the document. The defence asked to see the document as the defendant was anxious to check its accuracy, and the Judge refused the request. Held. The proper principles to be followed are:

1 It is convenient to remember that a document of this kind is supplied at the request of the defendant.

2 Except to the extent that the defendant's contention that he has given assistance is supported by the police, it will not generally be likely that the sentencing Judge will be able to make any adjustment in sentence. A defendant's unsupported assertion to that effect is not normally likely to be a reliable basis for mitigation.

3 The courts must rely very heavily upon the greatest possible care being taken, in compiling such a document for the information of the Judge. The Judge will have to rely upon it, without investigation, if police enquiries are not to be damaged or compromised and other suspects, guilty or innocent, are not to be affected. The document in the present case had not been prepared with sufficient care. Those who prepare such documents, and senior officers who verify them, must realise the importance of ensuring that they are complete and accurate.

4 Except in very unusual circumstances, it will not be necessary, nor will it be desirable for a document of this kind to contain the kind of details which would attract a public interest immunity application.

5 If very exceptionally such a document does contain information attracting a public interest immunity consideration, then the usual rules about the conduct of such an

application will apply. In particular, Crown Court (Criminal Procedure and Investigations Act 1996) (Disclosure) Rules 1997 1997/698 [which became Criminal Procedure Rules 2014 2014/1610 Rule 22. Ed.] will apply. The defence can and should be told of the public interest immunity application.
6 Absent any consideration of public interest immunity, which we take to be the general position, a document of this kind should be shown to counsel for the defence, who will no doubt discuss its contents with the defendant. That is not, we emphasise, because it will be necessary to debate its contents, but it is so that there should be no room for any unfounded suspicion that the Judge has been told something potentially adverse to the defendant without his knowing about it. A defendant is entitled to see documents put before the trial Judge on which he is to be sentenced. Expeditions to the Judge's chambers should not be necessary in these cases. There should never normally be any question of evidence being given, or of an issue being tried upon the question of the extent of the information provided.
7 If the defendant wishes to disagree with the contents of such a document, it is not appropriate for there to be cross-examination of the policeman, whether in court or in chambers. The policeman is not a Crown witness, he has simply supplied material for the Judge, at the request of the defendant. It would no doubt be possible, in an appropriate case, for a defendant to ask for an adjournment to allow any opportunity for further consideration to be given to the preparation of the document. Otherwise, if the defendant does not accept what the document says, his remedy is not to rely upon it. Cross-examination on the usefulness of the information would almost inevitably be contrary to the public interest. It would be likely to damage enquiries still in train, trials yet to come, suspects guilty or innocent and quite possibly the defendant in the instant case.
8 No doubt, the learned Judge should ordinarily disregard such a document, if asked by the defendant to do so. In such case, he will no doubt not then be minded to entertain any submission that the defendant has given valuable assistance to the police.
9 If the Judge does take the document into consideration he will, no doubt, say no more than is in accordance with the present practice, namely that he has taken into consideration all the information about the defendant with which he has been provided.
R v AXN and ZAR 2016 EWCA Crim 590, 2 Cr App R (S) 33 (p 341) LCJ Two defendants appealed their sentences saying not enough credit had been given for their offer/actual assistance. Held. We see no basis whatsoever for departing from the guidance in *R v X* 1999.

71.26 *Sentencing remarks*

Reasons for not following usual sentencing requirements
Criminal Procedure Rules 2015 2015/1490 Rule 28.1(1) This rule applies where the court decides:...

(d) to pass a lesser sentence than it otherwise would have passed because the defendant has assisted, or has agreed to assist, an investigator or prosecutor in relation to an offence.

(2) The court must explain why it has so decided, when it explains the sentence that it has passed.
(3) Where paragraph (1)(d) applies, the court must arrange for such an explanation to be given to the defendant and to the prosecutor in writing, if the court thinks that it would not be in the public interest to explain in public.
LEGAL REPRESENTATION: NEED FOR IN CUSTODIAL CASES see the **CUSTODY Defendants who have not been previously sentenced to custody** section at **28.19**.

71.27 *Appeals*

Guide to Commencing Proceedings in the Court of Appeal 2018 para A5-2. **Insufficient weight given to assistance to prosecution authorities** Where a ground of appeal against sentence is that the Judge has given insufficient weight to the assistance given to the prosecution authorities, the "text" which had been prepared for the sentencing Judge is obtained by the Registrar. Grounds of appeal should be drafted in an anodyne form with a note to the Registrar alerting him to the existence of a "text". The CAO will obtain the "text" and the single Judge will have seen it when considering leave as will the full Court before the appeal hearing and it need not be alluded to in open Court.

72 LABOUR MARKET ENFORCEMENT ORDER

72.1

Immigration Act 2016 s 20[909]

Post-conviction order Where a person has been convicted of a trigger offence, the court may make a Labour Market Enforcement Order, Immigration Act 2016 s 20(1) and (2). The order may include prohibitions, restrictions and requirements, Immigration Act 2016 s 21.

Stand-alone order A Magistrates' Court may make a Labour Market Enforcement Order where one of the trigger offences have been committed, Immigration Act 2016 s 18.

Test to apply The test for both types of order is whether the measure or order is 'just and reasonable', Immigration Act 2016 s 19(1)(b) and 20(2).

Variation and discharge Both parties may apply to vary and discharge a Labour Market Enforcement Order. The hearing is at the Magistrates' Court.

Breach of the order Failure to comply with an order without reasonable excuse is a criminal offence, Immigration Act 2016 s 27. The offence is triable either way. On indictment the maximum penalty is 2 years. The summary maximum is 6 months and/or an unlimited fine.[910]

72.2 ***What are the trigger offences?***

Immigration Act 2016 s 14(4) 'Trigger offence' means:

a) an offence under the Employment Agencies Act 1973 other than one under section 9(4)(b) of that Act;
b) an offence under the National Minimum Wage Act 1998;
c) an offence under the Gangmasters (Licensing) Act 2004;
d) any other offence prescribed by regulations made by the Secretary of State;
e) an offence of attempting or conspiring to commit an offence mentioned in paragraphs a) to d);
f) an offence under Serious Crime Act 2007 Part 2 in relation to an offence so mentioned;
g) an offence of inciting a person to commit an offence so mentioned;
h) an offence of aiding, abetting, counselling or procuring the commission of an offence so mentioned.

73 LICENCE CONDITIONS, JUDGE RECOMMENDING

73.1

Criminal Justice Act 2003 s 238

This is not a derelict power. It is just a forgotten power.

Appeals The inclusion of subsection 238(3) (see **73.2**) presumably means an appeal is not possible.

Example For an example of its use, see *R v Lodge* 2012 EWCA Crim 1906, 2013 1 Cr App R (S) 87 (p 467).

Probation The pre-privatisation probation service considers that there is a presumption that wherever possible all such recommendations will be included when a prisoner is

---

[909] In force 25/11/16, see Immigration Act 2016 (Commencement No 2 and Transitional Provisions) Regs 2016 2016/1037 para 4

[910] Immigration Act 2016 s 27(2) says the fine must not exceed the statutory maximum. As the offences with the statutory maximum now carry an unlimited fine, it could be argued that the section has been poorly drafted and that the fine is unlimited.

released on licence. If the Offender Manager assesses that the recommendations are not necessary or proportionate, they must consult with Probation Trust Contract Managers to seek authority to omit such conditions from the licence. Where the Probation Trust Contract Manager feels it is detrimental or inappropriate to include the court-recommended licence conditions, it will write to the sentencing judge to advise him or her of the decision and will provide reasons, National Offender Management Service PI 07/2011.

73.2 ***Power to order***

Power of court to recommend licence conditions for certain prisoners

Criminal Justice Act 2003 s 238(1) A court which sentences an offender to a term of imprisonment or detention in a Young Offender Institution of 12 months or more in respect of any offence may, when passing sentence, recommend to the Secretary of State particular conditions which in its view should be included in any licence granted to the offender under this Chapter on his release from prison.

(2) In exercising his powers under Criminal Justice Act 2003 s 250(4)(b) in respect of an offender, the Secretary of State must have regard to any recommendation under subsection (1).

(3) A recommendation under subsection (1) is not to be treated for any purpose as part of the sentence passed on the offender.

(4) This section does not apply in relation to a sentence of detention under Powers of Criminal Courts (Sentencing) Act 2000 s 91 or Criminal Justice Act 2003 s 228.[911]

74 LIFE IMPRISONMENT: BASIC PRINCIPLES/DISCRETIONARY LIFE

74.1

This chapter deals with the general principles about life imprisonment and one type of life imprisonment, discretionary life. This is where the 'dangerousness' provisions and the automatic life provisions do not apply. There are two types of discretionary life sentence. The first is where the offence was committed before 4 April 2005, so the dangerousness provisions do not apply. The second is where the offence has a maximum sentence of life imprisonment but the offence is not a specified offence in Criminal Justice Act 2003 Sch 15, see **56.18**. Two examples of the second type are class A drug supply and importation of class A drugs. For mandatory life sentences, which are only available in murder cases, see **287.1** in Volume 2.

Children and young offenders Life imprisonment can't be passed. What can be passed is set out at **74.3**.

Court Martial The Court may pass life imprisonment/custody for life for all ranks, ex-servicemen and women, and civilians. Detention for life is not available for officers, warrant officers and NCOs but is available for the other ranks, ex-servicemen and civilians, see *Guidance on Sentencing in the Court Martial 2018* Annex B.

Disqualification from driving Where the court passes a life sentence (other than one with a whole life order) with either obligatory disqualification, discretionary disqualification or disqualification under the totting up provisions, the court is required to select the appropriate period of disqualification and extend it by the length of the minimum term.[912] The section was designed to prevent offenders serving most of their disqualification periods in prison. The sections were amended by Criminal Justice and Courts Act 2015 s 30. For more detail see **41.16**.

Victim surcharge The court must impose a victim surcharge of £170, Criminal Justice Act 2003 s 161A-161B and Criminal Justice Act 2003 (Surcharge) Order 2012 2012/1696 as amended. There are exceptions, a) where a compensation order or an

[911] Repealed by Legal Aid, Sentencing and Punishment of Offenders Act 2012 Pt 3 s 123(d)

[912] Road Traffic Offenders Act 1988 s 35A(1)-(3) and (4)(a) and Powers of Criminal Courts (Sentencing) Act 2000 s 147A(1)-(3) and (4)(a) inserted by Coroners and Justice Act 2009 s 2 and Sch 16 paras 2 and 5. Schedule 16 is in force from 13/4/15.

Unlawful Profits Order or a Slavery and Trafficking Reparations Order is imposed, when a reduced amount or a nil amount can be ordered, see **17.67**, and b) where the offence was committed before 1 October 2012, when no surcharge can be made, see **115.3**. Where the offence was committed on or after that date and before 8 April 2016, the amount to be imposed is £120, see **115.4**. In non-mandatory life cases, for defendants who were aged 21+ when convicted but were, when the offence was committed, aged a) under 18, the amount is £20, and b) aged 18-20, the amount is £120, see **115.4**.
Rehabilitation period This sentence is excluded from rehabilitation.[913]
Release Release for prisoners serving CJA 2003 s 225 and 226/discretionary life, custody for life and detention for life sentences is via the Parole Board on expiry of the minimum term. The test is whether 'the prisoner's confinement is no longer necessary for the protection of the public', Crime (Sentences) Act 1997 s 28(6)(b). On release the prisoner is subject to supervision. Where a determinate term is imposed to run concurrently with an indeterminate term, release cannot occur until the release requirements of both sentences have been satisfied.
Removal from UK A prisoner who has served the minimum term of a life sentence and is liable to removal from the UK may be removed at any time. No direction from the Parole Board is required and a direction as to release does not prevent removal, Crime (Sentences) Act 1997 s 32A created and inserted by Legal Aid, Sentencing and Punishment of Offenders Act 2012 s 119. If, having been removed, he or she returns to the UK, he or she is to be treated as unlawfully at large and is liable to be detained pursuant to the sentence. If there has been a previous Parole Board direction as to release, he is to be treated as having been recalled, Crime (Sentences) Act 1997 s 32B.

74.2 ***Statistics England and Wales***
Life sentence

		Aged 10-17		Aged 18-20		Aged 21+		All		Total
		Ma	**Fem**	**Ma**	**Fem**	**Ma**	**Fem**	**Ma**	**Fem**	**Both**
All	2014	21	0	41	1	360	19	422	20	442
	2015	13	1	35	3	304	13	352	17	369
	2016	7	1	44	0	331	24	382	25	407
	2017	10	0	38	1	296	17	344	18	362
Mandatory	2014	17	0	38	1	259	18	314	19	333
	2015	12	1	29	3	211	10	252	14	266
	2016	6	1	34	0	226	22	266	23	289
	2017	9	0	35	1	190	15	234	16	250
Discretionary	2014	4	0	3	0	101	1	108	1	109
	2015	1	0	6	0	93	3	100	3	103
	2016	1	0	10	0	105	2	116	2	118
	2017	1	0	3	0	106	2	110	2	112

For explanations about the statistics, see page 1-xii.

74.3 ***The different orders***
R v Saunders and Others 2013 EWCA Crim 1027, 2014 1 Cr App R (S) 45 (p 258) LCJ There are now four situations in which the sentence of imprisonment for life arises for consideration.

(a) Mandatory life sentences arising from a conviction for murder.

[913] Rehabilitation of Offenders Act 1974 s 5(1)(a)

(b) Statutory life sentences arising from a conviction for a second listed offence, Criminal Justice Act 2003 s 224A [commonly called automatic life].

(c) Life sentences following a conviction for a specified offence, upon a finding of dangerousness, Criminal Justice Act 2003 s 225(1)-(2) [and section 226(1)-(2)].

(d) Life sentences where Criminal Justice Act 2003 s 225 [or 226] do not apply.

Note: There are two groups of para d) life sentences. One is life in historical cases, which include the historical sex offences (see para **74.5**). The other is offences which are not Criminal Justice Act 2003 specified offences, like class A drug importation and supply of class A drugs offences. For those two offences, judges invariably consider that, for exceptionally serious offences, very long determinate sentences are required rather than life sentences. Ed.

Order	Aged 10-17	Aged 18-20	Aged 21+
Mandatory life for murder only	Detention during HM's Pleasure,[914] see **287.77** in Volume 2	Custody for life[915]	Imprisonment for life[916]
Section 225/226 life and Discretionary life	Detention for life[917]	Custody for life[918]	Imprisonment for life[919]
Automatic life 2012	Not available[920]	Custody for life[921]	Imprisonment for life[922]

R v Wilson 2016 EWCA Crim 1555, 2017 1 Cr App R (S) 7 (p 35) D was convicted of causing GBH with intent and child destruction. The Judge found that the dangerousness provisions were made out. He also said that if they had not been made out he would have imposed a discretionary life sentence. Held. This case might then have been suitable for discretionary life but we don't have to decide that.

For more detail, see **295.2** in Volume 2.

For guidance on sentencing those aged under 21 to custody, see the **CHILDREN AND YOUNG OFFENDERS: CUSTODIAL SENTENCES** chapter.

74.4 *Statutory provisions/Time on remand/Curfew and tag discount*

Determination of tariffs.

Powers of Criminal Courts (Sentencing) Act 2000 s 82A(1) This section applies if a court passes a life sentence in circumstances where the sentence is not fixed by law.

(2) The court shall, unless it makes an order under subsection (4) below (see **74.16**), order that the provisions of Crime (Sentences) Act 1997 s 28(5)-(8) (referred to in this section as the 'early release provisions') shall apply to the offender as soon as he has served the part of his sentence which is specified in the order.

(3) The part of his sentence shall be such as the court considers appropriate taking into account:

(a) the seriousness of the offence, or of the combination of the offence and one or more offences associated with it,

---

[914] Powers of Criminal Courts (Sentencing) Act 2000 s 90 This applies when a person 'appears to the court to have been under 18 at the time the offence was committed', Powers of Criminal Courts (Sentencing) Act 2000 s 90.

[915] Powers of Criminal Courts (Sentencing) Act 2000 s 93

[916] Criminal Justice Act 2003 s 226(2)

[917] Powers of Criminal Courts (Sentencing) Act 2000 s 91(3) and Criminal Justice Act 2003 s 226(2)

[918] Powers of Criminal Courts (Sentencing) Act 2000 s 94(1)

[919] Powers of Criminal Courts (Sentencing) Act 2000 s 94(1) and Criminal Justice Act 2003 s 225(2)

[920] Criminal Justice Act 2003 s 224A(1)(a)

[921] Criminal Justice Act 2003 s 224A(2) inserted by Legal Aid, Sentencing and Punishment of Offenders Act 2012 s 122 entitles the order for those aged 18+ as 'imprisonment for life'. However, until Criminal Justice and Court Services Act 2000 s 61 is in force, Legal Aid, Sentencing and Punishment of Offenders Act 2012 Sch 19 para 24(2)(a) applies and this renames the order as 'custody for life'.

[922] Criminal Justice Act 2003 s 224A(2)

(b) the effect that the following would have if the court had sentenced the offender to a term of imprisonment:

(i) Criminal Justice Act 2003 s 240ZA (crediting periods of remand in custody),

(ii) Armed Forces Act 2006 s 246 (equivalent provision for service courts),

(iii) any direction which the court would have given under Criminal Justice Act 2003 s 240A (crediting periods of remand on bail subject to certain types of condition).

(c) the early release provisions as compared with Criminal Justice Act 2003 s 244(1).

(4) [see **74.16**]

(5)-(6) [Repealed]

(7) In this section:

"court" includes the Court Martial;

"life sentence" means a sentence mentioned in subsection (2) of section 34 of the Crime (Sentences) Act 1997 other than a sentence mentioned in paragraph (d) or (e) of that subsection.

(8) So far as this section relates to sentences passed by the Court Martial, section 167(1) [of the Powers of Criminal Courts (Sentencing) Act 2000] below [which stipulates that the Act only extends to England and Wales] does not apply.

Note: Criminal Justice and Courts Act 2015 s 15(1) substituted subsection 82A(3)(b).[923] Ed.

74.5 ***Criminal for life imprisonment*** ***Offences committed before the 2003 dangerousness provisions were in force***

R v Hodgson 1968 52 Cr App R 113 One condition for a life sentence was, 'the offence(s) are in themselves grave enough to require a very long sentence'.

R v Chapman 2000 1 Cr App R (S) 377 LCJ D pleaded to reckless arson and reports said he suffered from a personality disorder. The Judge set the minimum term at one year. Held. Life should never be imposed unless the circumstances are such as to call for a severe sentence based on the offence.

R v DP 2013 EWCA Crim 1143, 2 Cr App R (S) 63 (p 398) D pleaded to assault by penetration and other sexual offences. When the offences were committed, the Criminal Justice Act 2003 dangerousness provisions were not in force. D was sentenced to life. Held. para 15 The then criteria for the imposition of a discretionary life sentence are set out in *R v Hodgson* 1968 52 Cr App R 113 and in *Att-Gen's Ref No 32 of 1996* 1997 1 Cr App R(S) 261. In the second case, the Lord Chief Justice said there were two conditions to be satisfied before a discretionary life sentence could be passed. First, the offender should have been convicted of a very serious offence. Second, there should be good grounds for believing that the offender may[924] be a serious danger to the public for a period which cannot reliably be estimated at the date of the sentence. By 'serious danger' the court had in mind particularly serious offences of violence and serious offences of a sexual nature. Unless both of those conditions were fulfilled, a discretionary life sentence was not available. 'A very serious offence' is an offence, the degree of seriousness of which is such that it might properly be regarded as meriting a life sentence, see *R v JD* 2012 EWCA Crim 2370, at paras 13 and 23. In *Att-Gen's Ref No 43 of 2009* 2009 EWCA Crim 1925, 2010 1 Cr App R (S) 100 (p 628), this court, considering Criminal Justice Act 2003 in a judgment given by Lord Judge, expressed reservations as to whether cases where the specified minimum term was of the order of 4-6 years should have attracted a discretionary life sentence rather than an IPP sentence. Lord Bingham had said, in *Att-Gen's Ref No 32 of 1996* 1997 1 Cr App R(S) 261 at 265, that a sentence of discretionary life imprisonment should only be passed in the most exceptional circumstances. But in making that observation we note that he was

[923] In force 13/4/15, Criminal Justice and Courts Act 2015 (Commencement No 1, Saving and Transitional Provisions) Order 2015 2015/778 para 3 and Sch 1 para 11

[924] The judgment qualifies this by adding 'or may not be', which must be a typo.

embracing both limbs of the *Hodgson/Whittaker* criteria. If the threshold for a life sentence is not crossed then the second step is to decide whether in the appellant's case it was necessary to protect the public from serious harm from him in the future. If it was, then a longer than commensurate sentence could have been passed under Powers of Criminal Courts (Sentencing) Act 2000 s 82(2)(b), together with an extended licence period. Here both parts of the life sentence test have been made out.
See also: *R v D* 2012 EWCA Crim 2370, 2013 1 Cr App R (S) 127 (p 674) (An historical case. Old cases relied on. A minimum term of 3½ years upheld.)

74.6 ***Criteria for life imprisonment Offences committed before the 2003 dangerousness provisions were in force Procedure***
R v G 2014 EWCA Crim 1221 LCJ D was convicted of rape and other sex offences. Before the verdict the Judge warned counsel that he was considering a life sentence. Some of the offences were committed before the 2003 changes. Others were not. The Judge received no assistance from prosecution counsel. Counsel said to the Court of Appeal that the Judge was experienced and did not need any help. Held. Bearing in mind the time span over which the offences were committed and the significant changes made by legislation, a judge needs help. It is incumbent on the prosecution to assist the judge about his powers and remind him of the relevant authorities. The amendments to the legislation needed to be carefully analysed by the judge. We will ask the DPP to make sure that Crown counsel are reminded in cases of this gravity that assistance must be provided whatever view may be taken of the experience of the judge.

74.7 ***Criteria for life imprisonment Offences committed before the 2003 dangerousness provisions were in force Setting the minimum term***
R v Bell 2015 EWCA Crim 1426, 2016 1 Cr App R (S) 16 (p 113) D pleaded to manslaughter. The offence was in 2000. The defence sought to argue that European Convention on Human Rights art 7(1) and the principles in *R v Sullivan and Others* 2004 EWCA Crim 1762, 2005 1 Cr App R (S) 67 (p 308) applied so the Judge was bound to pass a sentence which was no more than what would have been imposed in 2000. Held. para 37, 47 and 54 *R v Sullivan* 2004 is plainly distinguishable as the case was manslaughter, which is determined by judicial discretion and murder is determined by Criminal Justice Act 2003 Sch 21, laid down by Parliament. para 50 *R v Sullivan* 2004 does not apply to discretionary life cases. paras 42-44 We apply *R v Secretary of State for the Home Dept ex parte Uttley* 2004 UKHL 38 to say the heavier penalty provision of article 7(1) applies to the maximum penalty. The Court should apply *R v H* 2011 EWCA Crim 2753, 2012 2 Cr App R (S) 21 (p 88), see para **242.31** in Volume 2. para 63 In discretionary life cases, the minimum term should reflect current sentencing practice. Appeal dismissed.

74.8 ***Failure to warn counsel that a life sentence is being considered***
R v Cross 2008 EWCA Crim 1194, 2009 1 Cr App R (S) 34 (p 193) para 8 It is desirable, unless there are particular reasons for not doing so, for a judge contemplating a discretionary life sentence to alert counsel to the fact that it is at least a sentencing option that he is considering. That will give counsel the opportunity, in particular, to raise any matters of law concerning the approach to such a sentence. That said, the lack of a warning to counsel could not of itself be a reason for allowing an appeal. It may lead to the existence of other grounds.

Setting the minimum term

74.9 ***Statutes and rules/Judicial task***
Criminal Practice Directions 2015 EWCA Crim 1567 para VII L.1 Powers of Criminal Courts (Sentencing) Act 2000 s 82A (see **74.4**) empowers a judge when passing a sentence of life imprisonment, where such a sentence is not fixed by law, to specify by order such part of the sentence ('the relevant part') as shall be served before the prisoner may require the Secretary of State to refer his case to the Parole Board. This is applicable to defendants under the age of 18 years as well as to adult defendants.

L.2 Thus the life sentence falls into two parts:

a) the relevant part, which consists of the period of detention imposed for punishment and deterrence, taking into account the seriousness of the offence, and
b) the remaining part of the sentence, during which the prisoner's detention will be governed by consideration of risk to the public.

L.3 The judge is not obliged by statute to make use of the provisions of section 82A when passing a life sentence. However, the judge should do so, save in the very exceptional case where the judge considers that the offence is so serious that detention for life is justified by the seriousness of the offence alone, irrespective of the risk to the public. In such a case, the judge should state this in open court when passing sentence.
L.4 In cases where the judge is to specify the relevant part of the sentence under section 82A, the judge should permit the advocate for the defendant to address the court as to the appropriate length of the relevant part. Where no relevant part is to be specified, the advocate for the defendant should be permitted to address the court as to the appropriateness of this course of action.
L.5 In specifying the relevant part of the sentence, the judge should have regard to the specific terms of section 82A and should indicate the reasons for reaching his decision as to the length of the relevant part.

74.10 ***Guilty plea, Discount for***
Reduction in Sentence for a Guilty Plea Guideline 2007, see www.banksr.com Other Matters Guidelines tab para 2.6 A reduction in sentence should only apply to the punitive elements of a penalty. para 5.1 Where a [dangerous offender] requires the calculation of a minimum term…the approach will be the same as for any other determinate sentence. para 7.1 For discretionary life, the fixing of the term is different from that followed for murder. The court first determines what the equivalent determinate sentence would have been. Accordingly the approach to the calculation of the reduction for a guilty plea should follow the process and scale adopted in relation to determinate sentences.
Note: There is a new guideline but it deals with mandatory life (see **287.25** in Volume 2) and not non-mandatory life. However, the statements in the old guideline would appear to reflect current practice. Ed.
R v Lang 2005 EWCA Crim 2864, 2006 2 Cr App R (S) 3 (p 13) para 10 The court must identify the notional determinate sentence which would have been imposed if a life sentence or IPP had not been required. In calculating the minimum term, an appropriate reduction should be allowed for a plea of guilty (see *Sentencing Guidelines Council Guideline on Reduction for a Guilty Plea* para 5.1). Half that term should normally then be taken.

74.11 ***Calculating the minimum term*** ***Dividing the notional term***
R v Szczerba 2002 EWCA Crim 440, 2 Cr App R (S) 86 (p 387) Judges should normally take half the notional term. There are circumstances in which more than half may well be appropriate. One example is *R v Haywood* 2000 2 Cr App R (S) 418 where a life sentence was imposed on a serving prisoner for an offence committed in prison. In such a case the term specified can appropriately be fixed to end at a date after that on which the defendant would have been eligible for release on licence from his original sentence. This may involve identifying a proportion of the notional determinate term up to two-thirds. Another example is where a life sentence is imposed on a defendant for an offence committed during licensed release from an earlier sentence, who is therefore susceptible to return to custody under Powers of Criminal Courts (Sentencing) Act 2000 s 116. In such a case the specified period could properly be increased above one-half, to reflect the fact that a specified period cannot be ordered to run consecutively to any other sentence. There may well be other cases where it is appropriate to specify a period greater than one-half. It would not, in our judgement, be helpful to seek to list all the circumstances in which the sentencing judge's discretion can properly be so exercised. But, unless there are exceptional circumstances, half the notional determinate sentence

should be taken (less, of course, time spent in custody) as the period specified to be served. If a judge specifies a higher proportion than one-half, he should always state his reasons for so doing.
Note: Since this case, judges invariably divide the notional term by two. There are, however, very rare exceptions such as *R v Rossi* 2014 below. Ed.
R v Williams 2016 EWCA Crim 1964 D pleaded to attempted murder. In September 2014, he stabbed a woman in the back of the head, shoulder and arms from behind. She required 147 stitches and was too scared to leave her home. In 1986, when D was aged 19, he pleaded to manslaughter on the basis of diminished responsibility. He stabbed a woman 15 times with a carving knife. D received life with a 3-year minimum term. D was not released until October 2014. Both offences were without provocation. D had an unstable personality disorder. The Judge started at 33 years and reduced it to 24 years with a full plea discount. He then took two-thirds of that because of the exceptional gravity of the offence, making 16 years. Held. D was clearly a very dangerous man. If there are exceptional circumstances the increase does not have to be to two-thirds. However, here there is no justification to depart from the 50% rule.
For more detail, see **288.17** in Volume 2.
See also: *R v Rossi* 2014 EWCA Crim 2081, 2015 1 Cr App R (S) 15 (p 120) (Early plea. Attempted armed robbery, firearm with intent and possessing ammunition. Carried loaded double-barrelled shotgun into bookmakers. Pointed gun at cashier. Later fired two shots in street. Aged 58, compliant but with appalling record. 1984, attempted murder (×3), robbery (×3) (life). 2001, firearm offence (life). Released from prison 16 months before these offences were committed. 10% plea discount making 18 years and a 12-year minimum term. D's history justified departing from normal practice of deducting half. So starting at 20 years, with plea discount 13 to 13½ years, making 9 years. [So about ⅓ deduction upheld.])

74.12 ***Don't add a period for public protection***
R v Sullivan and Others 2004 EWCA Crim 1762, 2005 1 Cr App R (S) 67 (p 308) LCJ S was convicted of murder. The Court of Appeal gave guidance about the then new statutory provisions. Held. The sentence for murder is, of course, fixed by law so Criminal Justice Act 2003 s 142 [which is about the purposes of sentencing, one of which is the protection of the public] does not apply to the determination of the minimum period in the case of a life sentence. However, the section is still important. This is because it underlines the very different task that a judge performs when deciding the length of a minimum term, having imposed a life sentence, from the task that he performs when he decides what should be the length of a determinate sentence. <u>In the case of the minimum term he is only directly concerned with 'seriousness', the protection of the public being provided by the imposition of the life sentence</u>. After the minimum term has been served, protection of the public becomes the responsibility of the Parole Board, which then decides when it is safe to release the offender on licence.
Note: The underlining is for emphasis. Ed.
R v Peters 2005 EWCA Crim 605, 2 Cr App R (S) 101 (p 627) In murder cases, the protection of the public, rightly regarded as the prime consideration, is achieved by the mandatory life sentence itself.
R v Jones 2005 EWCA Crim 3115, 2006 2 Cr App R (S) 19 (p 121) at 130 The guidance in Schedule 21 is to assist judges. The judge must have regard to the guidance, but each case will depend critically on its particular facts. If the judge concludes it is appropriate to depart from the guidance, he should explain his reasons. Protection of the public is not a relevant factor as that is the task of the Parole Board when considering release.
Note: All these cases are murder cases, but the principle applies to all life sentences. Ed.

74.13 ***The exercise is a balancing exercise not a mathematical one***
R v Peters 2005 EWCA Crim 605, 2 Cr App R (S) 101 (p 627) The reality, as the statute acknowledges, is that justice cannot be done by rote. This principle applies equally to

cases where the judge considers that the seriousness of the offence calls for a longer sentence than the normal starting point, as it does to cases where the proper minimum term is lower. One problem arising from the legislative framework is that the sentencing court may approach the decision, or be invited to do so, as if the ultimate sentence represents a mathematical calculation. It does not. The true seriousness of the offence, which the minimum term is intended to reflect, inevitably represents a combination, and simultaneously a balancing, of all the relevant factors in the case.
R v Ennis 2008 EWCA Crim 969 D was convicted of murder. There was a co-defendant. Held. This sentencing exercise was a broad-brush exercise. It is particularly unfortunate that the guidance prescribed by Schedule 21 was not followed so as to provide fact-finding and an assessment of the sentence for this defendant.
R v Beckford 2014 EWCA Crim 1299, 2 Cr App R (S) 34 (p 285) This Court has said on many occasions that the setting of the minimum term is not achieved by slavishly and mechanically following Criminal Justice Act 2003 Sch 21. Courts must achieve a just result.

74.14 ***Calculating the minimum term Pass a global sentence***
Criminal Justice Act 2003 s 225(2)(b) If…the court considers that the seriousness of the offence, or of the offence and one or more offences associated with it, is such as to justify the imposition of a sentence of imprisonment for life, the court must impose a sentence of imprisonment for life.
R v Lundberg 1995 16 Cr App R (S) 948 D pleaded to manslaughter, unlawful wounding and destroying property reckless as to whether life was endangered. He was sentenced to life. Held. The judge is entitled to sentence for the total of the offending.

74.15 ***Discount for time spent in custody***
Note: The proper approach for discount for time spent in custody when a discretionary life sentence is imposed is not specifically dealt with in Legal Aid, Sentencing and Punishment of Offenders Act 2012 s 110 or in any of the associated material. However, Criminal Justice Act 2003 s 269 as amended by Legal Aid, Sentencing and Punishment of Offenders Act 2012 s 110(10) determines that the old rules apply to mandatory life sentences. Judges: a) work out the appropriate minimum term, then b) deduct any period if there was a guilty plea, and then c) deduct the appropriate period for the days on remand and curfew and tag time in the unlikely event the defendant was on bail before his sentence. Ed.
R v A 2014 EWCA Crim 2483 D was convicted of oral and vaginal rape and given life. Held. para 55 The Judge must specifically adjust the sentence to take into account time spent on remand and qualifying curfews. The sentence might properly be announced by saying, the minimum term is 15 years less 6 months 18 days.
For the position in murder cases and the details of Criminal Justice Act 2003 s 269 see para **287.90** in Volume 2.

74.16 ***Whole life orders***
Powers of Criminal Courts (Sentencing) Act 2000 s 82A(4) If the offender was aged 21 or over when he committed the offence and the court is of the opinion that, because of the seriousness of the offence or of the combination of the offence and one or more offences associated with it, no order should be made under subsection (2) (the release provisions) above, the court shall order that the early release provisions shall not apply to the offender.
R v Jones 2005 EWCA Crim 3115, 2006 2 Cr App R (S) 19 (p 121) at 131 para 10 A whole life order should be imposed where the seriousness of the offending is so exceptionally high that just punishment requires the offender to be kept in prison for the rest of his or her life. Often, perhaps usually, where such an order is called for, the case will not be on the borderline. The facts of the case, considered as a whole, will leave the judge in no doubt that the offender must be kept in prison for the rest of his or her life. To be imprisoned for a finite period of 30 years or more is a very severe penalty. If the

case includes one or more of the factors set out in para 4(2) it is likely to be a case that calls for a whole life order, but the judge must consider all the material facts before concluding that a very lengthy finite term will not be a sufficiently severe penalty. Where a whole life order is called for, the case will not be on the borderline. If the judge is in doubt, this may well indicate that a finite minimum term which leaves open the possibility that the offender may be released for the final years of his or her life is appropriate.

R v Oakes and Others Re MR 2012 EWCA Crim 2435, 2013 2 Cr App R (S) 22 (p 132) para 87 LCJ MR was convicted of three rapes, two GBHs with intent, four burglaries (connected with the rapes) and other charges. The Judge sentenced him to whole life. Held. LCJ para 22 This Court has proceeded on the basis that, provided the court has reflected on matters of mitigation properly available to the defendant, a whole life order imposed as a matter of judicial discretion as to the appropriate level of punishment and deterrence following conviction for a crime of utmost seriousness would not constitute inhuman or degrading punishment. para 24 A whole life minimum term is a draconian penalty, indeed it is the order of last resort reserved for cases of exceptionally serious criminality. para 29 The whole life order, the product of primary legislation, is reserved for the few exceptionally serious offences in which, after reflecting on all the features of aggravation and mitigation, the judge is satisfied that the element of just punishment and retribution requires the imposition of a whole life order. If that conclusion is justified, the whole life order is appropriate, but only then. para 102 Without suggesting that the court is prohibited from making a whole life order, unless the defendant is convicted of at least one murder, such an order will, inevitably, be a very rare event indeed. **25-year minimum term** not whole life.

Att-Gen's Ref No 123 of 2014 2015 EWCA Crim 111, 2015 1 Cr App R (S) 67 (p 470) LCJ was convicted of three attempted murders and conspiracy to commit aggravated burglary. He pleaded to linked offences. As a 'hotel creeper' he entered a hotel room where he repeatedly struck V2 to the head with a hammer. D also attacked V1, smashing her skull six times with the hammer. V1 was struck even after she was unconscious and a whole side of her skull was destroyed, with part of her brain protruding and brain matter spread over her face. All the attacks occurred in front of V2's three children, one of whom was deeply distressed and covered in the victims' blood. D left the victims for dead and made off with a suitcase full of valuables. D was aged 32 and had 37 previous appearances for 62 offences, having begun offending aged 12. He first went to prison in 1997 for section 20 assault and had also been convicted of robbery (2½ years in 1998, his longest sentence), burglary and other assaults. D had also used a hammer during an affray in 2008. He was prone to losing his temper and had a 'mixed type' disorder. D had little insight into his offending, but did express remorse. Held. We would emphasise, as Lord Judge did in *R v Oakes* 2012 EWCA Crim 2435, 2013 2 Cr App R (S) 22 (p 132), that there may well be cases, exceptional though they may be, where, even if none of the victims has died, a whole life order might nonetheless be appropriate. We can envisage for an exceptional case of attempted murder such a sentence being passed. But this is not that case. Concurrent **life** sentences with a **27-year minimum**, not 18-year minimum.

Note: It may be that the gap between the sentences for attempted murder with horrific injuries and those for murder is closing. It may be that the aggravating features of the horrific injuries, the number of victims and the presence of children made a very large difference. Either way, the courts have no interest in placing ceilings on the sentences they can impose. Ed.

R v Andrews 2015 EWCA Crim 883 D pleaded at his PCMH to six rapes, kidnapping, section 18 and ABH. He lured a drunk woman to his flat and then imprisoned her. There was anal, oral and vaginal rape. After many hours he took her to a wood, abused her and threw her into a stream leaving her for dead. D had two manslaughter convictions and a similar indecent assault conviction. The Judge passed a whole life order, based on the

risk he posed. Held. That was flawed. We have had the benefit of an extensive analysis of cases where whole life has been imposed.[925] There is no case where one or more of the victims was not murdered. Although the door is not conclusively shut to whole life for non-homicide cases, the practice of this court has been against the imposition of such orders. *Att-Gen's Ref No 123 of 2014* 2015 EWCA Crim 111, 2015 1 Cr App R (S) 67 (p 470) is a striking example of this, see **288.10** in Volume 2. Courts should consider all the relevant circumstances and apply *R v Jones* 2005 and *R v Oakes and Others* 2012. Whole life should not have been imposed.
For ***Whole life orders and Article 3*** see **287.88** in Volume 2.
For examples of discretionary life orders, see the **MANSLAUGHTER *Life sentence Whole life orders*** para at **283.65** in Volume 2.

74.17 *Young offenders*

R v C 2012 EWCA Crim 1397 D was convicted of section 18. The Judge gave him IPP. Held. The finding of dangerousness was entirely right. It seems to us that the younger the offender, the more cautious the court must be in passing indeterminate sentences. There are two reasons for this. The first is that it is a very serious matter to deprive a young offender, however serious his offences, of any sense of hope or measurable prospects of release. The second is that the younger the offender, the more scope and potential there is for change over a shorter period of time than would be the case with someone who was, say, 10 years older. Because of new information, extended sentence instead.
Att-Gen's Ref No 33 of 2016, 2016 EWCA Crim 749 D pleaded to attempted murder and ABH. He viciously attacked a stranger in a shop causing dreadful injuries. Held. A life sentence is a sentence of last resort but particular reflection is required before imposing a life sentence on a young offender. However here, custody for life must be imposed, not an extended sentence.
For more details, see **288.21** in Volume 2.

Combined with other orders

74.18 *Offender of Particular Concern Order, Combined with*

Criminal Justice Act 2003 s 236A(1) Subsection (2) [the imposition of the an Offender of Particular Concern Order] applies where:..(c) the court does not impose one of the following for the offence:
(i) a sentence of imprisonment for life, or
(ii) an extended sentence under section 226A.
(2)-(4) [Not listed]
(5) The references in subsections (1)(c) and (2) to a sentence imposed for the offence include a sentence imposed for the offence and one or more offences associated with it.
For the full section, see **81.2**.
R v Fruen and DS 2016 EWCA Crim 561, 2 Cr App R (S) 30 (p 271)[926] para 127 The checklist is as follows:.. (d) Criminal Justice Act 2003 s 236A cannot apply if the court imposes life or an extended sentence for the offence or an associated offence.
R v Powell 2018 EWCA Crim 1074, 2 Cr App R (S) 34 (p 303) D was sentenced to three extended sentences, two Offender of Particular Concern Orders and 10 determinate sentences. Held. Having imposed an extended sentence, the Court was precluded from passing an Offender of Particular Concern Order on other counts, see section 236A(1)(c) and (5). *R v Fruen and DS* 2016 applied. We quash the Offender of Particular Concern Order.

74.19 *Sexual Harm Prevention Orders, Combined with*

R v Smith and Others 2011 EWCA Crim 1772, 2012 1 Cr App R (S) 82 (p 468) para 13 The usual rule ought to be that an indeterminate sentence needs no SOPO, at least unless

[925] I was defence counsel and the Schedule that was used was mine. It is at www.banksr.com Other Matters Other Documents tab Whole life section, Schedule of Whole life cases.
[926] Also known as *R v LF* 2016 EWCA Crim 561, 2 Cr App R (S) 30 (p 271)

there is some very unusual feature which means that such an order could add something useful and did not run the risk of undesirably tying the hands of the offender managers later.

R v MI 2012 EWCA Crim 1792 LCJ D was sentenced to IPP and a SOPO. He appealed the SOPO relying on *R v Smith and Others* 2011 EWCA Crim 1772, 2012 1 Cr App R (S) 82 (p 468). Held. As a result of *R v Smith and Others* 2011, it would be rare for the two orders to be made simultaneously. Rare does not mean never, but here we quash the SOPO.

Note: These cases overlook the problem of sex offenders who start contacting children etc. while they are serving their sentences. Some of the contact may not be prohibited by prison rules. The licence conditions only operate when a prisoner is released. For these offenders there is a strong need for a Sexual Harm Prevention Order from the day of sentence.

Although these cases deal with SOPOs, there is no reason why these principles shouldn't be applied in relation to SHPO cases. Ed.

Sentencing remarks

74.20 *Explain sentence, Judge must*

Criminal Justice Act 2003 s 174(1)[927] A court passing sentence on an offender has the duties in subsections (2) and (3).

(2) The court must state in open court, in ordinary language and in general terms, the court's reasons for deciding on the sentence.

(3) The court must explain to the offender in ordinary language:

(a) the effect of the sentence…

Judicial College's Crown Court Compendium Part II Sentencing June 2018 page 4-7

2D Passing a life sentence

15 The court must:

(1) Set out findings in relation to those matters described in paras 1-3 of [this guide] [Determining the seriousness etc.]

(2) State that the sentence is one of imprisonment/custody/detention for life.

(3) EITHER state that because of the [extreme] seriousness of the offence/ combination of offences, the early release provisions will not apply and that the sentence is a whole life order.

OR (in any other case) state the minimum term by explaining:

(a) what the determinate sentence would have been after a trial (taking account of any aggravating and mitigating factors);

(b) any reduction which would have been given for a guilty plea;

(c) that the minimum term is almost always one half of that notional sentence (explaining that this would have been the custodial element of a determinate term); and

(d) the deduction made for days spent on remand in custody and/or on qualifying electronically monitored curfew.

(4) Explain the consequences:

(a) The minimum term will be served in full before D is eligible to be considered for release by the Parole Board.

(b) The decision about whether or when he will be released will be taken by the Parole Board.

(c) If D is released he or she will be on licence for the rest of his/her life.

(d) The licence will be subject to conditions, which will be set at the time of his release, and if he were to break any condition he or she would be liable to be returned to prison to continue to serve his/her sentence and might not be released again.

[927] As substituted by Legal Aid, Sentencing and Punishment of Offenders Act 2012 s 64

Example
[As I have already told your advocate] I am satisfied that you present a significant risk of causing serious harm by committing further similar offences, a risk that is likely to carry on long into the future. I am satisfied that your offence is so serious that a sentence of life imprisonment is required; and that is the sentence which I impose.
As to the minimum term which you must serve: if I had been sentencing you to a determinate sentence, taking account of all of the aggravating and mitigating factors in this case, after a trial I would have sentenced you to 15 years' imprisonment. Giving you full credit for your prompt plea of guilty I would have reduced that to 10 years. Because you would have served up to half of that sentence in custody I fix the minimum term which you will serve at half of 10 years: that is 5 years. Finally I reduce that minimum term of 5 years by the number of days which you have spent on remand in custody: 71 days. This means that the minimum term which you will serve before the Parole Board may consider your possible release is one of 4 years and 294 days.
It is most important that you and everyone concerned with this case should understand what this in fact means. The minimum term is **not** a fixed term after which you will automatically be released but is the [initial] term that must be served before the Parole Board can undertake their first review of the case (including a review of the risk that you then present) and can consider whether you can properly be released from custody subject to licence at that stage and if so on what terms.
If and when you are released you will be subject to licence; and this will remain the case for the rest of your life. If for any reason your licence were to be revoked, you would be recalled to prison to continue to serve your life sentence in custody.
It follows that unless and until the Parole Board consider that your release is appropriate then you will remain in custody.

For ***Direction that evidence should be retained for parole hearings*** see **86.58**.

75 LIFE IMPRISONMENT: AUTOMATIC LIFE

75.1

Criminal Justice Act 2003 s 224A[928]

This is sometimes called statutory life, which is a bit confusing as the other life sentences are also statutory.

Children and young offenders The order is only available for those aged over 18. For offenders aged 18-20, the order is called automatic custody for life.

Commencement The order applies to offences which were committed on or after 3 December 2012.[929]

Court Martial Armed Forces Act 2006 s 218A is a corresponding section for defendants at the Court Martial, inserted by Legal Aid, Sentencing and Punishment of Offenders Act 2012 Sch 22 para 2.

Defendants under 21 The provisions also apply to defendants aged 18-20. These defendants are sentenced to custody for life, see next paragraph.

Extended disqualification from driving Where the court passes automatic life (other than one with a whole life order) with either obligatory disqualification, discretionary disqualification or disqualification under the totting up provisions, the court is required to select the appropriate period of disqualification and extend it by the length of the minimum term.[930] The section was designed to prevent offenders serving most of their disqualification periods in prison. The sections were amended by Criminal Justice and Courts Act 2015 s 30. For more detail see **41.16**.

---

[928] As inserted by Legal Aid, Sentencing and Punishment of Offenders Act 2012 s 122
[929] Criminal Justice Act 2003 s 224A(1)(a)-(b) and Legal Aid, Sentencing and Punishment of Offenders Act 2012 (Commencement No 4 and Saving Provisions) Order 2012 2012/2906
[930] Road Traffic Offenders Act 1988 s 35A(1)-(3) and (4)(a) and Powers of Criminal Courts (Sentencing) Act 2000 s 147A(1)-(3) and (4)(a) inserted by Coroners and Justice Act 2009 s 2 and Sch 16 paras 2 and 5. Schedule 16 is in force from 13/4/15.

Hospital Orders The automatic life provisions do not prevent a court from making a Hospital Order, Mental Health Act 1983 s 37(1A)(ba).
Victim surcharge The court must impose a victim surcharge of £170, Criminal Justice Act 2003 s 161A-161B and Criminal Justice Act 2003 (Surcharge) Order 2012 2012/1696 as amended. There are exceptions, a) where a compensation order or an Unlawful Profits Order or a Slavery and Trafficking Reparations Order is imposed, when a reduced amount or a nil amount can be ordered, see **17.67**, and b) where the offence was committed before 1 October 2012, when no surcharge can be made, see **115.3**. Where the offence was committed on or after that date and before 8 April 2016, the amount to be imposed is £120, see **115.4**. For defendants who are now aged 21+ but were, when the offence was committed, aged a) under 18, the amount is £20, and b) aged 18-20, the amount is £120, see **115.4**.
Old automatic life Those convicted on or after 1 October 1997 and before 4 April 2005 of a 'serious offence', who had been convicted of another 'serious offence', were liable for automatic life unless there were 'exceptional circumstances', Crime (Sentences) Act 1997 s 2. A 'serious offence' was defined by Crime (Sentences) Act 1997 s 2(5). The provisions were re-enacted by Powers of Criminal Courts (Sentencing) Act 2000 s 109 and 109(5) respectively.
Release Release for prisoners serving both the 2003 and 2012 automatic life sentences is via the Parole Board on expiry of the minimum term. The test is 'the prisoner's confinement is no longer necessary for the protection of the public', Crime (Sentences) Act 1997 s 28(6)(b). On release the prisoner is subject to supervision.
Removal from UK A prisoner who has served the minimum term of a life sentence and is liable to removal from the UK may be removed at any time. No direction from the Parole Board is required and a direction as to release does not prevent removal, Crime (Sentences) Act 1997 s 32A created and inserted by Legal Aid, Sentencing and Punishment of Offenders Act 2012 s 119. If, having been removed, he or she returns to the UK, he or she is to be treated as unlawfully at large and is liable to be detained pursuant to the sentence. If there has been a previous Parole Board direction as to release, he or she is to be treated as having been recalled, Crime (Sentences) Act 1997 s 32B.

75.2 *Statutory provisions*

Life sentence for second listed offence
Criminal Justice Act 2003 s 224A(1)[931] This section applies where:
(a) a person aged 18 or over is convicted of an offence listed in Part 1 of Schedule 15B,
(b) the offence was committed after this section comes into force, and
(c) the sentence condition and the previous offence condition are met.
(2) The court must impose a sentence of imprisonment for life or in the case of a person aged at least 18 but under 21, custody for life under Powers of Criminal Courts (Sentencing) Act 2000 s 94[932] unless the court is of the opinion that there are particular circumstances which:
(a) relate to the offence, to the previous offence referred to in subsection (4) or to the offender, and
(b) would make it unjust to do so in all the circumstances.
(3) The sentence condition is that, but for this section, the court would, in compliance with sections 152(2) [requirement not to pass a custodial sentence unless the offence was so serious that a fine or community order could not be justified, see **28.26**] and 153(2)

---

[931] As inserted by Legal Aid, Sentencing and Punishment of Offenders Act 2012 s 122. In force for offences committed after 3/12/12, Legal Aid, Sentencing and Punishment of Offenders Act 2012 (Commencement No 4 and Saving Provisions) Order 2012 2012/2906

[932] Criminal Justice Act 2003 s 224A(2) inserted by Legal Aid, Sentencing and Punishment of Offenders Act 2012 s 122 uses the expression 'imprisonment for life'. However, until Criminal Justice and Court Services Act 2000 s 61 is in force, Legal Aid, Sentencing and Punishment of Offenders Act 2012 Sch 19 para 24(2)(a) applies and the section is as listed.

[requirement that the sentence should be for the shortest term, see **28.32**], impose a sentence of imprisonment for 10 years or more or, if the person is aged at least 18 but under 21, a sentence of detention in a Young Offender Institution for such a period,[933] disregarding any extension period imposed under section 226A [provisions for extended sentences, see **56.5**].

(4) The previous offence condition is that:

(a) at the time the offence was committed, the offender had been convicted of an offence listed in Schedule 15B ('the previous offence'), and

(b) a relevant life sentence or a relevant sentence of imprisonment or detention for a determinate period was imposed on the offender for the previous offence.

(5) A life sentence is relevant for the purposes of subsection (4)(b) if:

(a) the offender was not eligible for release during the first 5 years of the sentence, or

(b) the offender would not have been eligible for release during that period but for the reduction of the period of ineligibility to take account of a relevant pre-sentence period.[934]

(6) An extended sentence imposed under this Act (including one imposed as a result of Armed Forces Act 2006) is relevant for the purposes of subsection (4)(b) if the appropriate custodial term imposed was 10 years or more.

(7) Any other extended sentence is relevant for the purposes of subsection (4)(b) if the custodial term imposed was 10 years or more.

(8) Any other sentence of imprisonment or detention for a determinate period is relevant for the purposes of subsection (4)(b) if it was for a period of 10 years or more.

(9) An extended sentence or other sentence of imprisonment or detention is also relevant if it would have been relevant under subsection (7) or (8) but for the reduction of the sentence, or any part of the sentence, to take account of a relevant pre-sentence period.

(10)-(11) [see **75.5**]

(12) Where an offence is found to have been committed over a period of two or more days, or at some time during a period of two or more days, it must be taken for the purposes of subsections (1)(b) and (4)(a) to have been committed on the last of those days.

Note: Subsection 224A(12) was inserted by Criminal Justice and Courts Act 2015 s 5(1).[935] Ed.

For the list of the Schedule 15B offences see the **Extended Sentences (EDS)** ***Schedule 15B Offences*** paras at **56.61**.

75.3 *Pre-sentence reports*

Criminal Justice Act 2003 s 156(1) In forming any such opinion as is mentioned in [various sections including section 153(2), the need for the custodial sentence to be for the shortest term, see **28.32**], a court must take into account all such information as is available to it about the circumstances of the offence or (as the case may be) of the offence and the offence or offences associated with it, including any aggravating or mitigating factors.

(2) [Not listed]

(3) Subject to subsection (4), a court must obtain and consider a pre-sentence report before:

(a) [Various sections about certain custodial sentences including section 153(2), see **56.44**]

(b) [About community sentences. Not listed, see **15.10**]

---

[933] Until Criminal Justice and Court Services Act 2000 s 61 is in force, Legal Aid, Sentencing and Punishment of Offenders Act 2012 Sch 19 para 24(2)(b) applies and the section is as listed.

[934] This legislative spaghetti appears to mean in (b) that if a defendant's minimum term before the discount for the plea of guilty was 5 years or more, that offence counts.

[935] In force 13/4/15, Criminal Justice and Courts Act 2015 (Commencement No 1, Saving and Transitional Provisions) Order 2015 2015/778 para 3 and Sch 1 para 5

(4) Subsection (3) does not apply if, in the circumstances of the case, the court is of the opinion that it is unnecessary to obtain a pre-sentence report.
(5)-(8) [Not listed, see **15.10** and **56.44**]
(9) References in subsections (1) and (3) to a court forming the opinions mentioned in sections 152(2) [about community orders, see **28.26**] and 153(2) [the need for the custodial sentence to be for the shortest term, see **28.32**] include a court forming those opinions for the purposes of section 224A(3) [automatic life sentence conditions, see **75.2**].

75.4 *Can automatic life be imposed when the offence does not carry life?*

Att-Gen's Ref No 27 of 2013 2014 EWCA Crim 334[936] LCJ para 8 [The application of section] 224A could lead in cases that may be rare to the imposition of a life sentence in respect of an offence which does not carry life as a maximum.
R v Cox 2018 EWCA Crim 1852 The Judge gave life for a Sexual Offences Act 2003 s 9 offence, which carries a 14-year maximum sentence. The defence appealed on other grounds. Held. This is one of those rare cases where a life sentence can be imposed regardless of the maximum sentence.

75.5 *Definitions*

Criminal Justice Act 2003 s 224A(10)[937] For the purposes of subsections (4) to (9):
'**extended sentence**' means:

(a) a sentence imposed under Powers of Criminal Courts (Sentencing) Act 2000 s 85[938] or under Criminal Justice Act 2003 s 226A, 226B, 227 or 228 (including one imposed as a result of Armed Forces Act 2006 s 219A, 220, 221A or 222), or
(b) an equivalent sentence imposed under the law of Scotland, Northern Ireland or a member State[939] (other than the United Kingdom),

'**life sentence**' means:

(a) a life sentence as defined in Crime (Sentences) Act 1997 s 34, or
(b) an equivalent sentence imposed under the law of Scotland, Northern Ireland or a member State (other than the United Kingdom),

'**relevant pre-sentence period**', in relation to the previous offence referred to in subsection (4), means any period which the offender spent in custody or on bail before the sentence for that offence was imposed,
'**sentence of imprisonment or detention**' includes any sentence of a period in custody (however expressed).
(11) An offence the sentence for which is imposed under this section is not to be regarded as an offence the sentence for which is fixed by law.
For the rest of the section, see **75.2**.
R v Frost 2001 2 Cr App R (S) 26 (p 124) In 1991, D, when aged 15, was found guilty of wounding with intent to resist arrest. D received a 12-month Supervision Order. In 2000, he was sentenced for another wounding with intent count. By this time D had collected a number of other convictions. The pre-sentence report had identified that D was 'a high risk to the public'. Because of the two wounding matters he qualified for and was given automatic life under Crime (Sentences) Act 1997 s 2. The Judge found no exceptional circumstances. On appeal it was argued that the 1991 finding was not a 'conviction'. The defence argued that because an offence would not be a conviction if there had been a probation order, it should not be a conviction when there was a Supervision Order. Held. That does not assist us. Applying Children and Young Persons Act 1933 s 59 the 1991 finding was a conviction. Because of the pre-sentence report, there cannot be exceptional

[936] This case is also known as *R v Burinskas* 2014 EWCA Crim 334.
[937] As inserted by Legal Aid, Sentencing and Punishment of Offenders Act 2012 s 122. In force for offences committed on or after 3/12/12
[938] Repealed on 4/4/05 by Criminal Justice Act 2003 Sch 37 para 1
[939] Presumably this means a member State of the European Union.

circumstances here. However, there was a legal anomaly because had he been two years older in 1991, the equivalent order would have been probation, which would not have counted as a conviction. The anomaly amounted to an exceptional circumstance.
Note: Since this case was heard, probation has been abolished. Although this case deals with the old automatic life sentence, the principles are likely to apply to the new automatic life sentence. Ed.

75.6 *Judicial guidance*

Att-Gen's Ref No 27 of 2013 2014 EWCA Crim 334[940] LCJ para 8 For a life sentence to be imposed under section 224A there is no requirement of a finding that the offender is dangerous within the meaning of Criminal Justice Act 2003, although it is likely that in most such cases he will be. It follows that the fact that an offender is not dangerous is not something that of itself would make it unjust to pass a life sentence under this section. Section 225(2)(b) does not apply to the relevant offence in section 224A. There is no requirement to consider whether the 'seriousness' threshold has been passed.
para 42 The first question to be considered in all cases where [the dangerousness] provisions apply is whether the offender is dangerous. Where section 224A may be relevant there will be a temptation to move straight to a consideration of that provision. That temptation should be resisted. It may lead to the omission of the crucial first question of whether the offender is dangerous.
para 43 The order in which a judge should approach sentencing in a case of this type is this:

(i) Consider the question of dangerousness. If the offender is not dangerous and the conditions in section 224A are satisfied then (subject to section 224A(2)(a) and (b)) a life sentence must be imposed.
(ii) If the offender is dangerous, consider whether the seriousness of the offence and offences associated with it justify a life sentence. Seriousness is to be considered as we have set out at para 22.
(iii) If a life sentence is justified then the judge must pass a life sentence in accordance with section 225. If section 224A also applies, the judge should record that fact in open court.
(iv) If a life sentence is not justified, then the sentencing judge should consider whether section 224A applies. If it does then (subject to the terms of section 224A) a life sentence must be imposed.
(v) If section 224A does not apply the judge should then consider the provisions of section 226A. Before passing an extended sentence the judge should consider a determinate sentence.

R v Saunders and Others 2013 EWCA Crim 1027, 2014 1 Cr App R (S) 45 (p 258) LCJ The new statutory life sentence[941] has not replaced IPP. Many offenders who represent a danger to the public may not 'qualify' for the statutory life sentence. Yet, for some offenders, the imperative of public protection continues undiminished, and is not wholly met by the 'new' extended sentence. Very long term public protection must therefore be provided by the imposition of a discretionary life sentence.

75.7 *Exception when sentence would be unjust*

Criminal Justice Act 2003 s 224A(2)[942] The court must impose a sentence of imprisonment for life unless the court is of the opinion that there are particular circumstances which:

(a) relate to the offence, to the previous offence referred to in subsection (4) or to the offender, and
(b) would make it unjust to do so in all the circumstances.

[940] This case is also known as *R v Burinskas* 2014 EWCA Crim 334.
[941] Also known as 'automatic life'. Ed.
[942] As inserted by Legal Aid, Sentencing and Punishment of Offenders Act 2012 s 122. In force for offences committed after 3/12/12, Legal Aid, Sentencing and Punishment of Offenders Act 2012 (Commencement No 4 and Saving Provisions) Order 2012 2012/2906.

For the rest of the section, see **75.2**.
Note: The test based on whether the sentence would be 'unjust' uses the same word in the test for minimum sentences in burglary cases, see **227.24** in Volume 2. This requirement is easier to meet than the more stringent test in the firearms minimum sentences, see **262.45** in Volume 2.

76 Life Imprisonment: Dangerousness, Based on

76.1

Mandatory order When the dangerousness criteria are satisfied and life imprisonment is justified, the judge has no discretion and he or she must pass a life sentence, Criminal Justice Act 2003 s 225(2)(a), see **76.2** and **76.3**.
Court Martial The Court may pass life imprisonment/custody for life for all ranks, ex-servicemen and women, and civilians. Detention for life is not available for officers, warrant officers and NCOs but is available for the other ranks, ex-servicemen and civilians, see *Guidance on Sentencing in the Court Martial 2018* Annex B.
Victim surcharge The court must impose a victim surcharge of £170, Criminal Justice Act 2003 s 161A-161B and Criminal Justice Act 2003 (Surcharge) Order 2012 2012/1696 as amended. There are exceptions, a) where a compensation order or an Unlawful Profits Order or a Slavery and Trafficking Reparations Order is imposed, when a reduced amount or a nil amount can be ordered, see **17.67**, and b) where the offence was committed before 1 October 2012, when no surcharge can be made, see **115.3**. Where the offence was committed on or after that date and before 8 April 2016, the amount to be imposed is £120, see **115.4**. For defendants who are now aged 21+ but were, when the offence was committed, aged a) under 18, the amount is £20, and b) aged 18-20, the amount is £120, see **115.4**.
Rehabilitation period This sentence is excluded from rehabilitation.[943]
Historical offences This sentence is only available for offences committed on or after 4 April 2005, see Criminal Justice Act 2003 s 225(1)(a) and Criminal Justice Act 2003 (Commencement No 8 and Transitional and Saving Provisions) Order 2005 2005/950.
Release Release for prisoners serving Criminal Justice Act 2003 s 225 and 226/ discretionary life, custody for life and detention for life sentences is via the Parole Board on expiry of the minimum term. The test is whether 'the prisoner's confinement is no longer necessary for the protection of the public', Crime (Sentences) Act 1997 s 28(6)(b). On release the prisoner is subject to supervision. Where a determinate term is imposed to run concurrently with an indeterminate term, release cannot occur until the release requirements of both sentences have been satisfied.
Removal from UK A prisoner who has served the minimum term of a life sentence and is liable to removal from the UK may be removed at any time. No direction from the Parole Board is required and a direction as to release does not prevent removal, Crime (Sentences) Act 1997 s 32A created and inserted by Legal Aid, Sentencing and Punishment of Offenders Act 2012 s 119. If, having been removed, he or she returns to the UK, he or she is to be treated as unlawfully at large and is liable to be detained pursuant to the sentence. If there has been a previous Parole Board direction as to release, he is to be treated as having been recalled, Crime (Sentences) Act 1997 s 32B.
See also the **Rehabilitation of Offenders Act 1974** chapter.

76.2 ***Statutory provisions Defendant aged 18+***
Meaning of "specified offence" etc.
Criminal Justice Act 2003 s 224[944]

[943] Rehabilitation of Offenders Act 1974 s 5(1)(a)
[944] These sections are listed as amended by Legal Aid, Sentencing and Punishment of Offenders Act 2012 Sch 21 and Criminal Justice and Immigration Act 2008 (Transitory Provisions) Order 2008 2008/1587 art 2(2)(b).

(1) An offence is a "specified offence" for the purposes of this Chapter if it is a specified violent offence, a specified sexual offence or a specified terrorism offence[945].
(2) An offence is a 'serious offence' for the purposes of this chapter if and only if:
(a) it is a specified offence [see above], and
(b) it is, apart from section 224A [automatic life, see **75.2**],[946] punishable in the case of a person aged 18 or over by:
(i) imprisonment for life or, in the case of a person aged at least 18 but under 21, custody for life, or
(ii) imprisonment (or, in the case of a person aged at least 18 but under 21, detention in a Young Offender Institution) for a determinate period of 10 years or more.
(3) In this chapter:
'serious harm' means death or serious personal injury, whether physical or psychological,
'specified violent offence' means an offence specified in Part 1 of Schedule 15 [see **56.19**],
'specified sexual offence' means an offence specified in Part 2 of that Schedule [see **56.20**].
'specified terrorism offence' means an offence specified in Part 3 of that Schedule [see **56.21**][947].
Criminal Justice Act 2003 s 225(1) This section applies where:
(a) a person aged 18 or over is convicted of a serious offence committed after the commencement of this section, and
(b) the court is of the opinion that there is a significant risk to members of the public of serious harm occasioned by the commission by him of further specified offences [see **56.23**].
(2) If:
(a) the offence is one in respect of which the offender would apart from this section be liable to imprisonment for life, and
(b) the court considers that the seriousness of the offence, or of the offence and one or more offences associated with it, is such as to justify the imposition of a sentence of imprisonment for life, the court must impose a sentence of imprisonment for life (or in the case of a person aged at least 18 but under 21, a sentence of custody for life).
(3)-(4) [Repealed[948]]
(5) An offence the sentence for which is imposed under this section is not to be regarded as an offence the sentence for which is fixed by law.
Note: There is a whole section of law about the meaning of 'significant risk' (see **56.24**), 'serious offences' and 'specified offences' (see **56.17**). It can be found in the 7th edition of this book. It was very relevant to IPP but will rarely be critical when a life sentence under the dangerousness provisions is considered. Ed.

76.3 ***Dangerousness provisions Statutory provisions Defendant aged under 18***
Detention for life for serious offences committed by those under 18
Criminal Justice Act 2003 s 226(1) This section applies where:
(a) a person aged under 18 is convicted of a serious offence [for definition, **76.2**] committed after the commencement of this section, and
(b) the court is of the opinion that there is a significant risk to members of the public of serious harm occasioned by the commission by him of further specified offences.
(2) If:

[945] 'or a specified terrorist offence' was inserted by Counter-Terrorism and Border Security Act 2019 s 9(2) In force 12 April 2019, Counter-Terrorism and Border Security Act 2019 s 27(3).
[946] Legal Aid, Sentencing and Punishment of Offenders Act 2012 Sch 19 para 16 substitutes '224A' for '225'.
[947] As inserted by Counter-Terrorism and Border Security Act 2019 s 9(2)(b) In force 12 April 2019, Counter-Terrorism and Border Security Act 2019 s 27(3).
[948] The subsections were repealed by Legal Aid, Sentencing and Punishment of Offenders Act 2012 s 123(a).

(a) the offence is one in respect of which the offender would apart from this section be liable to a sentence of detention for life under section 91 of the Sentencing Act,[949] and

(b) the court considers that the seriousness of the offence, or of the offence and one or more offences associated with it, is such as to justify the imposition of a sentence of detention for life,

the court must impose a sentence of detention for life under that section.

(3)-(4) [Repealed[950]]

(5) An offence the sentence for which is imposed under this section is not to be regarded as an offence the sentence for which is fixed by law.

Note: There is a whole section of law about the meaning of 'significant risk' (see **56.24**), 'serious offences' and 'specified offences' (see **56.17**). It can be found in the 7th edition of this book. It was very relevant to IPP but will rarely be critical when a life sentence under the dangerousness provisions is considered. Ed.

76.4 *Need to consider whether risk could be dealt with by an extended sentence*

R v A 2014 EWCA Crim 2483 D was convicted of oral and vaginal rape. He had a previous conviction for rape when he was aged 19 for which he received 5 years' YOI. The Judge found that the dangerousness criteria were made out and said that, having made that conclusion, she had to pass a life sentence. Held. para 23 If the Judge is considering a life sentence or an extended sentence he or she must address whether the offender will remain or may remain a threat to the public in future. If it is considered the offender will cease to be a risk in the predictable future, that militates against a life sentence. If not, that militates in favour of a life sentence which imports no backstop release date. para 27 Here the Judge did err in reaching the conclusion that she 'must' impose a life sentence [unless she had privately considered an extended sentence and rejected it]. Consequently we will go through the exercise. On the facts, life, not an extended sentence.

76.5 *Judicial guidance*

R v Chapman 2000 1 Cr App R (S) 377 LCJ D pleaded to reckless arson and reports said he suffered from a personality disorder. The Judge set the minimum term at one year. Held. Life should never be imposed unless the circumstances are such as to call for a severe sentence based on the offence.

R v Lang 2005 EWCA Crim 2864, 2006 2 Cr App R (S) 3 (p 13) para 8 The Court considered the 'dangerous offender' provisions. Held. Parliament has adopted the *R v Chapman* 2000 1 Cr App R (S) 377 criteria for the imposition of a discretionary life sentence for these new provisions.

R v Kehoe 2008 EWCA Crim 819, 2009 1 Cr App R (S) 9 (p 41) para 7 LCJ D pleaded to manslaughter on the basis of diminished responsibility and was sentenced to life imprisonment. Held. The cases decided before Criminal Justice Act 2003 came into effect no longer offer guidance on when a life sentence should be imposed. When a court finds that the defendant satisfies the criteria for dangerousness, a life sentence should be reserved for those cases where the culpability of the offender is particularly high or the offence itself particularly grave. It is neither possible nor desirable to set out all those circumstances in which a life sentence might be appropriate.

R v Wilkinson 2009 EWCA Crim 1925 LCJ [The decision to impose life,] like virtually every sentencing decision, [is] fact-specific. It is clear that as a matter of principle the discretionary life sentence under section 225 should continue to be reserved for offences of the utmost gravity. Without being prescriptive, we suggest that the sentence should come into contemplation when the judgement of the court is that the seriousness is such that the life sentence would have what Lord Bingham observed, in *R v Lichniak*

[949] Powers of Criminal Courts (Sentencing) Act 2000 s 91

[950] The subsections were repealed by Legal Aid, Sentencing and Punishment of Offenders Act 2012 s 123(b).

2001 EWHC 294 (Admin), would be a 'denunciatory' value, reflective of public abhorrence of the offence, and where, because of its seriousness, the notional determinate sentence would be very long, measured in very many years.

R v McDonald 2010 EWCA Crim 127 The question we ask is whether the facts of the present offence were so grave as to fall into that category of cases in which a sentence of life imprisonment was appropriate. Notwithstanding the justified words of the Judge to the effect that the public abhorred offences such as this, of importance to the consideration which we have had to make is the fact that the jury found the appellant not guilty of attempted murder. While the offences of which he stood convicted remained exceptionally serious, they did not, in our view, fall into the top bracket requiring a life sentence. We shall therefore quash the sentence of life imprisonment and substitute IPP.

R v Cardwell 2012 EWCA Crim 3030, 2013 2 Cr App R (S) 43 (p 284) D was convicted of possessing firearms with intent to enable others to endanger life. With others he imported firearms from the US for sale to criminals. He was given life with an 11-year term. Held. The principles in *R v Wilkinson* 2009 supplement the statutory process and do not replace it. One cannot assume from the seriousness of the offending alone that an offender is dangerous. The court must still consider the issue of dangerousness within the context of Criminal Justice Act 2003 s 229. In doing so, a greater significance must be given to the seriousness of the offending but the test remains the same and must be applied to the particular offender who is to be sentenced. Here it cannot be concluded that there was a significant risk to members of the public of serious harm being occasioned by the commission by D of further specified offences, so 22 years instead. For more detail see **260.6** in Volume 2.

R v Jenkin 2012 EWCA Crim 2557, 2013 2 Cr App R (S) 15 LCJ D pleaded to section 18. He gouged his partner's eyes out with his fingers. *R v Kehoe* 2009 applied. The *Kehoe* indications are not cumulative, they are alternative. Life and a Hospital Order with a Restriction Order were correct.

R v Saunders and Others 2013 EWCA Crim 1027, 2014 1 Cr App R (S) 45 (p 258) LCJ Neither Criminal Justice Act 2003 nor Legal Aid, Sentencing and Punishment of Offenders Act 2012 imposed any limit on the power of the court to order a sentence of life imprisonment. Some of these offences may involve a significant risk of serious harm to the public, but are not included within the list of 'specified' offences in the dangerousness provisions in the 2003 Act. One obvious example is the offender who commits repeated offences of very serious drug supplying which justifies the imposition of the life sentence. In circumstances like these the court is not obliged to impose the sentence in accordance with section 225(2), but its discretion to do so is unaffected. In reality, the occasions when this second form of discretionary life sentence is likely to be imposed will be rare. The 'denunciatory' ingredient identified to distinguish between the circumstances in which the discretionary life sentence rather than IPP should be imposed is no longer apposite. By that we mean that although the 'denunciatory' element of the sentencing decision may continue to justify the discretionary life sentence, its absence does not preclude such an order. As every judge appreciates, however, the life sentence remains the sentence of last resort.

Att-Gen's Ref No 27 of 2013 2014 EWCA Crim 334[951] LCJ para 15 Cases about life imprisonment before the December 2012 changes are now of limited assistance. para 17 We cannot interpret Criminal Justice Act 2003 s 225 as now enacted as though the sentence of IPP continues to exist. para 18 Save for automatic life, a life sentence remains a sentence of last resort. As IPP is no longer available, it is inevitable therefore that sentences of life imprisonment will be imposed more frequently than before. It is what Parliament intended and also ensures (as Parliament also intended), so far as is possible, [that] there is effective protection of the public. para 25 It should not be overlooked that Criminal Justice Act 2003 s 226A(4) makes the imposition of [an

[951] This case is also known as *R v Burinskas* 2014 EWCA Crim 334.

extended] sentence discretionary. As was the case under the previous regime, even where there is a finding of dangerousness, an ordinary determinate sentence is sometimes appropriate. Where a life sentence is not justified an extended sentence will usually, but not always, be appropriate. The option of a determinate sentence should not be forgotten.
para 22 The question in section 225(2)(b) as to whether the seriousness of the offence (or of the offence and one or more offences associated with it) is such as to justify a life sentence requires consideration of:

(i) the seriousness of the offence itself, on its own or with other offences associated with it, in accordance with the provisions of Criminal Justice Act 2003 s 143(1). This is always a matter for the judgment of the court,
(ii) the defendant's previous convictions (in accordance with Criminal Justice Act 2003 s 143(2)),
(iii) the level of danger to the public posed by the defendant and whether there is a reliable estimate of the length of time he will remain a danger,
(iv) the available alternative sentences.

For ***Direction that evidence should be retained for parole hearings*** see **86.58**.
For the ***Pre-sentence requirement*** see **56.44**.
LIFE IMPRISONMENT: MANDATORY LIFE, see the **MURDER** chapter in Volume 2.

77 MEDICAL REPORTS

77.1

For medical reports on mentally disordered defendants, see the **DEFENDANT *Mentally disordered defendants*** paras at **242.39** in Volume 2.

Hospital Orders There are additional powers to order reports where a court is considering a Hospital Order or a Guardianship Order, see the **HOSPITAL AND GUARDIANSHIP ORDERS Reports** section at **67.16**.

Remand time limits When Anti-social Behaviour, Crime and Policing Act 2014 Sch 1 para 5 is in force the maximum time a defendant may be remanded for a medical report after an alleged breach of the new civil injunctions is three weeks if he or she is in custody and four weeks if on bail.

77.2 *Procedure and rules*

Criminal Practice Directions 2015 EWCA Crim 1567 para R 3P[952]
paras 3P.1-3 [Not listed at they only set out general matters.]
3P.4 Where the court requires the assistance of such a report then it is essential that there should be (i) absolute clarity about who is expected to do what, by when, and at whose expense; and (ii) judicial directions for progress with that report to be monitored and reviewed at prescribed intervals, following a timetable set by the court which culminates in the consideration of the report at a hearing. This is especially important where the report in question is a psychiatric assessment of the defendant for the preparation of which specific expertise may be required which is not readily available and because in some circumstances a second such assessment, by another medical practitioner, may be required.
paras 3P5-9 [Not listed. They deal with timetabling and associated matters.]
3P.10 Guidance entitled 'Good practice guidance: commissioning, administering and producing psychiatric reports for sentencing' prepared for and published by the Ministry of Justice and HM Courts and Tribunals Service in September 2010 contains material that will assist court staff and those who are asked to prepare such reports: http://www.ohrn.nhs.uk/resource/policy/GoodPracticeGuidePsychReports.pdf
para 3P.10-16 [Not listed. They deal with funding and those in custody etc.]

[952] As inserted by Criminal Practice Directions 2015 Amendment No 7 2018 EWCA Crim 1760. In force 1/10/18

77.3 *Defendant relies on medical certificate and does not attend*
Note: The rules about what a medical certificate should contain, how the court is not bound by the certificate, examples of unsatisfactory explanations, how medical practitioners are liable to be summoned to court to justify their statements, defendant who have no date when they will be able to come court etc. are in Criminal Practice Directions 2015 EWCA Crim 1567 para I 5C. Ed.

77.4 *Court requested medical reports*
Criminal Procedure Rules 2015 2015/1490 Rule 28.8(1)[953] This rule applies where for sentencing purposes the court requires[:]
(a) a medical examination of the defendant and a report; or
(b) information about the arrangements that could be made for the defendant where the court is considering
(i) a hospital order, or
(ii) a guardianship order.
(2) The court must:
(a) identify each issue in respect of which the court requires expert medical opinion and the legislation applicable;
(b) specify the nature of the expertise likely to be required for giving such opinion;
(c) identify each party or participant by whom a commission for such opinion must be prepared, who may be:
(i) a party (or party's representative) acting on that party's own behalf,
(ii) a party (or party's representative) acting on behalf of the court, or
(iii) the court officer acting on behalf of the court;
(d) where there are available to the court arrangements with the National Health Service under which an assessment of a defendant's mental health may be prepared, give such directions as are needed under those arrangements for obtaining the expert report or reports required;
(e) where no such arrangements are available to the court, or they will not be used, give directions for the commissioning of an expert report or expert reports, including:
(i) such directions as can be made about supplying the expert or experts with the defendant's medical records,
(ii) directions about the other information, about the defendant and about the offence or offences alleged to have been committed by the defendant, which is to be supplied to each expert, and
(iii) directions about the arrangements that will apply for the payment of each expert;
(f) set a timetable providing for:
(i) the date by which a commission is to be delivered to each expert,
(ii) the date by which any failure to accept a commission is to be reported to the court,
(iii) the date or dates by which progress in the preparation of a report or reports is to be reviewed by the court officer, and
(iv) the date by which each report commissioned is to be received by the court; and
(g) identify the person (each person, if more than one) to whom a copy of a report is to be supplied, and by whom.
(3) [What the report should contain, see below.]

77.5 *Medical reports What they should contain*
Criminal Procedure Rules 2015 2015/1490 Rule 28.8(1)[954] A commission addressed to an expert must:
(a) identify each issue in respect of which the court requires expert medical opinion and the legislation applicable;

[953] Criminal Procedure (Amendment No 2) Rules 2018 2018/847 para 7 substituted a new Rule 28.8. In force 1/10/18
[954] Criminal Procedure (Amendment No 2) Rules 2018 2018/847 para 7 substituted a new Rule 28.8. In force 1/10/18

(b) include:
(i) the information required by the court to be supplied to the expert,
(ii) details of the timetable set by the court, and
(iii) details of the arrangements that will apply for the payment of the expert;
(c) identify the person (each person, if more than one) to whom a copy of the expert's report is to be supplied; and
(d) request confirmation that the expert from whom the opinion is sought:
(i) accepts the commission, and
(ii) will adhere to the timetable.

77.6 *Medical report, Court must have a*

Criminal Justice Act 2003 s 157(1) Subject to subsection (2), in any case where the offender is or appears to be mentally disordered, the court must obtain and consider a medical report before passing a custodial sentence other than one fixed by law.
(2) Subsection (1) does not apply if, in the circumstances of the case, the court is of the opinion that it is unnecessary to obtain a medical report.
Criminal Justice Act 2003 s 157(5) In this section 'mentally disordered', in relation to any person, means suffering from a mental disorder within the meaning of Mental Health Act 1983.
(6) In this section 'medical report' means a report as to an offender's mental condition made or submitted orally or in writing by a registered medical practitioner who is approved for the purposes of Mental Health Act 1983 s 12 by the Secretary of State as having special experience in the diagnosis or treatment of mental disorder.

77.7 *Failure to have a medical report Appeals*

Criminal Justice Act 2003 s 157(4) No custodial sentence which is passed in a case to which subsection (1) applies is invalidated by the failure of a court to comply with that subsection requirement for medical reports, but any court on an appeal against such a sentence:
(a) must obtain a medical report if none was obtained by the court below, and
(b) must consider any such report obtained by it or by that court.

77.8 *Contents of experts' reports*

Criminal Procedure Rules 2015 2015/1490 Rule 19.4…an expert's report must:
(a) give details of the expert's qualifications, relevant experience and accreditation,
(b) give details of any literature or other information which the expert has relied on in making the report,
(c) contain a statement setting out the substance of all facts given to the expert which are material to the opinions expressed in the report, or upon which those opinions are based,
(d) make clear which of the facts stated in the report are within the expert's own knowledge,
(e)[955] where the expert has based an opinion or inference on a representation of fact or opinion made by another person for the purposes of criminal proceedings (for example, as to the outcome of an examination, measurement, test or experiment):
(i) identify the person who made that representation to the expert,
(ii) give the qualifications, relevant experience and any accreditation of that person, and
(iii) certify that that person had personal knowledge of the matters stated in that representation.
(f) where there is a range of opinion on the matters dealt with in the report:
(i) summarise the range of opinion, and
(ii) give reasons for his own opinion,

[955] As substituted by Criminal Procedure (Amendment) Rules 2018 2018/132 para 9. In force 2/4/18

(g) if the expert is not able to give his opinion without qualification, state the qualification,
(h) include such information as the court may need to decide whether the expert's opinion is sufficiently reliable to be admissible as evidence,
(i) contain a summary of the conclusions reached,
(j) contain a statement that the expert understands an expert's duty to the court, and has complied and will continue to comply with that duty, and
(k) contain the same declaration of truth as a witness statement.

NON-MOLESTATION ORDERS, BREACH OF see **RESTRAINING ORDERS: HARASSMENT/ NON-MOLESTATION ORDERS: BREACH OF**

78 NOTIFICATION: SEX OFFENDERS

78.1
Sexual Offences Act 2003 s 80-92
Notification is automatic and is dependent on whether the statutory criteria are made out and not what a judge or magistrate says.[956] If the court explains the notification procedure incorrectly, that does not alter the defendant's obligations. If the statutory criteria are met and the judge or magistrate says nothing, notification still applies. The court is, however, under a duty to issue a certificate which sets out the facts of the conviction etc.[957] Where notification depends on the age of a person as in an indecent photograph case, the Court needs to rule on the age of the individual, see *R v George* 2018 EWCA Crim 417, 2 Cr App R (S) 10 (p 76) at **78.15**.
Children and young offenders Notification applies whatever the age of the offender.[958] Parental directions apply where the offender is aged 10-17.[959]
Court Martial The notification requirements are applied in the same way in the Court Martial as they are in the civilian courts, see *Guidance on Sentencing in the Court Martial 2018* para 5.10.4.
Parental Directions Order The only notification order the court can make is a Parental Directions Order, see **78.31**.
Stand-alone orders There are also stand-alone notification orders for sexual offenders.[960] Applications are made to the Magistrates' Court. This order is not dealt with in this book because it is not part of a court's sentence.

Who is subject to notification?

78.2 ***Statutory provisions***
Persons become subject to notification requirements
Sexual Offences Act 2003 s 80(1) A person is subject to the notification requirements of this Part for the period set out in section 82 ('the notification period') if:
(a) he is convicted of an offence listed in Sch 3 [see **78.4**],
(b) he is found not guilty of such an offence by reason of insanity,
(c) he is found to be under a disability and to have done the act charged against him in respect of a Sch 3 offence [see **78.4**], or
(d) in England and Wales or Northern Ireland, he is cautioned in respect of such an offence.
(2) A person for the time being subject to the notification requirements of this Part is referred to in this Part as a 'relevant offender'.

---
[956] *R v Longworth* 2006 UKHL 1, 2 Cr App R (S) 62 (p 401)
[957] Sexual Offences Act 2003 s 92
[958] Sexual Offences Act 2003 s 80
[959] Sexual Offences Act 2003 s 89
[960] Sexual Offences Act 2003 s 97-102

Persons formerly subject to Part 1 of the Sex Offenders Act 1997

Sexual Offences Act 2003 s 81(1)[961] A person is, from the commencement of this Part until the end of the notification period, subject to the notification requirements of this Part if, before the commencement of this Part:[962]

(a) he was convicted of a Sch 3 offence [see **78.4**],

(b) he was found not guilty of a Sch 3 offence by reason of insanity,

(c) he was found to be under a disability and to have done the act charged against him in respect of a Sch 3 offence, or

(d) in England and Wales or Northern Ireland, he was cautioned in respect of a Sch 3 offence.

(2) Subsection (1) does not apply if the notification period ended before the commencement of this Part.

(3) Subsection (1)(a) does not apply to a conviction before 1st September 1997 unless, at the beginning of that day, the person:

(a) had not been dealt with in respect of the offence,

(b) was serving a sentence of imprisonment, or was subject to a community order, in respect of the offence,

(c) was subject to supervision, having been released from prison after serving the whole or part of a sentence of imprisonment in respect of the offence, or

(d) was detained in a hospital or was subject to a guardianship order, following the conviction.

(4) Paragraphs (b) and (c) of subsection (1) do not apply to a finding made before 1st September 1997 unless, at the beginning of that day, the person:

(a) had not been dealt with in respect of the finding, or

(b) was detained in a hospital, following the finding.

(5) Subsection (1)(d) does not apply to a caution given before 1st September 1997.

(6) A person who would have been within subsection (3)(b) or (d) or (4)(b) but for the fact that at the beginning of 1st September 1997 he was unlawfully at large or absent without leave, on temporary release or leave of absence, or on bail pending an appeal, is to be treated as being within that provision.

(7) Where, immediately before the commencement of this Part, an order under a provision within subsection (8) was in force in respect of a person, the person is subject to the notification requirements of this Part from that commencement until the order is discharged or otherwise ceases to have effect.

(8) The provisions are:

(a) Sex Offenders Act 1997 s 5A (Restraining Orders),

(b) Crime and Disorder Act 1998 s 2 (sex offender orders made in England and Wales),

(c) Crime and Disorder Act 1998 s 2A (interim orders made in England and Wales),

(d), (e) and (f) [Scottish and Northern Irish provisions].

78.3 *Judicial guidance*

R v Longworth 2006 UKHL 1, 2 Cr App R (S) 62 (p 401) Lords Where someone was conditionally discharged before 1 May 2004 he was not liable to the notification requirements.

See also: *R v Wiles* 2004 EWCA Crim 836, 2 Cr App R (S) 88 (p 467) (D was sentenced to a 2-year extended sentence (6 months' custody 18 months' extended licence). Considering Powers of Criminal Courts (Sentencing) Act 2000 s 76 and 85, Crime and Disorder Act 1998 s 117 and Criminal Justice Act 1991 s 31, the relevant term was the total sentence and not the custodial part.)

---

[961] This section was brought into force by Sexual Offences Act 2003 (Commencement) Order 2004 2004/874. In force 1/5/04

[962] This section was brought into force by Sexual Offences Act 2003 (Commencement) Order 2004 2004/874. In force 1/5/04

What are the trigger offences?

78.4 ***Power to order What are the Schedule 3 offences?***

Sexual Offences Act 2003 Sch 3

Note: These offences are listed in chronological order. Ed.

Sexual Offences Act 1956

s 1 (rape)

s 5 (intercourse with girl under 13)

s 6 (intercourse with girl under 16), if the offender was 20 or over

s 10 (incest by a man), if the victim or (as the case may be) other party was under 18

s 12 (buggery) if: a) the offender was 20 or over, and b) the victim or (as the case may be) other party was under 18

s 13 (indecency between men) if: a) the offender was 20 or over, and b) the victim or (as the case may be) other party was under 18

s 14 (indecent assault on a woman) if: a) the victim or (as the case may be) other party was under 18, or b) the offender, in respect of the offence or finding, is or has been: i) sentenced to imprisonment for a term of at least 30 months, or ii) admitted to a hospital subject to a restriction order

s 15 (indecent assault on a man) if: a) the victim or (as the case may be) other party was under 18, or b) the offender, in respect of the offence or finding, is or has been: i) sentenced to imprisonment for a term of at least 30 months, or ii) admitted to a hospital subject to a restriction order

s 16 (assault with intent to commit buggery), if the victim or (as the case may be) other party was under 18

s 28 (causing or encouraging the prostitution of, intercourse with or indecent assault on girl under 16)

Indecency with Children Act 1960 s 1 (indecent conduct towards young child)

Criminal Law Act 1977 s 54 (inciting girl under 16 to have incestuous sexual intercourse)

Protection of Children Act 1978 s 1 (indecent photographs of children), if the indecent photographs or pseudo-photographs showed persons under 16 and: a) the conviction, finding or caution was before the commencement of this Part, or b) the offender: i) was 18 or over, or ii) is sentenced in respect of the offence to imprisonment for a term of at least 12 months

Customs and Excise Management Act 1979 s 170 (penalty for fraudulent evasion of duty etc.) in relation to goods prohibited to be imported under Customs Consolidation Act 1876 s 42 (indecent or obscene articles), if the prohibited goods included indecent photographs of persons under 16 and: a) the conviction, finding or caution was before the commencement of this Part, or b) the offender: i) was 18 or over, or ii) is sentenced in respect of the offence to imprisonment for a term of at least 12 months

Criminal Justice Act 1988 s 160 (possession of indecent photograph of a child), if the indecent photographs or pseudo-photographs showed persons under 16 and: a) the conviction, finding or caution was before the commencement of this Part, or b) the offender: i) was 18 or over, or ii) is sentenced in respect of the offence to imprisonment for a term of at least 12 months

Sexual Offences (Amendment) Act 2000 s 3 (abuse of position of trust), if the offender was 20 or over

Sexual Offences Act 2003

s 1 and 2 (rape, assault by penetration)

s 3 (sexual assault) if: a) where the offender was under 18, he is or has been sentenced, in respect of the offence, to imprisonment for a term of at least 12 months, b) in any other case: i) the victim was under 18, or ii) the offender, in respect of the offence or finding, is or has been: a) sentenced to a term of imprisonment, b) detained in a hospital, or c) made the subject of a community sentence of at least 12 months [For how to determine the length of a community order, see **15.15**]

s 4-6 (causing sexual activity without consent, rape of a child under 13, assault of a child under 13 by penetration)
s 7 (sexual assault of a child under 13) if the offender: a) was 18 or over, or b) is or has been sentenced in respect of the offence to imprisonment for a term of at least 12 months
s 8-12 (causing or inciting a child under 13 to engage in sexual activity, child sex offences committed by adults)
s 13 (child sex offences committed by children or young persons), if the offender is or has been sentenced, in respect of the offence, to imprisonment for a term of at least 12 months
s 14 (arranging or facilitating the commission of a child sex offence) if the offender: a) was 18 or over, or b) is or has been sentenced, in respect of the offence, to imprisonment for a term of at least 12 months
s 15 (meeting a child following sexual grooming etc.)
s 15A (sexual communication with a child)
This entry was inserted by Serious Crime Act 2015 Sch 4 para 66(2). In force 3 April 2017.
s 16-19 (abuse of a position of trust) if the offender, in respect of the offence, is or has been: a) sentenced to a term of imprisonment, b) detained in a hospital, or c) made the subject of a community sentence of at least 12 months [For how to determine the length of a community order, see **15.15**]
s 25-26 (familial child sex offences) if the offender: a) was 18 or over, or b) is or has been sentenced in respect of the offence to imprisonment for a term of at least 12 months
s 30-37 (offences against persons with a mental disorder impeding choice, inducements etc. to persons with mental disorder)
s 38-41 (care workers for persons with mental disorder) if: a) where the offender was under 18, he is or has been sentenced in respect of the offence to imprisonment for a term of at least 12 months, b) in any other case, the offender, in respect of the offence or finding, is or has been: i) sentenced to a term of imprisonment, ii) detained in a hospital, or iii) made the subject of a community sentence of at least 12 months [For how to determine the length of a community order, see **15.15**]
s 47 (paying for sexual services of a child) if the victim or (as the case may be) other party was under 16, and the offender: a) was 18 or over, or b) is or has been sentenced in respect of the offence to imprisonment for a term of at least 12 months
s 48[963] (causing or inciting child prostitution or pornography) if the offender: a) was 18 or over, or b) is or has been sentenced in respect of the offence to imprisonment for a term of at least 12 months
s 49 (controlling a child prostitute or a child involved in pornography) if the offender: a) was 18 or over, or b) is or has been sentenced in respect of the offence to imprisonment for a term of at least 12 months
s 50 (arranging or facilitating child prostitution or pornography) if the offender: a) was 18 or over, or b) is or has been sentenced in respect of the offence to imprisonment for a term of at least 12 months
s 61 (administering a substance with intent)
s 62-63 (committing an offence or trespassing, with intent to commit a sexual offence) if: a) where the offender was under 18, he is or has been sentenced in respect of the offence to imprisonment for a term of at least 12 months, b) in any other case: i) the intended offence was an offence against a person under 18, or ii) the offender, in respect of the offence or finding, is or has been: a) sentenced to a term of

[963] This offence was inserted by Sexual Offences Act 2003 (Amendment of Schedules 3 and 5) Order 2007 2007/296.

imprisonment, b) detained in a hospital, or c) made the subject of a community sentence of at least 12 months [For how to determine the length of a community order, see **15.15**]

s 64-65 (sex with an adult relative) if: a) where the offender was under 18, he is or has been sentenced in respect of the offence to imprisonment for a term of at least 12 months, b) in any other case, the offender, in respect of the offence or finding, is or has been: i) sentenced to a term of imprisonment, or ii) detained in a hospital

s 66 (exposure) if: a) where the offender was under 18, he is or has been sentenced in respect of the offence to imprisonment for a term of at least 12 months, b) in any other case: i) the victim was under 18, or ii) the offender, in respect of the offence or finding, is or has been: a) sentenced to a term of imprisonment, b) detained in a hospital, or c) made the subject of a community sentence of at least 12 months [For how to determine the length of a community order, see **15.15**]

s 67 (voyeurism) if: a) where the offender was under 18, he is or has been sentenced in respect of the offence to imprisonment for a term of at least 12 months, b) in any other case: i) the victim was under 18, or ii) the offender, in respect of the offence or finding, is or has been: a) sentenced to a term of imprisonment, b) detained in a hospital, or c) made the subject of a community sentence of at least 12 months [For how to determine the length of a community order, see **15.15**]

67A[964] (voyeurism: additional offences) (1) if a) the offence was committed for the purpose mentioned in section 67A(3)(a) (sexual gratification), and b) the relevant condition is met.

(2) Where the offender was under 18, the relevant condition is that the offender is or has been sentenced in respect of the offence to imprisonment for a term of at least 12 months.

(3) In any other case, the relevant condition is that—

(a) the victim was under 18, or

(b) the offender, in respect of the offence or finding, is or has been:

(i) sentenced to a term of imprisonment,

(ii) detained in a hospital, or

(iii) made the subject of a community sentence of at least 12 months.

[For how to determine the length of a community order, see **15.15**]

s 69-70 (intercourse with an animal, sexual penetration of a corpse) if: a) where the offender was under 18, he is or has been sentenced in respect of the offence to imprisonment for a term of at least 12 months, b) in any other case, the offender, in respect of the offence or finding, is or has been: i) sentenced to a term of imprisonment, or ii) detained in a hospital

Criminal Justice and Immigration Act 2008 s 63[965] (possession of extreme pornographic images) if the offender: a) was 18 or over, and b) is sentenced in respect of the offence to imprisonment for a term of at least 2 years

Coroners and Justice Act 2009 s 62(1)[966] (possession of prohibited images of children) if the offender: a) was 18 or over, and b) is sentenced in respect of the offence to imprisonment for a term of at least 2 years

Serious Crime Act 2015 s 69 (possession of paedophile manual) If the offender:

(a) was 18 or over, or

(b) is sentenced in respect of the offence to imprisonment for a term of at least 12 months.

Note: This entry was inserted by Serious Crime Act 2015 Sch 4 para 66(3).[967] Ed.

[964] Inserted by Voyeurism (Offences) Act 2019 s 1(3) In force 12 April 2019.

[965] Inserted by Criminal Justice and Immigration Act 2008 Sch 26 para 58(2)

[966] Inserted by Coroners and Justice Act 2009 Sch 2(3) para 62(2)

[967] In force 3/5/15, Serious Crime Act 2015 (Commencement No 1) Regulations 2015 2015/820 para 2

78.5 ***Service offences***
Sexual Offences Act 2003 Sch 3 [list continued]
(1) An offence under:
(a) Army Act 1955 s 70,
(b) Air Force Act 1955 s 70, or
(c) Naval Discipline Act 1957 s 42[968]
of which the corresponding civil offence (within the meaning of that Act) is an offence listed in any of the paragraphs (above).
(2) A reference in any of those paragraphs to being made the subject of a community sentence of at least 12 months is to be read, in relation to an offence under an enactment referred to in sub-para (1), as a reference to being sentenced to a term of service detention of at least 112 days.

78.6 ***Interpretation***
Sexual Offences Act 2003 Sch 3 (list continued)
1 A reference in a preceding paragraph to an offence includes:
(a) a reference to an attempt, conspiracy or incitement to commit that offence, and b) except in paragraphs 36 to 43, a reference to aiding, abetting, counselling or procuring the commission of that offence.
2 A reference in a preceding paragraph to a person's age is:
(a) in the case of an indecent photograph, a reference to the person's age when the photograph was taken,
(b) in any other case, a reference to his age at the time of the offence.
3 In this Schedule 'community sentence' has, in relation to England and Wales, the same meaning as in Powers of Criminal Courts (Sentencing) Act 2000.
4 For the purposes of paragraphs 14, 44 and 78:
(a) a person is to be taken to have been under 16 at any time if it appears from the evidence as a whole that he was under that age at that time,
(b) Protection of Children Act 1978 s 7 (interpretation) [applies as it] applies for the purposes of the Act.
Community orders For determining the length of a community order and therefore the length of notification, see **15.15**.

78.7 ***Detention and Training Order and notification***
R v M, B and H 2010 EWCA Crim 42 M and B were convicted of two counts of sexual activity with a child (Sexual Offences Act 2003 s 9(2) and 13). H was convicted of three counts of the same. H and B were aged 16 and M was aged 15. H was given an 18-month DTO and M and B received 12-month DTOs. The Judge initially stated that the defendants were subject to notification requirements, 10 years for H and 7 years for M and B. M's counsel said notification did not apply. The periods were halved for M and B. Held. The adult trigger period of notification was 12+ months. By virtue of Sexual Offences Act 2003 s 131, a period of detention under a DTO applies to an equivalent sentence of imprisonment. Powers of Criminal Courts (Sentencing) Act 2000 s 102 states that the period of detention under a DTO is one half of the term of the order. Therefore under Sexual Offences Act 2003 s 80, there would be no notification requirements as half the term of detention is less than 12 months.

78.8 ***Extended sentences and notification***
R (Minter) v Chief Constable of Hampshire 2011 EWHC 1610 (Admin) High Court In 2006 D was given a 4½-year extended sentence with an 18-month custodial term under the 2000 provisions. The Chief Constable determined it was a greater than 30-month sentence of imprisonment so making the period indefinite. Held. As Powers of Criminal Courts (Sentencing) Act 2000 s 85 refers to an extended sentence being the aggregate of

[968] Repealed on 31/10/09 by Armed Forces Act 2006 Sch 17 para 1

the two parts the period that matters is the total sentence. So notification was indefinite. Although we were not asked to decide the point we see no basis for a different analysis of a 2003 extended sentence.

How long is the notification period?

78.9 ***Statutory periods***

The periods Sexual Offences Act 2003 s 82(1) lists the notification period for a person within section 80(1) or 81(1). It does not list all the sentences which trigger notification.

Start date The period runs from the date of the sentence or caution, Sexual Offences Act 2003 s 82(6).

Youths and service personnel For service personnel and defendants aged under 21, 'imprisonment' in the table below includes the equivalent custodial sentence, Sexual Offences Act 2003 s 131.

Offender subject to a Sexual Harm Prevention Order Where the defendant is subject to a SHPO which will last longer than the period of notification, the notification will last for the length of the SHPO, see **78.12**.

Notification triggered by sentence length Sexual Offences Act 2003 Sch 3 lists the offences which trigger notification. Some of the listed offences only trigger notification if the sentence is of a certain length or the defendant and/or the victim are under a certain age. See **78.4** for more details.

Sexual Offences Act 2003 s 82(1) The notification period for a person within section 80(1) or 81(1) is:

Description of sentence for Sch 3 offence	**Notification period aged 18+**	**Notification period aged under 18**
Caution in England, Wales or Northern Ireland	2 years	1 year
Conditional discharge	The period of conditional discharge	The period of conditional discharge
Imprisonment for a term of 6 months or less	7 years	3½ years
Imprisonment for more than 6 months but less than 30 months	10 years	5 years
Imprisonment for Public Protection or Imprisonment of 30 months or more	An indefinite period	An indefinite period
Imprisonment for life	An indefinite period	An indefinite period
Hospital Order without a Restriction Order	7 years	3½ years
Hospital with a Restriction Order	An indefinite period	An indefinite period
An order of any other description	5 years	2½ years

Note: The wording in the table has been edited to make the table easier to understand. The table below does not feature in Sexual Offences Act 2003 s 82(1) and was drafted to assist. Ed.

Other sentences	
Description of relevant offence	**Method of calculating the term**
Community sentence[969]	Consider the 'an order of any other description' box in the table above.
Suspended sentence[970]	Apply the suspended custodial term to the table above.
Extended sentence (EDS) under Criminal Justice Act 2003 s 226A and 226B Extended sentence under Criminal Justice Act 2003 s 227-228	Apply the aggregate of the custodial term and the extended licence period to the table above.[971]

78.10 ***Offender convicted of two or more offences***

Sexual Offences Act 2003 s 82(3) Subsection (4) applies where a relevant offender within section 80(1)(a) or 81(1)(a) is or has been sentenced, in respect of two or more offences listed in Sch 3:

(a) to consecutive terms of imprisonment, or

(b) to terms of imprisonment which are partly concurrent.

(4) Where this subsection applies, subsection (1) has effect as if the relevant offender were or had been sentenced, in respect of each of the offences, to a term of imprisonment which:

(a) in the case of consecutive terms, is equal to the aggregate of those terms,

(b) in the case of partly concurrent terms (X and Y, which overlap for a period Z), is equal to X plus Y minus Z.

78.11 ***Defendant found to be under a disability then later tried***

Sexual Offences Act 2003 s 82(5) Where a relevant offender the subject of a finding within section 80(1)(c) or 81(1)(c) (offender found to be under a disability and to have done the act charged against him in respect of a Sch 3 offence) is subsequently tried for the offence, the notification period relating to the finding ends at the conclusion of the trial.

Notification and Sexual Harm Prevention Orders and Sexual Offences Prevention Orders

78.12 ***Notification and Sexual Harm Prevention Orders and Sexual Offences Prevention Orders Statute***

SHPOs and interim SHPOs: notification requirements

Sexual Offences Act 2003 s 103G(1) Where:

(a) a sexual harm prevention order is made in respect of a defendant who was a relevant offender immediately before the making of the order, and

(b) the defendant would (apart from this subsection) cease to be subject to the notification requirements of this Part while the order (as renewed from time to time) has effect,

the defendant remains subject to the notification requirements.

(2) Where a sexual harm prevention order is made in respect of a defendant who was not a relevant offender immediately before the making of the order:

[969] By virtue of Sexual Offences Act 2003 Sch 3 para 96, 'Community sentence' has the same meaning as in Powers of Criminal Courts (Sentencing) Act 2000. Section 33 of the 2000 Act has been amended so as to remove the definition of 'community sentence' (which was 'a sentence which consists of or includes one or more community orders'.) Criminal Justice Act 2003 s 147(1) defines community sentence as a community order or a Youth Rehabilitation Order.

[970] A suspended sentence is a custodial sentence for the purposes of notification, Criminal Justice Act 2003 s 189(6).

[971] See *R v Wiles* 2004 EWCA Crim 836, 2 Cr App R (S) 88 (p 467).

(a) the order causes the defendant to become subject to the notification requirements of this Part from the making of the order until the order (as renewed from time to time) ceases to have effect, and

(b) this Part applies to the defendant, subject to the modification set out in subsection (3).

(3) The "relevant date" is the date of service of the order.

(4) Subsections (1) to (3) apply to an interim sexual harm prevention order as if references to a sexual harm prevention order were references to an interim sexual harm prevention order, and with the omission of "(as renewed from time to time)" in both places.

(5) Where:

(a) a sexual harm prevention order is in effect in relation to a relevant sex offender (within the meaning of section 88A), and

(b) by virtue of section 88F or 88G the relevant sex offender ceases to be subject to the notification requirements of this Part,

the sexual harm prevention order ceases to have effect.

(6) and (7) [notification and applications for civil SHPOs]

78.13 ***Notification, Combined with General matters***

R v Hammond 2008 EWCA Crim 1358 When imposing a Sexual Offences Prevention Order in addition to a notification requirement under Sexual Offences Act 2003 Sch 3, the court should ensure that the terms of the order are consistent with the notification requirements. Excessively wide terms ought to be avoided.

R v Smith and Others 2011 EWCA Crim 1772, 2012 1 Cr App R (S) 82 (p 468) It is not normally proper to impose a SOPO so that the notification requirements are extended beyond the period prescribed by law. But it does not follow that the duration of a SOPO ought generally to be the same as the duration of notification requirements. Notification requirements and the conditions of a SOPO are generally two different things. The first require positive action by the defendant, who must report his movements to the police. The second prohibit him from doing specified things. Ordinarily there ought to be little or no overlap between them.

Note: These principles would appear to apply to SHPOs.

Other matters

78.14 ***Notification is not part of the sentence***

R v Longworth 2006 UKHL 1, 2 Cr App R (S) 62 (p 401) Lords Rule stated and applied.

78.15 ***Court paperwork wrong***

R v George 2018 EWCA Crim 417, 2 Cr App R (S) 10 (p 76) D pleaded to distributing an indecent photograph. He was conditionally discharged. The Court signed a form under Sexual Offences Act 2003 s 92 to say he had been convicted of a Sexual Offences Act 2003 Sch 3 offence [for notification proceedings]. D appealed his conviction, which was dismissed. The Registrar made enquiries and the prosecution said the photograph was not of a girl aged under 16 so it was not a Schedule 3 offence. Held. We have no power to deal with an appeal about the certificate so we dismiss the sentence appeal. Two of us reconstitute ourselves as the Divisional Court and quash the certificate.

78.16 ***European Convention on Human Rights, Compatibility with***

R (F) v Secretary of State 2010 UKSC 17 Supreme Court F, when aged 11, committed rape on a six-year-old and in 2005 he was convicted of this offence. He was given a 30-month prison sentence and was subject to automatic notification. He complained that the lack of an opportunity to review the requirements was a breach of his article 8 rights. Held. It was agreed that the notification did interfere with his article 8 rights and that it was directed at the legitimate aim of prevention of crime and the protection of the rights and freedoms of others. The issue was whether the requirements without a review were proportionate to that aim. The changes to notification requirements in Criminal Justice and Court Services Act 2000 and Criminal Justice Act 2003 s 84-91 will have given some of those subject to those requirements very good reason for wishing to have those requirements lifted because the requirements were capable of causing significant interference with their article 8 rights. It is obvious that it is necessary for the authorities that are responsible for the management and supervision of those convicted of sexual offences to be aware of the whereabouts of those who are subject to active management or supervision. For those that no longer pose any significant risk the requirements can only impose an unnecessary and unproductive burden on the responsible authorities. The Divisional Court and the Court of Appeal were correct to find that the notification requirements constitute a disproportionate interference with article 8 rights because they make no provision for individual review of the requirements. We repeat the declaration of incompatibility made by the Divisional Court.

R (Prothero) v Secretary of State for the Home Department 2013 EWHC 2830 High Court D was convicted of nine sexual offences. He was subject to the notification requirements. The Secretary of State made modifications to the notification requirements by Sexual Offences Act 2003 (Notification Requirements) (England and Wales) Regulations 2012 2012/1876 which required that those subject to the regime must notify the police of details of their bank accounts and any associated credit or debit cards. D argued that such provisions were incompatible with ECHR, particularly article 8. Held. There was no incompatibility. The means employed [to enable the police to quickly trace an offender] are not in any way inappropriate or disproportionate.

78.17 ***Can the notification contribute to a reduction/increase in sentence?***

Att-Gen's Ref No 50 of 1997 1998 2 Cr App R (S) 155 The sentencing Judge thought that nine months was appropriate for two counts of indecent assault. He said, "That would require registration for 10 years, which would be an absurd additional burden. I have no discretion." He passed a 6-month sentence which required 7 years of notification. Held. The Judge was wrong to reduce the sentence. It is the duty of judges to implement the sentencing powers that have been given to them by Parliament.

R v H 2007 EWCA Crim 2622 D pleaded to sexual assault contrary to Criminal Justice Act 2003 s 3 (30 months' detention under section 91, 30 months' extended licence under Powers of Criminal Courts (Sentencing) Act 2000 s 85). Owing to the sentence of 30 months or more, D would remain on the Sex Offender Register indefinitely (Criminal Justice Act 2003 s 82(1)). He entered a static caravan, which was occupied by V, aged 17, whilst V was in bed, naked. D, naked and sexually aroused, got into bed, asked for sex, said "please" and pushed V onto her back. They physically struggled and D eventually desisted. D had ejaculated onto her back. D, aged 17½, was effectively of good character. Reports raised concerns about reoffending based on cognitive distortions. It was argued that: a) the notification period should be calculated based on the custodial term rather than a combination of the custodial term and an extended licence period, and b) where a sentence is on the cusp of a regime that required notification for life, rather than for a more limited period of 5 years (as D was aged under 18), it fell to the Judge to consider whether he should not mitigate the effect of the sentence by reducing the 30-month term, if only by a short period. Held. a) We see considerable force in this submission but do not feel it is necessary to decide the matter. b) It cannot be said that it is appropriate to reduce that proper [custodial] term simply because [a defendant] is on the cusp of [two notification periods].

DPP v Clutterbuck 2006 EWHC 3447, 2007 2 Cr App R (S) 16 (p 72) The defendant was convicted of SOA 2003 s 3. The probation officer asked that an order of not less than 12 months should be imposed to enable the sex offender group work programme to be completed. The Magistrates sentenced him to an 11-month community order. The prosecution appealed, saying it would be improper to impose a sentence which would abrogate the notification scheme. Held. The Magistrates had behaved entirely properly.

R v Banham 2010 EWCA Crim 448 D, aged 17, pleaded to two offences of sexual activity with a willing 14-year-old girl, V. There was no pressure or significant harm. The pre-sentence report said he had respect for women. There were no relevant

convictions. Held. A community order would require D to be on the Register for 5 years. That is a significant punishment and a handicap to a young man seeking employment. There was no danger that required registration. Conditional discharge for 6 months.
R v M 2010 EWCA Crim 592 D, aged 15, pleaded to three rapes of a 9-year-old girl. He was of good character. D was sentenced to 2 years 9 months' detention, and served his sentence. A new report concluded that D suffered from Asperger's syndrome. Held. On the information the Judge had, the sentence cannot be criticised. Asperger's syndrome severely impairs responses to other people. D may well have misread what to another person would have been obvious signs of her attitude to what he was doing. The sentence made the notification period life. We do not consider that that is appropriate. If we reduce the sentence to 2 years 2 months, the notification period would be 5 years. That would be appropriate.

78.18 *Court must explain/Suggested sentencing remarks*

Criminal Procedure Rules 2015 2015/1490 Rule 28.3(1) This rule applies where, on a conviction, sentence or order, legislation requires the defendant:
(a) to notify information to the police…
(2) The court must tell the defendant that notification requirements apply, and under what legislation.
Judicial College's Crown Court Compendium Part II Sentencing June 2018 page 8.1
3 The court has two functions:
(1) to certify that the defendant has been convicted of a relevant offence and tell the defendant of his/her obligation to notify the police within 3 days of his/her conviction, if at liberty, or within 3 days of his/her release from custody of various personal particulars, including where he/she is living. See also CrimPR 28.3. (2) for offenders under 18, the court may also make a direction under s.89 of the SOA 2003 that the obligations imposed on the defendant are in fact to be imposed on the parent/guardian.

Example
I certify that you have been convicted of a sexual offence so that you must, for a period of {number} years from the date of your conviction/for the rest of your life, keep the police informed at all times of your personal particulars, the address at which you are living and any alteration in the name you are using. You will be given full details of these requirements on a form at the end of this hearing.

R v George 2018 EWCA Crim 417, 2 Cr App R (S) 10 (p 76) D pleaded to distributing an indecent photograph. He was conditionally discharged. The Court signed a form under Sexual Offences Act 2003 s 92 to say he had been convicted of a Sexual Offences Act 2003 Sch 3 offence [for notification proceedings]. D appealed his conviction, which was dismissed. The Registrar made enquiries and the prosecution said the photograph was not of a girl aged under 16 so it was not a Schedule 3 offence. Held. Two of us reconstitute ourselves as the Divisional Court and quash the certificate. Judges should be alive to those offences which are listed in Schedule 3 [but because of the age qualification are not ones requiring notification]. The Judge should determine the age of the child in question.

78.19 *Appeals*

R v Longworth 2006 UKHL 1, 2 Cr App R (S) 62 (p 401) Lords There was no appeal but it would be unhelpful if we did not indicate our view as to the point of law certified by the Court of Appeal.
R v Odam 2008 EWCA Crim 1087, 2009 1 Cr App R (S) 22 (p 120) D was convicted of exposure and sentenced to a community order with one term only, namely unpaid work of 120 hours. The Judge said he was subject to notification for 5 years. Held. Although there is no right of appeal against notification requirements it is appropriate to correct

any errors made in the sentencing remarks which may have misled D as to his position. D had not been sentenced to a community order of at least 12 months so notification did not apply.
R v Davidson 2008 EWCA Crim 2795, 2009 2 Cr App R (S) 13 (p 76) D appealed the Judge's order that notification requirements applied. Held. The Judge was correct to say notification requirements were applicable. If we had jurisdiction to hear the appeal we would have dismissed it. We give permission for the judgment to be reported.

What does notification entail?

78.20 ***Definition of 'relevant date'***
Sexual Offences Act 2003 s 82(6) In this Part, 'relevant date' means:
(a) in the case of a person within section 80(1)(a) or 81(1)(a) [see **78.2**], the date of the conviction,
(b) in the case of a person within section 80(1)(b) or (c) or 81(1)(b) or (c) [see **78.2**], the date of the finding,
(c) in the case of a person within section 80(1)(d) or 81(1)(d) [see **78.2**], the date of the caution,
(d) in the case of a person within section 81(7), the date which, for the purposes of Sex Offenders Act 1997 Part 1, was the relevant date in relation to that person.

78.21 ***Initial notification***
Notification requirements: initial notification
Sexual Offences Act 2003 s 83(1) A relevant offender must, within the period of three days beginning with the relevant date [see **78.21**], notify to the police the information set out in subsection (5).
(2)-(4) [see **78.22**]
(5) The information is:
(a) the relevant offender's date of birth,
(b) his national insurance number,
(c) his name on the relevant date [see **78.20**] and, where he used one or more other names on that date, each of those names,
(d) his home address[972] on the relevant date [see **78.20**],
(e) his name on the date on which notification is given and, where he uses one or more other names on that date, each of those names,
(f) his home address on the date on which notification is given,
(g) the address of any other premises in the United Kingdom at which, at the time the notification is given, he regularly resides or stays,
(h) any prescribed information.[973]
(6) When determining the period for the purpose of subsection (1), there is to be disregarded any time when the relevant offender is:
(a) remanded in or committed to custody by an order of a court or kept in service custody,
(b) serving a sentence of imprisonment or a term of service detention,
(c) detained in a hospital, or
(d) outside the United Kingdom.

78.22 ***Offender subject to notification immediately before conviction etc.***
Sexual Offences Act 2003 s 83(2) Subsection (1) does not apply to a relevant offender in respect of a conviction, finding or caution within section 80(1) if:

[972] Sexual Offences Act 2003 s 83(7) In this Part, 'home address' means, in relation to any person: a) the address of his sole or main residence in the United Kingdom, or b) where he has no such residence, the address or location of a place in the United Kingdom where he can regularly be found and, if there is more than one such place, such one of those places as the person may select.
[973] Sexual Offences Act 2003 s 83(5A) In subsection (5)(h) 'prescribed' means prescribed by regulations made by the Secretary of State.

(a) immediately before the conviction etc., he was subject to notification requirements as a result of another conviction etc. or an order of a court ('the earlier event'),
(b) at that time, he had made a notification under subsection (1) in respect of the earlier event, and
(c) throughout the period referred to in subsection (1), he remains subject to the notification requirements as a result of the earlier event.

(3) Subsection (1) does not apply to a relevant offender in respect of a conviction, finding or caution within section 81(1) or an order within section 81(7) if the offender complied with section 2(1) of the Sex Offenders Act 1997 in respect of the conviction, finding, caution or order.

(4) Where a notification order is made in respect of a conviction, finding or caution, subsection (1) does not apply to the relevant offender in respect of the conviction, finding or caution if:

(a) immediately before the order was made, he was subject to the notification requirements of this Part as a result of another conviction, finding or caution or an order of a court ('the earlier event'),
(b) at that time, he had made a notification under subsection (1) in respect of the earlier event, and
(c) throughout the period referred to in subsection (1), he remains subject to the notification requirements as a result of the earlier event.

For the rest of the section, see **78.21**.

78.23 *Requirement to notify changes*

Notification requirements: changes

Sexual Offences Act 2003 s 84(1) A relevant offender must, within the period of three days beginning with:

(a) his using a name which has not been notified to the police under section 83(1), this subsection, or Sex Offenders Act 1997 s 2,
(b) any change of his home address,[974]
(c) his having resided or stayed, for a qualifying period, at any premises in the United Kingdom the address of which has not been notified to the police under section 83(1), this subsection, or Sex Offenders Act 1997 s 2,
(ca) any prescribed change of circumstances,[975] or
(d) his release from custody pursuant to an order of a court or from imprisonment, service detention or detention in a hospital,

notify to the police that name, the new home address, the address of those premises, the prescribed details or (as the case may be) the fact that he has been released, and (in addition) the information set out in section 83(5).

(2)-(3) [see **78.24**]

(4) [see **78.25**]

78.24 *Notification can be given prior to change occurring*

Sexual Offences Act 2003 s 84(2) A notification under subsection (1) may be given before the name is used, the change of home address or the prescribed change of circumstances occurs or the qualifying period[976] ends, but in that case the relevant offender must also specify the date when the event is expected to occur.

---

[974] Sexual Offences Act 2003 s 83(7) In this Part, 'home address' means, in relation to any person: a) the address of his sole or main residence in the United Kingdom, or b) where he has no such residence, the address or location of a place in the United Kingdom where he can regularly be found and, if there is more than one such place, such one of those places as the person may select.

[975] Sexual Offences Act 2003 s 83(5A) In this section: a) 'prescribed change of circumstances' means any change: i) occurring in relation to any matter in respect of which information is required to be notified by virtue of section 83(5)(h), and ii) of a description prescribed by regulations made by the Secretary of State, b) 'the prescribed details', in relation to a prescribed change of circumstances, means such details of the change as may be so prescribed.

[976] Sexual Offences Act 2003 s 84(6) In this section, 'qualifying period' means: a) a period of 7 days, or b) two or more periods, in any period of 12 months, which taken together amount to 7 days.

(3) If a notification is given in accordance with subsection (2) and the event to which it relates occurs more than two days before the date specified, the notification does not affect the duty imposed by subsection (1).

78.25 *Notified change does not occur within three days*

Sexual Offences Act 2003 s 84(4) If a notification is given in accordance with subsection (2) and the event has not occurred by the end of the period of three days beginning with the date specified:

(a) the notification does not affect the duty imposed by subsection (1), and
(b) the relevant offender must, within the period of six days beginning with the date specified, notify to the police the fact that the event did not occur within the period of three days beginning with the date specified.

78.26 *Periodic notification Who does it apply to?*

Sexual Offences Act 2003 s 85(4) This subsection applies to the relevant offender if he is:

(a) remanded in or committed to custody by an order of a court,
(b) serving a sentence of imprisonment or a term of service detention,
(c) detained in a hospital, or
(d) outside the United Kingdom.

78.27 *Periodic notification What is required?*

Notification requirements: periodic notification

Sexual Offences Act 2003 s 85(1) A relevant offender must, within the period of one year after each event within subsection (2), notify to the police the information set out in section 83(5), unless within that period he has given a notification under section 84(1).
(2)-(3) [see **78.28**]

Sexual Offences Act 2003 s 83(5) The information is:

(a) the relevant offender's date of birth,
(b) his national insurance number,
(c) his name on the relevant date [see **78.20**] and, where he used one or more other names on that date, each of those names,
(d) his home address[977] on the relevant date [see **78.20**],
(e) his name on the date on which notification is given and, where he uses one or more other names on that date, each of those names,
(f) his home address on the date on which notification is given,
(g) the address of any other premises in the United Kingdom at which, at the time the notification is given, he regularly resides or stays,
(h) any prescribed information.[978]

78.28 *Periodic notification When is it?*

Sexual Offences Act 2003 s 85(2) The events are:

(a) the commencement of this Part (but only in the case of a person who is a relevant offender from that commencement),
(b) any notification given by the relevant offender under section 83(1) or 84(1), and
(c) any notification given by him under subsection (1).

(3) Where the period referred to in subsection (1) would (apart from this subsection) end whilst subsection (4) applies to the relevant offender, that period is to be treated as continuing until the end of the period of three days beginning when subsection (4) first ceases to apply to him.

---

[977] Sexual Offences Act 2003 s 83(7) In this Part, 'home address' means, in relation to any person: a) the address of his sole or main residence in the United Kingdom, or b) where he has no such residence, the address or location of a place in the United Kingdom where he can regularly be found and, if there is more than one such place, such one of those places as the person may select.

[978] Sexual Offences Act 2003 s 83(5A) In subsection (5)(h) 'prescribed' means prescribed by regulations made by the Secretary of State.

78.29 *Methods of notification*

Method of notification and related matters

Sexual Offences Act 2003 s 87(1)[979] A person gives a notification under section 83(1), 84(1) or 85(1) by:

(a) attending a police station in his local police area, and

(b) giving an oral notification to any police officer, or to any person authorised for the purpose by the officer in charge of the station.

(2) A person giving a notification under section 84(1):

(a) in relation to a prospective change of home address, or

(b) in relation to premises referred to in subsection (1)(c) of that section,

may give the notification at a police station that would fall within subsection (1) if the change in home address had already occurred or if the address of those premises were his home address.

The acknowledgement of notification must be in writing, see Sexual Offences Act 2003 s 87(3).

Where notification is given, the police or authorised person may take the person's fingerprints and photograph, Sexual Offences Act 2003 s 87(4).

78.30 *Notification of travel*

Notification requirements: travel outside the United Kingdom

Sexual Offences Act 2003 s 86(1) The Secretary of State may by regulations make provision requiring relevant offenders who leave the UK, or any description of such offenders[980] to comply:

(a) before they leave, with a notification under subsection (2),

(b) if they subsequently return to the UK, with a notification under subsection (3).

(2) A notification under this subsection must disclose:

(a) the date on which the offender will leave the UK,

(b) the country (or, if there is more than one, the first country) to which he will travel and his point of arrival in that country,

(c) any other information prescribed by the regulations which the offender holds about his departure from or return to the UK or his movements while outside the UK.

(3) A notification under this subsection must disclose any information prescribed by the regulations about the offender's return to the UK.

(4) [Repealed[981]]

The details of the requirements can be found in Sexual Offences Act 2003 (Travel Notification Requirements) Regulations 2004 2004/1220. The regulations provide for notification before an intended departure (Reg 5) and notification of the return to the UK (Regs 8 and 9) etc.

Parental directions

78.31 *Power to order parental direction*

Parental directions: variations, renewals and discharges

Sexual Offences Act 2003 s 89(1) Where a person within the first column of the following table ('the young offender') is aged under 18 when he is before the court referred to in the second column of the table…that court may direct that subsection (2) applies in respect of an individual ('the parent') having parental responsibility for the young offender.

---

[979] Sexual Offences Act 2003 s 88(3) 'Local police area' means, in relation to a person: a) the police area in which his home address is situated, b) in the absence of a home address, the police area in which the home address last notified is situated, c) in the absence of a home address and of any such notification, the police area in which the court which last dealt with the person in a way mentioned in subsection (4) is situated.

[980] Sexual Offences Act 2003 s 86(4) Regulations under subsection (1) may make different provision for different categories of person.

[981] Criminal Justice and Immigration Act 2008 Sch 28 Part 4.

Description of person	Court which may make the direction
A relevant offender within section 80(1)(a) to (c) or 81(1)(a) to (c), (notification after an SOA 2003 Sch 3 conviction).	The court which deals with the offender in respect of the offence or finding
A relevant offender within section 129(1)(a) to (c) (conviction for a breach of a Risk of Sexual Harm Order)	The court which deals with the offender in respect of the offence or finding
A person who is the subject of a Notification Order, Interim Notification Order, Sexual Offences Prevention Order or Interim Sexual Offences Prevention Order	The court which makes the order
A relevant offender who is the defendant to an application under subsection (4) (or, in Scotland, the subject of an application under subsection (5))	The court which hears the application

(2) Where this subsection applies:

(a) the obligations that would (apart from this subsection) be imposed by or under sections 83 to 86 (the notification requirements) on the young offender are to be treated instead as obligations on the parent, and

(b) the parent must ensure that the young offender attends at the police station with him, when a notification is being given.

(3) A direction under subsection (1) takes immediate effect and applies:

(a) until the young offender attains the age of 18, or

(b) for such shorter period as the court may, at the time the direction is given, direct.

(4) A chief officer of police may, by complaint to any Magistrates' Court whose commission area includes any part of his police area, apply for a direction under subsection (1) in respect of a relevant offender ('the defendant'):

(a) who resides in his police area, or who the chief officer believes is in or is intending to come to his police area, and

(b) who the chief officer believes is under 18.

78.32 *Parental directions Variations, renewals and discharges*

Sexual Offences Act 2003 s 90(1) A person within subsection (2) may apply to the appropriate court for an order varying, renewing or discharging a direction under section 89(1) (see above).

(2) The persons are:

(a) the young offender,

(b) the parent,

(c) the chief officer of police for the area in which the young offender resides,

(d) a chief officer of police who believes that the young offender is in, or is intending to come to, his police area,

(e) [Scottish provisions]

(f) where the direction was made on an application under section 89(4) (see above), the chief officer of police who made the application,

(g) where the direction was made on an application under section 89(5) (see above), the chief constable who made the application.

(3) An application under subsection (1) may be made:

(a) where the appropriate court is the Crown Court, in accordance with rules of court,

(b) in any other case, by complaint.

(4) On the application the court, after hearing the person making the application and (if they wish to be heard) the other persons mentioned in subsection (2), may make any order, varying, renewing or discharging the direction, that the court considers appropriate.

(5) In this section, the 'appropriate court' means:
(a) where the Court of Appeal made the order, the Crown Court,
(b) in any other case, the court that made the direction under section 89(1) (see above).

78.33 ***Review of notification***
R (F) v Secretary of State 2010 UKSC 17 Indefinite notification without a review is incompatible with European Convention on Human Rights art 8.
Sexual Offences Act 2003 (Remedial) Order 2012 2012/1883[982] inserts Sexual Offences Act 2003 s 91A-91F which provide that a person subject to an indefinite notification requirement may apply for a review to the relevant chief officer of police with an appeal from that decision to the Magistrates' Court. If the person is subject to a SOPO or Interim SOPO, no application can be made. No application can be made until after 15 years from the person's first notification. That period is reduced to 8 years when the person was aged under 18.

79 Notification: Sex Offenders: Breach of Requirements

79.1
Sexual Offences Act 2003 s 91
Mode of trial Triable either way
Maximum sentence Indictment 5 years. Summary 6 months and/or an unlimited fine.[983]
There are maximum fines for those aged under 18, see **13.44**.

79.2 ***Statutory offence***
Offences relating to notification
Sexual Offences Act 2003 s 91(1) A person commits an offence if he:
(a) fails, without reasonable excuse, to comply with:
(i) section 83(1) [initial notification requirement, see **78.21**,]
(ii) section 84(1) [requirement to notify changes, see **78.23**,]
(iii) section 84(4)(b) [requirement to notify changes did not occur, see **78.25**,]
(iv) section 85(1) [periodic notification, see **78.27**,]
(v) section 87(4) [duty to allow fingerprints and/or photographs to be taken, see **78.29**, or]
(vi) section 89(2)(b) [parental failure to ensure young offender attends police station, see **78.31**, or]
(vii) any requirement imposed by regulations made under section 86(1) [travel notification, see **78.30**,] or
(b) notifies to the police, in purported compliance with section 83(1), 84(1) or 85(1) [for details, see 78.23] or any requirement imposed by regulations made under section 86(1) (see above), any information which he knows to be false.
(2) A person guilty of an offence under this section is liable:
(a) on summary conviction, to imprisonment for a term not exceeding 6 months or a fine not exceeding the statutory maximum or both;
(b) on conviction on indictment, to imprisonment for a term not exceeding 5 years.
(3) A person commits an offence under para a) of subsection (1) on the day on which he first fails, without reasonable excuse, to comply with section 83(1), 84(1) or 85(1) or a requirement imposed by regulations made under section 86(1) (for reference details, see above) and continues to commit it throughout any period during which the failure continues, but a person must not be prosecuted under subsection (1) more than once in respect of the same failure.

982 In force 30/7/12
983 Legal Aid, Sentencing and Punishment of Offenders Act 2012 s 85(1) and (4) and Legal Aid, Sentencing and Punishment of Offenders Act 2012 (Commencement No 11) Order 2015 2015/504

(4) Proceedings for an offence under this section may be commenced in any court having jurisdiction in any place where the person charged with the offence resides or is found.

79.3 *Sentencing Council 2018 Guidelines*

Breach Offences Guideline 2018, see www.banksr.com Other Matters Guidelines tab In force 1 October 2018 page 39
Sexual Offences Act 2003 s 91

STEP ONE **Determining the offence category**

The court should determine the offence category with reference only to the factors listed in the tables below. In order to determine the category the court should assess **culpability** and **harm**.

Culpability

In assessing culpability, the court should consider the **intention** and **motivation** of the offender in committing any breach.

A	• Determined attempts to avoid detection • Long period of non-compliance
B	• Deliberate failure to comply with requirement
C	• Minor breach • Breach just short of reasonable excuse

Harm

The level of **harm** is determined by weighing up all the factors of the case to determine the harm that has been caused or was at risk of being caused. In assessing any risk of harm posed by the breach, consideration should be given to the original offence(s) for which the order was imposed and the circumstances in which the breach arose.

Category 1	Breach causes or risks very serious harm or distress
Category 2	Cases falling between Categories 1 and 3
Category 3	Breach causes or risks little or no harm or distress

79.4

STEP TWO **Starting point and category range**

Having determined the category at step one, the court should use the corresponding starting point to reach a sentence within the category range from the appropriate sentence table below. The starting point applies to all offenders irrespective of plea or previous convictions.

	Culpability		
Harm	**A**	**B**	**C**
Category 1	**Starting point** 2 years' custody	**Starting point** 1 year's custody	**Starting point** 36 weeks' custody
	Category range 1 year's to 4 years' custody	**Category range** 26 weeks' to 2 years' custody	**Category range** 26 weeks' to 1 year 6 months' custody

Culpability			
Harm	**A**	**B**	**C**
Category 2	**Starting point** 1 year's custody	**Starting point** 36 weeks' custody	**Starting point** High-level community order
	Category range 26 weeks' to 2 years' custody	**Category range** 26 weeks' to 1 year 6 months' custody	**Category range** Medium-level community order to 36 weeks' custody
Category 3	**Starting point** 36 weeks' custody	**Starting point** High-level community order	**Starting point** Low-level community order
	Category range 26 weeks' to 1 year 6 months' custody	**Category range** Medium-level community order to 36 weeks' custody	**Category range** Band B fine to medium-level community order

For the meaning of high-level, medium-level and low-level community orders, see **15.12**. For a Band B fine, see **58.28**.

79.5 [Aggravating and mitigating factors]

Page 42 The table below contains a **non-exhaustive** list of additional factual elements providing the context of the offence and factors relating to the offender. Identify whether any combination of these, or other relevant factors, should result in an upward or downward adjustment from the starting point.

In some cases, having considered these factors, it may be appropriate to move outside the identified category range.

Factors increasing seriousness
Statutory aggravating factors:
Previous convictions, having regard to a) the **nature** of the offence to which the conviction relates and its **relevance** to the current offence; and b) the **time** that has elapsed since the conviction
Offence committed whilst on bail
Other aggravating factors:
Breach committed shortly after order made
History of disobedience of court orders (where not already taken into account as a previous conviction)
Breach constitutes a further offence (where not separately prosecuted)
Offence committed on licence or while subject to post sentence supervision
Factors reducing seriousness or reflecting personal mitigation
Breach committed after long period of compliance
Prompt voluntary surrender/admission of breach or failure
Age and/or lack of maturity where it affects the responsibility of the offender
Mental disorder or learning disability where linked to the commission of the offence
Sole or primary carer for dependent relatives

STEP THREE to STEP EIGHT These are: Consider assistance to the prosecution, Reduction for guilty plea, Totality principle, Ancillary orders, Duty to give reasons and Consider time spent on bail with a tag.

79.6 ***Suggested approach to the guideline***

Note: I suggest the best approach is to give little weight to the old cases and simply apply the guideline. Ed.

79.7 ***Pre-guideline cases***

R v Piskadlo 2014 EWCA Crim 76 D pleaded to breaching his notification requirements. It was his sixth offence since August 2011. On his last release from prison he was given strict instructions to notify. Two weeks later he was found banging his head on some steps. He was taken to hospital and spat at a police officer (3 months consecutive, no appeal). D was aged 33 and an itinerant alcoholic. The Judge said the only solution was to lock him up and told him "When you choose a different way, things may change". Held. We start at 18 months. With plea that makes **12 months** and with the 3 months, 15 months.

R v Norton 2014 EWCA Crim 1275, 2 Cr App R (S) 79 (p 627) D pleaded (full credit) to failure to comply with notification requirements. These requirements were imposed after three rape convictions. Following release he was convicted on no fewer than 11 subsequent occasions for failure to comply. Shortly after last complying with the requirements he relocated unannounced and joined a team of tarmac layers with whom he partook in fraud. Both offences were committed during the operational period of a suspended sentence. Held. We take the view that D's history of persistent and wholesale disregard for the notification provision was a very serious aggravating feature and a deterrent sentence was entirely justified. Nevertheless, the absence of any evidence of relevant and substantive harm or threat of harm renders the sentence too high. **18 months** not 2 years (15 for the substantive offence, 3 for the activated suspended sentence).

See also: *R v Keeley* 2018 EWCA Crim 2089 (D pleaded to two notification offences. In 2013, eight months after his Court of Appeal case, D, in breach of his notification requirements, went on a circuitous route to the Philippines. In 2017, he was arrested there and was deported for posing a risk to children. The Judge started at 5 years and with plea moved to **40 months** concurrent on each. He reduced that by 4 months to 36 months because of the time D had spent in custody in the Philippines. The defence appealed on the issue of time served awaiting deportation, not the length of the sentence. The appeal was dismissed.)

For details of the deportation issue, see **39.13**. For details of the 2013 case, see *R v Keeley* 2013 EWCA Crim 1014 at **242.7** in Volume 2.

For more cases see para **79.6** in the 13th edition of this book.

79.8 ***Extending notification requirements on breach***

R v Evans 2012 EWCA Crim 519 D pleaded to four counts of breaching his notification obligations. The Judge told D that as a result of the new convictions D would have to sign the Register for the next 10 years. Held. That was wrong. As the offence was not listed in Schedule 3, see **78.4**, a further extension did not arise.

80 NOTIFICATION: TERRORISTS

80.1

Counter-Terrorism Act 2008 s 40-61

Duty of the court to explain The duty is at para **78.18**.

80.2 ***Power to order What are the trigger offences?***

The list can be found in Counter-Terrorism Act 2008 s 41-43. The main offences are:

(a) Terrorism Act 2000 s 11-12, 15-18, 38B, 54 and 56-61.
(b) Terrorism Act 2006 s 1-2, 5-6 and 8-11.
(c) Offences where the court has found a terrorist connection, Counter-Terrorism Act 2008 s 30.

80.3 ***Power to order Which individuals must notify?***
Counter-Terrorism Act 2008 s 45(1) The notification requirements apply to a person who in England and Wales:

(a) has been convicted of an offence and sentenced to:

(i) imprisonment or custody for life,

(ii) imprisonment or detention in a Young Offender Institution for a term of 12 months or more,

(iii) imprisonment or detention in a Young Offender Institution for Public Protection under Criminal Justice Act 2003 s 225,

(iv) detention for life or for a period of 12 months or more under Powers of Criminal Courts (Sentencing) Act 2000 s 91 (offenders under 18 convicted of certain serious offences),

(v) a Detention and Training Order for a term of 12 months or more under section 100 of that Act (offenders under age of 18),

(vi) Detention for Public Protection under Criminal Justice Act 2003 s 226 (serious offences committed by persons under 18),

(via) detention under Criminal Justice Act 2003 s 226B (extended sentence of detention for certain dangerous offenders aged under 18),[984] or

(vii) detention during HM's Pleasure, or

(b) has been:

(i) convicted of an offence to which this Part applies carrying a maximum term of imprisonment of 12 months or more,

(ii) found not guilty by reason of insanity of such an offence, or

(iii) found to be under a disability and to have done the act charged against them in respect of such an offence,

and made subject in respect of the offence to a Hospital Order.

Counter-Terrorism Act 2008 s 45(4) The references in this section to an offence carrying a maximum term of imprisonment of 12 months or more:

(a) are to an offence carrying such a maximum term in the case of a person who has attained the age of 18, and

(b) include an offence carrying in the case of such a person a maximum term of life imprisonment and an offence for which in the case of such a person the sentence is fixed by law as life imprisonment.

(5) In relation to any time before the coming into force of Criminal Justice and Court Services Act 2000 s 61 subsection (4)(a) above has effect with the omission of the words '(18 in relation to England and Wales)'.

80.4 ***European Convention on Human Rights, Compatibility with***
R (Irfan) v Secretary of State 2012 EWCA Civ 1471 D was sentenced to 4 years for assisting in an act of terrorism and his notification was fixed at 10 years. D appealed to the High Court and then to the Court of Appeal. It was contended that the failure to have the term reviewable was incompatible with article 8, relying on *R (F) v Secretary of State* 2010 UKSC 17, where the failure to review a life-long automatic notification was held to be incompatible with article 8. Held. The House of Lords in *R(F) v Secretary of State 2010* was deliberately confining [the decision] to life-time notifications. It was not binding authority that any notification without a right of review is disproportionate without more factors. Terrorism is different from sex offending. Notwithstanding the seriousness of sex offending, terrorism offences have unique features which compound concern. A single act can cause untold damage. Here there was nothing disproportionate.

80.5 ***Notification details***
Initial notification is set out in Counter-Terrorism Act 2008 s 47.
The notification of changes is set out in Counter-Terrorism Act 2008 s 48.

[984] Subsection 45(1) (a)(via) was inserted by Legal Aid, Sentencing and Punishment of Offenders Act 2012 Sch 21 para 33.

The notification for financial information and information about identification documents is set in Counter-Terrorism Act 2008 s 48A
Periodic re-notification is set out in Counter-Terrorism Act 2008 s 49.[985]
The method of notification is set out in Counter-Terrorism Act 2008 s 50.
The travel notification is set out in Counter-Terrorism Act 2008 s 51 and Counter-Terrorism Act 2008 (Foreign Travel Notification Requirements) Regulations 2009 2009/2493.
The notification periods are set out in Counter-Terrorism Act 2008 s 53.
The notification offences are set out in Counter-Terrorism Act 2008 s 54-55.
Notification after an absence from the UK is set out in Counter-Terrorism Act 2008 s 56.

81 OFFENDER OF PARTICULAR CONCERN ORDER

81.1
Also known as SOPC (Sentences for Offenders of Particular Concern).
Criminal Justice Act 2003 s 236A
Criminal Justice and Courts Act 2015 s 6 and Sch 1 introduces this new order.[986]
Availability/Children and young offenders Where: a) the offence is: i) listed in Criminal Justice Act 2003 Sch 18A, or ii) is a historical offence which would amount to a Schedule 18A offence,[987] b) the defendant was aged 18 at the time of the offence, c) the sentence was passed on or after 13 April 2015, and d) a life sentence or extended sentence is not imposed, the court must, if it imposes a custodial sentence, make an Offender of Particular Concern Order under Criminal Justice Act 2003 s 236A.[988]
Length Where the sentence is one of imprisonment, the length is 'the appropriate custodial term' and a further 1 year when the offender is on licence, Criminal Justice Act 2003 s 236A(2).
Indictments The Court of Appeal has said that it would be helpful in section 236A cases if indictments were drafted to include the fact that the victim was aged under 13 and that there was penetration. Failure to do that does not mean the order cannot be imposed. For these principles see *R v Fruen and DS* 2016 EWCA Crim 561, 2 Cr App R (S) 30 (p 271)[989] para 28.
There need not be a custodial sentence/Suspended sentences The sentence need not be a custodial sentence. A community sentence may be imposed. Where a suspended sentence is appropriate, the court should make a community order instead. For these principles see *R v Fruen and DS* 2016 EWCA Crim 561, 2 Cr App R (S) 30 (p 271) paras 12-13.
Maximum sentences The court may not exceed the statutory maximum that was in force at the time the offence was committed. Where the legislation imposes a maximum sentence, like 10 years, the maximum sentence that can be imposed is 9 years and the obligatory 1-year extended licence. For these principles see *R v Fruen and DS* 2016 EWCA Crim 561, 2 Cr App R (S) 30 (p 271) para 15. In *R v Stables* 2017 EWCA Crim 1856, a 4½-year order was unlawful when the maximum for the offence was 5 years.
Court Martial There is a corresponding service provision, Armed Forces Act 2006 s 224A, inserted by Criminal Justice and Courts Act 2015 Sch 1 para 8.
Release See **81.11**.

[985] Sections 47, 48 and 49, and travel notification requirement regulations were amended by Counter-Terrorism and Border Security Act 2019 s 12 and Sch 4 para 51. In force 12 April 2019, Counter-Terrorism and Border Security Act 2019 s 27(3). Section 48A was inserted by the same provisions.
[986] In force 13/4/15, Criminal Justice and Courts Act 2015 (Commencement No 1, Saving and Transitional Provisions) Order 2015 2015/778 para 3 and Sch 1 para 6 and 72
[987] Criminal Justice Act 2003 Sch 18A para 23
[988] As inserted by Criminal Justice and Courts Act 2015 s 6 and Sch 1
[989] Also known as *R v LF* 2016 EWCA Crim 561, 2 Cr App R (S) 30 (p 271)

81.2 *Statutory provisions*

Special custodial sentence for certain offenders of particular concern

Criminal Justice Act 2003 s 236A(1) Subsection (2) applies where:

(a) a person is convicted of an offence listed in schedule 18A (see **81.3**) (whether the offence was committed before or after this section comes into force),

(b) the person was aged 18 or over when the offence was committed, and

(c) the court does not impose one of the following for the offence:

(i) a sentence of imprisonment for life, or

(ii) an extended sentence under section 226A.

(2) If the court imposes a sentence of imprisonment for the offence, the term of the sentence must be equal to the aggregate of:

(a) the appropriate custodial term, and

(b) a further period of 1 year for which the offender is to be subject to a licence.

(3) The 'appropriate custodial term' is the term that, in the opinion of the court, ensures that the sentence is appropriate.

(4) The term of a sentence of imprisonment imposed under this section for an offence must not exceed the term that, at the time the offence was committed, was the maximum term permitted for the offence.

(5) The references in subsections (1)(c) and (2) to a sentence imposed for the offence include a sentence imposed for the offence and one or more offences associated with it.

(6)-(7) [Power to add to and vary list of offences, which is not listed.]

81.3 *List of trigger offences*

Criminal Justice Act 2003 Sch 18A

Terrorism offences

1-3 Offences Against the Person Act 1861

s 4 (soliciting murder) [when it] has a terrorist connection,

s 28 (causing bodily injury by explosives) [when it] has a terrorist connection,

s 29 (using explosives etc. with intent to do grievous bodily harm) [when it] has a terrorist connection.

4-6 Explosive Substances Act 1883

s 2 (causing explosion likely to endanger life or property) [when it] has a terrorist connection,

s 3 (attempt to cause explosion, or making or keeping explosive with intent to endanger life or property) [when it] has a terrorist connection,

s 4 (making or possession of explosive under suspicious circumstances) [when it] has a terrorist connection.

6A-10 Terrorism Act 2000

[The offences marked with a * were inserted by Counter-Terrorism and Border Security Act 2019 s 9(6) In force 12 April 2019, Counter-Terrorism and Border Security Act 2019 s 27(3).]

s 11 (membership of a proscribed organisation),*

s 12 (inviting support for a proscribed organisation).";s 54 (weapons training),*

s 56 (directing terrorist organisation),

s 57 (possession of article for terrorist purposes),

s 58 (collection of information likely to be of use to a terrorist),*

s 58A (publishing information about members of the armed forces etc.),*

s 58B (entering or remaining in a designated area),*

s 59 (inciting terrorism overseas).

11-13 Anti-terrorism, Crime and Security Act 2001

s 47 (use etc. of nuclear weapons),

s 50 (assisting or inducing certain weapons-related acts overseas),

s 113 (use of noxious substance or thing to cause harm or intimidate).

13A-18 Terrorism Act 2006

s 1 (encouragement of terrorism),*

s 2 (dissemination of terrorist publications),*
s 5 (preparation of terrorist acts),
s 6 (training for terrorism),
s 8 (attendance at a place used for terrorist training), *
s 9 (making or possession of radioactive device or material),
s 10 (use of radioactive device or material for terrorist purposes etc.),
s 11 (terrorist threats relating to radioactive devices etc.).

Sexual offences

19-20 Sexual Offences Act 2003
s 5 (rape of a child under 13),
s 6 (assault of a child under 13 by penetration).

Accessories and inchoate offences

21(1) Aiding, abetting, counselling or procuring the commission of an offence specified in the preceding paragraphs of this Schedule (a 'relevant offence'),
(2) An attempt to commit a relevant offence,
(3) Conspiracy to commit a relevant offence,
(4) An offence under Serious Crime Act 2007 Part 2 in relation to which a relevant offence is the offence (or one of the offences) which the person intended or believed would be committed.

22 An offence in the following list that has a terrorist connection:
(a) an attempt to commit murder,
(b) conspiracy to commit murder, and
(c) an offence under Serious Crime Act 2007 Part 2 in relation to which murder is the offence (or one of the offences) which the person intended or believed would be committed.

Abolished offences

23 An offence that:
(a) was abolished before the coming into force of section 236A, and
(b) if committed on the day on which the offender was convicted of the offence, would have constituted an offence specified in the preceding paragraphs of this schedule.

Meaning of 'terrorist connection'

24 For the purposes of this schedule, an offence has a terrorist connection if a court has determined under Counter-Terrorism Act 2008 s 30 that the offence has such a connection.

81.4 ***List of trigger offences*** ***Doubt about the age of the victim***

R v Clarke and Another 2017 EWCA Crim 393, 2 Cr App R (S) 18 (p 140) D was convicted of historical offences. Some counts had the victim's age as 'either 12-14 or 12 or 13. The Judge did not make an Offender of Particular Concern Order. Held. para 50 As the Judge had not been able to determine that the victim was aged under 13, he was right not to make the order.

81.5 ***Check list for imposing the order/Fixing the custodial term***

Criminal Justice Act 2003 s 236A(3) The 'appropriate custodial term' is the term that, in the opinion of the court, ensures that the sentence is appropriate.
For the rest of the section, see **81.2**.

R v Fruen and DS 2016 EWCA Crim 561, 2 Cr App R (S) 30 (p 271)[990] para 127 The checklist is as follows:
(a) Is the offence listed in Criminal Justice Act 2003 Sch 18A?
(b) If the offence is a repealed historical sexual offence, did it involve rape or penetration of a child aged under 13?
(c) Was the offender aged 18 or over when the offence was committed?
(d) Criminal Justice Act 2003 s 236A cannot apply if the court imposes life or an extended sentence for the offence or an associated offence.

[990] Also known as *R v LF* 2016 EWCA Crim 561, 2 Cr App R (S) 30 (p 271)

(e) A sentence is to be expressed as a single term comprising the custodial element and a further 1-year period of licence.
(f) Each offence qualifying for section 236A must be sentenced in the terms set out at e) above.
(g) Are the section 236A sentences to run concurrently or consecutively to one another? If concurrently, the overall custodial term for those offences plus a further 1-year period of licence should be stated at the end of sentencing.
(h) If consecutively, the total custodial term for those offences as well as the total further period of licence should be stated at the end of sentencing.

Note: Perhaps the first consideration is whether custody is appropriate, see Criminal Justice Act 2003 s 236A(2) at **81.2**. This section in rare cases enables Suspended Sentence Orders, Hospital Orders and community orders to be imposed instead. Ed.

R v Thompson and Others 2018 EWCA Crim 639, 2 Cr App R (S) 19 (p 164) (Five-judge court) para 7 The phrase 'appropriate custodial term' in section 236A does not require the court to approach the length of the custodial term other than as the shortest time that is commensurate with the seriousness of the offence.

81.6 ***Concurrent and consecutive sentences With determinate sentences***

R v Fruen and DS 2016 EWCA Crim 561, 2 Cr App R (S) 30 (p 271) para 17 Concurrent sentencing may involve counts involving ordinary determinate terms and section 236A sentences. No difficulty arises from those types of sentence running concurrently alongside one another. para 19 If there is a combination of ordinary determinate terms and section 236A sentences to be passed, no particular problem arises if the section 236A sentences are passed consecutively to the other counts. para 20 The consequence for judges is that they will need to give careful consideration to the structuring of their sentences as decisions as to whether to make sentences concurrent or consecutive will impact upon the length of the further licence period.

Note: Where this sentence is made consecutive to a determinate sentence, judges must pass the determinate sentence first and then pass the Offender of Particular Concern Order, *R v Clarke and Another* 2017 EWCA Crim 393, 2 Cr App R (S) 18 (p 140), *R v Stables* 2017 EWCA Crim 1856 and *R v T* 2017 EWCA Crim 1533.

81.7 ***Concurrent and consecutive sentences Offender of Particular Concern Orders, More than one***

R v Fruen and DS 2016 EWCA Crim 561, 2 Cr App R (S) 30 (p 271) para 20 There is nothing in section 236A which affects or limits the power provided by Powers of Criminal Courts (Sentencing) Act 2000 s 154(1) to impose a consecutive sentence. Moreover, in the analogous field of extended sentences under Criminal Justice Act 2003 s 226A this Court has held that it is permissible to pass consecutive extended sentences, [see **56.78**]. para 24 Where consecutive section 236A sentences are imposed, consecutive further periods of licence must follow. The consequence for judges is that they will need to give careful consideration to the structuring of their sentences as decisions as to whether to make sentences concurrent or consecutive will impact upon the length of the further licence period.

R v S 2016 EWCA Crim 2058, 2017 1 Cr App R (S) 41 (p 332) D pleaded to historical sex offences. For two of the counts the Judge passed concurrent Offender of Particular Concern Orders with a 25-year custodial term and a 2-year further licence. Held. para 11 Each sentence should have a 1-year further licence period, so as the sentences were concurrent we amend the order made so there was only 1 extra year's licence.

R v Mardon 2017 EWCA Crim 519 The Judge passed a series of concurrent and consecutive sentences. Held. The Judge failed to relate the 1-year extra licence to specific offences. We re-sentence, giving the offences which carry the Offender of Particular Concern Order a 1-year extra licence and making them concurrent.

Att-Gen's Ref 2018 Re Griffith 2018 EWCA Crim 977 D was convicted of 10 counts of indecent assault and an indecency count. Both had a maximum sentence of 10 years. The

Judge passed 12 years made up of three 4-year consecutive groups of sentences, with a total 3-year extended licence. Held. We increase each group to 5 years, making 15 years in all. [The 3-year extended licence remained.]

Combined with other orders

81.8 ***Extended sentences and life sentences, Combined with***
Criminal Justice Act 2003 s 236A(1) Subsection (2) [the imposition of the an Offender of Particular Concern Order] applies where:..(c) the court does not impose one of the following for the offence:
(i) a sentence of imprisonment for life, or
(ii) an extended sentence under section 226A.
(2)-(4) [Not listed]
(5) The references in subsections (1)(c) and (2) to a sentence imposed for the offence include a sentence imposed for the offence and one or more offences associated with it. For the full section, see **81.2**.
R v Fruen and DS 2016 EWCA Crim 561, 2 Cr App R (S) 30 (p 271) [991] para 127 The checklist is as follows:.. (d) Criminal Justice Act 2003 s 236A cannot apply if the court imposes life or an extended sentence for the offence or an associated offence.
R v Powell 2018 EWCA Crim 1074, 2 Cr App R (S) 34 (p 303) D was sentenced to three extended sentences, two Offender of Particular Concern Orders and 10 determinate sentences. Held. Having imposed an extended sentence, the Court was precluded from passing an Offender of Particular Concern Order on other counts, see section 236A(1)(c) and (5). *R v Fruen and DS* 2016 applied. We quash the Offender of Particular Concern Order.

81.9 ***Explain sentence, Judge must/Suggested sentencing remarks***
Judicial College's Crown Court Compendium Part II Sentencing June 2018 page 4-17

Example 1
You will serve one half of your custodial term in custody before your case is referred to the Parole Board for consideration of whether and on what terms it is safe for you to be released. You will be released at the direction of the Parole Board at some point not later than the end of the custodial term. You will then serve the remainder of the custodial term (if any) and 12 months on conditional licence and supervision. You must abide by the conditions of your release, or you will be liable to serve the rest of the sentence in custody.

Example 2
I have to sentence you for two offences. The sentence on the first count will be six years' imprisonment. The sentence on the second count will be two years' imprisonment, to run consecutively. That makes a total of eight years' imprisonment.
Both of your offences fall within s.236A of the Criminal Justice Act 2003. I am required by that section to impose on you a special custodial sentence for offenders of particular concern which will combine the custodial periods I have referred to and an extended licence period of one year in relation to each count.
This means that I impose custodial terms of eight years in total, together with further licence periods of two years in total, making 10 years in all.
The effect of this is that you will serve one half of your total custodial term in custody before your case is referred to the Parole Board for consideration of whether and on what terms it is safe for you to be released. In your case, this means you will serve at least four years' imprisonment before that reference to the Parole Board can take place. Whatever view the Parole Board takes you will be entitled to release as of right no later than the end of the custodial term, which in your case is eight years.
At whatever point you are released you will then serve the remainder of the custodial term (if any) and the additional licence period of two years in the community on conditional licence and subject to supervision. You must abide by the conditions of your release, or you will be liable to serve the full sentence in custody.

[991] Also known as *R v LF* 2016 EWCA Crim 561, 2 Cr App R (S) 30 (p 271)

R v Fruen and DS 2016 EWCA Crim 561, 2 Cr App R (S) 30 (p 271)[992] The Judge passed sentence on DS for 19 counts with some concurrent and some consecutive and some with the Offender of Particular Concern Order. Held. para 54 The Judge was in error to say the licence was for only 1 year and for failing to say which offences the 1-year extra licence extension applied to. He also failed to pass the new order on the historical offences [to] which it applied. Because it was clear that the total sentence was 15 years with the extra year licence extension period, the appeal is dismissed.
Note: Many might think it would have been better if the Court of Appeal had converted the sentences into what they should have been and told the defendant correctly what the sentences meant. The total would of course have remained the same. Ed.

81.10 *Appeals*

R v Fruen and DS 2016 EWCA Crim 561, 2 Cr App R (S) 30 (p 271)[993] The Judge failed to make an Offender of Particular Concern Order when the conditions were met. The sentence was not manifestly excessive. Held. para 29 It would not be right to replace the determinate term with such an order. Nor would it be right to reduce the term by a year and add the 1-year licence term as that would reduce the appropriate term. We leave the sentence alone, applying *R v Reynolds and Others* 2007 EWCA Crim 538, 2 Cr App R (S) 87 (p 553).
R v Thompson and Others 2018 EWCA Crim 639, 2 Cr App R (S) 19 (p 164) (Five-judge court) The Court considered four cases to determine the meaning of 'more severely dealt with'. Held. para 23 *R v Fruen and DS* 2016 EWCA Crim 561, 2 Cr App R (S) 30 (p 271) is not authority for the proposition that if a custodial term is reduced by at least a year, a sentence under Criminal Justice Act 2003 s 236A will necessarily satisfy the requirements of section 11(3). The issue of section 11(3) requires a detailed consideration of the impact of the sentence to be substituted which must involve considerations of entitlement to automatic release, parole eligibility and licence. If a custodial sentence is reduced, the addition of non-custodial orders (such as disqualification from driving or Sexual Offences Prevention Orders[994]) may be added but, in every case, save where the substituted sentence is 'ameliorative and remedial', that sentence must be tested for its severity (or potential punitive effect) compared to the original sentence.
For more details, see **4.74**.

81.11 *Release*

Release on licence of prisoners serving sentence under section 236A
Criminal Justice Act 2003 s 244A(1) This section applies to a prisoner ('P') who is serving a sentence imposed under section 236A.
(2) The Secretary of State must refer P's case to the Board:
(a) as soon as P has served the requisite custodial period, and
(b) where there has been a previous reference of P's case to the Board under this subsection and the Board did not direct P's release, not later than the second anniversary of the disposal of that reference.
(3) It is the duty of the Secretary of State to release P on licence under this section as soon as:
(a) P has served the requisite custodial period, and
(b) the Board has directed P's release under this section.
(4) The Board must not give a direction under subsection (3) unless:
(a) the Secretary of State has referred P's case to the Board, and
(b) the Board is satisfied that it is not necessary for the protection of the public that P should be confined.

[992] Also known as *R v LF* 2016 EWCA Crim 561, 2 Cr App R (S) 30 (p 271)
[993] Also known as *R v LF* 2016 EWCA Crim 561, 2 Cr App R (S) 30 (p 271)
[994] The Judge presumably meant Sexual Harm Prevention Orders.

(5) It is the duty of the Secretary of State to release P on licence under this section as soon as P has served the appropriate custodial term, unless P has previously been released on licence under this section and recalled under Criminal Justice Act 2003 s 254 (provision for the release of such persons being made by Criminal Justice Act 2003 s 255A-255C).
(6) For the purposes of this section:
'the appropriate custodial term' means the term determined as such by the court under section 236A,
'the requisite custodial period' means:

(a) in relation to a person serving one sentence, one-half of the appropriate custodial term, and

(b) in relation to a person serving two or more concurrent or consecutive sentences, the period determined under Criminal Justice Act 2003 s 263(2) and 264(2).

R v Fruen and DS 2016 EWCA Crim 561, 2 Cr App R (S) 30 (p 271) para 7 Those sentenced to the order cannot be released until the Parole Board is satisfied that it is not necessary for the protection of the public that the offender shall be detained in custody. If the Parole Board makes no such order the defendant is released after the end of the [custodial] term. para 6 If a prisoner were to be released after 3 years he or she would be released on licence of 4 years (3 years plus the extra 1 year).
Note: At para 8 of the judgment, the Court says when a defendant is released after serving the whole custodial term he or she is released unconditionally. In fact, the individual would be released subject to the 1-year obligatory licence. Ed.

82 PARENTING ORDERS/PARENTAL ORDERS

82.1
Parenting orders and parental orders can be made with a variety of orders. For a list of the orders, see the back index.

82.2 ***Statistics England and Wales***
Parenting Orders

	2012	2013	2014	2015	2016
Orders made	660	398	295	262	218

For explanations about the statistics, see page 1-xii. The MoJ no longer provides Banks on Sentence with these statistics.
Note: It is extremely unlikely that all parenting orders were recorded. Ed.

82.3 ***Procedure***
The Criminal Procedure Rules 2015 2015/1490 behaviour order rules apply, see the note at **27.2**.
For the procedure and for varying the order, see **84.14**.

82.4 ***Parents and guardians, Enforcing the responsibilities Guidelines***
Sentencing Children and Young People Guideline 2017, see www.banksr.com Other Matters Guidelines tab page 14 In force 1 June 2017
Section three: Parental responsibilities
3.1 For any child or young person aged under 16 appearing before court there is a statutory requirement that parents/guardians attend during all stages of proceedings, unless the court is satisfied that this would be unreasonable having regard to the circumstances of the case.[995] The court may also enforce this requirement for a young person aged 16 and above if it deems it desirable to do so.

[995] Children and Young Persons Act 1933 s 34A

3.2 Although this requirement can cause a delay in the case before the court it is important it is adhered to. If a court does find exception to proceed in the absence of a responsible adult then extra care must be taken to ensure the outcomes are clearly communicated to and understood by the child or young person.
3.3 In addition to this responsibility there are also orders that can be imposed on parents. If the child or young person is aged under 16 then the court has a duty to make a **parental bind over** or impose a **parenting order**, if it would be desirable in the interest of preventing the commission of further offences.[996] There is a discretionary power to make these orders where the young person is aged 16 or 17. If the court chooses not to impose a parental bind over or parenting order it must state its reasons for not doing so in open court. In most circumstances a parenting order is likely to be more appropriate than a parental bind over.
3.4 A court cannot make a bind over alongside a referral order. If the court makes a referral order the duty on the court to impose a parenting order in respect of a child or young person under 16 years old is replaced by a discretion.[997]

83 Pre-sentence Reports

83.1
Criminal Justice Act 2003 s 156-158
Purposes of probation These are listed in Offender Management Act 2007 s 1 and include giving assistance to the courts in determining the appropriate sentence, the supervision and rehabilitation of those charged and convicted of offences, and providing accommodation for offenders. For the purpose of pre-sentence reports, see **83.5**.

Types of report

83.2 ***Standard delivery reports***
Magistrates' Court Sentencing Guidelines 2008, see www.banksr.com Other Matters Guidelines tab page 190 Written reports may be standard delivery reports (SDRs). [These are:]
(a) based on a full OASys assessment,
(b) generally appropriate where a custodial sentence is being considered, although in some straightforward cases a fast delivery pre-sentence report may be sufficient,
(c) where community orders are being considered, generally appropriate for high seriousness cases.
[These] should normally be available within 15 working days, 10 working days if the offender is in custody.
For the purpose of probation, see **83.1**.
83.3 ***Oral reports***
Criminal Justice Act 2003 s 158(1A) Subject to any rules made under subsection (1)(b) and to subsection (1B), the court may accept a pre-sentence report given orally in open court.
(1B) But a pre-sentence report that:
(a) relates to an offender aged under 18, and
(b) is required to be obtained and considered before the court forms an opinion mentioned in section 156(3)(a), see **83.13**, must be in writing.
83.4 ***Fast delivery reports***
Magistrates' Court Sentencing Guidelines 2008, see www.banksr.com Other Matters Guidelines tab page 190 Written reports may be fast delivery reports (FDR). [These are:]
(a) completed without a full OASys assessment,
(b) where community orders are being considered, generally appropriate for low or medium seriousness cases and may be appropriate in some high seriousness cases.

[996] Powers of Criminal Courts (Sentencing) Act 2000 s 150 and Crime and Disorder Act 1998 s 8
[997] Crime and Disorder Act 1998 s 9(1A)

[These] should normally be available within 24 hours.

General matters

83.5 *Purpose of the pre-sentence report*

Magistrates' Court Sentencing Guidelines 2008, see www.banksr.com Other Matters Guidelines tab page 190 The purpose of a pre-sentence report is to provide information to help the court decide on the most suitable sentence. In relation to an offender aged 18 or over, unless the court considers a report to be unnecessary, it is required to request a report before deciding:

(a) that the community or custody threshold is passed,
(b) what is the shortest term of a custodial sentence that is commensurate with the seriousness of the offence,
(c) whether the restrictions on liberty within a community order are commensurate with the seriousness of the offence, and
(d) whether the requirements are suitable for the offender.

83.6 *Pre-sentence report, Definition of*

Criminal Justice Act 2003 s 158(1) In this Part, 'pre-sentence report' means a report which:

(a) with a view to assisting the court in determining the most suitable method of dealing with an offender, is made or submitted by an appropriate officer, and
(b) contains information as to such matters, presented in such manner, as may be prescribed by rules made by the Secretary of State.

83.7 *How to draft a pre-sentence report*

On 15 October 2014, the Youth Justice Board set out its instructions to youth offending teams and managers about how to draft reports for courts (referral panel reports and pre-sentence reports), see www.banksr.com Other Matters Other Documents. It is an exceptionally focused document giving a wealth of detailed instructions. Paragraph 2.12 prohibits a recommendation either way about the dangerousness of the offender.

The Ministry of Justice's *Guidance for Court Officers Report Writers and Offender Managers*, see www.banksr.com Other Matters Other Documents tab National Offender Management Service, contains the official instructions for writing pre-sentence reports.

Magistrates' Court Sentencing Guidelines 2008, see www.banksr.com Other Matters Guidelines tab page 190 Every report should contain:[998]

(a) basic facts about the offender and the sources used to prepare the report,
(b) an offence analysis,
(c) an assessment of the offender,
(d) an assessment of the risk of harm to the public and the likelihood of reoffending,
(e) a sentencing proposal.

83.8 *Using material in the pre-sentence report as a basis for sentence*

R v Tolera 1999 1 Cr App R (S) 25 D pleaded to possession of heroin with intent to supply. Held. If the defence want to rely on an account given in the pre-sentence report and ask to treat that as the basis of sentence, it is necessary that counsel expressly draw the relevant paragraphs to the attention of the court and that it be treated as the basis of sentence. It is very desirable that the prosecution be forewarned of this request.

R v Rocha 2007 EWCA Crim 1505 D pleaded to robbery. The Judge must by his assessment of the risk factor have disagreed with the psychiatrist. Held. He was not bound by that finding. However, we do not know his reasoning for that rejection. A defendant wants to know what his sentence is and does not want to hear a long speech from the judge, but an indeterminate sentence is a very serious matter and both the appellant and this Court need to be able to understand the judge's reasoning process. Sometimes that may be obvious, but if part of the process involves rejecting the opinion

[998] Probation Bench Handbook (2005)

of a suitably qualified expert, as it may be perfectly proper for the judge to do, the court needs to be able to understand the reason for the sentencing judge not accepting it. Considering the matter again we quash the IPP.

See also the **Extended sentences** ***Pre-sentence reports*** section at **56.44** and the ***Evidence Bad behaviour with no conviction for it Using reports*** para at **56.57**.

83.9 *Disclosure of the co-defendant's report/defence material*

R v Clarke 2009 EWCA Crim 47 D and his girlfriend, G, pleaded to supply counts. G told the police D was dealing in drugs and where drugs were concealed in their property. D was aged 25 and G was aged 19. The Judge was provided with pre-sentence reports and testimonials for both defendants. G's mother submitted a letter which made substantial criticism of D and which blamed D for G's predicament. G's pre-sentence report depicted G as a young woman influenced by D, who was six years older. G's mother's letter was not disclosed to D or his counsel. Held. No authority is cited to support a general proposition that the testimonials and other materials submitted on the part of one defendant are required to be disclosed to others. It is commonplace for the accounts given by one defendant to be at odds with the accounts of others. It is commonplace for pre-sentence reports, in setting out offence analysis and background analysis in respect of each of a number of defendants, to give very different accounts and paint very different pictures. But it is not general practice for the pre-sentence reports to be exchanged with other defendants, nor would we suggest the introduction of any such requirement. As a matter of general fairness, if a judge, reading material submitted on behalf of one defendant, considers that he may be persuaded to take it into account against the other defendant as an aggravating factor, then he must undoubtedly warn that defendant's counsel and disclose at least the thrust of the material and invite submissions upon it.

Note: This is an old case, but the principles expressed appear to be still correct. Ed.

83.10 *Reference to bad character where there is no conviction/Admissions in the pre-sentence reports*

R v Cunnah 1996 1 Cr App R (S) 393 D pleaded to five counts of indecently assaulting a female under the age of 16 and was sentenced to 2½ years' imprisonment. Five other counts were to remain on file. The victims were two young sisters, the daughters of a woman D was cohabiting with at the time of the assaults. The younger of the two girls first complained to the police. After his arrest, D admitted the offences but he disputed the girls' recollections of the incidents. His pleas of guilty were based on his police interviews, which substantially differed from the girls' complaints, which formed the basis of the Crown's case. D's acceptance of the prosecution case was limited. The Crown accepted D's pleas and as such the Judge did not feel a *Newton* hearing was necessary. Sentencing was adjourned for the production of a pre-sentence report. In order to assess the offender as suitable for probation the probation service requires that they are satisfied that the offender is being frank about his offending. The report disclosed D's complete frankness and acceptance of the girls' complaints. This was not raised by counsel in mitigation and the Judge did not raise it with counsel. Held. D appeared to be accepting the truth of the victims' statements. When fresh, highly relevant material of this nature appears in a pre-sentence report in cases of this nature there must be a discussion between counsel and the judge. This was particularly so in circumstances such as this, where pleas have been entered and accepted on a very narrow view of the facts indeed. That discussion is necessary so everybody is aware from that moment onwards upon what basis the judge thereafter will proceed. The sentence should be determined on the basis when the pleas were entered. D may not have fully understood what he was being asked by the probation officer.

R v Considine 2007 EWCA Crim 1166, 2008 1 Cr App R (S) 41 (p 215) D was convicted of two counts of making threats to kill. Held. *R v Farrar* 2006 EWCA Crim 3261, 2007 2 Cr App R (S) 35 (p 202) clearly did not decide that, absent a conviction, the court making the section 229 decision is precluded from considering evidence of previous misconduct which would amount to a criminal offence. Arguments advanced on the basis that it did so decide are ill-founded. The contrary is true, and in *R v Farrar* 2006, the end result was that material directly related to the earlier incident did in fact contribute to the conclusion that Farrar himself should properly be assessed as dangerous. For this purpose no conviction was necessary. Provided the judge could resolve the issue fairly, it was sufficient for the information to be contained in a psychiatric report.

R v JW 2009 EWCA Crim 390, 2 Cr App R (S) 94 (p 623)[999] D, aged 14, was convicted of attempted murder and possession of a firearm with intent to endanger life. The Judge had a pre-sentence report and a psychological report. Both authors of the reports considered D was not dangerous. The Judge considered the facts of the offences to be enough to conclude that D posed a significant risk. In his sentencing remarks he mentioned both reports and their conclusions but did not analyse those conclusions. Held. The court is not bound by the assessments made in reports. However, if the court asks for the assistance of experts, and having read their assessments is minded to reject their conclusions, the court should set out in some detail the reasons for so doing. That was not done here.

R v LE 2014 EWCA Crim 1939 D pleaded to having sex with an adult relative (×7) and perverting the course of justice, and was given extended sentences. The pre-sentence report said that D posed a risk to children and vulnerable adults. It was based, at least partially, on V's reports of abuse by the complainant which were the basis of the trial and when she was much younger, but the earlier abuse was not accepted. The report also relied on reports of abuse from former partners of D which were again denied. Held. It would not be right for this Court to take account of an assessment which was based, in part at least, on such disputed factors that had not been either admitted or been the subject of convictions. Pre-appeal report set aside. However, without that material, we conclude that the 'dangerousness' test was made out.

R (S) v Leicestershire & Rutland Probation Trust 2014 EWHC 3154 (Admin), 2015 1 Cr App R (S) 12 (p 95) High Court D was convicted of raping his step-daughter (×5) and indecently assaulting another girl. D appealed asking (amongst other matters) for references in the report to the facts for an offence for which a judge directed an acquittal to be removed and the report to record that D was acquitted of raping his ex-wife. D's concern was the use of the report at Parole Board hearings. After a High Court hearing the report was redrafted. D asserted that the new report should not refer to a) his ex-wife as a victim (because he was acquitted of this matter), and b) a police claim that there were indecent images on his computer when no charges were brought. Held. The OASys[1000] assessment in the report must contain all relevant facts, including those relating to an unpursued allegation, provided it is clearly and unequivocally stated that no charges were brought and no conviction ensued. A mere recitation of facts, however vigorously denied, is permissible. The same approach is adopted to the dropped rape charge as it is clear that the judge rejected it as there was no case to answer, a strong finding in favour of D. There is nothing in the report to suggest these matters were treated as correct [or relied on for their recommendations]. If the Parole Board draws an incorrect inference from this, judicial review proceedings could be pursued at least in theory. I reject this application as the inclusion of these matters is neither irrational nor unreasonable. D is able to raise matters of concern with the authorities.

83.11 *Correcting alleged errors*

R (S) v Leicestershire & Rutland Probation Trust 2014 EWHC 3154 (Admin), 2015 1 Cr App R (S) 12 (p 95) (For an example of someone taking judicial review proceedings to ensure a quashed conviction in his pre-sentence was properly dealt with, see **83.10**.)

[999] The Cr App R (S) list this case as 2009 EWCA Crim 107, which is in error.
[1000] Offender Assessment System

83.12 ***Defence cross-examining the author of the report***
R v Green 2002 EWCA Crim 2075 D pleaded to rape. The pre-sentence report said D posed a serious risk to the public. There was an issue whether the author of the report had misled the psychiatrist to obtain his report without the consent of the defence solicitors. Defence counsel asked the Judge not to accept the assessment in the report and he believed the Judge had accepted that submission. The Judge passed an extended sentence. The defence appealed saying had they known the assessment was accepted they would have applied to cross-examine the probation officer. Held. Where there is a challenge to the assessment of risk that is the appropriate procedure.

Court duty to have a pre-sentence report

83.13 ***Pre-sentence report, Court must have Statutory provisions***
Pre-sentence reports and other requirements
Criminal Justice Act 2003 s 156(1) In forming any such opinion as is mentioned in [Criminal Justice Act 2003] s 148(1) [need for offence(s) to be serious enough to warrant such a community sentence, see **15.9**] or (2)(b) [need for the restrictions a community sentence to be commensurate with the seriousness of the offence, see **15.9**], section 152(2) [offence must be so serious fine or community service order cannot be justified, **28.26**] or section 153(2) [the custodial sentence must be for the shortest term, see **56.44**], or in section 1(4)(b) or (c) of the Criminal Justice and Immigration Act 2008 (youth rehabilitation orders with intensive supervision and surveillance or fostering) [see **119.10**], a court must take into account all such information as is available to it about the circumstances of the offence or (as the case may be) of the offence and the offence or offences associated with it, including any aggravating or mitigating factors.
(2) In forming any such opinion as is mentioned in section 148(2)(a) [making community order and Youth Rehabilitation Orders requirements the most suitable, see **15.9**], the court may take into account any information about the offender which is before it.
(3) Subject to subsection (4), a court must obtain and consider a pre-sentence report before:

(a) in the case of a custodial sentence, forming any such opinion as is mentioned in Criminal Justice Act 2003:
s 152(2) [general restrictions on imposing discretionary custodial sentences, see **28.26**],
s 153(2) [length of a discretionary custodial sentence, see **28.32**],
s 225(1)(b) [the significant risk factor in the dangerousness provisions, see **56.24**],
s 226(1)(b) [the significant risk factor in the dangerousness provisions for those aged under 18, see **39.12**],
s 226A(1)(b) [the significant risk factor in the dangerousness provisions for 2012 extended sentences, see **56.24**], or
s 226B(1)(b) [the significant risk factor in the dangerousness provisions for 2012 extended sentences for those aged under 18, see **56.7**,[1001]] or

(b) in the case of a community sentence, forming any such opinion as is mentioned in:
Criminal Justice Act 2003 s 148(1) or (2)(b) [the restrictions on the liberty etc. considerations for community sentences, see **15.9**],
or in Criminal Justice and Immigration Act 2008 s 1(4)(b) or (c) [considerations whether the offence etc. is so serious to make a Youth Rehabilitation Order appropriate, see **119.10**],
or any opinion as to the suitability for the offender of the particular requirement or requirements to be imposed by the community order or Youth Rehabilitation Order.

(4) Subsection (3) does not apply if, in the circumstances of the case, the court is of the opinion that it is unnecessary to obtain a pre-sentence report.
(5) [see **83.15**]

[1001] The last two subsections dealing with subsections 226A(1)(b) and 226B(1)(b) were inserted by Legal Aid, Sentencing and Punishment of Offenders Act 2012 Sch 21 para 22. The subsection that dealt with the old extended sentences was repealed.

(6)-(8) [see **83.20**]
(9) References in subsections (1) and (3) to a court forming the opinions mentioned in sections 152(2) and 153(2) include a court forming those opinions for the purposes of section 224A(3).
(10) The reference in subsection (1) to a court forming the opinion mentioned in section 153(2) includes a court forming that opinion for the purposes of section 226A(6) or 226B(4).
For the need for a pre-sentence report in serious sexual offences, see **314.10** in Volume 2.

83.14 *Pre-sentence report, Should have Understanding the mitigation*
R v Ebbs 2019 EWCA Crim 175 D pleaded to affray. D struck out at a supporter of a rival football club at a tube station after a match. The defence asked for a pre-sentence report, which was refused. Held. A pre-sentence report should have been obtained. The suggestion the Judge had all the information in front of him is undermined by his minimal reference to the mitigation. The Judge would have learnt about D's wife's mental problems and D's support for her and her four young children. D was also the stepfather of two of his wife's children. Immediate release ordered.
For more detail, see **203.12** in Volume 2.

83.15 *Pre-sentence report, Court must have Defendant aged under 18*
Criminal Justice Act 2003 s 156(5) In a case where the offender is aged under 18, the court must not form the opinion mentioned in subsection (4) (see **83.13**) unless:
(a) there exists a previous pre-sentence report obtained in respect of the offender, and
(b) the court has had regard to the information contained in that report, or, if there is more than one such report, the most recent report.

83.16 *Court Martial Court must have a report*
Pre-sentence reports
Armed Forces Act 2006 s 256(1) Subject to subsection (2), a court must obtain and consider a pre-sentence report before:
(a) forming any such opinion as is mentioned in: section 242(1) or 243(2) (service detention), section 260(2) or 261(2) (custodial sentence), or section 265(1) (dismissal or dismissal with disgrace),
(b) forming any such opinion as is mentioned in section 270(1) or (2)(b) (community punishment) or any opinion as to the suitability for the offender of the particular requirement or requirements to be included in a community punishment, or
(c) forming the required opinion for the purposes of section 219(1), 219A(1), 221(1), or 221A(1) (sentences for dangerous offenders).[1002]
(2) Subsection (1) does not apply if, in the circumstances of the case, the court is of the opinion that it is unnecessary to obtain a pre-sentence report.
(3) Where the offender is aged under 18, the court must not form the opinion mentioned in subsection (2) unless:
(a) there exists a previous pre-sentence report obtained in respect of the offender, and
(b) the court has had regard to the information contained in that report, or, if there is more than one such report, the most recent report.
(4)-(9) [see **83.21**]
(10) The reference in subsection (1)(a) to a court forming any such opinion as is mentioned in section 260(2) or 261(2) includes a court forming such an opinion for the purposes of section 218A(4).
Guidance on Sentencing in the Court Martial 2018 para 2.14.1 The court must obtain and consider a pre-sentence report [section 256(1)] before passing:

[1002] This subsection is listed as amended by Legal Aid, Sentencing and Punishment of Offenders Act 2012 Sch 22 para 33(2).

i. a sentence of imprisonment, ii. a sentence of detention, iii. a sentence of dismissal or dismissal with disgrace, iv. a community sentence, v. a sentence in respect of a dangerous offender, or vi. a sentence in respect of violent or sexual offences.
para 2.14.2 However, if it is of the opinion that it is unnecessary [Armed Forces Act 2006 s 256(2)] the court may decide not to obtain and consider a PSR. For cases of Absence Without Leave (AWOL), where a period of detention is normally awarded, the court is likely to dispense with a PSR if there are no special circumstances, provided the defendant has legal representation and has had the opportunity to request a PSR.

Deciding whether to order a report

83.17 ***Principles to consider***
Imposition of Community and Custodial Sentences Guideline 2017, see www.banksr.com Other Matters Guidelines tab page 8 In force 1 February 2017
Whenever the court reaches the provisional view that:

- the custody threshold has been passed; and, if so
- the length of imprisonment which represents the shortest term commensurate with the seriousness of the offence;

the court should obtain a pre-sentence report, whether verbal or written, unless the court considers a report to be unnecessary. Ideally a pre-sentence report should be completed on the same day to avoid adjourning the case.
Magistrates: Consult your legal adviser before deciding to sentence to custody without a pre-sentence report.
Criminal Practice Directions 2015 EWCA Crim 1567 para I 3A.17 In a case in which the defendant, not having done so before, indicates an intention to plead guilty to his representatives after being sent for trial but before the Plea and Trial Preparation Hearing, the defence representative will notify the Crown Court and prosecution forthwith. … a Judge should at once request the preparation of a pre-sentence report if it appears to the court that either:

a) there is a realistic alternative to a custodial sentence; or
b) the defendant may satisfy the criteria for classification as a dangerous offender; or
c) there is some other appropriate reason for doing so.

R v Townsend 2018 EWCA Crim 875, 2 Cr App R (S) 30 (p 278) D pleaded to supplying class A drugs. The defence asked for a pre-sentence report. The Judge refused the request. The defence said the report would help about the extent of the duress and other matters. Held. para 14 It is the role of the advocate to put together the mitigation and anything else he or she considers will assist the judge in the sentencing exercise. It is not the role of the Probation Service to do that work. Statements of what a defendant says about his background carry no more weight because they are in a pre-sentence report than if they are put forward by an advocate. The role of the Probation Service is to offer a realistic alternative to custody to deal with issues of dangerousness or to deal with something specific within their area of expertise. The grounds for appeal here are unarguable.

83.18 ***Minimum sentences and pre-sentence reports***
R v Densham 2014 EWCA Crim 2552, 2015 1 Cr App R (S) 37 (p 279) D was convicted of possession with intent to supply. He had already served a 7-year minimum term. The defence argued that a pre-sentence report should have been ordered. D appealed. A report was obtained. Held. para 8 Unless a defendant can show that it would be unjust to impose a minimum term, the judge should adjourn for a pre-sentence report. That course should usually be taken where the burden is on the defendant to show that a minimum term should not be imposed. On the facts, appeal dismissed.
Note: The last Lord Chief Justice was very keen to reduce the obtaining of unnecessary reports. Ed.

83.19 ***Sending cases to the Crown Court/Committals***
Criminal Practice Directions 2015 EWCA Crim 1567 para I 3A.9 Where a Magistrates' Court is considering [a] committal for sentence or the defendant has indicated an intention to plead guilty in a matter which is to be sent to the Crown Court, the Magistrates' Court should request the preparation of a pre-sentence report for the Crown Court's use if the Magistrates' Court considers that:
a) there is a realistic alternative to a custodial sentence; or
b) the defendant may satisfy the criteria for classification as a dangerous offender; or
c) there is some other appropriate reason for doing so.

Appeals

83.20 ***Failure to have a report Appeals***
Criminal Justice Act 2003 s 156(6) No custodial sentence or community sentence is invalidated by the failure of a court to obtain and consider a pre-sentence report before forming an opinion referred to in subsection (3) [see **83.13**], but any court on an appeal against such a sentence:
(a) must, subject to subsection (7), obtain a pre-sentence report if none was obtained by the court below, and
(b) must consider any such report obtained by it or by that court.
(7) Subsection (6)(a) does not apply if the court is of the opinion:
(a) that the court below was justified in forming an opinion that it was unnecessary to obtain a pre-sentence report, or
(b) that, although the court below was not justified in forming that opinion, in the circumstances of the case at the time it is before the court, it is unnecessary to obtain a pre-sentence report.
(8) In a case where the offender is aged under 18, the court must not form the opinion mentioned in subsection (7) unless:
(a) there exists a previous pre-sentence report obtained in respect of the offender, and
(b) the court has had regard to the information contained in that report, or, if there is more than one such report, the most recent report.
R v Ozberkcan 2014 EWCA Crim 2377 D was convicted of affray. D and another male tried to enter a take-away restaurant. The doorman, V, said there was a private party and the other male repeatedly punched V. Meanwhile, D hit V on the back with a metal chair, forcing staff to intervene. D, aged 38, had a young family and was of good character. The Judge did not order a pre-sentence report and additional medical mitigation was not available to him. Held. As D had no relevant convictions and was facing a custodial sentence, a pre-sentence report should have been ordered. The question still had to be asked by us: what difference would a pre-sentence report have made? His depression would have been material but the prison report does not support it. **6 months**, not 9.
See also: *R v Milhailsens* 2010 EWCA Crim 2545 (D pleaded to ABH. He had only a caution. The Judge said a report was a waste of money. D received 6 months. ABH. Held. There should have been a report but the failure does not itself give rise to an appeal against sentence. Sentence reduced on other grounds.)

83.21 ***Failure to have a report Appeals Court Martial***
Armed Forces Act 2006 s 256(4) No sentence is invalidated by a failure of a court to obtain and consider a pre-sentence report before doing any of the things mentioned in paras a) to c) of subsection (1).
(5) However, any court on appeal against a custodial sentence in respect of a service offence, a sentence of dismissal or dismissal with disgrace, a sentence of service detention or a community punishment:
(a) must (subject to subsection (6)) obtain a pre-sentence report if none was obtained by the court below, and
(b) must consider any such report obtained by it or by that court.
(6) Subsection (5)(a) does not apply if the court is of the opinion:

(a) that the court below was justified in forming an opinion that it was unnecessary to obtain a pre-sentence report, or
(b) that, although the court below was not justified in forming that opinion, in the circumstances of the case at the time it is before the court it is unnecessary to obtain a pre-sentence report.
(7) Where the offender is aged under 18, the court must not form the opinion mentioned in subsection (6) unless:
(a) there exists a previous pre-sentence report obtained in respect of the offender, and
(b) the court has had regard to the information contained in that report or, if there is more than one such report, the most recent report.
(8) Subsections (5) to (7) do not apply to the Summary Appeal Court on an appeal to it.
(9) Subsections (1) to (4) do apply to the Summary Appeal Court in relation to a sentence of service detention, but as if the opinions referred to in subsection (1)(a) were any such opinion as is mentioned in section 242(4) or 243(3).

84 Preventive Orders

84.1

Owing to the proliferation of preventive orders, the rules for them have been collated into one chapter.

Warning This chapter brings together the cases for a large number of preventive orders, most of which have now been repealed. It is very important when considering the case reports to remember the order that is proposed and the danger the defendant poses. It is the details of the instant case that will determine whether an order is required and what terms are required. Earlier cases provide guidance only. The guidance must be seen in the context of the facts of that case and the order made or proposed. This is particularly so with prohibitions relating to the Internet, where standard terms can become out of date very quickly.

See also the **Sexual Harm Prevention Orders** and **Criminal Behaviour Orders** chapters.

The Behaviour Rules

84.2 ***Orders to which these Behaviour Rules apply***

Criminal Procedure Rules 2015 2015/1490 Rule 31.1(1) This Part applies where:
(a) a Magistrates' Court or the Crown Court can make, vary or revoke a civil order:
(i) as well as, or instead of, passing a sentence, or in any other circumstances in which other legislation allows the court to make such an order, and
(ii) that requires someone to do, or not do, something,
(b) a Magistrates' Court or the Crown Court can make a European protection order,
(c) a Magistrates' Court can give effect to a European protection order made in another European Union member State.
(2) A reference to a 'behaviour order' in this Part is a reference to any such order.
(3) [Deals with hearsay evidence, see **84.27**]
[Explanatory] Note: In the circumstances set out in the Acts listed, the court can make a behaviour order:
(a) on conviction, under:
(i) Football Spectators Act 1989 s 14A (Football Banning Orders),
(ii) Protection from Harassment Act 1997 s 5 (Restraining Orders),
(iii) Crime and Disorder Act 1998 s 1C and 1D ([the repealed] Anti-social Behaviour Orders and Interim Anti-social Behaviour Orders),
(iv) Crime and Disorder Act 1998 s 8-9 (Parenting Orders),
(v) Sexual Offences Act 2003 s 103A (Sexual Harm Prevention Orders),
(vi) Serious Crime Act 2007 s 19 or 21 (Serious Crime Prevention Orders),
(vii) Anti-social Behaviour, Crime and Policing Act 2014 s 22 (Criminal Behaviour Orders),

(viii) Modern Slavery Act 2015 (Slavery and Trafficking Prevention Orders),
(b) on acquittal, under:
(ix) Psychoactive Substances Act 2016 s 19 (prohibition orders),
(x) Immigration Act 2016 s 20 (labour market enforcement orders)[1003]
Protection from Harassment Act 1997 s 5A (Restraining Orders on acquittal), and
(c) on the making of a finding of not guilty by reason of insanity, or a finding of disability, under Modern Slavery Act 2015 s 14 (Slavery and Trafficking Prevention Orders), and
(d) in proceedings for a genital mutilation offence, under Female Genital Mutilation Act 2003 Sch 2 para 3 (female genital mutilation protection orders).
[There is a note about European Protection Orders]

General principles about making a preventive order

84.3 *Basic principles*

Magistrates' Court Sentencing Guidelines 2008, see www.banksr.com Other Matters Guidelines tab page 168 **Anti-social behaviour orders** The order must be proportionate to the legitimate aim pursued and commensurate with the risk guarded against. The court should avoid making compliance very difficult through the imposition of numerous prohibitions, and those that will cause great disruption to the subject should be considered with particular care.
R v McGrath 2005 EWCA Crim 353, 2 Cr App R (S) 85 (p 525) D pleaded to theft and the Judge made an ASBO. Held. In determining whether an ASBO is necessary, the Judge is entitled to take all of the offender's conduct into account, both before and after the commencement date. There is no requirement that acts prohibited by an ASBO should by themselves give rise to harassment, alarm or distress. The test for the grant of an ASBO is necessity. The terms of the ASBO should be commensurate with the risk to be guarded against and hence not disproportionate. What is disproportionate must depend on the facts of each case, having regard to both the restrictions to be imposed on the offender and the risk against which the ASBO is seeking to protect the public. The ASBO should be approached with a proper degree of caution and circumspection. They are not cure-alls. They are not lightly to be imposed.
R v Boness 2005 EWCA Crim 2395, 2006 1 Cr App R (S) 120 (p 690) D pleaded to burglary and the Judge made an ASBO. Held. Each separate order prohibiting a person from doing a specified thing must be necessary to protect persons from further antisocial acts by him. Not only must the court, before imposing an order prohibiting the offender from doing something, consider that such an order is necessary to protect persons from further antisocial acts by him, the terms of the order must be proportionate in the sense that they must be commensurate with the risk to be guarded against. This is particularly important where an order may interfere with an ECHR right.
R v Dyer 2010 EWCA Crim 2096 D pleaded to drug supply and the Judge made an ASBO. Held. The main question that a court has to consider is whether an order is necessary to protect relevant persons from further antisocial acts by him. With orders on conviction, an additional factor has to be considered, namely the impact of the sentence on the necessity for an order, since the one may make the other unnecessary. It is suggested that relevant considerations will be: a) the nature and length of the sentence, b) the order's likely effect on the defendant, c) the nature, length and effect (if any) of previous sentences, d) the duration, conditions and likely effect of any period of licence. It is always desirable for the judge to consider the book. Each case is fact-specific.
Note: Although these cases relate to ASBOs, it may assist with the new orders. However, it should be remembered that the test for many preventive orders varies. Ed.
R v Smith and Others 2011 EWCA Crim 1772, 2012 1 Cr App R (S) 82 (p 468) The Court gave guidance about SOPOs. Held. para 4 The SOPO offers a flexibility in

[1003] Added by Criminal Procedure (Amendment) Rules 2017 2017/144 para 6

drafting which is in one sense welcome because it enables the order to be tailored to the exact requirements of the case. That flexibility, however, must not lead draftsmen to an inventiveness which stores up trouble for the future. It will do this if it creates a provision which is, or will become, unworkable. That may be because it is too vague or because it potentially conflicts with other rules applicable to the defendant, or simply because it imposes an impermissible level of restriction on the ordinary activities of life. The SOPO must meet the twin tests of necessity and clarity. The test of necessity brings with it the subtest of proportionality.

84.4 ***The individual must be capable of complying with the order***

Wookey v Wookey 1991 3 WLR 135 A wife sought a Non-Molestation Order against her mentally ill husband, H. The Official Solicitor said H would be unfit to plead if charged with a criminal offence and was incapable of understanding an injunction. A Judge granted an injunction. The Official Solicitor appealed. Held. It is a well-established, general proposition for injunctions that the grant of an injunction is a discretionary remedy derived from the equitable jurisdiction which acts *in personam* (directed at a particular person) and only against those who are amenable to its jurisdiction, nor will the court act in vain by granting an injunction which is idle and ineffectual. An injunction should not, therefore, be granted to impose an obligation to do something which is impossible or cannot be enforced. The injunction must serve a useful purpose for the person seeking the relief and there must be a real possibility that the order, if made, will be enforceable by the process *in personam*. However, the courts expect and assume that their orders will be obeyed and will not normally refuse an injunction because of the respondent's likely disobedience to the order. In the view of the consultant psychiatrist, H was incapable within the McNaughten Rules of understanding what he was doing or that it was wrong. An injunction ought not to be granted against a person found to be in that condition since he would not be capable of complying with it. Such an order cannot have the desired deterrent effect nor operate on his mind so as to regulate his conduct. If the order can have no effect upon H, any breach by him cannot be the subject of effective enforcement proceedings since he would have a clear defence to an application for committal to prison for contempt.

R (Cooke) v DPP 2008 EWHC 2703 (Admin) High Court D was convicted under Public Order Act 1986 s 5 and he was fined. An ASBO was made prohibiting him from entering Northampton and begging etc. D had complex medical problems. The defence contended that D was incapable of understanding the ASBO. Held. The Court considered *Wookey v Wookey* 1991 3 WLR 135. An ASBO is not an injunction but there are obvious similarities. An ASBO should not be granted if the defendant is truly incapable of complying with it. That is because an ASBO is not necessary for the protection of the public in such circumstances, and it would be wrong to make one where the court knows that the defendant is not capable of complying with it. Justices should not refuse to make an ASBO on such grounds unless the defendant does not have the mental capacity to understand the meaning of the order, or to comply with it. If the Justices had concluded that the appellant's mental state was such that he was truly incapable of complying with the conditions of any ASBO that they were minded to make, they would have been wrong in law to make the order. If by reason of mental incapacity an offender is incapable of complying with an order, then an order is incapable of protecting the public and cannot therefore be said to be necessary to protect the public. Here D was capable of understanding the order.

Pender v DPP 2013 EWHC 2598 (Admin) High Court D pleaded to six begging offences. He was given an ASBO and appealed. The defence said D did not have the capacity to comply with it. D was aged 63 with numerous previous convictions for begging. The defence called a doctor, who said D a) did not have the capacity to comply with the order, b) suffered from schizophrenia, c) had a very severe cigarette addiction and d) was incapable of work. The Judge concluded that D did understand the order as he had tried to hide from the police. D appealed. Held. In *R (Cooke) v DPP* 2008 the

Court drew the important distinction between the lack of capacity to comply with an order and a personality disorder on account of which a person may be liable to disobey [the order]. That distinction will often be difficult to draw and is a matter of fact for the tribunal. The mere fact that it is almost inevitable that a person will disobey is not a basis for refusing to make an ASBO. It cannot be right that the courts decline to make an ASBO merely because someone suffers from an addiction that makes it difficult to obey an order and it is most likely that it will be disobeyed. The Judge was entitled to disagree with the expert but she must explain the basis of the disagreement. That basis was missing. There were no facts found justifying the factual conclusion that D was capable of complying with the order. Order quashed.

84.5 *European Convention on Human Rights art 9*

R v Uddin and Others 2015 EWCA Crim 1918, 2016 1 Cr App R (S) 57 (p 57) Nine defendants were sentenced for violent disorder and other public order offences arising out of a march and a fight near a stall on different days in central London. The defendants were all Sunni Muslims from Luton. A group of men were engaged in Da'wah, proselytising for Islam. They were manning a stall and giving leaflets to passers-by. They were all given ASBOs. para 15 The Judge imposed prohibitions about performing Da'wah (defined for the purposes of this order as proselytising in a public place (not a mosque). The terms prohibited [being] in the company of more than four other persons [also performing Da'wah], setting up a stall without first having informed the local authority and where necessary, having obtained written permission and being within 200 metres of any other group performing Da'wah. Held. para 39 Article 9 protects the right of everyone to 'freedom of thought, conscience and religion', including the freedom to manifest their religion in teaching alone or in community with others. This freedom is subject only to limitations prescribed by law and necessary in a democratic society in specified ways, including for the protection of public order and for the protection of the rights and freedoms of others but, in contrast with articles 10 and 11 not including the prevention of crime per se. There can be no doubt that the restrictions in the ASBO on the appellants' performance of Da'wah *prima facie* restrict their article 9 Convention rights. In particular, they prohibit the appellants from performing Da'wah together with more than four others and from setting up a stall for this purpose without first informing the local authority. The violence occurred not as a result of Da'wah or evangelism but as a result of personal confrontation between the defendants and a group of football supporters. The terms were neither a necessary nor a proportionate response to anything done by the defendants.

84.6 *Family issues Contact with children*

R v Cetin 2014 EWCA Crim 343 D pleaded to intimidation. He was involved in a domestic disturbance with his wife, V, who became a prospective witness in criminal proceedings. In breach of his bail, D travelled from Kent to Suffolk and V was terrified to see him. The Restraining Order imposed had a term that he was not to contact his daughter 'unless through lawyers'. Held. V must be protected. The issue of contact with the daughter is not capable of being adjudicated as a by-product of criminal proceedings on scant information, solely as a protective device to benefit V. A carefully drafted Restraining Order will be called for so it does not interfere with the child's right to respect for family life and D's rights are not disproportionally interfered with. Term amended to prohibit D from contacting either V or her daughter save through contact arrangements made through V's solicitors or by order of the Family Court.

R v Khellaf 2016 EWCA Crim 1297, 2017 1 Cr App R (S) 1 (p 1) D pleaded to three breaches of a Non-Molestation Order. There was a history of violence and harassment, mainly about D's contact with his child. Held. The authorities set out the following propositions: 1)-3) [see **93.7** and **93.15**], 4) Particular care should be taken when children are involved to ensure that the order does not make it impossible for contact to take place between a parent and child [even] if that is otherwise inappropriate.

84.7 *Family issues Contact with victim Victim has custody of defendant's children*
R v Kaddu 2015 EWCA Crim 2531 D pleaded late to ABH. At night he conducted a protracted, very serious, very frightening, sinister attack in a number of locations on his ex-partner, V, while their children slept. D had previous convictions for supply, robbery and firearms. Held. Due to considerable psychological harm to ex-partner and other factors, the Judge was able to make the offence Category 1 and to start at 4 years. The terms of the Restraining Order were likely to prove unworkable. We substitute, '1) except as provided in para 2, D must not contact V directly or indirectly, whether by himself or by any person acting on his behalf; 2) contact for the purpose of making arrangements in relation to the children of D and V may be made through a solicitor, through the relevant Social Services department or otherwise in accordance with any order of the Family Court.

84.8 *Family issues Family law protection orders for children may provide a better solution*
R v D 2005 EWCA Crim 3660 D pleaded to eight counts of sexual abuse of his daughter when she was aged between 10 and 13. The offences were three of indecent assault, two of attempted rape, two of indecent activity with a child and one of assault by penetration. He received 6 years in all. D was also subject to a SOPO, a condition of which prevented him from seeing his son, L. D appealed. Held. The word 'may' in the Act means the court has a discretion whether to make an order or not. The Judge's order does not have flexibility. It prevents D from contacting or approaching L without a limit on time. It does not take into account L's interests. In the legislation, L has no right to apply to vary, renew or discharge the order. Where a court is concerned with the inflexibility of a SOPO, it can be addressed by way of a link to family proceedings. SOPOs can cause problems when the abuse is contained within a family, particularly where the court must consider the protection of a child who was not the direct target of the abuse. In such situations, it may be desirable to draft the order in terms which provide a link to the court's family jurisdiction. There may be situations where a child's best interests can be better served by more than the blunt instrument of a SOPO alone. Order varied.

84.9 *Family issues Separating married couples*
R v Gowan 2007 EWCA Crim 1360 D pleaded to threats to kill, dangerous driving and other offences. GBH and ABH charges were left on the file. He punched, kicked and stamped on his wife, W. D then stormed out of his home in a rage shouting insults at W. He was under the influence of drugs. Although disqualified, he drove his car into his neighbour's parked cars, seriously damaging them. At the police station, D threatened to kill W and burn her. Later W retracted her statement and D and W were reconciled. The Judge gave D IPP with an 18-month term and an ASBO which prohibited him from having any contact with his wife or going within 200 metres of her house. After the sentence, W was prevented by prison staff from visiting D. Defence counsel said as they lived in the same household, the ASBO fell outside the terms of section 1C(2), because the section referred to the likelihood of harassment to person(s) 'not of the same household'. Held. It is clear from the terms of section 1C(2) that it was never intended that an ASBO should be made in circumstances such as here. D's licence on release will provide sufficient deterrence.

84.10 *Orders must consider subject's past conduct as well as the instant offences*
R v Uddin and Others 2015 EWCA Crim 1918, 2016 1 Cr App R (S) 57 (p 57) Nine defendants were given ASBOs. Held. The decisions to impose the ASBOs were taken without the prosecution presenting evidence about the appellants' past conduct, including in some but not all cases their past convictions, and, as we infer from the Judge's ruling, without consideration of the personal circumstances of each appellant. Usually a defendant's personal circumstances and previous behaviour would be highly relevant considerations when making an ASBO.

84.11 ***Orders are preventive measures not an additional punishment/sanction***

Magistrates' Court Sentencing Guidelines 2008, see www.banksr.com Other Matters Guidelines tab page 168 As the ASBO is a preventive order it is unlawful to use it as a punishment, so, when sentencing an offender, a court must not allow itself to be diverted into making an ASBO as an alternative or additional sanction.

R v Boness 2005 EWCA Crim 2395, 2006 1 Cr App R (S) 120 (p 690) The purpose of an ASBO is not to punish an offender, rather the requirement is that the order must be necessary to protect persons from further antisocial acts by him.

84.12 ***Imposing a preventive order to increase the maximum sentence if the defendant is convicted again of dangerous driving etc.***

R v Kirby 2005 EWCA Crim 1228, 2006 1 Cr App R (S) 26 (p 151) D pleaded to dangerous driving and disqualified driving. He had very many previous convictions, the vast majority for motoring offences. He had 17 convictions for taking vehicles without consent, of which six were for the aggravated form of that offence. He had numerous convictions for driving while disqualified. He had one previous conviction for dangerous driving. D was sentenced to 20 months and 5 months consecutive. The Judge made an ASBO saying that, "It would increase the penalty the courts can now impose on you". Held. Where the underlying objective was to give the court higher sentencing powers in the event of future similar offending, [that] is not a use of the power which should normally be exercised.

R v Williams 2005 EWCA Crim 1796, 2006 1 Cr App R (S) 56 (p 305) The defendant was sentenced for (presumably) disqualified driving, drink/driving and dangerous driving. He was sentenced to a Community Rehabilitation Order. He failed to keep his appointments and was subsequently arrested for theft. He was aged 36 with 223 convictions on 46 occasions. There were a very large number of convictions for driving while disqualified and a significant number for dangerous driving and drink/driving. He had an unfortunate background and had mental health problems. For the breach he was sentenced to 1 day's imprisonment, and an ASBO which prohibited him from driving was made. The Judge wanted to reinforce the disqualification order. Held. *R v Hall* 2004 EWCA Crim 2671, 2005 1 Cr App R (S) 118 (p 671) and *R v Kirby* 2005 EWCA Crim 1228, 2006 1 Cr App R (S) 26 (p 151) do not speak with one voice. Following the principles in *R v Kirby* 2005, the order should be quashed. We note, however, that *R v Kirby* does not rule out the possibility of making an ASBO because of problems with sentencing powers in exceptional circumstances.

R v Boness 2005 EWCA Crim 2395, 2006 1 Cr App R (S) 120 (p 690) We affirm the rule in *R v Kirby* but different considerations may apply if the maximum sentence is only a fine. The court must still go through all the steps to make sure that an ASBO is necessary.

R v Morrison 2005 EWCA Crim 2237, 2006 1 Cr App R (S) 85 (p 488) The defendant was in breach of an ASBO for being in the front seat of a motor vehicle. Held. An ASBO to restrain driving while disqualified alone would (usually at least) be unlikely to be within the terms of the statute. However, it might be appropriate against a man with an appalling record involving frequent offences of driving with excess alcohol. The behaviour against which ASBOs are directed must be behaviour which is likely to cause harassment, alarm or distress to persons outside the offender's own household.

Note: These are old cases. However, there is nothing to suggest the cases don't state the law correctly. Ed.

See also: *R v Lawson* 2005 EWCA Crim 1840, 2006 1 Cr App R (S) 59 (p 323) (*R v Kirby* 2005 EWCA Crim 1228, 2006 1 Cr App R (S) 26 (p 151) followed. Order quashed.)

84.13 ***Individual under 18 Welfare of the child as a primary consideration***

R (A) v Leeds Magistrates' Court 2004 EWHC 554 (Admin) High Court The police successfully applied for an interim ASBO in respect of a 16-year-old and 65 others to combat class A drug supply. Dealers and users associated in a particular area in Leeds, bringing with them linked crime. Held. In proceedings against children and young persons, the welfare of the child is a primary consideration but not the primary consideration. The interests of the public are themselves a primary consideration.

The application and pre-hearing duties

84.14 *Prosecution's application*

Application for behaviour and notice of terms of proposed order: special rules

Criminal Procedure Rules 2015 2015/1490 Rule 31.3(1) This rule applies where:

(a) a prosecutor wants the court to make one of the following orders if the defendant is convicted:

(i) an anti-social behaviour order (but this rule does not apply to an application for an interim anti-social behaviour order),

(ii) a Serious Crime Prevention Order,

(iii) a Criminal Behaviour Order, or

(iv) a prohibition order;

(b) a prosecutor proposes, on the prosecutor's initiative or at the court's request, a Sexual Harm Prevention Order if the defendant is convicted;

(c) a prosecutor proposes a Restraining Order whether the defendant is convicted or acquitted.

(2) Where paragraph (1)(a) applies, the prosecutor must serve a notice of intention to apply for such an order on:

(a) the court officer,

(b) the defendant against whom the prosecutor wants the court to make the order, and

(c) any person on whom the order would be likely to have a significant adverse effect,

as soon as practicable (without waiting for the verdict).

(3) A notice under paragraph (2) must:

(a) summarise the relevant facts,

(b) identify the evidence on which the prosecutor relies in support,

(c) attach any written statement that the prosecutor has not already served, and

(d) specify the order that the prosecutor wants the court to make.

Note [in the Rules]. The Practice Direction [2015] sets out a form of notice for use in connection with this rule. Under Serious Crime Act 2007 s 8 a Serious Crime Prevention Order may be made only on an application by the Director of Public Prosecutions or the Director of the Serious Fraud Office. See also Serious Crime Act 2007 Sch 2 para 2, 7 and 13. Sexual Offences Act 2003 s 107 describes the content and effect of a Sexual Offences Prevention Order. Under Crime and Disorder Act 1998 s 11, on an application for an Anti-social Behaviour Order the court may give a special measures direction under Youth Justice and Criminal Evidence Act 1999. Under Anti-social Behaviour, Crime and Policing Act 2014 s 31 the court may give such a direction on an application for a Criminal Behaviour Order.

Note: The first part says the form for making an application is in the Practice Direction. It isn't in the current directions, 2015 EWCA Crim 1567. It can, however, be found at www.justice.gov.uk/courts/procedure-rules/criminal/forms Part 31 or see www.banksr.com Other Matters Other Documents tab ASBOs. Ed.

R v W and F 2006 EWCA Crim 686 Two defendants were convicted of robbery and the Judge made ASBOs as requested. Held. The case summary attached to the application for the ASBOs did not set out the particular facts which the CPS relied on other than the facts constituting the robbery offence. Instead the application set out only a vague 'Overview of the Problem' and some 'Reasoning'. Therefore there was no summary of facts that the Judge could put to the offenders to see, quickly and easily, whether or not the facts were disputed by them. It was unfortunate that the prosecution did not assist the Judge or the defence in summarising the facts at the hearing when the ASBO was sought. The result was that the Judge was in no position to make findings of particular facts to support his general conclusion that the defendants had been guilty of antisocial behaviour, other than the facts of the robbery offence. ASBOs quashed.

R v Uddin and Others 2015 EWCA Crim 1918, 2016 1 Cr App R (S) 57 (p 57) Nine defendants were given ASBOs. Held. If the prosecution significantly depart from the intention stated in their notice, the defendant must have clear and specific notice of the change. Whatever the exact position about service of the prosecution's skeleton argument, we are satisfied that in this case the defendants were left unsure about what case they had to meet. Given the importance to them of the prohibitions imposed by the orders, we would allow the appeals on the [procedural unfairness] ground alone.

See also: *R v Howard* 2016 EWCA Crim 1906 (Mother subject to a Restraining Order after no evidence on stalking count concerning son. Held. para 14 The Court has repeatedly restated the importance of compliance with Rule 31.)

84.15 *Defendant's response*

Criminal Procedure Rules 2015 2015/1490 Rule 31.3(4) A defendant served with a notice under paragraph (2) (a notice from the prosecutor, see **84.14**) must:

(a) serve notice of any evidence on which the defendant relies on:[1004]

(i) the court officer, and

(ii) the prosecutor,

as soon as practicable (without waiting for the verdict), and

(b) in the notice, identify that evidence and attach any written statement that has not already been served.

Note: There is a note at the bottom of this rule which says the form for the reply is in the Criminal Practice Directions. It isn't in the current directions, 2015 EWCA Crim 1567. It isn't at www.justice.gov.uk/courts/ procedure-rules/criminal/formspage. It appears to have been withdrawn. Ed.

R v W and F 2006 EWCA Crim 686 Two defendants were convicted of robbery and the Judge made ASBOs as requested. Held. The case summary attached to the application for the ASBOs did not set out the particular facts which the CPS relied on other than the facts constituting the robbery offence. Instead the application set out only a vague 'Overview of the Problem' and some 'Reasoning'. Therefore there was no summary of facts that the Judge could put to the offenders to see, quickly and easily, whether or not the facts were disputed by them. It was unfortunate that the prosecution did not assist the Judge or the defence in summarising the facts at the hearing when the ASBO was sought. The result was that the Judge was in no position to make findings of particular facts to support his general conclusion that the defendants had been guilty of antisocial behaviour, other than the facts of the robbery offence. ASBOs quashed.

84.16 *Courts initiating the proceedings*

C v Sunderland Youth Court 2003 EWHC 2385 (Admin), 2004 1 Cr App R (S) 76 (p 443) High Court A Youth Court made an ASBO. Held. Elementary fairness requires a court, if it proposes to make an order of its own motion, to indicate: a) the basis on which it provisionally considers an order may be appropriate, and b) the material on which it proposes to rely so that the person potentially liable can make [proper] submissions.

R (McGarrett) v Kingston Crown Court 2009 EWHC 1776 (Admin) High Court At an appeal hearing in the Crown Court the Judge found the case proved, fined the defendant and without any application from the Council prosecutor imposed an indefinite ASBO. Held. There can be no objection to the court taking the initiative to consider whether or not an ASBO should be imposed. The statute entrusts the court with that power, despite the fact that the prosecution had not advanced the case for an ASBO. However, here the ASBO should be quashed because of procedural unfairness.

[1004] The Criminal Procedure (Amendment No 2) Rules 2016 2016/705 para 11(b)(iii) removes the requirement that the notice has to be in writing. In force 3/10/16

84.17 ***Prosecution must show statutory provisions are met***

R v Halloren 2004 EWCA Crim 233 Where the Crown invites a judge to make a Restraining Order of this nature, it is incumbent upon them to be familiar with the necessary statutory provisions and to be in a position to put before the judge the material which shows that the statutory provisions have been met.

84.18 ***Defence must have sufficient time to consider the application/ Representations, Right to make***

Behaviour orders: general rules

Criminal Procedure Rules 2015 2015/1490 Rule 31.2(1) The court must not make a behaviour order unless the person to whom it is directed has had an opportunity:

(a) to consider:

(i) what order is proposed and why, and

(ii) the evidence in support, and

(b) to make representations at a hearing (whether or not that person in fact attends).

(2) That restriction does not apply to making:

(a) an interim behaviour order, but unless other legislation otherwise provides such an order has no effect unless the person to whom it is directed:

(i) is present when it is made, or

(ii) is handed a document recording the order not more than seven days after it is made,

(b) a restraining order that gives effect to a European Protection Order, where rule 31.10 applies (Giving effect to a European Protection Order made in another EU member State).

R v Smith and Others 2011 EWCA Crim 1772, 2012 1 Cr App R (S) 82 (p 468) para 26 It is essential that there is a written draft, properly considered in advance of the sentencing hearing. The normal requirement should be that it is served on the court and on the defendant before the sentencing hearing. We suggest not less than two clear days before but in any event not at the hearing. It is sensible for it to be available in electronic form as well as paper form.

R v RM 2012 EWCA Crim 2805 We reiterate as forcefully as we can the desirability, indeed the necessity, of any proposed SOPO being served on the defendant's advisors before the day of the hearing so that any dispute about it can be the subject of discussion, and if the discussion does not result in a resolution of the dispute, to an informed debate before the judge, a debate that should in every case be informed by reference to *R v Smith* 2012.

84.19 ***Standard of proof***

R v Crown Court at Manchester ex parte McCann 2002 UKHL 39 Lords (A case concerning a stand-alone ASBO) The enquiry whether an order is necessary to protect persons from further antisocial acts by him does not involve a standard of proof. It is an exercise of judgement and evaluation.

R (Cleveland Police) v H 2009 EWHC 3231 (Admin) High Court H was made the subject of a stand-alone SOPO and appealed to the Crown Court. The order was quashed and the police appealed. Held. When one looks to see what the effect of the order is and the serious result that comes from it, and indeed when one considers that the acts in question may often, although not necessarily, amount to conduct which could be said to be in breach of the criminal law, it is, on the whole, desirable that the standard be the high one, which is indeed equivalent to the criminal standard.

Note: Applications are now judged on their merits and not on the consideration of burdens and standards of proof. Ed.

84.20 ***Court's power to shorten time limits and waive notice and application rules***

Court's power to vary requirements under this Part

Criminal Procedure Rules 2015 2015/1490 Rule 31.11 Unless other legislation otherwise provides, the court may:

(a) shorten a time limit or extend it (even after it has expired),
(b) allow a notice or application to be given in a different form, or presented orally.

The hearing

84.21 *Procedure General*

R v Lima 2010 EWCA Crim 284 The Judge made an ASBO. Held. It would seem the Judge either ignored or was entirely ignorant of the code. This case illustrates the need for observance of the Criminal Procedure Rules where an order significantly restricting the liberty of a person is envisaged. The procedure followed was unsatisfactory.

R v Aldridge and Eaton 2012 EWCA Crim 1456 LCJ D pleaded to indecent image offences. A SOPO was made. He was accused of breaching the order but the Judge dismissed the charge and then, without applying the Criminal Procedure Rules, made variations to the SOPO. A pre-sentence report account of an incident was relied on. Held. The entire process was inappropriately informal. We quash the variations save one which was not based on a procedural failure.

See also: *R v Trott* 2011 EWCA Crim 2395 (Order quashed because of procedural flaws.)

84.22 *The procedure must be fair*

R (McGarrett) v Kingston Crown Court 2009 EWHC 1776 (Admin) High Court D was fined at the Magistrates' Court for failing to comply with a noise abatement notice. At D's appeal hearing, the Judge found the case proved, fined the defendant and, without any application from the prosecution, imposed an indefinite ASBO. Held. The matter proceeded in a manner which breached the principles of procedural fairness. In particular, there were no findings of fact recorded by the Judge in his judgment. The Judge did not put precisely to D the concerns that he had about his behaviour. D's counsel attempted to make submissions to the Judge, for example about a witness statement, but the Judge seemed not to give them sufficient attention. ASBO quashed.

R v Uddin and Others 2015 EWCA Crim 1918, 2016 1 Cr App R (S) 57 (p 57) Nine defendants were given ASBOs. Held. In *W v Acton Youth Court* 2005 EWHC 954 (Admin), at para 30, the court said 'The actual and potential consequences for the subject of an ASBO make it…particularly important that procedural fairness is scrupulously observed.' We agree. After all, a defendant facing an application for an ASBO is exposed to hearsay evidence which would be inadmissible in criminal proceedings, but the case against him is not pleaded as it would be in civil proceedings for an injunction. The defendant's protection is the notice, together with the requirement that the prosecution attach to it any material on which the application is based (and specifically give notice of any hearsay evidence relied on). It follows that if the prosecution significantly departs from the intention stated in the notice, the defendant must have clear and specific notice of the change. Whatever the exact position about service of the prosecution's skeleton argument, we are satisfied that in this case the defendants were left unsure about what case they had to meet. Given the importance to them of the prohibitions imposed by the orders, we would allow the appeals on this ground alone.

84.23 *Proceeding in the absence of the defendant*

R v P 2004 EWCA Crim 287, 2 Cr App R (S) 63 (p 343) LCJ P pleaded to robbery and other offences. He was aged 15 at the time of the offences. The prosecution applied for an ASBO for 'quite some time' in P's absence. Held. The totality of the proceedings should have been in the presence of the appellant.

M v Burnley etc. Magistrates' Court 2009 EWHC 2874 (Admin) High Court R, aged 14 at appeal, and N, aged 13 at appeal, were given ASBOs. The boys then moved and seven months before the ASBOs expired, the police applied to vary them. The Court was notified that a trial of the issues would be necessary. On the hearing day, R's education authority arranged a taxi to take him to school. The authority was aware of the hearing date. The Magistrates found that N was unable to attend because his mother was indisposed. The Magistrates then considered the witnesses who had attended, the time since the application had been served and decided in the interests of justice to proceed.

The boys' solicitor did not have full instructions and felt that his role should be to take a note of the proceedings rather than take an active part in the application. The Magistrates varied the order to widen the geographical area and removed an association prohibition. Held. R had effectively been prevented from attending. N was unable to attend. The principle of *audi alteram partem* (everyone has a right to be heard) applies with no less force to civil proceedings generally than it does to criminal proceedings, in particular proceedings of this nature where an individual may be brought to court in order to answer a summons in respect of allegations against him of misbehaviour. It applies to an ASBO hearing. Plainly, a court considering whether to adjourn an application will need to be careful to distinguish genuine reasons for a defendant not being present, from those reasons which are spuriously advanced or designed to frustrate the process. However, if it should come to the conclusion that either of these two latter circumstances is the case, the court should say so. It cannot simply be inferred that a court has come to the conclusion that the excuse before them is spurious or designed to frustrate the process unless that is clearly stated by the Magistrates.

It cannot be said that a court must always adjourn where a defendant is not present. If a conclusion is open to the court, reasonably on the material before it, either to the effect that an excuse given is spurious, or if there is a truly compelling and exceptional reason for proceeding notwithstanding a good excuse for non-attendance, the court has the power to do so. This, however, would be an exceptional case. Because it has been recognised by the highest authority that it requires a very rare or exceptional case for the power to be exercised in this way, it is incumbent upon the court to draw attention to the factors which persuade it that the case before the court is within the very rare category to which Lord Bingham referred in *R v Jones* 2002 UKHL 5, 2 Cr App R 9 (p 128) at para 13. The public interest thus could not be said to be so great as to place this case into a wholly unusual category. The fact that the witnesses were present is an irrelevant consideration, as also was the fact that some time had gone past since the case had been listed. Neither of those are particularly unusual circumstances where application is made. In the obvious case of someone who for instance has suffered a vomiting infection that morning or had been involved in a car crash on the way to court or had been subject to various other problems which are not difficult to think of which might have prevented her or his attendance, it would be entirely unreasonable for a court to proceed, notwithstanding. Nothing seems to have been identified which could bring this case within the category into which it would have been required to be. The Magistrates ought to have recognised that it would only be in a rare case that it would be right to proceed in the absence of a defendant who, through no fault of his own, was unable to attend. The ASBOs are quashed.

See also the **PROCEDURE, SENTENCING Absent defendants** section at **86.24**.

84.24 ***Can the court aggregate group activity?***

Chief Constable of Lancashire v Potter 2003 EWHC 2272 (Admin) High Court D was a prostitute working in certain areas of Preston, where other prostitutes had caused and were causing substantial problems to the residents of the area. Much of the prostitution was carried out in order to fund drug habits. The problems were caused by the prostitutes as a whole, not by the actions of any particular prostitute. An application for an ASBO was refused on the basis that conduct could not be aggregated. Held. As a matter of practicality, it is permissible to aggregate conduct of others to a defendant. It is a step to finding that the defendant's conduct was likely to have the effect of causing harassment, alarm or distress.

The evidence

84.25 ***Evidence Duty to serve***

Criminal Procedure Rules 2015 2015/1490 Rule 31.4(2) A party who wants the court to take account of evidence not already introduced must:

(a) serve notice on:[1005]
(i) the court officer, and
(ii) every other party, as soon as practicable (without waiting for the verdict),
(b) in the notice, identify that evidence, and
(c) attach any written statement containing such evidence.

84.26 ***Right to challenge the evidence***
R v P 2004 EWCA Crim 287, 2 Cr App R (S) 63 (p 343) LCJ The procedure adopted in the Crown Court was defective in that the appellant was not given any opportunity to dispute the allegations contained in a witness statement. It is plainly the duty of a court making such an order to identify matters relied upon by the party seeking the order to give the defendant an opportunity to dispute the allegation.

84.27 ***Hearsay***
Civil Evidence Act 1995 s 1(2) Hearsay is a statement made otherwise than by a person while giving oral evidence in the proceedings which is tendered as evidence of the matters stated. Section 13 of that Act defines a statement as meaning 'any representation of fact or opinion, however made'.
Criminal Procedure Rules 2015 2015/1490 Rule 31.1(3) A reference to 'hearsay evidence' in this Part is a reference to evidence consisting of hearsay within the meaning of Civil Evidence Act 1995 s 1(2).
Criminal Procedure Rules 2015 2015/1490 Rule 31.6(1) A party who wants to introduce hearsay evidence must:
(a) serve notice on: (i) the court officer, and (ii) every other party directly affected, and[1006]
(b) in that notice:
(i) explain that it is a notice of hearsay evidence,
(ii) identify that evidence,
(iii) identify the person who made the statement which is hearsay, or explain why if that person is not identified, and
(iv) explain why that person will not be called to give oral evidence.
(2) A party may serve one notice under this rule in respect of more than one notice and more than one witness.
For the time limits, see **84.20**.

84.28 ***Hearsay Applications to cross-examine***
Criminal Procedure Rules 2015 2015/1490 Rule 31.7(1) This rule applies where a party wants the court's permission to cross-examine a person who made a statement which another party wants to introduce as hearsay.
(2) The party who wants to cross-examine that person must:
(a) apply in writing, with reasons, not more than seven days after service of the notice of hearsay evidence, and
(b) serve the application on:
(i) the court officer,
(ii) the party who served the hearsay evidence notice, and
(iii) every party on whom the hearsay evidence notice was served.
(3) The court may decide an application under this rule with or without a hearing.
(4) But the court must not:
(a) dismiss an application under this rule unless the applicant has had an opportunity to make representations at a hearing (whether or not the applicant in fact attends), or

[1005] The Criminal Procedure (Amendment No 2) Rules 2016 2016/705 para 11(c) removes the requirement that the notice has to be in writing. In force 3/10/16
[1006] The Criminal Procedure (Amendment No 2) Rules 2016 2016/705 para 11(e) removes the requirement that the notice has to be in writing. In force 3/10/16

(b) allow an application under this rule unless everyone served with the application has had at least seven days in which to make representations, including representations about whether there should be a hearing.

Note [in the Rules]. See also Civil Evidence Act 1995 s 3.

84.29 ***Hearsay*** ***Credibility and consistency***

Criminal Procedure Rules 2015 2015/1490 Rule 31.8(1)[1007] This rule applies where a party wants to challenge the credibility or consistency of a person who made a statement which another party wants to introduce as hearsay.

(2) The party who wants to challenge the credibility or consistency of that person must:

(a) serve notice of intention to do so on:

(i) the court officer, and

(ii) the party who served the notice of hearsay evidence

not more than seven days after service of that hearsay evidence notice, and

(b) in the notice, identify any statement or other material on which that party relies.

(3) The party who served the hearsay notice:

(a) may call that person to give oral evidence instead, and

(b) if so, must serve notice of intention to do so on:

(i) the court officer, and

(ii) every party on whom he served the hearsay notice

not more than seven days after service of the notice under paragraph (2).

Note [in the Rules]. Civil Evidence Act 1995 s 5(2) describes the procedure for challenging the credibility of the maker of a statement of which hearsay evidence is introduced. See also section 6 of that Act. The 1995 Act does not allow the introduction of evidence of a previous inconsistent statement otherwise than in accordance with Criminal Procedure Act 1865 s 5-7.

84.30 ***Hearsay*** ***Time limits***

Criminal Procedure Rules 2015 2015/1490 Rule 31.3(4) A defendant served with a notice under paragraph (2) [a notice from the prosecutor, see **84.14**] must:

(a) serve notice of any evidence on which the defendant relies on:[1008]

(i) the court officer, and

(ii) the prosecutor,

as soon as practicable (without waiting for the verdict), and

(b) in the notice, identify that evidence and attach any written statement that has not already been served.

84.31 ***Hearsay*** ***Judicial guidance***

Heron v Plymouth City Council 2009 EWHC 3562 (Admin) High Court H was a persistent shoplifter who targeted security officers and store detectives who sought to stop him etc. The Court imposed an ASBO. Held. Hearsay evidence is admissible and indeed may be of great value. However, magistrates must be careful not to rely upon mere allegation where the subject matter of that allegation is denied. If there is an allegation of an offence, then it must be proved.

84.32 ***Propensity evidence***

Birmingham City Council v Dixon 2009 EWHC 761 (Admin) High Court The Council applied for an ASBO against D and an Interim ASBO was made. Held. There is no reason why evidence showing propensity to behave in an antisocial manner should not be relevant.

84.33 ***Evidence available after the application is served, Admissibility of***

Birmingham City Council v Dixon 2009 EWHC 761 (Admin) High Court The Council applied for an ASBO against D and an Interim ASBO was made. The Council wished to

[1007] The Criminal Procedure (Amendment No 2) Rules 2016 2016/705 para 11(f)(i) removes the requirement that the notice has to be in writing. In force 3/10/16

[1008] The Criminal Procedure (Amendment No 2) Rules 2016 2016/705 para 11(b)(iii) removes the requirement that the notice has to be in writing. In force 3/10/16

adduce evidence that D had committed further acts of antisocial behaviour since the date of the application and while he was subject to the Interim Order. The District Judge ruled the evidence out. Before making an ultimate finding, the District Judge found the existing evidence insufficient to make an ASBO. The Council appealed against the preliminary ruling. Held. The provisions of Criminal Justice Act 2003 about bad character evidence do not apply to ASBO proceedings 'which are civil in nature'. There is no reason why evidence of later conduct showing propensity to behave in an antisocial manner should not be relevant to the question whether D had acted in an antisocial manner during the period covered by the complaint. It is still necessary to prove the allegations that are specified in the complaint itself. Evidence of post-complaint behaviour may assist in proving the allegations contained in the complaint, but it does not of itself enlarge the scope of the complaint. If the complaint is to be enlarged, that must be done by amendment. I would reject the submission that the complaint can itself be substantiated on the basis of later behaviour, even where the behaviour alleged in the complaint has not itself been proved. In the absence of an appropriate amendment to bring in the later behaviour as part of what is alleged in the complaint, it cannot assist in the way contended for by the Council's counsel.

In the present case, there was no application to amend the complaint. Accordingly, the evidence of later behaviour could have only the limited function that I have indicated. Proof of that later behaviour could not of itself enable the complaint to be substantiated. I have concentrated so far on section 1(1)(a), but post-complaint behaviour is also relevant, and plainly so, to the question in section 1(1)(b) whether an order is necessary to protect relevant persons from further antisocial acts. It is obvious that evidence that a defendant had turned over a new leaf or had, for example, become ill or suffered a disabling accident since the period covered by the complaint would be relevant to the question whether an order was necessary. It is equally obvious, in my view, that evidence of further antisocial behaviour since the period covered by the complaint is relevant to the need for an order. In a case where the antisocial behaviour during the period covered by the complaint was relatively limited, evidence of post-complaint behaviour might indeed tip the balance in favour of the need for an order. The Council's counsel was right to submit that more recent evidence may be of particular value in deciding whether an order should be made. The District Judge was wrong to hold that evidence of later behaviour was irrelevant to the questions he had to consider. The Council's appeal is allowed.

Disputes as to facts see the **FACTUAL BASIS FOR SENTENCING** ***Same rules apply when imposing ancillary orders*** para at **57.26**.

General principles about drafting the order

84.34 ***Who should write the draft order?***

R v Guest 2011 EWCA Crim 1542 The Court of Appeal considered an ASBO. Held. It is not appropriate [or] satisfactory that a non-legally qualified police officer, without any real input from counsel on either side, should draft the order.

R v Jackson 2012 EWCA Crim 2602 All too often in the Crown Court prosecuting counsel puts before the judge a proposed SOPO which has not been drafted by him or her but by whatever relevant unit. That unit seems to have been ignoring the decisions of this court as to what is appropriate.

It is essential that prosecuting counsel appreciate that they are responsible for an appropriate SOPO which meets the individual case and provides the necessary protection. It is not right and it certainly is a dereliction of counsel's duty if he or she fails to consider for him or herself when prosecuting what is indeed proportionate. The prosecuting counsel must appreciate that it is their responsibility to put before the judge provisions which are necessary and proportionate and which go no further than are necessary and proportionate to provide for protection in the future. If there is argument it is essential that the judge is referred to the leading authorities.

84.35 ***Order must be tailor-made and proportionate Do not use standard list of prohibitions***

Magistrates' Court Sentencing Guidelines 2008, see www.banksr.com Other Matters Guidelines tab page 168 [ASBO section] An order should not impose a 'standard list' of prohibitions, but should identify and prohibit the particular type of antisocial behaviour that gives rise to the necessity of an ASBO. Each separate prohibition must be necessary to protect persons from antisocial behaviour by the subject, and each order must be specifically fashioned to deal with the individual concerned. The order must be proportionate to the legitimate aim pursued and commensurate with the risk guarded against.

B v Chief Constable of Avon and Somerset Constabulary 2000 EWHC 559 (Admin) High Court If the [ASBO] is wider than is necessary for the purposes of protecting the public from serious harm from the defendant, the order will not meet the requirements of Crime and Disorder Act 1998 s 2(4) and will fall foul of the Convention requirement that the means employed, if restrictive of guaranteed rights, should be necessary and proportionate to the legitimate ends towards which they are directed.

R v Collard 2004 EWCA Crim 1664, 2005 1 Cr App R (S) 34 (p 155) D pleaded to seven counts of making indecent photographs or pseudo-photographs of children (1-7) and 16 counts of possession of indecent photographs or pseudo-photographs of children (8-24). Held. When a court makes a Restraining Order, its terms must be tailored to meet the danger that the offender presents. It must not be oppressive, it must be proportionate. Order varied.

R v McGrath 2005 EWCA Crim 353, 2 Cr App R (S) 85 (p 525) The terms of an ASBO must be clear, as the sanction for breach may well be imprisonment. They must be justified and commensurate. [Where the term is too wide] the party at risk of imprisonment should not be left to the discretion of the prosecution whether to prefer charges.

W v Acton Youth Court 2005 EWHC 954 (Admin) High Court The prohibitions can be very wide. Many prohibit what would be criminal behaviour but not all. Each condition imposed must be considered against this question: 'Does it appear to the court that this condition in these terms, taken together with other conditions to be imposed, is necessary to protect persons in any place in England and Wales from further antisocial acts by the defendant?' The words 'in these terms' underline that it may be necessary to consider not simply whether a particular kind of prohibition is necessary but how broad it needs to be.

R v Boness 2005 EWCA Crim 2395, 2006 1 Cr App R (S) 120 (p 690) para 29 Any order should be tailor-made for the individual offender, not designed on a word processor for use in every case, and the court must ask itself, when considering any specific order prohibiting the offender from doing something, 'Is this order necessary to protect persons in any place in England and Wales from further antisocial acts by him?'...para 38 The terms of the order must also be proportionate in the sense that they must be commensurate with the risk to be guarded against. This is particularly important where an order may interfere with an ECHR right protected by Human Rights Act 1998, e.g. articles 8, 10 and 11. Just because an ASBO must run for a minimum of 2 years, it does not follow that each and every prohibition within a particular order must endure for the life of the order. It may be necessary to include a prohibition which would need to be amended or removed after a period of time, for example when the offender starts work (provided that at least one prohibition is ordered to have effect for at least 2 years). We think that bail conditions provide a useful analogy. A defendant may be prohibited from contacting directly or indirectly a prosecution witness or entering a particular area near the alleged victim's home. The aim is to prevent the defendant trying to tamper with witnesses or committing a further offence. But the police do not have to wait until he has tampered or committed a further offence and thus committed a very serious offence. If he breaks the conditions even without intending to tamper, he is in breach of his bail

conditions and liable to be remanded in custody. The victim has the comfort of knowing that if the defendant enters the prescribed area, the police can be called to take action. The victim does not have to wait for the offence to happen again.
Note: Unfortunately the paragraph numbers in the Criminal Appeal Reports are one lower than in the official transcript. The paragraph numbers listed here are from the official transcript. Ed.
CPS v T 2006 EWHC 728 (Admin) High Court Each prohibition must be proportionate and commensurate with the risk to be guarded against.
R v Hemsley 2010 EWCA Crim 225 D was made subject to a SOPO. Held. It is essential that such orders are clear on their face, capable of being complied with without unreasonable difficulty and/or the assistance of a third party and free of risk of unintentional breach.
R v Smith and Others 2011 EWCA Crim 1772, 2012 1 Cr App R (S) 82 (p 468) The flexibility of the order must not lead draftsmen to an inventiveness which stores up trouble for the future. The prohibitions must not be vague nor conflict with the other rules applicable to the defendant. The twin tests are necessity and clarity. A subtest of necessity is proportionality. The real risk of unintentional breach must be avoided. When considering the imposition of SOPOs, it must be remembered that a defendant convicted of sexual offences is likely to be subject to at least three other relevant regimes. No SOPO is needed if it merely duplicates such a regime. Nor must a SOPO interfere with such a regime. The following regimes must be considered: a) the sex offender notification rules, b) disqualification from working with children, and c) licence on release from prison.
R v Parsons and Morgan 2017 EWCA Crim 2163, 2018 1 Cr App R (S) 43 (p 307) P and M appealed their SHPOs. Held. para 5 Any SHPO must be tailored to the facts. There is no one size that fits all factual circumstances.
R v Khan 2018 EWCA Crim 1472, 2 Cr App R (S) 53 (p 426) The Court of Appeal considered a Criminal Behaviour Order. Held. para 14 It is essential that the guidance in *R v Boness* 2005 EWCA Crim 2395, 2006 1 Cr App R (S) 120 (p 690) at paras 19-23[1009] should be borne in mind (see above). The terms of the order must be precise and capable of being understood by the offender. para 15 Because an order must be precise and capable of being understood by the offender, a court should ask itself before making an order, "are the terms of this order clear so that the offender will know precisely what it is that he is prohibited from doing?" Prohibitions should be reasonable and proportionate; realistic and practical; and be in terms which make it easy to determine and prosecute a breach.
See also: *R v Guest* 2011 EWCA Crim 1542 (Late plea to making (×4) and possessing indecent photographs of a child, and possession of extreme pornographic images (×3). Held. SOPO was disproportionate and oppressive. His conduct was only aimed at females, whereas the order prohibited contact etc. with any person under the age of 16. Order amended.)
Note: The above cases related to ASBOs and SOPOs but the principles seem to be of general application. Ed.

84.36 *Precise and capable of being understood, Order must be*

Magistrates' Court Sentencing Guidelines 2008, see www.banksr.com Other Matters Guidelines tab page 168 The court should avoid making compliance very difficult through the imposition of numerous prohibitions, and those that will cause great disruption to the subject should be considered with particular care. It is advisable to make an order for a specific period, and when considering the duration of an order imposed on a youth, the potential for the subject to mature may be a relevant factor.

[1009] It looks as if these paragraphs are not the ones the Court was referring to. It looks as if they are those listed in the case summary above.

B v Chief Constable of Avon and Somerset Constabulary 2000 EWHC 559 (Admin) High Court If anyone is the subject of a prohibitory court order for breach of which he is liable to severe punishment, that person is entitled to know, clearly and unambiguously, what conduct he must avoid to comply with the order. Such clarity is essential for him. It is scarcely less essential for any authority responsible for policing compliance with the order and for any court called upon to decide whether the terms of the order have been broken. The order should be expressed in simple terms, easily understood even by those who, like the appellant, are not very bright.
R v Boness 2005 EWCA Crim 2395, 2006 1 Cr App R (S) 120 (p 690) An ASBO must obviously be precise and capable of being understood by the offender. A court should ask itself before making an order: 'Are the terms of this order clear so that the offender will know precisely what it is that he is prohibited from doing?'
CPS v T 2006 EWHC 728 (Admin) High Court D, aged 13, was made subject to an ASBO which prohibited him from, amongst other things, 'acting in an antisocial manner in the city of Manchester'. Held. Each prohibition must be precise and must be targeted at the individual and at the type of antisocial behaviour it is to prevent. It must be expressed in simple terms so as to be easily understood. The prohibition lacked the essential element of clarity as to what D was and was not permitted to do. Such a wide provision as this without further definition or limitation should never be included in an ASBO again.
M v DPP 2007 EWHC 1032 (Admin) High Court An ASBO should be precise, clear and certain. The terms should be no wider than necessary.
R v Smith and Others 2011 EWCA Crim 1772, 2012 1 Cr App R (S) 82 (p 468) The Court gave guidance about SOPOs. Held. para 5 As to clarity, a convenient analogy is the framing of an injunction in a civil court, which also attracts the sanction of imprisonment. The terms of a SOPO must be sufficiently clear on their face for the defendant, those who have to deal with him in ordinary daily life, and those who have to consider enforcement, to understand without real difficulty or the need for expert legal advice exactly what he can and cannot do. Real risk of unintentional breach must be avoided, *R v Hemsley* 2010 EWCA Crim 225.
R v Parsons and Morgan 2017 EWCA Crim 2163, 2018 1 Cr App R (S) 43 (p 307) P and M appealed their SHPOs. Held. para 5 Any SHPO prohibitions imposed must be clear and realistic. They must be readily capable of simple compliance and enforcement. It is to be remembered that breach of a prohibition constitutes a criminal offence punishable by imprisonment. None of the SHPO terms must be oppressive and, overall, the terms must be proportionate.
See also: *Heron v Plymouth City Council* 2009 EWHC 3562 (Admin) (ASBOs should be clear, comprehensible and enforceable, otherwise they amount to no more than beating the wind. They must be precise and targeted.)
R v Douglas 2011 EWCA Crim 2628 (Order so vague and unworkable. Quashed completely.)
Note: The above cases related to ASBOs but the principles seem to be of general application. Ed.

Particular individuals

84.37 ***Animal rights activists On the facts, order necessary***
R v Avery and Others 2009 EWCA Crim 2670, 2010 2 Cr App R (S) 33 (p 209) B and six others were either convicted of, or pleaded to, conspiracy to commit blackmail. All the defendants were involved in an animal rights organisation whose primary purpose was to cause a life sciences company, H, to shut down. The animal rights organisation targeted H, individuals and other companies that had dealings with or were associated with H. Those targeted were subjected to various activities including hoax bombs, allegations of paedophilia, demonstrations at staff members' homes, threats of criminal damage to property which were often carried out, threats of physical assault, and threatening and

abusive telephone calls, emails and letters. Companies that were involved in dealings with H were threatened that the actions would continue until they severed all contact with H. The financial consequences of the criminal damage and the interference with company business were estimated at in excess of £20 million. Most of the defendants had a string of previous convictions including criminal damage, public order offences, assault and harassment. All the defendants were sentenced to terms of imprisonment ranging between 8 and 11 years and were made subject to an ASBO which prohibited them all indefinitely from participating in, organising or controlling any demonstration or meeting protesting against animal experimentation, sending any communication to any of the companies named in the schedule to the order, communicating directly or indirectly with any person associated with the business or any of the businesses listed in the schedule. Defence counsel said the orders were unnecessary because it was impossible to say how the sentence of imprisonment might affect the defendants and that their attitudes may well have changed following their release. The Judge said if there was a genuine change of attitudes they could always apply to have the orders varied or discharged on their release. Held. We accept that the right to protest and the right to participate in free debate are important rights, and in almost all circumstances it would be a severe matter to limit the right of an individual lawfully to participate in discussion or demonstrations. However, these circumstances were exceptional.

The Judge was uniquely well placed to assess the gravity of the offence, the part played by each of the defendants, and, most importantly, the need for public protection for those who had been the victims of their conduct. The Judge's assessment was, in our view, overwhelmingly supported by evidence and he was entitled to conclude that the orders should run for an indefinite period of time. The likelihood of a change of attitude following release from prison was slight but there was the safeguard of the right to apply to have the orders varied or discharged on their release from custody should their attitudes change. The fact that the defendants will be prevented from engaging in lawful campaigning is not a basis for the refusal to make an order. The crucial questions are: is the restriction proportionate to the aim to be achieved? Is there a legitimate aim? In this case the legitimate aim is to protect the public and in particular 'the prevention of disorder and crime and the protection of the reputation and rights of others'. For three defendants life was appropriate. For one defendant 5 years, not life.

84.38 ***Drug dealers*** ***On the facts, order unnecessary***

R v Lima 2010 EWCA Crim 284 D pleaded to supplying cannabis. D, aged 24, was a failed asylum seeker from Sierra Leone. He was selling wraps of cannabis and was found to be in possession of £30 in cash and two small bags of skunk cannabis. A further stash was discovered elsewhere which included 20 further bags of cannabis. D had been convicted of supplying cannabis or possessing cannabis with intent on seven previous occasions. A witness for the prosecution gave hearsay evidence that drug dealers in general constituted a nuisance in the streets around the market but did not specifically identify D as one of them. The Judge said D was a regular dealer and was without status in this country so was liable to automatic deportation in light of the sentence that he had in mind, although he would have recommended D's removal as a potential detriment to this country. The Judge also considered the imposition of an ASBO without giving notice to D or his counsel. D was sentenced to 18 months' imprisonment, was recommended for deportation and was given an ASBO. Held. The ASBO was simply not warranted. It was not shown that it was necessary for the protection of the public from antisocial behaviour and the procedure followed was unsatisfactory. It was wrong in principle to pass the order. ASBO quashed.

84.39 ***Speeding dangerously, Those*** ***Magistrate entitled to decline to order***

R (Gosport Borough Council) v Fareham Magistrates' Court 2006 EWHC 3047 (Admin) High Court. M was the owner of a jet-ski. Complaints were made that he had been riding it at speed, circling buoys and riding through the wash of a ferry. The

Council applied for an ASBO. Witness statements did not identify any individual who was caused harassment, alarm or distress, or that there were any swimmers in the water at the time. The Magistrate said M had acted immaturely and irresponsibly when dealing with the authorities, who were trying to regulate the use of power craft in that area, but he was not satisfied so that he was sure that M's activities had caused, or were likely to cause, harassment, alarm and distress. The Magistrate was therefore not satisfied that there were grounds to make an ASBO. Held. It had not been established to the criminal standard of proof that M's behaviour on any of the relevant days had actually caused or had been likely to cause harassment, alarm and distress to one or more of the persons not of the same household as himself. Where it cannot be shown that a potential victim was present, section 1(1)(a) is not complied with. The Magistrate was entitled to refuse the application.

84.40 ***Thieves On the facts, order necessary***
R v Vittles 2004 EWCA Crim 1089, 2005 1 Cr App R (S) 8 (p 31) D pleaded to a specimen count of theft, driving whilst disqualified and driving with no insurance. He asked for 12 thefts and three attempted thefts to be taken into account. The thefts were from cars to support his heavy drug use. Frequent thefts were from US servicemen's cars near an air base. He had stolen over £3,500 worth of goods. His record was terrible and was predominantly about similar thefts from vehicles. He was sentenced to 3 years 10 months. An ASBO with a geographical restriction for a particular District Council was imposed. Held. Exceptionally an ASBO was appropriate because of the vulnerable US victims specifically targeted. This was notwithstanding the substantial prison sentence. However, 5 years not life.
See also: *R v McGrath* 2005 EWCA Crim 353, 2 Cr App R (S) 85 (p 525) (Broke into a car. Aged 25. 112 convictions, mostly for dishonesty. ASBO was only just necessary.)
See also the ***Car Parks*** para at **84.45**.

Drafting particular terms

84.41
Warning The fact that a prohibition is or is not suitable in a reported case does not necessarily mean the same decision will be made in another case. When considering these cases it is important to remember the offences which the defendant was involved in and the preventive order that was involved. Each case will depend critically on its own facts. Some of the cases relate to repealed orders and that may be relevant. Ed.

84.42 ***Abusive, threatening or aggressive behaviour etc.***
JSB ASBO Guide for the Judiciary 2007 Appendix 2, Valid prohibitions, see www.banksr.com Other Matters Other Documents tab ASBOs
Note: The JSB guidance is old. Hopefully it will be updated soon. Ed.

Type of antisocial behaviour	Possible prohibitions	Comment
Threatening, abusive behaviour particularly when directed to public servants such as social workers, hospital staff or housing officers	Not to go within a specific distance of the offices of the relevant departments. Not to approach staff of the departments.	If included in a prohibition, the term 'antisocial behaviour' requires further definition or limitation so as to provide clarity to the defendant. Any prohibition relating to the commission of further 'acts causing harassment, alarm or distress' would not be appropriate without further limitation: *CPS v T* 2006 EWHC 728 (Admin).

Type of antisocial behaviour	Possible prohibitions	Comment
Persistent drunken, abusive behaviour within an identifiable area or neighbourhood	An order including prohibitions such as: Not to consume alcohol in a public place (defined if appropriate). Not to leave an identified property during prescribed periods of the day. Not to meet identified individuals.	Prevention is best achieved through prohibitions which are comparable to bail conditions, non-association, curfews, keeping out of defined areas. Care needs to be exercised over the extent and duration of prohibitions such as curfews. See *R (Lonergan) v Lewes Crown Court* 2005 EWHC 457 (Admin).

R v Davies 2008 EWCA Crim 3021 D pleaded to driving without due care. In 2007, D's brother was convicted of raping V's daughter. Nine months later, D drove his white van close behind V's car. V pulled over so D could drive past, which he did. V waited but D stopped further on. V was again following D who was driving slowly and braking. V's daughter, who was in the car, who was not the rape victim, screamed. D then waited at a junction and when V turned right D followed her. When D stopped, V 'drove round to him' and D drove towards her. V was forced to brake and reverse. Her daughter and her daughter's friend started crying. D drove off and the police were called. On arrest D said, "You can put me on life row, I'll kill her if she does my head in." In interview he agreed there was animosity towards V's family. He was fined £165 and an ASBO was made prohibiting D deliberately doing an act to or towards named members of V's family, to cause alarm, distress or fear etc. for 2 years. Held. The Judge was entitled to conclude V's family needed protection. The order was not too broad or too vague. It was not preventing merely criminal acts. The order only applied to deliberate acts so did not apply to inadvertent ones. It also only applied to acts which caused alarm, distress or fear. Therefore the order was sufficiently clear. The order was necessary and appropriate.

84.43 ***Abusive behaviour, Persistent drunken***

JSB ASBO Guide for the Judiciary 2007 Appendix 2, Valid prohibitions, see www.banksr.com Other Matters Other Documents tab ASBOs

Type of antisocial behaviour	Possible prohibitions	Comment
Persistent drunken, abusive behaviour within an identifiable area or neighbourhood	An order including prohibitions such as: Not to consume alcohol in a public place (defined if appropriate). Not to leave an identified property during prescribed periods of the day. Not to meet identified individuals.	Prevention is best achieved through prohibitions which are comparable to bail conditions, non-association, curfews, keeping out of defined areas. Care needs to be exercised over the extent and duration of prohibitions such as curfews. See *R (Lonergan) v Lewes Crown Court* 2005 EWHC 457 (Admin).

84.44 ***Begging***

JSB ASBO Guide for the Judiciary 2007 Appendix 2, Valid prohibitions, see www.banksr.com Other Matters Other Documents tab ASBOs

Type of antisocial behaviour	Possible prohibitions	Comment
Begging, particularly aggressive pursuit of donations where connected to drug misuse	The order might include a prohibition of begging or loitering for the purpose of begging in a clearly defined area. Consider a prohibition of entry into a defined area subject to controlled exceptions e.g. to attend drug rehabilitation treatment.	Caution should be exercised over prohibitions which apply over wide areas. Although the risk exists that the individual will relocate to beg in another area, wide area prohibitions may be disproportionate. Note the availability of Intervention Orders under Drugs Act 2005.

84.45 ***Car parks***

R v Boness 2005 EWCA Crim 2395, 2006 1 Cr App R (S) 120 (p 690) D was a persistent prolific offender and had admitted to drug misuse. There were three main aspects to his antisocial behaviour: threatening behaviour (two incidents), vehicle crime (three incidents) and other offences of dishonesty such as burglary and theft (three incidents and other incidents of handling stolen goods). On the other hand he was being sentenced to a custodial sentence of 3 years' detention and was thus subject to a period on licence and subject to recall or return to custody. D was prohibited from 'Entering any public car park within the Basingstoke and Deane Borough Council area, except in the course of lawful employment'.

It was submitted that: a) it was far from clear that it was necessary to make an ASBO in respect of D, b) the antecedent information does not state whether any of the vehicle crimes committed by the appellant took place in a public car park. However, it is submitted that it could sensibly be argued that a person intent on committing vehicle crime is likely to be attracted to car parks. The prohibition as drafted does not appear to allow the offender to park his own vehicle in a public car park or, for example, to be a passenger in a vehicle driven into a public car park in the course of a shopping trip. Thus, in the absence of evidence showing that the appellant committed vehicle crime in car parks, there would appear to be a question mark over whether the prohibition is proportional, particularly as the car park prohibition seems to be drafted with a view to allowing the appellant to ride a motorcycle. If the Court contemplated the lawful use of a motorbike as an activity which the appellant could pursue, then this prohibition would significantly limit the places he might be able to park it. It is of note that in *R v McGrath* 2005 the Court of Appeal held a similar prohibition to be too wide, although it covered a much larger geographical area. Held. We agree with both submissions. Even if the order was necessary to prevent antisocial behaviour by the appellant, it was not proportionate.

See also: *R v McGrath* 2005 EWCA Crim 353, 2 Cr App R (S) 85 (p 525) (Car thief being banned from Hertfordshire, Bedfordshire and Buckinghamshire car parks was unnecessarily draconian. He would not be able to use a supermarket car park.)

See also the ***Thieves On the facts, order necessary*** para at **84.40**.

84.46 ***Car racing***

JSB ASBO Guide for the Judiciary 2007 Appendix 2, Valid prohibitions, see www.banksr.com Other Matters Other Documents tab ASBOs

Type of antisocial behaviour	Possible prohibitions	Comment
Car racing on public roads, common land or on play area	Prohibitions which aim to curtail involvement in the activity are better than those which restate a pre-existing offence e.g. not to drive on land not forming part of the road. So include: Not to congregate with others to race motor cars. Not to associate with named persons (others known to race cars).	Courts have been criticised for imposing orders on persistent offenders in order to increase the potential punishment. The order must be justified on preventative grounds.

R v Boness 2005 EWCA Crim 2395, 2006 1 Cr App R (S) 120 (p 690) If a court wishes to make an order prohibiting a group of youngsters from racing cars or motorbikes on an estate or driving at excessive speed (antisocial behaviour for those living on the estate), the order should not (normally) prohibit driving whilst disqualified. It should prohibit, for example, the offender whilst on the estate from taking part in, or encouraging, racing or driving at excessive speed. It might also prevent the group from congregating with named others in a particular area of the estate. Such an order gives those responsible for enforcing order on the estate the opportunity to take action to prevent the antisocial conduct, it is to be hoped, before it takes place. Neighbours can alert the police, who will not have to wait for the commission of a particular criminal offence. The ASBO will be breached not just by the offender driving but by his giving encouragement by being a passenger or a spectator. It matters not for the purposes of enforcing the ASBO whether he has or has not a driving licence entitling him to drive.

84.47 *Child contact prohibitions Is the order appropriate?*

R v Hepworth 2012 EWCA Crim 48 D pleaded to two counts of sexual activity with a child. He met the victim at a train station and befriended her. They went to his house, where she stayed the night. They had consensual intercourse. He appealed his SOPO. Held. Adopting the proposed draft in *R v Smith* 2011 EWCA Crim 1772, 2012 1 Cr App R (S) 82 (p 468), the prohibitions were: a) using the Internet to contact or attempt to contact any female known or believed to be under the age of 16, b) having any unsupervised contact of any kind with any female under the age of 16, other than i) such as is inadvertent and not reasonably avoidable in the course of lawful daily life, or ii) with the consent of the child's parent or guardian, who has knowledge of his convictions. 10-year SOPO not indefinite.

R v Horn 2014 EWCA Crim 653 D pleaded to child sex image offences. About half of the 90 videos were Level 4 or 5. Some involved the rape of children aged as young as 6. D was a deputy headmaster of a primary school with specific responsibilities for child protection. The pre-sentence report said he was extremely remorseful and distressed. There was an assessment of a low risk of further offending. Held. There was no suggestion he had assaulted any children in his care. The low risk assessment related to image offences and not contact offences. The prohibition not to contact a child likely to be aged under 16 and having unsupervised contact with a child aged under 16 with the consent of the child's parents or guardian was quashed.

R v TS 2014 EWCA Crim 1848 D was convicted of sexual assault. He and his family lived opposite V, a 12-year-old girl. He was friendly with her and one day he stroked her bottom and thigh. The girl left. D was aged 51 and had only a caution for ABH in 2007. He had an IQ of 50 and it was possible he found it difficult to cope. He was given an 8-month suspended sentence. The SOPO said D could not have unsupervised contact with anyone under 16 nor undertake employment where he might have such unsupervised contact. Held. These terms were unnecessary and disproportionate.

R v Jones 2014 EWCA Crim 1859, 2015 1 Cr App R (S) 9 (p 68) D pleaded (full credit) to making indecent photos of a child (×10) and possession of indecent photos of a child. On D's laptop there were around 30 videos at Levels 1-4 and six cartoons and images at Level 5. One Level 4 video was of a girl of around 11 being penetrated anally to ejaculation. D was aged 64 at sentence. He had two previous convictions for similar offences, the last being in 2006 (custody). D was diagnosed with a 'disorder of sexual preference' but did not meet the criteria for paedophilia. The pre-sentence report noted that D's behaviour was part of an emerging pattern and not an escalation of behaviour. It also mentioned that D had never engaged in sexual activity with a child and identified research indicating that child pornography-only offenders have low rates of future contact sexual offences. Therefore D posed a low risk of carrying out contact sexual offences and he had also voluntarily removed his access to the Internet. The Judge imposed 2 years' imprisonment and a 10-year SOPO restricting D's Internet usage and prohibiting D from having any unsupervised contact with children aged under 16 other than in the presence of their parent or guardian who knew about his sexual convictions. Held. In the absence of an identifiable risk of contact offences, a prohibition on unsupervised contact with children aged under 16 cannot be justified. That element of the SOPO quashed.

See also: *R v Wille* 2012 EWCA Crim 1599 (Digital and oral sex with child. Abuse of trust. Good character. The term not to associate with those aged under 18 without full disclosure etc. was oppressive and not necessary. Term quashed.)

R v Juneidi 2014 EWCA Crim 996 Pleaded to seven indecent images offences. Pre-sentence report found no physical risk to children, but a worrying sexual interest in them. Term prohibited seeking employment in which he was likely to come into contact with children aged under 18, without permission of an officer. Employment prohibition was unnecessary in light of the automatic restrictions placed upon him by the ISA [Disclosure and Barring Service].

Old cases: *R v Hemsley* 2010 EWCA Crim 225 (One term was unnecessarily wide and was capable of prohibiting the defendant from working in any shop, or sending a Christmas card to a family member aged under 16. Another would arguably prevent the defendant from attending church or a football match. The terms were quashed.)

84.48 ***Child contact prohibitions Is the order appropriate? Are the notification requirements sufficient?***

R v Smith and Others 2011 EWCA Crim 1772, 2012 1 Cr App R (S) 82 (p 468) The Court gave guidance about SOPOs. Held. para 25 i) [Child prohibitions] must be justified as required beyond the restrictions placed upon the defendant by [what is now the Disclosure and Barring Service]. If there is a real risk that [the defendant] may undertake some activity outside the ISA prohibitions, then such a term may be justified. Otherwise it is not. What is covered by the Safeguarding Vulnerable Groups Act 2006 needs examination in each case. The key provisions are to be found in section 5 and Schedule 4 Part 1, which defines regulated activities relating to children. Generally speaking, para 2 prevents the defendant from engaging in any form of teaching, training or instruction of children, any form of care, advice, guidance or therapy, and from acting as a driver for children's activities. That will cover most unpaid as well as formal paid occupations which carry a risk of contact offences. It will for example cover football or other sports clubs and youth groups. We suggest that judges should ordinarily require the Crown to justify an application for a SOPO term relating to activity with children by demonstrating what the risk is which is not already catered for by the Safeguarding Vulnerable Groups Act 2006.

R v Sokolowski and Another 2017 EWCA Crim 1903, 1 Cr App R (S) 30 (p 216) D pleaded to making indecent photographs. Held. para 6(iii) Particular care must be taken when considering whether prohibitions on contact with children are really necessary; although such orders may be necessary to prevent the defendant from seeking out children for sexual purposes. Where a defendant is convicted of viewing child pornography, an SHPO should only contain provisions preventing contact, or permitting only supervised contact, with children where there is a real risk that the offending will progress to contact offences. It is not enough for the prosecution to assert, or for the court to assume, that such provisions are necessary on the safety-first principle, irrespective of how remote or fanciful the risk of such progression might be. Even when provisions are necessary, they must still be proportionate in their scope, see *R v Smith and Others* 2011 at para 22-24 and *R v Lewis* 2016 EWCA Crim 1020, 2017 1 Cr App R (S) 2 (p 5) at para 10.

(iv) A person subject to an SHPO is automatically subject to notification requirements. An SHPO must operate in tandem with the statutory notification scheme. It must not conflict with the notification requirements; and it is not normally a legitimate use of an SHPO to use it simply to extend the notification requirements.

See also: *R v Martino* 2017 EWCA Crim 2605 (Plea to 306 Category A images, 715 Category B images and over 81,750 Category C images with some moving images. Pre-sentence report said low risk of contact offences. Judge said there may still be a very small risk. Held. That was not a proper basis for child contact provisions, which we remove.)

84.49 ***Child contact prohibitions Appropriate form of words, The***

Judicial College's Crown Court Compendium Part II Sentencing June 2018 page 7-21

11. The Examples on the next page are based on those approved by the CACD in *R v Smith and Others* 2011 EWCA Crim 1772, 2012 1 Cr App R (S) 82 (p 468) and subsequent cases. However, it must be remembered that the order should be tailored to the individual, and that prohibitions on computer use should reflect current technology. That was particularly so in relation to risk management monitoring software, cloud storage and encryption software. See *R v Parsons and Morgan* 2017 EWCA Crim 2163, 2018 1 Cr App R (S) 43 (p 307) as to guidance on prohibitions containing such technology.

Example 2: Contact with children

The defendant is prohibited from having any unsupervised contact or communication of any kind with any female/male/child under the age of 16/18, other than:

(i) such as is inadvertent and not reasonably avoidable in the course of lawful daily life, or

(ii) with the consent of the child's parent or guardian (who has knowledge of his convictions) and with the express approval of Social Services for the area.

This order will last until {specify}/indefinitely.

Example 3: Living with children

The defendant is prohibited from:

1. living in the same household as any male/female/child under the age of 16/18 unless with the express approval of Social Services for the area;

2. having any unsupervised contact or communication of any kind with any male/female/child under the age of 16/18, other than:

(i) such as is inadvertent and not reasonably avoidable in the course of lawful daily life, or

(ii) with the consent of the child's parent or guardian (who has knowledge of his convictions) and with the express approval of Social Services for the area.

This order will last until {specify}/indefinitely.

R v Smith and Others 2011 EWCA Crim 1772, 2012 1 Cr App R (S) 82 (p 468) In cases where it really is necessary to impose a prohibition on contact with children (of whatever age) it is essential to include a saving for incidental contact such as is inherent in everyday life. SOPOs which prohibit the defendant from activities which are likely to bring him into contact with children must be justified as required beyond the restrictions placed upon the defendant by [what is now the Disclosure and Barring Service].

R v Neish 2012 EWCA Crim 62 LCJ D was convicted of sexual activity with a child (×3) and indecent assault. He received a SOPO. Held. The purposes of the order could be fully achieved by substituting a more precise and concise order. D was prohibited from:

a) going to, or remaining at, any address (including the address at which he resides) or place (other than a public place at which other adult members of the public are ordinarily present and are actually present) at which any female child whom he knows or believes to be under the age of 16 resides or is present unless i) the child is accompanied at all times by a person aged 18 years or more who has not been convicted of a sexual offence, an offence of indecency, or any offence against a child, and ii) the child's parent or legal guardian is aware of D's previous convictions and has given express permission for the appellant to go to, or remain at, the address or place while the child is present, or b) using any video, digital or photographic equipment, mobile telephones capable of storing pictures, or any other equipment knowingly to capture images of any female child under the age of 16 years.

R v Jackson 2012 EWCA Crim 2602 D pleaded to voyeurism, indecent photographs of a child and possession of extreme photographs. D was prohibited, among other matters, from working where a child aged under 16 worked. He appealed his SOPO. Held. The SOPO was, in many respects, entirely disproportionate to the offences D had committed. There was no suggestion that D had ever caused any problems outside his home. There has never been any suggestion of molestation of any sort or sexual advances to any child outside D's home. The prohibition relating to employment was unnecessary and disproportionate. The reference to 'persons under 18' was not suitable. We also substitute for an excessive term, 'Having any unsupervised contact of any kind with anyone under the age of 16 other than i) one such as is inadvertent and not reasonably avoidable in the course of lawful daily life; or ii) with the consent of the child's parent or guardian who has knowledge of his convictions.'

R v MF 2012 EWCA Crim 2645 D was given a five-paragraph set of prohibitions re children. Held. We substitute, 'The defendant is prohibited from having any unsupervised contact or communication with any person under the age of 16 other than a) such as is inadvertent and not reasonably avoidable in the course of lawful daily life, b) with the consent of the child's parent or guardian who has knowledge of his convictions, or c) such contact with his daughter as may be permitted by any court having jurisdiction to do so.'

R v PE 2013 EWCA Crim 1197 D pleaded to sexual assault of his step-granddaughter. He appealed his SOPO. Held. The order was to an extent vague, overly discursive and confusing. We substitute, 'D is prohibited from having any unsupervised contact of any kind with any female under the age of 16 other than: a) such as is inadvertent and not reasonably avoidable in the course of lawful daily life, or b) with the consent of the child's parent and guardian who has knowledge of his conviction.'

R v Angell 2014 EWCA Crim 1382, 2 Cr App R (S) 80 (p 631) D was recalled to prison and a SOPO was imposed preventing him from having any article etc. about the care and nurturing of children aged under 16. Police searched D's house, finding pregnancy and baby magazines and also soiled nappies. D pleaded to breaching the SOPO, receiving a 2-year community order. 11 months later, police found unused and clean nappies, baby cream and wipes. D was aged 63 and, in addition to breaching the SOPO before, had convictions for several sex offences against children. One was for unlawfully detaining a girl aged 13. The pre-sentence report said he had no experience of intimate relationships, but said he had a desire to look after children. Further, D could not accept the risks he presented, having no insight into his behaviour. He deliberately breached the SOPO, saying he would only abide by it if and when he had a child himself to look after which would be as a result of a 'sinister relationship' or an abduction. Held. His behaviour was related to some bizarre and sinister obsession. *Obiter* The condition [about articles] was too widely drawn. It is important to discourage any act which might foster or encourage D's obsession. However, it was difficult to see how an order prohibiting possession of entirely respectable child-rearing manuals or baby products could protect the public from serious harm. We think this condition should be reconsidered after an application [to vary].

R v W 2015 EWCA Crim 434 D was convicted of rapes of children aged under 13 and other sex offences. He was sentenced to 20 years and given a SOPO. Held. The SOPO was necessary, but it was too draconian. We substitute, 'W is prohibited from 1) having any unsupervised contact or communication of any kind with any female under the age of 16, whether or not under supervision from a person registered with the ISA [Disclosure and Barring Service] who is capable of supervising other persons, other than: a) such as is inadvertent and not reasonably avoidable in the course of lawful everyday life; or b) except in the presence of, and with the consent of, the child's parents or guardian (who has knowledge of his convictions).'
For prohibition 2), see **84.51**.
R v Parsons and Morgan 2017 EWCA Crim 2163, 2018 1 Cr App R (S) 43 (p 307) P appealed his SHPO. Held. para 74 As P's interest was in female children, we confine the prohibition to female children.
See also: *R v Davies* 2012 EWCA Crim 1633 (Plea to grooming. Began relationship with V, aged 15 years and 11 months, who was a vulnerable resident in a care home, managed by his partner's mother. Aged 25 at appeal. Restriction preventing D 'allowing any female child under 16 into his or any residence where he may stay unsupervised' was unnecessary and disproportionate. Order amended to permit seeing his daughter.)
R v Fryer 2014 EWCA Crim 775 (D pleaded to sexual activity with a child. V was aged 15. D was a long-standing family friend. They developed a full sexual relationship and V became pregnant. The Judge imposed a SOPO prohibiting him from, among other things, having any unsupervised contact of any kind with a person under the age of 16 other than inadvertent contact or with the child's parent/guardian's consent. Held. There was no suggestion that D took an interest in boys. Order amended to prohibit unsupervised contact with any female aged under 16 (other than inadvertent or with the child's parent's/guardian's consent).
R v H 2015 EWCA Crim 947 D was convicted of two sexual assaults on a younger male relative. He was given a SOPO which prohibited him from a) using any social networking site including Facebook, and b) having or using any device which had a webcam facility. Held. The condition would make it difficult for D to use any computer or other technical device. We substitute:
'2 Using any device capable of accessing the Internet unless (a) it has the capacity to retain and display the history of use and (b) the offender makes the device available on request for inspection by a police officer.
3 Using any device fitted with a camera to communicate via the Internet with any person unless (a) it has the capacity to retain and display the history of use and (b) the offender makes the device available on a request for inspection by a police officer.
4 Deleting the history referred to in either restriction 2 or 3 without the written permission of the Chief Constable of the police force for the area in which he is residing at the time.
5 Using any device by means of the Internet or otherwise to knowingly communicate with children under the age of 16 years by any means whatsoever.
6 Visiting any Internet site, including Internet chat rooms, specifically intended to be for the use of children under the age of 16 years.
7 Possessing any device capable of storing digital images unless he makes it available for inspection by a police officer and subject to a condition that it has the capacity to retain and display a history of its use.'
R v Hussain 2016 EWCA Crim 1017 (Two counts of sexual activity with a child. Defendant, D, now aged 26. Child, V, then aged 14. D was a friend of V's aunt. D has an extensive family. Held. Total ban on unsupervised access too wide. Limited to contacting the victim and seeking employment which might allow unsupervised contact with children under 16.)

84.50 ***Child contact prohibitions*** ***The appropriate age for prohibitions is 16***
R v Smith and Others 2011 EWCA Crim 1772, 2012 1 Cr App R (S) 82 (p 468) The Court gave guidance about SOPOs. Held. para 21 Any provision in a SOPO must be tailored to the necessity to prevent sexual offending which causes serious harm to others. The majority of offences relating to children are committed only when the child is under the age of 16. The exceptions are offences committed under Sexual Offences Act 2003 s 16-19 against those in respect of whom the defendant stands in a position of trust, as defined in section 21, together with family offences under sections 25 and 26. If the risk is genuinely of these latter offences, prohibitions on contact with children under 18 may be justified. Otherwise, if contact with children needs to be restricted, it should relate to those under 16, not under 18.
R v Jackson 2012 EWCA Crim 2602 D pleaded to voyeurism, indecent photographs of a child and possession of extreme photographs. Held. The reference to 'persons under 18' was not suitable. We substitute for an excessive term, 'Having any unsupervised contact of any kind with anyone under the age of 16 other than i) one such as is inadvertent and not reasonably avoidable in the course of lawful daily life; or ii) with the consent of the child's parent or guardian who has knowledge of his convictions.'
R v RM 2012 EWCA Crim 2805 D pleaded to causing a child aged under 13 to engage in sexual activity (×3). He was the maternal grandfather of the 7- or 8-year-old victim. A Sexual Offences Prevention Order was made prohibiting him from, among other things, allowing etc. a female aged under 18 into his residence or visiting or being present in a building etc. with a female aged under 18. The Sexual Offences Prevention Order was to run until further order. Held. Adopting the suggested formula in *R v Smith* 2011 EWCA Crim 1772, the age restriction on females aged under 18 would be reduced to 16 and the wording amended to account for inadvertent and reasonable contact.
R v Kimpriktzis 2013 EWCA Crim 734, 2014 1 Cr App R (S) 6 (p 23) D was convicted of eight sex offences relating to when he had oral and anal sex with a 13-year-old boy, V, when he was aged 21. D contacted V on a gay chat line and wore no protection when he knew he was HIV positive. D did not tell the boy that. He was given a SOPO. D was recalled on his licence when, in breach of his SOPO, he advertised items on eBay which would be of interest to children. Police secured amendments to his SOPO. D applied to vary it using forged letters. He pleaded to attempting to pervert the course of justice and was given a 6-month suspended sentence. A new SOPO was made which included a prohibition on child contact for those aged under 17. Held. D was a predatory paedophile. However, following *R v Smith* 2011 EWCA Crim 1772, 2012 1 Cr App R (S) 82 (p 468) the child age in a SOPO prohibition should be 'under 16'.
R v B 2016 EWCA Crim 488 D pleaded to child sex offences against V, who at the time of the offending was aged 14 and when D was aged 21. V was vulnerable. While V's relationship with D continued her relationship with her family deteriorated sharply. When bailed, D ignored a bail term and continued to have sex with V. V wrote supportive letters for D and refused to support the prosecution. The Judge found D had exercised controlling behaviour over V. D received 3 years 7 months. The prosecution asked that the SOPO should prohibit contact until V was aged 18 as V was particularly vulnerable and needed protection. The Judge did so. Held. We too want to protect the victim. However, we see no reason to depart from the clear guidance in *R v Smith* 2011 and have no option but to substitute 'aged 16' for 'aged 18'.
R v Parsons and Morgan 2017 EWCA Crim 2163, 2018 1 Cr App R (S) 43 (p 307) P appealed his SHPO. Held. para 74 We don't interfere with the prohibition restricting the contact to females aged under 18, because of the definition in the SHPO legislation, see **101.4**.
Note: As P's interest was in children it is hard to see what the purpose was of the 16- to 18-year-old prohibition. It would be unfair to P and administratively difficult for the police. The definition was inserted for other reasons, not for determining the age of the other party in prohibitions. Ed.

See also: *R v Juneidi* 2014 EWCA Crim 996 (Pleaded to seven indecent images offences. Pre-sentence report found no physical risk to children, but a worrying sexual interest in them. Term prohibited seeking employment in which he was likely to come into contact with children aged under 18, without permission of an officer. Employment prohibition was unnecessary in light of the automatic restrictions placed upon him by [what is now the Disclosure and Barring Service]).

84.51 *Child contact prohibitions Employment issues*

R v Kimpriktzis 2013 EWCA Crim 734, 2014 1 Cr App R (S) 6 (p 23) D was convicted of eight sex offences relating to when he had oral and anal sex with a 13-year-old boy, V, when D was aged 21. D contacted V on a gay chat line and wore no protection when he knew he was HIV positive. D did not tell the boy that. He was disqualified from working with children and given a SOPO. D was recalled on his licence when, in breach of his SOPO, he advertised items on eBay which would be of interest to children. Police secured amendments to his SOPO. D applied to vary it using forged letters. He pleaded to attempting to pervert the course of justice and was given a 6-month suspended sentence. A new SOPO was made which included a prohibition on undertaking any work, voluntary or paid, which was likely to bring him into contact with any male child save with the written permission of the relevant Chief Constable. The prosecution said that permission might well be withheld. Held. D was a predatory paedophile. The order would prevent D from obtaining any employment. We would not wish to condemn him to living off benefits for life. We will delete that condition. He is subject to his [Disclosure and Barring Service barring] term.

R v W 2015 EWCA Crim 434 D was convicted of rapes of children aged under 13 and other sex offences. He was sentenced to 20 years and given a SOPO. Held. The SOPO was necessary, but it was too draconian. We substitute, 'W is prohibited from 2) making an application for or occupying any employed or voluntary position, whether paid or not, which involves any contact with a female under the age of 16, save as in the exceptions within prohibition 1) [see **84.49**].

See also: *R v Juneidi* 2014 EWCA Crim 996 (Pleaded to seven indecent images offences. Pre-sentence report found no physical risk to children, but a worrying sexual interest in them. Term prohibited seeking employment in which he was likely to come into contact with children aged under 18, without permission of an officer. Employment prohibition was unnecessary in light of the automatic restrictions placed upon him by the Disclosure and Barring Service.)

R v H 2015 EWCA Crim 1105 (Three sex assaults against employee, aged 16, who was staying with H. Touching and rubbing. Aged 48 and no sex previous. H occasionally operated fairground attractions. Clause prohibiting employment which is likely to allow unsupervised access to children aged under 18 deleted and another clause adapted to allow H to do work.)

Old cases: *R v Hemsley* 2010 EWCA Crim 225 (One term was unnecessarily wide and was capable of prohibiting the defendant from working in any shop, or sending a Christmas card to a family member aged under 16. Another would arguably prevent the defendant from attending church or a football match. The terms were quashed.)

84.52 *Criminal activity*

Magistrates' Court Sentencing Guidelines 2008, see www.banksr.com Other Matters Guidelines tab page 168 The police have powers to arrest an individual for any criminal offence, and the court should not impose an order which prohibits the subject from committing an offence if it will not add significantly to the existing powers of the police to protect others from antisocial behaviour by the subject.

R v Boness 2005 EWCA Crim 2395, 2006 1 Cr App R (S) 120 (p 690) A court should be reluctant to impose an order which prohibits an offender from, or merely from, committing a specified criminal offence. The aim of an ASBO is to prevent antisocial behaviour. To prevent it, the police or other authorities need to be able to take action before the antisocial behaviour it is designed to prevent takes place. If, for example, a court is faced by an offender who causes criminal damage by spraying graffiti, the order should be aimed at facilitating action to be taken to prevent graffiti spraying by him and/or his associates before it takes place. An order in clear and simple terms preventing the offender from being in possession of a can of spray paint in a public place gives the police or others responsible for protecting the property an opportunity to take action in advance of the actual spraying and makes it clear to the offender that he has lost the right to carry such a can for the duration of the order. In *R (W) v DPP* 2005 EWHC 1333 (Admin), the Divisional Court held that a clause in an ASBO made for a young offender which prohibited him from committing any criminal offence was plainly too wide and unenforceable. There was a danger that W would not know what a criminal offence was and what was not. It was well established that an order had to be clear and in terms that would enable an individual to know what he could and could not do. A general restriction was not necessary where specific behaviour restrictions were in place. Brooke LJ said (para 8) that, given the offender's previous convictions for theft, a prohibition against committing theft 'might not have been inappropriate'. We have already expressed our reservations about such a prohibition. In *R v Werner* 2004 EWCA Crim 2931, the female defendant had committed a number of offences over a relatively short period of time which involved stealing credit cards, a cheque book and other items from hotel rooms while the occupants were out and using the cards to obtain services and goods. The Judge made an ASBO prohibiting her from entering any hotel, guesthouse, or similar premises anywhere within the Greater London area. It was submitted on D's behalf that this was an inappropriate and improper use of the power because the behaviour it sought to protect the public from was only antisocial in the sense that all criminal offences were antisocial and it was not the sort of behaviour that ASBOs were meant to target. The Court of Appeal declined to express a definitive view on this issue and quashed the order on a different ground, but they did make the following observations. The forms of conduct listed in the *Home Office Guide 2002* page 8 have a direct or indirect impact on the quality of life of people living in the community. They are different in character from offences of dishonesty committed in private against individual victims, distressing though such offences are to the victims. The Court said that it would not like to be taken to say that in no case could offences of this sort attract such an order.

There is another problem with the kind of order in *R v Werner* 2004. In the absence of a system to warn all hotels, guesthouses or similar premises anywhere within the Greater London area, there is no practical way of policing the order. The breach of the ASBO will occur at the same time as the commission of any further offence in a hotel, guesthouse or similar premises. The ASBO achieves nothing, as if she is not to be deterred by the prospect of imprisonment for committing the offence, she is unlikely to be deterred by the prospect of being sentenced for breach of the ASBO. By committing the substantive offence she will have committed the further offence of being in breach of her ASBO, but to what avail? The criminal statistics will show two offences rather than one. If, on the other hand, she 'worked' a limited number of establishments, it would be practical to supervise compliance with the order. The establishments could be put on notice about her and should she enter the premises the police could be called, whether her motive in entering the premises was honest or not.

The court should not impose an order which prohibits an offender from committing a specified criminal offence if the sentence which could be passed following conviction for the offence should be a sufficient deterrent. If following conviction for the offence the offender would be liable to imprisonment, an ASBO would add nothing other than to increase the sentence if the sentence for the offence is less than 5 years' imprisonment. But if the offender is not going to be deterred from committing the offence by a sentence of imprisonment for that offence, it may be thought that the ASBO is not likely further to deter and is therefore not necessary.

M v DPP 2007 EWHC 1032 (Admin) High Court The Youth Court included a term, 'Not to knowingly associate with a person or persons whilst such person or persons are engaged in attempting or conspiring to commit any criminal offence in England or Wales'. The Divisional Court considered whether it was capable of being understood. Held. Even if the clause was to be construed as the Magistrates intended, it would still be subject to the criticism that the prohibition called for an exercise in value judgement on the part of the appellant, who might have to take an instant decision as to whether those with whom he was associated were in the process of attempting to commit a crime, or had reached a stage where they were engaging in a conspiracy. That cannot be right, even on the construction which the Magistrates clearly intended. A clause of this nature is to be avoided just as, if for not entirely the same reasons, prohibitions in ASBOs as to the commission of criminal offences are to be avoided. This clause cannot stand.
Heron v Plymouth City Council 2009 EWHC 3562 (Admin) High Court The Magistrates imposed a condition on H that prohibited him from 'behaving in any way causing or likely to cause harassment, alarm or distress to any person'. H was a persistent shoplifter who targeted security officers and store detectives who sought to stop him etc. Held. This restriction does no more than repeat offences in Public Order Act 1986. It is neither precise nor targeted.
See also: *R (W) v DPP* 2005 EWHC 1333 (Admin) (W was prohibited from 'committing any criminal offence'. That was very plainly too wide. It was invalid and unenforceable. For more detail, see **26.15**.)
Old case: *R v P* 2004 EWCA Crim 287, 2 Cr App R (S) 63 (p 343) (LCJ We are by no means persuaded that the inclusion [of prohibitions against public order and possession of offensive weapon offences] is to be actively discouraged.)
Computer prohibitions see ***Internet/Computer prohibitions*** at **84.73**.

84.53 ***Curfews***
R v Boness 2005 EWCA Crim 2395, 2006 1 Cr App R (S) 120 (p 690) D was a persistent prolific offender and had admitted to drug misuse in the community. He was given 3 years' detention and an ASBO for 5 years which included a curfew. Held. Although curfews can properly be included in an ASBO, we doubt, as does the prosecution, that such an order was necessary in this case. Although the offences of interfering with a motor vehicle and attempted burglary were both committed between 10 pm and midnight on the same evening, there is no suggestion that other offences have been committed at night. Moreover, the author of the pre-sentence report states that D's offending behaviour did not fit a pattern which could be controlled by the use of a curfew order. Even if an ASBO was justified, a 5-year curfew to follow release is not, in our view, proportionate. Order quashed.
See also: *R (Lonergan) v Lewes Crown Court* 2005 EWHC 457 (Admin) (It is advisable for Magistrates' Courts to consider carefully the need for and duration of a curfew provision when making an ASBO.)

84.54 ***Damage, Causing***
R v Boness 2005 EWCA Crim 2395, 2006 1 Cr App R (S) 120 (p 690) D was a persistent prolific offender and had admitted to drug misuse in the community. D was prohibited from 'Doing anything which may cause damage'. The prosecution submitted that this prohibition, even if justified (which is far from clear), is far too wide and asked, "Is [D] prohibited from scuffing his shoes?" Held. We agree.

84.55 ***Demonstrations, Public/Freedom of peaceful assembly***
R v Uddin and Others 2015 EWCA Crim 1918, 2016 1 Cr App R (S) 57 (p 57) Nine defendants were sentenced for violent disorder and other public order offences arising out of a march and a fight near a stall on different days in central London. The defendants were all Sunni Muslims from Luton. A group of men were engaged in Da'wah, proselytising for Islam. Four were given an ASBO prohibiting each from being together or in company with, in any public place while attending any demonstration,

protest or rally, a number of named persons. They were also prohibited from attending a march where notification had not been given or approaching members of the public. Held. It was not disputed that the term engages the appellant defendants' article 10 rights, most obviously perhaps in that their freedom of expression is restricted by the prohibition on approaching members of the public. The Judge's reasoning does not explain how the prohibition reduces the risk of anti-social behaviour on the part of these three appellants so that it can be said to be necessary and proportionate to the risk of antisocial behaviour that would otherwise result from them attending a demonstration, rally or protest. It seems to us immaterial to the later disorder that the march was not authorised, just as the violence and disorder would not have been excused or the offenders' conduct mitigated if it had been. para 54 The term 'approaching members of the public' when attending a demonstration, protest or rally was unjustifiably restrictive. It is an ordinary part of any demonstration to hand out public leaflets, and a major restriction on freedom of expression to prohibit it. And the prohibition would cover such innocent conduct as asking about the nearest underground station to go home. The prohibitions were unjustified and disproportionately restrictive. Parts of them were also unclear.

84.56 ***Demonstrations, Public Political activity***

R v Avery and Others 2009 EWCA Crim 2670, 2010 2 Cr App R (S) 33 (p 209) B and six others were either convicted of or pleaded guilty to conspiracy to commit blackmail. All the defendants were involved in an animal rights organisation whose primary purpose was to cause a life sciences company, H, to shut down. The animal rights organisation targeted H, individuals and other companies that had dealings with or were associated with H. Those targeted were subjected to various activities including hoax bombs, allegations of paedophilia, demonstrations at staff members' homes, threats of criminal damage to property which were often carried out, threats of physical assault, and threatening and abusive telephone calls, emails and letters. Companies that were involved in dealings with H were threatened that the actions would continue until they severed all contact with H. The financial consequences of the criminal damage and the interference with company business were estimated at in excess of £20 million. Most of the defendants had a string of previous convictions including criminal damage, public order offences, assault and harassment. All the defendants were sentenced to terms of imprisonment ranging between 8 and 11 years and were made subject to an ASBO which prohibited them all indefinitely from participating in, organising or controlling any demonstration or meeting protesting against animal experimentation, sending any communication to any of the companies named in the Schedule to the order, communicating directly or indirectly with any person associated with the business or any of the businesses listed in the Schedule. Defence counsel said the orders were unnecessary because it was impossible to say how the sentence of imprisonment might affect the defendants and that their attitudes may well have changed following their release. The Judge said if there was a genuine change of attitudes then they could always apply to have the orders varied or discharged on their release. Held. We accept that the right to protest and the right to participate in free debate are important rights, and in almost all circumstances it would be a severe matter to limit the right of an individual lawfully to participate in discussion or demonstrations. However, these circumstances were exceptional.

The Judge was uniquely well placed to assess the gravity of the offence, the part played by each of the defendants, and, most importantly, the need for public protection for those who had been the victims of their conduct. The Judge's assessment was, in our view, overwhelmingly supported by evidence and he was entitled to conclude that the orders should run for an indefinite period of time. The likelihood of a change of attitude following release from prison was slight but there was the safeguard of the right to apply to have the orders varied or discharged on their release from custody should their attitudes change. The fact that the defendants will be prevented from engaging in lawful campaigning is not a basis for the refusal to make an order. The crucial questions are: is the restriction proportionate to the aim to be achieved? Is there a legitimate aim? In this case the legitimate aim is to protect the public and in particular 'the prevention of disorder and crime and the protection of the reputation and rights of others'. For three defendants, life was appropriate. For one defendant, 5 years not life.

84.57 ***Drug supply***
Example: *R v Hashi and Others* 2014 EWCA Crim 2119, 2015 1 Cr App R (S) 17 (p 135) D pleaded to 12 counts of class A drug supply. Other defendants to similar offences. They were street dealers. The Judge gave them ASBOs. Held. Orders upheld, save the association terms quashed.)

84.58 ***Drug paraphernalia***
R v Briggs 2009 EWCA Crim 1477 D pleaded to making an offer to supply crack cocaine. She had been implicated by an undercover operation to combat street dealing. She was given a community order and an ASBO. One of the terms prohibited her being in possession of drug paraphernalia, including foil, homemade pipes and hypodermic needles unless provided by a registered [drug] worker etc. D was aged 45 with 22 convictions including two for supplying class A drugs. She also had a drug habit. Held. The term was not necessary as a) it would not protect local residents from further offending by D, b) possession of the material would not prevent distress and c) use of the paraphernalia would be a criminal offence so an ASBO would be unnecessary.
See also: *R v Simsek* 2015 EWCA Crim 1268 (*R v Briggs* 2009 applied. Term quashed.)

84.59 ***Educational premises***
JSB ASBO Guide for the Judiciary 2007 Appendix 2, Valid prohibitions, see www.banksr.com Other Matters Other Documents tab ASBOs

Type of antisocial behaviour	Possible prohibitions	Comment
Attending school premises to cause nuisance	Order prohibitions which could include: Not to go to named schools or to go within a defined area around the schools. Not to approach staff or pupils of a named school.	Prohibitions must clearly address the type of behaviour and should prevent the opportunity to cause a nuisance arising in the first place. Delineation of areas should be supported by a map appended to the order.

R v Boness 2005 EWCA Crim 2395, 2006 1 Cr App R (S) 120 (p 690) D was a persistent prolific offender and had admitted to drug misuse in the community. There were three main aspects to his antisocial behaviour: threatening behaviour (two incidents), vehicle crime (three incidents) and other offences of dishonesty such as burglary and theft (three incidents and other incidents of handling stolen goods). He was sentenced to a custodial sentence of 3 years' detention and was thus subject to a period on licence and subject to recall or return to custody. D was prohibited from 'Entering any land or building on the land which forms a part of educational premises except as an enrolled pupil with the agreement of the head of the establishment or in the course of lawful employment'. It was submitted: "It is not clear what information provided the basis for making this prohibition. There is nothing in the appellant's previous offending history which suggests that he engages in antisocial behaviour in educational premises. It is submitted that the term 'educational premises' arguably lacks clarity, for example, does it include teaching hospitals or premises where night classes are held? There also appears to be a danger that the appellant might unwittingly breach the terms of the order were he, for example, to play sport on playing fields associated with educational premises." Held. We agree with this analysis. The order was not necessary and is, in any event, unclear.

84.60 *Employment restrictions*
R v Janes 2016 EWCA Crim 676, 2 Cr App R (S) 27 (p 256) D was convicted of fraud. He overcharged a man in his 80s for gardening work. D was aged 43 and in 2009 was given 2 years for consumer credit offences and money laundering. The Judge said it was pitiless daylight robbery of an elderly man. D was sentenced to 18 months and was given a Criminal Behaviour Order which had the effect of preventing him from touting for business. Held. The order did not stop D working. It just stopped touting. It was appropriate.

84.61 *Fly posting*
JSB ASBO Guide for the Judiciary 2007 Appendix 2, Valid prohibitions, see www.banksr.com Other Matters Other Documents tab ASBOs

Type of antisocial behaviour	Possible prohibitions	Comment
Fly posting	An order prohibiting the defendant from carrying posters, paste and any material designed for sticking publicity material on buildings and public facilities, or an order prohibiting the use of a motor vehicle containing these items and materials.	Could consider the use of disqualification under Powers of Criminal Courts (Sentencing) Act 2000 s 146, if the fly posting was carried out from a motor vehicle.

See also the ***Graffiti*** para at **84.66**.

84.62 *Football supporters etc. chanting etc.*
JSB ASBO Guide for the Judiciary 2007 Appendix 2, Valid prohibitions, see www.banksr.com Other Matters Other Documents tab ASBOs

Type of antisocial behaviour	Possible prohibitions	Comment
Noise nuisance caused by raves, rowdy games and chanting by gangs (e.g. football supporters)	Non-association clauses in ASBOs are more effective in enabling prevention of antisocial behaviour than orders not to cause nuisance. Exclusion from a defined area is effective.	Prohibition which attempts to prevent the possession of equipment for playing music or games can be effective but often the defendant is not the owner, but merely a participant in the rowdy behaviour.

84.63 *Geographical restrictions*
R v Beck 2003 EWCA Crim 2198 para 9 Orders should be framed in practical terms. In many cases it may be preferable to frame restrictions by reference to specific roads or rivers. The Court was unable to regard the 2 km radius restriction adopted in the present order as invalidating it. If it seemed likely to cause any problem, a map could have been prepared, or the matter referred back to the Court, by way of application for variation. In the event of an innocent minor infringement, due to failure to appreciate the precise boundary of a restriction, any court could also be relied upon to act proportionately and sensibly. Under domestic law it was the Judge's duty to take into account the drastic effect for the appellant of the Restraining Order in causing him to move home, and to have regard to considerations of proportionality. The appellant's conduct, however, was making the life of the complainant and her daughter in their home intolerable. The appellant had ignored a caution in 1998 and continued his harassment of the complainant. The Court had to balance the respective interests in their homes of the appellant, who was the guilty offender, and the complainant, whose life was being spoiled. The Restraining Order was not wrong.

W v Acton Youth Court 2005 EWHC 954 (Admin) High Court D was prohibited from entering certain areas and their 'environs'. Held. That was a word D was unlikely to understand.

R v Debnath 2005 EWCA Crim 3472, 2006 2 Cr App R (S) 25 (p 169) A radius restriction will not necessarily invalidate an order. If necessary, a map should be prepared.

R v Bradfield 2006 EWCA Crim 2917 D pleaded to burglary, theft, damaging property and harassment (Community Rehabilitation Orders and a Restraining Order). Police were regularly called out because of verbal abuse between D and his ex-partner, V. D broke into V's house following the dissolution of their relationship. He was captured on CCTV stealing underwear, going through drawers in various rooms, masturbating and ejaculating onto the bed sheets. The Restraining Order prevented him from coming within 500 yards of the road where V lived with their two children. It also prevented D from contacting V directly or indirectly. D lost his job and the Restraining Order became more onerous. D wished to vary or discharge the order on the grounds that the DHSS was a very short distance from the road. Further, the Jobcentre was within the 500-yard area and the order prevented him from seeking, obtaining or travelling to work and handicapped him on the labour market. He also said the railway station was within the prohibited area and many buses travelled through the prohibited area. V opposed the variation. Held. There was no evidence put before the Judge on behalf of the appellant. It is not surprising the Judge concluded, in the absence of detailed proposals for variation which addressed V's continuing anxieties and concerns, that her interests had to be given priority. The Judge was entirely correct to do so. If any application is made in future, D and those acting for him would be advised to support it with evidence.

Note: It can be inferred from the judgment that had: a) evidence been collected about the need to visit the Jobcentre etc. and b) variations been proposed which would have dealt with the ability to remain on a bus as it travelled through the prohibited area etc. some variations would have been made. Ed.

R v TS 2014 EWCA Crim 1848 D was convicted of sexual assault. He and his family lived opposite V, a 12-year-old girl. He was friendly with her and one day he stroked her bottom and thigh. The girl left. D was aged 51 and had only a caution for ABH in 2007. He had an IQ of 50 and it was possible he found it difficult to cope. He was given an 8-month suspended sentence. The SOPO said D could not enter V's road nor contact V. Held. D's family were very supportive of him. It would be very difficult for him to live on his own. The road prohibition was neither necessary nor proportionate.

DPP v Bulmer 2015 EWHC 2323 (Admin), 2016 1 Cr App R (S) 12 (p 74) para 22 B had a long record of antisocial behaviour offences and breaches of court orders, but she was unable to manage her chronic alcoholism. The vast majority of her offending was in the centre of York and the CPS wanted a prohibition preventing B from going within the area bound by the York outer ring road. The District Judge refused to make a non-conviction Criminal Behaviour Order because there was no positive requirement to assist her with her alcoholism and an order would not prevent her antisocial behaviour as she would just commit it outside the area. Held. para 40 One of the factors the courts have emphasised when considering exclusion areas in ASBOs is the clarity they provide as compared with prohibitions of certain sorts of behaviour. Such prohibitions are difficult to police and those subjected to them may find it difficult to assess whether they are breaching the order because of their disabilities or other problems, whether alcoholism, drug addiction or something else. para 43 It must, however, be emphasised that the order must be tailored to the specific circumstances of the person on whom it is to be imposed, and that assessments of proportionality are intensively fact sensitive. para 39 If the fact that she would simply move her antisocial activities to another location is seen as an important factor against making the order that was sought, the court would in effect be deciding not to protect those in her primary area of activity.

R v Cornish 2016 EWCA Crim 1450 The Restraining Order banned the defendant, D, from 'St Germans village or the surrounding area.' Held. para 19 The term 'St Germans village' itself lacked definition. The phrase 'or surrounding areas' was vaguer still. If D was to be prohibited from entering an area it [must] be clearly delineated. This is easily done by drawing a boundary on a map. Order quashed for procedural reasons.

R v Khan 2018 EWCA Crim 1472, 2 Cr App R (S) 53 (p 426) The Court of Appeal considered a Criminal Behaviour Order. Held. para 15 Exclusion zones should be clearly delineated (generally with the use of clearly marked maps, although we do not consider that there is a problem of definition in an order extending to Greater Manchester).

84.64 *Geographical restrictions Determining the area*

C v Sunderland Youth Court 2003 EWHC 2385 (Admin), 2004 1 Cr App R (S) 76 (p 443) High Court I do not suggest for one moment that an order may not properly relate to the whole of a local government area, but the Magistrates must give very careful consideration as to what is the appropriate area for an order. There is no evidence that they gave such consideration in the present case. Order quashed on this and other grounds.

R v Bowker 2007 EWCA Crim 1608, 2008 1 Cr App R (S) 72 (p 412) D pleaded to violent disorder. D was two days short of his 18th birthday and was involved in a violent altercation involving two rival groups outside a nightclub. The Judge made no distinction between the ages of the nine defendants, the others being aged 19 or older, and said D was at the forefront of those involved in the violence. All nine were made subject to an ASBO which was unlimited in time and prohibited them from entering Wigan town centre between 10 pm and 7 am every day of the week. Held. Although the duration of the order is of concern, an application can be made to the court at any time for the order to be modified. The restriction was not inappropriate.

Heron v Plymouth City Council 2009 EWHC 3562 (Admin) H was prohibited from entering part of Plymouth and the area was marked in red on a map. The defence said that was too wide and was not proportionate. Further, it would prevent H from finding work. Held. The restriction was necessary, sensible and proportionate. It did not prevent H from shopping or visiting the bus station, the railway station, the benefits office, the police station or the library. There is no evidence H has ever sought work. It might shift the problem elsewhere but H was likely to be caught [offending] in his local shops.

R v Ballard 2011 EWCA Crim 2210 D pleaded to false imprisonment. He was in a relationship of short duration with V. He accused V of seeing another man, frogmarched her to his nearby house and took her to the bedroom. D punched V in the face. The Judge imposed a Restraining Order prohibiting D from entering the Isle of Dogs, in east London. D, aged 27, had three convictions and four cautions. Held. A Restraining Order was necessary to protect V. However, the Exclusion Order in its current form was more onerous than necessary. A more limited exclusion order in that area would more satisfactorily provide protection for V. D would also be permitted to travel through the area by Docklands Light Railway. The period would be reduced from 5 to 3 years.

See also: *R v Whitehead and Others* 2013 EWCA Crim 2401 (Conspiracy to steal mountain bikes at car parks in Cumbria. Travelled from Liverpool in a van. Cutting tools used. Stole £13,850 worth of bikes. Items totalling £2,750 taken. Aged 27-41. Each had a poor record. Planning and targeting of high-value items. Short-lived conspiracy. Prohibitions included entering Cumbria save to travel through it on the M6 and visiting any property within Cumbria save for work when written permission obtained from property owner and police. Prohibitions were stark but necessary.)

R v Cook 2014 EWCA Crim 137 (Aged 63 with numerous previous convictions for sexual offences including two attempted rapes (6 years) and breaches of court orders. In breach by using a bus to visit a hospital. In 2013, D masturbated whilst on a London Underground train. Six days later, he wanted to go to hospital to get his hearing aid repaired. New term of 'Entering any train station or using on any public train or underground train unless authorised by [his] supervising police officer'. Held. The prohibition does not prevent him from travelling on a train, it requires him to notify the police of his intention to travel so that his movements can be monitored if necessary. Given the nature and extent of his offending, the additional prohibition was proportionate. Appeal dismissed.)

84.65 ***Geographical restrictions Prohibited from going home***

R v Richardson 2013 EWCA Crim 1905 D was convicted of witness intimidation, criminal damage and two breaches of a Restraining Order. There was a campaign of harassment against V over three years. At one time D worked in a fast-food outlet with V. D tried to become a friend of V on Facebook. Early on, D was involved in a parking dispute with V's aunt and others. V had made a witness statement about D's harassment. D had pleaded to harassment twice during the course of conduct. She was now in breach of a suspended sentence given for that harassment. V was now aged 49 with no other relevant convictions. The Judge noted D's utter refusal to comply with court orders or to desist from her vindictive and cruel campaign of harassment. The Judge gave D a 3-year sentence with the 16-week suspended sentence activated in full. The Judge made a new Restraining Order prohibiting D from entering the area in which she and V lived. He received confirmation that D would lose her tenancy because of her 3-year sentence but would be re-housed elsewhere on her release. The order prohibited her from visiting her mother, who was in poor health and in her mid-70s. She relied on D in part for care. V and her immediate family subsequently moved but retained ties to the area and regularly needed to visit friends and relatives living there. They wanted to return. V's mother, who also lived in the exclusion zone area, was also in poor health. Held. The position was that upon release from custody, D would not be able to visit her mother in the exclusion zone. Her mother would have to visit her. There was no reason why that could not be achieved. That had to be balanced against the risk that if no such order was made and D had free access to the exclusion area, there was a very real possibility that she would come into contact with V or her family, with the likelihood of further harassment. The Judge was correct to strike a balance. He applied the correct test of necessity and remarked that the order was proportionate. The order could not have been modified in any way so as to permit D to visit her mother within the exclusion zone whilst affording V and her family the peace of mind to which they were entitled. Unusual as this order may be, we are quite unable to say that in the exceptional circumstances of the case it was wrong in principle. Appeal dismissed.

R v F 2014 EWCA Crim 539 LCJ D was convicted of common assault and committing an offence with intent to commit a sexual offence against V, his neighbour. He asked for a blow job in payment for mowing her lawn. D grabbed V's arms and pulled her into the living room onto a couch. D said, "It won't take long" and "it's not that big". V managed to free herself and noticed his flies were unzipped. There was a bruise on one of V's arms. V felt she had no option but to move because of her apprehension if she stayed. D owned his house. Held. D was now prepared to move and live with his daughter. To police that willingness we vary the Restraining Order to add, 'not living within a mile of V's address'.

See also: *R v Howell* 2016 EWCA Crim 2061 (D threatened neighbours and bashed a fence with a machete. Very bad record. A Restraining Order banned D from returning home. The defence said it was in breach of his article 8 rights. Held. It wasn't, because there was an exception when an order was 'necessary…in the interests of preventing crime'. Some judges would have thought prison was appropriate. It was necessary to look at the whole sentence. Here, with the previous convictions and his earlier failure to comply with court orders, the term was necessary and proportionate.)

84.66 ***Graffiti***

JSB ASBO Guide for the Judiciary 2007 Appendix 2, Valid prohibitions, see www.banksr.com Other Matters Other Documents tab ASBOs

Type of antisocial behaviour	Possible prohibitions	Comment
Criminal damage through regular spray can graffiti	An order prohibiting the defendant from being in possession of any can of spray paint in a public place.	See *R v Boness* 2005 EWCA Crim 2395, below. Defining the geographical area of application can result in the offender committing further acts elsewhere.

R v Boness 2005 EWCA Crim 2395, 2006 1 Cr App R (S) 120 (p 690) If a court is faced by an offender who causes criminal damage by spraying graffiti, the order should be aimed at facilitating action to be taken to prevent graffiti spraying by him and/or his associates before it takes place. An order in clear and simple terms preventing the offender from being in possession of a can of spray paint in a public place gives the police or others responsible for protecting the property an opportunity to take action in advance of the actual spraying and makes it clear to the offender that he has lost the right to carry such a can for the duration of the order.
See also the ***Fly posting*** para at **84.61**.

84.67 *Groups, Congregating in*

R v Boness 2005 EWCA Crim 2395, 2006 1 Cr App R (S) 120 (p 690) D was a persistent prolific offender and had admitted drug misuse in the community. There were three main aspects to his antisocial behaviour: threatening behaviour (two incidents), vehicle crime (three incidents) and other offences of dishonesty such as burglary and theft (three incidents and other incidents of handling stolen goods). He was sentenced to a custodial sentence of 3 years' detention and was thus subject to a period on licence and subject to recall or return to custody. D was prohibited from 'Congregating in groups of people in a manner causing or likely to cause any person to fear for their safety or congregating in groups of more than six persons in an outdoor public place'. Held. Given D's previous history the first part of the prohibition can be justified as necessary. As the prosecution point out, the final clause would appear to prohibit the appellant from attending sporting or other outdoor events. Such a prohibition is, in our view, disproportionate. They also point out that D would be able to argue that he had a reasonable excuse for attending the event. This is an insufficient safeguard.

N v DPP 2007 EWHC 883 (Admin) High Court Following a conviction for disorderly conduct, D, aged 15, was made subject to an ASBO which prohibited him from, amongst other things, congregating in groups of three or more in a public place other than when with adults over the age of 21 years. Held. This prohibition was disproportionate and insufficiently clear. The order was re-drafted so that D was 'prohibited from congregating in a public place in a group of two or more persons in a manner causing or likely to cause any person to fear for their safety'.
See also: *R v Browne-Morgan* 2016 EWCA Crim 1903, 2017 1 Cr App R (S) 33 (p 279) (Drug dealer. 'Not to congregate in a public place in a group of two or more persons in a manner causing or likely to cause any person to fear for their safety', was acceptable.)
See also the ***Individuals, Being in the company of*** para at **84.70**.

84.68 *Hoods, masks etc.*

R v Boness 2005 EWCA Crim 2395, 2006 1 Cr App R (S) 120 (p 690) D was a persistent prolific offender and had admitted to drug misuse in the community. There were three main aspects to his antisocial behaviour: threatening behaviour (two incidents), vehicle crime (three incidents) and other offences of dishonesty such as burglary and theft (three incidents and other incidents of handling stolen goods). He was sentenced to a custodial sentence of 3 years' detention and was thus subject to a period on licence and subject to recall or return to custody. D was prohibited from 'In any public place, wearing, or having with you anything which covers, or could be used to cover, the face or part of the face. This will include hooded clothing, balaclavas, masks or anything else which could be used to hide identity, except that a motorcycle helmet may be worn only when lawfully riding a motorcycle'. It was submitted, "It is presumed that this prohibition was based upon the assertion that [D] is forensically aware and will use items to attempt to prevent detection. The terms of the prohibition are too wide, resulting in a lack of clarity and consequences which are not commensurate with the risk which the prohibition seeks to address. The phrase 'having with you anything which...could be used to cover the face or part of the face' covers a huge number of items. For example, it is not unknown for those seeking to conceal their identity to pull up a jumper to conceal part of the face, but surely the prohibition cannot have been intended to limit so radically the choice of clothing that the appellant can wear? It seems that the appellant would potentially be in breach of the order were he to wear a scarf or carry a newspaper in public." Held. We agree.

R (B) v Greenwich Magistrates' Court 2008 EWHC 2882 (Admin) High Court D and four others had been involved in public disorder when hoods or hats had been worn. D was prohibited by an ASBO from 'wearing any article of clothing with an attached hood in any public place in the London Borough of Greenwich, whether the hood is up or down'. The Judge said he was satisfied that a prohibition would reduce the swagger, menace and fear of antisocial behaviour. Held. The prohibition clearly satisfies the tests of clarity, necessity and proportionality. Application dismissed.

84.69 ***Inciting others to act in an antisocial manner***

R v Boness 2005 EWCA Crim 2395, 2006 1 Cr App R (S) 120 (p 690) D was a persistent prolific offender and had admitted to drug misuse in the community. para 77 D was prohibited from 'Acting or inciting others to act in an antisocial manner, that is to say, a manner that causes or is likely to cause harassment, alarm or distress to one or more persons not of the same household'. The prosecution submitted that this was a proper order to make and was in accordance with the Home Office guidance. Held. para 77 We would prefer some geographical limit, in the absence of good reasons for having no such limit.

84.70 ***Individuals, Being in the company of***

R v Boness 2005 EWCA Crim 2395, 2006 1 Cr App R (S) 120 (p 690) D was a persistent prolific offender and had admitted to drug misuse in the community. He was sentenced to a custodial sentence of 3 years' detention and was thus subject to a period on licence and subject to recall or return to custody. D was prohibited from 'Being in the company of eleven named individuals'. Held. We share those doubts whether a prohibition that prevents D from associating with any of the named individuals for five years after his release, even in a private residence where one or more resides, is disproportionate to the risk of [the] antisocial behaviour it is designed to prevent.

R v Dyer 2010 EWCA Crim 2096 D, who had serious convictions for drug trafficking, was prohibited from associating with named persons who were also arrested in the drugs operation D was arrested in. D claimed he did not know any of them. Held. The overwhelming likelihood is that drug dealers of this kind are known to each other, although maybe not by the name set out here but otherwise. Providing that sufficient identification is provided to this appellant so he knows who these people are, we consider that condition was necessary. We do not create a precedent.

Gueye and Sanchez v Spain 2011 C-483/09 ECJ The applicants were convicted of domestic violence and received ancillary orders prohibiting them from being within 1 km and 500 m of the victims. Both applicants began living with the victims and were subsequently apprehended for breach of the ancillary orders. The victims admitted that they had voluntarily resumed cohabitation with the offenders. The applicants sought a declaration that to resume living together with the freely given consent of their partners did not constitute an offence of failing to comply with the ancillary orders imposed. The victims joined the action in support. The question arose whether the right of the victim to be understood meant that the prosecution had a positive obligation to allow the victim to express her thoughts etc. on the direct effects on her life which may be caused by penalties imposed upon the offender, with whom she has a strong emotional relationship. Held. [Council of the European Union] Framework Decision 2001/220/JHA article 2(1)[1010] is intended to ensure that a victim can effectively and adequately take part in the criminal proceedings, which does not imply that a mandatory injunction to stay away cannot be imposed contrary to the wishes of the victims.

R v Khan 2018 EWCA Crim 1472, 2 Cr App R (S) 53 (p 426) The Court of Appeal considered a Criminal Behaviour Order. Held. para 15 Where a defendant is prohibited from contacting or associating with certain individuals, those individuals must be clearly identified.

See also: *Hills v Chief Constable of Essex* 2006 EWHC 2633 (Admin) (A prohibition against associating with this named individual was not unfair because the other individual didn't have a similar prohibition.)

R v Samad 2016 EWCA Crim 1766 (D was the organiser of a class A drug network. Received 19 years' custody. A Serious Crime Prevention Order had terms prohibiting him from associating with five of his co-defendants. Defence said they were close friends and the families interacted on a regular basis. Held. We accept the term will restrict D and his family within their Bengali community, but the term will assist in reducing the risk of further offences. Appeal dismissed.)

See also the ***Groups, Congregating in Groups*** para at **84.67**.

84.71 ***Image/Photographic prohibitions***

R v Hemsley 2010 EWCA Crim 225 D pleaded to 23 counts of making an indecent photograph or pseudo-photograph of a child (6 months' imprisonment on each, concurrent). A Sexual Offences Prevention Order was passed, one of the terms of which was, 'b) Not to own or possess any image of a naked child, under the age of 18, whether printed, digitally or electronically stored. This includes any image of a naked child under the age of 18 that has been published in any book or film that has been on general release within the UK. For the purpose of this prohibition naked child means any female under the age of 18 years who has their nipples, genitals or buttocks exposed or any male under the age of 18 years who has their genitals or buttocks exposed.' D, aged 27, was hitherto of good character. Held. Term b) cannot be described as necessary. It is clearly capable of unintentional breach because it is impossible to know whether, for example, a film on general release might include an image of the buttocks of a naked baby. It also criminalises possession of mainstream books, DVDs, art, archaeology, architecture and so on. There is no evidence enabling the conclusion to be reached that an order as wide as that which was made was necessary. The order was quashed and replaced with one just involving the Internet.

R v Mortimer 2010 EWCA Crim 1303 D was convicted of three counts of sexual assault on a child under the age of 13 and one count of causing or inciting a child to engage in sexual activity. He was sentenced to 3 years' IPP. D was on licence for previous sex offences and had befriended a woman with two girls aged four and eight, the elder of whom made the complaint in respect of three counts of sexual assault on a child aged under 13. A pre-sentence report indicated that D denied the offences. D, aged 37, had a history of sex offences against children, including three offences of gross indecency with a child and three offences of indecent assault against a female aged under 14, for which he received extended sentences of 32 months plus 3 years. D had been recalled from licence on four occasions. He was assessed as posing a high risk of reoffending, and that there was a very high risk of harm to children. The Judge described D as an exceptionally dangerous paedophile who presented a significant risk to young girls. He was satisfied the case called for IPP. He also passed a Sexual Offences Prevention Order, including the prohibition of: a) having in his possession any photo of a child aged under 16 unless with permission, b) possessing a computer, and c) using the Internet or its

[1010] See www.banksr.com Other Matters Other Documents tab.

successor for purposes other than work, study or seeking employment. D appealed against the order on the basis that the terms were too wide, insufficiently clear and for an indefinite period of time. Held. Considering the order, a blanket ban on possessing photographs is not justified. It is also very vague and indefinite.
See also: *R v Jackson* 2012 EWCA Crim 2602 (Plea to voyeurism, indecent photographs of a child and possession of extreme photographs. The camera prohibition was entirely inappropriate.)

84.72 *Internet/Computer prohibitions Basic principles*

R v Smith and Others 2011 EWCA Crim 1772, 2012 1 Cr App R (S) 82 (p 468) The Court gave guidance about SOPOs. Held. para 20 i) [Re blanket bans see **84.74**] ii) Although the *R v Hemsley* 2010 EWCA Crim 225 formulation restricting Internet use to job search, study, work, lawful recreation and purchases has its attractions, on analysis [it has] the same flaw, albeit less obviously. Even today, the legitimate use of the Internet extends beyond these spheres of activity. Such a provision in a SOPO would, it seems, prevent a defendant from looking up the weather forecast, from planning a journey by accessing a map, from reading the news, from sending the electricity board his meter reading, from conducting his banking across the web unless paying charges for his account, and indeed from sending or receiving e-mail via the web, at least unless a strained meaning is given to 'lawful recreation'. The difficulties of defining the limits of that last expression seem to us another reason for avoiding this formulation. More, the speed of expansion of applications of the Internet is such that it is simply impossible to predict what developments there will be within the foreseeable lifespan of a great many SOPOs, which would unexpectedly and unnecessarily, and therefore wrongly, be found to be prohibited.
iii) [Re police supervision of orders, see **84.78**.]
iv) There are fewer difficulties about a prohibition on Internet access without filtering software, but there is a clear risk that there may be uncertainty about exactly what is required and the policing of such a provision seems likely to be attended by some difficulty.
v) Of the formulations thus far devised and reported, the one which seems to us most likely to be effective is the one requiring the preservation of readable Internet history coupled with submission to inspection on request. There is no need for the SOPO to invest the police with powers of forcible entry into private premises beyond the statutory ones which they already have. It is sufficient to prohibit use of the Internet without submitting to inspection on request. If the defendant were to deny the officers sight of his computer, either in his home or by surrendering it to them, he would be in breach. One suitable form of such an order appears in [the case of Steven] Smith at para 53 [of this judgment].
vi) Where the risk is not simply of downloading pornography but consists of or includes the use of chatlines or similar networks to groom young people for sexual purposes, it may well be appropriate to include a prohibition on communicating via the Internet with any young person known or believed to be under the age of 16, coupled no doubt with a provision such as we mention in (v). In some such cases, it may be necessary to prohibit altogether the use of social networking sites or other forms of chatline or chatroom. For an example [see the order we made for Wayne] Clarke at para 33(3) of this judgment.
R v Parsons and Morgan 2017 EWCA Crim 2163, 2018 1 Cr App R (S) 43 (p 307) para 3 Following the introduction of SHPOs, the new questions to ask when considering an SHPO are posed in *R v NC* 2016 EWCA Crim 1448, 2017 1 Cr App R (S) 13 (p 87). They are: i) Is the making of an order necessary to protect the public from sexual harm through the commission of scheduled offences? ii) If some order is necessary, are the terms imposed nevertheless oppressive? iii) Overall, are the terms proportionate? *Re Encryption software* [para 26 The Court had heard evidence about this] para 28 As with cloud storage, a prohibition must not be a blunt instrument nor a trap for the unwary ([e.g.] simply using the default setting of a device in everyday legitimate use). It must be

targeted and aimed at the installation of encryption or wiping software on any device other than that which is intrinsic to its operation. We draft the orders accordingly, see **84.79**.

84.73 *Internet/Computer prohibitions Are they appropriate?*

R v Chamberlain 2011 EWCA Crim 517 D pleaded to possessing indecent photos of children (×2) and possessing extreme pornographic images. Police arrived at D's mother's address and found indecent images on his computer. There were 40 images, including six at Level 3 and 12 at Level 4. There were 18 moving images including one at Level 3 and six at Level 4. There were also four extreme images which included animals. His basis of plea was that they were downloaded in 2006 or 2007, when he was aged 16 or 17, he stumbled across them and never paid for any images. There was a pre-sentence report which described D as disgusted at his offences. A SOPO was imposed with an indefinite term to give an officer access. D, aged 20 at his appeal, was of good character. Held. A SOPO of this size and extent is not appropriate in this particular case. We have particularly in mind that for a young man in this position who has moved on, it would unnecessarily restrict his unfettered right to have access to the Internet for the purposes of education, entertainment, jobs etc. It does seem to us that perhaps insufficient regard was paid to the basis of plea and that really this was a period of experimentation that has been left long behind. Of course the essence of a SOPO is to protect the public from serious sexual harm, but on the other hand it should not be oppressive or disproportionate. There is no evidence here that he has ever touched a child inappropriately and in our view he is highly motivated to address this previous behaviour. It is our judgement that the addition of a SOPO was not necessary in this case.

See also: *R v Awad* 2014 EWCA Crim 1451, 2 Cr App R (S) 74 (p 577) (Pleas to relationship threats to kill V and ABH on V. Received 4 years. Held. Conditions not to contact V or seek to identify the whereabouts of V were enough. Terms to make available to police any computer and not to possess a computer capable of having its history removed were unnecessary.)

84.74 *Internet/Computer prohibitions Blanket ban*

R v Smith and Others 2011 EWCA Crim 1772, 2012 1 Cr App R (S) 82 (p 468) The Court gave guidance about SOPOs. Held. para 20 i) A blanket prohibition on computer use or Internet access is impermissible. It is disproportionate because it restricts the defendant in the use of what is nowadays an essential part of everyday living for a large proportion of the public, as well as a requirement of much employment. Before the creation of the Internet, if a defendant kept books of pictures of child pornography it would not have occurred to anyone to ban him from possession of all printed material. The Internet is a modern equivalent.

R v Parsons and Morgan 2017 EWCA Crim 2163, 2018 1 Cr App R (S) 43 (p 307) M appealed his SHPO, which had a blanket ban on M using the Internet. Held. We agree with the extract in *R v Smith* 2011 [see above]. The need for an individual to be able to access the Internet, and to possess devices capable of accessing the Internet, has become 'the established norm'. The Internet is now an integral part of social life, of commercial transactions and is very much encouraged in dealings between an individual and government departments or local authorities. The massive expansion of social media further highlights developments in this regard. We would be unwilling to say that a blanket ban on Internet use can 'never' be justified. Such a prohibition would be appropriate in [only] the most exceptional cases. In all other cases, a blanket ban would be unrealistic, oppressive and disproportionate, cutting off the offender from too much of everyday, legitimate living. M's blanket ban was that.

84.75 *Internet/Computer prohibitions Don't make them too wide*

R v Mortimer 2010 EWCA Crim 1303 D was convicted of three counts of sexual assault on a child under the age of 13 and one count of causing or inciting a child to engage in sexual activity. He was sentenced to 3 years' IPP. D was on licence for previous sex offences and had befriended a woman with two girls aged 4 and 8, the elder of whom made the complaint in respect of three counts of sexual assault on a child under 13. A pre-sentence report indicated that D denied the offences. D, aged 37, had a history of sex offences against children, including three offences of gross indecency with a child and three offences of indecent assault against a female aged under 14, for which he received extended sentences of 32 months plus 3 years. D had been recalled from licence on four occasions. He was assessed as posing a high risk of reoffending, and that there was a very high risk of harm to children. The Judge described D as an exceptionally dangerous paedophile who presented a significant risk to young girls. He was satisfied the case called for IPP. He also passed a Sexual Offences Prevention Order, including the prohibition of a) possessing a computer, and b) using the Internet or its successor for purposes other than work, study or seeking employment. D appealed against the order on the basis that the terms were too wide, insufficiently clear and for an indefinite period of time. Held. Prohibition of possession of a computer is draconian and is not necessary for the protection of the public or specific individuals. It is oppressive and not proportionate. The prohibition of using the Internet other than for the purposes of work, study or seeking employment is neither necessary nor is it proportionate. It is also almost if not wholly impossible to police.

R v Hall 2010 EWCA Crim 2373 D pleaded to seven counts of making photographs of a child and four counts of possessing indecent photographs of a child. He was also convicted after a trial of three counts of sexual assault of a child. D was made the subject of a Sexual Offences Prevention Order, of which one of the conditions was not to possess a computer with Internet access for five years commencing after release. D approached V, aged 11, whose mother he knew. He fondled V's penis, tried to kiss him and put his tongue inside his mouth. The activity occurred on more than one occasion. The Judge remarked that there was an element of breach of trust in that he had become a father figure for V and used the position to groom the boy. There was evidence that the abuse had resulted in V becoming disruptive at home. Held. These were serious sexual offences committed on a child 46 years younger than V. The prohibitions contained in the Sexual Offences Prevention Order must be considered against the questions that any court is obliged to ask itself when imposing such an order. First, is the order complained of necessary to protect the public generally, or any particular member of the public, from serious sexual harm? Second…are the particular terms of the order that has been made oppressive? Third, are the terms of the particular order made proportionate? The Court is persuaded that that condition is too wide.

R v Brown 2011 EWCA Crim 1223 D pleaded to serious sex offences against children. A Sexual Offences Prevention Order was made, including the provision 'save where to do so is inadvertent or unavoidable, not to possess any images of a child under the age of 16 years unless the prior permission of that child's parents or guardian has been obtained'. Held. That restriction would, for example, serve to criminalise the continued possession of a daily newspaper which happened to have an inoffensive photograph of a child in it unless it was disposed of straight away upon realisation that such a photograph was in the newspaper. It is not adequate to rely upon the good sense of prosecutors in cases of this type so that very widely drafted prohibitions can be incorporated. The provision is too widely drafted and shall be deleted.

R v Smith and Others 2011 EWCA Crim 1772, 2012 1 Cr App R (S) 82 (p 468) Although the *R v Hemsley* (2010) formulation restricting Internet use to job search, study, work, lawful recreation and purchases has its attractions, it seems to us on analysis to suffer from the same flaw, albeit less obviously. Even today, the legitimate use of the Internet extends beyond these spheres of activity. Such a provision in a SOPO would, it seems, prevent a defendant from looking up the weather forecast, from planning a journey by accessing a map, from reading the news, from sending the electricity board his meter reading, from conducting his banking across the web unless paying charges for his account, and indeed from sending or receiving e-mail via the web, at least unless a strained meaning is given to 'lawful recreation'. The difficulties of defining the limits of that last expression seem to us another reason for avoiding this formulation. More, the speed of expansion of applications of the Internet is such that it is simply impossible to predict what developments there will be within the foreseeable lifespan of a great many SOPOs, which would unexpectedly and unnecessarily, and therefore wrongly, be found to be prohibited. Some courts have been attracted to a prohibition upon the possession of any computer or other device giving access to the Internet without notification to the local police. Most defendants, like most people generally, will have some devices with Internet access, and a requirement that they be notified of it adds little of any value. There is no need for the SOPO to invest the police with powers of forcible entry into private premises beyond the statutory ones which they already have.

R v P 2011 EWCA Crim 1925, 2012 1 Cr App R (S) 79 (p 447) D was convicted of three counts of sexual activity with a child family member. He had regular sexual intercourse with V, his step-daughter, aged 16-17. She became pregnant and gave birth. The sexual intimacy persisted after V turned 18. D was 'prohibited from residing or knowingly being in any premises where any female person under the age of 18 is present without consent'. Held. The words 'is present' are quite remarkably and unacceptably wide. The Judge intended for the order to cover residence, not presence. Prohibition quashed.

R v Jackson 2012 EWCA Crim 2602 D pleaded to voyeurism, indecent photographs of a child and possession of extreme photographs. He appealed his SOPO. Held. The SOPO was in many respects entirely disproportionate to the offences D had committed. The accessing the Internet except under supervision of employer and owning any computer in his home prohibitions were entirely excessive. It is *prima facie* unreasonable to require anyone not to have any means of accessing the Internet in their home. Quite apart from anything else, many telephones nowadays will have that facility. The time is perhaps approaching when it may be most telephones will have that capacity. Those are not the only means whereby or the only devices through which such access can be achieved. Such prohibitions are generally to be regarded as inappropriate. We substitute, '1 Using any device capable of accessing the Internet unless i) it has the capacity to retain and display the history of Internet use; and ii) D makes the device available on request for inspection by a police officer. 2 Deleting any such history of Internet use'.

See also: *R v Stewart* 2011 EWCA Crim 807 (Don't make them too restrictive.)

R v Martin 2011 EWCA Crim 2182 (Plea to having an indecent photograph and making indecent photographs (×6). A SOPO was necessary and amended to prohibit using any device capable of accessing the Internet unless it has the capability to retain and display the history of Internet use.)

R v Barber 2012 EWCA Crim 2874 (New terms substituted as original ones were too wide.)

84.76 ***Internet/Computer prohibitions Risk management software***

R v Parsons and Morgan 2017 EWCA Crim 2163, 2018 1 Cr App R (S) 43 (p 307) P and M appealed their SHPOs. Held. para 14 *Risk management monitoring software* [A detailed explanation and analysis was given. Not listed.] para 18 Given the administrative burdens and police resources, we would be concerned about a prohibition which assumed that a police force would necessarily wish to insist on the installation of such software or which made the use of the device contingent on the approval by the police force of software already installed on it; the latter prohibition could unintentionally (and by the back door) become a ban on usage of the device.

The trigger should be notification by the offender to the police of his acquisition of a computer or device capable of accessing the Internet; the police cannot be expected to know otherwise. The device should have the capacity to retain and display the history of Internet use and the offender should be prohibited from deleting such history. The device should be made available immediately on request for inspection by a police officer (or employee) and the offender should be required to allow any such person to install risk management software if they so choose. The offender should further be prohibited from interfering with or bypassing the normal running of any such software. We draft the orders accordingly, see **84.79**.

84.77 ***Internet/Computer prohibitions Storage prohibitions***
R v Parsons and Morgan 2017 EWCA Crim 2163, 2018 1 Cr App R (S) 43 (p 307) P and M appealed their SHPOs. [The Court heard expert evidence and gave analysis which is not listed.] Held. The vice against which a prohibition should be targeted is not the default or automatic use of cloud storage, 'practically ubiquitous' in the devices available today. That would be too blunt an approach. A prohibition too widely worded would not only be unnecessary but could readily be a trap for the unwary user of (for example) a smartphone in mass usage. The vice is instead the deliberate installation of a remote storage facility, specifically installed by an offender without notice to the police and which would not be apparent from the device he is using, and not intrinsic to the operation of any such device. We draft the orders accordingly, see **84.79**.

84.78 ***Internet/Computer prohibitions Police supervision of***
R v Hemsley 2010 EWCA Crim 225 D entered an early guilty plea to 23 counts of making an indecent photograph or pseudo-photograph of a child (6 months' imprisonment on each, concurrent). It is noteworthy that the 6,592 images discovered spanned Levels 1-4 and of 71 moving images discovered, 29 were at Level 4. D was subject to a Sexual Offences Prevention Order including the following term: a) Not to own or use any computer, electronic, magnetic or optical device which has the capability of storing, receiving or transmitting data without permitting any police constable to enter the premises upon which they are kept in order that they can examine and if necessary remove any such device for the purpose of carrying out such an examination. Held. Term a) is an impermissible attempt to confer extensive powers of search and seizure upon the police pursuant to a statutory provision which only enables an order preventing something from being done to be made. Such orders should not create a situation in which police powers of search and seizure are extended with none of the procedural safeguards which usually and importantly regulate the exercise of such powers.
R v Smith and Others 2011 EWCA Crim 1772, 2012 1 Cr App R (S) 82 (p 468) para 20 iii) Some courts have been attracted to a prohibition upon the possession of any computer or other device giving access to the Internet without notification to the local police. It may be that this might occasionally be the only way of preventing offending, but the vast increase in the number and type of such devices makes it onerous both for defendants and the police. Its effect is, *inter alia*, to require the defendant to tell the police when he buys a new mobile telephone, or a PlayStation for his children. In most cases the police will need to work on the basis that most defendants, like most people generally, will have some devices with Internet access, and that a requirement that they be notified of it adds little of any value.
R v Parsons and Morgan 2017 EWCA Crim 2163, 2018 1 Cr App R (S) 43 (p 307) P and M appealed their SHPOs. Held. The device should be made available immediately on request for inspection by a police officer (or employee) and the offender should be required to allow any such person to install risk management software if they so choose. The offender should further be prohibited from interfering with or bypassing the normal running of any such software. We draft the orders accordingly, see **84.79**.

84.79 ***Internet/Computer prohibitions Specimen prohibitions***
Judicial College's Crown Court Compendium Part II Sentencing June 2018 page 4-22
11. The Examples on the next page are based on those approved by the CACD in *R v Smith and Others* 2011 EWCA Crim 1772, 2012 1 Cr App R (S) 82 (p 468) and subsequent cases. However, it must be remembered that the order should be tailored to the individual, and that prohibitions on computer use should reflect current technology. That was particularly so in relation to risk management monitoring software, cloud

storage and encryption software. See *R v Parsons and Morgan* 2017 EWCA Crim 2163, 2018 1 Cr App R (S) 43 (p 307) as to guidance on prohibitions containing such technology.

Example
Example 1: Internet access
The defendant is prohibited from:
1. Using any computer or device capable of accessing the internet unless:
(i) he/she has notified the police VISOR team within 3 days of the acquisition of any such device;
(ii) it has the capacity to retain and display the history of internet use, and he does not delete such history;
(iii) he/she makes the device immediately available on request for inspection by a police officer, or police staff employee, and allows such person to install risk management monitoring software if they so choose;
This prohibition shall not apply to a computer at his/her place of work, Job Centre Plus, Public Library, educational establishment or other such place, provided that in relation to his/her place of work, within 3 days of him commencing use of such a computer, he/she notifies the police VISOR team of this use.
2. Interfering with or bypassing the normal running of any such computer monitoring software.
3. Using or activating any function of any software which prevents a computer or device from retaining and/or displaying the history of internet use, for example using 'incognito' mode or private browsing.
4. Using any 'cloud' or similar remote storage media capable of storing digital images (other than that which is intrinsic to the operation of the device) unless, within 3 days of the creation of an account for such storage, he/she notifies the police of that activity, and provides access to such storage on request for inspection by a police officer or police staff employee.
5. Possessing any device capable of storing digital images (moving or still) unless he/she provides access to such storage on request for inspection by a police officer or police staff employee.
6. Installing any encryption or wiping software on any device other than that which is intrinsic to the operation of the device.
This order will last until {specify}/indefinitely.

Note: Specimen prohibitions need to be applied very carefully, because: a) the prohibitions should be determined by the perceived risk posed by the particular defendant the court is dealing with, b) each case is different, and c) specimen directions can fail to keep up with digital changes. Ed.

R v Williams 2012 EWCA Crim 1674 D was convicted of rape, anal rape and taking indecent photos involving a young girl. A SOPO prohibited him from 'downloading any material from the Internet, save downloading for the purpose of any lawful employment or study'. Held. The order was too wide and flawed on the grounds of uncertainty, proportionality and enforceability. It will be amended to, 'The applicant will be prohibited from: a) using any device capable of accessing the Internet which does not have the capacity to retain or display the history of Internet use, b) making any attempt to delete such history of Internet use, c) making any attempt to disable the capacity of the device to record and retain that history of Internet use, and d) refusing to show such a history of Internet use to a police officer if so requested.'

R v M 2012 EWCA Crim 2148 D pleaded to three counts of causing a child to watch a sex act. Held. Applying *R v Smith* 2009 we substitute: 'The defendant is prohibited from: 1 Using a device capable of accessing the Internet unless: i) it has the capacity to retain and display the history of Internet use, and ii) he makes the device available on request for inspection by a police officer. 2 Deleting such history. 3 Using the Internet to contact or to attempt to contact any female known or believed to be under the age of 16. 4 Possessing any device, including a mobile telephone, capable of storing digital images unless he makes it available on request for inspection by a police officer.'

R v Kimpriktzis 2013 EWCA Crim 734, 2014 1 Cr App R (S) 6 (p 23) D was convicted of eight sex offences relating to when he had oral and anal sex with a 13-year-old boy, V, when he was aged 21. D contacted V on a gay chat line and wore no protection when he knew he was HIV positive. D did not tell the boy that. He was given a SOPO. D was recalled on his licence when, in breach of his SOPO, he advertised items on eBay which would be of interest to children. Police secured amendments to his SOPO. D applied to vary that using forged letters. He pleaded to attempting to pervert the course of justice and was given a 6-month suspended sentence. A new SOPO was made which included a term prohibiting him from using devices 'capable of accessing the Internet…unless D made the device available on request for removal and inspection by a police officer'. Held. D was a predatory paedophile. However, our experience is that when a computer is removed it may take a long time for an inspection to be carried out. Further if the history had been deleted, which would be a breach of his SOPO, he could be arrested and his computer seized. The words 'removal and' should be deleted.

R v McDonald 2015 EWCA Crim 2110, 2016 1 Cr App R (S) 48 (p 307) The Judge imposed standard *R v Smith* 2011 EWCA Crim 1772, 2012 1 Cr App R (S) 82 (p 468) computer prohibition terms (see *R v M* 2012 above). The defence argued that police would be able to see e-mails from his solicitors. Held. para 20 Neither defence counsel or any member of this Court has found any authority in which the standard *R v Smith* 2011 approved prohibition has been challenged. Appeal dismissed.

R v Parsons and Morgan 2017 EWCA Crim 2163, 2018 1 Cr App R (S) 43 (p 307) M and P appealed their SHPOs. The Court considered a wide range of computer issues for an SHPO. Held. para 58 We substitute the following terms:

'M is prohibited from:

(1) using any computer or device capable of accessing the Internet unless:

(a) he has notified the police VISOR team within 3 days of the acquisition of any such device;

(b) it has the capacity to retain and display the history of Internet use, and he does not delete such history;

(c) he makes the device immediately available on request for inspection by a police officer, or police staff employee, and he allows such person to install risk management monitoring software if they so choose.

This prohibition shall not apply to a computer at his place of work, Jobcentre Plus, public library, educational establishment or other such place, provided that in relation to his place of work, within 3 days of him commencing use of such a computer, he notifies the police VISOR team of this use.

(2) Interfering with or bypassing the normal running of any such computer monitoring software.

(3) Using or activating any function of any software which prevents a computer or device from retaining and/or displaying the history of Internet use, for example using "incognito" mode or private browsing.

(4) Using any "cloud" or similar remote storage media capable of storing digital images (other than that which is intrinsic to the operation of the device) unless, within 3 days of the creation of an account for such storage, he notifies the police of that activity, and provides access to such storage on request for inspection by a police officer or police staff employee.

(5) Possessing any device capable of storing digital images (moving or still) unless he provides access to such storage on request for inspection by a police officer or police staff employee.

(6) Installing any encryption or wiping software on any device other than that which is intrinsic to the operation of the device.'

A similar set of prohibitions were substituted in P's SHPO.
See also: *R v Wiggins and Others* 2014 EWCA Crim 1433, 2 Cr App R (S) 72 (p 560) (Given 4 years for ABH on former partner. Making his phone available to police and not to possess a computer that has the facility to remove its history were unnecessary and an infringement of his rights.)
Superceded cases: *R v Hemsley* 2010 EWCA Crim 225 (Relied on software prohibitions.) *R v Lea* 2011 EWCA Crim 487 D (Relied on software prohibitions.) *R v Collins* 2011 EWCA Crim 965 (Relied on risk management software.)
Kerb crawling see the ***Prostitution*** para at **84.85**.

84.80 ***Knives***
Hills v Chief Constable of Essex 2006 EWHC 2633 (Admin) D, aged 12,[1011] was given a stand-alone ASBO. It included a prohibition from carrying any knife or bladed article. Defence counsel said that the prohibition amounted to something which was already prohibited by the criminal law. Held. The prohibition was necessary because it covered knives which were less than three inches long which were not covered by the bladed article offence.

84.81 ***Mobile phone restrictions***
R v Dyer 2010 EWCA Crim 2096 D, who had serious convictions for drug trafficking, was prohibited from carrying a mobile phone which is not registered to his own name and that the registered mobile phone must be registered with intelligence officers at Trinity Road Police Station. Held. As regards the first, although it has been rather unrealistically submitted to us that there is little evidence of use of a mobile phone by D, it is absurd to suggest that drug dealers do not use mobile phones. There is also plain evidence in this case that the initial contact was made by a mobile phone. It is well known that drug dealers do use mobile phones. The problem that occurs is that mobile phones are sometimes 'pay as you go' and not registered. It seems to us clear that if D is to be prevented from drug dealing in the future and this evil trade stopped as far as he is concerned, it is necessary that any mobile phone be registered in his name if he is to have one. We have considered whether it is right that such a mobile phone should be registered with intelligence officers. However, as the CPS have not seen fit to come along to this Court to justify that further requirement, we cannot see that we can uphold that. This has been rightly objected to as an intrusion into D's liberty. Unless there was some justification for it that is shown to us, we strike that part of the ASBO out. We do not create a precedent.
See also: *R v Hancox and Duffy* 2010 EWCA Crim 102, 2 Cr App R (S) 74 (p 484) (Counterfeiting of banknotes on a commercial scale. Mobile phone and Internet notification in Serious Crime Prevention Order. Held. We are acutely aware of the potential for interference in a private life with communication restrictions. However, the restrictions (few details given) were proportionate.)
R v Wiggins and Others 2014 EWCA Crim 1433, 2 Cr App R (S) 72 (p 560) (Given 4 years for ABH on former partner. Making his phone available to police and not to possess a computer that has the facility to remove its history were unnecessary and an infringement of his rights.)
See also: *R v Awad* 2014 EWCA Crim 1451, 2 Cr App R (S) 74 (p 577) (Pleas to relationship threats to kill V and ABH on V. Received 4 years. Held. Conditions not to contact V or seek to identify their whereabouts and not to possess a computer capable of having its history removed were unnecessary.)

84.82 ***Motorbikes etc. causing nuisance and dangers***
JSB ASBO Guide for the Judiciary 2007 Appendix 2, Valid prohibitions, see www.banksr.com Other Matters Other Documents tab ASBOs

[1011] The Court refused to make an anonymity order.

Type of antisocial behaviour	Possible prohibitions	Comment
Nuisance and dangers caused by the use of quad bikes, motorbikes, mini-motos and scooters	Prohibitions which prevent the defendant sitting on any type of vehicle clearly described. Non-association with other users (named) of similar vehicles.	The identity of others with whom the defendant must not assemble must be clearly noted in as much detail as possible in the ASBO.

84.83 ***Nuisance***

JSB ASBO Guide for the Judiciary 2007 Appendix 2, Valid prohibitions, see www.banksr.com Other Matters Other documents tab ASBOs

Type of antisocial behaviour	Possible prohibitions	Comment
Nuisance and dangers caused by the use of quad bikes, motorbikes, mini-motos and scooters	Prohibitions which prevent the defendant sitting on any type of vehicle clearly described. Non-association with other users (named) of similar vehicles.	The identity of others with whom the defendant must not assemble must be clearly noted in as much detail as possible in the ASBO.
Noise nuisance caused by raves, rowdy games and chanting by gangs (e.g. football supporters)	Non-association clauses in ASBOs are more effective in enabling prevention of antisocial behaviour than orders not to cause nuisance. Exclusion from a defined area is effective.	Prohibition which attempts to prevent the possession of equipment for playing music or games can be effective but often the defendant is not the owner, but merely a participant in the rowdy behaviour.

84.84 ***Premises/Land, Prohibitions from entering etc.***

R v McGrath 2005 EWCA Crim 353, 2 Cr App R (S) 85 (p 525) D, a car thief, was banned from 'Trespassing on any land belonging to any person whether legal or natural within Hertfordshire, Bedfordshire and Buckinghamshire'. Held. One only needs to test it. If D took a wrong turn on a walk and entered someone's property, he would be at risk of a 5-year sentence. It would be small comfort that there is a prosecutor's discretion.

R v Boness 2005 EWCA Crim 2395, 2006 1 Cr App R (S) 120 (p 690) at para 69 D was a persistent offender and had admitted to drug misuse in the community. There were three main aspects to his antisocial behaviour: threatening behaviour (two incidents), vehicle crime (three incidents) and other offences of dishonesty such as burglary and theft (three incidents and other incidents of handling stolen goods). He was sentenced to a custodial sentence of 3 years' detention and was thus subject to a period on licence and subject to recall or return to custody.

First prohibition: D was prohibited from 'Remaining on any shop, commercial or hospital premises if asked to leave by staff. Entering any premises from which barred'. The prosecution submitted that D had convictions for offences of dishonesty, including an attempted burglary of shop premises, and he has been reprimanded for shoplifting. Thus, there appears to be a foundation for such a prohibition. It is submitted that this term is capable of being understood by D and is proportionate given that it hinges upon being refused permission to enter/remain on particular premises by those who have control of them. Held. We agree, although we wonder whether D would understand the staccato sentence: 'Entering any premises from which barred'.

Second prohibition: D was prohibited from 'Entering upon any private land adjoining any dwelling premises or commercial premises outside of opening hours of that premises without the express permission of a person in charge of that premises. This includes front gardens, driveways and paths. Except in the course of lawful employment'. Held. It was pointed out that in *R v McGrath* 2005 [see above] the Court of Appeal held that a term which prohibited the appellant from 'trespassing on any land belonging to any person whether legal or natural within those counties' was too wide and harsh. If D took a wrong turn on a walk and entered someone's property, he would be at risk of a 5-year prison sentence. This prohibition, albeit less open to criticism than the one in *R v McGrath* 2005, is also too wide and harsh. Although certain pieces of land might easily be identified as being caught by the prohibition (such as a front garden, driveway or path) it might be harder to recognise, say, in more rural areas. The absence of any geographical restriction reinforces our view. Furthermore, there is no practical way that compliance with the order could be enforced, at least outside the appellant's immediate home area.

84.85 ***Prostitution***

JSB ASBO Guide for the Judiciary 2007 Appendix 2, Valid prohibitions, see www.banksr.com Other Matters Other Documents tab ASBOs

Type of antisocial behaviour	Possible prohibitions	Comment
Prostitution	The prohibition should prevent entry into a clearly defined area. The order might include a prohibition of loitering for the purpose of prostitution.	Prohibiting prostitutes from entering an area may lead to the problem arising in another area. However, care needs to be exercised over proportionality. The second prohibition might offend the principle that the prohibition should be preventative rather than add to the potential punishment for a criminal offence.
Kerb crawling	Exclusion from a defined area. Prohibition of approaching female pedestrians in a specific area.	Driving disqualification can be effective in cases such as this.

84.86 ***Public servants, Threatening abusing etc.***

JSB ASBO Guide for the Judiciary 2007 Appendix 2, Valid prohibitions, see www.banksr.com Other Matters Other Documents tab ASBOs

Type of antisocial behaviour	Possible prohibitions	Comment
Threatening, abusive behaviour particularly when directed to public servants such as social workers, hospital staff or housing officers	Not to go within a specific distance of the offices of the relevant departments. Not to approach staff of the departments.	If included in a prohibition, the term 'antisocial behaviour' requires further definition or limitation so as to provide clarity to the defendant. Any prohibition relating to the commission of further 'acts causing harassment, alarm or distress' would not be appropriate without further limitation: *CPS v T* 2006 EWHC 728 (Admin).

84.87 ***Raves, rowdy games etc.***

JSB ASBO Guide for the Judiciary 2007 Appendix 2, Valid prohibitions, see www.banksr.com Other Matters Other Documents tab ASBOs

Type of antisocial behaviour	Possible prohibitions	Comment
Noise nuisance caused by raves, rowdy games and chanting by gangs (e.g. football supporters)	Non-association clauses in ASBOs are more effective in enabling prevention of antisocial behaviour than orders not to cause nuisance. Exclusion from a defined area is effective.	Prohibition which attempts to prevent the possession of equipment for playing music or games can be effective but often the defendant is not the owner, but merely a participant in the rowdy behaviour.

84.88 ***Sexual activity prohibitions***

R v Boyd 2013 EWCA Crim 2384 D was convicted of manslaughter. D admitted to enjoying intercourse with transvestite men. He also admitted that he and others would have intercourse with his dog, which he had specifically trained for such a purpose. D had consensual sexual activity with V, the deceased. V suffered internal injury as a result of having an instrument or a hand inserted into his rectum. Expert evidence stated this would have measured at least 18 cm. A term in his SOPO prohibited: a) seeking or having sexual relationships of any kind with male transvestites and b) using advertisements or any Internet or telecommunications network for contacting male transvestites. Held. Both terms were flawed. They failed to distinguish between: a) homosexual activity between consenting male transvestites and b) dangerous sexual practice which resulted in this fatality. They were neither necessary nor proportionate.

84.89 ***Shoplifting***

Heron v Plymouth City Council 2009 EWHC 3562 (Admin) High Court H was a persistent shoplifter who targeted security officers and store detectives who sought to stop him etc. The Magistrates imposed a condition on H that sought to enable those who question or stop this offender to require him to prove that any item he has with him has been lawfully purchased. It read, 'Not to have with him or carry any packaged, wrapped, bagged, new or unused goods or objects not belonging to him, except food, in any public place without a valid receipt or the consent of the owner of the packaged, wrapped, bagged, new or unused goods or objects in Plymouth as marked in red on Map 2.' Held. Until I had assistance from counsel I did not know what on earth it meant. To one who does not claim to be a particularly frequent reader of the terms of ASBOs, it has an unpromising beginning if I cannot understand it. Whether H could understand it or not remains not so much a matter of speculation as certainty. It offends the need to keep the terms of an ASBO, of which, after all, the consequences of a breach could be imprisonment for as long as 5 years, as simple and as clear as possible. It is all too easy apparently for H to continue to steal without any apparent means of being successfully stopped. I strike it out.

84.90 ***Tools etc. for theft etc., Possession of***

R v McGrath 2005 EWCA Crim 353, 2 Cr App R (S) 85 (p 525) D, a car thief, was banned from 'having in his possession in any public place any window hammer, screwdriver, torch or any tool or implement which could be used for the purposes of breaking into motor vehicles'. Held. This was too wide. The meaning of the words 'any tool or implement' is impossible to ascertain. The prohibition also overlaps with the offence of going equipped.

R v Boness 2005 EWCA Crim 2395, 2006 1 Cr App R (S) 120 (p 690) D was a persistent prolific offender and had admitted to drug misuse in the community. There were three main aspects to his antisocial behaviour: threatening behaviour (two incidents), vehicle crime (three incidents) and other offences of dishonesty such as burglary and theft (three incidents and other incidents of handling stolen goods). He was sentenced to a custodial sentence of 3 years' detention and was thus subject to a period on licence and subject to recall or return to custody. D was prohibited from 'Having any item with you in public which could be used in the commission of a burglary, or theft of or from vehicles except that you may carry one door key for your house and one motor vehicle or bicycle lock key. A motor vehicle key can only be carried if you are able to inform a checking officer of the registration number of the vehicle and that it can be ascertained that the vehicle is insured for you to drive it'. If so, the order is neither clear nor proportionate. Held. We agree. The first part of this prohibition has been drafted too widely and lacks clarity. We agree there are many items that might be used in the commission of a burglary, such as a credit card, a mobile phone or a pair of gloves. Was D being prohibited from carrying such items? Order quashed on this and other grounds.

84.91 ***Tools etc. as potential weapons, Possession of***

R v Boness 2005 EWCA Crim 2395, 2006 1 Cr App R (S) 120 (p 690) D was a persistent prolific offender and had admitted to drug misuse in the community. There were three main aspects to his antisocial behaviour: threatening behaviour (two incidents), vehicle crime (three incidents) and other offences of dishonesty such as burglary and theft (three incidents and other incidents of handling stolen goods). He was sentenced to a custodial sentence of 3 years' detention and was thus subject to a period on licence and subject to recall or return to custody. D was prohibited from 'Having possession of any article in public or carried in any vehicle that could be used as a weapon. This will include glass bottles, drinking glasses and tools'. It was submitted that: a) the necessity for such a prohibition is not supported by the material put forward in support of the application, b) there is very little in the appellant's antecedent history which indicates a disposition to use a weapon, c) furthermore, it is submitted that the wording of the prohibition is obviously too wide, resulting in lack of clarity and consequences which are not commensurate with the risk, d) many otherwise innocent items have the capacity to be used as weapons, including anything hard or with an edge or point, e) this prohibition has draconian consequences and f) the appellant would be prohibited from doing a huge range of things including having a drink in a public bar. Held. We agree.

84.92 ***Vehicle prohibitions***

R v Boness 2005 EWCA Crim 2395, 2006 1 Cr App R (S) 120 (p 690) para 74 D was a persistent prolific offender and had admitted to drug misuse in the community. There were three main aspects to his antisocial behaviour: threatening behaviour (two incidents), vehicle crime (three incidents) and other offences of dishonesty such as burglary and theft (three incidents and other incidents of handling stolen goods). He was sentenced to a custodial sentence of 3 years' detention and was thus subject to a period on licence and subject to recall or return to custody. para 74 Prohibition 8 was, 'Touching or entering any unattended vehicle without the express permission of the owner'. It was submitted: 'D had previous convictions for aggravated vehicle taking and interfering with a motor vehicle, and has been reprimanded for theft of a motorcycle. Held. The prohibition is sufficiently clear and precise, and is commensurate with the risk it seeks to meet'.

para 86 Prohibition 13 was, 'Being carried on any vehicle other than a vehicle in lawful use'. Held. We are not convinced that this prohibition is sufficiently clear and proportionate. We do not find the expression 'lawful use' to be free from difficulty. If 'the carrying' is likely to constitute a specific criminal offence (e.g. one of the family of taking without consent offences), what does this order add? We would have preferred a geographical limit.

Making the order

84.93 ***Making the order***

Test to apply This issue is dealt with at the beginning of each chapter for the particular preventive orders.

Note: Most orders only enable the court to impose prohibitions whereas the Criminal Behaviour Order also enables the court to impose a term requiring the offender to do something, Anti-Social Behaviour, Crime and Policing Act 2014 s 22(5)(b), see **25.13**. Ed.

C v Sunderland Youth Court 2003 EWHC 2385 (Admin), 2004 1 Cr App R (S) 76 (p 443) The Magistrates' Court must act fairly and have regard to all relevant considerations. What fairness requires and what considerations are relevant will depend upon the circumstances of each particular case. There is the elementary requirement that there should be clarity as to the basis for any order made by the Magistrates under Crime and Disorder Act 1998 s 1C, particularly if the breach of such an order exposes a person to potential criminal penalties. The discretion conferred by section 1C, although broad, is not unfettered. It was particularly important that justice should be seen to be done.

84.94 ***The findings of fact must be recorded/Duty to give reasons***

Breach of ASBO Guideline 2008, see www.banksr.com Other Matters Guidelines tab page 13 para 3 ASBOs It is particularly important that the findings of fact giving rise to the making of the order are recorded by the court.

R v P 2004 EWCA Crim 287, 2 Cr App R (S) 63 (p 343) LCJ The findings of fact giving rise to the making of the order must be recorded.

W v Acton Youth Court 2005 EWHC 954 (Admin) High Court D was given an ASBO. Held. It is necessary for the magistrates to give reasons in some form on making an order. They may be given orally at the time of making an order. They should be sufficient to enable the person who is the subject of the order to understand why it has been made and to indicate to all that the Magistrates have applied their minds to the correct issues. Here it would seem that nothing was said by the Magistrates other than such words as were necessary to make the order.

R v W and F 2006 EWCA Crim 686 The judge should state his findings of fact expressly and they should be recorded in writing on the order made by the judge in the space provided on the form set out in the Practice Direction.

R (McGarrett) v Kingston Crown Court 2009 EWHC 1776 (Admin) High Court The Judge did not record any findings of fact. D appealed over this failure and other grounds. Held. We quash the ASBO over this failure and other procedural unfairness.

Heron v Plymouth City Council 2009 EWHC 3562 (Admin) High Court H was a persistent shoplifter and the Magistrates made an ASBO. The reasons given were as follows: 'They would address the more recent pattern of offending in the case law. They had read the case law.' Held. 'Plainly reasons need only be short and simple, but magistrates now are trained to and do in any case of conviction, or in cases such as these, give short reasons so that the offender or the person placed subject to an ASBO should know the reasons why it was imposed and what it is getting at.' These reasons given did not satisfy that requirement. The reasons in the case stated plainly do, but reasons need to be given at the time.

R v Uddin and Others 2015 EWCA Crim 1918, 2016 1 Cr App R (S) 57 (p 57) Nine defendants were given ASBOs. On the form with the order, the part on the back of the form for the facts to be stated was blank. Held. This court has previously emphasised that a judge should state his findings of fact and they should be recorded in the written order, see *R v W and F* 2006 EWCA Crim 686 at para 45. We repeat that.

For the general duty to give reasons, see **86.49**.

84.95 ***Explain sentence, Judge/Magistrate must/The exact terms of the order must be given in open court***

Criminal Justice Act 2003 s 174(1)(a)[1012] The court must state in open court, in ordinary language and in general terms, the court's reasons for deciding on the sentence.

(b) The court must explain to the offender in ordinary language:

(i) the effect of the sentence,

(ii) the effects of non-compliance with any order that the offender is required to comply with and that forms part of the sentence,

[1012] As substituted by Legal Aid, Sentencing and Punishment of Offenders Act 2012 s 64

(iii) any power of the court to vary or review any order that forms part of the sentence…

R v P 2004 EWCA Crim 287, 2 Cr App R (S) 63 (p 343) LCJ The order (an ASBO) must be explained to the offender. The exact terms of the order must be pronounced in open court and the written order must accurately reflect the order as pronounced.

R v Khan 2018 EWCA Crim 1472, 2 Cr App R (S) 53 (p 426) The Court of Appeal considered a Criminal Behaviour Order. Held. para 15 In the case of a foreign national defendant, consideration should be given to the need for the order to be translated.

84.96 ***Duty to explain if order not made when it could be***

Criminal Procedure Rules 2015 2015/1490 Rule 31.2(3) Where the court decides not to make, where it could:

(a) a Football Banning Order, or

(b) a Parenting Order, after a person under 16 is convicted of an offence,

the court must announce, at a hearing in public, the reasons for its decision.

How long should the order and prohibition(s) last?

84.97 ***How long should the order last?***

Magistrates' Court Sentencing Guidelines 2008, see www.banksr.com Other Matters Guidelines tab page 168 It is advisable to make an order for a specific period, [and] when considering the duration of an order imposed on a youth, the potential for the subject to mature may be a relevant factor. Not all prohibitions set out in an ASBO have to run for the full term of the ASBO itself. The test must always be what is necessary to deal with the particular antisocial behaviour of the offender and what is proportionate in the circumstances. At least one of the prohibitions must last for the duration of the order but not all are required to last for the 2 years that is the minimum length of an order.

R v Rampley 2006 EWCA Crim 2203 The Judge made the SOPO until further order. Held. There are advantages in the defendant knowing that there is a finite term to the order. 7 years substituted.

Note: The then relevant section, Sexual Offences Act 2003 s 107(1)(b), gave the court the power to make the order 'until further order'. Ed.

See also: *R v Whitehead and Others* 2013 EWCA Crim 2401 (Conspiracy to steal mountain bikes at car parks in Cumbria. Travelled from Liverpool in a van. Cutting tools used. Stole £13,850 worth of bikes. Items totalling £2,750 taken. Aged 27-41. Each had a poor record. Planning and targeting of high-value items. Short-lived conspiracy. 10 years from release reduced to **5 years.**)

Note: The best way to determine the appropriate length for an order is to carefully evaluate the factors in the case you are considering. Other cases will give little assistance. Ed.

84.98 ***A life order was appropriate***

An example: *R v Avery and Others* 2009 EWCA Crim 2670, 2010 2 Cr App R (S) 33 (p 209) (ASBOs For three defendants, **life** was appropriate. For one defendant, 5 years not life, see **84.37**.)

R v Collard 2004 EWCA Crim 1664, 2005 1 Cr App R (S) 34 (p 155) D pleaded to seven counts of making indecent photographs or pseudo-photographs of children (1-7) and 16 counts of possession of indecent photographs or pseudo-photographs of children (8-24). On counts 1-7 he received 1 year's imprisonment on each count and on counts 8-24 he received 2 years' imprisonment on each count. All sentences were to be served concurrently. 5,284 similar offences were taken into consideration. D was also subject to a Restraining Order under Sex Offenders Act 1997 s 5A, which prohibited him from owning, using, possessing or having any access to any personal computer, laptop or any other equipment capable of downloading any material from the Internet. The prohibition was not to apply to the lawful access to, and use of, the Internet in the course of lawful employment. D appealed. Held. Bearing in mind the nature of the material, the depth of

D's addiction or obsession and that there was nothing to indicate when D's proclivities might cease, an **indefinite order** was correct. He can apply to discharge the order at any time.

84.99 ***On the facts, order too long***

R v Vittles 2004 EWCA Crim 1089, 2005 1 Cr App R (S) 8 (p 31) D pleaded to a specimen count of theft, driving whilst disqualified and driving with no insurance. He asked for 12 thefts and three attempted thefts to be taken into account. The thefts were from cars to support his heavy drug use. Frequent thefts were from US servicemen's cars near an air base. He had stolen over £3,500 worth of goods. His record was terrible and was predominantly about similar thefts from vehicles. He was sentenced to 3 years 10 months. An ASBO with a geographical restriction for the whole of Forest Heath except to attend court was imposed. Held. Exceptionally an ASBO was appropriate because of the vulnerable US victims specifically targeted. This was notwithstanding the substantial prison sentence. However, **5 years** not life.

R v Whitton 2006 EWCA Crim 3229 D pleaded to three exposures. Within a 3-month period, D had committed 12 separate offences involving exposure to females between the ages of 11 and 24, with the victims predominantly in their early teens. A number of these offences occurred outside a school. D, aged 43, was assessed as posing a medium risk to children and the public. Held. The duration of the SOPO was excessive, however, and the appropriate term was **5 years** not 10.

R v Ward 2007 EWCA Crim 1436 D was convicted of attempted theft. He was sentenced to 3½ years' imprisonment and made subject to an ASBO which prohibited him from a) entering the London Borough of Kensington and Chelsea, and b) having in his possession any articles in connection with the removal of motor vehicle wheels or alloys. The order was to run indefinitely. D, aged 34, had 119 previous convictions including many offences of theft and vehicle interference. Held. Whilst it was appropriate to make the order both geographically and as to the activities proscribed, an indefinite order was disproportionately long. An order for **10 years** would have been appropriate.

See also: *R v Rush* 2005 EWCA Crim 1316 (ASBO **5 years** not 10)

R v Rampley 2006 EWCA Crim 2203 (SOPO Aged 53. On the facts, **7 years** not until further order.)

R v Avery and Others 2009 EWCA Crim 2670, 2010 2 Cr App R (S) 33 (p 209) (ASBO For one defendant **5 years** not life).

R v Ball 2010 EWCA Crim 1740 (ASBO ABH and railway offence. Attacked railway conductor. Abusive behaviour to others. Prohibition against using a train. **3 years** and not 10 so order lasts just over 2 years after his release.)

R v Jackson 2012 EWCA Crim 2602 D pleaded to voyeurism, indecent photographs of a child and possession of extreme photographs. He appealed his SOPO. Held. There have to be good reasons for extending the order beyond the reporting period. There may well be cases in which it would be entirely appropriate to do that. It is clear that there is no legal proscription which prevents the extension beyond that period. However, here **5 years** was proportionate.

R v Juneidi 2014 EWCA Crim 996 (D pleaded to seven indecent images offences. A pre-sentence report found he posed no physical risk to children, but had a worrying sexual interest in them. As D had sought to address his offending by paying for psychotherapy, **10 years** not an indefinite order.)

Combined with other orders

84.100 ***Custody, Combined with***

Magistrates' Court Sentencing Guidelines 2008, see www.banksr.com Other Matters Guidelines tab page 168 Where a custodial sentence of 12 months or more is imposed and the offender is liable to be released on licence and thus subject to recall, an order will not generally be necessary.

Note: This section of the guideline related to ASBOs. Ed.

R v Barclay and Others 2011 EWCA Crim 32, 2 Cr App R (S) 67 (p 385) On five occasions D sold £10 wraps of cocaine or heroin to undercover police officers posing as retail purchasers in St Pauls in Bristol. The purity of the drugs was around 29-30%. He was found with £1,735 cash when arrested. D, aged 19, had nine convictions for 15 offences including simple possession of class C (×3), class B (×2) and class A (×1). Police evidence was that the area had been taken over by drug gangs and the residents were intimidated and service providers had to have police escorts. The Judge imposed 4 years' YOI and an ASBO. The ASBO prohibited D from entering certain areas, associating with named individuals and carrying a mobile not registered in his name. It also required his mobile to be registered with an intelligence officer. It was argued that in light of the custodial sentence, the ASBO was not necessary, on the basis that whilst in custody, D would undertake courses to address his offending behaviour, and upon release would be subject to licence conditions. Issue was also taken with the prohibitions. The three other defendants were aged 19 (×2) and 24. They had varying past criminality. Held. There was an obvious basis for concluding that the custodial sentence might not dissuade D from future offending. In relation to the other defendants, the post-conviction ASBOs were not simply directed at future drugs offending by the appellants but also…at their involvement in the antisocial behaviour associated with the open street dealing of drugs. These ASBOs were also targeted at the nuisance, fear and intimidation which were conducive and preparatory to open drug dealing. The defendants had to be prohibited from contributing to this type of antisocial behaviour separate from, but essential to, the open market in drugs. The orders are upheld.

R v Smith and Others 2011 EWCA Crim 1772, 2012 1 Cr App R (S) 82 (p 468) The usual rule ought to be that an indeterminate sentence needs no SOPO, at least unless there is some very unusual feature which means that such an order could add something useful and did not run the risk of undesirably tying the hands of the offender managers later.

R v W 2015 EWCA Crim 434 D was convicted of rapes of children aged under 13 and other sex offences. He was sentenced to 20 years and given a SOPO. The issue of whether the SOPO was necessary arose. The prosecution said there was a lacuna in the law because the Disclosure and Barring Service barring applied to regulated activity which meant activity 'frequently carried out by the same person' on more than two days in any period of 30 days. They said if D on release was to work as a classroom assistant, sports instructor or scout master once or twice a month he would not be covered by the barring system. Held. The SOPO was necessary.

Old cases: *R v P* 2004 EWCA Crim 287, 2 Cr App R (S) 63 (p 343) LCJ (Where custodial sentences in excess of a few months are passed, and offenders are liable to be released on licence, circumstances in which there is demonstrable necessity to make ASBOs are likely to be limited.)

R v Vittles 2004 EWCA Crim 1089, 2005 1 Cr App R (S) 8 (p 31) (Exceptionally an ASBO was appropriate because of the vulnerable US victims specifically targeted. This was notwithstanding the substantial prison sentence.)

R v Frost 2006 EWCA Crim 2705 (Having regard to the imposition of a substantial custodial sentence with licence provisions following D's release, the requirement of necessity was not met in this case. ASBO quashed.)

Note: These principles for combining preventive orders and extended sentences and life would appear to apply to Sexual Harm Prevention Orders (SHPOs). However, the obvious advantage of having both orders is that an SHPO can prohibit and penalise activity in prison concerning children which is not or may not be prohibited by the prison, e.g. contacting children. A licence only comes into force when the prisoner is released. There is a lot to be said for making most SHPOs start from the date of sentence. Ed.

84.101 ***Extended sentences, Combined with***

Att-Gen's Ref No 55 of 2008 2008 EWCA Crim 2790, 2009 2 Cr App R (S) 22 (p 142)[1013] When exercising its judgement as to whether a sentence of IPP was appropriate, the court was entitled to and should have in mind all the alternative and cumulative methods of providing the necessary public protection against the risk posed by the individual offender. A Sexual Offences Prevention Order, with appropriate conditions attached, could form part of the total protective sentencing package when structured around a determinate or extended sentence. The primary question was the nature and extent of the risk posed by the individual offender and the most appropriate method of addressing that risk and providing public protection. If the overall sentencing package provided appropriate protection then IPP should not be imposed.

Note: This case may have been superceded or adapted by *R v Smith* 2011 below. The references to IPP have not been removed in case part of the context is lost. Ed.

R v Stocker 2013 EWCA Crim 1993 D was convicted of rape and other sexual offences. The Judge imposed an IPP sentence and a SOPO. The Judge found that a SOPO was necessary and would not be academic because if D appealed against sentence, the Court of Appeal might set aside the IPP sentence and substitute for it a determinate sentence. Held. On that interpretation of *R v Smith and Others* 2011 EWCA Crim 1772, 2012 1 Cr App R (S) 82 (p 468), a SOPO should be imposed in virtually all cases of dangerous offenders because there is always the possibility of an appeal. That cannot be right. The principle in *R v Smith* 2011 is clear. There is nothing exceptional about this case and, in the light of the indeterminate sentence of imprisonment, it was not necessary to make a SOPO. D will only be released from the indeterminate sentence when it is deemed 'safe' to do so and he will be subject to appropriate conditions. Order quashed.

Note: The principles for imposing SOPOs and IPP with other protective orders and extended sentences are similar. The note at the end of the previous case applies to this case. Ed.

84.102 ***Life sentences, Combined with***

R v Smith and Others 2011 EWCA Crim 1772, 2012 1 Cr App R (S) 82 (p 468) The usual rule ought to be that an indeterminate sentence needs no SOPO, at least unless there is some very unusual feature which means that such an order could add something useful and did not run the risk of undesirably tying the hands of the offender managers later.

R v I 2012 EWCA Crim 1792 LCJ D was sentenced to IPP and a SOPO. He appealed against the SOPO relying on *R v Smith* 2011 EWCA Crim 1772, 2012 1 Cr App R (S) 82 (p 468). Held. As a result of *R v Smith* 2011, it would be rare for the two orders to be made simultaneously. Rare does not mean never, but here we quash the SOPO.

R v Watts 2014 EWCA Crim 1211 D pleaded to the rape of a child and kidnapping. The Judge gave him life and a SOPO. The defence appealed. The prosecution pointed out there were differences between the sanction for breach of a licence and the penalties after a conviction for breach of a SOPO. He also said a breach of a SOPO would be more apparent on the record so life and a SOPO was appropriate. Held. We agree with the distinctions. We don't say the two orders can never be combined. Release is only on very considered terms. A breach of licence for a life prisoner is not likely to generate a short recall. We do not think there is the necessity of a further public trial rather than a prompt recall. The usual rule ought to be an indeterminate sentence needs no SOPO, unless there is some very unusual feature which means a SOPO could add something useful, rather than tying the hands of the offender managers later. We quash the SOPO because the conditions [D should be under] are best left when release is about to take place.

Note: The note at the end of para **84.100** may assist. Ed.

[1013] The title in the judgment is *R v C and Others* 2008 EWCA Crim 2790.

84.103 ***Youth Rehabilitation Orders***
F v Bolton Crown Court 2009 EWHC 240 (Admin) High Court D was convicted of possession of an imitation firearm with intent. He was aged 13 and was sentenced to a 2-year Supervision Order with a curfew. An ASBO was made. Defence counsel said there was no reason to believe that the Supervision Order together with the curfew would not be adequate to contain D's behaviour and as such the ASBO was unnecessary. Held. The ASBO was not necessary.

Varying and discharging preventive orders

Note: There is normally a section near the end of each preventive order that lists the powers to vary etc. Ed.

84.104 ***Applications to vary/discharge and service of material***
Applications to vary or revoke behaviour order
Criminal Procedure Rules 2015 2015/1490 Rule 31.5(2) A person applying under this rule must:
(a) apply in writing as soon as practicable after becoming aware of the grounds for doing so, explaining:
(i) what material circumstances have changed since the order was made, and
(ii) why the order should be varied or revoked as a result, and
(b) serve the application on:
(i) the court officer,
(ii) as appropriate, the prosecutor or defendant, and
(iii) any other person listed in paragraph (1)(b), if the court so directs.
(3) A party who wants the court to take account of any particular evidence before making its decision must, as soon as practicable:
(a) serve notice on:[1014]
(i) the court officer,
(ii) as appropriate, the prosecutor or defendant, and
(iii) any other person listed in paragraph (1)(b) on whom the court directed the application to be served, and
(b) in that notice identify the evidence and attach any written statement that has not already been served.
(4) The court may decide an application under this rule with or without a hearing.
(5) But the court must not:
(a) dismiss an application under this rule unless the applicant has had an opportunity to make representations at a hearing (whether or not the applicant in fact attends), or
(b) allow an application under this rule unless everyone required to be served, by this rule or by the court, has had at least 14 days in which to make representations, including representations about whether there should be a hearing.
(6) The court officer must:
(a) serve the application on any person, if the court so directs, and
(b) give notice of any hearing to:
(i) the applicant, and
(ii) any person required to be served, by this rule or by the court.
Note [in the rules]: The legislation that gives the court power to make a behaviour order may limit the circumstances in which it may be varied or revoked and may require a hearing. The hearsay rules apply to variation and discharge hearings.
R (Langley) v Preston Crown Court 2008 EWHC 2623 (Admin) High Court D was given a stand-alone ASBO. Held. The provisions of variation or discharge are in the Act to deal with change of circumstances or potentially with the passage of time, where the

[1014] The Criminal Procedure (Amendment No 2) Rules 2016 2016/705 para 11(d) removes the requirement that the notice has to be in writing. In force 3/10/16

offender is able to come back to the court and say he has mended his ways, left the area, got a job or any other consideration which may lead the court to think that the prohibition on him can be lifted.

84.105 ***Applications to vary or revoke Time limits***
Criminal Procedure Rules 2015 2015/1490 Rule 31.5(2) A person applying under this rule must:

(a) apply in writing as soon as practicable after becoming aware of the grounds for doing so, explaining:
  (i) what material circumstances have changed since the order was made, and
  (ii) why the order should be varied or revoked as a result, and
(b) serve the application on:
  (i) the court officer,
  (ii) as appropriate, the prosecutor or defendant, and
  (iii) any other person listed in paragraph (1)(b), if the court so directs.

Criminal Procedure Rules 2015 2015/1490 Rule 31.11 The court may:

(a) shorten a time limit or extend it (even after it has expired),
(b) allow a notice or application to be given in a different form, or presented orally.

Sadler v Worcester Magistrates' Court 2014 EWHC 1715 (Admin) High Court D was convicted of serious sexual offences in Romania including buggery of a young boy. D returned to the UK. On three occasions a 15-year-old boy, NP, had stayed at D's flat. An interim SOPO was made. The police subsequently found the boy at D's address. A stand-alone SOPO was made. D's appeal to the Crown Court was dismissed. After the 5-year limit had expired, D applied to discharge the order. The respondent called evidence that D had not undergone treatment and that on up to 50 occasions he had travelled to countries inferentially as a sex tourist. NP gave evidence that nothing sexual had occurred between D and himself, either before or after the imposition of the SOPO. The District Judge said that the starting point had to be that the SOPO was properly made and D could not seek to undermine the finding that in 2007 he posed a serious risk of sexual harm. The District Judge declined to discharge the order, but varied the order having regard to *R v Smith* 2011 EWCA Crim 1772, 2012 1 Cr App R (S) 82 (p 468). D's appeal to the Crown Court was again dismissed. The defence submitted that NP's evidence was highly relevant and the District Judge was wrong to ignore it because if it had been available in 2007, the order would not have been made. Held. The District Judge was correct to conclude that evidence should not be adduced to establish that the SOPO should not have been made. When the application is to discharge…a change of circumstances is necessary, otherwise the application is no more than an appeal against the original order. There was no change of circumstance since the order was made, so appeal dismissed.

84.106 ***Variation includes extending the order***
Leeds City Council v RG 2007 EWHC 1612 (Admin) High Court D, aged 13, was made subject to an ASBO following a stand-alone civil application. Leeds City Council sought a variation of the order to extend the term for a further 3 years. Held. In the case of an application to vary the length of an order the applying authority will have to persuade the magistrates that it is appropriate to vary the length of the existing ASBO, rather than make an application for a new one. The Magistrates were thus wrong to conclude that they had no power to vary the length of the ASBO in question.

84.107 ***Who can apply to vary?***
R v D 2005 EWCA Crim 3660 D pleaded to eight counts of sexual abuse of his daughter. D was subject to a Sexual Offences Prevention Order, a condition of which prevented him from seeing his son, L. D appealed. Held. In the legislation, L has no right to apply to vary, renew or discharge the order.

84.108 ***Should the Council etc. apply for a new order instead?***
James v Birmingham City Council 2010 EWHC 282 (Admin) High Court It was argued that because there was no appeal from a variation of an ASBO it would be fairer if a fresh order was applied for. Held. Where any fresh antisocial behaviour or other unacceptable conduct (such as breaches of that order) is closely interlinked with the original order, it may be desirable that the limitations imposed by the original order should stand, and it may be more sensible to vary rather than impose a fresh order. This is so even where the period of the order is varied by an extension of two years or more. Here the Court was entitled to consider that a variation was appropriate.

84.109 ***Need there be a fresh antisocial act?***
James v Birmingham City Council 2010 EWHC 282 (Admin) High Court There is no basis for saying that a variation requires the establishment of a fresh antisocial act. Frequently, ASBOs will be varied to reflect a change in circumstances which is wholly unrelated to the commission of any fresh antisocial act, such as, say, a defendant may obtain a job in the forbidden area or in circumstances where he will inevitably have contact with someone with whom he should not associate. No antisocial act need be established to justify the variation. There is in principle no basis for treating an extension of duration of the order any differently from any other terms.

84.110 ***Purpose of variation and discharge***
R (Langley) v Preston Crown Court 2008 EWHC 2623 (Admin) High Court D was given a stand-alone ASBO. Held. The provisions of variation or discharge are in the Act to deal with changes of circumstances or potentially with the passage of time, where the offender is able to come back to the court and say he has mended his ways, left the area, got a job or any other consideration which may lead the court to think that the prohibition on him can be lifted.

Appeals

84.111 ***Who can appeal?***
R v D 2005 EWCA Crim 3660 D pleaded to eight counts of sexual abuse of his daughter. D was subject to a Sexual Offences Prevention Order, a condition of which prevented him from seeing his son, L. D appealed. Held. In the legislation, L has no right to apply to vary, renew or discharge the order.

84.112 ***Test for the Court of Appeal***
R v Mortimer 2010 EWCA Crim 1303 D was convicted of three counts of sexual assault on a child under the age of 13 and one count of causing or inciting a child to engage in sexual activity. He was sentenced to 3 years' IPP. The Judge added a Sexual Offences Prevention Order. D appealed against the order on the basis that the terms were too wide, insufficiently clear and for an indefinite period of time. Held. There are three questions for us to consider: a) Is the order complained of necessary to protect the public generally or any particular member of the public from serious sexual harm? b) If it is necessary at all, are the particular terms of the order that has been made oppressive? c) Are the terms of the particular order proportionate?
DPP v Bulmer 2015 EWHC 2323 (Admin), 2016 1 Cr App R (S) 12 (p 74) para 22 B had a long record of antisocial behaviour offences and breaches of court orders, but she was unable to manage her chronic alcoholism. The District Judge refused to make a Criminal Behaviour Order because there was no positive requirement to assist her with her alcoholism and an order would not prevent her antisocial behaviour. Held. para 28 An appellate court is generally reluctant to interfere with findings of fact and evaluative judgments made by the primary decision-maker. This is particularly so where the decision-maker has heard oral evidence and has had an opportunity to assess witnesses. A degree of circumspection on the part of an appellate court will also be appropriate where, as in this case, the primary decision-maker makes findings on the basis of witness

statements and the other material before the court, [in this case[1015]] the schedule of convictions, and evaluates the evidence in those statements and that material. In this appeal by way of case stated, the appellant did not put those witness statements before this court. Generally speaking, this is not done and there is no need to do so. But the consequence is that this court is not in as good a position as the primary decision-maker to make the evaluation. Moreover, this court is primarily concerned with questions of law. para 36 The matter is not one of 'pure discretion'. Unless, however, the court hearing an appeal concludes that the judge has plainly erred in some way, either in his assessment of the facts or in applying the wrong test or leaving out of account matters which he was required to take into account, it should not interfere with his conclusion.

84.113 ***Appeals about applications to vary etc.***
Leeds City Council v RG 2007 EWHC 1612 (Admin) High Court para 11 D was made the subject of a stand-alone ASBO. The Council involved applied to the Magistrates' Court to extend the order. The Magistrates' Court refused to extend the order saying there was no power to do so. The Council appealed to the High Court. Held. The Magistrates were wrong to conclude there was no power to vary the order. The fact that there is no appeal from any variation is a matter which has caused us concern. But it seems to us this is insufficient in itself to justify a departure from the clear meaning of the subsection. The protection for a defendant is, in our view, provided by the fact that an application to vary, if it imposes more stringent obligations (such as greater length), on a defendant, can only succeed if the applying authority can put before the magistrates material which justifies the extension as necessary in order to achieve the statutory objective. The usual burden and standard of proof will apply to the determination of that question. Further, in an application to vary length, the applying authority will have to persuade the magistrates that it is appropriate to vary the length of the existing ASBO rather than make application for a new one. There would be a clear rationale, for example, for asking for an extension of an ASBO for less than two years, on the basis that the authority did not consider that it was necessary to have a further period as long as the minimum period of two years which would be necessary were a fresh ASBO to be ordered.
R (Langley) v Preston Crown Court 2008 EWHC 2623 (Admin) High Court D was given a stand-alone ASBO. Shortly before it expired, the Council applied to extend it and the application was granted. D appealed to the Crown Court and the Court decided there was no jurisdiction to hear the appeal. D appealed to the High Court. Held. An ASBO made in the Magistrates' Court on conviction is appealable to the Crown Court under Crime and Disorder Act 1998 s 4 in the same way as a free-standing ASBO but in neither case is there a right of appeal against a variation of the original ASBO. Case stated and judicial review are remedies available against the Magistrates' Court.

84.114 ***Appeals Individual consents at hearing***
R (T) v Manchester Crown Court 2005 EWHC 1396 (Admin) High Court T, aged 15, was made the subject of an ASBO after a series of complaints. T's mother consented to the making of the ASBO. The District Judge made the order after reading the papers. T appealed to the Crown Court on the basis that the order was not necessary. At the invitation of the advocate for the Council, the Judge dismissed the appeal citing no compelling reason to vacate the consent. T appealed and the Council did not contest the appeal. Held. It is clear that an order cannot be made merely on the basis of the consent of the person subject to it. The Court considering the making of an order must itself be satisfied to the required standard of proof...and, further, must exercise its own judgement. The Crown Court is not deprived of jurisdiction merely because the parent of the individual consented to the order in the Court below. Whether or not such consent was

[1015] The judgment has the word 'here' at this point. I am unsure what the Judge meant to say. It could have been 'hear' but that does not read well.

given, if a person subject to an order seeks to appeal, the appeal must be heard. However, if the claimant did consent in the Court below, that will be powerful evidence that there is absolutely nothing in the appeal. Order to strike out appeal quashed.

84.115 ***Judge fails to use appropriate test***
R v D 2005 EWCA Crim 3660 The Judge did not go through the appropriate steps before making a SOPO. Held. It therefore falls to this Court to exercise those powers afresh. On the facts, SOPO varied.

84.116 ***Can the Court of Appeal correct an invalid order?***
R v Monument 2005 EWCA Crim 30 D pleaded to 16 counts of making indecent photographs or pseudo-photographs of a child (8 months' imprisonment on each count, concurrent). D had downloaded 4,266 indecent images, notably 378 of which were at Level 4 and 23 at Level 5 (see *R v Oliver* 2002 EWCA Crim 2766). On the day of sentencing, no application was made for the imposition of a Restraining Order. Some 14 days later, the Crown made an application to re-list the case within the 28-day period under the slip rule in order to add a Restraining Order. That hearing was heard a week later. By this point, the legislation containing the provisions for the imposition of a Restraining Order had been repealed, and provisions allowing the imposition of a Sexual Offences Prevention Order had been enacted. This fact was overlooked by the parties. The Judge imposed a Restraining Order on D, stating he was not prepared to do so for a term exceeding 3 years and that it should take effect from that day. When the oversight was discovered, D appealed against the Restraining Order, arguing that it was invalid. The Crown argued that the order was valid as D was convicted prior to the earlier legislation being repealed. Held. What was purportedly 'done' under the earlier legislation could not have been done, as the legislation had been repealed. An argument that as a result of Interpretation Act 1978 s 17(2)(b) the effect of making a Restraining Order had the [same] effect as if a Sexual Offences Prevention Order had been made was unsustainable. Further, the Restraining Order could not be saved or preserved by Interpretation Act 1978 s 17(2)(b) as Sexual Offences Act 2003 s 104 did not re-enact the 1997 Act as: a) there were differences between the two orders, and b) the legislation had been repealed. The order was invalid. Finally, Criminal Appeal Act 1968 s 11(3)(b) precludes the substitution of a Restraining Order by a Sexual Offences Prevention Order as the legislation requires Sexual Offences Prevention Orders to be a minimum of 5 years, whereas the Restraining Order in question was for 3 years. Order invalid and set aside.
R v Aldridge and Eaton 2012 EWCA Crim 1456 LCJ E was given a 3-year SOPO. Later the Judge was told the minimum period was 5 years and he varied it to 5 years believing that was the order he made. The application for variation was out of time and no one attended. Held. The order was unlawful. The term could not be extended as that would be treating E 'more severely'. The order must be quashed.

84.117 ***Whether to appeal or vary/Old SOPOs***
R v Hoath 2011 EWCA Crim 274 LCJ H and S were given SOPOs and did not appeal the orders. Nearly 2½ years later H applied to vary the order. The Judge refused to vary the order saying it was too soon. S applied to vary 16 months later. The Judge said the challenge was to the breadth of the order and that was a matter for the Court of Appeal. He refused to vary the order. Held. Objections in principle to the terms of a SOPO imposed by the Crown Court should be raised by an appeal to the Court of Appeal and not by subsequent applications to vary to the Crown Court. Section 108(3) should be exercised where there was a change of circumstances. In our view the application as it is now put before the court is not an application for a variation at all. It is an appeal (substantially out of time) as to the ambit of the original order. However, where the defendant relies on particular and unanticipated difficulties arising from the form and/or wording of the order, those difficulties should be identified promptly (in writing and

with particularity) and sent to the prosecuting authority so as to see whether the matter can be put before the Crown Court on an agreed basis and in any event to narrow the area of dispute.

R v I 2012 EWCA Crim 1792 LCJ D was sentenced to IPP and a SOPO in 2006. He appealed against the SOPO relying on *R v Smith* 2011 EWCA Crim 1772, 2012 1 Cr App R (S) 82 (p 468). Held. As the case was heard long before *R v Smith* 2011, the SOPO was justified. We are not a review body for every SOPO.

R v Martin 2012 EWCA Crim 2272 D pleaded to indecent photographs and was in May 2010 given 30 months and a SOPO. On his release he applied to vary the SOPO and a draft revised order was agreed. The Judge, following *R v Hoath* 2011, refused. D appealed out of time. Held in October 2012. The order was disproportionately restrictive. We quash it and substitute another.

Note: There are thousands of individuals with inappropriate preventive orders and terms. Not to allow appeals may be judicially convenient but it is in everyone's interest that someone is able to review these unsuitable orders. The Lord Chief Justice may consider the order is something that happened long ago but a preventive order applies to the present and the future. It is very much in the interests of society and those who have to enforce these orders that the orders are proportionate and fair. It would be unfortunate that an individual whose advocate only concentrated on the prison term and failed to notice that the SOPO was too wide was stopped from appealing (because the application was out of time) and was stopped from varying (because he should have appealed). It would also create an anomaly. A defendant who reoffends would have the opportunity when sentenced for the fresh offence to argue for an appropriate SOPO. A defendant who does not reoffend would be in a less fortunate position. Ed.

84.118 ***Appeals to vary etc. Which court?***

R (Langley) v Preston Crown Court 2008 EWHC 2623 (Admin) High Court D was given a stand-alone ASBO. Shortly before it expired the Council applied to extend it and the application was granted. D appealed to the Crown Court and the Court decided there was no jurisdiction to hear the appeal. D appealed to the High Court. Held. *Obiter* Where an ASBO is made following a conviction in the Crown Court, an appeal lies to the Court of Appeal as it would be 'an order made by a court when dealing with an offender' and thus be appealable, Criminal Appeal Act 1968 s 50 (see also section 9 of that Act). Although we heard no argument on the point, a variation of an ASBO which was made by the Crown Court would, at least arguably, also fall within the description of an 'order made by a court when dealing with an offender' and thus also be appealable to the Court of Appeal. The provisions of the Criminal Appeal Act 1968 do not of course apply to a Magistrates' Court order. It would seem that the only right of appeal on the facts is by Crime and Disorder Act 1998 s 4. It was also accepted by all appearing before us that there would also be a right to appeal on the law by way of case stated and judicial review of any decision of the Magistrates relating to an ASBO. An ASBO made in the Magistrates' Court on conviction is appealable to the Crown Court under section 4 of the Act in the same way as a free-standing ASBO but in neither case is there a right of appeal against a variation of the original ASBO. Case stated and judicial review are remedies available against the Magistrates' Court.

We were told that there have been attempts to get round the absence of a right of appeal against the variation of an ASBO by seeking leave to appeal out of time against the original ASBO. This course was followed in *R v Bradfield* 2006 EWCA Crim 2917, which was a Protection from Harassment Act 1997 case. Where Parliament has decided not to grant a right of appeal against a variation, we would regard it, save in the most exceptional circumstances, as an abuse of process to allow an appeal to go forward out of time against the original order. European Convention on Human Rights art 6 was not violated by the lack of appeal.

85 Previous Convictions and Antecedents

85.1

Approach Each previous conviction is an aggravating factor, see **85.2**. However, it is important that a defendant is not punished twice for the same offence. Therefore, the courts should be careful not to increase a sentence disproportionately because of a defendant's criminal record. However, a criminal record is an important way of considering how a defendant has responded to previous sentences. If non-custodial sentences have not been effective, the options of the court will be limited. When the court is considering an extended sentence (EDS), particular bad character may be of crucial importance. Ed.

Persistent offenders For details of the persistent offender paragraphs in the various chapters, see the index.

For a definition of 'persistent offender' see the **Children And Young Offenders: Custodial Sentences *Persistent offenders Who are?*** para at **14.8**.

85.2 *Statutory provisions*

Determining the seriousness of an offence

Criminal Justice Act 2003 s 143(1) In considering the seriousness of any offence, the court must consider the offender's culpability in committing the offence and any harm which the offence caused, was intended to cause or might forseeably have caused.

(2) In considering the seriousness of an offence ("the current offence") committed by an offender who has one or more previous convictions, the court must treat each previous conviction as an aggravating factor if (in the case of that conviction) the court considers that it can reasonably be so treated having regard, in particular, to:

(a) the nature of the [previous conviction], and

(b) the time that has elapsed since the conviction.

(3) [Provision about committing offences on bail being an aggravating factor, see **242.3** in Volume 2]

(4) Any reference in subsection (2) to a previous conviction is to be read as a reference to:

(a) a previous conviction by a court in the United Kingdom,

(aa) a previous conviction by a court in another member State of a relevant offence under the law of that State,

(b) a previous conviction of a service offence within the meaning of the Armed Forces Act 2006 ("conviction" here including anything that under section 376(1) and (2) of that Act is to be treated as a conviction), or (c) a finding of guilt in respect of a member State service offence.

(5) [Foreign convictions, see **85.5**]

(6) For the purposes of this section:

(a) an offence is "relevant" if the offence would constitute an offence under the law of any part of the United Kingdom if it were done in that part at the time of the conviction of the defendant for the current offence,

(b) "member State service offence" means an offence which:

(i) was the subject of proceedings under the service law of a member State other than the United Kingdom, and

(ii) would constitute an offence under the law of any part of the United Kingdom, or a service offence (within the meaning of the Armed Forces Act 2006), if it were done in any part of the United Kingdom, by a member of Her Majesty's forces, at the time of the conviction of the defendant for the current offence,

(c) "Her Majesty's forces" has the same meaning as in the Armed Forces Act 2006, and

(d) "service law", in relation to a member State other than the United Kingdom, means the law governing all or any of the naval, military or air forces of that State.

85.3 ***Court Martial statutory provisions***

Deciding the seriousness of an offence

Armed Forces Act 2006 s 238(1) A court or officer dealing with an offender for a service offence ('the current offence') must in considering the seriousness of the offence:

(a) consider the offender's culpability in committing the offence and any harm which the offence caused, was intended to cause or could foreseeably have caused,

(b) if the offender has one or more previous convictions, treat as an aggravating factor each previous conviction that the court or officer considers can reasonably be so treated.

(2) In considering whether a previous conviction can reasonably be treated as an aggravating factor the court or officer must have regard (in particular) to:

(a) the nature of the offence to which the conviction relates and its relevance to the current offence, and

(b) the time that has elapsed since the conviction.

(3) Any reference in subsection (1) or (2) to a previous conviction is to be read as a reference to:

(a) a previous conviction of a service offence,

(b) a previous conviction by a court in the British Islands of an offence other than a service offence,

(c) a previous conviction by a court in a member State other than the United Kingdom of a relevant offence under the law of that State, or

(d) a finding of guilt in respect of a member State service offence.

(4) Nothing in this section prevents the court or officer from treating:

(a) a previous conviction by a court outside both the British Islands and any member State, or

(b) a previous conviction by a court in any member State (other than the United Kingdom) of an offence which is not a relevant offence or a member State service offence,

as an aggravating factor in any case where the court or officer considers it appropriate to do so.

(5) For the purposes of this section:

(a) an offence is 'relevant' if the offence would constitute an offence under the law of any part of the United Kingdom if it were done in that part at the time of the conviction in respect of the current offence,

(b) 'member State service offence' means an offence which:

(i) was the subject of proceedings under the service law of a member State other than the United Kingdom, and

(ii) would constitute an offence under the law of any part of the United Kingdom, or a service offence, if it were done in any part of the United Kingdom, by a member of Her Majesty's forces, at the time of the conviction of the defendant for the current offence, and

(c) 'service law', in relation to a member State other than the United Kingdom, means the law governing all or any of the naval, military or air forces of that State.

85.4 ***Service convictions in civilian courts***

Criminal Justice Act 2003 s 143(2) [This section deals with the requirement to treat previous convictions as aggravating factors, see **85.2**].

(3) [see **85.2**]

(4) Any reference in subsection (2) to a previous conviction is to be read as a reference to:

(a) [England and Wales law, see **85.2**]

(aa) a previous conviction by a court in another member State of a relevant offence under the law of that State,

(b) a previous conviction of a service offence within the meaning of the Armed Forces Act 2006 ('conviction' here including anything that under section 376(1) and (2) of that Act is to be treated as a conviction), or
(c) a finding of guilt in respect of a member State service offence.

Criminal Justice Act 2003 s 143(6) For the purposes of this section:
(a) [England and Wales law, see **85.2**]
(b) 'member State service offence' means an offence which:
(i) was the subject of proceedings under the service law of a member State other than the United Kingdom, and
(ii) would constitute an offence under the law of any part of the United Kingdom, or a service offence (within the meaning of the Armed Forces Act 2006), if it were done in any part of the United Kingdom, by a member of Her Majesty's forces, at the time of the conviction of the defendant for the current offence,
(c) 'Her Majesty's forces' has the same meaning as in the Armed Forces Act 2006, and
(d) 'service law', in relation to a member State other than the United Kingdom, means the law governing all or any of the naval, military or air forces of that State.

85.5 ***Foreign convictions***

Criminal Justice Act 2003 s 143(2) (This section deals with the requirement to treat previous convictions as aggravating factors, see **85.2**).
(3) [Provision about committing offences on bail being an aggravating factor, see **242.3** in Volume 2]
(4) Any reference in subsection (2) to a previous conviction is to be read as a reference to:
(a) a previous conviction by a court in the United Kingdom,
(aa) a previous conviction by a court in another member State of a relevant offence under the law of that State…[1016]
(5) Subsections (2) and (4) do not prevent the court from treating:
(a) a previous conviction by a court outside both the United Kingdom and any other member State, or
(b) a previous conviction by a court in any member State (other than the United Kingdom) of an offence which is not a relevant offence,
as an aggravating factor in any case where the court considers it appropriate to do so.

R v Luciano and Rothery 2016 EWCA Crim 195 In February 2014, R was sentenced in Spain to 9 years but had absconded before sentence. A European arrest warrant was issued. In December 2014, in England, R received 15 years. Both offences involved drug supply. The defence argued that the Judge had increased the sentence because R had avoided serving his Spanish sentence. Held. The Judge could not pass a consecutive sentence nor a sentence increased to reflect his avoiding the Spanish sentence. However, the Judge could increase the sentence because of the statutory aggravating factor of having a similar previous conviction. Doing that exercise, 10 years 8 months.

85.6 ***Overarching Principles: Seriousness Guideline 2004***

Overarching Principles: Seriousness Guideline 2004, see www.banksr.com Other Matters Guidelines tab

para 1.21 The lists below bring together the most important aggravating features with potential application to more than one offence or class of offences…

1.22 **Factors indicating higher culpability**: [In the list is] Previous conviction(s), particularly where a pattern of repeat offending is disclosed.

[1016] This subsection was inserted by Coroners and Justice Act 2009 Sch 17 para 6.

85.7 *Spent convictions*

Rehabilitation of Offenders Act 1974 s 7(2)(a) Nothing in section 4(1) [of this Act] [the effect of rehabilitation for spent convictions] shall affect the determination of any issue, or prevent the admission or requirement of any evidence, relating to a person's previous convictions or to any circumstances ancillary thereto:

(a) in any criminal proceedings before a court in England and Wales (including any appeal or reference in a criminal matter).

Criminal Practice Directions 2015 EWCA Crim 1567 para V 35A.1 The effect of Rehabilitation of Offenders Act 1974 s 4(1) is that a person who has become a rehabilitated person for the purpose of the Act in respect of a conviction (known as a 'spent' conviction) shall be treated for all purposes in law as a person who has not committed, or been charged with or prosecuted for, or convicted of or sentenced for, the offence or offences which were the subject of that conviction.

35A.2 Section 4(1) of the 1974 Act does not apply, however, to evidence given in criminal proceedings: section 7(2)(a).

35A.3 On conviction, the court must be provided with a statement of the defendant's record for the purposes of sentence. The record supplied should contain all previous convictions, but those which are spent should, so far as practicable, be marked as such. No one should refer in open court to a spent conviction without the authority of the judge, which authority should not be given unless the interests of justice so require. When passing sentence the judge should make no reference to a spent conviction unless it is necessary to do so for the purpose of explaining the sentence to be passed.

See also the **REHABILITATION OF OFFENDERS ACT 1974** chapter.

85.8 *Defendant convicted of other matters between date of offence and sentence*

R v Darrigan 2017 EWCA Crim 169, 1 Cr App R (S) 50 (p 397) D pleaded on the day his case was listed for trial to wounding with intent. On 16 August 2014, D, then aged 17, after drinking, pushed a broken bottle into his friend's face. At that time, D had two convictions. One was for battery when he was aged 11 (a Referral Order) and a little later, shoplifting (an absolute discharge). However, he was on bail for a) an affray (6 months' DTO), possessing class B drugs with intent (4 months' suspended YOI) and one not specified offence (concurrent DTO). 15 days after the offence, D committed battery and possession of an offensive weapon (Youth Rehabilitation Order). After his release from the DTO, D regularly committed offences. On 8 September 2016, three weeks after his plea, he was sentenced to 4½ years for the glassing offence. He was then aged 19. D then had about 3 months left to serve of a total term of 16 months' YOI. The Judge started at 4 years, raised it to 5 years for the previous convictions and then gave 10% for the plea. Held. The glassing offence pre-dated the first custodial sentence. His then two previous convictions did not justify a 12-month uplift although the glassing offence was committed when D was on bail. 3 years 9 months substituted.

Note: The real problem is that the rule that young offenders should have their trials held as soon as possible was not applied. It could be said that D had a lesser sentence for the offences that were passed between the date of the glassing offence and his sentence for that offence than he would have done if the glassing offence had been tried at the proper time. Ed.

85.9 *Persistent offenders and the maximum sentence*

R v Foulger and Others 2012 EWCA Crim 1516 Ba and Bu were convicted of conspiracy to steal a container of cigarettes. Ba, a professional criminal, had 11 convictions for 33 offences between 1998 and 2009. These included theft of a lorry containing goods worth £30,000 (2001) and of a lorry with a load worth £84,000 (2004). He also had an offence of handling 8 million cigarettes (2009). Held. It would be wrong for defendants who continue to commit this sort of serious offence to think that they will not receive the maximum sentence simply because it is possible to envisage cases with more serious facts.

The court bundle and basic principles

85.10 ***The standard format***
Criminal Practice Directions 2015 EWCA Crim 1567 para II 10A.2 The record should usually be provided in the following format:
Personal details and summary of convictions and cautions – Police National Computer [PNC] Court/Defence/Probation Summary Sheet
Previous convictions – PNC Court/Defence/Probation printout, supplemented by Form MG16 if the police force holds convictions not shown on PNC
Recorded cautions – PNC Court/Defence/Probation printout, supplemented by Form MG17 if the police force holds cautions not shown on PNC.
Criminal Practice Directions 2015 EWCA Crim 1567 para II 10A.7 Where the current alleged offence could constitute a breach of an existing sentence such as a suspended sentence, community order or conditional discharge, and it is known that that sentence is still in force, then details of the circumstances of the offence leading to the sentence should be included in the antecedents. The detail should be brief and include the date of the offence.

85.11 ***Full and proper material must be available***
Criminal Practice Directions 2015 EWCA Crim 1567 para II 10A.6 In the Crown Court, the police should also provide brief details of the circumstances of the last three similar convictions and/or of convictions likely to be of interest to the court, the latter being judged on a case-by-case basis.
R v Reynolds 1985 Unreported 25/1/85 Slang expressions and the making of general unparticularised derogatory assessments of character are unattractive and unhelpful.
R v Kinsella 1990 The Times 11/9/90 Crown Courts have an obligation to ensure that full and proper antecedent reports are available both for the judge and the Court of Appeal.

85.12 ***Updating the antecedents***
Criminal Practice Directions 2015 EWCA Crim 1567 para II 10A.6 In the Crown Court, the police should also provide brief details of the circumstances of the last three similar convictions and/or of convictions likely to be of interest to the court, the latter being judged on a case-by-case basis.
Criminal Practice Directions 2015 EWCA Crim 1567 para II 10A.8 On occasions the PNC printout provided may not be fully up to date. It is the responsibility of the prosecutor to ensure that all of the necessary information is available to the court and the Probation Service and provided to the defence. Oral updates at the hearing will sometimes be necessary, but it is preferable if this information is available in advance.

85.13 ***Cautions***
Criminal Practice Directions 2015 EWCA Crim 1567 para II 10A.1 The defendant's record (previous convictions, cautions, reprimands, etc.) may be taken into account when the court decides not only on sentence but also, for example, about bail, or when allocating a case for trial.
Note: So the implication is that cautions are matters the court can consider. In fact they regularly do so. Ed.

85.14 ***Community order breaches***
Criminal Practice Directions 2015 EWCA Crim 1567 para II 10A.7 Where the current alleged offence could constitute a breach of an existing sentence such as a suspended sentence, community order or conditional discharge, and it is known that that sentence is still in force, then details of the circumstances of the offence leading to the sentence should be included in the antecedents. The detail should be brief and include the date of the offence.

85.15 ***Defence contest the record***
Criminal Practice Directions 2015 EWCA Crim 1567 para II 10A.3 The defence representative should take instructions on the defendant's record and if the defence wish to raise any objection to the record, this should be made known to the prosecutor immediately.
85.16 ***Endorsable offences when their time limit has expired***
Chief Constable of West Mercia v Williams 1987 RTR 188 D had convictions for driving matters for which the time limit for being 'effective' under what is now Road Traffic Offenders Act 1988 s 45(5)(a) had expired. D sought to have the conviction not considered. Held. It cannot be contended that the effect of the subsection was to prevent the Magistrates from hearing and taking into consideration the previous record of D even if the matters did not appear on his licence.
For the rule about the power to impose a community order on a persistent offender who is aged 16 or over and has been fined on three or more occasions (which is not yet in force), Criminal Justice Act 2003 s 151(1) and (2), see **15.11**.

86 PROCEDURE, SENTENCING

86.1
Expert evidence The rules about expert evidence are in Criminal Practice Directions 2015 EWCA Crim 1567 para V 33A. For an example of a victim also being used as the psychiatric expert, see *Att-Gen's Ref 2017 Re Watts* 2017 EWCA Crim 1009, 2 Cr App R (S) 52.
For plea discussions in complex fraud cases, see the **FRAUD** ***Complex fraud, Plea discussions in*** para at **267.11** in Volume 2.
86.2 ***Judges sitting as district judges and Court of Appeal judges sitting as Crown Court judges Statute***
Courts Act 2003 s 66(1) Every holder of a judicial office specified in subsection (2) has the powers of a justice of the peace who is a District Judge (Magistrates' Courts) in relation to: a) criminal causes and matters, and b) [family proceedings].
(2) The offices are: a) judge of the High Court, b) deputy judge of the High Court, c) Circuit judge, d) deputy Circuit judge [and] e) recorder.
(2A) A qualifying judge advocate has the powers of a justice of the peace who is a District Judge (Magistrates' Courts) in relation to criminal causes and matters.[1017]
(3) For the purposes of Children and Young Persons Act 1933 s 45, every holder of a judicial office specified in subsection (2) is qualified to sit as a member of a Youth Court.
(4) [relates to family proceedings]
(5) In this section 'qualifying judge advocate' means:
(a) the Judge Advocate General, or
(b) a person appointed under Courts-Martial (Appeals) Act 1951 s 30(1)(a) or (b) [assistants to the Judge Advocate General].
(6) Subsection (2A) is without prejudice to the powers conferred by this section on a person within subsection (2) where that person is also a qualifying judge advocate.[1018]
Explanatory Note to the Act It is not expected that extensive use would be made of the provision, but it would be possible for a Circuit judge in the Crown Court to deal with a summary offence without the case having to go back to a Magistrates' Court. At present, certain summary offences can be included in an indictment. If the person is convicted on the indictment, the Crown Court may sentence him if he pleads guilty to the summary offence, but if he pleads not guilty the powers of the Crown Court cease. It is intended in such cases that the judge of the Crown Court should be able to deal with the summary offences then and there as a magistrate. He would follow Magistrates' Courts' procedure.

[1017] Added by Armed Forces Act 2011 Sch 2 para 6(a)
[1018] Added by Armed Forces Act 2011 Sch 2 para 6(b)

86.3 ***Judges sitting as district judges and Court of Appeal judges sitting as Crown Court judges Cases***

R v Ashton and Others 2006 EWCA Crim 794, 2 Cr App R (S) 15 (p 231) D was erroneously sent to the Crown Court for trial when the Court thought his burglary was a minimum sentence case when in fact it wasn't. D wanted his case to proceed so the Judge sat as a District Judge and dealt with the mode of trial. Summary trial was accepted and the defendant pleaded guilty. D was then sentenced for the burglary. D appealed his conviction. Held. This case provides a good illustration of how an inflexible invalidity rule is contrary to the interests of the accused and the prosecution, as well as running contrary to the public interest in the fair administration of criminal justice. The course adopted caused no identifiable injustice: to the contrary, it enabled the case (for the benefit of everyone directly involved and the public) to proceed without any material delay.

R (Hauschildt) v Highbury Corner Magistrates' Court 2007 EWHC 3494 (Admin) High Court The officer tricked D into coming back to the UK by saying he would be able to surrender and then return to care for his partner. In fact police had decided then not to keep the promise. D returned. The police opposed D's bail and he was brought before the Magistrates' Court and bail was opposed. D was remanded into custody. Held. This was a clear abuse of the process. The way to cure the abuse is for me to sit as a District Judge and hear a bail application with the abuse finding taken as a change of circumstances.

W v Leeds Crown Court 2011 EWHC 2326 (Admin) High Court W was committed for trial with an adult. The adult pleaded guilty and it was suggested the sentencing Judge should remit the case to the Magistrates Court for trial by rehearing the decision to commit. Held. The Court could not use the section 66 power here because the case was no longer at the Magistrates' Court.

R v Buisson 2011 EWCA Crim 1841 Where a committal is invalid in the Crown Court, a High Court judge and a Circuit judge can reconstitute the Court as a Magistrates' Court and exercise the powers of a District Judge. There is the same power at the Court of Appeal.

Note: The case is an example of: a) the Court of Appeal approving a Crown Court judge committing a case he had held to be invalidly committed, and b) the Court of Appeal judge acting as a District Judge to sentence the same person who had had another invalid committal. Ed.

R v Iles 2012 EWCA Crim 1610 D, aged 16, was committed for trial for arson and criminal damage. He appeared at the Magistrates' Court for two sets of other matters on different days and these matters were adjourned. At the Crown Court, the Judge decided to sentence the matters on indictment as a judge and sit as a Youth Court to sentence the other matters. He purported to vary a 'minimum term' when one was not available. Held. The criminal damage charge was valid. Detention was imposed for four offences when only a DTO was available. An extended sentence was unlawful as the offence was not a specified offence. There appears to have developed a practice under which the Magistrates' Courts adjourn summary only matters, knowing the offender is due to appear at a Crown Court on other matters, and invite the Crown Court to enable the summary cases to be dealt with at the same time by the expedient of arranging for a Circuit Judge to sit as a District Judge. Such a practice has advantages, but there are dangers. Therefore before this practice is followed, the Magistrates' Court must carefully consider whether this is in the interests of justice and ensure that there is the power to do so. A Crown Court judge who is invited to deal with two sets of proceedings in this way must decide whether it is appropriate in the light of submissions from both the prosecution and the defence. For this purpose it must be kept firmly in mind that when sentencing as a District Judge the sentence is imposed by the Magistrates' Court, and consideration must be given not only to advantages but also to dangers that may arise because: a) the judge would, as regards the Magistrates' Court matters, be limited to the powers of a Magistrates' Court, powers which must be carefully checked by counsel and the court;

and b) sentences that the judge imposes when sitting as a Magistrates' Court would have a different route of appeal from that applicable to sentences imposed by the judge when sitting in the Crown Court. If the invitation is accepted, then consideration must again be given to these dangers at the stage of deciding what sentence should be imposed by the judge when sitting as a Magistrates' Court.

R v Dillon 2017 EWCA Crim 2642, 2019 1 Cr App R (S) 22 (p 155) D was sent to the Crown Court with an adult, AD, on a £102,000 fraud charge. He pleaded guilty and his sentence was adjourned. The pre-sentence report recommended a Referral Order but it said that order would need a remittal to the Youth Court. The matter was put back and it was suggested the Judge could sit as a district judge. The Judge made a Youth Rehabilitation Order. Held. The pre-sentence report was correct about the Referral Order. The case should have been remitted immediately after the plea (see *R v Lewis* 1984 [above]) because there was no issue of disparity and there was no direct link with AD. The Youth Court is given exclusive competence to make a Referral Order and the Judge could not acquire that by sitting as a district judge. There would have been no extra delay as a pre-sentence report was required. At the Youth Court a Referral Order had to be made. Neither we nor the Crown Court can make a Referral Order. Given the delay, the errors and D's good performance with the Youth Rehabilitation Order, we substitute a conditional discharge.

For more detail, see **13.29**.

R v Ford 2018 EWCA Crim 1751 D was charged with section 18 and appeared at the Youth Court when aged 17. The case was adjourned so the defence could read the papers. On the next appearance D was aged 18. D pleaded to section 18 and possession of an offensive weapon. D was committed for sentence under Powers of Criminal Courts (Sentencing) Act 2000 s 3. At the Crown Court, D received 6½ years in all. Held. We assume the magistrates purported to commit D under section 3B because that is the section for those who require additional sentencing powers. To use Magistrates' Court Act 1980 s 24 (which enables those who turn 18 to be dealt with in the Youth Court) the defendant must be aged 17 when the court determines mode of trial, see *R v Islington North Juvenile Court ex parte Daley* 1982 75 Cr App R 280 (House of Lords). So, there was no power to take D's plea or commit him to the Crown Court. Everything after that was invalid, so we quash D's sentence, acting as Judges of the Divisional Court. One of the judges then sat as a District Judge at the Youth Court and committed the matter for trial. The same Judge sat as a Crown Court Judge and took the pleas, heard the case opened, listened to the mitigation, sentenced D to 4 years 8 months and passed some ancillary orders.

R v Potter 2019 EWCA Crim 461 D breached his Criminal Behaviour Order and the Judge gave him 30 days YOI and amended his Criminal Behaviour Order. Held. A Crown Court has no power to vary a Magistrates' Court order, even where the defendant is being sentenced for breaching the order. The Judge can't vary it by sitting as District Judge under Courts Act 2003 s 66, because the judge is still sitting as a Crown Court judge.

See also: *R v Frimpong* 2015 EWCA Crim 1933, 2016 1 Cr App R (S) 59 (p 395) (The Court considered whether a Judge could exercise the remittal powers that the Magistrates' Court had for the Criminal Courts Charge. Held. The Crown Court does not reconstitute itself as a Magistrates' Court. The Judge exercises the powers of the Magistrates' Court. Here the power could not be used as the Judge could not have specified herself as a Magistrates' Court and if the proposed order was made it would cut across the collection system, which is a matter for the Magistrates' Court. There are other procedural reasons why the power could not be used.)

86.4 *Open court, Cases must be heard in*

Criminal Practice Directions 2015 EWCA Crim 1567 para I 5B.1[1019] Open justice, as Lord Justice Toulson reiterated in the case of *R (Guardian News) v City of Westminster Magistrates' Court* 2012 EWCA Civ 420, is a 'principle at the heart of our system of justice and vital to the rule of law'. There are exceptions but these 'have to be justified by some even more important principle'. However, the practical application of that undisputed principle, and the proper balancing of conflicting rights and principles, call for careful judgments to be made.

Magistrates' Courts Act 1980 s 121(4) Subject to the provisions of any enactment to the contrary, a Magistrates' Court must sit in open court if it is: a) trying summarily an information for an indictable offence, b) trying an information for a summary offence, c) imposing imprisonment, d) hearing a complaint, or e) holding an inquiry into the means of an offender for the purposes of section 82 (imprisonment for default).

Note: The principles and the exceptions were extensively reviewed in the House of Lords in *Att-Gen v Leveller Magazine Ltd* 1979 68 Cr App R 342. The main exceptions to the open court rule are cases with children and young persons, and informants. For reasons of space these are not dealt with in this book. Some of the principles can be found in the next paragraph. Ed.

Re Guardian News Ltd 2016 EWCA Crim 11, 1 Cr App R 33 (p 527) LCJ The defendant, Erol Incedal, had parts of his trial heard in private, see **86.5**. The press appealed both before and after the trial. Held. para 47 The court proceeds on the basis that the principle of open justice is fundamental to the rule of law and to democratic accountability, *R (Mohamed) v Secretary of State for Foreign and Commonwealth Affairs (No 2)* 2010 EWCA Civ 158, 2011 QB 218 at paras 39 and 41. It is impossible to improve on the eloquent statements made in *Scott v Scott* 1913 AC 417 para 48. It has, however, always been recognised that there are exceptions which have been developed in cases over the years and to which it is again unnecessary to refer. The general principle is clearly expounded in *Att-Gen v Leveller Magazine Ltd* 1979 68 Cr App R 342 at para 354.

For the rule that sentencing remarks should be in open court, see **86.47**.

For the principles, see *Judicial College on Reporting Restrictions in the Criminal Courts May 2016*, www.banksr.com Other Matters Other Documents Reporting Restrictions page 7.

86.5 *Open court, Cases must be heard in Exceptions*

Criminal Practice Directions 2015 EWCA Crim 1567 para II 16B.1 Open justice is an essential principle in the criminal courts but the principle is subject to some statutory restrictions. These restrictions are either automatic or discretionary. Guidance is provided in the joint publication *Reporting Restrictions in the Criminal Courts*, issued by the Judicial College, the Newspaper Society, the Society of Editors and the Media Lawyers Association. The current version is the third edition and has been updated to be effective from June 2014. It is available at www.banksr.com Other Matters Other Documents tab.

Note: There then follows the procedure that should be followed. Ed.

European Convention on Human Rights art 6 …Everyone is entitled to a fair and public hearing…Judgment shall be pronounced publicly but the press and public may be excluded from all or part of the trial in the interest of morals, public order or national security in a democratic society, where the interests of juveniles or the protection of the private life of the parties so require, or the extent strictly necessary in the opinion of the court in special circumstances where publicity would prejudice the interests of justice.

[1019] As inserted by Criminal Practice Directions 2015 Amendment No 6 2018 para 2

Criminal Procedure Rules 2015 2015/1490 Rule 6 sets out the court rules for parties who wish to apply for an order that a trial be 'in private' or that all or part of a trial be held *in camera* for reasons of national security or for the protection of the identity of a witness or any other person.

Guardian News and Others v Incedal and Another 2014 EWCA Crim 1861 D and MR were charged with terrorism-related offences. The Judge ordered that the defendants' entire trial should be held *in camera* [in private]. The Guardian, BSkyB and others appealed. Held. The Rule of Law is a priceless asset of our country and a foundation of our constitution. One aspect of the Rule of Law, a hallmark and a safeguard, is open justice, which includes criminal trials being held in public and the publication of the names of defendants. Open justice is both a fundamental principle of the common law and a means of ensuring public confidence in our legal system; exceptions are rare and must be justified on the facts. Any such exceptions must be necessary and proportionate. However, open justice must give way to a yet more fundamental principle, that the paramount object of the court is to do justice. No more than the minimum departure from open justice will be countenanced. [Cases listed.] Order quashed in part, the swearing of the jury, reading the charges to the jury, part of the Judge's introductory remarks, part of the prosecution opening, the verdicts and the sentencing (subject to further argument) to be held in public. Accredited journalists could attend for [most] of the trial [but unable to report the content]. The defendants should be named. Although this was a preparatory hearing we permit publication of our hearing and this judgment (which did not refer to the evidence).

Re Guardian News Ltd 2016 EWCA Crim 11, 1 Cr App R 33 (p 527) LCJ Erol Incedal, see above, was convicted of some of the counts and the press applied for the material heard by the accredited journalists to be made public. Held. para 51 Where the reason for departing from the principle of open justice is based on reasons relating to national security, it is for the court and the court alone to determine if the stringent test has been met. It, and it alone, decides whether the evidence or material in question should be heard in public or not. para 57 The proper approach of the court is to examine the nature of the evidence and to determine the effect of hearing it in public. Deciding the issue on the basis that the DPP might not continue with the prosecution does not satisfy the test of necessity. para 68 The presence of the accredited journalists during significant parts of the trial made the management of the trial very much more difficult than if the trial had been conducted conventionally. para 69 A court should hesitate long and hard before it makes a similar order. paras 70 and 73 Although there was a strong public interest in the evidence that was heard in the presence of the accredited journalists being [reported], the orders were strictly necessary. [This case is not fully summarised.]

See also: *Times Newspapers v R* 2016 EWCA Crim 877 (Judge ordered defendant's evidence to be heard in private. Principles and procedures considered. Application by the press refused.)

For the principles, see *Judicial College on Reporting Restrictions in the Criminal Courts May 2016*, www.banksr.com Other Matters Other Documents Reporting Restrictions pages 8 and 18.

Anonymity/The press etc.

See also the **CHILDREN AND YOUNG OFFENDERS: GENERAL PRINCIPLES Reporting restrictions** section at **13.3**.

86.6 *Disclosure to press etc. Documents*

R (Guardian News) v City of Westminster Magistrates' Court 2010 EWHC 3376 (Admin) High Court An extradition case involved the allegation of bribery of Nigerian officials by a subsidiary company owned by a company associated with the Vice-President of the United States. *The Guardian* newspaper had the prosecution opening note and one of the defendant's skeleton arguments. A District Judge refused to permit reporters from the newspaper to inspect documents that were relied on by parties during an extradition hearing. The documents had been referred to in open court. The District Judge said that there was nothing relied on in the skeleton arguments that had not been repeated orally in open court. Held. Members of the public have no right to see any exhibit. Freedom of Information Act 2000 permits citizens to apply for information from public authorities with exemptions. Documents used in court proceedings are exempt. It would be strange if material exempt under statute could be applied for under common law. Neither the press nor the public have a right to inspect documents.

R v Marine A and Others 2013 EWCA Crim 2367 Court Martial Appeal Court and Divisional Court LCJ Afghan insurgent murder trial. The Court refused to release certain photographic stills. The press appealed. Held. para 37 Access to material used in court is governed by the common law principle of open justice. The default position is that access should be permitted to documents and other material which was evidence in the trial. para 49 Material presented in open court should generally be released to members of the public, including journalists, *R (Guardian News) v City of Westminster Magistrates' Court* 2012 EWCA Civ 420. Criminal Practice Directions 2014 EWCA Crim 1569 set out the principles. The court is bound to consider the rights of victims, parties, witnesses and third parties. para 54 There is a long-standing practice that recognises the press as a 'public watchdog' in a democratic society. *Observer and Guardian v UK* 1992 14 EHRR 153 makes special provision for guidance on access by legal representatives instructed by the media or accredited reporters who hold a card issued by the UK Press Card Authority Ltd. para 76 The Judge Advocate was entitled to refuse to release certain images. para 77 The Judge Advocate ordered that some images be released. The MoD did not appeal against that. We considered further images in the same category, on which the Judge Advocate made no decision. We order the further images to be released. para 80 In future where there has been a murder or violent attack and there is an application for the release of such images, it is expected that the advocate will draw the judge's attention to the likely impact on the victim's family.

Note: Criminal Practice Directions 2015 EWCA Crim 1567 para II 16B.1 says guidance about open justice reporting restrictions can be found in the joint publication *Reporting Restrictions in the Criminal Courts 2014*, issued by the Judicial College, the Newspaper Society, the Society of Editors and the Media Lawyers Association. The guidance is detailed and there are sections about disclosure to the press of court lists, documents on the court file, access to prosecution materials etc. Ed.

See also: Criminal Practice Directions 2015 EWCA Crim 1567 para I 5B.26

86.7 *Publicity is integral in the administration of justice*

R v Winchester Crown Court ex parte B 2000 1 Cr App R 11 Publicity is to be regarded as integral, not merely collateral, to the administration of justice.

R (Trinity Mirror plc) v Croydon Crown Court 2008 EWCA Crim 50, 2 Cr App R (S) 1 (p 1) A five-judge court. para 32 It is impossible to overemphasise the importance to be attached to the ability of the media to report criminal trials. In simple terms this represents the embodiment of the principle of open justice in a free country. An important aspect of the public interest in the administration of criminal justice is that the identity of those convicted and sentenced for criminal offices should not be concealed. Uncomfortable though it may frequently be for the defendant, that is a normal consequence of his crime.

86.8 *Postponement of publication of the proceedings*

Contempt of Court Act 1981 s 4(2) In any such proceedings [legal proceedings held in public] the court may, where it appears necessary for avoiding a substantial risk of prejudice to the administration of justice in those proceedings, or in any other proceedings pending or imminent, order that the publication of any report of the proceedings, or any part of the proceedings, be postponed for such period as the court thinks necessary for that purpose.

R v Sarker 2018 EWCA Crim 1341 LCJ The trial Judge postponed reporting of a doctor's trial for fraud. The BBC appealed the order. The Court of Appeal set out the relevant rules and authorities. Held. In section 4(2) cases, [the applicant must show] clearly (and ordinarily in writing): i) how contemporaneous, fair and accurate reports of the trial will cause a substantial risk of prejudice, and ii) why a postponement order would avoid the identified risk of prejudice. The default position is the general principle that all proceedings in courts and tribunals are conducted in public. This is the principle of open justice. Media reports of legal proceedings are an extension of the concept of open justice. Here, fair and accurate contemporaneous reporting of the trial would not have given rise to any risk of prejudice. Order quashed. [The rest of the careful and detailed guidance is not listed.]

R v Beale 2017 EWCA Crim 1012 B gave evidence in a rape trial. She was later put on trial for perjury and perverting the course of justice for making false rape claims. The Judge made an order under section 4(2), because otherwise it would deprive B of her right to anonymity. Held. The power given under section 4(2) has clear limitations: it is for the protection of the administration of justice in particular proceedings. Section 4(2) does not give power to make an order restricting publication for the purposes of protecting the administration of justice generally. The Judge accepted that naming B would not create a substantial risk of prejudice to the administration of justice in the current proceedings; and so there was no power to make the order. Also, section 4(2) cannot postpone the publication of proceedings indefinitely, see *Times Newspapers Limited v R* 2007 EWCA Crim 1925, 2008 1 Cr App R 16. para 19 Open justice and freedom of the press are fundamental principles. A reporting restriction under section 4(2) represents an interference with those principles and such a restriction can only be imposed where this is 'necessary'. para 20 The Judge failed to ask himself whether the restriction was 'necessary'. An order is only 'necessary' if it satisfies the requirements of European Convention on Human Rights art 10(2), that is to say, it is 'necessary in a democratic society' in pursuit of one or more of a number of specified aims. This includes the requirement that the measure be a proportionate means of achieving such aims. In order to avoid an unwarranted incursion into open justice, the step-by-step approach to making a section 4(2) order, identified in *R v Sherwood and Others* 2001 EWCA Crim 1075 at para 22, must be followed [not listed here]. Judge's order quashed.

See also **86.9**.

For the principles about postponements, see *Judicial College on Reporting Restrictions in the Criminal Courts May 2016*, www.banksr.com Other Matters Other Documents Reporting Restrictions pages 27 and 39.

86.9 *Anonymity of complainants Sex offenders*

Sexual Offences (Amendment) Act 1992 s 1(1) Where an allegation has been made that an offence to which this Act applies has been committed against the person, no matter relating to that person shall during that person's lifetime be included in any publication if it is likely to lead members of the public to identify that person as the person against whom the offence is alleged to have been committed.

Note: The Act applies to Indecency with Children Act 1960 s 1 (indecent conduct towards young child), all offences in Sexual Offences Act 2003 Part 1 except s 64-65 (sex with an adult relative), s 69 (intercourse with an animal) and s 71 (sexual activity in a public lavatory), most of the offences under Sexual Offences Act 1956 and some other offences, see Sexual Offences (Amendment) Act 1992 s 2. Ed.

R v Beale 2017 EWCA Crim 1012 B gave evidence in a rape trial. She was later put on trial for perjury and perverting the course of justice for making false rape claims. The Judge ruled he had no power to make an anonymity order under Sexual Offences (Amendment) Act 1992 s 1. Held. The Judge was right. Section 1 does not operate to prohibit a report of any criminal proceedings other than those in which a person is accused of the sexual offence in question, or in an appeal from such proceedings. para 3.2 of the Judicial College Reporting Restriction section [see below] is an accurate statement of the law.

See also **86.8**.

Judicial College on Reporting Restrictions in the Criminal Courts May 2016, www.banksr.com Other Matters Other Documents Reporting Restrictions para 3.2:

Victims of sexual offences

Victims of a wide range of sexual offences are given lifetime anonymity under the Sexual Offences (Amendment) Act 1992. The 1992 Act imposes a lifetime ban on reporting any matter likely to identify the victim of a sexual offence, from the time that such an allegation has been made and continuing after a person has been charged with the offence and after conclusion of the trial. The prohibition imposed by section 1 applies to 'any publication' and therefore includes traditional media as well as online media and individual users of social media websites, who have been prosecuted and convicted under this provision.[1020]

The offences to which the prohibition applies are set out in section 2 of the 1992 Act and include rape, indecent assault, indecency towards children and the vast majority of other sexual offences.

There is no power under the 1992 Act to restrict the naming of a defendant in a sex case. Complainants enjoy the protection provided by section 1 of the 1992 Act and it is for the media to form its own judgment as to whether the naming of a defendant in a sex case would of itself be likely to identify the victim of the offence.[1021] The same must be true for witnesses other than victims in sex cases.

A defendant in a sex case may apply for the restriction to be lifted if that is required to induce potential witnesses to come forward and the conduct of the defence is likely to be substantially prejudiced if no such direction is given.

There are three main exceptions to the anonymity rule. First, a complainant may waive the entitlement to anonymity by giving written consent to being identified (if they are 16 or older).[1022]

Secondly, the media is free to report the victim's identity in the event of criminal proceedings other than the actual trial or appeal in relation to the sexual offence. This exception caters for the situation where a complainant in a sexual offences case is subsequently prosecuted for perjury or wasting police time in separate proceedings.[1023] It appears to have been the intention of Parliament, however, that a complainant would retain anonymity if, during the course of proceedings, sexual offences charges are dropped and other non-sexual offence charges continue to be prosecuted.[1024]

Thirdly, the court may lift the restriction to persuade defence witnesses to come forward, or where the court is satisfied that it is a substantial and unreasonable restriction on the reporting of the trial and that it is in the public interest for it to be lifted.[1025] This last condition cannot be satisfied simply because the defendant has been acquitted or [there has been some] other outcome of the trial.[1026]

[1020] For example, individuals who posted on social network websites revealing the identity of a victim of rape by the former footballer Ched Evans were convicted of offences under this provision, see, for example, www.theguardian.com/uk/2012/nov/05/ched-evans-rape-naming-woman.

[1021] *R (Press Association) v Cambridge Crown Court* 2012 EWCA Crim 2434, paras 15-17

[1022] It is a defence to an offence of publishing identifying matter under Sexual Offences (Amendment) Act 1992 s 5 to show that the complainant gave written consent to the publication, see section 5(2).

[1023] Sexual Offences (Amendment) Act 1992 s 1(4)

[1024] Report of the Advisory Group on the Law of Rape (the Heilbron Committee), Cmnd 6352, paras 168-172. As the purpose of the anonymity provision is to encourage complainants in sexual offences cases to come forward, it would be inconsistent with the statutory purpose if dropping a sexual offence charge during the course of proceedings had the effect of removing anonymity. In addition, any interpretation that anonymity automatically falls away in such circumstances creates problematic conflicts, for example it could lead to sexual offences charges being maintained in order to ensure continued anonymity, in circumstances where dropping the charge (e.g. in a negotiated plea) was in the interests of justice.

[1025] Sexual Offences (Amendment) Act 1992 s 3

[1026] Sexual Offences (Amendment) Act 1992 s 3(3)

86.10 ***Reporting restrictions*** ***Behaviour rules***

Note: The behaviour rules for reporting restrictions are in Criminal Procedure Rules 2015 2015/1490 Rule 6. Ed.

See also the note at **86.6**.

86.11 ***Anonymity*** ***Defendant's***

R (Trinity Mirror plc) v Croydon Crown Court 2008 EWCA Crim 50, 2 Cr App R (S) 1 (p 1) A five-judge court. D pleaded to child pornography offences. The Judge issued an injunction preventing D's identity being disclosed, to protect his children's human rights. The press appealed. Held. para 30 The Crown Court has no general power to grant injunctions. There is no inherent jurisdiction to do so on the basis that it is seeking to achieve a desirable, or indeed a 'just and convenient' objective. para 32 It is impossible to overemphasise the importance to be attached to the ability of the media to report criminal trials. In simple terms this represents the embodiment of the principle of open justice in a free country. An important aspect of the public interest in the administration of criminal justice is that the identity of those convicted and sentenced for criminal offences should not be concealed. Uncomfortable though it may frequently be for the defendant, that is a normal consequence of his crime. From time to time occasions will arise where restrictions on this principle are considered appropriate, but they depend on express legislation, and, where the court is vested with a discretion to exercise such powers, on the absolute necessity for doing so in the individual case. There was no power to make this order. para 34 This Court is naturally concerned for the welfare of D's children. We accept the assessments of their mother, their head-teacher, their social worker and the consultant child psychiatrist. Nevertheless we must adopt a much wider perspective. All we can properly do in the interests of the children is, exceptionally, to announce our decision in advance both of the delivery of our judgment and of our setting aside of the Judge's order. Our intention was to create a period in which work might be done with the children, with a view to enabling them better to cope with the public identification of their father following its earlier postponement.

R (Press Association) v Cambridge Crown Court 2012 EWCA Crim 2434 D was convicted of five counts of rape. The Judge was concerned about the impact on D's family of the expected publicity about the conviction. He purported to order an unlimited prohibition on the publication of D's name. Held. para 17 We are wholly unpersuaded that [there is] any power in the 1992 Act which vests a judge with jurisdiction to make an order that a defendant should be given anonymity, even when the purpose of the order is to protect the anonymity of the complainant. Looking at the matter broadly, any such powers are not to be lightly inferred. There are very good reasons why defendants are not provided with anonymity, particularly after they have been convicted.

R v Marine A and Others 2013 EWCA Crim 2367 Court Martial Appeal Court and Divisional Court LCJ Marine A was convicted of murder and had his anonymity order lifted. He and others appealed. Held. para 87 The starting point is the duty of the court, as a public authority, to ensure compliance with the principles of 1) open justice, 2) that there be no interference with an individual's rights under European Convention on Human Rights arts 2 and 3, and 3) no unnecessary or disproportionate interference with: a) the rights of the public under European Convention on Human Rights art 10 (having regard to the position of the media under Human Rights Act 1998 s 12), and b) of any relevant individuals under European Convention on Human Rights art 8. As open justice is so important a principle, an order that a defendant be not identified will not be necessary if some other measure is available to protect those rights of the individuals, and that other measure would be proportionate. para 112 For Marine A, there is the greatest public interest in knowing who he was and his background, given his conviction. It would require an overwhelming case if a person convicted of murder in the course of an armed conflict were to remain anonymous. We consider the danger of being attacked in prison and the dangers to his family whom the MoD have taken steps to protect and the balance comes down very firmly on the side of open justice. [Position of other marines considered and orders made.]

Guardian News and Others v Incedal and Another 2014 EWCA Crim 1861 D and MR were charged with terrorism-related offences. The Judge ordered that the defendants' entire trial should be held *in camera* (in private). Held. The defendants should be named. For more details, see **86.4**.

See also: *A Local Authority v PD* 2005 EWHC 1832 (Admin)[1027] (High Court Family D's name ordered to be withheld because it was necessary to protect the rights and interests of D's children, applying European Convention on Human Rights arts 8 and 10.)

86.12 ***Anonymity Teachers***

Education Act 2002 s 141F[1028] provides teachers with anonymity after an allegation against them is made. The restrictions cease to apply 'once proceedings for the offence have been instituted', see Education Act 2002 s 141F(10).

86.13 ***Anonymity Witnesses***

Criminal Practice Directions 2015 EWCA Crim 1567 para V 18D[1029] sets out the procedure when an application is made.

Note: Coroners and Justice Act 2009 s 88-89 enables judges to prevent defendants ever knowing who the witnesses are. The power relates to trials. The power was considered in *R v Donovan and Kafunda* 2012 EWCA Crim 2749. Ed.

See also the **Children and Young Offenders: General Principles Reporting Restrictions** section at **13.20**.

86.14 ***Anonymity Defendants Appeals***

R v Marine A and Others 2013 EWCA Crim 2367 Court Martial Appeal Court and Divisional Court LCJ Marine A, when convicted of murder, had his anonymity order lifted. He and others appealed. Held. paras 38, 39 and 47 There is no appeal from the Court Martial to the Court Martial Appeal Court but there is an appeal to the Divisional Court.

It is necessary to give Armed Forces (Court Martial) Rules 2009 2009/2041 Rules 153 and 154 a broad and liberal construction in the light of their purpose. In *Re Central Independent Television* 1991 92 Cr App R 154 this Court took a similar liberal approach to the corresponding provision in Criminal Justice Act 1988 s 159 in the light of its legislative purpose.

Pre-sentence matters

86.15 ***Crown Court procedure/Plea and Trial Preparation Hearing***

Criminal Practice Directions 2015 EWCA Crim 1567 para I 3A.3 requires the defendant to fill in a Plea and Trial Preparation Hearing form. Para 3A.4 requires the prosecutor to serve:

(i) a summary of the circumstances of the offence,

(ii) any account given by the defendant in interview, whether contained in that summary or in another document,

(iii) any written witness statement or exhibit that the prosecutor then has available and considers material to plea or to the allocation of the case for trial or sentence,

(iv) a list of the defendant's criminal record, if any, and

(v) any available statement of the effect of the offence on a victim, a victim's family or others.

The details must include sufficient information to allow the defendant and the court at the first hearing to take an informed view:

[1027] The case is also known as *Local Authority, A v PD* 2005 EWHC 1832.

[1028] As inserted by Education Act 2011 s 13(1)

[1029] As inserted by Criminal Practice Directions 2015 Amendment No 7 2018 EWCA Crim 1760. In force 1/10/18

(i) on plea,
(ii) on venue for trial (if applicable),
(iii) for the purposes of case management, or
(iv) for the purposes of sentencing (including committal for sentence, if applicable).
The first hearing is a Plea and Trial Preparation Hearing.

86.16 ***The purposes of sentencing*** ***Defendant aged 18+***
Criminal Justice Act 2003 s 142(1) Any court dealing with an offender in respect of his offence must have regard to the following purposes of sentencing:
(a) the punishment of offenders,
(b) the reduction of crime (including its reduction by deterrence),
(c) the reform and rehabilitation of offenders,
(d) the protection of the public, and
(e) the making of reparation by offenders to persons affected by their offences.
(2) (Subsection (1) does not apply to offenders under 18, murder, dangerous offenders, minimum sentences, Hospital Orders etc.)
R v Nicholson 2014 EWCA Crim 2710 D pleaded to six counts of exposure. While exposing himself he made threats. He told one psychiatrist he would do serious harm if he could get hold of females. He posed a very high risk of harm and his offending was likely to lead to rape. He was also assessed as being incapable of engaging in treatment. The Judge said he had a poor understanding of his SOPO. Held. D was clearly dangerous. D possesses a continuing threat of a very serious nature and will do so unless and until he can receive treatment which currently he won't engage with. Protection of the public was a relevant consideration, Criminal Justice Act 2003 s 142(1). The Judge was entitled to take into account the dangers D posed. Using consecutive sentences, we start at **6 years**, so with plea 4 years not 4½ years in total. For more details including his extensive previous convictions, see **256.6** in Volume 2.

86.17 ***The purposes of sentencing*** ***Defendant aged under 18***
Note: Criminal Justice Act 2003 s 142A[1030] states that there are the same purposes for those aged under 18 as there are for those aged over 18 (see **86.16**, save 'the reduction of crime' is omitted). However, this section has not yet been commenced and it is thought that it may never be commenced. Ed.
Crime and Disorder Act 1998 s 37(1) The principal aim of the youth justice system is to prevent offending or reoffending.
Sentencing Children and Young People Guideline 2017, see www.banksr.com Other Matters Guidelines tab In force 1 June 2017 page 5
1.10 Criminal Justice Act 2003 s 142 sets out the purposes of sentencing for offenders who are over 18 on the date of conviction. That Act was amended in 2008 to add section 142A, which sets out the purposes of sentencing for children and young people, subject to a commencement order being made. The difference between the purposes of sentencing for those under and over 18 is that section 142A does not include as a purpose of sentencing 'the reduction of crime (including its reduction by deterrence)'. Section 142A has not been brought into effect. Unless and until that happens, deterrence can be a factor in sentencing children and young people although normally it should be restricted to serious offences and can, and often will, be outweighed by considerations of the child or young person's welfare.

86.18 ***All matters should be dealt with on the same occasion***
Criminal Practice Directions 2015 EWCA Crim 1567 para III 19D.1 The court at which the defendant is produced should, where practicable and legally permissible, arrange to have all outstanding cases brought before it (including those from different courts) for the purpose of progressing matters and dealing with the question of bail.

[1030] As inserted by Criminal Justice and Immigration Act 2008 s 9

R v Bennett 1980 2 Cr App R (S) 96 D was ordered to perform 200 hours of community work and later dealt with for earlier offences by 18 months' imprisonment. Held. It needs to be said, as firmly and as strongly as possible, that there is an obligation on solicitors, counsel and judges alike to do all within their power to ensure that as far as possible all outstanding charges against a defendant are dealt with in the same court, by the same judge upon a single occasion. This will enable a consistency in the sentencing of an individual person to be achieved and the kind of unsatisfactory situation such as now confronts this Court to be eliminated. The failure of solicitors, members of the Bar and of the judiciary to pay sufficient regard to this oft-recurring problem is also wasteful of time and money.

86.19 ***Defendant sentenced on different occasions for similar offences***
Att-Gen's Ref No 92 of 2009 2010 EWCA Crim 524 D was sentenced in 1987 to 7 years for child rape and other child sex offences. He was released and there was no further offending. He was then arrested in 2009 for repeated child rapes in 1973-74. He was given a suspended sentence. Held. When he was first arrested it was open to him to reveal he had abused another child. He did not do that. However, we do not lose sight of the principle of totality [which] would have been of far greater relevance had D been candid with the Court back in 1987.
R v S 2013 EWCA Crim 2091 D was sentenced for historical sex offences and released. He was then arrested for offences committed before those he had served a sentence for. He was convicted of those offences. Held. The court's task is to look at the offending as a whole and structure the sentences to be passed in such a way that they properly reflect the totality of the offending. We apply that rule.
R v Gooden 2016 EWCA Crim 2286 In March 2016, D pleaded to robbery committed in March 2012. In 2012, he was interviewed about robberies including this one. In July 2012, he received a 9 years 2 months' extended sentence (4 years 2 months' custody 5 years' extended licence) for some of the robberies. D was released and turned his life round. Held. The delay was inexcusable. The explanation given was wholly unacceptable. An immediate custodial sentence was wrong. The 21-month sentence (which had already been discounted) will be suspended and 150 hours' unpaid work added.
See also: *R v McKeown* 2015 EWCA Crim 535 (D was sentenced for separate offences at two different times. The defence argued that the Court should consider what he would have been sentenced to if the sentences had been imposed at the same time. Held. That is the correct approach. On the facts, sentences upheld.)
R v Slater 2015 EWCA Crim 2084 (In 2000, D was sentenced for sex offences against a pupil and received 3 years. In 2015, he was sentenced for sex offences against seven more pupils. D received 4 years 4 months in all. Held. That was more than he would have received if the matters had been dealt with at the same time. However, he could have told the police about the later matters in 2000. 3 years 3 months substituted.)
R v Murray 2018 EWCA Crim 1252, 2 Cr App R (S) 41 (M was serving 4 years for 11 burglaries. Held. Those defendants who do not volunteer their involvement in other offences run a risk. *R v Cosburn* 2013 EWCA Crim 1815 and *R v McLean* 2017 EWCA Crim 170 applied. 10 months consecutive for later offence of burglary upheld.)
R v Hadidi 2018 EWCA Crim 1392 (D pleaded to 34 thefts from persons (2 years on each). Three months earlier he had been sentenced to 30 months for eight similar offences and an attempted theft, both sets of offences consecutive. Held. We look at what sentence he would have received if he had been sentenced on the same occasion, so 3½ years in all.)
For more detail, see **344.28** in Volume 2.

86.20 ***Duty of legal representatives to tell the court of other matters awaiting sentence***
R v Bennett 1980 2 Cr App R (S) 96 D was ordered to perform 200 hours of community work and later dealt with for earlier offences by 18 months' imprisonment. Held. It needs

to be said, as firmly and as strongly as possible, that there is an obligation on solicitors, counsel and judges alike to do all within their power to ensure that as far as possible all outstanding charges against a defendant are dealt with in the same court, by the same judge upon a single occasion. This will enable a consistency in the sentencing of an individual person to be achieved and the kind of unsatisfactory situation such as now confronts this Court to be eliminated.

When a solicitor and a member of the Bar know that there are other charges against him to be dealt with than those before the court, they should ensure that an application is made to the judge to have the defendant they represent put back to be dealt with later at that Crown Court centre or be transferred to another Crown Court centre where the other outstanding charges lie. Since they are more likely than anyone else to have this kind of knowledge, solicitors especially should be alert to achieving this conclusion.

86.21 ***Defendant's right to be present and represented***

R v May 1981 3 Cr App R (S) 165 LCJ D was sentenced, for six offences, to 4 years on two counts and 2 years on four counts. The sentences were concurrent. After the hearing, defence counsel realised that D had been sentenced to 4 years for an offence that had a 2-year maximum. The clerk was told but the Judge had left the building. The defence counsel expected the unlawful sentence to be reduced. However, there was no hearing and the sentence was varied in chambers. D appealed and all parties were under the impression that the variation was to make all sentences 2 years save for one count which remained at 4 years. His sentence was reduced to 3 years. It was then realised that the Judge's variations were more extensive than had been thought as two of the sentences had been increased from 2 years to 4 years. The case was relisted. Held. The defendant is entitled to be present throughout every stage of the sentencing procedure. He is entitled to be represented. The variations were effected without D being apprised of the intention to carry them out. D should not have been deprived of his right to make representations. The variations were null and void. All the variations will be quashed except the unlawful sentence variation.

R v Hall 1981 Unreported 19/1/82 The defendants were sentenced separately. Held. The usual practice when sentencing co-defendants should be to hear all the evidence and submissions relating to sentence in the presence of all of them, before passing sentence on any of them. The practice should only be departed from in exceptional circumstances, for instance if serious violence were anticipated from the dock.

R v Allan and Others 2011 EWCA Crim 1022 Four defendants heard their mitigation and they were taken to the cells. They did not hear what mitigation was made for the other defendants. Held. There was no justification for that. Short of extreme circumstances or voluntary absence, each defendant should be present throughout the hearing.

R v Ali and Ishaq 2014 EWCA Crim 3010 After a trial, D was sentenced to 12 years without counsel being present. He or she was temporarily elsewhere on a professional commitment. Held. After a hard-fought trial, even though it may have appeared to the Judge that there was nothing by way of mitigation, it is particularly important that counsel who have represented the defendants have the opportunity to mitigate on behalf of their clients. We deprecate the way that the Judge dealt with the matter in the absence of counsel.

86.22 ***Campaigns, petitions, public opinion etc.***

R v Wilkinson 1987 9 Cr App R (S) 468 D pleaded to GBH and other counts. He drove his car at people leaving a disco. The Judge considered that an earlier Judge had 'more or less promised' that he would be put on probation if he did well in a hostel. However, he considered that he would be failing in his public duty if he did not pass a custodial sentence and that a lenient sentence might result in public outrage. Held. We understand the difficulty the second Judge faced and the feeling that there might be public outrage. However, that was a difficulty that he must be prepared to face. The sentence had to be varied to probation.

Att-Gen's Ref Nos 24 and 45 of 1994 1995 16 Cr App R (S) 583 LCJ The Court considered two death by dangerous driving prosecution appeals. Held. We must emphasise that this Court cannot be persuaded by campaigns or by clamour to pass extremely long sentences where the criminality of the offender does not justify it. The Court is primarily concerned with the criminality of the person who has caused the death.

86.23 ***Plea to lesser count Convicted/Plea to more serious count***

R v Cole 1965 49 Cr App R 199 LCJ D pleaded to handling and was convicted of armed robbery. The defence appealed the conviction saying the plea to handling stopped a trial for the robbery. Held. The procedure is that if a defendant is convicted of the more serious offence, the other count should remain on the file and there should be no sentence on it.

R v Bebbington 1978 67 Cr App R 285 LCJ D pleaded to possession of cannabis and was convicted of possession with intent to supply cannabis. He was sentenced to 18 months concurrent on the possession count. Held. We set aside the 18-month sentence and substitute no separate sentence, because otherwise D would be sentenced twice for the same offence.

R v Beckford 2018 EWCA Crim 3006 D pleaded to possession of heroin and was convicted of possession with intent to supply heroin. He was sentenced to 2 months concurrent on the possession count. Held. para 1.3 The usual practice is not to pass an additional sentence on the lesser count. We quash the 2-month sentence.

R v Mapstone 2019 EWCA Crim 410 D pleaded to section 18 on the day his trial was listed. [He presumably had pleaded to section 20 earlier.] The Judge imposed no penalty on the section 20. Held. para 10 The guilty plea to the section 18 offence made the section 20 fall away. It should not have attracted no penalty and it should have been left to lie on the file. We substitute that order.

Absent defendants

86.24 ***Defendant absconds***

Written Standards for the Conduct of Professional Work 2014 para 15.3.1[1031] If during the course of a criminal trial and prior to final sentence the defendant voluntarily absconds and the barrister's professional client, in accordance with the ruling of the Law Society, withdraws from the case, then the barrister too should withdraw. If the trial judge requests the barrister to remain to assist the court, the barrister has an absolute discretion whether to do so or not. If he does remain, he should act on the basis that his instructions are withdrawn and he will not be entitled to use any material contained in his brief save for such part as has already been established in evidence before the court. He should request the trial judge to instruct the jury that this is the basis on which he is prepared to assist the court.

15.3.2 If for any reason the barrister's professional client does not withdraw from the case, the barrister retains an absolute discretion whether to continue to act. If he does continue, he should conduct the case as if his client were still present in court but had decided not to give evidence and on the basis of any instruction he has received. He will be free to use any material contained in his brief and may cross-examine witnesses called for the prosecution and call witnesses for the defence.

Note: Defendants are regularly tried in their absence, *R v Jones* 2002 UKHL 5, 2 Cr App R 9 (p 128) and *R v O'Hare* 2006 EWCA Crim 471. The Plea and Trial Preparation Hearing form asks the advocate whether they have warned the defendant that the Judge may try the defendant in his absence. There is power to sentence in a defendant's absence. Ed.

For the penalties see the **BAIL OFFENCES** chapter.
For other issues about absent defendants, see **Absent defendants** in the back index.

[1031] Although this relates to trials, the same rules would apply to sentence hearings.

86.25 ***Defendant fails to attend Magistrates' Court***

Magistrates' Courts Act 1980 s 12(3) In proceedings to which this subsection applies, the court shall not in a person's absence sentence him to imprisonment or detention in a Young Offender Institution or make a Detention and Training Order or an order under Criminal Justice Act 2003 Sch 12 para 8(2)(a) or (b) that a suspended sentence passed on him shall take effect.

(3A) But where a sentence or order of a kind mentioned in subsection (3) is imposed or given in the absence of the offender, the offender must be brought before the court before being taken to a prison or other institution to begin serving his sentence (and the sentence or order is not to be regarded as taking effect until he is brought before the court).

(4) In proceedings to which this subsection applies, the court shall not in a person's absence impose any disqualification on him, except on resumption of the hearing after an adjournment under Magistrates' Courts Act 1980 s 10(3) above, and where a trial is adjourned in pursuance of this subsection the notice required by Magistrates' Courts Act 1980 s 10(2) above shall include notice of the reason for the adjournment.

(5) Subsections (3) and (4) apply to:

(a) proceedings instituted by an information, where a summons has been issued, and
(b) proceedings instituted by a written charge.

(6) Nothing in this section requires the court to enquire into the reasons for the accused's failure to appear before deciding whether to proceed in his absence.

(7) The court shall state in open court its reasons for not proceeding under this section in the absence of an accused who has attained the age of 18 years, and the court shall cause those reasons to be entered in its register of proceedings.

86.26 ***Defendant refuses to leave the cell***

R v De Havilland 1981 3 Cr App R (S) 165 LCJ D was convicted of two rapes. He refused to leave the cells. D was sentenced in his absence. Held. This was very unusual but there was power to do so.

The five parts of the procedure

The sentencing procedure falls into five principal sections. They are: a) The gathering of material, b) The prosecution case, c) The defence case, d) The sentencer's tasks, and e) Other matters.

The gathering of material (the court bundle and the basic principles)

86.27 ***The standard format***

Criminal Practice Directions 2015 EWCA Crim 1567 para II 10A.2 The record should usually be provided in the following format:

Personal details and summary of convictions and cautions – Police National Computer [PNC] Court/Defence/Probation Summary Sheet

Previous convictions – PNC Court/Defence/Probation printout, supplemented by Form MG16 if the police force holds convictions not shown on PNC

Recorded cautions – PNC Court/Defence/Probation printout, supplemented by Form MG17 if the police force holds cautions not shown on PNC.

Criminal Practice Directions 2015 EWCA Crim 1567 para II 10A.7 Where the current alleged offence could constitute a breach of an existing sentence such as a suspended sentence, community order or conditional discharge, and it is known that that sentence is still in force, then details of the circumstances of the offence leading to the sentence should be included in the antecedents. The detail should be brief and include the date of the offence.

86.28 ***Breaches of community orders, suspended sentences etc.***

Criminal Practice Directions 2015 EWCA Crim 1567 para II 10A.7 Where the current alleged offence could constitute a breach of an existing sentence such as a suspended sentence, community order or conditional discharge, and it is known that that sentence is still in force, then details of the circumstances of the offence leading to the sentence should be included in the antecedents. The detail should be brief and include the date of the offence.

86.29 ***Disclosure for a sentencing hearing***

Att-Gen's Guidelines on Disclosure 2013 para 71 In all cases the prosecutor must consider disclosing in the interests of justice any material which is relevant to sentence (e.g. information which might mitigate the seriousness of the offence or assist the accused to lay blame in part upon a co-accused or another person).

For the disclosure of a co-defendant's pre-sentence report/defence material see **83.10**.

86.30 ***Full and proper material must be available***

Criminal Practice Directions 2015 EWCA Crim 1567 para II 10A.6 In the Crown Court the police will provide brief details of the circumstances of the last three similar convictions and/or of convictions likely to be of interest to the court, the latter being judged on a case-by-case basis. This information should be provided separately and attached to the antecedents as set out below.

R v Reynolds 1985 Unreported 25/1/85 Slang expressions and the making of general unparticularised derogatory assessments of character are unattractive and unhelpful.

R v Kinsella 1990 The Times 11/9/90 Crown Courts have an obligation to ensure that full and proper antecedent reports were available both for the judge and the Court of Appeal.

86.31 ***Orders for reports should be in open court***

R v Kendall 1978 Unreported 8/5/78 D was convicted of wounding her husband. She was remanded for reports. The trial Judge, who had previous knowledge of the parties through divorce proceedings, wrote directly to the prison medical officer, setting out the history and asking for the officer's view. The officer sent back an unfavourable report. Held. The contents of the Judge's letter could not be criticised. However, it was undesirable for judges to obtain reports in that way. The proper course was to give directions in open court.

Note: There have been significant procedural changes since 1978 with an emphasis on swift justice and saving money. Whether this rule would be applied might depend on the circumstances of the individual case. Ed.

86.32 ***Law reports Citing and providing copies to the court***

Criminal Practice Directions 2015 EWCA Crim 1567 para XII D.14 **Provision of copies to the Crown Court and the Magistrates' Courts** When the court is considering routine applications, it may be sufficient for the court to be referred to the applicable legislation or to one of the practitioner texts. However, it is the responsibility of the advocate to ensure that the court is provided with the material that it needs properly to consider any matter.

D.15 If it would assist the court to consider any authority, the directions at paragraphs D.2 to D.7 (see para **4.19**) relating to citation will apply and a list of authorities should be provided.

D.16 Copies should be provided by the party seeking to rely upon the authority in accordance with Rule 37.12. This Rule is applicable in the Magistrates' Courts, and in relation to the provision of authorities, should also be followed in the Crown Court since courts often do not hold library stock. Advocates should comply with paragraphs D.8 to D.10 relating to the provision of copies to the court.

For citing authorities at the Court of Appeal, see para **4.19**.

See also the **PRE-SENTENCE REPORTS, MEDICAL REPORTS** and the **VICTIM PERSONAL STATEMENTS/VICTIM IMPACT STATEMENTS** chapters.

86.33 ***Law reports Crown Court decisions and press articles***

Att-Gen's Ref No 120 of 2015 and *R v Ziamani and Others* 2016 EWCA Crim 568, 2 Cr App R (S) 32 (p 304) LCJ The CPS had a practice of providing a schedule of cases including Crown Court decisions to the Judge at sentencing hearings. Held. para 1 It is not in the public interest that judges should be guided by unauthoritative decisions or by the use of such a schedule for sentencing. Open and fair justice requires that all guidance is in the public domain and given by either the Sentencing Council or decisions of this Court.

R v Thelwall 2016 EWCA Crim 1755 LCJ D pleaded to a Health and Safety offence. para 23 The Judge was referred by the defence to online Crown Court reports where suspended sentences had been imposed. They came from the Health and Safety Executive, the CPS and the press. Held. This was not permissible.

R v Sandu 2017 EWCA Crim 908 D pleaded to fire safety offences. Held. para 20 The Judge was shown some newspaper articles. Held. The practice of providing newspaper and other reports of cases must stop.

The prosecution case

86.34 ***Open, Duty to***

Criminal Practice Directions 2015 EWCA Crim 1567 para VII D.1 To enable the press and the public to know the circumstances of an offence of which an accused has been convicted and for which he is to be sentenced, in relation to each offence to which an accused has pleaded guilty the prosecution shall state those facts in open court, before sentence is imposed.

86.35 ***Contents of the opening***

R v Hobstaff 1993 14 Cr App R (S) 605 The prosecution referred to the effects on the victims without any material being served on the defence. Held. The way the court dealt with the effects is disturbing to a degree. What the prosecution said was wholly improper. It was clothed in colourful and emotive language. It is wholly improper for the Crown to inform the court of the effects of an indecent assault upon the complainant without submitting supporting evidence to the court in the appropriate form. The evidence had to be made available in a proper form such as an expert's report or a witness statement. Also: a) the evidence had to be served in advance to the defence, allowing defence counsel to deal with it as he saw fit, and b) the evidence had to form part of the judge's papers, allowing the judge to be fully informed. His judgment would not be influenced by prosecution information alone. Sentence reduced.

R v O'S 1993 14 Cr App R (S) 632 Following *R v Hobstaff* 1993, the danger…is that a case can be opened in a florid way on material which has not been available to the defence. If that is to be accepted by the judge, or the judge is to make assumptions not based on evidence but perhaps on his experience, then the defence may be, as a result, at a disadvantage.

Note: The prosecution will put before the court all relevant information. Previous convictions will be given to all parties and the prosecution advocate will outline the details of the convictions, see the **Previous Convictions and Antecedents** chapter and the **Factual Basis For Sentencing Bad character etc. for which there is no conviction** section at **57.6**. The prosecution are able to call witnesses, but unless there are complexities, the judge will expect the matters to be in written form with a succinct explanation from the prosecution advocate. If any offences are to be taken into consideration, they will be given to the judge at or before this stage. For more information, see the **TICs** chapter. Ed.

For determining the factual basis, see the **Factual Basis For Sentencing** chapter.

For what evidence can be used, see the **Factual Basis For Sentencing Evidence** section at **57.15**.

Where there is a dispute as to the facts, this will need to be determined. It will normally require a *Newton* hearing, see the **Factual Basis For Sentencing Dispute as to facts** section at **57.42**.

The defence case

86.36 ***Defence case***

Note: The defence can call witnesses but normally defence tactics in sentencing hearings are 'damage limitation' so witnesses are rarely called. However, a defendant's employer will create a better impression by giving live evidence than would be created by a written statement. If the defendant is aged under 18, witnesses as to his character may be critical in determining whether a custodial sentence can be avoided. Section 9 statements can carry more weight than letters.

The defence advocate (or if the defendant is unrepresented, the defendant himself or herself) has the opportunity to address the court. The skill is to diminish the aggravating factors and give prominence to the mitigating factors. A few advocates tell the tribunal what they should do. A much better tactic is to show that a particular course could be taken and point out the advantages of taking that course. Ed.

For the procedure for dealing with defence accusations about witnesses, see the **Derogatory Assertion Orders** chapter.

86.37 ***Right to make a speech in mitigation Judge should listen patiently***

R v Billericay JJs ex parte Rumsey 1978 Crim LR 305 D was convicted of threatening behaviour with intent to provoke a breach of the peace. The Justices immediately sentenced him to 3 months' imprisonment. Held. D was anxious that certain matters were put before the Court. The sentence will be quashed. However, we can rehear the matter. We do. We impose the same sentence.

R v Jones 1980 Crim LR 58 D was convicted of indecent assault on a boy aged 6. He claimed his confession had been forged. The Judge interrupted counsel's mitigation address several times and said counsel was in difficulty and the only way out of the difficulty was to say nothing. It was never easy to mitigate for a man who had forwarded a lying defence. But it was his duty to mitigate. The Judge should not have discouraged him but should have listened patiently, however difficult the defendant had made counsel's task by his defence.

R v Harris 1986 Unreported 26/6/86 The Judge's interruptions and offensive comments effectively prevented counsel from making a mitigation address. Held. Only if mitigation can properly be described as irrelevant should the judge not allow it to be presented.

86.38 ***Bias Asking judge to cease acting in a case***

R v Pigott 2009 EWCA Crim 2292, 2010 2 Cr App R (S) 16 (p 91) D was convicted of cheating the public revenue. During a hearing about some intelligence information, the Judge made some comments about D and during mitigation the Judge indicated D had had more money than was on the face of the documents and did not consider his studying for a degree at the Open University 'positive'. His counsel told her that it seems he cannot win. The defence asked the Judge to recuse herself from the case. Held. In assessing whether the Judge displayed bias, it is necessary to consider not simply what she said on each occasion when it is said she demonstrated bias, but also the cumulative effect of her remarks throughout the proceedings. [However, her comments during the mitigation] demonstrated scepticism, which turned out to be justified, but not bias. The second exchange (relating to D's Open University degree) did not indicate bias. It was simply the impression the Judge had obtained from the evidence in the case.

Stubbs and Others v R 2018 UKPC 30 Privy Council In 2002, S, D and E were tried for murder and linked offences. On appeal, the convictions were quashed. In 2007, a second trial, held before Isaacs J, was aborted on the first day of the summing up. In 2013, D and others were convicted of the offences. In 2015, an appeal was heard before Isaacs J and two other Judges. The defence invited Isaacs J to recuse himself on the grounds of apparent bias. The Court rejected that request. Held. The appearance of bias is a recognised ground for recusal, *Amjad v Steadman-Byrne* 2007 ECA Civ 625 and *Otkritie International v Urumov* 2014 EWCA Civ 1315. There is a thin line between case management and premature adjudication. The fact a judge has previously made a decision adverse to the interests of a litigant is not, of itself, sufficient to establish the appearance of bias. Here the appeal Court was required to address essentially the same issues that were ruled on in the Isaacs J trial. They were not, however, identical. The appellants were entitled to a hearing before an independent and impartial tribunal.

Although Isaacs J could hear another trial, different considerations apply with an appeal. The trial situation is about judicial continuity. That is not present at an appeal. The passage of time between the second trial and the appeal could have done little to diminish the concern. The fact there were other judges on the appeal was [not relevant as each] judge needed to consider the matters afresh. If one judge is affected by apparent bias, the whole decision would have to be set aside. It is necessary to stand firm against attempts to influence who was to sit on a case. Isaacs J's decisions during the second appeal would lead a fair-minded and informed observer to conclude that there was a real possibility that he had pre-judged issues. S, D and E did not have the appearance of a fresh tribunal of three judges to consider their appeals. We advise the convictions should be quashed.
Note: This was an appeal from The Bahamas, where there are few appellate judges. In the appeal courts here, a clean slate policy is applied. Ed.
See also: *R v Okokono* 2013 EWCA Crim 2321 (Counsel suggested Judge in the Crown Court was biased and appealed. The same counsel in another case had that Judge as a member of the Court. The Judge should not sit on the case.)
For the test to apply for bias, see *In Re Pinochet* 1999 UKHL 52 and *Magill v Porter* 2001 UKHL 67.

86.39 ***Burdens of proof for matters raised by defendant***
R v Guppy 1995 16 Cr App R (S) 25 A civil burden of proof rests on D where he puts forward extraneous issues in mitigation of doubtful validity, and he should be afforded the opportunity to call evidence in support. Ordinarily, a court would accept the accuracy of counsel's statement.

The sentencer's tasks

86.40 ***Overview***
Note: Judges are required to:

(a) make findings of fact where there is a dispute, see the **FACTUAL BASIS FOR SENTENCING Dispute as to facts** section at **56.37**,
(b) determine the provisional sentence, see **86.41**,
(c) if there has been a plea of guilty, make an appropriate discount, see the **GUILTY PLEA, DISCOUNT FOR** chapter,
(d) make appropriate ancillary orders like confiscation (often adjourned), penalty points, disqualification from driving, forfeiture and a Restraining Order,
(e) give reasons for the sentence, see **86.49**,
(f) explain the sentence, see **86.49**.

For more details, see the **Sentencing remarks** section at **86.47**.
If a judge wishes to reward members of the public who have assisted in the case or make commendations about those who were involved in the investigation process or presentation of the prosecution case, this is normally done immediately after the sentencing remarks and after the defendant has left court.[1032] Ed.

86.41 ***Must determine the seriousness of an offence/Determining the provisional sentence***
Determining the seriousness of an offence
Criminal Justice Act 2003 s 143(1) In considering the seriousness of any offence, the court must consider the offender's culpability in committing the offence and any harm which the offence caused, was intended to cause or might foreseeably have caused.
Note: Judges and magistrates choose a starting point. This is usually determined by taking a starting point or considering a range from a guideline. They then adjust the starting point or select a sentence from within or outside the range having considered the factors in the case. This is called the provisional sentence.

[1032] Criminal Law Act 1967 s 28-29

Consultation The Sentencing Council expects to issue a consultation document for 'seriousness' in June 2019 and aims to publish a definitive guideline in summer 2020.

86.42 ***The step-by-step approach for determining the provisional sentence***

Note: The court assesses:

(a) whether there is a statutory minimum sentence or mandatory sentence that must be imposed, e.g. life imprisonment for murder, 7 years for a third class A drug trafficking offence, 3 years for a third domestic burglary offence or 5 years for certain firearm offences,

(b) the legal framework for the particular offence or offences. This is found in the guidelines from the Sentencing Council and Sentencing Guidelines Council and Court of Appeal judicial guidance, see the **GUIDELINES** chapter. If the case is a serious example of the offence, the court will consider the maximum sentence available, see:
CUSTODY: ***Maximum must be reserved for the most serious cases*** at **28.15**,
CUSTODY: ***Maximum given with a plea of guilty*** at **28.17**,
CUSTODY: ***Maximum considered inadequate etc.*** at **28.17**, and
CONCURRENT OR CONSECUTIVE SENTENCES ***Grave cases/Maximum considered inadequate*** at **18.9**,

(c) the culpability of the defendant. Criminal Justice Act 2003 s 143(1) provides that the court must consider this, see **86.39**,

(d) the impact on the victim or potential victim. Even a tax fraud has a victim,

(e) in sexual cases and violent cases in particular, the risk posed by the defendant. This may be critical in determining whether preventive orders, like Criminal Behaviour Orders and Restraining Orders, are appropriate. It is also a main factor in determining whether an extended sentence is appropriate and is a main factor in considering whether a life sentence is appropriate, but not the length of the minimum term,

(f) the sentences of defendants connected with the case who have already been dealt with (if there are any),

(g) the aggravating and mitigating features of the offence, which includes assessment of his criminal record if there is one, see **86.43**.

(h) the defendant's personal mitigation, see **242.48** in Volume 2,

(i) whether the sentence should be discounted because:

(1) the defendant has given or will give evidence against his criminal associates, or

(2) the defendant has given assistance to the authorities.

For both these factors see the **INFORMANTS/GIVING EVIDENCE FOR THE PROSECUTION** chapter.

Taking into account a) to i), the court arrives at a provisional sentence. Then, if the defendant has pleaded guilty, the court will work out what the appropriate deduction should be for the plea of guilty, see the **GUILTY PLEA, DISCOUNT FOR** chapter.

The Judicial Studies Board had information about the structured approach to sentencing, which was available on its website. The Board became the Judicial College, the website changed to www.judiciary.gov.uk and it appears the information is not available to the public.

The sentencing in murder cases is slightly different, see the **MURDER Guilty pleas** section at **287.25** in Volume 2. Ed.

86.43 ***Aggravating and mitigating circumstances***

Note: These include:

(a) the list of aggravating and mitigating factors listed in the *Overarching Principles: Seriousness Guideline 2004*, www.banksr.com Other Matters Guideline tab para 1.20, see **64.21**. Some of them are:

(i) whether the offence was committed when the defendant was on bail, see the ***Bail, Offence(s) Committed when on bail*** para at **242.3** in Volume 2,

(ii) the defendant's previous convictions, which are a statutory aggravating factor, see the **PREVIOUS CONVICTIONS** chapter. For how to deal with other bad character see the ***Bad character etc. for which there is no conviction*** section at **57.6**,

(b) the list of aggravating and mitigating factors in the guideline for the offence,

(c) the pre-sentence, medical and education reports if there are any, see the **PRE-SENTENCE REPORTS** chapter and the **MEDICAL REPORTS** chapter,

(d) the good character of the defendant, where the offence is not subject to a guideline, see **242.26** in Volume 2. Ed.

86.44 ***Finding and interpreting comparable cases***

Note: Non-guideline reported cases are only an illustration of the basic sentencing principles. Some of them are influential, others less so. Recent cases are more useful than older ones. Some offences like manslaughter are very hard to index because of the variety of ways the offence can be committed. However, even if there is a very similar case, it does not mean that the same sentence will be passed as in a reported case. Magistrates' Courts normally pass lower sentences than Crown Courts. Many Crown Court judges pass lower sentences than the Court of Appeal judges. Judges differ in their approaches, and judges have a discretion when weighing up all the different factors before they pass sentence.

In *R v Erskine* 2009 EWCA Crim 1425, 2 Cr App R 29 the Lord Chief Justice sought to restrict the number of cases counsel copy and cite for the Court of Appeal. The fact that the Court of Appeal considers that a sentence is not manifestly excessive does not mean that that sentence is the sentence that they would have passed. Where the Court of Appeal is considering an appeal by the prosecution (which are cited as *Att-Gen's Ref No 43 of 2013* etc.) the sentence that is substituted will usually be less than the appropriate sentence to take into account the stress etc. of the defendant's being sentenced twice. However, this rule does not apply in prosecution appeals when considering the minimum term of life sentences.[1033] Ed.

Att-Gen's Ref Nos 73 and 75 of 2010 and 3 of 2011 Re P 2011 EWCA Crim 633[1034] LCJ These cases enable us to emphasise that the jurisdiction of this Court to amplify, to explain or to offer a definitive sentencing guideline of its own, [or] to issue guidelines, if it thinks fit, is undiminished. No guideline can require that an unjust sentence should be imposed. For more detail, see **64.20**.

See also the **APPEALS: COURT OF APPEAL** ***Citing authorities*** para at **4.19**.

86.45 ***Sentencing is not a mathematical exercise***

R v Martin 2006 EWCA Crim 1035, 2007 1 Cr App R (S) 3 (p 14) The sentencing decision does not represent a mathematical exercise, nor does it result from arithmetical calculation. We rejected the idea that each element relevant to the sentencing decision has or should have some notional length ascribed to it. The sentencing decision requires the judge to balance all the ingredients of the case whether aggravating or mitigating. There was no grid plan. There was no points system.

Att-Gen's Ref No 126 of 2006 2007 EWCA Crim 53, 2 Cr App R (S) 59 (p 362) D, aged 14, murdered a fellow schoolboy. The starting points were from Criminal Justice Act 2003 Sch 21. Held. It is clear that the appropriate sentence remains fact-specific. It is trite law that irrespective of the 'starting point', the end result may be a minimum term of 'any length', well below or well above the defined starting point. The court must take account of every aggravating and mitigating feature. These lists are not exhaustive. The same holds good [for the] definitive guidelines issued by the Sentencing Guidelines Council/Sentencing Council, or guideline decisions of this Court.

[1033] Criminal Justice Act 1988 s 36(3A) as inserted by Criminal Justice Act 2003 s 272(1) and amended by Criminal Justice and Immigration Act 2008 s 46(1)-(2)

[1034] In some reports this case is listed as *Att-Gen's Ref Nos 73 and 75 of 2010 and 3 of 2011* 2011 EWCA Crim 633.

86.46 ***Ancillary orders***
Note: The court will consider:

(a) whether costs should be awarded against the defendant, see the **COSTS** chapter,
(b) whether compensation is appropriate, see the **COMPENSATION ORDERS** chapter,
(c) whether an ancillary order should be made, such as a confiscation order, a destruction order for drugs found in the case, disqualification, forfeiture, or a Football Banning Order,
(d) the appropriate victim surcharge,[1035] see the **VICTIM SURCHARGE** chapter.

The court will then pass sentence. Frequently the confiscation order procedure (if there is one) will be adjourned. Ed.

Sentencing remarks

86.47 ***Sentencing remarks Must be oral and in open court***
Att-Gen's Ref No 96 of 2009 2010 EWCA Crim 350 LCJ D, aged 14, was 'educationally sub-normal' and had an IQ of 71, well below average. He was convicted of rape. The Judge in his sentencing remarks was mindful of the ability or otherwise of D to comprehend his sentencing remarks and kept them succinct. He informed both counsel that he would reduce his reasons to writing and that they would be made available to both sides within a few days. Held. It would have been better if the Judge had prepared his sentencing remarks in writing, available at the moment when he came to pass sentence. Handing them out later was wrong. We cannot think of any occasion when it can be appropriate for the reasons for a sentencing decision not to be given in open court. In principle, we cannot have sentencing decisions, or the reasons for them, announced behind closed doors. They should be read out publicly.
R v Billington 2017 EWCA Crim 618, 2 Cr App R (S) 22 (p 171) The Judge said he would provide reasons for his sentence in writing later. He then imposed an extended sentence. The defence received the reasons. The prosecution did not. Held. Sentencing can frequently be complex and technical and the analysis for extended sentences might require an adjournment. But it is crucial that the articulation of the reasoning takes place orally in public. This is to ensure that the public at large, which includes the press, are made fully aware of the reasons for the sentence passed. Transparency in the working of the justice system is integral to the maintenance of public confidence in that system. Transparency is equally critical in ensuring that the defendant knows exactly why the sentence has been passed and it facilitates consideration of possible grounds of appeal. For similar reasons, it enables the Crown to know whether they should oppose an appeal and, if so, upon what basis and even whether they would wish to challenge a sentence as unduly lenient. Criminal Justice Act 2003 s 174(2) stipulates that such reasons must be given in 'open court'. None of this, of course, prevents the increasingly common practice of the judge handing out printed copies of the sentencing remarks to those in court once they have been delivered.
R v Tinkler 2018 EWCA Crim 1243 D pleaded to death by dangerous driving and other offences. The following day, the Judge sent an e-mail reducing the disqualification from 12 to 11 years. Held. That approach, whilst no doubt an efficient one, is not appropriate. In the interests of open justice, any sentence, including consequential orders or corrections, should be announced in open court and on notice, *R v Billington* 2017, see above.
For the need for cases to be heard in open court, see **86.4**.
See also: **VARIATION OF SENTENCE** ***There must be a hearing in open court*** para at **112.17**.

86.48 ***Sentencing remarks Contents***
Note: The sentencing remarks should contain:

[1035] Criminal Justice Act 2003 s 161A-161B

(a) the facts the sentencer has found for the sentencing. Judges normally list key factors which have influenced the sentence(s),
(b) how the guidelines (which normally exist for the offence(s)) have been applied, see **64.18**,
(c) the sentencer's decision and reasons on any legal issue that have not been the subject of oral ruling,
(d) where there are mandatory orders, like for third class A drug trafficking offences, an explanation why the minimum sentence has or has not been imposed,
(e) the explanation and reasons for the sentence with reference to the statutory provisions, if appropriate. In extended sentences (EDS) and murder cases, the judge is required to give details of the various stages that led him or her to impose his or her orders,
(f) if there has been a guilty plea, the sentence that there would have been had there not been a plea and the reasons for a reduced discount if one was given, see the **GUILTY PLEA, DISCOUNT FOR** chapter,
(g) any ancillary orders with the reasons why they have been imposed or not imposed,
(h) the days that were served in custody awaiting sentence. The judge will normally refer to credit for these days in custody. Where a defendant has been tagged and on a curfew awaiting sentence the judge will normally give half a day's discount for each day. For both these principles, see the **CUSTODY: DISCOUNT FOR TIME SPENT IN/CURFEW DISCOUNT** chapter,
(i) if there is a custodial sentence, the expected date of release or the method of calculation for the date of release,
(j) the orders which apply automatically upon certain convictions, namely notification and the vulnerable groups barring orders, see the **NOTIFICATION** and **VULNERABLE GROUPS: BARRING** chapters. Ed.

R v Hagan 2012 EWCA Crim 1822, 2013 1 Cr App R (S) 90 (p 483) LCJ D was convicted of possessing a firearm with intent to endanger life. He was aged 16. The Judge believed D revelled in his membership of a gang. The Judge gave 9 years and said his sentencing remarks should be sent to the relevant people at D's school and to the Ofsted inspector, who he believed were insufficiently aware of the problem [of gangs]. Held. That direction ought not to have been included in the remarks.

For ***Sentencing remarks in extended disqualification cases***, see *R v Needham and Others* 2016 EWCA Crim 455, 2 Cr App R (S) 26 (p 219) at **41.16**.

86.49 *Reasons Judge must give reasons*

Note: Almost all sentencing orders require the judge or magistrate to give reasons why he or she made the order and an explanation as to what it entails. The requirement to explain the order is listed in the relevant chapter. Ed.

Duty to give reasons for and to explain effect of sentence

Criminal Justice Act 2003 s 174(1)[1036] A court passing sentence on an offender has the duties in subsections (2) and (3).

(2) The court must state in open court, in ordinary language and in general terms, the court's reasons for deciding on the sentence.

(3) The court must explain to the offender in ordinary language:
(a) the effect of the sentence,
(b) the effects of non-compliance with any order that the offender is required to comply with and that forms part of the sentence,
(c) any power of the court to vary or review any order that forms part of the sentence, and
(d) the effects of failure to pay a fine, if the sentence consists of or includes a fine.

For the duty to give reasons about how a guideline was applied or not applied, see **64.18**.

[1036] As substituted by Legal Aid, Sentencing and Punishment of Offenders Act 2012 s 64

For the duty to give reasons for children and young offenders, see the **CHILDREN AND YOUNG OFFENDERS: CUSTODIAL SENTENCES *Reasons, Sentencers must give Children etc.*** para at **13.50**.
For ***Suggested sentence remarks*** see the chapter for each relevant sentencing order. Ed.
For where a guideline is not followed, see the **GUIDELINES *Reasons Judge must give reasons if not following a guideline*** para at **64.18**.

86.50 ***Explain sentence, Sentencer must*** ***Time on remand/Curfew***
Note: Since Legal Aid, Sentencing and Punishment of Offenders Act 2012 s 108-109 (see **30.2**) was in force, the judge no longer has to order time on remand where there is a determinate custodial sentence. However, he or she has to deduct time where there has been a qualifying curfew and tag. In life cases the judge has to make the calculation for both matters before determining the minimum term. It is still appropriate to tell defendants that time on: a) remand, and b) curfew and tag has been/will be deducted. Ed.

86.51 ***Explain the sentence, Sentencer must*** ***Explanation wrong***
R v Ravel 2007 EWCA Crim 1091 The Judge passed an extended sentence with a 15-month custodial part on D. He then passed a 3-month consecutive sentence. He told D that he would only serve half of it. He had overlooked that D would not be released from the extended sentence until the Parole Board directed his release. After nine months D was not released. The case was relisted before the sentencing Judge and the Judge, expressing his concern, said he intended that D should serve 18 months and indicated he should be released forthwith. D then appealed. Held. The full Court in giving leave expressed concern that, when a judge had passed a sentence intending that the defendant should be released after nine months, that had not happened and that that had left D with an understandable grievance which should be considered by the full Court. If this Court had any discretion it might give effect to these concerns, but the reality is that neither the Judge at first instance nor this Court has any discretion. We have no alternative but to dismiss the appeal. We ask that the Parole Board should pay significant regard to the view expressed by the…Judge that D should be released at the end of nine months. That cannot of course be binding on the Parole Board, but we hope that they will [bear] that very much in mind when considering whether to release D and that they should also bear in mind as a matter of justice and fairness the expectation which was raised in D's mind by the indication given to him by the Judge at the time of sentence.
R v Bright 2008 EWCA Crim 462, 2 Cr App R (S) 102 (p 578) The Judge told D that he would be released after half his 7-year sentence whereas the 1991 release provisions applied, so he would serve longer before the prison was obliged to release him. The defence asked for the sentence to be reduced so D would be released after 3½ years under the 1991 provisions. Held. The submission is based on a fallacy. The actual sentence was 7 years' imprisonment. The release provisions did not and should not have affected the Judge's sentencing decision. What he was required to do was to explain the effect of the sentence in the context of the applicable statutory provisions relating to release. He did not 'intend' that D should be released after 3½ years, that would simply have been the consequence if the 2003 Act had applied to the sentence, and he was required to state that consequence in open court. Precisely the same applies to his observations when reconsidering the sentence. He knew that the appellant would be eligible for release after 3½ years, but not automatically entitled to it. He was entitled to say, as a Judge of considerable experience, that it would be very likely indeed that the defendant would in fact be released at the end of 3½ years. Again, that did not mean that he so 'intended'. The sentence of 7 years' imprisonment is not open to question on the basis that the order achieved a different result from that which the Judge intended.
R v Giga 2008 EWCA Crim 703, 2008 2 Cr App R (S) 112 (p 638) The Judge sentenced D to 6 years and explained that D would serve half his sentence. In fact the defendant was liable to serve two-thirds of the sentence. The defence asked that the sentence should be reduced to reflect the Judge's intention. Held. We do not accept that

submission. There was nothing in the Judge's remarks to suggest he was determining the correct sentence with his mind primarily directed to the question of release. We prefer the approach in *R v Bright* 2008 EWCA Crim 462, 2 Cr App R (S) 102 (p 578) to other cases. The judge determines the length of the sentence, not how long D will spend in custody. The fact that the Judge's explanation was inaccurate does not undermine his decision or provide grounds for saying that the sentence was wrong in principle or manifestly excessive, which it was not.

R v Dunn 2012 EWCA Crim 419 D was sentenced to 15 years each for 12 offences of rape. The Judge said D would be released after 7½ years. In prison he learnt that for the earlier offences he would not be entitled to be released until after 10 years. For the rest the release date would be 7½ years. The case was relisted but the time limit for variation had expired. The Judge wanted to reduce the sentences for the earlier offences so D would be released after 7½ years. It was agreed that D should appeal with an indication from the Judge that he wished the Court of Appeal to reduce the sentence for the earlier offences. The Judge told D that he did not want him to be disadvantaged and it was a procedural anomaly which was going to be resolved. Held. Early release provisions should not be considered. The Parole Board may release him after 7½ years. There was no injustice.

R v R 2012 EWCA Crim 709 D pleaded to various sex offences. All parties overlooked the fact that some of the older offences were under the pre-Criminal Justice Act 2003 regime. The case was brought back to court after the time limit for amending the sentence had expired. The Judge encouraged D to appeal. Held. If the Judge states the wrong release date that is most unfortunate, but the principle in *R v Dunn* 2012 EWCA Crim 419 must stand.

R v Hardy 2013 EWCA Crim 36 D was sentenced to 6 years and the Judge said he would serve half the sentence. In fact, as the offences were historical, D had to serve two-thirds. The defence said the sentence should reflect what the Judge had in mind as the correct period of custody. Held. There may be rare and exceptional circumstances where the Judge selects a length of sentence after which the defendant should be released. Here the Judge expressed no such intention. The sentence was not wrong.

For a judge recommending particular licence conditions, see the **LICENCE CONDITIONS, JUDGE RECOMMENDING** chapter.

Other matters

86.52 *Start date for sentences*

Powers of Criminal Courts (Sentencing) Act 2000 s 154(1) A sentence imposed by the Crown Court shall take effect from the beginning of the day on which it is imposed unless the court otherwise directs.

Court Martial A sentence of imprisonment generally runs from the date it is passed but where the offender is already serving a previous custodial sentence, the court may order that the new custodial sentence shall run consecutively from the expiry of the earlier sentence, Armed Forces Act 2006 s 188(3)(b), see *Guidance on Sentencing in the Court Martial 2018* para 3.1.6.

See also: *R v Kaplan* 1978 RTR 119 (D, the defendant, lost his appeal at the Court of Appeal and it followed that his disqualification would be reinstated. The Court was told D was driving when the appeal was dismissed. The Court ordered that the order should not be drawn up until 10.30 the next day.)

86.53 *Combining sentences Basic principles*

Note: Many of the chapters in this book have a section entitled **Combined with other orders**. This section is usually near the end of the chapter, before the appeals section if there is one. Ed.

R v Ithell 1969 53 Cr App R 210 This Court has emphasised that as a matter of sentencing practice, but not as a matter of law, it is almost invariably wrong to impose two conflicting penalties simultaneously.

R v Butters and Fitzgerald 1971 55 Cr App R 515 The defendants were subject to immediate imprisonment and suspended sentences at the same time. Held. That was undesirable as a matter of sentencing practice. In general courts should avoid mixing up sentences which fall into different categories. Here we make it one type only.

R v McElhorne 1983 5 Cr App R (S) 53 In general, courts should avoid mixing sentences which fall into well-established and different categories.

86.54 *Backdate sentences, Crown Court can't*

R v Gilbert 1974 60 Cr App R 220 The Court reviewed Courts Act 1971 s 11(1) (which has since been re-enacted in Powers of Criminal Courts (Sentencing) Act 2000 s 154(1), see above) and the earlier authorities. Held. There was not and never had been a power to order that a sentence should commence at a time earlier than the date upon which it was pronounced.

Note: The Court of Appeal can backdate a sentence, see **4.73**.

86.55 *Sentence unclear/Ambiguous*

R (Webb) v Swindon Crown Court 2011 EWHC 1507 (Admin) High Court D breached his licence by committing a burglary and the Judge made the burglary sentence consecutive to the recall period. D appealed his sentence and it was reduced by one year. The prison and the Crown Court Sentencing Enforcement Unit thought the recall period ran from the date of the new offence. The Court of Appeal and the defence counsel had assumed it ran from the date of the sentence. The prison then told the defendant he would serve the longer term. The defence wrote letters to the Crown Court and approached the CCRC. Eventually they appealed to the High Court. Held. The Judge's order was ambiguous, so the order must be read favourably to D. The shorter period is ordered.

Note: The High Court held that the action against the prison was not apt and the substance was, 'What order did the Judge make?' Therefore the appeal appears without jurisdiction as it 'related to trial on indictment', so it was barred, Senior Courts Act 1981 s 29(3). Ed.

See also: *R v Ketley* 1989 Unreported 22/11/89 (It was unclear whether the sentence was concurrent or consecutive to the existing sentence. Matter resolved in favour of the defendant.)

R v Watkins and P 2014 EWCA Crim 1677, 2015 1 Cr App R (S) 6 (p 41) (D pleaded to rape and other sex offences on babies. The Judge said he passed a 35-year extended sentence (15-year and 14-year consecutive custodial terms and a 6-year extended licence). Held. [The constituent parts of the sentence] were ambiguous so we resolve the dispute in D's favour so only the 14-year sentences were to be an extended sentence.)

86.56 *Written order different from judge's oral order*

R v Kent 1983 5 Cr App R (S) 171 There was a difference between the Judge's pronouncement and the court record. Held. It was the Judge's pronouncement that was the order. If the staff are in doubt as to the pronouncement, they should consult the judge.

R v Pelletier 2012 EWCA Crim 1060 D pleaded to breaching his SOPO. The defence later discovered that the Judge's oral term in his SOPO was different from the written order and D was not guilty of breaching the oral term. Held. To avoid this, judges should order draft orders to be issued. We quash the conviction.

R v Hamer 2017 EWCA Crim 192, 2 Cr App R (S) 13 (p 82) *R v Pelletier* 2012 held that the terms of the order are the ones the judge announced.

R v Cooper 2018 EWCA Crim 1958 The Judge ordered 2 years 109 days' disqualification. The Court record said 2 years. Held. The order is as pronounced by the Judge. We order the Court record be amended.

86.57 *Judge forgets to sentence*

R v G 2014 EWCA Crim 1221 LCJ The Judge forgot to sentence on some counts in a complicated indictment. Court staff pointed this out and the Judge indicated the sentence. Held. Yet again Crown counsel failed in their duty to point this failure out. The Judge should have returned to court and pronounced the sentences in open court.

86.58 *Direction that evidence should be retained for parole hearings*

R v Wilson 2012 EWCA Crim 386, 2 Cr App R (S) 77 (p 440) LCJ D pleaded to two rapes against 3-year-olds and 44 other sex offences against children. Held. Life with 13½-year minimum term. We endorse the Judge's direction that the material that was used for the sentence hearing should be retained for the time he is considered for parole.

86.59 *Procedural irregularities*

R v Ashton and Others 2006 EWCA Crim 794, 2 Cr App R (S) 15 (p 231) para 9 The prevailing approach to litigation is to avoid determining cases on technicalities (when they do not result in real prejudice and injustice) but instead to ensure that they are decided fairly on their merits. This approach is reflected in the Criminal Procedure Rules and, in particular, the overriding objective. Accordingly, absent a clear indication that Parliament intended jurisdiction automatically to be removed following [a] procedural failure, the decision of the court should be based on a wide assessment of the interests of justice, with particular focus on whether there was a real possibility that the prosecution or the defendant may suffer prejudice. If that risk is present, the court should then decide whether it is just to permit the proceedings to continue.

R v Ford 2018 EWCA Crim 1751 D was charged with section 18 and appeared at the Youth Court aged 17. The case was adjourned so the defence could read the papers. On the next appearance D was aged 18. D pleaded to section 18 and possession of an offensive weapon. D was committed for sentence under Powers of Criminal Courts (Sentencing) Act 2000 s 3. At the Crown Court, D received 6½ years in all. Held. We assume the magistrates purported to commit D under section 3B because that is the section for those who require additional sentencing powers. To use Magistrates' Court Act 1980 s 24 (which enables those who turn 18 to be dealt with in the Youth Court) the defendant must be aged 17 when the court determines mode of trial, see *R v Islington North Juvenile Court ex parte Daley* 1982 75 Cr App R 280 (House of Lords). So, there was no jurisdiction to take D's plea or commit him to the Crown Court. Everything after that was invalid. Acting as Judges of the Divisional Court we quash the committal. For details of what happened next, see **13.8**.

86.60 *Unlawful orders*

DPP v T 2006 EWHC 728 (Admin) High Court The normal rule is that an order of the court must be treated as valid unless and until it is set aside or varied on appeal or on an application to vary. During the intervening period it cannot be treated as a nullity and of no legal effect.

R v Miah 2011 EWCA Crim 1850 The first sentencing Judge revoked a Suspended Sentence Order when the defendant was not in breach. The second sentencing Judge, not knowing about the 'revocation', activated the Suspended Sentence Order. Held. There was no power for the first Judge to revoke the order. However, an invalid order remains in force until overturned on appeal. Therefore, the second Judge had no power to activate the order.

See also the **APPEALS: CROWN COURT APPEALS** ***Magistrates pass an unlawful sentence*** para at **5.25**.

87 REFERRAL ORDERS

87.1

Powers of Criminal Courts (Sentencing) Act 2000 s 16

Availability A Referral Order is available to the Youth Court or other Magistrates' Court dealing with an offender who is under 18 years of age.[1037] There are a number of conditions. The main one is that the defendant must have pleaded guilty. The order is not available in the Crown Court except when the court is hearing appeals. For more detail and when it is not available, see **87.3**.
Individual support order offences A Referral Order may not be made for these offences.[1038]
Meaning of the order A Referral Order is an order that the offender is referred to a youth offender panel. There are two types of order, one mandatory, see **87.4**, one discretionary, see **87.5**.
General matters The functions of the youth offending team are laid down in Powers of Criminal Courts (Sentencing) Act 2000 s 18(2).
The duties of the youth offending team are laid down in Powers of Criminal Courts (Sentencing) Act 2000 s 21.
There is a power for the youth offending team to permit victims and those 'capable of having a good influence over the offender' to attend a meeting, Powers of Criminal Courts (Sentencing) Act 2000 s 22(4)-(5).
The aims and terms of the order can be found at Powers of Criminal Courts (Sentencing) Act 2000 s 23(1)-(2).
The functions of the youth offending panel can be found at Powers of Criminal Courts (Sentencing) Act 2000 s 29.
Guilty plea As a referral order is a sentence that is only available upon pleading guilty there should be no further reduction of the sentence to reflect the guilty plea, *Sentencing Children and Young People Guideline 2017*, see www.banksr.com Other Matters Guidelines tab at para 5.15.
Electronic monitoring The programme may not include electronic monitoring, see Powers of Criminal Courts (Sentencing) Act 2000 s 23(3).
Rehabilitation period The period ends when the youth offender contract (including any extension) ceases to have effect. Where there is no contract, the period ends when the contract would have ceased.[1039]
See also the **REHABILITATION OF OFFENDERS ACT 1974** chapter.
Victim surcharge The court must impose a victim surcharge of £20, Criminal Justice Act 2003 s 161A-161B and Criminal Justice Act 2003 (Surcharge) Order 2012 2012/1696 as amended. Where a compensation order is imposed, a reduced amount can be ordered or no victim surcharge need be imposed, see **17.67**. Where the offence was committed on or after 1 October 2012 and before 8 April 2016, the amount is £15, see **115.4**.

87.2 ***Statistics England and Wales***
Referral Orders Magistrates' Court/Youth Court

	2012	2013	2014	2015	2016	2017
Number of orders	16,382	13,162	12,858	12,367	11,402	10,611

For explanations about the statistics, see page 1-xii.

Power to order/Test to apply

87.3 ***Mandatory orders Power to order***
Duty and power to refer certain young offenders to youth offender panels.
Powers of Criminal Courts (Sentencing) Act 2000 s 16(1) This section applies where a Youth Court or other Magistrates' Court is dealing with a person aged under 18 for an offence and:

[1037] Powers of Criminal Courts (Sentencing) Act 2000 s 16(1)
[1038] Crime and Disorder Act 1998 s 1AB(4)
[1039] Rehabilitation of Offenders Act 1974 s 4B-4C

(a) neither the offence nor any connected offence is one for which the sentence is fixed by law,
(b) the court is not, in respect of the offence or any connected offence, proposing to impose a custodial sentence on the offender or make a Hospital Order (within the meaning of the Mental Health Act 1983) in his case, and
(c) the court is not proposing to discharge him whether absolutely or conditionally in respect of the offence.[1040]

(2) If:
(a) the compulsory referral conditions are satisfied in accordance with section 17 below, and
(b) referral is available to the court,

the court shall sentence the offender for the offence by ordering him to be referred to a youth offender panel ('a Referral Order').

The referral conditions.

Powers of Criminal Courts (Sentencing) Act 2000 s 17(1) For the purposes of section 16(2) above and subsection (2) below the compulsory referral conditions are satisfied in relation to an offence if the offence is an offence punishable with imprisonment and the offender:
(a) pleaded guilty to the offence and to any connected offence, and
(b) has never been:
(i) convicted by or before a court in the United Kingdom of any offence other than the offence and any connected offence, or
(ii) convicted by or before a court in another member State of any offence.

Breach of ASBO Guideline 2009, see www.banksr.com Guidelines tab page 17 para 4 Where a young offender pleads guilty and is being sentenced for the first time, the court must impose a Referral Order unless either it considers the offence to be of such a nature that an absolute discharge or Hospital Order is appropriate or it considers the offence to be so serious that only a custodial sentence is appropriate. Such an order refers the offender to a youth offender panel, and the court may (or 'shall' in the case of a child aged under 16) require at least one parent or guardian to attend the panel meetings unless this would be unreasonable.[1041]

87.4 *Mandatory orders Court may not defer sentence*

Powers of Criminal Courts (Sentencing) Act 2000 s 19(7) Where section 16(2) of this Act requires a court to make a Referral Order, the court may not under section 1 of this Act defer passing sentence on him, but section 16(2) and subsection (3)(a) of this Act do not affect any power or duty of a Magistrates' Court under:
(a) section 8 of this Act (remission to Youth Court, or another such court, for sentence),
(b) Magistrates' Courts Act 1980 s 10(3) (adjournment for inquiries), or
(c) Mental Health Act 1983 s 35, 38, 43 or 44 (remand for reports, Interim Hospital Orders and committal to Crown Court for Restriction Order).

87.5 *Discretionary orders Power to order*

Powers of Criminal Courts (Sentencing) Act 2000 s 16(3) If:
(a) the discretionary referral conditions are satisfied in accordance with section 17 below, and
(b) referral is available to the court,

the court may sentence the offender for the offence by ordering him to be referred to a youth offender panel ('a Referral Order').

[1040] As amended by Legal Aid, Sentencing and Punishment of Offenders Act 2012 s 79(1). The change only applies to offences committed after 3/12/12, see Legal Aid, Sentencing and Punishment of Offenders Act 2012 s 79(4).
[1041] Powers of Criminal Courts (Sentencing) Act 2000 s 20

Powers of Criminal Courts (Sentencing) Act 2000 s 17(2)[1042] For the purposes of section 16(3) above, the discretionary referral conditions are satisfied in relation to an offence if:

(a) the compulsory referral conditions are not satisfied in relation to the offence, and
(b) the offender pleaded guilty:
(i) to the offence, or
(ii) if the offender is being dealt with by the court for the offence and any connected offence, to at least one of those offences.

87.6 *Sentencing Children and Young People Guideline 2017*

Sentencing Children and Young People Guideline 2017, see www.banksr.com Other Matters Guidelines tab In force 1 June 2017 page 2.

6.19 A referral order is the mandatory sentence in a Youth Court or Magistrates' Court for most children and young people who have committed an offence for the first time and have pleaded guilty to an imprisonable offence. Exceptions are for offences where a sentence is fixed by law or if the court deems a custodial sentence, an absolute or conditional discharge or a hospital order to be more appropriate.

6.20 A discretionary referral order can also be imposed for any offence where there has been a plea of guilty regardless of previous offending history. It should be remembered that they are not community orders and in general terms may be regarded as orders which fall between community disposals and fines. However, bearing in mind that the principal aim of the youth justice system is to prevent children and young people offending, second or subsequent referral orders should be considered in those cases where:

(a) the offence is not serious enough for a YRO but the child or young person does appear to require some intervention; **or**
(b) the offence is serious enough for a YRO but it is felt that a referral order would be the best way to prevent further offending (as an example, this may be because the child or young person has responded well in the past to such an order and the offence now before the court is dissimilar to that for which a referral order was previously imposed).

Referral orders are the main sentence for delivering restorative justice and all panel members are trained Restorative Conference Facilitators; as such they can be an effective sentence in encouraging children and young people to take responsibility for their actions and understand the effect their offence may have had on their victim.

6.21 In cases where children or young people have offended for the first time and have pleaded guilty to committing an offence which is on the cusp of the custody threshold, YOTs should be encouraged to convene a Youth Offender Panel prior to sentence (sometimes referred to as a 'pseudo-panel' or 'pre-panel') where the child or young person is asked to attend before a panel and agree an intensive contract. If that contract is placed before the sentencing Youth Court, the court can then decide whether it is sufficient to move below custody on this occasion. The proposed contract is not something the court can alter in any way; the court will still have to make a decision between referral order and custody but can do so on the basis that if it makes a referral order it can have confidence in what that will entail in the particular case.

6.22 The court determines the length of the order but a Referral Order Panel determines the requirements of the order.

Offence seriousness	Suggested length of referral order
Low	3-5 months
Medium	5-7 months

[1042] The Secretary of State may amend these conditions by regulation, Powers of Criminal Courts (Sentencing) Act 2000 s 16(3)-(4).

Offence seriousness	Suggested length of referral order
High	7-9 months
Very high	10-12 months

The YOT may propose certain requirements and the length of these requirements may not correspond to the above table; if the court feels these requirements will best achieve the aims of the youth justice system then they may still be imposed.

87.7 *Which courts can make an order?*

Powers of Criminal Courts (Sentencing) Act 2000 s 16(1) This section applies when a Youth Court or other Magistrates' Court is dealing with a person.

Note: Crown Courts may make the order when hearing appeals from Youth Courts. Ed.

R v Dillon 2017 EWCA Crim 2642, 2019 1 Cr App R (S) 22 (p 155) D was sent to the Crown Court with an adult, AD, on a £102,000 fraud charge. He pleaded guilty and his sentence was adjourned. The pre-sentence report recommended a Referral Order but it said that order would need a remittal to the Youth Court. The matter was put back and it was suggested the Judge could sit as a district judge. The Judge made a Youth Rehabilitation Order. Held. The pre-sentence report was correct about the Referral Order. The case should have been remitted immediately after the plea (see *R v Lewis* 1984 [above]) because there was no issue of disparity and there was no direct link with AD. The Youth Court is given exclusive competence to make a Referral Order and the Judge could not acquire that by sitting as a district judge. There would have been no extra delay as a pre-sentence report was required. At the Youth Court a Referral Order had to be made. Neither we nor the Crown Court can make a Referral Order. Given the delay, the errors and D's good performance with the Youth Rehabilitation Order, we substitute a conditional discharge.

Making the order

87.8 *Purpose of the order*

Breach of ASBO Guideline 2008, see www.banksr.com Other Matters Guidelines tab Annex C para 4 [When dealing with referral orders] panel meetings are intended to result in a youth offender contract, which is aimed at repairing the harm caused by the offence and addressing the causes of the offending behaviour (including requirements such as unpaid work in the community).

87.9 *Maximum and minimum length*

Powers of Criminal Courts (Sentencing) Act 2000 s 18(1) A Referral Order shall:

(c) specify the period [which must not be less than 3 nor more than 12 months].

Powers of Criminal Courts (Sentencing) Act 2000 s 24(4) Where the panel was established in pursuance of two or more associated Referral Orders, the length of the period for which the contract has effect shall be that resulting from the court's directions under section 18(6) (additional orders may not cause the aggregate to exceed 12 months).

87.10 *How long should the order be?*

Sentencing Children and Young People Guideline 2017, see www.banksr.com Other Matters Guidelines tab In force 1 June 2017 page 25

6.22 The court determines the length of the order but a Referral Order Panel determines the requirements of the order.

Offence seriousness	Suggested length of referral order
Low	3-5 months
Medium	5-7 months
High	7-9 months

Offence seriousness	Suggested length of referral order
Very high	10-12 months

The YOT may propose certain requirements and the length of these requirements may not correspond to the above table; if the court feels these requirements will best achieve the aims of the youth justice system then they may still be imposed.

87.11 ***Contents of the order***

Powers of Criminal Courts (Sentencing) Act 2000 s 18(1) A Referral Order shall:

(a) specify the youth offending team responsible for implementing the order,

(b) require the offender to attend each of the meetings of a youth offender panel to be established by the team for the offender, and

(c) specify the period for which any youth offender contract taking effect between the offender and the panel under section 23 is to have effect (which must not be less than 3 nor more than 12 months).

87.12 ***Sentencing for more than one offence***

Powers of Criminal Courts (Sentencing) Act 2000 s 18(4) and (5) Where, in dealing with an offender for two or more connected offences, a court makes a Referral Order in respect of each, or each of two or more, of the offences, the orders shall have the effect of referring the offender to a single youth offender panel. The provision shall accordingly be the same in each case, except that the periods specified under subsection (1)(c) may be different.

(6) The court may direct that the period so specified in either or any of the orders is to run concurrently with or be additional to that specified in the other or any of the others, but in exercising its power under this subsection the court must ensure that the total period for which such a contract as is mentioned in subsection (1)(c) above is to have effect does not exceed 12 months.

Parental orders (Parents to attend meetings)

87.13 ***Power to order/When order mandatory***

Making of referral orders: attendance of parents etc.

Powers of Criminal Courts (Sentencing) Act 2000 s 20(1) A court making a Referral Order may make an order requiring:

(a) the appropriate person, or

(b) in a case where there are two or more appropriate persons, any one or more of them,

to attend the meetings of the youth offender panel.

(2) Where an offender is aged under 16 when a court makes a Referral Order in his case:

(a) the court shall exercise its power under subsection (1) above so as to require at least one appropriate person to attend meetings of the youth offender panel, and

(b) if the offender is a child who is looked after by a local authority[1043] the person or persons so required to attend those meetings shall be or include a representative of the local authority.

(3) The court shall not under this section make an order requiring a person to attend meetings of the youth offender panel:

(a) if the court is satisfied that it would be unreasonable to do so, or

(b) to an extent which the court is satisfied would be unreasonable.

87.14 ***Parental orders Definition of appropriate adult***

Powers of Criminal Courts (Sentencing) Act 2000 s 20(4) Except where the offender is a child who [is looked after by a local authority] each person who is a parent or guardian of the offender is an 'appropriate person' for the purposes of this section.

(5) Where the offender [is a child who is looked after by a local authority] each of the following is an 'appropriate person' for the purposes of this section:

[1043] As defined in Powers of Criminal Courts (Sentencing) Act 2000 s 20(6)

(a) a representative of the local authority mentioned in that subsection, and
(b) each person who is a parent or guardian of the offender with whom the offender is allowed to live.

87.15 ***Parental orders*** ***Failure to attend meetings***

Powers of Criminal Courts (Sentencing) Act 2000 s 20(7) If, at the time when a court makes an order under this section:

(a) a person who is required by the order to attend meetings of a youth offender panel is not present in court, or
(b) a local authority whose representative is so required to attend such meetings is not represented in court,

the court must send him or (as the case may be) the authority a copy of the order forthwith.

For breaches of the order, see the **REFERRAL ORDERS: RE-SENTENCING Parent or guardian failing to attend meetings** section at **88.8**.

Combined with other orders

87.16 ***Absolute discharge, Combined with***

Powers of Criminal Courts (Sentencing) Act 2000 s 19(3) The court shall, in respect of any connected offence, either sentence the offender by making a Referral Order or make an order discharging him absolutely.

87.17 ***Bind overs, Combined with***

Powers of Criminal Courts (Sentencing) Act 2000 s 19(1) and (5)(a) Where the court makes a Referral Order, the court may not make an order binding him over to keep the peace or to be of good behaviour.

87.18 ***Bind overs of parents or guardians, Combined with***

Powers of Criminal Courts (Sentencing) Act 2000 s 19(1) and (5)(b) Where the court makes a Referral Order, the court may not make, in connection with the conviction of the offender for the offence or any connected offence: b) an order under section 150 of this Act (binding over of parent or guardian).

87.19 ***Conditional discharge, Combined with***

Powers of Criminal Courts (Sentencing) Act 2000 s 19(1)-(4)(d) Where the court makes a Referral Order, the court may not make an order discharging him conditionally.
Note: The section has been summarised. Ed.

87.20 ***Deferred sentence, Combined with***

Powers of Criminal Courts (Sentencing) Act 2000 s 19(7) Where the court makes a Referral Order, the court may not defer passing sentence on him.

87.21 ***Fine, Combined with***

Powers of Criminal Courts (Sentencing) Act 2000 s 19(1)-(4) Where the court makes a Referral Order, the court may not deal with the offender by ordering him to pay a fine.

87.22 ***Hospital and Guardianship Orders, Combined with***

Mental Health Act 1983 s 37(8) Where an order is made under this section, the court shall not:..make a Referral Order (within the meaning of the Powers of Criminal Courts (Sentencing) Act 2000) in respect of the offence.

87.23 ***Parenting Orders, Combined with***

Crime and Disorder Act 1998 s 9(1) and (1A) The requirement that a court shall make a parenting order when the conditions are satisfied does not apply to Referral Orders.

87.24 ***Reparation Order, Combined with***

Powers of Criminal Courts (Sentencing) Act 2000 s 19(1)-(4)(c) Where the court makes a Referral Order, the court may not make a Reparation Order in respect of him.
Powers of Criminal Courts (Sentencing) Act 2000 s 73(4)(b) The court shall not make a Reparation Order if it proposes to make a Referral Order.

87.25 *Street Offences Act 1959: Supervision of offenders, Combined with*
Powers of Criminal Courts (Sentencing) Act 2000 s 19(4) Where the court makes a Referral Order, the court may not make an order under Street Offences Act 1959 s 1(2A) (offender required to attend meetings with 'supervisor' when convicted of loitering or soliciting for the purposes of prostitution) in respect of the offender.

87.26 *Youth Rehabilitation Order, Combined with*
Powers of Criminal Courts (Sentencing) Act 2000 s 19(1)-(4) Where the court makes a Referral Order, the court may not deal with the offender by imposing a sentence which includes a Youth Rehabilitation Order.

Matters after order made

87.27 *Duty to explain the order*
Powers of Criminal Courts (Sentencing) Act 2000 s 18(3) On making a Referral Order the court shall explain to the offender in ordinary language:
(a) the effect of the order, and
(b) the consequences which may follow:
(i) if no youth offender contract takes effect between the offender and the panel, or
(ii) if the offender breaches any of the terms of any such contract.

87.28 *YOT programme*
Powers of Criminal Courts (Sentencing) Act 2000 s 23(2) The terms of the programme may, in particular, include provision for any of the following:
(a) the offender to make financial or other reparation to any person who appears to the panel to be a victim of, or otherwise affected by, the offence, or any of the offences, for which the offender was referred to the panel,
(b) the offender to attend mediation sessions with any such victim or other person,
(c) the offender to carry out unpaid work or service in or for the community,
(d) the offender to be at home at times specified in or determined under the programme,
(e) attendance by the offender at a school or other educational establishment or at a place of work,
(f) the offender to participate in specified activities (such as those designed to address offending behaviour, those offering education or training or those assisting with the rehabilitation of persons dependent on, or having a propensity to misuse, alcohol or drugs),
(g) the offender to present himself to specified persons at times and places specified in or determined under the programme,
(h) the offender to stay away from specified places or persons (or both),
(i) enabling the offender's compliance with the programme to be supervised and recorded.
(3) The programme may not, however, provide:
(a) for the electronic monitoring of the offender's whereabouts, or
(b) for the offender to have imposed on him any physical restriction on his movements.
(4) No term which provides for anything to be done to or with any such victim or other affected person as is mentioned in subsection (2)(a) may be included in the programme without the consent of that person.

Amending, discharging and revoking the order

87.29 *Amending the Referral Order Residence*
Powers of Criminal Courts (Sentencing) Act 2000 s 21(5) Where it appears to the court which made a Referral Order that, by reason of either a change or a prospective change in the offender's place or intended place of residence, the youth offending team…('the current team') either does not or will not have the function of implementing Referral

Orders in the area in which the offender resides or will reside, the court may amend the order so that it instead specifies the team which has the function of implementing such orders in that area ('the new team').

87.30 ***Extension of the youth offender contract***

Powers of Criminal Courts (Sentencing) Act 2000 Sch 1 para 9ZD(1) If it appears to the appropriate court that it would be in the interests of justice to do so having regard to circumstances which have arisen since the contract took effect, the court may make an order extending the length of the period for which the contract has effect.

87.31 ***Extension of youth offender contract Maximum extension***

Powers of Criminal Courts (Sentencing) Act 2000 Sch 1 para 9ZD(2) An order under sub-para (1):

(a) must not extend that period by more than 3 months, and

(b) must not so extend that period as to cause it to exceed 12 months.

(3) In deciding whether to make an order under sub-para (1), the court shall have regard to the extent of the offender's compliance with the terms of the contract.

87.32 ***Extension of the contract Offender must be present***

Powers of Criminal Courts (Sentencing) Act 2000 Sch 1 para 9ZD(4) The court may not make an order under sub-paragraph (1) unless:

(a) the offender is present before it.

87.33 ***Revocation of Referral Order 'in the interests of justice'***

Powers of Criminal Courts (Sentencing) Act 2000 s 27A(1) This section applies where, having regard to circumstances which have arisen since a youth offender contract took effect under section 23, it appears to the youth offender panel to be in the interests of justice for the Referral Order (or each of the Referral Orders) to be revoked.

(2) The panel may refer the offender back to the appropriate court requesting it:

(a) to exercise only the power conferred by Sch 1 para 5(2) to revoke the order (or each of the orders), or

(b) to exercise both:

(i) the power conferred by Sch 1 para 5(2) to revoke the order (or each of the orders), and

(ii) the power conferred by Sch 1 para 5(4) to deal with the offender for the offence in respect of which the revoked order was made.

(3) The circumstances in which the panel may make a referral under subsection (2) above include the offender's making good progress under the contract.

(4) Where:

(a) the panel makes a referral under subsection (2) in relation to any offender and any youth offender contract, and

(b) the appropriate court decides not to exercise the power conferred by Schedule 1 para 5(2) to this Act in consequence of that referral,

the panel may not make a further referral under that subsection in relation to that offender and contract during the relevant period[1044] except with the consent of the appropriate court.

Note: Further details of the referral powers can be found in Powers of Criminal Courts (Sentencing) Act 2000 Sch 1. Ed.

87.34 ***Revocation of Referral Order because of further offences***

Powers of Criminal Courts (Sentencing) Act 2000 Sch 1 para 14(1) This paragraph applies where, at a time when an offender is subject to referral, a court in England and Wales deals with him for an offence (whether committed before or after he was referred to the panel) by making an order other than:

[1044] In subsection (4) above 'the relevant period' means the period of three months beginning with the date on which the appropriate court made the decision mentioned in paragraph (b) of that subsection, Powers of Criminal Courts (Sentencing) Act 2000 s 27A(5).

(a) an order under paragraph 11 or 12 (extension of compliance period[1045]) above, or
(b) an order discharging him absolutely.

(2) In such a case the order of the court shall have the effect of revoking:
(a) the Referral Order (or orders), and
(b) any related order or orders under paragraph 9ZD, 11 or 12.

(3) Where any order is revoked by virtue of sub-paragraph (2), the court may, if it appears to the court that it would be in the interests of justice to do so, deal with the offender for the offence in respect of which the revoked order was made in any way in which (assuming section 16 of this Act had not applied) he could have been dealt with for that offence by the court which made the order.

(4) When dealing with the offender under sub-paragraph (3) the court shall, where a contract has taken effect between the offender and the panel under section 23 of this Act, have regard to the extent of his compliance with the terms of the contract.

87.35 ***Discharge of the Referral Order***

Powers of Criminal Courts (Sentencing) Act 2000 Sch 1 para 7(3) If:
(a) a contract had taken effect under section 23 of this Act, but
(b) the period for which it has effect has expired (otherwise than by virtue of section 24(6)),

the court shall make an order declaring that the Referral Order (or each of the Referral Orders) is discharged.

Note: There are other powers to discharge, Powers of Criminal Courts (Sentencing) Act 2000 Sch 1 para 8. Ed.

88 Referral Orders: Re-sentencing

88.1

Powers of Criminal Courts (Sentencing) Act 2000 s 22(2)

Re-sentencing in Referral Order cases is similar to sentencing in cases for the breach of other orders. For paragraphs about breach proceedings, see the back index.

88.2 ***Statutory powers to refer offender back to the court***

Powers of Criminal Courts (Sentencing) Act 2000 s 25(2) If, however, it appears to the panel at the first meeting or any such further meeting that there is **no prospect of agreement** being reached with the offender within a reasonable period after the making of the Referral Order (or orders):
(a) subsection (1)(b) above shall not apply, and
(b) instead the panel shall refer the offender back to the appropriate court.

(3) If at a meeting of the panel:
(a) agreement is reached with the offender but he does not sign the record produced in pursuance of section 23(5), and
(b) his failure to do so appears to the panel to be unreasonable,

the panel shall end the meeting and refer the offender back to the appropriate court.

Powers of Criminal Courts (Sentencing) Act 2000 s 22(2) If the offender **fails to attend** any part of such a meeting the panel may:
(a) adjourn the meeting to such time and place as it may specify, or
(b) end the meeting and refer the offender back to the appropriate court,

and subsection (1) above shall apply in relation to any such adjourned meeting.

Powers of Criminal Courts (Sentencing) Act 2000 s 26(4) At a progress meeting the panel shall do such one or more of the following things as it considers appropriate in the circumstances, namely:..
(b) discuss with the offender any breach of the terms of the contract which it appears to the panel that he has committed…

[1045] In this Part of this Schedule 'compliance period', in relation to an offender who is for the time being subject to referral, means the period for which (in accordance with section 24 of this Act) any youth offender contract taking effect in his case under section 23 of this Act has (or would have) effect, Powers of Criminal Courts (Sentencing) Act 2000 Sch 1 para 15(2).

(d) consider whether to accede to any request by the offender that he be referred back to the appropriate court.

(5) Where the panel has discussed with the offender such a **breach** in a progress meeting, the panel may decide to end the meeting and refer the offender back to that court.

Powers of Criminal Courts (Sentencing) Act 2000 s 26(8) If at a progress meeting:

(a) any such variation is agreed but the offender does not sign the record produced in pursuance of subsection (6), and

(b) his failure to do so appears to the panel to be unreasonable,

the panel may end the meeting and refer the offender back to the appropriate court.

Powers of Criminal Courts (Sentencing) Act 2000 s 26(10) Where the panel has discussed with the offender such a request as is mentioned in subsection (4)(d) (**request of offender** to be referred back to court), the panel may, if it is satisfied that there is (or is soon to be) such a change in circumstances as is mentioned in subsection (3)(a)(ii), decide to end the meeting and refer the offender back to the appropriate court.

Powers of Criminal Courts (Sentencing) Act 2000 s 27(4) Where at the final meeting the team **do not conclude** that the **contract has been satisfactorily completed** the panel shall refer the offender back to the appropriate court.

Note: The bolding is for emphasis. Ed.

88.3 *Duty of panel to explain reasons for referral back to court*

Powers of Criminal Courts (Sentencing) Act 2000 Sch 1 para 9ZC The panel shall make the referral by sending a report to the appropriate court explaining why the offender is being referred back to it.

88.4 *Powers on breach of Referral Orders*

Powers of Criminal Courts (Sentencing) Act 2000 Sch 1 para 5(4) Where any order is revoked under sub-paragraph (2) or by virtue of sub-paragraph (3), the appropriate court may deal with the offender in accordance with sub-paragraph (5) for the offence in respect of which the revoked order was made.

(5) In so dealing with the offender for such an offence, the appropriate court:

(a) may deal with him in any way in which (assuming section 16 of this Act had not applied) he could have been dealt with for that offence by the court which made the order, and

(b) shall have regard to:

(i) the circumstances of his referral back to the court, and

(ii) where a contract has taken effect under section 23 of this Act between the offender and the panel, the extent of his compliance with the terms of the contract.

Note: There is also a power to extend the compliance period, see Powers of Criminal Courts (Sentencing) Act 2000 Sch 1 para 10-13. The maximum extension is 12 months, see Sch 1 para 13(1). Criminal Justice and Courts Act 2015 s 43 adds a new para 6A to Schedule 1. It enables the court to continue the order with a fine or an extended term. Criminal Justice and Courts Act 2015 s 45 provides extra powers when the court is revoking the order because of a further conviction.[1046] Ed.

88.5 *Sentencing Children and Young People Guideline 2017*

Sentencing Children and Young People Guideline 2017, see www.banksr.com Other Matters Guidelines tab In force 1 June 2017 page 33

Breach of a referral order (referral back to court)

7.7 If a child or young person is found to have breached the conditions of their referral order the court can revoke the referral order and re-sentence the child or young person using the range of sentencing options (other than a referral order) that would have been available to the court that originally sentenced them. If the court chooses not to revoke the referral order then it is possible to:

[1046] In force 13/4/15, Criminal Justice and Courts Act 2015 (Commencement No 1, Saving and Transitional Provisions) Order 2015 2015/778 para 3 and Sch 1 para 43 and 45

- allow the referral order to continue with the existing contract;
- extend the length of the referral order up to a maximum of 12 months (in total); or
- impose a fine up to a maximum of £2,500.

7.8 If an offender has attained the age of 18 by the first court hearing then breach proceedings must be dealt with by the adult Magistrates' Court. If the court chooses to revoke the order then its powers are limited to those available to the court at the time of the original sentence.

Commission of further offences whilst on a referral order

7.9 The court has the power to extend a referral order in respect of additional or further offences. This applies to not only a first referral order but also to any subsequent referral orders. Any period of extension must not exceed the total 12-month limit for a referral order.

7.10 If the court chooses not to extend the existing referral order or impose a discharge they have the power to impose a new referral order (where the discretionary referral order conditions are satisfied) in respect of the new offences only. This order can remain or run alongside the new order or the court may direct that the contract under the new order is not to take effect until the earlier order is revoked or discharged. Alternatively, the court may impose an absolute or conditional discharge.

7.11 If the court sentences in any other way they have a discretionary power to revoke the referral order. Where an order is revoked, if it appears to be in the interests of justice, the court may deal with the original offence(s) in any way that the original court could have done, but may not make a new referral order. Where the referral contract has taken effect, the court shall have regard to the extent of the child or young person's compliance with the terms of the contract.

88.6 ***Magistrates' Court Sentencing Guidelines 2008***

Magistrates' Court Sentencing Guidelines 2008, see www.banksr.com Other Matters Guidelines tab page 147 When sentencing for the breach of any order for which there is not a specific guideline, the primary objective will be to ensure compliance. Reference to existing guidelines in respect of breaches of orders may provide a helpful point of comparison.

Note: The guideline deals with sentencing for breaches and in Referral Orders the procedure is re-sentencing, which is similar but not the same. Ed.

Appeals

88.7 ***Appeals after court re-sentences offender***

Powers of Criminal Courts (Sentencing) Act 2000 Sch 1 para 6 Where the court in exercise of the power conferred by paragraph 5(4) (powers after court upholds panel's decision) deals with the offender for an offence, the offender may appeal to the Crown Court against the sentence.

Parent or guardian failing to attend meetings

88.8

For the power to impose the order and where there is a duty to impose the order, see the **Referral Orders Parental orders (to attend meetings)** section at **87.13**.

88.9 ***Parenting Orders Power to make***

Powers of Criminal Courts (Sentencing) Act 2000 Sch 1 para 9D(1) Where the parent appears or is brought before the Youth Court under paragraph 9C, the court may make a Parenting Order in respect of the parent if:

(a) it is proved to the satisfaction of the court that the parent has failed without reasonable excuse to comply with the order under section 20 of this Act, and
(b) the court is satisfied that the Parenting Order would be desirable in the interests of preventing the commission of any further offence by the offender.

88.10 ***Parents and guardians Securing attendance***

Powers of Criminal Courts (Sentencing) Act 2000 s 22(2A) If:

(a) a parent or guardian of the offender fails to comply with an order under section 20 (requirement to attend the meetings of the panel, see **87.13**), and

(b) the offender is aged under 18 at the time of the failure,

the panel may refer that parent or guardian to a Youth Court acting in the local justice area in which it appears to the panel that the offender resides or will reside.

Powers of Criminal Courts (Sentencing) Act 2000 Sch 1 para 9C(1) Where the Youth Court receives such a report it shall cause the parent to appear before it.

(2) For the purpose of securing the attendance of the parent before the court, a justice acting in the local justice area in which the court acts may:

(a) issue a summons requiring the parent to appear at the place and time specified in it, or

(b) if the report is substantiated on oath, issue a warrant for the parent's arrest.

(3) Any summons or warrant issued under sub-paragraph (2) shall direct the parent to appear or be brought before the Youth Court.

88.11 ***Parents and guardians Duty of panel to explain reason for referral***

Powers of Criminal Courts (Sentencing) Act 2000 Sch 1 para 9B The panel shall make the referral by sending a report to the Youth Court explaining why the parent is being referred to it.

88.12 ***Parents and guardians Duty to obtain information about family***

Powers of Criminal Courts (Sentencing) Act 2000 Sch 1 para 9D(6) Before making a Parenting Order under this paragraph where the offender is aged under 16, the court shall obtain and consider information about his family circumstances and the likely effect of the order on those circumstances.

88.13 ***Parenting Orders What do they entail?***

Powers of Criminal Courts (Sentencing) Act 2000 Sch 1 para 9D(2) A Parenting Order is an order which requires the parent:

(a) to comply, for a period not exceeding 12 months, with such requirements as are specified in the order, and

(b) subject to sub-paragraph (4), to attend, for a concurrent period not exceeding three months, such counselling or guidance programme as may be specified in directions given by the responsible officer.

(3) The requirements that may be specified under sub-paragraph (2)(a) are those which the court considers desirable in the interests of preventing the commission of any further offence by the offender.

(4) A Parenting Order under this paragraph may, but need not, include a requirement mentioned in subsection (2)(b) in any case where a Parenting Order under this paragraph or any other enactment has been made in respect of the parent on a previous occasion.

88.14 ***Parenting Orders Maximum length***

Powers of Criminal Courts (Sentencing) Act 2000 Sch 1 para 9D(2) A Parenting Order is an order which requires the parent:

(a) to comply, for a period not exceeding 12 months, with such requirements as are specified in the order, and

(b) …for a concurrent period not exceeding 3 months, such counselling or guidance programme as may be specified in directions given by the responsible officer.

88.15 ***Parenting Orders Requirements***

Powers of Criminal Courts (Sentencing) Act 2000 Sch 1 para 9D(4) A Parenting Order under this paragraph may, but need not, include a requirement mentioned in subsection (2)(b) in any case where a Parenting Order under this paragraph or any other enactment has been made in respect of the parent on a previous occasion.

(5) A counselling or guidance programme which a parent is required to attend by virtue of subsection (2)(b) may be or include a residential course but only if the court is satisfied:

(a) that the attendance of the parent at a residential course is likely to be more effective than his attendance at a non-residential course in preventing the commission of any further offence by the offender, and
(b) that any interference with family life which is likely to result from the attendance of the parent at a residential course is proportionate in all the circumstances.

88.16 ***Parenting Orders do not affect Referral Orders***
Powers of Criminal Courts (Sentencing) Act 2000 Sch 1 para 9F(1) The making of a Parenting Order under paragraph 9D above is without prejudice to the continuance of the order under section 20 of this Act.

88.17 ***Parenting Orders, Breach of***
Powers of Criminal Courts (Sentencing) Act 2000 Sch 1 para 9F(2) Magistrates' Courts Act 1980 s 63(1)-(4) (power of Magistrates' Court to deal with person for breach of order etc.) apply (as well as section 22(2A) of this Act and this Part of this Schedule) in relation to an order under section 20 of this Act.

88.18 ***Parenting Orders Appeals***
Powers of Criminal Courts (Sentencing) Act 2000 Sch 1 para 9E(1) An appeal shall lie to the Crown Court against the making of a Parenting Order under paragraph 9D above.
(2) Crime and Disorder Act 1998 s 10(2)-(3) (appeals against Parenting Orders) apply in relation to an appeal under this paragraph as they apply in relation to an appeal under subsection (1)(b) of that section.

89 Rehabilitation of Offenders Act 1974

89.1
This Act introduced a set of rules which enabled less serious convictions not to be treated as convictions after a set period. Each less serious sentence has its rehabilitation period determined by the type and sometimes also by the length of the sentence imposed. Less serious offences or orders have their own period which do not keep earlier convictions 'alive'. Since 1974 the Act has been repeatedly amended and as a result the system has become needlessly confusing and complicated. I have tried to compile a table for the periods but the more the sections are examined, the more anomalies and uncertainties appear. Some of the details need an interpretation from a court for their extent to become known. Ed.
The 2012 amendments Legal Aid, Sentencing and Punishment of Offenders Act 2012 s 139 further amended the 1974 Act.[1047] The exclusions from rehabilitation of offences of 30 months or more was replaced by sentences of more than 48 months. There were a mass of further changes.

89.2 ***The principle of rehabilitation***
Rehabilitation of Offenders Act 1974 s 1(1) Subject to subsection (2) below, where an individual has been convicted, whether before or after the commencement of this Act, of any offence or offences, and the following conditions are satisfied, that is to say:
(a) he did not have imposed on him in respect of that conviction a sentence which is excluded from rehabilitation under this Act, and
(b) he has not had imposed on him in respect of a subsequent conviction during the rehabilitation period applicable to the first-mentioned conviction in accordance with Rehabilitation of Offenders Act 1974 s 6, a sentence which is excluded from rehabilitation under this Act,
then, after the end of the rehabilitation period so applicable (including, where appropriate, any extension under section 6(4) below of the period originally applicable to the

[1047] In force 10/3/2014

first-mentioned conviction) or, where that rehabilitation period ended before the commencement of this Act, after the commencement of this Act, that individual shall for the purposes of this Act be treated as a rehabilitated person in respect of the first-mentioned conviction and that conviction shall for those purposes be treated as spent.
(2), (2A) and (2B) [see **89.16** and **89.17**]
(3)-(4) [see **89.5**]

89.3 *General effect of rehabilitation*

Effect of rehabilitation.
Rehabilitation of Offenders Act 1974 s 4(1) Subject to Rehabilitation of Offenders Act 1974 s 7-8 below, a person who has become a rehabilitated person for the purposes of this Act in respect of a conviction shall be treated for all purposes in law as a person who has not committed or been charged with or prosecuted for or convicted of or sentenced for the offence or offences which were the subject of that conviction, and, notwithstanding the provisions of any other enactment or rule of law to the contrary, but subject as aforesaid:
(a) no evidence shall be admissible in any proceedings before a judicial authority exercising its jurisdiction or functions in England and Wales to prove that any such person has committed or been charged with or prosecuted for or convicted of or sentenced for any offence which was the subject of a spent conviction, and
(b) a person shall not, in any such proceedings, be asked, and, if asked, shall not be required to answer, any question relating to his past which cannot be answered without acknowledging or referring to a spent conviction or spent convictions or any circumstances ancillary thereto.
(2) Subject to the provisions of any order made under subsection (4), where a question seeking information with respect to a person's previous convictions, offences, conduct or circumstances is put to him or to any other person otherwise than in proceedings before a judicial authority:
(a) the question shall be treated as not relating to spent convictions or to any circumstances ancillary to spent convictions, and the answer thereto may be framed accordingly, and
(b) the person questioned shall not be subjected to any liability or otherwise prejudiced in law by reason of any failure to acknowledge or disclose a spent conviction or any circumstances ancillary to a spent conviction in his answer to the question.
(3) Subject to the provisions of any order made under subsection (4):
(a) any obligation imposed on any person by any rule of law or by the provisions of any agreement or arrangement to disclose any matters to any other person shall not extend to requiring him to disclose a spent conviction or any circumstances ancillary to a spent conviction (whether the conviction is his own or another's), and
(b) a conviction which has become spent or any circumstances ancillary thereto, or any failure to disclose a spent conviction or any such circumstances, shall not be a proper ground for dismissing or excluding a person from any office, profession, occupation or employment, or for prejudicing him in any way in any occupation or employment.
(4) [Powers of Secretary of State]
(5) For the purposes of this section and Rehabilitation of Offenders Act 1974 s 7, any of the following are circumstances ancillary to a conviction, that is to say:
(a) the offence or offences which were the subject of that conviction,
(b) the conduct constituting that offence or those offences, and
(c) any process or proceedings preliminary to that conviction, any sentence imposed in respect of that conviction, any proceedings (whether by way of appeal or otherwise) for reviewing that conviction or any such sentence, and anything done in pursuance of or undergone in compliance with any such sentence.

(6) For the purposes of this section and section 7 below 'proceedings before a judicial authority' includes, in addition to proceedings before any of the ordinary courts of law, proceedings before any tribunal, body or person having power:

(a) by virtue of any enactment, law, custom or practice,

(b) under the rules governing any association, institution, profession, occupation or employment, or

(c) under any provision of an agreement providing for arbitration with respect to questions arising thereunder,

to determine any question affecting the rights, privileges, obligations or liabilities of any person, or to receive evidence affecting the determination of any such question.

89.4 ***General effect of rehabilitation Court proceedings etc.***

Limitations on rehabilitation under this Act, etc.

Rehabilitation of Offenders Act 1974 s 7(1) [Saving provisions about pardons, fine enforcements etc., see **89.8**]

(2) Nothing in section 4(1) shall affect the determination of any issue, or prevent the admission or requirement of any evidence, relating to a person's previous convictions or to circumstances ancillary thereto:

(a) in any criminal proceedings before a court in England and Wales (including any appeal or reference in a criminal matter),

(b) in any service disciplinary proceedings or in any proceedings on appeal from any service disciplinary proceedings,

(bb) in any proceedings under Sexual Offences Act 2003 Part 2 [sexual notification] or on appeal from any such proceedings,

(c) and (cc) [Provisions about marriage, adoption and civil partnerships and Children Act 1989]

(d) in any proceedings relating to the variation or discharge of a Youth Rehabilitation Order under Criminal Justice and Immigration Act 2008 Part 1, or on appeal from any such proceedings,

(e) [Provisions about hearings under Social Work (Scotland) Act 1968]

(f) in any proceedings in which he is a party or a witness, provided that, on the occasion when the issue or the admission or requirement of the evidence falls to be determined, he consents to the determination of the issue or, as the case may be, the admission or requirement of the evidence notwithstanding the provisions of section 4(1).

(g) [Repealed]

(h) [Provisions about criminal memoirs etc.]

Criminal Practice Directions 2015 EWCA Crim 1567 para V 35A.1 The effect of Rehabilitation of Offenders Act 1974 s 4(1) is that a person who has become a rehabilitated person for the purpose of the Act in respect of a conviction (known as a 'spent' conviction) shall be treated for all purposes in law as a person who has not committed or been charged with or prosecuted for or convicted of or sentenced for the offence or offences which were the subject of that conviction.

35A.2 Section 4(1) of the 1974 Act does not apply, however, to evidence given in criminal proceedings: section 7(2)(a). Convictions are often disclosed in such criminal proceedings. When the Bill was before the House of Commons on 28 June 1974 the hope was expressed that the Lord Chief Justice would issue a Practice Direction for the guidance of the Crown Court with a view to reducing disclosure of spent convictions to a minimum and securing uniformity of approach. The direction is set out in the following paragraphs. The same approach should be adopted in all courts of criminal jurisdiction.

35A.3 [Provisions about trials]

35A.4 It is not possible to give general directions which will govern all these different situations, but it is recommended that both court and advocates should give effect to the general intention of Parliament by never referring to a spent conviction when such reference can reasonably be avoided.

89.5 *Sentence, Definition of*

Rehabilitation of Offenders Act 1974 s 1(3) In this Act 'sentence' includes any order made by a court in dealing with a person in respect of his conviction of any offence or offences, other than:

(za) a surcharge imposed under Criminal Justice Act 2003 s 161A [a victim surcharge],

(a) an order for committal or any other order made in default of payment of any fine or other sum adjudged to be paid by or imposed on a conviction, or for want of sufficient distress to satisfy any such fine or other sum,

(b) an order dealing with a person in respect of a suspended sentence of imprisonment,

(c) an order under Prosecution of Offences Act 1985 s 21A (criminal courts charge).[1048]

(3A) [Provision about fine enforcement]

(4) In this Act, references to a conviction, however expressed, include references:

(a) to a conviction by or before a court outside England and Wales, and

(b) to any finding (other than a finding linked with a finding of insanity) in any criminal proceedings that a person has committed an offence or done the act or made the omission charged,

and notwithstanding anything in Powers of Criminal Courts (Sentencing) Act 2000 s 14 (effect of an absolute or conditional discharge) or Armed Forces Act 2006 s 187 (conviction of a person discharged to be deemed not to be a conviction) a conviction in respect of which an order is made discharging the person concerned absolutely or conditionally shall be treated as a conviction for the purposes of this Act and the person in question may become a rehabilitated person in respect of that conviction and the conviction a spent conviction for those purposes accordingly.

89.6 *Statutory periods*

Rehabilitation of Offenders Act 1974 s 5 and 8A

Note: These periods are listed as amended by Rehabilitation of Offenders Act 1974 s 5(2)-(5). This section produces two tables. The text has been rearranged to make it easier to understand. Ed.

The general list

The periods are subject to a reduction by half for persons under 18 in most cases. See the table for details.

Legal Aid, Sentencing and Punishment of Offenders Act 2012 s 139 abolished all the previous periods. The new terms are set out in an amended Rehabilitation of Offenders Act 1974 s 5(2)-(5). The period starts from the date of conviction.[1049] The 'Section' column in the table below refers to the section of Rehabilitation of Offenders Act 1974 which determines the rehabilitation period. The terms, when rearranged, are as follows.

Sentence	Section (for all but one, Rehabilitation of Offenders Act 1974)	End of rehabilitation	
		Adult offenders	Those aged under 18 at date of conviction
Absolute discharge	s 5(4)(a)	There is no period, so the period is nil.	

[1048] As inserted by Criminal Justice and Courts Act 2015 Sch 12 paras 8-9

[1049] Rehabilitation of Offenders Act 1974 s 5(2)(a)

Sentence	**Section** (for all but one, Rehabilitation of Offenders Act 1974)	**End of rehabilitation**	
		Adult offenders	Those aged under 18 at date of conviction
Approved school	s 5(8)(b)	**Period A**	
Automatic life	s 5(1)(a)	Rehabilitation is excluded.	
Bind over	s 5(8)(b)	**Period A**	
Cautions: Conditional[1050]	s 8A and Sch 2 para 1	At end of relevant caution	
Cautions: Other		At the time caution is given	
Community order*	s 5(2)	12 months **Period B**	n/a
Compensation order	s 5(2)	The date when the payment is made in full	
Conditional discharge	s 5(8)(a)	**Period A**	
Custodial sentence* of more than 48 months	s 5(1)(b) and (d)	Rehabilitation is excluded.	
Custodial sentence* of more than 30 months but not exceeding 48 months	s 5(2)	7 years **Period C**	3½ years **Period C**
Custodial sentence* of more than 6 months but not exceeding 30 months	s 5(2)	4 years **Period C**	2 years **Period C**
Custodial sentence* of 6 months or less	s 5(2)	2 years **Period C**	1½ years **Period C**
DPP[1051]	s 5(1)(f)	Rehabilitation is excluded.	
Extended sentence (EDS) (Criminal Justice Act 2003 s 226A-226B)	s 5(1)(b) and 5(2)	The sentence is not specifically dealt with in the legislation. It is assumed that the period will depend on the length of the term of custody.	
Extended sentence (Criminal Justice Act 2003 s 227-228 only)[1052]	s 5(1)(f)	Rehabilitation is excluded.	
Fine	s 5(2)	12 months **Period D**	6 months **Period D**
Hospital Order under Mental Health Act 1983 Part 3 (with or without a Restriction Order)	s 5(8)(d)	**Period A**	

[1050] This period is subject to exceptions, see the later paragraphs of the Schedule.
[1051] This includes DPP sentences passed as a result of the application of Armed Forces Act 2006 s 219-222.
[1052] This includes extended sentences passed as a result of the application of Armed Forces Act 2006 s 219-222. The order was repealed by Legal Aid, Sentencing and Punishment of Offenders Act 2012 on 3/12/12.

Sentence	Section (for all but one, Rehabilitation of Offenders Act 1974)	End of rehabilitation	
		Adult offenders	Those aged under 18 at date of conviction
Immigration decision, Relevant[1053]	UK Borders Act 2007 s 56A(1)	Rehabilitation is excluded.	
Imprisonment, see Custodial sentences			
IPP[1054]	s 5(1)(f)	Rehabilitation is excluded.	
Life imprisonment, custody for life, detention for life[1055] and detention during HM's Pleasure	s 5(1)(a), (d) and (e)	Rehabilitation is excluded.	
Preventive detention	s 5(1)(c)	Rehabilitation is excluded.	
Referral Order under Powers of Criminal Courts (Sentencing) Act 2000 s 16	s 5(8)(e)	**Period A**	
Remand home/Committal to, custody of a remand home under Children and Young Persons Act 1933 s 54[1056]	s 5(8)(a)	**Period A**	
A relevant order*	s 5(2)	**Period A**	
Removal from HM's Service[1057]	s 5(2)	12 months **Period D**	6 months **Period D**
Reprimands or warnings under Crime and Disorder Act 1998 s 65[1058]	s 8A(2)(c) and Sch 2	At the time the reprimand or warning is given	
Service detention*	s 5(2)	12 months **Period E**	6 months **Period E**
Street Offences Act 1959 s 1(2A) order	s 5(8)(c)	**Period A**	
Suspended sentences/Suspended Sentence Orders	The period is the same as for an immediate sentence.[1059]		
Suspended sentences/Suspended Sentence Orders: Activated	The period to consider is the length that was originally imposed, see **89.13**.		

[1053] UK Borders Act 2007 s 56A(1), as inserted by Legal Aid, Sentencing and Punishment of Offenders Act 2012 s 140. Commencement was on 1/10/12.
[1054] This includes IPP sentences passed as a result of the application of Armed Forces Act 2006 s 219-222.
[1055] This includes sentences of: a) detention for life and detention during HM's Pleasure under Armed Forces Act 2006 s 209 and 218 and their corresponding equivalent under earlier armed forces statutes, see Rehabilitation of Offenders Act 1974 s 5(1)(d) and (1A) and b) those sentenced for murder in Scotland under Criminal Procedure (Scotland) Act 1975 s 205(2) or (3).
[1056] Repealed by Children and Young Persons Act 1969 s 72 Sch 6.
[1057] This means a sentence of dismissal with disgrace from HM's Service, a sentence of dismissal from HM's Service or a sentence of cashiering or discharge with ignominy, Rehabilitation of Offenders Act 1974 s 5(8).
[1058] Repealed by Legal Aid, Sentencing and Punishment of Offenders Act 2012 s 135
[1059] This is because a sentence of imprisonment is treated as an immediate sentence of imprisonment, Criminal Justice Act 2003 s 189(6).

Sentence	Section (for all but one, Rehabilitation of Offenders Act 1974)	End of rehabilitation	
		Adult offenders	Those aged under 18 at date of conviction
Youth Rehabilitation Order*	s 5(2)	n/a	6 months **Period B**
Any order which imposes a disqualification, disability, prohibition or other penalty and is not otherwise dealt with in [this] table or under subsection (3) (see above)	s 5(8)(g)	**Period A**	
All other sentences	s 5(4)(b)	There is no period, so the period is nil.	

* Statutory definitions of the terms with a * are in para **89.7**.
Period A The period is until the day provided for by or under the order as the last day on which the order is to have effect.
Period B The period is to the end of the period of [XX] months beginning with the day provided for by or under the order as the last day on which the order is to have effect.
Period C The period is from the end of the period of [XX] years beginning with the day on which the sentence (including any licence period) is completed.
Period D The period is to the end of the period of [XX] months beginning with the date of the conviction in respect of which the sentence is imposed.
Period E The period is to the end of the period of [XX] months beginning with the day on which the sentence is completed.
Rehabilitation of Offenders Act 1974 s 5(3) Where no provision is made by or under a community or youth rehabilitation order or a relevant order for the last day on which the order is to have effect, the rehabilitation period for the order is to be the period of 24 months beginning with the date of conviction.

89.7 ***Definitions***
Rehabilitation of Offenders Act 1974 s 5(8) In this section:
'Community or Youth Rehabilitation Order' means:
(a) a Community Order under Criminal Justice Act 2003 s 177,
(b) a Service Community Order or Overseas Community Order under Armed Forces Act 2006,
(c) a Youth Rehabilitation Order under Criminal Justice and Immigration Act 2008 Part 1, or
(d) any order of a kind superseded (whether directly or indirectly) by an order mentioned in paragraph (a), (b) or (c).
'Custodial sentence' means:
(a) a sentence of imprisonment. 'A sentence of imprisonment' includes a sentence of penal servitude (and 'term of imprisonment' is to be read accordingly),
(b) a sentence of Detention in a Young Offender Institution,
(c) a sentence of Borstal training,
(d) a sentence of youth custody,
(e) a sentence of corrective training,
(f) a sentence of detention under Powers of Criminal Courts (Sentencing) Act 2000 s 91 or Armed Forces Act 2006 s 209,
(g) a Detention and Training Order under Powers of Criminal Courts (Sentencing) Act 2000 s 100 or an order under Armed Forces Act 2006 s 211,
(h) any sentence of a kind superseded (whether directly or indirectly) by a sentence mentioned in paragraph (f) or (g).

Note: 'Custodial sentences' also includes detention under Criminal Procedure (Scotland) Act 1975 s 206 (detention of children convicted on indictment), Rehabilitation of Offenders Act 1974 s 5(1)(d). Ed.

'**Removal from Her Majesty's Service**' means a sentence of dismissal with disgrace from Her Majesty's Service, a sentence of dismissal from Her Majesty's Service or a sentence of cashiering or discharge with ignominy.

'**Relevant order**' means one of the orders which are included separately in the table with a **Period A** rehabilitation period:

(a) an order under Children and Young Persons Act 1933 s 54 committing the person convicted to custody in a remand home,

(b) an approved school order under section 57 of the same Act,

(c) an order under Street Offences Act 1959 s 1(2A),

(d) a Hospital Order under Mental Health Act 1983 Part 3 (with or without a Restriction Order),

(e) a Referral Order under Powers of Criminal Courts (Sentencing) Act 2000 s 16,

(f) an earlier statutory order, or

(g) any order which imposes a disqualification, disability, prohibition or other penalty and is not otherwise dealt with in the Table or under subsection (3) (see para **89.6** above),

but does not include a Reparation Order under Powers of Criminal Courts (Sentencing) Act 2000 s 73.

'**Sentence of service detention**' means:

(a) a sentence of service detention (within the meaning in Armed Forces Act 2006 s 374), or a sentence of detention corresponding to such a sentence, in respect of a conviction in service disciplinary proceedings, or

(b) any sentence of a kind superseded (whether directly or indirectly) by a sentence mentioned in para (a).

UK Borders Act 2007 s 56A(2) "relevant immigration decision" means any decision, or proposed decision, of the Secretary of State or an immigration officer under or by virtue of the Immigration Acts, or rules made under Immigration Act 1971 Sch 3 [immigration rules], in relation to the entitlement of a person to enter or remain in the United Kingdom (including, in particular, the removal of a person from the United Kingdom, whether by deportation or otherwise).

89.8 ***Enforcement of any process or any fine***

Rehabilitation of Offenders Act 1974 s 7(1) Nothing in Rehabilitation of Offenders Act 1974 s 4(1) above shall affect:

(a) [Provision about pardons etc.]

(b) the enforcement by any process or proceedings of any fine or other sum adjudged to be paid by or imposed on a spent conviction,

(c) the issue of any process for the purpose of proceedings in respect of any breach of a condition or requirement applicable to a sentence imposed in respect of a spent conviction, or

(d) the operation of any enactment by virtue of which, in consequence of any conviction, a person is subject, otherwise than by way of sentence, to any disqualification, disability, prohibition or other penalty the period of which extends beyond the rehabilitation period applicable in accordance with section 6 above to the conviction.

For the rest of the section, see **89.4**.

Service sentences

89.9 ***Service disciplinary proceedings***

Rehabilitation of Offenders Act 1974 s 2(1) For the purposes of this Act any finding that a person is guilty of an offence in respect of any act or omission which was the subject of service disciplinary proceedings shall be treated as a conviction and any punishment awarded or order made by virtue of Army Act 1955 Sch 5A or Air Force Act 1955 or Naval Discipline Act 1957 Sch 4A in respect of any such finding shall be treated as a sentence.

Rehabilitation of Offenders Act 1974 s 2(5) In this Act, 'service disciplinary proceedings' means any of the following:

(za) any proceedings (whether or not before a court) in respect of a service offence within the meaning of Armed Forces Act 2006 (except proceedings before a civilian court within the meaning of that Act),

(a) any proceedings under Army Act 1955, Air Force Act 1955, or Naval Discipline Act 1957 whether before a Court Martial or before any other court or person authorised thereunder to award a punishment in respect of any offence),

(b) any proceedings under any Act previously in force corresponding to any of the Acts mentioned in paragraph a) above,

(bb) any proceedings before a Standing Civilian Court established under Armed Forces Act 1976,

(c) any proceedings under any corresponding enactment or law applying to a force, other than a home force, to which Visiting Forces (British Commonwealth) Act 1933 s 4 applies or applied at the time of the proceedings, being proceedings in respect of a member of a home force who is or was at that time attached to the first-mentioned force under that section,

whether in any event those proceedings take place in England and Wales or elsewhere.

(6) Armed Forces Act 2006 s 376(1)-(3) ('conviction' and 'sentence' in relation to summary hearings and the SAC[1060]) apply for the purposes of this Act as they apply for the purposes of that Act.

Rules for calculating the period

89.10 *Offender convicted of more than one offence*

Rehabilitation of Offenders Act 1974 s 6(2) Where more than one sentence is imposed in respect of a conviction (whether or not in the same proceedings) and none of the sentences imposed is excluded from rehabilitation under this Act, then, subject to the following provisions of this section, if the periods applicable to those sentences in accordance with section 5 differ, the rehabilitation period applicable to the conviction shall be the longer or the longest (as the case may be) of those periods.

89.11 *Offender later convicted of a fresh offence*

Rehabilitation of Offenders Act 1974 s 6(4) Subject to subsection (5) below, where during the rehabilitation period applicable to a conviction:

(a) the person convicted is convicted of a further offence, and

(b) no sentence excluded from rehabilitation under this Act is imposed on him in respect of the later conviction,

if the rehabilitation period applicable in accordance with this section to either of the convictions would end earlier than the period so applicable in relation to the other, the rehabilitation period which would (apart from this subsection) end the earlier shall be extended so as to end at the same time as the other rehabilitation period.

(5) Where the rehabilitation period applicable to a conviction is the rehabilitation period applicable in accordance with Rehabilitation of Offenders Act 1974 s 5(8) above to an order imposing on a person any disqualification, disability, prohibition or other penalty, the rehabilitation period applicable to another conviction shall not by virtue of subsection (4) above be extended by reference to that period, but if any other sentence is imposed in respect of the first-mentioned conviction for which a rehabilitation period is prescribed by any other provision of Rehabilitation of Offenders Act 1974 s 5 above, the rehabilitation period applicable to another conviction shall, where appropriate, be extended under subsection (4) above by reference to the rehabilitation period applicable

[1060] I think this means Strategic Air Command (now United States Strategic Command).

in accordance with that section to that sentence or, where more than one such sentence is imposed, by reference to the longer or longest of the periods so applicable to those sentences, as if the period in question were the rehabilitation period applicable to the first-mentioned conviction.
Note: This rule is known as 'keeping a spent conviction alive'. Ed.

89.12 ***Consecutive custodial sentences***

Rehabilitation of Offenders Act 1974 s 5(7) For the purposes of this section:

(a) consecutive terms of imprisonment or other custodial sentences are to be treated as a single term,

(b) terms of imprisonment or other custodial sentences which are wholly or partly concurrent (that is terms of imprisonment or other custodial sentences imposed in respect of offences of which a person was convicted in the same proceedings) are to be treated as a single term.

Note: The rest of the subsection is not listed. Ed.

89.13 ***Suspended sentences, Activation of***

Rehabilitation of Offenders Act 1974 s 5(7)(c) No account is be taken of any subsequent variation, made by a court dealing with a person in respect of a suspended sentence of imprisonment, of the term originally imposed.

89.14 ***Breach of conditional discharges or probation***

Rehabilitation of Offenders Act 1974 s 6(3) Without prejudice to subsection (2) [see **89.10**], where in respect of a conviction a person was conditionally discharged or a probation order was made and after the end of the rehabilitation period applicable to the conviction in accordance with subsection (1) or (2) above he is dealt with, in consequence of a breach of conditional discharge or a breach of the order, for the offence for which the order for conditional discharge or probation order was made, then, if the rehabilitation period applicable to the conviction in accordance with subsection (2) above (taking into account any sentence imposed when he is so dealt with) ends later than the rehabilitation period previously applicable to the conviction, he shall be treated for the purposes of this Act as not having become a rehabilitated person in respect of that conviction, and the conviction shall for those purposes be treated as not having become spent, in relation to any period falling before the end of the new rehabilitation period.
Note: This is a classic example of how not to legislate. It appears that this means if an individual is sentenced for a breach after the rehabilitation period has expired, the period is governed by the breach sentence. Ed.

89.15 ***Foreign sentences***

Rehabilitation of Offenders Act 1974 s 5(7)(f) A sentence imposed by a court outside England and Wales is to be treated as the sentence mentioned in this section to which it most closely corresponds.

89.16 ***Defendant fails to comply with sentence***

Rehabilitation of Offenders Act 1974 s 1(2) A person shall not become a rehabilitated person for the purposes of this Act in respect of a conviction unless he has served or otherwise undergone or complied with any sentence imposed on him in respect of that conviction, but the following shall not, by virtue of this subsection, prevent a person from becoming a rehabilitated person for those purposes:

(a) failure to pay a fine or other sum adjudged to be paid by or imposed on a conviction, or breach of a condition of a recognisance or of a bond of caution to keep the peace or be of good behaviour,

(b) breach of any condition or requirement applicable in relation to a sentence which renders the person to whom it applies liable to be dealt with for the offence for which the sentence was imposed, or, where the sentence was a suspended sentence of imprisonment, liable to be dealt with in respect of that sentence (whether or not, in any case, he is in fact so dealt with),

(c) failure to comply with any requirement of a suspended sentence supervision order.

(2A) Where in respect of a conviction a person has been sentenced to imprisonment with an order under the [now repealed] Criminal Law Act 1977 s 47(1) [partly served and partly suspended sentences] he is to be treated for the purposes of subsection (2) above as having served the sentence as soon as he completes service of so much of the sentence as was by that order required to be served in prison.

89.17 ***Defendant fails to comply with sentence Confiscation Orders***

Rehabilitation of Offenders Act 1974 s 1(2B) In subsection (2)(a) [see para above], the reference to a fine or other sum adjudged to be paid by or imposed on a conviction does not include a reference to an amount payable under a confiscation order made under Proceeds of Crime Act 2002 Part 2 or 3.

90 Reparation Orders

90.1

Powers of Criminal Courts (Sentencing) Act 2000 s 73-74

Availability This order is only available for offenders aged 10-17, see **90.3**.

90.2 ***Statistics England and Wales***

Reparation Orders

	2012	2013	2014	2015	2016	2017
Orders made	565	270	198	139	114	83

For explanations about the statistics, see page 1-xii. For more detailed statistics, see www.banksr.com Other Matters Statistics tab.

Power to order

90.3 ***Statutory power to order***

Powers of Criminal Courts (Sentencing) Act 2000 s 73(1) Where any person aged under 18 is convicted of an offence other than one for which the sentence is fixed by law, the court may make an order requiring him to make reparation specified in the order:

(a) to a person or persons so specified, or

(b) to the community at large,

and any person so specified must be a victim of the offence or a person otherwise affected by it.

Powers of Criminal Courts (Sentencing) Act 2000 s 73(3) 'Make reparation' in sections 73 and 74 means make reparation for the offence otherwise than by the payment of compensation.

90.4 ***Need for a probation report***

Powers of Criminal Courts (Sentencing) Act 2000 s 73(5) Before making a Reparation Order, a court shall obtain and consider a written report by an officer of a local probation board, an officer of a provider of probation services, a social worker of a local authority or a member of a youth offending team indicating:

(a) the type of work that is suitable for the offender, and

(b) the attitude of the victim or victims to the requirements proposed to be included in the order.

Making the order

90.5 ***Requirements***

Requirements and provisions of reparation order, and obligations of person subject to it.

Powers of Criminal Courts (Sentencing) Act 2000 s 74(1) A Reparation Order shall not require the offender:

(a) to work for more than 24 hours in aggregate, or

(b) to make reparation to any person without the consent of that person.

(2) Requirements specified in a Reparation Order shall be such as are commensurate with the seriousness of the offence, or the combination of the offence and one or more offences associated with it.

(3) Requirements, as far as practicable, shall be such as to avoid:

(a) any conflict with the offender's religious beliefs, or with the requirements of any youth community order to which he may be subject, and

(b) any interference with the times, if any, at which he normally works or attends school or any other educational establishment.

90.6 ***Maximum term for the order***

Powers of Criminal Courts (Sentencing) Act 2000 s 74(1) A Reparation Order shall not require the offender: (a) to work for more than 24 hours in aggregate.

90.7 ***Reasons, Must give***

Powers of Criminal Courts (Sentencing) Act 2000 s 73(8) The court shall give reasons if it does not make a Reparation Order in a case where it has power to do so.

Criminal Procedure Rules 2015 2015/1490 Rule 28.1(1) This rule applies where the court decides:..

(b) not to make, where it could:

(i) a Reparation Order (unless it passes a custodial or community sentence)...

(2) The court must explain why it has so decided, when it explains the sentence that it has passed.

For the general requirement to give reasons, see **86.49**.

Revocation and amendment of a Reparation Order

90.8 ***Statutory power to revoke or amend the order***

Powers of Criminal Courts (Sentencing) Act 2000 Sch 8 para 5(1) The court may: a) make an order revoking the Reparation Order, or b) make an order amending it i) by cancelling any provision included in it, or ii) by inserting in it any provision which could have been included in the order if the court had then had power to make it and was exercising the power.

90.9 ***Application by responsible officer or supervisor***

Criminal Procedure Rules 2015 2015/1490 Rule 32.4(1) Except for Rule 24.8 (Written guilty plea: special rules) and 24.9 (Single justice procedure: special rules), the rules in Part 24, which deal with the procedure at a trial in a Magistrates' Court, apply:

(a) as if:

(i) a reference in those rules to an allegation of an offence included a reference to an allegation of failure to comply with an order, to which this Part applies,

(ii) a reference to the court's verdict included a reference to the court's decision to revoke or amend such an order, or to exercise any other power it has to deal with the defendant, and

(iii) a reference to the court's sentence included a reference to the exercise of any such power, and

(b) with the necessary consequential modifications.

(2) The court officer must serve on each party any order revoking or amending an order which this Part applies.

90.10 ***Applications by the defendant***

Criminal Procedure Rules 2015 2015/1490 Rule 32.3(1) This rule applies where:

(a) the defendant wants the court to exercise any power it has to revoke or amend an order to which this Part applies, or

(b) where the legislation allows, a person affected by such an order wants the court to exercise any such power.

(2) That defendant, or person affected, must:

(a) apply in writing, explaining why the order should be revoked or amended, and

(b) serve the application on:

(i) the court officer,

(ii) the responsible officer or supervisor, and

(iii) as appropriate, the defendant or the person affected.

90.11 ***Offender must be present for breach, revocation and amendment proceedings***
Powers of Criminal Courts (Sentencing) Act 2000 Sch 8 para 6(1) A court shall not make an order under paragraph 2 or 5(1) (breach proceedings or revoking or amending the order) unless the offender is present before the court.

90.12 ***Court must serve the order revoking or amending the order***
Criminal Procedure Rules 2015 2015/1490 Rule 32.4(2) The court officer must serve on each party any order revoking or amending an order to which this Part applies.

Combined with other orders

90.13 ***Custody, Combined with***
Powers of Criminal Courts (Sentencing) Act 2000 s 73(4)(a) The court shall not make a Reparation Order in respect of the offender if it proposes to pass on him a custodial sentence.

90.14 ***Referral Orders, Combined with***
Powers of Criminal Courts (Sentencing) Act 2000 s 19(1)-(4)(c) Where the court makes a Referral Order, the court may not make a Reparation Order in respect of him.
Powers of Criminal Courts (Sentencing) Act 2000 s 73(4)(b) The court shall not make a Reparation Order if it proposes to make a Referral Order.

90.15 ***Youth Rehabilitation Orders, Combined with***
Powers of Criminal Courts (Sentencing) Act 2000 s 73(4)(b) The court shall not make a Reparation Order in respect of the offender if it proposes to make in respect of him a Youth Rehabilitation Order.
Criminal Justice and Immigration Act 2008 Sch 1 para 30(4) A court must not make a Youth Rehabilitation Order in respect of an offender at a time when…a Reparation Order made under Powers of Criminal Courts (Sentencing) Act 2000 s 73(1) is in force in respect of the offender, unless when it makes the order it revokes the earlier order.

90.16 ***Youth Rehabilitation Orders, Combined with Imposed at different times***
Powers of Criminal Courts (Sentencing) Act 2000 s 73(4A) The court shall not make a Reparation Order in respect of the offender at a time when a Youth Rehabilitation Order is in force in respect of him unless when it makes the Reparation Order it revokes the Youth Rehabilitation Order.

91 REPARATION ORDERS: BREACH OF

91.1 ***Statutory powers***
Powers of Criminal Courts (Sentencing) Act 2000 Sch 8 para 2(2) Where Sch 8 para 2 applies (the order is breached), the court:

(a) whether or not it also makes an order under para 5(1)(i) may order the offender to pay a fine not exceeding £1,000, or
(b) if the Reparation Order was made by the Magistrates' Court, may revoke the order and deal with the offender for the offence in respect of which the order was made, in any way in which he could have been dealt with for that offence by the court which made the order, or
(c) if the Reparation Order was made by the Crown Court, may commit him in custody or release him on bail until he can be brought or appear before the Crown Court.

Powers of Criminal Courts (Sentencing) Act 2000 Sch 8 para 2(4) Where by virtue of (2)(c) (above) the offender is brought or appears before the Crown Court, and it is proved to the satisfaction of the court that he has failed to comply with the requirement in question, that court may deal with him, for the offence in respect of which the order was made, in any way in which it could have dealt with him for that offence if it had not made the order.
For breach proceedings, see the **COMMUNITY ORDERS: BREACH OF** chapter.

91.2 ***Sentencing Children and Young People Guideline 2017***
Sentencing Children and Young People Guideline 2017 see www.banksr.com Other Matters Guidelines tab In force 1 June 2017 page 32
7.4 If it is proved to the appropriate court that the child or young person has failed to comply with any requirement of a reparation order that is currently in force then the court can:

- order the child or young person to pay a fine not exceeding £1,000; or
- revoke the order and re-sentence the child or young person in any way which they could have been dealt with for that offence.

If re-sentencing the child or young person the court must take into account the extent to which the child or young person has complied with the requirements of this order.
7.5 If the order was made by the Crown Court then the Youth Court can commit the child or young person in custody or release them on bail until they can be brought or appear before the Crown Court.
7.6 The child or young person or a Youth Offending Team (YOT) officer can also apply for the order to be revoked or amended but any new provisions must be ones that the court would have been able to include when the original reparation order was given. There is no power to re-sentence in this situation as the child or young person has not been found to be in breach of requirements.
Even when an offender has attained the age of 18 breach of a reparation order must be dealt with in the Youth Court.

91.3 ***Magistrates' Court Sentencing Guidelines 2008***
Magistrates' Court Sentencing Guidelines 2008, see www.banksr.com Other Matters Guidelines tab page 147 When sentencing for the breach of any order for which there is not a specific guideline, the primary objective will be to ensure compliance. Reference to existing guidelines in respect of breaches of orders may provide a helpful point of comparison.

91.4 ***Part compliance***
Powers of Criminal Courts (Sentencing) Act 2000 Sch 8 para 2(7) In dealing with an offender, a court shall take into account the extent to which he has complied with the requirements of the Reparation Order.

91.5 ***Offender must be present for breach proceedings***
Powers of Criminal Courts (Sentencing) Act 2000 Sch 8 para 6(1) A court shall not make an order under paragraph 2 unless the offender is present before the court.

91.6 ***Power to order parent/guardian to pay fine etc. for breaches of orders***
Powers of Criminal Courts (Sentencing) Act 2000 s 137(2) Where but for this subsection a court would impose a fine on a child or young person under:..d) Powers of Criminal Courts (Sentencing) Act 2000 Sch 8 para 2(2)(a) (breach of Reparation Order),...the court shall order that the fine be paid by the parent or guardian of the child or young person instead of by the child or young person himself, unless the court is satisfied:
(i) that the parent or guardian cannot be found, or
(ii) that it would be unreasonable to make an order for payment, having regard to the circumstances of the case.

91.7 ***Parent/Guardian to pay fine etc. Offender under 16***
Powers of Criminal Courts (Sentencing) Act 2000 s 137(3) In the case of a young person aged 16 or over, subsections (1) to (2) of this section shall have effect as if, instead of imposing a duty, they conferred a power to make such an order as is mentioned in those subsections.

91.8 ***Parent/Guardian must have opportunity of being heard***
Powers of Criminal Courts (Sentencing) Act 2000 s 137(4) Subject to subsection (5), no order shall be made under this section without giving the parent or guardian an opportunity of being heard.

(5) An order under this section may be made against a parent or guardian who, having been required to attend, has failed to do so.

92 Restitution Orders

92.1

Powers of Criminal Courts (Sentencing) Act 2000 s 148-149

Children and young offenders The order is available whatever the age of the offender.

92.2 *Statistics England and Wales*

Restitution Orders

	2012	2013	2014	2015	2016
Orders made	151	138	71	55	65

For explanations about the statistics, see page 1-xii. The MoJ no longer provides Banks on Sentence with these statistics.

Applications and the procedure

92.3 *Application for a Restitution Order, service of application and extending the time limits*

Criminal Procedure Rules 2015 2015/1490 Rule 28.7(1) This rule applies where, on application by the victim of a theft, the court can order a defendant to give that person goods obtained with the proceeds of goods stolen in that theft.

(2) A person who wants the court to exercise that power if the defendant is convicted must:

(a) apply in writing as soon as practicable (without waiting for the verdict),
(b) serve the application on the court officer, and
(c) in the application:
  (i) identify the goods, and
  (ii) explain why the applicant is entitled to them.

(3) The court officer must serve a copy of the application on each party.

(4) [see **92.5**]

(5) The court may:

(a) extend (even after it has expired) the time limit under paragraph (2), and
(b) allow an application to be made orally.

92.4 *Application is not necessary*

Powers of Criminal Courts (Sentencing) Act 2000 s 149(1) The following provisions of this section shall have effect with respect to section 148 [see **92.6**].

(2) The powers conferred by subsections (2)(c) and (4) of that section shall be exercisable without any application being made in that behalf or on the application of any person appearing to the court to be interested in the property.

92.5 *Right to make representations*

Criminal Procedure Rules 2015 2015/1490 Rule 28.7(4) The court must not determine the application unless the applicant and each party has had an opportunity to make representations at a hearing (whether or not each in fact attends).

Making the order

92.6 *Power to order Recovery, restoration and recompense*

Powers of Criminal Courts (Sentencing) Act 2000 s 148(1) This section applies where goods have been stolen, and either:

(a) a person is convicted of any offence with reference to the theft (whether or not the stealing is the gist of the offence), or
(b) a person is convicted of any other offence, but such an offence as is mentioned in (1)(a) is taken into consideration in determining his sentence.

(2) Where subsection (1) applies, the court by or before which the offender is convicted may on conviction (whether or not the passing of sentence is in other respects deferred) exercise any of the following powers:

(a) the court may order anyone having possession or control of the stolen goods to restore them to any person entitled to recover them from him or her,

(b) on an application of a person entitled to recover any other goods directly or indirectly representing the stolen goods (i.e. the proceeds of disposal or realisation in whole or part), the court may order those other goods to be delivered or transferred to the applicant, or

(c) the court may order that a sum not exceeding the value of the stolen goods shall be paid out of any money of the person convicted which was taken out of his possession on his apprehension, to any person who, if those goods were in the possession of the person convicted, would be entitled to recover them from him.

92.7 ***Evidence and test to apply***

Powers of Criminal Courts (Sentencing) Act 2000 s 148(5) The court shall not exercise the powers conferred by this section unless in the opinion of the court the relevant facts sufficiently appear from evidence given at the trial or the available documents, together with admissions made by or on behalf of any person in connection with any proposed exercise of the powers.

(6) In subsection (5) above 'the available documents' means:

(a) any written statements or admissions which were made for use, and would have been admissible, as evidence at the trial, and

(b) such documents as were served on the offender in pursuance of regulations made under Crime and Disorder Act 1998 Sch 3 para 1.

92.8 ***Power to order Consequential victims***

Powers of Criminal Courts (Sentencing) Act 2000 s 148(4) Where the court on a person's conviction makes an order under subsection (2)(a) above for the restoration of any goods, and it appears to the court that the person convicted:

(a) has sold the goods to a person acting in good faith, or

(b) has borrowed money on the security of them from a person so acting,

the court may order that there shall be paid to the purchaser or lender, out of any money of the person convicted which was taken out of his possession on his apprehension, a sum not exceeding the amount paid for the purchase by the purchaser or, as the case may be, the amount owed to the lender in respect of the loan.

92.9 ***Power to order Crown money***

Powers of Criminal Courts (Sentencing) Act 2000 s 148(11) An order may be made under this section in respect of money owed by the Crown.

92.10 ***Magistrates' Court Sentencing Guidelines 2008***

Magistrates' Court Sentencing Guidelines 2008, see www.banksr.com Other Matters Guidelines tab page 163 para 1 A custodial sentence must not be imposed unless the offence 'was so serious that neither a fine alone nor a community sentence can be justified for the offence'.[1061] Guidance regarding this threshold and the approach to the imposition of custodial sentences is set out in the Sentencing Guidelines Council's definitive guideline *Overarching Principles: Seriousness Guideline 2004*.

2 The guideline emphasises that:

- the clear intention of the threshold test is to reserve prison as a punishment for the most serious offences,
- passing the custody threshold does not mean that a custodial sentence should be deemed inevitable; custody can still be avoided in light of offender mitigation or where there is a suitable intervention in the community which provides sufficient restriction (by way of punishment) while addressing the rehabilitation of the

[1061] Criminal Justice Act 2003 s 152(2)

offender to prevent future crime. However, where the offence would otherwise appear to warrant a term of imprisonment within the Crown Court's jurisdiction, it is for the Crown Court to make that judgement,

- the approach to the imposition of a custodial sentence should be as follows:
(a) Has the custody threshold been passed?
(b) If so, is it unavoidable that a custodial sentence be imposed?
(c) If so, can that sentence be suspended? (Sentencers should be clear that they would have imposed a custodial sentence if the power to suspend had not been available.)
(d) If not, impose a sentence which takes immediate effect for the shortest term commensurate with the seriousness of the offence.

92.11 ***'Goods', Definition of***
Powers of Criminal Courts (Sentencing) Act 2000 s 148(10) In this section and section 149 of this Act, 'goods', except in so far as the context otherwise requires, includes money and every other description of property (within the meaning of Theft Act 1968) except land, and includes things severed from the land by stealing.

92.12 ***'Stealing', Definition of***
Powers of Criminal Courts (Sentencing) Act 2000 s 148(7) Subject to subsection (9) below, references in this section to stealing shall be construed in accordance with Theft Act 1968 s 1(1) (read with the provisions of that Act relating to the construction of section 1(1)).
Powers of Criminal Courts (Sentencing) Act 2000 s 148(9) Theft Act 1968 s 24(1) and (4) (interpretation of certain provisions) shall also apply in relation to this section as they apply in relation to the provisions of that Act relating to goods which have been stolen.

92.13 ***Order limited to value of goods stolen***
Powers of Criminal Courts (Sentencing) Act 2000 s 148(3) Where the court has power on a person's conviction to make an order against him both under section 148(2)(b) and (c) [see **92.6**], with reference to the stealing of the same goods, the court may make orders under both paragraphs provided that the person in whose favour the orders are made does not thereby recover more than the value of those goods.

Combined with other orders

92.14 ***Absolute and conditional discharges, Combined with***
Powers of Criminal Courts (Sentencing) Act 2000 s 12(7) Nothing in this section shall be construed as preventing a court, on discharging an offender absolutely or conditionally in respect of any offence…from making in respect of the offence an order under Powers of Criminal Courts (Sentencing) Act 2000 s 148 (Restitution Orders).[1062]

92.15 ***Deferred sentences, Combined with***
Powers of Criminal Courts (Sentencing) Act 2000 s 148(2) Where this section applies, the court by or before which the offender is convicted may on the conviction (whether or not the passing of sentence is in other respects deferred) exercise any of the following powers: [the list of powers collectively making a Restitution Order].

Appeals

92.16 ***Order is automatically suspended until appeal period has passed***
Criminal Appeal Act 1968 s 30(1) The operation of an order for the restitution of property to a person made by the Crown Court shall, unless the court direct to the contrary in any case in which, in their opinion, the title to the property is not in dispute, be suspended until (disregarding any power of a court to grant leave to appeal out of time) there is no further possibility of an appeal on which the order could be varied or set aside, and provision may be made by rules of court for the custody of any property in the meantime.

[1062] As amended by Criminal Justice and Courts Act 2015 Sch 12 paras 8-9

Powers of Criminal Courts (Sentencing) Act 2000 s 149(4) Any order under that section [148] [the making of a Restitution Order] made by a magistrates' court shall be suspended:

(a) in any case until the end of the period for the time being prescribed by law for the giving of notice of appeal against a decision of a Magistrates' Court,

(b) where notice of appeal is given within the period so prescribed, until the determination of the appeal,

but this subsection shall not apply where the order is made under section 148(2)(a) or b) and the court so directs, being of the opinion that the title to the goods to be restored or, as the case may be, delivered or transferred under the order is not in dispute.

92.17 ***Court of Appeal's powers***

Criminal Appeal Act 1968 s 30(2) The Court of Appeal may by order annul or vary any order made by the court of trial for the restitution of property to any person, although the conviction is not quashed, and the order, if annulled, shall not take effect and, if varied, shall take effect as so varied.

Powers of Criminal Courts (Sentencing) Act 2000 s 148(7) Any order under this section shall be treated as an order for the restitution of property within the meaning of Criminal Appeal Act 1968 s 30 (which relates to the effect on such orders of appeals).

92.18 ***Supreme Court's powers***

Criminal Appeal Act 1968 s 30(3) Where the Supreme Court restores a conviction, it may make any order for the restitution of property which the court of trial could have made.

92.19 ***Appeals TICs***

Powers of Criminal Courts (Sentencing) Act 2000 s 149(3) Where an order is made under that section against any person in respect of an offence taken into consideration in determining his sentence:

(a) the order shall cease to have effect if he successfully appeals against his conviction of the offence or, if more than one, all the offences, of which he was convicted in the proceedings in which the order was made,

(b) he may appeal against the order as if it were part of the sentence imposed in respect of the offence or, if more than one, any of the offences, of which he was so convicted.

See also the **TICs** chapter.

Varying the order

92.20 ***Procedure***

Note: The Criminal Procedure Rules 2015 2015/1490 behaviour order rules apply, see the note at **27.2** and the **Criminal Procedure Rules: Behaviour Rules** chapter. All the rules are at www.banksr.com Other Matters Other Documents tab. Ed.

93 Restraining Orders: Harassment

93.1

Protection from Harassment Act 1997 s 5

Availability See **93.6** below.

Children and young offenders The order is available whatever the age of the offender.

Choosing which order to use A Criminal Behaviour Order can have mandatory requirements as well as prohibitions. Under a Restraining Order only prohibitions can be ordered. Breaches for both the orders carry the same penalty. Both orders provide protections for victims who have suffered harassment, alarm etc. As the test for making a criminal behaviour order (see **25.2**) is easier to meet than the test for a Restraining Order, it is hard to imagine why a prosecutor would ever apply for a Restraining Order, but they do.

93.2 ***Statistics England and Wales***

Restraining Orders: Harassment

	2013	2014	2015	2016
Number of orders made	18,630	19,318	20,594	23,047

For explanations about the statistics, see page 1-xii. The MoJ no longer provides Banks on Sentence with these statistics.

93.3 *Purpose of the order*

R v Debnath 2005 EWCA Crim 3472, 2006 2 Cr App R (S) 25 (p 169) The purpose of a Restraining Order is to prohibit particular conduct with a view to protecting the victim or victims of the offence and preventing further offences under section 2 or 4 of the Act.

R v Smith 2012 EWCA Crim 2566, 2013 2 Cr App R (S) 28 (p 191) The purpose of the legislation was to provide new criminal and civil remedies for the activity generally described as 'stalking', see the consultation paper *Stalking The Solutions: Consultation Paper*, published by the Home Office on 9 July 1996. Another purpose of a [Restraining Order] is to protect a person from harassment by a defendant. The Court must first be satisfied that the defendant is likely to pursue a course of conduct which amounts to harassment within the meaning of section 1.

93.4 *What activity does the order apply to?*

R v Smith 2012 EWCA Crim 2566, 2013 2 Cr App R (S) 28 (p 191) D was acquitted of criminal damage and interfering with the crew when he was travelling in an aircraft. The defence challenged whether the order was lawful. The Judge made a Restraining Order. One of the issues was what activity did this power cover. Held. The Home Office Minister said on 17 December 1996, defending the broad definition [in section 1] in the Commons, "Stalkers do not stick to activities on a list. Stalkers and other weirdos who pursue women, cause racial harassment and annoy their neighbours have a wide range of activity which it is impossible to define." In 1997 a minister said, "[Section] 1 is widely drafted and, for example, the activities of political activists, market researchers, telephone sales companies, evangelical religious organisations and journalists as well as activities such as begging, racial or sexual harassment, harassment by neighbours or harassment in the workplace could be covered by the Bill…The courts will look at each case individually on its merits and in time case law may offer more guidance on the type of conduct and the particular circumstances which might be covered by [section] 1." In construing section 1 of the 1997 Act, it is right to have regard to the type of mischief at which it was aimed. It is also right to have regard to what the ordinary person would understand by harassment. It does not follow that because references to harassing a person include alarming a person or causing a person distress (section 7(2)), any course of conduct which causes alarm or distress therefore amounts to harassment, *Thomas v News Group Newspapers* 2001 EWCA Civ 1233 at para 29. So to reason would be illogical and would produce perverse results. A person who habitually drives too fast in a built-up area may cause alarm to other road users, but conduct of that sort was not what Parliament was invited to consider and would not fall within the ordinary understanding of what is meant by harassment. In *R v Curtis* 2010 EWCA Crim 123 the court referred to the definition of the word 'harass' in the Concise Oxford Dictionary, as meaning to 'torment by subjecting to constant interference or intimidation'. Stalking is the prime example of such behaviour, but not the only possible form. It may occur, for example, between neighbours or in the workplace, *Majrowski v Guy's and St Thomas's NHS Trust* 2006 UKHL 341 para 18. Essentially it involves persistent conduct of a seriously oppressive nature, either physically or mentally, targeted at an individual and resulting in fear or distress, *Thomas v News Group Newspapers* 2001 at para 30.

Power of other courts to make orders

93.5 *High Court and County Court injunctions*

Protection from Harassment Act 1997 s 3A [Power of the High Court and County Court to make a harassment injunction is listed]

Power to order

93.6 *Power to order*

Protection from Harassment Act 1997 s 5(1) A court sentencing or otherwise dealing with a person (the defendant) convicted of an offence may (as well as sentencing him or dealing with him in any other way) make an order under this section.
(2) The order may, for the purpose of protecting the victim or victims of the offence, or any other person mentioned in the order, from further conduct which:
 (a) amounts to harassment, or
 (b) will cause fear of violence,
prohibit the defendant from doing anything described in the order.
R v Chinegwundoh 2015 EWCA Crim 109, 1 Cr App R (S) 61 (p 429) D was unfit to plead but found to have committed fraud and used a false instrument. D was a practising barrister but was disbarred for forging court documents. The Judge made a Restraining Order. Held. A finding that a person did the act is neither a 'conviction' nor an 'acquittal'. Restraining order quashed.

93.7 *Test to apply*

Protection from Harassment Act 1997 s 5(2) The order may, for the purpose of protecting the victim or victims of the offence, or any other person mentioned in the order, from further conduct which:
 (a) amounts to harassment, or
 (b) will cause fear of violence,
prohibit the defendant from doing anything described in the order.
R v Jose 2013 EWCA Crim 939 J was acquitted of having a bladed article and the Judge imposed a Restraining Order. Held. From *R v Smith* 2012 EWCA Crim 2566, 2013 2 Cr App R (S) 28 (p 191) the following principles emerge.
1) Since the purpose of an order under [Protection from Harassment Act 1997] section 5A [see **93.9**] is to protect a person from harassment by an acquitted defendant, the court must first be satisfied that the defendant is likely to pursue a course of conduct which amounts to harassment within the meaning of section 1 of the Act. See *R v Smith* 2012 at paragraph 29.
2) It does not follow that because references to harassing a person include alarming a person or causing a person distress, that therefore any course of conduct which causes alarm or distress amounts to harassment. Essentially harassment: '. . . involves persistent conduct of a seriously oppressive nature, either physically or mentally, targeted at an individual and resulting in fear or distress', see *R v Smith* 2012 at para 24.
3) The power to make an order under section 5A is circumscribed by the important words: 'necessary . . . to protect a person from harassment by a defendant.' The word 'necessary' is not to be diluted. To make an order prohibiting a person who has not committed any criminal offence from doing an act which is otherwise lawful on pain of imprisonment is an interference with the person's freedom of action which can be justified only when it is truly 'necessary' for the protection of some other person, see *R v Smith* 2012 at para 30.
R v Khellaf 2016 EWCA Crim 1297, 2017 1 Cr App R (S) 1 (p 1) D pleaded to three breaches of a Non-Molestation Order. There was a history of violence and harassment mainly about D's contact with his child. Held. The authorities set out the following propositions: 1) [see **93.15**], 2) An order should not be made unless the judge concludes that it is necessary to make an order in order to protect the victim. 3) The terms of the order should be proportionate to the harm that it is sought to prevent. 4) Particular care should be taken when children are involved to ensure that the order does not make it impossible for contact to take place between a parent and child [even] if that is otherwise inappropriate.[1063]

[1063] Without the insertion of the word 'even' the sentence makes no sense. It is hoped that is what the Judge wanted the judgment to say.

R v Taylor 2017 EWCA Crim 2209, 2018 1 Cr App R (S) 39 (p 273) D was acquitted of burglary. Held. We apply *R v Jose* 2013. Parliament has been careful to limit the circumstances in which such an order can be made, particularly since a breach of the order is criminal. It is easy to understand the caution of Parliament and the limits of the power given to the courts by Parliament in the context of an individual who has just been acquitted of any offence.
Note: Most of these principles are relevant to post-conviction orders. Ed.
Disputes as to facts see the **FACTUAL BASIS FOR SENTENCING** ***Same rules apply when imposing ancillary orders*** para at **57.26**.

93.8 ***There must be an identifiable victim***
Protection from Harassment Act 1997 s 5(2) The order may, for the purpose of protecting the victim or victims of the offence, or any other person mentioned in the order, from conduct which:
(a) amounts to harassment, or
(b) will cause a fear of violence,
prohibit the defendant from doing anything described in the order.
Protection from Harassment Act 1997 s 5(4) The prosecutor, the defendant or any other person mentioned in the order may apply to the court which made the order for it to be varied or discharged by a further order.
(4A) Any person mentioned in the order is entitled to be heard on the hearing of an application under subsection (4).
R v Smith 2012 EWCA Crim 2566, 2013 2 Cr App R (S) 28 (p 191) D was acquitted of criminal damage and interfering with the crew when he was travelling in an aircraft. He was given a Restraining Order. The defence challenged the order. Held. If D had been convicted, a Restraining Order under section 5 would have had to name those whom the order was intended to protect, see section 5(2). Any person named in the order would then have been entitled to be heard on an application to vary or discharge the order. Section 5A incorporates most of the provisions of section 5, but not section 5(2) for the obvious reason that there has not been an offence and therefore the language of section 5(2) could not apply. However, it could not be rationally supposed that an order under section 5A therefore need not identify the person, or possibly group of persons, whom the order is intended to protect.
The omission of the identification of any potential victim in the order made by the judge is not a matter of mere formality. The need for identification of the person who is to be protected reflects the underlying purpose of the provision. It is for the protection of a particular vulnerable person, or possibly an identifiable group of vulnerable persons. This order was for the protection of the world at large, or whoever might happen to be on any aircraft on which D might travel. Order quashed.

93.9 ***Acquittal, Power to make an order after an***
Protection from Harassment Act 1997 s 5A A court may make a Restraining Order for an acquitted defendant if it considers it is necessary to protect a person from harassment by the defendant.
R v Thompson 2010 EWCA Crim 2955, 2011 2 Cr App R (S) 24 (p 131) LCJ The order did not go beyond the verdict of the jury. It was carefully based on the evidence. Order upheld.
R v Major 2010 EWCA Crim 3016, 2011 2 Cr App R (S) 26 (p 139) LCJ D was acquitted and the Judge made a Restraining Order. Held. Save in the clearest of cases, to ensure that an impression is not given that the judge is going behind the verdict of the jury, the judge may wish to adjourn the case to the following day so that the matter can be fully considered. Where an individual had been acquitted of a harassment offence, it was open to a judge to impose a Restraining Order provided there was a factual basis for doing so, and the reasons were identified by the judge. The Court rejected the submission that such an order could only be made on uncontested facts, as that would

ignore the will of Parliament to protect the victim, provided there was a need for the order. Protection from Harassment Act 1997 s 5A was inserted by Domestic Violence, Crime and Victims Act 2004 s 12(5) in order to deal with cases where there was clear evidence that the victim needed protection but there was insufficient evidence to convict of particular charges. The ordinary civil standard of proof applies. Proof on the balance of probabilities does not contradict the verdict of the jury or suggest the defendant was in fact guilty. The order addresses a future risk. It is possible to admit evidence not heard at the trial. The evidence does not have to establish on the balance of probabilities there was harassment. The test is whether there is conduct which falls short of harassment which, if repeated, may amount to harassment so making the order necessary. The judge is required to identify the factual basis for imposing the order. The judge should state the reasons for making the order. Here we quash the order because there was no conclusion that the order was necessary. The court's form needs amending because it conflicts with section 5A(1) of the Act.

R v K 2011 EWCA Crim 1843, 2012 1 Cr App R (S) 88 (p 523) D pleaded not guilty to sexual assault and common assault. The Crown offered no evidence and the Judge directed an acquittal. V, D's estranged wife, did not make a statement. V's sister had given a statement. There were three earlier allegations made by V and also a caution against D in respect of an assault against V in 2005. No details or evidence were heard. It was alleged that D was trying to lift V's skirt, and that he held V's sister by both cheeks and kissed her. The Judge, of his own volition, explored the making of a Restraining Order, heard submissions and subsequently imposed such an order. Held. The Judge failed to consider that the allegations may have been false. He should have considered adjourning the hearing to allow the procedural requirements stated in Criminal Procedure Rules 2015 2015/1490 Rule 31 to be adhered to. Such limited evidence being before the court, there was no sound evidential basis upon which to make a Restraining Order. Order quashed.

R v Smith 2012 EWCA Crim 2566, 2013 2 Cr App R (S) 28 (p 191) D was acquitted of criminal damage and interfering with the crew when he was travelling in an aircraft, because of his insanity. D made a swift recovery. The Judge made a Restraining Order. The defence challenged the order. Held. The power to make an order under section 5A is circumscribed by the important words 'necessary…to protect a person from harassment by the defendant'. The word 'necessary' is not to be diluted. To make an order prohibiting a person who has not committed any criminal offence from doing an act which is otherwise lawful, on pain of imprisonment, is an interference with that person's freedom of action which could be justified only when it is truly necessary for the protection of some other person. The Judge used the section as if it were an adjunct to the Mental Health Act as a means of protecting the public against the possible effects of a possible recurrence of a mental illness. That is not the function of the section. The effect of the order was to impose an unlawful and unjustifiable restraint on D's ability to live a normal part of his life. Order quashed.

R v AJR 2013 EWCA Crim 591 D was acquitted of attempted murder by reason of insanity. He attacked his baby with a knife on an isolated occasion. The Judge imposed a Restraining Order. Held. para 20 There is no parallel provision [in section 5A] to section 5(2) conferring a power to protect a victim from conduct which 'will cause fear of violence'. Here, terrible though the events were, there was no relevant 'course of conduct' in either sense [of section 7(3)(a) and (b)]. The incident was a single one and did not satisfy the requirements of the Act as explained by Toulson LJ (see the above case). Further, the Judge recognised in his sentencing remarks that D was not suffering from the disability that pertained at the time of the attack on his daughter. Order quashed.

See also: *R v Lawrence* 2012 EWCA Crim 1164 (Order quashed because the Judge failed to state the factual background. It was necessary for the Judge to state his reasoning.)

R v McDermott and Others 2013 EWCA Crim 607, 2014 1 Cr App R (S) 1 (p 1) (Nasty group assault on a man who was the partner of the sister-in-law of two of the defendants. History of tension. The three defendants were acquitted in relation to the assault but Restraining Orders were made as the Judge found on the civil standard they had probably played a role in the assault. Those convicted of the assault had earlier had the Restraining Orders quashed on the basis they were counter-productive. Defendants appealed their Restraining Orders. Victim personal statement suggested continuing need for the orders. Disparity argument rejected. Restraining Order upheld.)
R v Hart 2015 EWCA Crim 389 (Judge excluded some evidence so the case collapsed. Over lunch there was an incident and through both counsel the Judge heard two different versions of it. The Judge made a Restraining Order. Held. There was no evidence, there were no findings and there were no reasons. Order quashed.)
R v Eduardo 2016 EWCA Crim 2097 (Defendant was given a Restraining Order after he was acquitted. Held. There must be due process. Order quashed because Judge failed to identify the factual basis and failed to give reasons.)

93.10 ***Acquittal, After Test to apply There must be a course of conduct***
Protection from Harassment Act 1997 s 1(1A) A person must not pursue a course of conduct:
(a) which involves harassment of two or more persons, and
(b) which he knows or ought to know amounts to harassment of the other.
Protection from Harassment Act 1997 s 7(3) A 'course of conduct' must involve:
(a) in the case of conduct in relation to a single person (see section 1(1)), conduct on at least two occasions in relation to that person, or
(b) in the case of conduct in relation to two or more persons (see section 1(1A)), conduct on at least one occasion in relation to each of those persons.
R v Smith 2012 EWCA Crim 2566, 2013 2 Cr App R (S) 28 (p 191) D was acquitted by reason of insanity. Held. The purpose of a [Restraining Order] is to protect a person from harassment by a defendant. The Court must first be satisfied that the defendant is likely to pursue a course of conduct which amounts to harassment within the meaning of section 1. Pursuit of a course of conduct requires intention.
In construing section 1 of the 1997 Act, it is right to have regard to the type of mischief at which it was aimed. It is also right to have regard to what the ordinary person would understand by harassment. It does not follow that because references to harassing a person include alarming a person or causing a person distress (section 7(2)), any course of conduct which causes alarm or distress therefore amounts to harassment, *Thomas v News Group Newspapers* 2001 EWCA Civ 1233 at para 29. So to reason would be illogical and would produce perverse results. A person who habitually drives too fast in a built-up area may cause alarm to other road users, but conduct of that sort was not what Parliament was invited to consider and would not fall within the ordinary understanding of what is meant by harassment. In *R v Curtis* 2010 EWCA Crim 123 the court referred to the definition of the word 'harass' in the Concise Oxford Dictionary, as meaning to 'torment by subjecting to constant interference or intimidation'. Stalking is the prime example of such behaviour, but not the only possible form. It may occur, for example, between neighbours or in the workplace, *Majrowski v Guy's and St Thomas's NHS Trust* 2006 UKHL 341 para 18. Essentially it involves persistent conduct of a seriously oppressive nature, either physically or mentally, targeted at an individual and resulting in fear or distress, *Thomas v News Group Newspapers* 2001 at para 30.

93.11 ***Corporations as victims***
R v Buxton and Others 2010 EWCA Crim 2923, 2011 2 Cr App R (S) 23 (p 121) LCJ The defendants pleaded to obstruction of a railway and were conditionally discharged and made the subject of a restraining order. They made an environmental protest on a

company's railway line. The defence contended that the order could not be made to protect a limited company. Held. We have heard nothing to persuade us a section 5 order cannot [protect] a company.

93.12 ***Domestic violence cases***

Domestic Abuse Guideline 2018, see banksr.com Other Matters Guidelines tab page 5 para 16. In force 24 May 2018.

16. The court should also consider whether it is appropriate to make a restraining order, and if doing so, should ensure that it has all relevant up to date information. The court may also wish to consider making other orders, such as a European protection order, sexual harm prevention order, criminal behaviour order (this is not an exhaustive list). Further details for restraining orders are set out below.

RESTRAINING ORDER

17. Where an offender is convicted of any offence, the court may make a restraining order (Protection from Harassment Act 1997, section 5).

18. Orders can be made on the initiative of the court; the views of the victim should be sought, but their consent is not required.

19. The order may prohibit the offender from doing anything for the purpose of protecting the victim of the offence, or any other person mentioned in the order, from further conduct which amounts to harassment or will cause a fear of violence.

20. If the parties are to continue or resume a relationship, courts may consider a prohibition within the restraining order not to molest the victim (as opposed to a prohibition on contacting the victim).

21. The order may have effect for a specified period or until further order.

22. A court before which a person is **acquitted** of an offence may make a restraining order if the court considers that it is necessary to protect a person from harassment by the defendant (Protection from Harassment Act 1997, section 5A).

Procedural rules/Making the order

93.13 ***Procedural rules***

R v K 2011 EWCA Crim 1843, 2012 1 Cr App R (S) 88 (p 523) After the Crown offered no evidence, the Judge on his own initiative made a Restraining Order. There was no adjournment. Held. Where no evidence has been offered and there is no established evidential basis for the order, different considerations apply than if a Judge proposes to make an order immediately following a trial, where evidence has been heard. Here, the Judge should have considered adjourning the matter so the procedural requirements could be met. There must be a proper opportunity to address the evidence.

R v Zakacura 2013 EWCA Crim 2595 D pleaded to ABH. Whilst on bail for an assault against V2, he attended V2's address, contrary to his bail conditions, and assaulted V1. After sentencing D, the Judge asked the prosecution whether they sought a Restraining Order. Counsel responded that he had not been asked to seek one, but that in his view it seemed appropriate. The Judge said, "Absolutely" and made the order. Held. No notice was given to D or his representative that an order would be sought or explaining the basis for any such application. It was not even clear whether the matter had been considered by the police or the prosecution, and if it had, what views they had formed and why. It was wholly unclear whether the victim's views had been sought and obtained. It wasn't clear upon what basis he advanced the application. The defence was not invited to make any representations before the order was imposed. The procedure was unfair and the making of the order was not properly founded on all potentially relevant information. The order must be quashed.

R v Khellaf 2016 EWCA Crim 1297, 2017 1 Cr App R (S) 1 (p 1) The views of the victim should be obtained. It is the responsibility of the prosecution to ensure that the necessary enquiries are made. For more detail, see **93.15**.

See also: *R v Brough* 2011 EWCA Crim 2802, 2012 2 Cr App R (S) 8 (p 30) (The Judge took too summary an approach to the application and erred in not conducting a proper examination of the evidence and not explaining his reasons.)
For the rule that shows that the Behavioural Rules apply, see **27.2**. For those rules, see **84.14**.

93.14 *Evidence*

Protection from Harassment Act 1997 s 5(3A)[1064] In proceedings under this section both the prosecution and the defence may lead, as further evidence, any evidence that would be admissible in proceedings for an injunction under section 3 (civil injunctions).
Criminal Procedure Rules 2015 2015/1490 Rule 31.4(2) A party who wants the court to take account of evidence not already introduced must:
(a) serve notice on:[1065]
(i) the court officer, and
(ii) every other party,
as soon as practicable (without waiting for the verdict),
(b) in the notice, identify that evidence, and
(c) attach any written statement containing such evidence.
R v Bradfield 2006 EWCA Crim 2917 D pleaded to burglary, theft, damaging property and harassment (Community Rehabilitation Orders and a Restraining Order). Police were regularly called out because of verbal abuse between D and his ex-partner, V. D broke into V's house following the dissolution of their relationship. He was captured on CCTV stealing underwear, going through drawers in various rooms, masturbating and ejaculating onto the bed sheets. The Restraining Order prevented him from coming within 500 yards of the road where V lived with their two children. It also prevented D from contacting V directly or indirectly. D lost his job and the Restraining Order became more onerous. D wished to vary or discharge the order on the grounds that the DHSS was a very short distance from the road. Further, the Jobcentre was within the 500-yard area and the order prevented him from seeking, obtaining or travelling to work and handicapped him on the labour market. He also said the railway station was within the prohibited area and many buses travelled through the prohibited area. V opposed the variation. Held. There was no evidence put before the Judge on behalf of the appellant. It is not surprising the Judge concluded, in the absence of detailed proposals for variation which addressed V's continuing anxieties and concerns, that her interests had to be given priority. The Judge was entirely correct to do so. If any application is made in future, the appellant and those acting for him would be advised to support it with evidence.
Note: It can be inferred from the judgment that had: a) evidence been collected about the need to visit the Jobcentre etc. and b) variations been proposed which would have dealt with the ability to remain on a bus as it travelled through the prohibited area etc., some variations would have been made. Ed.

93.15 *Victim's views*

R v Picken 2006 EWCA Crim 2194 D pleaded to putting a person in fear of violence and common assault. He was sentenced to 2 years and a 5-year Restraining Order was made. His relationship with the victim, V, was turbulent with incidents of violence. Around midnight, he threatened her with a sharp knife and she thought he would kill her. A few days later there was another nasty, similar incident. Before sentence, V visited D in prison and the Judge was told by the defence she did not want a Restraining Order. The Judge said that was a reason to make the order. Held. The Judge should have found out from the prosecution what the situation was. If V wanted to continue the relationship, an order was inappropriate. Order quashed.

[1064] Inserted by Domestic Violence, Crime and Victims Act 2004 s 12(2)
[1065] The Criminal Procedure (Amendment No 2) Rules 2016 2016/705 para 11(c) removes the requirement that the notice has to be in writing. In force 3/10/16

R v Khellaf 2016 EWCA Crim 1297, 2017 1 Cr App R (S) 1 (p 1) D pleaded to three breaches of a Non-Molestation Order. There was a history of violence and harassment mainly about D's contact with his child. Held. The authorities set out the following propositions:
1) A court should take into account the views of the person to be protected. We do not say that there will never be a case where it would be inappropriate to make a restraining order, even though the subject of the order does not seek one, but the views of the victim will clearly be relevant. Nor do we say that a court must have direct evidence of the views of the victim. That may prove impossible. The court may be able to draw a proper inference as to those views, or may conclude that a Restraining Order should be made whatever the views of the victim, although clearly if a victim does not want an order to be made because she wants to have contact, that may make such an order impractical. In normal circumstances the views of the victim should be obtained. It is the responsibility of the prosecution to ensure that the necessary enquiries are made. 2)-4) [See **93.7**.]
R v Herrington 2017 EWCA Crim 889, 2 Cr App R (S) 38 In November 2015, D was sentenced to 11 months for ABH against V. A matter of hours after his release he slapped V five to six times, and when a member of the public intervened he threatened to attack him. D was arrested. D was aged 37 and had 36 court appearances for 97 offences. In March 2017, at the sentencing hearing, the probation report said there was a very high risk to V, probation staff, the public and [V's child]. They asked for a Restraining Order. V was in Court supporting D and had refused to make a statement. D was sent to prison for 12 months and a Restraining Order was made. Held. We caused the police to contact her and she told them unambiguously that she wants this Restraining Order revoked. D is a violent and an unruly man. But we cannot prevent an adult from living with who[m] she wants. V has the right to live with him if she chooses. The child may require the protection of the court but the appropriate course is for proceedings in the family court. If the probation service is concerned about its staff it can apply for an order protecting them. We cannot protect its staff by keeping D and V apart. Order quashed.
See also: *R v Brown* 2012 EWCA Crim 1152 (*R v Picken* 2006 EWCA Crim 2194 applied. Order quashed.)

93.16 ***Length of the order***
Protection from Harassment Act 1997 s 5(3) The order may have effect for a specified period or until further notice.
See also: *R v Howard* 2016 EWCA Crim 1906 (Mother subject to a Restraining Order after no evidence on stalking count concerning son. Held. para 17 The test is not reasonableness but necessity. **5 years** not life.)

93.17 ***More than one order in force***
R v Beck 2003 EWCA Crim 2198 The defendant was given a Restraining Order. He breached it and was given a fresh one. Held. We set aside the first order.

Drafting the terms

93.18 ***Wording generally The order must be specific and precise***
R v Evans 2004 EWCA Crim 3102, 2005 1 Cr App R 32 (p 546) In *R v P* 2004 EWCA Crim 287, 2 Cr App R (S) 63 (p 343), an ASBO case, the Court said, 'The terms of the order must be precise and capable of being understood by the offender'. The same applies to a Restraining Order. However, even if the phrase 'abusive actions' was considered to be objectionably imprecise and even unintelligible, that would not afford a ground of appeal against any conviction.
R v Debnath 2005 EWCA Crim 3472, 2006 2 Cr App R (S) 25 (p 169) A Restraining Order must be drafted in clear and precise terms so there is no doubt as to what the defendant is prohibited from doing.

R v Mann 2000 Unreported 21/2/00 The defendant's order prohibited him from contacting any member of staff at the probation hostel. Held. The order should identify the persons for whom protection is sought. The two individuals were named in the order amended by the Court of Appeal.
For drafting the particular terms see the **Preventive orders** entry in the back index.

93.19 ***On the facts, order correct/incorrect***
R v Buxton and Others 2010 EWCA Crim 2923, 2011 2 Cr App R (S) 23 (p 121) LCJ The defendants pleaded to obstruction of a railway. They were conditionally discharged and made the subject of a Restraining Order. The 12 defendants made an environmental protest on a company's railway line from an open-cast coal mine to a power station. Two defendants chained themselves to the railway line and another superglued himself to the other two. Nine defendants were of good character and three had convictions. However, the Judge decided to treat them all the same. The Judge considered they were all intelligent and not criminals. The defence contended the order was unnecessary. Held. With some hesitation, we consider the Restraining Order was inappropriate.
R v Wall 2012 EWCA Crim 1576 D was convicted of three counts of fraud against a young woman and her parents. The offences were committed when he was on bail for identical offences. The Judge made a Restraining Order. Held. The order was not necessary against the victims as they would not want anything more to do with him. The third term does not refer to any victim and it should do. Order quashed.
R v Fraser 2013 EWCA Crim 799 D pleaded to possessing a firearm without a certificate. He was acquitted of attempted murder and section 18. D was in a relationship with L. That relationship was ended by D, but the two remained in contact. D subsequently wanted to resume their relationship but L did not. He sent her flowers and repeatedly asked her out for meals. L's house was subsequently damaged in an arson attack. Two months later, L was shot by someone using a 12-bore shotgun as she was leaving her house. L thought that it might be her former husband or D. D was a farmer and when the police were investigating, they found a single-barrelled shotgun and 40 cartridges hidden in some bales of hay. D received 8 months for the firearm offence. The Judge also made a Restraining Order. Held. D's attentions, though not wholly welcome, were of a relatively harmless kind and there was nothing to suggest that L indicated that she wished for the protection of the court. An order of this kind is likely to bear heavily on D as they live in the same area and have interests as well as friends in common. The order cannot be justified. Restraining Order quashed.
See also: *R v James* 2013 EWCA Crim 655, 2 Cr App R (S) 85 (p 542) (D was acquitted of sexual assault and convicted of ABH. All important matters had been resolved in D's favour. The order was wrong in principle.)
R v Deeds 2013 EWCA Crim 1624 (There was an overwhelming need for the order and, subject to one matter, the prohibitions were correct.)

93.20 ***Explain sentence, Judge/Magistrate must***
R v Major 2010 EWCA Crim 3016, 2011 2 Cr App R (S) 26 (p 139) LCJ D was acquitted and the Judge made a Restraining Order. Held. Judges are required to identify the factual basis for imposing the order. Judges should state the reasons for making the order.
R v Fraser 2013 EWCA Crim 799 D pleaded to possessing a firearm without a certificate. The Judge made a Restraining Order. Held. The Judge did not explain in any detail what the facts were on which he based the decision to make the Restraining Order. He simply said he had heard enough evidence to justify that course. The Judge should identify the facts which he considered provide sufficient basis for the order. For more detail of the case, see **262.12** in the **Firearms** chapter in Volume 2.
R v Jose 2013 EWCA Crim 939 D was acquitted of having a bladed article. D had been abusive and hostile to his ex-partner and it was claimed he had a knife. The prosecution asked for a Restraining Order. The Judge made no finding that the order was necessary,

just that it was reasonable. Held. It is always incumbent on the court imposing the order to state its reasons for doing so. That must not be overlooked, *R v Lawrence* 2012 EWCA Crim 1164.
For the general requirement to give reasons, see **86.49**.

Variation/discharge of the order

93.21 ***Power to vary or substitute or discharge an order***
Protection from Harassment Act 1997 s 5(4) The prosecutor, the defendant or any other person mentioned in the order may apply to the Court which made the order for it to be varied or discharged by a further order.
Protection from Harassment Act 1997 s 5(7)[1066] A court dealing with a person for an offence under this section may vary or discharge the order in question by a further order.
Shaw v DPP 2005 EWHC 1215 (Admin) High Court The District Judge stated that there had been no material change of circumstances since the hearing of the last application and dismissed the application. Held. There is no express requirement to satisfy the court that there has been a material change in circumstances since the making of the Restraining Order or the dismissal of any earlier application to discharge. In an application or further application to discharge the applicant must show that something has changed so that the continuance of the order is no longer necessary or appropriate. Unless that is so, the applicant would be entitled to have the merits of an earlier decision or decisions redetermined anew without having appealed them. The only question upon a subsequent application such as was made here is whether events have happened which, in contrast to the position which previously obtained, now mean that the order is no longer necessary or appropriate. The District Judge was quite right.
R v Debnath 2005 EWCA Crim 3472, 2006 2 Cr App R (S) 25 (p 169) The power of the court to vary or discharge the order in question by a further order under section 5(4) is an important safeguard to defendants. The Court of Appeal is unlikely to interfere with the terms of a Restraining Order if an application to the court which imposed the Restraining Order to vary or discharge was, in the circumstances, the appropriate course.

93.22 ***Procedure***
Note: The Criminal Procedure Rules 2015 2015/1490 behaviour order rules apply, see the note at **27.2**. For the rules themselves, see **84.14**. Ed.

93.23 ***Right of victims to make representation***
Protection from Harassment Act 1997 s 5(4A)[1067] Any person mentioned in the order is entitled to be heard on the hearing of an application under subsection (4), [see para **93.21**].
Note: The Explanatory Note to Domestic Violence, Crime and Victims Act 2004 which introduced section 5(4A) says the amendment means victims can make representations at breach hearings and the Rules of Court will ensure that the victims are notified of any applications to vary or discharge the order. Ed.

93.24 ***Appeals from variation hearings***
R v Bradfield 2006 EWCA Crim 2917 D pleaded to burglary and harassment and was given a Restraining Order. He lost his job, which made the Restraining Order more onerous. He applied to vary it. The issue of whether there was jurisdiction to appeal arose. Held. This issue is by no means straightforward. However, if we allow the appeal to be about the original order we do not have to resolve the issue. We would not want this case to be taken as authority for the proposition that the Court has jurisdiction to hear an appeal against a refusal to vary a Restraining Order.
R v Hall 2010 EWCA Crim 1919 D pleaded (full credit) to breach of a Restraining Order and an offence under Malicious Communications Act 1988. In July 2008 D was subject to a community order imposed for offences of harassment. He had made telephone calls

[1066] Inserted by Domestic Violence, Crime and Victims Act 2004 s 12(4)
[1067] Inserted by Domestic Violence, Crime and Victims Act 2004 s 12(3)

and sent text messages to an ex-partner. He threatened to smash windows. In November 2009, and in breach of the community order, he telephoned another ex-partner and threatened to "slit [her] throat". He pleaded to offences under Malicious Communications Act 1988 and Protection from Harassment Act 1997. He received 4 weeks' suspended for 12 months and was made subject to a Restraining Order. The order prohibited him from contacting the ex-partner or her family. In February 2010, D left a gift at a venue where the ex-partner was due to sing. The gift was for her son. He then telephoned twice, leaving a lengthy message and subsequently a threatening message. D claimed that he had been told by V's parents that giving a gift would be acceptable. A victim impact statement detailed V's stress and inability to work due to fear. D had 27 convictions for 53 offences, including violence. Held. The original sentence of 15 months for the breach of the Restraining Order and 4 months for the Malicious Communications Act 1988 offence related to the same behaviour. To add a further period of imprisonment in respect of the same behaviour seems to us to have been wrong in principle. So, **15 months** for the breach of the Restraining Order and **4 months concurrent** for the Malicious Communications Act 1988 offence. The suspended sentence was activated in full and consecutively (**4 weeks**) making **16 months**.

Appeals

93.25 ***Appeals***

R v Jose 2013 EWCA Crim 939 D was acquitted of having a bladed article. D had been abusive and hostile to his ex-partner and it was claimed he had a knife. The prosecution asked for a Restraining Order. The Judge made no finding that the order was necessary, just that it was reasonable. Held. We have to assess this order on the basis of those findings and not on the basis of findings which might have been made. Order quashed.

94 RESTRAINING ORDERS: HARASSMENT/ NON-MOLESTATION ORDERS: BREACH OF

94.1

Protection from Harassment Act 1997 s 5(5)

Family Law Act 1996 s 42A[1068]

Modes of trial Both offences are triable either way.

Maximum sentences For both offences: On indictment 5 years. Summary 6 months and/or and an unlimited fine.[1069] There are maximum fines for those aged under 18, see **13.44**.

Proving the breach

94.2 ***Statutory provisions Restraining Orders***

Protection from Harassment Act 1997 s 5(5) If without reasonable excuse the defendant does anything which he is prohibited from doing by an order under this section, he is guilty of an offence.

94.3 ***Defence of reasonable excuse Restraining Orders***

Protection from Harassment Act 1997 s 5(5) If without reasonable excuse the defendant does anything which he is prohibited from doing by an order under this section, he is guilty of an offence.

94.4 ***Mental element for the offence/ Forgetfulness***

R v Nicholson 2006 EWCA Crim 1518 D attended a demonstration and was in breach of her ASBO. She sought to raise a reasonable excuse defence because she had no recollection of ever having heard before, or at the demonstration, of any reference to one of the named premises she was prohibited from going to in her ASBO. The Judge ruled the offence was a strict liability offence. Held. It is not helpful to characterise an offence

[1068] As inserted by Domestic Violence, Crime and Victims Act 2004 s 1

[1069] Legal Aid, Sentencing and Punishment of Offenders Act 2012 s 85(1) and (4) and Legal Aid, Sentencing and Punishment of Offenders Act 2012 (Commencement No 11) Order 2015 2015/504

as one of 'strict liability' where the prosecution do not have to prove any sort of *mens rea*, but where there is a statutory provision for a defence or an evidential issue to be raised based on the presence or absence of some state of mind on the part of the defendant. The prosecution do not, as part of their case, have to prove knowing breach of such order. The fact the prosecution do not as part of their case have to prove knowing breach of such order means that there is not the same tension between proof by the prosecution of their case triggering considerations of an evidential issue of reasonable excuse (if it is raised) and acceptance of forgetfulness or misunderstanding as such an excuse. If a jury were to accept forgetfulness or misunderstanding in the circumstances as genuine and reasonable, say, because of chronic absent-mindedness or pressing distractions, we do not consider that it is necessary to combine it with another reason or to look for another one, 'in which forgetfulness plays its part' in the different statutory context of offences of possession of offensive weapons and possession of bladed articles.

94.5 *What constitutes a breach?*

R v Evans 2004 EWCA Crim 3102, 2005 1 Cr App R 32 (p 546) D, aged 78, was given a Restraining Order which prohibited her from being 'abusive by words or actions towards X, Y and Z and their respective families'. A plumber who came to do repairs for Mrs Z parked his van close to Mrs Z's car. D's car was parked in the same street. D drove her car close up behind the van, blocking it in. Breach proceedings were brought. D was convicted and the defence said driving a car could not be 'an abusive action'. Held. Looking at the meaning of words in a criminal context is no reason for giving them a narrow or strained meaning. The application of that meaning to the facts should be left to the fact-finding tribunal. It can make no difference that the offence in this case was being by action contrary to the terms of a Restraining Order, rather than contrary to a statutory provision which specifically prohibits such conduct. Either way, the approach elucidated in cases such as *Brutus v Cozens* 1972 56 Cr App R (S) 799 and *R v Associated Octel Ltd* 1996 EWCA Crim 1327, 1997 1 Cr App R (S) 435 should apply. The Judge was right to leave the case to the jury.

94.6 *Burdens of proof*

R v Evans 2004 EWCA Crim 3102, 2005 1 Cr App R 32 (p 546) D was convicted of breaching her Restraining Order. She appealed on the basis she had a reasonable excuse. Held. It is for the defendant to raise the evidential issue of reasonable excuse and then for the prosecution to prove lack of reasonable excuse. If a defendant said she believed the order permitted her to act as she did, then the prosecution would have to satisfy the jury that this belief, if it was held, was not a reasonable excuse.

R v Charles 2009 EWCA Crim 1570 D was convicted of breaching an ASBO. D had been made the subject of an ASBO which prohibited him from engaging in any behaviour which caused or was likely to cause harassment, alarm or distress to any person not of the same household as himself. D allegedly used a screwdriver to scratch a man's back and was charged with breaching the ASBO without reasonable excuse. The Judge said the legal burden was on D to show that he had a reasonable excuse for his actions. Held. It cannot have been the intention of Parliament to place any burden of proof on D under section 1(10) which criminalised conduct that Parliament itself had not criminalised and had not described the terms in which that could be done. The burden of disproving reasonable excuse was on the Crown where a defendant had raised the issue on the evidence before the court.

For ***Is there a defence that the term was invalid?*** see para **26.15**.

94.7 *Duplicity, Breach and*

S v Doncaster Youth Offending Team 2003 EWHC 1128 (Admin) High Court S was convicted of failing to comply with a Detention and Training Order. S had failed to reside where the YOT had instructed him to, and he had failed to report for four consecutive weeks. It was submitted that the information was bad for duplicity. Held. Sometimes it is difficult to distinguish between separate offences, on the one hand, and

different features of committing the same offence, on the other. There were two quite separate licence conditions of which the appellant was in breach. These were failing to keep in touch with his supervising officer and failing to live at the address approved by his supervising officer. These were two separate offences that should not have been tried on the same information.
Note: Although this case relates to a failure to comply with a different order, the principles to apply are likely to be the same. Ed.

Sentencing

Note: There are many similarities between a breach of a Restraining Order and breach of a Non-Molestation Order. However, there are a few differences. As ever, all cases should be treated as fact-specific. Ed.

94.8 ***Breach Offences Guideline 2018***
Breach Offences Guideline 2018, see www.banksr.com Other Matters Guidelines tab In force 1 October 2018 page 20
Restraining orders: Protection from Harassment Act 1997 s 5(5) and (5A)
Non-molestation orders: Family Law Act 1996 (section 42A)
Breach of a protective order (restraining and non-molestation orders)

STEP ONE **Determining the offence category**

The court should determine the offence category with reference only to the factors listed in the tables below. In order to determine the category the court should assess **culpability** and **harm**.
Culpability
In assessing culpability, the court should consider the intention and motivation of the offender in committing any breach.

A	• Very serious and/or persistent breach
B	• Deliberate breach falling between A and C
C	• Minor breach • Breach just short of reasonable excuse

Harm

The level of **harm** is determined by weighing up all the factors of the case to determine the harm that has been caused or was intended to be caused.

Category 1	Breach causes **very** serious harm or distress
Category 2	Cases falling between Categories 1 and 3
Category 3	Breach causes little or no harm or distress*

* Where a breach is committed in the context of a background of domestic abuse, the sentence should take care not to underestimate the harm which may be present in a breach.

94.9

STEP TWO **Starting point and category range**

Having determined the category at step one, the court should use the corresponding starting point to reach a sentence within the category range from the appropriate sentence table below. The starting point applies to all offenders irrespective of plea or previous convictions.

	Culpability		
Harm	**A**	**B**	**C**
Category 1	**Starting point** 2 years' custody	**Starting point** 1 year's custody	**Starting point** 12 weeks' custody
	Category range 1 to 4 years' custody	**Category range** High-level community order to 2 years' custody	**Category range** Medium-level community order to 1 year's custody
Category 2	**Starting point** 1 year's custody	**Starting point** 12 weeks' custody	**Starting point** High-level community order
	Category range High-level community order to 2 years' custody	**Category range** Medium-level community order to 1 year's custody	**Category range** Low-level community order to 26 weeks' custody
Category 3	**Starting point** 12 weeks' custody	**Starting point** High-level community order	**Starting point** Low-level community order
	Category range Medium-level community order to 1 year's custody	**Category range** Low-level community order to 26 weeks' custody	**Category range** Band B fine to high-level community order

The table above refers to single offences. Where there are multiple offences consecutive sentences may be appropriate – please refer to the [*TICs and Totality Guideline 2012: Crown Court*].

For the meaning of high-level, medium-level and low-level community orders, see **15.12**. For a Band B fine, see **58.28**.

94.10 [Aggravating and mitigating factors]

Page 24 The table below contains a **non-exhaustive** list of additional factual elements providing the context of the offence and factors relating to the offender. Identify whether any combination of these, or other relevant factors, should result in an upward or downward adjustment from the starting point.

In some cases, having considered these factors, it may be appropriate to move outside the identified category range.

Factors increasing seriousness
Statutory aggravating factors:
Previous convictions, having regard to a) the **nature** of the offence to which the conviction relates and its **relevance** to the current offence; and b) the **time** that has elapsed since the conviction
Offence committed whilst on bail
Other aggravating factors:
Breach committed shortly after order made
History of disobedience to court orders (where not already taken into account as a previous conviction)
Breach involves a further offence (where not separately prosecuted)
Using contact arrangements with a child/children to instigate offence and/or proven history of violence or threats by offender

Breach results in victim or protected person being forced to leave their home
Impact upon children or family members
Victim or protected subject of order breached is particularly vulnerable
Offender takes steps to prevent victim or subject harmed by breach from reporting an incident or seeking assistance
Offence committed on licence or while subject to post sentence supervision
Factors reducing seriousness or reflecting personal mitigation
Breach committed after long period of compliance
Prompt voluntary surrender/admission of breach or failure
Age and/or lack of maturity where it affects the responsibility of the offender
Mental disorder or learning disability where linked to the commission of the offence
Sole or primary carer for dependent relatives
Contact not initiated by offender – a careful examination of all the circumstances is required before weight is given to this factor

For additional aggravating and mitigating factors, see **94.13**.

STEP THREE to STEP EIGHT These are: Consider assistance to the prosecution, Reduction for guilty plea, Totality principle, Ancillary orders, Duty to give reasons and Consider time spent on bail with a tag.

94.7d *Suggested approach to the guideline*

Note: I have assumed that the *Breach of a Protective Order Guideline 2006* is in part superseded. If Judges find parts of the old guideline useful, I can see no reason why those parts should not be used if they are not inconsistent with the new guideline. I have removed most of the old tariff cases, but left some because they deal with legal principles. Those cases should be treated with care as the new guideline has a new structure which must be applied. The old cases should not determine the length of the sentence. That is determined by the guideline. Ed.

94.11 *Breach of a Protective Order Guideline 2006*

Breach of a Protective Order Guideline 2006, see www.banksr.com Other Matters Guidelines tab para B 2.1

Sentencing for breach

The facts that constitute a breach of a protective order may or may not also constitute a substantive offence. Where they do constitute a substantive offence, it is desirable that the substantive offence and the breach of the order should be charged as separate counts. Where necessary, consecutive sentences should be considered to reflect the seriousness of the counts and achieve the appropriate totality.

2.2 Sometimes, however, only the substantive offence or only the breach of the order will be charged. The basic principle is that the sentence should reflect all relevant aspects of the offence so that, provided the facts are not in issue, the result should be the same, regardless of whether one count or two has been charged. For example:

(i) if the substantive offence only has been charged, the fact that it constitutes breach of a protective order should be treated as an aggravating factor,

(ii) if breach of the protective order only has been charged, the sentence should reflect the nature of the breach, namely, the conduct that amounts to the substantive offence, aggravated by the fact that it is also breach of an order.

2.3 If breach of a protective order has been charged where no substantive offence was involved, the sentence should reflect the circumstances of the breach, including whether it was an isolated breach, or part of a course of conduct in breach of the order, whether it was planned or unpremeditated, and any consequences of the breach, including psychiatric injury or distress to the person protected by the order.

94.12 Factors influencing sentencing

Breach of a Protective Order Guideline 2006, see www.banksr.com Other Matters Guidelines tab

para C 3.3 Action in response to the breach should have as its primary aim the importance of ensuring that the order is complied with and that it achieves the protection that it was intended to achieve.

3.4 When sentencing for a breach of an order, the main aim should be to achieve future compliance with that order where that is realistic.

3.5 The nature of the original conduct or offence is relevant in so far as it allows a judgement to be made on the level of harm caused to the victim by the breach and the extent to which that harm was intended by the offender.

3.6 If the original offence was serious, conduct which breaches the order might have a severe effect on the victim where in other contexts such conduct might appear minor. Even indirect contact, such as telephone calls, can cause significant harm or anxiety for a victim.

3.7 However, sentence following a breach is for the breach alone and must avoid punishing the offender again for the offence or conduct as a result of which the order was made.

3.8 The protective orders are designed to protect a victim. When dealing with a breach, a court will need to consider the extent to which the conduct amounting to breach put the victim at risk of harm.

3.9 There may be exceptional cases where the nature of the breach is particularly serious but has not been dealt with by a separate offence being charged. In these cases, the risk posed by the offender and the nature of the breach will be particularly significant in determining the response. Where the order is breached by the use of physical violence, the starting point should normally be a custodial sentence.

3.10 Non-violent behaviour and/or indirect contact can also cause (or be intended to cause) a high degree of harm and anxiety. In such circumstances, it is likely that the custody threshold will have been crossed.

3.11 Where an order was made in civil proceedings, its purpose may have been to cause the subject of the order to modify behaviour rather than to imply that the conduct was especially serious. If so, it is likely to be disproportionate to impose a custodial sentence for a breach of the order if the breach did not involve threats or violence.

3.12 In some cases where a breach might result in a short custodial sentence but the court is satisfied that the offender genuinely intends to reform his or her behaviour and there is a real prospect of rehabilitation, the court may consider it appropriate to impose a sentence that will allow this. This may mean imposing a Suspended Sentence Order or a community order (where appropriate with a requirement to attend an accredited domestic violence programme).

3.13 Breach of a protective order will generally be more serious than breach of a conditional discharge. Not only is a breach of a protective order an offence in its own right but it also undermines a specific prohibition imposed by the court. Breach of a conditional discharge amounts to an offender failing to take a chance that has been provided by the court. A court will need to assess the level of risk posed by the offender. If the offender requires treatment or assistance for mental health or other issues, willingness to undergo treatment or accept help may influence sentence.

94.13 Aggravating and mitigating factors

Breach of a Protective Order Guideline 2006, see www.banksr.com Other Matters Guidelines tab page 5 para D 4.1 Many of the aggravating factors which apply to an offence of violence in a domestic context will apply also to an offence arising from breach of a protective order.

Note: The key aggravating and mitigating factors are in *Breach Offences Guideline 2018*, see **94.10**. As the aggravating and mitigating factors in the guideline are described as 'non-exhaustive', these factors may be of assistance. However, these factors may not be used to determine the offence category at step one of the new guideline. Ed.

Aggravating factors

para D 4.1

(i) **Victim is particularly vulnerable** 4.2 For cultural, religious, language, financial or any other reasons, some victims may be more vulnerable than others. This vulnerability means that the terms of a protective order are particularly important and a violation of those terms will warrant a higher penalty than usual. 4.3 Age, disability or the fact that the victim was pregnant or had recently given birth at the time of the offence may make a victim particularly vulnerable. 4.4 Any steps taken to prevent the victim reporting an incident or obtaining assistance will usually aggravate the offence.

(ii) **Impact on children** 4.5 If a protective order is imposed in order to protect children, either solely or in addition to another victim, then a breach of that order will generally be more serious.

(iii) **A proven history of violence or threats by the offender** 4.6 Of necessity, a breach of a protective order will not be the first time an offender has caused fear or harassment towards a victim. However, the offence will be more serious if the breach is part of a series of prolonged violence or harassment towards the victim or the offender has a history of disobedience to court orders. 4.7 Where an offender has previously been convicted of an offence involving domestic violence, either against the same or a different person, or has been convicted for a breach of an order, this is likely to be a statutory aggravating factor.

(iv) **Using contact arrangements with a child to instigate an offence** 4.8 An offence will be aggravated where an offender exploits contact arrangements with a child in order to commit an offence.

(v) **Victim is forced to leave home** A breach will be aggravated if, as a consequence, the victim is forced to leave home.

(vi) **Additional aggravating factors** 4.10 In addition to the factors listed above, the following will aggravate a breach of an order:

- the offence is a further breach, following earlier breach proceedings;
- the breach was committed immediately or shortly after the order was made.

Mitigating factors

Breach of a Protective Order Guideline 2006, see www.banksr.com Other Matters Guidelines tab

Mitigating factors page 6 para D i) **Breach was committed after a long period of compliance** para 4.11 If the court is satisfied that the offender has complied with a protective order for a substantial period before a breach is committed, the court should take this into account when imposing sentence for the breach. The history of the relationship and the nature of the contact will be relevant in determining its significance as a mitigating factor.

D (ii) **Victim initiated contact** para 4.12 If the conditions of an order are breached following contact from the victim, this should be considered as mitigation. It is important to consider the history of the relationship and the specific nature of the contact in determining its significance as a mitigating factor.

4.13 Nonetheless it is important for the court to make clear that it is the responsibility of the offender and not the victim to ensure that the order is complied with.

94.14 Key factors

Breach of a Protective Order Guideline 2006, see www.banksr.com Other Matters Guidelines tab

page 7 para E (a) When sentencing for a breach of a protective order (which would have been imposed to protect a victim from further harm), the main aim should be to achieve future compliance with that order.

(b) A court will need to assess the level of risk posed by the offender. If the offender requires treatment or assistance for mental health or other issues, willingness to undergo treatment or accept help may influence sentence.
page 7 1 **Key factors** a) The nature of the conduct that caused the breach of the order, in particular, whether the contact was direct or indirect, although it is important to recognise that indirect contact is capable of causing significant harm or anxiety.
(b) There may be exceptional cases where the nature of the breach is particularly serious but has not been dealt with by a separate offence being charged. In these cases the risk posed by the offender and the nature of the breach will be particularly significant in determining the response.
(c) The nature of the original conduct or offence is relevant to sentencing for the breach in so far as it allows a judgement to be made on the level of harm caused to the victim by the breach, and the extent to which that harm was intended by the offender.
(d) The sentence following a breach is for the breach alone and must avoid punishing the offender again for the offence or conduct as a result of which the order was made.
(e) Where violence is used to breach a Restraining Order or a molestation order, custody is the starting point for sentence.
(f) Non-violent conduct in breach may cross the custody threshold where a high degree of harm or anxiety has been caused to the victim.
(g) Where an order was made in civil proceedings, its purpose may have been to cause the subject of the order to modify behaviour rather than to imply that the conduct was especially serious. If so, it is likely to be disproportionate to impose a custodial sentence for a breach of the order if the breach did not involve threats or violence.
(h) In some cases where a breach might result in a short custodial sentence but the court is satisfied that the offender genuinely intends to reform his or her behaviour and there is a real prospect of rehabilitation, the court may consider it appropriate to impose a sentence that will allow this. This may mean imposing a suspended sentence order or a community order (where appropriate with a requirement to attend an accredited domestic violence programme).
(i) While, in principle, consecutive sentences may be imposed for each breach of which the offender is convicted, the overall sentence should reflect the totality principle.
For the meaning of a medium-level and a low-level community order see **15.12**.
A Band C fine is 150% of net weekly income. For more detail, see **58.28**.

94.15 ***Judicial guidance Pre-2018 guideline case***
R v Thomas 2011 EWCA Crim 2340 The court imposed 15 months' custody for breach of a Restraining Order, following numerous previous breaches. Held. The primary aim of sentencing in this context is to ensure compliance with the Restraining Order and thereby to protect the victim for whose help and assistance it is made.

94.16 ***Persistent offenders/Previous breaches***
R v Rashid 2016 EWCA Crim 1811 D was convicted in his absence of breaching his Restraining Order. He was in a relationship with P for about 2 years. It broke up in 2012 and since then he repeatedly harassed P and her adult daughter, V. Most but not all of the offending was on the telephone. In December 2011, for battery and abusive behaviour, D was conditionally discharged. In February 2014, for threatening words etc. directed at other family members, D was fined. In September 2014, for a course of conduct between February and August 2014, D was given 20 weeks and a Restraining Order. D was released in November 2014. In January 2015, D followed V and shouted abuse at her from his car. He made 11 phone calls and sent two texts to her. One referred to her boyfriend, although V did not understand the text. In April 2015, there were further calls to V. D was arrested. Just before the trial he told V he wasn't going to turn up. D was convicted in his absence and arrested as he tried to flee the country. D was now 56 and had angina. The pre-sentence report for the earlier offence said the offending was premeditated and predatory, motivated by revenge. Further, D made derogatory remarks

about V and expressed misogynistic views. Held. Importantly the breaches did not involve physical contact, although they caused significant anxiety and distress. The offending was just two months after his release. The new offending was exactly the same as before. We strike a balance between the nature of the breaches and the fact these were the first breaches and the fact D was offending again. We think **6 months** not 14, and 6 months consecutive for the bail offence as before.

R v Leigh 2017 EWCA Crim 1035 D was convicted of breaching his Restraining Order. In September 2012, D was made the subject of a Restraining Order. It prevented him from contacting V or her daughter, directly or indirectly, or entering the road in which they lived. D visited V's house at 2 am and banged on the door repeatedly. He was ignored but he returned in the afternoon on four occasions over a 4-hour period. Police attended, and D appeared to be intoxicated and was verbally aggressive to the officers. D was aged 44 at the time of the appeal and had a poor criminal record involving some 26 offences. He had breached this Restraining Order four times previously, receiving a 12-month prison sentence for the last breach. The breaches came only a month after D was released from prison. V lived in fear of D and suffered from panic attacks and psoriasis caused by stress. She had to change her route to and from work to avoid any unwanted attention from D and had suffered severe psychological harm which was continuing. He had once been given a Hospital Order. D's pre-sentence report showed that he had no intention of engaging with the probation service or in seeking assistance for what was then suspected to be a serious mental health problem. From D's repeated abusive behaviour throughout the trial, the Judge was satisfied that D was a man with a frightening demeanour. He said he would sentence outside the *Breach of a Protective Order Guideline 2006*. There was no psychiatric report at the time of sentencing. A report had since been obtained and it highlighted a significant past psychiatric history. D suffered from a schizo-affective disorder. After sentence, he was admitted to a secure psychiatric unit and medication was prescribed. The report said that D's condition was treatable at present in hospital and eventually with close monitoring in the community. Held. The Judge was entitled to move substantially higher than the starting point (26 to 39 weeks' custody for more than one breach). The persistent breaches of the order are at least in part attributable to D's medical condition. **2 years**, not 3.

R v Illing 2017 EWCA Crim 1347 D pleaded to four breaches of a Restraining Order and failing to notify. In October 2009, he received a short prison sentence for breach of a Restraining Order. In August 2012, D was convicted of a sexual offence. He received a prison sentence and a Restraining Order. In February 2015, D received 12 weeks' imprisonment for notification failures. In January 2016, he received another 12 weeks for further notification failures. In April 2016, D was given a non-conviction Restraining Order which prohibited him from contacting a named woman and prohibited him from entering Colchester. Early in May 2016, for offences of harassment and breach of a Restraining Order, D was given a 10-week suspended sentence. Soon after that offences were committed and in September 2016, D was sentenced to a total of 48 weeks for notification failures, breach of a Restraining Order and the activation of the suspended sentence. The day after his release, D went to Colchester to meet a friend, F. On the next day, again went to Colchester to meet F and stayed overnight. That was the notification failure as well as a breach. Three days later, D again visited F. The next day, he again went to Colchester to meet F. The Judge noticed that at the time of the offending, D was subject to post-sentence supervision. He arrived at 20 months for the notification failure, making 15 months after the plea discount. For the breaches he went outside the *Breach of a Protective Order Guideline 2006* and by the same route arrived at 15 months making 30 months in all. Held. There was a complete disregard for the orders of the court. Lengthy prison sentences had not deterred him. However, there was no allegation of contacting the woman named in the Restraining Order. Nonetheless, the court cannot simply ignore repeated breaches of court orders. A radical departure from the guideline was permissible. **2 years** on all the counts concurrent substituted.

See also: *R v Cliff* 2015 EWCA Crim 1091 (Plea during trial. In December 2013, breach of first order by texting former partner (10 weeks). New order made. In July 2014, breach of second order by texting former partner pretending to be his father. Domestic violence convictions in May 2012. Harassment in December 2013 and January 2014. **18 months suspended** was severe but it was designed to protect the victim.)

R v Brown 2015 EWCA Crim 1700, 2016 1 Cr App R (S) 22 (p 148) (Late plea to breach of a Non-Molestation Order. Case 1 Threats to kill and an assault on V, who was vulnerable (6 months). Case 2 Breach by approaching V's address (12 months). Three weeks after release, D called her on his mobile (no answer). **8 months** not 14.)

R v Greengrass 2015 EWCA Crim 1826 (Plea. Order to protect mother. Lived with his grandfather and mother. When awaiting sentence, granted bail. Breached bail and Restraining Order. Three breaches in all. History of violence and defiance of court orders. Consecutive sentences were essential. **14 months** in all not 22.)

R v Fell 2016 EWCA Crim 1983 (Plea. On one day the victim received four calls (not answered). She answered the next call and the defendant said, "Tick tock, Tick tock". The original offences were kidnapping and ABH (28 months). Aged 25. 38 previous convictions,.4 previous for breaches but not on this victim. Held. We start at 20 months not 22, so **18 months** not 20.)

Post-2018 guideline cases

R v O'Hagan 2018 EWCA Crim 272 D pleaded to breaching a Restraining Order. D and V were former partners. In 2006, an indefinite Restraining Order was made prohibiting D from contacting her. Since then D had breached the order eight times and had been given custody for the breaches. D had damaged V's car, threatened her with a knife and made threats over the phone. In 2016, D was released from prison and almost immediately went to V's place of work and said he loved her. Next, he went to her home and confronted V's new partner. D went back to the place of work three times in the next four days. V was extremely distressed about this. D was now aged 34 and had 39 previous convictions including robbery, threats to kill, ABH, malicious communications and the breaches. There were no non-breach offences against V for 10 years. The pre-sentence report said D posed a risk of serious harm to V. The Judge found V had suffered significant psychological harm. Held. We start at 18 months not 27, so with plea 12 months.

R v Saleem 2018 EWCA Crim 2398 D pleaded to breaching his Restraining Order at the Magistrates' Court. He was committed for sentence. D was now aged 51 and had been married for over 20 years. He and his wife, V, had five children. In May 2014, he received a conditional discharge for battery of V. In December 2014, D committed ABH on V and their eldest daughter. In August 2016, for that, with the breach of the conditional discharge, D received 28 months' custody. A Restraining Order prohibiting contact with V and their family was made. D contacted his son on Facebook and in June 2017, he was given a community order for that. In November 2017, he committed three harassment offences and [three] breaches of the Restraining Order. He: a) drove down the street where his family lived, b) visited his extended family around the country asking them to contact V, and c) approached his son. D received 9 months suspended for that. Four months later, V was with one of their daughters in a street when D shouted at them from a parked car saying, "I want to talk to you. I want to come home." V took her daughter into a supermarket. The Judge found the contact had a very serious impact on V and her daughter. Held. This was a 'single breach involving no/minimal contact', so in the lowest level of the then current guideline. We avoid an element of double accounting namely increasing the sentence for the repeated breaches and activating the suspended sentence consecutively for the past behaviour. We move to 6 months, so with plea, **4 months** not 12 consecutive to the 9-month suspended sentence activated in full, making 13 months not 21.

R v McFadyen 2019 EWCA Crim 340 D pleaded to two breach offences (one regarding V and one regarding S). From November 2016 to June 2017, D was in a relationship

with V. It ended because of D's violent assaults on V. That led to a conviction for battery in October 2017, resulting in a Restraining Order for V and her daughter, S. In November 2017, there was harassment against V and a breach (28 days' imprisonment). In December 2017, there was another harassment and breach (community order). From December 2017 to May 2018, D set up Facebook accounts in various names and sent V messages which frightened her, one of which was, "Wait until you bump into me". Some of the messages were abusive. Many were offensive. V suffered from PTSD and depression, which was made worse by this conduct. When interviewed, D said that 'all women were like this, trying to fuck him over and make him look bad'. He also falsely denied leaving voicemails. The victim statement from V described the intolerable effects of D's behaviour. D had in 2016 a conviction for harassment (4 weeks suspended). The Judge said the guideline faded into the margins because of D's utter failure to stop offending in this nasty way. For count 1, she moved to 3 years, and with the plea discount arrived at 31 months. For count 2, she started at 12 months and with a 25% plea discount and totality arrived at 7 months consecutive. Held. The Judge was right to identify two significant aggravating features, the misery caused to V and to a lesser extent S, and D's relentless refusal to comply with any court orders. V was particularly vulnerable because of her illness and the constant effect of D's behaviour. If this was D's first breach the suggested starting point would have been 26-29 weeks' custody. Accepting the messages were 'mild', we move, after totality, to 2 years on count 1 and 6 months on count 2. With plea that is 20 months and 4 months making **2 years** in all.
See also: *R v Green* 2018 EWCA Crim 2682 (D pleaded to two breaches of a Restraining Order. After his relationship with V ended, D harassed and stalked her and her seven-year old son. A Restraining Order was imposed. There were repeated breaches and D was given 18 weeks. Two weeks after D's release, D called V and asked to meet her. D made 298 calls to her which went to voicemail. Because of automatic delete features the number might have been about 400. On two days, D spoke to V at the store where she worked. D was aged 46 with 21 previous convictions, including a) burglary and arson (30 months) and b) harassment (2002, £100 fine; 2003, with breach, conditional discharge; 2004, £100 fine; 2005, £200 fine; May 2017, 18 weeks; November 2017, 1 month; and 2018, stalking with two breaches, 9 months consecutive to the 1 month). The earlier offences related to previous partners. Held. V had to be protected, but 3 years reduced to **2 years** with plea was well within the range.)

94.17 ***Sending electronic or postal messages/Phone calls Pre-2018 guideline cases***

R v London 2016 EWCA Crim 122 D pleaded to breach of a Restraining Order. D bombarded his ex-partner, V, with unwanted telephone calls, some of which were threatening, including threatening V's new boyfriend and anyone she began a relationship with. In less than 11 weeks he sent over 9,200 texts to her. On one occasion, D turned up at her place of work and put his arm around her and took a photo of them both. When arrested, D denied any knowledge of the Restraining Order. D, aged 36, had 53 appearances for sentence involving 106 convictions including public disorder, assaults and criminal damage. However, there was no history of physical domestic violence. In 2012, there were harassment and malicious communication offences involving the care proceedings for his nephew. In January 2014, D was given a conditional discharge for sending a threatening letter. In March 2014, he was given 6 weeks' imprisonment for offences against V. A Restraining Order was made. In May 2014, D breached the Restraining Order and was given a suspended 16-week sentence. He was in breach of that Suspended Sentence Order. His supervising officer said D had little respect for court orders and was not motivated to engage, believing he was hard done by by the courts. The pre-sentence report said, a) D was unable to move on because he wanted to exercise control over V, and b) the likelihood of reconviction was very high. V, who was pregnant with his child, asked for a lenient sentence. The Judge said the messages and the attendance at V's workplace must have caused a huge amount of psychological damage

and pressure. He also said this kind of offending was totally out of sync with the reality of the case. He considered the maximum sentence was a better guide to the sentence than the guideline. Appeal reports said, a) D had a dissocial personality disorder which was linked to his behaviour, b) to reduce the offending D's maladaptive personality traits had to be addressed, and c) D suffered from moderate depression. Held. The Judge was wrong to consider the psychological pressure was severe. We sentence outside the guidelines. We start at 27 months, so with plea **18 months** not 36, with 4 months, not 2, for the breach making 22 months not 38 months.
See also: *R v Farren* 2013 EWCA Crim 2571 (Plea. Sent a threatening text message to son. Previously breached the order by sending threatening text message to ex-wife. Was within the 100-metre exclusion zone of son's house on three occasions on same day. Used a disguise. Custodial sentence merited. Poor report from prison. Starting at 12 months, not 21, **8 months** not 14.)

95 Revocation of New Drivers' Licences

95.1

Road Traffic (New Drivers) Act 1995
Although this order is often called the disqualification of new drivers, the court does not order the defendant to be disqualified. The court instead sends the defendant's details to the Secretary of State, who revokes the driver's licence.
When drivers pass their driving test, they begin a two-year probationary period, see **95.3**. Penalty points that have accrued before the probationary period count in the same way as if 'totting up' were being considered for an adult. Points qualify for the probationary driver if the offence generating the points was within the probationary period but the conviction was after the period.

95.2 *What are the differences between revocation and disqualification until test is passed?*

Note: The main differences are:

(a) Disqualification is an order of the court and revocation is a mandatory administrative act by the Secretary of State.
(b) Disqualification is consequently part of the sentence (whether as a discretionary order or a mandatory order).
(c) There is an appeal in disqualification cases. There is no appeal in revocation cases, see **95.22**.
(d) If a driver who has been disqualified until he passes a test drives without observing the conditions for a provisional licence, he or she commits the offence of driving whilst disqualified. If a driver who has had his or her licence revoked drives without observing the conditions for a provisional licence, he or she commits the offence of driving otherwise than in accordance with a licence. Ed.

Revocation power

95.3 *Two-year probationary period for newly qualified drivers*

Probationary period for newly qualified drivers.
Road Traffic (New Drivers) Act 1995 s 1(1) For the purposes of this Act, a person's probationary period is, subject to section 7 [see **95.5**], the period of two years beginning with the day on which he becomes a qualified driver.
(2) [see **95.4**]
(3)-(4) [Re EEA definitions. Not listed]

95.4 *'Qualified driver' Definition*

Road Traffic (New Drivers) Act 1995 s 1(2) For the purposes of this Act, a person becomes a qualified driver on the first occasion on which he passes:

(a) any test of competence to drive mentioned in Road Traffic Act 1988 s 89(1)(a) or (c),
(b) any test of competence to drive conducted under the law of:

(i) another EEA State,[1070]
(ii) the Isle of Man,
(iii) any of the Channel Islands, or
(iv) Gibraltar.

[For the rest of the section, see **95.3**.]

95.5 *Termination of probationary period*

Early termination of probationary period.

Road Traffic (New Drivers) Act 1995 s 7 For the purposes of this Act a person's probationary period comes to an end if:

(a) an order is made in relation to him under Road Traffic Offenders Act 1988 s 36 (order that a person be disqualified until he passes the appropriate driving test),
(b) after his licence is revoked under section 3, he is granted a full licence following the passing of a test which is a relevant driving test for the purposes of section 4, or
(c) after his test certificate is revoked under Schedule 1 para 5, or his licence and test certificate are revoked under para 8 of that Schedule, he is granted a full licence following the passing of a test which is a relevant driving test for the purposes of paras 6 or 9 of that Schedule.

95.6 *Surrender of licences 6+ penalty points on licence*

Surrender of licences.

Road Traffic (New Drivers) Act 1995 s 2(1) Subsection (2) applies where:

(a) a person is the holder of a licence,
(b) he is convicted of an offence involving obligatory endorsement,
(c) the penalty points to be taken into account under Road Traffic Offenders Act 1988 s 29 (points to be taken into account on conviction) on that occasion number six or more,
(d) the court makes an order falling within section 44(1)(b) of that Act (orders for endorsement) in respect of the offence,
(e) the person's licence shows the date on which he became a qualified driver, or that date has been shown by other evidence in the proceedings, and
(f) it appears to the court, in the light of the order and the date so shown, that the offence was committed during the person's probationary period.

(2) Where this subsection applies, the court must send to the Secretary of State:

(a) a notice containing the particulars required to be endorsed on the counterpart of the person's licence in accordance with the order referred to in subsection (1)(d), and
(b) on their production to the court, the person's licence and its counterpart.

(3)-(4) [see **95.7**]

How the system works

95.7 *Surrender of licences Fixed penalty points*

Road Traffic (New Drivers) Act 1995 s 2(1)-(2) [see **95.6**]

(3) Subsection (4) applies where:

(a) a person's licence and its counterpart have been sent to the fixed penalty clerk under Road Traffic Offenders Act 1988 s 54(7), retained by a vehicle examiner under that section or delivered to the appropriate person in response to a conditional offer issued under section 75 of that Act,
(b) the offence to which the fixed penalty notice or the conditional offer relates is one involving obligatory endorsement,
(c) the appropriate person endorses the number of penalty points to be attributed to the offence on the counterpart of the licence,
(d) the penalty points to be taken into account by the appropriate person in respect of the offence number six or more,[1071]

[1070] Amended by Coroners and Justice Act 2009 Sch 21 para 62(5)
[1071] Amended by Coroners and Justice Act 2009 Sch 21 para 62(5)

(e) the licence shows the date on which the person became a qualified driver, and
(f) it appears to the appropriate person, in the light of the particulars of the offence endorsed on the counterpart of the licence and the date so shown, that the offence was committed during the person's probationary period.

(4) Where this subsection applies:
(a) the appropriate person may not return the licence and its counterpart under Road Traffic Offenders Act 1988 s 57(3) or (4) or 77(1), but
(b) unless the appropriate person is the Secretary of State, he must send them to the Secretary of State.

95.8 ***Pre-test points, Counting***
Adebowale v Bradford Crown Court 2004 EWHC 1741 (Admin) High Court D was awarded six points when a learner. He then passed his test and later received five further points. The DVLA then added the points together and revoked his licence. Held. It was correct. The test did not 'wipe the slate clean'.

95.9 ***What if a driver accumulates six points before passing the first test?***
Note: If a driver accumulates six points before passing his first test he will not have his licence revoked because the trigger offence must take place after he has passed his first test. However, if he receives penalty points after the passing of the test, his licence will be revoked if there are six points within the relevant period (three years). Ed.

95.10 ***What if a driver accumulates six points after passing the second test?***
Note: If a driver accumulates six points, has his or her licence revoked, passes a second test and then accumulates a further six points all within the two years after his or her first test, he or she will not have his or her licence revoked for a second time because his or her probationary period has ended, Road Traffic (New Drivers) Act 1995 s 7. The driver will, however, be liable to be disqualified under the totting up procedure. Ed.

95.11 ***Magistrates' Court Sentencing Guidelines 2008***
Magistrates' Court Sentencing Guidelines 2008, see www.banksr.com Other Matters Guidelines tab The guideline applies to the Magistrates' Court and to the Crown Court hearing appeals or sentencing for summary only offences.[1072]

New drivers
page 186 para 24 Drivers who incur six points or more during the two-year probationary period after passing the driving test will have their licence revoked automatically by the Secretary of State. They will be able to drive only after application for a provisional licence pending the passing of a further test.[1073]
para 25 An offender liable for an endorsement which will cause the licence to be revoked under the new [drivers] provisions may ask the court to disqualify rather than impose points. This will avoid the requirement to take a further test. Generally, this would be inappropriate since it would circumvent the clear intention of Parliament.

Court duties

95.12 ***Duty of the court to send material to Secretary of State***
Road Traffic (New Drivers) Act 1995 Sch 1 para 2(3) Part IV of this Schedule [which deals with the surrender and revocation of licences and test certificates] applies to a person who falls within sub-paragraph (4) or (5):
(4) A person falls within this sub-paragraph if:
(a) he holds a licence issued as a full licence in relation to a class or certain classes of vehicles,
(b) he is treated under Road Traffic Act 1988 s 98(2) as authorised by a provisional licence to drive another class or other classes of vehicles, and
(c) he holds a test certificate which relates to that other class of vehicles or any of those other classes of vehicles.

[1072] Added by Serious Crime Act 2007 Sch 6 para 63(2)
[1073] Serious Crime Act 2015 (Commencement No 1) Regulations 2015 2015/820 para 2

(5) A person falls within this sub-paragraph if he holds:
(a) a licence issued as a full licence in relation to a class or certain classes of vehicles and as a provisional licence in relation to another class or other classes of vehicles, and
(b) a test certificate which relates to that other class of vehicles or any of those other classes of vehicles.

Road Traffic (New Drivers) Act 1995 Sch 1 para 7(1) Where the circumstances mentioned in section 2(1) (see **95.6**) exist with respect to a person to whom this Part of this Schedule applies, sub-paragraph (2) applies instead of section 2(2).

(2) The court must send to the Secretary of State:
(a) a notice containing the particulars required to be endorsed on the counterpart of the person's licence in accordance with the order referred to in section 2(1)(d),
(b) on their production to the court, the person's licence and its counterpart, and
(c) on its production to the court, the person's test certificate.

(3) Where:
(a) the circumstances mentioned in section 2(3) (see **95.7**) exist with respect to a person to whom this Part of this Schedule applies, and
(b) the appropriate person has received the person's test certificate in accordance with paragraph 3(4),

sub-paragraph (4) applies instead of section 2(4).

(4) The appropriate person:
(a) may not return the person's licence and its counterpart under Road Traffic Offenders Act 1988 s 57(3) or (4) or 77(1), but
(b) unless the appropriate person is the Secretary of State, must send them and the person's test certificate to the Secretary of State.

Revocation of licence and test certificate

95.13 *Revocation of licence and test certificate*

Road Traffic (New Drivers) Act 1995 Sch 1 para 8(1) Where the Secretary of State:
(a) has received a notice sent to him under paragraph 7(2)(a) of particulars required to be endorsed on the counterpart of a person's licence or has received the licence and its counterpart under paragraph 7(2)(b) or (4)(b), and
(b) has received the person's test certificate sent to him under paragraph 7(2)(b) or (4)(b) or is satisfied that the person has been issued with a test certificate,

the Secretary of State must by notice served on that person revoke the licence and the test certificate.

(1ZA) Where paragraph 7(4) applies and the appropriate person is the Secretary of State, the Secretary of State must by notice served on the person to whom the fixed penalty notice or conditional offer was given or issued revoke that person's licence and test certificate.

(2) A revocation under this paragraph shall have effect from a date specified in the notice of revocation which may not be earlier than the date of service of that notice.

95.14 *Application of legislation to Crown servants*

The Crown.

Road Traffic (New Drivers) Act 1995 s 8 This Act applies to persons in the public service of the Crown.

95.15 *Obligatory revocation of licence*

Road Traffic (New Drivers) Act 1995 s 3(1) Where the Secretary of State receives:
(a) a notice sent to him under section 2(2)(a) of particulars required to be endorsed on the counterpart of a person's licence, or
(b) a person's licence and its counterpart sent to him in accordance with section 2(2)(b) or (4)(b),

the Secretary of State must by notice served on that person revoke the licence.

(1ZA) Where section 2(4)(a) applies but the appropriate person is the Secretary of State, the Secretary of State must by notice served on the person to whom the fixed penalty notice or conditional offer was given or issued, revoke that person's licence.
(2) A revocation under this section shall have effect from a date specified in the notice of revocation which may not be earlier than the date of service of that notice.

95.16 *'Appropriate person', Definition of*
Road Traffic (New Drivers) Act 1995 s 2(7) In this section and section 3:
'the appropriate person', in relation to a fixed penalty notice, means:
(a) if it was given by a constable or an authorised person, the fixed penalty clerk, and
(b) if it was given by a vehicle examiner or the Secretary of State, the Secretary of State, and
'the appropriate person', in relation to a conditional offer, means:
(a) where the conditional offer was issued under Road Traffic Offenders Act 1988 s 75(1), (2) or (3), the fixed penalty clerk, and
(b) where it was issued under Road Traffic Offenders Act 1988 s 75(1A) or (3B), the Secretary of State.

Surrender of test certificate

95.17 *Persons to whom duty to surrender applies*
Road Traffic (New Drivers) Act 1995 Sch 1 para 2(2) Part II and Part III of this Schedule applies to a person who holds:
(a) a licence issued as a provisional licence, and
(b) a test certificate.

95.18 *Duty of defendant to provide test certificate to the court*
Road Traffic Offenders Act 1988 s 7(1) A person who is prosecuted for an offence involving obligatory or discretionary disqualification and who is the holder of a licence must:
(a) cause it to be delivered to the proper officer of the court not later than the day before the date appointed for the hearing, or
(b) post it, at such a time that in the ordinary course of post it would be delivered not later than that day, in a letter duly addressed to the clerk and either registered or sent by the recorded delivery service, or
(c) have it with him at the hearing,
and the foregoing obligations imposed on him as respects the licence also apply as respects the counterpart to the licence.
Road Traffic (New Drivers) Act 1995 Sch 1 para 2(1) Part II (Schedule 1 para 3) of this Schedule applies to any person to whom Part III or IV of this Schedule applies (Schedule 1 paras 4-9).
Road Traffic (New Drivers) Act 1995 Sch 1 para 3(1) Sub-paragraph (2) applies where:
(a) a person to whom Part II of this Schedule applies is prosecuted for an offence involving obligatory endorsement, and
(b) the time at which the offence for which he is prosecuted is alleged to have occurred is a time during his probationary period.
(2) Any obligations imposed on the person under Road Traffic Offenders Act 1988 s 7 as respects his licence and its counterpart shall also apply as respects his test certificate.
(3) If, in a case where sub-paragraph (2) applies:
(a) the person is convicted in the proceedings in question of an offence involving obligatory endorsement, and
(b) he has not previously caused his test certificate to be delivered or posted it to the proper officer of the court,
he must produce his test certificate to the court.
Road Traffic (New Drivers) Act 1995 Sch 1 para 3(4) In a case where:

(a) the licence of a person to whom this Part of this Schedule applies has (with its counterpart) been sent to the appropriate person under Road Traffic Offenders Act 1988 s 54(7) or delivered to the appropriate person in response to a conditional offer issued under section 75 of that Act,
(b) the offence to which the fixed penalty notice or the conditional offer relates is one involving obligatory endorsement and occurring during his probationary period, and
(c) the person proposes to pay the fixed penalty to the appropriate person,
the person must ensure that when the fixed penalty is paid his test certificate is sent to the appropriate person.

95.19 ***Surrender of a test certificate***
Road Traffic (New Drivers) Act 1995 Sch 1 para 4(3) Where:
(a) the circumstances mentioned in section 2(3)(a) to (d) and (f) (see **95.7**) exist with respect to a person to whom this Part of this Schedule applies,
(b) the appropriate person has received the person's test certificate in accordance with para 3(4), and
(c) the test certificate shows the date on which the person became a qualified driver,
section 2(4) does not apply but if the appropriate person is the fixed penalty clerk sub-paragraph (4) applies instead.
(4) The fixed penalty clerk must send to the Secretary of State:
(a) a notice containing the particulars endorsed on the counterpart of the person's licence, and
(b) the person's test certificate.

95.20 ***A person who fails to provide test certificate commits an offence***
Road Traffic (New Drivers) Act 1995 Sch 1 para 2 (1) Part II (Schedule 1 para 3) of this Schedule applies to any person to whom Part III or IV of this Schedule applies (Schedule 1 paras 4-9).
Road Traffic (New Drivers) Act 1995 Sch 1 para 3(5) A person who without reasonable excuse fails to comply with sub-paragraph (3) or (4) is guilty of an offence and shall be liable on summary conviction to a fine not exceeding Level 3 on the standard scale.

95.21 ***Revocation of test certificate***
Road Traffic (New Drivers) Act 1995 Sch 1 para 5(1) Where the Secretary of State:
(a) has received a notice sent to him under para 4 of particulars required to be endorsed or endorsed on the counterpart of a person's licence, and
(b) has received the person's test certificate sent to him under para 4(2)(b) or (4)(b) or is satisfied that the person has been issued with a test certificate,
the Secretary of State must by notice served on that person revoke the test certificate.
(1ZA) Where section 2(4) is disapplied by para 4(3) and the appropriate person is the Secretary of State, the Secretary of State must by notice served on the person to whom the fixed penalty notice or conditional offer was given or issued revoke that person's test certificate.
(2) A revocation under this paragraph shall have effect from a date specified in the notice of revocation which may not be earlier than the date of service of that notice.
(3) The effect of the revocation of a person's test certificate is that any prescribed conditions to which his provisional licence ceased to be subject when he became a qualified driver shall again apply.

Appeals

95.22 ***Appeals***
Note: A defendant can appeal against the conviction or the sentence which triggers the revocation. However, the revocation is not subject to an appeal because the revocation is not an order of the court but a mandatory administrative task carried out by the Secretary of State. Ed.

Retests

95.23 *New licence not to be issued until driver passes retest*

Re-testing.

Road Traffic (New Drivers) Act 1995 s 4(1) Subject to subsection (5) and section 5, the Secretary of State may not under the Road Traffic Act 1988 Part III grant a person whose licence has been revoked under section 3 a full licence to drive any class of vehicles in relation to which the revoked licence was issued as a full licence…unless he satisfies the Secretary of State that within the relevant period he has passed a relevant driving test.

(2)-(3) [see **95.25**]

(4) In subsection (1) 'the relevant period' means the period beginning:

(a) after the date of the revocation of the licence, and

(b) not more than two years before the date on which the application for the full licence is made.

(5) [see **95.6**]

95.24 *'Relevant driving test', Definition of*

Road Traffic (New Drivers) Act 1995 s 4(2) In this section 'relevant driving test' means, in relation to a person whose licence has been revoked, any test which:

(a) falls within section 1(2)(a) or b), and

(b) is a test of competence to drive any vehicle included in any class of vehicles in relation to which the revoked licence was issued as a full licence.

(3) If the Secretary of State grants a full licence to a person who is required to pass a relevant driving test in order to be granted that licence, the licence granted must (subject to Road Traffic Act 1988 Part IV and Road Traffic Act 1988 s 92) be one authorising that person to drive all the classes of vehicles in relation to which the revoked licence was issued as a full licence.

For the rest of the section, see **95.23**.

Combined with other orders

95.25 *Disqualification, Combined with*

Note: The two procedures operate independently of each other if they apply at the same time or on different occasions. Ed.

95.26 *Disqualification until test is passed, Combined with*

Road Traffic (New Drivers) Act 1995 s 4(5) Subsections (1) and (1A) do not apply to a person whose licence has been revoked under section 3 if, before he passes a relevant driving test, an order is made in relation to him under Road Traffic Offenders Act 1988 s 36 (disqualification until test is passed).

For the rest of the section see **95.23**.

Note: The presumed purpose of this section is to ensure that a driver is not subject to two orders to pass a driving test. If a driver has his or her licence revoked because he or she has six penalty points on his or her licence and then is convicted of causing death by dangerous driving he or she must be ordered to be disqualified until he or she has passed his or her test. The effect of this section ensures that the sole order is the disqualification order. Ed.

95.27 *Totting up, Combined with*

Note: When a probationary driver has his or her licence revoked because they have accrued six penalty points, those points remain on his or her licence. Consequently the totting up procedure will remain applicable at any time the licence accumulates the relevant number of points. Ed.

Restoration of licence without retesting

95.28 *Individual appeals disqualification Licence restored*

Restoration of licence without re-testing in certain cases.

Road Traffic (New Drivers) Act 1995 s 5(1) If the Secretary of State receives notice that a person whose licence has been revoked under section 3 is appealing against a

conviction or endorsement which was the basis or formed part of the basis for the revocation, he must grant that person free of charge a full licence for a period prescribed by regulations.
(2) Regulations under subsection (1) may in particular prescribe:
(a) a period expiring when the appeal is finally determined or abandoned, or
(b) a period expiring on the date on which the revoked licence would have expired if it had not been revoked.
(3) [see **95.29**]
(4)-(5) [see **95.30**]
(6) [see **95.31**]
(7) Any licence granted in accordance with subsection (1) or (4) shall have effect for the purposes of the Road Traffic Acts as if it were a licence granted under Part III of the Road Traffic Act 1988.
(8) [Re Regulation making. Not listed.]
(9) [see **95.34**]

95.29 ***On appeal, Licence endorsed with 6+ points Licence revoked***

Road Traffic (New Drivers) Act 1995 s 5(3) If the regulations prescribe a period other than that mentioned in subsection (2)(a), a licence granted under subsection (1) shall be treated as revoked if:
(a) following the appeal, the penalty points taken into account for the purposes of section 2 are not reduced to a number smaller than six, or
(b) the appeal is abandoned.
For the rest of the section, see **95.28**.

95.30 ***Appeal Quashed conviction etc. Licence restored***

Road Traffic (New Drivers) Act 1995 s 5(4) If, in the case of a person whose licence has been revoked under section 3, the Secretary of State receives notice that a court:
(a) has quashed a conviction which was the basis or formed part of the basis for the revocation of the licence,
(b) has quashed an endorsement which was the basis or formed part of the basis for the revocation of the licence and has not on doing so ordered him to be disqualified, or
(c) has made an order which has the effect of reducing the penalty points taken into account for the purposes of section 2 to a number smaller than six,
then, subject to subsection (5), the Secretary of State must grant that person free of charge a full licence for a period expiring on the date on which the revoked licence would have expired if it had not been revoked.
(5) Subsection (4) does not require the Secretary of State to grant a licence to a person who has been granted a previous licence which has not been surrendered unless that person provides the Secretary of State with an explanation for not surrendering the previous licence that the Secretary of State considers adequate.
For the rest of the section, see **95.28**.

95.31 ***'New' licence must contain same entitlements as 'old' licence***

Road Traffic (New Drivers) Act 1995 s 5(6) If, in accordance with subsection (1) or (4), the Secretary of State grants a full licence to a person whose licence has been revoked under section 3, the licence granted must be one authorising that person to drive all the classes of vehicles in relation to which the revoked licence was issued as a full licence.
For the rest of the section, see **95.28**.

95.32 ***Regulations may make different provision for different cases***

Road Traffic (New Drivers) Act 1995 s 5(9) Regulations under this section may:
(a) include such incidental or supplementary provision as appears to the Secretary of State to be expedient,
(b) make different provision for different cases.
For the rest of the section, see **95.28**.

95.33 ***Restoration of licence on passing test***
Road Traffic (New Drivers) Act 1995 Sch 1 para 6(1) Subject to Part V of this Schedule, the Secretary of State may not under Road Traffic Act 1988 Part III grant a person whose test certificate has been revoked under para 5 a full licence…unless he satisfies the Secretary of State that within the relevant period he has passed a relevant driving test.
(2) In this paragraph 'relevant driving test' means, in relation to a person whose test certificate has been revoked, any test which:
(a) falls within paragraph (a) or (b) of section 1(2), and
(b) is a test of competence to drive any vehicle included in any class of vehicles that, immediately before his test certificate was revoked, he was permitted to drive without observing prescribed conditions.
Road Traffic (New Drivers) Act 1995 s 1(2)[1074] For the purposes of this Act, a person becomes a qualified driver on the first occasion on which he passes:
(a) any test of competence to drive mentioned in Road Traffic Act 1988 s 89(1)(a) or (c),
(b) any test of competence to drive conducted under the law of:
(i) another EEA State,
(ii) the Isle of Man,
(iii) any of the Channel Islands, or
(iv) Gibraltar.
(3) If the Secretary of State grants a full licence to a person who is required to pass a relevant driving test in order to be granted that licence, the licence granted must (subject to Road Traffic Act 1988 Part IV or section 92) be one authorising that person to drive all the classes of vehicles that, immediately before his test certificate was revoked, he was permitted to drive without observing prescribed conditions.
Road Traffic (New Drivers) Act 1995 Sch 1 para 10 Where:
(a) a person's test certificate has been revoked under paragraph 5 or his licence and test certificate have been revoked under paragraph 8, but
(b) before he passes a relevant driving test, an order is made in relation to him under Road Traffic Offenders Act 1988 s 36 (disqualification until test is passed),
paragraph 6(1) or, as the case may be, paragraph 9(1) shall not apply to him.

95.34 ***Retest Issuing a new licence Revocation of licence and test certificate***
Road Traffic (New Drivers) Act 1995 Sch 1 para 9(1) Subject to Part V of this Schedule, the Secretary of State may not under Road Traffic Act 1988 Part III grant a person whose licence and test certificate have been revoked under paragraph 8…a full licence to drive any class of vehicles mentioned in sub-paragraph (4), unless he satisfies the Secretary of State that within the relevant period he has passed a relevant driving test.
(2) In this paragraph 'relevant driving test' means any test which:
(a) falls within paragraph (a) or (b) of section 1(2) [see **95.4**], and
(b) is a test of competence to drive any vehicle included in any class of vehicles mentioned in sub-paragraph (4).
(3) If the Secretary of State grants a full licence to a person who is required to pass a relevant driving test in order to be granted that licence, the licence granted must (subject to Road Traffic Act 1988 Part IV and Road Traffic Act 1988 s 92) be one authorising that person to drive all the classes of vehicles mentioned in sub-paragraph (4).
(4) The classes of vehicles are:
(a) any class of vehicles in relation to which the revoked licence was issued as a full licence, and
(b) any class of vehicles:
(i) that he was treated under Road Traffic Act 1988 s 98(2) as authorised to drive under a provisional licence, or
(ii) in relation to which the revoked licence was issued as a provisional licence,

[1074] As amended by Crime (International Co-operation) Act 2003 Sch 5 para 56

and that, immediately before the test certificate was revoked, he was permitted to drive without observing prescribed conditions.
Road Traffic (New Drivers) Act 1995 Sch 1 para 10 Where:
(a) a person's test certificate has been revoked under paragraph 5 or his licence and test certificate have been revoked under paragraph 8, but
(b) before he passes a relevant driving test, an order is made in relation to him under Road Traffic Offenders Act 1988 s 36 (disqualification until test is passed),
paragraph 6(1) or, as the case may be, paragraph 9(1) shall not apply to him.

96 Risk of Sexual Harm Orders

96.1
Sexual Offences Act 2003 s 123-127
This was a stand-alone preventive order. It was repealed on 8 March 2015[1075] by Anti-social Behaviour, Crime and Policing Act 2014 s 113 and Sch 5 para 5. It was replaced by the Sexual Risk Order.
Variation/discharge There is power to vary, renew and discharge the order.[1076]
Offences If a person without reasonable excuse: a) does anything which he is prohibited under the order from doing or b) fails to surrender his or her passport, he or she commits an offence.[1077] The offence is an either way offence with a maximum sentence on indictment of 5 years or on summary conviction 6 months and/or a £5,000 fine for offences committed before 12 March 2015 and an unlimited fine thereafter.[1078] There are maximum fines for those aged under 18, see **13.44**.

97 Sample Counts/Specimen Counts/Representative Offences

97.1
Compensation orders For the rules about compensation orders and sample counts, see para **17.5**.

97.2 *How to draft the indictment*

R v A 2015 EWCA Crim 177, 2 Cr App R (S) 12 (p 115)[1079] D was convicted of rape and sexual assault by penetration of his wife, V. There was vaginal, oral and anal rape. During the period, V said she was raped every few days. The prosecution relied on three multiple incident counts relying on Practice Direction (Criminal Proceedings: Arraignment) 2008 IV 34.14. Held. If the indictment had been drafted alleging, 'on not less than five occasions' with another alternative count alleging a single incident, the Judge would have had a solid basis for sentencing. Here the Judge breached the requirement that the defendant should not be sentenced for crimes for which he had not been convicted. Sentenced reduced.

97.3 *Basic rules*

R v Burfoot 1991 12 Cr App R (S) 252 D pleaded to six counts of burglary and was convicted of a further 19 counts. D had indicated that he wished for an additional 600 counts to be taken into consideration, but later reneged. He was sentenced on the basis that the additional 19 counts were specimen counts. Held. At the time of sentencing, D's case was that he had not committed the other offences and D should have been sentenced only on the six counts to which he pleaded guilty, and the 19 counts on which he was convicted.
R v Canavan and Others 1998 1 Cr App R (S) 243[1080] LCJ The Court heard three unconnected cases to clarify the law for sample counts. Two cases involved indecent assaults. One involved witness intimidation. Held. A defendant is not to be convicted of

[1075] Anti-social Behaviour, Crime and Policing Act 2014 Sch 5 para 5(1)
[1076] Sexual Offences Act 2003 s 125 and Anti-social Behaviour, Crime and Policing Act 2014 s 114(2)(a)
[1077] Words inserted by Protection of Freedoms Act 2012 Sch 9 para 146(b)(i)
[1078] Inserted by Policing and Crime Act 2009 Sch 7 para 25(2)
[1079] This case is also known as *R v S* 2015 EWCA Crim 177.
[1080] This case is also known as *R v Kidd* 1998 1 Cr App R 243.

any offence with which he is charged unless and until his guilt is proved. These are basic principles. It is not easy to see how a defendant can lawfully be punished for offences for which he has not been indicted and which he has denied. It is said that the trial judge can form his own judgment of the evidence. But this is to deprive the appellant of his right to trial by jury in respect of the other alleged offences. Unless such other offences are admitted, such deprivation cannot in our view be consistent with principle. Sentences reduced accordingly.

Where a defendant is convicted on an indictment charging him with offences said to be representative of other similar criminal offences committed by him, it is inconsistent with the principle that the court should take into account such other offences so as to increase the sentence if the defendant does not admit the commission of other offences and does not ask the court to take them into consideration. Nor does statute legitimise the practice of sentencing for unindicted, unadmitted offences.

Att-Gen's Ref No 82 of 2002 2003 EWCA Crim 1078, 2 Cr App R (S) 115 (p 673) Provided that the admitted basis on which an offender pleads guilty embraces the wider course of conduct, then it was proper for a sentencing judge to proceed to pass sentence on that basis.

R v Tovey 2005 EWCA Crim 530, 2 Cr App R (S) 100 (p 606) LCJ The *R v Kidd* 1998 approach is not to be qualified based on reasonable inferences the judge can draw. We have no difficulty with *Att-Gen's Ref No 82 of 2002*. If there is a clear acceptance by the offender that the court can take into account the wider course of conduct, then it is the equivalent of an informal invitation to take into consideration the other offences. There is no requirement to be excessively technical as long as there is a clear admission or finding of guilt. In the majority of situations, the problem will be most satisfactorily alleviated by the appropriate framing of an indictment.

R v Hartley 2011 EWCA Crim 1299, 2012 1 Cr App R (S) 7 (p 91) D was convicted of two counts of sexual abuse committed in the 1980s. Each count related to a period of activity and not to identifiable incidents. The Judge was reminded that D was convicted of two offences only. However, the Judge sentenced for the 'whole period of time…involved here'. Held. If counts are framed which are extracted from an alleged course of conduct, conviction on those counts cannot be taken to be a conviction of multiple additional unframed counts which have never appeared on the indictment. That would deprive the defendant of the opportunity to have his guilt determined by a jury, see *R v Canavan and Others* 1998 1 Cr App R (S) 243.

R v A 2015 EWCA Crim 177, 2 Cr App R (S) 12 (p 115)[1081] D was convicted of rape and sexual assault by penetration of his wife, V. There was vaginal, oral and anal rape. During the period, V said she was raped every few days. The prosecution relied on three multiple incident counts relying on Practice Direction (Criminal Proceedings: Arraignment) 2008 IV 34.14. Held. There is a long established rule that it is for the judge to determine the factual basis for sentencing. It is for the jury to determine how many times the defendant committed the crime. It is not permissible to draft a single count to constitute an entire course of conduct. The Judge can only sentence for the offences which the jury had convicted the defendant of. A balance has to be struck between including sufficient counts to give the court adequate sentencing powers and not burdening the indictment. If the indictment had been drafted alleging, 'on not less than five occasions' with another alternative count alleging a single incident, the Judge would have had a solid basis for sentencing. Here the Judge breached the requirement that the defendant should not be sentenced for crimes for which he had not been convicted. Sentence reduced.

See also: *R v Younas* 2017 EWCA Crim 1, 1 Cr App R (S) 44 (p 348) (D pleaded to two anal rapes of a child. Nothing on the indictment to suggest either count was a sample count. First time matter raised was by the Judge in the prosecution opening. Defence

[1081] This case is also known as *R v S* 2015 EWCA Crim 177.

advocate acquiesced. Held. The Judge's approach was not permissible. It was likely that D thought he was pleading to two rapes. We proceed on the basis there were just two rapes.)

Old case: *Anderson v DPP* 1978 67 Cr App R 185 (Lords The Judge made a Criminal Bankruptcy Order based on incidents which were not subject to counts in the indictment. Held. It is essential that the practice should not be followed except with the express and unequivocal assent of the defendant himself.)

97.4 *Multiple incident counts*

Criminal Procedure Rules 2015 2015/1490 Rule 10.2(2) More than one incident of the commission of the offence may be included in a count if those incidents taken together amount to a course of conduct having regard to the time, place or purpose of commission.

Criminal Practice Directions 2015 EWCA Crim 1567 para II 10A.11[1082] Criminal Practice Rules 10.2(2) allows a single count to allege more than one incident of the commission of an offence in certain circumstances. Each incident must be of the same offence. The circumstances in which such a count may be appropriate include, but are not limited to, the following:

a) the victim on each occasion was the same, or there was no identifiable individual victim as, for example, in a case of the unlawful importation of controlled drugs or of money laundering;

b) the alleged incidents involved a marked degree of repetition in the method employed or in their location, or both;

c) the alleged incidents took place over a clearly defined period, typically (but not necessarily) no more than about a year;

d) in any event, the defence is such as to apply to every alleged incident. Where what is in issue differs in relation to different incidents, a single "multiple incidents" count will not be appropriate (though it may be appropriate to use two or more such counts according to the circumstances and to the issues raised by the defence).

10A.12 Even in circumstances such as those set out above, there may be occasions on which a prosecutor chooses not to use such a count, in order to bring the case within Proceeds of Crime Act 2002 s 75(3)(a) (criminal lifestyle established by conviction of three or more offences in the same proceedings): for example, because section 75(2)(c) of that Act does not apply (criminal lifestyle established by an offence committed over a period of at least six months). Where the prosecutor proposes such a course, it is unlikely that Criminal Procedure Rules Part 1 (the overriding objective) will require an indictment to contain a single "multiple incidents" count in place of a larger number of counts, subject to the general principles set out at paragraph 10A.3.

10A.13 For some offences, particularly sexual offences, the penalty for the offence may have changed during the period over which the alleged incidents took place. In such a case, additional "multiple incidents" counts should be used so that each count only alleges incidents to which the same maximum penalty applies.

10A.14 In other cases, such as sexual or physical abuse, a complainant may be in a position only to give evidence of a series of similar incidents without being able to specify when or the precise circumstances in which they occurred. In these cases, a 'multiple incidents' count may be desirable. If on the other hand the complainant is able to identify particular incidents of the offence by reference to a date or other specific event, but alleges that in addition there were other incidents which the complainant is unable to specify, then it may be desirable to include separate counts for the identified incidents and a 'multiple incidents' count or counts alleging that incidents of the same offence occurred 'many' times. Using a 'multiple incidents' count may be an appropriate alternative to using 'specimen' counts in some cases where repeated sexual or physical abuse is alleged. The choice of count will depend on the particular circumstances of the

[1082] As amended by Criminal Practice Directions 2015 Amendment No 2 2016 EWCA Crim 1714

case and should be determined bearing in mind the implications for sentencing set out in *R v Canavan and Others* 1998 1 Cr App R (S) 243. In *R v A* 2015 EWCA Crim 177, 2 Cr App R (S) 12 (p 115) the Court of Appeal reviewed the circumstances in which a mixture of multiple incident and single incident counts might be appropriate where the prosecutor alleged sustained sexual abuse.

R v A 2015 EWCA Crim 177, 2 Cr App R (S) 12 (p 115)[1083] D was convicted of rape and assault by penetration. The counts were multi-allegation counts. Held. There is a long-established rule that it is for the judge to determine the factual basis of sentencing, apart from the rare cases in which the jury is asked to return a special verdict. But there is an undoubted difference between establishing the facts that are relevant to the charge and deciding how many times a defendant [has] committed the crimes for which he is to be sentenced. Generally, when the prosecution allege that a defendant has perpetrated a number of similar acts on different occasions, it is impermissible for the accused to be charged with a single offence as representing, or constituting, the entire course of conduct for the purposes of sentence. The cardinal rule is that the judge may sentence only for those offences in respect of which the accused has been convicted, or which he has asked to be taken into consideration on sentence. para 47 The central answer to this problem [of determining the proper basis for sentencing] is to be identified in the purpose underpinning multiple counts. It is to enable the prosecution to reflect the defendant's alleged criminality when the offences are so similar and numerous that it is inappropriate to indict each occasion, or a large number of different occasions, in separate charges. When the prosecution fails to specify a sufficient minimum number of occasions within the multiple incident count or counts, they are not making proper use of this procedure. In cases of sustained abuse, it will often be unhelpful to draft the count as representing, potentially, no more than two incidents. Indeed, in this case, if there had been a multiple incident count alleging, for example, 'on not less than five occasions' with an alternative of one or more specimen counts relating to single incidents for the jury to consider if they were unsure the offending had occurred on multiple occasions, the judge would have had a solid basis for understanding the ambit of the jury's verdict and he would have been able to pass an appropriate sentence. Therefore, the prosecution needs to ensure that there is one or more sufficiently broad course of conduct counts, or a mix of individual counts and course of conduct counts, such that the judge will be able to sentence the defendant appropriately on the basis of his criminality as revealed by the counts on which he is convicted. In most cases it will be unnecessary for the counts to be numerous, but they should be sufficient in number to enable the judge to reflect the seriousness of the offending by reference to the central factors in the case, e.g. the number of victims, the nature of the offending and the length of time over which it extended. Therefore, in drafting the indictment, a balance needs to be struck between including sufficient counts to give the court adequate sentencing powers and unduly burdening the indictment. As the editors of Archbold Criminal Pleading Evidence and Practice 2015 at paragraph 1-225 have observed, the indictment must be drafted in such a way as to leave no room for misinterpretation of a guilty verdict and regard must be had to the possible views reached by the jury and to the position of the judge, so as to enable realistic sentencing. Because this wasn't done, the only fair way is to sentence D for just two incidents for each count.

For more detail see **314.55** in Volume 2.

R v H 2018 EWCA Crim 541 D pleaded to assault by penetration of a child under 13 and sexual assault on a person under 13. He accepted three assaults by penetration and five assaults. The prosecution summary set out a wider course of offending. The Judge did not address the factual dispute and sentenced for 'numerous incidents'. Held. The counts in the indictment did not specify that the counts were multi-incident. para 26 Absent an agreed basis going wider (for example, via TICs, or by way of an acceptance that the

[1083] This case is also known as *R v S* 2015 EWCA Crim 177.

charges are samples of the extent of overall offending admitted in interview), D would be liable to be sentenced only for the two offences to which he pleaded. Charges must make clear the course of conduct that is being alleged. The number of incidents was limited to the number admitted in interview.
For more detail, see **314.72** in Volume 2.
R v Hyde-Gomes 2018 EWCA Crim 2364 D was convicted of attempted rape and other historical sex offences. Held. para 28 It is necessary for the particulars for multiple offences to make clear the minimum number of occasions on which the offending took place. As that hadn't happened here, the number must be two only.

97.5 *The Barton approach*
Barton v DPP 2001 EWHC 223 (Admin) High Court An information which alleged theft of just over £1,300, over a period of years, did not offend against the rule that an information should only allege a single offence. There were 94 takings from the cash register. The prosecution's case was set out in a schedule with dates and amounts involved. Despite the fact that the individual appropriations were each capable of being separately identified, it was permissible to charge the whole course of conduct as a continuous offence because the defendant had no specific explanation for individual takings and put forward the same defence for all takings. The Magistrate accordingly was in a position to disregard any amount that he was unsure that the defendant had taken. If they had been charged as separate offences, the average amount would have been about £15. Even if there had been 10 informations the amount would still be under £200. It simply would not represent the overall criminality, which was over £1,300. Specimen counts/informations are no longer a possibility. To have 94 separate informations would have rightly been regarded as oppressive.
R v Tovey 2005 EWCA Crim 530, 2 Cr App R (S) 100 (p 606) at 615 LCJ The approach in *Barton v DPP* 2001 is perfectly acceptable. The approach should, however, not be stretched further to cases where the evidence for the prosecution and the defence raises different issues in relation to different counts. As to the Crown Court, in the appropriate circumstances, the same approach could appropriately be applied. This would be subject to no unfairness being caused to the defendant. It is ensuring fairness to the defendant that is at the heart of the *R v Kidd* 1998 approach. However, unless resort was had to special verdicts, depending on the facts of a particular case, it would not be known if the jury were only satisfied that some and not other offences had been committed. Bearing in mind the complications that can arise from special verdicts, the approach in *Barton v DPP* 2001 can only safely be used if the case of both the prosecution and the defence was the same in respect of all the acts said to be part of the same activity.

97.6 *Judge determining issue*
Domestic Violence, Crime and Victims Act 2004 s 17 The prosecution may apply to a judge for a trial to take place on the basis that the trial of some, but not all, of the counts included in the indictment may be conducted without a jury if:

(a) the number of counts is likely to mean that a trial by jury of all the counts would be impracticable,

(b) each count or group of counts to be tried by the jury could be regarded as a sample of the counts to be tried without a jury, and

(c) it is in the interests of justice for an order to be made.

Criminal Practice Directions 2015 EWCA Crim 1567 para II 10A.4 The Directions lay down the procedure for such trials.

98 SENDING CASES TO THE CROWN COURT AND COMMITTALS

98.1
Powers of Criminal Courts (Sentencing) Act 2000 s 3-7

Powers to send cases to the Crown Court/commit to the Crown Court

98.2 ***List of various powers***

Description	Statute	Details	Crown Court powers	Source of Crown Court powers
Cases where magistrates may/must decline jurisdiction				
Indictable and either way cases: Adults	Crime and Disorder Act 1998 s 51(1)	See **98.4**	Full Crown Court powers	–
Adults: Related matters	Crime and Disorder Act 1998 s 51(3)	See **98.5**	**Summary matters** If a guilty plea, Magistrates' Court powers only. If no plea, no power to deal with. **Other matters** Full Crown Court powers[1084]	Crime and Disorder Act 1998 s 6(4)-(5) see **98.28**
Children and young persons	Crime and Disorder Act 1998 s 51A(1)	See **98.6**	A wide variety of powers depending what the offence is and sometimes whether the defendant is a persistent offender.	–
Children and young persons: Related matters	Crime and Disorder Act 1998 s 51A(5)	See **98.7**	**Summary matters** If a guilty plea, Magistrates' Court powers only. If no plea, no power to deal with. **Other matters** Full Crown Court powers[1085]	Crime and Disorder Act 1998 s 6(4)-(5) see **98.28**

[1084] This is an assumption, as I can find no section that deals with the available powers, although it may be lost in all this legislative spaghetti.

[1085] Again, this is an assumption, as I can find no section that deals with the available powers, although it may be lost in all this legislative spaghetti.

Description	Statute	Details	Crown Court powers	Source of Crown Court powers
Children and young persons: With an adult	Crime and Disorder Act 1998 s 51(7)	See **98.8**	Indictable offences only, see Crime and Disorder Act 1998 s 5(7) at **98.6** A wide variety of powers depending what the offence is and sometimes whether the defendant is a persistent offender.	–
Where a notice has been given by DPP in certain cases involving children	Crime and Disorder Act 1998 s 51C	–	Full Crown Court powers	–
Plea indicated at the Magistrates' Court (this and those below are committals for trial)	Powers of Criminal Courts (Sentencing) Act 2000 s 4	See **98.13**	Crown Court powers when an either way offence, otherwise Magistrates' Court powers	Powers of Criminal Courts (Sentencing) Act 2000 s 4(5), see **98.13**
Plea indicated at the Magistrates' Court: Related offences	Powers of Criminal Courts (Sentencing) Act 2000 s 4(1)	See **98.13**	Crown Court powers when Powers of Criminal Courts (Sentencing) Act 2000 s 5(1) applies, otherwise Magistrates' Court powers[1086]	Powers of Criminal Courts (Sentencing) Act 2000 s 5(1), see **98.27**
Crown Court should deal with case: Offender aged under 18	Powers of Criminal Courts (Sentencing) Act 2000 s 3B[1087]	See **98.14**	Crown Court powers	Powers of Criminal Courts (Sentencing) Act 2000 s 5A, see **98.32**

[1086] Powers of Criminal Courts (Sentencing) Act 2000 s 4(5) and (5)(1), see para **98.31** and **98.26** respectively.

[1087] This section was amended by Criminal Justice and Courts Act 2015 s 53, which substituted a new Powers of Criminal Courts (Sentencing) Act 2000 s 3B(1), see **98.19**. In force 13/4/15, Criminal Justice and Courts Act 2015 (Commencement No 1, Saving and Transitional Provisions) Order 2015 2015/778

Description	Statute	Details	Crown Court powers	Source of Crown Court powers
Plea indicated at the Magistrates' Court: Related offences: Offender aged under 18	Powers of Criminal Courts (Sentencing) Act 2000 s 4A	See **98.15**	Crown Court powers	Powers of Criminal Courts (Sentencing) Act 2000 s 5A, see **98.32**
After magistrates have dealt with case				
Greater punishment required: Either way offences	Powers of Criminal Courts (Sentencing) Act 2000 s 3(2)	See **98.9**	Full Crown Court powers[1088]	Powers of Criminal Courts (Sentencing) Act 2000 s 5(1), see **98.26**
Greater punishment required: Additional offences	Powers of Criminal Courts (Sentencing) Act 2000 s 6(2)	See **98.11**	Crown Court powers when an either way offence, otherwise Magistrates' Court powers	Powers of Criminal Courts (Sentencing) Act 2000 s 6(2), see **98.11**
Specific orders/offences				
Many of the situations below can be committed under the general powers (sections 3(2) and 6(2)) above as well.				
Attendance Centre Order, Breach of	Powers of Criminal Courts (Sentencing) Act 2000 Sch 5 para 2(1)(c)	See **7.2**	Revoke the order. Re-sentence: £1,000 fine or custody	Powers of Criminal Courts (Sentencing) Act 2000 s 5(1), see **7.2**
Bail, Failure to surrender to	Bail Act 1976 s 6(6)	See **215.9** in Volume 2	12 months or a fine or both	Bail Act 1976 s 7, see **215.1** in Volume 2
Conditional discharge, Breach of	Powers of Criminal Courts (Sentencing) Act 2000 s 13(5)(a)	See **20.4**	The same powers as the court that imposed the order	Powers of Criminal Courts (Sentencing) Act 2000 s 13(6), see **20.6**
Community orders, Breach of	Powers of Criminal Courts (Sentencing) Act 2000 Sch 8 para 9(6)	See **16.18**	Criminal Justice Act 2003 Sch 19 para 6 Crown Court orders only.[1089] Crown Court powers	Criminal Justice Act 2003 Sch 8 para 10(1), see **16.8**

[1088] So, for example, if the defendant pleads guilty to arson at the Magistrates' Court, he or she can be sentenced to life.
[1089] Criminal Justice Act 2003 Sch 8 para 9(6)

Description	Statute	Details	Crown Court powers	Source of Crown Court powers
After trial, prosecution ask for a committal so a confiscation order can be made	Proceeds of Crime Act 2002 s 70	See **21.11**	a) if the Magistrates' Court state they would have committed under section 3(2), Crown Court powers, b) otherwise, Magistrates' Court powers	a) Proceeds of Crime Act 2002 s 70(5) and 71(2) b) Proceeds of Crime Act 2002 s 71(3), see **21.11**
Confiscation order: Additional matters	Proceeds of Crime Act 2002 s 70(2)-(3)	See **21.11**	a) if the Magistrates' Court state they would have committed under section 3(2), Crown Court powers, b) otherwise, Magistrates' Court powers	a) Proceeds of Crime Act 2002 s 70(5) and 71(2) b) Proceeds of Crime Act 2002 s 71(3), see **21.11**
Restriction Order, Offender committed with a view to making after a trial	Mental Health Act 1983 s 43	See **67.27**	a) Hospital Order with/without a Restriction Order, or b) if no such order made, Magistrates' Court powers only	Mental Health Act 1983 s 43(2), see **67.27**
Ditto	Mental Health Act 1983 s 44	See **67.22**	Where offender is committed under section 43 above, he or she may be committed to hospital as opposed to custody	Mental Health Act 1983 s 44(1) see **67.22**
Suspended Sentence Order, Breach of: Offences that trigger breach	Criminal Justice Act 2003 Sch 12 para 11(2)	See **107.7**	Crown Court orders only. If a summary only offence, the maximum. If an either way offence, Crown Court powers	This is from the maximums for the offences.[1090]

[1090] I am unable to find part of any statute that deals with this specifically.

Description	Statute	Details	Crown Court powers	Source of Crown Court powers
Youth Rehabilitation Order, Breach of	Criminal Justice and Immigration Act 2008 Sch 2 para 7(1)	See **120.12**	a) £2,500 fine (£250 if aged under 14) or b) Crown Court powers. Order must be: a) a Crown Court order and b) one with a Criminal Justice and Immigration Act 2008 Sch 1 para 36 order. For list, see **120.13**.	Criminal Justice and Immigration Act 2008 Sch 2 para 8(2), see **120.13**
Specific defendants				
Corporate defendants	Powers of Criminal Courts (Sentencing) Act 2000 s 3(5) and 6(1)	See **98.16**	Full Crown Court powers	Powers of Criminal Courts (Sentencing) Act 2000 s 5(1), see **98.26**
Serious and complex fraud cases	Crime and Disorder Act 1998 s 51B	–	Full Crown Court powers	–
Dangerous offenders (who may require an extended sentence or life)	Powers of Criminal Courts (Sentencing) Act 2000 s 3A(1)	See **98.18**	Crown Court powers[1091]	Powers of Criminal Courts (Sentencing) Act 2000 s 5(1), see **98.26**
Dangerous offenders: Defendant under 18	Powers of Criminal Courts (Sentencing) Act 2000 s 3C(1)	See **98.18** and **98.35**	Crown Court powers[1092]	Powers of Criminal Courts (Sentencing) Act 2000 s 5(1), see **98.26**
Dangerous offenders: Related offences	Powers of Criminal Courts (Sentencing) Act 2000 s 3C(3) and 6(1)	See **98.18**	If a summary only offence, the maximum. If an either way offence, Crown Court powers	This is from the maximums for the offences.[1093]
Note: Usually, dangerous defenders can be committed under the general powers listed above as well. Ed.				

98.3 ***Judicial comment***

R v Ruth 2014 EWCA Crim 546 The Court grappled with various Acts to determine the committal situation. Held. We must observe that the legislation is of a needless complexity, now common in legislation affecting the administration of criminal justice. Its wholesale revision, into a more readily comprehensible form, would be welcome.

[1091] Powers of Criminal Courts (Sentencing) Act 2000 s 3A(1)
[1092] Powers of Criminal Courts (Sentencing) Act 2000 s 3C and 5A
[1093] I am unable to find part of any statute that deals with this specifically.

98.4 *Sending cases to the Crown Court Adults*

Sending cases to the Crown Court: adults

Crime and Disorder Act 1998 s 51(1) Where an adult appears or is brought before a magistrates' court ('the court') charged with an offence and any of the conditions mentioned in subsection (2) below is satisfied, the court shall send him forthwith to the Crown Court for trial for the offence.

(2) Those conditions are:

(a) that the offence is an offence triable only on indictment other than one in respect of which notice has been given under Crime and Disorder Act 1998 s 51B or 51C below;

(b) that the offence is an either-way offence and the court is required under Magistrates' Courts Act 1980 s 20(9)(b), 21, 22A(2)(b), 23(4)(b) or (5) or 25(2D) to proceed in relation to the offence in accordance with subsection (1) above;

(c) that notice is given to the court under section 51B or 51C below in respect of the offence.

(3)-(11) [see **98.5** and **98.7**]

(12) In the case of an adult charged with an offence:

(a) if the offence satisfies paragraph (c) of subsection (2) above, the offence shall be dealt with under subsection (1) above and not under any other provision of this section or section 51A below;

(b) subject to paragraph (a) above, if the offence is one in respect of which the court is required to, or would decide to, send the adult to the Crown Court under:

(i) subsection (5) above; or

(ii) subsection (6) of section 51A below,

the offence shall be dealt with under that subsection and not under any other provision of this section or section 51A below.

98.5 *Sending cases to the Crown Court Adults Related matters*

Crime and Disorder Act 1998 s 51(3) Where the court sends an adult for trial under subsection (1) [see **98.4**], it shall at the same time send him to the Crown Court for trial for any either-way or summary offence with which he is charged and which:

(a) (if it is an either-way offence) appears to the court to be related to the offence mentioned in subsection (1) above; or

(b) (if it is a summary offence) appears to the court to be related to the offence mentioned in subsection (1) above or to the either-way offence, and which fulfils the requisite condition (as defined in subsection (11) below).

(4) Where an adult who has been sent for trial under subsection (1) above subsequently appears or is brought before a magistrates' court charged with an either-way or summary offence which:

(a) appears to the court to be related to the offence mentioned in subsection (1) above; and

(b) (in the case of a summary offence) fulfils the requisite condition,

the court may send him forthwith to the Crown Court for trial for the either-way or summary offence.

(5) and (6) [Re co-defendants arrested after a case is sent to the Crown Court]

(7)-(9) [see **98.8**]

(10) The trial of the information charging any summary offence for which a person is sent for trial under this section shall be treated as if the court had adjourned it under Magistrates' Courts Act 1980 s 10 and had not fixed the time and place for its resumption.

(11) A summary offence fulfils the requisite condition if it is punishable with imprisonment or involves obligatory or discretionary disqualification from driving.

Crime and Disorder Act 1998 s 51A(6) Where:

(a) the court sends a child or young person ("C") for trial under subsection (2) or (4) above; and

(b) an adult appears or is brought before the court on the same or a subsequent occasion charged jointly with C with an either-way offence for which C is sent for trial under subsection (2) or (4) above, or an either-way offence which appears to the court to be related to that offence,

the court shall where it is the same occasion, and may where it is a subsequent occasion, send the adult forthwith to the Crown Court for trial for the either-way offence.

(7) Where the court sends an adult for trial under subsection (6) above, it shall at the same time send him to the Crown Court for trial for any either-way or summary offence with which he is charged and which:

(a) (if it is an either-way offence) appears to the court to be related to the offence for which he was sent for trial; and

(b) (if it is a summary offence) appears to the court to be related to the offence for which he was sent for trial or to the either-way offence, and which fulfils the requisite condition.

(8) The trial of the information charging any summary offence for which a person is sent for trial under this section shall be treated as if the court had adjourned it under Magistrates' Courts Act 1980 s 10 and had not fixed the time and place for its resumption.

(9) A summary offence fulfils the requisite condition if it is punishable with imprisonment or involves obligatory or discretionary disqualification from driving.

Crime and Disorder Act 1998 s 51E For the purposes of sections 50A to 51D above:

(a) "adult" means a person aged 18 or over, and references to an adult include a corporation;

(b) "either-way offence" means an offence triable either way;

(c) an either-way offence is related to an indictable offence if the charge for the either-way offence could be joined in the same indictment as the charge for the indictable offence;

(d) a summary offence is related to an indictable offence if it arises out of circumstances which are the same as or connected with those giving rise to the indictable offence.

R v Osman 2017 EWCA Crim 2178 D was charged with affray and possession of a bladed article and was released on bail. He failed to attend court as required. He was then charged with two bail offences. He indicated that he would be pleading not guilty. The Magistrates declined jurisdiction on the other charges and D was committed for trial. The bail matters were purportedly committed under Crime and Disorder Act 1998 s 51(3). At the Crown Court, D pleaded to breach of bail. [It looks as if the alternative bail count was dropped.] Held. Bail offences under Bail Act 1976 s 6(1) and (2) are not strictly speaking 'summary' offences. They are only triable at the court where the bail [in question] had been granted. The bail offences were not related to the other offences. The committal was a nullity. Had D pleaded or been found guilty, the Magistrates could have committed the bail matters if they thought it appropriate. (The Court then reconvened itself as a Magistrates' Court and D pleaded to breach of bail. The Court passed a concurrent rather than a consecutive sentence for the bail offence.)

98.6 *Sending cases to the Crown Court Children and young persons*

Sending cases to the Crown Court: children and young persons

Crime and Disorder Act 1998 s 51A(1) This section is subject to Magistrates' Courts Act 1980 s 24A and 24B (which provide for certain offences involving children or young persons to be tried summarily).

(2) Where a child or young person appears or is brought before a magistrates' court ("the court") charged with an offence and any of the conditions mentioned in subsection (3) below is satisfied, the court shall send him forthwith to the Crown Court for trial for the offence.

(3) Those conditions are:

(a) [homicide, and certain minimum sentence];

(b) [Powers of Criminal Courts (Sentencing) Act 2000 s 91 offences];
(c) that notice is given to the court under section 51B or 51C below in respect of the offence;
(d) that the offence is a specified offence (within the meaning of Criminal Justice Act 2003 s 224) and it appears to the court that if he is found guilty of the offence the criteria for the imposition of a sentence under Criminal Justice Act 2003 s 226B [extended sentences] would be met.

(4) Where the court sends a child or young person for trial under subsection (2) above, it may at the same time send him to the Crown Court for trial for any indictable or summary offence with which he is charged and which:
(a) (if it is an indictable offence) appears to the court to be related to the offence mentioned in subsection (2) above; or
(b) (if it is a summary offence) appears to the court to be related to the offence mentioned in subsection (2) above or to the indictable offence, and which fulfils the requisite condition (as defined in subsection (9) below).

98.7 ***Sending cases to the Crown Court Children and young persons Related matters***

Crime and Disorder Act 1998 s 51A(5) Where a child or young person who has been sent for trial under subsection (2) above subsequently appears or is brought before a magistrates' court charged with an indictable or summary offence which:
(a) appears to the court to be related to the offence mentioned in subsection (2) above; and
(b) (in the case of a summary offence) fulfils the requisite condition,
the court may send him forthwith to the Crown Court for trial for the indictable or summary offence.

(6)-(7) [see **98.5**]

(8) The trial of the information charging any summary offence for which a person is sent for trial under this section shall be treated as if the court had adjourned it under section 10 of the 1980 Act and had not fixed the time and place for its resumption.

(9) A summary offence fulfils the requisite condition if it is punishable with imprisonment or involves obligatory or discretionary disqualification from driving.

(10) In the case of a child or young person charged with an offence:
(a) if the offence satisfies any of the conditions in subsection (3) above, the offence shall be dealt with under subsection (2) above and not under any other provision of this section or section 51 above;
(b) subject to paragraph (a) above, if the offence is one in respect of which the requirements of subsection (7) of section 51 above for sending the child or young person to the Crown Court are satisfied, the offence shall be dealt with under that subsection and not under any other provision of this section or section 51 above.

(11)-(12) [not listed]

Crime and Disorder Act 1998 s 51E For the purposes of sections 50A to 51D above:
(a) "adult" means a person aged 18 or over, and references to an adult include a corporation;
(b) "either-way offence" means an offence triable either way;
(c) an either-way offence is related to an indictable offence if the charge for the either-way offence could be joined in the same indictment as the charge for the indictable offence;
(d) a summary offence is related to an indictable offence if it arises out of circumstances which are the same as or connected with those giving rise to the indictable offence.

98.8 ***Sending cases to the Crown Court Children and young persons With an adult***

Crime and Disorder Act 1998 s 51(7) Where:

(a) the court sends an adult ('A') for trial under subsection (1), (3) or (5) [see **98.4** and **98.5**]; and
(b) a child or young person appears or is brought before the court on the same or a subsequent occasion charged jointly with A with an indictable offence for which A is sent for trial under subsection (1), (3) or (5) above, or an indictable offence which appears to the court to be related to that offence,

the court shall, if it considers it necessary in the interests of justice to do so, send the child or young person forthwith to the Crown Court for trial for the indictable offence.
(8) Where the court sends a child or young person for trial under subsection (7) above, it may at the same time send him to the Crown Court for trial for any indictable or summary offence with which he is charged and which:
(a) (if it is an indictable offence) appears to the court to be related to the offence for which he is sent for trial; and
(b) (if it is a summary offence) appears to the court to be related to the offence for which he is sent for trial or to the indictable offence, and which fulfils the requisite condition.

(9) Subsections (7) and (8) above are subject to Magistrates' Courts Act 1980 s 24A and 24B (which provide for certain cases involving children and young persons to be tried summarily).
(10) The trial of the information charging any summary offence for which a person is sent for trial under this section shall be treated as if the court had adjourned it under section 10 of the 1980 Act and had not fixed the time and place for its resumption.

98.9 ***General power Either way offences etc.***
Committal for sentence on summary trial of offence triable either way
Powers of Criminal Courts (Sentencing) Act 2000 s 3(1) Subject to subsection (4), see **98.17**, this section applies where on the summary trial of an offence triable either way a person aged 18 or over is convicted of the offence.
(2) If the court is of the opinion:
(a) that the offence or the combination of the offence and one or more offences associated with it was so serious that greater punishment should be inflicted for the offence than the court has power to impose, or
(b) in the case of a violent or sexual offence, that a custodial sentence for a term longer than the court has power to impose is necessary to protect the public from serious harm from him,

the court may commit the offender in custody or on bail to the Crown Court for sentence in accordance with section 5(1), see **98.26**.
(3) Where the court commits a person under subsection (2) above, section 6 below (which enables a Magistrates' Court, where it commits a person under this section in respect of an offence, also to commit him to the Crown Court to be dealt with in respect of certain other offences) shall apply accordingly.
Powers of Criminal Courts (Sentencing) Act 2000 s 6(1) This section applies where a Magistrates' Court ('the committing court') commits a person in custody or on bail to the Crown Court under any enactment mentioned in subsection (4) to be sentenced or otherwise dealt with in respect of an offence ('the relevant offence').
Powers of Criminal Courts (Sentencing) Act 2000 s 6(4) The enactments referred to in subsection (1) above are:..
(b) Powers of Criminal Courts (Sentencing) Act 2000 s 3-4A (committal for sentence for offences triable either way),

Magistrates' Court Sentencing Guidelines Update March 2012 page 18c, see www.banksr.com Other Matters Guidelines tab There is ordinarily no statutory restriction on committing an either way case for sentence following conviction. The general power of the Magistrates' Court to commit to the Crown Court for sentence after a finding that a

case is suitable for summary trial and/or conviction continues to be available where the court is of the opinion that the offence (and any associated offences) is so serious that greater punishment should be inflicted than the court has power to impose.
R v Sheffield Crown Court ex parte DPP 1994 15 Cr App R (S) 768 High Court Magistrates accepted jurisdiction and D and M pleaded to unlawful possession of a firearm and ammunition. The case was adjourned for reports. The matter was next before a Magistrate who considered his powers were inadequate and committed the defendants for sentence. The Crown Court accepted that the committal was invalid as all the aggravating factors were considered by the Magistrate. Held. The wording of the statute clearly allows a Magistrates' Court to form an opinion that the offence or offences ought to be committed to Crown Court, notwithstanding that the court has already accepted jurisdiction. The committal was valid. [The old rule was displaced by the statutory changes.]
R v North Essex JJs ex parte Lloyd 2001 2 Cr App R (S) 15 (p 86) High Court LCJ D pleaded to an offence under Insolvency Act 1986. He was committed for sentence on the basis that their sentencing powers (specifically, to fine D) were insufficient. Held. There is no reason why magistrates cannot take advantage of section 38 (now Powers of Criminal Courts (Sentencing) Act 2000 s 3(2)) if they consider that the appropriate punishment is a fine but that their powers to impose a fine are restricted by the statutory limit at a figure which is too low a punishment for the particular circumstances of the case which is before them.
For powers on committal under this section see **98.26**.
Note: Since this case was reported there are usually unlimited fines and new procedures for that, see **58.7**. Ed.

98.10 ***Greater sentencing powers required Other***
Committal for sentence in certain cases where offender committed in respect of another offence
Powers of Criminal Courts (Sentencing) Act 2000 s 6(1) This section applies where a Magistrates' Court ('the committing court') commits a person in custody or on bail to the Crown Court under any enactment mentioned in subsection (4) to be sentenced or otherwise dealt with in respect of an offence ('the relevant offence').
Powers of Criminal Courts (Sentencing) Act 2000 s 6(4) The enactments referred to in subsection (1) above are:
(a) Vagrancy Act 1824 (incorrigible rogues)
(b) Powers of Criminal Courts (Sentencing) Act 2000 s 3-4A [see **98.9** (committal for sentence for offences triable either way)],
(c) Powers of Criminal Courts (Sentencing) Act 2000 s 13(5) of this Act (conditionally discharged person convicted of further offence),
(d) [Repealed]
(e) Criminal Justice Act 2003 Sch 12 para 11(2) (committal to Crown Court where offender convicted during operational period of suspended sentence).
Note: In December 2013, the Government announced that it intended to repeal Vagrancy Act 1824 s 4. It has still not happened. Ed.

98.11 ***Additional offences***
Powers of Criminal Courts (Sentencing) Act 2000 s 6(2) Where this section applies and the relevant offence is an indictable offence, the committing court may also commit the offender, in custody or on bail as the case may require, to the Crown Court to be dealt with in respect of any other offence whatsoever in respect of which the committing court has power to deal with him (being an offence of which he has been convicted by that or any other court).
(3) Where this section applies and the relevant offence is a summary offence, the committing court may commit the offender, in custody or on bail as the case may require, to the Crown Court to be dealt with in respect of:

(a) any other offence of which the committing court has convicted him, being either:
(i) an offence punishable with imprisonment, or
(ii) an offence in respect of which the committing court has a power or duty to order him to be disqualified under Road Traffic Offenders Act 1988 s 34-36 (disqualification for certain motoring offences), or
(b) any suspended sentence in respect of which the committing court has under Criminal Justice Act 2003 Sch 12 para 11(1) power to deal with him.

R v Day 2018 EWCA Crim 2637 D was committed to the Crown Court for being in breach of his Crown Court 6-month suspended sentence (section 6). At the same time, D was committed for a burglary, two thefts and an attempted theft (section 6). He was sentenced to 12 months for the burglary. Held. That sentence was justified. However, the Crown Court was restricted to the Magistrates' Court powers for the burglary, so the maximum was 6 months, which we substitute.

Note: The exact committing power is not referred to. The alternative might have been to proceed in a robust way, see **98.43**, and ensure that an adequate sentence was passed. Ed.

98.12 ***Children and young offenders***

Committal for sentence of young offenders on summary trial of certain serious offences

Powers of Criminal Courts (Sentencing) Act 2000 s 3B(1)[1094] This section applies where on the summary trial of an offence mentioned in section 91(1) of this Act a person aged under 18 is convicted of the offence.

(2) If the court is of the opinion that:
(a) the offence, or
(b) the combination of the offence and one or more offences associated with it,
was such that the Crown Court should, in the court's opinion, have power to deal with the offender as if the provisions of section 91(3) below applied, the court may commit him in custody or on bail to the Crown Court for sentence in accordance with section 5A(1) below (see **98.35**).

(3) Where the court commits a person under subsection (2) above, section 6 below (see **98.11**) (which enables a Magistrates' Court, where it commits a person under this section in respect of an offence, also to commit him to the Crown Court to be dealt with in respect of certain other offences) shall apply accordingly.

R (DPP) v South Tyneside Youth Court 2015 EWHC Crim 1455 (Admin), 2 Cr App R (S) 59 D, aged 15, was charged with three oral rapes and a child sex offence against V aged 6-7. D was aged 14-15 at the time of the offences. Before the amendment to section 3B was in force, the District Judge at the Youth Court decided to retain jurisdiction, believing (wrongly) he had a general power of committal. The prosecution appealed saying the starting point was 10 years (for Category 3A) or 8 years (for Category 3B) reduced by half to one-quarter because of D's age and so the case should be committed for trial. Held. The law is complex and by no means straightforward. Before the amendments were made to section 3B (see above), there were only two routes for a child or young offender to be committed for sentence. First, where the offender indicated a plea of guilty for an offence in the Powers of Criminal Courts (Sentencing) Act 2000 s 91 list and second, using the powers in section 3B or where the dangerousness provisions were made out, using the powers in section 3C of the Act. Once the decision as to venue was made it was irrevocable. If the Court retained jurisdiction for trial, it had to retain jurisdiction for sentence. The District Judge's belief as to his powers was wrong. This changed on 13 April 2015. The Youth Court from then on had the power to commit if the Crown Court should [deal] with the offender.

Note: The Court also dealt with the relationship between this new power to commit and allocation decisions, which are not dealt with in this book. Ed.

[1094] As amended by Criminal Justice and Courts Act 2015 s 53. In force 13/4/15

98.13 ***Plea indicated at the Magistrates' Court (including related[1095] offences)***

Committal for sentence on indication of guilty plea to offence triable either way

Powers of Criminal Courts (Sentencing) Act 2000 s 4(1) This section applies where:

(a) a person aged 18 or over is before a Magistrates' Court ('the court') charged with a triable either way offence ('the offence'),

(b) he or (where applicable) his representative indicates under Magistrates' Courts Act 1980 s 17A, 17B or 20 that he would plead guilty if the offence were to proceed to trial,

(c) proceeding as if the Magistrates' Courts Act 1980 s 9(1) were complied with and he pleaded guilty under it, the court convicts him of the offence.

(1A) But this section does not apply to an offence as regards which this section is excluded by Magistrates' Courts Act 1980 s 17D (certain offences where value involved is small).

(2) If the court has sent[1096] the offender to the Crown Court for trial for one or more related offences, it may commit him in custody or on bail to the Crown Court to be dealt with in respect of the offence in accordance with section 5(1).

(3) If the power conferred by subsection (2) above is not exercisable but the court is still to determine to, or to determine whether to, send the offender to the Crown Court for trial under Crime and Disorder Act 1998 s 51 or 51A for one or more related offences:

(a) it shall adjourn the proceedings relating to the offence until after it has made those determinations, and

(b) if it sends the offender to the Crown Court for trial for one or more related offences, it may then exercise that power.

Note: The opening phrases in section 4(3) may be a parliamentary mistake, but that is what the Act says. Ed.

(4) Where the court:

(a) under subsection (2) commits the offender to the Crown Court to be dealt with in respect of the offence, and

(b) does not state that, in its opinion, it also has power so to commit him under Powers of Criminal Courts (Sentencing) Act 2000 s 3(2), or, as the case may be, section 3A(2),[1097] section 5(1) (see **98.27**) shall not apply unless he is convicted before the Crown Court of one or more of the related offences.

(5) Where section 5(1) (see **98.27**) does not apply, the Crown Court may deal with the offender in respect of the offence in any way in which the Magistrates' Court could deal with him if it had just convicted him of the offence.

(6) Where the court commits a person under subsection (2) above, Powers of Criminal Courts (Sentencing) Act 2000 s 6(1) (which enables a Magistrates' Court, where it commits a person under this section in respect of an offence, also to commit him to the Crown Court to be dealt with in respect of certain other offences) shall apply accordingly.

(7) For the purposes of this section one offence is related to another if, were they both to be prosecuted on indictment, the charges for them could be joined in the same indictment.

(8) In reaching any decision under or taking any step contemplated by this section:

(a) the court shall not be bound by any indication of sentence given in respect of the offence under Magistrates' Courts Act 1980 s 20 (procedure where summary trial appears more suitable), and

(b) nothing the court does under this section may be challenged or be the subject of any appeal in any court on the ground that it is not consistent with an indication of sentence.

[1095] 'Related' is not a word used by Parliament. Parliament uses the word 'other'. The word 'related' is used because the power to commit these offences requires another offence to be involved.

[1096] Word substituted by Criminal Justice Act 2003 Sch 3(1) para 24

[1097] Words inserted by Criminal Justice Act 2003 Sch 3(1) para 24(6)

R v Sallis 2003 EWCA Crim 233, 2 Cr App R (S) 67 (p 394) D indicated pleas of guilty to two offences of possession of a class A drug with intent to supply (heroin and crack cocaine). Being an either way offence, and D having indicated guilty pleas, the Magistrates' Court was required to proceed as if the proceedings were the beginning of a summary trial and D had pleaded (see Magistrates' Courts Act 1980 s 17A). D was committed under Powers of Criminal Courts (Sentencing) Act 2000 s 4 (where D had indicated pleas to one or more related offences). D received 3 years concurrent for each offence. Held. The Justices did not state that they felt that they had power to commit under Powers of Criminal Courts (Sentencing) Act 2000 s 3 (committal where the offence was so serious that greater punishment should follow than was available in the Magistrates' Court). Without such a statement, the Crown Court's powers are limited to that of the Magistrates' Court. Sentence reduced to 6 months consecutive.
R v Qayum 2010 EWCA Crim 2237 D was committed for trial for matters including a bladed article under Powers of Criminal Courts (Sentencing) Act 2000 s 3 (greater punishment required) and for theft under Powers of Criminal Courts (Sentencing) Act 2000 s 6 (related offence). At the Crown Court he received 2 years for the theft and 9 months consecutive for the bladed article. Held. This was unlawful as the maximum for the theft was 6 months, see Powers of Criminal Courts (Sentencing) Act 2000 s 7(1). The distinction between these two committal powers is critical and fundamental. We rearrange the sentence to 12 months for the bladed article consecutive to 6 months for the theft.
For powers on committal under this section, see **98.9** and **98.27**.
Children and young offenders see para **98.33**.

98.14 ***Plea indications given at the Magistrates' Court Offender under 18***
Committal for sentence of young offenders on summary trial of certain serious offences
Powers of Criminal Courts (Sentencing) Act 2000 s 3B(1)[1098] This section applies where on the summary trial of an offence mentioned in section 91(1) of this Act a person aged under 18 is convicted of the offence.
(2) If the court is of the opinion that:
(a) the offence; or
(b) the combination of the offence and one or more offences associated with it,
was such that the Crown Court should, in the court's opinion, have power to deal with the offender as if the provisions of section 91(3) below applied, the court may commit him in custody or on bail to the Crown Court for sentence in accordance with section 5A(1) below.
(3) Where the court commits a person under subsection (2) above, section 6 below (which enables a Magistrates' Court, where it commits a person under this section in respect of an offence, also to commit him to the Crown Court to be dealt with in respect of certain other offences) shall apply accordingly.
Powers of Criminal Courts (Sentencing) Act 2000 s 5A(1) Where an offender is committed by a Magistrates' Court for sentence under section 3B, the Crown Court shall inquire into the circumstances of the case and may deal with the offender in any way in which it could deal with him if he had just been convicted of the offence on indictment before the court.

98.15 ***Plea indications given at the Magistrates' Court Offender under 18: Related offences***
Crime and Disorder Act 1998 s 51 or 51A
Committal for sentence on indication of guilty plea by child or young person with related offences
Powers of Criminal Courts (Sentencing) Act 2000 s 4A(1) This section applies where:

[1098] As amended by Criminal Justice and Courts Act 2015 s 53(1) and (2). In force 13/4/15

(a) a person aged under 18 appears or is brought before a Magistrates' Court ('the court') on an information charging him with an offence mentioned in subsection (1) of section 91 below ('the offence'),

(b) he or his representative indicates under Magistrates' Courts Act 1980 s 24A or 24B (as the case may be) (child or young person to indicate intention as to plea in certain cases) that he would plead guilty if the offence were to proceed to trial, and

(c) proceeding as if section 9(1) of that Act were complied with and he pleaded guilty under it, the court convicts him of the offence.

(2) If the court has sent the offender to the Crown Court for trial for one or more related offences, that is to say one or more offences which, in its opinion, are related to the offence, it may commit him in custody or on bail to the Crown Court to be dealt with in respect of the offence in accordance with section 5A(1) [of this Act].

(3) If the power conferred by subsection (2) above is not exercisable but the court is still to determine to, or to determine whether to, send the offender to the Crown Court for trial under Crime and Disorder Act 1998 s 51 or 51A for one or more related offences:

(a) it shall adjourn the proceedings relating to the offence until after it has made those determinations; and

(b) if it sends the offender to the Crown Court for trial for one or more related offences, it may then exercise that power.

Note: The opening phrases in section 4A(3) may be a parliamentary mistake, but that is what the Act says. Ed.

(4) Where the court:

(a) under subsection (2) above commits the offender to the Crown Court to be dealt with in respect of the offence; and

(b) does not state that, in its opinion, it also has power so to commit him under section 3B(2) or, as the case may be, section 3C(2) above,

section 5A(1) below shall not apply unless he is convicted before the Crown Court of one or more of the related offences.

(5) Where section 5A(1) below does not apply, the Crown Court may deal with the offender in respect of the offence in any way in which the Magistrates' Court could deal with him if it had just convicted him of the offence.

(6) Where the court commits a person under subsection (2) above, section 6 below (which enables a Magistrates' Court, where it commits a person under this section in respect of an offence, also to commit him to the Crown Court to be dealt with in respect of certain other offences) shall apply accordingly.

(7) Section 4(7) above applies for the purposes of this section as it applies for the purposes of that section.

Powers of Criminal Courts (Sentencing) Act 2000 s 5A(1) Where an offender is committed by a Magistrates' Court for sentence under section 4A, the Crown Court shall inquire into the circumstances of the case and may deal with the offender in any way in which it could deal with him if he had just been convicted of the offence on indictment before the court.

Conditional discharges, Breach of see the **CONDITIONAL DISCHARGE, BREACH OF** ***Power to commit for breach of a conditional discharge*** para at **20.4**.

Community orders see the **COMMUNITY ORDERS** ***Committals to Crown Court for re-sentencing*** para at **16.18**.

98.16 ***Companies and public bodies as defendants***

Powers of Criminal Courts (Sentencing) Act 2000 s 3(5) The preceding provisions of this section shall apply in relation to a corporation as if:

(a) the corporation were an individual aged 18 or over, and

(b) in subsection (2) above, paragraph (b) and the words 'in custody or on bail' were omitted.

R v F Howe and Son (Engineers) Ltd 1999 2 Cr App R (S) 37 In the case of a company, magistrates can properly commit for sentence on the basis that their powers to fine are insufficient.

R v North Essex JJs ex parte Lloyd 2001 2 Cr App R (S) 15 (p 86) High Court LCJ D pleaded to an offence under Insolvency Act 1986. He was committed for sentence on the basis that their sentencing powers (specifically, to fine D) were insufficient. Held. There is no reason why D should not be committed where they consider a fine the appropriate penalty, but also consider the statutory limit is too low in light of the facts of the case.

See also the **COMPANIES AND PUBLIC BODIES AS DEFENDANTS** chapter.

98.17 ***Criminal damage Exception***

Powers of Criminal Courts (Sentencing) Act 2000 s 3(4) [Section 3] does not apply in relation to an offence as regards which this section is excluded by Magistrates' Courts Act 1980 s 33 (certain offences where value involved is small).

98.18 ***Dangerousness Criminal Justice Act 2003***

Committal for sentence of dangerous adult offenders

Powers of Criminal Courts (Sentencing) Act 2000 s 3A(1) This section applies where on the summary trial of a specified offence triable either way a person aged 18 or over is convicted of the offence.

(2) If, in relation to the offence, it appears to the court that the criteria for the imposition of a sentence under Criminal Justice Act 2003 s 226A[1099] would be met, the court must commit the offender in custody or on bail to the Crown Court for sentence in accordance with section 5(1) below.

Powers of Criminal Courts (Sentencing) Act 2000 s 3C(1) This section applies where on the summary trial of a specified offence a person aged under 18 is convicted of the offence.

(2) If, in relation to the offence, it appears to the court that the criteria for the imposition of a sentence under Criminal Justice Act 2003 s 226B[1100] would be met, the court must commit the offender in custody or on bail to the Crown Court for sentence in accordance with section 5A(1), see **98.32**.

(3) Where the court commits a person under subsection (2) above, Powers of Criminal Courts (Sentencing) Act 2000 s 6 below (which enables a Magistrates' Court, where it commits a person under this section in respect of an offence, also to commit him to the Crown Court to be dealt with in respect of certain other offences) shall apply accordingly.

R v Robson 2006 EWCA Crim 1414, 2007 1 Cr App R (S) 54 (p 301) D was aged 17 when he was convicted at the Magistrates' Court of two specified and serious offences. When he came to be sentenced in the Crown Court, he was aged 18. The Judge applied the dangerous offenders provisions. Held. The date that matters for determining the sentence was the date of conviction.

See also ***Dangerous young offenders*** para at **98.35**.

Mentally disordered defendants see the **HOSPITAL AND GUARDIANSHIP ORDERS** ***Magistrates' power to commit for sentence*** para at **67.27**.

Has the Court prevented itself from having a committal?

98.19 ***Committing case after jurisdiction has been accepted Magistrates' Court***

R v Sheffield Crown Court ex parte DPP 1994 15 Cr App R (S) 768 High Court Magistrates accepted jurisdiction and D and M pleaded to unlawful possession of a firearm and ammunition. The case was adjourned for reports. The matter was next before a stipendiary Magistrate who considered his powers were inadequate and committed the defendants for sentence. The Crown Court accepted that the committal was invalid as all the aggravating factors were considered by the Magistrates. Held. The wording of the

[1099] Words substituted by Legal Aid, Sentencing and Punishment of Offenders Act 2012 Sch 21 para 8
[1100] Words substituted by Legal Aid, Sentencing and Punishment of Offenders Act 2012 Sch 21 para 9

statute clearly allows a Magistrates' Court to form an opinion that the offence or offences ought to be committed to Crown Court, notwithstanding that the court has already accepted jurisdiction. The committal was valid. [The old rule was displaced by the statutory changes.]

98.20 ***Indication of summary disposal may prevent committal/Legitimate expectation***

R v Rennes 1985 7 Cr App R (S) 343 After an adjournment for a community service assessment, D was committed to Crown Court and sentenced to 12 months for offences of dishonesty. Held. Each case of this type depends on what the defendant has been led to expect. There can be no absolute rule that where a community service assessment is included among the reports, and where that assessment is favourable, a sentence of imprisonment will automatically be quashed. In practice it seems to me that magistrates would in every case be wise to give the sort of warning which I understand is usually given in these cases. D's legitimate expectation ought not be defeated. Imprisonment quashed.

R v Southampton Magistrates' Court ex parte Sansome 1999 1 Cr App R (S) 112 High Court It will not be sufficient to establish that a defendant merely held an expectation of a certain disposal. It will be necessary to show that the court had made a promise to the defendant, on which he formed a legitimate expectation.

R v Nottingham Magistrates' Court ex parte Davidson 2000 1 Cr App R (S) 167 High Court LCJ D committed an offence of aggravated vehicle taking. He admitted that offence and was bailed. He subsequently committed the same and admitted that offence. Having indicated that he would plead to the offences, the Magistrates' accepted jurisdiction. The case was adjourned for reports. Before a differently constituted bench, D was committed to Crown Court, and the Court rejected the contention that it was bound. Held. Where an indication had been given that a defendant will be disposed of summarily, without the express statement that a differently constituted bench could form an alternative opinion, the legitimate expectation created will bind the court.

Thornton v CPS 2010 EWHC 346 (Admin), 2 Cr App R (S) 65 (p 434) High Court No judicial review will lie on the basis of 'legitimate expectation' if the expectation was founded upon a decision of the bench which was so unreasonable as to be perverse, or was a decision that no reasonable bench, properly directing itself, could have reached. Where an expectation is based on an indication which is inconsistent with the Sentencing Guidelines Council guidelines, it may well be that a defendant does not have a legitimate expectation. It will depend on the facts.

Note: It may be that the changes to Powers of Criminal Courts (Sentencing) Act 2000 in 2015, see **98.14**, were designed to remove this principle, as the power to commit was widened.

Procedure: Magistrates' Court

98.21 ***Must inform defence of intention to commit***

R v North Essex JJs ex parte Lloyd 2001 2 Cr App R (S) 15 (p 86) LCJ It seems to me that it would be sensible if magistrates, in the situation which existed here where they were minded to commit an offender for sentence under section 38 (now Powers of Criminal Courts (Sentencing) Act 2000 s 3(2)), were to intimate that that is the course which they are considering before they actually take the decision to commit. This will enable advocates appearing on behalf of the offender to advance any arguments which they feel it would be useful to deploy in order to persuade the magistrates to take a different course.

98.22 ***Reasons? Is there a duty to give***

R v Leith 1983 JP 193 D pleaded to theft offences. He was a persistent thief. Magistrates committed him for sentence and sent a letter about his alcohol problems. They believed a longer sentence might deter him and other alcoholics from stealing. Held. When

committing a defendant to Crown Court for sentence, the Magistrates may communicate their reasons for doing so. However, they must: a) be stated in open court and b) be communicated to the appellate court, the appellant and the respondent.
R v Wirral Magistrates' Court ex parte Jermyn 2001 1 Cr App R (S) 137 (p 485) High Court A committal for sentence is not the sort of decision for which reasons have to be given, as any person so committed has the opportunity to make full representations to the sentencing court in due course as to the appropriate penalty.
R v North Essex JJs ex parte Lloyd 2001 2 Cr App R (S) 15 (p 86) LCJ High Court If an offender is committed for sentence on the basis that the powers of punishment in respect of the fine are inadequate, it would be helpful if the magistrates say so. Any statement would not bind a judge of the Crown Court, but it would be extremely valuable for him to know the basis upon which the committal had been made.

98.23 ***Bail position generally remains the same***
R v Rafferty 1998 2 Cr App R (S) 449 LCJ When committing a defendant to the Crown Court for sentence, the usual practice as regards bail will be to leave the situation unchanged. If he was in custody prior to the committal hearing, he should usually be committed in custody.

98.24 ***Papers to be sent to the Crown Court***
Criminal Practice Directions 2015 EWCA Crim 1567 para VII K.1 Criminal Procedure [Rules 2015] Rule 28.10 applies when a case is committed to the Crown Court for sentence and specifies the information and documentation that must be provided by the Magistrates' Court. On a committal for sentence any reasons given by the magistrates for their decision should be included with the documents. All of these documents should be made available to the judge in the Crown Court if the judge requires them, in order to decide before the hearing questions of listing or representation or the like. They will also be available to the court during the hearing if it becomes necessary or desirable for the court to see what happened in the lower court.
Criminal Procedure Rules 2015 2015/1490 Rule 28.10(1) This rule applies where a Magistrates' Court or the Crown Court convicts the defendant and:

(a) commits or adjourns the case to another court:
(i) for sentence, or
(ii) for the defendant to be dealt with for breach of a deferred sentence, a conditional discharge, or a suspended sentence of imprisonment, imposed by that other court,
(b) deals with a deferred sentence, a conditional discharge, or a suspended sentence of imprisonment, imposed by another court, or
(c) makes an order that another court is, or may be, required to enforce.

(2) Unless the convicting court otherwise directs, the court officer must, as soon as practicable:

(a) where paragraph (1)(a) applies, arrange the transmission from the convicting to the other court of a record of any relevant:
(i) certificate of conviction,
(ii) Magistrates' Court register entry,
(iii) decision about bail, for the purposes of Bail Act 1976 s 5,
(iv) note of evidence,
(v) statement or other document introduced in evidence,
(vi) medical or other report,
(vii) representation order or application for such order, and
(viii) interim driving disqualification.
(b) where paragraph (1)(b) or (c) applies, arrange:
(i) the transmission from the convicting to the other court of notice of the convicting court's order, and
(ii) the recording of that order at the other court;

(c) in every case, notify the defendant and, where the defendant is aged under 14, an appropriate adult, of the location of the other court.

Sentencing powers on committal

Note: For the sentencing powers for the specific committal powers, e.g. confiscation and breach of bail, see **98.2**.

98.25 ***Accepting jurisdiction does not limit Crown Court's powers, Accepting***

R v Lowes 1988 10 Cr App R (S) 175 The proposition that Magistrates' Courts Act 1980 s 38 (now Powers of Criminal Courts (Sentencing) Act 2000 s 3(2)) restricted the Crown Court's sentencing powers to that of the Magistrates' Court once summary jurisdiction had been accepted, prior to committal for sentence, was incorrect.

98.26 ***Greater punishment is required/Dangerous offenders/Related offence-s Crown Court powers***

Powers of Criminal Courts (Sentencing) Act 2000 s 5(1) Where an offender is committed by a Magistrates' Court for sentence under section 3 (greater punishment required) (see **98.9**), 3A (committal for dangerous offenders) (see **98.18**), or 4 (related offences), the Crown Court shall inquire into the circumstances of the case and may deal with the offender in any way in which it could deal with him if he had just been convicted of the offence on indictment before the court.

98.27 ***Indication of plea of guilty Related offences Crown Court's powers apply***

Powers of Criminal Courts (Sentencing) Act 2000 s 4(1) This section applies where:

(a) a person aged 18 or over is before a Magistrates' Court ('the court') charged with a triable either way offence ('the offence'),

(b) he or (where applicable) his representative indicates under Magistrates' Courts Act 1980 s 17A, 17B or 20(7) that he would plead guilty if the offence were to proceed to trial, and

(c) proceeding as if Magistrates' Courts Act 1980 s 9(1) were complied with and he pleaded guilty under it, the court convicts him of the offence.

(2) If the court has committed the offender to the Crown Court for trial for one or more related offences, it may commit him in custody or on bail to the Crown Court to be dealt with in respect of the offence in accordance with section 5(1).

For the rest of the section see **98.13**.

Powers of Criminal Courts (Sentencing) Act 2000 s 5(1) Where an offender is committed by a Magistrates' Court for sentence under section 3 (greater punishment required) (see **98.9**), 3A (committal for dangerous offenders) (see **98.18**), or 4 (committal on indication of guilty plea for triable either way offence), the Crown Court shall inquire into the circumstances of the case and may deal with the offender in any way in which it could deal with him if he had just been convicted of the offence on indictment before the court.

(2) In relation to committals under section 4 above, subsection (1) above has effect subject to section 4(4) and (5) [see **98.31**].

98.28 ***Summary only matters Procedure and powers of the Crown Court***

Crime and Disorder Act 1998 Sch 3 para 6(1) This paragraph applies where a magistrates' court has sent a person for trial under section 51 or 51A of this Act for offences which include a summary offence.

(2) If the person is convicted on the indictment, the Crown Court shall consider whether the summary offence is related to the indictable offence for which he was sent for trial or, as the case may be, any of the indictable offences for which he was so sent.

(3) If it considers that the summary offence is so related, the court shall state to the person the substance of the offence and ask him whether he pleads guilty or not guilty.

(4) If the person pleads guilty, the Crown Court shall convict him, but may deal with him in respect of the summary offence only in a manner in which a magistrates' court could have dealt with him.

(5) If he does not plead guilty, the powers of the Crown Court shall cease in respect of the summary offence except as provided by sub-paragraph (6) below.
(6) If the prosecution inform the court that they would not desire to submit evidence on the charge relating to the summary offence, the court shall dismiss it.
(7) The Crown Court shall inform the designated officer for the magistrates' court of the outcome of any proceedings under this paragraph.
(8) If the summary offence is one to which Criminal Justice Act 1988 s 40 applies, the Crown Court may exercise in relation to the offence the power conferred by that section; but where the person is tried on indictment for such an offence, the functions of the Crown Court under this paragraph in relation to the offence shall cease.
(9) Where the Court of Appeal allows an appeal against conviction of an indictable offence which is related to a summary offence of which the appellant was convicted under this paragraph:

(a) it shall set aside his conviction of the summary offence and give the clerk of the magistrates' court notice that it has done so; and
(b) it may direct that no further proceedings in relation to the offence are to be undertaken;

and the proceedings before the Crown Court in relation to the offence shall thereafter be disregarded for all purposes.
(10) A notice under sub-paragraph (9) above shall include particulars of any direction given under paragraph (b) of that sub-paragraph in relation to the offence.
(12) An offence is related to another offence for the purposes of this paragraph if it arises out of circumstances which are the same as or connected with those giving rise to the other offence.

98.29 ***Summary only matters Crown Court No indictable offence remains Adults***

Crime and Disorder Act 1998 Sch 3 para 7(1) Subject to paragraph 13 below, this paragraph applies where:

(a) a person has been sent for trial under Crime and Disorder Act 1998 s 51 or 51A but has not been arraigned; and
(b) the person is charged on an indictment which (following amendment of the indictment, or as a result of an application under paragraph 2 above, or for any other reason) includes no main offence.

(2) Everything that the Crown Court is required to do under the following provisions of this paragraph must be done with the accused present in court.
(3) The court shall cause to be read to the accused each remaining count of the indictment that charges an offence triable either way.
(4) The court shall then explain to the accused in ordinary language that, in relation to each of those offences, he may indicate whether (if it were to proceed to trial) he would plead guilty, or not guilty, and that if he indicates that he would plead guilty the court must proceed as mentioned in sub-paragraph (6) below.
(5) The court shall then ask the accused whether (if the offence in question were to proceed to trial) he would plead guilty or not guilty.
(6) If the accused indicates that he would plead guilty the court shall proceed as if he had been arraigned on the count in question and had pleaded guilty.
(7) If the accused indicates that he would plead not guilty, or fails to indicate how he would plead, the court shall decide whether the offence is more suitable for summary trial or for trial on indictment.
(8) Subject to sub-paragraph (6) above, the following shall not for any purpose be taken to constitute the taking of a plea:

(a) asking the accused under this paragraph whether (if the offence were to proceed to trial) he would plead guilty or not guilty;
(b) an indication by the accused under this paragraph of how he would plead.

(9) In this paragraph, a "main offence" is:

(a) an offence for which the person has been sent to the Crown Court for trial under section 51(1) of this Act; or
(b) an offence:
(i) for which the person has been sent to the Crown Court for trial under subsection (5) of section 51 or subsection (6) of section 51A of this Act ("the applicable subsection"); and
(ii) in respect of which the conditions for sending him to the Crown Court for trial under the applicable subsection (as set out in paragraphs (a) to (c) of section 51(5) or paragraphs (a) and (b) of section 51A(6)) continue to be satisfied.

para 8 [deals with defendants who are too disorderly to be in court]
para 9 [deals with how the Crown Court shall decide whether an offence is more suitable for summary trial or trial on indictment (see para 7(7) or 8(2)(d)).]
para 10(1) This paragraph applies (unless excluded by paragraph 15 below) where the Crown Court considers that an offence is more suitable for summary trial.
(2) The court shall explain to the accused in ordinary language:
(a) that it appears to the court more suitable for him to be tried summarily for the offence;
(b) that he can either consent to be so tried or, if he wishes, be tried on indictment; and
(c) in the case of a specified offence (within the meaning of Criminal Justice Act 2003 s 224), that if he is tried summarily and is convicted by the court, he may be committed for sentence to the Crown Court under Powers of Criminal Courts (Sentencing) Act 2000 s 3A if the committing court is of such opinion as is mentioned in subsection (2) of that section.
(3) After explaining to the accused as provided by sub-paragraph (2) above the court shall ask him whether he wishes to be tried summarily or on indictment, and:
(a) if he indicates that he wishes to be tried summarily, shall remit him for trial to a magistrates' court acting for the place where he was sent to the Crown Court for trial;
(b) if he does not give such an indication, shall retain its functions in relation to the offence and proceed accordingly.
para 11 If the Crown Court considers that an offence is more suitable for trial on indictment, the court:
(a) shall tell the accused that it has decided that it is more suitable for him to be tried for the offence on indictment; and
(b) shall retain its functions in relation to the offence and proceed accordingly.

R v McDermott-Mullane 2016 EWCA Crim 2239 D was charged with possession of an offensive weapon. The prosecution asked for it to be sent to the Crown Court and it was. The prosecution also asked for a summary assault and a summary only theft to be tried summarily. The defence asked for all matters to be dealt with in the same place and those offences were sent to the Crown Court too. The prosecution discontinued the offensive weapon before any hearing. At the first hearing, the prosecution discontinued the assault matter and D pleaded to the theft. Because of D's record, the Judge started at 2 years and with the plea gave D 15 months with 3 months consecutive for an activated suspended sentence. Held. The theft was always a summary only offence and the maximum was 6 months. It was not capable of being the only offence in an indictment so the indictment was a nullity. Here the practical solution would have been for the Judge to sit as a District Judge and deal with the theft charge. That was not done. As the Crown had no jurisdiction to deal with the matter, neither does the Court of Appeal. Therefore, we reconvene ourselves as the Administrative Court and quash the conviction and the activation of the suspended sentence.

For the power for the judge to sit as a district judge, see **86.2**.

98.30 ***Summary only matters Crown Court No indictable-only offence remains Children and young persons***

Crime and Disorder Act 1998 Sch 3 para 13(1) This paragraph applies, in place of paragraphs 7 to 12 above, in the case of a child or young person who:

(a) has been sent for trial under section 51 or 51A of this Act but has not been arraigned; and

(b) is charged on an indictment which (following amendment of the indictment, or as a result of an application under paragraph 2 above, or for any other reason) includes no main offence.

(2) The Crown Court shall remit the child or young person for trial to a magistrates' court acting for the place where he was sent to the Crown Court for trial.

(3) In this paragraph, a "main offence" is:

(a) an offence for which the child or young person has been sent to the Crown Court for trial under section 51A(2) of this Act; or

(b) an offence:

(i) for which the child or young person has been sent to the Crown Court for trial under subsection (7) of section 51 of this Act; and

(ii) in respect of which the conditions for sending him to the Crown Court for trial under that subsection (as set out in paragraphs (a) and (b) of that subsection) continue to be satisfied.

98.31 ***Indications of guilty plea Related offences Lesser offences***

Powers of Criminal Courts (Sentencing) Act 2000 s 4(4) Where the court:

(a) under subsection (2) commits the offender to the Crown Court to be dealt with in respect of the offence, and

(b) does not state that, in its opinion, it also has power so to commit him under section 3(2) or, as the case may be, section 3A(2),[1101]

section 5(1) shall not apply unless he is convicted before the Crown Court of one or more of the related offences.

(5) Where section 5(1) does not apply, the Crown Court may deal with the offender in respect of the offence in any way in which the Magistrates' Court could deal with him if it had just convicted him of the offence.

Powers of Criminal Courts (Sentencing) Act 2000 s 7(1) Where under section 6 (committal for related offences) (see **98.13**) above a Magistrates' Court commits a person to be dealt with by the Crown Court in respect of an offence, the Crown Court may, after inquiring into the circumstances of the case, deal with him in any way in which the Magistrates' Court could deal with him if it had just convicted him of the offence.

R v Bateman 2012 EWCA Crim 2518, 2013 2 Cr App R (S) 26 (p 174) D was given 12 months suspended. He breached the order by committing four beatings and was committed for sentence. The assaults were of some severity and against his partner. There were similar previous convictions. The Judge activated the suspended sentence and imposed 5 months' detention for the assault and made all the sentences consecutive. The Judge relied on Powers of Criminal Courts (Sentencing) Act 2000 s 7(2), 'section 7(1) does not apply where under section 6 a Magistrates' Court commits a person [to the] Crown Court in respect of a suspended sentence previously imposed by the Crown Court'. Held. That was wrong. The powers are the Magistrates' powers.

98.32 ***Young offenders***

Powers of Criminal Courts (Sentencing) Act 2000 s 5A(1) Where an offender is committed by a Magistrates' Court for sentence under section 3B [plea indicated, young offenders see **98.14**], 3C [dangerous young offenders, see **98.18**] or 4A [plea indicated,

[1101] Words inserted by Criminal Justice Act 2003 Sch 3 para 24(6)

related offenders, young offenders], the Crown Court shall inquire into the circumstances of the case and may deal with the offender in any way in which it could deal with him if he had just been convicted of the offence on indictment before the court.
(2) In relation to committals under section 4A above, subsection (1) above has effect subject to section 4A(4) and (5).

Offenders under the age of 18

98.33 ***Basic principles***
Magistrates' Courts Act 1980 s 24(1) Where a person under the age of 18 years appears or is brought before a Magistrates' Court on an information charging him with an indictable offence he shall, subject to Crime and Disorder Act 1998 s 51 and 51A [sending adults for trial and sending young offenders for trial for grave crimes] and to sections 24A and 24B below [similar provisions], be tried summarily.
CPS v South East Surrey Youth Court 2005 EWHC 2929 (Admin), 2006 2 Cr App R (S) 26 (p 177) High Court D, then aged 17, allegedly assaulted V in the face with a beer bottle, causing a wound. D was also arrested for an unrelated robbery where it was said a knife was used. The Youth Court sent the robbery to the Crown Court and on a later date the CPS also asked for the ABH to be sent, under Crime and Disorder Act 1998 s 51A(3)(d). This was on the basis that ABH was a 'specified violent offence': Criminal Justice Act 2003 s 224(3). The Court declined to commit because ABH was not a grave crime, so the provisions of Magistrates' Courts Act 1980 s 24(1) were not met. The CPS appealed. Held. We consider the obligations of a Youth Court when dealing with a potentially dangerous offender. Here the provisions are not merely labyrinthine, they are manifestly inconsistent with each other. Yet again, the courts are faced with a sample of the deeply confusing provisions of Criminal Justice Act 2003 and the satellite statutory instruments to which it is giving stuttering birth. Magistrates' Courts Act 1980 s 24(1) requires summary trial of a person under 18 unless the offence is grave and may require a sentence of long-term detention, in which case the defendant must be committed for trial. Crime and Disorder Act 1998 s 51A requires a child or young person to be sent to the Crown Court for trial if the offence is specified in Sch 15 and if convicted, it appears the criteria for the imposition of an indeterminate sentence or an extended sentence under Criminal Justice Act 2003 s 228[1102] would be met. Justices should bear in mind: a) those who are under 18 should, wherever possible, be tried in a Youth Court, which is best designed for their specific needs, *R (H) v Southampton Youth Court* 2004 EWHC 2912 (Admin) and *R (CPS) v Redbridge Youth Court* 2005 EWHC 1390, b) the guidance in *R v Lang* 2005 EWCA Crim 2864, 2006 2 Cr App R (S) 3 (p 13), particularly in para (iv) in relation to non-serious specified offences (see **56.26**), c) the need, when dealing with those aged under 18, to be particularly rigorous before concluding that there is a significant risk of serious harm by the commission of further offences. Such a conclusion is unlikely to be appropriate in the absence of a pre-sentence report following assessment by a youth offending team, d) in most cases where a non-serious specified offence is charged, an assessment of dangerousness will not be appropriate until after conviction when, if the dangerousness criteria are met, the defendant can be committed to the Crown Court for sentence, e) when a youth [aged] under 18 is jointly charged with an adult, an exercise of judgement will be called for by the Youth Court when assessing the competing presumptions in favour of i) joint trial of those jointly charged and ii) the trial of youths in the Youth Court. Factors relevant to that judgement will include the age and maturity of the youth, the comparative culpability in relation to the offence and the previous convictions of the two, and whether the trial can be severed without either injustice or undue inconvenience to witnesses. Therefore the Justices' approach, in

[1102] Repealed by Legal Aid, Sentencing and Punishment of Offenders Act 2012 s 123(d), in force 3/12/12

declining to consider Crime and Disorder Act 1998 s 51A(3)(d), was flawed. However, the conclusion that summary jurisdiction should be accepted for the purposes of trial is unimpeachable.

98.34 ***Defendant crosses age threshold***

Powers of Criminal Courts (Sentencing) Act 2000 s 7(4) Where, under section 6 above, a Magistrates' Court commits a person to be dealt with by the Crown Court in respect of an offence triable only on indictment in the case of an adult (being an offence which was tried summarily because of the offender's being under 18 years of age), the Crown Court's powers under subsection (1) in respect of the offender after he attains the age of 18 shall be powers to do either or both of the following:

(a) to impose a fine not exceeding £5,000,

(b) to deal with the offender in respect of the offence in any way in which the Magistrates' Court could deal with him if it had just convicted him of an offence punishable with imprisonment for a term not exceeding six months.

R v Robson 2006 EWCA Crim 1414, 2007 1 Cr App R (S) 54 (p 301) D was aged 17 when he was convicted at the Magistrates' Court of two specified and serious offences. When he came to be sentenced in the Crown Court, he was aged 18. The difference was crucial. Held. The manifest purpose of the provision was to ensure that the sentencing powers of the Crown Court were not limited to those of the Magistrates' Court. It is unnecessary for us to speculate what the word 'just' adds to the exercise. Magistrates' Courts Act 1952 s 29(3) allows the Crown Court to deal with an offender committed by the Magistrates' Court as if he had just been convicted on indictment. The effect of this section merely ensures that the sentencing powers of the Crown Court were not limited to those of the Magistrates' Court. It is sufficient for us to state that, having regard to Criminal Justice Act 2003 s 225-228, it did not require D to be sentenced under the regime applicable to those aged 18 or over solely because he would have been 18 years old on conviction if he had 'just' been convicted on indictment.

98.35 ***Dangerous young offenders***

Powers of Criminal Courts (Sentencing) Act 2000 s 3C(1) This section applies where on the summary trial of a specified offence a person aged under 18 is convicted of the offence.

(2) If, in relation to the offence, it appears to the court that the criteria for the imposition of a sentence under Criminal Justice Act 2003 s 226B[1103] would be met, the court must commit the offender in custody or on bail to the Crown Court for sentence in accordance with section 5A(1) [see **98.32**].

Powers of Criminal Courts (Sentencing) Act 2000 s 5A(1) Where an offender is committed by a Magistrates' Court for sentence under section 3C (committals for dangerous young offenders) (see above), the Crown Court shall inquire into the circumstances of the case and may deal with the offender in any way in which it could deal with him if he had just been convicted of the offence on indictment before the court.

Dangerous Offenders Guide for Sentencers and Practitioners 2008 para 6.5.3 The Youth Justice Board anticipates that normally the court would find a youth to be a dangerous offender only if he or she was assessed in a pre-sentence report to pose a very high risk of serious harm or, in a small number of cases and due to specific circumstances, a high risk of serious harm. However, the court is not bound by the assessment of risk in the pre-sentence report; it does not follow automatically that, because an offender has been assessed as posing a high risk or very high risk of serious harm, he or she is a dangerous offender.

R (W) v Caernarfon Youth Court 2013 EWHC 1466 (Admin) High Court D, aged 11, was charged with rape of a child under 13 (penetration of V's mouth), three counts of sexual assault of a child aged under 13 and common assault. V was aged 6. The District

[1103] Words substituted by Legal Aid, Sentencing and Punishment of Offenders Act 2012 Sch 21 para 9

Judge accepted jurisdiction and the matter was adjourned for trial. Before the trial date D pleaded to all counts. Reports were ordered which revealed: a) a likelihood he had been exposed to adult pornography, b) when aged 5 and 7, he had invited others to lick his penis, and c) at school he had pulled boys' trousers down. The District Judge committed D for sentence under section 3C, because of the significant risk the defendant posed. The defence brought judicial review proceedings claiming that as there had been no trial there could not be a committal under section 3C. Held. We cannot accept that submission. The word 'trial' includes defendants who plead. Here the change of decision about jurisdiction arose because of the report. The District Judge was entitled to exercise his residual powers which are exercisable in very exceptional circumstances to commit D for sentence. Further the acceptance of summary jurisdiction created no legitimate expectation he would be dealt with summarily. However, on the facts, it was not open to the District Judge to commit. Case remitted back to the Youth Court.

Procedure Crown Court

98.36 ***Proper evidence of conviction etc. required***

R v Jeffries 1963 Crim LR 559 Where a person is committed for sentence, proper proof of conviction and identity should be made. It is not satisfactory merely to ask the person if he admits the matters.

98.37 ***TICs***

R v Davies 1980 2 Cr App R (S) 364 This Court has no hesitation in saying that the appropriate time for the defendant to be asked if he wishes other offences to be taken into consideration is at the court which is to sentence him and that the court should ask the accused himself (not merely his counsel). If there is any dispute about the matter, the offences ought to be gone through one by one. Even, therefore, where an accused has asked magistrates to take offences into consideration, the accused should once more be given the opportunity to say whether he wishes or does not wish them to be taken into consideration at the Crown Court before he is sentenced.

98.38 ***Factual disputes***

Shaw v Hamilton 1982 4 Cr App R (S) 80 D was acquitted and the Magistrates imposed a bind over. D appealed and the Judge declined to allow the prosecution to call the three witnesses that gave evidence, saying that it was undesirable as that might make it appear that the issue of guilt was being reconsidered. The prosecution appealed. Held. That was wrong. It implied that, on an appeal to the Crown Court from a Magistrates' Court against sentence, it is not possible for sworn evidence to be heard. If there is a challenge which does not go to conviction and goes solely to sentence, it is open to the Crown Court to hear evidence.

Munroe v DPP 1988 152 JP 657 High Court D pleaded to ABH on a police officer. D was committed for sentence. The Court told the Crown Court that the plea version was materially different from the prosecution case. D claimed one punch with an open hand and the prosecution claimed four punches with a clenched fist. D said he had told the Magistrates about his version. Enquiries revealed that the Magistrates' Court had no record of the disagreement. The defence asked the Crown Court to remit the case to the Magistrates' Court to determine the factual basis and to consider again whether a committal was needed. The Judge said he had no power to do that. They considered the factual issue should be determined by the Crown Court. D appealed. Held. The Crown Court did have power to remit the case to find the correct version, *R v Mutford and Lothingland JJs ex parte Harber* 1971 55 Cr App R (S) 57. The Crown Court also has the jurisdiction to determine the issue itself. Which is appropriate depends on when the dispute arises. Where the dispute occurs in the Magistrates' Court, they should hear the evidence and determine the issue. If they commit they must ensure the Crown Court is told of their findings. The Crown Court should then sentence on the facts as found by the Magistrates and not allow the case to be reopened. If the dispute arises at the Crown Court, they should determine the issue.

Gillian v DPP 2007 EWHC 380 (Admin), 2 Cr App R 12 (p 148) High Court D pleaded to ABH at the Magistrates' Court. His basis of plea was not accepted and the Court held a *Newton* hearing before a Stipendiary Magistrate. He found in favour of the prosecution and committed the case. At the Crown Court D said he wished to dispute the facts. The Judge held he did not have the power to conduct one as it had previously been determined. D appealed. Held. The Crown Court has jurisdiction to hold a further *Newton* hearing if it is in the interests of fairness and justice to do so…that much is clear from the express terms of section 5(1) and the Crown Court's obligation to enquire into the circumstances of the case. In the ordinary way, I would not expect the judge in the Crown Court to exercise his discretion in favour of allowing a defendant to reopen the magistrates' findings of fact unless the defendant was able to point to some significant development or matter, such as (but not confined to) the discovery of important further evidence having occurred since the Magistrates' Court reached its conclusion on the facts. In saying that, I would not wish it to be thought that I was laying down any absolute or strict formula as to how the judge should exercise his or her discretion in any particular case. Everything will depend upon the facts and circumstances of the particular case. However, there was no feature of circumstance in this case which made it necessary in the interest of fairness to reopen the factual issue. Appeal dismissed.
For *Newton* hearings generally, see the **FACTUAL BASIS FOR SENTENCING *Newton* hearings Basic principles** section at **57.59**.

98.39 ***Newton hearings***
Gillian v DPP 2007 EWHC 380 (Admin), 2 Cr App R 12 (p 148) High Court The Crown Court has jurisdiction to hold a further *Newton* hearing if it is in the interests of fairness and justice to do so…that much is clear from the express terms of section 5(1) and the Crown Court's obligation to enquire into the circumstances of the case. In the ordinary way, I would not expect the judge in the Crown Court to exercise his discretion in favour of allowing a defendant to reopen the magistrates' findings of fact unless the defendant was able to point to some significant development or matter, such as (but not confined to) the discovery of important further evidence having occurred since the Magistrates' Court reached its conclusion on the facts. In saying that, I would not wish it to be thought that I was laying down any absolute or strict formula as to how the judge should exercise his or her discretion in any particular case. Everything will depend upon the facts and circumstances of the particular case.
For *Newton* hearings generally, see the **FACTUAL BASIS FOR SENTENCING *Newton* hearings Basic principles** section at **57.59**.

98.40 ***Can the case be remitted to the Magistrates again?***
R v Isleworth Crown Court ex parte Buda 2000 1 Cr App R (S) p 538 High Court D indicated a plea to importation of cocaine. It was subsequently discovered that the packages that he had swallowed contained bicarbonate of soda, not cocaine. It was argued that the decision of the Magistrates to commit was based on a wrong view of the facts. The case was remitted to the Magistrates' Court to allow them to reconsider the amended information. Held. Where a defendant is committed to Crown Court on an incorrect view of the facts of the offence, the proper approach would be to allow the defendant to change his plea. The consequence would be that the case would be remitted to the Magistrates' Court for consideration on a proper view of the facts. Where there is no application to change plea, there is no power to remit the case to the Magistrates' Court.

Procedural failures

98.41 ***Procedural failures General guidance***
R v Warren 1954 38 Cr App R 44 LCJ If a man who is committed for sentence desires to take the point that he was wrongly committed for sentence, the right course for him to take is to apply to the Queen's Bench Division for a prerogative writ, either a writ of

prohibition directed to quarter sessions to prevent them from proceeding, and he must do that before he is before the (Crown Court), or possibly, at a later stage, a writ of *certiorari*, to bring up the order of committal and quash it.

R v Ashton and Others 2006 EWCA Crim 794, 2 Cr App R (S) 15 (p 231) In separate appeals, judges of the Crown Court exercised the powers of a District Judge (as a judge of the Magistrates' Court) in order to overcome certain procedural failures during committal for sentence. Held. Whenever a court is confronted by failure to take a required step, properly or at all, before a power is exercised ('a procedural failure'), the court should first ask itself whether the intention of the legislature was that any act done following that procedural failure should be invalid. If the answer to that question is no, then the court should go on to consider the interests of justice generally, and most particularly whether there is a real possibility that either the prosecution or the defence may suffer prejudice on account of the procedural failure. If there is such a risk, the court must decide whether it is just to allow the proceedings to continue. On the other hand, if a court acts without jurisdiction – if, for instance, a Magistrates' Court purports to try a defendant on a charge of homicide – then the proceedings will usually be invalid.

R v Buisson 2011 EWCA Crim 1841 Where a committal is invalid in the Crown Court, a High Court Judge and a Circuit Judge can reconstitute the Court as a Magistrates' Court and exercise the powers of a District Judge, Courts Act 2003 s 66. There is the same power at the Court of Appeal.

Note: This case is an example of: a) the Court of Appeal approving a Crown Court Judge committing a case he had held to be invalidly committed, and b) the Court of Appeal Judge acting as a District Judge to sentence the same person who had had another invalid committal.

For the procedure when a Judge of the Court of Appeal sits as a District Judge see the **PROCEDURE, SENTENCING** ***Judge sitting as a District Judge*** para at **86.2**. Ed.

98.42 *Disputes as to which type of committal it was*

R v Murphy 2012 EWCA Crim 469 D was committed for sentence. He was unrepresented. The certificate didn't list the type of committal for the breach of the Crown Court Suspended Sentence Order. On the back under 'Offences and results' the form said: 'Possession of an offensive weapon committed under section 6'. A letter from the Magistrates' Court said the committal was not because the Magistrates' powers were insufficient. This was clarified to 'I only rely on my notes'. The CPS representative considered that to the best of her recollection the committal was because of the seriousness. Held. There was compelling evidence the offence was under section 3. It was the Crown Court powers for the offensive weapon offence which applied.

See also: *R v Mitchell* 2011 EWCA Crim 2030 (No plea made. Certificate said section 6. Held. In the absence of compelling evidence, we are bound by the certificate.)

98.43 *Committal invalid/Wrong section used/Memorandum wrong/Additional offences*

R v Ayhan 2011 EWCA Crim 3184, 2012 2 Cr App R (S) 37 (p 207) LCJ D's memorandum of conviction said the committal for the summary only offences was under section 3 (which is for either way offences). Enquiries revealed that the committal was under section 6 (the right section) and the memorandum was wrong. Held. The mistake does not invalidate the committal. When such issues arise again, they can be dealt with in a robust and practical way.

R v Hellyer 2015 EWCA Crim 1410 (Magistrates used section 3 when it should have been section 6. No injustice flowed so we say no more about it.)

R v Osman 2017 EWCA Crim 2178 Two bail offences were purportedly committed under Crime and Disorder Act 1998 s 51(3) at the same time as charges of affray and possession of a bladed article. Held. The bail offences were not related to the other offences. The committal for the bail matters was a nullity. Had D pleaded or been found guilty, the Magistrates could have committed the bail matters if they thought it appropriate. (The Court then reconvened itself as a Magistrates' Court and D pleaded to breach of bail. The Court passed a concurrent rather than a consecutive sentence for the bail offence.)

R v Day 2018 EWCA Crim 2637 D was committed to the Crown Court for being in breach of his Crown Court 6-month suspended sentence (section 6). At the same time, D was committed for a burglary, two thefts and an attempted theft (section 6). He was sentenced to 12 months for the burglary. Held. That sentence was justified. However, the Crown Court was restricted to the Magistrates' Court powers for the burglary, so the maximum was 6 months, which we substitute.

Note: If D pleaded guilty, which appears to be the case, the new sentence would be wrong if 6 months was the maximum as he should have had a discount. The exact committing power is not referred to. The alternative might be to proceed in a robust way, see above, and ensure that an adequate sentence was passed. However, I doubt whether the Court can pass a sentence in excess of the maximum the committing section provides. For a similar refusal to exceed the powers of the committing section, see *R v Rimmer* 2018 EWCA Crim 2972. Ed.

See also: *R v Hall* 1982 74 Cr App R 67 (D was committed for trial. Later the committal certificate was found to have the wrong section on it. That did not invalidate the committal.)

R v Russell 1998 2 Cr App R (S) 375 (The inaccuracy of the memorandum was lamentable. The committal was valid.)

Appeals

98.44 *Null/Invalid committals*

R v Ayhan 2011 EWCA Crim 3184, 2012 2 Cr App R (S) 37 (p 207) LCJ D's memorandum of conviction said the committal for the summary only offences was under section 3 (which is for either way offences). Enquiries revealed that the committal was under section 6 (the right section) and the memorandum was wrong. Held. The mistake does not invalidate the committal. When such issues arise again, they can be dealt with in a robust and practical way.

Appeals against conviction and committals for sentence

98.45 *The jurisdiction on committal is separate from the appeals proceedings*

R v Croydon Crown Court ex parte Bernard 1980 2 Cr App R (S) 144 High Court LCJ D was convicted at the Juvenile Court and was committed for sentence. D wanted to appeal against the conviction. The young barrister who represented D believed he was advised by someone from D's solicitors that they were against that. At the committal hearing at the Crown Court, the same barrister said D questioned the finding of guilt. After questioning, the barrister, without speaking to D, said he was not instructed to appeal. D was sent to Borstal. D wrote to the solicitors and an appeal was launched. Leave to appeal out of time was given. At the appeal hearing a different Judge said that, as the sentence had been determined, he was *functus officio* and there could be no appeal. D appealed to the High Court. Held. The Crown Court has two separate forms of jurisdiction: a) the task of determining committals for sentence, and b) appeals from the justices. We order the Court to hear the conviction appeal.

98.46 *A court hearing an appeal cannot commit a case to itself*

R v Bullock 1963 47 Cr App R 288 LCJ D was convicted and sentenced and he appealed. It was not clear whether he appealed solely against conviction or against conviction and sentence. His appeal against conviction was dismissed. The Court was of the opinion that the sentence was inadequate. Exercising the powers that the Magistrate had, the Court committed the case to itself and increased D's sentence. He appealed. Held. A court cannot commit to itself on an appeal. If the course taken by the Court was correct, defendants would be deprived of two safeguards against increased sentences: a) the opinion of two courts (that greater punishment is required) and b) the lower court has expressed a contrary opinion to that of the higher court, increasing the sentence.

99 SERIOUS CRIME PREVENTION ORDERS

99.1

Serious Crime Act 2007 s 1-43

These orders are either stand-alone orders made at the High Court or post-conviction orders made at the Crown Court.

Children and young offenders The order is only available when the offender is aged 18+, see **99.22**.

Financial Reporting Orders These orders were repealed by Serious Crime Act 2015 s 50(1).[1104] The repeal of the order does not affect orders made before the repeal date, Serious Crime Act 2015 s 86(7). In a parliamentary overview of the Serious Crime Bill, it was said that the then Bill consolidates Financial Reporting Orders into the Serious Crime Prevention Order. For detail about the orders, see the 10th edition of this book.

Power to order

99.2 ***Statutory power to order High Court (Stand-alone orders)***

Serious Crime Act 2007 s 1(1) The High Court in England and Wales may make an order if:

(a) it is satisfied that a person has been involved in serious crime (see **99.4**) (whether in England and Wales or elsewhere), and

(b) it has reasonable grounds to believe that the order would protect the public by preventing, restricting or disrupting involvement by the person in serious crime in England and Wales.

99.3 ***Statutory power to order Crown Court (post-conviction orders)***

Orders by Crown Court on conviction

Serious Crime Act 2007 s 19(1) Subsection (2) applies where the Crown Court in England and Wales is dealing with a person who:

(a) has been convicted by or before a Magistrates' Court of having committed a serious offence in England and Wales and has been committed to the Crown Court to be dealt with, or

(b) has been convicted by or before the Crown Court of having committed a serious offence in England and Wales.

(2) The Crown Court may, in addition to dealing with the person in relation to the offence, make an order if it has reasonable grounds to believe that the order would protect the public by preventing, restricting or disrupting involvement by the person in serious crime in England and Wales.

(2A) [The rule that a defendant can't have two orders at the same time, see **99.25**]

(3)-(4A) [Not listed. Northern Ireland]

(5) An order under this section may contain:

(a) such prohibitions, restrictions or requirements, and

(b) such other terms,

as the court considers appropriate for the purpose of protecting the public by preventing, restricting or disrupting involvement by the person concerned in serious crime in England and Wales.

(6) The powers of the court in respect of an order under this section are subject to sections 6 to 15 (safeguards).

(7) An order must not be made under this section except:

(a) in addition to a sentence imposed in respect of the offence concerned, or

(b) in addition to an order discharging the person conditionally.

(8) An order under this section is also called a serious crime prevention order.

[1104] The report states that he was concerned in fraudulently evading duty on a class B drug. Clearly this cannot be the case since there is no duty on class B drugs because they are prohibited. Consequently, it is assumed the suggestion of 'evading duty' was a typo.

99.4 *'Involved in serious crime', Definition of*

Serious Crime Act 2007 s 2(1) For the purposes of this Part, a person has been involved in serious crime in England and Wales if he:

(a) has committed a serious offence in England and Wales,

(b) has facilitated the commission by another person of a serious offence in England and Wales, or

(c) has conducted himself in a way that was likely to facilitate the commission by himself or another person of a serious offence in England and Wales (whether or not such an offence was committed).

(2) In this Part "a serious offence in England and Wales" means an offence under the law of England and Wales which, at the time when the court is considering the application or matter in question:

(a) is specified, or falls within a description specified, in Part 1 of Schedule 1 [see **99.5**]; or

(b) is one which, in the particular circumstances of the case, the court considers to be sufficiently serious to be treated for the purposes of the application or matter as if it were so specified.

(3) For the purposes of this Part, involvement in serious crime in England and Wales is any one or more of the following:

(a) the commission of a serious offence in England and Wales,

(b) conduct which facilitates the commission by another person of a serious offence in England and Wales,

(c) conduct which is likely to facilitate the commission, by the person whose conduct it is or another person, of a serious offence in England and Wales (whether or not such an offence is committed).

(4) For the purposes of section 1(1)(a), a person has been involved in serious crime elsewhere than in England and Wales if he:

(a) has committed a serious offence in a country outside England and Wales,

(b) has facilitated the commission by another person of a serious offence in a country outside England and Wales, or

(c) has conducted himself in a way that was likely to facilitate the commission by himself or another person of a serious offence in a country outside England and Wales (whether or not such an offence was committed).

(5) In subsection (4) "a serious offence in a country outside England and Wales" means an offence under the law of a country outside England and Wales which, at the time when the court is considering the application or matter in question:

(a) would be an offence under the law of England and Wales if committed in or as regards England and Wales, and

(b) either:

(i) would be an offence which is specified, or falls within a description specified, in Part I of Schedule 1, if committed in or as regards England and Wales, or

(ii) is conduct which, in the particular circumstances of the case, the court considers to be sufficiently serious to be treated for the purposes of the application or matter as if it meets the test in sub-paragraph (i).

(6) The test in subsection (4) is to be used instead of the tests in sections 2A(1) and 3(1) in deciding for the purposes of section 1(1)(a) whether a person has been involved in serious crime in Scotland or (as the case may be) Northern Ireland.

(7) An act punishable under the law of a country outside the United Kingdom constitutes an offence under that law for the purposes of subsection (5), however it is described in that law.

99.5 *'Serious offence', Definition of*

Serious Crime Act 2007 s 2(2) In this Part "a serious offence in England and Wales" means an offence under the law of England and Wales which, at the time when the court is considering the application or matter in question:

(a) is specified, or falls within a description specified, in Part I of Schedule 1, or
(b) is one which, in the particular circumstances of the case, the court considers to be sufficiently serious to be treated for the purposes of the application or matter as if it were so specified.

Serious Crime Act 2007 Sch 1

Note: The Schedule follows with some of the titles of the subsections altered to make it easier to find an offence. The subsections have been put in alphabetical order. Also some of the offences have been repealed. They no doubt remain in the list to deal with historical offences. Ed.

Armed robbery etc.

Serious Crime Act 2007 Sch 1 para 5(1) An offence under Theft Act 1968 s 8(1) (robbery) where the use or threat of force involves a firearm, an imitation firearm or an offensive weapon.

(2) An offence at common law of an assault with intent to rob where the assault involves a firearm, imitation firearm or an offensive weapon.

(3) In this paragraph: 'firearm' has the meaning given by Firearms Act 1968 s 57(1), 'imitation firearm' has the meaning given by Firearms Act 1968 s 57(4), 'offensive weapon' means any weapon to which Criminal Justice Act 1988 s 141 (offensive weapons) applies.

Blackmail and gangmasters

Serious Crime Act 2007 Sch 1 para 11(1) An offence under Theft Act 1968 s 21 (blackmail).

(2) An offence under Gangmasters (Licensing) Act 2004 s 12(1) or (2) (acting as a gangmaster other than under the authority of a licence, possession of false documents, etc.).

Corruption and bribery

Serious Crime Act 2007 Sch 1 para 9(1)[1105] An offence under any of the following provisions of Bribery Act 2010:

(a) section 1 (offences of bribing another person),
(b) section 2 (offences relating to being bribed),
(c) section 6 (bribery of foreign public officials).

Computer misuse

Serious Crime Act 2007 Sch 1 para 11A.[1106]

An offence under any of the following provisions of the Computer Misuse Act 1990:

(a) section 1 (unauthorised access to computer material),
(b) section 2 (unauthorised access with intent to commit or facilitate commission of further offences),
(c) section 3 (unauthorised acts with intent to impair, or with recklessness as to impairing, operation of computer etc.),
(d) section 3ZA (unauthorised acts causing, or creating risk of, serious damage to human welfare etc.),
(e) section 3A (making, supplying or obtaining articles for use in offence under section 1, 3 or 3ZA).

Counterfeiting

Serious Crime Act 2007 Sch 1 para 10 An offence under any of the following provisions of Forgery and Counterfeiting Act 1981:

(a) section 14 (making counterfeit notes or coins),
(b) section 15 (passing etc. counterfeit notes or coins),
(c) section 16 (having custody or control of counterfeit notes or coins),

1105 As substituted by Legal Aid, Sentencing and Punishment of Offenders Act 2012 s 64

1106 The report states that he was concerned in fraudulently evading duty on a class B drug. Clearly this cannot be the case since there is no duty on class B drugs because they are prohibited. Consequently, it is assumed the suggestion of 'evading duty' was a typo.

(d) section 17 (making or having custody or control of counterfeiting materials or implements).

Drug etc. trafficking

Serious Crime Act 2007 Sch 1 para 1(1) An offence under any of the following provisions of Misuse of Drugs Act 1971:

(a) section 4(2) or (3) (unlawful production or supply of controlled drugs),
(b) section 5(3) (possession of controlled drug with intent to supply),
(ba) section 6 (restriction of cultivation of cannabis plant),[1107]
(c) section 8 (permitting etc. certain activities relating to controlled drugs),
(d) section 20 (assisting in or inducing the commission outside the United Kingdom of an offence punishable under a corresponding law).

1A An offence under any of the following provisions of the Psychoactive Substances Act 2016:

(a) section 4 (producing a psychoactive substance),
(b) section 5 (supplying, or offering to supply, a psychoactive substance),
(c) section 7 (possession of psychoactive substance with intent to supply),
(d) section 8 (importing or exporting a psychoactive substance).[1108]

(2) An offence under any of the following provisions of Customs and Excise Management Act 1979 if it is committed in connection with a prohibition or restriction on importation or exportation which has effect by virtue of Misuse of Drugs Act 1971 s 3:

(a) section 50(2) or (3) (improper importation of goods),
(b) section 68(2) (exportation of prohibited or restricted goods),
(c) section 170 (fraudulent evasion of duty etc.).

(3) An offence under either of the following provisions of Criminal Justice (International Co-operation) Act 1990:

(a) section 12 (manufacture or supply of a substance for the time being specified in Schedule 2 to that Act),
(b) section 19 (using a ship for illicit traffic in controlled drugs).

Environmental offences

Serious Crime Act 2007 Sch 1 para 13(1) An offence under Salmon and Freshwater Fisheries Act 1975 s 1 (fishing with prohibited implements etc.).[1109]

(2) An offence under Wildlife and Countryside Act 1981 s 14 (introduction of new species etc.).

(3) An offence under Environmental Protection Act 1990 s 33 (prohibition on unauthorised or harmful deposit, treatment or disposal etc. of waste).

(4) An offence under Control of Trade in Endangered Species (Enforcement) Regulations 1997 1997/1372 Reg 8 (purchase and sale etc. of endangered species and provision of false statements and certificates).

Financial sanctions offences

Note: Policing and Crime Act 2017 s 151 amends Serious Crime Act 2007 Sch 1 Part 1 by adding paras 13B and 29A, which relate to financial sanction. For reasons of space and because the orders are rare, the full text is not listed. In force 1 April 2017. Ed.

Firearm offences

Serious Crime Act 2007 Sch 1 para 3

(1) An offence under any of the following provisions of Firearms Act 1968:

(a) section 1(1) (possession etc. of firearms or ammunition without certificate),
(b) section 2(1) (possession etc. of shotgun without certificate),
(c) section 3(1) (dealing etc. in firearms or ammunition by way of trade or business without being registered),
(d) section 5(1), (1A) or (2A) (possession, manufacture etc. of prohibited weapons).

[1107] As substituted by Identity Cards Act 2006 s 39(4)

[1108] Repealed by Extradition Act 2003 s 218 on 1/1/04

[1109] As amended by Identity Cards Act 2006 s 39(3), which substituted 'travel authorisation' for 'passport' (on 20/10/09) and Identity Documents Act 2010 Sch 1 para 17, which reversed that change (on 21/1/11).

(2) An offence under either of the following provisions of Customs and Excise Management Act 1979 if it is committed in connection with a firearm or ammunition:
(a) section 68(2) (exportation of prohibited or restricted goods),
(b) section 170 (fraudulent evasion of duty etc.).
(3) In sub-paragraph (2) 'firearm' and 'ammunition' have the same meanings as in Firearms Act 1968 s 57.
Fraud
Serious Crime Act 2007 Sch 1 para 7(1) An offence under Theft Act 1968 s 17 (false accounting).
(2) An offence under any of the following provisions of Fraud Act 2006:
(a) section 1 (fraud by false representation, failing to disclose information or abuse of position),
(b) section 6 (possession etc. of articles for use in frauds),
(c) section 7 (making or supplying articles for use in frauds),
(d) section 9 (participating in fraudulent business carried on by sole trader etc.),
(e) section 11 (obtaining services dishonestly).
(3) An offence at common law of conspiracy to defraud.
Intellectual property
Serious Crime Act 2007 Sch 1 para 12(1) An offence under any of the following provisions of Copyright, Designs and Patents Act 1988:
(a) s 107(l)(a), (b), (d)(iv) or (e) (making, importing or distributing an article which infringes copyright),
(b) s 198(l)(a), (b) or (d)(iii) (making, importing or distributing an illicit recording),
(c) s 297A (making or dealing etc. in unauthorised decoders).
(2) An offence under Trade Marks Act 1994 s 92(1), (2) or (3) (unauthorised use of trade mark etc.).
Money laundering
Serious Crime Act 2007 Sch 1 para 6 An offence under any of the following provisions of Proceeds of Crime Act 2002:
(a) s 327 (concealing etc. criminal property),
(b) s 328 (facilitating the acquisition etc. of criminal property by or on behalf of another),
(c) s 329 (acquisition, use and possession of criminal property).
Organised crime
Serious Crime Act 2015 s 45 (participating in activities of organised crime group).[1110]
People trafficking
Serious Crime Act 2007 Sch 1 para 2(1) An offence under Immigration Act 1971 s 25, 25A and 25B (assisting unlawful immigration etc.).
(2) An offence under any of [the following] sections of Sexual Offences Act 2003 s 57-59A[1111] (trafficking for sexual exploitation).
(3) An offence under Asylum and Immigration (Treatment of Claimants, etc.) Act 2004 s 4 (trafficking people for exploitation).
Prostitution and child sex
Serious Crime Act 2007 Sch 1 para 4(1) An offence under Sexual Offences Act 1956 s 33A (keeping a brothel used for prostitution).
(2) An offence under any of the following provisions of Sexual Offences Act 2003:
(a) s 14 (arranging or facilitating commission of a child sex offence),
(b) s 48 (causing or inciting child prostitution or pornography),
(c) s 49 (controlling a child prostitute or a child involved in pornography),
(d) s 50 (arranging or facilitating child prostitution or pornography),

[1110] As amended by Identity Cards Act 2006 s 39(3), which substituted 'travel authorisation' for 'passport' (on 20/10/09) and Identity Documents Act 2010 Sch 1 para 17, which reversed that change (on 21/1/11).
[1111] Legal Aid, Sentencing and Punishment of Offenders Act 2012 s 85(1) and (4) and Legal Aid, Sentencing and Punishment of Offenders Act 2012 (Commencement No 11) Order 2015 2015/504

[Serious Crime Act 2015 Sch 4 para 81(1)-(2) renames the section 48-50 offences.[1112] The offences become:]
s 48 (causing or inciting sexual exploitation of a child),
s 49 (controlling a child in relation to sexual exploitation),
s 50 (arranging or facilitating sexual exploitation of a child),
(e) s 52 (causing or inciting prostitution for gain),
(f) s 53 (controlling prostitution for gain).

Public revenue, Offences in relation to

Serious Crime Act 2007 Sch 1 para 8(1) An offence under Customs and Excise Management Act 1979 s 170 (fraudulent evasion of duty etc.) so far as not falling within paragraph 1(2)(c) or 3(1)(b) (see the Drug trafficking and Arms trafficking sections above).
(2) An offence under Value Added Tax Act 1994 s 72 (fraudulent evasion of VAT etc.).
(3) An offence under Taxes Management Act 1970 s 106A (fraudulent evasion of income tax).[1113]
(4) An offence under Tax Credits Act 2002 s 35 (tax credit fraud).
(5) An offence at common law of cheating in relation to the public revenue.

Slavery, forced labour etc.[1114]

Modern Slavery Act 2015 s 1 (slavery, servitude and forced or compulsory labour)
Modern Slavery Act 2015 s 2 [human trafficking]

Terrorism

[The following offences were inserted by Counter-Terrorism and Border Security Act 2019 s 14(2) In force 12 April 2019, Counter-Terrorism and Border Security Act 2019 s 27(3).]
An offence for the time being listed in section 41(1) of the Counter-Terrorism Act 2008 (offences to which Part 4 of that Act applies: terrorism offences). [Those offences are:]
(a) Terrorism Act 2000
section 11 or 12 (offences relating to proscribed organisations),
sections 15 to 18 (offences relating to terrorist property),
section 38B (failure to disclose information about acts of terrorism),
section 54 (weapons training),
sections 56 to 61 (directing terrorism, possessing things and collecting information for the purposes of terrorism and inciting terrorism outside the United Kingdom);
(b) an offence in respect of which there is jurisdiction by virtue of any of sections 62 to 63D of that Act (extra-territorial jurisdiction in respect of certain offences committed outside the United Kingdom for the purposes of terrorism etc.);
(c) an offence under section 113 of the Anti-terrorism, Crime and Security Act 2001 (use of noxious substances or things);
(d) Terrorism Act 2006
sections 1 and 2 (encouragement of terrorism),
sections 5, 6 and 8 (preparation and training for terrorism),
sections 9, 10 and 11 (offences relating to radioactive devices and material and nuclear facilities);
(e) an offence in respect of which there is jurisdiction by virtue of section 17 of that Act (extra-territorial jurisdiction in respect of certain offences committed outside the United Kingdom for the purposes of terrorism etc.).

[1112] Legal Aid, Sentencing and Punishment of Offenders Act 2012 s 85(1) and (4) and Legal Aid, Sentencing and Punishment of Offenders Act 2012 (Commencement No 11) Order 2015 2015/504

[1113] As amended by Identity Cards Act 2006 s 39(3), which substituted 'travel authorisation' for 'passport' (on 20/10/09) and Identity Documents Act 2010 Sch 1 para 17, which reversed that change (on 21/1/11).

[1114] As amended by Identity Cards Act 2006 s 39(3), which substituted 'travel authorisation' for 'passport' (on 20/10/09) and Identity Documents Act 2010 Sch 1 para 17, which reversed that change (on 21/1/11).

Inchoate offences

Serious Crime Act 2007 Sch 1 para 14(1) An offence of attempting or conspiring in the commission of an offence specified or described in this Part of this Schedule.

(2) An offence under Part 2 of this Act (encouraging or assisting) where the offence (or one of the offences) which the person in question intends or believes would be committed is an offence specified or described in this Part of this Schedule.

(3) An offence of aiding, abetting, counselling or procuring the commission of an offence specified or described in this Part of this Schedule.

(4) The references in sub-paragraphs (1) to (3) to offences specified or described in this Part of this Schedule do not include the offence at common law of conspiracy to defraud.

Earlier offences/Historical offences

Serious Crime Act 2007 Sch 1 para 15 (1) This Part of this Schedule (apart from paragraph 14(2) [see **Inchoate offences** above]) has effect, in its application to conduct before the passing of this Act, as if the offences specified or described in this Part included any corresponding offences under the law in force at the time of the conduct.

(2) para 14(2) has effect, in its application to conduct before the passing of this Act or before the coming into force of Serious Crime Act 2007 s 59, as if the offence specified or described in that provision were an offence of inciting the commission of an offence specified or described in this Part of this Schedule.

Scope of offences

Serious Crime Act 2007 Sch 1 para 16 Where this Part of this Schedule refers to offences which are offences under the law of England and Wales and another country, the reference is to be read as limited to the offences so far as they are offences under the law of England and Wales.

99.6 *'Has committed a serious offence' Statutory presumptions*

Serious Crime Act 2007 s 4(1) In considering for the purposes of this Part whether a person has committed a serious offence:

(a) the court must decide that the person has committed the offence if:

(i) he has been convicted of the offence, and

(ii) the conviction has not been quashed on appeal nor has the person been pardoned of the offence, but

(b) the court must not otherwise decide that the person has committed the offence.

99.7 *Facilitates the commission of a serious offence, Matters to ignore*

Serious Crime Act 2007 s 4(2) In deciding for the purposes of this Part whether a person ('the respondent') facilitates the commission by another person of a serious offence, the court must ignore:

(a) any act that the respondent can show to be reasonable in the circumstances, and

(b) subject to this, his intentions, or any other aspect of his mental state, at the time.

(3) In deciding for the purposes of this Part whether a person ('the respondent') conducts himself in a way that is likely to facilitate the commission by himself or another person of a serious offence (whether or not such an offence is committed), the court must ignore:

(a) any act that the respondent can show to be reasonable in the circumstances, and

(b) subject to this, his intentions, or any other aspect of his mental state, at the time.

99.8 *European Convention on Human Rights*

R v Hancox and Duffy 2010 EWCA Crim 102, 2 Cr App R (S) 74 (p 484) The defendants pleaded to conspiracies to produce large amounts of counterfeit banknotes. The Judge made a Serious Crime Prevention Order. Held. The necessity for orders to be proportionate also follows from the fact that they will almost inevitably engage European Convention on Human Rights art 8. They will satisfy the requirement in article 8(2) for the order to be made according to law, because they are made within a statutory structure, but, as that article is now understood, it requires further that they must be proportionate, see the authoritative expression in *EB (Kosovo) v SSHD* 2008 UKHL 41, 2009 1 AC 1159, at para 7, of the questions which arise under article 8:

a) Will the proposed (order) be an interference by a public authority with the exercise of the applicant's right to respect for his private…life?
b) If so, will such interference have consequences of such gravity as potentially to engage the operation of article 8?
c) If so, is such interference in accordance with the law?
d) If so, is such interference necessary in a democratic society in the interests of…the prevention of disorder or crime?
e) If so, is such interference proportionate to the legitimate public end sought to be achieved? That means that it is not enough that the order may have some public benefit in preventing, restricting or disrupting involvement by the defendant in serious crime. The interference which [the order] will create with the defendant's freedom of action must be justified by the benefit, the provisions of the order must be commensurate with the risk.

Procedure

99.9 *General matters*

The Criminal Procedure Rules 2015 2015/1490 Rule 31 behaviour order rules apply, see the note at **27.2**. For the rules, see **84.14**.

Serious Crime Act 2007 s 36(4) The Crown Court, when exercising its jurisdiction under this Part, is a criminal court for the purposes of Courts Act 2003 Part 7 (procedure rules and practice directions).

99.10 *Nature of the proceedings High Court (Stand-alone orders)*

Serious Crime Act 2007 s 35(1) Proceedings before the High Court in relation to serious crime prevention orders are civil proceedings.

99.11 *Nature of the proceedings Crown Court (post-conviction orders)*

Serious Crime Act 2007 s 36(1) Proceedings before the Crown Court arising by virtue of section 19 [making an order, see **99.19**], section 20 [varying an order, see **99.43**] or section 21 [varying an order in breach proceedings] are civil proceedings.

Serious Crime Act 2007 s 36(4) The Crown Court, when exercising its jurisdiction under this Part, is a criminal court for the purposes of Courts Act 2003 Part 7 (procedure rules and practice directions).

99.12 *Who may apply for an order?*

Serious Crime Act 2007 s 8 A serious crime prevention order may be made only on an application by:

(i) the Director of Public Prosecutions,
(ii) the Director of Revenue and Customs Prosecutions, or
(iii) the Director of the Serious Fraud Office.

99.13 *Application, Making*

Criminal Procedure Rules 2015 2015/1490 Rule 31.3(1) This rule applies where:

(a) a prosecutor wants the court to make one of the following orders if the defendant is convicted:[1115]
 (ii) a Serious Crime Prevention Order,
 (i) and (iii) [Not listed. About ASBOs and Criminal Behaviour Orders]
(b) [Not listed. About Sexual Harm Prevention Order]

(2) Where paragraph (1)(a) applies (order on application), the prosecutor must serve a notice of intention to apply for such an order on:

(a) the court officer,
(b) the defendant against whom the prosecutor wants the court to make the order, and

[1115] This Act came into force on 15/10/13, Prevention of Social Housing Fraud Act 2013 (Commencement) (England) Order 2013 2013/2622 para 2.

(c) any person on whom the order would be likely to have a significant adverse effect,
as soon as practicable (without waiting for the verdict).

(3) A notice under paragraph (2) must:

(a) summarise the relevant facts,

(b) identify the evidence on which the prosecutor relies in support,

(c) attach any written statement that the prosecutor has not already served, and

(d) specify the order that the prosecutor wants the court to make.

Note: For the Serious Crime Prevention Order application form, see www.banksr.com Other Matters Other Documents Serious Crime Prevention Orders. Ed

99.14 ***Defendant's response***

Criminal Procedure Rules 2015 2015/1490 Rule 31.3(4) A defendant served with a notice under paragraph (2) must:

(a) serve notice of any evidence on which the defendant relies on:[1116]

(i) the court officer, and

(ii) the prosecutor,

as soon as practicable (without waiting for the verdict), and

(b) in the notice, identify that evidence and attach any written statement that has not already been served.

99.15 ***Right to make representations High Court (Stand-alone orders)***

Serious Crime Act 2007 s 9(1) The High Court must, on an application by a person, give the person an opportunity to make representations in proceedings before it about the making of a serious crime prevention order if it considers that the making of the order would be likely to have a significant adverse effect on that person.

99.16 ***Right to make representations Crown Court (post-conviction orders)***

Serious Crime Act 2007 s 9(4) The Crown Court must, on an application by a person, give the person an opportunity to make representations in proceedings before it arising by virtue of section 19, 20, 21 or 22E[1117] if it considers that the making or variation of the serious crime prevention order concerned (or a decision not to vary it) would be likely to have a significant adverse effect on that person.

99.17 ***Evidence***

Serious Crime Act 2007 s 36(3)(a) The court is not restricted to considering evidence that would have been admissible in the criminal proceedings in which the person concerned was convicted.

99.18 ***Power to adjourn***

Serious Crime Act 2007 s 36(3)(b) The court may adjourn any proceedings in relation to a serious crime prevention order even after sentencing the person concerned.

Test to apply

99.19 ***Test to apply***

Serious Crime Act 2007 s 19(2) The Crown Court may make an order if it has reasonable grounds to believe that the order would protect the public by preventing, restricting or disrupting involvement by the person in serious crime in England and Wales.

R v Hancox and Duffy 2010 EWCA Crim 102, 2 Cr App R (S) 74 (p 484) The defendants pleaded to conspiracies to produce large amounts of counterfeit banknotes. The Judge made a Serious Crime Prevention Order. Held. Unlike some statutory provisions for the making of preventive orders e.g. Anti-social Behaviour Orders under Crime and Disorder Act 1998 s 1C and Sexual Offences Prevention Orders under Sexual Offences Act 2003 s 104, this one is not expressly couched in terms of necessity. But we doubt that the different form of words makes a significant difference in practice. It was common ground before us that the principles set out by this Court in *R v Mee* 2004 EWCA Crim 629, 2 Cr App R (S) 81 (p 434) (see **109.7**), in the context of the

[1116] As amended by Criminal Justice and Courts Act 2015 Sch 12 paras 8-9

[1117] The period was extended to 56 days by Criminal Justice and Immigration Act 2008 s 47 and Sch 8 para 28 on 14/7/08.

similarly worded power to make Travel Restriction Orders under Criminal Justice and Police Act 2001 s 33, apply equally to SCPOs. Such orders can be made only for the purpose for which the power was given by statute. It is a judgement and assessment of future risk and the order must be proportionate.

99.20 ***Standard of proof***

Serious Crime Act 2007 s 35(2) The standard of proof to be applied by the [High] Court in such proceedings is the civil standard of proof.

Serious Crime Act 2007 s 36(2) The standard of proof to be applied by the [Crown] Court in such proceedings is the civil standard of proof.

R v Hancox and Duffy 2010 EWCA Crim 102, 2 Cr App R (S) 74 (p 484) The defendants pleaded to conspiracies to produce large amounts of counterfeit banknotes. The Judge made a Serious Crime Prevention Order. Held. Section 36 provides that the standard of proof is the civil standard. We have heard no argument upon, and say nothing about, whether the House of Lords decision in *R (McCann) v Crown Court at Manchester* 2002 UKHL 39, 2003 1 AC 787 applies to require, on pragmatic grounds, the application of what is effectively the criminal standard. The CPS guidance assumes that it will.

Making the order

99.21 ***Order must be proportionate, practical, enforceable and precise***

R v Hancox and Duffy 2010 EWCA Crim 102, 2 Cr App R (S) 74 (p 484) The defendants pleaded to conspiracies to produce large amounts of counterfeit banknotes. The Judge made a Serious Crime Prevention Order. Held. Much of what this Court said in *R v Boness* 2005 EWCA Crim 2395, 2006 1 Cr App R (S) 120 (p 690) about Anti-social Behaviour Orders, will apply equally to SCPOs. In particular, that decision examines the application of the test of proportionality, and emphasises the importance of the order being practicable and enforceable and satisfying the test of precision and certainty. Preventive orders of this kind in effect create for the defendant upon whom they are imposed a new criminal offence punishable with imprisonment for up to 5 years. They must be expressed in terms from which he, and any policeman contemplating arrest or other means of enforcement, can readily know what he may and may not do.

R v Carey and Taylor 2012 EWCA Crim 1592 Whether they are necessary should be considered carefully. Their term should be restricted to that which is absolutely necessary. One order quashed here.

R v Hall and Others 2014 EWCA Crim 2046, 2015 1 Cr App R (S) 16 (p 127) (The fact that the defendants would be released on a licence which would last longer than the order was no reason not to make the order.)

R v McGrath 2017 EWCA Crim 1945 D was convicted of conspiracy to blackmail and controlling prostitutes for gain. He appealed his Serious Crime Prevention Order. Held. para 21 D should be entitled to use the full range of methods of communication now available on a mobile phone. Any concerns should be addressed in the other prohibitions in the order. The £1,000 cash limitation will stay as that is sufficient and D had used cash in his illegal activities. We reject most of the other appeal points.

Disputes as to facts see the **FACTUAL BASIS FOR SENTENCING** ***Same rules apply when imposing ancillary orders*** para at **57.26**.

99.22 ***Defendant's minimum age for making the order***

Serious Crime Act 2007 s 6 An individual under the age of 18 may not be the subject of a serious crime prevention order.

99.23 ***Order must be for a specified term***

Serious Crime Act 2007 s 16(1) A serious crime prevention order must specify when it is to come into force and when it is to cease to be in force.

99.24 ***Five-year maximum for the order***

Serious Crime Act 2007 s 16(2) An order is not to be in force for more than 5 years beginning with the coming into force of the order.

See also: *R v Deeds* 2013 EWCA Crim 1624 (An order to run for 5 years from the defendant's release from prison was unlawful (no doubt because it started at the date of sentence so was over 5 years).)

99.25 ***Can't have two orders at the same time***

Serious Crime Act 2007 s 19(2A)[1118] A court that makes an order by virtue of subsection (2) [see **99.3**] in the case of a person who is already the subject of a serious crime prevention order in England and Wales must discharge the existing order.

99.26 ***Commencement of the order***

Serious Crime Act 2007 s 16(1) A serious crime prevention order must specify when it is to come into force.

Serious Crime Act 2007 s 16(3) An order can specify different times for the coming into force, or ceasing to be in force, of different provisions of the order.

(4) Where it specifies different times in accordance with subsection (3), the order:

(a) must specify when each provision is to come into force and cease to be in force, and

(b) is not to be in force for more than 5 years beginning with the coming into force of the first provision of the order to come into force.

The prohibitions, restrictions and requirements

99.27 ***Power to add prohibitions, requirements etc. High Court***

Serious Crime Act 2007 s 1(3) An order under this section (see **99.2**) may contain:

(a) such prohibitions, restrictions or requirements, and

(b) such other terms,

as the court considers appropriate for the purpose of protecting the public by preventing, restricting or disrupting involvement by the person concerned in serious crime in England and Wales or (as the case may be) Northern Ireland.

99.28 ***Examples of provisions that can be made***

Serious Crime Act 2007 s 5(1) This section contains examples of the type of provision that may be made by a serious crime prevention order but it does not limit the type of provision that may be made by such an order.

(2) Examples of prohibitions, restrictions or requirements that may be imposed by serious crime prevention orders include prohibitions, restrictions or requirements in relation to places other than England and Wales.

(3) Examples of prohibitions, restrictions or requirements that may be imposed on individuals (including partners in a partnership) by serious crime prevention orders include prohibitions or restrictions on, or requirements in relation to:

(a) an individual's financial, property or business dealings or holdings,

(b) an individual's working arrangements,

(c) the means by which an individual communicates or associates with others, or the persons with whom he communicates or associates,

(d) the premises to which an individual has access,

(e) the use of any premises or item by an individual,

(f) an individual's travel (whether within the United Kingdom, between the United Kingdom and other places or otherwise).

(4) Examples of prohibitions, restrictions or requirements that may be imposed on bodies corporate, partnerships and unincorporated associations by serious crime prevention orders include prohibitions or restrictions on, or requirements in relation to:

(a) financial, property or business dealings or holdings of such persons,

(b) the types of agreements to which such persons may be a party,

(c) the provision of goods or services by such persons,

(d) the premises to which such persons have access,

(e) the use of any premises or item by such persons,

[1118] The provisions are no longer mandatory but the example illustrates the use of the power.

(f) the employment of staff by such persons.

(5) Examples of requirements that may be imposed on any persons by serious crime prevention orders include:

(a) a requirement on a person to answer questions, or provide information, specified or described in an order:

(i) at a time, within a period or at a frequency,

(ii) at a place,

(iii) in a form and manner, and

(iv) to a law enforcement officer or description of law enforcement officer, notified to the person by a law enforcement officer specified or described in the order,

(b) a requirement on a person to produce documents specified or described in an order:

(i) at a time, within a period or at a frequency,

(ii) at a place,

(iii) in a manner, and

(iv) to a law enforcement officer or description of law enforcement officer, notified to the person by a law enforcement officer specified or described in the order.

(6) The prohibitions, restrictions or requirements that may be imposed on individuals by serious crime prevention orders include prohibitions, restrictions or requirements in relation to an individual's private dwelling (including, for example, prohibitions or restrictions on, or requirements in relation to, where an individual may reside).

(7) In this Part:

"document" means anything in which information of any description is recorded (whether or not in legible form),

"a law enforcement officer" means:

(a) a constable,

(b) a National Crime Agency officer who is for the time being designated under section 9 or 10 of the Crime and Courts Act 2013,

(c) an officer of Revenue and Customs, or

(d) a member of the Serious Fraud Office, and

"premises" includes any land, vehicle, vessel, aircraft or hovercraft.

(8) Any reference in this Part to the production of documents is, in the case of a document which contains information recorded otherwise than in legible form, a reference to the production of a copy of the information in legible form.

99.29 ***Restrictions on oral answers***

Serious Crime Act 2007 s 11 A serious crime prevention order may not require a person to answer questions, or provide information, orally.

99.30 ***Legal professional privilege***

Serious Crime Act 2007 s 12(1) A serious crime prevention order in England and Wales or Northern Ireland may not require a person:

(a) to answer any privileged question,

(b) to provide any privileged information, or

(c) to produce any privileged document.

(2) A "privileged question" is a question which the person would be entitled to refuse to answer on grounds of legal professional privilege in proceedings in the High Court.

(3) "Privileged information" is information which the person would be entitled to refuse to provide on grounds of legal professional privilege in such proceedings.

(4) A "privileged document" is a document which the person would be entitled to refuse to produce on grounds of legal professional privilege in such proceedings.

(4A) [Not listed. Scotland]

(5) But subsections (1) and (4A) do not prevent an order from requiring a lawyer to provide the name and address of a client of his.

99.31 *Excluded material and banking information*

Serious Crime Act 2007 s 13(1) A serious crime prevention order may not require a person to produce:

(a) any excluded material as defined by Police and Criminal Evidence Act 1984 s 11.

(aa) and (b) [Not listed. Scotland and Northern Ireland]

(2) A serious crime prevention order may not require a person to disclose any information or produce any document in respect of which he owes an obligation of confidence by virtue of carrying on a banking business unless condition A or B is met.

(3) Condition A is that the person to whom the obligation of confidence is owed consents to the disclosure or production.

(4) Condition B is that the order contains a requirement:

(a) to disclose information, or produce documents, of this kind, or

(b) to disclose specified information which is of this kind or to produce specified documents which are of this kind.

99.32 *Disclosure is prohibited by other enactments, When*

Serious Crime Act 2007 s 14(1) A serious crime prevention order may not require a person:

(a) to answer any question,

(b) to provide any information, or

(c) to produce any document,

if the disclosure concerned is prohibited under any other enactment.

99.33 *Communication restrictions*

R v Hancox and Duffy 2010 EWCA Crim 102, 2 Cr App R (S) 74 (p 484) The defendants were involved in counterfeiting banknotes on a commercial scale. Mobile phone and Internet notification made in a Serious Crime Prevention Order. Held. We are acutely aware of the potential for interference in a [person's] private life with communication restrictions. However, the restrictions [few details given] were proportionate.

99.34 *On the facts, Order correct/Judge entitled to make the prohibitions*

R v Hancox and Duffy 2010 EWCA Crim 102, 2 Cr App R (S) 74 (p 484) H and D pleaded to conspiracies to produce counterfeit banknotes on a commercial scale. Over a nine-month period in Scotland and London both £20 and €50 notes were made. The exact amount was unknown but notes with over £2m face value were being manufactured or awaiting distribution. H's London flat was used for the crucial foiling process. H was also involved in counterfeiting DVDs and developed a 'franchising operation'. H was now aged 84 and had 15 dishonesty convictions. He had very serious health conditions which significantly limited his mobility. His heart condition made him breathless and there was a 10% risk of an acute attack. The Judge gave him a suspended sentence because of his frail health and age. He also made a Serious Crime Prevention Order. H's prohibitions and requirements included: a) buying, possessing photocopiers, printers and scanners, except one type and notification of any model acquired, and b) buying, possessing etc. foiling material. H was required to notify the Serious Organised Crime Agency of: i) premises owned, rented etc. ii) vehicles he had access to, and iii) changes of address. D had similar restrictions imposed including mobile phone and Internet notification. Held. Neither age nor his poor health prevented H from taking an active part in the conspiracies nor had he been prevented from travelling. The Judge was entitled to reach the conclusions he did for H. For D we are acutely aware of the potential for interference in a private life with communication restrictions. However, the restrictions [few details given] were proportionate.

R v Webb and Clark 2011 EWCA Crim 882 D pleaded to supplying cocaine, converting criminal property, infringing copyright and abetting the sale of a shotgun. The Judge made a Serious Crime Prevention Order with the following terms: a) he was not to have any more than £1,000 in cash on his person at any one time, b) he must not have more than one mobile telephone device at any one time, c) he must not have more than one vehicle, d) he must not have more than one bank account, e) he must not be away from his home address for more than five consecutive days without informing the police, and f) he must not associate with a man named Peter Henny. Held. We can see nothing wrong with these terms. It is always open for the defendant to apply to the Crown Court for the order to be relaxed.

Note: This case in no way indicates a template for these orders. The decision was simply that the Judge was entitled to make these prohibitions. The case is only listed because there are so few reported cases on this order. Ed.

See also: *R v Batchelor* 2010 EWCA Crim 1025, 2011 1 Cr App (S) 25 (p 169) (Jewellery con man who stole £230,000-£380,000 worth of jewellery from customers. Previous conviction for similar (5½ years). Some elderly victims. **5 years**. The order was entirely reasonable and utterly proportionate.)

R v Barnes and Orford 2012 EWCA Crim 2549 (Plea to drug supply. Members of a motorcycle gang used to front drug dealing in South Wales over several years. The orders banning association with certain clubs were necessary and proportionate. The preconditions for making the orders were made out.)

R v Deeds 2013 EWCA Crim 1624 (There was an overwhelming need for the order and, subject to one matter, the prohibitions were correct.)

R v Seale 2014 EWCA Crim 650 (D pleaded to various drug conspiracies involving large quantities of ecstasy, cocaine and other drugs. He was the principal link in acquiring and shipping them to the UK. He had a drug importation offence on his record (8 years). D was restricted to one mobile, one SIM card and one computer. He was not allowed to associate with 10 named individuals. He was banned from travelling abroad. These terms were not objectionable but that did not mean they would be necessary in other cases.)

99.35 ***On the facts, order incorrect***

R v Mangham 2012 EWCA Crim 973, 2013 1 Cr App R (S) 11 (p 62) D pleaded to three counts of unauthorised access to computer material with intent, Computer Misuse Act 1990 s 1 and one count of unauthorised modification of computer material, Computer Misuse Act 1990 s 3. D hacked into Facebook's computers and infiltrated Facebook employees' e-mail accounts and e-mail archives. He then gained access to their Phabricator server and therefore their source code. This was their unique software which gives Facebook its functionality. Facebook estimated its costs at $200,000, which included their time investigating, accessing and remedying the damage done. The FBI and the US Dept of Justice had three special agents working full time for about three weeks. The FBI sent two agents to the UK. D was aged 26 and of good character. He probably suffered from Asperger's syndrome, a personality disorder, social phobia and possibly major depression. He had exposed vulnerabilities at Yahoo. He was paid for this assistance. The Judge considered: a) D was possibly emotionally younger than 26, b) D had never intended to pass any of the information on or make any financial gain, c) the conduct was not harmless experimentation, d) Facebook's entire operation was potentially at risk, and e) the behaviour was persistent and sophisticated. The information had not been passed to anyone and there was no financial gain. The order was not proportionate. We quash it.

Combined with other orders

99.36 ***Absolute and conditional discharge, Combined with***

Serious Crime Act 2007 s 19(7) An order must not be made under this section except: (a) in addition to a sentence imposed in respect of the offence concerned; or (b) in addition to an order discharging the person conditionally.

Serious Crime Act 2007 s 36(5) A serious crime prevention order may be made in spite of anything in Powers of Criminal Courts (Sentencing) Act 2000 s 12 and 14 (power to make and the effect of an absolute or conditional discharge), see **1.3**, **19.1** and **19.5**.

99.37 ***Hospital Orders, Combined with***

R v Dunning 2018 EWCA Crim 3018 D pleaded to three threats to kill involving a particular school and the Judge passed a Hospital Order and a Serious Crime Prevention Order (SCPO) banning D from the area where the school was and schools generally. D told mental health staff he harboured plans to launch a Dunblane-style gun attack on the primary school's children. The defence said as there was a Restriction Order in place, the SCPO was wrong in principle. The prosecution said a mere breach of the condition of release from the Hospital Order would not itself justify recall and D might benefit from clear boundaries. There was nothing wrong with the Judge's conclusions.

Other matters

99.38 ***Order must be served on defendant***

Serious Crime Act 2007 s 10(1) The subject of a serious crime prevention order is bound by it or a variation of it only if:..

(b) a notice setting out the terms of the order…has been served on him.

(2) The notice may be served on him by:

(a) delivering it to him in person, or

(b) sending it by recorded delivery to him at his last known address (whether residential or otherwise).

(3) For the purposes of delivering such a notice to him in person, a constable or a person authorised for the purpose by the relevant applicant authority may (if necessary by force):

(a) enter any premises where he has reasonable grounds for believing the person to be, and

(b) search those premises for him.

99.39 ***Restrictions on using disclosed material***

Serious Crime Act 2007 s 15(1) A statement made by a person in response to a requirement imposed by a serious crime prevention order may not be used in evidence against him in any criminal proceedings unless condition A or B is met.

(2) Condition A is that the criminal proceedings relate to an offence under section 25.

(3) Condition B is that:

(a) the criminal proceedings relate to another offence,

(b) the person who made the statement gives evidence in the criminal proceedings,

(c) in the course of that evidence, the person makes a statement which is inconsistent with the statement made in response to the requirement imposed by the order, and

(d) in the criminal proceedings evidence relating to the statement made in response to the requirement imposed by the order is adduced, or a question about it is asked, by the person or on his behalf.

Guidance for defence and prosecution appeals can be found at *Guide to Commencing Proceedings in the Court of Appeal 2018* section **D18**.

Appeals

99.40 ***Appeals Court of Appeal***

Serious Crime Act 2007 s 23 This section deals with appeals from the High Court.

Serious Crime Act 2007 s 24 This section deals with appeals by the person subject to the order and the DPP and others from the Crown Court.

Serious Crime Act 2007 (Appeals under Section 24) Order 2008 2008/1863 para 4(2) The Court of Appeal will allow an appeal where the decision of the Crown Court was: a) wrong, or b) unjust because of a serious procedural or other irregularity in the proceeding in the Crown Court.

para 5(1) The Court of Appeal has all the powers of the Crown Court.

(2) The Court of Appeal may:

(a) make a serious crime prevention order,
(b) affirm, set aside or vary any order or judgment made or given by the Crown Court,
(c) refer any issue for determination by the Crown Court,
(d) order a new hearing in the Crown Court,
(e) make an order for costs in accordance with Part 3 (Costs),
(f) make an order for the payment of interest on those costs.

(3) The Court of Appeal may exercise its powers in relation to the whole or part of an order of the Crown Court.

Note: It appears these extensive powers would override the section 11(3) prohibition (see **4.74**). The order has extensive costs provisions, see paras 13-38 and 42. Appeals to the Supreme Court are dealt with in paras 39-43.

Note: A Serious Crime Prevention Order NG form and a respondent's notice form are to be used, see www.banksr.com Other Matters Other Documents Serious Crime Prevention Order. Ed.

Variation

99.41 ***Variation of the order***

R v Hancox and Duffy 2010 EWCA Crim 102, 2 Cr App R (S) 74 (p 484) The defendants pleaded to conspiracies to produce large amounts of counterfeit banknotes. The Judge made a Serious Crime Prevention Order. Held. There is no power in the Crown Court subsequently to vary the order, unless the defendant is brought back for breach or is convicted of a further serious offence (as defined), and then only at the instance of the applicant prosecutor, not the defendant, Serious Crime Act 2007 s 20-21 (for section 20 see **99.43**). The High Court has a more general power to vary any order made. Either the Crown or the defendant may apply for High Court variation, but the defendant has to show a change of circumstance before his application may be entertained, see sections 22(2) and 17(3) and (4).

99.42 ***Variation of the order High Court (Stand-alone orders)***

Serious Crime Act 2007 s 17(1) The High Court may, on an application under this section, vary a serious crime prevention order in England and Wales if it has reasonable grounds to believe that the terms of the order as varied would protect the public by preventing, restricting or disrupting involvement, by the person who is the subject of the order, in serious crime in England and Wales.

Note: The rest of the section contains the procedure etc. Ed.

99.43 ***Variation of the order Crown Court (Post-conviction orders)***

Serious Crime Act 2007 s 20(1) Subsection (2) applies where the Crown Court in England and Wales is dealing with a person who:

(a) has been convicted by or before a Magistrates' Court of having committed a serious offence in England and Wales and has been committed to the Crown Court to be dealt with, or
(b) has been convicted by or before the Crown Court of having committed a serious offence in England and Wales.

(2) The Crown Court may:

(a) in the case of a person who is the subject of a serious crime prevention order in England and Wales, and
(b) in addition to dealing with the person in relation to the offence, vary the order if the court has reasonable grounds to believe that the terms of the order as varied would protect the public by preventing, restricting or disrupting involvement by the person in serious crime in England and Wales.

99.44 ***Variation of the order Procedure***

The Criminal Procedure Rules 2015 2015/1490 Rule 31 behaviour order rules apply, see the note at **27.2**. For the rules, see **84.104**.

99.45 ***Other matters***
Serious Crime Act 2007 s 20(5)-(7) This section deals with the limits on the power to vary.
Serious Crime Act 2007 s 21 This section deals with the powers to vary on a breach.
Serious Crime Act 2007 s 22 This section deals with the inter-relationship between the High Court and the Crown Court.

99.46 ***Right to make representations General***
Serious Crime Act 2007 s 10(1) The subject of a serious crime prevention order is bound by it or a variation of it only if:..he is represented (whether in person or otherwise) at the proceedings at which the variation is made.

99.47 ***Right to make representations Crown Court***
Serious Crime Act 2007 s 9(4) The Crown Court must, on an application by a person, give the person an opportunity to make representations in proceedings before it arising by virtue of section 19, 20 or 21 if it considers that the making or variation of the serious crime prevention order concerned (or a decision not to vary it) would be likely to have a significant adverse effect on that person.
Serious Crime Act 2007 s 10(1) The subject of a serious crime prevention order is bound by it or a variation of it only if: a) he is represented (whether in person or otherwise) at the proceedings at which the order or (as the case may be) variation is made.

Discharge of the order

99.48 ***Statutory power to discharge the order***
Serious Crime Act 2007 s 18 [The power to discharge the order and restrictions on discharge are set out.]

100 SERIOUS CRIME PREVENTION ORDERS: BREACH OF

100.1
Serious Crime Act 2007 s 25(1) (failure to comply with a serious crime prevention order)
Mode of trial Triable either way
Maximum sentence Indictment 5 years. Summary 6 months and/or an unlimited fine.[1119] There are maximum fines for those aged under 18, see **13.44**.
Forfeiture There is a power to forfeit anything which is in the defendant's possession which was 'involved in the offence'.[1120]
Sentencing *Breach Offences Guideline 2018*, see www.banksr.com Other Matters Guidelines tab In force 1 October 2018 page 56 says, **'Other breach offences** Where an offence is not covered by a sentencing guideline a court is entitled to use, and may be assisted by, a guideline for an analogous offence subject to differences in the elements of the offences and the statutory maxima.'

100.2 ***Judicial guidance***
R v Koli 2012 EWCA Crim 1869, 2013 1 Cr App R (S) 6 (p 39) D was convicted of two breaches of his Serious Crime Prevention Order. Held. para 18 The court must take into account: a) the time between the imposition of the order and the date of the breach, b) any history of non-compliance, c) whether non-compliance has: i) been repeated and ii) come in the face of warnings and requests for information, and d) whether the non-compliance was inadvertent or deliberate. It is particularly important whether the breach was related to the commission of further serious offences and might lead to the conclusion that the failure to comply added to the risk that the particular subject of the order was likely to commit further offences. The court would also have to consider the harm caused by non-compliance for breach.

[1119] The provisions are no longer mandatory but the example illustrates the use of the power.
[1120] Repealed by Criminal Procedure (Insanity and Unfitness to Plead) Act 1991 Sch 4 para 1 on 1/1/92

100.3 ***Cases***

R v Koli 2012 EWCA Crim 1869, 2013 1 Cr App R (S) 6 (p 39) D was convicted of two breaches of his Serious Crime Prevention Order. His order was made in February 2011 when he received 3½ years for money laundering. He was required to provide notification of communication devices, vehicles and possession of cash. D failed to notify: a) at least one and possibly more than one mobile. The verdict was also apt to cover a laptop computer, and b) a Honda motor car. D had also been warned of his obligations. D was aged 36, intelligent and well aware of his obligations. D had been in breach of his licence by talking to his former co-defendant. The licence had been revoked. The effect of that was the equivalent of a 17-month sentence. The defence relied on the absence of any harm to the public. Held. No risk to the public was proved. Most of the failures arose because D did not treat the order seriously. That was the seriousness of the offending. **12 months** not 24 was correct.

101 SEXUAL HARM PREVENTION ORDERS

101.1

Sexual Offences Act 2003 s 103A-I as inserted by Anti-social Behaviour, Crime and Policing Act 2014 s 113 and Sch 5 para 4.

This order is the main replacement order for the Sexual Offences Prevention Order and the order came into force for all preventive order applications made on or after 8 March 2015.[1121]

It is a post-conviction only order.

Children and young offenders The order and Sexual Risk Orders are available whatever the age of the offender.

Court Martial The order applies to the Court Martial, Sexual Offences Act 2003 s 103A and 137(2).

Service Sexual Offences Prevention Orders This order was enacted by Armed Forces Act 2011 s 17, which inserted Armed Forces Act 2006 s 232A. The section has never been in force. As the Court Martial uses the Sexual Harm Prevention Order it can be assumed there is no intention to bring the order into force.

Interim Sexual Harm Prevention Orders These are available for stand-alone orders, see Sexual Offences Act 2003 s 103F. This may be because in criminal proceedings cases the judge has very wide powers to make bail conditions.

Sexual Risk Orders Sexual Offences Act 2003 s 122A-K, as inserted by Anti-social Behaviour, Crime and Policing Act 2014 s 113(1) and Sch 5 para 4, creates this civil preventive order. The order came into force for all applications commenced after 8 March 2015,[1122] Anti-social Behaviour, Crime and Policing Act 2014 s 114(2). Applications are made to the Magistrates' Court. The test is whether 'there is a reasonable cause to believe it is necessary for a Sexual Risk Order to be made'. Interim Sexual Risk Orders may be made under section 112E. Notification of the person's name(s) and home address within three days is part of the order, see section 122F. The penalty for a breach is the same as for a breach of a Sexual Harm Prevention Order namely, on indictment 5 years, and on summary conviction 6 months and/or an unlimited fine, see section 122H(3).

The procedure

101.2 ***Prosecution's application***

Criminal Procedure Rules 2015 2015/1490 Rule 31.3(1) This rule applies where:..

(b) a prosecutor proposes, on the prosecutor's initiative or at the court's request, a Sexual Harm Prevention Order if the defendant is convicted;

[1121] This is not clear in the judgment.

[1122] Armed Forces (Court Martial) Rules 2009 2009/2041 Rules 118-124

(c) a prosecutor proposes a Restraining Order whether the defendant is convicted or acquitted.[1123]

Criminal Procedure Rules 2015 2015/1490 Rule 31.3(5) Where paragraph (1)(b) applies, the prosecutor must:

(a) serve a draft order on the court officer and on the defendant not less than two business days before the hearing at which the order may be made,

(b) [Re Sexual Offences Prevention Orders],

(c) in a case in which a Sexual Harm Prevention Order is proposed, in the draft order specify those prohibitions which the prosecutor proposes as necessary for the purpose of:

(i) protecting the public or any particular members of the public from sexual harm from the defendant, or

(ii) protecting children or vulnerable adults generally, or any particular children or vulnerable adults, from sexual harm from the defendant outside the United Kingdom.

R v W and F 2006 EWCA Crim 686 Two defendants were convicted of robbery and the Judge made ASBOs as requested. Held. The case summary attached to the application for the ASBOs did not set out the particular facts which the CPS relied on other than the facts constituting the robbery offence. Instead, the application set out only a vague 'Overview of the Problem' and some 'Reasoning'. Therefore there was no summary of facts that the Judge could put to the offenders to see, quickly and easily, whether or not the facts were disputed by them. It was unfortunate that the prosecution did not assist the Judge or the defence in summarising the facts at the hearing when the ASBO was sought. The result was that the Judge was in no position to make findings of particular facts to support his general conclusion that the defendants had been guilty of antisocial behaviour, other than the facts of the robbery offence. ASBOs quashed.

Note: Although this case involved an ASBO, the principles are likely to apply to Sexual Harm Prevention Orders. Ed.

Power to order/Test to apply

101.3 *Post-conviction Statutory power to order/Test to apply*

Sexual harm prevention orders: applications and grounds

Sexual Offences Act 2003 s 103A(1) A court may make an order under this section (a 'Sexual Harm Prevention Order') in respect of a person ('the defendant') where subsection (2) or (3) applies to the defendant.

(2) This subsection applies to the defendant where:

(a) the court deals with the defendant in respect of:

(i) an offence listed in Schedule 3 or 5 (see **101.6**), or

(ii) a finding that the defendant is not guilty of an offence listed in Schedule 3 or 5 by reason of insanity, or

(iii) a finding that the defendant is under a disability and has done the act charged against the defendant in respect of an offence listed in Schedule 3 or 5,

and

(b) the court is satisfied that it is necessary to make a Sexual Harm Prevention Order, for the purpose of:

(i) protecting the public or any particular members of the public from sexual harm from the defendant, or

(ii) protecting children or vulnerable adults generally, or any particular children or vulnerable adults, from sexual harm from the defendant outside the United Kingdom.

Sexual Offences Act 2003 s 103B(5) For the purposes of section 103A, acts, behaviour, convictions and findings include those occurring before the commencement of this Part.

[1123] As amended by Legal Aid, Sentencing and Punishment of Offenders Act 2012 Sch 5 para 54. In force 1/4/13

R v Smith and Others 2011 EWCA Crim 1772, 2012 1 Cr App R (S) 82 (p 468) The Court gave guidance about SOPOs. Held. para 4 The SOPO offers a flexibility in drafting which is in one sense welcome because it enables the order to be tailored to the exact requirements of the case. That flexibility, however, must not lead draftsmen to an inventiveness which stores up trouble for the future. It will do this if it creates a provision which is, or will become, unworkable. That may be because it is too vague or because it potentially conflicts with other rules applicable to the defendant, or simply because it imposes an impermissible level of restriction on the ordinary activities of life. The SOPO must meet the twin tests of necessity and clarity. The test of necessity brings with it the subtest of proportionality. para 8 The questions to ask are: i) Is the making of an order necessary to protect from serious sexual harm through the commission of scheduled offences? ii) If some order is necessary, are the terms proposed nevertheless oppressive? iii) Overall are the terms proportionate? para 9 it must be remembered that a defendant convicted of sexual offences is likely to be subject to at least [two] other relevant regimes. No SOPO is needed if it merely duplicates such a regime. Nor must a SOPO interfere with such a regime. The following regimes must be considered: the sex offender notification rules and the licence provisions.

R v Boyd 2013 EWCA Crim 2384 D was convicted of manslaughter. D admitted to enjoying intercourse with transvestite men. He also admitted that he and others would have intercourse with his dog, which he had specifically trained for such a purpose. D had consensual sexual activity with V. V suffered an internal injury as a result of having an instrument or a hand inserted into his rectum. He died from blood loss. Expert evidence stated the internal injury would have been caused by the insertion of something into V's rectum which would have measured at least 18 cm. The Judge made a SOPO which prohibited D from owning or keeping a dog. The defence said that the prohibitions were required to protect members of the public. Held. This term was to protect humans because as the dog had been especially trained for this activity there was an obvious risk of 'serious psychological injury' to humans. The term was properly included.

Att-Gen's Ref 2016 Re NC 2016 EWCA Crim 1448, 2017 1 Cr App R (S) 13 (p 87) The Court considered an SHPO. Held. para 9. Whilst the statutory provisions for the imposition of SOPOs are different from SHPOs, in that such an order could only have been made to protect the public or a particular member of it from serious sexual harm, we do consider that, with slight amendment, the questions posed in *R v Smith* 2011 (above) para 8 remain relevant. Those are: i) Is the making of an order necessary to protect the public from sexual harm through the commission of scheduled offences? ii) If some order is necessary, are the terms imposed nevertheless oppressive? iii) Overall, are the terms proportionate?

101.4 *Definitions*

Section 103A: supplemental

Sexual Offences Act 2003 s 103B(1) In section 103A:

"**appropriate date**", in relation to a qualifying offender, means the date or (as the case may be) the first date on which the offender was convicted, found or cautioned as mentioned in subsection (2) or (3) below;

"**child**" means a person under 18;

"**the public**" means the public in the United Kingdom;

"**sexual harm**" from a person means physical or psychological harm caused:

(a) by the person committing one or more offences listed in Schedule 3, or

(b) (in the context of harm outside the United Kingdom) by the person doing, outside the United Kingdom, anything which would constitute an offence listed in Schedule 3 if done in any part of the United Kingdom;

"**qualifying offender**" means a person within subsection (2) or (3) below;

"**vulnerable adult**" means a person aged 18 or over whose ability to protect himself or herself from physical or psychological harm is significantly impaired through physical or mental disability or illness, through old age or otherwise.
(2)-(4) [see **101.5**]
(5) For the purposes of section 103A, acts, behaviour, convictions and findings include those occurring before the commencement of this Part.
(6)-(7) [see **101.5**]
(8) Subsection (9) applies for the purposes of section 103A and this section.
(9) In construing any reference to an offence listed in Schedule 3, any condition subject to which an offence is so listed that relates:
(a) to the way in which the defendant is dealt with in respect of an offence so listed or a relevant finding (as defined by section 132(9)), or
(b) to the age of any person,
is to be disregarded.

101.5 ***Who can be given an SHPO?/Insane defendants/Persons abroad***

Sexual Offences Act 2002 s 103B(2) A person is within this subsection if, whether before or after the commencement of this Part, the person:
(a) has been convicted of an offence listed in Schedule 3 (other than at paragraph 60) or in Schedule 5,
(b) has been found not guilty of such an offence by reason of insanity,
(c) has been found to be under a disability and to have done the act charged against him in respect of such an offence, or
(d) has been cautioned in respect of such an offence.
(3) A person is within this subsection if, under the law in force in a country outside the United Kingdom and whether before or after the commencement of this Part:
(a) the person has been convicted of a relevant offence (whether or not the person has been punished for it),
(b) a court exercising jurisdiction under that law has made in respect of a relevant offence a finding equivalent to a finding that the person is not guilty by reason of insanity,
(c) such a court has made in respect of a relevant offence a finding equivalent to a finding that the person is under a disability and did the act charged against the person in respect of the offence, or
(d) the person has been cautioned in respect of a relevant offence.
(4) In subsection (3), "relevant offence" means an act which:
(a) constituted an offence under the law in force in the country concerned, and
(b) would have constituted an offence listed in Schedule 3 (other than at paragraph 60) or in Schedule 5 if it had been done in any part of the United Kingdom.
For this purpose an act punishable under the law in force in a country outside the United Kingdom constitutes an offence under that law, however it is described in that law.
(6) Subject to subsection (7), on an application under section 103A(4) the condition in subsection (4)(b) above (where relevant) is to be taken as met unless, not later than rules of court may provide, the defendant serves on the applicant a notice:
(a) stating that, on the facts as alleged with respect to the act concerned, the condition is not in the defendant's opinion met,
(b) showing the grounds for that opinion, and
(c) requiring the applicant to prove that the condition is met.
(7) The court, if it thinks fit, may permit the defendant to require the applicant to prove that the condition is met without service of a notice under subsection (6).

Trigger offences

Note: These trigger offences apply to Sexual Harm Prevention Orders and notification. Ed.

101.6 ***Power to order What are the Schedule 3 offences?***
Sexual Offences Act 2003 s 103B(8) Subsection (9) applies for the purposes of section 103A and this section.
(9) In construing any reference to an offence listed in Schedule 3, any condition subject to which an offence is so listed that relates:
(a) to the way in which the defendant is dealt with in respect of an offence so listed or a relevant finding (as defined by section 132(9)[see below]), or
(b) to the age of any person,
is to be disregarded.
Sexual Offences Act 2003 s 132(9) In this section, 'relevant finding', in relation to an offence, means:
(a) a finding that a person is not guilty of the offence by reason of insanity, or
(b) a finding that a person is under a disability and did the act charged against him in respect of the offence.
Note: The effect of these subsections is to require the court to ignore the conditions in the Schedule that relate to: a) the sentence the defendant received, b) the age of the defendant, and c) the age of the victim. An example of all three of these conditions is the entry in the Schedule for the offence of Sexual Offences Act 2003 s 3 (sexual assault), see para **78.4**. The conditions remain in force for notification, which is based on the same schedule and is triggered automatically. The conditions are lifted for Sexual Harm Prevention Orders, which are discretionary orders. Ed.
Warning Because of the need to ignore the conditions (see the Note above), they have been removed from the Schedule so the Schedule is not as it is in the Act. To see the full Schedule see **78.4**. Ed.
Sexual Offences Act 2003 Sch 3
Note: These statutes are listed in chronological order. Ed.
Sexual Offences Act 1956
para 1 s 1 (rape)
2 s 5 (intercourse with a girl under 13)
3 s 6 (intercourse with a girl under 16)
4 s 10 (incest by a man)
5 s 12 (buggery)
6 s 13 (indecency between men)
7 s 14 (indecent assault on a woman)
8 s 15 (indecent assault on a man)
9 s 16 (assault with intent to commit buggery)
10 s 28 (causing or encouraging the prostitution of, intercourse with or indecent assault on a girl under 16)
11 **Indecency with Children Act 1960** s 1 (indecent conduct towards a young child)
12 **Criminal Law Act 1977** s 54 (inciting a girl under 16 to have incestuous sexual intercourse)
13 **Protection of Children Act 1978** s 1 (indecent photographs of children)
14 **Customs and Excise Management Act 1979** s 170 (penalty for fraudulent evasion of duty etc.) in relation to goods prohibited to be imported under Customs Consolidation Act 1876 s 42 (indecent or obscene articles), if the prohibited goods included indecent photographs of persons under 16[1124] and: a) the conviction, finding or caution was before the commencement of this Part.[1125]
15 **Criminal Justice Act 1988** s 160 (possession of indecent photograph of a child)
16 **Sexual Offences (Amendment) Act 2000** s 3 (abuse of a position of trust)

[1124] Repealed by Criminal Justice Act 1988 Sch 16 para 1 on 1/1/00
[1125] Subsection b) is not listed as Sexual Offences Act 2003 s 103(8) and (9) (see the beginning of this paragraph) requires the court to disregard the subsection.

Sexual Offences Act 2003

17 s 1-2 (rape, assault by penetration)

18 s 3 (sexual assault)

19 s 4-6 (causing sexual activity without consent, rape of a child under 13, assault of a child under 13 by penetration)

20 s 7 (sexual assault of a child under 13)

21 s 8-12 (causing or inciting a child under 13 to engage in sexual activity, child sex offences committed by adults)

22 s 13 (child sex offences committed by children or young persons)

23 s 14 (arranging or facilitating the commission of a child sex offence)

24 s 15 (meeting a child following sexual grooming etc.)

24A s 15A[1126] (sexual communication with a child)

25 s 16-19 (abuse of a position of trust)

26 s 25-26 (familial child sex offences)

27 s 30-37 (offences against persons with a mental disorder impeding choice, inducements etc. to persons with a mental disorder)

28 s 38-41 (care workers for persons with a mental disorder)

29 s 47 (paying for sexual services of a child)

Note: s 47 is also listed in Schedule 5, see **101.7**. Ed.

29A s 48[1127] (causing or inciting child prostitution or pornography)

29B s 49 (controlling a child prostitute or a child involved in pornography)

29C s 50 (arranging or facilitating child prostitution or pornography)

Note: s 51-53 and 57-59A are listed offences in Schedule 5, see **101.7**. Ed.

30 s 61 (administering a substance with intent)

31 s 62-63 (committing an offence or trespassing, with intent to commit a sexual offence)

32 s 64-65 (sex with an adult relative)

33 s 66 (exposure)

34 s 67 (voyeurism)

35 s 69-70 (intercourse with an animal, sexual penetration of a corpse)

35A **Criminal Justice and Immigration Act 2008** s 63[1128] (possession of extreme pornographic images)

35B **Coroners and Justice Act 2009** s 62(1)[1129] (possession of prohibited images of children)

35C **Serious Crime Act 2015** s 69 (possession of paedophile manual)

Service offences

para 93 1) An offence under:

(a) Army Act 1955 s 70,

(b) Air Force Act 1955 s 70, or

(c) Naval Discipline Act 1957 s 42,

of which the corresponding civil offence (within the meaning of that Act) is an offence listed in any of paragraphs 1-35B.[1130]

(2) A reference in any of those paragraphs to being made the subject of a community sentence of at least 12 months is to be read, in relation to an offence under an enactment referred to in sub-paragraph (1), as a reference to being sentenced to a term of detention of at least 112 days.

[1126] This entry was inserted by Serious Crime Act 2015 Sch 4 para 66(1) and (2). In force 3/4/17

[1127] Paragraphs 29A-29C were inserted by Sexual Offences Act 2003 (Amendment of Schedules 3 and 5) Order 2007 2007/296.

[1128] Inserted by Criminal Justice and Immigration Act 2008 Sch 26 para 58(2)

[1129] Inserted by Coroners and Justice Act 2009, Sexual Offences Act 2003 Sch 21 para 62(2)

[1130] Amended by Coroners and Justice Act 2009 Sch 21 para 62(5)

(3) In sub-paragraph (2), the reference to detention is to detention awarded under Army Act 1955 s 71(1)(e) or Air Force Act 1955 or Naval Discipline Act 1957 s 43(1)(e).[1131]

para 93A 1) An offence under Armed Forces Act 2006 s 42 as respects which the corresponding offence under the law of England and Wales (within the meaning given by that section) is an offence listed in any of paragraphs 1 to 35B.[1132]

(2) A reference in any of those paragraphs to being made the subject of a community sentence of at least 12 months is to be read, in relation to an offence under that section, as a reference to:

(a) being made the subject of a service community order or overseas community order under the Armed Forces Act 2006 of at least 12 months; or

(b) being sentenced to a term of service detention of at least 112 days.

(3) Armed Forces Act 2006 s 48 (attempts, conspiracy, encouragement and assistance and aiding and abetting outside England and Wales) applies for the purposes of this paragraph as if the reference in subsection (3)(b) to any of the following provisions of that Act were a reference to this paragraph.

para 94 A reference to an attempt, conspiracy or incitement to commit that offence, and b) except in paragraphs 36 to 43, a reference to aiding, abetting, counselling or procuring the commission of that offence.

para 94A A reference in a preceding paragraph to an offence ('offence A') includes a reference to an offence under Serious Crime Act 2007 Part 2 in relation to which offence A is the offence (or one of the offences) which the person intended or believed would be committed.[1133]

Note: When considering this Schedule for the Sexual Harm Prevention Order, the age and sentence qualifications have been removed and they should be ignored, Sexual Offences Act 2003 s 106(14), see entry at the beginning of this paragraph. Ed.

R v Hamer 2017 EWCA Crim 192, 2 Cr App R (S) 13 (p 82) There is no power to make an SHPO for a breach of a SOPO, because the offence is in neither Schedule 3 nor Schedule 5.

101.7 ***Power to order What are the Schedule 5 offences?***

Note: The statutes are listed in chronological order. Ed.

Other offences for the purposes of Part II

para 1 Murder

2 Manslaughter

3 Kidnapping

4 False imprisonment

4A Outraging public decency[1134]

Offences Against the Person Act 1861

5 s 4 (soliciting murder)

6 s 16 (threats to kill)

7 s 18 (wounding with intent to cause grievous bodily harm)

8 s 20 (malicious wounding)

9 s 21 (attempting to choke, suffocate or strangle in order to commit or assist in committing an indictable offence)

10 s 22 (using chloroform etc. to commit or assist in the committing of any indictable offence)

11 s 23 (maliciously administering poison etc. so as to endanger life or inflict grievous bodily harm)

12 s 27 (abandoning children)

[1131] Inserted by Armed Forces Act 2006 Sch 16 para 212(2)(b)

[1132] Amended by Coroners and Justice Act 2009 Sch 21 para 62(5)

[1133] Added by Serious Crime Act 2007 Sch 6 para 63(2)

[1134] This offence was inserted by Sexual Offences Act 2003 (Amendment of Schedules 3 and 5) Order 2007 2007/296 para 3(2).

13 s 28 (causing bodily injury by explosives)
14 s 29 (using explosives etc. with intent to do grievous bodily harm)
15 s 30 (placing explosives with intent to do bodily injury)
16 s 31 (setting spring guns etc. with intent to do grievous bodily harm)
17 s 32 (endangering the safety of railway passengers)
18 s 35 (injuring persons by furious driving)
19 s 37 (assaulting officer preserving wreck)
20 s 38 (assault with intent to resist arrest)
21 s 47 (assault occasioning actual bodily harm)

Explosive Substances Act 1883

22 s 2 (causing explosion likely to endanger life or property)
23 s 3 (attempt to cause explosion, or making or keeping explosive with intent to endanger life or property)
24 **Infant Life (Preservation) Act 1929** s 1 (child destruction)
25 **Children and Young Persons Act 1933** s 1 (cruelty to children)
26 **Infanticide Act 1938** s 1 (infanticide)

Firearms Act 1968

27 s 16 (possession of firearm with intent to endanger life)
28 s 16A (possession of firearm with intent to cause fear of violence)
29 s 17(1) (use of firearm to resist arrest)
30 s 17(2) (possession of firearm at time of committing or being arrested for offence specified in Schedule 1 to that Act)
31 s 18 (carrying a firearm with criminal intent)

Theft Act 1968

31A s 1 (theft)[1135]
32 s 8 (robbery or assault with intent to rob)
33 s 9(1)(a) (burglary with intent to steal, inflict grievous bodily harm or do unlawful damage)[1136]
34 s 10 (aggravated burglary)
35 s 12A (aggravated vehicle-taking) involving an accident which caused the death of any person

Criminal Damage Act 1971

36 s 1 [when] arson [only]
37 s 1(2) (destroying or damaging property) other than an offence of arson
38 **Taking of Hostages Act 1982** s 1 (hostage-taking)

Aviation Security Act 1982

39 s 1 (hijacking)
40 s 2 (destroying, damaging or endangering safety of aircraft)
41 s 3 (other acts endangering or likely to endanger safety of aircraft)
42 s 4 (offences in relation to certain dangerous articles)
43 **Mental Health Act 1983** s 127 (ill-treatment of patients)

Child Abduction Act 1984[1137]

43A s 1 (offence of abduction of child by parent etc.)
43B s 2 (offence of abduction of child by other persons)
44 **Prohibition of Female Circumcision Act 1985 s 1** (prohibition of female circumcision)[1138]

Public Order Act 1986

45 s 1 (riot)

[1135] This offence was inserted by Sexual Offences Act 2003 (Amendment of Schedules 3 and 5) Order 2007 2007/296.
[1136] As amended by Sexual Offences Act 2003 (Amendment of Schedules 3 and 5) Order 2007 2007/296
[1137] Sections 2 and 4 were inserted by Sexual Offences Act 2003 (Amendment of Schedules 3 and 5) Order 2007 2007/296. Sections 2A and 4A were inserted by Protection of Freedoms Act 2012 Sch 9 para 146.
[1138] The offence was repealed by Female Genital Mutilation Act 2003 s 7 from 3/3/04. However, the offence remains in the schedule for historical offences.

46 s 2 (violent disorder)
47 s 3 (affray)
48 **Criminal Justice Act 1988** s 134 (torture)

Road Traffic Act 1988

49 s 1 (causing death by dangerous driving)
50 s 3A (causing death by careless driving when under influence of drink or drugs)

Aviation and Maritime Security Act 1990

51 s 1 (endangering safety at aerodromes)
52 s 9 (hijacking of ships)
53 s 10 (seizing or exercising control of fixed platforms)
54 s 11 (destroying fixed platforms or endangering their safety)
55 s 12 (other acts endangering or likely to endanger safe navigation)
56 s 13 (offences involving threats)

Protection from Harassment Act 1997[1139]

56A s 2 or 2A (offences of harassment and stalking)[1140]
57 s 4 or 4A (putting people in fear of violence and stalking involving fear of violence or serious alarm or distress)[1141]

Crime and Disorder Act 1998

58 s 29 (racially or religiously aggravated assaults)
59 s 31(1)(a) or (b) (racially or religiously aggravated offences, Public Order Act 1986 s 4 or 4A)
60 Channel Tunnel (Security) Order 1994 1994/570 Part II (offences relating to Channel Tunnel trains and the tunnel system)
60ZA **Regulation of Investigatory Powers Act 2000** s 53-54 (contravention of notice relating to encrypted information or tipping off in connection with such a notice)[1142]
60A **Postal Services Act 2000** s 85(3)-(4)[1143] (prohibition on sending certain articles by post)

International Criminal Court Act 2001

61 s 51-52 (genocide, crimes against humanity, war crimes and related offences), other than one involving murder
61A **Communications Act 2003** s 127(1) (improper use of public electronic communications network)[1144]

Sexual Offences Act 2003

62 s 47 [paying for sexual services of a child] where the victim or (as the case may be) other party was 16[1145] or over
63 s 51-53 or 57-59A [exploitation of prostitution and trafficking for sexual exploitation][1146]
63A **Domestic Violence, Crime and Victims Act 2004** s 5 (causing or allowing a child or vulnerable adult to die or suffer serious physical harm)[1147]
63B **Modern Slavery Act 2015 s 2** (human trafficking)[1148]

Service offences

para 172 An offence under:
(a) Army Act 1955 s 70,

[1139] This offence was inserted by Sexual Offences Act 2003 (Amendment of Schedules 3 and 5) Order 2007 2007/296.
[1140] Inserted by Protection of Freedoms Act 2012 Sch 9 para 146(a)(i) and (iii)
[1141] Words inserted by Protection of Freedoms Act 2012 Sch 9 para 146(b)(i)
[1142] Inserted by Policing and Crime Act 2009 Sch 7 para 25(2)
[1143] This offence was inserted by Sexual Offences Act 2003 (Amendment of Schedules 3 and 5) Order 2007 2007/296.
[1144] This offence was inserted by Sexual Offences Act 2003 (Amendment of Schedules 3 and 5) Order 2007 2007/296.
[1145] Anti-social Behaviour, Crime and Policing Act 2014 requires the court to ignore the phrase 'the age of any person' listed in the Schedule. The effect of this entry in the Schedule is open to argument.
[1146] The section 59A entry was added by Protection of Freedoms Act 2012 Sch 9 para 140(4).
[1147] This entry was inserted by Domestic Violence, Crime and Victims Act 2004 Sch 10 para 59(2) and was amended by Domestic Violence, Crime and Victims (Amendment) Act 2012 Sch 1 para 5.
[1148] As inserted by Modern Slavery Act 2015 Sch 5 para 5(1) and (3)

(b) Air Force Act 1955 s 70, or
(c) Naval Discipline Act 1957 s 42,

of which the corresponding civil offence (within the meaning of that Act) is an offence listed in any of the paragraphs 1-63A.[1149]

para 172A(1) An offence under Armed Forces Act 2006 s 42 as respects which the corresponding offence under the law of England and Wales (within the meaning given by that section) is an offence listed in any of paragraphs 1 to 63A.

(2) Armed Forces Act 2006 s 48 (attempts, conspiracy, encouragement and assistance and aiding and abetting outside England and Wales) applies for the purposes of this paragraph as if the reference in subsection (3)(b) to any of the following provisions of that Act were a reference to this paragraph.

General

173 A reference in a preceding paragraph to an offence includes:
(a) a reference to an attempt, conspiracy or incitement to commit that offence, and
(b) a reference to aiding, abetting, counselling or procuring the commission of that offence. The making of an order.

173A A reference in a preceding paragraph to an offence ('offence A') includes a reference to an offence under Serious Crime Act 2007 Part 2 in relation to which offence A is the offence (or one of the offences) which the person intended or believed would be committed.

174 A reference in a preceding paragraph to a person's age is a reference to his age at the time of the offence.

Test to apply This is listed at **101.3**.

101.8 *Scope of the order*

Sexual Offences Act 2003 s 103C(1) A Sexual Harm Prevention Order prohibits the defendant from doing anything described in the order.

Sexual Offences Act 2003 s 103C(4) The only prohibitions that may be included in a Sexual Harm Prevention Order are those necessary for the purpose of:
(a) protecting the public or any particular members of the public from sexual harm from the defendant, or
(b) protecting children or vulnerable adults generally, or any particular children or vulnerable adults, from sexual harm from the defendant outside the United Kingdom.

(5) In subsection (4) 'the public', 'sexual harm', 'child' and 'vulnerable adult' each has the meaning given in section 103B(1) [see para **101.4**].

Note: **Electronic tag** In *R (Richards) v Teesside Magistrates' Court* 2015 EWCA Civ 7, 1 Cr App R (S) 60, D challenged a requirement of his stand-alone SOPO for him to wear a tag as there was no express provision in the legislation and the tag was an interference with his privacy, and it was not a prohibition etc. The Master of the Rolls in the Court of Appeal held that the tag requirement was lawful. Ed.

101.9 *The order must not be oppressive*

R v Collard 2004 EWCA Crim 1664, 2005 1 Cr App R (S) 34 (p 155) D pleaded to seven counts of making indecent photographs or pseudo-photographs of children (1-7) and 16 counts of possession of indecent photographs or pseudo-photographs of children (8-24). On counts 1-7 he received 1 year's imprisonment on each count and on counts 8-24 he received 2 years' imprisonment on each count. All sentences were to be served concurrently. 5,284 similar offences were taken into consideration. D was also subject to a Restraining Order under Sex Offenders Act 1997 s 5A which prohibited him from owning, using, possessing or having any access to any personal computer, laptop or any other equipment capable of downloading any material from the Internet. The prohibition was not to apply to the lawful access to, and use of, the Internet in the course of lawful employment. Held. When a court makes a Restraining Order, its terms must be tailored

[1149] As amended by Domestic Violence, Crime and Victims Act 2004 Sch 10 para 59(4)

to meet the danger that the offender presents. It must not be oppressive, it must be proportionate. In the instant case the terms were draconian. It would have sufficed for the order to have prohibited D from downloading material from the Internet which was not for the purpose of any lawful employment. Order varied.
See also: *R v Guest* 2011 EWCA Crim 1542 (Late plea to making (×4) and possessing indecent photographs of a child, and possession of extreme pornographic images (×3). Held. SOPO was disproportionate and oppressive. His conduct was only aimed at females, whereas the order prohibited contact etc. with any person under the age of 16. Order amended.)
Note: These cases relate to a Restraining Order and a SOPO. The test is now different. What is required is a balanced approach. Ed.

101.10 ***Is the order necessary?***
R v Allen 2018 EWCA Crim 108 D pleaded to four counts of sexual activity with a child. He was aged 29 and he corresponded with G, aged 15, on social media. They met in July 2015. In September 2015, they met at an 'event' and afterwards had sex in a hotel bedroom. There was no sex at the next two meetings. At the following meeting, they had sex in a car. After the next meeting, G's mother found messages and reported D to the police. D told the mother he loved G and wanted to marry her. D made full admissions. The pre-sentence report said D did not seem to have acted in a sexually predatory way and he did not seem to have an unhealthy interest in young teenage girls. D had three relationships with partners of his age or slightly younger. The risk of harm to children was assessed as medium. Held. The test of necessity was not met. We quash the order.
See also: *R v MSS* 2018 EWCA Crim 266 (D pleaded to sexual activity with a female member of his family. He developed a relationship with his step-daughter, V. The sexual element started when V was aged 17 and lasted nine years. D was of positive good character. Held. The SHPO was not necessary.)

101.11 ***Downloading indecent material, Defendant was Is an order necessary?***
R v Halloren 2004 EWCA Crim 233 D pleaded to a number of offences of making indecent photographs or pseudo-photographs of a child (8 years' imprisonment). Police officers executed a search warrant and seized D's computer, which was subsequently found to contain seven images at Level 1, one at Level 2, two at Level 3 and three at Level 4, one of which was a moving image showing a pre-pubescent girl giving oral sex to an adult male. A number of similar offences were taken into consideration. D, aged 32, was of previous good character and it was recommended by a pre-sentence report that a Community Rehabilitation Order be imposed. However, the author of the report recognised that a custodial sentence was likely to be passed. The report also noted that there appeared to be a low risk of reoffending. Held. There must be material before the judge to show that an order is indeed necessary as opposed, for example, to being desirable. There is no such material in this case. The legislation requires that the judge be satisfied of certain matters before making the order. This requires the judge expressly to consider the statutory criteria for making the order and before making the order, to indicate the basis on which they have been met in the case before him. 'We are unable to see…the need to protect the public from serious harm from D.' Order quashed.
R v Collard 2004 EWCA Crim 1664, 2005 1 Cr App R (S) 34 (p 155) D pleaded to seven counts of making indecent photographs or pseudo-photographs of children (1-7) and 16 counts of possession of indecent photographs or pseudo-photographs of children (8-24). On counts 1-7 he received 1 year's imprisonment on each count and on counts 8-24 he received 2 years' imprisonment on each count. All sentences were to be served concurrently. 5,284 similar offences were taken into consideration. D was also subject to a Restraining Order under Sex Offenders Act 1997 s 5A which prohibited him from owning, using, possessing or having any access to any personal computer, laptop or any other equipment capable of downloading any material from the Internet. The prohibition was not to apply to the lawful access to, and use of, the Internet in the course of lawful

employment. Held. When a court makes a Restraining Order, its terms must be tailored to meet the danger that the offender presents. It must not be oppressive, it must be proportionate. In the instant case the terms were draconian. It would have sufficed for the order to have prohibited D from downloading material from the Internet which was not for the purpose of any lawful employment. Order varied.

R v Terrell 2007 EWCA Crim 3079, 2008 2 Cr App R (S) 49 (p 292) D pleaded to four offences of making indecent images of a child, with 36 similar offences TIC'd. The offences involved single images at Levels 1, 2, 3 and 5 found on D's computer, of boys between 7 and 13 years of age. None of the boys appeared to be under any coercion or distress. D, aged 21, had convictions at the age of 16 for making indecent images of children. Then, over 1,200 images were discovered, mostly at Levels 1 and 2 (4-month DTO). He was sentenced to 5 months' IPP concurrent on each count. The Judge concluded that a Sexual Offences Prevention Order was only available where a sentence of imprisonment exceeding 12 months had been passed. D appealed, arguing that although there was a significant risk of reoffending in a similar fashion, and that downloading such images contributed to the market and thereby the harm done to children, Criminal Justice Act 2003 s 224-229 required a more direct link between offence and serious harm than was present here. Held. Following *R v Beaney* 2004 EWCA Crim 449 and *R v Collard* 2004 EWCA Crim 1664, 2005 1 Cr App R (S) 34 (p 155), the previous Restraining Order provisions (Sex Offenders Act 1997 s 5A) could be satisfied by the harm done through downloading such images and the same reasoning applied to Sexual Offences Prevention Orders. Downloading perpetuated the market and networks, so encouraging the making of further images. The assertion that if the 'dangerousness' provisions in Criminal Justice Act 2003 were not satisfied, those in Sexual Offences Act 2003 s 104 and 106 (Sexual Offences Prevention Orders) could not be satisfied, was wrong. *R v Richards* 2006 EWCA Crim 2519 distinguished the two provisions. It is plain that the threshold for an IPP sentence must be higher than for the imposition of a Sexual Offences Prevention Order. The seriousness of the harm required by Criminal Justice Act 2003 is emphasised by the words 'death or personal injury' and stands in contrast with Sexual Offences Act 2003. It may be possible for the statutory criteria to be satisfied in certain cases where the notional determinate sentence is relatively short, e.g. a matter of months. There was no evidence that D's role in perpetuating the market would become more significant or that he would play a more important role in a distribution network. It cannot reasonably be said, in the context of the statutory provisions, that there is a significant risk of D's reoffending occasioning harm to a child or children whether through perpetuating the market, or through further indecent images being taken, or through a child becoming aware of the indecent purposes to which photographs might be put. The link between the offending act and the possible harm is too remote to satisfy the requirement that it be D's reoffending which causes the serious harm. Perpetuating the market or distribution network for indecent images encourages others to commission, take or create indecent images of a level which may be capable of causing serious harm to children and the child or children who might be photographed could well become aware of the use to which these photographs would be put. The indirect and uncertain harm arising from the contribution to the harm which any downloading of indecent images may have does not necessarily fall outside the scope of Sexual Offences Act 2003 provisions, as discussed in *R v Beaney* 2004 and *R v Collard* 2004.

The Judge was wrong to suppose that a Sexual Offences Prevention Order could not be imposed in the absence of a 12-month minimum determinate sentence[1150] or possibly notional determinate sentence. No statutory provision imposes such a limit. The potential utility of a Sexual Offences Prevention Order does not mean that the tests in Sexual Offences Act 2003 s 104 are necessarily satisfied. IPP quashed.

[1150] This related to IPP, which is no longer available.

R v Lea 2011 EWCA Crim 487 D pleaded to making (×16) and possessing (×5) indecent images of children aged between 3 and 15 (predominantly 12-15). There were 11,869 images, of which 6,275 were capable of being viewed, 1,390 Level 4 images and 33 Level 5 images. It was apparent that D had been involved in the collection and viewing of this material over a period of about five years. The material had not been distributed to others. A Sexual Offences Prevention Order was imposed, prohibiting, among other things, unsupervised contact with a child aged under 16, unsupervised contact with his child whilst aged under 16, accessing the Internet without the permission of the police and possessing a camera etc. outside his place of residence. D, aged 45, had one conviction for an unrelated offence. The defence argued that the SOPO should be restricted to preventing inappropriate use of computers. Held. There was no suggestion that D would progress to contact offences. There is force in the defence submission. The order was far too wide given the test in *R v Mortimer* 2010 EWCA Crim 1303. It would be quashed and replaced by the conditions in *R v Hemsley* 2010 EWCA Crim 225: a) not to use the Internet for a purpose other than work, education or lawful recreation and the purchase of goods/services, and b) not to use, save at his place of employment or supervised public facility, any computer which does not have software installed designed to prevent accessing child pornography. The order would be for 10 years, the same duration as his notification requirements.

See also: *R v Beaney* 2004 EWCA Crim 449 (Individuals merely viewing photographs do contribute to the harm suffered by children and do pose a threat which needs to be protected against.)

R v Blyth 2011 EWCA Crim 2399 (Plea to making an indecent photograph of a child (×3) (126 images and 21 movies at Levels 1 and 2) and possessing an extreme pornographic image (bestiality). Children aged between 6 and 13. Aged 56. Good character. Considering *R v Smith and Others* 2011 and *R v Mortimer* 2010, no basis to make a SOPO. Order quashed.)

Note: These relate to Restraining Orders and SOPOs. However, the two orders and the Sexual Harm Prevention Order all have the test of necessity. Ed.

101.12 ***Internet contact***

R v Bingham 2015 EWCA Crim 1342, 2016 1 Cr App R (S) 3 (p 10) D pleaded to distributing an indecent photograph. Using a fake name, D made contact with V, a 17-year-old who functioned as a 12-year-old because of his autism. D showed V a video of an adult male with a female child. V asked how old the child was and D said seven. D asked V to show his penis to the child. V seemed disgusted. D had experienced shame, his relationship broke up, he lost contact with friends and family and he was in employment.[1151] The Judge gave D 16 months and made an SHPO. Held. It was a Category B offence. The image was distributed to engage V in sexual activity. Not every case of distribution will warrant an SHPO. Distribution to a 17-year-old will not necessarily demonstrate a risk to younger children. It depends on the facts. The requirement of necessity must not be diluted, but here there was distribution to a young person, a stranger, to make him expose his penis. There was the evidence to justify the SHPO.

101.13 ***Foreign travel prohibitions***

SHPOs: prohibition on foreign travel

Sexual Offences Act 2003 s 103D(1) A prohibition on foreign travel contained in a Sexual Harm Prevention Order must be for a fixed period of not more than 5 years.

(2) A 'prohibition on foreign travel' means:

(a) a prohibition on travelling to any country outside the United Kingdom named or described in the order,

[1151] D's age and whether he was of good character were not revealed.

(b) a prohibition on travelling to any country outside the United Kingdom other than a country named or described in the order, or
(c) a prohibition on travelling to any country outside the United Kingdom.
(3) Subsection (1) does not prevent a prohibition on foreign travel from being extended for a further period (of no more than 5 years each time) under section 103E.
(4) A Sexual Harm Prevention Order that contains a prohibition within subsection (2)(c) must require the defendant to surrender all of the defendant's passports at a police station specified in the order,
(a) on or before the date when the prohibition takes effect, or
(b) within a period specified in the order.
(5) Any passports surrendered must be returned as soon as reasonably practicable after the person ceases to be subject to a Sexual Harm Prevention Order containing a prohibition within subsection (2)(c) (unless the person is subject to an equivalent prohibition under another order).
(6) Subsection (5) does not apply in relation to:
(a) a passport issued by or on behalf of the authorities of a country outside the United Kingdom if the passport has been returned to those authorities,
(b) a passport issued by or on behalf of an international organisation if the passport has been returned to that organisation.
(7) In this section 'passport' means:
(a) a United Kingdom passport within the meaning of the Immigration Act 1971,
(b) a passport issued by or on behalf of the authorities of a country outside the United Kingdom, or by or on behalf of an international organisation,
(c) a document that can be used (in some or all circumstances) instead of a passport.

R v B 2015 EWCA Crim 2046 D was convicted of four indecent assaults and three gross indecencies. When he was aged 18, D was heavily involved with his local church and in his gap year, he went to the Philippines to work with disadvantaged children. There he met a woman, W, whom he brought back to the UK and then married. When aged 18 or 19, he sexually assaulted two girls aged 9-10 and V1, aged 13. The worst incident was when D put his hand up V1's skirt and touched the top of her inner thigh. D put her hand on his erect penis through his trousers. Both V1 and V2 were adversely affected by the experience, particularly V1. There was no offending since then although there was an incident in the Philippines in 1995, which could not be charged in the UK. D was now aged 50 and after the gap year he went to an ecclesiastical college and then was ordained. He had devoted himself to charitable work in the Philippines over 30 years, for which he was awarded an MBE. The Judge passed a sentence of 5 years in total and made an SHPO with a foreign travel prohibition, prohibiting travel to 11 countries associated with sex tourism, including the Philippines. Held. The order must be proportionate to the risk involved. D regards the Philippines as his home. There was no offending in the last 20 years. To stop D living in the Philippines would be disproportionate. Order quashed.

For full details of the case see **327.23** in Volume 2.

R v Cheyne 2019 EWCA 182 D pleaded to two counts of voyeurism and was committed for sentence. He then absconded for five years. D returned to the UK to renew his passport and was arrested. He was given a suspended sentence with a treatment programme and an SHPO. About three months later, the prosecution applied to add a foreign travel prohibition banning all foreign travel. They relied on: a) his convictions for burglary with intent to rape (5 years) and indecent assaults, b) his desire to return to Thailand, c) his links with hotels, casinos and bars in Thailand, d) the inability of the police to manage him if he was abroad, e) his day trips out of Thailand, the purpose of which was unknown, and f) the fact that Thailand was known for sexual exploitation and the lack of monitoring of sex offenders. The defence said the offending was not serious and it was a breach of D's privacy. Held. We look at the risk posed and the background. The order was properly made.

For the principle whether the applicant needed a change of circumstances to add this foreign travel prohibition, see **101.32**.

Drafting the prohibitions etc.

These are listed at the **PREVENTIVE ORDERS Drafting the particular terms** section at **84.41**.

How long should the SHPO be?

101.14 ***Minimum and maximum length***

Sexual Offences Act 2003 s 103C(2) Subject to section 103D(1), a prohibition contained in a Sexual Harm Prevention Order has effect:

(a) for a fixed period, specified in the order, of at least 5 years, or

(b) until further order.

(3) A Sexual Harm Prevention Order:

(a) may specify that some of its prohibitions have effect until further order and some for a fixed period,

(b) may specify different periods for different prohibitions.

101.15 ***How long should the order be? Judicial guidance***

R v Rampley 2006 EWCA Crim 2203 The Judge made the SOPO 'until further order'. Held. There are advantages in the defendant knowing that there is a finite term to the order. 7 years substituted.

R v Jackson 2012 EWCA Crim 2602 D pleaded to voyeurism, indecent photographs of a child and possession of extreme photographs. He appealed his SOPO. Held. There have to be good reasons for extending the order beyond the reporting period. There may well be cases in which it would be entirely appropriate to do that. It is clear that there is no legal proscription which prevents the extension beyond that period. However, here 5 years was proportionate.

R v Young 2015 EWCA Crim 2512 D pleaded to having indecent photos on his phone. He was given a community order. The Judge made an indefinite order. Held. We see no reason to depart from the general rule set out in *R v Hammond* 2008 EWCA Crim 1358 that the SOPO should run for the same period as the notification period. The order shall last until 5 January 2020 (so 5 years).

R v Moxham 2016 EWCA Crim 182 D pleaded guilty to indecent image offences. Held. We substitute a community order for 12-month custody. The 15-year Sexual Harm Prevention Order was wrong in principle. It should not have lasted longer than the relevant notification period. Because of the community order, the appropriate length for the SHPO was 5 years.

R v Sokolowski and Another 2017 EWCA Crim 1903, 1 Cr App R (S) 30 (p 216) D pleaded to making indecent photographs. Held. para 6(v) An SHPO should not be made for an indefinite period, unless the court is satisfied of the need to do so. It should not be made indefinite without careful consideration or as a mere default option. Where an indefinite order is made, unless it is obvious, reasons (even if brief) should be given as to why it is necessary, see *R v McLellan and Bingley* 2017 EWCA Crim 1464, 2018 1 Cr App R (S) 18 (p 107) at para 25. para 35 Here, the order should be no longer than the notification period, so 10 years.

101.16 ***On the facts, how long should the order be?***

R v Collard 2004 EWCA Crim 1664, 2005 1 Cr App R (S) 34 (p 155) D pleaded to seven counts of making indecent photographs or pseudo-photographs of children (1-7) and 16 counts of possession of indecent photographs or pseudo-photographs of children (8-24). On counts 1-7 he received 1 year's imprisonment on each count and on counts 8-24 he received 2 years' imprisonment on each count. All sentences were to be served concurrently. 5,284 similar offences were taken into consideration. D was also subject to a Restraining Order under Sex Offenders Act 1997 s 5A, which prohibited him from owning, using, possessing or having any access to any personal computer, laptop or any other equipment capable of downloading any material from the Internet. The prohibition

was not to apply to the lawful access to, and use of, the Internet in the course of lawful employment. D appealed. Held. Bearing in mind the nature of the material, the depth of D's addiction or obsession and that there was nothing to indicate when D's proclivities might cease, an indefinite order was correct. He can apply to discharge the order at any time.
R v Whitton 2006 EWCA Crim 3229 D pleaded to three exposures. Within a three-month period, D had committed 12 separate offences involving exposure to females between the ages of 11 and 24, with the victims predominantly in their early teens. A number of these offences occurred outside a school. D, aged 43, was assessed as posing a medium risk to children and the public. Held. The duration was excessive, however, and the appropriate term was 5 years not 10.
R v Moxham 2016 EWCA Crim 182 D pleaded guilty to indecent image offences. Held. We substitute a community order for 12 months' custody. The 15-year Sexual Harm Prevention Order was wrong in principle. It should not have lasted longer than the relevant notification period. Because of the community order, the appropriate length for the SHPO was 5 years.
See also: *R v Rampley* 2006 EWCA Crim 2203 (Aged 53. On the facts, 7 years not until further order.)
Note: Three of these cases relate to Restraining Orders and SOPOs. The principle would appear to apply to SHPOs. Ed.

Combined with other orders

101.17 ***Determinate custody, Combined with***
R v Smith and Others 2011 EWCA Crim 1772, 2012 1 Cr App R (S) 82 (p 468) The Court gave guidance about SOPOs. Held. para 14 A SOPO may plainly be necessary if the sentence is a determinate term or an extended term. In each of those cases, whilst conditions may be attached to the licence, that licence will have a defined and limited life. The SOPO by contrast can extend beyond it and this may be necessary to protect the public from further offences and serious sexual harm as a result.
See also the note at **101.20**.

101.18 ***Existing Sexual Harm Prevention Order***
Sexual Offences Act 2003 s 103C(6) Where a court makes a Sexual Harm Prevention Order in relation to a person who is already subject to such an order (whether made by that court or another), the earlier order ceases to have effect.
For the other rules about combining SOPOs and other orders, see the **PREVENTIVE ORDERS** Combined with other orders section at **84.100**.

101.19 ***Extended sentences (EDS), Combined with***
Example: *R v BD* 2015 EWCA Crim 1415 (Convicted of two rapes and a sex assault. Stepdaughter, aged 6 or 7. One of the rapes was with a punch. Raped a family friend, aged 14, who was babysitting. No previous sexual convictions. Held. It was unfortunate that neither counsel dealt with the interaction of the extended sentence and the SOPO. Here we think the SOPO would provide sufficient protection so we quash the extended sentence.)
Note: This case relates to a SOPO. The principle would appear to apply to SHPOs. Ed.

101.20 ***Life sentence, Combined with***
R v Smith and Others 2011 EWCA Crim 1772, 2012 1 Cr App R (S) 82 (p 468) para 13 The usual rule ought to be that an indeterminate sentence needs no SOPO, at least unless there is some very unusual feature which means that such an order could add something useful and did not run the risk of undesirably tying the hands of the offender managers later.
R v MI 2012 EWCA Crim 1792 LCJ D was sentenced to IPP with a SOPO. He appealed the SOPO relying on *R v Smith and Others* 2011 EWCA Crim 1772, 2012 1 Cr App R

(S) 82 (p 468). Held. As a result of *R v Smith and Others* 2011, it would be rare for the two orders to be made simultaneously. Rare does not mean never, but here we quash the SOPO.

Note: Although these cases deal with SOPOs, there is no reason why these principles shouldn't be applied in relation to SHPO cases. Ed.

Note: These cases overlook the problem of sex offenders who start contacting children etc. while they are serving their sentences. Some of the contact may not be prohibited by prison rules or may be done when the offender is temporarily released. The licence conditions only operate when a prisoner is released. For these offenders there is a strong need for a Sexual Harm Prevention Order from the day of sentence. Ed.

For ***Sexual Harm Prevention Orders and notification*** see **78.12**.

Disclosure and Barring Service

101.21 ***Order combined with barring***

R v W 2015 EWCA Crim 434 D was convicted of rapes of children under 13 and other sex offences. He was sentenced to 20 years and given a SOPO. The issue of whether the SOPO was necessary arose. The prosecution said there was a lacuna in the law because the [DBS] barring applied to regulated activity which meant activity 'frequently carried out by the same person' on more than two days in any period of 30 days. They said if D on release was to work as a classroom assistant, sports instructor or scout master once or twice a month he would not be covered by the barring system. Held. The SOPO was necessary.

Appeals

101.22 ***Statutory power to appeal***

SHPOs and interim SHPOs: appeals

Sexual Offences Act 2003 s 103H(1) A defendant may appeal against the making of a Sexual Harm Prevention Order:

(a) where the order was made by virtue of section 103A(2)(a)(i) (general power to order SHPOs), as if the order were a sentence passed on the defendant for the offence,

(b) where the order was made by virtue of section 103A(2)(a)(ii) or (iii) (SHPOs where there is a finding of insanity/disability), as if the defendant had been convicted of the offence and the order were a sentence passed on the defendant for that offence.

(2) A defendant may appeal to the Crown Court against the making of an Interim Sexual Harm Prevention Order.

(3) A defendant may appeal against the making of an order under section 103E (SHPO variations, renewals and discharges), or the refusal to make such an order:

(a) where the application for such an order was made to the Crown Court, to the Court of Appeal,

(b) in any other case, to the Crown Court.

(4) On an appeal under subsection…(3)(b) (Magistrates' Court orders), the Crown Court may make such orders as may be necessary to give effect to its determination of the appeal, and may also make such incidental or consequential orders as appear to it to be just.

(5) Any order made by the Crown Court on an appeal under subsection (1)(c) or (2) (other than an order directing that an application be re-heard by a Magistrates' Court) is for the purposes of [Sexual Offences Act 2003] s 103E(9) or s 103F(5) (respectively) to be treated as if it were an order of the court from which the appeal was brought (and not an order of the Crown Court).

101.23 ***Who can appeal?***

R v D 2005 EWCA Crim 3660 D pleaded to eight counts of sexual abuse of his daughter. D was subject to a Sexual Offences Prevention Order, a condition of which prevented him from seeing his son, L. D appealed. Held. In the legislation, L has no right to apply to vary, renew or discharge the order.

101.24 ***Test for the Court of Appeal***

R v Mortimer 2010 EWCA Crim 1303 D was convicted of three counts of sexual assault on a child under the age of 13 and one count of causing or inciting a child to engage in sexual activity. He was sentenced to 3 years' IPP and a Sexual Offences Prevention Order. D appealed against the order on the basis that the terms were too wide, insufficiently clear and for an indefinite period of time. Held. There are three questions for us to consider: a) Is the order complained of necessary to protect the public generally or any particular member of the public from serious sexual harm? b) If it is necessary at all, are the particular terms of the order that has been made oppressive? c) Are the terms of the particular order proportionate?

Note: The test is different but otherwise the principles would appear to apply to SHPOs. Ed.

101.25 ***Judge fails to apply appropriate test***

R v D 2005 EWCA Crim 3660 The Judge did not go through the appropriate steps before making a SOPO. Held. It therefore falls to this Court to exercise those powers afresh. On the facts, SOPO varied.

Note: This principle would appear to apply to SHPOs. Ed.

101.26 ***Can the Court of Appeal correct an invalid order?***

R v Monument 2005 EWCA Crim 30 D pleaded to 16 counts of making indecent photographs or pseudo-photographs of a child (8 months' imprisonment on each count, concurrent). D had downloaded 4,266 indecent images, notably 378 of which were at Level 4 and 23 at Level 5 (see *R v Oliver* 2002 EWCA Crim 2766). On the day of sentencing, no application was made for the imposition of a Restraining Order. Some 14 days later, the Crown made an application to re-list the case within the 28-day period under the slip rule in order to add a Restraining Order. That hearing was heard a week later. By this point, the legislation containing the provisions for the imposition of a Restraining Order had been repealed, and provisions allowing the imposition of a Sexual Offences Prevention Order had been enacted. This fact was overlooked by the parties. The Judge imposed a Restraining Order on D, stating he was not prepared to do so for a term exceeding 3 years and that it should take effect from that day. When the oversight was discovered, D appealed against the Restraining Order, arguing that it was invalid. The Crown argued the order was valid as D was convicted prior to the earlier legislation being repealed. Held. What was purportedly 'done' under the earlier legislation could not have been done, as the legislation had been repealed. An argument that as a result of Interpretation Act 1978 s 17(2)(b) the effect of making a Restraining Order had the [same] effect as if a Sexual Offences Prevention Order had been made was unsustainable. Further, the Restraining Order could not be saved or preserved by Interpretation Act 1978 s 17(2)(b) as Sexual Offences Act 2003 s 104 did not re-enact the 1997 Act, as: a) there were differences between the two orders, and b) the legislation had been repealed. The order was invalid. Finally, Criminal Appeal Act 1968 s 11(3)(b) precludes the substitution of a Restraining Order by a Sexual Offences Prevention Order as the legislation requires Sexual Offences Prevention Orders to be a minimum of 5 years, whereas the Restraining Order in question was for 3 years. Order invalid and set aside.

R v Aldridge and Eaton 2012 EWCA Crim 1456 LCJ E was given a 3-year SOPO. Later the Judge was told the minimum period was 5 years and he varied it to 5 years believing that was the order he made. The application for a variation was out of time and no one attended. Held. The order was unlawful. The term cannot be extended as that would be treating E 'more severely'. The order must be quashed.

Note: These principles would appear to apply to SHPOs. Ed.

Variations, renewals and discharges

101.27 ***Statutory power to vary, renew and discharge***

SHPOs: variations, renewals and discharges

Sexual Offences Act 2003 s 103E(1) A person within subsection (2) may apply to the appropriate court for an order varying, renewing or discharging a Sexual Harm Prevention Order.
(2) The persons are:
(a) the defendant,
(b) the chief officer of police for the area in which the defendant resides,
(c) a chief officer of police who believes that the defendant is in, or is intending to come to, that officer's police area,
(d) where the order was made on an application by a chief officer of police under section 103A(4), that officer.
(3) An application under subsection (1) may be made:
(a) where the appropriate court is the Crown Court, in accordance with rules of court,
(b) in any other case, by complaint.
(4) Subject to subsections (5) and (7), on the application the court, after hearing the person making the application and (if they wish to be heard) the other persons mentioned in subsection (2), may make any order, varying, renewing or discharging the Sexual Harm Prevention Order, that the court considers appropriate.[1152]
(5) An order may be renewed, or varied so as to impose additional prohibitions on the defendant, only if it is necessary to do so for the purpose of:
(a) protecting the public or any particular members of the public from sexual harm from the defendant, or
(b) protecting children or vulnerable adults generally, or any particular children or vulnerable adults, from sexual harm from the defendant outside the United Kingdom.
Any renewed or varied order may contain only such prohibitions as are necessary for this purpose.
(6) In subsection (5) 'the public', 'sexual harm', 'child' and 'vulnerable adult' each has the meaning given in section 103B(1) [see **124A**].
(7)-(8) [see **101.29**]
(9) In this section 'the appropriate court' means:
(a) where the Crown Court or the Court of Appeal made the Sexual Harm Prevention Order, the Crown Court,
(b) where an adult Magistrates' Court made the order, that court, an adult Magistrates' Court for the area in which the defendant resides or, where the application is made by a chief officer of police, any adult Magistrates' Court acting for a local justice area that includes any part of the chief officer's police area,
(c) where a Youth Court made the order and the defendant is under the age of 18, that court, a Youth Court for the area in which the defendant resides or, where the application is made by a chief officer of police, any Youth Court acting for a local justice area that includes any part of the chief officer's police area,
(d) where a Youth Court made the order and the defendant is aged 18 or over, an adult Magistrates' Court for the area in which the defendant resides or, where the application is made by a chief officer of police, any adult Magistrates' Court acting for a local justice area that includes any part of the chief officer's police area.
In this subsection 'adult Magistrates' Court' means a Magistrates' Court that is not a Youth Court.

101.28 *Appealing variations Which court?*
R v Aldridge and Eaton 2012 EWCA Crim 1456 LCJ *R v Hoath* 2011 EWCA Crim 274 was correctly decided. The appeal is to the Court of Appeal (Criminal Division) not (Civil Division).

[1152] Surprisingly, this is what the subsection says. If the first 'the' is replaced by 'an', and a comma is inserted after the first 'application', the subsection makes more sense.

101.29 ***Time limits for discharging the order***

Sexual Offences Act 2003 s 103C(7) The court must not discharge an order before the end of 5 years beginning with the day on which the order was made, without the consent of the defendant and:

(a) where the application is made by a chief officer of police, that chief officer, or

(b) in any other case, the chief officer of police for the area in which the defendant resides.

(8) Subsection (7) does not apply to an order containing a prohibition on foreign travel and no other prohibitions.

101.30 ***Crown Court can't vary a Magistrates' Court order***

R v Hadley 2012 EWCA Crim 1997 In 2006, D committed a serious offence. On his release in 2008, D was made the subject of a stand-alone SOPO, until further order. In 2011, he was sentenced for five breaches. He agreed to the adding of an Internet condition. Held. The offence was Sexual Offences Act 2003 s 113(1)(a), which is not in the Sch 3 list, see **78.4**. Therefore no SOPO could be made. As variations to a Magistrates' Court order had to be made at a Magistrates' Court (see Magistrates' Courts Act 1980 s 108(7)), no variation was possible. Condition quashed.

Note: This rule would appear to also apply to SHPOs as Sexual Offences Act 2003 s 103I (which creates the offence of breach of SHPOs and SOPOs after SHPOs came into force) is not listed in Schedule 3 either. Ed.

101.31 ***Evidence to undermine original order***

Sadler v Worcester Magistrates' Court 2014 EWHC 1715 (Admin) High Court D was convicted of serious sexual offences in Romania including buggery of a young boy. D returned to the UK. On three occasions a 15-year-old boy, NP, had stayed at D's flat. An interim SOPO was made. The police subsequently found the boy at D's address. A stand-alone SOPO was made. D's appeal to the Crown Court was dismissed. After the 5-year limit had expired, D applied to discharge the order. The respondent called evidence that D had not undergone treatment and on up to 50 occasions had travelled to countries inferentially as a sex tourist. NP gave evidence that nothing sexual had occurred between D and himself, either before or after the imposition of the SOPO. The District Judge said that the starting point had to be that the SOPO was properly made and D could not seek to undermine the finding that in 2007 D posed a serious risk of sexual harm. He varied the order having regard to *R v Smith* 2011. D's appeal to the Crown Court was again dismissed. The defence submitted that NP's evidence was highly relevant and the Judge was wrong to ignore it because if it had been available in 2007, the order would not have been made. Held. The District Judge was correct to conclude that evidence should not be adduced to establish that the SOPO should not have been made. When the application is to discharge…a change of circumstances is necessary, otherwise the application is no more than an appeal against the original order. There was no change of circumstance since the order was made, so appeal dismissed.

101.32 ***Does an applicant need a change of circumstances to vary an order?***

R v Cheyne 2019 EWCA 182 D pleaded to two counts of voyeurism and was committed for sentence. He then absconded for five years. D returned to the UK to renew his passport and was arrested. He was given a suspended sentence with a treatment programme and an SHPO. About three months later, the prosecution applied to add a foreign travel prohibition banning all foreign travel. The defence said that the prosecution would need a change of circumstances. The police said at the first hearing they had not investigated D's past fully and an officer deputed to monitor him raised questions about: a) D's activities in Thailand where he had been when he absconded, and b) who D had been associating with. Held. para 16 For a party merely to return to the court and say, "I would like a variation" would be wrong in principle, because it would undermine the finality of the original order. So, in general terms, a variation must have some basis, rather than be, in effect, an illegitimate attempt to appeal. However, it is not right that a variation is precluded as a matter of law by a requirement for change, even [when] the evidence which provides the basis for the variation in the order was not known by the court, but should have been. Here the Chief Constable has a continuing obligation to protect children and vulnerable adults. There would be a perfectly proper basis even if there was fault on the part of the police for the application for the variation as it was sought here. The order proceeds from a protective duty and [recent] knowledge does justify an application of this kind. We grant the application.

101.33 ***Orders with unforeseen difficulties***

R v Hoath 2011 EWCA Crim 274 LCJ Where the defendant relies on particular and unanticipated difficulties arising from the form and/or wording of the order, those difficulties should be identified promptly (in writing and with particularity) and sent to the prosecuting authority so as to see whether the matter can be put before the Crown Court on an agreed basis and in any event to narrow the area of dispute.

102 Sexual Harm Prevention Orders/Sexual Offences Prevention Orders: Breach of

102.1

Sexual Offences Act 2003 s 103I(1) and (2) (Breach of Sexual Harm Prevention Orders, Interim Sexual Harm Prevention Orders, Sexual Offences Prevention Orders, Interim Sexual Offences Prevention Orders and Foreign Travel Orders).

Modes of trial Triable either way

Maximum sentences Indictment 5 years. Summary 6 months and/or an unlimited fine.[1153] There are maximum fines for those aged under 18, see **13.44**.

Conditional discharge This order is not available for breaches of a SOPO.[1154]

Breach of Sexual Offences Prevention Orders There is no power to make an SHPO for a breach of a SOPO, because the offence is in neither Schedule 3 nor Schedule 5, see *R v Hamer* 2017 EWCA Crim 192, 2 Cr App R (S) 13 (p 82).

General principles

102.2 ***Is there a defence the term was invalid?***

R (W) v DPP 2005 EWHC 1333 (Admin) High Court W was prohibited from 'committing any criminal offence'. Breach proceedings were conducted and the issue arose whether the validity of the term affected the breach issue. Held. An ASBO is to be treated as a valid order unless and until it is varied. It is only if it is invalid, as opposed to an order which might have been made in some other form, that any question arises as to whether the court considering an allegation of breach of the order can take into account submissions relating to its validity. *Boddington v British Transport Police* 1999 2 AC 143 is authority for the proposition that if an order of this type is plainly invalid, then the magistrates can consider submissions to that effect in the same way as they can consider submissions that a bye-law was *ultra vires* without the necessity of prior proceedings or concurrent proceedings in the High Court for the purpose of identifying and declaring the invalidity. This would only apply to an order as plainly invalid as one which contains a restraint preventing a defendant from committing any criminal offence. There will be a danger of opening floodgates if challenges to ASBOs could be made in breach proceedings, but in all these cases there are exceptions which are as plain as the exception in this case. This prohibition was unenforceable.

Note: Although this case deals with an ASBO, the principles would apply to SHPOs. Ed.

102.3 ***Duplicity, Breach and***

S v Doncaster Youth Offending Team 2003 EWHC 1128 (Admin) High Court S was convicted of failing to comply with a DTO. S had failed to reside where the YOT had

[1153] Legal Aid, Sentencing and Punishment of Offenders Act 2012 s 85(1) and (4) and Legal Aid, Sentencing and Punishment of Offenders Act 2012 (Commencement No 11) Order 2015 2015/504

[1154] Sexual Offences Act 2003 s 103I(4)

instructed him to, and he had failed to report for four consecutive weeks. It was submitted that the information was bad for duplicity. Held. Sometimes it is difficult to distinguish between separate offences, on the one hand, and different features of committing the same offence, on the other. There were two quite separate licence conditions of which the appellant was in breach. These were failing to keep in touch with his supervising officer and failing to live at the address approved by his supervising officer. These were two separate offences that should not have been tried on the same information.
Note: Although this case deals with a failure to comply with a DTO, the principles would apply to breaches of SOPOs. Ed.

102.4 ***CRO should have details of the order breached***
Criminal Practice Directions 2015 EWCA Crim 1567 para II 8A.7 Where the current alleged offence could constitute a breach of an existing sentence such as a suspended sentence, community order or conditional discharge, and it is known that that sentence is still in force, details of the circumstances of the offence leading to the sentence should be included in the antecedents. The detail should be brief and include the date of the offence.

Sentencing: Guidance

102.5 ***Breach Offences Guideline 2018***
Breach Offences Guideline 2018, see www.banksr.com Other Matters Guidelines tab In force 1 October 2018 page 33
Breach of a sexual harm prevention order (also applicable to breach of a sexual offences prevention order and to breach of a foreign travel order)
Sexual Offences Act 2003 s 103I

STEP ONE **Determining the offence category**

The court should determine the offence category with reference only to the factors listed in the tables below. In order to determine the category, the court should assess **culpability** and **harm**.
Culpability
In assessing culpability, the court should consider the **intention** and **motivation** of the offender in committing any breach.

A	• Very serious or persistent breach
B	• Deliberate breach falling between Categories A and C
C	• Minor breach • Breach just short of reasonable excuse

Harm

The level of **harm** is determined by weighing up all the factors of the case to determine the harm that has been caused or was at risk of being caused. In assessing any risk of harm posed by the breach, consideration should be given to the original offence(s) for which the order was imposed and the circumstances in which the breach arose.

Category 1	Breach causes **very** serious harm or distress
Category 2	Cases falling between Categories 1 and 3
Category 3	Breach causes little or no harm or distress

102.6

STEP TWO **Starting point and category range**

Having determined the category at step one, the court should use the corresponding starting point to reach a sentence within the category range from the appropriate sentence table below. The starting point applies to all offenders irrespective of plea or previous convictions.

	Culpability		
Harm	**A**	**B**	**C**
Category 1	**Starting point** 3 years' custody	**Starting point** 2 years' custody	**Starting point** 1 year's custody
	Category range 2 to 4 years 6 months' custody	**Category range** 36 weeks' to 3 years' custody	**Category range** High-level community order to 2 years' custody
Category 2	**Starting point** 2 years' custody	**Starting point** 1 year's custody	**Starting point** High-level community order
	Category range 36 weeks' to 3 years' custody	**Category range** High-level community order to 2 years' custody	**Category range** Medium-level community order to 26 weeks' custody
Category 3	**Starting point** 1 year's custody	**Starting point** 26 weeks' custody	**Starting point** Medium-level community order
	Category range High-level community order to 2 years' custody	**Category range** Medium-level community order to 36 weeks' custody	**Category range** Band B fine to high-level community order

For the meaning of high-level, medium-level and low-level community orders, see **15.12**. For a Band B fine, see **58.28**.

102.7 [Aggravating and mitigating factors]

Page 36 The table below contains a **non-exhaustive** list of additional factual elements providing the context of the offence and factors relating to the offender. Identify whether any combination of these, or other relevant factors, should result in an upward or downward adjustment from the starting point.

In some cases, having considered these factors, it may be appropriate to move outside the identified category range.

Factors increasing seriousness
Statutory aggravating factors:
Previous convictions, having regard to a) the **nature** of the offence to which the conviction relates and its **relevance** to the current offence; and b) the **time** that has elapsed since the conviction
Offence committed whilst on bail
Other aggravating factors:
Breach committed immediately or shortly after order made

History of disobedience of court orders (where not already taken into account as a previous conviction)
Breach involves a further offence (where not separately prosecuted)
Targeting of particular individual the order was made to protect
Victim or protected subject of order is particularly vulnerable
Offender takes steps to prevent victim or subject harmed by breach from reporting an incident or seeking assistance
Offence committed on licence or while subject to post sentence supervision
Factors reducing seriousness or reflecting personal mitigation
Breach committed after long period of compliance
Prompt voluntary surrender/admission of breach
Age and/or lack of maturity where it affects the responsibility of the offender
Mental disorder or learning disability where linked to the commission of the offence
Sole or primary carer for dependent relatives

STEP THREE to STEP EIGHT These are: Consider assistance to the prosecution, Reduction for guilty plea, Totality principle, Ancillary orders, Duty to give reasons and Consider time spent on bail with a tag.

102.8 ***Suggested approach to the guideline***

Note: I have listed some old cases in this book, because they deal with legal principles. Those cases should be treated with care as the new guideline has a new structure which must be applied. The old cases should not determine the length of the sentence. That is determined by the guideline. Ed.

102.9 ***Judicial guidance***

R v Brown 2001 EWCA Crim 724, 2002 1 Cr App R (S) 1 (p 1) Police obtained a Sex Offender Order for the defendant. Held. It would be wholly illogical if, against the background that the order was for the protection of children, a judge did not have the protection of children foremost in his mind. The actual quality of the acts which constituted the breach are by no means the only consideration in determining its seriousness.

R v Fenton 2006 EWCA Crim 2156, 2007 1 Cr App R (S) 97 (p 597) D breached his Sex Offender Order. The Court considered the sentencing in breach of ASBO cases as instructive. Held. If the breach does not involve any real or obvious risk to that section of the public [which] it is intended should be protected by the order, a community penalty which further assists the offender to live within the terms of the order may well be appropriate, although repeated breaches will necessarily involve a custodial sentence, if only to demonstrate that the orders of the court are not to be ignored and cannot be broken with impunity.

R v Byrne 2009 EWCA Crim 1555, 2010 1 Cr App R (S) 65 (p 433) D was given 15 years and a SOPO for buggery. He breached the SOPO repeatedly. He chose deliberately to breach the child contact prohibition to prove he could be with children without abusing them. Held. para 17-18 The importance of whether an appellant has deliberately chosen to ignore a SOPO on a wholesale basis and persistently…goes to the question of culpability, which must always be considered in determining the seriousness of offending. The other aspect that informs an assessment of seriousness is that of harm. The question of an assessment of the risks run by the breach of the SOPO comes into play. That assessment includes not only a consideration of the immediate risks which were generated by the breach to the other people concerned, it also imports a consideration of the nature and magnitude of the underlying general risk posed by the offender, reflected in his previous offending.

R v Razaq and Razaq 2011 EWCA Crim 2677 D received 11 years for two sexual activity counts. He had previous convictions for the same offence. D breached his SOPO. Held. If [a SOPO] is contravened, serious punishment should follow. Compliance with the SOPO is not optional and no offender should imagine he has a number of chances to breach it before the law will crack down. This 3-year sentence (concurrent) sends a powerful message that first-time compliance is required.

R v Koli 2012 EWCA Crim 1869, 2013 1 Cr App R (S) 6 (p 39) D was convicted of two breaches of his Serious Crime Prevention Order. Held. para 18 The court must take into account: a) the time between the imposition of the order and the date of the breach, b) any history of non-compliance, c) whether non-compliance has i) been repeated and ii) come in the face of warnings and requests for information, and d) whether the non-compliance was inadvertent or deliberate. It is particularly important whether the breach was related to the commission of further serious offences and might lead to the conclusion that the failure to comply added to the risk that the particular subject of the order was likely to commit further offences. The court would also have to consider the harm caused by non-compliance for breach.

R v Bell 2012 EWCA Crim 2362 D pleaded to breach of a SOPO. Held. Any serious breach of a SOPO is likely to attract a substantial custodial sentence because: a) by the very nature of the order, a sexual crime has already been committed, b) the SOPO has been held to be a necessity, and c) it will have been flouted by the offender.

R v Pilling 2013 EWCA Crim 1944 D pleaded to 12 breaches of his SOPO. Many of the breaches amounted to sexual offences, which were not charged. Held. That charging was quite proper. Breaching the order attracts a higher sentence than any specific offence would have attracted.

For more detail see **102.12**.

102.10 ***Consecutive sentence for offending and SHPO is appropriate***

R v Stilwell 2016 EWCA Crim 1375 D pleaded to child sex offences and breach of his Sexual Offences Prevention Order. D received a global sentence taking into account the breach of the SOPO. para 31 The defence argued that the SOPO sentence should be concurrent because the commission of the child sex offence necessarily involved a breach of the SOPO. Once done the global sentence should be reduced. Held. 'The imposition of imprisonment for breach of a SOPO or SHPO consecutive to that for the offence, the facts of which give rise substantially but not entirely to the breach, is sound sentencing practice and it is to be encouraged subject to the principles of totality or, where it is necessary to front-load the sentences for the main offence in order, as could have happened in this case, to achieve a sentence to reflect the overall criminality of the appellant.'

102.11 ***Need for sentencer to address the behaviour as well as punish***

R v McGreen 2010 EWCA Crim 2776 D pleaded to possession of extreme pornographic images and other similar counts. The Judge sentenced D to imprisonment. Held. These are very difficult sentencing exercises. There is a public interest in punishing people who view and download this kind of material, but there is also a public interest to try to ensure that people who do commit such offending are dealt with in a way which is likely to reduce, rather than leave untreated, their need for this kind of imagery. Immediate release.

R v V 2013 EWCA Crim 488 D pleaded at the PCMH to breach of a SOPO and five counts of making indecent images. In 2010 he was sentenced to a 3-year community order and an indefinite SOPO for 31 offences of making indecent images. In 2011, police visited his home and found 46,000 indecent images on his computer. There were 3,220 at Level 1, 559 at Level 2, 313 at Level 3, 341 at Level 4 and 53 at Level 5. He made frank admissions. The first pre-sentence report discussed D's Community Sex Offender Group Work programme and how at the time of the offences, D had only just begun the programme, whereas when he was to be sentenced, he had nearly completed it. There was about 15 months' delay before sentencing during which time D had changed. The report recommended a suspended sentence as it would assist in addressing D's behaviour. Held. We agree with the comments in *R v McGreen* 2010 (see above). There is a public interest in trying, by appropriate measures, to reduce future offending as well as punishing past offending. The learned Judge on this occasion failed to address that particular element and the delay. Had he done so, he would have followed the recommendation of the PSR. We now do so. **16 months suspended** with a Sex Offender Treatment Programme, not 18 months.

Sentencing: Specific breaches

102.12 ***Being in the company etc. of those aged under 16 Pre-2018 guideline case***

R v Pilling 2013 EWCA Crim 1944 D pleaded to 12 breaches of his SOPO. In February 2010, he was given a community order and a SOPO for possession of indecent images of a child. The SOPO prohibited contact with girls aged under 18. From August 2011, he sent over 50 text messages a week to V, a 13-year-old girl, during a six-month period. Her actual age was not discussed. D tried to meet her. Also in August 2011, he sent 15-20 text messages to V2. There were requests to see her naked. V2's mother texted D to say V2 was only 14 years old. D said he was sorry and continued texting V2. He texted V3, who was a 15-year-old vulnerable girl who suffered from an attachment disorder. D used false names and pretended he was a doctor and that he had a 15-year-old daughter. D asked for naked pictures of her and she sent him indecent images of herself. They met and D attempted to kiss her. She pulled away and he left her at a railway station. Because of her autism she did not board a train and was missing for six hours. Six months later he picked her up from school and they went for a walk. D told her he wanted sexual intercourse. He touched her and kissed her but she pulled away. He pushed her and she was bruised. He became angry when she didn't drink enough of the vodka he had given her. He gave her £20 and left her at a railway station but she didn't catch a train. V3 was missing overnight. He also breached the order by having three mobiles with internet access. D was aged 59. He was assessed with having a high risk of harm to children. Held. D was exceptionally devious in his use of text messages. He was callously indifferent to V3's safety. In all **40 months** not 4½ years.

102.13 ***Computer/Internet breaches Pre-2018 guideline cases***

R v Bell 2012 EWCA Crim 2362 D pleaded to breach of a SOPO and distributing an indecent photograph of a child. In 2010, a community order and a SOPO were imposed for two exposures and inciting etc. a female child under 16 to engage in sexual activity (×2). The SOPO prohibitions included not communicating with, or attempting to do so, girls aged under 16 and an Internet access prohibition involving girls aged under 16. Less than a year later, D accessed 'TeenChat', an Internet chat room. A police officer posed as 'Amy', a 13-year-old girl. D asked Amy whether she was 'into spanking'. The conversation progressed onto Windows Live Messenger, where D claimed he was a 44-year-old single mother involved in an 'all mother spanking club' where girls were subjected to spanking and physical abuse. During the chat with Amy, D distributed a number of images online, one of which was a Level 1 indecent image of a female child aged 11-13. The child posed naked from the thigh upwards on a bed. In 1999, D had three convictions for indecent assault on females. The pre-sentence report concluded that there was a high risk of reoffending. Held. There were two flagrant breaches of the SOPO. A starting point of **18 months** was appropriate. With the aggravation and the plea, the sentence was **18 months** not 3 years. 2 months concurrent for the photograph would remain.

R v Draynor 2016 EWCA Crim 646 D pleaded (full credit) to breaching his SOPO. In 2004, police obtained a Risk of Sexual Harm Order for D after there was inappropriate

behaviour towards a young male, V. In 2010, D pleaded to five sexual activity counts involving a child aged between 12 and 15 and two breaches of his Risk of Sexual Harm Order. The activity involved masturbating and touching a boy. He was sentenced to 8 years and a SOPO was made. In 2011, the month after his release, he used Facebook to contact a 13-year-old boy. D was returned to prison. While in custody, the SOPO was amended to prohibit any access to social networking sites. In March 2015, D was released and his SOPO was explained to him on a home visit by his offender manager. In June 2015, D saw his probation officer and asked whether he could contact a website called Hi5. After making enquiries the officer told D it was prohibited. Later that day, D went to a library and contacted that site. In interview D admitted the breach and also admitted searching the profile of a brother of V. D had no other convictions and the pre-sentence report said he had complied well with all the programmes and courses he had attended in prison. Held. This was a deliberate and flagrant breach of the SOPO. We start at 30 months so with plea **20 months** not 32.
See also: *R v Eller* 2015 EWCA Crim 2340 (Breached Internet protection terms by using computer to direct child rape in Philippines. A consecutive sentence of **3 years** was not too long. The total sentence of 14 years was severe but upheld.)

102.14 ***Minor breaches Pre-2018 guideline cases***
R v Angell 2014 EWCA Crim 1382, 2 Cr App R (S) 80 (p 631) D was given a SOPO which prevented him from having any article etc. about the care and nurturing of children aged under 16. After serving the 5-year custodial term of his extended sentence for child sex offences, he was released. Police searched D's house, finding pregnancy and baby magazines and also soiled nappies. D was recalled to prison. He pleaded to breaching the SOPO, receiving a 2-year community order. 11 months later, police found unused and clean nappies, baby cream and wipes. D was aged 63 and, in addition to breaching the SOPO before, had convictions for several sex offences against children. One was for unlawfully detaining a girl aged 13. The pre-sentence report said he had no experience of intimate relationships, but said he had a desire to look after children. Further, D could not accept the risks he presented, having no insight into his behaviour. He deliberately breached the SOPO, saying he would only abide by it if and when he had a child himself to look after, which would be as a result of a 'sinister relationship' or an abduction. Held. His behaviour was related to some bizarre and sinister obsession. This was the second breach of the [baby prohibition]. There was no alternative to custody but the breaches were minor so **6 months consecutive** per breach making **12 months**, not 3 years, in all.
R v Lane 2017 EWCA Crim 1439 D, now aged 73, pleaded at the Magistrates Court to a breach of his SOPO. Following D's release from prison, he moved into sheltered accommodation for the elderly and the managers of the home were told D was not to have contact with children visiting residents. D befriended two residents and had contact with children. He then sent the children Christmas cards and presents. His invitation to the children to visit his accommodation was not successful. There was similar further contact two months later. These children were aged 9, 8, 5 and 3. He asked for their dates of birth, so he could buy them presents. D did give them presents. The residents gave them a photograph album containing photographs of children as a thank you gesture. This was the breach of the SOPO. D returned the photographs, saying he was not allowed them. D was arrested and admitted he had groomed the residents and that if he had been able to be alone with the children there was a 90% chance of sex offences taking place. D had 25 previous convictions. In 1996 for five sex offences against females aged under 13 and other sex offences he received 10 years. In 2003 police found images of children in his cell. In 2004[1155] a SOPO was made. It was breached in: 2006 (community order), 2007 (2 years) and 2010 (4 years). The Judge gave credit for the plea (but only 20%) and because he had handed the photographs back. The Judge also said it

[1155] The judgment says it was 2014, but that can't be right because of the dates given for when the order was breached.

was only a matter of time before D touched a child again, despite the long sentences he had been given. That meant the photographs were only a small part of what was going on, because D was grooming children with a view to abusing them. Wishing to protect children, the Judge said he would pass the same 4-year sentence again. Held. D was an entrenched paedophile. We should not start at the maximum for the offence. D needs full credit for his plea. We start at 4½ years, so with plea 3 years.

102.15 ***Notify address etc., Failure to*** ***Pre-2018 guideline case***

R v PSD 2013 EWCA Crim 2605 D pleaded to failing to comply with notification requirements of his SOPO (×2) and doing an act prohibited by his SOPO. D was convicted of rape and other sexual offences against his step-daughter in 2005. He received 8 years and was given a SOPO. He was released in 2011. He began a relationship with W, who had children and young granddaughters. W was unaware of D's convictions. He failed to notify the police that he was staying at W's address. On one occasion D took the children to a football match (the prohibited act offence). D was aged 44 at appeal. He had not engaged in offending treatment work. Held. That was of grave concern. Immediate custody was correct. There was part compliance and there were none of the extreme aggravating features identified in *R v Byrne* 2009 EWCA Crim 1555, 2010 1 Cr App R (S) 65 (p 433). Starting at 4 years was too high. With full credit for the plea, **18 months** not 2 years 8 months.

102.16 ***Persistent breaches*** ***Pre-2018 guideline cases***

R v Lazenby 2016 EWCA Crim 337 D pleaded (full credit) to eight offences of breaching a SOPO. D was an entrenched paedophile, with a particular interest in children aged under 5. On eight separate occasions he used a public library computer to search for pictures of such children. None of the pictures accessed were prohibited and were about potty training etc. D made full admissions. D was now aged 47 and was sentenced in 1984 for indecent assault (conditional discharge) and in 1993 for child sex offences (probation). In 2002, he was sentenced for child image offences to a 10-year extended sentence (6 years' custody 4 years' extended licence). On his release, photographs of children were found in his room at a hostel. He was recalled to prison. In his prison cell indecent sexual pictures were found. The day after his next release in 2010, he was found in possession of child images with written fantasies. He was recalled. In 2011 more pictures of children were found in his cell. The police then applied for a SOPO involving Internet prohibitions. In 2012, he was sentenced for a breach of that order to a 3-year community order. From that date the probation saw a change in his attitudes. He had completed courses and had 2 years without an incident. Held. There was something of a sea change in his attitude. He had now served 4 months of the 20-month sentence he had received. A tenancy was available to him which might not be if his appeal was dismissed. We substitute a fresh **12-month community order** with a rehabilitation requirement.

R v Pennant 2017 EWCA Crim 1180 D pleaded to three outraging public decency counts and three breaches of a SOPO. At various times throughout the day, D was seen sitting on an electricity box at the corner of a road in Nottingham. He was masturbating and seemed to take an interest in females as they walked past. D was subject to a SOPO which prohibited him from using 'sexual words or gestures towards any female with whom he is not in a relationship and without her consent…' D had previous convictions between 2007 and 2011 for 12 counts of exposure. In 2014, he committed a sex assault. In 2008 and 2014, he had breached court orders. This offending was whilst he was on licence. The Judge said that D was becoming a menace and passed 16 months on each indecency count consecutively, and 16 months for each breach, concurrent, making 4 years. Held. There can be no doubt that the Judge was entitled to pass a custodial sentence but we must consider totality. Before plea, 3 years would have been sufficient, so with the plea discount, **2 years** on all counts concurrent.

R v Lane 2017 EWCA Crim 1439 D, now aged 73, pleaded at the Magistrates Court to a breach of his SOPO. Following D's release from prison, he moved into sheltered accommodation for the elderly and the managers of the home were told D was not to have contact with children visiting residents. D befriended two residents and had contact with children. He then sent the children Christmas cards and presents. His invitation to the children to visit his accommodation was not successful. There was similar further contact two months later. These children were aged 9, 8, 5 and 3. He asked for their dates of birth, so he could buy them presents. D did give them presents. The residents gave them a photograph album containing photographs of children as a thank you gesture. This was the breach of the SOPO. D returned the photographs, saying he was not allowed them. D was arrested and admitted he had groomed the residents and that if he had been able to be alone with the children there was a 90% chance of sex offences taking place. D had 25 previous convictions. In 1996 for five sex offences against females aged under 13 and other sex offences he received 10 years. In 2003 police found images of children in his cell. In 2004[1156] a SOPO was made. It was breached in: 2006 (community order), 2007 (2 years) and 2010 (4 years). The Judge gave credit for the plea (but only 20%) and because he had handed the photographs back. The Judge also said it was only a matter of time before D touched a child again, despite the long sentences he had been given. That meant the photographs were only a small part of what was going on, because D was grooming children with a view to abusing them. Wishing to protect children, the Judge said he would pass the same 4-year sentence again. Held. D was an entrenched paedophile. We should not start at the maximum for the offence. D needs full credit for his plea. We start at 4½ years, so with plea 3 years.

103 SEXUAL OFFENCES PREVENTION ORDERS (REPEALED)

103.1

This order was repealed and replaced by Sexual Harm Prevention Orders and Sexual Risk Orders by Anti-social Behaviour, Crime and Policing Act 2014. The repeal was on 8 March 2015.[1157]

The details of the order can be found in the 9th edition of this book.

Breaches see the previous chapter.

103.2 ***Statutory power to vary, renew and discharge***

SOPOs: variations, renewals and discharges

Sexual Offences Act 2003 s 108 (1) A person within subsection (2) may apply to the appropriate court for an order varying, renewing or discharging a sexual offences prevention order.

(2) The persons are:

(a) the defendant;

(b) the chief officer of police for the area in which the defendant resides;

(c) a chief officer of police who believes that the defendant is in, or is intending to come to, his police area;

(d) where the order was made on an application under section 104(5), the chief officer of police who made the application.

(3) An application under subsection (1) may be made:

(a) where the appropriate court is the Crown Court, in accordance with rules of court;

(b) in any other case, by complaint.

(4) Subject to subsections (5) and (6), on the application the court, after hearing the person making the application and (if they wish to be heard) the other persons mentioned in subsection (2), may make any order, varying, renewing or discharging the sexual offences prevention order, that the court considers appropriate.

[1156] The judgment says it was 2014, but that can't be right because of the dates given for when the order was breached.

[1157] Anti-social Behaviour, Crime and Policing Act 2014 (Commencement No 8, Saving and Transitional Provisions) Order 2015 2015/373

(5) An order may be renewed, or varied so as to impose additional prohibitions on the defendant, only if it is necessary to do so for the purpose of protecting the public or any particular members of the public from serious sexual harm from the defendant (and any renewed or varied order may contain only such prohibitions as are necessary for this purpose).
(6) The court must not discharge an order before the end of 5 years beginning with the day on which the order was made, without the consent of the defendant and:
(a) where the application is made by a chief officer of police, that chief officer, or
(b) in any other case, the chief officer of police for the area in which the defendant resides.
(7) In this section "the appropriate court" means:
(a) where the Crown Court or the Court of Appeal made the sexual offences prevention order, the Crown Court;
(b) where a magistrates' court made the order, that court, a magistrates' court for the area in which the defendant resides or, where the application is made by a chief officer of police, any magistrates' court whose commission area includes any part of the chief officer's police area;
(c) where a youth court made the order, that court, a youth court for the area in which the defendant resides or, where the application is made by a chief officer of police, any youth court whose commission area includes any part of the chief officer's police area.
(8) This section applies to orders under:
(a) section 5A of the Sex Offenders Act 1997 (restraining orders),
(b) section 2 or 20 of the Crime and Disorder Act 1998 (sex offender orders made in England and Wales or Scotland), and
(c) Article 6 of the Criminal Justice (Northern Ireland) Order 1998 (sex offender orders made in Northern Ireland),
as it applies to sexual offences prevention orders.
Note: This section has been repealed but because of transitional provisions continues to apply to SOPOs made before they were replaced by SHPOs. Ed.

R v Hamer 2017 EWCA Crim 192, 2 Cr App R (S) 13 (p 82) At the bottom of the prosecution's written application, the 'officer in the case' and the 'supervisor's name' were identified. Held. Neither of those two are mentioned in Sexual Offences Act 2003 s 108(2), so there was no valid application and the Judge had no power to vary the order. Variation quashed.

R v Lane 2017 EWCA Crim 1439 D was convicted of fresh sexual offences and the Judge sought to vary D's existing SOPO. The application was not signed by the Chief Constable. Held. This error invalidated the application. The variations to the SOPO are quashed. [The prosecution said they would make a fresh application.]

For the required approach see the **SEXUAL HARM PREVENTION ORDERS** paras at **101.27**.

103.3 *Whether to appeal or vary/Old SOPOs*

R v Hoath 2011 EWCA Crim 274 LCJ H and S were given SOPOs and did not appeal the orders. Nearly 2½ years later H applied to vary the order. The Judge refused to vary the order saying it was too soon. S applied to vary it 16 months later. The Judge said the challenge was to the breadth of the order and that was a matter for the Court of Appeal. He refused to vary the order. Held. Objections in principle to the terms of a SOPO imposed by the Crown Court should be raised by an appeal to the Court of Appeal and not by subsequent applications to vary to the Crown Court. Section 108(3) should be exercised where there was a change of circumstances. In our view the application as it is now put before the Court is not an application for a variation at all. It is an appeal (substantially out of time) as to the ambit of the original order. However, where the defendant relies on particular and unanticipated difficulties arising from the form and/or wording of the order, those difficulties should be identified promptly (in writing and

with particularity) and sent to the prosecuting authority so as to see whether the matter can be put before the Crown Court on an agreed basis and in any event to narrow the area of dispute.
Note: It must be hoped this principle is not extended too far. There are thousands of individuals with inappropriate preventive orders and terms. Declining to deal with them may be judicially convenient but it is in everyone's interest that someone is able to review these unsuitable orders. The Lord Chief Justice may consider the order is something that happened long ago but SOPOs apply to the present and the future. It is very much in the interest of society and those who have to enforce these orders that the orders are proportionate and fair. It would be unfortunate that an individual whose advocate only concentrated on the prison term and failed to notice that the SOPO was too wide was stopped from appealing (because the application was out of time) and was stopped from varying it (because he should have appealed). It would also create an anomaly. A defendant who reoffends would have the opportunity when sentenced for the fresh offence to argue for an appropriate SOPO. A defendant who does not reoffend would be in a less fortunate position. Ed.
R v I 2012 EWCA Crim 1792 LCJ D was sentenced to IPP and a SOPO in 2006. He appealed against the SOPO relying on *R v Smith* 2011 EWCA Crim 1772, 2012 1 Cr App R (S) 82 (p 468). Held. As the case was heard long before *R v Smith* 2011, the SOPO was justified. We are not a review body for every SOPO.
R v Martin 2012 EWCA Crim 2272 D pleaded to indecent photographs and was in May 2010 given 30 months and a SOPO. On his release he applied to vary the SOPO and a draft revised order was agreed. The Judge, following *R v Hoath* 2011, refused. D appealed out of time. Held in October 2012. The order was disproportionately restrictive. We quash it and substitute another.
R v Hyde and Others Re C 2016 EWCA Crim 1031, 2 Cr App R (S) 39 (p 416) at para 87 In 2005 D was given a very widely drawn SOPO. The defence argued it should not have been made because D was sentenced to IPP. Held. We agree. *R v Smith* 2011 involved no real change in the law.

104 SPECIAL REASONS

104.1

The order applies to when the court thinks it is 'fit' not to disqualify and not to endorse a licence.
Road Traffic Offenders Act 1988 s 44(2) Where the court does not order the person convicted to be disqualified, it need not make an order under subsection (1) if for special reasons it thinks fit not to do so.
Road Traffic Offenders Act 1988
 s 34 (disqualification for certain offences)
 s 44(2) (orders for endorsement: special reasons)
Availability See **104.4**.
Loss of plea credit when application is unsuccessful, see **57.76**.

104.2 ***Drink/driving and drug/driving prescribed limits***
Drink/driving: Prescribed limits

	Breath µg (micrograms)	Blood mg (milligrams)	Urine mg (milligrams)
England and Wales	35	80	107
Scotland from 5/12/14	22	50	67

		Breath µg (micrograms)	**Blood mg (milligrams)**	**Urine mg (milligrams)**
Service personnel performing a regulated duty, see **247.15** in Volume 2	Reg 4 duty	35	80	107
	Reg 5 duty	9	20	27

Note: The information is taken from the Directgov Think! website http://think.direct.gov.uk/drink-driving.html. Ed.
For the ***Drug/driving: Prescribed limits*** see **247.9** in Volume 2.

Power to find/Test to apply

104.3 ***Power to find***
Road Traffic Offenders Act 1988 s 34(1) Where a person is convicted of an offence involving obligatory disqualification,[1158] the court must order him to be disqualified for such a period not less than 12 months as the court thinks fit, unless the court for special reasons thinks it fit to order him to be disqualified for a shorter period or not to order him to be disqualified.
Road Traffic Offenders Act 1988 s 44(2) Where the court does not order the person convicted to be disqualified, it need not make an order under subsection (1) if for special reasons it thinks fit not to do so.
Note: Whether facts are, or are not, capable of amounting to special reasons is a matter of law. Ed.

104.4 ***Test to apply***
R v Wickins 1958 42 Cr App R 236 D pleaded to driving whilst unfit through drink. Following *Whittall v Kirby* 1946 2 AER 552, a special reason must:
(a) be a mitigating or extenuating circumstance,
(b) not amount to a defence in law,
(c) be directly connected with the offence, and
(d) be a matter which the court ought properly to take into consideration when imposing punishment.
Hosein v Edmunds 1970 RTR 51 Every special reason must amount to a mitigating circumstance, but not every mitigating circumstance will amount to a special reason.
Holroyd v Berry 1973 RTR 145 LCJ It is well established that personal hardship affecting the defendant is not a ground for special reasons. For more detail, see **104.44**.
Nicholson v Brown 1974 RTR 177 LCJ D pleaded to driving without due care. He drove his lorry when it was raining and snowing. When he was in a line of traffic, not travelling fast, he passed over a patch of mud. He was forced to brake suddenly and he said his brakes failed to respond. He hit the car in front. The Magistrates found special reasons. Held. It was somewhat unfortunate that D pleaded guilty and did not fight the case because his plea was based on a mistaken belief that if you run into the car in front you must be guilty of careless driving, see *Scott v Warren* 1974 RTR 104. However well-intentioned the finding of special reasons was, it was not supported in law. A special reason must be something which amounts to a mitigating or extenuating circumstance not amounting in law to a defence. In this case, either D was guilty or not. If he was guilty his licence ought to be endorsed. If the *ratio* of the Scottish case *Smith v Henderson* 1950 JC 48 was that if the offence is a relatively minor one, that can amount to a special reason, I disagree.
Bullen v Keay 1974 RTR 559 LCJ D pleaded to driving while unfit through drugs. D drove to a lay-by and took a quantity of barbiturate tablets in order to take his own life. The following morning, he was seen driving in a very erratic fashion. He mounted a roundabout and demolished a sign. The Magistrates found special reasons, namely: a) he

[1158] Road Traffic Offenders Act 1988 Sch 2

had not intended to drive, he had intended to go into a coma and die, b) when he drove he was not in control of his actions, and c) the case fell within the four criteria for special reasons. D was not disqualified. The prosecution appealed. Held. The second was a suggested defence of automatism which could not be advanced as a special reason on a plea of guilty. A special reason cannot amount to a defence in law. None of the suggested special reasons were special reasons.

DPP v O'Connor and Others 1992 13 Cr App R (S) 188, RTR 66 High Court Five laced drink cases were heard together. When deciding special reasons magistrates should ask, following *R v Newton* 1974 RTR 451, a) on a balance of probability do the facts disclose in law a special reason, and b) if yes, is it right in all the circumstances that we should exercise our discretion and not disqualify?

DPP v Murray 2001 EWHC 848 (Admin) High Court D deliberately left his car at home before he went drinking. He travelled home on a motorised foot scooter. He was charged with excess alcohol and his case was adjourned until after the High Court had determined whether a foot scooter was a motor vehicle, thereby exposing D to disqualification. The High Court determined that it was a motor vehicle and D pleaded guilty. The Magistrates found special reasons. The prosecution appealed and the defence submitted that a reasonable and honest mistake as to the law could amount to special reasons. Held. There were no mitigating or extenuating circumstances directly connected with the commission of the offence. Any ignorance of the law by D was peculiar to him and not to the facts of the offence of excess alcohol. Ignorance of the law cannot as a matter of law amount to special reasons as it was not a mitigating or extenuating circumstance directly connected with the commission of the offence. The Magistrates were wrong to find special reasons.

Ng v DPP 2007 EWHC 36 (Admin), RTR 35 (p 431) High Court D pleaded to excess alcohol. D was required to provide a specimen of breath during which he belched. He alleged that this caused an artificially inflated reading and that this amounted to a special reason. The court found that D's contention was connected with the offender (i.e. D) and not the offence. D was disqualified and appealed. Held. D's contention went directly to the commission of the offence and if accepted could provide an explanation as to why the specimen exceeded the prescribed level. Case remitted for reconsideration.

104.5 *Burden of proof*

Pugsley v Hunter 1973 1 WLR 578 High Court D pleaded to excess alcohol. Held. The burden to prove the facts which D relies on as constituting special reasons, is on D. This burden is discharged when it is proved on the balance of probabilities.

Park v Hicks 1979 RTR 259 D pleaded to excess alcohol. D's wife had suffered brain damage and was advised not to get excited. D and his wife were at a party expecting their host to drive them home. An incident occurred and D was left with no choice but to drive his wife home for her own safety. No evidence was adduced relating to the wife's condition. Held. The onus is on D to set up the facts from which special reasons can be inferred. Far more substantial medical evidence was necessary before special reasons would be found.

See also: *DPP v O'Connor and Others* 1992 13 Cr App R (S) 188, RTR 66 (The court must consider whether D has shown on the balance of probabilities that his drink was laced.)

The procedure for special reasons

104.6 *Defence disclosure*

Pugsley v Hunter 1973 1 WLR 578 High Court Where D intends to call evidence to prove facts or medical opinion in support of a plea of special reasons, notice of the nature of the evidence ought to be given to the prosecution at a sufficient interval before the hearing.

DPP v O'Connor and Others 1992 13 Cr App R (S) 188, RTR 66 Where notice is not given by D, the prosecution should elicit this fact in cross-examination to allow the court to reflect on D's *bona fides* in raising the issue.

104.7 *Rules of evidence*

Pugsley v Hunter 1973 1 WLR 578 High Court Where D intends to call evidence to prove facts or medical opinion in support of a plea of special reasons, notice of the nature of the evidence ought to be given to the prosecution at a sufficient interval before the hearing. The exception is when a layman could reliably and confidently say that lacing is the only way in which excess alcohol had entered D's blood, otherwise medical evidence is required.

R v Croydon Crown Court ex parte Lenham 1974 RTR 493 High Court D pleaded to excess alcohol. An adjournment was sought in order to secure the presence of a witness. D's solicitors had been diligent in attempting to contact the witness, but they had not informed the court that they were not ready for trial. An adjournment was refused, despite the argument that refusal would effectively result in the disqualification of D. He appealed. Held. Even if D's solicitors had not been diligent, D should not bear the responsibility for this. A costs order would have been the correct punishment for D's solicitors. The case does not encourage belated applications for adjournment.

104.8 *Rules of evidence Hearsay*

The details about hearsay evidence are not dealt with, as this book is primarily about sentencing. Ed.

Criminal Justice Act 2003 s 114(1) In criminal proceedings a statement made not in oral evidence in the proceedings is admissible as evidence of any matter stated…if (certain provisions apply.)

Criminal Justice Act 2003 s 134 'Criminal proceedings' means criminal proceedings in which the strict rules of evidence apply.

Flewitt v Horvath 1972 RTR 121 D was convicted of driving with excess alcohol. In evidence, he asserted that 'someone' had told him that a third party had put vodka in his drink. Held. That evidence is hearsay evidence and not admissible. Any evidence called must not infringe the rule against hearsay evidence.

Pugsley v Hunter 1973 1 WLR 578 The strict rules of evidence apply to special reasons.

Note: It is suggested the effect of the 2003 Act is to make hearsay evidence admissible where: a) the conditions of the Act are satisfied and the court grants permission, b) both parties agree it can be admitted, c) the evidence falls into the rare category of automatically admissible hearsay evidence such as public documents, or d) the court is satisfied that it is in the interests of justice for it to be admitted. Ed.

Basic principles

104.9 *The court should only exercise its discretion in 'clear and compelling circumstances'*

Vaughan v Dunn 1984 RTR 376 A Detective Constable pleaded to excess alcohol. He drove his car into a lamp post. He asserted that there were special reasons present for not disqualifying him, namely that his police work involved undercover operations in licensed premises. Held. The exercise of the discretion to find special reasons should only be exercised in clear and compelling circumstances.

104.10 *Human Rights Act 1998 and delay*

Myles v DPP 2004 EWHC 594 (Admin), 2005 RTR 1 (p 1) High Court D was convicted for failure to provide a specimen after a reliable breath test sample could not be obtained. There was an unnecessary delay of 1 year and 8 months in the stating of the case, breaching D's right to a hearing within a reasonable time under European Convention on Human Rights art 6(1). Held. In relation to 'just satisfaction' for the breach of article 6(1), it could be reflected in D's sentence, however it could not be achieved by the finding of special reasons. It could not be accepted that Human Rights Act 1998 required the definition of special reasons to be extended.

104.11 ***Special reasons found Court can still disqualify***

DPP v O'Connor and Others 1992 13 Cr App R (S) 188, RTR 66 High Court Five laced drink cases were heard together. When deciding special reasons magistrates should ask, following *R v Newton* 1974 RTR 451, a) on a balance of probability do the facts disclose in law a special reason, and b) if yes, is it right in all the circumstances that we should exercise our discretion and not disqualify?

Donahue v DPP 1993 RTR 156 D pleaded to excess alcohol. He attended a function and asked to be served a non-alcoholic wine. He was unknowingly served alcoholic wine. When leaving the function he entered his car and drove. He immediately left the road and was subsequently breathalysed, showing 99 µg of alcohol per 100 ml of breath. He contended that there were special reasons not to disqualify. The court found special reasons but disqualified D for 12 months on the basis that he must have realised that he was unfit to drive. D appealed. Held. The court did not err in its decision. It approached the considerations correctly.

R v St Albans Crown Court ex parte O'Donovan 2000 1 Cr App R (S) 344 High Court D was convicted of driving with excess alcohol. He had 103 µg[1159] per 100 ml of breath and was disqualified for 20 months despite the court finding the presence of special reasons. The mandatory disqualification period was 12 months. D appealed to the Crown Court where his appeal was dismissed. D subsequently applied for judicial review. Held. Where special reasons exist and it has not been established, or even suggested, that D's driving posed a danger to anyone, it would be hard to justify a period of disqualification in excess of the mandatory 12 months. It would be unusual for a court to find special reasons for not disqualifying and subsequently disqualify. Appeal allowed.

R v Mander 2008 EWCA Crim 1521 D, a taxi driver, was convicted of dangerous driving.[1160] He had picked up five men and, upon reaching their destination, three of the men exited the taxi. Fearing he would not be paid, D drove to the police station. D failed to ensure the doors were shut before driving away and after travelling a short distance at approximately 30 mph, one passenger jumped out of the open door. He suffered serious head injuries from which he subsequently died. D was disqualified. He appealed, arguing that the Judge erred in not finding special reasons. Held. A court can find a special reason and go on to disqualify. The correct approach is to consider whether there is a special reason present, then consider whether to disqualify D for 12 months, or to disqualify him for less than 12 months. Appeal dismissed.

Special reasons and specific offences

104.12 ***Aggravated vehicle-taking***

Road Traffic Offenders Act 1988 s 34(1A) Where a person is convicted of an offence under Theft Act 1968 s 12A (aggravated vehicle-taking), the fact that he did not drive the vehicle in question at any particular time or at all shall not be regarded as a special reason for the purposes of subsection (1) [obligatory disqualification].

104.13 ***Failure to provide a specimen Basic principles***

Note: It is very unlikely that special reasons will apply. Ed.

R v Jackson 1969 2 AER 453, 1970 RTR 165 The court found it difficult to envisage what would constitute a special reason in relation to a failure to provide, since that failure had to be 'without reasonable excuse'.

Anderton v Anderton 1977 RTR 424 D refused to provide a specimen after being stopped by police due to the nature of his driving. D had sustained a serious cut to his hand and was driving to the hospital when stopped by police. He had consumed two or three glasses of mild beer. D contended that there were special reasons not to disqualify him as he had taken practical means to get medical attention. The prosecution contended that D had not shown that there was no alternative but to drive, that it was necessary for him to drive, or that he had explored other possible solutions. Held. The offence was failure to

[1159] Assuming I have corrected a typo correctly.

[1160] The judgment says the offence was dangerous driving, not causing death by dangerous driving.

provide, not driving with excess alcohol and therefore D's contentions are irrelevant because the special reason must relate to the failure to provide the specimen. Here the suggested special reason related to the reason for driving. There were no special reasons present.

Daniels v DPP 1992 13 Cr App R (S) 482 D was arrested on suspicion of stealing a motor-cycle. He was then asked to provide a sample. He refused to do so. He was cleared of the offence for which he was arrested but was convicted of refusing to supply a sample. He contended there were special reasons. Held. The fact that an offender has been found guilty of failing to provide a specimen of breath without a reasonable excuse does not necessarily mean that there cannot be a special reason for not disqualifying. The fact that there was no reasonable excuse for failing to provide a specimen meant that there were no special reasons.

104.14 ***Failure to provide a specimen On the facts, special reasons found***

Bobin v DPP 1999 RTR 375 D was charged with failure to provide a specimen. D was breathalysed and taken to a police station. He was then informed that the breathalyser at the station was not working correctly. Another officer asked him for a sample of blood or urine. D enquired whether a refusal would result in an automatic disqualification. The officer replied "No". On that basis, D refused. He was convicted and disqualified for 18 months. The Crown Court upheld the finding that there were no special reasons present. D appealed. Held. D's decision had been affected by inaccurate information and that was capable of amounting to a special reason. Case remitted to the Magistrates' Court for reconsideration.

104.15 ***Failure to provide a specimen On the facts, no special reasons***

Scobie v Graham 1970 RTR 358 D was charged with failure to provide a specimen. The car D had been driving was involved in a collision. When interviewed at the hospital, D refused to provide a specimen, but had understood what was being asked of him. The Court found the fact that: a) D was in hospital, b) in some considerable pain, and c) that he had received a blow to the head constituted special reasons. The prosecution appealed. Held. Being in hospital did not constitute special reasons. The only reason capable of being a special reason was that D had received a blow to the head. As the Court had found that D understood what was being asked of him, there was no reasonable excuse. The circumstances did not present a special reason.

Hockin v Weston 1972 RTR 136 D pleaded to failure to provide a specimen. D was involved in a serious accident in which his wife was critically injured. He was requested to provide a specimen and refused to do so. He had not had his injuries tended to, nor did he know whether his wife was alive. D contended that there were special reasons not to disqualify him. Held. This may have amounted to a defence of reasonable cause. However, as D had pleaded guilty, he had abandoned that contention and admitted he had no reasonable excuse. The facts could not amount to a special reason.

Bunyard v Hayes 1985 RTR 348 D was charged with failure to provide, failing to stop after an accident and driving without due care and attention. A lawful arrest is not a prerequisite to a charge of failure to provide a specimen. How the defendant had come to be at the police station is irrelevant, he had failed to provide a specimen and was guilty. See also: *Courtman v Masterson* 1978 RTR 457 (D consumed alcohol between the occurrence of a collision and a request to provide a specimen. That might lead to an acquittal but it cannot amount to a special reason.)

DPP v Daley (No 2) 1994 RTR 107 (D claimed he was incapable of providing a specimen. That might be a reasonable excuse but it is not a special reason.)

104.16 ***Failure to provide a specimen Defendant not driving***

R v Ashford Magistrates' Court ex parte Wood 1988 RTR 178 High Court D was found guilty of failure to provide a specimen and acquitted of three other driving offences on the basis that he was not driving. D failed to provide a specimen. His licence was endorsed. D appealed on the basis that there was a special reason present, namely that D was not driving the car. Held. As a matter of law, it is clear that the fact that D was not driving at the time can be a special reason. The Justices retained a discretion to endorse a licence where special reasons are present. The Justices had approached the issue correctly in law and exercised their discretion as they are entitled to do.

Special reasons and particular circumstances

104.17 ***Bail condition not to drive***
Note: This cannot be a special reason. Ed.
R v Kwame 1975 RTR 106 D was committed to the Crown Court to stand trial for a driving offence, and was bailed with a condition not to drive or attempt to drive until the trial. D pleaded guilty and submitted that the bail term was a special reason as otherwise he would be disqualified for more than the minimum term. He was disqualified for 12 months. D appealed. Held. a) The Magistrate was entitled as a matter of law to impose such a bail condition. b) The bail condition was not connected to the offence, but was connected with personal hardship. There were no special reasons.
Note: Where a defendant is subject to an interim disqualification order, the period of that interim order is deducted from the total period of disqualification, see **42.5**. Ed.
For ***Deemed defendant*** see the ***Nominated defendant*** para at **104.46**.

104.18 ***Drinking is part of defendant's employment***
Note: This cannot be a special reason. Ed.
Vaughan v Dunn 1984 RTR 376 A Detective Constable was charged with driving with excess alcohol after a specimen contained 100 μg of alcohol per 100 ml. D was involved in undercover work which required him to visit licensed premises. He was given a drinking allowance of £2 per day. Justices found that this constituted a special reason and did not disqualify him. The prosecution appealed. Held. Appeal allowed. There were no special reasons.

104.19 ***Driving a short distance Judicial guidance***
Note: This can be a special reason but only in very limited circumstances. Ed.
Chatters v Burke 1986 8 Cr App R (S) 222 D pleaded to excess alcohol. The car in which he was a passenger left the road and went into a field. He drove the car back onto the road. The driving on the road was only a few yards. Held. There are seven factors to consider when deciding whether or not to disqualify for driving with excess alcohol when the driving was for a short distance: a) how far the vehicle was driven, b) the manner in which it was driven, c) the state of the vehicle, d) whether the driver intended to drive any further, e) road and traffic conditions, f) whether there was any danger, and g) the reason for the vehicle being driven.
DPP v Bristow 1998 RTR 100 D pleaded to excess alcohol. He contended that he had only driven a short distance. The Magistrates found special reasons. The prosecution appealed. Held. The matter must be considered objectively and the quality and gravity of the crisis must be assessed in that way, The key question is: 'What would a sober, reasonable and responsible friend of the defendant, present at the time, but himself a non-driver and thus unable to help, have advised in the circumstances: drive or do not drive?'

104.20 ***Driving a short distance On the facts, special reasons made out***
Reay v Young 1949 1 AER 1102 There were special reasons not to disqualify D after a conviction for an offence of permitting the use of a motor vehicle which is uninsured and by an unlicensed driver. The car was driven 150 yards, very slowly, on moorland. It would have been an entirely different case if the car had been driven in the same circumstances in a town.
Chatters v Burke 1986 8 Cr App R (S) 222 D, who had been drinking, was a passenger in the car. The car rolled over and went into a field. D drove the car from the field and parked it on the road with no intention of driving it further. D pleaded to driving with

excess alcohol. The court found special reasons for not disqualifying him. The prosecution appealed. Held. The shortness of the distance driven was not the only factor taken into account. Special reasons upheld.

DPP v Corcoran 1991 RTR 329 D drove slowly with no lights on, with excess alcohol, for a distance of 40 yards at night. D parked the car in a pre-arranged parking space and the street was well lit with no traffic. He did not pose a danger to other road users. Special reasons for not disqualifying D were found. The prosecution appealed. Held. Each case turns on its merits. The short distance was only one factor. The major factor may have been the absence of danger (actual or potential) to other road users. The Justices were entitled to find as they did.

R v St Albans Crown Court ex parte O'Donovan 2000 1 Cr App R (S) 344 High Court D was convicted of driving with excess alcohol. He left a pub and proceeded to move his car in the car park to allow access to and from the car park. His driving was erratic. His reading was about three times the drink/driving limit. The court found special reasons, considering the seven factors in *Chatters v Burke* 1986 (see above), then proceeded to disqualify D for 20 months. This was upheld by the Crown Court. Held. Taking into account the special reasons, 12 months.

See also: *James v Hall* 1972 RTR 228 (D had been at his daughter's wedding and had been invited to stay overnight. He drove a few yards and parked in a friend's driveway. D was stopped by police. Justices entitled to find special reasons.)

104.21 *Driving a short distance On the facts, no special reasons*

R v Shaw 1974 RTR 225 D pleaded to excess alcohol. D drove his car a short distance down a private road, but the road was accessible to the public and was used by pedestrians. The council had shown no desire to exclude the public. D was disqualified and appealed. Held. The question of whether the public generally have access to a road in order to make it 'a road to which the public has access' within the legislation was rightly left to the jury. The short distance did not constitute a special reason.

Haime v Wallet 1983 5 Cr App R (S) 165 High Court D was convicted of driving with excess alcohol after driving 200 yards outside a pub. Justices found special reasons not to disqualify D. The prosecution appealed. Held. The mere chance that D had only driven 200 yards (which would have been dangerous to road users) did not constitute a special reason.

CPS v Humphries 2000 RTR 52 High Court D was convicted of attempting to drive a car whilst under the influence of alcohol. He admitted his intention was to steal the car that he was found in, but he was unable to start the engine. He had travelled two car lengths as a result of the car being pushed by a friend. The Court found special reasons not to disqualify him. The Crown appealed. Held. The Court should have considered what D intended to do, which by his own admission was to drive home intoxicated, not what he actually achieved. Because of his intention there was no special reason.

See also: *R v Agnew* 1969 Crim LR 152 (D had driven about 6 feet under the influence after an accident. Judge was entitled to disqualify him for 12 months because he considered D's reading of 126 was so high he should not have driven at all.)

Coombs v Kehoe 1972 RTR 224 (D was re-parking his lorry after drinking in a pub. 200-yard journey. No special reasons.)

104.22 *Driving at the request of a policeman*

Note: This can be a special reason but only in very limited circumstances. Ed.

R v McIntyre 1976 RTR 330 D pleaded to driving with excess alcohol and was disqualified from driving. D had parked his car outside a nightclub where it was causing an obstruction. Upon exiting the nightclub, a policeman advised him not to drive his car. D genuinely thought the policeman had asked him to move his car. Held. This was capable of amounting to a special reason. D would not be disqualified, as the trial Judge had indicated that he would not have disqualified D had he felt able to do so.

De Munthe v Stewart 1982 RTR 27 D was charged with excess alcohol. D had parked his car causing an obstruction and was asked by a policeman to move it. As he did so, the policeman suspected D had been drinking and required him to provide a specimen of breath. D was convicted and contended that there were special reasons for not disqualifying him, namely that he had driven at the constable's request. Held. In considering special reasons, account had to be taken of driving at the constable's request, but also of the voluntary driving following it. Distinguished *R v McIntyre* 1976. D's appeal was dismissed.

104.23 *Driving not impaired by alcohol*

Note: This cannot be a special reason. Ed.

Brown v Dyerson 1968 3 AER 39 *Obiter* The fact that D's driving was not impaired does not amount to a special reason.

Taylor v Austin 1969 1 AER 544 D's car collided with a taxi and he was found to be just over twice the prescribed limit of alcohol. He pleaded guilty but was not disqualified on the basis that a) his driving was not impaired, b) the accident was not his fault, and c) he would suffer undue hardship as his licence was essential for his work. The prosecution appealed. Held. There were no special reasons. Unimpaired driving may amount to a mitigating circumstance but not to a special reason. Appeal allowed.

See also: *R v Jackson* 1969 2 AER 453, 1970 RTR 165 (Evidence of impairment of driving ability is irrelevant.)

104.24 *Drugs etc. unknowingly adding to the effects of alcohol*

Note: This can be a special reason but only when the charge is driving whilst unfit and in very limited circumstances. It cannot be a special reason when the charge is driving with excess alcohol. Ed.

Chapman v O'Hagen 1949 2 AER 690 High Court D was charged with being unfit to drive through drink or drugs. He had been kicked in the leg by a horse and had taken painkillers, one of which was a dose appropriate for dogs and not humans. He was unaware that this was a larger dose. He consumed whiskey and beer, not knowing the combined effects of the two intoxicants. The Magistrates found special reasons. Held. The Court would not have come to the same decision, although there was evidence entitling them to do so. The moment in time when the Justices ought to have been considering the presence, if any, of special reasons entitling them to exercise their discretion not to disqualify D was the time he was found to be in charge of the car when unfit to do so, not at the time when he consumed the alcohol. Here the facts were capable of amounting to special reasons where the charge was 'unfit' but not where excess alcohol was charged. Appeal dismissed.

R v Holt 1962 Crim LR 565 D pleaded to driving under the influence of drink or drugs and was disqualified for 12 months. He contended there was a special reason for not disqualifying him, namely that he had been taking medication and had not been warned of the effect of combining the medication with alcohol. Held. This was capable of being a special reason. D had been misled into committing the offence.

R v Julien 1966 Crim LR 52 D pleaded to driving whilst unfit through drink or drugs. He had suffered a very severe electric shock at around 3 pm which had forced him to end work for the day. He drank three or four half pints of beer before driving at around 7 pm. A doctor gave evidence that alcohol could have a far greater effect on a person who had suffered such an electric shock. Held. Special reasons present.

R v Scott 1970 1 QB 661 D pleaded to excess alcohol. D was prescribed sleeping tablets and anti-depressants and proceeded to drink alcohol whilst on the medication. She knew of the dangers but had no idea that alcohol and medication would produce a more violent reaction than merely alcohol. Held. This could not be a special reason.

R v Ealing Magistrates' Court ex parte Woodman 1994 RTR 189 High Court D was convicted of driving whilst unfit through drugs. At trial, expert evidence was given to the effect that a hypoglycaemic attack was caused by excess insulin or insufficient food

intake. The Magistrate concluded that D had failed to follow medical advice and that the attack was caused by excess insulin. D was convicted and appealed. Held. There was insufficient evidence to establish that the effective cause of D's unfitness was excessive insulin administered by D. It could not be said that the insulin rather than the failure to eat properly had caused the attack. No special reasons present. However, appeal allowed.
Kinsella v DPP 2002 EWCA Crim 545 High Court D pleaded to excess alcohol. Held. There is clear authority that special reasons are not available when the defendant has been affected by an illness of which he has no knowledge. This is because in breathalyser cases the test is objective, namely whether the blood alcohol level is over the prescribed limit and the physical condition leading to the reading is a condition special to the offender and not the offence. D's condition (abnormal alcohol metabolism) was special to him (albeit unknown to him) and not the offence. D was aware he had been drinking and nevertheless chose to drive.

104.25 ***Earlier test negative***
Note: This cannot be a special reason. Ed.
DPP v White 1988 RTR 267 D pleaded to excess alcohol. Where a motorist who had consumed alcohol continues to drive after a negative breath test, and subsequently fails a second breath test, there are no special reasons.

104.26 ***Emergency Driving in an emergency General principles***
Note: This can be a special reason but only in very limited circumstances. Ed.
Brown v Dyerson 1968 3 AER 39 High Court While the High Court has been willing to recognise that an emergency is capable of amounting to a special reason, in every case so far reported, the High Court has emphasised that before an emergency can constitute a special reason, D must first show that there was no alternative but for him to drive and that he had explored every reasonable alternative before driving. The emergency must be real, not nebulous or manufactured. It is not sufficient emergency, if it can be shown that D should have anticipated the emergency arising.
Jacobs v Reed 1974 RTR 81 High Court D pleaded to excess alcohol. Held. An emergency may constitute special reasons for not disqualifying an individual guilty of driving with excess alcohol, but the emergency is to be considered objectively.
Taylor v Rajan 1974 RTR 304 High Court D pleaded to excess alcohol. He claimed he needed to travel because it was discovered that through another's illness he needed to travel to lock up his restaurant. Held. Magistrates must consider: a) the whole of the circumstances, b) the nature and degree of the crisis or emergency, and c) whether there were alternative means of transport. One of the important matters is whether the emergency was sufficiently acute to justify the driver taking out his car. Magistrates should only exercise their discretion in clear and compelling circumstances. In this and the joined case, there were no special reasons.
Thompson v Diamond 1985 RTR 316 High Court D pleaded to excess alcohol. D had been drinking at home with no intention of driving when he received a telephone call informing him that his mother had been taken to hospital as an emergency case. In fact there was no such emergency. Held. A medical or other emergency is capable of amounting to a special reason, but the test is objective as to whether such an emergency existed. It is unlikely that simply travelling to see a near relative because of some emotional need would ever amount to a special reason. There were no special reasons here.
DPP v Bristow 1998 RTR 100 High Court D pleaded to excess alcohol. D reacted to news that his daughter and her friend had been indecently assaulted and were being held against their will by driving to the address given to him immediately. He pleaded to driving with excess alcohol but asserted that there were special reasons present. Held. The key question to be answered in these so-called emergency cases was what a

reasonable, sober and responsible friend who was present at the time but a non-driver, would have advised in the circumstances: drive or not drive. Here that person would not have advised D to drive. There were no special reasons.
DPP v Ubhi 2003 EWHC 619 (Admin) High Court D pleaded to excess alcohol. D, a student, had been drinking with friends. After retiring for the night he was woken by the sound of his sister screaming. She had fallen in the bathroom and was in some considerable pain. D attempted to ring the hospital and a taxi firm but was left with the conclusion that he had to drive his sister to the hospital. He was stopped by police, who breathalysed him and called an ambulance for his sister. The Court found special reasons not to disqualify D. The prosecution appealed. Held. The Court held that the correct approach is to consider what a reasonable person would have done, or how a reasonable person would have reacted. The case was returned to the Magistrates' Court for reconsideration.

104.27 ***Emergency Driving in an emergency Medical***
Note: This can be a special reason, but it would normally be necessary to show there was no reasonable alternative and there is a real emergency rather than an inconvenience. Ed.
R v Lundt-Smith 1964 3 AER 225 High Court D pleaded to causing death by dangerous driving. He was an on-duty ambulance driver, who was instructed to take a woman in labour from one hospital to another. Both the nurse and the matron told him to hurry as she could give birth at any moment. With horn sounding and blue light flashing and at 40-50 mph, he drove to the next hospital. D approached a red light, saw no traffic and slackened his speed. The ambulance collided with a scooter, whose driver subsequently died. The scooter driver was crossing the junction on a green light. There was some evidence the scooter had poor lights. The prosecution conceded that the Court could find special reasons. Held. There was no defence to the charge. I am satisfied you looked both ways. The mother and baby's life depended on the speed of your driving. It would be very wrong to prevent you earning your living. The circumstances did constitute special reasons. D was not disqualified and 'discharged unconditionally'.
Evans v Bray 1977 RTR 24 High Court D pleaded to driving with excess alcohol but successfully argued the existence of special reasons not to disqualify him. He asserted that he had received an urgent telephone call from his wife, who needed to be driven 40 miles to collect some pills, without which she risked serious illness. The prosecution appealed. Held. The Court had failed to consider all the circumstances, in particular D's failure to consider an alternative course of action, and the high level of alcohol in his blood. There were no special reasons.
Anderton v Anderton 1977 RTR 424 High Court Driving due to a medical emergency can be a special reason for driving with excess alcohol etc., but it will not be a special reason for failure to provide a specimen.
Park v Hicks 1979 RTR 259 High Court D was charged with excess alcohol. His wife had suffered brain damage and was advised not to get excited. D and his wife were at a party expecting their host to drive them home. An incident occurred and D was left with no choice but to drive his wife home for her own safety. No evidence was adduced relating to the wife's condition. Held. The onus is on D to set up the facts from which special reasons can be inferred. Far more substantial medical evidence was necessary before special reasons would be found. Prosecution appeal allowed.
Thompson v Diamond 1985 RTR 316 D pleaded to excess alcohol. D had been drinking at home with no intention of driving when he received a telephone call informing him that his mother had been taken to hospital as an emergency case. In fact there was no such emergency. The prosecution appealed against the finding of special reasons. Held. A medical or other emergency is capable of amounting to a special reason, but the test is objective as to whether such an emergency existed. It is unlikely that simply travelling to see a near relative because of some emotional need would ever amount to a special reason. Prosecution appeal allowed.

DPP v Ubhi 2003 EWHC 619 (Admin) High Court D pleaded to excess alcohol. D, a student, had been drinking with friends. After retiring for the night he was woken by the sound of his sister screaming. She had fallen in the bathroom and was in some considerable pain. D attempted to ring the hospital and a taxi firm but was left with the conclusion that he had to drive his sister to the hospital. He was stopped by police, who breathalysed him and called an ambulance for his sister. The Court found special reasons not to disqualify D. The prosecution appealed. Held. The Court held that the correct approach is to consider what a reasonable person would have done, or how a reasonable person would have reacted. Returned to the Magistrates' Court for reconsideration.
See also: *DPP v Upchurch* 1994 RTR 366 (Three individuals with head injuries unable to get to hospital. The decision to find special reasons could not be faulted.)

104.28 ***Emergency, Driving in an National emergency***
Note: It is hard to conceive of a national emergency when there is no alternative but to ask someone under the influence to drive. Therefore special reasons are exceptionally unlikely. Ed.
Whittall v Kirby 1946 2 AER 552 High Court D pleaded to driving whilst unfit through drink. In circumstances of national emergency, considerations of public benefit may be taken into account and can amount to special reasons.
Gordon v Smith 1971 RTR 52 High Court D pleaded to driving whilst unfit through drink. He gave evidence that he was a driver in the Army and expected to be posted to Northern Ireland where he would be required to drive army vehicles. The Justices accordingly only disqualified him for one month. The prosecution appealed. Held. Military duties in Northern Ireland were in no sense an emergency or a national emergency of the type referred to in *Whittall v Kirby* 1946.
See also the ***National interest, Defendant needs to drive in the*** para at **104.44**.

104.29 ***Emergency, Driving in an Personal***
Note: This can be a special reason in very limited circumstances and only where there were no taxis or friends etc. to do the driving instead. Ed.
Aichroth v Cottee 1954 2 AER 856 High Court LCJ D was sentenced for driving whilst disqualified. D was told by telephone by his foreman that a dough mixing machine had broken down. D had the keys to the store where the special tools that were needed were kept. If the machine was not repaired, the morning's bread production for 5,000 retailers and 500 wholesalers would be spoilt. There were no taxis about. Held. Courts must consider the availability of public transport and taxis. It is a reasonable deduction from the example of a man going to a dying relative or a doctor going on an urgent call that a sudden emergency, provided it is serious enough and provided it cannot be reasonably dealt with in any other way, can amount to special reasons. There were special reasons here. Appeal allowed.
Reynolds v Roche 1972 RTR 282 High Court D pleaded to driving whilst unfit through drink. Having drunk alcohol, he rushed home in case the babysitter had left the child alone. Justices found this constituted a special reason. The prosecution appealed. Held. This did not constitute an emergency and was not a special reason.
Powell v Gliha 1979 RTR 126 High Court D pleaded to excess alcohol. D's husband was disabled and required a specially fitted lavatory. D and her husband attended a party with the intention of staying overnight. At the party she consumed alcohol. Her husband needed to go to the lavatory and D, being the less intoxicated of the two qualified drivers present, drove her husband home. Held. A 'crisis situation' was capable of providing special reasons, but it is important that no invented crisis should be accepted. Relevant considerations include whether D had acted reasonably and responsibly. D had not acted so, as she had failed to make provisions for her husband to use the lavatory whilst at the party. D was to be disqualified.
DPP v Heathcote 2011 EWHC 2536 (Admin) High Court D pleaded to excess alcohol. A quad bike was stolen and someone said, "Get into the van". D and another got into a

van following the sound of the quad bike. D was driving. After about 10 minutes and 1½ miles D stopped and approached some police officers and tried to report the theft of the bike. D was told to report the theft to a police station. D was then breath tested. D's test result was 57 μg and D was arrested. Held. No sober, reasonable or responsible friend of D would have advised him to drive. The danger to road users must have been obvious. The problem was theft and not imminent fear or threat to life and limb. The matter should have been left to the police. This was a very clear case of no special reasons. Finding quashed.
See also: *R v Baines* 1970 RTR 455 (D's business partner was stranded in the countryside with his ailing mother. No special reasons.)
Taylor v Rajan 1974 RTR 304 (No responsible person at D's restaurant. No special reasons.)
Robinson v DPP 1989 RTR 42 (Solicitor driving at 92 mph to make an appointment at his office. No special reasons.)
DPP v Doyle 1993 RTR 369 (D was assaulted by her former boyfriend when she returned to collect her car. No special reasons.)
DPP v Cox 1996 RTR 123 (With hesitation, club steward's special reasons for driving 150 yards on a public road to deal with a burglar alarm.)
DPP v Enston 1996 RTR 324 (Being blackmailed by woman saying otherwise she would claim rape. Magistrates entitled to find special reasons.)

104.30 ***Emergency, Driving in an*** ***Emergency over***
Note: This cannot be a special reason. Ed.
DPP v Feeney 1989 89 Cr App R 173 High Court D was sentenced for driving with excess alcohol. D had driven a friend home who had been involved in a situation which the Court found did constitute an emergency. D then drove himself 1,000 yards home during which he was stopped and required to provide a sample of breath. There was found to be over the prescribed limit of alcohol in his breath. Held. The second journey had occurred after the emergency and as such it could not be justified. D knew that he had been drinking. There were no special reasons for the later journey.
See also: *Fraser v Barton* 1974 RTR 311 (D, who had not intended to drive, was telephoned by a friend who was having serious domestic trouble. Drove home afterwards. No special reasons.)
DPP v Waller 1989 RTR 112 (D crashed into a wall and sought to argue special reasons on the basis he had no intention of driving. Drove home afterwards. No special reasons.)
DPP v Doyle 1993 RTR 369 (D was assaulted by her former boyfriend when she returned to collect her car. She was frightened to use public transport. No special reasons.)

104.31 ***Fatigue and lack of food***
Note: This cannot be a special reason. Ed.
Archer v Woodward 1959 Crim LR 461 High Court D pleaded to driving while under the influence of drink and dangerous driving. He was under the influence of alcohol to the extent that he could not properly control the car. The Magistrates found that a) D's condition was attributable as much to fatigue and lack of food as to drink, b) the quantity of drink was small, and c) he had behaved soberly earlier in the day after drinking. They found special reasons. The prosecution appealed. Held. None of these factors were capable of being special reasons.
Knight v Baxter 1971 RTR 270 High Court D pleaded to driving whilst unfit through drink. His work necessitated him visiting licensed premises and he ascertained that he would be under the legal limit after consuming two pints of beer. When arrested he had consumed two pints of beer but had not eaten. He contended this was a special reason not to disqualify him. Held. The fact that the level of alcohol in D's blood might have been lower had D eaten more food is not a special reason not to disqualify D.

R v Ealing Magistrates' Court ex parte Woodman 1994 RTR 189 High Court D was convicted of driving whilst unfit through drugs. At trial, expert evidence was given to the effect that a hypoglycaemic attack was caused by excess insulin or insufficient food intake. The Magistrate concluded that D had failed to follow medical advice and that the attack was caused by excess insulin. D was convicted and appealed. Held. There was insufficient evidence to establish that the effective cause of D's unfitness was excessive insulin administered by D. It could not be said that the insulin rather than the failure to eat properly had caused the attack. Special reasons not present. However, appeal against conviction allowed.

104.32 *Hardship, Personal*

Note: This cannot be a special reason. Ed.

Mullarkey v Prescott 1970 RTR 296 D pleaded to driving whilst unfit through drink. D was a disabled driver with no legs. He appealed an order for disqualification on the basis that it would cause undue hardship as he could only walk short distances with his artificial legs, and relied upon the fact he was only driving a quarter of a mile home, late at night with little traffic present, as a special reason. Held. This did not constitute a special reason.

Glendinning v Batty 1973 RTR 405 D pleaded to excess alcohol. He was seen by police officers driving without lights on. D was stopped and was breathalysed. A later test disclosed 83 mg alcohol/100 ml blood. D contended that the Justices find special reasons not to disqualify him. The Justices considered: a) he was married with four children and earned his living by driving, b) the triviality of the offence, and c) D was an inexperienced drinker and had miscalculated the quantity of alcohol which would put him above the statutory limit. Held. These clearly cannot amount to special reasons.

Old cases: *R v Steel* 1968 Crim LR 450 (Hardship related to the offender and not to the offence.)

Taylor v Austin 1969 1 AER 544 (Undue hardship was not a special reason.)

R v Jackson 1969 2 AER 453, 1970 RTR 165 (D was disabled and disqualification from driving would cause him hardship. This failed as a special reason because that related to the offender and not to the offence.)

104.33 *Ignorance of the law*

Note: This cannot be a special reason. Ed.

DPP v Murray 2001 EWHC 848 (Admin) High Court D deliberately left his car at home before he went drinking. He travelled home on a motorised foot scooter. He was charged with excess alcohol and his case was adjourned until after the High Court had determined whether a foot scooter was a motor vehicle, thereby exposing D to disqualification. The High Court determined that it was a motor vehicle and D pleaded guilty. The Magistrates found special reasons. The prosecution appealed and the defence submitted that a reasonable and honest mistake as to the law could amount to special reasons. Held. There were no mitigating or extenuating circumstances directly connected with the commission of the offence. Any ignorance of the law by D was peculiar to him and not to the facts of the offence of excess alcohol. Ignorance of the law cannot as a matter of law amount to special reasons as it was not a mitigating or extenuating circumstance directly connected with the commission of the offence. The Magistrates were wrong to find special reasons.

See also: *Scott v McKechnie* 1956 Crim LR 423 (Defendant unaware he had to be insured.)

DPP v Powell 1993 RTR 266 (Defendant unaware of motorised child's bike requiring registration.)

104.34 *Inhaling fumes containing alcohol*

Note: This can be a special reason but only in very limited circumstances. Ed.

Brewer v Metropolitan Police Commissioner 1969 1 WLR 267 High Court LCJ D pleaded to driving while unfit. D had consumed a small amount of alcohol which did not render him unfit to drive in itself. However, before consuming it, he had worked at the premises of an engineering firm degreasing a container used for storing a grease solvent for some hours with no extractor fan. Previously he had only performed this function in short periods and was therefore unaware of the effects of the fumes. Expert evidence was adduced to the effect that the fumes had rendered him unfit without his knowledge. D's argument as to the existence of special reasons was rejected. The Court accepted D's account but found that he was negligent in not enquiring as to the effects of the fumes. D appealed saying there was a special reason. Held. Whether it is a special reason or not depends on whether the individual knows their drink has been laced. Once it was accepted that D was unaware the fumes contained alcohol, the only possible way of fixing D with constructive knowledge was if there were circumstances fixing him with the knowledge of the alcohol content. Case remitted with direction that there was no reason D should be disqualified.

104.35 ***Insurance offences Believing insurance not necessary***
Note: This can be a special reason but only in very limited circumstances. Ed.
DPP v Powell 1993 RTR 266 High Court D was convicted of careless driving, driving with no insurance and driving without 'L' plates, after riding his child's mechanically propelled motorcycle along a road, striking a car. The Court accepted that D genuinely believed that the cycle was a toy and that no insurance was required to drive it. They decided not to endorse D's licence. The prosecution appealed. Held. The Court had correctly found special reasons for all offences except the careless driving.
DPP v Heritage 2002 EWHC 2139 (Admin) High Court D pleaded guilty to driving with no insurance. He bought a new car and after telephoning his insurers reasonably believed he was still insured to drive his old car. He parked his old car on the side of the road intending to clean it. Another car collided with it and it was discovered he was not insured to drive the car. The Court issued D with an absolute discharge and concluded that the short distance driven amounted to a special reason not to disqualify. The prosecution appealed, contending the issue was not the driving but the parking. Held. The Court was correct to look at the matter as a whole. The Magistrates were able to find special reasons.

104.36 ***Laced drinks Test to apply***
Note: This can be a special reason. Ed.
Pridige v Grant 1985 RTR 196 High Court The approach should be: a) Do the facts disclose the presence of a special reason? and b) Should D have realised he was unfit to drive through drink?
DPP v O'Connor and Others 1992 13 Cr App R (S) 188, RTR 66 High Court Five laced drink cases were heard together. D was convicted of a drink/driving offence but was not disqualified following a successful argument based on laced drinks. Held. People who lace drinks knowing that someone is to drive can be prosecuted. A driver who decides to mix drink with his driving does so at his peril. He has a very heavy responsibility to watch with extreme care the amount that he drinks and to see that he does not take more than is likely to be within the statutory limit. The responsibility for watching his drink is with him all the time, and it is a very heavy and important one. If his glass is being topped up, then he must watch his glass. To put his glass down and come back to it not knowing what may happen to it meanwhile does not show the measure of responsibility which is required. The correct approach is to consider the following questions: a) Has D shown on the balance of probabilities, using admissible evidence, the existence of special reasons, and b) If yes, has D shown that his is a case where disqualification should not be imposed? If D claims his drink was laced and relies on this as constituting a special reason, he must show: a) that his drink was laced, b) he did not know it was laced, and c) that he would not otherwise have exceeded the prescribed limit. Save cases that would be obvious to a layman, magistrates can expect to hear expert evidence.

Notice of this should be given to the prosecution. Even with the existence of special reasons, the court can disqualify if they feel D's driving was so erratic or his excess alcohol is such that he ought to have realised he was unfit to drive.
DPP v Sharma 2005 EWHC 879 (Admin) High Court D pleaded to driving with excess alcohol. D's friend bought her two Smirnoff Ice drinks, but unbeknown to D, he laced them with 100 ml of vodka each. Both D and the arresting officer gave evidence to the effect that D did not appear to be under the influence of alcohol, but her specimen registered at 83 µg of alcohol per 100 ml of breath, a little over twice the limit. D was not disqualified. The prosecution appealed. Held. D must demonstrate that she was unaware of the laced drink's impact. The Justices were entitled to find as they did.

104.37 ***Laced drinks Examples***
Brewer v Metropolitan Police Commissioner 1969 1 WLR 267 High Court D pleaded to driving while unfit to drive through drink and was disqualified for 12 months. Alcohol exacerbated by something else is capable of being a special reason. If someone laces another's drink, looked at loosely, it is capable of constituting a special reason. Here the Justices were entitled to find as they did.
For more details see **104.34**.
R v Shippam 1971 RTR 209 D pleaded to excess alcohol (84 mg per 100 ml blood). D argued special reasons on the basis that his lager and lime had been laced with vodka. D was disqualified. The question was whether the vodka had resulted in a quantity below the limit of 80 mg to exceed that limit. Held. Disqualification quashed.
R v Messom 1973 RTR 140 D pleaded to driving while unfit through drink. He visited a friend and was offered a drink. He asked for a small whiskey topped up with ginger beer. He was given a large brandy with a small quantity of ginger beer. Held. A lack of knowledge about the amount of spirit one is drinking can amount to a special reason. We quash the disqualification.
R v Newton 1974 RTR 451 D pleaded to excess alcohol. He had 127 mg of alcohol per 100 ml of blood. The Court was not convinced of the argument that D's drink was laced and disqualified D. Held. When a defendant puts forth a 'laced drink' argument as a special reason not to disqualify him [or her], the court should approach the issue in two stages. First, 'Do the circumstances disclose in law a special reason?' If 'yes', they should consider in all the circumstances (having particular regard to the defendant's own conduct) whether it would be right to take advantage of the existence of the special reason and not disqualify [him or her].
DPP v Barker 1990 RTR 1 High Court D pleaded to excess alcohol. D attended a party where she had unwittingly consumed vodka mixed with an orange juice drink. D subsequently drove and was arrested the following day. She provided two samples registering 109 and 110 µg of alcohol per 100 ml of breath. D was not disqualified due to, *inter alia*, expert evidence that alcohol consumed prior to her attendance at the party would not have exceeded the legal limit. The prosecutor appealed. Held. The facts as found meant D did not appreciate she had consumed alcohol. Appeal dismissed.
DPP v O'Connor and Others 1992 13 Cr App R (S) 188, RTR 66 D was convicted of a drink/driving offence but was not disqualified following a successful argument based on laced drinks. Held. In the existence of special reasons, the court can disqualify if they feel D's driving was so erratic or his excess alcohol is such that he ought to have realised he was unfit to drive.

104.38 ***Lack of knowledge***
Note: Whether it can be a special reason depends very much on what the lack of knowledge was of. Ed.
Barnett v French 1981 RTR 173 An information was preferred against D as a nominated defendant for having insufficient tread on his tyres. He was the principal transport officer in the Environment Agency. The Crown was the owner, and another individual the driver, of a public service vehicle which had operated contrary to an offence under

Motor Vehicles (Construction and Use) Regulations 1978 1978/1017. D was convicted by Magistrates. However, the Justices did not endorse his licence, finding special reasons for not doing so. D appealed his conviction. Held. D was rightly convicted. Road Traffic Act 1972 s 188(8) requires there to be a nominated defendant as the vehicle in question was a public service vehicle for the Crown. The Justices were also right not to endorse D's licence, finding special reasons in the absence of any culpability. Government departments should nominate John Doe born *circa* 1657.

DPP v O'Meara 1988 10 Cr App R (S) 56 D was convicted of driving with excess alcohol but was not disqualified. D had drunk the equivalent of six or seven pints the previous evening. He had had eight hours' sleep and had eaten a meal after he awoke. 12 hours had elapsed between his drinking and being stopped by the police. The Justices found that the elapsed time constituted a special reason. The prosecution appealed. Held. Ignorance as to the overnight effect of alcohol on breath levels could not constitute a special reason for not disqualifying a driver. It goes not to the offence, but to the offender.

DPP v Jowle 1997 163 JP 85 D was convicted of driving whilst over the prescribed limit. He had not consumed alcohol for a number of years, although he was addicted to mouthwash, which he knew gave him a 'lift', but claimed he was unaware it contained alcohol. The Court found special reasons and did not disqualify him. The prosecution appealed. Held. D had driven in an erratic manner and had consumed mouthwash, which, if he was unaware contained alcohol, he was aware it gave him a 'lift'. The Court was wrong to find the presence of special reasons.

See also: *R v Cambridge Magistrates' Court ex parte Wong* 1992 RTR 382 (D consumed wine and cough linctus then drove. A breath reading showed 40 µg of alcohol per 100 ml of breath. D claimed he was unaware that the cough linctus contained alcohol. Evidence showed that the cough linctus contained alcohol which would amount to 1.7 µg. The Magistrates did not find special reasons. D argued that the practice was not to prosecute where the reading was below 40 µg. Held. Case returned to the Magistrates for reconsideration.)

104.39 *Limit Defendant just over the limit*

Note: This cannot be a special reason. Ed.

Delaroy-Hall v Tadman 1969 1 AER 25 High Court D was charged with excess alcohol. Held. The fact that the quantity by which D was over the prescribed limit was small could not in any particular case constitute a special reason. The special reason must be something other than the commission of the offence. However, the fact that the excess is very small might be a reason not to prosecute at all.

See also: *Glendinning v Batty* 1973 RTR 405 (D, an inexperienced drinker, was 3 mg over the prescribed limit. Held. This was not a special reason.)

104.40 *Limit may not have been reached while defendant was driving*

Note: This cannot be a special reason. Ed.

Ferriby v Sharman 1971 RTR 163 High Court D pleaded to driving with excess alcohol. A blood specimen was taken 48 minutes after consumption of alcohol. D advanced special reasons that when the specimen was taken, the level may have been rising to its peak, whereas when D ceased driving, the level may have been below the prescribed limit. Held. The only material time to consider the level of alcohol in a driver's blood is the moment the specimen is taken.

104.41 *Lost specimen*

Note: This has been found to be a special reason but it is unlikely to ever be in the future. Ed.

R v Anderson 1972 RTR 113 D was 1 mg over the prescribed limit. D received a written and verbal notice that no prosecution would be brought. He was not told the expert said he was 1 mg over the limit. D destroyed the specimen he had retained. He was then prosecuted. Held. The defendant lost the opportunity to challenge the reading. The events leading up to D destroying his specimen were special to the offence and not special to him [so the special reason was not barred]. A special reason was present. No disqualification.

Harding v Oliver 1973 RTR 497 High Court D failed two breath tests and subsequently consented to a blood test to ascertain the level of alcohol in his blood. Three samples were taken, one of which was to be retained by D. He intended to have the sample tested as he did not believe that he was over the prescribed limit. D took the sample to a hospital, which subsequently lost it. He was convicted but not disqualified. The prosecution appealed. Held. The fact that the driver who drove with excess alcohol lost the specimen of blood provided by him cannot amount to a special reason not to disqualify him.

See also: *Doyle v Leroux* 1981 RTR 438 (Prosecution brought after D was informed there would be no prosecution. Special reasons were not present.)

See also the ***Nature of the prosecution*** para at **104.45**.

104.42 ***Mistake as to how much alcohol had been consumed***

Note: This can be a special reason but only in very limited circumstances. Ed.

Newnham v Trigg 1970 RTR 107 D pleaded to drink/driving. He had a cold and was served whiskey and ginger in bed by his wife. D was unaware of the proportion of whiskey to ginger. Justices did not disqualify him on the presence of a special reason. The prosecution appealed. Held. Ignorance of the exact quantity being consumed could not amount to a special reason.

Alexander v Latter 1972 RTR 441 D was charged with drink/driving. He consumed two small lagers and then visited a pub where the landlord suggested he try a diabetic lager. Unknown to D the diabetic lager was twice as strong as the lager he was accustomed to drinking. D consumed three bottles. D drove and subsequently pleaded to excess alcohol. Justices did not disqualify him on the basis the 'mistake' amounted to a special reason. The prosecution appealed. Held. The level of alcohol in his blood existed not merely due to his inattentiveness but as a result of the actions of a third person. Special reason present on the basis that it was not merely due to D's miscalculation.

DPP v O'Connor and Others 1992 13 Cr App R (S) 188, RTR 66 High Court Five laced drink cases were heard together. Held. A driver who decides to mix drink with his driving does so at his peril. He has a very heavy responsibility to watch with extreme care the amount that he drinks and to see that he does not take more than is likely to be within the statutory limit. The responsibility for watching his drink is with him all the time, and it is a very heavy and important one. If his glass is being topped up, then he must watch his glass. To put his glass down and come back to it not knowing what may happen to it meanwhile does not show the measure of responsibility which is required. For more detail see **104.36**.

See also: *R v Messom* 1973 RTR 140 (Plea to excess alcohol (132 mg of alcohol per 100 ml of blood). D asked for a small whiskey with a large quantity of ginger ale and was given a large brandy with a small quantity of ginger ale. *Alexander v Latter* 1972 cited. Special reasons present.)

Old case: *Adams v Bradley* 1975 RTR 233 (A person who chooses to combine drinking and driving is under a duty to observe the quality and quantity of drink he consumes.)

104.43 ***Minor offence***

Note: This cannot be a special reason. Ed.

Nicholson v Brown 1974 RTR 177 LCJ D pleaded to driving without due care. He drove his lorry when it was raining and snowing. When he was in a line of traffic, not travelling fast, he passed over a patch of mud. He was forced to brake suddenly and he said his brakes failed to respond. He hit the car in front. The Magistrates found special reasons. Held. It was somewhat unfortunate that D pleaded guilty and did not fight the case because his plea was based on a mistaken belief that if you run into the car in front you must be guilty of careless driving, see *Scott v Warren* 1974 RTR 104. However well-intentioned the finding of special reasons was, it was not supported in law. A special reason must be something which amounts to a mitigating or extenuating circumstance not amounting in law to a defence. In this case, either D was guilty or not. If he was guilty his licence ought to be endorsed. If the *ratio* of the Scottish case *Smith v Henderson* 1950 JC 48 was that if the offence is a relatively minor one, that can amount to a special reason, I disagree.

104.44 *National interest, Defendant needs to drive in the*

Note: It is very unlikely that special reasons could apply. Either the individual should not be drunk or there would be an alternative to that individual driving. It might, just might, be different in wartime. Ed.

Gordon v Smith 1971 RTR 52 D pleaded to driving whilst unfit through drink. He gave evidence that he was a driver in the Army and expected to be posted to Northern Ireland where he would be required to drive army vehicles. The Justices accordingly only disqualified him for one month. The prosecution appealed. Held. Military duties in Northern Ireland were in no sense an emergency or a national emergency of the type referred to in *Whittall v Kirby* 1946 2 AER 552.

Holroyd v Berry 1973 RTR 145 D, a doctor, was convicted of driving with excess alcohol. He submitted that there were special reasons why he should not be disqualified, namely that he used his car to visit patients in an area with very few doctors. If disqualified, he would have to resign. The Crown Court found no special reasons. Held. To interfere with the decision of the Crown Court that there were no special reasons present would widen the intentionally narrow escape route from mandatory disqualification. Appeal dismissed.

See also the ***Emergency, Driving in an National emergency*** para at **104.28**.

104.45 *Nature of the prosecution*

Note: It is very unlikely that special reasons will apply. If the case has been proved then the law applies. Ed.

R v Anderson 1972 RTR 113 D was 1 mg over the prescribed limit. D received a written and verbal notice that no prosecution would be brought. He destroyed the specimen he had retained. He was then prosecuted. Held. The events leading up to D destroying his specimen were not special to him. Special reason present. No disqualification.

Kerr v Armstrong 1974 RTR 139 D reported an accident himself which led to his prosecution for driving with excess alcohol. He was disqualified for one month only on the basis of the presence of special reasons. The prosecution appealed. Held. This cannot amount to a special reason for not imposing a mandatory disqualification.

See also: *Doyle v Leroux* 1981 RTR 438 (Prosecution brought after defendant was informed there would be no prosecution. Special reasons were not present.)

104.46 *Nominated defendant*

Note: Judges hope that nominated individuals will not be prosecuted. Special reasons apply. Ed.

Proceedings in respect of offences in connection with Crown vehicles.

Road Traffic Offenders Act 1988 s 94(1) Where an offence under the Traffic Acts is alleged to have been committed in connection with a vehicle in the public service of the Crown, proceedings may be brought in respect of the offence against a person nominated by the Crown.

(2) Subject to subsection (3) where any such offence is committed any person so nominated shall also be guilty of the offence as well as any person actually responsible for the offence (but without prejudice to proceedings against any person so responsible).

(3) Where any person is convicted of an offence by virtue of this section:

(a) no order is to be made on his conviction save an order imposing a fine,

(b) payment of any fine imposed on him in respect of that offence is not to be enforced against him, and

(c) apart from the imposition of any such fine, the conviction is to be disregarded for all purposes other than any appeal (whether by way of case stated or otherwise).

Barnett v French 1981 RTR 173 An information was preferred against D for having insufficient tread on his tyres. D was employed by the Department of Environment, charged with an offence relating to a public service vehicle. D was the nominated individual, as he was responsible for 3,500 vehicles. Held. In the absence of any culpability any endorsement of his licence would have been a travesty of justice. Special reason present.

See also: *Secretary of State for the Environment v Hooper* 1981 RTR 169 (It was wrong to convict the Secretary of State, who did not as such own or use any vehicles.)

104.47 ***No risk to others***

Note: This cannot be a special reason. Ed.

Milliner v Thorne 1972 RTR 279 D pleaded to drink/driving. He drove on a straight road with good visibility and no other road users were put at risk. Held. This could not amount to a special reason.

Old case: *Reay v Young* 1949 1 AER 1102 (D drove 150 yards on moorland very slowly. This could be a special reason.)

Note: This case appears to have been superceded by *Milliner v Thorne* 1972 and so should not be relied on. Ed.

104.48 ***Quantity of drink small***

Note: This cannot be a special reason. Ed.

Archer v Woodward 1959 Crim LR 461 D pleaded to driving while under the influence of drink and dangerous driving. The Magistrates found: a) D's condition was attributable as much to fatigue and lack of food as to drink, b) the quantity of drink was small, and c) he had behaved soberly earlier in the day after drinking. The prosecution appealed against the finding of special reasons. Held. None of the factors found by the Magistrates were capable of being special reasons. Held. The quantity of drink consumed is incapable of being a special reason.

See also the ***Limit Defendant just over the limit*** para at **104.39**.

104.49 ***Small person exceeding prescribed limit before a larger person would have done***

Note: This cannot be a special reason. Ed.

Knight v Baxter 1971 RTR 270 D pleaded to excess alcohol but contended that there were special reasons present for not disqualifying him, namely that he had drunk two pints of beer only, had not eaten and had not realised that, being a small man, this might have affected the level of alcohol in his blood. Held. This does not amount to a special reason.

Strong drink without warning, see the ***Mistake as to how much alcohol had been consumed*** para at **104.42**.

104.50 ***Unfitness only began during the journey***

Note: This cannot be a special reason. Ed.

Duck v Peacock 1949 1 AER 318 D was charged with drink/driving. He consumed alcohol, entered his car and began to drive. After approximately 10 minutes he became dizzy. He stopped the car and fell asleep with the engine running. The Court found that this constituted a special reason. The prosecution appealed. Held. There were no special reasons present to allow the Court to exercise its discretion not to disqualify.

Archer v Woodward 1959 Crim LR 461 D pleaded to driving while under the influence of drink and dangerous driving. He had consumed alcohol but was fit to drive when he began his journey. Held. This is not capable of being a special reason not to disqualify.

104.51 ***Unknown illness added to the effects of alcohol***

Note: This can be a special reason but only in very limited circumstances and not when the charge is driving with excess alcohol. Ed.

R v Wickins 1958 42 Cr App R 236 D was charged with being unfit to drive through drink or drugs. He suffered from diabetes, a fact which he was unaware of. He had consumed a small quantity of beer which, but for the diabetes, would not have affected his driving. Held. D had not taken sufficient drink to affect the mind of an ordinary man. It was the diabetes which caused the offence to be committed. This amounted to a special reason.
Goldsmith v Laver 1970 RTR 162 D was charged with excess alcohol, not being unfit to drive. He suffered from diabetes, a fact which he was unaware of. The Court found his diabetes constituted a special reason not to disqualify him. The prosecution appealed. Held. As D was charged with excess alcohol, the breath test showing he was almost three times the legal limit rendered the diabetes irrelevant. *R v Wickins* 1958 distinguished on the basis that D's diabetes made the effects of alcohol greater. In the present case, irrespective of the effect of the diabetes, D was almost three times over the legal limit.
Jarvis v DPP 2001 165 JP 15 D was convicted of dangerous driving. She was diabetic and suffered a hypoglycaemic episode whilst driving and contended that there were special reasons present for not disqualifying her, namely that she could not be held personally culpable for the offence. D was disqualified and appealed. Held. The physical condition was particular to the offender and not to the offence. There were no special reasons present.

Other matters

104.52 ***Court must state the grounds for finding special reasons***
Road Traffic Offenders Act 1988 s 47(1) [Where the court finds special reasons] it must state the grounds for doing so in open court.
Criminal Procedure Rules 2015 2015/1490 Rule 28.1(1) This rule applies where the court decides:..
(c) not to order, where it could…
(ii) the endorsement of the defendant's driving record
(iii) the defendant's disqualification from driving, for the usual minimum period or at all.
(2) The court must explain why it has so decided, when it explains the sentence that it has passed.
(3) [procedure for reasons to be given in writing when not in the public interest for them to be given in public.]
For the general requirement to give reasons, see **86.49**.

104.53 ***Appeals to the Crown Court Procedure***
DPP v O'Connor and Others 1992 13 Cr App R (S) 188, RTR 66 On the hearing of an appeal in the Crown Court from the Magistrates' Court, the appeal is a rehearing. In the normal way, relevant evidence should be called again as the Crown Court must decide: a) whether special reasons are present, and b) whether the court's discretion should be exercised. If the fact is agreed, or only a different finding is being challenged, then that might not be necessary.

105 Street Offences Act 1959: Supervision of Offenders

105.1
Street Offences Act 1959 s 1(2A)
This order was amended by Policing and Crime Act 2009 s 17. Strangely the order appears to have no name.

105.2 ***Power to order***
Street Offences Act 1959 s 1(1) It shall be an offence for a person (whether male or female) aged 18 or over[1161] persistently[1162] to loiter or solicit in a street[1163] or public place for the purpose of prostitution.[1164]

[1161] 'Aged 18 or over' was inserted by Serious Crime Act 2015 s 68(7). In force 3/5/15

Street Offences Act 1959 s 1(2) A person guilty of an offence under this section shall be liable on summary conviction to a fine of an amount not exceeding Level 2 on the standard scale, or, for an offence committed after a previous conviction, to a fine of an amount not exceeding Level 3 on that scale.
Street Offences Act 1959 s 1(2A) The court may deal with a person convicted of an offence under this section by making an order requiring the offender to attend three meetings with the person for the time being specified in the order ('the supervisor') or with such other person as the supervisor may direct.
Street Offences Act 1959 s 1(2C) Where the court is dealing with an offender who is already subject to an order under subsection (2A), the court may not make a further order under that subsection unless it first revokes the existing order.

105.3 ***Purpose of the order***

Street Offences Act 1959 s 1(2B) The purpose of the order is to assist the offender, through attendance at meetings, to a) address the causes of the conduct constituting the offence, and b) find ways to cease engaging in such conduct in the future.

105.4 ***Can't have two orders in place at the same time***

Street Offences Act 1959 s 1(2C) Where the offender is already subject to a subsection (2A) order, the court may not make a further order under that subsection unless it first revokes the existing order.

Combined with other orders

105.5 ***Combined with other orders General prohibition***

Street Offences Act 1959 s 1(2D) If a court makes an order under subsection (2A) it may not impose any other penalty in respect of the offence.

105.6 ***Referral Orders, Combined with***

Powers of Criminal Courts (Sentencing) Act 2000 s 19(1)-(4) Where the court makes a Referral Order, the court may not deal with the offender by making an order under Street Offences Act 1959 s 1(2A).

106 SUSPENDED SENTENCE ORDERS

106.1

Criminal Justice Act 2003 s 189-192
Availability The defendant must be aged 18+. For the conditions that must be satisfied, see **106.6**. For those aged 18-20 the sentence is a suspended term of detention in a Young Offender Institution, see **106.3**.
Maximum and minimum terms There is a 2-year maximum term and a 2-week minimum term, see **106.3**.
Court Martial The Court Martial has the power to impose suspended sentence orders for all servicemen and civilians, Armed Forces Act 2006 s 200, see **106.5**.
Historical offences For offences committed before 4 April 2005, a Suspended Sentence Order is not available, Criminal Justice Act 2003 (Commencement No 8 and Transitional and Saving Provisions) Order 2005 2005/950 para 2 and Sch 2 para 5. For these offences the court can pass a suspended sentence under Powers of Criminal Courts (Sentencing) Act 2000 s 118, however old the offence is.[1165] There is no power to add requirements. The suspended sentence had to be for not less than 1 year or more than 2 years,

---

[1162] Street Offences Act 1959 s 1(4)(a) For the purposes of this section conduct is persistent if it takes place on two or more occasions in any period of three months.
[1163] Street Offences Act 1959 s 1(4)(c) For the purposes of this section 'street' includes any bridge, road, lane, footway, subway, square, court, alley or passage, whether a thoroughfare or not, which is for the time being open to the public, and the doorways and entrances of premises abutting on a street (as hereinbefore defined), and any ground adjoining and open to a street, shall be treated as forming part of the street.
[1164] Street Offences Act 1959 s 1(4)(b) For the purposes of this section any reference to a person loitering or soliciting for the purposes of prostitution is a reference to a person loitering or soliciting for the purposes of offering services as a prostitute.
[1165] Although the section has been repealed, the saving provisions mean that the section applies to offences committed before 4 April 2005, see Criminal Justice Act 2003 (Commencement No 8 and Saving Provisions) Order 2005 2005/950 art 4 and Sch 2 para 5(2)(xii). For the operation of the rules, see *Att-Gen's Ref 2017 Re CGF* 2017 EWCA Crim 1987 para 6.

section 118(2). Where there are consecutive sentences the total must not exceed the 2-year maximum. A sentence of imprisonment had to be appropriate and there was a need for exceptional circumstances to justify the suspension, section 118(4). Fines and compensation orders could be passed at the same time but community sentences could not, section 118(5) and (6). Breaches of these orders are dealt with by Powers of Criminal Courts (Sentencing) Act 2000 s 119-120.

Offenders who become aged 21 at the breach hearing Where a defendant is in breach of a suspended sentence made when he or she was aged under 21 and the breach hearing is when the defendant is aged 21+, the court must pass a YOI order and not a prison sentence.[1166]

Victim surcharge The court must impose a victim surcharge, Criminal Justice Act 2003 s 161A-161B and Criminal Justice Act 2003 (Surcharge) Order 2012 2012/1696 as amended. There are exceptions, a) where a compensation order or an Unlawful Profits Order or a Slavery and Trafficking Reparations Order is imposed, when a reduced amount or a nil amount can be ordered, see **17.67**, and b) where the offence was committed before 1 October 2012, when no surcharge can be made, see **115.3**. Where the offence was committed on or after that date and before 8 April 2016, the relevant figure in brackets below applies, see **115.4**. The amount to be imposed is: for a sentence of 6 months or less, £115 (£80), and more than 6 months, £140 (£100). For defendants who were convicted when aged 18+ but were aged under 18 when the offence was committed, the amount is £30 (£20), see **115.4**.

Rehabilitation period The rehabilitation is the same as for an immediate term of imprisonment, see **89.6**.

106.2 *Statistics England and Wales*

Suspended Sentence Orders Aged 18+

	2012	2013	2014	2015	2016	2017
Number of orders	44,643	48,763	52,979	57,070	56,317	53,114

For an explanation about the statistics, see page 1-xii. For more detailed statistics, see www.banksr.com Other Matters Statistics tab.

106.3 *Power to order*

Suspended sentences of imprisonment

Criminal Justice Act 2003 s 189(1)[1167] If a court passes a sentence of imprisonment or, in the case of a person aged at least 18 but under 21, a sentence of detention in a Young Offender Institution for a term of least 14 days but not more than 2 years, it may make an order providing that the sentence of imprisonment or detention in a Young Offender Institution is not to take effect unless:

(a) during a period specified in the order for the purposes of this paragraph ('the operational period') the offender commits another offence in the United Kingdom (whether or not punishable with imprisonment), and

(b) a court having power to do so subsequently orders under paragraph 8 of Schedule 12 that the original sentence is to take effect.

(1A) An order under subsection (1) may also provide that the offender must comply during a period specified in the order for the purposes of this subsection ('the supervision period') with one or more requirements falling within section 190(1) and specified in the order.

[1166] Criminal Justice Act 2003 Sch 12 paras 8(2)(a) and (b). A similar community order provision was interpreted by the Court of Appeal in *R v Aslam* 2016 EWCA Crim 845, 2 Cr App R (S) 29 (p 267) at para 3.
[1167] Criminal Justice and Immigration Act 2008 Sch 1 para 32(1)

(1B) Where an order under subsection (1) contains provision under subsection (1A),[1168] it must provide that the sentence of imprisonment or detention in a Young Offender Institution will also take effect if:

(a) during the supervision period the offender fails to comply with a requirement imposed under subsection (1A), and

(b) a court having power to do so subsequently orders under paragraph 8 of Schedule 12 that the original sentence is to take effect.

Note: Until Criminal Justice and Court Services Act 2000 s 61 (the abolition of YOI and other sentences) is in force, the parts underlined in section 189(1) and (1B) are inserted by Legal Aid, Sentencing and Punishment of Offenders Act 2012 Sch 9 para 20. Ed.

106.4 ***Power to order Defendant aged 18-20***

Note: Legal Aid, Sentencing and Punishment of Offenders Act 2012 s 68 substituted a new subsection 189(1) (see para **106.3** above) and at first glance appears to remove the power to impose a suspended sentence on defendants aged 18-20. Not only is the power to order removed but also the amendment to the old section, Criminal Justice Act 2003 (Sentencing) (Transitory Provisions) Order 2005 2005/643 para 3(2)(a)(i), has been cancelled, see Legal Aid, Sentencing and Punishment of Offenders Act 2012 Sch 9 para 13. However, Legal Aid, Sentencing and Punishment of Offenders Act 2012 Sch 9 para 20, which deals with transitory provisions, inserts the wording underlined in the section until Criminal Justice and Court Services Act 2000 s 61 (which abolishes detention in a Young Offender Institution) comes into force. What a needlessly complicated way to legislate. Ed.

106.5 ***Court Martial***

Armed Forces Act 2006 s 200-202 deals with the imposition of Suspended Sentence Orders.

Guidance on Sentencing in the Court Martial 2018 para 3.1.7 The Court Martial may impose a suspended sentence order with or without community requirements in the same way as a civilian court, Armed Forces Act 2006 s 200. On one interpretation the legislation appears to make it possible for the Court Martial to impose community requirements with a suspended sentence of imprisonment but without dismissal. Such a sentence would frustrate the Services' policy that community orders are incompatible with continued service and should not be used.

106.6 ***When can suspended sentences be imposed? Conditions required***

Note: The conditions are:

(a) The offence must carry a sentence of imprisonment, section 189(1), see **106.3**.

(b) All the statutory requirements for passing an immediate sentence of imprisonment must be present. These are set out in the Custody section in the contents index, see section 189(6) and **106.8**.

(c) The defendant is either aged 21+ (for suspended imprisonment) or aged 18-20 (for suspended detention in a Young Offender Institution), see section 189(1).

(d) The custodial period must be 14+ days but not more than 2 years (not more than 6 months in a Magistrates' Court), see section 189(1).

(e) The supervision period, if any, must be 6+ months and not more than 2 years, see section 189(3).

(f) The operational period must be 6+ months and not more than 2 years, see section 189(3).

(g) The supervision period, if any, must not end later than the operational period, see section 189(4). Ed.

For the guideline about the four steps that can lead to a Suspended Sentence Order, see **28.3**.

[1168] Criminal Justice Act 2003 (Surcharge) Order 2012 2012/1696

106.7 *Magistrates' Court Sentencing Guidelines 2008*
Magistrates' Court Sentencing Guidelines 2008, see www.banksr.com Other Matters Guidelines tab
page 163 para 3 If the court imposes a term of imprisonment between 14 days and 6 months,[1169] it may suspend the sentence for between 6 months and 2 years (the 'operational period').[1170] Where the court imposes two or more sentences to be served consecutively, the power to suspend the sentence is not available in relation to any of them unless the aggregate of the terms does not exceed 6 months.[1171]
4 When the court suspends a sentence, it must impose one or more requirements for the offender to undertake in the community. The requirements are identical to those available for community orders.
6 There are many similarities between suspended sentences and community orders: requirements can be imposed on the offender and the court can respond to breach by sending him or her to custody. The crucial difference is that a suspended sentence is a prison sentence; it may be imposed only where the court is satisfied both that the custodial threshold has been passed and that it is not appropriate to impose a community order, fine or other non-custodial sentence.
7 A further difference is the approach to any breach; when sentencing for breach of a community order, the primary objective is to ensure that the requirements of the order are complied with. When responding to breach of a suspended sentence, the statutory presumption is that the custodial sentence will be activated.[1172]
9 When the court imposes a suspended sentence, it may also order that the sentence be reviewed periodically at a review hearing.[1173]

106.8 *Suspended Sentence Orders are subject to the same criteria as immediate imprisonment*
Criminal Justice Act 2003 s 189(6) Subject to any provision to the contrary contained in Criminal Justice Act 1967, Powers of Criminal Courts (Sentencing) Act 2000 or any other enactment passed or instrument made under any enactment after 31 December 1967, a suspended sentence[1174] which has not taken effect under paragraph 8 of Schedule 12 is to be treated as a sentence of imprisonment or in the case of a person aged at least 18 but under 21, a sentence of detention in a Young Offender Institution for the purposes of all enactments and instruments made under enactments.
New Sentences: Criminal Justice Act 2003 Guideline 2004, see www.banksr.com Other Matters Guidelines tab para 2.2.6 A suspended sentence is a sentence of imprisonment. It is subject to the same criteria as a sentence of imprisonment which is to commence immediately. In particular, this requires a court to be satisfied that the custody threshold has been passed.

The requirements that can be made part of a Suspended Sentence Order

106.9 *Generally*
Criminal Justice Act 2003 s 189-190 enable one or more of the requirements to be imposed as part of a Suspended Sentence Order. The requirements are listed at **15.16** onwards.

[1169] Criminal Justice Act 2003 s 189(1) as amended by Criminal Justice Act 2003 (Sentencing) (Transitory Provisions) Order 2005 2005/643 art 2(2)(a)
[1170] Criminal Justice Act 2003 s 189(3)
[1171] Criminal Justice Act 2003 s 189(2) as amended by Criminal Justice Act 2003 (Sentencing) (Transitory Provisions) Order 2005 2005/643 art 2(2)(b)
[1172] *Youth Justice: The Scaled Approach*, YJB 2009 www.yjb.gov.uk/scaledapproach
[1173] Criminal Justice and Immigration Act 2008 s 1(3) and 1(4), Criminal Justice Act 2003 s 174(2)(ca) and (cb). However, it may be imposed in other circumstances following a 'wilful and persistent' breach of a Youth Rehabilitation Order. (Note: Following the coming into force of Legal Aid, Sentencing and Punishment of Offenders Act 2012 s 64, a new Criminal Justice Act 2003 s 174 is substituted. The reference to Criminal Justice Act 2003 s 174(2)(ca) and (cb) now reads 'Criminal Justice Act 2003 s 174(8)(a)'.)
[1174] Criminal Justice Act 2003 s 148(1)

106.10 ***Guidelines***
New Sentences: Criminal Justice Act 2003 Guideline 2004, see www.banksr.com Other Matters Guidelines tab para 2.2.14 Whilst the offence for which a suspended sentence is imposed is generally likely to be more serious than one for which a community sentence is imposed, the imposition of the custodial sentence is a clear punishment and deterrent. In order to ensure that the overall terms of the sentence are commensurate with the seriousness of the offence, it is likely that the requirements to be undertaken during the supervision period would be less onerous than if a community sentence had been imposed. These requirements will need to ensure that they properly address those factors that are most likely to reduce the risk of reoffending.
Because of the very clear deterrent threat involved in a suspended sentence, requirements imposed as part of that sentence should generally be less onerous than those imposed as part of a community sentence. A court wishing to impose onerous or intensive requirements on an offender should reconsider its decision to suspend sentence and consider whether a community sentence might be more appropriate.
Imposition of Community and Custodial Sentences Guideline 2017, see www.banksr.com Other Matters Guidelines tab. In force 1 February 2017
page 9
Suspended Sentences: General Guidance
(i) The guidance regarding pre-sentence reports applies if suspending custody.
(ii) If the court imposes a term of imprisonment of between 14 days and 2 years (subject to magistrates' courts sentencing powers), it may suspend the sentence for between 6 months and 2 years (the 'operational period'). The time for which a sentence is suspended should reflect the length of the sentence; up to 12 months might normally be appropriate for a suspended sentence of up to 6 months.
(iii) Where the court imposes two or more sentences to be served consecutively, the court may suspend the sentence where the aggregate of the terms is between 14 days and 2 years (subject to magistrates' courts sentencing powers).
(iv) When the court suspends a sentence, it may impose one or more requirements for the offender to undertake in the community. The requirements are identical to those available for community orders on page 5.
(v) A custodial sentence that is suspended should be for the same term that would have applied if the sentence was to be served immediately.

106.11 ***Need there be requirements?***
Criminal Justice Act 2003 s 189(1A) An order under subsection (1) may also provide that the offender must comply during a period specified in the order for the purposes of this subsection ('the supervision period') with one or more requirements falling within section 190(1) and specified in the order.
Note: The new section 189(1) (see **106.3**) and (1A) above, both substituted by Legal Aid, Sentencing and Punishment of Offenders Act 2012 s 68, remove the need for a requirement to be imposed. Ed.

106.12 ***Compatibility***
Criminal Justice Act 2003 s 190(5) Before making a Suspended Sentence Order imposing two or more different requirements…the court must consider whether, in the circumstances of the case, the requirements are compatible with each other.

106.13 ***Religious beliefs/Educational timetable etc., Avoid conflict with***
Criminal Justice Act 2003 s 217(1) The court must ensure, as far as practicable, that any requirement imposed…is such as to avoid: a) any conflict with the offender's religious beliefs or with the requirements of any other relevant order to which he may be subject, and b) any interference with the times, if any, at which he normally works or attends any educational establishment.

(2) The responsible officer in relation to an offender to whom a relevant order relates must ensure, as far as practicable, that any instruction given or requirement imposed by him in pursuance of the order is such as to avoid the conflict or interference mentioned in subsection (1).

106.14 ***Offence warrants more than 2 years***

R v Phipps 2007 EWCA Crim 2923, 2008 2 Cr App R (S) 20 (p 114) D pleaded to burglary and asked for 14 burglary TICs to be considered. He was liable to a 3-year minimum sentence. The Judge took a merciful approach, found it unjust to pass the minimum sentence and passed a 12-month suspended sentence with two requirements. She hoped this would break his drug addiction. Shortly after, D left his drug rehabilitation centre and that was a breach of the order. He was taken to court. The sentencing Judge had retired and a new Judge sentenced D to 3½ years because he had thrown away his chance. Held. We don't criticise the merciful approach and the second Judge's approach could not be faulted. The sentence was well deserved. [For breach of community orders, Schedule 8 para 10 empowers the court to deal with him 'in any way in which he could be dealt with when the order was made'. No such power exists for Suspended Sentence Orders.] So 12 months was the maximum sentence [as that was the length of the order].

Note: Since this case was reported, the maximum period that can be suspended has increased to 2 years, so the principle would be applied less often now. Ed.

The requirements

For details of the requirements see the **COMMUNITY ORDERS The requirements that can be made part of the community order/Suspended Sentence Order** section at **15.16**.

The making of the order

106.15 ***Legally represented, The defendant must be The status of the order***

Powers of Criminal Courts (Sentencing) Act 2000 s 83(5) For the purposes of [the requirement that the defendant be legally represented] a previous sentence of imprisonment which has been suspended and which has not taken effect…shall be disregarded.

See also the **CUSTODY: GENERAL PRINCIPLES Defendants who have not been previously sentenced to custody section at 28.19**.

106.16 ***Decision making process***

New Sentences: Criminal Justice Act 2003 Guideline 2004, see www.banksr.com Other Matters Guidelines tab para 2.2.10 There are many similarities between the suspended sentence and the community sentence. In both cases, requirements can be imposed during the supervision period and the court can respond to breach by sending the offender to custody. The crucial difference is that the suspended sentence is a prison sentence and is appropriate only for an offence that passes the custody threshold and for which imprisonment is the only option.

para 2.2.11 The full decision making process for imposition of custodial sentences under the new framework (including the custody threshold test) is set out in paragraphs 1.31-1.33 of the [*Overarching Principles: Seriousness Guideline 2004*]. For the purposes of suspended sentences the relevant steps are: a) Has the custody threshold been passed? b) If so, is it unavoidable that a custodial sentence be imposed? c) If so, can that sentence be suspended (sentencers should be clear that they would have imposed a custodial sentence if the power to suspend had not been available)? d) If not, impose a sentence which takes immediate effect for the term commensurate with the seriousness of the offence.

106.17 ***The length of the suspended period of imprisonment and the suspension***

Criminal Justice Act 2003 s 189(1)[1175] If a court passes a sentence of imprisonment or, in the case of a person aged at least 18 but under 21, a sentence of detention in a Young

[1175] Criminal Justice Act 2003 s 148(5)

Offender Institution for a term of at least 14 days but not more than 2 years, it may make an order providing that the sentence of imprisonment or detention in a Young Offender Institution is not to take effect unless:..[1176]

Note: Legal Aid, Sentencing and Punishment of Offenders Act 2012 therefore increased the maximum term from 12 months to 2 years. Ed.

New Sentences: Criminal Justice Act 2003 Guideline 2004, see www.banksr.com Other Matters Guidelines tab para 2.2.6 A suspended sentence is a sentence of imprisonment. It is subject to the same criteria as a sentence of imprisonment which is to commence immediately. In particular, this requires a court to be satisfied that the length of the term is the shortest term commensurate with the seriousness of the offence.

New Sentences: Criminal Justice Act 2003 Guideline 2004, see www.banksr.com Other Matters Guidelines tab para 2.2.12 Before making the decision to suspend sentence, the court must already have decided that a prison sentence is justified and should also have decided the length of sentence that would be the shortest term commensurate with the seriousness of the offence if it were to be imposed immediately. The decision to suspend the sentence should not lead to a longer term being imposed than if the sentence were to take effect immediately. A prison sentence that is suspended should be for the same term that would have applied if the offender were being sentenced to immediate custody.

para 2.2.13 When assessing the length of the operational period of a suspended sentence, the court should have in mind the relatively short length of the sentence being suspended and the advantages to be gained by retaining the opportunity to extend the operational period at a later stage.

The operational period of a suspended sentence should reflect the length of the sentence being suspended. As an approximate guide, an operational period of up to 12 months might normally be appropriate for a suspended sentence of up to 6 months and an operational period of up to 18 months might normally be appropriate for a suspended sentence of up to 12 months.

106.18 *Consecutive suspended sentences*

Criminal Justice Act 2003 s 189(2) Where two or more sentences imposed on the same occasion are to be served consecutively, the power conferred by subsection (1) is not exercisable in relation to any of them unless [the total] does not exceed 2 years.[1177]

New Sentences: Criminal Justice Act 2003 Guideline 2004, see www.banksr.com Other Matters Guidelines tab para 2.2.21 It is expected that any activated suspended sentence will be consecutive to the sentence imposed for the new offence.

106.19 *Time served on remand Principles*

Criminal Justice Act 2003 s 240ZA(7) For the purposes of this section a suspended sentence:

(a) is to be treated as a sentence of imprisonment when it takes effect under paragraph 8(2)(a) or (b) of Schedule 12, and

(b) is to be treated as being imposed by the order under which it takes effect.

R v Mohammed 2007 EWCA Crim 2756, 2008 2 Cr App R (S) 14 (p 85) D was sentenced to a 2-year suspended sentence. He had served 13½ months on remand. The sentence was later activated. Held. A judge considering whether to impose a suspended sentence of imprisonment should at that stage take into account the time spent by D on remand. It is best, as this case reveals, if the fact that the judge has done so is made plain in the sentencing remarks. If a defendant has already spent such time on remand as is equivalent to the length of custodial sentence the judge is considering imposing, then, at least in general, a suspended sentence should not be imposed. Otherwise, as expressed in *R v McCabe* 1988 10 Cr App R (S) 134, the defendant is at risk [in fact, if not in theory] of double punishment. It does not at all follow from the mere fact that a defendant has

[1176] Criminal Justice Act 2003 s 148(3)(b)

[1177] As amended by Legal Aid, Sentencing and Punishment of Offenders Act 2012 s 68(2)

spent substantial time in custody on remand that a suspended sentence should not be imposed, the appropriate sentence may well reflect both the time on remand plus the length of the suspended sentence.
R v Rakib 2011 EWCA Crim 870, 2012 1 Cr App R (S) 1 (p 1) Where a Suspended Sentence Order is imposed and subsequently activated, it is to be treated as a sentence of imprisonment for the purposes of Criminal Justice Act 2003 s 240.[1178] Where the offender has spent time on remand to the effect that a section 240 direction will entirely swallow up the activated Suspended Sentence Order, the activation becomes an entirely empty exercise. The imposition of a Suspended Sentence Order in those circumstances is usually to be deprecated.
R v Hewitt 2011 EWCA Crim 885, 2 Cr App R (S) 111 (p 633) D was given a Suspended Sentence Order of 12 months for threats to kill etc. against his former girlfriend. He had spent 204 days on remand. Three months later, he committed more offences. The Court deferred sentence. A week later he committed more offences. The Judge activated the Suspended Sentence Order with a 2-month deduction for part compliance with the order making 10 months. The Judge ordered the later periods of custody to count but not the 204 days. Held. Ordinarily the judge should impose the sentence merited by the offence, and suspend it with an indication that if it was breached the defendant should expect a section 240 direction in his favour. If the judge has in mind an '*R v Whitehouse* 2010' sentence, the judge must make it very clear what he has done and why. The activating judge should not assume the days were taken into account when the sentence was imposed. However, where it is clear they have been it is open to the activating judge not to take them into account. There should be no double credit. The time on remand should have been deducted, even though it made the Suspended Sentence Order appear curious or empty.
R v Collier 2013 EWCA Crim 1132 D was given a 12-month suspended sentence. He had spent 180 days on remand which was not referred to in the sentencing remarks. He breached the order and was given a 2-month sentence consecutive to the suspended sentence activated in full. However, the Judge said the time spent on remand must have been a factor in deciding to impose the suspended sentence and declined to take the remand time into account. Held. Under section 240ZA(7) time on remand is automatically deducted when a suspended sentence is activated. That may not have happened because of what the Judge said. We dismiss the appeal and the Prison Service must deduct those days from the time to serve. In fact, D should have been released some time ago.
Note: This means the Judge should not factor in the time served on remand, except because of the length of the time on remand, when considering whether an immediate custodial sentence or suspended is appropriate in principle. Ed.
See also: *R v Hinds* 2018 EWCA Crim 749 (D pleaded. Summary only offence. Maximum 6 months. 29 days in custody, which nearly equated to a 2-month sentence. Given 6 weeks suspended. Held. The position is exactly the same as in *R v Hewitt* 2011 (see above). Conditional discharge substituted.)
See also the **SUSPENDED SENTENCE ORDERS: BREACH OF** ***Time on remand*** para at **107.27**.

106.20 *Time served on remand/curfew Whole sentence served*

Note: These principles should apply to occasions where the court is considering imposing a community order as well. Ed.
R v Waters and Young 2008 EWCA Crim 2538 W and Y pleaded to handling stolen goods. On two occasions a lorry was driven into a building in which an ATM was installed and the cash stolen. They received 44 weeks' imprisonment, suspended for 2 years with requirements of 2 years' supervision and 85 hours' unpaid work. W had spent

[1178] Such an order may be imposed following 'wilful and persistent failure to comply with a Youth Rehabilitation Order imposed for a non-imprisonable offence': Criminal Justice and Immigration Act 2008 Sch 2 para 6(12) and 8(12).

223 days on remand and Y 174 days. The Judge indicated the sentence should be 9 or 12 months' imprisonment. Because of the time served, he passed a sentence of 44 weeks suspended for 2 years, with supervision and 85 hours' unpaid work, because he considered the sentences would be meaningless if they were imposed. Held. The Judge should not have used the term 'suspended sentence supervision order'. If 9-12 months was the appropriate term that is what should have been imposed. It was not a meaningless sentence, it was a real sentence. The appropriate sentence was 9 months so effecting immediate release.

R v Barrett 2010 EWCA Crim 365, 2 Cr App R (S) 86 (p 551) D pleaded to threatening behaviour and other charges. He had served almost 4 months when sentenced. D told the probation officer that he would not engage with a community order because he had served his sentence. Held. The total sentence could not have exceeded 6 months. We can understand why the Judge wanted to impose a suspended sentence because she wanted to ensure the public had a measure of protection from D and D needed support. However, the suspended sentence was more severe in its impact than the maximum sentence. The Judge had to avoid that. The only way to avoid that would be to pass a sentence of immediate effect. To ensure that D is not more severely dealt with on appeal, conditional discharge substituted.

R v Hewitt 2011 EWCA Crim 885, 2 Cr App R (S) 111 (p 633) D was given a Suspended Sentence Order, which he breached. Held. If the defendant has already been in custody on remand for a period longer than that which he would serve in prison, then the judge must consider whether it would be appropriate to impose a suspended sentence at all. It is important that he does not impose a suspended sentence that may either be more severe in its custodial impact than the maximum appropriate sentence of immediate custody, or alternatively be of no practical effect on activation (and hence no incentive to comply) because of the effect of section 240. The judge should look elsewhere for an appropriate sentence, which might, for example, take the form of an immediate term of imprisonment (with a section 240 direction), a community order, or a conditional or absolute discharge.

R v Morgan 2013 EWCA Crim 2148 D pleaded to arson. He set fire to his bed. The fire was put out by his girlfriend and another. Later, D then lit another fire in the hallway. D admitted in interview that he set fires in an attempt to end his life. Whilst on remand D had been receiving effective treatment for his depression. The Judge originally thought that a 12-month sentence (before a full discount) was appropriate but realised that with time on remand that meant immediate release. This would mean an end to D's treatment. The Judge wanted D to have treatment and support. The defence said he would be liable to serve half the term if there was a breach. Held. Suspending a sentence should not lead to an increase in the term imposed if that sentence was immediate custody. The Judge's approach was wrong. 8 months, not 15, suspended, with the requirements remaining.

Note: The effect of this order was if there was a breach the court could impose a custodial sentence of up to 8 months. He would not have to serve it as the remand time would count, see **106.19**.

R v Williams 2018 EWCA Crim 2396 D was convicted of possession of an offensive weapon. He had served on a curfew the equivalent of 166 days on remand. The Judge sentenced him to 3 months suspended, with an unpaid work requirement. The defence on appeal asked for a conditional discharge, so there would be no supervision. Held. We impose an immediate sentence of 3 months' imprisonment because that is what the offence merited. [The time had been served.]

See also: *R v Maughan* 2011 EWCA Crim 787, 2 Cr App R (S) 89 (p 493) (Served the equivalent of 13 months. Worth 8 months. Suspended sentence wrong. Immediate release.)

R v Earl 2014 EWCA Crim 261 (A drowning had been charged as common assault. 54 days on remand. 59 days on curfew. **Community order with 8 months' supervision** not 4 months suspended with 18 months' supervision.)

Old case: *R v Hemmings* 2007 EWCA Crim 2413, 2008 1 Cr App R (S) 106 (p 623) (It is not right that the defendant should receive a substantial further punishment when he has already served the maximum sentence.)

106.21 ***Time served on remand Order substituted on appeal***
Consolidated Criminal Practice Direction 2011 para I 9.1 Where an appellate court substitutes a suspended sentence of imprisonment for one having immediate effect, the court should have in mind any period the appellant has spent in custody. If the court is of the opinion that it would be fair to do so, an approximate adjustment to the term of the suspended sentence should be made. Whether or not the court makes such adjustment, it should state that it had that period in mind. The court should further indicate that the operational period of suspension runs from the date the court passes the suspended sentence.
Note: Although this is officially revoked, the contents of this direction might be helpful. Ed.

106.22 ***Notify Must notify the defendant of the requirement/Court must give the defendant copies of the order***
Criminal Justice Act 2003 s 219(1) The court must provide copies of the order:
(a) to the offender,
(b) if the offender is aged 18 or over, to an officer of a local probation board assigned to the court or an officer of a provider of probation services acting at the court,
(c) if the offender is aged 16 or 17, to an officer of a local probation board assigned to the court, an officer of a provider of probation services acting at the court or to a member of a youth offending team assigned to the court, and
(d) where the order specifies a local justice area in which the court making the order does not act, to the local probation board acting for that area, or a provider of probation services acting.
Criminal Procedure Rules 2015 2015/1490 Rule 28.2(1) This rule applies where the court:
a) makes a Suspended Sentence Order,…
(2) The court officer must notify:
(a) the defendant of:
(i) the length of the sentence suspended by a Suspended Sentence Order, and
(ii) the period of the suspension,
(b) the defendant and, where the defendant is under 14, an appropriate adult, of:
(i) any requirement or requirements imposed, and
(ii) the identity of any responsible officer or supervisor, and the means by which that person may be contacted…

106.23 ***Licence Defendant serving a sentence for a revoked licence***
Criminal Justice Act 2003 Sch 12 para 9(2) The power to make an order under sub-paragraph (1)(b) (making an activated suspended sentence consecutive or immediate to another term of imprisonment, see **106.27**) has effect subject to section 265 (restriction on consecutive sentences for released prisoners).

106.24 ***Explain sentence, Judge must/Suggested sentencing remarks***
Judicial College's Crown Court Compendium Part II Sentencing June 2018 page 4-27
3) Passing the sentence
The court must:
1) Complete the steps set out in chapter S-3 [of this guide] [determining the seriousness].
2) State that:
(a) the seriousness of the offence is such that neither a fine alone nor a community order can be justified;
(b) the sentence of…is the least that can be imposed to mark the seriousness of the offence/s.

(c) Direct that the sentence will be suspended (for a period of not less than 6 months or more than 2 years): the 'operational period'.

3) Consider whether any requirement(s) from the list specified in Criminal Justice Act [2003] s 190 (identical to Community Order requirements: see chapter S 5-1) should be attached to the order to be completed within, or complied with for, a period of not less than 6 months or more than 2 years: the 'supervision period'. It is no longer mandatory to impose any requirement on a suspended sentence.

4) Explain the consequences of any further offending and/or breach of a requirement if one or more have been imposed and at which court any breaches will be considered. (Usually breaches of suspended sentences are retained by the Crown Court.).

5) If the court is ordering reviews, specify the date of the first review.

Example: with requirement for supervision (offence committed before 1 February 2015)
The sentence of…months/weeks* will be suspended for 2 years. If in the next 2 years you commit any offence you will be brought back to court and it is likely that this sentence will be brought into operation.
Also, for the next 12 months, you will be supervised by a Probation Officer. That means you must meet him when and where he requires and co-operate fully with him. If you fail to comply with this requirement you will be in breach of this order, which means that you will be brought back to court and you will be liable to serve the sentence.
Example: with requirement for Rehabilitation Activity Requirement (offence committed on or after 1 February 2015)
The sentence of…months/weeks* will be suspended for 2 years. If in the next 2 years you commit any offence you will be brought back to court and it is likely that this sentence will be brought into operation.
Also for the next 12 months you will be subject to a rehabilitation activity requirement. That means that you must meet with the office supervising this requirement as and when required and you must attend and co-operate fully with any activities arranged by him. If you fail to comply with this requirement you will be in breach of this order, which means that you will be brought back to court and you will be liable to serve the sentence.
[If reviews are ordered:..and you must return to court at {specify} on {date} when your progress will be reviewed. At that review the court will have a short report on your progress from your supervising officer. If you are doing well the order will continue, but if you are failing to comply with it, you will be in breach of this order and liable to serve the sentence.]
Note:
1. The original stipulation that a suspended sentence had to be expressed only in weeks no longer applies.
2. The possible consequences of reoffending/breach are simplified in the above example with a view to D being able to understand them. The court's full powers are set out in chapter S 9-3 [of this guide].

Note: There is no explanation of what the * means. I assume it means 'delete as appropriate' Ed.

Combined with other orders

106.25 ***Community sentences, Combined with***

Criminal Justice Act 2003 s 189(5) A court which passes a suspended sentence on any person…may not impose a community sentence…in respect of any other offence.

R v Robinson 2013 EWCA Crim 199 Rule applied. Community order quashed.

106.26 ***Compensation orders, Combined with***

TICs and Totality Guideline 2012: Crown Court, see www.banksr.com Other Matters Guidelines tab page 16 (*Magistrates' Court Sentencing Guidelines Update March 2012* page 18p) A compensation order can be combined with a Suspended Sentence Order.[1179]

[1179] Powers of Criminal Courts (Sentencing) Act 2000 s 118(5)

106.27 *Immediate imprisonment, Combined with*

R v Sapiano 1968 52 Cr App R 674 LCJ The court passed a 9-month term of imprisonment and a 9-month term of imprisonment suspended for three counts of handling. Held. This was a wrong sentence as it went against the intention of the Act, which was to avoid immediate custody, and was potentially impractical. All sentences suspended.

R v Butters and Fitzgerald 1971 55 Cr App R 515 The defendants were subject to immediate imprisonment and suspended sentences at the same time. Held. That was undesirable as a matter of sentencing practice, although there is no statutory bar to doing that. In general, courts should avoid mixing up sentences which fall into different categories. The sentences were rearranged so it was one or the other.

Note: Although these cases seem very old, the principle seems valid today. Ed.

106.28 *Licences Prisoners released on licence*

Criminal Justice Act 2003 Sch 12 para 9(1) When making an order under paragraph 8(2)(a) or (b) (activating a Suspended Sentence Order) that a sentence is to take effect (with or without any variation of the original term), the court:

(a) [Repealed]

(b) may order that the sentence is to take effect immediately or that the term of that sentence is to commence on the expiry of another term of imprisonment passed on the offender by that or another court.

(2) The power to make an order under sub-paragraph (1)(b) has effect subject to section 265 (restriction on consecutive sentences for released prisoners, see **18.21**).

106.29 *Sexual Harm Prevention Orders, Combined with*

R v Smith and Others 2011 EWCA Crim 1772, 2012 1 Cr App R (S) 82 (p 468) A SOPO may plainly be necessary if the sentence is suspended. Whilst conditions may be attached to the licence, that licence will have a defined and limited life. The SOPO by contrast will extend beyond the suspended sentence because a SOPO cannot be made unless prohibitions of at least 5 years are called for.

Note: There is no reason why this principle should not apply to Sexual Harm Prevention Orders. Ed.

Reviews of Suspended Sentence Order

106.30 *Power to review a Suspended Sentence Order*

Criminal Justice Act 2003 s 191-192 provide a power to review the order and the requirements with some exceptions where a court 'imposes one or more community requirements'.[1180]

106.31 *Power to amend and cancel community requirements*

Criminal Justice Act 2003 Sch 12 para 13(1) Where at any time while a suspended sentence order is in force, it appears to the appropriate court on the application of the offender or the responsible officer that, having regard to the circumstances which have arisen since the order was made, it would be in the interests of justice to do so, the court may cancel the community requirements of the Suspended Sentence Order.

(2) The circumstances in which the appropriate court may exercise its power under sub-paragraph (1) include the offender making good progress or his responding satisfactorily to supervision.

Criminal Justice Act 2003 Sch 12 para 15 At any time during the supervision period, the appropriate court may, on the application of the offender or the responsible officer, by order amend any community requirement of a Suspended Sentence Order: a) by cancelling the requirement, or b) by replacing it with a requirement of the same kind, which the court could include if it were then making the order.

[1180] Criminal Justice and Immigration Act 2008 s 1(4)(c)

Note: There are other powers of amendment: a) medical (Sch 12 para 16), b) drug reviews to be made without a hearing (Sch 12 para 17), and c) unpaid work requirements (Sch 12 para 18). The requirement for copies is at Sch 12 para 22. Ed.

106.32 ***No power to revoke***

R v Miah 2011 EWCA Crim 1850 D was subject to a Suspended Sentence Order. He was sentenced to 10 months. He was not in breach of the Suspended Sentence Order, but the judge purported to revoke it. Held. The Judge could amend the community requirements but he could not revoke the order.

R v Blakemore 2016 EWCA Crim 1396, 2017 1 Cr App R (S) 5 (p 24) D pleaded to eight counts, mostly of drug supply but also robbery and other charges. He was in breach of a 6-month Suspended Sentence Order. The Judge revoked that order. Held. As D had been convicted of further offences, the Judge had to activate the order in full or in part unless it was unjust so to do. It certainly would not have been unjust but revoking it was not an option. However, it was not open for us to activate it.

Note: The total sentence was reduced from 13½ years to 10½ years. There appears no reason why the Court should not have activated the order in full or in part. Even if the Court hadn't reduced the sentence, it could have activated the sentence in full as long as it made the sentences concurrent. The bar to increasing penalties at the Court of Appeal only applies to an increase when 'the case is taken as a whole', see **4.74**. Ed.

See also: *R v Shakari* 2008 EWCA Crim 3324 (There is no power to revoke a Suspended Sentence Order when resentencing if the defendant is not in breach.)

107 Suspended Sentence Orders: Breach of

107.1

Criminal Justice Act 2003 s 193 and Sch 12 para 8 (power to activate the suspended sentence in full, or for a lesser term, or to impose more onerous community requirements, or extend the supervision period etc., or impose a fine.)

Historical offences For offences committed before 4 April 2005, courts can pass a suspended sentence under Powers of Criminal Courts (Sentencing) Act 2000 s 118. Breaches of suspended sentences are dealt with by Powers of Criminal Courts (Sentencing) Act 2000 s 119-120. For more detail see **Historical offences** at **106.1**.

Victim surcharge It is the date of the offence for which the Suspended Sentence Order was imposed that matters. Where all the offences were committed after 1 October 2012, the court must impose the relevant victim surcharge for whatever sentence was passed.[1181] For more details see **115.6**.

Preliminary matters

107.2 ***Treatment/Drug rehabilitation requirements, Breaches of Exemption from breach proceedings***

Criminal Justice Act 2003 Sch 12 para 10(1) An offender who is required by any of the following community requirements of a Suspended Sentence Order:

(a) a mental health treatment requirement,

(b) a drug rehabilitation requirement, or

(c) an alcohol treatment requirement,

to submit to treatment for his mental condition, or his dependency on or propensity to misuse drugs or alcohol, is not to be treated for the purposes of paragraph 8(1)(a) as having failed to comply with that requirement on the ground only that he had refused to undergo any surgical, electrical or other treatment if, in the opinion of the court, his refusal was reasonable having regard to all the circumstances.

[1181] This is a restriction on consecutive sentences for released prisoners which has now been repealed.

107.3 *Duty of responsible officer to give a warning before proceedings begin*
Criminal Justice Act 2003 Sch 12 para 4(1) If the responsible officer is of the opinion that the offender has failed without reasonable excuse to comply with any of the community requirements of a Suspended Sentence Order, the officer must give him a warning under this paragraph unless:

(a) the offender has within the previous 12 months been given a warning in relation to a failure to comply with any of the community requirements of the order, or
(b) the officer causes an information to be laid before a justice of the peace in respect of the failure.

(2) A warning under this paragraph must:

(a) describe the circumstances of the failure,
(b) state that the failure is unacceptable, and
(c) inform the offender that if within the next 12 months he again fails to comply with any requirement of the order, he will be liable to be brought before a court.

New Sentences: Criminal Justice Act 2003 Guideline 2004, see www.banksr.com Other Matters Guidelines tab para 2.2.15 Where an offender has breached any of the requirements without reasonable excuse for the first time, the responsible officer must either give a warning or initiate breach proceedings.

107.4 *Failure to comply after a warning Breach proceedings are mandatory*
Criminal Justice Act 2003 Sch 12 para 5 If:

(a) the responsible officer has given a warning under para 4 (see above) to the offender in respect of a Suspended Sentence Order, and
(b) at any time within the 12 months beginning with the date on which the warning was given, the responsible officer is of the opinion that the offender has since that date failed without reasonable excuse to comply with any of the community requirements of the order, the officer must cause an information to be laid before a justice of the peace in respect of the failure in question.

New Sentences: Criminal Justice Act 2003 Guideline 2004, see www.banksr.com Other Matters Guidelines tab para 2.2.15 Where there is a further breach within a 12-month period, breach proceedings must be initiated.

107.5 *Power to issue warrant and summons Crown Court*
Criminal Justice Act 2003 Sch 12 para 7(1) This paragraph applies to a Suspended Sentence Order made by the Crown Court which does not include a direction that any failure to comply with the community requirements of the order is to be dealt with by a Magistrates' Court.
(2) If at any time while a Suspended Sentence Order to which this paragraph applies is in force it appears on information to the Crown Court that the offender has failed to comply with any of the community requirements of the order, the Crown Court may:

(a) issue a summons requiring the offender to appear at the place and time specified in it, or
(b) if the information is in writing and on oath, issue a warrant for his arrest.

(3) Any summons or warrant issued under this paragraph must direct the offender to appear or be brought before the Crown Court.
(4) Where a summons issued under sub-paragraph (1)(a) requires the offender to appear before the Crown Court and the offender does not appear in answer to the summons, the Crown Court may issue a warrant for the arrest of the offender.

107.6 *Power to issue warrant and summons Magistrates' Court*
Criminal Justice Act 2003 Sch 12 para 6(1) This paragraph applies to:

(a) a Suspended Sentence Order made by a Magistrates' Court, or
(b) any Suspended Sentence Order which was made by the Crown Court and includes a direction that any failure to comply with the community requirements of the order is to be dealt with by a Magistrates' Court.

(2) If at any time while a Suspended Sentence Order to which this paragraph applies is in force it appears on information to a justice of the peace that the offender has failed to comply with any of the community requirements of the order, the justice may:

(a) issue a summons requiring the offender to appear at the place and time specified in it, or

(b) if the information is in writing and on oath, issue a warrant for his arrest.

(3) Any summons or warrant issued under this paragraph must direct the offender to appear or be brought:

(a) in the case of a Suspended Sentence Order which is subject to review, before the court responsible for the order,

(b) in any other case, before a Magistrates' Court acting in the local justice area in which the offender resides or, if it is not known where he resides, before a Magistrates' Court acting in the local justice area concerned.

(4) Where a summons issued under sub-paragraph (2)(a) requires the offender to appear before a Magistrates' Court and the offender does not appear in answer to the summons, the Magistrates' Court may issue a warrant for the arrest of the offender.

Criminal Justice Act 2003 Sch 12 para 12 This paragraph contains the power of the original court to issue warrants or summonses where another court sentencing the defendant did not deal with the breach of the suspended sentence.

107.7 ***Committal to Crown Court***

Criminal Justice Act 2003 Sch 12 para 8(6) Where a Suspended Sentence Order was made by the Crown Court and a Magistrates' Court would (apart from this sub-paragraph) be required to deal with the offender [for the breach] it may instead commit him to custody or release him on bail until he can be brought or appear before the Crown Court.

Powers of Criminal Courts (Sentencing) Act 2000 s 7(2) Subsection (1) (the requirement that the Crown Court shall deal with the offender in any way the Magistrates' Court could) does not apply where under Magistrates' Courts Act 1980 s 6 a Magistrates' Court commits a person to be dealt with by the Crown Court in respect of a suspended sentence, but in such a case the powers under Criminal Justice Act 2003 Sch 12 para 8-9 (power of court to deal with suspended sentence) shall be exercisable by the Crown Court.

Criminal Justice Act 2003 Sch 12 para 11(2) Where an offender is convicted by a Magistrates' Court of any offence and the court is satisfied that the offence was committed during the operational period of a suspended sentence passed by the Crown Court: a) the court may, if it thinks fit, commit him in custody or on bail to the Crown Court, and b) if it does not, must give written notice of the conviction to the appropriate officer of the Crown Court.

107.8 ***CRO should have details of the order breached***

Criminal Practice Directions 2015 EWCA Crim 1567 para II 10A.7 Where the current alleged offence could constitute a breach of an existing sentence such as a suspended sentence, community order or conditional discharge, and it is known that that sentence is still in force, then details of the circumstances of the offence leading to the sentence should be included in the antecedents. The detail should be brief and include the date of the offence.

Court powers

107.9 ***Court powers on breach***

Powers of court on breach of community requirement or conviction of further offence

Criminal Justice Act 2003 Sch 12 para 8(1)(a)[1182] This paragraph applies where:

[1182] This section is as amended by Legal Aid, Sentencing and Punishment of Offenders Act 2012 s 69(2) Sch 9 para 10 and Sch 10 para 38(2).

(a) it is proved to the satisfaction of a court before which an offender appears or is brought under paragraph 6 or 7 or by virtue of section 192(6) that he has failed without reasonable excuse to comply with any of the community requirements of the Suspended Sentence Order, or
(b) an offender is convicted of an offence committed during the operational period of a suspended sentence (other than one which has already taken effect) and either:
(i) he is so convicted by or before a court having power under paragraph 11 to deal with him in respect of the suspended sentence, or
(ii) he subsequently appears or is brought before such a court.
(2) The court must consider his case and deal with him in one of the following ways:
(a) the court may order that the suspended sentence is to take effect with its original term unaltered,
(b) the court may order that the sentence is to take effect with the substitution for the original term of a lesser term,
(ba) the court may order the offender to pay a fine of an amount not exceeding £2,500,
(c) in the case of a Suspended Sentence Order that imposes one or more community requirements, the court may amend the order by doing any one or more of the following:
(i) imposing more onerous community requirements which the court could include if it were then making the order,
(ii) subject to subsections (3) and (4) of section 189, extending the supervision period, or
(iii) subject to subsection (3) of that section, extending the operational period.
(d) in the case of a Suspended Sentence Order that does not impose any community requirements, the court may, subject to section 189(3), amend the order by extending the operational period.
(3) The court must make an order under sub-paragraph (2)(a) or (b) unless it is of the opinion that it would be unjust to do so in view of all the circumstances, including the matters mentioned in sub-paragraph (4), and where it is of that opinion the court must state its reasons.
(4) The matters referred to in sub-paragraph (3) are:
(a) the extent to which the offender has complied with any community requirements of the Suspended Sentence Order, and
(b) in a case falling within sub-paragraph (1)(b), the facts of the subsequent offence.
(4ZA) A fine imposed under sub-paragraph (2)(ba) is to be treated, for the purposes of any enactment, as being a sum adjudged to be paid by a conviction.
(4A) Where a Magistrates' Court dealing with an offender under sub-paragraph (2)(c) would not otherwise have the power to amend the Suspended Sentence Order under paragraph 14 (amendment by reason of change of residence), that paragraph has effect as if the references to the appropriate court were references to the court dealing with the offender.
(5) Where a court deals with an offender under sub-paragraph (2) in respect of a suspended sentence, the appropriate officer of the court must notify the appropriate officer of the court which passed the sentence of the method adopted.
(6) Where a Suspended Sentence Order was made by the Crown Court and a Magistrates' Court would (apart from this sub-paragraph) be required to deal with the offender under sub-paragraph (2)(a), (b), (ba) or (c) it may instead commit him to custody or release him on bail until he can be brought or appear before the Crown Court.
Criminal Justice Act 2003 Sch 12 para 8(8) In proceedings before the Crown Court under this paragraph any question whether the offender has failed to comply with any community requirements of the Suspended Sentence Order and any question whether the offender has been convicted of an offence committed during the operational period of the suspended sentence is to be determined by the court and not by the verdict of a jury.

Note: Criminal Justice Act 2003 s 189(3)-(4) states: a) that the supervision period and the operational period must each be not less than 6 months and not more than 2 years, and b) the supervision period must not end later than the operational period. Ed.

107.10 ***Court powers on breach Magistrates' Court Guidelines***
Magistrates' Court Sentencing Guidelines 2008, see www.banksr.com Other Matters Guidelines tab page 163 para 5 If the offender fails to comply with a community requirement or commits a further offence, the court must either activate the suspended sentence in full or in part or amend the order so as to:[1183]

(a) extend the period during which the offender is subject to community requirements,
(b) make the community requirements more onerous, or
(c) extend the operational period.

Note: There is now the power to fine, see **107.9** at para 8(2)(ba). Ed.

107.11 ***Court powers on breach Judicial guidance***
R v Phipps 2007 EWCA Crim 2923, 2008 2 Cr App R (S) 20 (p 114) D pleaded to burglary and asked for 14 burglary TICs to be considered. He was liable to a 3-year minimum sentence. The Judge took a merciful approach, found it unjust to pass the minimum sentence and passed a 12-month suspended sentence with two requirements. She hoped this would break his drug addiction. Shortly after, D left his drug rehabilitation centre and that was a breach of the order. He was taken to court. The sentencing Judge had retired and a new Judge sentenced D to 3½ years because he had thrown away his chance. Held. We don't criticise the merciful approach and the second Judge's approach could not be faulted. The sentence was well deserved. [For breach of community orders, Schedule 8 para 10 empowers the court to deal with him 'in any way in which he could be dealt with when the order was made'. No such power exists for Suspended Sentence Orders.] So 12 months was the maximum sentence [as that was the length of the order].

R v Jones 2010 EWCA Crim 3298 D was given a suspended sentence with community requirements for 13 offences of taking etc. indecent photographs of children. Later he committed voyeurism and pleaded to it. The Judge activated the suspended sentence and made a Sexual Offences Prevention Order. Held. When activating a suspended sentence, the court may impose more onerous community requirements which the court could include if it were making the [original] order. A SOPO is not within the definition of a community requirement in Criminal Justice Act 2003. The Judge had no power to make the SOPO.

R v Bateman 2012 EWCA Crim 2518, 2013 2 Cr App R (S) 26 (p 174) D was given 12 months suspended. He breached the order for four common assault charges and was committed for sentence. The assaults were of some severity and against his partner. There were similar previous convictions. The Judge activated the suspended sentence, imposed 5 months' detention for the assault and made all the sentences consecutive. The Judge relied on Powers of Criminal Courts (Sentencing) Act 2000 s 7(2): 'section 7(1) does not apply where under section 6 a Magistrates' Court commits a person [to the] Crown Court in respect of a suspended sentence previously imposed by the Crown Court.' Held. That was wrong. The powers are the Magistrates' Court powers.

R v Ward 2012 EWCA Crim 3139, 2013 2 Cr App R (S) 35 (p 233) D pleaded to manslaughter and was given 9 years. He was in breach of a 9-month Suspended Sentence Order and the Judge made no order about it. Held. When a suspended sentence is breached, the court must order the sentence to take effect either in its original form or with a reduction unless it is unjust to do so. The 9 years is affirmed and we activate the sentence but concurrently with the 9-month sentence.

[1183] Criminal Justice Act 2003 Sch 12 para 8

Note: In such situations the court must: a) order the suspended sentence to take effect for i) the original term, or ii) a reduced term, or b) impose a fine not exceeding £2,500, unless it is of the opinion that it is unjust to do so,[1184] where it must state its reasons. Further, the court may amend the order by: a) extending the operational period, b) extending the supervision period, or c) imposing more onerous requirements. Ed.
R v H 2013 EWCA Crim 2115 D pleaded to section 20. About a year earlier he had received a Community Order at the Magistrates' Court. He appeared for breaching that order on five occasions, on the last of which the Community Order was revoked and a suspended sentence imposed. He breached the requirements of the order and proceedings were instituted. The Judge gave him 30 months and 2 months for breach of the suspended sentence. Held. The imposition of the suspended sentence was after the date for the section 20 offence and so there was no breach of the order because of a commission of an offence. Criminal Justice Act 2003 Sch 12 paras 6 and 8 make it clear that the summons for the breach must be issued by the court that imposed the sentence and that the same court must deal with the breaches of a requirement. The power of the Crown Court to deal with a breach of a suspended sentence imposed by magistrates is limited to breaches by [commission] of a further offence…which is governed by paragraph 9. The 2 months for the breach was unlawful.
R v Blakemore 2016 EWCA Crim 1396, 2017 1 Cr App R (S) 5 (p 24) D pleaded to eight counts, mostly of drug supply but also robbery and other charges. He was in breach of a 6-month Suspended Sentence Order. The Judge revoked that order. Held. As D had been convicted of further offences, the Judge had to activate the order in full or in part unless it was unjust so to do. It certainly would not have been unjust but revoking it was not an option. However, it was not open for us to activate it.
Note: The total sentence was reduced from 13½ years to 10½ years. There appears no reason why the Court should not have activated the order in full or in part. Even if the Court hadn't reduced the sentence, it could have activated the sentence in full as long as it made the sentences concurrent. The bar to increasing penalties at the Court of Appeal only applies to an increase when 'the case is taken as a whole', see **4.74**. Ed.
R v Bostan 2018 EWCA Crim 494, 2 Cr App R (S) 15 (p 112) In January 2017, D received four suspended sentences totalling 18 months. In October 2017, in breach proceedings, the Judge attempted to activate just one of them, a 3-month suspended sentence. Held. para 11 The suspended sentences were one single indivisible term of 18 months. It is not possible to activate part of the term. That means that contrary to what the Judge wanted, the whole term had been activated and on a later hearing no further activation was possible.
Att-Gen's Ref 2018 Re Usherwood 2018 EWCA Crim 1156, 2 Cr App R (S) 39 (p 337) D was sentenced for supply offences and for breach of a suspended sentence. The Judge passed no penalty. Held. para 20 The Judge should have dealt with it as required by Criminal Justice Act 2003 Sch 12 [**see 112.9**]. We activate the order in full and make it concurrent because of totality.
See also the SUSPENDED SENTENCE ORDERS ***No power to revoke unless there is a breach*** para at **106.32**.

Deciding what order to make

107.12 *The proper approach* *Pre-2018 guideline cases*

R v Ithell 1969 53 Cr App R 210 The proper approach where a fresh offence has been committed during the period of suspension of an earlier sentence is that the court should first sentence the defendant in respect of the fresh offence by punishment appropriate to that offence, and thereafter address itself to the question of the suspended sentence.
R v Levensconte 2011 EWCA Crim 2754, 2012 2 Cr App R (S) 19 (p 80) D was convicted of an offence committed during the operational period of a suspended

[1184] Criminal Justice Act 2003 Sch 12 para 8(3)-(4)

sentence. The Judge said that he treated that fact as an aggravating feature of the later offence. He activated the suspended sentence in full and made it consecutive. Held. He was wrong to treat it as an aggravating factor.

107.13 ***Presumption of activation***

Criminal Justice Act 2003 Sch 12 para 8(3)[1185] The court must make an order under sub-paragraph (2)(a) or (b) [activation of the full term or a lesser term, see **107.9**] unless it is of the opinion that it would be unjust to do so in view of all the circumstances, including the matters mentioned in sub-paragraph (4), and where it is of that opinion the court must state its reasons.

Breach Offences Guideline 2018, see www.banksr.com Other Matters Guidelines tab In force 1 October 2018 pages 8 and 10

[The same instruction appears for both types of breach.]

The court **must activate the custodial sentence** unless it would be unjust in all the circumstances to do so [see **107.16**].

107.14 ***Breach Offences Guideline 2018*** ***Conviction for a further offence***

Breach Offences Guideline 2018, see www.banksr.com Other Matters Guidelines tab In force 1 October 2018 page 8

Breach of a suspended sentence order

1) Conviction for further offence committed during operational period of order

The court **must activate the custodial sentence** unless it would be unjust in all the circumstances to do so [see **107.16**]. The predominant factor in determining whether activation is unjust relates to the level of compliance with the suspended sentence order and the facts/nature of any new offence. **These factors are already provided for in the penalties below which are determined by the nature of the new offence and level of compliance, but permit a reduction to the custodial term for relevant completed or partially completed requirements where appropriate.**

The facts/nature of the new offence is the primary consideration in assessing the action to be taken on the breach.

Where the breach is in the second or third category below, the prior level of compliance is also relevant. In assessing the level of compliance with the order the court should consider:

i) the overall attitude and engagement with the order as well as the proportion of elements completed;
ii) the impact of any completed or partially completed requirements on the offender's behaviour;
iii) the proximity of breach to imposition of order; and
iv) evidence of circumstances or offender characteristics, such as disability, mental health issues or learning difficulties which have impeded offender's compliance with the order.

Breach involves	Penalty
Multiple and/or more serious new offence(s) committed	Full activation of original custodial term
New offence similar in type and gravity to offence for which suspended sentence order imposed and:	

[1185] This section is as amended by Legal Aid, Sentencing and Punishment of Offenders Act 2012 s 69(2) Sch 9 para 10 and Sch 10 para 38(2).

Breach involves	Penalty
a) No/low level of compliance with suspended sentence order **OR**	Full activation of original custodial term
b) Medium or high level of compliance with suspended sentence order	Activate sentence but apply appropriate reduction* to original custodial term taking into consideration any unpaid work or curfew requirements completed
New offence less serious than original offence but requires a custodial sentence and:	
a) No/low level of compliance with suspended sentence order **OR**	Full activation of original custodial term
b) Medium or high level of compliance with suspended sentence order	Activate sentence but apply appropriate reduction* to original custodial term taking into consideration any unpaid work or curfew requirements completed
New offence does not require custodial sentence	Activate sentence but apply reduction* to original custodial term taking into consideration any unpaid work or curfew requirements completed **OR** Impose more onerous requirement(s) and/or extend supervision period and/ or extend operational period and/or impose fine

* It is for the court dealing with the breach to identify the appropriate proportionate reduction depending on the extent of any compliance with the requirements specified

107.15 ***Breach Offences Guideline 2018 Failure to comply with the requirements***
Breach Offences Guideline 2018, see www.banksr.com Other Matters Guidelines tab In force 1 October 2018 page 10

2) Failure to comply with a community requirement during the supervision period of the order

The court **must activate the custodial sentence** unless it would be unjust in all the circumstances to do so [see 112.15c]. The predominant factor in determining whether activation is unjust relates to the level of compliance with the suspended sentence order. **This factor is already provided for in the penalties below which are determined by the level of compliance, but permit a reduction to the custodial term for relevant completed or partially completed requirements where appropriate.**

The court must take into account the extent to which the offender has complied with the suspended sentence order when imposing a sentence.

In assessing the level of compliance with the order the court should consider:

i) the overall attitude and engagement with the order as well as the proportion of elements completed;
ii) the impact of any completed or partially completed requirements on the offender's behaviour; and
iii) the proximity of breach to imposition of order; and

iv) evidence of circumstances or offender characteristics, such as disability, mental health issues or learning difficulties which have impeded offender's compliance with the order.

Breach involves	Penalty
No/low level of compliance	Full activation of original custodial term
Medium level of compliance	Activate sentence but apply reduction* to original custodial term taking into consideration any unpaid work or curfew requirements completed
High level of compliance	Activate sentence but apply reduction* to original custodial term taking into consideration any unpaid work or curfew requirements completed **OR** Impose more onerous requirement(s) and/or extend supervision period and/ or extend operational period and/or impose fine

* It is for the court dealing with the breach to identify the appropriate proportionate reduction depending on the extent of any compliance with the requirements specified.

107.16 ***Breach Offences Guideline 2018 Meaning of 'unjust'***

Breach Offences Guideline 2018, see www.banksr.com Other Matters Guidelines tab In force 1 October 2018 pages 9 and 11 (where the entry is the same in each place)

Unjust in all the circumstances

The court dealing with the breach should remember that the court imposing the original sentence determined that a custodial sentence was appropriate in the original case.

In determining if there are other factors which would cause activation to be unjust, the court may consider all factors including:

- any strong personal mitigation;
- whether there is a realistic prospect of rehabilitation;
- whether immediate custody will result in significant impact on others.

Only new and exceptional factors/circumstances not present at the time the suspended sentence order was imposed should be taken into account.

In cases where the court considers that it would be unjust to order the custodial sentence to take effect, it must state its reasons and it **must** deal with the offender in one of the following ways:

(a) impose a fine not exceeding £2,500; OR

(b) extend the operational period (to a maximum of two years from date of original sentence); OR

(c) if the SSO imposes community requirements, do one or more of:

(i) impose more onerous community requirements;

(ii) extend the supervision period (to a maximum of two years from date of original sentence);

(iii) extend the operational period (to a maximum of two years from date of original sentence).

107.17 ***Amending suspended sentences instead of activation***

New Sentences: Criminal Justice Act 2003 Guideline 2004, see www.banksr.com Other Matters Guidelines tab para 2.2.22 Where the court decides to amend a Suspended Sentence Order rather than activate the custodial sentence, it should give serious consideration to extending the supervision or operational periods (within statutory limits) rather than making the requirements more onerous.

107.18 ***Part-compliance Judicial guidance Pre-2018 guideline case***
Note: The primary approach is the approach in the *Breach Offences Guideline 2018* at **107.15**. The following case must be treated with care as the guideline approach must not be undermined. Ed.
R v Ballard 2016 EWCA Crim 1173 D was in breach of his Suspended Sentence Order. Held. para 10 Compliance with an unpaid work requirement will normally justify a reduction, but dilatory and grudging compliance will not yield the same result. Similarly, if attendance on a course has not altered the defendant's thinking attitude, activation in full may be justified.
107.19 ***Part-compliance Order with unpaid work requirement Pre-2018 guideline cases***
See the note in para **107.18**.
R v Finn 2012 EWCA Crim 881, 2 Cr App R (S) 96 (p 569) In January 2010, D pleaded to theft and received 6 months' imprisonment and a full activation of his 9-month suspended sentence consecutively. In July 2010, D was given a further 100 unpaid work hours and an extended supervision requirement for theft. In November and December 2010, D breached his ASBO. Twice in December 2010 and once in January 2011 he committed shop thefts. He was given a curfew, a fine and another 100 hours' unpaid work. Also in January he committed another shop theft, the instant offence. D was aged 29 and had 86 convictions on 36 occasions. D had completed the 140 hours of unpaid work and was near the end of the supervision. The Judge considered there was a wholesale failure to comply with the 'Supervision Order' most often because of his offending. Held. The 6 months was not excessive. Suspended sentences must be complied with in full. The catalogue of breaches and failures to comply with the original order demonstrated that D never had any intention of refraining from his criminal activities. Some judges might have given modest credit for the unpaid work but it was not unjust to activate the suspended sentence in full. D has only himself to blame.
R v McDonagh 2017 EWCA Crim 2193 D pleaded to section 18. The offence was committed on 10 May 2016. He was sentenced to 54 months' custody. He was in breach of a suspended sentence for a section 20 offence with a very similar factual background. That was imposed on 15 February 2016. The order had 180 hours of unpaid work attached, which D had completed. The Judge said the suspended sentence had to be activated in full unless it was unjust to do so. He activated it in full. Held. There was a wider discretion than that. Because the breach occurred so soon after the suspended sentence was imposed and the second offence 'was identical in nature' the reduction for the work done should be modest. 14 months not 18 months activated.
See also: *R v Kavanagh* 2010 EWCA Crim 1737, 2011 1 Cr App R (S) 63 (p 395) (Breach of Suspended Sentence Order imposed for possession of cocaine, affray and counterfeiting offences. 32 weeks suspended. The defendant had completed 212[1186] of 200 hours unpaid work and 22 hours of classes. 70% of the operational period had expired. 8 weeks, not 32, concurrent with a sentence for drugs offences.)
R v Prime 2013 EWCA Crim 2525, 2014 2 Cr App R (S) 19 (p 131) (D sentenced to 1 year, suspended, with unpaid work. Six months later, D pleaded to harassment and received a 24-month community sentence. D's suspended sentence was to remain. A year on, D pleaded to breaching Non-Molestation and Restraining Orders and the Judge activated the suspended sentence. He had completed 165 of the 180 hours of his unpaid work. Held. D had a substantial record and the second substantive offence was committed on bail. Each offence was a separate breach of the suspended sentence. Activating 10 months out of 12 was at the upper end, but not excessive.)
R v Ansley 2014 EWCA Crim 1135 (Sentenced to 8 months suspended for fraud. 67 previous offences. 11 previous breaches of non-custodial sentences. Three breaches by failure to attend in 6 months. First breach within weeks of imposition of the order (10

[1186] This seems a bit unlikely and perhaps it should read '112'.

extra hours). Second breach (2 months tag). Had completed 55½ hours of 250 hours' unpaid work. Held. Judge entitled to activate the entirety of the suspended sentence. A suspended sentence is not a 'set-off' whereby defendants can trade a reduction in length by reference to partial compliance. He had wholly failed to engage with the order.)
R v Barratt 2017 EWCA Crim 1631 (D pleaded to controlling or coercive behaviour, affray, threatening behaviour, sending malicious communications, driving whilst disqualified, no insurance and due care. He was in breach of a 6-month suspended sentence with 150 hours which he had completed. The Judge gave him 30 months with the suspended sentence activated in full, making 36 months. Held. We note the hours worked. Given the number and seriousness of the offences that were committed during the operational period it was not wrong to activate in full.

107.20 ***Part-compliance Order without unpaid work requirement Pre-2018 guideline cases***
See the note in para **107.18**.
R v Collins-Reed 2012 EWCA Crim 2036, 2013 1 Cr App R (S) 95 (p 504) D pleaded to battery involving V, his then girlfriend, and was given a suspended sentence of 16 weeks suspended for 2 years. About 16 months later he committed ABH. This time the victim was V's boyfriend and the assault was more serious. There had been a supervision requirement and programme requirement, which D had completed. The pre-sentence report said he had an 'impressive commitment to the supervision process'. The Judge gave him 24 weeks and activated the suspended sentence in full. Held. The requirements had had no significant impact on his behaviour. The Judge was quite correct to implement the order in full.
R v Wolstenholme 2016 EWCA Crim 638, 2 Cr App R (S) 19 (p 168) D was convicted of common assault and committed for sentence. He punched and knocked out his then partner. D was aged 33 and had 'a bad record for violence particularly for similar assaults'. In 2014, D was 14 months into an 18-month Suspended Sentence Order for affray. It included a Thinking Skills Programme and alcohol treatment. The Judge found the Thinking Skills Programme had not worked. The pre-sentence report said there was some motivation to change. Held. D had gone back to alcohol assuming he had ever left it. The new assault was significant. D demonstrated a total failure to have gained any benefit from the Suspended Sentence Order. Although D had attended the courses he had not put what he had learnt into practice. Full activation upheld.
R v Ballard 2016 EWCA Crim 1173 D was convicted of going equipped (12 months) and a 6-month Suspended Sentence Order was activated in full for theft and aggravated vehicle-taking offences. The order was with various programmes. He had 10 convictions mainly for theft and vehicle taking. D had completed 20 months of the 24-month order and had failed to attend on three occasions (2 written warnings and a fine). The Judge heard the supervision had gone well. Held. We note the 20 months completed and the new similar offence to his previous offending. 4 months' activation not 6.
See also: *R v Abdille* 2009 EWCA Crim 1195, 2010 1 Cr App R (S) 18 (p 99) (D had attended courses but as he had continued to commit offences he had learnt nothing from them and there was no unpaid work requirement. Activation in full was correct.)
R v Pash 2013 EWCA Crim 576, 2014 1 Cr App R (S) 4 (p 14) (Plea to criminal damage and possession of a bladed article. In breach of a 12-month suspended sentence imposed for arson and theft etc. (no unpaid work requirement). He had complied with the requirements attached to it. Aged 34. Convictions for 28 offences between 1994 and 2011. Because of the minor nature of the offences and his compliance with the previous order, 5 months of the suspended sentence activated, not 12. Overall custody 8 months not 15.)
See also the **COMMUNITY ORDER: BREACH OF** *Part compliance* para at **16.25**.

107.21 ***New offence does not warrant custody***
Breach Offences Guideline 2018, see www.banksr.com Other Matters Guidelines tab In force 1 October 2018 page 8

New offence does not require custodial sentence	Activate sentence but apply reduction* to original custodial term taking into consideration any unpaid work or curfew requirements completed **OR** Impose more onerous requirement(s) and/or extend supervision period and/ or extend operational period and/or impose fine

For the rest of the guideline, see **107.14**.

107.22 ***New sentence should be consecutive to the activated suspended sentence***
Further provisions as to order that suspended sentence is to take effect
Criminal Justice Act 2003 Sch 12 para 9(1) When making an order under paragraph 8(2)(a) or (b) that a sentence is to take effect (with or without any variation of the original term) the court:

(a) [repealed]

(b) may order that the sentence is to take effect immediately or that the term of that sentence is to commence on the expiry of another term of imprisonment passed on the offender by that or another court.

(2) The power to make an order under sub-paragraph (1)(b) has effect subject to section 265 (restriction on consecutive sentences for released prisoners).
(3) For the purpose of any enactment conferring rights of appeal in criminal cases, each of the following orders:

(a) an order made by the court under paragraph 8(2)(a) or (b),

(b) an order made by the court under Prosecution of Offences Act 1985 s 21A (criminal courts charge) when making an order described in paragraph (a),

is to be treated as a sentence passed on the offender by that court for the offence for which the suspended sentence was passed.[1187]
New Sentences: Criminal Justice Act 2003 Guideline 2004, see www.banksr.com Other Matters Guidelines tab para 2.2.21 It is expected that any activated suspended sentence will be consecutive to the sentence imposed for the new offence.
TICs and Totality Guideline 2012: Crown Court, see www.banksr.com Other Matters Guidelines tab page 9 Offender sentenced to a determinate term and subject to an existing Suspended Sentence Order: Where an offender commits an additional offence during the operational period of a suspended sentence and the court orders the suspended sentence to be activated, the additional sentence will generally be consecutive to the activated suspended sentence, as it will arise out of unrelated facts.

107.23 ***Consecutive activated suspended sentences*** ***Summary only matters***
R v Chamberlain 1992 13 Cr App R (S) 525 The Magistrates' Courts Act 1980 s 133 limit on sentencing powers for consecutive sentences did not apply when activating a suspended sentence.
R v Hester-Wox 2016 EWCA Crim 1397, 2 Cr App R (S) 43 We apply the rule in *R v Chamberlain* 1992.

107.24 ***New offence relatively minor*** ***Pre-2018 guideline case***
R v Oduntan 2018 EWCA Crim 295 D pleaded to possession of a 'small amount of cannabis'. He was stopped in the street and admitted the offence immediately. D was aged 19 and had started university. He was in breach of two suspended sentences. One was for supplying heroin and cocaine (18 months), with 200 unpaid hours, which had been completed. The other was possession of a bladed article (6 months), with 100

[1187] Sub-paragraph 9(3) was substituted by Criminal Justice and Courts Act 2015 Sch 12 para 16. In force 13/4/15

unpaid hours, and 10 extra unpaid hours were added for the breach of the earlier order, 20 of which had been completed. The two orders were 13 months apart and the second order was six weeks before the cannabis offence. In between the suspended sentences he was given a community order for a false representation offence and no penalty for possession of cannabis. The Judge gave credit for the compliance with the terms of the order. When the last suspended sentence was ordered, D was told this was his last chance. The Judge imposed 1 month and activated the orders in full but made the sentences concurrent making 18 months in all. Held. There should have been a greater reduction, so 1 month for the offence, 9 months and 4 months concurrent, making 9 months in all.
Note: This sentence still seems disproportionate for so trivial an offence. The Court should not have interrupted or terminated his university education. The previous Judge saying "last chance" was before anyone knew the breach was going to be for possession of cannabis. With D's age and good response to the orders a more constructive approach would have been to fine D for the cannabis and extend the operational periods of both the suspended sentences. This was the solution in *R v Bathgate* 2016 EWCA Crim 930, where the defendant was a drug addict who breached three suspended sentences imposed on the same day by committing a possession of cannabis offence. There was no fine, just extensions of the terms. Ed.

107.25 ***New offence is non-imprisonable***
New Sentences: Criminal Justice Act 2003 Guideline 2004 para 2.2.22, see www.banksr.com Other Matters Guidelines tab If the new offence is non-imprisonable, the sentencer should consider whether it is appropriate to activate the suspended sentence at all. Where the court decides to amend a Suspended Sentence Order rather than activate the custodial sentence, it should give serious consideration to extending the supervision or operational periods (within statutory limits) rather than making the requirements more onerous.

107.26 ***Suspended Sentence Order nearly over***
Note: *Breach Offences Guideline 2018*, see www.banksr.com Other Matters Guidelines tab In force 1 October 2018 pages 8 and 10 (the sections are the same) requires the court when dealing with: a) a new offence which is less serious than the original offence but requires a custodial sentence and b) a new offence which does not require a custodial sentence, to consider the overall attitude and engagement with the order as well as the proportion of elements completed; and

(iii) the proximity of [the] breach to [the] imposition of the order.

paras (ii) and (iv) are not listed.
In these circumstances sentencers are advised to apply the guideline with these considerations in mind. Ed.
Old pre-2018 guideline case: *R v Carmody* 2015 EWCA Crim 1029 D pleaded to ABH and was in breach of an 18-month Suspended Sentence Order. The victim in each was the same. The Suspended Sentence Order had only 6 weeks left and he had complied fully with the requirements, including a 250-hour unpaid work requirement. Held. 4 months not 8 months activated consecutively, making 20 months not 24.

107.27 ***Time served on remand Post-LASPO changes***
Criminal Justice Act 2003 s 240ZA(7)[1188] For the purposes of this section a suspended sentence:

(a) is to be treated as a sentence of imprisonment when it takes effect under paragraph 8(2)(a) or (b) of Schedule 12, and
(b) is to be treated as being imposed by the order under which it takes effect.

[1188] This section was inserted by Legal Aid, Sentencing and Punishment of Offenders Act 2012 s 108(2).

Note: This means the judge who imposes a suspended sentence should not factor in the time served on remand, except when considering whether an immediate custodial sentence is appropriate. Ed.

R v Collier 2013 EWCA Crim 1132 D was given a 12-month suspended sentence. He had spent 180 days on remand which was not referred to in the sentencing remarks. He breached the order and was given a 2-month sentence consecutive to the suspended sentence activated in full. However, the Judge said it must have been a factor in deciding to impose the suspended sentence. Held. Under section 240ZA(7) time on remand is automatically deducted when a suspended sentence is activated. That may not have happened because of what the Judge said. We dismiss the appeal and the Prison Service must deduct those days from the time to serve. In fact, D should have been released some time ago.

For the position before Legal Aid, Sentencing and Punishment of Offenders Act 2012, see para **119.23** of the 10th edition of this book.

See also the **SUSPENDED SENTENCE ORDERS** ***Time served on remand*** para at **106.19**.

Giving reasons

107.28 ***Reasons Must give reasons if not activating***

Criminal Procedure Rules 2015 2015/1490 Rule 28.1(1) This rule applies where the court decides:..

(c) not to order, where it could,

(i) that a suspended sentence of imprisonment is to take effect…

(2) The court must explain why it has so decided, when it explains the sentence that it has passed.

For the general principles about giving reasons, see **86.49**.

107.29 ***Explain sentence, Judge must/Suggested sentencing remarks***

Criminal Justice Act 2003 s 174(2)[1189] The court must state in open court, in ordinary language and in general terms, the court's reasons for deciding on the sentence.

(3) The court must explain to the offender in ordinary language:

(a) the effect of the sentence,

(b) the effects of non-compliance with any order that the offender is required to comply with and that forms part of the sentence,

(c) any power of the court to vary or review any order that forms part of the sentence…

Judicial College's Crown Court Compendium Part II Sentencing June 2018 page 9-3

Example 1: where suspended sentence brought into operation following breach of requirement, with the term not reduced

It is clear that you have not cooperated with the {specify requirement} at all since the sentence of {specify terms of the suspended sentence} was passed and that you are unable or unwilling to do so. Because of this the suspended sentence will be brought into operation in full: you will serve the sentence of {length of sentence}.

Example 2: where suspended sentence brought into operation following breach of requirement, with the term reduced because of some progress

Although you are in breach of the {specify} requirement of the suspended sentence imposed on {date} and it is not unjust to bring the sentence into operation, I give you credit for the fact that {e.g. initially you cooperated with the curfew requirement/you have performed some unpaid work} by reducing the length of the sentence. The sentence you will now serve is one of {specify}.

[1189] As substituted by Legal Aid, Sentencing and Punishment of Offenders Act 2012 s 64

Example 3: where suspended sentence brought into operation following commission of a further offence, with the term reduced
The suspended sentence to which you were subject when you committed the offence of {specify} will be brought into operation but I take account of {e.g. your cooperation with the curfew requirement/the hours of unpaid work which you performed} by reducing the length of that sentence to {specify reduced term}. This will be served consecutively to the sentence of {specify} which you are to serve for {specify new offence/s}.
Example 4: where suspended sentence not brought into operation because it would be unjust to do so
Although you are in breach of the {specify requirement} of the suspended sentence passed on {date} I am satisfied that it would be unjust to bring the sentence into operation because {state reasons e.g. you only failed to do unpaid work on two occasions and you have since nearly completed all of the hours which were ordered}. In these circumstances instead of serving the sentence you will {specify e.g. do 20 extra hours of unpaid work/be fined £{amount}}.
[The effect of the order should then be explained as per examples given earlier in this work.]

Judicial College's Crown Court Compendium Part II Sentencing June 2018 page 4-36

Example 2: when suspended sentence brought into operation
The days which you spent on remand in custody before you were originally sentenced will automatically count towards the [part of the] sentence which I have now brought into operation.

108 TICs

(Offences taken into consideration)

108.1

The problems TICs are offences that the defendant wants the court to take into consideration when sentencing him or her. When the system is used properly the system is a quick way of dealing with offences fairly. When the system is used inappropriately it can cause problems, such as:

(a) offences being included which are too serious,
(b) offences being included that trigger orders like notification, or disqualification from driving, so the offences should have been specifically charged,
(c) offences which have been compiled so the police officer can inflate his or her force's clear-up rate when in fact the defendant was not involved in all the offences,
(d) offences being included which have insufficient information included with them so no party knows how serious the offence was. Also the judge or magistrate finds sentencing difficult as the nature of the offence is unknown,
(e) the defendant being pressurised to accept a list without him or her being clear what it is he or she is accepting,
(f) the police believing the TICs are agreed when months later they are told just before sentence they are not, so they are forced to either forget about the offences or start proceedings all over again.

If the rules are followed, the problems should be minimised. For more detail, see **108.9**.

General matters

108.2 ***Benefits of TICs***

CPS Legal Guidance: TICs, see www.banksr.com Other Matters Other Documents tab
The benefits [of the TIC system] include:

(a) the court has a fuller and more accurate picture of the offending and is able to give a longer sentence than it would if it were dealing only with the substantive charge,
(b) the defendant is able to 'clear the slate' to avoid the risk of subsequent prosecution for those offences and put the past behind him, which can support rehabilitation,
(c) Although the presence of TICs may increase the sentence, the additional penalty will be less severe than if the offences were prosecuted separately,

(d) the victim has an opportunity to claim compensation in respect of an offence admitted by the defendant, detected and acknowledged by the criminal justice system,
(e) the police gain valuable intelligence, increase clear-up rates, record a fuller picture of offending for possible use in future cases or to support applications for CR/ASBOs[1190] or other restrictive orders,
(f) the prosecution has a fuller and more accurate picture of the offender's criminal history when considering the public interest stage of the full Code Test, bail decisions, bad character, dangerousness etc.,
(g) resources are used efficiently, and
(h) the public's confidence in the criminal justice system is improved.

108.3 *Status*

R v Howard 1991 92 Cr App R 223 The question was whether an offence TIC'd was, for the purposes of Criminal Justice Act 1982 s 1(4)[1191] (restrictions on passing custodial sentences), a conviction. Held. TICs do not in law constitute a conviction. We cannot take it into account when considering whether the criteria are met because it is not a conviction.

Note: Therefore, the sentence which may be imposed may not exceed the statutory maximum for the offences which the offender is due to be sentenced for. Further offences which trigger an order like notification do not do so if the offence is only taken into consideration. However, they can form part of the factual background for an overall order like confiscation and compensation, due to specific statutory provisions. Ed.

R v Miles 2006 EWCA Crim 256 In some cases the offences taken into consideration will end up by adding nothing or nothing very much to the sentence which the court would otherwise impose. On the other hand, offences taken into consideration may aggravate the sentence and lead to a substantial increase in it.

108.4 *TIC must be for an offence the court may sentence for*

TICs and Totality Guideline 2012: Crown Court, see www.banksr.com Other Matters Guidelines tab page 3 (*Magistrates' Court Sentencing Guidelines Update March 2012* page 18e) The Magistrates' Court cannot take into consideration an indictable only offence. The Crown Court can take into account summary only offences provided the TICs are founded on the same facts or evidence as the indictable charge, or are part of a series of offences of the same or similar character as the indictable conviction offence.[1192]

R v Simons 1953 37 Cr App R 120 LCJ D was committed for trial for driving whilst disqualified. There was a difference of opinion about whether the charge could be committed and the prosecution suggested it should be TIC'd. The Judge and D agreed. The defence appealed on the basis that if there was no power to try the offence then it could not be taken into consideration. Held. This Court has laid down that driving offences ought not to be taken into consideration. Further if a court has no jurisdiction to try a particular offence, the court ought not to take that offence into consideration. On the facts there was nothing wrong with the sentence.

108.5 *Service offences Jurisdiction*

R v Anderson 1958 42 Cr App R 91 D, a soldier, was awaiting Court Martial proceedings for offences of larceny from other soldiers. D and his commanding officer requested that the offences be taken into consideration by the quarter sessions. Held. As these were civil as well as military offences, the quarter sessions were entitled to take them into account. Had they been military offences only, of course they could not have done so.

1190 This means criminal ASBO, known as a post-conviction ASBO.
1191 Now repealed
1192 Criminal Justice Act 1988 s 40

Compiling TICs/prosecution and court procedure

108.6 *Police procedure*

R v Walsh 1973 Unreported 8/3/73 Since the matter is essentially one of tacit agreement between the court and the accused person, it is essential that those administering justice, both the police in the pre-trial stage and the court at the trial stage, should ensure that the accused man understands what is being done, admits the offences and wishes to have each and every one of them taken into consideration. The safeguards that both police and courts can adopt are [as follows]:
The police have to prepare the list or the schedule which has to be served upon an accused. If it is known that he intends to plead guilty, this schedule can be served before arraignment. If he is going to plead not guilty, then it may be that such a list should not be served until after he has been found guilty. All that one can say of the standards to be observed by the police in the preparation and service of the list is that they should exercise meticulous care in the preparation of the list and they should ensure that when the list is given to him, his signature is obtained, and in so far as it is within the power of the police to ensure it, they should ensure that he gets an opportunity of studying the list before he signs it, and certainly, of course, before he has to deal with it in court.
R v Ali 2009 EWCA Crim 2396 For details about what the police should not say about TICs when dealing with a detainee, see para **108.24**.
R v Thompson 2012 EWCA Crim 1764 D received 2 years 8 months, in part because of his bad record. He was visited in prison by police and invited to help them 'clear the books'. Held. It is absolutely essential that when police officers invite defendants to admit wholesale past offences in the way that has been done here, no promises are made about the way in which the defendant will be dealt with. That is perhaps particularly important when a defendant is in custody. We doubt that this case called for any significant downward adjustment on the grounds that the defendant's admissions helped the victims. What it did call for was a significant downward adjustment in recognition of the fact that the defendant had provided the evidence against himself.

108.7 *Prosecution practice*

CPS Legal Guidance: TICs, see www.banksr.com Other Matters Other Documents tab
Procedure Procedural safeguards are now set out in the *TICs and Totality Guideline 2012: Crown Court* section [see below].
The police should include five copies of the TIC schedule with the prosecution file in accordance with the *Manual of Guidance*.
A copy of the TIC schedule should be included in advance information to the defence or pre-sentence information to the Probation Service.
There should be sufficient information in the case papers to enable the prosecution and defendant to decide whether to ask the court to take such offences into consideration and to enable the offence(s) to be properly outlined to the court.
Any interview record should include adequate and sufficient details of any admissions made by a defendant to offences appearing in the TIC schedule.
The TIC schedule must be served on the defendant who should be given a full opportunity to understand what he is being asked to accept. The defendant must admit the offence and should do so personally rather than through legal representatives. Special care should be taken with vulnerable and/or unrepresented defendants. The defendant must sign the schedule.
Two copies of the TIC schedule (MG18) and a Compensation schedule (MG19) should be presented to the Court when the defendant pleads guilty or is convicted so that the defendant can be asked whether he wishes the Court to take into consideration all or some of the offences included in the TIC schedule and so that compensation orders can be made where appropriate.
When the TICs are put to the defendant, the list need not be read out in full. It is sufficient if the judge confirms with the defendant that he has signed the list, that it

contains so many offences, that he agrees he committed those offences and he wishes them to be taken into consideration when sentence is passed for the substantive offence(s).

The number of offences which the defendant wishes to be taken into consideration should be endorsed on the file. The original schedule, suitably endorsed, should be retained by the Court and a copy supplied by the court to the police. A copy of the TIC schedule, clearly marked as to which offences were admitted by the defendant, should be retained in the file.

If there is any doubt as to which offences in a list the defendant wishes to have taken into consideration, the doubt should be resolved in open court, and if there is any doubt about his admission of a particular offence, it should not be taken into consideration.

If the defendant is committed to the Crown Court for sentence, then the Crown Court must follow the usual procedure, even if the defendant agreed to the schedule in the Magistrates' Court.

108.8 *Proper approach/procedure*

TICs and Totality Guideline 2012: Crown Court, see www.banksr.com Other Matters Guidelines tab page 3 (*Magistrates' Court Sentencing Guidelines Update March 2012* page 18e) A court should generally only take offences into consideration if the following procedural provisions have been satisfied:

(a) the police or prosecuting authorities prepared a schedule of offences (TIC schedule) that they consider suitable to be taken into consideration. The TIC schedule should set out the nature of each offence, the date of the offence(s), relevant detail about the offence(s) (including, for example, monetary values of items) and any other brief details that the court should be aware of,

(b) a copy of the TIC schedule must be provided to the defendant and his representative (if he has one) before the sentence hearing. The defendant should sign the TIC schedule to provisionally admit the offences,

(c) at the sentence hearing, the court should ask the defendant in open court whether he admits each of the offences on the TIC schedule and whether he wishes to have them taken into consideration,[1193]

(d) if there is any doubt about the admission of a particular offence, it should not be accepted as a TIC. Special care should be taken with vulnerable and/or unrepresented defendants,

(e) if the defendant is committed to the Crown Court for sentence, this procedure must take place again at the Crown Court even if the defendant has agreed to the schedule in the Magistrates' Court.

R v Walsh 1973 Unreported 8/3/73 Since the matter is essentially one of tacit agreement between the court and the accused person, it is essential that those administering justice, both the police in the pre-trial stage and the court at the trial stage, should ensure that the accused man understands what is being done, admits the offences and wishes to have each and every one of them taken into consideration. The safeguards that both police and courts can adopt are [as follows].

When the matter is dealt with in court, the best practice is that the police officer responsible for serving the list should be called to say that it was served, and that he had the document signed by the accused man. But in any event, it is the court's responsibility at this stage to ensure that the accused man, who after all in this matter is acting in concert and agreement with the court, understands the document that he has received, and has a proper opportunity, which means time, to consider the document. If necessary, time can be given by adjournment. Before proceeding to sentence, the court must be clear not only that he understands the document that he has received and has had time to study it, but that he accepts that the listed offences are offences which he has committed and that he desires them to be taken into consideration. If this conventional practice is to

[1193] *Anderson v DPP* 1978 67 Cr App R 185

continue to the benefit of the administration of justice and to the benefit of the accused person, the burden is on the court, and to a lesser extent on the police, to ensure that the man has a full opportunity of understanding what he is being asked to accept. If that is done, then the practice is of benefit to all concerned.
Note: What used to be done with TICs by police officers in the witness box is now done by the prosecution advocate to save time. Ed.
Anderson v DPP 1978 67 Cr App R 185 Lords If justice is to be done it is essential that the practice [of offences being taken into consideration] should not be followed except with the express and unequivocal assent of the offender himself. Accordingly, he should be informed explicitly of each offence which the judge proposes to take into consideration, and should explicitly admit that he committed them and should state his desire that they should be taken into consideration in determining the sentence to be passed on him.
R v Miles 2006 EWCA Crim 256 In relation to offences taken into consideration, we have these observations:
(a) The sentence is intended to reflect a defendant's overall criminality.
(b) Offences cannot be taken into consideration without the express agreement of the offender. That is an essential prerequisite.
(c) The offender is pleading guilty to the offences. If they are to be taken into account [and the court is not obliged to take them into account] they have relevance to the overall criminality.
(d) When assessing the significance of TICs, as they are called, of course the court is likely to attach weight to the demonstrable fact that the offender has assisted the police, particularly if they are enabled to clear up offences which might not otherwise be brought to justice.
(e) It is also true that co-operative behaviour of that kind will often provide its own very early indication of guilt, and usually means that no further proceedings at all need be started.
(f) They may also serve to demonstrate a genuine determination by the offender (and we deliberately use the colloquialism) to wipe the slate clean, so that when he emerges from whatever sentence is imposed on him, he can put his past completely behind him, without having the worry or concern that offences may be revealed so that he is then returned to court.
Note: The guidelines take precedence over these cases. Ed.

108.9 *Offences which should not be taken into consideration*
TICs and Totality Guideline 2012: Crown Court, see www.banksr.com Other Matters Guidelines tab page 2 (*Magistrates' Court Sentencing Guidelines Update March 2012* page 18d) It is generally undesirable for TICs to be accepted in the following circumstances:
(a) where the TIC is likely to attract a greater sentence than the conviction offence,
(b) where it is in the public interest that the TIC should be the subject of a separate charge,
(c) where the offender would avoid a prohibition, ancillary order or similar consequence which it would have been desirable to impose on conviction. For example: where the TIC attracts mandatory disqualification or endorsement and the offence(s) for which the defendant is to be sentenced do not,
(d) where the TIC constitutes a breach of an earlier sentence,
(e) where the TIC is a specified offence for the purposes of Criminal Justice Act 2003 s 224, but the conviction offence is non-specified, or
(f) where the TIC is not founded on the same facts or evidence or part of a series of offences of the same or similar character (unless the court is satisfied that it is in the interests of justice to do so).
CPS Legal Guidance: TICs, see www.banksr.com Other Matters Other Documents tab General Principles

A defendant should **not** be invited to have an offence taken into consideration in the following circumstances:

(a) if the public interest requires that it should be the subject of a separate trial,

(b) if the court has no jurisdiction to deal with the offence,

(c) if the offence attracts mandatory disqualification or endorsement and the offence(s) for which the defendant is to be sentenced do not,

(d) if the offence to be taken into consideration is likely to attract a greater sentence than the offence for which he is to be sentenced,

(e) if the offence to be taken into consideration is not similar to one of the offences for which he is to be sentenced (exceptionally a judge may take into consideration dissimilar offences if satisfied that it is in the interest of justice to do so),

(f) if the offence to be taken into consideration might, by virtue of its date, constitute a breach of an earlier sentence giving the court increased powers of sentence,

(g) if the offender would escape the possibility of an extended sentence being imposed, which would otherwise fall to be considered by the court, had the specified offence been charged as a substantive offence.

108.10 *TIC more serious than the prosecuted offences*

CPS Legal Guidance: TICs, see www.banksr.com Other Matters Other Documents tab General Principles

A defendant should **not** be invited to have an offence taken into consideration in the following circumstances:..If the offence to be taken into consideration is likely to attract a greater sentence than the offence for which he is to be sentenced.

It is generally undesirable for TICs to be accepted in the following circumstances:..where the TIC is likely to attract a greater sentence than the conviction offence.

R v Lavery 2008 EWCA Crim 2499 D pleaded to robbery (DPP minimum term of 30 months). He asked for five offences to be taken into consideration. The Judge noted that some of the offences were more serious than the instant offence. The Judge adjourned the case twice to allow the CPS to consider prosecuting D for these offences. The prosecution returned to court refusing to prosecute. The Judge considered four of the five offences admitted by D. They were all robberies. The Judge considered that, in light of the prosecution's refusal to prosecute, justice demanded that the offences be taken into consideration when sentencing and imposed DPP. Held. It will be open to a judge to refuse to take an offence into consideration if he forms the view that to do so would be to distort the sentencing exercise and lead to an unjust result and that the public interest requires that the offence be charged. But we recognise that it may be extremely difficult for a judge to decline to take offences into consideration when a defendant wants to wipe the slate clean. That underlines the importance of the prosecution following the *Code of Practice*, which states that D should not be invited to have an offence taken into consideration where the offence is likely to attract a greater sentence than the instant offence. However, there is no reason in principle why an offence to be taken into consideration, and which is of a more serious nature than the index offence or offences, should not result in a higher sentence than would otherwise have been the case, as the sentence will reflect the defendant's overall criminality.

108.11 *Offence subject to a charge*

CPS Legal Guidance: TICs, see www.banksr.com Other Matters Other Documents tab

Magistrates' Courts Cases and Offence[s] TIC'd which [were] previously charged in another Area

A Magistrates' Court may take outstanding offences into consideration. It must not take into consideration a charge which has been committed or sent to the Crown Court. A Magistrates' Court should obtain the consent of the relevant legal adviser to the Justices before taking into consideration a matter pending as a charge before another Magistrates' Court. As with Crown Court cases, the prosecutor also should liaise with the CPS in the other Area to check whether the offence is one that is suitable to be taken into consideration.

Offences TIC'd which were previously charged in another Area

Where TICs are dealt with in another Area to that from which the offences originate, it is essential that liaison takes place between police and CPS Areas, not only to ensure that it is appropriate to deal with the matters as TICs, but also to ensure that any necessary follow-up action is taken in the originating Area. For example, withdrawal of substantive proceedings and outstanding warrants, once taken into consideration elsewhere.

Crown Court Cases – TICs

A Crown Court judge may take other offences into consideration even though they have already been charged as offences and committed for trial or sent to that or another Crown Court. The judge should enquire whether there is any prosecution objection before doing so.

If the offence is charged in another CPS Area, the lawyer or caseworker should liaise with that Area in order to ascertain whether the offence is suitable to be taken into consideration.

If the other offence is too serious to take into consideration, it may still be appropriate for the proceedings to be transferred so that all are dealt with by one court.

When deciding whether or not it is appropriate for an offence that is charged to be taken into consideration, prosecutors should consider the factors set out above.

The Crown Court should not take into consideration an offence which it is not empowered to try e.g. a summary offence.

Where a defendant has been committed for sentence after asking for offences to be TIC'd by the Magistrates' Court, the Crown Court must follow the usual procedure and ascertain whether he wishes the offences to be TIC'd by the Crown Court. He may decide he no longer wishes them to be taken into account.

108.12 ***Compensation orders and offences taken into consideration***

Powers of Criminal Courts (Sentencing) Act 2000 s 130(1) A court by or before which a person is convicted of an offence, instead of or in addition to dealing with him in any other way, may, on application or otherwise, make a compensation order requiring him:..to pay compensation for any personal injury, loss or damage resulting from that offence or any other offence which is taken into consideration by the court in determining sentence.

Powers of Criminal Courts (Sentencing) Act 2000 s 132(5) Where a compensation order is made in respect of a TIC the order shall cease to have effect if the defendant successfully appeals against his conviction or all of the offences in the proceedings in which the order was made. The defendant may appeal against the order as if it were part of the sentence imposed in respect of the offence, or any of the offences he was convicted of.

Magistrates' Court Sentencing Guidelines 2008, see www.banksr.com Other Matters Guidelines tab page 165 para 2 Compensation may also be ordered in respect of offences taken into consideration.

CPS Legal Guidance: TICs, see www.banksr.com Other Matters Other Documents tab

Compensation

The court is required pursuant to Powers of Criminal Courts (Sentencing) Act 2000 s 130(1) to consider the question of compensation in respect of offences being taken into consideration. Evidence to support the extent of the compensation sought must be available in these circumstances and the relevant sections of the MG18 and MG19 completed.

In the Magistrates' Court, the total sum of a compensation order is limited under section 131 of the Act to (currently) £5,000 per offence in respect of which the offender has been formally convicted. Compensation orders in respect of TIC offences cannot therefore exceed those limits. For example, if the defendant is convicted of one offence and there are five TICs, the total compensation awarded cannot exceed £5,000. If the defendant is convicted of two offences and there are 10 TICs, the total compensation awarded cannot exceed £10,000.

There are no such limits in the Crown Court.

If a confiscation order is made against the defendant under Proceeds of Crime Act 2002, victims can be compensated using money derived from the confiscated sum. If it is clear that there would otherwise be insufficient means to compensate the victim, the court must order the shortfall to be paid from the confiscated sum. Victims of TIC offences are included in these provisions.

R v Crutchley and Tonks 1994 15 Cr App R (S) 627 C and T pleaded to numerous specimen counts and compensation orders were made for sums representing the entirety of C and T's offending, not just the amounts represented by the counts on the indictment. No offences were taken into consideration. Held. It was not open to the court to make a compensation order in respect of loss or damage arising from admitted offences which had not been charged or taken into consideration, on the ground that the offenders had admitted that the offences charged were sample counts representing a number of other offences.

R v Hose 1995 16 Cr App R (S) 682 LCJ D was sentenced for specimen counts. Held. A compensation order should only be made for the value represented by the counts with which the defendant has been convicted. Where the evidence clearly shows that, for example, the amount stolen was in excess of what is represented by the specimen counts, this did not mean that the offences had been taken into consideration in the formal meaning of the term (see *Anderson v DPP* 1978 67 Cr App R 185).

108.13 *Defendant acquitted of main charge*

CPS Legal Guidance: TICs, see www.banksr.com Other Matters Other Documents tab Acquittal

If the defendant is acquitted of the substantive offence and there is a schedule of TICs, the prosecution should still consider whether it is appropriate to charge some or all of the TICs as substantive offences. Where it is thought appropriate to proceed with new charges and where the defendant pleads guilty to those new charges, the court should be informed that the defendant had made early voluntary admissions to those charges.

Is a TIC appropriate?

108.14 *Breach of court order(s), Offence is*

CPS Legal Guidance: TICs, see www.banksr.com Other Matters Other Documents tab General Principles It is generally undesirable for TICs to be accepted in the following circumstances:..where the TIC constitutes a breach of an earlier sentence.

R v Webb 1953 37 Cr App R 390 LCJ D breached his probation and the breach was taken into consideration. Held. A court should not take into consideration a breach of a conditional discharge or probation. A separate sentence should be passed for the breach so that the conviction of the original offence, for which the conditional discharge was imposed, may rank as a conviction under Criminal Justice Act 1948 s 12.[1194]

108.15 *Extended sentences possible*

TICs and Totality Guideline 2012: Crown Court, see www.banksr.com Other Matters Guidelines tab page 2 (*Magistrates' Court Sentencing Guidelines Update March 2012* page 18d) It is generally undesirable for TICs to be accepted in the following circumstances:..where the TIC is a specified offence for the purposes of Criminal Justice Act 2003 s 240, but the conviction offence is non-specified.

CPS Legal Guidance: TICs, see www.banksr.com Other Matters Other Documents tab General Principles

[1194] Repealed by Powers of Criminal Courts Act 1973 Sch 6

A defendant should **not** be invited to have an offence taken into consideration in the following circumstances:..if the offender would escape the possibility of an extended sentence being imposed, which would otherwise fall to be considered by the court, had the specified offence been charged as a substantive offence.

108.16 ***Motor vehicle offences***

TICs and Totality Guideline 2012: Crown Court, see www.banksr.com Other Matters Guidelines tab page 2 (*Magistrates' Court Sentencing Guidelines Update March 2012* page 18d) It is generally undesirable for TICs to be accepted in the following circumstances:..where the offender would avoid a prohibition, ancillary order or similar consequence which it would have been desirable to impose on conviction. For example: where the TIC attracts mandatory disqualification or endorsement and the offence(s) for which the defendant is to be sentenced do not.

CPS Legal Guidance: TICs, see www.banksr.com Other Matters Other Documents tab General Principles

A defendant should not be invited to have an offence taken into consideration in the following circumstances:..if the offence attracts mandatory disqualification or endorsement and the offence(s) for which the defendant is to be sentenced do not.

R v Simons 1953 37 Cr App R 120 Motor car offences, that is to say, offences against the Road Traffic Acts in relation to the driving, insurance or otherwise of motor vehicles, ought not to be taken into account, but should be left for separate prosecution because the law requires magistrates to take certain steps with regard to endorsement[1195] or disqualification from holding a licence, which can only be done if there is a conviction. That cannot be done if the charge is only taken into account.

108.17 ***Restitution Orders, Cases attracting***

Powers of Criminal Courts (Sentencing) Act 2000 s 148(1) This section applies where goods have been stolen, and either:

(a) a person is convicted of any offence with reference to the theft (whether or not the stealing is the gist of his offence), or

(b) a person is convicted of any other offence, but such an offence as is mentioned in paragraph (a) above is taken into consideration in determining his sentence.

(2) Where this section applies, the court [may make a Restitution Order].

The hearing

108.18 ***Consent must be given at court***

R v Nelson 1967 51 Cr App R 98 Before offences are taken into consideration, there should be an explicit enquiry by the judge as to whether the defendant admits his guilt.

R v Davies 1980 2 Cr App R (S) 364 The appropriate time for the defendant to be asked if he wishes other offences to be taken into consideration is at the court which is to sentence him and that should be done by the court whether it be by the judge or the clerk of the court asking the accused himself (not merely his counsel) whether he wishes the offences to be taken into consideration. Even, therefore, where an accused may have asked magistrates to take other offences into consideration before he is committed to the Crown Court, the accused should once more be given the opportunity to say whether he wishes or does not wish them to be taken into consideration at the Crown Court before he is sentenced.

108.19 ***Defendant changes his or her mind***

CPS Legal Guidance: TICs, see www.banksr.com Other Matters Other Documents tab Rejected TICs

Where, in court, a defendant rejects previously admitted TICs, the CPS file should be clearly marked and immediate consideration given to prosecuting the now denied offences.

1195 A typo has been corrected.

Earlier in the process (preferably at the charging/review stage), prosecutors should have agreed with the police which TICs were to be proceeded with in the event of the defendant's refusal to accept them. That decision would have been based, in the usual way, on the sufficiency of evidence, the public interest test and the guidance provided in the Code for Crown Prosecutors, which provides, para 9.5: 'where a defendant has previously indicated that he or she will ask the court to take an offence into consideration when sentencing, but then declines to admit that offence in court, Crown Prosecutors will consider whether a prosecution is required for that offence. Crown Prosecutors should explain to the defence advocate and the court that the prosecution of that offence may be subject to further review, in consultation with the police or other investigators wherever possible.'

The defendant can be invited, in court, to give a reason for his denial of the previously admitted offences. Any explanation given should be taken into account by the prosecutor when deciding whether or not to proceed with charges.

Where possible, the prosecutor should immediately inform the court and defendant that the prosecution intends to proceed on the relevant denied offences and, if in the Magistrates' Court, lay information there and then. The police should be notified by the CPS that this has happened. If it is not possible to lay the relevant information there and then, for example in a Crown Court case, the police will need to be notified so that they can take the appropriate action.

Prosecutors should not ask for sentencing on the substantive offences to be delayed to await the outcome on the new offence(s). However, the new file should be fully endorsed to record the context in which the decision to prosecute was made so that, in the event of sentencing on the new offence(s), the court can be properly apprised and can sentence appropriately, reflecting the lack of credit for any guilty plea and the denial in court of a previously admitted TIC.

If a decision is made not to prosecute a denied TIC offence, the police should notify the victim, especially because the court will not be empowered to make a compensation order.

R v Davies 1980 2 Cr App R (S) 364 D told the Magistrates that he wished the offences to be taken into consideration. He was committed for trial. At the Crown Court counsel for D said D did not want them to be taken into account. The Judge ruled that D had already accepted the offences and they had been entered on the memorandum and that was an end to it. A number of them were taken into account and others not. Held. The appropriate time for the defendant to be asked if he wishes other offences to be taken into consideration is at the court which is to sentence him and that should be done by the court whether it be by the judge or the clerk of the court asking the accused himself (not merely his counsel) whether he wishes the offences to be taken into consideration. Even, therefore, where an accused may have asked magistrates to take other offences into consideration before he is committed to the Crown Court, the accused should once more be given the opportunity to say whether he wishes or does not wish them to be taken into consideration at the Crown Court before he is sentenced. If there is a dispute the offences should be gone through one by one. D should have been asked again. He should have been allowed to change his mind.

R v Nelson 1967 51 Cr App R 98 D had indicated that he wished the Court to take offences into consideration when sentencing him for larceny. D subsequently changed his mind and the Judge was informed that D no longer wished for the offences to be taken into consideration as he claimed that his statement admitting the offences was false. Held. The Court should have satisfied itself by an explicit enquiry. Sentence reduced [for what appears to be for this and other reasons].

108.20 *Defendant changes his or her mind Pressure from the judge*

R v Nelson 1967 51 Cr App R 98 D had indicated that he wished the Court to take offences into consideration when sentencing him for larceny. D subsequently changed his mind and the Judge was informed that D no longer wished for the offences to be taken into consideration as he claimed that his statement admitting the offences was false. The Judge then said to D, "Nelson, you have heard what your learned counsel has said. You have made a statement admitting other offences, you have signed a document asking for them to be taken into consideration by me today, and I can do so. If you do not wish that course to be taken, the prosecution are entitled to try you for them and, if you are convicted, you will be separately sentenced in respect of those other offences. Do you want me to take into consideration the offences which you have asked on that form I should take into consideration?" D then accepted the TICs. Held. That was a threat. It put pressure upon the defendant of an undesirable kind. The Court should have satisfied itself by an explicit enquiry. Sentence reduced [for what appears to be for this and other reasons].

108.21 *Dispute as to the number/which offences to be taken into consideration*

R v Urbas 1964 Crim LR 37 Where there is a doubt as to the number of offences that the defendant is admitting and asking to be taken into consideration, the doubt should be resolved in open court.

R v Davies 1980 2 Cr App R (S) 364 Where there is doubt as to which offences the defendant wishes to be taken into consideration, the offences ought to be gone through one by one so as to ascertain which the defendant wishes and which he does not wish to be taken into consideration.

108.22 *Judicial duties*

R v McLean 1911 6 Cr App R 26 LCJ Prior to acquiescing to the defendant's request to take an offence into consideration, the judge must be satisfied that neither the prosecution think it is desirable that there should be a public investigation into the other charges, nor that the public interest does not require any further investigation of the pending charge.

108.23 *Judicial discretion*

TICs and Totality Guideline 2012: Crown Court, see www.banksr.com Other Matters Guidelines tab page 2 (*Magistrates' Court Sentencing Guidelines Update March 2012* page 18d) The court has [a] discretion as to whether or not to take TICs into account. In exercising its discretion the court should take into account that TICs are capable of reflecting the offender's overall criminality. The court is likely to consider that the fact that the offender has assisted the police (particularly if the offences would not otherwise have been detected) and avoided the need for further proceedings demonstrates a genuine determination by the offender to 'wipe the slate clean'.[1196]

R v Lavery 2008 EWCA Crim 2499 D pleaded to robbery (DPP minimum term of 30 months). He asked for five offences to be taken into consideration. The Judge noted that some of the offences were more serious than the instant offence. The Judge adjourned the case twice to allow the CPS to consider prosecuting D for these offences. The prosecution returned to Court refusing to prosecute. The Judge considered four of the five offences admitted by D. They were all robberies. The Judge considered that, in light of the prosecution's refusal to prosecute, justice demanded that the offences be taken into consideration when sentencing and imposed DPP. Held. It will be open to a judge to refuse to take an offence into consideration if he forms the view that to do so would be to distort the sentencing exercise and to lead to an unjust result and that the public interest requires that the offence be charged. But we recognise that it may be extremely difficult for a Judge to decline to take offences into consideration when a defendant wants to wipe the slate clean. That underlines the importance of the prosecution following the Code of Practice, which states that D should not be invited to have an offence taken into consideration where the offence is likely to attract a greater sentence than the instant offence. However, there is no reason in principle why an offence to be

[1196] *Per* Lord Chief Justice, *R v Miles* 2006 EWCA Crim 256

taken into consideration and which is of a more serious nature than the index offence or offences should not result in a higher sentence than would otherwise have been the case, as the sentence will reflect the defendant's overall criminality.

108.24 ***Increasing the sentence to reflect the TIC(s)***

Powers of Criminal Courts (Sentencing) Act 2000 s 161(1) For the purposes of this Act, an offence is associated with another if:

(a) the offender is convicted of it in the proceedings in which he is convicted of the other offence, or (although convicted of it in earlier proceedings) is sentenced for it at the same time as he is sentenced for that offence, or

(b) the offender admits the commission of it in the proceedings in which he is sentenced for the other offence and requests the court to take it into consideration in sentencing him for that offence.

TICs and Totality Guideline 2012: Crown Court, see www.banksr.com Other Matters Guidelines tab page 3 (*Magistrates' Court Sentencing Guidelines Update March 2012* page 18e) The sentence imposed on an offender should, in most circumstances, be increased to reflect the fact that other offences have been taken into consideration. The court should:

1 Determine the sentencing starting point for the conviction offence, referring to the relevant definitive sentencing guidelines. No regard should be had to the presence of TICs at this stage.

2 Consider whether there are any aggravating or mitigating factors that justify an upward or downward adjustment from the starting point.

The presence of TICs should generally be treated as an aggravating feature that justifies an upward adjustment from the starting point. Where there [are] a large number of TICs, it may be appropriate to move outside the category range, although this must be considered in the context of the case and subject to the principle of totality. The court is limited to the statutory maximum for the conviction offence.

3 Continue through the sentencing process including:

(a) consider whether the frank admission of a number of offences is an indication of a defendant's remorse or determination and/or demonstration of steps taken to address addiction or offending behaviour,

(b) any reduction for a guilty plea should be applied to the overall sentence,

(c) the principle of totality,

(d) when considering ancillary orders these can be considered in relation to any or all of the TICs, specifically:

(i) compensation orders:[1197] in the Magistrates' Court cannot exceed the limit for the conviction offence,

(ii) restitution orders.[1198]

R v Ali 2009 EWCA Crim 2396 Thames Valley Police wrote to their officers about a new TIC scheme saying, 'The scheme has the full backing of both the Crown Courts and Magistrates' Courts in Thames Valley. Judge Hall (the resident Judge at Oxford Crown Court) has agreed that unless there are aggravating circumstances, from now on a defendant should not attract additional sentence[1199] for offences admitted by way of TIC. In fact, where it is confirmed by police in a statement, that without the admission police would have been unlikely to detect the crimes, a reduction in sentence may be forthcoming in recognition of the assistance given to the police and the victims.'[1200] Held. We most certainly profoundly disagree [with the latter part]. Judge Hall had exceeded his authority. Although the commission of multiple offences will obviously increase the seriousness of the position of the offender, the consequences will almost

[1197] Powers of Criminal Courts (Sentencing) Act 2000 s 131(2)
[1198] Powers of Criminal Courts (Sentencing) Act 2000 s 148
[1199] Presumably they meant punishment.
[1200] This extract is reproduced verbatim.

inevitably be far less severe if the offences are admitted, especially if the police accept that otherwise there was no prospect of the crime being detected. Offences taken into consideration are an important vehicle for clearing the slate and starting afresh at the conclusion of whatever sentence is then imposed and offenders should think hard about the advantage of making a clean breast of all criminality along with the mitigation to be derived from so doing.
R v Thompson 2012 EWCA Crim 1764 D received 2 years 8 months, in part because of his bad record. He was visited in prison by police and invited to help them 'clear the books'. Held. TICs are not simply ignored when it comes to passing sentence.

TICs accepted

108.25 ***TICs accepted Future prosecutions***
CPS Legal Guidance: TICs, see www.banksr.com Other Matters Other Documents tab Prosecuting admitted TICs
Although there is no conviction in respect of offences TIC'd and a plea of *autrefois convict* is therefore not available, the practice is not to proceed on an offence previously TIC'd by the court. If, exceptionally, the practice is not observed, the court should ensure no additional punishment is imposed on account of such offence. A CCP [a Chief Crown Prosecutor] should be consulted before any decision to prosecute is made in these circumstances. An attempt to proceed may be considered to amount to an abuse of process.
108.26 ***TIC accepted Conviction for main matter quashed***
R v Nicholson 1948 32 Cr App R 98 LCJ Where upon a conviction a defendant asks for an outstanding offence to be taken into consideration, there is no conviction for that outstanding offence. Where the conviction is quashed on appeal, the defendant cannot establish a plea of *autrefois convict* if he is prosecuted for the TIC.

109 Travel Restriction Orders

109.1
Criminal Justice and Police Act 2001 s 33
Availability See **109.3** below.
Children and young offenders The order is available whatever the age of the offender.
Compliance orders A Travel Restriction Order may be made under a compliance order ordered after a confiscation order has been made, see **21.148.**)
109.2 ***Statistics England and Wales***
Travel Restriction Orders

	2012	2013	2014	2015	2016
Number of orders	21	18	8	9	5

For explanations about the statistics, see page 1-xii. The MoJ no longer provides Banks on Sentence with these statistics.

Power to order

109.3 ***Power to order***
Criminal Justice and Police Act 2001 s 33(1) The power applies where:
(a) the offender has been convicted by any court of a post-commencement drug trafficking offence,
(b) the court deems it appropriate to impose a term of imprisonment for that offence, and
(c) the term of imprisonment considered appropriate by the court is 4 years or more.
Meaning of "drug trafficking offence"
Criminal Justice and Police Act 2001 s 34 'Drug trafficking offence' in section 33 includes aiding, abetting, counselling or procuring any of the following offences:

(a) an offence under Misuse of Drugs Act 1971 s 4(2) or (3) (production and supply of controlled drugs),
(b) an offence under Misuse of Drugs Act 1971 s 20 (assisting in or inducing commission outside the United Kingdom),
(c) any such other offence under the same Act as may be designated by order made by the Secretary of State,
(d) an offence under:
(i) Customs and Excise Management Act 1979 s 50(2) or (3) (improper importation),
(ii) Customs and Excise Management Act 1979 s 68(2) (exportation), or
(iii) Customs and Excise Management Act 1979 s 170 (fraudulent evasion), in connection with a prohibition or restriction on importation or exportation having effect by virtue of Misuse of Drugs Act 1971 s 3,
(e) an offence under Criminal Law Act 1977 s 1,
(f) an offence under Criminal Attempts Act 1981 s 1, and
(g) an offence under Misuse of Drugs Act 1971 s 19 or at common law of inciting another person to commit any of those offences.

Note: Surprisingly, money laundering in drugs cases is not included. Ed.

R v Alexander and Others Re C 2011 EWCA Crim 89 C was sentenced for conspiracy to supply cannabis and conspiracy to conceal the proceeds. C received 3½ years for the drug offence and 3 years consecutive for the concealing, making 6½ years. The Judge made Travel Restriction Orders of 2 years. Held. The statute refers to a single sentence of imprisonment of 4 years or more. There was no power to make the order.

The hearing and test to apply

109.4 *Procedure*

Note: The Criminal Procedure Rules 2015 2015/1490 behaviour order rules appear to apply, see the note at **27.2**. For the rules, see **84.14**.

R v Mee 2004 EWCA Crim 629, 2 Cr App R (S) 81 (p 434) The Judge in this case adopted a very full and fair procedure, which should be followed. In doing so he indicated to counsel that he was considering making an order and invited counsel to take instructions from the defendant as to any particular matters which could be relevant to his decision.

Disputes as to facts see the **FACTUAL BASIS FOR SENTENCING** ***Same rules apply when imposing ancillary orders*** para at **57.26**.

109.5 *Judicial duty to consider making an order*

Criminal Justice and Police Act 2001 s 33(2)(a) The court has a duty upon sentencing the offender to consider whether it would be appropriate to include a travel restriction order.

109.6 *Test to apply*

Criminal Justice and Police Act 2001 s 33(2)(b) If the court considers it is appropriate in all the circumstances to make a travel restriction order, an order must be made. Consideration can be taken of any other convictions of the offender for post-commencement drug trafficking offences in respect of which the court is also passing sentence.

R v Shaw and Others Re W and K 2011 EWCA Crim 98 D pleaded to conspiracy to supply cocaine. The conspiracy was a 'dry run' with no cocaine imported. D's offence involved no foreign travel. D was involved with others who were known to have made overseas trips in preparation to import large quantities of drugs. The Judge found no good reason for not imposing an order in each case. Held. The Judge was right to make the order. It was highly material that the involvement in the respective offences was with or through a co-defendant who demonstrated foreign links both with his present and past offending.

109.7 ***Test to apply Drug importers***
R v Mee 2004 EWCA Crim 629, 2 Cr App R (S) 81 (p 434) The powers must be exercised for the purpose for which they were granted and proportionally so. The length is not a substitute for the appropriate period of imprisonment. The purpose is to prevent or reduce the risk of reoffending after the defendant's release from prison. It is not confined to importation cases but by their facts such cases are likely to be most apt for the court to consider such an order. It is not possible to set out the broad range of facts which are likely to arise in individual cases. However, the courts should begin with a careful consideration of the circumstances with a view to making a realistic assessment of the risk which arises from the facts of the case. Principles of proportionality and fairness require a balanced approach when considering the length of time for which the restriction will be imposed. When considering an order, the court must have regard to the prejudice to the offender's future employment, a fact which the legislature must have contemplated. Such prejudice must be regarded as the necessary consequence of the imposition of an order for which the statute provides a specific regime of relief. A restriction on one's freedom to travel is a restriction on a significant aspect of modern life. It is not to be taken away from a person for a number of years without grounds for doing so as it may affect his right to live and work abroad, to visit his family etc. The mere fact that a defendant has imported drugs does not necessarily give rise to the risk that he will, upon release, engage in such activity again. Cases where there is a one-off importation of drugs would give rise to different considerations to that of a large, sophisticated importation from a country well known to be a source of supply.
See also: *R v Graham* 2011 EWCA Crim 1905, 2012 1 Cr App R (S) 57 (p 332) (2.1 kilos of cocaine. The Judge considered that the order would protect the public if she was tempted to import again. The 10-year sentence should do that. No sufficient basis for making the order.)

Making the order

109.8 ***Minimum term for the order***
Criminal Justice and Police Act 2001 s 33(3)(b) The order continues after the offender's release from custody for a period and continues after that time for not less than 2 years.

109.9 ***Order cannot exclude certain countries***
R v Mee 2004 EWCA Crim 629, 2 Cr App R (S) 81 (p 434) The drugs trade is truly international, which is the reason why Criminal Justice and Police Act 2001 does not contemplate a Travel Restriction Order that is linked to only certain parts of the world where the drugs trade flourishes with its greatest potency.

109.10 ***How long should the order be?***
R v Mee 2004 EWCA Crim 629, 2 Cr App R (S) 81 (p 434) para 14 'The length of the order is to be measured to the defendant.' Factors to consider by way of example are age, previous convictions, the risk of reoffending, family contacts, employment and so forth. The court should also consider the quality, quantity, and type of drug imported, degree of sophistication in the offence(s), D's prior travel pattern, D's contact with the drugs trade and D's role in the importation. The length should be what is required to protect the public in light of the assessment of the degree of risk which is presented by the facts. It is vital that it is tailored to each defendant to such a degree as the court feels able when balanced against the risk.
R v Campbell 2004 EWCA Crim 2333, 2005 1 Cr App R (S) 92 (p 520) D was convicted for importing cannabis. D returned to Heathrow airport from Kingston, Jamaica, carrying 13 packages of cannabis resin weighing just under 17 kilos in a suitcase bearing a fraudulent name and address. In interview, D denied checking in the bag in question. However, his documentation showed he checked in two bags and not one, as he had claimed. D, aged 47, had two convictions in the 1980s for drug offences in Jamaica. Additionally in 1984, he was imprisoned for 20 weeks for evasion of duty. In 1993, for importing a controlled drug, D was fined £120. In 1995, for importation, D received a

community service order. In 2001, for importing a class B drug,[1201] 27 months. The Judge considered that D was prepared to continue importing drugs. Held. The correct term of imprisonment was 6 years and not 7. D posed a real risk for future importations, therefore a Travel Restriction Order for a duration longer than the minimum was required. However, **5 years** not 10 was appropriate.
R v Sacco 2006 EWCA Crim 1391 D pleaded to conspiracy to import cocaine and was sentenced to 8 years' imprisonment. The Judge made a 5-year Travel Restriction Order. The conspiracy spanned four years and involved seven trips from Holland. He knew that the journeys concerned drugs and his role was to transport the money across the Channel. D never purchased drugs or brought drugs back to the United Kingdom and he was not involved in the sale of drugs in the United Kingdom. D later withdrew from the conspiracy. D had a wife and three children in Scotland and, save for one cousin, all of D's own family, who were in their 70s, lived in Italy. D's father was aged 81. D asserted that his wife and children spoke only English, his family in Italy only Italian. Visits to Italy without D were therefore impractical. His father was in poor health and both parents were elderly. Upon release D hoped to return to Italy to find work. He was a qualified surveyor in Italy but with insufficient English to practise here. D suffered an attempted attack whilst in custody. Held. The order was not wrong in principle. The Court considered that the length would provide undue hardship towards D and commented that this could be avoided if Italy could be excluded from the order. The legislation does not provide for this. **2 years** not 5.
See also: *R v Ferguson* 2010 EWCA Crim 2860 (10 years' imprisonment. 10-year Travel Restriction Order was not excessive.)

109.11 ***Duty to give reasons if order made***
R v Mee 2004 EWCA Crim 629, 2 Cr App R (S) 81 (p 434) Unless the exchanges between counsel and the court disclose clearly why the need to make an order arises, and…why a certain period is to be imposed, the judge should give succinct reasons explaining why he or she is imposing the order and for the specified period.
R v Ferguson 2010 EWCA Crim 2860 D pleaded to two conspiracy to supply drugs counts. The Judge made a Travel Restriction Order. He did not give reasons. Held. The statute does not expressly require the sentencing judge to give reasons for imposing a Travel Restriction Order. It is usually helpful for judges to give reasons where they exercise judicial discretion, and where a Travel Restriction Order is made, reasons for making an order ought usually to be given, unless they are obvious.
Note: For the general principles about giving reasons, see **86.49**. Ed.

109.12 ***Duty to give reasons if order not made***
Criminal Justice and Police Act 2001 s 33(2)(c) If the court considers an order is not appropriate, the court must state its reasons.
Criminal Procedure Rules 2015 2015/1490 Rule 28.1(1) This rule applies where the court decides:..

(b) not to make, where it could,…

(iii) a travel restriction order.

(2) The court must explain why it has so decided, when it explains the sentence that it has passed.

109.13 ***Explain sentence, Judge/Magistrate must***
Criminal Justice Act 2003 s 174(2)[1202] The court must state in open court, in ordinary language and in general terms, the court's reasons for deciding on the sentence.
(3) The court must explain to the offender in ordinary language:

(a) the effect of the sentence,

[1201] The report states that he was concerned in fraudulently evading duty on a class B drug. Clearly this cannot be the case since there is no duty on class B drugs because they are prohibited. Consequently, it is assumed the suggestion of 'evading duty' was a typo.
[1202] As substituted by Legal Aid, Sentencing and Punishment of Offenders Act 2012 s 64

(b) the effects of non-compliance with any order that the offender is required to comply with and that forms part of the sentence,
(c) any power of the court to vary or review any order that forms part of the sentence…

On the facts, order correct/incorrect

109.14 ***On the facts, order correct/within judge's discretion***

R v Mee 2004 EWCA Crim 629, 2 Cr App R (S) 81 (p 434) D pleaded to importing cocaine. D was stopped by Customs officers at Heathrow airport after arriving on a flight from Jamaica. After routine questioning he was allowed to claim his baggage. He passed through the green 'nothing to declare' channel and was stopped again and his luggage was searched. A quantity of cocaine was discovered valued at £150,000. D alleged that he had travelled to Jamaica for a two-week holiday but on meeting a girl there had stayed there for three months, continuing a romance. It became apparent that D had travelled to Jamaica in the February for a two-week holiday, returned to the United Kingdom and then shortly after travelled to Jamaica once more. D had bought a £600 ticket and made no attempt to change his original homeward-bound ticket. It was also apparent that D had travelled to Honolulu via mainland United States in the previous year. In interview, D claimed he had received approximately £10,000 from his salary as a result of illness and wanted to use the money to fund international trips once a year. Held. It would have been preferable had the Judge given his reasons for a period of 15 years. The following facts are relevant to the decision: a) the deliberate nature of the journey. D is not a one-off holidaymaker, b) the prior establishment of a connection in Jamaica which was not a romance but a decision to trade, c) the deliberate and sophisticated nature of the importation itself, d) D's unsatisfactory answers in interview in connection with the true circumstances of his journey, e) the suspicion under which his journeying elsewhere obviously fell and had to be considered. Substitute a period of 5 years for the period of 15 years.

R v Campbell 2004 EWCA Crim 2333, 2005 1 Cr App R (S) 92 (p 520) D was convicted for importing cannabis. D returned to Heathrow airport from Kingston, Jamaica, carrying 13 packages of cannabis resin weighing just under 17 kilos in a suitcase bearing a fraudulent name and address. In interview, D denied checking in the bag in question. However, his documentation showed he checked in two bags and not one, as he had claimed. D, aged 47, had two convictions in the 1980s for drug offences in Jamaica. Additionally in 1984, D received 20 weeks' imprisonment for evasion of duty. In 1993, for importing a controlled drug, D was fined £120. In 1995, for importation, D received a community service order. In 2001, for importing a class B drug,[1203] he was sentenced to 27 months. The Judge considered that D was prepared to continue importing drugs. Held. The correct term of imprisonment was 6 years and not 7. D posed a real risk for future importations, therefore a Travel Restriction Order for a period longer than the minimum was required. However, 5 years not 10 was appropriate.

R v Sacco 2006 EWCA Crim 1391 D pleaded to conspiracy to import cocaine and was sentenced to 8 years' imprisonment. The conspiracy spanned four years and involved seven trips from Holland. He knew that the journeys concerned drugs and his role was merely to transport the money across the Channel. D never purchased drugs or brought drugs back to the United Kingdom and was not involved in the sale of drugs in the United Kingdom. D then withdrew from the conspiracy. D had a wife and three children in Scotland and, save for one cousin, all of D's own family, who were in their 70s, lived in Italy. D's father was aged 81. D asserted that his wife and children spoke only English, his family in Italy only Italian. Visits to Italy without D were therefore impractical. His father was in poor health and both parents were elderly. Upon release D

[1203] The report states that he was concerned in fraudulently evading duty on a class B drug. Clearly this cannot be the case since there is no duty on class B drugs because they are prohibited. Consequently, it is assumed the suggestion of 'evading duty' was a typo.

hoped to return to Italy to find work. He was a qualified surveyor in Italy but with insufficient English to practise here. D suffered an attempted attack whilst in custody. The Judge made a Travel Restriction Order for a period of 5 years. Held. The order was not wrong in principle. The Court considered that the length would provide undue hardship towards D and commented that this could be avoided if Italy could be excluded from the order. The legislation does not provide for this. 2 years not 5.
R v Watson 2013 EWCA Crim 182 D pleaded to importing a little over 2 kilos of cocaine. She arrived by air from Jamaica with her children aged 16, 14 and 11. Customs found the drugs in some coffee and in tubes of cosmetics. A search of her home revealed documents relating to the flights to Jamaica and which showed she had significant financial difficulties. D was aged 35 and of good character. The Judge made a Travel Restriction Order and the defence contended that the order did not give weight to D's good character, the low risk of reoffending and the effect of the order on her children. Held. It was reasonable for the Judge to infer she was motivated by financial gain. There was nothing to suggest exploitation or that she was placed under pressure. Involving the children was a serious aggravating factor. The Judge had all the relevant factors in mind. The circumstances of the offence with the evident financial difficulties pointed firmly towards a need to restrict her travel. The order would have a limited effect on her children. The Judge was entitled to make the order.
See also: *R v Gonal* 2011 EWCA Crim 587 (D was convicted of conspiracy to supply cocaine. The Judge regarded D as the prime mover in a wide-ranging conspiracy lasting almost 4 years. D had a large number of previous convictions for drug offences. **10 years** was appropriate.)

109.15 *On the facts, order incorrect*

R v Fuller 2005 EWCA Crim 1029, 2006 1 Cr App R (S) 8 (p 52) D imported 570 grams of cocaine in two rum bottles from Jamaica. After an early guilty plea D was sentenced to 4 years' imprisonment with a 5-year Travel Restriction Order. D's estranged husband lived in Jamaica. Her parents lived there for around half of each year, and they had plans to increase the time they spent there. D's motive was her debts totalling £5,000. D was aged 25 and of good character. D was responsible for a 3-year-old child who had suffered from meningitis. Held. The offence was a one-off. The sentencing Court should have considered the position of D's child, specifically the location of the child's grandparents and the fact that the grandparents are unlikely to be able to afford to visit the child in the UK. The child cannot travel to Jamaica without his mother and as such the order would effectively ban the child from seeing his grandparents. The Court took the view that there was no risk of D offending again and that a Travel Restriction Order was not appropriate.
R v Onung 2006 EWCA Crim 2813, 2007 Cr App R (S) 3 (p 9) D pleaded to importing cocaine. Three weeks after his birth in the UK he travelled with his family to Nigeria. When aged 23 he returned to the UK in order to study. The following year D's mother's health deteriorated and he became involved in offending with a view to funding a ticket to visit his mother in Nigeria. D also had a partner in Nigeria who had been carrying his twins but suffered a miscarriage, and a 5-year-old niece for whom he should be responsible. None of D's family could afford to visit him in the UK. D arrived in London from Brussels by Eurostar. He was questioned by Customs officers and X-rayed, which revealed a number of packages present in his body. D passed 98 packages equating to 513 grams of cocaine at 100%, valued at a little over £66,000. He admitted in interview that he had knowingly brought into the UK controlled drugs, explaining that he was subjected to threats when in Amsterdam. D, aged 24 and of good character, was sentenced to 6 years' imprisonment. A Travel Restriction Order was imposed for a period of 5 years. The Judge gave no reasons for imposing the order or explanation for the 5-year period. Held. The offence was a one-off importation in which D, in his accepted basis of plea, was not criminally involved until he was already in Amsterdam. Considering D's personal circumstances, the Travel Restriction Order was quashed.

R v Edward 2012 EWCA Crim 3232 D pleaded in 2006 to conspiracy to supply. He supplied couriers with cocaine to transport. D, aged 52 at time of appeal, had convictions for the supply of controlled drugs. He had a child and grandchild in Majorca. There was no evidence of his being involved in the importation of drugs from abroad. A Travel Restriction Order was made for 10 years on the basis that he had property abroad. Held. Following *R v Brown* 2010, the making of this order must be proportionate and reasons ought to be given. The judge must focus sharply on the facts of the case. There was no evidence that D's properties in Majorca had been acquired through commercial activity in controlled drugs. Nor was it necessary to prevent further offences. The order was neither necessary nor appropriate.

Matters arising after order made

109.16 *What does the order entail?*

Criminal Justice and Police Act 2001 s 33(3)(a) A travel restriction order is an order which prohibits the offender from leaving the United Kingdom at any time in the period which begins with the offender's release from custody.

Criminal Justice and Police Act 2001 s 33(7) References in this section to the offender's first release from custody are references to his first release from custody after the imposition of the travel restriction order which is neither:

(a) a release on bail, nor

(b) a temporary release for a fixed period.

R v Sacco 2006 EWCA Crim 1391 D asserted that his wife and children spoke only English, his family in Italy only Italian. Visits to Italy without D were therefore impractical. His father was in poor health and both parents were elderly. Upon release D hoped to return to Italy to find work. He was a qualified surveyor in Italy but with insufficient English to practise here. Held. The Court considered that the length would provide undue hardship towards D and commented that this could be avoided if Italy could be excluded from the order. The legislation does not provide for this.

109.17 *Passports, Delivery and return of*

Criminal Justice and Police Act 2001 s 33(4) A travel restriction order may contain a direction to the offender to deliver up to the court, or cause to be delivered to the court, any UK passport held by him. Upon delivery, the court shall send any passport to the Secretary of State at such an address determined by the Secretary of State.

(5) Where the offender's passport is held by the Secretary of State by reason of imposing a travel restriction order, the Secretary of State:

a) may retain it for so long as the prohibition imposed by the order applies to the offender, and
b) shall not return the passport after the prohibition has ceased to apply, or when suspended, except where the passport has not expired and an application for its return is made by the offender.

Note: The Identity Cards Act 2006 s 39(3) substituted 'travel authorisation' for 'passport' (on 20/10/09) and the Identity Documents Act 2010 Sch 1 para 17 reversed that change (on 21/1/11). Ed.

109.18 *'UK passport', Definition of*

Criminal Justice and Police Act 2001 s 33(8)[1204] In this section "UK passport" means a United Kingdom passport within the meaning of Immigration Act 1971 (see section 33(1)).

109.19 *Defendant removed from UK*

Criminal Justice and Police Act 2001 s 37(2) A travel restriction order made in relation to any person shall remain in force, notwithstanding the exercise of any prescribed removal power in relation to that person, except in so far as either:

(a) the Secretary of State by order otherwise provides, or

[1204] As substituted by Identity Cards Act 2006 s 39(4)

(b) the travel restriction order is suspended or revoked under Criminal Justice and Police Act 2001 s 35.

Criminal Justice and Police Act 2001 s 37(3) No person shall be guilty of an offence under Criminal Justice and Police Act 2001 s 36 in respect of any act or omission required of him or her by an obligation imposed in the exercise of a prescribed removal power.

(4) A 'prescribed removal power' means any power as:

(a) consists in a power to order or direct the removal of a person from the United Kingdom, and

(b) is designated for the purposes of this section by an order made by the Secretary of State.

Criminal Justice and Police Act 2001 s 37(7) All references to a person's removal from the United Kingdom in section 37 include references to his deportation, extradition, repatriation, delivery up or other transfer to a place outside the United Kingdom.

Travel Restriction Order (Prescribed Removal Powers) Order 2002 2002/313 article 2 Each of the powers set out in the Schedule is designated as a prescribed removal power for the purposes of Criminal Justice and Police Act 2001 s 37.

Travel Restriction Order (Prescribed Removal Powers) Order 2002 2002/313 Sch 1

(a) Colonial Prisoners Removal Act 1884 s 3(1),

(b) United Nations Act 1946 (Powers to order or direct the removal of a person from the United Kingdom conferred by Orders in Council made in exercise of the power contained in section 1(1)),

(c) Backing of Warrants (Republic of Ireland) Act 1965 s 2(1),[1205]

(d) Immigration Act 1971 s 5(1) Sch 2, paras 8-14 and Sch 3 para 1,

(e) Mental Health Act 1983 s 86(2)(a)-(b),

(f) Repatriation of Prisoners Act 1984 s 1(1), 2 and 4(1),

(g) Extradition Act 1989 s 12(1) and Sch 1 para 8(2),

(h) Criminal Justice (International Co-operation) Act 1990 s 5,

(i) Immigration and Asylum Act 1999 s 10,

(j) Immigration (European Economic Area) Regulations 2000 2000/2326 Reg 21(3) and

(k) International Criminal Court Act 2001 s 5, 7, 15, 21, 32 and 43.

Revocation and suspension of Travel Restriction Orders

109.20 *Revoke, Statutory power to*

Revocation and suspension of a travel restriction order

Criminal Justice and Police Act 2001 s 35(1) Subject to the following provisions of this section, the court by which a travel restriction order has been made in relation to any person under section 33 may:

(a) on an application made by that person at any time which is:

(i) after the end of the minimum period, and

(ii) is not within three months after the making of any previous application for the revocation of the prohibition,

revoke the prohibition imposed by the order with effect from such date as the court may determine; or

(b) on an application made by that person at any time after the making of the order, suspend the prohibition imposed by the order for such period as the court may determine.

(2) [The test, see **109.22**]

(3)-(4) [Power to suspend, see **109.24**]

(5) [Duty to be in UK at end of suspension, see **109.25**]

(6) [Re suspension, see **109.23**]

[1205] Repealed by Extradition Act 2003 s 218 on 1/1/04

(7) The "minimum period":

(a) in the case of a travel restriction order imposing a prohibition for a period of 4 years or less, means the period of 2 years beginning at the time when the period of the prohibition began,

(b) in the case of a travel restriction order imposing a prohibition of more than 4 years but less than 10 years, means the period of 4 years beginning at that time, and

(c) in any other case means the period of 5 years beginning at that time.

109.21 ***Procedure for revocation and suspension***

The Criminal Procedure Rules 2015 2015/1490 behaviour order rules appear to apply, see the note at **27.2**.

Criminal Procedure Rules 2015 2015/1490 Rule 28.6(1) This rule applies where, on application by the defendant, the court can remove, revoke or suspend a disqualification or restriction included in a sentence (except a disqualification from driving).

(2) A defendant who wants the court to exercise such a power must:

(a) apply in writing, no earlier than the date on which the court can exercise the power;

(b) serve the application on the court officer; and

(c) in the application:

(i) specify the disqualification or restriction, and

(ii) explain why the defendant wants the court to remove, revoke or suspend it.

(3) The court officer must serve a copy of the application on the chief officer of police for the local justice area.

109.22 ***Test when revoking orders***

Criminal Justice and Police Act 2001 s 35(2) A court to which an application for the revocation of the prohibition imposed on any person by a travel restriction order is made shall not revoke that prohibition unless it considers that it is appropriate to do so in all the circumstances of the case and having regard, in particular, to:

(a) that person's character;

(b) his conduct since the making of the order; and

(c) the offences of which he was convicted on the occasion on which the order was made.

109.23 ***Suspend, Statutory power to***

Criminal Justice and Police Act 2001 s 35(1) Subject to the following provisions of this section, the court by which a travel restriction order has been made in relation to any person under section 33 may:

(a) [see **109.20**]

(b) on an application made by that person at any time after the making of the order, suspend the prohibition imposed by the order for such period as the court may determine.

Criminal Justice and Police Act 2001 s 35(6) Where the prohibition imposed on any person by a travel restriction order is suspended, the end of the period of prohibition imposed by the order shall be treated (except for the purposes of subsection (7)) as postponed (or if there has been one or more previous suspensions, further postponed) by the length of the period of suspension.

Note: This means that if the order is suspended, the time the order was suspended is added to the length of the order. Ed.

109.24 ***Test when suspending orders***

Criminal Justice and Police Act 2001 s 35(3) A court shall not suspend the prohibition imposed on any person by a travel restriction order for any period unless it is satisfied that there are exceptional circumstances, in that person's case, that justify the suspension on compassionate grounds of that prohibition for that period.

(4) In making any determination on an application for the suspension of the order in relation to a prohibition imposed on a person, a court (in addition to considering the matters in section 35(3)) shall have regard to:

(a) that person's character,

(b) his or her conduct since the making of the order,

(c) the offences of which he was convicted on the occasion on which the order was made, and

(d) any other circumstances of the case that the court considers relevant.

109.25 ***Duty to be in the UK at the end of a suspension etc.***

Criminal Justice and Police Act 2001 s 35(5) Where the prohibition is suspended, it shall be the duty of the person to whom the prohibition applies:

(a) to be in the United Kingdom when the period of suspension ends, and

(b) if the order contains a direction under Criminal Justice and Police Act 2001 s 33(4), to surrender, before the end of that period, any passport[1206] returned or issued to that person in respect of the suspension by the Secretary of State.

Combined with other orders

109.26 ***Removal powers, Combined with***

Criminal Justice and Police Act 2001 s 37(1) A travel restriction order made in relation to any person shall not prevent the exercise in relation to that person of any prescribed removal power.

Criminal Justice and Police Act 2001 s 37(7) All references to a person's removal from the United Kingdom in section 37 include references to his deportation, extradition, repatriation, delivery up or other transfer to a place outside the United Kingdom.

See also the **COMBINING SENTENCES** chapter.

110 TRAVEL RESTRICTION ORDERS: BREACH OF

110.1

Criminal Justice and Police Act 2001 s 36

The offences are below. (For the statute see **110.2**.)

(a) leaving the UK when subject to a travel restriction order,

(b) not being present in the UK when suspension period of an order ends, and

(c) failing to deliver up or surrender passport.[1207]

Modes of trial and maximum sentences For offences a) and b): Triable either way on indictment maximum sentence 5 years. Summary maximum 6 months and/or a £5,000 fine for offences committed before 12 March 2015 and an unlimited fine thereafter.[1208] There are maximum fines for those aged under 18, see **13.44**.

For offence c): Summary only, maximum 6 months and/or a £5,000 for offences committed before 12 March 2015 and an unlimited fine thereafter.[1209] There are maximum fines for those aged under 18, see **13.44**.

110.2 ***Statutory offences***

Criminal Justice and Police Act 2001 s 36(1) A person who leaves the United Kingdom at a time when he [or she] is prohibited from leaving it by a travel restriction order is guilty of an offence . . .

(a) and (b) [The penalties, see **110.1**]

[1206] As amended by Identity Cards Act 2006 s 39(3), which substituted 'travel authorisation' for 'passport' (on 20/10/09) and Identity Documents Act 2010 Sch 1 para 17, which reversed that change (on 21/1/11).

[1207] As amended by Identity Cards Act 2006 s 39(3), which substituted 'travel authorisation' for 'passport' (on 20/10/09) and Identity Documents Act 2010 Sch 1 para 17, which reversed that change (on 21/1/11).

[1208] Legal Aid, Sentencing and Punishment of Offenders Act 2012 s 85(1) and (4) and Legal Aid, Sentencing and Punishment of Offenders Act 2012 (Commencement No 11) Order 2015 2015/504

[1209] Legal Aid, Sentencing and Punishment of Offenders Act 2012 s 85(1) and (4) and Legal Aid, Sentencing and Punishment of Offenders Act 2012 (Commencement No 11) Order 2015 2015/504

(2) A person who is not present in the United Kingdom at the end of a period during which a prohibition imposed on him by a travel restriction order has been suspended commits an offence . . .

(a) and (b) [The penalties, see **110.1**]

(3) A person who fails to comply with:

(a) a direction in a travel restriction order to deliver up a passport[1210] to a court or to cause it to be delivered up or any duty to surrender a passport[1211] to the Secretary of State commits an offence.

110.3 *Duplicity, Breach and*

S v Doncaster Youth Offending Team 2003 EWHC 1128 (Admin) High Court S was convicted of failing to comply with a Detention and Training Order. S had failed to reside where the YOT had instructed him to, and he had failed to report for four consecutive weeks. It was submitted that the information was bad for duplicity. Held. Sometimes it is difficult to distinguish between separate offences, on the one hand, and different features of committing the same offence, on the other. There were two quite separate licence conditions of which the appellant was in breach. These were failing to keep in touch with his supervising officer and failing to live at the address approved by his supervising officer. These were two separate offences that should not have been tried on the same information.

Note: The application of the duplicity rules for a different order may provide assistance. Ed.

110.4 *Magistrates' Court Sentencing Guidelines*

Breach Offences Guideline 2018, see www.banksr.com Other Matters Guidelines tab In force 1 October 2018 page 56 says, '**Other breach offences** Where an offence is not covered by a sentencing guideline a court is entitled to use, and may be assisted by, a guideline for an analogous offence subject to differences in the elements of the offences and the statutory maxima.'

Magistrates' Court Sentencing Guideline, see www.banksr.com Other Matters Guidelines tab page 147 When sentencing for the breach of any order for which there is not a specific guideline, the primary objective will be to ensure compliance. Reference to existing guidelines in respect of breaches of orders may provide a helpful point of comparison.

110.5 *Judicial guidance*

R v Koli 2012 EWCA Crim 1869, 2013 1 Cr App R (S) 6 (p 39) D was convicted of two breaches of his Serious Crime Prevention Order. Held. para 18 The court must take into account: a) the time between the imposition of the order and the date of the breach, b) any history of non-compliance, c) whether non-compliance has i) been repeated and ii) come in the face of warnings and requests for information, and d) whether the non-compliance was inadvertent or deliberate. It is important to consider whether the breach was related to the commission of further serious offences and might lead to the risk that a particular subject was likely to commit further offences. The court would also have to consider the harm caused by non-compliance for breach.

Note: Although these remarks were given when a different breach was considered, the principles may assist. Ed.

[1210] As amended by Identity Cards Act 2006 s 39(3), which substituted 'travel authorisation' for 'passport' (on 20/10/09) and Identity Documents Act 2010 Sch 1 para 17, which reversed that change (on 21/1/11).

[1211] As amended by Identity Cards Act 2006 s 39(3), which substituted 'travel authorisation' for 'passport' (on 20/10/09) and Identity Documents Act 2010 Sch 1 para 17, which reversed that change (on 21/1/11).

111 UNLAWFUL PROFIT ORDERS

111.1

Prevention of Social Housing Fraud Act 2013 s 4-5[1212]

Definition It is an order requiring the offender to pay a landlord the profit from unlawfully sub-letting a tenancy, Prevention of Social Housing Fraud Act 2013 s 4(3) and 5(2).

Two types There are two types, post-conviction (Prevention of Social Housing Fraud Act 2013 s 4) and stand-alone orders (Prevention of Social Housing Fraud Act 2013 s 5).

Post-conviction orders The defendant must have been convicted of unlawfully sub-letting: a) a secured tenancy (Prevention of Social Housing Fraud Act 2013 s 1), or b) an assured tenancy (Prevention of Social Housing Fraud Act 2013 s 2).

Victim surcharges Where there are insufficient means to pay an Unlawful Profit Order and a victim surcharge, the victim surcharge can be reduced up to the full amount, Criminal Justice Act 2003 s 161A(3). For more detail, see **115.11**.

Maximum amount The maximum amount payable is the 'total amount received as a result of the conduct' less 'the amount paid as rent to the landlord', Prevention of Social Housing Fraud Act 2013 s 4(6).

Combined with an absolute or conditional discharge Powers of Criminal Courts (Sentencing) Act 2000 s 12(7) Nothing in this section shall be construed as preventing a court, on discharging an offender absolutely or conditionally in respect of any offence-…from making in respect of the offence an Unlawful Profit Order under Prevention of Social Housing Fraud Act 2013 s 4.[1213]

Combined with a fine Where a defendant has insufficient means to pay both an 'appropriate Unlawful Profit Order' and a fine, the court must give preference to the Unlawful Profit Order, Prevention of Social Housing Fraud Act 2013 s 4(8) and (9).

112 VARIATION OF SENTENCE

112.1

Magistrates' Courts Act 1980 s 142(1) (Magistrates' Court)

Powers of Criminal Courts (Sentencing) Act 2000 s 155(1) (Crown Court)

There seems no reason to treat the two powers of the courts differently, save that the Magistrates' Court power has no time limit. However, any delay in applying to either court may be critical in determining whether a variation is made.

Crown Court power

112.2 ***Crown Court power***

Powers of Criminal Courts (Sentencing) Act 2000 s 155(1) Subject to the following provisions of this section, a sentence imposed, or other order made, by the Crown Court when dealing with an offender may be varied or rescinded by the Crown Court within the period of 56 days beginning with the day on which the sentence or other order was imposed or made.

Note: This is often referred to as the 'slip rule'.

R v Iqbal 1985 7 Cr App R (S) 35 The statutory power is a continuation of the old common law powers.

112.3 ***Crown Court Extent of the power***

R v Reynolds and Others 2007 EWCA Crim 538, 2 Cr App R (S) 87 (p 553) The Court of Appeal considered eight separate cases together to give guidance about IPP and extended sentences. Held. para 7 Provided any mistake is identified quickly enough, the court can exercise its power under Powers of Criminal Courts (Sentencing) Act 2000

[1212] This Act came into force on 15/10/13, Prevention of Social Housing Fraud Act 2013 (Commencement) (England) Order 2013 2013/2622 para 2.

[1213] As amended by Criminal Justice and Courts Act 2015 Sch 12 paras 8-9

s 155(1) to vary the sentence within the period of 56[1214] days beginning on the day on which the sentence or other order was imposed. There is no doubt that this power can be exercised to reduce or increase the sentence: see *R v Hart* 1983 5 Cr App R (S) 25, *Commissioners of Customs and Excise v Menocal* 1980 AC 598, and *R v Hadley* 1995 16 Cr App R (S) 358. However, this Court has made it clear that the power to increase the sentence should be exercised with care, see *R v Woop* 2002 EWCA Crim 58, 2 Cr App R (S) 65 (p 281). The power to increase the sentence would be properly exercised if the mistake was that the court had failed to appreciate, for example, that the 'specified offence' was a 'serious offence', so that the mandatory[1215] provisions of section 225 or 227 required an indeterminate sentence as opposed to an extended sentence. Equally the power could be exercised where the mistake was a failure to recognise the offence as a 'specified offence', as a result of which an ordinary determinate sentence or other disposal has been imposed. Whatever inhibition there may be on increasing sentences cannot apply if the court is merely seeking to comply with its statutory obligations.

R v Aldridge and Eaton 2012 EWCA Crim 1456 LCJ E was given a 3-year SOPO. Later the Judge was told the minimum period was 5 years. The transcript showed the order was made for 3 years. The Judge thought he had made the order for 5 years and purported to make an administrative correction. Held. The Judge could not have varied the order under section 155 as it was out of time and no one attended. The 5-year order was unlawful. The Judge could not extend it and neither can we. Order quashed.

R v Catchpole 2014 EWCA Crim 1037, 2 Cr App R (S) 66 (p 516) D pleaded to theft and common assault and a robbery count was dropped. The Judge was very unhappy with this. The Judge gave D 3 months in all, which meant D was entitled to immediate release. Later in the day, a probation officer said he was not aware that D was appearing for sentence and that D was due to be sectioned under Mental Health Act 1983. The officer asked for an order that D should be assessed under the 1983 Act. The Judge said he was going to rescind the sentence totally and remand D in custody. Defence counsel was located. The Judge said he knew too little about D and there was no mention of mental health problems in the probation report. A psychiatric report was shown to the Judge and he ordered the sentence to be rescinded and remanded him to a hospital. Later, a different judge sentenced D to a Hospital Order. Held. The actions of the first Judge were lawful. There was no objection to the matter being heard by a different judge. Appeal dismissed.

R v Gross 2016 EWCA Crim 531 D was sentenced for three historical rapes and other sex offences to 16 years with a full discount. The Judge brought the defendant back to Court and increased the sentence to 18 years, saying that D had had many opportunities to volunteer his guilt so 25% credit was appropriate. Held. Recent cases indicate that the restrictive approach to variation in *R v Nodjoumi* 1985 7 Cr App R (S) 183 no longer applied. There is now a flexible approach in which fairness to the defendant and the public interest both have to be weighed. On the facts the Judge was not able to reduce the plea discount and so increase the sentence because D had not revealed his offending before. The first sentence was correct.

R v Warren 2017 EWCA Crim 226, 2 Cr App R (S) 5 After the Judge had passed his sentence, the prosecution told him that he had misstated the facts for D. The Judge said he would not increase the sentence. Later he learned that the prosecution were preparing to appeal the sentence. He then listed the case and increased the sentence from 6 years 8 months to 8½ years. Held. The current state of the law is as follows.

1) Where an error occurs in the factual basis of sentence it should be pointed out to the court as soon as possible and consideration should be given to correcting it at the earliest opportunity, preferably by revisiting [the] sentence on the same day rather than a subsequent day.

[1214] The period was extended to 56 days by Criminal Justice and Immigration Act 2008 s 47 and Sch 8 para 28 on 14/7/08.

[1215] The provisions are no longer mandatory but the example illustrates the use of the power.

2) A judge should not use the slip rule simply because there is a change of mind about the nature or length of the sentence but the slip rule is available where the judge is persuaded that he had made a material error in the sentencing process whether of fact or law. It is relevant in considering whether he had made a material error that that error might be corrected by the Court of Appeal on the Attorney General's application.
3) The sooner the slip rule is invoked in such a case, the better. The passage of time from the first decision to its revision is a material consideration as to how the power should be exercised, but there is a 56-day cut off in any event.
4) A judge should not be unduly influenced by the prospect of a reference being made to change the sentence that he thought was right at the time by the mere threat of a review by the Attorney General. If the judge concludes that the sentence was not wrong in principle and was not unduly lenient, he should not change his mind simply because there is the possibility of a reference. The judge can then use the opportunity at the further sentencing hearing to give any further explanations for the original decision for the sentence.
5) [See **112.18** (about the attendance of defendants).]
6) Although *R v Nodjoumi* 1985 7 Cr App (S) 183 no longer identifies the basic rule in such cases, the appearance of justice and the impact of the change on a defendant where an error has not been induced by anything that he has said or done is a relevant consideration and in appropriate cases it can be reflected in a modest discount to the proposed revised sentence to reflect this fact. This [was] done in this case. We consider that modest discount was appropriate and sufficient.
R v O'Connor 2018 EWCA Crim 1417, 2 Cr App R (S) 49 (p 397) D pleaded to robbery, ABH and other offences directed at his ex-girlfriend, G, her new partner, her mother and three police officers. D was aged 30 with 20 previous convictions, a number of them for violence. A psychiatrist considered that D had a severe anti-social personality disorder and a massive anger management problem. D had also attacked a prison officer, a prison inmate and a dock officer. [It looks as if at least two of these were after his arrest.] D said he wanted to kill G's family. For the robbery the Judge passed a sentence of 45 months with 4 months consecutive for three of the other offences. A week later, the Judge said he had approached the sentence wrongly. He changed the robbery sentence to an 8-year 1 month extended sentence (4 years 1 month's custody 4 years' extended licence). He also made the 4 months concurrent. Held. Sentencing is a much more complex matter than it used to be. There is the strongest public interest in addressing the risk D posed. We adopt *R v Warren* 2017 [see above]. There was no difficulty in the Judge correcting his error.
See also: *R v D* 2014 EWCA Crim 2340, 2015 1 Cr App R (S) 23 (p 168) (The Judge thought he could vary outside the time limit because it was an attempt. He could not. Sentence rearranged.)
Old cases: Other old cases are best ignored because the rules for variation have changed in recent years.

112.4 *Crown Court On the facts, suitable for variation*
R v Hart 1983 5 Cr App R (S) 25 LCJ D was sentenced to a suspended sentence for two common assaults (one on a female probation officer) and assault on a PC. The Judge said he was passing that sentence solely because he had been told that D had a chance to make a fresh start in Italy with his girlfriend where a job was available. Shortly after, the local newspaper ran an article in which D said he had conned the Judge and the claims were a concoction. The following week, in a further article, D asserted the claims were true. D was brought back to court and the Judge varied the sentence to 6 months' immediate imprisonment. Held. The Judge was absolutely right to review the sentence. This was a plain case for varying the sentence but it was done one day too late.
R v Evans 1985 7 Cr App R (S) 35 The Judge during the sentencing initially passed sentence for burglary and reckless driving and then indicated 12 months for some driving matters. He was told the maximum sentences for those were 6 months. The Judge then increased the sentences for the burglary from 9 to 12 months and the reckless

driving from 12 months to 18. The defence said it was inappropriate to make that alteration and it gave rise to a real sense of grievance. Held. If a court had decided that the appropriate sentence for a particular offence was, say, a year, it would be wrong to increase that sentence artificially above the proper level simply because the total sentence would be insufficient. That is not what happened in this case. There was no room for any legitimate grievance, nor are we persuaded that the Judge exercised his undoubted discretion incorrectly.

R v Sivyer and Others 1987 9 Cr App R (S) 428 The Judge varied the 18-month sentence to 12 months, reduced the company director disqualification from 4 years to 3 and imposed £5,000 costs. Held. It is impossible to single out one item in isolation. Orders affirmed.

R v McLean 1988 10 Cr App R (S) 18 D pleaded to robbery and wounding. The mitigation was that D was turning over a new leaf and this was supported by a letter from D to the Judge. This referred to D's determination to change his ways. D received 3 years and very shortly after, D escaped through an open door. The Judge re-listed the case and while D was still at large said he originally intended to pass a 5-year term but because of the remorse and his desire to make a new, honest life had reduced the sentence to 3 years. The escape had 'given the lie to that'. The sentence was increased to 4 years. Later D received concurrent sentences for other matters and 6 months consecutive for the escape. Held. Considering whether D had 'conned' the Court, the facts in *R v Hart* 1983 were clearer. But the Judge was entitled to find D's statements were utterly false. It was a proper exercise of the Judge's discretion and it could not be said that 4 years was excessive.

R v Reynolds and Others 2007 EWCA Crim 538, 2 Cr App R (S) 87 (p 553) The power to increase the sentence would be properly exercised if the mistake was that the court had failed to appreciate, for example, that the 'specified offence' was a 'serious offence', so that the mandatory[1216] provisions of section 225 or 227 required an indeterminate sentence as opposed to an extended sentence. Equally the power could be exercised where the mistake was a failure to recognise the offence as a 'specified offence', as a result of which an ordinary determinate sentence or other disposal has been imposed. Whatever inhibition there may be on increasing sentences cannot apply if the court is merely seeking to comply with its statutory obligations.

R v Imperio 2018 EWCA Crim 759 D was convicted of five child sex offences and pleaded to another. The Judge sentenced him to 1 year, 5 years, 7 years, 4 years, 7 years and 2 years. All were concurrent. The prosecution counsel then said, "The totality guidelines suggest there should be an element of consecutive sentences in these sorts of cases." The Judge said that was a good point and rose to consider it. He returned and made a distinction between some of the counts, reduced two of the sentences but made them consecutive and 10 years in all. The defence said there was no error of law or fact so the variation was unlawful. Held. The Judge's failure to consider the *TICs and Totality Guideline: Crown Court 2012* was a material error of law. The Judge was not only entitled to vary the sentence, but he was under a duty to do so.

R v Ochesanu 2018 EWCA Crim 2772 D and B pleaded to section 20. B was sentenced on the basis that he had: a) picked up the weapon in a street attack, b) used it on V, the victim, c) continued to kick and punch V, and d) kicked V in the head. D was sentenced on the basis he had not [held] the weapon, that he had not kicked V in the head and he was not the prime mover. B received 2 years 3 months. D received 2 years suspended. After the hearing, it was discovered on the CCTV that the person wielding the weapon and kicking V in the head could not have been B. The case was relisted 12 days after the sentences. The Judge found that D had launched himself at V, struck him over the head

[1216] The provisions are no longer mandatory but the example illustrates the use of the power.

and body and had kicked and punched V on the ground. D's sentence was varied to 2 years' immediate imprisonment. B's sentence was varied to 2 years suspended. Held. That was lawful, rational and fair.
See also: *R v Iqbal* 1985 7 Cr App R (S) 35 (Order for detention under section 91 substituted for youth custody, which was unlawful. Variation not wrong in principle.)
R v Miller 1991 12 Cr App R (S) 519 (After hearing, assets found. Judge able to vary the drug confiscation order from £0 to the value of the assets.)

112.5 ***Crown Court On the facts, not suitable for variation***
R v Cassidy 2010 EWCA Crim 3146, 2011 2 Cr App R (S) 40 (p 240) D was sentenced to a Suspended Sentence Order of 34 weeks for possession of amphetamine with intent to supply. He attended a non-enforceable appointment during which an argument developed. D made a number of unpleasant, abusive and threatening remarks to or about the staff. Breach proceedings were initiated. D admitted breaching the earlier order. The Judge, two weeks after the sentence, found that D had misled the court into believing that he would comply with the order, and was therefore not bound by the original order. Held. It is not possible to find on this occasion that the court was misled in the way contemplated by *R v Hart* 1983 5 Cr App R (S) 25. The course taken by the Judge was tantamount to sentencing D for an offence of which he had not been convicted. **34 weeks** not 12 months.
R v Hudson 2011 EWCA Crim 906, 2 Cr App R (S) 116 (p 666) D was convicted of rape and his conviction was quashed. He was reconvicted and the Judge considered 6 years was appropriate. Erroneously believing that the time before the first conviction would not count, he passed 3 years and 215 days. He was then told that because of Criminal Appeal Act 1968 Sch 1[1217] the days counted automatically. He then purported to vary the sentence, after the 56-day time limit, so the defendant would actually serve the sentence he thought was appropriate. He considered it was the equivalent to altering the days to count outside the limit. Held. It wasn't. It was a significantly different variation. Variation quashed.
See also: *R v Powell* 1985 7 Cr App R (S) 247 (After the defendant received 3 months' youth custody, he and others took part in rude and offensive behaviour. The Judge increased the sentence to 6 months. There was a clear procedure for dealing with contempts. It was wrong, so variation quashed.)

Magistrates' Court power

112.6 ***Magistrates' Court Statutory power***
Magistrates' Courts Act 1980 s 142(1) A Magistrates' Court may vary or rescind a sentence or other order imposed or made by it when dealing with an offender if it appears to the court to be in the interests of justice to do so, and it is hereby declared that this power extends to replacing a sentence or order which for any reason appears to be invalid by another which the court has power to impose or make.

112.7 ***Magistrates' Court Extent of the power***
Jane v Broome 1987 The Times 2/11/87 D pleaded to drink/driving. The Magistrates found special reasons and then considered they erred in law and varied the sentence to add 12 months' disqualification. Held. The Magistrates were entitled to act as they did.
Holmes v Liverpool City JJs 2004 EWHC 3131 (Admin) High Court D was convicted of dangerous driving. The victim of the bad driving was tossed into the air and received a head injury from which he would never recover '100%'. It appears the Magistrates said custody was not appropriate and imposed 50 hours' community service. The victim's mother-in-law wrote to Lord Justice Thomas expressing absolute disgust at the sentence and the total destruction of the lives of so many people. The letter was sent to the Magistrates' Court and an investigation occurred. It was discovered that the prosecution had decided not to provide the Magistrates with the statements from the neurologist and

[1217] Repealed by Criminal Procedure (Insanity and Unfitness to Plead) Act 1991 Sch 4 para 1 on 1/1/92

the husband (of the victim[1218]), taking the view that the sentence should be based on the driving. Some five months after the complaint was received, the matter was re-listed. The Magistrates, in a statement for the High Court, said that had they known the injuries and the appropriate law, they would not have imposed the sentence they did. They adjourned the case for a pre-sentence report and the defendant appealed to the High Court. Held. The effect on the victim is a material consideration. We apply *R v Croydon Youth Court ex parte DPP* 1997 2 Cr App R 411 (a conviction case). 'The purpose of the section was to rectify mistakes. It was generally and correctly to be regarded as a slip rule and the power under the section could not be extended to cover situations beyond those akin to a mistake. Thus it was wholly wrong to employ section 142(2) as a method by which a defendant could obtain a rehearing in circumstances where he could not appeal to the Crown Court by reason of his unequivocal plea of guilty. Nor was it in the interests of justice. That case indicates that the power is to be used in a relatively limited situation, namely one which is akin to mistake or, as the Court says, the slip rule. But there is no reason, on the face of it, to limit it further. If a court has been misled into imposing a particular sentence, and it is discovered that it has been so misled, then the sentence may properly be said to have been imposed because of a mistake; the mistake being the failure of the court to appreciate a relevant fact. That may well give power to the court to vary, but it does not indicate that that power should necessarily be used. Where it could be shown, for example, that magistrates had been misled by something put forward in mitigation by the defence into imposing a sentence which was more lenient than that which would have been appropriate had they known the true circumstances, that would be capable of triggering a variation. It would be easier to say that it was in the interests of justice to make use of that power. There is no doubt that the power can be exercised even if an increase in sentence is involved. It is very important to bear in mind the principle of finality in sentencing (see **112.20**). It is of some importance that the claimant has already served his 50 hours' community service. It must be recognised that Parliament has with the greatest care and circumspection indicated when and how there should be, in relation to the Crown Court, a power to increase sentences. The answer that it gives is only if the sentence can be regarded as unduly lenient, and then only in relation to a relatively small number of indictable offences. It is a jurisdiction clearly that has to be exercised with care. Furthermore, there is, undoubtedly, an element of double jeopardy that is recognised in all cases where the Court of Appeal is persuaded that a sentence was unduly lenient. It will not then impose the full sentence that would have been appropriate. There is always a significant discount to recognise the element of double jeopardy. The prosecution advocate very properly did not seek to argue that the circumstances of this case were such as on their facts to justify the use that the Magistrates sought to make. But he was concerned that we should not shut the door upon the use of section 142 in a situation where magistrates had, for whatever reason, been in ignorance, and thus mistaken, about material facts which led them to a particular sentence. The reason why they were unaware of the material facts would obviously be relevant in deciding whether it was in the interests of justice that the matter should be reconsidered, but it is certainly possible to envisage circumstances where the failure of the court to be aware of such material factors could enable variation to be properly made. It would only be in very rare circumstances that it would be appropriate to resort to section 142 to consider an increase in sentence, particularly if that increase, as here, brought the possibility of custody as opposed to another form of disposal.

Certainly the facts of this case do not come anywhere near justifying such a use of section 142. I am far from persuaded that the Magistrates were misled in any way as to what the appropriate considerations should be, and even if they were, this was not a case, on any view, where it should have made the difference between the sort of sentence they decided to impose, namely community service, and a different and more severe form of

[1218] This is not clear in the judgment.

sentence. The fact, if it be a fact, that they might have imposed a slightly longer period of community service, cannot conceivably be a proper reason to reopen the question of sentence. That would be marginal and an inappropriate use of section 142, even assuming it was proper to use it. The Magistrates were wrong and they should not have attempted to vary.

112.8 ***Magistrates' Court Don't delay***
Holmes v Liverpool City JJs 2004 EWHC 3131 (Admin) High Court D was convicted of dangerous driving. The victim's mother-in-law wrote to Lord Justice Thomas expressing absolute disgust at the sentence and the total destruction of the lives of so many people. The letter was sent to the Magistrates' Court and an investigation occurred. Some five months after the complaint was received, the matter was re-listed. They adjourned the case for a pre-sentence report and the defendant appealed to the High Court. Held. If the power is to be used to increase a sentence, it must be exercised very speedily. It is interesting to note that Parliament, when section 142 was first enacted, imposed a 28-day time limit upon the use of the powers. That time limit was removed in 1995 but the similar powers that the Crown Court has to reconsider sentences have to be exercised within 28 days (now 56 days). So if the case had been committed for trial there would have been no power for the Crown Court to vary the sentence outside the 28-day period. Of course, we have to recognise that the time limit has been removed by Parliament, but we must also recognise that it is essential that this power should be used very expeditiously.
See also the ***Crown Court Time limits*** para at **112.11**.

112.9 ***No power after appeal determined***
Magistrates' Courts Act 1980 s 142(1A) The power conferred on a Magistrates' Court by subsection (1) shall not be exercisable in relation to any sentence or order imposed or made by it when dealing with an offender if:
(a) the Crown Court has determined an appeal against:
(i) that sentence or order,
(ii) the conviction in respect of which that sentence or order was imposed or made, or
(iii) any other sentence or order imposed or made by the Magistrates' Court when dealing with the offender in respect of that conviction (including a sentence or order replaced by that sentence or order), or
(b) the High Court has determined a case stated for the opinion of that court on any question arising in any proceeding leading to or resulting from the imposition or making of the sentence or order.

112.10 ***Court Martial***
Armed Forces (Court Martial) Rules 2009 2009/2041 Rules 118-124 The court may vary a sentence imposed by it within the period of 56 days beginning with the day on which the sentence was imposed. The judge advocate may give a direction on his own motion or on application from the prosecution or defence. The full court will reconsider the matter but the judge advocate may direct that no lay members are present if they cannot be made available.
Guidance on Sentencing in the Court Martial 2018 para 2.25 After the Court Martial has passed a sentence, power exists[1219] for the court to vary the sentence during the 56 days after sentence. Variation proceedings may take place of the judge's own motion, or on the application of the prosecution or defence. The court comprises the same judge as at the sentencing proceedings and all the same lay members, or as many of them as can practicably attend in person or by live video link. The purpose of the variation proceedings is to correct legal errors in sentencing (such as a longer period of custody than the maximum for that offence, or a sentence which is not available for a person of

[1219] Armed Forces (Court Martial) Rules 2009 2009/2041 Rules 118-124

that rank). It is not intended to be used so that discretion can be exercised differently, or because opinions have changed. A defendant wishing to seek a variation should write to the Judge Advocate General giving reasons for his application. The JAG will forward the application to the judge who sat in the sentencing proceedings for a decision as to whether to list the case for variation proceedings. There is no appeal against a judge's decision not to proceed, but the sentence whether varied or not is still subject to appeal to the Court Martial Appeal Court.

Time limits

112.11 ***Crown Court Time limits***

Powers of Criminal Courts (Sentencing) Act 2000 s 155(1) A sentence imposed, or other order made, by the Crown Court when dealing with an offender may be varied or rescinded by the Crown Court within the period of 56 days beginning with the day on which the sentence or other order was imposed or made.

112.12 ***Crown Court Time limits No power to extend them/Late power to adjourn***

R v Reynolds and Others 2007 EWCA Crim 538, 2 Cr App R (S) 87 (p 553) Earlier judgments of this Court were restrained by *Commissioners of Customs and Excise v Menocal* 1980 AC 598 in considering whether it was possible to adjourn to a date outside the [now 56-day] period. We have come to the conclusion that we can and should revisit the question of whether or not the court is entitled, in pursuance of section 155 of the 2000 Act, to exercise the power to rescind and then exercise its common law power to adjourn. The consequential adjournment no more offends against the principle of certainty than a decision of the Crown Court to adjourn in the first instance. Clearly, as a matter of good sentencing practice, the defendant is entitled to know his sentence as soon as possible. But there may be many situations in which it would be in the defendant's own interest for there to be an adjournment. In our judgement, therefore, the Crown Court has power, after rescinding all or part of its original order, to adjourn final sentence to a later date.

Att-Gen's Ref No 79 of 2015 2016 EWCA Crim 448, 2 Cr App R (S) 18 (p 158) The Attorney-General applied for the sentence to be varied. At some stage, the victim told the police about something new and it was realised that the defendant had been sentenced on the wrong basis. The Judge was not available so the case was heard within the time limit by a different Judge, who adjourned the matter until the first Judge was available. The first Judge, after a further adjournment, varied the sentence, but after the time limit had expired. Held. There is no power to extend the 56-day time limit although it is open to the court to rescind the decision within the time limit and adjourn the re-sentencing to outside the time limit. Only the sentencing judge may vary the sentence, *R v Morrison* 2004 EWCA Crim 2705. The variation was invalid. Sentence varied under the reference procedure.

112.13 ***Time limits Crown Court Co-defendant exception***

Powers of Criminal Courts (Sentencing) Act 2000 s 155(7) [The] Criminal Procedure Rules:

(a) may, as respects cases where two or more persons are tried separately on the same or related facts alleged in one or more indictments, provide for extending the period fixed by subsection (1) above,

(b) may, subject to the preceding provisions of this section, prescribe the cases and circumstances in which, and the time within which, any order or other decision made by the Crown Court may be varied or rescinded by that court.

(8) In this section:

'sentence' includes a recommendation for deportation made when dealing with an offender, 'order' does not include an order relating to a requirement to make a payment under regulations under Legal Aid, Sentencing and Punishment of Offenders Act 2012 s 23 or 24.[1220]

Criminal Procedure Rules 2015 2015/1490 Rule 28.4(4) The court must not exercise its power in the defendant's absence unless:

(a) the court makes a variation:

(i) proposed by the defendant, or

(ii) the effect of which is that the defendant is no more severely dealt with under the sentence as varied than before, or

(b) the defendant has had an opportunity to make representations at a hearing (whether or not the defendant in fact attends).

112.14 ***Same judge must vary order*** ***Crown Court***

Powers of Criminal Courts (Sentencing) Act 2000 s 155(4) A sentence or other order shall not be varied or rescinded under this section except by the court constituted as it was when the sentence or other order was imposed or made, or, where that court comprised one or more justices of the peace, a court so constituted except for the omission of any one or more of those justices.

Att-Gen's Ref No 79 of 2015 2016 EWCA Crim 448, 2 Cr App R (S) 18 (p 158) The Attorney-General applied for the sentence to be varied. At some stage, the victim told the police about something new and it was realised that the defendant had been sentenced on the wrong basis. The Judge was not available so the case was heard within the time limit by a different Judge, who adjourned the matter until the first Judge was available. The first Judge, after a further adjournment, varied the sentence, but after the time limit had expired. Held. There is no power to extend the 56-day time limit although it is open to the court to rescind the decision within the time limit and adjourn the re-sentencing to outside the time limit. Only the sentencing judge may vary the sentence, *R v Morrison* 2004 EWCA Crim 2705. The variation was invalid. Sentence varied under the reference procedure.

R v Morrison 2016 EWCA Crim 2705 The Judge gave D 4 months concurrent with other sentences for interfering with a vehicle. The maximum sentence was 3 months. The mistake was noticed within the then 28-day slip rule time limit but the Judge had died. Another Judge reduced the sentence to 2 months. Held. That second Judge's review of the sentence was null and void. Only the sentencing Judge had power to review his or her sentences.

Procedure

112.15 ***Applications to vary etc. a sentence etc.***

Criminal Procedure Rules 2015 2015/1490 Rule 28.4(1) This rule:

(a) applies where a Magistrates' Court or the Crown Court can vary or rescind a sentence or order, other than an order to which rule 37.17 applies (Setting aside a conviction or varying a costs etc. order), and

(b) authorises the Crown Court, in addition to its other powers, to do so within the period of 56 days beginning with another defendant's acquittal or sentencing where:

(i) defendants are tried separately in the Crown Court on the same or related facts alleged in one or more indictments, and

(ii) one is sentenced before another is acquitted or sentenced.

(2) The court may exercise its power:

(a) on application by a party, or on its own initiative,

(b) at a hearing, in public or in private, or without a hearing.

(3) A party who wants the court to exercise that power must:

(a) apply in writing as soon as reasonably practicable after:

(i) the sentence or order that that party wants the court to vary or rescind, or

[1220] As amended by Legal Aid, Sentencing and Punishment of Offenders Act 2012 Sch 5 para 54. In force 1/4/13

(ii) where paragraph (1)(b) applies, the other defendant's acquittal or sentencing,
(b) serve the application on:
(i) the court officer, and
(ii) each other party, and
(c) in the application:
(i) explain why the sentence should be varied or rescinded,
(ii) specify the variation that the applicant proposes, and
(iii) if the application is late, explain why.
(4) [see **112.13**]
(5) [see **112.12**]

112.16 ***The case must be properly listed so all interested parties may attend***
R v Perkins and Others 2013 EWCA Crim 323, 2 Cr App R (S) 72 (p 461) D pleaded to historical sexual offences. The Judge sought, in D's absence, to vary downwards the sentences originally imposed. The case was not formally listed and neither counsel, who were present merely by coincidence, had their original papers. The Judge did not invite submissions from either counsel, observing that to require D to travel to court would be detrimental to his health, and he proceeded to order the variation. Held. It should be listed so that all the interested parties, not only the defendant, but the victims, the public and the media may be present if they wish. This variation hearing undoubtedly took place in open court, but if no one with a direct interest in the case had any idea that it was to be listed, for those most closely concerned, the hearing was effectively a private hearing. That should not happen.
R v Tinkler 2018 EWCA Crim 1243 D pleaded to death by dangerous driving and other offences. The following day, the Judge sent an e-mail reducing the disqualification from 12 to 11 years. Held. That approach, whilst no doubt an efficient one, is not appropriate. In the interests of open justice, any sentence, including consequential orders or corrections, should be announced in open court, on notice as stated in *R v Billington* 2017 EWCA Crim 618, 2 Cr App R (S) 22 (p 171), see **86.47**.
See also the **Procedure, Sentencing** ***Sentencing remarks Must be oral and in open court*** para at **86.47**.

112.17 ***There must be a hearing in open court***
R v H 2000 1 Cr App R (S) p 181 The Judge sentenced D, a serving prisoner, to 3½ years. He did not say whether the sentence was to be concurrent or consecutive to the existing sentence. The Young Offender Institution asked for clarification and the Judge said the sentence should be consecutive. There was no judicial enquiry about the existing sentence. This change made the total sentence nearly 4 years and 4 months. It also made D a long-term prisoner so he had to serve two-thirds of his sentence rather than half. Held. There should have been a hearing in open court so representations could have been made.
R v DH 2014 EWCA Crim 1108 D was sentenced and later the Judge thought some of the sentences were unlawful. His clerk told counsel by e-mail and he purported to vary the sentences. [On a later date], he reconstituted the court and gave both counsel an opportunity to comment about his earlier variation. He then confirmed the sentences. Held. To vary a sentence the Judge must reconstitute the court with the defendant present. The Judge did not properly vary his order on the day of the sentence.
R v G 2014 EWCA Crim 1221 LCJ The Judge forgot to sentence on some counts in a complicated indictment. Court staff pointed this out and the Judge indicated the sentence to them. Held. Yet again, Crown counsel failed in their duty to point this failure out. It is no part of the way justice is conducted that any sentence is imposed other than in open court. The Judge should have returned to court and pronounced the sentences in open court.
R v Cox 2019 EWCA Crim 71 D pleaded to driving and other offences. After communications, both parties were invited to comment about varying the order by an

agreed tag time discount and disqualification under the totting up rules. The parties did so and the sentences were varied to deduct 18 days of tag time and impose 10 months' disqualification. This was done without a hearing. The defendant appealed about the custodial period. Held. That period was not excessive. We see no objection to the agreed tag time being deducted without a hearing. The disqualification should not have been dealt with administratively. D was opposing an order being made. Despite both parties being content with the procedure, potential disqualification was a serious matter. It should have been dealt with in open court with the defendant present. The public should be able to [see justice being done]. The sentence remains valid and we uphold both variations, which the defence don't challenge.

R v Holland 2019 EWCA Crim 481 The Judge intended to apply a full plea discount but only applied a 25% discount. Defence counsel e-mailed the Judge pointing out the error. The Judge simply corrected the error without a hearing. The defence appealed on other grounds. Held. A hearing was necessary to ensure open justice. However, the fact there was no hearing did not render the variation a nullity.

Old case: *R v Dowling* 1989 88 Cr App R 88 (If a judge is minded to vary a sentence he has passed or even to clarify a doubt or ambiguity as to the effect of it, he should do so in open court. He should not do it behind the scenes or by transmitting a message. Only if the matter is finally resolved in open court will all concerned and the public hear the final decision from the judge himself and in his own terms. Only thus will a shorthand note be recorded and available.)

112.18 *Attendance of the defendant*

Criminal Procedure Rules 2015 2015/1490 Rule 28.4(4) The court must not exercise its power in the defendant's absence unless:

(a) the court makes a variation:

(i) which is proposed by the defendant, or

(ii) the effect of which is that the defendant is no more severely dealt with under the sentence as varied than before, or

(b) the defendant has had an opportunity to make representations at a hearing (whether or not the defendant in fact attends).

R v Cleere 1983 5 Cr App R (S) 465 The Judge passed a suspended sentence on D after hearing he had been reunited with his wife and was now in employment. D then went to Ireland and his wife wrote to the Court saying she was not reunited with D and D was not in employment. The case was re-listed. A lexigram was sent to D's home. At the hearing D was not present and his solicitors withdrew saying they could no longer act for him. The Judge decided D did not deserve a suspended sentence and changed the sentence to an immediate one. Held. The Judge should not have altered the sentence without giving D or his counsel an opportunity to address the Court. The sentence of immediate imprisonment was null and void.

R v Perkins and Others 2013 EWCA Crim 323, 2 Cr App R (S) 72 (p 461) D pleaded to historical sexual offences. The Judge sought, in D's absence, to vary downwards the sentences originally imposed. The case was not formally listed and counsel were present by coincidence. The Judge observed that to require D to travel to court would be detrimental to his health and he proceeded to order the variation. Held. The case should be listed so…the defendant [is] present. This was effectively a private hearing. That should not happen.

R v E 2014 EWCA Crim 1105 The defendant should have been present, see **112.17**.

R v Warren 2017 EWCA Crim 226, 2 Cr App R (S) 5 The defendant, D, was not brought to court because of an 'administrative slip'. The Judge increased D's sentence, saying his advocate was well able to make submissions. Held. Sentencing and re-sentencing should take place in the presence of the [defendant] and administrative convenience should not be allowed to degrade that principle. But if for one reason or another the defendant cannot be brought to court in the 56 days, there is a discretion to proceed in his absence

so long as there is an advocate who is properly instructed and is able to make pertinent submissions, [which D's] advocate was. Re-listing the case was the preferable course. However, the Judge could hear the application in the absence of D.
Note: Many would consider the defendant should have been able to hear why he will serve a longer term and the case should have been adjourned. A slip-up is the lamest of excuses for denying D his important right. If D is not there, justice is seriously eroded. Rule 28.4(4)(b) makes the rest of the rule worthless. Interestingly, the Judges' decision is contrary to the principle they stated. Ed.
For more detail see **112.3**.
R v Ghaus 2018 EWCA Crim 1209 After a muddled sentencing hearing, prosecution counsel pointed out an inconsistency. The Judge (a Recorder) then appeared to alter the sentence. Both counsel tried to work out what the sentence was and decided to go back into Court to seek help. In Court, without the defendant, the Judge said the sentence was 38 months. It wasn't clear whether this was a statement of what the sentence was or a variation. After that defence counsel were told that the Judge without the attendance of anyone had increased the sentence to 45 months. Held. The sentencing remarks were riddled with errors and contradictory findings. A section of them was deplorable. For the second hearing, the Court erred by increasing the sentence in the absence of the defendant, contrary to Rule 28.4(4). [There was another variation hearing on a later date in which the sentencing remarks were also defective.]
R v Cox 2019 EWCA Crim 71 Amending an order to deduct agreed tag time could be done without the defendant. Dealing with totting up should be dealt with in open court with the defendant present, see **112.17**.
Old case: *R v May* 1981 3 Cr App R (S) 165 (LCJ The defendant is entitled to be present throughout every stage of the sentencing procedure. He is entitled to be represented. These variations were null and void.)

112.19 *Crown Court Correcting mistakes after time limits have expired*

Lawrie v Lees 1881 7 App Cas 19, at 34-35 Under the original powers of the court, quite independent of any order that is made under the Judicature Act, every court has the power to vary its own orders which are drawn up mechanically in the registry or in the office of the court, to vary them in such a way as to carry out its own meaning, and where language has been used which is doubtful, to make it plain. That power is inherent in every court.
Re Swire 1885 30 Ch D 239 Court of Appeal We recognise that the court has an inherent jurisdiction over its own orders. The court has jurisdiction over its own records, and if it finds that the order as passed and entered contains an adjudication upon that which the court in fact has never adjudicated, then it has jurisdiction which it will in a proper case exercise, to correct its record, that it may be in accordance with the order really pronounced. Every court has inherent power over its own records as long as those records are within its power, and that it can set right any mistake in them. It seems to me that it would be perfectly shocking if the court could not rectify an error which is really the error of its own minister.
R v Michael 1976 QB 414 Crown Court Judge D was acquitted and asked for his costs. The order was granted but no reference was made to the costs of the committal proceedings. The taxing official refused to pay those costs and the case was re-listed after the time limits had expired. Held. It has long been recognised that a court may have power to alter or recall an order which it has made before that order has been perfected by entry in the court's records. This is a power which is well recognised in the civil courts. It would appear to have been a power exercised by courts of assize and quarter sessions, aided by the fiction that the order was not entered or perfected until the last day of the assizes or sessions. This power is reflected in Courts Act 1971 s 11(2) and accordingly there is considerable force in the argument that section 11(2) has by necessary implications limited the power to alter or recall an order in the Crown Court to the circumstances mentioned in that subsection.

Quite apart from the power to alter or recall an order before it has been perfected by entry, the cases show that the court can have an inherent jurisdiction to amend or rectify the order recorded in its record to make such record accord with the order intended by the court. I apply *Lawrie v Lees* 1881 7 App Cas 19 and *Re Swire* 1885 30 Ch D 239 where the Court of Appeal recognised that it has such an inherent jurisdiction over its own orders. The Court of Appeal, like the Crown Court, was created by statute and accordingly this decision establishes that statutory creation of a court is no bar to that court having that inherent jurisdiction.

R v Saville 1980 2 Cr App R (S) 26 LCJ The Judge made a Criminal Bankruptcy Order. He omitted to specify the 'amount of the loss or damage appearing to have resulted from the offences' as required by Powers of Criminal Courts Act 1973 s 39(3)(a).[1221] After the time limits had expired, the error was drawn to the Judge's attention and he made the necessary specification. The defence said the order was defective and it was too late to vary the order. Held. This case can be distinguished from earlier authorities such as *Customs v Menocal* 1980 by virtue of the total unimportance of the alteration performed. We are reinforced in our view by the first instance case of *R v Michael* 1976. The correction can be regarded as an adjustment of an inchoate order which at that moment existed.

R v Onwuka 1992 13 Cr App R (S) 486 The Judge made a confiscation order but failed to make a prison in default order, failed to issue a certificate for the amount as required and made other failures. Two years later when the order was known to be unenforceable, the prosecution asked the Judge to correct the errors made. The Judge did so, relying on *R v Saville* 1980. A prison in default term of 2 years was made. Held. It could not be said that the omission to impose a sentence in default of 2 years was 'of such a character that, if it had been mentioned before the order had been entered, the omission would have been supplied as a matter of course without further argument'. Here the sum ordered to be confiscated was at the lowest end of the bracket and most counsel would have contended, and many a sentencer would have agreed, that it would not be appropriate to impose the maximum term in default. Not only was an additional penalty imposed, but the term to be served in default of payment was greater than it need have been. The variation was in error so we quash the confiscation order.

R v Bukhari 2008 EWCA Crim 2915, 2009 2 Cr App R (S) 18 (p 114) The prosecution asked for confiscation proceedings to be conducted under Criminal Justice Act 1988 when it should have been made under Proceeds of Crime Act 2002. The Judge made such a confiscation order. The flaw was noticed and the case was brought back to court, but long after the then 28-day time limit had passed. The Judge accepted that the time limit was not elastic, but he sought to substitute a reference to the 1988 Act for a reference to the 2002 Act. The reasons given were: a) had the correct Act been used for the proceedings D would have consented to the order, and b) D was not disadvantaged by the variation. Held. Neither reason was valid. The order was unlawful. The variation was unlawful. Order quashed. However, applying Criminal Appeal Act 1968 s 11(3) (power to substitute sentences) and following *R v Lazarus* 2004 EWCA Crim 2297, 2005 1 Cr App R (S) 98 (p 552), the Court substituted a confiscation order under Proceeds of Crime Act 2002.

R v Aldridge and Eaton 2012 EWCA Crim 1456 LCJ E was given a 3-year SOPO. Later the Judge was told the minimum period was 5 years. The transcript showed the order was made for 3 years. The Judge thought he had made the order for 5 years and purported to make an administrative correction. Held. The Judge could not have varied the order under section 155 as it was out of time and no one attended. The 5-year order was unlawful. The Judge could not extend it and neither can we. Order quashed.

[1221] Repealed by Criminal Justice Act 1988 Sch 16 para 1 on 1/1/00

See also: *R v Lazarus* 2004 EWCA Crim 2297, 2005 1 Cr App R (S) 98 (p 552) (The confiscation order was made under the wrong Act. Applying Criminal Appeal Act 1968 s 11(3) (power to substitute sentences) the Court substituted a confiscation order under the right Act.)
Note: There are of course many cases indicating that it is not possible to vary outside the time limit and that principle should normally be applied. Ed.

112.20 ***Importance of finality in sentencing***
Holmes v Liverpool City JJs 2004 EWHC 3131 (Admin) High Court D was convicted of dangerous driving. The victim's mother-in-law wrote to Lord Justice Thomas expressing absolute disgust at the sentence and the total destruction of the lives of so many people. The letter was sent to the Magistrates' Court and an investigation occurred. Some five months after the complaint was received the matter was re-listed. Held. It is very important to bear in mind the principle of finality in sentencing. This is a matter which has been made clear by the House of Lords in *R v Secretary of State for the Home Dept ex parte Pierson* 1998 AC 539 at p 585, 'It is a general principle of the common law that a lawful sentence pronounced by a judge may not retrospectively be increased. The general principle of our law is therefore that a convicted criminal is entitled to know where he stands so far as his punishment is concerned. He is entitled to legal certainty about his punishment. His rights will be enforced by the courts. In enacting Criminal Justice Act 1991 s 35(2), with its very wide power to release prisoners, Parliament left untouched the fundamental principle that a sentence lawfully passed should not retrospectively be increased. The minimum standard of fairness does not permit a person to be punished twice for the same offence. Nor does it permit a person, once he has been told what his punishment is to be, to be given in substitution for it a more severe punishment.' That case was a challenge to the Secretary of State's exercise of a power that he believed he had to increase the tariff on life sentences following convictions for murder. The principle of finality is an important consideration. It must be recognised that Parliament has with the greatest care and circumspection indicated when and how there should be, in relation to the Crown Court, a power to increase sentence. The answer that it gives is only if the sentence can be regarded as unduly lenient, and then only in relation to a relatively small number of indictable offences. It is a jurisdiction clearly that has to be exercised with care. Furthermore, there is, undoubtedly, an element of double jeopardy that is recognised in all cases where the Court of Appeal is persuaded that a sentence was unduly lenient. It will not then impose the full sentence that would have been appropriate.
For more details, see **112.8**.
R v Bestel and Others 2013 EWCA Crim 1305, 2014 1 Cr App R (S) 53 (p 312) D and others applied to appeal their confiscation orders out of time following the decision in *R v Waya* 2012 UKSC 51, 2013 2 Cr App R (S) 20 (p 87). The Court considered an extensive selection of precedents. Held. para 23 The principle of finality was applied in *Serious Organised Crime Agency v O'Docherty* 2013 EWCA Civ 518, subject to the need to avoid substantial injustice. The Court found on the facts that there would be no substantial injustice in declining to permit the re-opening of a judicial decision on grounds which could have been but were not argued at the time it was made. The recent pronouncements in both divisions of the Court of Appeal and in the Supreme Court as to the importance and primacy of the principle of finality have the effect of requiring the most exceptional circumstances before an applicant may be permitted to argue that the new law should apply to his old case and that, otherwise, a substantial injustice will be caused. para 31 The principle of finality that decisions made under the law as it was then understood should not be disturbed unless substantial injustice would follow is well recognised and we must apply it.
For more detail see **4.14**.

112.21 ***No power until after an appeal is determined***
Powers of Criminal Courts (Sentencing) Act 2000 s 155(1A) The power conferred by subsection (1) may not be exercised in relation to any sentence or order if an appeal, or an application for leave to appeal, against that sentence or order has been determined.
Change in law see also the **CONFISCATION** ***Appeals after a change in the case law*** para at **21.152**.

Miscellaneous matters

112.22 ***When does the varied sentence take effect? Crown Court***
Powers of Criminal Courts (Sentencing) Act 2000 s 155(5) Subject to subsection (6) below, where a sentence or other order is varied under this section the sentence or other order, as so varied, shall take effect from the beginning of the day on which it was originally imposed or made, unless the court otherwise directs.

112.23 ***When does the varied sentence take effect? Notices of appeal***
Powers of Criminal Courts (Sentencing) Act 2000 s 155(6) For the purposes of:

(a) Criminal Appeal Act 1968 s 18(2) (time limit for notice of appeal or of application for leave to appeal), and

(b) Criminal Justice Act 1988 Sch 3 para 1 (time limit for notice of an application for leave to refer a case under section 36 of that Act),

the sentence or other order shall be regarded as imposed or made on the day on which it is varied under this section.

112.24 ***When does the varied sentence take effect? Magistrates' Court***
Magistrates' Courts Act 1980 s 142(5) Where a sentence or order is varied under subsection (1) above, the sentence or other order, as so varied, shall take effect from the beginning of the day on which it was originally imposed or made, unless the court otherwise directs.

112.25 ***Defendant appeals then sentence varied***
Example: *R v Egginton* 2016 EWCA Crim 1775, 2017 1 Cr App R (S) 20 (p 142) (Defendant, D, given 10 years. D appeals. Then Judge varies sentence to 6 years. Defence say they told the Court, which was not received. Single Judge unaware of variation, grants leave. Held. Leave was granted on a false basis. Counsel should have drafted revised grounds of appeal.)

113 VICTIM PERSONAL STATEMENTS/VICTIM IMPACT STATEMENTS

113.1
Code of Practice for Victims of Crime 2015 lays down a whole series of measures for victims with their entitlements and how their victim impact statements etc. should be dealt with by the court.
Criminal Practice Directions 2015 EWCA Crim 1567 para VII F refers to victim statements as 'victim personal statements'. Where there has been a fatality, members of the deceased's family may make a 'family impact statement'. Both these statements have been often called 'victim impact statements'. The new directions put 'community impact statements' on a formal basis. These statements are written by the police. Business impact statements are introduced.

113.2 ***Introduction***
Criminal Practice Directions 2015 EWCA Crim 1567 para VII F.1 Victims of crime are invited to make a statement, known as a victim personal statement (VPS). The statement gives victims a formal opportunity to say how a crime has affected them. It may help to identify whether they have a particular need for information, support and protection. The court will take the statement into account when determining sentence. In some circumstances, it may be appropriate for relatives of a victim to make a VPS, for example where the victim has died as a result of the relevant criminal conduct. The revised *Code*

of Practice for Victims of Crime 2013 gives further information about victims' entitlements within the criminal justice system, and the duties placed on criminal justice agencies when dealing with victims of crime.
Note: There is now a *Code of Practice for Victims of Crime 2015*. Ed.

113.3 ***Purpose***
R v Perkins and Others 2013 EWCA Crim 323, 2 Cr App R (S) 72 (p 461) The purpose of victim personal statements is to allow victims a more structured opportunity to explain how they have been affected by the crime. They are a way of ensuring that the court will consider, in accordance with Criminal Justice Act 2003 s 143, 'any harm which the offence caused'. They also identify a need for additional or specific support or protection for the victims of crime, to be considered at the end of the sentencing process. The *Guide for Police Officers, Investigators and Criminal Practitioners* is entirely consistent with the Practice Direction. It records: 'The VPS is the victim's chance to:
(a) explain in their own words how the crime has affected them, either physically, emotionally, financially or in any other way,
(b) express legitimate concerns, such as feeling vulnerable, fearful, intimidated or worried about the alleged offender being granted bail,
(c) say if they intend to seek compensation…,
(d) request referral to Victim Support or to other agencies who might help them.'

113.4 ***Need for victim impact statements***
Example: *R v Ismail* 2005 EWCA Crim 397, 2 Cr App R (S) 88 (p 542) LCJ The defendant was convicted of rape. He was sentenced without the Judge having a pre-sentence report. Held. That is regrettable. [It should be routine to obtain a victim impact statement in these cases.]

113.5 ***Making the statement***
Criminal Practice Directions 2015 EWCA Crim 1567 para VII F.2 When a police officer takes a statement from a victim, the victim should be told about the scheme and given the chance to make a VPS. The decision about whether or not to make a VPS is entirely a matter for the victim. No pressure should be brought to bear on their decision, and no conclusion should be drawn if they choose not to make such a statement. A VPS or a further VPS may be made (in proper s 9 form, see below) at any time prior to the disposal of the case. It will not normally be appropriate for a VPS to be made after the disposal of the case. There may be rare occasions between sentence and appeal when a further VPS may be necessary, for example, when the victim was injured and the final prognosis was not available at the date of sentence. However, VPS after disposal should be confined to presenting up-to-date factual material, such as medical information, and should be used sparingly.
Criminal Practice Directions 2015 EWCA Crim 1567 para VII F.3…b) Evidence of the effects of an offence on the victim contained in the VPS or other statement must be in proper form, that is a witness statement made under Criminal Justice Act 1967 s 9 or an expert's report.
The *Guide for Police Officers, Investigators and Criminal Practitioners* The VPS must not include the victim's [view] about how the offender should be punished. That is for the magistrate or judge to decide.
R v Perkins and Others 2013 EWCA Crim 323, 2 Cr App R (S) 72 (p 461) para 9 The decision whether to make a statement must be made by the victims personally. They must be provided with information which makes it clear that they are entitled to make a statement, but no pressure, either way, should be brought to bear on their decision. The process does not create an opportunity for the victim of crime to suggest or discuss the type or level of sentence to be imposed. The statement constitutes evidence. That is the basis on which it is admitted. It must therefore be treated as evidence. It must be in a formal witness statement.

113.6 *Victims should be advised that their opinions about the sentence are not relevant*
Criminal Practice Directions 2015 EWCA Crim 1567 para VII F.3…e) The opinions of the victim or the victim's close relatives as to what the sentence should be are therefore not relevant, unlike the consequences of the offence on them. Victims should be advised of this. If, despite the advice, opinions as to sentence are included in the statement, the court should pay no attention to them.
See also the VICTIMS ***Views of the victims about the sentence*** para at **113.6**.

113.7 *The statement must be served*
Criminal Practice Directions 2015 EWCA Crim 1567 para VII F.3…b) The VPS or other statement must be…served in good time upon the defendant's solicitor or the defendant, if he or she is not represented.
R v Perkins and Others 2013 EWCA Crim 323, 2 Cr App R (S) 72 (p 461) The VPS must be served on the defendant's legal advisors in time for the defendant's instructions to be taken and for any objection to the use of the statement, or part of it, if necessary, to be prepared. For one of the cases, the statement was handed over far too late in the process. Late service of the statements is wholly inappropriate and…wrong in principle. It must stop.

113.8 *Victim can read their statement or have it read for them*
Criminal Practice Directions 2015 EWCA Crim 1567 para VII F.3…c) At the discretion of the court, the VPS may also be read aloud or played in open court, in whole or in part, or it may be summarised. If the VPS is to be read aloud, the court should also determine who should do so. In making these decisions, the court should take account of the victim's preferences, and follow them unless there is good reason not to do so. Examples of this include the inadmissibility of the content or the potentially harmful consequences for the victim or others. Court hearings should not be adjourned solely to allow the victim to attend court to read the VPS. For the purposes of [the then] Criminal Practice Directions 2015 EWCA Crim 1567 para I 5B: Access to information held by the court, a VPS that is read aloud or played in open court in whole or in part should be considered as such, and no longer treated as a confidential document.
The *Code of Practice for Victims of Crime 2015* Part A para 1.20 provides similar instructions.

113.9 *Proper approach of the court*
Criminal Practice Directions 2015 EWCA Crim 1567 para VII F.3 If the court is presented with a VPS the following approach, subject to the further guidance given by the Court of Appeal in *R v Perkins and Others* 2013 EWCA Crim 323, 2 Cr App R (S) 72 (p 461), should be adopted:..b) Evidence of the effects of an offence on the victim contained in the VPS or other statement must be in proper form, that is a witness statement made under Criminal Justice Act 1967 s 9 or an expert's report, and served in good time upon the defendant's solicitor or the defendant, if he or she is not represented. Except where inferences can properly be drawn from the nature of or circumstances surrounding the offence, a sentencing court must not make assumptions unsupported by evidence about the effects of an offence on the victim. The maker of a VPS may be cross-examined on its content.
Criminal Practice Directions 2015 EWCA Crim 1567 para VII F.3…e) The court must pass what it judges to be the appropriate sentence having regard to the circumstances of the offence and of the offender, taking into account, so far as the court considers it appropriate, the impact on the victim.
Domestic Abuse Guideline 2018, see banksr.com Other Matters Guidelines tab In force 24 May 2018 page 4 para 10

10. A sentence imposed for an offence committed within a domestic context should be determined by the seriousness of the offence, not by **any** expressed wishes of the victim. There are a number of reasons why it may be particularly important that this principle is observed within this context:

- The court is sentencing on behalf of the wider public
- No victim is responsible for the sentence imposed
- There is a risk that a plea for mercy made by a victim will be induced by threats made by, or by a fear of, the offender
- The risk of such threats will be increased if it is generally believed that the severity of the sentence may be affected by the wishes of the victim.

Domestic Abuse Guideline 2018, see banksr.com Other Matters Guidelines tab In force 24 May 2018 page 5 para 23

VICTIM PERSONAL STATEMENTS

23. The absence of a Victim Personal Statement (VPS) should not be taken to indicate the absence of harm. A court should consider, where available, a VPS which will help it assess the immediate and possible long-term effects of the offence on the victim (and any children, where relevant) as well as the harm caused, whether physical or psychological.

R v H 1999 The Times 18/3/99 Statements from the victims will be approached with proper care. They necessarily reflect one side only of a complex situation.

R v Perks 2001 1 Cr App R (S) 19 (p 66) D pleaded to robbery. The Judge's papers included a document from the CPS, which said, 'The actions of this greedy, self-indulgent, irresponsible, mindless and spoilt thug have forever ruined the carefree life of a caring woman. What about the victim of this crime, she is totally and utterly innocent, yet she is going to pay for someone else's crime for the rest of her life. Why? Jail him! Make an example of him to others who think that drugs are socially acceptable. They are not!!' It was from the victim's husband and was not disclosed to the defence. Held. The Court shares the concern of defence counsel about the document. A number of propositions can be derived from the authorities: a) a sentencer must not make assumptions, unsupported by evidence, about the effects of an offence on the victim, b) if an offence has had a particularly damaging or distressing effect upon a victim, this should be known to and taken into account by the court when passing sentence, and c) evidence of the victim alone should be approached with care, the more so if it relates to matters which the defence cannot realistically be expected to investigate. It is to be hoped that in future 'victim impact statements' will be in proper form as envisaged by this court in *R v Hobstaff* 1993 14 Cr App R (S) 605.

R v Perkins and Others 2013 EWCA Crim 323, 2 Cr App R (S) 72 (p 461) The process does not create an opportunity for the victim of crime to suggest or discuss the type or level of sentence to be imposed.

113.10 *Use that can be made of the statement*

Criminal Practice Directions 2015 EWCA Crim 1567 para VII F.3…b) Except where inferences can properly be drawn from the nature of or circumstances surrounding the offence, a sentencing court must not make assumptions unsupported by evidence about the effects of an offence on the victim. The maker of a VPS [victim personal statement] may be cross-examined on its content.

R v Perkins and Others 2013 EWCA Crim 323, 2 Cr App R (S) 72 (p 461) In the selection of any passages for quotation or summary, the advocate and indeed the judge must be very sensitive to the position of the victim, and on occasions the need to respect the victim's privacy. The statement may be challenged, in cross-examination, and it may give rise to disclosure obligations, and as the case of one of these defendants underlines, may be used, after conviction, to deploy an argument that the credibility of the victim is open to question.

113.11 *Business impact statements*

Criminal Practice Directions 2015 EWCA Crim 1567 para VII I.1[1222] Individual victims of crime are invited to make a statement, known as a Victim Personal Statement ('VPS'), see CPD VII Sentencing F. If a victim, or one of those others affected by a crime, is a business, enterprise or other body (including a charity or public body, for example a school or hospital), of any size, a nominated representative may make an Impact Statement for Business ('ISB'). The ISB gives a formal opportunity for the court to be informed how a crime has affected a business or other body. The court will take the statement into account when determining sentence. This does not prevent individual employees from making a VPS about the impact of the same crime on them as individuals. Indeed, the ISB should be about the impact on the business or other body exclusively, and the impact on any individual included within a VPS.

I.2 When a police officer takes statements about the alleged offence, he or she should also inform the business or other body about the scheme. An ISB may be made to the police at that time, or the ISB template may be downloaded from www.police.uk, completed and emailed or posted to the relevant police contact. Guidance on how to complete the form is available on www.police.uk and on the CPS website. There is no obligation to make an ISB.

I.3 An ISB or an updated ISB may be made (in proper [section 9 form, see below, not listed]) at any time prior to the disposal of the case. It will not be appropriate for an ISB to be made after disposal of the case but before an appeal.

I.4 A business or other body wishing to make an ISB should consider carefully who to nominate as the representative to make the statement on its behalf. A person making an ISB on behalf of such a business or body, the nominated representative, must be authorised to do so on its behalf, either by nature of their position, such as a director or owner or a senior official, or by having been suitably authorised, such as by the owner or Board of Directors or governing body. The nominated representative must also be in a position to give admissible evidence about the impact of the crime on the business or body. This will usually be through first hand personal knowledge, or using business documents (as defined in section 117 of the Criminal Justice Act 2003). The most appropriate person will vary depending on the nature of the crime, and the size and structure of the business or other body and may for example include a manager, director, chief executive or shop owner.

I.5 If the nominated representative leaves the business before the case comes to court, he or she will usually remain the representative, as the ISB made by him or her will still provide the best evidence of the impact of the crime, and he or she could still be asked to attend court. Nominated representatives should be made aware of the on-going nature of the role at the time of making the ISB.

I.6 If necessary a further ISB may be provided to the police if there is a change in circumstances. This could be made by an alternative nominated representative. However, the new ISB will usually supplement, not replace, the original ISB and again must contain admissible evidence. The prosecutor will decide which ISB to serve on the defence as evidence, and any ISB that is not served in evidence will be included in the unused material and considered for disclosure to the defence.

I.7 The ISB must be made in proper form, that is as a witness statement made under section 9 of the Criminal Justice Act 1967 or an expert's report; and served in good time upon the defendant's solicitor or the defendant, if he or she is not represented. The maker of an ISB can be cross-examined on its content.

I.8 The ISB and any evidence in support should be considered and taken into account by the court, prior to passing sentence. The statement should be referred to in the course of

[1222] As substituted by Criminal Practice Directions 2015 Amendment 8 2019 EWCA Crim 495 para 7. In force 1/4/19.

the sentencing hearing and/or in the sentencing remarks. Subject to the court's discretion, the contents of the statement may be summarised or read out in open court; the views of the business or body should be taken into account in reaching a decision.
I.9 The court must pass what it judges to be the appropriate sentence having regard to the circumstances of the offence and of the offender, taking into account, so far as the court considers it appropriate, the impact on the victims and others affected, including any business or other corporate victim. Opinions as to what the sentence should be are therefore not relevant. If, despite the advice, opinions as to sentence are included in the statement, the court should pay no attention to them.
I.10 Except where inferences can properly be drawn from the nature of or circumstances surrounding the offence, a sentencing court must not make assumptions unsupported by evidence about the effects of an offence on a business or other body.

113.12 ***Community impact statements***
Criminal Practice Directions 2015 EWCA Crim 1567 para VII H.1 A community impact statement may be prepared by the police to make the court aware of particular crime trends in the local area and the impact of these on the local community.
H.2 Such statements must be in proper form, that is a witness statement made under Criminal Justice Act 1967 s 9 or an expert's report, and served in good time upon the defendant's solicitor or the defendant, if he is not represented.
H.3 The community impact statement and any evidence in support should be considered and taken into account by the court, prior to passing sentence. The statement should be referred to in the course of the sentencing hearing and/or in the sentencing remarks. Subject to the court's discretion, the contents of the statement may be summarised or read out in open court.
H.4 The court must pass what it judges to be the appropriate sentence having regard to the circumstances of the offence and of the offender, taking into account, so far as the court considers it appropriate, the impact on the local community.
Criminal Practice Directions 2015 EWCA Crim 1567 para VII H.6 It will not be appropriate for a community impact statement to be made after disposal of the case but before an appeal.
R v Skelton 2014 EWCA Crim 2409, 2015 1 Cr App R (S) 34 (p 265) D pleaded to possession of cocaine with intent to supply. 20 grams and 190 grams of cocaine were found with zip-lock bags and scales. He was in breach of a suspended sentence for supplying cannabis. A police officer wrote a community impact statement saying in effect that D was one of the biggest and nastiest dealers of cocaine and other drugs in the area and had been so over the last three to four years. The Judge said that she could not take such a view into account and also said [referring to the officer's remark] "it seems that everything that was said about [D] in that report has been borne out". Held. It was not appropriate to give the impression, albeit mistaken, that he was being sentenced [with that remark in mind]. These reports should be limited to expressing the effect of a particular crime in a particular community and most certainly should not be used as a character assassination of defendants. **6 years** not 7 for the cocaine.

113.13 ***Sentencing remarks and victim statements***
Criminal Practice Directions 2015 EWCA Crim 1567 para VII F.3…d) In all cases it will be appropriate for a VPS to be referred to in the course of the sentencing hearing and/or in the sentencing remarks.

113.14 ***Victim impact statements for the Court of Appeal***
R v Perkins and Others 2013 EWCA Crim 323, 2 Cr App R (S) 72 (p 461) para 12 It will seldom be appropriate for a statement to be introduced at a sentencing appeal if it was not before the sentencing court. Obviously there will be occasions when an update to the statement is appropriate. If so, the formalities must continue to be observed. In this court the purpose of the statement is unchanged. It cannot be used for the purposes of arguing that the sentence was excessive or lenient. Just because of the need for flexibility, there

will be occasions when, as in the Crown Court, the court will permit the victim of the crime (see para 50) to give evidence in the form of reading a properly prepared and timeously served further statement.

114 Victims

114.1

The *Code of Practice for Victims of Crime 2015* lays down a whole series of measures about their entitlements. It is based on the Directive on Victims' Rights 2012/29/EU and the *Code of Practice for Victims of Crime 2013*.

See also the **Victim Personal Statements/Victim Impact Statements** chapter.

114.2 ***AIDS Victim fears that he or she has contracted AIDS from the sex attack***

R v Malcolm 1988 9 Cr App R (S) 487 The victim was raped and feared that she might contract AIDS. There was no evidence she had. The Judge added 2 years to the sentence because of the fear. Held. That was not justified. Sentence reduced from 12 years to 10.

R v Twigg 1988 Unreported 8/6/88 D was convicted of inciting a boy to commit an act of gross indecency with a woman. There was no evidence that the woman had AIDS. Held. The risk that the woman had AIDS was so slight it should be ignored. Because of the Judge's remarks about it, the sentence was reduced.

See also the **Defendant *AIDS/HIV, Defendant has*** para at **241.1** in Volume 2.

114.3 ***Emergency workers***

Commencement This Act came into force on 13 November 2018.[1223]

Assaults on Emergency Workers (Offences) Act 2018 s 1 [Common assault offence, see **225.1** in Volume 2]

Aggravating factor

2(1) This section applies where:

(a) the court is considering for the purposes of sentencing the seriousness of an offence listed in subsection (3), and

(b) the offence was committed against an emergency worker acting in the exercise of functions as such a worker.

(2) The court:

(a) must treat the fact mentioned in subsection (1)(b) as an aggravating factor (that is to say, a factor that increases the seriousness of the offence), and

(b) must state in open court that the offence is so aggravated.

(3) The offences referred to in subsection (1)(a) are:

(a) an offence under any of the following provisions of the Offences against the Person Act 1861:

(i) section 16 (threats to kill);

(ii) section 18 (wounding with intent to cause grievous bodily harm);

(iii) section 20 (malicious wounding);

(iv) section 23 (administering poison etc);

(v) section 28 (causing bodily injury by gunpowder etc);

(vi) section 29 (using explosive substances etc with intent to cause grievous bodily harm);

(vii) section 47 (assault occasioning actual bodily harm);

(b) an offence under section 3 of the Sexual Offences Act 2003 (sexual assault);

(c) manslaughter;

(d) kidnapping;

(e) an ancillary offence in relation to any of the preceding offences.

(4) For the purposes of subsection (1)(b), the circumstances in which an offence is to be taken as committed against a person acting in the exercise of functions as an emergency

[1223] Assaults on Emergency Workers (Offences) Act 2018 s 4(2)

worker include circumstances where the offence takes place at a time when the person is not at work but is carrying out functions which, if done in work time, would have been in the exercise of functions as an emergency worker.
(5) In this section: "ancillary offence", in relation to an offence, means any of the following:
(a) aiding, abetting, counselling or procuring the commission of the offence;
(b) an offence under Part 2 of the Serious Crime Act 2007 (encouraging or assisting crime) in relation to the offence;
(c) attempting or conspiring to commit the offence; "emergency worker" has the meaning given by section 3.
(6) Nothing in this section prevents a court from treating the fact mentioned in subsection (1)(b) as an aggravating factor in relation to offences not listed in subsection (3).
(7) This section applies only in relation to offences committed on or after the day it comes into force.
Consultation The Sentencing Council expects to issue a consultation document for emergency workers in October 2019 and aims to publish a definitive guideline in early 2021.

114.4 *Emergency workers, meaning of*

Commencement This Act came into force on 13 November 2018.[1224]
Meaning of "emergency worker"
Assaults on Emergency Workers (Offences) Act 2018 s 3(1)-(2) In sections 1 and 2, "emergency worker" means:
(a) a constable;
(b) a person (other than a constable) who has the powers of a constable or is otherwise employed for police purposes or is engaged to provide services for police purposes;
(c) a National Crime Agency officer;
(d) a prison officer;
(e) a person (other than a prison officer) employed or engaged to carry out functions in a custodial institution of a corresponding kind to those carried out by a prison officer;
(f) a prisoner custody officer, so far as relating to the exercise of escort functions;
(g) a custody officer, so far as relating to the exercise of escort functions;
(h) a person employed for the purposes of providing, or engaged to provide, fire services or fire and rescue services;
(i) a person employed for the purposes of providing, or engaged to provide, search services or rescue services (or both);
(j) a person employed for the purposes of providing, or engaged to provide:
(i) NHS health services, or
(ii) services in the support of the provision of NHS health services, and whose general activities in doing so involve face to face interaction with individuals receiving the services or with other members of the public.
(2) It is immaterial for the purposes of subsection (1) whether the employment or engagement is paid or unpaid.

114.5 *Emergency workers Other definitions*

Commencement This Act came into force on 13 November 2018.[1225]
Assaults on Emergency Workers (Offences) Act 2018 s 3(3) In this section:
"custodial institution" means any of the following:
(a) a prison;

[1224] Assaults on Emergency Workers (Offences) Act 2018 s 4(2)
[1225] Assaults on Emergency Workers (Offences) Act 2018 s 4(2)

(b) a young offender institution, secure training centre, secure college or remand centre;
(c) a removal centre, a short-term holding facility or pre-departure accommodation, as defined by section 147 of the Immigration and Asylum Act 1999;
(d) services custody premises, as defined by section 300(7) of the Armed Forces Act 2006;

"custody officer" has the meaning given by section 12(3) of the Criminal Justice and Public Order Act 1994;
"escort functions":
(a) in the case of a prisoner custody officer, means the functions specified in section 80(1) of the Criminal Justice Act 1991;
(b) in the case of a custody officer, means the functions specified in paragraph 1 of Schedule 1 to the Criminal Justice and Public Order Act 1994;

"NHS health services" means any kind of health services provided as part of the health service continued under section 1(1) of the National Health Service Act 2006 and under section 1(1) of the National Health Service (Wales) Act 2006;
"prisoner custody officer" has the meaning given by section 89(1) of the Criminal Justice Act 1991.

114.6 *Exploited victims Their reluctance to report offences*

Att-Gen's Ref Nos 2-5 of 2013 2013 EWCA Crim 324, 2 Cr App R (S) 71 (p 451) para 5 Those who are exploited are always and inevitably vulnerable. Just because they are so vulnerable, [they are] profoundly reluctant to report what has happened or is happening to them. It is far from straightforward for them even to complain about the way they are being treated, let alone to report their plight to the authorities so that the offenders might be brought to justice.

114.7 *Hostility towards disabled, gay and transgender victims*

Increase in sentences for aggravation related to disability, sexual orientation or transgender identity

Criminal Justice Act 2003 s 146(1)[1226] This section applies where the court is considering the seriousness of an offence committed in any of the circumstances mentioned in subsection (2).
(2) Those circumstances are:
(a) that, at the time of committing the offence, or immediately before or after doing so, the offender demonstrated towards the victim of the offence hostility based on:
(i) the sexual orientation (or presumed sexual orientation) of the victim,...
(iii) the victim being (or presumed to be) transgender, or
(b) that the offence is motivated (wholly or partly):
(i) by hostility towards persons who are of a particular sexual orientation,...or
(iii) by hostility towards persons who are transgender.
(3) The court:
(a) must treat the fact that the offence was committed in any of those circumstances as an aggravating factor, and
(b) must state in open court that the offence was committed in such circumstances.
(4) It is immaterial for the purposes of paragraph (a) or (b) of subsection (2) whether or not the offender's hostility is also based, to any extent, on any other factor not mentioned in that paragraph.
(5) In this section 'disability' means any physical or mental impairment.
(6) In this section references to being transgender include references to being transsexual, or undergoing, proposing to undergo or having undergone a process or part of a process of gender reassignment.

[1226] This section includes the amendments made by Legal Aid, Sentencing and Punishment of Offenders Act 2012 s 65(4)-(6).

Note: Armed Forces Act 2006 s 241 contains an identical section save for a different description for the court. Ed.

Overarching Principles: Seriousness Guideline 2004, see www.banksr.com Other Matters Guidelines tab para 120 Factors indicating higher culpability [are]…4 Offence motivated by, or demonstrating, hostility to the victim based on his or her sexual orientation (or presumed sexual orientation).

Gay victims, see the **Rape and Assault by Penetration** ***Sexual orientation, Hostility to/Motivated against*** para at **314.58** in Volume 2.

114.8 *Gays treated as vulnerable victims*

Example: *R v Garner* 2014 EWCA Crim 926 (Plea to manslaughter and attempted robbery. There were a series of robberies on a towpath where gays met for casual sex. A group followed V5 and tried to rob him. That was frustrated and V5 was pushed in the canal and drowned. The Judge commented that the men who visited the area were vulnerable because those who preyed on them did so knowing that their victims were unlikely to complain because of their situation. 10 years upheld. For more detail, see **283.16** in Volume 2.)

114.9 *Hostility towards disabled, gay and transgender victims Sexual orientation-Meaning*

Public Order Act 1986 s 29AB In this Part [of this Act] 'hatred on the grounds of sexual orientation' means hatred against a group of persons defined by reference to sexual orientation (whether towards persons of the same sex, the opposite sex or both).

Equality Act 2010 s 12(1) Sexual orientation means a person's sexual orientation towards: a) persons of the same sex, b) persons of the opposite sex, or c) persons of either sex.

R v Pinchion 2013 EWCA Crim 242 D pleaded (full credit) to ABH. D and his co-accused wrongly believed V to be a paedophile. D sat astride V and punched him several times in the face, taunting him. Held. It was wrong to treat presumed paedophilia as coming within the Guideline's aggravating factor of an offence motivated by hostility based on sexual orientation.

R v B 2013 EWCA Crim 291, 2 Cr App R (S) 69 (p 443) D pleaded to ABH. He hit V, who he believed had sexually interfered with his stepgranddaughter. The Judge assessed D as having higher culpability because the attack was motivated by hostility towards V's [presumed] sexual orientation, namely D's belief that V was a paedophile. Held. That was not a factor which indicated higher culpability.

114.10 *Medical staff as victims Statute and judicial guidance*

Emergency workers Where the offence is committed on or after 13 November 2018 and is 'committed against' an emergency worker (which includes NHS staff) 'acting in the exercise of [his or her] function', the court is required to treat that fact as an aggravating factor, Assaults on Emergency Workers (Offences) Act 2018 s 2(1)-(3). For more detail and the definition of an 'emergency worker', see **114.4**.

R v McNally 2000 1 Cr App R (S) p 535 The public are rightly concerned about violence towards those employed in hospitals. Doctors, nurses and auxiliary staff often work long hours in difficult circumstances, which may be emotionally draining and are often marked by pressures of many kinds. Such people are entitled to whatever protection the courts can give and those who use physical violence against them should expect a sentence of immediate imprisonment.

Att-Gen's Ref No 69 of 2005 2005 EWCA Crim 3050, 2006 1 Cr App R (S) 130 (p 756) The defendant pleaded guilty to two counts of administering a noxious substance with intent to endanger life. He went to a doctor's surgery with a can of petrol threatening to burn the surgery. *R v McNally* 2000 1 Cr App R (S) p 535 applied.

R v McDermott 2006 EWCA Crim 1899, 2007 1 Cr App R (S) 28 (p 145) In general terms, assaults on medical staff require immediate custody.

114.11 *Mentally disordered victims, Hostility towards*

Criminal Justice Act 2003 s 146(2) Those circumstances are:

(a) that, at the time of committing the offence, or immediately before or after doing so, the offender demonstrated towards the victim of the offence hostility based on:

(i) the sexual orientation (or presumed sexual orientation) of the victim,

(ii) a disability (or presumed disability) of the victim, or

(iii) the victim being (or being presumed to be) transgender, or[1227]

(b) that the offence is motivated (wholly or partly):

(i) by hostility towards persons who are of a particular sexual orientation,

(ii) by hostility towards persons who have a disability or a particular disability, or

(iii) by hostility towards persons who are transgender.[1228]

(3) The court:

(a) must treat the fact that the offence was committed in any of those circumstances as an aggravating factor, and

(b) must state in open court that the offence was committed in such circumstances.

Criminal Justice Act 2003 s 146(5) In this section, 'disability' means any physical or mental impairment.

Note: Armed Forces Act 2006 s 241 contains an identical section for service courts, save for a different description of the court. Ed.

114.12 *Considering bereaved families*

Criminal Practice Directions 2015 EWCA Crim 1567 para VII G.1 In cases in which the victim has died as a result of the relevant criminal conduct, the victim's family is not a party to the proceedings, but does have an interest in the case. Bereaved families have particular entitlements under the Code of Practice for Victims of Crime. All parties should have regard to the needs of the victim's family and ensure that the trial process does not expose bereaved families to avoidable intimidation, humiliation or distress.

G.2 In so far as it is compatible with family members' roles as witnesses, the court should consider the following measures:

a) Practical arrangements being discussed with the family and made in good time before the trial, such as seating for family members in the courtroom; if appropriate, in an alternative area, away from the public gallery.
b) Warning being given to families if the evidence on a certain day is expected to be particularly distressing.
c) Ensuring that appropriate use is made of the scheme for victim personal statements in accordance with the paragraphs above. See also the **VICTIM PERSONAL STATEMENTS/VICTIM IMPACT STATEMENTS** chapter.

G.3 The sentencer should consider providing a written copy of the sentencing remarks to the family after sentence has been passed. Sentencers should tend in favour of providing such a copy, unless there is good reason not to do so, and the copy should be provided as soon as is reasonably practicable after the sentencing hearing.

114.13 *Status of victims in proceedings*

Council of Europe Directive Re Victims 2012 2012/29/EU (9) Crime is a wrong against society as well as a violation of the individual rights of victims. As such, victims of crime should be recognised and treated in a respectful, sensitive and professional manner without discrimination of any kind based on any ground such as race, colour, ethnic or social origin, genetic features, language, religion or belief, political or any other opinion, membership of a national minority, property, birth, disability, age, gender, gender expression, gender identity, sexual orientation, residence status or health. In all contacts with a competent authority operating within the context of criminal proceedings, and any service coming into contact with victims, such as victim support or restorative justice

[1227] Added by Legal Aid, Sentencing and Punishment of Offenders Act 2012 s 65(4)(b)

[1228] Added by Legal Aid, Sentencing and Punishment of Offenders Act 2012 s 65(5)(b)

services, the personal situation and immediate needs, age, gender, possible disability and maturity of victims of crime should be taken into account while fully respecting their physical, mental and moral integrity. Victims of crime should be protected from secondary and repeat victimisation, from intimidation and from retaliation, should receive appropriate support to facilitate their recovery and should be provided with sufficient access to justice.

Council of Europe Directive Re Victims 2012 2012/29/EU (17)...Women victims of gender-based violence and their children often require special support and protection because of the high risk of secondary and repeat victimisation, of intimidation and of retaliation connected with such violence.

Council of Europe Directive Re Victims 2012 2012/29/EU (26) When providing information, sufficient detail should be given to ensure that victims are treated in a respectful manner and to enable them to make informed decisions about their participation in proceedings. In this respect, information allowing the victim to know about the current status of any proceedings is particularly important.

Note: This is a very small part of the directive, which was the basis for the MoJ *Code of Practice for Victims of Crime 2013*, and which was updated to become the *Code of Practice for Victims of Crime 2015*. Ed.

Gueye and Sanchez v Spain 2011 C-483/09 ECJ The Framework Decision 2001/220/JHA does not impose an obligation on Member States to ensure that victims will be treated in a manner equivalent to that of a party to proceedings.

114.14 *Defendant attacking victims/complainants in the media*

Att-Gen's Ref No 38 of 2013 2013 EWCA Crim 1450 LCJ D, Stuart Hall, pleaded at his PCMH to 14 counts of indecent assault. He was a well-known, [formerly] popular and successful public figure through his TV and radio career. Upon being charged, he made a public statement to the media calling the allegations "pernicious – callous, cruel and above all, spurious". Held. This deliberate falsehood is a seriously aggravating feature. D was attempting to use the media for the purpose of possibly influencing potential jurors. Whatever it may or may not have done to potential jurors, we have a clear idea of what it did to the victims. One said she was absolutely incensed. D pleaded guilty but not at the first opportunity, but more importantly not before he had publicly and deliberately attacked the victims. There are two ways of approaching this: a) reduce the appropriate discount taken by the Judge by 25%, or b) add the aggravating feature to our starting point and then apply the appropriate discount for the plea. We consider the course consistent with current practice is the latter.

R v Clifford 2014 EWCA Crim 2245, 2015 1 Cr App R (S) 32 (p 242) D was convicted of eight indecent assaults. Four young vulnerable victims, one of which was aged under 16, were assaulted over a number of years. Some, under the pretence of entry into showbusiness, were made to remove clothing. The victims were groped and some were forced to masturbate D to ejaculation. D's actions had caused additional trauma to the victims by intentionally issuing press statements maintaining his innocence. Held. Great care needs to be taken not to elevate denials, albeit vehement, into something deserving of further punishment in the absence of some more explicit traducing of the victim. The court, of course, is perfectly entitled to reflect these matters in withholding available mitigation since the offender has shown no sign of remorse...but they should not have been used by way of positive aggravation.

114.15 *Restorative Justice Programme, The*

R v O'Brien 2004 EWCA Crim 2572 D pleaded at the Magistrates' Court to theft and burglary. The theft was when he visited his mother's house and, needing money for his drug addiction, stole perfume, a table lamp and a portable television. His mother was a stroke victim. She contacted the police. D was granted bail and shortly afterwards he entered a house where the occupant, who was upstairs, saw him going through a chest of drawers. She confronted him but he stole a bag containing binoculars of sentimental value. He was intent on taking more. He did not use any violence. D, aged 34, had a bad record for dishonesty including burglary. A pre-sentence report described his motivation to rid himself of drugs but spoke of a high risk of reoffending. He agreed to enter the Restorative Justice Programme and signed an Outcome Agreement. He met the victim, V, and apologised. He accepted that what he had done was serious and said that he intended to keep out of trouble. He agreed to take a drugs rehabilitation course in prison, employment training and to write to V. V, a 'thoroughly distinguished member of society', wrote to him saying her impression was that he had shown genuine remorse at the meeting and a positive wish to lead a more constructive life. In prison he kept away from drugs. He was moved to another prison where he did not settle, and a further probation report made dispiriting reading. That report was in stark contrast with what had been written about him earlier. Held. The Restorative Justice Programme is a significant matter and should be borne in mind in sentencing. The Judge failed to give sufficient credit for his attendance at the conference with V. Taking into account V's attitude and her clear and important impression, the sentences of **6 months** and **2 years** should run concurrently not consecutively. He should be grateful to V.

Victim impact statements, see the **VICTIM PERSONAL STATEMENTS/VICTIM IMPACT STATEMENTS** chapter.

114.16 *Views of the victims about the sentence*

Criminal Practice Directions 2015 EWCA Crim 1567 para VII F.3…e) The opinions of the victim or the victim's close relatives as to what the sentence should be are therefore not relevant, unlike the consequences of the offence on them. Victims should be advised of this. If, despite the advice, opinions as to sentence are included in the statement, the court should pay no attention to them.

R v Hayes 1999 The Times 5/4/99 [Notwithstanding the case name, this was an Attorney-General's reference.] D pleaded to robbing his great-grandmother, aged 95, with whom he lived. The two had an affectionate relationship. He went to her house wearing a mask, pushed her in the chest and caused her to stumble back and slide to the floor. He put his hand in her bag and stole her purse. She suffered some bruising. When re-interviewed he admitted the offence and said he had been ripped off in a drugs transaction. He was then aged 17. He showed profound remorse and was having difficulty in coping with custody. He had served 3 months. His great-grandmother had forgiven him, and they had resumed their normal relationship. His grandmother was finding it difficult to cope without him. He was normally kind and considerate. The two ladies did not feel anger towards him but were concerned for his welfare. He was given probation. Held. The sentence cannot depend on the wishes of those most affected by the crime. Crimes perpetrated against vengeful victims would be sentenced differently and much more severely than identical crimes committed against merciful victims. What is more, there are many crimes with more than one victim, and different victims of the same crime might, and sometimes do, take very different views. Many victims simply do not want to have the responsibility or be subject to the inevitable pressures that would be created on them if their views were reflected in the sentencing process. That, many of them feel, is a matter for the court, and they are right. The responsibility rests with the sentencing judge. He has an overall view of current sentencing considerations. None of that means or implies that the victim is to be ignored. An essential consideration is to assess the impact of the particular crime on the individual victim or victims. Rarely, the court is required to consider a refinement of this principle which arises when the imposition of a custodial sentence will add to the distress and concern suffered by the victim. That is a factor to which the court must also pay attention. The weight to be attached to it in a particular case and its practical impact on the sentencing decision depends of course on the crime itself and all the very many differing facets of the case which the judge has to balance. Here the Judge balanced the relevant considerations and was merciful. We should be profoundly troubled if it were thought that a judge could not temper justice with mercy. The sentence was courageous and justified but not unduly lenient.

R v Perks 2001 1 Cr App R (S) 19 (p 66) The opinions of the victim and the victim's close relatives on the appropriate level of sentence should not be taken into account. The court must pass what it judges to be the appropriate sentence having regard to the circumstances of the offence and of the offender subject to two exceptions: a) where the sentence passed on the offender is aggravating the victim's distress, the sentence may be moderated to some degree, and b) where the victim's forgiveness or unwillingness to press charges provide evidence that his or her psychological or mental suffering must be very much less than would normally be the case.

R v Dzokamshure 2008 EWCA Crim 2458, 2009 1 Cr App R (S) 112 (p 629) D pleaded early to kidnapping V. V did not wish to pursue the complaint. She did everything to assist D. She gave evidence for him and supported him at the Court of Appeal. Held. A public interest is involved in this case beyond that of the victim herself. The arrogance and disregard for other people and their privacy shown by D cannot be tolerated. The absence of previous convictions and the fulsome forgiveness of the victim do not render **18 months** inappropriate. It was appropriate.

Att-Gen's Ref No 99 of 2009 2009 EWCA Crim 181 LCJ D pleaded to the rape of his sister, V, when she was aged 12 and he 15½. D was now aged 41. Statements from the family suggested that V did not want a prison sentence imposed. The Judge didn't want to add to the burdens and unhappiness of the victim. He sought clarification, and the CPS thought that was inappropriate and asked for the case to be re-listed. The Judge said that he had directed that the woman should be asked whether the statements were true and that it was insulting for the prosecution to suggest that what he was seeking was the views of the victim. Held. We share the CPS's concerns. All this was most unfortunate. It had no bearing on the sentencing decision. There plainly was a misunderstanding which could have been cleared up. This case serves to highlight some of the dangers and difficulties which almost inevitably arise if victims are drawn into the sentencing decision.

For more detail, see the **Rape and Assault by Penetration** ***Historical cases*** para at **314.36** in Volume 2.

R v Fazli 2009 EWCA Crim 939 D pleaded to ABH, battery, criminal damage and possession of cannabis. Three of the offences were against his wife, who wrote a letter to the Court saying that she did not wish D to stay long in prison and she did not want her children to know their father was in prison because of her. The Judge said that the incarceration was entirely because of D, and feelings like this are a familiar consequence of controlling and intimidating behaviour of defendants. He disregarded the letter. Held. The Judge was right to observe this and to disregard the letter.

R v Odedara 2009 EWCA Crim 2828, 2010 2 Cr App R (S) 51 (p 359) D pleaded to causing death by dangerous driving. Held. Those who have to cope with this shattering blow may well be tempted to think, at least at the height of their loss, that imprisonment will provide some kind of solace but it rarely does and it is not its principal purpose. No sentence can bring back the departed. No sentence can or should attempt to put a price on a life.

Att-Gen's Ref No 38 of 2013 2013 EWCA Crim 1450 LCJ D pleaded to 14 counts of indecent assault. He was a well-known former TV celebrity. The Attorney-General appealed the sentences and the victims were concerned about the press publicity. The Court read all the information about the victims. Held. We must consider the harm done to victims, but victims do not and cannot decide sentences. We cannot have sentences which depend upon whether a victim feels particularly vengeful, moderately vengeful, not vengeful at all, filled with mercy, or even, as some do, believes that there should not be a prison sentence. The principles are set out in *R v Nunn* 1996 2 Cr App R (S) 136.

See also the **VICTIM PERSONAL STATEMENTS/VICTIM IMPACT STATEMENTS** ***Victims should be advised that their opinions about sentence are not relevant*** para at **113.6**, and the **RAPE AND ASSAULT BY PENETRATION** ***Victim does not want the defendant sent to prison/has forgiven him*** para at **314.86** in Volume 2.
For statements of principle about bereaved relatives (who make both positive and negative statements about the defendant), see the **DEATH BY DRIVING: GENERAL PRINCIPLES** ***Victims*** para at **237.16** in Volume 2.

114.17 ***Victim of sexual assault will lose contact with father, stepfather etc.***
Att-Gen's Ref No 2 of 2001 2001 2 Cr App R (S) 121 (p 524) D pleaded to seven counts of indecent assault against his stepdaughter when she was between the ages of 8 and 15. Held. The loss through imprisonment of her stepfather will bear hardly upon her and that can be taken into account.

115 VICTIM SURCHARGE

115.1
Criminal Justice Act 2003 s 161A-161B
(also known as the Statutory surcharge)
Background The Magistrates' Association had opposed the concept of the surcharge since the legislation appeared, arguing that, 'as a fixed sum, it fell hardest on the least well-off, and reduced judicial independence to sentence taking all an individual offender's circumstances into account. The principles of the surcharge and the way it was activated caused much anger and resentment among the magistracy, and indeed some decided they could not remain on the bench'.[1229]
Name of the order Strangely, the statute creating the order does not give the order a name. The Act just refers to a 'surcharge'. However, the order is universally known as a 'victim surcharge'.
Children and young offenders The order applies whatever the age of the offender.
Purpose When the order was introduced, it was said the money obtained would be spent on improving 'services for victims of crime'. Gillian Guy, Chief Executive of Victim Support, stated that "The money distributed through the surcharge has helped support witness care units, the victims fund, independent domestic violence advisors and…Victim Support".[1230]
Power to search There is a power to search 'a person' when a court is imposing a victim surcharge, Powers of Criminal Courts (Sentencing) Act 2000 s 142(1)-(2) and Magistrates' Courts Act 1980 s 80(1). For details see **58.15**.
Confiscation Where a Crown Court makes a confiscation order with a compensation order and it is believed that there is insufficient means to satisfy both orders in full, the court must direct that so much of the victim surcharge is to be paid out of the monies recovered, Proceeds of Crime Act 2002 s 13(5)-(6), see **21.143**.
Compensation orders The order remains mandatory, save where the court considers a compensation order or an Unlawful Profit Order or a Slavery and Trafficking Reparations Order is appropriate and there are insufficient means to pay the victim surcharge and one of those orders. In those circumstances the order can be reduced up to the full amount, Criminal Justice Act 2003 s 161A(3). For more detail see **115.11**.
Victim surcharge No victim surcharge applies to those found in contempt of court as the order is not a 'sentence of imprisonment', see *R v Yaxley-Lennon* 2018 EWCA Crim 1856 LCJ para 4 and 76.
Historical offences For all offences committed on or after 1 April 2007, a surcharge was required when the defendant was fined. The only exception to the requirement is the compensation exception (see above). When an offence was committed before 1 April 2007 no surcharge can be ordered.

[1229] 'The Surcharge – Three years on', *Magistrate*, Volume 66 Number 5 June 2010, page 2
[1230] 'The Surcharge – Three years on', *Magistrate*, Volume 66 Number 5 June 2010, page 3

Fixed penalties From 1 October 2012, all 'disorderly behaviour fixed penalties' had added to them half the relevant victim surcharge, Criminal Justice and Police Act 2001 s 3(2) and (2A) as amended by Domestic Violence, Crime and Victims Act 2004 s 15.[1231]
Who benefits? Initially it was revealed who received the money and the largest recipient was the CPS. Over the last seven years I have been able to find little information. In a document released by the MoJ in 2012, under a banner saying 'Transparency data', there is a list of organisations awarded funding from the Peer Support fund. The inference is that money comes from the victim surcharge. However, the accompanying list only shows the organisations that have been recommended for an award, which is not the same. The amount recommended to be awarded is only £250,000, and I have found no information as to where the bulk of the money goes. It is all rather unsatisfactory.

115.2 *Statistics*

Victim surcharge[1232]

	2012	2013	2014	2015	2016	2017
Total amount ordered	£14.1m	£30.5m	£37.6m	£41.6m	£46.9m	£51.8m

115.3 *Availability Determining which rules apply*

Age of defendant	Situation	Which rules and amounts
All ages	Offence on or after 1 April 2007 and before 1 October 2012[1233]	£15 when fined[1234]
	Offence on or after 1 April 2007 where the date of the offence straddles 1 October 2012	Old rules apply[1235]
	Date of offence could be before and after rules changed	The Judge should make an appropriate finding, see para **115.7**.
	Conspiracy straddles 1 October 2012	The [first] date in the particulars must be the first date on which a relevant act is alleged to have taken place. That date determines which regime applies.[1236]
	Breach of Suspended Sentence Order/community order etc.	The date to determine which rules apply is the date of the offence for which the order was imposed. If there is more than one offence, select the date of the earliest offence, see para **115.6**.
	The above principles would also apply when the court is deciding whether the new increases to the victim surcharge apply.	

[1231] Domestic Violence, Crime and Victims Act 2004 (Commencement No 15) Order 2012 2012/1697
[1232] The information below is taken from Lord Bach, then Parliamentary Under-Secretary of State, according to 'The Surcharge – Three years on', *Magistrate*, Volume 66 Number 5 June 2010, page 2 and *Hansard* 24 June 2010 Written Answers to Questions Column 280W.
[1233] Domestic Violence, Crime and Victims Act 2004 s 14(1)
[1234] For more detail see the 8th edition of this book.
[1235] *Att-Gen's Ref No 59 of 2014* 2014 EWCA Crim 1926
[1236] *Att-Gen's Ref No 28 of 2014* 2014 EWCA Crim 1723 para 30

Age of defendant	Situation		Which rules and amounts
All offences were committed when the defendant was aged over 18 or one or more of the offences were committed when the defendant was aged under 18	The offence(s) were committed on or after 1 October 2012	Same type of sentence for all the offences	Apply the relevant surcharge in the relevant column in para **115.4** below.[1237]
		Different types of sentences passed	Apply the highest single surcharge for any of the sentences in the relevant column in para **115.4** below.[1238]
Offence straddles the date the defendant reached the age of 18			The court is likely to treat the defendant as if he were aged under 18.[1239]

115.4 ***The amounts***

These amounts are from Criminal Justice Act 2003 (Surcharge) Order 2012 2012/1696 as amended by Criminal Justice Act 2003 (Surcharge) (Amendment) Order 2016 2016/398.

Crown Courts For offences committed on or after 8 April 2016 the surcharges below apply. For amounts payable before that date, see the 11th edition of this book.

Magistrates' Courts There is no victim surcharge at the Magistrates' Court when the defendant is given immediate custody[1240] for offences committed before 1 September 2014. For offences committed on or after that date, the surcharges below apply.[1241]

Order	Offender aged under 18 on the date of the offence	Offender aged 18-20 on the date of the offence	Offender aged 21+ on the date of the offence
Absolute discharge	No surcharge		
Community order Criminal Justice Act 2003 s 177(1)	£15 (£20 for offences committed before 8 April 2016*) #	£60 (£85 for offences committed before 8 April 2016*)	
Conditional discharge	£15*	£20* Where the defendant is not an individual the amount is also £20*	
Custody for life Powers of Criminal Courts (Sentencing) Act 2000 s 93 Murder only	£30 (£20 for offences committed before 8 April 2016) #	£170*	n/a
Custody for life Powers of Criminal Courts (Sentencing) Act 2000 s 94 Non-murder cases	£30* #	£170*	n/a
Deferred sentence	No surcharge		

[1237] Criminal Justice Act 2003 (Surcharge) Order 2012 2012/1696 para 4(1) and (2)(a)
[1238] Criminal Justice Act 2003 (Surcharge) Order 2012 2012/1696 para 4(1) and (2)(b)
[1239] *R v Hobbs* 2002 EWCA Crim 387, 2 Cr App R (S) 93 (p 425) and *R v S* 2007 EWCA Crim 1622, 2008 1 Cr App R (S) 47 (p 255)
[1240] Criminal Justice Act 2003 (Surcharge) Order 2012 2012/1696 Sch 1
[1241] Criminal Justice Act 2003 (Surcharge) (Amendment) Order 2014 2014/2120

Order	Offender aged under 18 on the date of the offence	Offender aged 18-20 on the date of the offence	Offender aged 21+ on the date of the offence
Detention and Training Order Powers of Criminal Courts (Sentencing) Act 2000 s 100	£30*	n/a	
Detention during HM's Pleasure Powers of Criminal Courts (Sentencing) Act 2000 s 90	£30*	n/a	
Detention for life Criminal Justice Act 2003 s 226	£30*	n/a	
Detention under section 91 Powers of Criminal Courts (Sentencing) Act 2000 s 91	£30*	n/a	
Extended sentence (EDS) Criminal Justice Act 2003 s 226A-226B	£30*	Presumably £170*	
Fine	£20*	10% of the fine, rounded up or down to the nearest pound, which must be no less than £30* and not more than £170*. The same rule applies when the defendant is not a natural person.	
Hospital Order and Guardianship Order Mental Health Act 1983 s 37	No surcharge		
Hybrid Order Mental Health Act 1983 s 45A	The order is an order of imprisonment with a direction, so the imprisonment/detention rules probably apply. Support for this can be found in *R v Poole* 2014 EWCA Crim 1641, 2015 1 Cr App R (S) 2 (p 7).		
Imprisonment	£30* # #	6 months or less: £115* More than 6 months to 24 months: £140* More than 24 months: £170*	
		All amounts # #	
Life imprisonment	£20 # #	£120 # #	£170*
Referral Order Powers of Criminal Courts (Sentencing) Act 2000 s 16(2) or 16(3)	£20*	n/a	

Order	Offender aged under 18 on the date of the offence	Offender aged 18-20 on the date of the offence	Offender aged 21+ on the date of the offence
Suspended Sentence Order Criminal Justice Act 2003 s 189(1)	£30* #	6 months or less: £115* More than 6 months to 24 months: £140*	
Young Offender Institution, Detention in an Powers of Criminal Courts (Sentencing) Act 2000 s 96	£30* #	6 months or less: £115* More than 6 months to 24 months: £140* More than 24 months: £170*	n/a
Youth Rehabilitation Order Criminal Justice and Immigration Act 2008 s 1	£20 *	n/a	

Note: 'n/a' means the sentence is not available for a particular age range.
To determine what sentences are available, it is the date of conviction that matters. This surcharge only applies to offenders who were aged 18 on the date of their conviction.
These amounts only apply to those who were aged 21 on the date of their conviction.
*These amendments only apply where all the offences were committed on or after 8 April 2016 and where the defendant was convicted on a date where he was able to be sentenced to the order in question.
This section has been written with the help of Sarah Mackie, to whom I am grateful. Ed.

Power to order

115.5 *Statutory power*

Court's duty to order payment of surcharge

Criminal Justice Act 2003 s 161A(1) A court when dealing with a person for one or more offences must also (subject to subsections (2) and (3)) order him to pay a surcharge.
(2) Subsection (1) does not apply in such cases as may be prescribed by an order made by the Secretary of State.
(3) Where a court dealing with an offender considers:

(a) that it would be appropriate to make a compensation order, but

(b) that he has insufficient means to pay both the surcharge and appropriate compensation,

the court must reduce the surcharge accordingly (if necessary to nil).

(4) For the purposes of this section a court does not 'deal with' a person if it:

(a) discharges him absolutely, or

(b) makes an order under Mental Health Act 1983 in respect of him.

115.6 *Breaching orders, Victim surcharge for*

R v Bailey and Others 2013 EWCA Crim 1551, 2014 1 Cr App R (S) 59 (p 376)[1242] para 15 D was dealt with for a breach of a suspended sentence. The original offence was committed before the new victim surcharge regime started. Held. para 4 In breach proceedings the relevant time for determining which rules apply is the date of the original offence. This is because the court is still 'dealing' with the sentence for the original offence. para 20 Order quashed.

[1242] The Cr App R (S) report does not include para 15.

See also: *R v Howell* 2014 EWCA Crim 1903 (It is the date of the original sentence that matters.)

R v Leigh 2015 EWCA Crim 1045, 2 Cr App R (S) 42 (p 332) (As the breach of the Suspended Sentence Order was for an offence before the changes came into force, order quashed.)

Note: It can be inferred that the amount payable is determined by the order made at the breach proceedings. Ed.

115.7 *Date of offence unclear*

R v Bailey and Others 2013 EWCA Crim 1551, 2014 1 Cr App R (S) 59 (p 376) para 5 Where there are difficulties in determining whether the offence took place before or after the rule change, the court should adopt the broad approach in *R v Harries and Others* 2007 EWCA Crim 1622, 2008 1 Cr App R (S) 47 (p 255). This case concerned the sentencing regime for dangerous offenders and was dependent on the commencement date, 4 April 2005. At para 12, the LCJ said, "...the judge, considering all the evidence, should make whatever findings are appropriate in the light of the evidence and give reasons for his conclusions, in particular, if in such a case the offence is found, on analysis of the evidence, to have taken place after 4 April."

By analogy, in relation to the victim surcharge, without taking undue time, the court should take a view on the evidence so that the appropriate order can be made. In the absence of a clear answer, lengthy analysis is utterly unnecessary and the issue should be resolved in the way least punitive to the offender.

115.8 *More than one offence*

R v Hemsworth 2013 EWCA Crim 916 D pleaded to burglary. He was in breach of a community order imposed in June 2012 for supply of class A drugs. The Judge re-sentenced D to 9 months for the supply, concurrent to 18 months for the burglary. He imposed the £100 victim surcharge as the burglary offence was committed after the Criminal Justice Act 2003 (Surcharge) Order 2012 2012/1696 came into force on 1 October 2012. Held. That was erroneous. Although the burglary offence was committed after the SI was in force, the transitional provisions expressly disapply the order where the court deals with an offender for more than one offence, any one of which is committed before the SI was in force. Since the court was also re-sentencing for the supply offence, it was dealing with D for matters before the SI was in force. Therefore, the surcharge is quashed.

115.9 *TICs*

R v Bailey and Others 2013 EWCA Crim 1551, 2014 1 Cr App R (S) 59 (p 376) para 8 References in the table to 'dealing with an offender' do not apply to TICs. TICs should be ignored when the surcharge is considered.

Making the order

115.10 *Making the order*

R v Bailey and Others 2013 EWCA Crim 1551, 2014 1 Cr App R (S) 59 (p 376) para 10 As with the impact of Criminal Justice Act 2003 s 240 (the old rules for time on remand), there is clearly room for mistakes which could add 'a wholly unnecessary and disproportionate expenditure of funds at the present time', see *R v Nnaji* 2009 EWCA Crim 468, 2 Cr App R (S) 107 (p 700) at para 9(i), endorsing the approach in *R v Gordon* 2007 EWCA Crim 165, 2 Cr App R (S) 66 (p 400). Similarly, on the basis that the identification of the size of the surcharge is driven entirely by the sentence, courts have adopted the approach of making an order in these terms, "The surcharge provisions apply to this case and the order can be drawn up accordingly".

R v Holden 2013 EWCA Crim 2017 D was sentenced. The Judge imposed a victim surcharge and then sat as a District Judge and ordered the surcharge to be remitted to 1 day's imprisonment and therefore deemed to have been served. Held. It is not permissible to fix a term in default in respect of the victim surcharge.

115.11 *Compensation order, Combined with*

Criminal Justice Act 2003 s 161A(3) Where a court dealing with an offender[1243] considers:

(a) that it would be appropriate to make one or more of a compensation order, an unlawful profit order and a slavery and trafficking reparations order, but

(b) that he has insufficient means to pay both the surcharge and appropriate amounts under such of those orders as it would be appropriate to make,

the court must reduce the surcharge accordingly (if necessary to nil).

Magistrates' Court Sentencing Guidelines 2008, see www.banksr.com Other Matters Guidelines tab p 151 Compensation takes priority over the victim surcharge where the offender's means are an issue.

R v Beckford 2018 EWCA Crim 2997 D pleaded to ABH. para 14 The Judge ordered that the victim surcharge was 'to be applied by way of compensation' to the victim. Held. The Judge had no power to make such a direction. The correct procedure under Criminal Justice Act 2003 s 161A was to make a compensation order in the sum of £140 and thereafter reduce the victim surcharge to enable the compensation to be paid. We substitute such an order.

115.12 *Other orders, Combined with*

Magistrates' Court Sentencing Guidelines 2008, see www.banksr.com Other Matters Guidelines tab p 151 para 31 Where the offender is of adequate means, the court must not reduce the fine to allow for imposition of the surcharge. Where the offender does not have sufficient means to pay the total financial penalty considered appropriate by the court, the order of priority is compensation, surcharge, fine, costs.

115.13 *Parent/guardian must pay the surcharge*

Powers of Criminal Courts (Sentencing) Act 2000 s 137(1A) Where but for this subsection a court would order a child or young person to pay a surcharge under Criminal Justice Act 2003 s 161A (duty to order payment of a surcharge), the court shall order that the surcharge be paid by the parent or guardian of the child or young person instead of by the child or young person himself, unless the court is satisfied:

(a) that the parent or guardian cannot be found, or

(b) that it would be unreasonable to make an order for payment, having regard to the circumstances of the case.

Appeals

115.14 *Errors/Unlawful orders General*

R v Stone 2013 EWCA Crim 723 D pleaded to benefit fraud. He and his partner, P, claimed a number of benefits totalling £21,800+. The new £100 surcharge did not apply, but the Judge erroneously made an order. Held. [Where there is an unlawful victim surcharge], at the application for leave stage the procedure which has been adopted on previous occasions when similar problems have arisen is appropriate. The application for leave against sentence should be considered by the single judge on the papers in the usual way. If leave to appeal on other grounds is given, the appeal will be listed before the full court for oral argument. If, however, the only ground upon which leave is given is the wrongful making of a victim surcharge order, then unless the application for leave is renewed on other grounds, the case should be listed as a non-counsel hearing at which the quashing of the victim surcharge order, if it is indeed unlawful, can be made publicly. On an appeal to this court in which no victim surcharge order has been imposed [where] it should have been, this court will have no power to make such an order if the effect would be to increase the ultimate overall penalty.

R v Bailey and Others 2013 EWCA Crim 1551, 2014 1 Cr App R (S) 59 (p 376) para 30 K pleaded to theft. Held. para 11 It is the duty of prosecuting and defence advocates to

[1243] Criminal Justice Act 2003 s 161A(4) For the purposes of this section a court does not 'deal with' a person if it: a) discharges him absolutely, or b) makes an order under Mental Health Act 1983 in respect of him.

ensure that the [surcharge] sum is correct, and this should be done on the same day that sentence is passed. We would expect it to be agreed and confirmed with the clerk of the court but, in the absence of agreement, the matter can be referred to the judge for a decision to be made. If compensation is to be ordered, however, and submissions addressed in relation to Criminal Justice Act 2003 s 161A(3), a judicial decision will be required. [Where the court follows the procedure in para **115.11**], and an error has been made in the record, we anticipate that the record can be corrected well within the appropriate time. If it is not and an appeal becomes necessary, the prosecution should be notified and an attempt made to agree the position. The application for leave to appeal should then state both the facts and the agreement. On receipt of [the application], the matter will be remitted by the Registrar direct to the [full] court for the error to be corrected. There will be no need for a representation order (and the expenditure of yet further money) and the offender should be informed that as no purpose would be served by attendance, the Court will assume that he does not intend to exercise his right to do so unless informed to the contrary within 28 days. This procedure follows that identified (in respect of time spent on remand) in *R v Normal* 2006 EWCA Crim 1792. para 13 Criminal Appeal Act 1968 s 11(3) will prevent the court from imposing or increasing a surcharge which is less than the order mandates unless it reduces some other element of the sentence. For successful appeals against substantive sentences, if the sentence alters (because a threshold is crossed, for example when a community order replaces a custodial sentence), the order of the court will reflect that reduction. In successful references by the Attorney General, the surcharge may increase. A surcharge should have been imposed here but [as we have affirmed the sentence] we cannot add one.

115.15 ***Order not appropriate***
R v Dos-Santos 2013 EWCA Crim 280 D pleaded to robbery. The Judge sentenced him to 20 months but omitted to order a victim surcharge. Held. We reduce the sentence to 16 months. We could also impose a victim surcharge, which was not made below. However, D had no money, was now in prison and his partner is expecting a baby. It seems to us in the circumstances that it would not be appropriate to impose that additional obligation.

116 Violent Offender Orders

116.1

Criminal Justice and Immigration Act 2008 s 98-112
As the order does not follow a conviction, the procedural details are not dealt with in this book.

Type of order This is a stand-alone preventive order.

Children and young offenders The order is available whatever the age of the offender.[1244]

Applications A chief officer of police may apply to a Magistrates' Court for an order for 'qualifying offenders'.[1245]

Qualifying offenders Those who have acted in such a way as make it necessary to make a Violent Offender Order for the purpose of protecting the public from the risk of 'serious violent harm' caused by the individual.[1246]

Interim orders There is a power to make an Interim Violent Offender Order, Criminal Justice and Immigration Act 2008 s 104-106.

Contents of the order The order and an interim order may contain prohibitions, restrictions and conditions.[1247]

[1244] Criminal Justice and Immigration Act 2008 s 99(4)(a)(i) lists one of the conditions as 'a sentence of imprisonment or other detention'.
[1245] Criminal Justice and Immigration Act 2008 s 99
[1246] Criminal Justice and Immigration Act 2008 s 101(3)
[1247] Criminal Justice and Immigration Act 2008 s 102

Notification Those subject to this order or an interim order must comply with the notification requirements[1248] within three days[1249] of the order coming into force.

116.2 *Breach*

Criminal Justice and Immigration Act 2008 s 113 (failure to comply etc. with a Violent Offender Order)
Mode of trial Triable either way
Maximum sentence Indictment 5 years. Summary 6 months and/or a £5,000 fine for offences committed before 12 March 2015 and an unlimited fine thereafter.[1250] There are maximum fines for those aged under 18, see **13.44**.
Sentencing *Breach Offences Guideline 2018*, see www.banksr.com Other Matters Guidelines tab In force 1 October 2018 page 56 says, '**Other breach offences** Where an offence is not covered by a sentencing guideline a court is entitled to use, and may be assisted by, a guideline for an analogous offence subject to differences in the elements of the offences and the statutory maxima.'
R v Koli 2012 EWCA Crim 1869, 2013 1 Cr App R (S) 6 (p 39) D was convicted of two breaches of his Serious Crime Prevention Order. Held. para 18 The court must take into account: a) the time between the imposition of the order and the date of the breach, b) any history of non-compliance, c) whether non-compliance has i) been repeated and ii) come in the face of warnings and requests for information, and d) whether the non-compliance was inadvertent or deliberate. It is important to consider whether the breach was related to the commission of further serious offences and might lead to the risk that a particular subject was likely to commit further offences. The court would also have to consider the harm caused by non-compliance for breach.
Note: Although these remarks were given when a different breach was considered, the principles may assist. Ed.

117 Vulnerable Groups: Barring

117.1

Safeguarding Vulnerable Groups Act 2006 as amended by Protection of Freedoms Act 2012
The Authority The Safeguarding Vulnerable Groups Act 2006 created the Independent Barring Board. This became the Independent Safeguarding Authority (ISA). The Authority had a massive task and the legislation and statutory instruments are extensive. As the inclusion in a barred list for a relevant offence is automatic and not dependent on any court order, the details are not set out in this book. Protection of Freedoms Act 2012 s 87-88 replaced the Independent Safeguarding Authority and the Criminal Records Bureau with the Disclosure and Barring Service (DBS), and gave the Secretary of State power to dissolve the ISA and transfer the functions of the ISA to the DBS. The DBS's website is www.gov.uk/dbs, its e-mail address for barring operations is dbsdispatch@dbs.gsi.gov.uk and its barring helpline is 01325 953795.
The different types of barring There are two ways an individual can be on a barred list. The first way is when an individual has been cautioned or convicted of an offence which appears in the list of relevant offences, see below. This is known as 'automatic barring' and requires no order of a court. The second way is when the DBS decides it is appropriate to add an individual to the list. This is known as discretionary barring and usually follows a referral from a third party, such as an employer.
The lists Where barring applies to an offence, an entry in the relevant chapter in Volume 2 states which list is applicable to the offence.
There are two lists. Each has two groups of trigger offences.

[1248] Criminal Justice and Immigration Act 2008 s 107-112
[1249] Criminal Justice and Immigration Act 2008 s 108(1)
[1250] Legal Aid, Sentencing and Punishment of Offenders Act 2012 s 85(1) and (4) and Legal Aid, Sentencing and Punishment of Offenders Act 2012 (Commencement No 11) Order 2015 2015/504

First list (i) Children's barred list with no right to ask to be removed from the list, see Safeguarding Vulnerable Groups Act 2006 (Prescribed Criteria and Miscellaneous Provisions) Regulations 2009 2009/37 Reg 3 and Sch para 1. An offence example is rape of a child.

(ii) Children's barred list with a right to ask to be removed from the list, see the same regulations 2009/37 Reg 4 and Sch para 2. An offence example is rape of an adult.

Second list (i) Adults' barred list with no right to ask to be removed from the list, see the same regulations 2009/37 Reg 5 and Sch para 3. An offence example is sexual activity with a person with a mental disorder, Sexual Offences Act 2003 s 30.

(ii) Adults' barred list with a right to ask to be removed from the list, see the same regulations 2009/37 Reg 6 and Sch para 4. An offence example is rape of a child.

For whether an offence is on any of the lists see the first paragraph of the chapter for that offence.

Sentencer's task when automatic barring applies The only task of the sentencer when sentencing a defendant is to tell him or her which list he or she will be included on and under what legislation, see **117.4**. It would be helpful if defendants are told whether they can make representations to be removed from the list.

Discretionary (Non-automatic) barring[1251] An individual may be barred by a decision of the DBS. There are two grounds for this: a) the individual has behaved in a way that has endangered a vulnerable person, and b) the DBS decides that the individual may behave in a way that would harm a vulnerable person or put that person at risk of harm. For discretionary (non-automatic) barring cases, if the DBS considers they are 'minded to bar' the person, he or she will be provided with all the information the DBS relied on in reaching that decision and they will be invited to make representations as to why they should not be barred.

Those aged under 18 Automatic barring applies when the defendant is aged 18 during part of the time his or her offence was committed.[1252] If the offence was committed when the defendant was aged under 18, automatic barring does not apply. This is irrespective of whether the conviction is before or after the defendant turns 18. However, the DBS may use its discretionary barring powers to include the person in a barred list.[1253]

117.2 *European Convention on Human Rights*

R (Wright) v Secretary of State for Health and Another 2009 UKHL 3 Lords Care Standards Act 2000 s 82(1) makes provision for keeping a list of people deemed unsuitable to work with vulnerable adults. Prior to determination of each reference to the Secretary of State under section 82(1), each claimant was placed on the list without a hearing. The claimants sought judicial review, arguing breaches of European Convention on Human Rights arts 6 and 8. Held. Allowing the appeal that: a) since the provisional listing of a care worker under Care Standards Act 2000 s 82(4)(b) could result in irreparable damage to the person's employment or prospects of employment in the care sector, it amounted to a determination of a civil right within article 6(1) notwithstanding that it was only an interim measure, b) that, given the possibility of such damage, it was necessary for the procedure of provisional listing to be fair, whereas the denial of an opportunity for care workers to answer allegations before being listed made section 82(4)(b) procedurally unfair and contrary to article 6(1), and c) that the listing of a person on suspicion of such serious misconduct as to indicate that he or she posed a risk to vulnerable adults could result in stigma so great as to constitute an interference with the right to respect for private life under article 8 of the Convention, which extended to the right to establish and develop relationships with others, including work colleagues. Declaration of incompatibility granted.

[1251] Safeguarding Vulnerable Groups Act 2006 s 2 and Sch 3
[1252] Safeguarding Vulnerable Groups Act 2006 Sch 3 para 24(7)
[1253] Safeguarding Vulnerable Groups Act 2006 s 2

R (Royal College of Nursing) v Secretary of State 2010 EWHC 2761 (Admin) High Court D pleaded to possession of indecent photos. Held. The ISA (now known as the DBS) placing individuals who have been convicted or cautioned for offences without the right to make representations prior to listing, is a breach of articles 6 and 8.
Note: It is open to the DBS to hear oral evidence but the ISA (as the body was previously called) said it had never done so, *ISA v SB* 2012 EWCA Civ 977. Ed.

117.3 ***Statutory instruments and notes***

The following documents are posted at www.banksr.com Other Matters Other Documents tab
Safeguarding Vulnerable Groups Act 2006, as enacted and as amended
The Explanatory Note
Safeguarding Vulnerable Groups Act 2006 (Prescribed Criteria and Miscellaneous Provisions) Regulations 2009 2009/37, which set out the four lists
Safeguarding Vulnerable Groups Act 2006 (Miscellaneous Provisions) Regulations 2009 2009/1548
The Explanatory Note for the 2009/1548 regulations
The Information Note with a schedule of all the offences
Safeguarding Vulnerable Groups Act 2006 (Prescribed Criteria) (Foreign Offences) Order 2008 2008/3050
Safeguarding Vulnerable Groups Act 2006 (Prescribed Information) Regulations 2008 2008/3265

117.4 ***Court must tell the defendant he is barred***

Criminal Procedure Rules 2015 2015/1490 Rule 28.3(1) This rule applies where, on a conviction, sentence or order, legislation requires the defendant:
(a) to notify information to the police, or
(b) to be included in a barred list.
(2) The court must tell the defendant that such requirements apply, and under what legislation.
Note: The defendant is given by the court a 'Notice of inclusion in the Children's Barred List or Adults' Barred List (or both)' form. The Magistrates' Court form number is 5626. The form provides some information about the barring system with details of the DBS's website (www.gov.uk/dbs), its barring e-mail (dbsdispatch@dbs.gsi.gov.uk) and its barring helpline (01325 953795). Ed.

118 Young Offender Institution, Detention in

118.1

Powers of Criminal Courts (Sentencing) Act 2000 s 96
Availability The defendant must be aged 18-20 on the date of conviction.[1254]
Minimum term Orders shall be for not less than 21 days, see **118.6**.
Breach proceedings Where a defendant is in breach of a suspended sentence or a community order made when he or she was aged under 21 and the breach hearing is when the defendant is aged 21+, and custody is appropriate, the court must pass a YOI order and not a prison sentence.[1255]
Victim surcharge The court must impose a victim surcharge, Criminal Justice Act 2003 s 161A-161B and Criminal Justice Act 2003 (Surcharge) Order 2012 2012/1696 as amended. There are exceptions, a) where a compensation order or an Unlawful Profits Order or a Slavery and Trafficking Reparations Order is imposed, when a reduced amount can be ordered or no victim surcharge need be imposed, see **17.67**, and b) where

[1254] Powers of Criminal Courts (Sentencing) Act 2000 s 96(a), see **118.3**
[1255] Criminal Justice Act 2003 Sch 12 paras 8(2)(a) and (b), 10(1)(b), 21(2)(b)(ii) and 23(2)(b)(ii). The community order provision was interpreted by *R v Aslam* 2016 EWCA Crim 845, 2 Cr App R (S) 29 (p 267) para 3. The exception to this rule is whether a defendant is in breach of a community order by failing to comply with it and the offence does not carry imprisonment then, where the defendant is aged 21+ at the breach hearing, the court must pass a prison sentence of 6 months or less and not YOI, see Criminal Justice Act 2003 Sch 12 para 10(1)(c).

the offence was committed before 1 October 2012, when no surcharge can be made, see **115.3**. Where the offence was committed on or after that date and before 8 April 2016, the amount is the relevant figure in brackets below, see **115.4**. The amount to be imposed is: for a sentence of 6 months or less, £115 (£80), more than 6 months to 24 months, £140 (£100), and more than 24 months, £170 (£120). For defendants who where convicted when aged 18+ but were aged under 18 when the offence was committed, the amount is £30 (£20), see **115.4**.

Rehabilitation period When the order is over 48 months the sentence is excluded from rehabilitation.[1256]

When the order is more than 30 months and not more than 48 months: 7 years

When the order is more than 6 months and not more than 30 months: 4 years

When the order is less than 6 months: 2 years[1257]

See also the **REHABILITATION OF OFFENDERS ACT 1974** chapter.

Release and supervision An individual is released after serving half their sentence. A 3-month supervision period applies to all YOI sentences of less than 12 months on release, Criminal Justice Act 2003 s 256B.[1258] The age of the offender on release is no longer a relevant consideration. Young offenders serving 12 months or more will be subject to licence for the second half of their sentence.

For a table showing the various custodial sentences for those aged under 21 with the maximum terms, see the **CHILDREN AND YOUNG OFFENDERS: CUSTODIAL SENTENCES** chapter.

118.2 *Statistics England and Wales*

Young Offender Institution, Detention in

	2010	2011	2012	2013	2014	2015	2016	2017
Males	12,273	11,276	9,266	7,522	6,235	5,649	5,346	5,906
Females	736	569	510	327	308	232	202	228
All	13,052	12,109	9,838	7,849	6,560	5,907	5,571	6,159

Many of the figures do not reconcile. It may be that for some entries the programmer did not specify the sex of the offender. For explanations about the statistics, see page 1-xii. For more detailed statistics, see www.banksr.com Other Matters Statistics tab.

For ***Pre-sentence reports***, see the **PRE-SENTENCE REPORTS** chapter.

Power to order

118.3 *Statutory power to order*

Detention in a young offender institution for other cases where offender at least 18 but under 21.

Powers of Criminal Courts (Sentencing) Act 2000 s 96[1259] Subject to section 90 (detention at HM's Pleasure), 93 (custody for life/murder), and 94 (custody for life/not murder) where:

(a) a person aged at least 18 but under 21 is convicted of an offence which is punishable with imprisonment in the case of a person aged 21 or over, and

(b) the court is of the opinion that either or both of paragraphs (a) and (b) of section 79(2) apply or the case falls within section 79(3) (both these subsections have been repealed),

the sentence that the court is to pass is a sentence of detention in a Young Offender Institution.

For the requirement that there be legal representation, see the **LEGAL REPRESENTATION: NEED FOR IN CUSTODIAL CASES** chapter.

[1256] Rehabilitation of Offenders Act 1974 s 5(1)(b)

[1257] Rehabilitation of Offenders Act 1974 s 5(2)

[1258] Inserted by Legal Aid, Sentencing and Punishment of Offenders Act 2012 s 115

[1259] There are no subsections in this section.

For ***Justified, Must be***, see the **CUSTODY: GENERAL PRINCIPLES *Offence must be so serious a fine or a community sentence cannot be justified*** para at **28.26**.

118.4 ***Power to order for defendants serving YOI who turn 21***
Powers of Criminal Courts (Sentencing) Act 2000 s 97(5) Subject to section 84,[1260] where an offender who:

(a) is serving a sentence of detention in a Young Offender Institution, and
(b) is aged 21 or over, is convicted of one or more further offence for which he is liable to imprisonment, the court shall have the power to pass one or more sentences of imprisonment to run consecutively upon the sentence of detention in a Young Offender Institution.

Making the order

For considerations about the ***Welfare of the offender, Must consider***, see the **CHILDREN AND YOUNG OFFENDERS: GENERAL PRINCIPLES Welfare** section at **13.38**.
For ***Mentally disordered defendants***, see the **DEFENDANT *Mentally disordered defendants*** para at **242.39** in Volume 2.

118.5 ***Maximum terms***
Powers of Criminal Courts (Sentencing) Act 2000 s 97(1) The maximum term of Detention in a Young Offender Institution that a court may impose for an offence is the same as the maximum term of imprisonment that it may impose for that offence.
Note: When life is imposed, the sentence is called 'custody for life'. Ed.

118.6 ***Minimum term***
Powers of Criminal Courts (Sentencing) Act 2000 s 97(2)[1261] A court shall not pass a sentence for an offender's detention in a young offender institution for less than 21 days.
For the requirement that the sentence must be for the shortest term, see the **CUSTODY: GENERAL PRINCIPLES *Custodial term must be for the shortest term*** para at **28.32**.

118.7 ***Consecutive terms General power***
Powers of Criminal Courts (Sentencing) Act 2000 s 97(4) Where an offender is convicted of more than one offence for which he is liable to a sentence of Detention in a Young Offender Institution, irrespective of whether he is serving a sentence of Detention in a Young Offender Institution, the court shall have the same power to pass consecutive sentences of Detention in a Young Offender Institution as if they were sentences of imprisonment.

118.8 ***Consecutive terms Young offender serving YOI turns 21***
Powers of Criminal Courts (Sentencing) Act 2000 s 97(5) Subject to section 84[1262] where an offender who: a) is serving a sentence of Detention in a Young Offender Institution, and b) is aged 21 or over, is convicted of one or more further offence for which he is liable to imprisonment, the court shall have the power to pass one or more sentences of imprisonment to run consecutively upon the sentence of Detention in a Young Offender Institution.
See also the **DETENTION AND TRAINING ORDERS: BREACH OF LICENCE *Concurrent and consecutive terms after breach of supervision*** para at **38.5**.

Combined with other orders

118.9 ***Prison in default of payment, Combined with***
Powers of Criminal Courts (Sentencing) Act 2000 s 139(5) Where a court orders a prison in default term it may be consecutive to a term being served.
Note: For assistance about other combinations, see the **CUSTODY: GENERAL PRINCIPLES Combined with other orders section at 28.34**.

[1260] This was a restriction on consecutive sentences for released prisoners, which was repealed on 4/4/05.
[1261] As amended by Criminal Justice Act 2003 Sch 37(7) para 1 on 1/5/13, Criminal Justice Act 2003 (Commencement No 30 and Consequential Amendment) Order 2012 2012/2905
[1262] This is a restriction on consecutive sentences for released prisoners which has now been repealed.

Duty to explain/Sentencing remarks

118.10 ***Explain sentence, Judge must/Suggested sentencing remarks***
Judicial College's Crown Court Compendium Part II Sentencing September 2016 page 4-22
3 **Passing the sentence**
The court must:
1) Set out findings in relation to those matters described in paras 1-3 of [chapter S3 of this guide] [which is determining seriousness etc.]
2) State that[:]
(a) the seriousness of the offence is such that neither a fine alone nor a community order can be justified. (These are the words of the statute but are commonly expressed in sentencing remarks as "the offence is so serious that only a custodial sentence can be justified");
(b) the sentence is the least that can be imposed having regard to the seriousness of the offence.
3) Explain the effect of the release provisions.

> **Example**
> The offence is so serious that only a custodial sentence can be justified and the least possible sentence I can impose having regard to the aggravating and mitigating factors of the case is one of…months/years detention in a Young Offender Institution of which you will serve up to half in custody…
> NOTE: here explain the effect of the release provisions, examples of which, dependent on length of sentence, are to be found in chapter S4-4 [of this guide] [determining seriousness].

118.11 ***Explain sentence, Judge must Consecutive sentences***
Consolidated Criminal Practice Direction 2011 para I.8.1 Where a court passes on a defendant more than one term of imprisonment the court should state in the presence of the defendant whether the terms are to be concurrent or consecutive. Should this not be done the court clerk should ask the court, before the defendant leaves court, to do so.
I.8.2 If a prisoner is, at the time of sentence, already serving two or more consecutive terms of imprisonment and the court intends to increase the total period of imprisonment, it should use the expression 'consecutive to the total period of imprisonment to which you are already subject' rather than 'at the expiration of the term of imprisonment you are now serving', lest the prisoner be not then serving the last of the terms to which he is already subject.
Note: This has now been repealed, but is still useful as guidance. Ed.

119 Youth Rehabilitation Orders

119.1
Criminal Justice and Immigration Act 2008 s 1-7
Children and young offenders The order is only available for those aged under 18, see **119.6**.
Length Not more than 3 years after the date on which the order takes effect, by which time all the requirements in the order must have been complied with,[1263] see **119.32**. For determining the length when it is uncertain, see **15.15**.
Victim surcharge The court must impose a victim surcharge of £20, Criminal Justice Act 2003 s 161A-161B and Criminal Justice Act 2003 (Surcharge) Order 2012 2012/1696 as amended. For offences committed before 8 April 2016, the amount is £15. Where a compensation order is imposed, a reduced amount can be ordered or no victim surcharge need be imposed, see **17.67**.
Rehabilitation period 6 months from the date when the order ceases to have effect.[1264]

[1263] Criminal Justice and Immigration Act 2008 Sch 1 para 32(1)
[1264] Rehabilitation of Offenders Act 1974 s 5(2)

The order has been in force from 30 November 2009.[1265]

119.2 *Statistics England and Wales*
Youth Rehabilitation Orders

	2013	**2014**	**2015**	**2016**	**2017**
Number of orders	10,505	8,777	7,628	6,605	6,001

For explanations about the statistics, see page 1-xii.

Preliminary matters

119.3 *Reports*
Criminal Justice and Immigration Act 2008 Sch 1 para 28 Before making a Youth Rehabilitation Order, the court must obtain and consider information about the offender's family circumstances and the likely effect of such an order on those circumstances. See also the **MEDICAL REPORTS** and the **PRE-SENTENCE REPORTS** chapters.

Outline of the order, power to order and test to apply

119.4 *Outline of the order*
Criminal Justice and Immigration Act 2008 s 1 provides for a single community sentence (the Youth Rehabilitation Order) within which a court may include one or more requirements.

119.5 *Statutory provisions*
Youth rehabilitation orders
Criminal Justice and Immigration Act 2008 s 1(1) Where a person aged under 18 is convicted of an offence, the court by or before which the person is convicted may in accordance with Schedule 1 make an order (in this Part referred to as a "youth rehabilitation order") imposing on the person any one or more of the following requirements:

(a) an activity requirement (see paragraphs 6 to 8 of Schedule 1), [see **119.14**]
(b) a supervision requirement (see paragraph 9 of that Schedule), [see **119.28**]
(c) in a case where the offender is aged 16 or 17 at the time of the conviction, an unpaid work requirement (see paragraph 10 of that Schedule), [see **119.29**]
(d) a programme requirement (see paragraph 11 of that Schedule), [see **119.25**]
(e) an attendance centre requirement (see paragraph 12 of that Schedule), [see **119.15**]
(f) a prohibited activity requirement (see paragraph 13 of that Schedule), [see **119.26**]
(g) a curfew requirement (see paragraph 14 of that Schedule), [see **119.16**]
(h) an exclusion requirement (see paragraph 15 of that Schedule), [see **119.21**]
(i) a residence requirement (see paragraph 16 of that Schedule), [see **119.27**]
(j) a local authority residence requirement (see paragraph 17 of that Schedule), [see **119.23**]
(k) a mental health treatment requirement (see paragraph 20 of that Schedule), [see **119.24**]
(l) a drug treatment requirement (see paragraph 22 of that Schedule), [see **119.18**]
(m) a drug testing requirement (see paragraph 23 of that Schedule), [see **119.17**]
(n) an intoxicating substance treatment requirement (see paragraph 24 of that Schedule), [see **119.22**] and
(o) an education requirement (see paragraph 25 of that Schedule) [see **119.19**].

(2) A youth rehabilitation order:
(a) may also impose an electronic monitoring requirement (see paragraph 26 of Schedule 1) [see **119.20**], and
(b) must do so if paragraph 2 of that Schedule so requires.

(3) A youth rehabilitation order may be:

[1265] Criminal Justice and Immigration Act 2008 s 1-7 and Sch 1-2 were enacted by Criminal Justice and Immigration Act 2008 (Commencement No 13 and Transitory Provision) Order 2009 2009/3074 para 2.

(a) a youth rehabilitation order with intensive supervision and surveillance (see paragraph 3 of Schedule 1) [see **119.11**], or
(b) a youth rehabilitation order with fostering [**119.10**] (see paragraph 4 of that Schedule).

(4) [Restrictions about making an order with fostering, see **119.10**]
(5) Schedule 1 makes further provision about youth rehabilitation orders.
(6) This section is subject to:
(a) sections 148 and 150 of the Criminal Justice Act 2003 (restrictions on community sentences etc.) [see **15.9** and **15.7**], and
(b) the provisions of Parts 1 and 3 of Schedule 1.

119.6 ***Power to order***
Criminal Justice and Immigration Act 2008 s 1(1) Where a person aged under 18 is convicted of an offence, the court may in accordance with Sch 1 make an order (a 'Youth Rehabilitation Order') imposing any one or more of the following requirements.

119.7 ***Test to apply***
Sentencing Children and Young People Guideline 2017, see www.banksr.com Other Matters Guideline tab In force 1 June 2017 page 25
6.25 The offence must be 'serious enough' in order to impose a YRO, but it does not need to be an imprisonable offence. Even if an offence is deemed 'serious enough' the court is not obliged to make a YRO.
6.26 The requirements included within the order (and the subsequent restriction on liberty) and the length of the order must be proportionate to the seriousness of the offence and suitable for the child or young person. The court should take care to ensure that the requirements imposed are not too onerous so as to make breach of the order almost inevitable.
6.27 [This lists the requirements and is not included.]
6.28 When determining the nature and extent of the requirements the court should primarily consider the likelihood of the child or young person re-offending and the risk of the child or young person causing serious harm. A higher risk of re-offending does not in itself justify a greater restriction on liberty than is warranted by the seriousness of the offence; any requirements should still be commensurate with the seriousness of the offence and regard must still be had for the welfare of the child or young person.
6.29 The YOT will assess this as part of their report and recommend an intervention level to the court for consideration. It is possible for the court to ask the YOT to consider a particular requirement.

	Child or young person profile	**Requirements of order**[1266]
Standard	Low likelihood of re-offending **and** a low risk of serious harm	Primarily seek to repair harm caused through, for example: • reparation; • unpaid work; • supervision; and/or • attendance centre

[1266] The examples provided here are not exclusive; the YOT will make recommendations based upon their assessment of the young offender which may vary from some of the examples given.

Enhanced	Medium likelihood of re-offending **or** a medium risk of serious harm	Seek to repair harm caused and to enable help or change through, for example: • supervision • reparation • requirement to address behaviour e.g. drug treatment, offending behaviour programme, education programme; and/or • a combination of the above.
Intensive	High likelihood of re-offending **or** a very high risk of serious harm	Seek to ensure the control of and enable help or change for the child or young person through, for example: • supervision • reparation • requirement to address behaviour • requirement to monitor or restrict movement, e.g. prohibited activity, curfew, exclusion or electronic monitoring; and/or • a combination of the above.

6.30 If a child or young person is assessed as presenting a high risk of re-offending or of causing serious harm but the offence that was committed is of relatively low seriousness then the appropriate requirements are likely to be primarily rehabilitative or for the protection of the public.

6.31 Likewise if a child or young person is assessed as presenting a low risk of re-offending or of causing serious harm but the offence was of relatively high seriousness then the appropriate requirements are likely to be primarily punitive.

Who are persistent offenders?

119.8 *Defendant aged under 15*

Criminal Justice and Immigration Act 2008 s 1(4) A court may only make [a Youth Rehabilitation Order with Intensive Supervision and Surveillance] if:..c) if[1267] the offender was aged under 15 at the time of conviction, the court is of the opinion that the offender is a persistent offender.

119.9 *Persistent offender previously fined*

Note: This is dealt with by Criminal Justice Act 2003 s 151 which, although amended, has never been brought into force. For a note about it and the full section, see **15.11**. Ed. For the rules about who is a persistent offender, see **14.8**.

The enhanced orders

119.10 *Fostering, Youth Rehabilitation Order with*

Note: There are three types of Youth Rehabilitation Order: a standard order, a Youth Rehabilitation Order with Fostering and a Youth Rehabilitation Order with Intensive Supervision and Surveillance. Ed.

Criminal Justice and Immigration Act 2008 s 1(3) A Youth Rehabilitation Order may be…a Youth Rehabilitation Order with Fostering.

Criminal Justice and Immigration Act 2008 Sch 1 para 4(6) A Youth Rehabilitation Order which imposes a fostering requirement is referred to as 'a Youth Rehabilitation Order with Fostering' (whatever other requirements mentioned in section 1(1) or (2) it imposes).

Test to apply Criminal Justice and Immigration Act 2008 s 1(4) A court may only make an order if:

(a) the court is dealing with the offender for an offence which is punishable with imprisonment,

[1267] There is a drafting error here. The Act only makes sense if the 'c)' is omitted and is replaced by an 'and' or better still para c) is made into a subsection. Further, the Act contains two 'ifs'.

(b) the court is of the opinion that the offence, or the combination of the offence and one or more offences associated with it, was so serious that, but for paragraph 3 or 4 of Sch 1, a custodial sentence would be appropriate (or, if the offender was aged under 12 at the time of conviction, would be appropriate if the offender had been aged 12), and

(c) if the offender was aged under 15 at the time of conviction, the court is of the opinion that the offender is a persistent offender.

Criminal Justice and Immigration Act 2008 Sch 1 para 4(2) If the court is satisfied:

(a) that the behaviour which constituted the offence was due to a significant extent to the circumstances in which the offender was living, and

(b) that the imposition of a fostering requirement (see para 18) would assist in the offender's rehabilitation,

it may make a Youth Rehabilitation Order in accordance with section 1 which imposes a fostering requirement.

Compulsory consultation Criminal Justice and Immigration Act 2008 Sch 1 para 4(3) But a court may not impose a fostering requirement unless:

(a) it has consulted the offender's parents or guardians (unless it is impracticable to do so), and

(b) it has consulted the local authority which is to place the offender with a local authority foster parent.

Requirements may not be consecutive Criminal Justice and Immigration Act 2008 Sch 1 para 31(5) The court may not direct that two or more fostering requirements are to be consecutive.

119.11 ***Intensive Supervision and Surveillance, Youth Rehabilitation Order with***

Note: There are three types of Youth Rehabilitation Order: a standard order, a Youth Rehabilitation Order with Fostering and a Youth Rehabilitation Order with Intensive Supervision and Surveillance. Ed.

Criminal Justice and Immigration Act 2008 s 1(3) A Youth Rehabilitation Order may be:
a) a Youth Rehabilitation Order with Intensive Supervision and Surveillance (see Schedule 1 para 3).

Definition Criminal Justice and Immigration Act 2008 Sch 1 para 3(2) The court, if it makes a Youth Rehabilitation Order which imposes an activity requirement, may specify in relation to that requirement a number of days which is more than 90 but not more than 180.

(3) Such an activity requirement is referred to in this Part of this Act as 'an extended activity requirement'.

(5) A Youth Rehabilitation Order which imposes an extended activity requirement (and other requirements in accordance with sub-paragraph (4)) is referred to in this Part of this Act as 'a Youth Rehabilitation Order with Intensive Supervision and Surveillance' (whether or not it also imposes any other requirement mentioned in section 1(1)).

Prohibited combinations of requirements Criminal Justice and Immigration Act 2008 Sch 1 para 5(1) A Youth Rehabilitation Order with Intensive Supervision and Surveillance may not impose a fostering requirement.

Test to apply Criminal Justice and Immigration Act 2008 s 1(4) But a court may only make an order mentioned in subsection (3)(a) or (b) if:

(a) the court is dealing with the offender for an offence which is punishable with imprisonment,

(b) the court is of the opinion that the offence, or the combination of the offence and one or more offences associated with it, was so serious that, but for paragraph 3 or 4 of Sch 1, a custodial sentence would be appropriate (or, if the offender was aged under 12 at the time of conviction, would be appropriate if the offender had been aged 12), and

(c) if the offender was aged under 15 at the time of conviction, the court is of the opinion that the offender is a persistent offender.

Compulsory requirements Criminal Justice and Immigration Act 2008 Sch 1 para 3(4) A Youth Rehabilitation Order which imposes an extended activity requirement must also impose:

(a) a supervision requirement, and

(b) a curfew requirement (and, accordingly, if so required by paragraph 2, an electronic monitoring requirement).

Maximum and minimum hours for activity requirement Criminal Justice and Immigration Act 2008 Sch 1 para 3

(2) The court, if it makes a Youth Rehabilitation Order which imposes an activity requirement, may specify in relation to that requirement a number of days which is more than 90 but not more than 180.

Length of the order Criminal Justice and Immigration Act 2008 Sch 1 para 32(3) In the case of a Youth Rehabilitation Order with Intensive Supervision and Surveillance, the minimum period specified for compliance with the requirements must not be shorter than 6 months after the date on which the order takes effect.

Those who fail to comply with pre-sentence drug testing Criminal Justice and Immigration Act 2008 Sch 1 para 5(2) Nothing in:

(a) section 1(4)(b), or

(b) Criminal Justice Act 2003 s 148(1) or (2)(b) (restrictions on imposing community sentences)

prevents a court from making a Youth Rehabilitation Order with Intensive Supervision and Surveillance in respect of an offender if the offender fails to comply with an order under Criminal Justice Act 2003 s 161(2) (pre-sentence drug testing).

119.12 *Intensive supervision and surveillance (curfew) requirement*

Criminal Justice and Immigration Act 2008 s 1(3) A Youth Rehabilitation Order may be:

(a) a Youth Rehabilitation Order with Intensive Supervision and Surveillance (see Schedule 1 para 3).

For details of the ***Intensive Supervision and Surveillance***, ***Youth Rehabilitation Order with*** see **119.11**.

The requirements

119.13 *What requirements can be imposed?*

Criminal Justice and Immigration Act 2008 s 1(1) Where a person aged under 18 is convicted of an offence, the court may in accordance with Sch 1 make an order (a 'Youth Rehabilitation Order') imposing any one or more of the following requirements (which are listed in the table).

List of requirements, restrictions on imposing etc.

Aged 10-17 unless otherwise stated

Youth Rehabilitation Order requirements	Maximum/minimum periods and restrictions etc.
Activity requirement, see **119.14**	Maximum period 90 days[1268]
Attendance centre requirement, see **119.15**	Aged 10-13: maximum 12 hours Aged 14-15: minimum 12 hours, maximum 24 hours Aged 16-17: minimum 12 hours, maximum 36 hours[1269] Ages relate to date of conviction

[1268] Criminal Justice and Immigration Act 2008 Sch 1 para 20(3)(a)

[1269] Criminal Justice and Immigration Act 2008 Sch 1 para 20(3)(c)

Youth Rehabilitation Order requirements	Maximum/minimum periods and restrictions etc.
Curfew requirement, see **119.16**	Maximum period: 12[1270] months[1271] Length: minimum 2 hours a day, maximum 16 hours[1272] a day[1273]
Drug testing requirement, see **119.17**	Offender must express willingness to comply[1274]
Drug treatment requirement, see **119.18**	Must be recommended[1275] and the offender must express willingness to comply[1276]
Education requirement, see **119.19**	Not to cover any period after offender reaches compulsory school-leaving age
Electronic monitoring requirement, see **119.20**	Where the court imposes a Curfew Requirement or an Exclusion Requirement, this requirement must be imposed unless inappropriate or offender does not consent
Exclusion requirement, see **119.21**	Maximum period: 3 months
Intoxicating substance treatment requirement, see **119.22**	Must be recommended The offender must express willingness to comply
Local authority residence requirement, see **119.23**	Maximum period: 6 months No part of the requirement may be when offender is aged 18+
Mental health treatment requirement, see **119.24**	The offender must express willingness to comply
Programme requirement, see **119.25**	Must be recommended
Prohibited activity requirement, see **119.26**	–
Residence requirement, see **119.27**	Offender must be aged 16+ at date of conviction The individual with whom the offender will reside must consent
Supervision requirement, see **119.28**	–
Unpaid work requirement, see **119.29**	Must be aged 16-17 only Length 40-240 hours in aggregate

The individual requirements

119.14 *Activity requirement*

Criminal Justice and Immigration Act 2008 Sch 1 para 6

Definition It requires the offender to, in accordance with instructions given by the responsible officer, present him or herself at the specified place, or participate in the specified activity on such days which may be specified.

Length of order The number of days specified must not in aggregate be more than 90. Note: There is power to impose between 90 and 180 hours. However, this becomes an extended activity requirement which then converts into a Youth Rehabilitation Order with Intensive Supervision and Surveillance (curfew) requirement, see **119.12**. Ed.

[1270] This was increased from 6 months to 12 months by Legal Aid, Sentencing and Punishment of Offenders Act 2012 s 81(3).
[1271] Criminal Justice and Immigration Act 2008 Sch 1 para 11(3)(a)
[1272] This was increased from 12 hours to 16 hours by Legal Aid, Sentencing and Punishment of Offenders Act 2012 s 81(2).
[1273] Criminal Justice and Immigration Act 2008 Sch 1 para 16(4)
[1274] Criminal Justice and Immigration Act 2008 Sch 1 para 16(2)
[1275] Criminal Justice and Immigration Act 2008 s 1(1)(c)
[1276] Criminal Justice and Immigration Act 2008 Sch 1 para 10(2)

119.15 *Attendance centre requirement*
Criminal Justice and Immigration Act 2008 Sch 1 para 12
Definition A requirement that the offender must attend an attendance centre specified in the order for such a number of hours as may be specified.
Court must have been notified arrangements have been made A court may not include an attendance centre requirement in a Youth Rehabilitation Order unless it has been notified by the Secretary of State that:

i) an attendance centre is available for persons of the offender's description, and
ii) provision can be made at the centre for the offender.

Centre must be reasonably accessible The court must be satisfied that the attendance centre proposed to be specified is reasonably accessible to the offender, having regard to the means of access available to the offender and any other circumstances.
Length of order (Ages relate to date of conviction)
Aged 10-13 years: maximum 12 hours,
Aged 14-15 years: 12-24 hours,
Aged 16-17 years: 12-36 hours.
Attendance per day An offender may not be required under this paragraph to attend at an attendance centre:

(a) on more than one occasion on any day, or
(b) for more than 3 hours on any occasion.

119.16 *Curfew requirement*
Criminal Justice and Immigration Act 2008 Sch 1 para 14
Definition A requirement that the offender must remain for periods specified at a place specified.
Length of order Maximum 12 months[1277] in length
Hours per day Minimum 2 hours and maximum 16 hours[1278] per day
Information to be considered Before making a Youth Rehabilitation Order imposing a curfew requirement, the court must obtain and consider information about the place proposed to be specified in the order (including information as to the attitude of persons likely to be affected by the enforced presence there of the offender).

119.17 *Drug testing requirement*
Criminal Justice and Immigration Act 2008 Sch 1 para 23
Definition A requirement that for the purpose of ascertaining whether there is any drug in the offender's body during the treatment period, the offender must, during that period, provide samples in accordance with instructions given by the responsible officer or treatment provider.
Court must have been notified arrangements have been made A court may not include a drug testing requirement in a Youth Rehabilitation Order unless the court has been notified by the Secretary of State that arrangements for implementing drug testing requirements are in force in the local justice area in which the offender resides or is to reside.
Compulsory requirements The court must also impose a drug treatment requirement.
Consent by offender The offender must express a willingness to comply with the requirement.
Details of terms A Youth Rehabilitation Order which imposes a drug testing requirement:

(a) must specify for each month the minimum number of occasions on which samples are to be provided, and
(b) may specify:
 (i) times at which and circumstances in which the responsible officer or treatment provider may require samples to be provided, and

[1277] This was increased from 6 months to 12 months by Legal Aid, Sentencing and Punishment of Offenders Act 2012 s 81(3).
[1278] This was increased from 12 hours to 16 hours by Legal Aid, Sentencing and Punishment of Offenders Act 2012 s 81(2).

(ii) descriptions of the samples which may be so required.

A Youth Rehabilitation Order which imposes a drug testing requirement must provide for the results of tests carried out otherwise than by the responsible officer on samples provided by the offender in pursuance of the requirement to be communicated to the responsible officer.

119.18 *Drug treatment requirement*

Criminal Justice and Immigration Act 2008 Sch 1 para 22

Definition A requirement that the offender must submit during a period or periods specified, to treatment by or under the direction of a person so specified having the necessary qualifications or experience with a view to the reduction or elimination of the offender's dependency on, or propensity to misuse drugs.

Availability A court may not include a drug treatment requirement in a Youth Rehabilitation Order unless it is satisfied:

(a) that the offender is dependent on, or has a propensity to misuse, drugs, and

(b) that the offender's dependency or propensity is such as requires and may be susceptible to treatment.

119.19 *Education requirement*

Criminal Justice and Immigration Act 2008 Sch 1 para 25

Definition A requirement that the offender must comply with approved educational arrangements during a period or periods specified.

Test to apply A court may not include an education requirement in a Youth Rehabilitation Order unless the inclusion of the education requirement is necessary for securing the good conduct of the offender or for preventing the commission of further offences.

Must consult local authority A court may not include an education requirement in a Youth Rehabilitation Order unless:

(a) it has consulted the local authority proposed to be specified in the order with regard to the proposal to include the requirement, and

(b) it is satisfied: i) that, in the view of that local authority, arrangements exist for the offender to receive efficient full time education suitable to the offender's age, ability, aptitude and special educational needs (if any).

Length of order Any period specified in a Youth Rehabilitation Order as a period during which an offender must comply with approved education arrangements must not include any period after the offender has ceased to be of compulsory school age.

119.20 *Electronic monitoring requirement*

Criminal Justice and Immigration Act 2008 s 1(2) and Criminal Justice and Immigration Act 2008 Sch 1 para 2 and 26

Obligation to impose The requirement must be imposed when there is a curfew requirement (whether by virtue of paragraph 3(4)(b) or otherwise), or an exclusion requirement, unless: a) in the particular circumstances of the case, the court considers it inappropriate for the order to do so, or b) the court is prevented by paragraph 26(3) or (6) from including such a requirement in the order, see CJIA 2008 s 1(2)(b) and Sch 1 para 2(2).

Definition A requirement for securing the electronic monitoring of the offender's compliance with other requirements imposed by the order during a period specified in the order or determined by the responsible officer in accordance with the order, see CJIA 2008 Sch 1 para 26(1).

Test A court must also impose an electronic monitoring requirement in a Youth Rehabilitation Order unless: a) in the particular circumstances of the case, the court considers it inappropriate for the order to do so, or b) the court is prevented by paragraph 26(3) (order impracticable) or (6) (no Secretary of State notification) from including such a requirement in the order.

Court must have been notified arrangements have been made The court must: a) have been notified by the Secretary of State that arrangements for electronic monitoring of offenders are available:

(i) in the local justice area proposed to be specified in the order, and

(ii) for each requirement mentioned in the first column of the Table in para 26(7) which the court proposes to include in the order, in the area in which the relevant place is situated, and

(b) is satisfied that the necessary provision can be made under the arrangements currently available, see CJIA 2008 Sch 1 para 26(6).

Consent is required Where: a) it is proposed to include an electronic monitoring requirement in a Youth Rehabilitation Order, but b) there is a person (other than the offender) without whose co-operation it will not be practicable to secure that the monitoring takes place, the requirement may not be included in the order without that person's consent, see CJIA 2008 Sch 1 para 26(3).

Duty to notify Where an electronic monitoring requirement is required to take effect during a period determined by the responsible officer in accordance with the Youth Rehabilitation Order, the responsible officer must, before the beginning of that period, notify: a) the offender, b) the person responsible for the monitoring, and c) any person falling within sub-paragraph (3)(b) of para 26, of the time when the period is to begin, see CJIA 2008 Sch 1 para 26(2).

119.21 *Exclusion requirement*

Criminal Justice and Immigration Act 2008 Sch 1 para 25

Definition A provision prohibiting the offender from entering a place specified in the order for a specified period.

Length of order The period specified must not be more than 3 months.

Prohibition for periods within the order An exclusion requirement:

(a) may provide for the prohibition to operate only during the periods specified in the order, and

(b) may specify different places for different periods or days.

Fostering, Youth Rehabilitation Order with, see **119.10**.

Intensive supervision and surveillance (curfew) requirement, see **119.12**.

For Court of Appeal cases about a community order's exclusion requirement, see **15.23**.

119.22 *Intoxicating substance treatment requirement*

Criminal Justice and Immigration Act 2008 Sch 1 para 24

Definition A requirement that the offender must submit during a period or periods specified in the order, to treatment by or under the direction of a person so specified having the necessary qualifications or experience, with a view to the reduction or elimination of the offender's dependency on or a propensity to misuse intoxicating substances.

Availability Where a person aged under 18 is convicted of an offence, the court may in accordance with Schedule 1 make an order (a 'Youth Rehabilitation Order') imposing any one or more of the requirements listed in Criminal Justice and Immigration Act 2008 s 1(1).

Court must be satisfied arrangements are in place A court may not include an intoxicating substance treatment requirement in a Youth Rehabilitation Order unless:

(a) the court is satisfied that arrangements have been or can be made for the treatment intended to be specified in the order (including, where the offender is to be required to submit to treatment as a resident, arrangements for the reception of the offender),

(b) the requirement has been recommended to the court as suitable for the offender by a member of a youth offending team, an officer of a local probation board or an officer of a provider of probation services, and

(c) the offender has expressed willingness to comply with the requirement.

Test to apply A court may not include an intoxicating substance treatment requirement in a Youth Rehabilitation Order unless it is satisfied:

(a) that the offender is dependent on, or has a propensity to misuse, intoxicating substances, and

(b) that the offender's dependency or propensity is such as requires and may be susceptible to treatment.

119.23 ***Local authority residence requirement***

Criminal Justice and Immigration Act 2008 Sch 1 para 17

Definition A requirement that, during the period specified in the order, the offender must reside in accommodation provided by or on behalf of a local authority specified in the order for the purposes of the requirement.

Availability Where a person aged under 18 is convicted of an offence, the court may in accordance with Sch 1 make an order (a 'Youth Rehabilitation Order') imposing any one or more of the requirements listed in Criminal Justice and Immigration Act 2008 s 1(1).

Test to apply A court may not include a local authority residence requirement in a Youth Rehabilitation Order made in respect of an offence unless it is satisfied:

(a) that the behaviour which constituted the offence was due to a significant extent to the circumstances in which the offender was living, and

(b) that the imposition of that requirement will assist in the offender's rehabilitation.

Duty to consult A court may not include a local authority residence requirement in a Youth Rehabilitation Order unless it has consulted:

(a) a parent or guardian of the offender (unless it is impracticable to consult such a person), and

(b) the local authority which is to receive the offender.

Length of order The order must not be longer than 6 months and not include any period after the offender has reached the age of 18.

119.24 ***Mental health treatment requirement***

Criminal Justice and Immigration Act 2008 Sch 1 para 20

Definition A requirement that the offender must submit, during a period or periods specified in the order, to treatment by or under the direction of a registered medical practitioner or a chartered psychologist with a view to improving the offender's mental condition.

Availability Where a person aged under 18 is convicted of an offence, the court may in accordance with Sch 1 make an order (a 'Youth Rehabilitation Order') imposing any one or more of the requirements listed in Criminal Justice and Immigration Act 2008 s 1(1).

Test to apply A court may not include a mental health treatment requirement in a Youth Rehabilitation Order unless:

(a) the court is satisfied, on the evidence,[1279] that the mental condition of the offender:

(i) is such as requires and may be susceptible to treatment, but

(ii) is not such as to warrant the making of a Hospital Order or Guardianship Order within the meaning of Mental Health Act 1983,

(b) the court is also satisfied that arrangements have been or can be made for the treatment intended to be specified in the order (including, where the offender is to be required to submit to treatment as a resident patient, arrangements for the reception of the offender), and

(c) the offender has expressed willingness to comply with the requirement.

119.25 ***Programme requirement***

Criminal Justice and Immigration Act 2008 Sch 1 para 11

Definition A requirement that the offender must participate in a systematic set of activities ('a programme') specified in the order at a place or places so specified on such number of days as may be so specified.

[1279] The requirement that the evidence had to be from a registered medical practitioner was repealed by Legal Aid, Sentencing and Punishment of Offenders Act 2012 s 82(2).

Availability Where a person aged under 18 is convicted of an offence, the court may in accordance with Sch 1 make an order (a 'Youth Rehabilitation Order') imposing any one or more of the requirements listed in Criminal Justice and Immigration Act 2008 s 1(1).
Test to apply A court may not include a programme requirement in a Youth Rehabilitation Order unless:

(a) the programme which the court proposes to specify in the order has been recommended to the court by:

(i) a member of a youth offending team,

(ii) an officer of a local probation board, or

(iii) an officer of a provider of probation services, as being suitable for the offender, and

(b) the court is satisfied that the programme is available at the place or places proposed to be specified.

Other persons must consent A court may not include a programme requirement in a Youth Rehabilitation Order if compliance with that requirement would involve the co-operation of a person other than the offender and the offender's responsible officer, unless that other person consents to its inclusion.
R v Price 2013 EWCA Crim 1283, 2014 1 Cr App R (S) 36 (p 216) D was given a community order with a 'General Offending Behaviour Programme'. This was contingent on the Probation Service taking the view that this was appropriate. Held. Leaving the programme to the Probation Service was unlawful. The programme must be specified.

119.26 *Prohibited activity requirement*

Criminal Justice and Immigration Act 2008 Sch 1 para 13
Definition A requirement that the offender must refrain from participating in activities specified in the order:

(a) on a day or days so specified, or

(b) during a period so specified.

Availability Where a person aged under 18 is convicted of an offence, the court may in accordance with Sch 1 make an order (a 'Youth Rehabilitation Order') imposing any one or more of the requirements listed in Criminal Justice and Immigration Act 2008 s 1(1).
Must consult local authority/certain bodies A court may not include a prohibited activity requirement in a Youth Rehabilitation Order unless it has consulted: a) a member of a youth offending team, b) an officer of a local probation board, or c) an officer of a provider of probation services.
R v Jacob 2008 EWCA Crim 2002 D was given a community order. Held. The primary purpose of a [prohibited activity] requirement is not to punish the offender but to prevent, or at least reduce, the risk of further offending. This requirement was disproportionate. Requirement quashed. For more details of the case see **15.23**.

119.27 *Residence requirement*

Criminal Justice and Immigration Act 2008 Sch 1 para 16
Definition A requirement that, during the period specified in the order, the offender must reside:

(a) with an individual specified in the order, or

(b) at a place specified in the order.

Age requirement A court may not include a place of residence requirement in a Youth Rehabilitation Order unless the offender was aged 16 or over at the time of conviction.
Matters to consider Before making a Youth Rehabilitation Order containing a place of residence requirement, the court must consider the home surroundings of the offender.
Must consult certain bodies/persons A court may not specify a hostel or other institution as the place where an offender must reside for the purposes of a place of

residence requirement except on the recommendation of: a) a member of a youth offending team, b) an officer of a local probation board, c) an officer of a provider of probation services, or d) a social worker of a local authority.
Consideration Before making a Youth Rehabilitation Order containing a place of residence requirement, the court must consider the home surroundings of the offender.

119.28 ***Supervision requirement***
Criminal Justice and Immigration Act 2008 Sch 1 para 9
Definition A requirement that the offender must attend appointments with the responsible officer [or another] at such times and places as determined by the responsible officer.

119.29 ***Unpaid work requirement***
Criminal Justice and Immigration Act 2008 Sch 1 para 10
Definition A requirement that the offender must perform unpaid work.
Test to apply A court may not impose an unpaid work requirement in respect of an offender unless:

(a) after hearing (if the court thinks necessary) an appropriate officer, the court is satisfied that the offender is a suitable person to perform work under such a requirement, and

(b) the court is satisfied that provision for the offender to work under such a requirement can be made under the arrangements for persons to perform work under such a requirement which exist in the local justice area in which the offender resides or is to reside.

Number of hours Between 40 and 240 inclusive, to be performed at such times appointed by the appropriate officer.
Length of order Unless revoked, a Youth Rehabilitation Order imposing an unpaid work requirement remains in force until the offender has worked under it for the number of hours specified in it.

Making the order

119.30 ***Statutory considerations***
Criminal Justice and Immigration Act 2008 Sch 1 para 29(1) Before making:

(a) a Youth Rehabilitation Order imposing two or more requirements, or

(b) two or more Youth Rehabilitation Orders in respect of associated offences,

the court must consider whether, in the circumstances of the case, the requirements to be imposed by the order or orders are compatible with each other.
(2) Sub-paragraph (1) is subject to para 2 (see **119.20**), 3(4) and 4(4).
(3) The court must ensure, as far as practicable, that any requirement imposed by a Youth Rehabilitation Order is such as to avoid:

(a) any conflict with the offender's religious beliefs,

(b) any interference with the times, if any, at which the offender normally works or attends school or any other educational establishment, and

(c) any conflict with the requirements of any other Youth Rehabilitation Order to which the offender may be subject.

(4) The Secretary of State may by order provide that sub-paragraph (3) is to have effect with such additional restrictions as may be specified in the order.

119.31 ***Requirements Consecutive Orders***
Criminal Justice and Immigration Act 2008 Sch 2 para 31(6) Where the court directs that two or more requirements of the same kind are to be consecutive:

(a) the number of hours, days or months specified in relation to one of them is additional to the number of hours, days or months specified in relation to the other or others, but

(b) the aggregate number of hours, days or months specified in relation to both or all of them must not exceed the maximum number which may be specified in relation to any one of them.

119.32 ***Length of a Youth Rehabilitation Order***
Criminal Justice and Immigration Act 2008 Sch 1 para 32(1)[1280] A youth rehabilitation order must specify a date (the end date), not more than 3 years after the date on which the order takes effect, by which all the requirements in it must have been complied with.
(2) If a youth rehabilitation order imposes two or more different requirements falling within Part 2 of this Schedule, the order may also specify a date by which each of those requirements must have been complied with; and the last of those dates must be the same as the end date.
(3) In the case of a youth rehabilitation order with intensive supervision and surveillance, the date specified for the purposes of sub-paragraph (1) must not be earlier than 6 months after the date on which the order takes effect.
(4) Subject to paragraph 10(7) (duration of youth rehabilitation order imposing unpaid work requirement), a youth rehabilitation order ceases to be in force on the end date.

119.33 ***Discount for time spent in custody***
Criminal Justice Act 2003 s 149(1) In determining the restrictions on liberty to be imposed by a community order or Youth Rehabilitation Order…, the court may have regard to any period for which the offender has been remanded in custody in connection with the offence or any other offence which was founded on the same facts or evidence.
R v Rakib 2011 EWCA Crim 870, 2012 1 Cr App R (S) 1 (p 1) D was charged with sexual assault and exposure (×2). He was remanded in custody. He received a community order, having spent nearly six months on remand (being the equivalent of an 11- or 12-month sentence). Held. Where an offender has served a significant period on remand, but in light of the duty under Criminal Justice Act 2003 s 142 (purposes of sentencing) a court considers a community order appropriate, the period on remand is not and cannot be (as *R v Hemmings* 2007 EWCA Crim 2413, 2008 1 Cr App R (S) 106 (p 623) suggests) a necessarily determinative factor in deciding what the appropriate sentence is. Section 149 states a court may have regard to any period spent on remand when considering restrictions on liberty to be imposed by a community order. Although Criminal Justice Act 2003 s 149 says 'may have regard to' such periods on remand, a sentencing judge should usually have regard to such periods. It may be that in some cases the significant period spent on remand is sufficient for a court to consider that no further punishment is necessary. Where the offender has served a period on remand equivalent to the maximum custodial sentence, there is still a discretion to impose a community order, even if that includes substantial restrictions. Appeal dismissed.

119.34 ***Crown Court para 36 direction***
Criminal Justice and Immigration Act 2008 Sch 1 para 36(1) Where the Crown Court makes a Youth Rehabilitation Order, it may include in the order a direction that further proceedings relating to the order be in a Youth Court or other Magistrates' Court (subject to para 7 of Sch 2).
(2) In sub-paragraph (1), 'further proceedings', in relation to a Youth Rehabilitation Order, means proceedings:

(a) for any failure to comply with the order within the meaning given by paragraph 1(2)(b) of Schedule 2, or
(b) on any application for amendment or revocation of the order under Part 3 or 4 of that Schedule.

119.35 ***Explain sentence, Judge must/Suggested sentencing remarks***
For the general principles, see para **86.48**.
Judicial College's Crown Court Compendium Part II Sentencing June 2018 page 5-7
4. Passing the sentence
The court must:
1) Complete the steps set out in chapter S3 [in this guide] [determining the seriousness].

[1280] This paragraph has the amendments made by Legal Aid, Sentencing and Punishment of Offenders Act 2012 s 83(1). In force 3/12/12

2) State that[:]
(a) the offence, or the combination offences, is serious enough to warrant such a sentence;
(b) the sentence is the least that is commensurate with the seriousness of the offence/s;
(c) (if it is the case) the court has had regard to time spent on remand/in secure accommodation in imposing the requirement/s attached to the order.
(3) Specify and explain the requirement/s attached to the order including the requirement that the offender keep in touch with the responsible officer in accordance with such instructions as he may be given by that officer.
Specify whether any breach of any requirement is to be dealt with in the Crown Court or the Youth Court and explain the court's powers in the event of any such breach or conviction of another offence.
NOTE: the example given for a Community Order in chapter S5-1 above may easily be adapted for a YRO [see **15.42**].
Note: Legal Aid, Sentencing and Punishment of Offenders Act 2012 s 64 inserted a new Criminal Justice Act 2003 s 174(8), which imposes a duty that when 'the offender is under 18 and the court imposes a sentence that may only be imposed in the offender's case if the court is of the opinion mentioned in: a) Criminal Justice and Immigration Act 2008 s 1(4)(a)-(c) and Criminal Justice Act 2003 s 148(1) (Youth Rehabilitation Order with Intensive Supervision and Surveillance or with fostering)…the court must state why it is of that opinion'. Ed.

Combined with other orders

119.36 *Detention and Training Orders (earlier order), Combined with*

Criminal Justice and Immigration Act 2008 Sch 1 para 30(2) If a Detention and Training Order is in force in respect of an offender, a court making a Youth Rehabilitation Order in respect of the offender may order that it is to take effect instead:
(a) when the period of supervision begins in relation to the Detention and Training Order in accordance with Powers of Criminal Courts (Sentencing) Act 2000 s 103(1)(a), or
(b) on the expiry of the term of the Detention and Training Order.

119.37 *Hospital and Guardianship Orders, Combined with*

Mental Health Act 1983 s 37(8) Where an order is made under this section, the court shall not: pass a Youth Rehabilitation Order (within the meaning of Criminal Justice and Immigration Act 2008 Part 1) in respect of the offence.

119.38 *Referral Order, Combined with*

Powers of Criminal Courts (Sentencing) Act 2000 s 19(1)-(4) Where the court makes a Referral Order, the court may not deal with the offender by imposing a sentence which includes a Youth Rehabilitation Order.

119.39 *Reparation Order, Combined with*

Powers of Criminal Courts (Sentencing) Act 2000 s 73(4)(b) The court shall not make a Reparation Order in respect of the offender if it proposes to make in respect of him a Youth Rehabilitation Order.
Criminal Justice and Immigration Act 2008 Sch 1 para 30(4) A court must not make a Youth Rehabilitation Order in respect of an offender at a time when…a Reparation Order made under Powers of Criminal Courts (Sentencing) Act 2000 s 73(1) is in force in respect of the offender, unless when it makes the order it revokes the earlier order.

119.40 *Youth Rehabilitation Order, Combined with another type of*

Note: There are three types of Youth Rehabilitation Order: a standard order, a Youth Rehabilitation Order with Fostering and a Youth Rehabilitation Order with Intensive Supervision and Surveillance. Ed.

Criminal Justice and Immigration Act 2008 Sch 1 para 31(1) This paragraph applies where the court is dealing with an offender who has been convicted of two or more associated offences.
(2) If, in respect of one of the offences, the court makes an order of any of the following kinds:
(a) a Youth Rehabilitation Order with Intensive Supervision and Surveillance,
(b) a Youth Rehabilitation Order with Fostering, or
(c) any other Youth Rehabilitation Order,
it may not make an order of any other of those kinds in respect of the other offence, or any of the other offences.
(3) If the court makes two or more Youth Rehabilitation Orders with Intensive Supervision and Surveillance, or with Fostering, both or all of the orders must take effect at the same time (in accordance with para 30(1) or (2)).
(4) Where the court includes requirements of the same kind in two or more Youth Rehabilitation Orders, it must direct, in relation to each requirement of that kind, whether:
(a) it is to be concurrent with the other requirement or requirements of that kind, or any of them, or
(b) it and the other requirement or requirements of that kind, or any of them, are to be consecutive.

119.41 ***Youth Rehabilitation Order is in force, Another***
Criminal Justice and Immigration Act 2008 Sch 1 para 30(4) A court must not make a Youth Rehabilitation Order in respect of an offender at a time when another Youth Rehabilitation Order…is in force in respect of the offender, unless when it makes the order it revokes the earlier order.

Matters after order made

119.42 ***Notify Must notify the offender of the requirements imposed***
Criminal Procedure Rules 2015 2015/1490 Rule 28.2(1) This rule applies where the court:
(b) imposes a requirement under:..
(ii) a Youth Rehabilitation Order, or…
(c) orders the defendant to attend meetings with a supervisor.
(2) The court officer must notify:
(a) [Not relevant],
(b) the defendant and, where the defendant is under 14, an appropriate adult, of:
(i) any requirement or requirements imposed, and
(ii) the identity of any responsible officer or supervisor, and the means by which that person may be contacted…
(c) [Deals with the requirement to tell the responsible officer or supervisor etc.]

119.43 ***Responsible officer/Qualifying officer, Definition of***
Meaning of 'the responsible officer'
Criminal Justice and Immigration Act 2008 s 4(1) For the purposes of this Part, 'the responsible officer', in relation to an offender to whom a Youth Rehabilitation Order relates, means:
(a) in a case where the order:
(i) imposes a curfew requirement or an exclusion requirement but no other requirement mentioned in section 1(1), and
(ii) imposes an electronic monitoring requirement,
the person who under paragraph 26(4) of Sch 1 is responsible for the electronic monitoring required by the order,
(b) in a case where the only requirement imposed by the order is an attendance centre requirement, the officer in charge of the attendance centre in question,

(c) in any other case, the qualifying officer who, as respects the offender, is for the time being responsible for discharging the functions conferred by this Part on the responsible officer.

(2) In this section 'qualifying officer', in relation to a Youth Rehabilitation Order, means:

(a) a member of a youth offending team established by a local authority for the time being specified in the order for the purposes of this section, or

(b) an officer of a local probation board appointed for or assigned to the local justice area for the time being so specified or (as the case may be) an officer of a provider of probation services acting in the local justice area for the time being so specified.

119.44 ***Duties of the responsible officer***

Responsible officer and offender: duties in relation to the other

Criminal Justice and Immigration Act 2008 s 5(1) Where a Youth Rehabilitation Order has effect, it is the duty of the responsible officer:

(a) to make any arrangements that are necessary in connection with the requirements imposed by the order,

(b) to promote the offender's compliance with those requirements, and

(c) where appropriate, to take steps to enforce those requirements.

(2) In subsection (1) 'responsible officer' does not include a person falling within section 4(1)(a) ('the responsible officer' where the order imposes a curfew or exclusion requirement and an electronic monitoring requirement)

(3) In giving instructions in pursuance of a Youth Rehabilitation Order relating to an offender, the responsible officer must ensure, as far as practicable, that any instruction is such as to avoid:

(a) any conflict with the offender's religious beliefs,

(b) any interference with the times, if any, at which the offender normally works or attends school or any other educational establishment, and

(c) any conflict with the requirements of any other Youth Rehabilitation Order to which the offender may be subject.

(4) The Secretary of State may by order provide that subsection (3) is to have effect with such additional restrictions as may be specified in the order.

(5)-(6) [see **119.45**]

119.45 ***Duties of the offender***

Criminal Justice and Immigration Act 2008 s 5(5) An offender in respect of whom a Youth Rehabilitation Order is in force:

(a) must keep in touch with the responsible officer in accordance with such instructions as the offender may from time to time be given by that officer, and

(b) must notify the responsible officer of any change of address.

(6) The obligation imposed by subsection (5) is enforceable as if it were a requirement imposed by the order.

Amending the order

119.46 ***Power to amend General power Crown Court***

Criminal Justice and Immigration Act 2008 Sch 2 para 14(4) The Crown Court may by order amend the Youth Rehabilitation Order:

(a) by cancelling any of the requirements of the order, or

(b) by replacing any of those requirements with a requirement of the same kind which could have been included in the order when it was made.

119.47 ***Power to amend General power Magistrates' Court***

Criminal Justice and Immigration Act 2008 Sch 2 para 13(4) The appropriate court (see para 13(6) below) may by order amend the Youth Rehabilitation Order:

(a) by cancelling any of the requirements of the order, or

(b) by replacing any of those requirements with a requirement of the same kind which could have been included in the order when it was made.

Criminal Justice and Immigration Act 2008 Sch 2 para 13(6) In this paragraph, 'the appropriate court' means:

(a) if the offender is aged under 18 when the application under sub-paragraph (1) was made, a Youth Court acting in the local justice area specified in the Youth Rehabilitation Order, and

(b) if the offender is aged 18 or over at that time, a Magistrates' Court (other than a Youth Court) acting in that local justice area.

119.48 ***Power to amend Change of residence Crown Court***

Criminal Justice and Immigration Act 2008 Sch 2 para 14(2) If the Crown Court is satisfied that the offender proposes to reside, or is residing, in a local justice area ('the new local justice area') other than the local justice area for the time being specified in the order, the court:

(a) must, if the application was made by the responsible officer, or

(b) may, in any other case,

amend the Youth Rehabilitation Order by substituting the new local justice area for the area specified in the order.

119.49 ***Power to amend Change of residence Magistrates' Court***

Criminal Justice and Immigration Act 2008 Sch 2 para 13(2) If the appropriate court (for definition see **119.47**) is satisfied that the offender proposes to reside, or is residing, in a local justice area other than the local justice area for the time being specified in the order, the court:

(a) must, if the application was made by the responsible officer, or

(b) may, in any other case,

amend the Youth Rehabilitation Order by substituting the new local justice area for the area specified in the order.

Criminal Justice and Immigration Act 2008 Sch 2 para 13(6) In this paragraph, 'the appropriate court' means:

(a) if the offender is aged under 18 when the application under sub-paragraph (1) was made, a Youth Court acting in the local justice area specified in the Youth Rehabilitation Order, and

(b) if the offender is aged 18 or over at that time, a Magistrates' Court (other than a Youth Court) acting in that local justice area.

119.50 ***Power to amend Change of residence Schedule 2 para 15 factor***

Criminal Justice and Immigration Act 2008 Sch 2 para 15(1) In sub-paragraphs 15(2) and (3) (see below), 'specific area requirement', in relation to a Youth Rehabilitation Order, means a requirement contained in the order which, in the opinion of the court, cannot be complied with unless the offender continues to reside in the local justice area specified in the Youth Rehabilitation Order.

(2) A court may not amend a Youth Rehabilitation Order which contains specific area requirements unless it either:

(a) cancels those requirements, or

(b) substitutes for those requirements other requirements which can be complied with if the offender resides in the new local justice area mentioned in paragraph 13(2) or (as the case may be) 14(2).

(3) If:

(a) the application was made by the responsible officer, and

(b) the Youth Rehabilitation Order contains specific area requirements,

the court must, unless it considers it inappropriate to do so, so exercise its powers that it is not prevented by sub-paragraph (2) from amending the order.

(4) The court may not amend a Youth Rehabilitation Order imposing a programme requirement unless the court is satisfied that a programme which:

(a) corresponds as nearly as practicable to the programme specified in the order for the purposes of that requirement, and

(b) is suitable for the offender,
is available in the new local justice area.

119.51 ***Defendant must consent to certain amendments***
Criminal Justice and Immigration Act 2008 Sch 2 para 16(3) The court may not under paragraph 13(4) or 14(4) (amending the order) impose:
(a) a mental health treatment requirement,
(b) a drug treatment requirement, or
(c) a drug testing requirement,
unless the offender has expressed willingness to comply with the requirement.
(4) If an offender fails to express willingness to comply with a mental health treatment requirement, a drug treatment requirement or a drug testing requirement which the court proposes to impose under paragraph 13(4) or 14(4), the court may:
(a) revoke the Youth Rehabilitation Order, and
(b) deal with the offender, for the offence in respect of which the order was made, in any way in which that court could have dealt with the offender for that offence (had the offender been before that court to be dealt with for it).
(5) In dealing with the offender under sub-paragraph (4)(b), the court must take into account the extent to which the offender has complied with the order.

119.52 ***Power to amend Extending unpaid work requirement***
Criminal Justice and Immigration Act 2008 Sch 2 para 17(1) Where:
(a) a Youth Rehabilitation Order imposing an unpaid work requirement is in force in respect of an offender, and
(b) on the application of the offender or the responsible officer, it appears to the appropriate court that it would be in the interests of justice to do so having regard to circumstances which have arisen since the order was made, the court may, in relation to the order, extend the period of 12 months specified in Schedule 1 para 10(6).

119.53 ***Amending Applications by responsible officer or supervisor***
Criminal Procedure Rules 2015 2015/1490 Rule 32.4(1) Except for Rules 24.8 (Written guilty plea: special rules) and 24.9 (Single justice procedure: special rules), the rules in Part 24, which deal with the procedure at a trial in a Magistrates' Court, apply:
(a) as if:
(i) a reference in those rules to an allegation of an offence included a reference to an allegation of failure to comply with an order to which this Part applies,
(ii) a reference to the court's verdict included a reference to the court's decision to revoke or amend such an order, or to exercise any other power it has to deal with the defendant, and
(iii) a reference to the court's sentence included a reference to the exercise of any such power, and
(b) with the necessary consequential modifications.
(2) The court officer must serve on each party any order revoking or amending an order to which this Part applies.

119.54 ***Amending Applications by the defendant***
Criminal Procedure Rules 2015 2015/1490 Rule 32.3(1) This rule applies where:
(a) the defendant wants the court to exercise any power it has to revoke or amend an order to which this Part applies, or
(b) where the legislation allows, a person affected by such an order wants the court to exercise any such power.
(2) That defendant, or person affected, must:
(a) apply in writing, explaining why the order should be revoked or amended, and
(b) serve the application on:
(i) the court officer,
(ii) the responsible officer or supervisor, and
(iii) as appropriate, the defendant or the person affected.

119.55 ***Court's duty to serve amended order***
Criminal Procedure Rules 2015 2015/1490 Rule 32.4(2) The court officer must serve on each party any order revoking or amending an order to which this Part applies.

Revoking the order

119.56 ***Statutory power to revoke***
Criminal Justice and Immigration Act 2008 Sch 2 para 11(1) This paragraph applies where:

(a) a Youth Rehabilitation Order is in force in respect of any offender,
(b) the order:
(i) was made by a Youth Court or other Magistrates' Court, or
(ii) was made by the Crown Court and contains a direction under Sch 1 para 36, and
(c) the offender or the responsible officer makes an application to the appropriate court under this sub-paragraph.

(2) If it appears to the appropriate court to be in the interests of justice to do so, having regard to circumstances which have arisen since the order was made, the appropriate court may:

(a) revoke the order, or
(b) both:
(i) revoke the order, and
(ii) deal with the offender, for the offence in respect of which the order was made, in any way in which the appropriate court could have dealt with the offender for that offence (had the offender been before that court to be dealt with for it).

(3) The circumstances in which a Youth Rehabilitation Order may be revoked under sub-paragraph (2) include the offender's making good progress or responding satisfactorily to supervision or treatment (as the case requires).
(4) In dealing with an offender under sub-paragraph (2)(b), the appropriate court must take into account the extent to which the offender has complied with the requirements of the Youth Rehabilitation Order.
(5) A person sentenced under sub-paragraph (2)(b) for an offence may appeal to the Crown Court against the sentence.

119.57 ***Crown Court powers to revoke***
Revocation of order with or without re-sentencing: powers of Crown Court
Criminal Justice and Immigration Act 2008 Sch 2 para 12(1) This paragraph applies where:

(a) a Youth Rehabilitation Order is in force in respect of an offender,
(b) the order:
(i) was made by the Crown Court, and
(ii) does not contain a direction under paragraph 36 of Schedule 1, and
(c) the offender or the responsible officer makes an application to the Crown Court under this sub-paragraph.

(2) If it appears to the Crown Court to be in the interests of justice to do so, having regard to circumstances which have arisen since the Youth Rehabilitation Order was made, the Crown Court may:

(a) revoke the order, or (b) both:
(i) revoke the order, and
(ii) deal with the offender, for the offence in respect of which the order was made, in any way in which the Crown Court could have dealt with the offender for that offence.

(3) The circumstances in which a Youth Rehabilitation Order may be revoked under sub-paragraph (2) include the offender's making good progress or responding satisfactorily to supervision or treatment (as the case requires).

(4) In dealing with an offender under sub-paragraph (2)(b), the Crown Court must take into account the extent to which the offender has complied with the Youth Rehabilitation Order.
(5) The person sentenced under sub-paragraph (2)(b) for an offence may appeal to the Crown Court against the sentence.
(6) No application may be made by the offender under sub-paragraph (1) while an appeal against the Youth Rehabilitation Order is pending.
(7) If an application under sub-paragraph (1) relating to a Youth Rehabilitation Order is dismissed, then during the period of three months beginning with the date on which it was dismissed no further such application may be made in relation to the order by any person except with the consent of the appropriate court.
Criminal Justice and Immigration Act 2008 Sch 2 para 12 [applies in Crown Court where no para 36 direction is made].
(5) No application may be made by the offender under sub-paragraph (1) while an appeal against the Youth Rehabilitation Order is pending.
(6) If an application under sub-paragraph (1) relating to a Youth Rehabilitation Order is dismissed, then during the period of three months beginning with the date on which it was dismissed no further such application may be made in relation to the order by any person except with the consent of the Crown Court.

120 Youth Rehabilitation Orders: Breach of

120.1
Criminal Justice and Immigration Act 2008 Sch 2 para 4
Guidelines *Breach Offences Guideline 2018*, see www.banksr.com Other Matters Guidelines tab In force 1 October 2018 page 56 says, '**Other breach offences** Where an offence is not covered by a sentencing guideline a court is entitled to use, and may be assisted by, a guideline for an analogous offence subject to differences in the elements of the offences and the statutory maxima.' For the guideline about the powers and the proper approach, see **120.16**.

Pre-hearing matters

120.2 ***Duty to give warning***
Criminal Justice and Immigration Act 2008 Sch 2 para 3(1) If the responsible officer is of the opinion that the offender has failed without reasonable excuse to comply with a Youth Rehabilitation Order, the responsible officer must give the offender a warning under this paragraph unless under para 4(1) or (3) the responsible officer causes an information to be laid before a justice of the peace in respect of the failure.

120.3 ***Warning, Contents of a***
Criminal Justice and Immigration Act 2008 Sch 2 para 3(2) A warning under this paragraph must:
- (a) describe the circumstances of the failure,
- (b) state that the failure is unacceptable, and
- (c) state that the offender will be liable to be brought before a court:
  - (i) in a case where the warning is given during the warned period relating to a previous warning under this paragraph, if during that period the offender again fails to comply with the order, or
  - (ii) in any other case, if during the warned period relating to the warning, the offender fails on more than one occasion to comply with the order.

120.4 ***Warning must be recorded***
Criminal Justice and Immigration Act 2008 Sch 2 para 3(3) The responsible officer must, as soon as practicable after the warning has been given, record that fact.

120.5 *'Warned period', Definition of*
Criminal Justice and Immigration Act 2008 Sch 2 para 3(4) In this paragraph, 'warned period', in relation to a warning under this paragraph, means the period of 12 months beginning with the date on which the warning was given.

120.6 *Warnings not heeded*
Criminal Justice and Immigration Act 2008 Sch 2 para 4(1) If the responsible officer:
(a) has given a warning ('the first warning') under paragraph 3 to the offender in respect of a Youth Rehabilitation Order,
(b) during the warned period relating to the first warning, has given another warning under that paragraph to the offender in respect of a failure to comply with the order, and
(c) is of the opinion that, during the warned period relating to the first warning, the offender has again failed without reasonable excuse to comply with the order,
the responsible officer must cause an information to be laid before a justice of the peace in respect of the failure mentioned in paragraph (c).
(2) But sub-paragraph (1) does not apply if the responsible officer is of the opinion that there are exceptional circumstances which justify not causing an information to be so laid.

120.7 *Issue of summons or warrant by Magistrates' Court*
Issue of summons or warrant by justice of the peace
Criminal Justice and Immigration Act 2008 Sch 2 para 5(1) If at any time while a Youth Rehabilitation Order is in force it appears on information to a justice of the peace that an offender has failed to comply with a Youth Rehabilitation Order, the justice may:
(a) issue a summons requiring the offender to appear at the place and time specified in it, or
(b) if the information is in writing and on oath, issue a warrant for the offender's arrest.
(2) Any summons or warrant issued under this paragraph must direct the offender to appear or be brought:
(a) if the Youth Rehabilitation Order was made by the Crown Court and does not include a direction under Sch 1 para 36 (see **119.34**), before the Crown Court, and
(b) in any other case, before the appropriate court.
Criminal Procedure Rules 2015 2015/1490 Rule 32.2(1) This rule applies where:
(a) the responsible officer or supervisor wants the court to:
(i) deal with a defendant for failure to comply with an order to which this Part applies, or
(ii) revoke or amend such an order; or
(b) the court considers exercising on its own initiative any power it has to:
(i) revoke or amend such an order, and
(ii) summon the defendant to attend for that purpose.
(2) Rules 7.2 to 7.4, which deal, among other things, with starting a prosecution in a Magistrates' Court,[1281] apply:
(a) as if:
(i) a reference in those rules to an allegation of an offence included a reference to an allegation of failure to comply with an order to which this Part applies, and
(ii) a reference to the prosecutor included a reference to the responsible officer or supervisor, and
(b) with the necessary consequential modifications.
Note: A Sch 1 para 36 order is that future proceedings should be in the Youth Court or another Magistrates' Court. Ed.

[1281] The words 'by information and summons' were deleted by Criminal Procedure (Amendment) Rules 2018 2018/132 para 14. In force 2/4/18

120.8 ***'Appropriate court'? What is the***
Criminal Justice and Immigration Act 2008 Sch 2 para 5(3) In sub-paragraph (2), 'appropriate court' means:
(a) if the offender is aged under 18, a Youth Court acting in the relevant local justice area, and
(b) if the offender is aged 18 or over, a Magistrates' Court (other than a Youth Court) acting in that local justice area.

120.9 ***'Local justice area'? What is the***
Criminal Justice and Immigration Act 2008 Sch 2 para 5(4) In sub-paragraph (3), 'relevant local justice area' means:
(a) the local justice area in which the offender resides, or
(b) if it is not known where the offender resides, the local justice area specified in the Youth Rehabilitation Order.

120.10 ***Failure to answer a summons***
Criminal Justice and Immigration Act 2008 Sch 2 para 5(5) Sub-paragraphs (6) and (7) apply where the offender does not appear in answer to a summons issued under this paragraph.
(6) If the summons required the offender to appear before the Crown Court, the Crown Court may:
(a) unless the summons was issued under this sub-paragraph, issue a further summons requiring the offender to appear at the place and time specified in it, or
(b) in any case, issue a warrant for the arrest of the offender.
(7) If the summons required the offender to appear before a Magistrates' Court, the Magistrates' Court may issue a warrant for the arrest of the offender.

Defences

120.11 ***Breach of mental health and drug and intoxicating substance treatment requirements, Defences***
Criminal Justice and Immigration Act 2008 Sch 2 para 9(1) Sub-paragraph (2) applies where a Youth Rehabilitation Order imposes any of the following requirements in respect of an offender:
(a) a mental health treatment requirement,
(b) a drug treatment requirement,
(c) an intoxicating substance treatment requirement.
(2) The offender is not to be treated for the purposes of paragraph 6 or 8 as having failed to comply with the order on the ground only that the offender had refused to undergo any surgical, electrical or other treatment required by that requirement if, in the opinion of the court, the refusal was reasonable having regard to all the circumstances.

120.12 ***Power to commit for sentence Crown Court orders***
Power of magistrates' court to refer offender to Crown Court
Criminal Justice and Immigration Act 2008 Sch 2 para 7(1) Sub-paragraph (2) applies if:
(a) the Youth Rehabilitation Order was made by the Crown Court and contains a direction under paragraph 36 of Sch 1, and
(b) a Youth Court or other Magistrates' Court would (apart from that sub-paragraph) be required, or has the power, to deal with the offender in one of the ways mentioned in paragraph 6(2) (see **120.14**).
(2) The court may instead: a) commit the offender in custody, or b) release the offender on bail, until the offender can be brought or appear before the Crown Court.
(3) Where a court deals with the offender's case under sub-paragraph (2) it must send to the Crown Court:
(a) a certificate signed by a justice of the peace certifying that the offender has failed to comply with the Youth Rehabilitation Order in the respect specified in the certificate, and
(b) such other particulars of the case as may be desirable,

and a certificate purporting to be so signed is admissible as evidence of the failure before the Crown Court.

Court powers

120.13 *Crown Court powers*

Note: Besides the powers listed below, there is the power to amend the order, see **120.28**. Ed.

Powers of Crown Court

Criminal Justice and Immigration Act 2008 Sch 2 para 8(1) This paragraph applies where:

(a) an offender appears or is brought before the Crown Court under paragraph 5 or by virtue of paragraph 7(2), and

(b) it is proved to the satisfaction of that court that the offender has failed without reasonable excuse to comply with the Youth Rehabilitation Order.

(2) The Crown Court may deal with the offender in respect of that failure in any one of the following ways:

(a) by ordering the offender to pay a fine of an amount not exceeding:

(i) £250, if the offender is aged under 14, or

(ii) £2,500[1282] in any other case…

(c) by dealing with the offender, for the offence in respect of which the order was made, in any way in which the Crown Court could have dealt with the offender for that offence.

Criminal Justice and Immigration Act 2008 Sch 2 para 8(12) The court may (when dealing with a failure to comply with an order) impose a Youth Rehabilitation Order with Intensive Supervision and Surveillance notwithstanding anything in section 1(4)(a) or (b).

(13) If:

(a) the order is a Youth Rehabilitation Order with Intensive Supervision and Surveillance, and

(b) the offence mentioned in sub-paragraph (2)(c) was punishable with imprisonment,

the court may impose a custodial sentence notwithstanding anything in Criminal Justice Act 2003 s 152(2) (general restrictions on imposing discretionary custodial sentences).

(14) If:

(a) the order is a Youth Rehabilitation Order with Intensive Supervision and Surveillance which was imposed by virtue of paragraph 6(13) or sub-paragraph (12), and

(b) the offence mentioned in sub-paragraph (2)(c) was not punishable with imprisonment,

for the purposes of dealing with the offender under sub-paragraph (2)(c), the Crown Court is to be taken to have had power to deal with the offender for that offence by making a Detention and Training Order for a term not exceeding 4 months.

Note: Legal Aid, Sentencing and Punishment of Offenders Act 2012 s 83(5) added Criminal Justice and Immigration Act 2008 Sch 1 para 16A, which enables a court to extend the order on breach. Ed.

120.14 *Magistrates' Court powers*

Note: Besides the powers listed below, there is the power to impose intensive supervision and surveillance, see **120.16**. Ed.

Powers of magistrates' court

Criminal Justice and Immigration Act 2008 Sch 2 para 6 (1)[1283] This paragraph applies where:

[1282] The maximum amount was increased from £1,000 to £2,500 by Legal Aid, Sentencing and Punishment of Offenders Act 2012 s 84(3).

[1283] As amended by Legal Aid, Sentencing and Punishment of Offenders Act 2012 s 83(2)

(a) an offender appears or is brought before a youth court or other magistrates' court under paragraph 5, and

(b) it is proved to the satisfaction of the court that the offender has failed without reasonable excuse to comply with the youth rehabilitation order.

(2) The court may deal with the offender in respect of that failure in any one of the following ways:

(a) by ordering the offender to pay a fine of an amount not exceeding £2,500.

(b) by amending the terms of the youth rehabilitation order so as to impose any requirement which could have been included in the order when it was made:

(i) in addition to, or

(ii) in substitution for,

any requirement or requirements already imposed by the order;

(c) by dealing with the offender, for the offence in respect of which the order was made, in any way in which the court could have dealt with the offender for that offence (had the offender been before that court to be dealt with for it).

(3) Sub-paragraph (2)(b) is subject to sub-paragraphs (6) to (9).

(4) In dealing with the offender under sub-paragraph (2), the court must take into account the extent to which the offender has complied with the youth rehabilitation order.

(5) A fine imposed under sub-paragraph (2)(a) is to be treated, for the purposes of any enactment, as being a sum adjudged to be paid by a conviction.

(6) Subject to sub-paragraph (6A), any requirement imposed under sub-paragraph (2)(b) must be capable of being complied with before the date specified under paragraph 32(1) of Schedule 1.

(6A) When imposing a requirement under sub-paragraph (2)(b), the court may amend the order to substitute a later date for that specified under paragraph 32(1) of Schedule 1.

(6B) A date substituted under sub-paragraph (6A):

(a) may not fall outside the period of six months beginning with the date previously specified under paragraph 32(1) of Schedule 1;

(b) subject to that, may fall more than three years after the date on which the order took effect.

(6C) The power under sub-paragraph (6A) may not be exercised in relation to an order if that power or the power in paragraph 8(6A) has previously been exercised in relation to that order.

(6D) A date substituted under sub-paragraph (6A) is to be treated as having been specified in relation to the order under paragraph 32(1) of Schedule 1.

(7) Where:

(a) the court is dealing with the offender under sub-paragraph (2)(b), and

(b) the youth rehabilitation order does not contain an unpaid work requirement,

paragraph 10(2) of Schedule 1 applies in relation to the inclusion of such a requirement as if for "40" there were substituted "20".

(8) The court may not under sub-paragraph (2)(b) impose:

(a) an extended activity requirement, or

(b) a fostering requirement,

if the order does not already impose such a requirement.

(9) Where:

(a) the order imposes a fostering requirement (the "original requirement"), and

(b) under sub-paragraph (2)(b) the court proposes to substitute a new fostering requirement ("the substitute requirement") for the original requirement,

paragraph 18(2) of Schedule 1 applies in relation to the substitute requirement as if the reference to the period of 12 months beginning with the date on which the original requirement first had effect were a reference to the period of 18 months beginning with that date.

(10) Where:

(a) the court deals with the offender under sub-paragraph (2)(b), and
(b) it would not otherwise have the power to amend the youth rehabilitation order under paragraph 13 (amendment by reason of change of residence),
that paragraph has effect as if references in it to the appropriate court were references to the court which is dealing with the offender.

(11) Where the court deals with the offender under sub-paragraph (2)(c), it must revoke the youth rehabilitation order if it is still in force.

(12) Sub-paragraphs (13) to (15) apply where:
(a) the court is dealing with the offender under sub-paragraph (2)(c), and
(b) the offender has wilfully and persistently failed to comply with a youth rehabilitation order.

(13) The court may impose a youth rehabilitation order with intensive supervision and surveillance notwithstanding anything in section 1(4)(a) or (b).

(14) If:
(a) the order is a youth rehabilitation order with intensive supervision and surveillance, and
(b) the offence mentioned in sub-paragraph (2)(c) was punishable with imprisonment,
the court may impose a custodial sentence notwithstanding anything in section 152(2) of the Criminal Justice Act 2003 (general restrictions on imposing discretionary custodial sentences).

(15) If:
(a) the order is a youth rehabilitation order with intensive supervision and surveillance which was imposed by virtue of sub-paragraph (13) or paragraph 8(12), and
(b) the offence mentioned in sub-paragraph (2)(c) was not punishable with imprisonment,
for the purposes of dealing with the offender under sub-paragraph (2)(c), the court is to be taken to have had power to deal with the offender for that offence by making a detention and training order for a term not exceeding 4 months.

(16) An offender may appeal to the Crown Court against a sentence imposed under sub-paragraph (2)(c).

Note: Legal Aid, Sentencing and Punishment of Offenders Act 2012 s 83(5) added Criminal Justice and Immigration Act 2008 Sch 1 para 16A, which enables a court to extend the order on breach. Ed.

120.15 ***Sentencing Children and Young People Guideline 2017***

Sentencing Children and Young People Guideline 2017, see www.banksr.com Other Matters Guideline tab page 33 In force 1 June 2017

7.12 Where a child or young person is in breach of a YRO the following options are available to the court:

- take no action and allow the order to continue in its original form;
- impose a fine (up to £2,500) (and allow the order to continue in its original form);
- amend the terms of the order; or
- revoke the order and re-sentence the child or young person.

7.13 If the terms of the order are amended the new requirements must be capable of being complied with before the expiry of the overall period. The court may impose any requirement that it could have imposed when making the order and this may be in addition to, or in substitution for, any requirements contained in the order. If the YRO did not contain an unpaid work requirement and the court includes such a requirement using this power, the minimum period of unpaid work is 20 hours; this will give greater flexibility when responding to less serious breaches or where there are significant other requirements to be complied with.

7.14 A court may not amend the terms of a YRO that did not include an extended activity requirement or a fostering requirement by inserting them at this stage; should these requirements be considered appropriate following breach, the child or young person must be re-sentenced and the original YRO revoked.

7.15 A court must ensure that it has sufficient information to enable it to understand why the order has been breached and should be satisfied that the YOT and other local authority services have taken all steps necessary to ensure that the child or young person has been given appropriate opportunity and the support necessary for compliance. This is particularly important if the court is considering imposing a custodial sentence as a result of the breach.

7.16 Where the failure arises primarily from non-compliance with reporting or other similar obligations and a sanction is necessary, the most appropriate response is likely to be the inclusion of (or increase in) a primarily punitive requirement such as the curfew requirement, unpaid work, the exclusion requirement and the prohibited activity requirement or the imposition of a fine. However, continuing failure to comply with the order is likely to lead to revocation of the order and re-sentencing for the original offence.

7.17 Where the child or young person has 'wilfully and persistently' failed to comply with the order, and the court proposes to sentence again for the offence(s) in respect of which the order was made, additional powers are available.

A child or young person will almost certainly be considered to have 'wilfully and persistently' breached a YRO where there have been three breaches that have demonstrated a lack of willingness to comply with the order that have resulted in an appearance before court.

7.18 The additional powers available to the court when re-sentencing a child or young person who has 'wilfully and persistently' breached their order are:

- the making of a YRO with intensive supervision and surveillance even though the offence is non-imprisonable;
- a custodial sentence if the YRO that is breached is one with an intensive supervision and surveillance requirement, which was imposed for an offence that was imprisonable; and
- the imposition of a DTO for four months for breach of a YRO with intensive supervision and surveillance which was imposed following wilful and persistent breach of an order made for a non-imprisonable offence.

The primary objective when sentencing for breach of a YRO is to ensure that the child or young person completes the requirements imposed by the court.

7.19 If an offender has attained the age of 18 by the first court hearing then breach proceedings must be dealt with by the adult Magistrates' Court. If the court chooses to revoke the order then its powers are limited to those available to the court at the time of the original sentence.

Commission of further offences during a YRO

7.20 If a child or young person commits an offence whilst subject to a YRO the court can impose any sentence for the new matter, but can only impose a new YRO if they revoke the existing order. Where the court revokes the original order they may re-sentence that matter at the same time as sentencing the new offence.

120.16 ***Magistrates' Court powers*** ***Intensive Supervision and Surveillance***

Criminal Justice and Immigration Act 2008 Sch 2 para 6(13) The court may impose a Youth Rehabilitation Order with Intensive Supervision and Surveillance notwithstanding anything in section 1(4)(a) or (b).

(14) If:

(a) the order is a Youth Rehabilitation Order with Intensive Supervision and Surveillance, and

(b) the offence mentioned in sub-paragraph (2)(c) was punishable with imprisonment,

the court may impose a custodial sentence notwithstanding anything in Criminal Justice Act 2003 s 152(2) (general restrictions on imposing discretionary custodial sentences).

(15) If: a) the order is a Youth Rehabilitation Order with Intensive Supervision and Surveillance which was imposed by virtue of sub-paragraph (13) or paragraph 8(12), and b) the offence mentioned in sub-paragraph (2)(c) was not punishable with imprisonment,

for the purposes of dealing with the offender under sub-paragraph (2)(c), the court is to be taken to have had power to deal with the offender for that offence by making a Detention and Training Order for a term not exceeding 4 months.

The hearing

120.17 ***Procedure***

Criminal Justice and Immigration Act 2008 Sch 2 para 4(3) If:

(a) the responsible officer is of the opinion that the offender has failed without reasonable excuse to comply with a Youth Rehabilitation Order, and

(b) sub-paragraph (1) does not apply (in a case not within sub-paragraph (2)), the responsible officer may cause an information to be laid before a justice of the peace in respect of that failure.

120.18 ***CRO should have details of the order breached***

Criminal Practice Directions 2015 EWCA Crim 1567 para II 10A.7 Where the current alleged offence could constitute a breach of an existing sentence such as a suspended sentence, community order or conditional discharge, and it is known that that sentence is still in force, details of the circumstances of the offence leading to the sentence should be included in the antecedents. The detail should be brief and include the date of the offence.

120.19 ***Breach to be determined by the judge***

Criminal Justice and Immigration Act 2008 Sch 2 para 8(15) In proceedings before the Crown Court under this paragraph any question whether the offender has failed to comply with the Youth Rehabilitation Order is to be determined by the court and not by the verdict of a jury.

120.20 ***Part compliance, Must consider***

Criminal Justice and Immigration Act 2008 Sch 2 para 8(4) In dealing with the offender under sub-paragraph (2), the Crown Court must take into account the extent to which the offender has complied with the Youth Rehabilitation Order.

120.21 ***Crown Court Different sentence imposed Must revoke YRO***

Criminal Justice and Immigration Act 2008 Sch 2 para 8(10) Where the Crown Court deals with an offender under sub-paragraph (2)(c), it must revoke the Youth Rehabilitation Order if it is still in force.

(11) Sub-paragraphs (12) to (14) apply where:

(a) an offender has wilfully and persistently failed to comply with a Youth Rehabilitation Order, and

(b) the Crown Court is dealing with the offender under sub-paragraph (2)(c).

120.22 ***Unpaid work not in original order***

Criminal Justice and Immigration Act 2008 Sch 2 para 6(7) Where:

(a) the court is dealing with the offender under sub-paragraph (2)(b), and

(b) the Youth Rehabilitation Order does not contain an unpaid work requirement, Sch 1 para 10(2) (see **119.29**) applies in relation to the inclusion of such a requirement as if for '40' (the minimum number of hours) there were substituted '20'.

(8) The court may not under sub-paragraph (2)(b) impose:

(a) an extended activity requirement, or

(b) a fostering requirement, if the order does not already impose such a requirement.

(9) Where:

(a) the order imposes a fostering requirement (the 'original requirement'), and

(b) under sub-paragraph (2)(b) the court proposes to substitute a new fostering requirement ('the substitute requirement') for the original requirement,

paragraph 18(2) of Sch 1 applies in relation to the substitute requirement as if the reference to the period of 12 months beginning with the date on which the original requirement first had effect were a reference to the period of 18 months beginning with that date.

(10) Where:

(a) the court deals with the offender under sub-paragraph (2)(b), and

(b) it would not otherwise have the power to amend the Youth Rehabilitation Order under paragraph 13 (amendment by reason of change of residence), that paragraph has effect as if references in it to the appropriate court were references to the court which is dealing with the offender.

120.23 ***Judicial discretion***

120.24 ***Parent/Guardian to pay fine etc. for breaches of orders***

Powers of Criminal Courts (Sentencing) Act 2000 s 137(2) Where but for this subsection a court would impose a fine on a child or young person under:

(za) Criminal Justice and Immigration Act 2008 Sch 2 para 6(2)(a) or 8(2)(a) (breach of Youth Rehabilitation Order),

…the court shall order that the fine be paid by the parent or guardian of the child or young person instead of by the child or young person himself, unless the court is satisfied:

(i) that the parent or guardian cannot be found, or

(ii) that it would be unreasonable to make an order for payment, having regard to the circumstances of the case.

120.25 ***Parent/Guardian to pay fine etc. Offender under 16***

Powers of Criminal Courts (Sentencing) Act 2000 s 137(3) In the case of a young person aged 16 or over, subsections (1) to (2) of this section shall have effect as if, instead of imposing a duty, they conferred a power to make such an order as is mentioned in those subsections.

120.26 ***Parent/Guardian must have opportunity of being heard***

Powers of Criminal Courts (Sentencing) Act 2000 s 137(4) Subject to subsection (5), no order shall be made under this section without giving the parent or guardian an opportunity of being heard.

(5) An order under this section may be made against a parent or guardian who, having been required to attend, has failed to do so.

Amending the order

120.27 ***Crown Court powers Amending the order***

Criminal Justice and Immigration Act 2008 Sch 2 para 8(2) The Crown Court may deal with the offender by:..b) amending the terms of the Youth Rehabilitation Order so as to impose any requirement which could have been included in the order when it was made: i) in addition to, or ii) in substitution for, any requirement or requirements already imposed by the order.

(3) Sub-paragraph (2)(b) is subject to sub-paragraphs (6) to (9).

(4) In dealing with the offender under sub-paragraph (2), the Crown Court must take into account the extent to which the offender has complied with the Youth Rehabilitation Order.

Criminal Justice and Immigration Act 2008 Sch 2 para 8(6) Subject to sub-paragraph (6A),[1284] any requirement imposed under sub-paragraph (2)(b) must be capable of being complied with before the date specified under paragraph 32(1) of Sch 1.

(6A) When imposing a requirement under sub-paragraph (2)(b), the Crown Court may amend the order to substitute a later date for that specified under paragraph 32(1) of Schedule 1.

(6B) A date substituted under sub-paragraph (6A),

(a) may not fall outside the period of six months beginning with the date previously specified under paragraph 32(1) of Schedule 1;

[1284] This phrase and sub-paragraphs (6A), (6B) and (6C) were inserted by Legal Aid, Sentencing and Punishment of Offenders Act 2012 s 83(3).

(b) subject to that, may fall more than three years after the date on which the order took effect.

(6C) The power under sub-paragraph (6A) may not be exercised in relation to an order if that power or the power in paragraph 6(6A) has previously been exercised in relation to that order.

(7) Where:

(a) the court is dealing with the offender under sub-paragraph (2)(b), and

(b) the Youth Rehabilitation Order does not contain an unpaid work requirement, paragraph 10(2) of Sch 1 applies in relation to the inclusion of such a requirement as if for '40' there were substituted '20'.

(8) The court may not under sub-paragraph (2)(b) impose: (a) an extended activity requirement, or b) a fostering requirement, if the order does not already impose such a requirement.

(9) Where: a) the order imposes a fostering requirement (the 'original requirement'), and b) under sub-paragraph (2)(b) the court proposes to substitute a new fostering requirement ('the substitute requirement') for the original requirement, paragraph 18(2) of Sch 1 applies in relation to the substitute requirement as if the reference to the period of 12 months beginning with the date on which the original requirement first had effect were a reference to the period of 18 months beginning with that date.

120.28 ***Magistrates amending the order***

Criminal Justice and Immigration Act 2008 Sch 2 para 6(2) The court may deal with the offender in respect of that failure in any one of the following ways…

(b) by amending the terms of the Youth Rehabilitation Order so as to impose any requirement which could have been included in the order when it was made:

(i) in addition to, or

(ii) in substitution for, any requirement or requirements already imposed by the order.

(3) Sub-paragraph (2)(b) is subject to sub-paragraphs (6) to (9).

(4) In dealing with the offender under sub-paragraph (2), the court must take into account the extent to which the offender has complied with the Youth Rehabilitation Order.

Criminal Justice and Immigration Act 2008 Sch 2 para 6(6) Subject to sub-paragraph (6A),[1285] any requirement imposed under sub-paragraph (2)(b) must be capable of being complied with before the date specified under Sch 1 para 32(1) (the 3-year maximum length, see **119.32**).

(6A) When imposing a requirement under sub-paragraph (2)(b), the court may amend the order to substitute a later date for that specified under paragraph 32(1) of Schedule 1.

(6B) A date substituted under sub-paragraph (6A):

(a) may not fall outside the period of six months beginning with the date previously specified under paragraph 32(1) of Schedule 1;

(b) subject to that, may fall more than three years after the date on which the order took effect.

(6C) The power under sub-paragraph (6A) may not be exercised in relation to an order if that power or the power in paragraph 8(6A) has previously been exercised in relation to that order.

120.29 ***Fixing the date for an amended order***

Criminal Justice and Immigration Act 2008 Sch 2 para 16A(1)[1286] The appropriate court may, on the application of the offender or the responsible officer, amend a Youth Rehabilitation Order by substituting a later date for that specified under paragraph 32(1) of Schedule 1.

[1285] This phrase and sub-paragraphs (6A), (6B) and (6C) were inserted by Legal Aid, Sentencing and Punishment of Offenders Act 2012 s 83(2).

[1286] This paragraph was inserted by Legal Aid, Sentencing and Punishment of Offenders Act 2012 s 83(5).

(2) A date substituted under sub-paragraph (1):

(a) may not fall outside the period of six months beginning with the date previously specified under paragraph 32(1) of Schedule 1;

(b) subject to that, may fall more than three years after the date on which the order took effect.

(3) The power under sub-paragraph (1) may not be exercised in relation to an order if it has previously been exercised in relation to that order.

(4) A date substituted under sub-paragraph (1) is to be treated as having been specified in relation to the order under Schedule 1 para 32(1).

Note: Subsection (5) defines 'the appropriate court' and subsection (6) provides that offenders aged 18+ are dealt with in the Magistrates' Court, not the Youth Court. Ed.

Appeals

120.30 ***Appeals from the Magistrates' Court New sentence imposed***

Criminal Justice and Immigration Act 2008 Sch 2 para 6(2) The court may deal with the offender in respect of that failure in any one of the following ways:

(a) [fining], see **120.14**,

(b) [amending the order], see **120.28**,

(c) by dealing with the offender, for the offence in respect of which the order was made, in any way in which the court could have dealt with the offender for that offence (had the offender been before that court to be dealt with for it).

Criminal Justice and Immigration Act 2008 Sch 2 para 6(16) An offender may appeal to the Crown Court against a sentence imposed under sub-paragraph (2)(c).

Contents Index

References are to paragraph numbers.